The OLIVER WENDELL HOLMES DEVISE
HISTORY OF THE SUPREME COURT
OF THE UNITED STATES

General Editor: PAUL A. FREUND

THE OLIVER WENDELL HOLMES DEVISE

HISTORY OF THE SUPREME COURT
OF THE UNITED STATES

General Editor: PAUL A. FREUND

THE

Oliver Wendell Holmes

DEVISE

HISTORY OF
THE SUPREME COURT
OF THE UNITED STATES

VOLUME VI
PART ONE

THE OLIVER WENDELL HOLMES DEVISE

History of the

SUPREME COURT

of the United States

VOLUME VI

Reconstruction
and Reunion
1864-88

PART ONE

By Charles Fairman

NEW YORK
The Macmillan Company

Collier-Macmillan Ltd.
LONDON

The Macmillan Company
866 Third Avenue, New York, N.Y. 10022
Collier-Macmillan Canada Ltd., Toronto, Ontario
Library of Congress Catalog Card Number: 70–169254

FIRST PRINTING

PRINTED IN THE UNITED STATES OF AMERICA

Contents

Illustrations

FOLLOWING PAGE 584

Andrew Johnson

William H. Seward

Gideon Welles

Orville H. Browning

Jeremiah S. Black

Robert J. Walker

Benjamin R. Curtis

Henry Stanbery

Reverdy Johnson

David Dudley Field

William M. Evarts

Benjamin F. Butler

Lyman Trumbull

Edwin M. Stanton

James Speed

William L. Sharkey

William P. Fessenden

John Sherman

Jacob M. Howard

Matthew Hale Carpenter

Charles Sumner

Thaddeus Stevens

John A. Bingham

Thomas A. Hendricks

Edward Bates

Montgomery Blair

Edgar Cowan

Augustus H. Garland

John A. Campbell

ILLUSTRATIONS

Amos T. Akerman

John B. Henderson

William M. Stewart

FOLLOWING PAGE 904

During the Passage of the Civil Rights Bill

Managers of the Impeachment of the President, 1868

James A. Garfield

Henry Winter Davis

George S. Boutwell

Samuel Shellabarger

Benjamin F. Wade

Timothy O. Howe

Zachariah Chandler

Simon Cameron

James M. Ashley

Burton C. Cook

James G. Blaine

Henry J. Raymond

Garrett Davis

James R. Doolittle

Frank P. Blair, Jr.

Herschel V. Johnson

Ira Harris

Frederick T. Frelinghuysen

James W. Grimes

Charles D. Drake

John William Wallace, the Reporter

Mrs. Myra Bradwell

Ward Lamon, U.S. Marshal

Richard C. Parsons, the Marshal

Illustrations

Congressman George C. McKee

Judge Richard Busteed

Governor William G. Brownlow

Charts, Tables, Documents

Foreword

W HEN OLIVER WENDELL HOLMES, JR., Associate Justice of the
Supreme Court, died in March 1935 at the age of ninety-three,
he left to the United States of America his residual estate, amounting to
approximately $263,000. Since such a bequest was unusual, there was
no ready formula for utilizing this money. The subsequent deliberations
among government leaders about a suitable disposition of the gift were
interrupted by the onset of the Second World War, with the result that
for many years the money remained in the Treasury, untouched and
uninvested. Finally, in 1955, an act of Congress (P.L. 84–246) established the Oliver Wendell Holmes Devise Fund, consisting of the
original bequest augmented by a one-time appropriation in lieu of
interest. The act also created the Permanent Committee for the Oliver
Wendell Holmes Devise to administer the fund. The Committee consists of four public members appointed by the President of the United
States for an eight-year term and the Librarian of Congress as Chairman
ex officio.

The principal project supported by the Holmes bequest, as
stipulated in the enabling act, has been the preparation and publication
of a history of the Supreme Court of the United States. The present
volume is part of that series. Intended to fill a gap in American legal
literature, the multivolume history has been planned to give a comprehensive and definitive survey of the development of the Court from
the beginning of the nation to the present. Paul A. Freund, Carl M.
Loeb University Professor, Harvard University, has served as editor
in chief. The authors, of whom Charles Fairman, Professor of Law
emeritus, Harvard Law School, is one, have devoted many years to
the research and writing.

The operation of the Permanent Committee has been dependent
upon the services of the distinguished men who have contributed their

time, their wisdom, and their practical assistance as members of the Committee. Their names appear below.

In the early days of the Committee, Joseph P. Blickensderfer was Administrative Editor and Special Assistant to the Chairman. Dr. Blickensderfer contributed much imagination, enthusiasm, and hard work to plans for the publication of the history of the Supreme Court and later to preparations for the Holmes Devise lecture series also supported by the Committee. Following Dr. Blickensderfer's death in 1960, the late Lloyd Dunlap served as Administrative Editor for the years 1961–64. Since then the responsibility for the office of the Permanent Committee has been assigned to Mrs. Elizabeth E. Hamer, Assistant Librarian of Congress, who is assisted by Mrs. Jean Allaway as Administrative Officer for the Devise.

As Chairman *ex officio* of the Committee that has sponsored this work, I am happy to see the plans for the Oliver Wendell Holmes history of the Supreme Court come to fruition. This volume and its companions will form an appropriate tribute to the great Justice whose legacy has made possible their publication.

> *L. Quincy Mumford*
> LIBRARIAN OF CONGRESS

PERMANENT COMMITTEE FOR
THE OLIVER WENDELL HOMES DEVISE

(TERMS OF EIGHT YEARS EXCEPT FOR INITIAL APPOINTMENTS)

Charles T. McCormick	1956–58 (two-year term)
Edward S. Corwin	1956–60 (four-year term)
George L. Haskins	1956–58 (six-year term but resigned 10/7/58)
Virgil M. Hancher	1956–64
Frederick D. G. Ribble	1958–66
Ethan A. H. Shepley	1959–67
Nicholas Kelley	7/8/60–7/22/60
Jefferson B. Fordham	1961–69
Harry H. Ransom	1964–72
Herbert Wechsler	1966–74
Robert G. McCloskey	1967–69
J. A. C. Grant	1970–78
Alfred H. Kelly	1970–78

Editor's Foreword

No MORE ANXIOUS RESPONSIBILITY could be faced by a court than to adjudicate controversies arising out of a civil war and its aftermath, in a time of turmoil that pitted not merely citizen against citizen but section against section and Congress against the Chief Executive. How the Supreme Court discharged that responsibility is a pervading theme of this volume, which covers primarily the period of the Chief Justiceship of Salmon P. Chase (1864–73), though its unity is defined by topics rather more than by dates.

Professor Fairman has mapped the terrain of his period on a spacious scale, enabling him to present the telling detail that gives color and verisimilitude to the narrative and conviction to his judgments. Supreme Court litigation appears as a stage in a cycle, a transforming station in the flow of a current that includes the political and social origins of a conflict as well as the consequences and repercussions of the Court's decision. For the litigation stage itself the author has taken in effect the model described by Maitland in writing of the Year Books: "What they [some nameless lawyers at Westminster] desired was not a copy of the chilly record, cut and dried, with the concrete particulars concealing the point of law: the record overladen with the uninteresting names of litigants and oblivious of the interesting names of sages, of justices, of sergeants. What they desired was the debate with the life-blood in it, the twists and turns of advocacy, the quip courteous and the countercheck quarrelsome. They wanted to remember what really fell from Bereford, C.J., his proverbs, his sarcasms . . . ." We are able in this volume to savor the personal as well as professional qualities of the protagonists in litigation, coming to know many of them as familiars. And through exposure to the minutes of the Court and personal journals we gain revealing glimpses into the management of the Court's business.

Litigation, as I have said, is only one phase of the contests, great and small, reaching the Court for judgment. The contests are recounted and analyzed with an intimacy made possible by prodigious labors of scholarship. From this intimacy arise new insights. Some of the great conflicts, notably Reconstruction, have been fought over by historians until the battlefield seems barren. What Professor Fairman has done to invigorate the subject is to explore the interrelations of Court, Congress, and state legislatures, revealing, for one thing, the effects of tall talk and obiter dicta in judicial opinions on the hardening of positions in the local editorial offices and legislative halls. Other conflicts of the period, notably the extensive controversies over municipal financing of railroad expansion in the western states, have been grossly neglected by historians. In order to assess the right of the matter as between the holders of repudiated bonds and the municipalities that repented of their frenzied finance, Professor Fairman has done a major original work of historical reconstruction. Here, as in the study of Reconstruction itself, he has wrung from legislative journals, court records, memoirs, and newspaper files the figures of politicians, publicists, litigants, and the interests behind litigants that are vital characters in the drama.

The whole work immerses us deeply in the affairs of Court and country. It is rich and penetrating, the product of many years of single-minded scholarly dedication.

Paul A. Freund

Preface

THIS FIRST OF TWO VOLUMES allotted to the period of Reconstruction and Reunion, 1864 to 1888, records the affirmation of
universal freedom and the framing and adoption of the Fourteenth
Amendment. Upon the basis of this new security for the protection of
all persons, by March 1870 the last of the secessionist States had been
restored to representation in Congress. In April 1873 in the *Slaughter
House Cases* the Court made its initial construction of the new Amendment. A few weeks later Chief Justice Chase died, while the Court was
in adjournment. This makes a convenient point at which to interrupt
the main thread of the account. Some topics, however, have been
carried to their conclusion, long after 1873—notably the discussion of
the adjustment of private relationships affected by the war, and the
controversies over municipal bonds issued in aid of railroad projects.

Some readers may expect that a book about the Supreme Court
will be entirely a composition in lofty strains. But to be truthful it must
be pointed out that in this period the Court's work as determined by
the Judiciary Act included a mass of commonplace litigation on matters
of private right, differing from what came before the State courts in
nothing save that the parties must be citizens of different States. And
only in exceptional circumstances did a matter of criminal justice reach
the Court. Enough is said in the present volume to substantiate these
observations. The Court's contributions to the growth of the common law
and to the special subjects of federal cognizance are reserved for consideration in the volume to follow.

It will be evident that the writing has been based upon bedrock:
the transcripts of record and briefs, the Court's Docket and Minutes,
sometimes the case files in the National Archives. For the States undergoing reconstruction, the proceedings of their constitutional con-

ventions, their session laws, and the legislative journals underlying the session laws received painstaking examination.

Records and briefs for the terms covered by the present volume are available in collections so few that one does not count beyond the fingers of one hand. I have been happy to work from microfilm produced according to my requirements. The set of paper books at the Michigan State Library at Lansing begins with those that belonged to Justice Bradley, which are enriched by his notes as he worked his way through the cases. My selections from that source crowd five reels of microfilm.[1]

Throughout the book the reader will recognize the value of the papers of Chief Justice Chase, some preserved by the Historical Society of Pennsylvania and some by the Library of Congress; those of Justice Davis, deposited with the Illinois State Historical Society at Springfield, and available by photoduplication at the Chicago Historical Society; and the letters of Justice Miller to his brother-in-law. I am obliged to the Library of Duke University for supplying from their Herschel V. Johnson papers the items quoted in the discussion of the *Cotton Tax Case*. It is by permission of the Harvard College Library that quotation is made from Charles Sumner papers there collected. Twenty reels from the Library of Congress microfilm of the Andrew Johnson papers, for years of his Presidency, were examined. This time-consuming exercise was undertaken because there was a fair prospect that it would prove useful: in the outcome it yielded some pertinent items, and a mass of observations of considerable cumulative effect. This is illustrative of numerous ventures, prudently undertaken, which as it turns out may return an abundance, or a trifle, or nothing at all.

Gatherings from many newspapers figure prominently in text and footnotes. We are concerned with a period that had nothing comparable to the present *New York Times* with its wide coverage and comprehensive *Index*. One must select, from what is available, such files as seem promising, and put them to the test. The preservation of old newspapers on microfilm has progressed so far as to make that the scholar's chief reliance.[2] Conditions in the South during the war and reconstruction were not favorable to the orderly production or to the preservation of newspapers. Enterprises were often short-lived, changes in ownership and in editorial policy were common; there are numerous gaps, small and large. Often the files of a journal of a century ago had so far deteriorated that it is only by aid of a magnifying glass that one

[1] I am grateful to Professor Samuel Krislov for drawing it to my attention that these books bore the comments of Justice Bradley; to Miss Charlotte C. Dunnebacke, the Librarian, for her courtesy and patience; and to the Michigan State Records Center for the execution of a difficult assignment.

[2] *Newspapers on Microfilm*, 6th edition 1967, compiled under the direction of George A. Schwegmann, Jr., and published by the Library of Congress.

can decipher. Amassing details for the chapters on municipal bonds involved a wearisome quest for newspapers reporting on communities affected. It seemed a great discovery to find that the *Missouri Republican*, published at St. Louis, had comprehensive reports of activities throughout the State in the years when resistance to judicial enforcement was most stubborn.

In the pursuit of newspapers and other materials I visited State archives, historical societies, and university libraries, selecting for photocopy useful papers, and learning from their collections of microfilm what it would be profitable for me to procure for examination in my study at home. I recall with gratitude the courtesy and helpfulness of the archivists and librarians along my way.

It was recognized from the beginning that the Library of Congress would provide "a center of information." The earliest report of the Permanent Committee promised that the authors' investigations "will reach far into collateral fields, in order to set the Court at all stages firmly in the political, economic, and intellectual context of the moment." That has involved the calling forth of materials from the far corners of that great repository, to be woven together at the author's desk. The Library has lent books, provided photoduplication of many items, and fulfilled numerous requests for specific bits of information. My file of correspondence, several inches thick, suggests the extent of the traffic.

The arrangements entered into in the summer of 1957 contemplated that an author would be able to complete his book within four years, with a semester or perhaps a year of leave from academic duties. It soon became manifest that for a due performance of my undertaking a far more persistent effort must be made. Thanks to Guggenheim and Social Science Research Council fellowships, and a share in grants made to the Committee by the Rockefeller Foundation, it was possible to be on leave from January 1960 to June 1962—and the work has continued incessantly since that time. In 1966 the Committee agreed that two volumes be allowed for my period.

Books and articles about the Court and the Justices are beyond numbering and, like the stars, "one differeth from another in brightness." Reconstruction has been the subject of spirited reinterpretation, and the outpouring of essays has quickened while the present volume was being written. Few of these titles will be mentioned in my chapters. To have expressed admiration for particular writings would have suggested a lack of appreciation for others. To have pronounced an adverse judgment without giving reasons would have sounded presumptuous; to have composed critical reviews would have been uncongenial and space-consuming. It has seemed the proper course simply to allow every tub to rest upon its own bottom. I have been busy hooping my barrel as tightly as skill permitted.

Every volume of the Reports bears evidence that while the Justices are sworn to "do equal right" there will yet be divergence in their conclusions. It must be patent that when one individual undertakes to appraise the work of the Bench over a period of years—and an exceedingly controversial one at that—it is beyond belief that all of his judgments will command universal assent. I have been mindful of the responsibility imposed by participation in the writing of our *History*, and have taken time to arrive at conclusions "according to the best of my abilities and understanding."

Charles Fairman

Reconstruction and Reunion
1864-88

PART ONE

CHAPTER I

Chief Justice Chase

W HEN THE SUPREME COURT began its term on the first Monday
in December 1864, the life of the Confederacy was ebbing.
Lee's Army of Northern Virginia was wasting behind the earthworks at
Petersburg. Sherman, marching from Atlanta to the sea, was approaching Savannah. The end of the struggle was at hand.

Amid these events the coming in of the Court was of small interest. The *National Intelligencer*—the capital's best newspaper—waited
until January 20, 1865, to make this mention:

> The present term of the Supreme Court of the United States
> commenced on Monday, the 5th ultimo, with the chair of the Chief
> Justice vacant, occasioned by the death of the Hon. Roger B. Taney.
> His successor, the Hon. Salmon P. Chase, took his seat on the bench
> on Thursday, the 15th of December last, and the Court was thus
> constituted, the Associate Justices ranking by seniority, as follows:
>
> Mr. Chief Justice Salmon P. Chase
> Mr. Justice James M. Wayne
> Mr. Justice John Catron
> Mr. Justice Samuel Nelson
> Mr. Justice Robert C. Grier
> Mr. Justice Nathan Clifford
> Mr. Justice Noah H. Swayne
> Mr. Justice Samuel F. Miller
> Mr. Justice David Davis
> Mr. Justice Stephen J. Field.
> The Reporter of the Court is J. W. Wallace, Esq., of Pennsyl-
> vania.
> Clerk—D. W. Middleton, Esq.
> Marshal—W. H. Lamon, Esq.

The *Intelligencer* recalled that the 37th Congress in 1863 had enlarged the Court to ten and had rearranged the circuits, providing an additional Justice to perform circuit duties in the Pacific States. The account explained the grouping of the States into circuits, to each of which was assigned a Justice who went about trying cases during the months from spring to late autumn when the Supreme Court was not in session. The Chief Justice presided over the Fourth Circuit, which extended from Delaware to North Carolina and West Virginia. Justice Wayne was assigned to the Fifth, comprising the Southeastern States; Justice Catron to the Sixth, stretching from Kentucky to Texas. Progress through these circuits had, of course, been interrupted by the war.

The Court, the *Intelligencer* continued, had begun its term with a docket of three hundred and sixty cases, sixty of which came from the South and were being passed over until peace was restored.[1] It might have explained that normally a case after being filed had to wait about two years before in turn it came up for argument. Thereupon it was considered in conference, assigned to a Justice for the writing of an opinion, and finally announced in open court as a decision. At this period of the Court's history the cases, in the main, were not difficult; ordinarily agreement came easily, and judgment might be rendered within perhaps three weeks after argument.

The 38th Congress also met on the first Monday in December, in its Second Session, that would expire on March 3, 1865. President Lincoln's message drew attention to the proposed amendment to the Constitution, abolishing slavery; it had passed the Senate, and now in the recent national election the people had clearly declared their will that it be adopted. On January 31, the House concurred with the Senate, and thus the Thirteenth Amendment was submitted to the States for ratification by their legislatures.

Chief Justice Taney had died on October 12, 1864. On December 6, shortly after the reading of the President's message, the Senate went into executive session, where it considered and forthwith consented to the nomination of Salmon P. Chase to be the Chief Justice. The appointment had been expected and gave general satisfaction.

CHASE'S ASSOCIATES

WHEN CHASE TOOK HIS SEAT, on December 15, 1864, he joined a group widely varied in age, experience, and talents. James M. Wayne of Georgia, the senior Associate Justice, had come to the Court in 1835,

---

[1] Infra, p. 135.

by appointment of President Jackson. Now venerable, calm, steadfast in his devotion to the Union under the Constitution, he awaited the day when "with a spirit exempt from the corruptions of party, our country will again be what it was before it became distracted by rebellion and scourged by civil war."[2]

John Catron of Tennessee, at seventy-eight the eldest of the Justices, was absent throughout the term and died on May 30, 1865. His place was not filled and, as will presently be seen, Congress in 1866 reduced the size of the Court.

Samuel Nelson, seventy-two, was completing twenty years on the Supreme Bench, after an even longer service on the courts of New York. Nelson walked straightly in the settled paths of the law, fearful of the precipitate course of the party in power.

Robert Cooper Grier, old at seventy, had spent more than thirty years in judicial office—on an inferior court of Pennsylvania and, since 1846, on the Supreme Court. He was forthright, even rugged, and a stanch Unionist. Thanks to a thorough classical education and a tough mind, his opinions had been vigorous and admirably concise.

Nathan Clifford of Maine, sixty-one years of age, came last among those appointed by Lincoln's Democratic predecessors. His mental habits showed the pinch of early circumstance. *Nathan Clifford, Democrat*, is the title justly given to his biography;[3] he held fixedly to the tenets of that party, seemed little moved by the nation's new birth of freedom, and was a narrow constructionist opposed to expansive judicial movements.

Chase's other four brethren were Swayne, just turned sixty, and Miller, Davis, and Field, all in their late forties. Noah H. Swayne, Virginia-born but opposed to slavery, had early hung up his shingle in Ohio. He had been United States Attorney under President Jackson, and thereafter had held high rank at the Columbus bar. Lincoln appointed him to the Court as successor to Justice McLean, in January 1862.[4] Swayne was affable and ingratiating, well-connected among Ohio Republicans, and highly regarded by the bar of his circuit. His opinions, sometimes sententious, showed a marked regard for authority, especially of the English cases.

Samuel Freeman Miller was one of the most remarkable men ever to reach the Supreme Bench, and certainly one of the greatest.

---

[2] 2 Wall. xii.

[3] Philip G. Clifford, *Nathan Clifford, Democrat (1803–1881)* (New York and London: G. P. Putnam's Sons, 1922).

[4] John McLean (1785–1861) of Ohio, Postmaster General under Presidents Monroe and John Quincy Adams, was appointed to the Court by President Jackson in 1829. He was assigned to the Seventh Circuit, in what was then the Northwest.

Born in Kentucky in 1816, he had practiced medicine in a village near Cumberland Gap, belatedly read law, and in 1847 was admitted to his new profession. After Kentucky rejected gradual emancipation, in 1850 he moved with his wife and children to Keokuk, Iowa, a growing town of 2,500 at the head of low-water navigation on the Mississippi. Thanks to a natural bent for the law, a vigorous intellect, and sustained application, by 1862 he stood at the head of the Iowa bar. He took leadership, too, among the State's active Republicans. Here was an authentic representative of the great Northwest, a section entitled to a major voice in the national councils. With no false modesty, Miller sought a place on the Court, and with united support from his State attained it, in July 1862.

David Davis, of Bloomington, Illinois, was a Marylander by birth; he had attended Kenyon College in Ohio, read law in New England, and begun practice in Illinois. For fourteen years he had been judge of the Eighth Judicial District, in central and eastern Illinois, where Lincoln practiced. He had managed Lincoln's interests in the Chicago convention in 1860. To obtain for Davis an appointment to the Supreme Court had been the sustained endeavor of the lawyers of the old circuit, and at long last the President's judgment concurred in that desire. To Judge Davis, a seat on the Court was a place, not a calling; he had professed to prefer the District Judgeship for Northern Illinois, "because I know I could discharge the duties of the one satisfactorily, but am diffident about the other."[5] Never renouncing politics, he developed an obvious preoccupation with the Presidency, and in 1877 left the Court to become a Senator through the votes of Democrats and Independents. Justice Davis was absent by reason of illness throughout the December term, 1864.

In 1863, when Congress created a tenth seat on the Court, the President appointed Stephen Johnson Field, the Chief Justice of California—a strong judge and in politics a War Democrat. Field had grown up in a New England parsonage. On graduating from Williams College he read law and then practiced with his brother, David Dudley Field, in New York City. In 1849 he sailed for California via the railroad at Panama—a route he was to pass and repass as a Justice until, in 1869, the transcontinental railroad was opened. He remained on the Court until his resignation in 1897. Field sat with Wayne, who had sat with Marshall, and Marshall had come to the Court in 1801. Three overlapping periods of service thus spanned almost a century of judicial history.

---

[5] Willard L. King, *Lincoln's Manager, David Davis* (Cambridge, Mass.: Harvard University Press, 1960), 191.

4

THE PRESIDENT REFLECTS ON
THE CHIEF JUSTICESHIP

THERE HAD BEEN NO NEED for the President to act before the Senate convened. In the meantime, with characteristic shrewdness and propriety, he held the matter in suspense.[6] As Secretary of the Treasury in Lincoln's Cabinet, Chase—assuming a lofty superiority in ability and in moral perception—had never given an unqualified support to his chief.[7] He had been more than receptive to a movement among impatient Republicans to put Lincoln aside and make Chase their candidate. On June 29, 1864, on the occasion of a difference with the President in the matter of an appointment, Chase offered his resignation (as he had at other junctures) and was chagrined when, this time, it was accepted.[8]

---

[6] He could have made no more than a *recess* appointment, which must expire by the end of the Senate's next session. Constitution, Art. II, Sec. 2, cl. 3. Or he could have announced what nomination he purposed to make when the Senate convened.

When Taney died, on Wednesday, October 12, the Presidential canvass was in full swing. On October 11, State elections in Indiana, Ohio, and Pennsylvania had shown a preference for Republicans—substantial, moderate, and narrow, respectively. The great test would come on Tuesday, November 8. Chase, now a private citizen, was bestirring himself in the canvass.

For Lincoln to designate Chase prior to the election would have made further campaigning on his part improper and would have tended to alienate conservative Unionists.

(Two years before, in October 1862, after months of waiting, Lincoln had given David Davis a recess appointment to the Court—an action that gave great satisfaction in Illinois. King, *Davis*, 199. However, when the Court came in on Monday, December 1, Davis did not present himself. He waited until December 10, when he offered letters patent of his permanent appointment, made on December 8 with the advice and consent of the Senate. Minutes of the Supreme Court.)

[7] An illustration is the Administration's crisis in December 1862, when Republican Senators sought to subordinate the President's action to the "combined wisdom" of a Radical-minded Cabinet—aiming to exclude Seward and make Chase the central figure. In bringing about this situation, Chase—in Professor Allan Nevins' words—"had spread his poison into every channel he could reach." *The War for the Union* (New York: Charles Scribner's Sons, 1959, 1960), II, 350–63. By contriving a meeting where Chase was brought face-to-face with the Senators he had incited and where he made a miserable showing, Lincoln managed to restore his own authority with a Cabinet representing the various shades of Unionist sentiment.

[8] "Chase you see hung on as long as possible and dropped off at last like a rotten pear unexpectedly to himself & everybody else. He supposed he would bully Lincoln by threatening to resign unless he was permitted to make the Treasury appts. without control . . . ." So wrote rancorous Francis P. Blair, Sr., to his son, Frank, Jr., on July 4, 1864. Ford Collection, New York Public Library. The enmity of the Blair family toward Chase would soon have something more to feed upon, when he was appointed to the Chief Justiceship coveted by Blair's other son, Montgomery.

He spent two months sojourning in New England, "peddling his griefs in private ears, and sowing dissatisfaction about Lincoln," at a season of despair when men were scheming to force Lincoln to withdraw in favor of some new candidate who might inspire confidence.[9] But September saw Republicans carry elections in Maine and Vermont—victories by Sherman at Atlanta and Sheridan at Winchester—and a new resolution by Chase to join in the effort to win the election for Lincoln.[10]

The death of Taney, at eighty-seven, had seemed imminent for months. At the time of Chase's departure from the Cabinet, Lincoln had given visitors to understand that he might have the Chief Justiceship when it became vacant. As soon as that moment arrived, Chase and his supporters became importunate.

Among these Senator Sumner was the most persistent, although neither he nor any other advocate had any dominant influence upon Lincoln. Under date of October 12, Sumner wrote from Boston, calling on the President to act:[11]

> Providence has given us a victory, in the death of Chief Justice Taney. It is a victory for Liberty & for the Constitution.
>
> Thus far the Constitution has been interpreted for Slavery. Thank God! it may now be interpreted surely for Liberty. The importance of this change cannot be exaggerated.
>
> Still further, the powers of the govt. in the conduct of the war, may now be vindicated, whether as regards the rebels or foreign nations.
>
> To this end, the successor of Chief Justice Taney must be a person, who, besides an acknowledged mastery of his profession, is an able, courageous, & determined friend of Freedom, who will never let Freedom suffer by concession or hesitation, & he must also have an aptitude for public law.

[9] The comment is from Samuel Bowles of the *Springfield Republican*. George S. Merriam, *Life and Letters of Samuel Bowles* (New York: Century Co., 1885), I, 413; James Ford Rhodes, *History of the United States from the Compromise of 1850* (New York: Macmillan Co., 1893–1906), IV, 527–29; James G. Randall and Richard N. Current, *Lincoln, the President: Last Full Measure* (New York: Dodd, Mead, 1955), 210–31.

[10] Chase's diary entry of September 17, in Jacob W. Schuckers, *The Life and Public Services of Salmon Portland Chase* (New York: D. Appleton and Co., 1874), 511; also in David Donald, ed., *Inside Lincoln's Cabinet. The Civil War Diaries of Salmon P. Chase* (New York, London, Toronto: Longmans, Green and Co., 1954), 254–55. Letter of October 2 to John Sherman, in Sherman, *Recollections of Forty Years* (Chicago, New York, London, Berlin: Werner Co., 1895), I, 340–42.

[11] Lincoln Papers, L.C. Taney died at about 11 P.M. on the twelfth. Carl B. Swisher, *Roger B. Taney* (New York: Macmillan Co., 1936), 577. Hence Sumner wrote in anticipation or instantly upon advice by telegraph— or misdated his letter.

At this moment, I think Mr. Chase fulfills more of these requirements than any other person, & I write at once to express my hope that he may be nominated. Let it go forth that he is Chief Justice & our cause will gain every where.

In a letter of October 14, Sumner informed Chase that he had promptly written to the President and had "urged anew the considerations to which he yielded last spring in favor of your nomination"; now, he wrote, "accept, & complete our great reformation by purifying the Constitution, & by upholding those measures through which the Republic will be saved."[12]

Chase's reply, from Cincinnati on the nineteenth, contained this passage:

It is perhaps not exactly *en règle* to say what one will do in regard to an appointment not tendered to him; but it is certainly not wrong to say to you that I should accept. I feel that I can do more for our cause & our country & for the success of the next Administration in that place than in any other. Happily it is now certain that the next Administration will be in the hands of Mr Lincoln from whom the world will expect great things. God grant that his name may go down to posterity with the two noblest additions historian ever recorded—Restorer and Liberator.[13]

Sumner copied this ingratiating profession and sent it to the President, in a letter of October 24; anti-slavery men, he wrote, were "trembling" lest the opportunity be lost of appointing a Chief Justice who would sustain the War Powers and "deal a death-blow to Slavery"; no "old-fashioned lawyer who has accepted for years pro-Slavery glosses can do this."[14] Also on October 24 he wrote to Chase, advising him of a reported effort on behalf of Justice Swayne:

I do not think this possible. It so happened that the Presdt. last spring mentioned Judge Swayne to me as the ablest of the new judges & a candidate for C.J. I spoke very frankly of the effect of such an appointment, & insisted that he had not the elements required for the head of the bench now. It was after this conversation that he said that he would tender the place to you, & I understand he has repeated this determination since, especially to the Senate Com^ttee when it visited him to know the occasion of your resignation. He then con-

---

12 Chase Papers, L.C.
13 Ibid.
14 In a third urgent letter, on November 20, he repeated his call for an announcement for Chase: "I thought it ought to have been made on the evening of Taney's funeral." Lincoln Papers, L.C.

fessed that you & he could not get along together in the Cabinet, but that he should be glad to make you C.J. John Sherman knows about this conversation.[15]

CANDIDACIES

THE ARRAY OF QUOTATIONS that follow will serve two purposes: to afford a narrative, and to demonstrate what were the qualifications regarded as important. As is usual when a seat on the Court is to be filled, names were suggested that never entered into the reckoning. Three candidacies are to be kept in view: that of Chase, sometime Senator, Governor, and recently Cabinet officer, and foremost public figure; that of Justice Swayne, senior among Lincoln's appointees to the Court; and —seemingly contingent upon Chase being passed by—that of William M. Evarts of New York, active practitioner who had distinguished himself in a wide range of public matters.

Evarts was then forty-six; Chase was fifty-six; Swayne would reach sixty in December.

Orville H. Browning—recently a Senator from Illinois, now busy with law and politics in Washington—on the morning after Taney's death called on Secretary Fessenden at the Treasury Department and inquired whether he would accept the Chief Justiceship if his friends procured it for him. As Browning recorded in his diary, Fessenden rejected the proposal, decisively; he said that

> he knew that the place was designed for Mr Chase, and that the appointment would be tendered to him, and accepted by him—that when Mr Chase resigned as Secretary of the Treasury, and [ex-Governor] Tod, of Ohio, was nominated to the vacancy he, Fessenden, as Chairman of the Finance Committee of the Senate called on the President to induce him to withdraw Tod's nomination and reinstate Mr Chase—that the President refused to do so, and showed a determination not to take him back into the cabinet, but remarked that he had great respect for Mr Chase, and that if the Chief Justiceship of the Supreme Court was now vacant he would appoint him to that place—that previously when it was thought the Chief Justice was near his end, he had made up his mind, in the event of his death to appoint Mr Chase, and that he had not changed his mind, and would appoint him now if the place was vacant. . . .[16]

---

[15] Letter of Oct. 24. Chase Papers, L.C. Senator Sherman was a member of the Committee on Finance, and William Pitt Fessenden (now Secretary of the Treasury, *vice* Chase) had then been its chairman.

[16] *Diary of Orville Hickman Browning* (Springfield: Illinois State Historical Library, Vol. I [1850–64], Theodore C. Pease and James G. Randall, eds., 1925; Vol. II [1865–81], Randall, ed., 1933). Entry for Oct. 13, 1864. I, 686–87.

(Tod had promptly declined; whereupon the President nominated Fessenden, without his knowledge.[17])

Browning's objective was to avert the appointment of Chase. Of like mind was the venerable Thomas Ewing of Ohio—former Senator, Cabinet officer, and recently Browning's partner in a practice that consisted largely in influencing action within the Government.[18] Henry Stanbery, Ewing's friend and former partner, recommended Swayne, with an implication adverse to Chase.[19] Glancing ahead, in 1866 Stanbery and Browning would sit together in Andrew Johnson's Cabinet, while Ewing would be his trusted counsellor. Reactions to the prospect of having Chase as Chief Justice have a close correlation with later attitudes on the issues of Reconstruction and the future status of the Negro.

Edwin M. Stanton was gladdened by the thought that the President might now relieve him of the burden of the War Department by a transfer to Taney's place. Justice Grier, well acquainted with Stanton's great power as a lawyer, encouraged him in that thought by the following letter from Philadelphia on October 13:

> I have just received your telegraph [*sic*] announcing the death of Chief Justice Taney. Although often differing in opinion with him I had the highest respect and esteem for him & sincerely lament his loss.
>
> I see speculations are already rife as to his successor. It is a question in which I feel a deep interest. I know of no man more competent to fill the place, or who *deserves it so much* as yourself. You have been wearing out your life in the service of your country & have fulfilled the duties of your very responsible & laborious office with unexampled ability, and I think the president owes it to you & that you should be suffered to retire in this honorable position.
>
> I see the papers are already beginning to put forward the name of Mr Chase, but I presume the president will not be persuaded thereby, that he is the choice either of the bar or the people—or attend to the dictation of the *journalocracy*.
>
> It would give me the greatest pleasure and satisfaction to have you preside on our bench. I am sure you would be the *right man* in the *right place*.[20]

---

[17] Carl Sandburg, *Abraham Lincoln; The War Years* (New York: Harcourt, Brace and Co., 1939), III, 109–17.

[18] Belatedly, Ewing on December 3 advised the President that Chase "would not be acceptable to the Bar of Ohio . . . . He is a politician rather than a lawyer" and, Ewing feared, would be "intriguing & trading for the Presidency." Lincoln Papers, L.C.

[19] He wrote of Swayne: "I do not know of any one in this region of the Country whose appointment . . . would give such general satisfaction . . . ." Letter from Cincinnati on Oct. 31. Lincoln Papers, L.C.

[20] Stanton Papers, L.C.

By invitation, Browning called on Mrs. Stanton on Sunday, October 16. (The Secretary was then at Grant's headquarters—where he learned that the general wanted him to stay at the War Department.) Mrs. Stanton expressed a strong desire that her husband be appointed Chief Justice. Next day Browning urged the President to name Stanton. He learned that Attorney General Bates wanted the place.[21]

Ex-Governor Tod wrote to Lincoln on October 17,

> to advise that you leave the Chief Justiceship vacant until after the fall of Richmond and then tender the position to Stanton. "I know whereof I speak. ". . .[22]

Secretary Fessenden—responding to an inquiry from Chase—sent this reassurance on October 20:

> . . . I think there can be no doubt about it. The Prest said to me of his own motion that he "had not forgotten" our conversations, but as things were going on well he thought it best not to make any appointment, or say any thing about it, until the election was over.
> Do not give yourself any anxiety, whatever you may see in the papers. Neither Stanton nor I will allow our names to be used. *So far*, you are safe, at least, & I believe all is right.

On November 18 he replied to another note from Chase: "I have no doubt you will be C. J. . . ."[23]

Stanton—also replying to a letter from Chase—wrote on November 19, disclaiming any desire to have the office for himself.

> In regard to the chief-justiceship, I learn from outside sources that Swayne is the most active and Blair the most confident of the candidates. My belief is that you will be offered the appointment, if it has not already been done. . . .[24]

Montgomery Blair's candidacy may be dismissed in short order. He had been dropped from his place as Postmaster General in September, to placate the Radical Republicans. Now he and his father, Francis

---

[21] *Diary*, I, 687–88. Benjamin P. Thomas and Harold M. Hyman, *Stanton: The Life and Times of Lincoln's Secretary of War* (New York: Alfred A. Knopf, 1962), 336–39.

[22] Lincoln Papers, L.C. He did not explain: perhaps an intimation from Stanton?

Tod and Stanton had long been acquainted in prewar Democratic politics in Ohio. Tod had been a Douglas delegate to the National Democratic Convention in 1860. On the position of the Negro he was not nearly so advanced as Chase.

[23] Chase Papers, Hist. Soc. of Pa.

[24] Schuckers, *Chase*, 512–13; Thomas and Hyman, *Stanton*, 338.

P. Blair, Sr., craved his appointment as a vindication. Gideon Welles, Secretary of the Navy, gave him support: he told the President that the Chief Justice should possess such qualifications as "a judicial mind," "not a partisan, but one who was impressed with the principles and doctrines which had brought this Administration into power"—and that among the candidates, Blair "best conformed to these requirements."[25] Actually, as the next few years proved, Blair—like his father, and brother Frank, Jr. (for the family acted as a unit)—was unsafe in judgment, an inveterate partisan, an enemy of the Civil Rights Act, a defender of government by white men only, a fanatical opponent of Congressional Reconstruction.[26] If, in the account of strained relations between Congress and the Court presently to be pursued, one were to imagine that Blair, rather than Chase, had been made Chief Justice, the dangers would seem appalling. But it is not to be supposed that Lincoln ever had the slightest thought of appointing Blair.

THE JUSTICES PROPOSE SWAYNE

THE RISE AND FALL of Swayne's candidacy was recorded by Justice Davis in a letter of December 12, 1864, to his brother-in-law, Judge Julius Rockwell of Massachusetts. Davis was at that moment at his home in Illinois, where for some weeks he had been confined to bed. He wrote at length:

> . . . I much desired the appointment of Judge Swayne, & have done all that was proper in his behalf. After I heard of the death of Chief Justice Taney, while quite sick, I dictated a letter to the Presᵈᵗ earnestly recommending Judge Swayne, & for fear that he had not received the letter I wrote again on the eve of the meeting of Congress.[27] As soon as I saw an intimation in the papers, that

---

[25] *Diary of Gideon Welles* (Boston and New York: Houghton Mifflin Co., 1911), II, 181–82, entry for Nov. 26, 1864.

[26] Montgomery Blair's political management during one brief period bulks large in *Politics, Principle, and Prejudice, 1865–66* (New York: Free Press of Glencoe, 1963), by LaWanda and John H. Cox.

[27] Letters of Oct. 22 and Nov. 29, 1864. Lincoln Papers, L.C.

The salient points on behalf of Swayne were that "Although of decided political views he has never been an active partisan," and that "Judge Swayne is a good Lawyer, well grounded in the principles of the common law, but not a mere book Lawyer. He is not a narrow man, yet careful of precedent, giving it always its great and due weight, but wearing no chains whatever. He has *good temper*, an important requisite, and unless my brother judges have changed since last winter, his appointment would be very agreeable to many of them. . . ." The qualification, to *many of* them, was added as a correction.

my name was talked of, I wrote to Gov Dennison (Judge Swayne's intimate friend) advising him of what I had done, & that I was not a candidate.[28]

If the Pres^{dt} took any one from the bench, it was eminently proper that he sh^d select Judge Swayne. He was his first appointee, & by all odds the best lawyer among his appointees.

Last winter when it was supposed that Judge Taney might die at any moment the majority of the Court desired Judge Swayne's app^t and I went at their instance to the Pres^{dt} and so told him, adding my own wishes on the subject, & begging him not to appoint Chase.

I received a letter, on Saturday [Dec. 10] from Washington, stating that Judge Grier went to the Pres^{dt} on last Monday [Dec. 5], & stated that the appnt of Judge Swayne w^d be very acceptable to the Court.

I understand that of the Cabinet, Seward, Wells [sic], Usher[29] & Dennison were earnest for Swayne & against Chase. (I dont know how the others stood). *They* did not know that Chase's name was sent in, or determined on, until after the event.

It is also said that the Blairs were taken wholly by surprise.

Although *I* would not have appointed Mr Chase and although I think the Pres^{dt} ought not to have done so, yet as it is done, it is the part of good philosophy to bear it well, & not to fret about it. I dont propose to disturb myself about it at all.

I congratulate myself that I was not in Washington, for I should have been conspicuous in opposing him. I hope for the best & have no doubt that by the time I get there that the Court will be moving along smoothly, & that all will be harmonious.[30]

"Last winter," Davis here wrote, at a moment when Taney's death seemed imminent, he had gone to the President on behalf of "a majority" of the Court. (The Minutes show that Taney was absent from December 14, 1863, until April 8, 1864.) And then on December 5, 1864, Grier had gone to reiterate that Swayne would be very acceptable. (We have seen Grier's expression of his desire that Stanton be appointed.[31]) Doubtless the senior Justices, all Democrats, had an aversion to the advent of Chase—and in that context would have welcomed the promotion of Swayne. Miller and Field will be mentioned presently; each recorded his support of Chase.[32]

---

[28] William Dennison, who like Swayne resided in Columbus, Ohio, had been Chase's successor as Governor; now he was Postmaster General, in succession to Montgomery Blair.

[29] Secretary of the Interior.

[30] Davis Papers, Ill. State Hist. Soc.

[31] Supra, p. 9.

[32] Infra, pp. 14, 15, 16.

SUPPORT FOR CHASE

RECOMMENDATIONS TO LINCOLN about the Chief Justiceship, when read critically, are instructive. Spontaneity, eagerness and even zeal marked the messages in support of Chase. Justice Jacob Brinkerhoff of the Supreme Court of Ohio wrote on October 14:

> I think I cannot be mistaken in saying that at least ninety nine in every hundred of the loyal men of Ohio wish—strongly wish—to hear that he has been designated . . . .
>
> . . . In all the qualities of a lawyer fitting him for the adjudication of the ordinary run of cases, he has in my opinion no superior on the bench or off of it; while he is at the same time *preeminently* fitted to take a leading part in the decision of the numerous and most important judicial questions of a political character which must arise out of the rebellion.[33]

Brinkerhoff, it should be explained, was devout in the anti-slavery cause —as he had shown in his service in Congress (1843–47) and on the Ohio bench, where in a dissenting opinion in 1859 he had declared the Fugitive Slave Law unconstitutional.[34] Perhaps to the Judge's way of thinking, the category of "loyal men" was somewhat strictly confined.[35]

Worthy of particular attention is the letter of Timothy Danielson Lincoln of Cincinnati—eminent at the bar, and well known to the President. (Seven years earlier they had been on opposite sides in the important Rock Island Bridge litigation, tried before Justice McLean.[36]) Like a prudent counsellor, he cautioned that "Very many of the measures which Congress and you as the Chief Magistrate . . . have been compelled to adopt to carry us through this struggle" would soon be tested in suits—concerning the draft, the currency, credit and revenue, and many other matters.

> They will be pressed with great pertinacity, if not bitterness and it is very important that some one familiar with & friendly to these measures be in this place.

---

[33] Lincoln Papers, L.C.

[34] *Ex parte* Bushnell, 9 Ohio St. 77, 221.

[35] Compare what Senator Henry S. Lane later advised the President: "Every Union man in Indiana *desires* Gov Chase's appt. & every Democrat *expects* it." Quoted by Speaker Colfax to Chase in a letter of Dec. 5, 1864. Chase Papers, Hist. Soc. of Pa.

[36] In the federal Circuit Court at Chicago. See Albert J. Beveridge, *Abraham Lincoln 1809–1858* (Boston and New York: Houghton Mifflin Co., 1928), I, 598–601; *Collected Works of Abraham Lincoln*, Roy P. Basler, ed. (New Brunswick, N.J.: Rutgers University Press, 1953), II, 413–22.

Furthermore, for three decades the Supreme Court "was willingly being floated along in the current" of pro-slavery Democratic rule.

> Now it seems to me to be the duty of the President to select for the Presiding Judge of that Court one who has well defined and deep seated anti-Slavery views and whose construction of the Constitution will be in that spirit. We want a man who is an able lawyer, has broad views of public policy, and whose private and public character stands high before the World . . . . Few of the old Judges of that Court have any sympathy with those principles which underlie the whole drift of events . . . toward an obliteration of Slavery, and none of the new ones, except Mr. Justice Miller, had any push until this struggle commenced: nor have any of them breadth of mind and strength of will and long and well considered contemplation of the subject from this stand point . . . .

Chase, he continued, was the man for whom the country now was looking to fill the Chief Justiceship.[37] The author had been an ardent opponent of slavery, yet he was writing with a cool head.

Stanley Matthews (who had read law in Chase's office) and other leading Cincinnatians instantly busied themselves in support of Chase.[38] (Matthews was appointed to the Supreme Court in 1881, upon the resignation of Swayne.) From San Francisco came a telegram from Governor F. F. Low and Justice Field, expressing their opinion that the appointment of Chase would be "eminently judicious & highly satisfactory to the loyal people of the Pacific Coast."[39] At New York City, David Dudley Field wrote the President a quite energetic request for the appointment of Chase: "His position as a lawyer will justify it, while his integrity, candor, and devotion to the cause of human freedom, made it eminently fit . . . ."[40] William Curtis Noyes, another leader at that bar, described Chase as "eminently qualified to discharge judicial duties and especially those so important as the many great ones that come before the Supreme Court."[41]

Judge Bland Ballard, whom Lincoln had appointed to the District Court for Kentucky in 1861, wrote that Chase was preeminently quali-

---

[37] Letter of October 17. Lincoln Papers, L.C. T. D. Lincoln described himself as "a constant and steadfast friend of your Administration at all times, and as one who has felt personally friendly with you"—which was meaningful. To Chase, in a congratulatory letter on December 10, T. D. Lincoln recalled their association in the early '40's, when "to be called an Abolitionist was to be tabooed in so-

cial, business and political relations. What a change—indeed what a glorious change!!" Chase Papers, L.C.

[38] Communications sent to Postmaster General Dennison were forwarded to the President without comment. Lincoln Papers, L.C.

[39] Lincoln Papers, L.C.

[40] Letter of Oct. 14. Ibid.

[41] Letter of Oct. 22. Ibid.

fied to serve on the Court in the period then at hand. "The times require a man of firmness and deep conviction as well as one of learning and ability."[42] Members of the judiciary and bar of Connecticut wrote that Chase, "while possessing the high esteem of the great mass of his loyal fellow citizens," was also the one "most likely to command . . . the confidence and respect of judges and lawyers . . . ."[43]

The four Justices of the Supreme Court of Iowa urged the selection of Chase. The significant point to note is their statement of the qualifications they regarded as important:

> We need not say that Govr Chase is an able lawyer. He is more than this, and it is chiefly because he is more that we are solicitous for his appointment. He has in our opinion that strength of intellect—that intimate and thorough knowledge of the great and fundamental principles underlying the national structure—and is so fully in sympathy with the right view of those questions which at the present crisis are rendered difficult & intricate—that he would come to their consideration not as the mere lawyer, but also as the able and far seeing statesman. Such a man, we humbly submit we need in this position at this time, and for years to come. . . .[44]

John Sherman (Chase's successor as Senator from Ohio) went campaigning in Iowa, where he encountered Justice Miller; he wrote to the President from Des Moines on October 22 to report:

> In a conversation with Judge Miller of the Supreme Court last evening he authorized me to say to you that he preferred the appointment of Gov. Chase as Chief Justice to any one named—and that he knew Judge Field concurred in this.
> He said he felt some delicacy in writing you as last winter he concurred in authorizing Judge Davis to say for him that the appointment of Judge Swayne would be acceptable—but subsequent reflection satisfied him that the public service would be best promoted by the selection of Gov. Chase. As the hearty concurrence of the newly appointed Judges is vitally important I deem it proper to inform you of these facts . . . .

This accords with Justice Davis' account of the message he had carried to the President the previous winter, in the letter to Rockwell, quoted

---

[42] Letter of Nov. 2. Ibid.

[43] Lincoln Papers, L.C. Dated "November, 1864." Among the signatories were ex-Chief Justice Henry M. Waite and ex-Judge William W. Ellsworth: the son of the former became, and the father of the latter had been, Chief Justice of the Supreme Court of the United States.

[44] Ibid. Dated December 5, it arrived after the nomination had been made: but that is irrelevant to the point for which it is here quoted. Two of the signers were outstanding as Judges: George G. Wright and John F. Dillon. Infra, pp. 923, 941, 990.

above.[45] That incident will be considered in a moment. Now returning to Sherman's letter to the President:

> I can assure you with great confidence that the profession in the States West of the Mississippi generally agree that Chase will bring more Judicial Strength to the Bench than any one named. I telegraphed you from Chicago in consequence of very decided opinions expressed there in favor of Chase.[46] With no personal preference between Chase & Swayne it is my firm conviction that Chase will reflect higher honor in the exalted position of Chief Justice than Judge Swayne & his appointment could be justified by obvious political reasons.[47]

Schuyler Colfax of Indiana, Speaker of the House of Representatives, was campaigning through eight Western States. He informed the President that there was a "general desire" for the appointment of Chase, and repeated Justice Miller's statement of his preference.[48]

Consider now what had happened "last winter," when the Justices, anticipating Taney's death, authorized Davis to suggest to the President that Swayne would be acceptable to them when the time came.[49] On reflection, such action is quite understandable. The four senior Associate Justices, old Democrats, doubtless would much prefer a "mere lawyer" (the Iowa Judges' phrase) to any "far seeing statesman" Lincoln would be likely to choose. They had found their Brother Swayne to be a well-read lawyer, courteous and amiable from first meeting. The old Justices could expect nothing more agreeable than that the succession be quietly settled upon him. (Public attention had not then been focused upon Taney's replacement. Chase was busy running the Treasury Department;

---

[45] Supra, p. 12.

[46] Telegram of Oct. 19. Lincoln Papers, L.C.

[47] Lincoln Papers, L.C.

In Sherman's *Recollections*, I, 340–43, are letters of this period from Chase to Sherman. That of November 12 shows that he was very anxious about the appointment, although he professed to "give little heed" to reports. Sherman, replying on November 27 after an absence in New York City, reported that "*all* our leading friends *who were not candidates* desired your nomination . . . ." Chase Papers, Hist. Soc. of Pa.

[48] Letters from South Bend, Indiana, Oct. 23, and (after seeing Justice Miller at Keokuk) from Quincy, Illinois, on Nov. 3. Lincoln Papers, L.C. From the same places, on Oct.

24 and Nov. 3, Colfax wrote encouraging letters to Chase. Chase Papers, Hist. Soc. of Pa.

[49] Taney, in a message to Davis on Wednesday, December 16, 1863, wrote: "I was so hoarse [at conference] on Saturday [December 12] that I was unable to discuss any of the cases before us as I wished to do . . . . And the cold air from the broken pane of glass at the court room, did its work so effectually upon my head, that I have been obliged to lie quietly in bed for the last three days. I am up today . . . . I hope to be in Court on Friday." Davis Papers, Ill. State Hist. Soc.

Actually he did not return until April 8, ten days before the term was closed.

his thoughts for his own advancement were fixed upon the Presidency.) Davis held Swayne in admiration, and had formed sympathetic attachments among the older Justices; he did not want the war to lead to any sweeping change in constitutional development. Being close to Lincoln, he was the only appropriate messenger for the majority. How heartily Miller may have concurred, what may have been Field's position, *quaere*.[50] Doubtless it would have been embarrassing, and perhaps seemingly inexpedient, to take a stand against the promotion of this colleague.

So far as Justice Miller was concerned, just at that moment something happened in his relations with Swayne. On December 16, 1863, the Court heard argument in *Gelpcke v. Dubuque*[51]—which became the leading case establishing the enforceability in federal courts of municipal railroad-aid bonds notwithstanding that by State court decisions they were invalid. On January 11, 1864, this decision was announced, by Justice Swayne. His opinion closed with this sentiment: "We shall never immolate truth, justice, and the law, because a State tribunal has erected the altar and decreed the sacrifice."[52] Justice Miller dissented, and warned: "What this may lead to it is not possible now to foresee, nor do I wish to point out the field of judicial conflicts, which may never occur . . . ." But bitter and protracted conflicts did occur, with the highest courts of Iowa, Wisconsin, Michigan, Missouri and, with less intensity, with others, including the courts of Illinois and New York. The cleavage within the Court widened, with Swayne protecting the bondholders and Miller sustaining the taxpayers. In 1878 Miller referred to the course of the majority in these words:

> It is the most painful matter connected with my judicial life that I am compelled to take part in a farce whose result is invariably the same, namely to give more to those who have already, and to take away from those who have little, the little that they have.[53]

Wherever the merits may appear to lie—and the examination is intricate and toilsome[54]—the difference was so important that one would

---

50 Davis' statement was that "the majority of the Court" desired Swayne.

51 1 Wall. 175. Infra, p. 935.

52 The State tribunal in this case was the Supreme Court of Iowa. The remark remained "a barbed arrow that will long rankle and wound," said Beck, J., in 1869. This was in Holman v. Fulton, a habeas corpus case where the Iowa Judge released county supervisors from the custody of a United States Marshal executing a writ of attachment from a federal Circuit Court. *Keokuk Gate City*, March 30, 1869. Infra, p. 969.

53 To his brother-in-law, William P. Ballinger, January 13, 1878. Charles Fairman, *Mr. Justice Miller and the Supreme Court, 1862–1890* (Cambridge, Mass.: Harvard University Press, 1939), 231.

54 Infra, chs. 17 and 18.

suppose that Miller would thenceforth be unwilling to see Swayne become Chief Justice.

Whatever Justice Field's position may have been at the time of Davis' mission in favor of Swayne, it seems that in April 1864 he professed his desire that Chase become Chief Justice. This appears in a letter from Chase to Field, written in 1866:

> Do you remember when, just before the end of the term, in the spring of 1864, you met me on the avenue, and expressed your warm wish that I might fill the place I now occupy? If you have forgotten it, I have not, nor shall I ever forget it. It took me by surprise, but was very grateful to my feelings.[55]

When the place became vacant, six months thereafter, Field sent the telegram already quoted, endorsing Chase.[56]

SUPPORT FOR SWAYNE

SUPPORT FOR JUSTICE SWAYNE—aside from the gestures by his brethren—appears to have come largely from admiring practitioners within his circuit, plus some adventitious benefit from men bent upon stopping Chase. The recommendations of Swayne preserved among the Lincoln Papers lack the warmth and spontaneity found in many of those on behalf of Chase. From Detroit, Ross Wilkins, Judge for the Eastern District of Michigan, wrote on October 24 that he had "been informed" that Swayne had been proposed "by his associates & by prominent statesmen & jurists"; he wished to join in commending one so "well qualified by professional habitude & eminent ability." The District Attorney, Alfred Russell, on November 7 added that the appointment could "give perhaps greater satisfaction to the Profession and the Country" than any other. H. H. Emmons (appointed Circuit Judge in 1870) wrote on

---

[55] Robert B. Warden, *An Account of the Private Life and Public Services of Salmon Portland Chase* (Cincinnati, Ohio: Wilstach, Baldwin and Co., 1874), 647. The Chief Justice wrote on April 30, 1866. On April 3 the Court had adjourned, and Field, setting out to hold his Circuit Courts on the Pacific Coast, had been taken quite ill—as Chase learned from Cyrus W. Field, the Justice's brother. In words of personal affection such as Chase seldom addressed to a colleague, he wrote:

You must take the best care of yourself, not only for the sake of your family, but of your country, which now needs true patriotism as well as legal learning upon the bench. I feel all the interest of warm personal friendship in your welfare. It is not in my nature to forget friends, even where serious differences of judgment and political affinities come in to make separation; and no such differences come between us. . . . Then followed the recollection quoted in the text.

[56] Supra, p. 14.

November 14 that "with all the leading members of our bar I feel a great desire" for Swayne's appointment. From Cincinnati, Judge Humphrey H. Leavitt of the Southern District of Ohio wrote on October 30 that there was "no one, in my judgment, more eminently qualified . . . , or whose appointment would be more acceptable to the Bar and the Public."[57] He dwelt upon Swayne's learning, "acceptable manners," and "entirely orthodox and reliable" views on "great constitutional questions" then arising. He added, pointedly, "Nothing, I am persuaded can ever induce him while on the bench to enter the arena of political strife. . . ." Judge Hiram V. Willson of the Northern District of Ohio on November 10 forwarded his statement that there were "but few if any judges or lawyers in the 7th federal Circuit, who do not desire the appointment" of Swayne. He mentioned Swayne's "large and long practice," "his remarkable memory of English & American adjudged cases," and "his great amenity of manner."

Particular interest attaches to the letter of Morrison R. Waite, from Toledo on October 22. (Ten years later, when next the Chief Justiceship was to be filled, the choice would fall upon him.)

> Having been for many years familiarly acquainted, socially and professionally, with Judge Swayne . . . , I beg leave to recommend him for appointment to the office of Chief Justice. He has always stood in the front rank of the profession, and his appointment as Associate Justice was, so far as my knowledge extends, universally approved by his brethren. His promotion . . . would, I am quite sure, be equally acceptible [*sic*].

One infers that this was induced by some of Swayne's more insistent friends.[58] If Waite had felt any eagerness for the appointment of Chase, he would not have given even so restrained an endorsement of Swayne.[59]

---

[57] On the clash Judge Leavitt had had with Governor Chase, see p. 30.

[58] Compare what General Rutherford B. Hayes was thinking in his camp in Virginia on December 12: "I am very glad Governor Chase is Chief Justice. I had almost given up his appointment. I received letters from Swayne's friends urging me to write in his behalf. I heard nothing of the kind from friends of Governor Chase. I suppose they felt safe." *Diary and Letters of Rutherford Birchard Hayes* (Columbus: Ohio State Archeological and Historical Soc., 1922–26), II, 547.

In 1855, in the case of Rosetta, a slave girl brought from Kentucky to Ohio, wherein Chase won her release on habeas corpus from the State court, he had as associate "R. B. Hayes, a young lawyer of great promise," who "acquitted himself with great distinction." So Chase wrote on March 19, 1864, to J. T. Trowbridge—in one of a series of letters supplying material for his popular biography, *The Ferry-Boy and the Financier*, published in 1864. Warden, *Chase*, 344–45.

[59] In 1862 Waite had accepted the nomination for Congress as candidate of pro-Administration moderates, in opposition to the choice of the radical wing of the party, James M. Ashley, who would make abolition the pri-

The pith of these letters was that Swayne was a learned and amiable judge, and that lawyers who tried cases before him desired his promotion (notwithstanding the candidacy of Chase).

SUPPORT FOR EVARTS

IF THE PLACE were to be filled from the active bar, William M. Evarts had the most impressive credentials.[60] The case was well put by Justice Horace Gray of the Supreme Judicial Court of Massachusetts, in a statement to his associate, Justice Ebenezer R. Hoar (Evarts' cousin), and by him sent on to the White House. (From 1881 to 1902, Horace Gray sat on the Supreme Court: successor to Clifford, predecessor to Holmes.)

> I have no hesitation in agreeing with you that if for any reason the President should not appoint Mr Chase Chief Justice, Mr Evarts is the fittest of those who have been prominently named for that great place, and his nomination the most satisfactory to the profession that could be made.
>
> I know of no man who combines so large and assured a grasp of the law of nations with so thorough an education and experience in municipal law, or from whom better hopes could be entertained of an upright, high toned and brilliant judicial career, and of a firm and successful carrying out of the great principles which have been the corner stones of the policy of this administration.

Chief Justice George T. Bigelow of the same court wrote that he knew of no one "who in every aspect is so well qualified to fill the office" as Evarts.

---

mary goal. Ashley received 39 percent of the votes and was elected; Waite 32 percent, and the Peace Democrat 29 percent. C. Peter Magrath, *Morrison R. Waite: The Triumph of Character* (New York: Macmillan Co., 1963), 67–71.

In 1864, Ashley was urging the appointment of Chase: it "would give great satisfaction to the earnest union men of the country, & I feel confident our cause would be safe in his keeping . . . ." Letter of Nov. 14 to the President. Lincoln Papers, L.C.

[60] On October 15, 1864, Evarts wrote to Richard Henry Dana, Jr., of Boston, acknowledging Dana's offer of support: "I am willing to take the office and willing to be presented as the candidate of the profession and of public opinion for the place even if I should not get it. . . . A good deal of interest has been spontaneously shown here [in New York] . . . by persons of the *highest* political influence. . . ." Evarts had been "on the point of writing" to Dana on that subject. Brainerd Dyer, *The Public Career of William M. Evarts* (Berkeley: University of California Press, 1933), 156–57. The quotation is from a letter among the Evarts Papers in the possession of the family.

He is in the prime of life, possessed of abundant learning and professional ability, of a spotless integrity, great energy of purpose & administrative talent, & perfectly sound in his political views & principles.

Bigelow's concluding comment reflected the recent decline in confidence in the Court: he observed that the appointment of Evarts would
.
secure a just, wise and liberal interpretation of the Constitution of the United States, adapted to carry forward and establish the principles of regulated liberty, & would restore & preserve the confidence of the people of the whole country in our highest judicial tribunal.[61]

The seven Judges of the New York Court of Appeals certified their "entire confidence" in Evarts' qualifications—referring to "his extended and varied juridical learning and his position in the front rank of the Bar of this State"; also "the refinement, courtesy and dignity of his manners." Nothing was said about soundness of political views or needed changes in constitutional doctrine: the signatories were not of one party, and they spoke of qualities that were above controversy.[62] Like points had been made, with considerable elaboration, in a letter from Alexander S. Johnson, a former Chief Judge, who observed that Evarts' experience had extended to some of "the largest public questions with which the human intellect is ever called to deal."[63]

---

[61] Gray's letter of Nov. 14 to Hoar, and Bigelow's of Nov. 17 to the President, are in the Lincoln Papers, L.C.

[62] Lincoln Papers, L.C. The statement was sent to the President under cover of a letter of November 21 from Judge Henry E. Davies; the statement is in his handwriting.

[63] Letter of Nov. 7. Ibid. Johnson— a grandson of President John Adams —had sat on the Court of Appeals from 1852 to 1860. He cited three of Evarts' greatest cases: Lemmon v. People, 20 N.Y. 562 (1860); United States v. Baker et al., Fed. Case No. 14,501 (C.C.S.D.N.Y. 1861); and the Prize Cases, 2 Bl. 635 (1863).

Lemmon, a citizen of Virginia, had brought slaves to New York en route to Texas. Upon their release on habeas corpus, an appeal was carried to the State's highest court. Charles O'Conor, retained by the State of Virginia, argued for a right of passage through a free State. (This was in accord with his personal view that slavery was just and beneficent.) On O'Conor in Reconstruction matters, see infra, pp. 386–389, 607–12.

Evarts, engaged by the State of New York, argued that neither the United States Constitution (in particular, Privileges and Immunities Clause of Art. IV, and Commerce Clause) nor statutes, nor the constitution or statutes of New York, nor the principles of the law of nations, gave legal cause for restraint of human liberty in New York. The Court of Appeals sustained the release.

Appearing for the petitioner in first instance was John Jay—grandson of the first Chief Justice, and a leader in the anti-slavery cause. See infra. Associated with Evarts was Chester A. Arthur, later the President. Sherman Evarts, Arguments and Speeches of William Maxwell Evarts (New York: Macmillan Co., 1919), I, 3–13, Chester L. Barrows, William M.

21

THE PRESIDENT'S MISGIVINGS ABOUT CHASE

LINCOLN WAS FULLY COGNIZANT of Chase's great powers: he made handsome acknowledgment to visitors, and made it clear that he would overlook all personal vexations. He was mindful of the large place Chase had taken in public expectation about the appointment. He felt assured—so far as a President properly could be when choosing a Judge—that Chase would sustain the war measures. But he had one great misgiving: Chase's consuming ambition to be President.[64] An authentic statement is that of Speaker Colfax, writing to Chase on Monday, December 5, the day Congress assembled. He had had "a long talk" with the President on Friday; Sumner had seen him on Saturday; Senator

---

Evarts (Chapel Hill: University of North Carolina Press, 1941), 83–87.

United States v. Baker, the Trial of the Savannah Pirates, was an indictment, under the Piracy Statute, of officers and crew of a ship, commissioned as a privateer by the Confederate President, who had captured the ship of citizens of the United States. Evarts led for the prosecution. The jury failed to agree.

In the Prize Cases the question was whether the President might lawfully blockade ports in the possession of the rebels, without a declaration by Congress that war existed. Evarts argued that "the Government is to be guided and controlled . . . by the facts that are before it"; that it had lawful power to meet the rebellion "by means that were appropriate to the actual front and power, and threat of force in war, that were moved against the Government . . . ." The majority, per Grier, J., sustained the captures, in language similar to Evarts'. *Speeches*, I, 214, 220–23, 269–70.

Counsel for the claimants included James M. Carlisle, a leading figure.

Associated with Evarts in the Prize Cases was, among others, Richard Henry Dana, Jr., then United States Attorney for the District of Massachusetts.

Judge Hoar and Dana called on Lincoln in November 1864 to talk about the Chief Justiceship—but said that if he had determined to appoint

Chase they would proceed no further. Rhodes, *History of the U.S.* V, 45–46—recording Hoar's recollection of Lincoln's comments: high respect for Chase's ability—determination to overlook their personal troubles and Chase's supercilious criticism—hesitation by reason of Chase's restless desire for the Presidency.

John Jay, mentioned above, wrote to Chase on November 23: he had been in communication with Sumner; he had heard of Dana's meeting with Lincoln (supra); he understood that Swayne's candidacy was supported by men who hoped to receive his place as Associate Justice; he regarded Evarts as not sufficiently anti-slavery; "the popular verdict on the Slavery question in the Presidential election fairly entitles us to a recognition" in the choice of a Chief Justice—which would be Chase. Jay's letter of congratulation on December 7 was in that spirit. Chase Papers, L.C.

[64] George S. Boutwell, *Reminiscences of Sixty Years in Public Affairs* (New York: McClure, Phillips Co., 1902), II, 29; Hugh McCulloch, *Men and Measures of Half a Century* (New York: Charles Scribner's Sons, 1888), 186–88; Sherman, *Recollections,* I, 343–44; recollection of Judge Hoar, quoted in Rhodes, *History of the U.S.,* V, 45–46. Although recorded long afterward, it is not doubted that it was substantially correct.

Lane of Indiana had gone to him that morning: Lincoln appeared to remain undecided. The Speaker was urging members of Congress to go to the White House—Garfield, Wilson of Iowa (Chairman of the Judiciary Committee),[65] and others. Lincoln had repeated to Colfax "various objections he had heard, which he added, did not influence him"; Colfax had replied that they were "unworthy"; one objection, however, he saw fit to pass on to Chase, in these admonitory words:

> that your ambition was the Presidency, & that a Pres¹. candidate should not be C.J. to use it as a stepping stone, impairing the strength & impartiality of the Judiciary. I asked Mr. Lincoln if you had not yourself once told him your preference to be C.J. rather than President. He replied Yes; & I added that, if appointed, I felt certain you would dedicate the remainder of your life to the Bench. . . .

Colfax added, "I did not say it to the President, but I may say it here frankly, that I never did fancy C.J. [*sic*] McLean being a candidate for President."[66]

It was on the next day after this anxious letter that the President nominated Chase. He had remained mistrustful to the end. In the years that followed, Lincoln's misgivings were abundantly confirmed.[67]

ADMIRERS AND EXPECTATIONS

LETTERS OF CONGRATULATION, like the recommendations, contained discriminating comments. Justice Gray assured Chase that "the opportunity" was afforded of "the most magnificent civil career which the future of the Country discloses."[68] William Cullen Bryant expressed the thought more emphatically: Chase's new post would be "more important to the country, for many years after the war shall have ended, than

---

[65] By reason of this position, Wilson is a significant figure in the history of the Court.

[66] Chase Papers, Hist. Soc. of Pa. McLean, Circuit Justice of the Seventh Circuit, supra, had been perennially available, and attractive by reason of his anti-slavery views. Even in 1860 he aspired to the Republican nomination, although he had ceased to be effective on the Court, and died one month after Lincoln's inauguration.

[67] When the Lincoln Papers in the Library of Congress were opened to the public in 1947, it became possible to examine new material on the appointment of a Chief Justice in 1864. Letters there lodged were used, according to their respective needs, by Randall and Current, *Lincoln, the President: Last Full Measure*; David M. Silver, *Lincoln's Supreme Court* (Urbana: University of Illinois Press, 1956); and Thomas and Hyman, *Stanton.* Willard L. King, in his *Davis* (1960), made effective use of Justice Davis' Papers as well as those of Lincoln.

[68] Dec. 7. Chase Papers, L.C.

the Presidency itself."[69] Alphonso Taft wrote, "To be Chief Justice . . . is more than to be President, in my estimation. I rejoice . . . that, now, the momentous interests of *Liberty*, will be protected in that High Court."[70]

Chase's close affinity with the spokesmen of organized religion is illustrated by these letters: Henry W. Bellows, outstanding Unitarian clergyman and founder of the Sanitary Commission, wrote that the earthly position of Chief Justice "nearest resembles in dignity and responsibility that of the Supreme Arbiter";[71] and the fervent Bellamy Storer, Judge of the Superior Court of Cincinnati and professor in the local law school, foresaw Chase "vindicating the principles of constitutional liberty, as understood by the spirit of the age, and the truth of God."[72]

Dr. J. E. Snodgrass of New York, formerly editor of the *Baltimore Saturday Visitor*, recalled his association with Chase in proclaiming "the glorious axioms" of the anti-slavery movement, which would "become the settled doctrine of the Courts of Justice as well as the all-pervading conviction of legislative bodies."[73]

Joseph Medill wrote that now "I feel confident that [the Constitution] will be expounded in accordance with the principles of Freedom and Human Rights . . . . Securing the Chief Justiceship is victory No. 2, only second in importance to the election of Lincoln, and so the loyal part of the Country regards it." Medill was the publisher of the *Chicago Daily Tribune*, the great voice of Radical Republicanism in the Northwest.[74]

General Henry B. Carrington, at Indianapolis, rejoiced that "the representative man of True Liberty takes the place of *Marshal[l]*! Thank God, the good cause lives and thrives and Slavery comes to an end! . . . A holy mission is in our hands; and I cannot tell you how rejoiced I am at your new position." The writer—lawyer, anti-slavery advocate, Republican organizer, Adjutant General of Ohio under Governors Chase and Dennison—had recently exposed the activities of the Sons of Liberty in the Northwest: he added that Chase would be glad to learn that General Heintzelman [until recently in command of the Northern Depart-

---

[69] Dec. 10. Chase Papers, Hist. Soc. of Pa. Bryant and his *New York Evening Post* will figure prominently, infra, pp. 344–55.

[70] Dec. 7. Chase Papers, L.C. The same preference was later entertained by Taft's son, who he'd both offices.

[71] Dec. 13. Ibid. The United States Sanitary Commission, established in 1861, developed an elaborate or-

ganization for the care of sick and wounded soldiers and of dependent families.

[72] Dec. 7. Ibid. Judge Storer will be mentioned infra, pp. 1312–18.

[73] Dec. 12. Ibid. Dr. Snodgrass was an occasional and devoted correspondent.

[74] Dec. 9. Chase Papers, Hist. Soc. of Pa.

ment], Speaker Colfax and others were saying that by "my efforts, the North-west had been spared the horror of civil war."[75]

It resulted from Carrington's report that certain leaders among the Sons of Liberty were brought to trial before a military commission—whence arose the case of *Ex parte Milligan* in the Supreme Court.[76]

Supporters of Chase had stressed that he was deeply committed to the war measures of the Government—including the Legal Tender Act. Now in his congratulations William H. Y. Hackett, Portsmouth financier and Presidential Elector for New Hampshire, recalled Chase's monetary policies: "So far as fame is concerned you will have secured enough by having restored to the General Government its rightful and necessary control over the currency . . . ."[77] When Judge Samuel A. Foot expressed his satisfaction that Chase would now have a large part in "the moulding into form of our institutions on the basis of universal freedom,"[78] he had good reason to believe that the ex-Secretary was clear in his own mind that the legal tender legislation he had advocated was sustainable under the Constitution. In June 1863, when that issue was being litigated in the New York Court of Appeals, Foot (a former Judge of that court) in association with David Dudley Field, had attended and presented a defense of the statute, pursuant to instructions from Secretary Chase.[79]

A final quotation, this from Richard C. Parsons, Collector of Internal Revenue at Cleveland: "The dearest wish of my heart has been fully gratified . . . ."[80] Chase early sought to make Parsons the Marshal of the Supreme Court and in 1867 succeeded.

Parsons is here introduced as representative of a band of loyal men appointed by Chase while Secretary of the Treasury, who thereafter were ever vigilant to advance the interests of their chief.[81] Among these adherents were the Treasury agents sent into the Southern States as the

---

[75] Dec. 7, Hq. Draft Rendezvous, Indianapolis. Chase Papers, L.C. Carrington, a graduate of Yale College and a student at the law school there, had practiced law with Aaron F. Perry and William Dennison, before being drawn into the work of organizing the militia.

[76] Infra, p. 195.

[77] Dec. 13. Chase Papers, L.C. Hackett will presently be mentioned in connection with municipal bond decisions. Infra.

[78] Dec. 10. Ibid.

[79] Infra, p. 693.

[80] Dec. 7. Chase Papers, L.C.

[81] Another of this group was Colonel William B. Thomas, Collector of the Port of Philadelphia. On May 17, 1867, the Chief Justice, in acknowledging the expression of approval of a decision from J. Glancy Jones (Democratic politician) added that "My friend, Col. Thomas, of Phila., hopes to see you before long." And Jones, writing to the Chief Justice on July 9, 1868, said that "I have devoted all my faculties for 18 mos. to secure your nomination . . . ." Chase Papers, L.C. Thomas worked toward making Chase President in 1868 and then in 1872. Infra, p. 391, n. 75.

armies advanced, to carry out the involved economic measures with which the Department was charged; from them the Chief Justice continued to receive a stream of reports on political developments in the South.

In the authorship of these letters one may discern certain types of relationship. There were men of eminence, qualified to convey an assurance that in their judgment Chase indeed stood foremost among the nation's leaders. There were others who were proud to recall association in some of his worthy accomplishments. And there were his devoted henchmen. Notably lacking was the relationship of colleague, where men have worked in concert on the basis of equality and mutual respect. Chase had had virtually no experience with such association, certainly not in Lincoln's Cabinet. Nor was his egocentric nature easily adaptable to it.

THE PRESIDING OFFICER OF THE COURT

THESE LETTERS may have given an exaggerated notion of the power inherent in the Chief Justiceship. The office was still identified with John Marshall, as though his unique personal ascendancy might be assumed by a successor. Men's image of Taney was that he was the embodiment of pro-slavery jurisprudence; he was indelibly tagged with the statement that black men "had no rights which the white man was bound to respect."[82] To put Chase in Taney's place seemed to amount to a contradiction of that proposition. It so happened that this was Lincoln's fifth appointment, thereby making a new majority.

The office of Chief Justice was referred to by T. D. Lincoln, who knew the Court at first hand, as that of "the Presiding Judge."[83] How Chase was obliged to adapt himself to that relationship to his associates was recalled by Justice Miller in 1878, five years after Chase's death:

> He liked to have his own way: but when he came upon the bench it was admirable to see how quietly and courteously the Court resisted his imperious will, never coming to direct conflict, and he finally had to

---

[82] That had been said in Dred Scott v. Sandford, 19 How. 393, 407 (1857). On the jurisdictional question, whether Scott, a Negro, had been entitled to sue as a citizen of the United States, Taney held that members of his race were not citizens within the meaning of the Constitution—and in that connection, in a sweeping generalization about what had been understood when the Constitution was framed, he used the words quoted. Nevertheless, Taney had gone on to rule upon the substantive issue, holding that Congress had no power to exclude slavery from a territory of the United States. Hence the Missouri Compromise of 1820 was pronounced unconstitutional.

[83] Supra, p. 14.

take the position which he held, that he was the Moderator and presiding officer over the Supreme Court, and not possessed of any more authority than the rest of the Bench chose to give him.[84]

The manner in which the Chief Justice functions will appear more precisely when the working of the Court comes to be examined.[85]

CHASE'S QUALIFICATIONS

THE QUALIFICATIONS supposed to be important for appointment to the Court should be brought more clearly into focus. The Iowa Judges said, *not* a mere lawyer, but a far-seeing statesman—one with a grasp of the fundamental principles of the national structure. The Chief Justice of Massachusetts called for one who would give a wise and liberal interpretation of the Constitution, establishing principles of regulated liberty. Justice Gray said that he should have a command of the law of nations as well as of municipal law. T. D. Lincoln spoke of sympathy with the current of events that was sweeping toward the obliteration of slavery. Many said that there should be the prospect that the great principles of Lincoln's Administration would be maintained.

Foremost practitioners, such as D. D. Field and W. C. Noyes, commended Chase's large legal attainments. One should take account of what they were. In September 1827 he had begun to read law, under the guidance of William Wirt, Attorney General of the United States.[86] Although supervision was somewhat casual, the student was self-directive and ambitious. He had close touch with causes before the Supreme Court. Thus his diary for February 14, 1829, records attendance at the argument of *Wilkinson v. Leland*,[87] where Wirt was opposed by Senator Daniel Webster. Starting with the administration of a decedent's estate, the argument developed into a claim to judicial disallowance of what Webster represented to be an instance of "flagrant acts . . . subverting the great principles of republican liberty and of the social compact; such as giving the property of A to B."[88] While denying that anything of that sort had occurred, Justice Story for a unanimous Court observed that

---

[84] Newspaper clipping of an interview, retained among Justice Miller's papers.

[85] Infra, pp. 62–67.

[86] Wirt (1772–1834) held that office from November 1817 to March 1829, under Presidents Monroe and John Quincy Adams. Concurrently he carried on a large private practice.

[87] 2 Pet. 627 (1829).

[88] A New Hampshire executrix had sold land in Rhode Island without probate there, and used the proceeds to pay the debts of what was virtually an insolvent estate; on petition of the executrix, but without notice to the heirs, the Rhode Island legislature confirmed the sale, doing what the probate court of Rhode Island would properly have done.

"The fundamental maxims of a free government seem to require, that the rights of personal liberty and private property should be held sacred. . . ." It would be the duty of the Judiciary, if occasion arose, to enforce such a limitation upon legislative power. These were words that Justice Field would quote when, in 1871, he and Chase, Nelson, and Clifford, dissenting, pronounced the Legal Tender Act of 1862 unconstitutional;[89] he would repeat in *Munn v. Illinois* in 1877, when, again in dissent, he denied the power of a legislature to fix charges of grain elevators.[90]

Surely this was instruction of a very high order. Chase noted that Webster preferred to argue "from general principles, seldom descending into minute analysis . . . . He is remarkable for strength rather than dexterity, and would easier rend an oak than untie a knot. . . ." If, Chase concluded, "any degree of industry would enable me to reach his height, how day and night should testify to my toils!"[91]

In December 1829 Chase was examined by Chief Judge Cranch and his associates in the Circuit Court for the District of Columbia and was enrolled as an attorney. Removing to Cincinnati, he was admitted to the Ohio bar the following June.

There he practiced until his election to the Senate in February 1849.[92] While clients still were few he undertook a compilation of the untidy Statutes of Ohio and of the Northwestern Territory, 1788-1833, a highly useful work in three volumes, published in 1833-35. Its quality

---

[89] The Legal Tender Cases, 12 Wall. 457, 671.

[90] 94 U.S. 113, 148.

[91] Warden, *Chase* 166.

[92] One index to the extent and nature of his practice is found by noting the instances in the Ohio Reports wherein Chase or the firm of which he was head made appearances. For comparison, like figures are shown for Swayne and his firm. For December 1846 to 1849, as reported in 15, 16, 17, and 18 Ohio Reports:

	Chase, or his firm	Swayne, or his firm
15 Ohio	2	4
16 Ohio	2	2
17 Ohio	4	2
18 Ohio	4	4
Total	12	12

Chase's cases were in commercial law and banking, real property, trusts, and pleading and practice.

The most interesting litigation within the above enumeration had to do with efforts by an adherent to the "Old School" of the Presbyterian Church to force the ouster from professorships in Lane Seminary of Lyman Beecher and Calvin E. Stowe, of the more ardent "New School." (Beecher was father of Henry Ward Beecher and Harriet Beecher Stowe; Stowe was the latter's husband.) In *State ex rel. Kemper v. Beecher*, 16 Ohio 358, the court held that proceedings by quo warranto must fail, not having been brought within the three-year limit set by the statute. In *Kemper v. Trustees of Lane Seminary*, 17 Ohio 293, the court adopted Chase's argument that plaintiff, merely as a donor to the seminary, had no such interest as would support a suit to control the trustees in their administration. Thus no case had been made for a judicial determination of a difference between religious communities. Compare *Watson v. Jones*, 13 Wall. 679 (1872), infra, pp. 907-17.

won the praise of Chancellor Kent and Justice Story.[93] In 1836 he appeared in the Supreme Court and won its judgment in *Voorhees v. Jackson*—thereafter a leading authority on the presumption of validity to be accorded to the judgment of a court of competent jurisdiction, notwithstanding that the record fail to show compliance with all statutory requirements.[94]

In March 1837 Chase was retained on behalf of Matilda, who had been seized as a fugitive slave when found in the household of James G. Birney. Her owner had been taking her from Virginia en route to Missouri; when the steamboat docked at Cincinnati she escaped. In habeas corpus proceedings in the Court of Common Pleas, Chase argued without success that, having been brought by her master into a free State, Matilda could not thereafter be treated as a slave. Chase's argument was printed and circulated. Then Birney was indicted under an Ohio statute forbidding the harboring of a slave. Chase was retained for the defense. A conviction was reversed by the State Supreme Court for a defect in the indictment Chase had chosen not to raise. The Court directed, however, that Chase's argument, to the effect that Matilda had ceased to be a slave, be included in the report of the case.[95]

Much more of this sort of work followed; Chase became known as the "attorney general for runaway slaves."

In *Jones v. Van Zandt*, decided by the Supreme Court in 1847, Chase and William H. Seward argued, unsuccessfully, for a construction of the Fugitive Slave Act which the Court said would have vitiated its effect; their challenge of the constitutionality of the Act was also rejected.[96] These services were performed without a fee. Chase's 108-page argument was reprinted.

Formerly a Whig, Chase in 1841 adhered to the Liberty Party, and in 1844 supported its candidate, Birney, his erstwhile client. He presided at the Free-Soil Convention in 1848, and was chief draftsman of its platform: "our calm but final answer is, 'No more slave States and no more slave territory.'"

During his term in the Senate, after Congress in its Compromise

---

[93] Schuckers, *Chase*, 35–37. Kent wrote, "how you could endure the task . . . I can hardly conceive, with all my own habits of perseverance."

[94] 10 Pet. 449, affirming Fed. Case No. 939 in the Circuit Court for the District of Ohio. A State court's judgment confirming a sale under a writ attaching the land of an absent debtor had been attacked collaterally, long afterward, for failure to show compliance with certain provisions of an Act of 1805, Chase's Ohio Laws 462.

[95] Warden, *Chase*, 282–84, gives Chase's account of the Matilda and Birney cases, in a letter of March 16, 1864, to John T. Trowbridge. Birney v. Ohio, 8 Ohio 230.

[96] 5 How. 215. Chase's account is in a letter of March 18, 1864, to Trowbridge. Warden, *Chase*, 296–98. The original action and a companion case between the same parties are reported in Federal Cases Nos. 7501 to 7505, in the Circuit Court for Ohio.

of 1850 passed a more effective Fugitive Slave Act, Chase argued the case of *Norris v. Crocker* in the Supreme Court, winning a decision that the new law, by implication, had repealed the Act of 1793, and that pending actions for a penalty under the old statute were barred.[97] Chase's argument was dwelt upon eighteen years later when, in *Ex parte McCardle*, counsel were contending over a statute whereby Congress withdrew a category of the Court's jurisdiction with effect upon a pending appeal that menaced the Reconstruction Act.[98]

Upon leaving the Senate, Chase served three terms—six years—as Governor of Ohio. Repeated clashes between agents for the return of fugitive slaves under the Act of 1850 and State officers hostile to their efforts—with writs of habeas corpus issuing from both State and federal courts—brought Governor Chase into protracted controversy with District Judge Leavitt. The *Cincinnati Enquirer*, the leading Democratic journal in Southern Ohio, called it "a war on the part of Chase and his abolition crew against the United States courts."[99] This experience was reflected in Chief Justice Chase's dissent in *Tarble's Case* in 1872, when the Court, per Field, J., held that a State judge has no authority to issue habeas corpus for the discharge of a person held by an officer of the United States under claim of federal authority.[100]

From Governor, Chase progressed to Secretary of the Treasury. Much of his work there was highly relevant to his service as Chief Justice. He was the designer of the national bank system; and controversies concerning banks and the taxation of bank shares were numerous. Wartime legislation, concerning commercial intercourse with States in rebellion, and the treatment of captured, abandoned, and confiscable property, directed that the Secretary of the Treasury prescribe necessary regulations, and through his agents carry out the controls. Out of this came an enormous volume of litigation after the war.

Such was the record which, judges and lawyers declared, made Chase particularly well qualified for appointment to the Supreme Court. His years at the bar, although far behind him, had demonstrated capacity for coping with major legal problems. Since then he had acquired, what the Iowa Judges particularly mentioned, a wide practical acquaintance with the working of the governmental system. Swayne had practiced law steadily for twice as long, and had an outstanding acquaintance with the English and American authorities: and yet that did not seem to meet the demands of the occasion. Even though ordinary private litigation then consumed much of the time of the Court,[101] men foresaw that large new issues were impending.

---

[97] 13 How. 429 (1851).
[98] 7 Wall. 506 (1869), infra, p. 492.
[99] Schuckers, *Chase*, 171–82; War-

den, *Chase*, 344–51.
[100] 13 Wall. 397, infra, pp. 1424–26.
[101] Infra, ch. 2.

In the discussion of the vacancy, nothing was said about previous judicial experience: no one suggested that the work of a Justice could only, or best, be learned by apprenticeship on a lower bench. History taught no such lesson.

A CAVEAT

A WORD OF CAUTION is in order. Chase's supporters were sometimes men who, wrapped in consciousness of their own moral rectitude, took little account of the sentiment of others. Recall, for instance, Judge Brinkerhoff's assurance that ninety-nine out of every hundred loyal men in Ohio strongly desired Chase's appointment.[102] But ex-Governors Dennison and Tod, Morrison Waite and Judge Leavitt, Tom Ewing and Stanbery, and doubtless hundreds of other Republicans, and War Democrats, were loyal men who did not share Brinkerhoff's eagerness. Enthusiasts rejoiced that with Chase on the Court, "Freedom," "Human Rights," "constitutional liberty, as understood by the spirit of the age, and the truth of God" would now prevail. But such highly subjective expressions from one quarter obscured fundamental disagreements that would soon be brought into open controversy before the Court—"with great pertinacity, if not bitterness."[103]

---

[102] Supra, p. 13.

[103] As T. D. Lincoln had remarked to the President. Supra, p. 13.

CHAPTER II

The Work of the Supreme Court

C HASE FOUND HIS BRETHREN proceeding tranquilly with an un-
exciting docket of cases. Never again would there be a term
wherein so few questions of importance were answered as in that of
1864–65. Review of judgments in Circuit Courts of the United States
made up the bulk of the work, and in the large majority of these no
issue of federal law was involved; the cases were of federal cognizance
only because the litigants were citizens of different States. Let the matter
in dispute exceed the value of $2,000, and the judgment of the inferior
federal tribunal could be carried to the Supreme Court. So in large part
the Justices spent their days on the law of real property, contracts, commercial transactions, trusts and equitable remedies—the same sort of
business that came before the State appellate courts. Their expositions of
the law would be received with respect by State courts, and contribute
bit by bit to the development of private law.

Although some of these decisions would have considerable importance, this part of the Court's work was far from spectacular. For example, *Providence Tool Company v. Norris*,[1] where Justice Field spoke for
the Court, held that an agreement to compensate for procuring a contract
with the Government—here a War Department order for rifles—is unenforceable as being against public policy. This was familiar as to lobbying
with a legislature, and the Court said that the principle applied to procuring action by an executive department as well. As Justice Holmes,
fifty years later, expressed the teaching of this case, "contracts that
obviously and directly tend in a marked degree to bring about results
that the law seeks to prevent cannot be made the ground of a successful
suit."[2]

---

[1] 2 Wall. 45 (1865).
[2] Sage v. Hampe, 235 *U.S.* 99, 105
(1914).

The *Providence Tool* case has often
been cited and applied. For example
in Trist v. Child, 21 Wall. 441, 449

II: *The Work of the Supreme Court*

Marine Bank of Chicago v. Fulton County Bank[3] and related cases called for a determination which of two banks—the collecting bank, or its principal—must bear the loss of depreciating currency. In late 1860 and 1861 most banks of Illinois, whose notes were secured in part by bonds of Southern States, were collapsing. The Chicago bank, on collecting notes for its New York correspondent, had mixed the proceeds with its ordinary funds. The Court held that it thereby made itself its correspondent's debtor, not its agent, and was not entitled, when demand was made, to make its creditor bear the further depreciation of Illinois notes. Characteristically, after applying the rule, Justice Miller added, "let us look for a moment at the equity of defendant's position," and showed that the Court was reaching the just result.

In *Drury v. Foster et ux.,*[4] a married woman had signed a mortgage wherein material elements—the name of the mortgagee, the sum of money involved, and the times of payment—were left blank; she acknowledged this paper before a notary. The husband filled in the blanks and obtained a loan. In a suit to foreclose, the Circuit Court sustained the defense that the wife had not joined in the deed as required by the State statute.[5] An appeal to the Supreme Court was argued by Wheeler H. Peckham against James M. Carlisle.[6] Justice Nelson's opinion held

---

(1875), lobbying for an appropriation; Meguire v. Corwine, 101 U.S. 108, 111) (1880), claim to share of the fee of Richard M. Corwine, for whom Meguire had procured employment by the Treasury as special counsel in United States v. Farragut, 22 Wall. 406 (1875), litigation on behalf of officers and crews in respect of prize money for captures at New Orleans; Oscanyan v. Arms Co., 103 U.S. 261, 273 (1881), where the consul general of the Ottoman Government claimed payment for his services in inducing his Government to purchase arms from defendant.

[3] 2 Wall. 252 (1865).

[4] 2 Wall. 24 (1865).

[5] Minn. Comp. Statutes, c. 36, sec. 13, provided that "a married woman may bar her right of dower in any estate conveyed by her husband . . . by joining in the deed of conveyance, and acknowledging the same . . ." as prescribed by the statutes.

[6] Wheeler H. Peckham (1833–1905), born in Albany, had prepared for the bar in the Albany Law School and in the office of his father, Rufus W. Peckham (1809–73), later a Judge of

the Court of Appeals. The son, after practicing in Iowa and then in Minnesota, returned in 1864 and thereafter had his office in New York City. President Cleveland nominated him to be an Associate Justice in 1894; he failed of confirmation when the Senators from New York invoked "Senatorial courtesy."

In 1895 his brother, Rufus W. Peckham (1838–1909), then Judge of the New York Court of Appeals, was nominated and confirmed as an Associate Justice.

James M. Carlisle, counsel for the appellee, will be mentioned frequently hereafter.

The Circuit Court for Minnesota, whose decree was here affirmed, was held by District Judge Rensselaer R. Nelson (1826–1904), son of Justice Nelson. Appointed by President Buchanan in 1858, he served until 1896, becoming the senior in point of service among all District Judges.

These personal references suggest what becomes a strong impression when one has worked in the period to be covered by this book: that so far as public life was concerned, America

that the wife could not by words authorize her husband to complete the instrument, because the statute disabled her from doing so. Her acknowledgment was of no help, because what she acknowledged was only an ineffective piece of paper. For the Court to hold otherwise would amount to "a virtual repeal of the statute" for the protection of the married woman's property "and also a denial of the disability of the common law that forbids the conveyance of her real estate" by another on her behalf.

> Losses of the kind may be guarded against, on the part of dealers in real estate, by care and caution; and we think that this burden should be imposed on them, rather than that a sacrifice should be made of the rights of a class who are dependent enough in the business affairs of life, even when all the privileges with which the law surrounds them are left unimpaired.

Chase found his new work rather boring. He had abandoned large public affairs to return to the law, in which he had become rusty. Even so, now and then his days at the bar would be brought familiarly to mind, as when in *Harvey v. Tyler*,[7] discussing the presumption of validity to be accorded to the judgment of a court of competent jurisdiction, reliance was placed on the "remarkably similar" case of *Voorhees v. Jackson* in 1836—Chase's early success in the Supreme Court.[8] Now to concentrate on facts and issues, on records and briefs, as the just decision of cases demands, seemed a chore: "Working from morning till midnight, and no result, except that John Smith owned this parcel of land or other property instead of Jacob Robinson; I caring nothing, and nobody caring much more, about the matter."[9]

Tobey v. Leonards,[10] argued during Chase's first week on the bench, shows what he had in mind. The question was this: when Jonathan Tobey and his wife conveyed their entire estate to their son-in-law Leonard, to induce Leonard and Leonard's father to purchase the Tobey homestead from the foreclosing mortgagee, was their conveyance made subject to an oral agreement that equity should now enforce, that the estate would be reconveyed when Tobey found the means to repay the Leonards? Justice Clifford on the circuit had concluded that complainant failed to establish the alleged agreement,[11] and now an appeal was brought. The case was opened on December 21, and occupied the entire

---

was still a rather close community— so interwoven are the associations one observes.

[7] 2 Wall 328 (1865).

[8] Supra, p. 29.

[9] David Donald, ed., *Inside Lincoln's Cabinet. The Civil War Diaries of*

Salmon P. Chase (New York, London, Toronto: Longmans, Green and Co., 1954), 261.

[10] 2 Wall. 423 (1865).

[11] Fed. Case No. 14,067 (C.C.D. Mass. 1861).

sitting on December 22. Sidney Bartlett began the argument; already distinguished, he lived to become a legendary figure at the bar. Opposing was Richard Olney: three decades later as Attorney General he would be submitting to the Court the momentous issues of the *Income Tax Case*,[12] the *Sugar Trust Case*,[13] and the strike injunction case of *In re Debs*.[14] In *Tobey v. Leonards*, however, he was arguing a cause of no moment to the country and of no consequence as a precedent. It was no more than an angry family controversy that had caught up the neighborhood of New Bedford, Massachusetts—as Reporter Wallace recounts in his chatty statement of facts. Only by residence across the line in Rhode Island had the complainant been enabled to come into the federal court. An appeal in equity brought up the whole case, not merely alleged errors on points of law. Here the Court must pick its way through a record of 348 pages, seeking amid eighty depositions a conclusion whether there had in truth been a private agreement that the Leonards would restore the land. Justice Wayne's opinion held that there had, and that equity should enforce it. Justices Clifford and Grier noted dissent. No important principle was propounded; the decision made no perceptible mark upon the law.[15]

As these illustrations suggest, much of the Court's work at this time was quite pedestrian. Senator Reverdy Johnson explained to his colleagues how the Justices must spend their time:

> I think I am safe in saying that at least one half the cases in the Supreme Court are more or less troublesome because of their obligation to examine into the facts. That is almost solely the case in equity causes. The records are generally very large, the testimony being generally very voluminous, and as the court is obliged, as the law now stands, to examine into the whole record in order to pass judgment upon the facts as well as the law, it takes a great deal of their time. The same remark is applicable to cases in admiralty. . . .[16]

The time was close at hand when, by reason of controversies growing out of Reconstruction, the Court would no longer be working at a quiet pattern. But even when the chapters are given over to matters of high dramatic quality, it should be borne in mind that there was always a mass of humdrum litigation.

---

[12] Pollock v. Farmers' Loan & Trust Co., 157 U.S. 429 (1895); 158 U.S. 601 (1895).

[13] United States v. E. C. Knight Co., 156 U.S. 1 (1895).

[14] 158 U.S. 564 (1895).

[15] On "Shepardizing" the case, that is, consulting Shepard's *United States Citations*, it appears that Tobey v. Leonards was never cited by the Supreme Court.

[16] Cong. Globe, 39–1, 1718. April 2, 1866.

RENEWED IMPORTANCE OF INTERNATIONAL LAW

INTERNATIONAL LAW, and in particular the law of prize, now rose to be once again a major concern of the Court. In Marshall's time, what with the Napoleonic Wars and then the wars of independence in Latin America, the powers of belligerents and the rights of neutrals had bulked large in Wheaton's Reports. Justice Story's scholarly mind had been directed to the Court's need: his anonymous notes on the principles and practice in prize causes, appended to 1 and 2 Wheaton (February terms, 1816 and 1817), amounted to a restatement of the law.[17] This was an important subject for practitioner and student. When the first volume of Chancellor Kent's *Commentaries on American Law* appeared in 1826, Part I on the law of nations (treating largely of prize law), and Part II on the constitutional law of the United States, were of about equal length; and whereas the former could be supported with a wealth of decided cases, the latter was scarcely more than textual explanation. How different the relative positions when Chase came to the bench: the Court had developed an imposing body of constitutional jurisprudence, while in the meantime only very rarely had there been occasion to think about questions of prize.

Now the Justices must restudy prize law, as cases came up from federal courts. A contemporary list of "Law Books to be purchased (10 copies) for the use of the Judges," found among the Chief Justice's papers, makes the point. These were the books the Justices chose to have within arm's-reach, and more than one-fourth of the titles pertained to the law of nations.[18]

---

[17] In 1854 his work was published in London as *Notes on the Princip'es and Practice of Prize Courts; with documents and forms used in the High Court of Admiralty in England.* Edited by F. T. Pratt, it made a book of 286 pages.

[18] Chase Papers, L.C. While the list bears no date, references in various letters among the Justices show that it was under active consideration in 1866.

In international law, the list included the treatises by Vattel, Wheaton, Phillimore, Halleck, and Woolsey; several works on blockade and prize; and the English Admiralty Reports (9 vols.).

In the municipal law fields, the list included the various treatises by Story and by Parsons; Kent's *Com-* *mentaries;* Greenleaf on Evidence; Greenleaf's Edition of Cruise's *Digest of the Laws of England respecting Real Property;* Washburn on Real Property; Angell and Ames on Corporations; several works on Equity Pleadings and Equity Jurisprudence; Chitty on Contracts; Sedgwick on Damages; Phillips on Insurance; the works of Burge and Theobald on Suretyship; on Patents, George Ticknor Curtis' treatise, Robb's *Patent Cases,* and Law's *Digest of American Cases;* also Curtis' *Law of Copyright.*

Smith's Leading Cases, and *American Leading Cases* (4th ed. 1857, by J. I. C. Hare and John William Wallace, the Reporter) were useful tools, as were the law dictionaries of Bouvier and Jacob.

These titles in municipal law rein-

Most appropriately, the Chief Justice assigned to himself the important cases of prize. Here he had a great advantage over his brethren: as Secretary of the Treasury he had borne a major part in the Administration's conduct of economic warfare. His first full opinion was in *The Circassian*,[19] an appeal from the District Court for the Southern District of Florida. A neutral ship had been captured on May 4, 1862; its papers disclosed a purpose to go on to the port of New Orleans, in breach of the blockade. The point was that Union troops had begun the occupation of the city on May 1, three days before the capture. Notwithstanding culpable intent, concededly a hostile blockade would end when the place ceased to be hostile. The Court took the view that at the moment of capture only the city, not the port and the district commercially dependent upon it, had been restored to the Government's grasp. Accordingly the capture was sustained. Justice Nelson, pointing

---

force the statement in the text, that the Justices were in large part concerned with the same types of problem as came before the State courts.

Particularly of federal concern, the list included the Opinions of the Attorney General, and Conkling's *Organization, Jurisdiction and Practice of the Courts of the United States, with appendix containing rules and forms*. The 4th edition, 1864, was a book of 882 pages. The scope of *federal jurisdiction* was necessarily an ever-present concern in the United States courts. The author, Alfred Conkling, had been Judge for the Northern District of New York from 1825 to 1852. Roscoe Conkling, his son and sometime law student, will reappear as Congressman, Senator, and twice recipient of a tender of a place on the Supreme Court.

The list of books each Justice should have at hand began, "*All* the reports of cases decided in the several circuit courts, and district courts of the United States." Such reports as then existed were the product of individual initiative in collecting and publishing. Almost continuous reports for the First Circuit covered the years from 1812 to 1856. (1 Clifford did not appear until 1869.) For the Second Circuit there were only two volumes prior to Blatchford's Reports running from 1845. There were several volumes of reports for the Third Circuit;

John William Wallace had now brought out two of the three volumes wherein he reported decisions from 1842 to 1862.

For the South and West, federal reports were rare indeed: one volume contained some of Marshall's decisions in Virginia and North Carolina. (The single volume of Taney's decisions in Maryland did not appear until 1871.)

Justice McLean had published six volumes of his decisions in the Seventh Circuit.

Judge Cranch published in 1852–53, six volumes of decisions of the Circuit Court for the District of Columbia.

Add a volume of federal cases in Arkansas and one of Circuit Court decisions in California, and one has substantially covered Circuit Court reporting to 1866.

Perhaps not so large a library was provided at this time. Justice Swayne, in a letter of August 24, 1866, to the Chief Justice, sent a list—much smaller than that described above—with the explanation that "the means are so limited, which can be applied to their purchase." Chase Papers, Hist. Soc. of Pa.

Each Justice would be supplied with a set of the United States Reports, and the Statutes at Large.

[19] 2 Wall. 135 (1865).

to General Butler's assertion of possession in a proclamation dated May 1 (but not published until May 6), concluded that federal authority had already been restored; he felt it his duty to record his dissent, because of "a conviction that there is a tendency . . . to press the right of blockade beyond its proper limits," making precedents that might some-day prove embarrassing. Counsel for the owners had placed their case in the context of the American Government's historic defense of neutral rights in periods of European war.

The result in *The Circassian* turned on an appreciation of the factual situation in New Orleans. After the war the British-American Mixed Commission by divided vote made an award to the owners.[20]

Three other opinions by Chase at that term affirmed other prize decrees by the same District Court. In *The Venice*,[21] restoring a ship captured near New Orleans after national authority had been firmly re-established, the Chief Justice inserted a sentence that glanced toward the future; from the action of Congress and the Executive he deduced

> a general purpose which seeks the re-establishment of the national authority, and the ultimate restoration of States and citizens to their national relations, under better forms and firmer guaranties, without any views of subjugation by conquest. . . .

The Baigorry[22] had sailed on May 26, 1862, from a Louisiana port still within Confederate hands; it was condemned for violation of the blockade. *The Andromeda* and cargo[23] were held good prize on a finding that the contrivance of neutral ownership was only colorable; moreover, the sailing from Texas had been in breach of blockade, even though no watch was apparent at the time of egress.

The much-cited case of *Mrs. Alexander's Cotton*[24] was an appeal in prize from the District Court for the Southern District of Illinois, sitting at Springfield—surely an unusual quarter for such a proceeding. During Banks' expedition up the Red River, a party from a gunboat had gone ashore and captured cotton on a plantation. The Court held the cotton to have been enemy's property, liable to capture as the very sinews of rebel strength; Banks' foray had been too brief to efface the hostile relation created by three years of rebellion. The captors, however, took no prize money: although the Navy had, in Lincoln's phrase, made its tracks wherever the ground was a little damp, Congress had excluded property on land from the award of prize. Instead, the cotton must be handed over to the Treasury agent, as provided in the Abandoned and

---

[20] John Bassett Moore, *Digest of International Law* (Washington: Government Printing Office, 1906), VII, 840–42.

[21] 2 Wall. 258 (1865).
[22] 2 Wall. 474 (1865).
[23] 2 Wall. 481 (1865).
[24] 2 Wall. 404 (1865).

Captured Property Act.[25] As to the contention that Mrs. Alexander had remained loyal to the United States: that was immaterial, since on familiar principle the character of the property was governed by the place where it lay; Congress had provided a proceeding in the Court of Claims whereby an owner might recover the proceeds on proof of never having given aid to the rebellion. The Chief Justice wrote the opinion; it was a matter with which he was thoroughly conversant.

Chase also spoke for the Court in *The Slavers (Kate)*,[26] one of several appeals against condemnation under laws to suppress the slave trade. In 1860 and thereafter the District Attorney for the Southern District of New York had filed libels against ships there fitted out and sailing for the African coast ostensibly to traffic in merchandise. The inference of guilt fairly sprang from the records. The critical question was, what measure of proof must be met? District Judge Betts, a great figure in maritime law, distinguished between indictable crimes and other offenses, like the present, that involved only pecuniary penalties or a forfeiture; after an extensive review of reported cases and of admiralty practice, he applied the "uniform and distinct" view of his court that where the Government's evidence created strong suspicion, the burden lay on the claimant. He decreed forfeiture and, on appeal to the Circuit Court, Justice Nelson affirmed. In this and companion cases before the Supreme Court, able counsel, including Evarts, argued that the Government must show positive proof of a guilty intention. The Chief Justice's opinion announced simply that "The case . . . bears upon it such indications of the guilty purpose . . . that we should require clear explanation by convincing proof to repel the conclusion . . . ."

THREE IMPORTANT PRECEDENTS

OF A SCORE OF PRIZE CASES decided during the next two terms, three merit notice in historical perspective: *The Bermuda*,[27] *The Springbok*,[28] and *The Peterhoff*,[29] for their development of the law of continuous voyage. The British Government, by "the rule of the War of 1756", had declared that neutrals would not be permitted to engage in time of war in trade from which they were excluded in time of peace, in particular, between a Continental country and its colonies.[30] During the Napoleonic Wars, when American shipowners sought to evade the rule by sailing between France and her colonies via an American port, the

---

[25] Infra, p. 787.
[26] 2 Wall. 350 (1865).
[27] 3 Wall. 514 (1866).
[28] 5 Wall. 1 (1867).
[29] 5 Wall. 28 (1867).

[30] Considered by Chancellor Kent in his survey of the law of nations, in Part I of his *Commentaries on American Law*, at I, *81–87.

English prize court held that this must be regarded as one continuous voyage, and condemned. When the American Civil War broke out, a blockade of the Southern ports was declared and effectively maintained. A neutral ship sailing with intent to breach the blockade was liable to capture at any point on its voyage. Neutrals remained free, however, to carry even military stores from one neutral port to another, and there to offer them for sale to any who would buy. A tremendous traffic sprang up whereby supplies essential to the Confederacy were carried to some near-by neutral port, such as Nassau in the Bahamas, and thence through the blockade to Charleston, Savannah, or Wilmington. The Federal Government by naval action sought to deny this resource to the enemy, and by its law officers sought to induce the judiciary to sustain its captures as lawful. But, said Chief Justice Chase, expressing a view maintained in Anglo-American prize law, "we administer the public law of nations, and are not at liberty to inquire what is for the particular advantage or disadvantage of our own or another country."[31] The pressure of argument on behalf of the Government now ran counter to the traditional national policy of restricting belligerent rights.

The problem was posed in *The Dolphin*,[32] heard by the loyal District Judge who remained at Key West. Cases of "hardware" that proved to be rifles and swords had been shipped from Liverpool to Nassau—which concededly would be lawful commerce. "But if," said Judge Marvin, "it was the intention of the owner that the vessel should simply touch at Nassau, and should proceed thence to Charleston, or some other port of the enemy," the enterprise would violate the belligerent rights of the United States. "The cutting up of a continuous voyage into several parts . . . may render it more difficult for cruisers and prize courts to determine where the ultimate terminus is intended to be"; but if that was in the Confederacy, the entire venture was unlawful. He cited English cases. "Nassau furnishes no market for any such cargo as this. It is a small town. . . . Probably not three merchant steamers ever arrived at that port from any part of the world until after the present blockade was established, except the regular government mail steamers. Was her cargo to be sold in Nassau, including the 920 rifles and the 2,240 swords?" On a finding that a continuous voyage through the blockade had been intended, condemnation was decreed. Other District Courts followed.

The Supreme Court established that line of reasoning in *The Bermuda*.[33] The ship, purportedly British, had made one round trip

---

[31] The Peterhoff, 5 Wall. 28 (1867). Accord, Story, J., in The Schooner Adeline, 9 Cr. 244, 284 (1815). The leading British affirmation is The Zamora [1916] 2 A.C. 77.
[32] Fed. Case No. 3975 (S.D.Fla. 1863).
[33] 3 Wall. 514 (1866).

through the blockade, but of course that offense was purged when it had been completed. Next she sailed from Liverpool to Bermuda, thence for Nassau, on which run the capture was made. The alleged British owner-ship seemed only a sham; the venture had been managed entirely by Confederate agents at Liverpool. A large part of the cargo was contra-band; many articles were by their mark intended only for a Confederate destination. Spoliation of the ship's papers confirmed the misrepresenta-tion. Argument was heard on January 9, 10, 13, and 14, 1865; then, "because of the desire of the Court to have all the aid that counsel could give in the examination of the important questions of fact and law," reargument was ordered, and heard on January 8 and 9, 1866. Evidently there had been no intention that the cargo should become a part of the common stock at Bermuda or Nassau; transshipment to a fast light steamer had been contemplated. Clearly the real destination had been the Confederacy. "Our conclusion is that both vessel and cargo, even if both were neutral, were rightly condemned . . . ." That established the doctrine. This was on March 12, 1866.

The Springbok[34] had been argued at the close of the reargument of *The Bermuda*, but was held under consideration until January 3, 1867. On the facts, the case for the captors was not strong. A British ship had been chartered to carry to Nassau; the shipowners appeared to have no interest in the cargo, "and there is no sufficient proof that they had any knowledge of its alleged unlawful destination." So the ship was restored. The cargo was owned by British merchants. "A part of it, small in comparison with the whole, consisted of arms and munitions of war . . . . Another and somewhat larger portion consisted of articles useful and necessary in war . . . ." There were army buttons and navy buttons. If any property was liable to condemnation, on established principle it "infected" all belonging to the same owner. But, said the Court, "we repeat, contraband or not, it could not be condemned, if really destined for Nassau and not beyond; and, contraband or not, it must be condemned if destined to any rebel port, for all rebel ports are under blockade." The difficulty was to show that the owners' purpose had been to send their goods on to the Confederacy. The contents of many of the packages had not been disclosed in the bills of lading. The goods were consigned to order or assignees, which suggested that no sale to anyone at Nassau was in view. The trial court had permitted the captors to "invoke" the records in two other cases where goods of the same owners had been condemned.[35] And "If these circumstances were insufficient grounds," another, it was said, might be found in the presence

---

[34] 5 Wall. 1 (1867).
[35] To invoke, in prize procedure, was to call in evidence from a parallel case, or from the papers of a sister ship of the same owners.

at Nassau of a certain blockade runner known to be owned by the claimants. (Critics later pointed out that this blockade runner had been elsewhere at that moment.)[36] Inferring a guilty intent from these circumstances, the Court affirmed the condemnation of the cargo.

The Peterhoff,[37] British, was captured on a voyage to Matamoros, Mexico, near the mouth of the Rio Grande, opposite Brownsville, Texas. Access to Matamoros was not subject to blockade; goods really intended for sale in the market there would go free. Moreover, inland trade between Mexico and Texas, even in military supplies, was innocent. But as to that portion of the cargo that was contraband, such as artillery harness and military shoes, the Court said that "There is nothing in this case which tends to convince us" that Matamoros was their real destination, "while all the circumstances indicate that these articles, at least, were destined for the use of the rebel forces . . . ." Contraband "destined in fact" to the enemy was liable to capture even though "primarily destined to Matamoros" and even though its further transportation in the interior would have violated no blockade. Other goods of the same ownership were infected.

For half a century *The Springbok* and *The Peterhoff* continued to provoke dissent, especially in neutral countries. Their doctrine lay like a stepping stone whereby a strong naval power in time of war might advance to a more commanding position on belligerent rights. The British prize court took that step early in the First World War:

> The doctrine of "continuous voyage" was first applied by the English Prize Courts to unlawful trading. There is no reported case in our Courts where the doctrine is applied in terms to the carriage of contraband; but it was so applied and extended by the United States Courts against this country in the time of the American Civil War; and its application was acceded to by the British Government of the day; and was, moreover, acted upon by the International Commission which sat under the Treaty between this country and America, made at Washington on May 8, 1871 . . . .

This was *The Kim*,[38] where British forces had captured neutral vessels carrying meat products from America to Denmark, itself a food exporter. Evidently the "highly probable destination" was Germany. Refusing "to be blinded to the realities," the court condemned.

At the time of the Civil War it was proper to say—as Grier, J., did in the *Prize Cases*[39]—that war was "that state in which a nation

---

[36] Moore, *Digest of International Law*, VII, 724.
[37] 5 Wall. 28 (1867).
[38] Law Reports [1915] Probate 215.

In the High Court of Justice, Probate, Divorce and Admiralty Division.
[39] 2 Bl. 635, 666 (1863).

prosecutes its right by force"; also it could be said that when this remedy by self-help was being followed, the duty of strangers to the dispute was to "pursue a conduct friendly and impartial toward the belligerent powers."[40] A century has brought a marked advance. The nations of the world have united "to ensure . . . that armed force shall not be used, save in the common interest."[41] In 1950 the General Assembly of the United Nations, finding "that international tension exists on a dangerous scale," adopted a Uniting for Peace plan, to increase the prospect of effective action to suppress acts of aggression.[42] It is needless to say that the hope has not been fulfilled. But it is true that impartial neutrality is no longer regarded as the normal and proper attitude when the peace of nations is endangered. The world has moved far from the ground on which questions of prize were argued before Chase and his brethren. Yet at that time these cases were of high importance, inasmuch as they concerned not only captors and claimants, but also the relations of the United States with foreign powers, in particular, Great Britain.

SOME CATEGORIES OF THE COURT'S BUSINESS

ONLY A SMALL FRACTION of the prize condemnations were appealed to the Supreme Court, and most of those could be affirmed on clear principles. On behalf of *The Duoro*,[43] running cotton out of Wilmington, North Carolina, nothing could be said more than that she reached the open sea before the blockading vessel began the chase, which was no defense at all. Nevertheless Charles Edwards, experienced counsel often engaged by British claimants, made bold to take an appeal to the Supreme Court. "It is impossible to imagine a plainer case for condemnation," said the Chief Justice. He added a sharp rebuke: "We impose penalties when writs of error merely for delay are sued out, in cases of judgments at law for damages; and if the rule were applicable to the case before us we should apply it." The Court had built up its rules without system, and in using the technical expression "writ of error," applicable to cases at law, it had made no provision to penalize dilatory "appeals" in cases of equity and admiralty.

While prize litigation dried up quickly after the 1866 term, normal instances of admiralty jurisdiction, notably collisions, remained a considerable part of the Court's work. Admiralty is exclusively a concern of

---

[40] President Washington's Neutrality Proclamation of April 22, 1793. 11 Stat. 753. Am. State Papers: Foreign Relations (Washington: Gales and Seaton, 1832–61), I, 140.

[41] Preamble of the Charter of the United Nations (1945).
[42] U.N. General Assembly, Fifth Sess. Doc. A/1481, Nov. 4, 1950.
[43] 3 Wall. 564 (1866).

the federal courts, and the District Court heard cases in first instance. Appeal lay to the Circuit Court; then the Judiciary Act allowed a further resort to the Supreme Court, whose review once again covered the whole case, facts as well as law. Often it might be said, in the words of Justice Nelson, that "On looking into the proofs in the case, which are very voluminous, it will be found that the testimony of the master and hands on board of the respective vessels, as usual, is contradictory . . . ."[44] (The ethics of the sea instills loyalty to ship and shipmates.) So the Reports are full of talk about lights and lookouts, tacking and luffing— lore to which many appointees to the Court had never been initiated. Chief Justice Chase tended to assign these cases to Justice Clifford, who lived among sailors, and found the business congenial. By the Act of February 16, 1875,[45] Congress limited review in admiralty cases to questions of law, and raised the jurisdictional minimum from $2,000 to $5,000.

Litigation over Spanish and Mexican land grants in California was a special category of the Court's business. Chase's first term saw several instances, among them the *Sutter Case*,[46] involving the immense estate of New Helvetia where gold had been discovered in 1848. The United States by the treaty of peace with Mexico had pledged to respect existing grants of land. To give effect to that undertaking, Congress in 1851 provided that claims be determined by a board of commissioners, with review by the District Court and appeal to the Supreme Court. The tracts involved were vast and, after the discovery of gold, very valuable. The grants were identified by crude maps—"rough daubs called desiños"—[47] which often did not agree with the terrain. The controversies abounded in "extensive frauds, with forged grants and perjured witnesses," "squatters and champertous attorneys."[48] Leaders at the bar in Washington—commonly such of them as had political entrée—were engaged to press these matters in the Executive offices and before the Court. By reason of his California background, Justice Field was most conversant with Mexican land law and was frequently selected to write the opinion.

Railroad receiverships in the federal courts were another special matter, illustrated at the 1864 term by several instances concerning the LaCrosse and Milwaukee Company.[49] That line had been forced into

---

44 Wells v. The Ann Caroline, Fed. Case No. 17,389 (S.D.N.Y. 1859); subsequently carried to the Supreme Court where the decree was modified. The Ann Caroline, 2 Wall. 538 (1865).
45 18 Stat. 315.
46 United States v. John A. Sutter, 2 Wall. 562 (1865).
47 Grier, J., in United States v.

Billing, 2 Wall. 444, 448 (1865).
48 Grier, J., dissenting in United States v. Vallejo, 1 Bl. 541, 556 (1862).
49 R.R. Co. v. Soutter, 2 Wall. 440 (1865); R.R. Co. v. Soutter, 2 Wall. 510 (1865); Minnesota Co. v. St. Paul Co., 2 Wall. 609 (1865); *Ex parte* Fleming, 2 Wall. 759 (1865).

what Justice Miller, out of court, called "the fiercest fight I ever saw,"[50] running back and forth for years between the Circuit and the Supreme Court. The rough and tumble of railroad operations makes a considerable part of the history of the Court after the Civil War.

SECTION 25 OF THE JUDICIARY ACT

HALF A DOZEN CONSTITUTIONAL QUESTIONS came before the Court at Chase's first term—not all of which could then be answered. Three of these came up from a State court, under Section 25 of the Judiciary Act of 1789. That great section, an indispenable girder in the federal structure, gave a resort to the Supreme Court in any case where a claim of federal right had been finally rejected by the judiciary of a State.[51] *Hawthorne v. Calef*[52] raised the contention that a statute of the State of Maine, as construed by its highest court, had impaired the obligation of a contract, in violation of the Contract Clause of the Constitution. Plaintiff had given credit to a corporation at a time when a stockholder was liable, to the extent of his stock, for corporate debts. Various repeals and revisions, as the Maine court worked out their effect,[53] had left the creditor without this secondary remedy. Should "contract" in the constitutional sense be read large enough to include this additional security beyond the creditor's right against the principal debtor? Benjamin R. Curtis, for the plaintiff, invoked the broad construction that he himself had expressed for the Court when he was one of its members:[54]

---

[50] Charles Fairman, *Mr. Justice Miller and the Supreme Court, 1862–1890* (Cambridge, Mass.: Harvard University Press, 1939), 240.

[51] In material part Section 25 provided:

That a final judgment or decree in any suit, in the highest court of law or equity of a State in which a decision in the suit could be had,

[1] where is drawn in question the validity of a treaty or statute of, or an authority exercised under the United States, and the decision is against their validity; or

[2] where is drawn in question the validity of a statute of, or an authority exercised under any State, on the ground of their being repugnant to the constitution, treaties or laws of the United States, and the decision is in favour of such their validity; or

[3] where is drawn in question the construction of any clause of the constitution, or of a treaty, or statute of, or commission held under the United States, and the decision is against the title, right, privilege or exemption specially set up or claimed by either party . . . ,

may be re-examined and reversed or affirmed in the Supreme Court of the United States upon a writ of error . . . .

[52] 2 Wall. 10 (1865).

[53] Coffin v. Rich, 45 Me. 507 (1858).

[54] Curran v. Arkansas, 15 How. 304, 319 (1853), quoted in his Opening Argument for the Plaintiff, 8.

The obligation of a contract, in the sense in which those words are used in the Constitution, is that duty of performing it, which is recognized and enforced by the laws. And if the law is so changed that the means of legally enforcing this duty are materially impaired, the obligation of the contract no longer remains the same.

The Court agreed. Without becoming involved in Maine's tangled statutes, it said simply that the repealing act, by depriving the creditor of an important remedy, had impaired his contract.

Throughout the years the Contract Clause, as applied by the Court, had done much to protect economic arrangements against popular restlessness. Presently it would become of relatively less significance, when the Fourteenth Amendment added the more pervasive guarantee of due process and equal protection of the laws.

GOVERNMENT BONDS AND STATE TAXES

IN THE *Bank Tax Case*, argued and decided in January, 1865,[55] the Justices were in accord that where a State tax was imposed on the bank's capital (rather than on its corporate franchise, or on some privilege), it could not be applied to such part of that capital as was invested in United States securities. This was an application of a principle firmly established in the time of Marshall, that the exercise of a national power—in this case, "to borrow Money on the credit of the United States"[56]—must be free and unembarrassed.[57]

During the war, Congress established a system of national banks. A central feature of the plan was that each bank would invest in United States bonds, which it could then use as the basis for issuing national bank notes that would circulate as currency. By the National Bank Act of 1864,[58] Congress declared that nothing therein would prevent State taxation of the shares of such banks, with these limitations: the tax must not be "at a greater rate than is assessed upon other moneyed capital in the hands of individual citizens," and must not "exceed the rate imposed upon the shares" of State banks.

The New York Legislature changed the form of its tax to take advantage of this Act of Congress. *Van Allen v. The Assessors*[59] was brought by an owner of shares in the First National Bank of Albany, all of whose capital was invested in United States securities. He said that

---

[55] 2 Wall. 200. Twenty-five cases were decided together, the principle of one opinion being applicable to all.

[56] Constitution, Art. I, Sec. 8, cl. 2.

[57] McCulloch v. Maryland, 4 Wheat. 316 (1819); Weston v. Charleston, 2 Pet. 449 (1829).

[58] Act of June 3, 1864, 13 Stat. 99, amending and reenacting the Act of Feb. 25, 1863, 12 Stat. 665.

[59] 3 Wall. 573 (1866).

shares were simply portions of the capital and could no more be taxed than could the capital itself; to avoid constitutional objections, the Act of Congress ought not to be so construed as to mean otherwise. After hearing the case argued "at great length and with eminent ability,"[60] the Court, by divided vote, held that the interest of a shareholder was "a distinct, independent interest," something apart from the capital owned by the corporation. The Act of Congress was construed to permit State taxation of the whole of that interest, and as so construed, was free from constitutional defect. The Court pointed out that along with ownership of the bonds had come "new uses and new privileges"; in particular, the bank was enabled to issue its own notes, which should bring great benefits to the shareholders. Justice Nelson spoke for the majority.

The Chief Justice (Wayne and Swayne, JJ., joining with him) insisted upon a different view. "It may well be questioned . . . whether Congress has power under the Constitution to authorize State taxation of national securities, either directly or indirectly." First, unless Congress had authorized such taxation when the bonds were issued, tax-exemption might be *inferred*—so that State taxation would impair a term which should be read into the contract between the United States and the bondholder. Actually, Congress had declared that these bonds were free from State and municipal taxation: could Congress then authorize indirect taxation upon the shares of a corporation whose capital was invested in them? The power was so questionable that the Court should not suppose that Congress intended to exercise it.

> And were the power to authorize such taxation clear, a superior question would remain—the question of good faith, of public virtue, of national honor.

Aside from this contractual aspect, the Chief Justice referred to "great principles already established by the decisions of this Court," which Congress must have had in view: that States cannot tax the agencies of the United States, or United States securities in the hands of an individual or when part of the capital of a corporation. Accordingly, when Congress conceded that shares might be taxed at a rate not

---

[60] Three cases were argued together, on January 31, February 1, 2, and 5, 1866. Evarts, Charles B. Sedgwick (Republican Congressman, 1859–63), Lyman Tremain (formerly Attorney General of New York, prominent Republican, Congressman 1873–75), and others appeared for the shareholders. The tax was defended by Francis Kernan (formerly Reporter of the Court of Appeals, and Democratic Congressman, later a Senator) and Amasa J. Parker (formerly a Congressman, Judge sitting in the Court of Appeals, a founder of the Albany Law School, and leading War Democrat).

greater than that assessed upon other moneyed capital, and not to exceed that imposed upon State bank shares, it must be taken to have meant only assessment *after* investments in United States securities had been deducted. Only by that construction would "sound principle and perfect faith" be observed.

Van Allen v. The Assessors became a leading case,[61] often applied in the reasoning of the Court, and still more often examined in learned discussion of the persistent problem of intergovernmental immunities in the federal system. It may be remembered for this practical result: that it brought "a vast amount of property within the taxing power of the States, which would have been excluded" had the distinction between corporate property and shares of stock not been made.[62]

Chase, the architect of the national banks, wanted to exalt his creations. He presented, not a rigorous analysis of the problem, but rather an impressive development of the conviction he must have held from the outset. He suggested constitutional difficulties: an implied exemption which States must not impair, a denial of power in Congress to permit State taxation even though Congress judged it to be expedient. He saw a superior question, even if the power of Congress were clear: there would still be limitations of good faith, public virtue, national honor—moral tests, beyond the Constitution, which seemingly the Court should apply to the acts of a coordinate branch of the Government.[63] These objections he merely suggested, by the way, without insisting upon them. One may recall Justice Miller's comment, that Chase had "an imperious will"—he "liked to have his own way."[64] Here the majority had refused to accept a view which the ex-Minister of Finance regarded as a matter of great importance. His reaction was to assume a lofty moral position and to defend it by objections which only attentive examination will remove.[65]

---

[61] Actually, in that case the Justices were united in holding the New York statute invalid, in that in one respect it failed to treat shareholders in national banks as favorably as shareholders in State banks. But, said Nelson, J., "The defect may be readily remedied," as indeed it was, a month later. Foreseeing such amendment, he had gone on to rule upon "the main and important question."

After the legislature had cured the defect, in People v. The Commissioners (and ten other cases), 4 Wall. 244 (1867), Evarts and other counsel returned to the attack, over old ground and new. The Court reaffirmed its holding, and Chase, Wayne, and Swayne noted dissent.

[62] As White, J., observed in Owensboro Nat. Bank v. Owensboro, 173 U.S. 664, 680 (1899).

[63] This sounds like the invocation of a "Higher Law," which had figured prominently in anti-slavery discussion.

[64] Supra, p. 26.

[65] The matter is here dwelt upon with an eye to consideration presently of Hepburn v. Griswold and its overruling in the Legal Tender Cases, infra, ch. 14.

Of course an undertaking actually given by the United States to lenders should be honored. Of course the States should not be allowed, by taxation or otherwise, substantially to embarrass the proper functioning of the Federal Government. Beyond that, there was no merit in allowing holders of shares in banks to enjoy exemption from nondiscriminatory taxation by State and local government. It was a problem to be solved, not by absolute constitutional propositions and appeals to national honor, but by candid analysis.

"Have you read the opinion and the dissent in the Bank Tax cases together?" So the Chief Justice closed a letter to Justice Field on April 30, 1866.[66] The judgment had been announced on March 26. The Court had adjourned on April 3, and Field had set out for California. Now printer's proofs had been revised, and the Clerk had distributed copies among the Justices. Chase hoped that Field would be impressed when he read the dissenting opinion in print.

Copies of the opinions were widely in demand, by reason of the many interests affected.[67]

It was impracticable for the States to collect the tax on shares sustained in the *Van Allen* case, if the shareholder lived out-of-State. Accordingly States required the national banks to withhold the tax and remit to the collector, and the Court found this unobjectionable.[68]

Van Allen showed that the Court was prepared to make nice distinctions to find a sound adjustment in the federal system where one sovereign's power to borrow must be reconciled with another sovereign's power to tax. A State may tax the corporate franchises it confers, whether at a fixed sum or according to some measure of use. In *Society for Savings v. Coite*,[69] *Provident Institution v. Massachusetts*,[70] and *Hamilton Manufacturing Co. v. Massachusetts*[71]—all decided on March 30, 1868—the Court upheld such a tax on savings banks measured by a percent of total deposits, and on a manufacturing company according to

---

[66] Robert B. Warden, *An Account of the Private Life and Public Services of Salmon Portland Chase* (Cincinnati, Ohio: Wilstach, Baldwin and Co., 1874), 647, 649.

[67] In the Senate on May 7, Sherman obtained an order for printing three thousand copies. He explained, "It is unusual for the Senate to print decisions of the Supreme Court; but there are a multitude of cases pending . . . , and I have a great number of applications for this decision . . . . Cong. Globe, 39–1, 2414. *The Stockholder*, 4:536 of July 3, 1866, told of ques-

tions on the application of the decision, and set out a circular of rulings by the State Comptroller, of June 28. A decision such as that in *Van Allen* had effects that were felt throughout the financial community.

[68] National Bank v. Commonwealth, 9 Wall. 353 (1870); Lionberger v. Rouse, 9 Wall. 468 (1870); Van Slyke v. Wisconsin, 154 U.S. 581, 20 L. Ed. 240 (1871).

[69] 6 Wall. 594.

[70] 6 Wall. 611.

[71] 6 Wall. 632.

the market value of its capital stock, notwithstanding that the deposits and the capital were in part invested in United States securities.[72]

Oliver Wendell Holmes, Jr., in an annotation to his twelfth edition of Kent's *Commentaries*, observed that in these decisions the Court had "gone very far" in sustaining the corporate franchise tax.[73] Years later, when himself on the Court, he joined in following them where they seemed applicable, through a moment of eclipse[74] and on to their restoration to authority.[75]

STATE AND NATIONAL INTERESTS IN PILOTS AND BRIDGES

AT DECEMBER TERM 1864 the Court had very real difficulty with two cases of State regulation affecting interstate commerce. *Steamship Company v. Joliffe*[76] questioned the validity of California's regulation of pilotage for the port of San Francisco. In 1852 Congress had passed an Act for the better security of lives on steam vessels, in the course of which it provided for federal licensing of pilots. California in 1861 made its own regulations for licensing pilots for San Francisco and required all vessels to pay pilotage fees. The Pacific Mail Steamship Company, then the great carrier between California and the East Coast, tested the law by refusing to pay. The case, after having been held over for reargument,[77] was heard by seven Justices. Four, speaking by Field, J., held that the statutes could be reconciled. "Pilot" in maritime usage had two meanings: a member of the crew who steered the ship on

---

[72] In each case Chase, C.J., Grier and Miller, JJ., dissented, "on the ground that the tax was on the property and not upon the franchises and privileges . . . ."

In 1890, when of the participants only Justices Field and Miller remained, these cases were cited and followed in Home Insurance Co. v. New York, 134 U.S. 594, per Field, J.; Miller and Harlan, JJ., dissenting: the Court sustained a tax upon corporations, measured by dividends, where the dividends were derived from interest on government bonds.

In the two cases from Massachusetts, Sidney Bartlett and Representative Henry L. Dawes appeared for the Provident Institution and the Hamilton Co., respectively. The State was represented by its Attorney General, Charles Allen, who will appear presently as the author of a powerful brief sustaining the Louisiana statute involved in the Slaughter House Cases. Infra, pp. 1346–47.

[73] I, *429 n.l (1873).

[74] Macallen Co. v. Massachusetts, 279 U.S. 620 (1929), Stone, J., dissenting with Holmes and Brandeis, JJ.

[75] Educational Films Corp. v. Ward, 282 U.S. 379 (1931); Pacific Co. v. Johnson, 285 U.S. 480 (1932).

[76] 2 Wall. 450 (1865).

[77] When it came up at the 1863 term, the case was put over to permit California by its Attorney General to defend its statute. Minutes, Feb. 23, 1864.

her voyage, and also a mariner skilled in guiding ships into and out of port. They read the Act of Congress as applying only to the former, thereby leaving the latter to be controlled by local law. Justices Miller, Wayne, and Clifford, dissenting, foresaw invidious regulations productive of a "piebald, conflicting and incongruous system . . . ." What if every town on the inland lakes and rivers required steamboats to pay for a local pilot? When in 1871 the federal statute was revised,[78] wisdom was drawn from both opinions. No State charge, it was enacted, could be laid upon a steamer having a federally licensed pilot; the State remained free, however, to apply its pilotage laws to other vessels.

The other case of State regulation produced an equal division within the Court. This was the *Albany Bridge Case*,[79] a suit in the Circuit Court to enjoin the building of a bridge over the Hudson River as authorized by a statute of New York, on the ground that complainant, a citizen of Massachusetts, would be denied a federal right to engage in the coasting trade with a point above the proposed bridge. If State power in this situation were denied, it would require Congressional action to permit the bridging of any stream bearing interstate commerce. If State bridge laws were sustained, some water-borne commerce would be destroyed. In 1862 in this and in the *Passaic Bridge Case*,[80] as one finds in the Minutes for January 27, the Justices had been equally divided. Now once more the Court found itself unable to give an opinion to guide the court below. (The two judges in the Circuit Court having themselves been divided, the outcome was that nothing could be done for the complainant.) At the 1865 term, in the *Schuylkill Bridge Case*,[81] a majority was mustered on the side of sustaining State bridge laws. Justices Clifford, Wayne, and Davis dissented. Justice Nelson, whose objection to such laws was already well known, took no part in the case. Here were three Democrats and one Republican who, differing with their brethren, held the view that federal authority, even though unexercised, excluded State action.

The decision gave lasting satisfaction. The States remained free to act in local situations where it would have been difficult to engage the attention of Congress. When presently it appeared that the federal interest should be safeguarded, Congress provided an administrative examination to avert any "unreasonable obstruction of the free navigation."[82]

---

[78] 16 Stat. 440, 455.

[79] 2 Wall. 403 (1865), wherein was repeated the equal division reported in Silliman v. Hudson River Bridge Co., 1 Bl. 582 (1862).

[80] Milnor v. New Jersey R.R., 3 Wall. Appendix 782.

[81] Gilman v. Philadelphia, 3 Wall. 713 (1866).

[82] Act of Mar. 3, 1899. 30 Stat. 1121, 1154.

THE COURT INVALIDATES AN
ENACTMENT OF CONGRESS

AT CHASE'S FIRST TERM the Court held one section of an Act of Congress to be unconstitutional, the fourth such occasion in the Court's history.[83] This was done so unobtrusively, however, that one has to look closely to discover what happened. In 1855 Congress created the Court of Claims, whose function it would be to examine certain categories of claims against the United States and to report its findings to Congress. Prior to that time the matter had been left to the uncertain political process of private bill legislation. In 1863, when a mass of claims were arising out of war contracts, Congress established an orderly process whereby that court would not merely *report*—it would *decide*, and enter a judgment between the claimant and the United States; furthermore, by Section 5 of the statute, an appeal to the Supreme Court was authorized.[84] In the 1790's, at the very outset of government under the Constitution, it had been established, quite obscurely on that occasion too, that the federal judicial courts could not be charged with *reporting* on claims to other branches of government:[85] the judicial power was a power only to determine with finality. Did the Act of 1863, in the section directing the Supreme Court to hear appeals from the Court of Claims, repeat the old error? Section 14 of the statute enacted

> That no money shall be paid out of the treasury for any claim passed on by the court of claims till after an appropriation therefor shall have been estimated for by the Secretary of the Treasury.

Would the Supreme Court, if it heard and decided an appeal in such a case, be entering an effective judgment, or would it only be making a finding subject to control by another branch of government?

Gordon contended that the United States owed him money. The Court of Claims held that he had shown no valid cause of action. On December 2, 1863, he filed an appeal.[86] The Supreme Court, recognizing that its jurisdiction was questionable, made an order on April 4,

---

[83] Gordon v. United States, 2 Wall. 561 (1865). Counting as the first United States v. Yale Todd (1794), n. 85. Then came Marbury v. Madison, 1 Cr. 137 (1803), and next, Dred Scott v. Sandford, 19 How. 393 (1857).

[84] Act. of Mar. 3, 1863. 12 Stat. 765.

[85] This is the conclusion to be derived from Hayburn's Case, 2 Dall. 409 (1792) and its sequel, United States v. Yale Todd, decided in 1794 and reported in a note to United States v. Ferreira, 13 How. 40 (1851).

[86] Gordon v. United States, 2 Wall. 561 (1865).

1864, that the case be continued and that the question of constitutional jurisdiction be argued at the next term. All parties interested in the question were invited to participate.[87]

Without waiting to hear that argument, Chief Justice Taney prepared a draft of what he regarded as the proper answer. The critical passages are these:

> nor can Congress authorize or require this Court to express an opinion on a case . . . where its judgment would not be final and conclusive upon the rights of the parties, and process of execution awarded to carry it into effect.
>
> The award of execution is a part, and an essential part of every judgment passed by a court exercising judicial power. . . .

No payment would be made unless the Secretary submitted an estimate and Congress made an appropriation. So, as Taney saw it, the "ultimate judicial power will . . . be exercised by the Legislative Department . . . ." The Supreme Court could not participate in such a proceeding.[88]

Death deprived Taney of an opportunity to use his draft opinion.

At the December term 1864, the Court set the first Tuesday in January as the time when it would hear argument on this constitutional issue. It was so argued, by counsel sustaining the jurisdiction. On March 10, 1865, the last day of the term, the Court dismissed the appeal for want of jurisdiction. Chief Justice Chase, in a brief per curiam opinion, said:

> We think that the authority given to the head of an Executive Department by necessary implication in the 14th section of the amended Court of Claims Act, to revise all the decisions of that court requiring payment of money, denies to it the judicial power from the exercise of which alone appeals can be taken to this Court.[89]

The reasons for this conclusion, he added, "may be more fully announced hereafter," which was never done. Dissent by Justices Miller and Field was noted.

Congress hastened to meet the Court's objection: it repealed Sec-

---

[87] Minutes of the Court, Apr. 4, 1864. Chief Justice Waite, in United States v. Jones, 119 U.S. 477 (1886), erroneously gives the date as April 10 (a Sunday).

[88] This draft opinion was published long afterward in 117 U.S. 697, at a time when the Court was called upon to reexamine the question of its jurisdiction on appeal from the Court of Claims. In United States v. Jones, 119 U.S. 477 (1886), Chief Justice Waite recounted the events at the 1863 and 1864 terms.

[89] 2 Wall. 561.

tion 14.[90] Thereupon, at December term 1866, the Court began to hear appeals from the Court of Claims—a jurisdiction it has been exercising ever since.[91]

Taney's draft opinion took the ground that *the award of execution* was an essential part of every judgment passed by any court exercising the "judicial power of the United States" established by Article III of the Constitution. That view went beyond what the Court actually decided. For certainly the execution of any money judgment against the United States must be dependent upon an appropriation by Congress. "No money shall be drawn from the Treasury, but in Consequence of Appropriations made by Law."[92] Surely the Court would not sustain a levy upon property of the United States as a means of satisfying a judgment. Here is a matter where the judiciary, having declared with finality what right and justice require, must look to another branch of government for supporting action.[93] Presumably it was this reflection that caused Justices Miller and Field to dissent from the holding that the presence of Section 14 made unconstitutional the grant of a review under Section 5.

The issue suggested in Gordon's case was speculative; no actual collision was even remotely threatened. The Court was not invading an area claimed by Congress; rather it was declining to enter an area that Congress had assigned to it. Congress cheerfully removed the obstacle so that the Court might act. One pauses for a moment to view this subdued scene of understanding and accommodation. Soon litigants would be urging the Court to advance upon political ground Congress had seized and was determined to maintain for itself alone. Soon Congress would be legislating to forbid, not to invite, the Court's action.

---

[90] By the Act of Mar. 17, 1866, c. 19, 14 Stat. 9. In explaining this measure, Senator Trumbull, chairman of the Judiciary Committee, recalled that the Court had objected to "departmental supervision under the fourteenth section. Now, there is no such supervision exercised; it is not in point of fact done; but the judgments are paid out of the appropriation which we make; and the sole object of the bill is to repeal that fourteenth section." Cong. Globe, 39–1, 771 (1866).

[91] De Groot v. United States, 5 Wall. 419 (1867).

[92] Constitution, Art. I, Sec. 9, cl. 7.

[93] Reporter Wallace, in his headnote in Gordon v. United States, inac-

curately stated that the case held that "no appellate jurisdiction over the Court of Claims could be exercised by this Court . . . ." *Could not* expressed the upshot of Taney's draft opinion, but it was not what the Court decided.

A contention that review by the Court was precluded merely by the potential control of Congress over payments was rejected in *United States v. Jones*, 119 U.S. 447 (1886). It was raised there by a claimant who had won in the Court of Claims and sought to prevent a review by the Supreme Court, which might (and did—121 U.S. 89) reverse the judgment of the Court of Claims.

AN ABORTIVE CASE ON A SENSITIVE ISSUE

SHORTLY BEFORE THE CLOSE of December term 1864 a case was made challenging a position where the Lincoln Administration was most vulnerable: its action in detaining accused or suspected persons without trial. Here was an issue that had remained imminent since April 1861;[94] the Government had anxiously contrived to avoid any occasion demanding a decision by the Supreme Court. And now, in February 1865, a case had reached the docket. Since the Reports show nothing more than a three-sentence per curiam opinion on a point of procedure,[95] one must look to other sources to re-create the episode. Early in 1864, an Army paymaster had been robbed; John Dugan and Christopher V. Hogan, government police officers, were charged with complicity and held, by order of the Secretary of War, without being brought to trial. In January 1865 the Supreme Court of the District of Columbia granted petitions for habeas corpus, directed to the Superintendent of the Old Capitol Prison. The respondent respectfully declined to comply, "by reason of the order of the President of the United States endorsed upon said writ." The indorsement was, in Dugan's case:

> The within named John Dugan was arrested on and is imprisoned by my authority. This writ of *habeas corpus* is suspended, and the officer having Dugan in custody is directed not to produce his body, but to hold him in custody until further notice, giving this order on your return to the Court.
>
> Jan. 23, 1865   A. Lincoln

The petition in Dugan's behalf had been based upon the statute of March 3, 1863, wherein Congress, in authorizing the suspension of the writ of habeas corpus, provided that if when the federal grand jury met it failed to indict, the prisoner would be entitled to release upon taking an oath of allegiance.[96] (Much more will be said of that statute when

---

[94] *Ex parte* Merryman, Fed. Case No. 9487, where Taney, C.J., in habeas corpus had ordered the release of one seized by the Executive for participating in the obstruction of army forces coming through Baltimore to the defense of the Government. President Lincoln had refused to comply. "Are all the laws *but one* to go unexecuted, and the Government itself go to pieces lest that one be violated?" So the President responded, in his message to the Special Session of Congress on July 4, 1861. *Collected Works of Abraham Lincoln*, Roy P. Basler, ed. (New Brunswick, N.J.: Rutgers University Press, 1953), IV, 421, 430.

[95] *Ex parte* Dugan, 2 Wall. 134 (1865).

[96] 12 Stat. 755.

Ex parte Milligan is reached.[97]) Two grand juries, it was alleged, had come and gone since Dugan's arrest, and a third term had been going on for six weeks. The District of Columbia court held that power to suspend the writ in time of rebellion was by the Constitution vested in the President alone;[98] that the statute was enacted out of abundant caution, "to justify such exercise of authority if, as claimed by some, the provision should be finally declared to be a grant of legislative power." Accordingly the return was held sufficient.[99] This was on Saturday, February 11.

On Monday the thirteenth counsel filed an action in the Supreme Court of the United States, No. 6 Original, in the matter of Dugan; this was a petition for habeas corpus, and for certiorari directed to the Supreme Court of the District of Columbia to send up the record for appellate review.[100] On February 17 a like action, No. 7 Original, was brought on behalf of Hogan. At that time counsel filed in each case a transcript he had obtained of the record in the court below.

The Administration became alarmed. Many prisoners, of high and low degree, were being detained, on order of the Secretary of State or of the Secretary of War. A decision in favor of Dugan and Hogan would lead to a general jail delivery, unless the President put himself in open defiance of the Court. Secretary Welles' diary reports at length the wild rumors and suspicions blowing through the Executive offices. "Some intimation comes through Stanton, that His Honor the Chief Justice intends to make himself felt by the Administration when he can reach them. I shall not be surprised, for he is ambitious and able. Yet on that subject he is as much implicated as others." (Welles always took a rancorous view of Chase.) Attorney General Speed "is apprehensive Chase will fail the Administration . . . . The President expresses, and feels, astonishment. Calls up the commitals of Chase on these measures." "Seward thinks Chase, if badly disposed, cannot carry the court, but this

---

[97] 4 Wall. 2 (1866), infra. Contemporaneously with this case there was a significant debate in Congress. See infra.

[98] Art. I (dealing generally with Congress) provides in its Sec. 9, clause 2, that "The Privilege of the Writ of Habeas Corpus shall not be suspended, unless when in Cases of Rebellion or Invasion the public Safety may require it."

[99] *In re* John Dugan, 6 Mackey 131.

[100] The writ of habeas corpus commanded the person detaining another to produce the body of his prisoner, with the cause of the detention. The writ of certiorari commanded the inferior court to send up the record in a proceeding before it. "As the certiorari alone removes not the body, so the habeas corpus alone removes not the record itself, but only the prisoner with the cause of his commitment . . ." Bacon's *Abridgment*, title Habeas Corpus, B 3. Hence the need for the writ of certiorari in aid of the Supreme Court's appellate jurisdiction in habeas corpus. See infra, pp. 443–44.

is mere random conjecture."[101] This is evidence of what the President and Cabinet were thinking, not of the state of the Chief Justice's mind.

On February 27 the Court granted certiorari "returnable forthwith." It would take the court below a little time to comply with this command that it certify and return a copy of the record, and the Supreme Court was close to its adjournment. (On February 17 it had announced that it would hear no arguments after March 3.) The instant this point was gained, counsel for the petitioners made another request. He had already obtained a copy of the record, and had filed it on February 17. On the twenty-seventh, as the Minutes show, he asked the Court, "upon the admission of the Attorney-General that the copy was a correct one, to hear the case without a return from the court below. *The Attorney-General, on the other hand*, while admitting the copy of the record to be correct, moved the court, for reasons he had laid, to continue the case."

What response should be made? Personal liberty was at stake; application for habeas corpus always has peremptory overtones. It would have been dramatic to say, Let not the sun set on any man unjustly held in prison. But then the great constitutional issue was not susceptible of hasty disposition. There were many controversial points to explore— about the powers of the President, the powers of Congress, the power of the judiciary; after argument the Justices doubtless would need much time in conference. The day was close at hand when the Court should adjourn to permit the Justices to go on their circuits. As Dugan's petition made clear, these petitioners had bided their time: the same case could have been made as soon as the first grand jury had adjourned. Doubtless for their own good reasons they had waited for a propitious moment; now their counsel asked the Court to take a short cut.

The Court announced this ruling:

> We think it the better, as well as the more regular practice, to await the return of the court below before taking any action on the merits. The *certiorari* will, therefore, be now awarded. Upon the coming in of the return the case will be regularly before us; and the motion for continuance made by the Attorney-General will then be disposed of.[102]

On March 3, 1865, it was "Ordered by the Court that these cases be and the same are hereby continued to the next term of this Court."

They were not brought up at the next term; the only subsequent

---

[101] *Diary of Gideon Welles* (Boston and New York: Houghton Mifflin Co., 1911), II, 242–43, 245–46. Entries for Feb. 21 and 22, 1865, wherein recent happenings were recalled.

[102] 2 Wall. 134.

entry is that for December 10, 1866, when on motion of counsel for the petitioners it was ordered that the petitions be dismissed at the cost of the petitioners. Evidently Dugan and Hogan had been released. The Court had declined to hasten its step to reach the issue, and in the outcome the question became moot.

THE IRON-CLAD OATH

WE COME TO THE TOUCHY issue of test oaths. On March 10, 1865, the last day of the term, the Court made a notable amendment to its rules. It required that all thereafter practicing at its bar take an oath that they had never voluntarily borne arms against the United States, or given aid or encouragement to persons in armed hostility thereto, or exercised the functions of any office under any authority or pretended authority hostile to the United States. The Court was thus bringing its rules into accord with a recent Act of Congress.

By the Act of July 2, 1862,[103] Congress had prescribed the above "iron-clad" oath for civil and military officers of the United States. In the First Session of the 38th Congress, on January 25, 1864, Senator Sumner had introduced S. 72, to amend the statute so as also to require the oath of all seeking admission to the bar of any federal court or appearing there by reason of previous admission. The Judiciary Committee reported adversely, near the close of the session.

At the Second Session, on December 21, 1864, Sumner remarked on the committee's "unaccountable" rejection of his bill; he would ask the Senate's early attention.[104] That he did, the next day, with the result that his bill carried by a vote of 27 to 4. Senator Reverdy Johnson of Maryland, Democrat, explained that it had been "the almost unanimous opinion of the committee that it was not at all necessary to the security of the country that this oath should be required"; that it could with as much reason "be prescribed to every man in the United States"; as the Senator from Massachusetts, however, seemed to think that the condition of the country would be less perilous if the members of the bar took the oath, he was willing to silence his own fears on that subject and let the bill pass.[105] The House readily concurred, 66 to 26, and Sumner's bill became law on January 24, 1865.[106]

When the Court amended its rule to conform it was merely recognizing the presumptive validity of an Act of Congress. If an adjudication on constitutionality was to be made, it would be only when the issue was raised by some interested party.

---

[103] 12 Stat. 502.
[104] Cong. Globe, 38–2, 91.

[105] Cong. Globe, 38–2, 109.
[106] 13 Stat. 424.

II: *The Work of the Supreme Court*

That occasion was not long in arising. In the first week of the next term, on December 8, 1865, Reverdy Johnson sought an early hearing for *Ex parte Garland*, No. 6 Original, [107] an application by a pardoned Confederate for leave to resume his practice at the Supreme Court bar, notwithstanding the statute. Here was the beginning of a great case on test oaths, that would end in January 1867, in a judgment that Sumner's statute was unconstitutional. By that time the Court would have been drawn into the vortex of political controversy.[108]

The basic requirement for admission to the Supreme Court's roll of attorneys, since the Court was organized in February 1790, had been that the applicant had for three years past been admitted to practice before the highest court of the jurisdiction to which he belonged, and was of good character. It was in order, at any sitting of the Court, for a member of its bar to move the admission of a qualified applicant. The first to be admitted at December term 1864 was James Speed of Louisville, Kentucky: this was the new Attorney General, who a week later reappeared to produce his commission and his oath of office. Three of those admitted at this term were destined to become members of President Grant's Cabinet: George S. Boutwell, of Massachusetts; George H. Williams, of Oregon; and Edwards Pierrepont, of New York. On December 22, 1864, Charles D. Drake of St. Louis was admitted: a relentless Radical, in the months immediately thereafter he was foremost in the framing of Missouri's "Drakonian Constitution" that required an oath of unbroken loyalty from lawyers and clergymen as well as from office-holders. When the Court next came in, there would be awaiting on its docket *Cummings v. Missouri*,[109] the appeal of a Catholic priest who performed the rites of his church without taking the State's new test oath, a companion case to *Ex parte Garland*.

The most interesting admission at that term, however, was that of John S. Rock of Boston, a member of the Massachusetts bar. This was a man of color. Senator Sumner, his sponsor, had consulted the Chief Justice in advance: "I know not how far the Dred Scott decision may stand in the way."[110] On February 1, 1865, the motion was made, and

---

[107] 4 Wall. 333 (1867). It had been filed on December 4, 1865.

[108] Infra, pp. 143–44, 240–42.

[109] 4 Wall. 277 (1867), infra, p. 134. It had been filed on November 8, 1865.

[110] Letter of Dec. 21, 1864. Chase Papers, Hist. Soc. of Pa. Submitting Rock's papers, Sumner pointed out that the applicant was "cordially recommended by Govr. Andrew & others in the public service. . . . " Sumner's thoughts ran on to a sweeping conclusion:

Of course the admission of a colored lawyer . . . would make it difficult for any restriction on account of color to be maintained any where. Street cars would be open afterwards.

Rock had been admitted to the Massachusetts bar on September 14, 1861. Also, it appears he had the M.D. degree: Rock to Sumner, June 6, 1856. Sumner Papers, Harvard Library.

granted, without question. It was interpreted as a sign and portent.[111] At that same moment the constitutional amendment to abolish slavery left Congress on the course of ratification. This event was observed by services in the chamber of the House of Representatives on Sunday, February 12. The Reverend Henry H. Garnet—who, born a slave, had escaped to freedom—quoted from Matthew 23:4 words spoken of the scribes and Pharisees: "they bind heavy burdens and grievous to be borne, and lay them on men's shoulders; but they themselves will not move them with one of their fingers." It was the first time a member of his race had conducted services within the halls of Congress. It did begin to seem "that Kingdom's coming and the year of Jubilee."[112]

JUSTICE DAVIS EXPRESSES SOME VIEWS

To JUSTICE DAVIS, detained at Bloomington by illness, Rock's admission to the Supreme Court's bar appeared an unseemly exhibition. To his brother-in-law, Julius Rockwell (a Superior Court judge in Massachusetts, and once briefly Sumner's colleague in the Senate), he wrote with his usual forthrightness:

> Mr Sumner is running his radicalism athwart every body's prejudices. What object of swearing in the negro man, as an attorney of U.S. Supreme Court. He had no business there & never would. It was all for effect & cui bono? The negro can never be elevated to social & political rights in this country & all wise statesmen know it. But republics make politicians & not statesmen. . . .[113]

Davis entertained rather definite views about the legal consequences of winning the war. In the summer of 1863 he had read an important letter from William Whiting, Solicitor of the War Department, to the Union League of Philadelphia, in which these propositions were developed:

---

[111] Justice Wayne's biographer notes that the Minutes show that Wayne was absent on the day Rock was admitted, and infers that it had been more than the Judge "could stomach." Alexander A. Lawrence, *James Moore Wayne, Southern Unionist* (Chapel Hill: University of North Carolina Press, 1943), 194. But the Minutes further show that Wayne was absent from January 16 through the twenty-fourth, and again from February 1 until Monday, February 13, which repels the inference. Wayne was not a Judge who made resentful demonstrations. For example, he did not, as Taney did, omit to make the usual call upon the President on New Year's Day, 1862. Lawrence, *Wayne*, 184.

[112] The allusion is to "Kingdom Coming" (1861), words and music by Henry Clay Work (1832–84), of abolitionist antecedents, whose war songs buoyed the nation; "Marching through Georgia" is his best-remembered song.

[113] Letter of Feb. 19, 1865. Davis Papers, Ill. State Hist. Soc.

Do not permit [the seceding States], without proper safeguards, to resume in your councils in the Senate and in the House the power which their treason has stripped from them. . . .

. . . The character of a public enemy having once been stamped upon them by the laws of war, remains fixed until it shall have been, by our consent, removed. . . .

Allow the inhabitants of conquered territory to form themselves into States, only by adopting Constitutions such as will forever remove all cause of collision with the United States, by excluding slavery therefrom, or continue military government over the conquered district until there shall appear therein a sufficient number of loyal inhabitants to form a republican government, which, by guaranteeing freedom to all, shall be in accordance with the true spirit of the Constitution of the United States.[114]

Davis commented disapprovingly:

He distinctly announces, that no State must be permitted to come back unless its Constitution is altered. The doctrine will astonish a good many, & especially, if it is supposed to be endorsed by the administration. . . . If the rebel States lay down their arms, how is any *treaty* to be made with them. All political questions, growing out of the war must be settled by the Courts. . . .[115]

To Davis' mind, "Whatever the *Law is*—and it seems to me . . . very clear," must govern the position of the Southern States when fighting ended; "I shall decide, fearlessly & honestly."[116]

Would the Southern States, once their rebellion was crushed, immediately be entitled to representation in Congress? Would the Constitution for the future be no different from what it had been in 1860, save as any amendment might be ratified by "three fourths of the several States,"[117] with participation by the seceding States just as they emerged

---

[114] Ann. Cyc. 1863, 836–38. William Whiting (1813–73), a Boston lawyer, was Solicitor of the War Department from 1862 to 1865. His *War Powers Under the Constitution of the United States* ran through many editions. (43d ed., Boston: Lee and Shepard, 1871.) Whiting was elected to the 43rd Congress, but died before Congress met.

Richard Henry Dana, Jr., United States District Attorney for Massachusetts, in an address before the Republican State Convention in October 1863, deprecated "closet work, abstract speculations" about reconstruction as producing division when the war had still to be won. *National Intelligencer*, Oct. 14, 1863.

Attorney General Bates found Dana's speech an "admirable" reply to "the wild theories of Sumner, Boutwell, Whiting, and the like—that the revolted States being *out of the Union*, and to be ruled as conquered territory . . ." *Diary of Edward Bates* (Washington: Government Printing Office, 1933), 309, Oct. 15, 1863.

[115] Letter to Rockwell, Aug. 19, 1863.

[116] Letter to Rockwell, Sept. 16, 1863.

[117] Constitution, Art. V.

from the war? Would the status of the Negro remain, as in the past, a domestic question for each State?

When the time came, would the nation really allow the political issues growing out of the war to be settled by the Court? Suppose a venerable majority of the Justices, once again disdaining to "falter in the path of duty,"[118] acted on such a view: Would they pronounce another *Dred Scott* decision? All this was imminent when Chase became Chief Justice, even though at the moment it seemed to him that the Court had little better to do than say "that John Smith owned this parcel of land or other property instead of Jacob Robinson."[119]

THE COURT, IN SESSION AND IN CONFERENCE

NOT ONLY WAS CHASE'S FIRST TERM relatively unimportant: it was also brief. Adjournment came after only fourteen weeks, on March 10, 1865. The Court's practice was to sit from Monday through Friday, coming in at 11 A.M. and remaining until 3 P.M. Hearings moved slowly. The Court's unhurried rule was that "Only two counsel shall be permitted to argue for each party, plaintiff and defendant, in a cause"; no counsel might speak more than two hours, save by special leave in advance.[120] (In 1871 the allowance was cut to "two hours on each side.") A "printed brief or abstract of the case . . . , together with the points intended to be made, and the authorities intended to be cited . . ." must be filed with the Clerk at least three days before the case was called; "and no other book or case" was to be referred to in argument.[121] Commonly on one, or on each side, only one counsel would argue. Perhaps one or both parties would submit on the printed argument alone. If they agreed to submit, and the printed arguments were filed within the first ten days of the term, the Court would consider the case without regard to its place on the docket—with the prospect of an early decision.[122]

From December term 1860 until 1935 (when its separate building was completed), the Court sat in what theretofore had been the Senate

---

118 Taney, C.J., in Dred Scott v. Sandford, 19 How. 393, 426 (1857).
119 Supra, p. 34.
120 Rule 21. Two Counsel—Two Hours—Briefs. Rules of court revised at December term 1858. 21 How. v, xii.
A grant of extra time was not confined to occasions where some major problem of law must be probed; an allowance was made in Tobey v. Leonards, the case of the family feud mentioned above. Supra, pp. 34-35.
121 Fifteen copies of the brief were to be deposited: nine for the Court, one for the Reporter, one to be retained by the Clerk, and the residue for counsel. Rule 21.
122 Rule 20.

chamber. This was on the Capitol's main (or second) floor, north of the central rotunda and on the east side of the building. The chamber (still preserved) is bow-shaped, with a length of 75 feet and a maximum width of 45 feet.[123] A platform on the flat side supported the long bench at which the Justices sat in arm-chairs, backs to a row of green marble pillars. Behind these pillars, along the east wall, ran a corridor by which the Justices reached the bench. A spread eagle, poised above the Chief Justice's chair, looked out—over the chairs and tables for counsel, and the benches for spectators that lined the semicircular wall —toward the chamber's main entrance. Affixed to this wall were the busts of former Chief Justices—Jay, Rutledge (brief tenant under a recess appointment), Ellsworth, and Marshall. (Taney would not be so commemorated until he had been joined in death by Chase, and time had mollified resentment over the *Dred Scott* case.)[124]

In the robing room the Justices would don their black gowns[125] and proceed to the corridor behind the pillars, entering the chamber through parted curtains as the Marshal announced the Court. The senior Associate Justice would be at the Chief Justice's right hand, the next at his left, and so on alternately in order of appointment. When each was at his place the Crier, responding to a glance from the Chief Justice, would proclaim that the Court was open: "God save the United States and this Honorable Court." The Justices seated themselves for a session that would continue for four hours without interruption.

When a new Justice had been appointed he would appear and take the judicial oath: to administer justice without respect to persons, to do equal right to the poor and to the rich, and faithfully and impartially to perform his duties to the best of his abilities and understanding, agreeably to the Constitution and the laws of the United States.[126] (If

---

[123] Compare with the Court's present chamber, a rectangle of 82 by 91 feet.

[124] In 1865, H.R. 748, a bill to provide a bust of Taney for the Supreme Court Room was hooted down by Sumner and his associates. "Let such a vacant space in our court-room testify to the justice of our Republic. Let it speak in warning to all who would betray liberty." Cong. Globe, 38–2, 1012–17. Feb. 23, 1865.

In 1874, the 1st Session of the 43rd Congress (Republican in both branches) passed without debate S.61, to provide busts of both Taney and Chase. Sumner's S.300, to honor Chase alone, was "indefinitely postponed."

[125] Assisted over many years by Archie Lewis, a freedman from Virginia, who served the Court from 1849 until his death in 1913. *Washington Post* and *Washington Star*, Nov. 23, 1913. Letters from the Justices to the Clerk often refer to reliance upon Archie Lewis for attending to their personal effects, for arranging for their return to their lodgings in Washington, and the like.

[126] Judiciary Act of 1789, sec. 8. 1 Stat. 76. Now 28 U.S. Code, sec. 453.

A Judge must also take the oath required generally of civil and military officers—then the iron-clad oath of 1862. Supra, p. 58.

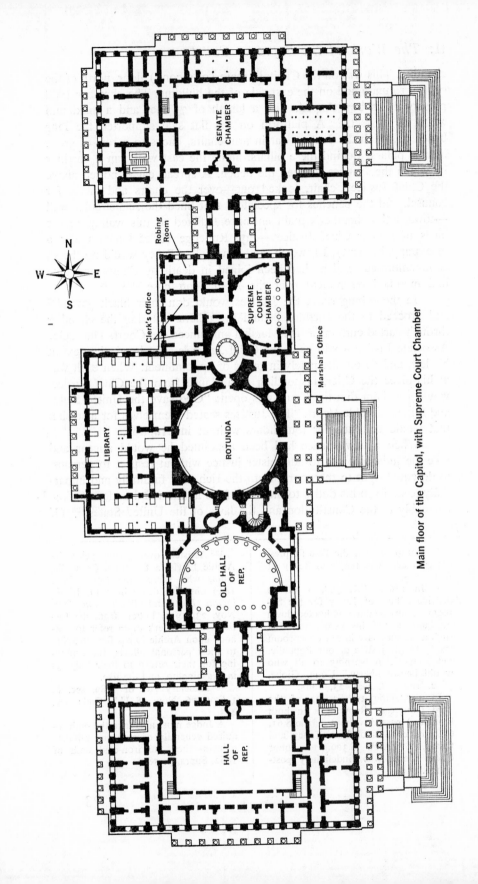

Main floor of the Capitol, with Supreme Court Chamber

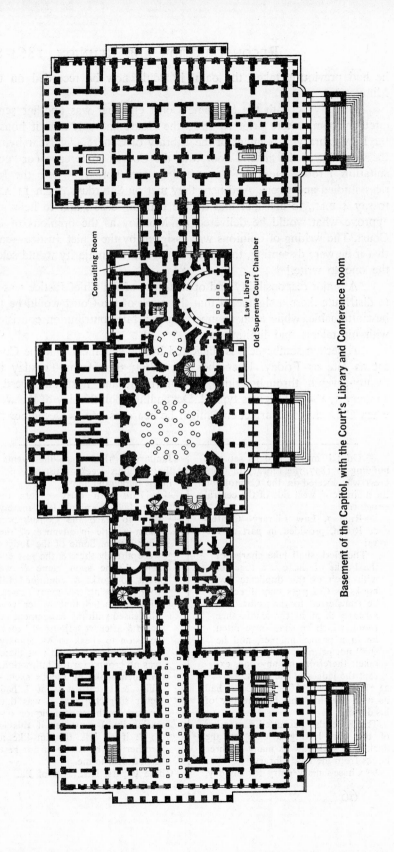

Consulting Room

Law Library
Old Supreme Court Chamber

Basement of the Capitol, with the Court's Library and Conference Room

he had previously taken the oath, it would now be recorded on the Minutes.)

Directly beneath the Supreme Court chamber was another semi-circular room, where prior to 1860 the Court had sat; now it housed the Law Library, a segment of the Library of Congress.[127] Near by, on the west side of the ground floor, was the Court's conference (or "consultation") room. Here the Court had its own library;[128] here the Justices studied and wrote. And here they met on Saturdays, from 11 A.M. to say 4 P.M., to consider and decide pending cases, and to hear and approve what would be delivered on Monday as the opinions of the Court. The writing of opinions was assigned by the Chief Justice—save that if he were dissenting, the senior Justice in the majority would select the one to write.[129]

A major responsibility and opportunity of the Chief Justice was so to distribute these assignments that the work of the Court would be the best attainable, while each member made a fair contribution consistent with his talents and limitations.

A certain somberness is suggested by the statement that the Court sat as late as Friday, December 23, 1864; then from Tuesday the twenty-seventh through Friday, the thirtieth; and next on Tuesday, January 3, 1865. This was typical. Depending upon the day of the week when Christmas fell, arguments might be heard as late as December 24,

---

[127] Until it moved into its separate building in 1897, the Library of Congress was located in the Capitol, on the main floor, west side of the central structure.

[128] Rule 7, Law Library—Conference Room, provided in part as follows:

The clerk shall take charge of the books of the court, together with such of the duplicate law books as Congress may direct to be transferred to the court, and arrange them in the conference room, which he shall have fitted up in a proper manner; and he shall not permit such books to be taken therefrom by any one, except the judges of the court.

21 How. vii, viii. After the Court had its own Marshal, this became one of his duties.

The Rule also permitted a member of the bar, having a case on the docket, to withdraw as many as three books from the Law Library.

[129] Chase's diary entry for Sunday, January 7, 1866—recalling events in the previous week—illustrates points in the paragraph above.

[Talk with early callers on Saturday morning] left merely time to reach the Consultation room a little in advance of the hour eleven. Some of the Judges were already there & the rest except Wayne soon came & we went to work; & continued till four disposing of many cases. Field intimated that Miller was displeased with my assignment of cases & after we adjourned I took occasion to speak to M. frankly on the subject & found that there was no ground for the intimation. M. then spoke of Field's excitability & I learned what I had never suspected that it was due in part to the use of liquor occasionally. I must see if this is so & if so talk to him like a brother; for he is one of our best men & dear to me.

Chase Papers. Hist. Soc. of Pa.

and as early as the twenty-sixth. Normally the interruption at the New Year would be equally brief. At the 1867 term, Tuesday, December 24, and Thursday, the twenty-sixth, were both work-days; then at the close of business on Monday, the thirtieth, the Court adjourned to Monday, January 6, 1868. On every New Year's Day the President and his lady held open house. The Justices would come early in the reception, next after the diplomatic corps. For this occasion the Marshal would provide carriages; on leaving the White House the Justices might drive about, perhaps two or three together, to make official and personal calls.

THE JUSTICES FIND LODGINGS

FOR THE SOJOURN IN WASHINGTON a Justice would rent rooms in a boarding-house, commonly at Morrison's (No. 23, Four-and-a-half Street, N.W.) or at Taylor's (on C Street at the corner of Third, N.W.). Justice Wayne (who by reason of the war did not return to Georgia) made his home at No. 2 Franklin Place, near I Street between Thirteenth and Fourteenth, far uptown as that then seemed. There Justice Davis had gone in December 1862, to his immediate regret:

> The rooms I engaged did not suit at all. Judge Wayne enticed me up there, but he gave me bad advice. Judge Nelson advised me by all means to come to Morrison's, where four other Judges were boarding & where the Library is.[130]

Upon making this change, Davis described his new lodgings to his wife:

> I . . . am in the 3rd story of the House, with two fair rooms. The stairs are pretty steep. There is a door between me & the adjoining occupant, & we have to talk pretty low. The quarters in this city, generally are not very good. These Judges are going to try to get a public Ladies parlor for next winter, & bring their wives here. There is no parlor. And if I have to take these rooms for next winter, I will take all 3, so that no one can interfere with your privacy and mine.[131]

---

[130] Letter of Dec. 22 to Rockwell. Davis Papers, Ill. State Hist. Soc.

[131] Letter of Dec. 12, 1862. Davis Papers, Ill. State Hist. Soc.

Apropos of the lack of privacy: December term 1865 found Justices Clifford and Davis boarding at Taylor's; Mrs. Davis had accompanied her husband. Writing to her sister on March 5, 1866, she related that a young woman teacher was also lodging at Taylor's. "It seems she invited 75 persons to come here tonight and dance—the performance is to come off . . . in the dining room which is in the basement. [Justice Clifford had been asked for the use of his front room for the party.] The Judge has two rooms with folding doors in fact the parlors of the house. We

He felt he had done well to move to Morrison's. "The Judges are pleasant & agreeable. Some of them are learned men—others not. I feel my want of learning lamentably but will try & get along by study."[132] "The society of the Judges is a good deal, & the Library is everything."[133]

By the late '60's the Justices were advancing to the somewhat greater comfort of a hotel; Nelson, Clifford, Miller, and Davis stayed at the National, on the corner of Pennsylvania Avenue and Sixth Street. Willard's on Pennsylvania at Fourteenth, with its crowded bar and public rooms, seemed ill-suited to the mode of life—and to the pocketbook —of a Justice of the Supreme Court. (The salary was then $6,000, with $500 more for the Chief Justice.[134]) Davis, after social calls there, commented that "Willards is like a village—1000 people they say eat at the House every day—and 800 sleep in it. The life is pleasant enough for young people, only one would tire of it soon . . . ."[135]

Chase, on returning as Chief Justice, had made his home in the fashionable residence of his daughter Kate and her husband, Senator William Sprague of Rhode Island, at Sixth and E Streets. "Kate Chase" was rather beautiful, commanding, and consumed by a passion that her father attain the Presidency. Sprague had youth, a dashing appearance, and inherited wealth, but in character he was insecure; at home he found neither love nor respect, and among Senators he was never

---

eat in the front one, and he writes and studies there—the back one is his *bed* room. He said he did not well see how he could give up the room— and we agreed with him. If they used it as a room to put their hats and cloaks—and a dressing room—they would of course come in late when they went home and disturb him— and it seemed quite undignified and out of place for him to have them there more especially as his wife was away. . . . We are saved much vexation by having a private table . . . ." Davis Papers, Ill. State Hist. Soc.

[132] Letter to his wife, Dec. 14, 1862.

[133] Letter to his wife, Dec. 16, 1862.

[134] The salary of an Associate Justice had been fixed at $3,500 by the Act of September 23, 1789, 1 Stat. 72; $4,500 by the Act of February 29, 1819, 3 Stat. 484; $6,000 by the Act of March 3, 1855, 10 Stat. 655. By the Act of March 3, 1871, 16 Stat. 494, the salary was raised to $8,000, equal to that which the heads of Executive Departments had been receiving since 1853.

In the general raising of salaries by the Act of March 3, 1873, 17 Stat. 485, 486—whereby the President's salary was set at $50,000, the first increase from the original $25,000—the Justices were allowed $10,000. That figure remained until by the Act of February 12, 1903, 32 Stat. 825, the salary was raised to $12,500.

At all these times the Chief Justice received $500 more than his associates.

In a boarding house, in 1864–65, Justice Clifford paid $180 a month for self and wife. Letter to Clerk, Aug. 19, 1865. National Archives.

In September 1873, after careful inquiry Clifford reported to Justice Davis that "We cannot get rooms at the Arlington—Willard's—Ebbitt House, or Wormleys, short of $400 per month. I will not give it." The Justices might return to the rooms they had occupied at the National, where "The price will be $250. per month as last year." Letter of Sept. 17, 1873. Davis Papers, Ill. State Hist. Soc.

[135] Letter to his wife, Feb. 7, 1863.

taken very seriously. One must consider this strange situation when one seeks to penetrate the character of the Chief Justice.[136]

THE COURSE OF HEARING, DECIDING, AND OPINION-WRITING

JUSTICE DAVIS REMARKED on the convenience of having a working set of books at the boarding-house. That enabled one to do more of his opinion-writing in his room (with record and briefs at hand), away from the Court's library in the Capitol. When satisfied with what he had written, a Justice would read his opinion at conference; upon approval there, he would deliver it the following Monday.

An understanding of the workings of the Court is essential. After docketing, a case would wait some two or three years before in turn it was called for oral argument. That was a persistent shortcoming—a condition that prevailed throughout the service of Chief Justice Chase (1864 to 1873) and of Waite (1874 to 1888): any change to promote expedition would be offset by the increase in the volume of litigation, arising from the expansion of the country and from legislation by which the federal jurisdiction was broadened. No adequate remedy was provided until 1891 when Congress created a system of intermediate appellate tribunals, the Circuit Courts of Appeals, as a barrier to reduce the flow of business into the Supreme Court.[137]

While this waiting was too long, the process of consideration was too cursory. Ordinarily the interval between argument and announcement of the decision was about a month; sometimes it was even less. When a session lasted about seventeen weeks, more or less, opinions must be turned out with dispatch.[138] Ordinarily the Court would discuss and vote on a case on the Saturday next after argument. The Justice to whom it was assigned would write his opinion, over say two or three weeks. Then he would bring his manuscript to conference, and his brethren would listen to his reading of it. (A case might, of course, be

---

[136] Thomas G. and Marva R. Belden did this with remarkable perception and high literary skill in *So Fell the Angels* (Boston and Toronto: Little, Brown and Co., 1956).

[137] Act of Mar. 3, 1891. 26 Stat. 826.

[138] The median duration between December term 1859 and December term 1867 was seventeen weeks. At December term 1868 the Court broke off on April 15, 1869, to meet in an adjourned session on October 4— thereby putting in two months of work before the opening of the statutory term in December 1869. Adjourned sessions in October continued until, by the Act of January 24, 1873, 17 Stat. 419, Congress enacted that the term should begin on the second Monday in October. Throughout Waite's period the Court convened on that day in October and adjourned some time in the first half of May, save that in 1887 it continued to May 27.

held for further study, or a reargument might be ordered; but that would be unusual.) This practice gives pause: the other Justices would generally have no opportunity to read the opinion and to reflect upon the drafting. On a Saturday there would be a discussion and then a vote on cases theretofore undecided, plus the listening to prepared opinions. That statement "shows to a demonstration" (one of Justice Clifford's phrases) that the Court as a body could not have scrutinized opinions to weigh the import of expressions and omissions. So long as the Justices were satisfied on the major points, the author was pretty free, one gathers, to choose his language. It follows that, as compared with what might be supposed, one is less warranted in attributing to the Court the very language used, and better entitled to treat the composition (for praise or blame) as showing the quality of the author. Evidently there was not a very high sense of corporate responsibility.[139]

There might be dissent from the Court's decision, or from a holding on some particular point; but individual notations of disagreement or doubt merely about implications or dicta were exceedingly rare.

REPORTING THE COURT'S OPINIONS

WHEN A JUSTICE had read his opinion, in full or in summary, from the bench, the further course of the manuscript was governed by the Court's Rule 25. This began,

> 1. All opinions delivered by the court shall immediately, upon the delivery thereof, be delivered over to the clerk to be recorded. And it shall be the duty of the clerk to cause the same to be forthwith recorded, and to deliver the originals, with a transcript of the judgment or decree of the court thereon, to the reporter, as soon as the same shall be recorded.

The Clerk, it should be explained, would have each opinion set in type; proof would be sent to the Justice who wrote it, for his examination, and if need be a revise would be sent, before final printing.[140] For a fee the Clerk would supply a certified copy. Rule 25 continued:

---

[139] A striking illustration of this is the Chief Justice's opinion in Texas v. White, infra, at pp. 646–48.

[140] The following letters to the Clerk from Justice Clifford, at Portland, Maine, illustrate. On April 12, 1866, he wrote: "I return proof of my opinion by this mail. It is exceedingly well done but I think you had better send a revise so as to have it perfect. . . ." Then on April 20:

"I return the proof of my opinion in U S v Dashiel [3 Wall. 688, decided April 3.] It is perfect. I think your proof reader is very proficient. I hope you will keep him as long as possible. He is a credit to your office. . . ." National Archives. Papers from the Clerk's Office.

2. And the opinions of the court, as far as practicable, shall be recorded during the term, so that the publication of the reports may not be delayed thereby.

3. The original opinions of the court, delivered to the reporter, shall be filed in the office of the clerk of the court, for preservation, as soon as the volume of reports for the term, at which they are delivered, shall be published.

At this point a brief explanation of the duties of the Reporter is in order. He would have the original opinions, and the text of the Court's judgment or decree.[141] Also he would have his copy of the transcript of record and of each brief, and whatever notes he had taken during the argument (while seated at his desk, below the extreme left of the bench). To prepare his reports for the printer he must see that each case had an accurate headnote; a statement of such facts as were material to the decision; and whatever summary of the arguments of counsel seemed needful for an understanding of the case. Then would follow the opinion for the Court, and any dissent. The Reporter's contribution called for clarity of perception, concise and accurate statement, and sound judgment on how to attain effectiveness and utility. The author of the opinion would have made some statement of facts at the outset; the Reporter might consider that sufficient, or expand it, or compose a completely new statement. Here was a field where the Justices and the Reporter might collide—as they did, with bruising impact, in the early volumes of Wallace's Reports, from 1864.

A headnote is meant to express exactly what propositions the case establishes; it should be concise and perspicuous. Where, as sometimes happened, a Justice framed his own headnote, a lack of confidence was implied.

John William Wallace (1815–84), Reporter for twelve terms beginning with that for December 1863, came of a family of Philadelphia lawyers, and was well schooled for the bar. He did not, however, engage in active practice. He became a law librarian, an editor, a sojourner in Europe. He reported *Cases in the Circuit Court of the United States for the Third Circuit*—one volume appearing in 1849, the second in 1854—and the third in 1871. His earlier work showed him to be a copious rather than a concise reporter; even so, one could hardly have foreseen what he did upon becoming Reporter of the Supreme Court.

Wallace was appointed on March 21, 1864, in place of Jeremiah S. Black, whose resignation was that day accepted.[142] The change at

---

[141] The Rule used the two nouns, because in equity and admiralty a judgment is termed a "decree."

[142] In the first edition of 1 Wallace at vii the year is inaccurately given as 1863. Black (1810–83), sometime

that juncture was inconvenient; the appointee must report a term that had run four-fifths of its course when he took his oath to perform his duties "according to the best of my abilities and understanding." His understanding and abilities were soon to be called in question.

Wallace was old-fashioned, an aristocratic gentleman who cherished polite learning and wrote in stilted phrases.[143] With high heart he set out to adorn his statements of fact with extraneous bits of information, as if to entertain an audience of dilettantes. Thus in a case on the duty of a municipality to maintain safe thoroughfares, he began with these picturesque details:

> Among the festal anniversaries of the city of Providence, R.I., is that known as "Commencement Day." Upon this occasion Brown University gives its degrees; and citizens and strangers throng the town. Upon the anniversary of 1859, Miss Babcock, of Connecticut, visited Providence and was participating in the spectacle. A procession was passing through one of the streets in a central part of the city, and Miss Babcock, who was walking in the same street, then filled with people, fell through an opening in the pavement which gave entrance into a cellar below, whereby she was severely injured.[144]

In *The Bermuda*, a circumstance tending to show a Confederate destination was reported in this elegant passage:

> So among the persons that embarked on the Bermuda, at Liverpool, were certain gentlemen residents of Charleston, but perfectly well known in circles of gentility and pleasure, both North and South, before the rebellion began. Among these, as was noted by counsel, was the late amiable Mr. John Julius Pringle, a gentleman of education and fortune, resident in South Carolina during the winter, but at Newport, Rhode Island, in summer, and in that agreeable resort

---

Chief Justice of Pennsylvania, Attorney General and briefly Secretary of State under Buchanan, had been nominated to be an Associate Justice, but failed of confirmation by a vote of 25 to 26 on February 21, 1861. His fortunes being at a low ebb, he accepted the office of Reporter, and brought out 1 and 2 Black. He will figure conspicuously as counsel before the Supreme Court.

[143] Here is a typical conclusion to a letter, of May 27, 1875, to Chief Justice Waite:

Command me to any extent in the matter at hand; & believe me
Dear Sir,
    With sincerest regard,
Your obliged servt.

        John Wm. Wallace.

Waite Papers, L.C.

[144] The City v. Babcock, 3 Wall. 240 (1865). The points decided, and they were elementary, were that the Court would not consider alleged errors not presented by the record; that insufficiency of the evidence to sustain

of taste and fashion by many pleasingly, and with regrets, remembered. . . .[145]

The reports abounded in this sort of amiable gentility.

It was more serious when the Reporter cast doubt on the integrity of a bench of State judges. In *Havemeyer v. Iowa County (Wisconsin)*, a suit brought in the Circuit Court to enforce municipal bonds, the question carried up to the Supreme Court was whether to respect a decision of the Wisconsin court in 1859 on the meaning of a "general law" as used in the State constitution; if it were followed, Havemeyer's bonds would be unenforceable. But if, instead, the federal court applied what in 1858 the Wisconsin court had *assumed*, in a case where both parties had treated a bonding statute as a *private* law, the bonds would be good. Wallace's statement of facts ended with this comment upon the State court's change of position:

> how far this departure from precedent was owing to a truer conception of the nature of general and particular laws, and how far to the fact, that the judiciary of Wisconsin was a body elected by popular suffrage at short intervals, and which might have come to the bench suffused with the feelings and ideas and wishes of a constituency wishing to disown an obligation which it had found much easier to contract than to pay, was a matter not seen perfectly alike by all sides.[146]

In March 1867, when Congress was informed that *two* volumes would be needed to report the decisions at the current term of the Supreme Court, and a larger appropriation was requested, Representative Ithamar C. Sloan of Wisconsin spoke out: "I hope the House will not consent to any increase of compensation to the present reporter . . . for the reason that he is unfit for the position . . . ." He specified:

> in the case of Havemyer [sic] vs. Iowa county . . . he has taken occasion to indulge in a gratuitous and unfounded statement insulting to the judges of the supreme court of our State, and through them to the judges of other States where they are elected by the people. . . .

the verdict was ground for a motion for a new trial, but not for a writ of error; that an instruction withdrawing from the jury the right to determine matters of fact was properly refused. Brown and its commencement had nothing to do with the questions.

[145] Supra, pp. 40–41.

[146] 3 Wall. 294, 296 (1866). Particulars are set out in chapter 18, note 21.

The intimation that the Wisconsin judges "were influenced to make the decision they did by a desire to court popular favor" was "without the slightest foundation in truth. . . ."[147]

Certainly Wallace's remark had been completely out of order.

John Chipman Gray (1839–1915) and John C. Ropes (1836–99), keen young Boston practitioners who in 1866 established the *American Law Review*, promptly visited upon Wallace's Reports their lofty reprobation.[148] They wondered whether the unfortunate Miss Babcock "was a blonde or a brunette." "We charge Mr. Wallace with inexcusable prolixity in his statements of facts and his reports of arguments. . . . [T]he reader will be struck with the loose and heedless way in which his head-notes are constructed. . . . We . . . concede that there are abundant marks in his volumes of anxious and careful labor. But this very fact tells conclusively against his fitness for his place. . . . To insure against such reports in the future, nothing less will suffice, than that Mr. Wallace should cease to be reporter. If this cannot be, then we demand in behalf of the profession, an entire change in his theory and practice of reporting. . . ."

The *New York World*—Copperhead and carping—took up the complaint in an editorial on "A Supreme Court Fool."[149] It took exception to Wallace's "cheap patriotism," in his comment that "The capture of the ironclad Atlanta was one of the early evidences that the rebel confederacy could not stand at all before the power of the government . . . ."[150] It pronounced his reporting "a disgrace to the American bar," and called upon the Court to remove him at once. "Yet here even, perhaps, the Chief Justice would dissent"—a slur because Chase was among the Justices who did not join in the majority opinions in *Ex parte Milligan*[151] and the *Test Oath Cases*,[152] where the expressions of the Court had been highly pleasing to the *World*.

The review of 1, 2, and 3 Wallace in the *Richmond Enquirer*, however, was so glowing that it could be used as an advertisement.[153] Such "marked aptitude for reporting," it was there said, "encourages us to hope that with Mr. Wallace's volumes has dawned a new era in American reporting." Now at last "full justice" was being done to the argument of counsel; "the desire of appearing to advantage in the

---

[147] Cong. Globe, 39–2, 1724, March 2, 1867. The provision made for the second volume, by the Act of March 2, 1867, 14 Stat. 471, is given at p. 79.

[148] "Wallace's Reports. *Am. L. Rev.*, 1: 229–37. January 1867.

[149] January 23, 1867.

[150] The Ironclad Atlanta, 3 Wall. 425, 427 (1866). It was a question of the division of prize money: Which vessels "made the capture"? The Reporter's editorializing was improper.

[151] *Infra*, p. 209.

[152] *Infra*, p. 241.

[153] In the *National Intelligencer*, Apr. 3, 1867.

volumes of so learned and discriminating a reporter will incite many a gentleman to greater diligence and research."

With kindly Justice Wayne (generally presiding during Taney's last months), Wallace's relations were exceedingly cordial. Grier had been his sponsor. Davis was his "amiable friend."[154] With Miller there was unbroken friendship. To Field he was "largely indebted for assistance" with California land cases.[155] But with Swayne and Clifford there soon was trouble.[156]

Swayne had written an important opinion on the law of evidence in *Blackburn v. Crawfords*.[157] David Crawford had died intestate. If his deceased brother's offspring were legitimate, they would take the estate. Their mother testified there had been a marriage, after the birth of two of the children. As Justice Swayne wrote, "The fact of this marriage was the central and controlling question in the case"—the question, that is, before the jury in the Circuit Court. What the writ of error brought before the Supreme Court was several specific issues— whether the trial court had erred in this or in that ruling upon evidence or in granting this or in refusing that instruction. (The estate was valuable and the contest acute.) As Justice Swayne wrote his opinion, each point was properly isolated for solution. In the result the judgment was reversed and a new trial ordered.

But when the case came to the Reporter, he constructed what he considered to be a proper statement of the facts, subordinating Justice Swayne's opinion to his own scheme. He expanded on evidence given by the children's mother, including how, on a priest's advice, she had summoned her paramour and told him "that the salvation of her soul was of more importance to her than all things else in this world; that she must separate from him if he would not marry her." Whereupon, she testified, a secret marriage took place. The Reporter then drew attention to what he seemed to believe to be the question before the Supreme Court:

> This was a narrative sufficiently touching, and quite circumstantial, no doubt. But was it true? Was the case one of a marriage solemnized in form, and kept secret for five and twenty years; a romance, per- haps—discovered only in the end, by relatives not enriched, to be a

---

[154] Wallace's expression, in letter to the Clerk, Mr. Middleton, Apr. 17, 1866. National Archives, Papers from office of the Clerk of the Supreme Court.

[155] Preface to 1 Wall. at xv and xvi on Field and Wayne.

[156] After he had ceased to be Re-

porter, and when they neared the end of their judicial service, Wallace held the performance of these two in low esteem. Fairman, *Mr. Justice Miller*, 382, quoting Wallace to William A. Maury, Nov. 9, 1880.

[157] 3 Wall. 175 (1866).

reality—perhaps a *mésalliance* simply? Or was it one of those less regular relations,—affairs, *mutato nomine*, of every day, and out of which men elaborate such infinite vexation for themselves from the pure element of the affections—misdirected?

When in early October 1866 Justice Swayne received a copy of 3 Wallace, just off the press, he discovered how his opinion had been mutilated. He wrote to the Clerk:

> If you can possibly do so, please send me a copy of my opinion in Blackburn v. Crawfords. If you have them—I shall also be greatly obliged if you will send one to Messrs Johnson Brent Merrick & Alexander *Each*.
> *I will cheerfully pay for them.*[158]
> My opinion in 3rd Wallace is butchered. I cant stand it. It shall not occur again. I will do as Judge Clifford does—have the opinion published in every case just as it is delivered to the Reporter.[159]

When presently there was a need for further printings of Wallace's earlier volumes, the Reporter took occasion to give his text a very light pruning. His subsequent work showed the benefit of the chastening he had undergone.[160]

---

[158] The Clerk was entitled to a fee for a certified copy of a recorded opinion. Even an Executive Department must pay. For example, when the Assistant Secretary of the Interior, Otto, requested on April 8, 1868, a copy of the opinion in United States v. Alire, 6 Wall. 573, decided on April 6, there was a charge of $3.92. Papers of the Clerk's Office, National Archives, Record Group No. 267.

[159] Letter from Columbus, Ohio, October 8, 1866. Papers of the Clerk's Office, National Archives. On October 11 Clerk Middleton replied: "It so happened that I had on hand, exclusive of my filed copy, just the number of copies you desired, which I take pleasure in *presenting* to you."

[160] After Wallace's death (on January 12, 1884), J. Hubley Ashton, able practitioner at the Supreme Court bar and formerly Assistant Attorney General, wrote the following significant comment to ex-Justice Davis:

> I suppose you have heard of the death of our old friend, John William Wallace, who, I know, had a great regard for you while he was here as Reporter of the Court. . . . Very few people knew how much labor he bestowed on his Reports . . . . Whether his ideas as to the duty of a Reporter were in all respects correct or not, he was certainly in his work one of the most conscientious men I ever knew. . . .
> Do you recollect the circumstances of his appointment as Reporter?
> Judge Grier nominated him; but he was little known, if at all, to the other Judges, I believe. I recollect that Judge Swayne wrote a letter to Judge [William D.] Kelley, who was then in the House, to know what his politics were. Judge Kelley did not happen to know much about him, as he [Wallace] had been in Europe a number of years, and sent Judge Swayne's letter to me, in Philadelphia, and asked me to give him the necessary information. It so happened

II: *The Work of the Supreme Court*

Disaccord between Justice Clifford and the Reporter was quite another matter. We may start with a note Clifford wrote to the Clerk, from Portland on April 3, 1865. He was sending corrected proof of three opinions,[161] and added,

> Be sure & give a copy of that dissent [by Clifford, in *Lowber v. Bangs*][162] to the reporter as I have reason to think he will omit to publish it *if he can find any excuse*—Make it certain that he has it.[163]

He was referring to an important case on the construction of a contract of affreightment; the Court had reversed a decision by Clifford on the circuit,[164] and now he was dissenting at great length and with characteristic fullness of quotations.

In his day Clifford was at once the most prolix and most pedestrian member of the Court. Only a man devoid of humor could have opened an opinion with such an utterance as this:

> Experience shows that ships and vessels engaged in navigation are liable to be exposed to collision when approaching each other from opposite directions, or on intersecting lines, or even when approaching on parallel lines proximate to each other, and that seasonable precautions are indispensable, under such circumstances, to avoid such disasters, and to prevent the destruction of property and to save the lives of those employed in such important and perilous pursuits.[165]

---

that I had shortly before made the acquaintance of Mr Wallace, and I was able to write such a letter to Judge Kelley as satisfied Judge Swayne, who gave Mr Wallace his vote. The fact was that Mr Wallace returned to this country from Europe, because he believed it was the *duty* of every citizen to be at home when the country was in trouble. He was an old fashioned Federalist, and his politics, as he used to say, were those of Washington & Hamilton. He believed in a strong and rather aristocratic Government. He would have voted, at any time for a President for life, if he could have been sure of having a strong man in the office. . . . Letter of Jan. 24, 1884. Davis Papers, Ill. State Hist. Soc.

161 The Slavers (Sarah), 2 Wall. 366; The Slavers (Weathergage), 2 Wall. 375; and The Slavers (Reindeer),

2 Wall. 383. These were companion cases to The Slavers (Kate), 2 Wall. 350, supra, p. 39, decided per Chase, C.J.

162 2 Wall. 728 (1865).

163 Papers from the Clerk's Office. National Archives.

164 Bangs v. Lowber, Fed. Case No. 840 (C.C.D.Mass. 1862).

165 The Sea Gull, as the original opinion is set out in 23 L. Ed. 90, 92 (1875). This and some other passages were omitted from the report in 23 Wall. 165.

Sometimes Clifford supplied headnotes for his opinions. They were very long, running to perhaps a fourth as many words as the opinion itself. The Reporter, however, exercised his authority to write his own headnotes. For example, compare United States v. Dashiel, 3 Wall. 688 (1866) and 18 L. Ed. 268; Hamilton Mfg. Co. v. Massachusetts, 6 Wall. 632 (1868) and 18 L. Ed. 904. Clifford's method

Clifford practiced one notable economy in the use of words: he had an aversion to the article *the*. So he would write: "Master of the Wells testifies . . . . Vessel of the claimants was . . . . Excuse for the sudden change is . . . . Principal question of fact, therefore, is . . . ."[166] Habitually, when at length he had finished his quotation of authorities, after perhaps eighteen or twenty pages, Justice Clifford would signal the end of his opinion by saying that "Viewed in the light of these suggestions"—or "Tested by these considerations"—or "Governed by these views"—the decision must be so and so.

"As a mere matter of economy," so wrote the editors of the *American Law Review* in their criticism of Wallace's first three volumes,[167] "the profession have a right to demand that no superfluous matter should swell the costly volumes which are indispensable to them in their business."

Wallace stated in 1866 that

> The sales of the United States Supreme Court Reports are not large, so many of the cases are of local interest only; so many on fact alone; the reports of the State courts have become so numerous and come so immediately home to the daily business of the bar that sales of much more than one thousand copies are not to be counted on. . . .[168]

On January 22, 1868, Representative Michael C. Kerr, Democrat, who from 1862 to 1865 had reported the decisions of the Supreme Court of Indiana, introduced a resolution reciting that "many of the decisions of the Supreme Court of the United States possess no intrinsic value for the profession or the country," wherefore let the Judiciary Committee consider the expediency of charging the Court to select what decisions were of enough value that they should be reported.[169] Nothing came of this proposal.

From the foregoing three statements, certain observations arise. The judiciary legislation brought to the Supreme Court many controversies that were of no general interest; often the report was of a case wherein the Justices had been required to examine the entire record

---

was, not simply to identify the issues and state the precise holding thereon, but rather to list every legal proposition, whether contested or not, involved in the Court's line of reasoning. See The Wanata, 95 U.S. 600 (1877), as reported in 24 L. Ed. 461. A schooner had collided with a pilot boat at anchor: Clifford's ten headnotes (over six hundred words) set out detailed holdings on points of

admiralty and the rules of navigation.

[166] The Ann Caroline, 2 Wall. 538 (1865).

[167] Supra, p. 74.

[168] Letter of Feb. 25, 1866, to the Secretary of the Interior. Cong. Globe, 39–1, 3130.

[169] Cong. Globe, 40–2, 693. He had reported 18 through 22 Indiana. Kerr was a man of ability and became Speaker.

anew to make their own determination of the facts.[170] Such cases, quite aside from the drain upon the Justices, would encumber the Reports with much that had "no intrinsic value." While certainly the Reporter should learn to forego irrelevance, "the main objection" continued to be—what some of the Justices would never recognize—"that the opinions are far too long," as Justice Miller wrote in 1879.[171]

The office to which Wallace came was still governed by a statute of 1842.[172] In return for a salary of $1,300 the Reporter would supply the Government with 150 copies of the volume for each annual term. Occasionally two volumes had been required, and Congress had doubled the compensation. The Reporter would sell to the public, at a price not to exceed $5. Wallace, like Black, charged $4; but with the mounting cost of paper he reported in February 1866 that he was scarcely recovering his expenses. In accordance with his modest request, Congress raised the salary to $2,500 in return for 300 copies,[173] with an additional $1,500 whenever the Court directed the publication of a second volume in any year.[174] The time allowed for the publication of the decisions was increased from six months to "eight months after they are made."[175]

---

[170] Such review of the facts was involved in equity appeals and (until 1875) in appeals in admiralty. In January 1872 the House passed H.-R. 891, "to further regulate the appellate jurisdiction of the Supreme Court," whereby (along with other measures to relieve the Court) in cases not tried by jury, the court below would make findings of fact, and the Supreme Court would review only questions of law. This died in the Senate Judiciary Committee. The bill was drawn by Justice Miller, and had the concurrence of his brethren. Fairman, *Mr. Justice Miller*, 403.

The editors of the *American Law Review*, in an article on "The Supreme Court" in July 1875, remarked that

> The court which first hears the cause is at least as competent as the court above to decide the facts; and when the evidence before the former is given *viva voce* in open court, it has an advantage which is never possessed by the latter. . . . It is said that these cases are an immense addition to the work of the court; and one can hardly suppose that it would

be otherwise when one remembers how voluminous the evidence in them usually is. The labor thus laid upon the Supreme Court brings no particular advantage, either to the parties or to others . . . . 9:668, 671–72.

[171] Letter of Oct. 29, 1879, to William P. Ballinger, telling of a committee on reporting. Fairman, *Mr. Justice Miller*, 408–9.

[172] 5 Stat. 545. As he recalled in the letter of Feb. 25, 1866, to the Secretary of the Interior, supra, n. 168. He went on to explain why Congress should be asked to make a better provision.

[173] Appropriations Act of July 23, 1866. 14 Stat. 205.

[174] Act of Mar. 2, 1867. 14 Stat. 471.

[175] Act of May 21, 1866, 14 Stat. 51. The provisions are brought together in Rev. Stats., secs. 681, 682. Wallace counted on four months to prepare the text, and two months for printing and binding, but felt anxiety at the possibility of delay in the mechanical production. "The court, in approving of the bill drawn for eight months, knew that I should get

When Wallace wrote in February 1866 that "sales of much more than one thousand copies" could not be counted on,[176] he did not reckon on the demand there soon would be for volumes reporting major constitutional decisions arising out of the war. When 4 Wallace —containing *Ex parte Milligan* on trial by military commission[177] and the *Test Oath Cases*[178]—appeared, "its first edition of some fifteen hundred copies was absorbed by the legal profession almost as soon as issued."[179]

When Wallace resigned in 1875 he was receiving the salary of $4,000 for two annual volumes, and was understood to be making from four to eight thousand dollars from sales.[180] At that time the salary of an Associate Justice had recently been raised to $10,000.

THE OFFICE OF CLERK

THE CLERK OF THE SUPREME COURT, from December term 1863 until his death in 1880, was Daniel Wesley Middleton; he had been employed in the business of the Clerk's office since 1825. He was, said Chief Justice Waite, "courteous . . . , dignified . . . , faithful in every duty, and never unmindful of the confidential relations he had with the Court"; "even a whisper of complaint against him, in any particular, has never reached our ears."[181] The recital of some of the Clerk's duties will throw light on the internal administration of the Court. One was to keep the Docket. Each case lodged with the Court was entered in order on a new page in the docket book; then every action concerning it would be posted to that page, ending ordinarily with the issue of a mandate to carry out the judgment.

The Minutes were a cognate responsibility. This journal opened each day with a list of the Justices present; then were recorded the events of that day, in particular, admissions to the Court's bar; the arguments heard; any order that was entered; judgments rendered (ordinarily on Mondays); any rules promulgated; and from time to time a new allotment of the Justices to the various circuits. When one works through the Minutes one thinks by moments rather than by topics; often it is striking to observe that a variety of tough cases, not

---

my work done at the very earliest day practicable . . . ." Letter of Feb. 28, 1866. Sen. Misc. Doc. 75, 39–1 (1866).

[176] Supra, p. 78.

[177] Infra, pp. 207–08.

[178] Infra, p. 241.

[179] Advertisement of W. H. & O. H. Morrison, the law publishers at Washington, in the *National Intelligencer*, Oct. 24, 1867, offering a second printing.

[180] John L. Cadwalader to J. C. B. Davis. Cablegram, text repeated in letter from Cadwalader to Chief Justice Waite, Oct. 27, 1875. Waite Papers, L.C.

[181] Minutes, May 10, 1880.

ordinarily associated in one's mind, were all being pressed upon the Justices at one time.

Transcripts of record of proceedings in the court below, the briefs of counsel, and in general all papers for the Court, would be filed with the Clerk. Communication with counsel, notably advice on when their cases would reach the call of the docket, was through him. Certificates of admission to practice at the Court's bar bore the seal of the Court and the signature of the Clerk; here was the occasion for one of the fees to which the Clerk was entitled.[182]

The Clerk's office, lodged on the main floor of the Capitol on its west side, directly opposite the Supreme Court chamber, would remain active even when the Court was adjourned. The Clerk would always be in touch with the Justices, and ready to supply their varied requests. He would send printer's proof of their opinions, for revision; the Reporter must be notified of any change. A direction from Justice Field at San Francisco, on August 18, 1868, recalls the state of communication; it had taken a month for a letter from the Clerk to reach him:

I believe I requested you a year ago to mark letters for me "per Steamer," as more reliance could then be placed [upon mail by steamer, via the Isthmus of Panama]. Since then matters have greatly changed in this respect. Owing to the great extension of the Pacific Railway, communication is had regularly between New York and San Francisco every fourteen days. I will therefore ask you to send all my letters hereafter by the overland mail. . . .[183]

Indeed on May 10, 1869, the gap between the railroad lines from the East and from the West was closed.

The Clerk's office performed innumerable personal services for the Justices, such as forwarding salary payments, aiding in arrange-

---

[182] Until 1883 the Clerk's compensation was by fees. The Act of March 8, 1792, 1 Stat. 275, 277, allowed him "ten dollars per day for his attendance in court, and for his other services . . . , double the fees of the clerk of the Supreme Court of that State in which the Supreme Court of the United States shall be holden." This was substantially repeated in the Act of February 28, 1799, 1 Stat. 624, 625, when the seat of the Government was about to be removed to the District of Columbia. The bill of fees thereupon adopted was based upon those allowed by the laws of Maryland to the clerk of its Court of

Appeals. Per Bradley, J., in Florida v. Anderson, 131 U.S. App. cxxxv, 23 L. Ed. 461 (1876).

The Act of March 3, 1883, 22 Stat. 631, permitted the Clerk to retain as personal compensation only $6,000 in any year out of fees from litigated cases. He continued to receive the entirety of admission fees until that was cut down by the Court's order of Oct. 10, 1921.

The Court now fixes the compensation of its officers. Revised Title 28 U.S.C. (1949), secs. 671–675.

[183] Papers of the Clerk's Office. National Archives.

Philadelphia
October 15 1866

L W Middleton Esqr
Dear Sir

I have received the third vol. of Wallace's reports sent by you to me — I had before, received one from the Secy of the Interior Was not that one intended for my library — No. 3 in Washington?

What is my prospect of being able to get a room in the capitol? I should know as soon as possible So that if I must, I can make other arrangements.

Judge Wayne, who called to see me lately, said he would attend to have the matter arranged — I mentioned the subject also in a letter to the chief justice — but have heard nothing thus far — so that I presume there is some difficulty in the case. Please let me hear from you. Very truly yours, R C Grier

46

Justice Grier to Clerk Middleton

He has received a copy of 3 Wallace's Reports, in addition to the one supplied by the Secretary of the Interior. What is the prospect of his being able to lodge in the Capitol?

ments for their lodging, and seeing to it that the Justice's desk and books were in place for his arrival. Consider the correspondence with Justice Grier in preparation for December term 1866.

Grier, now seventy-two years old and in failing health, wrote to the Clerk from Philadelphia on August 31, 1866: "I have just returned from the sea shore—*somewhat better*—*I hope rather* than *expect* to be with you next winter[.] the great difficulty will be *getting up stairs*. . . ."[184]

Justice Grier conceived the idea—astonishing as it seems—that he might go to live in the Capitol. On October 9 he broached this to the Chief Justice:

> If I could have a *room in the Capitol* on the *level* of our court room, so as not to be compelled to "*get up stairs*" I could attend to my duty at Washington as usual, if my health continues. The Clerk tells me that the Marshal has a room allotted to him in the Capitol, which he has no great use for—could he be prevailed upon to yield it to me?[185]

Inquiry addressed to the Clerk brought a reply, however, that upon examining the Marshal's office, he was "impressed with the belief that it would not answer your purpose for many reasons."

> In the first place it is too small to enable you to be comfortable in it, and being excluded from the sun, except for a very short time early in the morning, it is necessarily quite damp, and I think it would be running a great risk for you to sleep in it at night. Your Library could not, in any way, be accommodated in it, which of course would put you to considerable inconvenience. . . .

The Chief Justice, he said, agreed in this conclusion.

During the previous winter, both Grier and Field had lived at No. 6 North A Street, approximately the spot where the northwest corner of the Supreme Court building now rests. If Grier would arrange to have the room there, on the ground floor, previously occupied by Field, that—the Clerk suggested—would be more practicable:

> my idea is that you would be vastly more comfortable by having a room on the first floor at Capt. Wells' house, as I am sure an easy mode, could be adopted to convey you to and from the Capitol. . . .[186]

So it was arranged. "I can walk or ride the short distance to the Capitol—I can easily attend consultation in the library," Grier assured

---

[184] Ibid.
[185] Chase Papers, Hist. Soc. of Pa.

[186] Clerk's reply of Oct. 16 to Grier's inquiry of Oct. 15. National Archives.

the Chief Justice. "I need the exercise both of *mind* and *body*—which sitting in court would afford me. . . ."[187] On November 26 came requests to the Clerk, about preparations to be made for his arrival: that the Marshal's men have wood cut and stored in the cellar; that the proprietor have a fire burning in his room; that "a *warm supper* on Monday evening" be in readiness.[188]

As the Minutes show, Justice Grier was in his seat on Tuesday, December 4, when the Court began the call of the docket.

This episode does more than illustrate one of the services of the Clerk: it also lays a foundation for reporting the mental failure of Grier and his resulting resignation, while the constitutionality of the Legal Tender Act was under consideration in the Court.[189]

THE MARSHAL

PERFORMING THE DUTIES OF MARSHAL, when Chase came to the bench, was Ward H. Lamon, who as a young lawyer in Danville, Illinois, had once had a local partnership with Lincoln. By a provision of the original Judiciary Act, then still in force, the United States Marshal for the district wherein the Supreme Court sat would, in addition to his other duties, attend the Supreme Court.[190] Lamon had accompanied Lincoln on the trip to Washington in 1861, and had been appointed Marshal for the District of Columbia, a post closely related to guarding the President's life. (In times of supposed danger, Lamon slept just outside Lincoln's bed-chamber.) In the "confederated factions" that had made up the Republican party in Illinois,[191] Lamon was prominent in the wing furthest removed from the Abolitionists. On Lincoln's death, Lamon resigned and formed a partnership with Jeremiah S. Black, whose political outlook he shared.[192] Lamon and Justice Davis had been close friends since their days on the circuit in Illinois, and presently sympathetic relations developed between Black and Davis.[193]

[187] Letter of Oct. 22, 1866. Chase Papers, L.C.
[188] Papers of the Clerk's Office. National Archives.
[189] Infra, pp. 713–19.
[190] 1 Stat. 87.
[191] Willard L. King, *Lincoln's Manager, David Davis* (Cambridge, Mass.: Harvard University Press, 1960), 127.
[192] On February 26, 1866, after President Johnson's veto of the Freedmen's Bureau Bill had been sustained only by a narrow vote in the Senate, Lamon wrote to assure Johnson that his policy was indeed that which Lincoln would have pursued. Johnson Papers, L.C.
[193] Mrs. Davis in a letter of January 28, 1866, referred to "Judge Black—who by the way stays late but [is] the pleasantest talker I know of." A letter of February 25, 1866, records that "Judge Black and Lamon came in . . . and are still here in the Study—Tis nearly bed time . . . ." Davis Papers, Ill. State Hist. Soc.

To the vacancy caused by Lamon's resignation the President appointed David S. Gooding of Greenfield, Indiana, who at that moment and thereafter was busy at beating the bushes to bring out support for Johnson. It was in accord with practice that the United States Marshal would be an active partisan; but it was not appropriate that one so engaged also serve the Supreme Court as its Marshal.

By the Act of March 2, 1867, Congress created the office of Marshal of the Supreme Court, to which the Court itself would appoint.[194] The first occupant was Richard C. Parsons, already introduced as a personal intimate of the Chief Justice and recently a Collector of Internal Revenue.[195] Parsons entered upon his duties on April 3, 1867, and continued until December 16, 1872, resigning upon being elected to Congress. (When in 1869–70 Chase purchased and remodeled a large old house, about an hour's walk north of the Capitol, Parsons took charge of the reconstruction.)

John G. Nicolay was next appointed Marshal, and continued in that office through the year 1887. His letter of resignation explained that "the literary and historical labors upon which I am engaged as a co-worker will during the next few years require the whole of my time."[196] He was referring, of course, to the great undertaking on which he and John Hay, President Lincoln's secretaries, were engaged, the ten volume *Abraham Lincoln: A History* that was published in 1890. In the long years of his service with the Court, Nicolay had been using his spare time on this biographical work.

THE JUSTICES GO ON CIRCUIT

WHEN CHASE'S FIRST TERM CLOSED, on March 10, 1865, the Justices set out to make the rounds of their respective circuits, as far as was practicable in a country still engaged in civil war. It was the duty of every Justice once each year to attend the Circuit Court for each District within his circuit. Otherwise each Circuit Court would be held by the District Judge for that District sitting alone. The Circuit Court was the important federal court of first instance. (The District Court,

---

[194] 14 Stat. 443. The salary was $3,500.

[195] Supra, p. 25.

On Sunday, April 7, 1867, Justice Davis wrote to his wife:

By invitation yesterday morning I walked an hour with the Chief Justice before breakfast, and then had breakfast with him. He is very polite, but no political sub-ject was broached between us. It is generally understood that he is a candidate for the Presidency, with what success remains to be seen. The Court app^t his man, Col Parsons . . . Marshall [*sic*]. He is evidently a gentleman of culture & refinement & lives in Cleveland. Davis Papers.

[196] Minutes, Jan. 4, 1888.

held only by the District Judge, had jurisdiction in admiralty, including prize; of revenue and postal matters; and of lesser offenses against the United States.) In practice, the tendency was to hold more important matters for hearing by the two Judges, or by the Circuit Justice alone, save that where the Justice was old and infirm there might be a lasting inability to perform circuit duty.[197] In serious criminal cases it was of great importance to bring the matter before a bench of two Judges: if they differed in opinion they could certify the questions to the Supreme Court; otherwise the ruling of the court could not be tested by an appeal.[198] (Not until 1889 did Congress provide a review of right by the Supreme Court in criminal cases, and then only at the suit of one convicted of a capital offense.[199])

Chief Justice Chase, after holding the Circuit Court in Baltimore, was back in Washington when, on April 14, President Lincoln was shot. During what proved to be Lincoln's last days, Chase had written him two letters on the reconstruction of the Southern States. In particular he was concerned that the President insist upon suffrage for the Negroes:

> This way is recommended by its simplicity, facility & above all, justice. It will be, hereafter, counted equally a crime & a folly if the colored loyalists of the rebel states shall be left to the control of restored rebels, not likely, in that case, to be either wise or just, until taught both wisdom and justice by new calamities.[200]

---

[197] This was coming to be the case with Justice Grier. He had given up circuit work in the summer of 1862, and thereafter the situation became chronic. Letter of Aug. 9, 1862, to Justice Clifford. Clifford Papers, Me. Hist. Soc. *Pittsburgh Legal J.*, 17:36 (1870).

[198] This had been strikingly illustrated in *Ex parte* Nathaniel Gordon, 1 Bl. 503, decided on February 17, 1862. Gordon, a citizen of Maine, had been taken while carrying slaves from Africa; he was tried for piracy under the federal statute, in the Circuit Court for the Southern District of New York, and sentenced to die by hanging on February 7, 1862. The trial judges refused to certify any division of opinion. President Lincoln refused to commute the sentence, but stayed execution until February 21. Application was made to the Supreme Court for writs of prohibition and certiorari. Taney, C.J., pointed out that "in criminal cases, the proceedings and judgment of the Circuit Court cannot be revised or controlled here"; the only situation where the Supreme Court was "authorized even to express an opinion" was where the Judges below certified a question, which they could not properly do if they "agreed in opinion, and did not think there was doubt enough to justify them in submitting the question" to the Supreme Court.

Gordon is said to have been "the only slave-trader ever convicted and hanged in accordance with federal law"; in numerous cases juries had failed to convict. *Collected Works of Abraham Lincoln*, V, 47, 128–29.

[199] Act of Feb. 6, 1889. 25 Stat. 655, 656. See United States v. Sanges, 144 U.S. 310, 319–22 (1892), and Cobbledick v. United States, 309 U.S. 323, 324–25 (1940).

[200] Letter written in Baltimore, April 11, 1865. *Collected Works of Abraham Lincoln*, VIII, 399.

The Chief Justice pressed the same view on President Johnson. He offered a draft of what he hoped would become a "new and crowning proclamation . . . securing equal and universal suffrage in reorganization." Johnson was understood to profess agreement, but was recorded as concluding "I dont see how I can issue such a document now. I am new and untried and cannot venture what I please."[201] Johnson suspended judgment for some weeks before he settled upon his policy for reconstruction. When he made up his mind, it was not from the Chief Justice that he drew inspiration.

THE CHIEF JUSTICE ON A SOUTHERN TOUR

GENERAL JOHNSTON'S SURRENDER TO SHERMAN, in late April, made it possible for Chase to undertake a tour of inspection in the South. Bearing letters from the President in furtherance of his journey, he set forth on board a revenue cutter bound for New Orleans. He visited principal cities along the coast, and returned via the Mississippi River, reaching Washington in mid-August. Along the way he made speeches, and what he said was widely reported. He talked casually with many men, and snatches of these conversations were caught up by newspapers all over the country. At Charleston he told a large audience of Negroes that if all men thought as he did, universal suffrage would be established. "But there is not that agreement. Having nothing to do with politics, I am not prepared to say what will be the action of the Government." He counselled industry and perseverance.[202] At New Orleans, "he thought it was better, on account of his position in the Supreme Court, to decline the invitation" to make another address, but responded in a public letter that repeated his views.[203] Thus the name of the Chief Justice appeared, constantly and everywhere, in political discussion throughout the anxious months between Lincoln's death and the convening of the 39th Congress.

Chase had come to a Court that enjoyed no commanding moral authority. During the long controversy over slavery it had fallen low in public confidence, and the period of the war was not a time for any substantial recovery. It was plainly to be foreseen that when at last arms were silenced, issues resulting from the war would come crowding before the Court—and that it could best serve the nation if it met them from a position of calm detachment.

---

[201] Diary entry of Apr. 29, 1865. *Inside Lincoln's Cabinet. The Civil War Diaries of Salmon P. Chase*, 271–72.

[202] Ann. Cyc. 1865, 765.
[203] *New Orleans Tribune*, June 6 and 10, 1865; Ann. Cyc. 1865, 515.

That however was not the call as it sounded in the ears of the Chief Justice. He could not stifle the outpouring of his own lofty sentiments, to bide the occasion when he and his brethren would be called to speak responsibly on such of the impending questions as pertained to the tasks of the Supreme Court.

CHAPTER III

Reconstruction—by Lincoln and by Johnson

A CONTRAST IS TO BE NOTED. Time has brought an ever-increasing popular interest in the Civil War, and among specialists a discriminating familiarity with its participants and their battles. It has been quite otherwise with Reconstruction: that experience cannot yet be viewed objectively; acquaintanceship has seldom been free from bias. Even as the Reconstruction Act was being put into operation, "Love and tears for the Blue,/Tears and love for the Gray" could be sung feelingly—and the years have only strengthened the sentiment.[1] But even a century after Reconstruction, the nation cannot sincerely sing in unison that "Black and white together,/We shall overcome."

Yet upon that dark period a history of the Supreme Court must dwell. Those who lost in battle early sought sanctuary in appeals to the Court; the portents it gave out were such as to bring upon it the menaces of Congress. For a season, judicial authority was openly defied. Then in the outcome, when the country was wearied and the politicians had withdrawn, it was left to the Court to say what effect the Reconstruction statutes and constitutional amendments were to have. The time would come when one would hear the lament, If only the Court had

---

[1] The quotation is of the concluding lines of "The Blue and the Gray," appearing in the *Atlantic Monthly* of September 1867, and quickly reprinted and recited, North and South. It was prompted by a report that at Columbus, Mississippi, women had "strewn flowers alike on the graves of the Confederate and of the National soldiers." The author was Francis Miles Finch (1827–1907), subsequently a Judge of New York's Court of Appeals, dean of Cornell Law School, and president of the State Bar Association. Andrew D. White, his friend, said that "all the orations and sermons and appeals for the restoration of kindly feeling between the two sections have been exceeded in real effect upon the national heart by this simple poem." See D. A. B.

It may be found in William Cullen Bryant's *Family Library of Poetry and Song* at 533; the second stanza is in *Bartlett's Familiar Quotations*.

then done its duty, what travail the nation would have been spared! Perhaps that is too severe toward the Court and too indulgent toward the nation. It is a matter to be probed critically.

Unless one has patiently examined the involved chronology—to distinguish between what was cause and what was consequence—and has looked squarely at the hard alternatives inherent in the facts, he cannot know the context within which the Court acted. Without full knowledge a responsible judgment may not be made. But what, in this tangle, is truth? Historiography has had its moods. All must concede that Southern whites resorted to lawless violence: some will excuse on the ground that they were only protecting themselves against the vindictive Radicals led by Thad Stevens. All must concede that the Radicals ran to excesses: some will explain that Southern intransigence made this inevitable. Conclusions have been governed by what one was prepared to condone and what to condemn.

Then prepossessions have become the basis for criticism of the Court, leading to impressionistic judgments that one action was wise and valorous and some other decision was an inglorious retreat from duty. A rigorous reexamination is in order, scanning as much of the scene as comes within the background when the focus is upon the Supreme Court.

When Congress met in December 1865, President Johnson during almost eight months had had a free hand to shape events. Congress had to reckon, what should now be done? Simply readmit the Southern States to representation, said the President, and "thereby complete the work of restoration"; look to the States to "provide adequate protection and remedies for the freedmen."[2] Congress was unwilling to accept so minimal a settlement. Its bill to enlarge the protective powers of the Freedmen's Bureau was killed by a veto. President Johnson denounced leading Radicals in a vulgar tirade. A Civil Rights Bill was then carried over his veto. There were race riots, in Memphis and in New Orleans. Congress framed a Fourteenth Amendment, stating propositions essential to a post-war Constitution.

The election of 1866 was a test of strength between Johnson and Congress; the latter emerged triumphant. Meanwhile it was rumored that the Supreme Court was going to hold loyalty oaths unconstitutional, and so it turned out. The Court released prisoners condemned in wartime by a military commission, and in doing so uttered a dictum that conveyed an immediate threat to Congress. The Southern legislatures, organized under the President's patronage, spurned the Fourteenth Amendment, virtually to a man.

The Second Session of the 39th Congress, meeting in December

---

[2] Message to Congress. Cong. Globe, 39–1, App., 1.

1866, was faced with a factual situation that was sharply defined and inexorable. It should be marked well. Either Congress and the country must accept the line on which the President and the Southern States had taken their stand—in substance, settle for the Constitution as it had been in 1860, minus "slavery"—or else that position must be breached.

Moving against that barrier, Congress set about reconstruction anew, by admitting black citizens to participate with whites in forming new governments, in place of those dedicated to rule by white men only. Leaders of the South, refusing to conform, pinned wild hopes on the Supreme Court getting their people out of their predicament. Congress made clear that it would brook no interference. Only by a series of hair-breadth escapes was an outright collision between Court and Congress averted.

At the outset one needs to understand how matters stood at the time of Appomattox, and then examine developments over twenty months to the convening of the Second Session of the 39th Congress, when the second Reconstruction was instituted.

WHAT TO DO ABOUT THE FREEDMEN

"WITHOUT SLAVERY the rebellion could never have existed":[3] Lincoln might have added that if the rebellion were suppressed, slavery too would perish. The Emancipation Proclamation of January 1, 1863, was a war measure applicable only to places in rebellion; its validity was disputed. To abolish slavery everywhere, the Thirteenth Amendment was proposed; between February 1 and December 6, 1865, it received the necessary ratifications. So slavery was ended: but what was to be the status of the Negro? Was that question to be answered by the several States—or should federal protection be provided, by statute or by further constitutional amendment? If it were left to the States, would not a new "peculiar institution" be created, a rigid status lifted above the old no higher than was supposed to satisfy the Thirteenth Amendment? Was the Negro to be permitted to work his own way, by industry, character, and intelligence, without limit because of race? In the autumn of 1865 the answers were not obvious.

Looking back, one can see that a mighty national effort was in order, to meet the four million freedmen in the plight where emancipation found them, and afford such advancement as was practicable for the long road ahead. Given the circumstances, such an undertaking

---

[3] Lincoln's Message to Congress, Dec. 1, 1862. *Collected Works of Abraham Lincoln*, Roy P. Basler, ed., (New Brunswick, N.J.: Rutgers University Press, 1953), V, 518, 530

would have been far more exacting than any of the operations carried on by the United States since World War II in relief of foreign peoples, or in programs for opening economic opportunities to the under-privileged at home. The Freedmen's Bureau, created in 1865, was woe-fully unequal to the task—in conception and scope, in administrative capacity, and in appropriations. Over four years its resources amounted to about three dollars per freedman.[4] Yet by those who would not lift a finger, it was derided as "the largest and most expensive eleemosynary institution that ever existed." "Congress has no power to pass laws to organize a vast system of poor-houses, to endow them, and to establish and support in them the paupers of the United States, black and white . . . ."[5]

A nation of self-helpers had no proper conception of organized social service. Even had there been general sympathy for a public com-mitment to afford to freedmen the means of attaining economic inde-pendence, the American people lacked the skill requisite to such an enterprise. The governmental system rested upon law and politics, but was utterly deficient in administration. The conduct of the Civil War had been a monument to that inadequacy.[6] Private efforts, notably to satisfy the universal thirst for education, were commendable and even heroic, but for so plentiful a harvest, the laborers were few.[7]

---

[4] Receipts from January 1, 1865, to August 1, 1869, were $12,965,395.40. Not all of its expenditures were for freedmen. Thus in accordance with a Joint Resolution of March 30, 1867, food was issued to those suffering from crop failures in the South and Southwest, without regard to color. Report of the Commissioner (General O. O. Howard) of Oct. 20, 1869, in Annual Report of the Secretary of War, House Ex. Doc. 1, pt. 2, 41st Cong., 2d Sess., pp. 497 et seq.

See letter of Chief Justice Chase to Governor Patton of Alabama, Mar. 11, 1867, infra, pp. 311–12.

George R. Bentley, *A History of the Freedmen's Bureau* (Philadelphia: University of Pennsylvania Press, 1955), examines the experience in detail.

[5] Senator Garrett Davis of Ken-tucky, supporting President Johnson's veto of the bill to enlarge the powers of the Bureau. Cong. Globe, 39–1, 933–36. Feb. 20, 1866.

[6] "It was wonderful how well Lin-coln managed matters on which he thought deeply; it was also wonderful how completely he refused to think about some matters at all. Adminis-tration was one of them." Allan Nevins, *The War for the Union, 1862–1863* (New York: Charles Scrib-ner's Sons, 1960), 364. Homely illus-tration may be seen in the mass of his notes to department heads, re-sponding to the importunities of a stream of callers. Willard King in his biography of Justice Davis comments that Davis' "badgering of Lincoln with requests for minor appointments in the depths of the President's misery over the war makes one cringe, but Davis had not the slightest conscious-ness of any wrongdoing." *Lincoln's Manager, David Davis* (Cambridge, Mass: Harvard University Press, 1960), 308.

[7] In November 1861 federal forces took the fine harbor of Port Royal, South Carolina, and the Sea Islands thereabout. At the approach of the expedition, white folk withdrew to Charleston; the slaves remained on these rich cotton lands, which con-

III: *Reconstruction—by Lincoln and by Johnson*

In 1867, after proposals to admit qualified Negroes to the suffrage had been repelled, Congress called all adult blacks to share in voting. The result was a woeful disparity between political equality conferred by statute and "labor's utter nakedness"[8] in respect of education and economic opportunity.[9] To point to this deficiency is not to affirm that Thad Stevens' program to confiscate and distribute the lands in "rebeldom" was worthy of acceptance; a work thus conceived in hatred and uncharitableness did not commend itself to the people of the North.[10]

An opinion, widely proclaimed throughout the South and seriously considered in the North, was that "the colored race is destined to speedy extinction, crowded out of existence" under the conditions of

---

tinued under military occupation throughout the war. Philanthropic bodies in Boston, New York, and Philadelphia dispatched "evangels" to bring guidance and education to these people.

What ensued is related with rare skill and discernment by Mrs. Willie Lee Rose in *Rehearsal for Reconstruction: The Port Royal Experiment* (Indianapolis, Ind.: Bobbs-Merrill Co., 1964). Here one finds, in miniature, the basic problems and the varied types that figured in Reconstruction. The evangels—unlike the Peace Corps volunteers a century later—received no preparatory instruction in the mores of the natives. The situation as seen at Beaufort proved far more complex than it had seemed at Boston. Port Royal became "a mecca for assorted planners, reporters, and radical thinkers . . . ."

Broadly, the slaves performed well. Many acquired title to land at sales for taxes due to the United States. See De Treville v. Smalls, 98 U.S. 517 (1879).

In a few years, the North became tired, and "concluded that in granting the franchise the national obligation to the freedmen had been fulfilled." In Mrs. Rose's epilogue, "Revolutions May Go Backward," one reads that by the turn of the century, "The islanders could no longer vote, but in a signal respect they were more fortunate than other Negroes of the South. They owned their own land, and on it they could support themselves. . . . The Sea Islanders had learned the lessons of freedom, and

they became, in their own way, as self-governing as many a small New England town. The church remained for them a greater force in the conduct of men than man-made law . . . ."

[8] John Greenleaf Whittier's "To the Thirty-ninth Congress," *Poetical Works* (Boston: Houghton Mifflin Co., 1882), 388.

[9] The *New York World*, the organ of responsible Northern Democracy, made this point in an editorial on "The Future of the Negroes," January 28, 1867:

The ballot can do little for the freedmen, inasmuch as it cannot place them on anything like an equal footing with the white laboring classes . . . . The ballot cannot gain them admission into the various trades-unions; it cannot compel skilled artisans to receive them as apprentices; it cannot force the proprietors of establishments to give them employment when their white hands object; it cannot give negroes the tenure of land and make them independent small farmers against the growing tendencies of agriculture to cultivation on a large scale. Those who wish to benefit the negroes, and not merely make political capital out of them, must study their prospects from the new stand-points of the white laboring classes. . . .

[10] On the Confiscation Acts of 1861 and 1862, in litigation before the Court, see infra, ch. 15.

freedom.[11] Greeley's *New York Tribune*, on the contrary, expressed confidence in the freedman's ability to survive and, if permitted, to advance. "America owes the black man a debt, whose arrears run back two hundred years. To give him schools and a chance of manhood is not to attempt payment, but only to acknowledge the obligation."[12]

WHAT TO DO ABOUT SOUTHERN "STATES"

How to deal with the rebellious States was another basic problem. Here men caught in conceptual modes of thought were unable to put the problem in terms of practicable operations. A State consists of people dwelling within given boundaries and submitting to some machinery of government. How get hold of such an entity for purposes of restoration? Take Louisiana as the most convenient example. Its people had voted 20,448 for secession, 17,296 against,[13] although their convention passed the ordinance by overwhelming vote. When in May 1862 New Orleans was occupied by federal forces, local groups sought to restore normal relations with the Union—an object the President encouraged. Congressional elections were held, and two Representatives were seated on February 17, 1863, in the closing days of the 37th Congress. (No further representation was admitted until July 1868.)

The year 1863 was filled with conflicting movements to restore Louisiana. Conservatives, like the planter Bradish Johnson[14] and the lawyer J. Q. A. Fellows,[15] stood on the State's old constitution and sought simply to go on as in the past. The Free State group, whose

---

[11] *The Nation*, 1:106, July 27, 1865, reprinting a letter from a traveler in South Carolina. Also ibid., 1:325, Sept. 14, 1865. "Slavery is abolished now, but in a hundred years the negro himself will be abolished," said the *Clarion*, then published at Meridian, Mississippi, August 17, 1865. The *Jackson Clarion* spoke of mortality more temperately, December 25, 1866. Persons then born would live to "find a negro rather an uncommon spectacle," prophesied the *Cincinnati Enquirer*, June 11, 1867. On the same theme, *Augusta Chronicle and Sentinel*, Jan. 28, 1866; *New York Herald*, Jan. 14, 1867; B. F. Perry, letter in *Columbus* (Georgia) *Sun*, May 22, 1867; *Rich-* mond *Enquirer and Examiner*, April 18, 1868; *New Orleans Picayune*, April 27, 1873.

Vernon L. Wharton reports and comments on such opinions, in *The Negro in Mississippi, 1865–1890* (New York: Harper & Row, Harper Torch books, 1965), at 54–55.

[12] Mar. 26, also Mar. 11 and Apr. 30, 1869.

[13] Ann. Cyc. 1861, 431.

[14] Later to appear in Dow v. Johnson, 100 U.S. 158 (1880), seeking to recover from a Union general for the alleged carrying away of personal property.

[15] Later to appear as counsel for the butchers in the *Slaughter House Cases*, 16 Wall. 36 (1873).

leader was Thomas J. Durant,[16] called for a larger deliverance: they would frame a new constitution and establish Negro suffrage. Others stood between these positions. In the relatively favorable climate of New Orleans, many free men of color had acquired property and education. Well-edited newspapers expressed their aspirations, in excellent English and French, with apt allusions to the classics. Their case was simply this: "We are men, treat us as such."

Here were the loyal and the disillusioned, seeking to undo secession, by different paths and with conflicting objectives. In Arkansas as well, after Little Rock was occupied in September 1863, action was in progress to restore the State. Such movements tended to pull down the Confederacy and to build up national authority; they were to be fostered, and could not be left to themselves. It was a proper responsibility of the President, incident to the conduct of the war, to guide and support them. In a State much of whose soil was still dominated by Confederate forces, those who made bold to act could represent only a minority of the State's population: Were they to be told that steps toward restoration must wait until resistance was at an end?

When the need for a plan became urgent, Lincoln put one forward, "as a rallying point," in a proclamation of December 8, 1863, concurrent with his annual message to Congress. He offered pardon to any who took an oath thenceforth to be loyal and to support the statutes and Executive proclamations with reference to slavery so long as they had not been held invalid by the Supreme Court.[17] (In Lincoln's expectation, the Court would eventually settle the effect of those measures: hence his concern when a Chief Justice was selected.) When well-disposed persons, to a number as great as one-tenth of the State's voters in the election of 1860, joined to set up a government, the Executive would support it as the government of that State. Whether representation from a State so restored would be seated in Congress was a matter for the respective Houses. The President added

> that any provision which may be adopted by such State government in relation to the freed people of such State, which shall recognize and declare their permanent freedom, provide for their education, and which may yet be consistent, as a temporary arrangement, with their present condition as a laboring, landless, and homeless class, will not be objected to by the national Executive. . . .

---

[16] See infra, pp. 270, 290.

[17] *Collected Works of Abraham Lincoln*, VII, 53.

Certain exceptions were made: civil and senior military officers of the Confederacy, those who had left the federal judiciary or Congress or the military service to aid in the rebellion, those who had mistreated Union servicemen.

The words were carefully chosen: Lincoln always distinguished between the distant goal and the immediately practicable advance, and kept both in view.

In that part of Louisiana within Union lines, containing about one-third of the total population, the plan was promptly put into execution. On February 22, 1864, Michael Hahn, a moderate, was elected Governor, by a vote considerably greater than the total for his opponents, the Free State candidate who sought Negro suffrage and the Conservative, Fellows, who sought compensation for slaveowners. Delegates were chosen to frame a constitution, which would abolish slavery. It was at this juncture that Lincoln sent his memorable letter to Hahn:

> I congratulate you on having fixed your name in history as the first-free-state Governor of Louisiana. Now you are about to have a Convention which, among other things, will probably define the elective franchise. I barely suggest for your private consideration whether some of the colored people may not be let in—as, for instance, the very intelligent, and especially those who have fought gallantly in our ranks. They would probably help, in some trying time to come, to keep the jewel of liberty within the family of freedom. But this is only a suggestion, not to the public, but to you alone.[18]

In the matter of Negro suffrage, the President was leading gently: he saw no constitutional authority for insisting, and his suggestion was far in advance of political practice. In only five States—New England, except Connecticut—was the qualification "white" omitted from the suffrage laws.

Louisiana's new constitution fell short of Lincoln's hopes: while it abolished slavery and called for the education of all children, it gave the vote only to whites, with a clause empowering the legislature to extend the suffrage to others who "by military service, by taxation to support the Government, or by intellectual fitness may be deemed entitled thereto." In the next legislature, on November 15, 1864, a bill thus to extend the suffrage was rejected on first reading, by a vote of 15 to 5.[19]

This was a portentous decision. Professor John R. Ficklen, in his *History of Reconstruction in Louisiana*, spoke tardy wisdom when, in a conclusion contrary to the tendency of his study, he said that "had Lincoln's advice been followed the South would doubtless have been spared the horrors of congressional reconstruction . . . ."[20] Here was a

---

[18] Letter of March 13, 1864. *Collected Works of Abraham Lincoln*, VII, 243.

[19] Louisiana Senate Journal 1864–65, 59.

[20] Baltimore, Md.: Johns Hopkins Press, 1910, at 64.

community of African blood, quite outstanding in respect of wealth, culture, and accomplishments. Beyond question it would have supplied voters of high intelligence. Yet the lawmakers, well advised that their decision would set a course for Southern restoration, deliberately refused to allow any person of color to qualify for a voice in government. This should be marked as a capital mistake.

Concurrently the President's plan was being carried out in Arkansas, with similar result. A convention met in Little Rock in January 1864. There was great irregularity in the appointment of delegates, since the Confederates controlled part of the country and made communication perilous. The new constitution abolished slavery, but gave the suffrage only to whites. The new Governor, Isaac Murphy, was a Unionist who as a delegate in 1861 had stood alone in opposing secession. Those who participated in the reorganization amounted to about one-fourth of the voters at the election of 1860.

Representatives were elected to the 38th Congress, one of them being a colonel in the Union Army. When they appeared in January 1864, the House refused to receive them. In June the Senate likewise refused to seat two claimants. They represented only a minority of the people of Arkansas, Sumner objected. Moreover, the present organization of Arkansas was "revolutionary in character. Nay, more, it may all be traced to a *military order*."[21] The point was that an Executive, not a Congressional, plan was being followed. Congress was then considering the Wade-Davis bill for reconstruction, and the Radical Republicans thought no Southern State was ready for representation until it had undergone the rigorous course that plan prescribed. For a different reason, Conservative Democrats joined in rejecting: they would wait until delegations truly representative of the old South could be seated. These claimants, said Willard Saulsbury of Delaware, came from "a rotten borough government established by Abraham Lincoln, and not by the people of Arkansas."[22] Only half a dozen opposed when Republicans and Democrats joined to reject the Arkansans.[23]

Representative Henry Winter Davis of Maryland was brilliant, self-assured, and at odds with the Administration; he was "well fitted to lead, but not always safe to follow; . . . his views on reconstruction were no whit behind those of the foremost radical in Massachusetts."[24] Senator Benjamin F. Wade of Ohio, bluff and acrimonious, was bent upon bringing the conduct of the war under the close supervision of Congress. Their bill, in opposition to Lincoln's plan, expressed the Radicals' program for dealing with Southern States. Had it become law,

---

[21] Cong. Globe, 38–1, 2897. June 13, 1864.
[22] Ibid., 2903.

[23] Ibid., 3368.
[24] Obituary in *The Nation*, 2:33, Jan. 11, 1866.

it would have authorized the President to appoint in each rebellious State a provisional governor who would administer law as it had existed before the State was overthrown (save as to slavery), and collect and expend taxes. After resistance had been suppressed, and a majority of white male citizens had taken the oath of allegiance, delegates to a constitutional convention would be chosen. Office holders under the Confederacy and all who had voluntarily borne arms were to be excluded from voting and from serving as delegate. When the constitution, amended to forbid slavery, repudiate the war debt, and exclude from suffrage and office all who had held a place (other than one merely ministerial, or below the rank of colonel) under the usurping power, had been ratified at an election, it would result that upon the assent of Congress the State would be entitled to choose Senators and Representatives.

Davis took his stand on Article IV, Section 4: the United States guarantees to every State "a Republican Form of Government." That, he declared confidently, vests in Congress "a plenary, supreme, unlimited political jurisdiction, paramount over courts, subject only to the judgment of the people of the United States, embracing within its scope every legislative measure necessary and proper to make it effectual."[25] By enacting his bill Congress would establish "law" where now there was only "the dictation of military . . . [i.e., the President's] authority." He purposed not only to abase the President, but to elude the judiciary as well. What Congress prescribed in securing republican governments could not be questioned by any court: here *Luther v. Borden*[26] was cited. "If gentlemen say the Constitution does not bear that construction, we will go before the people . . . and by their judgment we will abide." There was a revolutionary cast to Davis' speech.

Here one catches early rumblings of the storm that was to break over the Supreme Court, three years later.

What qualifications were to be required for participation in a restored State, as voter and as office holder, was another basic problem in Reconstruction. The Wade-Davis bill answered, exclude all who had held important office in the Confederacy. Here the Radicals would collide with one of the toughest facts of Reconstruction: the rank and file of the Southern people would not accept—still less consent by their own hands to impose—any rule that would disqualify those who had led them into rebellion. "Loyalty" lay deep in Southern mores. If anybody was to be penalized, they would take their stand beside their chiefs. And the old leaders had no thought of immolating themselves.

The Wade-Davis bill was passed at the very end of the session,

---

[25] Cong. Globe, 38–1, App. 82. Mar. 22, 1864.

[26] 7 How. 1 (1849). Infra, p. 395.

by modest majorities, some Republicans and all Democrats opposing. Lincoln let it fail by a pocket veto, but issued a proclamation to say that if the loyal people in any State chose to carry out the Wade-Davis plan, the President would perform his part.[27] Davis and Wade, in exasperation, published an intemperate "protest."[28] The President should "suppress by arms armed rebellion, and leave political reorganization to Congress."

An attempt was renewed to carry the bill at the Second Session of the 38th Congress, that met in December 1864, a month after Lincoln had been reelected. Some former supporters had now turned critics. In the outcome the bill was put aside, and on March 3, 1865, that Congress ended. So the President was left free to shape a course.

Tennessee at that moment was choosing a governor and legislature under a revised constitution that abolished slavery. This was the culmination of three years of labor. In March 1862, after the Confederates evacuated Nashville, the President had commissioned Andrew Johnson, then a Senator, to be Military Governor.[29] In May 1862, Justice Catron came to Nashville and reopened the Circuit Court. But the people were divided in loyalty, rebel incursions were effective, and it was not until the spring of 1865 that the Unionists were able to establish an administration. The bitterness of the struggle was reflected in the oath prescribed for any voter whose loyalty was challenged: he was to swear that he "ardently desired" the suppression of the rebellion, "sincerely rejoiced" in Union victories, "cordially opposed" a negotiated peace, and would "heartily aid" in all loyal measures. The legislature promptly limited the franchise to unconditional (white) Unionists, to be tested by an oath almost as intrusive.

Tennessee was held, precariously, by a Republican administration under Governor William G. (Parson) Brownlow; there was some prospect that the party might continue to win elections. Accordingly the Radicals in Congress regarded Tennessee with an indulgence not extended to Arkansas or Louisiana.

The restoration of Virginia was a case by itself. Throughout the war the State's name was borne by a loyal government, recognized by Congress as well as by the President. In the western part of the Old Dominion the people had refused to be carried out of the Union. They organized a government at Wheeling, with Frank H. Pierpoint as Governor. This Virginia was represented in both Houses of the 37th Congress (1861–63). With the consent of the legislature at Wheeling, West

---

[27] *Collected Works of Abraham Lincoln*, VII, 433.

[28] Edward McPherson, *The Political History of the United States of America, during the Great Rebellion*, 2d ed. (Washington: Philp & Solomons, 1865), 332.

[29] The only Senator who did not withdraw when his State seceded.

Virginia came into being as a State; it was represented in the 38th Congress and thereafter. Governor Pierpoint moved his administration to Alexandria. The legislature consisted of representatives from the residue of Virginia, including districts occupied by Union forces. Virginia was represented in the Senate of the 38th Congress; the House rejected claimants from three districts because of the slender vote—a considerable part of each district had lain within the Confederate lines.

Upon Lee's surrender at Appomattox, Governor Pierpoint moved to Richmond, and acted with notable forbearance. Under his leadership his little legislature extended the suffrage to all persons otherwise qualified who took an oath thenceforth to be loyal. Negro suffrage was not provided. By an amendment to the Alexandria Constitution of 1864, ex-Confederates became eligible to office. Anticipating such amendment, a legislature truly representative of the white population was elected; it convened at Richmond in December 1865. Thus when the 39th Congress was meeting, Virginia was herself again, with a representative body consisting largely of former Whigs not prominent in secession.

LINCOLN'S THOUGHTS AFTER APPOMATTOX

BETWEEN LEE'S SURRENDER on April 9, 1865, and Booth's shot five days later, Lincoln was fixing his thoughts upon reconstruction. At his last Cabinet meeting, on the fourteenth, "He remarked that this was the great question now before us, and we must soon begin to act. Was glad Congress was not in session."[30] Reconstruction had been the subject of important remarks on April 11, responding to a serenade. To argue whether the Southern States were now in or out of the Union—the theme of ceaseless disputation in Congress—was, he said, to pursue "a merely pernicious abstraction," with no effect "other than the mischievous one of dividing our friends." The substantial thing was to get the States back into "their proper practical relation" with the Union. (Those were helpful phrases for inducing constructive thought.)

> I believe it is not only possible, but in fact, easier, to do this, without deciding, or even considering, whether these states have ever been out of the Union, than with it. Finding themselves safely at home, it would be utterly immaterial whether they had ever been abroad. . . .

---

[30] *Diary of Gideon Welles* (Boston and New York: Houghton Mifflin Co., 1911), II, 281.

III: *Reconstruction—by Lincoln and by Johnson*

He recalled what had been done in Louisiana:

> The amount of constituency, so to speak, on which the new Louisiana government rests, would be more satisfactory to all, if it contained fifty, thirty, or even twenty thousand, instead of only about twelve thousand, as it does. It is also unsatisfactory to some that the elective franchise is not given to the colored man. I would myself prefer that it were now conferred on the very intelligent, and on those who serve our cause as soldiers. Still the question is not whether the Louisiana government, as it stands, is quite all that is desirable. The question is, "Will it be wiser to take it as it is, and help improve it; or to reject, and disperse it?" "Can Louisiana be brought into proper practical relation with the Union *sooner* by *sustaining*, or by *discarding* her new State Government?"

It was the beginning of an effort upon which loyal white and Negro could unite until they had caused it to ripen to a complete success.

With regard to the future,

> What has been said of Louisiana will apply generally to other States. And yet so great peculiarities pertain to each state, and such important and sudden changes occur in the same state; and, withal, so new and unprecedented is the whole case, that no exclusive, and inflexible plan can safely be prescribed as to details and collaterals. . . .

It might become his duty to make some new announcement to the people of the South: "I am considering, and shall not fail to act, when satisfied that action will be proper."[31]

Lincoln had an instinct for the essential. It was not some true constitutional theory that must be established: the men of the North could not have united upon one, much less gain agreement from the South. Human sentiments and emotions, and especially attitudes toward black people, must be reckoned with, matters that would respond only to an all-embracing wisdom. The President's task, as in the war, was to persuade the reluctant, to restrain the impetuous, and to advance by steps having a workable measure of support.

---

[31] *Collected Works of Abraham Lincoln*, VIII, 399. This was one of the most penetrating and thoughtful of Lincoln's formal speeches. But to his audience, assembled for a victory celebration, it was disappointing. The *New York Tribune* reported that it "fell dead." Sumner, on reading it, saw "confusion and uncertainty in the future, with hot controversy. Alas! alas!" Sandburg recreated the occasion, *Abraham Lincoln: The War Years*, 4 vols. (New York: Harcourt, Brace and Co., 1939), IV, 219–25.

Letters written to Lincoln on April 12 show two representative points of view within the Republican party. James Dixon, Senator from Connecticut, was a conservative: a man of education and philosophic breadth, an old Whig who had stood firm against the spread of slavery, he now sought a magnanimous restoration of the Union. Lincoln's response to the serenade, he said, "does equal honor to your head and heart." At Hartford, "it is the subject of universal approbation." "Depend upon it, Sir, the people want no manifestations of a vengeful spirit."[32]

Then came a statement that expressed what seems to have been widely and warmly held throughout the North at this triumphant moment:

> The truth is, you have thus far conducted the war so wisely & successfully, that the people are willing to trust you to conclude it according to your best judgment. No man in power had ever before so confidant & grateful a constituency. They now hope you will be merciful as well as just. Your kindness has endeared you to the popular heart as much as your firmness & fidelity.

Chief Justice Chase, holding court at Baltimore, had also read the speech. He had been urging the President to require the Southern States to establish suffrage for *all* loyal citizens. Instead, Lincoln had made a veiled reference to Chase by recalling that "this [reconstruction] plan [of December 8, 1863] was, in advance, submitted to the then Cabinet, and distinctly approved by every member of it." Now Chase responded that "I . . . was willing, if I could not get exactly the plan I thought best, to take the plan you thought best, & to trust the future for modifications."[33]

> I most earnestly wish you could have read the New Orleans papers for the last few months. Your duties have not allowed it. I have read them a good deal—quite enough to be satisfied that, if you had read what I have, your feelings of humanity & justice would not let you rest till *all* loyalists are made equal in the right of self protection by suffrage.
>
> Once I should have been, if not satisfied, reasonably contented by suffrage for the more intelligent & for those who had been soldiers; now I am convinced that universal suffrage is demanded by sound policy and impartial justice alike.

The Senator, confidently, had urged the President to be merciful and just; the Chief Justice, mistrustfully, appealed to his humanity and

---

[32] Lincoln Papers, L.C.

[33] *Collected Works of Abraham Lincoln*, VIII, 399–401n.

justice. But what was justice in these circumstances? The President himself, at the Cabinet meeting on April 14, displaying the mobility of his thinking, said that he "had perhaps been too fast in his desires for early reconstruction."[34] Lincoln had always preserved a freedom to move in the light of events, and he was considering what next should be done.

The situation had indeed changed. Before Appomattox, Lincoln had been fostering liberation movements which tended to hasten the collapse of the rebellion. For 10 percent of the people of a State to reject the Confederacy and to emancipate constituted a substantial moral advance. After the Confederacy had fallen it was no more than the universal desire at the South to receive amnesty and be restored to the benefits of the Union as easily as possible.

In his proclamation of December 8, 1863, offering amnesty to those who would set their hands to the work of reconstruction, the President's points had been permanent freedom, provision for education, and his acquiescence in reasonable temporary arrangements in accordance with the freedmen's "present condition as a laboring, landless, and homeless class." That was what was proposed if the people of a State would desist from rebellion. It showed no willingness definitively to remit the freedmen to the grace of Southern whites; rather it said, let the local legislatures have an opportunity to show how they would provide for the transition. He was offering them an opportunity to "adopt some practical system by which the two races could gradually live themselves out of their old relation to each other, and both come out better prepared for the new. Education for young blacks should be included in the plan."[35] Consistently he urged that the suffrage be extended to those who could use it intelligently, especially to those who had borne arms.

It was the Southern people, such as they were—subject to such change in outlook as it was possible to induce—that were to be restored to the Union. Lincoln had no thought of erecting regimes manned by ever-loyal Unionists; they were few in number, and generally ineffectual; ex-rebels would never break ranks to join them. Neither would Lincoln seek suddenly to impose universal suffrage. Indeed it was unfair to the Negro people, unprepared as most of them were for effective citizenship, thus to try them by so severe a test. Lincoln understood the obduracy of the problem, and viewed it in the

---

[34] Chase's diary entry for Apr. 15, 1865, quoting what Attorney General Speed had told him. David Donald, ed., *Inside Lincoln's Cabinet. The Civil War Diaries of Salmon P. Chase* (New York, London, Toronto: Long-mans, Green and Co. 1954), 268.

[35] Letter of Aug. 5, 1863, to General N. P. Banks, with copy to three civilian leaders in Louisiana. *Collected Works of Abraham Lincoln*, VI, 365.

perspective of time. He was willing to begin with short steps where there was the prospect of continuing advance.

A President wise and skillful as Lincoln would have set goals the Southern people would be expected to meet. How well they would have responded is questionable. There is much reason to believe, however, that they were far more amenable to guidance immediately after Appomattox than they proved to be in December.[36]

Lincoln's moral authority was such that, it seems highly probable, he could have created in the North an opinion that the goals he set for the South should be accepted as adequate. The matter was new and thinking was fluid.

A wise President would never have allowed his own position to be compromised by any shortcomings of the South. He would have kept it clear to the Southern people that they would have to satisfy the Houses of Congress before they would be restored to representation. The President's duty was to the entire nation, not forgetting the mass of new citizens whose future was about to be settled by white men. From a position somewhat removed he might, perhaps, bring about an accord. But in any event he must maintain his hold upon that part of the nation that had preserved the Union; no settlement could be made that did not satisfy their sense of what was right. Between the Abolitionists and the Copperheads stood a mass of citizens whose good opinion a wise President would have regarded as indispensable.

It was not given to Andrew Johnson to be wise. Courage he had in a high degree, and devotion to the Union as he knew it: those qualities had brought him far. But he thrived on controversy, reducing it to the level of personal denunciation. He relied confidently on his understanding of the common people: but he proved insensitive to the moral earnestness of millions from Maine to Kansas who, notwithstanding some invidious laws on their own books, were determined that the black people should be given a chance. Johnson was, moreover, a lifelong Democrat, a stranger to the party that had elevated him to the Vice Presidency. He staked his policy on the work of the Southern leaders, who responded by yielding to his influence not a whit more than seemed absolutely necessary. He allowed a break with the majority in Congress to become inevitable, even as the more responsible Republicans were striving to avert it. Unreason in the South went unrestrained, while resolution was building up in Congress.

By the time the jurisdiction of the Supreme Court was invoked, "passion governed the hour."[37]

---

[36] Witness after witness before the Joint Committee on Reconstruction in the early months of 1866 expressed this opinion.

[37] Justice Miller's expression in a letter of Jan. 19, 1868. Infra, p. 463.

III: *Reconstruction—by Lincoln and by Johnson*

PRESIDENT JOHNSON INAUGURATES A POLICY

SIX WEEKS AFTER COMING TO OFFICE, President Johnson set his policy in motion. He offered amnesty to those who would swear to support the Constitution and the Union, and the laws and proclamations on emancipation.[38] Certain classes were excluded, but on application, clemency would be "liberally extended." In practice, pardon was abundant. He began the appointment of Provisional Governors for the seven Southern States not already on the road toward restoration. Each governor was to call a convention, the delegates to be chosen by those qualified by the law in force in 1861 and loyal within the benefit of the amnesty proclamation. This meant that, ignoring the urging of Chief Justice Chase, the President would not attempt to impose any form of Negro suffrage. He did presently recommend that a qualified suffrage be granted by State action—advice that received not the slightest consideration. Three obvious matters—the undoing of secession, the abolition of slavery, and the repudiation of the rebel debts—were formalities of expiation; boggling by the conventions would augur ill. Even if smoothly performed, they did not touch the substantial matter, what provision would be made for the future, by the conventions and by the legislatures that followed, particularly with regard to the freedmen.

During the summer and autumn of 1865, people of the North were hopeful and expectant—willing, even eager, to put the best construction on the President's acts. "We all endorse President Johnson," said Senator Lot Morrill of Maine as he set forth for the convening of Congress. "He is probably the most popular President in our history. All parties do him homage."[39] When Johnson recalled his battles for the Constitution and the Union, asked for confidence, and avoided specifics, people assured themselves that this puzzling business of restoration was really in safe hands. Presently, however, their credulity was disturbed as reports came out of the South, in particular of the actions of the conventions and legislatures.

The action of those lawmaking bodies, in the autumn and winter of 1865, is a crucial point. If they were making conscientious efforts to cope with sudden emancipation, then it might be argued that things were going well until the Radicals in the 39th Congress malevolently upset the President's program for prompt restoration. If—more truly—it must be said that these responsible bodies were taking positions that

---

[38] Proclamation of May 29, 1865. 13 Stat. 758. Edward McPherson, *The Political History of the United States of America during the Period of Re-* construction, 3d ed. (Washington: James J. Chapman, 1880), 9.
[39] *Augusta* (Maine) *Kennebec Journal*, Dec. 8, 1865.

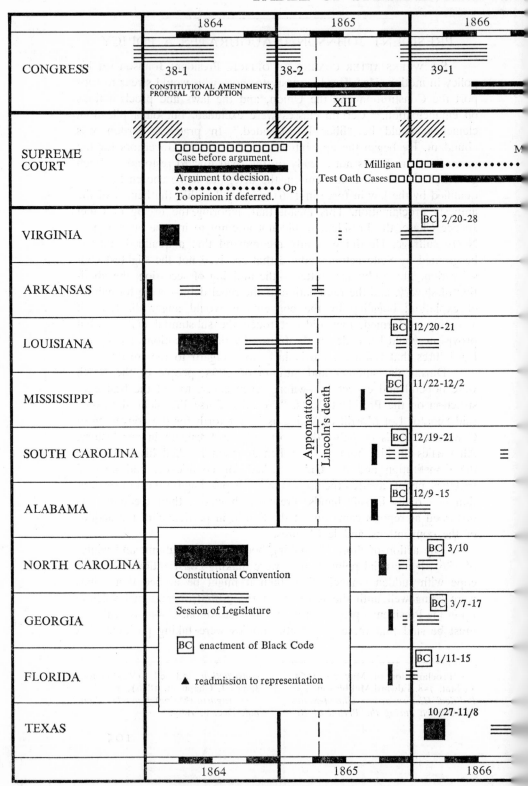

	1864	1865	1866
CONGRESS	38-1 CONSTITUTIONAL AMENDMENTS, PROPOSAL TO ADOPTION	38-2 XIII	39-1
SUPREME COURT	Case before argument. Argument to decision. Op To opinion if deferred.	Milligan Test Oath Cases	M
VIRGINIA			BC 2/20-28
ARKANSAS			
LOUISIANA			BC 12/20-21
MISSISSIPPI		Appomattox / Lincoln's death	BC 11/22-12/2
SOUTH CAROLINA			BC 12/19-21
ALABAMA			BC 12/9-15
NORTH CAROLINA	Constitutional Convention Session of Legislature BC enactment of Black Code ▲ readmission to representation		BC 3/10
GEORGIA			BC 3/7-17
FLORIDA			BC 1/11-15
TEXAS			10/27-11/8

| | 1864 | 1865 | 1866 |

1867	1868	1869	1870
40-1 40-1 40-1	40-2	40-3 41-1	41-2

XIV

XV

Mudd, Arnold, Spangler □■

on ■

.v □■••••••••••••••Op
on

Ga. v Grant □□□□□□□□□□□□□ Op

McCardle □□

Yerger □
jur. aff.

▲ 1/26

▲ 6/22

▲ 7/9

▲ 2/23

▲ 7/9

▲ 7/13

▲ 7/4

▲ 7/15

▲ 6/25

▲ 3/30

Congressional Reconstruction

1867	1868	1869	1870

boded ill for any renewed national understanding, then it was indeed proper for the incoming Congress to seek such further guarantees as were needed. There was a transcendent national interest in the terms on which the Republic, redeemed at so great a cost, was thenceforth to be governed, an interest not to be foreclosed by what the rebel States, with the concurrence of the President, saw fit to offer. Interpretation of the entire course of Reconstruction turns on this point.

Mississippi led the way, holding its convention in August. Alabama and South Carolina followed in September; in October came conventions in North Carolina, Georgia, and Florida. Each lasted about a fortnight. The Provisional Governor of Texas, seeking to learn from mistakes elsewhere, deferred that State's convention to February 1866.

Dwelling upon the proceedings of these conventions, one observes how unready were their members to accept a new order. This was true even though, in the main, those chosen had not been active secessionists; many described themselves as old line Whigs. An examination of local newspapers shows that the debates were being followed very closely and that it was easy politics to talk proud defiance and wave the stars and bars. Secession was gone forever: by what formula should that fact be acknowledged? Generally delegates became exercised over the choice between repealing the ordinance of 1861, declaring it void, and declaring it to have been void from the beginning. There was solicitude to avoid any "reflection upon [the] intelligence and patriotism" of those who had led in secession and to "conciliate the feelings of our people at home."[40] In Texas, controversy over the *ab initio* question went on for weeks.

Slavery too was beyond recall, yet again feelings ran high over the formula: abolish it, or—less hurtful to pride—declare as a fact that it had been destroyed by the United States Government? Some cherished a hope that Congress would still make some compensation: the convention should do nothing to weaken the claim. Some even hoped that the Supreme Court would hold invalid the proclamation and laws on emancipation.[41]

"It is exactly such arguments . . . that paralyze and strike down the arm of the Executive . . . and place a weapon in the hands of the Radicals," warned Judge William Yerger, one of Mississippi's moderates.[42] He pointed to the bright side—Negroes would now count in full for congressional apportionment and the South would gain in represen-

---

[40] *Journal of the Proceedings and Debates of the Constitutional Convention of the State of Mississippi, August 1865,* at 176 and 191.

[41] Among these was Judge Robert

S. Hudson in the Mississippi convention. Ibid., at 74, 85. He appears later as chairman of the commission to draft that State's code for freedmen.

[42] Ibid., at 152.

tation. Another important figure, Amos R. Johnston, formerly a "steadfast Whig," also dwelt upon the need to "look realities in the face."

> Gentlemen talk sometimes about an adjudication from the Supreme Court, touching compensation. Are not gentlemen aware that there is nothing to hope from a Supreme Court composed of Black Republicans and Radicals, with a Chief Justice traveling the country as a disgusting itinerant preacher of the doctrine of negro suffrage?[43]

He pointed to a fair prospect, if delegates would forgo contention over the immaterial: united with Conservatives of the North, they might elect a Conservative President and Congress; compensation for slaves would have a fair hearing. They could form "a great party, irresistible in its power . . . . There is no chance for a Southern man to occupy the Presidential chair. We should be well satisfied with a Northern President possessed of conservative sentiments, and willing to accord to the revolted States their political rights and civil privileges."[44]

Such was the counsel of a Mississippi moderate. The debates, however, showed resistance on every point, whether substantial or only sentimental. These things were reported in the press throughout the country.

President Johnson's recommendation on Negro suffrage was made known at the opening of the Mississippi convention: extend the franchise to those who could read the Constitution and write their name, or who paid taxes on real property to the value of $250. Such action "would completely disarm the adversary and set an example the other States will follow. This you can do with perfect safety, and you thus place the Southern States, in reference to free persons of color, upon the same basis with the free States."[45] (One notes Johnson's implication that he viewed the Radicals as "the adversary" and the Southern leaders as his friends.)

What the President thus urged received no serious consideration in any convention. In Texas, Provisional Governor A. J. Hamilton sounded an unwelcome note when he suggested that possibly in the future the freedmen could attain such intelligence as would merit the suffrage; to permit them gradually to qualify, there should be a rule on future admission applicable equally to black and white.[46] In late February 1866, the moment when Congress was about to take up the

---

[43] Ibid., at 87, 93.
[44] Ibid., at 90, 96.
[45] Sen. Exec. Docs. 39th Cong., 1st Sess., No. 26, Provisional Governors, 229; Ann. Cyc. 1865, 581.
[46] *Journal of the Texas State Convention, 1866*, at 26.

proposed Fourteenth Amendment, one delegate argued that the vote should be given to all males who could read and write. This found no support.[47]

In accord with the well-nigh universal view was the statement of Provisional Governor B. F. Perry to the South Carolina convention: those of the North who support equal suffrage on the basis of literacy and property "forget that this is a white man's government, and intended for white men only; and that the Supreme Court of the United States has decided that a negro is not an American citizen under the Federal Constitution."[48] It was in character that this inflexible doctrinaire would regard *Dred Scott* as sound law. A Unionist in 1860, Perry became foremost in the movement for total resistance after 1865.

In all the discussion in these conventions and legislatures of 1865 there is virtually no suggestion that with freedom the Negro people would ever be able substantially to improve. One status had been destroyed; a new status must now be established wherein the freedmen thenceforth would remain. There was some range of opinion on what the incidents of the new status ought to be—how far the code of slavery could safely be relaxed. That was a matter to be settled by "a white man's government."

In several States—notably Mississippi, South Carolina, and Georgia—the convention provided for a commission to prepare, for the coming legislature, a draft code on the rights of Negroes.

THE LEGISLATURES ENACT "BLACK CODES"

EIGHT SOUTHERN LEGISLATURES were in session at some time in December 1865. Each addressed itself to the status of the Negro. The Mississippi legislature, opening in October, enacted the bulk of its code in late November. South Carolina finished its work by Christmas; Alabama and Georgia had made a start. In Louisiana the Houses had passed their bills; the most important of these, to regulate labor contracts, failed by reason of the Governor's opposition. Florida completed its legislation in January, Virginia in February, North Carolina in March. The Southern States had spoken, and the impact was felt in Congress from the moment it assembled.

In a major aspect, the problem was economic. To make his crop, a planter must have workers from early in the year until Christmas. How could he be assured a labor supply? Typically the statutes constrained the freedman to find employment by a certain day in January,

---

[47] Ibid., at 81–91.
[48] *Journal of the Convention of the* *People of South Carolina, 1865,* at 14.

and regulated the relation of master and servant. ("Master and servant" was not a debasing expression peculiar to the South; it came from the common law on domestic relations, along with "husband and wife" and "parent and child."[49]) Normally the incidents of employment were borrowed from the practices of the plantation: toil from sunrise to sunset, except on Sunday; industrious performance of tasks, according as the laborer was rated full hand, three-fourths-hand, etc.; orderliness in quarters, hours of permitted absence; and the like. If the terms seem hard, as they were, one should in fairness recall the toil of men, women, and children in Northern factories at that period. It was inescapable that a mass of menial laborers suddenly released from bondage be subject to comprehensive legal controls.

Statutes on apprenticeship should be viewed in the context of the time. Normally persons under age, not enjoying the care of a parent, would be bound to service. How the code for blacks differed from the general law on apprentices was the significant point.

Vagrancy bulks large in the black codes. But laws against "vagrancy" have been common throughout the country; they are notoriously indefinite, and frequently are allowed to slumber out of sight. So when one finds alarming provisions in Southern codes for Negroes one should understand that analogs could be found in the North. The extent and manner of their enforcement would be significant.

In other respects the criminal law was enlarged to strike at offenses to which Negroes were supposed to be especially prone.

Viewed in another aspect, the task of the Southern legislatures was to confer civil rights upon the Negro. The Georgia constitution was amended to charge the legislature "to provide by law for the government of free persons of color; for the protection and security of their persons and property, guarding them and the State against any evil that may arise from their sudden emancipation . . . ." Benevolent statements of this sort were common. From the point of view of the legislators, they were passing "civil rights" statutes conferring capacities theretofore unknown—even though, to other eyes, these appeared to be shocking denials of common right.

These observations are essential to a fair understanding, as one turns to an examination of the particulars of the black codes.[50]

---

[49] Blackstone, *Commentaries on the Laws of England*, bk. 1, ch. 14; Kent, *Commentaries on American Law*, pt. 4, lecture 32.

[50] The discussion that follows proceeds from a painstaking examination that went behind the codes to the legislative journals, to learn how these statutes came to be framed as they were—what alternatives, milder or more severe, were considered—what range of opinion was represented—how amenable were the legislators to moderating suggestions from President Johnson?

The Mississippi legislature convened on October 16, 1865, after an election campaign in which the question of permitting the Negro to testify against the white had been a major issue. The legislators took up the report of the convention's committee to prepare a draft code. The report conceded that "some of the proposed legislation may seem rigid and stringent to the sickly modern humanitarians," but said that the wayward and vicious "must be smarted, governed, reformed and guided by instincts and morals higher and holier than theirs . . . ."[51]

With this draft before it, a joint select committee under the chairmanship of Horatio F. Simrall[52] prepared a civil rights bill. Section 1 conferred a right to acquire and dispose of personal property; the freedman was not to be permitted to own land. Even this was cut down by a proviso that the section should not be construed to allow the freedman to rent or lease land or tenements, except in incorporated places where the authorities "shall control the same."[53]

So it entered into the Act to confer Civil Rights on Freedmen.[54] William L. Sharkey—formerly chief justice, lately Provisional Governor, then Senator-elect (never seated)—called this "a foolish provision": "I warned them of the folly of committing this terrible error . . . ."[55]

The really stubborn matter lay in Section 4, competence to testify. As the law stood, Negroes (including persons of one-eighth Negro blood) "shall be incapable of being witnesses in any case whatever, except for or against each other."[56] The House went no further than to allow the Negro to testify against the white where the witness was *himself* a party to the action or was the victim of the crime.[57] There it halted, for tactical advantage. Governor Humphreys advised the President that the legislature "seem willing to extend to the freedman the right to testify in court, if assured the troops would be withdrawn. Members fear that one concession only leads to another. What assurances can I give on this subject?" The President, who must have been tried by the mulish response to his efforts, declined to bargain. He hoped the

---

[51] Mississippi House Journal, App. 15 (1865).

[52] See infra, ch. 6, n. 110.

[53] Miss. House J., 209 (1865).

[54] Laws of 1865, 82.

[55] Testifying before the Joint Committee on Reconstruction, Mar. 8, 1866. House Report No. 30, 39th Cong., 1st Sess., Part III, 133. Some historians have denied that such was the law—but it was, however, what Judge Sharkey stated in precise detail.

The *Jackson Clarion* of December

6, 1865, found the statute inconsistent with the State constitution's new mandate "for the protection and security of the person and property of the freedmen," and reported that the President had directed that the prohibition on purchasing or leasing real property be disregarded. It set out a telegram to that effect from General Howard of the Bureau to the local administrator.

[56] Miss. Rev. Code 1857, 510.

[57] Miss. House J., 210–13 (1865).

legislature would "appreciate the suggestions" he made.[58] The Governor reinforced the President's suggestions with an emphatic message. He said flatly that the Negro should be allowed to be a witness just as was the white—it was "the most common privilege of freedom." It was "an insult to the intelligence and virtue of our courts and juries of white men" to suspect that they could not protect the innocent "against the falsehood and perjury of black witnesses."[59]

Very certainly the legislators could not have supposed that local juries would be unduly credulous of Negro testimony. Only a symbolic value was at stake: that the law should continue to affirm that the Negro's word was not as good as a white man's.

The House relaxed just a little: it modified the bill to permit a Negro to testify where *a* Negro—not necessarily the witness—was a party or a victim. It did this after its committee reported that there was reason to believe that such modification would lead to the removal of the Freedmen's Bureau and the Union garrison. So the bill passed, 58 to 31.[60]

The Senate proved even less tractable. A tough dozen in the membership of thirty-one would have scrapped the civil rights bill and substituted a scheme whereby the county board of police as the Negro's agent and "next friend" would have the most drastic powers over his contracts and his person.[61] After much resistance the bill was carried, 16 to 13, and on November 25, 1865, became law.

In the debate, one of the objectors proposed an additional section: if any white man was arrested, under the provision permitting the Negro to complain of a crime whereof he was the victim, and the charge appeared false and malicious, the court might summarily impose a fine up to $50 and imprisonment for as much as 20 days.[62] This measure, making it exceedingly hazardous for a black man ever to accuse a white, was passed as the Act Supplemental of December 2, 1865.[63]

The provisions on labor made by far the most substantial part of Mississippi's legislation for the Negro. In effect, he was compelled by early January to bind himself for a year's work; "if the laborer shall quit the service of the employer, before expiration of his term of service, without good cause, he shall forfeit his wages for that year . . . ."[64] A deserter incurred heavy costs for recapture, to be paid by the employer and set against wages.[65]

---

[58] Humphreys' dispatch, and President's reply of Nov. 17, in Ann. Cyc. 1865, 585.

[59] Miss. House J., App. 44, 45 (1865).

[60] Miss. House J., 282, 284 (1865).

[61] Miss. Sen. J., 223–26 (1865).

[62] Miss. Sen. J., 231 (1865).

[63] Laws of 1865, 194.

[64] Act to confer Civil Rights on Freedmen, Sec. 6. Laws of 1865, 82, 83–84.

[65] Secs. 7, 8.

113

The statute on Negro apprentices[66] applied to all under the age of eighteen who were orphans, or whose parents failed to support them. The probate court would bind them, giving preference to the former owner. The master's duty was to feed and clothe, to treat humanely, and to teach to read and write if the apprentice was under fifteen. There was no requirement that the apprentice be taught any trade or calling, or that he receive anything when at majority his service was completed; thereby the statute departed significantly from the law on white apprentices.[67]

The Act to amend the Vagrant Laws[68] defined the class much more widely than theretofore, for example, to include those who "misspend what they earn," and then (as to Negroes only) those "with no lawful employment or business . . . ." Vagrancy was subject to a summary trial. This statute went on to establish a scheme for the support of indigent Negroes: it imposed a head tax, not to exceed one dollar, on every Negro between eighteen and sixty years of age, to create the Freedmen's Pauper Fund; failure to pay the tax was prima facie evidence of vagrancy.[69]

A bill striking at a variety of practices by which freedmen might disturb the community became law on November 29, 1865.[70] This punished, among other things, "insulting gestures, language or acts," "exercising the function of a minister of the Gospel, without a license from some regularly organized church," and "committing any other misdemeanor, the punishment of which is not specifically provided for by law." Further, all penal laws applicable to slaves were reenacted as applicable to all Negroes, save as the mode of trial and punishment had been changed by law.

New county courts were established, proceeding more summarily than did the circuit courts, to try cases of petit larceny, assault, and a range of smaller offenses. Punishment, besides penalties otherwise provided, extended to "corporal punishment, by suspending the party convicted by the thumbs, not more than two hours in twenty-four, nor more than ten days . . . ."[71]

---

66 Laws of 1865, 86.

67 On white apprentices, Rev. Code 1857, 213–14.

68 Laws of 1865, 90.

69 The *Jackson Clarion* of December 9 commented that the Legislature had "made [the freedmen] vagrants if they do not have homes, and at the same time denied them the right to seek a home in the ordinary way. . . .

If the laws of the present Legislature were regarded, slavery would be restored in a far worse form than it was before." The Legislature "in its overtopping anxiety to feed the prejudices of a certain class of people" had caused the promising start on restoration to be "hopelessly marred."

70 Laws of 1865, 165.

71 Laws of 1865, 66–81.

It was made unlawful for any railroad to allow a Negro to ride in any first class car used by whites.[72]

Such was the body of law to provide for "the protection and security" of the freedmen.[73] So far as the legislative journals disclose, the bills, save in the matter of competency to testify, went through without a hitch other than debate on details. The Negro's place was made clear: he was to be a laborer, chiefly a plantation laborer, bound by the year; his wage would, in practice, be set by the employers; to be without employment would lead to severe sanctions. It was not contemplated that the Negro would progress, for the roads were barred. No public education was provided. Poor relief was a charge only upon the Negroes.[74]

Mississippi, like other Southern States at this moment, hastened to reorganize the militia.[75] It also authorized the organization of volunteer companies.[76]

---

[72] Laws of 1865, 229, 231.

[73] An impressive judgment was pronounced by J. H. Jones, in his paper on "Reconstruction in Wilkinson County," *Publications of the Mississippi Historical Society*, VIII, 153–75 (1904):

It must be confessed that the Mississippi Legislature of 1865 and 1866, assembled under President Johnson's plan of reconstruction, afforded good reasons for the belief in the minds of the ignorant negroes that their old masters were secretly conspiring against their newly acquired freedom, and only waited for an opportunity to put their plans into effect. Looking back upon the methods by which that Legislature undertook to deal with the negro problem, one is amazed at such stupidity; at such a display of monumental folly committed by men of ordinary intelligence. Its members seem to have been asleep, like Rip Van Winkle, during the war, and when awakened from their long nap, they began to legislate in relation to negroes just where the code of 1857 left off. . . .

He traced salient provisions of the legislation, with severe comments, and concluded:

When I read these laws . . . , presumably enacted by the best intelligence of the State, I was not at all surprised that bitter Abolitionists like Thad Stevens, . . . should have believed that the reconstruction acts were necessary to the proper administration of justice in the South.

To identify J. H. Jones one turns to the *Biographical and Historical Memoirs of Mississippi*, 2 vols. (Chicago: Goodspeed Publishing Co., 1891), I, 1055–57. He graduated from the University of Mississippi in 1858, with first honors in his class, and then read law. Entering the Confederate army as a private, he emerged as colonel of a regiment that had suffered heavy losses; he himself had been wounded. Three of his brothers, all in their teens, were killed in battle. Colonel Jones later served in both houses of the legislature, and in the constitutional convention of 1890. His high position in Mississippi was "attained rather by native talent than by tact."

[74] Laws of 1865, 90, 92, creating the Freedmen's Pauper Fund.

[75] Act of Dec. 2, 1865. Laws of 1865, 96–137.

[76] Act of Nov. 3, 1865. Laws of 1865, 164.

On December 2, two days before the 39th Congress convened, Mississippi rejected the Thirteenth Amendment.[77] Governor Humphreys had recommended that Section 1 be ratified but that Section 2 be rejected, "as its adoption, will open the door to that wide range of construction that would centralize in the Federal Government all the powers of government intended by the framers of the Constitution to be 'reserved to the States or to the people.' "[78]

A joint committee reported that such a ratification would be wholly "inoperative," and recommended that nothing be done. It was "the anxious desire of the people of Mississippi to withdraw the Negro race from National and State politics"; to authorize Congress to pass "appropriate" legislation would "open a subject which your committee had believed extinct, as theme for radicals and demagogues . . . ."[79] The Houses agreed to take no action.[80]

The legislature passed a number of resolutions on federal relations, of a sort that were generally adopted throughout the South.[81] On December 6 it recorded its confidence in President Johnson's administration "so far as its public course has been developed,"[82] approbation which could only tend to disparage the President in the eyes of Congress.

South Carolina's legislature acted along similar lines, albeit somewhat less insensibly. Here too the work started with a draft prepared by a commission: Provisional Governor Perry commended it as "a perfect system of law adapted to our new state of affairs." Enactment should enable the President to declare South Carolina "to be entitled to her position once more as a member of the Federal Union."[83] Although the person of color might own property, real or personal, he was forbidden to follow any occupation other than that of farmer or servant save by an annual license and on payment of a tax, one hundred dollars to be a storekeeper or peddler, ten dollars to engage in any other calling.[84] Fees and fines went into a District Court Fund which, after deduction on account of the judge's salary, was available for relief of indigent Negroes. For the same purpose, a tax was laid on Negroes of working age.[85] A conception pervading the legislation of this period is that

---

[77] Laws of 1865, 270–74.

[78] House J. 311, Sen. J., 241–42 (1865).

[79] House J., 317–19 (1865).

[80] House J., 333–36 (with some support for ratification of Sec. 1); Sen. J., 297–99.

[81] Requesting the President to withdraw "all garrisons and other bodies of the army" from the South, Laws of 1865, 254–55; that Jefferson Davis be liberated and amnestied, ibid., at 280–84; that Congress repeal the

ironclad oath for office-holders, ibid., at 274–78. During the war, this last memorial said, "There was then to be found in the broad South no man with soul so dead as not to stand up and take sides with his own, his native land . . . ."

[82] Laws of 1865, 247.

[83] S.C. House J., 25 (Extra Sess. 1865).

[84] Laws of 1865, 299.

[85] Laws of 1865, 301–3.

whatever might be spent for Negro relief or education must be collected from Negroes.

The black codes of the other Southern States were enacted in December 1865 and the weeks following. (Texas alone was moving slowly.)

SOUTHERN DELEGATIONS ARE
NOT SEATED IN CONGRESS

THE HASTE WITH WHICH RESTORATION had been pushed, save in Texas, looked to a great consummation: to have Senators and Representatives take their seats in the 39th Congress, meeting on the first Monday in December 1865. It would be "the imperative duty" of the Clerk of the House, so Provisional Governor Perry advised the South Carolina legislature, to call the names of all who had presented their credentials, at the organization of the House of Representatives.[86]

The delegations from the South included a considerable number of Confederate colonels, generals, and Congressmen; also Vice President Alexander H. Stephens.

Of course that is not how it happened. Clerk McPherson included only the loyal States in the rollcall, and the Republicans proceeded to organize the House, electing the Speaker by 139 to 36 votes. (Had the Southerners been admitted, the Republicans would still have had a large majority, but less than the two-thirds necessary to override a veto.) The Senators from the South were not seated.

The great problems, commented *The Nation*, were two: the terms on which the States would be readmitted, and "indissolubly connected with it," the future status of four million freedmen. The former, it explained, could not be determined by the Executive alone:

> What is called "the reconstruction policy" of President Johnson is merely tentative and initiatory, and it remains for the legislative branch of the Government to take a deliberative survey of the whole field, to confirm or annul such acts of the Executive as do not rest upon positive law, and to fix, by appropriate legislation, the whole policy of the future.[87]

This expressed a general view in the North: what the President had done was tentative; now Congress must deliberate upon the settlement. *The Nation* continued: the recent legislation in the South "forced upon the early attention of Congress" the question how the liberties of the black race were to be made secure. Certainly "the Supreme Court as at

---

[86] S.C. House J., 16 (Extra Sess. 1865).

[87] 1:710. Dec. 7, 1865.

present constituted would enforce the essence of the Constitutional Amendment," with or without "appropriate legislation." Even so, Congress should act: the protection of the freedmen should not be postponed "to the remote contingencies of a judicial decision."

In ultimate significance for the Supreme Court, what the House and Senate did at this First Session of the 39th Congress would prove far more important than anything the Court decided at its December term 1865. The historian of the Court should keep his watch in the halls of Congress, not linger within the chamber of the Court.

THE JOINT COMMITTEE ON RECONSTRUCTION

ON DECEMBER 4, quickly after the organization of the House, Thaddeus Stevens moved for a joint committee of fifteen to inquire into the condition of the States which formed the Confederacy. The Senate concurring, there came into being the Joint Committee on Reconstruction. This group fashioned the words that became the Fourteenth Amendment; giving meaning to those words presently became the momentous task of the Supreme Court.

The President's message to the new Congress sounded reassuring. "Gradually and quietly, and by almost imperceptible steps," he had "sought to restore the rightful energy of the Government and of the States."[88] With the adoption of the Thirteenth Amendment (completed on December 6), "it would remain for the States whose powers have so long been in abeyance, to resume their places in the two branches of the national Legislature . . . ." He implied that the Houses *ought* to seat the Southern delegations—still their proper authority was expressly recognized. Good faith, the message continued, required that the freedman be secure in his liberty, including his choice of his occupation; it was best that adequate protection be provided by the States themselves. Be not anxious to read the future, he cautioned; questions about the destiny of the freedman might quietly settle themselves. So calm a message tended to allay misgivings.

Chief Justice Chase fairly itched to put his own hands to the work of reconstruction. Situated as he was, he could only impress his advice upon the participants. Witness his diary entry for Monday, December 11, 1865:

> Thaddeus Stevens & Charles Sumner to dinner—both accidentally. Much talk about restoration. I could not adopt Stevens view about holding States as Territories with view to constitutional amend-

---

[88] Cong. Globe, 39–1, App. 1, 2.

ments but very willing he should bring them forward, thinking the right ground might perhaps be easiest found when extreme views most fully before Country.[89]

Stevens' extreme view was that the rebel States "severed their original compacts, and broke all the ties that bound them" to the Union; "being now conquered," they were "subject to the absolute disposal of Congress."[90] Their hope for the future lay in the constitutional provision that "New States may be admitted by Congress into this Union." This conceded that secession had, in a sense, been successful, that South Carolina and the others had indeed dissolved their relation to the Union.[91]

The struggle on the part of the United States had been a war of conquest, so Stevens insisted. He scoffed at the idea that Confederates were liable to punishment for treason:[92] they were recognized belligerents who had been defeated and whose property could be confiscated.[93] Stevens proposed four constitutional amendments. Three dealt with points to which the Joint Committee would soon be giving attention: the rebel debt, equality before the law, and representation.[94] For apportioning Representatives, the Constitution counted free inhabitants and "three-fifths of all other Persons"; now the "other Persons" had become free and in consequence the allotment to the late slave States would be, not seventy Representatives, but eighty-three.[95] If measures were not taken, the Southern States when readmitted, joining with their allies the Northern Democrats, would presently control the Government. Stevens would base representation upon legal voters: the Southern States must either enfranchise the freedman or suffer a sharp reduction in Representatives and in electoral votes.

A fourth amendment sought by Stevens would repeal the constitutional prohibition of a tax on exports; for years to come the South would yield little internal revenue, and he proposed to reach its people by a tax on their cotton; ten cents a pound might produce $100,000,000 a year. The matter of the cotton tax became a large issue, in politics and

---

[89] Chase Papers, Hist. Soc. of Pa.

[90] Speech of December 18, 1865. Cong. Globe, 39–1, 72–75.

[91] Three years later, Chase gave the Court's rejection of that view, in Texas v. White, 7 Wall. 700 (1869). Infra, ch. 13.

[92] On this see United States v. Jefferson Davis, infra, pp. 175–77, 607–12.

[93] On the matter of confiscation, see infra, ch. 15.

[94] On the Fourteenth Amendment, see infra, ch. 20.

[95] No actual change would come until the Census of 1870 had been taken and Congress had made a new apportionment, and then numbers would depend upon what was fixed as the total membership of the House. The results of the proposed Amendment, on the basis of the Census of 1866, were presented by Conkling in the House on Jan. 22, 1866. Cong. Globe, 39–1, 357.

in litigation, as will be explained in discussing the great unreported case of *Farrington v. Saunders,* on which in 1871 the Supreme Court found itself equally divided.[96]

The Chief Justice's other dinner guest on December 11, Senator Sumner, was dearly hoping to be put at the head of the Joint Committee. However—as recorded by Senator Fessenden, who did receive that place —"standing as he does before country, and committed to the most ultra views, even his friends declined to support him, and almost to a man fixed upon me. . . . I think I can see my way through, and if Sumner and Stevens and a few other such men do not embroil us with the President, matters can be satisfactorily arranged—satisfactorily, I mean, to the great bulk of Union men throughout the States."[97]

Earlier in the year Chase had written, "I have so long taken an active part in *shaping events* that I feel the task of *adjudicating cases* however important, as somewhat irksome."[98] The discontent was sharper, now that Congress had the challenging task of restoration. It must never have occurred to Chase, as he plied Senators and Representatives with advice, that in the end it would be the Supreme Court that brought the enduring values out of the text contrived by Congress. His diary entry for December 18, 1865, tells a story. At dawn he was "earnest in prayer for God's direction through day [*sic*]." Chase was a man of deep piety. Presently "Walked to Capitol with John Sherman" and talked politics. "To S. C. Reception Room—all Judges there but Wayne. A couple of motions for admission . . . ."[99] Then Chase sat through the argument of two cases, one of which was of considerable importance.[100] Then,

> Going home overtaken by [Senator Henry] Wilson & went to his room—he gave me probable names of Senate Committee on Reorganization [Reconstruction]—Fessenden, Grimes, & others—said Sumner cᵈ not be made Chairman—spoke of interviews with President who will concede, he thinks, all that is substantial—said Stevens was making great speech in House—wanted me to see Bingham,[101]

---

96 Infra, ch. 16.

97 Fessenden's letter home, Dec. 24, 1865. Francis Fessenden, *Life and Public Services of William Pitt Fessenden,* 2 vols. (Boston and New York: Houghton Mifflin and Co., 1907), II, 20.

98 Letter of March 30, 1865, to General Irwin McDowell. *Library of Congress Quart. J. of Acquisitions,* XIX, 10 (1961).

99 The Court's Minutes show that Attorney General Speed made the motion for Joseph H. Choate—who thirty years later would achieve a spectacular triumph in persuading the Court to hold the income tax unconstitutional. Caleb Cushing moved the admission of William E. Chandler of New Hampshire, then Assistant Secretary of the Treasury (see Texas v. White, infra), later Senator and Secretary of the Navy.

100 The Binghamton Bridge, 3 Wall. 51 (1866).

101 Representative John A. Bingham

who inclined to impracticable views. Sent to Binghams [*sic*] room. He was not in. Came home . . . Gen Garfield came in & remained till after dinner—long talk—explained my theory of reorganization based on universal suffrage as a logical consequence of the facts which have already taken place. He accepts it & thinks of making a speech based on these views. . . .

The "great speech" by Stevens on December 18 contained the "extreme views" with which Chase disagreed.[102] There seems to be no reason to suppose that Chase's conversations had appreciable effect upon the drafting of Section 1 of the Amendment. It is to be noted that, in the expectation of Fessenden and Wilson, Republican leaders, a satisfactory arrangement could be reached with the President.

CONGRESS GROPES WITH A HARD PROBLEM

"THE PREPONDERANT FEELING in Congress is buoyant and hopeful"—so ran a dispatch of December 9 to *The Nation*.[103] "Whatever elements of division and controversy may be latent in the great Union party, which holds so heavy a majority of both Houses, no token of such division was manifested in the first week of the session." "About half the representatives constituting the House (ninety out of one hundred and eighty-three members) are new to our legislative halls. They represent, not a well-drilled and thorough-paced party majority, but they represent the people." The feeling was strong against seating Southern delegations "in advance of any guaranty that the results of the war" were secure. "The New England members are no more determined in this sentiment than are those from the great Middle and Western States."

But what were, or should be, "the results of the war"? Certainly provision must be made for the Negro's future: to promise fairness in the administration of justice; the means of improving himself as capacity and character would permit; freedom to enter any gainful employment and to sell his labor in an open market. The statutes and bills in the Southern legislatures, as well as concerted private action that was more potent than government itself, made Congress acutely aware that national principles must be imposed. What those principles should be was seen only in part; any enumeration would start with the right to sue, to contract, to hold property, to receive equal treatment at the bar of justice. How much further the enumeration should be carried, and by what

---

of Ohio, who became a member of the Joint Committee and took the leading part in drafting Section 1 of the Fourteenth Amendment. Infra, pp.

1270–90. Both Wilson and Bingham were lodging at the Washington House.
[102] Cong. Globe, 39–1, 72–75.
[103] 1:739. Dec. 14, 1865.

governmental mechanics such principles should be made effective, posed an entirely novel problem, difficult even to apprehend.

Congress might legislate for the Southern States as a group, on the view that it was still dealing with the rebellion; but eventually those States would be readmitted, and thereupon become as free as the other States. Congress had new power to enforce the Thirteenth Amendment by "appropriate legislation," but how far did that extend? Governor Perry had expressed apprehension that Congress might "claim the right to legislate for the negro after slavery was abolished." Secretary Seward, for the President, replied that the objection was "querulous and unreasonable"; the powers of Congress were restrained, not enlarged, by Section 2.[104]

Perry, reporting to the legislature, hailed this tart reply as a triumph; it confirmed "the plain, honest construction of the language," that when slavery was abolished, the power to legislate would be ended.[105] Surely Seward was unsound in construing Section 2 as a restraint. Doubtless Perry was wrong in limiting the Amendments to the mere abolition of ownership of the body. The river Jordan had been crossed, must the freedman be abandoned at the margin? Yet any large construction of Section 2 ran into this objection: How could the power to enforce the abolition of slavery be made to reach discriminations widely made against Negroes in States where slavery never existed? Some of the provisions in the Southern black codes had long existed on Northern statute books.

Senator Henry Wilson of Massachusetts was one whose devotion to liberty was not matched by discernment how to secure it. On December 13, 1865, he precipitated debate by moving to take up his S. 9, to declare that all laws in the rebel States whereby inequality in civil rights was imposed on the basis of color, were void, and that anyone attempting to make or enforce such a law would be liable to fine and imprisonment.[106] "As a matter of justice and humanity," Wilson asked that his bill be passed instantly, without reference to committee; there was danger of bloody outbreaks at Christmas, a few days hence.

Objection was voiced on all sides. Reverdy Johnson of Maryland said that the bill raised questions about which the Senate should be "very closely advised." Once the Southern States were readmitted, Wilson's measure would lose all effect. Sherman and Trumbull explained, with patient indulgence, why a bill of this character should be considered in committee—the problem was more complicated than the bill suggested. Saulsbury of Delaware derided the "insane effort to elevate the

---

[104] Sen. Exec. Doc. No. 26, 39th Cong., 1st Sess., 198 (1866).
[105] S. C. House J., 69–70 (Extra Sess. 1865); McPherson, *History of Reconstruction*, 22–23.
[106] Cong. Globe, 39–1, 39.

African race to the dignity of the white race." When the bill was further considered on the twentieth, Sumner made a long speech, quoting from letters from his numerous correspondents, in one Southern State after another, all going to show the enormity of what was going on there. He urged "Pass the bill now under consideration; pass any bill; but do not let this crying injustice rage any longer. An avenging God cannot sleep while such things find countenance."[107] Nothing came of Wilson's effort.

These were characteristic performances all around: the Massachusetts Senators, whose zeal was coupled with a lofty disdain of practicalities; Reverdy Johnson, quick to point holes in their scheme; Trumbull and Sherman, responsible men seeking prudent courses; and William Saulsbury, who would rail at anything that would advance the black man.

On December 19, Trumbull, chairman of the Judiciary Committee, gave notice that he would introduce legislation to enlarge the powers of the Freedman's Bureau and to protect all persons in the enjoyment of their civil rights.[108] This he did on January 5, 1866, by S. 60, the Freedmen's Bureau Bill, and S. 61, the Civil Rights Bill. These measures, it will be seen, led to a break between the President and the Republican party, something that thoughtful members of the party had striven to avoid.

In the meantime, the Joint Committee on Reconstruction was considering what further constitutional amendment was needed.

The problem before the Congress, and relations between Congress and President, would have been difficult enough even had it been possible to proceed in good order. Nothing so wholesome was to be. Thad Stevens—notwithstanding that as a member of the Joint Committee he would have the opportunity to exert his force effectively—seized an early occasion to controvert the views in the President's message.[109] Speaking for himself alone and trusting that "the Republican party will not be alarmed at what I am saying," he reiterated his thesis that the Southern States were mere conquered provinces to be dealt with at discretion. Two obnoxious Democrats rushed in to stand beside the President, thus making it inexpedient for any Republican to say a favorable word.[110] The President, responding to a request by the

---

[107] Cong. Globe, 39–1, 90–95.

[108] Cong. Globe, 39–1, 77.

[109] Cong. Globe, 39–1, 72–75. Dec. 18, 1865.

[110] Cong. Globe, 39–1, 115, 117–120. Dec. 21, 1865.

The two were Finck of Ohio ("representing a political school whose friendship to the Administration at this time was a millstone about its neck"—James G. Blaine, *Twenty Years of Congress*, 2 vols. [Norwich, Conn.: Henry Bill Publishing Co., 1884, 1886] II, 131) and Voorhees of Indiana.

Senate for information, reported that in nearly all the Southern States "measures have been adopted or are pending, to confer upon freedmen rights and privileges which are essential to their comfort, protection and security."[111] Sumner called this "whitewashing," and a wrangle ensued until Trumbull urged that "this unprofitable debate may cease." "At a time like this, when great questions are before us," it was harmful to provoke controversy.[112] Actions such as these by Stevens and Sumner hastened the day when the irascible side of Andrew Johnson would assert itself.

JUSTICE MILLER VIEWS THE SCENE

ON JANUARY 11, 1866, six days after Trumbull's bills had been introduced, Justice Miller surveyed the prospect, in a letter to a kinsman, a reluctant Confederate, residing in Galveston, Texas. Miller, it will be seen, had been shocked by the black codes. But he had a sense of practicality, and from his life in Kentucky had known the Negro people at close hand. Now the letter:

> The discussion on reconstruction is just opened in both houses, and promises to be able, and somewhat bitter. As far as I can form an opinion the President will not break with the majority in Congress if he can avoid it. That is he will make every concession consistent with any due regard to his personal dignity, and his own convictions of his duty. I believe he will assent to almost any means of securing the civil rights of the negro, short of imposing negro suffrage on the states in rebellion against their will. There is also a large body of influential republicans who are determined that the civil rights of the negro must be rendered safe, before the members from those states are permitted to take part in the legislation of Congress; but who are quite anxious to prevent a rupture with the President. I hope much from them and him. There are however three other classes of

[111] Sen. Exec. Doc. No. 2, 39th Cong., 1st Sess. December 19, 1865. He transmitted, as requested, the detailed report Carl Schurz had made on a tour of inspection he had made, at Johnson's request, between July and October 1865. Schurz concluded that "If nothing were necessary but to restore the machinery of government," progress was satisfactory. "But if it is required that the southern people should accommodate themselves to the war in point of spirit," it was otherwise. They recognized no more than that the old form of chattel slavery was ended.

To counteract this impressive document, the President sent along a report General Grant had made on a recent tour of a week's duration. Grant concluded, from conversations he had had, that "the mass of thinking men of the South accept the present situation" and "were anxious to return to self-government, within the Union, as soon as possible."

[112] Cong. Globe, 39–1, 80. Dec. 19, 1865.

men, who desire this rupture and whose powers of mischief are very great.

The most potent of these are certain ultra negro suffrage impracticables, who have no faith in the President giving any aid to their policy, and who desire to precipitate a rupture while they are yet as they suppose themselves to be, the leaders of the majority. The next most mischievous class is composed of certain men who are republicans, but are anxious to signalise themselves as special friends of the President and his policy, in order that they may monopolise the executive patronage. These while claiming to speak for the President and thus making him as far as they can, responsible for their utterances, really know but little more of his views than I do. The third class are those who were elected distinctly as democrats, and whose only hope of a return of their party to power, is in the break up of the great party which has suppressed the rebellion, against their wishes and efforts. The prospect ahead is not cheering. One thing however I think is clear. There is no hope for southern members being admitted into this Congress, unless some security is given against the manifest intent thus far shown by every southern state, to refuse to place the negro on an equality with the white man in all his civil rights. The power to make laws which are to operate on the black man and not on the white, will be taken from those states, before the present Congress will admit their delegations. This may be relied on.

The laws proposed by Mississippi, Alabama, South Carolina, &c do but change the form of the slavery. As it *was*, the individual slave belonged to, and laboured for the individual white man. As it is *proposed to be*, the whole body of the negro race in each state, must belong to and labour for the whole body of the white people of that state, under compulsion of law.

The pretence is that the negro wont work without he is compelled to do so, and this pretence is made in a country and by the white people, where the negro has done all the work for four generations, and where the white man makes a boast of the fact that *he* will *not* labour.[113]

THE FREEDMEN'S BUREAU BILL

S. 60, THE FREEDMEN'S BUREAU BILL, would strengthen and prolong that institution and, with an eye to recent Southern legislation, would enact that wherever the Negro was denied civil rights accorded to whites, "military protection and jurisdiction" would be extended over him. Further, if any person under color of local law deprived any Negro

---

[113] Charles Fairman, *Mr. Justice Miller and the Supreme Court, 1862–1890* (Cambridge, Mass.: Harvard University Press, 1939), 128–29.

of any civil right enjoyed by whites, the offender would be liable to trial and punishment by the officers of the Bureau. The bill was passed by straight party votes, 37 to 10 in the Senate, 136 to 33 in the House. On February 19 the President vetoed in a message that conceded nothing on the score of injustice in Southern legislation and asserted that competition for the Negro's labor "will enable him to command almost his own terms. He also possesses a perfect right to change his place of abode," a right to be exercised if in any locality he failed to find "a mode of life suited to his desires."[114] This was an exasperating disregard of plainest facts. The concluding portion of the veto message asserted "another very grave objection": whereas the Constitution imperatively declares that each State shall be represented in the House and the Senate, yet here the States most concerned in the legislation had been denied that right. In the President's view, most of the Southern States "have already been fully restored, and are to be deemed as entitled to enjoy their constitutional rights as members of the Union."

This denied the very competence of Congress to act until the representatives of the South were seated. The practical consequence would have been that the Republican majority could accomplish nothing more than pleased the President, who was now identifying himself with the Southern States and their Democratic friends in Congress.

When the bill was reconsidered in the Senate, Trumbull said he was "greatly surprised" by the veto. That was true: he had been consulting the President and believed that common understanding had been reached. To Johnson's callous suggestion that freedmen might simply move to a more congenial locality, Trumbull retorted, "they cannot read the finger-boards by the wayside."[115] On the question of overriding the veto, 30 answered yea and 18 nay; it was less than the requisite two-thirds. Dixon, Doolittle, and a few other conservative Republicans were unwilling to go against the President, at least on this bill. From that moment until the failure of impeachment, two years and three months later, it was constantly a question how many Senators on this wing of the party would go to the aid of the President.

On the evening of February 22 a crowd came to the White House to express their approval of the veto. Responding extemporaneously, Johnson lapsed into the mode of speech he had used back in Tennessee; when he was finished he had sealed his breach with the party. In times past he had fought the enemies of the Union at the South and, he cried out, he would fight the enemies of the Union today. Name them: he said Thaddeus Stevens; he said Charles Sumner. There was talk, he went on, that he should be beheaded: Did not the blood of Lincoln appease the

---

[114] Cong. Globe, 39–1, 915–17.

[115] Cong. Globe, 39–1, 936–42. Feb. 20, 1866.

opponents of Government? But if his blood too must be given for the Union, so be it.[116]

"Bad in substance, bad in language, bad in style," "such a speech as no President could make without suffering in the estimation of thoughtful men," was the comment of Hugh McCulloch, Secretary of the Treasury, who had particularly cautioned Johnson against such an error.[117]

THE CIVIL RIGHTS BILL IS CARRIED OVER A VETO

S. 61, THE CIVIL RIGHTS BILL, had a larger significance than the companion that had fallen. Passed over the President's veto, it became the Act of April 9, 1866;[118] it remains the source of some provisions in the United States Code. The key to the statute was in the declaration of Section 1 that citizens of every color were entitled in each State to the civil rights there enjoyed by white citizens—those rights being to sue, be parties and give evidence; to take, hold and dispose of real and personal property; and to have the benefit of all laws for the security of person and property. In these respects, the Negro should have whatever rights the white man had: that was the theme. Before this principle, the greater part of the new black codes would fall. So too would numerous provisions on Northern statute books. Since the bill applied to all the States it must, to be sustained, find support in some constitutional provision of general application. Theretofore it had belonged to each State to declare the civil rights of those within its borders; it was free to make distinctions. Now Congress said that color must be no bar.

Whence came the power to do this new thing? Senator Trumbull, opening debate on January 29, found authority in the Thirteenth Amendment.[119] That was intended to give "practical freedom" to every person within the United States. "Liberty and slavery are opposite terms." An unjust encroachment upon civil liberty was, in fact, "a badge of servitude which, by the Constitution, is prohibited." This was a bold construction of the Amendment; it was recognized that for the protection of the individual against unjust action by his own State, a more solid constitutional ground should be sought. Indeed the Joint Committee was working on that problem while the Civil Rights Bill was being debated. Out of its labors came the measure which, on June 13, 1866, Congress proposed to the States as the Fourteenth Amendment.

---

[116] McPherson, *History of Reconstruction*, 58–63.

[117] *Men and Measures of Half a Century* (New York: Charles Scribner's Sons, 1888), 393. So too, it seems, Senator Doolittle had warned.

Diary of Gideon Welles, 3 vols. (Boston and New York: Houghton Mifflin Co., 1911), II, 647.

[118] 14 Stat. 27.

[119] Cong. Globe, 39–1, 474.

In the meantime, dividing on party lines, the two Houses passed the Civil Rights Bill. The President vetoed, his long list of objections ending with the assertion that the bill would frustrate the happy adjustment of race relations and unduly centralize power in the national Government.[120] This time Senate Republicans mustered 33 against 15, and the House voted 122 to 41, thus overriding the veto.

Presently another Freedmen's Bureau Bill was introduced, passed, and on July 16, vetoed and promptly carried by the requisite majorities. The President's message renewed his objections to the extension of military jurisdiction to civilians in time of peace, warned of conflicts between military authorities and State courts, and referred to recent instances of corruption within the Freedmen's Bureau.

The Civil Rights veto made it clear beyond any further delusion that Johnson would not go with the Republican party. For him, the Thirteenth Amendment was enough, and it had executed itself. No more than in the past should the citizen have federal rights against his State. The Amendment's one significant consequence for the future would be greater Southern representation in Congress. Consider what was the most advantageous settlement a participant in the rebellion could have asked: except for a slight hope of compensation for slaves, that very happiest outcome was virtually what President Johnson was insisting upon.

That was where the Democratic party stood in the campaign of 1866.

The Joint Committee was proceeding on a different view: the Constitution needed further amendment, and their first concern was with representation. "Representatives . . . shall be apportioned among the several States . . . according to their respective numbers . . ." said the Constitution; the provision for reckoning slaves at three-fifths had cancelled out. Either the freedmen should be given the vote, or else their effect on the basis of representation should in some way be reduced: that seemed evident to the Republicans. Sumner and those who stood with him accepted only the former of these solutions, but they were far in advance of prevalent opinion.[121]

SENATOR STEWART'S NOTEWORTHY PROPOSAL

FOR A MOMENT, in mid-March, it seemed that Congress and the Southern people might possibly reach an understanding along the lines

---

[120] Cong. Globe, 39–1, 1679–81.
[121] In the autumn elections of 1865, the voters of Connecticut, Minnesota, and Wisconsin rejected proposals to extend the suffrage to Negroes, in each case by about 55

of a proposal by Senator William M. Stewart of Nevada.[122] General amnesty and restoration to representation would be accorded to any State that would amend its constitution to do away with racial discrimination in civil rights and would extend the suffrage to black and white on equal terms, save that no one qualified to vote in 1860 would lose the franchise. The State could fix any educational or property test it chose— yet the Negro would have, as the majority in Congress appeared to want, "an opportunity ultimately to be enfranchised." The Senator quoted the President's dispatch to Provisional Governor Sharkey on August 15, urging that the vote be given to Negroes who were literate or who paid taxes on $250 worth of property; the plan now proposed seemed in accord with that thought. The South, Stewart declared, "cannot be governed except by a majority of its people"; he sought to give them an opportunity "to assent to this proposition, because I believe that this is about the sense of the country." The Senators from Massachusetts were quick to accept: "with open arms," cried Sumner; "universal liberty, universal justice, universal suffrage, and universal amnesty," chorused Wilson.[123] Of course it was not universal suffrage. An educational test might bar nine-tenths of the freedmen, observed *The Nation*'s correspondent, who pointed to the possibility that a State might take the benefit of the bargain and then revert to discrimination. Editorially that journal said that to insure permanence the settlement should be made "irrevocable by a Federal guarantee"; nevertheless, the proposal had been an "exciting incident" and might open "a pleasant road out of a very embarrassing position."[124]

The *National Republican* of Washington, which cultivated the appearance of reflecting President Johnson's views, said it would "not violently oppose" the plan "should the South exhibit sense enough to adopt it," which seemed unlikely; it would prefer, however, to do as the President advocated: seat the Southern delegations and leave the suffrage to the States.[125]

The *Richmond Dispatch*, a relatively moderate journal, said that the Stewart plan might "quiet the demands of the Radicals"; it concluded, however, that "the bitter pill of equal suffrage . . . will hardly be swallowed," even though it would make no difference in the outcome of

---

percent of the vote. Ann. Cyc. 1865, 304, 577, 823.

In 1867, Ohio rejected such an amendment by 54 percent, Kansas by 65 percent, and Minnesota by 51 percent. McPherson, *History of Reconstruction*, 353–54.

[122] S. J. Res. 48, introduced Mar. 16, 1866. Cong. Globe, 39–1, 1437.

[123] Cong. Globe, 39–1, 1438.

[124] 2:353–55. Mar. 22, 1866.

[125] Mar. 19, 1866.

The *National Republican* (Simon P. Hanscom, editor) carried at its masthead one sentiment by Lincoln and three quotations from Johnson. The President, it seems, agreed with Secretary Welles in reposing "no confidence" in the editor. Welles' *Diary*, II, 653.

elections.[126] Two days later it dismissed the proposal as "not worth a discussion."

The *Montgomery Daily Mail* said "no, a thousand times no." "By this offer . . . the Southern States will be placed in the position of purchasing the lives of Mr. Davis and other of our prominent statesmen, at the price of a surrender of certain rights of the States." It was an "atrocious proposition."[127]

Confederate brigadier William M. Browne of Athens, Georgia, commented to Howell Cobb:

> I think Stewart's proposition more infamous than Stevens's subjugation or Sumner's compulsory nigger suffrage scheme, because it affects benevolence and invites us to eat dirt to please the radicals. If I have to eat it, I want to be compelled to do it, not to be hospitably invited to do it as a desirable meal.[128]

A proffer for accommodation had met disdain.[129] The test was simple: Would the South accept the principle that the black man would be admitted to vote when he met the standard set for whites? No effect on elections was to be expected for years to come. The point was not yielded; Southerners told themselves that the President would prevail over Congress and get for them everything they wanted. Johnson was aware of "the favorable reception of Stewart's resolutions" in Congress,[130] but said not a word to promote acceptance. A week later he vetoed the Civil Rights Bill and dispelled all hope of accommodation. "The sternly loyal people of the country are justly incensed," said the *Kennebec Journal* of Augusta, Maine,[131] organ of James G. Blaine, which up to that time had argued against "a permanent breach between the President and the party which elected him."[132]

Southern leaders were emboldened; they displayed the spirit of Howell Cobb's correspondent: stand firm—compulsion is preferable to concession. Within a year they would learn that Johnson could not be their deliverer; then their hopes would be fixed upon the Supreme Court.

---

[126] Mar. 21, 1866.

[127] Mar. 25, 1866.

[128] Letter of Mar. 28, 1866. Correspondence of Toombs, Stephens and Cobb, in Annual Report of Am. Hist. Assn. for 1911, II:677, 678.

[129] Additional comments on the Stewart proposal are to be found in Eric L. McKitrick, *Andrew Johnson and Reconstruction* (Chicago: University of Chicago Press, 1960), 341–43, and in Joseph B. James, *The Framing of the Fourteenth Amendment* (Urbana: University of Illinois Press, 1956), 94–96.

[130] *Diary of Gideon Welles*, II, 457, for Mar. 20, 1866.

[131] Mar. 30, 1866.

[132] On March 2, 1866, apropos of Johnson's intemperate exhibition on February 22, the *Kennebec Journal* said mildly that he "would have shown more wisdom" had he refrained from replying to "the violent assaults of his accusers," but placed the blame on Thad Stevens, a "shattered old man" no longer fit for leadership.

Stewart's proposal looked to an understanding which, it was supposed, would obviate the need to amend the Constitution. That failing, he cast his proposal into a constitutional amendment, in place of the measure on which the Joint Committee had been working.[133] But the fleeting moment had been lost.

THE JOINT COMMITTEE REPORTS A FOURTEENTH AMENDMENT

ON APRIL 30, 1866, the Joint Committee reported to the Houses a measure which, emerging from Congress on June 13, was submitted to the States as the proposed Fourteenth Amendment.

Section 1,[134] whose promise of due process and equal protection in time became *the* Fourteenth Amendment and one of the Constitution's two most important provisions in terms of Supreme Court adjudication, was at the moment regarded as less controversial and of less consequence than the next two sections, now virtually forgotten.

Section 2 dealt with representation in Congress. When the right to vote was denied to any of the adult male citizens of a State, the basis of representation would be reduced "in the proportion which the number of such male citizens shall bear to the whole number of male citizens twenty-one years of age in such State." Suppose that State law allowed no Negro to vote: by means of the census, Congress might determine what was the proportion of adult male Negroes to the total of adult male citizens, and in that measure reduce the State's apportionment of seats in the House of Representatives. After the Fifteenth Amendment was adopted in 1870, however, color could no longer be made an express bar. Section 2 did not touch exclusion by private action—by physical violence, economic pressure, or threats. A State might set requirements—as by poll tax, property qualification, or literacy test—applicable in principle to all. That, according to Section 2, would have led to a reduction in the basis of representation. Actually, however, Section 2 was never enforced; when examined closely it proved quite impracticable.[135] But to the men of the 39th Congress, it seemed of the highest importance.[136]

Section 3, as the proposed Amendment went to the States, dis-

---

[133] S. J. Res. 62, Cong. Globe, 39th Cong., 1st Sess., 1906, Apr. 12, 1866; Kendrick, *Journal of the Joint Committee of Fifteen on Reconstruction*, 82, Apr. 16, 1866.

[134] Infra, pp. 1282–98.

[135] Infra, pp. 1265–69.

[136] "The second section I consider the most important in the article," said Stevens in presenting the measure to the House. Cong. Globe, 39–1, 2459, May 8, 1866. Senator Howard, introducing the proposal to the Senate on May 23, pp. 2764–71, discussed the second section at greater length than any other.

qualified from federal and State office all who, having previously sworn as office holders to support the Constitution, thereafter had engaged or aided in rebellion. "But Congress may by a vote of two-thirds of each House, remove such disability." In potency to arouse resentment throughout the South, this provision was enormous. The other sections were objectionable enough, but this was considered degrading in a point of honor. It would exclude men "who themselves are not more guilty than we are," reported the Committee on Federal Relations of Florida's House of Representatives;[137] "and it coolly asks us to be the executioners," said the committee of the lower house in Texas.[138] The attempt to separate leaders from followers was ill-conceived, and on balance, harmful. Soon Congress would be removing disabilities on a large scale;[139] but Southern resistance had been heightened, and so it remained.

Section 4 declared the validity of the public debt to be beyond question, and forbade the payment of the rebel debt or of claims for the loss of slaves.

Section 5 declared that Congress would have power to enforce by appropriate legislation.

In Tennessee, Governor Brownlow promptly summoned the legislature. It voted ratification on July 19; then Tennessee was readmitted to representation on July 24, 1866. Twenty-three months would pass, Congressional reconstruction would have worked its transformation, before another State—Arkansas—was readmitted.

"The proposed amendments to the Constitution . . . appear to me to be just what we need," wrote Justice Field from California on June 30, 1866, to the Chief Justice.[140] He continued:

> I think all members of the Union party can unite cordially in their support. If the President withholds his approval he will sever all connection with the Union party. Two things are certain—the American people do not intend to give up all that they have gained by the war—and they do intend that loyal men shall govern the country.

---

[137] Fla. House J., 79 (1866).

[138] Texas House J., 580 (1866).

[139] Batches of names were included in private bills, notably Acts of Dec. 14, 1869, 16 Stat. 607, and Mar. 7, 1870, 16 Stat. 614. By the Act of May 22, 1872, 17 Stat. 142, disabilities were removed from all except those who had served the United States as members of the 36th or 37th Congresses, officers in the judicial, military or naval services, heads of Departments, or ministers to foreign countries.

Aside from the constitutional disability which only Congress could remove, on July 4, 1868—a few days before ratification of the Fourteenth Amendment was completed—President Johnson, supplementing earlier proclamations, granted pardon to every participant in the rebellion except those under indictment. 15 Stat. 702. A final proclamation on December 25, 1868, granted pardon without reservation. 15 Stat. 711.

[140] Chase Papers, L.C.; Carl B. Swisher, *Stephen J. Field* (Washington: Brookings Institution, 1930), 145.

President Johnson did indeed disapprove. In a message to Congress[141] he questioned "the constitutional validity of the proceedings," and expressed "grave doubts . . . whether the action of Congress is in harmony with the sentiments of the people . . . ." This message, commented *The Nation*, tended "to impress the South more strongly than ever with the belief that it is foully wronged, and that the passage of this amendment will be a fresh outrage, and that Andrew Johnson is their only earthly friend."[142]

Events kept putting the President more and more in the wrong. At Memphis, in early May, there had been riots between Negro soldiers and local police; more than forty lives were lost—all Negro. More significant, and more damaging to the President's policy, was the riot at New Orleans in late July. In a confused political context, Louisiana Unionists, with the support of Governor J. Madison Wells, sought to hold a convention. The lieutenant governor, the mayor, and the party of amnestied rebels were opposed, and used the city police to prevent the meeting. About forty Unionists, white and black, were killed, and many more were wounded. The President's secretary, in releasing a report by General Sheridan, suppressed a sentence that accused the mayor of acting "in a manner so unnecessary and atrocious as to compel me to say that it was murder." Later Johnson put the blame on the Radicals.

In late August and early September the President made his "Swing around the Circle" in defense of "My Policy." His speeches were numerous, repetitious, and very much in character. Lacking dignity himself, the President was greeted with indignities. It was a monumental disaster.[143]

The result for the Republicans in the autumn elections was described as "the most decisive and complete victory ever won in American politics."[144] In each House of the 40th Congress there would be the two-thirds majority requisite to override a veto.

The 39th Congress would be emboldened by that success when it met for its Second Session on December 3,—the point to which we shall come at the opening of Chapter V.

---

[141] Cong. Globe, 39–1, 3349. June 22, 1866.

[142] 2:801. June 25, 1866.

[143] The New Orleans riot and the "Swing around the Circle" had politi-

cal effects, accurately evaluated by McKitrick, *Andrew Jackson and Reconstruction*, ch. 13.

[144] *The Nation*, 3:390. Nov. 15, 1866.

CHAPTER IV

December Term 1865: The Current Quickens

LIKE CONGRESS, the Court convened on the first Monday in December 1865. For the Court, as for Congress, expectancy was in the air, modulated, however, because conflicts are slowed in their approach to the court of last resort. Augustus H. Garland, recently a Confederate Senator from Arkansas, was petitioning for leave to resume his place at the Court's bar, without taking the loyalty oath required by the late Congress.[1] This stood No. 6 among the matters of original jurisdiction. Robert H. Marr of Louisiana filed a like petition, No. 8, which was heard and decided with *Garland*. After hearing arguments on December 15 and 22, on the preliminary matter of leave to file, the Court set the cases down for an early hearing on the merits. On the appellate docket were cases from the Supreme Court of Missouri wherein Cummings, a priest, and Garesche, an attorney, challenged the test oath imposed on their professions by that State's new constitution.[2] At the request of Attorney General Speed and the Attorney General of the State, these Missouri cases were advanced for argument next after *Garland*.[3]

The matter of the "Indiana treason trials" had just been placed before the Court. During the summer, when Justice Davis was holding the Circuit Court at Indianapolis, writs of habeas corpus had been

[1] *Ex parte* Garland, 4 Wall. 333 (1867).

[2] Cummings v. Missouri, 4 Wall 277 (1867).

[3] Supreme Court Minutes, Fri., Feb. 23, and Mon., Feb. 26, 1866. A motion by Reverdy Johnson on behalf of the plaintiffs to take their cases out of turn had been denied on Dec. 11. When the Court first made its rule on taking a case out of turn, at January Term 1830, it required that "special and peculiar circumstances" be shown. Whereas counsel for the private parties could speak only for the personal concern of their clients, the responsible law officers could show public interests that called for an early determination.

sought by Lambdin P. Milligan and others, Copperheads tried by military commission for conspiracy and inciting insurrection and sentenced to death.[4] Davis and the District Judge had certified a division of opinion—not, it seems probable, because of any disagreement on the law, but because of Justice Davis' sense of the importance of getting the case into the Supreme Court. Also certified to the Court, from the Circuit Courts for Indiana and Wisconsin, were two prosecutions for obstructing the draft, a subject not theretofore considered.[5]

Cases challenging the validity of war-time Legal Tender Acts now appeared on the docket—*McGlynn v. Magraw*[6] and then *Hepburn v. Griswold*:[7] four times continued from term to term, their eventual decision on February 7, 1870, holding such Acts invalid, would lead to one of the most controversial episodes in the annals of the Court.

President Johnson, in his message of December 4, 1865, had referred to the power of Congress to regulate commerce among the several States:

> It is of the first necessity, for the maintenance of the Union, that that commerce should be free and unobstructed. No State can be justified in any device to tax the transit of travel and commerce between States. . . .[8]

He urged Congress, "while the country is still young," to take action that would "prevent any selfish impediment to the free circulation of men and merchandise." Within the month, *Crandall v. Nevada*,[9] challenging just such a transit tax, was filed with the Supreme Court. Actually two decades passed before Congress made any large exertion of its power under the Commerce Clause. In the meantime it became a major problem for the Court: how large was its conception of "commerce among the several States," what State exactions should be struck down as inconsistent with that clause.

Thus the Court was being drawn toward the quickening main stream.

SOUTHERN APPEALS: THE CHIEF JUSTICE ANNOUNCES AN ORDER

AT THIS TERM the Court resumed the consideration of Southern appeals, in abeyance during hostilities. One of these was *Newell v.*

---

[4] *Ex parte* Milligan, 4 Wall. 2 (1866).
[5] United States v. Scott, 3 Wall. 642 (1866), and United States v. Murphy, 3 Wall. 649 (1866). Infra, pp. 140–41.
[6] 8 Wall. 639 (1870).
[7] 8 Wall. 603 (1870).
[8] Cong. Globe, 39–1, App. 1, 3.
[9] 6 Wall. 35 (1868).

Norton & Ship,[10] from the Eastern District of Louisiana. Six years had gone since it was filed in the Supreme Court by Robert H. Marr: now he was ineligible to appear, and it must be argued by other counsel. The case is notable for its early statement of what is called the "two-court rule." Here was a libel in admiralty, decided by the District Court, whose judgment had been affirmed in the Circuit Court by Justice Campbell. Now picking up the record Justice Grier found "more than a hundred depositions . . . . In these there is the usual conflict of testimony which always attends such cases. The issue is one entirely of fact . . . ." "It would be a very tedious as well as a very unprofitable task" for the Justices to work through this mass of conflicting depositions to decide whether the two lower courts in agreement had been wrong. "Parties ought not to expect this court to revise their decrees merely on a doubt raised in our minds as to the correctness of their judgment, on the credibility of witnesses, or the weight of conflicting testimony." In a variety of contexts the Court through the years has applied its "seasoned and wise rule"[11] that, save upon an exceptional showing of error, it will accept the concurrent findings of two inferior federal courts.[12]

Another case from the Circuit Court for Louisiana, waiting on the docket since 1860, presented the attempt by a purchaser of slaves to rescind the transaction for alleged defects.[13] In this as in *Newell v. Norton* and two other Southern cases, the parties who had been hailed up to the Supreme Court were asking that without further delay a day for hearing be set. Orville H. Browning entered and argued the motions in respect of two of these,[14] as did James M. Carlisle in respect of the other two.[15]

On February 13, 1866, the Chief Justice announced that the Court would hear the cases, on proof of notice to the respective adverse parties or to their counsel *qualified as an attorney & counsellor under the existing rules*:[16] that meant that the usual notice to counsel

---

[10] 3 Wall. 257 (1866).

[11] Comstock v. Group of Institutional Investors, 335 U.S. 211, 214 (1948).

[12] The Richmond, 103 U.S. 540, 543 (1881). So far as admiralty appeals were concerned, a statute of 1875, 18 Stat. 315, relieved the Court of the labor of reviewing evidence. Supra, p. 35.

[13] Andrews v. Hensler, 6 Wall. 254 (1867).

[14] Andrews v. Hensler, and Simpson v. Dall, 3 Wall. 460 (1866). The latter case, alleging error in a judg-

ment by the Circuit Court for Eastern Tennessee, was an action to establish liability for obstructing plaintiff's prosecution of an attachment suit. The Court, per Davis, J., reversed a judgment for the plaintiff.

[15] Newell v. Norton, and De Sobry v. Nicholson, 3 Wall. 420 (1866). In a suit by an out-of-State contractor, Louisiana defendant's objection to the jurisdiction for alleged absence of diversity of citizenship was pleaded too late, and moreover was without merit.

[16] Minutes for Feb. 13, 1866.

of record [where now barred from practice in a federal court by the test oath for attorneys] would not suffice.[17]

Justice Davis thereupon spoke up emphatically to say that that was *not* his understanding of what had been decided in conference. The matter went over, and next day the Chief Justice announced that the Court directed that the order be modified to read "on proof of notice by either party to the other or to the counsel of such other party appearing of record in this Court or to the attorney of record in the Court from which the cause is brought." Chase recorded his dissent.[18]

Thereafter he noted dissent when each of these four cases was decided: it could hardly have been that he disagreed with all of the decisions on the merits.

In *Andrews v. Hensler*, the case on the rescinding of a contract, nothing was made of the circumstance that the transaction was for *slaves*. The case was cited by Justice Swayne in 1872 for its recognition of a right of action on a contract for the sale of slaves, if valid where made.[19]

The incident of the Chief Justice's announcement and forced modification next day, is noteworthy for several reasons. It illustrates Justice Miller's statement that the Associate Justices "resisted his imperious will" and constrained him to recognize that his authority was only such as the rest of the Bench chose to give him.[20] It reflects, moreover, Chase's firm attachment to the test oath for attorneys. As will presently appear, after the Court had held the requirement unconstitutional, Chase was unwilling to bow to the decision.[21]

It was Justice Davis who raised his voice against the Chief in open court. The incident produced a certain estrangement,[22] which

---

[17] *Ex parte* Garland, holding invalid the test oath for attorneys, was not decided until January 14, 1867. Among counsel of record for the several plaintiffs in error were Pierre Soulé and Judah P. Benjamin.

[18] Minutes for Feb. 14, 1866.

[19] Osborn v. Nicholson, 13 Wall. 654, 657, where Chase, C.J., dissented. Infra, pp. 859-60.

[20] Supra, p. 26.

[21] Infra, pp. 766-67.

[22] Orville H. Browning made this diary entry for February 14, 1866:
Just after 3 P.M. Judge Davis of the Supreme Court sent for me to meet him at the room of the Clerk of the Sup. Court, Mr Middleton. I went over. He wanted to talk with me about a

motion I had entered and argued some three weeks ago to set down for argument one case from Tennessee, and one from Louisiana. Yesterday Chief Justice Chase delivered the opinion of the court setting the cases down for argument, but said, in doing so, that we must give notice to any attorney of the other party who could appear in this court under the present rules, before the cases would be heard. Judge Davis became very much excited, and stated from the bench that such was not his understanding of the decision of the Court—but that we were entitled to be heard upon giving notice to the opposite party, or

was effaced by further association and by an exchange of cordial letters initiated by Chase in the summer of 1867.[23]

The incident shows that the Chief Justice might be wrong and wilful in his announcement of an action by the Court. Here the difference was small, and was promptly settled. Suppose the constitutionality of an important statute were at stake, and a challenge to the accuracy of an announcement by the Chief Justice found the Justices deeply divided: that situation arose four years later, when the validity of the Legal Tender Act was before the Court.[24]

THE COURT LOOKS TO THE LIMITS
OF ITS JURISDICTION

WE NOW ENTER A PERIOD of hard questions of jurisdiction, where the Court must pause, on the threshold, to consider whether it has authority to hear and decide the particular case. One might, impatiently, brush aside this topic as "merely technical," concerned with minutiae, not going to the substance of right and justice. That would misconceive. There are limits to the judicial power, just as there are to the powers of the President, and the powers of Congress. The Supreme Court, in the American system, marks those limits. It should be especially conscientious when it must declare what are its own powers, for here it is judge in its own case. Before it considers redress for alleged illegality elsewhere it should make sure that it itself is acting within the law. That is basic to the Court's integrity.

Daniels v. Railroad Company[25] presented a question of jurisdiction, in a low key. In the Circuit Court for Northern Illinois, Daniels, a

---

the Counsel who was engaged in the Court below. This morning, at the opening of the Court, Ch J Chase announced that the decision was as stated by Judge Davis on yesterday, and that we should be heard upon giving notice to the opposite party or the Counsel who appeared for him below, but entered his protest against the decision.

Judge Davis told me of the scene in the Consultation room, and then told me to beware of Judge Field—that he was a d m d rascal and dmd rouge [rogue], and to be very cautious about what I said before him. Browning's diary entry for the previous Saturday, February 10, records that

In the evening dined at Mr Middletons in company with judges of Supreme Court, Atto Genl. Secy of War, Reverdy Johnson, Mr Carlisle &c.

Perhaps Justice Davis' caution arose out of something that had been said on that occasion.

Diary of Orville Hickman Browning (Springfield: Illinois State Historical Library, Vol. I [1850–64], Theodore C. Pease and James G. Randall, eds., 1925; Vol. II [1865–81], Randall, ed., 1933), II:61–62.

[23] Infra, ch. 11, n. 7.

[24] Infra, pp. 747–52.

[25] 3 Wall. 250 (1866).

citizen of Connecticut, sued an Illinois railroad corporation for personal injuries suffered in Illinois, resulting, it was alleged, from the negligence of the engineer. Daniels had been permitted to make a trip of interest to himself on undertaking to fire the engine. Was he, as he contended, a passenger, or, as the company argued, had he been working as an employee? Here was an "important question of fact, not without difficulty," which had to be resolved before one reached the legal question what principle of liability was applicable. At the July (1864) term of the Circuit Court, Justice Davis (who was new to the work) and District Judge Drummond (who was not) in effect certified the whole case, fact and law, to the Supreme Court. Should the Supreme Court take such a case? Its jurisdiction is conferred by the Constitution, but "with such Exceptions, and under such Regulations as the Congress shall make."[26] Congress in 1802 had made a regulation: that whenever any *question* should occur before a Circuit Court, upon which the opinions of the judges were *divided*, the *point* on which they disagreed might be certified to the Supreme Court for its decision.[27] What had been sent up here, said Justice Swayne, was not a question on a point of law, but the entire controversy, "as if we were called upon to discharge the twofold functions of a court and jury." The Court dismissed for want of jurisdiction and sent the case back with an order "to proceed in it according to law"; the trial court must decide, on the evidence, what had been the relation between Daniels and the railroad.[28] The Court, Justice Swayne recalled, had always resisted attempts during the pendency of a trial to send up "the whole case, instead of an isolated point," for decision.[29] It had frowned upon, but occasionally tolerated,

---

[26] Art. III, Sec. 2, cl. 2.

[27] 2 Stat. 160.

[28] If on the facts plaintiff was an employee, the question would have arisen, what defense was available in the fellow-servant rule adopted in England in 1837, Priestly v. Fowler, 3 Mees. & Wels. 1, and by the Massachusetts court in 1842, Farwell v. Boston & Worcester Ry., 4 Met. 36? (Fellow-servants were deemed to have *assumed* the risk of one another's negligence—so that the employer would escape liability.) Apparently the Supreme Court had never considered this significant rule: no such case was cited. (Cf. Philadelphia & Reading R.R. v. Derby, 14 How. 468, 484 (1852): the *Farwell* case had "no application to the present.") Counsel for the plaintiff said that "in those States where it has arisen, the widest diversity of opinion" had been expressed as to its scope. Brief in Supreme Court, 19. Examination of the briefs shows that on neither side did counsel say, This case is governed by the common law of Illinois, the place where the injury occurred. Plaintiff's citations were from other jurisdictions; defendant cited Illinois cases "lastly," to round out the survey. The Supreme Court was then following the doctrine of Swift v. Tyson, 16 Pet. 1 (1842): where the federal court had jurisdiction by reason of diversity of citizenship, it was not bound by the common law of the particular State, save in matters "strictly local." Infra, p. 938.

[29] Marshall, C.J., in United States v. Bailey, 9 Pet. 267, 274 (1835).

a certification pro forma that the judges differed on a point "when in truth they both rather seriously doubted than differed about it."[30] Now the Court recognized its duty scrupulously to stay within the limits Congress had imposed, even though the parties and the judges below sought its ruling. It is for Congress, said Justice Swayne,

> to determine how far, within the limits of the capacity of this court to take, appellate jurisdiction shall be given, and when conferred, it can be exercised only to the extent and in the manner prescribed by law. In these respects it is wholly the creature of legislation.

This was a simple case between private parties, and the Court found it easy to say, "it is for Congress to determine how far . . . appellate jurisdiction shall be given." But two years later Congress would be limiting the Court's appellate jurisdiction for the very purpose of preventing a decision on the power of Congress to enact its Reconstruction legislation—and the path of judicial duty would not be so plain.[31]

OBSTRUCTION OF THE DRAFT

TWO INDICTMENTS for obstruction of the war-time draft gave the Court an occasion to speak on the Conscription Act of 1863 as amended in 1864.[32] The most significant observation is that the Court calmly applied the canons of construction appropriate to penal statutes generally, with the result that the accused went free. By the first statute, Congress provided that persons subject to military service should be *enrolled*; then the President was authorized to *draft* them. Anticipating

---

[30] Taney, C.J., in United States v. Stone, 14 Pet. 524, 525 (1840).

In Webster v. Cooper, 10 How. 54 (1850), however, Taney recorded the Court's determination to put an end to "the irregularity and evil tendency" of a practice that "would, if sanctioned, convert this court into one of original jurisdiction . . . , instead of being, as the Constitution intended it to be, an appellate court to revise the decisions of inferior tribunals."

As to criminal cases, see supra, p. 86.

A notable instance of indulgence had been in Jones v. Van Zandt, 5 How. 215 (1847), an action for a penalty under the Fugitive Slave Act

of 1793, where Chase and Seward had been of counsel. Supra, p. 29. There Justice McLean and the District Judge had certified fourteen questions, not because they disagreed, but—as the Supreme Court observed—"because the questions involved could not otherwise be brought here; and they possessed so wide and deep an interest, as to render it desirable that they should come under the revision of this court."

[31] Infra, pp. 467-70.

[32] United States v. Scott, 3 Wall. 642 (1866), and United States v. Murphy, 3 Wall 649 (1866), supra, n. 5.

some obstruction, it imposed penalties for resisting the *draft*. Experience showed that trouble might come at the earlier stage of *enrolment*. So in 1864 Congress amended the statute to punish resistance to enrolment: the maxima were much higher; if an enrolling officer was killed, the penalty would be death. Sarah Murphy and others were charged with assaulting an officer making an enrolment, in 1863, when the statute reached those resisting the draft. Scott was charged with a capital offense under the amendment of 1864 in that he had killed an officer making the draft; but the death penalty added in 1864 referred to interference with enrolment.[33] The problems were not quite so simple as this statement implies; each penal clause admitted of a larger reading. Although interference with conscription had been a major threat to the survival of the nation, the Justices read these criminal statutes fairly—just as in ordinary cases—and gave the accused the benefit of what doubtless was an inadvertence on the part of Congress.

The constitutionality of the Civil War draft never came before the Supreme Court. Chief Justice Taney, when infirmity prevented his attendance at court, wrote out his "Thoughts on the Conscription Law of the U. States," concluding that it was invalid as an infringement on State power: if the federal Government could draft some it might draft all of the State's citizens except the Governor, and thus bring the State to naught.[34] (In the Confederacy, fighting for State Rights, the courts of half a dozen States upheld the central Government's conscription law.[35]) The chief discussion on the Northern side was in the Supreme Court of Pennsylvania, which by the narrowest majority, on a rehearing, sustained the statute.[36] During World War I, when the *Selective Draft Cases*[37] came before the Supreme Court, the objections urged before the Pennsylvania court in 1863 were renewed; Chief Justice White, speaking for a unanimous Court, pronounced them "too frivolous" for serious consideration.

It is not to be doubted that if the Civil War draft had been tested before the Court of that day, it would have been sustained; but in the condition of thought then prevailing the objections could not have been treated as "frivolous."

---

[33] Justice Davis, who sat with the District Judge in the Circuit Court, wrote to his brethren for their views —apparently without success. Willard L. King, *Lincoln's Manager, David Davis* (Cambridge, Mass.: Harvard University Press, 1960), 251n.

[34] Carl B. Swisher, *Roger B. Taney* (New York: Macmillan Co., 1936), 570–71.

[35] Cited in Selective Draft Cases, 245 U.S. 366 (1918).

[36] Kneedler v. Lane, 45 Pa. St. 238 (1864). Judges Strong and Read, reinforced by Judge Agnew, recently elected, produced a majority. This Judge Strong was appointed to the Supreme Court of the United States in 1870. Infra, pp. 719–20.

[37] 245 U.S. 366 (1918).

TRADING WITH THE ENEMY

ECONOMIC WARFARE against the Confederacy had always been plagued by domestic traffickers in licenses—"bloodsuckers who propose to make use of the blockade as a machine to enrich themselves," Secretary Welles called them.[38] A case in point was *The Reform*,[39] the libel of a small vessel and cargo, seized en route from Baltimore to a point in Confederate Virginia. In 1861 Congress had forbidden commerce with places in insurrection, subject to such licenses as the President saw fit to grant; this intercourse, so far as licensed, could be carried on only under regulations prescribed by the Secretary of the Treasury. On February 13, 1862, Congress appropriated $3,000 for the purchase of cotton seed, under the superintendence of the Secretary of the Interior, for general distribution. The Secretary by letter authorized one Hodge "to procure a cargo of the same in Virginia, and bring it to Baltimore." Hodge contracted with Penniman for the latter to carry out the enterprise. Penniman sent a cargo to a hostile point and received another on the return trip, but the Government got no cotton seed. Another attempt was being made by the *Reform* when arrested. The vessel had cleared for Alexandria, a friendly port, but was bound for a hostile port; it carried many articles not disclosed on the manifest. The report of the Secretary of the Interior showed that he construed the statute of 1862 to mean that the cotton seed was to be obtained at some place under the control of the Government;[40] there were such places in Virginia. If it were held, however, that this minor authority to buy cotton seed was intended pro tanto to supersede the nonintercourse policy of the statute of 1861—and if a license to go for cotton seed implied permission to engage in forbidden trade in other things—and if a license to Hodge to make one trip would justify Penniman in making two—and if a false manifest and fraudulent clearance and other discrepancies did not vitiate the claim of bona fides—if all of these points were resolved in favor of the claimants, then restitution was in order. Judge Giles in the District Court for Maryland had dismissed the libel, the Circuit Court had affirmed, and the Government appealed. The Supreme Court, however, speaking through Justice Clifford, was unanimous in directing a decree for forfeiture. The holding seems obvious. The striking feature of the incident is that the judgment of the Circuit Court, found to be clearly erroneous, had been pronounced by the late Chief Justice. With deep sincerity, Taney had consistently taken the very narrowest view of the power to fight the war for the Union.

---

[38] *Diary*, I:166. Oct. 10, 1862.
[39] 3 Wall. 617 (1866). And see

infra, p. 786.
[40] Government's brief, 10.

THE *MILLIGAN* AND *TEST OATH* CASES ARE HEARD

THE PRAYER OF MILLIGAN'S PETITION to the Circuit Court sought release from military custody "under the act of Congress approved March 3, 1863,[41] entitled 'An act relating to habeas corpus, regulating judicial proceedings in certain cases.'" That statute had declared that, during the rebellion, the President, whenever in his judgment the public safety required it, "is authorized" to suspend the privilege of the writ of habeas corpus.[42] The words were apt: if, as some contended, the President by his own proper authority under the Constitution might suspend the writ, the Act of March 3 could be read as declaratory of that view; if on the other hand only Congress could permit the writ to be suspended, the Act conferred the requisite authority. Section 2 of the Act provided that political prisoners, if a federal grand jury should thereafter meet and fail to indict them, would upon taking an oath of allegiance be entitled to their discharge. Should the Circuit Court issue the writs? On the facts stated, were petitioners entitled to be discharged? Did the military commission have jurisdiction to try them? Those were the questions certified to the Supreme Court. The hearing was set for Monday, March 5, 1866. At the outset the Court ordered "that three hours be allowed each counsel in the argument of these cases. That four counsel may appear and argue the cases on the part of the petitioners; and the Attorney General, and two associates for the United States in opposition to the petitioners."[43]

Appearing for the petitioners were Jeremiah S. Black, Attorney General under Buchanan; Joseph E. McDonald, loyal Indiana Democrat, who had defeated Milligan to become his party's nominee for governor in 1864; David Dudley Field, Justice Field's eldest brother; and James A. Garfield, arguing his first case in the Supreme Court. Black, astutely, had invited this distinguished Union soldier and Representative to join in the case, and Garfield had accepted to defend the proposition that even a disloyal man could be tried only by a lawful tribunal. For the Government, Attorney General Speed was supported by Henry Stanbery (who shortly succeeded to the Attorney Generalship) and Benjamin F. Butler. Argument ran from March 5 through 9, and was continued on March 12 and 13.

On April 3, the last day of the term, the Chief Justice announced the Court's ruling on the three questions certified: the writ of habeas corpus should be issued; petitioners ought to be discharged according

---

[41] 12 Stat. 755.
[42] Cited in connection with *Ex parte* Dugan, 2 Wall. 134 (1865),

supra, p. 55.
[43] Minutes, Monday, March 5, 1866.

to the Act of March 3, 1863; the military commission had been without jurisdiction. This was the result without any reasons. The Chief Justice said that the opinion of the Court would be read at the next term, "when such of the dissenting judges as see fit to do so will state their grounds of dissent."[44] The Minutes of the Court set out merely the answers to the questions certified—"per Mr Ch: Jus: Chase." No dissents were recorded. (As it turned out, Chase, C.J., and Wayne, Swayne and Miller, JJ., concurred specially: that is, while agreeing with the judgment of the Court, they dissented from some of the propositions in the Court's opinion, which was written by Justice Davis.)

The action of the Court occasioned little notice at the moment. There was no knowing what ground the opinion would take, or what might be said in dissent. The country had more interesting things to think about, such as the Civil Rights Bill which had been vetoed and was awaiting the action of the Senate.[45]

On March 13, 14, and 15, 1866, immediately after the argument in *Milligan*, the Court heard *Ex parte Garland* and *Ex parte Marr*, on the federal test oath. The test oath cases from Missouri followed on March 15, 16, 19, and 20. Opposing one or both of the oaths were David Dudley Field and Reverdy Johnson. Attorney General Speed and Stanbery defended the congressional requirement; Senator John B. Henderson and George P. Strong of Missouri sustained the provision in their State constitution. In these cases the Judges did not reach a firm conclusion by the time set for adjournment. When that day came the cases were continued to the next term: *curia advisari vult*, the formula for saying that the Court would consider the matter further. The federal cases differed from those from Missouri; different powers and limitations were involved. First exchange of views at conference had disclosed sharp differences of opinion. The whole business was put over. In the meantime, while an election campaign was being fought, the country would remain uninformed, barring some breach in the secrecy of the conference.

Thus involved, but not yet committed on the issues of Reconstruction, on April 3, 1866, the Court adjourned to the first Monday in December.

HIGH HOPES IN THE SOUTHERN PRESS

SOUTHERN NEWSPAPERS, raising high hopes on frail foundations, began to suggest that heroic deeds might soon be expected from the Justices. The *Richmond Dispatch*,[46] in an editorial on "The Supreme

---

[44] 18 L. Ed. 291.
[45] Supra, p. 127.

[46] March 28, 1866.

Court and the Rights of States," recalled that Sir Thomas More had won immortality and glorified his judicial office by withstanding Henry VIII, and that Sir Edward Coke had nobly declared the law in the teeth of James I; perhaps the Justices would acquit themselves as bravely. Two cases decided on March 26, it was said, might mark a trend. In *Van Allen v. The Assessors* the Court had affirmed the power of the State to tax an individual's shares in a national bank,[47] and in *McGuire v. Commonwealth of Massachusetts* it had held that payment of a federal license tax on dealing in intoxicants gave no freedom from a State's prohibition law.[48] Did not these show a movement toward State's rights? The *New Orleans Picayune*[49] professed to see that the *McGuire* decision had "a very important bearing on other constitutional questions." A later issue asserted "the hope, which some of the decisions of the Supreme Court . . . quicken almost into expectancy, that the [Civil Rights Act] will be pronounced unconstitutional by that body, beyond which there is no further power of appeal."[50] The finality of the Court's decisions on constitutional questions was a favorite Southern theme at that moment.

On April 2, 1866, President Johnson declared that insurrection in the Southern States was at an end.[51] One of the recitals in the long argumentative preamble ran as follows:

> . . . standing armies, military occupation, martial law, military tribunals, and the suspension of the privilege of the writ of *habeas corpus* are, in time of peace, dangerous to public liberty, incompatible with the individual rights of the citizen, contrary to the genius and spirit of our free institutions, and exhaustive of the national resources, and ought not, therefore, to be sanctioned or allowed, except in cases of actual necessity, for repelling invasion or suppressing insurrection or rebellion . . . .

Did this mean, as the *Augusta Chronicle and Sentinel* understood, that "the State of Georgia is now . . . in the same condition, as to the

---

[47] Supra, pp. 46–48.

[48] 3 Wall. 387. The statute laying the tax had provided expressly that such license should not be construed to authorize the carrying on of any occupation prohibited by State law. Therefore it was "not material" to consider what might otherwise have been its effect.

The Nation reported that "About twenty-five hundred persons are said to be affected by this decision, and to owe the State, in consequence, nearly half a million of dollars in accumulated fines." 2:418, Apr. 5, 1866.

[49] Apr. 3, 1866.

[50] Apr. 8, 1866.

[51] 14 Stat. 811. Texas was omitted. A further proclamation on August 20, 1866, made a like finding as to Texas, and declared that peace and civil authority prevailed throughout the United States. 14 Stat. 814.

exercise of all its civil rights, as the State of Massachusetts"?[52] Did the Freedmen's Bureau lose the jurisdiction it had been exercising for the protection of colored persons? Military commissions had been trying persons charged with outrages upon freedmen and Unionists in places where in fact State courts would afford no remedy. Was that power now withdrawn? On January 12, 1866, the War Department had instructed commanders in the rebellious States to protect from prosecution in the State courts persons charged for acts done under federal military authority. Could such persons henceforth be hailed before a State court?[53] When questions were raised, the Administration responded that the proclamation did not have such effects.[54]

The *Picayune*, again vaulting to a conclusion, announced that if the Justices of the Supreme Court now entered upon circuit duties, that would be "a decisive act of judicial recognition" that "no change had been worked, by the events of the late years, in the constitutional relations of the Southern States as integral members of the Union." "The course which the Supreme Court is evidently taking . . . brings an immense weight . . . against the self-will and factiousness of Congress."[55]

SOUTHERN MATTERS ARISING IN THE CIRCUITS

EVENTS ON THE CIRCUIT, between spring and autumn 1866, became matters of great moment. First, the South. In October 1865, responding to an inquiry by the President, the Chief Justice had said that he and Justice Wayne thought it would be unbecoming for Justices of the Supreme Court to attend circuits in States still in insurrection.[56] In March 1866, in a letter to Judge George W. Brooks of the federal court for North Carolina, the Chief Justice had made it clear that his unwillingness was based not upon any doubt about jurisdiction, but only on his conception of propriety for a Justice of the Supreme Court:

> My objections to the holding of Circuit Courts where the habeas corpus is still suspended and martial law yet enforced do not apply with so much force to the District Judges as to the Chief Justice and

[52] Apr. 11, 1866.

[53] See Coleman v. Tennessee, 97 U.S. 509 (1879), and Dow v. Johnson, 100 U.S. 158 (1884).

[54] Adjutant General's Office to General O. O. Howard, Apr. 17, 1866, and the President's Acting Private Secretary to Governor Worth of North Carolina, Apr. 27, 1866. Edward McPherson, *The Political* History of the United States of America during the Period of Reconstruction, 3d ed. (Washington: James J. Chapman, 1880), 17n.

[55] Apr. 13, 1866.

[56] Jacob W. Schuckers, *Life and Public Services of Salmon Portland Chase* (New York: D. Appleton and Co., 1874), 535–36.

Justices of the Supreme Court of the United States. I should waive them I think if I were a District Judge, but representing for the time as I do the Supreme Judicial Power of the Nation, it has seemed to me best not to hold courts where my judicial action might come in conflict with the military power. As soon as the President, who wields the Supreme Military Power of the Nation, shall think it wise and safe to revoke the suspension of the habeas corpus, and with it martial law, as to all acts of the Judicial Tribunals of the Nation, my objections to the holding of courts by the Justices of the Supreme Court will be entirely removed, and I shall hold such courts, in the Circuit assigned to me, which, as you know, includes, at present, Virginia, and North Carolina.

His advice to the District Judge, who was competent to hold the Circuit Court alone, was that

If I were in your place I would do so, and if conflict with military power should occur, should submit for the occasion referring the matter to the President. Of course I should take care to avoid all unnecessary conflict.[57]

The Chief Justice thus evidenced his view that, as a consequence of the rebellion, the Southern States were subject to military government: to that basic fact the administration of federal justice must, if need be, adapt itself.[58]

---

[57] Letter of Mar. 20, 1866. Copy in Andrew Johnson Papers, L.C.

[58] Chase framed a notable statement of the methods and objectives permitted to the National Government in preparing the rebel States for restoration, in his address to the grand jury in North Carolina, where he held court in June 1867. He said in part:

Under these circumstances [at the close of hostilities] it became the duty of the National Government to provide for the reorganization of republican governments in the States, in a form and upon principles which should guarantee its permanence and its adhesion to the Union.

The general powers of the National Government include many derivative and auxiliary powers. The power to suppress a rebellion includes the power to reestablish order upon stable foundations.

The power to enfranchise, as a military measure, a great population held as slaves, includes the power and imposes the duty of providing for the safety, and the welfare of the enfranchised people. The power to guarantee a republican form of government to each State in the Union includes the power, when a State government has been overthrown [,] to provide for its reestablishment upon the enduring foundation of Equal Rights and impartial justice.

When, therefore, the termination of active hostilities found the State without constitutional Government and without constitutional civil functionaries, it became the duty of the National Government to secure order and protect rights by Military Government or other provisional government until the great end of

The President's proclamation of April 2, as the Chief Justice first understood it, put an end to military government; he determined to attend the Circuit Court for Virginia.[59] Shortly, however, Executive instructions appeared, inconsistent with that view,[60] and he abandoned his purpose.

EGAN'S CASE: JUSTICE NELSON'S DICTUM

IN A CASE HEARD IN CHAMBERS in May 1866, Justice Nelson pronounced a portentous dictum: that "the moment the rebellion was suppressed" and a rebel State's government had been reorganized under the superintendence of the President, "the ancient laws resumed their accustomed sway" and once again "the State [was] in the full enjoyment, or entitled to the full enjoyment, of her constitutional rights and privileges." This was said in deciding In re Egan [or Eagan], releasing on habeas corpus a prisoner held in the penitentiary at Albany, New York, under sentence of a military commission, which had found that he murdered a Negro boy at Lexington, South Carolina, in September 1865.[61]

The Southern press hailed this as "an important decision"[62]—

---

restoration could be fully and satisfactorily accomplished.

The powers of the National Government under these abnormal circumstances, are not to be determined by rules framed for ordinary conditions. The powers called into action are not ordinary powers; and the ends to be accomplished are not common ends.

Chase Papers, Hist. Soc. of Pa.

With this outlook compare that of Nelson, J., in the case of Egan, next to be introduced.

[59] There is a lengthy statement of his views in letter of Sept. 24, 1866, to Schuckers. Schuckers, Chase, 540–42.

[60] Supra, n. 54.

[61] In the Matter of Eagan, 6 Parker's Reports of Decisions in Criminal Cases, 675, setting out the writ (returnable May 4, 1866) and the decision "At Chambers. Cooperstown, N.Y., May 16, 1866." Amasa J. Parker, the reporter, had represented the petitioner; his report is doubtless accurate.

The same case is reported as In re Egan, Fed. Case No. 4303—C.C.N.D.N.Y., June 22, 1866. (The writ might be granted by a Justice at chambers, or by a Circuit Court—see infra, pp. 440–42. Sometimes the reports confused.)

Under the practice then followed, federal prisoners were committed to some State prison (Rev. Stats., Secs. 5536–50 (1875).)—in this case, that at Albany, which was within Justice Nelson's circuit.

Amasa J. Parker (1807–90) was a very able lawyer, and also a leading Democrat. While supporting the war, he had been critical of arbitrary arrests. In the present case he seems to have acted like a lawyer zealous for his client's deliverance—rather than as a partisan seeking a political effect. I am grateful to Ernest M. Breuer, Esq., State Law Librarian, and Mrs. Mildred M. Leddy of the New York State Library, for diligent search in quarters I asked to have explored.

[62] Richmond Dispatch, June 2, 1866.

"sound, cogent and conclusive";[63] it was "a hopeful sign" when such men as Nelson "came forward to light up the old beacons."[64] Reverdy Johnson quoted Nelson's opinion at some length in the Senate on June 8, dwelling on its affirmation that the Southern States were now entitled to the full enjoyment of constitutional rights.[65] The Fourteenth Amendment, recently voted by the House, was then being debated in the Senate; Johnson was contending that, in the absence of spokesmen for the Southern people, Congress ought not to proceed with "a measure which is contrary to what we know they would do if they were not by compulsion forced to take it."

In holding that the military commission that sentenced the petitioner was without jurisdiction, it had not been at all necessary for Justice Nelson to make his pronouncement about "the full enjoyment" of constitutional rights: that was exactly what the President had been insisting and Congress had been denying.

As senior among those in the majority in the *Milligan* case, Nelson had selected Davis to speak for the Court. On September 3, replying to a letter from Davis, he sent "a newspaper copy of the opinion referred to."[66]

HABEAS CORPUS CASE IN DISTRICT COURT FOR DELAWARE

A SIMILAR DECISION in the District Court for Delaware, on November 17, 1866, also had political significance.[67] In South Carolina in October 1865, an army guard had been posted over certain cotton. Three soldiers of the guard were attacked and, with hands tied, were shot; their bodies were thrown into the Savannah River. After extensive investigation, Keys and three other civilians were charged with murder; after a trial before a military commission, lasting from January to April 1866, the accused were convicted. As recommended by the commission, sentences of death were commuted to life imprisonment.[68]

The president of the commission was Major General Charles Devens (1820–91), subsequently Attorney General in the Hayes Cabi-

---

[63] *Augusta Chronicle and Sentinel,* June 6, 1866.

[64] *New Orleans Picayune,* June 8, 1866.

[65] Cong. Globe, 39–1, 3030.

[66] Davis Papers, Ill. State Hist. Soc.

[67] United States v. Commandant of Fort Delaware, Fed. Case No. 14,842. Facts in greater detail, and a more extended opinion, are found in the (Wilmington) *Delaware Gazette,*

November 16, 20, and 23, 1866.

[68] *The Charleston Daily News,* in an editorial on December 7, said that the evidence for the prosecution "was purely circumstantial" and that the public, "who were perfectly familiar with the whole history of the trial, were unanimously agreed that they were unjustly convicted." (This did not say that the public believed the men innocent.)

net, and a Justice of the Supreme Judicial Court of Massachusetts (1873–77, 1881–91).

Orville H. Browning, retained as counsel, argued before the President that the prisoners should be sent to some place where they would be within the habeas corpus jurisdiction of a Northern court. (Browning was a close political friend of Johnson; at one of their conferences on the South Carolina matter, the President invited Browning to become Secretary of the Interior, an appointment that was made next day.[69]) Presently the prisoners were sent to Fort Delaware, a congenial spot.[70]

Writs of habeas corpus were promptly sought from District Judge Hall.[71] Appearing for the petitioners was Thomas F. Bayard, consistently an opponent of the war and of Republican policies.[72]

In ordering the discharge of the prisoners, Judge Hall said that when the military commission had been appointed, South Carolina had already been restored to its constitutional relation to the Union and was "in the exercise of its civil functions." Contrasting the disadvantage of the trial to which petitioners had been subjected with a trial by civil court in South Carolina, Judge Hall said:

> In so small a body, comparatively, as the army, so associated, with so much in common, so sensitive, there must be an esprit de corps that will not allow us to expect impartial justice from this collision with citizens, while the broad ground of citizenship is not liable to this objection. . . .

But the trouble was that the white citizens of the South were so associated, with so much in common, so sensitive, with such esprit de corps, that their courts would not punish those who murdered or otherwise injured Union soldiers or white Unionists or Negroes. No constitutional theory could budge that hard fact.

"How far the opinion is correct," the *American Law Review* commented after reporting Judge Hall at length, "and how far con-

---

[69] *Diary*, II, 79–85. His fee was $1,000. H. R. Rep. No. 23, 39th Cong., 2d Sess., 3, of February 22, 1867. "Murder of Union Soldiers."

[70] It is indicative of predominant sentiment in this border State that the Thirteenth, Fourteenth, and Fifteenth Amendments were all rejected when proposed. (All were ratified in 1901.)

[71] Willard Hall (1780–1875), Massachusetts-born and a graduate of Harvard College, had resided in Delaware since 1803. He had held various State offices and been a Representa-

tive in Congress. Appointed District Judge by President Monroe in 1823, he served until December 1871.

[72] Bayard (1828–98) had characterized the war as "this great *John Brown* raid"; the wise course was "to give it aid in no way whatever, but by *passive resistance* to impede its progress." Letter of July 26, 1864. Bayard Papers, L.C., quoted by Charles C. Tansill, *The Congressional Career of Thomas Francis Bayard, 1869–1885* (Washington: Georgetown University Press, 1946), at 18.

formable with the actual state of affairs as declared to exist in the South by Acts of Congress, we do not undertake to judge: it is certainly matter of grave doubt."[73]

When Congress met in December 1866, Representative Frederick A. Pike drew attention to the murders and to Judge Hall's decision, and called for a select committee to investigate.[74] (Pike came from Maine, as had the victims.) At the request of other members, the inquiry was widened to include other incidents. The outcome was that Pike and his Republican colleague, Farnsworth of Illinois, recommended "intervention of the authority of the general government in the only practicable mode in which it can be exerted, and that is through its military forces." The minority member, Cooper of Tennessee, said that the remedy was "such legislation, founded upon high and broad liberality, as will restore brotherly feeling . . . ."[75]

The need for federal protection against resentful acts of violence practiced and condoned in Southern communities would be one of the major considerations leading to the passage of the Act for the more efficient government of the rebel States, of March 2, 1867.[76]

POLITICAL CONTEST IN MISSOURI: LEAKS IN THE SUPREME COURT

IN THE ELECTORAL CAMPAIGN in Missouri in the summer of 1866, no topic was of greater importance than the test oath imposed by the constitution of 1865. That Radical document, adopted by a narrow majority, prescribed a detailed test of loyalty, which must be met not only by State and local officers, but also by voters; by jurors; by officers of corporations; by professors and school teachers; by attorneys; by clergymen and church trustees. The Conservatives sought a legislature that would initiate a repeal. More timely relief was hoped for through a judicial determination that the requirement violated the Federal Constitution; it would be the height of good fortune if such a decision could be made known before the autumn election.

But the appeals of Cummings, the priest, and Garesche, the attorney, had been left undecided, as we know, when the Supreme Court adjourned on April 3, 1866.[77] At that moment a third suit, *Blair v.*

---

[73] 1:576–78, Apr. 1867. In the meantime, an Act of Congress of March 2, 1867, had declared that "no legal State governments or adequate protection for life or property now exists" in ten rebel States, and had expressly authorized trial by military

commission when found necessary. Infra, pp. 285–309.
[74] Cong. Globe, 39–2, 28. Dec. 6, 1866.
[75] H. R. Rep. No. 23, 39th Cong., 2d Sess., at 3, 9. Infra.
[76] Infra, pp. 253–54.
[77] Supra, p. 144.

Thompson and Ridgely, was pending in the Missouri courts.[78] General Francis P. Blair, Jr., recently a corps commander in Sherman's army, was challenging the test oath as to voters: he declined to take it on the ground that in 1861, in defense of the Union, he had taken arms against the government of Missouri, then under a rebel governor.[79]

On May 1, 1866, John Hogan, Democrat seeking reelection to Congress,[80] said in a speech in St. Louis:[81]

> Now I say that the Supreme Court has decided that the oath of Missouri is an unconstitutional oath. While I don't know it from any written opinion which they have published, I have it . . . from the judges themselves that made the decision; that decision is now on record in the court.

This threw the Republicans badly off balance.

Senator Henderson (who had appeared for the State in the Supreme Court) consulted the Chief Justice, and on his advice went to the Minutes—a public record—and read the Court's order: that the cases be continued under advisement to the next term.[82] Henderson sent back to Missouri a letter of May 28, quoting the order and saying that "it is not possible that they are 'decided.' " It was *not* like *Milligan,* which had been decided although an opinion was awaited.[83] But then Hogan, also in Washington, published a letter of May 30 from Senator Reverdy Johnson, who recalled that he and David Dudley Field had argued that the requirement was ex post facto and a bill of attainder. Continuing,

> To this conclusion a majority of the court came, as was well known a few days before the close of the term. It was also known, certainly was known to me, that the failure to announce the decision was not

---

[78] See infra, pp. 613–17.

[79] The Blair family have already been introduced in connection with Montgomery Blair's aspiration to be appointed Chief Justice in 1864. Supra, p. 11.

[80] (1805–92). Irish-born, a Methodist preacher, wholesale grocer, postmaster of St. Louis under Buchanan, and member of the 39th Congress. He supported President Johnson in his policy "for bringing back the Southern States, with as much of the manhood of the people retained, as is possible." As candidate for the 40th Congress, he was defeated by William A. Pile,

also a Methodist preacher, and Brevet Major General in the war.

[81] (St. Louis) *Missouri Republican* (Democratic journal), May 2, 1866.

[82] Supra, p. 144.

[83] The letter appeared in the *Hannibal* (Missouri) *Courier* (apparently not now available); was quoted by (inter alia) the *Jefferson City State Times* (apparently not now available); whence it was quoted in the *Chillicothe Spectator* (Radical), of June 28, 1866. This recital illustrates how local newspapers of a hundred years ago may no longer be accessible to scholars; also, how such an item of news might be spread about.

because any one of the Judges constituting the majority then doubted upon the question; but I suppose it was mainly owing to the fact that the Judge selected to deliver the opinion had not time before the close of the term to prepare such a one as the importance and gravity of the question required. That this will be done during the recess, and that it will be delivered at the next term, I have no doubt. And I cannot forbear to add that, when it will be done, the cause of constitutional liberty and religious freedom will be secured against all attempts to strike at either that may be made in periods of temporary excitement, and oblivion of the rights of the citizen and the true interests of the country.[84]

Garesche, the litigant, published a card to say, "I reassert it that the oath has been voted on, has been decided illegal, for reasons which annul it for every class of the community, and that at the next term of the Supreme Court such will be the decision." That made a further claim on which Democrats were insisting: that the decision in favor of the priest and the attorney would be so broad as to strike down the oath even as to voters. Garesche urged those who could not take the oath nonetheless to go to the polls and force a record to be made of each rejection; also to sue any officer who rejected. "Unless at the approaching election the returns come in more rapidly than heretofore, the decision of the Court will be known before the results of the election, and thus wrongs can be righted."[85]

The election would be held on Tuesday, November 6; the Court would meet on Monday, December 3. It was indeed sanguine for Democrats to expect some prompt utterance from the Court so sweeping as to condemn the test oath for voters.

Justice Miller, on his circuit, saw the publication of Reverdy Johnson's letter, and on June 5 wrote to the Chief Justice about it:[86]

I call your attention to the statement of Mr. Johnson in the enclosed slip. Whatever may be our guesses at the individual conclusions of the members of the Court, it is certainly false that the Court ever decided the case, or even took a vote upon it. Not only so but there are several members of the Court, who have never as far as I know *expressed* any opinion on the subject.

---

[84] (Washington, D.C.) *National Intelligencer*, June 1, 1866; copied by (inter alia) the (Columbia) *Missouri Statesman*, June 8, 1866—a journal that carried at its masthead "Stand by the President."

[85] *Missouri Statesman*, June 15, 1866. The (St. Louis) *Missouri Democrat* (Republican journal) in its tri-weekly edition of June 13 pointed to the "persistent" attempt being made to create the impression that the test oath for voters was before the Supreme Court. The *Chillicothe Spectator* of June 7 made this point in an editorial on "Political Mendacity."

[86] Written from Keokuk. Chase Papers, L.C.

A very animated political contest is now going on in the State of Missouri, between the radicals and their opponents, the latter including every returned rebel in the State. This contest is looked upon by both parties as settling the future of that State for years to come, not only in its political relations, but as affecting the personal safety of the respective parties.

In this contest the stringent character of the oath prescribed by the Missouri Constitution, which was before us in the case referred to by Mr. Johnson, is made a strong point in the attack upon the radicals; and the assertion, that the Sup. Court of the United States has decided it to be in conflict with the Constitution is telling with fatal effect on the radicals.

Undoubtedly this was the purpose aimed at by the motion of Judge Field, that we should decide this case, and postpone the Congressional oath case. This move you will remember was defeated by my appeal to the Court not to decide this case if they passed the other, which succeeded by the good feeling and sense of justice of our brother Grier.

Now shall this falsehood be permitted to work successfully its injurious effects or shall it be contradicted? The Honorable Mr. Hogan is asserting the same thing everywhere in public speeches and so is Genl Blair. It was certainly a violation of judicial propriety for any Judge to state what Mr. Johnson says he knows, and I do not believe any Judge has said it, because it is false.

But it seems to me that while we may well feel restrained from stating what *did* take place, there is no wrong, but a manifest propriety in contradicting the assertion that the Court has decided an important case, or an important principle when it has done no such thing.

I think if any of the radicals of reputable standing should ask me, I should feel bound to contradict the statement, but I believe they are afraid to do so, lest the story of Johnson and Hogan might be confirmed.

I write this in private confidence, to learn your views, and also to suggest that such a confidential conversation between yourself and Senator Henderson, or Brown,[87] or Genl Loan,[88] as would at least enable them to claim as boldly as Hogan and Johnson assert, might do a great deal of good without committing any impropriety; if you concur with me in this matter.

The Chief Justice, at Washington, replied in a long letter on June 9.[89] He had been on the point of writing to Miller on the same

---

[87] B. Gratz Brown (1826–85), Senator from Missouri. He entered into the Liberal movement, and was elected Governor in 1870; at the same election, constitutional amendments were adopted, doing away with the test oaths.

[88] Benjamin F. Loan (1819–81), Missouri Congressman; Brigadier General in the State Militia, 1861–63.

[89] Chase Papers, Hist. Soc. of Pa.

subject. Reverdy Johnson's letter seemed "a gross violation of all propriety, even if the facts were as stated by him." "I have no memoranda of what took place"; his "impression" was that the Congressional test oath had been discussed at length, the Missouri cases not at all. He recalled Field's motion, Miller's "strong appeal," and Grier's joining with Swayne, Davis, Miller, and the Chief in voting to postpone. He knew of no consultation on the Missouri cases. "If there was any by members of the Court, as a caucus or conference separate from the other Judges . . . I know nothing of it. I should be sorry to believe there was any such private arrangement or understanding . . . ."

Chase recalled that after the Court adjourned (April 3) he had taken the train to New York City; Justice Clifford was on the cars and "we had a good deal of talk." Clifford had been told by Nelson "either just before or immediately after we took our seats on the Bench the last day that Judge Grier had consented to withdraw his vote on postponement & the case could therefore be decided; to which he, Judge Clifford, replied that he should not have anything to do with disturbing what was already settled." [The account is obscure—at second–, third–, and fourthhand; as repeated, it sounds as though there had been some hope at this very last moment of pronouncing a judgment against the Missouri test oath.]

Chase continued: "Now I shall be very glad to hear from you whose memory is so much more accurate than mine an exact account of what did actually transpire. It may be important that I be able to state the facts exactly hereafter."

Then Chase came to the point of Miller's letter. Despite several inquiries, he had refrained from making a statement for publication: it seemed to have been assumed that he was in favor of sustaining the test oaths, and "such an answer would therefore be imputed to mere partizanship."

> My conscience would acquit me, for *nothing* is the object of more earnest desire with me than to know the sense of the Constitution just as it was known by those who made & adopted it, & to declare this sense —just this & this only—in every case that comes before us. . . .

(Chase's letters abound in this sort of protesting: the world will impute wrong motives, but his conscience will acquit him.) He went on to relate that he had already made some responses:

> I have only said in conversation that the record shows that the two Missouri cases were continued *under advisement* & that I know nothing that contradicts the statement. In only one letter to a friend in St Louis have I said that no such decision was made by the Court; whatever may have been concluded out of the Court by Judges

among themselves: and this was in private to avoid the imputation I have mentioned. ...

A public statement coming from Justice Miller would, he wrote, be "far less" liable to an imputation of partisanship.

In conclusion on the topic of test oaths, Chase wrote:

> I shall speak to Henderson whom I have already referred to the record on the subject. He was counsel on one side & Johnson on the other, & has a right to know that Johnson has had no information which was denied to him.

Apparently Miller acted on his own advice, for soon it was published that "one of the Judges positively declares" that the question had not been settled in conference.[90] The Conservative press retorted that no matter what an "ignorant" Judge from Iowa had to say, Hogan and Blair had a positive statement to the contrary from "one of the most distinguished members" of the Court.[91] Why did not Senator Henderson produce a letter from the Chief Justice? "The latter would not be reticent on such an important point if he could aid his Radical friends in Missouri."[92] Presently the Republicans quoted the Chief Justice indirectly to that effect.[93]

On June 26 the *Missouri Democrat*—the leading Republican organ—announced "A Sockdolager." It published a letter to Senator Drake from Gustavus Koerner, sometime justice of the Supreme Court of Illinois, lieutenant governor, and (as Lincoln once wrote), "one of the most reliable of men."[94] Koerner had conversed with a Justice of the Supreme Court, who had assured him that no question broader than the validity of the test oath as applied to attorneys and clergymen had been involved in the litigation before the Court, and had added, "with great animation, that even that question was not decided *by the Court, that no vote had ever been taken on it*, and that it was simply continued under advisement." Evidently this was Justice Davis: among his papers is a letter of June 28 from Miller at Keokuk, inclosing the

---

[90] *Missouri Democrat*, tri-weekly ed., June 22, 1866.

[91] *St. Louis Dispatch*, quoted and derided by the *Missouri Democrat*, tri-weekly ed., June 29, 1866.

[92] *Jefferson City People's Tribune*, June 20, July 11, 1866.

[93] *Missouri Democrat*, tri-weekly ed., June 29, 1866. Joel F. Asper, editor of the *Chillicothe Spectator*, Union veteran, and subsequently Radical member of the 41st Congress, had written the Chief Justice on June 18: "I would like to know whether any decision has been arrived at, and if proper I would like permission to use the information in such a way as would be of service in our fight here." Chase Papers, L.C.

[94] Collected Works of Abraham Lincoln, IV, 476.

"Sockdolager" article and rejoicing "at the bold and courageous manner" in which Davis had contradicted the falsehood. Miller related that "being asked by Genl. Pope at Leavenworth about a month ago, I gave an emphatic contradiction, as you did to Koerner . . . ."[95]

As an incident in the political canvass, the Johnson statement may be dropped at this point. The Missouri Radicals were overwhelmingly successful in November, winning a solid delegation to Congress.

When word reached Justice Field, he telegraphed to the Chief Justice from San Francisco on June 30: "Have read with amazement Reverdy Johnsons letter to Hogan on Missouri Case does it require any notice from Judge Please answer."[96] On the same day he wrote, condemning the "singular indelicacy" of Johnson's statements, "even if they were in fact true." Certainly there had been no decision—the only vote was on postponing—events might contradict Johnson's estimate. "I suppose he got what he knows on the subject from Judge Nelson with whom he was very intimate—mingled up known with other matters. I do not regret that I was never intimate with him."[97]

In a letter to Miller on July 3, Chase returned to Reverdy Johnson's statement, and quoted the telegram from Justice Field:

> I suppose "Judge" means "Judges." I have not replied, hardly knowing what to say. Johnson's statement may well *amaze* anybody, unless there was, what I will not believe, a secret arrangement among five of the Judges that the Congress-Attorney-oath cases should be postponed and that the Missouri oath case should be decided against the oath without any opportunity for prior consultation among the Judges, and one or more of the parties to the understanding were sanguine enough to take the success of the scheme for certain & spoke of what was agreed to be done as a fact accomplished. If you can imagine any other explanation of Johnson's confident assertion that the conclusion of the majority was well known. If it be true as he says that a Judge was selected to prepare the opinion this also must have been agreed on in the caucus! Is it possible? Can it be possible? On the other hand how could Johnson have manufactured the story from whole cloth?[98]

These two letters from Chase give rise to reflections. He had made "no memoranda" of what transpired in conference. He had "an impression": Miller's recollection was "so much more accurate" than his own. Danger attended this way of doing business, especially

---

[95] Davis Papers, Ill. State Hist. Soc. Miller told of his exchange of letters with the Chief Justice; "I sent him at his request memoranda from my note book in which I have a full statement of the whole affair noted down at the time."

[96] Chase Papers, L.C.

[97] Chase Papers, L.C.

[98] Chase Papers, Hist. Soc. of Pa.

in any situation where Chase had a strong personal concern for the outcome.

Of deeper significance, the letters reveal a want of mutual confidence within the Court. Chase really believed that possibly some of his brothers were meeting in caucus and planning to announce a decision invalidating the Missouri requirement—even without prior consultation in the full Court. Johnson's supposition about "the Judge selected to deliver the opinion" was taken as an affirmation and treated as a substantiating detail. Clifford's statement about Nelson's remark confirmed Chase's suspicion.

What should one conclude? First, evidently the practice of the Court in reaching decisions was somewhat loose. This comes home to the Chief Justice. He presides at the conference and guides discussion; the keeping of a record of business is peculiarly his responsibility. Chase's successor, Chief Justice Waite, was far more attentive in this respect.

Apparently some intention persisted to condemn the Missouri test oath before the Court adjourned. Whatever may have been going on, Clifford represented that he learned of it from Nelson just as the Justices were going on the bench on April 3. (They sat side by side.) But it had become impracticable at that late moment to carry out any scheme. (Surely one must reject as too fantastic the possibility of a preconcerted outburst when the Chief Justice reached *Garesche* and *Cummings*, the last cases mentioned that day, and announced that they were being held under advisement.) At any rate, Clifford would not countenance a disturbance of what had been settled. (Nathan Clifford was simple, free from guile, not one to join in any cunning little combination.) The most important conclusion to be drawn is that the Court was deficient in corporate solidarity. Chase's reiteration that he does not believe the story reveals that he could not dismiss a fear that there was some truth in it. The specter of a decision in caucus was a threat to his authority as the Court's presiding officer.

Even as he was disquieted by this misgiving, the Chief Justice himself was deep in negotiations he had initiated with members of the two Judiciary Committees, on matters of major concern to the entire Court, about which he had not consulted his brethren. This will be explained in a moment.

Reverdy Johnson's statement really does not raise a great mystery. It proved to be substantially true, and it was in accord with disclosures already made by some of the Justices. On March 25 Orville H. Browning noted in his diary that Justice Grier had told him what the Court was going to do in the *Milligan* and *Test Oath* cases: that Wayne, Nelson, himself, Clifford, and Field were "against the Missouri test oaths." (So it turned out.) On April 3 Browning recorded that

Justice Nelson informed him that it was thanks to Grier's vote that a decision was postponed. On April 7 Justice Field told him that "Miller made a personal appeal to have the test oath case from Missouri postponed till next term, and that Grier in the kindness of his heart consented, but was afterwards very sorry for it."[99]

Justice Miller, writing to his brother-in-law in Texas on July 31, 1866, added a note, telling of the argument of the test-oath cases:

> As to the probability of the final decision, I can only say that while no vote was taken on either case, it was apparent that the court was nearly equally divided. There was four in favor of supporting the oath and four against it. Of the future vote of those eight if they shall all be present I am reasonably sure they will be as they then indicated. But there was one Judge, who said that if a vote was taken he should sustain the Congressional oath, but should hold the Missouri oath which is almost identical void as in conflict with the federal Constitution!! He made an earnest effort to have the vote taken on the latter proposition, but insisted on postponement in the former.
>
> What a Judge will do next winter who could come to such conclusions and who could desire such action as he desired of course no man can tell from any thing he then said. This of course is strictly confidential.[100]

This adds something to think about. The Judge who made an earnest effort to have a vote on the Missouri cases but to postpone the Congressional oath cases must have been Field: only he satisfies the statements in the letters between Miller and Chase. And now Miller quotes this Judge as professing that he would sustain the Congressional oath if a vote on that issue must be taken. In the outcome, Field wrote the opinion for the majority in both cases, holding both oaths invalid, and a reader would not suspect that he had ever been of unsettled mind.

Note too that aside from the uncertain Judge, Miller feels "reasonably sure" about four who will vote one way and four who will vote the other. The Justices were approaching the issues of Reconstruction with their own political opinions, strongly held and freely expressed to their intimates.

But Miller's prediction was qualified: "if they shall all be present." For the older members of the Court, life tenure had become precarious. Justice Wayne survived less than a year. Nelson would soon be seventy-four. Grier had just suffered a stroke; Chase's letter of July 3 had brought this information:

---

[99] Browning's *Diary*, II, 67, 69–70.
[100] Charles Fairman, *Mr. Justice Miller and the Supreme Court, 1862–1890* (Cambridge, Mass.: Harvard University Press, 1939), 130–31.

This morning I had a letter from Wallace [the Reporter] in which he spoke of Grier's paralytic affliction as quite serious, though it did not at all affect his mind, nor indeed any part of his body save his lower limbs. He says that brother G bears the calamity bravely. He has gone to the seashore & I shall try to visit him.

For the eventful three years that follow, one should keep Justice Grier's wasting condition in mind. Without his vote, the Justices would have stood four against four on the test oaths. Either those cases must have been continued without decision, or else the judgments of the Missouri court must have been affirmed, and the applications of Garland and Marr must have been denied, "by an evenly divided Court." Then Justice Wayne's death would have left a majority that *sustained* the test oaths.

Until early in 1870, the outcome of great constitutional issues is going to depend on the rate of deterioration of Justice Grier's body and mind.

TWO JUDICIARY BILLS

TWO RELATED MEASURES before the First Session of the 39th Congress now come under review.

One was S. 103, to reorganize the judiciary, by Senator Ira Harris of New York, second ranking member of the Judiciary Committee. He had introduced a bill on the first day of the session; had subsequently taken account of similar bills, notably those by Senators Henderson and Stewart; had corresponded extensively with federal Judges: now on January 29, 1866, he introduced a revised draft, which was referred to the Judiciary Committee.[101] The Harris bill would create an intermediate appellate court within each circuit, manned by the Circuit Justice and the District Judges, any three of whom would constitute a quorum. Appeals thence to the Supreme Court would be limited to categories of important litigation. The plan would permit a prompt review of judgments in federal courts of first instance, and would reduce the business of the Supreme Court, then nearly three years in arrears.

The scheme had been suggested some two decades earlier. It had been actively discussed, under the sponsorship of Senator Douglas, in the 33d Congress, in 1854 and 1855. Senator Trumbull had revived the proposal in the 38th Congress.[102]

---

[101] Cong. Globe, 39–1, 472.

[102] The history of the movement for an intermediate appellate court, from 1848 to enactment in 1891, is traced in Felix Frankfurter and James M. Landis, *The Business of the Supreme Court* (New York: Macmillan Co., 1927), at 70–85, 97–101.

On March 16, 1866, Harris reported S. 103 out of committee. He had consulted the Justices repeatedly: all except Clifford approved his bill.[103] Debate on April 2, 3, and 4 showed that the merits of the plan were appreciated by the Senate, which thereupon passed the bill by a vote of 23 to 6.[104] This was done just as the Court adjourned.

As the Justices went about their circuits, the Harris bill lay on the table of the Judiciary Committee of the House. If it became law, they need never again hold trials in first instance; the duty of each Justice, while the Supreme Court was in adjournment, would have been to preside on the bench of the appellate court, held at one place within his circuit. However, as events turned out, S. 103 never emerged from the House Judiciary Committee.

The other bill was H.R. 334, to fix the number of Judges of the Supreme Court and accordingly to change certain circuits. This became the Act of July 23, 1866,[105] and as will appear, threw the Justices into considerable confusion.

The authorized membership of the Court, originally fixed at five, had been increased to seven in 1807, to nine in 1837, and to ten by a statute of 1863. Justice Catron, absent throughout December term 1864, died in May 1865. The President allowed the next term to pass without making a nomination.

On February 26, 1866, Representative James F. Wilson of Iowa, chairman of the Judiciary Committee, introduced H.R. 334, and on March 8 reported it out of committee. It would restore the authorized strength of the Court to nine. He recalled that some had foreseen that the increase to ten "would be rather detrimental" to the working of the Court; now the existence of a vacancy made this an opportune moment. "I know that some of the members of that court are confirmed in that opinion that the court is too large." He added,

> I should be in favor myself, from information I have from some of the members of the court, of still further reducing the number if another vacancy now existed; and I think that in the judiciary amendment act [presumably meaning Senator Harris' bill, pending in the Senate] it might be well to provide for a further reduction if vacancies should occur.

Without comment from any other member, and without a division, the House voted assent.[106] On the same day, March 8, the Senate sent the bill to its Judiciary Committee, where it remained for three months.

---

[103] Infra, p. 164.
[104] Cong. Globe, 39–1, 1711–19; 1738–42; 1762–64.

[105] 14 Stat. 209.
[106] Cong. Globe, 39–1, 1259.

These were eventful months. On March 27 the President vetoed the Civil Rights Bill. Congress overrode that veto, and went on to override the veto of a second Freedmen's Bureau Bill. The Fourteenth Amendment was debated in May and early June, and submitted to the States.

On April 16, the President nominated Henry Stanbery of Cincinnati, Ohio, to be an Associate Justice, vice Catron. As counsel associated with the Attorney General, Stanbery had participated in the argument of *Ex parte Milligan*, which was concluded on March 13; then on the fourteenth had appeared in the *Garland* case. On March 14 the Civil Rights Bill was sent to the President; and Stanbery became the principal draftsman of the veto message.[107] Welles' *Diary* records Johnson's "desire to get a sound man on the bench, one who was right on fundamental constitutional questions. Stanbery, he says, is with us thoroughly, earnestly."[108]

The Nation, quite accurately, described the nominee as "a man of the very highest character, and a lawyer of very unusual attainments."[109] Also relevant, however, was the fact, then "pretty well known," that Stanbery "was the gentleman who supplied Mr. Johnson with his legal objections to the civil rights bill." The editors had "on general principles the strongest objection to seeing enquiries instituted into a man's political views for the purpose of ascertaining his fitness for a seat on the judicial bench"; even so,

> the truth is that the Supreme Court does not simply declare the law; it to a certain extent shapes the polity of the country, and the opinions of its judges as to the fundamental structure of the Government are, and will be for some time to come, of the last importance. . . .

The conclusion was that this was not a suitable appointment.

The nomination of Stanbery reposed in the Senate. On July 23, 1866, the President signed H.R. 334, reducing the authorized membership of the Court, so that there was no longer a vacancy. On the same day, he nominated Stanbery to be Attorney General, as successor to Speed, who a week earlier had quit the Johnson Administration.

One needs to follow closely to discern what happened in the matter of judiciary legislation during some weeks prior to July 23. There

---

[107] "Andrew Johnson and His Ghost Writers: An Analysis of the Freedmen's Bureau and Civil Rights Veto Messages," *Miss. Valley Hist. Rev.*, 48:460, 473–78 (1961), by John H. and LaWanda Cox, who examined the drafts in the Johnson Papers and identified the handwriting.

[108] *Diary of Gideon Welles*, 3 vols. (New York: Houghton Mifflin Co., 1911), II, 487.

[109] 2:514, Apr. 26, 1866.

was the "Senate Bill"—Harris' well-considered measure to reform the judicial system—resting in the House Judiciary Committee. And there was the "House Bill"—Wilson's uncontested measure to reduce the Court to nine—waiting in the Senate Judiciary Committee. We shall be examining letters between Justice Miller at Keokuk and the Chief Justice in Washington. Miller's heart was set on the Senate bill, a measure that would have enormously facilitated the administration of justice. Chase had interests of his own, which presently he expressed in draft amendments to be fastened to one or other of the bills—objectives which evidently he had not disclosed to his brethren.

Miller's letter of June 5,[110] apropos of Reverdy Johnson's statement about the test oath cases, bore this postscript: "Cant you say a word to some senators & mem. of the house for our judiciary bill"— that is, the Senate bill for intermediate appellate courts.

Chase's reply of June 9,[111] after discussion of the test oath matter, made this response to Miller's postscript:

> The Judiciary Committee of the House has the Court bill under consideration. It has been in the hands of my friend Judge Lawrence of Ohio[112] as a Subcommittee who has conferred freely with me, and it is now in a very satisfactory shape. If the Committee agree to the amendment & the House sanction the bill I think the whole country will be benefitted.

A colleague on the Court was entitled to be answered openly: What were the improvements the Chief Justice was undertaking to make through the agency of his friend on the committee?

Still greater misgiving was inspired by Chase's letter of June 15,[113] abruptly propounding a new objective for judiciary legislation:

> It is very important—if it is important that adequate salaries should be paid to the Judges of the Supreme Court [—] that the number of Judges should be reduced proportionately as vacancies may occur, to seven. I think that the salaries of the highest Judicial Officers of the Nation ought not to be less than those of the highest Military Officers: and at least an approximation might be made if

---

[110] Supra, p. 153.

[111] Supra, p. 154.

[112] William Lawrence (1819–99), sometime judge of the court of common pleas. In 1863, at Chase's request Lincoln had appointed him District Judge for Florida—a post Lawrence declined. *Collected Works of Abraham Lincoln*, ed. Roy P. Basler (New Brunswick, N.J.: Rutgers University Press, 1953), VI, 363n, 517–18; David Donald, ed., *Inside Lincoln's Cabinet: The Civil War Diaries of Salmon P. Chase* (New York, London, Toronto: Longmans, Green and Co., 1954), 182, 311.

[113] Chase Papers, Hist. Soc. of Pa.

the number were not so large, and especially if by the reduction of the number the means of increase would ultimately be supplied.

If you concur in this view please write to Wilson [Chairman of the House Judiciary Committee] and press it on him, without naming me in this connexion however.

There is one connexion though, in which it may be well to name me. The House Judiciary Committee has before it the Judiciary bill [S. 103] from the Senate and in respect to this I should like to have Wilson confer with me freely. So far it has been in the charge of Judge Lawrence, who has now been called home by the death of his father. Your relation as friend & constituent to Wilson[114] will warrant you in asking him to confer with me and your knowledge of the bill warrants you in assuring him that I shall be most happy to give any assistance in making the bill what it ought to be.

There was a postscript:

If you think it wise pray write to Swayne & Davis to write to any members they are on such terms with, as to make it proper.

This was awaiting Miller when on June 26 he reached home after attending his circuit courts. Next day he replied:[115]

. . . .

I have written by the same mail that carries this to Wilson in the matters that you suggest.

I fear our Judiciary bill will fail. The session draws near its close. The bill had full consideration in the Senate. Judge Harris submitted it repeatedly to the Judges, and it was approved by all except Clifford.[116]

If it is attempted to remodel it now, at the close of the session, with no opportunity to consult with the Judges of the Supreme or District Courts, it may be doubted if it will succeed or if it will be generally satisfactory.

The bill as it passed the Senate had the approval of all the district judges, of all the Judges of the Sup Court but one—Clifford. Can it be hoped that serious changes can now be introduced in the house, without dissatisfaction and danger of defeat. Beside the Senate

---

[114] In the 1st Congressional District of Iowa.

[115] Chase Papers, L.C.

[116] The reason for Clifford's stand does not appear. But he had a bias against innovation, and was never alert to hastening needs. His circuit duties were performed agreeably within the 150 miles from his home at Portland to Providence, always within sight of the Atlantic, save for a term at Exeter, nine miles inland. He could have had no appreciation of the problems of administering justice in the South and the expanding and litigious West.

as a body, is much more inclined to respect the views of the members of our Court than the House, and it was there you could have exerted yourself to perfect the bill with more success. If this fails I shall trouble myself no more with efforts to procure legislation. I have suggested to Mr Wilson, that he should call on you on the subject, and have also made mention of salaries in connection with a reduction of the number of Judges. I have done this with some reluctance, as I have a great indisposition to seem to ask for legislation for mere personal advantage to myself.

But in reference to the Judiciary bill I have been painfully conscious of the delay of Justice in the Sup. Court. I commenced agitating the subject before you came on the bench, in a long communication to the Chairmen of the Judiciary Com. of both houses. I thought when I left Washington there was strong prospect of fair fruit for these exertions, in the passage of the Senate bill. I am of course aware that no bill can embody all that every person may desire. But as none of the Court expressed dissatisfaction with that bill, except Clifford, as it passed the Senate with nearly unanimity I had some ground to hope it would be accepted by the house, and pass. I know not what modifications you wish to make. From your sound sense I infer they must be wise ones. If they result in defeating the bill, either by delay or by the contests they provoke I shall doubt if they are worth that sacrifice.

You will excuse this frankness as that quality is one of the great pleasures of our intercourse. I am so deeply interested in the passage of the bill I could not say less.

Miller's reiteration of his objections reflects exasperation at the Chief Justice's intervention.[117]

The ends Chase hoped to achieve by amendment of one or other of the pending bills are disclosed by a draft in his scrawl, so much

---

[117] On June 28, 1866, he wrote to Justice Davis: "What do you hear of our judiciary bill? The telegrams I see about it are unsatisfactory, and I fear the Chief Justice and some members of the House committee have so modified the Senate bill, that it will not pass the House, or if it does will not meet either the approval of the President or of the original authors and friends of the bill." Davis Papers, Ill. State Hist. Soc.

This disappointment came at a moment when Miller felt concern for his own ability to continue in effective judicial service. In his letter of June 9 to the Chief Justice he had

remarked, "I have suffered this spring from fulness of blood in the head; but shall be through with my spring terms soon when I hope, quiet will restore me." The Chief Justice, in reply, suggested that they plan to meet for a vacation on Lake Superior.

But the symptoms of overwork continued to cause alarm. Mentioning this in a letter of July 2 to his brother-in-law, Miller wrote: "You know I was about thirty when I commenced reading law, and from that time to this, say twenty years, few men of my acquaintance, have given as many hours to study, to hard intellectual labour as I have."

corrected and interlined as to defy typographical reproduction. It is accompanied by a clean draft in a fair hand.[118]

The latter begins:

> § No vacancy in the office of Associate Justice of the Supreme Court shall be filled by appointment until the number of Associate Justices shall be reduced to six; and thereafter the said Supreme Court shall consist of a Chief Justice of the United States & six Associate Justices, any four of whom shall be a quorum . . . .

H.R. 334 as proposed by Wilson and passed by the House had simply reduced to *eight* Associate Justices. Chase, in pursuit of higher salaries, wanted the number of Associate Justices to be reduced to *six*. And he took the occasion to refer to his own office, not as that of "Chief Justice of the Supreme Court of the United States" to which he had been appointed, but by a more distinguished title, "Chief Justice of the United States."[119]

Section I of the clean draft concludes: "The annual compensation of the Chief Justice shall hereafter be twelve thousand dollars, and that of each Associate Justice shall be ten thousand dollars, payable quarterly." In Chase's original drafting, this had stood out as a separate section, and the number of thousands had been left blank; then he had drawn a sweeping line, to tuck it in at the end of Section I. The figures he had in mind appear in the clean draft.

The letter of June 15 disclosed his objective: judicial salaries "not less than those of the highest Military Officers." This had a special significance at the moment. On May 4 the House by overwhelming vote had passed H.R. 3, to revive the grade of General of the United States Army. The purpose was to confer upon Grant a higher title. As Lieutenant General his pay and allowances came to $16,800 a year; as the bill passed the House, they would be $17,640.[120] On July 17

---

[118] In the Chase Papers, Hist. Soc. of Pa.

[119] Immediately following the fair-hand draft of Chase's proposal came the following—evidently addressed to those in Congress who would be considering the matter, and intended to show consistency in his advocacy of a reduction of the size of the Court:

In January 1855 I moved to reduce the number to six. [Andrew P.] Butler [of South Carolina] the Chairman of the Judiciary Committee expressed himself personally in favor of it, though he voted against it. The votes for it included the best lawyers in the Senate Badger [of North Carolina], Cooper [of Pennsylvania], Fessenden [of Maine], Foot [of Vermont] and Pearce [of Maryland]. It was not at all sectional or party, Badger, Me. [sic: copyist's error], Bell, Tenn., Pearce of Md., and Rusk of Texas voting with Fessenden, Sumner and Wade.

Cong. Globe, 1854–55, p. 240.

[120] Cong. Globe, 39–1, 2387. May 4, 1866.

the Senate passed the bill, with some increment in allowances, and so it became law on July 25. At once Grant was appointed, and Sherman was promoted to the vacancy.

At that period the Justices received only $6,000, with an additional $500 for the Chief (the difference that had existed from the beginning).[121] As an argument for increments to $10,000 and $12,-000, Chase would have the Court reduced to seven.

Section 2 of Chase's draft provided: "The Chief Justice with the approval of the Court may appoint a Marshal . . ." whose salary would be $3,000. The Judiciary Act of 1789 had authorized "the Supreme Court" to appoint its Clerk. Chase, after a little scribbling and scratching, had rejected that form and settled on the provision above. He had his own man in mind.

On July 3 Chase acknowledged receipt of Miller's letter of June 27, the one saying, in effect, that he hoped Chase would forbear to meddle with the Harris Intermediate Appellate Court Bill by offering amendments, whatever they might be. Now Chase replied:

> You are quite right about the Court Bill. No amendments should be suffered to interfere with its progress and this is what I say to our friends on the Committee.
>
> The three amendments which I feel most concerned in are (1) the Appointment of a Marshal for the Court by the Chief Justice with the sanction & approval of the Court (2) the reduction of the number of Judges to 7 by direction that no new appointments of Associates be made till the number reduced to that figure (3) application of money saved by reduction to increase of salaries. I am quite willing to give them all up rather than lose the bill.
>
> The greatest danger, however, is not from amendments but from delay. The Judiciary Committee has not been called since the bill was referred to it, & the opposition of some of the Eastern Members makes it impossible for the Committee to get consent to report it out . . . . Lately there has been even a majority against it in Committee; but that majority has been overcome so far that it will be reported. What Wilson said to me yesterday led me to hope that it would be reported today, and it may be—or may have been, as it is now about 4 P.M. If actively pressed it need not fail but my fears are greater than my hopes. If ever through the House it will be safe.[122]

But S. 103 was not reported out of the House Committee, then or thereafter.

---

[121] Supra, p. 68n.

[122] Chase Papers, Hist. Soc. of Pa. At some places in the passage above the letterpress copy is indis-tinct. I do not doubt, however, that with knowledge of the subject matter I have read correctly.

In the Senate, on June 13 Trumbull reported H.R. 334 with an amendment: his committee differed with the House regarding the combinations whereby the States would be regrouped in the reduction of the circuits from ten to nine.[123]

On July 10, Trumbull moved that the Senate begin consideration; but now he was instructed to report a *further amendment* to reduce the Court to *seven* members, pending which no vacancy as Associate Justice would be filled.[124] The bill would for the present arrange the States into nine circuits; further regroupings would have to be made from time to time as the number of Justices fell.

Sherman of Ohio—without referring to the proposed reduction to seven, and consequent enlargements of the circuits from time to time—objected to the committee's arrangement as it would affect his State. Ohio and Michigan then comprised a circuit. The House, in reducing to nine, had added West Virginia. But now the Senate Judiciary Committee would put Kentucky and Tennessee in the circuit with Ohio and Michigan. Trumbull replied that the circuits would be "necessarily large"; however, "The Senator from Ohio is aware that a bill has passed the Senate and is pending in the other House to relieve the supreme judges entirely from circuit duty and establish an intermediate court of appeals."[125] He added that the court "will be held in but one place" in the circuit. Sherman replied that as S. 103 passed the Senate, Cleveland had been designated; a change in the composition of the circuit would mean inconvenience, perhaps even the building of a new courthouse. Howard of Michigan reinforced these objections.

Nevertheless the amendment was agreed to.

Then Trumbull moved the further amendment: to strike out the House version of Section 1 and insert new language. What he read proves to be the Chief Justice's draft—*without, however, the concluding sentence to increase compensation.* Without a word from any Senator, the amendment was accepted.

Trumbull said nothing about authorship. Nor did he notice the insinuation of a new title. Nor was there any comment on those matters in debate.

This further amendment, to reduce the Court to seven, originated after June 13, but earlier than July 10. That accords with Chase's letter of June 15 to Justice Miller, suddenly proposing pressure for higher pay, with a drastic reduction of the Court as an inducement.[126]

Then Senator Harris proposed an additional section; and here he offered Chase's provision for a Marshal, verbatim. He insisted that

---

123 Cong. Globe, 39–1, 3134.
124 Ibid., 3697.

125 Ibid., 3698.
126 Supra, p. 163.

"the judges" had suggested it to him. Reverdy Johnson said it was "singular"; he had "never heard from any of the judges" any complaint about the existing practice. Trumbull objected that it had never been considered in committee: "I have heard nothing of it until it is now proposed for the first time . . . ." Without division, the proposal was rejected. Then the bill as amended was passed.[127]

In the House on July 18, H.R. 334 came up as the next business: Would the House accept the Senate's amendments? Chairman Wilson asked concurrence at once.[128] Randall (Dem.) made the point that there was no report from the Judiciary Committee. Wilson said, "but the members of the committee have consulted about it and a majority of them recommend concurrence." Spalding (Rep.) of Ohio repeated the objection Sherman had made in the Senate; he asked for time for discussion.

Woodbridge (Rep.) of Vermont observed:

> I simply wish to say that I am opposed to the bill at present. If the bill to reorganize the judiciary [S. 103] should pass the House, then I might possibly be in favor of this bill, but unless that does pass it seems to me it would be very unwise for us to adopt the provisions inserted by the Senate.

Woodbridge was saying that *if* the Intermediate Appellate Court Bill were to pass, then *possibly* it would appear that seven Justices would suffice. Woodbridge was a member of the Judiciary Committee. He treats the passage of S. 103 as doubtful.

Wentworth (Rep.) of Illinois asked whether this bill would abolish the place to which the President had recently made a nomination. Wilson answered yes: it would even reduce the number of Associate Justices to six. "I know that a number of the members of the Supreme Court think it will be a vast improvement." The bill had first "passed the House before any nomination was made." (Actually, it had passed thirty-nine days before the President nominated Stanbery.)

On agreeing to the bill as amended by the Senate, the vote was 78 yeas (Republicans, including one "Administration Republican") to 41 nays (19 Democrats, 3 "Administration Republicans," and 19 Republicans).

The President signed, and it became the Act of July 23, 1866.[129]

On July 28 the First Session ended, without the Senate bill having been considered by the House.

---

[127] Cong. Globe, 39–1, 3699. July 10, 1866.
[128] Ibid., 3909. That one page sufficed to record discussion and passage.
[129] 14 Stat. 209.

CONCLUSIONS ON THE TWO BILLS

IF S. 103 HAD BEEN ENACTED in 1866, that would have initiated a reform of enormous benefit. (As it turned out, not until 1891 was the system of intermediate appellate courts established.) From the favorable winds that carried it through the Senate, there did seem a reasonable hope that it would be accepted by the House. When so great a prospect was in view, it was a time to avoid the least confusion over lesser things.

Wilson's bill to return the Court to a membership of nine, as it had been so long, was meritorious. In the three years during which the authorized strength was ten, there had been only five days—December 7 to 11, 1863—when that many Justices were present. It was desirable that there be an odd number, to avoid an evenly divided Court. Too many Judges would encumber the process of consultation. Too few would unduly increase the burden of opinion-writing, and afford too little variety in talents, background, and experience. Nine able Judges, present in mind and body, seemed to be the optimum.

The idea of a Court of seven was ill considered. Chase propounded it only as an inducement to win higher pay. Gradual reduction would recurrently have produced widespread inconvenience. (This was averted by a restoration of the Court to nine in 1869.[130]) As Trumbull had observed, circuit boundaries must have been redrawn with each change in the actual number of members, upsetting the ways of Judges, counsel, and litigants. Seven circuits would not have been adequate to the needs of the country: this would be evident if one were to examine the matter with old railroad maps and timetables in hand.

As an expedient to preclude appointments by President Johnson, the reduction to seven was unnecessary. In a Senate where the Republican strength was well over twice that of Democrats and Johnson's friends combined, confirmation of any unsatisfactory nominee could be prevented. It is no wonder that the President made no contest over the bill.

Chase's performance shows him to have been imperceptive in his dealing with his brethren. When he parted with them at the close of the term, he had not consulted them, either about the size of the Court or about a request for higher compensation. These were matters in which the interest of each was as great as his own; all should have been consulted, and a collective judgment sought.

---

[130] Infra, pp. 487–88.

A substantial increase in salary could have been abundantly justified; but it was not something to be sought covertly, or at the sacrifice of effective judicial organization.

In the pursuit of a large increase in compensation, Chase failed. The salary of the Chief Justice was raised from $6,500 to $8,500 in 1871, and to $10,500 by an Act of March 3, 1873, two months before Chase's death.[131]

The more pretentious title secreted in the Act of July 23, 1866, brought him no prestige, since the public knew nothing of it.[132] Melville W. Fuller, appointed in 1888, was the first whose commission bore the title "Chief Justice of the United States."

For the Court to have its own Marshal was an appropriate, but minor, objective. Chase was seeking a bit of patronage. It was authorized at the Second Session, by a bill introduced by Senator Wade of Ohio; before passage, however, the words "upon recommendation of the Chief Justice" were struck out.[133]

In his approach to Congress, Chase worked through his friend, Representative Lawrence, to put S. 103 into "very satisfactory shape." Disclosing to Miller what he wanted in the matter of salaries, he asked him to propose the idea to the Chairman of the House Judiciary Committee, "without naming me in this connexion," and to enlist Swayne and Davis in supporting appeals. (Despite "a great reluctance," Miller felt constrained to approach Wilson; apparently he did not involve his associates.) Evidently Chase used his friend, Senator Harris, in an effort to engraft his amendments upon H.R. 334. His draft of the section to reduce the Court to seven appears in Trumbull's further amendment of July 10: it is not disclosed whether Trumbull knew the source, or whether he had knowledge of the basic desire for higher pay. He did not know about the proposal for a Marshal: evidently Harris was acting guardedly in striving to satisfy Chase's desires.[134]

---

[131] The amounts successively provided down to 1903 were stated in chapter 2, note 134. The provision in the Judiciary Act of 1789 was simply "to the Chief Justice." 1 Stat. 72. That in 1819 was "to the Chief Justice of the United States." 3 Stat. 484. Later provisions were "to the Chief Justice of the Supreme Court . . . ." 10 Stat. 655 (1855); 16 Stat. 494 (1871); 17 Stat. 486 (1873); 32 Stat. 825 (1903).

[132] But see p. 738, where in 1870 the new title was brought to light by Senator Drake.

[133] Cong. Globe, 39–2, 694, 1439. 14 Stat. 433. This was S. 534, a bill to empower the Court to allot the Justices to Circuits; see infra, p. 175.

[134] Two years later, after Harris had been supplanted in the Senate by Roscoe Conkling, he called upon Chase to help him obtain a Judgeship in the Court of Claims—not as the best post to which he might aspire, but chiefly because it would enable him to settle his family in Washington. On June 13, 1868, he wrote to Chase: "I believe you can secure the place for me. The President is under great obligations to you. I am sure he can but realize it. I think he is kindly disposed towards me. . . ." He went on to express gratification at

This was hardly an exemplary way for a Chief Justice to proceed in presenting to Congress a request for judiciary legislation.[135]

CONFUSION IN THE CIRCUITS

THE OBSCURE ACTION AND INACTION in Congress had left the Judges in a state of uncertainty. Justice Davis explained this in a letter of August 9, 1866, to his brother-in-law, Judge Rockwell. While the Senate bill to reorganize the judicial system had been allowed to sleep in the House,

> a bill was passed, reducing the number of Judges to 7, which puzzled me a good deal. Is it to be a permanent policy: if so, the Supreme Judges will be relieved from circuit duty and will be stationary at Washington, because 7 Judges cannot perform the Circuit duty of the United States. But I have supposed the bill was passed simply to prevent the Presdt fr appointing Supreme Judges & that it might be changed hereafter. If the Supreme Judges are to be an appellate Court at Washington and nothing else, I wd be glad to know for the knowledge wd affect very materially my future arrangements. But I cant be enlightened at present. I must patiently wait & see.[136]

In the business of amending and enacting H.R. 334, an important matter had been overlooked: *there was no provision for allotting the Justices among the new Circuits.* (*If* S. 103 had been enacted, *it* would have made such a provision for the new Circuit duties therein contemplated.)

Section 2 of the new statute, in brief, suppressed (Catron's) Sixth Circuit and distributed its five States; Circuits theretofore numbered

---

the rapid development of sentiment to make Chase President: "I regard it as almost a *moral certainty* that you are to be nominated and elected." Chase Papers, Hist. Soc. of Pa.

Chase wrote to the President on July 17, urging the appointment. He marked the letter "Private," and asked, "Please don't let this note go in the Judiciary file; but consider it as the suggestion of one who wishes from your action nothing but credit to yourself." Johnson Papers, L.C.

The President appointed his friend, Judge Samuel Milligan of Tennessee.

Harris did not spell out the reasons why, in his view, the President was "under great obligations" to the Chief Justice. However, the latter had presided at the trial of the impeachment, which had closed on May 26, 1868.

Chase was mindful of "the friendship the Judge [Harris] has consistently shown for me." Letter to his daughter Nettie, July 11, 1867. Chase Papers, L.C.

[135] When Chase was appointed to the Court, Gideon Welles commented in his diary that he was "politically ambitious and restless, prone to, but not very skillful in, intrigue and subtle management." II, 192–93.

[136] Davis Papers, Ill. State Hist. Soc.

Seventh to Tenth were redesignated Sixth to Ninth respectively. Arkansas was added to the Eighth (formerly the Ninth, to which Justice Miller had been allotted); Kentucky and Tennessee went into the Sixth (formerly Swayne's Seventh); and Louisiana and Texas were placed in the Fifth (Wayne's). To offset these additions, the Fifth would lose South Carolina to the Fourth (the Chief Justice's), and the Fourth would lose Delaware to the Third Circuit (Grier's). Wisconsin would be grouped with Illinois and Indiana to make the Seventh (formerly Davis' Eighth). The statute provided that the First and Second Circuits (comprising the New England States and New York) "shall remain as now constituted."

In the past, Congress had made provision for new allotments as they were needed. It had charged the Court to act whenever a new Justice was appointed. But now, in reducing the Circuits, it had done nothing about assigning the Justices. Should the Chief Justice, for example, say that he was still competent to act throughout the Fourth Circuit—no matter that its composition was altered? Should Justice Field say that really he had been allotted to the Pacific coast—no matter that that area had a new number? Could Swayne, Davis and Miller, respectively, properly act in the Circuit wherein each now found himself, although neither in number nor in composition was it that to which he had been allotted?

The prescribed terms of the Circuit Courts, in the main, did not fall in the late summer; the Justices normally attended them in the months immediately after the Supreme Court adjourned, and resumed in the autumn.

"As soon as I read the law," Justice Davis recalled, "I saw that a question of jurisdiction would arise as to the Circuits whose numbers were changed, and therefore considered it with reference to my own action. . . ."[137] By the most recent order of the Court, he had been allotted to the Eighth Circuit:[138] that had then consisted of Illinois and Indiana. Now Illinois, Indiana, and Wisconsin comprised the Seventh Circuit. He was urged to attend the September term in Wisconsin, where important litigation was pending.[139] Did he have jurisdiction?

---

[137] Retained draft, in Davis Papers, of letter to the Chief Justice on Oct. 22, 1866. The text in the Chase Papers, Hist. Soc. of Pa., varies somewhat.

[138] Minutes of Jan. 17, 1865—consequent upon the appointment of a Chief Justice.

[139] Matt. H. Carpenter had written him from Milwaukee, on July 19:

The bill rearranging the Cir-

cuits has passed & we are in yr ct.

Harris Bill will probably not pass. Our Sept Term is the 2d Monday Sept.

For five years the railroad fight here has monopolized the court, & all the important causes of a general nature have been accumulating. There are for hearing in Sept several very

Davis consulted Swayne, Miller, Nelson, and Clifford. Swayne sent to Chase a copy of his reply. Presently Chase sent a detailed analysis to each of his brethren, arguing strongly that all allotments, except those of Clifford and Nelson to the First and Second Circuits, had been superseded. He asked their views: Could the several Justices now act?

In the exchange of opinions, Justice Clifford was the only one who answered yes to each of these situations; he would construe the Act to achieve what Congress doubtless expected. All the other views on record agreed that Swayne, Davis, Miller, and Field no longer had a Circuit. As to the situation where the numerical designation remained but the composition was altered: Chase and Grier felt that they had no authority to act; Swayne and Davis were inclined to think otherwise; Miller and Nelson found it very doubtful and said that it would certainly be imprudent to act. Grier could "find no way of *evading* the conclusion at which you [Chase] have arrived"; he would go on to hear argument in the case before him, provisionally, but would "abstain from making any order or decree . . . ."

Miller's reply to Chase was most responsive and helpful. He had "no difficulty" in concluding that Justices formerly allotted to Circuits Sixth to Tenth could perform duty nowhere. While his opinion was not firmly settled "on the abstract question of law" as to Circuits Third to Fifth, "I have a very decided opinion as to the duty of a Judge in your situation." He supposed the Chief Justice had invited an expression on more than the bare legal problem, and took the responsibility for straightforward counsel:

> In consideration of the great doubt of your authority to hold such courts, and some of the very serious matters on which you would probably be required to act if you held them, with the fact that the District Judge can hold such courts without question, it is my opinion that it is *not* your duty to hold them, and that the strongest considerations of conscience and delicacy, require you to abstain from the exercise of a doubtful authority . . . .

He trusted that Chase would attribute this frankness to "a sincere friendship."[140]

---

heavy Equity Causes, and municipal bond cases to a very large amount.

Now my dear Sir, cant you do us the great favor to come up ten days and hear these causes? Davis Papers, Ill. State Hist. Soc.

[140] The letters quoted and summarized above are found in the Chase Papers, Hist. Soc. of Pa., and the Davis Papers, Ill. State Hist. Soc. Among the former: Swayne to Chase, Aug. 24, inclosing copy of his letter to Davis, Aug. 23; Swayne to Chase, Oct. 2; Chase's draft of letter to the Justices, dated Oct. 5 (some copies sent on other days); Grier to Chase, Oct. 9; Miller to Chase, Oct. 11; Clif-

At the Second Session of the 39th Congress the Circuit difficulty was cured by an Act of March 2, 1867,[141] providing that allotments when required from time to time would be made by the Court, and out of term by the Chief Justice—substantially the law today.[142] It was in this statute that the Court was authorized to appoint a Marshal.[143]

JEFFERSON DAVIS, DEFENDANT

MILLER'S COUNSEL had particular reference to a situation in which the Chief Justice was then involved. Because of Jefferson Davis, Chase had been caught in a difficult position, conspicuously and unavoidably. Unmentioned, that had been an element in the Circuit problem.

Jefferson Davis was then imprisoned at Fortress Monroe; a federal grand jury in Virginia had indicted him for treason.[144] Trial would be

---

ford to Chase, Oct. 13; Nelson to Chase, Oct. 18; Davis to Chase, Oct. 22. Also, District Judge Giles to Chase, Oct. 17.

Among the Davis Papers: Miller to Davis, Aug. 22, responding to a "short note" from Davis; Nelson to Davis, Sept. 3; Clifford to Davis, Sept. 17; Chase to Davis, Oct. 3, inclosing circular; Miller to Davis, Oct. 12; Davis to Chase, Oct. 22, retained copy. Also, District Judge Drummond to Davis, Oct. 16.

The views of Wayne and Field do not appear.

[141] 14 Stat. 433.

[142] 28 U.S.C., Sec. 42.

[143] Supra, p. 171.

[144] On May 14, 1866—before the Act of July 23 had injected the uncertainty about jurisdiction to sit in a Circuit Court—Chase had written to his daughter Nettie:

The President has not yet issued any proclamation to abrogate martial law & restoring the writ of Habeas Corpus & it is still uncertain whether I shall hold the Courts in Virginia & North Carolina.

An indictment has been found against Davis for treason, but it is under a statute which does not make death the penalty.

Chase Papers, L.C.

In the second sentence above, Chase had reference to a significant amendment to the law of treason. The Constitution, by Art. III, Sec. 2, makes a definition:

Treason against the United States, shall consist only in levying war against them, or in adhering to their Enemies, giving them Aid and Comfort. . . .

It is for Congress (subject to a limitation, infra, p. 780) to prescribe the punishment. By a statute of 1790, one convicted "shall suffer death." 1 Stat. 112.

But on July 17, 1862, Congress passed an Act to Suppress Insurrection; to punish Treason and Rebellion . . . . 12 Stat. 589. By its Sec. 1 the trial court was given a discretion to impose a lesser punishment: not less than five years at hard labor and a fine of not less than $10,000.

Then in Sec. 2 the statute of 1862 denounced the crime of inciting or engaging in rebellion, or giving aid or comfort thereto: the punishment would be imprisonment for not more than ten years and a fine of not more than $10,000.

Each section imposed a disability to hold office under the United States.

Justice Field had had occasion to construe the Act of 1862, in United States v. Greathouse *et al.*, Fed. Case No. 15,254 (C.D.N.D. Calif. 1863). The defendants had fitted out and set sail in the schooner *J. M. Chapman*, with intent to engage in privateering

in the Circuit Court there. While as a matter of law the District Judge (John C. Underwood[145]) could sit alone, it was unthinkable that that trial be held without the Circuit Justice. (Here it should be recalled that until 1889 there was no review by the Supreme Court of criminal cases, but that if two Judges sat in the Circuit Court they could certify a division of opinion.[146])

The popular demand that Jefferson Davis be punished brought a rash of proposed resolutions at the First Session of the 39th Congress, calling for a speedy trial. The President was at pains to keep the record clear that delay, if it occurred, was not by any fault of his. Chase's unwillingness to hold court where military control prevailed had done service in the autumn of 1865.[147] That position he maintained in the spring of 1866: he would not go upon the circuit until the President had proclaimed that the writ of habeas corpus was in full efficiency, so that he would have no apprehension of "conflict real or apparent between the [federal] judiciary & the military authorities."[148] The Chief Justice submitted to the President a draft of such a proclamation, as he assured Gerrit Smith (whose eccentric philosophy had led him to aid John Brown in 1859 and was now prompting concern for Jefferson Davis). The President did issue such a proclamation on August 20, 1866, declaring that "peace, order, tranquility and civil authority now exist in and throughout the whole of the United States . . . ."[149]

---

against the United States. The effect of the statute, he held, was to make treason, when it consisted in engaging in rebellion, punishable only by the reduced penalty provided by Section 2.

In the light of this construction of the law, one understands the concluding remark in Chase's letter of May 14, quoted above. Writing to Nettie on May 19, Chase said that Jefferson Davis had been indicted for levying war in 1864, "which if Judge Field's construction of the statute is sustained is only punishable by imprisonment not exceeding ten years or fine not over $10,000, or both; and which upon any construction can at most be punished by any amount of fine & imprisonment or by death at the discretion of the Court."

In a letter of November 20, 1867, advising District Judge Brooks in North Carolina, Chase wrote: "It may be well to remind the people that there is such a crime as treason & to give the Grand Jury the law

on the subject as modified by the Act of 1862. I incline to the opinion expressed by Judge Field in the Chapman case . . . ." Letters in Chase Papers, L.C.

[145] See infra, at p. 608.

[146] Supra, p. 86.

[147] Johnson to Chase, Oct. 2, 1865, and Chase's reply of Oct. 12, Ann. Cyc. 1865, 513–14.

[148] Letter of Mar. 20, 1866, to District Judge Brooks—of which the President had a copy—supra, pp. 146–47; letter to Nettie, May 14, 1866, supra, n. 144. The words quoted above are from a fragment of a letter which (from internal evidence) was written to Nettie in early June 1866.

[149] 14 Stat. 814, 817. Attorney General Stanbery on October 12 had advised the President that there was no impediment to the full exercise of the jurisdiction of the federal court in Virginia in Jefferson Davis' case. Doubt had arisen whether, considering the Act of July 23, the Chief Justice could sit in the Circuit Court:

But by that time the Act of July 23 had, in Chase's view, rendered him incompetent to act as Circuit Justice.

When the President's speech-making "Swing around the Circle" got out of hand, hecklers would cry "Hang Jeff Davis," and Johnson would retort, "Why don't Judge Chase . . . —why don't he try him?"[150] In the face of such a public demand, Chase's line of reasoning that he could not hold court in Virginia because Delaware had been taken from and South Carolina had been added to his circuit, must have sounded like the most paltering excuse.

Chase was reluctant ever to hold the trial, but ever anxious not to appear to be in the wrong.[151] It was in this situation, where concern for his public image might affect Chase's consideration of judicial duty, that Justice Miller gave his forthright judgment.[152]

In the end, there never was a trial.[153]

TWO CONVENTIONS

A NATIONAL UNION CONVENTION, to affirm support for the policies of President Johnson, met at Philadelphia on August 14–16, 1866. The initiative had come from Johnson Republicans, such men as Secretary Seward, Senators Doolittle and Dixon, and Orville H. Browning. They were joined by Democrats, Northern and Southern, who hoped by an appearance of moderation to win over enough Republican voters to elect a Fortieth Congress wherein, at least, vetoes by the President could not be overridden.

Chase commented on this in a letter of July 2 to his daughter Nettie, then in Europe:

> . . . We all hoped that the President would cease his war on Congress when the [Fourteenth] Amendment was proposed. But it is not so. The war continues, and grows more & more bitter. The Presidents servants have called a National Convention, and the so called

---

however that might be, "it is certain that the Executive cannot interfere . . . ." Case of Jefferson Davis, 12 Ops. Atty. Gen. 69.

Chase wrote to Smith on May 31 that "several weeks ago" he had submitted a draft. Chase Papers, L.C.

[150] McPherson, *History of Reconstruction*, at 135 and 140, sets out some of the speeches.

[151] District Judge Thomas Drummond, whose opinion Justice Davis solicited, commented that "He [Chase] undoubtedly wishes to justify himself before the Country for his refusal to try the Monroe Prisoner, but if I were you I would let him stand on his own bottom." Letter of October 16. Davis, replying briefly to Chase on October 22, expressed the view that as to those States that "*were* and *are* in the 4th Circuit & were allotted to the Chief Justice, his power still exists to hold Courts in them." Chase Papers, Hist. Soc. of Pa.

[152] Supra, p. 174.

[153] Infra, pp. 607–12.

Democrats approve and doubtless there will be a large attendance in Philadelphia in August. It will be just what patronage, with the help of hungry democrats can make it. But it will represent no ideas— nothing but platitudes and will not have the sympathies of the papers & will fail.

Just now Tennessee is the battle ground of conflict. Gov. Brownlow has called the Legislature to meet on the 4th of July. If it meets it will ratify the amendment and the Senators & Representatives of the State will be at once admitted. So the Administration is straining every nerve to prevent the Legislature from coming together, or, if it assembles, from action. Strange policy this! to profess great anxiety for the readmission of the States to Congress and yet to do everything possible to prevent them from accepting an amendment admitted to be fair & reasonable, upon the acceptance of which their Senators & Representatives to be at once admitted.[154]

On August 9, when the meeting of the National Union delegates was at hand, Justice Davis wrote to his brother-in-law on a wide range of topics. Touching on politics,

Johnson & Congress are in antagonism, & cannot of course ever again unite. The Johnson party in this State will be very weak. Many men believe that his notions of policy are right, but disapprove wholly of a union with the democracy. The distinctive feature of politics here is to do anything to prevent rebels from again getting into power. I keep aloof from politics & know very little that is going on . . . . But we will soon see whether the incongruous elements at Philadelphia will unite & what *that* body will thunder forth.[155]

The "arm-in-arm convention"—so called from the opening scene where delegations from South Carolina and Massachusetts came down the aisle in pairs—was a spectacle whose success depended upon the strictest stage management. Vallandigham of Ohio, chiefest of all Copperheads, was forced, most unwillingly, to get out of town. Southern leaders kept their delegations on their best behavior, with a total abstention from oratory. Alexander H. Stephens, Vice President of the Confederacy, found "that peculiar circumstances of an antecedent nature made his non-participation as an active delegate more advisable than otherwise."

Henry J. Raymond—Republican member of Congress, editor of the *New York Times*, and associate of Thurlow Weed and Seward in

---

[154] Chase Papers, L.C.
On July 19, 1866, Tennessee ratified the Amendment—the third State to do so. By joint resolution of July 24 it was readmitted to representation.

[155] Davis Papers, Ill. State Hist. Soc.

the conservative wing of New York Unionists—prepared the resolutions. The President was acclaimed; the seating of Southern delegations in Congress was demanded; and to the recital that slavery was abolished it was added (words first voiced by Judge William Yerger of Mississippi) that "there is neither desire nor purpose on the part of the Southern States that it should ever be re-established." The pending Fourteenth Amendment was not mentioned; Southern spokesmen would not tolerate so much as a suggestion that perhaps there should be "some enlargement" of federal power "in the respects covered" by the Amendment.[156]

When Senator Reverdy Johnson's committee presented the resolutions to the President, the latter, heedless of the harmony so painfully contrived at Philadelphia, went off into a condemnation of the "body called, or which assumes to be, the Congress of the United States, but in fact a Congress of only a part of the States." (These and other words then spoken would be quoted, in February 1868, in the tenth Article of Impeachment of the President.[157])

President Johnson, between August 28 and September 15, was on an electioneering tour to Chicago, with return via St. Louis, "mortifying his best & sincerest friends," as Chase noted.[158] "Probably no orator of ancient or modern times ever accomplished as much by a fortnight's speaking as Mr. Johnson has done," said *The Nation*.[159]

Elections on October 9 in Pennsylvania, Ohio, Indiana, and Iowa proved Republican victories; "the moral effect of their combined action upon elections in the other States is absolutely irresistible," *The Nation* rightly forecast.[160]

Justice Miller, writing to Justice Davis on October 12, commented:

> The recent elections seem to have extinguished the Johnson, Philadelphia Convention party; the members of which are rapidly taking their places like Weed among the Copperheads, or Raymond among the Republicans.
>
> I have strong hope that the November elections will take from Johnson all hope of a revolutionary Congress which he can pretend to recognise, and that however violent the political contest in future may be, it will be determined by ballots.

---

[156] "Three Days in Philadelphia," by John R. Dennett, in *The Nation*, 3:152–54, Aug. 23, 1866; Ann. Cyc. 1866, 754–57; "Extracts from the Journal of Henry J. Raymond," *Scribner's Monthly*, 20:275–80, June 1880. McKitrick traces the organization and the course of the convention, in *Andrew Johnson and Reconstruction* (Chicago: University of Chicago Press, 1960), 403–16.

[157] Supplement to Cong. Globe, 40–2, Proceedings of the Senate, at 4.

[158] Diary entry for Sept. 3. Chase Papers, Hist. Soc. of Pa.

[159] 3:241. Sept. 27.

[160] 3:311. Oct. 18.

I ardently wish, I can hard[ly] say I hope, that enough of the Southern States may adopt the constitutional amendment to make it the law of the land. In that event I should insist hereafter on the admission of all the States to Congressional representation, and to a liberal exercise of the power conferred on Congress as regards excluded rebels.[161]

On September 3, Southern Loyalists convened at Philadelphia, in response to a call that declared that Congress must now exert its powers to secure equal protection to all citizens. Among those who signed the call were Judge Underwood of Virginia and Andrew J. Hamilton and George W. Paschal of Texas.[162] Thomas J. Durant of Louisiana presided at the organization; James Speed, recently Attorney General, became permanent chairman. His address revealed to the country how wide a breach had developed within the Administration. (Postmaster General Dennison had now withdrawn; at the Interior, James Harlan of Iowa had been succeeded by Browning.)

Responding to the Southern Loyalists' invitation, Republican delegations from Northern States came to Philadelphia: Governors and ex-Governors; Senators; influential editors such as Greeley, Schurz, and Forney; Garfield, Hayes, Stanley Matthews, and Robert C. Schenck from Ohio. Also present was Chase's adherent, Richard C. Parsons, who presently became Marshal of the Supreme Court.

George W. Paschal, named above, was already preparing the suit of *Texas v. White*, pursuant to the direction of Hamilton, who had just then ceased to be Provisional Governor. The suit would be filed in the Supreme Court in February 1867. Durant soon moved to Washington, and appeared as counsel in *Texas v. White*, the *Slaughter House Cases*, and other important litigation before the Court.

Into this hive of political activity the Chief Justice descended for a sojourn of three and a half days. His concern for Southern Unionists was deep;[163] he wanted to impress his guidance upon their leaders. He recorded in his diary for September 3:

---

[161] Davis Papers, Ill. State Hist. Soc.

[162] Ann. Cyc. 1866, 756–59; James G. Blaine, *Twenty Years of Congress*, 2 vols. (Norwich, Conn.: Henry Bill Publishing Co., 1884, 1886), II, 223–28.

[163] "My heart is made to ache every day by the tales of distress suffered by the Union men, black and white, in the rebel States," he had written to his daughter Nettie on May 19, 1866. He had received callers from Virginia, including three of the grand jurors who had indicted Jefferson Davis. "All agreed that sympathy with the Union cause was now regarded as a disgrace & offence—& that Union-men were as far as possible being crushed out." Chase concluded that "treason & rebellion are at the top; Unionism and loyalty are at the bottom." Then hopefully, "But it will not always be so. The country is becoming more and more in earnest. The President must recede

This is the day of the Southern Loyalists Convention & there was an immense concourse of people at Philadelphia. Of course I could not take part, but I could not help feeling deep sympathy and interest. . . . These loyalists have come together to . . . say what further they think necessary to the real restoration of the lately rebel States & to the security of loyal men in them . . . .[164]

Even though he did not participate on the floor, Chase attended political dinners, received numerous callers, and gave advice, such as this:

Had a good talk with Gov. Hamilton & Mr Durant & recommended to them earnestly to make the Cong. Amendment the platform for the Campaign, expressing my full belief that though not all we desire or need, still it was a sufficient basis of reconstruction and a bridge over which we can pass to final & decisive victory.[165]

Chase allowed himself to become very sanguine about ratification of the Fourteenth Amendment. Writing to a daughter on October 15, he explained his reckoning:

I think it now certain that this amendment will become a part of the Constitution . . . . The whole number of States being now 36 the votes of 27 (three fourths) are required for ratification. There are 21 original free States which may be set down as sure to ratify. This leaves 6 wanting from the late slave States; of these Tennessee has ratified & Missouri will. If Maryland is carried she will make the third. Delaware will probably go the same way as Maryland & will make the fourth. It cannot be doubted I think that two more will be found, which will be enough. The rest of the unreconstructed States will doubtless follow. And this great agony will be over. Then will follow universal or at least impartial suffrage.[166]

If Chase had taken heed of the spirit that dominated the National Union Convention, his judgment would have been more sound. What if the "doubtless" and the "ifs," piled upon what seemed "sure," all failed to materialize? This was the problem that Congress had to face at its next session. And soon the Court had to play a responsible part in the unfolding conflicts.

---

from his position of antagonism to Congress, and withdraw opposition to the guarantee amendments of the Constitution which it proposes," or he would find himself more odious than Tyler or Buchanan had become. Chase Papers, L.C.

[164] Chase Papers, Hist. Soc. of Pa.
[165] Diary, Sept. 5.
[166] Letter to Nettie. Chase Papers, L.C.
Compare Justice Miller's estimate of Oct. 12, supra, pp. 179–80.

CHAPTER V

The Milligan *and* Test Oath *Cases*

THE 39TH CONGRESS met on December 3, 1866, for its short session, to run to March 4. The Republicans had received an inspiriting vindication at the autumn polls, after what had been essentially a contest between the President and the Congress. They would have, in the 40th Congress, a preponderance of nearly 3 to 1 in the House, nearly 4 to 1 in the Senate. Before the elections, an ardent contributor to *The Nation* had prayed that when the 39th Congress reassembled it would be "supported by the popular verdict, strengthened by contact with the people, comforted by their sympathy, to take a bolder and higher stand in behalf of the great cause of human rights for which it has shown so true a regard!"[1] Now that was what the election seemed to mean.

President Johnson's message to Congress ignored the recent canvass. Far from suggesting any practicable adjustment, he insisted once again that the Southern States be readmitted, just as they were. If, after that, it appeared that the Constitution needed change in any particular, let it be sought by the appointed method. The Southern States, he informed Congress, had "proceeded in good faith, to the enactment of measures for the protection and amelioration of the condition of the colored race"; evidently that was to be regarded as exclusively a concern of the States. The President called for a "return to the ancient landmarks" in order to assure "the perpetuity of our free institutions," and for a restoration of "fraternal feeling."[2]

In the usage of the period—and often in the comment of his-

---

[1] Thomas G. Shearman in *The Nation*, 3:90, 91, Aug. 2, 1866. The writer was a New York lawyer and reformer, associated with David Dudley Field in the movement for codification; he was also interested in minority groups, in free trade, and in the single tax.

[2] Cong. Globe, 39–2, App., 1–5.

torians—"fraternal feeling" carries a silent condition that the freedman be left to local law and custom.[3]

The legislatures of the Southern States (other than Tennessee) consistently were scorning the Fourteenth Amendment. If those ten States held out, the Amendment must fail for want of the requisite three-fourths of the thirty-seven States.[4] (That would be true even if every loyal State, including Kentucky, Maryland, and Delaware, were to ratify.[5]) *Stand firm!* was the word that had been passed about the South in the summer and autumn of 1866.[6] This pending Amendment "never could have been matured and passed, if all the States had been in Congress by their Representatives . . . ." It "seeks to degrade and disfranchise the ablest and purest men of the State . . . ." So ran the resolutions adopted by the men of Augusta County, Virginia.[7] Other objections were made, but those two themes were most common. "We do not believe that there is a single respectable and intelligent man in the State who is willing that our Legislature should give the consent of the old Commonwealth to the indignity and desecration" of the Fourteen Amendment, said the *Chronicle and Sentinel* of Augusta, Georgia.[8] From November 1866 to February 1867, as the legislatures met and took up the Amendment, they rejected out of hand, by virtually unanimous votes. This was treated as a matter of honor. The few men who spoke the voice of reason went unheard.[9]

---

[3] For example, in a letter of March 11, 1866, to his brother-in-law, Judge Julius Rockwell, Justice Davis wrote:

This country needs quiet and rest; fraternal relations should be cultivated, instead of hatred engendered; our industrial interests should be cherished, and our finances watched, protected & guarded. These things are not to be. The idea that the negro must have suffrage, & all other rights in the opinion of Sumner and that class of men, rides higher than all material things. And hence we are to have agitation, double distilled. And if this agitation continues until the next Presidential election, it will be fearful. . . .

Davis Papers, Ill. State Hist. Soc.

[4] Nebraska, the thirty-seventh state, was admitted to the Union on March 1, 1867.

[5] Kentucky rejected on Jan. 10, 1867; Delaware on Feb. 1; and Maryland on Mar. 23.

[6] For example, *Richmond Daily Enquirer*, June 18; *New Orleans Picayune*, June 26; *Little Rock Gazette*, July 16; *Augusta Chronicle and Sentinel*, Oct. 30.

[7] *Richmond Enquirer*, July 2, 1866.

[8] Oct. 22, 1866.

[9] A dispassionate analysis was made by Governor Pierpoint in presenting the proposed Amendment to the Virginia legislature in his message of December 3, 1866. An effort was being made, he said, "by politicians who support the President's policy, to induce the legislatures of the nonrepresented States to reject the constitutional amendment, in the hope that in another contest before the people, they may be more successful." But when one considered "the favorable auspices for the President's policy under which the late political contest was inaugurated"—with the aid of an able Cabinet, shrewd politicians, and the extensive use of federal patronage—and the decisive defeat that had ensued, "it

Thus Congress, with an impressive majority of the loyal people behind it, faced the President and the Southern States, across the issue of the Fourteenth Amendment.

Such was the tightly drawn situation when the Supreme Court began its term on December 3.

---

is not likely that another campaign can be so favorably inaugurated for the supposed interests of the southern states as the one just closed." He warned against relying upon Northern Democrats.

Congress now was supported "by far the greater portion of the property and intelligence of the country and by the independent laboring classes of the manufacturing and agricultural districts. It now embraces the flower and strength of both the old political parties in the northern states, brought together by the late war, and now held together by a common sentiment and sympathy. Young men arriving at the age of manhood, naturally fall into, and thus swell its ranks. It will become stronger for many years to come. This may be termed the *dominant* party, led by the ardent and cultivated intellects now representing it in congress. A glance at the details of the late elections will convince the most skeptical of the correctness of the views as to the composition of the two parties above taken." "As you approach the great agricultural and manufacturing districts, where education is as common as children— where people read and think—you find the great strength of the congressional party."

The practical question for the legislature, said the Governor, was whether, by rejecting the Amendment, "you are likely to place *the people* of our state in a better condition. If the views I have presented be correct, there is no hope of better terms."

It should not be regarded as dishonorable for a people "disarmed and unable to resist" to submit to the disqualifications imposed by Section 3 of the Amendment. "The disqualifications proposed, practically, do not go to the army that surrendered at Ap-

pomattox courthouse. I suppose not five per cent of the individuals who composed that army, will be affected . . . ." The disqualifications fell chiefly upon the class that "did not expose their persons in the strife to secure victory in a war they so largely contributed to inaugurate. There were few at Appomattox who had been active in bringing on the war." "For the sake of securing peace and its blessings, may it not be an act of exalted patriotism for a portion of the old and middle-aged citizens to yield gracefully to a necessity they cannot avert?" Va. Sen. J., 1866–67, 28–34.

But the Governor was an outsider; his appeal was ignored. The House of Delegates voted to reject, 74 to 1; the Senate, 27 to 0. House J., 1866–67, 108; Sen. J., 101.

In Arkansas, Governor Isaac Murphy told the legislature that "Judging from the results of the late elections, and from the decided tone of public sentiment in the States that subdued the insurrection, it is not probable that better terms will be granted. The effect of rejection on the prosperity and happiness of the people of the State, demands solemn consideration." Message of Nov. 8, 1866. Ark. Sen. J., 1866–67, 51; House J., 44. But in Arkansas as in Virginia, the ex-Confederates had taken control of the legislature; Murphy too was an outsider. On December 15 the Senate voted to reject, 24 to 1; two days later the House concurred, 68 to 2. Sen. J., 1866–67, 262; House J., 290–91.

Of the governors who were on terms of kinship with their legislatures, Robert M. Patton of Alabama was the first to urge the prudence of ratifying. Patton was a practical businessman, who was getting along very well with General Wager Swayne, in charge of the Freedmen's Bureau—

Its first business of importance would be to agree upon and announce an opinion setting forth the reasons for the answers it had made on April 3 to the questions certified in Milligan's case.[10]

A PREFACE TO *MILLIGAN*

JAMES A. GARFIELD, arguing before the Supreme Court the absence of legal authority for the trial of Milligan by military tribunal, had drawn attention "to a circumstance showing the sentiment on this subject of the House of Representatives of the Thirty-eighth Congress," and in particular to the stand taken by "one of the noblest, ablest, and most patriotic men that have honored this nation during the war,—that great man, so lately taken from us, Henry Winter Davis, of Maryland."[11]

The occasion to which Garfield referred, presented in full view, provides a background against which *Ex parte Milligan* may be viewed in perspective.

Representatives John Ganson and Francis Kernan, New York Democrats, had obtained unanimous consent to resolutions directing the Committee on Military Affairs to inquire and report on the confinement of prisoners by military authority.[12] In support of such inquiry, Representative Davis drew attention to the Act of March 3, 1863, to the effect that the President was authorized, during the rebellion, to suspend the privilege of the writ of habeas corpus: however, the Secretaries of State and War were there directed to furnish to the Judges of the Circuit and District Courts lists of all persons, citizens of loyal States, held as political prisoners; where a grand jury had adjourned without finding an indictment, such a person would be entitled to his discharge, upon taking an oath of allegiance.[13] (Where a list had not been furnished, discharge might be sought by establishing the facts upon oath.)

---

a "liberal, just and honorable" officer, in the Governor's words. House J., 1866–67, 5. At the outset, in his message of Nov. 12, 1866, Patton had expressed the view "that this amendment should not be ratified." House J., 36. On Dec. 6, however, he advised the legislature that "events of vast importance" were transpiring; there was "an unmistakable purpose on the part of those who control the National Legislature, to enforce at all hazards their own terms of restoration." "We should look our true condition full in the face." He urged the legislature to consider "the necessity of the case." Ala. Sen. J., 1866–

67, 176. Next day, however, the Senate voted to reject, 28 to 3; the House concurred, 69 to 8. Sen. J., 183; House J., 213.

[10] Supra, pp. 143–44.

[11] Samuel Klaus (ed.), *The Milligan Case* (New York: Alfred A. Knopf, 1929), 116; Burke A. Hinsdale (ed.), *The Works of James Abram Garfield*, 2 vols. (Boston: James S. Osgood and Co., 1882), I, 143, 176.

[12] Cong. Globe, 38–2, 189 (January 10, 1865), and 316 (January 18).

[13] 12 Stat. 755.

(Just at that moment the statute was invoked by counsel for Dugan and Hogan, in habeas corpus proceedings, already mentioned, in the Supreme Court for the District of Columbia.[14])

"I know of no such list as the law requires ever being furnished . . . , nor of any one discharged . . . ," said Davis.[15] S. S. Cox, Ohio Democrat, caused the statute to be read at length, and called for an inquiry "whether there has been any attempt made to carry out the law. . . ."[16] Several members told of specific instances of detention without trial. Garfield (a member of the Military Affairs Committee) said "I have this moment arrived in the Hall, after a visit of two hours to one of the prisons . . ."; what he had observed made him the more concerned that the inquiry be pursued.[17]

Davis made a speech, notable for what he conceded as well as for what he claimed. He was outspoken in support of the suspension of the privilege of habeas corpus by the Act of March 3, 1863: but that statute provided a remedy where detention was unjustifiably prolonged. He was prepared to accord the President an even wider discretion, to meet cases where "persons of great influence" were "supposed to entertain sinister designs . . . against the Government," mentioning Vallandigham; he was "ready here to-day to modify" the statute of 1863; but "while it is the law let it be obeyed."[18]

The session was near its end, and no further action was taken by the House.

On March 2, just before the session (and Davis' service in Congress) would come to an end, he moved to amend the Miscellaneous Appropriation Bill by adding this section:

> That no person shall be tried by court-martial, or military commission, in any State or Territory where the courts of the United States are open, except persons actually mustered, or commissioned, or appointed in the military or naval service of the United States, or rebel enemies charged with being spies . . . .[19]

His purpose was to reassert the supremacy of the law in a matter where, "amid the general acclaim of the people," it had increasingly been ignored. His amendment was drawn "not to cast imputation upon any administration or any officer," but to recognize and correct "the

---

[14] Supra, pp. 55–57.
[15] Cong. Globe, 38–2, 318. Jan. 18, 1865.
[16] Ibid., 318–19.
[17] Ibid., 320.
[18] Ibid., 318.
[19] Cong. Globe, 38–2, 1323. As introduced, it went on to declare that all proceedings theretofore had contrary to this provision were vacated, and that all persons affected must be discharged or delivered to the civil authorities for trial. Later he carried a motion to strike out this concluding provision. P. 1332.

error which the people as well as the Government have in common committed against the foundation of their own safety . . . ."[20]

In the outcome, after a pertinent debate, the House accepted Davis' amendment by vote of 75 to 64; and so the bill went to the Senate, on the evening of March 2.[21] There, following a spirited discussion that ran into the early hours of March 4, a motion to strike Davis' section was carried by 20 votes to 14.[22] Conference showed an inability at that late moment to reach agreement, and so the entire bill failed.[23]

Davis performed brilliantly in maintaining his position that while the President might "*hold* [suspects] under the precautionary discretion conferred by law," he must "not try, not convict . . ." by military court.

Dawes of Massachusetts, in accord with Davis' motion, drew attention to the breadth to which Congress had extended the jurisdiction of naval courts-martial over civilians performing functions related to the Navy. He told of the case of the Smith brothers, businessmen of Boston, who had recently been tried by naval court-martial on a charge of defrauding the Government: he apprehended conviction and a heavy sentence. Now, Dawes said, he was protesting against things that had been done under legislation he himself had supported.[24] (The allegations against the Smith brothers, and the mode of trial, had for months been a matter of controversy between the Massachusetts delegation in Congress and the Secretary of the Navy; it had, inevitably, been carried to the President. On March 18, 1865, a fortnight after Dawes' speech, the President set aside the sentence with a bit of Lincolnian reasoning: if with a million dollar contract they had intended to defraud, surely their gain would have been much greater than was reflected by the record.[25]

---

[20] Ibid., 1324.
[21] Ibid., 1330, 1332.
[22] Ibid., 1380.
[23] Ibid., 1421–23.
[24] Ibid., 1324–25.
[25] *Collected Works of Abraham Lincoln*, Roy P. Basler, ed., (New Brunswick, N.J.: Rutgers University Press, 1953), VII, 522–23; VIII, 240, 364; *Diary of Gideon Welles*, 3 vols. (Boston and New York: Houghton Mifflin Co., 1911), II, 7, 53–57, 60, 90, 124, 224–25, 231, 238, 260–64, 266, 334, 359; Carl Sandburg, *Abraham Lincoln: The War Years* (New York: Harcourt Brace and Co., 1939), III, 460–62; IV, 124–27. Sandburg relates how Sumner on March 17, 1865, insisted that Lincoln "ought not to sleep on the case." Lincoln heard him from 11 P.M. to 12:20 A.M., and told Sumner to return at 9 A.M.—when Lincoln read the order stated above, and treated Sumner to a reading from the humor of Petroleum V. Nasby. Sandburg observes that the Assistant Secretary, in his eagerness to protect the Navy from fraudulent contractors, had employed a detective whom Welles distrusted as "a cormorant, searching papers, utterly reckless." After the President had dismissed the case, Welles pointed out to Sumner incriminating matters unknown to Sumner. Whatever the guilt of the Smith

George H. Pendleton of Ohio, Democrat, wanted to know "how men who are confined under sentence of military commissions or courts-martial are to obtain their constitutional rights," having regard to the habeas corpus statute of 1863. His colleague Schenck answered, "By application to the courts." He conceded that, in a situation where the President had exercised his power to suspend the privilege, as he had in "the matter [that] came before a court in this city a short time since" (meaning Hogan and Dugan),[26] the remedy would not be available.[27]

George H. Yeaman, Unionist of Kentucky, wanted to insert, after "spies" in Davis' section, "or enemies charged with a violation of the laws of war." His concern was to preserve the military jurisdiction over unlawful combatants—"these vagabonds, cut-throats, and robbers, who have to-day become the greatest scourge to the States of Missouri, Tennessee, and Kentucky." He explained that "in three fourths of Kentucky we have no courts of justice, because from the acts of these men we cannot hold them": courthouses had been burned, officers of the courts could not attend, jurors and witnesses could not be summoned.[28] Davis' reply was that "If there is room to hold a military court there is room to hold a civil court."

In the Senate, Lane of Indiana moved to strike the section, and went into a somewhat excited defense of the resort to a military tribunal to try those implicated in the "treasonable organization" that recently sought "to revolutionize the north-western States."[29] (Milligan and co-defendants had been tried the previous autumn; their application to the Circuit Court for writs of habeas corpus had not yet been made.)

Senator Reverdy Johnson, in reply, said that military commissions had disregarded "all the safeguards and rules of evidence, adopted after the experience of centuries . . . ." Hundreds had been held without trial, in violation of the provision in the Act of March 3, 1863. "That law has been utterly disregarded."[30]

Senator Trumbull said that "just such acts as this section seeks to avoid" had weakened the Government in the North. "If you would be strong, be strong under the banner of the law and the Constitution." On the failure to report to the federal courts those who were detained in

---

brothers, and whatever the scope of the statutory jurisdiction granted to naval courts-martial, surely this was a case that should have been handled by indictment and trial in the federal court.

26 Supra, pp. 55–57.
27 Cong. Globe, 38–2, 1325.
28 Ibid., 1325, 1327. Yeaman was a

man of high character, and certainly no Radical. Having failed of reelection, he was appointed Minister to Denmark by Johnson; subsequently he taught constitutional law in Columbia College.

29 Ibid., 1369–71.
30 Ibid., 1370–71, 1372.

prison, he exculpated the Secretary of War: Stanton had promptly charged the Judge Advocate General to see that the Act of March 3, 1863, was observed. He quoted the Secretary to the effect "that these arrests . . . by subordinate officers had given him more pain than almost anything else that had occurred during the war . . . ."

But while concurring in Davis' purpose, Trumbull reiterated his concern that the language be more guarded. It should recognize that persons "employed" in the service (such as workers in arsenals, and teamsters), as well as those "enlisted," were subject to military jurisdiction. The Senate accepted this amendment. Trumbull said that the section "should be so framed as not to impair the efficiency of the Government in carrying on this war . . ."; it should permit military trial of "offenders connected with the military service."[31] Trumbull, who as chairman of the Judiciary Committee felt a special responsibility, was evidently uneasy about tacking this section to an appropriations bill, without reference to the appropriate committees and with no adequate examination of what the effect might be.[32]

Senator Hendricks of Indiana made an earnest reply to the somewhat wild discourse of his colleague Lane. The acts for which certain citizens of Indiana had been tried by a military commission were offenses punishable in the federal court under the statute to suppress treason and insurrection, of July 17, 1862:[33] the accused should have had a civil trial. The statute of March 3, 1863, while authorizing the President to suspend the privilege of the writ, afforded "a substitute" by its provisions whereby a prisoner could be brought before a Judge and, upon a proper showing, have his discharge. He quoted at length. This was a law "which will not allow the President to put any man on his trial before a military court unless he be properly answerable before such a court." "The trouble is not in the law. Senators, the law is plain." Now Congress should "go further than that" by making the specific prohibition of military trials contained in the Davis amendment.[34]

Stewart of Nevada resented the proposal as calling for "a vote of condemnation upon the Administration," an admission "that our enemies were right and we were wrong." By the recent elections the

---

[31] Ibid., 1373.

[32] Davis' measure permitted the military trial of enemies only if "charged with being spies." "A spy is a person who secretly, in disguise or under false pretense, seeks information with the intent of communicating it to the enemy." Art. 88, Instructions for the Government of the Armies of the United States in the Field (1863). One whose intent was, rather, to liberate prisoners, or to damage life or property, would not be "a spy," and by Davis' provision would have been beyond the military jurisdiction. Yeaman pointed to a class of unlawful belligerents who would have been excluded. Prisoners of war who rose against their guards would not have been triable.

[33] 12 Stat. 589. Supra, p. 175, n. 144.

[34] Cong. Globe, 38–2, 1374–75.

people had affirmed their belief "that the Constitution, when fairly construed, does enable this Government to defend itself against its enemies."[35] Howard of Michigan said, "away with this mawkish, affected sensibility in regard to courts-martial. If there is any fault connected with them, . . . it is that they have not been used with sufficient vigor and vigilance."[36] Conness of California had "little respect for these croakings and these pretentious exhibitions of regard for constitutional law."[37]

Trumbull reprehended these "extraordinary remarks." The proposition before the Senate was "that hereafter in the loyal States, where the courts are open, no person not in some way connected with the military service shall be tried by court-martial or military commission. . . . It is prospective in its operation." He thought that there had been "more obstacles thrown in the way of an efficient prosecution of this war, by the attempt to do things that need not have been done, and by giving an advantage to these secret sympathizers, than in any other way." He was carried on to a fervid affirmation "that I do care for the Constitution and for law and for liberty, and that I am for preserving them all, and the country and the Union also, for it is the Constitution and liberty that make the Union worth preserving."[38]

Lane's motion to strike was carried by the vote of 20 (Republicans) to 14 nay votes (6 of which were cast by Republicans).[39]

When the Miscellaneous Appropriation Bill went to a conference committee, the result, as reported by Henry Winter Davis, was that the conferees from the upper chamber stated "that while a majority of the Senate concurred in the principle involved," the section would not be accepted as an addition to the appropriation bill, nor "in the present state of feeling and temper" could it be passed as a separate bill. Whereupon a majority of the House conferees said that their sense of duty "would not allow them to provide for any pecuniary appropriations at the expense of so grave a reflection upon the fundamental principles of the Government."[40]

Accordingly the affected activities of the Government had to be "carried on on faith" until a new Congress made the appropriations.[41]

The incident gives rise to various reflections, and may be used to support different conclusions. Certainly it was not sound practice for a member, some hours before the end of the Congress, to impose an important provision as a rider on an appropriation bill—to say that "I am not willing to change one word"[42]—and let the appropriation fail if

---

35 Ibid., 1372.
36 Ibid., 1373–74.
37 Ibid., 1374.
38 Ibid., 1379–80.

39 Ibid., 1380.
40 Ibid., 1421.
41 Cong. Globe, 39–1, 856.
42 Cong. Globe, 38–2, 1327.

that provision was not accepted. That was not a satisfactory way to legislate, even in the name of "the fundamental principles of the Government."

The burden of rational discussion was that there were serious abuses to correct; but evidently fault lay in no single quarter. Davis said that "the people as well as the Government" had fallen into error. Dawes' complaint went to what the Navy had done in pursuance of statutory authority. Speaker after speaker dwelt upon failure to comply with the statute of 1863: but surely the members of Congress had not suddenly discovered what had been going on at the Old Capitol Prison in plain view nearby on First Street. Nor could Stanton escape responsibility by an assignment to the Judge Advocate General. Congress showed concern over the ramified problem, even though the Houses failed at the moment to agree on Henry Winter Davis' prescription.[43]

Samuel S. Cox, Ohio Democrat who had joined in the debate, later wrote that Davis' audacious action was "worthy of the parliamentary heroism in the time of the Stuarts and their prerogative. . . . Amidst the wildest applause, the three years of arbitrary arrogance and flagrant violation of our Magna Charta was buried beneath the reprobation and scorn of the American House of Representatives." It was "worthy of the great liberators of mankind . . . ."[44] And yet only a few weeks earlier in the session, Representative Cox had opposed the Amendment to abolish slavery as "dangerous and inexpedient"—"the culmination of this suicidal policy" that had carried on the war.[45]

Throughout the troubled years to follow one will constantly observe the semblance of devotion to civil liberty and, on the obverse side of the coin, a determination to withhold the blessings of liberty from others.

---

[43] A note apropos of Davis' views that the power of the Executive had increased and ought to be diminished. Davis, as chairman of the Committee on Foreign Affairs, had carried through the House in April 1864 a resolution declaring that the policy of the United States was opposed to a monarchical government in Mexico. The President, however, handled the delicate matter of the French occupation in his own way. At the Second Session, Davis reported a resolution to the effect that Congress has a constitutional right to an authoritative voice in declaring and prescribing the foreign policy of the United States. When the House defeated the proposal, he asked to be excused from further service on the committee. This was denied. Cong. Globe, 38–1, 2475; 38–2, 48–53.

When at the Second Session the House declined to enact a revised version of the Wade-Davis measure on Reconstruction which Lincoln had pocket-vetoed after the First Session, Davis lamented that the "Government of law" had lately become "a Government of personal will." Cong. Globe, 38–2, 970.

[44] *Three Decades of Federal Legislation*, (Providence, R.I.: J. A. & R. A. Reid, 1886), 234.

[45] Cong. Globe, 38–2, 238–42. Jan. 12, 1865.

MILLIGAN'S CASE

DURING THE SUMMER OF 1866, Justice Davis had been writing his opinion to give the Court's reasons for its order of April 3.[46] Pursuant to that order, Milligan had been liberated on April 10.[47]

On Monday, December 14—a fortnight after the Justices had convened, and the first day when decisions on the merits were announced —Justice Davis delivered the opinion of the Court. The Chief Justice read a concurring opinion in which he was joined by Wayne, Swayne, and Miller.

Now to view the case in its entirety, we go back to the beginning.

Lambdin P. Milligan was a Peace Democrat: he would concede Confederate independence and stop the fighting. Among the most outspoken of that wing of the party were Congressmen Alexander Long of Cincinnati—who for a speech advocating recognition of the independence of the Confederacy was declared to be "an unworthy member of the House"[48]—and Clement L. Vallandigham of Dayton, Ohio, who was defeated for reelection in 1862.[49]

---

[46] Supra, pp. 143–44.

[47] Milligan v. Hovey, Fed. Case No. 9605 (C.C.D. Ind. 1871).

[48] Cong. Globe, 38–1, 1634, Apr. 14, 1864. He failed of reelection. In 1868, Long and Chief Justice Chase were in close communion in seeking the latter's nomination for President by the National Democratic Convention. Infra, pp. 525–57.

[49] By reason of the relationship he, and the litigation in which he had been involved, bear to matters discussed in the present book, a full statement is in order.

Vallandigham (1820–71) was self-righteous and fanatical in his principles, which included opposition to fanatical Abolitionists. He had supported the war with Mexico, but would not vote one dollar or shed one drop of blood for the war to preserve the Union. He was convinced that in 1859 John Brown was supported by a widespread conspiracy— and four years later was himself in a like predicament. To advance his principles he courted martyrdom.

General Burnside (who after his disaster at Fredericksburg had in March 1863 been sent to the Department of the Ohio), on April 13, 1863, issued his G.O. No. 38: ". . . The habit of declaring sympathies for the enemy will not be allowed in this department . . . ." Vallandigham staged a parade and rally at Mount Vernon, Ohio, on May 1, where in the course of a prepared speech he spat and stamped upon a copy of G.O. No. 38; he declared that propositions to restore the Union had been rejected by "Lincoln and his minions" prior to Fredericksburg; that it was a war to crush liberty and erect despotism, to free the blacks and enslave the whites; that he firmly believed that the men in power were attempting to establish a despotism more oppressive than had ever been known before.

(S. S. Cox, mentioned above at p. 191, spoke from the same platform, and later asserted that *his* words were erroneously attributed to Vallandigham. *Three Decades of Federal Legislation*, 83, 197.)

Burnside caused Vallandigham to be seized at his home at night, and brought before a military commission. On May 16 he was sentenced to be imprisoned for the duration

V: *The* Milligan *and* Test Oath *Cases*

In Indiana, Illinois, and neighboring States, stubborn, dogmatic men of that persuasion formed a secret society which was, in effect, a military branch of the Peace Democrats. In 1863 they styled themselves the Order of American Knights, and after February 22, 1864, the Sons

of the war. *The Trial of Hon. Clement L. Vallandigham . . . and the Proceedings Under his Application for a Writ of Habeas Corpus . . .* (272 pages) was published at Cincinnati in 1863. The president of the commission was Brigadier General Robert B. Potter, a member of the New York bar. See D.A.B. One of the members was Major John Mason Brown of Kentucky: a Yale classmate of Justices David J. Brewer and Henry B. Brown, he was prominently mentioned for the place on the Court to which the former was appointed, as well as for the Attorney Generalship in Harrison's Cabinet. Another was Major Richard M. Corwine, a Cincinnati lawyer, mentioned in chapter 2, note 2. He was well known to Lincoln. *Collected Works*, IV, 36, 47–48; VIII: 323.

Burnside did all this without consulting his superiors in Washington to learn whether the Administration approved of this move to stifle its most conspicuous critic.

Habeas corpus was promptly sought in the federal Circuit Court at Cincinnati, held by Judge H. H. Leavitt, already identified. Supra, p. 19.

The President, embarrassed, talked with members of his Cabinet. Stanton urged the suspension of the writ of habeas corpus in this particular case. Seward and Chase thought otherwise. Lincoln sent a note to Stanton on May 13:

Chase thinks the case is not before Judge Swaine [Swayne], that it is before Judge Levett [sic], that the writ will probably not issue, whichever the application may be made before; and that, in no event, will Swaine commit an imprudence. His chief reason for thinking the writ will not issue, is that he has seen in a newspaper that Judge Levett stated that Judge Swaine & he refused a similar application last year.

Collected Works, VI, 215.

After a full hearing, Judge Leavitt denied the writ; he was following the action of Swayne, J., and himself in the similar case of Bethuel Rupert, unreported, at the October term 1862. *Ex parte* Vallandigham, Fed. Case No. 16,816, May 16, 1863. On Swayne's view in the Rupert case, see infra, ch. 12, n. 12.

As the best means out of the difficulty, Lincoln caused an order to be sent to Burnside on May 19: that Vallandigham be sent "beyond our military lines."

With Vallandigham no longer in custody, there was no basis for seeking review *by habeas corpus* in the Supreme Court.

Counsel took a new approach: on January 14, 1864, George E. Pugh filed an original proceeding in the Supreme Court, a petition for a *writ of certiorari* directed to the Judge Advocate General of the Army, directing him to send up a copy of the record of the military commission. This motion was argued on January 22; on February 15 the writ was denied for want of jurisdiction, per Wayne, J. The Court refrained from any dictum on the merits of the case. *Ex parte* Vallandigham, 1 Wall. 243.

The question of jurisdiction—a technical matter—is explained infra, ch. 10, n. 202. The ruling is confirmed by *In re* Vidal, 179 U.S. 126 (1900), where on similar facts the writ was denied, per Chief Justice Fuller (who himself, as a Democratic politician in Illinois, had in 1863 supported a condemnation of "the flagrant and monstrous usurpations" of the Lincoln Administration, and Burnside's suppression of the *Chicago Times*. Willard L. King, *Melville Weston Fuller* (New York: Macmillan Co., 1950), 47–60.

On the occasion of the Vallandigham affair, as Carl Sandburg writes, "A duplex clamor went into the

of Liberty. Vallandigham was named Supreme Commander.[50] Milligan was "major general" of the Northeastern Division of Indiana; William A. Bowles had command of members in the Southeastern.[51]

Leaders from Indiana, Illinois, Kentucky, and Missouri, meeting as the Council of the Order in Chicago in July 1864, planned "to

President's ears, the Peace Democrats in one key and tempo, the antislavery radicals in another." *Abraham Lincoln: The War Years*, II, 172. He sets the context at 150–77. Lincoln responded to the Peace Democrats by two notable letters: that to Erastus Corning and others at Albany, New York, on June 12, and that to Matthew Birchard and his committee from the Ohio Democratic State Convention on June 29, 1863. *Collected Works*, VI, 260, 300.

The Ohio Democrats on June 11 made Vallandigham their candidate for Governor, and Pugh, his counsel, for Lieutenant Governor. The election in October yielded (with the soldiers' votes) about 288,000 for Brough, Unionist, to 187,000 for Vallandigham. Ann. Cyc. 1863, 730–731.

Vallandigham had gone through the Confederacy to Windsor, Ontario (opposite Detroit).

On June 15, 1864, he appeared at a Democratic convention at Hamilton, Ohio. The Administration did not touch him. He secured a plank in the national platform of 1864 declaring that the war had been "four years of failure" and calling for "immediate efforts . . . for a cessation of hostilities with a view to an ultimate convention of all the States . . . ." McClellan, accepting the nomination for President, declared that "the Union must be preserved at all hazards."

[50] While sojourning in Canada he was cooperating with Jacob Thompson, agent of the Confederacy. Wood Gray, *The Hidden Civil War. The Story of the Copperheads* (New York: Viking Press, Compass Books, 1964), 166–69, 179, 187–88. First published in 1942 and reprinted on the occasion of the centennial of the Civil War, this is an impressive work of scholarship.

Frank L. Klement's *The Copperheads in the Middle West* (Chicago: University of Chicago Press, 1960), takes as its thesis that "the midwestern Copperheads were conservatives who opposed changes which the war was bringing to America"—that they have falsely been "viewed as men whose hearts were black"; much that has been accepted is branded as "mythology."

The judicious account of Kenneth M. Stampp in "The Milligan Case and the Election of 1864 in Indiana," *Miss. Valley Hist. Rev.*, 31:41–58 (1944), and in *Indiana Politics during the Civil War* (Indianapolis: Indiana Historical Bureau, 1949), views the conspiracy as a fantastic enterprise whose chief significance was in Indiana politics—a boon exploited by Governor Morton and an embarrassment to the loyal leadership of the Democratic party.

George Fort Milton's *Abraham Lincoln and the Fifth Column* (New York: Vanguard Press, 1942) is also to be noted.

James D. Horan's *Confederate Agent: A Discovery in History* (New York: Crown Publishers, 1954) is a lively account of the activities of young Captain Thomas H. Hines, CSA, in Canada, in aid of a Copperhead revolution in Illinois, Indiana, and Ohio in 1864. A collaborator there was Joshua F. Bullitt, Chief Justice of the Court of Appeals of Kentucky, a commander in the Sons of Liberty who had escaped from federal arrest. For a year after Appomattox, at Toronto, Hines read law under Bullitt's instruction. Twenty years later he too became a Justice and Chief Justice of the Court of Appeals.

[51] Testimony of Thomas Heffren, a lawyer of Salem, who was "Deputy Grand Commander" for Indiana. Proceedings of the Military Commis-

release the [Confederate] prisoners on Johnson's Island [in Sandusky Bay, of Lake Erie]; at Camp Chase, near Columbus, Ohio; at Camp Morton [at Indianapolis], and also at Camp Douglas [south of Chicago], and that the prisoners at Camp Douglas, after their release, were to go over and release those at Rock Island [in the Mississippi River]. At the same time there was to be an uprising at Louisville, at which the Government stores, etc., were to be seized."[52]

Governor Oliver P. Morton,[53] and Brigadier General Henry B. Carrington, in command of the District of Indiana, kept informed of the movement, in particular through a detective who joined the order and became Grand Secretary for Kentucky. In October 1864 charges were brought against Milligan, Bowles, and others. By the account of Morton's biographer,

> General Carrington, who had collected the evidence against the accused, was in favor of trying them in one of the Federal courts, but Secretary Stanton and Governor Morton determined that more drastic measures were required.[54]

---

sion, in appendix to *The Milligan Case*, edited by Samuel Klaus, 251, at 330, 333, 344–47. Originally Heffren was a co-defendant. During the trial, proceedings against him were withdrawn and he was released. P. 330.

[52] Testimony of Joseph J. Bingham before the military commission. Klaus (ed.), *The Milligan Case*, 288, 293, stating what Harrison H. Dodd, Grand Commander for Indiana, had told him, about Aug. 2 or 3, 1864. Bingham was editor of the *Indiana State Sentinel* of Indianapolis, and chairman of the Democratic State Central Committee. He testified: "I joined an order which was called the American Knights, in the latter part of October or the beginning of November, 1863"; however, "I did not consider myself a member of the organization since [February 16, 1864], and have not been a member, though my having been a member in the order gives me the confidence of the members, and I have learned many things that I otherwise should not have known." Pp. 288, 291.

On cross-examination Bingham said that he had heard indirectly that the proposal for revolution had been voted down by the Council at Chicago. P. 298.

[53] (1823–1877). Professor William B. Hesseltine concluded that he "had zeal and ingenuity and administrative skill, but his emotions were unstable, and he was frequently filled with unwarranted terror." *Lincoln and the War Governors* (New York: Alfred A. Knopf, 1948), 391.

[54] William D. Foulke, *Life of Oliver P. Morton*, 2 vols. (Indianapolis: Bowen-Merrill Co., 1899), I, 419.

Looking for verification, I found in the Archives at the Indiana State Library a book made up of unnumbered typewritten pages, apparently compiled, long after the event, by Carrington.

About the middle of the book, appears the following:

Governor Morton urged the immediate arrest of citizens named in my Official Report to him, as members of said Sons of Liberty, and their trial by a Military Commission.

Having been forbidden by the Department Commander, to make such arrests, except [upon requisition of higher authority], and believing that the Federal Courts, then open, backed by Military Authority could more wisely adjudicate the cases, and

This determination was made upon political grounds. Unlike the military trial of Vallandigham, initiated by General Burnside's own bad judgment, that of Milligan was decided on by two civil organizers of victory. They made a capital mistake. Within eight months, Morton would be beseeching Johnson not to allow the sentences of the commission to be executed.[55]

The charges were (1) conspiracy against the Government, (2) affording aid to rebels, (3) inciting insurrection, (4) disloyal practices, and (5) violation of the laws of war.[56] The acts specified constituted offenses denounced in the statutes and punishable in the federal courts.

Proceedings before the military commission at Indianapolis ran from September to December 1864, concurrently, be it noted, with the electoral campaign.[57] Milligan, Bowles, and one Horsey were found guilty on all charges and sentenced to be hanged.

Joseph E. McDonald (1819–91) of Indianapolis was engaged to save the condemned men. Formerly a Congressman and the State's Attorney General, he was a loyal Democrat and a highly respected lawyer. He had defeated Milligan to win his party's nomination for Governor in 1864;[58] in joint debates with Morton each candidate had appealed to his followers to avoid turbulence. Now in his clients' behalf

---

with less political excitement, I declined to make such arrests without Orders from the War Department, which I failed to receive, upon submission of the entire subject matter.

Carrington's account goes on to relate that by arrangement between Secretary Stanton and Morton, in late August, 1864, General Alvin P. Hovey, who strongly sustained the jurisdiction of a military commission, was placed in command of the District of Indiana.

Carrington (1824–1912) had been educated at Yale College and law school. At the Ohio bar he practiced with William Dennison, presently Governor. As Adjutant General under Governors Chase and Dennison, his effective organization made it possible to send militia to save West Virginia for the Union, before volunteers could be raised. For this service, Carrington was commissioned colonel in May 1861; later he was promoted to brigadier general. Professor Wood Gray finds that he lacked the qualifications for interpret-

ing the reports of informers; that he sought to gain attention, and to provide support for the Republican party. *The Hidden Civil War*, 134.

Carrington's letter to Chase on the latter's appointment as Chief Justice has been quoted. Supra, pp. 24–25.

[55] Infra, pp. 197–99.

[56] Klaus (ed.), *The Milligan Case*, pp. 67–73.

[57] The trial of Harrison H. Dodd, Grand Commander for Indiana, began in September, and ended abortively when he escaped—from what looks like intentionally negligent custody. The trial of Milligan, Bowles *et al.* went from October 21 to December 6.

In the State election on October 11, Morton received 152,084 votes and his opponent, Joseph E. McDonald, 131,210.

At the Presidential election on November 8, Lincoln received 150,422 and McClellan 130,233.

[58] Receiving 1,097 votes in the State convention to 167 for Milligan. Foulke, *Life of Morton*, I, 301.

McDonald called upon President Lincoln, who went over the record of trial, found certain errors because of which it should be sent back for correction, and hoped that by the time the papers came back to him there would be "such a jubilee over yonder" in Virginia that "we shall none of us want any more killing done"; "I'll keep them in prison awhile to keep them from killing the Government."[59]

But then Lincoln was assassinated, and Johnson's earliest mood was to "make treason odious." He approved the sentences; an order of May 2, 1865, directed that Milligan, Bowles, and Horsey be executed on Friday, May 19.

(On May 1, the President, pressed by Stanton and supported by the opinion of Attorney General Speed, had directed that the persons implicated in the murder of President Lincoln be tried by military commission. The trial lasted from May 13 to June 29. Four were sentenced to death, and executed on July 7. Dr. Samuel A. Mudd and three others were sentenced to imprisonment. They will continue to be of interest, when applications for habeas corpus are made, in December 1866, and again in the autumn of 1868.[60]

(Speed subsequently filed an opinion,[61] beginning with the proposition that the Constitution recognizes the law of nations, which includes the laws of war. [So far, accord: *Ex parte Quirin*, 317 U.S. 1 (1942).] Indeed, so the opinion affirmed, "the laws of war constitute the greater part of the law of nations." By the laws of war, an army deals with secret as well as open enemies. Then, the big jump in the argument, those who in time of war assassinate the President in a city defended by fortifications and soldiers are to be assimilated to bushwackers. Booth's cry, "Sic semper tyrannis," was said to show that he acted as a public foe. Accordingly, those accused "not only can, but ought to be, tried before a military tribunal.")

On May 10, 1865, counsel for Milligan et al. appeared in the Circuit Court at Indianapolis, held by Justice Davis and District Judge David McDonald, seeking writs of habeas corpus.

Frantic efforts were now made to move the President to clemency. Governor Morton sent the Speaker of the Indiana House of Representatives to Washington, bearing an open letter which concluded, "I protest against these executions."[62]

Peculiar interest attaches to a letter, doubtless written by Justice Davis, which he and Judge McDonald sent on May 11 to the President:

---

[59] McDonald's and Justice Davis' accounts, in William H. Herndon and Jesse W. Weik, *Herndon's Lincoln*, 3 vols. (Chicago: Belford, Clarke and Co., 1889), ch. 19.

[60] Infra, pp. 237–39, 488.
[61] 11 Ops. Atty. Gen. 297, dated "July 1865."
[62] Foulke, *Life of Morton*, I, 428–31.

We learn that, under a conviction by a Military Commission in this city last autumn, William A. Bowles, Lambdin P. Milligan, and Stephen Horsey are to be executed here on the 19th instant.

We beg leave to present you a few suggestions touching our opinion of the wisdom and policy of the course adopted in this matter.

We do not call in question the guilt of these men. We are satisfied that their trial had a most salutary effect on the public mind by developing and defeating a most dangerous and wicked conspiracy against our government. But, as the object of that trial has been fully attained, and as the whole aspect of things has since so entirely changed, we respectfully suggest that it may well be doubted whether it would be a safe and wise policy now to execute this sentence.

The Court which pronounced the sentence is a new tribunal unknown to the Common Law. There is no denying the fact that many learned lawyers doubt its jurisdiction over citizens unconnected with the military, as these men were. We express no opinion on this question. It is due, however, to ourselves to say that we have given it sufficient consideration to be satisfied that it is not clear of difficulty. No citizen yet tried by a military tribunal has, we believe, been executed. Would it not be wiser to defer the execution of these men until the Supreme Court of the United States have passed on the question of the jurisdiction of the court that tried them?

If these men are executed now, and the Federal Judiciary should hereafter deny the jurisdiction under which they were tried, the government would be justly chargeable with lawless oppression.

We understand that the parties convicted intend to institute proceedings by which the question of jurisdiction can be tested in the Supreme Court of the United States, if the execution be delayed long enough for a hearing there. We would most respectfully but earnestly urge the wisdom and justice of giving them time to be heard before that tribunal. In this case, we cannot see how a few months delay can be prejudicial to the cause of public justice. But we can very well see that if these men are executed now, and if hereafter the authority of the Military tribunal, on whose sentence the execution is had, should be judicially denied, a stain on the national character would be the consequence.

This, too, is a mode of conviction so unusual and extraordinary among our people, that, no doubt, many of our good citizens would deem it harsh and revolting; whereas, if it had been in the usual course of criminal justice in our civil courts, we do not doubt that the people would very generally acquiesce. And the same would be true if the execution were delayed till the Supreme Court has adjudged that the sentence ought to be executed.

We beg leave also most respectfully to state that, aside from the legal question, which we press most earnestly, we doubt the policy of the proposed execution. We fear its effect upon the public mind in Indiana. By many, these men will be regarded as political martyrs. Every thing now, in this State, is quiet and peaceable.

We ardently pray for the success of your administration, and for the restoration of the authority of the government. And, actuated by a sincere desire that no error may be committed on the part of the United States which might hereafter be regretted, we have felt it our duty as your friends, as judicial officers, and as citizens, in all good faith and good will to lay the foregoing suggestions before you.[63]

It will be seen that, for the attainment of their objective, there was need for special care in drafting, inasmuch as the President had on May 1 committed himself to the trial, before such an extraordinary tribunal, of persons unconnected with the military service, charged with murder, in a place where the civil courts were freely in operation.

On May 16, Johnson commuted Horsey's sentence to life imprisonment, and respited Milligan and Bowles to June 1. On May 30 Secretary Stanton telegraphed that the President had commuted all sentences to life imprisonment at hard labor; the penitentiary at Columbus, Ohio, was designated as the place of imprisonment. On June 3 that order was executed.

The Circuit Court had proceeded forthwith on the petition of May 10, asking that the writ issue;[64] formally there was no return by a respondent. Hence it was later argued that there had been no opportunity to present such reasons as the Government might give to justify the detention. Actually, however, as the record showed, the United States District Attorney participated actively and had the opportunity to be heard on all the issues.[65]

On the day next after the close of the hearing, Justice Davis and Judge McDonald certified that they differed in opinion and thereby, as

---

[63] National Archives. Papers from the Office of the Judge Advocate General: Indiana Treason Trials.

[64] The subsequent commutation does not enter into the case: there was no occasion to consider that after June 3, 1865, the detention was at a place *outside* the territorial jurisdiction of the Circuit Court for Indiana. Compare the problems in *Ex parte* Endo, 323 U.S. 283 (1944), and Ahrens v. Clark, 335 U.S. 188 (1948).

[65] See *Ex parte* Endo, 323 U.S. 283, 305 (1944), where the Court said: "The fact that no respondent was ever served with process or appeared in the proceedings is not important. The United States resists the issuance of a writ. A cause exists in that state of the proceedings and an appeal lies from denial of a writ without the appearance of a respondent. *Ex parte* Milligan, 4 Wall. at 112; *Ex parte* Quirin, 317 U.S. 1, 24."

In *Ex parte* Quirin the Court recognized the practice of granting a rule to show cause why the writ should not be issued—as sanctioned in Walker v. Johnston, 312 U.S. 275, 284 (1941). That practice is now specifically authorized by 28 U.S.C. sec. 2243 (1948).

permitted by the statute of 1802,[66] put their questions before the Supreme Court. They were these:

> 1st. On the facts stated in said petition and exhibits, ought the writ of habeas corpus to be issued?
> 2nd. . . . ought . . . Milligan to be discharged . . . ?
> 3d. Whether . . . the military commission . . . had jurisdiction legally to try and sentence Milligan . . . ?[67]

Chronology is to be noted, from the Supreme Court's Docket and Minutes. The transcript of the *Milligan* record was filed on December 27, 1865.[68] On February 5, 1866, the Court, acting on a motion by Jeremiah S. Black, set the first Monday in March (the fifth) for argument; that is, it would take up the case at once, out of turn. On March 2, Attorney General Speed moved to dismiss for want of jurisdiction; the Court directed that that matter be heard along with the argument on the merits. On March 5 it ordered that four counsel might appear for the petitioners, and that the Attorney General and two associates would be heard in opposition; three hours would be allowed each counsel. Also on March 5, on Black's motion, James A. Garfield was admitted to the bar of the Court.

THE ARGUMENTS IN *MILLIGAN*

THE GOVERNMENT'S PRELIMINARY CONTENTION about want of jurisdiction may be dismissed briefly. It rested upon a very close construction of statutory language. Thus the Act of 1802, authorizing the certificate of division of opinion, spoke of certifying "upon the request of either party"; it contemplated a "cause" between adverse parties; but the Judges below had acted with only the petitioner before them: "the record hardly exhibits the Attorney of the United States, Mr. Hanna, as taking any part." Without an actual issue of the writ and a respondent formally on the record, so it was contended, the situation was not within the Act of 1802.

When Justice Davis was writing his opinion in the summer of 1866, he apprehended, as foreshadowed by the Chief Justice's remark when on April 3 he announced the Court's ruling,[69] that there would be dissenters and that they would strike at this point. Accordingly he was at pains to show why the "literal and technical" critique of the

---

[66] 2 Stat. 159, 160. See supra, p. 139.
[67] 4 Wall. at 108.
[68] That of Bowles was filed on Jan. 12, 1866; that of Horsey on Mar. 1.

The three cases became, respectively, Nos. 350, 365, and 376, and were heard and decided together.
[69] Supra, pp. 143–44.

Circuit Court's action in May 1865 should be rejected. On this he solicited Justice Clifford's counsel.

But the apprehended dissent turned out to be nothing more than a preliminary paragraph in the Chief Justice's concurring opinion, observing that there was some difficulty with the Act of 1802—but "we are willing to resolve whatever doubt may exist in favor of the earliest possible answers to questions involving life and liberty. . . ."

It is sometimes asserted, in popular criticism and in historical writing, that in some situation the Court used some "merely technical" pretext to escape from plain duty. Instances of this complaint will presently appear. Commonly this springs from a failure to appreciate something really essential, or from disappointment because the Court did not overleap all barriers to crush the object of the critic's unhappiness. In *Milligan*, however, the challenge to jurisdiction was, indeed, "merely technical," and was rejected. No Justice took that ground to avoid the substantive issue.

Henry Stanbery presented the Government's argument on jurisdictional points.[70] On the merits, its case was conducted by the Attorney General and Benjamin F. Butler. They spoke of the President's "sovereignty in carrying on war." They contended, in language suited to the royal Stuarts in times before the prerogative had been bound by the law and custom of the constitution, that once war had come, the President was "the sole judge of the exigencies, necessities, and duties of the occasion . . . . During the war his power must be without limit . . . ." The Constitution's provisions for a trial in the civil courts were said to be inapplicable: "These, in truth, are all peace provisions of the Constitution, and . . . are silent amidst arms . . . ." The Third Amendment (soldiers shall not be quartered in any house . . . in time of war, except in a manner to be prescribed by law) was said to be the only constitutional restraint upon the President in carrying on a war.

A competent Attorney General would never have permitted such an outlandish argument to be made, or rendered such an opinion as that already referred to, sustaining the trial by military commission of those charged as Booth's accomplices. But Speed was not up to his job. Justice Miller, in a private letter of March 4, the day before argument in *Milligan* began, had said that "the session of the Court has developed his utter want of ability as a lawyer—He is certainly one of the feeblest men who has addressed the Court this term."[71]

---

[70] Save where otherwise indicated, comments that follow are based on the reports, 4 Wall. 2 and 18 L. Ed. 281, and on Klaus (ed.), *The Milligan Case.*

[71] Charles Fairman, *Mr. Justice Miller and the Supreme Court, 1862–1890* (Cambridge, Mass.: Harvard University Press, 1939), 118.
In accord with this was the advice

Black, McDonald, Ex parte: On the matter of   Certificate of division

Garfield.   Lambdin P. Milligan.   Circuit Court

                 Petitioner   Indiana

Stanbery, Att. Gen.
Butler.

1865 Dec: 27	Record received and filed
1866 Jan: 24	Motion of Mr Black to set day for argument filed.
1866 Feb: 5	Ordered to be set for argument on the first monday of march.
1866 Mar: 2	Agreement of Counsel filed.
1866 Mar: 2	Motion of Attorney Gen. &c. to dismiss, filed, and ordered for argument with the merits.
1866 Mar: 5	Three counsel granted each counsel.
1866 Mar 5	Argument commenced
1866 Mar 6	Argument Continued
1866 Mar 7	Argument Continued
1866 Mar 8	Argument Continued
1866 Mar 9	Argument Continued
1866 Mar 12	Argument Continued
1866 Mar 13	Argument Concluded
1866 April 3	Answered in favor of petitioner

Docket page for *Ex parte Milligan*, commencing when the case was filed.

Ex parte: In the matter of
350 L. P. Milligan. Petitioner

On consideration of
the application of
counsel, it is now

Ex parte: In the matter of
365 W. A. Bowles. Petitioner
and
Ex parte: In the matter of
376 Stephen Horsey

here ordered by the
Court that three
hours be allowed
each counsel in
the argument
of these cases.

That four counsel may appear and argue
the cases on the part of the petitioners; and
the attorney General, and two associates
for the United States in opposition to the
petitioners.

Ex parte: In the matter of
350 L. P. Milligan. Petitioner

The arguments
of these cases
was commenced
by Mr McDonald
of Counsel for
the petitioners.

Ex parte: In the matter of
365 W. A. Bowles. Petitioner
and
Ex parte: In the matter of
376 Stephen Horsey. Petitioner

Page from the Minutes for March 5, 1866, when additional time was
granted and argument began.

In Ben Butler, Speed had an associate whose war-time record and professional character gave assurance of a loose, brash performance, such as would never gain the confidence of the Justices.[72]

Garfield for the petitioners examined relevant English and American materials to distinguish what situations fell within and what without the jurisdiction of military tribunals. He showed that the acts with which the petitioners had been charged were punishable under the criminal statutes. The Act of March 3, 1863, permitted detention of suspected persons until the civil authorities could examine the nature of their acts, but went no further. He dwelt on the debate on Henry Winter Davis' motion, specifically to restrain trial by military commission: it showed the view of the House, and "almost every Senator" acknowledged the justice of the proposition. Garfield made an admirable presentation—pertinent, persuasive, and candid.

Black followed; and Orville H. Browning, who attended throughout the *Milligan* hearing, made this comment: "He did not look at a book or a note, but made, I think, the finest argument, and the most magnificent speech to which I ever listened."[73]

A few excerpts will suggest Black's method. The case presented "a single point, and that an exceedingly plain one": did "this strange tribunal" have jurisdiction? No: neither of the subject-matter nor of the parties, "and the Act of Congress of March 3, 1863, which was passed with express reference to persons precisely in the situation of these men, declares that they shall be delivered up for trial to the proper civil authorities."

He turned to the "very elaborate official paper which [the Attorney General] published last July," and in accord with it the position taken in the Government's brief in *Milligan*. Black took opposite ground: the Government's thesis would contravene the Constitution's provisions on "the judicial power of the United States" and its several particulars whereby the administration of punitive justice was carefully guarded.

---

of Thomas Ewing the elder to President Johnson, in a letter of March 15, 1866: "It is of the utmost importance that you have a stronger man in that place—it is due to yourself and also to the Court, for Mr. Speed is not a competent legal adviser especially on the present critical condition of affairs—and I know that the Court does not rely on him—I believe he is loyal and you ought not to turn him adrift but make him a District Judge some-where, say in Mississippi." He urged the President to name Stanbery to the place; "he stands with the head of the Bar in the West—'if not first, in the *very first* line.' " Johnson Papers, and retained copy in Ewing Papers, L.C.

[72] The Argument of Benjamin F. Butler . . . was separately printed, Lowell, Massachusetts, 1866; it is not set out in Klaus.

[73] *Diary of Orville Hickman Browning* (Springfield: Illinois State Historical Library, Vol. I [1850-64], Pease and Randall, eds., 1925; Vol II [1865-81], Randall, ed., 1933), II, 65. Mar. 7, 1866.

He said that "these provisions exist in full force, unchangeable and irrepealable." He did not need "by a long chain of legal argumentation, nor by the production of numerous books with the leaves dog-eared and the pages marked," to show that these ancient rights remained in force. Yet, according to "the doctrine of the Attorney General's Office ever since the advent of the present incumbent," "The Constitution is repealed, or its operation suspended, in one State because there is war in another." Black contrasted the "most precarious position" to which the rights of the citizen had lately been reduced with the security in which they had been maintained during "the War of 1812, [when] the man emphatically called the Father of the Constitution was the supreme Executive Magistrate. Talk of perilous times! There was the severest trial this Union ever saw. That was no half-organized rebellion on the one side of the conflict, to be crushed by the hostile millions and unbounded resources of the other."[74]

As Black progressed he became more scornful of the Attorney General, whose "idea of humanity as well as law is embodied in the bureau of military justice, with all its dark and bloody machinery." Black prodded with his own special weapons: quotations from the Old Testament and from Shakespeare. "Come, Mr. Attorney, 'gird up thy loins now like a man; I will demand of thee, and thou shalt declare unto me if thou hast understanding.' " Speed was being tried like Job. The next moment, for his "despotic and lawless" doctrine he was classed with the "oppressors of mankind"—he was one of those who could "set the murderous Machiavel to school."

One sees that Black felt very much at home in the Supreme Court. As Justice Miller commented, he was "strong in argument and imperious, and . . . all the Judges of the Sup. Court know his great powers."[75] He would, indeed, have been sitting on its bench, if in the Senate on February 21, 1861, there had been as many as twenty-six, instead of only twenty-five, in favor of confirmation. That is a solemn

---

[74] Black, as Attorney General in the Buchanan Administration, had taken the very narrowest view of the power of the Federal Government in the event of an attempted secession. Thus in an opinion of Nov. 20, 1860, 9 Ops. Atty. Gen. 516, he had advised: "But what if the feeling in any State against the United States should become so universal that the Federal officers themselves . . . would resign their places? . . . In that event troops would certainly be out of place, and their use wholly illegal. . . . Without the exercise of those [judicial] func-

tions which belong exclusively to the civil service, the laws cannot be executed in any event . . . ."
Throughout Reconstruction, in counselling President Johnson and in argument before the Court, Black will be found to minimize the significance of the Civil War and the power of the United States in consequence of it.

[75] Letter of June 17, 1869, to his brother-in-law, who was about to argue a case in the Circuit Court in association with Black. Fairman, *Mr. Justice Miller*, 233.

thought when one reflects upon the relation of the Court to the issues of preserving and restoring the Union.

David Dudley Field spoke the last words from the bar, on March 12 and 13, 1866. He excluded, at the outset, matters that were *not* involved in the case: "it is not a question respecting the power of a conqueror over . . . conquered States. What may or may not be the rightful interference of the military in the States lately in rebellion—to what extent they may go, how long continue, and when and how cease to act—are not questions in this case. . . . Nor is it a question how far the *legislative department* of the Government can deal with the question of martial rule. Whatever has been done in these cases has been done by the executive department alone. . . ."

(A moment's pause, to glance ahead: presently Congress established a policy for the reconstruction of the States lately in rebellion, and chose the army to be the agent for carrying it into effect. Congress provided that civilians might be tried by military tribunal if, by reason of the ineffectiveness of local civil tribunals, that appeared necessary. When one McCardle was charged before a military commission with impeding the execution of the Acts of Congress, the validity of that procedure would be challenged before the Supreme Court, and again Black and Field would appear against the Government. And in March 1868, Field would declare:

> I must say . . . that the argument for the exercise of military power in such a case was exhausted in the Milligan case. . . . It is idle . . . — it is presumptuous, to come into the court and reargue that matter again, as if anything more could be said. The discussion . . . is closed in this tribunal.[76]

Soon, it will be seen, Justice Davis felt stung by criticism that in his opinion in Milligan he had gone out of his way to prejudge the power of Congress in dealing with the rebel States.[77] Relevant to that matter is the variance between Field's statement of what was *not* involved when Milligan was being argued, and what two years later he said the Court had there settled beyond any further question.)

Field, so Browning commented in his diary,[78] made "an interesting, well considered argument, and did justice to the case." Evidently Browning found Black's style more gratifying to his own sentiments. Field indulged in no invective. In rational order, he dealt with every issue in the entire case, in a thorough, lawyer-like manner. On the sub-

---

[76] *National Intelligencer*, Mar. 6, 1868. See infra, p. 455.

[77] Infra, pp. 231–34.
[78] II, 66. Mar. 13.

stantive question: "The discussion of the competency of the military commission is first in order, because, if the petitioners were lawfully tried and convicted, it is useless to inquire how they could be released from an unlawful imprisonment." He concluded that, "upon the text of the original Constitution, as it stood when it was ratified, there is no color for the assumption that the President, . . . without Act of Congress, could create military commissions for the trial of persons not military . . . ."

But to quiet apprehensions and to guard against possible dangers, a Bill of Rights had been added: he found in those provisions specific reinforcements of his conclusion.

The Government had built its argument upon the alleged authority of the Executive to declare martial law: accordingly Field pursued that subject exhaustively, to exclude it as a justification for what had been done to Milligan.

It remained to consider the petitioners' remedy, under the Act of March 3, 1863. Since a grand jury had met, and adjourned without finding an indictment, petitioners had been entitled to be brought before the Circuit Court; and, since the conviction by the military commission was invalid, they had been entitled to their discharge.

The positions taken by counsel, as attention has been directed to them, will take on particular significance when the opinions of Justice Davis and the Chief Justice come to be examined.

THE OPINION FOR THE COURT

"THE CONTROLLING QUESTION," said Justice Davis, was this: "Upon the *facts* stated in Milligan's petition . . . had the military commission . . . *jurisdiction*, legally, to try and sentence him?" "The provisions of [the Constitution] on the administration of criminal justice are too plain and direct, to leave room for misconception or doubt of their true meaning." He cited Article III's prescription of trial by jury; the Fourth Amendment (no unreasonable searches and seizures; warrants to issue only on probable cause); the Fifth (grand jury, except in cases arising in the land and naval forces, or in the militia in actual service); and the Sixth (speedy and public trial by an impartial jury). *Now* the attempt was made to avoid what the Founders, foreseeing troublous times, had "established by irrepealable law." Here Justice Davis made a memorable answer to the extreme doctrine advanced on behalf of the Government: "The Constitution of the United States is a law for rulers and people, equally in war and in peace, and covers with the shield of its protection all classes of men, at all times, and under all circumstances. No doctrine, involving more pernicious consequences, was ever invented by the wit of man," he added, than that constitutional rights could be suspended because of war. "[T]he Government, within the Constitution, has all the powers granted to it which are necessary to preserve its existence," as had been proved by the outcome of the recent war.

Had Milligan been denied rights guaranteed by the Constitution? There was, first, the provision on "the judicial power of the United States." The "laws and usages of war," whatever they might be, could not sanction a military trial of a citizen in civil life, in no wise connected with the military service, where the courts were open. "Congress could grant no such power," and had never attempted to do so.

Other guarantees of freedom were broken when Milligan, a civilian, was denied the protection of grand jury and trial jury.

On the side of the Government, it had been argued that in time of war the commander of a force had power, subject to the President, to suspend all civil rights and to subject civilians to *his will*. Justice Davis answered: "Not one of these [constitutional] safeguards can the President, or Congress, or the Judiciary disturb, except the one concerning the writ of habeas corpus." It was not a question of the power to proclaim martial law where the courts and civil authorities had been overthrown, nor of the power of a commander in places in rebellion. However,

> Martial law cannot arise from a *threatened* invasion. The necessity must be actual and present; the invasion real, such as effectually closes the courts and deposes the civil administration.
>
> . . . Martial rule can never exist when the courts are open, and in the proper and unobstructed exercise of their jurisdiction. It is also confined to the locality of actual war. Because, during the late Rebellion it could have been enforced in Virginia, where the national authority was overturned and the courts driven out, it does not follow that it should obtain in Indiana, where that authority was never disputed, and justice was always administered. . . .

The third question, then, must be answered in the negative: the military commission that tried Milligan was without jurisdiction.

The first question should be answered in the affirmative. "The suspension of the privilege of the writ of habeas corpus does not suspend the writ itself. The writ issues as a matter of course; and on the return made to it the court decides whether the party applying for it is denied the right of proceeding any further with it."

The second question should also be answered in the affirmative: on the facts stated in the petition, Milligan was entitled to be discharged by the terms of the Act of March 3, 1863.

V: *The* Milligan *and* Test Oath *Cases*

THE CONCURRING OPINION

CHIEF JUSTICE CHASE reached the same result by a much shorter route and with the least agitation: "The act of Congress of March 3d, 1863, comprises all the legislation which seems to require consideration in this connection. The constitutionality of this act has not been questioned and is not doubted." He sketched its provisions. First it authorized the President to suspend the privilege of the writ of habeas corpus. Section 2 required that lists of prisoners be sent to the Judges. If a grand jury adjourned without finding an indictment a prisoner would be entitled to be brought before the court and to have his discharge upon the terms provided therein. Section 3 provided that where a list had not been supplied, a prisoner might, upon allegation of the facts verified by oath, similarly obtain his discharge.

Milligan came "within the precise letter and intent" of the statute. The Chief Justice's construction gave the words a decisive effect: "the Act seems to have been framed on purpose to secure the trial of all offences of citizens by civil tribunals, in States where these tribunals were not interrupted in the regular exercise of their functions." David Dudley Field in his argument had not claimed so much.[79] He had said, the competency of the military commission must first be determined: if Milligan had been lawfully tried and convicted, that would be the end of the matter. But if the answer to that was No, "then the means of relief become subjects of inquiry," and for that he looked to the Act of 1863.

The Chief Justice, however, said that the entire inquiry should begin and end with the Act of 1863:

> These provisions obviously contemplate no other trial or sentence than that of a civil court, and we could not assert the legality of a trial and sentence by a military commission, under the circumstances specified in the Act and described in the petition, without disregarding the plain directions of Congress.

Thus Question 1, Ought the writ to issue?, must be answered Yes.

Question 2, On the facts stated, ought Milligan be discharged?, must also be answered Yes.

And as "an unavoidable inference from affirmative answers to the other two," the third reply must be that the military commission did not have jurisdiction.

"We do not think it necessary to look beyond these provisions

---

[79] Supra, pp. 206–07.

[that is, the Act of March 3, 1863]. In them we find sufficient and controlling reasons for our conclusions."

This was an exceedingly generous construction of the statute that authorized the suspension of the privilege of the writ of habeas corpus—imputing to Congress an intention at the same time to prohibit the military trial of civilians in States where the administration of the laws was unimpaired. *If* that was what the statute meant, then—on familiar principle—the Justices should rest their ruling on that basis, refraining from a gratuitous pronouncement upon what the Constitution would or would not countenance.[80]

Let it be supposed, however, that Sections 2 and 3 of the Act were taken to mean that one imprisoned was entitled to a judicial hearing, whereupon an order would be made: for his discharge, unconditionally, or otherwise, as there provided—*or* for his remand in the event a lawful sentence or other cause for detention were shown. On such a construction, the court should, in the circumstances of Milligan, proceed to determine whether—by Executive authority, absent any authorization by Congress—the military trial of a citizen in a loyal State under the prevailing conditions had been lawful. That would have left out of consideration what the powers of *Congress* would be under hypothetical circumstances.

Actually—inasmuch as the majority had ruled against the power of Congress, by propositions with which the concurring Justices did not agree—the latter proceeded to make their own pronouncements upon the same matters. The Chief Justice said:

> We by no means assert that Congress can establish and apply the laws of war where no war has been declared or exists.
>
> Where peace exists the laws of peace must prevail. What we do maintain is, that when the nation is involved in war, and some portions of the country are invaded, and all are exposed to invasion, it is within the power of Congress to determine to what States or districts such great and imminent public danger exists as justifies the authorization of military tribunals for the trial of crimes and offences against the discipline or security of the army or against the public safety.

"In Indiana, the judges and officers of the courts were loyal to the government." Chase picked up Davis' remark, and turned it around: "But it might have been otherwise. In times of rebellion and civil war it may often happen, indeed, that judges and marshals will be in active sympathy with the rebels, and the courts their most efficient allies."

---

[80] Justice Brandeis' concurring opinion in Ashwander v. Tennessee Valley Authority, 297 U.S. 288, 341 (1936), sets out the classic statement of canons.

We have confined ourselves to the question of power. It is for Congress to determine the question of expediency. And Congress did determine it. That body did not see fit to authorize trials by military commission in Indiana, but by the strongest implication prohibited them. With that prohibition we are satisfied, and should have remained silent if the answers to the questions certified had been put on that ground, without denial of the existence of a power which we believe to be constitutional and important to the public safety—a denial which . . . seems to draw in question the power of Congress to protect from prosecution the members of military commissions who acted in obedience to their superior officers, and whose action, whether warranted by law or not, was approved by that upright and patriotic President under whose administration the Republic was rescued from threatened destruction.

COMMENT

THAT *Ex parte Milligan* wears several faces may be discerned from a close reading of key sentences in Charles Warren's appreciation:

This famous decision has been so long recognized as one of the bulwarks of American liberty that it is difficult to realize now the storm of invective and opprobrium which burst upon the Court at the time when it was first made public. [He quoted contemporary editorials.] . . . That this decision, which has since been recognized by all men as the palladium of the rights of the individual, should at the time of its rendition have been so generally compared with the *Dred Scott Case* is a striking commentary on the passionate political conditions of that era.[81]

. . . .

The Democratic papers naturally applauded the decision. . . .[82]

While "the verdict of history," Warren continued, had validated "the immortal opinion of Judge Davis in support of the right of the citizen to protection against arbitrary military action,"

there has always been considerable sympathy . . . towards that part of the decision of the four Judges which distinguished the question of Congressional power from Executive usurpation . . . . That the doctrine asserted by the majority is "calculated to cripple the constitutional powers of the Government and to augment the public

---

[81] See comment infra, pp. 214–21.
[82] *The Supreme Court in United States History*, rev. ed., 2 vols. (Boston: Little, Brown and Co., 1928), ch. 22, "The Milligan Case."

dangers in times of invasion and rebellion" (in the words of Chief Justice Chase) is . . . unquestionable . . . [W]hatever may be the view as to the law so laid down, there was a serious and well-founded criticism of the propriety of the Court's action in expressing any opinion whatever on the power of Congress . . . .

Justice Davis' opinion is indeed a landmark of constitutional liberty. The propositions in the Government's brief—that in time of war the powers of the Executive "must be without limit," that the restraints of the Constitution "are silent amidst arms"—were utterly at variance with the national inheritance and traditions, and called for the most emphatic contradiction. Justice Davis' statement that the Constitution is a law for rulers and people, in war and in peace, protecting all classes of men, at all times and under all circumstances, is as fine a sentence as can be found anywhere in the United States Reports.

There was ground for apprehension that in some categorical propositions in the opinion there was latent danger to the Government in event of an invasion or rebellion. In 1917, on the occasion of World War I, Charles Evans Hughes spoke on "War Powers Under the Constitution" before the American Bar Association.[83] He advised that some of the sentences in the Milligan opinion should not be taken literally: "Certainly, the test should not be a mere physical one, nor should substance be sacrificed to form."

Early in World War II the Court was confronted with a concrete situation.[84] Eight men trained in sabotage were landed, secretly at night, by a German submarine; they buried their uniforms and set forth in civilian dress, armed with explosives, on a mission to destroy war industries. When apprehended they were brought before a military commission convened by the President, charged with "Violation of the law of war." Appointed counsel instituted habeas corpus proceedings in the District Court for the District of Columbia, and by appropriate steps brought the matter to the Supreme Court, which met in a Special Term. Counsel for the petitioners relied on *Ex parte Milligan*: they could not be tried by military commission "where the courts are open and their process unobstructed." It was a case not "arising in the land or naval forces," and accordingly it was argued that the petitioners could be proceeded against only upon indictment by a grand jury, and by jury trial. But the Court was unanimous in holding that the *Milligan* opinion was "inapplicable to the case presented by the present record." Combatants who enter secretly without uniform to wage war are "offenders against the law of war subject to trial and punishment by military tribunals."

---

[83] 42 A.B.A. Rep. 232; Sen. Doc. No. 105, 65th Cong., 1st Sess.

[84] *Ex parte* Quirin, 317 U.S. 1 (1942).

V: *The* Milligan *and* Test Oath *Cases*

While Congress had not "undertaken to . . . enumerate or define by statute all the acts which that law condemns," it had by the Articles of War recognized that they were triable by military commission.[85] The Court held that petitioners were in lawful custody.

In short, the very words of the *Milligan* opinion should not be taken as precise tests for all future emergencies. They might allow too little, and they might invite too much.[86]

The criticism that the opinion went out of the way to limit the power of Congress will recur constantly in the pages that follow; and what Justice Davis said in retrospective justification will be set forth.

That the opinion immediately raised a storm and was likened to

---

[85] The Court in a footnote cited numerous pertinent instances during the Civil War.

It was a novel feature of the *Quirin* case that acts of unlawful belligerency were committed, not "on the theater of active military operations," but at points far removed. Even so, the gist of the offense was not a crime made punishable in a District Court.

[86] In some situations perhaps too little: Normally a commander in an area of active operations would sustain and rely upon the courts and the several branches of civil administration—interfering with their functions no more than appeared necessary for the accomplishment of the mission with which he was charged. Yet he might need to impose regulations that were not enforceable in the courts under either federal or State law.

Perhaps more to be feared in the future—as one looks ahead, a century after *Milligan*—is that an uncritical attachment to the words of the opinion might seem to invite too much.

The nation now has reason to fear a nuclear attack, from the air—resulting in a staggering loss of life, destruction of homes, stores, offices and factories, and utter dislocation of the processes of government and of the economy—of production, marketing, finance, transportation and communications. Recuperation, it is firmly believed, would be a task for *civil* administration, under effective national leadership that reached down to the people through established State and municipal agencies.

This comment is made with some emphasis, lest *Milligan* be supposed to teach that wherever the courts are closed (as doubtless many would be on the morrow of a nuclear attack), martial rule becomes appropriate. *Ex parte Milligan* was concerned with a situation where Union and Confederate armies advanced and retreated over contested ground: a commander must be allowed a certain authority over men and things in the immediate vicinity—not because he was well qualified to govern, but simply because that was essential to doing his job. Henceforth one must contemplate the possibility of attack upon places remote from any operations on land—where there would be no need to permit military control in order to keep the civil population out of the army's path.

How to organize recovery from atomic attack calls for fresh, constructive thinking. The solution is not to be found in the thoughts present in the minds of the Justices in 1866.

I discussed this matter in "Government Under Law in Time of Crisis," at the Marshall Bicentennial Conference in 1955. Arthur E. Sutherland, ed., *Government Under Law* (Cambridge, Mass.: Harvard University Press, 1956), 232–86. Also in Hearings before Subcommittee of the Committee on Government Operations of the House of Representatives, on Civil Defense for National Survival, at 279–340, 84th Cong., 2d Sess. (1956).

Dred Scott[87] will not be difficult to understand when one comes to know the context. In the remembrance of *Ex parte Milligan,* much has been forgotten.

THE RECEPTION OF THE *MILLIGAN* OPINION

THE TWO OPINIONS were read on December 17, 1866. The Court, however, "in order to prevent an imperfect synopsis from going forth, denied the reporters present the usual privilege of taking notes", so the *New York Times*[88] reported. It was not until January 1 that the opinion appeared in the newspapers.

Even before the text became known to the public, the opinion for the majority received a conspicuous application by President Johnson, in a case about which the country was already exercised. This was such a single instance as seemed to typify a pervasive condition.

In November a Negro driving down a road in Virginia had collided with the vehicle of Dr. James L. Watson, wherein the doctor's wife and daughter were riding, breaking the wheels. Next day the doctor sought out the Negro and shot him to death. An examining court of five magistrates discharged the killer. General John M. Schofield, in charge of the Bureau in Virginia, thereupon directed that Watson be tried before a military commission, under the Freedmen's Bureau Act.[89] On December 19 the general respectfully declined to comply with a writ of habeas corpus out of a State court.[90]

At once the bearing of the *Milligan* case upon Watson's was discussed. "The Supreme Court of the United States has rendered a decision which fully sustains the position of counsel [for Watson]," declared the *Richmond Enquirer* on December 19. The leading editorial in the *Richmond Dispatch* for that day was on "The Case of Dr. Watson as it is Affected by the last Decision of the Supreme Court." It concluded that "there is not one inch of ground upon which the commission can base a claim to jurisdiction . . . ." Its second editorial, "White and

---

[87] Infra, pp. 216, 225–29, 232, 236.
[88] Dec. 27, 1866; *National Intelligencer,* Jan. 15, 1867.
[89] Sen. Exec. Docs., 39th Cong., 2d Sess., No. 29. Violations of the Civil Rights Bill, 17–37.
The Freedmen's Bureau Act, passed over a veto on July 16, 1866, provided that in the rebel States the Bureau would "extend military protection and have military jurisdiction over all cases and questions concern-

ing the free enjoyment" of the rights there secured—which included "equal benefit of all laws and proceedings concerning personal liberty, personal security . . . ."
[90] Ann. Cyc. 1866, at 765, gives the text of the return. The writ issued from the Circuit Court for the City of Richmond, and was served by James Lyons, a leading figure at the Virginia bar and in Democratic politics.

Black" said that "if [the Negroes] depended upon the 'Freedmen's Bureau,' they would be in evil plight indeed." "[T]he less we are troubled and worried by Freedmen's Bureaus and the sensational legislation of Washington, the sooner and more completely shall we succeed in establishing just and cordial and beneficent relations between the two races."

On December 21, 1866, four days after the *Milligan* opinion was delivered, the President, on the advice of Attorney General Stanbery, directed that Dr. Watson be discharged. It was announced in the press that the action was "in accordance with the recent decision of the Supreme Court."[91]

"Well done, Mr. Johnson," said the *Dispatch*; praise, too, to the Supreme Court, which "in rendering this decision has postponed for a time at least that destruction of republican government which will have taken place when the military shall become superior to the civil authorities."[92] Its neighbor, the *Enquirer*, said that "It has been decided by the Court that Congress has *no power* to authorize a military commission." Further, "The upright action of the Supreme Court has inspired the country with new hope of a speedy tranquilization. The revolutionary proceedings of Congress are promised a check which has been little counted on."[93] The Little Rock *Arkansas Gazette* said that the *Milligan* decision, at last, "encourages the belief that the Supreme Court would become a barrier to the sweeping progress of a ruthless fanaticism"; already it had produced a good result in the release of Dr. Watson.[94] The *Chronicle and Sentinel* of Augusta, Georgia, said that the federal military authority had been "dragging one of [Virginia's] best and most esteemed citizens to trial before a forum which is declared to be illegal and revolutionary" by the *Milligan* decision.[95]

But, asked the *Jackson* (Michigan) *Citizen*, "Where is this thing to end? . . . It is certain that no punishment will be administered by the civil courts. Mr. Johnson has taken care that none shall be administered in any other way."[96] *The Nation* gave an account of Dr. Watson's case and its outcome; it continued:

> We hope the case will not be suffered to rest there. Courts such as now exist in the South are no more protection to the freedmen than if they did not exist, and we cannot and ought not to suffer so large a proportion of our population to remain without the protection of law of some kind. . . .[97]

---

[91] *National Intelligencer*, Dec. 24.
[92] Dec. 22, 29.
[93] Dec. 19, 21.
[94] Dec. 29.
[95] Dec. 22.
[96] Jan. 1, 1867.
[97] 3:510, Dec. 27.

In the House of Representatives on January 3, 1867, Thad Stevens came at once to "the late decision of the Supreme Court" and the release of Dr. Watson "under this most injurious and iniquitous decision." He said that Congress must now carry out Reconstruction, free from Executive or Judicial restraint.[98]

Chase's friend, John Jay,[99] wrote on January 5, 1867, to the Chief Justice, expressing his concern upon reading the opinion for the majority:

> If, as the public begin to fear, their denial . . . of the powers of Congress, is any index of the view they are prepared to take of the great questions that will come before them in reference to reconstruction, our situation is certainly a grave one, & it will require more wisdom than the Republican managers have sometimes shewn, to surmount gracefully the formidable opposition, no longer of a simply obstinate President defying the will of the people, but of an Executive furnished with a Constitutional standpoint by the Supreme Judiciary, giving validity to his acts, & checkmating Congress at the most eventful moment by denying its power & annulling its legislation.
>
> I cannot yet consent to believe that we are to be brought into this dilemma—& that appointees of Mr. Lincoln are ready to imitate the late Chief Justice in making the Court the chief support of the advocates of Slavery & the Rebellion. . . .[100]

True to his heritage, John Jay was a worker for human freedom, and for other objectives justly falling within the description of "liberalism."[101] By his lights, there was danger that the majority would emulate Chief Justice Taney, who by his dictum in *Dred Scott* had invoked the Bill of Rights to declare the slaveholder's constitutional privilege to take his property into any Territory of the United States: the attempt by Congress to limit the spread of slavery was unconstitutional.[102] In effect Jay was asking, Whose liberty is it that the Court is going to protect?

---

[98] Cong. Globe, 39–2, 251.

[99] Supra, ch. I, n. 63.

[100] Chase Papers, L.C.

[101] See D.A.B. on Chief Justice John Jay; his son, Judge William Jay; and his grandson, John Jay (1817–94).

[102] 19 How. 393 (1857).

Taney had held that free Negroes "cannot become citizens, within the meaning of the Federal Constitution"; therefore Scott's suit had not been within the diversity jurisdiction of the Circuit Court.

But not stopping there, he had gone on to pronounce—in order to avoid "serious mischief and injustice in some future suit"—that the Missouri Compromise Act of 1820 whereby Congress purported to exclude slavery from certain territory was unconstitutional. Such a statute, "which deprives a citizen of the United States of his liberty or property, merely because he came himself or brought his property into a particular Territory of the United States . . . could hardly be dignified with the name of due

V: *The* Milligan *and* Test Oath *Cases*

In the fortnight before the texts became available, comment was ill informed. The *Washington Chronicle*, whose proprietor, John W. Forney, was Secretary of the Senate, and an advanced Radical, said hastily that "Treason . . . has at last found a secure shelter in the bosom of the Supreme Court."[103] The conservative *National Intelligencer* flew to the other extreme: "neither in the breadth of the issue, the extravagance of cotemporary heresies on the subject, nor the magnitude of the stake, could any past cause before that high court compare with this." It deprecated the fact that four Justices had gone out of the way to pass upon a "speculative question."[104] With the same slant of view, the *New Orleans Picayune* lamented that there was dissent from the proposition, "which is expressed with emphatic distinctness, that Congress cannot . . . authorize military commissions to try and punish civilians" where the courts are open. Happily these dissenters were "overruled by the majority, in some golden sentences, which stand out in noble contrast to the loose declamatory passages" of Chief Justice Chase's opinion.[105]

The *Chicago Tribune*, leading Republican journal of the Middle West, said on January 4 that the text of the opinions was now at hand; it proceeded to discuss the case rather fully in important editorials. It concluded that

> the only difference between the Judges is precisely on this point, *whether a law that Congress did not enact would have been constitutional if it had really been enacted.*

---

process of law [guaranteed by the Fifth Amendment]." Such an enactment was said to be analogous to one establishing a religion or prohibiting the free exercise thereof, or abridging the freedom of speech or of the press, or the right peaceably to assemble and petition the Government [First Amendment]; or to denying the right to keep and bear arms [Second Amendment]—or the right to trial by jury [Sixth Amendment]—or freedom from compulsory self-incrimination [Fifth Amendment]. So Taney's opinion—although a ruling on the point was not called for—was a memorable affirmation of the citizen's liberty: his liberty to bring his slave into any Territory of the United States.

This was the first occasion where the Court declared an Act of Congress invalid for violating one of the guaranties of the Bill of Rights.

Justice Wayne, "concurring . . . entirely in the opinion," said that the Court was performing its proper function when it took this occasion to affirm "constitutional principles of the highest importance, about which there had become such a difference of opinion, that the peace and harmony of the country required the settlement of them by judicial decision."

This attempt, by a gratuitous judicial pronouncement, to settle the slavery question, was surely the worst mistake the Justices ever made.

[103] Dec. 19, 1866. In the Senate next day Reverdy Johnson called it "indefensible for any one holding a public capacity to assail the integrity of the Supreme Court." Cong. Globe, 39–2, 210. No Senator came to Forney's defense.

[104] Dec. 20.

[105] Jan. 10.

Explaining that an *obiter dictum* on a matter not before the court established no precedent, the editor said that

> Such a stepping aside from the case in hand was, we think, unnecessary, uncalled for and unwise, and will do much to revive the unfavorable impression of the tribunal, which rested upon the public mind after the Dred Scott decision, and which has only been obliterated by the war because it has been supposed that the present Court is in sympathy with the principles of liberty and the spirit of the age.

Putting on a brave air, the *Tribune* assured its readers that the decision

> disturbs neither the Civil Rights or the Freedmen's Bureau Bill, even by implication. It declares no law of Congress unconstitutional. It settles nothing. Hence all the hullabaloo raised about it comes to an end.[106]

At the same time the *Concord* (New Hampshire) *Monitor* was recalling "the Dred Scott dictum" that had "defied the inherent sense of justice that reigns in the heart of the American People"; there was an "ugly squint" in the *Milligan* opinion, suggesting that perhaps again a majority of the Court would undertake to "set up their dicta against the solemn purpose of the People, vindicated upon the battle-field and enforced at the ballot-box."[107]

The *Alton* (Illinois) *Telegraph* apprehended, hopefully, that, when the question came squarely before it, the Court would not deny the Federal Government power to exercise military jurisdiction over the States recently in rebellion.

> But one thing is certain, . . . and that is that the American people have determined to preserve our free institutions, the unity of the States and the equal rights of all men, and neither the President nor the Supreme Court will long be permitted to stand in the way of these great ends.[108]

In Justice Davis' home town, the *Pantagraph* ran an editorial on "The Milligan Case: What it Settles and What it Threatens." It concluded:

> We do not complain of the court for having decided to discharge Milligan; for after having determined that military [martial] law did not prevail in Indiana at the time of his arrest, and that he was therefore entitled to the benefit of the statute, they could do

---

[106] Jan. 4, 5.   [107] Jan. 4.   [108] Jan. 11.

no less. But with Chief Justice Chase, we think the court should have stopped here, and not volunteered opinions which give alarm to all but rebels and their sympathizers.[109]

The *Keokuk Gate City* devoted an editorial to the thesis that throughout the course of English history the struggle for popular rights had been by the people and Parliament against the Crown supported by obsequious judges; so too in the colonial period. And now,

> A Supreme Court that tries after the events of these six years to preserve a scintilla of the spirit of that [*Dred Scott*] decision . . . should have no agency in moulding the new Union to grow out of the late war, a Union founded in justice and the rights of man.[110]

When one reads the comment of the *New York Times* one should bear in mind that this was the organ of Henry J. Raymond (1820–69), then serving his one term in Congress. Raymond was innately moderate, fair, reflective; he was holding aloof from the Radicals. The *Times* said that, instead of expressing "the common sense doctrine that the Constitution provides for the permanence of the Union, and for such exercise of authority by Congress as may be necessary to preserve the National existence," the Court "throws the great weight of its influence into the scale of those who assailed the Union and step after step impugned the constitutionality of nearly everything that was done to uphold it. . . . The whole Copperhead press exults over the decision. . . . The newly declared reliance of the President and the Southern States upon the interposition of the Supreme Court has a certain apparent justification in this decision."[111] But the *Springfield Republican*, whose editor, Samuel Bowles, was also an independent Republican, and mild on the subject of Reconstruction, viewed *Milligan* as "simply a reaffirmation of the sacred right of trial by jury"; it deprecated "popular alarm or partisan animosity."[112] That reaction was exceptional.

The Democratic press indeed found cause for jubilation. The *New York World*, under Manton Marble, had been the inveterate foe of the Lincoln Administration. Now it said that the Court's "decision on a matter which was the main topic of controversy between the

---

[109] Jan. 8. On the twelfth, however, the entire Court was taken to task for discharging the petitioners.

The *Pantagraph*'s editors sought "hearts that beat in unison with the cadences of the Song of Human Liberty." "We do not take much stock in the political soundness of the Supreme Court. There are three or four members who will do their best to make conscientious decisions in favor of the Union side, but the balance are men who may be expected to side with the rebels on every possible occasion." Jan. 1.

[110] Jan. 8.

[111] Jan. 3.

[112] Jan. 2, 5.

Democratic party and its opponents during the war, is the final judgment of the law, as it will be the verdict of history, that the obloquy heaped upon Democrats for their opposition to the arbitrary exertions of authority, was undeserved. . . . If a majority of the Court dare stand for the Constitution on this question, there is solid ground for trusting its steadfast fidelity on all others."[113] The *Cairo Democrat*, published in southernmost Illinois, in a town that voted Democratic three-to-one, reprinted the *World*'s comment and rejoiced that the Supreme Court "is the final arbiter of all questions properly before it." It professed to believe that "this decision is wholly free from partisan bias."[114] The *Detroit Free Press* made much of the thought that the Court had vindicated the party's war-time position, and that more could be expected.

> The same Supreme Court has declared null and void the infamous "test oath" act, against which the Democracy also protested in vain . . . , and that same Supreme Court will nullify every unconstitutional act of the fanatical Rump which disgraces the nation.[115]

The *Louisville Democrat*'s correspondent wrote that the Court's action gave assurance "that in the worst days of party insanity and misrule, there is one conservative department of the Government unawed and uninfluenced by the arbitrary power of Jacobinism . . . *God save the Union and the Supreme Court*." The *Democrat*'s editor added that "It is said the Radicals, of the legal persuasion, grow sick at heart when they contemplate the decision."[116]

The *Jackson* (Mississippi) *Clarion* hailed the *Milligan* opinion as "A Ray of Hope." "It vindicates individual right and destroys radical hopes of carrying into effect the various revolutionary schemes projected for our humiliation and oppression. . . . They not only desire to turn negroes into white men, but in order to do that, they are compelled to assail our own republican system of government . . . ."[117]

For a season the Court was the object of fulsome praise by Democratic editors: it was the band at Thermopylae;[118] it was "the great point of immediate attack" that would not be beaten down;[119] it was "like a lion in the path of those who would contemn the Constitution";[120] it would "not cower before the breath of the majority in the

---

[113] Dec. 18, 19, 21, 25, 1866; Jan. 5, 12, 1867.
[114] Dec. 23; Jan. 9.
[115] Dec. 21, 1866. Actually the *Test Oath Cases* were not decided until January 14; but the vote in conference had already been taken.
[116] Jan. 5.

[117] Jan. 5. A similar editorial on January 11 said "We have from the first believed that our only hope rested on the judiciary."
[118] *Cairo Democrat*, Dec. 23, echoing the *New York World*.
[119] *Cincinnati Enquirer*, Jan. 7.
[120] *National Intelligencer*, Jan. 17.

Northern States";[121] it would "resist the overwhelming tide" that was sweeping away the Constitution";[122] it was "the great constitutional umpire";[123] it was "a monument of American wisdom and patriotism" that would keep "every other power of the Government in its proper place."[124] The editor of the *Picayune* said that "This emerging of the Supreme Court above the atmosphere of partisan strifes and tumultuous popular passions into the region of calm and unclouded justice is the rising above the waters of the Ararat, on which the ark of the constitution may repose in security."[125]

But the *Dayton* (Ohio) *Journal,* commenting on this "wonderful reverence" from the Democracy, said that

> They do not reverence the Court because of its exalted position as a judicial body—but because it has done something which pleases the Southern rebels and themselves as well. The Democracy find material for party use in every thing which strengthens the rebellious spirit at the South, and places obstacles in the way of enforcing submission to the national authority.[126]

A string of editorial comments call for an evaluation: What does all this go to show? It is a notable fact that in the discussion of the *Milligan* opinion, very little was said about Milligan—much less than was said about Dr. Watson. The Court's order of April 3, 1866, and the resulting release on April 10, had occasioned only slight casual interest. In December and January, comment was largely concerned with applications to the immediate future. The opinion was read as indicating that the Court was prepared to hamper Congress in the matter of restoring the Union, something in no wise presented by the record of Milligan's trial in Indiana in 1864. In a moment Justice Davis will be quoted as protesting that there was "not a word said in the opinion about reconstruction";[127] but South and North, that inference was drawn. It was by reason of that implication that Democratic and Republican editors expressed their delight or dismay over the Court's opinion.

Some Radical editors used the case to whip up partisan animosity. Around the first of the year, alarming dispatches were filed in Washington, of which the following to the *Newark* (New Jersey) *Evening Courier* is an illustration:

---

[121] *Augusta* (Georgia) *Chronicle and Sentinel,* Dec. 30.
[122] *Little Rock Gazette,* Dec. 29.
[123] *Raleigh Sentinel,* Jan. 16.

[124] *Meridian* (Mississippi) *Gazette,* Mar. 19, 1867.
[125] Jan. 8.
[126] Jan. 25.
[127] Infra, p. 232.

Every Republican member of Congress with whom I have conferred on the subject is out and out for abolishing the Supreme Court at once, upon the ground that if Congress does not abolish it, it will abolish Congress, for the President stands ready to execute its nefarious decision with an iron hand.

The Secretary of War [Stanton], one of the best lawyers in the United States, regards the Milligan decision as striking at the roots of the Freedmen's Bureau law, and as leading directly to its entire abrogation, as well as other legislation looking to the protection of loyal men, white and black, by the Federal Government, from the persecution of the disloyal and rebellious, whose bogus State power is thus confirmed to them.

I find that the decision of the whole court is as offensive to the Republicans of Congress as that of the majority. All confidence in the court is gone. . . .

The correspondent admits that he has not read the opinions, and is reporting what he has been told by people who heard them. If this much is bad, he continues, "what will the country say when the test oath decision comes to light!"

All the leading Republican journals, East and West, are following the lead of the Washington Chronicle and the Newark Courier, in this exposure of the treason and renegadism of the Supreme Court, thus exhibiting a healthful condition of public mind, which repudiates treason on the bench as well as in the White House.[128]

Of course this was not factual reporting. Forney's *Chronicle* had sent up a cry that the Court was "sheltering treason";[129] now the attempt was by reiteration to induce the country to believe the "exposure."

BLACK'S JACKSON DAY SPEECH

WHILE THE RADICAL JOURNALISM of Forney and the like was mischievous, doubtless more damage was done by Democrats who contrived to make it appear that they had captured the Court. On January 8, 1867, the anniversary of the Battle of New Orleans, Jackson Day was celebrated in Washington at a dinner under the auspices of the National Democratic Resident Committee.[130] President Johnson attended and spoke. High on the list of toasts came "The Supreme Court of the United States: the great conservative power of the government; never

---

[128] Jan. 2, 1867.   [129] Dec. 19, 22, 29.   [130] *National Intelligencer*, Jan. 9.

more needed or better appreciated than now." Jeremiah S. Black, leading counsel for Milligan, made the response. The Court, he said, was being "vilified, and abused, and slandered." He defended it against "the organs of disunity and anarchy [which] publicly proclaim their determination to disregard the [Milligan] decision . . . because it confines their power by limits inconveniently narrow." He dwelt upon the spokesman for the Court, praising his "irresistible logic" and "the felicity of illustration which makes the whole subject blaze with light"; by this one opinion he had attained "a position to which no earthly station can add any dignity." His had become

> One of the few, the immortal names
> That were not born to die.[131]

The occasion was widely noticed. *The Nation* commented that

> the fulsome laudation of Justice Davis delivered at a late "banquet" by Mr. Black, who is a practising attorney at the bar of Judge Davis' court, was in sufficiently bad taste, and has helped to get credence for a report which Mr. Black may like to have credited, but in which Judge Davis probably takes not much delight. . . .

The "report" was that Black had become "the fountain whence Mr. Justice Davis draws his legal and political opinions."[132]

Gossip, with an element of substance, was repeated in a letter of January 16 from the *Chicago Tribune*'s Washington correspondent. At the time, he had not supposed that Black's speech was worth mention; he found, however, that it was causing comment. Its pith lay in the extravagant compliment to Justice Davis.

> These words . . . cause much talk in some social and political circles, because they give point and significance to an assertion frequently made during the last year and a half. It is known to everybody who has cared to inquire or observe, that Justice Davis and Judge Black are on very intimate terms; and Western men who knew Mr. Davis before he was named to the Supreme bench, have been in the habit of saying, sometimes jocularly and sometimes indignantly, that "Judge Davis has taken old Black as his constitutional adviser. . . ."

The *Tribune*'s correspondent added that this impression had now been somewhat affected by the fact that in the *Test Oath Cases* decided on January 14, Davis had been with the Republican minority that would

---

[131] The *National Intelligencer* of January 10 reported the speech at length.

[132] 4:62. Jan. 24.

sustain the oaths, exchanging places with Justice Wayne in the 5-to-4 division of the Court.[133]

Social intercourse between Justice Davis and Black had for some time been rather intimate.[134] Normally, friendship between a member of the Court and a counsellor at its bar would be politically noncommittal. But Jerry Black was a man apart—so dogmatic in his opinions and so persistent in his political zeal that it was reasonable to infer that one who frequently shared his company probably shared his outlook.

JUDICIAL PRUDENCE IN CONSTITUTIONAL LITIGATION

THE NEW *American Law Review*[135] in its issue for April 1867 discussed the *Milligan* case from the point of view of judicial method in constitutional litigation. This journal stood alone among contemporary periodicals in respect of the high professional standard set by its critiques. The *Review* said in part:

> That the President had no power to establish a military commission to try civilians in a part of the country not invaded by hostile armies nor in a state of insurrection, but in which the regular courts of law were in full and uninterrupted operation, was decided unanimously by the court, and the prisoner was discharged. . . . Had this unanimous opinion been given simply and directly, it would have established for ever a solid principle of law, on which, in all troublous times, the country could have relied. . . . It would have commanded universal respect, and would have enlisted in its support the sound judgment and the common sense of the nation.

[133] *Chicago Tribune*, Jan. 22, 1867. "From Washington. One of the Powers Behind the Supreme Court. A Significant Speech."

[134] On October 7, 1866, Black had written Davis apropos of the latter's memorial remarks on General William W. Orme of Bloomington, who had died on September 13. Black wrote of friendship, linking himself with Davis: "judges who do their duty, and lawyers who use no falsehood." Then of his uncertain hope of a Democratic victory in the approaching election:

One thing is certain: if Johnson had taken what you called his "golden opportunity" of setting forth his plans and principles in his annual message and never attempted to unfold them in any thing below the dignity of a state paper or official document of some kind we would have swept radicalism from the face of the earth. Presidential stump speaking is a failure at least in comparison to what might have been achieved by the brighter sharper and more ponderous weapon of a message.
Davis Papers, Ill. State Hist. Soc.

[135] I:572. The editors were identified supra, p. 74.

But the court did not deliver a unanimous opinion. They divided on a point that was not before them for adjudication . . . . Instead of approaching the subject of the powers of the co-ordinate branches of the government as one of great delicacy, . . . they have seemed eager to go beyond the record, . . . to lay down the principles on which they would decide other questions, not now before them, involving the gravest and highest powers of Congress. They have seemed to forget how all-important it is for the preservation of their influence that they should confine themselves to their duties as judges between the parties in a particular case; how certainly the jealousy of the co-ordinate departments of the government and of the people would be excited by any attempt on their part to exceed their constitutional functions; and how, the more a case before the Supreme Court assumes a political aspect, the more cautious should be the judges to confine themselves within their proper limits.

If in *Milligan* the Justices had taken that austere view of their duty, the occasion for the outcry and for the adulation would have been avoided. In the House on January 4, 1867, in general debate on the President's message, Representative John Wentworth of Illinois, a Republican, and on occasion an ardent partisan, made this statement on *Ex parte Milligan*:

I have read both the majority and minority opinions of the court, and I find that for the most part they are both based upon the law of 1863. . . . I cannot well see how respectable lawyers can attack that decision of the Supreme Court after having read that law. I refer to the points where both the majority and minority agree. I do not see how they could have done any less than give that decision under that law. . . .[136]

Such an acknowledgment of rectitude from the side whence complaints had been coming was more to be prized than Black's gloating praise.

Where there is unanimity in the result, normally it is worth a great effort to reach unanimity in exposition. It has been a precept that the Court will not anticipate a question of constitutional law in advance of the necessity of deciding it; nor will it formulate a rule of constitutional law broader than is required by the precise facts to which it is to be applied. This, said Justice Matthews, has been found to be "the dictate of wisdom."[137] Normally the Court will show reticence on points about which another branch would have reason to be sensi-

---

[136] Cong. Globe, 39–2, 286.
[137] Liverpool, N.Y. & Phila. S.S. Co. v. Emigration Comm'rs., 113 U.S. 33, 39 (1885).

tive.[138] And generally, good practice calls for all practicable economy in ruling on points on the way to reaching a decision.[139]

Justice Davis said at the outset, "The controlling question in the case is this: . . . had the military commission . . . *jurisdiction* . . .?" If not, "it is our duty to declare the nullity of the whole proceedings." Quite so: if such affirmative justification was not established, the proceedings were a *nullity*. That would be a proper place to stop. If, on the other hand, the conclusion in some particular situation were that some tribunal that proceeded without the common-law juries *did* have jurisdiction, then that jurisdiction should be recognized.[140] Because, as Chief Justice Taft once explained, although "the Constitution of the United States is in force . . . wherever and whenever the sovereign power of that government is exerted," yet it "contains grants of power, and limitations which in the nature of things are not always and every-

---

[138] For example, *Ex parte* Quirin, 317 U.S. 1 (1942), considered above. Upon the sudden emergency in that case—the arrest of German saboteurs—the President by proclamation had declared that such foreign enemies were denied access to the courts. The Court, however, simply passed over the obvious constitutional objection; it said that it "saw nothing in the Proclamation to preclude access to the courts for determining its applicability to the particular case," and went on to decide upon applicants' contentions.

[139] No Justice has had a finer sense of this than Chief Justice Hughes. Consider his opinion in Sterling v. Constantin, 287 U.S. 378 (1932)—a case having a resemblance to *Milligan*. A federal District Judge had issued a temporary order restraining Texas authorities from limiting production of oil at certain wells. Thereupon the Governor proclaimed that the areas concerned were in a state of insurrection, declared "martial law," and continued the limitation. The Chief Justice's opinion is a model. It kept saying that "we need not undertake to determine" this and that matter along the way; giving the Governor's proclamation "all the weight" to which it was entitled—conceding "a permissible range of honest judgment"—noting and passing by two cases where the Court had used exuberant language—he said that "what are the allowable limits of military discretion, and whether or not they have been overstepped in a particular case, are judicial questions"; in the instant case, the findings of fact "leave no room for doubt that there was no military necessity which, from any point of view, could be taken to justify the action of the Governor . . . ." The controversy was decided—and a field of law that abounded in wild claims was set in order—without a single superfluous statement.

[140] *In re* Ross, 140 U.S. 453 (1891), sustaining jurisdiction of United States consular court to try American seaman charged with murder on American ship in Japanese harbor: guaranties of grand and trial juries not applicable.

Ex parte Mason, 105 U.S. 696 (1882), denying relief on habeas corpus to soldier sentenced by court-martial for assault with intent to kill prisoner in Washington, D.C., jail, over whom soldier was guard. (The prisoner was Guiteau, assassin of President Garfield.)

Coleman v. Tennessee, 97 U.S. 509 (1879). Soldier in army occupying rebel State during war, had been convicted by court-martial for murder. Held: military jurisdiction was exclusive; prisoner should be delivered to military authorities.

where applicable . . . ."[141] Thus in the case of the German saboteurs[142] their counsel argued "that even if the offenses with which they are charged are offenses against the law of war, this trial is subject to" the jury and grand jury requirements of Article III, Sec. 2, the Fifth and the Sixth Amendments. The Court answered No: those constitutional provisions "cannot be taken to have extended the right to demand a jury to trials by military commission . . ."; such trials were "never deemed to have been within their terms."[143] Common-law safeguards such as trial by jury are indeed "prized privileges of our system of government,"[144] which is one among the reasons why any extraordinary jurisdiction should be confined within its proper bounds as determined by courts exercising "the judicial power." As soon, however, as it could be determined that one in Milligan's situation was *not* within the jurisdiction of the military commission, the "controlling question" had been answered, and there was no occasion to enumerate the consequential detriments to which he would otherwise have been exposed.

Black in his argument had said that the constitutional safeguards in criminal prosecutions were "unchangeable and irrepealable." That was axiomatic, absent an amendment of the Constitution. Justice Davis, following, said that they were "established by irrepealable law." He went on to pronounce that "Congress could grant no such power." But the only action of Congress involved in Milligan's case was the helpful Act of 1863 upon which in fact he grounded his application. The sweeping pronouncement was intentional. Presently—when Justice Davis' own statement is set out at length—it will be seen that he felt a need to combat "the prevalent idea, that the legislative dept of the govt can override everything."[145]

The statement that *during the late Rebellion* military jurisdiction might properly be exercised *in Virginia* implied pointedly that it was no longer permissible there. But the Freedmen's Bureau Act of July 16, 1866, had declared that the Bureau would "have military jurisdiction over all cases concerning the free enjoyment" of the freedmen's rights. The burden of President Johnson's veto message was that that provision was unconstitutional. There lay an issue of major importance. In Dr. Watson's case, the President acted on the view that that provision had already been condemned by the *Milligan* opinion.[146]

---

[141] Balzac v. People of Porto Rico, 258 U.S. 298 (1922). For an alleged misdemeanor, B. had been tried without jury, pursuant to the Penal Code of Porto Rico as it then stood. Held: that in a territory not "incorporated into the Union," the constitutional provisions for jury trial did not apply, although "the guaranties of certain fundamental personal rights . . . had from the beginning full application . . . ."

[142] *Ex parte* Quirin, supra, pp. 212–13.

[143] 317 U.S. 1, 40, 41.

[144] Duncan v. Kahanamoku, 327 U.S. 304, 307 (1946).

[145] Infra, p. 232.

[146] Supra, p. 215.

The District Court for Delaware had recently held that murder of soldiers on guard duty in South Carolina was triable only in the civil courts,[147] in effect, in courts manned entirely by ex-rebels. Seemingly the dictum in *Milligan* now confirmed that view. On February 22, 1867, a Select Committee of the House, after inquiry into that and similar incidents, recommended that Congress meet the problem "in the only practicable mode . . . , and that is through its military forces."[148]

Also on February 22, 1867, the House was debating H.R. 859, to declare valid certain proclamations of the President, and acts done in pursuance thereof. Proceedings or acts done or had by military commissions under authority of the President would be "approved . . . , legalized, and made valid . . . to the same extent . . . as if . . . done under the previous express authority and direction of the Congress . . . ." Representative James F. Wilson of Iowa, chairman of the Judiciary Committee, had charge of the bill. It was true, he observed, that the majority of the Court had already denied the power of Congress to authorize trial by military commission:

> But this is a piece of judicial impertinence which we are not bound to respect. No such question was before the court in the Milligan case, and that tribunal wandered beyond the record in treating of it. Its discussion . . . was out of place, uncalled for, and wholly unjustifiable. Milligan presented no point in his case upon which Mr. Justice Davis and his concurring associates can hang an excuse for this unnecessary examination of the powers of Congress. All the court said upon this subject brought neither benefit nor harm to Milligan . . . .[149]

The indemnity bill became law on March 2.[150] The vote was 96 to 27 in the House, 36 to 8 in the Senate. It is not surprising that President Johnson approved: it covered those who had participated in the military commission which, directly under his authority, had tried and condemned those charged with complicity in the assassination of President Lincoln.[151] H.R. 859 had been introduced by Representative John A. Bingham, who as assistant judge advocate had participated in the prosecution.

Presently, in the Circuit Court for Indiana, Milligan sued for false arrest and imprisonment, naming as defendants General Alvin P. Hovey, District commander, and members of the military commission. They set up in defense the Indemnity Act of March 2, 1867; but Judge

---

147 Supra, pp. 149–50.
148 Supra, p. 151.
149 Cong. Globe, 39–2, 1484. He went on to give an interesting critique of the majority opinion.
150 14 Stat. 432.
151 Supra, p. 197.

Drummond reduced that statute to zero, because the majority in the Supreme Court had already decided that Congress could not have authorized such a trial.[152] However, by a statute of indemnity and limitations of March 3, 1863, Congress had cut off the right to recover at two years after an allegedly wrongful official act; hence, while the jury found for the plaintiff, only nominal damages were awarded.[153] Doubtless Congress may not deny all recovery for civil damages for an act it could not have authorized in advance; that limit was observed in the Act of March 2, 1867, as Senator Trumbull had pointed out in debate.[154] But surely the Government and the defendants ought to have had an opportunity to argue, as a bar to the damages action, that Congress did have power to authorize such a military trial, without that issue being prejudiced by a dictum of the Supreme Court.

Also on March 2, 1867, a bill for the More Efficient Government of the Rebel States became law, notwithstanding the objections of the President. When in *Ex parte McCardle* the validity of that statute in respect of its authorization of trial by military commission came before the Court, David Dudley Field, as has been noted, said that this had already been settled by the *Milligan* opinion.[155]

It was Executive action against which Milligan sought relief: yet the opinion managed to rule against Congress in respect of pending matters about which Congress felt most concerned and most sensitive.

JUSTICE DAVIS' CORRESPONDENCE

JUSTICE DAVIS was not thick-skinned; he set great store upon the good opinion of others. *Milligan* was the greatest case that would ever be confided to him; he had worked hard to make his opinion all that it should be. And now he was bitterly attacked. It hurt. He sent copies of his opinion to his friends, rejoicing at every response that brought approval, and marking with disappointment every one who remained silent.

District Judge Thomas Drummond at Chicago gave staunchest support in long letters of December 27, January 4, 30, and 31, February 15 and 26.[156] On January 4, upon reading the two opinions, he wrote:

---

[152] Milligan v. Hovey, Fed. Case No. 9605, in May 1871. Plaintiff was represented by Senator Thomas A. Hendricks; defendants by Benjamin Harrison, later President.

[153] Sec. 7 of the statute, 12 Stat. 756, 757. Milligan brought suit on March 13, 1868; therefore recovery was barred for acts prior to March 13, 1866. But Milligan had been discharged on April 10, 1866.

[154] Cong. Globe, 39–2, 1961. Mar. 2, 1867.

[155] Supra, p. 206; infra, p. 455.

[156] Davis Papers, Ill. State Hist. Soc.

I think you have put the points strongly & comprehensively, and with an impressiveness worthy of the transcendent importance of the questions involved. I have no fears of the ultimate issue of any controversy as to the two opinions & the weight to be attached to each. You must bear in mind that your opinion clashes with the acts of men performed & justified under feelings of high excitement . . . .

Drummond reprehended the partisan comment of the *Chicago Tribune*, which at the outset had "been trying to mislead . . . , to make people think that the radical part of the Court headed by the C.J. were against the Decision." But, he assured Davis, "you cannot be attacked without attacking all."[157] "The Tribune seems to have become the organ of the Jacobins & to go for topsy-turvyism generally."[158] As "the Supreme Court was in Jefferson's way in former times [so] it is now in the way of the worshippers of the 'Vox Populi.' I hope you are not disturbed because there are comparatively few come to the rescue of the Constitution. . . ."[159]

> I believe among the great majority of the Bar there is a conviction that you are right even now & that Congress is going too far, but it is the flood time of radicalism & after all it takes a man of nerve & pluck to stand up against an excited people.[160]

When it was reported that Stanton had declared that he believed Milligan was properly convicted, Drummond commented: "If Stanton had admitted that the Milligan conviction was illegal he would have spoken his own condemnation, because he was an active agent in originating that mode of trial. . . ."[161]

Most highly prized were these words from Thomas Ewing: "I can only say of the opinion that it is sound in every particular & the sound constitutional law is laid down in happily appropriate language." Ewing, Davis reminded his wife, was "the last of the great men of the Whig party." (He was also a confidant and adviser of President Johnson.) Davis sent his wife a copy of a letter from Dr. John F. Henry of Burlington, Iowa, who praised the opinion and added, "I have read with great pleasure Judge Black's high commendation . . . and his glowing eulogium of yourself . . . . Any man might be proud of his endorsement . . ." But, Davis cautioned his wife, "Don't show it, because you

---

157 Letter of Dec. 27.
158 Letter of Jan. 30.
159 Letter of Feb. 15.
160 Letter of Jan. 30. "I think what you say is true—that Johnson has to some extent *wilted* i.e. he is afraid. I hope Grant will not *wilt* too."

Drummond believed that "Grant might do a great deal of good if he would take a decided stand, but he hates politics." Senator Trumbull, he feared, "bends to the blast."
161 Letter of Feb. 26.

know [Dr. Henry's] sentiments have not been esteemed very loyal. His letter is certainly a high compliment." Also valued was the commendation of William H. Hanna of the Bloomington bar: "You are altogether in the right—*Dictum* and all." J. E. McClun, sometime Probate Judge, acknowledged receipt of the opinion with the comment,

> You know my fears that our troubles would end in a military despotism. This decision I say gives me hope. I have no confidence in Congress . . . . I have no faith in the Radicalism of the day. The party is rampant crazy & full of blood & Congress is simply the reiterator of the passion of the hour . . . .

Davis' opinion should "do much . . . to crush and subdue the reckless & revolutionary spirit . . ."[162]

"Having been attacked so much in the papers, I thought that Judge Rockwell wd have written me but as he has not I conclude that he does not like my opinion." So Justice Davis confided to his wife on January 30. When on January 31 this brother-in-law in Massachusetts did write, his reaction was, as Davis had feared, disappointing:

> the four Judges, seem to have done all that Milligan's case required, and to have done it upon sufficient reason. Then the question between them and the majority of the Court, is perhaps this; was it necessary & judicious in Milligan's case, to deny the authority of Congress, to authorize the Military Commission in Indiana. Happily, I am not called upon to decide that question, and I apprehend, it must be left a while, to ascertain, which opinion will "stand the test of talents & of time."
> But I think it is generally admitted that when a case shall arise, which shall require a decision of that question, this dictum, (if it be so) will be likely to ripen into a valid decision. At any rate, I think there is no doubt it will be found to be fairly and thoroughly argued, with great felicity of language and the true spirit of Judicial dignity and candor, in the opinion of the majority of the Court by Mr Justice Davis.[163]

When Davis replied on February 24, he was still suffering from the unexpected reprobation his opinion had aroused: only two days before, the chairman of the Judiciary Committee of the House had condemned the majority for "thrusting upon the country without warrant

---

[162] Ewing wrote on Jan. 20; McClun on Jan. 19; Dr. Henry and Hanna on Jan. 22; Davis' letters to his wife were on Jan. 27 and 30. Davis Papers, Ill. State Hist. Soc.

[163] Davis Papers, Ill. State Hist. Soc.

in the record" their views on "the gravest questions of constitutional law."[164] Davis set out his own justification, for a kinsman and able judge whose approbation he coveted. It merits quotation at length.

My dear Rockwell,

I regret that I have been so busy that I could not sooner acknowledge the receipt of your letter. I understand the point of it, though delicately expressed. Let us see about it. I had to prove that military trials were illegal. The Law of Congress, of course, only authorized the discharge of Milligan if his trial was illegal. If rightly convicted, he could not be discharged under that or any other Law. We held that the Amendments to the Constitution forbid any one not connected with the military service, in States where courts were open, and in the proper exercise of their jurisdiction, to be tried for crime, except by an established court or jury.

The right to try by a military tribunal was claimed as an Executive power. We held that the provisions of the Constitution were irrepealable and could not be suspended. Did it not logically follow, that Congress could not repeal. Believing as we did, that the whole thing was fundamental, wd it not have been unmanly, & unworthy a court, to have confined the denial to the Executive, and wd it not at once have been claimed, that we admitted Congress could do it. How can a provision be irrepealable, & yet Congress repeal it, disregard it, or suspend it. The whole argument, such as it is, is to show the irrepealable character of the Amendments—nothing else. I used the words "Congress could grant no such power" in the wrong place, but in the subsequent part of the opinion, I think I proved it, and we could only deny the military right to try Milligan through the provisions of the Constitution. These we had, therefore, to interpret, & we interpreted them, as binding on all, for ever. The opinion wd have been worth nothing for future time, if we had cowardly toadied to the prevalent idea, that the legislative dept of the govt can override everything. Cowardice of all sorts is mean, but judicial cowardice is the meanest of all. Not a word said in the opinion about reconstruction & the power is conceded in insurrectionary States, & yet the Republican press every where has denounced the opinion as a second Dred Scott opinion, when the Dred Scott opinion was in the interest of Slavery, & the Milligan opinion in the interest of liberty. I did not suppose the Republican party would endorse such trials after the war is over. Yet they do it, & have had printed in pamphlet form the strictures of Holt,[165] the head of the Military Bureau on this

---

[164] Cong. Globe, 39–2, 1485. Feb. 22, 1867. He was presenting the Indemnity Bill, supra, p. 228.

[165] Joseph Holt (1807–94) of Kentucky, had served in the Buchanan Administration as Postmaster General and, in 1861, as Secretary of War. He was made Judge Advocate General in September 1862; the Bureau of Military Justice, of which he be-

opinion, & are scattering them broadcast. I abide the judgment of *time*. The people are mad now, and, if they dont recover soon, civil liberty will be entirely gone. During the war I was afraid it wd be all gone. If saved at all, I believe that two years longer of war wd have buried it out of sight. The judgt of the whole Court is being attacked, & if any other man than Chase was at the head of it, the minority wd have been attacked boldly for agreeing that Milligan was wrongly convicted. They *now* stab the opinion by charging it on me when Chase agreed to every thing that they are condemning. *He* wrote for an object. Whether he will gain it or not remains to be seen.[166] Recollect, the majority did not know, what part of the majority opinion the minority would attack. We supposed when we separated last spring that the question of jurisdiction would be attacked. *That* was apparently the great question, & I took some pains to set that right.

Stanton is denouncing the opinions of the minority & majority, and says, that the minority cant be defended at all. That the power is a war power, belonging to the Executive. And just read this morsel. Think of a man swearing to the Law, & how will the Chief Justice like it.

[Here Justice Davis pasted a newspaper clipping, "Secretary Stanton on the Milligan Decision," wherein Stanton was quoted as having told a Congressional committee that "I believe that Milligan was properly convicted . . . ."]

Congress claims omnipotent power like the British Constitution. Why then a written Constitution. Majorities dont need any. Our ancestors were not willing like Chief Justice Chase to trust the virtue and intelligence of the people. They believed in the necessity of written, irrepealable guaranties to protect minorities against the aggressions of majorities. I believe in the doctrines of the Milligan opinion, as necessary in times of civil commotion, to protect American citizens as much as I believe in the revealed will of God.

. . . .

During the fierceness of the attack on me, no body wrote me, but since it is wearing out, or rather, abating I have recd a good many letters & among the rest one from Mr Ewing, a copy of which I enclose you. I ought to except Judge Drummond of Chicago, from the list of those who did not write. He wrote me promptly and ap-

---

came head, was created by Act of Congress of June 20, 1864.

Justice Davis refers to a twenty-four-page pamphlet, "Review of the Decision of the United States Supreme Court in the cases of Lambdin P. Milligan and others," *The Indiana Conspirators*, published by the Union Congressional Executive Committee. It had first appeared in the *Washington Chronicle*. It was of-

fered as "a complete refutation to the reasoning by which the decision of the majority of the Court was sought to be sustained."

[166] Presumably he imagined that Chase was guided by his hope of gaining the Republican nomination for the Presidency. But that would not explain the attitude of Wayne, Swayne, and Miller.

provingly, & the tone, temper & sympathy of it I shall not soon forget. It wd be folly to say that I am indifferent to criticism, but I can conscientiously say, that I do not *wilt* under it. It is a little remarkable that a year ago my cousin, Henry Winter Davis, was nearly deified by the radical party in Congress, & yet I have not advanced one idea, principle, or sentiment that he has not over and over again promulgated in his seat in Congress.[167] And if he was alive now, such stumpets as Forney, and Jacobins as Holt, wd not have the public ear as they do.

My intellectual & moral nature are conservative and this Court wd be a hell on earth to me, unless I can decide questions according to the light which God has given me. I hope that God will give me strength to utter my convictions & never to quail before any political tempest. Courts are made to interpret the will of the people as manifested through Laws & Constitutions. I did not suppose that it was their business to interpret that will as manifested by an election.

The people can change their Constitution, but until it is done all attempts to evade it, override it, or disregard it, end either in anarchy or despotism.

I have no faith in the purposes and aims of the extreme men of the dominant party, & they control legislation. Independence of thought & action are buried beneath the tyranny of party caucus.

I see no hope except in the disintegration of the dominant party. For the Democratic party have a taint about them, which will always prevent their replacement in power & justly so. But I will not *bore* you with my speculations about politics. I talk politics with no one, for I can do no good. I never before wished for the gift of high power. If I had the genius & power of extemporaneous debate that my poor cousin was blessed with, I wd resign my office & try if I could not by a great missionary effort wake up the common people of the West to a sense of their danger. . . .[168]

In mid-January, Justice Davis solicited Benjamin R. Curtis to prepare a defense of the opinion of the majority; he supplied him with

---

[167] Henry Winter Davis died on December 30, 1865.

Justice Davis held in high admiration this handsome, eloquent, captivating, uncompromising and impetuous kinsman. "My first *opinion* I brought down for Henry Davis to look at & he commends it & only altered the phraseology of a few sentences," Justice Davis wrote to his wife on Christmas day, 1862, when a guest at his cousin's home in Baltimore. Davis Papers, Ill. State Hist. Soc.

On the episode "a year ago," in the 38th Congress, see supra, pp. 185–91.

Apropos of Justice Davis' resistance to "the prevalent idea, that the legislative dept of the govt can override everything," who contributed more to that idea than Henry Winter Davis? For example, by insisting that Reconstruction belonged exclusively to Congress, free from judicial control. And by his attempt to subordinate the President's direction of foreign affairs to an authoritative voice of Congress. See supra, p. 191, n. 43.

[168] Davis Papers.

the briefs and other papers in the case, and newspaper comments. Curtis purposed to comply. He wrote on January 17:

> At present the question is whether Congress can destroy the Executive power. That question must assume some more definite shape before it can be possible to attract the attention of the people to a calm & dispassionate statement of the office of the Su. Ct. in our gov^t & to what the Court has done in this great decision. . . .

He added this counsel:

> do not allow yourself to be disquieted by newspapers any more than you can help. I venture to give this advice because I have been in a similar condition & subject to similar attacks.[169]

Davis' turning to Curtis was appropriate. Besides his position of authority in his profession and as a former Justice of the Supreme Court, Curtis had published a pamphlet on Executive Power in October 1862, arguing that the President had usurped power in suspending the privilege of the writ, and in the preliminary proclamation of emancipation. "It has never been doubted that the power to abolish slavery within the States . . . was reserved to the States." Curtis had remonstrated with Stanton, but found that "strange man" to be sincerely unmoved.[170]

When Curtis replied to Davis that the most immediate danger was that Congress would attempt to destroy the Executive, he had in mind the action of the House on January 7, 1867, when it authorized its Judiciary Committee to inquire and report whether the President had committed offenses for which impeachment would lie.[171]

Curtis wrote again on February 25:

> Mr. Stanton is, of course, ready to swear to the law under which he has caused people to be hanged: for if there *is* no such law *what has he done*!
>
> The Supreme Court must rely on the *final* judgment of the people to support its decision, & I hope & yet believe that final judgment will be right. I know the advantage which the radical party have in being *in the field & equipped for aggression.* . . .
>
> I have not the least doubt that *the Bar* of this country can be & will be wholly persuaded that the decision is right, if not one word beyond your opinion should be written on the subject. . . .

---

[169] Davis Papers, Ill. State Hist. Soc.

[170] Benjamin R. Curtis, ed., *A Memoir of Benjamin Robbins Curtis,* 2 vols. (Boston: Little, Brown and Co., 1879), I, 350–60; II, 306–35.

[171] Cong. Globe, 39–2, 321. Moved by Ashley of Ohio.

At the moment, he had neither time nor strength to prepare a pamphlet in support of Davis' opinion in *Milligan*.[172]

It is noteworthy how much of the applause of the *Milligan* opinion went at once to the point that it put a restraint upon *Congress*. Davis believed that the occasion called for the imposition of such restraint, that Republican control of Congress created a danger worthy of a great missionary effort. To his distinction, that *Dred Scott* was in the interest of Slavery but that *Milligan* spoke for Liberty, it could be rejoined that *Dred Scott* asserted a Fifth Amendment liberty, whereas *Milligan* was read throughout the Southern States as a new affirmation that Congress would not be allowed to interfere with their own peculiar institution. Of course that is far from being the whole truth about *Milligan*: but it is a *part* of the truth, a part which has commonly been overlooked.

IN RETROSPECT

STANTON AND GOVERNOR MORTON erred gravely when they determined to bring Milligan and co-defendants before a military commission. Then an Attorney General of cloudy judgment, with an associate who proceeded by effrontery, filed a lawless brief. Not one of the Justices would accept such stultifying propositions.[173] That afforded Black an occasion to which his style of advocacy was best suited—to treat his opponent's case with scorn as utterly preposterous.

The exorbitance of the Government's pretensions gave a semblance of justification for Justice Davis to go beyond the question of jurisdiction, to insist upon the admonition that the provisions of the Constitution could not be "repealed" by any branch of the Government.

In the context of the moment, the opinion came as a shock, a breach of the comity between the Court and Congress. It gave warning that as Congress was about to deal with intransigent Southern States supported by the President, it must reckon with an unfriendly Court.

Study and reflection have led to the conclusion—not suspected

---

[172] Davis Papers, Ill. State Hist. Soc.

[173] The only plausible line of argument would have been that the Executive must be accorded a discretion, commensurate with the occasion, to meet immediate danger—going on to submit to the judgment of the Court that, in the light of the circumstances, what had been done should not be held to have been ex-cessive. Such cases as Martin v. Mott, 12 Wheat. 19 (1827); Luther v. Borden, 7 How. 1 (1849); and Mitchell v. Harmony, 13 How. 115 (1852), could have been invoked for what they were worth. It is not supposed that this would have proved convincing—but counsel could thus have kept within the bounds of intellectual respectability.

at the outset—that the needless breadth of the language in *Milligan* should be reckoned as the starting point in the sequence of actions and reactions that led to the statute of March 27, 1868,[174] whereby Congress took away the Court's jurisdiction in *Ex parte McCardle*,[175] deliberately to forestall a decision on the constitutionality of the Reconstruction Acts. Far from inducing Congress to act with greater restraint, the effect of the opinion was rather to put party leaders into a more revolutionary frame of mind. The Court had impaired its own standing as authentic expositor of the Constitution.

The Nation of January 10, 1867, carried a perceptive article on "Political Questions in the Supreme Court."[176] Its editor, Godkin, while Radical on Reconstruction, was fair-minded, a man of understanding. The editorial began,

> The Supreme Court of the United States is just now the subject of lively popular interest and discussion. It has recently been, and will soon be again, called upon to decide questions which have been made political issues between hostile parties; and concerning which few men are able to think impartially. All the issues of the war, and of the era of reconstruction succeeding the war, will be submitted to the judgment of this court; and a strenuous effort will be made to secure from it decisions which will nullify the will of the people, and vindicate the rejected policy of Mr. Johnson. There is great danger that, whatever may be the decision of the court, its action may fail to command public confidence; that if the decision is against the views of the majority, it will be ascribed to partisanship, and that if it is with them, it will be thought to have been influenced by fear.

In *Milligan*, the editorial went on to say, the majority opinion was "deserving of criticism" for its needless statement denying Congress a power it had not attempted to exercise. "Such an opinion is calculated to arouse a suspicion that the court is anxious to express its views upon these great questions before they are legitimately presented to it."

THE CASE OF DR. MUDD

OF THE EIGHT TRIED FOR COMPLICITY in John Wilkes Booth's assassination of President Lincoln,[177] four were sentenced to hard labor: Dr. Samuel A. Mudd, Samuel Arnold, and Michael O'Laughlin for life,

------

[174] 15 Stat. 44.
[175] 6 Wall. 318 (1868); 7 Wall. 506 (1869). Infra, pp. 460, 464–65.

[176] 4:30.
[177] Supra, p. 197.

Edward Spangler for six years. Presently they were confined at Fort Jefferson, on the Dry Tortugas, in Florida.

Dr. Mudd, at his home in Maryland, had set Booth's broken leg. He had standing in his community; efforts to secure his release on writ of habeas corpus, or by clemency, were unremitting. He will linger on the margin of the history of the Court, and occasionally will make a significant appearance, until at the end of the Johnson Administration clemency rendered his and companion cases moot. Applications on his behalf are relevant to other matters of habeas corpus before the Justices.

The holding in *Milligan* on December 17, 1866, that where the courts are open, trial by military commission is invalid, gave hope to Dr. Mudd. Application for habeas corpus was made to Justice Wayne, whose circuit included Florida, the place of confinement. Failing there, counsel turned to the Chief Justice. As reported in a Washington dispatch of December 19, 1866, appearing in the *New York Herald* of the twentieth:

> Application was made today before Chief Justice Chase for a writ of habeas corpus in the case of Dr. Mudd, imprisoned at the Dry Tortugas for complicity in the assassination of Mr. Lincoln. The application was made by A. Sterett Ridgely, of the Baltimore bar. Hon. Reverdy Johnson is retained in the case.[178]

Andrew Sterett Ridgely was Reverdy Johnson's son-in-law.

The application was based on a provision in Section 14 of the Judiciary Act of 1789: "either of the justices of the supreme court, as well as judges of the district courts, shall have the power to grant writs of habeas corpus for the purpose of inquiry into the cause of commitment" where the detention was under claim of the authority of the United States.[179] Could a Justice send a writ to a place outside the circuit to which he was allotted?

Ridgely, writing to Chief Justice Chase on December 28, urged that the answer was Yes; he read the statute to mean that while a District Judge could issue a writ to run only to the extent of his District, the power of a Justice of the Supreme Court was "co-extensive with the whole United States." He added, "This is the view entertained by your predecessor the late Chief Justice."[180] Ridgely gave his authority for citing Taney:

---

[178] One reads of the application in the *National Intelligencer*, December 27, 1866; *The Nation*, 4:2, January 3, 1867; and Nettie Mudd, *Life of Dr. Samuel A. Mudd* (New York and Washington: Neale Publishing Co., 1906), 214–16, 219, 225, 228–30.

[179] 1 Stat. 82.

[180] Chase Papers, L.C.

V: *The* Milligan *and* Test Oath *Cases*

> In the case of Merryman, the application was addressed to him
> . . . as Chief Justice of the United States and Presiding Judge of the
> Circuit Court for Maryland. He, however, struck his pen through the
> latter part of the address, and caused the writ to issue by order of the
> Chief Justice of the United States . . . .

This referred to the memorable case, *Ex parte Merryman*, in May
1861.[181] Petitioner was held at Fort McHenry, Baltimore, on the
ground that he was a lieutenant in a secessionist company, in readiness
to cooperate with the rebels. Maryland was a part of the Circuit to
which Taney was assigned; the District of Columbia was not. That the
Chief Justice made the writ returnable at Baltimore, he stated, was not
on any supposition that his power in the premises was confined to his
Circuit, but only to avoid calling the respondent, General Cadwalader,
away from his place of duty.

If, now, Chase had any doubt of his jurisdiction to issue the writ
in respect of Dr. Mudd in Florida, would he set a date when Reverdy
Johnson and Ridgely could argue the question? Argument was heard,
whereupon the Chief Justice denied the application. No opinion was
filed.[182] Reverdy Johnson understood, however, that the Chief Justice
based his denial on the view that "he had no power himself to issue
such a writ to be executed outside his own circuit."[183] There, for the
moment, the matter ended. Dr. Mudd remained in Fort Jefferson, where
presently he rendered heroic service in an epidemic of yellow fever that
carried off many soldiers and also O'Laughlin, one of the co-defendants.

Two years later, however, a fresh attempt would be made on
behalf of Mudd and his two surviving companions; this case would
reach the Supreme Court and have a considerable importance, even
though it never came to a decision and is unknown to the Reports.[184]
And still later, Chief Justice Chase would have to reconsider his position, when petitions for habeas corpus were presented on behalf of
Yerger in Mississippi, and Brown and others in Texas, prisoners held
for trial by military commission under the Reconstruction Act.[185]

In the period of Reconstruction, each item seems to be related to
everything else.

---

[181] Fed. Case No. 9487.

[182] In 1949, in connection with an
article I was then writing, I requested
the Clerk of the Supreme Court to
cause a search to be made in the
files of the Court. He advised that
no copy was found. Nor have I come
upon one in my work with Chase
Papers.

[183] As Johnson stated in the Senate
on Jan. 25, 1867, Cong. Globe, 39–
2, 730. This was during discussion
of H.R. 605, the bill that became
the memorable Act of February 5,
1867, 14 Stat. 385, giving appeals to
the Supreme Court in habeas corpus
cases—the statute involved in *Ex
parte* McCardle. Infra, p. 448.

[184] Infra, pp. 488–92.

[185] Infra, pp. 565–78.

THE TEST OATH DECISIONS

WHEN THE COURT met in December 1866 it was expected that judgments would presently be rendered in *Ex parte Garland*,[186] challenging the Congressional test oath for practitioners in the federal courts, and *Cummings v. Missouri*,[187] on the State's test for clergymen. To loyalists in the ex-rebel States, the outcome for the Congressional requirement was of great practical interest. They sought a reargument in which they might be heard, to supplement the effort by Attorney General Speed and Stanbery the previous March. On December 11, as the Minutes record, Lorenzo Sherwood of Texas moved for a reargument of Garland. On the fourteenth it was announced that the motion was overruled. The *New York Evening Post* explained that Sherwood's object had been "that he and Governor Hamilton might argue it on behalf of the loyal people of the South."[188] Judge Sherwood had been prominent in the Southern Unionists' Convention at Philadelphia in September.

When on January 14, 1867, the Court spoke, each requirement was held unconstitutional, by a majority of five to four.[189] The division differed from that in *Milligan* in that Justice Wayne joined his Democratic brethren, while Justice Davis joined in the dissent.

The Court rescinded its own rule requiring the test oath.[190]

In each case, the issue was plain. Congress is forbidden to pass any bill of attainder or ex post facto law.[191] A like prohibition is laid upon the States.[192] If the requirement of a test oath were held to be a *punishment* for acts of disloyalty already committed, then it added an additional penalty after the act, and could be held to fall under the ban. If however the requirement were viewed as a *qualification* for the exercise of a calling of public significance, a security for the future, then it could be upheld—no matter that the Justices might think it

---

[186] 4 Wall. 333.

[187] 4 Wall. 277.

[188] Dec. 14, 1866.

Garland was *not* argued at December Term 1866. Lawyers' Edition (which I have found ordinarily to be accurate as to dates of argument and of decision) is in error in reporting *Garland*, 18 L.Ed. 366. It was not argued on December 15, 1866: it was argued, as stated in the text, on December 15 and 22, 1865, on the matter of leave to file, and on the merits on March 13, 14, and 15, 1866.

[189] In *Ex parte* Marr, supra at the same time as in *Ex parte* Garland, it was ordered that the prayer be granted.

In Garesche v. Missouri, supra the case on the attorney's oath, which stood on the same footing with *Cummings* and had been argued with it, no formal disposition was made until on April 24, 1867, on motion of Reverdy Johnson for plaintiff in error, the writ of error was dismissed.

[190] Minutes for Monday, Jan. 14, 1867.

[191] Art. I, Sec. 9, cl. 3.

[192] Art. I, Sec. 10, cl. 1.

New Orleans
10 Dec' 1866

My Dear Mr Middleton

We have contradictory ac-
counts of the action of the Sup Court
upon the Test oath to attorneys. Will
you tell me whether attorneys are
permitted to appear before the Sup
Court or admitted to the bar without
taking the oath under the act of
Jan'y 1865.

Has any action been taken by the
Court on the subject?

Will you inform me by title
given of any action?

Please inform my
friend Mr Meehan that Austin on
jurisprudence & several of his
other friends were buried in
the boxes, which my excellent
friends Archie & Tom preserved for
me. I will make a negociation
with Mr M. for exchange of prisoners
or restitution of captured property
on the most liberal terms of
reciprocity, known to belligerents
when I finish my unpacking

Most Truly yrs
J A Campbell

Hon D w Middleton
Clerk of Sup Court

Ex-Justice Campbell to the Clerk
What has the Court decided about the federal test oath? Terms for
restoring Austin on Jurisprudence, fallen into his hands.

unwise. It did not follow that because a new qualification would work a hardship it must be held to impose a penalty. But it could be argued that the constitutional prohibition should not be read narrowly, and that a test that barred the attorney from at least a part of his practice, and the clergyman from his ministry, was in effect highly penal. Garland pleaded further that he had received a pardon: but the significance of that turned on the same question, was the test a punishment?

Justice Field wrote the opinions for the majority. The Constitution, he said,

> deals with substance, not shadows. Its inhibition was levelled at the thing, not the name. It intended that the rights of the citizen should be secure against deprivation for past conduct by legislative enactment, under any form, however disguised. . . .[193]

In each case, it was held, the requirement had visited a new punishment, and hence came within the condemnation of the Constitution.

For the dissenters, Justice Miller urged that there was not such incompatibility as would warrant the Court in overriding the law-making power.[194] He stressed the importance of the attorney's role; one who had supported the rebellion had exhibited a trait of character that would permit a court, without aid of a statute, to declare him unfit to practice before it. As to the clergyman in Missouri: Justice Miller recalled how largely the Constitution had left the subject of religion to the State's own understanding. The Court in the past had respected this allocation of authority, even where the case seemed hard. However great the hardship resulting to Cummings from the requirement, the minority would have had the Court forbear to interpose between the State and its citizen.[195]

---

[193] Cummings v. Missouri, 4 Wall. at 325.

[194] 4 Wall. at 382.

[195] Justice Miller dwelt upon the instructive case of Permoli v. First Municipality of the City of New Orleans, 3 How. 589 (1845). Since 1827 the Municipality had had an ordinance—based upon the need to prevent the spread of yellow fever—that funerals be held in an appointed obituary chapel and not in parish churches. Father Permoli had been convicted of a violation. On writ of error, this was challenged before the Supreme Court as an infringement of religious liberty—an intrusion of government into matters of faith and doctrine. Justice Catron, for a unanimous Court, said that "before proceeding to examine the merits of the controversy, it is our duty to determine whether this Court has jurisdiction of the matter." The conclusion was that "The Constitution makes no provision for protecting the citizens of the respective States in their religious liberties: this is left to the State constitutions and laws . . . ." Since "the question presented by the record is exclusively of State cognizance," the Court dismissed for want of jurisdiction.

Note: The Fourteenth Amendment —with its latent possibilities in the field of religious liberty—was then

V: *The* Milligan *and* Test Oath *Cases*

These opinions, as recorded stenographically in the courtroom, at once became available for publication. The *National Intelligencer* explained how this came about:

> The United States Supreme Court, when their opinion in the Indiana military commission cases was announced, prohibited reports being made for publication, but the rule has been relaxed on condition that the publishers state that the reports are from reporters' notes, and not from the official manuscripts of the judges.[196]

The Court was unaccustomed to playing at the center of the public stage. Whether, as with *Milligan*, there was a fortnight of uncertainty and conjecture about what the Court had said, or, as now with the *Test Oath Cases*, stenographic reporting was permitted with the likelihood of garbling, there were some unfortunate results.[197]

The actual importance to the Government of the matters at stake in these cases was not great. So far as the requirement for practitioners at the federal bar was concerned, the Government lost nothing of present value. It had been enacted late in the war, only because Senator Sumner had become aroused at the sight of rebel sympathizers practicing law in the District of Columbia.[198] The requirement had already been held invalid by federal judges in the South.[199] On January 15, 1866, before

---

pending before the State legislatures. (*Missouri's Radical legislature ratified a fortnight after* Cummings *was decided.*) *And those who most desired the Supreme Court to deny the power of the State to impose a test oath belonged to the party which, in the name of State rights, was resisting the adoption of the Amendment.*

Some correspondence may be seen between Justice Field's rejection of Missouri's interference—on what he found to be unwarrantable grounds—with its citizens' pursuit of their callings, and his rejection of Louisiana's interference with the practice of its butchers in the *Slaughter House Cases*, 16 Wall. 36 (1873), the first great interpretation of the Fourteenth Amendment.

There is a correspondence, too, between Justice Miller's position, writing for the dissenters in *Cummings*, and that he took as spokesman for the Court in *Slaughter House*: in each he would respect the State's autonomy as regarded local government, and would have the Court for-

bear—notwithstanding the seeming unwisdom of the State's legislation—from what he regarded as an undue exercise of federal judicial power.

[196] Tuesday, Jan. 15, 1867. On the fifteenth and sixteenth the two opinions by Justice Field and the dissenting opinion by Justice Miller were published, and "some hundreds of copies extra" were run.

[197] The *National Intelligencer* of January 16 said that the account published by its rival, John W. Forney's *Chronicle*, was "materially incorrect." The *New Orleans Picayune's* correspondent stated that some reports of the Test Oath Cases were "neither clear nor satisfactory"; that it was preferable, as in Milligan's case, to exclude stenographers and wait for the official printed opinions. Feb. 6, 1867.

[198] Supra, p. 58.

[199] *In re* Baxter, Fed. Case No. 1118, C.C. E.D. Tenn. 1865, Trigg, J.; *In re* Shorter, Fed. Case No. 12,-811, D.C. Ala. 1865, Busteed, J.; *Ex parte* Law, Fed. Case No. 8126,

Garland was argued on the merits, Thad Stevens offered a resolution to instruct the Judiciary Committee to inquire into the expediency of allowing attorneys to practice without taking the oath; now that the war was at an end he saw no objection. The resolution was carried, 82 to 77; almost half of the majority were Republicans.[200] No action resulted.

Justice Miller concluded his dissent with the statement that

> I have endeavored to bring to the examination of the grave questions of constitutional law involved in this inquiry those principles alone which are calculated to assist in determining what the law is, rather than what, in my private judgment, it ought to be.[201]

To his kinsman in Texas, barred from pursuing his practice in the federal courts, Miller wrote his inner thoughts:

> I have felt bound by my clear convictions thus to vote and I am not sorry that the result is adverse to my opinion, on your account and generally because I think the requirement unnecessarily harsh at present.[202]

Indeed after Appomattox, heads of the Executive Departments found that to restore services at the South they were obliged to fill subordinate posts with appointees who could not take the iron-clad oath.[203]

REACTION TO THE TEST OATH DECISIONS

IT COMMONLY HAPPENS that on the morrow of a controversial decision by the Court, precipitate measures to strike back are introduced in Congress. So it was after the Test Oath decisions in January 1867. A bill by Representative Thomas Williams of Pennsylvania would have required a unanimous bench to invalidate a federal statute.[204]

D.C. Ga. 1866, Erskine, J. William M. Robinson, Jr., *Justice in Grey,* (Cambridge, Mass.: Harvard University Press, 1941), 596–98, gives additional details.

[200] Cong. Globe, 39–1, 234.

[201] 4 Wall. at 399.

[202] Letter of Dec. 8, 1866. Fairman, *Mr. Justice Miller,* 134. He wrote that "Today in consultation the court decided the congressional oath exacted of Attorneys to be void. . . . The opinions may not be read for two weeks yet and you will regard this as strictly confidential . . . ."

[203] Ann. Cyc. 1866, 738–39. Secretary Welles noted the Cabinet discussion on August 11, 1865: "the result was unanimous that the appointments should be made; that the current business of the Administration and the country must go on, notwithstanding unwise and ill considered legislation." II:358; also 318, 445, 450.

[204] Cong. Globe, 39–2, 616. Jan. 21, 1867.

That died in committee. Boutwell of Massachusetts reported from the Judiciary Committee a bill to exclude from the federal bar all guilty of a felony or of engaging in or encouraging rebellion.[205] An attempt to secure instant passage brought an all-night resistance by a "small, but red hot Gideon's band of Copperheads,"[206] who obtained one hour for debate. Then the bill was carried, 108 to 42.[207] "The Republicans are advancing apace on the road to absolute tyranny," said the *New York World*. "The Democratic members did well to make a resolute stand for the right of debate."[208] In the Senate, Boutwell's bill was allowed to die.

The Republican press had some difficulty in finding a basis for indignation over *Garland* and *Cummings*. Often the comments were misinformed. The *New York Tribune* had Justice Davis "of Indiana" among the majority and Justice Wayne with the minority, evidently supposing the division in *Milligan* had been maintained. It said that the Court's action "prevents Congress or the States from making loyalty a qualification of office,"[209] which it did not. The *New York Herald* made a like exaggeration, and came out strongly for the Williams bill.[210] The respectable *Cincinnati Gazette* said, "It is imperatively necessary now, when a bare majority of the Court . . . have attempted to usurp the legislative power, and to rescue the belligerent rebel States from the just terms of peace which the nation demands."[211] The *Chicago Tribune* said that the recent decisions showed "that it is the deliberate purpose of the Supreme Court to usurp the legislative powers of the Government, to defeat the will of the loyal men of this nation . . ." It too hailed the Williams bill.[212] The *Burlington* (Vermont) *Free Press* voiced a prevalent thought when it deplored another decision that "gave great comfort to the copperheads."[213]

The *Dayton Journal* noted that the decisions made former rebels and Democrats "ecstatic" and destroyed what returning confidence Unionists felt in the Court. It explained:

> The five years of war . . . kept the Supreme Court out of sight. The Dred Scott decision was reversed as a relic of barbarism [by the Thirteenth Amendment]. The Supreme Court, as was believed, would profit by the lesson taught by this great decision by the people. But it has not done so. . . .

---

[205] Cong. Globe, 39–2, 646. Jan. 22.

[206] *Columbus* (Ohio) *Morning Journal*, January 28.

[207] Cong. Globe, 39–2, 685. Jan. 23.

[208] Jan. 24.

[209] Jan. 15.

[210] Jan. 16, 23.

[211] Jan. 23.

[212] Jan. 17, 22.

[213] Jan. 16.

The *Journal* favored a requirement of unanimity, or at least two-thirds, to invalidate an Act of Congress.[214]

It was not that anything thus far decided was of any serious consequence to the party in power. When Milligan and his associates had been released on April 10, 1866, the country took it quietly, and Congress made no outcry. What was lost in *Garland* was no more than Thad Stevens and many other Republicans wanted to concede. The alarm was for substantial matters in the immediate future. Take the comment of *The Nation*, a journal not given to wild apprehension. While agreeing with the minority in the *Test Oath Cases*, it urged editors and orators to avoid "revilings and threatenings" that tended "to stimulate the growing want of respect both for judges and law." But as it read the portents, the people might soon face "the momentous problem whether they will allow the Government to be jeopardized, and the form of polity on which the nation has resolved, and for which 200,000 men have laid down their lives, to be set aside by any tribunal, however eminent and respectable." It concluded: "Questions which affect a nation's destiny that nation only can answer: and no nation worthy of the name will ever allow anybody else to answer them."[215]

THE TEST OATH DECISIONS MEET DISRESPECT

THE DECISION IN *Ex Parte Garland* was flouted by the Supreme Court for the District of Columbia. This was a new court, created by a statute of March 3, 1863. Its tone was set by its Chief Justice, David K. Cartter of Ohio, a political lieutenant of Senator Ben Wade and, as characterized by Attorney General Bates, "a fierce partizan, an inbred vulgarian and a truculent ignoramus."[216] By this court's first rule, adopted in 1863, an oath was prescribed for applicants to practice at its bar; this oath was identical with the iron-clad formula prescribed for federal officers by the statute of July 2, 1862. Allen B. Magruder had practiced in the predecessor court, the Circuit Court for the District of Columbia. He had followed the Confederacy, had been pardoned, and promptly after the *Garland* decision had applied for admission in the District of Columbia court, without taking the oath. That court turned its response into a demonstration against the Supreme Court of the United States. It drew a distinction between Garland, deprived by statute of an advantage to which he had already been admitted, and Magruder, a newcomer who must meet the qualifications set by the court

[214] Jan. 31.
[215] 4:41. Jan. 17.
[216] *Diary of Edward Bates 1859–1866* (Washington: Government Printing Office, 1933), 310, for Oct. 17, 1863. Accord: *Diary of Gideon Welles*, II, 359; III, 160, 286, 294.

in the exercise of its inherent power. But aside from that, the *Garland* case was said to show merely that five eminent lawyers had taken one view while four equally eminent lawyers and the Congress had taken another. The District of Columbia court would take its stand with Congress and the minority. This defiant response was widely noted in the press.[217]

West Virginia was a State whose very existence, during the war, depended upon the prevalence of loyalty to the Union. The test oath was given a wide application, and was continued after armed conflict had given way to political strife. A statute of February 14, 1866,[218] required an oath of constant loyalty as a condition to practicing law. This was challenged at the July term, 1866, of the Supreme Court of Appeals by a number of lawyers, "many of whom averred their readiness and ability to take [the oath], but denied the power of the legislature to prescribe additional oaths to attorneys who had been duly admitted in this State before the passage of the act."[219] The case was held over, in anticipation of the decision by the federal Supreme Court. Shortly after that came, however, the West Virginia court at its January term, 1867, affirmed the validity of the statute. The judges said they found nothing in Justice Field's opinion to unsettle their own clear conviction.[220]

A year later, a circuit judge was impeached and removed because, following the Supreme Court of the United States, he had granted an admission without the test oath.[221]

Further litigation, and a new constitution in 1872, would presently bring the West Virginia court into accord with the Supreme Bench. This will be considered, later on.[222] So too will Frank Blair's challenge to Missouri's requirement of an oath for voters, and a companion case, *Woodson v. State of Missouri ex rel. Attorney General*, on the test for office-holders.[223] Keeping company with them will be *Ridley v. Sherbrook* from Tennessee, where a pardoned Confederate sought mandamus to establish his right to vote without an oath.[224] Substantially it would be time, not the Court, that stilled these disputes. After Justice

---

[217] Reported, inter alia, in the *National Intelligencer* and in the *New York Tribune* of Feb. 13, 1867. The opinions of Cartter, C. J., and Wylie, J., may be found in Edward McPherson, *The Political History of the United States of America during the Period of Reconstruction*, 3rd ed. (Washington: James A. Chapman, 1880), 234–39. Magruder was admitted on June 20, 1874, upon taking the oath then prescribed by rule of court. The minutes of the court do not make clear just when the iron-clad oath was abandoned.

[218] W. Va. Acts of 1866, ch. 30, p. 19.

[219] Reporter's note, 2 W. Va. at 186.

[220] *Ex parte* Hunter, 2 W. Va. 122.

[221] Ann. Cyc. 1868, 763.

[222] Infra, p. 618.

[223] Supra, pp. 151–52; infra, pp. 613, 616.

[224] Infra, pp. 612, 616.

Wayne's death in July 1867, the Court would for two and a half years be held by eight Justices, equally divided in their approach to test oaths. In the meantime, Missouri and Tennessee, like West Virginia, would be moving toward the day when a new constitution would put an end to such requirements.

THE GREY JACKET: BEN BUTLER AND CALEB CUSHING

AT DECEMBER TERM 1866, quite aside from the spectacular constitutional causes, the Supreme Court was concerned with a load of matters of large significance to the public, or at least to private interests. A few of these should be mentioned.

Besides *The Springbok* and *The Peterhoff*, already noticed,[225] the Court at this term rendered a dozen other decisions in prize. Among these was *The Grey Jacket*,[226] wherein Ben Butler figured, in true character, as manipulator as well as counsel. Ship and cargo had been condemned for running the blockade, from Mobile toward Havana; it was a clear case. Butler was engaged, for a large contingent fee, to do what he could to salvage something at Washington. He propounded the theory, supported by belated professions by the claimant, that here was a loyal Unionist who in December 1863 was making a determined effort to break away from the Confederacy and come with his property to some loyal State; Butler undertook to induce the Government to remit the forfeiture. If this was a case of prize, then under the statute the proceeds would go half to the officers and men who made the capture and half to the naval pension fund. If however the Supreme Court could be induced to view this rather as a seizure pursuant to the Non-Intercourse Act of July 13, 1861, [227] the property would be forfeited to the United States, and the Secretary of the Treasury could remit to the claimant. Butler's approach was repelled by the Secretary of the Navy, who put him down as "reckless, avaricious, unscrupulous."[228] Attorney General Speed, slowly, saw through Butler's attempt to impose upon him. Then, according to Welles' diary,

> Failing at these points, Butler commenced intriguing at the Treasury, where he was listened to by [First Assistant Secretary W. E.]

---

[225] Supra, pp. 39–43.

[226] 5 Wall. 342 (1867).

[227] 12 Stat. 255. All goods coming from a State or section in insurrection into other parts of the United States, together with vessel or vehicle conveying the same, would be forfeited to the United States; but forfeitures and penalties might be mitigated or remitted by the Secretary of the Treasury.

[228] *Diary of Gideon Welles*, II, 469–70. Mar. 31, 1866.

Chandler, and finally Caleb Cushing was employed at Chandler's suggestion to give a written opinion, General Butler being the prompter. Cushing was timid, hesitated to present his opinion unsustained, and General Butler drew up a preamble and resolution which he procured Thad Stevens to present and procured to be passed under the previous question, without debate, to the effect that cases of this description should be suspended until the judgment of the Supreme Court should be obtained next winter [*i.e.*, at December term 1866] . . . . Stevens's resolution was passed on the 9th [of April, 1866],[229] and Cushing's opinion is dated on the 11th. The whole thing is disgraceful even to a lobby agent . . . .[230]

Stevens' extraordinary resolution recited that "whereas the question is now pending before the Supreme Court, whether such property so captured should be forfeited to the United States, or for the benefit of the captors" and "because of the press of business in said court" could not be determined until the next term, therefore "in the opinion of this House" the Treasury should withhold distribution to the captors—that is, to the officers and men of the Navy. This "expression of the opinion of the House" was hurried through by Thad Stevens in combination with two inveterate Democrats—enough in itself to excite a lively suspicion.

When *The Grey Jacket* was reached for argument, the Court was confronted with this unusual sight: Ben Butler appearing for the claimant; the Assistant Attorney General and an associate for the United States and the captors; and Caleb Cushing, for the Treasury Department, seeking to argue that the Attorney General was wrong and the claimant was right. Should the Court give ear to another branch of the United States Government, in contradiction of the Attorney General? The Court took the matter under advisement, and on Monday, January 7, 1867, the Chief Justice gave its answer:

that in causes where the United States is a party, and is represented by the Attorney General, or the Assistant Attorney General, or special counsel employed by the Attorney General, no counsel can be heard in opposition on behalf of any other of the Departments of the Government.

The Chief Justice went on to say that in this case, by reason of the impression at the bar and because the Court desired light, counsel for the Treasury would be heard.[231]

---

[229] Cong. Globe, 39–1, 1856.
[230] *Diary of Gideon Welles,* II,
492–93. Apr. 25, 1866.
[231] Minutes, and 5 Wall. 370, 371.

Certainly it was a sound rule, that the Government would speak only by its chief law officer or by counsel under his authority.[232]

When Justice Swayne announced the Court's opinion in *The Grey Jacket*, he found "nothing persuasive," "no redeeming feature," in Butler's appeal.

The Grey Jacket is a reminder that the Justices, being astute, saw many things that one would hardly guess from the Reports. This mention of the case has also shown the association between Ben Butler and Caleb Cushing, both of Massachusetts. The latter, once Attorney General, was now practicing in Washington; those who had some claim upon the Government were likely to seek his services. Hugh McCulloch, then Secretary of the Treasury, noting Cushing's varied talents, added that "he lacked only one thing . . . —convictions."[233] Cushing will reappear at a tense moment when, in 1874, President Grant sought to make him Chief Justice.

SOME OTHER BUSINESS AT DECEMBER TERM 1866

AT THIS TERM the Court decided a large California land case, *De Haro v. United States*,[234] wherein were engaged Stanbery, Attorney General; Cushing and Black, ex-Attorneys General; William M. Evarts, soon to become Attorney General; Montgomery Blair, ex-Postmaster General; and William M. Stewart, Senator from Nevada. These names, the fact that at the Attorney General's request it was heard as early as practicable, and the four days duration of the argument, suggest the magnitude and importance of this litigation to establish title to a tract within the city of San Francisco.[235]

One notes also a cluster of controversies between bondholders and cities and counties in the Northwest—Kenosha, Galena, Quincy, Rock Island, Burlington—brought to enforce securities issued in aid of railroads, whose validity was now contested. The tendency of the Court in such cases to deny all defenses produced a mounting resentment

---

[232] The Attorney General's authority became more clear when in 1870 his office became the Department of Justice. The post of Solicitor General was then created, under him, particularly to argue cases in the Supreme Court.

In " 'Inconsistency' in Government Litigation," *Harv. L. Rev.* 64:759 (1951), Robert L. Stern explained the practice in varied situations where agencies of the Government take different views of some question with which they respectively have a concern. The ICC and some other agencies have by statute been given autonomy in litigation.

[233] *Men and Measures of Half a Century* (New York: Charles Scribner's Sons, 1888), 24.

[234] 5 Wall. 599 (1867).

[235] It was filed on January 12, 1867, argued on April 8, 9, 10, and 11, and decided on May 13.

which would culminate, two years later, in outright defiance by communities in the otherwise loyal State of Iowa.[236]

Two opinions rendered at this term considered the extent of the liability of a municipality, New York and Chicago respectively, for injuries due to failure to maintain safe sidewalks.[237]

Also, the Court recognized the power of the Connecticut legislature to authorize a variation from the provisions of a charitable trust, where by reason of the growth of Hartford it had become impracticable to use the land in accord with the donor's instructions.[238] Evarts, seeking a forfeiture to the heirs, and B. R. Curtis, counsel for the trustees, had filed voluminous briefs. In these cases one catches glimmerings of future problems of urban land use and municipal responsibility.

Of the nation's population of 37 millions at that moment, less than one-eighth dwelt in cities—say 22 in all—of more than 50,000 inhabitants.[239]

One who observed, perceptively, in the Supreme Court chamber would learn enough to chronicle the annals of America—political, economic, and social.

It is reassuring to discover, often in seemingly little cases, that the Court was alert on points of practice and procedure, just as it is disturbing when one finds looseness or inattention. *Semple v. Hager*[240] teaches that where it is patent that the Court has no jurisdiction of the case, it will *dismiss* on the motion of the appellee, without waiting for the case to come up in its turn. Otherwise, said Grier, J., it would lie within the power of an appellant "by a frivolous pretense" to stall the execution of a judgment for some three years. In another case the same crusty judge censured counsel who had framed "a bill of exceptions (so called)" which was only "a sort of abstract or index" that failed to point what was the supposed error the Court was asked to review. "Protesting against attempts at mystifying the merits of a case by such records," Justice Grier addressed himself to what seemed to be the contested point.[241]

The Judiciary Act permitted appeals from a Circuit Court "when the matter in dispute exceeds the sum or value of two thousand dollars,

---

[236] Infra, chs. 17, 18.

[237] Mayor v. Sheffield, 4 Wall. 189 (1867); Robbins v. Chicago, 4 Wall. 657 (1867).

[238] Stanley v. Colt, 5 Wall. 119 (1867).

[239] There were twenty-five such cities by the Census of 1870.

[240] 4 Wall. 431 (1867).

[241] Evans v. Patterson, 4 Wall. 224 (1867), on writ of error to the Circuit Court for the Western District of Pennsylvania. Grier, J., and McCandless, District Judge, had heard the case; the District Judge had signed the bill of exceptions.

exclusive of costs." Therefore a judgment for exactly $2,000 could not be reviewed. "This court has no appellate jurisdiction, except as is defined by Congress," said the Chief Justice. This was *Walker v. United States*,[242] where the United States had recovered against the surety of William Walker, the filibustering adventurer charged under the Neutrality Act. Walker eluded the United States only to meet death before a Honduran firing squad.

In *Insurance Co. v. Ritchie*,[243] a Massachusetts corporation had asked the federal Circuit Court in that State to enjoin local officers of the federal internal revenue from collecting a tax they alleged to be due. Federal jurisdiction in such a suit had been established by an Act of Congress in 1864, which authorized appeal to the Supreme Court. The Circuit Court sustained the revenue officers and dismissed the bill. In the meantime, by the Act of July 13, 1866, Congress—ineptly— repealed the statute of 1864, without any saving clause for cases pending; it remitted taxpayers to another course of litigation. Insurance Co. nevertheless went up to the Supreme Court; the case was docketed on December 3, 1866. Could the Court consider an appeal, when the jurisdictional statute had been repealed while the litigation was pending? The Attorney General obtained early consideration. The Court's decision was that Congress had indeed cut off its power to proceed: "The appeal in this case must therefore be dismissed for want of jurisdiction."[244]

What if Congress were to abolish a category of the Court's appellate jurisdiction, after an appeal had been entertained, and patently in order to keep the Court from passing upon the constitutionality of a statute? That was the question in *McCardle's Case*, one year later.[245]

---

[242] 4 Wall. 163 (1866).
[243] 5 Wall. 541 (1867).
[244] The result of this tinkering by Congress was that, in such a situation as this (where there was no diversity of citizenship), plaintiff must start in a State court; the revenue officer might then remove to the Circuit Court; and appeal would lie to the Supreme Court. The Assessors v. Osbornes, 9 Wall. 567 (1870). Felix Frankfurter and James M. Landis, *The Business of the Supreme Court* (New York: Macmillan Co., 1927), 61–62, note 22.
[245] Infra, ch. 10.

CHAPTER VI

*Congressional Reconstruction:
Legislation—
The Act of March 2, 1867*

To BE THOROUGHGOING, a study of the Court's part in Congressional Reconstruction, 1867–70, must inch along, tracing action and reaction. Congress deliberated and acted—in response to the President's course, to Southern developments, to Northern sentiment, and to intimations from the Supreme Court. Presently it spoke, in the Act of March 2, 1867, "to provide for the more efficient Government of the Rebel States."[1] Thereafter, in successive efforts to induce the Court to deliver the Southern people from the grasp of Congress, the statute's vulnerable points were exposed and attacked. What follows will lay a foundation for appraising the action of the Court; where a matter is dwelt upon, its relevance will ultimately appear.

What now to do about the South was the great question when the Second Session of the 39th Congress opened on December 3, 1866.[2] The insecurity of life for loyal men, white and black, was one urgent concern.[3]

This from the speech of Frederick A. Pike of Maine is typical of what was being said:

---

[1] 14 Stat. 428.

[2] Supra, pp. 133, 182–84.

[3] Notable among instances coming to the attention of Congress were the riots at Memphis in early May, and at New Orleans in late July. Supra, pp. 182–84. The latter came immediately after the adjournment of the First Session. On December 6 the House appointed a select committee (Thomas D. Eliot of Massachusetts, chairman) to go to New Orleans to investigate, and "to report such appropriate legislative action as may be required in view of the condition of affairs in the State of Louisiana." Cong. Globe, 39–2, 28–29. On the resulting "Louisiana Bill," see infra, pp. 288–91.

The decision of Justice Nelson in chambers in May, *In re* Egan, supra, pp. 148–49, followed in November by that of the District Judge in the federal court for Delaware, supra, pp. 149–51, heightened the sense of urgency.

253

I am informed at the Freedmen's Bureau that in Georgia during the last year there have been about one hundred and fifty murders of freedmen and not a single punishment. The Watson case in Virginia[4] indicates the state of opinion there.

It is useless to go into details. The statements could be duplicated almost everywhere in the rebel States.[5]

More profoundly disturbing was the fact that the Southern States were uniformly refusing to accept the Fourteenth Amendment: two rejected before the Second Session opened; five during December, two in January, and the tenth in February. The President was encouraging this resistance. In the Alabama legislature, it seemed in early December that possibly ratification could be carried, until emphatic advice to reject came from Washington; and when in January the President was informed that a new effort was being made, he paralyzed it by this telegram:

What possible good can be obtained by reconsidering the constitutional amendment? I know of none . . . . There should be no faltering . . . .[6]

---

[4] Supra, pp. 214-16.

[5] Cong. Globe, 39-2, 255. Jan. 3, 1867. Pike was chairman of the Select Committee on the Murder of Union Leaders. Supra, p. 15.

What could be said in reply may be judged by the effort of Senator Cowan of Pennsylvania, Conservative Republican supporter of the President's policy:

Now, I aver that all this is sheer fabrication of the most flimsy character, and that not a single negro has been killed in the South because he was a Union man. If killed at all he has been killed for some sufficient reason, which that is not. . . .

I suppose if the whites kill the negroes now, they do so because they hate them. Will they love them any better when they find you have come to their rescue in such a terrible fashion [as the Military Reconstruction Bill]? . . .

Speech of Feb. 16, 1867. Cong. Globe, 39-2, App., 154.

This illustrates the outlook of one deeply attached to the Constitution as he had understood it in the past, who would deny any federal concern with civil relations within a State even in respect of the mass of men freed by the Thirteenth Amendment.

Cowan will appear among counsel for the complainant in Georgia v. Stanton, infra, p. 371.

[6] Telegram of January 17, 1867, to Lewis E. Parsons, former Provisional Governor. The exchange was introduced in the prosecution of the impeachment of the President. Trial of Andrew Johnson, Cong. Globe, 40-2, Supplement, 90. Also Edward McPherson, *The Political History of the United States during the Period of Reconstruction*, 3d ed., (Washington: James J. Chapman, 1880), 352-53.

The facts of the rejection in December are set out supra. Letters of General Wager Swayne to Chief Justice Chase, November 27 and December 10, 1866, report how sentiment for acceptance had been mounting until a dispatch urging rejection came from Parsons (then in Washington). "The cry was raised, 'we can't desert *our* President' . . . ." Chase Papers, L.C.

The attempt to bring a reconsidera-

VI: *Congressional Reconstruction*

In the meantime, as Northern legislatures convened, ratifications came pouring in: nine in January, five in February, bringing the count to twenty. However, as was to be expected, Kentucky, Delaware, and Maryland rejected.[7]

An amendment to the Constitution must be "ratified by the Legislatures of three fourths of the several States . . . ."[8] With the prospect of thirteen rejections in sight, the *New York World*—the organ of Northern Democracy—declared confidently that the Amendment was "as dead as Julius Caesar." It said this on November 17, 1866; and to impress the portent of the message, repeated its editorial on January 12:[9]

> Thirteen is one-fourth of fifty-two. The number of States must therefore reach fifty-two before such an amendment can be ratified. Where are the sixteen new States to come from?

"There is no likelihood that so many will ever be added"—not even in a hundred years.

Gloating, the *World* posed this challenge:

> The Constitution remaining, in spite of the Republicans, unaltered, will they condescend to tell us *what they propose to do about it?* That they can proceed no farther against the South by mere congressional legislation, they have confessed. Why else do they demand amendments? . . . No congressional sway can be more complete than a two-thirds majority of both Houses, capable of riding roughshod over the veto of the President. . . . As against the Supreme Court, a two-

---

tion in January brought the telegram quoted above, from Johnson to Parsons (then at Montgomery).

And see Eric L. McKitrick, *Andrew Johnson and Reconstruction* (Chicago: University of Chicago Press, 1960), 469–72.

[7] On Jan. 8, Feb. 7, and March 23, respectively. Delaware eventually ratified—on Feb. 12, 1901.

[8] ". . . or by Conventions in three fourths thereof, as the one or the other Mode of Ratification may be proposed by the Congress . . . ." Constitution, Art. V. See infra, n. 16.

[9] The *World* stood "foremost in ability and in the influence which it exerts over the mind of its party," said the *Jackson Clarion* of August 8, 1867—contrasting it with other Northern journals that "flourish by

pandering to the passions and prejudices of the Southern people."

The *World* claimed a circulation of 35,000 daily, and 75,000 for its weekly edition. Geo. P. Rowell & Co.'s *American Newspaper Directory* (New York, 1869), 71. It was edited by Manton Marble (1835–1917), and largely influenced by Samuel L. M. Barlow (1826–89). Each was a mover in Democratic politics. Barlow had an important law practice, and highly remunerative connections with business—particularly in railroad promotion.

On Marble, Barlow, and the *World*, see McKitrick, *Andrew Jackson and Reconstruction*, passim, and LaWanda Cox and John H. Cox, *Politics, Principle and Prejudice, 1865–66* (New York: Free Press of Glencoe, 1963), passim.

thirds majority avails nothing, potent as it is against the President. The Republican party, then, has proceeded as far as it can go by mere congressional action; and it can neither amend the Constitution to get more power, nor punish States for defeating proposed amendments.

The *New York Daily News* also gave advice, on December 1, 1866, in "Masterly Inactivity the Policy of the South," an editorial whose words reverberated in Southern discussion for months to come. The *News* was published and edited by Benjamin Wood (1820–1900), brother of ex-Mayor Fernando Wood (1811–81). Both had served in Congress, and would serve there again. Both had magnified the South's power to resist throughout the war, and now asserted that it could prove invincible as against Congress.[10] The *News* was a Tammany organ of low price and wide circulation, "generally limited to the tenement-house districts";[11] while it was unworthy of serious consideration, its slogans expressed what many Southern editors were happy to hear. What should the South do?

> We answer, let them do nothing, so far as political action is concerned. Let them simply watch and wait. A masterly inactivity[12] is the best policy they can adopt. Time, that will gradually teach the masses of the North the necessity of redeeming the republicanism of the country, will work out the problem in the interests of the South. The Radicals demand negro suffrage and the ratification of the Constitutional Amendment. They can get neither except by the consent of the Southern States and the suffrages of the Southern people. . . .

Yield nothing, and Congress would find itself "powerless to compel obedience." The Houses could continue to exclude Southern delegations—

> but let them do their worst, and the condition of the South will not be worse than it has been since the cessation of hostilities. . . . There is much virtue in passive resistance,[13] when the influence of time is in favor of those who passively resist. . . .[14]

If indeed Congress was caught in the toils as these editors asserted so confidently, the Civil War would have brought no advance

---

[10] On Fernando Wood, see infra, n. 228.

[11] Frank L. Mott, *American Journalism. A History: 1690–1960* (New York: Macmillan Co., 1962), 354.

[12] This phrase came from James Macintosh's *Vindicae Galliae* (1797), a reply to Burke's *Reflections on the French Revolution*.

[13] This phrase came from Scott's *The Heart of Midlothian*.

[14] The *Charleston Daily News* of December 6, 1866, quoted the editorial, which "well expressed" the Charleston journal's views.

beyond the mere abolition of "slavery." Indeed since the "other persons" of Article I, Section 3, had now become "free persons," the States of the Confederacy would be entitled to a larger voice in Congress and in the election of the President. Constitutional development would halt right where President Johnson and the Southern legislatures had drawn the line. Unless, that is, Congress brought about some drastic change in the basis on which those States were organized. Or, possibly, Congress could adopt and enforce the view that ratification by three-fourths of the States then represented in Congress would suffice.[15] In the circumstances, much could be said for that proposition; even so, it sounded revolutionary to bend the basic rules in order to get around a hard fact. And, in a larger view, it would be unavailing: recalcitrance would not cease; Southern governors, legislatures, judges, editors, and people generally would not suddenly bow before an Amendment thus proclaimed.[16] Even in the North, there would have been such an outcry as would have left the Amendment questionable and infirm.[17] And what would be the response of the Supreme Court when, as doubtless would happen, the existence of the Amendment came to be challenged?[18]

But Congress was not going to be stopped by Democratic editors' exposition of the rules. It would choose a way to get on with reconstruction, and immediately to provide some security for Union men in the communities of ex-rebels. Any trouble with the Supreme Court would be matter for another day.

---

[15] A joint resolution affirming that view was offered by Representative H. P. H. Bromwell of Illinois on January 21, 1867. On a Democratic demand for a roll-call, leave was granted by a vote of 94 to 33, on party lines. Cong. Globe, 39–2, 615–16. That such was the true view was repeatedly affirmed during the Second Session, in debate on Reconstruction legislation.

[16] Compare the *Pirates of Penzance*:
We yield at once, with humble mien,/Because, with all our faults, we love our Queen.

[17] The *Cincinnati Commercial*— edited by Murat Halstead, independent Republican—pronounced this scheme "ultra and objectionable"; it also dissented from the proposal that the Southern States be reorganized as Territories "with a basis of suffrage to be prescribed by act of Congress." But then it discovered "a key to unlock our difficulty." Article V permitted ratification by conventions. Supra, n. 8. Congress, the editorial asserted, would be free to "prescribe the qualifications of electors as well as of the persons elected" to such conventions; thereby it could "appeal from the bigoted prejudices of the State Legislatures to the sovereign judgment of the people." Editorial on "How to Put the Constitutional Amendment," Dec. 24, 1866.

The *Commercial* saw nothing "ultra" in its idea that, in this one situation, Congress would be free to disregard the basis of suffrage established by State law. Futhermore, Congress would have had to prescribe a very specially qualified electorate if it was to get a result different from the action of the legislatures. Commonly the legislators were themselves limited by the "bigoted prejudices" of the voters. For example, the situation in Alabama noted above.

[18] Infra, p. 432.

BASIC DIFFICULTIES

IF CONGRESS WERE TO CHARGE THE ARMY to protect loyal citizens in disaffected communities, it would have to prescribe the means by which that task was to be accomplished. By the Freedmen's Bureau Act of July 16, 1866, "military protection" and "military jurisdiction" had been extended over freedmen: but then, in Dr. Watson's case, the President had declared that in obedience to the *Milligan* opinion such jurisdiction could not be maintained.[19] What then should be done? In Congressional debate, reference was constantly made to *Milligan*—with an occasional question about the ultimate authority of the Supreme Court in the field of reconstruction.

To reconstruct—rather than simply to restore, as President Johnson demanded—bristled with practical difficulties. Some of these should be marked, before turning to the debates.

If the States were to be reconstructed on a broader base, with impartial suffrage and new guarantees of equal protection, Congress must choose whether to look to the existing governments to carry out this transformation, or else itself to create provisional authorities for that purpose. The admission of freedmen as voters, and the making of a constitution, would require registration and elections, under some supervision: these would be vital and complicated operations where a mass of inexperienced and unwelcome voters were to be introduced.

At the outset, moderate thought in Congress preferred to call upon the governments then in being to make such changes as were required. But was it sensible to expect a government solidly controlled by ex-rebels to preside over the liquidation of their old regime? No, it was replied: they already possessed all the means of influence—the press, the men of education, the clergy; they would so direct proceedings as to perpetuate their own power; "the timid people, black and white, . . . will be the sport of disloyal men."[20]

If some provisional authority was to be created, how would its members be selected? The Constitution provides that officers shall be appointed by the President, subject to confirmation by the Senate; the appointment of "inferior Officers," however, may be vested "in the President alone, in the Courts of Law, or in the Heads of Departments."[21] To allow President Johnson to select provisional officers to carry out the policy of Congress seemed a mockery; even if Congress were to prescribe stringent qualifications, and require submission to the Senate for con-

---

[19] Supra, p. 215.
[20] Representative Boutwell of Massachusetts. Cong. Globe, 39–2, 1209. Feb. 13, 1867.
[21] Art. II, Sec. 2, cl. 2.

firmation, the objection would be reduced but not removed. Alternatives were proposed—such as appointment by the Speaker and the President of the Senate,[22] or by the Chief Justice.[23] If Congress resorted to a military administration, it could require that general officers be put in charge; even then, President Johnson could take his pick within that class. What if appointment were vested in the General of the Army (Grant): Would he nevertheless take direction from the President? That point was debated.[24]

Merely to provide for the appointment of a provisional governor or a commission would not suffice: Congress must find registrars of voters and judges and clerks of election on whom it could rely, and must provide support for their operations.

And in the months while the transformation was going on, by whom would the State be governed? Would the existing regime continue in authority, or would Congress sweep it away and set up its own agency for the interim? Not clearly foreseen in the debates was the question whether, if the existing officers were allowed to remain, they would use their position to obstruct the execution of the Congressional program.

If rule by white men only must give way, who would be called to participate in the new start; and who if any would be excluded? Stewart's proposal in March 1866 will be recalled: suffrage without racial discrimination, save that those qualified in 1860 need not meet the test.[25]

That idea had been spurned in the South. The pending Fourteenth Amendment did not provide affirmatively for Negro suffrage: it

---

[22] Representative Isaac R. Hawkins of Tenn., Cong. Globe, 39–2, 1123.

[23] H.R. 856 by Representative Hamilton Ward of New York. It was not found in the L.C. microfilm collection. However, this feature is mentioned in the *Jackson Clarion* of December 13, 1866, and in the *Cincinnati Commercial* of December 15. The latter commented:

If Judge Kelley's bill, vesting in the Chief Justice the appointment of Internal Revenue officers, becomes a law, and that of Mr. Ward, of New York, authorizing him to appoint Provisional Governors of the unrepresented States, goes through, the Chief Justice may as well throw off the judicial ermine, and assume the imperial purple. . . .

Kelley's H.R. 831, to create and organize a Department of Internal Revenue, died in committee.

However, H.R. 598, to establish a uniform system of bankruptcy, was then pending, and became law on March 2, 1867—and it provided that appointment of registers in bankruptcy would be made "upon the nomination and recommendation of the Chief Justice of the Supreme Court . . . ." Infra, pp. 355–56.

[24] Infra, pp. 297–98.

[25] Supra, pp. 128–29. Stewart was son-in-law and sometimes law partner of Henry S. Foote, formerly Governor of Mississippi and Senator from that State; later Representative from Tennessee in the Confederate Congress. Stewart was outstanding as one who, while seeking really to get on with the reformation of the Union, was sincerely concerned with Southern conciliation.

said that if adult male citizens were denied the right to vote, the State's basis of representation would be proportionately reduced. When the Second Session came to grips with the need for further measures, it seemed evident that the freedmen must positively be admitted to share in governing. How else could any transformation be achieved?

As to exclusions, the starting point was Section 3 of the Amendment. It would, whenever it came into force, disqualify from holding State or federal office (but not from voting) all who, having taken an official oath to support the Constitution, had thereafter "engaged in insurrection or rebellion . . . or given aid or comfort to the enemies . . . ." The exact number thereby disqualified was undetermined, and practically undeterminable: it had seemed a fair estimate that possibly eighteen thousand pre-1860 officeholders were affected.[26] "Disqualified by the Fourteenth Amendment" was a phrase that might be used in other contexts to refer to this group. But one should not think in stereotypes: some of those affected were now disposed to serve loyally and helpfully, while the most irreconcilable rebels would not be disqualified if they had held no office before the war.

Another group defined by a formula consisted of those who could take the iron-clad oath of 1862—the affirmation of unbroken loyalty.[27] This would include the mass of freedmen, but comparatively few Southern whites, and few among those would be accorded leader-

---

[26] Practically undeterminable: consider, for instance, United States v. Powell, Fed. Case No. 16,079 (C.C.-D.N.C. 1871), under a statute to punish the holding of office by persons disqualified by the Fourteenth Amendment. In that case the jury must consider (1) Did P. actually take an oath of allegiance when he served as constable before the war? (2) When he offered a substitute for Confederate service, was he, as he now contended, overcome by such force as would excuse his conduct? (3) When he held office as justice of the peace, did he perform some act that aided the rebellion? The charge was by Circuit Judge Hugh L. Bond, a stout Unionist, not disposed to any captiousness in construing a statute to enforce the Fourteenth Amendment.

Senator Sherman, in debate on the Reconstruction Bill, estimated that "ten or fifteen thousand leading rebels" were affected—and a moment later said "from six to ten thousand."

Cong. Globe, 39–2, 1625, 1626. February 20, 1867. Blaine, in his *Twenty Years of Congress*, 2 vols. (Norwich, Conn.: Henry Bill Publishing Co., 1884, 1886), wrote that when the Amendment was under discussion, "the total number affected was estimated at fourteen thousand, but subsequently it was ascertained to be much greater." II, 511.

A participant who was pardoned before the adoption of the Amendment (that is, before July 21, 1868) was held *not* to have been disqualified. 18 Ops. Atty. Gen. 149 (1885).

Sec. 3 concluded: "But Congress may by a vote of two-thirds of each House, remove such disability." After many, singly or in batches, had been relieved, Congress by an Act of June 6, 1898, 30 Stat. 432, removed the disability entirely. It was then guessed that the total originally affected had been about 18,000. Cong. Rec., 55–2, 5405.

[27] Supra, p. 59.

ship by their communities. To reform State governments on the basis of participation only by the ever-loyal was subject to very grave objection. Senator Sherman put it bluntly:

> no proposition can ever pass this Congress, and no bill can ever be sanctioned by the American people which will disfranchise the white population of the southern States, with very few exceptions, and place the power of ten States in the hands of ignorant, emancipated freedmen. We want neither black nor white oligarchies. . . .[28]

Senator Sumner, at the opening of the Second Session, offered resolutions "declaring the true principles of reconstruction."[29] He called for "excluding all disloyal persons," while affirming that new governments must be founded on the "fundamental truths" of the Declaration of Independence: "that all men are equal in rights" and "that all just government stands only on the consent of the governed." As abstract ideas, to exclude the disloyal, and to govern by the consent of the governed, might sound fair enough—if each were considered in isolation. To reconcile them in some measure was quite another matter. Congress considered various proposals for separating as many ex-rebels as might safely be allowed to vote from such others as should be treated as virulent. There was need to look closely at the actual operation of any such formula.

Thaddeus Stevens evolved a system, which figured largely in Congressional groping: all persons of age on March 4, 1861, who had held office under or sworn allegiance to the Confederacy, would be declared to have *forfeited citizenship* and renounced allegiance: they would not be entitled to vote or hold office until five years after the filing of an application to be reinvested with citizenship. However, that ban would not apply to anyone who swore that on March 4, 1864, and at all times thereafter he would willingly have complied with the requirements of the President's proclamation of December 8, 1863 (offering amnesty and a plan for setting up a loyal State government[30]) had there been a safe opportunity to do so; and that thereafter he had been opposed to the continuance of the rebellion, had voluntarily given it no encouragement, but had earnestly desired the success of the Union, etc.[31]

---

[28] Cong. Globe, 39–2, 1563. Feb. 19, 1867. See infra, n. 206.

[29] Cong. Globe, 39–2, 15. Dec. 5, 1866. The Senate agreed to his motion to print.

[30] Supra, p. 95.

[31] Cong. Globe, 39–2, 250. Jan. 3, 1867.

Some background will be useful. As the proposed Fourteenth Amendment had been reported from the Joint Committee on April 30, 1866, its Section 3 provided that *until July 4, 1870, all who had voluntarily adhered to the rebellion would be excluded from voting for Representa-*

The objections to this were manifold. Representative Jehu Baker of Illinois pointed out that the attempt to revoke citizenship ran counter to the definition in the opening sentence of the Amendment.[32] And Julian of Indiana, who regarded Stevens' proposal as too lenient, demanded, "of what value would be such an oath?" How could perjury be proved; how (on the other hand) could "the hidden purpose or the secret intention" be established?[33]

This and other tests that would have turned upon some particular state of mind all came to naught.

It had been implicit in Congressional thought, when at the First Session the Fourteenth Amendment was devised, that terms were being set which the Southern States *would* accept in order to be readmitted.[34] Instead, they balked. Now, when the Second Session considered what next to provide, there was concern lest ex-rebels rush back through loop-holes. But what if, instead, the rank and file disdained to accept the terms proposed, and rallied around their proscribed chiefs? Would another Congressional effort thus be frustrated?

H.R. 543 IN THE FIRST SESSION, 39TH CONGRESS

HAVING IDENTIFIED some of the basic difficulties, we set out to trace, with no more detail than seems essential, legislative history leading to the statute of March 2, 1867.

In the First Session, on April 30, 1866, when Stevens reported from the Joint Committee the proposed Fourteenth Amendment, he also reported a companion measure, H.R. 543, "a bill to provide for restoring the States lately in insurrection to their full political rights." It

---

tives in Congress or electors for the President. Cong. Globe, 39–1, 2286.

In debate, Stevens hailed this as "the most popular" and "vital" provision in the Amendment. "Without that, it amounts to nothing." Cong. Globe, 39–1, 2460, 2544. Bingham, on the other hand, said that it could "bring no strength to the amendment." P. 2543. Stevens replied tartly that Bingham wanted to "kill this amendment." P. 2544.

In the Senate, this provision was stricken out, without debate, by a vote of 43 to 0. P. 2869. Later the provision that now stands in Section 3 was inserted.

When the Amendment as thus amended came up for concurrence by the House, Stevens lamented that the

change "endangers the Government . . . and may give the next Congress and President to the reconstructed rebels." P. 3148.

Undaunted, in the Second Session, Stevens was seeking to impose his provision for forfeiture, which would exclude a great mass of ex-Confederates, for the longer period of *five* years, from voting for *State* as well as federal officers.

[32] Cong. Globe, 39–2, App., 75–77. Jan. 17, 1867. "All persons born or naturalized in the United States, and subject to the jurisdiction thereof, are citizens of the United States and of the State wherein they reside."

[33] Cong. Globe, 39–2, App., 77, 78. Jan. 28, 1867.

[34] See infra, n. 41.

recited that it was expedient that they should be restored "at the earliest day consistent with the future peace and safety of the Union"; accordingly the bill would enact that when (1) the proposed Amendment should have become part of the Constitution, and (2) a State had ratified the same, and (3) had modified its constitution and laws in conformity therewith—Senators and Representatives might be admitted to Congress.[35]

The number 543 should be kept in view: in the Second Session there will be a fight about substituting and amending until, on January 28, 1867, H.R. 543 is sent back to the Joint Committee and, like a tattered banner, is withdrawn from the fray.

In the First Session, after the House had voted the proposed Amendment, H.R. 543 came up for consideration on May 15.[36] Stevens held back: it would be "very awkward to proceed" when the Senate had not acted upon the Amendment; he moved to postpone. John A. Bingham opposed delay: he said that the American people expected Congress to present "a system of measures full and complete for the restoration of the States lately in insurrection." "Let the House do its duty." An ugly scene followed. Stevens said Bingham "never agrees long" to anything settled in the Joint Committee; Bingham said that Stevens was confused. On a test of strength, 73 voted with Stevens and 55 with Bingham.[37] The losers were all Republicans, generally of moderate or conservative tendencies. The victors comprised 42 Republicans, generally of the ardent sort, and 31 Democrats.

On May 28, Stevens introduced a bill of his own, H.R. 623, "to enable the States lately in rebellion to regain their privileges in the Union": reciting that they had "forfeited all their rights," it prescribed a complete overhauling, with Negro suffrage, whereby they would fit themselves to be "reinstated" in the Union.[38]

These facts foreshadow the story of the Second Session.

Stevens, because he was chairman of the House delegation to the Joint Committee, appeared in the guise of sponsor of the committee's bill looking to readmission on the basis of the Amendment. But Stevens had never taken much stock in the Amendment, and was pertinaciously bent upon treating the rebel States as conquered territory, outside the pale of the Constitution.[39] He had his own bill, H.R. 623, running on his own theory.

Bingham, also a member of the committee, was devoted to the

---

[35] On the same day, Fessenden introduced an identical bill, S. 292, in the Senate.

[36] Cong. Globe, 39–1, 2598–99.

[37] Ibid., 2599. May 15, 1866.

[38] Ibid., 2858. The text, as modi-fied by Stevens to July 25, is set out at p. 4157; as further modified on July 28, the last day of the session, at pp. 4303–04.

[39] Supra, p. 119.

Fourteenth Amendment, especially to Section 1, in which he felt the pride of authorship. If the Southern States as then organized would only accept and carry out the principles of the Amendment, they would, in his view, be fit for restoration.

Stevens was wrong, and personally offensive, when he said that Bingham was out of line with the Joint Committee; rather, it was Stevens who was perverse when, abusing his position as sponsor of H.R. 543, he sought to impose his own measure as a substitute.[40]

In the 73-to-55 division just cited, Bingham had the majority of the Republicans on his side; Stevens won only by the aid of the Democrats, who detested the Fourteenth Amendment and opposed restoration on that basis.[41]

Suppose—looking ahead to the Second Session—that the Democrats and Stevens' band were to vote together at certain critical junctures: perhaps the Democrats could thereby keep the majority party divided and unable to carry out a program, and so gain time for the country to "come to its senses" and return the Democrats to power. Or perhaps, as Stevens planned, such maneuvres might show that the Republicans, if they were to enact any measure, would have to accept his extreme views.

But then, perhaps, it might turn out that neither the Democrats nor Stevens had calculated aright. Perhaps, rather than that the Second Session be allowed to end in failure, practical Republicans would come together upon some measure, more exacting than what the Joint Committee had proposed, less extreme than Stevens' plan, and make that the Congressional Reconstruction Act. Then the Southern States would have to live with something more distasteful than what the greater part of the majority party had set out to require—thanks to their own resistance in the first place, and secondarily because the Democrats in the House had shortsightedly played politics in company with Thaddeus Stevens. That is what happened: but it was charged that "the Radicals" had done this to the South.

---

[40] Infra, pp. 267–68.

[41] The First Session did not record a firm promise that acceptance of the Amendment would insure readmission. It did, however, on July 24, 1866—four days before its adjournment—readmit Tennessee, even though the Fourteenth Amendment had not yet become a part of the Constitution. The resolution recited the State's ratification of the Thirteenth and Fourteenth Amendments, and "other acts proclaiming and denoting loyalty." Actually, Tennessee had not removed the color bar on the suffrage.

How strong was the implication that prompt acceptance of the Amendment would suffice for readmission was the subject of much incidental discussion at the Second Session. It seems highly probable that it would have had that result. Also it seems very highly probable that enactment of H.R. 543 at the First Session would not have induced the Southern legislatures to ratify the Amendment.

H.R. 543 IN THE SECOND SESSION, 39TH CONGRESS

THAT THE RECONSTRUCTION ACT merits a new and penetrating examination is evidenced by recent studies. In Dr. W. R. Brock's *An American Crisis: Congress and Reconstruction, 1865–1867*,[42] this vexed matter is viewed afresh through English eyes. One of the author's comments is that

> Generalizations about Radicalism do not tell one who the Radicals were, and many historians . . . have fallen into the easy habit of calling "radical" everyone whom they dislike. If it is necessary to show that the Radicals were conspirators forcing an unwelcome policy upon an unsuspecting nation they become a small vindictive minority, but if it is desired to discredit the Republican party the Radicals are swollen into a controlling majority. . . .

"Opportunities of separating Radicals from moderates are rare," he continues, "but there is one vote in the second session which appears to have divided them"—when on January 28, 1867, moderates, assisted for one moment by the Democrats, carried a motion by Bingham to send Stevens' bill to the Joint Committee.[43]

Still closer attention was drawn to the Reconstruction Act when Professor David Donald published his lectures, *The Politics of Reconstruction, 1863–1867*.[44] In the concluding chapter, "The Pendulum of Legislation," he analogized the framing of the statute of 1867 to four cycles of oscillation over a narrowing arc, as accommodation was sought within the range of Congressional opinion. The pendulum is said to come to rest when a moderate measure by Senator Sherman, made somewhat more "radical" by amendments by Representatives Wilson of Iowa and Shellabarger, is accepted by both Houses. If Democrats had consistently worked with moderate and conservative Republicans, accord might have been reached on a settlement more tolerant toward the South.

At the Second Session, when on January 3, 1867, the Joint Committee's H.R. 543 came up in the order of business, Stevens moved to substitute the text of a bill of his own, filed on December 19.[45] This was basically the "forfeited rights" measure he had introduced at the

---

[42] London: Macmillan and Co., 1963.

[43] At 69–70; he goes on, at 71–94, to classify and characterize members of Congress.

[44] Baton Rouge: Louisiana State University Press, 1965.

[45] Cong. Globe, 39–2, 209, 250.

First Session, on May 28—with modifications he had introduced from time to time.[46]

He had started by providing that all adult male citizens, without regard to color, could vote: but that all who had sworn allegiance to the Confederacy were deprived of citizenship, and could not be reinstated for five years. (In effect, voting would have been limited to white

---

[46] Supra, p. 263.

Concern in Radical quarters that the Second Session start out with something more drastic than Joint Committee's H.R. 543 is reflected in the following letter from Representative John M. Broomall of Media, Pennsylvania—whom Blaine described as "independent," "inflexible in principle, untiring in effort." *Twenty Years of Congress*, 2:120. On October 27, 1866, he wrote to Stevens:

I have received and read yours of Oct 16th with a good deal of interest and thought much of the plan you propose. If a consultation could be brought about among fifteen or twenty of the radical members and Senators without its appearing that the remainder were excluded I can see that great good might result from it. A caucus of the entire party would result in nothing, as we both well know. Bingham and myself would agree upon nothing. You would help me to disagree. I take it that the inevitable question—whether all the adult males of the South are to be consulted in the reconstruction will find you the leader on one side and Bingham on the other. This question will make the coming political parties and I think it will divide our party in the coming session.

Now if we could get together those who would be upon *our* side of that question alone I would like it very much but after the first dozen who can tell who they are. Would it not be better if you agree with me in thinking this to be the great question coming for us to communicate by letter with Boutwell,

Kelly [W.D. Kelley of Pa.], [Thomas] Williams [of Pa.], Wilson of Iowa and such others as we feel sure of, and getting an interchange of views without a Caucus which if general will amount to nothing and if selected will look like forestalling opinion in the party.

I regret that the public press persisted in putting forth the Constitutional Amendment as the terms of reconstruction. I never assented to that proposition. It will go hard with me to consent to any reconstruction against the will of the loyal men of the South of either race. The Amendment is the means of protection of the Government and the North. It will do no good to the loyal majority of the South, three fourths of whom are disfranchised. [That is, by State law as it then stood.]

Please think of these things and write me. If you still think a conference desirable I will yield to your better judgment and aid in bringing it about.

Stevens Papers, L.C.

Whatever his method of consultation, Stevens' substitute had first "been submitted to many leading men." See infra, n. 161.

Broomall on December 4 offered a resolution that looked to a bill to be drawn on a somewhat different theory: that the Committee on Territories consider the expediency of establishing territorial governments in the ex-rebel States, and giving equal political rights to all adult male citizens who had not participated in the rebellion. P. 11. See the measure introduced by Representative Ashley, chairman of the Committee on Territories, infra, p. 268.

loyalists, Negroes, and such ex-rebels as had not been in either military or civil service.) For presentation at the Second Session, he had widened eligibility to admit such participants in the Confederacy as would swear to having had an intent loyal to the United States on March 4, 1864, and at all times thereafter.[47] At one time he had left the summoning and election of a constitutional convention to the existing State government. Recognizing that that was a weak point, he had amended to provide that the President would make the call; and that local election officers would be chosen by the voters who were on hand at the polls at 9 A.M. on election day.[48]

In his substitute of December 19, 1866, Stevens shifted from reliance on the President to a provision that the carrying out of the transformation in each State would be entrusted to a commission of three. He had written that "Congress shall elect" them; but when the matter came up on January 3, Stevens changed to "The Supreme Court of the District of Columbia shall appoint" the commissioners.[49] The commission would appoint election officials, make regulations, and procure the materials necessary to conduct elections.[50]

Quite a number of other reconstruction measures were introduced at the Second Session; but no more will be mentioned than is needful.

Stevens made a speech to launch his substitute.[51] He said that the action of the Supreme Court in *Ex parte Milligan*—the opinion had been published two days earlier[52]—showed that prompt legislation on the government of the rebel States was "absolutely indispensable." *Milligan* might appear "not as infamous as the Dred Scott decision," but in truth it was "far more dangerous" by reason of "its operation upon the lives and the liberties of the loyal men," black and white, in the South. The President's discharge of Dr. Watson[53] showed what *Milligan* meant in practice. His bill was "designed to enable loyal men, so far as I could discriminate them in these States, to form governments which shall be in loyal hands, that they may protect themselves from such outrages . . . ."

He went on to affirm certain propositions as basic. Congress was "the sole guardian" of the sovereignty of the people; no officer, from the President and the Chief Justice down, could do any act save as

---

[47] Supra, pp. 261–62.
[48] Draft of July 28, 1866. Cong. Globe, 39–1, 4303–4. In that draft, citizenship would be forfeited by those who had *voluntarily* taken the Confederate oath of allegiance; and it might be recovered after *three* years.

[49] That court was reliably Radical: consider its defiance of the Supreme Court in the matter of the test oath for attorneys. Supra, pp. 246–47.
[50] Cong. Globe, 39–2, 250.
[51] Ibid., 251–53. January 3, 1867.
[52] Supra, p. 214.
[53] Supra, p. 215.

directed by the legislative power. "Congress," he asserted, "denies that the old rebel States have any existence which gives them any rights under the Constitution." "I know of no Republican who does not ridicule what Mr. Seward thought a cunning movement, in counting Virginia and the other outlawed States" among those ratifying the Thirteenth Amendment. "It is to be regretted," he said pointedly, "that inconsiderate and incautious Republicans should ever have supposed that the slight amendments already proposed to the Constitution . . . would satisfy the reforms necessary for the security of the Government." The Negroes must be allowed to vote; they and the loyal whites would work together, and "the two united would form a majority, control the States, and protect themselves." This would insure the ascendancy of the Union party, on which "depends the safety of this great nation."

Audaciously, Stevens was declaring his own extreme positions to be the principles of the Republicans in Congress. In disparaging the Fourteenth Amendment as "slight" he was repudiating the Joint Committee's H.R. 543 that was based upon it.

At once the floor was taken by James M. Ashley, chairman of the Committee on Territories. He moved to amend Stevens' substitute by striking out all after the enacting clause and inserting a text of his own devising.[54] This would declare that existing State governments "are not valid . . . ." Then proceeding as though organized Territories were to be enabled to prepare for Statehood, his bill "invited" qualified adult male citizens to follow the steps indicated. "A mass convention, in each representative district" would send a delegate to a convention, which would select a Committee of Public Safety. That Committee would invite the voters to elect delegates to a constitutional convention; also it would appoint "sub-provisional committees" and judges and clerks to conduct elections. When the constitutional convention met, it would select a provisional governor and other officers for the interim; then it would frame a new fundamental law, wherein certain guarantees for the future must be incorporated. Upon its ratification by the voters and approval by Congress, admission to the Union would follow.[55] To qualify as a voter, the citizen must take an elaborate test oath.

---

[54] Cong, Globe, 39–2, 253–56 Jan. 3. Ashley, representing the Toledo district from 1859 to 1869, was an advanced Radical—a leader in attaining the Thirteenth Amendment, and also in impeaching the President. See supra, ch. I, n. 59.

[55] Should a convention decline to proceed by these steps, it was "invited" to submit to Congress a plan of its own. Sec. 7.

In accord with the territorial theory on which the bill was drawn, Sec. 14 provided that the convention in Texas might—after ceding to the United States roughly the western third of the territory that had been Texas—proceed to divide the remainder so as to produce a new State of Texas in the eastern portion, and another (unnamed) State in the central portion. In that event the con-

Julian of Indiana criticised this "extraordinary measure" as being too complicated; it was a "cunningly designed scheme . . . to meet the ugly fact that we have a bad man in the presidential chair . . . ."[56]

When Congress dared not trust either the Chief Executive or the existing State regimes, it must be perplexed to devise administrative machinery whereby new governments could be brought into being. Stevens' unsureness in drafting was evidence of this. So too was Ashley's amendment in 511 lines of print:[57] the Founders had written an entire Constitution in considerably smaller compass.

Bingham, defender of the original H.R. 543, moved to send Stevens' substitute and Ashley's amendment to the Joint Committee.[58] Stevens resisted. (He was hoping to force the House to accept his measure whenever he sensed he could command a majority.) Bingham's motion remained pending, while general debate ran on, until on January 28 the question was put—and the motion to refer was carried.[59]

It was incumbent on Bingham to support his position in a major speech, and that he did on January 16.[60] He saw in the Stevens and Ashley measures a "manifest departure from the spirit and intent" of the "great amendment for equal rights and equal protection." He urged, Stand by the Fourteenth Amendment: "There is strength in it . . . . There is peace in it . . . ."

But then Stevens asked, How many of the Southern States have rejected? And Bingham could make only a lame reply: "it does not follow that they will not yet accept it." Besides, he added, all along he had been saying that ratification by three-fourths of the States represented in Congress would suffice to make the Amendment binding. (In the light of this exchange, one may see that the situation now called for a deeper treatment than what Bingham had been advocating; presently he will add suffrage for the freedmen to his prescription.[61])

Resuming debate next day, Baker of Illinois, a conservative Republican and a lawyer, addressed himself "rigorously to a mere statement of . . . objections" to show why Stevens' substitute should be "referred for more mature consideration."[62] Look at its provision declaring that the existing regimes would be "acknowledged as valid governments for municipal purposes until the same shall be duly altered . . .": but if perchance Stevens' plan failed to be effectuated, Congress would find itself "in the awkward position of having recog-

---

vention would accordingly resolve itself into two bodies.

[56] Cong. Globe, 39–2, App., 77, 79. Jan. 28, 1867.

[57] H.R. 543. Ashley's Modified Amendment of Jan. 16, 1867. Printer's No. 367.

[58] Cong. Globe, 39–2, 256. Jan. 3, 1867.

[59] Infra, p. 275.

[60] Cong. Globe, 39–2, 500–505.

[61] Infra, p. 285.

[62] Cong. Globe, 39–2, 536, and App., 75–77.

nized in advance" the validity of all those regimes. Paine of Wisconsin had already hit hard at that provision.[63] Now Stevens rose and said that he would strike that section from his bill.[64]

Forfeiture of the rebel's citizenship was another feature at which Baker directed his critique.[65] He concluded, "I want to put some consistency, some law, some common sense into our vigor. I go for hooping our tub before putting water in it."

Quite otherwise was the comment of Josiah B. Grinnell of Iowa —abolitionist, clergyman, and promoter of Western enterprise. Grinnell's seat was at Stevens' left hand, in congenial proximity. The need, he said, was "for action rather than for hypercriticism."[66] He dwelt upon the "murders and outrages" daily inflicted upon loyal men, black and white; he indorsed the appeal of Thomas J. Durant of New Orleans, leading Southern Unionist, that Congress "authorize the loyal and true men, regardless of race or color, to organize governments . . . ." Congress, Grinnell concluded, should hasten to do "what the suffering implore, what justice demands, and what I believe God will approve."

Judge Rufus P. Spalding[67] made one point in few words. If the disloyal States would not accept the Amendment, then Congress should reconstruct them by the votes of loyal citizens without regard to color. But Stevens' measure would be inadequate during the period when it was being put into operation: "it does not afford any protection to that loyal class of the inhabitants . . . who are to perform these high functions. Why, sir, these colored men . . . are to be in jeopardy of being shot down like so many dogs when they attempt to visit the polls." He asked Stevens to accept a new section: to suspend the privilege of the writ of habeas corpus in the ex-rebel States, and to hold them under martial law until reconstructed.[68] Stevens at once made the change. (Even so, Spalding joined in sending Stevens' substitute to the Joint Committee.[69])

Spalding's was "a monstrous proposition," said Lawrence S. Trimble, Kentucky Democrat.[70] He quoted what had been said in *Milligan* by the Supreme Court, that "last citadel of liberty." He prayed that the Court might "continue . . . as the shield and protector of the

---

[63] Ibid., 499. Jan. 16.
[64] Ibid., App., 75, and p. 536.
[65] Supra, p. 261.
[66] Cong. Globe 39–2, 536–37. Jan. 17.
[67] (1798–1886). Graduating from Yale College, he read law with Zephaniah Swift, Chief Justice, and great systematizer of Connecticut's law. Spalding married one of his mentor's

daughters. Coming to Ohio, he sat on its Supreme Court, 1849 to 1852, and thereafter practiced in Cleveland.
William Rufus Day, Justice of the Supreme Court from 1903 to 1922, was Spalding's grandson.
[68] Cong. Globe, 39–2, 594. Jan. 19.
[69] Infra, p. 275.
[70] Cong. Globe, 39–2, App., 63–66. Jan. 21, 1867.

weak and the innocent through all time." His colleague, Judge Hise, declared that the "only hope of the preservation of a free Government is . . . in the decisions of the Supreme Court."[71]

Lewis W. Ross, Illinois Democrat, represented a district immediately west of Lincoln's Sangamon County; his home county (Fulton) had been a seat of Copperhead strength. He said that he deplored partisan denunciation of the Court, and of Justice Davis in particular, "for making a decision which nine hundred and ninety-nine out of every thousand lawyers in this country would have made before this rebellion took place."[72] Eldridge of Wisconsin said that the *Milligan* decision had brought "glad tidings to the depressed and despairing people"; neither "the clamor of disappointed demagogues, nor the malignant howl of crazy fanatics can ever dim the luster it has shed upon American jurisprudence."[73]

Michael C. Kerr of Indiana spoke on the theme "Once a State always a State" with the "inalienable right of local self-government."[74] He drew strength from the "honest, loyal, immortal words" of Justice Field in *Cummings v. Missouri*; from the truths "so bravely and earnestly uttered" by Justice Davis in *Milligan*; and "of like import," from Justice Nelson's declaration in the *Egan* case, that South Carolina was entitled to the full enjoyment of all her constitutional privileges.[75]

Samuel L. Warner, Connecticut Republican (who had studied law at both Yale and Harvard), told the House that he had "learned to place but little reliance upon the dogmas of that [Supreme] court . . . upon any question touching the rights of humanity . . . . As it has been administered that court has been but the chain which bound humanity to the rock of pretended constitutional immutability . . . ." He hoped that the present Court would not be "hasty to array itself against the spirit of the age . . . ."[76] Pike of Maine, drawing upon what he was then learning as chairman of the Select Committee on the Murder of Union Soldiers, said that Congress should establish new governments founded upon loyalty and universal suffrage. "I notice that a decision [by the Supreme Court] is threatened against such action . . . . But the court should recollect that it has had bad luck with its political deci-

---

[71] Ibid., App., 66, 69. Jan. 21, 1867. Elijah Hise, born in 1802, took his seat in Congress on December 3, 1866, as successor to Henry Grider, deceased. He was appointed to Grider's place on the Joint Committee on Reconstruction. Hise had been Justice and Chief Justice of the Kentucky Court of Appeals, 1851 to 1854. He committed suicide on May

8, 1867—"ill and despondent over his inability to help his country." D.A.B.
[72] Cong. Globe, 39–2, 778, 780. Jan. 26, 1867.
[73] Ibid., 561, 562. Jan. 18, 1867.
[74] Ibid., 622–25. Jan. 21, 1867.
[75] Fed. Case No. 4303 (1866), supra, p. 148.
[76] Cong. Globe, 39–2, 564, 569. Jan. 18, 1867.

sions. The people . . . thus far have preferred to govern the country themselves and let the court attend to its law business."[77]

On both sides of the House, there was a strong impression that the Court had already given a clear intimation of its attitude on the matter now pending.

William E. Dodge, Republican from New York City, was "not a constitutional lawyer"; he would look at the problem "in a common-sense way."[78] Actually this was a forward-looking businessman, and a reformer free from fanaticism.[79] In various contexts, Dodge observed, the Southern States had been treated as being still within the Union. He deeply regretted their rejection of the Amendment; he mentioned, as contributing to this folly, the misleading advice they had had from "high quarters"; the evil influence of the National Union Convention[80] and the expectation "that there would be another party in the country which would sustain the policy of the President."[81] The loyal people of the country had been "almost universally satisfied with the report of the [Joint Committee]"; he thought they would not approve what Stevens and Ashley now proposed. But the great need, he said, was for reconciliation—"something that will secure quiet and better feeling between the North and the South, and at the same time better feeling between southern men and the freedmen." He did not doubt that freedmen were being "shot down, imprisoned, whipped, and deprived of their rights under the law." "It was hardly to be expected—it would have been a miracle if it had not been so—" that immediately after emancipation such wrongs would not be committed. But consider Stevens' proposal "to disfranchise nearly the entire white population" and to give the colored people "virtual control" in the State: "as a dictate of common sense, taking mankind as we find them, . . . is it natural to suppose that the passage of such a law as this will be calculated to promote increased friendly relations" between North and South, or between the white and the colored population?

Speaking from his large experience, Dodge stressed that manufacturing, commerce, and agriculture would "measurably stand still" so long as reconstruction remained unsettled. If Congress would seek repose on the basis of the Amendment, and would strengthen the

---

[77] Ibid., 254, 255. Jan. 3, 1867—two days after the Milligan opinion was published.

[78] Ibid., 627–29. Jan. 21.

[79] Dodge (1805–83) was a founder of Phelps, Dodge & Co., dealers in metals; also interested in lumbering and in railroads. He was a leader in the peace movement and in temperance reform; an anti-slavery man who

had joined in the Peace Conference in February 1861. Dodge had successfully contested the election of James Brooks, bitter Democratic editor, who at the opening of the 39th Congress had been his party's nominee for Speaker.

[80] Supra, p. 177.

[81] Supra, p. 179.

economy, it would result that the condition of the freedmen would be elevated, as wage-earners and as citizens. But to degrade the Southern whites and to elevate the freedmen above them was not, Dodge thought, "calculated at all to promote the best interests of either."

Henry J. Raymond spoke late in the debate: his address was long, carefully prepared, and magisterial in tone; he asked not to be interrupted.[82] It was now clear, he said, that the people looked to Congress to prescribe something beyond what the President had proposed. Raymond explained his objections, however, to Stevens' bill, and to Ashley's, and to Spalding's amendment, and to Bingham's proposition that the Southern States need not be counted in amending the Constitution. He even objected to some of what the Supreme Court had said in the *Milligan* opinion: while he refrained from "too abstract a discussion," he regretted that the Court had seemed to say that the text of the Constitution must ever be the absolute rule of national life—whereas, Raymond said, "emergencies may arise . . . in which the sovereignty of the nation may transcend the authority of the Constitution without violating the law of national life, in which, indeed, that law itself may demand such an appeal from the Constitution to the nation which created and maintains it." He recalled instances, such as the purchase of Louisiana, where "the facts of history" had been accepted by the Court. He added: "If the Supreme Court is wise now, it will thus accept as accomplished and irreversible . . . the processes and results of our recent war."[83] (As Raymond had read Justice Davis' opinion in *Milligan*, it seemed to say that the Constitution had a precise meaning, given once for always: and Raymond was protesting that "The Constitution exists for the nation, not the nation for the Constitution."[84])

---

[82] Cong. Globe, 39–2, 715–20. Jan. 24, 1867. Raymond (1820–69) was editor of the *New York Times*—a political associate of Secretary Seward—and draftsman of the resolutions at the National Union Convention, August 1866. He served only in the 39th Congress; he had already lost his standing in the Republican party.

[83] Ibid., at 717.

[84] Raymond's idea has been aptly expressed in opinions by great Judges.

"[I]n determining whether a provision of the Constitution applies to a new subject matter," Justice Stone once said for the Court, "it is of little significance that it is one with which the framers were not familiar." They sought to establish "an enduring framework of government" adequate "for an indefinite future and in all the vicissitudes of the changing affairs of men"; as "a continuing instrument of government" it should be so construed as would "effectuate the Constitutional purpose." This was in United States v. Classic, 313 U.S. 299, 316 (1941). In particular, to effectuate the Constitution's purpose that the voters in each State should freely choose their Representatives, Congress might provide for punishing fraud in counting ballots at a *primary* election to choose candidates, no less than at the election of Representatives. No matter that the Framers had no thought of party primaries—any more than they contemplated that interstate commerce would include electric communication.

In a kindred vein, Justice Holmes

Raymond was better at making a critique than at devising constructive solutions. In the instant situation, he proposed that the pending Fourteenth Amendment be revised, by striking out Section 3 with its irritating and needless disqualifications, and by adding a section to declare that any future attempt to secede would result in forfeiture of the State's representation during the pleasure of Congress. He would declare that when three-fourths of all the States had ratified the Amendment as thus revised, the Southern States would be restored. He believed that this would receive prompt and cheerful acceptance, and that the Union would then stand on a "firm and enduring basis."

On Thursday, January 24, Stevens announced that, seeing "such diversity of opinion on this side of the House," he would—"if I do not change my mind"—move tomorrow to lay the whole reconstruction business on the table.[85] The situation was that only five weeks remained; presumably the President would veto, and might take the full ten days in doing so. Actually, Stevens was not on the point of giving up: instead he was about to start a hard drive to carry his bill.

On Saturday he announced that on Monday he would ask Ashley and Bingham to withdraw their motions: if they did so, his substitute would be open to amendment, and he hoped it could quickly be made acceptable and passed.[86] Ashley promptly agreed. At this point Roscoe Conkling, himself a member of the Joint Committee, made his first appearance in the debate; he took on the defense of Bingham's motion, and denied allegations by Stevens and Ashley that reference to the committee would kill all hope of legislation at the Second Session.

When H.R. 543 was reached on Monday the twenty-eighth, George W. Julian told why he could not agree to Stevens' measure, and yet would not vote to refer to the Joint Committee.[87] Julian was a stiff-necked and censorious Radical. The Fourteenth Amendment, he said, showed "cold-blooded ingratitude to our black allies." What the South needed was "*government*, the strong arm of power, out-stretched from the central authority here in Washington, making it safe [for freedmen, for loyalists, for Northern capital, and labor], and thus

observed in Missouri v. Holland, 252 U.S. 416, 433 (1920), that in construing the Constitution "we must realize that [its words] have called into life a being the development of which could not have been foreseen completely by the most gifted of its begetters. It was enough for them to realize or to hope that they had created an organism; it has taken a century and has cost their successors much sweat and blood to prove that they created a nation. The case be-

fore us must be considered in the light of our whole experience and not merely of what was said a hundred years ago." The holding was that the protection of migratory birds was a proper subject for the exercise of the federal power "to make Treaties": the federal authority was paramount over the State's interest in the birds while within its borders.

[85] Cong. Globe, 39–2, 721.
[86] Ibid., 781.
[87] Ibid., 813, and App., 77–80.

found a Christian civilization and a living democracy amid the ruins of the past. . . . Under this educational process I would have these rebellious districts trained in the way they should go . . . ," no matter how many years that might require. "This policy, by nationalizing the South, . . . would tend powerfully to make our whole country homogeneous."

Dodge of New York had counselled progress through reconciliation, until the freedmen's worth as workers and as citizens came to be recognized and the whites freely accorded them the treatment to which they were entitled.[88] Julian on the other hand would improve the rebels, by years in a "political *purgatory*," until they "shall wash away their guilt in their tears of genuine contrition." Dodge and Julian had one point in common: each said that the right way must take a long time.

Bingham's motion, brought to a vote on January 28, posed this alternative: Should Stevens' substitute go forward as the basis for any reconstruction legislation at this Session; or should the matter be remitted to the Joint Committee, where, Stevens and Ashley insisted, it would die? The Democrats voted to refer: they wanted no legislation at all. Conservatives and moderates, whose aims (whatever they might be) fell far short of Stevens', would vote with Bingham. And even one who favored energetic action, like Judge Spalding, might vote to refer because he appreciated the need for careful study. But those who were content with Stevens' bill—subject perhaps to slight amendment—or at any rate, like Julian, could expect nothing more to their liking, would vote against the motion. And a compelling consideration with some was their apprehension that reference to the Joint Committee really would be consignment "to the tomb of the Capulets."[89] When the division came, there were 88 yeas and 65 nays. The House clearly did not want Stevens' bill. It was a decisive vote.[90]

THE "NORTH CAROLINA PLAN," JANUARY-FEBRUARY 1867

WHILE DEBATE ON H.R. 543 went on, a number of more sober Southern leaders, heedful of impending doom, joined in an effort to find some new basis of settlement. A group met in Washington throughout the latter half of January. Among them were Governor Orr of South Carolina; former Provisional Governors, Sharkey of Mississippi, Marvin of Florida, and Parsons of Alabama; Nathaniel Boyden, unbending North Carolina Unionist and later Republican Congressman; and

---

[88] Supra, p. 272.
[89] Comment of William B. Allison of Iowa, later explaining why he had
voted with Stevens. Cong. Globe, 39–2, 1180. Feb. 12, 1867.
[90] Cong. Globe, 39–2, 817. Jan. 28.

Lewis Hanes, who had been denied a seat in the 39th Congress when he appeared as a Representative from North Carolina. These men prepared a plan which called upon the Southern States to offer more than they had yet been willing to concede, and upon Congress to propose a new form of Amendment which, they hoped, the Southern legislatures would be willing to ratify. On January 30 and 31 this was considered in conference with the President, and brought into conformity with his suggestions.[91]

Chief Justice Chase heard of the plan, as he mentioned in writing to a daughter on Thursday, January 31: on Monday he had had

> a call & talk with Gov. Orr of South Carolina on reconstruction. He says they are trying to arrange a counter proposition to that of Congress—admitting most of its features except disfranchisement, & adding by way of State action a law allowing impartial suffrage. North Carolina is to take the initiative in this. I wish them good progress but don't hope for much from anything except a ratification of the amendment.[92]

Succinctly, the proposal was that each Southern State would amend its constitution to admit to the suffrage every adult male who "can read the Constitution of the United States in the English language, and can write his own name, or may be the owner of $250 worth of taxable property"; provided, however, that no person would be excluded who was then legally qualified to vote. In consideration of this, Congress would submit a new measure, differing from the pending Fourteenth Amendment in several ways: notably, it would omit the objectionable Section 3 (which excluded from office those who had joined the rebellion after having taken an official oath of allegiance to the United States), and Section 5 (giving Congress power to enforce by appropriate legislation).

On February 6, Senator Dixon of Connecticut, conservative Republican supporter of the President, presented the plan to the Senate.[93]

---

[91] Notes of Colonel W. G. Moore, Private Secretary to President Johnson, 1866–68, in *Am. Hist. Rev.*, 19:98, 104 (1913).

[92] Chase to daughter Nettie (in Europe), letter written on Jan. 31 and Feb. 1. Chase Papers, L.C.

[93] Cong. Globe, 39–2, 1045, where the text is set out. He introduced it formally as S. Res. 169 on February 11. P. 1149.

The preamble recited that the ex-rebel States had not ratified the pending Amendment, but that "there is reason to believe" that they would ratify the proposal to follow, and that they would "by the voluntary action of the Legislatures and people" amend their respective constitutions [by the provision on suffrage sketched above]; wherefore the resolution asked than an amendment to the Constitution be proposed:

Sec. 1. (Perpetuity of the Union; secession precluded.)

Sec. 2. (Public debts: less far-

VI: *Congressional Reconstruction*

Here was another attempt, like Senator Stewart's "universal amnesty and universal suffrage" of March 1866,[94] to find some settlement acceptable to the South and satisfactory to Congress and the nation. This "North Carolina" or "Southern Plan" withered more rapidly than Stewart's, and has scarcely been remembered even as a footnote to history.

"The patrons of the measure," the *Richmond Enquirer* reported on February 4, "have indicated a solicitude to keep it out of the newspapers, and thus prevent, for a while, at least, any public discussion of its merits." The *Enquirer* had, however, received a copy with leave to publish—which it did.[95] "Those among us who counsel total inaction, and still more those who intensify the situation and increase the difficulty by words of abuse and insult, incur, we think, a very grave responsibility." The *Enquirer* found in the plan "some points that may be properly yielded": that the Union was perpetual and that the national debt would be held sacred. "The remaining provisions . . . embrace what we must consider an unnecessary surrender of important interests," which surely referred to qualified Negro suffrage, the plan's really interesting feature.

The proponents had contemplated that North Carolina would take the lead in supporting their proposal.[96] The very respectable *Raleigh Sentinel*[97] on February 5 published "The Plan of Adjustment," giving

---

reaching than Sec. 4 of the Fourteenth Amendment; there was no prohibition of compensation for loss of slaves.)

Sec. 3. (Almost identical with Sec. 1 of Fourteenth Amendment.)

Sec. 4. (Varying from Sec. 2 of Fourteenth Amendment: when a State excluded from voting on account of color, "the entire class of persons so excluded" would be excluded from the basis of representation. No property qualification of more than $250 of taxable property; no educational qualification more than ability to read the Constitution and to sign one's name.)

McPherson, *Reconstruction*, 258–59, gives a text, allegedly as "submitted to the Legislature of North Carolina." In truth, the measure laid before the Senate of North Carolina on March 1, 1867, and withdrawn after debate, differs at certain points from McPherson's version. N.C. Sen. J., 1866–67, 387–90.

The measure before the North

Carolina Senate recited in its preamble the proposed amendments to the United States and the State constitutions; then in its operative part it would have pledged that North Carolina would "adopt the aforesaid proposition by a Convention of her people."

The *New York Times* of February 5 set out substantially the version to be found in McPherson, *Reconstruction*.

[94] Supra, p. 129.

[95] The text was substantially identical with that placed before the North Carolina Senate on March 1. Supra, n. 93. Other Southern newspapers learned the terms from the *Enquirer*'s report.

[96] In Colonel Moore's notes on discussions with the President it was styled "The North Carolina Plan." Supra, p. 91.

[97] One of its two editors was Seaton Gales (1828–78)—son of Joseph Gales and nephew of William W. Seaton, proprietors over five

277

the text as supplied by Lewis Hanes. It explained that the framers had been of the opinion that the relations between the President and the Congressional leaders were such that neither would offer a compromise and that the South was caught between them. It asked open-minded consideration of the plan. On the seventh the *Sentinel* discussed the several sections, temperately and tentatively; it emphasized that this should be viewed as a *compromise*: there must be some surrender on each side. Evidently it was seeking to conciliate and lead public opinion.

On February 11 the *Sentinel* reported that Northern Democratic newspapers were advising the South to stand still, to make no surrender of principle. So, too, the papers in Virginia and North Carolina generally opposed. Nevertheless, it counselled, the South ought to accept such an adjustment if it came as a *finality*. The intense activity of Stevens, Ashley and others in Congress, and of "Southern loyalists"—"many of whom we regard as the worst men in the country"—showed that *true* Southern men should bestir themselves. Opportunely, it added, the State Senate had that day referred the proposal to its Committee on Federal Relations.[98]

But when at last the matter was considered by the North Carolina Senate, debate resulted in its withdrawal. Instead, the legislature took the utterly unrealistic line of calling for a convention of the States to propose constitutional amendments which by mutual concession would "lead to a restoration of our former happy relations."[99]

In South Carolina, the *Charleston Courier*—an old and important journal—covered the proposal in well-informed reports from Washington and in editorials, between February 8 and 18. At the outset it said that Southern judgment might well be reserved "until the temper and tone

---

decades of the *National Intelligencer.* Seaton, the surviving partner, had given up control of the *Intelligencer* on December 31, 1864. Seaton Gales spoke for moderation, and presently for acceptance of the Reconstruction Act.

[98] N.C. Sen. J., 1866–67, 260.

The *Charlotte* (North Carolina) *Western Democrat* of February 12 exclaimed that whereas the proposed Fourteenth Amendment left suffrage to regulation by the States, this plan would actually degrade the Southern whites to equality with the blacks. "We warn the people that many of their Representatives in the Legislature, and political tricksters and demogogues generally, are doing a great deal of harm, and are unworthy of public confidence. We say, without

any sort of hesitation, that the great mass of the people are being deceived by so called 'leading men.' . . ."

The *Wilmington* (North Carolina) *Journal* of February 15 said: "If this matter is forced to a vote, beyond doubt the resolution will and should be rejected. There is hardly a member of the Legislature who would feel himself authorized to vote for such propositions."

[99] N.C. Sen. J., 1866–67, 365, 377, 387–91; H. of Commons J., 1866–67, 434–35.

The Constitution, Article V, provides that "Congress . . . on the Application of the Legislatures of two thirds of the several States, shall call a Convention for proposing Amendments . . . ."

of the Republican party" was disclosed. A dispatch of February 12 said that the proposal had found "much favor" in Washington—but told also of renewed pressure to force enactment of a "Military Bill"[100] and also a "Bill to Establish a Territorial Government in Louisiana."[101] An editorial of the thirteenth said that it now seemed "fallacious" to expect that Senator Dixon's resolution would "afford a common platform" upon which President and Congress could meet.

The *Athens* (Georgia) *Southern Watchman* commented that "We are asked to yield every thing and in return receive nothing"; it was "unfortunate that any of [the South's] citizens should have voluntarily offered" a settlement.[102]

In Alabama, the plan was on February 15 "submitted to the superior wisdom of the Legislature." (Governor Patton was noncommittal: he had suffered a rebuff in January when he had done his best to induce favorable action on the Fourteenth Amendment.[103]) In the House, the Committee on Federal Relations recommended that "no further action be taken"—and so it was. In the Senate, an adverse report was adopted, by 14 votes to 6.[104]

The *Montgomery Mail*—the more militant of the capital's two Democratic newspapers—had been opposing compromise of any sort. Rejection of the Fourteenth Amendment was hailed in an editorial on "Noble Alabama."[105] "The Supreme Court Stands Firm," on December 22, applauded the decision in *Ex parte Milligan* and (three weeks prematurely) the invalidation of the attorneys' test oath. The Court, it said, was declaring "to Congress that the mad waves of bigotry and malice will dash in vain against the walls of the Judiciary." When the Governor sought to turn public sentiment toward acceptance of the Amendment, an editorial on "Gov. Patton vs. the Supreme Court" pronounced it folly to surrender when the Court's "recent decisions stand arrayed like mailed giants between the Radicals and the accomplishment of their threats."[106] The *Test Oath Cases*, it was said, made certain that "The Point of Danger is Passed!"[107] Editorials derided the North Carolina plan: "New Scheme a Bribe and a Jumble"—a pitiful surrender of "vital principle" to appease "the madness of the Mongrel party"—by "Smart Politicians," "Orr, Sharkey & Co." "It is impossible to compromise" on State Rights. "Masterly inactivity" was recommended.[108]

---

[100] Infra, p. 287.
[101] Infra, p. 290.
[102] Feb. 13, 1867.
[103] Supra, ch. 5, n. 9.
[104] Ala. House J., 1866–67, 456, 472–73; Sen. J., 363, 409–10.
[105] Dec. 9, 1866.

[106] Jan. 1, 1867; in like vein, editorials on Dec. 23 and 30.
[107] Jan. 16, 1867.
[108] Feb. 15, 16, 19, 1867. On the phrase "masterly inactivity," see supra, n. 12. The editorial approved the *Louisville Journal*'s comment that the plan was "an insult" and "an outrage."

This illustrates the line that many Southern papers, more especially those in smaller communities, would take throughout the period of Congressional Reconstruction.

The *Montgomery Advertiser*—"not among those who would reject every plan of pacification"—considered the pros and cons, and concluded: "Do nothing." "With singular unanimity, the Southern press advises that no action be taken upon the new plan . . . ." The *Advertiser*, too, advocated "masterly inactivity" in politics, along with hard work to restore the State's economy.[109]

In Mississippi, when Governor Humphreys received the propositions from Judge Sharkey, he transmitted them to the Legislature with the statement, "I disapprove them entirely." While the Legislature was quite unwilling to take any initiative, the Houses did, after heated debate, adopt a report undertaking that the propositions "would be taken into most careful deliberation, if they came before the Legislature in the shape of a final disposition of the subject, and would thereby bring stability and repose." The *Jackson Clarion*—the State's most important newspaper—said that "Now that a rupture has unhappily occurred between the Federal Executive and Congress, it would be most unwise, in our situation, . . . to place ourselves in an attitude of hostility to either." The Legislature did well to refrain from "any expression of opinion respecting a plan of settlement . . . not coming from the controlling power . . . ."[110]

Governor James W. Throckmorton of Texas, in private correspondence, expressed the opinion that "Our people will not object"— "for the sake of peace and quiet"—"if there is any manifestation that it will satisfy the radical majority." The Legislature, however, was not in session.[111]

Had a settlement on some such basis as the North Carolina plan been energetically pressed by the President in 1865, and had it been sincerely embraced by the South, it would surely have received very respectful consideration by Congress and the country. But time had run. On the day Senator Dixon presented the measure—February 6,

---

[109] Feb. 8, 14, 16, 1867. On the *Advertiser*, see infra, pp. 371–74.

[110] Miss. Sen. J., 1866–67, 293, 312–13; *Jackson Clarion,* Feb. 6 to 21, 1867, reporting the progress of the plan, the discussion in the legislature, and the proceedings of the Houses.

The report, presented by H. F. Simrall, argued that the Southern people were still entitled to rely on President Lincoln's proclamation of December 8, 1863, offering terms to those who, in the midst of war, would abandon the rebellion and renew their loyalty. Supra, p. 95.

[111] Letter of Feb. 20, 1867, "private," to Benjamin H. Epperson, claimant to a seat in the 39th Congress, and the Governor's agent in the East. Epperson Papers, Univ. of Texas Library.

1867—a "Military Bill," H.R. 1143, was reported from the Joint Committee.[112] Dixon's resolution was brushed aside: Saulsbury of Delaware announced Democratic opposition and said he hoped that no Southern State would so degrade itself as to accept;[113] Sumner on the other side said "I regard it as a delusion and a snare."[114] It was never debated.

H.R. 1143 became the Reconstruction Act of March 2. Critics have expatiated upon its severity, and have deplored the Court's failure to strike it down. The abortive North Carolina plan has been neglected: yet its brief story is noteworthy, because it shows authentically what was the state of ruling Southern opinion at the moment Congress acted. Even qualified Negro suffrage was opposed as a surrender of principle —and "honor" forbade any concession; "masterly inactivity," "passive resistance" was the approved course; the Supreme Court was counted upon to "arrest the tide of faction" and make Congress "impotent to destroy" the State governments as then established.[115]

JUSTICE MILLER'S LETTER OF FEBRUARY 6, 1867

SENATOR DIXON'S RESOLUTION was the occasion for a remarkable analysis of the partisan context within which the Court must now function, in a letter Justice Miller wrote to his kinsman, William Pitt Ballinger of Galveston, Texas. In early January, Ballinger had written his prescription for a settlement: suffrage for Negroes qualified by education or property; "a special jurisdiction to give protection to the

---

[112] Infra, p. 287.

[113] Cong. Globe, 39–2, 1046–47. Feb. 6.

[114] Ibid., 1149. Feb. 11.

[115] *Montgomery Mail*, Dec. 23, 1866.

In a discussion having the focus indicated above, it is needless to evaluate the North Carolina scheme, or to recount at length its reception in the North. The most obvious of numerous flaws was that the Southern States would have been free presently to repeal the grant of qualified suffrage.

The *Boston Advertiser* (February 7) stressed the "immaturity and insufficiency" of the proposal. Halstead's *Cincinnati Commercial* (February 9) examined critically and found it disappointing; its significance was that it showed "considerable prog-

ress" on the part of "influential men of the South" toward the position Congress had taken in the Fourteenth Amendment. The *Springfield Republican* (February 5) found it "encouraging as a mark of advancing opinion." It quoted what the editor of the *Columbia South Carolinian* had said on February 1, that there were "thoughtful men, leading men in the State," who were coming to think that qualified Negro suffrage would be the "final consummation of the purpose of the war" and "an essential element of our material and political prosperity." Raymond's *New York Times* (February 7) found the scheme "unsatisfactory," but welcome as "the first token of an awakening at the South to the realities of the situation."

negroes," which the States themselves would undertake; a constitutional amendment forbidding secession and including all the sections in the pending Fourteenth Amendment except the offensive Section 3. Did Miller think such a settlement would be acceptable to Congressional leaders?

On February 6, 1867, Justice Miller replied,[116] inclosing a newspaper clipping reporting what Senator Dixon had that day proposed. Miller commented:

> I have no hesitation in saying that in the shape of an amendment to the federal Constitution it is as acceptable to me as any basis of reconstruction which I have seen offered. I am not now and have not been at any time in favour of negro suffrage as a principle or for its own sake. I am not in favour on principle of any extension of the elective franchise. I think we had better see if it will sustain itself as it is before we extend it further. . . .

Miller was disturbed by the program of the Radicals who would overturn two of the great primary departments of the Government because their action did not conform to the wishes of the third; yet, even so,

> with all its faults, and all the dangers on which I see it driving, the Republican party is the only one from which I can have any hope for the country. The Democratic party of the North could not be in full power two years before Mr. Davis would be their candidate for the Presidency, and with the Southern States capable of casting their votes and the democracy as strong in the North as the republicans now are, he would be elected. It would happen thus. The moment their power was assured, the party would submit to its old leaders. Mr Vallandigham, Pendleton, Jerry Black, J. C. Breckinridge and that class of men, would again become its leaders. More moderate men might struggle against it but they could not prevent it.
>
> With these views you must see that my hopes for the future are not bright. Unquestionably the republican party is going it at a killing pace. It is true also that some of its leaders are reckless, and not over honest or patriotic. But there are men and strong men among them who if they could find in the flood that is drifting them along against their will a rock or other footing on which they could make a stand would do it manfully and I hope successfully. But here is their condition.

---

[116] He misdated the letter, February 6, 1866. Miller wrote "under pressure of other duties . . . ." Concluding, he cautioned "I have not time to revise, you must supply omissions and guess at words you cant make out."

VI: *Congressional Reconstruction*

The democratic party is utterly odious to the voting majorities every where. Mr. Johnson is now more odious than the democratic party. Any thing coming from them . . . cuts itself off from all sympathy with the dominant party. Not only so but makes it as much as a mans political existence is worth to do or say anything for them. This is just what you southern people are doing all the time. If a committee comes here they go and have a powow with Seward and Johnson, and forthwith publish it to the world, that they and the President are firm in their resistance to radicalism, that is, to the governing majority who alone can do them any good. They then call on that old political prostitute Reverdy Johnson, Saulsbury, Tom Florence,[117] Charles Mason, Cham[.] of Executive National Democratic Committee,[118] &c &c all of whom are hated by all loyal men worse a thousand times than they hate many honest rebels. All this is known and published over the land and makes the majority more determined, more bitter, more exacting than ever. These men never call on moderate republicans. Sometimes for form's sake they call on Thad Stevens, Wade, or Sumner that they may report at home how hostile and offensive they are.

Of course there is a large class of men in the North who seeing these things swear that so long as it remains so, and so long as your folks cling to these political associates they can remain without political power; But there is a large class of republicans who can overlook all this, who would be willing to incur the hazard even of a return to power of the allied democratic and rebel parties, rather than risk what we are risking, the eventual destruction of some of the best principles of our existing constitution; But who are still unwilling to trust you, I mean the Southern people, with full power over the negro, and the Union man of the South.

I wish to call your attention to this proposition strongly because it is one which governs quite enough votes at any time to overturn the republican party and also because it is one [to] which you in your letters never allude, and which all the good men I have seen from the South shirk or belittle. We cannot in the face of the events that have occurred since the war trust the South with the power of governing the negro and Union white man without such guarantees in the federal Constitution as secure their protection. Now you will say this is unjust. Let us see. Of course I do not believe that all the stories I

---

[117] Thomas B. Florence (1812–75), Democratic Congressman from Pennsylvania (1851–61), then editor and publisher of the (Washington) *Constitutional Union.*

[118] (1804–82), graduate of the United States Military Academy; formerly editorial writer on the *New York Evening Post*; Chief Justice of the Supreme Court of the Territory of Iowa; then practicing in Washington, and Chairman of the National Democratic Committee. See McKitrick, *Andrew Johnson and Reconstruction*, 68–74.

see in the papers about killing, beating, shooting these men are true. If you are fair minded you must admit that many of them are true. You will say that they are done by low degraded men who are found in all communities, and that your leading men disapprove of it. That is what is always said in reply. Show me how you disapprove of it. Show me a single white man that has been punished in a State court for murdering a negro or a Union man. Show me that any public meeting has been had to express indignation at such conduct. Show me that you or any of the best men of the South have gone ten steps out of their way to bring such men to punishment or to take any steps to prevent a recurrence of such things. Show me the first public address or meeting of Southern men in which the massacres of New Orleans or Memphis have been condemned or any general dissent shown at *home* at such conduct. You may say that there are two sides to those stories of Memphis and New Orleans. There may be two sides to the stories, but there was but one side in the party that suffered at both places, and the single truth which is undenied that not a rebel or secessionist was hurt in either case, while from thirty to fifty negroes and Union white men were shot down precludes all doubt as to who did it and why it was done.

Now as *I* feel and think, so large numbers of men who are not politicians think and feel. I am for Mr. Dixon's plan for settlement. I am for your plan. I am for universal amnesty and universal suffrage, not because any one of these are the best in themselves, but because we are losing what is more valuable than any of these things in the struggle which is demoralizing us worse than the war did. In my way, as I think it timely and useful to try to moderate my party friends, and work to bring about good results. But there are two parties to the settlement and your friends need quite as much working with as mine do. If I could be able to say tomorrow See here, they have hung a rebel in Texas for killing a negro, it would be the most effective speech that has been made since the war ended. Or if I could say see here what a former rebel said on this subject to his own comrades face to face, and then could point [to] a public outspoken condemnation of some such conduct it would have effect. That is the place for you and your true friends to work, as holding back with a steady hand is mine. May we both do our duty where it will be most effectual. I do not believe it will be found in the concoction of terms of settlement.[119]

These are the thoughts of the Justice who, six years later, would be spokesman for the majority in giving the Court's initial construction of the Fourteenth Amendment, wherein he strove to avert what

---

[119] Charles Fairman, *Mr. Justice Miller and the Supreme Court, 1862–* | *1890* (Cambridge, Mass.: Harvard University Press, 1939), 190–193.

seemed, in the words of this letter, "the eventual destruction of some of the best principles of our existing constitution."[120] On that account, and because of the accuracy of Justice Miller's perception, the letter is a document of highest importance.

THE "MILITARY BILL" AND THE "LOUISIANA BILL"

THE JOINT COMMITTEE, to which H.R. 543 had on January 28 been referred, met on Saturday, February 2, 1867. On Stevens' motion his substitute was read; then on Bingham's motion the original text was read. What should now be done?[121]

Stevens wanted to proceed on the basis of Enabling Acts, to authorize particular States to frame a new constitution and establish a new government. (That is, he wanted to start from his premise that the rebel States had forfeited their rights; to be readmitted to the Union, each must be reformed—with impartial suffrage, coupled with the exclusion of a large portion of the participants in the Confederacy. What such an Enabling Act might provide will be seen in a moment, when the "Louisiana Bill" is introduced.[122])

Bingham wanted to proceed from H.R. 543 as the committee had framed it at the First Session;[123] now he would add one further requirement: that the State "secure impartial suffrage to the male citizens of the United States." Existing governments would not be superseded; Congress would impose no proscription beyond what Section 3 of the Amendment provided about office-holding.

Without deciding upon any course, the committee adjourned before noon (when sessions of the two Houses would begin), to meet on Wednesday morning.

On Monday, February 4, Senator George H. Williams of Oregon, a member of the Joint Committee, introduced S. 564, "A bill to provide for the more efficient government of the insurrectionary States."[124] It recited that "the pretended State governments of the late so-called Confederate States" were affording no adequate protection of life and property, etc.; wherefore, in order that peace and good order might be enforced until loyal and republican governments could be established,

---

[120] Slaughter House Cases, 16 Wall. 36 (1873); infra, ch. 21.

[121] Journal of the Joint Committee, in Benjamin B. Kendrick, *The Journal of the Joint Committee of Fifteen on Reconstruction* (New York: Columbia University Studies in History, Economics and Public Law, 1914), 122.

[122] Infra, p. 290.

[123] Supra, pp. 262–63.

[124] Cong. Globe, 39–2, 975.

the bill would create military districts, each under a general officer; it would be the duty of such commander to give protection, to suppress disorder, and to cause criminals to be punished—by the local courts or, if he judged necessary, by military commission,[125] "anything in the

---

[125] This referred to a tribunal then familiar to those in responsible position.

Chief Justice Chase had observed in *Ex parte* Milligan, 4 Wall. 2 (1866), supra (in a passage about which there was no disagreement) that "There are under the Constitution three kinds of military jurisdiction." He distinguished them:

(1) *Military law*—briefly, the code for the government of soldiers—"is found in the Acts of Congress prescribing rules and articles of war, or otherwise provided for the government of the national forces." One of the enumerated powers of Congress, Art. I, Sec. 8, cl. 14, is "to make rules for the government and regulation of the land and naval forces." The *court-martial* is the tribunal provided by this code.

(2) *Military government* is "exercised in time of foreign war without the boundaries of the United States [as during the Mexican War: Leitensdorfer v. Webb, 20 How. 176 (1858)], or in time of rebellion and civil war within States or districts occupied by rebels treated as belligerents." In *The Grapeshot*, 9 Wall. 129 (1870), the Court said: "it became the duty of the National Government, wherever the insurgent power was overthrown, and the territory which had been dominated by it was occupied by the national forces, to provide as far as possible, so long as the war continued, for the security of persons and property, and for the administration of justice." Also Handlin v. Wickliffe, 12 Wall. 173 (1871); Pennywit v. Eaton, 15 Wall. 382 (1873); Burke v. Miltenberger, 19 Wall. 519 (1874) (above cases recognizing authority of courts appointed under military government); New Orleans v. Steamship Co., 20 Wall. 387 (1874) (sustaining lease of water front for ten years, made by municipal officers appointed under military

government); United States v. Diekelman, 92 U.S. 520 (1876) (no recovery where military governor detained foreign merchant vessel until it removed cargo he reasonably believed to be contraband).

(3) "Martial law proper" (or better, *martial rule*)—military control recognized to be lawful to the extent found actually necessary in the theater of active military operations—as considered in connection with *Ex parte* Milligan.

In the practice of the United States, the tribunal for the trial of criminal cases in the latter two situations is termed a *military commission*. Applicable principles of law were laid down in the Instructions for the Government of the Armies of the United States in the Field, War Department General Orders No. 100 of April 24, 1863, "prepared by Francis Lieber, LL.D., and revised by a board of officers . . . ." War of the Rebellion, Official Records, ser. 3, III.

The jurisdiction of a military commission extends to crimes as defined by the law of the place being occupied; offenses against the laws of war (a branch of international law); and violations of regulations imposed by the occupying power. The sentence of a commission is not subject to appellate review by the judiciary. *Ex parte* Vallandigham, 1 Wall. 243 (1864); *In re* Vidal, 179 U.S. 126 (1900). Habeas corpus lies, however, to test the jurisdiction of such commission. The cases of Milligan, McCardle, Martin and Gill, Yerger, and Brown *et al.*, as well as *In re* Egan and United States v. Commandant of Fort Delaware, are examples. See *Ex parte* Quirin, 317 U.S. 1 (1942).

By the statute of July 16, 1866, 14 Stat. 173, to continue the Freedmen's Bureau, enacted over a veto, the Executive was directed to "extend military protection and have military

constitutions or laws of the so-called States to the contrary notwith-standing."[126]

When the committee met on Wednesday, Representative Conkling moved that Senator Williams' bill be taken as the basis of discussion.[127] That was accepted; the committee went on to make small changes in drafting. Bingham sought, unsuccessfully, to remove the derogatory expressions. On Stevens' motion, it was voted to report this measure to the House.

That afternoon the bill—becoming H.R. 1143—was introduced and given first and second reading. Because it dealt, not with recon-struction, but only with security, to be provided by employment of the army, it was dubbed the "Military Bill." Stevens told the House, "I think I shall ask that it be put upon its passage to-morrow."[128]

On that same afternoon, at the other end of the capitol, Senator Dixon presented the North Carolina Plan.[129] It offered too little, and came too late.

As it turned out, debate on H.R. 1143 was not ended until February 13, a week after Stevens introduced it. In the meantime, familiar arguments were repeated. Pike and Farnsworth, the majority members of the Select Committee on the Murder of Union Soldiers, dwelt upon the credible testimony there adduced.[130] On the other side, Rogers of New Jersey said that "the very moment the rebellion ceased these States were entitled to all the rights under the Constitution that

---

jurisdiction over all cases" concern-ing the free enjoyment of the rights of personal liberty and security therein declared.

That statute supported the action of General Schofield in holding Dr. Watson for trial by military commis-sion in Virginia. Supra, p. 128. But then came the dictum in *Milligan*, and the President's order for Dr. Watson's release, in purported obedience to the Court's opinion.

Congress was thus well acquainted with the military commission when, in the Reconstruction Act of March 2, 1867, it made it the duty of each District commander to protect all persons and to cause disturbers of the peace and criminals to be pun-ished: "and to this end he may allow local civil tribunals to take jurisdic-tion . . . , or, when in his judgment it may be necessary . . . , he shall have power to organize military tribunals . . . ." It was under this authority that McCardle, Martin and Gill, Yerger, and Brown *et al.*, presently to be met, were brought to trial.

Colonel William W. Winthrop, *Military Law and Precedents*, 2d ed., revised and enlarged (Government Printing Office, 1920), discussed the military commission at 831–46, and "Military Authority and Jurisdiction under the Reconstruction Acts of 1867" at 846–62. This is a work of accuracy and authority. It first ap-peared in 1886; 2d ed. in 1896.

[126] The text, derived from the *New York Herald* of February 5, is set out in Kendrick, *Journal of the Joint Committee*, 380–82.

[127] Kendrick, *Journal of the Joint Committee*, at 124.

[128] Cong. Globe, 39–2, 1036–37. Feb. 6.

[129] Supra, p. 276.

[130] Cong. Globe, 39–2, App., 94–96 and 99–101, respectively, on Feb. 7.

they possessed before the war commenced."[131] To this effect he cited Justice Nelson in the *Egan* case.[132] He quoted Justice Davis in *Milligan* for the proposition that the right to trial by jury could not be constitutionally denied.[133] Judge Hise of Kentucky said that "these military satraps" would be used to protect "negroes . . . [who] have been taken by force from their masters, contrary to the Constitution . . . ."[134]

Rogers and Hise were members of the Joint Committee; but they had absented themselves from the meeting on February 6, when Bingham, with support from Senator Johnson and others, had sought to moderate the language of the bill.

Samuel Shellabarger (1817–96) of Springfield, Ohio—"one of the ablest lawyers in the House," "his mind possessed many of the qualities which distinguished Mr. Lincoln"[135]—said that "if [he] agreed with the other side of this House in regard to the state of fact," he would agree also that it would be "monstrous for us to pass this bill . . . ." In fact, however, although hostility was no longer flagrant, it had not yet ceased; life was insecure, even though courts were sitting. The Government must "exercise such extraordinary powers as are necessary to the preservation of the great life of the nation." H.R. 1143 was a bill for "the employment of the armies of the United States as a mere police force until we can establish civil governments, based upon the loyal suffrages of the people there"; only as an accompaniment to the "rapid and immediate establishment" of such governments could he support this bill.[136]

Shellabarger had already addressed himself to the contention that the Constitution, just as it was written, now entitled the ex-rebel States to all the constitutional rights and privileges. If the text were subject to no qualification by reason of the rebellion, then—if a State could not secede—it would follow that throughout the war the Confederate States

---

[131] Ibid., App., 83, 84. Feb. 7. LeBlond of Ohio used virtually the same words. "The executive, legislative, and judicial functions of each State continued in full operation during that period." P. 1077. Feb. 7.

[132] *In re* Egan, supra, p. 148.

[133] Trimble of Kentucky gave notice of an amendment to add to the bill a proviso requiring grand jury and trial jury, in words drawn from the Fifth and Sixth Amendments. Cong. Globe, 39–2, 1084. Feb. 7.

[134] Ibid., App., 96, 98. Feb. 7. Finck of Ohio asked, "Have we . . . forgotten the sermon of our divine Redeemer on the Mount? Are we to act as men who have no love or charity in their hearts?" P. 1079. Feb. 7. Stevens replied that the teachings on the Mount "refer simply to private offences, to personal transgressions, where men can well forgive their enemies and smother their feelings of revenge without injury to anybody. But what has that to do with municipal punishment? . . . ." P. 1214, Feb. 13.

[135] George F. Hoar, *Autobiography of Seventy Years*, 2 vols. (New York: Charles Scribner's Sons, 1903), I, 321; Blaine, *Twenty Years of Congress*, I, 328.

[136] Cong. Globe, 39–2, 1099–1100. Feb. 8.

were entitled to participate in Congress and in the election of the President. Since that was absurd, the text must be subject to qualification in the light of the actual situation. Shellabarger cast the Democrats' contention into the language of an imaginary Article in the original Constitution —not to "caricature or exaggerate," but to demonstrate "the appalling results of this position." "This is not the law of your nation's existence."[137]

The contrast between a letter-bound reading of the Constitution and reading it as a charter adequate to preserving "the life of the nation"—prominent throughout the war[138]—figured persistently in discussion of post-war problems: in editorials, in Congressional debates, in argument before the Court, and in judicial decision (e.g., the *Legal Tender* litigation[139]). Reprobation of the "life of the nation" theme drew strength from the looseness with which some Radicals would invoke it.

On the problem of how to provide even-handed justice in States governed by recent rebels, one proposed amendment to H.R. 1143 is here to be mentioned: Representative William Lawrence of Ohio wanted to provide that in each State the United States District Court and its Judge would have jurisdiction "to hear and determine all causes, proceedings, and rights of action at law, in equity and otherwise, and all matters of probate and testamentary jurisdiction . . ." as fully as they could have been heard and determined by State courts and judges prior to the rebellion. Further, the laws in force in the District of Columbia defining and punishing crimes would be extended to the affected States, and the United States Courts and Judges would have jurisdiction to enforce them. Lawrence's remarks indicated that he meant this to be exclusive of the State judiciary.[140]

That a careful practicing lawyer should have imagined that a Court manned by one Judge could perform such a feat is astounding. Later on the implications of the proposal will be examined.[141]

Of H.R. 1143 as conceived by the Joint Committee, Stevens said: "It was not intended as a reconstruction bill. It was intended simply as a police bill to protect the loyal men from anarchy and murder . . ." until Congress, "taking a little more time," could settle on "a bill for the admission of those rebel States upon the basis of civil government."[142]

---

[137] Ibid., 720–21. Jan. 24. Shellabarger made this analysis immediately following Raymond's editorial essay on Justice Davis' mode of thought in *Milligan*. Supra, p. 273. Without mentioning *Milligan*, Shellabarger had taken the common lawyer's approach.

[138] Supra, p. 273.
[139] Infra, pp. 713–15, 760–63.
[140] Cong. Globe, 39–2, 1083–84. Feb. 7.
[141] Infra, pp. 592–95.
[142] Cong. Globe, 39–2, 1214. Feb. 13.

Actually a bill for the admission of one rebel State—Louisiana—on the basis of civil government went sailing through the House in two days, February 11 and 12. To explain: the Select Committee on the New Orleans Riot, created on December 6, had been charged to make inquiry on the ground and to report such legislative action as seemed to be required in view of conditions in Louisiana.[143] The majority members, Thomas D. Eliot and Shellabarger, sponsored the "Louisiana Bill," H.R. 1162, which in regular order was called on Monday, February 11.[144] In the congested state of the calendar, it appeared that if consideration were postponed there would be little hope of its passage. Accordingly the House, interrupting its debate on H.R. 1143, proceeded with the Louisiana Bill and, with little debate, passed it.[145]

Although, as it turned out, the Louisiana Bill was never brought to a vote in the Senate, it is a document that will have great significance in the discussion that follows. The Republicans of the House, save for a few moderate or conservative members, voted for it; it was well received in the Senate; the Southern Republican Association (the organization of Loyalists, with Thomas J. Durant at their head) "heartily" endorsed it and petitioned Congress to legislate "for the reorganization of the other unreconstructed States on the same principle."[146]

Whenever, as the story unfolds, the "Military Bill" that Congress did enact on March 2, 1867, comes up for criticism, one may profitably compare it with the civil government bill which came near to enactment.

Here was a measure whereby a State would be enabled to re-establish itself within the Union, with every step being entrusted to civilians. It was capably drawn—apparently by Shellabarger—in little more than half the space used by Ashley's territorial bill of January 3.[147] By H.R. 1162 the President would appoint, upon confirmation by the Senate, a Provisional Governor, and a Provisional Council of nine—all citizens of the State, whose unbroken loyalty must meet tests even more searching than the iron-clad oath of 1862. The Provisional Governor and Council would exercise "all legislative power"; the Governor would see that State and federal laws were executed and, with the consent of the Council, would appoint State officers.

In June 1867 an election would be held for Governor, Senate and House, and other State officers, including judges. Then the all-important provision on qualifications for voting: adult male citizens, without

---

[143] Ibid., 28–29.
[144] Ibid., 1128–29.
[145] Infra, pp. 291–92.
[146] Cong. Globe, 39–2, 1171. Among the signatories were George W. Paschal, Andrew J. Hamilton, and Lorenzo Sherwood of Texas; Rufus Waples of Louisiana; James W. Hunnicutt and John Hawxhurst of Virginia.
[147] Supra, p. 268.

regard to color, who could take the iron-clad oath of 1862; provided, that one otherwise qualified who had never voluntarily given aid to the rebellion, other than as a private soldier, might be admitted by a Court of the United States if supported by the testimony of ever-loyal persons that the applicant had never given voluntary aid to the rebellion after March 4, 1864. The Secretary of War would make rules, and appoint officers to register voters and conduct elections.

In October 1867, delegates to a constitutional convention would be chosen: they must meet the test of loyalty prescribed for the Provisional Governor. The constitution must not "permit any distinction in the rights of men on account of race or color." If approved by a majority of the qualified voters, the constitution would be presented to Congress as the basis for the admission of the State to representation.

The President would appoint a general officer to be military commander within the State, and would place under him a military force adequate to the accomplishment of his duties. A militia, whose members must meet the qualifications for voters, would be organized, and would be under the direction of the military commander.

Shellabarger made the principal speech, cogently supporting the bill.[148] The vote was then called, and the bill carried by 113 to 47, 30 not voting.[149] It was almost a straight party vote: only six Republicans, Bingham among them, voted nay.

This was a plan for reorganization by *loyal* citizens. The provisional regime, from top to bottom, would be in safe hands. The Secretary of War would control registration and elections. Only loyalists, white and black, plus a segment of the least consequential of ex-Confederates, would be allowed to vote. Jurors and militiamen must meet that same test.

Even then, the bill took additional precautions. The general officer assigned to command was charged, whenever the civil authorities failed to enforce all the laws for the punishment of crimes, to "arrest and hold . . . offenders" until the civil authorities prosecuted. He would render such support, in the enforcement of all laws, State and federal, "as shall insure the full, speedy, and impartial enforcement of all such laws and of equal justice, and this without regard to race or color." The section thus summarized was quite striking in its draftsmanship. While the commander was to "support" the civil authorities, strong precatory words called upon him to act most energetically, if need be, to make sure that the purposes of the statute were indeed fulfilled. Just how he could *insure* that equal justice would be done by the civil authorities was left unanswered. (Louisiana had many loyalists who, as events

---

[148] Cong. Globe, 39–2, 1173–75. Feb. 12.   [149] Ibid., 1175.

since 1863 had shown, did not concede racial equality.) Evidently the draftsman hoped, by this residuary provision, to make it a little more probable that the plan did not fail.

As soon as the Louisiana Bill was out of the way, on February 12, the House returned to the Military Bill, and in an evening session and the following afternoon, disposed of it. Bingham urged an amendment that would set a course whereby a State undergoing reconstruction could be assured that it would be restored to representation in Congress. He would add a section to enact, in substance, that Senators and Representatives might be admitted—

[1] when the Fourteenth Amendment had become part of the Constitution; and

[2] when a State had given its assent and had conformed its constitution and laws thereto; and

[3] *when it shall have provided by its constitution that the elective franchise shall be enjoyed equally and impartially by all male citizens of the United States twenty-one years old and upward, without regard to race, color, or previous condition of servitude,* except such as may be disfranchised for participating in the late rebellion, or for felony at common law; and

[4] when the constitution shall have been *submitted to the voters as thus defined,* for ratification or rejection; and

[5] when the constitution, if ratified by the popular vote, shall have been submitted to Congress for examination and approval.[150]

Representative Blaine also offered an amendment, with the identical provision outlined above.[151] Bingham accepted Blaine's proposal;[152] the feature outlined above was thenceforth called "the Blaine amendment." After being rejected by the House, and then accepted in modified form by the Senate, it emerged in Section 5 of the Reconstruction Act of March 2, 1867.

---

[150] Ibid., 1211–12. Feb. 13. He had previously given notice of his proposal, in somewhat different form. Pp. 1176–77. Feb. 12.

[151] Ibid., 1213. Feb. 13. As originally proposed on February 12, Blaine's amendment provided that when the Fourteenth Amendment should have become part of the Constitution *by the ratification of three-fourths of the States now represented in Congress, etc.* He wanted thus to show the Southern States that their assent was *not* necessary to bring the Amendment into effect; ratification by them would be "merely an evidence both moral and legal of good faith and loyalty on their part." P. 1182, Feb. 12. This feature he abandoned.

And whereas Bingham had preferred to set out the text of the Fourteenth Amendment in the preamble—to place his proposition at the head of the bill—and to add the military part at the end, as a regime pending readmission (pp. 1176–77), Blaine, more tactfully, had simply offered his proposal as "an additional section" to go at the end of the Military Bill. P. 1182.

[152] Cong. Globe, 39–2, 1212. Feb. 13.

Boutwell of Massachusetts—Stevens' sturdy ally—pointed to a weakness in the Bingham-Blaine plan: in each State the existing government, remaining tightly under rebel control, would preside over the calling of the convention and the framing of the constitution; and then "these nine States [that is, other than Louisiana] will appear here with their constitutions framed as you demand, the constitutional amendment adopted, and negro suffrage provided for, but every officer in the States will be a disloyal man." He contrasted this with the "utmost security" that would be attained by the Louisiana Bill.[153]

Four courses, Boutwell said, were open. One was to admit the Southern States under the Bingham-Blaine plan—leaving their governments in the hands of rebels.

Or Congress could do nothing—and let the "grand carnival of disquiet . . . and murder" continue.

A third was to proceed as in the case of Louisiana; he mentioned North Carolina and Arkansas as perhaps ready. (Only where there was a substantial core of loyal men—sufficient to dominate the State and administer its offices—would it have been practicable to attempt this method.[154])

Fourth, for the meantime, "some sort of government . . . which shall protect the people in their rights" should be provided; and he knew of "no means whatever except to employ for that purpose the military force of the Government."

Hence, Boutwell said, there would be need for the Military Bill until the method of the Louisiana Bill could safely be applied to each of the remaining Southern States.

Bingham attempted to reply; but he was made to face the reality that only those already qualified to vote would choose the delegates to the convention; impartial suffrage would first be practiced at the election on whether the constitution should be ratified.[155]

Stevens, in his closing speech, said that to accept the Blaine amendment "would be an entire surrender of those States into the hands of the rebels." He reiterated that he had "no respect for" the Fourteenth Amendment.[156]

The House must now make a critical choice: Should Blaine's proposal be added to the Military Bill? If it were, the prospect would be held out of restoring the States on the basis of the Fourteenth Amendment with impartial suffrage. (Boutwell's criticism and Stevens' derision had advertised how easy that path could be for ex-rebels, if

---

[153] Ibid., 1207–10. Feb. 13.
[154] Senator Wilson wanted "to try the experiment" in Louisiana "where we have a loyal Governor and where the rebels are out of power." Cong.

Globe, 39–2, 1511. Feb. 18. And see Fessenden, infra, p. 295.
[155] Cong. Globe, 39–2, 1210–12. Feb. 13.
[156] Ibid., 1213–14. Feb. 13.

only they would follow it.) Or, as Stevens urged, the House might pass H.R. 1143 as it stood, "simply as a police bill," and let another Congress legislate for admitting the rebel States on the basis of civil governments firmly in loyal hands (and, in Stevens' mind, after some confiscation of rebels' property had been provided).

Blaine's effort was defeated: it drew only 69 yeas to 94 nays.[157] Stevens had a majority, by reason of the accession of twenty-three Democrats. Five of these came from New York, and four each from Pennsylvania and Illinois. Not solicitude for Southern friends, but the scoring of partisan advantage, was their motive. The *New York World* explained the strategy: "to force the dominant party to . . . retreat again, as they have for days past, in a demoralized condition."[158] (Within a few days, three of these strategists would be lamenting their inability, by dilatory tactics, to prevent the bill they had thus supported from becoming law.[159]) Blaine's motion had the support of seventeen Democrats—including five from Tennessee and Judge Hise of Kentucky —who were voting straightforwardly. If the Democrats who teamed with Stevens had, instead, joined the moderate and conservative Republicans in their effort to provide a mode of escape from military control, Blaine's motion would have carried (92 to 71).[160]

Then the bill itself was put to a vote, and carried by 109 (all but one of them Republicans) to 55 (Democrats and 13 conservative Republicans). Both Bingham and Blaine voted for the bill.[161]

---

[157] Ibid., 1215. Feb. 13.

[158] Feb. 14, 1867.

[159] Infra, n. 234.

[160] When Stevens introduced H.R. 1143, the *Cleveland Plain Dealer*— self-styled "Only Democratic Daily in Northern Ohio"—warned that the Radicals would have the South under permanent military rule. It quoted with approval what the *Philadelphia Age* said about the bill: "the sword and bayonet gleam in each paragraph . . ." Feb. 8. But when House Democrats enabled Stevens to exclude the Blaine amendment, the *Plain Dealer*, uncandidly reporting "No Terms to the South," said that "A considerable number of Republicans voted for making this provision a part of the Stevens bill, but a large majority of them opposed." Feb. 15.

[161] An interpretation quite different from the foregoing would result if one were to accept as guide Henry Van Ness Boynton, Washington correspondent of the *Cincinnati Gazette*

—the advanced Republican journal of Whitelaw Reid and Richard Smith. In a long letter of February 14, 1867, published in the *Gazette* of the nineteenth, he told how "old Thad" had been "fiercely attacked without cause, misrepresented and abused." Stevens' bill had been "rewritten four times" to embody views on which Republicans were substantially agreed. "The key to the bitterness" that developed was that Bingham "had undertaken to wrest the leadership of the House," from Stevens, and would ruin if he could not rule. It was "a severe commentary, . . . and yet it is too true," that Bingham and Blaine had gone over to the Democratic side of the House to solicit support.

Boynton did not mention that Stevens had abandoned the Joint Committee's bill of which he was nominally sponsor—or that he had been acting most wilfully in seeking to fasten his own extreme views upon his party in the House—or that he

SENATOR SHERMAN'S SUBSTITUTE

H.R. 1162, THE LOUISIANA BILL, and H.R. 1143, the Military Bill, came to the Senate on Wednesday, February 13—the one at the opening of the day, the other at the evening session.[162] There was hesitation which to take first. "I think they are both most excellent bills," said Wade of Ohio.[163] Sumner was expansive:

> Each is excellent. One is the beginning of a true reconstruction; the other is the beginning of a true protection. . . . The two should go on side by side the guardian angels of this Republic. . . . I accept them both with all my heart . . . .[164]

Precedence was settled on Thursday, in accord with the advice of Senator Fessenden (chairman of the Joint Committee): he was "decidedly of the opinion" that H.R. 1143 should be taken first; it was the one that "has general application to all these States." Only "by accident" had the Louisiana Bill been given precedence in the House; "it is but a local measure, having a comparatively narrow application . . ."; it was "regarded as in the nature of an experiment . . . ."

---

had won on February 13 only by the use of Democratic allies.

Boynton was a partisan journalist. Thus his loyalty to General Thomas, his old chief, led him to write a book attacking General Sherman.

When Boynton's father, Rev. Charles B. Boynton, was elected Chaplain of the House, the "great distinction" of his son's military service was mentioned as one of his qualifications. Cong. Globe, 39–1, 8–9. Dec. 5, 1865. His prayers—as was sometimes remarked in the press—had all the political ardor the leaders in the House could desire.

On Stevens' title to leadership in the House, compare with Boynton's letter the view of the *Cincinnati Commercial*, organ of the independent Murat Halstead:

> Mr. Thaddeus Stevens snorts and stamps the ground as though he were King of the Cannibal Islands. He has gone up to the Capitol with the impression, evidently, that the people have indorsed his doings and sayings. And that is where Mr. Thaddeus

Stevens makes a grand mistake. The people indorsed in the recent election what Mr. Stevens did not indorse in the last Congress, and what he tried hard to defeat, till he found resistance useless. The people accepted the constitutional amendment as the basis upon which all the States are to be admitted to representation, and an end put to the confused and perplexing state of things in which our national affairs are involved. It becomes Mr. Stevens to proceed with some modesty. He will find before the session has far advanced, that he is not the leader of the House, and that its practical men will refuse to follow him in an antic dance of rampant Radicalism.

Editorial comment of Dec. 7, 1866. And so it turned out.

[162] Cong. Globe, 39–2, 1223, 1239.

[163] Ibid., 1302. Feb. 14.

[164] Ibid., 1303. Feb. 14. Compare infra, p. 303.

On the merits of H.R. 1143, Fessenden was emphatic:

> It is a bill predicated on the principle of giving military government to the States which formed the late confederate States, an idea which I have always supposed to be the correct idea as applicable to those States until they become in a better condition. . . .

He thought that this bill, with the addition of the Blaine amendment —favored by "a majority of our friends" in the House—would commend itself to the Senate:

> it is about as perfect a remedy as anything that can be produced at the present time, and, in my judgment, we had better proceed with it.[165]

Senator Williams at once announced that he intended to propose an amendment:[166] when in print this proved to be the Blaine amendment. But when the Senate met next day—Friday the fifteenth of February—Williams had changed his mind: he would press for prompt passage, without amendment and with "little discussion."[167] His retreat, as he presently disclosed, was made in obedience to advice from "persons of the highest authority" in the House of Representatives, that such an amendment would "probably, if not certainly" be fatal to the bill.[168] Sherman said, sternly, that such "observations or threats made by persons in the House" should never be mentioned or considered in the Senate.[169]

Reverdy Johnson, in order to render the bill "less objectionable," at once adopted the Blaine amendment as his own.[170]

Stewart of Nevada spoke earnestly for the amendment: without it he could not accept the bill. Now, as a year ago, he wanted universal suffrage at once—and universal amnesty, too, as soon as practicable. More must be required than would have been acceptable if the Southern States had promptly ratified the Amendment; now

> it is manifest to everybody, that we must either give to all men in the South the ballot or we must resort to the military. . . .

Stewart had an unquestioning faith that suffrage was the means whereby "the black man may protect himself"; also he had a deep aversion to military rule:

---

[165] Ibid., 1302, 1303–04. Feb. 14. Compare infra, p. 303.
[166] Ibid., 1304. Feb. 14.
[167] Ibid., 1360–61. Feb. 15.

[168] Ibid., 1369. Feb. 15.
[169] Ibid., 1369.
[170] Ibid., 1360–61.

SUPREME COURT IN 1865.

Clerk Middleton, Justices Davis, Swayne, Grier, Wayne, Chase, C.J., Nelson, Clifford, Miller, and Field.

(Library of Congress)

SUPREME COURT CHAMBER in 1916.
The busts are of Chief Justices Rutledge (1795),
Marshall (1801–35), Chase (1864–73), and Fuller (1888–1910).
On the other side of the room were busts of Chief Justices Jay (1789–95),
Ellsworth (1796–1800), Taney (1836–64), and Waite (1874–88).
(Architect of the Capitol)

Chief Justice Chase, as he looked early (left)
and late in his service on the Court.
(Library of Congress)

William Sprague,
when Governor of Rhode Island.
(Library of Congress)

Kate Chase Sprague.
(Library of Congress)

Justice James M. Wayne.
(Library of Congress)

Justice Samuel Nelson.
(Library of Congress)

Justice Robert C. Grier.
(Library of Congress)

Justice Nathan Clifford.
(Library of Congress)

Justice Noah H. Swayne.
(Library of Congress)

Justice Samuel F. Miller.
(Library of Congress)

Justice David Davis.
(Library of Congress)

Justice Stephen J. Field.
(Library of Congress)

THE ROBING ROOM.
(Architect of the Capitol)

Justice William Strong.
(Library of Congress)

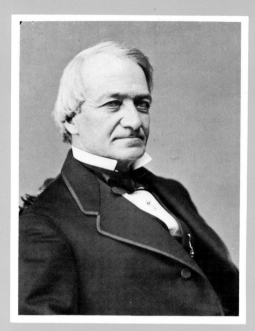

Justice Joseph P. Bradley.
(Library of Congress)

Attorney General Ebenezer R. Hoar.
(G. A. F. Corporation)

Justice Ward Hunt.
(Library of Congress)

THE LAW LIBRARY.
(Architect of the Capitol)

THE MARSHAL'S OFFICE.
(Library of Congress)

while I am willing to subject these people to this fearful ordeal that they have brought upon themselves, I am anxious at the same time to point to them a road of escaping it. . . .

The amendment, he reiterated, offered the "road of escape."

If you want men to rally around you in the South you must state the terms of restoration. The terms proposed in this amendment are all that humanity demands. Make that statement and my word for it you will have a party in the South eager to avoid this military rule and accept the terms of restoration which you propose.[171]

(But time was going to show that to many Southern leaders, military rule was not nearly so detestable as Negro suffrage.[172])

Senator Henderson of Missouri resembled Stewart in many qualities: each was young and vigorous, self-assured, forthright. Henderson too had complete confidence in the efficacy of the ballot, and profound misgivings about reliance upon military power. "The disease [of the South] was aristocracy"; and there had never been but one remedy: "if we intend to retain [the Negroes in this country], we must give them civil and political rights. . . . If we have made up our minds to reconstruct the South there is no other way . . . , and we need not send the military there."[173]

Henderson added "that this is not a palatable measure to the Union men of the southern States"; "some of the most radical," he understood, "regard it as a very dangerous measure." He feared (as did Stewart) that the army officers sent to administer the plan would succumb to Southern "blandishments and allurements." Would it not be President Johnson who selected and directed them? Howard of Michigan (who wanted "to govern these States by military power," without any "insidious" amendment,[174] and who in the Joint Committee had brought about the deletion of the words "under the authority of the President") said that "the whole duty" would rest with the General of the Army and that "U.S. Grant will do his duty." Henderson persisted: "but does he understand it as I understand it? [Laughter.] That is the practical question." Howard replied that he had confidence that the general's understanding would be "right"; whether that would be in

---

[171] Ibid., 1361, 1364–65, 1367–69. Feb. 15.

[172] Infra, pp. 369, 411, 505.

[173] Cong. Globe, 39–2, 1370–72. Feb. 15. He recalled that when he had sought to secure Negro suffrage in the Fourteenth Amendment, many

Senators derided the remedy as no more effective than sarsaparilla tonic. The Fifteenth Amendment, proposed at the 3rd Session of the 40th Congress, owed much to both Henderson and Stewart.

[174] Ibid., 1365. Feb. 15.

accordance with the President's policy, or with the policy of Congress, Howard had "nothing to say."[175]

Debate continued, through Friday evening (February 15) and on until 3 A.M., and then on Saturday afternoon and evening. Democrats did most of the talking.

In the meantime the Republicans, in caucus, appointed a committee to frame a measure upon which they might unite. Sherman was made chairman; Fessenden, Trumbull, Sumner, Howard, Frelinghuysen, and Howe were his colleagues. They withdrew to a committee-room and, as Sherman later recalled, together analyzed every proposition.[176] The preamble of H.R. 1143 as it came from the House spoke of "pretended State governments of the late so-called Confederate States": this was changed to declare that "no legal State governments or adequate protection for life or property now exist in the rebel States. . . ." Thus the committee got rid of the objectionable implication of "so-called States," and affirmed that the governments brought into being by President Johnson were *not legal*: "loyal and republican State governments" were to be established.

By Section 1, the *rebel* States were divided into five districts and made subject to the military authority of the United States, as in the bill from the House.

Section 2 made it the duty of *the President* [not of the General of the Army] to assign commanders and to detail sufficient forces.

Section 3 retained the provision that the District Commander would protect all persons—would suppress insurrection, disorder, and violence—and would punish, or cause to be punished, disturbers of the peace and criminals, by allowing local civil tribunals to try them "or, when in his judgment it may be necessary for the trial of offenders, he shall have power to organize military commissions . . . ." All interference under color of *State* authority with the exercise of military authority under this act would be void. (The bill from the House had purported to nullify *all* judicial control, thereby including the federal judiciary.)

Section 4 of the caucus committee's draft preserved certain salutary limitations on the exercise of military jurisdiction, drawn from Sections 4 and 5 of the House bill, while removing language that would seriously have beclouded the habeas corpus jurisdiction of the federal courts.

So far, it seems, all seven Senators were in agreement.

Then they took up the matter of the Blaine amendment, with its

---

[175] Ibid., at 1371. Compare Howard's presentation of the proposed Fourteenth Amendment, on May 15, 1866: he commended the new provision on privileges and immunities— "whatever they may be . . ."; only the courts could say. Cong. Globe, 39–1, 2765.

[176] Cong. Globe, 41–2, 1181–82. Feb. 10, 1870.

central proposition that in the States to be reconstructed, suffrage must be impartial, without regard to race. For that there was impressive support on the Republican side of the House.[177] In the Senate, Reverdy Johnson, Democrat, had stepped forward to sponsor it.[178] Debate had shown that there were three points to consider in the introduction of impartial suffrage: (1) whether it was prescribed for the election preliminary to the constitutional convention; (2) whether it was secured for the future in the constitution itself; and (3) as a minimum, that it would be applied in the election on ratification of the constitution. The Blaine amendment prescribed it at only the second and third of these points: hence Boutwell's criticism that ex-rebels would frame the constitution and contrive to perpetuate their control.[179] Senator Frelinghuysen had proposed—and the Senate had agreed without division—that Reverdy Johnson's amendment be broadened to prescribe impartial suffrage for the election of delegates.[180]

Thus when the Republican caucus committee met, the principle of impartial suffrage as a requirement for reconstruction had been recognized. Some of the committee, however, felt strongly that Congress ought not to direct that this be written into the new constitutions, inasmuch as most States of the North had not yet brought their own constitutions to that point.[181] When Sumner insisted that the statute require

---

[177] In the vote on February 13, supra at p. 294. "It is not true that our friends in the House are opposed to this amendment," said Stewart in the Senate on February 15. "It is true that some did not vote at all, because the whip and lash were a little too severe; but sixty-nine Union men did vote for it. . . ." Cong. Globe, 39–2, 1366.

[178] Supra, p. 296.

[179] Supra, p. 293.

[180] Cong. Globe, 39–2, 1392, at an early hour on Saturday morning.

[181] Senators had not yet recovered from the strain of debate on the bill for the admission of Nebraska into the Union, which became law, notwithstanding a veto, on February 9, 1867. 14 Stat. 391. This prescribed, as a "fundamental condition" to admission, that the Legislature by public act declare that there should be no denial of the elective franchise or of any other right by reason of race or color.

The rule of impartial suffrage for the District of Columbia had become law on January 8, 1867, 14 Stat. 375;

for the Territories on January 25, 1867, 14 Stat. 379. Sentiment had been strong to impose the same rule for the admission of Nebraska (S. 456) and for the admission of Colorado (S. 462—which did not survive the President's veto of January 28, 1867). On the Nebraska bill, debate had been animated over the propriety and the constitutional validity and effect of requiring that impartial suffrage be provided in the constitution —of requiring that it be a "fundamental condition" revocable only by consent of Congress—of making admission contingent upon acceptance by *the legislature* of such "fundamental condition."

Sumner had said "It passes my comprehension how we [will be able to] require Equal Rights in the rebel States [if we] sanction the denial of Equal Rights in a new State, which is completely within our jurisdiction . . . ." Cong. Globe, 39–2, 329. Jan. 8, 1867.

But Sherman had inquired, "Why should we in Ohio sneer at Nebraska for inserting the word 'white' in her

such a provision, Fessenden replied that inasmuch as impartial suffrage was prescribed for the election of delegates and then for ratification, and in the end the constitution would be submitted to Congress for its approval, no more should be or need be required. The majority agreed with Fessenden.

But when the caucus met to hear the report, Sumner, renewing his insistence, said that if Congress did not settle the question in advance, "every State and village between here and the Rio Grande would be agitated by it."[182] He won his point, by a majority of two.[183]

Sherman presented the measure as approved by the caucus, as a

---

constitution when in Ohio we have the same provision?" Pp. 129–30. Dec. 14, 1866. Howard denied that nondiscrimination in the suffrage was requisite to "a republican form of government": look how many of the States do not admit Negroes to the suffrage. He could not assent to the idea that Congress would impose such a condition upon Nebraska. Pp. 184–88, 219. Dec. 19, 20, 1866. Howe said that if Congress had the power to impose the condition—which he thought doubtful—it ought not to be exercised in the instant situation. Pp. 314–17. Jan. 7, 1867.

And see infra, pp. 327–31.

[182] Sumner's account, in a letter to John Bright, May 27, 1867. Edward L. Pierce, *Memoir and Letters of Charles Sumner*, 4 vols. (Boston: Roberts Brothers, 1894), IV, 320.

[183] The foregoing account of the caucus and its committee is based largely upon statements subsequently made in the Senate. On February 19, 1867, Sumner and Fessenden had rather a falling out with their colleagues, and in that connection some facts were recalled. Cong. Globe, 39–2, 1556–64.

Early in the First Session of the 40th Congress, at a trying moment, Sumner reprobated the Reconstruction Act in whose drafting he had participated—which produced shock and resentment on the part of Senators with whom he had associated. Infra. Bitterness endured.

Still later, while the bill for the readmission of Virginia was being debated, Trumbull and Sumner had a bitter exchange, when circumstances

in the passage of the Reconstruction Act were reviewed. Sumner said, in part, "I am the author of the provision in that Act conferring suffrage; and when I brought it forward the Senator from Illinois was one of my opponents . . . ." Cong. Globe, 41–2, 640. Jan. 21, 1870.

This was a season of bitter personal animosities in the Senate. Stewart, with record in hand, made a well aimed attack on Sumner on February 10, 1870, while the bill to readmit Mississippi was under discussion. Cong. Globe, 41–2, 1176–83. He traced the progress of the Reconstruction Act of 1867, and recalled the important contributions that others beside Sumner had made to its provision for impartial suffrage. Sherman recounted what had been done in the caucus committee. Pp. 1181–82. Sumner quoted speeches he had made for Equal Rights, from 1862. Pp. 1179–82.

Stewart's retort, in part, was that "Everybody admits . . . that he has made more speeches advocating the general principle than anybody else . . . . [But] I reckon if there had not been more practical brains than he has, to put them in shape and get them adopted, the poor black man would still be without the ballot . . . . He is a theorist, a grand, gorgeous, extensive theorist, but he is not a practical man, and my experience is that he has failed utterly to help us get practical measures. . . ." P. 1183.

Trumbull said that the members of Sherman's committee were "unanimously in favor of conferring suffrage on the colored people of the

substitute for H.R. 1143, about midnight.[184] He pointed to salient features. The governments set up by the Executive in the rebel States had always been "provisional . . . , dependent for their validity solely upon the action of Congress." Now Congress prescribed how those States could set up loyal governments "and find their way back to these Halls. . . . All that it demands . . . is to extend to all their male citizens, without distinction of race or color, the elective franchise. It is now too late in the day to be frightened by this simple proposition."

At the same time it was the duty of Congress to protect loyal men, white and black, against violence and wrong. Sherman noted that the substitute removed, from the military provisions, the limitation on the power of the federal judiciary, while all interference under color of State authority was denied validity. He said that the bill's authorization of trial by military commission was, in principle, "nothing . . . that is not now and has not been done every month within the last twelve months by the President . . ."; he construed the *Milligan* opinion as recognizing "that these tribunals might have been, and might now be, organized in insurrectionary States."

The substitute was accepted in place of the House bill, by vote of 32 to 3.[185] Buckalew of Pennsylvania, Garrett Davis of Kentucky, and Saulsbury of Delaware were following the line of the Democrats of the House; Hendricks of Indiana, whose authority and sense of responsibility appeared throughout the debate, voted for the substitute because it was "less objectionable than the bill."[186] Amendments proposed by the minority were rejected, except one to declare that no sentence of death by a military tribunal would be executed without the approval of the President.[187] Notwithstanding lateness and fatigue, the intemperate Senator McDougall of California spoke at length, warning the majority of the vengeance that awaited "when you go down to Hades, all of you."[188] Then the Sherman substitute was passed, 29 to 10, and the Senate adjourned at 6:22, Sunday morning.[189]

Fessenden and Sumner—it will soon be material to recall—hours earlier had gone to their beds. The former, ill, was paired with Reverdy

---

South, and it was only a question of the most practicable and best way of doing it." P. 1184.

Stewart's characterization of Sumner becomes relevant in various chapters of the history of the Court.

[184] Cong. Globe, 39–2, 1459, 1462. Hendricks promptly said that "It is now about the commencement of the Sabbath day." Labor on Sunday should be avoided. His motion to adjourn was defeated. P. 1459.

[185] Ibid., 1467.
[186] Ibid., 1466–67.
[187] Ibid., 1468. The vote was 21 (from both parties) to 16 (Republicans). Sherman pointed out that, without any such provision, "a single order" by the President would suffice to hold all such sentences to await the result of his review.
[188] Ibid., 1468–69.
[189] Ibid., 1469.

Johnson.[190] Sumner later explained that, after the caucus, "fatigued and not well," "feeling that there was nothing more for me to do, after midnight I withdrew."[191]

RESISTANCE, CONCESSION, AND ENACTMENT

WHEN THE SHERMAN SUBSTITUTE came to the House on Monday, Stevens moved to refuse concurrence and request a conference.[192] The old man, laboring under physical inability and moral depression,[193] struck out with unreasoning violence. "The House," he said, had thought it wise to postpone reconstruction until another Congress had had "a long time to consider the whole question"; accordingly its bill had "but a single object, the protection of the loyal men of the South" from anarchy and oppression. Now the Senate would give a pledge "to all the traitors in rebeldom"; "these outlawed communities of robbers, traitors, and murderers" would be enabled "to introduce these disloyal men among us." The Senate bill would "open the flood-gates of misery"; it would bring universal amnesty; billions of dollars in property that should be confiscated would be handed back to enrich traitors, while "our friends whose houses have been laid in ashes . . . are to suffer poverty and persecution . . . ."

Effective replies were made: by Blaine and Bingham, of course; by Farnsworth of Illinois (now a member of the Joint Committee); by Schenck, Garfield, and others. Wilson of Iowa answered Stevens with particularity; he concluded that the bill as it now stood "presents a liberal plan to the loyal people . . . upon which they may act under the protection of the military arm of this Republic in the formation of a State government of just such character as may to them seem best"—it went "far beyond anything which the most sanguine of us hoped for a year ago."[194]

At the outset, Stevens had said that he would call for a vote at four o'clock; but then he kept yielding, bit by bit, to Democratic bluster, until during the evening session he proposed—unexpectedly to the friends of the bill—that debate go on and that the House meet at 11 A.M. to vote. LeBlond promptly accepted for the Democrats.[195]

---

190 Ibid.

191 Cong. Globe, 41–2, 640. Jan. 21, 1870. See note 183.

192 Cong. Globe, 39–2, 1313, 1315, 1317. Feb. 18, 1867.

193 Self-characterization on Feb. 13. Ibid., 1213. He was nearing his seventy-fifth birthday.

194 Ibid., 1318–19.

195 Ibid., 1317, 1321–22, 1323, 1324, 1325. A detailed account of Stevens' collaboration with the Democrats, in a dispatch of February 19, appearing in the New York Evening Post of February 20, is here accepted as accurate.

The outcome on Tuesday morning was that the House refused to concur with the Senate. The count was 98 to 73.[196] But note the combination whereby Stevens' victory was achieved: 56 advanced Republicans who had gone against the majority of their party were joined by 42 Democrats to defeat a measure which, Stevens had insisted, would permit the South to vote for the Democratic candidate at the next presidential election. The correspondent of the *New York Evening Post* reported: "LeBlond, of Ohio, who was the manager on the Democratic side of the House, hastened over to shake hands with and congratulate Mr. Stevens over their mutual success.[197]

When the Senate met on Tuesday, Sumner presented a petition from the Southern Republican Association (Thomas J. Durant, president)—in addition to the one already presented in the House[198]—asking Congress to apply the Louisiana Bill to *all* the unreconstructed States.[199]

Soon a message arrived from the House, announcing its nonconcurrence and asking for a conference.[200] Fessenden wanted to accede: "there will be no difficulty, probably, in an agreement on something that will be satisfactory to both Houses."[201] So too did Sumner. Both Senators now picked faults in the Sherman bill—framed scarce three days agone in the caucus committee of which each had been a member. (Years later, Sumner recalled how the bill "was debated and matured sentence by sentence, word for word" in the committee.[202]) Fessenden now complained that the Blaine amendment "did not go far enough. . . . I did not think we were safe under it." But he had been ill and had "yielded to the will of the majority."[203]

Sumner said that now Fessenden "was right in asking more. . . .

---

[196] Ibid., 1340. Feb. 19.

[197] Feb. 20.

On the nineteenth, the *Evening Post*, referring to the tactics of the House Democrats, said "Such friends are enough to ruin any cause, and the sooner the men lately in rebellion cut loose from these thickheaded 'friends' of theirs the sooner they will relieve themselves of a burden they cannot afford to drag around."

The Radical *Cincinnati Gazette* of February 20—maintaining the theory propounded by their Washington correspondent, Boynton (supra, n. 161)—said that legislation had failed, largely because Bingham had attempted to wrest the leadership from Stevens. It concluded, "As it is this Congress is about to wind up in general failure . . ."—because it had refused to follow Stevens.

[198] Mentioned supra at p. 290—the petition presented in the House by Representative Eliot on February 12, 1867. Cong. Globe, 39–2, 1171.

[199] Ibid., 1553, Feb. 19, 1867. Sumner also presented a memorial from the Union League of Winchester, Virginia, asking that the terms of the Louisiana Bill be extended to Virginia.

[200] Ibid., 1554. Feb. 19.

[201] Ibid., 1556.

[202] Cong. Globe, 41–2, 640. Jan. 21, 1870—when he was expanding on his own contribution. Supra, n. 161.

[203] Cong. Globe, 39–2, 1559. Feb. 19, 1867.

All the good of the bill cannot make me forget its evil. . . . It is horribly defective. You cannot use too strong language in characterizing a measure with such fatal defects." The bill merely declared that the existing governments were not "legal," and provided for their replacement: but that was not enough—it left "the machinery and motive power" in the hands of rebels. Again, the bill required that the new constitutions secure suffrage without color bar, and permitted the disfranchisement of rebels: but that was not enough—"You must say that they *must* be disfranchised. Without this you surrender everything to them."[204]

It seems fair to suppose that importuning by Southern loyalists led Sumner thus suddenly to repudiate the work in which he had joined. The Sherman bill was defective in that it failed to transfer power immediately into loyalists' hands—such was the complaint of Durant's message to Sumner. And as Sumner later asserted, that legislation be made "agreeable to the Unionists of the South . . . with me is a rule of conduct."[205]

The Senate was in no mood to knuckle under to Thaddeus Stevens. Sumner and Fessenden, urging a conference, were answered pretty bluntly by surprised colleagues.[206] Lane of Indiana analyzed the division that had just taken place in the House: the "vast majority" of Republicans were in accord with the Senate—the opposition came from "extreme Radicals" plus "the whole Democratic party *en masse.*" "There is nothing to confer about."[207]

Here it was Tuesday, February 19; March 3 would fall on Sunday, and on March 4 the term of the 40th Congress would begin. (On January 22, 1867, Congress had enacted that the new Congress should meet at noon on that day.[208]) To apprehensions that the President would defeat the bill by a pocket veto, Hendricks replied that the Democratic Senators wanted the issue to be "squarely met" and saw "no reason to expect that the President will decline to act if Congress allows him time to do it." Further, he opposed a committee of conference: under the circumstances, that would simply "allow the House to have

---

[204] Ibid., 1562–63. Feb. 19.

[205] Cong. Globe, 40–1, 166. Mar. 16, 1867.

[206] Sherman recalled how long the Senate had heard Sumner declaim about the ballot for the colored citizen: at last that would be attained by this bill—and yet it was condemned because not enough whites would be excluded. Cong. Globe, 39–2, 1562–64. It was at this point that Sherman made the remark quoted above, that the American people would not stand for disfranchising the mass of whites while enfranchising the freedmen. Supra, p. 261.

Wilson of Massachusetts, following Sherman, opposed a conference and said that this bill was "the greatest by far of the measures of the session . . . ." Pp. 1564–65.

[207] Ibid., 1557.

[208] 14 Stat. 378. The power thus to "appoint a . . . Day" was clear. Art. I, Sec. 4, cl. 2.

its way . . . ."[209] Senator Cowan also made a contribution when he repelled imputations that the President would be lax in enforcing the bill if it became law.[210]

Saulsbury of Delaware expressed disgust that Senators of a "great, superior race" would listen to any "miserable, petty story" about mistreatment of Negroes.[211] McDougall of California was dismayed that Senators "who think there is a God, would undertake to place the barbarians of Mississippi and South Carolina in command of that country."[212] But Hendricks intervened to suggest that such "general discussion" be postponed to "let this vote be taken."[213]

Thereupon, without any notation of dissent, the Senate voted to insist upon its bill.[214]

The House, meeting at 7:30 P.M., spent a dilatory evening under Democratic management, with some contribution by Stevens' Radicals.

But when the House met on Wednesday, the Republicans had pulled themselves together. A pending amendment by Wilson of Iowa,[215] further amended on motion of Shellabarger, made the Sherman bill acceptable. With Republicans united, it was carried by 126 to 46.[216]

The concessions to win Stevens' followers were not very substantial. Wilson's modification was that those disqualified from office-holding by Section 3 of the Fourteenth Amendment would also be excluded from serving as delegate and from voting for delegates to the convention. (Such a person, however, would not thereby be excluded from voting on the ratification of the constitution.) Where the bill in its preamble recited that the existing governments were not "legal," Shellabarger's amendment added an express statement that until a rebel State was admitted to representation, any civil government therein would be provisional only, and subject to the paramount authority of Congress; further, that persons disqualified by Section 3 of the Amendment could not vote for officers, or hold office, under a provisional government.

The Senate could now rest and be thankful: the changes made by the House were tolerable. Sherman said it was a small matter; his "only material objection" was that several thousand leading rebels would be barred—needlessly, he thought—from voting at one election.[217] Sumner said that, on the contrary, this was "a great matter"; the exclusion of those rebels was an important safeguard.[218] Wilson of Massachusetts

---

[209] Cong. Globe, 39–2, 1557.
[210] Ibid., 1565–67.
[211] Ibid., 1568.
[212] Ibid., 1569.
[213] Ibid.
[214] Ibid., 1570.
[215] Ibid., 1356.

[216] Ibid., 1399–1400.
[217] Ibid., 1625. Feb. 20.
[218] Ibid. To show his consistency, he read at length from a speech he had made in Massachusetts in 1865, with its embellishments from Horace, Shakespeare, Milton, and LaFontaine.

regretted the amendments by the House; he sought universal amnesty and universal suffrage: "I am for lifting all men up, and against casting any down."[219] Hendricks said that no Senator, other than Sumner, had favored such an exclusion as the House had imposed. Sherman replied that "more than two thirds of the Union members of the House" agreed with Hendricks; it was Democratic tactics that had "compelled the friends of the measure to yield to these amendments."[220]

Doolittle of Wisconsin—one of four Republican Senators supporting the President—moved to amend by a proviso: that nothing in the act would bar from voting or holding office any person who had been pardoned or amnestied; otherwise the bill would be "in violation of the express decision of the Supreme Court on this very question." He quoted from Justice Field in *Ex parte Garland*,[221] including the statement that the effect of a pardon is to relieve "from all penalties and disabilities."[222] Edmunds of Vermont—a newcomer who for a quarter century would command the Senate's attention in speaking on constitutional issues—replied that while a pardon purges of guilt in a legal sense, the selection of those to be entrusted with resuscitating the rebel States was "a matter of political expediency over which the Supreme Court has no control."[223]

Doolittle's amendment was rejected, by 33 nays to 8 yeas.[224]

Reverdy Johnson gave notice that he would vote for the bill. From the outset he had been "ready to agree to any proposition which . . . would result in bringing the southern States back," however he might regret the conditions attached. He was unwilling that this Congress adjourn "without the adoption of some measure that holds out a hope . . . ."[225]

On the question of concurring in the amendments by the House, there were 35 yeas and 7 nays.[226]

The President returned the bill with his objections—on Saturday, March 2, early enough to permit the Houses to act.[227]

In declining to let the bill die—although the 39th Congress would end before the expiration of "ten days (Sundays excepted)"—the President ignored the advice of militants who wanted him to stage a battle.[228]

---

219 Ibid., 1626.
220 Ibid., 1639.
221 Supra, p. 242.
222 Cong. Globe, 39–2, 1636–38.
223 Ibid., 1638.
224 Ibid., 1645.
225 Ibid., 1627.
226 Ibid., 1645. On the night of Wed., Feb. 20. The Senate then adjourned at 10:47.

227 Ibid., 1728.
228 On February 21, Fernando Wood of New York—soon to take his seat in the 40th Congress—had written peremptorily:
Your own position in history —your consistent defence of the Constitution, and the welfare of our common country demand that you should *not* permit the

VI: *Congressional Reconstruction*

The preparation of the veto message was the work of Jeremiah S. Black and Attorney General Stanbery.[229] The former has been mentioned in several contexts, including his remarkable outpouring at the Jackson Day dinner on January 12.[230] In a letter of January 22, he had urged the President to make "a written address to the people" to explain "the crisis which is manifestly approaching, . . . the obligation of all to obey the constitution, your efforts to save it," the points of disagreement with Congress "and a vindication of your views . . . ." He offered himself as draftsman, his authorship to be "a confidential secret."[231] Stanbery has been mentioned as author of the message vetoing the Civil Rights Bill on March 27; as nominee on April 16 to a Supreme Court place that ceased to be; and as Attorney General in office since

---

Military Reconstruction bill to become a law. Its fate is in your hands, & the people will hold you responsible. *Let it die the death*, and to the next Congress March 4th you can discuss the question & once more endear yourself to the friends of constitutional liberty by maintaining your position as the great defender of their cause. This can be done in your annual message. Whatever else you lose preserve your manhood. Andrew Johnson Papers, L.C.

Francis P. Blair, Sr., writing the President on February 24, described the bill as a scheme "sacrificing the constitution & the South together—& our white to the black race"; the President should use "every delay that the Constitution makes possible" to cause the bill to "slide into non:entity with the broken Congress that gave birth to the monster—the begotten of an illegitimate caucus . . . ." Then he should take the occasion to state to the incoming 40th Congress his views on all the "momentous questions" involved. "To retreat before furious dogs," Blair wrote, "invites pursuit."

"I think the true plan to meet the exigency is a clean sweep of the present Cabinet as a concession to the discontents of the country. . . . The appointment of the most important, impartial & patriotic men of the leading States of the North, complying as far as possible with the popular will in each, would save the Constitution. . . ." Andrew Johnson Papers, L.C.

With the above advice, contrast that of Robert J. Walker, sometime Senator from Mississippi, and Secretary of the Treasury under President Polk. On February 22, 1867, he wrote confidentially to Reverdy Johnson a letter to be passed on to the President. He counselled: "1st Let his veto go in ample time for both Houses to act on the bill. 2d Whilst he repeats his constitutional objections let him *declare* his determination to *enforce the law* & advise the South to submit. . . . It is as much the duty of the President to *enforce* a vetoed bill, repassed by the two thirds vote, as any other. He should *say so clearly*." On Feb. 25 he wired the Senator: "Every hour since I wrote you adds to the popular current in favor of those views. . . ." The Senator passed these papers to the President. Andrew Johnson Papers, L.C.

Note that Walker later argued Mississippi v. Johnson and Mississippi v. Stanton on behalf of the State. Infra, ch. 8.

[229] John H. and LaWanda Cox, "Andrew Johnson and His Ghost Writers," *Miss. Valley Hist. Rev.*, 48:460, 468; *Diary of Gideon Welles*, 3 vols. (Boston and New York: Houghton Mifflin Co., 1911), III, 51, 54.

[230] Supra, pp. 222–23.

[231] Andrew Johnson Papers, L.C.

July 23, 1866.[232] Black soon became the leading counsel in attacks upon the Reconstruction Act.

Several themes were entwined in the message.[233] The sole objective in the Civil War, it said, had been to enforce the Constitution; the moment resistance ceased, States and individuals resumed all their rights. "No fallacy could be more transparent" than that Congress derived new powers in the premises. The rebellion had been simply one more insurrection: true, there had been ordinances of secession—but these were "mere nullities."

The preamble's recital of "no adequate protection of life" was brushed aside. Sometimes, North and South, offenders went unpunished: "occasionally, perhaps, by the inefficiency of courts or the prejudice of jurors."

Besides, said the message, good order was not what Congress had in view. The evident purpose was to compel "the adoption of organic laws" and to "force the right of suffrage out of the hands of the white people and into the hands of negroes," thereby "Africanizing the southern part of our territory." This violated "the universally acknowledged rule of constitutional law which declares that the Federal Government has no jurisdiction . . . to regulate such subjects for any State."

The means chosen, said the message, were in palpable conflict with the provisions of the Constitution and utterly destructive of those great principles of liberty and humanity for which the men of our race in every age had fought. In time of peace, where the courts were open, this bill would—contrary to what was laid down in *Ex parte Milligan*—deny rights to jury and grand jury and numerous other express guaranties; the message enumerated the particulars wherein "hundreds of thousands" would be degraded "from the rank of freemen to the condition of slaves."

The Constitution, just as it stood, supplied all that the country needed. Let Congress simply admit all States to representation: that would "send a thrill of joy throughout the land," and "speedily bring tranquillity to the public mind."

The message marshalled the manifold objections to the bill so fully that, later, counsel attacking it before the Court could do little more than reiterate and expatiate. But it offered nothing whatsoever either as to protection or as to institutional reform in the South. Indeed it denied that there was any need. "The Constitution, in its whole integrity and vigor, . . . is the best of all compromises."

Without ado, the House overrode the veto, by vote of 135 to 48 —far more than the requisite two-thirds.[234]

---

232 Supra, p. 162.
233 Cong. Globe, 39–2, 1969.

234 Ibid., 1733. March 2. Democratic leaders said that they would have

The Senate took more time to reach the same result.

Reverdy Johnson put on record the reasoning that led him to vote for the bill.[235] While such use of military force was in his view unconstitutional, the Supreme Court might hold this "to be a political question, to be decided exclusively by the political department of the Government, by Congress . . . ." Already, he pointed out, the South was subjected to military power, by the Freedmen's Bureau Act. Had the Southern States promptly accepted the Fourteenth Amendment, they would already, he firmly believed, be represented in Congress. The present bill offered more exacting terms for restoration. If this failed, "one of a much more harsh and unjust character would be adopted," leading to confiscation; what the Supreme Court might say of that, he had no "assured conviction." He trusted that "the reflecting and intelligent men of the South" would see the wisdom of organizing promptly under the present bill.

Saulsbury of Delaware rose to say he hoped that no Southern man would "participate in his own disgrace, degradation, and ruin: let them maintain their honor."[236]

The bill was passed by 38 votes to 10—and thereupon became law.[237]

---

filibustered, had the House rules not made that impracticable. (During the last ten days of the session, a two-thirds vote would permit immediate action on any bill.) P. 1732.

[235] Ibid., 1972–73, 1975. Mar. 2.
[236] Ibid., 1973.
[237] Ibid., 1976. Mar. 2.

CHAPTER VII

Supplementary Legislation; Reflections

W HAT THE RECONSTRUCTION ACT OF MARCH 2 had to say about *reconstruction*—as distinguished from *military protection*—was compressed in its hard-won concluding sections, 5 and 6. The former declared "That when the people . . . shall have formed a constitution . . . ," etc., the State would become "entitled to representation in Congress": but the Act did not prescribe the steps by which the constitution was to be framed (save as it set qualifications for participating). There was no command that any such effort be made. Although the existing State governments would be "deemed provisional only," a legislature might (so far as the Act was concerned) take the initiative and call a convention, conformably to the Act. (Thereby the enactment would be acknowledged to be an operative fact.) Or, conceivably, a spontaneous popular movement—doubtless led by white Unionists and supported by freedmen—might in some way produce a constitution which Congress would be asked to approve.[1] There was still another

---

[1] Senator Sherman had said:

No machinery is provided, it is true; but we have three examples already in our history of States being organized by the people without any previous enabling act. Here is an invitation to the people. They can call their party conventions, their State conventions, and finally by a movement of the people, without regard to their local Legislature or local tribunals, a constitutional convention can be convened, elected by all the people, and they can form a constitution. . . .

Cong. Globe, 39–2, 1564. Feb. 19, 1867.

His "three examples," presumably, were Tennessee (where delegates framed a constitution of February 1, 1796, claiming admission, which Congress granted on June 1, 1796); California (whose constitution of 1849, requesting admission "into the American Union," was framed by a convention called by General Bennett Riley, commanding the Pacific department and provisional governor; admission came on September 9, 1850); and Kansas (admitted on January 21, 1861, in accordance with the request of the Wyandotte con-

possibility, as the *New York Evening Post* later recalled in an historical review: "Matters might be left to go on as they were and meantime a case could be made up, on which the Supreme Court would decide that the new law was unconstitutional. Such was the course which some recommended."[2]

In Georgia, Joseph E. Brown, the war Governor,[3] at once urged compliance: the Governor and legislature should "order an election for delegates to a convention, to act upon the proposition now submitted by Congress."[4] Renewing this advice in an address at Atlanta on March 4, he gave reasons why it seemed vain to wait for a decision by the Supreme Court. "As the issues involved . . . are political ones, it is hardly to be expected they will be decided by that tribunal." Moreover, Justices Wayne, Nelson, and Grier "cannot be expected long to occupy their positions." The Court was two years in arrears, and could avoid a decision until cases challenging the Act were reached in order.[5]

In Alabama, Governor R. M. Patton had been repulsed in his effort to lead the people and the legislature to an acceptance of the Fourteenth Amendment.[6] He had worked in close accord with General Wager Swayne, and through Swayne had been brought into communication with Chief Justice Chase. Sometime in mid-February, when Congress was about to act on the Military Bill, Patton had consulted Chase about the consequences in the event the legislature were now to ratify the Amendment. Waiting until the bill had been enacted, Chase replied on March 11—putting the Southern situation in a large frame:

> This law has in some respects changed the aspect of affairs. Had the Constitutional Amendment been adopted as you recommended, there is little room for doubt that the ratifying States would have been promptly allowed representation in Congress and the disabling clause would have been so modified as to relieve very many,—

---

stitution framed and adopted in 1859).

The protracted ordeal of "Bleeding Kansas" was enough to show the impracticability of spontaneous organization among people separated by a mutual repugnance.

The *Charleston* (South Carolina) *Courier* of March 1, 1867, carried a letter from their Washington correspondent, of February 25 (when the bill was before the President) making this observation:

> The Bill makes it no one's business to call a Convention. A body of freedmen or a single individual may call it. They may

call, but will the Convention come when called? This will depend upon the disposition of the influential portion of the communities. It is already stated that Virginia will immediately reorganize under this Act . . . .

[2] June 26, 1867.

[3] (1821–94). Elected in 1857, he had served until June 1865. Chief Justice, 1868–70; United States Senator, 1880–91.

[4] Public letter of Feb. 23, in the *Athens* (Georgia) *Southern Watchman* of Mar. 6. See infra, pp. 411–12.

[5] *Charleston Courier*, Mar. 9, 1867.

[6] Supra, ch. 5, n. 9.

all, indeed, who should manifest a sincere and hearty good will to the Union and the National Government. The rejection of the amendment made the recent law inevitable; as all foresaw who understood the condition of things.

And now it seems to me that the advice given by Ex Gov. Brown of Georgia[7] is the best for all the unrepresented States. The sooner they avail themselves of the mode of obtaining representation given by the Act the better it will be for all concerned. . . . When [the question of suffrage was thus] settled & with representation restored won't a great revival of material prosperity take place [?] Capital will flow in to stimulate labor; and all parts of the country will take hold once more in active efforts for the good of all.

Nor have I the least doubt that the kind feeling which now finds expression in the appropriation of a million of dollars (I wish the sum were five millions & believe it would have been the best possible investment of the sum) for the relief of destitution in the unrepresented States would find further expression in the relief of many & perhaps nearly or quite all from the disability imposed by the amendment.

Let there be trust, confidence & loyalty & all will be well.[8]

Another significant estimate of the situation was made by Senator Sherman in a letter of March 12, replying to a citizen of Georgia who was solicitous that Southern whites promptly move to carry out the statute. Sherman wrote:

The bill . . . was passed in the earnest hope that it would tend to the full restoration of all the States to their rights in the Union. The

---

[7] Supra, p. 311.

[8] Chase Papers, L.C.
On March 9 the Senate had passed S. Res. 16, to appropriate one million dollars for food to be distributed by the Bureau of Refugees, Freedmen and Abandoned Lands, for the relief of the destitute in Southern and Southwestern States where crops had failed. Cong. Globe, 40–1, 39, 48. In the House this ran into difficulty —on both sides. Fernando Wood said that he knew of no Southern whites who asked for alms. P. 83. Williams of Indiana (Rep.) protested against taxing limbless Union veterans to pay the women and children of rebels. P. 83. Chanler of New York (Dem.) said the money would be used "to keep up a political machine." Ben Butler wanted to pay the money to the widows and orphans of soldiers who died in rebel prisons. P. 86. Judge Van Trump of Indiana (Dem.) could not find a shred of authority for giving public money to "a simple, naked, and unqualified charity." Pp. 233–35.

As it became law on March 30, the resolution authorized the Secretary of War to "apply as much as he may deem necessary" for such relief, out of appropriations already made. The Army Appropriation Act of March 2, 1867, had provided $1.5 million for commissary stores for the work of the Bureau.

As an incident in the administration of the Bureau, this is discussed in George R. Bentley, A History of the Freedmen's Bureau, (Philadelphia: University of Pennsylvania Press, 1955), 140–41.

sixth section I think too harsh, but it was put in in the House as the result of opposition from both extremes. At the request of large numbers from the South, we are passing a supplementary act to provide machinery of reconstruction. The original bill left all this to each State, but there was danger of double organizations and conventions, and therefore, to avoid further strife or difference, this new act will be passed. It is merely a scaffolding.

My earnest conviction is, that the South should not forego this opportunity to be restored to representation, and you may rely upon it, that a majority in both Houses will adhere to this offer, and execute it in good faith, and to the letter, if your people will do likewise. Neither section can be prosperous while the present conditions of military surveillance prevails.[9]

Uncertainty about proceeding came to an end when the 40th Congress on March 23 passed the Supplementary Act[10] which Sherman's letter forecast. That will be explained presently.[11] It is worth a glance, however, to note some reactions during that brief moment when existing governments were free to take the initiative.

A MOMENT FOR SPONTANEOUS ACTION

IN VIRGINIA, Governor Pierpoint addressed the legislature in a noteworthy message of March 4,[12] urging prompt action in pursuance of the Act of March 2. He surveyed the unhappy course of events since the fall of the Confederacy: as the President had freely granted clemency, the Southern press had taken on a bold and vindictive tone; there had been "inflammatory lectures, orations and essays," reported in the North; "some of our legislation has not been of the most fortunate character"; there had been murders of freedmen, "scarcely noticed by the officers of the law"; the Fourteenth Amendment, a "most magnanimous offer," had been rejected, "almost unanimously." Now Congress had passed this statute, and the Governor—hoping to secure tranquility and to avert new evils—called upon the legislature, "*in good faith,* to carry out the requirements of the law, . . . at once. . . . It is proper that the proposed convention shall be ordered by the general assembly. Any

---

9 To William K. DeGraffenreid of Macon, Georgia, who caused it to be published in the local *Journal.* Reprinted in *Columbus Enquirer* of Mar. 23, *Montgomery Weekly Advertiser* of Mar. 26, and doubtless in numerous other journals.
10 15 Stat. 2.

11 Infra, pp. 317–25.
12 Va. Sen. J., Extra Session 1867, pp. 328–33. As a historical document it has the same high quality as the message of December 3, 1866, urging ratification of the Fourteenth Amendment. Supra, pp. 183–84n.

other mode would be irregular, and may . . . result in the worst consequences. . . ."

In the lower House, a motion to appoint a committee to inquire into the expediency of calling a convention was denied a prompt hearing.[13] In the Senate, a bill to provide for electing a constitutional convention was carried by 25 to 4 votes; in the House the measure was tabled.[14]

A committee of the Senate was sent to Washington to inquire whether such initiative by the State would be acceptable;[15] it reported that this demonstration in favor of framing a constitution had "a most salutary effect in softening the asperity of prevailing opinion . . . ."[16] Actually nothing came of the effort; Congress was already well on the way to framing a measure that would supersede State action.

The *Richmond Dispatch* gave a grudging assent to Governor Pierpoint's message. In an important editorial on March 5 it regretted that he had put blame on the Southern press; "just and deliberate opinion, unbiassed by prejudice or passion, would never presume to visit a vast community with pains and penalties for the impulsive and crude diatribes of a few excitable editors."

But then the *Dispatch* gave advice, precisely in accord with the Governor's. Let the present government hasten to call a convention, in conformity with the Act of Congress. Otherwise, very certainly, the work would be carried out "by those who mean to visit us with pains, penalties, and disfranchisements such as the body of the people now little dream of."

The editor turned to those who dreamed of intervention by the Supreme Court:

> The Supreme Court is literally dead. So dead—and so proved to be by numerous events of late—that it is utterly impotent against Congress. The President has clearly indicated his intention to enforce the law. . . . Should the court be resorted to, its decision, rendered after two years, will be treated with utter contempt. . . . The Supreme Court, at best, would only give one majority for the protection of the States, while there are two members now whose physical condition is such that they may never again take their seats on the bench. [Doubtless referring to Wayne and Grier.]
>
> Even this argument is supererogatory. Congress does not intend that the Supreme Court shall obstruct its policy. The impotency of that tribunal alone protects it from an act for its reorganization. . . .

---

[13] House J., Extra Session 1867, pp. 7, 8. Mar. 4. Another motion called for a test of the constitutionality of the Act before the Supreme Court. P. 7.

[14] Sen. J., 344, 345, Mar. 6 and 7; House J., 31, 39, Mar. 11 and 13.
[15] Sen. J., 354. Mar. 11. The vote on sending was 12 to 8.
[16] Report of Mar. 15. Sen. J., 366.

VII: *Supplementary Legislation*

The editor added a persuasive thought: in calling a convention the legislature could be considered to be acting under duress, "and therefore inflicting no dishonor on us. . . ."

On March 18, when the Houses of Congress were approaching agreement on the Supplementary bill, the *Dispatch* reprinted and indorsed this comment by the *New York Times* on "Wait and See":

> These "wait-and-seeites," as our correspondent styles them, are only hurting themselves by their sullen inactivity. Action will be taken under the Act of Congress. The loyal whites and the enfranchised blacks will take steps to elect delegates to a constitutional convention, under the direction of the Military Governor. . . . If the disloyal whites do not choose to exercise the power left to them, they merely leave the whole field open to the rest of the inhabitants, who will thus be enabled the more thoroughly to have their own way. . . .

Then the *Times* editorial made this striking point: that "the practical effect of the do-nothing policy" would be equivalent to what would have resulted from the Louisiana Bill—the measure so ardently desired by the Southern loyalists.[17]

The *Richmond Enquirer* was among the wait-and-seeites. On February 25—while the Reconstruction Bill was before the President—its editorial on "The Indispensable Duty" declared that it was *imperative*, to test, at the earliest moment, the validity of the Sherman Shellabarger law." It would be wrong to call a convention until the federal judiciary had settled that question. The editor busied himself with the names of eminent Virginia lawyers to whom the Commonwealth might look "to prosecute her suit for *life*, and for *the right to live!*"

The *Enquirer* on March 6 contradicted what the *Dispatch* of the day before had said in the editorial quoted above. No good would be attained by haste to call a convention.

> Does any one really dream, that a constitution which might contain one single restriction, covert or overt, direct or indirect, on negro suffrage, would be accepted by Congress? . . .

In the end, "if the complexion of our politics does not please," Congress would find some pretext for refusing to readmit.

> We are, therefore, opposed to this jack-with-a-lantern chase after reconstruction . . . only to find ourselves bogged at last. Let us wait awhile. Let us see what the military are going to do. There is nothing,

---

[17] Supra, pp. 290–91.

in any event, to be lost by a little delay, and we shall see our way the clearer.[18]

In Arkansas, the legislature—now dominated by ex-rebels[19]—replied to the Act of Congress with a declaration that the existing government was "republican in form," the State's "true and proper government," which "cannot be properly changed, save in the manner pointed out by its own constitution." Unauthorized efforts to effect a change, by citizens voluntarily assembled, were condemned.[20]

The legislature had been emboldened by the report of a committee of ten who had been sent to Washington. On January 22 members listened "with breathless attention"[21] to the committee's firm conclusion that in the controversy between Congress and the President, the latter would maintain "with unabaiting earnestness" the proposition that the Southern States were "entitled to all their constitutional rights."[22]

The committee gave the reason for confidence that Congress would be curbed:

> The Supreme Court, another department of the Government, is looked to now as the umpire in the controversy; and your committee are unanimously of the opinion that the view taken on that question by the Executive will be sustained by this high judicial tribunal.

---

[18] It quoted, in order to refute, an editorial from the *New York Evening Post* of March 4, on the theme "If they know what is for their best good, they will make haste to reconstruct their State governments under the Act of Congress . . ."

[19] Supra, p. 184n.

[20] Joint Resolution of Mar. 13, 1867. Ark. Acts 1866–67, 557–59. Ark. House J., 832–34, 864; Sen. J., 743. The vote in the House was 48 to 8; in the Senate, 15 to 6.

[21] *Little Rock Gazette*, Jan. 24, 1867.

[22] Ark. House J., 1866–67, 392–97. The committee had arrived in Washington on January 1; they had conferred with the President; had been introduced at a meeting of the Cabinet; had dined with Secretary Seward; had conferred with Cabinet officers, Senators and Representatives, and others—of "different shades of opinion." Secretary Welles noted: "Told them I knew of nothing they had to reconstruct. . . . In regard to the Constitutional Amendment, assured them I was opposed to it . . . ." *Diary of Gideon Welles*, 3 vols. (Boston and New York: Houghton Mifflin Co., 1911), III, 1–8, entries for January 4 and 5; also *Diary of Orville Hickman Browning* (Springfield: Illinois State Historical Library, vol. I (1850–64), Pease and Randall, eds., 1925; vol. II (1865–81), Randall, ed., 1933), II, 122, for the same days. At that moment, decision of the Test Oath Cases was anticipated; also, the President was preparing what became his message of January 7, vetoing S. No. 1, to regulate the elective franchise in the District of Columbia. (On January 8 the bill became law, establishing suffrage "without any distinction on account of color.") In short, the Arkansans were steeped in the opinions of the President and his Cabinet.

The committee could give good reasons for coming to this conclusion, but they do not deem it proper to say more in this report than
to give the conclusions at which they arrived, from having frequent
interviews with distinguished individuals connected with the different
departments of the Government.

Having reached the above conclusion, we feel justified in expressing the opinion that the present State Government in Arkansas—
so generally acquiesced in by the people—will be sustained and preserved, despite all the efforts made to destroy it by disappointed office
seekers in our midst.

Congress might pass legislation "territorializing the Southern States;
but the Supreme Court, we confidently believe, will decide that Congress
has no power . . . ; and should Congress attempt to do so, contrary to
the decision of the Supreme Court," the " 'sober second thought' of the
country" would not sustain it. Already the Radical party was "beginning to disintegrate."[23]

This composite of the impressions of these ten Arkansans was
more credible than ordinary stories in the newspapers. Doubtless they
had heard what various Justices were understood to think about the
questions of the day. But later on, when Congressional sentiment had
crystallized in a statute, and action in some particular form had been
brought, the Justices must address themselves to more narrow issues—
for example, whether the question raised was of a sort that Judges ought
to decide; or whether the remedy sought was one which, on principle,
ought to be allowed. That a Justice had been heard to express disgust
that Congress was acting excessively or even "unconstitutionally" might
not indicate what his ruling would be upon some immediate issue. But
the Arkansans, like many other Southerners at that moment, were
counting wishfully on the mighty things the Court would do as the
great "umpire."

SUPPLEMENTARY ACT OF MARCH 23, 1867

On March 7, 1867, Senator Henry Wilson of Massachusetts introduced S. 18, "Supplementary to" the Act of March 2. It was referred
to the Judiciary Committee.[24]

---

[23] The House, overcoming some resistance, ordered that 5000 copies of
the report be printed; the Senate
ordered 3000 copies. House J., 397–
98; Sen. J., 351. The *Little Rock*

Gazette, with a circulation of some
1000 for its daily and 2500 for its
weekly edition, promised to reprint
in full. Jan. 24, 1867.
[24] Cong. Globe, 40–1, 13.

This bill should be tagged for later notice. It will have particular interest by reason of its draftsman: Chief Justice Chase.[25]

Also on March 7, Representative Kelley of Pennsylvania moved that the House instruct its Judiciary Committee to report a bill for calling conventions to reorganize the rebel States and providing for registration of voters and for elections.[26] The resulting measure, H.R. 33, was promptly passed by the House. In the Senate, the Judiciary Committee substituted the language of Senator Wilson's bill (by Chief Justice Chase), and in that form H.R. 33 went through the Senate. Presently conference led to the passage of the Senate substitute as amended. President Johnson vetoed, but the bill was nevertheless made law on March 23—the vote in the House being 114 to 25, and in the Senate, 40 to 7.[27]

The Commanding General in each District would cause a registration of voters to be made, and would appoint boards of registration; he would call and conduct elections, within a range of time allowed by the statute. His duties were prescribed with as much particularity as was practicable.[28]

There is no need to trace chronologically the debates and votes. It will suffice to identify certain major issues, and to note considerations urged and conclusions reached. Discussion in the main was pertinent and useful.

A moment after Kelley's motion was adopted, Shellabarger presented the memorial of loyalists of Alexandria, Virginia, complaining that in a local election, disloyal election officers had excluded loyal men (largely discharged soldiers), with the result that disloyal men had wrongly been declared elected. The petitioners urged that legislation akin to the Louisiana Bill[29] be enacted for all the unreconstructed States. "A loyal reconstruction is possible only through the assistance of loyal election officers."[30]

When Wilson of Iowa, chairman of the House Judiciary Committee, introduced H.R. 33, Representative Fernando Wood[31] promptly attacked it for taking away the people's right through their own elected

---

[25] Infra, p. 324.

[26] Cong. Globe, 40–1, 17.

[27] Ibid., 302–03, 314. 15 Stat. 2.

[28] The *Richmond Dispatch* in an editorial of March 18, 1867, pointed to the unusual problem of registration where "the great body" of freedmen had had no surname "until since the fall of the Confederacy, and they are not very well known by names they may since have adopted." Place of residence, too, might be un- certain. "Congress seems to consider that [registration] must be done with some degree of system, as much to protect [the freedmen] as the community."

[29] Supra, p. 290.

[30] Cong. Globe, 40–1, 17. The first signature was that of John C. Under- wood—the United States District Judge for Virginia. See infra, pp. 601– 07, 823–28.

[31] See supra, ch. 6, n. 228.

officers to initiate proceedings for a convention; this was a bill "to establish a military despotism"—to permit military commanders "to establish governments for these States as Louis Napoleon established an empire for France, as Maximilian proposed to establish an empire in Mexico."[32]

Compare: Wood called for civil supremacy as represented by the governments in being; the Alexandria petitioners reported how that worked in practice, and called for a transfer of power to loyal hands, black and white. Congress, seeking impartial registration and elections, chose neither: it enacted that the administration would be conducted under a general officer selected by the President. "So that," Blaine replied to Wood, "no one in possession or out of possession is to be prejudiced by any action of ours, but we intend to secure to everybody entitled to vote at all an even start in the race."[33]

What Blaine here said was the key to the Congressional program.

Samuel S. Marshall of Illinois chided the Republicans for having advanced so audaciously that now they were advocating measures that probably not ten of their number would have countenanced when the 39th Congress began. (Quite likely that was true—but not fairly to be imputed as a fault. Alarming developments in the South, painful disillusionment with Andrew Johnson, and then the frustration of expectations based on the Fourteenth Amendment: these had brought the party to the determination that the all-white regimes must be breached and that elections must be supervised.) Now Marshall was reproaching the Republicans for irresolution: "Why did Congress go on blundering from month to month, from folly to folly, until the close of the Thirty-Ninth Congress, before passing any bill that looked to restoration?" His conclusion was "Having placed themselves in opposition to the constitutional, reasonable, and patriotic policy of the President, they were utterly unable for more than a year to present any plan of their own . . . ."[34]

Marshall and Wood were Democratic spokesmen: the former had just received his party's votes for Speaker; the latter received a like compliment in the 43rd Congress. While affecting concern for constitutional principles, they shared their party's detestation of what Marshall called "these miserable mongrel governments fastened on the country."

Wilson was quick to catch up Marshall's reference to the President's "constitutional, reasonable, and patriotic policy": that was an indorsement of the Act of March 2.[35] So far as encroachment upon the freedom of State governments was concerned, the parallels were striking: in 1865 President Johnson had called conventions to frame

---

[32] Cong. Globe, 40–1, 62–63. Mar. 11.
[33] Ibid., 63. Mar. 11.

[34] Ibid., 64–66. Mar. 11.
[35] Ibid., 65, 66.

new constitutions—had fixed qualifications for voting, and for serving as delegate—had dictated that certain provisions be incorporated—and had called for the ratification of a pending constitutional amendment. So Wilson had reason for saying that "the Executive undertook to exercise the precise power that Congress exercised when it passed the act of March 2, 1867."[36] Southerners were prone to explain that, effectively, what was done in 1865 had been by the people themselves through their representatives; the directions of the President merely served to facilitate.

Now Congress sought the framing of new constitutions, such as would achieve a difficult (if indeed not an impossible) consensus—based upon participation by the community of whites, joined by Unionists and the mass of freedmen. How substantial should be the required manifestations of assent? Somehow there should be an ascertainment of willingness to make a constitution in accordance with the Act of March 2; somehow there should be a mode of election of delegates, somehow a vote on ratification. As the Senate substitute was drawn, (1) delegates would be elected "by a plurality of the votes cast"; (2) when the delegates assembled, they would first determine . . . whether it was the wish of the people . . . to frame a constitution . . . , and if so, . . . proceed . . ."; (3) for acceptance, there must be ratification "by a majority of the votes of the electors qualified"—which, Trumbull explained, meant *not* "by a majority of those who vote," but "by a majority of all the registered voters."[37]

Drake, the new Senator from Missouri, wanted a vote by the people, yes or no, whether to proceed under the statute: otherwise candidates might falsely promise to vote for a convention and then cheat and defraud the loyal people.[38] Howard of Michigan agreed: "it will render it more difficult" for "perfidious persons" to impose upon voters who had "little knowledge" of "their real situation."[39]

Fessenden offered "an improvement": the *existing governments* ought by formal enactment to request a convention. These disaffected men had made so many "complaints"—he repeated the word, over and over—about being excluded from representation: now he would force them openly to choose, so that they could not turn around and complain

---

[36] This point was made with cogency in the *Jackson* (Mississippi) *Clarion*, July 4, 1867. Arguing at that moment that white men should join in carrying out the Acts of March 2 and 23, the editor wrote: "How is it that some persons who applauded the extra constitutional acts of the President in 1865, . . . are so shocked at the plan which has been proposed by Congress? . . ." The editor went on to compare in detail, concluding that "as a question of PRINCIPLE," Congress had better authority to prescribe a plan of reconstruction than had the President.

[37] Cong. Globe, 40–1, 94–95. Mar. 14, 1867.

[38] Ibid., 95. Mar. 14.

[39] Ibid., 95–96.

"that they have been forced back."[40] Howard at once adorned that proposal: the legislatures then in office represented "the malignity of unrepentant rebels"; "I wish to see these same Legislatures, humiliating as it may be to their pride, and the more humiliating the better, brought down to the stool of repentance . . . ."[41]

Stewart replied that he would not leave it to "a bad minority" to say whether the majority should go forward.[42] Sumner shared Fessenden's spirit, but knew that Union men of the South would not approve of the proposal; he favored Drake's idea.[43]

The outcome was that the statute prescribed that the people themselves would vote, *for* or *against* a convention.

In providing for the initial election, to put the Congressional program in motion, and for the final election, on ratification of the constitution, discussion ranged between two positions: that a *majority of votes cast* should suffice, or that there should be a *majority of the entire number of registered voters*. There was apprehension that disaffected whites might keep freedmen from the polls—or on the other hand that they might "get registered and then by staying at home have the advantage" of frustrating the program.[44] Congress had to reckon that either might occur.

Bingham—whose unfaltering trust in the words of the Fourteenth Amendment permitted him to disdain other prudential devices—called for a mere majority of votes cast.[45] Representative Wilson explained that the Judiciary Committee had concluded that there should be a majority of the total number registered, on this ground:

> that in the rebel States the whites being in the possession of political power might by threats and intimidation prevent the colored citizens from voting, . . . and adopt a constitution which would not be free and equal in its operation . . . .[46]

Boutwell, also of the Judiciary Committee, added:

> we ought in the beginning to assert the doctrine that a majority of the people of these States shall assent to the work done by the conventions, and show that they are ready to sustain the frame-work of

---

[40] Ibid., 96–97, Mar. 14; 109–111, Mar. 15.

[41] Ibid., 112. Mar. 15.

[42] Ibid., 113. Mar. 15.

[43] Ibid., 117–18. Mar. 15.

[44] Senator Trumbull, ibid. at 150. Mar. 16.

[45] Ibid., 63, 64. Mar. 11. "I undertake to say that with the express grant

of powers put for the first time into the Constitution of your country it is utterly impossible, so long as the Representatives of the people are true to the trust committed to them, that any advantages shall be taken in all the years to come of these men called freedmen . . . ."

[46] Ibid., 63. Mar. 11.

government thus set up in harmony with the Constitution of the United States.[47]

Bingham's amendment won only 38 votes, against 70.[48]

The Senate was deeply troubled over the same problem. Oliver P. Morton, Indiana's war Governor, now Senator, proposed that a majority of votes cast on the question of ratifying would suffice. Why should "sullen rebels" and "stay-at-homes" defeat those who wanted to go forward? Congress had established a military government: "It is not in the interest of this Republic to have that government continued one day longer than is necessary."[49]

Stewart said, "I fully concur . . ."; "I do not wish to place any more clogs upon this machinery."[50]

Reverdy Johnson said, "I entirely agree . . . ." He dissented from the idea that "no government can be republican which does not consult in the first instance the will of all . . . ." "I am exceedingly unwilling to govern these States by military rule. . . . These people may become attached to military rule; the people of the United States may believe that it is the best mode of governing the South . . . ." He repeated the faith he had expressed on March 2 when the President's veto was defeated: that "the reflecting men of the South . . . have been, to a great extent, in favor of this measure. They are willing to live disfranchised if the people of their States are permitted to come in . . . . Why not let them come in?"[51]

(There were, indeed, some such "reflecting men": from time to time they did appear, to great advantage. But their number and influence proved to be far less than Reverdy Johnson anticipated.)

Roscoe Conkling—now a Senator—argued the opposite side, giving his new colleagues a sample of his haughty, vigorous style. It was to be foreseen, he said, that a large number of disloyal men would "turn away in disdain, as they have done from other propositions"; they would refuse even to register. If then a convention were called, and presently a constitution adopted, by minorities "so small as to be contemptible," there would be an outcry from Maine to California "that by the bayonet we are forcing upon an unwilling people a minority government. Is it worth while, sir?" *Time*, he said, was not so important as *manner* in this work of reconstruction.[52]

Howard, too, foresaw the possibility of many whites refusing to register; "we may have governments in which only negroes participate;

---

47 Ibid.
48 Ibid., 66.
49 Ibid., 97, Mar. 14; 146, Mar. 16.
50 Ibid., 98. Mar. 14.
51 Ibid., 98–99. Mar. 14.

52 Ibid., 148. Mar. 16. Conkling's election to the Senate superseded his reelection to the House. In the Senate he succeeded Ira Harris, elsewhere mentioned. Supra, pp. 160, 168–71.

the white population in the mean time standing entirely aloof from them. Is this desirable?" New governments should be based on a showing that a majority of the entire voting population wanted to "come back into the Union."[53]

Morton's amendment—requiring merely a majority of the votes cast—was adopted by 22 against 21.[54]

Edmunds, after more debate, won a proviso: that at least half of the registered voters should have voted on ratifying the constitution.[55]

The pertinent provisions, as they emerged in the Supplementary Act, should be marked for reference. In the election on calling a convention,

> If a majority of the votes given on that question shall be for a convention, then such convention shall be held as hereinafter provided; but if a majority of said votes shall be against a convention, then no such convention shall be held under this act; *Provided*, That such convention shall not be held unless a majority of all such registered voters shall have voted on the question of holding such convention.

And on ratification:

> the constitution shall be ratified by a majority of the votes of the registered electors qualified as herein specified, cast at such election, at least one half of all the registered voters voting upon the question of such ratification . . . .

Inasmuch as this would have permitted ratification by a bare majority of a bare majority of all registered voters, a safeguarding qualification was framed in conference committee, and accepted:

> and if it shall moreover appear to Congress that the election was one at which all the registered and qualified voters in the State had an opportunity to vote freely and without restraint, fear, or the influence of fraud, and if the Congress shall be satisfied that such constitution meets the approval of a majority of all the qualified electors in the State . . . .

The last clause was a loose formula to surmount a difference between the Houses: By what means could Congress satisfy itself that a majority of all approved if only a lesser number had voted approval? At any rate, power was reserved to meet a contingency.

A number of Senators and Representatives went on Southern tours

---

[53] Ibid., 147. Mar. 16.
[54] Ibid., 149. Mar. 16.

[55] Ibid., 151. The vote was 24 to 14.

in the late spring while Congress was in recess, endeavoring by speech and conference to guide proceedings under the statutes. Most widely noticed were the doings of Senator Wilson and Representative Kelley.

CHIEF JUSTICE CHASE DRAFTS A SUPPLEMENTARY BILL

SENATOR WILSON, near the close of his three-volume *History of the Rise and Fall of Slave Power in America*, had a chapter on "Congressional Reconstruction." He summarized the deliberations that led to the statute of March 2. At that point, "the purpose was clearly enough defined, . . . but . . . the processes by which such a result could be effected had not been marked out. That must be attended to." Then, speaking of himself in the third person:

> Accordingly, upon the assembling of the XLth Congress in March, at its first session, a bill, drawn up substantially by Chief Justice Chase, was introduced into the Senate on the 7th by Mr. Wilson, supplementary to the above-mentioned act. It provided [summarizing his S. 18[56]] . . . . It was also provided that the acting governor of any State, by taking the proper oath, might discharge these duties of the commanding general, with the consent of the latter.[57]

Wilson's statement that Chief Justice Chase was substantially the draftsman of S. 18 is confirmed by an item among the Chase Papers at the Historical Society of Pennsylvania: a single sheet bearing, in Chase's hand, his draft of the bill, from enacting clause through two lines of Section 3, with corrections and interlineations; the remainder of his draft is missing.

This invites some critical comments about Chief Justice Chase.

It is useful, and often necessary, that there be communication between members of the Court and members of the Congress—to provide a cure for difficulties arising in the application of the statutes governing the jurisdiction and procedure of the federal courts and to facilitate judicial administration. It will be recalled that during the 39th Congress there had been the problem of fixing the size of the Court, resulting in the Act of July 23, 1866.[58] It has been explained that on that occasion the Chief Justice supplied a draft—and that in doing so he sought to induce Congress to make other provisions: to increase the salaries of the Justices; to exalt his own station; and to create the office

---

[56] Supra, p. 317.
[57] Wilson, *Rise and Fall of Slave Power*, III, 619. The three volumes were published at Boston, between 1872 and 1877.
[58] Supra, p. 169.

of Marshal, to be appointed by himself.[59] The omission of any provision
for allotment to the new Circuits led to embarrassment in the summer
and autumn of 1866—and, in Chase's situation, the appearance of
shirking duty in the pending matter of Jefferson Davis.[60] At the
Second Session there was Senator Wade's measure to remove the allotment difficulty, and to give the Court a Marshal—something on which
Chase had set his heart. This became law on March 2, 1867.[61]

In these matters, as well as in his preoccupation with Reconstruction and with politics, Chase's concern for the Court, for the country,
and for his own advantage had kept him in constant communication
with members of the 39th Congress.

And now as the 40th Congress opened he busied himself with
drafting a Supplementary Bill to effectuate the purposes of the Reconstruction Act of March 2. It was a bill that called for no judicial skill:
it simply provided for a registration and for elections.

The Reconstruction Act was now the very center of partisan controversy. Its validity, in whole or in respect of a particular provision,
would be fought over before the Supreme Court. Certainly the world—
if it had known—would have had no doubt that a Chief Justice who
thus intermeddled with supplementary details must already feel a deep
commitment to the basic Act.

The impropriety is heightened by the context of the moment. On
December 13, 1866, the *National Intelligencer*—conservative, and normally grave—published a "Pot-Pourri in the House." This reported "the
introduction of a multitude of measures intended to curtail the constitutional powers of the Executive"—leading toward an "inextricable
confusion" of Legislative, Executive, and Judicial powers. It added,

> It was suggested to-day that the anxiety manifested to thrust upon
> the Supreme Court a large portion of the executive patronage pro-
> posed to be taken away from the President was a bribe to that hitherto
> incorruptible and irreproachable body to participate in the division
> of the spoils and become the ally of Congress in setting aside the
> Constitution.
>
> The unscrupulous assailants of the President and the Constitu-
> tion . . . seem to regard the Supreme Court as the only formidable
> obstacle in their way. . . .

Congress—reacting against its relative loss of authority during
the war, and mindful of the need to combat Johnson's policies—was
braced to encroach upon the powers of the President, or even to remove
him. Indeed on December 17, Ashley of Ohio called for an inquiry

---

[59] Supra, pp. 165–67. [60] Supra, pp. 175–77. [61] Supra, p. 175.

looking toward an impeachment.[62] This was therefore a time of times when the Supreme Court should be exemplary in conforming to the Constitution's allocation of functions. This was especially applicable to the Chief Justice, who must preside over the Senate in the event the House impeached the President.

The Pot-Pourri's reference to "patronage" may have referred to Representative Hamilton Ward's H.R. 856, introduced on December 10: it provided for provisional governors in the ex-rebel States, to be appointed by the Chief Justice. As we know, nothing came of that proposal.[63]

At any rate, the reporter doubtless was thinking of the pending Bankruptcy Bill, which would provide for the appointment of one or more registers in bankruptcy in each Congressional district. Chase's estimate was, "say three hundred & fifty or sixty" appointments.[64] On December 14, Senator Poland for the Judiciary Committee moved to take up this bill. The resulting Bankruptcy Act of March 2 retained, notwithstanding stiff opposition in the Senate, the provision for nominations by the Chief Justice.

Soon, but too late, Chase would regret this mark of favor on the part of the majority party. His memorable experience with judicial cooperation under the Bankruptcy Act will receive particular attention in a moment.[65]

Not only was it improper for the Chief Justice to engage in framing a Supplementary Reconstruction Bill: he was not even a prudent adviser. His draft concluded with this provision:

> That the duties hereby imposed upon the commanding general in each district, and the powers conferred, may, with his consent, be performed and exercised by the acting governor of any State, who shall take an oath or affirmation faithfully to keep and perform the same.[66]

By "the acting governor" the draftsman meant the head of the State government, which the Act of March 2 had pronounced to be "provisional only." Upon mature consideration, Congress had rejected the idea of entrusting registration and elections to the all-white governments in office. It confided the task to general officers to be assigned by the President, because they were believed to give the best promise of a faithful execution of the Congressional purpose. But here the draftsman proposed to authorize the general in his discretion to hand over

---

[62] Cong. Globe, 39–2, 154.
[63] Supra, p. 259.
[64] Letter of Mar. 20 to his daughter Nettie. Chase Papers, L.C.

[65] Infra, p. 259.
[66] Sec. 6 of S. 18, referred to by Senator Wilson, *Rise and Fall of Slave Power*, supra, p. 324.

his trust to a governor whom Congress in its discretion had not seen fit to trust. If the general's delegation proved to yield disappointing results, could he revoke it? The statute made no such provision. Be that as it may, devesting would have been impracticable. The governor's oath would have been binding only in the forum of his own conscience. The entire conception was so unsound as to reflect upon the draftsman. When the Senate Judiciary Committee substituted the language of Senator Wilson's bill in H.R. 33,[67] it deleted this provision for delegation.

DEBATES ON FURTHER CONDITIONS— "FUNDAMENTAL" AND OTHERWISE

"EQUALITY OF CONSTITUTIONAL RIGHT and power is the condition of all the States of the Union, old and new," observed Justice Field for the Court in 1883.[68] The Constitution provides that "New States may be admitted by Congress into this Union:"[69] *this* Union, the Court has stressed—"a Union of States, equal in power, dignity, and authority . . . ." (Hence a provision in the enabling act whereby the new State must not move its capital for a certain time would cease to control after the moment of admission "on an equal footing with the original States."[70]) The principle had been recognized in 1845, in the case of *Pollard v. Hagan*, relating to the status of Alabama.[71]

But Congress in the 1860's, in its concern to secure freedom and equal treatment for the Negro in new States, was not paying much attention to this doctrine of the Supreme Court. Of States for which enabling acts were passed in 1864, Nevada was admitted that year subject to an "irrevocable ordinance" made "in obedience" to the statute;[72] Nebraska entered in 1867 upon its acceptance of a "fundamental condition";[73] and the effort to add Colorado to the Union was stopped with the veto, in 1867, of a bill which would also have imposed such conditions.[74]

It seemed very appealing, when Congress was framing terms for the wayward States, to impose salutary requirements, never to be revoked without the consent of Congress. Ashley put such covenants

---

[67] Supra, p. 318.

[68] Escanaba & L.M. Transp. Co. v. Chicago, 107 U.S. 678, 689.

[69] Art. IV, Sec. 3, cl. 1.

[70] Coyle v. Smith, 221 U.S. 559, 567 (1911), relating to the power of Oklahoma.

[71] 3 How. 212. Held: Alabama had the same right and power over the shores of navigable waters and the soil beneath them as did the other States respectively—notwithstanding a disclaimer exacted by Congress in the Enabling Act.

[72] 13 Stat. 30, 749.

[73] 13 Stat. 47; 14 Stat. 391. And see Bolin v. Nebraska, 176 U.S. 83 (1900).

[74] Cong. Globe, 39–2, 360–64, 481–82, 818, 1928.

for equal and impartial laws, and for free schools "from which no child shall be excluded because of race," into his substitute for H.R. 543 in January.[75] And now in the new session, Senator Drake proposed that the Supplementary Act contain such a prescription of voting by closed ballot.[76] Conkling objected that "this would be especially awkward in view of the fact that the Supreme Court has decided . . . that any such compact would be utterly and absolutely void for all purposes." Shortly he produced a copy of 3 Howard and cited *Pollard v. Hagan*.[77] "That decision has never been doubted," said Reverdy Johnson. But, Fessenden asked Conkling, suppose the House were to refuse to seat Representatives chosen in disregard of such a requirement: "what could the Supreme Court do about it?" Conkling replied: "I should say that the Supreme Court could do nothing, and that Congress could do everything"; each House could refuse to seat, either because it was "the Judge of the Elections, Returns and Qualifications of its own Members,"[78] or because the election was "at the instant a flagrant violation of one of the vital terms" upon which the State was to be readmitted to representation. But, he concluded, if a State removed such a provision after members had been seated, "we could never turn them out."[79] Doolittle thought that "we have no power to bind any State in the future" to anything more than what the Constitution itself imposed. Morton said, "We cannot bind any State not to amend [its] constitution . . ."; but Drake's requirement would be efficacious for a moment, and, in practice, once the secret ballot was in effect it would thereafter protect itself. Henderson thought Drake's proposal "inexpedient," but in any event "we cannot require it in all time to come of these States."

Drake removed the "shall never be changed" clause; even so, his amendment was rejected without a record vote.[80]

Senator Sumner wanted to go much further in prescribing fundamental conditions to be written into new State constitutions, beyond the nondiscriminatory suffrage required by the Act of March 2. On March 5 he gave notice of a bill to guarantee a republican form of government—Senate Bill No. 7—wherein he listed seven provisions, never to be changed without the consent of Congress. This was allowed to lie on the table: Sumner had no desire to bury it in the Judiciary

---

[75] Supra, p. 268.
[76] Cong. Globe, 40–1, 99. Mar. 14. Debated, 99–105.
[77] Supra, p. 327.
[78] Constitution, Art. I, Sec. 5, cl. 1.
[79] Cong. Globe, 40–1, 100. The reply was somewhat loose. Seemingly by "could never" he meant only "could not properly . . . ." The debate failed to distinguish between the House, whose members were popularly elected, and the Senate, whose members (prior to the Seventeenth Amendment, adopted in 1913) were chosen by State legislatures.
[80] Ibid., 109. Mar. 15.

Committee.[81] On the seventh he introduced "Resolutions declaring certain further guaranties required . . . ," and on the eleventh explained them to a critical audience.[82] And on March 16, a Saturday, at 10:30 P.M., when after three days of debate it seemed that a weary Senate was about to pass the Supplementary Bill, he moved an amendment to require that State constitutions provide for a system of nondiscriminatory public schools.[83]

The "Resolutions"—theses, and to Sumner virtually axioms—opened with the statement that Congress, in prescribing suffrage without regard to race, had "set an example for itself": now it should likewise require universal public education, and a homestead for every head of a family among the freedmen. Also—in response, one supposes, to the adverse reaction of loyalists to the Act of March 2—he now demanded that the existing State governments be utterly swept away—"vacated"—"so that they can have no agency in the work of reconstruction, and will cease to exercise a pernicious influence." In their stead, provisional governments should be constituted, to superintend the transition to permanent governments based upon "loyalty, beyond suspicion"; "every possible precaution must be adopted against rebel agency or influence in the formation of these governments."

Here let it be remarked that public schools, and still more free homesteads, were large substantive propositions; that Sumner's proposals came inopportunely when Senators were hastening to pass a Supplementary Bill needed to implement the Act of March 2; further, that they went beyond what majority sentiment would sustain; and still further, that before the Senate could responsibly resolve that homesteads "must be secured," it would have to study seriously by what means such an enormous commitment could be realized.

For Congress to vacate existing offices and to ordain that only the "loyal, beyond suspicion" could participate in reconstruction, would repudiate the conception on which the Act of March 2 had been based: that Congress was directing its own disinterested agency to administer elections wherein everybody entitled to vote would receive fair treatment.[84] To Sumner this vacating was an urgent matter: he told of letters from Virginia, reporting the movement whereby the legislature would call a convention—thereby, it was said, placing loyal men under the control of the most malignant of the late rebel leaders.[85]

The only one of Sumner's points having a prospect of immediate

[81] Ibid., 6, 9–10. At 165–67, on March 16, he discussed it at length. See infra, pp. 329–31.

[82] Ibid., 15, 49–56. He brought them up again on July 3. Pp. 467–68.

[83] Ibid., 165.

[84] Supra, pp. 258–59, 319.

[85] Cong. Globe, 40–1, 50, 51. Mar. 11. See supra, pp. 313–16.

acceptance was that which he proposed as an amendment to the Supplementary Bill—late on Saturday night, March 16:

> That the constitution shall require the Legislature to establish and sustain a system of public schools open to all, without distinction of race or color.[86]

Did this mean "that each and every school shall be open to children of both races?" Sumner replied that "according to the true principle, . . . the schools, precisely like the ballot-box or the rail cars, should be open to all. But the proposition is necessarily general in its character; it does not go into details. . . ."[87] Nor did the proposition declare that this could "never to be changed without the consent of Congress"—but Sumner made clear that that was what he wanted.[88]

He supported his amendment in a speech—studied, eloquent, oracular, and as it developed, highly provocative.[89] At once he condemned the Act of March 2:[90]

> I speak frankly. Let me then confess my regret that Congress chooses to employ the military power for purposes of reconstruction. The Army is for protection. . . .

But Congress had given the Army an initiative in instituting new governments:

> I regret this. . . . I would not see new States born of the bayonet. . . . I would intrust reconstruction to provisional governments, civil in character and organized by Congress. . . .

From the beginning, he asserted, he had maintained these views:

> At the last session I insisted upon the Louisiana bill in preference to the military bill. In the earliest moments of the present session I introduced a bill of my own . . . .

and here he held up Senate Bill No. 7, to guarantee a republican form of government, etc.[91] He elaborated upon that measure: there would be a provisional governor and a council of thirteen, appointed by the President; appointment and removal must have the approval of the

---

[86] Ibid., 165.
[87] Ibid., 169.
[88] Ibid., 166.
[89] Ibid., 165–67.
[90] Framed by the caucus committee of which he had been a member— where, he later recalled, it was "debated and matured sentence by sentence, word for word . . . ." Cong. Globe, 41–2, 640. Jan. 21, 1870. See supra, pp. 298–300.
[91] Supra, p. 328.

Senate; they would be bound by an oath, loaded with promissory clauses about policies to be pursued; appointees to inferior offices, jurors, militiamen, must all qualify by this same oath; so too must all admitted to participate, as voters or as members of the constitutional convention. The constitution must include seven "fundamental conditions," including schools "open to all without distinction of race or color."

> But if this bill cannot be adopted, then I ask that you shall take at least one of its provisions. Require free schools as an essential condition of reconstruction. . . .

He anticipated the objection that Congress should not add to the requirements made by the Act of March 2:

> It is only a few days old, so that whatever may be its character, nothing is as yet fixed under its provisions. It contains no compact, no promise, no vested right, nothing which may not be changed if the public interests require. . . . Seize the present moment. Grasp the precious privilege. . . .

He pronounced an apostrophe to Education. He contrasted the high proportion of literates in the North with the blight of ignorance among Southern whites, and consequently their failure to comprehend a republican government. He sought "a new triumph for civilization."

> For a military occupation, bristling with bayonets, I would substitute the smile of peace. But this cannot be done without education. As the soldier disappears his place must be supplied by the schoolmaster. The muster-roll must be exchanged for the school register, and our headquarters must be in a school-house.

The peroration came to an end with

> The Old must give way to the New, and the New must be worthy of a Republic, which, ransomed from Slavery has become an example to mankind. Farewell to the Old! All hail to the New!

All this aroused some indignation, promptly voiced by Senator Frelinghuysen.[92] The Senate, he said, had been engaged for weeks with measures for reconstruction,

> and now, when the work is about consummated, late on Saturday night, when we are about to take the final vote . . . , [Senator Sumner]

---

[92] Cong. Globe, 40–1, 167. Debate followed, 167–171.

with all the power of his influence gives it out to the world that we are establishing States that are to be born of the bayonet. No, sir; no. The constituents of these States are as free to form constitutions or not to form them as any community that ever existed, and I for one will not submit to be charged with being a party to the formation of States by the bayonet. What has the bayonet to do with it? . . .

The commander would conduct elections as Congress directed; but "Is there any bayonet pricking voters up to the polls to adopt our sentiments?"

Coming to the merits of the schools proposal, Frelinghuysen said that the Fourteenth Amendment, which would bar racial discrimination generally, must come into force before any rebel State could be restored; to require more than that was beyond the proper function of the Federal Government. Further, good faith forbade the adding of new conditions—now schools, and next it would be homesteads—to what the 39th Congress had set as terms of settlement in the Act of March 2. He quoted from the 15th Psalm: the upright man "sweareth to his own hurt, and changeth not": so too should an upright nation stand by its engagements.

Senator Conness said: "the civil government of the State of California was the product of a military order; and it is not now less free . . . for that reason."[93]

Senator Stewart resented Sumner's denouncing of the Act of March 2 after he had supported it; the "born of the bayonet" remark would be "continually repeated" by the Democrats. This was confirmed in a moment when Buckalew of Pennsylvania, Democrat, said that Sumner's "figure of speech represents nothing but the actual, honest, notorious, indisputable truth"; he had observed that Sumner was "the pioneer man" whose extreme positions soon came to be adopted by his party. Hendricks thought that Congress had no rightful power to make a constitution for a State; but aside from that, he saw "no fair dealing, no honesty," in adding this new condition to the Act of March 2, which had been regarded as "a finality." Sumner had waited to the last moment to add this "ornament, the dome upon the capitol of this restoration policy."

Morton of Indiana spoke for the amendment: "I regard the education of these people as essential to reconstruction. . . . I would have been in favor of having the colored people of the South wait a few years until . . . they were to some extent educated; but . . . the condition

---

[93] Ibid., 168. On the initiative for the organization of a State govern- ment, see supra, n. 1.

of things required that they should be brought to the polls at once; . . . but now let us provide against the danger by making provision for this steady education of these people. . . ." Cole of California recalled that for many years Southern States had made it a penal offense to educate Negroes; that in itself would justify the requirement. James W. Patterson of New Hampshire, experienced in school administration, raised the question whether it would be possible to maintain a common-school system without dividing large estates into small homesteads, "so that there may be small landholders who shall support these schools by the taxation which is laid upon them?"

On the vote, 20 Senators—including Wade, President pro tem., and others of the more hardy sort—voted for the amendment, and 20 others opposed; 13 were absent. So the amendment failed.

Then the Supplementary Bill was passed, by 38 to 2, and a spent Senate adjourned at 11:50 Saturday night.[94]

Within the next week, as has been recorded,[95] by conference the two Houses reached agreement, the President vetoed and the bill was nevertheless enacted and became the Supplementary Act of March 23, 1867.[96]

REFLECTIONS ON THE TWO STATUTES

THE DEBATES LEADING TO THE ACT OF MARCH 2 have now been summarized—from the origin in the latter part of the First Session, through Stevens' unsuccessful effort to carry his substitute for H.R. 543 in January 1867, to the process of reaching accord on H.R. 1143, with concurrent consideration of the Louisiana Bill. Then the 40th Congress provided the necessary supplement of March 23. If the narration has seemed long, that was unavoidable in a fair presentation of this large matter. Along with cries of outrage from obdurate Democrats, and fanatical demands by some extreme Radicals, there was an enormous body of pertinent, constructive discussion. It is remarkable how many men had a firm hold on some aspect of many-sided truth.

These little-known debates in the Second Session of the 39th Congress may appropriately be compared with the First Session's debates on the Fourteenth Amendment. In bulk, those of 1867 occupy about one and a half times as much space in the Congressional Globe as do those of 1866; in quality they are not inferior.[97] Indeed the two may

---

[94] Ibid., 171.
[95] Supra, p. 318.
[96] 15 Stat. 2.
[97] The history of the framing of the Fourteenth Amendment will be closely examined in Chapter 20, in preparation for Chapter 21's discussion of the *Slaughter House Cases*, where the Amendment's Section 1 was first construed by the Court.

In the framing of the Amendment, discussion in the Joint Committee

be viewed together as a continuing pursuit of one persistent problem: On what basis should the Union be restored—and what should be done when the South rejected the proffered basis?

Laying aside—if one can—preconceptions drawn from school books, novels, and folklore, let the options before the 39th Congress be recalled for candid appraisal—with insight sharpened by latter-day experience in the securing of civil rights.

I. There was President Johnson's stand, in his first message to Congress, on December 4, 1865: already, he said, he had restored the rebel States to their "rightful authority"; when the Thirteenth Amendment came into force (December 6) and when the Houses had seated Southern delegations, "the work of restoration" would be complete.

Consider the state of the law at that point. Until the Thirteenth Amendment abolished slavery, civil status had been entirely a matter of State concern. Thus when Chancellor Kent[98] discussed "The Rights of Persons" to "Personal Liberty and Security" and to "Religious Opinion and Worship," he was not dealing with rights that flowed from the Constitution or laws of the United States: he told of State constitutions and laws, and English origins. The provisions of the Federal Constitution's Bill of Rights, the Supreme Court had said, "must be understood as restraining the power of the general government, not as applicable to the States."[99] Among the matters of civil status, governed by State law, Kent discussed the relations of "Master and Servant": that is, of slaves, of "hired servants" [the field that has come to be largely covered by the National Labor Relations Act of 1935, as amended], and of apprentices. After telling about the law of slaves, Kent said in a footnote that "The African race, even when free, are essentially a degraded caste, of inferior rank and condition in society"—with a long citation of statutes and decisions to illustrate how widely the free Negro was denied equality of status with the white.[100]

By the Thirteenth Amendment, the State's exclusive authority over internal institutions was limited in one respect: that "slavery" was abolished. Congress was given one new power: to enforce that prohibi-

---

played a large part—and debate in the Houses was thereby accelerated. In the Second Session, the Joint Committee figured only for a moment, in framing H.R. 1143, the Military Bill.

Both in dealing with the Amendment and with H.R. 1143, the Republican Senators went into caucus and there reached accord. The result in each instance was to reduce debate on the floor of the Senate.

[98] *Commentaries on American Law* (1826), and numerous editions thereafter.

[99] Marshall, C. J., in Barron v. Baltimore, 7 Pet. 243, 247 (1833). He spoke in particular of the clause of the Fifth Amendment prohibiting the taking of private property without just compensation, but the proposition was applicable generally. On this matter, see infra, p. 1124.

[100] II, *258, note (a).

tion. And the federal courts, in the exercise of their established jurisdiction over controversies arising under the Constitution, would give effect to this new provision as occasion might arise.

By the Civil Rights Act of April 9, 1866,[101] Congress made bold to strike at some of what have been termed the "incidents of slavery": it declared that in every State *all* citizens would thenceforth have the same right to contract, to sue, to testify, to hold property, and to enjoy the equal benefit of the laws, as the State allowed to white citizens. But the constitutionality of this was denied, or questioned, even by men sincerely devoted to the objects of the statute. (Thus, Bingham and Raymond, on constitutional scruples, voted against the bill.) President Johnson's veto pronounced it an invidious discrimination "against the white race" and an invasion upon the "rights of the States." (Only after the Fourteenth Amendment had been adopted, and Congress had reenacted the provisions of the Civil Rights Act,[102] were these new rights understood to have a really solid foundation.)

By the original Constitution, "The Citizens of each State shall be entitled to all Privileges and Immunities of Citizens in the several States."[103] As Kent explained, citizens going from their own into another State "are entitled to the privileges that persons of the same description are entitled to in the state to which the removal is made, and to none other."[104] Thus the citizen of Massachusetts, visiting, say, South Carolina, had just as much right when there to preach Abolition as South Carolina allowed its own citizens. Although "slavery" was abolished by the Thirteenth Amendment, in other respects the Negro's "rank and condition in society" would be entirely governed by State law. (How wide or narrow was the reach of the Amendment would be open to future controversy.) A Negro travelling from State to State would in each be entitled to "the privileges that persons of the same description" there enjoyed.

So far, then, as the Constitution of the United States was concerned, a State in 1866 was subject to few restraints of any sort. (1) It must not transgress Article I, Section 10, "No State shall . . .": most important of these prohibitions being that it pass no "Law impairing the obligation of Contracts." (2) It must not obstruct the lawful operations of the United States or the exercise of rights flowing from it—such as a right to engage in interstate commerce. (3) And from 1866, it must not maintain slavery. With substantial accuracy it may be said that, aside from these rather simple limitations, a State was free to govern its own people as its own constitution and laws might provide; as to citi-

---

[101] 14 Stat. 27.
[102] Act of May 31, 1870, sec. 16. 16 Stat. 140, 144.

[103] Art. IV, Sec. 2, cl. 1.
[104] II, *71.

zens of other States, it must treat them no worse than it treated its own under like circumstances. Freedom of speech, freedom of the press, religious liberty, would have been concerns of each State for itself. The quality of its justice, the fairness of its administration, would have remained exclusively the State's own business—so long as none of the few federal rights were drawn in question.

Under the spreading branches of the Fourteenth Amendment men have come to find "equal protection" and "liberty" so pervasive, so familiar and seemingly so essential, that only by a jolt can one even dimly appreciate the significance of the fact that Congress insisted upon its adoption. It refused to join President Johnson in restoring the Union on the basis merely of the Thirteenth Amendment.

II. We come to the position taken by the Joint Committee on Reconstruction, in its report of April 30, 1866: along with the proposed Fourteenth Amendment it presented H.R. 543, which would have enacted that when an ex-rebel State had adopted and conformed to the Amendment, and the Amendment had come into force, Senators and Representatives might be seated.

The First Session adjourned, to be sure, without acting upon H.R. 543. Much was made, in retrospect, of the point that when Congress submitted the Amendment it failed to declare that acceptance would effect a *final* settlement.[105] (While in truth some Republicans at no time considered the Amendment as going far enough, there were strong expressions at the Second Session to the effect that *if* the Amendment had been accepted, promptly and sincerely, restoration on that basis must have followed.[106]) One may concede that, in dealing with States so recently at war with the United States, Congress did well not to preclude a change in its own position while they remained free to dicker indefinitely. The adequacy of any basis of settlement was to be judged in the light of the spirit with which the South approached it.

Distinctly, the response of the Southern legislatures was that they would not accept the Fourteenth Amendment.

III. Then recall Stevens' substitute for H.R. 543—as it stood on January 28, 1867, when the House refused to go forward with it: adult male citizens, without regard to color, were to choose delegates to a constitutional convention. "Citizen" *excluded* adherents to the Confederacy, save that a soldier below the rank of lieutenant might escape the forfeiture upon a determination that at all times after March 4, 1864, he had "earnestly desired the success of the Union," etc.[107]

Since the proposal lost its significance, it may be treated somewhat

---

[105] Supra, p. 264, n. 41.
[106] Recall Chief Justice Chase's estimate, as expressed in his letter to

Governor Patton, supra, pp. 311–12.
[107] Cong. Globe, 39–2, 250, 536, 594, 816, 817.

lightly as an interesting bit of Stevensiana. At best, its author could not look for enactment before, say, March 1. Yet it would have set the election of delegates on the first Tuesday in May (the seventh)—or, that failing, the third Monday of that month. Only those few weeks were allowed for organizing, nominating and campaigning within the innovated electorate of white Unionists—and Negroes, mostly freedmen—and the penitents from the Confederate ranks. (These reluctant ones, to win remission, would have had to go to a "court of record of the United States"—which in practice would mean travelling to the place where, and at a time when, the United States District Judge held court, and there taking oath and producing such evidence by ever-loyal persons as would satisfy the court that the applicant was so entitled. How he might have fared thereafter in his home community, *quaere*.)

When Stevens introduced his substitute on January 3, he said that the revolution begun by secession must not be suffered "to subside without erecting this nation into a perfect Republic."[108] But Congress did not pursue this option. Neither did it pursue Ashley's more elaborate scheme, offered as a substitute for Stevens' measure.[109]

IV. Next came the "Military Bill," H.R. 1143, reflecting Stevens' success within the Joint Committee: military districts would be established, and the commander would be charged to "protect all persons," "to suppress insurrection, disorder, and violence, and to punish, or cause to be punished" disturbers of the peace and criminals. There was no provision for reconstruction—nothing beyond what the preamble vaguely implied by its declaration that peace and good order must be enforced in the "so-called States until loyal and republican State governments can be legally established." It was a bill that led to nowhere.

Thanks to the House Democrats, Stevens was able to defeat the attempt to add the Bingham-Blaine amendment providing for a State's escape and restoration.

Had the Democrats' strategy succeeded, their party could have said: the "Radicals" who dominated the 39th Congress offered an Amendment that can never be adopted, and then became hopelessly demoralized—all because they refused to obey the Constitution's plain statement that each State shall have Senators and Representatives. When secession was abandoned and slavery was abolished, nothing more could justly be demanded. And the latest of Radical follies is this regime of military satraps.

Responsible men in Congress apprehended that if the 39th Congress expired with nothing better than the enactment of the Military Bill, it might result that the South would live under it indefinitely—and not too unwillingly, inasmuch as the exclusion of the freedmen from the

---

[108] Ibid., 251.   [109] Supra, p. 268.

political system could thus be maintained. The Southern way of life need not have been disturbed: the commander would have no mandate to subvert the existing regime—the freedmen had no political rights for him to enforce; he was simply to suppress disorder if it occurred, and to see that crimes were punished, with resort to military commissions if shortcomings of the local authorities made that seem necessary.

Prevailing Republican sentiment was that the 39th Congress must not end with so poor an accomplishment.

V. The Louisiana Bill was designed for that State alone. Because Southern loyalists called for its application elsewhere, and in this found some Congressional support, H.R. 1162 was soon thought of as the model for reconstructing—if, with regard to any other State, Congress saw fit to oust the existing all-white regime and transfer government into the hands of local Unionists.

Louisiana was a special case. New Orleans had been occupied by federal forces in May 1862. The people had abolished slavery in 1864, by the very first sentence in their new constitution. Since March 1864 there had been an elected governor loyal to the Union (even though ex-rebels had been capturing other offices). Free men of color had long been a substantial component of the population.

Under these circumstances, the bill would establish a reconstructed State government under officers who could take the iron-clad oath, with an electorate limited to Unionists, white and black, and private soldiers who had served unwillingly in the Confederate army. State judges must have been ever-loyal; jurors must meet the qualifications of electors. This gave promise that Unionists, including Negroes, would receive justice. Even so, as a further precaution, the military commander would be charged with an extraordinary responsibility in this field.[110]

While the House readily passed the Louisiana Bill, and some Senators spoke warmly of it, even if it had been enacted, still for nine other States the Military Bill would have been demanded in order to protect Unionists. Presumably in some States this need would have been protracted.

The attractiveness of the Louisiana Bill lay in its presenting a well-designed method for establishing a civil government under Unionist officers. It is no wonder that Southern loyalists wanted Congress to turn things upside down and place them on top. But before that could safely be attempted in any State, Congress needed to be satisfied that the plan would be supported by well-disposed men, substantial and numerous enough to perform the duties of State and local office, to provide acceptable jurors, and generally to carry on an effective administration in an unfriendly environment. The idea of governing by loyal men, when

---

[110] Supra, pp. 291–92.

faced squarely, involved the formidable task of finding sheriffs and justices of the peace, clerks, coroners, treasurers, assessors and collectors, and election officers, who besides having such loyalty must at least be literate.

Senator Wilson of Massachusetts, who at this period proved to be quite fair-minded, spoke hopefully in favor of applying the method of the Louisiana Bill. But first, he wanted to amend it "so as to make it equal and just," "so as to extend suffrage to the mass of the people in that State . . . ." Then "I want to try the experiment during the next few months . . . where we have a loyal Governor . . . ," "where we have a strong, earnest, and devoted class of Union men," and where offices could be filled by men "who, if not entirely loyal, are earnest men and will do justice." If successful, this would be "of incalculable value to the cause of the Union, . . . of liberty, and . . . of justice . . . ."[111]

This experimental proposal for Louisiana was the best scheme that Congress was able to devise for protecting Unionists from abuse by ex-rebels through the agency of civil courts and for transferring power forthwith to loyal civil officers.

The Senate, realizing that it must deal with the general problem, put the Louisiana Bill aside and turned its attention to the Military Bill—adding to it a method for reconstruction applicable to all the Southern States.

VI. This review of options ends with the course that Congress did adopt—by the Act of March 2, 1867, as supplemented by the Act of March 23. This provided a method of restoration, far more effective than Bingham's too-trustful proposal,[112] yet not so drastic as to place the Unionists in power. Having become convinced that the existing all-white regimes must be broken—that those who had made the war could not be permitted to defeat adequate guaranties for the future—Congress now called *all* adult male citizens to participate in framing a new constitution, excepting from the call only those who, having held public office, had thereafter joined in the rebellion.[113] This was far more generous to ex-rebels than the Louisiana Bill.

Registration and voting in this great constituent effort would be of critical importance. Congress was not content to entrust this business to the all-white governments in office. Neither did it turn it over to Southern loyalists. Recall Blaine's words: "no one in possession or out

---

[111] Cong. Globe, 39–2, 1511. Feb. 18, 1867.

[112] Supra, pp. 263, 269.

[113] Substantially those disqualified from holding office by Sec. 3 of the Fourteenth Amendment—conjecturally, say eighteen thousand.

Supra, ch. 6, n. 26. Bingham, who had opposed such exclusion, estimated that "not more than twenty-five thousand, all told" out of a million and a quarter in ten States, were disfranchised. Cong. Globe, 40–1, 542. July 9, 1867.

of possession is to be prejudiced by any action of ours"; "we intend to secure to everybody . . . an even start . . . ."[114] The military commander—who by the Act of March 2 had been given only a mission to protect against disorder and injustice—was by the Supplementary Act charged with conducting the registration and elections.

By reason of Sumner's success in the Republican caucus,[115] Congress prescribed that the constitution give the suffrage to all adult males, without regard to color, "except such as may be disfranchised for participation in the rebellion, or for felony at common law." Doubtless he was right in saying that if Congress did not lay down that rule in advance, the matter would be agitated in every village from the Potomac to the Rio Grande. (In retrospect, it seems fair to suppose that it would have been bandied about, much as Negro testimony had been a year and a half earlier. Even so, conservative delegates elected in pursuance of the statutes might have affected to ignore this prescription on the ground that in their view it was patently unconstitutional.[116] Encouraged by Democratic gains in Northern elections, they would be trusting that what Congress had enacted would not prove the last word.)

Refraining from measures that would have made a clean sweep of ex-rebels in office, Congress chose rather to continue the existing governments for the time being, as "provisional only, and in all respects subject to the paramount authority of the United States at any time to abolish, modify, control or supersede the same . . . ."[117] But in each State there would be the military commander, charged "to protect all persons in their rights." The President's veto of March 2, showing Jeremiah Black's gift for heightened statement, said that the commander would have the power "of an absolute monarch. His will is to take the place of all law."[118] But then Attorney General Stanbery gave an opinion on June 12, 1867, showing what that conservative lawyer could do by strict construction: he advised that it was merely a power "to sustain the existing frame of social order and civil rule, and not a power to introduce military rule in its place. In effect, it is a police power . . . ," to be used only in a contingency where a State had failed.[119]

Obviously these two Executive constructions were miles apart. One, or both, must be wrong.[120]

When in the same State there was a government that was "provi-

---

114 Supra, p. 319.
115 Supra, p. 300.
116 Infra, p. 426.
117 Made express by the Shellabarger amendment, supra, p. 305.
118 Supra, p. 308.
119 12 Ops. Atty. Gen. 182.
120 The *Cincinnati Enquirer* (a leading Democratic organ) pronounced both to be right, and elucidated: "The President interpreted the law according to its political intention . . . ," while the Attorney General was in duty bound to "interpret it according to its legal intention . . . ." June 20, 1867.

sional only," and also an agent of the "paramount" government, charged with accomplishing certain results, there was the possibility of collision.[121] This became a likelihood if there were not on both sides a purpose to make a success of the statutory scheme. Surely the agent of the government that was paramount would not be bound to accept the views of the government that was provisional on, say, what respect was to be paid to the Reconstruction Act itself. Surely the paramount representative charged to protect all persons in their rights was not necessarily constrained by the opinion of a provisional judge concerning what those rights were—for example, under the Civil Rights Act. If, notwithstanding disagreement, the officer of the provisional government went right on governing according to his own views, what was the agent of the paramount government to do? The Attorney General, in the opinion cited above, held that the commander had no authority to remove a State officer, or to suspend him from his functions, or to control the administration of the laws. Also, that in so far as civil rights came "within the cognizance of civil courts as contradistinguished from criminal courts," they were of no concern to the commander. He must not interfere when State courts selected jurors according to the old rules, giving no effect to the Civil Rights Act. In short, the commander could touch no function of the State "save only its criminal jurisdiction," and that only "when a necessity for such interference may happen to arise."

By the Supplementary Act, certain categories of participants in the rebellion were excluded from voting. In many instances it would be a nice question whether an individual came within the ban. (For example, had he been "an executive or judicial officer in any State" by reason of holding some municipal post, or by being a notary public, or an attorney? How much was embraced in "giving aid or comfort to the enemies of the United States"?) The district commanders raised questions, and the Attorney General gave two opinions to serve as guides.[122]

---

[121] General J. M. Schofield, on assuming command in the First District on March 13, by Order No. 1 called upon all officers of the Provisional Government of Virginia to continue to perform their duties, according to law; it was desirable that the military power "be exercised only so far as may be necessary to accomplish the objects for which that power has been conferred"; he appealed to the people of Virginia, and especially to magistrates and other civil officers, "to render the exercise of this power as slight as possible" by strict obedience to the laws and by the impartial administration of justice. Ann. Cyc. 1867, 757-58.

Other district commanders issued similar statements.

[122] 12 Ops. Atty. Gen. 141, May 24, 1867; ibid., 182, June 12, 1867. His views were examined at length in the Cabinet. Johnson Papers, L.C., record votes given "In Cabinet, June 18, 1867." This appeared in the press: *New York Tribune*, June 21. Welles' *Diary*, III, 107, 109-14. By direction of the Presi-

The statutory boards of registration, said the Attorney General, had no authority to inquire into an applicant's qualifications; if he took the oath he must be registered—with no sanction other than the possibility of an indictment for perjury.

To overcome the Attorney General's opinions and to remove obstructions, Congress passed a Second Supplementary Act, on July 19, 1867.[123] This affirmed the power of a district commander to suspend or remove from office whenever that appeared necessary for the proper administration of the statute; removals already made were confirmed. Boards of registration were expressly authorized to make inquiry and to determine an applicant's qualification to vote.

It was not that Congress had been legislating carelessly, that this Second Supplementary Act was required: a thousand columns of close print in the Congressional Globe bear evidence to the contrary. The trouble was that, once again, what it hoped to achieve had been checkmated; and, to avoid frustration, Congress must go still deeper into an unwelcome situation.

If Congress had seen fit to legislate for the South on the principles of the Louisiana Bill, doubtless collisions between civil and military authorities would have been very largely avoided. Ex-rebels would have been governed by loyalists. In court, they would have faced iron-clad judges and Unionist jurors selected without regard to color. If the commander, charged to "support" these civil authorities, had ever had occasion to act under his duty to "insure" "equal justice" and "impartial enforcement" of the laws, it might well have been to come to the aid of ex-rebels.

Experience demonstrates that it is always a perplexing and touchy undertaking when the United States Government must step in to secure to its citizens the enjoyment of their rights in the face of hostile forces entrenched behind local law and custom. This is true even when those rights have been fully established by the Supreme Court and when President and Congress are united in a determination to make them respected. How much more trying was the situation in 1867. Congress must reckon with a President who had met every critical measure with a veto, and who, while adhering to his duty to enforce the statutes, would yet give them the narrowest construction. The Court had not placed its authority behind the statutes: indeed it was widely believed to stand ready to condemn the entire effort. State officers were not merely evading federal laws by subterfuge: at critical junctures they proclaimed

---

dent, the substance of the Attorney General's opinions was communicated by the War Department to

Department commanders on June 20. Ann. Cyc. 1867, 739.
[123] 15 Stat. 14.

them to be unconstitutional and refused obedience. What Congress did in the prosecution of its effort to restore the Union on the basis of the Fourteenth Amendment is entitled to a far more discriminating consideration than it has generally received.

VIEWS OF BRYANT'S *NEW YORK EVENING POST*

BECAUSE HISTORICAL JUDGMENTS about the Court have reflected stubborn prepossession about Reconstruction, it will be useful once more to sweep over the field—this time to observe how William Cullen Bryant's *New York Evening Post* viewed the action of the 39th Congress. That journal, of slender circulation, has not been widely accessible to historians (as examination of Gregory's *Union List of Newspapers*, and *Newspapers on Microfilm* will show), and has not been quoted as commonly as Horace Greeley's strong-voiced *Tribune*, Henry J. Raymond's *Times*, Manton Marble's *World*, James Gordon Bennett's inconstant *Herald*, or Samuel Bowles' widely distributed *Springfield Republican*. William Cullen Bryant (1794–1878), however, as Allan Nevins wrote for the *Dictionary of American Biography*,

> brought to his editorial chair some qualities which no editor of his time possessed in equal degree. In culture and scholarship he surpassed Raymond, Bowles, and Greeley, while in dignity and adherence to moral principle he was far in advance of Bennett and Dana.[124] Few men of his time did half so much to lift journalism from a vulgar calling to a place of high honor and national influence. . . .

His editorials "were for the few and not the many."

One does not need to establish that the author of "Thanatopsis" was a man of pure spirit. A like fidelity to high ideals must be accorded to Parke Godwin (1816–1904), Bryant's editorial associate, son-in-law, and eventually his biographer. It is enlightening to observe how these men, with fixed ideas about public policy, reacted to the problems before the 39th Congress.

Bryant had been ardently anti-slavery. In his support of the Civil War he had been on the radical side, adhering rather to his friend Chase than to Lincoln. Johnson's approach to restoration, however, received the *Post*'s blessing. In a letter of December 25, 1865, Godwin assured the President of "hearty approval" of his course and his sentiments.

---

[124] Charles A. Dana in 1868 acquired the *New York Sun* and made it a colorful journal, with low price and wide popular appeal.

343

Our republican friends are admirable in their purposes, which are, to protect loyalty and liberty, but they must not be allowed to override that peculiarity of our system which makes the States equal self-governing communities.[125]

Bryant was prominent in the mass meeting of February 22, 1866, called to demonstrate approval of the President at a moment when his veto of the Freedmen's Bureau Bill was widening his breach with Congress.[126]

When on July 16, 1866, the Second Freedmen's Bureau Bill became law, notwithstanding another veto, the *Post* said that the President's objections were still valid.[127] The statute's authorization of "military protection" and "military jurisdiction over all cases and questions concerning the free enjoyment" of the freedman's rights seemed "so pernicious and so full of danger to the liberties of the country" that it would be "better to suffer some temporary inconvenience . . . ." If any citizen was denied justice in a State court he could resort to a court of the United States for protection under the Civil Rights Act (which had become law on April 9, over the President's veto).

It may be said that the blacks do not know how to do this, or are too poor and ignorant and friendless to do it. But they are not friendless; let private effort and private agencies be employed to help them, if that is necessary. . . . The government ought not to do this. . . .[128]

The editorial warned that resort to "paternal government" was the worst of expedients:

If men are to be fed by the government because they are starving, or to be clothed by it because they are in rags, or are to be coddled and specially protected by it because they are ignorant, then

---

[125] Johnson Papers, L.C.

[126] Bryant and other leading citizens of New York (David Dudley Field and William M. Evarts among them) were to carry the record to Washington. But in the light of the President's wild extemporaneous outburst in Washington on that same evening, a less conspicuous transmittal was adopted, and the President's invitation to dinner was declined. Francis B. Cutting and Henry Clews to the President, Mar. 5, 1866. Johnson Papers, L.C.

On the significance of this veto, see supra, pp. 126–27.

[127] Leading editorial on July 18.

[128] Bryant had taken part in the philanthropic support of the mission for the relief and education of the Negroes at Port Royal, South Carolina—in 1862, after landowners had withdrawn as Union forces occupied that area. Willie Lee Rose, *Rehearsal for Reconstruction. The Port Royal Experiment* (New York: Random House, Vintage Books, 1967), 42n.

government simply offers a premium to idleness, ignorance and unthrift. . . . The American doctrine is that if a man cannot take care of himself—the laws being just and equal—it is because he does not use the faculties God has given to all men, and it is therefore right that he should suffer. Neither the negroes nor the manufacturers have any right to special protection. . . .

Bryant was at that moment president of the American Free Trade League. In his aversion to paternalism, he viewed protection of the freedmen and protection of "infant industries" in the same aspect. The editorial next following was an attack on the protective tariff.

By September—when Johnson's "Swing around the Circle" had produced revulsion, and early elections foreshadowed a popular vindication of Republican leadership[129]—the editors were put on the defensive. "The President and the People" regretted Johnson's vituperation and his attachment to Copperheads: instead of scolding the Radicals he ought to disarm them by wiser conduct.[130] What the country needed was not more action by Congress, but greater individual initiative to enforce "dozens of laws on the statute book unexecuted." Southern loyalists, instead of coming North with their complaints, ought to resort to their local courts and have their assailants put under bond to keep the peace.[131] If men would only use the Civil Rights Act, would not liberty be secure everywhere? The object of the Constitution was to *limit* government: now that the war was won, the nation had a glorious opportunity to adhere to constitutional forms and to avoid new legislation.[132]

"The Constitutional Amendment—A Few Words to Southern Men," on September 24, said that the Amendment was undoubtedly right and just; even Section 3's disqualification of rebel leaders was not too severe if they escaped trial for treason. The editors still held that Southern delegations should be seated at once. However, the North would insist upon ratification before readmission—but also would insist on readmission if the Southern States would now ratify. Make a virtue of necessity: the Amendment would be adopted "in a very few years" in consequence of the admission of new States in the West, even without Southern ratifications.[133] Returning to the theme next day, the editors said that if only the Southern States would promptly ratify, and thereby clear the way for the consideration of the nation's economic problems,

---

[129] Supra, p. 179.
[130] Sept. 11, 1866.
[131] Referring to the Southern Loyalists' Convention, opening on Sept. 3 at Philadelphia. Supra, pp. 180–81.

[132] Editorials on Sept. 7, 10, 11, 20, 21.
[133] Compare this wild prediction with the estimate of the *New York World*, supra, p. 255.

the country would not forget what it owed them for so doing. The President would act wisely if he used his influence to that end.[134]

When in September the South Carolina legislature passed a statute substantially repeating Section 1 of the federal Civil Rights Act of April 9, the *Post* hailed this as a great event, confirming its faith "in the reforming influence of free institutions."[135] The federal statute "is no longer necessary in that State; the local laws henceforth will protect the freedman." Go on, it urged, and ratify the Amendment.[136]

From October 1866 to August 1867, Bryant was in Europe and Godwin was in charge.

Brutal facts now began to challenge editorial precept. In Mississippi a freedman, James Lewis, had been convicted of carrying a firearm; in default of payment of a fine of one dollar and costs, he had been committed to jail for five days and, still failing, would be hired to any white man who would make payment.[137] Habeas corpus was sought on the ground that the statute, in denying to Negroes the rights enjoyed by whites, was invalid under the federal Civil Rights Act; but Handy, C.J., to whom the application was made, held the federal Act unconstitutional.[138] The editor demanded, Is this case to end there? Quite likely Lewis did not have the means to go up to the Supreme Court:

> We hope the friends of equal rights will at once raise a sum of money to defray the necessary expense of employing the ablest counsel, to carry the case of Lewis at once before the Supreme Court of the United States. If that court decides the Civil Rights act to be con-

---

[134] "Complete the Work of Reconstruction," *New York Evening Post*, Sept. 25.

[135] The governor, having called a special session, observed in his message of September 4 that if such a law were enacted, the State would get rid of the military courts then being held under the Freedmen's Bureau Act. S. C. House J., Extra Sess. 1866, 9. Act. No. 4798, to declare the Rights of Persons la'ely known as Slaves and as Free Persons of Color, became law on September 21. Stats. at Large, Acts of General Assembly at the Extra Session of 1866, 393. In consequence, the General Commanding the Department of the South directed that the military courts be discontinued and that all cases be turned over to the State courts. Annual Report of October 30, 1866. Cong. Globe, 39–2, App., 34, 36.

[136] "Another Word to the South," *New York Evening Post*, Sept. 26.

[137] This was in accord with Secs. 1 and 5 of the Act to punish certain offenses [by Negroes], of November 29, 1865—a part of the "Black Code." Miss. Laws of 1865, 165. Supra, p. 114.

[138] In the *New York Times* of October 26, a correspondent reported that the Freedmen's Bureau at Jackson had caused the writ to be sued out, and had "employed eminent counsel . . . ." On the same page the *Times* set out Judge Handy's opinion. He quoted Kent's *Commentaries* on the status of members of the African race. (See supra, p. 334.) He held that the Thirteenth Amendment merely put an end to "slavery" and that the power of Congress went no further than to make abolition effective.

stitutional, it will settle a most important question, and the law will then be enforced as a matter of course, everywhere, without delays or appeals to state courts. So long as the matter is left in doubt, there will be appeals, loss of time, and injustice.[139]

Godwin was not simply a man of letters: he had actually been admitted to the Kentucky bar. And yet he remained so credulous as to suppose that as soon as the Civil Rights Act—on which he had been hanging his editorials—was sustained by the Supreme Court, the statute would be observed, "of course, everywhere." Every citizen's federal rights should be enforced, even "if to do so required the exercise of the whole power of the United States government."

Presently it came to national attention that in Maryland, upon conviction of a crime, Negroes were being "sold . . . for such term as a white man for the same offence would be sentenced to a penitentiary" —in accord with long-standing provisions of the Maryland Code.[140] Shocked, the *Post* demanded, What had the federal District Attorney been doing? Congress should investigate.[141]

When the annual reports of the army's department commanders were published for the incoming Session of Congress,[142] the editor took note of what those from the South had to say about the situation of the freedmen. These were even-tempered factual accounts—telling where conditions showed improvement as well as where they were bad. An editorial commented:

> The most terrible thing about the southern question is that the white people of that region appear to have no sense of justice, truth or fair-dealing, where the negro is concerned. . . .
> It is not that we read there of frequent or cruel outrages, but

---

[139] Editorial of Oct. 18, 1866, *New York Evening Post.*

[140] Art. 30, Secs. 194, 195.

[141] "Slavery in Maryland," Dec. 22, 1866. Representative Schenck had already drawn the practice to the attention of the House on December 17; Sumner raised it in the Senate on January 3, 1867. Each House referred to its Judiciary Committee. Cong. Globe, 39–2, 153–54, 238–39. Reverdy Johnson acknowledged that some judges, "conscientiously, I am satisfied," did adjudge "the sale of black people into a limited slavery," P. 1380, Feb. 15. H.R. 956, a joint resolution declaring the meaning of the Thirteenth Amendment, was introduced by Kas-

son of Iowa on January 7, 1867; his purpose was to show "that no such thing as selling a man into slavery" by judgment of a court "can possibly exist in the present condition of the Constitution," and to "strengthen the grounds on which the United States judiciary can decide this to be the right construction . . . ." The House passed this, by vote of 121 to 25, on January 8. Cong. Globe, 39–2, 324, 344–48. In the Senate, the Judiciary Committee thought that "the whole subject is covered by the civil rights bill"; accordingly consideration was "postponed indefinitely" by the Senate. P. 1866, Feb. 27.

[142] Cong. Globe, 39–2, App., 19–37.

these reports show the existence, in the South, of a contemptuous, malignant, beastly spirit of inhumanity on the part of white men towards the blacks, and towards Union men, which would be incredible, were it not presented in the calm and business-like official reports of commanding generals. As will be seen by the extracts we make below, where this spirit rules, laws are useless, courts and juries are a farce, and constitutions are as blank paper. . . .

In a community thus monstrously debased, civil government becomes impossible. . . .

Among the extracts was this passage from the report for the Department of the South:

These irregularities do not occur where persons of consideration are sufficiently interested in the proceedings to insist upon the proper action. . . .[143]

The editor commented:

It is notorious that the mass of the southern whites are, to an almost incredible degree, under the influence of the planter class.

The editorial ended with an appeal that funds be subscribed, counsel retained, and "at least one case . . . in every state" carried to the Supreme Court.[144]

When the President's message to the Second Session disclosed not the least willingness to bow to the recent elections, the *Post* said that a statesman of broader mind would have yielded personal opinion, and would have urged the Southern States to accept the Fourteenth Amendment, as they had accepted the Thirteenth at his bidding.[145] When the Houses passed the District of Columbia Elective Franchise Bill, an editorial praised Congress and regretted that Conservative Republican Senators had seen fit to vote against it. Manhood suffrage, it said, had become an essential development of American republicanism. This action of Congress was "a final settlement of the position and principles of the parties of the future."[146]

An editorial on "Congress and the Southern States," on December 18, said:

It is strange the Southern men do not see that to reject the Amendment is to subject themselves to harder terms. Already several

---

[143] Ibid., App., 34, 36.
[144] "The 'Persons of Consideration' in the South," *New York Evening Post*, Dec. 7, 1866.

[145] "The President's Message," *New York Evening Post*, Dec. 4.
[146] Dec. 14, 1866. The bill became law, over a veto, on January 8. 14 Stat. 375.

plans of reconstruction are broached . . . . Congress will not wait very long. As soon as it is satisfied that the Southern States will not have the Amendment, it will proceed to other measures.

It is useless to argue against such a course; the people in the recent elections have demanded and justified it. It is no use to show that the whole proceeding is extra-constitutional for the people reply that defiant and unpunished traitors shall not take advantage of constitutional forms to gain unfair advantage; they will not have such a condition of things as makes a vote in the South represent twice as much as in the North; they will in some way exclude from power the leaders and originators of the rebellion . . . .

If the Southern States must now be reorganized, Congress should see to it that *all* of the people participate.[147]

On December 20 and 24 the *Post* repeated its call: let the Southern States accept the Amendment before it is too late.

With the new year came a new tone of determination: "the insane and pig-headed folly of the southern leaders," encouraged by the President, was condemned; this spirit *"cannot be trifled with."*[148] The President's plan—*if* it had been in wiser hands, *if* he had insisted on universal liberty and equal rights, *if* he had acted in accord with the wisest leaders of his party—would (the editor believed) have sufficed. But that had fallen through, by the President's own fault. What next? The people wanted *no half measures*: their desire now was

that [Congress] shall reconstruct, beginning at the bottom, and that it shall devise such a measure as shall secure equal justice and equal rights in the southern states.

This was strictly in conformity with the Constitution: *Congress* must guarantee a republican form of government.[149]

Comment on *Milligan* and the *Test Oath Cases* was in a low key, and undistinguished. Presently the *Post* said that

While hasty and extreme men show considerable vexation at some recent decisions by the Supreme Court, the more temperate

---

[147] Next day, December 19, the *World* replied in an editorial, "Is the Constitution Obsolete?" It answered, Certainly not—and that it was strengthened in this belief by the Supreme Court's decision in *Ex parte* Milligan. "The country has everything to hope from the firmness, independence, and fidelity . . . of that august tribunal." Congress could easily pass its reconstruction bills over a veto: "But when the Court declares them null . . . , it will be the duty of the President to use the whole army and navy, if necessary, to make [those solemn judgments] respected."

[148] *New York Evening Post*, Jan. 5, 8, 1867.

[149] "What Next?", *New York Evening Post*, Jan. 5, 1867.

and sensible part of the community, we are glad to see, accept them as inevitable, because in strict conformity with the Constitution. Of course, when we accept the decisions of a court we do not take them with the mere extra judicial opinions which may be added to them, and which possess no authority or binding force.

It added that

At the same time there is undoubtedly considerable uneasiness in the country at what is called the attitude of the Supreme Court, and impatience at what is felt by some to be its restraint of possible Congressional action. . . .

It was not surprising, said the editor, that Copperheads sought and won some decisions where the Government had gone too far: if the Republicans were as active in suing to enforce the Civil Rights Act, they might find Supreme Court decisions on *their* side.[150]

The *Post* followed the legislative history leading to the Act of March 2 in sympathetic editorials and in remarkably useful dispatches from Washington. An example of the latter is this comment on the Sherman substitute as passed by the Senate on February 17: the most valid objection—subsequently cured by the Supplementary Act of March 23—was that it did not command any action within the Southern States. This point was made by Southern men, *not* loyalists:

These men say, "We cannot be expected to cut off our own heads, but we are willing that you should order them cut off. . . . If you want our state reconstructed on the basis of universal suffrage say so, order it done, prescribe the manner in which it shall be done, and then we can do it. But for us to volunteer action in that direction would be to excite a storm against ourselves."[151]

The editor hoped that the Republicans in Congress would stand firm on the Sherman substitute—"this sensible and generally acceptable bill"—and would overpower Stevens' opposition; there were signs that they were getting tired of this coalition of "a few impracticables in their own ranks and the democrats." The President, if he was wise, would seek to ally himself with the main body of Republicans "in carrying out a suitable and safe plan of reconstruction."[152] It was important for the public good that he *accept* it, in the right spirit, and thereby cause

---

150 "The Supreme Court," Jan. 16.
151 *Evening Post*, Feb. 20. Dispatch of Feb. 19.

152 "Reconstruction—Who Stands in the Way?", Feb. 20.

Southern opposition to disappear.[153] "What is there in this bill that he ought not to approve?" Reviewing both military and civil features, no valid objection was perceived.[154]

When the veto message came, the *Post* said that in objecting to the setting aside of the Southern regimes the President was merely repeating arguments decisively rejected by the country.

> He seems to forget that in doing this Congress has done exactly what he did himself in ignoring existing governments which were not authorized by the Constitution, while it has used its rightful powers of legislation in doing what he assumed to do without constitutional powers—legislation being the exclusive prerogative of Congress.[155]

The President's message claimed that the bill was condemned by what the Court had said in *Ex parte Milligan*: but the editorial replied,

> The *dicta* of the Supreme Court will not be regarded as decisive of the question on which he quotes them. They are but opinions, and are opposed by the contrary opinions of many judicial persons of the highest standing. . . .

On March 7, in "A Word to the People of the South," the editor hoped that sensible counsels there would lead to early reorganization. The more the new Act was considered,

> the wiser all its provisions will appear, and the more completely fitted to put an end to the present ruinous state of affairs in the southern states and build up new governments there on the safe foundation of justice.

In the days that followed, the *Post* noted with approval that white and colored men were meeting together to prepare for action under the statute;[156] it said that some members of Congress were "doing too much" when they called for further requirements,[157] and thereby supplied Southern disorganizers with a plausible argument. It hoped that the Republican party would build up a strong Southern wing; a two-party system there would lead to free discussion and a quick advance in liberal sentiments.[158]

---

[153] *New York Evening Post*, Feb. 21.

[154] "Why the President Ought to Sign the Bill," *New York Evening Post*, Feb. 23.

[155] *New York Evening Post*, Mar. 4.

[156] Ibid., Mar. 8, 21: Apr. 24.

[157] See supra, pp. 327–33.

[158] *New York Evening Post*, March 7, 8.

The importance of reliable machinery for carrying out the Congressional plan, as provided in the Supplementary Act, was the subject of another editorial. New voters would need "the most faithful instruction and the most impartial counsel as to their rights and duties"; no person should be appointed as a register "unless his personal sentiments are known to be fully in favor of the Reconstruction act," to make doubly sure that the purpose of Congress was carried out. It was vitally important

> that the registry shall be perfect and complete; that all the lawful voters shall have their names entered; that none shall be deterred by fear or rejected by prejudice; so that each state shall be reorganized by the expressed will of the whole people—those only excepted whose crimes properly exclude them.[159]

The editor's propositions should be considered reflectively. Should "personal sentiments" in favor of the Act be required of all employed in carrying it into effect? What of an agent whose personal sentiments caused him to favor "great principles of American liberty" different from what Congress had in view?[160] Should it suffice that the agent, without regard to personal sentiment, would faithfully seek to achieve the Congressional purpose? After the Attorney General had minimized the statute,[161] Congress enacted that its agents, without being bound by any such opinion, would apply the Act "liberally."[162] The questions are enough to show that, under the very special circumstances, the path of duty was not plain, or easy to follow. History has praised those officers who most tempered the wind to the lambs recently shorn of power; those who showed special concern for black lambs have not fared so well.[163]

Another problem, presently to be met: the *Post* said that lawful voters should not be deterred by fear. Suppose that, in a town where dominant sentiment was that Congressional reconstruction should be

---

[159] Ibid., April 4.

[160] The phrase comes from General Winfield S. Hancock's order of November 29, 1867, on assuming command of the Fifth Military District. Edward McPherson, *The Political History of the United States of America during the Period of Reconstruction*, 3d ed. (Washington: James J. Chapman, 1880), 324. In context, the order was so much in accord with President Johnson's sentiments that on December 18 he sent a message to Congress, suggesting "some public recognition of General Hancock's patriotic conduct." Cong. Globe, 40–2, 256, 264.

In the Democratic National Convention of 1868, General Hancock stood highest on several ballots. In 1876 he received 58 votes. In 1880 he was nominated for President on the third ballot.

[161] Supra, p. 340.

[162] Second Supplementary Act of July 19, 1867. 15 Stat. 14.

[163] See infra, pp. 501–04.

frustrated, the editor of the leading newspaper called upon "every decent white man" to "STAY AWAY FROM THE POLLS," and offered a reward for the name of any "sneak" who voted; "we shall publish the names of these voters if we can obtain them." Whether each voter was free to act would have consequence for all people within the State, and was vital to the Congressional purpose. Was the editor within his rights?[164]

In "Progress of Reconstruction. An Historical Review," on June 26, the *Post* remarked how some leaders in the South were facilitating and some were obstructing the Congressional plan. It made this observation:

> With the military rule placed over them the people of the ten states have generally expressed satisfaction; and the acts of the district commanders have usually been approved, as tending to promote peace and prosperity. Indeed, a large class have declared a preference for the continuation of military rule rather than accept the reconstruction which is its alternative. . . .

The last sentence is to be noted: rather, that is, than accept Negro suffrage. The veto message of March 2 said that "No master ever had a control so absolute over his slave" as this bill gave to the commanders. Black would resume that line of argument when he came to challenge the statute before the Court.[165] He knew the weakest point in Congressional Reconstruction, and was making the most of it. But one should know that Black's arguments were chosen for argument's sake—not as candid submissions in the pursuit of truth. Actually, Southern leaders most bitterly opposed to Reconstruction preached that it was preferable to live under the statute's military regime indefinitely—"two years longer, or, if need be, ten years"[166]—rather than to have civil government with universal suffrage. Recall Reverdy Johnson's word of caution: he wanted reconstruction carried out even if it might not be based upon "the will of all," lest the people, holding out, might "become attached to military rule."[167]

One concluding selection, the editor's estimate as he looked back upon "The Thirty-Ninth Congress."[168] Many years later, as the Fourteenth Amendment came to be more deeply appreciated, the image of the First Session was enhanced, while the Second, because of its Reconstruction Act, has been seen darkly. But First and Second Session

---

[164] See infra, pp. 420–21.
[165] Infra, p. 452.
[166] B. F. Perry, letter in *Charleston Courier*, Apr. 19, 1867.

[167] Supra, p. 322.
[168] *New York Evening Post*, Mar. 5, 1867.

comprised the same people—and the editor saw them at closer range. He wrote:

> The Thirty-ninth Congress was an honest body of men. The number of men ruled by their private interests or subject to corrupt influences was uncommonly small. It was a sober and moral body— there were fewer habitual or occasional drunkards or profligates in it than in any Congress for the last dozen years. . . .

He could not say that it was "an able body"—"but it had true instincts . . . ."

> A very few ignorant and unscrupulous extremists, and men carried away by personal feeling and interest, helped to give the Congress a bad name by introducing wild and extreme measures, and by the use of violent and indecorous language. . . .

The 39th Congress was determined on general propositions but greatly divided on details.

> It was timid, yet as tenacious as though all its members had possessed the courage of Stevens. It had the reputation of extreme radicalism, but was in fact a singularly conservative body. . . .

It was commonly supposed that this Congress was controlled by Thad Stevens and Charles Sumner: in truth, they had had comparatively little power,

> and were perhaps oftener and more severely disappointed in getting their measures through, than any other members . . . . Mr. Stevens was called the leader of the House, but he led an army which refused to follow, except where it suited itself, and he had not unfrequently to depend upon the democrats to help him check or disable his own side.

Then came this judgment by an editor who in December 1865 had believed that the President was entitled to "hearty approval."

> On the question of reconstruction [Congress] was careful and hesitating; yet determined to come to some conclusion. The mass of its members sought to follow the country rather than to lead it; they came to Washington favoring the President's policy, but quickly discovered, what the country did not so soon know, that the conditions under which the policy would be safe and just could not be attained, but were forbidden by the manner in which the President was determined to administer it. It is now plain that Mr. Johnson

determined to abandon, not only the party which had elected him to office, but also the principles which it was supposed he had adopted when he permitted the Republican party to take him for its candidate. . . .

Reluctantly yielding to the logic of the facts by which the 39th Congress was controlled, the *Post* had come a long way in fifteen months.

THE CHIEF JUSTICE AND THE BANKRUPTCY ACT

ON MARCH 28, 1867, the unprincipled *New York Herald* posed a question:

Shall Chief Justice Chase be Impeached?

The occasion was his supposed refusal to make nominations for the several hundred appointments as register, under the Bankruptcy Act of March 2. This was some of the "patronage" mentioned above, as supposedly prompted by a Congressional desire to induce judicial acquiescence in setting aside the Constitution.[169]

Here is an incident that merits exploration: as an illustration of the confusion of governmental functions during the period of Reconstruction—as an unfortunate experience of a Justice's acceptance of an extrajudicial task—and for what it reveals about Salmon P. Chase.

Exercising its power to establish "uniform Laws on the subject of Bankruptcies throughout the United States,"[170] Congress had passed such a statute in 1800 and repealed it in 1803; it had passed another in 1841 and repealed it in 1843. In the 38th and 39th Congresses, a Select Committee under the leadership of Representative Thomas A. Jenckes of Rhode Island had matured a Bankruptcy Bill. As passed by the House on May 22, 1866, it provided that registers in bankruptcy, to assist the District Courts in the administration of the system, would be nominated by the Chief Justice.[171]

Normally such an appointment would be confided to the Judge of the District Court, since it was under his supervision that the register would work. Or it could be made by the Circuit Court, where the Justice assigned to that Circuit would preside. As Senator Fessenden commented,

Those in favor of having the appointments given to the district judges I suppose are those residing in districts where the district

---

[169] Supra, p. 325 and p. 259, n. 23.
[170] Constitution, Art. I, Sec. 8, cl. 4.
[171] Cong. Globe, 39–1, 2655, 2742.

judges are of their way of thinking, and those who want to give them to the circuit judges are those in districts where the circuit and not the district judges are of their way of thinking. Thus arises a controversy over a very small matter.[172]

But if it was made the duty of the Chief Justice to *nominate*, it would be of little moment which court made the formal appointment.

On January 19, 1867, Senator Poland, on behalf of the Judiciary Committee, moved to strike out the provision for nomination by the Chief Justice, which as the bill then stood would vest appointment in the District Court.[173] These registers, he said, would be "perhaps about as important in rank as deputy sheriffs, and it certainly seems to me to be very small business to be belittling the office of the Chief Justice. . . ." Reverdy Johnson, too, "thought it altogether unfit": to assign such business to the Chief Justice

> is calculated very materially to diminish the influence which he ought to have in the judgment of all the country—not of a party, but of all.

Hendricks of Indiana asked, How could the Chief Justice know anything about the qualifications of members of the various local bars?

On a division, however, the Committee's amendment failed: there were 14 yeas, 16 nays.[174]

Hendricks, for the committee, tried again on February 5. This time the division was 21 to 21: again the amendment failed.[175] The political significance of this patronage was not overlooked: the Democrats and the Conservative Republicans were among those who voted to strike.

As the bill became law on March 2, 1867, it provided

> That it shall be the duty of the judges of the district courts . . . to appoint in each congressional district . . . , upon the nomination and recommendation of the Chief Justice of the Supreme Court of the United States, one or more registers in bankruptcy, to assist the judge of the district court . . . .[176]

The Supreme Court was in recess from February 28 until April 1, 1867: hence communication between the Chief Justice (who remained in Washington) and his brethren was by letter.

---

[172] Cong. Globe, 39–2, 587. Jan. 19, 1867.
[173] Ibid., 587. Debated, 587–90.

[174] Ibid., 590.
[175] Ibid., 1011.
[176] 14 Stat. 517, 518.

VII: *Supplementary Legislation*

The Associate Justices were being asked to use their influence in the matter of nominations. Evidently Grier had written in that connection, as shown by Chase's reply on March 11:

> I have your letter and have put it on file. I do not yet know that I shall nominate anybody to the District Judges but rather think I shall, though I heartily wish the duty had been imposed on anybody else.
>
> I have made up my mind to require evidence on these points.
>
> 1. Competency as a lawyer.
> 2. Integrity as a man.
> 3. Capacity and industry as a business man.
>
> When more than one such is recommended I will make the best choice I can.[177]

At the same time he wrote to Justice Miller (and also to Swayne), asking an opinion:

> I want you to give me the benefit of your best judgment on the question, Can Congress Constitutionally authorize the nomination of Registers in Bankruptcy to the District Court by the Chief Justice or any Associate Justice of the Supreme Court? I have asked Swayne for his advice and as yet no one else beside yourself. I shall not, probably, act in any case before April, but shall be glad of your views as soon as you can consider the matter.
>
> I wish most heartily that Congress had put the duty of nomination on some one else; but am inclined to perform it, if the putting it on me is not unconstitutional.
>
> . . . [He had recovered from a "dreadful cold."] But my new duties have pressed me so much that I have had no time for study. I tried to get to the Capitol to-day and shut myself up, but could not make my escape till four this afternoon. I am writing in the Conference Room.[178]

There was, indeed, at least a semblance of constitutional difficulty, and other objections of great weight: that this business would consume time needed for judicial duties; that the Chief Justice really could not make well-informed selections; and that it gave him a large patronage which inevitably had partisan significance. Reverdy Johnson had mentioned the constitutional point during the second debate on deleting the provision:

---

[177] Chase Papers, L.C.
[178] Chase Papers, L.C.: Robert B. Warden, *An Account of the Private Life and Public Services of Salmon* | *Portland Chase* (Cincinnati, Ohio: Wilstach, Baldwin and Co., 1874), 653–54.

> The Constitution provides . . . that Congress may . . . vest the appointment [of inferior officers] in a head of a Department or in a court. There is no authority to vest it in any individual member of a court; but this clause, so far from vesting the appointment in the [district] courts . . . , gives them merely a negative upon the nomination of the Chief Justice. . . .

Quite aside from the provision being "perhaps liable to that constitutional objection," he opposed it "principally" on the ground that the District Courts could far more properly perform the duty.[179]

If Chase had been doubtful or unwilling upon any ground, he should have made timely objection. Surely if he had tried he could have brought about the deletion. Yet he had stood by while a monumental statute was being enacted, and now put it in jeopardy by an affectation of scruple and unwillingness. It seems significant that for counsel at that point he turned to the two members of the Court whose partisan sentiments (if they allowed them to enter) would be least disturbed by the practical results of the patronage.

Writing to a daughter, Chase complained—"Oh! horror"—that the parade of would-be registers began when his breakfast was scarcely finished: "many come to present their applications in person, & many friends come to support them."[180]

It had turned out to be "an elephant." That is what Justice Davis wrote to his brother-in-law, Judge Rockwell, explaining why he could be of no help in promoting a certain nomination.

> The Chief Justice unquestionably laments the action of Congress, but his associates have no personal interest in, except so far as it mingles the judiciary with appointments that must be more or less political. The Judges are recommending no one—taking no part or lot in the matter—and will not volunteer any recommendations. . . . It is announced today that the New York City appointments will be made in a few days. I asked Judge Nelson if he knew anything about them. He said nothing whatever. . . .
>
> I had for myself to establish a rule to recommend no one, although it has been in many instances painful to me to deny valuable friends. The reasons for refusal are obvious, & need not be stated. The Chf Jus. has drawn an "elephant" & has so found out. He ought to have known it in season to have arrested the provision in the Senate last winter, for he was advised in relation to it.
>
> The applications are exceedingly numerous. I understand that

---

[179] Cong. Globe, 39–2, 1011.

[180] To Nettie, Mar. 20. Chase Papers, L.C.

there are 4 or 5 clerks constantly employed arranging letters, and digesting every case. . . . The new Marshal of the Court—Col Parsons—a devoted friend of the Chief Justice, has the oversight of the matter. The machinery looks like that of a regular bureau.[181]

(For David Davis it was hard indeed to be unable to help a friend in search of an office. As he once reminded Jeremiah S. Black, "You know, My Dear Friend, that I esteem social fidelity as a very high virtue." This was in a letter in August 1867, supporting Ward Lamon, Davis' close friend and Black's law partner, in his aspiration to become Postmaster General upon an anticipated reorganization of Johnson's Cabinet.[182])

The Chief Justice did indeed lament—within three weeks—that he had ever become involved in this bankruptcy business. In following his unsuccessful effort to extricate himself one observes how, in consequence of his failure to make timely objection, difficulties became compounded.

The 40th Congress sat from March 4 to March 30, and then recessed to July 3.

On March 21, Senator Trumbull introduced S. 95, to repeal the clause requiring the nomination of registers by the Chief Justice; then appointments would be made by the District Court in its own discretion.

I will state that in introducing this bill I consider myself authorized to say that it meets the approval of the Chief Justice, who thinks that this is imposing an unusual burden upon him, and it is with his approbation . . . that I introduce it. . . . I shall desire to call it up as soon as an opportunity offers.[183]

But next day, when Trumbull sought an easy passage, Conkling made trouble. The latter had been a Senator for almost three weeks, and already had made his weight felt.[184] Now he moved to send S. 95 to the Judiciary Committee, of which he was a member. Trumbull, the chairman, had said that "it was informally considered" there; but that did not suit Conkling, who wanted to kill the bill. He said that the House (of which he had been a member) had "very carefully" provided for nomination by the Chief Justice, and would not now consent to a repeal. Able lawyers there had satisfied themselves that there was "no

---

181 Letter of Apr. 2. Davis Papers, Ill. State Hist. Soc.
182 Letter of Aug. 16. Davis Papers.

Supra, ch. 10, n. 271.
183 Cong. Globe, 40–1, 241.
184 Supra, pp. 322, 328.

question" of constitutionality. As to the supposed burden, he could not believe "that the selection . . . would occupy more than two days . . ."; the Chief Justice had simply to accept the names supplied by the Senators and Representatives concerned.[185]

By this suggestion, the Chief Justice's role would be reduced to serving as a mere conduit of political favors.

Roscoe Conkling is a man to watch: in 1873, upon Chase's death, President Grant gave him first refusal of the office of Chief Justice.

Reverdy Johnson replied. He said that he was "very anxious" that Trumbull's bill be passed.

> I see it stated that [the Chief Justice] has declined acting until the Supreme Court shall be in session. I infer from that . . . that he proposes to take the opinion of that court as to the constitutionality of this provision, and I am by no means certain that the judges will not hold that Congress have no authority to impose this duty upon any one of the judges. . . .

He recalled, without citing, the circumstances of *Hayburn's Case* in 1792,[186] where the Judges on circuit had held that it was not within the power of Congress to require the Judiciary to perform other than judicial duties—in that instance, to report on claims for pensions.

There was no office in the gift of the Government, he concluded, that required "more close and exclusive attention" than that of a Justice;

> I think their whole time ought to be taken in studying the great questions which they are called upon to decide, in becoming masters of jurisprudence in all its branches; and to place either of them in a position which apparently gives him political power is to injure the country and at the same time injure the judge. . . .[187]

Senator Edmunds seized upon the report that the Chief Justice would delay action until he could consult his brethren, and in ten minutes had magnified it into a grave and complicated constitutional crisis.

He said that, notwithstanding the objections he had felt about the constitutionality and propriety of imposing the duty upon the Chief Justice, that provision was a part of the law. Now it was reported that he refused to perform this "executive duty" until he had had a consultation, in private, with the other Justices.

---

[185] Cong. Globe., 40–1, 277–78.
Mar. 22.

[186] 2 Dall. 409.
[187] Cong. Globe, 40–1, 278.

I wish to enter my protest in advance against the Chief Justice or . . . the President of the United States or the General of the armies, or whoever he may be, undertaking to get the opinion of the Supreme Court . . . in advance and *ex parte*. And in my judgment there would be no more justification in the Chief Justice refusing to obey what this law requires him to do, after such a consultation and after such advice, than there would before . . . . The practice of the Government, I believe, so far has been, and the only practice upon which Government can be securely administered, to obey the law which the law-making power passes . . . until on a proper case, with regular parties . . . it shall be held to be invalid.

. . . It is the business of the Supreme Court to decide causes, not to act as counsel even for one of their fellows; and the fact that this officer happens to be the Chief Justice is no more reason for his getting an *ex parte* opinion in advance than it is for any other citizen—not a particle. . . .[188]

In the circumstances of the moment there was reason why the report about Chase should provoke such an outburst. This one clause in the Bankruptcy Act of March 2 was unwise and of questionable constitutionality; and it appeared that the Chief Justice might refuse to act until the Justices in private consultation had affirmed its validity. But there was the Reconstruction Act of March 2: it was widely held to be utterly odious and patently unconstitutional, and the President had so affirmed in his veto message. What if the President were to take a stand like that reported of the Chief Justice! (Certainly he had been counselled to do just that.[189]) Edmunds did not spell this out—the implication was obvious. Now he was determined that the Chief Justice should march straight down the path of duty.

Senator Sherman was a practical legislator who kept his eye on the essentials. He admonished Conkling—just as he had admonished Williams when the Reconstruction Bill was being considered five weeks earlier[190]—that the Senate ought not to be told what the House of Representatives would or would not do. Avoiding the complexities raised by Edmunds, he said simply that (as he understood) the Chief Justice

is overrun by visitors who, having no knowledge of the precious character of his time, prevent him from performing the ordinary functions of his office . . . .

. . . It seems to me that this is a duty which we ought to relieve him from and relieve him promptly.[191]

---

[188] Ibid., 278–80. Mar. 22.
[189] Supra, pp. 306–07, n. 228.

[190] Supra, p. 296.
[191] Cong. Globe, 40–1, 279.

But, said Senator Fessenden, many members of Congress had already gone to their homes; while he would gladly relieve the Chief Justice, it seemed too late to amend the statute.[192]

The motion to send S. 95 to the Judiciary Committee was carried; and there it ended.

It is remarkable that Chase had been quite content to have this patronage, until it proved to be "an elephant"; and that it fell to Senator Johnson to protect the independence of his office—to Sherman to guard his "precious time"—and to Edmunds to inculcate a fastidious attention to duty—whereas the Chief Justice himself had been concerning himself with less relevant things, such as drafting a Supplementary Reconstruction Bill.

At the moment when Trumbull's bill was sent to the Judiciary Committee, Senator Anthony broached a measure of his own, to amend the Bankruptcy Act in another particular. The point may be stated briefly. The Act had become *operative* at once upon enactment, on March 2; by its concluding Section 50, however, *no petition* in bankruptcy should be *filed* until June 1. (Section 35, nevertheless, rendered void any preference given by an insolvent to a creditor within four months *prior* to the filing of a petition.) Now Senator Anthony wanted to amend the Act so that it would not become *operative* until June 1.[193] (The import, said Fessenden, would be that "You can do anything you please between now and June."[194]) Then on March 26 Senator Sprague moved to amend Anthony's proposal so as to declare that the Act would not operate until January 1, 1868.[195] Both proposals were rejected.[196]

(The Court presently had occasion to hold that the Act did reach back to render void a preference given by an insolvent prior to June 1. This was in a case where the assignee in bankruptcy, whose position was affirmed, was represented by Melville W. Fuller, the future Chief Justice.[197])

This leads us back to the *New York Herald's* editorial of March 28: "Shall Chief Justice Chase be Impeached?"[198] It seemed strange, it said, that at the moment when the Radicals were clamoring for the impeachment of President Johnson,

---

192 Ibid., 280.

193 Ibid., 281. Mar. 22.

194 Ibid., 351, Mar. 26.

195 Ibid., 347.

196 Ibid., 351, Mar. 26, and p. 433, Mar. 27.

197 Traders' Bank v. Campbell, 14 Wall. 87 (1872); Sec. 50's reference to June 1 applied only to the bringing of proceedings—not to the time when the preference was given. The case below was Campbell v. Traders' Nat. Bank, Fed. Case No. 2370 in the N.D. Ill.—Drummond, J., in the District Court, affirmed by Davis, Cir. J., in the Circuit Court.

198 Supra, p. 355. The policy and influence of the *Herald* at this period are examined infra, pp. 429–32.

the very man who is their candidate for the Presidency, has committed the impeachable offense of refusing to execute the laws and obstructing their execution. . . .

The first count was that "under the merest pretext" Chase had "refused to hold a court for the trial of Jeff Davis."[199] Now there was "a stronger case," in that he was evading his duty to nominate registers in bankruptcy. As evidence tending to confirm the rumor of Chase's refusal, the editorial cited Senator Sprague's motion to amend the Bankruptcy Act, on Tuesday, March 26.[200] (Sprague was the husband of Chase's daughter Kate; the Chief Justice was residing in their home.)

> Efforts have been made by the friends of Mr. Chase to relieve him from the duty imposed by Congress. As late as Tuesday last Mr. Sprague, his son-in-law, made a motion in the Senate to amend the Bankrupt bill, by striking out the 1st of June and inserting the 1st of January. This would extend the time for the law to go into effect six months. There can be no doubt as to the object of this motion. Mr. Sprague evidently wanted to relieve his father-in-law from a dilemma. . . .

The *Herald* gave its reason why Chase was obstructing the execution of the Bankrupt Act. He was the author of the system of National Banks. Many of his "pet institutions" were in a "rotten condition," as would be exposed if they were forced into bankruptcy. But Chase "expects to be carried into the White House by their influence." He wanted to keep the people from discovering "the enormities and dangers of [this] monstrous and unscrupulous monopoly." Would Congress permit him to frustrate its mandate?

> It would be better for [Ben Butler and his radical friends] to drop Mr. Johnson, at least until they have a case against him, and turn their attention to Chief Justice Chase.

The *Herald*'s animus is patent, and its reasoning wrong from start to finish. Thus Sprague spoke out of a concern for certain "business interests";[201] his amendment would only have postponed, not removed, the Chief Justice's duty to nominate registers.

Often the Court, or one of the Justices, is pilloried for action which, if fairly examined, would be found to have been strictly within the conscientious performance of duty. Chase's delay in the trial of

---

[199] Supra, pp. 175–77.
[200] Supra, p. 362.

[201] His remarks, Cong. Globe, 40–1, 347, at 348. Mar. 26, 1867.

Jefferson Davis may be so explained.[202] *Ex parte McCardle*, it will presently be made clear, was an instance where the Court was acting with strict propriety, and yet was roundly abused.[203] But in this matter of the nomination of the registers, Chase first erred by acquiescing, and so got into the position that Senator Edmunds censured. Since his yearning for the Presidency was obvious in much that Chase said and did, it resulted that anything he said or did would be exposed to that imputation.

In various connections the Bankruptcy Act was entwined with Reconstruction. Thad Stevens had said, when the bill was before the House, "But this is not the time, when all rebeldom is in debt to us, to pass a law to free them from their debts. . . ."[204] With the same concern, Sumner wanted to require that a citizen petitioning for voluntary bankruptcy subscribe to an oath, not simply of allegiance, but of unbroken loyalty.[205]

The Act did require that a register be qualified by the iron-clad oath of 1862. Consequently in the South the Chief Justice's selections would in effect be confined to a small class of lawyers who were foremost in Radical politics. Thus the *Jackson Clarion* of June 11, 1867, reported that "we learn from the Republican"—Vicksburg's Radical newspaper, wherein official announcements by the United States Government were published—that George C. McKee "has been appointed by Chief Justice Chase . . . ." Thereby the aspect of political patronage being dispensed by the Chief Justice was accentuated. McKee's name will figure in connection with *Ex parte McCardle*[206]—and as an officer in the Republican organization, leader in the constitutional convention, and successful candidate for Congress.[207]

It is striking how the leading figures in Reconstruction keep reappearing in new contexts. Among the records of the District Court for the Southern District of Mississippi may be found the final oath in bankruptcy of Edward M. Yerger: "I was on the 10th day of February A D 1869 upon my own petition duly declared a Bankrupt . . ."; it bears the indorsement "Filed 2 Aug 1869 Geo C McKee Reg."[208] But while in these proceedings Yerger was gaining freedom from his creditors, he killed the officer serving as mayor of Jackson—was brought before a military commission—and was denied release on habeas corpus; now able lawyers were seeking a way to raise his case in the

---

[202] Infra, pp. 607–12.
[203] Infra, pp. 478–80.
[204] Cong. Globe, 39–1, 846. Feb. 14, 1866.
[205] Cong. Globe, 39–2, 1005, 1012, 1186. Feb. 5, 12, 1867.
[206] Infra, pp. 420–21.
[207] Infra, ch. 9, n. 81, p. 429.
[208] Now in the Federal Record Center, Atlanta, Georgia.

Supreme Court. Perhaps, it seemed, this would be the occasion for condemning at least one feature of the Reconstruction Act.[209]

At last we may discharge the Chief Justice in this matter of the Bankruptcy Act. By his direction, the Clerk of the Supreme Court, under date of April 5, 1867, had published through the press a statement of the procedure to be followed in making nominations as register. Into this the Chief Justice wove an explanation of his delay:

> The duty of recommending and nominating to the District Courts . . . suitable persons for appointment is imposed on the Chief Justice of the United States [*sic*],[210] and Congress having now adjourned without acting upon the Bill introduced into the Senate to repeal this provision, he will proceed to carry it into effect.[211]

Thereby Chase removed the cause of Edmunds' alarm, and the pretext for the *Herald*'s envenomed editorial.

---

[209] Infra, pp. 580–81, 591.

[210] Referring to himself by a title he had unsuccessfully sought to obtain from Congress. Supra, p. 166.

[211] Letters among the Chase Papers, L.C., illustrate correspondence the Chief Justice had with District Judges in the matter of his nominations. To Judge R. A. Hill of Mississippi, June 1, 1867, he recommended a form of certificate to be recorded: "On consideration of the foregoing nomination made by the Chief Justice of the United States, it is determined by the Court that the said ———— be appointed . . . ." To Judge Wm. F. Giles of Maryland, May 31: "The action of the District Judge is wholly independent of mine. . . ." To Judge Edward H. Durell of Louisiana, May 27 and June 3: "I dissent from the doctrine that the District Judges are at all bound by the nomination of the Chief Justice." But as to two nominees whom Judge Bland Ballard of Kentucky had declined to appoint, Chase asked, "Would it not be well however to reconsider your action . . .?" Letter of June 22.

CHAPTER VIII

The Court and Congressional Reconstruction: March to May 1867

"WHAT WILL THE SOUTH DO?" The *New York World* posed the question on February 23, 1867, after the Houses had passed the Reconstruction Bill by overwhelming majorities. (It was only six weeks since the *World* supposed it was demonstrating that the Fourteenth Amendment was dead, and that Congress could do nothing more against the South.[1] But that was before H.R. 1143 had been introduced.) Now its editorials urged the South to take advantage of the "unequivocal Congressional pledge that the States shall be restored" upon compliance with the conditions.[2]

If the States would reorganize promptly, the prospect was that "the sixty or seventy Southern electoral votes" could be counted in the Presidential election of 1868, which "would in all probability turn the scale."

Negro suffrage would be quite manageable:

> In every State except South Carolina, the whites outnumber the blacks, and if they are united they can elect all the officers. . . . The skill of the Southern politicians will enable them to control the negro vote as they have always controlled the white vote . . . .

—if only they would begin at once, "before the Radicals manipulate the negro mind into subserviency . . . ." The blacks could easily be made to perceive a common interest with the whites, in such matters as opposition to the protective tariff and the Cotton Tax. "A tax of three cents a pound on cotton is as bad for the black cotton-grower as for the white."[3]

Discussing "The Supreme Court—Its Relations to the Pending

---

[1] Supra, pp. 255–56.   [2] Feb. 23, 26, 27; Mar. 8.   [3] See infra, p. 877.

Conflict," the *World* said that in the actual position of affairs, the Court "is of more value to the South than the President": it could not be overridden by majorities in Congress. Even so, "this advantage is too limited, is held by too frail a tenure, to be an important element in any long-sighted political calculation"—"the oldest men, appointees of former Democratic Presidents, being . . . in the usual course of nature, most likely to die." Moreover, the Act of July 23, 1866, had provided that membership would be reduced to seven as vacancies occurred.[4] Hence, "The Supreme Court is, at best, but a temporary dyke to help stay the floods while we are building a more permanent embankment. . . ."

The *World*, characteristically, was making a cool-headed analysis of Democratic interests: if Southern leaders could only "control their honest indignation," they would recognize the wisdom of prompt reorganization in pursuance of the statute.

In a situation so traumatic, Southern reactions varied. Some saw wisdom in prompt reorganization according to the Congressional program. Many chose defiance: some by ignoring the plan entirely, some by so acting under it as would (they hoped) defeat the calling of a convention. Some said, wait until the Supreme Court has spoken. Some would hold aloof to await Democratic victories in Northern elections. With such varied impulses at work, events took a wayward course.

A MOVEMENT FOR ACCEPTANCE

FOR SOME MONTHS, reports abounded of old and new citizens meeting in concord to prepare for reconstruction. In Columbia, capital of South Carolina, on March 18 colored citizens marched to a square where they heard General Wade Hampton, and other leaders, "setting forth the identity of the real interests of whites and blacks . . . , and counselling the latter to seek affiliation with those whites whose interest and desire it was to build up again the material prosperity of the South." Beverly Nash, colored, made a response widely reported in the South. He regretted that the Reconstruction law "disfranchises gentlemen in whom we have more confidence than anybody else."

I want to see everybody vote, except the women. I believe . . . we are not prepared for the suffrage. But we can learn. Give a man tools, and let him commence to use them, and, in time, he will learn a trade. So it is with voting. We may not understand it at the start, but, in time, we shall learn to do our duty.[5]

---

[4] Supra, pp. 168–69.
[5] *New York Herald*, Mar. 21, re-

printing from *Columbia Phoenix* of Mar. 19; *Montgomery Weekly Adver-*

The *Charleston Courier*, the State's oldest newspaper, said calmly that "now that universal suffrage has been decreed, the only object of all should be that it should be exercised with judgment, and with a view to the harmony . . . of the races." It urged "unity and tranquility."[6]

> As for the Supreme Court, it sits shivering in the wind. . . . The sounds that reach us are that its tendencies are to declare that it is for Congress alone to determine the political status of commonwealths.[7]

The *Courier* reported what William W. Boyce, sometime Representative in the federal and then in the Confederate Congress, was writing from Washington to his old constituents: he warned that either to stand aloof or to vote against holding a convention would be disastrous; act promptly and in good faith to carry out the statute, and there would be "nothing to fear from the votes or other action of the colored people."[8]

---

tiser, Mar. 26; Ann. Cyc. 1867, 691.

The *Herald*, applauding, said that "By such a movement the whole South could be brought back into the Union before the next Presidential election, and the disfranchised whites would have as complete political control . . . as if the ballots remained in their own hands and the shackles were still on the arms of their former slaves."

Beverly Nash, born a slave, was then a Columbia barber. He sat in the constitutional convention of 1868, and thereafter was a State Senator. In a corrupt job in 1872, he accepted $5,000 and railroad scrip for his vote, as he himself testified. Report of the Joint Investigating Committee on Public Frauds and Election of Hon. J. J. Patterson to the United States Senate, made by the General Assembly of South Carolina at the Regular Session 1877–78, p. 32. Testimony of Hon. William Beverly Nash. It was a time when, as Matthew C. Butler (formerly Major General, C.S.A., later United States Senator) testified, "If I had land to sell, and a senator would . . . say, 'I will buy that if you will give me $500,' I would buy him up as I would buy a mule." Report of the Joint Select Committee to inquire into the Condition of Affairs in the late Insurrec-

tionary States, Sen. Rep. No. 41, 42nd Cong., 2d Sess., vol. 4, 1185, 1192, 1207 (1872).

[6] Mar. 26, May 6, 1867.

[7] Mar. 28.

[8] May 30. The letter was widely noticed.

Boyce (1818–90), then practicing in Washington, had established friendly relations with the Chief Justice. Chase's diary for September 24, 1866, records a conversation with Boyce: Chase urged adoption of the Fourteenth Amendment; they "agreed that the black citizen must vote sometime—I urged why postpone the inevitable? . . ." Chase Papers, Hist. Soc. of Pa.

The Andrew Johnson Papers, L.C., show Boyce to have been urged for appointment as Provisional Governor; he sought an early accommodation and restoration. James L. Orr and others to the President, June 29, 1865; Boyce to the President, July 9 and 12, 1865. To Frank P. Blair, Sr., Boyce wrote on October 7, 1865, that he was proposed for Senator; he claimed "I was always ardently attached to the Union"; "I was certainly the leader of the peace party in my own State if not in the entire South."

On Boyce in the Reconstruction case *Ex parte* Brown, see infra, p. 581.

But other South Carolinians counselled resistance—and none other so effectively as B. F. Perry, recently the Provisional Governor.[9] He sent forth a stream of letters, which were reprinted throughout the South. His message was, register if you can—vote for the most trustworthy men—but also vote "No Convention." If a convention were averted, "We shall remain as we are . . . until there is a reaction at the North. It has already commenced in Connecticut . . . ."[10] There was "glorious news" in mid-April that Mississippi and Georgia had appealed to the Supreme Court.[11] How could "an educated, refined and gallant people" submit to government by "an inferior race, utterly ignorant and debased!" "Better—far better—to remain as you are, under the military rule of your conquerors," than to be guided by "that bastard virtue, called prudence."[12]

In North Carolina, the *Raleigh Sentinel* and the *Wilmington Journal*, papers of high standing, threw themselves into the movement for acceptance. Seaton Gales, co-editor of the *Sentinel*, speaking at a meeting of colored citizens, assured them that under the Reconstruction Act, "your civil privileges, your perfect political equality, are fully established." "Beware of those who would excite animosities between the two races." Both journals minimized the prospect of relief from the Supreme Court, or from an early political reaction in the North.[13]

---

[9] Supra, pp. 110, 117, 123.

[10] On the elections, see infra, p. 400.

[11] Infra, pp. 370, 378.

[12] Perry told his readers that "it is generally believed that the military commanders . . . will exercise their despotic powers wisely and humanely. . . . A despotism, wisely, justly and virtuously administered, is the most perfect government that can be established. . . ."

These typical expressions are extracted from letters in the *Charleston Courier*, April 19; *Montgomery Mail*, May 7 and 22; *Athens* (Georgia) *Southern Watchman*, May 1 and 15.

The *Montgomery Advertiser* commented: "His letters are self-refuting"; his course "is the one above all others to create the proscriptiveness which he deplores." Weekly edition, July 2. It reprinted a reasoned refutation by the *Charleston News*.

[13] *Journal*, Mar. 15, Apr. 19, 26, May 3; *Sentinel*, Apr. 15, 29. On Seaton Gales, see p. 277, n. 97. Joseph A. Engelhard (1832–79), senior publisher and editor of the *Journal*, was a well-educated lawyer and, at the

time of his death, North Carolina's Secretary of State. Each, at the close of the war, had been adjutant general on a brigade staff, C.S.A.

The language quoted above was in an address at Raleigh on April 22. Thomas W. Conway, an organizer for the Union League of America, was present, and next day sent a report to Chief Justice Chase:

Yesterday Governor Worth and his friends assembled with the colored citizens at Capitol Square in this town. The object was the same as that at Richmond [see pp. 407–08], namely to influence the vote of those men but it failed most beautifully. They paid respectful attention to all that was said to them but occasionally put in such responses as to greatly trouble the speakers.

One thing can be said of Governor Worth, Major Gales, and Mr. [R. H.] Battle [Jr.]—the three who spoke on the occasion. They were kind in their language as well as in their temper, and did not abuse us of the North in

The *Richmond Dispatch*, the voice of Virginia moderates, invoked the authority of General Lee in urging the people to "accept the situation fully."[14] The *Dispatch* reiterated its counsel of "complete compliance . . . . Anything short of that only prolongs our troubles . . . ." The Supreme Court was "utterly impotent against Congress." It professed "not a great deal of anxiety" at the prospect of "enfranchising the blacks," "believing that, with ordinary prudence and good sense, the process . . . will be without any serious disturbance of our social or industrial order. . . ."[15]

The *Richmond Enquirer*, however, rallied the opponents of cooperation. It said that "it is plain that in an appeal to the Supreme Court lies our only defence"; it advised, avoid the snare of compliance and "await, in patience, [such] a change in Northern sentiment . . . as will remove or overawe the party in power."[16]

GEORGIA GOES TO COURT

GOVERNOR CHARLES J. JENKINS promptly committed his State to challenging the Reconstruction Acts. To that end he hastened to Washington where, after a month of preparation, on April 10, 1867, he issued an address to the people of Georgia.[17] He began with a version of recent history, in accord with the line being taken in Georgia's bill of complaint in the Supreme Court.[18] "During the late civil war you were distinctly informed," by the President and the Congress of the United States, "that it was waged against you . . . solely for the maintenance of the Union."

> With these ideas in your minds (actuated by what considerations it matters not) in April, 1865, you, in good faith, . . . made full submission. . . .

From that arose "an undeniable right" to expect "speedy restoration to the position in the Union from which you had essayed to withdraw."

---

the manner of Judge Daniel & Marmaduke Johnson of Richmond. A very large audience was expected but how great was their disappointment when only between two and three hundred persons were to be seen on the ground!

The colored people are wide awake even down here and it is impossible to lead them to vote for their former Masters. Chase Papers, L.C.

[14] Expressing this view in private letters, Lee preferred that his name be not "unnecessarily brought before the public." Douglas S. Freeman, *R. E. Lee*, 4 vols. (New York: Charles Scribner's Sons, 1934–35), IV, 313–15.

[15] Feb. 25, Mar. 5, 9, 23.

[16] Apr. 13.

[17] *Columbus Enquirer*, Apr. 16; *Columbus Sun*, Apr. 16; *Athens Southern Watchman*, Apr. 24.

[18] Infra, n. 64.

But Congress had refused to receive Senators and Representatives. Rejection of the Fourteenth Amendment by Southern legislatures "seems to have stimulated the ire of the national legislators." The Acts of March 2 and 23 were then passed.

I hesitate not to say to you that they are palpably unconstitutional and grievously oppressive.

What then should Georgia do? Two courses had been discussed: prompt acquiescence, and "a firm, but temperate, refusal."

But, wrote the Governor, he saw a third course: to seek relief from "the Judicial Department—the great conservator of the supremacy of the Constitution." Unwilling to trust his own judgment, he had come to Washington to consult "jurists able and pure, who would view the whole subject from a different standpoint. I have done so, and, by such men, my proposed course has been approved. Before you read this the cause of Georgia will be in that august tribunal, hitherto true to the Constitution—the bulwark of our Liberties." He warned, however, that the attempt to make a case within the jurisdiction of the Court might fail.

Counsel retained by the Governor were J. S. Black, who had written the veto message;[19] Charles O'Conor of New York; [20] Edgar Cowan of Pennsylvania, Conservative Republican who had failed of reelection to the Senate;[21] and Robert J. Brent, an experienced practitioner at the Supreme Court bar.

These counsel were now on the point of filing the suit of *Georgia v. Stanton*.[22] (After that effort had failed, Governor Jenkins at the next term of the Court would try again with the suit of *Georgia v. Grant, Meade, et al.*[23])

A STAND FOR ACCEPTANCE IN ALABAMA

WITH NO HESITATION the *Montgomery Advertiser* had taken its stand: "Obey the Law." It rejected "masterly inactivity,"[24] and the wrongheaded counsel of James Brooks' *New York Express*, "Endurance, submission and political slavery under military rule."[25] "If we must

---

19 Supra, pp. 307–08.
20 O'Conor (1804–84) was an eminently skillful New York practitioner and ardent Irish Democrat. He had defended slavery, and denied that there was authority to coerce a seceding State. Now he was counsel for Jefferson Davis. Infra, p. 608.

21 Supra, pp. 254n., 305.
22 Infra, p. 384.
23 Infra, p. 433.
24 Supra, p. 256.
25 James Brooks (1810–73) had shown himself to be a pugnacious Copperhead in the 38th Congress. At the opening of the 39th, he was his

save ourselves," the *Advertiser* insisted, "we must avail ourselves of every right"; there was "no room for passion or prejudice—it is simply a question of common sense." It was a "delusion" to expect deliverance from the Supreme Court.[26]

The *Advertiser* reported that "nearly all of our exchanges" agreed with it; it marshalled such editorials. It presented approvingly the assembly at the capitol on March 25, where "many of the truest and most substantial men of Montgomery" joined with "a great many colored people" in adopting resolutions:

> That we consider it the duty of good citizens to unite to carry out with earnestness and harmony the requirements of the Military Reconstruction bill.
>
> . . . .
>
> That all men have a cordial welcome to political equality upon this basis.

Similar meetings were reported: a mixed crowd of two or three thousand at Mobile; a "Half-and-Half Party" at Selma; a dense stream of humanity pouring into Hayneville; a gathering at Tuskegee—all tending to show that moderate whites were accepting the new order. The *Advertiser* pronounced this "the proper and only sensible course." It conceded that

> An unimportant few with more prejudice than wisdom, have temporarily hesitated to enter into a political affiliation with the colored people. But all reflecting men see that in popular governments, where there is political equality, there must not only be affiliation, but active co-operation among voters to secure the administration of affairs for the common good. . . .[27]

Here was a journal whose directors were doing their best to develop a rational response in a touchy situation: there were indeed many whites who scorned affiliation—and many blacks who were rallying to join the Republican party.

---

party's candidate for Speaker. His seat was contested, and in April 1866 was awarded to William E. Dodge (Rep.). Brooks was elected to the 40th Congress, and served thereafter until his death.

[26] *Weekly Advertiser*, Mar. 19, 26. The weekly edition is quoted where the file of the daily is broken.

To the *Advertiser* had recently come William Wallace Screws (1839–1913): "as editor of the most important Democratic paper in the State, he directed the policies of the party for half a century." D.A.B.

[27] *Cincinnati Commercial*, Apr. 23, quoting *Montgomery Advertiser* of Apr. 16; *Columbus* (Georgia) *Enquirer*, Apr. 17, on the Hayneville meeting.

VIII: *The Court and Congressional Reconstruction*

In late May, when registration was coming into view, the *Advertiser* carried an important article:[28]

Mississippi and Alabama

We are proud to be ably and consistently supported in the line of policy which we have marked out for ourselves, by the Jackson, Mississippi, Clarion, edited by Hon. E. Barksdale, the leading exponent through the press of the views of Mississippi, before the war, and the fast friend and supporter of Mr. Davis, in the Confederate Congress.

Ethelbert Barksdale (1824–93) had been a Representative in the Confederate Congress from beginning to end.[29] Hodding Carter writes that he "symbolized for years the challenge of liberal Democrats to Bourbon control of the party."[30] The *Advertiser* then quoted from an editorial Barksdale had published in the *Jackson Clarion* of May 9:

The writer has had recent opportunity of interchanging views with many intelligent and leading citizens of eastern and southern Mississippi, and is gratified to be able to state with entire confidence that the great Conservative Reconstruction party is rapidly absorbing every other element. In some of the counties it will meet with but little, if any, organized opposition. Multitudes who were on first impulse, disinclined to take part in the Reconstruction movement inaugurated by Congress, . . . have, under the salutary influence of the sober, second thought, fully determined to accept the situation as they find it, and to enroll themselves and vote for a Convention, and for good and true men, pledged to reorganize the State Government, preparatory to admission into the Union. They plainly see that the work will eventually be accomplished; if not by them, by others less informed of the momentous interests at stake . . . . In some localities, it is to be regretted that a scheme to array the colored voters, as a class, in a position of antagonism to the whites, is being industriously prosecuted, but we trust it will be successfully counteracted by the vigilance and properly directed efforts of intelligent and patriotic people . . . . In every community there are discerning blacks who have detected the designs of these iniquitous plotters, and are warning the voters of color against them. . . .

The plans of the disorganizers, who are for the most part

---

[28] *Weekly Advertiser*, May 21.

[29] He was a delegate to Democratic National Conventions in 1860, 1868, 1872, and 1880; an elector in 1876; and a Congressman from 1883 to 1887, failing to win renomination in 1886.

[30] *The Angry Scar* (Garden City, N.Y.: Doubleday and Co., 1959), 352. His brother, General William Barksdale, fought with great distinction, until mortally wounded at Gettysburg.

emissaries from other regions, have been greatly aided by the counsels of the impracticables at home, who first advised the suicide policy of "masterly inactivity," but now advise that the people register their names and vote the anti-Convention ticket. It will be an easy task, however, for our Conservative friends to convince the new voters that there is a medium ground . . . between the Impracticables on the one hand and the Radicals on the other. It is the policy of prompt compliance with the requisitions of the Government as embodied in the Reconstruction Measures. . . .

Picking up Barksdale's concluding thought, the *Advertiser* said that the great need now was to steer between "the Scylla of Northern Radicalism . . . and the Charybdis of Southern Impracticables . . . ."

MODERATES AND IMPRACTICABLES IN MISSISSIPPI

THE *Jackson Clarion* spoke for an impressive group of responsible leaders, and sought the concurrence of local journals in the numerous county towns.

In the camp of the Impracticables, leadership was assumed by Colonel Edward M. Yerger, then editor of the *Jackson Mississippian*. This was a spirited, complex, and darkly dangerous man—memorable for his killing of the army officer acting as mayor of Jackson in 1869 and for the resulting case, *Ex parte Yerger*, in the Supreme Court.[31]

Promptly upon enactment of the Reconstruction statute, Barksdale pointed out in the *Clarion* that the President had seen that "further resistance would be fruitful only of evil." The people should be "disabused as speedily as possible of the delusion that any practical result can come from the Supreme Court."[32]

The *Clarion* of March 14 published a letter from Judge Wiley P. Harris[33] expressing the view that "Negro suffrage . . . must be regarded as one of the conditions on which we are to have civil government here. . . . If the white citizens of the State whose rights are still preserved to them, (and they comprise the great mass of our white male population) should decline to co-operate in the measures which shall be taken to organize civil government here, their refusal to act will be a virtual

---

[31] Yerger (1828–75) was in 1865 the publisher of the *Jackson News*, an ephemeral paper, while he had the work of State Printer; he brought out the *Journal of the Constitutional Convention* of that year. His title is said to reflect service on the staff of Major General Earl Van Dorn in the lower Mississippi valley. Further information appears infra, ch. 12, n. 17.

[32] Mar. 6 and 14.

[33] (1818–91). Sometime Democratic Congressman, and circuit judge; in later years "the acknowledged leader and mentor of the Mississippi bar." See D.A.B.

surrender of the civil power into the hands of those who will surely employ it to perpetuate their power by further proscriptions." Judge Harris continued:

> I take the occasion to say, that there is no power in the Supreme Court at the instance of the State to prevent the law from taking effect. I do not see how the State Government can make a case for *judicial action*, which can only be invoked in controversies . . . which are not purely political. The power of recognizing the existence of a State Government has, by that Court, been held to be a political, and not a judicial question—and to pertain to Congress; and although a controversy may arise in which that Court may be called on to decide the validity of some of the powers conferred on the military commanders, it is a matter of grave doubt whether it will ever venture to declare the political status of the existing government here, or any that may hereafter succeed it; and should the Court venture hereafter to do so, its decision would not be respected, and it would have no power to enforce it.

Accordingly citizens should "take an active part in all elections under the new order of things," and give "the full weight of their influence in creating and controlling the Government under which they are destined to live."

The hopelessness of a suit by the existing State government to enjoin the execution of the Reconstruction Act was also pointed out in a letter from Judge William Yerger.[34]

Thomas J. Wharton, formerly the State's Attorney General—describing himself as a life-long "EXTREMIST" in the "school of State Rights," and until lately an advocate of "masterly inactivity"—wrote that "there is more than a doubt whether it is possible for [a suit by the State in the Supreme Court to challenge the statute] to come within its jurisdiction," and that in any event there would be long delay. Prompt acceptance offered "the best hope of safety."[35]

"Masterly inactivity," "dying in the last ditch, and all that sort of thing," wrote Barksdale, "would only result in the formation, by freedmen and Radicals, of a State government thoroughly radical in all its features." Negro suffrage was an accomplished fact: talk of undoing it

---

[34] (1816–72). Judge of the State's highest court from 1851 to 1853; a lawyer of ability and independence. A Whig in pre-war politics, he had opposed secession; in the convention of 1865 he had a moderating influence. Supra, p. 108. There is a memoir in D.A.B.

Colonel Edward M. Yerger was his nephew.

The broken file of the *Clarion* now available does not contain Judge Yerger's letter, but its import is stated in the issues of March 19 and May 15.

[35] Mar. 16.

was as futile as a proposal to restore slavery. Let all white men now exert themselves to guide the new voters.[36]

To counteract the legal opinions in the *Clarion*, Colonel Yerger's *Mississippian* now published a letter from Chief Justice Handy, whose contention was that

> When a State has once become a member of the Union, her rights, as such, are fixed, under the Constitution . . . . No word or syllable of that instrument looks to the disintegration of the Union, or to the rejection of any State embraced in it . . . . Such a doctrine is alike inconsistent with its history, its spirit and objects, and its positive provisions. . . .[37]

This was high language from one who, six years earlier, had been a busy secessionist.[38]

To Judge Handy, and to Colonel Yerger, this demonstrated that the Southern States were entitled to be treated precisely like the loyal States. The Reconstruction Act was an absurdity.

And the Supreme Court would be bound so to hold. Refuting the opinions of "distinguished gentlemen" in the *Clarion*, Judge Handy pointed to the Constitution's specific provision that that Court had original jurisdiction "In all Cases . . . in which a State shall be Party":[39] *all* cases—the Court was the sole arbiter between the States and Congress, and was under a special duty to assure "the sacred

---

[36] Apr. 19, 24.

[37] Letter in the *Mississippian* of Mar. 10, reprinted in the *Columbus* (Georgia) *Sun.*, Apr. 12.

Because the *Mississippian* for this period has not been preserved, one must rely on quotations found in other journals.

[38] On Alexander H. Handy (1809–83), see the D.A.B. He had won election to the Court of Errors and Appeals in 1853, defeating the incumbent, Judge William Yerger. See infra. He became Chief Justice in 1864, and resigned on October 1, 1867, in protest against Congressional Reconstruction.

As Commissioner from the State of Mississippi to the State of Maryland, he had said in a speech in Baltimore on December 19, 1861: "Our plan is for the Southern States to withdraw from the Union for the present, to allow amendments to the Constitution

to be made, guaranteeing our just rights . . . . This question of slavery must be settled now or never. Many remedies have failed, we must try amputation to bring it to a healthy state. We must have amendments to the Constitution, and if we cannot get them we must set up for ourselves." Ann. Cyc. 1861, 55, 442–43.

His holding that the Civil Rights Act of 1866 was unconstitutional has been mentioned. Supra, p. 346.

Judge Sharkey, testifying on conditions in Mississippi before the Joint Committee on Reconstruction, on March 8, 1866, had said: "The judiciary department has fallen into bad hands . . . . The judges of the high court of errors were all secessionists. . . . [Their election] was a very sore thing for many of us. . . ." Report of the Joint Committee, Pt. III, 137.

[39] Art. III, Sec. 2, cl. 2.

observance of the rights of the States." The idea that the existing State government might not be able to test the Reconstruction Act in the Supreme Court "appears to be scarcely less monstrous than the act itself."[40]

The *Missouri Republican*, St. Louis' excellent Democratic journal, on May 17, 1867, carried this critical comment on the advice being given by Colonel Yerger and other Southern editors:

The Military Bill in the South.

The Daily *Mississippian*, published at Jackson, Mississippi, names eighteen papers in that State opposed to the acceptance of the military bill as a basis of reconstruction. It remarks that there are about fifteen papers which have not as yet defined their position, but the indications are that a large majority will finally oppose the military bill. The same paper quotes an editorial from a Northern paper entirely destitute of respectability or influence, calling upon the Southern people to refuse all action under the bill, but to wait for some future time when justice will be done.

It is noticeable that the leading papers of the South in all the larger cities have taken a practical view of this military bill. They perceive clearly all its odious features and its utter illegality. But they perceive equally clearly that the people of the late insurrectionary States have no power of choice. Distasteful as the military bill is, unjust as it is in its outrages upon constitutional rights, yet there appears to be no other way of recovery of the privileges of the States. . . . If those who ought to exercise the political power of the South and to direct it decline to organize under the military bill, matters will not remain *in statu quo*. There will be organization without them. The colored people with the Radical whites will engage actively in the work of reconstruction. They will register, vote, elect delegates, frame a Constitution and become the paramount controlling power sustained by Congress. . . . Conservatives of the North have an interest in this question, and they look with concern upon the action of the South. With the Southern States reorganized upon a Conservative basis the day is not remote when the Radical party will be in a hopeless minority, and the Government will be restored to the hands of those who revere the Constitution and the Union, and prize both above mere party ascendency. If through the apathy or the unintelligent pride, or the inaction of those in the South who ought to act, then ten States are permitted to fall into the hands of mendicant Southern loyalists and the deluded colored race, the Radical party will rule the nation for a generation to come. Let the full truth be told by Southern journals when they say, "wait—do nothing."

---

[40] There will be occasion presently to glance back at the opposing opinions of Chief Justice Handy and Judge Yerger. Infra, pp. 397-98.

There must be prompt and united action unless the determination is to resign all political power to the supreme control of the Radicals and the blacks.

This was the warning of a thoughtful conservative journal.

MISSISSIPPI v. JOHNSON

WHILE COUNSELS WERE THUS DIVIDED, the possibility of stopping Congressional Reconstruction by a decree of the Supreme Court was tested. Southern efforts to draw the Court into the situation were unremitting. The beginning was on April 5, 1867, when Judge Sharkey, as authorized by Governor Humphreys, presented the suit of *Mississippi v. Johnson*.[41] The end was not reached until March 11, 1870, when *Ex parte Yerger*[42] was dismissed. Congress reacted with a statute to repeal a grant of jurisdiction, and considered further proposals to deny the Court the power to pass upon Reconstruction.[43] While resistance to the Congressional program was pressed in other quarters, hope was not abandoned that a judgment might be obtained that would condemn "all that has been done towards Africanizing the excluded States," as the *Little Rock Gazette* put it.[44]

On April 5, 1867—Friday, the Court's day for motions—Judge Sharkey was present in the Supreme Court, ready to seek an injunction to restrain the President from executing the Reconstruction Acts.[45] At his side was Robert J. Walker, prepared to argue the motion.[46] The President had had notice, and the Cabinet had met that morning: Attorney General Stanbery wanted a consultation. "Attorney General was directed to object to the motion,—the President, as the representative of the United States, cannot be sued": such was Secretary Welles' note on the conclusion.[47] Even though the President utterly disapproved

---

[41] 4 Wall. 475.

[42] 8 Wall. 85.

[43] Infra, pp. 459–69, 587–88.

[44] Jan. 16, 1868.

[45] William L. Sharkey (1798–1873) had been Chief Justice of the High Court of Errors and Appeals from 1833 to 1851, after which he practiced at Jackson. He opposed secession. After the war he was Provisional Governor. Sharkey had been admitted to the Supreme Court's bar, on motion of Reverdy Johnson, on January 28, 1867, while he was in Washington in connection with the "Southern Plan," supra, pp. 275–81.

[46] Walker (1801–69), Pennsylvania-born, had been a Senator from Mississippi, and Secretary of the Treasury under Polk. Thereafter he practiced in Washington, specializing in matters that called for political facilitation, such as claims, and the sale of Alaska to the United States. He was a Union Democrat.

[47] *Diary of Gideon Welles*, 3 vols. (Boston and New York: Houghton Mifflin Co., 1911), III, 80–81. In accord, *Diary of Orville Hickman Browning* (Springfield: Illinois State Historical Library, vol. I (1850–64), Pease and Randall, eds., 1925; vol.

of the legislation, he and his Cabinet were clear that the Executive duty "to take care that the laws be faithfully executed" ought thus to be vindicated.

Mr. Sharkey said:

> If the Court please, I desire to make an application to the court this morning for an injunction on behalf of the State of Mississippi against Andrew Johnson and others. I desire at this time to file the bill . . . .[48]

He asked the Court to set an early date for the hearing.

Attorney General Stanbery was on his feet at once:

> This is an original case, and I believe the practice is to obtain leave of the court to file the bill. . . . I wish to appear at the first moment such an application is presented and object to the court entertaining jurisdiction of it, even *in limine*.

That is, he wanted to stop the proceeding "at the threshold."[49]

Accordingly, Sharkey moved for leave to file, and the hearing on that point was set for Friday, April 12.

In the meantime, on the eleventh, O'Conor in open court filed a motion for leave to docket the complaint of the State of Georgia against Stanton, Secretary of War, Grant, General of the Army, and Pope, commanding the Third Military District.[50] This was the matter Governor Jenkins had confided to J. S. Black and associates.

On Friday the twelfth, Sharkey asked that his motion in *Mississippi v. Johnson* be now heard, and the Chief Justice responded:[51]

> Before you proceed, perhaps it is well to state that a motion to file a bill is usually granted as a matter of course in this court. . . .

II (1865–81), Randall, ed., 1933), II, 142; "Notes of Col. W. G. Moore, Private Secretary to the President, 1866–1868," in *Am. Hist. Rev.*, 19:98, 107 (1913).

[48] *National Intelligencer*, April 6, 1867, gives a stenographic report. The text of the bill was set out in the *Jackson Clarion*, April 12.

[49] The Rules of the Supreme Court are now specific: "The initial pleading in any original action shall be prefaced by a motion for leave to file such pleading . . . ." A brief in support of the motion may be filed. Notice must be served on the ad-

verse party, who may file a brief in opposition. *Revised Rules of the Supreme Court* (1970), Rule 9. 398 U.S. 1011, 1019.

If it appears that the action will not lie, leave to sue will be denied—as it was where the Principality of Monaco sought to sue the State of Mississippi on defaulted bonds. 292 U.S. 313 (1934). See infra, p. 397.

[50] Minutes of the Court for that day.

[51] Proceedings were reported in full in the *National Intelligencer*, April 13.

In this case the Attorney General objected to the bill *in limine* as containing matter unfit to be received. That is the only point which can now be considered . . . . As the Attorney General takes the affirmative on this point the Court will hear him first.

Can the Court properly entertain a bill to restrain the President from carrying into effect an Act of Congress, alleged to be unconstitutional? That was the question.

In all the history of the Government, said the Attorney General, there had been no precedent for such a suit. Counsel in their brief had claimed support from a few analogies: the closest was an incident in the trial of Aaron Burr before the Circuit Court in Virginia, where Chief Justice Marshall had granted a subpoena to require the President to produce a certain letter.[52] President Jefferson had made no response. And the Chief Justice had refused any effort to compel the President: it had become apparent, said Stanbery, "that a very great error had been committed." There was only one jurisdiction to which the President was answerable for any supposed dereliction of duty—the process of impeachment. What would the consequences be if the Court were to attempt to subject the President to its process and if—as the Attorney General would advise—he refused to obey? Attach him for contempt? The thought was preposterous. Mississippi's attempt was "a suit not fit to be brought, and which no court in the United States can for a moment sustain."

The President, concluded the Attorney General, having vetoed these measures, had done everything he intended to do to oppose them. "From the moment they were passed over his veto there was but one duty in his estimation resting on him, and that was faithfully to carry out and execute these laws."[53]

Walker, in reply, started from the constitutional provision that

> In all Cases . . . in which a State shall be Party, the supreme Court shall have original Jurisdiction. . . .[54]

All cases, he insisted—"any case in which a State was a party, unless expressly restrained by other provisions of the Constitution." States "might be affected with most disastrous results if there was not one great tribunal to which they might hasten . . . ."

> Are not the facts that are now transpiring a commentary that is most significant upon the importance of conferring upon this court immediately . . . the right to decide at once all cases in which a State

---

[52] United States v. Burr, Fed. Case No. 14,692d (1807).

[53] Walker, it will be recalled, had urged that course. Supra, ch. 6, n. 228.

[54] Art. III, Sec. 2, cl. 2.

is a party . . .? The very foundations of the Government are now rocking on their base; and it may be that if this Government is to be saved at all, . . . it may well be that such a result can only be accomplished by the interposition of this court.

On Monday, April 15, the Chief Justice announced the decision of the Court: leave to file Mississippi's bill against the President was denied.

As to the case of Georgia against certain officers:

> The Attorney General who appears on behalf of E. M. Stanton & U. S. Grant makes no objection to the filing of this bill. The President is not made a party & no injunction is prayed for against him. The bill may be filed.[55]

Judge Sharkey announced that Mississippi's bill would be reformed to meet the' objection of the Court, and would be presented again. (From this emerged the suit of *Mississippi v. Stanton, Grant and Ord.*[56])

The Chief Justice's opinion, for a unanimous Court, in *Mississippi v. Johnson*, followed the line of Stanbery's argument. An attempt by the Judicial Department to control the performance by the President of his duty to execute the laws would, in words Marshall had used in *Marbury v. Madison*, be "an absurd and excessive extravagance."[57] Consider, Chase reasoned, how often in the nation's history Congress had passed a law whose constitutionality was vehemently denied: "but no one seems to have thought of an application for an injunction against the execution of the Act by the President." Consider what internal conflicts would arise if the Judicial Department sought to restrain the President:

---

[55] Minutes of the Court. The words quoted are from the file of papers in the case, preserved in the National Archives. This item illustrates the sort of memorandum the Chief Justice would scribble, to guide him in making an announcement.

On the same paper is also this note of an order made that day: "Ordered that the Court will adjourn on Thursday next till Monday, & that motions for Friday of this week be heard on Monday. [To observe Good Friday.]"

[56] Infra, p. 384.

[57] 1 Cranch 137 (1803).

Counsel had contended that in executing the Reconstruction Acts the President was performing merely "ministerial duties, in the exercise of

which no one is above the law"—as contrasted with duties involving the exercise of discretion. Even if for a moment it could be supposed that any duty of the President could be so regarded, certainly those under these Acts were not of that character. Refutation may be found in President Johnson's Papers, which are full of requests that this officer be detailed and that officer be relieved, that certain directions be given, and the like. Also the choice of means is reflected in the wide disparity between the natural import of the words of the law and the narrow construction given by the Attorney General. 12 Ops. Atty. Gen. 141, May 24, 1867; ibid., 182, June 12, 1867. Supra, pp. 340-42.

if he refused to obey, that must be the end of the matter; if he did obey, he might be impeached. Could the Court restrain the Senate from sitting as a court to try the impeachment? What a "strange spectacle" that would be!

So ended the first attempt to obtain a judgment holding the Reconstruction Acts invalid.

Some historians have said that in *Mississippi v. Johnson* the Justices "evaded," "looked about for some means of escape," "turned their backs on the brave argument of their *Ex parte* Milligan decision and retreated behind technicalities." Such comment takes no account of the fact that President Johnson—stubbornly courageous, and bitterly opposed to the legislation on grounds of constitutionality as well as policy—after taking counsel of his Cabinet, deliberately chose to resist Mississippi's motion.[58] It was highly creditable that he thus acted to maintain the authority of his office where in doing so he went in the teeth of his dearest political objective. And what the Court did was precisely in accord with the well-grounded submission of the Government's chief law officer.

On the day he left office—March 4, 1869—President Johnson in an address "To the People of the United States" made the following proposal for an amendment to the Constitution:

> The veto-power is generally exercised upon constitutional grounds, and whenever it is so applied, and the bill returned with the Executive's reasons for withholding his signature, it ought to be immediately certified to the Supreme Court of the United States for its decision. If its constitutionality shall be declared by that tribunal, it should then become a law; but, if the decision is otherwise, it should fail, without power in Congress to reënact and make it valid.[59]

If the bill in *Mississippi v. Johnson* had been accepted, the rational implication would have been that already it lay within the power of any State aggrieved by an Act of Congress to interpose a suspensory veto, so that before the measure could be put into operation its constitutionality must first be submitted to the Supreme Court. Thus in an attempt to

---

[58] Secretary Browning's diary, supra at note 47, records that "with the exception of Mr Stanton we all advised him to protest most earnestly against the proceeding. . . . Mr Stanton thought he should simply let them alone, and do and say nothing, and see how the lawyers moving for the injunction would get along. He was, however, overruled, and Mr Stanbery was instructed as Amicus Curia[e], in the name of the President, to enter his solemn protest against the whole proceeding."

That is, Stanton would simply have ignored the effort as utterly without foundation, and left it to the Court on its own prompting to make proper response. Surely what was done was far more seemly.

[59] Ann. Cyc. 1869, 589, 591. Infra, p. 497.

prevent the subversion of the government of Mississippi as then established, something very fundamental to the constitutional system of the United States would have been subverted.

If later writers have sometimes failed to discern the enormous implications of Mississippi's suit, it is not surprising that commentators of the moment also misconceived. The *Cincinnati Enquirer*—strongly Democratic, and bitter toward Chase—said that "the whole thing has about it an air of dodging and pettifoggery . . . . A Congress that wants obstacles cast in the way of the trial of its acts by the organic standard, is a Congress of scoundrels, or a Congress of revolutionists. . . . There is no escaping the conviction that [Chase] is temporizing and procrastinating and inventing reasons for a delay which is disreputable to the Court, to the country, and to himself."[60] On such a fundamental ruling on the extent of the Court's jurisdiction, it was to be expected that the Chief Justice, if he joined in it, would make himself the spokesman. But the old conservative Justices on whom the Democrats had been counting so much, plus Field, J., also a Democrat, were numerous enough to cause the suit to be entertained, had they thought it right to do so.

Partisan editors have ever been prone to applaud or malign the Court according to the crude test of what interest was immediately benefitted by one of its decisions.

The *National Intelligencer*—conservative and opposed to Congressional Reconstruction—was more discerning: it said that with an "ability befitting a question so unprecedented and momentous," the Attorney General had "vindicated the prerogative of the sovereign people of the Union against the power of any litigant in a private suit to suspend the vast machine of the Great Republic at his pleasure."[61]

---

[60] Apr. 17, 1867.
[61] Apr. 18.

The *New York World*, the organ of responsible Democratic opinion in the North, also made intelligent comments on Mississippi v. Johnson—and on Georgia v. Stanton, next to be discussed in the text. On April 11 it supposed "that not even Judge Sharkey himself has any sanguine hopes. . . . The Supreme Court will probably decide that this question is political, and that it has therefore no jurisdiction. . . ."

On April 17 it recalled that down to the war, the South had "refused to recognize the Supreme Court as the ultimate arbiter between the States and the federal government

. . ."; now the applications of Mississippi and Georgia should be appreciated as "a signal token of the great change public opinion has undergone in the South."

In April 24 it published a letter from George Ticknor Curtis, arguing that it had been a part of the Constitutional design that the Supreme Court would be the arbiter before which a State could assert its every right against the federal Government. In the close discussion of judicial power and of the jurisdiction of the Supreme Court, in Curtis' *Commentaries on the Jurisdiction, Practice, and Peculiar Jurisprudence of the Courts of the United States*, vol. I (1854), this theme did *not* appear.

GEORGIA v. STANTON

As RECORDED ABOVE, leave to file Georgia's bill against the Secretary of War and others had been granted on April 15[62]

On Thursday, April 18, Walker presented Mississippi's bill as reformed: it now named as defendants Stanton, Grant, and Ord (commanding the Fourth Military District). He thought it was "precisely similar" to Georgia's bill. Leave was granted.

Next the Attorney General: ". . . I have come to the conclusion that it is my duty to appear . . . . It is a duty that I would not seek, but it is one that I cannot avoid. . . ." He moved to dismiss the bills for want of jurisdiction. He—and he understood opposite counsel—would be prepared to argue the motion on Friday of next week (April 26).

The Chief Justice responded that the Court would hear them on that day; it would consider the two cases as one (which, by Rule 21, meant that "only two counsel" would be heard on a side).

O'Conor said he had hoped that two counsels would be heard on behalf of Georgia: the Court had had reason to observe that the *Georgia* and *Mississippi* cases were separate—"conducted by different counsel and with a different policy, as to the views taken of the law of the land." However, "we submit of course . . . ."[63] (It will be seen that, at the argument, the Court did not enforce the normal limit of two hours to each counsel.)

The complaint which counsel for Georgia sought to maintain was in the form of a suit for an injunction, the familiar mode of relief which courts of equity had fashioned for situations where irreparable

---

Curtis (1812–94), brother of Benjamin R. Curtis (1809–74), was devoted to President Johnson's policy of reconstruction, and was prepared to turn his pen to pamphleteering. (The work cited above was not continued beyond volume I. It is not to be confused with the smaller book, Benjamin R. Curtis' *Jurisdiction, Practice, and Peculiar Jurisprudence of the Courts of the United States*; edited, with notes, by G. T. and B. R. Curtis, Jr. [1880]. The latter was based on lectures at Harvard Law School, 1872–73.)

Ex-Chief Judge G. F. Comstock of New York, in a letter of April 25 to the *World*, argued that the Court should hear Georgia's case on the merits.

The *World* said, however, that it would not, for the sake of momentary political advantage, abandon the traditional Democratic attitude of checking the Supreme Court; it would be shortsighted now to magnify the Court when its conservative members must soon pass away. Apr. 24 and May 11.

On May 17 it said "We are not sorry that the attempt was made [by Mississippi and Georgia] . . . , for its failure must convince all the citizens of the Rebel States of the absolute necessity of submission."

[62] Supra, p. 381. Georgia v. Stanton, 6 Wall. 50. Mississippi v. Stanton is reported with it.

[63] *National Intelligencer*, Apr. 19.

injury was threatened and there was no adequate remedy in a court of law. It was available to prevent injuries to property, or breaches of trust, or invasions of certain analogous types of legal interest. Now Georgia asked the Court to protect its scheme of government, by restraining Stanton and others from registering voters, administering oaths, conducting elections, and holding a convention, as Congress had prescribed.

Did judicial power go to that extent?

Georgia's bill showed: that under its constitution of 1865,

> the only persons competent or qualified to vote . . . are the free white male citizens . . . ; and . . . no person is competent to hold any office . . . who is not one of the said electoral class . . . .

Moreover, the State owned a capitol and an Executive mansion, and other valuable property.

Further, there were inhabiting the State

> many thousands of black men of African descent, . . . in all respects qualified and competent, according to the terms of the said acts of Congress, to vote at any and every election assumed to be authorized or sanctioned by the said acts of Congress . . . ;

however;

> no one of such black men, nor any other black man, ever was, or now is, authorized by the constitution or laws of the said State of Georgia to vote at any election . . . or participate in any political power . . . .

Moreover there were inhabiting the State

> many thousands of free white male citizens . . . competent and qualified to vote . . . under the constitution and laws thereof, . . . who . . . are good, true, and honest men, . . . firmly and earnestly devoted to perpetuating the Union of the United States, faithful to the Constitution thereof, . . . who, nevertheless, could not truthfully take the oath or affirmation prescribed [by Congress] . . . and who are therefore precluded from registration . . . and from voting . . . .

The design of the Acts manifestly was

> to cause to be set aside . . . the said present existing State of Georgia and to cause to be erected and substituted in its place . . . another distinct and hitherto unknown State, to be called and designated the State of Georgia . . . .

The President intended, through the officers named as defendants, to carry out the Acts "whilst they remain unimpeached by any judicial court competent authoritatively to advise him." To prevent irreparable injury to the State, its government and proprietary rights, complainant sought a decree by the Supreme Court, and in the meantime a preliminary injunction.[64]

When the *Georgia* and *Mississippi* cases against Stanton, now respectively Nos. 13 and 14 Original, were called on Friday, April 26, the scene, as described in next day's *National Intelligencer*, was "of intense interest":

> The court-room, simple in its appointments and limited in its accommodations, is crowded. The Judges make their appearance, as

---

[64] The text of the bill appeared in the *National Intelligencer* of April 11, in the *Jackson Clarion* of April 24, and in full or in part in various other newspapers.

Mississippi's bill, and Georgia's, had each recited historical facts to establish the State's entry and then existing membership in the Union. There was a marked contrast, however, in the treatment of the Civil War.

By Mississippi's account, upon admission in 1817, "forever after it was impossible . . . to dissolve that connection with the other States, and any attempt to do so . . . was a nullity . . . ."

> The said State admits that by the wrongful acts of part of her citizens, and the neglect of the federal authorities to protect the loyal, her government became temporarily disorganized in reference to its relations to the Federal Government, but she claims that this evil has been corrected in the proper manner by the people of the State.

General Albert Pike, writing in the *Memphis Appeal*, deplored this as "humiliating"; the gallant State "had been made to say that her people were all rebels, but *she* remained all the time in the Union; for, if she did so, her sons fought against her also . . . and were undeniably guilty of treason"—which it was shameful to admit. Pike's alarming sentiments

were quoted and adopted by the *Jackson Clarion*, April 16, 1867.

On Pike as an advocate before the Supreme Court, see infra, p. 637.

The *Clarion* later declared that "indignation knew no bounds, when [R. J. Walker's] petition was published making up an infamously false record of the action of the State . . . ." It contrasted Walker with J. S. Black, "one of the first legal men and purest patriots in the country." Feb. 19, 1868.

Black's bill in Georgia v. Stanton was not jarring to Southern readers. It said that Georgia and certain other States "essayed to withdraw from the Union"; then

> That the Executive and Legislative Departments of the Government of the United States, thereafter, and now, in fact, administered by the remaining States, denied the right of the said States . . . so to withdraw; and on this issue a civil war ensued.

President and Congress had declared that war was waged against the seceding States solely to preserve the Union. In reliance on these representations, Georgia and the others had laid down their arms.

The *Jackson Chronicle* called this "a splendid display of jurisprudential skill." Apr. 24, 1867.

The disparity between these two versions, while meaningful to Southern pride, made not a whit of difference in the outcome.

usual, save that Justice Grier, whose health is feeble, takes his seat in advance of the court, aided by his colored servant. Within the bar are the Attorney General, his assistant,[65] the eminent counsel for Georgia—Messrs. Black, O'Conor, and Cowan; for Mississippi—Messrs. Walker and Sharkey; and near are Senators Johnson [of Maryland], Patterson [of Tennessee], Morgan [of New York], Stewart [of Nevada], and Fowler [of Tennessee], and a number of distinguished lawyers, among whom we recognized the Hon. Thomas Ewing,[66] Chief Justice Cartter of the Supreme Court [of the District of Columbia],[67] Philip R. Fendall,[68] and others known to the country.

The Attorney General opened by saying that if the policy of reconstructing according to the Congressional measures—the question which now divided the people of the United States into two great parties—were actually before the Court for decision, "I would rather choose to take my place by the side of the opposite counsel." But that was something to be settled by the political processes of government; it was "not one of those . . . controversies that your Honors can take cognizance of." "It is alleged that Georgia has certain political rights and privileges, and also that she has certain property. I can see very well where my learned friends were tending when they came to that part of the case. . . . They saw the necessity of founding the equity jurisdiction upon the State of Georgia as a corporation whose franchises and rights were about to be disturbed, and therefore entitled to preventive relief, as an individual would be to protect his property and his rights from irreparable mischief and injury." But protection of the State's property rights was not at all the object of this suit; the object was to prevent the carrying on of a registration, an election, a convention, a submission of a constitution to the people, whereby perhaps Georgia as then constituted would be supplanted by a new government. The Attorney General discussed precedents sustaining his position, and distinguished cases relied on by his opponents. "The great, stubborn question which now unhappily agitates the country from one end to the other," he concluded, "cannot be settled by the judgment of this court."

O'Conor replied for the State of Georgia. "In the case before your Honors," he said, "it should be understood at the outset what we mean by State." A State, "in a political juridical sense," was only "the electoral body—those who vote for the legislature . . . ." "The State of Georgia stands before this court as being a State . . . composed exclusively . . . of white male citizens above the age of twenty-one

---

65 L. E. Mills, for defendant Pope.
66 Supra, pp. 9, 230.
67 Supra, p. 246.
68 (1794–1868). Washington lawyer

and sometime District Attorney. Chairman of the meeting on Feb. 22, 1866, where President Johnson denounced the Radical leaders. Supra, pp. 126–27.

years . . . ." "There are in that State . . . a population, composed of persons who never had those qualities, who are not members of the State, nearly equal to the white population; and the question before this court of course is," whether those persons were to be allowed to grasp political power, "constituting a new and different State altogether from that which has heretofore existed, and wipe out of existence the Georgia of 1776 and the Georgia of today. . . . That is the question." Was that not an evil in law against which Georgia was entitled to be protected by the Court?[69]

Argument on behalf of Mississippi went over to the following Friday, May 3.

On that day Walker began at 11:15, and was allowed to continue without interruption to 2:35, commanding, it was reported, "the profound attention of all present."[70] He contested as too narrow the Attorney General's view of the Court's jurisdiction; each State could come to the Court "as the ultimate arbiter in all cases"—not merely to raise "questions of title to a tract of land or a sum of money, but as to all the great questions which involve the constitutionality of laws of Congress . . . ." *All* questions—that was his theme on the matter of jurisdiction.

In the beginning, Walker went on, it had been established "that each State should decide for itself who should have the right to vote." But now this Act of Congress "extends the right of suffrage to three or four millions of people excluded by the State constitutions, and excludes tens of thousands by classification who are entitled to it under the State constitutions—the broadest bill of attainder or of pains and penalties ever enacted." "But it was said that there had been a great rebellion in these States . . . . True, but what then?" The acts of secession were "mere nullities"—the work of "mere assemblages of traitors and

---

[69] *National Intelligencer*, Apr. 27.

The *Cincinnati Enquirer* on Apr. 30 told its readers that O'Conor had made a "decisive and overwhelming reply" to the Attorney General. But the *Charleston Courier*'s Washington correspondent reported that "His friends claim that he did not do himself justice . . . . He certainly did not impress the audience very favorably, but that was probably because the case affords no opportunity for oratorical display." May 3.

In the same dispatch the *Courier*'s correspondent made other observations. Of Stanbery: "He has an easy flow of language, uses terse and forcible English, and speaks in a mild,

pleasant voice . . . . He is certainly all lawyer and none of the politician." Of the Court: "Chief Justice Chase took pretty full notes . . . , but the majority of the Court seemed rather indifferent, very much as though the question was an old one and had been decided before. A decision adverse to the petitioners is generally expected." May 3, 1867. See infra, p. 391.

The *Courier* on April 12 had foreseen a holding that the subject was "entirely within the control of the political department."

[70] *National Intelligencer*, May 4, continuing the stenographic report; *New York Evening Post*, May 3.

insurgents, without the least particle of legal or constitutional authority . . . ." "It seemed perfectly clear, then, that State constitutions and laws which preexisted the rebellion . . . were in full force . . . ." The people of Mississippi could not be deprived of their old constitution.

By the time Walker closed, the hour was so late that the Court said it would hear the Attorney General's reply on Monday.[71]

In his closing argument, Stanbery resumed the theme that jurisdiction must be "the first fundamental question in every case." Counsel had claimed that the State had standing not only to speak in its own behalf, but also to assert the political rights of its citizens. "How do we know that the State of Georgia is the *parens patriae* of all the citizens of Georgia? . . . Have [counsel] consulted the citizens of Mississippi? . . . Recollect, not a portion of its citizens. That will not do. [W]hen a State in its *parens patriae* power comes to represent its citizens as citizens, it must represent them all, and cannot represent one set at the expense of another."[72]

The suggestion that the State as "father of the people" was entitled to sue on behalf of some of its citizens in controverting the power of Congress to confer equal rights upon others of its citizens was worthy of no consideration, and the Court gave it none.

On May 13 Georgia's bill was dismissed for want of jurisdiction. The opinion would come later.

It bears emphasis that the gist of Georgia's complaint—and of Mississippi's—was that the existing body politic was threatened with the introduction of black citizens to share in its affairs. The Secretary of War and subordinates were named as defendants, because they were the agents charged to administer the statutes. Walker's argument made reference to military government as a feature of the Congressional program—but the attack was aimed at the objective rather than at the agency by which it was accomplished. These were suits to preserve to the States their all-white systems of government.

The Mississippi suit took one turn more: on May 10 Walker asked leave to amend the bill. Counsel wanted to set forth an additional ground: an apprehension that General Ord would take possession of the State's treasury.[73] The Attorney General opposed. On May 16, the last

---

[71] Walker's performance was the subject of "much comment and admiration." *Charleston Courier*, May 7 and 8.

[72] *National Intelligencer*, May 7, reporting stenographically.

Black did not participate in the oral argument. The statement by him set out in 18 L.Ed. at 722 is a "summary of the points" made "for the con-

venience of the Attorney General and the judges." *National Intelligencer*, May 7.

[73] In Arkansas, also within the Fourth Military District, General Ord had directed the removal or suspension of the State Treasurer, on the ground that he was disqualified by Sec. 6 of the Reconstruction Act, and because of information that he would

day the Court sat, the motion was denied by an equally divided court. The suit was then dismissed for want of jurisdiction.[74]

Replying on May 17 to a Pennsylvania Democrat, formerly a member of Congress, the Chief Justice made this comment on *Georgia v. Stanton* and *Mississippi v. Stanton:*

---

improperly dispose of the State funds. Ann. Cyc. 1867, 49. (By the concluding provision of Sec. 6 of the Act of Mar. 2, 1867, no person should hold office in a provisional State government if he would be disqualified by Sec. 3 of the proposed Fourteenth Amendment: this was a part of the "Shellabarger amendment." Supra, p. 305.)

[74] The Minutes of the Court show that Justice Grier had been present as late as May 15, the day next prior to that on which the motion was denied.

The *National Intelligencer* of May 23 carried an Associated Press dispatch containing the following passage:

. . . from what has transpired since [the Court's] adjournment, there seems to be no doubt of the fact that the Justices who denied the filing of an amended bill . . . did so on the ground that it had no relevancy to the original bill, and was not supported by proof that General Ord intended to seize the property of the State; and besides, it was considered that if such a course should be pursued by General Ord, the remedy would be in an application for an injunction apart from considerations connected with the reconstruction acts, as in the case of the State of Texas, to which an injunction was granted on the basis of [a showing by] the complainant, who prayed that the writ might issue to restrain the payment of certain Texas bonds represented to have been fraudulently obtained during the rebellion.

That sounds so plausible that one supposes it to be accurate.

At the term just closed, Texas v. White, No. 12 Original, 7 Wall. 700

(1869), and the *Georgia* and *Mississippi* cases, Nos. 13 and 14 Original, had all engaged the Court's attention. On May 16, Texas had been granted an injunction to protect it, during the litigation, in its claim to receive payment from the Treasury. Virginia v. West Virginia, No. 11 Original, 11 Wall. 39 (1871), was also before the Court. Potentially, each involved the question whether a State undergoing Reconstruction had standing to bring suit in the Supreme Court.

The *Texas* and *West Virginia* cases are discussed infra, ch. 13.

The Attorney General did not question the standing of Georgia and Mississippi to sue—which of course is as one would expect, considering his position on the Reconstruction Acts. Nor did the Court need to broach that question in deciding whether the issue those States raised was "political" and not judicial.

Subsequently, in Texas v. White, Justice Grier made it clear that in his view, a State undergoing Reconstruction did *not* have standing to sue. It is not surprising that, holding that view, he avoided taking part in the ruling on Mississippi's motion for leave to amend its bill so as to litigate this new issue.

The indecisive conclusion of Mississippi's effort seemed to tease. *The Nation* commented, "thus the question whether the court can interfere to protect the public *property* of a State remains undecided." 4:405, May 23, 1867.

Ten months later, the *Montgomery Daily Mail*, indignant at the Court's "subterfuges," said that "Last year the Supreme Court evaded a decision upon the Reconstruction Acts by the happy accident of a belly-ache on the part of old Judge Grier." Mar. 24, 1868.

390

I am glad of your gratification in the result of the Georgia case. A similar decision in the Mississippi case was made yesterday. I do not doubt that they [are] as sound in law as beneficial to restoration.

Most earnestly do I hope that all patriotic men of the South will now proceed to the work of reorganization upon the basis of universal suffrage & equal justice for all. Then may we hope for restored prosperity & real peace.[75]

Seemingly the thought within the Court, all along, had been that the bills brought by Georgia and Mississippi could not be sustained. That is implicit in remarks Justice Miller interjected in a letter to his brother-in-law on April 24—that is, after leave to file had been granted, and prior to argument. He wrote:

How is reconstruction going in Texas? Will the State adopt the programme laid down by Congress? It is in my opinion as necessary for the North as it is for the South, that this should be generally adopted by the Southern States.

The strain upon constitutional government, from the pace at which the majority is now going, is one which cannot be much longer continued without destroying the machine. Yet as long as there is Southern resistance, there is no power in the North capable of arresting the onward course of public affairs. Of this you may rest assured.

The very force and power of State organizations which enabled the Southern people to organize a government of such power in so short a time, also enables the majority in the North however small in each State to control the whole country. As the loyal men or antisecessionists of the Southern States, were swallowed up by the majorities there, and could get no help from their friends in the North, so the minorities in the North, can render their friends in the South no service.[76]

The reasons for dismissing the applications of Georgia and Mississippi were not given until, in the middle of the next term, on February 10, 1868, Justice Nelson delivered the opinion of the Court.[77] "[T]he rights, for the protection of which our authority is invoked, are rights of sovereignty, of political jurisdiction, of government, of corpo-

---

[75] Chase Papers, L.C. To J. Glancy Jones (1811–78) of Reading, a clergyman-turned-lawyer, who often assured President Johnson, by letter or by personal visit, of support "in the noble & inflexible stand you have taken to save your country." In Johnson Papers, L.C.—for example letters of Apr. 18, 1865; Oct. 12, Nov. 6 and 21, 1867; Jan. 14, 1868.

Chase's letter to Jones concluded:

"My friend, Col. Thomas of Phil^a., hopes to see you before long." William B. Thomas was one of Chase's political adherents. Infra, p. 25, n. 81.

[76] Part of this appears in Charles Fairman, *Mr. Justice Miller and the Supreme Court, 1862–1890* (Cambridge, Mass.: Harvard University Press, 1939), 138.

[77] Georgia v. Stanton, 6 Wall. 50.

rate existence as a State," he observed—not personal or property rights such as are the familiar subjects of litigation. Complainants relied on *Rhode Island v. Massachusetts*,[78] where the Court had determined the boundary between two States: but that had been like fixing the line between separate tracts of land; sovereignty and jurisdiction were only incidental in such a case: they were dependent upon the main issue, the settling of the boundary. How different was the prayer in this case, that officers be enjoined from carrying out an Act of Congress, on the ground that the effect of the statute would be to abolish the existing government of Georgia and establish a different one in its place. That was a matter, said Justice Nelson, that did not belong to the jurisdiction of a court.

> The distinction between judicial and political power is so generally acknowledged in the jurisprudence both of England and of this country, that we need do no more than refer to some of the authorities on the subject. . . .

He cited four cases: two in the English chancery, two in the Supreme Court.

Ironically, the most apposite precedent was *Cherokee Nation v. Georgia*,[79] where in 1831 the Court had rejected a suit for an injunction to restrain the enforcement of a statute whereby Georgia was proceeding to deprive the Cherokees of the protection of their own laws and to suppress their system of self-government as guaranteed to them by treaties with the Federal Government. On that occasion Georgia had defied the Court, disdaining even to plead to the suit. "If courts were permitted to indulge their sympathies," wrote Chief Justice Marshall, "a case better calculated to excite them can scarcely be imagined." The Court, however, had dismissed the claim for want of jurisdiction: the Cherokee Nation was neither a "State" of the Union nor a "foreign State" within Article III's grant of judicial power; they were a "domestic dependent nation." Further, the Chief Justice had said in a memorable dictum, "a serious additional objection exists to the jurisdiction of the court. Is the matter of the bill a proper subject for judicial inquiry and decision? . . . The bill requires us to control the Legislature of Georgia, and to restrain the exertion of its physical force. The propriety of such an interposition by the court may well be questioned. It savors too much of the exercise of political power to be within the proper province of the judicial department. . . ."

What Marshall had said of the political action of Georgia in 1831

---

[78] 12 Pet. 657 (1838).   [79] 5 Pet. 1.

was what in effect the Court said in 1868 of the political action of Congress:

> If it is true that wrongs have been inflicted, and that still greater are to be apprehended, this is not the tribunal which can redress the past or prevent the future.[80]

The circumstance that the opinion on this fundamental question of the Court's jurisdiction was written by Nelson, the senior Associate Justice, rather than by the Chief, is attributable to a factor thus stated in the Reports:

> Mr. Chief Justice Chase:
> Without being able to yield my assent to the grounds stated in the opinion just read for the dismissal of the complainant's bill, I concur fully in the conclusion that the case made by the bill is one of which this Court has no jurisdiction.

Perhaps the explanation lies in some sentences Chase wove into his opinion in *Texas v. White* at the next term. "The new freemen necessarily became part of the people, and the people still constituted the State . . . ." It was the State, as thus constituted, that must be brought into constitutional relations with the Union; and this, "without a new election of officers, was obviously impossible; and before any such election could be properly held, it was necessary that the old constitution should receive such amendments as would conform its provisions to the new conditions created by emancipation . . . ."[81] O'Conor, it will be recalled, had declared that "The State of Georgia stands before this court as being a State . . . composed exclusively . . . of white male citizens . . . ." If "the State of Georgia," in Chase's thought, must henceforth be a society wherein the new freemen were necessarily a part, it might be said that the Court should not entertain a suit by the entity which Governor Jenkins purported to represent, to interfere with the organization of that new society which must be. Perhaps the Chief Justice had wanted to make this thought the basis for dismissing the bills.

THE PRINCIPLE IN *GEORGIA v. STANTON*

JUSTICE NELSON essayed no close analysis. He reiterated the distinction between "political" (with the related words "sovereignty and

---

[80] 5 Pet. 1, 20.   [81] 7 Wall. 700, 728–29, infra, p. 639.

jurisdiction") and "judicial" (and "rights of person and property"), as though repetition sufficed to explain. Undeservedly the case has always borne a semblance of mere expediency.

It is useful to start from what is elementary. Although all branches and officers of government are subject to law, and law in the main is interpreted by courts, yet there are some types of questions whose answer belongs on the political side of government. This may be the case because the Constitution says as much, expressly. For example, "Each House shall be the Judge of the Elections, Returns and Qualifications of its own Members . . . ." Art. I, Sec. 5, cl. 1.[82] It may be inferable from the Constitution. For example, the Court held that the duty to render up a fugitive from justice, Art. IV, Sec. 2, cl. 2, was "left to depend on the fidelity of the State executive" and was not judicially enforceable.[83]

When did the Civil War begin, when did it end? We must "refer to some public act of the political departments of the government to fix the dates," said Chase, C.J., in *The Protector*.[84] The Chief Justice had acted on that view in reaching a conclusion whether he should go on his circuit in the South.[85] When was the conquest of California completed, thereby cutting off the power of Mexican officials to make valid land grants? "[I]n this respect the Judiciary follows the action of the Political Department."[86] "Who is the sovereign, *de jure* or *de facto*, of a territory is not a judicial, but a political question. . . ."[87] In 1867 Alaska was acquired, and Congress forbad the killing of seals "within the limits of Alaska Territory, or in the waters thereof." A seizure was made fifty-seven miles from land, and the jurisdiction of the United States at that point was challenged. The Court would not "review the action of the political departments" upon this question of the national boundary.[88]

The laws refer to dealing with the "Indian Tribes." Justice Miller said, "In reference to all matters of this kind, it is the rule of this Court to follow the action of the Executive and other Political Departments of the Government, whose more special duty it is to determine such affairs. If by them those Indians are recognized as a tribe, this Court must do the same."[89]

"The United States shall guarantee to every State in this Union a

---

[82] Compare Powell v. McCormack, 395 U.S. 486 (1969).

[83] Kentucky v. Dennison, 24 How. 66 (1861).

[84] 12 Wall. 700 (1872). Accord, Lamar v. Browne, 92 U.S. 187 (1876).

[85] Supra, pp. 145–48.

[86] Field, J., in United States v. Yorba, 1 Wall. 412 (1864). Accord, United States v. Lynde, 11 Wall. 632 (1871).

[87] Gray, J., in Jones v. United States, 137 U.S. 202 (1890), citing applications in the English courts as well as the Supreme Court's own precedents.

[88] *In re* Cooper, 143 U.S. 472 (1892).

[89] United States v. Holliday, 3 Wall. 407 (1866).

Republican Form of Government . . . ." Art. IV, Sec. 4. As has been seen, Henry Winter Davis asserted "a plenary, supreme, unlimited jurisdiction, paramount over courts," which this constitutional provision gave to Congress in the matter of Reconstruction.[90] He rested upon the opinion of Taney, C.J., in the great case of *Luther v. Borden* in 1849.[91] Taney had there said that "under this Article of the Constitution it rests with Congress to decide what government is the established one in a State. . . . And its decision is binding on every other department of the government . . . ." That case arose in Rhode Island, where Dorr's movement had set up a popular government based upon universal manhood suffrage, to supplant the established charter government. The latter declared "martial law," under which authority Borden broke and entered the house of Luther, of the popular party. Moving to Massachusetts, Luther sued Borden in the federal Circuit Court; he offered testimony to prove that the Dorr government rested on the support of a large majority of the adult males. From a judgment for the defendant, the case was brought to the Supreme Court. Counsel for Luther asked the Court to give effect to a fundamental American principle, that "a majority of the community hath an indubitable, inalienable, and indefeasible right" to set up a new government. In explaining why this was not a matter for judicial determination, Taney made the statement about the Guaranty Clause, quoted above.

Robert J. Walker had been engaged on the side of this popular right in *Luther v. Borden*. Now as counsel for Mississippi in its suit against Stanton, Grant, and Ord he was contending that the overthrow of an established government by vote of a majority of the community, as authorized by the Act of Congress, was wrongful, and that it was the business of the Court to interfere.

In a latter-day effort to bring the single instances of a "political question" into rational order, the Court found these distinguishing marks: "a textually demonstrable constitutional commitment of the issue to a coordinate political department; or a lack of judicially discoverable and manageable standards for resolving it; or the impossibility of deciding without an initial policy determination of a kind clearly for nonjudicial discretion; or the impossibility of a court's undertaking independent resolution without expressing lack of the respect due coordinate branches of government; or an unusual need for unquestioning adherence to a political decision already made; or the potentiality of embarrassment from multifarious pronouncements by various departments on one question."[92]

As this language suggests, the concept of a "political question"

---

[90] Supra, p. 98.
[91] 7 How. 1.

[92] Baker v. Carr, 369 U.S. 186, 217 (1962).

runs to shadowy boundaries. Notions of the role of the Judiciary change through the years, in response to the pressure of men's demands. At the end of a century after *Georgia v. Stanton*, professorial discussion of "justiciability" and of "standing" to litigate had come to a high level of discrimination. To pursue that topic would carry this commentary far out of bounds.[93]

---

[93] A major development was Baker v. Carr, cited above, where in 1962—after State constitutional mandates for fair apportionment of legislative seats had long gone unheeded, and appeared not to be judicially enforceable—the Court at last assumed competence in the thorny field of legislative apportionment. The Court there treated Georgia v. Stanton, however, as still in good repute: it said that in the claim for judicial control of apportionment "Of course . . . any reliance on [the Guaranty Clause] would be futile." P. 227. The Court now found judicial power in the premises in the Equal Protection Clause of the Fourteenth Amendment.

Justice Douglas filed a concurring opinion, however, wherein he said that "The category of the 'political' question is, in my view, narrower than the decided cases indicate." "*Georgia v. Stanton* . . . involved the application of the Reconstruction Acts to Georgia—laws which destroyed by force the internal regime of that State. Yet the Court refused to take jurisdiction. . . . *Georgia v. Stanton* . . . expresses a philosophy at war with *Ex parte Milligan* . . . . The dominance of the civilian authority has been expressed from the beginning. . . ." 369 U.S. at 246–47 n. 3.

But the gravamen of Georgia's complaint would in no essential have been different if, instead of employing the army as its agent, Congress had enacted, say, that the *Chief Justice* should appoint *civil* Provisional Governors [as was proposed by H.R. 856, 39th Cong., 2d Sess., p. 259] and then had charged each Governor to conduct the registration and elections whereby the internal regime would have been transformed by admitting colored citizens to vote along with whites. If one reads Georgia's bill, one may see how easily it could have been recast to recite the appointment of the civil Governor, and complainant's apprehension of ruinous consequences.

In the view of the concurring opinion noted above, the Court in 1867 should have taken jurisdiction and (by clear implication) should have enjoined enforcement of the Reconstruction Acts. That is, it should have sustained the contention that "the State" was entitled to remain as it then was, "composed exclusively . . . of white male citizens." (O'Conor's argument, p. 387.) Such a pronouncement in 1867—had it been respected—would have been fatal to the pending Fourteenth Amendment with its promise of "equal protection." Yet it was that provision which, through Baker v. Carr, became the means whereby the Court in Gray v. Sanders, 372 U.S. 368, in 1963 invalidated Georgia's county-unit system of counting votes, where a vote in some counties had had a far different weight from that in others. "The conception of political equality from the Declaration of Independence, to Lincoln's Gettysburg Address, to the Fifteenth, Seventeenth, and Nineteenth Amendments can only mean one thing—one person, one vote," said Justice Douglas for the Court. That proposition of 1963 was in accord with what Congress was enforcing by the Reconstruction Acts of 1867—and in Georgia v. Stanton the Court said it would not stand in the way.

What Congress did in 1867 was an unprecedented assertion of authority, to meet a very difficult situation; so too did the Court go to unprecedented lengths in Baker v. Carr and Gray v. Sanders.

A SINGULAR CONFIRMATION

IT WAS REMARKED ABOVE that the strongest precedent against Georgia in 1867 was the case of *Cherokee Nation v. Georgia* in 1831.[94]

Now it is worth taking a moment to relate how Mississippi's contention in 1867 was, in the fullness of time, confuted by Mississippi.

In 1853, in *State v. Johnson*, the High Court of Errors and Appeals held the State liable on bonds issued to the Mississippi Union Bank.[95] "Millions of dollars" were involved and also, plaintiff contended, Mississippi's "good faith, truth, honor, and justice." The decision, as the judges had foreseen, gave rise to popular resentment. Judge Yerger failed of reelection; A. H. Handy was chosen in his place.[96]

The State, through the years, defeated every attempt to collect on such bonds.

In 1933, hopeless holders donated some of the bonds to the Principality of Monaco. *They* could not hail Mississippi into court—[97] but perhaps a *foreign State* could. In 1934 Monaco went into the Supreme Court, asking leave to file a suit against Mississippi.[98] It contended—as Chief Justice Handy had insisted in his letter in the *Mississippian* in 1867,[99] and as Walker had argued in *Mississippi v. Stanton et al.*[100]—that the Court had jurisdiction, by Section 2 of Article III, "in *all* cases in which a State shall be party." Mississippi's law officers answered—as the law officer of the United States had answered in 1867—that the case sought to be filed was not "justiciable." And the Court agreed: leave to file was denied.

"Manifestly," said Chief Justice Hughes, "we cannot rest with a mere literal application of the words . . . . Behind the words . . . are postulates which limit and control. . . ." One of these was that the controversy must be "justiciable"—(which was the ground for dismissing in 1867). Another postulate was that a nonconsenting State was not liable to suit by a foreign State.[101]

---

[94] Supra, p. 392.

[95] 25 Miss. 625. C. P. Smith, C.J., and William Yerger, J., wrote opinions. Each concurred in the opinion of the other, and E. S. Fisher, J., concurred in both.

[96] On Yerger and Handy, see pp. 374–78.

[97] The Eleventh Amendment provides: "The Judicial power of the United States shall not be construed to extend to any suit in law or equity, commenced or prosecuted against one of the United States by Citizens of another State, or by Citizens or subjects of any Foreign State." This cut into Article III's definition of judicial power: but the Eleventh Amendment did not *expressly* strike out the grant of jurisdiction "between a State . . . and foreign States . . . ."

[98] Principality of Monaco v. State of Mississippi, 290 U.S. 606, 291 U.S. 643. (Rule to show cause, and return made.)

[99] Supra, pp. 376–77.

[100] Supra, p. 388.

[101] Principality of Monaco v. State of Mississippi, 292 U.S. 313 (1934).

Here was the answer to the *"all"* suits" interpretation which in 1867 Chief Justice Handy had asserted so confidently in Colonel Yerger's newspaper,[102] against the opinions of Judge Harris and Judge Yerger.[103]

THE SITUATION AFTER DISMISSAL

HAVING PASSED the Supplementary Act of March 23, 1867 the 40th Congress recessed for three months. By mid-May the cloud raised by the Georgia and Mississippi suits had been removed, and the Court had adjourned. No Southern legislature was in session; none would sit again until a convention had met and a new start had been made under a new constitution. From the Potomac to the Rio Grande, the course prescribed by Congress was being carried out.

At this juncture there appeared in the Southern press a letter, written on the morrow of the dismissal of *Georgia v. Stanton*, by Judge William Marvin, who had held the federal Court at Key West notwithstanding secession, and subsequently had served as Provisional Governor of Florida.[104] He had written:

> I have been in Washington a number of days, and have had the opportunity to talk with a number of the Judges of the Supreme Court and other intelligent gentlemen, and the general wish seems to be that the South should reconstruct and get herself represented in Congress as soon as possible.[105] It is said that such is also the desire of the President. The most able and intelligent men see no way to get the country out of its present difficulties, but that for the South to fall in with the Congressional plan . . . .[106]

When *Georgia v. Stanton* was dismissed, the *Jackson Clarion* said that the decision should "convince all our people that there is no authority which can interpose . . . ." Now, it asked, would the white people participate in carrying out the Congressional plan—or were they going to wait for something worse?[107] It made a particularly impressive effort to convince the people of Mississippi of "The Necessities of the Hour":

---

[102] Supra, pp. 376–77.
[103] Supra, p. 375.
[104] United States District Judge, 1839–63; during the war he there decided many prize cases, "perhaps more than all the other courts put together." His testimony before the

Joint Committee on Reconstruction. Report, Pt. IV, 6. See supra, pp. 37, 40.
[105] See supra, pp. 311–17.
[106] *Jackson Clarion*, June 9; *Meridian Gazette*, June 13.
[107] May 15.

No consideration of timidity, no argument of pride—the certain forerunner of a downfall—no suggestion of prejudice, no unavailing attachment to old customs, will serve to excuse the conduct of any man who refuses to recognize the existing political power of the negro and to put forth every energy of his mind to wield it for wise and beneficial ends. That the negro has the privilege to vote when the pending elections occur, is as certain as that another day will succeed the present. You cannot prevent it by refusing to think of it. . . . It cannot be done by the senseless decrial of the negro, nor by stupid and unmeaning declamation in regard to the horrors of "negro rule." You will not have "negro rule" if you will strive to avert it, by according to him fully and freely what the laws of *the Government have awarded to him and what it is determined he shall have*, and by the gentle but potent influence of reason adapted to his feeble understanding, and of just and kind treatment. . . . Delays are dangerous. We must have a system of efficient organization, so as to combine the whole conservative element of the State and concentrate its whole power to the advancement of the one great end.[108]

The *Charleston Courier* said that the dismissal of the suits was "a fixed fact,"[109] and thereafter dwelt constantly on the importance of registering.

Journals that had held high hopes for relief by the Supreme Court joined in the call. "Register! Register!!" cried the *Richmond Enquirer*. Since many of its readers might be reluctant, it pointed out that

The act of registering will not *require* him to vote; but it will secure him *the option* of voting or not as may seem expedient in the future. . . . No man is wise enough in these times to know positively what it may be best to do months ahead. . . .[110]

The *Montgomery Mail* spoke peremptorily: "The man who fails to register and vote, votes against the peace and safety of the State."[111]

The Supplementary Act of March 23 had directed that registration be made before September 1, 1867; when that had been completed, at least thirty days' notice must be given of the election on calling a convention, and for the choice of delegates. Registration and elections now loomed as inevitable. Whether a convention was called would depend upon the result of the election: (1) a majority of those registered must come to vote, and (2) a majority of those voting must cast ballots "For a Convention."[112]

---

[108] June 11, 1867.
[109] May 24.
[110] June 17.

[111] May 18.
[112] Supra, pp. 323, 339–40. Infra, p. 404.

CHAPTER IX

The Background of Further Litigation

DEMOCRATIC GAINS IN NORTHERN ELECTIONS, culminating in November 1867, gave increasing encouragement to Southern resistance to the Congressional program.

First came Connecticut, on April 1. The Republican platform called for impartial suffrage, and declared the pending Fourteenth Amendment to be just. The Democrats condemned Congress' treatment of the South, and—expectantly—hailed the Supreme Court for demonstrating that it would "perform, without fear or favor, its high and solemn duties." Despite a major effort, the Republicans saw their Governor turned out and a Democrat installed. "The plain, naked, ugly reason," said *The Nation*, was that "a considerable body of the Connecticut Republicans did not want negro suffrage . . . ."[1]

In September, California chose as Governor a War Democrat critical of Congressional policy, to succeed a Republican. In Maine, the Republican majority was substantially reduced.

"I think there is a steady flow of public opinion against the abolition party," J. S. Black wrote on September 23. "I feel at this moment more hopeful than I have done for a long time. . . ." He looked forward, with guarded hope, to the elections in Pennsylvania, Ohio, and New York.[2]

On October 8, Pennsylvania elected a Democrat to its Supreme Court; in each House the Democrats improved their position.

In Ohio on the same day, while Rutherford B. Hayes was elected Governor by a narrow margin, the Democrats took control of both branches of the legislature. At the same election, a constitutional amend-

---

[1] 4:294, Apr. 11.
[2] Writing to Howell Cobb in Georgia. Toombs, Stephens, Cobb

Correspondence. *Ann. Report of Am. Hist. Assn. for 1911*, 2:687–88 (1913).

ment to admit colored men to the suffrage was rejected by a majority of more than fifty thousand. (The issue, however, was not clean cut, since the proposal would also have disfranchised those who had borne arms in support of the rebellion, or had moved to avoid the draft, or had deserted.[3])

On November 5, in New York the Democrats elected their State ticket and did very well with local offices. In New Jersey, the Republicans lost control of each House.

While Republican corruption, heedless management and unfortunate collateral issues could be offered as partial explanations, the returns seemed to show that the people were opposed to Negro suffrage and to the Congressional policy toward the South.

On November 13 a crowd of celebrants came to serenade the President. Responding, he said:

> I confess I am gratified, but not surprised, at the result of the recent elections. I have always had undoubting confidence in the people. . . . And thank God they have come, and that our republic may yet be saved. [Tremendous cheering.]
>
> . . . With abiding confidence in their patriotism, wisdom, and integrity, I am still hopeful that in the end the rod of despotism will be broken, the armed heel of power lifted from the necks of the people, and the principles of a violated Constitution preserved. The people have spoken in a manner not to be misunderstood. Thank God! . . .[4]

The cumulative effect of these developments was greatly to discredit the counsels of Southern moderates urging cooperation with the

---

[3] It was bad management to permit the central issue to be thus embarrassed.

Chief Justice Chase had demonstrated his concern by going home to vote. The defeat was widely reckoned as fatal to his aspirations for the Presidency in 1868.

The *New York Herald*—which at *that* time was bitter toward Chase and ardently supporting Grant—made the most of the defeat, notably in its issues of October 21 and 22, 1867. It wrote:

The republican State of Ohio, the hotbed of Western radicalism, the home of Chief Justice Chase, who is the nigger-radical candidate for the Presidency, has emphatically refused to give

the negroes the suffrage. . . . It means that the superior white race . . . will not degrade the country and government by admitting an inferior race to equality with themselves. . . .

The *Herald* reprinted, in order to deride, an editorial from the *Cincinnati Commercial* which, evidently striving to repair Chase's position, pointed out that Chase favored *universal* suffrage, and for the South would couple suffrage with amnesty, and that he had opposed confiscation and the impeachment of President Johnson.

[4] *New York Herald*, Nov. 14; Impeachment Investigation, House Judiciary Committee, 39th Cong., 2d Sess. and 40th Cong. 1st Sess., 1175.

new citizens. The *Charleston Courier* of November 20 gave this reading
of the portents:

> A re-action of public sentiment . . . is sweeping over the land . . . .
> The Radical programme to perpetuate or secure their domination, by
> *negroizing* the Southern States, and rendering Congress unconstitution-
> ally supreme over a patriotic and resisting President and a subservient
> judiciary, has revolted popular feeling and met with popular con-
> demnation. Let the Democracy then plant themselves uncompro-
> misingly on the Constitution, as formed *by* the white race and *for*
> the white race, and uphold the rightful supremacy of that race, as
> founded alike on its great predominance of numbers and superiority
> of intelligence; and they will, ere long, seal the destruction of
> Radicalism. . . .

The editorial closed with an outcry against the impending *"negroized*
Conventions in the South."

The Nation discussed Negro voting in thoughtful articles. It began,

> There are no advocates of equal suffrage whose conviction of
> its inherent justice, and of its necessity in order to secure a safe
> reconstruction of the country, can much exceed our own. . . .

In working toward that end, however, the Republicans had made mistakes, "erring alike in being too bold, and yet not bold enough." The
39th Congress at its last session *should* have submitted a constitutional
amendment to establish equal suffrage throughout the land.[5]

> Experience has repeatedly shown that there are almost twice as many
> men who will vote for a legislature that they know will enact equal
> suffrage as there are that will vote for the proposition directly. . . .

While the defeat in Ohio would work "little practical injustice" there, it
had greatly increased the difficulty of establishing equal suffrage in the
South, where to leave power in the hands of the whites alone "involves
the most enormous practical injustice." A "single labor" to carry an
amendment to the federal Constitution would avoid local issues and
voters' prejudices.[6]

The Nation returned to the problem, in these reflections on "God's
Will in Politics":

> . . . The misfortune of the Republican party has been that it
> has had to enter on the discussion . . . under the leadership of some

---

[5] See supra, pp. 296–300.

[6] *The Nation*, "Means and Ends," 5:334, Oct. 24, 1867.

men who have been bred in anti-slavery agitation and were therefore unfamiliar with the use of the ordinary political instruments—who
have so long been accustomed to dealing with moral considerations
solely that they were unable to see the force of any other. They
therefore set about preaching equal suffrage with as lofty an indifference to the prejudices or opinions or traditions of the mass of
the public as if they had been offering the gospel to a set of
heathen. . . .[7]

Democratic success caused Republican leaders to become more
determined, more united, more daring. Now they must get on with the
business of Reconstruction, with an eye to placing their party in a
strong position in the South.

Justice Miller, well acquainted with the practical leaders of the
party, described the situation in a letter of December 22, 1867, to his
brother-in-law in Texas:

There seems to be doubt that Grant will be the nominee of the
convention called to meet at Chicago next May.

Many thinking men among the Republicans doubt whether
even his name can secure a victory. There are also many Republicans
who now regret the extreme policy of the reconstruction acts, in the
question of suffrage. But the strict party men,—the coolest among
them—feel as did Macbeth, that they have waded so far into this
sea of radicalism, that it were easier (and safer), to go over than turn
back. Negro Suffrage in the North will probably be abandoned as
a party platform but the experiment of reconstruction on the Congressional basis will probably be adhered to. 1st because the party cannot
turn back, second because it affords the only chance for a republican
party in the South.

I speak of these things with no feeling, and hardly a wish. I
think the progress of Congress in invading the functions of the
Executive and Judicial branches of the Government, was only less
dangerous than a return to power of the democratic party, with
absolute control of ten rebel States, governed by exasperated rebels,
and their party in the North under their control, as they always have
been, even during the rebellion.

I feel more than I ever did in my life indifference to party
success, and surely if it be desirable that a Judge should not be a
partisan, I am quite as near possessing that qualification, as any man
on the bench.[8]

---

[7] *The Nation*, 5:396, Nov. 14, 1867.
[8] Charles Fairman, *Mr. Justice Miller and the Supreme Court, 1862–*
1890 (Cambridge, Mass.: Harvard
University Press, 1939), 139–40.

These events and interpretations serve as background for a view of the course of Congressional Reconstruction in four States: Alabama, Virginia, and—sources of litigation in the Supreme Court—Georgia and Mississippi.

THE SITUATION NOW BEFORE THE SOUTH

THE SUPPLEMENTARY ACT had directed that in each State there be a registration, before September 1, of those eligible to vote. Then an election would be held, for or against calling a convention:

> *Provided*, That such convention shall not be held unless a majority of all such registered voters shall have voted on the question of holding such convention.[9]

At the same time, there would be an election of delegates to serve if a convention were called.

In this there lurked the possibility of bringing the Congressional program to a halt. Let all opponents *register*, so far as they were eligible. Then let them *stay away from the election. If* the stay-at-homes numbered as many as half of the total registration, no convention would be held: the State would remain under military administration; Negro suffrage would be averted; Congress would be checkmated. Success in this gamble, if possible at all, required concert among the conservatives. Every one who abstained would run the risk of the constitution being written by Radicals, black and white.

Or, opponents might attend and vote "No Convention": at the same time they could vote for candidates in whom they had some trust.

If, however, conservatives failed to agree, and some aimed at a majority of absentees while others aimed at a majority of "no" votes, they would contribute to a result which all dreaded.

The moderates who have been quoted above[10] had not the least affection for the Congressional program: they said simply that cooperation would lead to a better outcome than would resistance, and that the situation would be quite manageable *if* white men would act sincerely on their profession that they were the freedmen's best friends. They counted on a large stock of good will—*if* it was properly cultivated.

ALABAMA

THE *Montgomery Mail*—an anti-Reconstructionist organ—saw fit in May to call for a maximum registration by conservatives:

[9] Supra, pp. 320-21.   [10] Supra, pp. 366-78.

its importance has been greatly increased since the refusal of the Supreme Court to take jurisdiction of the questions involved in the military act leaves us completely at the mercy of that law. We cannot avoid or postpone the call of a convention either by apathy or refusal to register. . . . We have a clear conservative majority of twenty thousand . . . , and if we fail to poll our strength we shall deserve to suffer. . . .

The editor professed confidence "that Alabama will elect an honorable Convention of statesmen . . . ."[11]

But by September 29 the *Mail*, in the light of recent developments, had reversed its position:[12] now it said,

Do not vote on the Question of Calling a Convention!—Now that it is manifest that the people of the North do not desire reconstruction upon the Radical programme, and will not permit unconstitutional measures to be forced upon the people of the South, it becomes the duty of our people to come to the aid of our Northern friends and defeat the Reconstruction Scheme by every means left in our power. . . . If we do not desire to fasten the iniquity upon ourselves we must take care that we do not do anything to aid the designs of the Radicals. . . .

It calculated that if all opponents—plus conjectural overconfident Radicals—stayed at home, the convention would fail for want of a majority of the total number registered. It concluded:

Every vote given "against a Convention" increases the chances of the Convention being held, while every such vote withheld diminishes those chances.[13]

The *Montgomery Advertiser* held to its position that it would be "madness— . . . utter ruin—for the Southern States to postpone reconstruction until the Democratic party comes into power." "The wildest calculators" must know that a convention would be called; the question then was, "what class of men are to represent us?"[14]

Observing that on the first day of the election "hundreds of black voters crowded to the polls" while "the white people remained away," the *Advertiser* conceded that

---

[11] "Importance of Registration," May 23, 1867.

[12] Besides the Democratic victory in California, two other developments are relevant. On a large scale, whites had refrained from registering. And in Louisiana—whose election, on September 27–28, was the first to be held under the Reconstruction Act—the conservatives had inaugurated the policy of abstention from voting.

[13] Sept. 29, 1867, quoted in the *Mail* of Jan. 24, 1868.

[14] *Weekly Advertiser*, Sept. 17, 24.

influences brought to bear upon [the freedmen] have been greater than their old masters and friends could counteract, and for the time being they listen to other counsellors. . . .[15]

The figures for Alabama were these:
Registration:

61,295 whites
104,518 colored
———————
165,813 total

Voting on calling a convention:

For: 18,553 whites   Against: 5,583 whites
     71,730 colored   0 colored
     —————   —————
     90,283 total   5,583 total

Hence a convention would be called. Of the white registrants, 39 percent had come to the polls; of the colored, over 68 percent.

Alabama had cast 89,572 votes in the election of 1860. A census in 1866 showed 261,004 white males and 214,253 colored. Even allowing for disfranchisement, there must have been many whites who failed to register. Further, as the *New York Herald* commented, "the registered whites, excepting a few . . . , abstained from voting . . . ."[16] It was estimated that of 100 delegates elected, 96 (including 17 blacks) were Radicals.[17]

The *Mail* had said in the beginning, "if we fail to poll our strength we shall deserve to suffer."

VIRGINIA

THERE WAS HERE AN ACTIVE REPUBLICAN PARTY with a moderate and an extreme wing. The leaders of the latter would have been gratified if, instead of the Military Bill which became the Act of March 2, the scheme of the Louisiana Bill had been applied to Virginia, thereby placing the government in their itching hands.[18] The freedmen were welcomed into this membership.

Very few men of family and position would cross class lines to offer leadership to the new citizens. The notable exceptions in Virginia were John Minor Botts—former Whig in Congress, constant Unionist, and bondsman for Jefferson Davis—and Alexander Rives—long a mem-

---

[15] *Weekly Advertiser*, Oct. 1, 8.
[16] Nov. 5.
[17] Here, and in discussions that follow, the returns on registration and elections set out in Edward McPherson's *Political History of the United States of America during the Period of Reconstruction*, 3d ed. (Washington: James J. Chapman, 1880), 374, are used. Some additional data are derived from the Annual Cyclopedia.
[18] Supra, pp. 288–92.

ber of the legislature, briefly a judge of the State's highest court, and later, from 1871 to 1882, United States District Judge for the Western District of Virginia. Rives was thus described by the moderately conservative *Richmond Dispatch*:

> This gentleman has occupied a position bordering on isolation because of his opposition to secession . . . . He has not at all mended his hold upon the sympathies of the people since the war, as he has chosen to identify himself with the so-called "Union" men and Republicans. In thus tenaciously adhering to his peculiar views, and not seeking to restore his former politico-social relations with his people, he has made a great sacrifice of peculiar force to one raised a gentleman and possessed of decided social virtues and accomplishments. Withal, the Judge is a man of learning and dignity of character . . . .[19]

The attempt of these men to lead the Republican party of Virginia along a sober, rational course soon ended in failure. The freedmen were captivated by unscrupulous and relentless men, too unworthy even to be supported by the Radicals in Congress.[20] Foremost of these was the Reverend James W. Hunnicutt, from South Carolina, an embittered zealot "governed by a narrow desire to keep the Republican party of the State under his own control."[21] Conspicuous also was John C. Underwood, United States District Judge for Virginia from 1864 to his death in 1873.

As candidates for the constitutional convention in 1867, both Botts and Rives were defeated: the former by a conservative, the latter by a Negro—illiterate, it was said, and "of proscriptive sentiments."[22]

Both Judge Underwood and Judge Rives figure largely in the history of the Supreme Court.[23]

From many platforms, conservative Virginians early gave the new voters instructions on their civic duties. A typical occasion was the "immense concourse of white and colored citizens" meeting at Richmond, under the auspices of a Negro committee, on April 15, 1867. Among those invited to speak was Raleigh T. Daniel, a reluctant Confederate who was then building up the Conservative party, dedicated to maintaining white supremacy.[24] As reported in the *Dispatch*,

---

[19] Oct. 25, 1867.
[20] Infra, pp. 598–601.
[21] *The Nation* 5:354, Oct. 31, 1867.
[22] *Richmond Dispatch*, Oct. 25, 1867; *New York Herald*, Nov. 1.
[23] On Underwood, see infra, pp. 599–607, 823–28.
Rives' name is made memorable by

Virginia v. Rives, 100 U.S. 313, and *Ex parte* Virginia, 100 U.S. 339, decided on March 1, 1880, with other leading cases on the Fourteenth Amendment.
[24] Daniel (1805–77) had been trained in the law office of his uncle, Justice Peter V. Daniel; he was Attorney General of Virginia from 1872

He asked his hearers if they would vote against their own white people whether or no? They had a majority in very few localities, and why doom themselves to a perpetual minority. [Voice.-"Shall we vote de Democratic ticket?"] If they did vote against us, what would be the result? An employer would say to his servants, "You don't have anything to do with me, you don't come about me, and when I ask about voting you run off to a secret meeting. You have no confidence in me, and I can employ you no longer." And will your new friends make up your losses? Where have they done anything to provide for your well-doing? [A Voice.-"Dey fed us all de winter."] But they will not feed you all your lifetime, my friend, and you will feel much more like a gentleman when you sit down to eat your own meals in the consciousness that you have earned what you eat.[25]

The conservatives were to discover, in October, that this sort of talk won no votes.

From the seclusion and safety of the Eastern Shore, a correspondent predicted in July that

If *left alone*, our former servants, trained well in the school of past servitude, and still attached to us (we continuing to treat them well, as we are bound by gratitude for the past as well as present interest) would be found in nothing hostile to that section in which they live . . . .[26]

In mid-October, however, the *New York Herald*'s correspondent reported from Richmond that

Since the recent elections in the North . . . , a marked change has come over the whites of the South. Many prominent newspapers and men who, despairing of any better terms, were preparing to advise or were advising acquiescence in the will of Congress and favoring the calling of a convention, are now opposing that measure. A reaction pervades every political circle, and at present all is involved in chaos . . . . The radical blacks have become infected . . . , and disorder and confusion exist in their ranks. . . .[27]

The *Richmond Enquirer and Examiner*—"unequivocal advocate of white supremacy"—announced on October 17 that "the turn in the

---

to his death. With James Lyons, Robert Ould, and others, he purchased the old *Enquirer* and the lately burned-out *Examiner* to launch the *Richmond Enquirer and Examiner* as the "defender of the conservative patriotism of the State," first appearing on July 15, 1867.

[25] Apr. 16. The *Dispatch* was publishing such items as "A Sensible Darkey Tells How He Became Free," and "A Colored Preacher Gives Some Good Advice." Apr. 15.
[26] *Dispatch*, July 18.
[27] Letter of Oct. 12, in *Herald* of Oct. 19.

angry, roaring, cruel tide of Northern sentiment has at last commenced."
On October 21, the day before the election began, it gave this "Advice
to Respectable Freedmen":

> nine-tenths of the freedmen in this city depend upon the white pop-
> ulation for their daily bread, as well as for shelter. Without the
> patronage and employment of the whites they must starve or seek
> their livelihood elsewhere.

If, contrary to advice, they voted for the Radicals, "they will have none
but themselves to blame when they pay the penalty for their folly."[28]
On the morning of election day, the *Dispatch* urged the freedmen
to adhere to their true friends, their late masters who had "parted with
their former servants in friendship and good will"—"the world never
beheld so mild a system of slavery"; they should desist from following
"strangers—the descendants of those who captured the native Africans
to make slaves of them . . . ."[29]
Registration had shown:

$$
\begin{array}{r}
120,101 \text{ whites} \\
105,832 \text{ colored} \\
\hline
225,933 \text{ total}
\end{array}
$$

Many whites had refrained from registering. Pursuant to the statute,
the Department commander apportioned 105 places in the convention
(equal to the number in the lower house of the legislature) among the
cities and counties, giving one delegate to each unit or, if need be, to
two or more contiguous units. Large surplus fractions were recognized
by giving an additional delegate to two or three units together. The
outcome was that 58 delegates were allotted to districts wherein there
was a colored majority and 47 to those where whites were more numerous.[30]

Evidently the hope for a convention with moderate outlook lay in
a full participation by the whites and in the possibility that some freedmen would accept prudent leaders.

---

[28] Oct. 21.
[29] Oct. 22.
[30] The figures on registration and
voting, by counties and towns, are
set out in Doc. No. 5, *Documents of
the Constitutional Convention*, Richmond, 1867, at pp. 51–56.
General Schofield reported to General Grant: "This apparently anomalous fact results from the unequal
distribution of the colored population
as compared with the white over the
State, the white majorities in the

western counties being very large,
while the colored majorities in the
central and eastern counties are comparatively small." *Richmond Dispatch*, Oct. 31, 1867. The *Dispatch*
absolved General Schofield from "the
least blame" for the result.
In some Eastern counties, the
colored majority was as small as 25,
61, 70, 86. In some Western counties,
the entire Negro registration was only
5, 9, 47, 56, 58, and 65.

The election on October 22-24 on calling a convention resulted as follows:

For:	14,835 whites	Against:	61,249 whites
	92,507 colored		638 colored
	107,342 total		61,887 total

Of the whites registered to vote, 63 per cent had come to the polls; of the colored, 88 per cent.

At the same time, delegates were chosen: 80 whites and 25 colored men; 70 were Republicans (almost all Radicals) and 35 were Conservatives.

The *Dispatch* pronounced this post mortem:

> The white voters remained at home throughout the State, Richmond being almost the only exception. Counties having large white majorities, as Bedford . . . have sent down Radical delegations.[31]

This, it said, was the result of "so much clashing counsel."[32]

The *New York Herald*'s correspondent at Richmond wrote on October 26:

> The whites, who had thirteen thousand and upwards registered majority, feel keenly the degradation of their boasted State; and all through their own apathy and neglect—the passive do nothing policy so strenuously and effectively advocated by the press here. The very papers here that were mainly the cause of defeat have raised a howl that is ridiculous beyond measure. . . .

Those chagrined were throwing "a liberal share of censure" on General Schofield.[33]

The correspondent reported, further, that the feeling of the whites toward the colored people was "now one of bitter animosity . . . . Already large numbers are discharged from work . . . ." The *Herald* reprinted editorials from half a dozen Virginia newspapers, urging that that penalty be applied.[34]

---

[31] Bedford had 2,408 white and 2,110 colored registrants. Voting at the election were 1,676 whites (less than 70 percent) and 1,900 colored (90 percent). Two Radicals were elected.

Quite a number of instances might be cited where white majorities by default suffered Radicals to be elected.

[32] Oct. 26.

[33] *Herald*, Oct. 30.

The Nation of November 14 took note of allegations of fraud and mismanagement thrown up by white citizens of Richmond. It commented that one who read their protest and the carefully detailed reply would appreciate "the difficulties with which the district commanders labor" in dealing with "the most perverse and obstinately foolish of communities." 5:386.

[34] Oct. 29, 30.

The *Nation* commented,

> Of course the Conservatives themselves are largely to blame for this result. It is they who first made the issue one of race. They have left nothing unsaid or undone to convince the negroes that what they sought was . . . the absolute exclusion of all colored persons from a share in the Government, and this the negroes, of course, resented in the only way in their power. . . . The greatest misfortune of all is . . . that the negroes thus provoked should fall into the hands of leaders like Hunnicutt. . . . [T]hey are now, thanks to him and his coadjutors, arrayed against all whites, some of their own best friends included.[35]

On December 3, 1867, the convention met; it chose Judge Underwood as its president. In four and a half months it framed a constitution with some remorseless provisions.

On December 11 and 12, some eight hundred Conservatives met in Richmond and organized to defeat the prospective constitution. The central proposition, in the resolutions it adopted, was that while all men should be equal before the law, "the governments of the States and of the Union were formed by white men to be subject to their control"; and that was how they should remain. R. M. T. Hunter, sometime United States Senator, and Confederate Secretary of State, made the principal speech. He regarded Negro suffrage as meaning control by the colored race; "he had no hesitation in saying that he preferred the military control" to submitting to the "decree of Congress": "Under military government he was controlled by men of his own race; educated men who acted under the responsibility of their commission and in some degree under the control of the President . . . ."[36]

Not until 1870 would Virginia achieve a painful accommodation.[37]

GEORGIA

GOVERNOR JENKINS' SUIT in the Supreme Court had been dismissed on May 13, 1867.[38] Now what would the people do?

From the outset, ex-Governor Joseph E. Brown had been urging compliance.[39] He quoted the Sermon on the Mount: "Agree with thine adversary quickly." "This vexed question may soon be permanently settled upon the best terms which we will ever be able to get." "We have

---

[35] 5:346, Oct. 31.
[36] Ann. Cyc. 1867, 763; "Correspondence of Robert M. T. Hunter," *Ann. Report of Am. Hist. Assn. for* *1916*, 2:353 (1918).
[37] Infra, pp. 598–601.
[38] Supra, p. 389.
[39] Supra, p. 311.

entered upon a new era. We need capital and labor. Neither will come till our difficulties are settled . . . ."[40]

More acceptable by far were the voices of ex-Governor Herschel V. Johnson[41] and Benjamin H. Hill,[42] urging resistance. The latter, after exhorting whites to register but *not* to vote, declared in a peroration that "it is better that we suffer [the Radicals] to dig ten millions of graves and hide within them the . . . Southern people uncoffined and forgotten, than that we . . . should dig one grave for our sense of honor . . . ."[43]

As in Virginia and Alabama, so in Georgia: Democratic victories in the North brought a toughening of resistance. The election would begin on October 29; on the twenty-sixth the *Augusta Chronicle* reported that

> The conservatives of Georgia, encouraged by the action of their friends in Alabama, have adopted the plan by which the latter came so near winning victory. Their press and leading men have, with singular unanimity, advised the people not to vote on the convention question . . . .

Only by that strategy, it was reckoned, could the "scheme for Africanizing the State" be defeated.[44]

The *Macon Journal*, when the election was at hand, urged abstention:

> Tyranny has left you but one weapon. Seize it. . . . Remember the 8th of October and the votes of Ohio and Pennsylvania. When New York and New Jersey speak let not your action be as a gag on their shout of victory.[45]

The advice was followed. "The returns from all parts of the State indicate that the conservatives took no part . . . ."[46]

Again this strategy failed. The returns from registration had been

$$
\begin{array}{rl}
96,333 & \text{whites} \\
95,168 & \text{colored} \\
\hline
191,501 & \text{total}
\end{array}
$$

---

[40] *Athens Southern Watchman,* Mar. 6; *Charleston Courier,* Feb. 28, Mar. 9; Ann. Cyc. 1867, 362.

[41] (1812–80). He had been candidate for Vice President on the Douglas ticket in 1860; Confederate Senator. He was denied admission as United States Senator in 1866.

Johnson will figure prominently in the attempt to win from the Supreme Court a holding that the Cotton Tax was unconstitutional. Infra, pp. 879–81, 889–95.

[42] (1823–82). Confederate Senator; after the war a Representative in Congress and then Senator.

[43] *New York Herald,* Oct. 1, quoting speech in Georgia on Sept. 11.

[44] Quoted in *New York Herald,* Oct. 29.

[45] Oct. 25, quoted in *New York Herald* of Oct. 29.

[46] *New York Herald,* Oct. 30, 31.

Of those registered, only 106,411 came to the polls. They voted as follows on calling a convention:

For:	32,000 whites	Against:	4,000 whites
	70,283 colored		127 colored
	102,283 total		4,127 total

Of the white registrants, 37 per cent came to vote; of the colored, 74 per cent. The great mass of conservative whites had abandoned constitution-making to the Radicals.

The convention met on December 9. When it attempted to obtain from the State Treasury an advance of money to defray expenses, Governor Jenkins refused. Out of this a controversy arose, which led to the suit of *Georgia v. Grant, Meade et al.*, filed in the Supreme Court on March 16, 1868. This further challenge to the Reconstruction Acts will be considered presently.[47]

MISSISSIPPI

THE DIVISION BETWEEN THOSE, represented by Barksdale's *Jackson Clarion*, who saw wisdom in embracing the Congressional program, and those who disdained it, whose strongest voice was Colonel E. M. Yerger, has been explained.[48]

On June 5, 1867, Colonel Yerger became editor of the *Vicksburg Herald*, a post he held until late in January 1868.[49] He persisted in arguing that the Southern States were then and there the "constitutional peers" of the loyal States, unaffected by the "void act of individuals" and the "pretended" elections by which the organization "called the Confederate States" had been created. The Constitution was a contract, and "No State shall pass a law impairing the obligation of a contract."[50] Reflecting pre-war political differences, he affirmed that it was the same old "diabolical, jesuitical, secession party machinery for

---

[47] Infra, pp. 433–37.

[48] Supra, pp. 374–78.

[49] From June 5 to August 25 the journal bore the title *Herald and Mississippian*.

[50] Editorials of June 20, 26, 29; July 4, 11. He maintained this position, commented the *Clarion*, "with a gravity which would be ludicrous, if the occasion were not too serious for jest." June 27.

Yerger claimed support from what Chief Justice Chase at that moment said in an opinion in the Circuit Court for North Carolina: "On no occasion, however, and by no act, have the United States ever renounced their constitutional jurisdiction over the whole territory and over all the citizens of the republic . . . ." Shortridge v. Macon, Fed. Case No. 12,812, holding that compulsory payment of a debt to a receiver under the Confederate sequestration laws did not defeat the right of the creditor. See infra, pp. 629n., 861.

hoodwinking the people" that once again would "push us on to ruin"—this time by bowing to Congressional Reconstruction.[51]

"Our Platform," he announced, was "The supremacy of the Constitution over State and Federal governments . . . ," "Opposition to all coerced amendments . . ." and to interference with "suffrage or other matters of rightful State administration." He would secure the citizen's "right to the blessings of civil government, trial by jury, and the administration of law in the civil courts"; also "equal protection to the freedmen by just laws impartially administered . . . ." And most emphatically, "Opposition to a Convention under the provisions of the 'Sherman Military Bill' . . . ."[52] He would not "elevate the negro beyond the standard God intended": let all men be warned that

> when they vote for a Convention they vote for the initiation of a war of races which when commenced will end in the extermination or banishment of the negroes. . . .[53]

While the Impracticables preached defiance, the Moderates were holding meetings where experienced leaders talked to mixed audiences. Their efforts worked up to a dinner held at Terry on July 4, where ex-Governor A. G. Brown told his colored friends that it was "by the finger of God," and not by the work of the Republicans, that they had attained their freedom. George Harris, responding, expressed thanks to the All-Wise Ruler of the Universe for hardening the heart of Mr. Davis so that he rejected the emancipation of Mr. Lincoln.[54]

Such a coming together exposed its promoters to "misrepresentation." Yerger's *Vicksburg Herald* called it "a grand amalgamation barbecue," "the most unbecoming, unfortunate move ever sanctioned by white men in this country."[55] The *Clarion*, in defense, assured its readers that "strict decorum and a due regard for social usages" had been observed: refreshments had been eaten at *separate* tables. It asked,

---

[51] "Wire Pulling at Jackson," July 12, 1867.

William C. Harris' *Presidential Reconstruction in Mississippi* (Baton Rouge: Louisiana State University Press, 1967) gives major attention to distinguishing ante-bellum affiliations of the leading figures of 1865–67. Former Whigs, such as E. M. Yerger and George L. Potter "appeared to delight in associating their old Democratic foes with Northern radicalism."

He comments that this "oversimplified party alignment on reconstruction and Negro suffrage." Pp. 243–44.

[52] Carried at the masthead, July 20 and thereafter.

[53] June 14, 18.

[54] *Clarion*, July 6.

[55] June 16, July 9—pointing out that it had been promoted by "ex-secession leaders—they have domineered in the South long enough . . . ."

> If the negro is not to be taught, and counselled with, by our own
> Southern people, are we to censure him if he seeks information of
> those who would strive to lead him in the way he should not go?[56]

That put the matter neatly. Intransigents might rail at mixed assemblies arranged by the "Assistant Radicals," the "mongrel party"—but where, otherwise, would black citizens be going to hear talk about their new rights?

Colonel Yerger's acrimonious remarks about others, and his hot temper when repaid in kind, brought him into several affairs of honor with other journalists[57]—as when the *Clarion* retorted that "Prince Beautiful has a very sore head," and again when Yerger charged by innuendo that editors urging acceptance of the statute were apostates motivated by a desire to win federal patronage.[58]

The *Vicksburg Times*—competitor of the *Herald*—originally took the position that neither by more fighting nor by more arguing could the people of Mississippi remedy their grievances;

> It is only by getting back into the Union . . . , and, do as they may,
> there is but one way of getting back—the way indicated by the Military
> bill. . . .[59]

But a month later a new editor was appointed, with a very different point of view: Colonel William H. McCardle.

As Colonel Yerger is being dwelt upon because he became a petitioner in the Supreme Court,[60] so the far more important case of *Ex parte McCardle*[61] is reason for scrutinizing the conduct of the new editor of the *Vicksburg Times*.[62]

---

[56] July 6.

[57] *Clarion*, July 11, 18, 21, 1866; Apr. 4 and 7, July 11 and 17, 1867; *Meridian Gazette*, Apr. 6, 1867; *Columbus* (Georgia) *Enquirer*, Apr. 9, 1867, quoting *Vicksburg Herald* of Apr. 2; *Vicksburg Herald and Mississippian*, July 12 and 17, 1867. Of five affairs here noticed, only one went so far as an exchange of shots, and in that neither party was struck.

[58] By Sec. 7 of the Appropriations Act of March 2, 1867, it was made the duty of the Clerk of the House of Representatives to select, in the Southern States, the newspapers in which official publications would be made. See infra, p. 440.

[59] Quoted in the *Clarion*, May 9, 1867.

[60] Infra, ch. 12.

[61] Infra, ch. 10.

[62] Born at Maysville, Kentucky, June 1, 1815, McCardle went to Mississippi as a youth and engaged in journalism. In politics he was then a Whig. He died at Jackson, April 28, 1893.

His name appears in *War of the Rebellion: Official Records of the Union and Confederate Armies*. On April 8, 1862, his "gallantry and good conduct" were mentioned by his division commander, Brigadier General Charles Clark. Again, in Lieutenant General J. C. Pemberton's report of

McCardle's editorials urged the whites "to resist despotism and despots," to maintain "the rights of the people who were born free";[63] they should refuse to participate in the infamous Congressional scheme. He made the *Times* a "racy journal" (Yerger's characterization[64])— less heavily freighted than the *Herald*, but excelling in vituperation. A sample is his denunciation of "The Scoundrelism of Satraps" in an editorial of November 6, 1867—an item that figured in the military proceedings that led to his appeal to the Supreme Court:

> We said a few days since that to be a military satrap, in the poor down-trodden South, was, ex necessitate rei, to be a scoundrel. As there is a good God in Heaven, we believe it; and we believe also that there is not a single shade of difference between Schofield, Sickles, Sheridan, Pope, and Ord,[65] and that they are each and all infamous, cowardly, and abandoned villains, who, instead of wearing shoulder straps and ruling millions of people, should have their heads shaved, their ears cropped, their foreheads branded, and their precious persons lodged in a penitentiary.[66]

Yerger reproved McCardle for giving circulation to an unfounded report of harsh action on the part of the District commander: "Our

---

August 25, 1863, McCardle's "constant performance of . . . arduous and responsible duties" was noted. These services were as assistant adjutant general, at Corinth and then at Vicksburg. Ser. I, vol. X, pt. I, 414, 415; vol. XXIV, pt. I, 249, 293.

President Davis charged Pemberton to hold Vicksburg; but then his immediate commander, General Joseph E. Johnston, instructed him to abandon the city and hold his army for a concentrated attack upon Grant. Pemberton remained in Vicksburg, and on July 4, 1863, surrendered.

Recriminations followed; and McCardle went into print in defense of his chief. In a letter to the *Mobile Register and Advertiser* he pronounced Pemberton to be "chiefest among those deserving of honor." Later he withdrew imputations against one of Pemberton's subordinates.

Johnston complained of McCardle to the War Department: his account contained "an untruth and a great exaggeration." Ser. I, vol. XXIV, 1061–66.

Subsequently McCardle was colonel and adjutant general of Missis-

sippi on the staff of Governor Charles Clark, his old chief. Ser. IV, vol. III, 308–9.

[63] "The New Year." Jan. 1, 1868. McCardle's editorials prior to 1868 cannot be followed closely: the broken file of the *Times* has a gap for all of 1867. Occasional quotations appear, and one may judge from his editorials in 1868.

[64] *Herald*, Sept. 19, 1867.

[65] The general officers then in charge, respectively, of the First, Second, Fifth, Third and Fourth Military Districts under the Reconstruction Act.

[66] *Ex parte* McCardle, Transcript of Record, p. 11.

"You stimulate my intellect & fecundate my thoughts," L. Q. C. Lamar once wrote to McCardle, "almost coveting" his trenchant style. Letter of May 31, 1875. McCardle was "a journalist . . . who has not abused the privileges of the press, but has zealously labored to exalt its mission," Lamar wrote to President Cleveland on April 7, 1885, urging an appointment. Letters in Mississippi Department of History and Archives.

neighbor of the Times seems to think that Gen. Ord is his special private property, and that no one else has a right either to abuse or defend him." While the general had done some things that Yerger regarded as "unnecessary and unconstitutional," still "as a courteous gentleman and one desirous of performing his unpleasant duties with as little oppression as possible towards our people, we believe him to be above reproach . . . ."[67]

Yerger constantly urged—and McCardle derided—the idea that Southern conservatives should now unite in a new Constitutional Union party, casting off the Democratic party and its old leaders who had carried the South into secession.[68]

The rival Vicksburg editors were agreed, however, in objective: to stand upon the Constitution as it was in the past, without the Fourteenth Amendment; to maintain government by white men only; and to frustrate the Congressional plan. They urged voters to register, and then to vote *against* a convention.

The differences between those who would vote *for* a convention and seek to enlist the freedmen in choosing *moderate* delegates supporting impartial suffrage, and on the other hand those who would spurn a convention, were argued at well-advertised assemblies, such as that at Brandon on August 26, when Albert G. Brown opposed George L. Potter in a four-hour debate. Brown—who as a Democrat had been elected as Congressman, Governor, and Senator, and then had served in the Confederate Senate—urged the importance of meeting Congress on its own platform.[69] Potter, formerly a Whig, "too old to learn [the new] negro minstrelsy of Union," argued that the void acts of secession could not destroy the Union or the rights of the States. It was not the work of rebels, it was the action of Congress, that now deprived them of their rights. The status of the Southern States had been recognized when the proposed Fourteenth Amendment was submitted for their consideration—and for good reason they had rejected it. How perverse and illogical now for Congress to subject them to military government, like conquered provinces, and at the same time demand that as States they ratify the Amendment! The real purpose was to put the Southern

---

[67] *Herald*, Oct. 11, 13, 1867.

[68] The idea was "Quixotic, . . . crazy and impracticable," said the *Times* on January 8, 1868. "Simply absurd," said the *Clarion*, January 14.

[69] Throughout the post-war period he urged moderation. Thus in 1874 he rejected the idea of a "white man's party:" "Give [the Negro] full justice, and he may no longer lend a willing ear to those who are his worst enemies." Edward Mayes, *Lucius Q. C. Lamar: His Life, Times, and Speeches,* 2d ed. (Nashville, Tenn.: Publishing House of the Methodist Episcopal Church, South, 1896), 246. The triumph in Mississippi of ideas he opposed led Brown to withdraw from politics in disgust. See D.A.B.

States under black rule, so that the Radicals could control them. "Our only hope . . . is to vote against this plan of military reconstruction."[70]

In late September, when the election was five weeks away, a State Central Reconstruction Club was formed at Jackson. Judge William Yerger was chosen president; Ethelbert Barksdale was chairman of the platform committee.[71] Although the Reconstruction program was "oppressive," rejection would lead to "accumulated oppressions." Without questioning the motives of those promoting a Constitutional Union party (Colonel Yerger, Potter, and their following), the success of their course would only incite Congress to impose terms "more stringent and humiliating." The Reconstruction Club sought the "prosperity of the colored population," with no discrimination; there should be an "efficient system of public schools for all classes." Capital should be attracted, and immigration from the North and from Europe should be encouraged; labor should be protected. The federal Cotton Tax—which bore heavily upon the "freedmen, who have commenced life anew in an untried capacity"—should be repealed. Such was the policy the voters of Mississippi were asked to support. The formation of county organizations was urged.

Looking toward "The Approaching Elections," one month thence, the *Clarion* observed:

> We have not believed that there would be any separate and distinct organization of the negro voters on an exclusively caste basis, unless a pretext for such an organization should be furnished by the consolidation of the whites into a separate party with a view to deprive the former of the privilege conferred upon them by Congress. . . .
>
> If there were not exciting causes to intensify the spirit of antagonism, the ascendancy of the negro element would be of necessity, ephemeral. . . .[72]

---

[70] The debate was reported in the *Clarion* of August 29. Potter's reply was dismissed in few words. The account above draws upon the full report of a speech he had made at Raymond on August 17, reported in the *Herald* of August 28-31.

Potter had been one of the most intractable members of the constitutional convention of 1865. In the debate over the formula for abolishing slavery, he wanted to go no further than a declaration that whereas certain authorities of the United States regarded the slaves as emancipated, but had failed to honor the obligation to compensate, the good people of Mississippi, reserving all rights, would for the time being submit to the view enforced by the federal authorities. Mississippi then stood "precisely as she stood on the day when she was admitted in the year 1817." *Journal of the Proceedings and Debates*, 55-56, 70. Supra, pp. 108-09. James W. Garner, *Reconstruction in Mississippi* (New York: Macmillan Co., 1901), 87.

[71] *Clarion*, Sept. 28. Others of the committee were Judge Wiley P. Harris, Amos R. Johnston, Thomas J. Wharton, and Fulton Anderson (a prominent lawyer, and brother-in-law of Colonel Yerger).

[72] Oct. 5.

IX: *The Background of Further Litigation*

In plain reason, wrote the *Clarion* on October 30, one week before the election, we

> cannot expect the freedmen to vote against [the convention], or to declare their unworthiness to accept the rights with which they have become invested; but it is to be expected that they will vote for men to serve in that body who have capacity, experience and intelligence . . . .

The freedmen should "understand distinctly" that the local candidates of the Reconstruction party were "fully committed to conform . . . to the requirements of the Military Bill"—specifically, to insert in the constitution a clause securing them the suffrage.

"STAY AWAY FROM THE POLLS"

THE RECALCITRANTS had been counting heavily on Democratic gains in the North, and, it will be recalled, elections in Ohio and Pennsylvania on October 8 confirmed those hopes.[73] When these returns were known, a bold change in tactics was adopted: instead of going to the polls and voting No on a convention, let conservatives *abstain* from voting. If a majority of the registered voters did not come to the polls, there could be no convention. But, the tacticians argued, even if a majority did come to the polls, and a convention were called, and even if a bogus constitution were to be framed, still the recent elections in the North showed that the voters there were "determined to be rid of the tyranny, usurpation and extravagance of the mongrel party. . . . The grand shield of the Constitution is held over us by the conservatives of the North . . . [where] our friends are imploring us to be firm and reject the poison that is offered us in the cup of reconstruction."[74]

Colonel McCardle later boasted that the *Times*—not Colonel Yerger's *Herald*—"was the FIRST JOURNAL IN THE STATE to advise the white men of Mississippi not to vote at the Convention election."[75] In pursuit of this objective he took steps which led to his being charged before a military commission with "Impeding the reconstruction of the Southern States under the Reconstruction Acts"—whence arose the case of *Ex parte McCardle*.[76]

---

[73] Supra, p. 400.
[74] *Herald*, Oct. 20. The *Herald* from October 11 was filled with this theme.
A convention of the Constitutional Union Party at Jackson on October 15 adopted the policy "to abstain from any participation whatever in the election . . . ." *Herald*, Oct. 17.
[75] *Times*, Jan. 8, 1868.
[76] Infra, p. 437.

The election opened on Tuesday, November 5; it would continue in each county as the board of registration progressed through its several precincts, one day or if need be more being allowed in each precinct.[77] The publication of two editorials in the *Times* on the morning of November 6 was specified as the acts of impeding:[78]

> STAY AWAY FROM THE POLLS.—We again urge every decent white man, every honorable gentleman of the Caucasian race, to avoid Gen'l Ord's election as he would avoid pestilence and a prison. As this advice does not apply to, and is not intended for the white sneaks of the loyal league, we shall expect to see these last-named despicable vermin out in all their strength. We should like to see the scoundrels in procession in daylight. We would engage Herrick to take their photographs.[79] They would make an addition to the rogues' gallery; and if our neighbor Clarke would only have them transferred to the Police Gazette, the transaction would ensure his fortune.[80]

The second editorial was:

> THE IMMORTAL EIGHT.—We are gratified to be able to announce to the readers of the *Times*, that at the court-house yesterday, the

---

[77] G.O. No. 31, Hq. Fourth Mil. Dist., of September 26, 1867, is reprinted in Ann. Cyc. 1867, 53–54.

[78] Transcript of Record, *Ex parte* McCardle, 11–12.

[79] Herrick & Dirr, local photographers.

[80] H. C. Clarke, local bookseller, conducted a Newspaper and Periodical Agency, and constantly supplied Vicksburg editors with periodicals, including the *National Police Gazette*. In return they mentioned him in their columns.

With McCardle's STAY AWAY FROM THE POLLS, compare the account in Robert Lowry and William H. McCardle's *History of Mississippi* (Jackson, Miss.: R. H. Henry, 1891), at 372–73. (The exclusions to which they refer were the result of the Act of Congress, not of the General Order; so too the admission of Negroes to vote.)

General Ord . . . issued an order . . . for an election of delegates to a Convention . . . .

In selecting delegates to that Convention a large number of the most intelligent white citizens in the State were excluded from participation in the election, by test oaths, penalties, etc., while negroes, ignorant and unscrupulous, knowing nothing of the responsibility attaching to the elective franchise, were made the docile instruments of an equally ignorant and more corrupt and worthless class of white men than ever cursed a free country.

This motley assemblage, known to this day as the "Black and Tan Convention," was called to order January 7th, 1868, by Alston Mygatt, who appeared there as the "so-called" representative of the people of Warren County. He delivered an address overflowing with venom against the people of his own race . . . .

There were a number of able, patriotic and true men in the Convention, but they were . . . powerless to accomplish good— confronted as they were by an overwhelming majority of characterless adventurers and ignorant negroes . . . .

Robert Lowry, the co-author, had been a Brigadier General, C.S.A., and was Governor from 1882 to 1890.

only place open to the white people, there were cast the votes of eight white people only!! We tried to get the names of the interesting sneaks who voted, but failed, though the *Times* office was and is prepared to pay a dollar for the name of each voter. We shall publish the names of these voters if we can obtain them, and some day we shall; but if we do not, we shall with pride chronicle the fact that in the heroic city of Vicksburg, the gallant Saragossa of the South, there were only eight cowards, dogs and scoundrels of the Mygatt and McKee stripe.[81]

Challenging the military authority to hold McCardle on this and other charges, habeas corpus proceedings were brought in the federal Circuit Court, held by District Judge Robert A. Hill. The result was that on November 25 McCardle was remanded to custody. He promptly took an appeal to the Supreme Court, and at once was admitted to bail.

Ex parte McCardle, as a momentous legal controversy—over the constitutionality of the Reconstruction Acts, and then over the power of Congress to withdraw a pending case from the jurisdiction of the Supreme Court—will presently receive minute examination.[82] For the moment, Reconstruction in Mississippi will be traced somewhat further.

In Mississippi there was a small numerical preponderance of

---

[81] Alston Mygatt was president, and McKee was secretary, of the Republican party in Mississippi. They were delegates to the constitutional convention from Warren County, and took leading parts in its proceedings.

Mygatt, a Northern man who had come to the State before the war, then operated a cotton gin at Vicksburg, was a State Senator from 1870 through 1873.

George C. McKee (1837–90), then practicing law at Vicksburg and a Register in Bankruptcy, was a Representative in the 41st, 42d, and 43d Congresses, where he sought legislation to refund the Cotton Tax—a matter greatly desired in the South. *Infra*, pp. 893–94.

McKee was born in Illinois, and attended Knox College. Admitted to the bar in 1858, he practiced at Centralia, in the southern part of the State. During the war he rose from private to the command of the 11th Illinois Infy.; his service was in the Mississippi valley, including the Vicksburg campaign. His name appears frequently in the *War of the Rebellion: Official Records*; repeatedly there is mention of gallantry and bravery. Ser. I, vol. XXXII, pt. I, 315–31; pt. III, 562 et seq.; vol. XLVIII, pt. I, 1027; pt. II, 257. He appears in April 1865 as Brigadier General commanding Enrolled Militia: 1st and 2d Mississippi, and 1st Mississippi Freedmen.

Robert J. Walker, in his argument in Mississippi v. Stanton on May 3, 1867, made a puzzling allusion to "the battalions from Mississippi who shed their blood in defence of the Constitution and the Union." *National Intelligencer*, May 4. He may have had reference to McKee's brigade of militia.

Lowry and McCardle, in their *History of Mississippi* (1891) say: "General McKee, having invested his means here, like the manly fellow he was, determined to stick by the State. He made many friends and died in the year 1890, after a long struggle with disease, sincerely lamented by the general public, political friends and foes alike." P. 631.

[82] *Infra*, ch. 10.

blacks over whites. An enumeration conducted by the State in 1866 showed

$$343,460 \text{ whites}$$
$$381,258 \text{ blacks}$$
$$\overline{724,718} \text{ total[83]}$$

If whites would exert a preponderance in influence, it behooved all eligible males to register. In this they might expect to be more alert than the freedmen. And they might induce a considerable number of freedmen to follow the advice of their "true friends."

Yet in mid-October the *Hinds County Gazette*—published in Raymond, in the same county as Jackson, the capital—observed a "lamentable picture": "many thousands of white men" had failed to register.[84] It pointed to the registration figures (then incomplete):

$$46,636 \text{ whites}$$
$$60,167 \text{ blacks}$$
$$\overline{106,803} \text{ total[85]}$$

The *Gazette* continued: "In the year 1860, over 69,000 white men voted in the State for President, while the total vote has gone as high up as 86,000. Look at Hinds County, for instance: in 1860 we cast 2,146 votes; in 1867 the total number of whites registered is 1,551 . . . ." Those who had failed to register bore "a weight of responsibility": the black majority "could have been, and would have been overcome, had every one registered who was and is entitled to do so under the laws of Congress."

Among the whites who did register, those who would go to the polls and vote *against* a convention, would still be able to join with moderates in voting for well-qualified delegates. But if they stayed away, and yet a convention were called, it would surely be dominated by those whom they branded as utterly unfit.

The mid-October shift by anti-Reconstructionists—from voting *against* a convention to *abstaining*—was actually a surrender of constitution-making to the Radicals. It was desperate to seek, by persuasion or threats, to keep enough men away from the polls to hold the total vote below a majority of the total registration. The most substantial hope these tacticians could have entertained, such as it was, lay in keeping the situation unsettled until Democratic victories in the North forced an abandonment of the Congressional program.

In the Fourth Military District, the published returns from the

---

[83] *Clarion*, July 17, 1867. Ann. Cyc. 1866, 521–22, gives incomplete figures.

[84] Quoted in the *Clarion*, October 16.

[85] Ann. Cyc. 1867, 517.

completed registration of voters and from the election made no distinction by color. For Mississippi the figures were:

Registered: 139,690

The total number voting at the election was 76,016.

On calling a convention, the division was

For: 69,739   Against: 6,277[86]

Notwithstanding the effort to avert it, a majority of those registered— 54 per cent—had come to the polls. Of those who came, 92 per cent voted *for* a convention.

As previously in Louisiana, in Alabama, in Virginia, and in Georgia, now once again those who would frustrate Reconstruction by abstention had been defeated. And those who hoped to go forward with a convention inclined to moderation had been disappointed. Radicals would frame the constitution, and would adopt measures to exclude their opponents from voting and from holding office.

Colonel McCardle, after a brief interruption, returned to the *Times*; thereafter he displayed a new device at the mast-head: "Remanded by Judge Hill."[87]

When the returns presently showed that there would be a convention, and that Radicals would have a large majority, the conservative groups made common cause. The "Yerger–Potter–Constitutional–Pop-gun–Party"[88] disappeared. Colonel Yerger accepted a place on the Democratic Central Committee, where he sat with Judge Yerger, Barksdale, Judge Harris, and John W. C. Watson, the leading conservative member of the constitutional convention.[89] When delegates were chosen for the National Democratic Convention meeting in New York City on July 4, Colonel Yerger was named from the State at large; and

---

[86] Ann. Cyc. 1867, 519–20.

[87] To avoid a misunderstanding that has sometimes occurred, it should be explained that McCardle was soon in more trouble with the military authorities. He and Colonel James Dugan, Radical editor of the *Vicksburg Republican*, had exchanged such "libelous assaults" as threatened, in the judgment of the District commander, to disturb the peace. On December 5 he directed that both be arrested and held, subject respectively to release on giving $1,000 bond to keep the peace. Each editor made bond. On January 27, 1868, General A. C. Gillem (Ord's successor) revoked the order and discharged the bonds. S.O. No. 198, Jr. Ser., Hq. 4th Mil. Dist., Dec. 5, 1867; S.O.

No. 17, Jan. 27, 1868. This episode had no relation to *Ex parte* McCardle.

The *Mobile Register*, confusing the two incidents, supposed that the order of January 27 was a cunning device to render the appeal moot. McCardle explained: "Quite a number of Ord's puppies had been snapping and barking fiercely *at us, while we were in prison* . . . . To save his puppies from a larger share of contempt and scorn, and for fear that they might *get hurt*, the big *dog* . . . required us to give bonds to keep the peace . . . ." *Times*, Feb. 16, 1868.

[88] *Times*, January 18, in a final vindictive thrust which McCardle promptly disavowed.

[89] See infra, pp. 424–26.

from the 4th District, Barksdale would be a delegate and McCardle an alternate.[90] Potter became Democratic candidate for Congress, opposing Colonel McKee.

CONSEQUENCES OF THE NONACTION POLICY

THE *Clarion* in a significant editorial of January 3, 1868, took account of developments. Without insisting unduly on the theme of we-told-you-so, it said:

> Whatever differences of opinion may exist as to past policy, it is now conceded that the Clarion was right in advising all the Conservative people in the State so far to waive their disgust at the enactment of the Military bills as to register their names as voters under them, and to vote for Conservatives to represent them in the Convention, no matter whether they were in favor of calling a Convention or not, or of reconstruction or not.—We may not have had wisdom to foresee the popular uprising in the Northern States which would spare our people the necessity of choice between reorganizing under the terms of these bills, or submitting to more stringent measures; but we did not underrate the importance of their voting in the election and voting for Conservative men to represent them in that body in case the opposition to calling it should fail of success.
>
> On this ground there might have been, and ought to have been concert of action among Conservatives: and there would have been, but for the change in tactics which was adopted a short time previous to the election, by a portion of the anti-reconstruction party.
>
> In the few counties where concentrated efforts were made to defeat the Radicals, the best results attended them. Notwithstanding the divisions to which we have referred, there will be from twenty-five to thirty Conservatives in the Convention, nearly one-third of the body.[91] Suppose, that following the example of the counties which have secured Conservative delegates, a united effort had been made in all the counties . . . from the seashore to the Tennessee line, in which the white element numerically predominates, is it not evident that the Convention would have been under the entire control of Conservatives? And in the hands of such a body how securely from the assaults of Radical agrarianism the people would have reposed? But it is idle to repine at past errors, or to indulge in crimination and recrimination, when all were prompted by a patriotic desire to do what they believed to be right. . . .

[90] *Clarion*, Feb. 21, 25; *Times*, Feb. 22.

[91] Garner counted only nineteen as Conservatives, out of one hundred members. *Reconstruction in Mississippi*, 187. But in the election of a president, Watson, Conservative, received 33 votes, to 53 for Eggleston, the leading Radical. *Journal of the Proceedings*, 7.

It was not by the design of Congress, but by the tactics of the defiant ones, that this one-sided result had occurred. But that fundamental truth would henceforth be conveniently ignored, and presently forgotten.

The *Clarion's* editorial of January 3 then turned to the immediate future:

> It is earnestly desired that the Conservatives elected to the Convention will be at their posts, every man of them, when it assembles on the 7th inst.—By entire union and concert among themselves, they may be the instruments of effecting much good . . . . Prominent among them, and one to whom the eyes of the people are turned with no ordinary interest, is the Hon. J. W. C. Watson, of Marshall County. . . . He is the leader of the "forlorn hope" in the ensuing struggle. . . .[92]

The convention, concerning itself with many things beside framing a constitution, ran from January 7 to May 18. It asked Congress for authority to vacate all State offices and fill them with loyal appointees. It had difficulty in raising funds for current expenses.[93] McCardle commented:

> Ord's convention has as much *right to* levy a tax upon the people of Mississippi, as a lot of drunken Choctaws have. . . . If they want pay for their invaluable services, let them do as the negroes in the Georgia Convention have done, go and *black boots* at a hotel . . . .[94]

The *Times* gave a daily report of proceedings, under such captions as "Ord's Nigger Convention,"[95] and "The Chain-Gang Convention."

In the Reconstruction Act of March 2, Congress had said that, to conform to its program, a new constitution should extend the suffrage to all adult male citizens, "except such as may be disfranchised for

---

[92] Watson, of Holly Springs in northern Mississippi, appears in the D.A.B.

He had striven to defeat secession; in the last year of the war he served as a Confederate Senator. In the convention of 1865 he sought to avoid antagonizing the North.

In 1885 he successfully argued the Railroad Commission Cases, 116 U.S. 307 (1886), where the Court held that the State's power to fix reasonable rates for railroads (established in Chicago, B. & Q. R.R. v. Iowa, 94 U.S. 155 in 1877) was not sur-

rendered by the grant of a charter that authorized the railroad "to fix . . . tolls and charges." Opposed to him were John A. Campbell, Wiley P. Harris, and other able counsel.

[93] So too did other conventions. Thus arose Georgia v. Grant, Meade *et al.* Infra, pp. 434-37.

[94] *Times,* Jan. 15. The Supplementary Act of March 23 authorized the convention to levy a tax—but that produced no ready funds.

[95] Garner puts the number of colored delegates at seventeen. *Reconstruction in Mississippi,* 187.

participation in the rebellion, or for felony at common law."[96] In the Mississippi convention, the majority wanted far-reaching disqualifications. The Conservative minority would not bow to the statute; J. W. C. Watson regarded it as "not obligatory upon me or upon the people of the State. So flagrant a violation of the rights of the State has never, in my judgment, been perpetrated . . . ." The minority would grant suffrage to whites only.[97]

In the outcome, the article on "Franchise" provided that to be eligible one must swear that he was not disqualified by the Reconstruction Acts and that "I admit the political and civil equality of all men." In the section on holding office: all who had supported secession—except such as had advocated the assembling of the convention of 1868 and continuously advocated the acts of the same—would be ineligible; provided, however, that only by reason of having voted for or signed the ordinance of secession would a private soldier in the Confederate army be barred by this section.

Upon the adoption of this article, Watson and most of the other Conservatives resigned from the convention.[98]

Meanwhile, in the Supreme Court, a motion to dismiss *Ex parte McCardle* for want of jurisdiction had been overruled. Argument on the merits would begin on March 2. The *Vicksburg Times* of February 19 reported the editor's reaction: "Of the result we have no doubt . . . . Rumors, speculations and conjectures from Washington, never disturbed our confidence or shook our faith."

McCardle himself was at that moment on the morning train bound for Jackson, to attend the convention of the "Democratic White Man's Party."[99] Resolutions were there adopted: one promised the colored people "safety of person and property, and full guarantees against oppression and injustice as freedmen"; voting and office-holding were denied, because of "ignorance and incompetence."[100]

Hopes for a great deliverance by judgment of the Supreme Court were dashed when *Ex parte McCardle* was put over to the December term. Congress by a statute of March 27 had repealed the grant of jurisdiction under which McCardle's appeal had been brought.[101]

On May 19, the day following the adjournment of Mississippi's constitutional convention, an order was published, calling an election to begin on June 22.

To defeat the "mongrel constitution," the Democrats counted on

---

[96] Supra, p. 300. This was the provision for which Sumner had contended.
[97] The *Clarion*, Mar. 20, reported Watson's speech at length.
[98] *Journal of the Proceedings*, for

Apr. 16 and 17; *Clarion*, Apr. 17 and 18.
[99] *Times*, Feb. 19.
[100] *Clarion*, Feb. 21; Ann. Cyc. 1868, 512.
[101] Infra, p. 465.

the 63,674 registered voters who had failed to vote in November. "Under the non-action policy," said the *Clarion*, "this vast army . . . remained away from the polls. This reserve force will now come to the front, and do what they are able to save the liberties and civilization of the white race . . . ."[102]

Colored citizens would be voting on the constitution, and now the Democrats besought them to vote to *reject*, because it was unfair to whites. The Democratic Central Committee professed that in the future "Special attention will be given to the protection and security of freedmen in their Constitutional rights of person and property and to their instruction in all matters pertaining to the public interest."[103] Grand barbecues and picnics were organized and free transportation provided, for "every man who can attend—white and black, Conservative or Republican." Negro Democratic clubs were promoted, and welcomed to join in torchlight processions. White and colored speakers were heard. "Judge Sharkey proved to [the freedmen] conclusively that it was alone to the Democratic party that they must look for the preservation of all the rights with which they are vested." Colonel Yerger "explained the fallacy of supposing universal suffrage and universal liberty went together";

> Upon the question of negro suffrage, he declared that the people of Mississippi had never yet formally expressed their sentiments. He warned the black man that he was now on trial, and as the States finally would settle the matter of suffrage, it depended entirely upon the justice and wisdom displayed now by the black voters whether they would hereafter enjoy the right upon a firm basis. . . .

If they carried the proposed constitution, they would raise "a storm which would finally sweep them from the face of the earth."[104]

Colonel McCardle—so forward in urging the tactics which had produced the present situation—now appeared on platforms where black and white were called to unite to extricate the white men from their plight. Far more credible in this effort, however, were such thoughtful men as Judge Yerger and Judge Harris, who had forewarned of what would result and had done their best to avert it. Among the Democratic speakers were L. Q. C. Lamar[105] and Horatio F. Simrall.[106]

---

[102] May 20.

[103] *Vicksburg Herald*, Apr. 7, 1868.

[104] *Herald*, June 5, 6, 7, 12, 16, 17, 20, 23, 25, 27.

[105] Then the sole professor in the Law School of the University of Mississippi. He conducted the two-year course by means of daily oral examinations on assigned parts of standard texts, with explanations and lectures, supplemented by moot courts. Advertisement in the *Clarion*, Aug. 24, Oct. 8, 1867, and other dates.

[106] As representative from the southwesternmost county in the State,

The Loyal League, composed of Radicals, white and black, was pressing the freedmen to go to the polls and vote for the constitution. To combat this influence, the Democratic party warned of the penalty for criminal conspiracy. An opinion by Judge William Yerger was published everywhere. He wrote:

All confederacies or leagues whatever, wrongfully to prejudice third persons or the public, are highly criminal at the common law.

On the illegal purpose:

The free exercise of the right to vote . . . is of the utmost importance to the public. On it depends the maintenance of free governments and the safety of the State. Any attempt to interfere with its exercise, by fear, threats or intimidation of any kind, or to deceive and defraud the voter as to his rights and duties is a great public wrong, and cannot be too highly stigmatized or punished. . . .[107]

(This may be used to test what, before the tables had been turned, Colonel McCardle had done by his editorials.[108])

---

in the legislature of 1865 he was chairman of the Joint Select Committee that framed the Act to confer Civil Rights on Freemen, and other measures comprised in the "Black Code." Supra, p. 112. In 1867 he brought in the report of a Joint Committee on the "North Carolina Plan." Supra, p. 280n.

His part in reaching the solution whereby Mississippi was presently readmitted to representation was effective.

In the Republican administration of Governor James L. Alcorn, Simrall was appointed a Justice of the Supreme Court. There he delivered the opinion in Donnell v. The State, 48 Miss. 661 (1873)—here mentioned because in the case of Bell v. Maryland, 378 U.S. 226 (1964), concerning Negro sit-in demonstrators in a restaurant, the import of the Mississippi case was debated between Goldberg, J., and Black, J. At 290–91, 298–99, 304–5, 307n, 340–41n.

Donnell had been convicted of refusing to sell to a Negro a ticket to a theatrical performance in a public hall, because of color, in violation of the State's Civil Rights Act of 1873. In habeas corpus, he contended that the statute was unconstitutional in that respect, as taking private property for public use without compensation, in violation of the State's Bill of Rights. The court held that the provision as to admission to theaters did not infringe the State constitution.

In the course of his opinion, Judge Simrall observed that "Events of such vast magnitude" had occurred within the last decade "that the public mind is not yet quite prepared to consider them calmly and dispassionately." "The 13th, 14th and 15th amendments are the logical results of the late civil war . . . . The fundamental idea and principle pervading [them], is an impartial equality of rights and privileges, civil and political," to all citizens. He said that "The statute deals with subjects which have always been under legal control"— and then mentioned resort to places of popular amusement along with service by common carriers and innkeepers.

[107] Clarion, June 13; Herald, June 17.
[108] Supra, pp. 420–21.

Inasmuch as McCardle has been quoted on McKee, it is fair to quote the latter—at a "Grand Mass Meeting" at Vicksburg on June 1: "Who is this McCardle? . . . This lying braggart always vaunting his own bravery, and anxious to bring difficulties to settlement by the duelist's pistols . . . ." Further particulars were still less flattering.[109]

At the election in June 1868 on the proposed constitution, the number voting was 120,091. (Compare this with the situation in November 1867: total registration was 139,690, of which 76,016 came to the polls.[110])

On the ratification of the constitution, the division was

　　　　For:　　56,231　　　　　Against:　　63,860

Thus it had been rejected.[111]

By about the same numbers, Democratic candidates for State office defeated Republicans. Four Democrats, and McKee, were successful in Congressional contests. However, since the defeat of the constitution meant that the State would remain under military control, the balloting to fill offices came to naught.

After much bitterness, an arrangement was reached at Washington in March and April 1869, whereby the President was authorized to submit the constitution at another election, with separate votes to be taken on the several proscriptive features.[112] At an election on November 30 and December 1, 1869, these features were rejected; otherwise the constitution was adopted. The readmission of Mississippi followed on February 23, 1870.[113]

INFLUENCE OF THE *NEW YORK HERALD*

THAT THERE WAS A SUBSTANTIAL MOVEMENT among thoughtful Southerners promptly to accept the Congressional program, is a significant fact. But once again, intransigence defeated accommodation and led to more travail. In reflecting on how this had come about, the editor of the *Jackson Clarion* pointed to the *New York Herald* as a considerable factor:

> No journal has done more to give impetus to the tide of opposition to radicalism in the North than the New York Herald, and none has had a more powerful agency in confirming the purpose of the whites in the South not to reorganize their State governments under

---

[109] *Vicksburg Weekly Republican* ("Official Journal of the United States"), June 2, 1868.
[110] Supra, p. 423.
[111] Ann. Cyc. 1868, 515.

[112] Act of April 10, 1869. A delegation of moderate Democrats, led by ex-Governor A. G. Brown and H. F. Simrall, had prepared the ground.
[113] Infra, p. 589.

the Congressional plan. Its terse and pungent articles exposing the injustice of the military bills, and predicting that more lenient terms would eventually be accorded the South by the Northern people, were circulated by the local press and read with avidity and hopefulness, and consequently have contributed largely to the result . . . .[114]

This well informed judgment merits attention.

The *Herald*, then under the direction of the younger James Gordon Bennett (1841–1918), had this to say on "The Influence of the Herald—No Mystery About It":

> Affiliating with no party, we are at liberty to speak, as no partisan journal can, of great public questions freely and frankly. Our enterprise and views and constant habit of keeping time with the footsteps of progress enable us to be ahead of all other papers in the punctuality and variety of our news. Our correspondents are to be found where ever any events are transpiring which can be of the least interest to the public . . . .[115]

One preoccupation of the *Herald* in 1867 was constantly to disparage the black people, a "barbarous" and "degraded race"—as in editorials on "Nigger Rights and Nigger Wrongs," and "The Nigger Question and the Republican Party."[116] It carried much special correspondence from the South, giving strongly bent interpretations of local developments. It reprinted editorials from all over the South, of like tendency. (Some have been quoted in the foregoing text.) Consider the appreciation by its correspondent in Canton, Mississippi:

> The appearance of your welcome sheet is always hailed with delight by the people in this portion of the satrapy of General Ord who are fortunate enough to get hold of it, and particularly since they believe it to contain the true sentiments of the mass of the Northern people concerning the disposition of the South in the future. Had the people believed that the conquering North would impose negro suffrage upon them, the constitutional amendment would long since have been adopted; but sane men in this land of the sun could not understand how their brethren up North of cooler and more thoughtful temperament would be willing to see intelligence and virtue succumb to ignorance and vice.

---

[114] Nov. 29, 1867.
[115] Oct. 6, 1867. Reprinting and complimenting itself upon appreciative editorials in the *New Orleans Picayune* and the *New Orleans Times* of Sept. 29, which had quoted and

relied upon what the *Herald* had said in an editorial of Sept. 27: that the North condemned "the radical policy of Africanizing the South."
[116] Oct. 14, 28.

. . . You may rest assured that blacks will vote *en masse* for the Convention, and extreme radical members thereof, the whites will as a general rule not vote at all. . . .[117]

Thus at a period that was critical for the future of the South, the *Herald* exerted a pervasive influence confirming the innate local disposition to resist.

The *Herald* did not cater to a thoughtful clientele.[118] It was not concerned about consistency. Having turned against President Johnson,[119] it condemned both him and the 40th Congress: both would pass away "and that will be the last of them."[120] The *Herald*'s solution was to go back to the Fourteenth Amendment, which it credited with having had "an overwhelming popular majority" from Maine to California. In editorials on "What Ought to be Done," "What is the Duty of Congress,"[121] it recalled what the 39th Congress had proposed—which, "if we are not mistaken, . . . has been ratified by three-fourths of the States represented in and constituting the government of the United States":

All, therefore, that is needed to give it effect as a part of the supreme law of the land is a resolution or bill from Congress declaring the ratification. . . .

That, the *Herald* supposed, would suffice: "Why can't we have the views of 'Old Thad Stevens' upon this question?"[122] No matter that the rebel States had rejected the Amendment:

Try them again, then, and they will be wiser. They will be glad to take it, on the sober second thought. Thus, within six months of the meeting of Congress the whole business may be settled, and permanently, too . . . .[123]

---

[117] *Herald*, Oct. 30.

Madison County, of which Canton is the seat, had by a census of 1866 a population of 4,457 whites and 13,789 colored, a total of 18,246.

The registration was 3,496, of whom 2,300 came to the polls.

The *American Citizen*, published at Canton, was a leading anti-Reconstruction organ.

[118] At the moment it was catching attention by a new policy: "We shall no longer publish in the Sunday HERALD any notices or criticisms of the Devil's doings at the theater. On

the contrary, our readers may purify and prepare themselves for religious notices . . . ." Oct. 20, 1867; also Oct. 27.

[119] It was urging a movement for Grant, which would upset the politicians, and make the country "perfectly safe against all extremists, radicals or copperheads." Oct. 22, 1867.

[120] Dec. 4, 1867.

[121] Oct. 19, Nov. 23.

[122] Nov. 23, 1867.

[123] Oct. 19, 1867.

It was a brash assumption to say that ratification by three-fourths of the States represented in Congress would suffice.[124] To proceed upon that line would doubtless have led to a challenge to the existence of the Amendment. Would the Supreme Court hold that whether a sufficient number of States had ratified was a "political question" to be determined by Congress? If not, then on the merits would the Court hold that a sufficient number had ratified? That would touch upon the delicate question whether indeed the Constitution had established "an indestructible Union of indestructible States."[125] Critics of Congress had dilated on its disregard of specific provisions of the Constitution: now the *Herald* announced that "the whole business" could be settled by conjuring away the specific provisions of Article V on the amending process.

But the *Herald*, by its remark, "Try them again," seemed to recognize that acceptance of the Fourteenth Amendment by the Southern States was requisite. To carry out its proposal, legislatures elected under the all-white constitutions would have had to be recalled, to express their "sober second thought." Waiving the impracticability, would they now, with Congress in retreat, accept what they had spurned a year earlier? As recently as February, when the "North Carolina Plan" had proposed a settlement on the basis of a greatly attenuated variation of the Amendment, the reaction at home had been discouraging.[126]

When the freedman was just beginning his painful ascent, the *Herald* did all it could to push him down. When thoughtful Southerners were striving to lead their people out by going forward, the *Herald* exerted a "powerful agency" in encouraging recalcitrance. When, in consequence of Southern rejection of the Amendment, the country was committed to a perilous course, the *Herald* spread confusion by its fatuous counsel. In contrast to the *Evening Post*, with its "adherence to moral principle,"[127] and the *World*, with its clearheaded calculation of Democratic interests[128]—examples of responsible journalism—the *Herald* was only adding to the unreason and bitterness of the moment.

---

[124] Supra, p. 257.
[125] See Texas v. White, which had been filed in the Supreme Court on Feb. 15, 1867, infra, pp. 638–40.

[126] Supra, pp. 275–81.
[127] Supra, pp. 343–55.
[128] Supra, pp. 255, 366–67.

CHAPTER X

Ex parte McCardle *and* Georgia v. Grant, Meade et al.

REGISTRATION IN THE VARIOUS STATES was held in the late summer or early autumn of 1867. Elections followed, being completed by late November. In every State, the vote was in favor of calling a convention. First meetings came between November 1867 and February 1868. (Texas is excepted from the above: it moved about three months later.)

If Congressional Reconstruction could yet be stopped by a judgment of the Supreme Court, certainly to be effective it should be won during the session that opened in December 1867.

Jeremiah S. Black was the central figure in this endeavor. The cases on which he fixed his hopes were two: *Ex parte McCardle*, an appeal from the denial of release on habeas corpus by the Circuit Court for Mississippi;[1] and *Georgia v. Grant, Meade and others*, an original suit growing out of Governor Jenkins' refusal to permit money in the State Treasury to be advanced to meet the expenses of the convention.[2] McCardle's appeal had been docketed on December 23, 1867. Counsel moved for leave to file *Georgia v. Grant* on February 12, 1868.

Let it be said at once that Black's efforts failed. Fighting right up to the end of the term, he was unable to bring either case to a conclusion; each went over—which in itself was fatal—and in the end each was dismissed.

In June and July 1868, long before the Court met in its next December term, six of the ten States would have been readmitted to representation in Congress under their new constitutions.

We shall be examining, with minute care, what transpired in the Reconstruction cases at the term that opened on December 2, 1867.

---

[1] 6 Wall. 318 (1868); 7 Wall. 506 (1869). Supra, pp. 419–21.

[2] 6 Wall. 241 (1868). Supra, p. 413.

433

This would close on the first Monday (the sixth) of April: the Chief Justice announced an order to that effect on February 10.

GEORGIA v. GRANT, MEADE et al.

GEORGIA'S NEW SUIT began just as *Georgia v. Stanton* closed. On Monday, February 10, 1868, Justice Nelson delivered the Court's opinion in the suit to enjoin the Secretary of War.[3] Next morning's *National Intelligencer*, after reporting that opinion, at once told of

a new bill in behalf of the State of Georgia against Generals Grant, Meade, Ruger, *et al.* It is understood that this bill will avoid all the difficulties encountered in the former argument, and raises distinctly a question of property, to wit: the Treasury of the State. An injunction to protect this is prayed for.

When Georgia's convention met on December 9, 1867, it faced the problem of meeting its expenses. The Supplementary Act had authorized the levy and collection of taxes for that purpose;[4] by an ordinance of December 20, a tax was laid; and to provide funds in the meantime, the State Treasurer was "authorized and directed" to advance $40,000.[5] General Meade, commanding the District, by letter of January 7 requested Governor Jenkins to issue a warrant for that sum; he was "clearly of the opinion" that this action of the convention was authorized by the Reconstruction Acts, and was "informed" that there was a precedent in appropriations made by the convention of 1865.[6]

On January 10 the Governor, in a reasoned letter, declined to comply. Such a payment would not be "by appropriation made by law," as required by the Constitution of 1865. Even the Reconstruction Acts provided only for raising money by a tax, not by an advance. Finally,

---

[3] Supra, pp. 389, 391.

[4] Sec. 8 of the Act of March 23, 1867, provided:

That the convention for each State shall prescribe the fees, salary, and compensation to be paid to all delegates and other officers and agents herein authorized or necessary to carry into effect the purposes of this act not herein otherwise provided for, and shall provide for the levy and collection of such taxes on the property in such State as may be necessary to pay the same.

[5] *Journal of Proceedings*, 564. General Pope, then commanding the Third District, had assured his support, before the ordinance was enacted. *Journal*, 65, 72–74.

The Treasurer, however, on December 21 refused to comply.

There the matter stood when, by War Department order of December 28, Pope was relieved and General Meade was assigned to the Third District.

[6] The entire correspondence pertinent to this matter was published in the *Milledgeville Federal Union* of January 21—contained in the case file in the National Archives.

compliance would leave him without funds for the State government's own needs. (At the same time, by executive order he suspended the collection of State taxes until May 1.)

The Governor made no reference to the precedent of 1865. Actually, that convention had consistently authorized payments to be made out of the State Treasury; one such action was initiated and carried through by Jenkins himself, who had been that body's unquestioned leader.[7] The convention of 1865, meeting pursuant to President Johnson's call and acting in accordance with terms set by him, had had no more standing in preexisting State law than did that now meeting in pursuance of the Acts of Congress.

By letter of January 13, the general removed the Governor, "Both of us," he wrote, "are acting from a conscientious sense of duty, but this issue is so plain and direct that all hope of harmonious action must be abandoned." He appointed General Ruger to serve as Governor, and Captain Rockwell as Treasurer.[8]

Thereupon Jenkins caused the suit of *Georgia v. Grant, Meade, Ruger and Rockwell* to be initiated in the Supreme Court. (He also carried the State's money to New York. Thus frustrated, the military authorities reached out for some other State property that would yield some revenue, and seized a State-owned railroad.)

The convention promptly adopted a resolution declaring that Jenkins' suit, purporting to be brought by the State, was unauthorized and would not be litigated; it asked the Court to dismiss it.[9]

The bill named the several defendants as citizens of States other than Georgia. It asserted that Georgia "is, and of right ought to be, a free and independent State; that she possesses all the faculties and powers of self-government, except those ceded to the United States; and that in the exercise of her autonomy she has organized for herself a political system which secures to her people, and to all persons in her Territory, the best and safest protection of their rights which, under the circumstances, could be given." Further, complainant owned a lot of

---

[7] *Journal of the Constitutional Convention of 1865*, at 54, 188, 245, 254, 257, 258.

[8] The power to remove a civil officer, and to fill a vacancy, had been conferred expressly by the second Supplementary Act of July 19, 1867, 15 Stat. 14—after Attorney General Stanbery had given an opinion that the power was not to be found in the original Reconstruction Act. 12 Ops. Atty. Gen. 182, of June 12, 1867. The Act of July 19 further provided that District commanders would not

be bound by any opinion of a civil officer of the United States: it left them to use their own best judgment, with an instruction to construe the legislation "liberally, to the end that all the intents thereof may be fully and perfectly carried out."

[9] *Journal of Proceedings*, 314–16, Feb. 14, 1868. The vote was 105 to 24. With the majority was Amos T. Akerman, whose name will appear as Attorney General of the United States, 1870–71. The resolution was filed with the Court on March 18.

land whereon was the State capitol, a railroad, and funds in its Treasury. Defendants, without lawful authority, had arbitrarily appropriated this property as far as it was accessible, and had attempted to get possession of the money in the Treasury. Only the Supreme Court could protect complainant from irreparable injury. It prayed for an injunction and an accounting. The bill was signed by Jeremiah S. Black, James M. Carlisle, and Montgomery Blair.

Here at last was a suit asking for relief such as a court could give. Even so, the way was not clear. Was Georgia, then under a military administration, a "State" within the benefit of Article III's grant of jurisdiction? (The same problem was involved in *Texas v. White*, already awaiting its turn on the docket.[10]) And was Jenkins, removed from his office, competent to bring the complaint?

Attorney General Stanbery had notified Secretary of War Stanton that he would not appear in cases challenging the Reconstruction Acts.[11] His effective appearance in the injunction suits had been to protect the Government on jurisdictional points; on the merits, his opposition to the legislation was well known. Congress accordingly passed a resolution authorizing the Secretary of War to employ counsel to defend the officers named in the Georgia suit "and any other officer or person intrusted with the enforcement of the reconstruction acts . . . ." This became law, without the President's signature, on February 22, 1868. The Secretary retained Senator Trumbull and, at his request, Matt. H. Carpenter of Wisconsin. James Hughes, until recently a judge of the Court of Claims, was associated with them.

It was a question, when Black moved for leave to file the Georgia suit, whether the Court should first hear argument on the jurisdictional questions noted above, or should let the case be docketed and then take up all questions at one time. The press—which as usual learned about deliberations in conference—reported that it was over the dissent of some of the Justices that the latter course was decided upon.[12] The Minutes for March 9 show that the Chief Justice then gave the Court's response. This, as reported in 6 Wallace 241, was that opposing counsel would not be heard on the motion for leave to file; the "peculiar circumstances" in *Mississippi v. Johnson* had caused the Court to depart from its usual practice. (When leave to file *Texas v. White* was sought

---

[10] 7 Wall. 700. Docketed Feb. 15, 1867; argued February 5, 8 and 9, 1869; decided Apr. 12. Infra, pp. 638–40.

[11] This was by letter of December 31, 1867, after *Ex parte* McCardle had been docketed. The circumstances and resulting action are set out in Cong. Globe, 42–2, 1702–3. Mar. 15, 1872.

[12] *Boston Advertiser*, Mar. 28, 1868. It reported that Carpenter had expected to argue the point on the status of Georgia, and Trumbull the point on Jenkins.

and granted on February 15, 1867, no question had been raised by the respondents or suggested by the Court.)

So Black was permitted to file his bill, leaving the jurisdictional question to be resolved when the case came to be heard on its merits.

PROCEEDINGS AGAINST McCARDLE

AT THIS SAME TIME, Black had charge of McCardle's appeal from the order of the Circuit Court for Mississippi, which in habeas corpus proceedings had remanded him to military custody. McCardle's case would presently occasion a memorable test of nerve between the Congress and the Court.

By order of General E. O. C. Ord, commanding the Fourth District, McCardle had been arrested and confined on November 8, 1867; a military commission was directed to convene at Vicksburg on November 20 for the trial of certain charges against him. These were based upon editorials he had published in the *Vicksburg Times* between October 2 and November 6.[13] They were, (1) Disturbance of the public peace in violation of the Reconstruction Act of March 2, and (2) Inciting insurrection, disorder, and violence, in violation of that Act. Thereunder the same two editorials were specified: "The Insolence and Despotism of a Small Satrap"[14] and "A Startling Rumor."[15] Charge 3 was Libel: by an editorial on "A Bureau Beauty";[16] by the "Small Satrap" editorial; and by "The Scoundrelism of Satraps," expressing the editor's belief

> that there is not a single shade of difference between Schofield, Sickles, Sheridan, Pope, and Ord, and that they are each and all infamous, cowardly, and abandoned villains, who, instead of wearing shoulder straps and ruling millions of people, should have their heads shaved,

---

[13] The election on calling a convention opened on November 5; it was to continue as long as need be to permit the commissioners of election to proceed promptly from precinct to precinct within their respective counties. G.O. No. 31, Hq. Fourth Mil. Dist., Sept. 26. Ann. Cyc. 1867, 53, 517.

[14] On November 1. A "bogus sheriff" appointed by the military authority had declined to release a prisoner on the order of a State judge until he could consult his commander; the editor said that if *he* had

been in the place of the State judge, he would have imprisoned "this minion of a vile minion" and held him until compelled to release "by force of the bayonet."

[15] On Oct. 15. The rumor was that General Ord was going to remove Governor Humphreys: in that event, the latter should not surrender until the former used the bayonet.

[16] On Oct. 2. Captain Pratt of the Freedmen's Bureau was a "blackguard"; "Some of the antics of this low-bred creature . . . would disgrace any convict in the land."

their ears cropped, their foreheads branded, and their precious persons lodged in a penitentiary.[17]

Charge 4 was "Impeding reconstruction" by editorials of November 6 that have previously been set out: "Stay Away from the Polls" and "The Immortal Eight," threatening to publish the names of "scoundrels" and "sneaks" who voted at "Gen'l Ord's election."[18]

On November 11, in the federal Circuit Court at Jackson, held by District Judge Robert A. Hill,[19] counsel sought a writ of habeas corpus, alleging that McCardle's "arrest and detention is in contravention of the Constitution and laws of the United States."[20] By those words they invoked an Act of February 5, 1867, presently to be examined.[21]

The writ issued, returnable on November 21. At that time General A. C. Gillem, commanding the Sub-District of Mississippi, produced the prisoner. The hearing continued on the twenty-second and twenty-third. Appearing for the petitioner were Judge Sharkey; Walker Brooke, former United States Senator and Confederate Representative; and T. A. Marshall, sometime the State's Attorney General.

When on Monday, November 25, the Judge ruled against the petitioner, an appeal was taken—as authorized by the Act of February 5, 1867. Agreeably to that statute, the court ordered that the petitioner be admitted to bail, which it fixed at $2,000.[22]

In this opinion,[23] Judge Hill traced the measures taken by the United States since the attempted secession was subdued. The President, for the purpose of securing to citizens their rights under the Constitution and laws of the United States, had appointed Judge Sharkey to be Provisional Governor and vested him with the authority necessary to attaining the desired objects.

Congress had refused to permit the States to resume their relations to the Union on that basis, and had established its own method by the Act of March 2—"the powers thus intended to be conferred

---

[17] On Nov. 2. The general officers there named were then in command of the First, Second, Fifth, Third and Fourth Districts, respectively.

[18] Supra, p. 353.

[19] (1811–1900). Born in North Carolina, he had settled in Mississippi before the war. Formerly a Whig, he had taken no part in secession, although he continued in the office of probate judge. He sat in the convention of 1865. In 1866 he was appointed District Judge. For many years he was a trustee of the University of Mississippi—which is mean-

ingful for his standing with the people of the State.

[20] Transcript of Record in *Ex parte McCardle*, 1.

[21] Infra, p. 448.

[22] Next day he produced his bond, with S. McD. Vernon (a proprietor of the *Times*) as surety, and went free.

[23] The case is not reported in Federal Cases. Judge Hall's opinion was published in full in the *Jackson Clarion* of November 26 and in the *Meridian Gazette* of November 27. Of course it appears in the Transcript of Record, at 16–22.

upon the commander of the district being similar in purpose though differing in detail from those conferred upon Governor Sharkey by the appointment of the President." The judicial tribunals constituted by Governor Sharkey had derived their validity, "not by means of any express provision of the constitution [of Mississippi], but as growing out of the provision of the State . . . . Such being the case, it is difficult to perceive any substantial distinction between that case and the present. . . ."

> In the former case, the power was conferred by the President upon a civilian; in this, it is conferred by Congress upon a commanding general of the army. If it is the duty of the government of the United States in any one or all of its departments, to protect the citizens in their rights of person and property, and as a means of doing which, to provide for the punishment of disorder and crime, in the absence of a practical State government, then the choice of means must be made by the power conferring such authority.

It resulted that "I cannot come to that clear conviction of mind necessary . . . to pronounce this act repugnant to the Constitution . . . ."

Second, on the authority of the District commander to bring the petitioner to trial before a military commission on these charges: counsel had argued that the arrest violated the freedom of speech and of the press secured by the Mississippi constitution. That freedom, said Judge Hill, was as fully available here as in any other State: but it did not protect the speaker or publisher from the penalty prescribed for abuse. "It is admitted that the publications are libelous, and that under the laws of the State would subject the petitioner to indictment, and if found guilty, to punishment . . . ." He did not doubt that numerous safeguards —such as a speedy and impartial trial, with the right to have counsel and to call witnesses—were intended by Congress: but the statute had authorized the commander to bring cases before a military commission rather than before a judge and jury. It was ordered that the petitioner be remanded.

Judge Hill concluded: "I am gratified that the law [of February 5, 1867] has provided a direct appeal to the Supreme Court, which meets in the Capitol on Monday next, where any error I may have committed can be corrected. . . ."

The foregoing statement of the *McCardle* case bristles with issues, some of which will presently be mentioned.[24] Much greater discernment and restraint should have been exercised by those who drew the charges and by General Ord who approved them. One should keep one's eye on the substantial complaint that McCardle was using editorials of com-

---

[24] *Infra,* pp. 453–59.

pulsive power to intimidate citizens to keep them from going to the polls.

The position of the Southern press in 1867 was peculiar. Congress sought to open a tightly closed society to participation by a rejected class of new citizens—ignorant, propertyless, inured to servitude. Editors such as McCardle were determined that this should not be done; by threats which had support from the white community they were doing all in their power to prevent the exercise of rights which Congress had conferred. Even though the message was only that "every white man" forego his right to vote, the objective in view was of profound consequence to every citizen of the State, and indeed to the entire nation. In the Senate, Howe of Wisconsin read the two editorials specified in Charge 4, with the comment that "it is not surprising that you find the number of your registered voters largely reduced."[25] "To a few obstinate, short-sighted, and tolerably malignant editors," commented *The Nation*, "we are indebted for most of the delay in settling the terms of readmission."[26]

THE WRIT OF HABEAS CORPUS UNDER THE JUDICIARY ACT OF 1789

AT THIS POINT the narrative must halt, to permit an explanation of the writ of habeas corpus. Everyone knows that the great writ of liberty is one of the "bright constellation" of guiding stars of the Republic, as Jefferson said in his first inaugural. One might suppose that so invaluable a boon would be readily available. Actually its functioning was caught up in intricate difficulties. One who would appreciate the Court's protection of individual liberties must not disdain the mechanism by which the ends were reached. Since this is a recurring topic, it is in order here to lay the basis for references throughout the book.

---

[25] In debate on a Supplementary Reconstruction Bill, on Jan. 31, 1868. Cong. Globe, 40-2, 881.

[26] 5:142. Aug. 12, 1867.

The award of public printing and designation as "official journal" by State and municipal administrations threw substantial advantages to favored publishers. Among such beneficiaries in 1865 had been E. M. Yerger—State Printer, and publisher of the *Journal of the Proceedings and Debates of the Constitutional Convention of Mississippi*.

On the side of Congress, in order to nurture struggling Republican organs, it was provided by the Appropriations Act of March 2, 1867, that the publication of federal statutes and notices in the unrepresented States would be allocated by the Clerk of the House of Representatives (Edward McPherson, closely allied to Thad Stevens). See supra, ch. 9, n. 58.

In Moncure v. Zunts, 11 Wall. 416 (1871), it was held that this provision did not supersede an earlier statute directing federal courts to conform to the practice in the State courts in the matter of publishing judicial notices.

X: Ex parte McCardle

By the Great Writ, known by the characteristic words in its Latin formula, one who held another in custody was called upon to produce the body of his prisoner, and submit to the court the cause of the detention. To understand what went on in *Ex parte McCardle*, and in many cases thereafter, one must look closely at the constitutional and statutory provisions governing the issue of the writ—some applicable generally to the federal courts, others pertaining to the Supreme Court in particular. In 1806 Chief Justice Marshall acknowledged "some obscurity in the act of Congress" and "some doubts . . . as to the construction of the Constitution."[27] In 1890 Justice Miller observed that habeas corpus in the federal courts "has always been clouded with more or less doubt and uncertainty."[28] That is fair warning from two Judges who were outstanding for their effort to keep the law as simple and rational as could be.

> The Privilege of the Writ of Habeas Corpus shall not be suspended, unless when in Cases of Rebellion or Invasion the public Safety may require it.

So the Constitution provides, in Article I, Section 9.

Section 14 of the Judiciary Act of September 24, 1789, sought to make the constitutional guarantee effective. It contains three sentences. First, the courts of the United States

> shall have power to issue writs of . . . habeas corpus, and all other writs not specially provided for by statute, which may be necessary for the exercise of their respective jurisdictions . . . .

That seems to confer no new jurisdiction, but merely to make clear that a federal court may use the tools needful for doing whatever it is otherwise authorized to do. To illustrate, there was a form of habeas corpus for bringing into court a prisoner wanted for trial, and another to call a prisoner to testify.[29]

Second,

> either of the Justices of the Supreme Court, as well as Judges of the District Courts, shall have power to grant writs of habeas corpus for the purpose of an inquiry into the cause of commitment.

---

[27] *Ex parte* Burford, 3 Cranch 448.
[28] *In re* Burrus, 136 U.S. 586. Uncertainty persisted: Ahrens v. Clark, 335 U.S. 188 (1948); Johnson v. Eisentrager, 339 U.S. 763 (1950).
[29] Habeas corpus ad prosequendum and ad testifcandum, respectively— distinct from the Great Writ of Liberty, habeas corpus ad subjiciendum. Carbo v. United States, 364 U.S. 611 (1961).

To inquire into "the cause of commitment" was the function of the Great Writ. But doubt lurked in the language: it gave power to Justices and Judges, off the bench, "in chambers"—but it specified nothing about *courts*.

The drafting of the third sentence is better understood when one recalls that under a companion statute of September 23, 1789, federal prisoners would normally be lodged in a State institution;[30] now to preclude unwarranted intrusion by the federal judiciary it was

> Provided, that writs of habeas corpus shall in no case extend to prisoners in gaol, unless where they are in custody, under or by colour of the authority of the United States, or are committed for trial before some court of the same, or are necessary to be brought into court to testify.

Detention, allegedly unlawful, under claim of *federal* authority was going to be the major field of operation of Section 14.

In *Ex parte Bollman and Swartwout*[31] in 1807, the Court considered what was the power of the federal courts—as distinguished from the Justices and Judges—to issue the Great Writ. It recognized that courts of the United States have no common law jurisdiction; for them "the power to award the writ . . . must be given by written law." Marshall's opinion reasoned somewhat boldly that not only did each federal court have power to issue the writ in aid of a jurisdiction otherwise vested (Sentence 1), but must be understood also to share in the power given by Sentence 2 to Justices and Judges to grant the writ "for the purpose of an inquiry into the cause of commitment." "It would be strange if the judge, sitting on the bench, should be unable to hear a motion for this writ where it might be openly made, and openly discussed, and might yet retire to his chamber, and in private receive and decide upon the motion." By the larger interpretation of Section 14 the Court would give "life and activity" to the constitutional guarantee.

This discussion dealt with the power of the federal judiciary generally under Section 14. But the Supreme Court must always keep within this provision of Article III:

> In all Cases affecting Ambassadors . . . , and those in which a State shall be Party, the Supreme Court shall have original Jurisdiction. In all the other Cases . . . [within the judicial power of the United States], the Supreme Court shall have appellate Jurisdiction . . . , with such Exceptions, and under such Regulations as the Congress shall make.

---

[30] 1 Stat. 96. [31] 4 Cranch 75.

Here the great case is *Marbury v. Madison*,[32] in 1803. The plaintiff started an action in the Supreme Court, to compel the Secretary of State to deliver a commission. He pointed to Section 13 of the Judiciary Act:

> . . . The Supreme Court . . . shall have power to issue . . . writs of mandamus, in cases warranted by the principles and usages of law, to any courts appointed, or persons holding office, under the authority of the United States.

But as the Court construed Article III, whereas Congress could *except* from the *appellate*, it could not *add* to the Court's *original* jurisdiction. "It is the essential criterion of appellate jurisdiction, that it revises and corrects the proceedings in a cause already instituted," said Marshall. In obedience to Article III, the Court must refuse to entertain Marbury's original action.

Three years later came the case of *Bollman and Swartwout*, already cited. They had been committed by the Circuit Court for the District of Columbia on a charge of treason.[33] Contending that the commitment was illegal, counsel turned to the Supreme Court for writs of habeas corpus. As explained above, Marshall construed Section 14 to authorize any federal court to issue the writ to inquire into the cause of commitment. Furthermore, in the instant situation the Supreme Court would be revising the judgment of an inferior court; "therefore," he concluded, this application was "appellate in its nature." On this view, the writ was granted (and eventually the prisoners were discharged). Justice Johnson, dissenting, thought that this sort of proceeding could not properly be regarded as appellate. He added that Justice Cushing (absent through illness) supported his view.

Reverting for a moment to the first sentence of Section 14, federal courts could issue "all other writs not specially provided for" as might be needed in the exercise of jurisdiction. One such writ was certiorari, whose function is to call upon an inferior court to send up the record of its proceedings. Habeas corpus and certiorari worked together: thus counsel for Bollman and Swartwout sought and obtained not only habeas corpus to direct the Marshal for the District of Columbia to produce the prisoners, but also certiorari to bring up for review the record of commitment in the Circuit Court. "Habeas corpus aided by certiorari"[34] thus became a mode by which the appellate jurisdiction of the Supreme Court might be invoked; it was in addition to the ways

---

[32] 1 Cranch 137.
[33] United Staets v. Bollman *et al.*,

Fed. Case No. 14,622 (1807).
[34] Supra, ch. 2, n. 100.

expressly provided in the Judiciary Act as amended, which were the "appeal" in cases of equity, of admiralty and maritime jurisdiction, and of prize, and the "writ of error" in actions at common law. In 1802 Congress authorized still another mode, whereby when Judges holding a Circuit Court differed in opinion, they might "certify" the question to the Supreme Court.

Through the years, the cases on the Supreme Court's jurisdiction in habeas corpus were not very numerous. Sharp dissents showed that the path was not clear. Habeas corpus makes a challenge to official power—often in a context of public excitement. Bollman and Swartwout[35] were being pursued by President Jefferson for complicity in the Burr conspiracy. Justice Johnson, newly appointed, was protesting at what he regarded as the shaky reasoning by which Marshall got hold of the case. Near the end of his thirty years of service Johnson maintained "I have always opposed the progress of this exercise of jurisdiction, and will oppose it so long as a hope remains to arrest it";[36] he agreed with his Brother Baldwin that (aside from the "special provision" for a certificate of division of opinion) "there seem to me to be only two cases in which the appellate jurisdiction of the Supreme Court can be exercised: appeals and writs of error,"—the modes of review specifically authorized by Congress.[37]

Tobias Watkins—public defaulter and Presidential intimate who brought discredit upon an Administration[38]—was in jail under sentence of the Circuit Court; the Supreme Court denied habeas corpus on the ground that, inasmuch as it had been given no direct appellate jurisdiction in criminal cases,[39] surely it had no authority to exercise an indirect review by habeas corpus.

Thomas Dorr[40] had set out to overturn the Government of Rhode Island; now he was so tightly immured in the State prison that he could not send word to carry to the Supreme Court his contention that he had been denied rights under the federal Constitution. When a friend asked the Supreme Court to bring him out of durance by habeas corpus, the response was that under the third sentence of Section 14, no federal court could grant the writ for a State prisoner in this predicament.

---

[35] Supra, pp. 442–43.

[36] Dissenting in *Ex parte* Watkins, 7 Pet. 568, 581 (1833).

[37] Dissenting in *Ex parte* Crane, 5 Pet. 190, 205–6 (1831).

[38] *Ex parte* Watkins, 3 Pet. 193 (1830); John Quincy Adams, *Memoirs*, 12 vols. (Philadelphia: J. B. Lippincott, 1874–77), VII, 141, 144, 290.

[39] United States v. More, 3 Cranch 159 (1805); see United States v. Sanges, 144 U.S. 310, 319–22 (1892), and Cobbledick v. United States, 309 U.S. 323, 324–25 (1940). Supra, p. 86.

[40] *Ex parte* Dorr, 3 How. 103 (1845). See discussion of Luther v. Borden, 7 How. 1 (1849), supra, p. 395.

X: Ex parte McCardle

Metzger[41] was held for extradition to France on a charge of forgery; the order was made, pursuant to the treaty, by District Judge Betts at chambers, after protracted argument by able counsel.[42] Upon motion for habeas corpus in the Supreme Court it was held that in acting under such a treaty the District Judge "exercises a special authority, and the law has made no provision for the revision of his judgment." It was declared broadly that "this Court can exercise no power, in an appellate form, over decisions made at his chambers by a Justice of this Court, or a Judge of the District Court"—a proposition soon questioned,[43] which as Chief Justice Chase's correspondence shows proved embarrassing,[44] and which presently was consigned to oblivion.[45]

Kaine[46] was an Irish fugitive whom a United States Commissioner, acting under the extradition treaty, had committed for delivery to the British consul. Upon a full hearing in habeas corpus in the Circuit Court for the Southern District of New York (Betts, D.J.)[47] —a hearing marked by "the excited temper of the auditories which thronged the court" and by such threats "that he would be rescued from the custody of the law by a mob" that it was not safe to bring the prisoner into court—it was ordered that he be remanded. Thereupon Nelson, Circuit Justice—invoking the power which Section 14 vested in each Justice—granted habeas corpus "in consequence of the difficult and important questions involved," and made the writ returnable "before all the Justices of the Supreme Court of the United States, in banc, at the beginning of the next term."[48] (This was in imitation of the practice in the King's Bench in England.) Not trusting to this alone, counsel also moved in the Supreme Court for that Court's writs of habeas corpus and certiorari.

The conclusions of the Justices may be sorted out as follows. All agreed that the power vested in the individual Justice could not serve as a fulcrum by which to hoist a case into the Supreme Court. (But as a later Court said in the *Habeas Corpus Cases* in 1880,[49] "if the Justice who issued the writ found the questions involved to be of great moment and difficulty, and could postpone the case here for the consideration of

---

[41] *In re* Metzger, 5 How. 176 (1847).

[42] *In re* Metzger, Fed. Case No. 9511 (S.D. N.Y., 1847).

[43] *In re* Kaine, 14 How. 103, 133 (1852).

[44] Infra, p. 572.

[45] *Ex parte* Yerger, 8 Wall. 85, 99 (1869); *Ex parte* Virginia, 100 U.S. 339, 341 (1880).

[46] *In re* Kaine, 14 How. 103 (1852).

[47] *In re* Kaine, Fed. Case No.

7598 (1852). Counsel for petitioner were Brady, Busteed & Emmet—leading names, reflecting the importance of the case to Irish nationalists. Richard Busteed was appointed District Judge for Alabama in 1863, in which office he gave a very disturbing performance. Infra, pp. 828–32.

[48] *In re* Kaine, Fed. Case No. 7597a (1852).

[49] *Ex parte* Clarke, 100 U.S. 399; also *Ex parte* Siebold, 100 U.S. 371.

the whole court without injury to the petitioner, we see no good reason why he should not have taken that course, as he did. It had merely the effect of making the application for a discharge one addressed to the court, instead of one addressed to a single Justice." So it turned out to be only a matter of being more fastidious in the use of words; counsel must put a new address at the head of the application. Seldom can jurisdictional difficulties be removed so easily.)

Further in Kaine's case, concerning the attempt to obtain review by means of the Supreme Court's own writ of habeas corpus: here Justice Curtis, alone, stoutly contended that where the Circuit Court had refused to discharge a prisoner from *the commitment by the Commissioner*, that refusal could not be regarded as the "cause of commitment" by an inferior court which the Supreme Court (consistently with Section 14 and Article III) could review;[50] only where an inferior court had itself ordered the commitment did the Supreme Court have jurisdiction. Before setting this down to finicking technicality, recall that this was Benjamin R. Curtis, a mind too powerful to be servile to form, yet utterly submissive to the sense of duty. The notion that a judge could manipulate rules to get results would have seemed an affront to integrity. He was looking at the substance of things. The entire process of extradition, as he saw it, pertained to the Executive—the Court had been given no authority in the premises. Upon reflection, Curtis renewed his admonition that, notwithstanding "the bias, which I suppose every one has in favor of [habeas corpus]," the Court ought not to allow it "to unsettle the nicely adjusted lines of jurisdiction, and produce conflict and disorder" in the administration of the criminal laws of the United States or in the "action of the divided sovereignties by which our country is governed."[51]

Justice Nelson (Taney, C.J., and Daniel, J., concurring) disagreed with this stiff reasoning. He swung into a spirited encomium on the Great Writ:

---

[50] "The cause of commitment is to be looked for in the warrant under which it began, and has been continued, and not in the decision of a court pronouncing that warrant valid." 14 How. at 123.

[51] *Ex parte* Wells, 18 How. 307 (1856). Campbell, J., appointed since the *Kaine* decision, joined in this dissent.

Until 1889 there was no right to a review by the Supreme Court in criminal cases. Supra, p. 86. Curtis meant that the Court should not use habeas corpus as a means to review where it could not review directly.

The reference to federal relations doubtless had in view the federal legislation for the interstate rendition of fugitives from justice and of fugitive slaves. By the rationale against which Curtis was arguing, the denial of habeas corpus by a Circuit Court in such a case would itself be regarded as the "cause of commitment" and subject to review in the Supreme Court.

I cannot, therefore, consent to cripple or limit the authority conferred upon this Court by the Constitution and laws to issue it, by technical and narrow construction; but, on the contrary, prefer to follow the free and enlarged interpretation always given, when dealing with it by the courts of England, from which country it has been derived. They expound the exercise of the power benignly and liberally in favor of the deliverance of the subject from all unlawful imprisonment . . . .

Coming from one so undemonstrative as Samuel Nelson, this was quite a display of feeling.

On the merits, these three Justices held that in committing Kaine for extradition, the Commissioner had acted without authority.

The other four Justices, without stopping to consider the question of jurisdiction, held that the Circuit Court had been right in sustaining the Commissioner. "We are not disposed, under the circumstances, to exercise the jurisdiction of this Court in the case."

Did that mean that seven Justices held that the Supreme Court did have jurisdiction in this situation—or was it only three?[52]

In 1869, when Attorney General Hoar was fighting hard to keep the Court from getting its hands on the Reconstruction Act,[53] he planted himself on the ground Justice Curtis had defended: "the decision In re Kaine has no bearing," he contended. Counsel for petitioner Yerger replied: on the jurisdictional question the four Justices *did* agree with the three—look, they said, they were "not disposed" in *that* case "to exercise *the jurisdiction of the Court*."[54]

These illustrations suffice to show that as a mode of reaching the Supreme Court, habeas corpus was "very clumsy"[55]—"attended by some inconvenience and embarrassment"[56]—"cumbrous."[57]

How much simpler and surer it would be if Congress were to authorize a straightforward "appeal" in place of this anomalous procedure.

---

[52] Thereafter Justice Nelson, in chambers, said: "there having been a dismissal of the case without any decision upon the merits, I am left to follow out my own convictions and conclusions . . . ; and being satisfied of the soundness of them, I must enforce them . . . ." Thereupon he ordered that Kaine be set free. *In re* Kaine, Fed. Case No. 7597 (1853).

[53] *Ex parte* Yerger, 8 Wall. 85, 93. Infra, pp. 575, 577, 582.

Yerger had been committed for trial by the military commission, and —as in Kaine's case—the Circuit Court had remanded to custody.

[54] Phillips' Brief in *Ex parte* Yerger, 6.

[55] Curtis, J., dissenting, in *Ex parte* Wells, 18 How. 307, 330 (1856).

[56] Chase, C.J., in *Ex parte* McCardle, 6 Wall. 318, 324 (1868).

[57] Hoar, Atty. Gen., arguing *Ex parte* Yerger, 8 Wall. 85, 93 (1869).

447

APPEAL IN HABEAS CORPUS CASES,
PROVIDED IN 1867

BY A STATUTE OF FEBRUARY 5, 1867, amending the Judiciary Act, Congress authorized an *appeal* to the Supreme Court in habeas corpus. This enacted:

> That the several courts of the United States, and the several justices and judges of such courts, within their respective jurisdictions, in addition to the authority already conferred by law, shall have power to grant writs of habeas corpus in all cases where any person may be restrained of his or her liberty in violation of the constitution, or of any treaty or law of the United States . . . . From the final decision of any judge, justice, or court, inferior to the circuit court, an appeal may be taken to the circuit court . . . and from the judgment of said circuit court to the Supreme Court of the United States . . . .[58]

The immediate concern was to enforce the grant Congress had made by a resolution to encourage enlistments, in 1865: where a slave volunteered, his wife and children should be forever free.[59] But it was discovered that if the master still held them to service, the federal judiciary had no authority to issue habeas corpus. Accordingly the House instructed its Judiciary Committee to report a bill, which it did by H.R. 605 in the 39th Congress, whose broad effect was "to enlarge the privilege of the writ of habeas corpus, and to make the jurisdiction of the courts and judges of the United States co-extensive with all the powers that can be conferred upon them."[60] If the detention was in violation of some federal right, the writ was now available. Moreover, there was a direct line of "appeal" to the Supreme Court.

Like the rain, the law impartially blesses the just and the unjust. Congress had set out to protect the wife and children of the Negro soldier—and within the year 1867 counsel for ex-Confederate McCardle would grasp the statute in an effort to prostrate Congressional Reconstruction, and preserve white supremacy.

The words "within their respective jurisdictions" are to be noted. It will be recalled that in December 1866, when Chief Justice Chase

---

[58] 14 Stat. 385. "This act shall not apply to the case of any person who is or may be in the custody of the military authorities of the United States, charged with any military offense, or with having aided or abetted rebellion against the Government of the United States prior to the passage of this act."

This did not exclude from the protection of the statute one who, like McCardle, was not charged with an offense against the articles of war governing those in the military service (triable by court-martial).

[59] 13 Stat. 571.

[60] Cong. Globe, 39–1, 87, 4151 (1865–66).

denied habeas corpus in the case of Dr. Mudd, imprisoned in Florida, apparently he was under the apprehension that the power of a Justice under Section 14 of the Judiciary Act was limited to cases within his allotted circuit.[61] In January 1867, when H.R 605 was under consideration in the Senate, Reverdy Johnson—of counsel to Mudd—drew attention to this point. The result of a colloquy with Senator Trumbull, chairman of the Judiciary Committee, was that the limiting phrase was inserted and became part of the statute.[62]

Whether Chase's apprehension in December 1866 was correct— that a Justice's jurisdiction in habeas corpus was limited to the circuit to which he was assigned—became an essential question when in 1869 counsel for Yerger, held in Mississippi, were pressing the Chief Justice to grant the writ.[63]

The powers granted in 1867 were "in addition to the authority already conferred by law." Then if Congress were to take away this right to *appeal* to the Supreme Court under this new statute, could the Court resume its old practice of granting *habeas corpus aided by certiorari* as a means of exercising appellate review? That question, too, would become critical in *Ex parte Yerger*.[64]

EX PARTE McCARDLE BEFORE THE SUPREME COURT

WITH THIS LONG EXPLANATION of the intricacies of habeas corpus —every bit of which will at some point be essential to understanding— we return to McCardle's appeal, filed on December 23, 1867.

Here was a suit, unembarrassed by any suggestion of contrivance, where a party who certainly had standing was challenging the Reconstruction Acts. One possibility was that the Court might hold that the provision for military trials was inconsistent with specific constitutional guarantees, without condemning the entire scheme. Then Congress must have looked to civil trials before local juries. Even if limited to that point, such a decision would have impaired the protective aspect of the Congressional program;[65] moreover, Southern resisters and Democrats generally would have been emboldened when they could boast that "the Reconstruction Act is unconstitutional." The Republicans in Congress appreciated the seriousness of any adverse decision.[66]

---

[61] Supra, pp. 237–39.
[62] Cong. Globe, 39–2, 730, 790 (1867).
[63] Infra, pp. 566–76.
[64] Infra, pp. 581–83.
[65] How seriously will be considered below, in connection with *Ex parte Yerger*. Infra, p. 580.

[66] At this moment—January 1868 —in Virginia the Executive Committee of the convention of Conservatives had found a plaintiff to suit their purpose, one Churchwell Combs, held by the military authorities on a charge of murder. He made his "X" at the foot of a petition for habeas

On December 30, 1867, Judge Black moved that the Court set a day for the hearing of McCardle's case.[67] The motion was argued on January 17, 1868. Trumbull, opposing, "could not imagine any reason" for advancing the case; the petitioner was on bail, and would not suffer by waiting until his case was reached in the regular order. Judge Black, the *National Intelligencer* reported, "completely riddled" this contention. "With an eloquence that commanded a death-like stillness, and a cogency that carried universal conviction," he stressed that this was a criminal case, and should be heard without delay; "he wanted to know if the Court would take the responsibility of postponing a decision for three years in a case of such transcendant importance." Judge Sharkey added that numerous cases, some capital, awaited the outcome of McCardle's appeal.[68]

Four days later the Chief Justice announced that a majority of the Court thought the case should be advanced; it was set for hearing on the first Monday in March.

Trumbull's efforts to stall the *McCardle* appeal reflect how

---

corpus, which members of the committee then presented to District Judge Underwood in the Circuit Court. *Richmond Dispatch*, Jan. 25, 1868.

(Underwood was president of the State's constitutional convention, then engaged in framing a highly proscriptive constitution. Supra, p. 411.)

The applicants solemnly told the Judge that "without attempting to anticipate" what his decision might be, they did not doubt that "a subject so grave and so long before the country" had already engaged his attention; accordingly they submitted the case without argument. (They were in a hurry to be on their way to the Supreme Court.)

The Judge, with equal insincerity, promised "to keep his mind open." *Richmond Enquirer and Examiner*, Jan. 27, 1868; *National Intelligencer*, Jan. 28.

The order book of the Circuit Court shows that on February 10, 1868, it was "ordered that the said Petition and writ be dismissed and the prisoner remanded . . . ." Also *Enquirer and Examiner*, Feb. 11.

As it turned out, no appeal was taken: the progress being made with *Ex parte* McCardle made it needless.

[67] The Court's rule on Call of the

Docket provided: "Criminal cases may be advanced by leave of the court on motion of either party."

The *Richmond Enquirer and Examiner* of January 14, 1868, said that "The public mind is becoming intensely excited" in its desire for "a speedy decision" on the constitutionality of the Reconstruction Act. "But already we have intimations that partisans on the bench are employing their arts to evade or delay the question." "The shepherds are conspiring with the dogs to devour the sheep they are set to foster and defend. The deed which Congressmen perjure themselves to commit, and which judges will perjure themselves if they even connive at, is a tyranny the most intolerable in civilized annals."

[68] Jan. 18, 1868.

On the same day the *Washington Chronicle* said that the object of Black's motion was "palpably a political one"; it was "scarcely supposable that [the court] will so far lose sight of its proper functions as to grant the motion."

The *Chronicle* was edited by John W. Forney—who was also Secretary of the Senate from July 15, 1861, to June 4, 1868. The *Chronicle* was the strident voice of intemperate Radicalism.

critical the matter appeared to the leaders in Congress. He now made a further obstruction: he moved to dismiss for want of jurisdiction. That matter was argued on January 31 and February 7—Fridays and hence motion days. One contention was that, for reasons assigned, the *Circuit Court* had not had jurisdiction under the habeas corpus statute of February 5, 1867.[69] The Chief Justice replied that that matter would be considered when the case was heard on its merits, "while the question before us upon this motion to dismiss, must necessarily be limited to *our* jurisdiction *on appeal* [italics supplied]."[70] Trumbull's other contention was this: the 1867 statute as quoted had given an appeal (1) from an individual Judge or District Court to the Circuit Court, and (2) from the Circuit Court to the Supreme Court; he argued that only a case *appealed to* the Circuit Court—not one brought there in the first instance—could be carried up to the Supreme Court. To this the Chief Justice said No—surely Congress did not mean *two* appeals in one situation and *none* in the other. This unanimous holding was announced on February 17, 1868.

(At this moment, McCardle was busy with the organization of the all-white Democratic party in Mississippi,[71] and with the writing of spirited editorials.[72] He was enjoying a new preeminence as "one of the most fearless and forcible writers in the South."[73])

Ex parte McCardle, it now seemed, was the case whereby Congressional Reconstruction was really being brought to book. Argument on the merits was heard on March 2, 3, 4, and 9, 1868; the Court allowed six hours to each side—three times the normal amount.[74]

---

[69] His argument was that the statute of 1867 declared that it conferred authority "in addition to" that already conferred; therefore it did not apply to any case already covered; but McCardle was imprisoned "under or by color of the authority of the United States" and so the writ *could* have been sought under the Judiciary Act; therefore (Trumbull argued) the Circuit Court did *not* have jurisdiction under the Act of 1867—and therefore this was not a case which, under the Act of 1867, could be appealed to the Supreme Court.

[70] *Ex parte McCardle*, 6 Wall. 318.

Accord: Order of the Court, per Taney, C.J., on Apr. 9, 1858, in Nelson v. Leland, 22 How. 48 (1860), when motion to dismiss for want of jurisdiction in the court below was overruled. And see Marshall, C.J., in Canter v. American Ins. Co., 2 Pet. 554 (1829).

[71] Supra, p. 426.

[72] For example, "The Late Fraudulent Election," denouncing the recent election as conducted by General Ord "and his scoundrelly Registrars" as "an unmitigated swindle." Jan. 11.

[73] Tributes collected in the *Vicksburg Times* of Feb. 2, 4, 7, 13.

[74] The account that follows is based upon the briefs; the reports of oral arguments by Carpenter (83 pages) and by Trumbull (29 pages) taken stenographically and printed by the Government Printing Office; and the reports in the *National Intelligencer*. (The issue of that newspaper on March 14 said that it was "the only paper in the country which has published reports of all the arguments in the McCardle case." Portions had been summarized, but in the main the stenographer's record was set out in full.)

This was "one of the greatest cases that has ever been heard before any tribunal" said Judge Black in opening. If the work of Congress was not struck down, he warned, "I think it is pretty nearly over with us. I do not believe that anything that amounts to the semblance of free government will last another year more. . . ." Then, with one of those sardonic flashes with which he enlivened his arguments, "Yes, this is the third day of March; it may last a year and a day.[75] But certainly it cannot survive that period."

Black professed to be "extremely embarrassed" in his argument —because the case was so very simple, and the law was all on his side! It was "necessary only that you take the Constitution in one hand and the obnoxious statute in the other, and compare the two . . . ."[76] His client had been denied what the Constitution guaranteed, a trial by jury. The *Milligan* case, he said, had established "that no man could, under any pretense, be deprived of his right to trial by jury so long as the courts of the United States shall continue to exist." To be sure, not all of the Justices had agreed; but now

> the principle of *stare decisis*, which involves the honor of the Court as well as the interests of the Court [country?] and the stability of law, requires that it should not be regarded as open after it has been definitely settled; and . . . it is now as binding on the conscience of those who did not concur as upon those who did.

Even the minority had said that "where peace exists the laws of peace must prevail."

As Black saw it, the Federal Government and the State of Mississippi, both republican in form, had been working harmoniously side by side until, by the Act of March 2, 1867, on the pretext of guaranteeing a republican form of government, Congress had trampled it all in the dust and on the ruins had erected "a government more absolute and more unendurable than anything that exists this side of Constantinople." He dilated on the enormity—without mentioning the fact that those on the side he represented had preferred to continue under "this Asiatic system" rather than to go forward without racial discrimination and thereby bring the regime to an end. A stranger listening to the argument would hardly have guessed that there had

---

[75] President Johnson's term would end on March 4, 1869.

[76] Long afterward, Justice Roberts oversimplified by the same figure of speech when spokesman for the majority in United States v. Butler, 297 U.S. 1, 62 (1936), where the first Agricultural Adjustment Act was invalidated. Jesting at such professions of automation, Thomas Reed Powell commented that the dissenting Justices, Brandeis, Stone, and Cardozo, "must have been without the right kind of precision instruments." *Vagaries and Varieties in Constitutional Interpretation* (New York: Columbia University Press, 1956), 42–43.

ever been a War of the Rebellion; Black merely said that where such an attempt had been put down, the Government could thereafter do no more about it than to prosecute any participant in the courts.

Judge Black, admirers said, had "pronounced the most powerful and magnificent political speech of the day."[77] Certainly it was political, and in its way, powerful; Black always fashioned his arguments with hammer on anvil.

Matt. H. Carpenter,[78] opening for the Government, displayed his peculiar powers: he was abundantly prepared, acute, tenacious of every strong point. He was defending an extraordinary statute; his "line of argument [was] not fashionable,"[79] and the Bench was not friendly.[80] He contended: "That the decision of the political power, that Mississippi is without any State government which can be recognized by the United States, is binding and conclusive upon this court, although the judges may think the decision erroneous."[81] In carrying out the guarantee of a republican form of government, ". . . Congress is the EXCLUSIVE judge of what means are necessary in a given case."[82]

Even the courts, he warned, were subject to the temptation to usurp power.[83] In a tone notably less deferential than what was usually heard in that chamber, he said

> The judges of this court, like the Apostles of our Lord, are men of like passions and infirmities with other men. The bar stands in much the same relation to the court that the Prophets held to the ruling powers of the ancient dispensation. It is our duty, when occasions require, to admonish and warn, *and that too whether courts will listen, or whether they will refrain. . . .*[84]

While repelling the "metaphysical abstractions" that would now accord the rebel States a normal status because their secession was "null,"[85] Carpenter avoided (as he explained to Secretary Stanton)[86]

---

[77] *National Intelligencer*, Mar. 11, 1868.

[78] (1824–81). Senator from Mar. 4, 1869, to Mar. 3, 1875, and from Mar. 4, 1879, until his death two years later. There is a good biography by E. Bruce Thompson, *Matthew Hale Carpenter, Webster of the West* (Madison: State Historical Society of Wisconsin, 1954), which at 84–99 tells of his performance in *McCardle*.

[79] Argument, 82.

[80] He said that from Judge Black's air of unconcern, he was led to "fear he knew what decision would be rendered here. But, knowing that he cannot read the secrets of your Honors' hearts," of course that could not be true. Argument, 5.

[81] Brief, 18.

[82] Brief, 34.

[83] Brief, 19.

[84] Argument, 5.

[85] Brief, 6. Sharkey's brief argued that it "only required the action of the sovereign authority—the people—[declaring that the attempt to secede was abandoned] to restore her to her former condition in all respects." P. 3.

[86] Letters of Feb. 10, 1868. Stanton Papers, L.C., quoted by Thompson, *Carpenter*, 95.

"all talk of the *right of conquest,* a theme that's very unpalatable to that court; and unsound in itself, I think . . . ." He claimed all the support he could find in decided cases, particularly what might be done in guaranteeing "a republican form of government,"[87] as developed by Taney in *Luther v. Borden.* "May not Providence have inspired this court to declare in advance, and by the lips of a southern man, revered by *all* men, the great constitutional doctrines necessary to guard this government against the perils of all subsequent times?"[88] It had there been affirmed that "Congress must necessarily decide" what was the rightful government in a State, "and its decision is binding on every other department."[89] That opinion had countenanced "a military government . . . intended merely for the crisis . . .": so here, "if Congress attempts to protect the people of such State by a military supervision, *ad interim,*" the courts must not interfere and release the persons taken into custody. Taney had said, "If the judicial power extends so far, the guarantee . . . [of a republican form of government] is a guarantee of anarchy and not of order."[90] Carpenter cut *Milligan* down to what was actually decided, and distinguished *McCardle,* where the State was *out* of the Union and where Congress *had* authorized trial by military commission. He was "undisturbed by the ghost of Milligan"—he thought it had "no bearing whatever on this discussion."[91]

"I am praised nearly to death," he wrote to his wife; "I had half the Senate for an audience. Miller's face was the face of an angel radiant with light and joy; Davis and Field looked troubled; Nelson, Clifford and Grier dead against me. But I shook them up and rattled their dry bones."[92]

Senator Trumbull's main effort was to induce the Court to acknowledge that Congress in reconstructing the rebel States was exercising a power not subject to judicial control. (A bill whereby Congress would make that declaration, and forbid the Court to take such a case, was waiting on the table of Trumbull's Judiciary Committee at that moment.[93]) He dwelt upon situations where the Court had held itself bound to follow the political branches, and sought to fit the present case into the reasoning of those precedents. If, however, the Court did not confine itself to such a holding, then he said that the Reconstruction

---

[87] Art. IV, Sec. 4.
[88] Argument, 34.
[89] 7 How. 1, 42. Supra, p. 395.
[90] 7 How. 1, 43.
[91] Argument, 5, 58–59.
[92] Frank A. Flower, *Life of Matthew Hale Carpenter* (Madison, Wis.: D. Atwood and Co., 1883), re-

counts Carpenter's part in *McCardle* at 108–16. Stanton requested that he consult William Morris Meredith (1799–1873), former Secretary of the Treasury, and foremost practitioner at the Philadelphia bar—who pronounced it remarkably able.
[93] Infra, p. 464.

Acts generally were not before the Court—only so much as applied to the trial of McCardle.[94] The provisions of the Bill of Rights, such as trial by jury, were not absolute. The Second Amendment declared that "the right to keep and bear arms shall not be infringed": Could the people of Vicksburg have set that up against General Grant? After the rebel armies had been dispersed, "thousands of Union men" were persecuted in the South; the nation must not "abandon its defenders to such a fate."[95]

David Dudley Field, concluding for the petitioner, drove at once at the most critical point.[96] The question was, could Congress subject a citizen, not connected with the military service, to trial by military tribunal? The provisions of the Bill of Rights were "prohibitions upon the exercise of power for any object whatever—for the exercise of power for a permitted end even, for otherwise it would have been unnecessary, because Congress could pass no act for any but a permitted end." The requirements of grand jury and trial jury went to the root of Congressional power. But that had already been settled by *Milligan*—"a judgment which has given the Court a new title to the respect of the world, and which will stand forever as one of the bulwarks of constitutional freedom." It was idle—it would be presumptuous—to reargue a matter so firmly established. Congress could not impose a military government upon the people—not in Alaska, just acquired, and not in Mississippi.

Field's argument on March 5 was interrupted when "the Chief Justice announced that he had been notified to attend the Senate and the Court adjourned." This is a reminder that, on another field, the Radicals were gathering for a decisive battle. The House of Representatives had impeached the President, and on March 5 the Senate was being organized as a court to try the impeachment. As the Constitution directed, "When the President of the United States is tried, the Chief Justice shall preside." It was not until March 30 that the trial got under way.

Resuming on March 9, Field considered and rebutted the theories advanced—in Congressional and popular discussion as well as in Carpenter's argument—to justify the extraordinary regime over the Southern States. He concluded, Mississippi was certainly a State in the Union, and her people had the rights of citizens; but in any event, military government could not be justified.

During these remarks Field had aimed a shaft at Justice Miller. "I deny that in a state of absolute anarchy the State of Iowa can be forced to take the institutions of New York; . . . her form of municipal

---

[94] Argument, 25.
[95] Argument, 23, 26.

[96] *National Intelligencer*, Mar. 6, 1868.

455

government . . . is for Iowa to determine for herself." As will appear in a weighty chapter,[97] at that moment counties in Iowa were resisting the enforcement of judgments on bonds improvidently granted to railroad promoters. On January 13, 1868, the Court had held it to be the duty of the Circuit Court by the writ of mandamus to compel municipal officers to collect taxes to satisfy judgments, notwithstanding that State courts had held the bonds invalid and had enjoined tax collection.[98] Justice Miller had recorded a hard-hitting dissent. Even while *McCardle* was being argued, the newspapers told of popular meetings to concert resistance to the enforcement of federal court orders. Thus from Iowa, so steadfast in the war for the Union, came talk that sounded like nullification.

This interjection serves as a reminder that while the Court was considering *McCardle*, it had other matters of capital importance to decide. If one studied the Court week by week, rather than topic by topic, the variety of major problems about which each Justice must be thinking would be impressive.

So far as appears, counsel arguing *McCardle* were not interrupted by questions from the bench. The issues were clear and familiar. One supposes that no Justice was still making up his mind.

The strategy of Black and his associates was nothing less than to free the Old South from the grasp of Congress: they did not aim merely to free McCardle from the general. Had it been otherwise, there was much ground they might have contested before making an attack upon the Reconstruction Act, even in its provision authorizing trial by military commission. Section 3 of the statute had made it the duty of the District commander (*a*) to protect all persons in their rights of person and property; (*b*) to suppress insurrection, disorder, and violence; and (*c*) to punish, or cause to be punished, all disturbers of the public peace and criminals. Could the editorials specified in Charges 1 and 2 be held to disturb the peace, or incite to insurrection? McCardle urged State officers to stand firm on his view of the law: then the military authorities must either back down, or themselves resort to "the bayonet."[99] Charge 3 alleged criminal libel of a captain, an appointed sheriff, and the five general officers commanding Districts. The misdemeanor of criminal libel—defamation made punishable because of its tendency to provoke a breach of the peace—is itself an unusual offense.[100] There were weighty reasons why the Court would hesitate to hold that Section 3 authorized a District commander to try and punish for this peculiar offense in respect of defamation of himself or of

---

[97] Ch. 17.
[98] Riggs v. Johnson County, 6 Wall. 166.

[99] Supra, n. 14.
[100] See Garrison v. Louisiana, 379 U.S. 64 (1964).

X: Ex parte McCardle

others engaged in enforcing the statute—unless, that is, the Justices were unwilling to observe what was later referred to as "a cardinal principle," "that this Court will first ascertain whether a construction of the statute is fairly possible by which the question [of constitutionality] may be avoided."[101]

While interference with the citizen's exercise of the right to vote (Charge 4) might well deserve punishment, Congress had not made it an offense, and it might have been argued cogently that before a commander could properly punish such interference he should first have published an order giving notice of the conduct which thenceforth would be punishable.

Raymond v. Thomas,[102] a later case on the Reconstruction Acts, shows the mode of approach the Court might take. Purchaser of a small property in South Carolina in 1863 had given the seller a mortgage; foreclosure after the war resulted in the loss of the property and a substantial money judgment besides. The District commander, General Canby, annulled that decree, relying on the large powers Congress had conferred. But when further litigation reached the Supreme Court, Swayne, J., observed: "It was not an order for mere delay. It did not prescribe that the proceeding should stop until credit and confidence were restored, and business should resume its wonted channels. It wholly annulled a decree . . ." where no adequate reason appeared. "The clearest language would be necessary to satisfy us that Congress intended that the power given by these Acts should be so exercised." Then came this canon of construction: "It is an unbending rule of law, that the exercise of military power, where the rights of the citizen are concerned, shall never be pushed beyond what the exigency requires."

Judge Sharkey filed a brief in *McCardle* which is notable for what he seemed eager to concede. He said at the outset that

> the acts under which these charges were made . . . are so broad, so comprehensive, and so complete for the establishment of absolute, unrestrained military supremacy, that it may be conceded the Military Commander had a right to arrest for anything deemed by him to be an offense, and to punish as he might think proper . . . .[103]

"The constitutionality of the reconstruction acts is the question to be determined by this Court," he insisted. He asked, "how could [Mississippi] get out of the Union by an act admitted on all hands to

---

[101] Brandeis, J., concurring in Ashwander v. T.V.A., 297 U.S. 288, 341 at 348 (1936).

[102] 91 U.S. 712 (1867).

[103] P. 2. Contrast with Attorney General Stanbery's strict construction in opinions of March 24 and June 12, 1867. 12 Ops. Atty. Gen. 141, 182. Supra, pp. 340–42.

be a nullity?" As soon as the people, with President Johnson's aid, had reorganized their State government, "the power of the United States . . . ceased."[104]

Not before page nineteen of a twenty-four-page brief did Sharkey come to the guaranties of the Bill of Rights and in particular the free-dom of speech and of the press—and here he represented that it was *Congress* that had transgressed:

> And we now proceed to show in what particulars Congress departed from the rule laid down in McCulloch vs. The State of Maryland,[105] by employing means which are not only prohibited by the Constitution, but utterly inconsistent with its letter and spirit. In order to do this we may, with propriety, look to the practical workings of the government so established, *all of which are justified as within the scope of its powers* by the body that created it. The Constitution declares that Congress shall make no law "abridging the freedom of speech or of the press." . . . What is the case before the Court? A citizen, not connected with the army or navy, was arrested and imprisoned by a military officer, not for any crime known to any law, but because he published certain articles which criticised severely the acts of that military officer as commander of the Military District. . . . [The commander] thus established a censorship of the press—nay more; he asserted and exercised a right which is totally destructive of the liberty of the press . . . . *These acts authorize all this* . . . .[106] [Italics supplied.]

Black, Field, and Sharkey did not attempt to magnify "the freedom of speech, or of the press," as Field had magnified "bill of attainder" when he argued *Cummings v. Missouri*.[107] Whether in 1867–68 anything more could have been made out of this guaranty of the First Amendment—more than Blackstone's definition, the absence of *previous* restraint[108]—is conjectural. It was not until after World War I that it received any considerable development by the Supreme Court.[109] Although the roots are deep in history, the flowering is quite recent. But even as the protection has been broadened, still one man's freedom does not extend to the utterance of threats calculated to compel another to abandon the exercise of his own rights.[110]

---

[104] Brief for Appellant, pp. 3–4.

[105] 4 Wheat. 316 (1819), the great case on "implied powers."

[106] Brief, 19–20.

[107] 4 Wall. 277 (1867).

[108] *Commentaries*, IV, 151.

[109] Compare Patterson v. Colorado, 205 U.S., 454, 462 (1907), with Schenck v. United States, 249 U.S. 47, 51 (1919), Holmes, J., speaking for the Court in each case.

[110] In the Reconstruction Acts, Congress was concerned with the in-equality between the freedmen and the whites in whom alone had lain the power to govern. In 1935, in pass-ing the National Labor Relations Act, Congress was concerned with "the inequality of bargaining power" between employees and their em-

X: Ex parte McCardle

Certainly McCardle did not want his appeal to be placed on grounds narrower than a frontal attack upon the entire Reconstruction Act. As he saw it, the matter at stake was whether the Court would halt the Radicals, who "hope to trample the Southern people into acquiescence of negro domination, and negro despotism"; "to arrest and impeach President Johnson"; and "to degrade the Supreme Court."[111]

REACTION IN CONGRESS: MEASURES TO CURB THE COURT

ON MONDAY, MARCH 9, at the close of Field's argument, the Court took *McCardle* under advisement. Action in Congress, however, soon became an element—the decisive element—in the case. By a bill hurried to enactment on March 27, 1868, the habeas corpus statute of February 5, 1867,[112] was repealed insofar as it permitted an appeal to the Supreme Court.

We leave *McCardle* in the hands of the Court, to trace related developments in Congress.

Here a note should be inserted, to set out the chronology of the impeachment of President Johnson—concurrent with the movement to restrain the Supreme Court.

The first effort to impeach, beginning with Ashley's motion of

---

ployers. In enforcing the latter Act, the Court observed that the publisher of a newspaper "has no special privilege to invade the rights and liberties of others." Associated Press v. NLRB, 301 U.S. 103, 132–33 (1937). "Slight suggestions as to the employer's choice" how the employees voted might be an "unfair labor practice" within the prohibition of the statute. Int'l Ass'n of Machinists v. NLRB, 311 U.S. 72, 78 (1940); NLRB v. Virginia Elec. & P. Co., 314 U.S. 469, 477 (1941).

The proposition in Giboney v. Empire Storage & Ice Co., 336 U.S. 490, 502 (1949), that "it has never been deemed an abridgment of freedom of speech or press to make a course of conduct illegal merely because the conduct was in fact initiated, evidenced or carried out by means of language, either spoken, written, or printed," has been applied in various situations. Building Service Employees v. Gazzam, 339 U.S. 532, 540 (1950); Int'l Brotherhood of Team-

sters v. Vogt, 354 U.S. 284, 291–92 (1957); Cox v. Louisiana, 379 U.S. 536, 555 (1965).

[111] *Vicksburg Times*, Feb. 7, 1868—commenting on Trumbull's motion to dismiss for want of jurisdiction, in an editorial on "Confession of Guilt." If the Radicals had even a remote *hope* that the Court would uphold the Acts, he wrote, they would *"desire"* a decision which should put the vexed question to rest."

His part in challenging Congress would be McCardle's particular claim to attention as an alternate at the National Democratic Convention in July. The ill-disposed *Vicksburg Weekly Republican* later reported that E. M. Yerger had been the only member of the Mississippi delegation who attracted respectable attention, and that as a consequence the "hero of the McCardle case" had been paying Yerger "backhanded compliments." Aug. 16, 1868.

[112] Supra, p. 448.

December 17, 1866,[113] had led to the taking of testimony during the Second Session of the 39th Congress. That effort ended when, on December 7, 1867, a resolution by Boutwell to impeach received only 57 yeas to 108 nays.[114]

Then on January 27, 1868, the Committee on Reconstruction (Thad Stevens, chairman) was authorized to inquire into attempts to obstruct the execution of the laws.[115]

The Tenure of Office Act—which, like the Reconstruction Act, became law notwithstanding a veto on March 2, 1867—forbade the removal, without the consent of the Senate, of officers appointed with such consent; provided, however, that Department heads would have such tenure during the term of the President by whom they were appointed and for one month thereafter.[116] Notwithstanding that statute, President Johnson on February 21, 1868, removed Secretary Stanton. On February 24 the House voted to impeach, and on March 3 agreed upon eleven articles.

Proceedings came as follows:

March 30 to April 20—Ben Butler presented the case for the Managers; evidence for the prosecution; B. R. Curtis opened for the defense; evidence for the defense.

April 20 to May 6—Argument of counsel, closed by Bingham for the prosecution.

May 7, 11—Senate determined rules for voting.

May 16—vote on Article XI: guilty, 35; not guilty, 19. The Chief Justice: Two-thirds not having pronounced guilty, the President is acquitted on this article.

May 26—like results on Articles II and III. The Senate as a court of impeachment adjourned sine die.[117]

Thus as we follow the steps leading to the Act of March 27, 1868, which took away the Court's jurisdiction to decide the *McCardle* appeal, we shall be aware of the movement to remove the President, leading to the trial that opened on March 30. Congress, and especially the House, was advancing with determination.

For a year—ever since *Milligan* with its dictum, followed closely by *Garland*—the Court had loomed as a menace to the Congressional majority. This was the obverse of the fact that as viewed from the South it offered a sanctuary. The hopeful adulation of the Court by the Southerners and their allies—the conservative views, openly declared, of some of the Justices—the uncertain foundation on which Congres-

---

[113] Supra, p. 235, n. 171.
[114] Cong. Globe, 40–2, 68.
[115] Cong. Globe, 40–2, 784–85.
[116] 14 Stat. 430. See ch. 11, note 20.

[117] The *Proceedings* were published as a Supplement to the Congressional Globe, 40th Cong., 2d Sess.

sional Reconstruction was based—all this, and the Radicals' own daring which grew with each bold advance, had brought their determination to the sticking point: the Court must be curbed. The Second Session of the 40th Congress, which began in December 1867, saw a number of measures to that end: one must step warily in picking one's way among them.

A leader in this movement was Representative John A. Bingham of Ohio, who in the preceding Congress had been the chief exponent of the First Section of the Fourteenth Amendment. Bingham is a marked man in constitutional law, whose performance on any occasion is to be watched—for the reason that his peculiar conceptions have come to be treated in some quarters as significant in interpretations of the Amendment.[118] Now in January 1868 he reported from the Committee on Reconstruction H.R. 439, a bill additional and supplemental to the Reconstruction Act: it would command that "the so-called civil governments" in the rebel States "shall not be recognized" by the Executive or the Judiciary—a point to be examined below in connection with *Texas v. White*[119]; second, the conduct of Congressional Reconstruction would have been taken from the President and vested in his subordinate, the General of the Army (Grant). "A bill to elect a President," the minority report dubbed it.[120] Briefly, this bill sailed through the House, but in the Senate was soon lost to view in the engrossing business of trying the impeachment of the President. In a debate that ranged widely over Radical objectives, Bingham defended "the party which, under God, saved the nation's life," and in particular its great handiwork, the Fourteenth Amendment then in the course of ratification:

> There is not an intelligent man in America but knows that to secure the rights of all citizens and free persons in every State was the spirit and intent of the Constitution from the beginning. There is not an intelligent man in America but knows that this spirit and intent of the Constitution was most flagrantly violated long anterior to the rebellion, and that the Government was powerless to remedy it by law. That amendment proposes hereafter that this great wrong shall be remedied by putting a limitation expressly into the Constitution, coupled with a grant of power to enforce it by law, so that when either Ohio or South Carolina or any other State shall in its madness or its folly refuse to the gentleman or his children or to me or to mine any of the rights which pertain to American citizenship or to a common humanity, there will be redress for the wrong through the power and majesty of American law.[121]

---

[118] Infra, ch. 20, n. 275.
[119] Infra, pp. 640–41.
[120] Cong. Globe, 40–2, 510, 511.

[121] Cong. Globe, 40–2, 514–15. Jan. 14, 1868.

As Bingham saw the march into the future, it was the Congress, rather than the Court, that was to be Valiant-for-Truth; through legislative power to enforce the Amendment would the rights of citizenship and common humanity be made secure. (The day before, in supporting another Radical measure that would have required the vote of two-thirds of the full Court to invalidate an Act of Congress,[122] Bingham said that of late the Court had "dared to descend from its high place in the discussion and decision of purely judicial questions to the settlement of political questions which it has no more right to decide for the American people than has the Court of St. Petersburg."[123] He even supported a proposal to require the concurrence of all the Justices before "the validity of any statute or of any authority exercised by the United States" could be denied.[124])

Democratic criticism conceded the "eloquent words," "warm utterances," "the fancy" and "the rhetoric" of Bingham's speech, but found no "substantial reasons which could justify the extraordinary legislation he proposed." Even if Congress were to forbid the Court to recognize the "so-called" governments in Southern States, it would nonetheless be the Court's duty, "on well settled principles," to adjudicate upon the validity of any provision of the Reconstruction Acts involved in a case before it.[125]

Familiarity brings one to know Bingham as an ardent rhetorician, not a man of exact knowledge or clear conceptions or accurate language.[126]

---

[122] S. 163 as House Judiciary Committee amended. Infra, p. 463.

[123] Cong. Globe, 40–2, 483. Jan. 13, 1868.

[124] Ibid., 489. Infra, p. 463.

[125] John V. L. Pruyn of New York. Cong. Globe, 40–2, 639. Jan. 20, 1868. While a staunch Democrat, Pruyn was also an acute lawyer of wide experience; his comments were consistently discriminating. Michael C. Kerr of Indiana, opposing Bingham's Reconstruction Bill, referred to the "magnificent or maudlin rhetoric and limping logic." Cong. Globe, 40–2, 578. Jan. 16.

[126] In his speech on January 14 Bingham launched into a flight in praise of Daniel Webster, "who, living, stood alone among living men, and who, dead, sleeps alone in his tomb by the sounding sea . . . ." Cong. Globe, 40–2, 511. This was

a favorite ornament: he had used it on February 4, 1862, in a debate on the Legal Tender bill, when he argued that Webster—despite his categorical statements to the contrary —was really to be reckoned as supporting the power to emit paper money. Cong. Globe, 37–2, 636–40. The expression was used again on February 28, 1866, when Bingham claimed that a speech by Webster supported his view that the federal Bill of Rights had always been obligatory upon the States even though not judicially enforceable against them. Cong. Globe, 39–1, 1091. But that was not at all what Webster had been saying. Charles Fairman, "Does the Fourteenth Amendment Incorporate the Bill of Rights? The Original Understanding," Stanf. L. Rev., 2:5, 35 (1949).

X: Ex parte McCardle

Coming now to the steps by which the Radicals did manage to put a curb upon the Court, the march starts with S. 163, a meritorious little bill introduced by Senator Trumbull on December 4, 1867; it would declare that *five* Justices—no longer *six*—would suffice for a quorum. By the Act of July 23, 1866, the Court was to be allowed to fall to a Chief and six Associate Justices, and *thereafter four* would be a quorum. In the meantime, Trumbull explained, "One or two of the judges at this time are unwell, and of the whole number, eight, it requires six to constitute a quorum . . . ."[127] The change was "very desirable," said Reverdy Johnson; "the Court was very near being without a quorum to-day, and the probability is, in the present condition of things, that it may be often without a quorum during the session."[128] So the Senate passed the bill instanter.

In the House the Judiciary Committee added a section to require that no Act of Congress be held invalid without the concurrence of two-thirds of all the members of the Court. (That would be six out of eight: in the probabilities of the moment, only if both Chase and Davis joined Nelson, Grier, Clifford, and Field could the Reconstruction Acts be invalidated.) Thomas Williams, a Pittsburgh lawyer of impatient Radicalism, wanted to go even further: he revived the proposal he had made just a year before, immediately after *Ex parte Garland*, to require unanimity to invalidate. That won the support of only twenty-five determined Radicals such as Bingham, James M. Ashley, and Logan; even members as advanced as Boutwell, Schenck, and James F. Wilson, along with steady men like Garfield and Dawes, voted with the Democrats to defeat that proposal. Then the bill with the two-thirds requirement was swept along by the usual partisan division.[129]

At this juncture Justice Miller was writing to his brother-in-law:

> The political situation looks to me more gloomy than it has ever looked. I never thought a separation by success of the rebellion the worst misfortune that could occur. But in the threatened collision between the Legislative branch of the government and the Executive and Judicial branches I see consequences from which the cause of free government may never recover in my day. The worst feature I now see is the passion which governs the hour in all parties and all persons who have controlling influence. In this the Supreme Court is as fully involved as the President or House of Representatives.

---

[127] Cong. Globe, 40–2, 19. Dec. 4, 1867. The reference was to Justices Nelson (then 75) and Grier (approaching 74).

This section of the Act of 1866, it will be recalled, had been drafted by the Chief Justice. Supra, p. 166.

[128] Ibid.

[129] The final vote was 116 to 39, with 33 not voting. Ibid., 489. Jan. 13, 1868.

. . . May God deliver us from narrow statesmen and bitter partisans of both sides. . . .[130]

When S. 163 as amended was returned to the Senate the Judiciary Committee laid it aside while a measure of its own was presented, attacking the problem from a different angle.

On February 17—the day the Court was overruling his motion to dismiss *McCardle* for want of jurisdiction[131]—Trumbull introduced S. 363 and asked that it be referred back to his Judiciary Committee. This was a bill to define the jurisdiction of the courts in certain cases. It would declare that the Reconstruction Acts were political in character and that no court was competent to question their validity. Congress would thus be asserting in its own behalf an authority which normally is conceded without question to the Court: competence to pronounce upon the Court's competence.

This bill was like the cocking of a gun, audible in the nearby Supreme Court chamber, where on March 4 Trumbull returned to argue that Reconstruction was a "political" matter where the Court should concede that it was bound by the action of Congress.[132]

Trumbull's S. 363 was never carried out. Instead the Radicals' object was gained through a bit of craftiness. S. 213, to amend the Judiciary Act, had started as a simple bill to permit the Supreme Court to review judgments under the internal revenue laws. (The Court's jurisdiction in such cases had been cut back, inadvertently, by a statute of July 13, 1866;[133] now the Treasury Department had prepared this bill to correct the situation.) It went through the Senate without question. When it reached the House, Representative James F. Wilson, chairman of the Judiciary Committee, once more saw the possibility of tacking on an amendment—this time one to repeal so much of the habeas corpus statute of 1867[134] as gave an appeal to the Supreme Court. That should put a stop to the *McCardle* case. Representative Schenck, in charge of the bill, yielded the floor; Wilson offered his amendment; and the bill with this addition was snapped through in an instant, on March 12. The Democrats did not perceive what was going on. (Later, when they cried out against this sharp practice, Wilson explained that "Gentlemen know I never trouble the House with any unnecessary remarks";[135] Schenck said that the spokesman of a bill was under no duty to "wake

[130] Letter of January 19, 1868. Charles Fairman, *Mr. Justice Miller and the Supreme Court, 1862–1890* (Cambridge, Mass.: Harvard University Press, 1939), 140.

[131] Supra, p. 451.

[132] Supra, p. 454.

[133] Supra, p. 252.

[134] Supra, p. 448.

[135] Cong. Globe, 40–2, 2060. Mar. 21.

up the slumbering."[136]) Back in the Senate, the amended bill was taken up late on the same day. Senator Buckalew, Democrat, sensed at once that the amendment must be "very important"; "I do not know what the effect of it is." George H. Williams, in charge, replied that it "explains itself." Buckalew, suspicion aroused, sought delay until the next day. "I should like to have time to read the law which it is proposed to repeal." The motion to postpone failed, and the bill was passed, 32 to 6.[137]

This day, March 12, 1868, should be marked for reference when we return to the action of the Supreme Court. On that day the bill to end appeals in habeas corpus was passed by both Houses. Upon being enrolled it would be sent to the President. A veto would surely be over-ridden.

Whitelaw Reid, in a dispatch of March 20, explained how the situation had appeared to the Radicals:

> The apprehension has been almost universal, among Republicans, that the decision [in *McCardle*] would pronounce the Reconstruction laws unconstitutional, and that, on the strength of this, Mr. Johnson would at once withdraw the troops from the Southern States. The current belief has been that five out of the eight Judges would so decide—Nelson . . . , Grier . . . , Clifford . . . , Field . . . , and Davis . . . . Mr. Davis is known to have expressed disapproval of some of the reconstruction legislation; but it is not certain that he will go to the length of pronouncing it all unconstitutional. . . .
>
> On the other hand, Justices Swayne . . . and Miller . . . are believed to regard the reconstruction legislation as constitutional, and to be certain so to decide. Mr. Chief Justice Chase's position has been much questioned . . . . [I]t may be considered certain that he will take counsel . . . solely of his judgment and his conscience. But he is known to have said that the most ardent desire of his life was to see the Southern States restored to their normal relations to the Union, under the reconstruction policy of Congress. And in the decision in the case of the Indiana conspirators, he has put on record his opposition to the trial of citizens before military courts, in time of peace. From these two facts it might perhaps be inferred that his decision would be adverse to the right of military trials, but not to the general reconstruction policy.[138]

Reid was known to be one of Chase's intimates. He hints broadly what "perhaps" the Chief Justice thought about a pending question—

---

[136] Ibid., 1884. Mar. 14.
[137] Ibid., 1847. Mar. 12.
[138] "Agate"—Reid's pen-name—in the *Cincinnati Gazette* of Mar. 24, 1868, copied in the *National Intelligencer* of Mar. 26.

on the basis of views which Chase, indeed, was then broadcasting among his numerous correspondents.

The next chapter will be devoted to the Chief Justice's pursuit of the Presidency in 1868. When it became apparent that Grant would be the Republicans' choice, Chase sought to ingratiate himself with the Democrats. He protested that "I am neither candidate nor aspirant. All I want is strength, wisdom & courage for whatever duty reason & conscience show me."[139] Where it seemed useful he would add such aims as "the complete restoration of the States lately in rebellion," "currency good enough to pay all debts whether to bondholders or working men," and "resistance to the attempts which have lately become so alarming, to subjugate the Executive and the Judicial Departments of the Government to the unlimited control of the Legislature . . . ."[140] To one acquaintance[141] he recalled that he had been "a steady friend to the congressional policy of reconstruction so far as it contemplated equal rights for all"; but he did not "believe that any thing had been accomplished by military supremacy in the rebel States that could not have been as well, if not better, accomplished by civil supremacy, authorized and regulated by Congress, with military subordination." This last he wrote on March 16, 1868—a week after counsel in *McCardle* had submitted that very matter to the judgment of the Court.[142]

It is no wonder that Reid, his well-wisher, felt a need to insist that a Chief Justice so deeply implicated in politics would yet judge with utter serenity.

---

[139] Letter of Mar. 23 to Jacob Heaton, long a correspondent. During the war Heaton had been Special Agent of the Treasury at Cincinnati. Chase Papers, L.C.

Compare Chase's letter of March 25 to John D. Van Buren, whom Chase came to regard as his agent in negotiations with New York Democratic leaders. Infra, p. 523.

[140] Letter of May 25 to Richard Gaines, his "old friend," recalling their political association in the past. "I was a Democrat then; too democratic for the Democratic party of those days, for I admitted no exception on account of race or color or condition, to the impartial application of democratic principles to all measures and to all men. Such a Democrat I am to-day." Chase Papers, L.C. Robert B. Warden, *An*

Account of the Private Life and Public Services of Salmon Portland Chase (Cincinnati, Ohio: Wilstach, Baldwin and Co., 1874), 690–91.

[141] Letter to J. E. Snodgrass of New York. Chase Papers, L.C. Jacob W. Schuckers, *The Life and Public Services of Salmon Portland Chase* (New York: D. Appleton and Co., 1874), 575; Warden, *Chase*, 681.

Virginia-born, Snodgrass had for a time edited the *Baltimore Saturday Visitor*, opposed to slavery; he maintained an active interest in politics and was a leader in various social groups.

[142] Doubtless it was a preference for the Louisiana Bill, rather than the Sherman Bill, supra, p. 295, that enabled Chase now to write as he did in criticism of the means Congress had chosen.

X: Ex parte McCardle

THE COURT DURING A TENSE MONTH

WE GO BACK TO THE COURT, to trace as precisely as may be the chronology of its doings between March 9, 1868, when it took *McCardle* under advisement, and April 6, when it continued that and other Reconstruction cases to the next term, and adjourned. The Court's Dockets (the Original and the Appellate) and Minutes record its more important formal actions. Newspaper accounts enable one to fill in details; but they must be read critically, and collated, to exclude error. And there are some personal papers to be quoted. Masses of commentary have been pronounced over the *McCardle* case: it is worthwhile to set out the facts, according to the best evidence available.

The Court's earliest conference day after the close of argument was Saturday, March 14. It appears that the *McCardle* case was not reached—which is not surprising, considering the accumulation of business near the close of a term.

When the Court next met for conference on Saturday, March 21, the bill to repeal its jurisdiction had for a week been awaiting action by the President. It was decided, under the circumstances, to postpone consideration of *McCardle*. This was over the opposition of Justices Grier and Field.

As was usual in matters of such interest, the Justices talked, so that the vote to postpone, and Grier's and Field's dissent, leaked out.[143]

---

[143] Welles, Secretary of the Navy, wrote in his diary for Monday, March 23: "The Judges of the Supreme Court have caved in, fallen through, failed, in the McCardle case. Only Grier and Field have held out like men, patriots, judges of nerve and honest independence." *Diary of Gideon Welles*, 3 vols. (Boston and New York: Houghton Mifflin Co., 1911), III, 320.

Browning, Secretary of the Interior, recorded in his diary for April 9 what he had heard at a lawyers' dinner:

Judge Field said the McCardle case had not been decided—that the judges refused to take it up for consideration in the consultation room on the ground that they did not wish to run a race with Congress, where it was understood a bill was pending to take away their jurisdiction— Grier & Field opposed this view and wished to proceed, which it was clearly the duty of the Court to do, but they were overruled by the others. This exhibition of cowardice on the part of the Court, and their readiness to surrender the inalienable rights of the citizen to the usurpation and tyranny of Congress is among the alarming symptoms of our times.

Field says that if the Court could have been brought to a decision the rights of the citizen would have been sustained by all the Court except Swayne. . . .

Diary of Orville Hickman Browning (Springfield: Illinois State Historical Library, vol. I (1850–64), Pease and

On March 25 came a veto message. The bill, wrote the President, "establishes a precedent which, if followed, may eventually sweep away every check on arbitrary and unconstitutional legislation."[144] Certainly the veto would be overridden: the minority in each House would do well even to gain a little time for debate.

At this point the remarks of Reverdy Johnson in the Senate were discriminating. On all that touched the Court he spoke with unique authority. As usual, he was well informed on what had transpired. There was no need, he said, to cut off debate: the Court was forbearing to make any test of speed in disposing of *McCardle*:

> I speak knowingly when I say—and I do not regret, for one, that the Supreme Court has come to that determination—that as long as this bill is pending it is not their purpose to dispose of a case which has already been argued, and which is before the court under the authority of the act which the bill upon your table proposes to repeal. It has, I know, been urged upon them that they should disregard the pendency of this measure and proceed to announce whatever decision they may have formed, if they have formed any, upon the case which is before them; but they have determined, as they have done upon former occasions, not to pursue such a course . . . .[145]

He recalled a comparable situation three years earlier. The statute admitting Nevada to the Union made no provision for disposing of appeals from the territorial court then pending in the Supreme Court. Large interests were involved. Those who had won below asked the Court to dismiss the appeals, inasmuch as there was no longer any court to which it could direct its mandate. Those who had brought the appeals besought Congress to correct the oversight. And the Court postponed a hearing on the motion to dismiss, "in order," Justice Grier had explained, "that the omission to provide for such cases in the original Act might be supplied by further legislation . . . ."[146] In both situations, said Senator Johnson, he thought the Court had acted becomingly when it withheld action while a bill affecting its decision was pending—in one case a bill to revive, in the other a bill to destroy the Court's power to decide.

The Senators in the minority were strong in reason, weak in

Randall, eds., 1925; vol. II (1865–81), Randall, ed., 1933), II, 191–92.

Apparently Field was expressing an estimate of how his brethren would have voted if *McCardle* had been considered on its merits and a vote had then been taken. Browning's note is not to be accepted as indubitable

—because Field was an ardent man where his feelings were aroused, and because he may have been imperfectly understood.

[144] Cong. Globe, 40–2, 2094.

[145] Ibid., 2095. Mar. 25.

[146] Freeborn v. Smith, 2 Wall. 160 (1865).

numbers. Trumbull, on the defensive, said that the bill was "of very little importance, in my judgment."

> When the Senator from Maryland says that this is repealing a law which gives the Supreme Court jurisdiction of a case now before it, and a great case, he assumes the very point in dispute. There is no such case before the Supreme Court, in my judgment, nor has the court decided that there is any such case.[147]

This finger-crossing "in my judgment" did not save this from being a gross prevarication,—and an unavailing one, too, since Senator Doolittle at once stated the actual situation.[148] Stewart of Nevada said that it was wise to repeal a statute that caused the Court to hear "long arguments upon a matter of trifling importance" when it was already "two or three or four years behind with its business and the vast interests of the country are delayed . . . ." But Hendricks of Indiana forced the admission that Stewart knew of no habeas corpus appeal other than McCardle's that had "overburdened" the Court.[149] Hendricks drew a contrast between the liberality of giving an appeal in civil cases where more than $2,000 was involved, and this shabby bill to take away the remedy of persons imprisoned—and liable perhaps even to capital punishment—allegedly in violation of the Constitution.[150] James A. Bayard of Delaware, of staid mentality, talked of a vested right in an appeal; the Court might hold that a repeal did not apply to a case already docketed. He hoped, at any rate, that the Court "would still pronounce their opinion on the law as it then existed, though they might add to that opinion that the legislative body had deprived them of the power to give the redress to the citizen to which he was entitled. Such would be my course . . . ."[151] What Bayard advocated was a gratuitous pronouncement, unavailing to the petitioner but invaluable to the Democratic party in discrediting the Republican program.

The bill was passed over the veto, and became law on March 27, 1868.[152]

---

[147] Cong. Globe, 40–2, 2096. Mar. 25.

[148] "The Supreme Court decided that they had jurisdiction of the decision of the court below and the right to review it, and review the whole of it; but the question as to whether the court below had jurisdiction of the case or not they would not decide until they came to decide on the merits." Ibid., 2097. See supra, p. 451.

[149] Cong. Globe, 40–2, 2097. Mar. 25.

[150] Ibid., 2115–18. Mar. 26.

[151] Ibid., 2124. Mar. 26.

[152] 15 Stat. 44. In the Senate the vote was 33 to 9, with 12 absent; in the House, 114 to 34, with 41 not voting. Cong. Globe, 40–2, 2128, 2170.

The *New York Times* correspondent reported that "No one pretended to doubt the legality of the bill and there was but little excitement over its passage." Mar. 27.

The Court had chosen not to hurry to a decision while yet it could, and now Congress had withdrawn its jurisdiction, with effect upon "appeals which have been . . . taken." In years to come, several aspects of this episode would be debated, often without distinguishing one from another. There was the basic question of the constitutionality of the Reconstruction Act; there was the propriety of the Court's delay; and there was the matter of the repeal of jurisdiction in a pending case —in respect of validity, and of constitutional morality. These several issues should be segregated in one's mind. An additional circumstance was that the trial of the impeachment of the President would soon begin, and would necessitate the attendance of the Chief Justice for a considerable period. And the Court must soon adjourn so that the Justices could go on their circuits.

The prospect in *McCardle* was bleak; but there remained *Georgia v. Grant, Meade et al.* On Friday, March 20, on Black's motion, the Court ordered that process issue to defendants, returnable on the first Monday in December. Then Black moved for a preliminary injunction, to command the respondents to desist from what they were doing until the case could be decided. If the Court would now grant that relief, Reconstruction in Georgia would be halted and an important point would be scored. The Court took this motion under advisement.

On Monday the Court ordered that notice of the motion be served on the defendants. At the close of the day, Secretary Stanton telegraphed to General Meade at Atlanta:

> This morning the Supreme Court fixed Friday of this week for hearing the motion for injunction on Jenkins Bill but require personal service of notice on the defendants. If you and General Ruger and the other officer named have any business in Florida or elsewhere the notice cannot be served personally, and I think the Court would be glad of it, so as to let the matter stand over until December. Can you take an inspection tour immediately, the others going elsewhere in different directions and let your destination be known only to yourself.[153]

Black persisted: he asked that argument might proceed on giving information to the respondents, without the delay necessary to effect personal service. Stanton advised Meade by another telegram, on the evening of the twenty-fourth:

> The Supreme Court refused to hear a motion for an injunction today on the Bill filed by Jenkins in the name of the State of Georgia and made the subpoenas against you & General Grant and others

---

[153] Stanton Papers, L.C. Telegram sent in cipher.

returnable on the first Monday of December next. Jenkins and his lawyers Black Blair and Fields [*sic*] were present in full force. Nothing was said in opposition to the motion but the Court took the matter in hand and indicated by their ruling their determination not to depart from the settled practice for the purpose of aiding Jenkins.[154]

Thus the *Georgia* case was snagged on an elementary point: proper service must be made on all adverse parties.[155]

It was reported in the press that "Mr. Black and his associates are immensely disgusted, as they have nothing whatever to show except defeat for the elaborate preparations and expense attending their attempts to defeat the reconstruction law in the Supreme Court. . . ."[156]

The conduct of the Court here was similar to that in *Ex parte Dugan*, when near the moment of adjourning in 1865 it refused to take a short cut in order to reach the question of the President's power to suspend the writ of habeas corpus.[157]

This delay was fatal. The emergence of a reconstituted Georgia, pursuant to the Congressional program, was so near at hand that the suit must be abandoned.[158] The graphic vocabulary of Black's disgust will be sampled in a moment.[159]

At this juncture when *McCardle* and the *Georgia* suit were fast waning, a third case suddenly appeared on its brief and uncertain course. This was *Ex parte Hamilton Martin and William E. Gill*, the petition of prisoners charged with the murder of a Negro and brought before a military commission; the Circuit Court for the Northern District of Florida had denied the writ. Their counsel was William G. M. Davis of Appalachicola, sometime Confederate brigadier. An earlier application to the Supreme Court had been put off: evidently this case

---

[154] Stanton Papers, L.C. Telegram sent in cipher.

[155] "The service of all subpoenas shall be by delivery of a copy thereof by the officer serving the same to the defendant personally" (or by leaving a copy at the place of abode); moreover, the injunction was grantable only upon "reasonable previous notice to the adverse party, or his attorney." Act of Mar. 2, 1793, 1 Stat. 334; Rules of Practice of the Courts of Equity of the United States, Rules 13, 55; State of New York v. State of Connecticut, 4 Dall. 1 (1799). The papers in the case file in the National Archives show that on March 25 Grant was served at Washington; that service on Meade was made on June 2 at Atlanta (Hq., 3rd Mil. Dist.), and on Ruger and Rockwell on June 3 at Milledgeville (then capital of Georgia).

[156] *Boston Advertiser*, Mar. 28.

[157] Supra, pp. 55–58.

[158] The Act of June 25, 1868, authorized the admission of Georgia to representation in Congress. Representatives were seated on July 25, 1868. But then the expulsion of Negroes from the Georgia legislature —see ch. 11, note 42—caused Congress to delay formal readmission until July 15, 1870.

On January 4, 1869, the Court ordered that Georgia v. Grant, Meade *et al.* stand dismissed.

[159] Infra, p. 478.

should await the outcome of *McCardle*.[160] But now Congress had doomed the *McCardle* appeal. Davis' clients were charged with a capital offense: it behooved him to renew his request.

On Friday, March 27, according to the Minutes,

> The motion filed by Mr. Davis for leave to docket this cause and to fix a day for hearing at the present term was argued by him in support of the motion. Whereupon this Court not being now here sufficiently advised of and concerning what order to render in the premises took time to consider.

Friday was the Court's day for motions; normally they would be considered in conference on Saturday, and answered on Monday.

The morning paper on Monday, March 30, carried a report that the Justices had decided to postpone the *McCardle* case, Grier and Field objecting.[161] This told the public what was already well known to persons within the circle of the Court.

This Monday, March 30, proved to be eventful. The Court met at the usual hour, 11 A.M., Chief Justice Chase presiding. (He must leave in time to enter the Senate Chamber at 12:30, when the trial of

---

[160] A note will explain why this is a puzzling case. It first appears in this entry on the Court's Minutes for Friday, February 14, 1868:

Ex parte	The motion filed
Hamilton	by Mr. Wm. G.
Martin	M. Davis for
and	leave to docket
Ex parte	this cause, and
Henry [*sic*]	a d v a n c e t h e
E. Gill	same for argu-

ment, at the present term, was argued by him, in support of the same, and by Mr. Attorney General Stanbery in opposition thereto—Whereupon this Court not being here sufficiently advised of and concerning what order to render in the premises took time to consider.

This was brought as an original proceeding—not as an appeal under the Act of February 5, 1867, as was *McCardle*.

The Minutes for Monday, February 17, show that the Court gave this answer: "On consideration of the motion filed by Mr. Davis for leave to docket this cause—It is now" But there the copying clerk reached the bottom of a page, and, alas, his attention wandered: at the top of the next page he jumped to another matter. Normally by resort to the Docket one would find posted, on the page assigned to a given case, a note of the order first recorded in the Minutes. Evidently leave to file was denied, for there is no Docket entry for *Ex parte* Martin and Gill until it was filed on April 6 as No. 12 Original, a petition for habeas corpus and certiorari—as suggested by the Court on March 31. Infra, p. 477.

It is needless to speculate at this point what was Davis' theory of jurisdiction when he first addressed the Court on February 17. Whatever he wanted, the Court must have told him to wait for the decision in *Ex parte* McCardle.

[161] *National Intelligencer*. The report, incorrectly, was that the Court in conference "decided" in favor of the appellant, only one Justice dissenting; and that subsequently it was determined, Grier and Field dissenting, not to "promulgate" its "decision."

the President would open. Then Justice Nelson would preside.) A number of decisions were announced from the bench, and the Chief Justice withdrew. The Court turned to current business, and then important events transpired, of a sort not recorded in the formal Minutes; one looks to reports in the press. The principal actors are Jere. S. Black —then Justice Grier—and finally Mr. Davis. Quoting the *National Intelligencer*,[162]

Judge Black brought to the notice of the Court a report that the promulgation of the decision in the McCardle case had been delayed to await the passage of an act of Congress intended to impair the power of the Court, and that since the passage of this act by Congress the Court had, in conference, determined not to promulgate its decision in this case before the adjournment. Chief Justice Chase was not upon the bench. Justice Nelson inquired of Judge Black what proposition he desired to make, and whether he wished to argue the effect of the repealing law. Without specifying any definite action desired, Judge Black professed a willingness to argue the matter spoken of either now or at the pleasure of the Court. Justice Nelson then asked Mr. Carpenter, the counsel of the War Department, if he had anything to say. He replied that he did not understand that there was any specific motion before the Court, but when one was made touching the interests of his clients, he would, upon proper notice, respond.

Now Justice Grier's intervention:

During this colloquy Justice Grier, with a manifestation of much emotion, observed, in substance, that he felt called upon to vindicate himself from whatever obloquy or censure may attach to any one in this matter; that he thought the failure to decide the McCardle case will be considered as a design on the part of the Court to wait for legislation to relieve them from the performance of an unpleasant duty.
      Justice Field inquired of Judge Black what authority he had for stating that the Court had determined not to promulgate the decision in the McCardle case. [To this no answer is recorded.]

Later the prepared text of Justice Grier's statement became available.

In re
McArdle [*sic*].
                                                Protest of Mr. Justice Grier.
      This case was fully argued in the beginning of this month. It is a case that involves the liberty and rights not only of the appellant,

---

[162] Mar. 31.

but of millions of our fellow-citizens. The country and the parties had a right to expect that it would receive the immediate and solemn attention of this court. By the postponement of the case we shall subject ourselves, whether justly or unjustly, to the imputation that we have evaded the performance of a duty imposed on us by the Constitution, and waited for legislation to interpose to supersede our action and relieve us from our responsibility. I am not willing to be a partaker of the eulogy or opprobrium that may follow; and can only say:

> "Pudet haec opprobria nobis,
> Et dici potuisse; et non potuisse repelli."
>
> R. C. Grier.

I am of the same opinion with my brother Grier, and unite in his protest.

> Field, J.

Apparently Grier then translated the passage from Ovid's *Metamorphoses*,[163] with adaptation to the occasion: "I am ashamed that such opprobrium should be cast upon the Court, and that it cannot be refuted."[164]

Now Davis stepped forward, to renew his insistence on the motion he had made on Friday. The *National Intelligencer*'s account continues:

> At this point General Davis made application to the Court to be allowed to proceed with an argument in the case of *ex parte* Martin and Gill, a case of habeas corpus, in which he desired to make an argument upon the effect of the recent act of Congress. Justice Nelson said that the application was under consideration by the Court. This case is even a stronger one than that of McCardle, involving the same questions, but involving also the lives as well as the liberty of two citizens, who may be unjustly tried, convicted, and executed before the next term of the Supreme Court, unless its decision is rendered now. It is expected that before the Court adjourns it will hear the argument in behalf of these parties in regard to the effect of the recent act of Congress repealing the habeas corpus act under which the case was brought into the Court.

---

[163] Book I, lines 758–59.

[164] The *National Intelligencer*, when on April 6 it published the text of this protest, said that it was "now lodged in the files of the Court, as an everlasting memorial to the honor of the venerable Mr. Justice Grier."

Whatever may have been done with this paper, a search of the Supreme Court files at the National Archives failed to find it. Reply of Sept. 14, 1964, from the Clerk of the Supreme Court, transmitting negative report of the National Archives.

The text given above is taken from *Some Account of the Work of Stephen J. Field as a Legislator, State Judge, and Judge of the Supreme Court of the United States* (1881), 49–50. On this book see infra, n. 275.

X: Ex parte McCardle

On Tuesday, March 31, the Court was ready with its answers, to Davis and to Black. First, its order in *Ex parte Martin and Gill*:

> On consideration of the motion filed by Mr. Davis on the 26th ultimo for leave to docket these appeals—It is now ordered by the court, that said motion be, and the same is hereby denied.

While the Court declined to hear what Davis had to say, it had something very encouraging to tell him. Here one turns to the account in the newspapers. Justice Nelson said that

> It was proper to suggest that the remedy, if the relators are entitled to any, [was] by a writ of habeas corpus from this Court . . . and a writ of certiorari under the fourteenth section of the Judiciary Act of 1789. This was the conclusion of the Court. It remained for the counsel to proceed accordingly if they saw proper. . . .[165]

It is significant that the Court thus volunteered its advice that, notwithstanding the abolition of the *appeal*, the old path remained. It was not certifying that the way was surely open, but it offered a meaningful "suggestion." This held out hope for prisoners under the Reconstruction Act—but it did nothing for Judge Black in his drive for a timely condemnation of the entire Congressional program.

Justice Nelson then turned to Black's request of yesterday for an argument on the validity of the repealing statute as it applied to the pending case of *McCardle*. The press dispatch gave a detailed account of what now passed between bench and bar. It merits quotation in full, because—to repeat—the *McCardle* case has been a controversial subject, and it is important to get down to facts. One point to be noted is that Judge Black absented himself when he might have been heard.

> Judge Nelson said a motion was made yesterday by Mr. Black for leave to argue the McCardle case, under the aspect it presents, in view of the recent act of Congress. One of the counsel, Mr. Black, was not in Court, but the conclusion of the Court was that if there was no objection, the Court would hear the argument at the opening of Court on Wednesday.
>
> It should here be stated that Judge Black, on making the motion yesterday, said that he did not think the recent act of Congress, withdrawing from the Court jurisdiction in this class of cases, was of any effect as to the McCardle case.

---

[165] Identical—and somewhat garbled—dispatches in *New York Times, New York Herald, Indianapolis Journal*, and *Chicago Republican*, Apr. 1, 1868.

Mr. Carpenter objected to argument to-morrow, as it was a case of much importance, and he should like more time.

Justice Miller asked Mr. Carpenter how much time he wanted.

Mr. Carpenter replied that if the subject went over to-morrow, it would necessarily go over for the term.

Judge Nelson said that the Court would let the question stand till counsel (Mr. Black) came in.

After waiting for the arrival of Judge Black, Mr. Sharkey said that he saw no necessity for arguing the McCardle case any further, and so far as he was concerned, he should merely like the privilege of filing a few authorities for himself in the absence of Judge Black. He was willing to submit it on a memorandum.

Judge Miller asked Mr. Carpenter whether he was satisfied with that?

Mr. Carpenter did not think that he was. The matter ought to be presented on both sides.

Judge Miller understood Mr. Carpenter to suggest, yesterday, that the matter should not be argued, but that the Court should settle the matter for itself.

Mr. Carpenter replied that he did not suggest what course should be pursued.

Mr. Sharkey remarked that Judge Black was not there.

Judge Clifford asked why.

Mr. Sharkey said he had got out of a sick bed to come here. He repeated that he had a little memorandum, and handed it to the Court. He did not wish to interfere with Judge Black.

The Court, after consideration, said that inasmuch as the Court was now approaching the end of the session, it must of necessity go over till next term. This was the opinion of the Court.[166]

Thus the Justices made it clear that they were willing to make time for Black, although so far as their own enlightenment was concerned they did not seek the benefit of argument. He might have used the opportunity to hurl some of his thunderbolts. Apparently, however, he now recognized that Congressional Reconstruction really could not be stopped—and suddenly quit trying.

After March 31 the Court met only in conference, until Monday, April 6, when it sat to announce a mass of decisions, and to continue to the next term all cases not decided—including *Georgia v. Grant, Meade et al.,* and *Ex parte McCardle.* The last disposition was as follows:

---

[166] *New York Times, New York Herald, Indianapolis Journal,* and *Chicago Republican,* Apr. 1.

X: Ex parte McCardle

Ex parte Hamilton Martin and William E. Gill 12 Original Petitioners	On consideration of the petition filed by Mr. W. G. M. Davis of counsel in behalf of the petitioners —It is considered, ordered, and

adjudged by this Court that a writ of Habeas Corpus be issued directed to the Marshal of the United States for the Northern District of Florida, commanding him to have the body of the said Hamilton Martin, and the body of the said William E. Gill, with the day, and the cause or causes of their detention before this Court on the first Monday of December next, to do, receive, and submit to all and singular those things, which the Court shall consider concerning them in this behalf, and to have then and there the said writ with his doings thereon.

And it is further ordered by this Court that a writ of certiorari do issue, to be directed to the Judges of the Circuit Court of the United States for the Northern District of Florida requiring and commanding them that they do send under the seal of the said Circuit Court, a full true and complete transcript of the proceedings had in said court in said cause, together with all things touching the same, to this Court, on the first Monday of December next.

And it is further ordered that all further proceedings in said Circuit Court in this case be stayed until the further order of this Court made in the premises.

per Mr. Justice Nelson.

Davis had followed the Court's suggestion, and here was the result. But the Court can be in error when it tries to be helpful, even in a matter of its own jurisdiction.[167] Whether this mode of review had

---

[167] Compare what the Court "suggested" in Wales v. Whitney, 114 U.S. 564 (1885), with what it decided in Cross v. Burke, 146 U.S. 82 (1892). Whitney, Secretary of the Navy, had ordered Wales to confine himself to the City of Washington (pending trial by court-martial). Habeas corpus being denied by the Supreme Court of the District of Columbia, counsel sought review in the Supreme Court of the United States by writ of habeas corpus—pursuant to the dictum in *McCardle*, infra, and the ruling in *Yerger*, 8 Wall. 85 (1869), infra, pp. 582–83. But on March 3, 1885, Congress restored the *appeal* in habeas corpus it had created in 1867 and repealed in 1868. 23 Stat. 437. "On a suggestion from the Court," counsel withdrew the application for the writ of habeas corpus, and took an appeal—which the Court entertained. Thereupon, on the merits, it affirmed the decision below. (This was all done in a hurry: the Secretary's order was on February 28, 1885, and the Supreme Court's judgment was on May 4, 1885, the last day of the term. The Minutes and Docket fail to show how the "suggestion" was made.)

In Cross v. Burke, where again an appeal was taken from denial of habeas corpus in the Supreme Court of the District of Columbia, Fuller, C.J., pointed out that—ignored by the Court in Wales v. Whitney—another Act of March 3, 1885, had limited appeal from the District of Columbia to cases where more than $5,000 was involved—which excluded matters, such as habeas corpus, where the right at stake could not be valued in money. [Such was the effect of Kurtz v. Moffitt, 115 U.S. 487 (1885).] Accordingly the appeal must be dismissed for want of jurisdiction.

survived the Act of March 27, 1868, would still have to be tested; doubtless the Government would oppose.

The Supreme Court, the *Springfield* (Massachusetts) *Republican* commented, "will not meddle with congressional reconstruction till after the presidential election, when nobody will ask its interference."[168] Nobody, it should have said, except an actual prisoner. While a decision against the constitutionality of the Reconstruction Act would be hailed as vindication by the Democrats, from now on it would be too late to interfere with the Congressional program.

THE COURT IS DENOUNCED AND DEFENDED

BLACK POURED OUT HIS DISAPPOINTMENT in a letter to Howell Cobb, the unpardoned and uncompromising Georgian, his old colleague in the Buchanan Cabinet:

[Washington, D.C., April, 1868.]

My Dear Sir: Forgive me for every apparent inattention. I never forget your interests for a moment. My heart yearns to serve you and I thought I could do you and many others some good. But there is nothing here that I can see besides corruption and tyranny. This whole government is so rotten and dishonest that I can only protest. It is drunk with blood and vomits crime incessantly. The convictions of six judges would have compelled them to give judgment against the infamous system of tyranny established over the South; but Congress interposed, and though the Court might have done its duty in McCardle's case, it has not and will not. The act which takes away the jurisdiction is a legislative decree, an exercise of judicial power, and therefore not constitutional. I asked for a judgment as if the act had not passed, but the question is laid over until,—when do you think? Next December. . . . The court stood still to be ravished and did not even hallo while the thing was getting done. . . .[169]

---

[168] Apr. 1, 1868.

[169] Correspondence of Toombs, Stephens, and Cobb. *Ann. Report of Am. Hist. Assn. for 1911,* 2:694 (1913).

Cobb, in a letter of Jan. 4, 1868, for the observance of Jackson Day in Washington, had called for faith in President Johnson and in a "Judiciary whose unspotted record has never yet been tarnished with a base subserviency to the unholy demands of passion and hatred." Ibid., 690, 694.

Black had until very recently been

on cordial terms with the President. Writing to him on November 25, 1867, apropos of the Annual Message to be sent on December 2, his letter contained these sentiments: "The mass of the people are *determined* to compel respect to the constitution. They will not consent to put it in the keeping of negroes. . . . Your ship will ride triumphant on the wave which submerges Chase & Grant both. Let Chase spend his money & Grant beat his drums to all eternity —the truth has got a start and if you

The Democratic press now cried shame upon the Court whose valor it had hailed so proudly a year before. "Ermine-clad Crawfishes," commented the *Montgomery Mail* when the Court refrained from forestalling Congress.[170] Henry Watterson's *Louisville Courier-Journal* ran an editorial on "Shirking a Decision," which said that the Court had not "possessed half the nerve that belongs to many a justice of the peace."[171] The *Richmond Enquirer and Examiner*, deploring "The Cowardice of the Supreme Court," said "the citizen whose life and liberty were in jeopardy expected the court . . . would at once decide" this "most sacred" appeal. (McCardle's life was not in jeopardy; to Martin and Gill, who were in danger, the Court had volunteered an invaluable suggestion.) The *Enquirer and Examiner* disclosed its real grievance: "The white race in ten States expected to see the whole fabric of negro rule crushed by the weight of judicial authority . . . ." But alas the country discovered that "The Supreme Court . . . is cowed, it trembles in the presence of the lawless body whose unconstitutional acts it was created to pronounce null and void." Honor to Grier and Field, the editor exclaimed; but "Shame, deep shame to the veteran Nelson, who has dimmed forever his previous high repute for courage and honesty by turning craven at the last. . . ."[172] (Ordinarily it was safe for Southerners to reckon that Justice Nelson would be on their side.)

A member of the Court's bar, signing simply as "X"—actually James M. Carlisle, one of the most experienced practitioners[173]—now sent a statement to the press, seeking "to put the public right with respect to [the Court's] action in the McCardle case." The matter had been carried forward most expeditiously from the time it was docketed

---

keep it going it will distance all competition. The document for Monday next is *plain* as you had it prepared when I saw you—and plain speaking is exactly what is needed. . . . Let them see if they can find you *guilty of violating the constitution. . . .*" Johnson Papers, L.C.

But when Black wrote to Cobb in April 1868 he had come to be at odds with all three branches of the Government. After he had entered upon the defense of the President, a long-standing matter of the claim of clients to the Alta Vela guano island became acute, and Johnson refused to take the protective action Black urged. On March 19 Black informed the President that he found himself "in a situation where I may be compelled to do what your counsel can-

not and ought not to do." Accordingly he withdrew from his engagement in the impeachment trial. Professor William N. Brigance in his *Jeremiah Sullivan Black* (Philadelphia: University of Pennsylvania Press, 1934), at 180–196, examined the involved and controverted matter in detail, and exonerated Black from any improper action toward the President.

To pursue an independent inquiry here would wander far out of bounds.

[170] Mar. 27.
[171] Apr. 14.
[172] Apr. 15.
[173] See Justice Davis' letter of Apr. 22, 1868, infra, p. 484. Carlisle has been mentioned as counsel for the petitioner in Georgia v. Grant, Meade *et al.*, supra. He will figure prominently in *Ex parte* Yerger, infra, pp. 566–85.

[December 23, 1867] to March 31, when no one was prepared to argue further. Carlisle continued:

> Perhaps there could be no more convincing proof that the Court has kept itself within the bounds of strict judicial propriety than is to be found in the fact that the *ultra* men in both political parties have concurred in the common object of attempting to weaken its just hold upon the confidence and affection of the people because of its action, and equally of its non-action, in this case. When it was ordered to be advanced upon the docket, . . . the Radical party cried out with one accord that the Court was lending itself to political objects. When it refused to run a race with the other co-ordinate branches of the Government, but proceeded with a decent respect to duty and to them, the extremists of the other side have not scrupled to accuse it of faltering in its high place. Both charges are unjust, and equally without foundation in fact.
>
> The judicial office makes any defence by the judges themselves out of the question; but they may safely rely upon the enlightened and generous press of the country, and upon the bar, who are, after all, the most competent and jealous critics of their conduct, to protect them from unmerited aspersion.[174]

Carlisle had made a praiseworthy effort to let the public understand exactly what the Court had done. His hortatory profession of confidence in the press was, however, unwarranted. The *Springfield Republican*, which ranked high in its sense of responsibility, observed merely that there was a "chapter of excuses" for the Court's failure to decide *McCardle*, and concluded that "the case is of little consequence, and to whom the blame justly belongs of much less."[175]

Comment on the Court commonly attaches undue weight to valorous utterances, particularly when in dissent. So it has been with *McCardle*: on the basis of Grier's protest, critics have represented that the Court acted ingloriously. But here we have heard Reverdy Johnson and then Carlisle, each seizing an opportunity to proclaim that in this equivocal situation the Court had acted with strict judicial propriety. They spoke out of a sense of their responsibility as leaders at the Supreme Court bar. In Taney's time these men had been his close intimates; they were free from the least taint of partiality for Radical schemes; professionally they had recently been engaged on the Southern side. No testimonial could have been more worthy of acceptance than theirs.

---

174 *National Intelligencer*, Apr. 11, 1868.   175 April 8, 1868.

X: Ex parte McCardle

JUSTICE DAVIS ON MANY THINGS

WHEN THE COURT ADJOURNED on April 6, 1868, elections on newly framed constitutions were near at hand (or had just been completed) in most of the Southern States. Justice Davis hastened to Aiken, South Carolina, where his family were sojourning, and arrived in time to observe the election at the place on April 14 to 16. In a long letter to Judge Rockwell he "rattled on," as he said, giving his views on many things.[176] "I have told you my convictions, & if they do not coincide with yours, I know you will excuse the frankness . . . . They are honestly entertained." He commented upon the election, and the plight of the freedmen—on Congressional Reconstruction, and the two political parties—on President Johnson's conduct, and the impeachment trial then in progress—and on the Court's recent action in *Ex parte McCardle*. The letter enables one to take a reckoning of conditions at the moment, as seen by this Justice who held an independent position on the Bench of eight.

Aiken, South Carolina
April 22nd 1868

My Dear Brother,

I ought to have written to you fr Washington, but I actually had not time. A judge of the Supreme Court, in order to discharge his duties creditably, has to work all the time in Washington, and gets pretty tired, when it is time to leave.

This place is on the route from Washington to Augusta & Savannah, by way of Richmond & Wilmington, and I got here in about 44 hours from Washington. . . .

(Aiken stands on high ground, sixteen miles from the Savannah River at Augusta, Georgia. The route lay by steamboat from Washington to Aquia Creek, Virginia; thence south and west, some six hundred miles over six railroads with three different gauges. One notes the inconvenience of transportation, only three years after Appomattox.)

. . . Plenty of negroes here, and a good many idle. There are no disturbances, that I can hear of, any where. The election last week passed off quietly, but when I saw the degraded ignorance of the poor creatures, who were voting at the instance of those, who dont care a rush about them except to get their votes for the offices

---

[176] Davis Papers. Ill. State. Hist. Soc.

they want to fill, I felt sad. The problem of negro suffrage, necessarily involving all political and social equality, may prove a measure of wisdom and good statesmanship, but I dont believe it. It seems to me that no candid man could believe it who saw the plantation hands voting, & the kind of men fr the North who solicit their votes. I was raised among negroes, & I have great kindness for the race, & in my soul I believe the thrusting on them political rights is to their injury. . . .

(In this election on South Carolina's constitution, 72 per cent of the votes cast were for adoption. Despite massive white abstention—both from voting on delegates in November 1867, and now on the proposed constitution—the votes for adoption amounted to 53 per cent of the total registration. The elected governor, James L. Orr—formerly Speaker of the federal House of Representatives, colonel of a South Carolina regiment, and Confederate Senator—had warned, unavailingly, against this refusal to participate under the Congressional plan.)

Resuming the letter: Justice Davis pronounced a sober judgment, in retrospect. It was that "Qualified, intelligent suffrage would have been better for them, & better for the whites, & I am sorry for both that it was not adopted. . . ." Looking ahead to the approaching Presidential contest in 1868, he wrote:

There is more repugnance to negroes at the West than here—repugnance I mean to any and every idea of equality, and if the Republicans would insert in their platform at Chicago, what they mean—equality in all political rights—they would be beaten in every Western State. But they wont do it, although their leaders mean it. The negroes, throughout the South have behaved well. They are a docile race of people, and if let alone by political adventurers would get along pretty well.

Both parties have run into extremes, and middle men are crushed out. The Democrats, instead of recognizing the war & its issues, & placing in the lead men who were for the war, and when the war was over were for settling it up, are placing in the lead men who were agt the war & whose sympathies were agt the Government. The Republican party, I mean the leaders are doing everything to keep up hate & intensify it—and want to do every thing to degrade these Southern people.

Is there wisdom or statesmanship in all this? If Mr Lincoln had have lived, he wd have encountered the hostility of the very men now controlling the Congress, but his hold on the people were such that any basis of settlement that he might have proposed would have been accepted by the people. The effect of the death of Mr Lincoln in continuing the unfortunate strife in the Country, cannot be overstated.

482

X: Ex parte McCardle

That was a significant estimate, on a matter where Justice Davis'
opinion is entitled to great weight. Could Lincoln have carried the
nation to a just and forward-looking Reconstruction, that would have
been a triumph of leadership comparable to the preservation of the
Union. Davis turned to Lincoln's successor:

> Johnson had no prestige & unfortunately his obstinacy & combat-
> iveness have postponed all chance of a wise settlement & been the means
> of injuring these Southern people, beyond the power of words to tell.
> *They* shd have accepted the Constitutional Amendment & wd have
> done it, if Johnson had advised them to do it. After the elections
> of 1866, if Johnson had had any good statesmanship he wd have
> advised the Southern States to have accepted it & thus avoid the worse
> measures in behalf of restoration which have been since imposed
> on them. But being actuated by no spirit of compromise, he could
> not see an inch beyond the time being. . . .

(Whether President Johnson can justly be held to have *injured* the
Southern people, considering how intractable were their own leaders, is
questionable. Certainly the responsibility was shared. Otherwise Justice
Davis' judgment was sound.)

> I believe the President to be an honest man and true patriot, but
> with qualities, totally unfitting him for the ruler of a people in the
> fix we are in. Obstinate, self willed, combative, slow to act, with
> no executive ability, and no proper appreciation of the dignity of his
> office. His speeches on his tour to Douglas' tomb wd have ruined
> even a *wooden man*. . . .

Davis turned to the impeachment trial.[177] He had been "amazed
at the weakness of the prosecution," amazed too "at the rejection of
evidence by the Senate, offered by the defence on the point of *intent.*"
"If there is any Slavery in the known world—Slavery of the Soul—
equal to that demanded by party, I dont know where it is." It would
take "heroism" for a Senator to act conscientiously on the impeachment.
"What a contrast" between the conduct of the defense, led by B. R.
Curtis, and that of the prosecution! "Butler, coarse as he is, has more
brains than the other managers, & on account of this, the lead has
naturally fallen to him."

> The influence of party is observable in the denunciation of the Chief
> Justice. Because he said this trial was a judicial proceeding he was
> denounced, and at every impartial ruling this denunciation has con-

---

177 See infra, pp. 521–26.

483

tinued & today in Washington, he is hated intensely by those in the lead of the Republican party. . . .

(Here Davis recalled *Ex parte Milligan*—still a sore point—and then went on to the recent experience with *Ex parte McCardle*.)

> I told him [the Chief Justice] he was getting a little taste of what I recd when I delivered the Milligan opinion, & I thank God today, that there was an opportunity for the Supreme Court to say what it did, on the subject of military trials. If this country lives as a free government, the wonder will be in after times, that there was any need in this age of the world to reaffirm the cardinal principles of civil liberty. I suppose Congress was unwilling to risk the Supreme Court on a subject akin to this and they repealed the law allowing a decision to be made in the McCardle case. By the way, the inability of the Supreme Court to satisfy the parties of the day in their course of action is exemplified in the McCardle case. It was advanced on the docket to be heard as all criminal cases are under the rules and for this the Court was denounced by the Republican press. The case was heard and argument closed on Monday 9th of March. On next Saturday, the day of consultation the case was not reached, & no one anticipated that it would be considered by Congress before the next consultation. But it was & the bill was passed repealing jurisdiction, & it was in the hands of the President when the next consultation was had. The Court—Grier & Field dissenting—thought it was unjudicial to run a race with Congress, and especially as the Bill might be signed at any moment by the President. They therefore did not take the case up & decide it (for an opinion could not have been written until the Presdt & Congress had acted.[)] For thus waiting, they have been denounced by the democratic press. So you see that nothing that they can do will satisfy the extreme views of party. Each wants some decision that will help them, rather than the law pronounced. I cut out from the National Intelligencer & send to you a communication on the subject said to be written by Mr. Carlisle a distinguished lawyer of Washington.

The clipping was the letter from "X," quoted above.

Davis' concluding thought was for the preservation of the federal system:

> Believing as I do, that in our extended Country, the preservation of the rights of the States is essential to the preservation of Liberty, I must confess to feeling great alarm at the tendency to consolidated Govt manifested by the Republican party. This alarms me more than all other things besides . . . .

The Southern States, said Justice Davis, *should* have accepted the Fourteenth Amendment, to avoid the worse measures Congress had imposed; in particular, universal suffrage. But he voices no exultation over the new security of liberty and equality the Amendment promises to bring. As he sees it, liberty is being *lost*—through the tendency to shift power from State to Nation, and the extremes to which both political parties have run.

A century later, many would be exulting that liberty was being *expanded* through the consolidated power of the Nation's highest Court, by means of the Fourteenth Amendment—an Amendment in derogation of the rights of the States, achieved by a headstrong Congress, despite a hostile Chief Executive and in defiance of the authority of the Supreme Court. This suggests a pause for reflection—and discernment in the deposit of one's faith. The "Blessings of Liberty" are multiform; appreciation has varied according to time and circumstance. Their fulfillment has been secured through no single feature of the constitutional system.

CHIEF JUSTICE CHASE ON THE *McCARDLE* CASE

AN ADDITIONAL ITEM is to be considered: a letter of April 5, 1868, from Chase to John D. Van Buren.[178] This was Sunday. During the week past, the Chief Justice had been presiding at the trial of the President. On Monday the Supreme Court would dispose of its final business and adjourn to December.[179] At this moment Chase was being appraised by Democratic leaders as a possible nominee; their convention would meet on July 4. Chase thanks Van Buren and Manton Marble (editor of the *New York World*) for a copy of an article to the effect that Chase was not seeking the nomination.[180] He says that he hopes no one "expects anything from me except the honest and impartial discharge of my duties as presiding officer." He proceeds to explain his position in the *McCardle* case, and to express sentiments on current matters—particularly his earnest desire for the early restoration of the Southern States. Our immediate concern is with the following paragraphs:

> In the McCardle case I agreed with all the Judges except two (Grier and Field), who have made public their dissent, that it would not become the Supreme Court to *hasten* their decision of an appeal for the purpose of getting ahead of the legislation of Congress. The Constitution gives the Supreme Court jurisdiction on appeals only

---

[178] Chase Papers, Hist. Soc. of Pa. It was in the clear handwriting of Chase's secretary—which commonly signifies that it was something regarded as important.
[179] Supra, p. 476.
[180] See infra, pp. 532–33.

"with such exceptions and under such regulations as the Congress shall make." Congress, therefore, had the undoubted right to except such cases as that of McCardle from its appellate jurisdiction; and it would have been, as we thought, an indecency to run a race in the exercise of *that* jurisdiction with the Legislature.

Whether Congress can *oust* an appeal already taken and perfected is another question. There are cases which support this view; but I should have been glad to have had the question argued. I was not present when it was decided to postpone the argument of it to the next term, having been necessarily absent in the Court of Impeachment all the week. I had previously proposed an adjournment to June, but met no support.

It was especially desirable to me to have the case decided; for it is highly probable that I shall meet the question on the Circuit; and I should feel better if I had a decision to guide and support me.

This introduces a new element in the controverted matter of the Court's conduct in *McCardle*: "*I had previously proposed an adjournment to June, but met no support.*" (It was to be expected that by June the Chief Justice would no longer be detained in the Senate.) No other mention of such a proposal has come to light.[181] Without questioning the truth of the sentence, it is to be viewed guardedly. To "propose" could be anything from urging to merely casual mention as a possibility. Throughout the letter, Chase's aim is evidently to justify and commend himself to these Democratic politicians.

The question Chase wanted to have argued in June was whether Congress could "oust an appeal already perfected. There are cases which support this view . . . ." When on April 12, 1869, that question came to be decided, Chase for a unanimous Court said that although counsel for the petitioner had offered citations to sustain their contention that jurisdiction in this instance was not affected by the repeal, "none of them, in our judgment, afford any support to it." It was found to be "quite clear" that the Court's jurisdiction had been ousted.[182]

Chase's next paragraph: it was especially desirable "to have the case decided," because it was "highly probable" he would "meet the question on the Circuit." But the particular question whether it was the duty of the Supreme Court—notwithstanding the Act of March 27, 1868—to decide an appeal already docketed, was not anything that required a ruling by the Circuit Court: that statute had not affected the Circuit Court's jurisdiction. However, *if* the Supreme Court had decided the question of its own jurisdiction *contrary* to the view it subsequently

---

[181] So far as the author recalls.

[182] *Ex parte* McCardle, 7 Wall. 506. Infra, p. 492.

found to be "quite clear" and *if* it had thereupon gone on to decide whether McCardle was entitled to his release, *then* it would have decided a question that might arise on the Circuit. And *if* it had decided that a military commission was without lawful power over a civilian in McCardle's situation, then surely the Chief Justice himself would have written the opinion; and if the outcome could be announced before the Democratic convention made its nomination, then certainly Chase's prospects would have been enormously enhanced.

The evidence of Chase's own correspondence, summarized in the next chapter, teaches one to look for ulterior motives.

THE COURT'S DECEMBER TERM 1868

BOTH THE CONGRESS AND THE COURT convened on the first Monday in December 1868. Unlike the situation a year earlier, when Congressional Reconstruction was vulnerable—and unlike the situation that would be presented in December 1869, when nervous Radicals would see a new scare in *Ex parte Yerger*[183]—this Third Session of the 40th Congress in December 1868 expressed nothing but solicitude for the well-being of the Court. The crisis had passed in April, when the Court had adjourned without a decision on *McCardle*. Since that time the Republicans, carried along on the personal popularity of General Grant, had won a national election, comfortably though not spectacularly. In the 41st Congress their strength would be better than 2 to 1 in the House, and 5 to 1 in the Senate.

The measure of the party's good will is the ease with which Senator Trumbull carried through a bill to increase the membership of the Court to nine, and to create for each of the nine Circuits the office of Circuit Judge, to relieve the Justices of some of the burden of trial work.[184] And when that failed for want of the President's signature— "only by accident, we believe," according to Henry Adams[185]—the First Session of the 41st Congress, convening at once on March 4, 1869, passed the measure in even better form, by adding the provision that any federal judge, having held his commission for at least ten years and having attained the age of seventy would, upon resignation, receive

---

[183] Infra, p. 586.

[184] S. 784. The Senate passed it on February 23, 1869, after little debate, without a record vote. The House passed it on March 3, without debate, by a vote of 93 to 22. Cong. Globe, 40–3, 1489, 1895.

[185] "The Session," *No. Am. Rev.* 108:610, 621 (1869). President Johnson let late bills be brought to him at the White House, where he sat until the moment his successor had been inaugurated.

his salary for life. This became effective on the first Monday in December, 1869.[186] Nowhere in the debates does one find a hostile sentiment toward the Justices.

In the Court, at the opening of the December term, 1868, Black appeared to ask leave to argue the effect upon *McCardle*'s case of the repeal of the Court's jurisdiction. This was granted; but the matter was not really urgent, and it was not until March 19, 1869, that argument was heard.[187]

In the meantime, other events are to be noticed. First, *Ex parte Martin and Gill* disappeared as casually as it had come onto the docket.[188] The return to the certiorari was filed on December 10. But then on January 4, 1869, when the Court was calling the Original Docket, this case was reached, and it was "Ordered by the court that this cause do stand dismissed with costs unless cause to the contrary be shown to the court on or before the first Friday in February next." The proceeding had been abandoned—apparently Martin and Gill had been put out of danger.

At this point Dr. Mudd reappears.[189] He had continued to serve at Fort Jefferson, Florida, the sentence imposed by the military commission at Washington in 1865. On July 4, 1868, President Johnson extended amnesty to those who had participated in the late rebellion. Invoking that grant, Mudd sought a writ of habeas corpus from District Judge Thomas J. Boynton of the Southern District of Florida. So too did his co-defendants, Samuel Arnold and Edward Spangler.[190] Relief was denied in an opinion that made two points: the assassination of the President for a political motive in time of civil war was (in Judge Boynton's view) properly triable by military commission—as an act of unlawful belligerency, which the Judge likened to the clandestine killing of the commanding General in a fortified city—and was not within the reasoning of the *Milligan* case; further, the crime of being accessory to the assassination was not embraced within the amnesty.[191]

On February 9, 1869, Philip Phillips[192] asked and obtained the Supreme Court's leave to file petitions for habeas corpus on behalf

---

[186] Act of Apr. 10, 1869, 16 Stat. 44.

[187] Infra, p. 492.

[188] Supra, pp. 471, 477.

[189] Supra, pp. 237–39.

[190] The fourth, Michael O'Laughlin, had died of yellow fever on September 23, 1867.

[191] Fed. Case No. 9899, Sept. 1868. It reports "opinion not now accessible." Actually the opinion was published in the *National Intelligen-*cer, October 5, 1868—and is among the papers in the pardon file, National Archives. The Judge commented that while it was "a matter of public notoriety" that there had been much doubt whether the evidence at the trial had been sufficient to convict, that was a matter that could not be considered on a petition for habeas corpus.

[192] Identified in connection with *Ex parte* Yerger, infra, p. 568.

of Mudd, Arnold, and Spangler.[193] Three days later the petitions were filed for the latter two. (The case of Mudd drops out at this point; his attorney had filed an application for pardon on September 5, 1868, and it was reported in the press that his deliverance was at hand.[194]) On February 15, 1869, the Chief Justice announced this order:

> The Court will hear argument upon the question whether it had jurisdiction to allow the writs of Habeas Corpus as prayed for. And also upon the question whether the jurisdiction of this Court in respect to the writ of Habeas Corpus is original or appellate.
>
> And the counsel for the petitioners will give notice of this order to the Attorney General.

On Phillip's motion, with the consent of Attorney General Evarts, a hearing was set for February 26.

The second sentence of the order was arresting: something important was afoot. Were there Justices prepared to hold that Congress *could* add to the Court's original jurisdiction (overruling *Marbury v. Madison*[195] on this point)—that it *had* done so by Section 14 of the Judiciary Act of 1789, and very properly, too, considering the guaranty of habeas corpus in Article I, Section 9 (here throwing away as no longer needed the labored theory of appellate jurisdiction by habeas corpus, in *Ex parte Bollman*)—and perhaps, still more boldly, that by force of the constitutional guarantee, Congress could not take away this jurisdiction except "in cases of rebellion or invasion . . ."? Certainly the Court would not on its own motion have raised the question of original jurisdiction if there had not been some interest in that topic.

Suspense may be relieved at once: the Court did not repudiate John Marshall. Nothing resulted beyond what Chase wrote in this musing paragraph in his opinion in *Ex parte Yerger*, eight months later:

> If the question were a new one, it would, perhaps, deserve inquiry whether Congress might not, under the power to make exceptions from this appellate jurisdiction, extend the original jurisdiction to other cases than those expressly enumerated in the Constitution; and especially, in view of the constitutional guaranty of the writ of habeas corpus, to cases arising upon petition for that writ.[196]

But, the Chief Justice hastened to say, what had been decided in *Marbury* and in *Bollman*[197] had not since been drawn into question.

---

[193] Docketed respectively as Nos. 12, 13 and 14, Original. Phillips' action was reported fully in the *New York Tribune*, February 10, 13, 1869.

[194] *New York Tribune*, Feb. 10, 12.
[195] Supra, p. 443.
[196] 8 Wall. 85, 97 (1869).
[197] Supra, p. 443.

Phillips did not choose to put his clients' case on the footing that the Court could exercise original jurisdiction. His brief, entitled "Appellate Power of Supreme Court United States to Issue the Writ of Habeas Corpus," was written and printed in time to be filed on February 19; it bears evidence of haste. He said that in creating "one Supreme Court," the Constitution contemplated that it should have "a general supervisory jurisdiction" over inferior tribunals. Marshall had classified a court-martial as "one of those inferior courts of limited jurisdiction, whose judgments may be questioned collaterally."[198] "Appellate jurisdiction" did not necessarily connote a power of direct review, leading to affirmance or reversal; it might be "a power to arrest the *execution* of a void judgment," as by releasing from imprisonment under a sentence imposed without jurisdiction. The Supreme Court, using its power under Section 14, could discharge Arnold and Spangler if it found that the military commission lacked jurisdiction, or if they were within the clemency of December 25, 1868.

Phillips' brief made no mention of the circumstance that an application had been denied by the District Judge. Apparently he saw no prospect that the Court could be induced to do, what in *Metzger's* case in 1847 it had said it could not do—review the decision of a Judge at chambers.[199] He thought it better to argue that a military commission was comparable to a territorial court, not invested with "judicial power" but yet subject to the appellate power of the Supreme Court.[200]

"Since the preparation of the foregoing brief," Phillips wrote under the heading "Additional," "my attention has been called by the court to the consideration of the act 5th February, 1867, . . . 'amendatory' of the act of 1789." He proceeded to argue persuasively that the Court could still exercise its old powers.

"Points of the Attorney General", signed by Evarts and Assistant Attorney General J. Hubley Ashton, replied that "This court cannot exercise any appellate control . . . over the Military Commission . . . , nor has this court power in any form or by any procedure to revise the proceedings of that Commission in the case of the petitioners."[201]

Oral argument in *Ex parte Arnold and Spangler* was heard on February 26, 1869. Attorney General Evarts, who would be out of office on March 4, left the matter in the able hands of Assistant Attorney General J. Hubley Ashton. Phillips and Ashton contended

---

[198] *Ex parte* Watkins, 3 Pet. 193, 209 (1830), explaining Wise v. Winters, 3 Cranch 331 (1806).

[199] *In re* Metzger, 5 How. 176, supra, p. 445.

[200] American Insurance Co. v. Canter, 1 Pet. 511 (1828).

[201] This brief was incorporated in that filed by Attorney General Hoar in *Ex parte* Yerger, 8 Wall. 85, eight months later; it is substantially reproduced in 19 L. Ed. at 333-35, reporting *Ex parte* Yerger. Infra, pp. 581-82.

over rough ground, before a Court that must have been mindful that only by a violent break with the past could it assume power to review on habeas corpus the sentence of an extraordinary body, not properly a *court*.[202]

Seemingly the Court was stirred by some roving thoughts, which a decision in *Ex parte Arnold and Spangler* would probably have brought into the open.[203]

Once again, however, the bright prospect of a memorable decision suddenly vanished. On March 1, just before he left office, President

---

[202] In the briefs, neither side cited *Ex parte* Vallandigham, 1 Wall. 243, where in 1864 the Court had held that it had no authority to issue the writ of certiorari to call up from the Judge Advocate General of the Army the record of a trial by military commission. The writ of habeas corpus was not there involved: that was precluded by the circumstance that Vallandigham was no longer in custody. Supra, p. 193n. (The Circuit Court for the Southern District of Ohio had denied habeas corpus. *Ex parte* Vallandigham, Fed. Case No. 16,816 (1863). The President, greatly embarrassed that the trial had ever been started, sent Vallandigham to the Confederate lines.) The Supreme Court held, quite properly, that certiorari was one of those "other writs not specially provided for by statute" which Section 14 of the Judiciary Act authorized the courts to issue only so far as "may be necessary for the exercise of their respective jurisdictions." See the language of Section 14, supra, p. 441. The same view was taken *In re* Vidal, 179 U.S. 126 (1900).

Habeas corpus, on the other hand —as Section 14 was construed in *Ex parte* Bollman—could be issued not only in aid of jurisdiction, but broadly "for the purpose of an inquiry into the cause of commitment" where the prisoner was held under color of the authority of the United States. With Vallandigham no longer in custody, habeas corpus had been out of the question. But Arnold and Spangler were in custody, and Phillips was arguing that, consistently with the Constitution and Section 14 of the Judiciary Act, the Supreme

Court did have jurisdiction to review their detention. If that were true, of course certiorari would be available in aid of the inquiry.

In his brief Phillips assumed that a military commission (emanating from the authority of the Executive) could be assimilated to a court-martial (established by Congress under its power to provide for the government of the land and naval forces): he spoke of "military tribunals" generally, and argued that they were "inferior courts" subject to the appellate jurisdiction of the Supreme Court. So, too, counsel for Vallandigham had started from his "Point I. A Military Commission is a Court of regular authority, but its jurisdiction is limited and special."

[203] Apparently uncertainty persisted, for in 1882, when the Court was asked by habeas corpus to review the judgment of a court-martial, Waite, C.J., announced that "upon this question there is not entire unanimity of opinion among the members of the Court, and we purposely withhold any decision at this time with respect to it." *Ex parte* Mason, 105 U.S. 696, 697. A soldier of the guard had been convicted of attempting to kill Guiteau, the assassin of President Garfield. All Justices agreed that there could be no discharge where, as here, the court-martial had jurisdiction to try the accused for the offense charged and the sentence was one which that court could lawfully impose.

Chief Justice Waite's Docket Book, in the Ms. Div., L.C., reflects no division of opinion in the vote on this case.

Johnson pardoned Arnold and Spangler, along with Dr. Mudd. On March 19 Phillips brought this to the attention of the Court, and the petitions were dismissed.

Also on March 19, McCardle's weary case was called, for argument on the contention that the repeal of jurisdiction could not affect a pending case. This time Judge Black did not appear; the argument devolved upon Judge Sharkey, who on March 31, a year before, had sought no more than "the privilege of filing a few authorities."[204] Carpenter opposed. He relied upon the principle the Court had recognized in *Norris v. Crocker* in 1851, sustaining "the exhaustive argument of the present Chief Justice, then at the bar," that the repeal of a statute barred a pending action.[205]

On April 12 the Chief Justice announced a unanimous decision. Article III allowed Congress to "make exceptions to the appellate jurisdiction . . . ." The Court would not inquire into motives. "Jurisdiction is the power to declare the law, and when it ceases to exist, the only function remaining to the court is that of announcing the fact and dismissing the cause."[206]

---

[204] Supra, p. 476.

[205] 13 How. 429. Supra, p. 30. This was an action for a penalty under Fugitive Slave Act of 1793. In 1850 Congress passed a more effective Fugitive Slave Act which covered the same ground and, the Court found, by necessary implication repealed the earlier statute. Held, that the instant action, pending in the Circuit Court when the new statute became law, was barred.

[206] *Ex parte* McCardle, 7 Wall. 506.

Often in one's preoccupation with a great cause, one does not think to inquire what action was taken in consequence of it. The Circuit Court's remand to custody had been stayed, pending the outcome of McCardle's appeal. Now the Supreme Court had dismissed the appeal for want of jurisdiction. Certainly—as will be apparent in a moment—the Government had no desire to lay hands on his person. Precisely how it got rid of him does not appear. A competent search of the Minute Book of the Circuit Court from April 1869 to its Special Term of January 24, 1870, found no mention of McCardle. The author's search at National Archives in the various series of orders of

Headquarters 4th Military District and in the ledger-books of that headquarters wherein communications were recorded, revealed no disposition. This negative result was confirmed by a reference service report. The broken file of the *Vicksburg Times* gave no answer. (By this time McCardle had ceased to be its editor; he was planning to publish a new daily, "The Forum"—which apparently never materialized.) The remaining numbers of the *Herald* and of the *Jackson Clarion* were unresponsive.

Perhaps nobody made any move and McCardle simply remained free, without formality. Perhaps the military authority advised the Circuit Court that it waived any further claim.

Much had transpired since McCardle took his appeal and was admitted to bail in November 1867.

The military commission had been adjourned sine die by order of Hq. 4th Mil. Dist. of January 2, 1868. Its president, Brevet Major General Galusha Pennypacker had been ordered to another station, leaving "a host of friends" in Vicksburg. *Herald*, Mar. 6 and 29, 1868. (On Pennypacker [1844–1916] see D.A.B.

X: Ex parte McCardle

It is to be remembered that the decision was unanimous. The dissent Grier and Field had announced from the bench a year before had concerned the postponement of consideration in conference, not the effect of a repeal.

The Chief Justice's opinion closed with this pregnant statement:

> Counsel seem to have supposed, if effect be given to the repealing Act in question, that the whole appellate power of the Court, in cases of habeas corpus, is denied. The Act of 1868 does not except from that jurisdiction any cases but appeals from circuit courts made under the Act of 1867. It does not affect the jurisdiction that was previously exercised.

It was, certainly, most unusual to declare prospectively that the Court would have jurisdiction in a certain situation. On this point, however, the Court had made its own examination before making the "suggestion" in *Martin and Gill*,[207] and then had heard the matter argued in the abortive case of *Arnold and Spangler*, as recently as February 26.

McCardle or anyone else, if need be, could still invoke the Supreme Court's jurisdiction in habeas corpus.

A POSTSCRIPT ON *McCARDLE*

On May 1, 1869, the Chief Justice wrote to District Judge Hill in Mississippi. He was sending a copy of his opinion in *Texas v. White*,[208] decided on April 12, the day when *Ex parte McCardle* was

---

Enlisting at the outbreak of the war, his distinguished gallantry had brought promotion to Brigadier General before his twenty-first birthday; in 1891 he was awarded a Medal of Honor.)

General Gillem, Ord's successor, was relieved of the command of the 4th Military District in March 1869 —a month before McCardle's appeal was dismissed. (He received a "testimonial of respect" from a meeting of citizens, presided over by General Wirt Adams, C.S.A. *Vicksburg Times*, March 11; *Jackson Weekly Clarion*, March 18.)

Congress by the Act of April 10, 1869, authorized the President to resubmit the constitution rejected in June 1868: he might—and did— designate particular provisions for separate vote. This looked to the restoration of Mississippi with a constitution admitting to the suffrage without racial discrimination, but shorn of the proscriptive features.

It now appeared that Congressional Reconstruction was no longer in jeopardy—and on that footing, McCardle had his quittance.

[207] Supra, p. 475.

[208] 7 Wall. 700. It affirmed the capacity of Texas, as a State in the Union, to bring an original suit in the Supreme Court. (That suit had been filed in February 1867.) The Chief Justice's opinion held that, although their rights had been "suspended" during the war, the Southern States had never been "out of the Union." Infra, pp. 638-40.

dismissed. Chase rejoiced at the Judge's report of progress in Mississippi:

> I am not surprised that at last common sense & practical views resume their sway, and that so large a majority of the educated & intelligent recognize that suffrage for both whites & blacks is best for all. If this simple truth had been recognized when I first urged its recognition on Southern men in 1865 hundreds of millions of dollars would have been saved & great suffering spared.[209]

On the margin the Chief Justice made a disclosure of the highest interest: "P.S. I may say to you that had the merits of the McCardle Case been decided the Court would doubtless have held that his imprisonment for trial before a military commission was illegal."

The Chief Justice wrote, "doubtless": he was relating, not a fact, but what he apprehended would have happened. There had been no occasion to take a vote on the merits—still less to settle the grounds on which a decision would be placed. His conclusion resulted, doubtless, from what he had observed of the individual views of his brethren. The Court, then, would have held that so much of the Reconstruction Act of March 2 as authorized trial by military tribunal was unconstitutional. Seemingly, in the Chief Justice's belief, it would not have invalidated the legislation in respect of its principal feature: the reorganization of the "rebel States" by the agency and on the basis therein provided. It is implicit in Chase's triumphant paragraph on universal suffrage that he regarded that principle as established.

A holding for the appellant on that narrow ground would still have been, practically, a defeat for Black and his associates. In political argument, however, the judgment could have been exploited for more than its true significance.

One hazards nothing in supposing that in such a decision the Chief Justice would have been joined at least by the Democrats (Nelson, Grier, Clifford, and Field) and by Justice Davis.[210]

The Chief Justice was confiding what he understood to be the state of mind among the Justices; even so, the validity of the provision for trial by military tribunal remained formally an open question.

---

[209] Chase Papers, L.C.

[210] In Texas v. White—which, as just noted, was decided on the same day that *Ex parte* McCardle was dismissed—Justice Grier (Swayne and Miller concurring) had declined "to join in any essay to prove Texas to be a State of the Union, when Congress have decided that she is not." That does not signify that Grier would have upheld the Reconstruction Act as it had been applied to McCardle: even when legislating for places not "within" any State, Congress remains under constitutional limitations. Swayne and Miller said that the status of Texas was a matter where the Court "is bound by the action of the Legislative Department."

X: Ex parte McCardle

Within a few weeks—on June 8, at Jackson, Mississippi—Edward M. Yerger killed the officer assigned to act as mayor. Would the Court on his behalf exercise the jurisdiction it had asserted in the dictum in *Ex parte McCardle*? If yes, would it go on to decide what the Chief Justice said it "doubtless" would have decided on the merits in *McCardle*?[211]

HOW THE COURT VIEWED ITS OWN JURISDICTION

CONTEMPORANEOUS WITH *Ex parte McCardle* one finds numerous inconspicuous reminders that the Court would look straitly, never indulgently, at questions of its own competence. "Nothing could be treated by this Court as merely technical, and for that reason to be disregarded, which was prescribed by Congress as the mode of exercising the Court's appellate jurisdiction," said Justice Miller in 1869, paraphrasing words of Chief Justice Taney—in cases that enforced strictly the limits of time for taking an appeal.[212] To the Court it was an everyday truth that its appellate jurisdiction was bounded by the Acts of Congress. This is not to be deprecated as illiberal. It has been given to the Supreme Court to mark the limits of all other authorities; it is proper that it be ever mindful of the statutes that limit its own.

Ordinarily it has been helpful, not invidious, for Congress to reduce the Court's jurisdiction, with application even to pending cases. The purpose may simply have been to enable the Court to keep its head above water.[213] Thus a statute of 1879 raised from $1,000 to

---

[211] Infra, pp. 584–85.

[212] Edmonson v. Bloomshire, 7 Wall. 306; United States v. Curry, 6 How. 106 (1848). The Court, said Taney, "does not feel itself authorized to treat the directions of an act of Congress as it might treat a technical difficulty growing out of ancient rules of the common law."
Other examples are Millingar v. Hartupee, 6 Wall. 258 (1868), where Jeremiah S. Black unavailingly urged the Court to give a wide reading to Sec. 25 of the Judiciary Act, authorizing a limited review of State court decisions; Austin v. The Aldermen, 7 Wall. 694 (1869), declining to pass upon a State statute at the suit of one not injured; *The Alicia,* 7 Wall. 571 (1869), and *The Lucy,* 8 Wall. 307 (1869), applying rigorously technical reasoning to reject appeals where

Congress in changing the prize law had produced confusion it doubtless had not intended. And "no consent of counsel can give jurisdiction." *The Lucy.*

[213] By an Act to Facilitate the Disposition of Cases in the Supreme Court, in 1875, 18 Stat. 315, findings of fact by the Circuit Court in admiralty cases were made final; review by the Supreme Court was limited to questions of law—the purpose being "to relieve us from the great labor of weighing and considering the mass of conflicting evidence which usually filled the records in this class of cases," said Waite, C.J., in *The Abbotsford,* 98 U.S. 440 (1879). When the point was challenged, it was declared specifically that the Supreme Court's "actual jurisdiction under the [appellate] power is con-

$2,500 the jurisdictional amount for taking appeals from the District of Columbia, thereby giving relief the Justices had for years been seeking.[214] The bar fell upon a litigant that had suffered judgment for $2,250, whose writ of error—after the normal wait of two and a half years—was just on the point of being argued. Had it not been for the statute, he might have had judgment on the merits on the very day he was turned out of court. However, Chief Justice Waite reminded, no one had a vested right to resort to the Supreme Court:

> Such a privilege once granted may be taken away, and if taken away, pending proceedings in the appellate court stop where the rescinding act finds them . . . . [W]e dismiss the suit, because our jurisdiction is gone.[215]

PRESIDENT JOHNSON ON THE *McCARDLE* CASE

THUS FAR *Ex parte McCardle* has been treated in a modulated tone—as the Court chose to treat it.[216] Yet the incident had high constitutional significance. Deliberately, Congress had commanded that the Court desist from the decision of a pending case involving the constitutionality of a statute—and the Court had bowed in acquies-

---

fined within such limits as Congress sees fit to prescribe." *The Francis Wright*, 105 U.S. 381 (1882), per Waite, C.J.

[214] 20 Stat. 320.

A bill drawn by Justice Miller, H.R. 891, 42nd Cong., 2d Sess., would have reduced drastically the intake of appeals; in particular, the minimum for cases brought up from the Supreme Court of the District of Columbia would have been raised from $1,000 to $5,000. The bill, approved by all the Justices, passed the House on January 31, 1872, but died in the Senate Judiciary Committee. A special friend of the District of Columbia recalled that its people "have immemorially had the right to appeal to the Supreme Court"; to which Ben Butler, sponsor of the bill, retorted that the Supreme Court was "almost as convenient to them as a county court to the people of a State." Cong. Globe, 42–2, 713, 732.

At this time Representative Michael C. Kerr of Indiana, leading Democrat, sought, unsuccessfully, to restore

the appeal in habeas corpus as established in 1867 and taken away in 1868. Ibid., 733. (It was restored by an Act of March 3, 1885, supra, n. 167.)

[215] Railroad Co. v. Grant, 98 U.S. 398 (1879). This case, No. 196 at October term 1878, had been docketed on October 7, 1876. The statute was enacted on February 25, 1879. The motion to dismiss was argued on April 1 and 2; the decision to dismiss was made on April 14. To illustrate the so-near-and-yet-so-far aspect of the case: Nos. 197 and 198, docketed on the same day as No. 196, were reached for argument on April 2, and were decided on their merits on April 14. Calhoun County v. Galbraith, 99 U.S. 214, and Railroad Co. v. Varnell, 98 U.S. 479.

[216] In *Ex parte* Yerger, looking back at *McCardle*, the Chief Justice said simply that "legislation of this character is unusual and hardly to be justified except upon some imperious public exigency." 8 Wall. 85, 104 (1869).

cence. It was a breach of constitutional order: normally one branch of government ought not to prevent another from exercising its proper functions.

How stridently this might be decried may be seen in a passage in President Johnson's valedictory, "To the People of the United States," of March 4, 1869.[217] After much in the familiar vein of self-exaltation (using "I" more than a score of times), he said that the usurpations of the majority in Congress had not been limited to inroads upon the Executive.

> By unconstitutional and oppressive enactments, the people of ten States of the Union have been reduced to a condition more intolerable than that from which the patriots of the Revolution rebelled. Millions of American citizens can now say of their oppressors, with more truth than our fathers did of British tyrants, . . . [listing grievances named in the Declaration of Independence].[218]

> This catalogue of crimes, long as it is, is not yet complete. The Constitution vests the judicial power of the United States "in one Supreme Court," whose jurisdiction "shall extend to all cases arising under this Constitution" and "the laws of the United States." Encouraged by this promise of a refuge from tyranny, a citizen of the United States, by the order of a military commander, given under the sanction of a cruel and deliberate edict of Congress, had been denied the constitutional rights of liberty of conscience, freedom of the press and of speech, personal freedom from military arrest, of being held to answer for crime only upon presentment and indictment, of trial by jury, of the writ of habeas corpus, and the protection of civil and constitutional government—a citizen, thus deeply wronged, appeals to the Supreme Court for the protection guaranteed to him by the organic law of the land. At once a fierce and excited majority, by the ruthless hand of legislative power, stripped the ermine from the judges, transferred the sword of justice to the general, and remanded the oppressed citizen to a degradation and bondage worse than death.

His veto, he wrote, had been rendered nugatory by the partisan majority in each House; the Constitution should be amended to provide that a bill, vetoed on constitutional grounds, would "be immediately certified to the Supreme Court of the United States for its decision," the bill to become law or fail according to that ruling.[219]

---

[217] Ann. Cyc. 1869, 589–92.
[218] Including a charge that Congress had "protected [soldiers] by a mock trial from punishment for any murders which they should commit on the inhabitants of these States."
[219] Supra, p. 382.

497

THE SITUATION REVIEWED

GIVEN THE CONDITIONS IN THE SOUTH as they were—the President as he was—and the Supreme Court as it appeared to be—before one pronounces a conclusion on the outcome in *Ex parte McCardle* one should consider attentively the situation presented to the Second Session of the 39th Congress, in the early months of 1867. The South had solidly rejected the proposed Fourteenth Amendment, after making clear that even qualified Negro suffrage, and any federal concern for civil status, were intolerable. The President's annual message expressed his firm stand that the Thirteenth Amendment was the final provision on the freedman; also that the Southern delegations ought to be seated without further delay, thereby making restoration complete. The line thus drawn by the President and the ex-rebel States would restore "the Union as it was," except that "slavery" was forbidden—and as a consequence those States would have enhanced strength in the House.[220] Each State would remain free to regulate its domestic institutions: that meant that the suffrage would be limited to whites, and that the Negro's civil status would be whatever the ruling class provided, short of "slavery." The war would have produced no enlargement of constitutional rights throughout the Union: the ex-rebel States would not allow it, and for a long, indefinite future they could block ratification by the requisite three-fourths. In Northern memory there still rankled the case of Samuel Hoar: retained by the Commonwealth of Massachusetts in 1844 to go to South Carolina to claim the protection of the law on behalf of colored seamen, citizens of Massachusetts, who were systematically held in jail while their vessel was in port, Hoar had been driven away by the menace of mob violence.[221] (Ebenezer Rockwood Hoar, Attorney General 1869–70,[222] was this man's son.) Thus in the past the Slave States had sealed themselves against expressions of moral indignation—and now they would not allow the Constitution to be amended to ameliorate the old situation.

Those who supposedly had lost the war, and their Northern

---

[220] Supposing a reapportionment on the basis of the Census of 1860, the seceding States (other than Arkansas and Florida) would each gain a seat, while the Northern States would correspondingly lose nine seats—a net gain for the Slave States of 18 in a House of 241 members. The computation was presented by Conkling during debate on the Fourteenth Amendment. Cong. Globe, 39–1, 357–58. Jan. 22, 1866. Actual reapportionment would wait until, after the taking of the Census of 1870, Congress enacted what would thereafter be the total number of seats in the House, and distributed them among the States.

[221] See article in D.A.B.; John Quincy Adams, *Memoirs*, XII, 119.

[222] Infra, p. 1123.

allies, found this to be in accord with true constitutional principles—and a very agreeable prospect as well.

Standing firmly on that line, at the opening of 1867, the President and ten Southern States confronted the Congress. On its side, Congress held one strong point: its Houses could not be *compelled* to seat any delegation. Should it not simply have declared what the Southern States must do, and bided its time for compliance—thereby avoiding any action that could have been adjudged unconstitutional? Time was not on the side of Congress: rather than yield on the Negro—for that was the core of the matter—the Southern States would have waited indefinitely, if need be, for something to turn up, notably Democratic victories in the North. It was utterly impracticable for the majority in Congress and their constituents to admit such impotence.[223]

If the war was to bring "a new birth of freedom," Congress must now preside over Reconstruction. It was idle any more to say that Johnson was carrying out Lincoln's method, or to thrash the question whether Lincoln had had better reason than Wade and Davis in 1864.[224] Lincoln was always moving forward, as rapidly as was practicable; under Johnson, the war would have resulted in transferring the black man from one fixed status to another, and in leaving the forces of reaction in an entrenched position. When one takes account of the moral fervor the struggle had unpent, the increased devotion men now felt toward the Nation they had preserved, and the material energies that had been released in the North, one sees that it really was unthinkable that these new impulses should now be denied, and that the country should settle down to accept what President Johnson called the "free institutions" of the past. It was imperative that Congress now speak for the Nation.

Congress spoke in the Reconstruction Act of March 2, 1867—after protracted and searching deliberations.[225] It resolved to break the all-white political communities by calling the new citizens to parti-

---

[223] *The Nation* had put this forcefully in an editorial of February 7, 1867, "Immediate Reconstruction a Duty." The South could not revive economically, it said, while its political situation remained unsettled. "How can [capitalists] safely lend money to governments which may at any day be overthrown?" Politically, "the perils of delay seem intolerable. The whole question is put at issue every alternate year. A single defeat would be irremediable; for if the Southern States are once recognized, the act can never be undone. And every year would add to the strength of the existing governments at the South; since toleration would amount to a half recognition, and vast pecuniary interests would become involved with them. Add to these considerations the possibility that at any moment the validity of these governments, as the only ones in existence may be asserted by the Supreme Court, and the danger that delay will result in a triumph for the South does not seem small." It concluded, "Now let [Congress] act, and act without delay." 4:110.

[224] Supra, pp. 97–99.

[225] Supra, pp. 333–43.

cipate with the old in laying a new constitutional foundation. Whether one regarded universal suffrage with enthusiasm (as did Chief Justice Chase[226])—or with misgiving (as did Justice Miller[227])—or with aversion (as did Justice Davis)[228]—this at any rate was true: that the existing regimes had clearly shown their unwillingness to establish *impartial* suffrage.[229] In that obdurate situation, reorganization by citizens "of whatever race" seemed unavoidable.

As to the method by which this transformation would be effected: it might have been entrusted to the governments then in office—*or* Congress might command that provisional governments composed of loyal men be organized. The former seemed fatuous.[230] The latter was impracticable, save as it might be tried experimentally in Louisiana and, conceivably, in one or two other States.[231] Refraining from either of these solutions, and taking account of the Constitution's provisions on appointment to office,[232] Congress turned to the Army as the best agency available for a faithful execution of the Congressional program.

The provisions charging District commanders with specific duties, in registering voters and conducting elections, came in the Supplementary Act of March 23—based on a draft bill prepared by the Chief Justice.[233] When in the spring of 1868 he made profession of his preference for "civil supremacy, authorized and regulated by Congress,"[234] was he impeaching his own handiwork?

The clause in Section 3 of the Act of March 2 authorizing trial by military commission arose out of an independent concern among members of Congress to protect loyal men—white Unionists, freedmen, soldiers of the garrison—in ex-rebel communities where they were the objects of hatred and where peace officers, judges, and juries would not protect them.[235] This, the most vulnerable feature of the Reconstruction Act, was something apart from the main purpose of reconstituting Southern political communities. This item will be considered later, after Attorney General Hoar's views in Weaver's case[236] and *Ex parte Yerger*[237] have been examined. It put the Reconstruction Act at a grave disadvantage, because it permitted "white man's government" to hold its ground by a vigorous denunciation of "drum-head courts."

Then let this clause of Section 3 be put aside for the moment. For reasons that had nothing to do with military trials, Congress saw fit to use general officers as its agents, in preference to either the ex-rebel regimes then in being or provisional governments to be raised up from

---

226 Supra, pp. 102, 105, 494.
227 Supra, p. 282.
228 Supra, pp. 481–82.
229 Supra, pp. 129, 277.
230 Supra, p. 258.
231 Supra, pp. 338–39.

232 Supra, p. 258.
233 Supra, p. 324.
234 Supra, p. 446.
235 Supra, pp. 150, 287.
236 Infra, pp. 561–63.
237 Infra, pp. 564, 575.

Southern Unionists, white and black. The nub of Southern grievance about "satraps" was exposed in these words in a letter by Robert Tyler, editor of the *Montgomery Advertiser*, to President Johnson: "they appear to have the idea that it would reflect upon their character as *soldiers* not to *execute* the Reconstruction Acts . . . ."[238] The "despotism" commonly decried proves generally to have been nothing more than what was inherent in executing faithfully, in the teeth of local defiance, the policy Congress had laid down.

EXAMINATION OF ONE CASE OF SUPPOSED "DESPOTISM"

IT SEEMS ENLIGHTENING to set out the facts in one of the best remembered of the instances: the encounter between Judge Alfred P. Aldrich of South Carolina[239] and General Edward R. S. Canby, commanding the Second District. The latter, as was his duty, published an order, G.O. No. 89 of September 13, 1867, to this effect:

> All citizens assessed for taxes, and who shall have paid taxes for the current year, and who are qualified, and have been, or may be, duly registered as voters, are hereby declared qualified to serve as jurors.

This meant that color, in itself, would be no bar. The Civil Rights Act of 1866,[240] applicable to all of the country, required this by its assur-

---

[238] Letter of Nov. 29, 1867. Johnson Papers, L.C. The import of the letter was summarized in a secretary's endorsement;

Deplores the unsettled and wretched state of political affairs in said State and denounces Genls Pope and Swayne as mere partizans of the Radical party and crazy upon the subject of Nigger suffrage and equality.

General Pope, commanding the Third Military District, and General Swayne, in charge of the Freedmen's Bureau in Alabama, were removed by direction of the President on December 28, 1867.

The former was not well suited to the work, but the latter is not to be disparaged.

Wager Swayne (1834–1902) was a son of Justice Swayne; after graduating from Yale College and Cincinnati Law School he practiced with his father. He entered the army as major of an Ohio regiment, participated in much heavy fighting, lost a leg, and rose to Major General of Volunteers. In 1893 he received the Medal of Honor for his action at Corinth.

Swayne administered the Reconstruction Acts with the intention to make them effective. He managed to maintain a good understanding with the elected Governor, R. M. Patton, and what one reads of him in the source material is highly creditable. For example, his testimony before the Joint Committee on Reconstruction, Testimony, Part III, 138–41. He was a correspondent of Chief Justice Chase. Supra, p. 311.

He retired in 1870, and his career thereafter confirms the view that he was a man of character and ability. After 1881 he had an important practice in New York City, in partnership with John F. Dillon, formerly Circuit Judge for the Eighth Circuit. See D.A.B.

[239] See infra, pp. 502–04.

[240] 14 Stat. 27.

ance to all citizens of "the full benefit of all laws and proceedings for the security of person and property as is enjoyed by white citizens." G.O. No. 89 was in accord with Chief Justice Chase's recent order for selecting federal jurors within his circuit, which included South Carolina. General Grant, in communications of August 14 and 15, 1867, had reminded District commanders of their duty to secure justice to all classes in jury selection.[241]

When Judge Aldrich opened the Court of Common Pleas and General Sessions at Edgefield, in the western part of the State, on October 7, he read G.O. No. 89, and announced that he would "carry into due and faithful execution the Act of the General Assembly, commonly called the Jury Law, passed A.D. 1831 . . . ."

> Believing, as I do, that the present Congress is an usurping body, and that its attacks upon the co-ordinate departments of government, and the United States and State Constitutions, are fast reducing the country to a position of party vassalage, I cannot retain my self-respect, conscientiously perform the obligations of my oaths of office, and lend my aid to support and perpetuate the tyranny of which we complain.

After more in this vein, he announced: "I cannot and will not execute this order."

The *Edgefield Advertiser* of October 9, 1867, published a full report under the caption "A Fearless Venerator and Upholder of the Constitution"; the Judge had set "a sterling example to his brethren throughout the State."

When the Judge confirmed that he had been accurately reported, General Canby suspended him from office[242]—which was precisely in accord with the Supplementary Act of July 19, 1867—and called upon the Governor "to provide by an assignment of the Judges . . . for the holding of the terms" of the court.

Then followed another theatrical performance. Judge Aldrich read in open court the order of suspension; promised "if God spares my life" to return with "ermine . . . unstained"; and directed, "Mr. Sheriff, let the court stand adjourned while the voice of justice is stifled." "You can imagine the scene. I cannot describe it," wrote a reporter who was carried away by the spirit of the moment.[243]

General Canby, reporting to the Chief of Staff his suspension of the Judge, commented that "his devotion is not to the Constitution of

---

[241] Army communications herein mentioned are preserved in the National Archives, Record Group No. 108.

[242] S.O. No. 183, Oct. 19, 1867.
[243] *Charleston Mercury*, Oct. 23, 1867.

the United States, but to the constitutions that perished with the Rebellion . . . ."

This was not, as has commonly been represented, a situation where civil authority was overborne by what Judge Aldrich chose to call "the tyranny and insolence of military despotism."[244] The issue was whether a judge in this ex-rebel State would be permitted to put a stop to the execution of the legislation of Congress—the Civil Rights Act and the Reconstruction Acts.

General Canby had deferred the issue of the order on juries to permit a careful consideration of the effect it would have in seaboard counties, where freedmen were in large preponderance; the matter was "very fully discussed" with Governor Orr.

After Orr had complained to the President, Canby explained to General Grant that "there could be under the order no injurious enlargement of jury lists": in practice, few Negroes could qualify.[245]

That the Civil Rights Act of 1866, reenacted by the Enforcement Act of 1870, [246] which became Sec. 1977 Rev. Stats., did forbid exclusion from jury service on ground of color was affirmed by the Supreme Court in 1880.[247]

Nota bene: repeated search of the South Carolina statutes enacted in 1831 discloses *no jury law*. A century earlier, in 1731, the legislature passed "An Act confirming and establishing the ancient and approved method of drawing juries by ballot, in this Province . . . ."[248]

It is significant that, amid all the worshipful accounts of the incident in 1867, apparently no thought was given to identifying the "Jury Law of 1831" so passionately vindicated.

Judge Aldrich had established a record in the constitutional convention of 1865: he was one of three voting against a motion to declare that the ordinance of secession "is hereby repealed," and one of eight voting against a motion to declare that "slavery shall never be re-established."[249] In *The Story of Reconstruction*, Ralph Henry Selph (who, while strongly attached to the Southern cause, based his judgments on a thorough acquaintance with the facts, and used legal materials with discrimination) notes "a contumacious resolution offered by A. P. Aldrich, calling on the people . . . to 'endure patiently the evils of,' and 'to await calmly deliverance from unconstitutional rule,' " which was rejected by all "sensible ex-Confederates."[250]

In the legislature of 1865, Aldrich was elected Speaker of the House, by 79 out of 80 votes.[251]

---

[244] Ibid.
[245] Letter of Oct. 12, 1867.
[246] 16 Stat. 140, 144.
[247] Strauder v. West Virginia, 100 U.S. 303.

[248] 3 *Cooper's Statutes at Large of South Carolina* . . . (1838), 274–87.
[249] Journal, 27 and 64.
[250] P. 87.
[251] House J., Extra Sess. 1865, 5.

General Canby (1817–73), a regular army officer, had a widely varied experience in civil affairs, during and after the war. *Harper's Weekly* said of him, "Among our veteran officers, there is probably none who, for fidelity, integrity and hard service, has more claims upon the gratitude of our people . . . . No officer in the Army can produce a cleaner record. None is more respected and beloved by the soldiers of his command."[252]

He was sent to troubled spots in Congressional Reconstruction, commanding the Second Military District, September 1867 to July 1868; the Fifth, November 1868 to April 1869; and the First, April 1869 until Virginia was readmitted in 1870. When he was sent to the Second, *The Nation* pointed out that "General Canby in Louisiana had the good opinion of every loyal man, and if he had none of the plaudits, he had the respect of all the disloyal. In all cases he appears simply desirous of doing his duty without the least regard for party considerations."[253]

Orville H. Browning, Secretary of the Interior and acting Attorney General in the Johnson Cabinet, wrote in his diary that "Genl Canby is a sensible and just man, and a very good lawyer . . . ."[254] The unbroken confidence of President Johnson and his Cabinet is significant.[255]

---

[252] 9:225. Apr. 15, 1865.

[253] 5:266. Oct. 3, 1867.

[254] *Diary*, II, 198, May 19, 1868.

[255] Professor Max L. Heyman, Jr., in *Prudent Soldier: A Biography of Major General E. R. S. Canby, 1817–1873* (Glendale, Cal.: A. H. Clark, 1959), examines his administration of the three Districts at 306–47, and finds that he had "the confidence of all except the extremists of both parties . . . ." Canby is mentioned frequently in James E. Sefton, *The United States Army and Reconstruction, 1865–1877* (Baton Rouge: Louisiana State University Press, 1967).

In 1866 Judge Aldrich had on his own initiative ceased to hold his courts, under the following circumstances.

South Carolina's Act to amend the Criminal Law, of December 19, 1865, in its Section IV, Means of Punishment, authorized, inter alia, imprisonment for terms from three months to ten years; also corporal punishment. "But no punishment more degrading than imprisonment shall be imposed on a white person for a crime not infamous." Acts of 1864–1865, 271, 273. This was one among the "Black Laws." Supra, p. 116, and infra, ch. 20, n. 58.

General Sickles, commanding the Department of South Carolina, by G.O. No. 1 of January 17, 1866, gave directions that overrode the recently enacted statutes, in the spirit that "All laws shall be applicable alike to all the inhabitants." By paragraph XVII, corporal punishment as a sentence was forbidden. Edward McPherson, *The Political History of the United States of America during the Period of Reconstruction*, 3d ed. (Washington: James J. Chapman, 1880), 36, 37; Walter L. Fleming, *Documentary History of Reconstruction*, 2 vols. (Cleveland: A. H. Clark Co., 1906, 1907), I, 207, 209.

Judge Aldrich's reaction is reported in a letter from Governor Orr to William H. Trescot, agent for the State at Washington, among the Andrew Johnson Papers, L.C. On March 27, 1866, Orr wrote: Judge Aldrich "declines to hold the remain-

X: Ex parte McCardle

CONTINUING THE REVIEW OF THE SITUATION IN 1867–68

IT HAS SEEMED PLAUSIBLE to accept editorial condemnations of Congress for "the overthrow of civil liberty" and the substitution of "military tyranny"—as, for example, in the *Richmond Enquirer and Examiner* of October 29, 1867. But read further, and one finds the editor's real grievance: that the white people were not "permitted to maintain that supremacy of the Caucasian race which God intended . . . ." He went on to express a sentiment prevalent in ruling Southern circles—admiration for what he called "the intelligence, courtesy and gallantry" of those regular army officers who were imbued with the "conservatism" of West Point. Indeed,

> if the people of Virginia felt assured of a continuance of military rule for a decade, the prosperity of the State would be placed upon an infinitely more secure footing than it is at present. . . . Who would not endure a century of Schofield rather than an hour of Hunnicutt and his negro associates.

---

ing courts on his circuit in consequence of the interference of the Military Authorities in Charleston in prohibiting the execution of his sentence of Whipping . . . . I am very sorry that Judge Aldrich has taken this course . . . ." At any rate, Orr wrote, there was no penitentiary or jail "so constructed as that a prisoner can be put to labor therein." Trescot was to explain the situation to the President, asking for a modification of Sickles' order.

Governor Orr called an extra session of the legislature, to meet on September 4, to consider legislation so to modify the law concerning persons of color that the courts of the State would be able to exercise jurisdiction in all cases. In his message of September 5 he pointed to the discriminatory features, which he urged should be removed. House J., Extra Sess. 1866, 9–15.

By the Act to declare the Rights of Persons lately known as Slaves and as Free Persons of Color, of September 21, 1866, equality of civil rights was established, substantially in the language of Section 1 of the Civil Rights Act of 1866. Acts of the General Assembly at Extra Session 1866, 393.

By. G.O. No. 15, Dept. of South Carolina, of October 1, 1866, General Sickles recognized this legislation and directed that all cases in which the parties were civilians be turned over to the State courts. Fleming, *Documentary History*, I, 211.

Instances such as these in which Judge Aldrich was involved need to be carefully examined, before one enters a judgment of "despotism." Even so well-intentioned a book as Hodding Carter's *The Angry Scar, The Story of Reconstruction* (Garden City, N.Y.: Doubleday and Co., 1959), states without specification that "The principal offense of the generals was their often wanton usurpation of civil administrations," and includes Sickles and Canby as "among . . . the worst . . . ." Pp. 146–47.

But government by extremists such as Hunnicutt was precisely what was to be expected if Congress had imposed a civil administration by loyalists as provided in the Louisiana Bill.[256]

While General Ord was not the very model of a military governor, undue credence has been given to McCardle's denunciations. It comes therefore as a surprise to read what Barksdale of the *Clarion* had to say in "A Retrospect," two years after Ord's departure. He was lamenting that through "blind faith in the stupid policy of 'non-action,' . . . and a reliance upon the interposition of the Supreme Court," the people of Mississippi had refused promptly to reorganize their government under the Reconstruction Acts.

> At that time [April 1867] the carpet-bag emissaries of mischief had not swarmed into the State. A District Commander [Ord] was in control who exercised his enormous powers sparingly and with a commendable regard for the sensibilities of the people. All the officers elected by them under their own laws, from Governor to the most inferior, were permitted to hold their places. . . .

But the refusal, and the "vain appeal from Congress . . . to Andrew Johnson . . ." had led from bad to worse. At the end of 1869, Mississippi had still not been readmitted to representation.[257]

Acceptance of the new citizens, removal of color as a basis for disqualification, had been the critical issue all along. On that ground, most of the faultfinding about details may be dismissed as unfounded or of only secondary importance.

From the moment Congress laid its hold upon the Southern States, it was inevitable that every effort would be made to induce the Court to break the grip. It seemed likely that unless Congress—and the country—were prepared to see the Reconstruction program invalidated, the Court would have to be defied.

The Nation had seen this from the start. More than any other journal, it was distinguished for penetration, disinterestedness, liberal-mindedness. The constitutional objectives it sought have now been authenticated by a century of history. That consideration entitles its

---

[256] At that moment *The Nation*, 5:354, October 31, 1867, described the Rev. James W. Hunnicutt as "foremost" among white demagogues in Virginia. "Originally, no doubt, a well-meaning man, zealous for liberty and loyalty, he has been perverted by the prospect of power which his great influence among the colored people opened to him, and embittered by the hatred of his white neighbors. His public language has sometimes had an affectation of liberality, but it is manifest that his actions have all been governed by a narrow desire to keep the Republican party of the State under his own control. . . ."

[257] *Jackson Weekly Clarion*, Dec. 16, 1869.

editorials to a certain authority in reaching a judgment on *Ex parte McCardle*. On January 24, 1867, it had looked to the immediate future:

> We *predict* that the North, having fought for and won the right of reorganizing the Union on the sure and lasting foundation of certain great principles, will respect the forms of law and the decisions of the Supreme Court so long as there is a fair prospect of gaining its ends in the regular constitutional way, but that whenever it shall appear that there is no hope of reaping the fruits of the war by regular means, the majority will not be bound by the opinions of the court on great questions of public policy. . . .[258]

The President, it said in September, was taking the view that any conditions other than those he thought proper to impose upon the South were unconstitutional. Congress disagreed, and regarded this as a matter vital to the safety of the nation. Unlike most collisions in the past, this had gone beyond negotiation. In this extremity, should it be admitted that it belonged to the Supreme Court finally to interpret the Constitution in all circumstances? The *Dred Scott* experience said No. If, *The Nation* argued, the majority in Congress became satisfied "that if it obey the judges the ends for which judges exist will be defeated," the majority should refuse obedience. "The Supreme Court is simply, when the destiny of a nation is at stake, nine elderly men."[259]

After Congress reconvened, an editorial on "Congress and the Supreme Court"[260] took note of S. 163 as amended, which would require a two-thirds vote of the full Bench to invalidate a statute.[261] "The proximate cause of this legislation is well known to be the report —we presume well founded—that five judges of the court hold the Reconstruction act to be unconstitutional." The editorial expressed reservations on the principle of this bill—deplored the tone of its supporters—and yet did not flinch from the conclusion that the Court must not be allowed to interfere with Reconstruction:

> Whatever we may think of the wisdom or constitutionality of the proceeding, too many calm and able men, including a large number of lawyers, have voted for it, to allow us to treat the result with anything but consideration and respect. We say this in the teeth of the fact that the debate previous to the vote was anything but calm or judicial in its tone, and, considering the excited state of the public mind, very unlikely to inspire confidence out of doors. The bill is one of the gravest that ever came before Congress, and yet the

---

[258] 4:72.
[259] 5:210. Sept. 12, 1867. Actually only eight men since Justice Wayne's death on July 5, 1867.
[260] 6:44. Jan. 16, 1868.
[261] Supra, p. 463.

principal speech in support of it—Mr. Bingham's[262]—was a violent harangue, very largely made up of coarse abuse of the court. Unless "the citizens of the Republic who keep watch at the gates of the morning, and the citizens of the Republic who keep watch at the going down of the sun," as he grandiloquently calls the people of the United States,[263] have greatly changed within a very few months, we venture to assert that it is not by rhetoric of this sort their approval can be won for changes of such moment as this bill covers.

The editorial hastened to add,

> We admit fully—we have done so more than once already— that any interference of the Supreme Court with the process of reconstruction, as Congress is carrying it on, would be *legislation*, and legislation of the highest order, no matter by what name it was called. . . . It would be in reality the assumption by the court—nay, by five members of the court acting under no responsibility to the country—of power to decide on what terms and conditions peace should be made . . . . Nothing could make an act of this sort anything but a political act. . . .

Accordingly the majority in Congress should not be censured for taking "precautions against the assumption by the court of legislative powers."

The Nation thought that Trumbull had gotten on "the right track" with his S. 363, to declare that Reconstruction was a political matter, where the judiciary must recognize the competence of Congress.[264]

On March 26, 1868—one day before S. 213, repealing jurisdiction in the *McCardle* situation, became law—*The Nation* once more affirmed its support of the method Congress had chosen for restoring the ex-rebel States:

> We are now of the same opinion with regard to the original Reconstruction bill we have been from the beginning. We believe it to be the best and only true one. . . . We are in favor of Congress carrying it out as it stands, in spite of the President and the Supreme Court and everybody else. . . .[265]

The next issue noted that the bill had become law. To avoid a possible collision over Reconstruction, Congress "very properly" had repealed the grant of jurisdiction made in 1867.[266]

---

[262] Supra, pp. 461–63.
[263] Cong. Globe, 40–2, 483. Jan. 13, 1868.

[264] 6:142. Feb. 20, 1868.
[265] 6:244–45.
[266] 6:262. Apr. 2, 1868.

X: Ex parte McCardle

In February and March 1868 it was generally supposed, and on good reason, that if the Court had an opportunity to decide a case involving the Reconstruction Acts it would pronounce the program as a whole to be unconstitutional. That had been the objective in *Georgia v. Grant, Meade et al.*—a case that went astray because of the time required to make service.[267] While *McCardle* exposed a more limited point of military trials, counsel for the appellant had worked for nothing less than a condemnation of the entire program.[268] Chase's postscript to Judge Hill, more than a year later, said that the Court "doubtless" would then have held the military trial illegal:[269] but even if he spoke advisedly and precisely of the attitude of the Justices at that late moment, it was reasonably to be supposed, in February and March 1868, that if the Court had an opportunity to speak it would condemn all. Justice Nelson had gratuitously announced in 1866 that the Southern States were even then entitled to all their constitutional rights.[270] Clifford's adherence to Democratic fundamentalism was beyond question. Grier and Field were understood to be hostile—which presently their protest over delay in *McCardle* confirmed. Davis' dictum in *Milligan* had cast its long shadow over the entire period: after his pronouncement against Congress where Congress had not acted, it was reasonable to expect that he would condemn the Reconstruction legislation in its entirety. Since *Milligan*, Davis and Judge Black had visibly drawn together—an association made easier by the circumstance that Ward Lamon, close friend of the one, was law partner of the other.[271]

That came to a majority ready to disallow the Congressional purpose, quite aside from any calculation about a Chief Justice who seemed always to be making calculations of his own.

It was not to be doubted that a judgment condemning the Reconstruction Acts would be followed promptly by a direction by the President that the army officers desist from their execution.[272]

The truth may be put in this arresting proposition, where latter-

---

[267] Supra, pp. 434–37.

[268] Supra, p. 456.

[269] Supra, p. 494.

[270] *In re* Egan, supra, p. 148.

[271] Seemingly Justice Davis had been pleased at the singular acclaim by Black at the Jackson Day celebration, January 8, 1867. *National Intelligencer*, Jan. 10, 1867; supra, pp. 222–24.

In August 1867, when a reorganization of the Cabinet was rumored and Lamon was suggested for Post-master General, Davis telegraphed an offer of support. Lamon replied on August 12, saying that "Judge Black desires me to . . . ask you to write *him* . . . the strongest letter you can in my favor . . . ." On August 16, Davis wrote Black such a letter. Davis Papers. Ill. State Hist. Soc.

[272] The dictum in *Ex parte* Milligan had been followed by a direction in Dr. Watson's case that jurisdiction under the Freedmen's Bureau Act be withdrawn. Supra, p. 215.

day readers may look at it squarely: one must believe that if Congress had failed to bring the weight of its authority to bear upon the ten States as then organized, there would have been no Fourteenth Amendment.

So long as "the State"—an obscurant phrase at this point—meant simply the white citizens who had been thwarted in their rebellion,[273] "the State" would never choose to ratify the Amendment or anything like it; it claimed the right simply to resume its place in the Union. After the new citizens had been admitted to participation, under Congressional compulsion, "the States" as thus reconstituted ratified with overwhelming approval. White citizens who chose to act on Alexander H. Stephens' view—"The best way to defeat a convention is to have nothing to do with it."[274]—were excluded by nothing but their own refusal to participate.

The unyielding outlines of the situation in 1867 and 1868 have been obscured by the mists of time. Military administration of the Southern States has seemed unconstitutional on its face. Men have found it easy to condemn Congressional defiance of the Court as a partisan excess—and then have gone on to praise the new freedom secured by the Fourteenth Amendment, with never a thought of any inconsistency.[275] But to be honest with the facts, one may not extol the benefit yet repugn the cost.

---

[273] Recall O'Conor's definition, arguing Georgia v. Stanton, supra, pp. 387–88.

[274] Letter of Oct. 22, 1867, to J. Barrett Cohen. Correspondence of Toombs, Stephens, and Cobb, *Ann. Rep. of Am. Hist. Assn. for 1911*, 2:688 (1913).

[275] Take John Norton Pomeroy, the jurist, as an example. *The Nation* for February 20, 1868, carried an unsigned article by him on "The Use of the Supreme Court to the Union." He found it "utterly inexplicable" that leaders in the party of the Union were concerting measures to thwart the Court, "the one department of the General Government which has uniformly been ranged on the side of the sovereign people, one and indivisible . . . ." 6:146–47.

Turn then to Pomeroy's "Introductory Sketch" in *Some Account of the Work of Stephen J. Field as a Legislator, State Judge, and Judge of the Supreme Court of the United States*, a book published in 1881—evidently compiled as a campaign document for 1880 if Field had captured the Democratic nomination for the Presidency. There Pomeroy praised Field's "high view concerning the supremacy of the United States Government," as exhibited in his stand on the Fourteenth Amendment when it first came to be construed in the *Slaughter House Cases*, 16 Wall. 36 (1873). Infra, pp. 1355–60. In that case, rejecting the "narrow interpretation" of Justice Miller for the majority, Field had "asserted in the strongest terms the universality of the amendment, its application to all classes of persons. He denied that its operation was confined to negroes. It afforded the same protection to *all* persons against local oppressive laws; it secured to all persons the equal protection of the laws. In a word, the XIVth Amendment was enacted to supply a great want, which had existed since the foundation of the government." Pomeroy went on in praise of Field's "broad, liberal and national interpretation . . . ." Pp. 54–55.

X: Ex parte McCardle

LATTER-DAY INTEREST IN *EX PARTE McCARDLE*

OVER THE YEARS the Court unhesitatingly cited *McCardle* to the point that the repeal of a court's jurisdictional grant, without a saving clause, cut off its power to decide. There seemed to be no question that, as Justice Frankfurter wrote in 1949, "Congress . . . may withdraw appellate jurisdiction once conferred and it may do so even while a case is sub judice. Ex parte McCardle. . . ."[276] But when in 1962 Justice Harlan repeated that proposition, there was a nervous reaction within the Court. Justice Douglas saw "great mischief"—"There is a serious question whether the McCardle case would command a majority view today."[277] Actually Congress had made no such attempt: the exchange arose out of a wholly different matter. Justice Harlan spoke also for Brennan and Stewart, JJ.; Justice Douglas had the support of Justice Black. The incident gave notice that some Justices were prepared to claim ground that for years had been conceded to Congress.

When Justice Frankfurter cited *McCardle* in 1949, that case was a matter of current public interest. Former Justice Roberts was advocating a constitutional amendment to prevent a repetition of *McCardle*.[278] Indeed he professed the opinion that in that case "The Court might well have said that, jurisdiction having existed when the case was submitted and the case now being in the bosom of the Court, it was too late for Congress to take away its jurisdiction."[279]

Justice Roberts would have amended the Constitution to declare:

> The Supreme Court shall have appellate jurisdiction in all cases arising under the Constitution of the United States, both as to law and fact, with such exceptions and under such regulations as the Court shall make.[280]

---

[276] National Mutual Insurance Co. v. Tidewater Transfer Co., 337 U.S. 582, 655. He wrote for himself and Justice Reed.

[277] Glidden Co. v. Zdanok, 370 U.S. 530, at 567 and 605n.

[278] "Now is the Time: Fortifying the Supreme Court's Independence," *A.B.A.J.*, 35:1 (1949).

[279] The period when a case can be said to rest "in the bosom of the Court" is subject to many casualties. Once docketed, a case may be advanced, or deferred, for a variety of reasons. At the time of *McCardle*, the Court's rules provided for consideration at once if counsel submitted on printed briefs. Sometimes

the Court decided, then rescinded its judgment, heard reargument, and made a new decision. Infra, pp. 662, 1452–53. It seems unsound to suggest that the power of Congress fluctuates according as a case is "in" or "out of" the Court's bosom.

[280] *A.B.A. Rep.*, 74:438–39 (1949); ibid., 75:116 (1950). Justice Roberts' proposal would also have fixed the membership of the Court at nine; retirement would be compulsory at seventy-five; a Justice might hold no other civil office; nor might he be a candidate for President or Vice President until five years after retirement or resignation.

Justice Roberts had known, responsibly, the crisis of 1937:[281] indeed he had made a considerable contribution to its solution.[282] But he had accepted uncritically the traditional impression of the crisis of 1868: that Congress had withdrawn jurisdiction "for political reasons and in a supposed emergency." He did not understand that if Congress had failed to maintain its authority in Reconstruction—if the ten Southern States had been left in the hands of the class that had fought and lost the war—the Fourteenth Amendment would not have been adopted. It was thanks to what Congress then did that, for instance, Justice Roberts and his brethren were able in 1937 to disallow the conviction of one whose agitation for "Equal rights for the Negroes" had by its "dangerous tendency" brought a long term in a State prison.[283] So, too, when the Court relieved a distributor of religious tracts from compliance with a requirement that permission be first obtained from the chief of police[284]—and when it set free colporteurs who had been convicted under a loose statute making it a felony to disseminate any teaching "which reasonably tends to create an attitude of stubborn refusal to salute, honor, or respect the flag . . . ."[285] It was, in Justice Roberts' opinion, one of the "privileges or immunities of citizens of the United States" under the Fourteenth Amendment to speak on matters of national concern, without license from the local authorities.[286] These are now accepted as platitudes of American freedom.

In two decades following Justice Roberts' resignation in 1945, the Court went on to larger connotations of "liberty" and "equal protection." Whereas in *Betts v. Brady*[287] in 1942 it had held that the Fourteenth Amendment imposed no absolute requirement that the State provide counsel to an indigent defendant in a case not capital, in *Gideon v. Wainwright*[288] in 1963 that holding was reversed; the Court

---

[281] When President Roosevelt had by his Message to Congress, on February 5, 1937, proposed that the Court be enlarged, to permit it to "function in accord with modern necessities." Sen. Rep. No. 711, 75th Cong., 1st Sess. 25.

[282] His vote in West Coast Hotel Co. v. Parrish, 300 U.S. 379, decided on March 29, 1937, made it possible to sustain a minimum wage law, overruling Adkins v. Children's Hospital, 261 U.S. 525 (1923). His vote in NLRB v. Jones & Laughlin Steel Corp., 301 U.S. 1, decided on April 12, 1937, made it possible to sustain the National Labor Relations Act's provisions for collective bargaining.

[283] Herndon v. Lowry, 301 U.S. 242, per Roberts, J.

[284] Schneider v. New Jersey, 308 U.S. 147 (1939), per Roberts, J.

[285] Taylor v. Mississippi, 319 U.S. 583 (1943), per Roberts, J. This statute of March 20, 1942, made a felon, inter alia, of one "who gives information as to the . . . military secrets of the nation or this State, by speech, letter, map or picture which would incite any sort of racial distrust, disorder, prejudices or hatreds. . . ." [Sic.]

[286] Hague v. C.I.O., 307 U.S. 496 (1939).

[287] 316 U.S. 455, per Roberts, J.

[288] 372 U.S. 335.

agreed with the submission of twenty-two States as amici curiae that *Betts v. Brady* had been "an anachronism." This was representative of numerous advances in the field of criminal law.

Relaxing its insistence that a plaintiff have "standing" to litigate a constitutional issue, the Court heard and sustained challenges to religious exercises—prayers[289] and Bible reading[290]—in the public schools. It found that there was a "penumbral right" of privacy, "emanating" from the Constitution, which was invaded by a Connecticut statute dating from 1879 that penalized the use of contraceptives.[291] Whereas it had seemed that a complaint of unfairness in legislative apportionment was "not meet for judicial determination,"[292] in *Baker v. Carr*[293] in 1962 that bar fell, and shortly the Court found in the Equal Protection Clause a command of "one person, one vote."[294]

This powerful movement is mentioned here for only one point: that in supplying judicial remedies for injustices and deficiencies not removed by the methods of democratic political action, the Court has gone far in establishing as law what it found implicit in or "peripheral" to the Constitution. This puts in somewhat different light the question whether the Court should be made secure against the possibility of there ever being a repetition of the *McCardle* experience.

What Justice Roberts proposed was, essentially, to declare the Court infallible on constitutional questions. But as the reach of the Constitution is widened through interpretation, the incidence of that proposal would be widened. What effect it might come to have upon the Justices' conception of their function,[295] what the consequences

---

[289] Engle v. Vitale, 370 U.S. 421 (1962).

[290] School District of Abington Township v. Schempp, 374 U.S. 203 (1963).

[291] Griswold v. Connecticut, 381 U.S. 479 (1965).

[292] Colegrove v. Green, 328 U.S. 549 (1946).

[293] 369 U.S. 186. Supra, p. 395.

[294] Gray v. Sanders, 372 U.S. 368 (1963). Supra, p. 396.

[295] Charles P. Curtis commented on Justice Roberts' proposal in characteristically bright language:

I start with the proposition that the power of the Court rests on nothing but its prestige, or, from our point of view, our respect for it, which are the bases of obedience to its decisions. We are equally anxious for the Court to make decisions and to have them obeyed. The best way to obtain both is to have the Court not only wise, but also wary and circumspect. We are only too well aware of the danger the Justices run of going arrogant on us . . . .

. . . [T]he Congress and the President have all the force, if they dare to use it, and the Court has all our, but nothing but our, respect, if it does not abuse it. We want to make mighty certain that it won't. And the best way is for the Court to operate under the constant apprehension that Congress can take away its jurisdiction. Let the Court live dangerously, so that it may act wisely. . . .

Letter to Harrison Tweed, quoted by

might be for American democracy, would need to be considered.

Our constitutional system was, in the language of the *Federalist*, so contrived that "its several parts may, by their mutual relations, be the means of keeping each other in their proper places."[296] Submission to the Court as the true voice of the Constitution presupposes an established confidence in the lofty disinterestedness of its members—something that at the time of *McCardle* the Court did not enjoy and did not deserve.

---

him in *Provisions of the Constitution Concerning the Supreme Court of the United States. The Gaspar G. Bacon Lectures on the Constitution of the*

United States, 1940–1950 (Boston: Boston University Press, 1953), 487, at 530–31.

[296] No. LI.

CHAPTER XI

Chief Justice Chase and the Presidency, 1868

NORMALLY ONE WOULD NOT STOP in the pursuit of a line of cases in the Supreme Court to take note of a Presidential candidacy. But the situation in 1867–68 was not normal. At a moment when partisan differences turned upon constitutional issues, the Chief Justice was angling for a nomination to the Presidency—by the Republican party so long as that seemed possible, and thereafter by the Democrats.

Looking back in 1876, Justice Miller made this characterization of Chase:

> Religious by training and conviction, and outward discipline, endowed by nature with a warm heart and vigorous intellect, but all these warped, perverted, shrivelled by the selfishness generated by ambition. I doubt if for years before his death, his first thought in meeting any man of force, was not invariably how can I utilize him for my presidential aspirations.
>
> But he was a great man and a better man than public life generally leaves one, after forty years of service.[1]

That judicious comment sets the tone for this chapter. And since our concern is to understand the character of the Chief Justice, rather than the intricacies of Republican and Democratic maneuvers, we may let selections from Chase's correspondence tell the story.

Daughter Nettie was in Europe: on the evening of Monday, May 27, 1867, Chase wrote her an account of his pleasurable day. (The Court had adjourned on the sixteenth, and his time was his own.)

> And one person after another has come in; first a Dr. [Samuel] Bard, who was in the rebel army all through the war and is now

---

[1] Charles Fairman, *Mr. Justice Miller, and the Supreme Court, 1862–* 1890 (Cambridge, Mass.: Harvard University Press, 1939), 251–52.

very thoroughly reconstructed and editor of a paper in Georgia [the *Atlanta New Era*, Republican] which advocates reconstruction under the military bill, and he talked and talked very well too and said many things I should wish to report if I had time . . . . And then came Judge [Edwards] Pierrepont of New York . . . and we all talked, and said a great many sensible things . . . . And after [Mr. Bard] went Judge Pierrepont talked about politics & I held off, and he expressed the opinion that at last the question would narrow down to the General [Grant] & the Chief Justice, and I said I thought a good many men would be spoken of, and a good deal more was said to me which would bear repetition if I had time . . . . Judge Pierrepont went away leaving me under the impression that he was a very smart man & not under any very strong impression that he thought likewise of me . . . .

Edwards Pierrepont (1817–92), a War Democrat, had in 1866 joined in the effort to create a National Union party of conservatives from both parties, in support of President Johnson. In 1868, he hoped that the Democrats would choose Chase; when the convention nominated Seymour and Blair, he went to the support of Grant. Whatever Pierrepont's purpose and however interesting his talk, this was a cool appraiser—not one of the devoted admirers to whom Chase was more accustomed.

Other visitors included General Robert K. Scott (1826–1900) of Ohio, Assistant Commissioner of the Freedmen's Bureau for South Carolina; Judge Nathan Sargent (1794–1875), "my old friend the Commissioner of Customs"; and Judge William T. Otto (1816–1905), "a real gentleman & so well cultivated," then Assistant Secretary of the Interior, subsequently Reporter of the Supreme Court. "And . . . then at ten o'clock another came, an old gentleman who wants me to be President & Genl. Howard [of the Freedmen's Bureau] Vice President; and the good old man—he is that—talked & I did not, & at last he went away . . . ."[2]

That the editor of a struggling Southern Republican newspaper (which came to an end in 1871), and the head of a division of the Freedmen's Bureau would come to see the Chief Justice was in accord with Chase's well-known endeavors to bring the new citizens into the political life of the South.[3] He had recently been elected President of the American Freedmen's Union Commission.[4]

---

[2] Chase Papers, L.C.

[3] For example, consider the report he had recently received from Thomas W. Conway, then touring the South as an organizer for the National Council of the Union League.

Supra, ch. 8, n. 13.

[4] Telegram of Hugh L. Bond of Baltimore, Oct. 10, 1866. Chase Papers, L.C. Bond (1828–93) was appointed in 1870 to the newly created office of United States Cir-

XI: *Chief Justice Chase and the Presidency*

William P. Mellen, war-time Treasury Agent at Cincinnati and an intimate friend, was traveling through Illinois in Chase's behalf in June and July 1867. At Jacksonville he visited Richard Yates (1818–1873), formerly Governor, now Senator. He reported to Chase:

> To use his own words, he "entertains higher respect and regard for you than for any other public man in the nation, and considers you to be the fittest man to be its next President." But he does not wish to be considered as absolutely committed at present. . . . He thinks Illinois, Wisconsin, Iowa & Missouri are likely to be united in the Convention for you. He is outspoken in opposition to the fitness of General Grant.
>
> I saw Col. [G.P.] Smith too of the "daily Jacksonville Journal." He is enthusiastically for you and is ready at any time with his paper to say and do whatever will advance your interests. He says you will remember him as the "Abolition Smith" who was driven out of West Virginia years ago. . . .

At Quincy, Mellen's visits included one with General Reuben C. Rutherford (1823–95): he was told that sentiment thereabouts was strong for Speaker Colfax, "much stronger than [for] General Grant";[5] he was cautioned that he seemed too sanguine about Chase's prospects. However, Mellen assured the Chief Justice,

> I have not talked with a republican since I left home, in Railroad cars, Hotels or elsewhere, that has not considered you the best man for the place. But some think General Grant or some other Military man sure to be nominated. Others think somebody else besides you will be selected. But is it possible that when there is such concurrence of individual preference, there is likely to be failure in aggregate expression?[6]

A fortnight later, at Chicago, Mellen wrote of an interview with Leonard Swett (1825–89), faithful friend of Lincoln and Justice Davis:

> He was especially denunciatory of you in 1864. His convictions are not induced by any friendly prepossessions.
>
> He said he had become satisfied that you are the man above all others who ought to be next President. That there is no man in

---

cuit Judge for the Fourth Circuit; he became a major figure in the administration of federal justice in the South. See D.A.B.

[5] In 1865, when Colfax, campaigning in that same territory, had been urging support for Chase as Chief

Justice, he had written to Chase frankly that "I felt certain you would dedicate the remainder of your life to the Bench." Supra, p. 23.

[6] Written at Burlington, Iowa, June 27, 1867. Chase Papers, L.C.

the Country comparable to you in the qualities required at this
time. . . .

Mellen enlarged upon "your magnanimity . . . , your hatred of slavery
and its results, modified by your broad views . . . , your sympathy with
the convictions of the loyal people of the country . . . ."

> He told me that he had a conversation with Judge Davis a few
> days ago and that he expressed himself decidedly in your favor. . . .[7]

Chase returned to his engrossing topic in a letter to Nettie on
July 11. He was at Albany, where he had gone to attend the wedding
of the daughter of ex-Senator Harris.[8]

> My compagnon de voyage was a young Mr. Cummins, of Oregon, to
> whom I had an opportunity of showing a kindness some half dozen
> years ago, and who is now bent on securing for me the support
> of all the Pacific States in the next Presidential nomination.[9] And

---

[7] Letter of July 9, 1867. Chase Papers, Hist. Soc. of Pa. Mellen supposed that the name was Leonard "Sweet," which suggests obtuseness.

Davis had written to his wife, on Sunday, April 7, 1867,

> By invitation yesterday morning I walked an hour with the Chief Justice before breakfast, and then had breakfast with him. He is very polite, but no political subject was broached between us. It is generally understood that he is a candidate for the Presidency, with what success remains to be seen. . . .

Davis Papers. Ill. State Hist. Soc. Davis had been opposed to Chase's appointment; and there had been an actual collision on the bench in February 1866. Now Chase was mending their relations. His writing on June 24, 1867, an overture—"because—well, because I like you . . ."—was not received by Davis until August, and thus did not contribute to the expression quoted by Swett.

[8] Chase Papers, L.C. Harris had done his best to achieve the legislation Chase desired in 1866. Supra, pp. 161–69.

[9] Presumably John Cummins (1838–1916), Indiana-born, who had come

to McMinnville, Oregon, where he taught school, was admitted to the bar, and in 1862 was elected to the legislature in a Radical triumph. In 1866–67 he sat on the Supreme Court of Idaho Territory and published Cummins' Reports. In first instance he held, and then spoke for the Court in affirming, that the Legal Tender Act of 1862 did apply to taxes, and that the statute was constitutional. Haas v. Misner & Lamkin, Cummins 203 (1867), 1 Idaho 170 (1867). (In Lane County v. Oregon, 7 Wall. 71 (1868), Chase, C.J., spoke for the Court in holding that the Act did not apply to State taxes. Infra, p. 704.)

Subsequently, it appears, John Cummins and his brother Henry were Radical lobbyists in Washington, D.C. Chase's reference to "a kindness some half dozen years ago" seems to correspond to a mention in his diary for September 12, 1862, that in the evening "Mr. Cummings" was among his callers. David Donald, ed., *Inside Lincoln's Cabinet: The Civil War Diaries of Salmon P. Chase* (New York, London, Toronto: Longmans, Green and Co., 1954), 137.

I am indebted to the Library of the Oregon Historical Society for identifying "a young Mr. Cummins, of Oregon."

it does look now that, if there were no military names before the public, the choice of the people might fall upon me. But very many seem to think that the nomination of a military candidate is a predestinated event, which must take place anyhow, and against which it is useless to make opposition. There are it is true many who think otherwise and who are zealous for me. But there are other non-military men who have also zealous friends; and I can easily see that I am not much more likely to be preferred than I was in 1860 or 1864. So I make myself contented—or try to. It is true that it does seem to me that I could accomplish, if I had the power, much that would be beneficial to the country and I am not insensible to the distinctions of the Chief Magistracy. But if the people dont want my services, I have no right to complain & if the distinctions are not mine, I shall, by no means repine. No man has any *claim* to such distinctions in a country like ours.

Congress is engaged in amending the reconstruction laws.[10] It is to be hoped, and I think the hope will be realized, that the amendments will be so framed as to ensure the earliest possible reorganization, under Constitutions securing to all equal rights & equal security for rights. . . .

Ohio's rejection of universal suffrage, at the election on October 8, 1867, was widely regarded as putting an end to Chase's prospects for the Presidency.[11] The *Cincinnati Commercial* refuted this in its leading editorial on October 15—virtually a brief on his behalf. He was "one of the most truly conservative men in the country." Chase opposed confiscation and impeachment. He did not insist upon Negro suffrage in the Northern States; in the South it was to be justified because there it was essential to public safety—but amnesty should be coupled with it. Chase's scheme of national banks had been essential to the war effort—but doubtless it should now be revised to meet changed conditions. He did not favor payment of the national debt in greenbacks—but neither did he approve Secretary McCulloch's contraction of the currency. Chase would so invigorate the public credit as to make greenbacks as good as gold.

Chase's candidacy became involved in an emerging controversy about fiat money. The Legal Tender Act of February 25, 1862, in addition to authorizing an issue of $150,000,000 in legal tender notes ("greenbacks"), also authorized the issue of $500,000,000 in bonds, redeemable at the pleasure of the Government after five years, and payable after twenty years ("5–20s"). The legal tender paper was made receivable in payment "of all claims and demands against the United

---

[10] This refers to what became the Supplementary Act of July 19, 1867.

Supra, p. 342.
[11] Supra, pp. 400–01.

States, of every kind whatsoever, except interest upon bonds and notes, which shall be paid in coin": but it was not expressly declared that greenbacks could not be used to pay the principal.[12] In 1867 the earliest issue of 5–20s became redeemable. The "Ohio idea," propounded by George H. Pendleton,[13] was that repayment be effected simply by a further emission of greenbacks—using "the same currency for the bond-holder as for the plough-holder." While this inflationary proposal was viewed as threatening a breach of faith by dominant thought in the East, it had an instant appeal in the debt-burdened West, and was supposed to have contributed to Democratic successes there in the autumn elections of 1867. Chase, as architect of the national banking system, was identified as the exponent of sound finance.

Such is the background of the letter General N. B. Buford wrote at Rock Island, Illinois, on October 12, 1867, asking Chase to put him "in intimate connection with your friends in the North Western States":[14]

I hope to see you, the honest men's candidate. The insidious attempt of the Democratic leaders in the West to gain popularity by appeals to the basest passions of men by violating the public faith can be more successfully thwarted by you than by any other man.[15]

Chase replied on the seventeenth:

Your very kind letter reached me yesterday. Accept my warm thanks for the continued confidence and affection which it manifests. I value such tokens from good & faithful men far beyond any official distinction.

Since our election in Ohio, in which the Republicans lost so

---

[12] Secretary McCulloch, in his annual report dated November 30, 1867, Cong. Globe, 40–2, App., 23, 30, explained that "The public judgment had not then been perverted by an irredeemable currency, and a proposition that indicated a long-continued departure from the specie standard would have found few supporters in Congress or among the people." Little was said in the Congressional debates, he reported, about the payment of principal, "apparently for the reason that no one supposed that they would or could be paid in anything else than in the heretofore recognized constitutional currency of the country. . . ."

[13] (1825–89), of Cincinnati: Democratic Congressman, 1857–65, a leader of the peace wing of his party, candidate for Vice President in 1864.

[14] Buford (1807–83), a man of character and substance, had after the war been Commissioner of Indian Affairs, and was then a special commissioner to inspect the Union Pacific Railroad. He was related to Orville H. Browning, then Secretary of the Interior.

[15] Chase Papers, L.C.

heavily, there is a strong tendency to seek political refuge in the shadow of a great military name. It seems to me that a careful [?] adhesion to principles and organization, & men fairly representing both, would better become Republicans and be more likely to secure the success politicians so much covet. But it may be that my personal interests blind me. I confess it would gratify me if the hopes you express could be realized, and I might have the opportunity of consummating the greatest work to which my life has been dedicated—the establishment of Union on the basis of equal rights for all, secured by just laws sanctioned by universal suffrage and the establishment of national & individual prosperity on the basis of uniform currency & inviolable faith. But I shall be satisfied if the results are attained, whoever may be chosen to lead & direct.[16]

Chase was realistic in saying that poor success in the elections impelled the Republicans to seek refuge in a great military name.[17] In mid-November, *The Nation* forecast that "The Republicans will pretty certainly nominate Grant."[18] The Democrats, it continued, would probably nominate either Pendleton or ex-Governor Horatio Seymour of New York.[19] "Their difficulty is that the former cannot carry the East, and the latter cannot carry the West . . . . We presume that Pendleton is the favorite; but New York and Pennsylvania are too important to be risked, and if they declare with emphasis that they cannot carry a repudiationist, the Democratic Convention cannot refuse to be guided by their advice."

It now appeared that Chase's best hope for the Presidency lay in the possibility that the Democratic party would make a bold new departure—casting behind it the issues of the war, rising above its present divisions, and fastening its choice upon him, an outsider.

TRIAL OF THE IMPEACHMENT OF PRESIDENT JOHNSON

On March 2 and 3, 1868, the House of Representatives agreed upon articles of impeachment of President Johnson. Representatives Bingham, Boutwell, James F. Wilson, Benjamin F. Butler, Thomas Williams, John A. Logan, and Thad Stevens were elected as managers.

---

[16] Chase Papers, L.C.
[17] Recall Miller's comment, p. 403.
[18] 5:395–96. Nov. 14.
[19] (1810–86). Gentlemanly, well to do and conservative, elegant in appearance, long a conciliator within the party; as war-time Governor he was loyal to the Union, but an opponent of emancipation, conscription, and other energetic measures.

Articles I to VIII were based on the attempted removal of Stanton, Secretary of War, in alleged violation of the Tenure of Office Act of March 2, 1867.[20]

Article IX charged that the President had given an order directly to an army officer, contrary to a provision in the Army Appropriation Act of March 2, 1867, requiring that "all orders . . . shall be issued through the General of the Army . . . ."[21]

Article X charged an attempt to bring "disgrace, ridicule, hatred . . ." upon the Congress by "intemperate, inflammatory, and scandalous harangues" in August and September 1866 (the time of the Swing Around the Circle).

Article XI made generalized charges drawn from the foregoing.

On March 5 and 6, the Chief Justice being in the chair, the Senate organized as a court to try the impeachment. Senator Hendricks challenged the competence of Senator Wade to sit, on the ground of interest in the outcome. (Wade was President pro tem. of the Senate. There being then no Vice President, he stood next in succession under a statute of 1792.[22]) After extensive debate, generally adverse to Hendricks' contention, the challenge was withdrawn.[23]

The President's answer was filed on March 23.[24] On March 31 the taking of evidence began. Counsel on behalf of the President were Stanbery, Benjamin R. Curtis, Evarts, Thomas A. R. Nelson of Ten-

---

[20] 14 Stat. 430. Repealed in 1887, 24 Stat. 500. It provided that the designated Cabinet officers "shall hold their offices respectively for and during the term of the President by whom they may have been appointed and for one month thereafter, subject to removal by and with the advice and consent of the Senate." To bring Stanton within this provision, the managers contended that he was still acting by appointment of President Lincoln and for the term for which he had been elected.

In Myers v. United States, 272 U.S. 52 (1926), this restraint upon the action of the President was held to have been unconstitutional.

[21] 14 Stat. 487.

[22] The Constitution, Art. II, Sec. 1, cl. 6 provides:

In Case of the Removal of the President from Office, or his Death, Resignation, or Inability to discharge the Powers and Duties of the said Office, the Same shall devolve on the Vice President, and the Congress may by Law provide for the Case of Removal, Death, Resignation, or Inability, both of the President and Vice President, declaring what Officer shall then act as President, and such Officer shall act accordingly, until the Disability be removed, or a President shall be elected.

The Act of March 1, 1792, placed the President pro tem. of the Senate next in succession, and then the Speaker of the House. James Madison, then a Representative, questioned whether these were "officers" within the meaning of the constitutional provision.

[23] Cong. Globe, 40–2, 1671 (Mar. 5), 1700 (Mar. 6).

[24] Proceedings were reported in a Supplement to the Congressional Globe, 40th Cong., 2d Sess. Answer at 12–18.

nessee, and William S. Groesbeck of Ohio (in place of Black who, having fallen out with the President, had withdrawn from the case[25]).

Chase had given careful study to his duties in this unique trial. His conclusion was that he was not entitled to vote upon all questions; nor on the other hand was his function merely to announce the decisions of the Senate, to which all questions must first be submitted. Rather, in the Chief Justice's view,

> he simply takes the place which the Vice President fills when other civil officers are tried and . . . can only vote in the case of a tie. His duty is limited except in that case to the decisions of questions of order and perhaps of incidental questions of evidence; an important duty to be sure, but not the source of power—since every decision is subject to be overruled by the Senate.

He wrote this on March 25 to John D. Van Buren, New York Democratic leader, in whom Chase reposed complete confidence while in pursuit of the party's nomination. He was explaining that "the extent of the power of the Chief Justice is vastly misconceived" by the public.[26]

His power to make rulings upon questions of evidence—which he had qualified with a "perhaps"—was soon tested. On March 31 Butler was examining his own witness, and Stanbery objected to the line of questioning. Chase said, "The Chief Justice thinks the testimony is competent, and it will be heard unless the Senate think otherwise." Instantly Senator Drake objected: the question should be submitted to the Senate, without any ruling by the Chief Justice. Then Butler claimed that as a manager he was entitled to join in the debate; even though this ruling had been in his favor, he wanted to contest the pretension of the Chief Justice. The Senators debated. Sumner proposed a resolution that the Chief Justice had no right to vote on any question, and could pronounce a decision only as the organ of the Senate, with its assent. This was rejected, by 26 votes to 22. In the end, the power of the Chief Justice to make rulings was sustained, subject to decision of the whole body if a Senator (but not counsel) asked for a vote.[27]

---

[25] *Supra,* ch. 10, n. 169.

Among the Evarts Papers in the Library of Congress is a copy of a statement, "Henry Stanbery in acct with the Fund contributed for Defence of President in Impeachment Case": Received from Secretary Seward, $7500; from Postmaster General Randall, $500; from Secretary Browning, $100; from Edward Cooper of Tennessee, $3000. Expenditures: to each of the five counsel named above, $2125; payment for other services, $475—balancing the account at $11,100.

[26] Chase Papers, L.C.

[27] *Cong. Globe,* 40–2, Supp. 59–63.

"Mr. Sumner's motion yesterday alarmed me," Chase wrote to Gerrit Smith. "Happily I was not compelled to decide" what duty would have required had the resolution been adopted.[28]

In the trial of an impeachment, "no Person shall be convicted without the Concurrence of two thirds of the Members present."[29] There were then 54 Senators; hence 36 votes were necessary for a conviction. None would come from the 9 Democrats, or from the 3 Johnson Republicans. There were 42 regular Republicans, and if as many as 7 voted to acquit, there would be no conviction. The Radical leaders were driving hard to get rid of Johnson. One consequence of the struggle was that Chase, presiding with impartiality, became increasingly estranged from Senators with whom he had formerly been in accord—and that his nomination by the Democrats became increasingly less improbable.

On April 17 and 18, Secretary Welles being in the witness chair, Evarts repeatedly sought to develop what had transpired at Cabinet meetings, in order to establish that the Cabinet advised that the Tenure of Office Bill was unconstitutional, and that the framing of a veto message "was devolved on Mr. Seward and Mr. Stanton"; that "Mr. Stanton and the other Secretaries who had received their appointments from Mr. Lincoln were not within the restrictions upon the President's power of removal"; that "it was considered by the President and Cabinet that a proper regard to the public service made it desirable that upon some proper case a judicial determination of the constitutionality of the law should be obtained"; that when the President removed Stanton and appointed General Thomas *ad interim* the President had stated that Mr. Stanton acquiesced.[30] The Chief Justice thought these inquiries to be proper, but the Senate consistently voted to exclude.

On April 19 Chase wrote again to Gerrit Smith:

> To me the whole business seems wrong, and if I had any option under the Constitution I would not take part in it. . . .
>
>   . . . In case a law, believed by the President to be unconstitutional, is passed, notwithstanding his veto, . . . it seems to me that it is his duty to execute it precisely as if he held it to be constitutional, except in the case where it directly attacks & impairs the Executive power confided to him by the Constitution. In that case it seems to me to be the clear duty of the President to disregard the law, so far at least as may be necessary to bring the question of its constitutionality before the Judicial Tribunals.

---

[28] Letter of April 2. Chase Papers, L.C. Robert B. Warden, *An Account of the Private Life and Public Services of Salmon Portland Chase* (Cincinnati, Ohio: Wilstach, Baldwin and Co., 1874), 683. Chase wrote "yesterday," but the proceedings show that it was on March 31.

[29] Art. I, Sec. 3, cl. 6.

[30] *Proceedings*, 225, 231–32, 233.

How else, he asked, could the President fulfil his oath to preserve, protect, and defend the Constitution? So it was proper for counsel to introduce evidence with a view to showing that in removing Stanton the President acted "not in wanton disregard" of a valid statute but "for the purpose of bringing the question before the Supreme Court."

> I was greatly disappointed & grieved, therefore, when the Senate, yesterday, excluded the evidence of Members of the Cabinet as to their consultations & decisions (in some of which Mr Stanton took a concurring part,) and the advice given by them to the President in pursuance thereof. I could not conceive of evidence more proper to be received . . . .
> The vote, I fear, indicated a purpose which, if carried into effect, will not satisfy the American People, unless they are prepared to admit that Congress is above the Constitution.[31]

On the same day Chase used much the same language in a letter to Alexander Long, lawyer and Democratic politician at Cincinnati, who had recently opened correspondence looking to the nomination of Chase for the Presidency.[32]

The letter to Gerrit Smith closed with this significant suggestion:

> Have you looked at the question, whether in the event of conviction the President pro tempore of the Senate is an "officer" who under the Constitution can *"act* as President"? & whether if such an "officer" he must *remain* such while acting as President? My own mind answers the last question in the affirmative & inclines to a negative answer to the first.
> It seems to me that you ought to give the public the American view of these questions, if you can find time to consider them.

The trial was nearing its close; divisions on significant questions suggested that if the President escaped conviction, it would be only by the closest margin. The Radical program was that by the statute of 1792, the President pro tem. of the Senate—Ben Wade—would succeed and become President,[33] and thereupon would name his own Cabinet. To this program, Chase now posed obstacles. In the context of the Constitution, a very strong argument could be made that the Act of 1792 did not accord with the Constitution's provision that Congress

---

[31] Chase Papers, L.C. Jacob W. Schuckers, *The Life and Public Services of Salmon Portland Chase* (New York: D. Appleton and Co., 1874), 577–78; Warden, *Chase*, 684–85.

Quotation directly from the manuscript.
[32] Chase Papers, L.C. Infra, p. 527.
[33] Supra, p. 522.

should make provision "declaring what Officer shall then act as President . . .";[34] elsewhere members of the Legislative Branch are not "officers." Chase "inclined" to that view; in any event he was clear that there would not be a new President, but rather that the designated officer would retain his old place and merely *act* as President. He invited Smith to drop this bombshell into public discussion.

Gerrit Smith (1797–1874) had during a long life given generous and enthusiastic support to many causes—abolition, peace, woman suffrage, foreign missions, observance of the Sabbath, temperance, the ending of capital punishment, vegetarianism, and reform in dress. Quite recently he had advocated moderation toward the South, and had become Jefferson Davis' bondsman. If this did not qualify him to speak on a point in constitutional interpretation, at any rate it insured that a paper from him would command attention.

The eventuality never arose. On May 16 a vote on Article XI showed 35 Guilty, 19 Not Guilty. The Chief Justice announced an acquittal on that charge.[35] After an adjournment for ten days, the same division was maintained on Articles II and III.[36] Fessenden of Maine, Fowler of Tennessee, Grimes of Iowa, Henderson of Missouri, Ross of Kansas, Trumbull of Illinois, and Van Winkle of West Virginia had followed conscience to join with the Johnson Republicans and the Democrats. The court adjourned without day. The impeachment had collapsed.

Chase, as well as the seven courageous Senators, became the object of public abuse. Among his papers is a long memorandum, dated May 18, 1868, wherein he repelled accusations in an article on "The Chase Conspiracy," published in the *Washington Chronicle* that morning.[37] He took satisfaction, however, from the letter of Professor Emory Washburn of Harvard Law School, to the effect that "our best & most discreet lawyers"

> feel that the dignity of office has been sustained, the purity of justice preserved, and the claim to confidence & respect vindicated by your rulings, your judicial bearing & the independence which you have maintained with so much impartiality. . . .[38]

---

[34] Art. II, Sec. 1, cl. 6.
[35] *Proceedings*, pp. 411–12.
[36] Ibid., pp. 414–15.
[37] Chase Papers, L.C. The article was republished from *The Spirit of the Times,* journal of the irresponsible George Wilkes (see D.A.B.). It alleged that Chase had made rulings on purpose to defeat the prosecution;

had applied undue persuasion to hesitant Senators; and that he was seeking such a Democratic platform as would conform to his own principles.
[38] Letter of Apr. 27. Chase Papers, L.C. Washburn (1800–1877), formerly a State judge and governor, was a great figure in the law. See D.A.B.

On May 26, Stanton notified the President that, in view of the outcome of the trial, "I have relinquished charge of the War Department . . . ." The President nominated General John M. Schofield to be his successor, and the Senate confirmed.

The National Republican Convention at Chicago on May 21 was unanimous in nominating General Grant on the first ballot. Schuyler Colfax was nominated for the Vice Presidency. Grant's terse letter of acceptance closed with "Let us have peace." In pledging "the utmost good faith to all creditors," the platform was resolute. On the other leading issue, it was equivocal:

> The guarantee by Congress of equal suffrage to all loyal men at the South was demanded by every consideration of public safety, of gratitude, and of justice, and must be maintained, while the question of suffrage in all the loyal States properly belongs to the people of these States.

Radical revolutionary fever had reached its high point and had broken. Johnson would remain in office, without power to do serious harm. Between June 22 and July 13, Arkansas, Florida, North Carolina, South Carolina, Louisiana, and Alabama—reconstructed in pursuance of the Congressional program—were readmitted to representation. It seemed a time for pause, to await a new Administration under Grant, which presumably would result from the autumn elections. Unless, that is, the Democratic party underwent some bold renovation, such as would persuade a mass of independent voters that it could more safely be entrusted with power.

CHASE'S PRINCIPLES AND THE DEMOCRATIC PARTY

If SO IMPROBABLE A TRANSFORMATION were to be attempted, Chase was the most probable selection as Presidential nominee. Yet before Chase and the Democracy could embrace, major adjustments must be made. What would each sacrifice to win the other?

Alexander Long of Cincinnati was already in correspondence with Chase, with a view to promoting him as a candidate. This was an incongruous association. Long (1816–86) had been a leader among Copperheads, second only to Vallandigham, whereas Chase's strength had lain in the impatient advance element of the Republican party. After a preliminary response that "I am neither aspirant or candidate myself. I want no more political distinction or position,"[39] Chase got down to terms in a letter of April 19:

---

[39] Chase to Long, Apr. 8, 1868. Warden, *Chase*, 684.

It appears to me quite unlikely that such a union, as is essential to success, can be brought about among those who agree in opposition to military commissions and military ascendancy in the government.

The Democratic party, no doubt, could insure such a union by proclaiming anew its old creed of Equal & Exact Justice for all men and declaring itself for the full restoration of the States, now unrepresented, on the basis of universal suffrage & universal amnesty, but against military government & military commissions, & the whole train of related doctrines such as State Suicide, State subjugation, confiscation and the like. Of such a union, so brought about, I should certainly desire the success. I should wish as earnestly now as I did in 1849 for the success of the Democracy united on such a basis. I could not wish otherwise & be faithful to my antecedents.[40]

With these sentiments I should not be at liberty to refuse the use of my name in the contingency you refer to. I see, however, very slight indications that such a contingency will occur; and I have, certainly, no desire for a nomination. I greatly prefer to remain disconnected from all political responsibilities save that of casting my vote.

I have no doubt however that such a union as you desire would be attended with complete success. Nor is there any reason stronger than prejudice why it should not take place. The restoration of the Southern States on the basis of universal suffrage is now certain. Every one of them will have adopted Constitutions, recognizing the right of every citizen, not disfranchised, to vote before the present Congress ends—most of them certainly & all of them probably before the Presidential election. The United Democracy, frankly conceding the permanence of these Constitutions & the rights of suffrage secured by them, and appealing to the sentiments of justice and generosity & enlightened interest for universal amnesty & the removal of all political disfranchisements, would carry two thirds if not more of these States: whereas, without the union suggested & upon the antiquated issues the Democratic Party can hardly hope to carry one of them, and its success seems impossible.[41]

---

[40] The allusion to 1849 recalled Chase's endeavor, through an alliance of Liberty men with Barnburner Democrats, to attain a balance of power and thereby lead the Democratic party to adopt Free-Soil principles. In Ohio, the result of party disruption was that the legislature remained unorganized for several weeks; one outcome of protracted negotiations was that Chase was chosen Senator by vote of all the Democrats (Alexander Long among them) plus two Independent Free-Soilers. Albert Bushnell Hart, *Salmon Portland Chase* (Boston and New York: Houghton, Mifflin and Co., 1899) explains the situation, at 104–112. Chase's representative in effecting his election was Stanley Matthews, Justice of the Supreme Court from 1881 to 1889.

[41] Chase Papers, L.C. Warden, *Chase*, 686–87. The quotation is made directly from the manuscript.

"I am not a candidate." But "I would not be at liberty to refuse the use of my name." Those two sentences appear over and over in letters to numerous correspondents.

Chase's terms contemplated a platform that accepted as an accomplished fact the reorganization of the Southern States with constitutions framed in pursuance of the Reconstruction Acts. (At that moment, eight such constitutions had been framed, of which four had also been ratified; Mississippi's convention was still in session, while that for Texas was yet to meet.) This transformation the Democrats were to accept, calling in return for universal amnesty and the removal of all disfranchisements. For that party, it would indeed have been a giant step.[42] Colored people would thus be assured that their new-won suffrage would not be the object of attack. (Chase fancied that, in this event, some of them would affiliate with the Democratic party.[43]

Denunciation of "military government & military commissions" struck a note to which Democrats would respond. But that regime would cease the instant a State was readmitted to representation—something that was "now certain" and indeed only a few weeks or months away—*if* no hitch developed. It seems significant that it was between March and June 1868 that Chase sounded this reproach against Congress[44]—rather than a year earlier when the legislation was being

---

[42] A few straws will indicate the direction of Democratic thought. In South Carolina, the Democratic convention that met on April 3, 1868—seeking a rejection of the proposed constitution at the election then at hand—had recognized the colored population "as an integral element of the body politic" and expressed a willingness "to grant them, under proper qualifications as to property and intelligence, the right of suffrage." This concession was attacked by Judge A. P. Aldrich (on whom, see supra, pp. 501–04). In reply the Central Executive Committee gave assurance that "political control of this State, and the country at large, [by the white race] is a right which must never be given up." Ann. Cyc. 1868, 596–99.

In Georgia, where during the summer the old leaders had been out in full force (infra, n. 116), the legislature in September 1868 expelled all colored members. Infra, ch. 12, n. 3.

In the States of the North West: Democratic State conventions in Ohio (Jan. 8, 1868), Indiana (Jan. 8),

Illinois (Apr. 15), and Iowa (Feb. 26) opposed Negro suffrage and denied the power of Congress to interfere. Ann. Cyc. 1868, 603, 377, 349–350, 385.

[43] Letter to James Gordon Bennett, Sr., May 22, 1868. Chase Papers, L.C. Infra, p. 535.

[44] Letter of Mar. 10, 1868, to William B. Thomas, Warden, *Chase*, 680–81; of Mar. 16 to Dr. J. E. Snodgrass, Warden, *Chase*, 681–82; of Apr. 19 to Theodore Tilton, Schuckers, *Chase*, 579; of Apr. 29 to Colonel William Brown, Warden, *Chase*, 690; of May 5 to Richard Gaines, Schuckers, *Chase*, 580–81; of May 29 to Hiram Barney, Schuckers, *Chase*, 583; of May 30 to August Belmont, Schuckers, *Chase*, 584–86; of June 18 to James Lyons, Schuckers, *Chase*, 586–88. Also full and seemingly accurate reports on the views of the Chief Justice, in a letter of April 24 from Washington to the *Cincinnati Commercial* (apparently written by its senior editor, Murat Halstead), reprinted in the *Richmond Dispatch*, Apr. 30, and the *Little*

framed and enacted, and when Chase was in such close contact with Congressional leaders that he supplied them with the draft of a Supplementary Bill.[45] Here was a complaint that he and the Democrats could utter in unison. But truth to tell, Chase's alternative must have been civil administration by Southern Unionists, whereas the Democrats' real grievance was that Congress had not allowed the ex-rebels to remain in power.

The Chief Justice was condemning features of Congressional Reconstruction that were involved in *Ex parte McCardle*, still pending before the Court. If it should be held that the Act of March 27 did not avail to bar a decision on the merits, then a judgment must be pronounced, at least on the jurisdiction of the military commission—if indeed the Court did not go so far as to condemn the entire Congressional scheme.

Prudently, Chase in his letter to Long laid down no proposition on the currency. Pendleton of Ohio stood for greenbacks, and his candidacy was now well organized. The question was, Could he at the convention muster enough delegates to meet the party's two-thirds rule? Only if he failed would there be any chance for Chase. Eastern Democrats needed no assurance that Chase stood for sound finance.

Platforms recently adopted in Ohio and in Indiana—those of the Republicians as well as those of the Democrats—reflected popular sentiment in the West. In Ohio the Democratic convention of January 8, 1868, called for payment of the 5–20 bonds in paper money, and condemned "the monopoly granted to the National Banks." The Republican convention of March 4 also called for redemption of the bonds in legal tender money, and opposed any contraction of the currency.[46] In Indiana, the two parties adopted planks similar, respectively, to those above.[47]

It was after these conventions had acted that Chase on March 10 wrote to William B. Thomas—Collector of the Port of Philadelphia while Chase had been Secretary, and now his active supporter. There was the usual disclaimer: "Whatever I may have formerly thought or even desired in connection with the Presidency, I wish now to have my name completely disconnected from it." He was satisfied that he was "not a suitable candidate for either party." Continuing,

A year ago—even six months ago I did not anticipate the present condition of affairs. But impeachment has come; the constitutionality of trials of civilians in the late rebel States by military commission is

---

Rock Gazette, May 7; and in a further account in the *New York Herald* of June 3, reprinted in the *National Intelligencer* of June 4.

[45] Supra, pp. 324–27.
[46] Ann. Cyc. 1868, 603–4.
[47] Ann. Cyc. 1868, 377–78.

before the Court; new doctrines are promulgated by Republican as well as Democratic conventions of disregard to public faith; and, in respect to these, the question of the constitutionality of the legal tender law assumes new importance. And in regard to all these matters I have a not unimportant voice. I prefer, in this state of things, to dismiss every thought which might incline the scale of judgment. Do what I may I cannot hope to escape imputations. I hope only to avoid giving any just occasion for them. The rest I leave to Him [who] alone judgeth righteously.[48]

"The question of the constitutionality of the legal tender law assumes new importance"—in the light of a popular demand for further issues of paper money. Quite so: the *National Intelligencer* of February 21 had told of *Hepburn v. Griswold*, and mentioned related cases on legal tender, then pending. It explained that

> These cases involve questions of great importance and of vital interest to the commercial world. It is rumored that the court is divided in opinion on these questions. This may or may not be true.
> But it is a subject of anxious inquiry by capitalists and bondholders what position the Chief Justice can take . . .

—considering that when Secretary of the Treasury he had expressed the opinion that the law was constitutional.

Now, the letter to Thomas shows, the Chief Justice was looking forward to speaking his "not unimportant voice."

The immediate problem before Chase, however, was going to be, how far would he sacrifice his principle of universal suffrage in an effort to make himself acceptable to the Democratic party?

"THE CHASE MOVEMENT"

In mid-March the *New York Sun*, recently acquired by Charles A. Dana, proposed that the Democrats nominate Chase for President; with him pitted against Grant the voters could choose between the country's two foremost men.[49] The *Sun* kept up a discussion, with quotations from other editors.[50] Then at Cincinnati, Murat Halstead's

---

[48] Chase Papers, L.C. Warden, *Chase*, 680–81.

[49] Dana (1819–97) had become editor in January. He declared that the *Sun* would be independent—favored Grant for President, and called for prompt restoration of the Southern States.

[50] Chase's obvious efforts to attain the Presidency had been a subject of constant comment throughout the press, with a running debate on his chances of success. When the impeachment trial was at hand, *The Nation* said that this had been "a great scandal"; "he was destroying the

Commercial, and the *Gazette*—journals known to be close to Chase—began to promote the nomination. The *Gazette*'s leading editorial on March 23, on "Chase and the Presidency," said "One thing is certain, and for this statement we have the highest authority, that if the Democrats run Mr. Chase, they must come to him, and stand upon his platform. He will not go to them." To any knowledgeable person that would mean that Whitelaw Reid was quoting his good friend the Chief Justice.

The *New York World*, which spoke with authority for the Democrats, on March 26 called the idea "a fitter topic for derision than for argument." For conducting himself like an upright judge, Chase had been "falling into disfavor with the Republican party"; even so, it would be inconsistent with his judicial office "to pass suddenly from one political party to the other at a time when so much party interest is attached to judicial proceedings in which he must necessarily bear a part. . . . [H]e and the Democrats alike scorn the shallow impertinence of the recent reports and speculations."

The *Chicago Tribune*—voice of Western Radicalism—on March 23 said that the proposal could no longer be ignored. Even supposing that Democratic politicians would swallow Chase in order to gain party spoils, the rank and file could not be dragged to the polls to vote for him. "The *Commercial* might as well preach to the pillar of salt on the city limits of Sodom, as to the Copperhead party of the United States."

James Gordon Bennett's *New York Herald* said on April 13 that "As for the small attempt to get up Chief Justice Chase for the democracy, it was all moonshine and green cheese." Admiral Farragut, it announced, was "the only available man who can neutralize the war popularity of General Grant."

The *Herald* was at that moment reporting the impeachment trial from the point of view of its detestation of Radical measures. As was its wont, it reduced conflict to simple terms and told its readers whom to applaud. The Chief Justice was the hero—"the man who looms up most prominently in his high station as the chief of the judiciary, presiding in the most important trial known in our history." (It seemed to believe that the Senators had merely the role of jurors.) The Chief Justice would "insist upon closing the impeachment trial . . . with a charge from the bench or withdraw from the mockery of a court"; it supposed he might demand an acquittal "on the clear point of law that there is no

---

popular respect for his office, and diminishing the popular confidence in his judicial integrity." 6:222. Mar. 19, 1868.

A few important citations are set out in the text; but their number could be multiplied. A larger selection is given in Professor Charles H. Coleman's *The Election of 1868. The Democratic Effort to Regain Control* (New York: Columbia University Press, 1933).

case to go to the jury." Suddenly the *Herald* discerned "The Golden Opportunity of the Conservatives." "Let them nominate Chase for the Presidency," with some "sterling soldier" for Vice President, "and they will rally the masses of the country . . . and . . . crush out the radicals and the copperheads together."[51]

The *Herald* was persistent in telling its readers that Chase was "the people's candidate." "Having apparently dismissed the Presidency from his thoughts, he is immeasurably nearer to that high office now than he ever was during the years he sought it." The *Herald* explained: until a short time ago, Grant seemed "the broad, grand, national" man —"Chase was the leading radical."

> But what a change a few weeks have made! Grant . . . has said enough to satisfy radicalism that he is a candidate to suit it; . . . he is seen to be . . . the tool, if not the bond slave of the nigger supremacy faction; while Chase stands supremely above all public men of the country; the one whom parties cannot make a tool. . . .
> Impeachment has done all this . . . .[52]

Set up Chase to oppose Grant, and "none can fail to recognize the constitution and the laws arrayed against revolutionary force."[53] For the Democratic party, the alternative was "Chase or Pendleton—Win or Lose is the Question."[54]

Meanwhile the Chief Justice was writing letters and giving interviews. A few examples will suffice.

On April 5 he wrote again to Van Buren, agent for the New York Democratic leaders.[55] He acknowledged receipt of an article from the *World*, asserting that he was not seeking the nomination:[56] it would "do much to disabuse the public." But then Chase went on to explain his position in recent matters—in terms pleasing to the Democrats. In *McCardle*, he had desired that the case be decided, and to that end had proposed that the Court meet in June—but he "met no support."[57] "[H]ad I been present in the District [of North Carolina] when the process of the [Circuit] Court was interfered with by the military, the judicial authority would have been maintained. . . . Certainly no fear of the consequences would have deterred me from the performance of my duty."[58] He went on to affirm, "Most earnestly do

---

[51] May 5, 6.
[52] May 7.
[53] June 4.
[54] June 12.
[55] His letter of Mar. 25 was quoted supra, p. 523.
[56] Supra, p. 532.
[57] Supra, pp. 485–86.

[58] General Sickles, commanding the Second District under the Reconstruction Act, had issued an order to stay execution of judgments for money in causes of action arising during the war. The Circuit Court (Chase, Cir. J., presiding) rendered judgment in disregard of this order; the local com-

I long for the complete restoration of peace and union." "[E]verybody ought to be willing to allow the right [to vote] to everybody else. . . . If this disposition could now be wrought into the Southern mind, peace and prosperity would speedily return . . . ."[59]

Edwards Pierrepont, who on March 27 in 1867 had forecast that the Republican choice would lie between the General and the Chief Justice,[60] wrote just a year later that "if things continue to drift as they are now doing," it seemed likely that the Democratic choice would fall on Chase. "The East is for it. If the Pendleton men West do not prevent, it will almost certainly be done."[61]

August Belmont, New York financier and chairman of the Democratic National Committee, wrote to explore Chase's views. A response at length was made on May 30. "For more than a quarter of a century," Chase said, "I have been, in my political views and sentiments, a Democrat." He traced his claim to that title. Looking to the future, "The slavery question, as you say, is now settled." He had no doubt of the authority of the National Government, under the clause of the Constitution guaranteeing "a Republican Form of Government," to reestablish State Governments in the South, with universal suffrage. But Congress was wrong, in the Reconstruction Acts, "in the establishment of despotic military governments" and "in the exclusion from suffrage of certain classes of citizens." However, "it has been and is impossible to get these reconstruction acts amended," and now it was desirable without delay to restore the States to the Union with their new constitutions. If "the white citizens hitherto prominent in affairs will simply recognize [the colored citizens'] right of suffrage," the leadership of the former would be joyfully accepted. And "if the Democratic party will give such assurance in any way that [the colored citizens] can understand and rely on, a majority if not all the Southern States may be carried for the Democratic candidates at the next election."[62]

This letter became something of a public document.[63]

---

mander interfered with execution. Sickles' support of his subordinate led to his replacement by General Canby. Chase, in a friendly letter to Sickles on September 19, 1867, said "I think it was a mistake that you did not at once . . . direct your subordinate to refrain from all interference with the process of the Courts of the United States. The reconstruction acts, in my judgment, contemplated no such interference . . . ." Chase Papers, L.C. Ann. Cyc. 1867, 547–48; Sefton, *The United States Army and Reconstruction 1865–1877* (Baton Rouge:

Louisiana State University Press; 1967), 158–60.
[59] Letter in the handwriting of his secretary (a wise precaution where the message was of highest importance)—original in Chase Papers, Hist. Soc. of Pa.; letter-press copy, with small modifications, in Chase Papers, L.C.
[60] Supra, p. 516.
[61] Letter of Mar. 27, Chase Papers, L.C.
[62] Schuckers, *Chase*, 584–86.
[63] The Annual Cyclopaedia for 1868, under "United States," reprinted

Chase was most anxious that Democrats accept his thesis that if Southern whites would only assure the colored people that their security as established under the new constitutions would not be assailed, the colored voters would fall into the Democratic ranks. On May 22 he wrote a letter—"*Private*"—to James Gordon Bennett, Sr.: "I cannot any longer forbear saying to you how much I feel myself indebted for the kind things which the Herald has lately said of me." Then he outlined this "wise and noble policy," which he hoped the *Herald* would advocate.[64]

The *Herald* on June 3 reported an interview, "Chief Justice Chase on the Situation." "As parties are now organized he is for the democratic party. He differs from them upon only one point—that of universal manhood suffrage." If he were elected he would carry out the platform faithfully, and would labor to make the party one of permanent usefulness. It quoted Chase to the effect that

> . . . There is no constitutional authority to hold [the Southern States] in subjugation, and if there were it would be alike unwise and unjust. . . . He thinks freedom and manhood suffrage should be an unquestioned right, but he controverts the idea that any other power than the States themselves can confer it. He holds that the general government has no control over the question and that the power rests in the States, where alone it should reside.

He would remove the political disabilities from every man in the nation.[65]

If Chase had really gone so far, he had yielded the essential point. He could go on protesting his devotion to universal suffrage as a policy: but if only the States could confer it, that was all that mattered. However, this was only a correspondent's story. Party leaders would insist upon a much better authenticated commitment.

---

a considerable portion of the letter in its narrative of major public events, with the explanation that it was "shown to several influential Democrats, and there is little doubt that its outspoken expressions in some points lessened the chances of Mr. Chase's nomination." At 750.

[64] Chase Papers, L.C. This too was in his secretary's clear handwriting.

In June 1867—after the *Herald* proposed that the Chief Justice be impeached, supra, p. 355—Chase had written to John Russell Young of the *New York Tribune*: "I seldom read the Herald." He thought it could do him

no real harm, "and its causeless and persistent personal hostility is better unread than read." Chase Papers, L.C. Letter of June 26; Warden, *Chase*, 667, giving date of June 29.

[65] Some disabilities were imposed by new constitutions. Then there were those which would be imposed by Section 3 of the Fourteenth Amendment: these could be removed only by the vote of two-thirds of each House. The Amendment was declared to be in effect by Joint Resolution of July 21, 1868—seven weeks after this interview.

The *Atlanta Constitution* in its leading editorial on June 21, "Principles on the Market," forecast that Chase would write a letter to the Democratic Convention, accepting the party's terms while urging his "opinion" in favor of universal suffrage. It concluded: "The [Republican] Chicago Convention found a man without a policy or a principle. The Democrats cannot risk one who abandons the policy and principles of a life-time for a nomination."

"A FOLDED BANNER"

As CHASE COMPROMISED HIMSELF more deeply with the Democrats, his old admirers cried in shock and disbelief. The most striking public expression came in an editorial in *The Independent* on April 16: "A Folded Banner." Theodore Tilton, the editor, was a dedicated friend of equal rights, and long an advocate of Chase's election to the Presidency as the Republican nominee. Coming from an interview, he had set down his unhappy conclusions: that Chase could no longer be a Republican leader, and that he would accept a Democratic nomination. Even so, "No one who knows the man will expect him ever to change, modify, or compromise his life-long and ineradicable convictions in favor of Liberty, Justice, and Political Equality."

Chase, feeling hurt, wrote Tilton a long, reproachful letter on April 19: he was "surprised by your confident expression of opinion that I would accept the Democratic nomination. I refused to say to you that I would not accept it. But I did not say that I would . . . ."[66]

In June, Chase received a letter from John T. Trowbridge, author of *The Ferry-Boy and The Financier*. The publisher proposed to issue a new edition, and Trowbridge thought "some addition quite necessary at this time, when your very prominent position is in much danger of being grossly misunderstood."[67] In preparation for this book, Trowbridge had in 1863–64 been Secretary Chase's house guest and companion; he had received detailed autobiographical letters. What might have become a campaign biography in 1864 appeared as a book "intended particularly for boys' reading"[68]—with an Appendix

---

[66] Chase Papers, L.C. Warden, *Chase*, 687–89; Schuckers, *Chase*, 579–80. Compare Chase's letter to Alexander Long on the same day, supra, pp. 527–28.

[67] Letter of June 19. Chase Papers, L.C. On Trowbridge (1827–1916), prolific author, and contributor particularly to magazines for children,

see D.A.B. *The Ferry-Boy and The Financier* (1864) had had a large sale.

[68] Characterization by Jacob W. Schuckers, Chase's secretary, in his *Chase*, 11n. Schuckers made use of the letters for his biography, especially for Chase's youth.

(pp. 311–32) devoted to Chase's anti-slavery cases and his financial policies, in fine print which juvenile readers might skip.

If Chase had received the nomination in 1868, the publisher would have seen a profit in running a revised edition. Certainly the passage that began, "Mr. Chase has been called 'the father of the new Republican party . . .' " would have had to be amended.

Correspondence initiated by James Lyons, prominent among Virginia Democrats and at the Richmond bar, drew Chase into a somewhat greater concession. (When holding court at Richmond, the Chief Justice had been a guest at Lyons' table.) On June 16 the latter made a request for clarification:

> As I understand your platform, the principal features of it are, First, Advocacy of universal suffrage by yourself. Secondly, Reference of the suffrage question to the States, as the only competent arbiters of it, Congress having no Constitutional power to define the right of suffrage in the States. Thirdly, A general amnesty. Fourthly, Immediate restoration of all the States to the Union with the abolition of all military government and control. . . .

Upon that platform, Lyons could give a cordial support. For, he explained, while he did not advocate universal suffrage for either whites or blacks, "I would not withhold my support from a statesman of great ability and experience who does advocate it, but concedes to the States the right to decide whether it shall prevail within their limits . . . ." Would Chase confirm, and allow Lyons to publish his reply?[69]

Prompt response was made on June 18. Chase did not desire the nomination; he gave no letters for publication, since they "would be regarded as evidence of such a desire." But Lyons was free to impart what he wrote.

Amid the husks, the kernel of Chase's answer was this:

> Of the reference to the suffrage question to the States, there can be no doubt in general of its wisdom and expediency. I am not prepared, however, to say that Congress, under the thirteenth and fourteenth amendments, should the latter be ratified, as now seems certain, will not have *any powers* in relation to the suffrage in the States . . . .

At this point he threw out a suggestion appealing to Lyons and his conservative friends: Was Virginia to be reckoned as one of the States

---

[69] Chase Papers, L.C. See infra, n. 73.

which, having no valid government at the close of the war, were subject to reorganization without distinction of color? It "may well be questioned."[70]

Writing further on June 20 and 21, Lyons sought to close the gap, now "so slight." Secession was a nullity: therefore the Southern States were entitled to continue with "the same Republican form of Government which they had before." The Democrats could not come to Chase without surrendering "a great Constitutional principle"—whereas Chase could come to them merely by forbearing to insist upon a policy, "in consideration of the great Public good you would accomplish." "If you are not nominated, Grant will probably be elected, and the South Africanized or the negro destroyed." He expanded on the degradation that must result. Surely the successor of Marshall and Taney would "never consent to offer up the sons and daughters of the South."[71]

One further letter from Lyons, of July 24, remains to be mentioned. By that time, despite Chase's surrender of principle to the Democratic leaders, the party convention had ignored him. After that experience, his mood was that he wanted it understood "that my position removed me from active participation in party strife"; he was uncertain how, or whether, he would vote at the election. This he wrote to his secretary, Jacob W. Schuckers, on July 20.[72] At that juncture Lyons resumed the correspondence, reporting that "newspaper scribblers continue to attack you" for failure to promise to support the nominees. Would Chase permit Lyons to publish their correspondence, "with an assurance from me that you will support the ticket on the Platform?" He held out an inducement: "It will be of great service to you four years hence to put a stop now to these false suggestions and insinuations."[73]

---

[70] Schuckers, *Chase*, 586–88.
[71] Chase Papers, L.C.
[72] Schuckers, *Chase*, 590.
[73] Chase Papers, L.C.
The *Richmond Enquirer and Examiner* (of which Lyons had become part owner when it was begun by merger in July 1867) carried a long editorial on "Chief Justice Chase" on August 17. It noted his "unprecedented reticence" in failing to make a "frank disclosure" whether he supported the Democratic ticket. It was not that his help was essential to Democratic victory in November: rather it was Chase who could not afford that history should record that he had abandoned his "faithful friends, who essayed a task so thankless in a cause so doubtful—to secure his nomination in July—and who were "now everywhere accused of the most criminal attempt to betray the Conservative cause . . . ."

It then reprinted "letters addressed to the Chief Justice by a distinguished citizen of Virginia"—Lyons' letters of June 20 and 21 (incorrectly dated June 18 and 19).

This was insolent treatment—and Chase had exposed himself to it.

CHASE COMES TO THE DEMOCRATIC POSITION

CHASE'S FORMAL SUBMISSION was effected by an exchange of letters. Thomas Ewing, Sr., wrote to his son on June 22, expressing what he said he understood to be Chase's position—notwithstanding what the *Cincinnati Commercial* [of June 20] represented it to be.[74] This interpretation was passed to Chase, who recorded his agreement, and the two letters were published on Monday morning, July 6, just as the Democratic Convention was getting down to business.

The *New York Herald*, which for days had been loaded with items favorable to Chase, gave this report:

> Important Letter from Chief Justice Chase—His Views on the Suffrage Question.
> The following letter from a distinguished statesman of Ohio, addressed to a gentleman in this city, was sent to Chief Justice Chase last week:—
>
> June 25 [*sic*], 1868.
> There is a growing disposition among the democracy of the West to accept Chief Justice Chase as their candidate. If cordially

---

[74] Ewing Papers, L.C. General Thomas Ewing, Jr. (1829–96) was then practicing law at Washington.

On June 18 he had written his father:

The Eastern Democrats do not believe Pendleton can be nominated. They talk of [General John A.] Dix [of New York], Hancock, [Governor James E.] English [of Connecticut] & [railroad magnate Asa] Packer (of Pa.) all of whom were strong war men. They believe that when Pendleton is beaten in convention his friends will support one of these four *eastern* men. . . .

It was in the light of that unpromising prospect that Ewing Sr. wrote his letter of June 22, pointing to the availability of Chase.

On June 30 the son replied:

. . . I saw the Chief Justice & told him what you say. He was much pleased & flattered, & says you properly stated his views. He has great hopes of getting the

nomination—but there is really no chance that he will get it. Were he nominated Pendleton or some like man would run as a third Candidate. So if Pendleton were nominated, I believe Chase would run independent. Neither will be nominated. . . .

We will have a great Soldiers Convention. I have had a great deal to do in arranging preliminaries for it. . . .

A conservative Soldiers' and Sailors' Convention met in New York City concurrently with the Democratic National Convention. Speaking to veterans, Ewing told how, "to maintain its grasp on the country," the Republican party had "enfranchised every negro. . . . The constitutional amendment . . . was one of the means by which it sought to accomplish this object . . . ." Under "the radical military reconstruction," one saw "the pampered negro fed in idleness, the white population reduced to poverty." *New York Herald*, Sun., July 5.

received by the party his election will be certain, and it is the safest and best we can do. I see the *Commercial* doubts his consenting to leave the question of suffrage, without distinction of race, to the States and considers it a departure from his long avowed principles. This I do not perceive. Chase is in favor of two things—the constitution of the United States and the rights of the States under it and suffrage without distinction of race; and I think he has never said he would violate the first in order to secure the last, and it is not an inconsistency or a departure from principle to refuse the attainment of an end, however desirable, by an assumption of ungranted powers.

In returning the foregoing letter to the gentleman to whom it was addressed the Chief Justice very clearly and tersely defines his position on the question of suffrage in relation to national politics, as follows:—

July 1, 1868.

Please say to your friend that he is entirely right as to my views of suffrage and States rights. What I desire for the Southern States is peace and prosperity, with all disfranchisements and disabilities removed and all rights restored to all citizens. But the practical disposition of the question of suffrage, as well as all other domestic questions, is for the people of the States themselves, not for outsiders. On this question I adhere to my old States rights doctrines. In the event of nomination and success I trust I should so act that neither the great party which makes the nomination, nor the great body of patriotic citizens whose co-operation would insure success, would have any cause to regret their action. It is an intense desire with me to see the democratic party meeting the questions of the day in the spirit of the day, and assuring to itself a long duration of ascendancy. It can do so if it will.

Yours truly,

S. P. Chase.[75]

Preparing its readers for this announcement, the *Herald* on July 2 had carried as its leading editorial, "Universal Nigger Suffrage—The Great Issue of the Campaign": "if Mr. Chase becomes the candidate

---

[75] Aside from the error in date, the printed letter contained insignificant variations from the original.

On July 31 the son wrote to the father:

Enclosed is a letter from Chief Justice Chase—an extract from which, & one from your letter to me which I sent him & which was the occasion of his letter, were published in the N.Y. papers on Monday July 7th [the sixth]. I sent you the publication marked. It attracted general attention, & pleased the Chase men greatly. No name was given, but you were guessed to be the author of the letter. . . .
Ewing Papers, L.C.

... he will recognize it as the issue and sustain the constitution and the legitimate right of the States as the true law. We can announce from the best authority that he will do this. ..."

The Constitution left suffrage to the States, and the Chief Justice would not violate the Constitution even for a desirable end. Ewing's letter made it sound simple. But Chase's opinion—tenaciously held and widely professed—had been that in reconstituting the rebel States, "loyal citizens without regard to complexion" should be called to frame "constitutions securing suffrage to all citizens of proper age and unconvicted of crime." In the last days of Lincoln's life, the Chief Justice had pressed him to command this by an assertion of Executive power— without any action by Congress and before there was a Thirteenth Amendment abolishing slavery.[76] That position he had maintained.

As recently as August 1867, in an exalted moment, he had given this sweeping import to the Thirteenth Amendment:

> Can any thing be clearer than that the National Legislature charged with the duty of "enforcing by appropriate legislation" the condition of universal freedom, is authorized and bound to provide for universal suffrage? Is not *suffrage* the best security against *slavery* and *involuntary servitude?* Is not the legislation which provides the *best* security the most *appropriate?*[77]

It had been Chase's peculiar distinction that he seemed always to take his stand on the highest moral ground—from which, his admirers were convinced, he could never be moved. He himself had asserted this in a notable passage in a letter of May 29, 1868, to Hiram Barney:

> My convictions are fairly represented by my record, and I cannot change them. I believe I could refuse the throne of the world if it were offered me at the price of abandoning the cause of equal rights and equal justice to all men. Indeed, "what should it profit a man to gain the whole world and lose his own soul?"[78]

---

[76] Letters of Apr. 11 and 12, 1865. Schuckers, *Chase*, 514–18. Supra, p. 102.

[77] Letter of Aug. 8, 1867, to George William Curtis, editor of *Harper's Weekly*, who had sent him a copy of a speech in favor of universal suffrage. Chase Papers, L.C.

[78] Schuckers, *Chase*, 583.

Barney, Collector of the Port of New York during Chase's tenure of the Treasury, was an ardent political aid; he loaned Chase money and helped manage his interests. When corruption was found within the customhouse, and Lincoln wanted to place Barney elsewhere, Chase stood firm against it. This was one of the difficulties over Chase's subordinates in New York that culminated in Chase's resignation being tendered and accepted. *Collected Works of Abraham Lincoln*, ed., Roy P. Basler (New Brunswick, N.J.: Rutgers University Press, 1953), VII, 120, 181, 268–69, 412–14, 419. See Thomas G. and Marva R. Belden, *So Fell the Angels* (Boston: Little, Brown and Co., 1956), using index.

THE CONVENTION

FOREMOST AMONG THE CANDIDATES was Pendleton of Ohio. The great question was, Could he poll as many as 212—two-thirds of the 317 delegates? Lesser candidacies depended on the outcome. The *Herald* of July 4 reported that

> The Ohio delegation presents a threatening front to all the scouts and friends of Chase, and maintains an eternal clamor in favor of the apostle of plentiful greenbacks. However weak they may secretly feel their cause to be they contrive to conceal their forebodings in violent denunciations of Grant and in abuse of Chase and Hancock. Many of the members have resolved to bolt from the party should an attempt be made to force the nomination of Chase . . . .

First on the Ohio list was General George W. McCook (1821–77): when the nomination of Pendleton had to be abandoned, it was he who announced Ohio's vote for Seymour, thereby forestalling any boom for Chase. Notable among other straight party men were Allen G. Thurman (1813–95), recently defeated for Governor and then elected United States Senator; ex-Senator George E. Pugh (1822–76), formerly Pendleton's law partner; and Judge Philadelph Van Trump (1810–74), then a Representative in Congress. Their adherence to Pendleton was unqualified.

President Johnson hoped to receive the nomination. In a statement of July 2 he declared that he remained, as he had ever been, "in the hands of the people, and at their disposal." His struggle for "constitutional liberty and human rights" must be continued.[79] On July 4 he extended amnesty for acts of treason and adherence to the enemy in the late war, except as to persons under indictment. Johnson's effort, by the Philadelphia Convention of August 1866,[80] to form a National Union party had been unsuccessful. He had refused to turn over the patronage to the Democratic politicians. If nominated now he would bring with him an accumulation of liabilities. He was put forward by Thomas A. R. Nelson, his counsel at the recent trial. On the first ballot he received 65 votes—second only to Pendleton's 105; thereafter his support faded away.

Thomas A. Hendricks of Indiana had been exercising responsible leadership during his term in the Senate; he had a wide appeal within the party. Although his strength mounted steadily to 132 votes, the opposition of the Pendleton forces proved insuperable.

---

[79] Ann. Cyc. 1868, 746.   [80] Supra, pp. 177–79.

General Winfield Scott Hancock had made a truly distinguished record in the war. In politics, he had endeared himself to the party by his pronouncement of adherence to "the great principles of American liberty" on November 29, 1867, when he assumed command of the Fifth Military District and found that "peace and quiet reign."[81] He advanced somewhat irregularly, and had 135 ½ votes on the twenty-first ballot, just before the convention swarmed to Seymour.

Ex-Governor Seymour had sincerely declared himself not to be a candidate. He was chosen to preside over the convention. Seymour had professed a preference for Chase, and was counted upon to bring the New York delegation to initiate a grand movement for him when other candidacies had lost their momentum. There was supposed to be strong latent support throughout the convention that would manifest itself at this signal. Samuel Tilden and Sanford E. Church were powerful New Yorkers who did not share this sentiment; they would presently join the leaders of the Ohio delegation in stopping Chase by selecting Seymour.

Francis P. Blair, Jr. (1821–75) of Missouri aimed to promise much, offend none, and emerge as the nominee when others had failed. He showed his quality in one deliberate madcap act that provided the Republican party with an invaluable campaign issue. On June 30 he addressed a letter to James O. Broadhead, chairman of the Missouri delegation. The two men had acted together in saving Missouri to the Union in 1861. The letter, published on July 3, noted that the Reconstruction program of Congress would soon be completed; Negro suffrage would be established, and Carpetbaggers would be installed in Congress. There was no hope of undoing this by legislative action: "It can only be overthrown by the authority of the Executive, who is sworn to maintain the Constitution . . . ." Here was the course Blair would pursue:

> There is but one way to restore the Government and the Constitution, and that is for the President elect to declare these [Reconstruction] acts null and void, compel the army to undo its usurpations at the South, disperse the carpetbag State governments, allow the white people to reorganize their own governments and elect Senators and Representatives. . . .

Northern Democrats in the House would admit the Representatives elected by the Southern whites; then this Democratic House and the Democratic President would compel the Senate (notwithstanding its majority of Republicans) to submit once more to the Constitution. This was "the real and only issue in this contest": "we must have a

---

[81] Supra, ch. 7, n. 160.

President who will execute the will of the people by trampling into the dust the usurpations of Congress . . . ."[82]

That was how Blair proposed, if elected, to undo the "palpable violation of [the Constitution's] fundamental principles."

The roster of delegates bore several names memorable in the annals of the Court. These were Garland of Arkansas and Garesche of Missouri, victors in the *Test Oath Cases*. McCardle, alternate from Mississippi, had recently become a household word. In another year, Colonel Yerger would attain a like distinction. As spokesman for the Mississippi delegation he carried a message that the men from the South had not come to impose the nomination of any particular candidate, but to claim the restoration of Southern rights.[83] Vallandigham of Ohio was conspicuous. The credulous secretary of Chase's "Committee of 100" reported that Vallandigham seemed "a sincere friend of yours," and Chase described Vallandigham as "a man of whose friendship one may well be proud."[84] J. D. Giddings of Texas will be mentioned shortly as one who really derived a profit from the great case of *Texas v. White*—after those who had fought to secede were in a position once more to control their indestructible State.[85]

George Washington Woodward's name led all the rest of the Pennsylvania delegation. Nominated to the Supreme Court by President Polk, he had failed of confirmation in 1846 by a vote of 20 for, 29 against. Then Justice Grier was appointed. In the light of events, this substitution may be reckoned a substantial contribution to the Lincoln Administration's conduct of the Civil War.[86] Woodward had visited the Blairs, father and son, on June 28: he was opposed to nominating Seymour, and hoped to see Frank Blair, Jr., on the ticket.[87]

---

[82] Smith, *The Francis Preston Blair Family in Politics*, 2 vols. (New York: The Macmillan Company, 1933) 2:-406–7. Ann. Cyc. 1868, 746–47.

[83] *New York Herald*, July 4; Smith, *The Blair Family*, 2:403.

[84] Frederick A. Aiken to Chase, July 3, in Chase Papers, L.C.; Blaine, *Twenty Years of Congress*, 2:395.

[85] Infra, pp. 668–75.

[86] In the *Prize Cases*, 2 Black 635 (1863), Grier, J., spoke for a bare majority in affirming that "The President was bound to meet [the rebellion] in the shape it presented itself, without waiting for Congress to baptize it with a name"; in particular, it was lawful for him to institute a blockade of rebel ports. Woodward would doubtless have gone with the other Democratic Justices to make a majority *contra*.

As a Judge of the Supreme Court of Pennsylvania, Woodward had been in the minority in Kneedler v. Lane, 45 Pa. St. 238 (1863), where the power of Congress to conscript was sustained. Supra. Again he was in the minority in Shollenberger v. Brinton, 52 Pa. St. 9 (1866), where the power of Congress to issue treasury notes and make them a legal tender was sustained. Supra, p. 141. In each case the decision was by three to two. Judge William Strong, appointed to the Supreme Court in 1870, was in the majority in each case.

Judge Woodward is quoted in the discussion of municipal bonds, infra, pp. 944–45.

[87] Smith, *The Blair Family*, II, 404.

Delegates from South Carolina included General Wade Hampton and ex-Provisional Governor B. F. Perry; also James Chestnut, first Senator to withdraw upon Lincoln's election; and Judge A. P. Aldrich, whose scrupulous fidelity to the Constitution as he understood it—as evidenced by his refusal to follow the Civil Rights Act in his court—had recently produced a memorable encounter with the District commander.[88] General N. B. Forrest of Tennessee; Georgia's dashing hero, J. B. Gordon; and ex-Governor Vance of North Carolina, were understood to hold exalted rank in the newly organized Ku Klux Klan.

Even though there were leading men and substantial numbers who were anxious to nominate Chase,[89] the more prominent and seemingly more representative personages were of a sort that would not willingly tolerate him.

The platform represented a Pendleton victory: it called for payment of all Government obligations in "lawful money" save where it had been otherwise expressly provided; also for "equal taxation" to include "government bonds and other public securities." The Reconstruction Acts were declared to be "unconstitutional, revolutionary, and void"; the Freedmen's Bureau should be abolished. It condemned "military despotism and negro supremacy," the repeal of part of the Court's jurisdiction, and the "atrocious calumnies" heaped upon the Chief Justice.[90]

On the fourth day and the twelfth ballot, when Pendleton's strength had begun to wane, the California delegation announced a ½ vote for Chase. Thereupon, according to the Proceedings, "prolonged cheering rose from the galleries and the hall. As it began to subside, several hisses were heard, which immediately caused a more enthusiastic renewal of the applause, which continued for several minutes."[91] The ½ vote appeared again on the thirteenth, the seventeenth, and the eighteenth ballots.

Next morning—Thursday, July 9—when Pendleton was out of the running, Broadhead put Blair's name before the convention.

The California delegation presented Justice Field, describing him

---

[88] Supra, pp. 501–03.

Sandburg's *Lincoln* relates that upon receipt of intelligence of the election of Lincoln, Aldrich had asked, "who ever waited for the common people when a great movement was to be made? We must make the move . . . ." *Abraham Lincoln: The War Years* (New York: Harcourt, Brace and Co., 1939), I, 5.

[89] Notable among them was Josiah G. Abbott (1814–91), distinguished at the Massachusetts bar; as a Repre-

sentative in the 44th Congress he sat on the Electoral Commission of 1877. He had lost two young sons in the war, officers in Massachusetts regiments. The younger, Major Henry L. Abbott, was one of the most intimate comrades of Oliver Wendell Holmes, Jr. See *Touched with Fire*, ed., Mark De Wolfe Howe (Cambridge, Mass.: Harvard University Press, 1947), 40–41.

[90] *Official Proceedings*, 58–60.

[91] Ibid., 119.

as "a wall of fire against the encroachments of Radical domination," "the guardian of the Constitution of his country against all the power of the Radical party...."[92]

The nineteenth ballot followed: Hancock received 135½ votes; Hendricks 107½; Blair 13½; Field 15;[93] again Chase received only the ½ vote from California. On the twenty-first ballot, Hancock again had 135½. Hendricks, whom the New York delegation was then supporting, had risen to 132; New York would not abandon him at this point. Chase on this one ballot received 4 votes, all from Massachusetts. Field was down to 8, all from his Circuit.

At the Chase command post, dominated by Kate Sprague, with Alexander Long and Schuckers (the Chief Justice's secretary) at her side, it seemed that the critical moment was at hand. But Colonel Van Buren (whom Chase imagined to be *his* agent dealing with the New York delegation, rather than a free but friendly politician) had faded away. And at the juncture when, in her expectation, Seymour would bring the New York delegation to announce for Chase, a much better organized counterplan was neatly executed. On the twenty-second ballot the Ohio delegation cast its vote for Seymour. Seymour stepped forward and directed the secretary not to receive the vote; he withdrew from the rostrum. Vallandigham of Ohio insisted that the vote must stand. Francis Kernan, a leading New York delegate, supported that view. One delegation after another fell into line. At the end, Tilden explained that New York had bowed, as it was free to do, to the demand of Ohio. The nomination was unanimous.

For the Vice Presidency, Blair was chosen on the first ballot.

Evidently the party was not going to rise above its past.

REACTIONS

"YOU HAVE BEEN MOST CRUELLY DECEIVED & shamefully used," Kate wrote to her father; "Mr Tilden and Mr Kernan have done this work & Mr Van Buren has been *their tool*"; "at the critical juncture," Van Buren could not be found. "Your name is a watch word with the people, & they have been outraged & deceived."[94]

"I am still depressed by the failure of the great movement," wrote Van Buren on July 16; "Gov: Seymour failed, from mere lack of will,

---

92 Ibid., 143.

93 They were 3 from California, 3 from Nevada, 2 from Oregon—all in his Circuit; and 7 from New Jersey, which had dropped its favorite son, ex-Governor Joel Parker.

94 Letter of July 10 (misdated *June*). Chase Papers, L.C.

to avail himself of a rare opportunity to attain a position of unrivalled greatness—such as even the Presidency cannot confer."[95]

"You are the victim either of the most outrageous duplicity or of the most contemptable [*sic*] imbecility of your leading friends out of the convention or in it," wrote William B. Thomas on July 11. "If they had proceeded upon presentation of your name, immediately upon the assembling of the convention on the 9th, as was desired by the entire Tennessee & Wisconsin delegations and as urged by myself, the convention would have been carryed [*sic*] (in my opinion) without difficulty."[96] "I am disgusted with the democratic party & with party politics generally, but remain your faithful friend & servant," wrote Hiram Barney on July 10. (When Thomas and Barney, like others who had been his subordinates in the Treasury, professed to be "faithful friends," it was an enduring sentiment: as the election of 1872 came into view they would be busily engaged in a renewed effort to win the great prize for Chase.[97])

"I have not written you since our signal defeat at New York in which we were so completely outwitted and out-generaled"—so Alexander Long wrote as he resumed his correspondence on September 10. Long was "quite willing" to take the blame. "My object in writing you at this time is to suggest that which may appear to be among the impossibilities and yet may be possible." He had been talking with Vallandigham, who was approaching the conclusion that the Democrats had a hopeless ticket. Long had a new idea: that if the party made a

---

[95] Chase Papers, L.C.

[96] Chase Papers, Hist. Soc. of Pa. "My friend, Col. Thomas of Phila., hopes to see you soon," Chase had written to J. Glancy Jones, Pennsylvania Democrat, in a letter of May 17, 1867, quoted above. Doubtless the meeting concerned the Presidency— for on July 8, 1868, when the Democratic convention had passed Chase by, Jones wrote in lament: "I have devoted all my faculties for 18 mos. to secure your nomination." "The times called for a man to meet the crisis & bridge a chasm; Passion not cool Judgment, has rushed in . . . ." Chase Papers, Hist. Soc. of Pa.

[97] Chase Papers, Hist. Soc. of Pa. Thomas, in a long letter of October 24, 1871, to Chase, was laying plans for making him the "candidate of the *people* without distinction of

party." He had enlisted the interest of Samuel J. Randall, leading Democratic Congressman from Pennsylvania, later Speaker. Chase Papers, L.C. And on January 6, 1872, Barney writes Chase that Thomas has called at his office. Barney has had several visits from Alexander Mitchell of Wisconsin—Democratic Congressman and president of the Chicago, Milwaukee & St. Paul Railroad. "He is your friend & is satisfied with your health . . . ." Chase Papers, L.C. The Chief Justice's serious illness and protracted absence from the Court during December term 1870 had created misgivings. During the summer of 1871, Chase had recuperated in Wisconsin, where he received Mitchell's attentions, including a railroad pass.

poor showing in Maine (on September 14) and in Pennsylvania, Ohio, or Indiana (on October 13) perhaps Seymour could be induced

> to tender his resignation as a candidate to the National Democratic Executive Committee in your favor and issue an address to the Democracy recommending you as a candidate upon the platform you are said to have approved . . . .[98]

That glittering prospect will be considered in a moment.
The Nation on July 16 commented that

> The only person who can really be said to have suffered seriously at the hands of the Convention is Chief-Justice Chase. In spite of all his efforts, and in spite too of the amazing readiness . . . to swallow Democratic propositions, no matter how bristly or how sinuous, he did not obtain any higher recognition than four votes. Had he got the nomination he would have incurred dislike and contempt in about equal proportions. As it is, . . . we fancy the contempt largely preponderates in the popular feeling about him. . . .

The editor added that "he has destroyed popular confidence in his decisions"; "no weight whatever will hereafter attach to any judgment of his on any one of the great constitutional questions arising out of the rebellion and reconstruction . . . ."

Already, the editorial continued, there were rumors that Chase might still be run as a candidate: but for the Democratic leaders to attempt such a maneuver would be "a confession of imbecility."[99]

Not all, even within the Court, shared *The Nation*'s disdain for the Chief Justice's performance. Justice Field could hardly have censured: his conduct in judicial office had been cited in the convention as showing his qualification for the Presidency.

Justice Davis saw nothing improper, as one infers from the purely political appraisal of Chase's conduct in a letter to Justice Clifford on November 2:

> The Country was ripe for a change, when the Convention met in N Y. but it was plain on account of the quasi hostility of the Democratic party to the war, that one who had acted with the Republicans during the war must be the standard bearer—and the Chief Justice, through the events of last winter, was properly disciplined for the race. There was great anxiety out here that he shd be nominated, by conservative men. His nomination wd have split the [Republican] party in pieces. Chase & Adams[100] should have been the ticket, or

---

[98] Chase Papers, L.C. Infra, pp. 549–50.
[99] 7:41.

[100] Charles Francis Adams (1807–86), who had resigned as Minister to

Chase & Hendricks. Gov Seymour wanted Chase nominated, & a man who could not say *no* when pressed to take the nomination—knowing that Chase was the available man—is now the *man* for the crisis.

As if the very Devil was in it—Frank Blair, a common Loafer, with no moral character, with his revolutionary letter to Broadhead, is nominated by Southern men, who go home & make speeches to infuriate the Northern people. People—plenty of them—are voting agt the Democratic party getting power as they fear some evil, & they are not voting because they approve of what the Republican party has done, & yet the election will be considered as an endorsement in full of everything, & the Leaders—the progressive men, will press extreme measures to the bitter end.[101]

Four years later, Justice Davis would himself be seeking a nomination to the Presidency, to arrest the course he now foresaw.

Justice Nelson entered into the political talk in a letter to Justice Clifford on October 22:

I agree with you that the democracy seem doomed. I have great regard for Seymour: and would rejoice to see him President: but he has hard to carry weight [*sic*]: and I have feared the result, ever since I heard Blair was his associate. . . . Some of my friends were offended in N.Y. because I would not consent to be a candidate, but I had no desire for it; and, no confidence in the leaders. Indeed, was not in the particular confidence of those who would control the policy of the party in the campaign and had no feeling I could influence it. . . .[102]

The idea of a Nelson-for-President movement may be dismissed lightly. Evidently Nelson did not think of his position as a Justice as presenting any impediment. Then there was another objection he did not mention: on election day in November he would be within one week of his seventy-sixth birthday.

THE "CHASE MOVEMENT" REVIVED

WITHIN THE WEEK FOLLOWING the adjournment of the convention, observant Democrats began to conclude that a fatal mistake had been made, as *The Nation* reported on July 16. Long's letter of September

---

Great Britain and returned to the United States in June 1868. In 1872 he and Justice Davis were leading possibilities for nomination as Liberal Republican candidate for the Presidency.

[101] Clifford Papers, Me. Hist. Soc.
[102] Ibid.

10 quoted Vallandigham's statement "in strict confidence" that he would despair if the Republican majority in Maine's election on September 14 exceeded 18,000. In the event, it exceeded 20,000. On October 13, in elections for State officers, Democratic candidates were defeated in Pennsylvania by 9,000 votes, and in Ohio by over 17,000. In Indiana, Hendricks lost the election for Governor, albeit by less than 1,000 votes; 7 Republicans and 4 Democrats were elected to Congress.

In the light of these results, Manton Marble's *New York World* set out to induce the party to make a bold change. On October 15, in a double-leaded editorial on "The Youthful, Indomitable Democracy," it spoke with pride of the party that had made "so gallant a fight" and come so close to success. Two reasons appeared, "in the absence of either of which our triumph would have been certain": these were "the military prestige of General Grant" and "the perversions of General Blair's position." The latter had led to an impression that the party was "virtually pledged to overthrow the new State governments by force." In spite of misfortune,

we may succeed yet if we can remove or neutralize these adverse influences . . . . We have still nearly three weeks . . . .

Prompt and judicious action might yet accomplish wonders:

if there is any impediment to success which can be removed by noble daring or self-sacrificing virtue, or a bold stroke of policy, now is the hour for action . . . . *L'audace! l'audace! toujours l'audace!*

Thereupon in political parlance, Seymour and Blair became "the impediments."

Next day the *World* resumed the argument in "The Ever-Vigorous Democracy." It concluded, "This is a time for plain talk, and we trust we have spoken intelligently enough for those whom it most concerns to take our meaning."

Plainly it was urging the Democratic National Executive Committee to get rid of Seymour and Blair and substitute a new ticket. It could hardly be doubted that this meant Chase.

Washington McLean's *Cincinnati Enquirer* (which had been Pendleton's strong support) spoke guardedly on October 17: at the moment there were "strong evidences . . . that the nomination of Mr. Chase, as the opponent of the Radical policy and candidate, would be acceptable to the great mass of the Democratic party"; it doubted, however, whether "any important results will come" from the attempt to change candidates. On the same day the *Ohio Statesman*, party organ at Columbus, spoke of the suggestion as "the very height of foolishness";

the party had been growing rapidly since the war, and would soon be victorious "if the party shall only be true to itself."

In New York, the *Sun* commented: "The World has arrived at the point which the Sun occupied months ago." It would be well to retire Seymour and Blair at once. Grant would be in office for the next eight years: "And the movement to elect his successor may as well be begun at once."[103]

The *Times* recalled that the *World* had warned the convention against acceding to the demands of the extremists, "the repudiators . . . and the nullifiers": yet that was exactly what the convention had done. Now the *World* was arraying itself against "the governing forces of the Democracy." It would not succeed.[104]

The *Tribune* said that the Democratic party might have placed "a great statesman at its head"; even had it done so, success seemed unlikely. Now Chase would know "that his candidacy would not change the fell spirit of the rebel Democracy . . . ."

> Much as the nation has trusted him, he knows that it would scorn his promises if he stood on the Democratic platform . . . . His enemies say he might do much to attain the Presidency; his worst enemies never accused him of a disposition to sell himself for nothing. . . .[105]

Bryant's *Evening Post* offered "Advice Gratis": to substitute Grant and Colfax in place of Seymour and Blair;

> then, to set to work and improve the Grant-Colfax platform, . . . insisting upon impartial suffrage everywhere, and laying this down as a cardinal point of the Democratic faith in every State. . . .[106]

The *Herald* had taken a new line of uncritical thought: "The intelligence of the American people is equal to all emergencies." The people had carried Lincoln through the war, and now were "satisfied that in General Grant we shall have a safe, sound, conservative President." Nothing remained but a "formal registering" of their conclusion.[107]

The *Cincinnati Commercial's* comment on the *World's* proposal was, "Gentlemen, it is *too late*. Your opportunity is lost. . . . Even the name of Salmon P. Chase would have no magic in it now."[108]

---

[103] Oct. 16.
[104] Oct. 16.
[105] Oct. 16.
[106] Oct. 16.
[107] Oct. 16.
[108] Oct. 16. One may notice in the same issue a telegram from Frank-

fort, Kentucky, to the effect that General John M. Harlan and Colonel John Mason Brown would address a Republican mass meeting to celebrate the victories in Indiana, Ohio, and Pennsylvania. Harlan was appointed to the Supreme Court in 1877. Brown

Chase's response in this contingency may be learned by juxtaposing a dispatch from Cincinnati in the *New York Times* of October 26 and a letter of November 2 from Alexander Long to Chase. The *Times* published a letter dated October 23 wherein a correspondent (J. Q. Thompson) recounted a conversation he had had on October 21 with Long. His report, loosely written, was in part untrue—particularly in setting out a supposedly "reliable copy" of a letter he had not seen. The purported letter was of October 17, from Chase to Long; one sentence was, "Should our friends urge my acceptance, in the event of Mr. Seymour's withdrawal, I should stand as a candidate in his stead . . . ." *This was a fabrication; there was no such letter.* Chase wrote to Long on October 27, with an enclosure—presumably the *Times* article, or a letter of denial. Long's reply of November 2 gave his report of the incident, with references to communications he had had from Chase. Doubtless his statement of the substance of such communications is true.

Thompson had called at Long's office on October 21 with a letter of introduction from a local Republican; he was anxiously seeking information for his private and individual benefit, as to the prospects for a change of candidates. Here is Long's account:

> I thereupon said to him, there would be no change: that Gov. Seymour would not withdraw and that unless he did so, no change could take place. I said to him, that Seymour was the only obstacle in the way, and that I had telegraphed to Manton Marble, that the position of the New York World was indorsed by ninety-nine out of every hundred Democrats in Ohio; that it was the last and only hope of constitutional liberty; that Gov. Seymour was the only obstacle in the way, and must yield to the great necessity.
>
> He then asked me if I had any assurance that Mr Chase would consent to become a candidate on the Democratic platform, if Gov. Seymour did decline?
>
> I told him I had not, but on the contrary, I knew he would not and that it would only result in defeat if he did. In that, Mr Thompson fully concurred with me.
>
> He then asked me how Mr Chase could become the candidate of the Democratic party, unless he accepted the platform?
>
> My reply was: that if Gov. Seymour would decline, there would be a universal demand among Democrats, in all parts of the country, for Mr Chase as the candidate with Genl. Franklin,[109]

---

has been mentioned as a member of the military commission that tried Vallandigham in 1863. Supra, ch. 5, n. 45.

[109] Major General William Buel Franklin (1823–1903) stood No. 1 in the class of 1843 at the Military Academy; Grant stood in the middle of the same class. Franklin was then in business in Connecticut. He was an elector, voting for Tilden, in 1876. See D.A.B.

Ewing, Hancock or Adams, for Vice President, on Mr Chase's own platform, and whether the National executive committee were willing or unwilling, the people would make the nomination, and that it only required three hours notice, after the announcement of the withdrawal of Gov. Seymour, to fill the largest space, in which a meeting could be held in this City, in the interest of Mr Chase.

He asked me if I had any assurance, that Mr Chase would accept such a nomination at this late day on his own platform.

I then informed him that my law partner, Mr Hoeffer, was in Washington—that he had reached there on last Saturday [October 17]—had an interview with Mr Chase and had sent me a telegram in cipher, to the effect; that if Seymour & Blair declined, and Mr Chase was nominated on his own platform, he would not feel at liberty to decline, and that within an hour after the telegram, Mr Hoeffer had written me a letter, which I had in my pocket, to the same effect.

But I now say; that I did not mention, suggest or intimate to him, a solitary sentance [*sic*], syllable or word contained in the letter more than to say, that it was to the same effect as the telegram in cipher; and I say further; that neither the letter of Mr Hoeffer, or his telegram, contains a sentence or word that appears in the printed letter of the Times.

He asked me if I referred to Mr Chase's platform, as that which was published in the Cincinnati Commercial of that morning? I said I did.[110]

---

[110] "Mr. Chase's platform" appears as Part II of "MR. CHASE'S VIEWS," a pamphlet printed shortly subsequent to the convention. The copy in the library of the Historical Society of Pennsylvania bears the handwritten date, August 1, 1868. The pamphlet —to which Long's letter presently refers—is here quoted or summarized:

MR. CHASE'S VIEWS

To correct misapprehensions, and to enable fair-minded citizens to form sound opinions, some of Chief Justice Chase's friends have thought it advisable to print together the several statements of political principles and measures to which, and to which alone, he has given his assent, within the last two months . . . .

The statements follow in their chronological order: the first having been published some time in June, the last on one of the first days of July.

I.

The first statement consists of three paragraphs, and expresses views which a number of intelligent Democrats thought would be accepted by the party, and is as follows:

1. Universal suffrage is a democratic principle, the application of which is left, under the Constitution of the United States, to the States themselves; [universal amnesty and complete removal of disabilities are necessary].

2. [No military government, or trial of private citizens by military commission.]

3. [Taxes should be reduced;] and, while all national obligations should be honestly and exactly fulfilled, no special privileges should be allowed to any classes of individuals or corporations.

[This 3-paragraph statement

He asked me if I had any letter from Mr Chase, on the subject of the proposed change of candidates? I told him *distinctly I had not*, but that I had full confidence in Mr Hoeffer, and again repeated, "Mr Seymour is the only obstacle in the way." He then went on to speak of the manner in which Seymour had been nominated; the corruption of New York politicians, and their foolish obstinacy in keeping Seymour on the track.

His statement in the correspondance [*sic*]—"the positive assurance that Judge Chase would accept the *race*; and an hour after Mr ——— left the Chief Justice, Mr. Chase wrote me a letter, which I have in my pocket" &c; after I had distinctly informed him in answer to his inquiry; that I had no letter from you on the subject, is as deliberate a falsehood, as was ever written down by mortal man.

[Long went on to point out other falsehoods, and to tell of a statement in the *Cincinnati Enquirer* of October 17 reporting an alleged telegram from Chase to the effect that in the event Seymour and Blair withdrew, Chase would consent to run as an independent candidate.]

Before Mr Hoeffer started for Washington, it was agreed between him and myself; that in case you should be willing to accept the position, he should telegraph me, "Case Settled," and if you would under no circumstances accept: to telegraph "Case cannot be Settled," and if you would accept upon terms, conditions or modifications, he should telegraph, in such manner as to indicate the conditions &c. Accordingly after his interview with you, he telegraphed me as follows: "Case can be Settled upon the printed terms which you have."

---

appears in Schuckers, *Chase*, 567.]

II.

[On "the platform," the following statement in Appleton's Annual Cyclopaedia, 1868, at 750, gives this explanation: "A few days before the assembling of the convention, at an interview sought for the purpose, by and in behalf of Democrats who desired his nomination, the subject of the possible agreement of the party and himself in a declaration of principles was discussed, and the Chief Justice expressed his willingness to accept a nomination upon the following platform, which was found to be acceptable to many of the delegates and to other prominent men of the party": then follows a 15-paragraph

document, covering a wide range of national issues in carefully balanced sentences.

[Coleman, *The Election of 1868*, at 137, discusses the origin of the "platform." "It seems probable that Van Buren actually wrote it, possibly in Washington with the assistance of Chase."

[The text appears in Schuckers, *Chase*, 568–70.]

III.

[This contains the pertinent extract from Ewing's letter, and Chase's acceptance on July 1. Supra, pp. 539–40.]

[MR. CHASE'S VIEWS then quotes Chase's letters of April 11 and 12 to President Lincoln, urging the President to impose universal suffrage as the basis for restoration. See supra, p. 102.]

This telegram no one could suspect or understand. Of course you would have known that "the printed terms," referred to what are known as "Chase's Views."[111] Consequently, you will I think, agree with me, that Mr Hoeffer's telegram stated more conditions or contingencies upon which alone you would accept, than you do yourself in your last letter, since in it, you required only your platform which is but the II. Statement of "Chase's Views" while his telegram informed me, that 1. & 3. Statements were alike conditions, and equally necessary to be first assented to by the Democracy.

All of this prearrangement, however, was based upon the condition, as a matter of course, that Seymour & Blair would retire and that the Democracy would demand your nomination, of all which, at the time, there was here the most enthusiastic proof. Geo. E. Pugh,[112] stood almost alone, opposed to it. At a meeting of the State central committee Judge Thurman,[113] who has a place for the next six years in the Senate and Judge Van Trump[114] who represents a Democratic district with over six thousand majority, opposed any change and declaired [sic] they would take the stump against you if you became a candidate in place of Seymour. This intimidated men of less influence and no position and that which is still worse [,] without either courage or judgment to do right and hence the proposition looking to a change was voted down and the result telegraphed to Gov. Seymour.

Tomorrow [election day] will teach them all a lesson in the School of experience and on Wednesday, will go up all over the land an exclamation of mortification and regret by the Democracy; Oh! we made a great mistake in not nominating Chief Justice Chase!![115]

The *New York Times* on October 28 announced that "Chief Justice Chase gives a very distinct and emphatic denial of the authenticity of the letter . . . . We shall expect to receive from our correspondent some satisfactory explanation . . . ." The *Cincinnati Commercial* next day said that "J.Q.T." had been "guilty of an extraordinary and disgraceful audacity."

When the denials and explanations have been duly noted, and the correspondent has been censured, for present purposes the matter may be reduced to this: what Long had in his pocket was not a letter that *Chase* had *written*, but a letter that *Hoeffer* had written reporting what Chase had *said*. And what Hoeffer stated—and what "you do yourself in your last letter"—was that, had Seymour and Blair retired, Chase was prepared in October to make the race upon the platform he had accepted in early July. Long had been accurate in telling the *Times*'

---

[111] Supra, n. 110.
[112] Supra, pp. 193n., 542.
[113] Supra, p. 542.

[114] Supra, pp. 312n., 542.
[115] Chase Papers, Hist. Soc. of Pa.

correspondent that, in those circumstances, once again Chase "would not feel at liberty to decline."

In that event, would he have resigned his office? That seems in the highest degree unlikely. Would he in the three weeks remaining have made campaign speeches? If he had, he would merely have said in a loud voice what he had been uttering in conversations and in letters.

THE OUTCOME

THE DEMOCRATIC LEADERS meeting in Tammany Hall on October 19 rejected the *World*'s demand for a change in the ticket. The straight party men—like Pugh, Thurman, and Van Trump in Ohio—had opposed it. But a change in strategy was adopted. Thus far Seymour had remained at home, and Blair had done the speaking: he had proclaimed that Congressional Reconstruction must be overturned by Executive action; and the responding rebel yell had given the country a bad scare.[116] Now Blair was to be hushed; Seymour sallied forth to engage in the canvass in person. President Johnson sent his greetings: "Let the living principles of the violated Constitution be proclaimed and restored . . . ."[117] Seymour traveled widely and spoke reassuringly and elusively on a variety of new topics.

While Blair had been denouncing "the fragment of a Congress" for trampling on "the fundamental charter of our liberties,"[118] Con-

---

[116] Old Southern leaders, such as Wade Hampton, Howell Cobb, Robert Toombs, Benjamin H. Hill, and Zebulon B. Vance had hailed expectantly a Democratic victory. That had driven prudent voters to the candidate who said, "Let us have peace."

Cobb has been introduced above as Jere Black's correspondent. Supra, p. 478. At a Democratic rally at Atlanta on July 23, Cobb, Toombs, and Hill all spoke, and the occasion was widely reported. "A Friend of the Cause" wrote to Cobb from New York on August 3:

About the most telling arguments used here by the Radical party are furnished by such men as yourself and Genl. Toombs. Your speech in Atlanta endorsing the candidates is extensively circulated and used as proof of the temper of the South. . . . I

notice in that speech the following language: "And raising the banner of Constitutional liberty and equality, we hurl into their teeth today the same defiance and bid them come on to the struggle. We are ready if they are. Snatch the old banner from the dust and give it again to the breeze, and if needs be to the God of battles, and strike one more blow for Constitutional liberty." . . .

The writer urged, "Do for the sake of the cause" stop this inflammatory speech-making; that at Atlanta would cost the Democratic ticket 50,000 votes.

Toombs, Stephens, Cobb Correspondence. *Ann. Report of Am. Hist. Assn. for 1911*, 2:702 (1913).

[117] *Ann. Cyc.* 1868, 752.

[118] Acceptance speech on July 13. *Ann. Cyc.* 1868, 752.

gress declared on July 21 that the Fourteenth Amendment had been adopted—imposing on the State a new duty of equal protection of every person within its jurisdiction.

Thaddeus Stevens died on August 21, and was buried in a cemetery not subject to racial discrimination—to "illustrate in my death the principles which I have advocated through a long life: Equality of Man before his Creator."

A Joint Resolution of July 20 directed the exclusion of electoral votes from States not yet reorganized and entitled to representation. The effect was that no votes were received from Virginia, Mississippi, and Texas. When the time came, the status of Georgia being undetermined,[119] Congress directed that the result be announced in the alternative. This was that Grant had received 214 electoral votes, and that Seymour had received 80 or 71.[120]

Emboldened by the election, Congress on February 26, 1869, proposed a Fifteenth Amendment:

> The right of citizens of the United States to vote shall not be denied or abridged by the United States or by any State on account of race, color, or previous condition of servitude.

That would enact the proposition that Chase had preached on all occasions—until in 1868 he had brought himself to say that "wisdom and duty require that the application of this principle be left . . . to the people of each State, without interference by the national Government."[121]

---

[119] Supra, pp. 434–38.

[120] Cong. Globe, 40–3, 1063. Feb. 10, 1869.

Of popular votes, Grant received 3 million to 2.7 million for Seymour. Grant received the electoral votes of Alabama, Arkansas, Florida, North Carolina, and South Carolina: Would conditions be such that that could be repeated? Louisiana showed a Democratic preponderance of more than 2 to 1: but it was alleged that this was the result of fraud. At the moment of victory, Republicans who looked closely saw reason to view the future with concern.

[121] "Mr. Chase's platform," par. 4.

CHAPTER XII

Ex parte Yerger, *and the Close of Congressional Reconstruction*

O N MARCH 4, 1869, Chief Justice Chase administered the oath of office to President Grant; he trusted that the day would "be ever associated in American remembrance with the perfected restoration of peace...."[1]

On the same day the 41st Congress met in its First Session, which continued to April 10.[2] Restoration had been so far perfected that Arkansas, Florida, North Carolina, South Carolina, Louisiana, and Alabama had all been readmitted to representation during the preceding Congress, although some of the seats, in Senate or House, were not occupied at this First Session of the new Congress. The readmission of Georgia had also been authorized; but then the houses of its legislature chose to expel their Negro members, with the consequence that formal readmission was delayed until July 15, 1870.[3] (Military control, however, was not reimposed.)

---

[1] Letter to Mrs. Grant, presenting the copy of the Bible used on that occasion. Robert B. Warden, *An Account of the Private Life and Public Services of Salmon Portland Chase* (Cincinnati, Ohio: Wilstach, Baldwin and Co., 1874), 718.

[2] The Constitution provided in Art. I, Sec. 4, cl. 2, that Congress would meet annually "on the first Monday in December, unless they shall by Law appoint a different Day." The Act of January 22, 1867, 14 Stat. 378, provided that in addition a new Congress would meet on the day its term began. (The Twentieth Amendment, in 1933, established "the 3d day of January" instead of the original pro-

vision.)

[3] Readmission had been authorized by Act of June 25, 1868. Representatives were seated on July 25, 1868.

But the lower House of the Legislature on September 3, by vote of 83 to 23, declared its colored members ineligible. The Senate on September 12 took like action, by vote of 24 to 11. House J. 1868, 242–43; Sen. J., 277–78. These proceedings were followed closely and applauded by the *Atlanta Constitution* (established in June, and dedicated to supporting the claims of white Georgians) and the *Augusta Chronicle and Sentinel.*

A convention of colored people,

XII: Ex parte Yerger

Mississippi, Texas, and Virginia remained under the Reconstruction Act until 1870, and from each came litigation presently to be considered. By an Act of April 10, 1869, Congress now provided for the restoration of those three States. The President was authorized to submit the constitutions already framed in Virginia and Texas, and to submit again that already rejected in Mississippi—selecting particular provisions, if he saw fit, for separate vote. (That would permit rejection of proscriptive provisions that had aroused the most vehement objection.) The negotiations leading to this legislation, and the action resulting from it, reflected an awareness of the need for accommodation.[4]

THE ACT TO AMEND THE JUDICIAL SYSTEM

THE IMPORTANT JUDICIARY STATUTE of April 10, 1869, has already been mentioned.[5] Now it should be examined in detail. First it enacted

> That the Supreme Court of the United States shall hereafter consist of the Chief Justice of the United States and eight associate justices, any six of whom shall constitute a quorum; and for the

meeting at Macon on October 6–8, addressed Congress—the only "power on earth to which we could appeal for help, with the hope of any degree of success"—in a closely argued and exceedingly able memorial. It was signed by their president, Henry M. Turner (1834–1915), an expelled member of the House. See D.A.B. A native South Carolinian, he was commissioned in 1863 as chaplain of the 1st Rgt., U.S. Colored Troops; member of the constitutional convention of 1868; subsequently bishop of the A.M.E. Church for Georgia. The memorial appears in Cong. Globe, 40–3, 2–4.

Against one colored Senator there was an independent ground for expulsion: Aaron Alpeoria Bradley had been convicted of a felony. He had already been expelled from the constitutional convention of 1868 on the basis of certified copies of records that showed a conviction for seduction by the City Court of Brooklyn, New York, in 1851, and that in 1856 he had been stricken from the roll of attorneys by the Superior Court of

Suffolk County, Massachusetts, for contempt of court and malpractice. *Journ. of Proc. Ga. Con. Con.* (1868), 271.

On April 4, 1870, the United States Supreme Court acted upon Bradley's application for admission to its bar. It referred the matter to a committee of three. On April 8 one of the committee—who had apparently been the sponsor—moved to withdraw the motion and supporting papers, and this was granted. Minutes, Apr. 4 and 8, 1870.

[4] In Virginia—see infra, pp. 598–601 —an election was held on July 6, 1869; the separate provisions were all rejected, and the constitution was adopted. In Texas, no separate questions were presented; the constitution was adopted at an election on November 30–December 3, 1869. In Mississippi—see supra, p. 429—at an election on November 30–December 1 the constitution was adopted, and all except one of the separate provisions were rejected.

[5] 16 Stat. 44. Supra, pp. 487–88.

purposes of this act there shall be appointed an additional associate justice of said court.

That got rid of the bungled legislation of July 23, 1866.[6]

Second, for each of the nine Circuits there would be a Circuit Judge, with the same power and jurisdiction therein as the Circuit Justice. Thenceforth a Circuit Court might be held by either of these Judges or by a District Judge, sitting together or apart. The salary of the Circuit Judge would be $5,000.

Henceforth it would be the duty of the Justice to attend at least one term of the Circuit Court in each District of his Circuit during every period of *two* years. (In practice, the press of important litigation would still demand his presence in some of the courts every year.)

For decades the Court had been weakened by the chronic decrepitude of some of its members—evident at the moment in Justices Grier and Nelson.[7] Now Congress sought to improve the effectiveness of the federal judiciary by the following provision:

> That any judge of any court of the United States, who, having held his commission as such at least ten years, shall, after having attained the age of seventy years, resign his office, shall thereafter, during the residue of his natural life, receive the same salary which was by law payable to him at the time of his resignation.

This is the beginning of legislation now codified in the Judicial Code in its chapter on Resignation and Retirement of Judges.[8]

This enactment became effective upon the first Monday of December 1869. The choice of new Circuit Judges would profoundly affect the quality of federal justice: this would be an important responsibility of the new Attorney General.

ATTORNEY GENERAL HOAR

EBENEZER ROCKWOOD HOAR (1816–95) of Massachusetts appears at this critical juncture as the Government's chief law officer. Like Evarts, whom he succeeded in the office of Attorney General, he was a grandson of Roger Sherman, signer of the Declaration of Independence,

---

[6] Supra, pp. 160–69.

[7] Charles Fairman, "The Retirement of Federal Judges," *Harv. L. Rev.*, 51:397 (1938).

[8] Since 1937 it has been possible under the same conditions to "retire from regular active service," remaining a Judge and receiving the salary of the office. Also a Judge may retire after attaining the age of sixty-five and after serving at least fifteen years. Such service need not have been continuous, nor upon one federal court.

of the Articles of Confederation, and of the Constitution. *Mutatis mutandis*, one might describe Hoar as John Adams had described the grandfather: "an old Puritan, as honest as an angel and as firm in the cause of American Independence as Mount Atlas."[9]

The great American cause in the grandson's time had been resistance to the encroachments of the slave power: he early declared that he would rather be a Conscience Whig than a Cotton Whig— thereby coining a slogan as well as establishing his devotion to human rights above economic or partisan advantage. James Russell Lowell, when he published the second series of his *Bigelow Papers* in 1867, dedicated the collection to Hoar, and made reference to him as

> . . . the Jedge, who covers with his hat
> More wit an' gumption an' shrewd Yankee sense
> Than there is mosses on an ole stone fence.

Hoar had served as Judge of the Common Pleas from 1849 to 1855; he sat on the Supreme Judicial Court from 1859 until he resigned in 1869 to enter the Grant Administration. Here was a judicious lawyer and a consistent friend of liberty. It is important to establish that character at the outset, before turning to the problems on which he was called to take a stand.

WEAVER'S CASE

JAMES WEAVER, a citizen of Texas, had there been sentenced to death by a military commission, for the murder of a freedman. The Reconstruction Act provided, however, "that no sentence of death . . . shall be carried into effect without the approval of the President." The proof was strong, and Johnson was unwilling to disapprove the sentence; nor yet would he approve what had been done under the statute he had denounced as unconstitutional. He sent the papers back to the War Department without action, and left the case for the incoming administration.[10] On March 24, 1869, Secretary Rawlins submitted the file to the Attorney General.

There was a large background in recent Texas history. In late 1867 and early 1868, Provisional Governor Pease had insisted that the white majority were so "embittered against the Government" as to make it necessary in some situations that law be enforced by military commission. General Winfield S. Hancock, commanding the Fifth Military

---

9 Charles F. Adams, Ed., *Familiar Letters of John Adams and His Wife,* (New York: Hurd and Houghton, 1876), 251.
10 *Baltimore Sun*, June 7, 1869.

District, declared however that "perfect peace prevailed," and rejected the request.[11]

The insecurity of life remained a partisan issue in Texas; the Democrats viewed the condition "with sorrow" but attributed it to "general demoralization resulting from the war." The *New York Tribune* of January 27, 1869, published one report of a common situation under the caption "Texas—The State of Society There—Murderers and Assassins Unpunished—The Rebellion Not Conquered." An editorial note explained that "Texas escaped the ravages of the war, and has never yet been able rightly to understand which side won it. We hope, within a month or two, that some easy lessons for learners may quicken her understanding and improve her conduct." (This was an admission contrary to the tenor of the *Tribune*'s editorial policy; it had been urging national reconciliation through moderation on both sides, and professed to believe that except for some bad spots, as in Texas, the law-abiding citizen was generally as secure in the South as he would be in Iowa or Massachusetts.[12])

After holding the Weaver case under advisement for more than two months, on May 31, 1869, Hoar rendered his opinion.[13] (The Supreme Court had dismissed *McCardle* on April 12; it would not be pronouncing on the Reconstruction Act at that time.) The papers showed:

> A freedman who had been at work for Weaver, having chosen to leave his employment to go to work for another man, went to him . . . to ask for the wages which were due him. Weaver seized an ox-band, beat him severely with that, and then sent his hired man . . . for a double-barreled gun, . . . and on his return shot the freedman through the head, killing him instantly. There appears to have been neither provocation nor resistance . . . .

The State judge had informed the commander of the Military District (General J. J. Reynolds) that a proper trial could not be had in the local court; he asked that a military commission be convened. The record indicated that the trial there had been "fairly and carefully conducted."

The Attorney General's opinion was that

> Having suppressed the rebellion as far as it was maintained by an armed force, it became the duty of Congress to re-establish the broken

---

[11] Ann. Cyc. 1868, 727–28. Supra, p. 352.

[12] Mar. 11, 1869. On the theme of moderation and reconciliation, there were editorials on January 14, 21, 23, 27, 1869.

[13] 13 Ops. Atty. Gen. 59.

relations of the State with the Union; and the same authority which recognized the existence of the war is, in my judgment, the only authority having the constitutional right to determine when, for all purposes, the war has ceased. The rights of war do not necessarily terminate with the cessation of actual hostilities. I can have no doubt that it is competent for the nation to retain the territory and the people which have once assumed a hostile and belligerent character "within the grasp of war"[14] until the work of restoring the relations of peace can be accomplished; that it is for Congress, the department of the national Government to which the power to declare war is entrusted by the Constitution, to determine when the war has so far ended that this work can be safely and successfully completed. . . .

In the meantime, the Government might employ "the means belonging to war" to vindicate the national authority and to restore republican governments.

The *American Law Review* was edited by very able men—John Chipman Gray and John C. Ropes—whose method was to subject even large constitutional questions to very straight legal analysis.[15] They published this comment on the Attorney General's opinion:

> It sustains the legality of the Reconstruction Act on what we have long been persuaded is the only consistent hypothesis; whether it is a correct hypothesis is another and a very different thing. On that we give no opinion, but only present this opinion as an intelligible and intelligent argument in support of one side of a grave constitutional question on which there has been talked no end of nonsense.[16]

---

[14] This phrase had become current after an address by Richard Henry Dana, Jr., at Faneuil Hall, Boston, on June 21, 1865, called to consider "Re-organization of the Rebel States." *"We have a right to hold the rebels in the grasp of war until we have obtained whatever the public safety and the public faith require."* Richard H. Dana (3d), ed., *Richard Henry Dana, Jr.: Speeches in Stirring Times* . . . (Boston and New York: Houghton Mifflin Co., 1910), 234, 247.

[15] Supra, pp. 74, 224.

[16] 4:170. Oct. 1869.

The *New York World* argued the other side in an effective editorial, "States or Not," published on July 4. It recalled that in Texas v. White,

decided on April 12, the Supreme Court had declared that Texas continued to be a State in the Union, with standing to sue. (7 Wall. 700, infra, pp. 638–40). But now the effect of the Attorney General's opinion was that "It is no State when its citizens' lives are to be protected and civil order maintained. . . . It . . . cannot say a word when strangers seize [its inhabitants], and, after a mock trial, hang them." The editorial warned against "the evils of a centralized authority"—corruption, tyranny, and "the bitterness of the passions it fosters in sections and in parties." The Attorney General's opinion had been "taken hot from crazy Butlerisms and Sumnerisms in Congress."

It was the responsibility of the chief law officer to view the problem in its large implications—a responsibility that loomed more starkly when, nine days after the *Weaver* opinion, the *Yerger* case arose in Mississippi.

YERGER'S CASE

AT JACKSON, MISSISSIPPI, on June 8, 1869, Edward M. Yerger accosted and stabbed to death Major Joseph G. Crane, an army officer assigned to act as mayor. The occasion was that the mayor had caused a piano to be seized under a warrant of distress for city taxes.[17]

[17] On his own petition, Yerger had been declared a bankrupt in February 1869. Supra, p. 364. Now he had a grievance against the city on the ground that by reason of inadequate culverts the home property had been damaged. At the time the piano was seized, Yerger was attending a National Commercial Convention at Memphis, where he was promoting a scheme for immigration from abroad, which he believed would make him "not only rich but magnificently rich." Testimony of Amos R. Johnston before the military commission. *Jackson Weekly Clarion*, June 3, July 22, 1869.

He was a man of great expectations. In June 1867, when a fund was being solicited to provide Jackson with a steam fire engine, Yerger made a subscription of $100—one of seven in so large an amount. Substantial citizens—including some who were his counsel in 1869—contributed $25. Yet concurrently in the *Clarion* one also reads the warning of the Tax Collector [*not* a military appointee] of an impending "CITY TAX SALE! ! !" —and Yerger's deficiency of $202.50 exceeded all others. *Jackson Clarion*, from June 4 to July 14, 1867.

In 1869, when Yerger's homicide was being discussed in the press, the *Montgomery Mail* asked, "What shall we say of the petty tyranny of this military despot at Jackson stealing the piano of a girl under the forms of carpet-bag law, and rousing the father to the desperate deed of cutting the tyrant to the heart?" Quoted in *The Nation*, 8:485, June 24, 1869. (By way of apology, it has been said that the piano had belonged to Mrs. Yerger before her marriage: but even supposing it to have been her separate property at the time of the killing, that would have afforded no defense.)

The *Louisville Courier-Journal* termed the killing "a personal matter" —"there was not the shadow of anything political about it." Ignoring the consideration that an officer had been killed for something done in the line of duty, the editor chided the *New York Tribune* for saying that the incident showed the need for military rule. "This is indeed most shameful. No night passes in the city of New York without the commission of a greater number of atrocities within the municipal limits than are perpetrated throughout the entire State of Mississippi or Georgia in a whole month." "Why should New York City be governed by the laws of peace and Mississippi by the laws of war?" June 18, 1869.

The *Jackson Clarion*, whose editor was acquainted with Yerger's addiction to irrational resentment and violence (p. 415), reprinted what the *Journal*, at Crane's home town, Dayton, Ohio, had said of him: that while Crane "was of mild, placable disposition, not given to violent expression of his sentiments, and prone to avoid controversy, it would be hard to select a man more careful to avoid offense. He was a gentleman in the true sense of the word . . . ." *Weekly Clarion*, June 19. Crane came of a distinguished ancestry: his father, Joseph H. Crane, had been a member

XII: Ex parte Yerger

Under authority granted by the Reconstruction Act, Yerger was promptly brought before a military commission on a charge of murder. Able counsel, including Judge William Yerger, the defendant's uncle, entered a plea to the jurisdiction: that the accused was a civilian; that the crime, if committed, was an offense only against Mississippi law; that he was entitled to the privileges of grand jury and trial jury.[18]

The Judge Advocate, in reply, cited the Attorney General's recent opinion in *Weaver's Case* as sustaining the jurisdiction. The commission overruled the plea and proceeded to hear testimony.

Yerger's unprovoked homicide was abundantly proved. The trial ran on for twenty-nine days, however, before being discontinued; during that time evidence was introduced whose object was to exclude "malice aforethought" and even to establish irresponsibility by reason of a moment of "moral insanity." Kinsmen and others testified to many acts of unreasoning violence and to Yerger's lack of self-control when his opinion was crossed. A colleague on the executive committee of the Democratic party recalled his "disposition generally to have his own way about everything, and to construe any opposition to his peculiar views into something aimed personally at himself . . . ."[19] His onetime newspaper partner instanced an outburst when Provisional Governor Sharkey urged that the law be changed to permit Negroes to testify.[20] Ironically, it was the testimony of a Negro that seemed best to substantiate the defense of insanity: Pamela Yerger, long a household slave, recounted a history of irrational conduct, as when the accused as a young man had without cause shot a Negro boy summoned to dance for the family. Yerger's sisters testified to the high credibility of this witness.

While the trial went on, an application for habeas corpus was made to Justice Swayne (who at that moment had the Fifth Circuit as an additional assignment), and by him denied. He acquiesced, however, in a renewal of the application before Chief Justice Chase.[21]

---

of Congress and a judge of Ohio's Supreme Court; his great-grandfather, Stephen Crane, represented New Jersey in the Continental Congress, 1774–76.

[18] The proceedings were reported in the Jackson Clarion, and subsequently in a book of 122 pages, *Trial of E. M. Yerger . . .* (1869).

[19] Amos R. Johnston. See supra, pp. 109, 564n.

[20] Jones S. Hamilton.

[21] Swayne's ground for denying the writ does not appear.

In the unreported case of Bethuel W. Rupert (a civilian held by military authority on a charge of disloyal conduct), Swayne, J., in the Circuit Court for the Southern District of Ohio, at October term 1862, "distinctly held that this court would not grant the writ of habeas corpus, where it appeared that the detention or imprisonment was under military authority," Leavitt, D.J., observed in *Ex parte* Vallandigham, Fed. Case No. 16,816 (1863), at 920. See p. 193n.

The *Cincinnati Enquirer* of November 7, 1862, in its account of Swayne's remarks the day before,

MAY A JUSTICE GRANT THE WRIT OF HABEAS CORPUS IN A CASE NOT ARISING WITHIN HIS CIRCUIT?

JUDGE EPHRAIM S. FISHER[22] found the Chief Justice on his circuit, at Richmond. What ensued can best be told by correspondence preserved among the Chase Papers at the Historical Society of Pennsylvania. It presents a serious question about the power to issue the writ of habeas corpus.

When in December 1866, immediately after the *Milligan* opinion, application had been made on behalf of Dr. Mudd, Chase had taken the view that a Justice had no authority to send the writ outside his own circuit;[23] now he was called upon to reconsider. He wrote to Justices Nelson and Clifford, for their experience and judgment:

Richmond Va. June 22, 1869

My dear Judge.

You are doubtless aware that a number of persons are imprisoned in Mississippi & Texas under the sentences of Military Commissions. One of them, at least, is under sentence of death; and, I presume, you have seen the opinion of the Attorney General asserting the validity of this sentence,[24] & the statement in the public

shows that he accepted Horace Binney's reasoned defense of Lincoln's view that it was competent for the President in time of war to judge of the necessity for suspending the writ, as against Taney's opinion that the power belongs exclusively to Congress. (Horace Binney, *The Privilege of the Writ of Habeas Corpus under the Constitution* [1862]; *Ex parte* Merryman, Fed. Case No. 9487 [1861], Taney, C.J.) Swayne found it singular that so much was being said about protecting the citizen from governmental interference, "and so little about the preservation and perpetuity of our glorious Union." The account is, however, too loose to show precisely what Swayne thought about judicial duty with respect to habeas corpus. The *Enquirer* was ardent in its support of Vallandigham. An editorial on "What will the Judiciary do?" ended with a warning that "there is no statute of limitations to run against the memory of an act of judicial unfaithfulness." Nov. 28, 1862.

[22] He had been an Associate Justice of the High Court of Errors and Appeals of Mississippi from 1851 to 1858, in part concurrently with Judge William Yerger. He took no part in the war. The constitutional convention of 1865, informally, gave him a sort of nomination for governor. He was defeated, however, by Benjamin G. Humphreys, a distinguished soldier who, on Brigadier General William Barksdale's death, had succeeded to his command.

[23] Supra, pp. 237–39.

[24] In the matter of Weaver, 13 Ops. Atty. Gen. 59, of May 31, 1869. Supra, pp. 561–64.

prints that the President, whose sanction of such a sentence is made by law indispensable to the execution of it has in this case given the required sanction.

Quite recently E. M. Yerger of Mississippi has been arraigned before a Military Commission in that State upon a charge of murder & the trial is now proceeding.

Application has been made in behalf of Yerger to Mr. Justice Swayne, who you remember was assigned by an order made last term to that Circuit in addition to his own regular Circuit for a writ of habeas corpus; but he has declined to allow the writ, expressing however to the gentlemen who made the application his perfect willingness that the application should be made to me & granted or denied according to my views of the law.

An application has been made to me accordingly; and under the circumstances I have no doubt of my duty, if I have the power. I find no instance in which a Justice of the Supreme Court has ever allowed a writ of habeas corpus to bring before him a person imprisoned in any district not included in the Circuit to which he was allotted. Has or has not a Justice of the Supreme Court power to allow the writ for that purpose?

The gentleman Judge Fisher of Mississippi who represents Mr. Yerger brings me an opinion of Mr. [Philip] Phillips of Washington, in which Mr. [James M.] Carlisle concurs, affirming the power.[25]

This opinion puts the power upon the ground that the constitutional privilege is universal & that the grant of the power to issue the writ to "either of the Justices of the Supreme Court as well as judges of the District Courts" is without limitation in the [Judiciary] act of 1789.[26] It puts the supposition that the laws providing for allotment to Circuits may be repealed & the Justices of the Supreme Court relieved of all Circuit Court duty, & asks would such repeal affect the power to issue writs of habeas corpus? It quotes the grant of jurisdiction in the act of Feb. 5, 1867 "that the several Courts of the United States and the several justices and judges of such Courts within their jurisdictions, in addition to the powers already conferred by law shall have power to grant writs of habeas corpus in all cases where a person may be restrained of his liberty in violation of the Constitution or any treaty or law of the United States,"[27] and it interprets the description "within their respective jurisdictions" as applicable only to the "Courts"; and infers that as the jurisdiction of the Supreme Court is coextensive with the Union the power of the Justices to issue writs of Habeas Corpus must have the same extent.

---

[25] The authority of a Justice to send the writ outside his circuit was also sustained in an opinion of June 21 rendered to Fisher by Robert J. Walker. On Walker, see supra, ch. 6, n. 228, pp. 378–91.

[26] Supra, p. 441.

[27] Supra, p. 448.

As I desire your judgment entirely irrespective of my own I merely state the question & what has been urged upon me, & beg your counsel.

With the greatest respect & esteem

Most Sincerely yours
S. P. Chase.

Such was the retained draft of letters "sent to Judges Nelson & Clifford June 22, 69, directed respectively to New York & Boston with request to P.M. to forward." (A Justice must attend to a mass of business while moving about during the summer, such as arranging for hearings in chambers; he looked to the postmasters to forward mail to the appropriate point.)

The authors of the opinions summarized by Chase should be identified: over many years they were trusted counsellors at the bar of the Court. The career of Philip Phillips (1807–84)[28] included these points: youth in South Carolina, where in the convention of 1832 he opposed nullification; removal to Mobile, and one term (1853–55) in the House of Representatives; thereafter practice in Washington, interrupted by a Southern sojourn from 1861 until the *Garland* decision in 1867. A series of articles he contributed to the *National Intelligencer* helped to bring about the establishment of the Court of Claims in 1855. His *Statutory Jurisdiction and Practice of the Supreme Court* ran through several editions. In 1876 he could record that for some years he had had cases in the Court "to a greater number, the Clerk informs me, than any lawyer has ever had."[29] In memorial proceedings, Senator L. Q. C. Lamar remarked that "a peculiar personal relation seemed to have grown up" between this counsellor and the members of the Court. Chief Justice Waite, in response to resolutions, noted "the candid courage of clear convictions."[30]

James Mandeville Carlisle (1814–77), already mentioned, was, in Justice Miller's characterization, "at once the most accomplished lawyer and cultivated warm hearted gentleman in Washington."[31] After preparing for the District of Columbia bar under the casual guidance of the great William Wirt—as had Chase—Carlisle had climbed to preeminence both in the local courts and at the Supreme Court bar. Over the years he enjoyed an intimate association with the Justices in that

---

[28] Supra, p. 448.
[29] "A Summary of the Principal Events of My Life," written in June 1876. Copy in Ms. Div., L.C. Whatever an exact count might show, certainly his practice was extensive, with much business from the South.

[30] *Proceedings of the Bar . . . on the Death of Philip Phillips* (1884).
[31] Supra, pp. 479–80; Letter of July 30, 1869, in Charles Fairman, *Mr. Justice Miller*, 112.

era when practitioners and judges went calling and dining at one another's homes.[32]

With this introduction one can appreciate the good understanding implicit in the following letter from Carlisle to Chase:

436 D Street
Washington
21 June 1869

My dear Mr. Chief Justice

Premising that I am not, in any professional sense, counsel for Mr. Yerger,[33] I write to add, informally, a remark or two to an opinion of mine, appended to one of Mr. Phillips, which Judge Fisher will exhibit to you. During the war—I think in *1861*, Judge Wayne, on a petition presented by the late Mr. R. S. Coxe, awarded a Hab. Corp, in the case of an enlisted man, and made it returnable before him, at the Supreme Court Room, at the Capitol here, on a convenient day—and on the return of the writ it was argued before him, for both sides, and *jurisdiction* was not questioned—under the act of 1789.

If you think the Petition makes a proper case (as it seems to me) there can be no difficulty in making the writ returnable in the same manner, or at *first Monday in October*—when you would have the advantage of conferring with your brethren if you desired it—and there could be no impropriety in referring to such conference in the opinion.

I am sure you will pardon these suggestions in favour of the motive which prompts them, even if they are superfluous, or indiscreet.

With great respect & warm regard

J M Carlisle

Mr. Ch. J. Chase

JUSTICE WAYNE IN THE UNREPORTED CASE OF STEVENS

THE CASE IN WHICH JUSTICE WAYNE granted the writ, notwithstanding that the restraint occurred outside his proper circuit, was

---

[32] It had been Carlisle's custom to visit Taney every Sunday evening, according to the "Recollections" of William A. Maury, sometime Assistant Attorney General—a typewritten account of 121 + 2 pages, examined in the office of the late John Spalding Flannery in 1936. Justice Davis in his letters and Orville H. Browning in his *Diary* record attending dinners for the Justices and others at Carlisle's home. *Diary of Orville Hickman Browning* (Springfield: Illinois State Historical Library, vol. I [1850–64], Pease and Randall, eds.; vol. II [1865–81], Randall, ed., 1933).

[33] At that time he had merely given an opinion to Judge Fisher on the jurisdiction of an individual Justice. Subsequently he did become counsel.

Ex parte Edward A. Stevens—recorded in a thick file which Wayne deposited in the Clerk's Office, and which is now preserved in the National Archives.[34]

Stevens was a soldier in the 1st Minnesota Infantry, a regiment mustered into the service on April 29, 1861, for a term of three months. He participated in the battle at Bull Run on July 21 (where the 1st Minnesota suffered the highest losses of any regiment engaged).[35] Along with others, he demanded—and was refused—release when the three months had expired. On his behalf, Richard S. Coxe (1792–1865), a distinguished practitioner experienced in habeas corpus,[36] applied to Justice Wayne. The writ issued, and Colonel Willis A. Gorman, the regimental commander, made return that the petitioner, along with the entire regiment, had subsequently volunteered and been mustered for three years or the duration of the war. Counsel for the Government was Edwin M. Stanton, who five months later became Secretary of War.

Justice Wayne heard argument in the Supreme Court chamber on August 23 and 24, at the conclusion of which he discharged the writ and remanded the petitioner to military duty. Subsequently he filed an opinion.[37]

Carlisle found the record, and notified the Chief Justice in a letter of June 22:

> I have been, this morning, at the Clerk's office, and have examined the case to which I referred in my hasty note of yesterday—of which I found a complete and formal record, from the petition to the final order remanding petitioner—including an attachment by which Col. Gorman was brought before the judge, and purged himself of the supposed contempt.[38] The case is entitled "Ex parte

---

[34] Record Group No. 267, Records of the Supreme Court, Habeas Corpus Cases heard at Chambers.

[35] Boatner, *Civil War Dictionary*, 553 (1959).

[36] He had appeared for petitioner in the leading cases of *Ex parte* Watkins, 3 Pet. 193 (1830), against Berrien, Atty. Gen.; *Ex parte* Watkins, 7 Pet. 568 (1833), against Taney, Atty. Gen.; and *In re* Metzger, 5 How. 176 (1847), against Clifford, Atty. Gen.

[37] There had been some disregard of departmental regulations, and of the Articles of War prescribed by Congress. "Has the Government a right to hold volunteers for three years who have not been enlisted in accordance with the method pre-

scribed in the Army Regulations?"—thus Stevens stated the question, in a letter to the editor of the *Washington Star*, to correct an inaccurate report of the case. He added that he had applied for the writ "at the instance of nearly all the members of the regiment."

Justice Wayne held that compliance in these respects was "not essential to the validity of the contract of enlistment where there had been an actual mustering into the service of the U.S. and service rendered by the soldier under it . . . ."

[38] Issued on August 10, the writ set noon on the fourteenth as the time when return should be made. Gorman's affidavit showed that it was served on him on the thirteenth, about

Edward A Stevens" Mr Edwin M Stanton appeared for Col Gorman (& the War Department generally)—& Mr. R. S. Coxe for the Petitioner. It appears by the record that the Petitioner was with his regiment at Edwards' Ferry, in Maryland, when the writ was awarded —Col Gorman was then in command. The jurisdiction was not questioned by Mr Stanton and the case was dismissed on its merits, upon proof controverting the matter set up in the petition.

In the event of your determining to award the writ in this case, I have thought that the order made by Judge Wayne, and upon which the proceeding was conducted to the end, might be useful to you, & Mr Middleton [Clerk of the Supreme Court] at my request has had a copy made, which is enclosed herewith. The record, as I said, is fully made out, & is preserved in the files of the office, in a separate package, stitched together after the fashion of the transcripts from the lower courts—with Judge Wayne's opinion at length, upon the merits, on the proofs taken before him. The final order was made on the 22' Aug I think. . . .

On June 23 Chase advised Nelson and Clifford of this information about Wayne's action.

It is not surprising that Stanton had made no contest over jurisdiction. The Government felt anxiety on account of the wide implication of the *Stevens* case, and doubtless counted it good fortune to have a hearing before a judge so disinclined to captiousness as Justice Wayne.[39]

UNCERTAINTY REMAINS

THE CHIEF JUSTICE saw objections to his granting the writ in Yerger's case, as Carlisle urged so confidently. Without denying the application, he advised Judge Fisher to go back to Mississippi and apply to the Circuit Court, whose jurisdiction was free from doubt. Then Chase wrote to District Judge Hill to explain his thoughts:

3 P.M., at the place where he was on duty with his regiment, forty miles from Washington; that he hastened to Washington as soon as duty permitted, arriving on the evening of the fourteenth after the attachment had been ordered.

Gorman was in civil life a lawyer, sometime Democratic Congressman from Indiana, and Territorial Governor of Minnesota."

[39] A. A. Lawrence, in his *James*

Moore Wayne, Southern Unionist, (Chapel Hill: University of North Carolina Press, 1943), 187, quotes the *Boston Advertiser*, as reprinted in the *National Intelligencer* of September 18, 1861: this "exile from home" had "honestly and frankly met a case which, had he chosen, might have given him an opportunity for cavilling at and embarrassing the proceedings of the Government."

Richmond, Va. June 22, 1869.

My dear Judge,

An application has been made to me on behalf of E. M. Yerger for a habeas corpus on the ground that he has been arrested by military authority & is now held for trial before a Military Commission.

I have advised that the application should be made to the Circuit Court or to you as District Judge authorized to hold the Circuit Court and I have no doubt that [it] is your duty to allow the writ. Your authority to do so under the law cannot be questioned: and your duty is a necessary inference from your authority.

When the writ is returned you can discharge or remand as you think the law requires. On this point I do not wish to make any suggestion.

If you think it your duty to discharge there will be an end of the case for I do not think that the military authorities will disregard a judicial decision. If on the other hand you think it your duty to remand an application can be made for a writ of certiorari with habeas corpus under the act of 1789, & a decision of the Supreme Court upon the legality of the imprisonment can be had.[40]

I shall still hold the application to me under consideration. My chief reason for not allowing the writ immediately is a doubt as to my power to take jurisdiction in habeas corpus outside of the limits of my Circuit. If the imprisonment were within my Circuit I should allow the writ without hesitation: though I should still prefer an allowance by a Circuit Court or by a Judge having authority to hold a Circuit Court because the judgment in that case if against the prisoner could certainly be revised in the Supreme Court of the United States, while this is, perhaps, not so certain as to a decision of a Supreme Court Judge.[41]

Faithfully your friend
S. P. Chase

Hon R. A. Hill
   U.S. District Judge Dis of Mississippi
   Oxford Mi.

The Chief Justice received answers from his brethren at their respective homes. First Justice Nelson's:

Cooperstown [N.Y.] June 28/69

My dear Ch Justice,

I answered yours of the 22 and 23d inst. yesterday and directed it to Washington.

But, afterwards, seeing that yours was dated at Richmond, it

---

[40] As had been said in the dictum at the end of the *McCardle* opinion. Supra, p. 493.

[41] See *In re* Metzger, 5 How. 176 (1847), supra, p. 445.

may be you expect the letter there: and hence write you of the fact.

My conclusions were 1—That the power conferred by the 14 §[42] was unrestricted, and as ample as respects the Justices as in respect to the Sup. Ct. which it is conceded is coextensive with the Union.

2d That no other Act of Congress, so far as I know or can find, imposes any restriction. . . .

3. The power conferred by the 14 § being unlimited, unless some subsequent reservation can be shewn, it follows that it exists coextensive with the Union.

Yours truly
S. Nelson

Clifford wrote with characteristic fullness:

Portland. July 6 1869

Dear Sir—

I closed my court at Providence R.I. on the 24th of June and went directly into N.H. to visit a sick sister and did not return till Saturday last [July 3] which is the reason that your letters have not received earlier attention. Since that time I have carefully considered the question whether a justice of the Supreme Court has the power to grant the writ of *Habeas Corpus* to bring a person before him who is imprisoned under federal authority out of the circuit to which he is allotted.

My opinion is that the Chief Justice and the Associate Justices of the Supreme Court under the Constitution and laws of Congress are authorized to act in three characters or capacities.

1 as a Supreme Court

2 as separate justices of that Court

3 as Circuit Judges

1 they cannot act as Supreme Court except when they are in session as such

2 They may grant writs of error to the State courts and issue writs of *Habeas Corpus* to relieve from federal imprisonment &c as separate justices, and their authority in that behalf is coextensive with the Union.

It includes *Territories* as well as States and is not affected by any allotment

3 They cannot do any act as Circuit Judges out of their circuits.

Governed by these propositions my conclusion is that you as Chief Justice of the Supreme Court (not as Circuit Judge) may issue the writ in the case mentioned in your letter.

Judge Wayne's case is distinctly in point and you will find a case where Judge Campbell granted a writ of error to a State court

---

[42] Quoted supra, pp. 441–42.

out of his circuit—my recollection is that it was to the Supreme Court of Tennessee.

    I regret the delay in answering your letter but it was unavoidable

Very Respectfully

Your Obt. Servant

Nathan Clifford

P S Mr. Middleton [the Clerk] will find the Tennessee case I think.

If Yerger's counsel had been content to apply to the Circuit Court they would have gone there in the first place. It would be held by District Judge Hill, who had denied relief to McCardle, and thereafter had held his ground although "strongly pressed" in other cases.[43] Certainly he would do no better for Yerger. And after that—even counting upon the Supreme Court to stick to its assertion at the end of the *McCardle* opinion—might not a sentence by the military commission be approved and executed before the Court could act? Might not Congress, when it met in December, cut off jurisdiction here as it had in *McCardle*?

RENEWED APPLICATION TO THE CHIEF JUSTICE

IT WAS DECIDED TO PRESS ANEW the application pending before the Chief Justice. On July 12 Chase set the matter for hearing on July 14, at the Supreme Court chamber; notice was given to the Attorney General.

At the appointed hour, 11 o'clock on that summer day, the Supreme Court chamber was "intolerably hot" and the Chief Justice expected to hold the hearing in less discomfort in the conference room; that proved impracticable because "a large number of auditors were present, including nearly all the prominent members of the bar of the District of Columbia." This one learns from the *Baltimore Sun*, which carried a rather full report.[44]

---

[43] Judge Hill had written on August 16, 1868, to Chase: "It has been repeatedly stated and urged that the Supreme Court have made up the decision in the McCardle case reversing the decision made by the Circuit Court, and broadly holding the Acts of Congress to be unconstitutional, and only withheld the opinion on account of the pressure of time." (This is another illustration of how persistently Southerners looked to the Supreme Court to make their troubles go away.)

Hill sought, as he wrote in this letter, "to convince the public mind, that whilst the Government demanded obedience to its laws, it desired the oppression of none. So far as party politics are concerned I have abstained from any active participation . . . ."

Chase Papers, Hist. Soc. of Pa.

[44] July 13, 1869. Substantially the same account appeared in the *Milwaukee Evening Wisconsin* of July 15, and the *Louisville Courier-Journal* of July 16, and presumably elsewhere.

Philip Phillips, opening, advanced the views he and Carlisle had expressed in their opinion.[45] He relied on Justice Wayne's action in the *Stevens* case.

Attorney General Hoar replied, earnestly and forthrightly. Conscientiously he saw it as his duty to fend off any judicial interference with the enforcement of the Reconstruction Act; throughout the Yerger litigation he was skillful in his strategy to avert such an outcome. He confessed "some embarrassment" to imagine "by what right, or under what duty, he appeared"—implying that the Chief Justice should feel a like embarrassment in supposing that he had any power in the premises. Hoar attended out of "his personal and official respect for the tribunal of which his Honor was the head and presiding officer." He argued that

> The Stat. of 1867 only confers the power on the judges "within their respective jurisdictions." If the 14 sect. of the Stat. of 1789 is not construed with the same limitations, then it has no limitation, and is literally applicable to every case of domestic restraint, the ordinary cases of husband and wife, parent and child, master and servant, guardian and ward, insane persons and the like, all over the Union, and the Chief Justice of the U.S. can be called on in his vacation to settle such questions by bringing them all to Washington [To produce this dilemma, Hoar was making the worst out of the imprecision of Section 14 and the absence of any decision by the Supreme Court rejecting his startling alternative.[46]] We admit the Stat of 1867 gives power to issue the writ, because the imprisonment is alleged to be in violation of the Constitution; but that only allows it to [be] issued in the districts and circuits respectively by the judges having judicial functions therein.[47]

On the merits, the Attorney General repeated the views expressed in his opinion of May 31 in the matter of *Weaver*.[48] "Sixteen hundred murders in Texas, stimulated by vindictive and rebellious hate," showed that peace had not yet been reestablished.

Carlisle, in turn, deplored the "spirit of disputation" in the Attorney General's argument. He maintained that the Reconstruction Act was unconstitutional; "it was a strange way to fit the people for republican government by putting them under the heel of military authority."

The hearing continued for four hours.

---

[45] Supra, p. 567.
[46] In 1890, *In re* Burrus, 136 U.S. 586, 593–94, the Court said: "The whole subject of domestic relations of husband and wife, parent and child, belongs to the laws of the States and not to the laws of the United States."
[47] Supra, p. 448.
[48] Supra, pp. 561–63.

Evidently the Chief Justice decided to issue the writ, directing the military authorities to produce the prisoner "on Saturday, the 9th of October, at the Supreme Court Room in the Capitol of the United States at the City of Washington, then and there to abide by, and perform whatever may be determined in that behalf by me, as Chief Justice, or by any Associate Justice of said Supreme Court of the United States." Among his papers is an order to that effect, prepared for his signature.[49] Inasmuch as the Supreme Court would convene on the first Monday in October for an adjourned session, the Chief Justice would have an opportunity to confer with his brethren.

STIPULATION OF COUNSEL

ACTION BY THE CHIEF JUSTICE was superseded, however, by an agreement on July 16 between the Attorney General and Messrs. Carlisle and Phillips:

> it is hereby stipulated, the Chief Justice approving, that the present proceedings be suspended without prejudice to the petitioner, and that an application in the mean time may be made in his behalf to the Circuit Court of the U S for the Mississippi District or the District Judge holding said Court for a writ of Habeas Corpus in the premises with a view that the question of the petitioner's right to the same may be brought before the Supreme Court of the U.S.

The Attorney General had authority to say that pending the outcome of this appeal, no sentence of the military commission would be executed.[50]

It was implicit in the agreement that without doubt the Circuit Court would deny the application.

(One may be disposed to ask, if it seemed certain that the case would reach the Supreme Court anyway, why must counsel go through the form of touching base in the Circuit Court? But surely the mere circumstance that one litigant's case patently merits the attention of the Supreme Court does not waive the jurisdictional requirements fixed by

---

[49] There are three relevant documents. First, in his own hand, is an opinion beginning with a decision to grant the writ, and setting out the Attorney General's objections; there the writing stops. Next there is a fair copy of the above, with amendments inserted in Chase's hand. Third, there is an order, drawn by the same copyist, to direct the production of the prisoner. Chase Papers, Hist. Soc. of Pa.

[50] Chase Papers, Hist. Soc. of Pa.; set out in *Trial of E. M. Yerger, before a Military Commission . . .*, at 120.

Congress and applicable to litigants generally.[51] Congress may—and by a statute of 1925 did—repose in the Court a large discretion to select the cases that deserve its consideration; but it is not for the Court to assume such a power without regard to law.)

Accordingly application was made to the Circuit Court at Jackson. On July 20 Judge Hill granted the writ. What followed was in routine, reduced, in this case, to formal acts. On July 22 the prisoner was brought under guard to the courthouse door, and then presented in court. The court ordered the Marshal to take custody. Judge William Yerger read the petition; the Judge Advocate made return; the case was submitted without argument; Judge Hill promptly held that the return showed sufficient cause, and ordered that the prisoner be turned back to the military custody.[52]

Now the appellate jurisdiction of the Supreme Court could be invoked. And if the Attorney General contended (as he would) for Justice Curtis' view in the *Kaine* case—that the inferior court's refusal to discharge one held by some other authority was *not* such "cause of commitment" as the Supreme Court was authorized by the Judiciary Act to review[53]—counsel would reply: Yerger was taken into custody of the court; when the court remanded him, its decree became the "cause of commitment."

On October 8, 1869, Yerger's counsel docketed in the Supreme Court a petition for habeas corpus aided by certiorari.

A COMPANION CASE: *EX PARTE BROWN*

AT THIS POINT a case from Texas entered into the stream of events. Filed on the same day was a like petition on behalf of Benjamin Brown and six others, held for trial by military commission on a charge of the murder of a Dr. Maxwell. In the Circuit Court for the Western District of that State, Judge Thomas H. Duval[54] had denied habeas

---

[51] As is illustrated in *Ex parte Quirin*, 317 U.S. 1 (1942), the wartime "Saboteurs' Case," where members of the German armed forces secretly passed through the defense lines of the United States and, discarding their uniforms, set out to commit hostile acts. They were brought to trial before a military commission appointed by the President, on charges of unlawful belligerency. The District Court for the District of Columbia, after a hearing, denied applications for leave to file petitions for habeas corpus; appeal was taken to the Court of Appeals; and the Supreme Court, in proceedings on certiorari in accordance with the Judicial Code, affirmed the orders of the District Court.

[52] Transcript of Record, of 6 pages; *Jackson Weekly Clarion*, July 29, 1869.

[53] Supra, p. 446.

[54] Appointed in 1857, he remained loyal to the Union, and at the close of hostilities reopened his court.

corpus on August 17, 1869. Counsel had then applied to the Chief Justice, whom he found in New England. On September 6 Chase made an order: he noted that there was "no good reason to apprehend that the sentence of the Military Commission," if against any of the petitioners, would be executed "until the questions arising upon this Petition shall have been determined by the Supreme Court of the United States" either in the *Yerger* case or upon a similar application to review the denial by the Circuit Court for Western Texas; accordingly he postponed action "until the second Monday of October next at chambers in the City of Washington...."[55]

CRITICISM BY THE PRESS

THE CHIEF JUSTICE, the Attorney General, and counsel had all been acting with fidelity to their respective duties. Novel questions of jurisdiction, the constitutionality of a provision of the Reconstruction Act, and human life were all involved. The best way had been found to bring this matter before the full Bench, and in the meantime to preclude the execution of a sentence.

But newspapers can make short work of legal complexities. The *Baltimore Sun*'s correspondent, "Data," reported "much disappointment" when the Chief Justice failed to decide the Yerger case: "the transfer of the matter to the Supreme Court is considered as shirking the very evident duty . . . to decide the vitally important legal questions, which necessarily affect political questions of great moment." On the merits of Yerger's case, he continued, "there is no variance of opinion among sound, unbiased lawyers"—it would be murder if he were executed by sentence of a military commission.[56] The "political questions" dependent upon the outcome of Yerger's case doubtless existed in the yearning of Southern diehards and Democratic leaders; certainly neither Congress (not then in session) nor President Grant was in any hurry to have a judicial decision.

---

[55] This order in Chase's hand, and other papers in *Ex parte* Brown *et al.*, are in Record Group No. 267 at the National Archives—Records of the Supreme Court, Habeas Corpus Cases heard at Chambers.

The order of the Chief Justice was reported to the press in a dispatch of September 7 from Norwich, Connecticut. *Atlanta Constitution,* September 9, 1869. Also in a dispatch of September 8 from Washington. *Baltimore Sun,* September 9.

Local counsel, D. U. Barziza, had called on Attorney General Hoar, who, while entering into no agreement, "thought there would be no danger until the meeting of the Supreme Court"; "President Grant also stated to me that the Yerger case was to be a precedent for similar cases." Statement filed Sept. 7 with the Petition for Habeas Corpus in the Supreme Court. Case File, National Archives.

[56] July 17, 1869.

XII: Ex parte Yerger

This loose comment was repeated in the *Richmond Dispatch*,[57] and perhaps elsewhere; one item of this sort might travel far.

The *Louisville Courier-Journal* renewed its taunt of judicial cowardice.[58] It said that it had expected all along that Chase would fail in *Yerger*, just as he had failed in *McCardle*; "We don't think that he has the courage to confront Congress squarely in the discharge of his functions. But, if he means to be a candidate for the Presidency, he had better have all sorts of courage." If the Chief Justice would not exercise jurisdiction, the editorial continued, "might not the whole Supreme Court be persuaded to exercise it? But probably the question is vain, for, if Grant means to have Yerger hung, he will probably order the ugly job dispatched without awaiting the action of the court." In that event, "the comparative insignificance" of Yerger's murder of Major Crane "would be quite lost in the tremendousness" of murder by the Government.[59]

Yerger's counsel had an informative and chastening talk with "Data," whereupon he sent a further dispatch to censure the report he himself had originated. Now he said that "the position of Chief Justice Chase" had been "misstated in nearly every instance" in the press: in truth he had not been unwilling to act; rather, the opposing counsel on their own initiative had agreed that it was wiser to have Yerger's case "brought up in the regular form from the Mississippi Circuit . . . ." "Those who charge Judge Chase with a disposition to shirk the decision do him injustice."[60] That, of course, did not undo the mischief.

The *Chicago Tribune*—unreasoning in its Radicalism—attacked the Chief Justice from the opposite quarter. In a captious editorial on "Mr. Chase's Mysterious 'Figuring' "[61] it supposed that he had intended to seize the occasion to discharge Yerger, and to decide that military trials were illegal and the Reconstruction Acts unconstitutional —hoping thereby to win Democratic and Conservative Republican support for the Presidency in 1872. A decision "that carpet-baggers and Northern officials in Southern States have no rights which the chivalry are bound to respect, would raise a howl of demoniac exultation from the whole rebel, Democratic and Copperhead crew." So apprehensive were the President and the Attorney General that "they humbly solicited . . . a delay and submission of the question to the full bench . . . , and obtained it only by stipulating" that in the meantime no sentence would be executed.

---

[57] July 19.
[58] Supra, p. 479.
[59] July 20.
[60] *Baltimore Sun*, July 22.

[61] Aug. 23, 1869, inspired by an alarming story from the Washington correspondent of the *Cincinnati Gazette* (Republican).

579

AN ANTICIPATED COLLISION BETWEEN COURT
AND CONGRESS: DUTY OF THE EXECUTIVE

THE YERGER BATTLE would be renewed when the Supreme Court met in adjourned session in October. Hoar looked forward with apprehension, as is shown by his letter of September 24 to Senator Sumner, written upon returning to Washington from his home at Concord, Massachusetts:

> I wanted very much to have a talk with you about the duty of the Executive in case the Supreme Court attempts to interfere with the military government of the unreconstructed States by Habeas Corpus, on which I have some pretty decided views:—but found no opportunity. I wish you would give me your ideas on the subject, both as to substance & form. . . .[62]

Since March 4 the Executive had been in accord with the Congress on the basic issue. What now would be "the duty of the Executive in case the Supreme Court attempts to interfere . . ."; what ought the Executive to do if the Court adjudged to be unlawful that which Congress had commanded to be done, when in the view of the Executive, Congress had acted *intra* and the Court had gone *ultra vires*? Hoar's letter to Sumner shows that, in his view, submission to the Court was not obviously the right answer.

This would not be the ordinary situation where the Court, in the performance of an admitted function, has found the action of another branch to be invalid. The instant problem had to do with the reconstruction of the Union, an unprecedented matter, over which—in the view of Congress and the Executive—Congress had primary authority: it would be the duty of the Judiciary to dispose of any litigation (if properly brought before it) upon the basis of such determination as Congress had made. Yet there was reason to apprehend that the Court, rejecting that view, would pronounce that what Congress had done was unconstitutional. Not only was the occasion unprecedented—so too was the cause to be defended. While the Fourteenth Amendment had been proclaimed to be in force in July 1868, and the adoption of the Fifteenth was in sight by the close of 1869, even so an eleventh-hour decision condemning the Reconstruction Act would brand with illegitimacy all that had been accomplished. The possible consequences—legal, political, and moral—were incalculable; they might have proved catastrophic.

---

[62] Sumner Papers, Harvard Univ. L.

XII: Ex parte Yerger

One may reflect, how passing strange if Yerger's malevolent blow —so representative of that wanton violence long condoned in the South[63] which the framers of the Fourteenth Amendment aspired somehow to exorcise—chanced at the last moment to be the means of unsettling the whole work of Reconstruction!

If such a judgment were pronounced by the Court, the Executive would need already to have reached a deliberate conclusion whether it was going to bow to the Court or stand with the Congress.

Very evidently, however, the Attorney General ought, if he properly could, to prevent that situation from arising. In the account that follows one will observe how he bent his efforts to that end. Fortunately, opposing counsel had a fine sense of what was due to the country and the Court, as well as of fidelity to client. The duties of all participants, rightly understood, could be—and were—reconciled.

On October 4, 1869, the Court met in adjourned session. On Friday the eighth, Carlisle and Phillips moved for leave to file for habeas corpus and certiorari. (At the same time, a like motion on behalf of *Brown et al.* in Texas was made by William W. Boyce, sometime Representative from South Carolina in the federal and then in the Confederate Congress, now practicing in Washington.[64]) "Upon the suggestion of the Attorney General," the Court set *Ex parte Yerger* down for argument on the question of the Court's jurisdiction. (*Ex parte Brown* was ordered to be passed over, to abide the decision in *Yerger.*) It was appropriate that jurisdiction be settled in advance.

EX PARTE YERGER: THE COURT SUSTAINS ITS JURISDICTION

AT THE HEARING ON OCTOBER 15, the Attorney General argued: for this Court to address the writ to the military commander would be an exercise of *original* jurisdiction (inconsistent with Article III of the

---

[63] The *Jackson Clarion* for Saturday, April 18, 1868—a little more than a year before Crane was stabbed to death—carried the following items in a single column:

Divine services to-morrow in all of our city churches.

— * —

The gunsmithing business has been unusually brisk, in Jackson, this week.

— * —

The Fighting Week.—This may be appropriately termed the fighting week in the history of Jackson.

— * —

SABBATH SCHOOL NOTICE.— Teachers and scholars of the several Sabbath Schools to meet to-morrow at 5 to practice hymns for approaching Sabbath School Celebration.

[64] Supra, p. 368.

Constitution[65]); it would not be an exercise of appellate jurisdiction over the Circuit Court, since that court "simply . . . left [Yerger] where it found him."[66] (Here the Attorney General was contending for the view Justice Curtis, dissenting, had maintained, *In re Kaine*, in 1852.[67]) And "this court cannot exercise any appellate control . . . over the military commission . . . ."[68] Moreover, the Attorney General argued, when the Act of March 27, 1868, repealed so much of the Act of February 5, 1867, as gave an appeal to the Supreme Court where the detention was alleged to be in violation of the Constitution, etc., it took away the Court's entire power in that field. "It did not mean merely to substitute a cumbrous and inconvenient remedy [under the Judiciary Act of 1789] for a direct and simple one." Here he was saying that the dictum at the close of *McCardle* was wrong.

The Chief Justice delivered the Court's opinion on Monday, October 25, ten days after argument. (Presumably the Justices agreed upon the decision at the earliest Saturday conference, and approved the opinion at the next. After *Dugan and Hogan*,[69] *Martin and Gill*,[70] *Arnold and Spangler*,[71] as well as *McCardle*, the subject must have been very familiar.) The objections were all brushed aside. "The great and leading intent of the Constitution and the law" in the matter of habeas corpus was "that every citizen may be protected by judicial action from unlawful imprisonment." "We regard as established upon principle and authority that the appellate jurisdiction by habeas corpus extends to all cases of commitment by the judicial authority of the United States, not within any exception made by Congress." (That was broad enough to cover the controverted matter of review of a denial of the writ by an individual Justice or Judge.)

> . . . It is unimportant in what custody the prisoner may be, if it is a custody to which he has been remanded by the order of an inferior court of the United States. . . .
>
> We are obliged to hold, therefore, that in all cases where a Circuit Court of the United States has, in the exercise of its original jurisdiction, caused a prisoner to be brought before it, and has,

---

[65] Supra, pp. 442-43.

[66] 8 Wall. 92-93, and nine-page memorandum, Points of the Attorney General.

[67] Supra, p. 446.

[68] This was in accord with what the Court had decided in *Ex parte Vallandigham*, 1 Wall. 243 (1864), supra, p. 491n., and with what was held in *In re* Vidal, 179 U.S. 126 (1900)— that military tribunals are not in-

ferior courts that come under the appellate review of the Supreme Court. Phillips had sustained a contrary view in arguing *Arnold and Spangler*, on which no decision had been made because the question became moot. Supra, p. 492.

[69] Supra, pp. 55-58.

[70] Supra, pp. 471-72, 474, 477.

[71] Supra, pp. 488-92.

after inquiring into the cause of detention, remanded him to the custody from which he was taken, this court, in the exercise of its appellate jurisdiction, may, by the writ of habeas corpus, aided by the writ of certiorari, revise the decision of the Circuit Court, and if it be found unwarranted by law, relieve the prisoner from the unlawful restraint to which he has been remanded.

As to the effect of the repealing statute of 1868, the Court now adjudged that its old power as granted by the Judiciary Act of 1789 could still be exercised.

Justice Miller dissented. While he filed no opinion, it seems likely that he agreed with the Attorney General's contention as to the effect of the repeal of 1868.

The Court, freeing itself from the perplexities that had arisen out of the obscure drafting of Section 14,[72] read the statute in the light of the Constitution, and took the eminently sensible view expressed in the language quoted above. Whether the inferior federal court had itself ordered the commitment, or had refused to interfere with imprisonment by some other authority, in either situation the Supreme Court had appellate jurisdiction.[73]

The power established in Ex parte Yerger remained the basis on which the Court was able to act until, in 1885, Congress restored the "appeal" it had authorized in 1867 and taken away in 1868.[74] In the meantime, it was thanks to the solution in Yerger that the Court was able to make some memorable decisions in defense of civil rights.[75]

---

[72] Supra, pp. 446–47.

[73] Ex parte Yerger, 8 Wall. 85.
Learned comment has noted that here the Court took a step in advance. Hart and Wechsler, The Federal Courts and the Federal System (Brooklyn: Foundation Press, 1953), 282; Oaks, "The 'Original' Writ of Habeas Corpus in the Supreme Court," Supreme Court Review 1962, 153, 163. This is not surprising. There would have been few occasions of the latter sort prior to the Civil War. That the Court would not have been disposed to interfere with the imprisonment of soldiers and sailors held pursuant to the statutory system of military justice is indicated by Dynes v. Hoover, 20 How. 65 (1858), an action for false imprisonment, where Carlisle had appeared unsuccessfully against Attorney General Cushing.

If Ex parte Dugan and Hogan, instituted in 1865, had come to judgment, that would have called upon the Court to consider its power to review in habeas corpus where the inferior court had denied relief to prisoners held by order of the Secretary of War.

[74] Act of Mar. 3, 1885, 23 Stat. 437. "From the final decision in such circuit court an appeal may be taken to the Supreme Court in the cases described in [Sec. 763 Rev. Stats.]"— that is, in habeas corpus where it was alleged that the restraint was in violation of the Constitution, a law, or a treaty of the United States.

[75] Notably in Ex parte Virginia, 100 U.S. 339 (1880); Ex parte Siebold, 100 U.S. 371 (1880); Ex parte Clarke, 100 U.S. 399 (1880); and Ex parte Yarbrough, 110 U.S. 651 (1884).

A DECISION ON THE MERITS IS AVOIDED

EACH SIDE NOW SURVEYED ITS POSITION. What follows is an elaboration upon conjecture.

For the Government, at this late date there was no compelling reason to fight a battle over *Yerger* and *Brown*. The program of Congressional Reconstruction was all but completed, and the Fourteenth Amendment was secure. In pursuance of the Act of April 10, Virginia had already adopted its constitution; in Texas and Mississippi, elections would be held on November 30. Before the Court could decide *Yerger* on the merits, there might well be no State to which the decision applied. There was no apprehension that another war of secession would ever arise—no need on that score to establish the Congressional power here at stake.

And on a candid estimate, a decision on *Yerger* would probably go against the Government; indeed in a substantial sense the Government could not possibly win. The Bench was at least as forbidding as it had appeared to Carpenter when arguing *McCardle* in March 1868.[76] Of the eight Justices, Nelson, Grier, Clifford, and Field must be counted as hostile. The Chief Justice in 1868 had scattered throughout the land his pronouncements that "Congress was . . . wrong . . . in the establishment of despotic military governments for the States and in authorizing military commissions for the trial of civilians in time of peace"[77]— although in performing his judicial duties he would "dismiss every thought which might incline the scale of judgment either way."[78] Since Justice Davis' dictum in *Milligan*, he must be reckoned as unfriendly. Even suppose for a moment that the Attorney General were to win as many as four of the Justices: a decision by an equal division would leave in force the Circuit Court's denial of relief—but that would be only a technical victory, actually a great moral defeat. Suppose the Court put the case over for reargument after a ninth Justice had come to the place recently created:[79] how vindictive it would have seemed to pursue these murderers after the Congressional regime was ended, when punishment would not longer serve to deter. And if, as was to be expected, the Government lost: that would impugn the new constitutional foundation, as well as the new Southern governments. Evidently the Government ought to settle out of court.

---

[76] Supra, pp. 453–54, 494.
[77] Letter to August Belmont, May 30. Jacob W. Schuckers, *The Life and Public Services of Salmon Portland Chase*, (New York: D. Appleton and Co., 1874), 584, 585.
[78] Letter to William B. Thomas, Mar. 10. Schuckers, *Chase*, 574–75; Warden, *Chase*, 680–81.
[79] Supra, pp. 487, 559–60.

Andrew Johnson.
(Library of Congress)

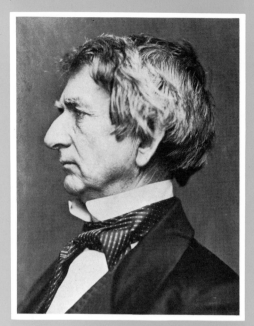

William H. Seward.
(Library of Congress)

Gideon Welles.
(Library of Congress)

Orville H. Browning.
(Library of Congress)

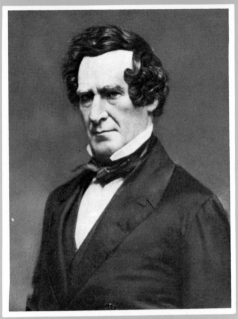

Jeremiah S. Black.
(Library of Congress)

Robert J. Walker.
(Library of Congress)

Benjamin R. Curtis.
(Library of Congress)

Henry Stanbery.
(Library of Congress)

Reverdy Johnson.
(Superior Court Room, Baltimore)

David Dudley Field.
(Library of Congress)

William M. Evarts.
(Library of Congress)

Benjamin F. Butler.
(Library of Congress)

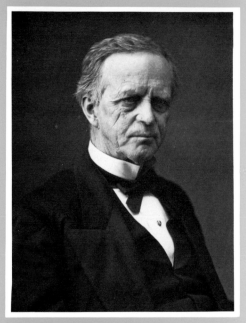

Lyman Trumbull.
(Library of Congress)

Edwin M. Stanton.
(G. A. F. Corporation)

James Speed.
(Library of Congress)

William L. Sharkey.
(U.S. Signal Corps)

William P. Fessenden.
(Library of Congress)

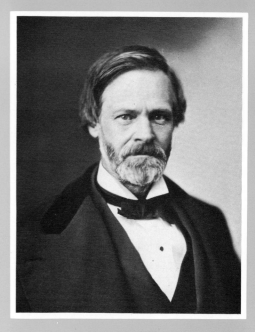

John Sherman.
(Library of Congress)

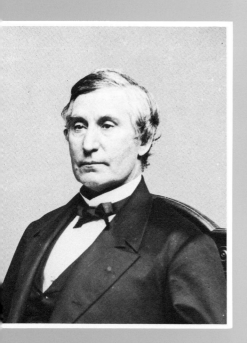

Jacob M. Howard.
(Library of Congress)

Matthew Hale Carpenter.
(Library of Congress)

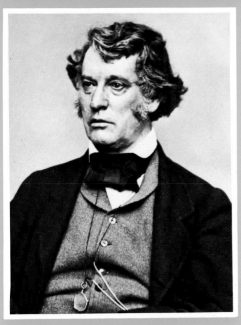

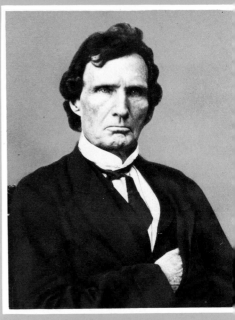

Charles Sumner.
(Library of Congress)

Thaddeus Stevens.
(Library of Congress)

John A. Bingham.
(U.S. Signal Corps)

Thomas A. Hendricks.
(U.S. Signal Corps)

Edward Bates.
(U.S. Signal Corps)

Montgomery Blair.
(Library of Congress)

Edgar Cowan.
(Library of Congress)

Augustus H. Garland.
(Library of Congress)

John A. Campbell.
(Library of Congress)

Amos T. Akerman.
(Library of Congress)

John B. Henderson.
(Library of Congress)

William M. Stewart.
(Library of Congress)

XII: Ex parte Yerger

It did not follow that because the Government could not win, Yerger could not lose. Carlisle and Phillips had been retained to rescue their client, not the Southern cause; it would have been imprudent to risk a battle when the Attorney General held open a path to safety.

Congress would convene in early December. If at that time the *Yerger* case held a serious menace, in the view of the Radicals, quite likely they would do something violent—hurtful to Yerger, to the Court, and to the country. Hoar as well as Carlisle and Phillips would deplore such an outcome.[80]

These considerations pointed to the propriety of a settlement whereby the *Yerger* case would not be brought to a hearing, and the prisoner would be surrendered for trial to the local authorities as soon as Mississippi was readmitted. This is reflected in the following item from the Court's Minutes for Tuesday, October 26, 1869:

Ex parte Edward M. Yerger, Petitioner

Mr. Phillips stated to the Court that on account of an arrangement in progress between the Attorney General and the counsel of petitioner, no motion will be made this morning for further proceedings but if there be no objection on the part of the Court, counsel will postpone moving until a subsequent day of the term.

The Chief Justice said, It is undoubtedly matter of discretion with the counsel for the petitioner to move for the writ of Habeas Corpus. The point of jurisdiction having been determined, the Court will hear a motion for the writ whenever counsel shall see fit to make it.

UNWARRANTED CRITICISM BY THE PARTISAN PRESS

DEMOCRATIC NEWSPAPERS PROMOTING an encounter wherein Congressional Reconstruction would be laid low were indignant when the adversaries shirked a fight. The *Louisville Courier-Journal*'s special correspondent called it "mere legal quibbling" when Yerger's counsel made clear that they asked no more than a ruling against military trials; he thought "the whole question" of the Reconstruction Act ought to be decided.[81] Writing on October 20 the correspondent of the *Richmond Dispatch* foretold "a masterly and exhaustive opinion from the learned Chief Justice" after the "wise, impartial, and incorruptible judges" had

---

[80] Hoar had his own reasons to know the Radicals' power for mischief: he was having to fight to secure good appointments to the new office of Circuit Judge. In that he was successful; and they in turn were successful in preventing Hoar's confirmation for the new place on the Supreme Court. Infra, pp. 727, 730.

[81] Oct. 20, 1869.

done their duty.[82] On the twenty-fifth he reported Chase's "able and unanswerable" opinion wherein "the flimsy sophistries of the Attorney General . . . were completely overturned, and the Constitution recognized as the supreme law of the land."[83] But when the editor got hold of the text of the opinion and discovered that "it does nothing more than affirm the jurisdiction," he wrote in disgust that "we do not choose to cumber our columns with it."[84] The *Augusta Chronicle & Sentinel* represented that this was a decision "denying the constitutionality of the Reconstruction Laws—at least in so far as they attempt to destroy the jurisdiction of the *civil* courts of the United States"; it purported to see proof that the Court was "unawed by the threats of Radical officials and the angry lashings of a partisan press."[85]

The *St. Louis Republican* supposed that the agreement not to press the *Yerger* case had been made "between the Supreme Court and the Executive," for the reason that "the Attorney General is convinced that the decision would be adverse to the Government." This was "most extraordinary." "We believe it has no parallel in the history of the Republic. It would be difficult to conceive a more humiliating attitude than the Government is made to occupy in such a bargain." The event showed that the political branches were "sufficiently powerful to force the [Supreme Court] to abstain from its sworn official duties."[86]

Whether one thinks of the disturbed state of mind of these newspaper men—or of their misrepresentation of responsible parties—or of the corruption of public understanding induced by such misinformation—this was lamentable reporting.

REACTION IN CONGRESS

THE 41ST CONGRESS met on December 6, 1869, for the second of its three sessions. As in the 39th Congress in early 1867, after the *Milligan* and *Garland* decisions—and as in the 40th Congress a year later, when *McCardle* threatened the Congressional program—now once again Radicals rushed to the battlements and made hostile gestures toward the Supreme Court. This time there was much less cause for alarm. Senator Drake of Missouri introduced S. 274, further to define and regulate the jurisdiction of the federal courts. In a prepared speech he said that he had reexamined the asserted power of the judiciary to

---

[82] Oct. 22.
[83] Oct. 26.
[84] Oct. 27.
[85] Oct. 28.

[86] Nov. 17, 1869. This was, of course, a Democratic newspaper. Next day its comment was repeated in the *Louisville Courier-Journal*.

pass upon the validity of Acts of Congress; he had concluded that Marshall had been wrong in *Marbury v. Madison*.[87] His bill would enact that no federal court could exercise such power.[88] The *Chicago Tribune* reported that the bill "is regarded by every thinking man as a monstrous piece of imbecile assurance." Drake's proposal was condemned in an editorial on "Abolishing the Constitution."[89] "His argument can scarcely be said to have been listened to by his colleagues," wrote *The Nation*.[90] Edmunds of Vermont answered Drake forthrightly. The greatest safeguard of liberty, he said, lay in the fundamental laws being administered by an independent and fearless judiciary.[91] Drake's bill died in committee.

Senator Sumner filed S. 280, in relation to the appellate jurisdiction of the Supreme Court: it would abolish *all* its appellate jurisdiction in habeas corpus cases. He asked the Judiciary Committee to act promptly: "There are interests in question which are well known to the Senate and the country that may be seriously affected . . . ."[92] One may read between the lines. At that moment the federal judges in the Southern States could be counted on to enforce the Radical program. (And some, it may be added, by their disgraceful conduct were adding substance to the complaints of Southern whites against the exercise of federal authority in their affairs.) They would deny relief to the Yergers and Ben Browns, whereas resort to the Supreme Court would, quite likely, result in their release. The Senator was not restrained by any forethought that some day the situation might be reversed and that Congress ought to establish justice on an enduring foundation.

Sumner introduced another "very good bill," S. 341, to enact a long philosophical declaration that the three branches of Government "each in its appropriate sphere only is authorized to pronounce officially the conclusions of the Government in the matters on which it is required to act"; such conclusions could not be held invalid by another branch.[93] He did not consider the manifold difficulties inherent in that proposition—for example, Did each branch determine conclusively what was "its appropriate sphere"? Sumner had been captivated by the constitutional draftsmanship of Continental Europe. He found it superior to Anglo-American thought, which held that the common law as understood by the judges was "the golden met-wand and measure to try the causes of the subjects,"[94] even as against the pretensions of the Crown

---

[87] 1 Cranch 137 (1803).

[88] Cong. Globe, 41–2, 86–93. Dec. 13, 1869.

[89] Dec. 14.

[90] 9:525. Dec. 16.

[91] Cong. Globe, 41–2, 94–96.

[92] Cong. Globe, 41–2, 3. Dec. 6.

[93] Text in Cong. Globe, 41–2, 2895–96.

[94] Sir Edward Coke to James I, the Case of Prohibitions del Roy, 12 Coke's Reports 63 (1607).

—which in American practice had been carried to the point that the judiciary applied the measure of the Constitution even to enactments of the legislature. Sumner now sought by a mere declaration of the Congress to reject that sturdy development in favor of an alien mode of theorizing. The Judiciary Committee obtained a discharge from considering this proposal.

That committee had its own ideas. It took Sumner's first bill, S. 280, struck out everything, and substituted the provision Trumbull had been urging nearly two years earlier, when *McCardle* had been the menace: as reported on December 9, 1869, it declared that the Reconstruction Acts were political in character and that no court might question their validity. Furthermore, until Reconstruction had been completed, the Supreme Court's appellate jurisdiction in habeas corpus would be suspended.[95]

Thurman of Ohio said that it would be utterly unprecedented for Congress to wrest from the Court competence to decide whether a question was "political."[96] He countered with a proposal to request the Attorney General to inform the Senate whether any arrangement existed whereby Yerger would be discharged or turned over to the civil authorities of Mississippi "in case Congress by any legislation should take away or restrict the jurisdiction of the Supreme Court," or any arrangement had been made to delay the hearing of the pending case.[97] Evidently this Democratic leader did not want his party to be deprived of the enormous benefit it would gain from a decision condemning the Reconstruction Act.

Trumbull, urging instant enactment of his bill, said that it was the Court's bad practice of "going out of the record and giving a dissertation on the powers of Congress . . . that has subjected the court to attack." He instanced the pronouncements in *Dred Scott* and *Milligan*. On behalf of the committee he offered an amendment, to declare that no Justice or Judge might grant habeas corpus outside his proper circuit or district: that would correct the view held by some Justices that their power extended throughout the country.[98]

Debate on December 16 was interrupted to make way for the bill on the restoration of Georgia. Congressional Reconstruction was drawing to a close. Yerger's case was not being pressed. Democratic objections sufficed to prevent Trumbull's bill from coming to a vote; Republican objections checkmated Thurman's call for information.

---

[95] Cong. Globe, 41–2, 45, 167. See supra, p. 464.

[96] Ibid., 96. Dec. 13.

[97] Ibid., 164. Dec. 16.

[98] Ibid., 167–9. As recorded, the amendment would have allowed the writ to be issued only "in the circuit or district *court* . . . ," but Trumbull's explanation implied no such limitation.

XII: Ex parte Yerger

THE *YERGER* AND *BROWN* CASES ARE DISMISSED ON MOTION OF PETITIONERS

SOON IT WAS ALL OVER. Mississippi was readmitted on February 23, 1870. On that day Phillips wrote to Judge William Yerger:

> We had this morning an interview with the Attorney Genl in reference to Mr. Yerger—He said to us "be quiet wait until the excitement is over in the Senate where Davis is hammering over the senators credentials[99] you will find that orders have been sent down to turn the prisoner over to the state authorities, but we shall furnish a guard to see that he does not escape." I have jotted down as near as may be the words used—We have no doubt it is all right— Let us hear from you if any order has been executed.[100]

Pursuant to orders, the military authorities with some formality delivered their prisoner to the civil authorities of Hinds County; he was charged with murder, and committed to the local jail.[101]

Phillips' further letter of March 12 reported the end of the case in the Supreme Court:

> . . . on yesterday (Friday) we called up the case for Habeas Corpus, stating to the Court that we had authentic information that Mr. Yerger had been delivered up by the military to the Civil authorities of the State and as the object of the petition was thus accomplished we moved to dismiss the same. The Court ordered the dismissal to be entered as with the consent of the Attorney General—This we believe ends our professional connection with the case. The movement has been a fortunate one as without doubt it has saved the life of the applicant.[102]

---

[99] Garrett Davis of Kentucky was objecting to the seating of the new Senators, one of whom, Hiram R. Revels, was the first Negro to sit in Congress. He took the place vacated by Jefferson Davis. Revels (1822–1901), born free in North Carolina, had gone North, where he obtained an education and became a minister of the African Methodist Church. He aided in recruiting Negro troops, and served as chaplain of a Mississippi regiment. In the Senate he was a moderate, and supported the removal of disabilities of white Southerners. Returning to Mississippi, he became president of Alcorn University. In 1875 he was active in aiding the Democrats to overthrow Carpetbag government. "My people are naturally Republicans," he wrote to President Grant, "but as they grow older in freedom so do they in wisdom. A great portion of them have learned that they were being used as mere tools . . . ." Ann. Cyc. 1875, 517.

[100] Phillips to Judge William Yerger, Phillips' Letterbook, 1870–71, 53. Ms. Div., L.C.

[101] *Jackson Weekly Clarion*, Mar. 3, 1870.

[102] Phillips' Letterbook, 1870–71, 76. L.C.

Ex parte Brown et al.—wherein the petition for habeas corpus aided by certiorari had been passed over to abide the decision of *Ex parte Yerger*[103]—now disappeared from the docket in like manner. Texas was readmitted on March 30, 1870, and on April 22 counsel informed the Court "that [petitioners] are no longer deprived of their liberty, and that civil authority is restored in the State of Texas." Accordingly the case was dismissed.

A POSTSCRIPT ON YERGER

ONE DOES NOT LOSE INTEREST in so memorable an individual as Yerger the moment he is dropped from the docket. After a few days in jail he escaped, apparently by tricking his guardians.[104] The new legislature (under Republican control) voted to investigate.[105] But then Yerger walked back into jail, after a week of hunting and fishing. An application for release on bail, before Chief Justice Thomas G. Shackelford (holding over under his appointment by General Gillem) was successful; the judge dwelt upon the liberality of Mississippi law in such cases, and set bail at $15,000.[106] The legislature was indignant; a joint address to remove the Chief Justice collapsed, however, when a select committee reported that, in its opinion, by the new constitution Shackelford had not been continued in office.[107] As the *Clarion* cheerfully observed, the commotion in the legislature had turned into "a ludicrous affair."[108] The local correspondent of a Northern paper reported that Governor Alcorn was "mortified," but "powerless in the premises"; the legislature's procrastination had prevented him from appointing a new Chief Justice. Now "Yerger, the irrepressible Yerger, is again at large upon the streets, airing his fine person in a new suit of clothes."[109]

In May 1871, when the pending prosecution was before the local circuit court, Yerger's counsel argued for dismissal on a plea of double jeopardy—the first peril consisting of the abortive proceedings before the military commission, proceedings which counsel therefore had denounced as a nullity.[110] In the meantime Yerger moved to Baltimore: one wonders whether this was not for security against prosecution in a State where the political climate was no longer congenial?

---

[103] Minutes for Oct. 11, 1869; supra, p. 581.

[104] *Jackson Weekly Clarion*, Mar. 17, 1870.

[105] Miss. Sen. J. 76 (1870); House J. 87.

[106] *Weekly Clarion*, Apr. 28.

[107] Sen. J. 196, 219–20 (1870); House J. 248.

[108] *Weekly Clarion*, May 5.

[109] *Eau Claire* (Wisconsin) *Free Press*, May 19.

[110] *Weekly Clarion*, May 25 and June 1, 1871.

There he engaged in an unsuccessful newspaper venture—in politics supporting the Liberal Republican movement.[111] And there he died on April 22, 1875.[112]

THE PROBLEM OF CRIMINAL JUSTICE IN EX-REBEL STATES

THE PROVISION IN SECTION 3 of the Reconstruction Act of March 2, 1867,[113] authorizing trial by military commission has been the feature least susceptible of a favorable interpretation at the bar of history. Before one pronounces judgment, however, the situation as seen by Congress and the obduracy of the problem should be understood.

During the war the armies of the United States occupying hostile territory exercised jurisdiction over crimes—not acts of legitimate warfare—to the prejudice of those forces or of the inhabitants of the occupied territory.[114] Acting as a guerrilla or "bushwhacker" by committing murder and pillage was a familiar incident of the Civil War; it was subject to trial by military commission in accordance with the common law of war—a branch of international law.[115] (The Confederate Government would doubtless have acted on a like view, following American precedents, had occasion arisen. Confederate presence within States loyal to the United States, however, was generally by brief invasion not amounting to occupation.) By the Reconstruction Act, Congress found that in the ten Southern States there were "no legal State governments"—which was a matter of political judgment—"or adequate protection for life or property"—for which there was abundant evidence within the knowledge of Congress. To meet this latter deficiency it authorized the continued exercise of the war-time jurisdiction if local civil tribunals proved ineffective. The legal defense for that

---

[111] Infra, p. 1471.

[112] *Baltimore Sun*, Apr. 24; *Weekly Clarion*, Apr. 28.

[113] Supra, pp. 298, 309.

[114] Winthrop, *Military Law and Precedents*, 2d ed., rev. and enl. (Government Printing Office, 1920), 831–46, "Trial and Punishment of Offences under the Law of War— the Military Commission."

This treatise by William Woolsey Winthrop (1831–99) is entitled to great respect. The author graduated from Yale College, and attended its law school and then that of Harvard. His family background had the best of cultural advantages: he was a descendant of Governor John Winthrop of Massachusetts, and of Jonathan Edwards, the theologian. Theodore Dwight Woolsey, Yale's president, was his uncle. He practiced at the New York bar from 1854 to the outbreak of the war. Enlisting at once, he became an officer in the 1st U.S. Sharpshooters. In 1863 he was assigned to the office of the Judge Advocate General. He was the deputy to that officer from 1884 to his retirement in 1895. He did his writing in the spirit of a sound, discriminating lawyer.

[115] *Ex parte* Quirin, 317 U.S. 1, 27 (1942).

591

action was expressed in Attorney General Hoar's opinion in the *Weaver* case.[116]

The alternative to the course Congress adopted should be scrutinized.

Soldiers, civilians loyal to the Union, and freedmen were the objects of murder and other criminal acts, after the organized attempt to secede had been abandoned. Were such crimes now cognizable only in the State courts? Such was the teaching of *In re Egan*[117] and *United States v. Commandant of Fort Delaware*.[118] But juries of yesterday's rebels would not convict their own people of outrages against such outsiders. That was a rock-bottom fact when Congress passed the Reconstruction Act.

Southern judges were only too eager, in a forum where they themselves declared the law, to maintain old pretensions and denounce Congress and its agents. Some cherished folklore of Reconstruction clusters about that situation.[119]

But if State courts would not do justice where Negroes, Unionists, or soldiers were set upon, still—as has often been remarked—the federal courts were open. Hence, it has been inferred, there was no reason for Congress to authorize trial by extraordinary tribunals.

That reflects a failure to penetrate a problem so deep that it would not be solved in a hundred years. Certainly the federal judges

---

[116] Supra, pp. 561–63.

Winthrop (see note 114) at 853–855, gives this authoritative statement of the extent to which the jurisdiction was exercised:

In the majority of cases indeed crimes and disorders, where without political significance, were allowed to be disposed of by the State judiciary. [Citing orders announcing that policy.] The trials by military commission under the Reconstruction Laws were in all not much over two hundred in number. [At some of these trials, however, a number of accused were joined in the same charge—twenty-three in one instance.] . . . .

As to *offences,* those taken cognizance of by military commission were:—*first* and principally, crimes and disorders made punishable by the local or common law, such as murder, manslaughter, robbery, larceny, "lynching," criminal conspiracy,

assault with intent to kill, assault and battery, burglary, obtaining money under false representations, false imprisonment, malicious mischief, breach of the peace and disorderly conduct, embezzlement, and malfeasance in office [by a deputy sheriff, and by two agents of the Freedmen's Bureau]; *second*, acts punishable by U.S. statutes, as purchasing arms, clothing, &c., from soldiers, forgery of checks on the Treasury, stealing public property, &c.; *third*, breaches of military orders regulating the selling of liquor to soldiers, forbidding the carrying of concealed weapons, securing rights to colored persons, &c.

[117] Supra, pp. 148–49.

[118] Supra, pp. 149–50.

[119] To document one instance, the encounter between Judge A. P. Aldrich and Gen. Canby has been set out at length. Supra, pp. 501–04.

then in office were not disaffected. Nor could it be said that federal grand jurors would not indict, or that petit jurors would not convict: they could be tested by the iron-clad oath of unbroken loyalty.[120] United States courts, however, have no general common law jurisdiction;[121] Congress must first pass a statute, based upon some adequate constitutional power, whereby crimes such as murder and robbery are made punishable in the federal courts. Recall the proposal of Representative William Lawrence of Ohio when the Reconstruction Bill was being debated.[122] He would have had Congress enact that the United States District Courts would thenceforth have jurisdiction in all matters which formerly had pertained to the courts of the States undergoing reconstruction. To that end the criminal laws in force in the District of Columbia would be put into force in those States. The District Court might sit at any time or place within the State "as may be necessary for the administration of justice."

The power of Congress thus to supplant a State's judiciary and to impose a code of criminal law would have been contestable—just as the imposition made by the Reconstruction Act was contested before the Supreme Court. Certainly a vastly greater number of Judges and prosecutors must have been authorized and installed, if such an undertaking was to be performed effectively. To satisfy Article III, the Judges must have been appointed to hold office "during good behavior" —even though the occasion would end when the State was restored. (Arkansas and Florida, which proceeded most expeditiously, were readmitted to representation in less than sixteen months after the Reconstruction Act became law.) Since a new criminal law must not operate ex post facto, crimes committed before its enactment could not be reached. As a means for the timely repression of future acts of malevolence, the scheme could not have been effective.

A belated proposal was framed by leading men of Boston, while the *Weaver* case[123] was before the Attorney General, and shortly after Hoar had been sojourning in Massachusetts. The group included Sidney Bartlett and George Otis Shattuck (Oliver Wendell Holmes' respected senior), distinguished at the bar; John M. Forbes and Edward Atkinson, industrialists of large public spirit; and Alexander H.

---

[120] Act of June 12, 1862, 12 Stat. 430; Rev. Stats. Secs. 820, 821. Moreover, in practice the Marshal could summon jurors ready for the job at hand; for years that was a serious complaint against federal justice in the South.
"The United States Marshal can practically pick out the jurors and fix up every jury to suit him," asserted the *Jackson Weekly Clarion*, April 18, 1872.

[121] United States v. Hudson and Goodwin, 7 Cranch 32 (1812); United States v. Coolidge, 1 Wheat. 415 (1816).

[122] Cong. Globe, 39–2, 1083–84. Feb. 7, 1867. Supra, p. 289.

[123] Supra, pp. 561–63.

Rice, sometime mayor and Congressman, later Governor. Under date of April 9, 1869, they submitted the following:

> In view of the legal doubt of the power of courts martial [military commissions] in time of peace, lynch law or total anarchy now threatens in the unreconstructed states unless Congress shall provide for the due execution there of some code of criminal law. For the protection of the people of these states and of citizens visiting there we respectfully urge your honorable bodies not to adjourn without taking action in this matter.
>
> We are assured from various sources of the pressing necessity of such action.[124]

Congress adjourned on April 10, before the petition could be presented.

These men of ability pointed to an evil that had already continued for four years—and here was what they would have Congress do about it.

"Some code of criminal law": What should it provide? Congress might have legislated on either of two lines. Suppose it made it a crime *against the United States* to injure, in an unreconstructed State, persons specially in need of federal protection. Who should be included: the Negro—(or only the freedman)—the Unionist—the soldier—the visitor from out-of-State? The definition of a crime must at all points be very specific. And exactly what class would be forbidden to commit this new crime: all whites who had supported the Confederacy? What specific intent would the statute require? What about double jeopardy, since in principle the act would already be punishable under State law? Without attempting a fine focus, it is evident that there would have been tremendous difficulties in devising so novel a statute—not to mention a sea of troubles in applying it.

A second approach would have been to make certain *State crimes* triable in a *federal court* where the situation as to actor and victim was such as Congress sought to reach. But if only a State grand jury could initiate a prosecution, the short answer was that indictments would not be found against local whites who preyed upon Negroes and Yankees.[125] Removal into a federal court on the defendant's motion was a

---

[124] Text found among the Sumner Papers, Harvard Univ. L.

[125] General Grant's memorandum of January 29, 1867, to the Secretary of War spoke of "the great number of murders of Union men and freedmen in Texas, not only as a rule unpunished, but uninvestigated . . . ."

Edward McPherson, *The Political History of the United States of America during the Period of Reconstruction*, 3d ed. (Washington: James J. Chapman, 1880), 298. Five weeks later the Reconstruction Act authorized trial by military commission in such a situation.

useful device where by reason of local prejudice a federal officer might be unfairly prosecuted in a State court[126]—but removal had no utility where the classes needing federal protection were being victimized by private violence in a disaffected community.

Perhaps members of Congress in that day engaged in no such refined cogitation. When they framed the Reconstruction Act they were coping with a transitory period. It was beyond question that Negroes and Unionists were being killed with impunity; a deterrent was needed, then and there. If anything was to be done about it, then, said Representative M. Russell Thayer, a Philadelphia lawyer,

> This bill proposes to extend to them the only protection which we can at present give them. It proposes to protect them by the strong arm of power until they shall be protected by equal laws and just and impartial tribunals.[127]

Thayer had shown a strong determination to insure that civil rights were given federal protection in the ex-rebel States—but he was not among the extreme Radicals.

It seems remarkable, looking back, how little these participants reckoned on the persistence of the basic conflict, how hopefully they spoke of the early advent of equal laws impartially applied.

Representative Henry J. Raymond was leaning just as far as intelligence and candor would permit to the support of President Johnson. Yet on the evidence before Congress he had to admit that it was clear "that life, liberty and property are not properly guarded by law, are not safe throughout those southern States." Even so, he opposed a military jurisdiction; the Reconstruction Bill looked like "the last resort of a decayed and dying republic." Ingenuity should devise something "of a civil nature adequate to the emergency."

> I would even prefer that this Congress, if it be deemed necessary, should appoint civil commissioners for each State. Name them in the bill if you are not willing to trust the naming of them to the chief Executive. Let those commissioners organize tribunals of some sort, and then let the Army support their decrees.[128]

The impracticability of this prescription is evident. Of course Congress could not, consistently with the Constitution, appoint any officers. The improvising of "tribunals of some sort" which by their decrees would make life safe was grandly vague.

---

[126] Tennessee v. Davis, 100 U.S. 257 (1880).

[127] Cong. Globe, 39–2, 1098. Feb. 8, 1867.

[128] Ibid., 1101–3. Feb. 8, 1867.

Garfield found inapposite Raymond's allusions to "the decadence and death" of ancient republics.[129] The bill was indeed "severe"; he had "many misgivings." But the Southern States had rejected the Amendment with its guarantees of liberty. "It is now our turn to act." Congress "must lay the heavy hand of military authority upon these rebel communities, and hold them in its grasp," to establish "law and peace where anarchy and violence now reign," to make it "both safe and honorable to have been loyal in the midst of treason," to permit the "humblest citizen . . . to travel in safety from the Ohio river to the Gulf." The bill was "not a proposition to commit the liberties of the Republic into the hands of the military." Rather, Congress was "commanding the Army to return to its work of putting down the rebellion . . . . [W]e are commanding them, as public servants, to do this work in the interest of liberty."

Garfield, it will be recalled, had spoken out against confining men without trial in the Old Capitol Prison; on ground of conscience he had argued *Milligan*'s case in the Supreme Court.[130] He had established his devotion to civil liberty. And now he made clear that, in his view, the substance of liberty would be served by this provision in the Reconstruction Bill.

Representative John Augustus Griswold of New York, War Democrat turned conservative Republican, recognized fully that "the rights and liberties of loyal men, both white and black, are totally ignored" in the South.[131] Here were his answers to the issues in the debate: he thought that military rule led to "greater danger than is justified by the evils we seek to correct"; he would "prefer giving those States further opportunity to exhibit a spirit of obedience and loyalty . . . ."

The denial of justice in communities of recent rebels could not be gainsaid. The foregoing quotations give a fair sampling of rational opinion on what should be done about it.

When the sands of a century had run, the nation would still have failed to establish adequate protection for the Negro and the outsider against violence tolerated by the community. Comment on the severity of what Congress did in 1867 should be viewed against that towering fact.

In 1865 it was the South that must "accept the situation." In 1867 the Radicals were so sanguine as to believe that they would soon achieve "republican governments based upon the will of the whole loyal people,"[132] with "equal laws and just and impartial tribunals."[133]

---

[129] Ibid., 1103–4.
[130] Supra, pp. 185–86.
[131] Cong. Globe, 39–2, 1100–101.

[132] Ibid., Garfield's phrase, at 1104.
[133] Thayer's phrase, Cong. Globe, 39–2, 1098.

XII: Ex parte Yerger

The mores, however, proved tougher than the Reconstruction Acts; presently it was the nation that must "accept the situation."

How *The Nation* bowed to the persistency of the problem is instructive, because this was the great organ of intelligent, liberal thought at the North.

From the outset the editors had given strong endorsement to the Congressional program. On February 28, 1867—while the Reconstruction Bill was awaiting Johnson's ineffective veto—an editorial on "Dangerous Precedents" said that although the extension of military rule over the South was a serious matter, still

> The unavenged massacre in New Orleans, the applauded murders of Union soldiers in Georgia, the boasted "disappearance" of Northern men from Texas, the atrocious acquittal of Dr. Watson in Virginia, are but examples of a state of affairs constituting a precedent more damaging to republican government than any period of temporary military rule can be. . . .[134]

It had adhered to that point of view, notably in "Good Sense About Reconstruction" in April 1868.[135] As late as June 1869 *The Nation* pronounced Attorney General Hoar's opinion in the *Weaver* case to be sound; otherwise "colored men hold their lives at the mercy of the white man's gun and knife." "We hope . . . that the sentence [in Weaver's case] will be carried out." It hoped, too, that the commission trying Yerger would go on to convict, and that "the citizens of Jackson" would be given the "moral spectacle" of "an incorrigible ruffian brought to the gallows . . . ."[136]

Then suddenly the vane whirled; evidently a new hand was allowed to write editorials. On July 29, 1869, a long article on "The Case of Colonel Yerger" wholly rejected the Attorney General's opinion that Congress could still exercise war powers in unreconstructed States.[137] "The local courts are open in these districts; the United States judges hold their circuits within them; . . . society as such is quiet; the only disturbance and breaches of peace are individual and sporadic." Under the doctrine of the majority in *Milligan*, which "must be taken as fully established," there was no "possible foundation" for military jurisdiction. Concede even that the Southern States had "been reduced to the condition of Territories": still, it had been "expressly affirmed in the Dred Scott case" that the Constitution's "muniments of civil liberty" applied in the territories.

The civil liberty with which Taney's opinion was concerned in

---

[134] 4:170.
[135] 6:264. Apr. 2.

[136] 8:445, 466. June 10 and 17.
[137] 9:86.

Dred Scott[138] was the citizen's right to be protected in taking his slave into any territory of the United States. Now that opinion was confidently invoked to support the proposition that if Weaver was charged with killing a freedman or Yerger with the killing of a soldier of the garrison, he was subject to punishment only upon indictment by a grand jury and conviction by a trial jury of the vicinage.

The Nation's editorial urged that the evil of the day should be patiently endured, in order to avoid creating what might on some morrow serve as a dangerous precedent—as though the morrow would not be sufficient unto its own problems:

> It may well be that there is some ill-will among the Southern people. It may well be that convictions are hard to obtain from Southern juries. These are grave evils, but they always must for a while follow the suppression of a great rebellion. It is better to endure them, and to await with patience the soothing effects of time; it is better that a few wretches like Yerger should escape their merited punishment, than that a weapon should be put into the hands of some future Government which may be effective in destroying the liberties of the nation.[139]

The choice before Congress was to act as it did or to suffer the evil as it was. No other practicable means of dealing with it was perceived. Whatever judgment is to be pronounced, that was the underlying factual situation.

"THE NEW MOVEMENT" IN VIRGINIA

WHAT WITH CONSERVATIVE INTRANSIGENCE and Radical irresponsibility, Virginia had come to a sorry pass. In 1865 under Governor Pierpoint it had had the prospect of early restoration under the most favorable auspices. Later, under Congressional Reconstruction, it had been guided by a most helpful District commander—one whose assignment had been requested by the unanimous voice of the legislators.[140]

---

[138] Scott v. Sanford, 19 How. 393 (1857). Supra, p. 26.

[139] Compare the demands of other editors a century later, that the Government use all the weapons in its hands to preserve the liberties of the nation; that it should "Enforce the Constitution" and protect the rights of equal citizenship by using "troops and bayonets, and for that matter tanks and grenades" (*The Nation*, 99:1, July 13, 1964); that it

should exercise "The Power to Protect" and "apply force . . . to protect and stop outrages that no civilized nation should tolerate" (*New Republic*, 152:5, Mar. 20, 1965).

[140] Andrew Johnson Papers, L.C. Letter of Pierpoint of Mar. 8, 1867, transmitting "a petition of all the members present," with sixty-three signatures, for General John M. Schofield, then commanding the Army's Department of Virginia.

XII: Ex parte Yerger

Yet the Republican party of Virginia had fallen under the leadership of envious destructionists; and through Conservative refusal to participate in the Congressional program, constitution-making had been surrendered to the extremists.[141]

When the constitutional convention, presided over by District Judge John C. Underwood, adjourned on April 17, 1868, it offered a document whereby suffrage was extended to adult males—with no limitation as to literacy, owning property, or paying a poll tax; paupers were not excluded. Then, cutting into this grant, was a great disqualifying exception of those who had held office and thereafter had participated in rebellion or given aid to the enemies of the United States; but the legislature by three-fifths vote might remove this disability. (Section 3 of the Fourteenth Amendment—the feature most bitterly resented at the South—had imposed such a disqualification on *office-holding*; the Virginia convention extended it to the *suffrage*.)

For office-holding the convention imposed a test of unbroken loyalty, comparable to the federal iron-clad oath of 1862, involved in *Ex parte Garland*.[142] More than that, an oath was required that one recognized the civil and political equality of all men before the law.[143]

Eligibility to serve on a jury was determined by eligibility to vote and hold office.

General Schofield warned the convention in April that it would be "practically impossible to carry on a government" with such disqualifications; in some counties there were very few men, of either race, who could read and write and take the test oath.[144]

At this juncture the press was reporting the "astonishing growth of the K.K.K.," whose members were flitting mysteriously from town to town, "everywhere kindling a spirit of patriotic ardor for the [old] constitution"; "the rapid increase of this secret society" gave warning to the Radicals that their program of "proscribing, disfranchising and

---

[141] Supra, pp. 406–11.

The *New York Times* of March 27, 1868, commented that the policy of the Conservatives in Virginia had been to show "contempt for the whole thing":

> their leaders have been chiefly young men of wit and power of repartee, of personal courage and family prestige, but lacking in that practical, sober judgment, and art of managing men, which were so requisite to their cause.

Thus they had played into the hands of the Radical leaders.

[142] Supra, pp. 58–59.

[143] Ben Butler, addressing the convention on January 14, had warned against a test oath: "It catches and holds in its meshes . . . those men who are conscientious and upright, while it lets the rascally ones through. And especially is that so, when men think an oath is imposed upon them that ought not to be imposed, and about the observance of which they are at liberty to use their own judgment. . . ." *Debates and Proceedings of the Constitutional Convention, 1867–68*, at 437–38.

[144] Ann. Cyc. 1868, 759.

pillaging the white men" would be resisted by force.[145] It was a question, said the *Richmond Dispatch*, "whether there is a possibility of a change in the disposition of the negro—of his giving up his prejudices and intolerance towards the only men who can . . . restore industry and the public welfare . . . . If he can't, the people of Virginia must necessarily accept the war of races the negroes have initiated . . . . The victory is not doubtful."[146]

Then came a lull when, on April 24, 1868, the commanding general announced that for want of appropriations by Congress the holding of an election on the proposed constitution was adjourned indefinitely.[147]

In the meantime the Conservatives had been looking to the Supreme Court for their deliverance. They had found a petitioner in whose name they could challenge the Reconstruction Act, and had met an expected rebuff from Judge Underwood in the Circuit Court. Appeal to the Supreme Court was abandoned when *Ex parte McCardle* was being prosecuted for the same objective.[148]

By the end of 1868 it was evident that neither by the Supreme Court nor by Democratic victories in the North would Congressional Reconstruction be arrested. Accommodation came at last through "the New Movement," launched by A. H. H. Stuart, a Virginian whose character and public service placed him above reproach. Universal suffrage, he observed, was inevitable; let us accept it, yet seek relief from the most objectionable features of the Underwood constitution.[149] Despite the usual objections,[150] the movement managed to succeed. Stuart was chairman of a committee of nine who visited Washington and prepared the ground for the Act of April 10, 1869, whereby the President would submit the proposed constitution to the voters—selecting provisions, if he deemed best, for separate vote.[151]

The election was held on July 6, 1869. President Grant designated, for separate votes, the disfranchising clause, and the test oath for officers. In the canvass for State officers, the moderate wing of the Republican party broke from the Radicals and put up its own "True

---

[145] *Richmond Enquirer and Examiner*, Mar. 26 and 31, 1868; similarly Mar. 27 and Apr. 18.

[146] Apr. 16, 1868.

[147] Ann. Cyc. 1868, 760.

[148] Supra, ch. 10, n. 66.

[149] Letter in *Richmond Dispatch* and *Richmond Whig* on Dec. 25, 1868.

Stuart (1807–97), formerly a Whig Congressman, and Secretary of the Interior under Fillmore, had opposed secession in the convention of 1861. He was a delegate to the Conservative Convention at Philadelphia in 1866.

[150] That it was dishonorable to compromise with principle, but not so to bow to compulsion. "Let [Virginia] take death, I say, rather than dishonor," wrote the high-strung ex-Governor, Henry A. Wise. *Richmond Enquirer and Examiner*, Jan. 18, 1869.

[151] Supra, p. 559.

Republican" ticket. The Conservative candidates then withdrew, to permit members of their party to vote for True Republicans. At the election, the constitution was ratified by more than 20 to 1; the disfranchising and test oath clauses were rejected, 3 to 2; the True Republican slate was elected by a vote of nearly 6 to 5. In the new legislature, the Radicals held less than one-third of the seats.[152] The Fourteenth, and the recently proposed Fifteenth Amendment, were quickly and almost unanimously ratified. On January 26, 1870, Virginia was readmitted to representation. It had been a long, hard experience.

DISTRICT JUDGE UNDERWOOD

JOHN C. UNDERWOOD (1809–73), born in New York and educated at Hamilton College, had studied law in Virginia while serving as tutor in a family, one of whose members became his wife. He had practiced law and Free-Soil politics, in New York and in Virginia, and in 1864 was appointed District Judge. Underwood's quality may be appraised by considering his charge to the federal grand jury on May 6, 1867:

> I have sometimes feared that by the usages of this State, which have given the selection of juries to the sheriffs and marshals, or, in professional language, have packed juries instead of drawing them from a box of names selected by other officers, as is done in most States, there was danger of getting indifferent persons upon the panel; but the care and rare judgment which our marshals have always shown in their selections prove my fears unfounded, and I am truly gratified to find so many gentlemen of public and private worth upon the present jury.[153]

"Care and rare judgment" had included prominent Republican politicians—including John Hawxhurst, foremost in leading the party to extremes. Judge Underwood went on to charge the grand jury on

---

[152] The results were not officially announced until September 9. The Radicals, convening on November 24, called upon Congress to order a new election, or to provide other relief whereby they might regain control.

The low standing of the Virginia Radicals among Republicans is indicated by an editorial in the *Chicago Tribune* of November 27: it condemned their effort to prolong military rule, and concluded: "no change is so much needed as the resumption of self-government by the people of that State."

[153] *Richmond Dispatch*, May 7, 1867.

The Act of Congress of July 20, 1840, 5 Stat. 394, Rev. Stats. § 800, directed that the selection of jurors in the federal courts should conform to the laws and usages of the State wherein the court sat. (It is now governed directly by provisions of 28 U.S. Code, §§ 1861–69.)

matters in nowise within their competence. He described Richmond as a city

> where licentiousness has ruled until probably a majority of births were illegitimate or without the forms of law; where the fashionable and popular pulpit had been so prostituted that its full-fed ministering gay Lotharios generally recommend worship of what they most respected—pleasure, property, and power . . . .

He then launched into an encomium upon Thad Stevens, whom successive Congresses "acknowledged as a leader and father with a deference that neither Clay, Fox, the Pitts, nor even Cicero, had ever known." Now this noble man was bitterly assailed for urging the confiscation of the property of leading rebels.[154]

In a series of habeas corpus cases—on behalf of Sally Anderson, Caesar Griffin, Jeter Phillips, and Sam Baker—this wayward Judge disturbed the commonwealth at a moment when repose was needed. Presently the Supreme Court was driven to an unusual expedient to correct him.

Here is how it came about. The Fourteenth Amendment came into effect in July 1868. Its Section 3 declared that "No person shall . . . hold any office . . . under any State" who, having taken an oath to support the Constitution, had thereafter engaged in the rebellion. At that moment the public functions of Virginia were in considerable measure being performed by officers who fell under that ban. Were they instantly swept from office, and their power brought to an end? Or, pending legislation to put Section 3 into operation, would their acts continue to be effective? That was the issue.

Sally Anderson had been convicted of arson and sentenced to hanging by a county court, one of whose justices, it was alleged, was disqualified by the Fourteenth Amendment. Habeas corpus was sought from Judge Underwood. Under the statute he could (1) issue the writ from the District Court, or (2) make it returnable at his chambers, or, (3)—since a District Judge was qualified to hold the Circuit Court— it was possible to issue the writ there. If he acted in the District Court, or in chambers, an appeal could be taken to the Circuit Court, where the Circuit Justice could sit to review. But if the District Judge, in the absence of the Circuit Justice, heard the matter alone in the Circuit Court, then a decision releasing a petitioner would be subject to no review whatsoever, inasmuch as the appeal to the Supreme Court, provided by the Act of February 5, 1867, had now been abolished.

---

154 *The Nation* commented that "the cause both of justice and good government would be served if the fountains of his eloquence could be sealed up." 4:365. May 9, 1867.

XII: Ex parte Yerger

In August 1868 Judge Underwood exploited that possibility. He allowed the Sally Anderson petition to be heard in the Circuit Court, before himself alone, without the knowledge of Chief Justice Chase, his Circuit Justice. He proceeded to hold that Section 3 of the Amendment operated of its own force, at once, to remove every disqualified person from office; accordingly the trial had been invalid and the petitioner could not be held. The Conservative organ, the *Enquirer and Examiner* on September 1, foreseeing what the decision would be, warned that it would lead to "a general jail delivery throughout the Commonwealth"; it threatened that as a consequence, "the people will, for their necessary defence, form vigilance committees, and administer the swift and sanguinary, but often substantial justice of lynch law . . . ."

Caesar Griffin was charged with assault with intent to kill, and on conviction had been sentenced to two years in the penitentiary. The same counsel as in Sally Anderson's case sought a writ of habeas corpus from Judge Underwood. Learning of this, Chief Justice Chase wrote from Washington on November 19:

> Dear Judge,
> The papers say that you are holding the Circuit Court at Richmond with a Grand Jury and are just now hearing an important habeas corpus case. . . .
> In the District Court or as District Judge you have undoubted jurisdiction of the Habeas Corpus case, and perhaps the writ is returnable before that Court, or before yourself at Chambers. If returnable to the Circuit Court would it not be best to postpone the decision till next week & then we can confer on the subject.[155]

Thus admonished, Judge Underwood heard the case in chambers.[156] Counsel in a swarm appeared to resist the release of the pris-

---

[155] Underwood Papers, L.C.

Chase's main point was that if the report in the press was true, "you are holding, doubtless, an adjourned term, and the legality of it becomes important." He pointed to an Act of Congress of May 21, 1866, 14 Stat. 51. That statute provided that the Circuit Court hold terms in Richmond on the first Monday in May and the fourth Monday in November; special or adjourned terms might be held "as may be ordered and prescribed by the Chief Justice of the Supreme Court of the United States . . . ." Normally it was a power common to all courts to adjourn to a future day. Mechanics Bank v. Withers, 6 Wheat. 106, 108 (1821). But was not the legal effect of the statute to qualify that power? "Next week"—Monday, November 23—the regular term would open "& then we can confer" on the habeas corpus case.

[156] Even so, "Owing to the strange condition of the papers of the case it was not surprising that the impression prevailed that the cause was pending in the Circuit Court." Thus the press quoted Chase, Cir. J., when he was holding court at Richmond. *Richmond Dispatch*, Dec. 3, 1868.

oner and to protect the State against having its courts put out of business. On December 7, 1868, Judge Underwood announced his decision: once more he held that Section 3 of the Amendment operated to render the trial a nullity. An appeal to the Circuit Court was entered at once.[157]

A few days thereafter a petition was sought for Jeter Phillips, condemned to death in a State court: his point was that the Court of Appeals, which had affirmed the conviction, contained judges who were disqualified by the Fourteenth Amendment. And early in January, 1869, came the petition of Sam Baker, also sentenced to death.[158] These petitioners were all Negroes—but that was not involved in the question of law. If the Fourteenth Amendment by its own force nullified the action of a disqualified judge, that result would apply to all convictions—and logically to all civil judgments as well. This alarming prospect prompted Chase to send another cautionary letter to the District Judge:

Washington, Jany 14 1869

Dear Sir,

In our conversation some weeks ago just after your decision in the Case of Sally Anderson I expressed my regret that you did not hear the case at chambers, so that an appeal might have be[en] taken, as in the Caesar Griffin Case, and the case argued before us both in the Circuit Court. I also stated that I entertained very serious doubts in regard to the correctness of the decision in those two cases; not being prepared to affirm that by the operation [of] the Fourteenth Amendment every Judge in the State . . . was at once deprived of all judicial character & authority, so that judgments & decrees & motions rendered by him became absolutely null & void. It is difficult to measure the consequences of such a determination: and the great possibility that the most serious evils may result from it though by no means proving its incorrectness, seems to justify & demand great care & circumspection in proceeding.

I have today seen a statement in the [Richmond] State Journal of yesterday that an application had been filed for an injunction restraining the collection of a judgment on the ground that it was issued by a court the members of which are disabled from holding office under the Fourteenth Amendment. If any such application has been made I will join you in hearing it. It may be heard here if you can attend. If not let it be postponed till I can come to Richmond.

The best and quickest way of obtaining an authoritative & final decision of the point which has arisen is to certify to a division

---

[157] The proceedings were reported fully, in the *Richmond Dispatch* and the *Enquirer and Examiner*, between November 18 and December 8, 1868.
[158] *Richmond Enquirer and Examiner*, Jan. 7; *Dispatch*, Jan. 8.

of opinion in the Caesar Griffin case now in the Circuit Court on appeal. If you think, as I do, that it is proper & expedient to certify this division you can have the necessary certificate made out & entered, as of any day when I was in Richmond in November or December last. As the division has arisen in a criminal case the case can be heard here as soon after the record comes up, as counsel are ready to argue it at some time during the present term.[159]

Please give this whole matter your early & considerate attention.[160]

The State Government now sought to put a stop to this menacing course of decisions: it filed an original proceeding in the Supreme Court. On Friday, January 29, 1869, "On the suggestion and motion of the State of Virginia" in open court, a writ of prohibition was sought, to be directed to Judge Underwood, "prohibiting him from further proceedings" in the cases of Anderson, Griffin, and Phillips.[161] This application was subject to very serious objections.[162] The Court set the matter down for an early hearing, and directed that in the meantime "no further proceeding be taken" in any of the cases.[163]

Argument was heard on Friday, February 12, when James Lyons

---

[159] The Court's rule on advancing criminal cases is set out supra, ch. 10, n. 67.

[160] Retained draft, in Chase Papers, Hist. Soc. of Pa. There is much rewriting and interlining, showing that the Chief Justice was exercising care and restraint. The letter as sent may have varied somewhat from the draft.

[161] *Ex parte* The State of Virginia, No. 11 Original.

The petition narrated what had been done in the three cases; then it alleged that in the *Phillips* case Judge Underwood "has awarded the said writ of habeas corpus returnable before the Circuit Court of the United States, at Richmond, on the ninth day of February, when the said Underwood will be the only judge in court, thereby transcending his authority as a judge of a court of the United States, improperly interfering with the administration of justice in the State of Virginia, one of the United States, and arresting the execution of the lawful judgments and sentences of her lawful courts, in derogation of the Constitution of the United States, and the constitu-

tion and laws of the State of Virginia, a State duly organized and recognized as one of the United States of America." *Richmond Enquirer and Examiner*, Feb. 2, 1869.

[162] Supposing that Virginia in her then condition had standing to maintain a suit (see Virginia v. West Virginia, infra, pp. 624–25, and Texas v. White, infra, pp. 636–40), even so, the remedy sought was not the appropriate way for getting at the trouble. The writ of prohibition goes to the situation where jurisdiction is lacking, not to mere errors in its exercise or censurable manoeuvers not transcending the judge's power. And, as the Supreme Court had said in a recent case, "If a thing is already done"—as it was, in *Sally Anderson's* case—"it is manifest the writ of prohibition cannot undo it." Nor would it be issued as a means of instructing the inferior court about cases that had not yet arisen. United States v. Hoffman, District Judge, 4 Wall. 158 (1867).

[163] Minutes of Friday, Jan. 29, 1869. The order was reported in full in the *Richmond Enquirer and Examiner*, February 2, 1869.

of Richmond spoke an hour and a half in support of the motion.[164] "If Judge Underwood could set aside the judgments of the State courts in these cases, he might do so in all cases, thus in effect overthrowing the Judiciary. . . . Virginia had therefore asked for a writ of prohibition to prevent these enormous ills, and to protect the people in the liberties and rights which the Constitution was intended to secure." If the District Judge could not be restrained, "criminals could be scattered all over the land."[165]

On Monday next, Justice Nelson announced:

> The Chief Justice, who holds by allotment the Circuit Court for the District of Virginia, has informed the court that before the pending motion for prohibition was made, he signified to the district judge his dissent from the opinion expressed by him in favor of the allowance of the writs of habeas corpus complained of in the petition; and that he has advised the district judge now holding the circuit court, to direct that this division of opinion in respect to the motion for the writ now pending in the case of Jeter Phillips, be certified to this court.[166]
>
> There is nothing in the provisional order, staying further proceedings by the district judge, which can be properly construed as prohibiting this course; and it is expected that the certificate will be filed at an early day.[167]

On February 26 the Court granted leave to the District Judge to file a supplemental return, and on April 15 put the case over to an adjourned session in October.

On Monday, May 3, the Circuit Court met in its regular term at Richmond. Chief Justice Chase held the court, and in *Griffin's Case* reversed the order of the District Judge.[168] It was, he said, "impossible to measure the evils" that would result from the construction in the decision under review. Reasons of good sense led to the conclusion that the Fourteenth Amendment did not instantly put disqualified per-

---

[164] He has previously been mentioned as counsel for Dr. Watson in 1866, and in connection with Chase's effort to win the Democratic nomination in 1868.

[165] From summary of his argument, *New York Tribune*, Feb. 13, 1869. Counsel for Phillips was present, but took no part. Judge Underwood was not in court.

[166] Chase had done this by letter of February 5—"which only repeats what I said this morning . . ."; and by another letter on Sunday, Feb-

ruary 14, presumably in the light of Saturday's conference. Underwood Papers, L.C.; rough draft of letter of February 14 in Chase Papers, Hist. Soc. of Pa.

[167] The text is in the Minutes for February 15, 1869—reprinted in 19 L. Ed. 153, which erroneously states that it was announced by the Chief Justice.

[168] Fed. Case No. 5815, decided May 10. *Enquirer and Examiner,* and *Dispatch,* May 11, 1869.

sons out of office; "legislation by Congress is necessary to give effect to the prohibition, by providing for such removal."[169]

The Chief Justice's opinion concluded with this remarkable announcement:

> This subject received the consideration of the Judges of the Supreme Court at the last term, with reference to this and kindred cases in this District, and I am authorized to say that they unanimously concur in the opinion that a person convicted by a judge de facto acting under color of office, though not de jure, and detained in custody in pursuance of his sentence, can not be properly discharged upon habeas corpus.[170]

It was most unusual to hear a Justice on circuit declare that he was authorized to announce the opinion of the Justices of the Supreme Bench on a matter pending in the Circuit Court. But the occasion was unusual. Here a District Judge, persisting in an abuse of power, was menacing the authority of the State judiciary. The question was simple; the Justices were clear that the District Judge was wrong. Prompt action was needed. The Court took this direct way to assert its supervisory power and put an end to the mischief.

The objective of *Ex parte Virginia*, to stop Judge Underwood, was thus accomplished. On the docket of the Court, the last entry was that for April 15, 1869, when it was ordered to be held under advisement.

UNITED STATES v. JEFFERSON DAVIS

How THE PROSECUTION of Jefferson Davis crawled its way to the Supreme Court docket made a long story, which for present purposes

---

[169] He noticed that action by Congress had confirmed that view. By Joint Resolution of the 40th Congress, 3d Session, officers of the provisional governments of Virginia, Texas, and Mississippi who could not take the iron-clad oath of 1862 "shall . . . be removed" unless their disabilities had been lifted; "but this resolution shall not take effect until thirty days from and after its passage." It was received by the President on February 6, 1869, and became law through his inaction. 15 Stat. 344.

[170] "Rapped on the Knuckles," commented the *New York Herald* on May 12: "Master Underwood, the exuberant but rather empty-headed personage who is United States Judge in the district of Virginia, some time ago discovered a mare's nest. [It related the *Caesar Griffin* case.] Underwood had better take the advice of his lawyer before he renders any more decisions."

The *Chicago Tribune* of May 13 reported that the Chief Justice was holding the Circuit Court for Virginia, "and, as usual, the most of his time is occupied in reversing the decisions of . . . Judge Underwood . . . ." It recounted the *Griffin* case: "Of course Judge Chase had to reverse this remarkable judgment . . ."; what he did was "no more than any rational person might expect . . . ."

may be cut short.[171] Captured in Georgia in May 1865, the Confederate President was confined at Fortress Monroe. After much uncertainty within the Johnson Administration—which at first was inclined to bring him before a military commission—Davis was indicted for treason by a federal grand jury in Virginia.[172] William M. Evarts and others had been retained by the Government as special counsel; before the case was closed, Evarts himself had become Attorney General. Davis was represented by an array of counsel, led by Charles O'Conor of New York.[173] In October 1865 President Johnson wrote Chief Justice Chase to inquire whether he would be holding the Circuit Court in Virginia during the autumn or early winter. Chase's reply took a position he had maintained for some time: that it was inappropriate for a Justice of the Supreme Court to go on circuit "in States which have been declared by the executive and legislative departments . . . to be in rebellion . . . ."[174] Both to the Government and to defense counsel it seemed indispensable that Chase, as the Justice assigned to the Fourth Circuit, should hold the court when Jefferson Davis was tried; and since the proceeding would probably be protracted, a considerable period must be found when Chase would not be occupied on the Supreme Court.

The unavoidable delay has been explained above: first Chase's scruples against his attendance until peace and civil authority had been restored—then the obstacle unwittingly created by Congress when it reduced the number of Circuits by the statute of July 23, 1866.[175] That was removed by the Act of March 2, 1867—but the Chief Justice's available time that autumn was not sufficient for a long trial.

On Saturday, November 23, 1867, he wrote from Baltimore (where he was holding court) to Judge Underwood:

> I have come reluctantly to the conclusion that I ought not to attempt to attend the Circuit Court at Richmond next week. I could in no event do more than charge the Grand Jury, for my duties in the Supreme Court make it impossible for me to be absent from Washington more than four or five days of next week, & wrong to be absent so long. I have work indeed for that Court which will use up every moment of the time until the session actually commences next Monday week. Of course I *cannot* take part in any trial at Rich-

---

[171] The narrative by Roy F. Nichols, "United States vs. Jefferson Davis," *Am. Hist. Rev.*, 31:266–84 (1926), leaves nothing to be desired. Bradley T. Johnson reported the prosecution fully in Chase's Circuit Court Decisions 1, Fed. Case No.

3621a.

[172] There is no need here to distinguish between the indictments found at different times.

[173] Supra, p. 371.

[174] Supra, p. 146.

[175] Supra, pp. 172–77.

mond likely to consume more than three four or five days of next week, & ought [not] to attempt to take part in any.[176]

From March through May 1868, Chase was presiding at the impeachment trial of the President. When in June he appeared on the bench at Richmond and professed his readiness to proceed with the Davis case, he found that Evarts (who had just completed a mighty effort

---

[176] Underwood Papers, L.C. The Chief Justice added these paragraphs:

Judge Giles [of the District Court for Maryland] has just left my room. He tells me that he has a letter from the late Chief Justice in which he questions the propriety if not the right of the District Judge to try a capital case in the absence of the Circuit Judge. He has promised to send me the letter & I shall send you a copy.

I have never considered the point, but have always supposed that a Circuit Court held by a District Judge had all the jurisdiction that it could have if held by both judges.

Next day he sent a copy of the Taney letter, and a charge to be read to the grand jury at Richmond. Underwood Papers, L.C.

A copy of Taney's letter of October 7, 1862, in the handwriting of Chase's secretary, is among the Chase Papers at the Historical Society of Pennsylvania. It made these points: inasmuch as capital cases were made triable in the Circuit instead of in the District Court, it was implied in reason that they should not be tried by the District Judge alone—"that the law intended to give the party standing on trial for his life the right to be heard before a Judge of the Supreme Court." Further: "If both Judges are present, any question that arises may be certified to the Supreme Court . . . ." The statute gave an appeal from the District Court "in civil cases of small comparative moment": hence Congress could hardly have intended that the District Judge have competence

to decide finally "in cases of life and death."

Taney doubted whether he had strength enough to come from Washington to Baltimore to hold court: "I have not been outside of my own room more than half a dozen times since the adjournment of the Supreme Court" [on March 24, six and a half months previously].

Behind this novel construction of the Judiciary Act lay a history. Marylanders supporting Southern secession had rioted on April 19, 1861, in resisting the passage of troops to the defense of Washington. To meet the opposition of which this was typical, President Lincoln authorized the suspension of the privilege of the writ of habeas corpus at any point along the line between Philadelphia and Washington as might be found necessary for the public safety. See Ann. Cyc. 1861, 55–59, 442–48; *Collected Works of Abraham Lincoln*, IV, 340–343, 344; 347; 421, 429–31; V, 24.

Out of this situation arose *Ex parte Merryman*, related above, where the Chief Justice—unavailingly—denied the power of the President thus to suspend the privilege of the writ. Fed. Case No. 9487. He pointed out that the Constitution "provides that the party accused shall be entitled to a speedy trial in a court of law."

Presently the Unionists (Henry Winter Davis and Judge Hugh L. Bond being prominent among them) gained the ascendancy in Maryland. They won the election for governor in November 1861. When the authority of the United States was secure, the District Attorney pressed for a trial of those charged with disloyal acts. And Taney and District Judge Giles exerted themselves successfully

in the defense of President Johnson) had arranged with O'Conor to let the case go over.

In July 1868, the Fourteenth Amendment was adopted. Also, Evarts became Attorney General. Each event had consequences for Jefferson Davis. Evarts made known to the Cabinet what he and his associate, Richard Henry Dana, had already concluded: that no benefit would be derived from prosecuting Jefferson Davis and that the case ought to be *nol. prossed.*

The bearing of the Amendment lay in its Section 3, disqualifying from office all who had served the Confederacy after having taken an oath to support the United States. O'Conor learned from one of his associates, who had talked with Chase, that Chase took the view that Section 3 imposed a punishment and precluded any further penalty. On that basis O'Conor moved to quash the indictment. Davis had taken an oath as a Member of Congress in 1845 (one of several occasions that could have been proved); by Section 3, counsel argued, he had suffered one, and the only, punishment that could be imposed. The *Test Oath Cases*,[177] they said, had established that disqualification because of past acts was punishment. To construe Section 3 as cumulative would make it ex post facto and offensive to basic constitutional principles. Rather it should be given a beneficent construction: it fixed a lighter punishment, which was the whole punishment, and nullified all conflicting statutes. Dana, who was always effective in dealing with questions of public law, advanced the strongest reasons against such a construction. It would be illogical, he pointed out, to exculpate persons who had held office and rebelled, while leaving punishable the host whose rebellion had not been aggravated by the breach of an oath. The *Test Oath Cases* were inapposite: there men had been debarred from the pursuit of private livelihood—whereas Section 3 sought to exclude from public office those deemed unfit, something quite apart from punishment for crime.

O'Conor, on the other side, said that "sound minds" had devised Section 3 "as a method of extricating the administration from a perplexing dilemma"—whether to "keep up a war of indictments against the Southern leaders" or to abandon all thought of retribution. Their solution was to impose the new and lesser punishment of disqualification from office. "Such was, undoubtedly, the intent of its framers; and, if so expounded by the courts, its operation will be as benign as its conception was just, wise, and politic. . . ."

---

to prevent these cases from being brought to trial. In the end the prosecutions were abandoned. Carl B. Swisher, *Roger B. Taney*, (New York: Macmillan Co., 1936), 556–60.

Taney's letter of October 7, 1862, was a part of this obstruction. He continued to find himself unable to attend the Circuit Court.

[177] Supra, pp. 240–44.

XII: Ex parte Yerger

One may pause to take note of this early ascription of purpose to the "sound minds" who wrote the Fourteenth Amendment. How many an advocate, in years to come, would assert, with no less assurance, that the view he found congenial "was, undoubtedly, the intent of [the Fourteenth Amendment's] framers"! O'Conor conveniently ignored the fact that no such wise and benign purpose was discerned in 1866, when to Southern eyes Section 3 had seemed the most degrading feature of a thoroughly unacceptable Amendment.[178]

O'Conor—tongue in cheek, since to him slavery had seemed "just, benign and beneficent"[179]—added brightly that "All honest admirers of that universal suffrage which has been established through this great civil war, earnestly desire that it should be accompanied by an amnesty as nearly perfect as possible . . . ."

On Saturday, December 5, 1868, the Chief Justice announced a failure to agree: he thought the indictment should be quashed, while Judge Underwood opposed. A certificate of their difference was sent up at once.

How paradoxical it would be if the absolution of Jefferson Davis became the first fruit, plucked from the most obnoxious branch, of the Fourteenth Amendment!

Presumably the Justices in the majority in *Ex parte Garland*[180] —Nelson, Grier, Clifford, and Field—would have found it congenial to accept O'Conor's theory of punishment coupled with amnesty. (Wayne, the fifth of the majority, was now dead.) But Chase had been among the dissenters who had maintained that the Congressional test-oath had been "purely a qualification, exacted in self-defense . . . and that it was not passed for the purpose of inflicting punishment, however merited, for past offenses." In that view Chase had remained steadfast: on April 1, 1867, two and a half months after *Garland* was decided, he had written to District Judge Giles: "I adhere to the dissent of the minority in the case before the Supreme Court, and am not willing . . . to countenance any supposition that I have changed my opinion."[181] He could not with consistency have explained two years later that

---

[178] For example, the message of Governor Daniel S. Walker of Florida, submitting the proposed Amendment to the legislature: "And who are those whom we are asked thus to disgrace with official disfranchisement? . . . Are they not those whom we have loved and trusted above all other men in the State? . . . And will their State now turn round and repay their devotion by putting a mark of infamy upon them? Perish for ever so base a thought! . . ." Fla. Sen. J. 5, 12–13 (1866); House J. 8, 16–17 (1866). Further on the contemporary understanding of the Fourteenth Amendment, see infra, ch. 20, n. 275.

[179] Article on O'Conor in D.A.B.

[180] Supra, p. 240.

[181] Chase Papers, L.C. The occasion for this statement will be explained infra, p. 767.

Section 3 of the Fourteenth Amendment did indeed both punish and at the same time cast oblivion over statutory crimes. Yet that result would have been precisely in accord with Chase's view of policy in 1868, when he was courting the approval of the Democratic party.

The problem disappeared when, at Christmas 1868, President Johnson removed the last exception to amnesty for participation in the rebellion. Accordingly on February 19, 1869, the case was dismissed from the Supreme Court docket. The punishment of Jefferson Davis, subject of so much clamor throughout the land, had become moot.

TEST OATH CASES—FROM TENNESSEE, MISSOURI, AND WEST VIRGINIA

THE DISCUSSION OF THE *Test Oath* decisions of January 1867 left a sign pointing to subsequent litigation on related issues.[182]

One reads of one of these suits in an arresting statement in the *Cincinnati Commercial* of March 11, 1869:

> The case of Broomfield [Bromfield] L. Ridley vs. Freeman Sherbrook, now in the Supreme Court of the United States, is the most important cause that ever went up from Tennessee, or, perhaps, from any other State. It involves the constitutionality of the Franchise Law, and upon its decision rests the fate of a hundred thousand disfranchised white men.

There is no *Ridley v. Sherbrook* in the United States Reports: how did it happen that this "most important case" has been lost to view?

Picking up the entry in the Court's Docket and Minutes, and examining the Transcript of Record, this is identified as the *Ridley v. Sherbrook* that had been decided by the Supreme Court of Tennessee in 1867.[183] It was a test oath case which—along with companions, *Blair* and *Woodson* from Missouri—remained for two years stuck in a deadlocked Court, until at last it was disposed of, inconclusively and inconspicuously. During all this time Democratic editors kept fussing at the Court for its delay.

It has been explained in sketching the restoration of Tennessee, that when in 1865 the hard-used Unionists were able to meet in convention, they proposed constitutional amendments to make themselves secure—and resolved that only citizens who could take a searching test oath might vote on ratification.[184] (The proposed amendments were

---

[182] Supra, pp. 247–48.   [183] 3 Coldwell (43 Tenn.) 569.   [184] Supra, p. 99.

ratified by vote of 21,104 to 40—which suggests the small base on which the Union movement rested.) The amendments provided that qualifications for the suffrage might be fixed by the legislature *which shall first assemble under the amended constitution*. Accordingly this first legislature did act, by limiting suffrage to white males who could meet a test of constant loyalty to the Union. This was done by the Franchise Law of May 3, 1866. Ridley, a Confederate early pardoned by President Johnson,[185] promptly sued to compel the registrar, Sherbrook, to accept his ballot without the test oath. At stake was the control of Tennessee: if the disfranchised rebels won, Parson Brownlow's days were numbered; his henchmen would be voted out of office, and the Radical newspapers would wither for want of official printing. When the case came before the Tennessee Supreme Court at its December term 1866, "all the office holders who had money enough, came to Nashville to . . . create a pressure in favor of a decision affirming the validity of the law."[186]

The Supreme Court at Washington was also in its December term 1866 when it decided *Cummings v. Missouri*, on January 14, 1867. The Tennessee judges took note—"as well as we can understand from the newspaper report"—and went right ahead to sustain the Franchise Law, on March 21. The three judges were unanimous. Justice Field's opinion in *Cummings* had stressed the proposition that one had a property in his means of livelihood, of which he must not be deprived by a test oath; but that reasoning, said the Tennessee court, did not apply to the elective franchise, which might be extended or restricted by the sovereign people.

Ridley obtained a writ of error, and docketed his case in the Supreme Court on July 6, 1867.

On its heels came two cases from Missouri: the suit of Frank P. Blair against Thompson and Ridgely, wherein the State court had sustained the test oath as to voters,[187] and *State ex rel. Wingate, Attorney General v. Warren Woodson*, which upheld the test for eligibility to hold office.[188] The Missouri judges, like those of Tennessee, distinguished *Cummings* as being based on one's property in his profession or calling; at the same time they praised Justice Miller's dissent as "an opinion which for ability, logic, and admirable juridical criticism, has rarely been excelled even in that august tribunal."[189]

---

[185] Pardoned on July 26, 1865; an old acquaintance, he was thenceforth a warm supporter, as is reflected by several letters from Ridley in the Andrew Johnson Papers, L.C.

[186] *Cincinnati Commercial*, Mar.

11, 1869.

[187] 41 Mo. 63 (Mar. term, 1867), supra, pp. 151–52, 247.

[188] 41 Mo. 227 (July term, 1867), supra, p. 247.

[189] 41 Mo. at 170.

In the Supreme Court the three cases fared together, so that one need not particularize. At December term 1867 the Court denied Blair's motion to advance out of turn. (Under the rule, "special and peculiar circumstances" must be shown: even supposing that the four Democrats saw good reason, there must be five votes to grant the motion.) If the cases had been taken up at once, and if a decision adverse to the test oaths had been made at that term, there would have been an immense benefit to the Democratic party in time for the election of 1868.[190] The Missouri Democrats in that year's platform protested that

> though the reasoning of the United States Supreme Court in the adjudication of cases proves the Missouri test-oath unconstitutional, null, and void, this [Radical] party of proscription still requires the oath to be administered . . . .[191]

In November, Grant carried the State by about 26,000 (while the Republican candidate for Governor won by a narrow margin); the number excluded by the test oath was more, perhaps far more than Grant's majority.[192] In Tennessee, of a total vote of 83,000, Grant had a majority of 30,000—which apparently was less than the number of the disfranchised.[193]

In March 1869, in their turn, the three cases were argued before the full bench of eight Justices. In the Missouri suits, Montgomery Blair and William M. Evarts attacked and Senator Charles D. Drake defended the proscriptive requirement.

Frank Blair and Drake, the protagonists in the struggle over Radicalism in Missouri, stood in marked contrast. The one had been foremost in frustrating pro-slavery Governor Jackson's effort to bind Missouri to the Confederacy in 1861. Thereafter he distinguished himself before Vicksburg, led a corps in Sherman's march to the sea, and worked for Lincoln's reelection. Now he was a belligerent Democrat. Drake had made an even more remarkable progress in the opposite direction. In 1860 he supported Douglas for President and Jackson for Governor. Becoming a convert to the Republican party, he adhered to its "Jacobin" wing in a factional quarrel that brought Lincoln to despair.[194] Presently he led a delegation of eighty-eight fault-finders to Washington, to quicken Lincoln's perception of the moral issues of

---

[190] It will be recalled that Blair was the nominee for Vice President at that election. Supra, p. 546.

[191] Ann. Cyc. 1868, 521.

[192] Ann. Cyc. 1868, 521, where it is estimated that about 30,000 were disfranchised.

[193] Ann. Cyc. 1868, 725; cf. 1870, 710, and 1872, 755.

[194] "I have been tormented with it beyond endurance for months, by both sides." Lincoln to Drake and others, May 15, 1863. *Collected Works of Abraham Lincoln*, VI, 218.

the war—with brass bands and anti-slavery committees greeting their progress at train stops along the way.[195]

Missouri's loyalty oath was Drake's particular handiwork. In 1867 he was elected to the Senate, where he stood for "radical Radicalism"—without, however, attaining a position of leadership.

Blair, returning from the war, undertook to break the Radicals' hold upon the State. At the election in November 1865 he professed an inability to swear that he had never "been in armed hostility to the United States . . . or to the government of this State," inasmuch as he had taken arms against the pro-Confederate governor. He sued the officers who refused to accept his ballot.

Arguing before the Supreme Court, Drake said that that contention was "most extraordinary"; in fighting to keep the State from being carried out of the Union, General Blair "was not acting in violation of law, but in obedience to it, and [his] refusal . . . to take the oath was owing to his own perverse and obstinate will."[196] He had not scrupled to take the oath at the election in 1868. Montgomery Blair interrupted to say, "that was true, but the oath was taken under protest as unconstitutional."[197] Evarts (who had just ceased to be Attorney General at the close of Johnson's Presidency) told the Court that this was "a case of greatest importance"; when General Blair came home from the war he found that he had been deprived of the right to vote by a law in the nature of a bill of attainder.

The Court held the test oath cases under advisement until October next, when it would resume at an adjourned session.[198]

The *Louisville Courier-Journal*, impatient, said that the Court had "lost much of its claim to public confidence"; "it lacks the courage

---

[195] Carl Sandburg describes the scene when, with his delegation marshalled around three sides of the East Room, Drake in stentorian tones read his lecture. To Lincoln it was a most depressing experience; one of his responses was that "I desire to so conduct the affairs of this administration that if, in the end . . . I have lost every other friend on earth, I shall at least have one friend left, and that friend shall be down inside of me."
The following evening Secretary Chase opened his home to the delegates, and "told them he was heartily in sympathy with their mission." *Abraham Lincoln: The War Years*, (New York: Harcourt, Brace and Co., 1939) II, 401–9. David Donald, ed.,

Inside Lincoln's Cabinet: The Civil War Diaries of Chase, (New York, London, Toronto: Longmans, Green and Co., 1954), 207. Entry for Sept. 30, 1863.
[196] The argument was summarized in the *New York Tribune*, Mar. 26, 1869.
[197] After the decision in Cummings v. Missouri, "it was argued by Democratic newspapers and orators that no citizen would be guilty of legal perjury who should take the oath . . . ." But a statute of 1868 established a system of boards of registration, which upon evidence or upon their own knowledge could reject the vote of one who took the oath. Ann. Cyc. 1868, 518–21.
[198] Order of Apr. 15, 1869.

to bring itself into collision with the dominant political party." And presently—typical of Henry Watterson's pungent remarks—the Court "has no more nerve than a mass of dough or a bowl of pig's-foot jelly."[199] The *Jackson Clarion* was confident that when the Court did speak, "the whole brood of tyrannical laws . . . to exclude freeborn men . . . will fall to the ground to the utter shame and consternation of their guilty authors."[200]

On January 31, 1870—Grier's last day on the bench—the situation within the Court was disclosed: it was announced that the Missouri court's judgment in *Blair v. Thompson* was affirmed *by an equally divided court.*[201] (Shortly thereafter, *Missouri v. Woodson*, and the Tennessee case, *Ridley v. Sherbrook*, were dismissed with costs.[202]) Throughout the three years the Court had consisted of eight. Now Congress had raised the membership to nine; soon President Grant would make two appointments. But unlike the pending question of legal tender,[203] which was of continuing importance, the constitutionality of test oaths for voters and office-holders could well be laid aside, unresolved—along with the old fighting issue of punishment for Jefferson Davis. Affirmance of the judgment below by an equal division ended the litigation without leaving a trace in the United States Reports.

---

[199] Mar. 30, Dec. 15, 1869.

[200] *Weekly Clarion*, Mar. 25, 1869.

[201] The *Cincinnati Enquirer*, bitterly partisan, carried an editorial on February 3 on "The Missouri Test-oath and Chief Justice Chase." Many, it said, had "expected better things of the Court . . . . But the Court appears to have been frightened by the bill of Senator Drake, of Missouri, which strikes directly at their most important jurisdiction . . . ." (On Drake's bill, see supra, pp. 586–87.)

Chief Justice Chase is for the test-oaths. This, we presume, will put him in line with the Republican party again, and, perhaps, will make him its candidate for President in 1872.

Alexander Long sent a clipping to Chase, who replied on February 10:

The article is founded wholly on misapprehension.

No doubt the Missouri oath is detestable, but that was not the question: but can the State regulate suffrage? There was so much injustice, and needless harshness in the extent of the right to challenge, and in the oath by which the challenged voter could relieve himself from the challenge, that one was naturally inclined to go as far as possible against it; but I thought and still think it safer not to interfere with the right of the State to regulate her own internal concerns. I am glad to see that the People of Missouri are about to wipe out the blot from their Constitution.

As to putting himself into line with any party, Chase wrote that "I would not compromise my principles for fifty Presidencies." Chase Papers, L.C.

[202] While their cases were pending, both Woodson and Ridley died. In the case of the former, who claimed an office, his administrator continued the litigation until, on February 3, 1870, it was dismissed on motion of Blair, his counsel. Ridley was suing only to establish the personal right to vote; appropriately the representative of his estate was not substituted; the case was dismissed on December 7, 1870.

[203] Infra, p. 677.

XII: Ex parte Yerger

The people of the border States were moving toward moderation. In Tennessee, in May 1869 the State Supreme Court held invalid legislation by which the Executive had been empowered to set aside the registration of voters.[204] That led to the election, in August, of a governor and legislators who favored the abolition of the disabilities; and that in turn led to the adoption in March 1870, by a vote of almost 3 to 1, of a new constitution that put an end to test oaths.[205]

In Missouri, a liberal movement led by B. Gratz Brown and Carl Schurz developed within the Republican party; its objectives were universal suffrage and amnesty, and reform in government. The legislature of 1869 chose Schurz for Senator, over the Radical candidate supported by Senator Drake. The year 1870 saw the utter rout of the Radicals. The Democrats, discouraged by the Supreme Court's failure to decide *Blair v. Thompson* as they had hoped, nominated no candidates for State office. The Radicals (who indorsed the Grant administration) and the Liberal Republicans (who did not) put up opposing tickets; the latter, supported by the Democrats, elected Brown as Governor. Constitutional amendments to do away with the test oaths were adopted. All this was done by overwhelming majorities. In December Drake accepted Grant's appointment to become Chief Justice of the Court of Claims, and withdrew from the Senate; but not until he and Schurz had engaged in a memorable exchange on Missouri's experience with the test oath and on what each thought of the part played by the other.[206] To the place Drake vacated, the Missouri legislature elected Frank P. Blair.[207]

In West Virginia, it will be recalled, the Court of Appeals had in 1867 refused to bow to the Supreme Court's ruling in *Cummings v. Missouri*.[208] In 1870 the State court maintained its stand, in a decision that held further that the pardon of the President was no answer to the

---

[204] State v. Staten, 6 Coldwell (46 Tenn.) 233.

[205] Ann. Cyc. 1869, 661–66; 1870, 703–6.

[206] Schurz created the occasion by proposing a resolution to the effect that disqualification had been imposed upon rebels by imperative necessity; but that as soon as such necessity ceased, fundamental principles of our government demanded their removal. He spoke on December 15, 1869. Cong. Globe, 40th Cong., 3d Sess., 118–28. Drake replied next day, in a speech entitled "Betrayal of the Republican party in Missouri." He said that the Liberal

Republican movement was "a measure of war against the administration of General Grant. . . . Sir, does the honored Republican party, indeed, need a new birth?" Cong. Globe, 40th Cong., 3d Sess., App. 1–8.

[207] He served from January 20, 1871, to March 3, 1873—"an insignificant brief term" as *The Nation* observed. 21:34, July 15, 1875.

Andrew Johnson, who returned to the Senate on March 4, 1875, died on December 6, 1875.

These items suggest the softening effects of time.

[208] Supra, p. 247.

State's requirement.[209] At the same time it sustained the suitor's test oath: whereas West Virginia law gave a rehearing to one whose property had been taken on an attachment, an Act of February 11, 1865,[210] imposed a test oath before one could exercise this right to sue.[211]

But when in 1873 the federal Supreme Court struck this down in two sentences, citing *Cummings* and *Garland*,[212] the State court promptly conformed.[213] Already, by a new constitution adopted in 1872, the State had prohibited political tests as a prerequisite to the enjoyment of civil and political rights; "Nor shall any person be deprived by law, of any right, or privilege, because of any act done prior to the passage of such law."[214]

The country was emerging from the preoccupations of the war, and once-lively issues were being laid to rest.

---

[209] *Ex parte* Quarrier and Fitzhugh, 4 W. Va. 210.

[210] Acts of 1865, ch. 29.

[211] Peerce v. Carskadon, 4 W. Va. 234. "When a government makes war upon its enemies, the right to confiscate their property as a war measure is unquestionable; and it is the same whether its enemies be citizens or aliens . . . ." The court relied on Virginia's confiscation of the property of British enemies, as sustained by Judge Roane in Read v. Read, 5 Call [Va.] 161 (1804).

[212] Pierce v. Carskadon, 16 Wall. 234. Bradley, J., noted dissent, "on the ground that the test oath in question was competent as a war measure in time of civil war."

[213] Peerce v. Carskadon, 6 W. Va. 383 (1873).

[214] Art. III, Bill of Rights, cl. 11.

CHAPTER XIII

A Union of "Indestructible States": Virginia v. West Virginia and Texas v. White

W HEN A STATE was denied representation in Senate and House, when in the eyes of Congress it had "no legal government" and was "made subject to the military authority of the United States" (to quote the Reconstruction Act of 1867), did such an entity have standing to litigate its rights as "a State" within the meaning of Article III, the Constitution's article on the judiciary? *Commonwealth of Virginia v. State of West Virginia,*[1] docketed in the Supreme Court in December 1866, must confront that difficulty. So too must *Texas v. White,*[2] filed in February 1867. The problem had been inherent in suits by Mississippi and Georgia, already discussed,[3] but each had gone off on some other preliminary point.

Virginia's case, advanced for early argument in May 1867, produced an equal division among the eight Justices; it was put over, and remained undecided until March 1871.

Texas v. White came along like a tortoise and was decided in April 1869.

These two cases will be considered in the order in which they came to the Court.

STATEMENT OF THE CASE

VIRGINIA'S SUIT against West Virginia was brought to reestablish jurisdiction over the counties of Berkeley and Jefferson, the easternmost tip of West Virginia.[4] In the outcome, the claim was denied by a

---

[1] 11 Wall. 39 (1871).
[2] 7 Wall. 700 (1869).
[3] Supra, ch. 8.
[4] This was distinct from the more celebrated controversy over West

Virginia's share in Virginia's public debt, which as Virginia v. West Virginia was litigated before the Supreme Court, from 206 U.S. 290 (1907) to 246 U.S. 565 (1918).

majority of four Justices (Miller, Swayne, Strong, and Bradley); Justices Davis, Clifford, and Field dissented. Chase, C.J., and Nelson, J., were absent by reason of illness.[5]

This case involved the application of the Compact Clause—which in itself makes it noteworthy. Benjamin R. Curtis led for the claimant, Reverdy Johnson for the respondent—which assured highly effective advocacy. Each side had a tenable position, as the close division within the Court reflected. Democratic sympathies would incline toward the old commonwealth, while West Virginia, born of loyalty to the Union, had an especial appeal to Republicans. The litigation was quite out of the ordinary, and repays examination.

By act of May 13, 1862, the loyal legislature of Virginia (then at Wheeling) gave consent to the formation of the State of West Virginia, to be composed of certain counties. Furthermore, Section 2 consented to the inclusion of the counties of Berkeley and Jefferson, and others named, whenever the voters thereof ratified the West Virginia constitution. Correspondingly, the constitution of the new State of West Virginia provided for the inclusion of those counties upon such vote. With this constitution, but with Berkeley and Jefferson not yet annexed, West Virginia was admitted to the Union pursuant to an Act of Congress of December 31, 1862.[6]

Elections were held in Berkeley and Jefferson in May 1863 under the Virginia statute, which had made it the duty of the Governor to ascertain and certify the result. In each case Governor Pierpoint determined that the vote had been in favor of annexation; he so certified to the Governor of West Virginia. The West Virginia legislature accepted the transfer and incorporated the counties.

The Constitution is so straightforward a document that it is unusual for any problem of textual intricacy to arise. In the transfer of these counties, however, there was a catch. The Constitution, in providing for the admission of new States, declares (Article IV, Section 3) that "no new State shall be formed or erected within the Jurisdiction of any other State . . . without the Consent of the Legislatures of the States concerned as well as of the Congress." For the formation of West Virginia, Congress and the Virginia legislature had given the consent required. But then there is the so-called Compact Clause (Article I, Section 10, clause 3), which provides that "No State shall, without the Consent of Congress, . . . enter into any Agreement or Compact with another State . . . ." Had *that* been complied with in respect of Congressional consent to transfer

---

[5] The appointment of Justices Strong and Bradley is related at length, infra, pp. 719–37; the illness of Chase and Nelson at pp. 655, 657.
[6] 12 Stat. 633.

Berkeley and Jefferson? West Virginia's leaders had supposed that nothing further was necessary: Congress had admitted their State with a constitution that contemplated the annexation.

But when the Confederates came home from the war they made trouble. The Virginia legislature that met in Richmond in December 1865—while claiming, for every beneficial purpose, direct succession from the loyal government that had sat at Wheeling and then at Alexandria—represented in spirit the same Virginia that had been fighting to secede. Instantly it repealed the legislation of 1862 and 1863 consenting to a transfer. West Virginia now urgently requested that Congress expressly declare its consent to the compact for the transfer. The House Judiciary Committee brought in a joint resolution to that effect. Virginia, it reported, could not now revoke its executed grant, accepted and acted upon by the grantee. It noted, too, the practical consideration that "the great thoroughfare for trade and travel of those two counties is the Baltimore and Ohio railroad. They have no direct railroad or other connexions with Richmond or any other part of the State of Virginia, except the [Shenandoah] valley counties adjacent to them."[7] The measure, its sponsor said, was "merely for the purpose of settling the controverted question . . . ."[8] Representative Andrew Jackson Rogers of New Jersey, combative Democrat, replied that by reason of Virginia's recent action there was no longer an agreement—nothing to which Congress could now add its consent. From his corner, Thad Stevens made sport of the report; Virginia, he said, was conquered territory, so what its legislature did was immaterial. In the end, by party votes, it was resolved "that Congress hereby recognizes the transfer . . . and consents thereto."[9]

Of course that could not settle the controversy. If Congress did not consent until 1866, how meet the point that Virginia had withdrawn from the agreement in 1865? The Judiciary Committee had talked contract law; but surely that could not avail against the Constitution's specific command that States shall not enter into agreements without the consent of Congress. If it were conceivable that, while Congressional action was awaited, such an agreement might have a certain binding force between the two States, then Virginia's bill alleged such "false suggestion" inducing Governor Pierpoint's certificate as should, it was argued, permit Virginia to withdraw.

West Virginia demurred: it said that the bill itself failed to make a

---

[7] H.R. Rep. No. 6, 39th Cong., 1st Sess. Jan. 12, 1866.

[8] Cong. Globe, 39–1, 689. Feb. 6, 1866.

[9] J. Res. 12 of Mar. 10, 1866; 14 Stat. 350. Cong. Globe, 39–1, House at 698, Feb. 6; Senate at 1205, Mar. 6.

case. The statutes as set out had vested in the Governor authority to ascertain and certify. Congress had consented when it admitted West Virginia with a constitution providing for the annexation.

B. R. CURTIS FOR VIRGINIA

ARGUMENT WAS HEARD on May 7 and 8, 1867. The Reconstruction Act was barely two months old; now counsel would be discussing its effect upon Virginia, which stood in a unique position among Southern States because there had always been a government loyal to the Union. The oral arguments of the several counsel were transcribed and each was separately printed, to be considered by the Justices along with the briefs.

As was his wont, Curtis proceeded as though he were solving a problem by logical demonstration. He would say, "we have advanced so far as this upon firm ground," and then move to the next position. His client, the Commonwealth of Virginia, throughout the war and that "complete restoration" that ensued, had had a government "recognized by Congress and the executive as in harmony with the Union, and at all times at peace with the United States . . . ."[10] Such was Virginia's unbroken record down to March 1867, when Congressional Reconstruction was imposed. That regime was said to be supported by "what is glibly called the 'war power.' " "Why is this supposed war power exerted to destroy the government of the State and expel the State from the Union?" The only possible reason was that "during the rebellion," the authority of "this lawful, recognized and friendly government of Virginia" had been defied and set at naught by rebels. "But whose fault was that? Were not the United States bound by the Constitution to maintain and uphold, and make effectual throughout the entire geographical territory of Virginia," the authority of this lawful and loyal government? By the express words of the Constitution, the United States was bound to protect Virginia against invasion and insurrection.

> And having failed in the performance of this clear duty, can the United States attribute it as a fault of the lawful government of Virginia, that this duty was not performed, and attach to its own failure of performance the penalties of destruction of that lawful government, and the expulsion of the State from the Union [?] . . .
>
> I deny the power of Congress thus to destroy the State of Virginia; and if it shall be found that this recent legislation of Congress has that extent, I respectfully insist and submit to this Court that Congress exceeded its power.

---

[10] Oral argument, 32.

622

But it did not seem absolutely necessary so to interpret the Reconstruction Act, "and certainly this Court will go no further in this direction than it shall find to be absolutely necessary."[11] (Curtis was ever the prudent counsellor; unlike Jeremiah S. Black in *Georgia v. Stanton, Georgia v. Grant, Meade et al.*, and *Ex parte McCardle*, Curtis had no mission to seek a condemnation of Congress.)

Thus, as Curtis would have it, the fault all along had lain with the "United States," which had failed to perform its duty toward the ever-loyal "State of Virginia." This showed what conceptual analysis might do by means of "pernicious abstractions."

On the merits of Virginia's claim, Curtis fastened upon the words of the Constitution: no State shall, without the consent of Congress, *enter into* any agreement with another State. This did not mean that Congress would *ratify* an agreement already made: it was a prohibition to contract. States might *negotiate*—but *contract* they might not until Congress had consented to their doing so.[12]

In any event, an essential of the supposed agreement had been withdrawn before Congress declared its consent. Curtis "confidently submitted" that Virginia was not estopped by the certificates made by the Governor in 1863. Virginia's willingness was always subject to a fundamental condition, that in fact a majority of the inhabitants elected to be transferred. When it found "that the means devised for ascertaining its performance had proved to be ineffectual through fraud and deception," there was no breach of faith in withdrawing from the proposed compact.[13]

REVERDY JOHNSON FOR WEST VIRGINIA

REVERDY JOHNSON REPLIED effectively to what Curtis had had to say on the merits. The mode and time of Congressional consent to an interstate compact was not prescribed by the Constitution. It might be given before, simultaneously with, or subsequent to the compact. "All that is required to render the compact valid between all parties is that Congress shall in fact consent.[14]

That Virginia's conditions had been met was settled conclusively by the Governor's certificate, as expressly provided in Virginia's statute. The other party, West Virginia, "was bound to rely upon such information. She had no right to go behind it and inquire into the facts. To have done so would have been merely impertinent." Acting upon that determination, West Virginia had accepted the counties and their

---

[11] Ibid., 33–34. [12] Ibid., 9–19. [13] Ibid., 37. [14] Ibid., 11.

inhabitants. "Under these circumstances to permit Virginia to regain them upon the allegation . . . that the certificate of the Governor was untrue . . . (especially in the absence of any pretense that West Virginia had committed or been privy to any fraud in obtaining the certificate) would be to suffer Virginia to perpetrate a fraud upon the new State." When West Virginia acted upon this assurance, the compact became binding, and neither could withdraw without the consent of the other.[15]

(Johnson's argument would come home to West Virginia eighty years later, when that State claimed to free itself from an interstate compact then in operation, on the basis of its assertion that its acceptance had been inconsistent with its own constitution. Rejecting this pretension, the Court cited *Virginia v. West Virginia* as having established the proposition that "Where the States themselves are before this Court for the determination of a controversy between them, neither can determine their rights *inter sese,* and this Court must pass upon every question essential to such a determination, although local legislation and questions of State authorization may be involved."[16])

Besides his reliance on the obligation of good faith essential to the scheme of interstate compacts, Johnson also invoked the authority of several recent decisions in a somewhat comparable matter. In *Knox County v. Aspinwall*[17] and cases that followed it, a statute had enacted that the governing board of a county might subscribe to railroad stock and issue bonds, provided that upon notice a majority of the voters approved; in a suit on such bonds, the Court had held that the determination whether the conditions had been complied with had been left to the board, and that purchasers of bonds were entitled to rely upon the board's certificate. With even more force, said Johnson, that reasoning should be applied where the Governor had made a certificate in execution of an express provision of the statute.

(The *Aspinwall* case, it will presently appear, became a bloody angle in the bitter struggle between bondholders and the taxpayers in communities, especially in the trans-Mississippi West, that had issued bonds in consideration of the promises of railroad promoters.[18])

Johnson advanced a second reason why the bill should be dismissed: that Virginia was not then "a State" qualified to bring the suit. By the Reconstruction Act, Congress had established the status of Virginia, and the Court should accept that political determination. Johnson

---

[15] Ibid., 7.
[16] West Virginia v. Sims, 341 U.S. 22, 29 (1951), quoting Hughes, C.J., in Kentucky v. Indiana, 281 U.S. 163, 176 (1930). The consideration of good faith on which Reverdy Johnson re- / lied was the basis on which Justice Jackson placed his concurring opinion. 341 U.S. at 35.
[17] 21 How. 539 (1859).
[18] Infra, pp. 931-33.

made clear that his personal opinion had not been in accord with the judgment of Congress.

In the Senate, two months later, when the Second Supplementary Reconstruction Bill was under consideration,[19] Johnson gave this explanation of the matter raised before the Court:

> the other point that I made—and I wanted the question decided— . . . was that Virginia was not a State . . . . I said . . . that upon a question of that kind, State or no State, which was a question in its nature political, it was to be submitted exclusively to the jurisdiction of Congress . . . ; and as they had decided by the [Reconstruction Act] that these States were not entitled to representation . . . , that was binding on the judiciary.

Johnson then gave his estimate of what the Court would say to that argument:

> The case is now held under advisement. I do not know certainly what the opinion of any one of the judges is upon that particular question, but I have reason to believe that again they are unanimous in believing that there is nothing in the point; that Virginia is as much a State now as she was the day she passed her ordinance of secession, and is, consequently, as much entitled now to claim the original jurisdiction of the Supreme Court as she would have been if she had never gone into the rebellion.[20]

In short, Johnson felt confident that his contention on this point would be rejected.

On May 16, 1867, a week after the argument in the *West Virginia* matter, the Court adjourned. That summer Justice Wayne died. And on January 21, 1868, as the Minutes show, the Chief Justice announced that the Court "is equally divided on the demurrer, and equally divided also upon the order which should be made in consequence of that division." (If this had been an appeal from a subordinate court, an equal division would have resulted in affirming what had been done below: but *Virginia v. West Virginia* had originated in the Supreme Court.) So the matter stood still until—after the resignation of Justice Grier and the appointment of Justices Strong and Bradley—on April 8, 1870, Curtis asked that it be set down for another argument.

In the meantime, in April 1869, the Court had decided in *Texas v. White* that a State undergoing Congressional Reconstruction was nonetheless qualified to maintain a suit. Grier, Swayne, and Miller, JJ.,

---

[19] Supra, p. 342.   [20] Cong. Globe, 40-1, 580. July 11, 1867.

had dissented on that point.[21] Also, on January 26, 1870, Virginia was readmitted to representation in Congress.

REARGUMENT

REARGUMENT WAS HEARD on February 13, 14, 15, and 16, 1871, before a Bench of seven.[22] Reverdy Johnson was now joined by Charles J. Faulkner of Berkeley County, distinguished as a lawyer, diplomat, and Confederate soldier.[23] A feature of this second presentation was a "Supplemental Argument" filed by Benjamin Stanton on behalf of West Virginia, to the effect that here was a "political question," not within the grant of "judicial power."[24] The distinction, he said, had been discussed "very fully" in *Georgia v. Stanton*, subsequent to the first argument in *Virginia v. West Virginia*.

Stanton had a point worthy of consideration, even though, fortunately, it won the assent of none of the Justices. In the great case of *Rhode Island v. Massachusetts*,[25] a suit contesting a boundary fixed in colonial times, Daniel Webster had denied the Court's jurisdiction: the judicial power extended only to "cases in law and equity"; that, he argued, excluded cases that were "political, or involving questions of sovereign power between States." Only Chief Justice Taney had accepted that view. Justice Baldwin, for the majority, had said that a decision on a boundary was in no wise more difficult than one "on lines between separate tracts of land . . . ." Putting the Court's jurisdiction on a broad foundation, he had said that inasmuch as States of the Union could neither go to war nor make settlement wait upon their pleasure, a resort to the judiciary was their only practicable course. Whether their controversy concerned "boundary, jurisdiction, or any other cause whatever," it was to be decided by the Court, according to a "solemn consideration of the rules of law appropriate to its nature as a judicial question . . . ." But, Stanton now pointed out, Virginia's complaint presented "no question of fact, affecting the boundaries of the State; . . .

---

[21] Infra, p. 640.

[22] Supra, pp. 619–20.

[23] (1806–84), former Congressman, Minister to France under Buchanan, and officer on Stonewall Jackson's staff. See D.A.B.

He pointed out that Virginia had now been readmitted to representation "with a constitution asserting no claim to any such territory." Brief of Chas. J. Faulkner (1870), p. 4.

[24] Stanton (1809–72), a cousin of the War Secretary, had been a Whig Congressman from Ohio in four Congresses before the war. After the war he had practiced at Martinsburg, West Virginia, the seat of Berkeley County, and then settled in Wheeling.

The argument was congenial to Stanton. In Congress on January 12, 1857—after the *Dred Scott Case* had been submitted—he had warned the Justices that they ought not to pass upon "great political questions." Cong. Globe, 34–3, 300–301.

[25] 12 Pet. 657 (1838).

no question of law arising upon the construction of deeds, charters, or title papers . . . ." "The relief prayed for is *not* the restoration of any rights of property, legal or equitable, but jurisdiction and sovereignty.[26] Congress, which could act upon considerations of which the Court could not take cognizance, had consented to the transfer. Stanton asked the Court to regard that as definitive.

THE DECISION

ON MARCH 6, 1871, it was announced that West Virginia's right was sustained and the bill was dismissed. The contention that Stanton had argued, however, was expressly rejected.

Justice Miller spoke for the majority. West Virginia's challenge to the Court's jurisdiction, he said, could not be sustained "without reversing the settled course of decision in this Court"; the Court's jurisdiction had been "satisfactorily sustained" in the elaborate opinion of Justice Baldwin in *Rhode Island v. Massachusetts.*

Coming to the merits, the consent of Congress to a compact between States need not be "express and formal"; here "an inference clear and satisfactory" was found that in admitting West Virginia, Congress had noticed and consented to the agreement making the accession of the two counties dependent upon a popular vote. Now Virginia contended that no valid election had ever been held—that Governor Pierpoint had been misled when he made his certificate. The answer was, Virginia's statute had "rested . . . the whole question on his judgment and in his hands . . . . She can have no right, years after all this has been settled, to come into a court of chancery to charge . . . that her own subordinate agents have misled her Governor, and that her solemn act transfering these counties shall be set aside . . . ."

Justice Davis, for the dissenters, said: "To my mind nothing is clearer than that Congress never did undertake to give its consent to the transfer" until March 1866—and that came too late.

Virginia v. West Virginia was different from the ordinary interstate controversy over a boundary, for reasons Stanton had pointed out. Where the object of the suit is to establish a line, then sovereignty follows as a consequence; here, however, the Court must decide which State had authority to rule over the territory and inhabitants of the two counties, and it would be the boundary that followed as a consequence. It was well that the Court made nothing of this distinction, being "content" to accept Justice Baldwin's large conception whereby the power of the Court was commensurate with the needs of the federal system.

---

[26] Supplemental Argument, 2.

MISSOURI v. KENTUCKY

WITHIN A FEW WEEKS the Court decided a boundary suit of the ordinary sort, in *Missouri v. Kentucky*.[27] The complainant laid claim to Wolf Island in the Mississippi River, then possessed and governed by Kentucky. The boundary had been defined as the middle of the main channel, and Kentucky was able to convince the Court that at all material times in the historical chain of title the main current had run to the west of the island. The suit had been filed on February 11, 1859; the Docket contains eighty-two entries of depositions, documents and maps, motions made, agreements entered, and the like. Argument was heard from January 25 to February 2, 1871—a part of each of five days and all of two more. Montgomery Blair and Franklin A. Dick[28] appeared for Missouri against Senator Garrett Davis and Henry Stanbery. Justice Davis delivered the opinion. He was always at his best in cases that called for practical experience. Here he went through the testimony of rivermen, settlers, explorers, and army engineers,[29] tested this by the known characteristics of the Western rivers, and thereupon confirmed Kentucky's title. Testimony had shown that the main channel was shifting and would ultimately run between Wolf Island and the Kentucky shore—which indeed did come to pass.

TEXAS' STANDING TO SUE

Texas v. White[30] is celebrated by reason of one memorable sentence—the most enduring thing Chase ever said: "The Constitution, in all its provisions, looks to an indestructible Union, composed of indestructible States."[31] This has become a national motto. But to appreciate its significance in 1869 one must recall the context.

In debating whether the erring States were "in the Union" men were seeking a simple premise that would yield answers to complex problems.[32] If the States were "in," it could be argued that as a logical

---

[27] 11 Wall. 395, decided Mar. 27, 1871.

[28] Dick, formerly an active Unionist at St. Louis, and Blair, in association, were constantly before the Court throughout the next ten years.

[29] "In a controversy of this nature, where State pride is more or less involved, it is hardly to be expected that the witnesses would all agree in their testimony."

[30] 7 Wall. 700 (1869).

[31] In the *Oxford Dictionary of Quotations* (1955 ed.) this is one of three of Chase's utterances; in Bartlett's *Familiar Quotations* (1955 ed.) it is one of two.

[32] Much as after the acquisition of insular possessions in 1899, the resulting problem of their place in the constitutional system was oversimplified by the question, "Does the Con-

consequence they should at once be treated exactly like the other States. If they were "out," then the Union and the Confederacy, like the fighters in Lincoln's story, had finished with each clad in the other's greatcoat. On the circuit, in 1867, Chase had found occasion to declare that

> these acts [of secession] did not effect, even for a moment, the separation of North Carolina from the Union, any more than the acts of an individual who commits grave offenses against the state by resisting its officers and defying its authorities, separate him from the State. Such acts may subject the offender even to outlawry, but can discharge him from no duty and can relieve him from no responsibility.[33]

Now in *Texas v. White* he was saying for the Court that, whatever the consequences of rebellion might be, at any rate the State had not withdrawn from the Union.

Chase had written on this theme in 1865, to guide his political friend Murat Halstead and associates of the *Cincinnati Commercial*. Here is the text of his draft:

> To the Proprietors of the Commercial
> Gentlemen,
>   Please allow me a few words about what is variously called "reconstruction"—"reorganization"—"restoration." I prefer the term "reorganization," as best expressing my idea of what is to be done in order to restore the relation of the States which have been [in] rebellion with the United States & the National Government.
>   As the starting point for what I have to say I take this proposition: the pretended Acts or Ordinances of Secession were absolutely null & all acts in furtherance of them . . . are equally null.
>   From this proposition it follows logically that no State has ever been withdrawn from the Union or from the authority of the National Government by any such acts or Ordinances; but each State, with its former boundaries & with its entire population remains, in the Union & subject to its constitutional authority as before attempted Secession.

---

stitution follow the flag?" Downs v. Bidwell, 182 U.S. 244 (1901); De-Lima v. Bidwell, 182 U.S. 1 (1901); Dooley v. United States, 182 U.S. 222 (1901).

[33] Shortridge v. Macon, Fed. Case No. 12,812 (C.C.D.N.C., June 1867). Citizens of Pennsylvania sued a citizen of North Carolina on a note executed in 1860. Held, compulsory payment of a debt under the Con-federate sequestration laws was no defense.

Chase's declaration in Shortridge v. Macon had been quoted by John Van S. L. Pruyn in the House on January 20, and by Reverdy Johnson in the Senate on January 27, 1868. Cong. Globe, 40–2, 639 and 775, apropos of the Supplementary Reconstruction Bill, H.R. 439.

But it does not follow that the *entire* population of a rebel State remains in the *same condition* or the *same relation* to the Nation & the National Government.

Precisely at this point comes in the error, as I think it, of those who insist that the rights of suffrage in reorganization are to be ascertained by the terms of the constitutions of the rebel States existing at the time of rebellion.

Indeed it is difficult to see upon what ground of reason it can be asserted that the Constitution & Laws existing before the rebellion must determine such relations as those of citizenship & suffrage without conceding at the same time that they determine who may be elected & to what offices; & without conceding moreover the validity of elections in pursuance of them. Consequently the legal existence of State organizations & State officials, created or claiming authority under them. If one class of relations must exist because the Constitutions & Laws before rebellion recognized it, why not all classes?[34]

The objective of this composition evidently was the dissemination of Chase's firm opinion that for the South's new day, suffrage ought not to be limited by the laws of the past. (He had pressed that view upon Lincoln, and then upon Johnson.) By general admission, a new start was to be made in choosing those who would govern the people: then why was it supposed that the old law established the class of people who were eligible to choose them? Unlike Thad Stevens, Chase did not want a theory (that of conquest) which would permit a redistribution of rebels' property; the theory should, however, require that the new citizens resulting from the war participate in making the new start. It will be seen that presently he wrote that view into the opinion in *Texas v. White*.

THE FACTS

IN 1851 TEXAS HAD RECEIVED $5,000,000 in United States bonds, as indemnification for boundary claims. Each bond was for $1,000, payable to the State or bearer, and redeemable after December 31, 1864.[35] The Texas legislature, by a statute of December 16, 1851,

---

[34] Draft, dated merely "1865," in Chase Papers, Hist. Soc. of Pa.

[35] At some points in the discussion it will be useful to know the exact form of the bonds:

It is hereby certified that the United States of America are indebted unto the State of Texas or bearer, in the sum of one thousand dollars, redeemable after the thirty-first day of December, 1864, with interest at five per centum per annum, payable semi-annually on the first days of January and July in each year, at the Treasury of the United States, on presentation and surrender of the proper coupon hereto annexed.

This debt is authorized by the act of Congress approved September 9th, A.D. 1850; it is re-

directed that the Comptroller of Public Accounts proceed to Washington and receive the bonds, and deposit them in the Treasury of the State of Texas; "provided that no bond . . . shall be available in the hands of any holder until the same shall have been indorsed in the city of Austin by the Governor of the State of Texas." The immediate purpose of this proviso was evidently to protect the State in getting the bonds to Austin; what further effect, if any, it should be given became a contested point in litigation.

At the outbreak of the rebellion, 782 of these bonds, unindorsed, remained in the State Treasury. By a statute of 1862, the Governor and certain other officers were constituted the Military Board, with "power to provide the defence of the State, by means of any bonds and coupons which may be in the treasury on any account." At the same time the statute of 1851 was repealed.

By a contract of January 12, 1865, the Military Board (1) sold to George W. White and John Chiles 135 of these bonds "now in the State treasury," with coupons attached, principal and interest amounting to $156,200; (2) also 76 bonds with coupons, amounting to $87,400, "said . . . bonds and coupons supposed to be upon deposit with Droege & Co., England." (In April 1862, 300 bonds had been sent to Europe, to support the purchase of supplies in aid of the rebellion. Peabody & Co., London bankers, purchased 149 in June 1862; the others remained in the hands of Droege & Co.[36] More on this will appear presently.) In consideration of (1) the 135 bonds at Austin, White & Chiles undertook to supply cards[37] and medicine; (2) for the 76 bonds they would also furnish cards and medicines "upon the same terms and conditions."[38] Our immediate concern is with the 135 bonds that were in the treasury.

When Governor Pendleton Murrah and his associates of the Mili-

---

corded in the office of the Register of the United States Treasury, and is transferable on delivery.

Washington, January 1st, A.D. 1851.

Coupons, extending to December 31, 1864, were for $25 for designated six months' interest, payable to bearer.

[36] Bill in equity in Texas v. Geo. Peabody & Co. *et al.*, filed by Geo. W. Paschal in the Supreme Court, Oct. 18, 1869.

[37] A card was a tool for combing out fibers of cotton, wool, etc. Its importance to the Confederate effort is indicated by the following:

The Board received through Droege Oetling & Company . . .

twelve thousand pair of cotton and wool cards which they immediately offered for distribution to the various counties . . . at as near cost in currency as they could make it—$10 per pair . . . .

Many a mother, wife, sister has been made happy having been able through these cards to provide clothing for their loved ones absent in the army . . . .

Report of the Military Board [in 1863, Gov. F. R. Lubbock, chairman], House Journal of the Tenth Legislature, Regular Session, 233, at 246, 247.

[38] Transcript of Record in Texas v. White, 8. Exhibit A.

tary Board made this contract, the Confederacy was about to crumble. Delivery of the bonds at Austin was made on March 15, less than a month before Lee's surrender. Quite aside from what, from the point of view of the United States, might be said against this contract as being in aid of the rebellion, it was also a job put upon the people of Texas. Gold bonds of the United States were turned over to White & Chiles upon their undertaking that "should they fail to execute such contract . . . they will pay said board for such bonds and coupons of the United States, rating them at eighty (80) cents upon the dollar, in 7 or 8 per cent. bonds of the State of Texas, or treasury warrants of the State of Texas at par." "In other words swap 8 cents, the price at which the State bonds were then selling, for one hundred cents, the value of U. S. bonds, if paid at the national treasury"—so commented Provisional Governor Andrew J. Hamilton when the papers disclosing this "swindle" by the "guardians of the State" were found scattered on the floor of the capitol.[39] A year later Governor J. W. Throckmorton, ex-Confederate, advised the legislature that the terms of the contract "were certainly very singular, and would indicate any thing but a just transaction."[40]

White & Chiles failed to deliver the supplies; their tender of depreciated State bonds and warrants was refused by Governor Hamilton.

Hamilton appointed George W. Paschal (1812–78), a leading Texas lawyer and steadfast Unionist, to go to Washington as the State's agent to do all that might be done to recover all the bonds alienated by the rebel Board—for which he was to charge such fees as the service rendered proper.[41] (Early in the war, indeed, Paschal had pointed out the danger to the Secretary of the Treasury, with the result that Chase gave instructions that coupons from unindorsed bonds were not to be redeemed.[42])

Paschal arrived in Washington in mid-September 1865 and thenceforth busied himself, notably before the Treasury and the President, in

---

[39] Transcript, 80. Letter to Paschal, Sept. 11, 1865.

White had cautioned a member of the Board on June 12, 1865: "It is important that the feds should not get possession of the contract . . . ." Transcript, 78.

[40] House Journal of the Eleventh Legislature, 83. Message of Aug. 20, 1866.

This was not the only transaction in which zeal for the service of the people of Texas did not control those who acted on behalf of the Board. Others are recorded in the Report of the Military Board, supra, note 37, at 235–38; Report of Messrs.

Pease and Palm on the Treasury, Texas House Journal (1866), 3–4.

[41] In re Paschal, 10 Wall. 483 (1871), Answer of Respondent with Affidavits, Exhibits, and Proofs, 2–3. It is not surprising that the retainer was not put into writing, or that the compensation was not fixed: the matter was urgent and uncertain—what might be involved could not be foreseen.

[42] Letter of June 21, 1861, written in view of the fact that coupons would become due on July 1, in Transcript of Record in National Bank v. Texas, 72. Also, the bill in Texas v. Geo. Peabody & Co., 5.

seeking to establish the title of Texas to all unindorsed bonds. He found that the Comptroller of the Treasury, Robert W. Tayler, had advised Secretary McCulloch, in a carefully reasoned opinion, that it was proper now to redeem bonds presented by bona fide holders.[43] Payments presently began to be made, upon examination and approval by the Comptroller.

Paschal also found that White (sometime citizen of Tennessee, and a resident of Austin, Texas) was already in Washington, and "seemed to be one of the influential men at the White House, having access at all times." Paschal demanded that the President arrest White with a view to his being sent to Texas on a charge of treason, but found Johnson "unwilling 'to administer the affairs of Texas,' as he termed it."[44] After persistent efforts to overcome Comptroller Tayler's opinion, Paschal obtained an order from Secretary McCulloch halting the redemption of unindorsed bonds. He caused notices to be published in the press, to warn against dealing in such bonds, notably by a "Caution to the public" in the *New York Tribune* of October 10, 1865.[45] Among the bonds whose payment was arrested were those that had been presented on behalf of Geo. Peabody & Co.

Paschal took a prominent part in the convention of Southern loyalists that met at Philadelphia on September 1, 1866, under a call which asserted that Congress should exert its authority to reconstruct the

---

[43] Texas Indemnity Bonds, Report of the Comptroller of the Treasury to the Secretary, made Aug. 15, 1865. A separately printed document of twenty-six pages. That able paper will figure in later discussion.

[44] *In re* Paschal, Answer of Respondent with Affidavits, Exhibits, and Proofs, 3–4.

The Andrew Johnson Papers in the Library of Congress contain the following communications from White to Johnson:

Letter written at Washington, Dec. 11, 1865. His home in Austin had been occupied by federal military authorities: he asked the President to order its restoration immediately.

Letter from New Orleans, Feb. 5, 1866. He passed on reports from Texas "that the white people, except a few Radicals, heartily indorse your policy."

Telegram from Austin, Feb. 3, 1866, urging pardon for one elected to the Texas convention.

Letter from Nashville, Tennessee, Sept. 27, 1866, urging parole for Williamson S. Oldham, Confederate Senator from Texas, then in Toronto, Canada. (See D.A.B.: Oldham was allowed to return to Texas, but refused to apply for a pardon. White and Oldham had been law partners.)

Telegram from Lynchburg, Virginia, January 7, 1868: had missed railroad connection; would be in Washington tomorrow.

Letter written at Washington, June 11, 1868—rejoicing at report that the President would nominate a conservative, and not a carpet-bagger, as collector of customs at Galveston.

Letter from Winchester, Tennessee, Oct. 13, 1869, reporting activities in aid of the election of Johnson as United States Senator for the term commencing Mar. 4, 1871. (After four days of balloting, Johnson was defeated by a vote of 55 to 51. Johnson did become a Senator on March 4, 1875.)

[45] Transcript in Texas v. White, 48.

Southern States on the basis of national protection of equal rights for all citizens.[46] So too did Andrew J. Hamilton and ex-Governor Elisha M. Pease. In the election in June, the latter had run for Governor against James W. Throckmorton, who had voted against secession but had later served the rebel government as a brigadier. Throckmorton was elected by a four-to-one majority, and was inaugurated in August.[47] Texas was uncongenial to men who had maintained that the Union is indestructible. Paschal moved his law office to New York.

Throckmorton removed Paschal from his employment as Agent and in his place employed Benjamin H. Epperson. Presently he engaged Richard T. Merrick, J. R. Brent, and George Taylor, conservative Washington practitioners, to bring suit on the White & Chiles bonds; their fee would be 25 percent of whatever was recovered by suit, compromise, or otherwise.[48]

In October 1866, Attorney General Stanbery gave an opinion that inasmuch as Peabody & Co., it appeared, had purchased their bonds for value in the market in 1862, with no knowledge that the selling broker was the State's agent to raise funds to aid the rebellion, the holder was entitled to payment.[49] No attention was given to the want of indorse-

---

[46] Ann. Cyc. 1866, 756–59. Supra, pp. 180–81.

[47] Texas House Journal, 1866, 16, 18.

[48] The contract with counsel, dated February 1, 1867, is set out in connection with *In re* Paschal, Answers of Respondent with Affidavits, Exhibits, and Proofs, 23. Exhibit B.

Epperson was politically in accord with Throckmorton; in November 1866 he won election to Congress as a conservative, but (in common with others in Southern delegations) was not seated. The Epperson Papers in the Library of the University of Texas include correspondence on the recovery of the Indemnity bonds. The following items, in letters to him from Governor Throckmorton, are here pertinent:

Of November 23, 1866:
I desire our Delegation in Washington to use every means in their power to prevent any payment on these bonds by the Government. I will make a fair & liberal settlement with all the parties—and if they will not so settle I will endeavor to get the government to cancel them. Texas

had better lose all than be beaten in a dishonorable manner.

I am specially desirous to get the *numbers* of the White & Chiles Bonds. The Military Board here kept no statement of the numbers. . . .

I will bring suit against White & Chiles if no other means will do and I wish the numbers.

Of December 12:
I will write you soon on the subject of the European Bonds, and if National troubles do not forbid, I think of appointing you the Agent to go to London, to arrange the matter.

And of February 20, 1867:
In regard to your compensation, I have to say you must look for that to whatever may be recovered. . . .

Upon Throckmorton's departure from office in August 1867 (see infra at p. 635), Epperson's agency ceased. Thereafter he was occupied as president of the Memphis, El Paso & Pacific, which projected a transcontinental railroad across Texas.

[49] 12 Ops. Atty. Gen. 72. Oct. 15, 1866.

ment by a loyal Governor. Thereupon the Treasury redeemed the 149 bonds with coupons for $167,625. (Presently Paschal, restored, would file an original suit against Peabody & Co. for an accounting.)

For the First National Bank of Washington and its cashier, Huntington, the Treasury also redeemed unindorsed Texas bonds—a few before the temporary suspension and a greater number thereafter. These will figure in *Huntington v. Texas*[50] and *National Bank v. Texas*,[51] suits prosecuted by Paschal after the State had won in *Texas v. White & Chiles.*

TEXAS v. WHITE IS FILED

ON FEBRUARY 15, 1867, Merrick and his associates filed in the Supreme Court the original suit of Texas against White and Chiles, and others to whom counsel sought to trace the bonds. An injunction was granted on May 16, to restrain defendants from receiving payment pending the outcome of the litigation.[52]

After a year in office, Governor Throckmorton was removed by an order of July 30, 1867, as an impediment to reconstruction. General Sheridan did this under the authority of the recent Congressional legislation; he appointed E. M. Pease to the place.[53] Pease restored Paschal to his former position as Agent; the latter came to Washington to resume charge. He "did not deem it consistent with honor, propriety, or the interest of the State to attempt to remove" the counsel retained by Throckmorton.[54] They on their part recognized "the zeal and fidelity with which [Paschal] sought to protect the interests of Texas" and "his great familiarity with the State legislation . . . and with the history of the bonds . . . ."[55] They all worked in association in *Texas v. White & Chiles*, while Paschal also gathered evidence to be used against the National Bank and Huntington.[56]

Here let it be recalled that in the latter half of January 1868, the House and then the Senate were considering Bingham's Supplementary Reconstruction Bill, which would have declared that "the so-called civil governments" in the States undergoing Reconstruction "shall not be recognized" by the Executive or the Judiciary.[57] To "recognize" is a verb of divers meanings. In one aspect, a State would be "recognized" if, under Article III, the Court took jurisdiction of a case "in which a State shall be Party."

---

[50] 16 Wall. 402 (1873). Infra, p. 650.
[51] 20 Wall 72 (1874). Infra, p. 650.
[52] Transcript, 12.
[53] Ann. Cyc. 1867, 715.
[54] *In re* Paschal, Answers of Respondent . . . , 8.
[55] Ibid., 105, 112. Affidavits of Brent and Merrick, respectively.
[56] Ibid., 8.
[57] Supra, p. 461.

On January 17 and 24, 1868, the Court heard Merrick argue against defense counsel who raised the bar that "The State of Texas has no such status in the Federal Union as authorized her to prosecute this suit in this court." On February 10 the Court made this disposition: the point was "reserved for further argument at the final hearing of the case."[58] There was a serious question to be examined—calmly, after the excited talk at the two ends of the capitol had died away.

ARGUMENT, ON THE STATUS OF TEXAS AND ON THE MERITS

A YEAR AND MORE LATER, on February 5, 8, and 9, 1869, the Court heard argument, both on the preliminary point and on the merits. Paschal opened and Merrick closed for Texas; the several respondents were heard by their respective counsel. On April 12 came the decision, in an opinion by the Chief Justice: Texas was in the Union and qualified to sue. On the merits, the contract with White & Chiles was declared to be void; White and Chiles, and all claiming to act in their behalf, were perpetually enjoined from asserting any right under the same. After the announcement of the decision, opposing counsel spent considerable time in framing the decree.[59] It left open a problem presently to be noticed in *Texas v. Hardenberg*:[60] the effect upon a holder who had received payment from the Treasury prior to the service of process. The decree came to be scanned again in 1875, when Chiles was found in contempt for having violated it.[61]

We turn back to the arguments in *Texas v. White*. A history of the Supreme Court should appraise the work of counsellors at its bar.[62]

An argument on behalf of a defendant in this case unavoidably showed a certain disaccord. The first position was that Texas, in its then condition, had no standing before the Court. That was a work of denigration. But for the contingency that the Court would hold otherwise, it must be argued that the rebel government's transaction with White & Chiles was valid and effective. That was a theme of exaltation, to show that the Texas of 1861–65 "dared do all that may become" a state.

Chiles put his case in the hands of Albert Pike and associates.

---

[58] Minutes, Mon., Feb. 10, 1868; Transcript, 32–34.

[59] Minutes, Apr. 12, 1869; 7 Wall. at 741–43. Merrick's Affidavit, In the Matter of Geo. W. Paschal. Answers of Respondent . . . , 112.

[60] 10 Wall. 68 (1869). Infra, p. 648.

[61] *In re* Chiles, 22 Wall. 157. Infra, p. 667.

[62] Paschal as Reporter of the Supreme Court of Texas in 1869 issued Volume XXV Supplement, which at pp. 434 to 621 reports Texas v. White—not only what appears in 7 Wallace 700 to 743, but also (at 485–591) extensive selections from oral arguments and briefs.

The account that follows uses the Transcript of Record and the full briefs.

Pike was a contentious man, who had resigned his commission as Confederate brigadier after a disagreement with the commander of his district, and then had aired his grievances to the public. Varied learning contributed to a diffuse style. And he could not refrain from refighting the war. His brief was a tract of ninety-six dense pages, with never a caption to point the way. It was laden with allusions to other uprisings—by Joshua and by Jereboam, Spartacus and Cataline, Cromwell, the French in La Vendée, the Irish Fenians, and much more, in exuberant irrelevance. Although Congress "had no *right* to establish a military despotism in Texas," yet that in fact it had done: even so, cognizance of that great outrage lay only "in God's chancery."[63] If nevertheless the Court concluded that it had jurisdiction, then it should declare that "the United States are estopped to assert principles contrary to the Declaration of Independence"—the right to revolt must be conceded.[64] (What an unruly proposition that would have been![65]) So long as hostilities were in progress the United States had recognized that Texas was "an existing and organized State, with a lawful government entitled to compel the obedience of all [its] inhabitants"; on that basis "all its acts, the making of the contract here in question included," must be held to have been valid.[66] If, however, Texas could now avoid any of its contracts, it would be only such as were harmful to the United States—whereas the contract with White & Chiles had been for harmless implements of household industry and medicine for the destitute.[67]

It was inconsiderate to ask the Justices to work through such a trackless wilderness of words—and unwise to suppose that this was effective advocacy.[68]

Philip Phillips, for White, went over the ground in a brief of thirteen pages, of which less than two were devoted to the question of jurisdiction. He relied on *Hepburn v. Ellzey*, where Chief Justice Marshall had said that the District of Columbia was not a "State" as that expression was used in the Constitution—pointing out that a State had Representatives and Senators and chose Presidential Electors, which the District did not.[69] Fastening upon those remarks as if they constituted

---

[63] Brief, 13.
[64] Brief, 53.
[65] The notion of invoking the Declaration of Independence to control a constitutional question, however attractive it may sound, needs to be viewed very critically. While Pike would make it defend the ordinances of secession, Timothy Farrar used it to demonstrate that thereafter, in law, slavery could not exist. *Manual of the Constitution of the United States of America* (Boston: Little, Brown

and Co., 1867), 53–62.
[66] Brief, 88.
[67] Brief, 89.
[68] Another brief of the same authorship and of like character will be met in the *Cotton Tax Case*, infra, pp. 885–86.
[69] 2 Cranch 445 (1804). The question was whether a citizen of the District had the same right as the citizen of a State to invoke the diversity of jurisdiction of the federal courts. Held, that he did not.

a definition, Phillips argued that when Texas did not have representation in Congress and did not choose electors it could not be a "State" within the jurisdictional grant of Article III, Section 2, clause 2.

Merrick, in a reply brief, wrote that "the State" and the government are not the same:

> The governments of those States were usurping governments, established upon the overthrow of the governments *de jure*, and organized for the purpose of hostility to the Union. And the object of the war was to overthrow these hostile and usurping governments, and re-establish the governments *de jure* in their legitimate authority, and at the same time restore the supremacy of the Federal Constitution in States that never had been and could not be withdrawn from the Federal Union.
>
> Wherever the flag of the Republic was unfurled, it exhibited on its folds the evidence of the existence and indestructibility of each and all of the States.[70]

This resort to imagery—the number of stars on the field of the flag— suggests how elusive was the issue whether Texas was a "State" within the original jurisdiction of the Supreme Court.

CHASE'S OPINION

APPROPRIATELY, Chase assigned to himself the writing of the opinion; in this case no other Justice could have spoken with such authority. The occasion called for some definitive statement on the result of attempted secession.

Was Texas one of the United States when the bill was filed? The Court was aware of "the difficulty, not to say impossibility of so disposing of [the question] as to satisfy the conflicting judgments of men equally enlightened, equally upright and equally patriotic." Chase began with the observation that the Constitution uses the word "State" in more than one sense: sometimes it refers to a geographical unit—(a Representative shall be an inhabitant of the State); sometimes it refers to the people—(the United States shall guarantee to every State a republican form of government); most frequently it expresses "the combined idea of people, territory, and government." The Colonies had formed a union which the Articles of Confederation declared to "be perpetual"; then the Constitution established "a more perfect union." Efforts to secede had not broken the bonds: "Our conclusion . . . is, that

---

[70] Brief printed in 1869, evidently filed after the argument, at p. 7.

Texas continued to be a State, and a State of the Union," notwithstanding the acts of rebellion. But while obligations remained unimpaired, relations changed: surely while Texas was controlled by a government engaged in hostilities it was not entitled to representation in Congress, nor could it have maintained a suit in the Supreme Court.[71]

> The government and the citizens of the State, refusing to recognize their constitutional obligations, assumed the character of enemies, and incurred the consequences of rebellion.
> These new relations imposed new duties upon the United States. The first was that of suppressing the Rebellion. The next was that of re-establishing the broken relations of the State with the Union . . . .

Here the Chief Justice wove into the opinion a line of thought to which he had always attached capital importance: the national responsibility for the freedmen. "A great social change increased the difficulty of the situation." The Emancipation Proclamation began and the Thirteenth Amendment confirmed the abolition of slavery. "The new freemen necessarily became part of the people . . . . And it was the State, thus constituted, which was now entitled to the benefit of the constitutional guaranty" of a republican form of government. There being no State government having constitutional relations with the Union, it became the duty of the United States to provide for the restoration. Before new officers could be elected, the State's constitution must "receive such amendments as would conform its provisions to the new conditions created by emancipation, and afford adequate security to the people of the State."

The opinion recalled that first the President had appointed a Provisional Governor and provided for the assembling of a convention. "Whether the action then taken was, in all respects, warranted by the Constitution, it is not now necessary to determine." (One questionable action had *not* been taken, although Chase had importuned Lincoln and then Johnson: the President had refused to take it upon himself to *impose* universal suffrage.[72]) "But the power to carry into effect the clause of guaranty is primarily a legislative power . . . ." Congress, "after long deliberation," has adopted measures for restoration, by the Reconstruction Acts. "Nothing in the case requires the Court to pronounce judgment upon the constitutionality of any particular provi-

---

[71] Nor could an individual or a business association in hostile territory have maintained a suit in the courts of the United States; but the right of action would merely be suspended, and "the restoration of peace removes the disability, and opens the doors of the courts." Hanger v. Abbott, 6 Wall. 532 (1868).

[72] Supra, pp. 86–87.

sion . . . ."[73] (As has been noted, Chase had felt free to express his personal views to correspondents in 1868, when his eye was on the Democratic nomination for President.[74]) Most of the Southern States had now completed that course of restoration.

But Texas was not of that number; it remained subject to the declaration of the Reconstruction Act that its government was not "legal" but "provisional only . . . ." "It suffices to say," the Chief Justice continued, "that the terms of the Acts necessarily imply recognition of existing governments; and that in point of fact, the governments thus recognized, in some important respects, still exist." The Provisional Governor, the elected Governor, and the latter's successor appointed by the military commander, had all sanctioned this litigation. The conclusion was that the suit was properly brought and was within the original jurisdiction of the Court.

Then in the substantive part of the case, the line of reasoning—to be examined in a moment[75]—led the Court to decree that the White & Chiles contract was of no effect, and that defendants were forbidden to assert any claim under it.

DISSENTS

JUSTICE GRIER DISSENTED, on the jurisdictional point and on the merits. On the former he said, "This is to be decided as a political fact, not as a legal fiction . . . . If I regard the truth of history for the last eight years, I cannot discover the State of Texas as one of these United States." Accepting Phillips' argument, he took Marshall's language in *Hepburn v. Ellzey* as the test, and said that Texas did not qualify.

Justice Swayne (Miller, J., with him) noted dissent on the point of "the incapacity of the State of Texas in her present condition, to maintain an original suit in this court. The question, in my judgment, is one in relation to which this court is bound by the action of the Legislative Department of the Government."[76]

---

[73] A fault-finding editorial in the *New York World* fastened upon that sentence. If the government of Texas that had maintained this suit was "legal enough to receive recognition at the hands of the Supreme Court," then the Court ought to have come right out and declared that the Reconstruction Acts had been unconstitutional. "Law means logic; logic means sense. . . . [W]hat law, logic, or sense is there in any such decision" as that in Texas v. White? Apr. 15, 1869.

The *World* was, of course, criticising from its point of view as the great Democratic organ, craving a condemnation of Congressional Reconstruction.

[74] Supra, pp. 533–35.

[75] Infra, p. 646.

[76] Thus to dissent did not signify disagreement with the Chief Justice's general proposition that the Constitution looks to an indestructible Union of indestructible States. Justice Swayne expressed that same thought three

COMMENT

ONE NEED NOT follow the commentators who have dwelt upon *Texas v. White* as an exegesis of constitutional theory; the result may be justified quite simply. The Constitution, framed in high hope, allowed for amendment but not for dissolution; it did not speak to the situation where secession in arms had been attempted.[77] It was most faithful to the Constitution's purpose to say that there had always remained a place in the circle of the Union for each erring State.[78] Moreover, to take jurisdiction here contravened no Congressional policy. Even while Congress deferred readmission to representation, it was insisting that the formerly rebel States were competent to act upon a constitutional amendment. To permit Texas to assert its claim to property would not retard—indeed it tended to advance—the Congressional program.

The Court's answer was far better than Thad Stevens' notion that the States had put themselves beyond the pale and had become merely conquered provinces.[79] It was better, too, than to profess Sumner's

---

years later, in a case that did not involve the technical point—standing to maintain a suit—present in Texas v. White. In White v. Hart, 13 Wall. 646 (1872), Swayne, J., said: "At no time were the rebellious States out of the pale of the Union. Their rights under the Constitution were suspended, but not destroyed. Their constitutional duties and obligations were unaffected and remained the same." The case was that the Georgia constitution of 1868 denied enforcement of any debt where a slave had been the consideration. To meet the objection that the application of this provision to a note given in 1859 infringed the Contract Clause, it was argued that when the constitution of 1868 was adopted, Georgia was outside the Union and so not bound by the Contract Clause. It was in rejecting that contention that Justice Swayne used the language quoted. The Court held that the provision could not constitutionally be applied to impair the obligation of contracts made prior to its adoption. Chase, C.J., dissented without opinion. See infra, pp. 858–60.

[77] The makers of the Constitution "called into life a being the develop-

ment of which could not have been foreseen completely by the most gifted of its begetters. It was enough for them to realize or to hope that they had created an organism; it has taken a century and has cost their successors much sweat and blood to prove that they created a nation. The case before us must be considered in the light of our whole experience and not merely in that of what was said a hundred years ago." Missouri v. Holland, 252 U.S. 416 (1920). So spoke Justice Holmes, who in the Civil War had contributed his full share to that development.

[78] "It was in aid of that process [of healing the wounds of the sanguinary conflict] that this Court formulated the doctrine expressed in the famous sentence in Texas v. White . . . . This theory served as a fruitful means for dealing with the problems for which it was devised. . . ." United States v. Florida, 363 U.S. 121, 131–32 (1960), concurring opinion of Frankfurter, J., in which three other Justices joined.

[79] Stevens died on August 11, 1868. Chase had said—in Shortridge v. Macon, Fed. Case No. 12,812, supra, n. 33 —that although the conquered pro-

theory that by attempting secession a State worked the instant extinction of its Statehood and dropped to the rank of a territory, from which it could ascend only by being admitted anew;[80] there was no need to contrive so scholastic a doctrine to meet this anomalous and transitory situation.[81]

Texas v. White was "a famous victory"—however vague may be the understanding what "this great fight did win." Sometimes a sentence uttered by the Court *is* important, quite aside from what may have been decided. In actual outcome, if the views of the dissenters had prevailed, Texas would have had to wait until its readmission to representation—which occurred on March 30, 1870, a year after the Court's decision—before it would have had standing to bring its suit. That may not seem a very important result. Yet the *National Intelligencer* expressed a prevalent estimate when it hailed *Texas v. White* as "emphatically the great case of this session . . . ." The Court's opinion, it continued, "will gladden the hearts of millions of our countrymen. It is evidence that this great bulwark of our liberties of the people has not been subordinated to

---

vince theory was supported by men "distinguished by abilities and virtues," it must be rejected.

[80] His "Resolutions declaratory of the relations between the United States and the territory once occupied by certain States," introduced on Feb. 11, 1862. Cong. Globe, 37–1, 736.

[81] It sounds like the *capitis diminutio* which figured largely in Roman law, denoting one's loss of liberty, or of citizenship, or of family status.

Professor John W. Burgess, in his *Reconstruction and the Constitution, 1866–1876* (New York: Charles Scribner's Sons, 1902), pronounced this theory of Sumner and other Radicals to be "sound political science and correct constitutional law" (p. 60), whereas Lincoln's conception had been "crude and erroneous" (p. 13). This magisterial pronouncement has influenced others in their notion of what constitutional law should be. Burgess supplied the key to his own understanding by his opening sentence: "The key to the solution of the question of Reconstruction is the proper comprehension of what a 'State' is in a system of federal gov-

ernment." Burgess had filled his mind with *staatsrechtswissenschaft*, and professed an arid formalism, as may be seen in his *Political Science and Comparative Constitutional Law* (Boston: Ginn Co., 1890). He did not grasp the common-sense practicality which Lincoln exemplified and which has been the strength of American constitutional law. "How do we read the Constitution? Is it not a practical instrument?" So spoke McLean, J., dissenting, in Dred Scott v. Sandford, 19 How. 393, 544 (1857); he was maintaining the authority of Congress to exclude slavery from a territory, in which the nation had theretofore acquiesced.

With Burgess' assumption of superiority over Lincoln on this constitutional problem, recall Professor Francis Lieber's superiority in the matter of Lincoln's use of English: "Why did the presdt. not give his message to some one to correct the language?"—used in the first Message to Congress, July 1861. Frank B. Freidel, *Francis Lieber, Nineteenth Century Liberal*, (Baton Rouge: Louisiana State University Press, 1947), 308.

legislative dictation. In this case it has risen to the highest dignity, and shown that it is unwilling to avoid any of the great responsibilities resting upon it."[82]

With this may be contrasted what other newspapers were saying by reason of another action taken by the Court on that same April 12— the dismissal of *Ex parte McCardle*.[83] That, declared the *Atlanta Constitution*, showed that "this last refuge of American liberty was sadly and shamefully evacuated by its lawful defenders, and its doors slammed in the faces of the weak and persecuted who fled to its altars."[84] Actually *McCardle* had ceased to be of critical importance a year and more past, when decision had been postponed.

The *National Intelligencer*, in a further editorial in praise of the opinion in *Texas v. White*, said that it was "acknowledged to be one of the ablest and most exhaustive and conclusive ever emanating from that highest tribunal of justice."[85] If—which has not been common—one goes on to study attentively what *Texas v. White* decided, beyond the preliminary question of jurisdiction, one will discover that "exhaustive and conclusive" is exactly what it was *not*. On the merits, the holdings now to be recounted were soon questioned and, when the test came, were held to have been erroneous.

FACTUAL BACKGROUND OF THE SUBSTANTIVE QUESTION

BEFORE ONE CAN UNDERSTAND the substantive part of the opinion in *Texas v. White*, some background must be acquired.

It was right that, to frustrate use by the rebels, the Treasury Department refuse throughout the war to redeem unindorsed bonds or their coupons. But when, hostilities having ceased, holders of such bonds pressed for payment, the matter was reconsidered. To protect the war effort of the United States had been one thing; to deny the claim of a purchaser for value in order to protect the people of Texas from the consequences of their own rebellion was something quite different.

By the report of August 15, 1865, already cited, the Comptroller of the Treasury, Robert W. Tayler, advised payment to those who had purchased in good faith.[86] He started with the instrument itself: the United States promised to pay the State or bearer in a bond that on its face was "transferable on delivery." The Court had recognized that

---

82 Apr. 13, 1869.
83 Supra, p. 492.
84 Apr. 20, 1869.

85 Apr. 17, 1869.
86 Supra, p. 633.

public bonds were commercial securities;[87] that meant that "possession of such paper carried the title with it to the holder. The possession and title are one and inseparable."[88] The Comptroller reasoned that it had not been within the power of the State to interfere with that contract. The statute of 1851 might be construed as merely the State's direction to its own officers, without affecting a bona fide purchaser. When the more than a dozen subsequent statutes were examined wherein the legislature had disposed of Indemnity bonds without any reference to indorsement by the Governor, the conclusion was that the statute of 1851 had been intended to be no more than a transitory measure. The Comptroller recommended that bona fide holders of Texas Indemnity bonds now be paid. The "new and loyal organization of the State government" would not be able to defeat such rights—but that only illustrated the truth "that such grave errors as have been committed by the State are never allowed to pass without severe losses."

An item in Texas' troubled story was the fact that Provisional Governor Andrew J. Hamilton, in New York on June 25, 1865, had rendered the following opinion: "In reply to your question about Texas indemnity bonds, issued by the United States, I can assure you they are perfectly good, and the government will certainly pay them to the holders."[89] As a fee for rendering this opinion, Hamilton received ten of the White & Chiles bonds. That was prior to the discovery of the papers disclosing the terms of the White & Chiles contract.

In accordance with Comptroller Tayler's report of August 15, the redemption of unindorsed bonds was commenced, each presentation being referred to the Comptroller, who must be satisfied that the holder had been loyal to the United States and had purchased for value.[90]

The propriety of this course found support in the reasoning of an opinion of Attorney General Speed on September 4, 1865, that—to quote the headnote—"an innocent holder of a 'seven-thirty' treasury

---

[87] Citing Moran v. Comm'rs of Miami County, 2 Bl. 722 (1863), a case of county bonds issued in aid of a railroad.

[88] Quoting Murray v. Lardner, 2 Wall. 110 (1865), per Swayne, J., sustaining the right of the holder of stolen bonds, purchased without knowledge of the theft. Infra at p. 647. Swayne was borrowing the language of Clifford, J., in the leading case of Goodman v. Simonds, 20 How. 343 (1858), wherein Stanley Matthews had appeared for the bona fide holder. Justice Matthews, twenty-seven years

later, spoke for the Court when, sustaining the right of a bona fide purchaser, Texas v. White was overruled. Morgan v. United States, 113 U.S. 476. Infra, p. 661.

[89] To J. Richard Barret. Chiles had offered to pay a debt to Barret in such bonds. Transcript of Record in Texas v. White, 105–6 (answer of Barret) and 29–30 (answer of White).

[90] Transcript of Record in National Bank of Washington v. Texas, 20 Wall. 72 (1874). Deposition of ex-Secretary McCulloch, at 66, and that of Tayler, at 29.

note, transferable by delivery, which was stolen and transferred when past due, is entitled to payment, as against the party from whom it was stolen."[91]

When the papers disclosing the unconscionable terms of the White & Chiles transaction were discovered, copies were dispatched to Judge Paschal, who forcefully represented to the Treasury Department that the State should be protected against this swindle. But the serial numbers of the White & Chiles bonds were not known; the parties had seen to that. To identify and locate these bonds, and then to determine whether the holders were affected with such knowledge as might defeat their claim of title, was a puzzle for Paschal, and for the Comptroller of the Treasury —and presently for the Justices.

"It is the desire of the department to protect the interest of the State so far as practicable," Comptroller Tayler wrote to the Treasurer on May 17, 1866, seeking more specific information.[92] The Comptroller found in discussion that counsel for the State seemed to concede that their case depended upon showing a want of good faith on the part of the holders. (It is notable that the State's representatives thought that that necessity must be admitted: in a moment we shall find the Chief Justice declaring that the world was chargeable with notice that by the Texas statute of 1851, an unindorsed bond was not negotiable.[93]) On January 19, 1867, the Comptroller notified counsel that if they did not within a week start legal action against the bondholders, he would advise the Secretary to redeem.[94]

On February 15, *Texas v. White* was initiated in the Supreme Court.[95]

John A. Hardenberg, one of the defendants, was in a special situation. He had presented thirty-four bonds for redemption in November 1866. On February 16, 1867, after *Texas v. White et al.* had been filed but before service of process, his counsel, Samuel S. Cox,[96] pro-

---

[91] 11 Ops. Atty. Gen. 332, Rights of *Bona Fide* Holders of Treasury Notes. The influence of that opinion upon the Department's attitude on Texas Indemnity bonds is reflected in the Transcript of Record in National Bank of Washington v. Texas, infra at p. 657, depositions of ex-Secretary McCulloch at 67, of former Assistant Secretary William E. Chandler at 86–87, and of Comptroller Tayler at 38.

[92] Transcript of Record in Texas v. White, 81–82.

[93] Infra, p. 646.

[94] Transcript in Texas v. White, 95.

[95] Supra, p. 635.
Texas v. McCulloch, a suit to enjoin the Secretary from making payment, had hurriedly been brought in the District of Columbia court. On February 19 it was dismissed. 7 Wall. at 714.

[96] Cox (1824–98), author of *Three Decades of Federal Legislation* (Providence, R.I.: J. A. and R. A. Reid, 1886), was a leading Democratic Congressman—from Ohio, 1857–65, and from New York, 1869–73 and 1886 until his death.

cured the redemption of these bonds under an arrangement by which other Government bonds of equal value were deposited with the Comptroller.

CHIEF JUSTICE'S OPINION ON THE SUBSTANTIVE ISSUE

INFORMED BY THIS BACKGROUND, we return to the Chief Justice's opinion where, having held that Texas was competent to bring the suit, he addressed himself to the merits of the case.

His first proposition was that "if a State, by a public Act of her Legislature, imposes restrictions upon the alienation of her property, . . . every person who takes a transfer of such property must be held affected by notice of them. Alienation, in disregard of such restrictions, can convey no title to the alienee."

This was saying that before anyone, anywhere, could safely purchase this Government bond, he must first satisfy himself that nowhere, among the acts of the State legislature, was there a provision purporting to restrict alienation; even though he had never heard of it, the Chief Justice said he was *affected by notice.*

This, it will appear, was branded a mere dictum in 1874, and overruled in 1885.[97]

Had the restriction of 1851 been effectively repealed by the statute of 1862, to provide for the defense of the State?[98] The Chief Justice said that doubtless effect must be given to some rebel legislation, such as was necessary for peace and good order among the citizens. But this statute of 1862 "was intended to aid rebellion . . . . We can give no effect, therefore, to this repealing Act."

If that meant what it said, the case was ended right there. (It will be seen, in a moment,[99] that in 1873 the Chief Justice "explained and qualified": he had not meant that the repealing statute was "absolutely void"; "on the contrary, it may be fairly inferred from what was said in *Texas v. White,* that if the bonds were issued and used for a lawful purpose," the holder's title would be unassailable. To recover, the State must prove unlawful issue and use, *plus* notice of that fact to the holders. Then it was *not* true that an alienee could take no title to an unindorsed bond.)

Next, as though ignoring the effect of what he had just said, the Chief Justice went on to consider the position of those among the

---

[97] National Bank of Washington v. Texas, 20 Wall. 72, 83 (1874), infra at p. 658; Morgan v. United States, 113 U.S. 476, 496 (1885), infra, p. 661.
[98] Supra, p. 631.
[99] Infra, p. 653.

defendants who insisted that they were innocent holders who had taken the bonds without notice of anything unlawful. In the recent case of *Murray v. Lardner*[100] the Court had laid down a rule strongly protective of the holder of a negotiable instrument. It had said:

> The party who takes it before due for a valuable consideration, without knowledge of any defect of title and in good faith, holds it by a title valid against all the world.
>
> Suspicion of defect of title or the knowledge of circumstances which would excite such suspicion in the mind of a prudent man, or gross negligence on the part of the taker, at the time of the transfer, will not defeat his title. That result can be produced only by bad faith on his part.
>
> The burden of proof lies on the person who assails the right claimed by the party in possession.

The Court, said the Chief Justice, remained "entirely satisfied with this doctrine." Had the State shown that these defendants had had notice of the want of title to the White & Chiles bonds? Yes, there was "evidence which might fairly be held to be sufficient proof of notice . . . ." That was stated simply as a conclusion, without detailing any particulars from the record.

Evidently it was left to Reporter Wallace, when during the summer he came to prepare his statement of the case, to extract from the depositions and summarize—as he did—the evidence supporting the Court's conclusion.

But, the Chief Justice hastened on to say, the rule in *Murray v. Lardner* had no application to *matured* obligations. "Purchasers of notes or bonds past due take nothing but the actual right and title of the vendors." And the Texas Indemnity bonds must be regarded as having been purchased when past due, inasmuch as they had been *redeemable* after December 31, 1864. He continued:

> In strictness, it is true they were not payable on the day when they became redeemable; but the known usage of the United States—to pay all bonds as soon as the right of payment accrues, except where a distinction between redeemability and payability is made by law and shown on the face of the bonds—requires the application of the rule respecting overdue obligations . . . .

So *redeemability* was assimilated to *payability*: the buyer should beware —as if that circumstance suggested some defect. It followed that the purchasers had taken no better title than White and Chiles.

---

[100] Supra, n. 88.

In 1875 the Court expressed "grave doubt" about that proposition, and in 1885 repudiated it.[101]

Aside, then, from the discussion of the jurisdictional point, for which *Texas v. White* is gladly remembered, the reasoning simply did not stand up. A similar want of rigor in analysis—but one productive of infinitely greater mischief—will be found in the Chief Justice's treatment of the cases on legal tender.

TEXAS v. HARDENBERG

THE STATE'S CLAIM against Hardenberg—the defendant whose bonds had been redeemed on February 16, 1867, one day after *Texas v. White et al.* was filed, upon a deposit of other bonds in their place—[102] was put over for further argument.[103] His contention was that the prayer for relief did not reach his situation. The Court replied that "it would savor of extreme technicality" to read the State's bill so narrowly. It held that the State's equity attached to the substituted bonds. As to Hardenberg's being affected with notice that his bonds came from the illegal White & Chiles transaction, the Court reaffirmed its conclusion in *Texas v. White* that he had known.

The decree was that Comptroller Tayler, as special master, sell substituted bonds to such amount as would satisfy the judgment for the State, with costs.

CONSEQUENCES OF TEXAS v. WHITE

TO NARRATE the consequences of *Texas v. White* involves the pursuit of two lines of inquiry, which at times run along together. One looks to its doctrine—how the Court qualified, questioned, and repudiated. The other inquiry looks to the bonds, and to the lawyers Texas employed to recover them—an eventful story with an ironic ending. *Texas v. White* is remembered for its conceptual distinction between the State which remained in the Union and the government and people who were fighting to be out. In the end, the Texas that recovered the bonds and distributed rewards was anything but an abstraction in the clouds.

As soon as *Texas v. White* was won, in April 1869, Paschal turned his attention to exploiting the proposition that unindorsed bonds had remained the property of the State. He sought to make that effective as to bonds sent to Europe, and other bonds at home.

---

[101] Vermilye v. Adams Express Co., 21 Wall. 138, 145 (1875), infra, pp. 659–60; Morgan v. United States, 113 U.S. 476, 496 (1885), infra, p. 661.

[102] Supra, p. 636.
[103] Texas v. Hardenberg, 10 Wall. 68, argued on Nov. 12 and decided on Nov. 29, 1869.

XIII: *A Union of "Indestructible States"*

In Texas, meanwhile, Radical Republicans (led by Edmund J. Davis) and moderates (led by A. J. Hamilton and Governor Pease, and enjoying the support of Democrats) fell into violent disagreement. General J. J. Reynolds, commanding the Military District, wrote to President Grant in support of the Radicals. His letter became a feature in the public discussion preceding the election where the people would vote on the new constitution and would choose between Davis and Hamilton for Governor. Pease resigned the governorship; Davis was appointed to succeed him, and thereafter took office by virtue of the election, which he had won by a very narrow margin.

Once again, Texas politics disturbed the pursuit of Texas bonds. On January 27, 1870, Provisional Governor Davis telegraphed to Judge Paschal: "Your appointment as agent for the State of Texas was revoked yesterday. Please account for amounts received."[104] In his place as agent the Governor appointed Thomas J. Durant, sometime Free State leader in Louisiana, now practicing in Washington.[105]

Davis' demand that Paschal turn over to Durant all that had been recovered in *Texas v. White*—$47,325 in gold—led to *In re Paschal*, a memorable case on the Court's power over the members of its bar, and on the attorney's lien on the funds of his client.[106]

Durant joined with Merrick in the further pursuit of Texas bonds. But then in 1873 Davis was voted out and Richard Coke, a Democrat, was voted into the office of Governor—with consequences that brought to the Supreme Court the suit of Merrick and Durant against Giddings, Coke's appointee as agent.[107]

These and other matters coming before the Court, presently to be introduced, belong to the inquiry about bonds and attorneys.

But first we take the line of cases that tested and rejected the doctrine in *Texas v. White*.

TEXAS v. WHITE AS A PRECEDENT

READERS SERIOUSLY INTERESTED in the Supreme Court should not be spared some exposure to the travail that may be produced by a remiss performance.

It has been noted that the Treasury had redeemed Texas Indemnity bonds for the First National Bank of Washington and its cashier, William S. Huntington.[108] As soon as *Texas v. White* was decided, Paschal, Merrick, and Brent began litigation in the District of Columbia court to establish the State's title to these bonds.

---

[104] *In re* Paschal, Answers of Respondent . . . , 13.
[105] Supra, pp. 94–95, 270.

[106] 10 Wall. 483 (1871). Infra, pp. 665–67.
[107] 115 U.S. 300 (1885).
[108] Supra, p. 635.

In one case, known in the United States Reports as *Huntington v. Texas*,[109] the State brought an action in trover, charging that defendants had converted to their own use thirty-seven bonds, property of the State. The Treasury had redeemed these bonds, some in July 1865, the others in January 1866. Some of these the Bank had purchased; the rest it had merely presented for redemption on behalf of holders to whom the Bank had made advances.

The second case, *National Bank of Washington v. Texas*,[110] was a suit in equity concerning nineteen bonds, alleged to be part of the White & Chiles parcel, purchased by the Bank between December 3, 1865, and September 27, 1866: these bonds the Treasury had redeemed on February 27, 1867 (after *Texas v. White* had been filed), but not until an equivalent deposit of other securities had been made with the Comptroller. The terms upon which that deposit had been made became an issue: was it "meant to be substituted as and for the proceeds of said bonds so nominally redeemed"[111]—or was it "intended alone as personal indemnity to the . . . Secretary [of the Treasury]"?[112]

There had been looseness in the transaction. The State, on the basis of *Hardenberg*'s case,[113] sought a decree that the Comptroller pay Texas out of the substituted securities.

The State's two cases started together, but—because one was a common law action for a money judgment in respect of bonds already redeemed, while the other was a suit in equity to reach substituted bonds held in trust by the Comptroller—the two had quite different adventures.[114] At one time, it will appear, the Supreme Court seemed to be pronouncing inconsistent judgments.

First, *Huntington*: since this was a "suit at common law where the value in controversy shall exceed twenty dollars," the Seventh Amendment guaranteed the right to trial by jury. But this was also a case "in which a State shall be Party": accordingly, by Article III of the Constitution, "the Supreme Court shall have original jurisdiction." If Texas had insisted on its rights in each of these respects, a most unusual spectacle

---

[109] 16 Wall. 402 (1873).

[110] 20 Wall. 72 (1874).

[111] As the State alleged. Transcript of Record, 12.

[112] The Bank's answer. Transcript, 21.

[113] Supra, p. 648.

[114] The State named both the Bank and Cashier Huntington as defendants in each case; the party first named in the respective complaints

gave the case its title in the United States Reports.

Texas v. White had been decided on April 12, 1869. The Huntington action was initiated in the Supreme Court of District of Columbia on May 1, 1869. The equity suit against the National Bank proceeded on an amended bill filed April 28, 1869. (The original bill had been filed on May 8, 1868.)

would have been produced—the Supreme Court sitting with a jury to try a common law action![115]

The State was not so inconsiderate; instead, it invoked the concurrent jurisdiction of the Supreme Court of the District of Columbia. The jury there were instructed in accordance with what was supposed to be the teaching of *Texas v. White*: if they found that the bonds were alienated by the usurping government in Texas, or had not been indorsed by a loyal Governor, no title passed. However, if defendants had merely collected by assignment the proceeds of bonds which others had presented for redemption, defendants would not be liable as converters. The jury found the defendants liable as to thirteen bonds, and not liable as to the remaining twenty-four. Judgment against bank and cashier was for the value of thirteen bonds in currency, at the date of redemption, with interest: $24,369.17 in all.[116]

Defendants and the State took out cross writs of error.

In the meantime, the equity suit had resulted in a decree in favor of the State for nineteen bonds with coupons, $21,075 in gold coin, plus interest from February 27, 1867, the date when the bank received payment; if the bank did not pay, the Comptroller would sell deposited securities to make that total.[117] (In short, the judge was following *Texas v. Hardenberg*.)

National Bank appealed.

The *Huntington* case on the cross writs of error was filed in the Supreme Court on November 28, 1871; the Bank's appeal on December 11. On motion of Thomas J. Durant, now representing the State,[118] over the opposition of J. Hubley Ashton, the Court ordered both matters to be advanced; argument was heard on April 8, 1872.[119]

---

[115] The Seventh Amendment provides:

In suits at common law, where the value in controversy shall exceed twenty dollars, the right of trial by jury shall be preserved, and no fact tried by a jury shall be otherwise re-examined in any Court of the United States, than according to the rules of the common law.

Even before that became part of the Constitution in 1791, provision for a jury trial in the Supreme Court had been made by Sec. 13 of the Judiciary Act of 1789: "And the trial of issues of fact in the Supreme Court, in all actions at law against citizens of the United States shall be by jury."

This was perpetuated as Sec. 689 of the Revised Statutes of 1875, and as Sec. 1872 of Title 28, United States Code, "Judicial Code and Judiciary," enacted in 1949.

The action of the State of Georgia v. Brailsford was tried by jury in the Supreme Court in 1794. 3 Dall. 1.

[116] Transcript of Record in Huntington v. Texas, 4.

[117] Transcript of Record in National Bank v. Texas, 94.

[118] Supra, p. 649.

[119] Huntington v. Texas and First National Bank of Washington v. Texas, 131 U.S. App. cx, 20 L. Ed. 550, Feb. 5, 1872.

Counsel for Texas had invoked a recent statute of June 30, 1870, 16

At the trial in *Huntington*, it seems, "no evidence was offered . . . to show that the bonds in controversy were a part of those involved in the White & Chiles transaction."[120] Under the instructions to the jury, brought up on the writ of error, the State could recover without establishing that point.

In *Texas v. White* the opinion as it rolled along had declared (1) that one took no title in an unindorsed bond; anyhow, (2) defendants took no title because they had notice that these were tainted bonds from White & Chiles; and (3) even if they hadn't known of the taint, they had taken overdue bonds and so had no better title than White & Chiles. Now in examining the instructions in *Huntington* the Court must isolate the first of these reasons and answer, true or false?

Counsel for Huntington made a persuasive demonstration that the statute of 1851—no bond shall be "available in the hands of any holder until the same shall have been indorsed in the city of Austin by the Governor"—"was evidently designed simply to secure the safe delivery of the bonds into the Treasury of Texas"; in years thereafter the legislature had "authorized the negotiation of various amounts of these bonds, without the slightest reference to the Governor's endorsement," to an aggregate exceeding the entire $5,000,000.[121] (This history had been traced by Comptroller Tayler in his report of August 15, 1865, already noticed.[122] That document had been cited to the Court in *Texas v. White*, but had not been made a part of the record. Phillips' brief for White had devoted less than a page to arguing that the statute of 1851 should be put out of the case; he had written simply that "this whole subject is considered in an elaborate report" by the Comptroller, where "the discussion . . . is so thorough and satisfactory that nothing remains to be added thereto."[123] It proved unwise to present the point so lightly. Pike's erudite brief for Chiles never got down to anything so practical.)

In any case where the Supreme Court is going to consider the effect of a State statute, there is a latent danger that it will construe by the words alone, without full understanding of the context and purpose. Now counsel for Huntington dwelt insistently upon the entire history of

---

Stat. 176, which gave priority in courts of the United States to cases "wherein a State is a party, or where the execution of the revenue laws of any State may be enjoined," "on sufficient reason shown." The Chief Justice noticed that "it is stated by the Governor of the State that the money represented by the bonds is very much wanted for the schools. This seems to us sufficient reason for advancing the causes."

Quite aside from the statute, the Court's Rule 26, Call and Order of the Docket, recognized that a case might be taken out of order "under special and peculiar circumstances to be shown to the Court." This carried forward a rule adopted in 1830.

[120] Statement and Brief of Ashton and Walter S. Cox, 2.

[121] Statement and Brief, 10.

[122] Supra, n. 43.

[123] Brief for White, 8–9.

this Texas legislation, "whereas in the White & Chiles case it was not the subject of argument by counsel, nor was it considered in the opinion of the Court."[124]

Counsel for Texas used only two sentences to say that this was an attempt to procure a revision of principles established in *Texas v. White*, which "in the absence of any intimation from the court that reargument would be desirable, we do not think it necessary to discuss."[125]

It was not until March 3, 1873—ten and a half months after argument—that the Chief Justice announced the Court's decision in the *Huntington* case.[126] Without admitting error on his part, he backed away from *Texas v. White*. Now he said it might be "fairly inferred" from the earlier opinion that if unindorsed bonds had been used for a legitimate purpose, such as schools, the purchaser would take a good title. "[T]he validity of [the State government's] alienation must depend on the object and purpose of it." The jury should have been instructed that only if "illegal issue and use, and the further fact of notice to the defendants" had been established, could they find for the State.

The trial court had been right, however, in its instruction that defendants were not liable for merely receiving the proceeds of bonds redeemed for others.

For the erroneous instructions too favorable to the State, the judgment must be *reversed and remanded*.

A fortnight later in the equity suit against the National Bank, the lower court's judgment in favor of the State was *affirmed, by an equally divided Court*.[127] While that was not necessarily contradictory of *Huntington*, it seemed surprising and had the appearance of inconsistency.

Justice Bradley scrawled the division on the cover of his copy of the Transcript:[128]

Reverse:	Miller	Affirm:	Chase
	Field		Clifford
	Strong		Swayne
	Bradley		Davis.

Before inquiring into the disaccord, the immediate practical significance of Texas' defeat in the *Huntington* case should be explained. Pending in the Supreme Court since October 1869 had been the original suit of *Texas v. Geo. Peabody & Co. et al.*, wherein Paschal had set out

---

[124] Statement and Brief, 2–3.

[125] Brief of Counsel for the State of Texas, at p. 2 of three pages.

[126] Huntington v. Texas, 16 Wall. 402.

[127] Minutes, Mar. 17, 1873. Justice Ward Hunt, who had come to the Court subsequent to the argument, took no part.

[128] In his set of Records and Briefs, in the Michigan State Library.

after the bonds sent to Europe in 1862. The opinion in *Texas v. White* had permitted him to take a very strong line. "I regret that you do not seem to comprehend the views of Chief Justice Chase . . . ," he had written to Peabody & Co. in July 1869. He quoted from the opinion: the State's restriction of 1851 requiring indorsement " 'gave notice to all the world.' " "Allow me to call your attention to this language . . . . This is all that I meant, gentlemen, by saying you were charged with notice. I did not mean actual or personal notice; but that notice which the public law engrafted upon the instruments themselves, and which affects purchasers as plainly as if these statutes had been printed in the bonds." This, Paschal insisted, was the *controlling* principle in *Texas v. White*—no matter that the Chief Justice had gone on to talk about actual knowledge, and to contrast the position of purchasers *ante* due and that of purchasers *post* due. Peabody & Co. were in no better position, wrote Paschal, than if they had paid money for a stolen watch.

> Pardon the plainness of the analogy. You will see from my speech that I have not the highest veneration for the distinction in favor of "innocent purchasers" of commercial paper. I value the necessities of commerce. But at last, in good morals, all property . . . should be taken in subordination to the rights of the rightful owners; and, with rare exceptions, . . . the law and good morals run together.[129]

That was a hard line, based on taking the Court at its word. But after that had come the decision in *Huntington*, which showed that if Texas was to recover from Peabody & Co., it would have to prove that there had been actual notice of illegal issue and use. (In the end, it will be found, that suit was dismissed.[130])

Now to inquire how the Court could sustain, by an equal division, a decree in favor of the State on one lot of bonds, right after its judgment against the State on another. The incident was symptomatic: for several years there had been signs that the Court was acting unsteadily— attributable in part to the infirmity of Grier, Nelson, and now Chase, with protracted absences from the bench.

The Bank asked for a rehearing. This was granted, as recorded in the Minutes for May 1, 1873:

> Ordered that the decree entered by this Court on the 17th day of May last be, and the same is hereby rescinded and annulled. And

---

[129] In the Matter of George W. Paschal. 10 Wall. 483 (1871). Answers of Respondent with Affidavits, Exhibits, and Proofs, 77–81. Letter of July 21, 1869. Similarly to Dabney, Morgan & Co., Peabody's agents in New York, in letters of June 24 and 26, 1869. Ibid., 66–68, 69–72. Paschal was then seeking a settlement, without the necessity of bringing a suit.

[130] Infra, p. 663.

that this cause be, and the same is hereby ordered for re-argument at the next term. per Mr. Chief Justice Chase.

That was the last day of the term—and, as it turned out, Chase's last day on the bench: he died on May 7.

A year later, on April 20, 1874—with Waite, C.J., in place of Chase, and Hunt, J., succeeding Nelson—a unanimous Court would *reverse* the judgment Texas had won in the court below.

The Bank's appeal brought up the whole record: plaintiff's bill; defendant's answer, sworn to be true; the depositions of witnesses on each side, taken out of court, upon interrogatories and counter-interrogatories; and the proceedings in court, resulting in the decree. Whereas in *Huntington*, on writ of error, it sufficed merely to decide whether the exceptions to the lower court's instructions to the jury were well founded, in the Bank's appeal in equity each Justice must work through the record, with the aid of the opposing briefs, to make up his mind what facts had been proved, and to consider how the law bore upon those facts.[131]

The bill alleged that the Bank's bonds were unindorsed: but now the *Huntington* decision established that Texas could not recover on that ground.

Further, the bill charged that the Bank had purchased "with express notice of the circumstances and manner in which the same had been obtained and converted by . . . White & Chiles . . . ."[132]

Should a Justice conclude, from the evidence in this 95-page record, that the State had proved this allegation?

At that time it was still the rule in equity that an answer under oath could be overcome only by the testimony of two witnesses, or of one witness sustained by corroborating circumstances.[133]

---

[131] On January 31, 1872, the House of Representatives had passed H.R. 891, a bill "to further regulate the appellate jurisdiction of the Supreme Court, and to prevent delays therein." One of its provisions for the relief of the Court was that, in cases where the facts were not found by a jury, the trial court would make findings of fact (as was done by the Court of Claims), and the Supreme Court would review only on questions of law. Justice Miller had drawn this bill, and his brethren approved. It went through the House rather easily, only to perish in the Senate Judiciary Committee. Charles Fairman, *Mr. Justice Miller, 1862–1890* (Cambridge, Mass.:

Harvard University Press, 1939), 403–4.

[132] Transcript, 11.

[133] The rule had recently been stated and applied in Slater v. Maxwell, 6 Wall. 268 (1868).

The rational basis for the rule had been denied by Bentham in his *Rationale of Judicial Evidence* (1827), Bowring's edition of his *Works*, VII, 530. Story sustained the rule in his *Equity Jurisprudence*, sec. 1528 (1836). It was abandoned for the federal courts by Rule 11, *Federal Rules of Civil Procedure* (1938)—if not indeed by the Equity Rules of 1912. See *Wigmore on Evidence*, 3d ed. 1940, sec. 2047.

The answer of the defendants, by the cashier under oath, denied knowledge that these were White & Chiles bonds, and also denied that in fact they were; inquiry at the Treasury before purchase had disclosed that no one there could identify the lot; defendants bought actually believing they were getting bonds not there included; they had paid a full consideration—98 percent in gold for most of the bonds.[134]

The *Bank* case illustrates strikingly what was involved in the proposition that in an equity appeal *the facts* were brought under review by the Justices. There had been 782 unindorsed bonds. Of these, 135 bonds (serial numbers unrecorded) had gone into the hands of White & Chiles. Had the State proved that the 19 here in suit had been among that 135? That was a great puzzle; and now it was the duty of the Justices to decide whether the State's contention should be sustained.

Comptroller Tayler, the State's leading witness, had testified, in part:

> From all the circumstances, my opinion is, those were of the White & Chiles bonds. That is only an opinion, however.[135]

---

[134] Transcript, 19–23.
[135] Transcript, 29.

It seemed that the unindorsed bonds were Nos. 4219 to 5000. Of these, 148 had been delivered to the Southern Pacific Railroad Company pursuant to legislation enacted prior to the rebellion. That left 634 that apparently had gone to the use of the Military Board. Of these, 300 had been sent to England; 112 others had been recovered by the United States forces at the close of hostilities and restored to the State authorities. That left 222 that apparently had been in the hands of the Military Board for use within the country. Conjecture as to the serial numbers of these bonds was chiefly by inference from such identification as could be made of bonds not tainted. But 34 of the Southern Pacific's bonds had been delivered to the Military Board in substitution for 34 of their own. (The latter thereby became purged. As to 25 of these, see 12 Ops. Atty. Gen. 78, Oct. 29, 1866. Texas Indemnity Bonds—Claim of Messrs. Mills.)

Comptroller Tayler deposed that he had "some means" of ascertaining the serial numbers of the bonds delivered to White & Chiles, "but not of the highest certainty as to all of them."

"I believe, however, that I may safely name the following as those delivered to White & Chiles, viz. . . ." Transcript, 34, 35.

Justice Bradley combed over the depositions, making extensive notes. He wrote on the cover of the Transcript, apparently on April 18, 1872— the date of the first argument:

> Reverse—not sufficient evidence they were issued in aid of the rebellion
>
> R.R. Co. had 148 bonds—Mr Tayler only guesses which they were

As he had examined the *Huntington* and the *National Bank* cases, he had noted his disagreement with the opinion in Texas v. White:

> I do not think the endorsement of the Governor was requisite to transfer the title to the bonds. Nothing appeared on their face, or by endorsement, to indicate this; but they were expressly payable to bearer, and transferable on delivery. . . .

Also,

> I do not think that the doctrine of *caveat emptor* can be applied to an innocent purchaser of the bonds, though he obtain them after Dec 31st 1864—because

XIII: *A Union of "Indestructible States"*

And Paschal had testified:

> I feel confident that the bonds redeemed for the bank, described by Mr. Tayler, were a part of the bonds which passed through the hands of White & Chiles, and I judge this from the circumstances which he has stated . . . .[136]

"From all the circumstances," that was their *opinion*: a mystery lay enshrouded within that inexplicit statement. That four of the eight Justices upon the first hearing voted to decide in favor of the State seems to have resulted from accepting these opinions as evidence.

When the cases against Huntington and the Bank were argued in April 1872, Justice Nelson was ill and had ceased to come to court. In November he resigned. His successor, Ward Hunt, sat for the first time on January 9, 1873. Then had come the business of affirming the judgment for Texas in the *Bank* case, and then rescinding and ordering a reargument. Then Chase died. The Court, convening in October, ordered that the Bank's appeal be not called before January 1, 1874.[137] That allowed inadequate time for President Grant's unbelievable ineptitude in finding a Chief Justice.[138] At last Waite took his seat on March 4; at once reargument was set for March 24.[139]

E. R. Hoar, until recently Attorney General, led for the Bank on the reargument. His twenty-page brief covered the essentials with complete effectiveness, and a crisp dispatch that seemed to say, Now let's have no muddling. This came properly enough from a counsellor of clear conceptions and forthright speech, who but for the ill-temper of some Senators would himself have been sitting on the Court.

The response matched Hoar's effort. On April 20 Justice Miller announced a unanimous decision in favor of the Bank. The terms on which the Bank had deposited other securities with the Comptroller proved "immaterial in the view we take of the case." Whether the bonds

---

they were not absolutely payable then, but only *redeemable* at the option of the U. S. Their not being redeemed was *no evidence of* dishonor. They were like bank bills, transferable hand to hand at all times, after as well as before that date.

[136] Transcript, 42.

[137] Minutes for Oct. 24, 1873.

[138] The place was offered to Senator Roscoe Conkling on November 8, 1873; he replied on November 20 that he was not interested. On December 1, Attorney General George H. Williams was nominated.

This aroused indignation; his ability was not of a high order, and his administration of the Department of Justice was involved in scandal. On January 8, 1874, the nomination was withdrawn.

Next day the President nominated Caleb Cushing, born in January 1800. Adverse reaction led to the withdrawal of that nomination on January 13.

On January 19, Morrison R. Waite was nominated; he was promptly confirmed, by vote of 63 to 6.

[139] Minutes for Mar. 6, 1874.

were "overdue" was waived for the moment, and did not need to be answered. The main allegation had been that these bonds were of the White & Chiles parcel. And on that the State's evidence had been "an absolute failure"—nothing more than the mere *opinion* of Tayler and Paschal. "As the matters on which this conclusion was founded were . . . all of them capable of being proved, no reason is perceived why the witness should be substituted for the court in weighing these facts, and making the proper inferences."

Then counsel for the State had placed reliance on the want of indorsement. But, Justice Miller replied, what the "eminent judge" in *Texas v. White* had said on that score had been "unnecessary to the decision of that case, and the soundness of the proposition may be doubted." The same judge, in *Texas v. Huntington*, had qualified his earlier statement, and the *Huntington* case, "on a careful examination of it, must be held to dispose of the one before us." Concluding, "there is no proof either of the unlawful issue or use, or purpose, nor of any notice to defendants of the probable existence of these facts." The decree below was reversed, with directions to dismiss the bill.

Justice Swayne (who according to Justice Bradley's memorandum had at first voted to affirm) now concurred in an opinion longer than Miller's, wherein he pronounced against Chase's positions in *Texas v. White* on point after point. "The repeal [in 1862] touching the Governor's indorsement was an act of ordinary legislation," and valid. But even if there had been no repeal, still the restriction in the statute of 1851 would have been ineffective, because "Texas could not restrain [the bonds'] transferability in the markets of the world" without bringing home actual notice to the buyer. Then he enlarged upon the proposition that the Bank's title would not have been affected even if the bonds could be considered "overdue"—a point on which he cast doubt.[140]

The two opinions illustrate the characteristic method of the respective Justices. Miller gains unanimity on the proposition that (without need to pursue intriguing conjectures) actually Texas had not *proved* that the Bank's bonds were tainted, much less that the Bank had been affected with knowledge. On that basis right could be done without making any more pronouncements on a subject where there had already been too many.

---

[140] Citing the opinion of Attorney General Speed, 11 Ops. Atty. Gen. 332 (1865), Rights of *Bona Fide* Holders of Stolen Treasury Notes, supra, pp. 644–45. Also a strong statement by Attorney General Black, 9 Ops. Atty. Gen. 413 (1860), Negotiability of Treasury Notes: "To hold that treasury notes, when transferred after maturity, are subject to equities between previous parties" would "impair their negotiability after maturity" and be "clearly inconsistent with the general intent of the law . . . ."

Swayne on the other hand writes a full opinion that passes upon points "involved" in the case although not necessary to a decision; he likes to cite authorities—and he is the great protector of the holders of negotiable instruments.

TEXAS v. WHITE IS OVERRULED

To REACH THE DEMISE of the doctrine in *Texas v. White*, two more decisions must be recorded, as well as certain fiscal statutes. An Act of Congress of March 3, 1865, authorized the borrowing of $600,000,000 by bonds or Treasury notes.[141] The latter were promises to pay "three years after date" with interest at 7.30 percent. (Hence they were called "7–30 notes.") Also bonds were issued, bearing 6 percent interest, "redeemable after five and payable twenty years from date." (Hence they were "5–20 bonds." The 5–20s, of this and earlier issues, became the largest category of national obligations, until they were called in the course of a refunding operation, soon to be mentioned.) Some of the 7–30 notes were convertible into 5–20 bonds at the pleasure of the holder.[142]

In *Vermilye v. Adams Express Co.*,[143] 7–30 notes payable on July 15, 1868, had been stolen from the Express Company in a train robbery on May 22, 1868. Promptly the Company cautioned the Treasury and banking houses, including Vermilye & Co., giving the serial numbers. On April 9 and 12, 1869, Vermilye purchased the stolen notes in the ordinary course of business and at fair prices. The Treasury refused to redeem. By bill of interpleader in the Circuit Court for the Southern District of New York, the United States called upon Adams and Vermilye to litigate between themselves the question which one was entitled to be paid. Judge Blatchford decided for Adams,[144] and Vermilye appealed.

Affirming, Justice Miller for the Court said that there was no adequate reason to except this situation from the rule that the purchaser of overdue paper takes subject to the right of an antecedent holder. Here the notes on their face were absolutely payable in three years, not merely redeemable as in *Texas v. White*. But, he warned pointedly, the Court implied no approval of that case. It was to be doubted that bonds,

---

[141] Act to provide Ways and Means for the Support of the Government, 13 Stat. 468. The Treasury notes there authorized were marketed rapidly after the fall of the Confederacy; the proceeds were used immediately for the heavy expenses of disbanding the Army. Ann. Cyc. 1865, 336.

[142] In National Bank of Washington v. Texas, supra at p. 657, the deposit with the Comptroller had at first been 7–30s, presently converted into 5–20s.

[143] 21 Wall. 138 (1875).

[144] United States v. Vermilye *et al.*, Fed. Case No. 16,618 (1872).

"redeemable but not payable at a certain date, except at the option of the government, do become overdue in the sense of being dishonored if not paid or redeemed on that day."

Further legislation must be mentioned, in approaching *Morgan v. United States*,[145] decided by the Court in 1885, per Matthews, J., who as a Senator had played a controversial part in the refunding operations to which that case made reference.

The Refunding Act of July 14, 1870,[146] authorized the Secretary of the Treasury to refund the national debt, by exercising the Government's option to call 5–20 bonds, and by issuing new bonds bearing lower interest. Three months after publication, interest on a called bond would cease. The Specie Resumption Act of January 14, 1875,[147] declared that from January 1, 1879, all legal tender notes would be redeemable in coin. To attain reserves adequate to make and maintain resumption, the Secretary would issue bonds of the description authorized by the statute of 1870, for gold at par.

A considerable part of the bonds to be retired were held in Europe. Secretary Sherman marketed new issues in 1878 and 1879 through a syndicate of bankers in New York and London, among whom was the house of Morgan. The Secretary had the delicate task of so adjusting the calling of old bonds and the sale of new as to maintain the calling of old bonds and the sale of new as to maintain at all times a gold reserve adequate to the uncertainties of resumption, while avoiding as far as possible the payment of double interest.

Morgan v. United States[148] had to do with 5–20s dated 1865, which on their face were redeemable after five years and payable after twenty. They had been called on July 30, 1878, and certain later days. On October 27, 1878, the bonds in question were stolen from the Manhattan Savings Institution. They turned up in London, where in 1879 Morgan purchased them from another bank of high respectability, and transmitted them to the Treasury in the course of the refunding operations. The Department refused payment, and, as permitted by Section 1063 of the Revised Statutes, submitted to the Court of Claims the question of its obligation to Morgan. Manhattan came in as an adverse claimant, and won the judgment of that court.[149] Morgan appealed.

---

[145] 113 U.S. 476.

[146] 16 Stat. 272.

[147] 18 Stat. 296. This was the so-called deathbed repentance of the Republican party, which had been overwhelmingly defeated in the November elections. The measure was carried by a straight party vote, in the lame-duck session of the 43rd Congress.

[148] 113 U.S. 476 (1885).

[149] L. Von Hoffman & Co. v. United States, and Manhattan Savings Institution v. United States, 18 Ct. Cls. 386 (1883).

XIII: *A Union of "Indestructible States"*

For Manhattan, counsel said: these bonds were overdue—*Texas v. White* and *Vermilye v. Adams* settle the case in our favor.

For Morgan, the brief by J. Hubley Ashton[150] ignored *Texas v. White. Vermilye* was distinguished: the notes there were overdue on their face, and the purchaser had ignored the notice of larceny. Then, wisely, he stressed the practical aspect:

> Congress knew that these bonds were held, in large amounts, in almost every civilized country, and by thousands who never would hear of the "calls" until after the interest on their bonds had ceased, and to whom the full and complete negotiability of the bonds, after that time, would be of the greatest importance, as enabling them readily to obtain the money for their securities when they wanted it, by negotiating the bonds, in the market, instead of incurring the risk and expense of sending them to the Treasury. And Congress knew that unless the bonds were freely negotiable, as commercial paper, everywhere, after, as well as before, the "calls" matured, their payment never could be effected, by the Government, without the use and transfer of gold, and the most serious disturbance of the money markets of America and Europe.[151]

Justice Matthews as spokesman for the Court wrote a lucid opinion, reviewing the long story of *Texas v. White* and its sequelae, and at last putting the law into order. The point about the State legislature being able to restrict negotiability "must be regarded as overruled." Also overruled was the proposition that as soon as a government bond became redeemable it must be regarded as overdue and non-negotiable. In the instant situation, while the Government's call for redemption would cause the interest to cease in three months, there was no reason why the bond should not circulate freely in commerce; a bona fide purchaser for value, prior to the date fixed for ultimate payment, would take a good title. That was what the contract imported, and moreover it was in accord with the practicalities of the market and the convenience of the United States. The judgment of the Court of Claims was reversed.

IN CONCLUSION ON *TEXAS v. WHITE*

THIS CRITICAL EXAMINATION yields significant reflections. Chase's sentence—this is an indestructible Union of indestructible States—was a noble utterance, although it had taken more than the Court's saying it

---

[150] Who had represented Huntington and the National Bank of Washington in their successful defense against the claims of Texas.

[151] Brief, 17.

to make it so. Earlier, undeterred by the prospect that on some occasion the Court would be called upon to rule upon the status of the Southern States, Chase had solicited the press to disseminate his theory on that subject. He could never suffer his moral talents to be "lodged in him useless." In *Texas v. White*, when he came to the merits, while he reached the right judgment—because White & Chiles' co-defendants were indeed chargeable with knowledge—he gave plural solutions, each erroneous and troublesome. That this opinion was allowed to pass by Chase's brethren—who soon thereafter showed that they knew better—tends to confirm the belief that the exercise of corporate responsibility for the work of the Court was badly needed at that period. Instances of deciding, then rescinding, and presently deciding the other way—as in *National Bank v. Texas*—strengthen the impression that this was a time of loose practice.

TEXAS PURSUES THE BONDS

WE TURN BACK to pick up the line of inquiry as to the State's bonds and its attorneys[152]—in the course of which we find illustration of two inherent powers of the Court: to hold members of its bar to an honest performance of professional duties, *In re Paschal*;[153] and to punish a contempt of its decrees, *In re Chiles*.[154]

When on January 27, 1870, Governor Davis removed Paschal as Agent and directed him to turn over all the moneys in hand to his successor, Thomas J. Durant,[155] the blow came inopportunely for the orderly prosecution of the State's claims. The decree in *Texas v. White* had been won on April 12, 1869; that as to *Hardenberg* on November 29. Paschal was just on the point of repelling an effort to reopen the case as to co-defendant George W. Stewart, holder of four bonds, who had made no contest when *Texas v. White et al.* was being tried. On February 7 the Court ordered Stewart to settle within thirty days.[156] Pending in the District of Columbia court were *Texas v. Huntington* and *Texas v. National Bank of Washington*. And on October 18, 1869, Paschal had filed in the Supreme Court the original suit of *Texas v. George Peabody & Co., Dabney, Morgan & Co., and Droege & Co.*, in respect of the three hundred bonds the Military Board had sent to England in 1862. At the moment of his removal, Paschal had reason to believe he was near to an advantageous settlement of this claim. All had been proceeding in good order.

---

152 Supra, p. 648.
153 10 Wall. 483 (1871).
154 22 Wall. 157 (1875).

155 Supra, p. 649.
156 131 U.S. App. xcv; 19 L. Ed. 532.

Peabody & Co., it should be explained, was the great London banking house founded by George Peabody (1795–1869), onetime grocer's apprentice of Danvers, Massachusetts, whose discriminating philanthropy reached both sides of the Atlantic, and included the Peabody Education Fund for the betterment of the South.[157] Dabney, Morgan & Co. of New York were agents for the Peabody bank. Droege & Co., composed of Prussian subjects, were bankers at Manchester, England, and in New York City; during the war their branch at Matamoros, Mexico, had dealt in contraband. The bill in *Texas v. Peabody & Co. et al.* sought an accounting for the 149 bonds which the Treasury had redeemed for Peabody on October 31, 1866,[158] and the surrender of the rest, believed to remain in the hands of Droege. (Without ever being brought to a decision, this suit remained on the docket until— Droege & Co. having surrendered the bonds in their hands—the case was dismissed on April 23, 1877, for want of prosecution. *Texas v. White, Chiles et al.*, and a related case, *Texas v. Chiles*, were dropped at that same time.[159])

Durant, the new Agent, on November 4, 1870, filed his authority to represent the State, and submitted two motions with regard to Paschal.[160] One asked for an order that he pay over the moneys he had received in *Texas v. White*; the other that he be no longer recognized as counsel in *Texas v. George Peabody & Co.*

Paschal's answer admitted the receipt of $47,325 in gold money.[161] Out of this he had paid to Merrick and associates $11,738, their fee of 25 percent under their agreement with Governor Throckmorton. He had disbursed $1,626 for costs and expenses in the several suits.[162] That left a balance of $33,961, out of which Paschal claimed a fee of $20,000 "for his services in regard to the White & Chiles bonds, and about the other bonds before the Treasury Department, the Presi-

---

[157] After his death on November 4, 1869, the firm went into liquidation. Peabody's executors were made parties to the record.

[158] In accord with the opinion of Attorney General Stanbery of Oct. 15, 1866. 12 Ops. Atty. Gen. 72. Texas Indemnity Bonds—Claim of Peabody & Co.

[159] Minutes for that day.

[160] *In re* Paschal, 10 Wall. 483 (1871).

[161] The Answers, a document of twenty pages, was under oath of November 23, 1870. It forms the first part of a 118-page document entitled In the Matter of George W. Paschal.

Answers of Respondent with Affidavits, Exhibits and Proofs.

Of this total, $8,000 had come from Birch, Murray & Co., and $37,175 from Hardenberg—co-defendants in Texas v. White. Paschal had not received the payment Stewart had been directed to make by the Court's order of February 7, 1870, supra, p. 649.

[162] These are itemized in Exhibit C, Answers of Respondent with Affidavits . . . , 23–26. All seems proper and incontestable. For example, $453 to Comptroller Tayler, his allowance as Special Master appointed by the Court under the decree in *Hardenberg.*

dent, and the country."[163] His understanding with Governor Hamilton had been "that he should charge such fees as the responsibility, the expense, the time, the learning necessary, and the services should render proper."[164] Those services had extended from the autumn of 1865 until early in 1870, except for Governor Throckmorton's year in office. He appended a statement by Edwin W. Stoughton that "in my opinion such charge is reasonable,"[165] along with similar estimates by other leading counsel.

Next the answer turned to the three hundred bonds sent to England; Paschal's exertions in that matter were recorded, with pertinent correspondence. Here he relied upon an agreement with Governor Pease, never reduced to writing, that he should have 25 percent of whatever was recovered on the Peabody bonds and 20 percent of the recovery from Droege.[166] Quite aside from the bonds, he had claims against the State for other legal services.[167] Paschal urged the Court to recognize that an attorney has a lien upon the papers and moneys of his client until his fees are settled (citing cases in Texas and elsewhere). That was particularly just in this instance, he maintained, inasmuch as he would be unable to bring a suit against the State.[168]

Paschal put his case in the hands of Albert G. Riddle (1816–1902), onetime Republican Congressman from Ohio who was practicing in Washington and often appeared before the Supreme Court. Riddle told the Court that he had advised Paschal to retain the money and papers until the matter was adjusted, "and I was informed by [ex-Justice Benjamin R. Curtis] that he gave the same advice and that he was still of opinion that such a course on the part of the respondent was right and proper."[169]

---

[163] Answers, 10.

[164] Answers, 3.

[165] Answers of Respondent with Affidavits, 115.

[166] Answers, 12.

[167] He claimed $17,577 for reporting, printing, and delivering 400 copies of each of these Texas Reports: vols. 25 Supp., 29, 30 and 31. Also $1,000 for each of the two suits brought in 1860. Answers, 23–26.

[168] Answers, 27.

[169] Answers, 110.

Riddle described his performance in the course of a chatty letter to the Chief Justice, on Sunday, December 11, 1870. The two had long been friends. Chase, recuperating from a paralytic stroke, had been absent throughout the term.

Now I trust you will take your own good time and get fully restored and then stay and refresh yourself, and enjoy recovered health, and come back to us when it pleases you, altho I must confess we sadly miss you, and the Supreme Court seems sadly diminished, and almost common.

I've been before it two or three times during its recent sittings, and was boreing it awfully on Friday [In re Paschal]. My speech was long at best, and I fear it seemed longer for [lacking] depth and breadth; and 3 oclock came before the end, and Mr Justice Nelson says "Mr Riddle your two hours are up." Yes I knew I had been up two hours, and I am sure it seemed all of that to every body else; so that the an-

And so the Court decided, in a notable opinion by Justice Bradley.[170] This matter was "in the nature of a proceeding as for a contempt. The application is based upon the power which the court has over its own officers to prevent them from, or punish them for, committing acts of dishonesty or impropriety calculated to bring contempt on the administration of justice." It was the alleged misconduct on which the Court's jurisdiction was grounded; "if no dishonesty appears the party will be left to his action" in an ordinary trial. The Court held, as the headnote accurately stated, that

> The attorney or solicitor, who is also counsel in a cause, has a lien for moneys collected therein for his fees and disbursements in the cause, and in any suit or proceeding brought to recover other moneys covered by the same retainer.

Where, as here, the attorney had "a fair and honest set-off, which ought in equity to be allowed by the complainant," that circumstance bore on the question of misconduct. And where, as here, the attorney could not bring his client into court, "it would seem to be against all equity to compel him to pay over the funds in his hands, and thus strip him of all means of bringing his claims to an issue." The State, on the other hand, could bring suit, and the defendant could have a jury trial on the validity of his demands, according to his contract or for the reasonable value of his services.

Durant had also moved that Paschal be forbidden to interfere with the suit of *Texas v. Peabody & Co.* Here Justice Bradley said that certainly a party was free to change his attorney, and a rule for that purpose would be granted—leaving to the displaced attorney, however, the advantage he had in holding the moneys and papers of his client as security for his fees and disbursements.

SIGNIFICANCE OF *IN RE PASCHAL*

TO APPRECIATE WHY this case is a landmark one must for a moment step into the past. Blackstone explained the distinction between

---

nouncement tho' accurate was unnecessary—and if the Chief J. had [been presiding] he would have announced in the blandest way that the time for adjt. had come, and regretfully suggest that I must suspend—however he may have felt. . . .

If this bores you think of what your associates have suffered and are threatened with at my hands, & how little they can help themselves.

Chase Papers, L.C.

If the Court appeared "almost common," so too must much of the argument at its bar at that period when the allowance of time was, by the present standard, prodigal.

[170] *In re* Paschal, 10 Wall. 483, decided Jan. 23, 1871.

the attorney at law (and the solicitor in chancery) whom one engaged "to manage his matters of law" and on the other hand the barrister who, upon instructions, appeared as an advocate to argue at the bar of a court. Barristers took upon themselves "the protection and defence of any suitors, whether plaintiff or defendant; who are therefore called their *clients*, like the dependents upon the ancient Roman orators. Those indeed practiced *gratis*, for honour merely, or at most for the sake of gaining influence: and so likewise it is established with us, that a counsel can maintain no action for his fees . . . "; he could expect only an honorarium, "a mere gratuity, which a counsellor cannot demand without doing wrong to his reputation . . . ."[171]

Had this stilted usage been adopted in republican America? In 1819 Chief Justice Tilghman of Pennsylvania had affirmed that in this respect "the law which our ancestors brought with them" remained unaltered; he denied recovery by an attorney for services both in and out of court. (In Pennsylvania, as in other States except New Jersey, the English distinction between attorney and counsel had not been maintained.[172]) This holding was repudiated, however, in 1830;[173] in 1835, Chief Justice Gibson condemned "the artificial structure and practical injustice" of his predecessor's opinion.[174] And Gibson's successor, Jeremiah S. Black, in a case in 1852—laying out principles which, Justice Bradley said, "strongly commend themselves for their good sense and just discrimination"—had held that an attorney was entitled to recover whatever his services were reasonably worth; he might retain such a fee, and the payment of the balance was all that could lawfully be demanded.[175] Ruling decisions in New York[176] and Texas[177] were to a like effect. The conclusion was that Paschal had done "nothing to call for the summary interposition of this court." Whether (as the Court was

---

[171] *Commentaries*, bk. III, ch. III.

[172] Mooney v. Lloyd, 5 Serg. & Rawle 412. He noted, however, that whereas physicians were on this same "honourable footing" in England, in Pennsylvania they could sue for fees.

William Tilghman (1756–1827) had been a Loyalist during the Revolution. On March 3, 1801—President Adams' last day in office—he had been appointed Chief Judge of the Third Circuit, an office he held until the first Congress during Jefferson's administration abolished the Circuit Courts by the Act of April 29, 1802. He became Chief Justice of Pennsylvania's Supreme Court, where he presided until his death.

[173] Gray v. Brackenridge, 2 Penr. & W. 75. "Gibson, C.J.—Expressed his satisfaction in over-ruling that case [Mooney v. Lloyd]."

[174] Foster v. Jack, 4 Watts 334.

[175] Balsbaugh v. Frazer, 19 Pa. St. 95.

[176] Stevens & Cagger v. Adams, 23 Wend. 57 (1840) in the Supreme Court of New York, where Samuel Nelson was then Chief Justice; affirmed in Adams v. Stevens & Cagger, 26 Wend. 451 (1841) in the Court for Trial of Impeachments and Correction of Errors.

[177] Casey v. March, 30 Texas 180 (1867), and several other cases cited.

inclined to believe) the case should be governed by the law of Texas, where the original retainer was made, or the Court should judge a member of its bar by what it "deems to be the prevailing rule in this country," on either view the result would be the same.

IN RE CHILES

Texas v. White was held on the Court's docket—moving up until it stood No. 1 Original—for the reason that the execution of the decree remained subject to the supervision of the Court; each party had leave to move for further orders. The case reported as *In re Chiles*, in 1875,[178] was an incident in that supervision. The Court's judgment holding Chiles in contempt was—it will soon be seen—of decisive effect in bringing the pursuit of the bonds to a close in 1877.

It is to be recalled that the bill of complaint in *Texas v. White* set out the contract whereby White & Chiles were to receive 135 bonds held at Austin, and also 76 bonds "in England, in the hands of Droege & Co."[179] The decree, responsive to the prayer for relief, was that the contract was void; that White and Chiles were enjoined from claiming any right under it; and that "the complainant is entitled to recover and receive the bonds and coupons mentioned in said contract."[180]

George W. White and John Chiles had gone their separate ways. After the commencement of the suit, a compromise was made between Governor Throckmorton and White, purporting to represent White & Chiles, under which the State received $12,000 in currency, as well as 8 bonds on file in the Treasury, and White & Chiles released their claim to bonds in England; in consideration whereof the State released all claim on White & Chiles and their sureties. When Chiles heard of this he notified the Governor that he did not recognize the settlement.[181]

At the moment when Paschal was ousted by Governor Davis, it appeared that he had brought Droege & Co. to a willingness to surrender the bonds in their hands upon allowance of their actual disbursements.[182]

But then Chiles asserted title to bonds deposited in England, including the seventy-six embraced in the White & Chiles contract: he based this on what he alleged to be a wholly different contract of March 4, 1865, between the Military Board and himself alone. He warned Droege not to settle the Texas claim without his authority.

---

[178] 22 Wall. 157.
[179] Supra, p. 631.
[180] Decree in 7 Wall. at 741–43.
[181] Transcript of Record in Texas v. White, 61–64. Supplemental answer of John Chiles.
[182] Answer of Respondent in the Matter of Paschal, 98–103.

Thus Chiles became the key to the problem. Fortunately for Texas, he was within the reach of the Supreme Court. If the power of the Court could effectively be brought to bear, that would be infinitely preferable to creating a holiday for English solicitors and counsel by litigating the State's claim in the English court. In November 1874, Richard T. Merrick and Durant, now working in association, explained the situation to Governor Coke of Texas, and were directed by him to proceed in the Supreme Court.[183]

Richard Coke (1828–97)—sometime secessionist, Captain CSA, and Supreme Court judge removed by General Sheridan—had been elected Governor in 1873 in a two-to-one Democratic triumph. The defeated candidate, Governor Davis, had vacated the office only after President Grant advised him "to yield to the verdict of the people."[184] Coke found an empty treasury. To collect the bonds, by suit or compromise, he appointed new agents, politically congenial to himself—the brothers Jabez D. and DeWitt C. Giddings, lawyers and bankers long identified with the development of Texas. The latter had served in the Confederate Army throughout the war and was now a Member of Congress.[185] The Governor assured Merrick and Durant, however, that the Giddingses were only "outside aids" in conducting the litigation against Chiles. (Eventually Coke's generous settlement with the agents

---

[183] Transcript of Record in Merrick *et al.* v. Giddings, 115 U.S. 300 (1885), at 19–20.

In the Archives in the Texas State Library, in the Letterpress Books of Governor Coke, is the following to Merrick and Durant, of November 22, 1874:

I enclose Letter of atty. to proceed against John Chiles in the matter of his claim to Texas indemnity bonds. This office shows no intimation of or allusion to any such claim as he sets up in his answer, a copy of which has been sent me by the Messrs Giddings. I have no doubt but that it is a fraudulent pretense, trumped up in the hope of forcing a compromise, and if I am right, I mean to see to it that results thoroughly disappoint his hopes.

At the same time Coke wrote to J. D. and D. C. Giddings that he regarded Chiles' claim "as an infamous attempt to swindle and blackmail"; he had instructed Merrick and Durant

"to take all necessary judicial proceedings to set aside his claim."

[184] Ann. Cyc. 1873, 740.

[185] He had been seated in the 42nd Congress, on May 13, 1872, upon the unanimous report of the Committee on Elections (McCrary of Iowa, Republican, being chairman)— notwithstanding that Governor Davis had given his certificate to the Republican candidate (William T. Clark, Brevet Major General, U.S.A.) after rejecting the returns from several counties on the ground of irregularities, fraud and violence. Cong. Globe, 42–2, 340–49, 3384–85. Giddings was reelected to the 43rd Congress, and again to the 45th.

Prominent in defending Giddings' claim to be seated was Representative William M. Merrick, Maryland Democrat, and brother of the attorney, Richard T. Merrick, who presently would be in controversy with Giddings over the division of compensation for the recovery of the Texas bonds.

and his niggardly treatment of counsel led to a controversy, *Merrick's Executor v. Giddings*,[186] decided by the Supreme Court in 1885. The record in that case throws light on the contempt proceeding against Chiles.)

Pursuant to their retainer by Governor Coke, in November, 1874 Merrick and Durant moved for a rule upon Chiles to show cause why he should not be dealt with as guilty of contempt by disobeying the Court's decree (in *Texas v. White*, still pending), and why he should not be ordered to convey to the State the bonds he claimed in the hands of Droege. Albert Pike, for Chiles, filed an answer, and the matter was argued on March 1 and 2, 1875.

Had Chiles' notice to the English bankers amounted to disobedience of the decree in *Texas v. White*? Pike argued strenuously that the object of the original suit had been only to annul the White & Chiles contract; the decree and the injunction should be construed as no wider than that object; they did not bar Chiles from asserting title under a different contract. In any event, merely to assert that he had a right without taking any action to enforce it, should not be held to violate the injunction.

The Court, per Justice Miller, rejected that narrow view. By its suit, Texas asserted its ownership of all the bonds that lay in its treasury at the time of the rebellion; Chiles and the other defendants had been called upon to defend their respective claims of title. Equity seeks to do complete justice; it would trifle with the court for a defendant to hide a part of his defense in order that it might serve as an excuse for evading the decree. Further, without determining how far "mere loose verbal assertion" might violate the injunction, certainly a written notice of claim of ownership, with threat of judicial proceedings, did amount to a violation. For this a fine of $250 was imposed. Field and Hunt, JJ., noted dissent.

The petition had also asked that Chiles be ordered to execute a conveyance to the State of his claim to the bonds. (That would have facilitated their release by the English bankers.) But, said the Court, that had not been required by the original decree, and it would not make such an order prospectively as part of this proceeding for contempt.

This was on March 29, 1875.

TEXAS v. CHILES

IN FACT A NEW BILL, *Texas v. John Chiles*, No. 6 Original on the Court's docket, had already been filed by Merrick and Durant on December 4, 1874. In aid thereof they asked that a subpoena issue to

---

[186] 115 U.S. 300. Infra, pp. 673-75.

Chiles summoning him to give his deposition to questions propounded by the State.[187]

Should the subpoena be granted: Could Chiles be required to testify in this controversy to which he was a party? Here one finds a reminder of what bright threads may be involved in what superficially appears to be a dull little case. The answer lay in something Congress had done in the Civil Appropriation Act of 1864, in a section looking to the prosecution of counterfeiters, by a proviso that achieved an important Benthamite reform in the law of evidence, and at the same time one of Senator Sumner's objectives for doing justice to the Negro.[188] How this concatenation of incongruous elements served to promote the recovery by Texas of its bonds is worth a moment's explanation.

This pertinent provision of the statute of 1864 became Section 858 of the codification known as the Revised Statutes (1875). It enacted that "In the courts of the United States no witness shall be excluded in any action on account of color, or in any civil action because he is a party to or interested in the issue tried . . . ." The second branch of that statement—a party to a suit may be called as a witness—was the result of what Charles Warren described as "one of the most necessary revolutions in the old Common Law doctrines"; he was referring to "the great reform in the law of evidence—especially in the removal of the rules which barred a witness from testifying because of interest, and because of being a party." He explained:

> The old Common Law bar of interest had become absurd in its application to modern trials. It resulted in many instances in the complete exclusion of the truth as to the facts of a case. In other instances, it was a direct inducement to fraud, as persons desired as witnesses, and likely to be excluded on grounds of interest made releases of their interest before the trial, only to receive a regrant of the interest so released, after the trial was over. . . .[189]

Jeremy Bentham's "keen and truculent attacks upon the system"[190] led to its overthrow by Parliament—by Lord Denman's Act in

---

[187] 21 Wall. 488 (1875). Chiles' Disclaimer and Answer, of January 18, 1875, was that before this bill was filed, and after he had made answer to the rule to show cause why he should not be punished for contempt (the rule was issued on November 4, 1874), he had assigned his interest in the bonds to William Hoffman of New York City, in consideration of mining and other stocks of face value

of $50,000. Case file in the National Archives.

[188] Act of July 2, 1864, 13 Stat. 351.

[189] History of Harvard Law School and of Early Legal Conditions in America, 3 vols. (New York: Lewis Publishing Co., 1908), II, 257–58.

[190] James Bradley Thayer, Legal Essays (Cambridge, Mass.: Harvard University Press, 1908), 311.

1843, which removed the bar as to "persons interested,"[191] and by Lord Brougham's Act in 1851, which admitted "the parties" to testify.[192] This, like other reforms then being made in the law of England, was widely adopted by American legislatures. Congress, by an Act relating to the law of evidence in the District of Columbia, of July 2, 1864, enacted almost verbatim the two English statutes.[193]

Running along with this measure for the District of Columbia—in a weary Congress that was holding evening sessions while the thermometer soared to 93°—was the Sundry Civil Appropriations Bill. One item would make an appropriation for the detection of counterfeiters. There Senator Sumner saw his last opportunity to gain an objective he had been cherishing throughout the session: he offered an amendment to provide "That in the courts of the United States there shall be no exclusion of any witness on account of color."[194] This "surely is germane" to convicting counterfeiters, he insisted; also he read a letter from District Judge Underwood of the federal court in Virginia,[195] urging that without the testimony of Negroes, "several confiscation cases" there pending might fail. When Senator Sherman, who agreed with the principle of the proviso, begged Sumner not to delay an appropriation bill with this controversial measure, the latter replied "I believe it is always time to do an act of justice." Carlile, conservative Unionist from Virginia, protested that "nothing would more outrage the public sentiment in a slave State than the fact that the property of one of its citizens had been confiscated upon negro testimony"; and Willard Saulsbury of Delaware added that "imagination can scarcely conceive the deplorable results."[196] The enormous significance of Negro testimony as a symbol has already been noticed[197]—quite aside from its importance in the administration of justice. Buckalew of Pennsylvania, Democrat, seeking to hobble Sumner's effort, managed to carry an amendment to add the words "nor in civil actions because he is a party to or is interested in the issue tried." (The like provision for the District of Columbia had been reported to the Senate ten days before.) But Sumner's amendment as amended was adopted, and the House concurred, the division in each chamber being along party lines.

Thus when Texas sought to compel Chiles to testify about the bonds it was able to invoke the provision Sumner sought for the benefit of the Negro. Defense counsel contended that the new statute gave

---

191 6 & 7 Vict., c. 85.

192 14 & 15 Vict., c. 99.

193 13 Stat. 374. This particular borrowing from England was noticed by Justice Gray in Hopkins v. Grimshaw, 165 U.S. 342 (1897).

194 Cong. Globe, 38–1, 3259. June 25, 1864.

195 On Judge Underwood and confiscation in Virginia, see infra, pp. 823–28.

196 Cong. Globe, 38–1, 3260, 3261.

197 Supra, pp. 112–13.

"merely a privilege to each party which may be availed of or not as a matter of choice, without conferring the right upon either to compel the other to testify." The Court, however, rejected that as "too narrow"; "the plain import of the words" was clear. "But if there were a doubt on the subject, the statute being remedial in its character, the doubt should be resolved in a liberal spirit in order to obviate as far as possible the existing evils."

This defeat for Chiles on April 5, 1875—coming one week after the Court had found him guilty of contempt[198]—was most discouraging to his prospects. Yet for Texas the problem was, how to get payment for the bonds held by Droege & Co. in England.

BRINGING HOME THE BONDS

DURANT AND MERRICK had already moved on that point. To the Congress that met in December 1874 they submitted on the part of the State a petition wherein they detailed what had been done to recover the bonds; of the 300 sent to Europe, 149 purchased by Peabody had been redeemed by the Treasury; as to the 151 bonds with coupons held by Droege and claimed by Chiles—wrongfully, according to *Texas v. White* —the petition asked that Congress direct the Secretary of the Treasury to pay their full amount to Texas. Thereby the State would be spared from having to submit to a foreign court "the most important and delicate questions of American polity and constitutional law . . . ."[199]

Representative Giddings presented this petition, and introduced H.R. 4001 to carry it into effect.[200] He had already been employed by Governor Coke to collect the bonds;[201] but what a Member of Congress does in the course of his legislative duties is not to be reckoned as work in the performance of a contract. The House passed the bill,[202] but it died in the Judiciary Committee of the Senate.

Even so, it now seemed evident that no one other than the State would be able to collect the bonds with coupons in Droege's hands. That was the result of the work, in and out of court, of Paschal, of Merrick and of Durant. After checks imposed upon Chiles in the spring of 1875, the task of collection should not prove difficult.

In late July, Giddings went to Europe; two months later he was

---

[198] Supra, p. 669.
[199] Cong. Record, 43–2, 79, 755–756.
[200] Ibid., 72, 79.

[201] Supra, p. 668.
[202] Cong. Record, 43–2, 1291–92. Feb. 15, 1875.

back with the bonds, which he redeemed at the Treasury for $339,240 in currency. He renewed previous statements to Merrick and Durant that the fund would not be surrendered to the State until their fees were paid. Presently he went to Austin and made a settlement with Governor Coke, at variance with those statements.

FORTUNE'S BUFFETS AND REWARDS

THE UNINSPIRING ACCOUNT that follows is based upon the Governor's report to the legislature;[203] the sworn statement to the Court, *In re Paschal*;[204] and the Transcript of Record in the suit of Merrick and Durant in the District of Columbia court, culminating in a decision by the Supreme Court in 1885.[205]

First, Governor Coke:

> During the eleven years which have elapsed since the first effort was made for the recovery of these bonds, not a dollar has ever been realized by the State until Col. Giddings went to Europe and made the settlement detailed in his report.

Out of the more than $339,000 Giddings had brought home, Coke continued, $300,000 had been paid into the State Treasury; what was left he had divided, $8,000 to Merrick and Durant and the rest to Giddings. He considered that Merrick and Durant had been "liberally paid for their services"—that Merrick and associates had received from Paschal $14,675 for their work in *Texas v. White*,[206] and Durant had received $1,954 from Governor Davis. He construed their contract with Governor Davis for a 20 percent fee as applicable only to money collected by judicial process, and "not one dollar . . . has been collected in that way . . . ." They had failed in their attempt to get a bill through Congress. Still, by their litigation against Chiles they had "exerted a moral influence in aid of Col. Giddings' direct efforts upon the holders of the bonds . . . ." He had offered them a choice between an allowance of $8,000 upon giving a receipt in full, and taking nothing and looking to the legislature. They had accepted the former alternative. "I cannot close this report without expressing the conviction that the State is indebted

---

[203] Texas Senate Journal, April 1876, 88–92. Apr. 26, 1876.

[204] Answers of Respondent with Affidavits, Exhibits, and Proofs. Especially Exhibit C, at 23–25.

[205] Merrick's Executor v. Giddings, 115 U.S. 300.

[206] This was shared by Merrick, R. J. Brent, and George Taylor.

to the prompt and vigorous action of Col. Giddings for the large amount of money realized."

The Governor made no reference to the services of Merrick and Durant in the suits of Texas against Huntington and the National Bank of Washington.[207] Doubtless there too their fees were to be contingent upon success, so that when the State lost they took nothing for their labor.

In 1874, when Coke instructed Merrick and Durant to pursue the litigation to prevent Chiles from further assertion of a claim to the bonds he described Giddings' position as that of "outside aid"; in 1875 he said that the former had contributed merely "a moral influence" in aid of the latter's direct and successful efforts. The allowance to Giddings was almost four times that to Merrick and Durant. What Giddings received for his two months of work in Europe was not far short of what Paschal had in hand in 1870 after four years of devoted professional exertions.

Merrick and Durant protested against the Governor's treatment, even as they accepted his settlement of $8,000. At once they appealed to the legislature to do justice,[208] and presently amended their memorial to request submission to a court for a determination of the facts independent of the settlement.[209]

When that proved fruitless they sued Giddings in the District of Columbia, seeking to establish that, under the particular circumstances, he breached a duty to them when he broke a promise "that he would hold and not pay over to the State or the Governor the fund thus collected . . . until the said compensation was paid . . . ."

Giddings deposed that any promise he had made was upon Governor Coke's assurance that he would settle all fees. But when Giddings went to Austin to settle, Coke said "the State must have $300,000"; that "he did not intend this money should go into their [Merrick and Durant's] hands, or that they should be in a position to dictate a settlement . . . ." Giddings testified further,

> I remonstrated that his allowance for fees was not sufficient, and told him that Merrick and Durant claimed twenty per cent. under their contract, and that I had earned [from] the State that amount; when the Governor said with emphasis that he had considered that matter fully, and that Merrick & Durant were not entitled to one cent under their contract, but, as I had reported that their services

---

[207] Supra, pp. 653, 657.
[208] Texas Senate Journal, April 1876, 87; and see index thereto under

Merrick & Durant.
[209] Senate Journal, April 1876, 844, 847–48.

had aided me in making the settlement, he would allow them $8,000, though he thought that $5,000 was enough, and he would allow me, or J.D. and D.C. Giddings, the balance of the excess of collection over the $300,000 . . . .[210]

The fact that Merrick and Durant had given a full discharge stood as a bar to a further recovery. The District of Columbia court gave judgment for the defendant,[211] and the Supreme Court, with evident reluctance, affirmed.[212]

Justice Harlan said that *In re Chiles*,[213] resulting in the judgment for contempt, had removed "the sole impediment in the way of prompt recognition" by Droege & Co. of the State's right. Further, "the evidence justifies the conclusion that it was in the minds of all the parties, including the Governor of Texas and the defendant, that the attorneys should be deemed to have participated in any collections made in England, provided it appeared that those collections were the result of the suit . . . ." Under the circumstances shown in the record, it might be that "for the violation of [his] promise, the defendant was responsible to [plaintiffs] in damages." But then Merrick and Durant had accepted $8,000 as full compensation. "That settlement, we are constrained to hold, swept away the very foundation of their demand against the defendant."

By the time that decision was announced, on November 8, 1885, Durant and Merrick were both dead.

The State of Texas—indestructible as a concept but mutable in its manifestations—in pursuing the bonds of which it had been dispossessed "by a certain unlawful combination of individuals in armed hostility to the Government of the United States,"[214] proved ungrateful to Paschal, the constant Unionist, and unjust to Merrick and Durant, by whose efforts its rights had been established. At the end, however, it showed partiality in rewarding "the prompt and vigorous action of Col. Giddings"[215] who, when "the sole impediment" had been removed, did —with the assistance of "Brother George"[216] (formerly the Texas

---

[210] Transcript of Record, 15.
[211] 12 D.C. (1 Mackey) 394 (1882).
[212] 115 U.S. 300 (1885).
[213] 22 Wall. 157 (1875), supra, pp. 667–69.
[214] Bill of Complaint in Texas v. White, Transcript, 3.
[215] When commanding the 21st Texas Cavalry, his "chivalry and daring" won special commendation from

Major General John A. Wharton, commander of cavalry in the Red River campaign of 1864. Mrs. R. E. Pennington, *The History of Brenham and Washington County*, (Houston, Tex.: Standard Printing and Lithographing Co., 1915), 70, 73.

[216] D. C. Giddings to Merrick, Nov. 4, 1874. Transcript of Record in Merrick v. Giddings, 23.

Military Board's agent with the Confederate Government at Richmond[217])—bring home half of the bonds the Military Board had sent to Europe.

> But things like that, you know, must be
> At every famous victory.

---

[217] Statement of Paschal to Comptroller Tayler, letter of Sept. 26, 1865, in Answers of Respondent with Affidavits . . . , 45–46, *In re* Paschal. Paschal proposed that George H. Giddings and others who disposed of Texas Indemnity bonds "all be ordered or sent to Austin and directed to make a full, fair and complete statement of their whole agencies and action in the premises."

In the Report of the Military Board [in 1863, Gov. F. R. Lubbock, chairman], supra, note 37, the first action reported is that, in consequence of letters from the Confederate Secretary of War, the Texas Senators, and Postmaster General John H. Reagan of Texas, the Board had delivered one hundred Texas Indemnity bonds to George H. Giddings to be used to secure arms and munitions of war; "but Mr. Giddings failed in the objects of his mission and the United States Bonds have been faithfully returned." House Journal of the Tenth Legislature, Regular Session, 233.

CHAPTER XIV

The Legal Tender Cases

W E COME TO ONE of the most controverted matters in the history of the Court. The controversy, however, must yield to the facts—when at length they have been laid out for candid examination.

On February 7, 1870, the Court held the Legal Tender Act of 1862 unconstitutional as applied to preexisting debts. The case was *Hepburn v. Griswold.*[1] Chief Justice Chase wrote the opinion, and Nelson, Clifford and Field, JJ., joined with him, Justice Miller wrote a dissenting opinion in which Swayne and Davis, JJ., concurred.

On the same day and at about the same hour, President Grant nominated William Strong of Pennsylvania and Joseph P. Bradley of New Jersey to be Justices. When they had been confirmed and had taken their seats, they joined with the three dissenters to grant Attorney General Hoar's motion for a further argument of the constitutional question, in cases still awaiting decision.

In the outcome, on May 1, 1871, in the *Legal Tender Cases*[2] the statute was sustained by a division of five to four.

Add to this that Chief Justice Chase, spokesman for those deeming the Act invalid, had when Secretary of the Treasury in 1862 advised Congress that reluctantly but decidedly he had come to "the conclusion that the legal tender clause is a necessity" and that he supported it "earnestly."[3]

---

[1] 8 Wall. 603.
[2] 12 Wall. 457.
[3] Letter of Feb. 3, 1862, to Rep. Elbridge G. Spaulding, in charge of the bill. Spaulding, *History of the*

Legal Tender Paper Money Issued During the Great Rebellion, 2d ed. (Buffalo: Express Printing Co., 1875), 59.

The Court's authority as expositor of the Constitution was seriously impaired by this unfortunate business. The present chapter will trace what happened and assess responsibility.

CIVIL WAR FINANCE

THE EMISSION OF a forced paper currency was the most questionable expedient of Chase's administration of the Treasury—as the creation of the national banking system was his most impressive accomplishment.

When Chase came to the Department in March 1861 he found that the treasury was empty, and that in the latter part of Buchanan's Administration the Government's credit had been shattered. Six percent bonds had fallen to 84; outgo exceeded income in the ratio of 4 to 1. To meet expenses until the new Congress met in special session on July 4, the Secretary managed with sixty-day loans.

In his first report to the Congress, the Secretary estimated that expenditures for the fiscal year ending on June 30, 1862, would be 320 millions. (As it turned out, the figure was 475.) He recommended that this be met by 80 millions from internal taxes and new customs duties, and 240 millions from loans. Congress responded with authority to borrow 250 millions: by 7 percent twenty-year bonds to be sold not below par, or by 7.3 percent three-year notes, or by demand notes (not to exceed 50 millions) issued as money and bearing no interest. To produce revenue it took these measures: a direct tax of 20 millions; an income tax, to be levied in April 1862; and higher duties on coffee, tea, sugar, and the like, expected to yield 22.5 millions. These measures were slow and inadequate. Of the direct tax, of course only that portion that fell on the loyal States could be realized—12 millions, minus the cost of collection.[4] The levy of a flat 3 percent on the excess of incomes over $800 would not take hold until almost the end of the fiscal year. The actual intake from customs and internal revenue proved far below expectations —only 52, not 80 millions.

"The striking feature of the plan of finance thus recommended at the commencement of the war by the secretary of the treasury, and adopted by Congress, was the reliance upon borrowing to meet all extraordinary military and naval expenditures." So wrote Wesley Clair

---

[4] Apprehension among the Founders led to the constitutional requirement that no direct tax be laid unless in proportion to the census. Art. I, Sec. 9, cl. 4. It now resulted that the people of Missouri must contribute almost as much as the people of Massachusetts, although they possessed only half as much property. Vermont, with far less wealth than Rhode Island, must yield almost twice as great a tax.

Mitchell in his monumental *History of the Greenbacks*,[5] adding, "Nothing shows more forcibly the inadequacy of this policy than the quickness with which the necessity for increased taxation made itself apparent." "In the development of a tax system appropriate to the events and conditions of the war, Chase took no leadership": so wrote Professor Davis R. Dewey in his standard *Financial History of the United States*.[6] The Secretary, like most others, erred in counting on a short war. Accordingly he favored three-year notes over long-term bonds. James G. Blaine, explaining in retrospect the "inadequate" and "laggard" action taken at the special session, recalled that

> There was a wide-spread opposition among the strongest advocates of the war, to all measures which would, at an early stage, render the contest pecuniarily oppressive, and hence make it unpopular.
> . . . As the struggle proceeded, it was demonstrated that those calculated most justly who relied most completely on the popular purpose to make every sacrifice to maintain the national integrity. This was however the period of depression after the first battle of Bull Run, of hesitation before casting every thing into the scale for patriotism.[7]

When, in the light of that reverse, Justice Grier wrote that it would be "a *long war*," and added, "We must conquer this rebellion . . . if it should cost 100,000 men & 1000 millions of money,"[8] he supposed he was expressing the highest measure of determination and sacrifice; yet by the tally of 1865 the cost in lives and treasure exceeded three times Grier's brave figures.

"After the disastrous battle of Bull Run, and when Washington was closely beleaguered, and the avenue thence to New York through Baltimore was intercepted by the enemy, Mr. Chase, then Secretary of the Treasury, came to [New York] via Annapolis, and immediately invited all persons . . . who were supposed to possess or to control capital to meet him on the evening of August 9th, at the house of John J. Cisco, Esq., then Assistant Treasurer of the United States in New York." So recalled George S. Coe, president of the American Exchange Bank, a leading figure in Civil War finance.[9] In a letter of October 8, 1875, to Elbridge G. Spaulding, he was tracing in detail events, as he had seen them, leading to the resort to legal tender paper in 1862. The

---

[5] (Chicago: University of Chicago Press, 1903), 18.

[6] (New York: Longmans, Green, 1934), 300.

[7] *Twenty Years of Congress*, 2 vols.

(Norwich, Conn.: Henry Bill Publishing Co., 1884, 1886), I, 403.

[8] Letter of July 24, 1861, to Justice Clifford. Clifford Papers, Me. Hist. Soc.

[9] On Coe (1817–96), see D.A.B.

addressee, a banker at Buffalo, New York, had been a member of the 37th Congress and chairman of a subcommittee of Ways and Means charged with currency legislation; the name of "father of the greenbacks" had been fastened upon him. Spaulding published in 1869 a *History of the Legal Tender Paper Money*. In 1875 he was preparing a second edition, to which Coe's letter became an appendix.[10]

The position of Cisco, Assistant Treasurer in charge of the New York Sub-Treasury, should be explained. The Act of August 6, 1846,[11] had established an "Independent Treasury" with a Sub-Treasury in designated cities. "Moneys received from whatever source for the use of the United States" went, under further legislation, into the Government's vaults at the Treasury or a Sub-Treasury; the Government did not entrust its money to any bank. (However, by a Supplementary Act of August 5, 1861,[12] the Secretary was permitted "to deposit any of the moneys obtained on any of the loans now authorized by law . . . in such solvent specie-paying banks as he may select . . . .")

Chase's call to the meeting on August 9 "drew together a large number" of financiers. Coe's account continues:

> During the discussion which ensued, I suggested the practicability of uniting the banks of the North by some organization that would combine them into an efficient and inseparable body, for the purpose of advancing the capital of the country upon government bonds in large amounts, and . . . to distribute them in smaller sums among the people . . . . This suggestion met the hearty approbation of the assembled company, and arrested the earnest attention of the Secretary. At his request it was presented to the consideration of the banks at a meeting called . . . on the following day . . . .

A plan prepared by a committee led to an undertaking by the banks of New York, Boston, and Philadelphia in concert[13] to take 50 millions in three-year 7.3 percent notes, with a promise to take like amounts in October and December; they would resell to the public without charge. The associated banks, with a capital of 120 millions, in mid-August had over 63 millions in coin. Thus at the moment they were in a strong position. To make the plan effective and to preserve the specie standard, it was essential that coin paid out would quickly flow back to the banks.

---

[10] App., pp. 89–96. On Spaulding (1809–97), see D.A.B.

[11] 9 Stat. 59.

[12] 12 Stat. 313.

[13] "It was greatly desired to include also the banks of the West, but it was found impracticable to secure the cooperation of the state banks of Ohio and Indiana, and the state banks of Missouri, the only other organization under a compacted system, were surrounded by combatants."

Accordingly it was at once proposed to the Secretary that he should suspend the operations of the Sub-Treasury Act in respect to these transactions, and following the course of commercial business, that he should draw checks upon some one Bank in each city representing the Association, in small sums as required, in disbursing the money thus advanced. By this means his checks would serve the purpose of a circulating medium, continually redeemed, and the exchanges of capital and industry would be best promoted. This was the more important in a period of public agitation when the disbursement of these large sums exclusively in coin, rendered the reserves of the Banks all the more liable to be wasted by hoarding. To the astonishment of the committee, Mr. Chase refused. Notwithstanding the act of Congress of August 5th,[14] which it seemed to us was passed for the very object then presented, . . . he declared upon his authority as finance minister, and from his personal knowledge of its purpose, had no such meaning or intent. This issue was discussed from time to time with much zeal, but always with the same result. . . . In the light which has since been shed upon the act of Congress referred to, it is evident that undue weight was given to the views of the Secretary, and that the Banks would have conferred an incalculable benefit upon the country, had they adhered inflexibly to their opinions. But the pressure of startling events required prompt decision, and the well known intelligence and patriotism of the Secretary, gave his judgment overwhelming power. . . .

In consequence, the banks' coin reserves were dissipated. "This first great error . . . certainly precipitated the adoption of that most unhappy expedient"—legal tender notes.

A further adverse effect upon the coin reserves resulted from the Secretary's decision to act under the grant of authority to issue up to 50 millions in demand notes bearing no interest. They were issued in small denominations—$5, $10, and $20—and were used, for example, to pay the troops. By November 30 Chase had put out 24 millions. The banks, as Coe recalled, "could not decline them without diminishing public confidence in the Government credit [nor could they] give them currency without impairing their own specie strength. . . . As soon as these notes thus appeared the reflux of coin to the banks at once sensibly diminished. . . ."

The Trent Affair—growing out of the seizure of Mason and Slidell, Confederate envoys, from the British steamer of that name—threatened in December to lead to hostile action by the British Government. The resulting strain, before the seizure was disavowed, impaired the government's credit.

---

[14] Supra, p. 680.

Another shock came with the publication of the Secretary's report to the incoming session of Congress. Revised estimates put revenue 25 millions below what had been expected, expenditures 214 millions higher. He asked for further taxes to produce 50 millions, and submitted with deference to Congress the question how further borrowing was to be effected. He drew attention to the weakness of the system whereby the country depended for currency upon the notes emitted by a multitude of State-chartered local banks of unknown solvency. He urged instead a system of national banks which would make large purchases of United States bonds, using them in turn as security for the issue of national bank notes. This would give the Treasury a market for its bonds, and give the country a uniform and secure currency. The plan was sound, but obviously would meet stiff opposition from the State banks. (Presently Congress did adopt it, by a statute of February 25, 1863; then by a statute of March 3, 1865, it suppressed the issue of State bank notes by striking them with a 10 percent tax.[15]) What was needed in December 1861, however, was a program immediately effective, adequate for financing a great war, and such as would satisfy the people that the government was firmly set on a sound course. In that respect the Secretary's report was a failure, and actually had an adverse effect.

"Taxation, heavy and universal, is felt to be the only solution of our present difficulties . . . ." So wrote Charles F. Dunbar, the able commentator on economic topics, in the *Boston Advertiser* of January 11, 1862.[16] "He recommends himself most to the public who grapples with questions like this boldly and confidently, and who dares to say to the people that the time has come when they must consent to feel the pressure of the war . . . ." On February 4 the *Advertiser* commented that "the country presents the spectacle of a people praying to be taxed."[17] Appletons' Annual Cyclopaedia for 1861 recorded the following as the reaction to Chase's statement to Congress:[18]

It was supposed that the annual report of the Secretary would present some practical and well-digested plan of finance that would restore confidence. When the document appeared, however, public expectation was disappointed at a moment when the greatest anxiety prevailed in respect to the relations with England, growing out of the capture

---

[15] Veazie Bank v. Fenno, 8 Wall. 533 (1869). Infra, p. 711.

[16] Dunbar (1830–1900), trained in the law, was then associate editor and part owner of the *Advertiser*. In 1869, when President Eliot came to Harvard, Dunbar was made professor of political economy, in which post he served for thirty years.

[17] Mitchell, *History of the Greenbacks*, 18–19, and Don C. Barrett, *The Greenbacks and Resumption of Specie Payments, 1862–1879*, (Cambridge, Mass.: Harvard University Press, 1931), 36–39, cite a range of contemporary comment to that effect.

[18] At p. 66, in its article on Banks.

of the Trent. The Secretary had no plan, a foreign war threatened, and the banks were loaded with securities they could not sell. . . .

By December the participating banks had resold scarcely more than a third of the notes they had purchased. Their specie during that month fell from 42 millions to less than 24 millions. On December 30 the New York banks suspended specie payments; banks throughout the country followed.

It is no reproach to Chase to say that he was not a master of finance. In ordinary times it had required no special competence to be head of the Treasury in a country where customs duties and receipts from the sale of public lands produced a surplus, so that the people paid no visible taxes to the national government. Chase had been brought into Lincoln's Cabinet because of his position in the Republican party. His patriotism and intelligence commanded respect; as Hugh McCulloch recalled, "he had few equals in analyzing difficult questions."[19] But his efforts were diffused. He was concerned with the general direction of the war. With a high sense of his own ability and a rather poor opinion of those about him, he extended himself to compensate for their short-comings. Meanwhile the Administration's financial operations went badly, as its early military operations went badly, because those in charge were unequal to their task.

The House Committee on Ways and Means referred the Secretary's recommendation for a national currency to Spaulding's subcommittee. The Treasury had not drafted a bill to effect its proposal; Chase asked Spaulding to prepare one. This was done: the bill was framed by late December. The chairman saw that so important and detailed a measure could be passed, at best, only after months of debate. Then to organize national banks, and to bring their notes into use, would take more time. Spaulding concluded that provision must be made for the immediate needs of the Government, while the national bank plan went forward. (The Government was then spending nearly one and a quarter millions a day.) On December 30—the day the New York banks suspended specie payments—he introduced a bill to authorize the issue of another 50 millions of treasury notes. These, however, were to be a legal tender in payment of all debts, public and private. It was a stopgap measure.

The lack of integrated governmental effort at this critical juncture is illustrated by the following circumstance. Attorney General Bates gave an informal opinion that the bill was constitutional, on the evening of January 6, 1862, in response to a request Spaulding had made "this afternoon." "I have given the subject such attention as the very brief

---

[19] *Men and Measures of Half a* *Century*, (New York: Charles Scribner's Sons, 1888), 181.

interval afforded . . . ." He gave his opinion "as a private man, and a professed constitutional legist"; in official counselling he was confined to requests within the Executive Branch of the Government. Certainly Chase should have prepared legislation adequate to his Department's needs, and should himself have obtained all the assistance the Attorney General had to offer. As it was, a Treasury measure, momentous in its economic consequences and dubious as to constitutionality, was launched with an unofficial opinion written "with all brevity and without argument, for the time does not allow elaborate consideration."[20] A striking contrast is to be marked between this skimpy attention when the currency was about to be put upon a paper basis, and the arduous disputation over the question, between 1868 and 1871, within the Court over which Chase had come to preside. A contrast is also to be drawn between the aloofness with which Chase as Secretary left it to Congress to bear the responsibility for meeting the crisis in the field of public finance, and the intrusion of Chase when Chief Justice into Executive and Congressional handling of Reconstruction—even going as far as to draft a Supplementary Reconstruction Bill.[21]

THE FIRST LEGAL TENDER ACT

BY ITS FIRST Coinage Act in 1792[22] Congress established a mint and provided that the gold and silver coins therein authorized—these and these alone—would be "a lawful tender in all payments whatsoever." That bimetallic standard had remained, although in 1834 Congress debased the gold dollar by about 6 percent, and after the discovery of gold in California depreciated the silver coins. The proposal now for the first time to give the Government's paper notes the quality of a tender which in law would discharge a debt ran counter to deep convictions. The Ways and Means Committee stood evenly divided; then one member withdrew his opposition in order that a bill might go to the House. H.R. 240, introduced on January 22, called for the issue of 100 millions, in addition to the 50 millions of notes authorized in July 1861.

Debate lasted a month. Was it within the concluding clause of the Constitution's grant of legislative power—"To make all Laws which shall be necessary and proper for carrying into Execution the foregoing Powers"—such as to raise and support armies, to provide and maintain a navy, to borrow money on the credit of the United States, and to regulate commerce? As a matter of policy, was there no better way to

---

[20] Bates to Spaulding, Cong. Globe, 37–2, 525; Spaulding's *History of the Legal Tender Paper*, 15.

[21] Supra, pp. 324–27.
[22] 1 Stat. 246.

meet the Government's pressing needs? Admittedly gold could be obtained for bonds if they were sold for what they would bring; but that went against the dogma that the United States ought never to sell its bonds below par. The laying of vigorous taxes would in time produce money and would immediately show the Government's determination and thus would strengthen its credit. Congress adopted a resolution declaring its purpose to impose taxes to yield a total of not less than 150 millions a year;[23] but it was not until July 1 that a tax bill became law. The minority in the Ways and Means Committee urged a substitute: issue 100 millions in 3.65 percent notes to be paid in two years, receivable for internal taxes and debts to the United States, and fundable in 7.3 percent bonds on which the interest would be in coin and which would be redeemed at the pleasure of the Government after ten years. In denominations not less than $5, they would circulate as money. In the outcome, this alternative was rejected.[24] There was much uncertainty about the relative efficacy of notes with and notes without the quality of legal tender.

Chase was opposed in principle to legal tender paper: but so was everyone else. The question was, what to do to meet the exigency of January and February 1862. The Secretary had remitted the problem to Congress, and Spaulding's bill was the result. It gathered support because a majority came to believe that it could not be avoided. Chase, touching up the bill, returned it on January 22, "regretting exceedingly" that it was found necessary, "but heartily desiring to co-operate with the Committee . . . ."[25]

On the twenty-ninth he committed himself more unreservedly, in a letter to Thad Stevens, chairman of the Ways and Means Committee:

> The provision making United States notes a legal tender has doubtless been well considered by the committee, and their conclusion needs no support from any observation of mine. I think it my duty, however, to say, that in respect of this provision my reflections have conducted me to the same conclusions they have reached. It is not unknown to them that I have felt, nor do I wish to conceal that I now feel, a great aversion to making anything but coin a legal tender in payment of debts. . . .

It had, however, become "indispensably necessary" that there be a further issue of United States notes and unavoidable that they be given the quality of legal tender.[26]

---

[23] Passed, 133 to 6, in the House on Jan. 15; in the Senate, 30 to 1, on Jan. 17.

[24] The House voted 95 nays to 55 yeas—and then passed the legal tender bill by 93 to 59.

[25] Spaulding, *History of the Legal Tender Paper*, 27.

[26] Cong. Globe, 37–2, 618.

Then on February 3 he wrote urgently to Spaulding:

> Mr. Seward said to me on yesterday that you observed to him, that my hesitation in coming up to the legal tender proposition embarrassed you, and I am very sorry to observe it, for my anxious wish is to support you in all respects.
>
> It is true that I came with reluctance to the conclusion that the legal tender clause is a necessity, but I came to it decidedly, and I support it earnestly. I do not hesitate when I have made up my mind, however much regret I may feel over the necessity of the conclusion to which I have come. . . .
>
> Immediate action is of great importance. The Treasury is nearly empty. I have been obliged to draw the last installment of the November loan; so soon as it is paid, I fear the banks generally will refuse to receive the United States notes. You will see the necessity of urging the bill through without more delay.[27]

It had been the Secretary's responsibility all along to point to a better way if he knew one. Now he not only asked—he was importunate: "The Treasury is nearly empty."

On February 6 the House passed the bill,[28] amended to make the issue 150 millions and to retire the 50 millions of notes authorized in July 1861. Of the 59 who voted against the bill, a score were Republicans—among them Roscoe Conkling and his brother Frederick, a New York banker; Owen Lovejoy of Illinois, whose zeal was tempered with wisdom; and Justin S. Morrill of Vermont, a specialist in finance, who said that the measure was "not blessed by one sound precedent." George H. Pendleton, anti-war Democrat, argued that the bill had "no solid foundation in the Constitution": by 1867 he had become the great Greenbacker, and in 1868 his view was imposed on the Democratic National Convention. Of the majority of 93, only half a dozen were Democrats.

On February 12 the Senate passed the bill by vote of 30 (of whom 5 were Democrats) to 7 (of whom 3 were Republicans).[29]

Differences were resolved in conference, and on February 25, 1862, the bill became law.

In a letter of February 4, 1862, Chase had explained his position to William Cullen Bryant:

> Your feelings of repugnance to the legal tender clause can hardly be greater than my own; but I am convinced that, as a temporary measure, it is indispensably necessary. From various motives—some

---

[27] Spaulding, *History of the Legal Tender Paper*, 59–60.

[28] Cong. Globe, 37–2, 695.
[29] Ibid., 37–2, 804.

honorable, and some not honorable—a considerable number, though a small minority of the business men or people, are indisposed to sustain the United States notes by receiving and paying them as money. The minority, in the absence of any legal tender clause, may control the majority to all practical intents. To prevent this, which would at this time be disastrous in the extreme, I yield my general views for a particular exception. To yield does not violate any obligation to the people, for the great majority, willing now to receive and pay their notes, desire that the minority may not be allowed to reap special advantages from their refusal to do so; and our government is not only a government of the people, but is bound, in an exigency like the present, to act on the maxim: *Salus populi suprema est lex.*

. . . .

In giving this consent, I feel that I am treading the path of duty, and shall cheerfully, as I have always done, abide the consequences. I dare not say that I care nothing for personal consequences, but I think I may say truly that I care little for them in comparison with my obligations to do whatever the safety of the country may require.[30]

STANDARDS OF JUDGMENT

Was the Legal Tender Act "necessary and proper"? Was it necessary? These are quite distinct inquiries, though often confounded. The one refers to the Constitution; the other is a subject for economists.

"Necessary and proper" does not mean "indispensably necessary," Marshall had concluded in an early opinion; Congress may choose any means, not prohibited, "which are in fact conducive" to the exercise of a granted power.[31] "The Constitution as a continuously operative charter of government does not demand the impossible or the impracticable." So wrote Chief Justice Stone for the Court in 1944, sustaining the Emergency Price Control Act as amended by the Inflation Control

---

[30] Godwin, *Biography of William Cullen Bryant,* 6 vols. (New York: D. Appleton and Co., 1883–84), II, 165.

On June 30, 1864—the day his resignation was accepted—Chase wrote to Bryant that "Looking back, I can see now no measure which my judgment condemns, except that required by the New York banks, to issue legal-tender coupons." "With this act [of resignation] terminates, I trust, my whole connection with official life. There has never been any thing for me but opportunity for

work; and I gladly surrender all claims upon it to those who may prize it more. . . ." Schuckers, *The Life and Public Services of Salmon Portland Chase* (New York: D. Appleton and Co., 1874), 404.

[31] United States v. Fisher, 2 Cr. 358 (1804), sustaining a statute giving the United States a priority over other creditors in bankruptcy. Marshall's classic statement, in McCulloch v. Maryland, 4 Wheat. 316 (1819), will be introduced later in the discussion. Infra, pp. 713–14.

Act.[32] The Constitution contemplates that those chosen to govern shall meet needs as they arise by the lights that then prevail: it does not demand that they attain a high proficiency in statecraft. Justice Holmes described the test to be applied by the Court in these words, when sustaining the statute of 1919 by which Congress controlled rents in the District of Columbia: the end being proper,

> we have no concern of course with the question whether those means were the wisest, whether they may not cost more than they come to, or will effect the result desired. It is enough that we are not warranted in saying that legislation that has been resorted to for the same purpose all over the world, is futile or has no reasonable relation to the relief sought.[33]

The performance of the Justices in judging the performance of the war-time Congress will in turn be judged when presently *Hepburn v. Griswold* (1870) and the *Legal Tender Cases* (1871) are reviewed.

Able economists have shown that the expedient of making paper money a legal tender could have been avoided, and that it worked seriously to the disadvantage of the Government and the people. (Still later economists might somewhat rephrase the earlier criticisms, in the light of recent experience in the management of the currency.) Energetic taxation promptly imposed—a willingness to pay high interest rates—greater use of interest-bearing certificates of indebtedness: these are among the points that have been made. The critics have found that 3.65 percent two-year treasury notes, advocated by the minority of the committee, would have served better than the issue of legal tender paper. They point out, finally, that it took so long to effect the printing of the greenbacks that they did not become available until April; it was by other means that the Treasury survived the crisis of February. Let all this be freely admitted: it goes to show that the responsible parties in 1861 and 1862 were not so adept as those who later made a systematic analysis of their problem. Similar critiques could be pronounced upon most of the operations by which the Civil War was waged and won.

FURTHER ISSUES

A SECOND LEGAL TENDER ACT, authorizing another 150 millions, was enacted on July 11, 1862, in response to the Secretary's statement

---

[32] Yakus v. United States, 321 U.S. 414, 424. He had used similar language in sustaining the Fair Labor Standards Act of 1939, in Opp Cotton Mills v. Administrator of the Wage and Hour Division, 312 U.S. 126, 145 (1941).

[33] Block v. Hirsh, 256 U.S. 135, 158 (1921).

that "The condition of the Treasury renders prompt action highly desirable." A third statute of March 3, 1863, supplementing a Joint Resolution of January 17, 1863, added still another 150 millions. The pinch at that moment was to make a long overdue payment of the troops. Resistance diminished with repetition. Amasa Walker (1799–1875), business man turned economist and a lecturer at Amherst College, was then in Congress: after dwelling upon the evils of irredeemable paper, he concluded: "But it will be asked what can be done, and whether it is not, in the present emergency, indispensable to issue an additional amount of these notes? I suppose it is, sir. I see no alternative."[34]

Upon the earlier issues there had been impressed the privilege of converting at face value into 5–20 6 percent gold bonds. At Chase's urging, this was omitted from the third issue, and as to the earlier greenbacks the right was cut off at July 1, 1863. The Secretary wanted to borrow at less than 6 percent. "This ill-fated action as to 'conversion', prevented the currency from purifying itself by a natural process at the close of the war"—so wrote Professor Barrett in his monograph on *The Greenbacks and Resumption of Specie Payments*—for the reason that "with the rise of government bonds above par, greenbacks would have flowed profitably into the funded debt and disappeared permanently from circulation."[35] Spaulding, writing in 1875, called it "the great mistake—greater than all other mistakes in the management of the war."[36] (Understandably, he was smarting under the lofty language with which Chase, become Chief Justice, had reprobated the entire legal tender experience.) And John Sherman, in retrospect, said that "the most essential legal attribute of the note was taken away . . . . [F]or my part in acquiescing in and voting for it I have felt more regret than for any [other] act of my official life."[37]

CHASE ON THE STUMP

IT IS RELAXING to turn for a moment from these complexities, to see how simple and right the resort to legal tender notes was made to appear in a speech by Secretary Chase at Cincinnati on October 12, 1863.[38] It was the eve of the State election, and he spoke in a popular vein. "At the outset of this struggle . . . the London Times said that Mr. Chase would very soon find himself in want of money . . . , and then

---

[34] Cong. Globe, 37–3, 339. Jan. 15, 1863.

[35] At p. 67.

[36] Introduction to his second edition, at p. 8.

[37] Cong. Globe, 44–1, 1473. Mar.

6, 1876. Senator Sherman was insisting that the Government was pledged to return to specie payments.

[38] Reported at length in the *National Intelligencer*, Oct. 20, 1863.

England would not let him have any, and then we would see what would become of our vaunted Republic!" But the green isle could sink into the depths of the sea before he would go there to borrow. [Cheers.]

Well, what was next to be done? I borrowed all the gold there was in the country. In this way I obtained about one hundred and seventy five millions of dollars in gold, and it didn't come back quite as fast as it went; and the banks and the capitalists who had furnished the gold began to say to me, "We cannot supply you with specie any longer unless you will agree to pay us such prices for it as will enable us to buy in Europe to replace it." This would not do . . . . Now what would you have had me do? You would have said to me, "Here am I, Mr. Smith, a farmer, and here am I, Mr. Jones, a mechanic, and here am I, Mr. Robinson, a merchant; take us instead of stock: base the currency of the country on us; go to work and make 'green-backs.' " I knew that was what you would have advised me to do, and, therefore, as my business was only to interpret your will, I went to work and made "greenbacks," and a good many of them at that. I had some handsome pictures put upon them too, and as I like to get pretty near to the people, and as the engravers thought me rather good looking, I told them they might put me on the end of the one dollar bills. [Laughter.]

Well, at first, a great many people thought this was a bold and hazardous experiment, and a good many of the banks said it was sure to fail . . . . A great many disloyal men thought they would be able to break us down. Some banks and persons refused to take the currency. What was to be done next? You would have told me to do exactly what I did do. You would have said, "If any bank is unwilling to take this money, it *shall* take it or get nothing at all." So we made it a legal tender, not quite so tender as they desired, but still *legally* so. [Laughter.] So the thing went on, and after awhile we agreed that we would issue bonds, and that if the people wished to invest in them they could do it and we would pay the interest in gold. That makes the currency sound. It is simply the love and gratitude of the people toward their Government put into the form of money. . . .

One thing more was needed to put the currency on an enduring basis: "and so we devised and carried out the national banking system."

"It is a very simple thing," the Secretary said in conclusion on this topic; "It is common sense and courage—that is all."

SOME CONSEQUENCES OF RESORT TO LEGAL TENDER PAPER

IN THE LONG RUN the nation paid dear for the experience. Of the public debt of 2.8 billions in August 1865, it is estimated that more than a fifth was attributable to the substitution of paper for metallic money.[39] The people suffered the myriad consequences of an irredeemable currency whose gold value ranged from an average of 93.90 for June 1862 to 62.30 for February 1863, recovered to 79.50 in August after Gettysburg and Vicksburg, then plunged to 38.70 during the next twelve months. Wages lagged behind prices, with the result that workers lost perhaps a fifth or a sixth in real income.[40] The profits from productive industry were less attractive than the brilliant possibilities of dealing in gold, in stocks, and in commodities. The greenbacks "must be charged with offering inducements to abandon agriculture and manufactures for the more speculative forms of trade." A new class of capitalists appeared, spending and wasting conspicuously. "The enlarged consumption of wealth which the paper currency made possible for the fortunate few was therefore contrasted with a diminished consumption on the part of the unfortunate many on whose slender means the greenbacks levied contributions for the benefit of their employers."[41] The American character was affected for the worse by this new type who, as Justice Miller wrote bitterly, "engage in no commerce, no trade, no manufactures, no agriculture. They *produce nothing.*"[42]

Greenbackers became a force in politics; paper money originally justified as necessary to the war effort was perpetuated to enable debtors more easily to discharge their obligations. After ten years of indecision, Congress by the Act of January 14, 1875, declared that specie payments would be resumed on January 1, 1879; to that end it directed that the circulation of greenbacks be gradually reduced to $300 millions. Thus the Republicans, having been soundly defeated in the election of 1874, did at the short term of the 43rd Congress what they knew the Democrats would not allow to be done at the 44th. Opponents of specie resumption were able by the Act of May 31, 1878, to stop contraction at the point where it was at that moment—with $346,681,000 of greenbacks outstanding. The statute directed that these notes be reissued and kept in circulation. But could an emission of legal tender paper in time of peace be squared with the Constitution? In 1884 the Court answered in the affirmative, as will be explained later in this chapter.[43] The campaign for cheap money went to a decisive defeat in the Battle of the Standards —the national election of 1896. Meanwhile, with paper dollars, gold dollars, and after 1877 silver dollars in the reckoning, conceptions

---

[39] Mitchell, *History of the Greenbacks*, 419.

[40] Ibid., 351.

[41] Ibid., 397, 400.

[42] Letter of Apr. 28, 1878, in Charles Fairman, *Mr. Justice Miller,* *and the Supreme Court, 1862–1890* (Cambridge, Mass.: Harvard University Press, 1939), 67.

[43] Juilliard v. Greenman, 110 U.S. 421. Infra, pp. 771–75.

of what was right in meeting obligations became obscure.[44] The crusade for cheap money was parallelled by the repudiation of State debts and by deep-seated resistance to the payment of municipal bonds. Public faith was a major concern in the work of the Court for the remainder of our period.

LEGAL TENDER CASES IN STATE COURTS

SHORTLY AFTER THE PASSAGE of the Legal Tender Act of February 25, 1862, suits were brought which tested its applicability and validity in a variety of situations. The Supreme Court of Indiana was the earliest of the courts of last resort to speak: it ruled in favor of the statute, in a wry opinion. The Bank of Indiana, with its twenty branches, existed under a charter providing that any branch whose obligations were not met in specie was liable to be closed. Its president, Hugh McCulloch— later Secretary of the Treasury under Lincoln, Johnson, and Arthur— called upon Justice Samuel E. Perkins, "a Democrat of the strictest order," and pointed to the serious consequences if the bank could not safely use the legal tender notes; an early decision to permit such use was needed.[45] A case was promptly made. On April 1 a demand for coin was refused; the Circuit Court sustained the bank, and at May term the Supreme Court ruled on an appeal. Perkins, J., pointed out the bank's dilemma, argued that the Act was unconstitutional, and then announced that, pro forma, the court would consider the Act valid "till the Federal Court shall determine the question otherwise."[46]

Two years later, the same Judges repeated this performance: they held the Act invalid, and then in the last paragraph gave judgment to

[44] For example, Senator Stanley Matthews—who became a Justice of the Supreme Court in 1881—introduced what became the Concurrent Resolution of January 25, 1878, declaring that all bonds of the United States were payable in silver dollars of 412 ½ grains, and that to restore such dollars as a full legal tender for that purpose was not a violation of public faith. (This referred to the weight of the silver dollar fixed by statute in 1837. After 1840 the silver dollar disappeared from circulation, its content having become more valuable than the gold dollar. In 1873, coinage of the long unused silver dollar was discontinued.) What Mat-

thews advocated ran counter to President Hayes' view that even if the right to pay in silver could be sustained, it would be a mistake thus to override the honest convictions of the public creditors. And the Secretary of the Treasury, Sherman, had given public assurance that the bonds would be paid in gold. By the Bland-Allison Act of February 28, 1878, passed over Hayes' veto, the silver dollar was again made a legal tender, and a limited coinage directed.

[45] McCulloch, *Men and Measures of Half a Century*, 136–38.

[46] Reynolds v. The Bank of the State of Indiana, 18 Ind. 467 (1862).

the contrary. A petition for rehearing, it was added, would keep the question open.[47]

In October 1864, in accordance with the constitution of 1851, an entire bench of judges was elected for a term of six years. A wholly new and Republican court was chosen. On a rehearing, the Legal Tender Act was unanimously sustained.[48]

New York's constitution forbade the legislature "to pass any law sanctioning in any manner, directly or indirectly, the suspension of specie payments" by any bank; that precluded relief by statute such as was given in some States. Henry H. Van Dyck, Superintendent of the Bank Department,[49] accordingly arranged litigation to determine whether the banks were protected by the Legal Tender Act. The most important of all State court pronouncements on the legal tender question was that in the companion cases of *Metropolitan Bank v. Van Dyck* and *Meyer v. Roosevelt*, argued before the Court of Appeals in 1863.[50] The high authority of this court was enhanced by the consideration that it established law for the country's center of finance and commerce.

Secretary Chase engaged David Dudley Field to appear on behalf of the Government; Field took as his associate Samuel A. Foot.[51] Their arguments were submitted to the Judges at their chambers in Albany on June 26 and 27—informally, "it being thought best that the government should not appear to have been concerned in the cases." "I have no doubt," Field assured the Secretary, "that the decision will be unanimous, in support of the law."[52] Field added, apprehensively, "What is the meaning of the movements in Pennsylvania and Maryland?"—referring

---

[47] Thayer v. Hedges, 22 Ind. 282 (1864). Judge Perkins' opinion in this case attained some notoriety. Consulting the Bible, he announced that "Historically considered, we find that the Almighty, and his Prophets and Apostles, were for a specie basis; that gold and silver were the theme of their constant eulogy. . . ." He referred to Abraham, Solomon and Jeremiah.

[48] Thayer v. Hedges, 23 Ind. 141 (1864).

[49] Van Dyck (1809–88) became Assistant Treasurer of the United States in place of John J. Cisco, supra at p. 680, in 1864, as a result of the disagreement between Chase and President Lincoln over Chase's subordinates in New York, which led to the acceptance of Chase's resignation and Cisco's as well. Supra, p. 5.

[50] 27 N.Y. 400 (1863).

Meyer and Roosevelt had stated an agreed case: that on a bond of 1854 to pay a certain sum "in lawful money of the United States," Meyer on June 11, 1862, tendered principal and interest in Treasury notes, which Roosevelt refused to accept.

[51] (1790–1878), who had sat on that bench. Supra at p. 25.

[52] Letter of June 29, 1863. Chase Papers, Hist. Soc. of Pa.

Under date of June 26, 1863, Foot filed a four-page memorandum of "points and propositions presented . . . on behalf of the Treasury Department . . . ," with an Appendix (pp. 5–9) wherein five New York bankers affirmed their belief in the practical necessity of resort to legal tender notes.

to the marches of Lee's and Meade's armies, whose convergence resulted in the battle of Gettysburg on July 1–3. The army must be better directed, he admonished, "or the people will become disheartened. Their confidence in the management of the war by both the Army and Navy Departments has nearly vanished. Can't something be done to revive it?" Things were done shortly in actions at Gettysburg and at Vicksburg, which in their way also sustained the Legal Tender Act.

At this moment the President was being bedevilled by anti-Administration Democrats, making all they could out of the embarrassment Burnside had produced by his arrest of Vallandigham.[53] The Administration was still feeling the effect of a decision on January 13 by the Supreme Court of Wisconsin, denying that it lay within the power of the President to suspend the privilege of the writ of habeas corpus.[54] In March it had won the *Prize Cases*, upholding the President's blockade of rebel ports in April 1861, by the narrowest of margins.[55] On April 4 one bench of the Supreme Court of New York had abundantly sustained the constitutionality of the Legal Tender Act, in a decision Chase hailed as equal to a victory in the field.[56] But if the Court of Appeals, the State's highest court, were to take a different view, the conduct of the war would indeed suffer a shock.

When the decision in *Metropolitan Bank v. Van Dyck*, and *Meyer v. Roosevelt*, was announced at September Term, it appeared that the Court of Appeals had sustained the statute by a 6 to 2 division.

> The power to borrow money on the credit of the United States carries with it, it seems, the power to attach the quality of legal tender to the notes issued, when, in the judgment of Congress, it is necessary to make them effectual for the purpose of borrowing.

So ran the headnote. One judge sustained the statute under the power to regulate commerce. Chief Judge Denio (with whose conclusions Judge Henry R. Selden concurred), dissenting, found it beyond the power of Congress to make paper money a legal tender. These were conscientious judges of high standing. The Chief Judge wrote:

> I shall be well satisfied if a majority of my brethren, and the federal court in which our decision will ultimately be reviewed, can

---

[53] Supra, ch. 5, n. 49.
[54] *In re* Kemp, 16 Wis. 359 (1863). After being beset by challenges of this sort, on September 15, 1863, the President issued a new proclamation based upon the specific authority of the Act of March 3, 1863. Supra, pp. 143, 185.

[55] 2 Bl. 635, decided Mar. 10, 1863. Supra, ch. 1, n. 63.
[56] Hague v. Powers, 39 Barbour (N.Y.) 427. A "very important decision," commented the *American Law Register*, 2 (n.s.):497, June 1863. See article in D.A.B. on Erasmus Darwin Smith, the presiding Justice.

reconcile the legislation . . . with a reasonable interpretation of the Constitution of the United States. It is not to be denied that it constitutes a part of a plan of public finance which, whether wisely organized or not, it is extremely important in the present crisis to maintain if it can properly be done. . . .

THE PUZZLING CASE OF *ROOSEVELT v. MEYER*

COUNSEL FOR ROOSEVELT (the creditor who declined to accept paper money) took his case to the Supreme Court, where on December 11, 1863, the record was filed. On the same day, counsel for Meyer, defendant in error, entered a motion that the case be dismissed. Argument was set for December 18. Was the party defeated below entitled to bring his case to the Supreme Court? Section 25 of the Judiciary Act of 1789[57] had provided that a decision by the highest State court wherein the case might be heard was subject to review by the Supreme Court "[1] where is drawn in question the validity of a . . . statute of . . . the United States, and the decision is against [its] validity; . . ." Counsel for the debtor pointed to the question which the parties, under the New York Code of Procedure, had submitted to the court of first instance: "Were the said notes of the United States a legal tender on the part of the plaintiff?" He said that "the validity of the act of 25th of February, 1862, alone was drawn in question," and that the decision "was *in favor* of its validity . . . ." It was immaterial that in the course of the argument the creditor had referred to various constitutional provisions.[58]

But his opponent relied upon another clause of Section 25: "[3] where is drawn in question the construction of any clause of the constitution . . . or statute of . . . the United States, and the decision is against the title, right, privilege or exemption specially set up or claimed by either party . . . ." He pointed to the certificate of the New York Court of Appeals: that defendant relied upon Article I, Section 8, clause 5 [the grant of power *to coin Money*] and on the Fifth, Ninth, and Tenth Amendments as constitutional grounds whereby he could not be paid against his will in anything but gold or silver coin, "and that the said claim . . . was overruled and disallowed by this court." Clause [3] was "much broader" than clause [1], and afforded a review wherever, as here, a right claimed under federal Constitution or statute had been denied.[59]

Argument on the motion to dismiss was heard on Friday, Decem-

---

[57] This great provision was introduced above. Supra, p. 45.

[58] Transcript of Record, 5; Brief of Defendant in Error, on Motion to Dismiss, 2, 5.

[59] Transcript of Record, 3; Points of Plaintiff in Error on Motion to Dismiss.

ber 18, before nine Justices. (Chief Justice Taney was absent; Justice Field had been seated on December 7.) On Monday next Justice Wayne, presiding, announced the decision: dismissed for want of jurisdiction.[60]

Eight years later, in another legal tender case, *Trebilcock v. Wilson*,[61] it was conceded that this had been erroneous. The Court, Justice Field explained rather lamely, "confined its attention to the first clause . . . and . . . appears to have overlooked the third clause . . . ."

Here is a tantalizing puzzle. The Court gave the wrong answer to what seems an elementary problem: Shall we attribute it to gross inattention? Or shall we conclude, they must have done it on purpose— evidently this was a dodge to spare the Legal Tender Act from the hazard of judicial scrutiny? Or shall we say that what seems obvious to us was not so to them—it was a case of first impression and they were following old lights?

Justice Wayne's short opinion cited four cases, to the point that "if the decision of the State court be in favor of the privilege claimed under the Act of Congress," the Supreme Court had no jurisdiction to review. In one of those cases, alien defendants had asked to remove the litigation into the federal court, as permitted by Section 12 of the Judiciary Act.[62] In another, a title to land under an Act of Congress was set up.[63] In two, defendants had pleaded a discharge under the federal Bankruptcy Act.[64] In each instance, the State court had *sustained* the federal right—and the Supreme Court had had no authority to review, for the reason Justice Wayne had given. It was the same as to Meyer's claim under the Legal Tender Act. But here there was something more, something not present in the cases Justice Wayne had cited. Here Roosevelt had asserted a right that belonged to him, under the United States Constitution, a right which the Court should protect even against a denial by Congress. The New York court certified distinctly that it had considered and rejected the creditor's contention. Certainly under clause [3] the Supreme Court ought to have taken the case.

Through the years, the most conspicuous applications of Section 25 had been in situations where the highest court of some State had flouted the Constitution, or a treaty or statute of the United States. State judges had been resentful: Section 25 was the great symbol of federal

---

[60] Roosevelt v. Meyer, 1 Wall. 512. The report records that Nelson, J., dissented. The Minutes contain no such statement. Wallace was not appointed until March 21, 1864, after Black's resignation; in much of 1 Wallace he was reporting decisions of which he had no firsthand knowledge. Supra, p. 71.

17 L. Ed. 500 is in error in record-ing that both argument and ruling were on December 21.

[61] 12 Wall. 687 (1872).

[62] Gordon v. Caldcleugh, 3 Cr. 268 (1806).

[63] Fulton v. McAffee, 16 Pet. 149 (1842).

[64] Strader v. Baldwin, 9 How. 261 (1850); Linton v. Stanton, 12 How. 423 (1851).

superiority. One tended to think of that provision, therefore, as "intended to protect the General Government in the free and uninterrupted exercise of the powers conferred on it by the Constitution," as Taney once put it.[65] Lurking in that statement was the implication that, conversely, where the power of the General Government was sustained, Section 25 did not apply. Perhaps the Justices in *Roosevelt v. Meyer* were reacting from habit when, seeing that the Legal Tender Act had been sustained, they denied their power to review.

It was, indeed, unusual that Section 25 was invoked where a State court had sustained an Act of Congress against a charge of unconstitutionality. The very able George W. McCrary cited no such precedent when in *Trebilcock v. Wilson*[66] he asked the Court to disregard *Roosevelt v. Meyer*. On reflection, this should not seem too surprising. Over the years, Congress had done little that was open to serious question on constitutional grounds.[67] Now it had passed a vulnerable statute. That this battle over federal power should be fought before State judges seems out of the ordinary; that State judges resolved grave doubts in favor of the national power is also remarkable. (Here State judges and Congress were at one in their devotion to the preservation of the Union; that made this somewhat different from many constitutional struggles in the past.) Apparently the novelty of *Roosevelt v. Meyer* caught the Justices unawares.

If they had stopped to reason they might have recalled a proposition early established: where opposing parties A and B claimed some benefit—say a grant of land—under an Act of Congress, so that a State court decision in favor of either would deny the claim of the other, the defeated party could take the case to the Supreme Court.[68] By parity of reasoning, where A relied on an Act of Congress and B relied on the Constitution itself, if the Court decided for A, surely B was entitled to a review by the Supreme Court.

The motion to dismiss was argued Friday, doubtless was decided in conference on Saturday, and was granted on Monday. It could have had only routine consideration.

Any notion that the Justices deliberately chose to dodge the legal tender question encounters serious objections. First, it would have been a breach of duty wilfully to deny a litigant's right to be heard. That

---

[65] Commonwealth Bank of Kentucky v. Griffith, 14 Pet. 56, 58 (1840).

[66] Supra, p. 696.

[67] Between Marbury v. Madison, 1 Cr. 137, in 1803, and Gordon v. United States, 2 Wall. 561, in 1865, the *Dred Scott Case*, 19 How. 393, in 1857, was the only instance where the Supreme Court held an Act of Congress invalid.

[68] Matthews v. Zane, 4 Cr. 382 (1808); Buel v. Van Ness, 8 Wheat. 312 (1823); Ross v. Barland, 1 Pet. 655 (1828).

would be something quite different from the matter of advancing a hearing or of deferring a decision. Review under Section 25 was a matter of right, not of judicial discretion. Moreover, one can hardly suppose that a majority of the Taney Court felt any tenderness toward the dubious and controversial Legal Tender Act. Indeed, had the constitutional question then been heard before the full bench of ten Judges, it seems unlikely that a majority would have been mustered to sustain the statute.

Seemingly *Roosevelt v. Meyer* should be explained by saying that a view which experience had made obvious to us was not obvious to those who first considered that case.[69]

All along, it is well to keep such a possibility in mind.

A suit testing the Act might, of course, have arisen in an inferior federal court, whence resort to the Supreme Court would have been clear. But during the war no such appeal was heard.

OTHER LEGAL TENDER CASES IN STATE COURTS

FROM THE NEW YORK COURT in 1863 to the Supreme Court of reconstructed South Carolina in 1869, fifteen courts of last resort, in passing upon the Legal Tender Act or at least in applying it, treated it as valid.[70]

---

[69] This explanation finds support from a comment in *Am. L. Rev.*, 1:750, 752, July 1867. The editors, Ropes and Gray, were taking the Supreme Judicial Court to task for its action in Essex Co. v. Pacific Mills, 14 Allen (96 Mass.) 389 (1867), where it was said that the Judges considered it improper, in the absence of a decision by the Supreme Court of the United States, "to treat the constitutionality of [the Legal Tender Act] . . . as an open question." See infra, note 70, item 13.

The editors commented: "the court, by deciding in favor of the law, so decides the case as to take away the defendant's right to appeal to the United States Court." Roosevelt v. Meyer was not cited: seemingly the editors regarded it as obvious that a writ of error would not lie.

[70] 1. Metropolitan Bank v. Van Dyck, and Meyer v. Roosevelt, 27 N.Y. 400, Sept. T. 1863. 6 to 2.

2. Breitenbach v. Turner, 18 Wis. 140. Jan. T. 1864. Unanimous.

3. Lick v. Faulkner, 25 Cal. 404. July T. 1864. Unanimous.

4. Thayer v. Hedges, 23 Ind. 141. On rehearing at Nov. T. 1864. Unanimous.

5. George v. Concord, 45 N.H. 434. Dec. T. 1864. Unanimous.

6. Hintrager v. Bates, 18 Iowa 174. Dec. 23, 1864. Unanimous.

7. Whetstone v. Colley, 36 Ill. 326. Jan. T. 1865. Unanimous.

8. Maynard v. Newman, 1 Nev. 271. Apr. T. 1865. Unanimous.

9. Van Husen v. Kanouse, 13 Mich. 303. May 13, 1865. Unanimous.

10. Shollenberger v. Brinton, 52 Pa. St. 9. May 24, 1865. Sustained by Strong, Read and Agnew, JJ., (Republi-

One court put itself in opposition to this current of decision. The Court of Appeals of Kentucky, on June 17, 1865, held the Act unconstitutional. This was in *Griswold v. Hepburn*[71]—a case destined for celebrity when Hepburn, debtor on a note made prior to the Legal Tender enactment, went up to the Supreme Court on writ of error. Of

cans); Woodward, C.J., and Thompson, J. (Democrats) dissented.

11. Appel v. Woltmann, 38 Mo. 194. Mar. T. 1866. Unanimous. Missouri's constitutional convention in 1865 adopted an ordinance vacating all judicial offices on May 1 of that year, and authorizing the governor to appoint to these vacancies. It was the new bench that sustained the Legal Tender Act.

12. Carpenter v. Northfield Bank, 39 Vt. 46. Aug. T. 1866. The court was unanimous, in a brief opinion holding the statute valid, until finally settled by the Supreme Court.

13. Essex Co. v. Pacific Mills, 14 Allen (96 Mass.) 389. Jan. T. 1867. Hoar, J., said for the court: "We do not regard it as consistent with the duties of this court to undertake at this time to consider or pass upon this question, as an original question of constitutional right. These notes practically constitute, and for five years have constituted, the money of the country. Pecuniary transactions of the whole people have been adapted to this state of things, and interests of an incalculable amount are affected by it. The validity of the acts of congress under which they were issued has been affirmed, so far as we are aware, by every judicial tribunal in which the question has been presented; and has been recognized in various

ways by the action of the state governments. There have been other acts of the national government which, however disputable on original principles, must be taken to be practically settled by public acquiescence, and the magnitude of the interests involved. The duty of deciding the limits of the constitutional powers of congress, where they affect private rights, belongs particularly to the supreme court of the United States; and it is enough for us to say that, in the absence of any decision by that tribunal, it does not seem to us proper for a state court, upon any views of construction which they may entertain, to treat the constitutionality of a statute of the United States, which so deeply affects all the relations of property in the community, and has been so long in operation, as an open question."

One of this unanimous bench was Horace Gray, J., who in Juilliard v. Greenman, 110 U.S. 421 in 1884, spoke for the Supreme Court in affirming the power of Congress to make treasury notes a legal tender even in time of peace. Infra, pp. 771–74.

14. Johnson and Taylor v. Ivey, 4 Cold. (44 Tenn.) 608. Dec. T. 1867. Unanimous.

15. O'Neil v. McKewn, 1 S.C. 147. Apr. T. 1869. Unanimous.

[71] 2 Duval (63 Ky.) 20.

699

the four Kentucky judges, apparently three participated in the decision: one of these, an Unconditional Unionist, dissented.

About seventy judges had taken part in these sixteen decisions. It was substantially true that all Republicans—except Selden, J., of New York—sustained the statute, while the Democratic judges—in Indiana, New York, Pennsylvania, and Kentucky—regarded it as invalid.[72] As will appear, reasoning toward *either* conclusion could be supported by weighty considerations, and was troubled by grave objections. If one accepted as first principle that the government of a Union intended to be perpetual was invested with power adequate to its own preservation, a conclusion to sustain the statute came naturally. Moreover, as Justice Hoar had said for the Supreme Judicial Court of Massachusetts, the very magnitude of the disruption that might result from an adverse decision must give pause to responsible judges.

APPROACHING THE CONSTITUTIONAL QUESTION

WHEN THE RECORD in Hepburn's case was filed on December 30, 1865, four other cases involving legal tender had already been docketed during that year.[73]

Hepburn v. Griswold was not decided until February 7, 1870, more than four years later.

In the meantime, three of the earlier cases would have been decided—without a ruling on the constitutional question.

In the meantime, also, three other cases involving legal tender would have come on the docket, and would have been decided—they too without a ruling on the constitutional question.

As these cases come to be introduced in the pages that follow, the order of their filing will be indicated in brackets, [1st] to [8th].

One will observe how the Court deliberated—how it held some cases over for further argument, and how, when in each case the issues presented by the record had been distinguished, and an appropriate solution had been reached, the decision in that matter was announced.

---

[72] Included in this generalization are a very few for whom it was impracticable positively to establish a party affiliation—in which case what seemed probable was accepted. The Illinois court, in the case cited above, gave effect to the Legal Tender Act without having need to pronounce upon constitutionality. This court was composed of Pinkney H. Walker, C.J., a Democrat appointed by a Republican governor and thrice elected from a normally Republican district; Judge Sidney Breese, a Democrat who had been much buffeted within his party, whom Douglas had branded a "deserter" in the Lincoln-Douglas debates; and Judge Charles B. Lawrence, Republican.

[73] Another case, Mandelbaum v. The People, had been docketed in December 1864. Eventually it was decided without reference to the legal tender point. See infra, n. 85.

XIV: *The* Legal Tender Cases

Thompson v. Riggs [1st][74] was the suit of customers who, prior to the Legal Tender Act, had deposited gold and silver coin in the Riggs bank. After that enactment, the bank refused to pay their balance in specie. Applying its recent statement of the rule that, absent special agreement, a bank becomes the owner of money deposited,[75] the Court held that the debt could be discharged in any legal tender money. Plaintiffs had failed effectively to save the question of constitutionality in the bill of exceptions on which they came to the Supreme Court. Argument was heard on May 8 and 9, 1867. On May 16, the last day of the term, the judgment in favor of the bank was affirmed. The promptness of the decision reflected the simplicity of the problem.[76]

Lane County v. Oregon [2d], in the regular call of the docket, was argued on December 26 and 30, 1867.[77] Oregon law directed that county officers render to the State its taxes "in gold and silver coin." Did the Legal Tender Act supersede this requirement? Senator George H. Williams of Oregon, appearing for the County, argued that it did, and that the Act was constitutional.[78] Senator Reverdy Johnson, for the State, argued that "debts" as used in the Legal Tender Act did not include taxes.[79] If the Act meant otherwise, it would constitute an unconstitutional interference with the State's internal organization.

Broderick's Executor v. Magraw [3d][80] was heard on January 22,

---

[74] 5 Wall. 663 (1867), on writ of error to the Supreme Court of the District of Columbia, whose decision is reported at 6 D.C. 99 (1864). Joseph H. Bradley of the District of Columbia bar, who appeared for the Thompsons in both courts, is not to be confused with Joseph P. Bradley of New Jersey, appointed to the Supreme Court in 1870.

[75] Marine Bank v. Fulton County Bank, 2 Wall. 252 (1865), where the rule had worked to the bank's disadvantage. Supra, p. 33.

[76] To put this in step with matters already discussed: the argument here followed immediately after the first argument in Virginia v. West Virginia, supra at p. 622; on the same day as this decision, Texas was granted an injunction to restrain White and Chiles, supra, p. 635—and Mississippi v. Stanton was dismissed for want of jurisdiction, supra, pp. 389–90.

[77] 7 Wall. 71 (1869), on writ of error to the Supreme Court of that State. The Docket records argument on those two days; the Minutes omit mention of the opening on the 26th.

The report in 19 L. Ed. 101 records "Argued Dec. 26, 1867, Mar. 2, 1868." There was no argument on the latter day—only an order that the case be continued, with leave to re-argue next December. Infra, p. 703.

[78] The Court had held that a State may not embarrass the means employed by the General Government in the exercise of its powers: Williams cited Bank of Commerce v. New York, 2 Bl. 620 (1863) (which the Court had applied in the *Bank Tax Case*, 2 Wall. 200 (1865), supra at p. 46. Sustaining the constitutionality of the Act, he cited Metropolitan Bank v. Van Dyck, 27 N.Y. 400 (1863), supra at p. 694, and Thayer v. Hedges, 23 Ind. 141 (1864), p. 693.

[79] To this effect he cited Perry v. Washburn, 20 Cal. 350 (1862), decided when Justice Field was Chief Justice of the California court.

[80] 8 Wall. 639 (1870), on writ of error to the Supreme Court of California, whose decision is reported at 26 Cal. 421 (1864).

David C. Broderick (1820–59), United States Senator, was mortally

1868. Broderick in 1858 made a note to pay a sum in "dollars," which was held by Magraw. In 1859 Broderick died. In probate proceedings, the executor set up a tender in "lawful money of the United States." Magraw answered on two grounds: that the executor had collected debts due to the estate in coin, and was bound as a trustee to pay in the same medium; also that the debt had been contracted prior to the passage of the Legal Tender Act, and for that reason could be satisfied only in coin.

Willard v. Tayloe [4th][81] was argued on January 23 and 27, thus following closely upon *Broderick's Executor*. Complainant in 1854 had leased the "Mansion House" in Washington, D.C., for ten years, with an option to purchase for a certain sum. Near the end of the period he accepted, tendered Treasury notes for the amount named, and on meeting refusal, sued for specific performance. Benjamin R. Curtis and Luke E. Poland (formerly Chief Justice of Vermont, now a Representative in Congress) appeared for the complainant. They argued that the money named in the covenant in the lease became a debt when Willard signified his option to purchase; that this was a "debt" within the meaning of the Legal Tender Act; and that the Act was within the powers of Congress. They called in aid the power of Congress "to exercise exclusive legislation" over the District of Columbia.[82]

Hepburn v. Griswold [5th],[83] from Kentucky, had on January 6 been submitted to the Court on written briefs—an unpretentious introduction for what would turn out to be a celebrated case.

Bronson v. Rodes [7th][84] alleged error by the New York Court of Appeals in holding that a debt contracted in 1851 to pay $1,400 "in gold or silver coin, lawful money of the United States," could be discharged in legal tender notes. This case, too, was submitted to the Court on briefs, on January 6.

Thus the Court was deeply involved in questions of legal tender. It had not, however, had the benefit of adequate oral argument. Upon the suggestion by Attorney General Stanbery of the great public importance of the constitutional issue, the Court on March 2, 1868, took the following action as to *Hepburn v. Griswold* and *Bronson v. Rodes*: it

---

wounded in a duel with David S. Terry (1823–89), who had resigned his office as Chief Justice to send the challenge. Each was well known to Justice Field. Terry's enmity toward Field, in another matter, was the cause out of which arose the great case of *In re* Neagle, 135 U.S. 1 (1890), sustaining the discharge from State custody of a United States deputy marshal who, in protecting Justice Field while on circuit duty,

had killed Terry as he made an assault.

[81] 8 Wall. 557 (1870), on appeal from the Supreme Court of the District of Columbia.

[82] Constitution, Art. I, Sec. 8, cl. 17.

[83] Supra, p. 699.

[84] 7 Wall. 229 (1869). The case below is Rodes v. Bronson, 34 N.Y. 649 (1866).

was "Ordered by the Court that these cases stand continued for re-argument by counsel at bar on the first Tuesday of the next Term of this Court: and that the Attorney General have leave to be heard on the part of the United States." At the same time, *Lane County, Broderick's Executor,* and *Willard* were continued "with leave to counsel to re-argue the same if they see fit on any question common to them and to [*Hepburn* and *Bronson*]...."[85]

REARGUMENT, AND CLOSER APPROACH TO THE QUESTION

BEFORE THE FULL BENCH of eight, reargument began on Tuesday, December 8, 1868; it continued on the ninth and tenth.

Henry Adams, then residing in Washington, writing on public affairs, attended all the arguments and reported for *The Nation*.[86] He expressed "a certain feeling of disappointment," "very little having . . . been made of the argument against the law."

> Mr. Curtis's argument, which opened the case, was, as usual with him, one that will be admired by lawyers rather than by the public . . . . Mr. Curtis argues with such severity, such perfect logical sequence, such clearness, with so much of the judicial spirit, with such caution against assumptions of fact or law, and, above all, with such absence of any appeal to feelings that might disturb and mislead the judgment, that one hesitates to criticise . . . .
>
> . . . Mr. Curtis spoke little longer than an hour, and the essential part of his argument can be stated very concisely. Congress, he said, has the power to borrow money, and as an incident to this power Congress has the choice of means for its exercise, subject, however, to two limitations. . . .

Those were that the means must be appropriate to a proper end, and must not be prohibited by the letter or any just implication of the Con-

---

[85] Also included in this latter order was Mandelbaum v. The People of the United States in the Territory of Nevada, an action to collect taxes, which on writ of error to the Supreme Court of the Territory had been docketed in the Supreme Court on December 8, 1864. This had been submitted on briefs on January 24, 1867, and had been continued at the end of the term.

Counsel did not join in the oral argument of the legal tender question.

On December 13, 1869, the judgment below was reversed on a wholly independent ground: that it appeared the trial court had struck an answer wherein defendant had presented a perfect defense. 8 Wall. 310.

[86] 7:501–2. Dec. 17, 1868. Having accompanied Charles Francis Adams as secretary when in 1861 the latter became Minister to Great Britain, the son had recently returned to America when the father ended that service.

stitution (what Marshall had said in a great sentence in *McCulloch v. Maryland*[87].)

Attorney General Evarts, Adams reported, argued with "vehemence" and an excess of "audacity."

> For two hours he heaped argument on sarcasm and persuasion on ridicule to prove that legal tender was a matter of no consequence at all, an incidental power subordinate to mere purposes of government; or, if not this, then a power essential to national existence, not to be placed among the substantive powers of the Constitution, but above them.

Adams was alarmed at this "magnificent contempt for the very idea of a government that should propose to itself the strict observance of law and right in times of national peril." Nor did the Government's case "seem to be helped by Mr. Evarts' afterthought that the Fourteenth Amendment, declaring that the validity of the debt should never be questioned, covered the legal tender clause as well as the debt."

Clarkson N. Potter (1825–82), New York Democrat (who had just been elected to the next Congress), seemed "not of the force necessary for supporting . . . against such advocates the weight of so burdensome a cause." His argument "contained many clever points," but "was discursive, loosely constructed, unequal, and not on a level with the occasion." Adams thought it a "disaster" that Curtis had not been met by counsel of comparable power.

The constitutional issue remained in suspense for fourteen months —until February 7, 1870. The Justices saw their way clear, however, to dispose of some pending matters. *Lane County v. Oregon* was decided on February 8, 1869.[88] The State's demand for specie was upheld: abundant reasons were found for holding that Congress had not attempted to intrude upon so vital a function as the State's raising of its revenue.

One week later came *Bronson v. Rodes.*[89] The New York Court of Appeals had held that a bond to pay "in gold or silver coin, lawful money of the United States," had been made solvable in United States notes of the same nominal value.[90] That decision was reversed. Chief

---

[87] 4 Wheat. 316, 421 (1819).

[88] 7 Wall. 71, per Chase, C.J. Supra, p. 701.

[89] 7 Wall. 229. Supra, p. 702.

[90] Rodes v. Bronson, 34 N.Y. 649, Sept. T. 1866, affirming the decision of the Supreme Court in Kimpton v. Bronson (and Rodes v. Bronson), 45

Barbour (N.Y.) 618, May 7, 1866.
The Court of Appeals had said, in part:
If the contract in question is to be excepted from the operation of the act of 1862, on the ground that it specifically provides for payment *in coin*, the constitu-

XIV: *The* Legal Tender Cases

Justice Chase started with the proposition that "It is the appropriate function of courts of justice to enforce contracts according to the lawful intent and understanding of the parties." Here, he said, the intent was clear: that payment be made "in coined lawful money." The contract was, "in legal import, nothing else than an agreement to deliver a certain weight of standard gold, to be ascertained by a count of coins . . . ." "We cannot suppose that it was intended by the . . . Currency Acts to enforce satisfaction . . . by the tender of depreciated currency . . . equivalent only in nominal amount to the real value . . . of the coined dollars. . . ." Assuming for the instant case that the legal tender clause was warranted by the Constitution—Chase's words were somewhat pointed—still gold and silver coins remained a legal tender. The Acts, reasonably construed, did not permit an express contract for coined dollars to be satisfied in another medium.

Justices Davis and Swayne each added a statement that he concurred in the ruling on this particular type of obligation, but assented to no larger implication in the opinion.

Justice Miller dissented in a concise opinion. When the contract was made, gold and silver coin was the only legal tender: *everyone* who accepted a note payable in dollars contemplated that it would be so paid. He supposed that the particular words here were chosen to make clear that payment in State bank notes was precluded. He rejected the Chief Justice's effort to impose the presumed intention of the parties as a controlling element in construing the Legal Tender Acts.

> As I have no doubt that it was intended by those Acts to make notes of the United States . . . a legal tender for all private debts then due, or which might become due on contracts then in existence, without regard to the intent of the parties on that point, I must dissent

---

tional power of congress . . . may be completely annulled in the future by inserting a similar provision in all contracts for the payment of specified sums of money. The contract is to be read now precisely as it would have been read previously to the passage of that act, to wit, as a contract creating a debt, in a specified sum, payable in lawful money . . . .

It is said that this view of the case is unjust to the creditor. But it is not so, unless the interests of creditors are more to be regarded than the rights of debtors, and are paramount to even the vital needs of the government. . . . As with contracts for future delivery of a commodity, said the court, so it was with a contract for a specified sum of money at a future date: the parties took the risk, respectively, of appreciation and of depreciation. Moreover, they were subject to the exercise of the powers of Congress, which in this instance had met an "extreme peril." "Unquestionably," said the court, Congress might have debased the gold and silver coins, with an effect upon creditors similar to that resulting by the issue of paper money.

from the judgment of the Court, and from the opinion on which it is founded.[91]

The *New York Tribune*'s correspondent, observing that the decision in *Bronson v. Rodes* did not pass upon the constitutionality of the Legal Tender Act, added: "I am authorized to state that the Court has not yet decided relative to its opinion upon this question." Editorial comment inferred that where coin had not been expressly mentioned, the Court would apply the Act.[92]

The Nation, however, trusted that the words "lawful money" used before the passage of the Act would be held to require coin. Applauding the *Bronson* decision, it said that

> One or two more in the same direction will completely sober most of the currency madcaps and put greenbacks before us in their real character—as a makeshift which it was excusable to resort to at the outbreak of the war, but which is the source of incalculable evils, and whose disturbing influence on trade and on private and public morals should, now that the war is over, be kept within the narrowest possible limits till we finally get rid of them. . . .[93]

---

[91] The Great Depression brought a sweeping away of the principles on which Chief Justice Chase founded his opinion.

By the Joint Resolution of June 5, 1933, 48 Stat. 112, Congress sought to assure a *uniform* value to coins and currencies of the United States; to that end it declared that any obligation purporting to require payment in gold or in a particular kind of coin would be discharged on payment, dollar for dollar, in *any* legal tender money. By the Gold Reserve Act of January 30, 1934, 48 Stat. 337, and a proclamation of the President next day in pursuance of that Act, the weight of the gold dollar was reduced from 25.8 to 15 5/21 grains nine-tenths fine.

In Norman v. Baltimore & Ohio R.R. Co., 294 U.S. 240 (1935), the invalidation of the gold clause in private contracts and in obligations of States, municipalities and their political subdivisions was sustained. Chief Justice Hughes, for a majority of five, distinguished the situation from that in Bronson v. Rodes, inasmuch as Congress in 1862 had permitted *two* descriptions of lawful money to exist concurrently: thus a contract payable specifically in one had been enforced. He dismissed as dictum so much of Chase's opinion as said that a contract for gold coin was in effect a contract for bullion. The Joint Resolution of 1933 declared such a contract to be contrary to public policy. And the Court, sustaining Congress, viewed the gold clause as a contract for money, and held that Congress had power thus to regulate the value of money.

The New York Court of Appeals in Rodes v. Bronson, supra, n. 90, had sought to protect the power of Congress against being annulled by private agreement; in the *Norman* case the Supreme Court upheld the exercise of that power.

[92] Feb. 16, 1869.

[93] 8:121 and 145–46, Feb. 18 and 25, 1869.

On August 27, 1868, it had expressed confidence that such would be the line taken by the Court, in accordance "with equity, common sense, and the requirements of an exalted statesmanship." 7:164. It held to that view, and deplored the reopening of the question, and the overrul-

Butler v. Horwitz [6th],[94] decided on March 1, 1869, concerned an annual ground rent of "fifteen pounds current money of Maryland, payable in English golden guineas . . . ."[95] It was agreed in the trial court "that the current pound of the State of Maryland was equal to $2.66 2/3, and therefore that the fifteen pounds spoken of as payable in gold and silver is equal to $40 in gold and silver"; also that on January 1, 1866, the day when the rent was due, "gold was worth 145 per cent. in currency . . . ," and that on that day Butler tendered and Horwitz refused $40 in greenbacks.[96]

Horwitz conceded the constitutionality of the Legal Tender Act: at issue was its operation on the facts agreed.

The Court of Common Pleas held that the Act should be so construed as not to impair a contract for the payment of gold and silver; it would give judgment for the payment with interest of the sum specified, to be satisfied by payment of its equivalent in currency. Accordingly on June 27, 1866, judgment was entered for Horwitz in the sum of $59.71 with costs.[97]

Butler brought up the case on writ of error—in order "to sustain the law of the land in its full force and integrity."[98] On the main point, the Court, per Chase, C.J., sustained the conclusion below, for reasons set out in *Bronson v. Rodes.* For error in assessing damages, however, the Court reversed and remanded: "judgment should have been entered in coin . . . ."[99]

Dwelling upon the terms of this covenant of 1791, the Chief Justice wrote that "the obvious intent, in contracts for payment or delivery

---

ing of *Hepburn.* 10:215, 218, and 263, Apr. 7 and 28, 1870; 12:281, Apr. 28, 1871.

[94] 7 Wall. 258.

[95] The full description was "fifteen pounds current money of Maryland, payable in English golden guineas, weighing five pennyweights and six grains, at thirty-five shillings each, and other gold and silver at their present established weight and rate, according to the act of assembly . . . ." Transcript of Record, 4.

The lease was of February 18, 1791 —before Congress by the Mint Act of 1792 established the dollar as the monetary unit.

As explained in the Brief of Plaintiff in Error, "There were Maryland shillings, the issue of the Proprietary, 35 of which equalled a £ sterling, or English guinea [of 20 shillings]. And when a £ Maryland was spoken

of, it meant a £ 4/7 the value of a sterling £ . . . ." P. 4.

[96] Transcript of Record, 4.

[97] Ibid., 5, 8.

[98] As counsel expressed it in the Brief for Plaintiff in Error, 9.

[99] Miller, J., dissented: "I understand the original contract to have been an agreement to pay in English guineas, as a commodity, and their value was, therefore, properly computed in the legal tender notes which by law would satisfy the judgment."

The case had been commenced in a Justice Court, and the Court of Common Pleas was the highest State Court wherein an appeal therefrom could be heard.

The Transcript of Record had been filed on December 15, 1866. On February 3, 1869, counsel submitted on briefs.

of coin, or bullion, to provide against fluctuations in the medium of payment, warrants the inference that it was the understanding of the parties that such contracts should be satisfied, whether before or after judgment, only in tender of coin . . . ." He completed the sentence with a dictum on the inference that arose from the *absence* of such a stipulation. What he wrote at this time should be viewed in juxtaposition with what he wrote eleven months later in *Hepburn v. Griswold:*

Butler v. Horwitz:	Hepburn v. Griswold:
. . . the absence of any express stipulation . . . , in contracts for payment in money, generally warrants the opposite inference of an understanding between the parties that such contracts may be satisfied, before or after judgment, by the tender of any lawful money.	Contracts for the payment of money, made before the Act of 1862, had reference to coined money, and could not be discharged, unless by consent, otherwise than by tender of the sum due in coin. Every such contract, therefore, was, in legal import, a contract for the payment of coin.

This is enough to put one on guard.

LETTERS FROM JUSTICES NELSON, GRIER, AND MILLER

In the summer of 1869, Elbridge G. Spaulding, chairman of the subcommittee wherein the Legal Tender Bill was framed, brought out his *History of the Legal Tender Paper Money Issued During the Great Rebellion.*[100] Complimentary copies were acknowledged by Justices Nelson, Grier, and Miller, in letters which Spaulding published in the second edition, in 1875.[101] Nelson wrote from Cooperstown on August 14; on a brief examination he found the book "to be very accurate." He continued:

We shall dispose of this question, I presume, in the due course of our coming session of the court, which begins 1st [Monday] of October. I have always regretted that the greenbacks were made a Legal Tender, and I think the Chief Justice now is of opinion that the *omission* would not have had much effect one way or the other, in its operation upon the bills. Not at least as much as he thought at the time the bill was passed. That the necessities of the government and business interests of the country would have given them all the credit, important or material.

---

[100] Supra, p. 680.   [101] Appendix at pp. 58–59.

I am very much obliged to you for this authentic record of one of the most important measures growing out of the war, and difficult to deal with since.

One might infer that probably Nelson would hold the Act invalid, and that he expected Chase to take that view.

Grier, after his summer vacation, wrote from Philadelphia on August 26:

> On my return home I am pleased to find a copy of your history . . . . It is a valuable historical document, and I am thankful for your kindness . . . , and concur with you fully in the views you take on the subject. Why our court has for two years *postponed* their consideration of the question, is unknown to me, and I don't feel any responsibility for its postponement. Excuse my pencil. I write with difficulty.

While the statement that he concurred fully with Spaulding's views was loose, it would appear to mean that Grier regarded the Legal Tender Act as a necessary and proper measure for meeting the war-time exigency. He seems ready to vote on the constitutional question, and is impatient that it has not already been settled.

Miller, writing from Keokuk on August 17, thanked Spaulding both for the book and for a letter that had accompanied it. His reply was frank, and significant:

> I read the book with much interest, because it gives the first clear view, as a whole, of the financial measures of the Government during the war, that I have had; but mainly because it gives an accurate and full account of the relation of the Chief Justice, while he was Secretary of the Treasury, to those measures; and especially to the legal tender clause, about which there was some uncertainty and much curiosity.
>
> A careful examination of all that is to be found in your book on that subject, leaves the impression on my mind that he had never had any doubt as to the constitutionality of that measure, but doubted its policy or expediency. This doubt seems to have been entirely removed, and his conviction of the necessity of that provision to enable him to carry on the department of the government under his charge, made him at last an advocate of it.
>
> If judicial propriety admitted of it, I could not give you any reliable opinion of the probable action of the Supreme Court. Of course I know the views of some of its members, but there are enough whose views I do not know (some of them are probably undetermined in their own minds), to make the matter as uncertain to me as to you. I have a very strong impression that the opinion of the majority of

the court, if rendered while constituted as it now is, will be such as the Chief Justice shall think it ought to be, when delivered. But with all my intimacy with him, and some knowledge of his character and habits of thought, I have no idea what that will be. . . . [The ellipsis is by Spaulding.]

A reader would not have doubted that Miller was going to uphold the statute. He was gratified to find responsibility pinned so firmly on the Secretary. Miller was evidently mistrustful of Chase's vagarious mode of thought, and apprehensive about his influence upon some of the Justices.

Miller spoke of the Court "while constituted as it now is": by the Act of April 10, there would be a ninth place on the first Monday in December, and the possibility of further change by the resignation of Grier (which seemed likely) or of Nelson.[102] Evidently judgment on the legal tender question was hanging in the balance; and evidently a change in the membership of the Court might produce a change in the outcome.

The Court met in an adjourned term, called for October 4, 1869, but—contrary to the expectation in Nelson's letter—it did not dispose of the great issue. It did reach and decide *Bronson v. Kimpton* [8th in the order of filing mentioned above[103]], the case of a bond given in 1859 for a payment "in gold or silver coin, lawful money of the United States." It was indistinguishable from *Bronson v. Rodes*, and was decided on its authority.[104]

POWER TO PROVIDE A CURRENCY

Two DECISIONS AT THIS TIME demonstrated the power of Congress to secure a sound and uniform currency. *Bank v. Supervisors*, decided January 16, 1869, settled this point: that greenbacks were among those "securities of the United States" which Congress in 1862 and 1863 had declared "shall be exempt from taxation by or under State authority."[105] Chief Justice Chase spoke for the Court in holding that these were indeed securities—obligations to pay in coined dollars, secured by a pledge of the national faith—within the meaning of the statute. To the contention that, if so construed, the provision was invalid, he replied:

---

[102] Supra at pp. 559–60.

[103] Supra, p. 700.

[104] 8 Wall. 444, decided Nov. 29, 1869. Kimpton came on writ of error to the Court of Appeals of New York; no counsel appeared for defendant in error.

Kimpton v. Bronson in the Supreme Court of New York had been reported at 45 Barbour 618, May T.

1866: and Rodes v. Bronson had been decided with it, at 634.

[105] 7 Wall. 26, reversing the Court of Appeals of New York, 37 N.Y. 21. This is another in the line of decisions on intergovernmental relations in the field of taxation, introduced supra at p. 46. Most of such cases at this time came from New York.

> And we think it clearly within the discretion of Congress to determine whether . . . their usefulness, as a means of carrying on the government, would be enhanced by exemption from taxation; and within the constitutional power of Congress . . . to provide by law for such exemption.

Here then was one quality—immunity to State taxation—that Congress could impress upon these notes as a means more effectively to exercise its power "to borrow money on the credit of the United States." Whether it could give them the quality of legal tender "belongs to another discussion."

More significant was the leading case of *Veazie Bank v. Fenno*, decided on December 13, 1869.[106] In instituting the system of national banks by the Act of February 25, 1863,[107] Congress provided a third type of currency, besides specie and greenbacks: national bank notes, secured by the deposit of United States bonds. By the Internal Revenue Act of July 13, 1866, Congress hit the circulation of State bank notes with a 10 percent tax.[108] This would destroy their use and give the field to national bank notes. Was this imposition invalid as a direct tax, not apportioned according to the census as required by Article I, Section 9, clause 4? Did the tax unconstitutionally impair the exercise of a power reserved to the States?[109]

On October 18, 1869, Caleb Cushing and Reverdy Johnson argued for the Bank, against Attorney General Hoar.

The Chief Justice sustained the tax in a good opinion. "Much diversity of opinion has always prevailed upon the question, what are direct taxes?" Chiefly, if not exclusively, they were taxes upon land and appurtenances, and capitation taxes. The tax on bank note circulation, at any rate, was not "direct."[110]

---

[106] 8 Wall. 533. On certificate of division of opinion by the Judges of the Circuit Court for Maine.

[107] 12 Stat. 670, supra, p. 682.

[108] 14 Stat. 146, reenacting and extending a provision of the Act of Mar. 3, 1865, 13 Stat. 484.

[109] Resisting an attempt to include such a tax in the Internal Revenue Bill of 1864, H. H. Van Dyck, Superintendent of Banking of the State of New York, supra at p. 693, had written an argument to the *New York Evening Post*. He wrote, in part: The Secretary of the Treasury, not content to leave his favorite scheme to the vindication of time and experience, invokes vindictive legislation . . . for the pur-

pose of "taxing out of existence" institutions that have been recognized since the formation of the Government as the legitimate offspring of the State legislation, the rightful possessors of State privileges, and constitutionally amenable only to State control. . . . Letter of Apr. 19, 1864. Cong. Globe, 38–1, 1934. Apr. 28, 1864.

[110] Reference was made to the discussion in Pacific Insurance Co. v. Soule, 7 Wall. 433 (1869), per Swayne, J. The Internal Revenue Act of July 13, 1866, required that incomes be estimated at their value in legal tender currency; the insurance company challenged this, unsuccessfully, as a direct tax.

Next, had Congress acted ultra vires by laying a tax whose purpose was to prevent the exercise of a faculty pertaining to the State's reserved powers? Counsel for the bank had argued that the prohibitive rate disclosed an unconstitutional purpose, which the Court should condemn. The Attorney General cited *Ex parte McCardle* to the point that the Court would not inquire into the motive prompting Congress to exercise its powers.[111]

The Chief Justice developed the thought that Congress could provide a circulation of coin; that it might emit bills on the credit of the United States; that it might make its bills "a currency, uniform in value and description, and convenient and useful for circulation."

> Having thus, in the exercise of undisputed constitutional powers, undertaken to provide a currency for the whole country, it cannot be questioned that Congress may, constitutionally, secure the benefit of it to the people by appropriate legislation. . . .

To that end,

> Congress may restrain, by suitable enactments, the circulation as money of any notes not issued under its authority. Without this power, indeed, its attempts to secure a sound and uniform currency for the country must be futile.

Nelson and Davis, JJ., dissented.

---

[111] Supra, p. 492.

Apropos of the Attorney General's proposition, a contrasting observation by the editors of the *American Law Review* may be mentioned, as showing how unfamiliar lawyers then were with the use by Congress of granted powers to attain results by indirection. In their comment on the *Hepburn* case they found fault with both majority and dissenters for having gone "outside of their proper sphere" in debating the necessity of resort to the legal tender clause: instead, "The intent [of Congress] is the first thing to be passed upon by the court, and we believe the court should hold Congress to a strict account as respects a lawful *intent* . . . ." *Am. L. Rev.* 4:604, 609 (April, 1870). Ropes and Gray did not reflect upon the problems to which their prescription would lead.

In 1904 in McCray v. United States, 195 U.S. 27, sustaining a federal excise on oleomargarine, ten cents a pound if colored to imitate butter and one-quarter of a cent if not so colored, White, J., said that "The decisions of this Court from the beginning lend no support whatever to the assumption that the judiciary may restrain the exercise of lawful power on the assumption that a wrongful purpose or motive has caused the power to be exerted." "Inquiry into the hidden motives which may move Congress to exercise a power constitutionally conferred upon it is beyond the competency of courts," said Stone, J., for the Court in Sonzinsky v. United States, 300 U.S. 506, 513 (1937), sustaining an excise on dealers in firearms. To pursue this topic would carry the footnote too far afield.

XIV: *The* Legal Tender Cases

The principle to be deduced is that Congress may take measures to make effective the exercise of its powers—going so far, in this instance, as to drive out of circulation the notes which State banks had been issuing under valid State franchises. Upon the same principle might Congress give to United States notes the quality of legal tender? The Chief Justice remarked that it was "not important here to decide" that question.

THE CONSTITUTIONAL QUESTION:
HEPBURN v. GRISWOLD

AT LAST, in *Hepburn v. Griswold*,[112] the Justices faced the constitutional question. On a note for "dollars" made in 1860 the debtor had tendered Treasury notes and the creditor had sued for coin.

On February 7, 1870, the Chief Justice, speaking also for Justices Nelson, Clifford and Field, held the Legal Tender Act unconstitutional as it applied to preexisting debts. He concluded with the statement that

> It is proper to say that Mr. Justice Grier, who was a member of the Court when this cause was decided in conference, Nov. 27, 1869, and when this opinion was directed to be read (Jan. 29, 1870), stated his judgment to be that the legal tender clause, properly construed, has no application to debts contracted prior to its enactment; but that upon the construction given to the Act by the other Judges he concurred in the opinion that the clause, so far as it makes United States notes a legal tender for such debts, is not warranted by the Constitution.

In accord with Grier's views, and with the then inclination of Field's mind,[113] the ruling was confined to preexisting debts. It resulted that instead of going to the crux of the matter—whether Congress had power to emit legal tender notes—the Chief Justice argued that the exercise of such power was unwarranted as it fell upon obligations previously contracted.

Admittedly, if a power to make notes a legal tender existed, it must be by reason of being "necessary and proper for carrying into execution" powers elsewhere granted. Chase turned to Marshall's gloss in *McCulloch v. Maryland*:[114]

> Let the end be legitimate, let it be within the scope of the Constitution, and all means which are appropriate, which are plainly adapted to that

---

[112] 8 Wall. 603.
[113] Infra, p. 716.
[114] 4 Wheat. 316, 421 (1819), sus-

taining the power to charter the Bank of the United States.

end, which are not prohibited, but consist with the letter and spirit of the Constitution, are constitutional. . . .

Chase bore down heavily upon certain words. Had the legal tender clause been *plainly adapted, really calculated* to effect a constitutional object? Eminent writers, Chase wrote, took the view that the quality of legal tender added nothing to the credit of the Government's notes. If it were conceded that some advantage was gained, this was far more than outweighed by the evils of irredeemable paper money.

(That was an estimate which the Secretary of the Treasury in 1862 might well have urged upon Congress, for the efficacy of a proposed measure was a matter belonging to that body.)

Then there was another view which to Chase seemed "decisive." Marshall had spoken of means consistent with the letter and *spirit* of the Constitution. To make the Legal Tender Act operate on debts already contracted was contrary to that spirit. It was unjust, whereas the Constitution was ordained to establish justice. It impaired the obligation of contracts, whereas States were forbidden to do so. And such legislation should be regarded as a deprivation of private property within the prohibition of the Fifth Amendment.

Dissenting, Justice Miller—Swayne and Davis, JJ., joining with him—rebutted the points made by the Chief Justice. He quoted Marshall's language in context, to the effect that where a measure was not prohibited it was for the legislature—not the judiciary—to judge of the degree of its necessity. He dwelt upon the plight to which the Government had been brought in 1862, and on the imperative need for what was done at that time. If, as had been held in *Veazie Bank* two months earlier,

Congress can, . . . under its implied power, protect and foster this currency by such means as destructive taxation on State bank circulation, it seems strange, indeed, if it cannot adopt the more appropriate and the more effectual means of declaring these notes of its own issue, for the redemption of which its faith is pledged, a lawful tender in payment of debts.

To condemn the statute because of its "indirect effect" upon contracts, wrote Miller, "is too vague for my perception." A declaration of war or the abolition of a tariff might have consequences no less severe upon private interests—yet no one would suggest that such a measure could be condemned as violating the Fifth Amendment.

The argument of the injustice of the law—"an injustice which, if it ever existed, will be repeated by now holding it wholly void"—was "too abstract and intangible" to be used as a test of the action of

Congress. "It substitutes our ideas of policy for judicial construction, an undefined code of ethics for the Constitution, and a court of Justice for the National Legislature."

Broderick's Executor v. Magraw[115] was dispatched on "the principles in the decision just rendered."

In retrospect, the *American Law Review* commented that *Hepburn v. Griswold* "presented the curious spectacle of the Supreme Court reversing the determination of Congress on a point of political economy."[116] Undoubtedly these were the words of its then editor—Oliver Wendell Holmes, Jr.

The Chief Justice's performance had at once struck the acute young Holmes as faulty. His own instinct for the jugular was shown in a communication published in the *American Law Review* for July 1870,[117] which as restated in a note to his twelfth edition of Kent's *Commentaries*[118] ran as follows:

> the power to "coin money" means to strike off metallic medals (*coin*), and to make those medals legal tender (*money*); if the Constitution says expressly that Congress shall have power to make metallic legal tender, how can it be taken to say by implication that Congress shall have power to make paper money legal tender?

Holmes could not see "how a limited power which is expressly given, and which does not come up to the desired height, can be enlarged as an incident to some other express power . . . ."

That contention went to the root of the matter—the existence of Congressional power to make the Government's notes a legal tender. If the answer was No, that would be decisive as to transactions *both before and after* the enactment.

The opinion of the Court, however, had been placed on a less substantial ground. No one, Chase had written, questions the constitutionality of the legislation by which a note currency had been authorized: "The doubt is as to the power to declare a particular class of these notes to be a legal tender in payment of pre-existing debts." Five times the issue was identified, twice the holding was stated, and always it was the *retroactive* operation of the legal tender clause that was said to be the point on which the case turned.[119]

That left open the question whether the statute could constitutionally be applied to obligations incurred *after* its enactment.

---

[115] 8 Wall. 639, decided Feb. 7, 1870.
[116] 7:146 (1872).
[117] 4:768.

[118] 1:[271–72] (1873).
[119] P. 606, initial sentence; 610, l. 27; 613, l. 1; 615, l. 24; 619, l. 30; 625, l. 16; 626, l. 4.

WHAT TRANSPIRED WITHIN THE COURT

THE CIRCUMSTANCES under which *Hepburn* and *Broderick's Executor* came to be decided were extraordinary. Events may be recreated, because some weeks later the two groups of Justices prepared recriminating accounts which, while soon withdrawn, subsequently became available.[120] At conference on Saturday, November 27, 1869, the *Hepburn* case was taken up. All of the eight Justices who then constituted the Court participated in a discussion that lasted three or four hours. When a division was taken, Chase, Nelson, Clifford and Field voted to affirm—Grier, Swayne, Miller and Davis to reverse. A question was made whether Grier really meant to vote as he did. He replied that he understood the Kentucky court to have held the legal tender statute unconstitutional, and that he voted to reverse. So *Hepburn v. Griswold* was declared to be affirmed by an equally divided court.

An even division would establish no principle.

Then *Broderick's Executor v. Magraw* was considered. Here Justice Grier made some remarks inconsistent with the vote he had just given. This was brought to his attention. He was reminded that in conversation with another member of the Court he had taken a view differing from that of any of the other Justices. The upshot was that he changed his vote in the *Hepburn* case, thus making a 5–to–3 decision against the statute as applied to preexisting debts.

As Chase stated in a letter written in 1871,[121]

> of the five Judges who concurred in the judgments and in the opinion, one, at least, Mr Justice Grier, regarded the act as constitutional in respect to contracts made after its passage. Judge Field was then inclined to the same view. The opinion was therefore confined to the effect of the act on pre-existing contracts. On this point the five Judges had no doubt. The minority consisted of three Judges. The full Court then consisted of eight Justices.

Recall now that—with Grier and Nelson particularly in mind—Congress by the Act of April 10, 1869, had provided salary for life to any Judge who resigned having attained the age of seventy and having served at least ten years.[122] That statute became effective on the first Monday in December. His colleagues now conveyed to Justice Grier

---

120 Infra, p. 739.
121 Letter of May 1, 1871—the day when the Court decided the *Legal Tender Cases*—to John Randolph Tucker of Virginia. Chase added that, if health permitted, he would file a

dissenting opinion. "I wish to leave my settled judgment on this great question upon the public records." Secretary's copy, in Chase Papers, L.C.
122 Supra, p. 560.

their unanimous view that he should take the benefit of the statute. On December 15 he resigned, effective January 31.

The Act of April 10 had also increased the Court to its old membership of nine. Thus on Monday, December 6, one vacancy existed —and with Grier's resignation on the fifteenth, there would be another on February 1.

On December 15 President Grant nominated Attorney General Hoar to the newly created ninth place. On December 20 he nominated Edwin M. Stanton to become a Justice in succession to Grier. But Stanton (after confirmation on December 20) died on December 24. Hoar's nomination was rejected on February 3, by vote of 24 to 33. Again there were two places to fill.

On February 7, the President nominated William Strong of Pennsylvania and Joseph P. Bradley of New Jersey to be Justices. These nominations, together with the resignation of Grier and the rejection of Hoar, will be canvassed later in this chapter.

At conference on Saturday, January 29, the Chief Justice presented his opinion in *Hepburn*, which was accepted by those on the prevailing side. Normally it would have been delivered on Monday, January 31—which was Grier's last day. The dissenters desired time, however, to prepare an opinion giving their reasons for disagreement. So the matter went over to Monday, February 7, when the prevailing and dissenting opinions were read.

The Transcript of Record in *Hepburn v. Griswold*, in the set of Records and Briefs preserved in the Library of Congress, was the copy distributed to Justice Grier. On the front cover, in his shaky handwriting, are pencilled several notations—the amount of the note, the pages where the two opinions in the Kentucky court were to be found, and the dates of submission and argument. At the foot of the cover he had written these words:

Legal Tender—pure & simple
prerogative of rascality

Here one may see an epithet—seemingly an admission of power—and the mark of a crotchety mind.

Statutory construction may blend subtly into constitutional interpretation, by way of the Court's refusal to give a statute "a retrospective operation, whereby rights previously vested are injuriously affected,"[123] and by its mode of construing to avoid "grave doubts" on the score of constitutionality.[124] Seemingly it was in this area that Grier lost his way

---

[123] Chew Heong v. United States, 112 U.S. 536, 559 (1884).

[124] United States v. Jin Fuey Moy, 241 U.S. 394, 401 (1916); Brandeis, J., in Ashwander v. T.V.A., 297 U.S. at 348 (1936).

at the conference on November 27. In a case on the circuit in 1864 he had so construed the Legal Tender Act as to avoid ruling on its constitutionality—there being an intimation, however, that he regarded it as valid.[125]

Moreover it appears that Grier had expressed his views to Noah Davis, a Republican Congressman from New York and member of the Judiciary Committee.[126] He was understood to hold (1) that the Act should be construed as inapplicable to debts already incurred, but (2) that Congress *could* constitutionally have made it apply to them. The basis for this statement is a passage in a letter from Judge Henry E. Davies (law partner of Noah Davis), written March 22, 1870, to Justice Bradley, congratulating him upon his appointment. Judge Davies wrote:

> Permit me to say that I also hope you will obtain from Judge Grier his reasons for affirming the judgment in the Kentucky legal tender case. He read them to Judge Noah Davis, who is on the Judiciary Com^t. H.R. and he put his concurrence solely upon the point that the act of Feb. 25, 1862, was not by its terms retroactive and made applicable to then existing debts. I understand that he conceded, it was in the power of Congress to have made it so applicable, and if in terms it had so declared, it would have been constitutional, both as to existing and subsequent debts.

Henry E. Davies (1805–81) had been a Judge of the New York Court of Appeals from 1860 to 1867; he had written the leading opinion in *Metropolitan Bank v. Van Dyck, Meyer v. Roosevelt*, upholding the Legal Tender Act. Noah Davis (1818–1902) served only

---

[125] In Philadelphia & Reading R.R. v. Morrison, Fed. Case No. 11,089 (C.C.E.D. Pa., Nov. 1864), plaintiff railroad company sought to compel the defendants to release their right to a ground rent upon payment of the principal in legal tender notes. District Judge Cadwalader identified two questions: (1) whether the statute was constitutional, and (2) whether, if the statute was constitutional, a ground rent was a "debt" within its meaning. Judge Cadwalader expressed his opinion on the first question—that the statute was unconstitutional. He said that he and the Circuit Justice (Grier) "seem to differ at present upon the first point, though there has not, as yet, been a full interchange of our views upon it. . . ."

Because Judge Cadwalader owned some ground rents, he withdrew from the bench to allow the Circuit Justice to decide the case alone.

Grier then delivered his opinion: the Act was "doubtful in policy and dangerous as a precedent" and should be construed strictly. He then held that the principal of a ground rent was not a "debt" and so was not within the statute.

[126] What follows comes from Fairman, "Mr. Justice Bradley's Appointment to the Supreme Court and the Legal Tender Cases," *Harv. L. Rev.*, 54:977–1034, 1128–55 (Apr. and May, 1941), at 1134. This article brings together a mass of letters and other material to which reference will be made from time to time in this chapter.

in the 41st Congress, from March 4, 1869, to July 15, 1870. During that time there was a First Session from March 4 to April 10, and the Second Session beginning on December 6, 1869. The time of the alleged conversation between Grier and Davis does not appear; *Hepburn* was settled in conference on November 27, before Congress met in its Second Session. Grier, it is said, "read" his reasons: perhaps there was some memorandum; no written opinion by him is mentioned in other accounts. Davis was a lawyer of distinction, and a strong Judge on the New York Supreme Court from 1857 to 1868, 1873 to 1887; his sentiments were firmly fixed. While Davis and Davies were lawyers of clear mind, there was room for misunderstanding in the transmission of the message to Bradley. At any rate, the episode tends to confirm that Grier had wobbled badly.

Whatever Grier may have said, or meant, on various occasions, evidently he was not up to the work at hand. Yet four of his brethren were willing, while he remained, to count his vote against the validity of a statute. Without his vote, those who would declare the Act unconstitutional were less than a majority of the full Bench. And by a canon laid down by the Court in 1834, only by a majority of the full Court ought a constitutional question be decided.[127] From what transpired at the conference it should have been recognized that the Court was then in no condition to settle the legal tender question. Certainly it would be unfortunate that the issue turn on the votes of Justices appointed after the division within the Court had occurred; even so, that would be preferable to declaring an Act of Congress invalid by the vote of a confused mind. It was to be expected that *any* person appointed to the Court at that time would have an outlook favorable to sustaining the war measures, including the Legal Tender Act. The same sort of considerations that had been pressed so conscientiously upon Lincoln when a Chief Justice was to be appointed in 1864 would now operate upon Grant—even if the division within the Court had remained a complete secret. The four Justices were determined to go ahead and assert their strength while yet they could.

The chief responsibility for this must surely be placed upon Chase.

APPOINTMENT OF STRONG AND BRADLEY

IT IS USEFUL at the outset to establish the character of the new appointees, and to trace their selection and confirmation.

William Strong (1808–95) grew up in a Connecticut parsonage, the eldest of eleven children. Family roots lay deep in New England; sons

---

[127] Per Marshall, C.J., in Mayor of New York v. Miln, 8 Pet. 122.

commonly attended college (generally Yale), and became lawyers (sometimes judges) or ministers. Strong graduated in 1828, with a reputation for devotion to serious study and an indebtedness that had enabled him to complete the course. He taught school, presently at an academy in New Jersey, where concurrently he read law with Garret D. Wall, later a Senator and judge of the State's highest court. When finances permitted he completed his preparation at Yale Law School.

Late in 1832 he opened his office at Reading, Pennsylvania. Here he prospered in his profession, married and raised a family, served on the city council and the school board, was director of a bank and an officer in two local railroads. As "a Democrat of the Old School" he represented his district in Congress from 1847 to 1851. When in 1857 he was elected to the Supreme Court of Pennsylvania, he was described as being "greatly beloved as a man, and greatly trusted and admired as a jurist."[128] He resigned in 1868, and engaged in a lucrative practice in Philadelphia.

On the issues that arose from the Civil War, Strong's convictions brought him into accord with the Republican party. He was one of a bare majority on the Pennsylvania bench that sustained the draft;[129] it was so, too, with the legal tender legislation.[130] In this he stood with Judge John Meredith Read, a stanch Republican, who in 1869 became importunate in urging that Strong be appointed to the Supreme Court.[131] He had been at work before Stanton was nominated; upon Stanton's death he resumed his efforts, as in this letter of December 25 to Senator Sumner:

> The lamented death of Judge Stanton creates a vacancy which should be filled by Judge Strong who is thoroughly master of our Pennsylvania system of law, which requires a Pennsylvania lawyer for the third circuit, composed of one great Republican State, that has ratified the 15. amendment, and two small democratic States [New Jersey and Delaware] that will reject it.[132]

---

[128] *Pittsburgh Legal News*, 5:279, Dec. 26, 1857, quoting the *Philadelphia Press*. Two vacancies were filled at that time, one of which was caused by the resignation of Jeremiah S. Black to become Attorney General in Buchanan's Cabinet.

[129] Kneedler v. Lane, 45 Pa. St. 238 (1864). Supra, p. 141.

[130] Shollenberger v. Brinton, 52 Pa. St. 9 (1865). Supra, n. 70.

[131] Read (1797–1874) had himself been nominated for a seat on the Court—in February 1845, at the close of Tyler's Administration. The Senate did not act.

[132] Sumner Papers, Harvard Univ. Lib.

This and most of the other letters on the appointments of 1870 are drawn from my article on "Mr. Justice Bradley's Appointment . . . ," cited in note 126 above. In large part, the correspondence came from the retained papers of Justice Bradley, which subsequently were deposited in the New Jersey Historical Society.

What follows also skims from my

XIV: *The* Legal Tender Cases

When on February 7 the President nominated Strong and Bradley, he made no distinction between the vacancy produced by Grier's resignation and the ninth place created by the Act of April 10. Pennsylvanians supporting Strong were fearful—needlessly—that Bradley might be preferred and receive the Court's allotment to the Third Circuit. Hence this letter from F. Carroll Brewster to Senator Sumner:

(Private)

Office of the Attorney General,
PENNSYLVANIA
Harrisburg, Feb: 10*th* 1870.

Hon: Charles Sumner
Senator
Sir,

. . . .

That slight acquaintance may be my apology for addressing you upon a subject which the Penna: Judiciary & Bar have much at heart—viz: the confirmation of Judge Strong for the Supreme Bench.

I hear of a rumor that an effort may be made to defeat him in order that Judge Bradley may be assigned here instead of to Georgia.

In common with thousands of our citizens who respect Judge Bradley we trust that no slight will be put upon Judge Strong.

An absurd report is also started that he is not a Republican. If years of unfaltering devotion to our principles can give claim to that title—Judge Strong has certainly earned it.

Of pure character—spotless integrity—high-toned patriotism & profound learning—I know no Jurist or Republican who has stronger claims.

. . . .

One who came to have an intimate acquaintance with Justice Strong left this accurate characterization: he was

tall and of unusually fine appearance, with a head of silvery hair and exceedingly courteous and winning demeanour. His countenance was expressive of great dignity and benevolence, and he was very

---

detailed accounts in "The Education of a Justice. Mr. Justice Bradley and Some of His Colleagues," *Stanf. L. Rev.*, 1:217–55 (1949), and my lectures on "What Makes a Great Justice? Mr. Justice Bradley and the Supreme Court, 1870–1892," in Boston University *Bacon Lectures on the Constitution of the United States, 1940–1950* (Boston: Boston University Press, 1953), 425–85; *Boston Univ. L. Rev.*, 30:49–102 (1950). Reference is also made to my lecture on Bradley at the University of Chicago Law School, included in their collection, *Mr. Justice* (Kurland & Dunham, eds.), pp. 69–95 in the edition of 1956, pp. 65–91 in the edition of 1964.

modest, unassuming and gracious. He was a deeply religious man, and perhaps somewhat excessive in the strictness with which he regarded his religious duties, and the careful observance of the Lord's Day. He was indeed a pillar in the church, and for many years was president of the American Tract Society.[133]

When by reason of the stress resulting from the war, some men felt a need to place the nation upon a deeper spiritual foundation, Strong became president of an association to secure an amendment to the Constitution's Preamble, to insert an acknowledgement of "Almighty God as the source of all authority and power in civil government, the Lord Jesus Christ as the Ruler of all nations, and His revealed will as the supreme law of the land . . . ." Presently the association published a journal, *The Christian Statesman.*

What might be viewed as Justice Strong's unaffected piety became, to other eyes, a threatening intolerance. Thus one of Senator Sumner's correspondents, reading of "the almost certain appointment" of Strong, wrote to urge that he should not be confirmed:

> I enter my protest . . . as a Jew, because Judge Strong is the head and front of a body of gentlemen [advocating the amendment] to acknowledge the Christian Religion *only* as the sole religion of the nation, . . . thereby excluding Jews & others from the benefits which the constitution now gives to all of every creed.[134]

To oppose Strong's association a Liberal League was formed, with a publication, *The Index.* In that journal for 1873 there appeared an article, "Who is Judge Strong?", by Elizur Wright. It was a tirade against the overturning of *Hepburn v. Griswold,* with which he merged his antipathy toward Strong's effort to amend the Constitution. The *Hepburn* decision, he wrote, had seemed to make the resumption of specie payments a necessity. "But the voice of Wall Street (clink of dollars) was too potent to allow the promise to be performed. . . . [By a reversal] the millennium of gold-gamblers, cornerers, and sharp-bargainers could be indefinitely prolonged. It was done by finding two lawyers who were smart enough to argue the seal from the face of a bond, and who could be depended on for the still more difficult job of reversing with some show of argument the Chief Justice's almost self-evidently righteous decision. Their names were STRONG and BRADLEY." "Having judicially dethroned and beheaded honesty, [Strong] seeks politically

---

[133] Theron G. Strong, *Landmarks of a Lawyer's Lifetime* (New York: Dodd, Mead and Co., 1914), 22. The author's father, Judge Theron R.

Strong (1802-73) of New York, was Justice Strong's first cousin.

[134] Edward J. Mawson of Philadelphia, Jan. 3, 1870. Sumner Papers, Harvard Univ. Lib.

to enthrone and establish religion by law. Have the followers of the Lamb made up their minds to rush into politics under the leadership of the fox?"

Wright (1804–85), like Strong, came of an old Connecticut family, had worked his way through Yale and graduated with distinction, had taught in an academy, and then had thrown himself into the advocacy of Abolition. Presently he turned upon the unsound practices of life insurance companies as a "lobby for the widow and orphan." In this field his work was uniquely constructive.

While the diatribe was unreasoning and wholly unfounded, in moral earnestness Elizur Wright was fully the equal of William Strong. In the collision of men of such worth one may see the vindication of a Constitution that secures tolerance for religious belief and disbelief. One may see, too, the need for the greatest reserve when one reads allegations of corruption on the Supreme Court.[135]

The rise of Joseph P. Bradley (1813–92) makes a still more remarkable story. Born on a small farm in the town of Berne, near Albany, New York, he was the eldest of twelve children in a family of sturdy colonial stock. An extraordinary power to think through problems, and a yearning for an education, were early displayed. In the autumn of 1831—after he had devoured all the books within reach, and had raised himself far beyond what the country school afforded—he declared his bold decision: he would go to New York City, obtain a clerkship, and by his earnings proceed to an academic education. An early freeze caused the last steamboat to depart ahead of time, just as the youth arrived at the Albany wharf! Returning to Berne, he encountered the new dominie of the Reformed Dutch Church, one of his former teachers, "who had always predicted that I would turn out something above the common run of country boys." The upshot was that the youth was taken under the minister's roof and prepared for Rutgers, the college fostered by the Reformed Dutch.

Bradley looked strange indeed when he arrived at college, clad in a home-made, homespun suit. His worth, however, was soon recognized; the faculty permitted him to complete the course in less than three years.

---

[135] Wright's letter, dated Boston, February 23, 1873, appeared in *The Index* of that year, at p. 132. On him, and on the editor of *The Index*, Francis E. Abbot, there are articles in the D.A.B.

The immoderacy of Wright's judgments is reflected in his participation in a movement to substitute Frémont for Lincoln as candidate in 1864. Ann. Cyc. 1864, 791.

The movement for a religious amendment is related in Philip Schaff's "Church and State in the United States," *Papers of the Am. Hist. Assn.*, 2:385 (1888). The effort to secure such an amendment has persisted through a century.

Wright's contribution to the regulation of the insurance business is mentioned infra, pp. 1398–99.

Among his classmates of 1836 were Frederick T. Frelinghuysen (1817–1885), later Senator and Secretary of State, and Cortland Parker (1818–1907), later president of the American Bar Association—lifetime associates.

He served his apprenticeship for the bar in the office of a Newark lawyer. However, as Bradley recalled, "I adopted my own course of study and frequently had mutual examinations with Frelinghuysen . . . . The result was that when we were examined for Attorney's license in November 1839, I had no difficulty in answering all questions propounded . . . ."[136]

In recalling his entry into practice, Bradley mentioned details that become relevant to his appointment, thirty years later.

> [In 1840] I received a proposal from John P. Jackson Esq. to enter into partnership with him in Newark. He was secretary and attorney of The New Jersey Railroad and Transportation Company, and practically the Superintendent of the road. Being unable to attend to all his engagements, he desired the association of some young man who would do the professional work required by his law business, and share with him the emoluments. This was exactly what I desired. . . . The cases which . . . came into my hands, soon brought me into notice; and from that day forth I never lacked employment in my profession. My connection with railroad cases took its origin from that partnership, and brought me to the notice of other institutions—the Camden and Amboy, and Morris and Essex Companies,—from which I afterwards received frequent employment.

Camden & Amboy, the most important of Bradley's clients, was grantee of an exclusive right to transport by rail across the State, on the line from New York toward Philadelphia and Washington. As was his professional duty, Bradley defended his client's interest—notably during and after the war, when in the New Jersey courts and before Congressional committees, he resisted the efforts of rival interests (supported by an aroused public) to break the New Jersey monopoly and establish a national "air route" between New York City and the Capital.

The Pennsylvania Railroad, with terminus at Philadelphia, wanted access to New York without dependence upon Camden & Amboy. Senator Simon Cameron of Pennsylvania had a large personal stake in the matter. By 1869, when Bradley began actively to seek a judicial appointment, it appeared that the conflict of interest between the Pennsylvania and the United Companies of New Jersey (which included Camden & Amboy) would be reconciled by a lease to the former of the

---

[136] The muscularity of his self-discipline is illustrated in "The Education of a Justice . . . ," cited in note 132 above.

entire properties of the latter. Until the Pennsylvania was made secure, however, Cameron would oppose appointment to the Court of the counsel of Camden & Amboy, who might as a Justice take the same restrictive view of the Congressional power over interstate commerce that he had been presenting in arguments in the New Jersey courts and before Congress.[137]

In tracing Bradley's approach to a judgeship we go back to Senator Trumbull's bill, introduced on Monday, January 18, 1869, to increase the membership of the Supreme Court to nine, and to create nine Circuit Judgeships.[138] Although that failed for want of President Johnson's signature, a similar measure, which also carried the provision for salary after resignation, became the Act of April 10, 1869. George Harding (1827–1902), an able Philadelphia lawyer with excellent political connections, was in Washington at the moment Trumbull's bill was filed; it occurred to him that the Circuit Judgeship might serve as a stepping stone whereby his friend Bradley could reach the Supreme Court as Grier's successor. On Sunday evening, January 17, he wrote:

D[r] Bradley

A bill will be introduced tomorrow in both houses with the sanction of the Supreme Court providing for 9 new Circuit Judges—1 for each circuit—They are to hold all circuit courts just as the Supreme Judges do—but not sit at Washington. The Supreme Judges will hold longer sessions & assist in holding Circuits only when they see fit—As soon as I heard about this bill (which will go through) I thought of you—& went up to see Grier & named you—He was delighted with the idea then I touched on his intention as to resigning. He is feeling very well just now & says if he resigns he will die for want of something to do—so we agreed that if you will take the Circuit Judgeship when created, *he* will go up to Grant and ask it of him for you as a personal favor & get the endorsement of the bench if need be. I will get Philad[a] and Bakewell[139] shall get Pittsburg to ask it.

If you take this place now Grier says as soon as he feels a little weaker he will resign in your favor on condition that Grant raises you from Circuit Judge to Supreme Judge.

Now Grier told me I might write this to you. Aint he a trump? We can put it through like a streak.[140]

. . . .

[137] I have explained in detail in "Mr. Justice Bradley's Appointment . . . ," cited in note 126 above.

[138] Supra, p. 487.

[139] William Bakewell, a leading patent lawyer of Pittsburgh; a Whig and later a Republican.

[140] Harding expected that Grier would have "much influence" with Grant, soon to be inaugurated.

As the D.A.B. article explains, Harding had become a foremost patent lawyer. It remains his unhappy distinction that he and his associate Edwin M. Stanton were the disdainful Eastern lawyers whose treatment

Harding was pertinacious and adept in marshaling support, as his numerous bulletins to Bradley make evident. Thus on March 15 he told of a reconnaissance in Washington. It appeared that the bill creating the Circuit Judgeships would pass. "Not only will Judge Grier urge you; but the whole court will be brought to unite on you. Judge Swayne said, It would be a great satisfaction to us all to have Mr Bradley on this bench, we entertain the highest opinion of him. . . . Stanton's son promised me to keep his father informed so that at the proper moment he would put in his oar."

Interest in the Circuit Judgeship was based on the calculation that it would lead to the Supreme Bench.

In late March, George M. Robeson, Attorney General of New Jersey (and three months later a member of Grant's Cabinet) carried to Washington this recommendation from the Judges of the State's highest court:

> To His Excellency, Ulysses S. Grant
>> President of the United States
>
>> The undersigned members of the Court of Errors and Appeals of the State of New Jersey do respectfully recommend Joseph P. Bradley Esq of New Jersey as a proper and suitable person to be appointed as a Circuit Judge of the United States under the reorganization of the Federal Courts.
>
>> He is a Scholar and a man of culture. He has long been distinguished for the extent and accuracy of his legal knowledge, and for the marked clearness and strength of his intellect in the application of his learning. He joins to these the power of discrimination, and the practical common sense which are as necessary to a judge as learning and power. His known integrity and high toned principle will place him in that regard above suspicion.
>
>> We have each of us known him well and personally for years. Some of us as his associates at the bar, others as a Counsellor in our Courts. And we earnestly recommend the appointment as one that will secure to the country a most able and efficient judge, and that will secure to his ability and merits an appropriate and well deserved reward.
>
>> Trenton March 1869

---

of Abraham Lincoln, retained as their associate in the McCormick Reaper case before Justice McLean in the Circuit Court at Cincinnati in 1855, led the latter to exclaim, "I am going home to study law! . . . These college bred fellows have reached Ohio, they will soon be in Illinois, and when they come, . . . I will be ready for them."

Beveridge, *Abraham Lincoln, 1809–1858*, 2 vols. (Boston and New York: Houghton Mifflin Co., 1928), I, 576–83.

The Philadelphia Inquirer, leading Republican daily, was published by Harding's brother, as successor to their father.

XIV: *The* Legal Tender Cases

Among Bradley's papers was a copy of this recommendation, dated March 31:

To His Excellency
Ulysses S. Grant
    President of the United States
Dear Sir

I understand that a bill has passed or is about to pass Congress providing for the appointment of nine new Circuit Judges.

Presuming that the result of my observation of the men practising in the 3rd Circuit may be of some value to you in making your selection, I take the liberty of stating to you that Mr. Joseph P. Bradley of Newark N. J. seems to me to be very thoroughly fitted for one of those Judgeships. He is an accomplished and sound lawyer —and is especially conversant with matters of Federal Law coming before the Courts of the United States. He would make a most excellent Judge.

                                    Very Respectfully
                                        Yours
                                        R. C. Grier

The Act of April 10, creating the nine Circuit Judgeships and authorizing salary after retirement, would not go into effect until December; and Attorney General Hoar was unwilling to discuss appointments until autumn. Harding learned from Justice Swayne that he and Justice Davis wondered "whether we had not better look direct to the Supreme Judgeship at first." He quoted Stanton as suggesting that it might be well to seek the ninth place on the Supreme Court instead of aiming at Grier's seat [for which, as it turned out, Stanton was himself nominated and confirmed on December 20]. Harding was watching closely; on July 19 he wrote:

> Grier got thro' his fishing & now is down at Deal. He is reported to be in good health. He cannot resign so as to obtain the benefit of the late Act before December next. The other Judges would like him & *Nelson* to take advantage of it & resign immediately thereafter & *they* will bring all their influence to bear to that end.
>
> A kind of pledge was made that he w^d. resign if the bill was passed in its present form. On the other hand the human nature in Grier may tempt him to hold on—It is conceded that his mind is perfectly strong but that the infirmity in his limbs is increasing—
>
> This is the condition of things now. We have plenty of time to watch however for nothing will be done until late in the fall—

In late August Bradley sailed for Europe and, concluding his travels, spent October 4 to 7 at Liverpool, chiefly in the company of

Thomas H. Dudley, the American Consul. Dudley, who had formerly practiced law at Camden and taken a conspicuous part in the organization of the Republican party, was familiar with Bradley's desire for judicial office and with the practical considerations bearing on its achievement. The J. Edgar Thomson mentioned in the following letter of November 6 from Dudley to Bradley was the president of the Pennsylvania Railroad; he and Bradley, according to Bradley's diary, had met in conference as recently as May 12.[141] Dudley wrote:

> I have before me a letter from my friend J Edgar Thomson dated Octr 25 in answer to one I wrote him about you in which he says. *"I am acquainted with Mr. Bradley and will do what I can to favour his confirmation. I can influence Mr Scott*[142] *but Cameron may [oppose] on account of Camden & Amboy having failed in their promises to aid him in his contest with Mr. Garrett of the B & O R R Co.; still I will see what can be done with him."*
>
> Mr Thomson means what he says & no doubt will do all that he can to promote your appointment.

Dudley urged Bradley to hasten the amalgamation of the United Companies of New Jersey with the Pennsylvania Railroad.

Hoar desired a place on the Court, preferably Grier's. Grier was reluctant to quit. William McKennan of Pittsburgh, a solid Republican and a friend of Grant's, was seeking the Circuit Judgeship.[143] For Bradley, this was a tight situation. On Wednesday, November 17, Harding wrote from Philadelphia:

> Dr Bradley
>
> As the time draws nigh I get nervous. I ran down Tuesday night to look the coast over. Called on Judge Grier saw Mrs Beck [a daughter] & him for an hour. They are moving on to Capitol Hill— He feels his oats & doesnt talk of resigning. I sounded him but he wouldnt respond to my touch. I saw Swayne—Nelson, & Davis— They are greatly exercised at his not resigning—They declared they were going to crowd him about Dec 1 '69. He sleeps on the bench, drops his head down & looks very badly. Congress will also crowd him if he dont resign—. . . . The president personally would like to appoint McKennan of Westn Penna on the Circuit. Hoare [*sic*] has

---

141 Thomson will figure prominently in the account of litigation to enforce municipal bonds issued in aid of railroad construction. Infra, ch. 17.

142 John Scott, Republican, sat in the Senate from 1869 to 1875; thereafter he was general counsel of the Pennsylvania Railroad. Harding advised Bradley that Scott "is only another name for Cameron"—his senior colleague. But in the end he supported confirmation.

143 McKennan (1816–93) received the appointment, and served until 1891.

determined to take the Southern Judicial Seat if Grier dont resign before Dec 10—He would much prefer however that Grier should resign first & he take Grier's place and then give you the Southern Circuit—He is thoroughly unselfish *you perceive*—

. . . .

Nelson, Davis & Swayne are loud in calling for you & they mutter at Grier saying how long—how long—

It is supposed that Mrs Smith [Grier's other daughter] & Mrs Beck support Grier in his wish to remain on the bench with a view to maintain their social status another winter in Washington—The Court are provoked at this—much of their time being spent in canvassing the subject.

All hands agree that you do well not to press for the Circuit Court Judgeship in the present condition of things. We are now watching the succession of the Atty Generalship. . . .

If, as appeared possible, the President selected William Strong to be Attorney General in place of Hoar, and McKennan became Circuit Judge, that would facilitate the appointment of Bradley, a Jerseyman, to the Supreme Court. Harding concluded:

Perhaps it will all be for the best if Hoare gets slid into the Southern Circuit & then you are left alone when Grier resigns. Perhaps this may be a Providential delay on Grier's part. . . .

George M. Robeson, now Secretary of the Navy, wrote to Bradley on December 8 that "I think the President is set on his friend McKennan for *Circuit* Judge. That dont hurt you at all—If Grier would only resign we could fix it all up in a week." Robeson continued:

The only possible chance against you is *Stanton*—He I think wants the Sup. Judgeship I dont think he can get it but at all events his chances are weakened by McKennan's appt—You are *on the list* as Grier's successor and only Stanton can hurt you—This is all strictly private . . . .

When on December 8 the President sent to the Senate his nominations for the Circuit Judgeships, McKennan was on the list. With the ninth seat on the Court supposedly reserved for Hoar, the attention of Bradley and his supporters became focused upon Justice Grier.

On December 9—less than a fortnight after Grier's strange performance at the conference where *Hepburn v. Griswold* was decided[144] —Chase and Nelson carried to him the message indicated by the following note from Mrs. Beck to George Harding:

---

[144] Supra, p. 716.

Washington:

Dec. 9ᵗʰ/69–

My dear Mr Harding,

The Chief & Judge Nelson waited on Pa this mor'g. to ask him to resign saying that the politicians are determined to oust him, & if he don't, they will repeal the law giving the retiring salaries.

Pa told them if they wished him to resign he would do so, to take effect the 1" of Feb.

What do you say to all this? Do you think he ought to do so? Excuse this rapid scribble—. . . .

Harding enclosed the note in a letter of December 11 to Bradley. He had hastened to Washington: "I saw Grier immediately at his rooms —the result is that he has agreed with me to put his resignation in your favor into Robeson's hands . . . ." (Of course a Justice could not effectively resign in another's favor.) Harding reported further:

The only troubles now are 1st Grier wishes to resign *now to take effect* February 1. Can Grant now appoint to such a vacancy. 2*ndly* Robeson dreads a little that possibly Stanton may be pressed in certain quarters. I have always looked forward to Stanton being Chief Justice when the time arrives & I hardly think his health will admit of his now being made a judge—I shall not change *my* programme.—Judge Hoar does not yet know of Grier's intended resignation nor does any one—He awaits my direction—I wish I could get him to send it in as of this date but fear I cannot without pulling him too hard—He has taken his rooms in Washn until 1st of Febry—. . . .

Developments now crowded one upon another. On December 15 Hoar was nominated to the new seat on the Court. On December 20 Stanton was nominated to become a Justice on February 1, *vice* Grier, resigned; this nomination was confirmed instanter, by vote of 46 to 11. On December 22 the Senate Judiciary Committee reported adversely on Hoar, and after debate in Executive Session the nomination was laid on the table. On December 24 Stanton died.

Once more, Strong and Bradley were leading contenders.

While it was not until February 3 that Hoar was actually rejected (by vote of 24 to 33), it had been evident since December 22 that a majority of the Senators were hostile. On December 28 Senator Lot Morrill of Maine wrote to his colleague Sumner:

The opposition to Judge Hoar is all wrong & frightfully *impolitic*. Can he not be confirmed upon sober second thought?

If the Sup. Court can not be made a break water, through such material as the lamented Stanton, & Hoar, who can predict the mischief that may come to the nation from unfriendly interpretation of the war & reconstruction measures of Congress?[145]

This reflects the pervading awareness of the magnitude of impending constitutional issues on which the opinions of the two new Justices—whoever they might be—would probably be decisive.

With the new year came a development from a new quarter: Senators from the recently readmitted States—all Republicans—were demanding representation from their section on the Court. They insisted that Hoar of Massachusetts was not acceptable for the place which almost certainly would carry with it assignment to the Fifth, or Southern, Circuit. Other Senators who had reasons of their own for disliking Hoar[146] gladly made this sectional objection an excuse for voting to reject. But the Southerners' program went further. As had been forecast in the press a fortnight earlier,[147] Senator Benjamin F. Rice of Arkansas, a member of the Judiciary Committee, introduced on January 13 a bill to alter the judicial system by breaking up the Third Circuit, and erecting an additional Circuit in the South by a separation of those States into a Southeastern and a Southwestern group.[148] One purpose in the minds of some was to produce a situation wherein Judge Henry Clay Caldwell of the federal District Court for Arkansas would become the logical appointee to one of the vacancies on the Court. Caldwell (1832–1915) was a man of upright character and marked ability, an Iowa lawyer who had marched into Little Rock as a colonel of cavalry and had remained as a Judge by appointment of President Lincoln. He was receiving the support of Justice Miller and the Iowa delegation.[149]

---

[145] Sumner Papers, Harvard Univ. Lib.

[146] Such as his "peculiar sweetness of temper," mentioned in the Washington dispatch, *New York Herald*, Feb. 8, 1870. The *Boston Advertiser* —which catered to refined and intelligent people—published on March 22 a news letter wherein Hoar was described as "the official who, more than any one else, has frustrated the plans and schemes of office jobbers and trading politicians." Specifically, the Attorney General had insisted upon first-rate appointments to the Circuit Judgeships. On June 20, upon leaving office, he wrote to Justice Bradley: "there is no service which I have been able to render to the country which I look back upon with such entire satisfaction, as upon the share which I have had in filling the judicial positions . . . ."

[147] Washington dispatch, *New York Tribune*, Jan. 1, 1870.

[148] S. 387, 41st Cong., 2d Sess.

[149] On December 31, 1869, Miller wrote to his brother-in-law in Texas:

I am making a strenuous effort for a circuit composed of Texas Arkansas Louisiana and Mississippi for which I hope to have my friend Caldwell appointed.

The case of Hoar is hopeless. There is no chance of his confirmation.

Fairman, *Mr. Justice Miller*, 344. Judge Caldwell is frequently mentioned therein.

On February 7, 1870—while the Rice Bill was under reference to the Judiciary Committee—the President sent to the Senate the nominations of Bradley and Strong to be Associate Justices.

CONFIRMATION OF STRONG AND BRADLEY

THE SENATE, without division, confirmed the nomination of Strong on February 18. But then Senator Rice moved to reconsider; that kept Strong in suspense until, on March 1, Rice gave up and withdrew his motion. On Monday, March 14, Strong took the oath required of all officers, and the oath prescribed for Judges, and was seated.[150] On Monday next, after the Saturday conference, the Court made a new order of allotment: Strong was assigned to the Third Circuit, while the Fifth Circuit was left open.

On March 21 Bradley's nomination was confirmed by vote of 46 to 9. The nine opponents comprised eight Southern Republicans and

---

[150] Chase's diary for March 14 recorded:

At Capitol—our new associate Judge Strong appeared—the test oath was administered in the Reception room by the Clerk in the presence of all the Judges—the regular oath at the Clerks table after Court opened—he going in with us & pausing there—he then took his seat extreme right.

The diary for 1870 is in the Library of Congress.

The judicial oath, prescribed by the Judiciary Act of 1789, has been explained. Supra at p. 63. It remains to this day. 28 U.S. Code, sec. 453.

The "test oath" to which Strong subscribed was the oath required generally of those entering upon an office under the United States—then the iron-clad oath of July 2, 1862, 12 Stat. 502. This remained notwithstanding *Ex parte* Garland, 4 Wall. 333 (1867): that decision applied only to the statute of January 24, 1865, which extended the requirement to attorneys in federal courts.

An Act of July 11, 1868, 15 Stat. 85, permitted one relieved of disability by Congress to enter upon a federal office upon taking only the prospective part of the oath: that he would support and defend the Con-

stitution and bear true faith and allegiance. This corresponded with Section 3 of the Fourteenth Amendment which, while disabling those who had joined in the rebellion after having taken an oath of office to support the Constitution, had permitted this disability to be removed "by vote of two-thirds of each House." The Fourteenth Amendment was declared to be in effect on July 21, 1868.

An anomaly resulted: the oath of 1862 remained applicable to such as had not taken an oath of office prior to engaging in the rebellion. The Act of February 15, 1871, 16 Stat. 412, enabled such persons to enter upon federal office upon taking the prospective part of the oath.

The Revised Statutes of 1875 prescribed the iron-clad oath in Section 1756—then in Section 1757 permitted the exceptions provided in 1868 and 1871.

By the Act of May 13, 1884, 23 Stat. 21, 22, Section 1756 was repealed; all entering upon an office were directed to take the oath prescribed in Section 1757. Justice L.Q.C. Lamar, confirmed in 1888—the Court's first ex-Confederate—was also the first after 1862 to take the short form of oath.

Senator Cameron of Pennsylvania.[151] Bradley took his oaths and was seated on March 23. On Monday, April 4, a new order was entered whereby he was allotted to the Fifth Circuit.

These statements tell the outcome of entangled efforts now briefly to be explained.

On February 8 the Senate referred the two nominations to its Judiciary Committee.

On February 9, Chairman Trumbull reported the Rice Bill, S. 387, with an amendment. Besides changing the Circuits so as to give two to the South at the expense of the existing Third, the Judiciary Committee would add this section:

> That the justices of the Supreme Court of the United States shall be residents of their respective circuits, and vacancies now or here-after existing in said court shall, in every case, be filled by a resident of the circuit: *Provided*, That the Chief Justice may preside in any circuit to which he may be allotted without a change of residence.[152]

This meant that, in the appointment of an Associate Justice, the President's selection would have been confined to the persons already resident within the Circuit which at the moment had no Circuit Justice; and by implication, an Associate Justice must not change his residence to any place outside the Circuit to which he belonged.[153] Moreover, this would apply to *existing* vacancies: *two* when the bill with the amendment was reported to the Senate, *one* when, on March 3, S. 387 first came up for debate.

At once Senator W. T. Willey of West Virginia moved to amend the amendment to read "That the justices of the Supreme Court of the United States shall reside in their respective circuits: *Provided*, That the Chief Justice may preside in any circuit to which he may be allotted without a change of residence."[154] This would have left the President free to choose from the entire country. An Associate Justice could comply with the statute by changing his residence, if need be, to some place within the Circuit to which the Court allotted him.

---

[151] The actions of the Senate on these nominations are recorded in the *Journal of the Executive Proceedings of the Senate*, volume 17, between pp. 359 and 402.

[152] Cong. Globe, 41–2, 1127 (Feb. 8, when the bill was reported), 1651 (Mar. 3, when it was first discussed).

[153] Being extemporized, the measure and the Committee's amendment disclosed a failure adequately to consider implications. One inconvenience in the proposed rearrangement of the Circuits appeared at once. William B. Woods, ex-Ohioan who had settled in Alabama after the war, had just been confirmed as Circuit Judge for the *Fifth* Circuit; but as S. 387 was drawn, his residence would be within the proposed *Fourth*. To meet this difficulty the Committee would amend the bill to interchange those numerical designations. Ibid., 1651.

[154] Ibid., 1651. Mar. 3.

Willey's amendment remained pending until, when S. 387 came up for further debate on May 31, it was adopted without opposition.[155] By that time Bradley had been holding his courts in the Fifth Circuit, disposing of difficult cases with masterly expedition[156] and commanding the admiration and confidence of the bar.[157]

On February 14 the Judiciary Committee reported favorably on the two nominations. Thenceforth Rice endeavored to block consideration until Congress acted on his S. 387. On February 18 Cameron obtained the confirmation of Strong—but Rice held that in suspense under his motion to reconsider, until March 1. Next day Rice moved to postpone consideration of Bradley to March 21, and that was carried by a narrow vote.

Throughout these days, Bradley's friends were vigilant. Particularly effective was Frederick T. Frelinghuysen. While he had ceased to be a Senator on March 3, 1869—being succeeded by John P. Stockton, Democrat—he had easy access to his old colleagues. Bradley was on excellent terms with Stockton, who, however, had to take care lest approbation from him react prejudicially. As he wrote, "I say . . . that you have been considered at the head of the bar since I have been at it, but you are an *extreme politician* in your views." He added that "Old 'Cameron' is mad, he thinks that you didn't stand up to some Rail Road contract . . . ."

Frelinghuysen at once assured Senators that Bradley would not "contest with Strong for circuits"; also that "you thought you could best discharge your duties by residing in the Cir.ᵗ & that you intended to." Some Senators, he explained, had placed their opposition to Hoar on the

---

[155] Ibid., 3942.

[156] Including a phase of the *Slaughter House Cases*, infra, pp. 1327–35.

[157] He held the Circuit Court for the Eastern District of Texas, at Galveston, from May 9 to 25. William P. Ballinger, Justice Miller's brother-in-law and a leader at that bar, gave this report:

he did a great deal of business, holding court several days until nearly dark. He was a new dispensation to us—contrasting very strongly with our manner of judges for a long time past. I like him extremely—and that was the sentiment of the Bar. He is a thorough ready lawyer, and the most complete *business man* I have ever seen on the bench—becomes the perfect master of the

case, down to its minutiae, with a facility and dexterity very admirable. His anxiety to get through here rendered him a little impatient in some instances; but he seemed ready to admit any mistake into which he might fall, and commanded the utmost confidence of the bar. We were unprepared—didn't expect him to do anything—and I was conscious that the Bar didn't show to good advantage, professionally, before him; but still I think, he was pleased with its deportment and judged favorably of its ability.

Letter to Justice Miller, quoted in my lecture on Bradley, in *Mr. Justice*, cited in note 132 above. P. 84, ed. of 1956; p. 80, ed. of 1964.

ground that he did not reside in the Fifth Circuit and would not agree to do so; they were anxious that Bradley relieve them from embarrassment on that point.

Senators wanted assurance concerning Bradley's outlook on constitutional issues—on which Frelinghuysen could speak from intimate association. Thus, as he wrote Bradley on February 16, "[Senator] Howard [of Michigan] told me he would like to have voted for you but he must have written evidence of how you stood on important questions —I remembered you had told me you had written to George [Harding] —I drove down & got letter gave it to Howard—& he is well satisfied & goes you strong." Senator Drake wanted like evidence, but Frelinghuysen left it to Howard to satisfy him.

What Bradley had written to Harding is not known; none of the correspondence moving in that direction has been found. In 1862 he had run for a seat in Congress on the Administration Union ticket—unsuccessfully, in a Democratic stronghold. On that occasion the *New York Evening Post* described him as "an eminent lawyer . . . [who] has never been, before this canvass, actively engaged in politics"; a Whig and then a Republican. "When the rebels took up arms he became an earnest supporter of the war, and has steadily opposed any rose-water treatment of the rebellion."[158] In 1868, as Republican candidate for presidential elector, he took an active part in the campaign. The retained notes from which he spoke disclose a thoroughgoing nationalist defending "the measures of the great Union party"; among these he particularly supported "the National legal tender."

During the war, when the exclusive rights of the Camden & Amboy and Baltimore & Ohio between New York and Washington had provoked nationwide indignation, rival railroad interests besought Congress to create a national "air-route" overriding the exclusive grants by the New Jersey and Maryland legislatures. In 1863 and 1864, when that proposal was being considered by committees of the 37th and the 38th Congress, Bradley was repeatedly appearing to argue his client's case against such legislation.[159]

In the Second Session of the 41st Congress, H.R. 19, to authorize the building of a military and postal railway from Washington to New York, was being actively debated in the House on March 3, 9, 10 and 16, 1870—the moment when Bradley's nomination was pending in the Senate. Representative Thomas Swann, Democrat—former mayor of Baltimore, governor, and president of the Baltimore & Ohio —was telling the House that

---

[158] Nov. 3, 1862.
[159] This is explained more fully in "Mr. Justice Bradley's Appointment ,

. . . ," cited in note 126 above. See pp. 981–88, 1030–33.

This power over their own soil in the construction of roads and canals, the States have always claimed and exercised. The Federal Government has never seen fit to interfere with it. Our whole system of internal improvement has grown up under State laws. . . .

"No State would be safe" if Congress could grant a right of way over her soil without her consent.[160]

What did the former counsel of Camden & Amboy really think on that question? Senator Zach Chandler of Michigan raised this with Frelinghuysen, who on March 9 wrote from Newark:

Friend Chandler—

You asked me the other day whether Mr Bradley was as heretical on the question of the power of Congress to make internal improvements as I was.

Let me say a word on that subject. It has never been adjudicated directly by the courts . . . & is therefore a fair question for counsel to argue about as may best suit their sides. . . . [At some length he set out considerations pro and con, without expressing a personal conclusion.] The doctrine of internal improvements is an old Whig doctrine & I am an old Whig & so is Mr. Bradley. I would not now ask Mr Bradley to authorize an expression of opinion on these vexed questions, but I can say as I told you the other day, that more than a year ago he advised me not to take ground in the Senate that Congress did not possess *power* to make internal improvements without the consent of the states. . . .[161]

Two names, now to be mentioned, should be identified. Albert W. Markley of Camden was an important figure in the United Companies of New Jersey: he went to Washington to assist Harding and Frelinghuysen. Absolom B. Woodruff was an attorney at Paterson: he made a trip to the capital, and reported:

> Arlington House
> March 16/70

(Private
&
Conf)
Dear Bradley,

I had an interview with Cameron today—I think he is inclined to go against you. He said that he told Mr. Markley that if you would sign a letter to the effect that your opinions did not coincide with the opinion by Ch. J. Chase, on the legal tender act lately delivered—& that you did not think the Constitution prohibited Con-

---

[160] Cong. Globe, 41–2, 1845. Mar. 10.   [161] Chandler Papers, L.C.

gress from chartering a railroad from here to New York—there would be no difficulty in your confirmation. That all he required was to *see* the letter & that Mr. Markley might do as he pleased with it afterwards.

He said if you would write such a one to me, or to any one else, under the same conditions he would have no difficulty in advocating your confirmation that he felt disposed to do all he conscientiously could for you &c &c.

I told him that asking a pledge from a candidate for a judicial office was a very delicate matter—& suggested that your former whig principles, and your opinions generally known to your friends & acquaintances, as to the general construction that ought to be given to the Constitution, I thought ought to be satisfactory to Senators.

He *seemed* to be very earnest in his opinion that there was danger we might have the Sup. Court so constituted, as that they would nullify practically all the results of the sacrifices of the Republicans in the late war. I assured him that no one in the country entertained stronger opinions than yourself, during the struggle as to the propriety of the energetic measures taken by the general Government. He *appeared* to be pleased to hear this, & said he would see me again.

I saw Mr. Chandler, who is manifestly *tinctured* at least with the same fears expressed by Senator Cameron, but expressed himself very much pleased with the strong Republican character I gave you, & said he did not think you ought to be required to give pledges. But, he did not *say* he would vote for your confirmation. I think he will on a *direct* vote, but, I think he supposes he can get a Southern man by means of his Districting Bill [S. 387]. . . .

On that same day—March 16—Senator Stockton wrote to explain the delay resulting from Rice's motion to defer action on Bradley until March 21: "The object of postponing was to press the bill [S. 387] first, the strength of the bill united with it the Southern vote and Cameron and national R.R. interests." But now it was clear that S. 387 could not pass, at any rate not before March 21. He mentioned eight Senators who in the meantime had come over to Bradley's side—among them, Chandler and Howard of Michigan. "Cameron has behaved badly, but we have gained by his treachery a strong personal hold on the Senate." "Stewart and Edmunds have just told me that we must succeed. . . . I have just told Stewart I would have every one in my command [that is, the Democrats] in their seats on Monday [March 21] at 3 o'clock and he says he will then make the move."

And so at last the question of confirmation was carried, over the opposition of Cameron and eight Southern Republicans. "The selection of Mr. Bradley," commented *The Nation*, "is probably as good a one as could have been made had the bar been searched over."

"There is, perhaps, nothing in which Grant's Administration has won such honorable distinction as in its judicial appointments." The carpet-bag Senators had been "unscrupulous" and "unblushing" in their treatment of Hoar and then Bradley.[162]

S. 387, having failed of its immediate purpose, was of little further interest. With Willey's amendment (to require the Associate Justices to reside within their respective Circuits) it was passed on June 1 and sent to the House—which accepted the report of its Judiciary Committee that the measure should be tabled.[163]

One brief incident, however, is worth recording. It concerns Senator Drake, the implacable. He had discovered that, prior to his advent, "in 1866, doubtless by inadvertence, there crept into an act of Congress an improper and illegal designation of the Chief Justice of the Supreme Court of the United States. . . ."[164] In the Act of July 23, 1866, to fix the number of Justices, there appeared the title "Chief Justice of the United States"; the error had been repeated in the Act of April 10, 1869. He found that Chase had so styled himself in the impeachment proceedings.

Thus what Chase had accomplished covertly[165] was brought into view (although his agency in achieving "this impropriety" was not mentioned).

Drake proposed an additional section to S. 387, to correct the statutes of 1866 and 1869 and to declare that the title was "Chief Justice of the Supreme Court of the United States." Without a word, the amendment was accepted. But then this failed when the House tabled S. 387.

FURTHER ARGUMENT IS ORDERED

ON FRIDAY, MARCH 25, 1870, Attorney General Hoar made motions for the early hearing of certain cases wherein the Government had a special concern. Two of these, involving legal tender, had thrice been "passed for the present" while the Court was sorting out the issues in the other cases mentioned above: they were *Latham's and Deming's Appeals* from the Court of Claims, wherein contractors sought the difference between the gold and the paper money value of claims on which they had already been paid in Treasury notes.[166] Hoar was frank in saying to the nine Justices that he sought another argument on the constitutional question.

---

[162] 10:200. Mar. 31.
[163] Cong. Globe, 41–2, 3977, June 1; 4864, June 27.
[164] Ibid., 41–2. 3976. June 1.
[165] Supra, pp. 166, 171.

[166] 1 Ct. Cls. 149 and 190 respectively; docketed on Aug. 17 and Nov. 26, 1866, respectively, they now stood Nos. 6 and 7. See infra, p. 743.
The other matters for which the

Before recreating the struggle that ensued within the Court, let the primary materials be identified. First, we have the Court's Minutes. From the side of the Chief Justice and his Brothers Nelson, Clifford, and Field there is a protest written by the Chief Justice, which was filed—and soon thereafter withdrawn. Two copies, twelve pages long and virtually identical, lie among the Chase Papers in the library of the Historical Society of Pennsylvania. Chase's diary has already been cited. Chapter twenty-eight of the biography by Schuckers, sometime secretary to the Chief Justice, interprets events from the subject's point of view.

Justice Miller on behalf of the new majority, in order to controvert the "very singular paper filed by the Chief Justice in these cases," prepared a counter-statement of facts, which under date of April 30 was signed by the five Justices. When he learned of this the Chief Justice withdrew his own statement from the files.

Justice Miller's original draft contained an account of how "an aged and infirm member of the Court" had changed his vote, and had subsequently been advised to resign.[167] "We do not say he did not agree to the opinion. We only ask, of what value was his concurrence, and of what value is the judgment under such circumstances?" To avoid pain to Grier should the paper come to his knowledge, this entire passage was omitted from the revised draft. Miller preserved it, however, along with the signed statement. Upon his death in 1890, the statement, with the excised passage, was obtained by Justice Bradley and, in accord with ex-Justice Strong, "A statement of facts relating to the order of the Supreme Court of the United States for a re-argument of the Legal-Tender question, in April, 1870," was "printed for private use."[168] In 1902, when all the Justices concerned were dead, the

---

Attorney General sought, and obtained, an order to advance were the then urgent cases of United States v. Tynem, 11 Wall. 88 (1871), and Blyew *et al.* v. United States, 13 Wall. 581 (1872). In the former, certified from the Circuit Court for California, it was held that the Act of Congress of July 14, 1870, to punish crimes against the Naturalization Laws had, by covering the field of a statute of 1813 and imposing new and additional penalties, operated as a repeal; and, there being no reservation as to offenses already committed, an indictment under the earlier statute must be dismissed. Norris v. Crocker, 13

How. 429 (1851), supra, p. 30, was cited and followed.

Blyew, which had been docketed only a week before Hoar's motion, raised a fundamental question under the Civil Rights Act of 1866. See infra, p. 846.

[167] Supra, pp. 716–17.

[168] Long ago I compared, and found the printed copy to be exact, save for a few changes in punctuation.

Also in the Bradley Papers was an undated note from Strong: he wished to share in the cost of printing, and suggested that Hoar, Wager Swayne (the Justice's son), and Justices Harlan, Gray, and Blatchford each be supplied with a copy.

statement appeared in *Miscellaneous Writings of the late Hon. Joseph P. Bradley, edited by a son.*

Then there is a letter of April 21 from Justice Miller to his brother-in-law, referring to the struggle. Other items will be introduced as the account proceeds.

When the Attorney General made his motion, James M. Carlisle, counsel for Latham, was present: he told the Court that he wished an early hearing, "but hoped that the legal tender question would not be reconsidered in his case."

> *He did not at that time intimate in any manner that there had been any agreement of counsel, or any action of the Court, which precluded that question in his case.* [Majority statement, italics in original.]

When the Justices met next day in their weekly conference, Chase made the assertion that an order had been made whereby *Latham and Deming* were to be governed by the decision to be made in *Hepburn v. Griswold*. To quote Chase's diary for Saturday, March 26:

> At Conference—all the judges present—Called up Attorney Generals mo. to assign day for hearing Latham v U.S. & Deming v Same—explained that order was made that the legal tender question, so far as involved in these cases, should be argued in Bronson v Rodes & Hepburn v Griswold, & not in these which were passed on that account: and that the effect of this order was that these cases as to these questions should abide the decision in those. To my surprise this statement though supported by Judges Nelson, Clifford & Field, was controverted by Judges Swayne, Miller & Davis; and to my greater surprise the new Judges, undertook to decide the point against the majority of their brethren. [Next sentence is partly undecipherable.] An order was made against our remonstrance to assign the cases for hearing on Monday Apr. 4.

On Monday, before the Justices went on the Bench, Chase said that if there was no objection he would not announce the order voted on Saturday until there was further conference after adjournment that day. He produced a letter from Mr. Carlisle, insisting that he had a right to expect that what was decided in *Hepburn* would govern his case as well. Postponement of the announcement was agreed, "though with some manifestations of dissatisfaction." After Court opened, a telegram was received from Justice Bradley at Newark: "A violent storm prevented my returning to Washington last evening . . . ."[169]

---

[169] Chase Papers, Hist. Soc. of Pa.

Reply was made that there would be a conference at 3 P.M. Tuesday, pending which Saturday's order was suspended. [Diary and Majority statement.]

The result of the conference was that, in deference to Carlisle's statement, it was agreed to give a hearing on Thursday, March 31.

On that occasion the Attorney General, supporting his motion, referred to the *Hepburn* decision as one that had been made possible by "the judicial opinion of a single man";

> and if (which is a supposable case), it turned out that it was an opinion about which even the deciding Judge . . . had entertained a different opinion at some other time, it would come down to the point that on the differing opinions at different times of his life, of a single man, the whole constitutional power of Congress . . . was to be subverted and set aside . . . .

Hoar's remarks were reported in full in the *New York Tribune* of April 1. While Chase's change of view would fit within the Attorney General's "supposable case," it seems quite possible that he was making a veiled reference to Grier's confusion, in order to press the point later expressed in Justice Miller's statement: Of what value was *Hepburn v. Griswold* under such circumstances?

Carlisle, opposing, gave his view of the history of the legal tender cases in the Court, and renewed his contention that Hepburn should conclude the issue of constitutionality. *"But he did not state or rely on any agreement with counsel for the government . . . , or any express order of the court to that effect."*

> Mr. [A.L.] Merriman, the senior counsel in Deming's case, was present at this argument. He took no part in it. He made no objection to the argument of the legal-tender question in his case, and did not then claim, nor has he ever claimed in court, that that question was precluded by any action of the court, or agreement of counsel. [Majority statement.]

In the conference that was held after the Court rose that Thursday afternoon, as Chase recorded in his diary—

> I recited briefly the facts—Stated the circumstances under which the Court refused to hear the legal tender question argued in these cases . . . . That they were passed because it was doubted if that question really arose in them & expressly because it was directed to be argued in Hepburn v Griswold & Bronson v Rodes in which the decision would be conclusive . . . . That counsel were so informed when the order to pass was made—that no rehearing of a case could be had except on mo of one the maj—that this was an attempt to do by indirection what cannot be done directly. . . .

741

The Chief Justice was here resting his opposition upon two grounds: (1) an alleged order when Latham and Deming were passed over, and (2) a proposition that the Court would not grant a rehearing of a case except on motion of some Justice who had been in the majority. Each point will be examined presently.[170]

Swayne, Miller, Davis and the two new Justices stood their ground. The result was that at the opening of the Court on Friday the Chief Justice announced an order: ". . . that these cases be set down for hearing on all the questions involved in the record on the 2nd Monday in April of this term." Dissent by himself and Nelson, Clifford and Field was noted. [Minutes of April 1.]

When the Court convened on Monday, April 11, Mr. Carlisle was not present. He had sent a letter saying that "he had not had time to prepare for the argument, and that he had an engagement to try a case in New York on Tuesday, which he had not been able to postpone . . . . A telegram was also read stating Mr. Merriman's illness." [Majority statement.] Clarkson N. Potter, on behalf of Carlisle, suggested a postponement. Attorney General Hoar opposed, "and in the course of his remarks spoke of the necessity for an early hearing and decision, because the country is disturbed and will continue to be disturbed until the whole question at issue is settled. . . ." So he was reported in a press dispatch, which related that the Chief Justice had interrupted "with evident feeling"; that Miller replied "with equal feeling"; that Nelson "came to the rescue of the Chief Justice, and Justice Davis spoke up, saying he concurred with Justice Miller." It was "a very lively scene . . . , the oldest lawyers practicing there having witnessed nothing like it . . . ."[171]

The Chief Justice's version of what transpired was recorded in the following memorandum, preserved among the Chase Papers of the Historical Society of Pennsylvania:

Substance of remarks of the Chief Justice and Mr. Justice Nelson; Mr. Potter's suggestion of postponement of argument of Court of Claims cases, made at instance of Mr. Carlisle, being under discussion.

Attorney General, having referred to the cases as being left open for argument on the question of legal tender, the Chief Justice interrupted him to say:

It is proper to say, Mr. Attorney General, that counsel in these cases were distinctly informed, when they were called and passed heretofore, both before and after the argument of those cases in which the legal tender question was decided, that this Court would not hear

---

[170] Infra, pp. 749–50.
[171] *Boston Daily Advertiser,* Apr.

12; (Springfield) *Illinois State Journal,* Apr. 13.

that question argued in these cases: in as much as that question would be or had been disposed of in the others. Neither the Chief Justice nor any one of the majority of the judges then on the bench and now here regarded the question as open after this order was announced to counsel.

Mr. Justice Nelson. I wish to add, Mr. Attorney General, that I understood distinctly that these cases, so far as the legal tender question was involved, were to abide the result in the other cases.

The Chief Justice, after some observations by Justices Miller and Davis to the effect that their recollections did not correspond to his, said:

I made the statement because the Attorney General seemed to labor under a misapprehension of facts. It is the duty of the Chief Justice to announce the Common orders of the Court, and I cannot be mistaken in the fact that the order I have mentioned was announced as I have stated it.

The upshot was that it was

Ordered by the Court that these cases be postponed until Monday next, the 18th instant.[172]

Actually, *Latham and Deming* were not reached until Wednesday, April 20.[173] At that time L. S. Chatfield, of counsel for Latham, moved that his client's appeal be dismissed. A. L. Merriman made a like motion as to Deming's appeal. Objection was made by the Attorney General, and Justices Miller and Bradley suggested doubts as to the right of appellants to withdraw the appeals. Upon request of Justice Miller the Court retired for consultation. There it was settled that the dismissal would be allowed. Upon the return to the bench, the Chief

---

[172] The case next called was Blyew *et al.* v. United States, supra, note 166. It was continued, and set down for argument "on the first Tuesday of the next term, after the cases already assigned for that day." Minutes of Apr. 11, 1870.

[173] On Monday, April 18, opinions were delivered in six cases, and then the Court resumed the hearing of a case wherein argument had begun on the previous Thursday: Merchants National Bank of Boston v. State National Bank, 10 Wall. 604 (1871). Argument ran on into Tuesday—that being the only case heard that day. Evarts, Sidney Bartlett and Josiah G. Abbott were opposed by B. R. Curtis and Benjamin F. Thomas (formerly a Judge of Massachusetts' highest court, and a powerful lawyer). The eminence of the counsel, and the fact that decision did not come until January 30, 1871, suggest the importance of the case. The Court, per Swayne, J., held defendant bank liable on a check certified by its cashier, the other party having taken it in good faith and without knowledge of defect in the agent's powers. Justice Clifford (whose decision on the circuit was reversed) dissented in an opinion in which Davis, J., concurred.

It bears repetition and illustration that even when caught up in a matter of high moment, the Justices must attend to a diversity of litigation.

Justice announced that the appeals were dismissed. [Minutes; Schuckers, p. 264.]

That put an end to Hoar's attempt to obtain a reversal of *Hepburn* in these cases. The Court stood ready, however, to hear the constitutional question argued anew when an occasion arose.

Next after the dismissal of *Latham and Deming*, the Chief Justice announced an order:

> that the Court will adjourn for this term, or to a day to be hereafter named, on Saturday the 30th instant . . . .

On April 21 Justice Miller was writing to his brother-in-law in Texas. Concluding,

> We have had a desperate struggle in the secret conference of the Court for three weeks over two cases involving the legal tender question. The Chief Justice has resorted to all the stratagems of the lowest political trickery to prevent their being heard, and the fight has been bitter in the conference room. Finally the new Judges and the minority in Hepburn v Griswold having withstood all assaults public and private, when the cases were called for argument yesterday, the Appellants dismissed their appeal. No doubt they had been paid to do it as their claims were not large and a decision in their favour hardly probable.[174]

---

[174] The Lathams, at the conclusion of a long and complicated controversy over payment for the construction of two custom-houses under contracts of 1855 and 1856, had sued for $47,231.37 with interest from March 9, 1863, that being the difference between what they had been paid in Treasury notes and what they claimed to be payable in coin. Transcript of Record, 10. From a dismissal in the Court of Claims, 1 Ct. Cls. 149, March 6, 1865, they appealed.

Deming, prior to the passage of the Legal Tender Act, had contracted to furnish rations for the Marine Corps; he sued for the difference in value between $13,172.56 as paid in Treasury notes and that figure as claimed in gold and silver, which difference the Court of Claims found to have been $3,182.04. Transcript of Record, 6. The claim was rejected. 1 Ct. Cls. 190, Dec. 5, 1865.

It was reported that the Lathams "had made such arrangements as would secure a successful prosecution of the said two claims in Congress,"

and had induced Deming's counsel to join in asking for dismissal. *Legal Gazette*, 2:380 (1870).

Among the papers preserved by Justice Bradley was a hand-written copy of a document, endorsed "Petition of the Lathams to *Congress* Stating the Circumstances under which the Legal Tender Cases were reopened." On this was written in red ink, semble by Justice Bradley, "But very untrue & one-sided."

The petition alleged that on the occasions when Latham v. United States was continued, the Chief Justice announced that it was to abide the decision in other cases. There followed pages of assertions of fact, hearsay, rumor and suspicion, concluding that

> knowing these facts and circumstances as above related, we became convinced that we had no fair show for justice before the Court as then organized; and therefore concluded to withdraw our case, and under the reserved rights of the Constitution we would make an appeal to your

The excitement has nearly used me up. It has been fearful; and my own position as leader in marshalling my forces, and keeping up their courage, against a domineering Chief, and a party in Court who have been accustomed to carry everything their own way, has been such a strain on my brain and nervous system as I never wish to encounter again.[175]

At the concluding session on April 30, the Justices, in inverse order of seniority, announced some thirty decisions. Then orders were made in some pending cases—in particular, *Knox v. Lee* was "continued and set down for re-argument, on the first Tuesday of the next

---

Honorable Body for justice, according to the merits of our claim.

Respectfully yours
O.B. & O.S. Latham
by O.B. Latham.

Among the Chase Papers in the Historical Society of Pennsylvania is a copy of an affidavit by O.B. Latham on Tuesday, April 26, 1870:

that A L Merriman Esqr Counsel in the case of Deming vs the United States, No. 7, of this Term which appeal was dismissed on Wednesday last, yesterday informed this deponent that Howard Esquire, of Philadelphia, representative of the Pennsylvania Central Rail Road, was now in Washington with a view to seeing if the said appeal could not be reinstated & argued & had offered in behalf of said rail road to pay Deming the face of his claim & to pay him the said A L Merriman Esquire, his counsel fee & more & that the Attorney General was ready & desirous to argue the said case, & that these statements were afterwards repeated to this deponent by both the said A L Merriman & the said Deming in the most exact & positive manner & further deponent saith not.

William J. Howard was general solicitor of the Pennsylvania Railroad Company. Two months earlier it had been reported in the press that he had come to Washington to consult the Attorney General about a reargument of the legal tender question, as soon as the new Justices were seated. *New*

York Herald, Feb. 25; *The Nation*, 10:130, Mar. 3. On Howard and the Pennsylvania Railroad, see infra, p. 770.

At the next term, Deming was back in the Supreme Court: as the Minutes for November 7, 1870, record, "Mr. Lander of counsel for appellant, filed motion to vacate the order heretofore made, dismissing this cause, and to reinstate this cause on the docket . . . ." On Friday, November 11, Lander argued for his motion, and written consent by Attorney General Akerman was filed.

On Monday, November 14, the motion was denied. Deming's Appeal, 10 Wall. 251. Justice Swayne, speaking for a unanimous Court, said in part:

It appears by the affidavit of Deming that he was aware of the dismissal very shortly after the order was made. This must necessarily have been so. It was announced in the proceedings of the Court published the next day. Nothing is produced from his counsel who made the motion. Deming states in his affidavit, that counsel acted without his knowledge or consent. Granting this to be so, his silence after the facts came to his knowledge, must be held to amount to acquiescence and ratification. . . .

He pointed out that the United States could suffer no prejudice by the overruling of the motion. (Actually, *Knox v. Lee* was then awaiting reargument.)

[175] Fairman, *Mr. Justice Miller*, 170–71.

745

term, after the cases already assigned for that day." Then the Court adjourned "until the last Monday of October next [the 31st] at twelve o'clock."

Knox v. Lee, on writ of error to the Circuit Court for the Western District of Texas, had been docketed on January 11, 1868. It appeared to contain a point on legal tender.[176] In its regular turn it had been argued on November 17, 1869, by John A. Wills for the defendant in error; George W. Paschal had submitted for the plaintiff in error on printed argument. Now it was to be reargued—destined to become one of the two *Legal Tender Cases* wherein, by a five-to-four division, the Court on May 1, 1871, affirmed the constitutionality of the statute.[177]

Hoar would not participate in that culmination of his effort to vindicate the power of Congress: on June 23, 1870, he was succeeded in the office of Attorney General by Amos T. Akerman of Georgia.[178]

---

[176] See infra, n. 194.

[177] 12 Wall. 457.

[178] On July 1, 1870, the Department of Justice came into existence— in succession to what since 1789 had been merely the Attorney General's Office. Act of June 22, 1870, 16 Stat. 162. "One of the objects," explained Representative Thomas A. Jenckes, who reported the measure from the Joint Select Committee on Retrenchment, "is to establish a staff of law officers sufficiently numerous and of sufficient ability to transact this law business of the Government in all parts of the United States"—instead of the practice of employing outside counsel. For this purpose the office of Solicitor General was created: he should be "a man of sufficient learning, ability and experience that he can be sent . . . into any Court wherever the Government has any interest in litigation, and there present the case of the United States as it should be presented." The other object was to undo a development that had gone on over several decades of "creating law officers in the different departments . . . who are entirely independent . . . of the Attorney General . . . ." "It is for the purpose of having unity of decision . . . in the executive law of the United States, that this bill proposes that all the law officers therein provided for shall be subordinate to one head." Explaining H.

1328. Cong. Globe, 41–2, 3035–36. Apr. 27, 1870. Thus the several departmental Solicitors were transferred to the new Department. The two posts of Assistant Attorney General were continued. See Cummings and McFarland, *Federal Justice* (New York: Macmillan Co., 1937), ch. XI.

Amos T. Akerman (1821–80) became Attorney General at the moment this measure was enacted. Born in New Hampshire, he had attended Phillips Exeter Academy, graduated from Dartmouth, and then gone South to teach. While a tutor in the household of John M. Berrien, Senator and ex-Attorney General, he prepared for the bar. Thereafter he was a busy country lawyer in northeastern Georgia. Reluctantly he "followed his State." In 1863 he joined the State Guard, serving chiefly as a quartermaster. He was among the first to urge acceptance of Congressional Reconstruction. As a member of the convention of 1868 he worked for moderation—"a hard and probably a thankless effort to do good to our stiff-necked people." In December 1869, Congress removed his disabilities and he was appointed District Attorney. Six months later he became Attorney General.

It was without forewarning that Hoar received the President's request for his resignation. In June 1870 Grant was bent upon a vain effort to

XIV: *The* Legal Tender Cases

MINORITY AND MAJORITY STATEMENTS

THE MATTER OF the opposing statments[179] should now be examined—attentively, but without need to exhaust the discrepancies. The protest against the "unprecedented" action of the new

secure the ratification of a treaty to annex the Dominican Republic; he sought by giving Hoar's place to the South to win the votes of Southern Republican Senators. See Storey and Emerson, *Ebenezer Rockwood Hoar*, (Boston and New York: Houghton Mifflin Co., 1911), 206–14. Such was the occasion for the unlikely appointment of Akerman.

The new chief law officer proved to be a man of strong moral fiber— which led to his departure under circumstances similar to his predecessor's. On August 30, 1871, Akerman wrote to his wife of "a new effort which I am satisfied is going on to oust me from office because I will not subserve certain selfish interests. . . . I am right in my principles of action on the subject in question, and I believe I am right in my views of the law . . . ." In rendering opinions to the Secretary of the Interior, Columbus Delano, he maintained that "The head of a Department should not dispose of public lands or issue the bonds of the nation in aid of any enterprise, however meritorious, without an unequivocal direction from the legislature." Central Branch Union Pacific Railroad Company, 13 Ops. Atty. Gen. 430, 439 (1871). Other limiting opinions were rendered in Oregon Central Railroad Company, 13 id. 382 (1871), and Western Pacific Railroad Company, 13 id. 387 (1871). Disappointed interests, actively supported by Secretary Delano, brought pressure upon the President. Grant yielded, and on December 13, 1871, wrote a confidential letter to Akerman:

> Circumstances convince me that a change in the office you now hold is desirable, consulting the best interests of the Government, and I therefore ask your resignation. [He recognized Aker-

man's "zeal, integrity, and industry," and tendered a Judgeship in Florida or Texas, or a foreign mission if one arose.] . . . My personal regard for you is such that I could not bring myself to saying what I say here any other way than through the medium of a letter. Nothing but a consideration for public sentiment could induce me to indite this.

(The quotations come from a biographical sketch, based upon Akerman's papers, in the *Cartersville* (Georgia) *Courant*, March 26, 1885 —a copy of which was supplied to me by a member of the family.)

Next day George H. Williams (1823–1910), recently a Senator from Oregon, was appointed Attorney General, effective January 10, 1872. Presently both he and Delano brought discredit upon the Administration, precisely because they lacked that high sense of public trust that led to Akerman's removal.

The first Solicitor General was Benjamin H. Bristow (1832–96) of Kentucky—a man of sterling character and excellent professional ability. Formerly a colonel who had seen hard fighting, and a vigilant District Attorney, he was in private practice in partnership with John M. Harlan when the appointment was made. In December 1871, Bristow submitted his resignation, but the President persuaded him to remain; when he left in November 1872 he carried with him a letter of high praise. Bristow returned as Secretary of the Treasury in June 1874. His breaking up the Whiskey Ring made him attractive as a possible reform candidate for the Presidency—and led to his separation from the Grant Administration in June 1876.

[179] Supra, p. 739.

majority was placed upon two contentions: that it was in breach of an order, and that it was in derogation of a rule about rearguments dating from 1852.

Take the first: that (at December term 1867)

> The two cases of Lathams v. The United States and Deming v. The United States were called, and were continued under an order of the Court announced by the Chief Justice, though not entered on the minutes, that the question of legal tender, so far as it might arise in them, would be argued in other cases, and that argument upon it would not be heard in these. The counsel for the Government as well as the counsel for the defendants [*sic*] were present when this order was made, and asquiesced in it.

Later on it is alleged that it was "in the month of March, 1868" that this took place.

Now to go to the Minutes and the Docket: the Court did make an order on March 2, 1868, for the purpose of an orderly approach to the constitutional question.[180] *Hepburn v. Griswold* and *Bronson v. Rodes* were to be reargued; and counsel in certain named cases, previously argued or submitted, were given leave to participate in the hearing if they saw fit. *Latham and Deming were not included. They had not yet reached the call of the docket.* On January 4, 1869, when Latham was first reached, the Minutes show the following:

	O B & O S Latham	Ordered by the
20	Appellants	Court on motion of
	vs.	Mr Carlisle on
	The United States	account of
		sickness of counsel

—that this cause be, and the same is hereby passed for the present.

On January 12, No. 39, *Israel Deming v. United States*, was called—and the Minutes show:

> On motion of Mr Talbot of counsel for the appellees and consent of Mr. Merriman for the appellant, Ordered by the Court that this cause be argued with No. 20.

(Thomas H. Talbot was an Assistant Attorney General.)

An Adjourned Term opened on October 4, 1869. On October 7 the Court made one order embracing *Latham* and *Deming*: "that these causes be passed for the present."

---

[180] Supra, pp. 702–03.

XIV: *The* Legal Tender Cases

The statutory term opened on Monday, December 6, 1869. On December 8 it was again ordered that the two cases, now Nos. 6 and 7, be "passed for the present."

It is not surprising that memories about details became dim. At the Chief Justice's request, Clerk Middleton searched the Minutes: he reported the orders made on March 2, 1868 [wherein Latham and Deming did not appear], adding that "These are the only orders in reference to the re-argument of the legal tender cases made by the Court."[181] *Latham* and *Deming* were each passed over on three occasions: there is no telling what incidental remark may at some time have been made by the Chief Justice. His protest quoted Carlisle's letter as follows:

> I was in court when my case was called and I distinctly understood, and so did Mr. Merriman, as he informed me, that these cases were from time to time, while the case of Hepburn v. Griswold was under advisement, passed by the order of the court and with the assent of counsel for the Government (Mr. Dickey and Mr. Talbott [*sic*]) to abide the decision in Hepburn v. Griswold upon the principal point involved in them.

(T. Lyle Dickey was also an Assistant Attorney General.)

Carlisle's letter was imprecise: he tells what he *understood*—and what Merriman said that he had *understood* about the import of what transpired when *from time to time* the cases were continued. The Majority statement replied that this was no more than an "expectation, usual and generally well founded," that what was decided in one case would govern like cases: but this "confers no absolute right."

When the Court had parallel cases before it, and saw fit to put one aside to abide the decision in the other, it would properly make an order specifically to that effect. A contemporary illustration has already been mentioned: on October 11, 1869, the Court ordered that *Ex parte Brown et al.* "be passed for the present, and abide the decision on the petition of Edward M. Yerger."[182]

Chase alleged a "distinct remembrance" of his announcement when the cases from the Court of Claims were postponed, "on several

---

[181] Chase Papers, Hist. Soc. of Pa.
[182] Minutes. Supra, p. 581.
From the Docket and Minutes one may learn that County of Douglas v. State of Oregon was filed on January 4, 1868, and with it a stipulation of opposing counsel that it abide the decision in Lane County v. Oregon. *Lane County* was decided on February 8, 1869, supra, p. 704, and on

February 19, on motion of counsel for the State, judgment in the *Douglas County* case was entered in accordance with the stipulation, per Chase, C.J.

The matter of one case "abiding the decision" in another was not the casual, informal practice one might suppose from the Chief Justice's protest.

occasions." The radical flaw is that the Chief Justice has no authority to announce such an order save upon consideration and direction by the Court. But, if he had presumed to make this announcement distinctly enough to be comprehended by his brethren on the Bench, "it would certainly have attracted the attention of the Judges who did not agree to that opinion [in *Hepburn v. Griswold*], and would have met with a denial on their part so emphatic as to be remembered." So Justice Miller wrote in his reply. Evidently he was thinking of the action on December 8, 1869—the third time that Latham and Deming were passed over, which was *after* the *Hepburn* case had been decided in conference on November 27: but presumably objection would have been voiced if an unauthorized announcement had been made on the earlier occasions when those cases were passed over.[183]

The Chief Justice—who was not attentive in the matter of keeping a record, and whose cast of mind was not such as to fasten retentively upon details[184]—had failed to make good on his first contention.

His second contention was that in reopening the constitutional question the new majority infringed "the settled rule of the court announced in 1852." This referred to *Brown et al. v. Aspden's Administrators.*[185] In December 1852 the decision below had been affirmed by an equally divided Court. In February 1853, appellants petitioned for a rehearing. In refusing, Chief Justice Taney said:

> the rule of the Court is this: that no re-argument will be heard in any case after judgment is entered, unless some member of the Court who concurred in the judgment afterwards doubts the correctness of his opinion, and desires a further argument on the subject. And when that happens, the Court will, of its own accord, apprise the counsel of its wishes, and designate the points on which it desires to hear them.

It should be interjected that on March 7, 1870, the Court, per Chase, C.J., stated a qualification of Taney's language—as was essential if counsel were to have the means of drawing attention to what were believed to be the Court's errors:

> Where the Court does not on its own motion order a rehearing, it will be proper for counsel to submit without argument, as has been

---

[183] Recall how Justice Davis had spoken up when, on February 14, 1866, the Chief Justice had misstated an order agreed upon in conference. Supra, pp. 136–38.

[184] Recall his statement when, in the summer of 1866, a question arose about what had transpired when the *Test Oath Cases* were discussed at conference the previous spring. Supra, pp. 155, 157–58.

[185] 14 How. 25.

done in the present instance, a brief written or printed petition or suggestion of the point or points thought important. If upon such petition or suggestion, any Judge who concurred in the decision thinks proper to move for a rehearing, the motion will be considered. If not so moved, the hearing will be denied as of course.[186]

In the Statement for the minority, Chase protested that what Taney had said in *Brown v. Aspden's Administrator* "not only in spirit but in letter" precluded a new argument on the constitutionality of the Legal Tender Act. This ignored the patent difference between reconsidering the *judgment* that had been entered in a cause and reconsidering a *question of law* that had been involved in it. The Attorney General's motion did not affect the judgment that had been entered between Hepburn and Griswold; the new majority did not purpose to disturb it. The object of the strict limitation of rehearings, Taney had explained, was to discourage the carelessness in preparing for the first argument, and the expense, delay and uncertainty that might otherwise arise. In thus seeking to protect the administration of justice there was no thought whatever of preventing the Judges who sat in some later case from freely examining the legal issues involved.

Accurately to express the Court's rule on rehearings, one should include a further limitation: the Court invariably refused all applications for rehearing made after the adjournment of the term at which the judgment was rendered.[187]

Chase's statement for the minority held that "we are obliged to regard the order opening that [legal tender] question for reargument

---

[186] Public Schools v. Walker, 9 Wall. 603. That case had been argued on Jan. 19, 20, and 21, 1870, decided on Feb. 14, and reported at 9 Wall. 282.(The dates shown in 19 L. Ed. 576 are inaccurate.) Montgomery Blair and F. A. Dick petitioned for a rehearing. The Minutes for March 7 record that it was after opposing counsel had been heard upon this point that rehearing was denied.

A Washington dispatch of April 8, 1870, in the *New York Herald* of April 9, reported that Representative James B. Beck of Kentucky moved in the Supreme Court "today" for a rehearing of Hepburn v. Griswold; that Potter started to reply, whereupon the Chief Justice said that the question was not debatable; that the motion was taken under advisement, but would be granted only if a Justice who voted for the judgment desired

a rehearing. The Minutes make no mention of such motion.

[187] The words are Justice Miller's in Bronson v. Schulten, 104 U.S. 410 (1882), citing Brown v. Aspden and other cases.

In its Rules promulgated on January 7, 1884, the Court incorporated this statement of its practice, in Rule 30, Rehearing:

A petition for rehearing after judgment can be presented only at the term at which the judgment is entered, unless by special leave granted during the term; and must be printed, and briefly and distinctly state its grounds, and be supported by certificate of counsel; and will not be granted, or permitted to be argued, unless a justice who concurred in the judgment desires it, and a majority of the court so determine.

as made not only in disregard of the settled practice of the court, but in clear violation of its positive rule." Certainly Chase could not derive from *Brown v. Aspden* a proposition that only if he or Nelson or Clifford or Field desired it could the question in *Hepburn v. Griswold* ever again be examined. The most that could have been claimed with any show of reason was that inasmuch as the *Hepburn* judgment itself was not to be reopened without such assent, the same issue ought not to be reconsidered in another case during that term. One could not have sustained a proposition that the rule in *Brown v. Aspden* forbade the majority to continue a pending case to the next term when surely the Court would be free to reconsider the issue. One of the reasons for the Court's practice, Taney had explained, was to avoid a perpetuation of "uncertainty and confusion."

But in truth it should be said that the manner in which a decision in *Hepburn v. Griswold* had been attained was enough to carry this matter beyond the range of the Court's normal practice in the disposition of cases.

As recently as December 20, 1869, Chase and Field had concurred with what Justice Miller said in a dissenting opinion in *Washington University v. Rouse*:

> With as full respect for the authority of former decisions, as belongs, from teaching and habit, to judges trained in the common law system of jurisprudence, we think that there may be questions touching the powers of legislative bodies, which can never be finally closed by the decisions of a court . . . .[188]

So flawed is Chase's protest as to suggest special caution when presently his position on *Hepburn v. Griswold* comes to be scrutinized.[189]

REARGUMENT IS HINDERED

IT TOOK MORE than the order of April 30, 1870, actually to bring about a reargument.[190] Impediments caused announced hearings to be postponed, and dates fixed in conference to be abandoned.

At last, on April 18 and 19, 1871, argument was made before a full Bench; on May 1, judgments were rendered affirming the constitutionality of the Legal Tender Act.

To explain the delay: the Chief Justice was absent until April 17. A stroke in the late summer, then a long recuperation, removed him from active life. He was turned into an old man. Justice Miller told of

---

[188] 8 Wall. 439, 444.   [189] Infra, pp. 765–67.   [190] Supra, pp. 745–46.

this in a letter of November 6, 1870: "The more recent indications are that the Chief will recover. Whether he will be able to serve efficiently may remain doubtful. . . ." Miller expected that he could be no more than "a figure head to the Court. . . ."[191]

And Justice Nelson, whose seventy-eighth birthday came in November: he did not attend the Adjourned Term, October 31 to December 2. At the Regular Term he was present, and presided, from December 5 through February 8. After that he sat only nine days: February 16, 17, 20, 21, 23 and 24; April 3, 18 and 19. (He was engaged in the work of the Joint High Commission for the settlement of differences between the United States and Great Britain.[192] Ill health was also a factor.)

And Justice Field was indisposed and absent for four weeks, between March 20 and April 17, save for his appearance on two Mondays.

Of the new minority, only Clifford was constantly in attendance. In the absence of Chase and Nelson, he presided.

On November 21 the reargument of *Knox v. Lee* was postponed to the first Tuesday in February (the seventh), it having been ascertained that neither Chase nor Nelson would be present at the time previously designated. Actually the argument was on February 23, before the eight Associate Justices. George W. Paschal, who had had a large part in winning *Texas v. White*,[193] represented the plaintiff in error. Appearing on the other side was John A. Wills of the District of Columbia bar, well educated and experienced, with a notable ability to make an effective presentation. *Opposing counsel agreed that the Legal Tender Act was valid.*[194]

---

[191] Fairman, *Mr. Justice Miller*, 251. To his brother-in-law.

[192] The Commission held conferences from time to time between February 27 and May 8. The American commissioners were Secretary of State Hamilton Fish; Nelson; Robert C. Schenck, Minister to Great Britain; E. R. Hoar, late Attorney General; and ex-Senator Geo. H. Williams of Oregon. The resulting Treaty of Washington of May 8, 1871, provided, inter alia, for the submission of the "Alabama claims" to arbitration, under rules framed by the High Commission.

[193] Supra, ch. 13.

[194] How the Legal Tender Act was involved in this case is somewhat elusive.

Mrs. Lee, a citizen of Pennsylvania,

owned a flock of sheep in Texas. In 1863 it was confiscated under the Confederacy's Sequestration Act; Knox was the purchaser. In 1866 Lee sued for conversion, in the Circuit Court for the Western District of Texas. The court instructed the jury that the sale under the Sequestration Act gave no title. That was the first of two alleged errors carried up to the Supreme Court.

The second point concerned legal tender. There was evidence that the sheep were worth an estimated sum in specie. Plaintiff offered to prove what was the difference in value between specie and greenbacks, in order that the jury might take that into account. Defendant objected: the Legal Tender Act had made them equal in law. The court sustained the objec-

In the meantime, *Parker v. Davis*, a legal tender case from the Supreme Judicial Court of Massachusetts, had been reached in the regular order of the docket, and on December 13 had been passed over. The case was this: in 1857 Parker agreed to sell to Davis a lot, so much down and balance in thirty days. Tender of the balance was refused. In 1867 the Supreme Judicial Court decreed specific performance. Davis paid legal tender notes into court; Parker demanded gold. A further decree supported Davis' contention: payment could be

---

tion, and plaintiff took no exception. Then, in the final paragraph of his charge, the Judge instructed: "In assessing damages, the jury will recollect that whatever amount they may give by their verdict, can be discharged by the payment of such amount in legal tender notes of the United States." An exception by the defendant was overruled. Transcript of Record, p. 21.

Before the Supreme Court, Paschal made a desperate effort to get around Texas v. White. He said that while it was there held that *State* acts in aid of rebellion were void, yet the Confederate States of America had maintained a government of paramount force whose decree of condemnation should be recognized as effective. Rebel Confiscation and Legal Tender Laws. Argument for Plaintiff in Error, pp. 2–9.

Wills replied that the fact that the States had set up a Confederacy did not endow their creation with powers which Texas v. White had denied to the State. Supplementary Brief of Defendant in Error, pp. 1–3.

If his first point was not sustained, Paschal continued, then he maintained that the Judge's instruction *assumed* that the Legal Tender Act was *invalid*: "he left it to the jury to infer that [legal tender notes] could only be forced upon the creditor at the rate they would bring in gold." Argument, p. 11. In effect the Judge was saying, "You will assess that [specie] value and add to it the known premium which it requires to buy that much gold with paper." Argument, p. 11.

Paschal launched into an acute critique of the Chief Justice's recent

opinions, culminating in *Hepburn*. Argument, pp. 11–45.

Concerning the instructions, Wills replied: the Judge "merely *reminded* the jury of what had already been *admitted* by the defendant, and had been *decided* on the trial," namely, that the damages, if any, could be paid in legal tender notes. Moreover, the jury had not been misled into giving excessive damages. Brief, p. 8.

The constitutionality of the Legal Tender Acts was maintained by the defendant in the court below; "it was decided by that court in his favor and at his instance." "The defendant in error (plaintiff below) acquiesced in that decision as correct, and took no bill of exceptions to that ruling." Supplemental Brief, pp. 6–9.

Wills therefore submitted "that no constitutional question can arise on this record." P. 11. But, if mistaken in this, he relied "confidently on the able constitutional argument presented by the counsel for the plaintiff in error"—and, if more were needed, on the dissenting opinion in Hepburn v. Griswold, and the majority opinions in the Supreme Court of Pennsylvania in Shollenberger v. Brinton, 52 Pa. St. 9 (1865), supra, n. 70, per Strong and Agnew, JJ. Ibid., pp. 11–12.

In closing he remarked on "the *strange anomaly*" that one side asked the Court to reverse and the other asked it to affirm the judgment below "for *the same reason, viz, that the legal-tender laws of the United States are constitutional, notwithstanding the late decision of the court.*" Ibid., p. 12.

"either in coined money of the United States or in the treasury notes of the United States."[195]

On February 13, 1871, counsel submitted *Parker v. Davis* on printed statements. For the former, Benjamin F. Thomas'[196] points were that the sum to be paid did not constitute a "debt" within the meaning of the Legal Tender Act; but if it did, it was a debt contracted prior to the enactment and not affected by it. Benjamin F. Butler, for Davis, submitted that no debt accrued until the court had entered its judgment, which was long subsequent to the enactment; and that the State court's decree of specific performance on terms that to it seemed equitable presented no question for the Supreme Court.

Thus at the close of the argument of *Knox v. Lee* on February 23, the situation was this: the Court had had oral arguments by counsel who *agreed* that the Legal Tender Act was constitutional, and printed statements from counsel whose points *evaded* the constitutional question.

Then—quoting what Justice Swayne recalled in a subsequent statement from the Bench[197]—

> At the close of the argument [in *Knox v. Lee*], Hon. Clarkson N. Potter[198] asked to be heard upon the constitutional question involved in the cases. The Attorney General [Akerman] expressed a desire to be heard also, if Mr. Potter were heard. These requests were taken into conference, and both promptly acceded to. . . .

But then Justice Nelson began his participation in the Joint High Commission; and in March, Field's absences began. On April 3, Clifford announced that on Monday, May 1, the Court would adjourn to Monday, October 16. Evidently, without very insistent pressure by the majority the reargument would have been stalled for a year.

On Monday, April 10, Justice Clifford announced an order by the Court—but allowed his personal feelings to be reflected in the form of words: the *majority* of the Court make the following order in *Knox v. Lee* and *Parker v. Davis*:

> that Mr Potter and the Attorney General will be heard in these cases on the twelfth instant upon the following questions.
>
> 1st. Is the act of Congress known as the legal tender act constitutional as to contracts made before its passage?

---

[195] Transcript of Record, pp. 27–28. 14 Allen (96 Mass.) 94. Judge Hoar and Judge Horace Gray were members of the court. The case was docketed in the Supreme Court on Nov. 30, 1868.
[196] Supra, n. 173.
[197] Infra, p. 756.
[198] Supra, pp. 704, 742.

2nd. Is it valid as applicable to transactions since its passage?

Mr Potter will open. The Attorney General will reply, and Mr Potter will close.

Clifford added:

> I dissent from the order of the Court in these cases, especially from that part of it which opens for re-argument the question whether the act of Congress, known as the legal tender act is constitutional as to contracts made before its passage—as I hold that that question is conclusively settled by the case of Hepburn v. Griswold, 8 Wall. 603, in which the opinion was given by the Chief Justice. And I am requested to say that Mr Justice Nelson, and Mr Justice Field concur in this dissent.[199]

But when April 12 came, only six Justices were present. Field sent a note to the "Acting Chief Justice," asking that the argument be put over to October.[200]

When the Court opened, as the Minutes record,

> Mr Justice Clifford informed the bar that Mr Justice Nelson was too unwell to attend court to-day, and that in consequence of his absence the hearing in these causes assigned for argument this morning would be further postponed, adding that notice would hereafter be given to the counsel when they could be heard.

Justice Swayne then delivered some prepared remarks, with considerable energy. He detailed the delays that had occurred, and how at last the request of Mr. Potter and the Attorney General had been acceded to. "On Monday last the announcement designating to-day was made. We were advised that it would suit the convenience of Mr. Justice Nelson to be present. . . ."

> It is due to this court and to the public, that both these cases shall be decided, and the important question which they present be put at rest as speedily as can be done with propriety. It is to be hoped that the early restoration of the health of Mr Justice Nelson will enable us to hear the further argument and announce our conclusion within the residue of the term.[201]

There had been no legal bar to proceeding to a hearing and decision: six Justices constituted a quorum. To have done so in this matter, however, would have appeared unseemly. The old majority, by

---

[199] Minutes, Apr. 10; 20 L. Ed. 290.
[200] Clifford Papers, Me. Hist. Soc.

[201] Minutes, Apr. 12; 20 L. Ed. 290.

Grier's impaired assent, had produced a situation where the full Bench must either acquiesce or seem to violate constitutional usage. Now the new majority could not let it appear that they had pressed on to overrule *Hepburn* while venerable members were too ill to attend.

Swayne's insistence proved effective. On April 18 and 19 the Bench was full—for the first time since April 26, 1870.

THE REARGUMENT

CLARKSON POTTER had not been brought into this case by the retainer of a litigant: he was a Democratic Congressman who volunteered in order to defend a cause—of metallic money, strict construction and limited government. *Hepburn v. Griswold* had given him a victory; now he addressed himself insistently to the Justices who had declined to be bound by that decision. What he said was promptly printed in a pamphlet of seventy-eight pages.[202]

From time immemorial—he cited Abraham's purchase, in Genesis 23:16—coins of precious metal, according to their intrinsic value, had been the medium of exchange. Congress had no power to create any other. What was "necessary and proper," even by Marshall's construction in *McCulloch v. Maryland*,[203] was strictly limited. To make Treasury notes a legal tender involved the exercise of a "substantive power," not something merely incidental such as might be allowed as a means to the exercise of a granted power.[204] The legal tender power was "not consistent with the letter and spirit of the Constitution, and was prohibited." "Some of your Honors have remarked that 'the argument is too vague for your perceptions' "—he quoted Miller's comment that a declaration of war or the lifting of a tariff might affect private property as much as had the Legal Tender Act: but, Potter answered, such consequences would be indirect, whereas here Congress was making a "sale of licenses to let men pay in short measures."[205] Congress had no power to impair the obligation of a contract: although the dissent had pointed out that this was not

---

[202] "Argument against the Power of Congress to Make United States Treasury Notes a Legal Tender. Washington," 1871.

[203] Supra, pp. 713–14.

[204] He based his distinction on what Marshall had said in *McCulloch*, sustaining the incorporation of the Bank of the United States: "The power of creating a corporation . . . is not, like the power of making war, or levying taxes, or of regulating commerce, a great substantive and independent power, which cannot be implied as incidental to other powers, or used as a means of executing them. It is never an end for which other powers are exercised, but a means by which other objects are accomplished. . . ." 4 Wheat. 316, 411 (1819).

[205] "Argument against the Power of Congress . . .", p. 45–46.

expressly forbidden, yet the express authority to "make uniform laws on the subject of bankruptcies" showed that no general power existed.[206]

On the Court's second question, he said that even as applied to subsequent transactions the statute was ultra vires. Congress had power "to borrow money on the credit of the United States." If it were still open to argument, Potter would not concede that this carried with it even a power to put Treasury notes into circulation; to give them the quality of legal tender went too far. The result was a currency of fluctuating value, whereas the power of Congress was only to provide *a fixed and uniform standard of value.*[207]

There he rested to hear the Attorney General's reply.

Attorney General Akerman submitted the brief his predecessor had prepared for *Latham's and Deming's Appeals* a year before (wherein Hoar had reprinted Evarts' brief in *Hepburn v. Griswold*, supplemented by Hoar's own observations in criticism of the opinion for the majority in that case[208]). Akerman proceeded, succinctly and in felicitous language, to answer Potter and to sum up the case for sustaining the judgment of Congress.[209]

Potter concluded on April 19. In his argument in *Hepburn* he had conceded gratuitously that in an extreme emergency the political branches of the Government might be justified in taking measures *beyond* the limits of the Constitution: Akerman had recalled and had repelled that idea. Potter admitted his reference to a "higher law," but said that "These, however, are considerations that cannot be addressed to your Honors."[210] (Potter's concession sounded like Chase's *salus populi* defense of the Legal Tender Bill in his letter of February 4, 1862, to Bryant.[211] To postulate that some action, necessary for the preservation of the Union, might be justifiable by, but only by, a higher law outside the Constitution, while insisting that the "necessary and proper" clause be so narrowly construed as to exclude it, really did not make good sense.)

This, Potter said in closing, "is the supreme crisis of the Republic"—greater than that when the scales of war hung poised. If the Legal Tender Act were sustained, the outcome would be that "instead of the limited and localized system of government established by our

---

[206] Ibid., at 51–54.

[207] Ibid., at 58–62.

[208] Evarts' brief is set out in the report of Hepburn in 19 L. Ed. 513–517. Hoar's Supplementary observations are set out in the report of the Legal Tender Cases, 20 L. Ed. 304–305, under Akerman's name.

[209] "Argument of the Attorney General on the Constitutionality of the Legal Tender Act of Congress of 1862." Pp. 14. Government Printing Office, 1871.

[210] P. 68.

[211] Supra, pp. 686–87.

fathers, we shall pass irretrievably into a centralized, consolidated, absolute government."[212]

DECISION OF THE *LEGAL TENDER CASES*

On May 1, 1871, amid the mass of decisions at the close of the term, Justice Strong announced that the judgments in *Knox v. Lee* and *Parker v. Davis* were affirmed, the Chief Justice and Nelson, Clifford, and Field dissenting. The delivery of opinions was deferred.

In mid-January 1872 two matters appear on the Minutes which for a moment may be considered together—one memorable as a beginning, the other as a close. On the eleventh and twelfth the Court heard argument in the *Slaughter House Cases*[213]—the first great test of the meaning of the Fourteenth Amendment. Arguing on the side that would magnify the new federal protection against State abuses were J. Q. A. Fellows, Conservative Louisiana Unionist,[214] and John A. Campbell, who in 1861 had resigned from the Supreme Court to follow the Confederacy. Advocating a narrow construction that would concede a larger freedom to the States were Matt. H. Carpenter[215] and Thomas J. Durant,[216] who on other occasions had exalted the power of the national Government. Only eight Justices were present. Justice Nelson, ill, was absent throughout that year of the Court, and on November 28, 1872, resigned. His place was taken by Ward Hunt of New York, who heard the reargument of *Slaughter House* and cast the momentous deciding vote.

The other event was the delivery on January 15, 1872, of the opinions in the *Legal Tender Cases*. Each of these historic decisions had the support of only a bare majority. In *Slaughter House* the dissenters were Chase and Field, Swayne and Bradley. New occasions bring new groupings. This is a helpful reflection as we come to the end of the embittered contest over legal tenders.

Let the Chief Justice relate what happened on Monday, January 15, as posted in his diary. He was writing at "Edgewood," the home he had recently purchased, on high ground about two and a quarter miles north of the capitol.

> Morning as usual [which included family prayers]—after bkft went to Capitol. Judge Strong read the opinion of majority (five) & I the opinion of the minority (four) on the constitutionality of the legal tender clause in the currency act of '62. Bradley read a separate opinion for & Clifford & Field separate opinions against constitutional-

---

[212] P. 78.

[213] Infra, pp. 1341–42.

[214] Supra, p. 94.

[215] Supra, pp. 436, 453.

[216] Supra, pp. 94, 270, 290.

ity. The opinion of the majority reverses Hepburn v. Griswold 5 to 3. It is I think a sad day for the country & for the cause of constitutional government. The consequences of the sanction this day given to irredeemable paper currency may not soon manifest themselves but are sure to come. The only thing I regret in connection with my administration of the Treasury is that I ever expressed even a qualified opinion that the making the United States notes a legal tender was necessary. It was a sad mistake into which I was drawn by my anxiety for the passage of the bill then pending. I regard this as the one blot upon my financial system.

The reading of the opinions took five hours and a half. Field had not concluded when I left the Capitol at half past four. It was past five when I arrived at Edgewood.[217]

Justice Strong's opinion may be regarded as the most important he ever rendered for the Court. He pointed to the large consequences that must follow if the Legal Tender Acts were held invalid. The Government would be denied a power that in some contingency might become indispensable, even if it was not so when these Acts were passed. Also there would be "great business derangement, widespread distress, and the rankest injustice": doubtless the major portion of existing indebtedness had been contracted after the Act of 1862 and in reliance upon it. The "fundamental question" was, "can Congress constitutionally give to Treasury Notes the character and quality of money?" There was "no well founded distinction" between the constitutionality of such a statute as it applied to *all* debts and as it applied only to such as were afterward contracted: the effects might vary, but not the question of constitutionality.

He turned to the mode by which the Constitution should be construed. All the powers therein provided were "means for a common end": the establishment of "a government, sovereign within its sphere, with capability of self-preservation, thereby forming a union more perfect than that which existed under the old Confederacy." It was not indispensable that a power be either expressly granted or directly traceable to some one specific power. He gave a variety of illustrations. The power to suspend the writ of habeas corpus was to be deduced from no express grant, but was recognized by the provision that the privilege could be suspended only in certain defined contingencies. It had been argued that the specific authority "to coin money" excluded an implied power to make anything other than gold and silver a legal tender: Strong countered by pointing out that notwithstanding specific authority to punish piracy and counterfeiting, statutes had from the beginning been enacted to define and punish many other crimes. From

---

[217] Chase Papers, Hist. Soc. of Pa.

"the earliest period of our existence as a nation," Congress had been accorded a wide choice of means conducive to the exercise of powers granted by the Constitution.

It had been argued that Treasury notes without the legal tender quality would have sufficed. "What then?" It was for Congress to judge the degree of necessity. Justice Strong went on, however, to assert affirmatively that, "to our view," other measures would not have sufficed.

As to the operation of the Act upon obligations previously incurred: "Every contract for the payment of money, simply, is necessarily subject to the constitutional power of the government over the currency . . . ."

Accordingly *Hepburn v. Griswold* was overruled. "The other questions raised in the case of Knox v. Lee were substantially decided in Texas v. White."[218]

Justice Bradley, while concurring in the opinion, made some "additional observations." A few key sentences will illustrate the style of this Judge who for twenty years would exert a powerful influence within the Court.

> The United States is not only a government, but it is a National Government, and the only government in this country that has the character of nationality. . . .
> Such being the character of the General Government, it seems to be a self-evident proposition that it is invested with all those inherent and implied powers which, at the time of adopting the Constitution, were generally considered to belong to every government as such, and as being essential to the exercise of its functions. . . .[219]

No one any longer doubted the power of the Government to emit bills of credit:

> This being conceded, the incidental power of giving such bills the quality of legal tender follows almost as a matter of course.

This was "entirely distinct" from the power "to coin money . . . ."

---

[218] See supra, p. 646.

[219] Clarkson had argued, "This is a limited Government. . . . Far from requiring that the new Government should possess all the powers usual to Sovereigns, [the framers] expressly forbade some most sovereign powers, and refused to grant others." Argument, pp. 35, 36.

The proposition that the National Government may exercise some powers that "inhere in sovereignty," without deriving them from particular grants in the Constitution, was thereafter occasionally echoed in the Reports, never more strikingly than in an opinion by Justice Sutherland for the Court in United States v. Curtiss-Wright, 299 U.S. 304 (1936), where he was stressing the amplitude of the Government's competence in dealing with international affairs.

It was argued that the Government might raise money by offering its bonds for sale: but that might be "too tardy and inefficient."

By its right of eminent domain the Government might take the farmer's cattle and horses and corn and give him only its certificates of indebtedness: Why could it not make such certificates receivable by the farmer's creditors? Was that anything more than putting the capitalist on the same platform with the farmer?

> No one supposes that these government certificates are never to be paid—that the day of specie payments is never to return. . . .

It was for the Legislative Department to say when specie payments should be resumed. Perhaps many thought it had been too long delayed. It might subserve the public good if the Court were now to hasten resumption by declaring the Legal Tender Act invalid.

> But what a miserable consideration would that be for a permanent loss of one of the just and necessary powers of the government . . . .

Bradley had a deep awareness of "the fundamental political conditions" on which citizens enjoyed the benefits of an ordered society:

> There are times when the exigencies of the state rightly absorb all subordinate considerations of private interest, convenience, or feeling; and at such times, the temporary though compulsory acceptance by a private creditor of the government credit in lieu of his debtor's obligation to pay, is one of the slightest forms in which the necessary burdens of society can be sustained. Instead of being a violation of such obligation, it merely subjects it to one of those conditions under which it is held and enjoyed.

In this controversy where the Court had been told that to rescue creditors from "this rising flood of centralization" was just as critical as had been the taking of Vicksburg or Gettysburg,[220] Bradley seemed to be lifting the national emblem high above all private interests. His words accented the greatly enhanced authority resulting to the United States from the triumph of the Union.

The Chief Justice read a dissent that went over the old ground. Clifford and Field, while joining with him, also delivered opinions. Nelson also dissented.

The opinions of Clifford and Field each ran to some 18,000 words—about three times as long as that by the Chief Justice. Each

---

[220] Clarkson's Argument, 77-78.

adduced arguments drawn from constitutional history to show that only gold and silver coin, whose value was intrinsic, could be made a legal tender. From that it followed that the Act was invalid not only as to preexisting debts—the holding in *Hepburn*—but as to debts subsequently contracted as well.

That of Justice Field was especially forceful. The express power "to coin money" precluded the existence of an implied power to make anything but coin a legal tender.[221] Where Bradley had shown that the Revolution had been fought on a paper currency and that Franklin had called it "a wonderful machine," Field read history as showing that the Founders had barred the door against a repetition.[222]

Concluding, Field repelled the intimation that to hold the Legal Tender Act invalid reflected a spirit adverse to the cause at stake in the war and to the men who had directed it:

> To them belong the greatest of all glories in our history—that of having saved the Union, and that of having emancipated a race. . . . But I do not admit that a blind approval of every measure which they may have thought essential to put down the rebellion is any evidence of loyalty to the country. The only loyalty which I can admit consists in obedience to the Constitution and laws made in pursuance of it. It is only by obedience that affection and reverence can be shown to a superior having a right to command. So thought our great Master when he said to his disciples: "If ye love me, keep my commandments."

[221] He made, in similar language, the point Holmes had made in his communication to the *American Law Review*, 4:768, July 1870. Supra, p. 715. And Holmes, in his twelfth edition of Kent's *Commentaries* (1873), took note that Field had done so "with great force." I: [271–72]. Thereafter the mention of Justice Field brought this incident to his mind.

[222] The Convention of 1787 had had under consideration a draft authorizing Congress "to borrow money and emit bills on the credit of the United States." After a debate in which a variety of opinions were expressed, it was voted to strike out the provision for bills of credit. Now to read this as depriving Congress of power to issue bills of credit would prove too much, since (in the words of Chase, C.J., in Veazie Bank v. Fenno, 8 Wall. 533, 548, supra at p. 712) "by the uniform practice of the government and by repeated decisions" that power had been put beyond question. Rather, Field—following Madison—held that the result had been to withhold from Congress the power to give its bills the quality of legal tender. But as Justice Gray later observed, Madison had "not explained why he thought that by striking out the words 'and emit bills' would leave the power to emit bills, and deny the power to make them a tender in payment of debts." Juilliard v. Greenman, 110 U.S. 421, 443 (1884), infra, pp. 771–74. When Professor James Bradley Thayer in 1887 examined the same material, he concluded that on this point "no argument [against the power of Congress] can be drawn from the action of the Convention . . . ." *Harv. L. Rev.*, 1:73 (1887), and his *Legal Essays* (Cambridge, Mass.: Harvard University Press, 1908), 69.

SUCCESSOR CASES

ONE WEEK after the reading of the *Legal Tender* opinions, the Court announced its decision in *Trebilcock v. Wilson*: that where a contract called for payment "in specie," a tender in paper money would not suffice.[223] This meant that the limited construction of the Legal Tender Act which the Court had adopted in *Bronson v. Rodes*[224] in 1869 was being maintained. Justice Miller reasserted his dissent. Justice Bradley also recorded his disagreement:

> In all cases where the contract is to pay a certain sum of money of the United States, in whatever phraseology that money may be described (except cases specially exempted by law), I hold that the Legal Tender Acts make the Treasury Notes a legal tender. Only in those cases in which gold and silver are stipulated for as bullion can they be demanded in specie, like any other chattel. . . .

In his concurring opinion in the *Legal Tender Cases*, Bradley had already announced that "I differ from my brethren" in the *Trebilcock* case (which evidently had already been decided in conference). Then he had commented:

> I do not understand the majority of the Court to decide that an Act so drawn as to embrace, in terms, contracts payable in specie, would not be constitutional. Such a decision would completely nullify the power claimed for the government. For it would be very easy, by the use of one or two additional words, to make all contracts payable in specie.[225]

---

[223] 12 Wall. 687, reversing the decision of the Supreme Court of Iowa in Wilson v. Trebilcock, 23 Iowa 331, at Dec. Term 1867.

This case has already been mentioned in connection with Roosevelt v. Meyer, supra, pp. 696–97.

Wilson in 1861 had given his note, payable "in specie," secured by a mortgage. In 1865 he brought suit, setting forth a tender in paper money, and praying for a decree to discharge the mortgage. The Iowa courts held the Legal Tender Act to be applicable, and constitutional.

In the Supreme Court, counsel for the debtor sought dismissal for want of jurisdiction, relying on Roosevelt v. Meyer. George W. McCrary, for Trebilcock, sustained his client's right

to a decree for payment in specie. Justice Field, for the Court, upheld its jurisdiction under clause [3] of the Judiciary Act: the creditor had claimed a right under a construction of the Constitution, and the State court had decided against that claim. Roosevelt v. Meyer had reached the wrong conclusion. Also, in substance the creditor had claimed a right under the statutes of the United States: he had contended that when the Legal Tender Act was construed in connection with the statutes that made gold and silver coin a legal tender, he was on that basis entitled to payment in coin.

[224] Supra, p. 705.

[225] 12 Wall. at 566–67.

XIV: *The* Legal Tender Cases

In the Joint Resolution of June 5, 1933, with respect to the "gold clause" in private contracts, Congress asserted the power which Miller and Bradley had vindicated, and in sustaining that action Chief Justice Hughes quoted and followed Bradley's language.[226]

The dissenters did not bow to the decision of the new majority in the *Legal Tender Cases.* In *Dooley v. Smith,*[227] where a tender in greenbacks on a note made in January 1862 was held good, Justice Field, in a dissent in which Chase and Clifford concurred, said

> We are . . . compelled by every consideration of duty which may be supposed to govern judicial officers on this Bench, to express on all proper occasions our dissent from what we regard as a wide departure from the limitations of the Constitution. . . .

Substitute "powers" for "limitations," and one has the proposition on which the new majority acted in refusing to be bound by *Hepburn v. Griswold.*

ADHERENCE TO EARLIER DECISIONS: A POLICY WITH QUALIFICATIONS

"STARE DECISIS IS NOT, like the rule of res judicata, a universal inexorable command." So Justice Brandeis began a much-cited passage collecting dozens of instances where the Court had overruled an earlier decision.[228] In many matters, he conceded "it is more important that the applicable rule of law be settled than that it be settled right." He pointed to a case on the priority of mortgages, where Justice Field had said that "Judicial decisions affecting the business interests of the country should not be disturbed except for the most cogent reasons . . . . If there should be a change, the Legislature can make it with infinitely less derangement . . . , for statutory regulations would operate only in the future."[229] "But," Justice Brandeis continued, "in cases involving the Federal Constitution, where correction through legislative action is practically impossible, this Court has often overruled its earlier deci-

---

226 Norman v. Baltimore & Ohio R.R., 294 U.S. 240, 306–7 (1935). See infra, p. 774.

227 13 Wall. 604, decided Feb. 5, 1872. The "duty to express . . . dissent" was professed again in Railroad Co. v. Johnson, 15 Wall. 195 (1873).

228 Burnet v. Coronado Oil & Gas Co., 285 U.S. 393, 405 (1932). He was one of four Justices, dissenting, who called for the overruling of Gil-lespie v. State of Oklahoma, 257 U.S. 501 (1922), wherein a tax-exemption had been created, over the dissent of three Justices. In 1938 the *Gillespie* decision was overruled in Helvering v. Mountain Producers Corp., 303 U.S. 376, 387, per Hughes, C.J., two Justices dissenting.

229 National Bank v. Whitney, 103 U.S. 99, 102 (1881). He spoke for a unanimous Court.

sions. The Court bows to the lessons of experience and the force of better reasoning . . . ." He quoted what Justice Miller (Chase and Field concurring) had said in the passage from his dissent in *Washington University v. Rouse*, set out above.[230] Also something that Justice Field had once said on behalf of the Court in construing a grant of public lands, where prior decisions were distinguished and explained away: "It is more important that the Court should be right upon later and more elaborate consideration of the cases than consistent with previous declarations. Those doctrines only will eventually stand which bear the strictest examination, and the test of experience."[231]

Chase and those who stood with him in the contest were not really challenging the proposition Taney had expressed in 1849: "that [the Court's] opinion upon the construction of the Constitution is always open to discussion when it is supposed to have been founded in error . . . ."[232] Their judgment was at the moment distorted by the miscarriage of their attempt to settle the legal tender question notwithstanding that it could be done only by the vote of a Justice who by common agreement was no longer fit to serve. Chase in particular was bent upon securing a condemnation of the statute. It will be recalled that on March 10, 1868—just after the Court had made its order for the oral argument of *Hepburn v. Griswold*—Chase had written William B. Thomas, who was promoting his nomination by the Democrats, that "the question of the constitutionality of the legal tender act assumes new importance."[233]

Harper's Weekly, which maintained that the new majority had acted wisely in upholding a necessary war power even at the cost of overruling *Hepburn v. Griswold*, was "sorry to add, what is universally understood," that "The circumstances of the [*Hepburn*] case unmistakably indicate that except for certain political hopes and expectations that opinion would probably not have been rendered. Even the Supreme Bench is not free from the soliciting whispers of political ambition."[234]

Chase's indignation at the overruling was inconsistent with his own attitude in 1867 when he was in the minority in the 5–to–4 decisions in the *Test Oath Cases*.[235] On March 1, 1867, he had written to District Judge Hill in Mississippi: "The decision of the majority of the Court [in *Ex parte Garland*] is law until reversed and you do right in conforming your action to it. . . ." But he construed the ruling to condemn the test oath requirement only as it had operated *retrospec-*

---

[230] Supra, p. 752.
[231] Barden v. Northern Pacific R. Co., 154 U.S. 288, 322 (1894).
[232] The Passenger Cases, 7 How. 283, 470.

[233] Supra, p. 531.
[234] "The Supreme Court and Legal Tender," 15:450. May 20, 1871.
[235] Supra, p. 240.

tively—"only as denying the right to impose the oath as a condition of continuing to exercise an office or profession."[236] Seemingly he indulged a hope that *Garland* might be overruled. This is borne out by Chase's letter of April 1, 1867, to District Judge Giles of Maryland. Apparently Giles had submitted the draft of an order to be entered by the Circuit Court, to bring its rules into accord with *Garland*. Chase gave the reasons why he declined to join in such action:

> I return the order you enclosed to me. You have full authority to make it, holding as you do the Circuit Court with complete jurisdiction. I shall find no fault if you direct it to be entered: but I cannot unite in the direction; first, because until the new allotment is made I have no jurisdiction as a Judge of the Circuit Court for Maryland;[237] and, secondly, because I adhere to the dissent of the majority in the case before the Supreme Court, and am not willing, by an act which on my part would be extra-jurisdictional to countenance any supposition that I have changed by opinion.[238]

THE OVERRULING OF *HEPBURN* WAS ANTICIPATED

"THE DECISION [in *Hepburn*] only partially disposed of a great question to which it related, and has not been received by the profession or by the public as conclusive of the matter." So wrote Justice Miller in the statement on behalf of the new majority.[239] "The course of public and private discussion . . . shows that there is little disposition to accept it as final . . ." was the *Boston Daily Advertiser*'s report from Washington.[240] Editorially that journal, well informed on economic matters, expressed the view that "the argument of the Attorney-General in favor of . . . [a] rehearing was unanswerable." Explaining, it observed that

> As to the scope of the actual decision of the court, we think it is much greater than its defenders admit. The amount of contracts out-

---

[236] Chase Papers, L.C. Judge Hill had written on January 20 that while he disagreed with the decision, he was acting in accordance with it. "It is contended by many here that that decision declared the test oath required by the act of 1862 as to all officers unconstitutional. I do not so understand it; if I am wrong would like to be corrected. . . ." Chase Papers, L.C.

[237] It will be recalled that the Act of July 23, 1866, to fix the number of Judges of the Supreme Court, and to change certain Judicial Circuits, had created an impediment, which Congress removed by the Act of March 2, 1867. Supra at pp. 172–75. Not until April 8, 1867, did the Court make a new order of allotment.

[238] Chase Papers, L.C.

[239] Supra, p. 739.

[240] Apr. 11, 1870.

standing which were created before the war, is believed to be in hundreds of millions. As we predicted when the decision was made public, payment of these in coin has been generally refused at the risk of litigation, and we believe that if the decision is maintained the resultant evil will be far greater than to allow the precedents of eight years to stand until general resumption. . . .[241]

On February 19, 1870, Representative George W. McCrary introduced a bill to stay execution of judgments in the federal courts on debts contracted prior to the second Legal Tender Act of July 11, 1862, unless the creditor would accept currency.[242] The Judiciary Committee took no action: even supposing a favorable disposition, events soon made it appear that the *Hepburn* ruling would not stand.

The Commissioners of the Sinking Fund of the State of Pennsylvania, in a public notice of February 24, 1870, asserted that in consideration of the division within the Court and the fact that the State's legislation authorized the payment of her indebtedness only in legal tender currency, "it would not be advisable for the State Treasurer to make any change in the present mode of paying the obligations of the commonwealth."[243] The General Assembly, however, passed a statute enacting

That the state treasurer, under the direction of the commissioners of the sinking fund, is hereby authorized, in his collections and payments, to conform to the decisions by said [Supreme] court, or such other decisions as may from time to time be made, anything in any act of assembly to the contrary notwithstanding.[244]

The Maine legislature passed a resolve, approved March 23, reciting the *Hepburn* decision and declaring

That while the said judicial opinion stands as the authoritative judgment of the said court, all such contracts made by this state prior to

---

[241] Apr. 22, 1870.

[242] H.R. 1265, 41st Cong., 2d Sess. The stay was to be graduated: one year on judgments for not more than $1,000, and so on to four years on judgments for more than $3,000; it would become terminable in the event the United States resumed and maintained specie payments.

McCrary has been mentioned as counsel for the creditor in Trebilcock v. Wilson, 12 Wall. 687 (1872), supra, n. 223.

[243] *The Stockholder*, 8:313, Mar. 15, 1870. The notice showed misin-formation as to the size of the Court and the number of Justices supporting the decision. The article went on to quote a letter that Reporter Wallace had sent to a Philadelphia journal, correcting erroneous statements, and adding that "on no great constitutional question where professional and public opinion has been largely divided, do I recall a case for many years where the Judges were unanimous, or nearer unanimity than in the present one. . . ."

[244] Laws, 1870, No. 47.

the date aforesaid [February 25, 1862], should be paid at maturity, in coin, or its equivalent in currency, and the treasurer of state is hereby authorized to act accordingly.[245]

Whatever may have been the magnitude of outstanding indebtedness contracted prior to the Legal Tender Act—on the nation's farms (two million in number, with an estimated value of seven billion dollars) and on town lots and buildings, by borrowings for business and industry, and by State and municipal bond issues—certainly the obligations of railroads constituted the most conspicuous interest affected by the *Hepburn* decision.[246] To test how boards of directors estimated the situation resulting from *Hepburn*, in respect of maturing bonds and interest coupons, resort was had to the records of a number of leading corporations.[247]

Some boards decided to go on paying in paper money. Thus on February 22, 1870, the directors of the Chicago, Burlington and Quincy Railroad voted "that our coupons be paid in currency as heretofore, and that nothing be paid under protest." The seconder of the motion was Sidney Bartlett, the highly respected Boston lawyer.[248] Next day the directors of the Erie Railway Company, with the advice of their counsel, adopted a resolution reciting that "it is understood that Railroad Companies generally will adhere to the policy of paying interest in legal tender currency" and directing the treasurer to continue that course.

Some voted to continue payment in paper, but to give a statement concerning the future. Thus the Joint Board of the United Companies of New Jersey, meeting on February 26,

> Resolved, That the Treasurers of the United Companies be directed to pay interest coupons on bonds issued prior to February 25th 1862, and other obligations created prior to that time, in the usual currency of the country as heretofore; but to notify the parties interested that the difference between the value of said currency and gold at the time of payment, will be hereafter paid by the Companies should the right to require the same become the settled law of the land.

---

[245] Acts and Resolves 1870, Resolves c. 195.

[246] *The Commercial and Financial Chronicle* for February 12, 1870, 10:198, estimated that "Probably not less than three hundred and fifty millions of state, city and railroad bonds will thus become specie paying." The *Boston Evening Transcript* reported that "It makes some hundreds of millions of railroad bonds and an immense aggregate of State and city bonds payable in coin, both principal and interest . . . ." Feb. 8, 1870.

[247] What follows restates some of the matters set out in the article on "Mr. Justice Bradley's Appointment . . . , *Harv. L. Rev.*, 54:1140, 1147–54, cited in note 126 above. The search was made at my request by officers of the several corporations.

[248] Supra, p. 35.

The Lehigh Coal & Navigation Company owed almost $137,000 of principal on March 1, 1870. The directors voted to pay in legal tender, with a certificate for the gold premium payable, with interest, "if said alleged right [to gold] be confirmed by lawful authority, within sixty days from the date of such confirmation, and within one year from the date hereof, unless said alleged right be denied by said lawful authority." The Lehigh Valley Railroad Company paid interest coupons in currency, with an undertaking to pay the gold premium "if the present decision of the Supreme Court of the United States is not reversed within a year." The Philadelphia & Reading owed $381,800 on April 1. It paid in currency, with a certificate for the gold premium: but on July 13—after the Court had adjourned without overruling *Hepburn*—the directors voted to redeem the certificates, and "that payment be made in gold or its equivalent for all obligations of the Company made prior to the passage of the legal tender act."

The prominence of the Pennsylvania Railroad made its reaction especially noteworthy. Interest on bonds would fall due on April 1 and on July 1. On February 12 the board of directors instructed its finance committee to secure the advice of counsel. On March 22 Chapman Biddle, solicitor for the Company's First District, rendered an opinion in which Theodore Cuyler, general counsel, and William J. Howard, general solicitor, concurred. Frequent conferences, it was reported, had been held with other transportation companies, but uniformity of action had not been attained. Continuing,

> The Committee are aware that since the decision in Hepburn vs. Griswold, the composition of the S.C. has undergone a change; two additional Judges have been confirmed (one of whom has already taken his seat) and by many persons it is assumed that the views of the new Judges do not harmonize on this constitutional question with those of their brethren who concurred in that Judgment. If this impression be well founded the existing law in regard to money contracts anterior to Feb. 1862, may before the lapse of a great while be materially modified, as it is understood that there is at least one case pending in the S.C. of the U.S. in which the same question is involved as in the case recently adjudicated. There appear to be but three ways which the Company can adopt in paying its obligations (created prior to Feb. 25/62).
>
> 1. By paying them in coin.
> 2. By paying them in currency, and at the same time agreeing by a suitable memorandum to pay the difference between coin and currency within a specified time thereafter, in currency, in case the Supreme Court shall affirm its recent decision. And
> 3. By refusing to pay except in currency.

It may be safely left to the wisdom of the Board of Directors to determine which of these modes will best promote the interests of the Comp'y.

On March 22 the board decided unanimously that the second course be followed. When, however, *Latham's* and *Deming's Appeals* were dismissed, the board concluded that "a readjustment of the question" was "not likely to be had within the period of one year from April 1, 1870"—the delay specified in the memorandum—and instructed the treasurer to redeem in coin.

The board of the Boston & Maine voted on February 26 to pay interest in coin. The directors of the Eastern Rail Road Company of Massachusetts instructed the treasurer to pay in gold "for the present and until otherwise instructed by this Board." Apparently this course was not invariably followed, however, for the minutes for February 16, 1871, record that several suits had been brought against the company for non-payment of interest and principal in gold.

At a meeting of the board of the Illinois Central Rail Road Company in New York on March 28 those present voted unanimously to comply with *Hepburn* in respect of certain interest coupons, some of which would fall due on April 1; this resolution was not to be made public until March 31, however, to permit a further meeting in case absent directors expressed dissent. No such meeting was held.

These items give substance to the observation with which Justice Bradley concluded his opinion: that the prompt action in granting a reargument of the issue in *Hepburn* had "had the effect of apprising the country that the decision was not fully acquiesced in, and of obviating any injurious consequences to the business of the country by its reversal."

THE CONTRIVED CASE OF *JUILLIARD v. GREENMAN*

It has been related above that Congress in 1875 directed that specie payments be resumed on January 1, 1879, and that meantime the circulation of Treasury notes be gradually reduced to $300 million.[249] It has also been noted that soft-money men carried the Act of May 31, 1878, whereby notes when received in the Treasury "shall be reissued and paid out again, and kept in circulation."[250] Two Congressmen—Democrat Ben Butler, who branded gold as the money of despots, and Republican Simeon B. Chittenden, New York business-

---

[249] Act of Jan. 14, 1875, 18 Stat. 296. Supra, p. 691.   [250] 20 Stat. 87.

man, who denounced greenbacks as a sham and a fraud—agreed to set up a case to settle their difference over the Act of 1878.[251] Augustus D. Juilliard of New York—wealthy textile manufacturer, sound-money advocate, and public benefactor—in 1879 sold cotton to Greenman, a citizen of Connecticut, for $5,122.90. (By the Act of February 16, 1875, for the relief of the Supreme Court, the money limit for taking up an appeal had been raised from $2,000 to $5,000.[252]) In payment, Greenman tendered $22.50 in gold, forty cents in silver, and Treasury notes—one for $5,000 and one for $100, identified as having been reissued under the Act of 1878. (The Resumption Act of 1875 had gone into operation: it took $5,100 in gold to get the notes thus tendered.) The tender was refused "on the sole ground that said $5100 was not tendered in gold coin of the United States."[253] Such was the frame of the suit of *Juilliard v. Greenman*.[254]

The Nation reported the arrangement between Butler and Chittenden and, as a defender of sound money, doubted the wisdom of thus needlessly procuring a decision. If the Court sustained the reissue, "the inflationists will be greatly encouraged"; an adverse decision, on the other hand, might precipitate such a rush to convert notes into gold as would imperil what had been accomplished under the Resumption Act.[255]

In the Circuit Court for the Southern District of New York, Circuit Judge Samuel Blatchford heard argument on June 7, 1879, and on June 11 gave judgment for the defendant.[256] On writ of error the case was filed in the Supreme Court on July 9. Senator George F. Edmunds (chairman of the Judiciary Committee, and leader in the enactment of specie resumption), and William Allen Butler of the New York bar,[257] represented the plaintiff.

Almost five years elapsed between docketing and decision—two years more than the normal wait. This was chiefly due to the fact that Justice Ward Hunt, who had come to the Court in 1872 as Justice Nelson's successor, was absent by reason of illness from Decem-

---

[251] [Ben] *Butler's Book* (Boston: A.M. Thayer and Co., 1892), 954–56, Charles Henry Butler, *A Century at the Bar of the Supreme Court* (New York: G. P. Putnam's Sons, 1942), ch. 5. The latter, Reporter of the Supreme Court from 1902 to 1916, was the son of William Allen Butler, who had managed the test case on behalf of the plaintiff, Juilliard.

[252] 18 Stat. 316.

[253] Transcript of Record, stipulation annexed by Addition to Record.

[254] 110 U.S. 421 (1884).

[255] 28:173, Mar. 13, 1879. The policy of the Treasury was to hold a specie reserve of at least 40 percent of the note circulation. Ann. Cyc. 1880, 267.

[256] Transcript of Record 6–7.

[257] (1825–1902); in 1885, president of the American Bar Assn. See D.A.B.

ber 24, 1878, until he resigned on January 27, 1882. Judge Blatchford, his replacement, was seated on April 3.

First, a motion by Edmunds to advance the case for an early hearing was denied on January 5, 1880. According to the press, it was understood that the Court was waiting for a full Bench.[258] But even if that objection had not been present, it is not to be supposed that the Court would have perceived in this artificial controversy such "special and peculiar circumstances" as Rule 26 required for taking a case out of its order on the docket. Then when the case was reached it was passed, on January 13, 1882, agreeably to a stipulation of counsel. (This was a fortnight before Hunt's resignation, mentioned above.) On October 11, 1882, on motion of William Allen Butler, it was passed again. (Justice Field was absent until October 16.) Next, motions by Edmunds to assign the case for hearing out of turn were denied, on January 8 and February 5, 1883. So it went over to the next term—when, on October 9, 1883, on motion of William Allen Butler, it was "passed and assigned for argument on the first day in January, 1884, that the Court is in session." When January 2 came, however, opposing counsel submitted on their printed arguments.

By this time the affair had become rather pointless. Legal tender notes had long been as acceptable as gold. The Greenback party had reached its crest in the elections of 1878. (In 1884 its candidate for the Presidency, Ben Butler, polled only 175,000 votes, and the party then disappeared.)

Counsel for Juilliard pressed the view that the decision in 1871 had upheld the Legal Tender Acts only "as WAR MEASURES"; they suggested that "the patriotic sentiment of the period" had "turned the scales of justice." They made the point that ten Justices in all had heard argument, and five had voted against the statute—an unimpressive effort to count Justice Grier in the balance. Now "with a single honored exception," all the voices in opposition "have been silenced

---

[258] *The Nation*, 30:19, Jan. 8, 1880.
Edmunds' motion had been filed on December 22, 1879. *The Nation* of December 25 observed, "Weak-kneed Congressmen of both parties will enjoy the holiday recess all the more because of the motion submitted to the Supreme Court on Monday by Senator Edmunds, in his capacity of counsel for the plaintiff in the made-up Chittenden-Butler suit . . . . Mr. Edmunds asked for its advancement, and if it could be argued and decided

adversely to the legal tenders this winter it would relieve both parties of a burden which they will find it difficult to carry in the next Congress." 29:432. President Hayes in his message of December 1, 1879, had called for the retirement of legal tender notes from circulation, and in the Finance Committee Senator Bayard, Democrat, was urging a resolution to that effect. Each party in Congress was divided and embarrassed.

by death." Counsel dwelt upon the variety of situations where the power of Congress depended upon facts and circumstances subject to judicial inquiry. What the Court had said of martial rule in the *Milligan* case[259] was quoted as applicable to legal tender paper: "as necessity creates the rule, so it limits its duration."[260]

On one point all the Justices agreed: no distinction was to be drawn between the issue in time of war and the reissue in time of peace. And all except Justice Field supported the decision in the *Legal Tender Cases.* Justice Horace Gray—who had been appointed in 1881 as successor to Justice Clifford—spoke for the Court. He began by emphasizing the wide scope that had been given to implied powers. In particular the power "to borrow money on the credit of the United States" was not to be read narrowly as it would be in a penal statute or in a private contract. From the power to borrow, together with the power to establish a uniform national currency (which resulted from various clauses), the Court drew the conclusion that the National Government—like other sovereign governments—could impress on its notes the quality of legal tender. It being determined that Congress did have that power, the decision whether it would be expedient to exercise it was "a political question, to be determined by Congress when the question of exigency arises, and not a judicial question, to be afterwards passed upon by the courts."

Justice Field had lost nothing in the vigor of his dissent. The power "to borrow" was unambiguous: it required a willing lender; the borrower, even though it were the Government, could not rightly give its notes a potency affecting strangers to the loan. The United States had a government of limited powers: What then had been the pertinence of recounting that the Emperor of Austria and other foreign sovereigns had made their paper money a legal tender?

Evils which Justice Field predicted did not arise; Congress did not abuse its power. All currency was maintained at the gold standard until, in the Great Depression, Congress found that it must devaluate the dollar and, "to assure uniform value to the coins and currencies of the United States," must render unenforceable all contracts, theretofore or thereafter made, for payment in gold. In *Norman v. Baltimore & Ohio R.R.,*[261] Chief Justice Hughes, speaking for a majority of five, started with what had been established in the *Legal Tender* decisions, and went on to sustain the position that Justices Miller and Bradley had taken in *Trebilcock v. Wilson*:[262] that Congress might validly

---

[259] Supra, p. 208.
[260] Brief for Plaintiff in Error, 6, 26, 57, 63.

[261] 294 U.S. 240 (1935).
[262] Supra, p. 764.

declare that contracts stipulating for a particular kind of money would be satisfied by whatever money had been made a legal tender. "Parties cannot remove their transactions from the reach of dominant constitutional power by making contracts about them."[263]

The overturning of *Hepburn v. Griswold* had been vindicated.

---

[263] 294 U.S. at 308.

CHAPTER XV

Consequences of the Confederacy I:
Confiscation, Clemency, and Contracts

T HE MATTER TO BE CONSIDERED in the next two chapters will sound strange because, happily, the nation has had little occasion to remember. Early in the Civil War, Congress sought to suppress rebellion by measures of confiscation. This shifted and unsettled estates, raised up informers, brought numerous and hard cases to the Court, and in the end showed no benefit commensurate with the detriments that resulted.

Another topic is the interdiction of trade with the enemy, subject to license by the Executive, and the appropriation of captured and abandoned property—an inept exercise, as it proved and one attended by much corruption.

Pardon and amnesty flowed copiously: How far did Executive clemency efface the effects of the measures just mentioned?

Then there were a host of suits to question, in a variety of contexts, what effect should be allowed to the laws of the Confederacy and of its member States.

Consequences of the war made a major item in the Court's business throughout the 1870's; indeed as late as 1892 it was solving puzzles under the Confiscation Act of 1862.[1] And as a precedent, *Miller v. United States*,[2] where in 1871 the Court sustained that Act, was relied upon as bedrock when the Court came to pass upon the seizure of German assets under the Trading with the Enemy Act of 1917.[3]

---

[1] Jenkins v. Collard, 145 U.S. 546; United States v. Dunnington, 146 U.S. 338.

[2] 11 Wall. 268.

[3] White v. Mechanics' Securities Corp., 269 U.S. 283 (1925). Said

Justice Holmes for the Court: "The funds were seized adversely by the United States in time of war. They are in its hands; it has been declared by an Act of Congress what shall be done with them, and that is the end

Then the matter of *Farrington v. Saunders*, the *Cotton Tax Case* of 1871, will be presented. At the time this was spoken of as "by far the most important suit that has ever been submitted to the Supreme Court of the United States."[4] The 39th Congress had laid a tax "upon all cotton produced within the United States."[5] Thad Stevens said, "I think there is a very good reason why this one article should pay a very large portion of the taxation which we are obliged to raise."[6] But was this a "direct tax," falling within the condemnation of the Constitution because not apportioned according to the population? Was it within the prohibition of a tax on exports? The Circuit Court for Western Tennessee sustained the statute in a suit to recover from the collector, and the case was brought to the Supreme Court. After two arguments, the judgment was affirmed by an equally divided Court. As was then the practice in such a situation, the matter was not included in the United States Reports.

A determination by the Court whether this was a "direct tax" within the meaning of the Constitution would, certainly, have been of enormous significance as a precedent; in 1895 the construction of that expression in a five-to-four ruling resulted in the invalidation of the income tax.[7] Yet *Farrington v. Saunders*, which came so near to being a momentous case, has been virtually unknown.[8]

Watson v. Jones,[9] decided in 1872, will round out the selection of representative decisions illustrating the work of the Court in quieting controversies resulting from the nation's great ordeal. A Presbyterian congregation at Louisville was rent by a schism over slavery; the General Assembly, highest judicatory of that church, supported emancipation. In a suit to gain control of the church property—brought in the federal court on the basis of diversity of citizenship—the Court, per Miller, J., held it to be the duty of the civil tribunal to accept and apply the ruling of the highest judicatory of the church. Only occasionally thereafter did the Court have occasion to deal with such a matter.

Then suddenly *Watson v. Jones* was brought sharply into focus

---

of the matter. There is no question that such a seizure and disposition are within its powers. Brown v. United States, 8 Cranch 110, 129; Miller v. United States, 11 Wall. 268." At p. 300.

[4] *Louisville Courier-Journal*, Dec. 26, 1869, quoting the *New Orleans Commercial Bulletin*.

[5] Act of July 13, 1866, 14 Stat. 98.

[6] Cong. Globe, 39–1, 2473. May 8, 1866.

[7] Pollock v. Farmers' Loan & Trust Co., 157 U.S. 429 and 158 U.S. 601.

[8] Warren's *Supreme Court in United States History*, new and rev. ed. 2 vols. (Boston: Little, Brown and Co., 1928), in Chapter 31, "The Legal Tender Cases," identifies it in a footnote, in explanation of a quotation from the *New York World* naming it as one of three most "important litigations arising out of the war."

[9] 13 Wall. 679.

by *Presbyterian Church in the United States v. Hull Church*,[10] decided in 1969. A dispute over control of church property arose when congregations at Savannah seceded from the parent body on the ground that the latter in its pronouncements on social and political matters had abandoned the fundamental tenets of the Presbyterian faith. Counsel for the parent body, resisting the claim for judicial interference, told the Court that "We think Watson vs. Jones and this case are very similar on the facts. . . . Watson involved the statement by the church on the question of slavery. This case involves the statement of the church on civil rights . . . ."[11] Thus issues from the Civil War may still reverberate in the Supreme Court chamber.

RESORT TO CONFISCATION

THE CONFEDERATE CONGRESS, by an Act of May 21, 1861 forbad Southern debtors to pay Northern creditors during the war.[12] So much was only an application of the rule that war stops commercial intercourse. The statute went on, however, to authorize debtors to pay what they owed into the Confederate Treasury, receiving in return a certificate bearing interest and redeemable on the restoration of peace. That, however, was consistent with eventual payment to the Northern creditors.

The United States Congress, by an Act of August 6, 1861, declared that all property suffered by the owner to be used in aid of the insurrection would be subject to capture, and to condemnation in a federal court.[13] Proceedings would be brought by the Attorney General or by the District Attorney for the district wherein the property was found or into which it was brought. Further, any person might file an information, "in which case the proceedings shall be for the use of such informer and the United States in equal parts." The statute would confiscate the property because of rebel *use*, not on the basis of a conviction of the owner. After Bull Run, when it was understood that the Confederates were using slaves to build earthworks and for other military tasks, the bill was expanded by the insertion of a section to forfeit the claim of the owner to any slave so used. This gave the person thus freed a defense, available in any court recognizing the

---

[10] 393 U.S. 440. On certiorari to the Supreme Court of Georgia.

[11] Transcript of oral argument, Dec. 10, 1968, at 47.

[12] Laws of the Provisional Congress, Sess. II, ch. 53, p. 151. Exception was made as to creditors in Delaware, Maryland, Kentucky, Missouri, and the District of Columbia.

[13] An Act to Confiscate Property Used for Insurrectionary Purposes, 12 Stat. 319.

authority of the United States, whenever the master asserted his claim to service.

Then the Confederate Congress passed its Act of August 30, 1861, for the sequestration of the property of alien enemies.[14] This opened with a recital that the Government and people of the United States had "departed from the usages of civilized warfare in confiscating and destroying the property of the people of the Confederate States . . . ," and that the only protection lay in such retaliation as would indemnify Confederate citizens: accordingly the lands, goods, rights and credits of alien enemies were to be sequestrated. "This was good war propaganda, but at that stage of the game hardly accurate," comments William M. Robinson, Jr., in his thoroughly competent study. "Confiscation and sequestration were in the minds of both parties equally from the commencement of the struggle."[15]

An amendatory statute of February 15, 1862, spoke of "confiscation" and made clear that the appropriation was definitive.[16] Section 7 provided that the next of kin, direct ascendants or descendants of the alien enemy, might have the property decreed to them as if the alien enemy were dead. Thus the property of Justice Wayne was promptly vested in fee in his son, the adjutant general of Georgia.[17] As will be seen presently, laws in aid of the rebellion fell with the Confederacy; orders of sequestration were held utterly void: "they gave no rights . . . , and took none from the legal owners."[18] On Justice Wayne's death his property passed under a will made on April 12, 1865, naming his son as one of his executors.[19]

The Confederate sequestration was vigorously enforced. Mr. Robinson reports that "the number of sequestration cases in most of the district courts ran well into the thousands and the proceeds into the millions of dollars. The law was economically administered, more than ninety per cent of the gross proceeds being covered into the Treasury."[20]

---

[14] Laws of the Provisional Congress, Sess. III, ch. 61, p. 201. As in the statute of May 21, exception was made for citizens of slaveholding States.

[15] *Justice in Grey* (Cambridge, Mass.: Harvard University Press, 1941), 495.

[16] Laws of the Provisional Congress, Sess. V, ch. 71, p. 260, at 266.

[17] Robinson, *Justice in Grey*, 244; Lawrence, *James Moore Wayne, Southern Unionist* (Chapel Hill: University of North Carolina Press,

1943), 189–90.

[18] Dewing v. Perdicaries, 96 U.S. 193, 195 (1878).

[19] Admitted to probate by the Orphans' Court of Washington County, District of Columbia, on July 20, 1867; a certified copy was filed in the Ordinary's Court of Chatham County, Georgia, on Aug. 5, 1867.

[20] *Justice in Grey*, 626. During half of the life of the statute, 7.5 millions came to the Treasury. The final amount cannot be determined. Ibid., 262–64.

SECOND CONFISCATION ACT

RETALIATION INVITES RETALIATION. On the opening of the session of Congress on December 2, 1861, Senator Trumbull introduced a bill to confiscate the property of rebels, and to give freedom to persons they held in slavery. So began an effort that culminated on the last day of the session in the Act of July 17, 1862.[21] The course of the debate was marked by sharp encounters between ultra and conservative supporters of the Union. The issues over which they contended reappeared when the question of constitutionality came to be argued before the Court in 1870 and 1871.[22]

The title of the Act expressed a purpose "to punish Treason and Rebellion" and "to seize and confiscate the Property of Rebels." Read "rebels" as referring to public enemies, and one may discern the two aspects in which Congress viewed those who participated in the Confederacy: as traitors, who might be dealt with as provided by municipal law; and as belligerents, liable to such measures as were sanctioned by the law of nations. "Treason against the United States," the only crime defined in the Constitution,

> shall consist only in levying War against them, or in adhering to their Enemies, giving them Aid and Comfort. No person shall be convicted of Treason unless on the Testimony of two Witnesses to the same overt Act, or on Confession in open Court.

Article III, Section 3, further provides:

> The Congress shall have Power to declare the Punishment of Treason, but no Attainder of Treason shall work Corruption of Blood, or Forfeiture except during the Life of the Person attainted.

The words of the defining sentence came from the Statute of Treasons, 25 Edw. III, Stat. 5, Ch. 2, of 1351. As the crime is uniquely heinous, so its definition and application are most narrowly confined. The statute of crimes in 1790 made the death penalty mandatory.[23]

Of course, as Trumbull said,

> Nobody expects to try for treason the two or three hundred thousand men now in arms against the Government, every one of whom is a legal traitor; but we will give them the rights of belligerents . . . .[24]

---

[21] 12 Stat. 589.
[22] Miller v. United States, 11 Wall. 268, argued Feb. 1 and 2, 1870, and again on Feb. 10 and 11, 1871. When on April 3 its validity was sustained, per Strong, J., Field and Clifford, JJ., dissented. See infra, pp. 801–03.
[23] 1 Stat. 112.
[24] Cong. Globe, 37–2, 943. Feb. 25, 1862.

The Government should, however, act as it might against a foreign enemy—by confiscating such property of adherents as came within its reach, and in particular by taking their slaves. Senator Cowan of Pennsylvania, skilful in debate and inveterately conservative, challenged this as "vicious reasoning": "In this way the constitutional guarantees . . . would all be nullified . . . . We then might forfeit all their property upon a judgment against them as belligerents, and afterwards hang them on the ground of their treason."[25]

But was it true that the law of nations sanctioned such confiscation? The negative was sustained by Representative Benjamin F. Thomas of Massachusetts, Conservative Unionist, recently a judge on the Supreme Judicial Court. "To give a plausible aspect to the proposition, the advocates of this bill have gone back to Grotius and to Bynkershoek for the rules of war . . . ."[26] But, Thomas insisted, "Commerce, civilization, Christian culture, have tempered and softened the rigor of the ancient rules . . . ." To be sure, confiscations had figured largely in the Revolution: the treaty of peace had pledged "no future confiscations" and an earnest recommendation to the State legislatures to restore what had been taken. Chief Justice Marshall, in a case during the War of 1812, had said that war gives to the sovereign the right to confiscate the property of the enemy; that humane mitigations had not impaired the right itself.[27] The actual decision, however, had been that no condemnation could be decreed until Congress directed. So Thomas dismissed Marshall's statement as an *obiter dictum;* at any rate, he said, the jurisprudence of nations now acknowledged a milder rule.

To prosecute for treason, the accused must first be found within the jurisdiction of a court of the United States; he must have a trial by jury, and the protection of the two-witness requirement; and in the event of conviction a forfeiture of property could be imposed for no longer than his life. The bill sought to avoid all this by exercising a belligerent's power over the property of the enemy. Jurisdiction would be acquired by libeling the thing when found or brought within a judicial district; the action would be *in rem*—just as it is against a ship or a cargo in admiralty, or against goods held for violation of the revenue laws. Thomas derided this expedient: "Magna Charta is soiled

---

[25] Ibid., 1053. Mar. 4, 1862.

It was a year later that Justice Grier, speaking for the majority in The Prize Cases, 2 Bl. 635, affirmed that it was not to be doubted "that the belligerent party who claims to be sovereign, may exercise both belligerent and sovereign rights."

[26] Cong. Globe, 37–2, App., 218–20. May 24, 1862.

Thomas belonged to an era when workers for peace hoped to narrow the scope of hostilities and to render noncombatants ever more exempt from the ravages of war.

[27] Brown v. United States, 8 Cranch 110 (1814).

and worm-eaten. The Bill of Rights, the muniments of personal freedom, habeas corpus, trial by jury, what are they all worth in comparison with this new safeguard of liberty, the proceeding *in rem*?"

It was apparent throughout the debate that the radicals were itching for a Congressional direction of the war, and for minimizing the leadership of the President. Senator Browning of Illinois, one of the most effective critics of the bill, asked, "If we begin by denuding the Executive, how long will it be before the judiciary is stripped of its ermine, and all power concentrated in the hands of an irresponsible legislature?"[28] It was a well-posed question.

Sumner, reacting, declared that "The war powers of Congress are derived from the Constitution, but, when once set in motion, are without any restraint from the Constitution . . . . The Senator knows very well . . . that by the Constitution of the United States, Congress may make all laws to regulate the duties and powers of the commander-in-chief. . . ."[29]

The bill as enacted took several lines. By way of defining crimes and punishments, Section I made treason punishable by death *or* imprisonment, and in addition the traitor's slaves would be free. Section 2 created the lesser offense of engaging or assisting in rebellion. By Section 3, one convicted of either of these crimes was made ineligible to hold office under the United States. Then, grasping the powers of a belligerent, the bill in Section 5 made it the duty of the President to cause the seizure of all the property of certain categories—First to Sixthly—of persons engaged in rebellion: officers of the armed forces; leading civil officers of the Confederacy; certain State officers; finally, those who, owning property in a loyal State or Territory or the District of Columbia, should thenceforth give aid to the rebellion.

Further, by Section 6, if any person in any insurrectionary State, being engaged in rebellion, did not within sixty days after a warning proclamation by the President, cease such aid and return to his allegiance, all his estate would be liable to seizure.

On July 25, 1862, that warning proclamation was issued.

Section 7 established the procedure for condemnation. Proceedings *in rem* against seized property would be brought in a court of the United States,

which proceedings shall conform as nearly as may be to proceedings in admiralty or revenue cases; and if said property, whether real or personal, shall be found to have belonged to a person engaged in rebel-

---

[28] Cong. Globe, 37–2, 2924. Jan. 25, 1862.

[29] Ibid., 2963, 2966. June 27, 1862.

lion, or who has given aid or comfort thereto, the same shall be condemned as enemies' property and become the property of the United States . . . .

The Act of 1862—unlike that of 1861—made no provision for informers.

The courts were authorized "to allow such fees and charges of their officers as shall be reasonable and proper in the premises."

Sections 9 to 12 struck at slavery, but less energetically than the more ardent had hoped. The slaves of a rebel, escaping to the Union lines or found in a place occupied by Union forces, would be deemed captives of war, and set free.

The President—so Section 13 enacted—was authorized to grant to rebels a pardon and amnesty, "with such exceptions and at such time and on such conditions as he may deem expedient for the public welfare." Inasmuch as the Constitution gave the President the power to pardon, it was questionable what function, if any, this section performed. President Lincoln referred to it when on December 8, 1863, he issued the proclamation offering pardon to those who would desist from rebellion and take an oath thenceforth to be loyal and to support the laws and proclamations with reference to slavery.[30]

(In its animosity toward President Johnson, the 39th Congress at its Second Session voted to repeal the above Section 13. The President received the bill on Wednesday, January 9, 1867, and by holding it for "ten days, Sundays excepted," allowed it to become law without his signature. In the meantime, on January 14, the Court announced its decision in *Ex parte Garland*.[31] Justice Field said that "This [pardoning] power is not subject to legislative control." The scope and consequences of Executive clemency, however, remained to be settled in further litigation.)

This Second Confiscation Bill reached President Lincoln late on July 14, 1862. Congressional leaders were anxious to adjourn. Lincoln let it be known that he had objections; the upshot was that the Houses hurriedly passed a Joint Resolution "explanatory" of their bill. The most significant feature was a direction that the measure should not be "so construed as to work a forfeiture of the real estate of the offender beyond his natural life." Taking the bill and the resolution together, the President signed both on July 17, at the same time sending to the Houses the draft he had prepared to express his objections.[32] To take

---

[30] See supra, p. 95. Infra, pp. 843, 845.
[31] 4 Wall. 333. See supra, pp. 241–42.
[32] The Confiscation Act is at 12 Stat. 589; the Joint Resolution at 12 Stat. 627. Lincoln's message is in S.

Exec. Doc. No. 70 and *Collected Works of Abraham Lincoln*, ed., Roy P. Basler (New Brunswick, N.J.: Rutgers University Press, 1953), V, 328–31.

the fee of the land of an enemy, when only a forfeiture for life could have been inflicted on the same man as a traitor, seemed inconsistent with the Constitution. "Again," commenting on the mechanics of enforcement,

> this act, by proceedings *in rem* forfeits property, for the ingredients of treason, without a conviction of the supposed criminal, or a personal hearing given him in any proceeding. That we may not touch property lying within our reach, because we can not give personal notice to an owner who is absent endeavoring to destroy the govern [ment,] is certainly not very satisfactory; still the owner may not be thus engaged, and I think a reasonable time should be provided for such parties to appear and have personal hearings. Similar provisions are not uncommon in connection with proceedings *in rem*.

This defect the Joint Resolution did not cure; presently it caused trouble.

TRADING WITH THE ENEMY

ECONOMIC WARFARE is beset with certain peculiar difficulties. Regulations, however well founded in reason and essential to the government's strategy, are never so firmly supported in public opinion as are laws against acts clearly *mala in se*. Dispensations and evasions yield enormous profits, while nobody in particular seems to be hurt. Violations are looked upon by many as only venial offenses, involving no disgrace. In this respect the experience of the Confederacy was akin to that of the North. One side wanted cotton, the other suffered from a want of things that cotton could procure. Need and greed worked on both sides.[33]

An Act of Congress of July 13, 1861, forbad commercial intercourse between loyal States and the States and parts of States declared to be in insurrection.[34] All goods moving in contravention of this ban

---

[33] Robinson, *Justice in Grey*, 150–152, 176–77. Where cotton could be traded for medicines and other things needed for the Confederate army, even commanders in the field might countenance violations of law. And where a community was beyond the protection of the Confederate forces, barter with the Federals was "almost inevitable and excusable," wrote Secretary of War Seddon. "Thus," Robinson concludes, "the crime of trading with the enemy came to be more generally regarded as an offense against the revenue laws than as an act of treason."

[34] An Act further to provide for the collection of duties on imports, and for other purposes. 12 Stat. 255.

were liable to forfeiture upon proceedings in a federal court. The President might, however, permit such transactions as, in his discretion, were deemed conducive to the public good; trade so licensed must conform to regulations to be prescribed by the Secretary of the Treasury. A supplementary Act of May 20, 1862, authorized the Secretary to stop the shipment of goods believed to be intended to reach the rebels, or directed to points where there was imminent danger of their falling into rebel hands.[35] Pursuant to this legislation, Secretary Chase on August 28, 1862, issued Regulations concerning Internal and Coastwise Commercial Intercourse. "No goods . . . , whatever may be the ostensible destination thereof, shall be transported to any place now under control of the insurgents; . . . nor to any place on the north side of the Potomac, and south of the Washington and Annapolis railroad . . . without a permit . . . ." From the eastern shore of the Chesapeake to the country west of the Mississippi, areas easily accessible to the Confederates were subjected to this same requirement.

Chief Justice Taney in the Circuit Court viewed this business with an unfriendly eye. In *United States v. Box of Dry Goods, Geo. W. Carpenter, Claimant,*[36] goods were to be shipped from Baltimore to Charles County, Maryland—which fronts on the Potomac where it bends deep into Virginia. On a charge that fraud had been committed in obtaining the permit, forfeiture was sought in the District Court. A decree for the Government was, however, reversed on appeal to the Circuit Court. "A civil war, or any other, does not enlarge the powers of the Federal Government over the States or the people, beyond what the compact has given to it in time of war." That meant that the war power was subject to the limitations applicable to the Commerce Clause—narrowly construed at that.

The Act of July 13, 1861, provided that "all goods . . . coming from said [insurrectionary] State or section into the other parts of the United States, and all proceeding to such State or section . . . shall, together with the vessel or vehicle conveying the same, . . . be forfeited to the United States . . . ." In *United States v. Two Thousand Bushels of Wheat, Penn and Mitchell, Claimants,*[37] it appeared that grain from Virginia had been taken across the Potomac into Maryland's southernmost county, and thence shipped to Baltimore. Taney in the Circuit Court construed the statute to mean that the liability of goods

---

[35] 12 Stat. 404.

[36] Unreported decision of June 19, 1863, summarized by District Judge Giles in United States v. The Francis Hatch, Fed. Case No. 15,158, D.C.

Md. 1864; part of Taney's opinion is set out in Ann. Cyc. 1863, p. 202.

[37] Unreported decision in June 1863, summarized by Giles, J., in United States v. The Francis Hatch, cited in the footnote 36 above.

and of vessel "adheres to them while they remain . . . in transitu between the forbidden places and no longer." No doubt he was analogizing with the rule in prize law: the neutral ship breaching blockade is purged if it completes the voyage without being caught.[38] The spy may not be penalized if he has returned into his own lines. (In baseball, a runner may steal a base if he succeeds in getting there before being tagged out.) Those are the rules. But a sovereign declaring law for persons who owe it obedience is not playing games: one charged with transporting stolen goods does not escape punishment by showing that he deposited his load before the arrest was made. It is not to be doubted that, had these holdings come to a review in the Supreme Court, there would have been a rejection of Taney's narrow construction of the non-intercourse law—which, it has been seen, was the result in the comparable case of *The Reform*.[39]

Thus far Congress had made confiscable certain property, movable and immovable: for *use in aid of the rebellion* under the Act of August 6, 1861, and by reason of *rebel ownership* under the Second Confiscation Act of July 17, 1862. Enforcement of this legislation was primarily the concern of the Attorney General,[40] the chief law officer of the Government. Then the *non-intercourse statute* of July 13, 1861, supplemented by that of May 20, 1862, provided for the forfeiture of goods and chattels, and vessels and vehicles, in forbidden trade with the enemy. This ban was primarily a concern of the Secretary of the Treasury—there was a close analogy to enforcing the revenue laws. But some commanders in the field, notably General Lew Wallace at Baltimore, took such matters into their own hands. Attorney General Bates complained in his diary of "the frequent instances of needless, groundless and wanton interference of the military . . . ."[41] And Secretary Chase, in his annual report of December 10, 1863, stated that it had been found "difficult to act with much efficiency or usefulness, and the regulation of trade was assumed almost exclusively by the military authorities."[42]

---

[38] As the Court had occasion to hold in *The Wren*, 6 Wall. 582 (1868).

[39] 3 Wall. 617 (1866), discussed supra, p. 142.

[40] He was particularly charged with responsibility by the President's orders of November 13, 1862, and January 8, 1863. *Collected Works of Abraham Lincoln*, V, 496; VI, 45. On January 8, 1863, Bates issued General Instructions to District Attorneys and Marshals relative to Proceedings under the Acts of Congress for Confiscation.

He said, in part, "The issuing of the order of seizure is trusted to the discretion of the District Attorney; and while he ought to be vigilant to execute the law he ought to be careful to avoid hasty and improvident seizures. . . ." The instructions are summarized in Ann. Cyc. 1863, 219.

[41] *The Diary of Edward Bates 1859–1866* (Washington: Government Printing Office, 1933), 350, entry of Mar. 22, 1864.

[42] Cong. Globe 38–1, App., 4 at 9.

ABANDONED AND CAPTURED PROPERTY

BY A STATUTE OF MARCH 12, 1863, Congress provided "for the Collection of abandoned Property and for the Prevention of Frauds in insurrectionary Districts within the United States."[43] This took account of two new categories of property: that which was *abandoned*, and that which was *captured* (other than as maritime prize). The Secretary of the Treasury was to appoint Special Agents to receive and collect such property within the rebel States. By the implementing Treasury Department Circular of July 3, 1863, the Secretary defined these categories. Abandoned property was such as had been deserted by the owners, or voluntarily abandoned by them to the civil or military authorities of the United States. Captured property was that which had been seized or taken from hostile possession by the armed forces of the United States. Such property, Congress directed, was to be either appropriated to the public use, after due appraisement, or forwarded to a place within the loyal States for sale at auction. By Section 3,

> And any person claiming to have been the owner of any such abandoned or captured property may, at any time within two years after the suppression of the rebellion, prefer his claim to the proceeds thereof in the Court of Claims; and on proof to the satisfaction of said court of his ownership of said property, of his right to the proceeds thereof, and that he has never given any aid or comfort to the present rebellion, to receive the residue of such property [after lawful expenses had been deducted].

That opened the door of the Court of Claims to a mass of suitors, chiefly cotton claimants. And after it was established that claimant

---

[43] 12 Stat. 820. President Lincoln approved the bill on March 12, notwithstanding that the 37th Congress had expired on March 4. This was contrary to the practical construction his predecessors had given to Article I, Section 7, of the Constitution. In the 38th Congress, the House Judiciary Committee reported that the measure was not in force. Cong. Globe, 38–1, 2880. H.R. Rep. No. 108, June 11, 1864. Nevertheless, Congress recognized its effectiveness when it passed a statute *in addition* to it, on July 2, 1864, 13 Stat. 375.

In La Abra Silver Mining Co. v. United States, 175 U.S. 423 (1899), the Court held that a bill signed by the President while the Houses were *in recess* had become law; it reserved the question, which was not before the Court, whether the same would be true where approval came after final adjournment. In Edwards v. United States, 286 U.S. 482 (1932), the Court, per Hughes, C.J., construed the pertinent provision as securing to the President ten days to consider and approve a bill, regardless of the recess or the adjournment of the Congress.

and Government alike could go on through the door into the Supreme Court,[44] the construction of the Abandoned and Captured Property Act became in the early 1870's a significant branch of the Court's work. Then this business dropped off; one notes a decision as late as 1888,[45] and then a straggler in 1919.[46]

The Special Agents appointed by Secretary Chase formed a group who remained devoted to his interests: they continued to supply him with information about conditions in the South, and to support his Presidential aspirations.

AMNESTY

PRESIDENT JOHNSON, it should here be recalled, issued four proclamations of amnesty. That of May 29, 1865, excluded numerous classes (among them, the owners of $20,000 worth of property); also, in restoring property rights, it excepted cases where confiscation proceedings were pending. That of September 7, 1867, admitted to the same benefits most, but not quite all of those earlier excluded. In the meantime, thousands of individual pardons had been given. The general amnesty of July 4, 1868, excluded only those under indictment, and in restoring rights of property excepted such property as had been legally divested. On Christmas Day, 1868, when impeachment lay behind and the end of his term was close at hand, Johnson threw open the gates and granted a full pardon for the offense of treason to all participants in the rebellion.

It remained to be determined how this clemency would bear upon the rights of persons affected by the various war measures.

---

[44] The Abandoned and Captured Property Act, approved March 12, 1863, did not specify that appeal would lie to the Supreme Court; but a statute of March 3, 1863, which reorganized the Court of Claims had provided in general language that appeals might be taken from the one to the other court. The Court of Claims took the view, however, that the Act of March 12 created a new jurisdiction, outside the scope of the appeal created by the Act of March 3.

Thereupon Congress, alarmed at the prospect that millions of dollars in claims might be allowed without any review by the Supreme Court (Senator Edmunds, Cong. Globe, 40–2, 2764), enacted that *the Govern-*

ment would have an appeal. Act of June 25, 1868, 15 Stat. 75.

In *Ex parte* Zellner, 9 Wall. 244, decided March 15, 1870, the Supreme Court held, however, that all along there had been a right of appeal under the basic statute of March 3, 1863. Accordingly mandamus was granted directing the Court of Claims to allow a claimant's appeal. So, too, in *Ex parte* Pargoud, 154 U.S. 577, 19 L. Ed. 620 (1870).

Some appeals involving the Abandoned and Captured Property Act came up through courts other than the Court of Claims.

[45] United States v. Johnson, 124 U.S. 236.

[46] O'Pry v. United States, 249 U.S. 323.

So much explanation has been needed, to lay a foundation for understanding problems that would occupy a considerable amount of the Court's attention.

EARLY PROBLEMS

SEVERAL ELEMENTARY POINTS were settled in *Mrs. Alexander's Cotton*, decided on March 10, 1865—a case that has been recounted in the early outline of the work of the Court.[47]

Questions on the two Confiscation Acts, on the standing of a rebel in a federal forum, and on the effect of a pardon, were brought to the Court's threshold when, on October 9, 1865, *United States v. LeRoy M. Wiley* was docketed; the Government sought the reversal of a judgment by Justice Nelson in the Circuit Court. In the end the case was disposed of without opinion, upon the consent of counsel that the judgment below be affirmed. There is no mention in the United States Reports: one learns of the incident from reports of proceedings below, from the Transcript of Record and other papers filed with the Supreme Court, and from the Court Docket and Minutes.[48]

Wiley, resident in Alabama, owned shares in the Great Western Railroad Company, an Illinois corporation, whose stock transfer books were kept in New York City. On August 23, 1863, the District Attorney for the Southern District of New York filed a libel on behalf of the United States and an informer. He sought a forfeiture of the shares under the Confiscation Acts of 1861 and 1862, alleging that Wiley had given aid to the rebellion, and that the shares had been used in aid of the rebellion.[49] To make a case under the Act of 1861, it must be shown that the shares were *used* in aid of the rebellion—something that was utterly wanting in the depositions offered. And if it were shown to be a case within the Act of 1862, the informer took no moiety. Wiley had disappeared into the Confederacy. Attempts to answer were made by Jeremiah Larocque, who had been his counsel in other matters, and by the corporation itself through Daniel Lord, its

---

[47] 2 Wall. 404. See supra, pp. 38–39.

[48] The case below was United States v. One Thousand Seven Hundred and Fifty-Six Shares, Fed. Case No. 15,960a (1863) and 15,960b (1864) in the District Court for the Southern District of New York; No. 15,961 (1865) on appeal in the Circuit Court. The proceedings before Judge Betts are reported in Ann. Cyc.

1863, 220–21, in its survey on "Confiscation."

[49] Transcript of Record, 2–6.

E. Delafield Smith (1826–78), the District Attorney, was a lawyer of distinction and an active Republican. One of his notable cases was United States v. Gordon, Fed. Case No. 15,-231 (1861), resulting in the conviction and execution of the master of a slave ship. See supra, p. 86, n. 198.

counsel: they challenged the court's jurisdiction, on the ground that the shares were not within the Southern District nor was the Great Western. Both answers were struck. District Judge Betts held that an inhabitant of a State in hostility with the United States was an "alien enemy" and hence "disqualified and inhibited from becoming a party to the pending action." Two witnesses from the South deposed that Wiley was notoriously a rebel sympathizer who sent his slaves to work on intrenchments; one witness had actually seen one slave so employed. The court decreed that the corporation cancel the old and issue a new share certificate, and that the proceeds be divided equally between the United States and the informer.[50]

An appeal to the Circuit Court was argued by Larocque and Lord, against William M. Evarts and Charles Donohue for the United States. Justice Nelson reversed the judgment below. There had been "some confusion of ideas" in the suit: "the libel of information and the decree are under the act of August 6, 1861, while the proofs are all under the act of July 17, 1862." More fundamental than that, the court had never acquired jurisdiction: the property consisted of an interest in an Illinois corporation, and its situs was in that State. Coming to what Justice Nelson regarded as "the most important question," even if Wiley was an alien enemy, he was entitled—what was familiar in prize adjudications—to appear as a claimant and contest the allegations. The libel must be dismissed. This was decided on July 21, 1865. (It was not until March 6, 1871, in *McVeigh v. United States*,[51] that the Supreme Court had occasion to affirm the same proposition of the alien enemy's right to defend.)

On July 20, 1865, the President had given Wiley a full pardon. Counsel for the Government did not allow that to deter them from taking the case to the Supreme Court, where it was docketed on October 9. (Also they began anew in Illinois, where the Great Western had its home office.) Now there was one more question: What was the effect of a pardon upon a proceeding under the Confiscation Acts?

On the first motion day—Friday, December 8—Larocque asked the Court to dismiss the appeal. The point at issue was stated next morning in the *National Intelligencer,* under the heading "Important Legal Discussion." On the following Friday, Attorney General Speed

---

[50] Decree filed Apr. 25, 1864. Transcript, 28-29.

The order was first to pay the lien of a debt owed by Wiley to Richard M. Blatchford, who intervened as authorized by the Act of March 3, 1863, 12 Stat. 762, a statute to protect liens on property condemned under laws relating to the rebellion.

Blatchford, an eminent member of the New York bar, was represented by his son, Samuel Blatchford—who became Judge Betts' successor as District Judge in 1867, Circuit Judge in 1878, and a Justice of the Supreme Court in 1882.

[51] 11 Wall. 259. See infra, pp. 798, 823-24.

argued in opposition to the motion. On that same day, argument began in *Ex parte Garland*, and there too a pardon was set up as an alternative ground for relief.[52] Decision in that case, it will be remembered, was deferred until January 14, 1867. It is as one would expect, then, that the Court denied Larocque's request for an early disposition. On January 8, 1866, it directed that the matter of the pardon go over until the case came to be heard on its merits.

At New Orleans, where the effect of a pardon was a subject of urgent concern, the *Picayune* of December 20, 1865, in "Questions Before the United States Supreme Court," gave details of *Wiley's* case, told of Garland's application, referred to a question "agitated here before Judge Durell," and hailed a decision Judge Busteed had just made in the federal court in Alabama holding the test oath for attorneys to be invalid.

After Stanbery became Attorney General, at December term 1866 he filed a suggestion in *United States v. Wiley,* conceding that the District Court had never acquired jurisdiction of the *res*, and also that its decree had been erroneous as to the informer; that conclusion made it needless to consider the effect of the pardon. On that basis, on May 15, 1867, the Court affirmed the judgment of the Circuit Court. Nothing had been gained in almost four years of litigation.

As cases came on during the next few years, issues were sorted out and decided. Several points on the Confiscation Act of 1861 were settled in decisions announced on March 25, 1868. In *Union Insurance Co. v. United States,*[53] the Court construed the Act of 1861 to mean that proceedings should be "in general conformity to the course in admiralty," adding that in seizures on land, "issues of fact, on the demand of either party, must be tried by jury." This was a suit to forfeit land in New Orleans, which the owner had leased to manufacturers of arms, and had then mortgaged to the Insurance Company. The latter intervened: as to the alleged use, "the intervenor is ignorant, and cannot either admit or deny the same . . . ."[54] The Court thought there was "no reasonable doubt" that the owner knew the use to be made of the property; but as to the Insurance Company there was no proof of consent except such as was suggested by the taking of the mortgage, which was not sufficient to support a forfeiture.

Armstrong's Foundry[55] brought up a decree forfeiting another

---

[52] 4 Wall. 333. See supra, pp. 240–42.
[53] 6 Wall. 759.
[54] Transcript of Record, 6.
[55] 6 Wall. 766.
Appearing for the claimant at the argument on January 29, 1868, was Humphrey Marshall (1812–72)—

sometime Whig Congressman from Kentucky, later Brigadier General, C.S.A., and a member of the Second Confederate Congress. He had been pardoned on December 18, 1867. His grandfather, whose name he bore, was John Marshall's cousin.

property at New Orleans that had been devoted to enemy use. The brief of Attorney General Stanbery, urging affirmance, opened with this acrid comment: "The proceedings had upon this information appear to have been conducted with most uncommendable conformity to that very peculiar system of procedure and practice which seems to prevail, in this class of cases in the federal court at New Orleans . . . ." The record was understandable only to one "versed in the mongrel methods" there employed in confiscation cases.[56]

The District Attorney who brought these proceedings on behalf of the United States and an informer was Rufus Waples—whose name will reappear presently.

While the appeal was pending in the Supreme Court, Armstrong received a pardon. That had no effect on this proceeding, said Stanbery: the Constitution spoke of "pardons for *offences*," whereas this was "a forfeiture of property . . . in virtue of the unlawful *predicament* in which the property may be found . . . ." This view was reinforced by a comparison with the Confiscation Act of 1862, which "expressly subjects property to confiscation *on account* of the personal criminality of the owners . . . ."[57]

Chase, C. J., for the Court rejected that reasoning: "We think it clear the statute regarded the consent of the owner to the employment of his property in aid of the Rebellion as an offense, and inflicted forfeiture as a penalty. . . ." The pardon relieved the owner of so much of the penalty as accrued to the United States. On the Attorney General's further point, that at any rate the pardon "cannot operate to remit the moiety which accrues to the informer,"[58] the Court thought it "unnecessary to express any opinion at present." (The case was being sent back for a new trial.) Justice Miller noted dissent.

St. Louis Street Foundry[59] was a companion case from New Orleans instituted by District Attorney Waples on behalf of the United States and an informer. Here Cronan, the owner, had entered a plea that before this libel was brought he had renewed his allegiance by subscribing to the oath required by President Lincoln's amnesty proclamation of December 8, 1863.[60] The Court held that, upon proper pleading and proof that he was not within any of the exceptions made by that proclamation, he would be entitled to the same benefit as if he had received a pardon.

---

[56] Government brief, 1.
[57] Ibid., 4, 9.
[58] Ibid., 11.
[59] 6 Wall. 770.

[60] Transcript of Record, 16. On the offer of amnesty, and the exceptions, see supra, p. 95, and infra, p. 845.

INFORMERS UNDER THE ACT OF 1861

THE RIGHT OF THE INFORMER became the one issue, as it turned out, in the *Confiscation Cases*,[61] decided on March 22, 1869. Here was a bundle of fifteen appeals from the Circuit Court for the Eastern District of Louisiana. Each had been initiated on information by one Charles Black, Sr., alleging that a named steamboat had been used in aid of the rebellion. Almost all the libels had been filed by District Attorney Waples, on June 20, 1865, or within a few days thereafter. The vessels had served under Confederate "orders," but the degree of constraint was a rather hazy matter. In one case appealed by the United States, Attorney General Evarts and Assistant Attorney General Ashton observed in their brief that

> There is no evidence whatever that physical force or restraint was at any time used to compel the employment of the boat in the service of the confederacy. . . .[62]

Judge Durell had decided nine of these cases against the Government, while in six it was the claimant that now appealed. As Ashton wrote in his brief in *Steamer General Beauregard v. United States,*

> In some of the cases the court below acquitted the property, and in others, not perceptibly different in their essential character, entered decrees of condemnation. We are not informed by any opinion of the district judge what rule or principle of decision was applied by him in the determination of this class of cases.[63]

Early in December term 1868, three of these appeals were argued: Ashton against Thomas J. Durant in two,[64] and in the third, Ashton for the United States and B. F. Butler for the informant against James M. Carlisle and his partner, John D. McPherson.[65] Thereafter, as the Minutes show, when companion cases were called they were "passed for the present," as Ashton had requested. Attorney General Evarts was reaching a conclusion about what the Government ought to do.

---

[61] 7 Wall. 454.
[62] Government Brief in United States v. *The Steamer T. S. Connolly*, 2.
[63] Ibid., pp. 1–2.
[64] On Dec. 10, No. 35, United States v. *The Nina Simmes*, and No. 44, United States v. *The General Beauregard*.
[65] On Dec. 14, No. 48, *The Capitol* v. United States.

This came up at the Cabinet meeting on January 12, 1869. O. H. Browning, Secretary of the Interior, wrote this account in his diary:[66]

> Mr. Evarts, Atto Genl, asked advice as to the course proper for him to pursue in respect to confiscation cases now pending. He stated that there were a number of such cases on the docket of the Supreme Court—most of them brought there by the United States, they having been cast on the trials below. He said these cases had been stimulated by informers who now claimed a right to have counsel, and be heard in the cases—that they had no right to be heard—that it was not becoming either the dignity or justice of the government to maintain a partnership with informers, who were wholly mercenary, but that it should at all times, retain absolute control of such cases, and dispose of them as public interests seemed to require. He thought confiscation should be no longer pursued and advised that all pending prosecutions. [sic] The President and Cabinet gave this their unanimous consent and authorized him to exercise his discretion in all the cases. Mr Seward and Mr McCulloch were the only ones who hesitated, but they assented.

The transcripts of record in these cases show the appraisals on the basis of which the several steamboats were released: they range from something less than $5,000 to more than $10,000. The informer might make a handsome winning for reporting to the District Attorney what must have been widely known.

Secretary Welles' diary for January 12 adds significant comments on the discussion in the Cabinet:[67]

> Evarts brought forward the subject of confiscation, which certain robbers, Radical disunionists, are pressing. He thought the subject had been pursued far enough. . . .

Seward wanted a schedule of the amount that might accrue to the Government. Welles "said there had been enough of persecution,—let us have peace." Browning and Postmaster General Randall concurred. Secretary of War Schofield said it would have been well if confiscation had been dropped two years earlier, "but as things were now situated, it would be best to let Congress . . . decide what should be done."

---

[66] *The Diary of Orville Hickman Browning* (Springfield: Illinois State Historical Library, vol. I (1850–64), Pease and Randall, eds., 1925; vol. II (1865–81), Randall, ed., 1933) II, 234–35.

[67] *The Diary of Gideon Welles*, 3 vols. (Boston and New York: Houghton Mifflin Co., 1911), III, 504–5.

Evarts asked if this view had not gone far enough. Why was Congress to absorb and take to itself the executive branch of government entirely? Were we doing our duty in yielding everything? . . .

Thus this relatively small matter was viewed in a large setting: what deference should be shown to the policy expressed in a statute—what was due to "the dignity and justice" of the United States—and whether this occasion should be taken to stand up against the increasing power of the Congress.

The conclusion is reflected in the Minutes of the Court. On Monday, March 1, 1869, the Attorney General's motion to dismiss all the appeals brought by the Government was granted; and in the cases where claimants had appealed, "a decree of reversal will be entered . . . upon the filing of the proper stipulation by counsel." However, if counsel for the informer desired to be heard, "they may proceed this morning."

Thereupon Caleb Cushing spoke in opposition, and Carlisle and Durant spoke in support of the motions.

Cushing, then sixty-nine years old, had been Attorney General under Pierce, and in 1860 a leading supporter of Breckinridge, the Southern Democratic candidate for the Presidency. Recently he had been enjoying a large practice in Washington. His affiliation with Ben Butler in extraordinary exertions to overturn the forfeiture of the *Grey Jacket* has been recounted.[68] In legal attainments Cushing was distinguished—but in his long public life he had failed to establish himself as a man of principle. How unthinkable it would have seemed at that moment that within five years President Grant would endeavor to place him in the center of the Supreme Court bench!

On March 22, 1869, Justice Clifford spoke for a unanimous Court in giving effect to the Attorney General's motions.[69] He affirmed that officer's complete authority over the conduct of all suits in which the Government was a party. This was supported by statute,[70] by usage, and by the recent ruling in *The Grey Jacket*.[71] Notwith-

---

[68] See supra, pp. 248–50.
[69] The Confiscation Cases, 7 Wall. 454.
[70] Including an Act of Aug. 2, 1861, charging him with "general superintendence and direction of the attorneys and marshals of all the districts . . . as to the manner of discharging their respective duties." 12 Stat. 285.
[71] 5 Wall. 370 (1867).
In another recent case, Francis v.

United States, 5 Wall. 338 (1867), the Court had held that one claiming to have been an informer under the Confiscation Act of 1861 "cannot thrust himself into a proceeding instituted by the Attorney General, for the sole use of the government, when it is resisted by such officer, who denies all his allegations, and refuses any further partnership with him."

standing some "unguarded expressions" in the past, the informer had no more than a conditional interest in what might eventually be decreed.

It was timely at that moment emphatically to affirm the authority of the Government's chief law officer. Throughout the country a good many things were being done in the name of federal justice that needed a strong correcting hand. When the Attorney General's Office was transformed into the Department of Justice under the Act of June 22, 1870,[72] that officer was enabled more effectively to discharge his responsibility.

FUNDAMENTAL PROBLEMS UNDER THE ACT OF 1862

THE SECOND CONFISCATION ACT gave rise to persistent difficulties. It was not to be "so construed as to work a forfeiture of the real estate of the offender beyond his natural life."[73] If the purchaser after condemnation took only an estate for the life of the offender, in whom in the meantime was the naked fee vested? Suppose the tenant committed waste or failed to pay the taxes: Who could protect the interest of those who would eventually be entitled as the offender's heirs? Could the offender exercise the rights of an owner who had granted only an estate for life? What would be the situation if the offender were pardoned: before condemnation and sale—or after the estate for his life had vested?

After the war, as confiscation cases were moving toward the Supreme Court, the *Vicksburg Herald & Mississippian* of July 13, 1867, reported what "A Strong Voice from the Yazoo Valley" had to say: "Confiscation Humbug Exposed." A "Distinguished Jurist" demonstrated that there was really nothing to fear—no need to sacrifice honor and accept amalgamation in the hope of averting the loss of "our poor old wasted . . . fields." He explained: nothing more than the life estate could be confiscated—and before that could happen, the owner must be indicted, tried, and convicted of treason, and even then, nothing could be done if he had a pardon or amnesty. Actually, confiscation

> will not embrace one acre in one hundred thousand acres, and to that only the lifetime title of some post-meridian rebel, already tottering toward the grave, and who is, by the act of confiscation, joyfully and gloriously relieved from federal, state, county, special taxes . . . the balance of his days, and the title secured to his children and heirs, unencumbered, at his death . . .

---

[72] 16 Stat. 162. See supra, ch. 14, n. 178.

[73] Joint Resolution of July 17, 1862, "explanatory" of the measure. 12 Stat. 627. See supra, pp. 783–84.

while the purchaser, after paying taxes and keeping the property in good repair, would walk away *broke*. So Mr. Rebel laughed in his heart at Mr. Radical: "Now ain't he green?"

The jurist would stake his life, "to-day before the *Radical* Supreme Court" that this demonstration was sound.

Federal Judge Underwood of the Eastern District of Virginia was enforcing a different view of the law. "Looking for light and guidance to the tribunal of Eternal Justice," he was giving a new twist to the Constitution's provision that "no Attainder of Treason shall work . . . Forfeiture except during the Life of the Person attainted": that meant "that the forfeiture must be perfected *during*, and not *after*, the lifetime of the party attainted." And Congress, he said, had set no narrower bounds than what the Constitution required. So he was decreeing that "all right, title, interest and estate" was confiscated and that the Marshal would deliver such a deed to the highest bidder.[74]

But the courts of Virginia refused to follow what Judge Underwood was doing, and in *Bigelow v. Douglas F. Forrest*[75] the Supreme Court had to say which was right. This became a landmark.

French Forrest, father of the defendant in error, had quit the United States Navy in 1861 and become a captain in the Confederate service.[76] His home was in Alexandria, Virginia. On November 9, 1863, in the District Court at Alexandria, "all the right, title, interest and estate" was condemned.[77] Bigelow became the owner of whatever was conveyed by that decree. Captain Forrest's death in November 1866 gave an early occasion to test whether the sale had carried the fee. The son and heir brought an action of ejectment in the State court, where Bigelow's petition to remove to the friendly federal forum was denied. Judgment for the plaintiff was affirmed on appeal. Thence the case was taken to the Supreme Court, where it was argued on March 15, 1870, and decided on March 28. Justice Strong, writing his first opinion, sustained the State court's judgment.

First, the claim to remove: an Act of March 3, 1863,[78] authorized any person sued on account of arrests, imprisonments, "or other trespasses or wrongs" done under color of authority from the President or Congress to have the suit or prosecution heard in a federal court. But, said Justice Strong, manifestly this had in view only personal

---

[74] McPherson, *Political History of the United States of America, during the Great Rebellion*, 2d ed. (Washington: Philp & Solomons, 1865), 206; *National Intelligencer*, Dec. 28, 1863, "A Constitutional Question." Attorney General Bates' *Diary* for November 19, 1863, p. 316, took note

of a mention in that day's *National Intelligencer* of Judge Underwood's decision "that confiscation of land is of the Fee simple."

[75] 9 Wall. 339 (1870).
[76] See article in D.A.B.
[77] Transcript of Record, 3-4.
[78] 12 Stat. 755.

actions—not possessory actions for real property. The State court had made no error on that point. And on the merits, it had been right in its construction of the Confiscation Act and the Joint Resolution that went with it: "they admit of no doubt" that an estate for the life of the rebel was all that could be condemned. Whatever the District Court might have attempted, that was the limit of its power, and purchasers "were bound to know" the legal effect of its decree. One further point: the Confiscation Act, after enumerating the classes of persons whose property was to be seized, purported to bar the suit of any such person for the possession or use of his property. Even though, as found in a special verdict, the defendant in error, Douglas Forrest, fell within this class, he had had no interest in the land when it was condemned; he could not have been heard in opposition to the decree; and he could not now be denied his right without a trial. Justice Strong closed by saying that the Court declined to pursue "curious speculations" about the "anomalies" produced by a statute that forfeited property for life but left the fee floating in uncertainty.

THE CONSTITUTIONALITY OF THE ACT OF 1862

CHIEF JUSTICE CHASE, on the circuit in May 1868, observed that although the question had not been litigated, he thought it "a fair conclusion that neither at the bar nor upon the bench was the constitutionality of the act [of 1862] doubted."[79] Yet inevitably an assault would be made: the legislation did not seem impregnable, and there were many interested in attacking it.

By the end of December 1868 there were on the Court's docket the cases of Garnett (one concerning real and another concerning personal property)—McVeigh—Miller—and *Tyler v. Defrees*. These were heard at December term 1869, and continued for a reargument, which took place between February 8 and 13, 1871. Among counsel participating were Attorney General Hoar replying to Benjamin R. Curtis and Cushing at the first hearing; at the second, Attorney General Akerman, Solicitor General Bristow, and Senator George F. Edmunds against Cushing. The first arguments began just as Justice Grier left the Court, and were heard by seven Judges. The second round was before Justices Clifford, Swayne, Miller, Davis, Field, Strong and Bradley; the Chief Justice took no part, while Nelson sat only on February 8.

The Court's decision in *McVeigh v. United States*[80] established the standing of the owner to be heard in confiscation proceedings.

---

[79] Semple v. United States, Fed. Case No. 12,661 (C.C.E.D. Va.).

[80] 11 Wall. 259 (1871). The case is discussed in much greater detail infra, pp. 823–28.

In 1863 McVeigh's home in Alexandria with its furnishings, was libelled in the District Court for Virginia.[81] An answer put in by counsel on McVeigh's behalf was stricken, on the ground that he was a resident of Richmond, within the Confederate lines.[82] Condemnation, purportedly of "all the right," etc., followed, and the property was sold.[83]

The Circuit Court, held by the Chief Justice, affirmed in November 1868, and instantly a writ of error was granted and the case was on its way to the Supreme Court.[84]

Justice Swayne, in a terse opinion for a unanimous Court, said that the District Court had committed "a serious error" in refusing to hear the answer:

> It is alleged that he was in the position of an alien enemy, and hence could have no *locus standi* in that forum. If assailed there, he could defend there. The liability and the right are inseparable. A different result would be a blot upon our jurisprudence and civilization. . . .

Justice Swayne made no reference to the Due Process Clause of the Fifth Amendment as securing the right to be heard; in correcting an inferior federal court it was not essential that a point under the Constitution be made. He did say that to condemn without a hearing "would be contrary to the first principles of the social compact, and the right administration of justice"—a mode of speech that would soon be going out of fashion.[85]

So the judgment of the Circuit Court was reversed and remanded for further proceedings.

Justice Swayne had observed that "our opinion will be confined" to the point that sufficed for the disposition of *McVeigh*. And

---

[81] Transcript of Record, 7. Judge Underwood ordered that notice be given by publication in the *Virginia State Journal* (a short-lived local Republican organ) and by posting on the courthouse door. P. 10.

[82] Ibid., 13–15.

[83] Ibid., 16–19. This was in March 1864. Notice of the sale was published in the same local paper and in the *National Republican* at Washington. (The latter was a Republican journal which had been designated for the publication of notices from the Executive Departments, in addition to the two with largest permanent subscriptions, which by statute were entitled to such business. *Collected Works of Abraham Lincoln*, IV, 328.)

[84] Transcript, 19.

[85] He cited Calder v. Bull, 3 Dall. 386 (1798), where Justice Samuel Chase in an individual opinion had spoken of "the great first principles of the social compact" as controlling even the legislative power.

Compare Justice Miller's reference to "the social compact" in Loan Association v. Topeka, 20 Wall. 655 (1875), infra, pp. 1105, 1108–12.

During World War I the Court referred to the holding in *McVeigh* as being "of course," an elementary proposition. Brandeis, J., in Watts, Watts & Co. v. Union Austriaca di Navigazione, 248 U.S. 9 (1918).

in the two cases of *Garnett v. United States*,[86] the Court reversed and remanded on another preliminary point, without coming to the constitutionality of the Confiscation Act.

In the *Garnett* case affecting real property, a libel filed in the District Court of the District of Columbia resulted in July 1863 in a decree forfeiting two lots "for and during the life of the said A. Y. P. Garnett."[87] A writ of error seeking review by the Supreme Court of the District of Columbia was dismissed in June 1868 on the ground that the appellate jurisdiction could not be invoked in that way.[88] Garnett took the case to the Supreme Court of the United States where, as has been related, it was twice argued.

In the meantime, in a wholly different matter, the Court had in effect made it clear that the District Court of the District of Columbia was subject to a writ of error from the Supreme Court of the District.[89]

The consequence was that the Court, instead of considering the problem of confiscation, remanded the *Garnett* cases to the Supreme Court of the District of Columbia with directions to proceed to exercise its appellate jurisdiction.

That left it to *Miller v. United States*[90] to become the leading case on the constitutionality of the Confiscation Act of 1862. On April 3, 1871, Justice Strong spoke for the Court in sustaining the statute. Justice Field dissented in an opinion in which Justice Clifford joined. Justice Davis agreed to sustaining the statute, but found reversible error in the proceedings below.[91]

The central issue was this: Was the legislation to be viewed as the action of a belligerent proceeding against its enemy—or, rather,

---

[86] 11 Wall. 256, disposing of cases Nos. 14 and 15. The former concerned certain real estate, and interests in personal property related thereto; the latter case concerned only personal property. The point on which the Court reversed was present in each case.

Alexander Y. P. Garnett (1819–88) left his medical practice in Washington in 1861 to go to his native Virginia, where he directed army hospitals and attended President Davis. In 1865 he returned to Washington, where as practitioner and professor of medicine he labored to raise the standards of the profession. See D.A.B.

[87] Transcript of Record in No. 292 —which became No. 14—at 6.

Garnett's lots were bought at the public sale by Alexander R. Shepherd. Transcript of Record, 19. Shepherd (1835–1902), an active Republican, was already embarked on a career in municipal politics that eventually won him the title of "Boss" and a statue on Pennsylvania Avenue. See D.A.B.

[88] Transcript of Record, 23–24.

[89] *Ex parte* Bradley, 7 Wall. 364, decided Mar. 30, 1869.

[90] 11 Wall. 268.

[91] Both the Chief Justice and Justice Nelson had been present at the first argument, and absent from the second. Chase remained absent when the decision was made. Nelson, however, reappeared on the Bench on April 3, for the first time since February 24. The Minutes contain no statement of abstention on his part— but that is not conclusive.

had Congress been denouncing crimes and prescribing penalties, in which case all the rights secured to an accused must be observed. All of the Justices agreed that Congress might rightly pursue either line of action.

Justice Strong maintained that these were indeed the measures of a belligerent and that they were sustainable as such. As to the Act of 1861, that could scarcely be denied: it defined no crime, but struck directly at property used in war against the United States.[92] And the Act of 1862, in the sections here pertinent, proceeded against enemies: it took their property as a means to the speedy termination of the war. To be sure, Congress had said "rebels" instead of "enemies": but in the context the two words were synonymous; "we are not to strain the construction of an Act of Congress in order to hold it unconstitutional."

Justice Field said that "the power to prosecute war granted by the Constitution, as is well said by counsel, is a power to prosecute war according to the law of nations, and not in violation of that law."[93] He cast doubt upon the permissibility of confiscation, by "the modern

---

[92] In Kirk v. Lynd, 106 U.S. 315 (1882), Waite, C.J., found the Confiscation Act of 1861 "manifestly an exercise" of the power "to make Rules concerning Captures on Land and Water." Art. I, Sec. 8, cl. 11. The property was not taken to punish the owner, but to lessen the warlike strength of the enemy. The purchaser of real property confiscated under the Act of 1861 took the fee.

[93] He was quoting the words of Benjamin R. Curtis. Argument for Plaintiffs in Error by Hon. B. R. Curtis in the United States Supreme Court, January 31, 1870. Reported by D. F. Murphy. At 7–8.

Field—borrowing from Curtis—assumed that "the rules and limitations prescribed by that law [of nations] were in the contemplation of the parties who framed and the people who adopted the Constitution"—and thus constituted restraints upon the granted powers which the Court should enforce.

If this were to be taken as more than an argumentative device for the case at hand, it would have to be treated as a very large proposition indeed. It would apply to such powers as the making of treaties, and the regulation of foreign commerce.

Certainly, as Marshall, C.J., said in Murray v. *Schooner Charming Betsy*, 2 Cr. 64, 118 (1804), "an act of Congress ought never to be construed to violate the law of nations if any other possible construction remains." Compare Cunard S.S. Co. v. Mellon, 262 U.S. 100 (1923), holding the National Prohibition Act applicable to foreign merchant ships when within the territorial waters of the United States.

It is firm constitutional law, as the Court has consistently declared, that "an Act of Congress may supersede a prior treaty," and that "the consequences in all such cases give rise to questions which must be met by the Political Department of the Government. They are beyond the sphere of judicial cognizance." *The Cherokee Tobacco*, 11 Wall. 616 (1871). Notable affirmations of this view are found in the *Head Money Cases*, 111 U.S. 580 (1884), per Miller, J.; Whitney v. Robertson, 124 U.S. 190, (1888), per Field, J.; and the *Chinese Exclusion Case*, 130 U.S. 581 (1889), per Field, J.

In the zeal of dissent, Field might defend positions that were only specious. Consider his dissent in the *Slaughter House Cases*, infra, pp. 1355–60.

law of nations"—following the line Judge Thomas had taken in the debate in the House of Representatives.[94]

But, Field continued, the Act of 1862 was "not directed against enemies at all, but against persons who have committed certain overt acts of treason." It was because this was a criminal measure that Lincoln had insisted on limiting the forfeiture of real property. The Act imposed punishment without trial, and was unconstitutional.

He went on to explain why, in his view, the proceedings in this instance had not met the requirements of the Constitution.

Miller's stock had been condemned with no notice to him other than by service upon an officer of the corporation and publication in a newspaper in the North. But, said Field,

> The doctrine that notice to the owner is given by seizure of the thing, rests upon the presumption that the owners of property retain possession of it themselves, or place it in the care and management of persons who will represent them and communicate to them any proceedings taken against their interest in relation to it. In this case this doctrine is entirely disregarded. The notice given to the president of one company and the vice president of the other might, with equal propriety, have been given to any other strangers to the owner. . . . Shares or stock in companies can only be seized in virtue of statutory provisions, which prescribe a mode of seizure equivalent to actual taking of possession. . . .

Justice Davis, too, would have reversed on the ground that no adequate notice had been given to the owner.

Circumstances drawn from the record—not mentioned in the opinion of the Court—will enable one to appreciate the objections to the procedure whereby Miller had been stripped of his property without any means of knowing what was going on.

EXAMINING THE TRANSCRIPT IN
MILLER v. UNITED STATES

ON FEBRUARY 27, 1864, a libel of information was filed in the District Court for Eastern Michigan by the District Attorney, against shares in two railroads incorporated in Michigan, property of Samuel Miller of Virginia, a rebel citizen, who had knowingly *used* the same in aid of the rebellion: wherefore the shares were subject to confiscation under the Act of 1861. By direction, the Marshal had seized the shares—by serving notice upon M. L. Sykes, Jr., vice president of one

---

[94] Supra, pp. 781–82.

corporation and president of the other.[95] John H. Browning, resident in New York City, had on November 19, 1863, filed an information on which the allegations were based.

Next the libel alleged that at times since July 17, 1862 [the date of the Second Confiscation Act] Miller had been an officer of the Confederate army and of the navy, a member of Congress, a Judge, a State legislator, etc., etc.—the particulars being to the attorney as yet unknown. (These allegations were not based on anything the District Attorney had reason to believe: he was simply running through Section 5 of the statute and putting Miller into every category—from First to Sixthly—of the persons whose property had been made at once confiscable.) Next it was alleged that, notwithstanding the President's proclamation of July 25, 1862, in pursuance of Section 6 of the Act of July 17, warning those in rebellion to return to their allegiance within sixty days, Miller had in Virginia and in South Carolina continued to aid the rebellion. (This was to make it appear that his property was confiscable under Section 6.)

By virtue of the *two* statutes, libellants asked for a decree that the shares be cancelled on the corporate books, that new certificates be issued to purchasers at auction, and that distribution of the proceeds be made *to the informer* and the United States in equal shares.[96]

District Judge Ross Wilkins set the first Tuesday in April, 1864, for a hearing, and directed that notice be published in the *Detroit Free Press*, twice a week for two weeks.

On March 24, 1864, John M. Thatcher, resident in New York City, there gave a deposition to the effect that about July 1, 1863, he had conversed with Miller at the latter's home in Virginia; Miller had said that the ultimate success of the Confederacy was certain, and that he would bear any sacrifice to achieve it; that he was giving one-tenth of his income to support the army, and also making large contributions to soldiers' wives and children—"as much . . . as all the rest of the county put together." Deponent believed that Miller had no attorney or agent in the Northern States.[97]

On the basis of that deposition, the District Court on April 5, 1864, decreed confiscation as prayed in the libel.[98]

At a public auction by Deputy Marshal H. B. Brown on April 23, sale was made to various bidders for a total of $37,891.76.[99] But

---

[95] Transcript of Record, 2–5; document of eight pages which by stipulation was added to the record. There were 200 shares in the Michigan Southern & Northern Indiana R.R., and 343 shares in the Detroit, Monroe & Toledo.

[96] Ibid., 5–6.
[97] Ibid., 15–17.
[98] Ibid., 17–18.
[99] Ibid., 21.

Henry Billings Brown (1836–1913), then practicing law at Detroit and serving both as Assistant District At-

then Sykes, now president of both companies, refused to make the transfer on the books; and upon a hearing for contempt, the court declined to compel him to do so, and instead ordered a new sale. This time the bids came to only $2,715. On July 18, 1864, the court ordered the distribution of the proceeds, after payment of costs, *to the informer and the United States.*[100]

In its decree the court entered the default of any appearance—made no finding of facts—and did not indicate under which statute the confiscation was adjudged.

Almost a year and a half later—after hostilities had ceased and communication had been restored—on December 5, 1865, counsel for Miller came into court with a petition to open and set aside the decree.[101] Miller therein asserted under oath that he was seventy-three years old, and for the past ten years had been infirm and unable to travel; he had held no office under the Confederacy or any State thereof —had not used his property in aid of the rebellion—had given no aid other than the taxes he had been compelled to pay; he had always been loyal to the United States Government.

He had first heard of the suit about August 26, 1865, whereupon he at once started an investigation. The certificates of stock had at all times been in his possession in Virginia. The statements of Thatcher were false, as he could prove.

He charged that it was with fraudulent intent that Sykes had refused to transfer the stock as ordered by the court; that Sykes and those who purchased at the second sale had corruptly combined to prevent a fair competition, that the purchase had been at less than one-fifteenth of the fair market value, and that shares so acquired had been transferred to one of the railroad companies. It was submitted that "no rights were acquired by said purchasers, by reason of the corrupt and fraudulent means used by them . . . ."

The petition further exhibited a pardon from the President, dated June 26, 1865.

The petition was supported by eight affidavits, asserting with considerable particularity Miller's constant loyalty to the United States. One came from a physician, now postmaster at Lynchburg, and another from a major and quartermaster in the United States army.[102]

The court ordered that copies be served on the District Attorney. After repeated continuances, argument was heard on four days in July 1867, the District Attorney, counsel for the purchasers, and

---

torney and as Deputy Marshal, was appointed District Judge in 1875, and Associate Justice of the Supreme Court in 1890.

[100] Ibid., 23–33.
[101] Ibid., 33–40.
[102] Ibid., 41–49.

Miller's counsel participating. On October 17, 1867, the motion to reopen was denied.

On June 9, 1868, the judgment was affirmed by the Circuit Court.[103]

Such was the situation at which the two dissenting opinions were directed. In admiralty and revenue cases, Justice Davis observed, seizure of the tangible thing was regarded as equivalent to personal service, on the ground that the person whose property was seized had entrusted it to some one who would represent him. But it was otherwise with intangible property such as shares: service on the officers of the corporation gave no notice to the owner, nor were they his agents with a duty to defend his interests. In this case, it appeared that their interest was in direct hostility to his. Publication in a newspaper gave no notice to one who dwelt in an insurgent State, with which communication was forbidden. "It is a *casus omissus*," calling for legislation establishing in advance the method of condemnation.[104] Counsel for Miller had invoked the Fifth Amendment, and evidently Davis had the Due Process Clause in mind.

But apart from that objection, "fatal to the recovery in this case," in Davis' view, was the fact that the decree divided the proceeds with the informer, which was authorized only under the Act of 1861. Yet if Thatcher's implausible affidavit tended to prove anything, it was that the property was within the Act of 1862. That irregularity he would have treated as an adequate ground for remanding for a new trial.

Davis was a down-to-earth Judge, alert to the practical aspects of doing justice. On his circuit, he had early insisted that there must at any rate be procedural fairness in enforcing confiscation.[105]

This examination of the record in the leading case shows how confiscation might work in practice. In defending the outcome in this instance, the Attorney General and the Solicitor General argued some pretty bald propositions. "It was not essential to the validity of the information, or other proceedings, that the name of Samuel Miller, or

---

[103] Ibid., 59. The transcript does not show what Judge sat in the Circuit Court. However, the bond and the citation on the writ of error to take the case to the Supreme Court were signed by Justice Swayne, which suggests that he had held the Circuit Court.

[104] Davis had accepted the reasoning, and at places adopted the language, of the Brief for Plaintiff in

Error by William P. Wells and Samuel T. Douglass of Detroit.

[105] In the unreported case of United States v. Two Second-hand Steam Engines, summarized in Ann. Cyc. 1864, page 204, reversing a judgment of District Judge Caleb B. Smith, he had held that in case of default after notice by mere publication, there must be a hearing, and actual proof of disloyalty, before condemnation could be pronounced.

any other person, should have been introduced. The information would have been good if it had alleged that the property seized belonged to an *unknown enemy*. . . . The recital of his name in the information, and the monition, and the judgment, does not make him a party to the suit or the judgment." "If he fail to appear and make his claim, he must be deemed to have renounced his interest in the *res*, and it is no excuse to say that he did not have actual notice, or that he could not appear. . . ."[106]

"It was not material *which* enemy owned [the property], but only that *an* enemy did," said Senator Edmunds, who had been retained by the purchasers of the shares. "Whether it was disposed of as the statute required, was . . . solely a question between the Government and its officers." Nor need it be more than stated, he concluded, that the decision of the District Court upon the petition to reopen the case "is not before this court, and not in anywise the subject of review."[107]

Even Miller's counsel recognized that the fact that judgment was given in accord with the Act of 1861, whereas the only proof offered tended to make it a case under the Act of 1862, "may be regarded as a mere irregularity."[108]

The opinion for the Court did not bring up the details that stir one's sense of justice. Formal points had been raised—such as will be considered in *Tyler v. Defrees*—and Justice Strong had busied himself in meeting them. In the result, the dismissal of technical objections leaves substantial ones unsuspected.

First, the seizure had been effective to give the District Court jurisdiction. The Act of 1862 spoke of the seizure of "stocks," and it was to be concluded that the mode intended was such as was adapted to that end. Justice Strong showed instances where, in admiralty practice, intangibles were attached by notice to the debtor or holder.

Second, there was such hearing and proof as was requisite to a valid decree. The information averred all that was necessary to warrant confiscation. There had been a seizure, a monition to appear, and a default—by which the facts averred were considered to be confessed. Moreover, the court did examine the depositions.

After default there was no fact to be ascertained—hence there was nothing to be tried by jury.

Where McVeigh had had actual notice of the suit to confiscate his real property, the Court had declared loftily that he must be allowed to defend himself in court. Justice Strong cited that in affirming Miller's

---

[106] Brief for the United States, 9, 12.

[107] Brief for the Purchasers of the Property, 1, 8, 11.

[108] Brief of W. P. Wells and Samuel T. Douglass, at December Term, 1870, 11.

right to sue out the writ of error. But no consideration of "the first principles of the social compact, and of the right administration of justice" had availed to give him any warning that his shares were threatened with confiscation.

A final note. Miller did not live to hear the outcome. On November 9, 1869, as the Docket shows, his death was reported to the Court and, on motion, his administrator, Nathaniel M. Page, was substituted.[109]

---

[109] According to local histories, Samuel Miller was born near Charlottesville, Virginia, in 1792, and died in March 1869. In his youth he came to Lynchburg where through frugality he became a tobacco dealer. Thanks to shrewdness, good fortune, and close attention to information gleaned from newspapers, he amassed wealth in widely diversified investments. He withdrew to a farm outside town where, in eccentric independence, he minded his affairs. The deposition of an old acquaintance that "I have never heard of his investing one cent . . . in securities of the so-called confederate government; except the purchase of . . . certificates to pay taxes . . . ." (Transcript of Record, 46) seems in accord with Miller's hardheadedness.

In later life and by his will he disposed of his wealth according to his own sense of values: notably, he established an industrial school in his native county and an orphanage for white girls at Lynchburg. A granite shaft was erected over his place of burial on the orphanage grounds.

The only evidence of Miller being attached to the rebellion, Justice Davis observed suspiciously, was "an affidavit, made in New York, of one John M. Thatcher (who, in some way not disclosed in the record, was able to get down to Virginia in 1863, hunt up Miller, and have a private conversation with him) . . . ." Actually the record does not even show that he *got down*—only that he deposed "I reside in New York city" and that he knew Miller and "saw him about the 1st of July, 1863, at his home near Lynchburg . . . ." Perhaps he originated in Virginia and found his way to New York. Commissioner Betts,

who took Thatcher's deposition, described him as being "about the age of forty-five years," which suggests that the deponent may not have known his own age. His residence in New York City did not come to the notice of the compilers of *Trow's New York Directory* of May 1, 1864, or that of May 1, 1865.

The word of this implausible character is all there was on which to base confiscation.

The informer was John H. Browning, a resident of New York City. According to the directory, that must have been the clothing dealer of that name, with business at 326 Broadway and house on Fourth Avenue at the corner of 94th Street. This man of rising prominence was born in Orange, New Jersey, on December 25, 1841, son of John Hazard and Eliza Smith (Hull) Browning, well-to-do natives of Connecticut. By the time of his death on October 26, 1914, John Hull Browning had long retired from his clothing business, and had served as officer or director of numerous corporations, been active in charities, and twice cast his ballot as a Republican presidential elector.

The first sale of Miller's shares had been made to Latham Hull and in lesser amounts to William A. Moore, Jesse Ingersoll, and Calvin Wright, for a total of $37,891.76. That proved abortive by reason of the refusal of M. L. Sykes, Jr., to make the transfer.

The second sale was to Henry M. Johnson and Charles H. Hibbard for a total of only $2,715.

The given name "Latham" recurred in the family of John Hull Browning's mother; she had a cousin, Latham Hull, born in 1812. Whatever relation-

TYLER v. DEFREES

IN REVENUE CASES—on which confiscation proceedings were to be modeled—an executive officer (normally the Collector of Customs or the Collector of Internal Revenue) would first seize the property sought to be forfeited; then upon the filing of a libel of information in the District Court, a monition would be issued, directing the Marshal to attach the property and hold it until the further order of the court, and to give notice to all claimants to appear at a certain time. It was this second seizure, by the Marshal, that brought the property under the jurisdiction of the court. Now in executing the Confiscation Acts, Attorney General Bates, acting by direction of the President, gave instructions that "All seizures are to be made by the Marshal upon the written authority of the District Attorney"; thereupon the District Attorney would start judicial proceedings. The course then would be that the court would issue a monition to its Marshal, substantially as in revenue cases. However, inasmuch as he already held the property in his custody, the Marshal might fail to observe the formality of a second, or "judicial" seizure. Would the omission of this detail affect the validity of a condemnation? The statute called for conformity "as nearly as may be" to proceedings in admiralty or revenue cases; but, said Justice Field, a statute so highly penal should be construed very narrowly.

Here was the central point at issue in *Tyler v. Defrees*,[110] wherein the decision was announced on April 10, 1871—one week after *Miller v. United States*.

Major Henry B. Tyler of the Marine Corps had gone South and become a colonel in the Confederate Navy. In June 1863 proceedings were brought to confiscate his house in the District of Columbia. Ward Lamon, Marshal for the District, made his certificate that he had given notice to the occupant and had seized as directed by the District Attorney. But the record did not show a second seizure, in execution of the monition of the court. Forfeiture of the estate for the duration of Tyler's life was decreed, and in September the Marshal sold that interest

ship, if any, there may have been between the informer and the first purchaser, this observation is to be noted: the petition on behalf of Miller alleged that the amount of the second sale was less than one-fifteenth of fair market value of the shares; that would put the value at over $40,725. The bids of Latham Hull and associates were not very far out of line with this estimate.

Whatever further inquiry might disclose concerning relationships and motivations, this conclusion is incontestable: the United States confiscated say $40,000 worth of property from Samuel Miller, and in the end received $1,167.08 for its effort.

[110] 11 Wall. 331 (1871).

to John Van Riswick.[111] Presently it was purchased by John D. Defrees (a leading Indiana Republican, and Superintendent of Public Printing).

In January 1867 Tyler brought an action to eject Defrees. Since he was attacking the judgment of condemnation collaterally, success depended upon showing that it had been rendered without jurisdiction: errors, such as might have been ground for reversing on appellate review, would be of no avail unless they went to the very root of the power to decide.[112] Here was a matter of major concern to ex-Confederates; as the *Columbus* (Georgia) *Enquirer* reported hopefully, "the decision of the case will therefore be of much interest."[113] The District of Columbia court gave judgment for the defendant, and Tyler went up to the Supreme Court.

Robert J. Brent and Richard T. Merrick appeared for the plaintiff in error, against Albert G. Riddle, recently a Republican Congressman from Ohio, and L. Madison Day, a Louisiana Unionist who figures prominently in confiscation cases.

Had the Marshal's failure to make a "judicial seizure" of what he had already seized left the court without jurisdiction, so that its decree had been void? Rejecting that contention, Justice Miller for the Court said that

> Undoubtedly, by the individual, whose property is thus seized and condemned for acts of hostility to his government, the course pursued will be scrutinized with an eye quick to detect errors, and it is not strange that this critical spirit should affect the argument here. When to this is added the belief, long inculcated, that the Federal

---

[111] Transcript of Record, 15.

[112] Earlier in that term Justice Miller had discussed this principle—which "takes rank as an axiom of the law"—in the much cited case of Cooper v. Reynolds, 10 Wall. 308 (1870). In a Tennessee court Brownlow had sued Reynolds for false imprisonment; defendant having left the State or gone into hiding, jurisdiction was obtained by attaching his land and publishing notice. Judgment went by default and the attached property was sold; Cooper took his deed from that sale and was put in possession. Later Reynolds, as a citizen of Illinois, brought ejectment in the Circuit Court for Eastern Tennessee. Reversing the judgment there, the Supreme Court held that the State court had obtained jurisdiction by attachment of the res, and that in this collateral proceeding its judgment could not be held void for irregularities preliminary to the attachment.

Field, J., dissented, on the ground that the State court had not acquired jurisdiction. Later, in Pennoyer v. Neff, 95 U.S. 714 (1878), Field recalled that while he had "considered that some of the objections to the preliminary proceedings . . . were well taken and, therefore dissented from the judgment," the doctrine "received the approval of all the judges."

Brownlow was the militant Unionist, later Governor, who early in the war had been imprisoned for his loyalty. Joseph A. Cooper was a Unionist, and Major General in the army. President Grant appointed him a Collector of Internal Revenue.

[113] May 17, 1867.

Government, however strong in a conflict with a foreign foe, lies manacled by the Constitution and helpless at the feet of a domestic enemy, we need not be surprised that both the power of Congress to pass such a law as the one in question, and the capacities of the courts to enforce it, should meet with a stout denial.

The Court, however, would not be bound "by a system of procedure so captious, so narrow, so difficult to understand and to execute, as to amount to a nullification of the statute." Here "the point raised seems to be as narrow and unsubstantial as the second seizure would be useless."

Justice Field (Justice Clifford concurring) filed a dissent; Justice Davis noted that he did not agree to all that had been said in the opinion.

At the close of a supplemental brief, Riddle and Day drew the Court's attention to an accompanying pamphlet by Day on "The Constitutionality and Legality of Confiscations in Fee, Under the Act of July 17, 1862." This was a production of 107 pages, opening with the proposition that "Congress had power to confiscate the property of rebels and traitors, in fee, for treason." Here we meet for the first time Day's theory of the law on confiscation.

The constitutional text, Article III, Section 3, clause 2, must be brought back into focus:

> The Congress shall have Power to declare the Punishment of Treason, but no Attainder of Treason shall work Corruption of Blood, or Forfeiture except during the Life of the Person attainted.

To meet President Lincoln's scruples against imposing, on a different ground, what was greater than could constitutionally be inflicted for treason, the Joint Resolution accompanying the Confiscation Act directed that it should not be "so construed as to work a forfeiture of the real estate of the offender beyond his natural life."[114]

But now Day would read the constitutional text in a new light: it did *not* limit the power of Congress to prescribe the punishment of treason. At Common Law, he explained, perpetual forfeiture *resulted of course* from a sentence of death for treason; the "but no Attainder" provision said simply,

> in the absence of Congress making any express provision as to forfeiture of real estate for treason, that on the party receiving sentence . . . the *resulting* consequence therefor . . . shall not produce of itself a forfeiture of real estate beyond the lifetime of the offender. . . .

---

[114] Supra, p. 783.

The effect was merely to bar what might have been adjudged in the silence of Congress. If the framers of the Constitution had intended to limit "the broad and comprehensive words of the grant," surely they would have made it "too clear to admit of doubt or controversy."[115]

Furthermore, confiscation under the Act of 1862 was not a punishment for treason—it was directed at enemies' property, proceeded against *in rem*. "Confiscation of enemies' property is not limited to a mere life by the joint resolution." It was true that in *Bigelow v. Forrest* the Supreme Court had held otherwise:[116]

> But that was a case of first impression . . . , and seems to have been framed on a misapprehension of the true mode of applying the law to the facts of the case.

He claimed that the legislative history of the Joint Resolution demonstrated his proposition. Senator Clark of New Hampshire, author of the amendment to prescribe that the statute should not be construed to work a forfeiture, etc., had said, "I present the amendment to meet what I believe to be the objection of the President. That is it exactly." Day's summary continued:

> The *sole* objection of the President to the bill as stated by Senators Harris, King, Trumbull, and Howard, (*and to whose statements no one dissented*) was, that Congress, according to his view, could not constitutionally confiscate real estate for treason, beyond the life of the traitor. . . .

But, Day's argument went on, it was only Section 1 that *punished treason*—so it was "this provision, and this provision alone, . . . which gave rise to doubt in the mind of the President . . . ." Therefore the provisions on confiscation of enemies' property, in Sections 5 and following, extended to the taking of the entire interest in real as well as in personal property.[117]

Brent and Merrick added an appendix to their brief, to acquaint the Court with what Charles M. Conrad of the New Orleans bar had argued in other litigation on the Confiscation Act. (On May 28, 1870, he and Day had met in the argument of *Conrad v. United States* before Bradley and Woods, JJ., in the Circuit Court in New Orleans—one of the *Confiscation Cases*, soon to be discussed, that were decided by the

---

[115] Pp. 2–5, 11.
[116] 9 Wall. 339, decided Mar. 28, 1870. Supra, pp. 797–98.
[117] Day's pamphlet on *The Con-*

stitutionality and Legality of Confiscations in Fee . . . , (New Orleans, 1870), at 77–82.

Supreme Court in May 1874.[118] Doubtless it was in that connection that each had put his contentions into print.) Conrad had insisted, at point after point, upon a compliance with very stiff legal interpretations. Among them,

> It is clear, therefore, that to sustain the proceedings *in rem*, it was necessary to show that the owner of the property proceeded against had *taken part in the rebellion*.
>   The only legal mode of showing this was by trying and convicting him.[119]

This was the sort of argument at which Justice Miller's remarks were aimed. Conrad was fighting hard: his own land was at stake. And Day was fighting to save his winnings.

PARTIES IN INTEREST

NEW ORLEANS was a city where there was much to confiscate, and workers eager for the harvest. Among the proceedings we shall note those brought against the property of Judah P. Benjamin, successful lawyer, and Confederate Secretary of War and then Secretary of State; of John Slidell, once United States Senator, later Confederate diplomatic agent at Paris; of Charles M. Conrad, sometime Congressman and Cabinet officer under the United States, a Representative in the Confederate Congress; of Duncan F. Kenner, another Representative, who in 1861 proposed the confiscation of enemies' assets, and who in 1865 carried to England the Government's offer to emancipate slaves in exchange for recognition. Other Confederate officers whose property was libelled were Frank H. Hatch, vigilant Collector of Customs at New Orleans; Senator Thomas J. Semmes[120] who, early pardoned, was prominent in litigation both as party and as counsel; and General Harry T. Hays, who fought on in the Trans-Mississippi Department when all else was lost.

Outstanding among purchasers at confiscation sales were District Attorney Waples,[121] and James Graham, the Marshal. L. Madison

---

[118] The Confiscation Cases, Fed. Case No. 3097 (1872); 20 Wall. 92. That Conrad and Day had met in argument on May 28, 1870, is shown by the transcript of record in the *Conrad* case—as well as in Justice Bradley's diary for that day.

[119] Brief of Plaintiff in Error, at 19.

[120] In 1886 Semmes was elected president of the American Bar Association. He was a cousin of Captain Raphael Semmes of the raider *Alabama*.

[121] Waples (1825–1902) was born in Delaware. In 1849 he emigrated to New Orleans, where he graduated from the law department of the University of Louisiana. From 1852 he practiced there, in partnership with his brother, Stephen H. Waples, and

Day, already introduced, figures prominently. This was a lawyer who would not take No for an answer: it was in confiscation cases carried up by him that the Supreme Court first applied its rule for affirming, on motion by the defendant in error, State court judgments where

> it is manifest the writ was taken for delay only, or that the question on which the jurisdiction depends is so frivolous as not to need further argument.[122]

Still another was Edward Warren Burbank, wholesale grocer: the Court had recently rejected an evasive objection he had raised against a judgment for fraud in business dealings.[123] We shall come in a moment to *Ex parte Graham and Day* and *Ex parte Waples and Burbank*, at December Term 1870.[124]

---

successively with others. On the outbreak of the war he removed to Delaware, and presently went to Washington—making speeches against slavery.

In May 1863 he returned and entered upon the office of District Attorney; fourteen months later he was removed. He was active in Republican politics, held numerous offices, and was a member of the constitutional convention of 1868.

In 1878 Waples settled in Ann Arbor, Michigan, where he wrote several treatises on the law. Especially to be noted is *Proceedings in Rem* (Chicago: Callaghan and Co., 1882). Infra, p. 823.

See *Who Was Who in America, 1897–1942*.

[122] This addition to Rule 6, Motions, was announced on May 8, 1876.

The Minutes show that on November 20, 1876, Thomas A. Clarke moved to dismiss the following cases brought up on writ of error to the Supreme Court of Louisiana: No. 417, Davis [Davies] v. Slidell; No. 435, Huppenbauer v. Slidell; and Nos. 668 and 669, Ames v. Slidell. Opposing were Day, T. J. Durant and C. W. Hornor, and D. C. Labatt. On November 27, 1876, the judgments were all affirmed with costs—"under the practice authorized by the amendment to Rule 6, section 3, promul-

gated at the last Term." 23 L. Ed. 871.

Bradley endorsed on the transcripts: "Affirm under new rule as frivolous."

[123] Burbank v. Bigelow, 154 U.S. 558, 19 L. Ed. 51, decided Jan. 11, 1869.

E. B. Bigelow and Thomas S. Burbank were in partnership. Bigelow sued his partner and Edward W. Burbank (the partner's brother), charging fraud between the two to defeat plaintiff's rights; that EWB owed the firm a certain sum of money, one-half of which plaintiff asked the court to compel EWB to pay him.

TSB, before answering, filed a peremptory exemption, and the suit was dismissed as to him.

EWB filed a general answer; then on the day set for trial before a jury, he filed a peremptory exemption, praying that the case be dismissed as to him because the partner had not been made a party. The trial court overruled the exception because it "came too late."

The Supreme Court affirmed, following Breedlove v. Nicolet, 7 Pet. 413, 432 (1833).

That E. W. Burbank paid the judgment of $13,864.34 appears in Burbank v. Bigelow, 92 U.S. 179 (1876).

[124] *Ex parte* Waples and Burbank is reported at 154 U.S. 579, 19 L. Ed. 981. Discussed infra, pp. 817–18.

Attorney General Bates' diary entry for July 4, 1863, reflects his distaste for the situation in New Orleans:

In the forenoon, comes Cuthbert Bullitt, to have a talk about La. affairs. I propose to make him Marshal, in place of Graham, and some other good man Dist Atty vice *Waples*.

How the President will take it, I know not; but if he'll just let me "take the responsibility," I'll make short work of Mr. Chase's knot of ignorant and rapacious swindlers, from the Balise to C[a]iro.

Mr. Bullitt tells me that the officers (of Revenue &c) down to clerks, occupy the best houses, (ready furnished) in N. O—without contract or rent, as far as he knows—Mr. Flanders, for instance, lives in Mrs. Fiske's palace, furnished with great magnificence.[125]

Graham was removed; Bullitt was on July 6 appointed in his place. Waples was also removed.

Presiding in the District Court was Edward H. Durell (1810–1887), a Northerner who had graduated from Harvard Law School in 1832. He settled in New Orleans in 1836, and after secession lived in retirement. Lincoln appointed him to the Judgeship in 1863. In the post-war reconstruction of Louisiana his judicial action was so extraordinary that—had he not resigned in 1874—it seems that he would have been impeached.[126]

In *Day v. Micou*,[127] lots belonging to Benjamin had been condemned, and purchased by Day, in 1865. The property, however, had been mortgaged in 1858 to Mrs. William C. Micou.[128] The deed authorized by the District Court gave Day a title in fee. Moreover, an order made by Judge Durell on District Attorney Waples' motion had

---

[125] *The Diary of Edward Bates*, 382.

Bullitt, in business at New Orleans, was a loyalist in the President's confidence; he was acting Collector of Customs after the federal authority was restored.

Balise was a small settlement at Pass à la Outre, where lower Mississippi pilots were taken on and discharged. From that extremity to Cairo, southernmost city in Illinois, was the range within which the Special Agents of the Treasury Department carried on their operations.

Benjamin F. Flanders (1816–96) was then Special Agent at New Orleans. Born in New Hampshire, after graduating from Dartmouth

College he moved to New Orleans, where he was an editor, alderman, school superintendent, and officer of a railroad company. The war caused him to leave, but he returned when the federal forces had taken the city. Thereafter he held a variety of offices.

[126] See infra, p. 837.

[127] 18 Wall. 156, decided Jan. 19, 1874.

[128] Benjamin and Micou had practiced in partnership until the latter's death in 1854. Micou was nominated to be a Justice of the Supreme Court by President Fillmore on February 24, 1853. The Senate did not act, and when Pierce became President the appointment of John A. Campbell followed promptly.

provided that wherever real estate was condemned, the Marshal would cause all mortgages to be cancelled.[129] In the State courts, the Micou heirs won a judgment that their mortgage subsisted and was enforceable upon the property.[130] Day took a writ of error.

In part this went back over the ground in *Bigelow v. Forrest*; the matter of the mortgage was new. Day argued his own cause, along with two others that sought a reversal of judgments won by the heirs of John Slidell.[131]

Day had set the tone by inserting this as the opening passage of his brief:

MAY IT PLEASE THE COURT: When the "Bonnie Blue Flag"[132] went down before "The Star Spangled Banner," and that glorious emblem of "The Union, the Constitution, and the Enforcement of the Laws," again waived [*sic*] in triumph
"From Maine's dark pines and crags of snow
To where Magnolian breezes blow,"
it was fondly hoped that civil strife and contention were at an end, and that peace, quiet and repose had returned to bless the land.
. . . .
. . . . [But some] who would theoretically, merely,
"Die for the cause they could not save,"
rushed into the courts, renewed the contest in another form, and we are here to-day on a writ of error to the Supreme Court of Louisiana to reverse a victory obtained by the *new mode* of hostility and attack upon the power and authority of the United States and the rights of one which are firmly based upon the same.

But when Day was done, the Court told opposing counsel, Thomas Allen Clarke, that it would not call upon him to reply. It was unusual that an appeal was so clearly unmeritorious that it could be said at once that it had failed.

Justice Strong wrote the opinion. *Bigelow v. Forrest* was reaffirmed. As to the claim to be free from the encumbrance, the Act of 1862 affected only such interest as the enemy had in the property. This was to be distinguished from admiralty and revenue cases, where

---

[129] Transcript of Record in Day v. Micou, at 38. Authority was supposed to be derived from the provision in Section 8 of the Act of 1862 that courts would "have power to make such orders . . . as shall fitly and efficiently effect the purposes of this act, and vest in the purchasers . . . good and valid titles . . . ."

[130] 26 La. Ann. 718.
[131] Brugere v. Slidell, and Heath v. Slidell, 154 U.S. 598, 21 L. Ed. 862, decided with Day v. Micou. The former affirms 27 La. Ann. 70.
[132] The song of 1861, "Hurrah for the Bonnie Blue Flag!," referred to the secession flag of South Carolina.

there was reason to treat the thing itself as the offender or the debtor, and where condemnation generally passed the entire title.[133]

For years thereafter, Day was importuning Congress to give back his money.[134]

AN ILLUSTRATIVE CASE

THE *Confiscation Cases* decided on May 4, 1874, comprised a cluster that had come up together from the Circuit Court for the District of Louisiana.[135] To afford an acquaintance with the mode of operation, we shall follow one of them—*Ten Lots of Ground, Property of Charles M. Conrad*—from the beginning.[136]

On August 7, 1863, District Attorney Waples filed his libel of information. He used a printed form he had prepared for general use, with blank spaces to be filled in by hand. The page and two-thirds provided for the description of the property had to be crowded to include the description of the ten lots. On page 3 were printed paragraphs, prepared to correspond to the particulars of Sections 5 and 6 of the Act of 1862. Thus paragraph V alleged that ———— [and here the name of Charles M. Conrad was inserted] did after July 17, 1862, "act as an officer of the army or navy of the rebels . . . , or as a member of Congress, or as a judge of a court, or as a cabinet officer, or as a foreign minister, or as a commissioner, or as a consul" of the Confederacy. Paragraphs VI, VII, and VIII alleged a variety of other things the said Conrad had done in carrying on the rebellion. [Presently this mode of pleading will receive judicial attention.] Wherefore the condemnation of the ten lots was sought. The monition and publi-

---

[133] In *The Hampton*, 5 Wall. 372 (1867), it was held that capture as prize overrides previous liens. Miller, J., explained why the claim of a loyal mortgagee could not be allowed: "If it were once admitted . . . , there would be an end of all prize condemnations. As soon as a war was threatened, the owners of vessels and cargoes which might be so situated as to be subject to capture would only have to raise a sufficient sum of money on them, by *bona fide* mortgages, to indemnify them in case of such capture"; thereafter both owner and mortgagee could be indifferent.

This holding was applied in *The Battle*, 6 Wall. 498 (1868). Also on the occasion of the war with Spain, in *The Carlos F. Roses*, 177 U.S. 655 (1900).

[134] Of the following reports on his claim, all but the first were favorable: S. Rep. No. 7, 44th Cong., 1st Sess. (1876); H.R. Rep. No. 308, 44th Cong., 1st Sess. (1876); S. Rep. No. 389, 44th Cong., 1st Sess. (1876); S. Rep. No. 505, 45th Cong., 2d Sess. (1878); H.R. Rep. No. 50, 45th Cong., 3d Sess. (1878); H.R. Rep. No. 9, 46th Cong., 2d Sess. (1879); S. Rep. No. 240, 47th Cong., 1st Sess. (1882); H.R. Rep. No. 694, 47th Cong., 1st Sess. (1882); S. Rep. No. 167, 48th Cong., 1st Sess. (1884); S. Rep. No. 66, 49th Cong., 1st Sess. (1886).

[135] *The Confiscation Cases (Slidell's Land)*, 20 Wall. 92. Companion cases are cited infra, n. 143.

[136] For purposes of this narrative

cation followed, and on September 1, 1863, default was found and the libel was taken to have been confessed. After interventions had been disposed of, on February 3, 1865, the ten lots with all the buildings and improvements were condemned, and public sale ordered.

The Marshal's return showed that Waples had bought five of the lots for $8,700. E. W. Burbank took one item, an undivided half interest in a lot with improvements, for $1,075. One Stephenson purchased four lots for $450. Total receipts thus came to $10,225. After the allowances to the court's officers and accumulated taxes had been disbursed, the balance payable into the Treasury was $5,699.[137]

After the war Conrad made efforts to recover his property. In 1868 a motion to correct the Marshal's return was entered, and presently dismissed. In February 1869 a bill of review was filed, asking the District Court to reopen the case and set aside the decree. In November that was amended to make Waples and Burbank parties. The court allowed the libel to be filed, and summoned Waples and Burbank to appear.

Parallel to these actions were those being made for a review of the decree in *Sixteen Lots of Ground, Property of Kenner*, with Graham and Day being made parties.

To put a stop to this line of action, petitions were filed in the Supreme Court for writs of prohibition: *Ex parte Graham and Day*,

---

there is no need to cite to the pages of printed transcript. Actually these proceedings appear in the transcript of record of other cases where it was requisite to set out what had been done in the original proceeding.

Normally for this period one may find, in the Case File in the National Archives, the handwritten collection of items—extracted from the Minutes of the District and Circuit Courts—from which the printed transcript was set in type. In the narrative I have, in part, used the handwritten record for *Ex parte* Waples, No. 10 Original, decided with the reported case of *Ex parte* Graham, No. 9 Original, 10 Wall. 541 (1871). It was there that I noticed that District Attorney Waples used a printed form listing the multiplicity of rebel activities in which the owners of libelled property were alleged to have engaged—resulting in the "extreme ambiguity" on which Justice Bradley animadverted in the Circuit Court. See infra, pp. 818–19.

[137] Taxation of costs—Extract from Minutes of Apr. 5, 1865. (Somewhat condensed.)

To District Attorney [Waples] for services to	
June 30, 1864 at 2%	204.50
District Attorney, subsequent	25.00
Ex-Clerk and Clerk	76.40
U.S. Commissioner	20.00
Marshal Graham	93.44
Marshal Bullitt	385.74
Registrar 1%	102.25
	907.33

Taxes	
U.S. Direct Tax	103.56
City, 1862–64	2342.00
State, 1861–64	1132.60
Drainage	32.02
Clerk's and Sheriff's fees	8.50
	3618.68

Total deducted from proceeds of sale	$4526.01

No. 9 Original,[138] and *Ex parte Waples and Burbank*, No. 10 Original,[139] at December term 1870.

The theory of these moves was that Section 13 of the Judiciary Act authorized the Supreme Court to issue writs of prohibition "to the district courts, when proceeding as courts of admiralty . . ."; and the Confiscation Act directed that confiscation proceedings "conform as nearly as may be to proceedings in admiralty or revenue cases . . . ." The Court heard argument on December 20, 1870, and on January 9, 1871, denied the motions. "It is too clear to admit of doubt," said Swayne, J., that confiscation cases were *not* cases in admiralty.

In the meantime, in December 1869 Conrad sued out a writ of error to take the decree against his property into the Circuit Court. At about the same time, Slidell, Kenner, and Hatch also sought writs of error.[140]

These cases were awaiting Justice Bradley's advent on his first circuit, in May 1870.[141] After a full hearing on all points, it was announced that "for reasons assigned, the court withholds its decision until the next term of the Supreme Court of the United States." This reflects the fact that *Miller v. United States*, testing the constitutionality of the statute, was pending there and awaiting a reargument.

The *Slidell, Conrad,* and *Hatch* cases stood still until Justice Bradley next held court there, in June 1872. In the meantime, Slidell had died, and Clarke, his executor, was substituted.

The case against the 844 lots and 10 squares of Slidell was much the largest and was taken first in the opinion. The decree was that the libel of information was dismissed; the executor was entitled to be paid the net proceeds of the property, less encumbrances paid, but the sale stood confirmed. The cases of Conrad and Hatch were disposed of on the same basis.

Bradley had by now become well acquainted with Radical goings on at New Orleans, and with the legal work in that behalf. His standard of professional performance was high: not so his patience. That emerges in his opinion supporting the decree.

Many of the points, including the constitutional issue, had now

---

138 10 Wall. 541.

139 154 U.S. 579.

140 In *The Confiscation Cases*, Fed. Case No. 3097, Bradley, J., speaking of Slidell's case, said "The final judgment of condemnation was rendered on the 18th of March, 1865, and the writ of error was sued out on the 17th of March, 1870. It was sued out, therefore, just in time to save the statute of limitations."

Sec. 22 of the Judiciary Act of 1789 provided generally that writs of error must be brought within five years. 1 Stat. 84–85. See *The Protector*, 12 Wall. 700 (1872). By Sec. 2 of the Act of June 1, 1872, the limit was shortened to one year for review by the Circuit Court and two years for review by the Supreme Court.

141 See infra, ch. 21, n. 86.

been settled: he ran over them. "There is one objection, however, that has given me some trouble." He referred to the libel Waples had drawn, alleging through four paragraphs that the owner of the property had done this or that, and this or that, etc.[142] "It is one of the most remarkable specimens of loose pleading and uncertain statement that I remember ever to have seen," said the Justice. "Now, from this allegation, can any mortal man tell what John Slidell did?" "The whole information," he concluded, "is substantially defective, and the judgment must be reversed." So, too, with *Conrad* and *Hatch*.

Two years later the Supreme Court, eight Justices participating, decided by vote of five to three that the confiscation must be sustained.[143] Concededly, said Justice Strong, in a criminal case such loose allegations would be "wholly insufficient." But "mere formal faults" which under the circumstances "cannot have injured any one" would not warrant reversing the decree. Clifford and Field each made a brief statement of dissent. Davis noted his dissent.

Justice Bradley, it was recorded, "did not sit in the argument of this case and took no part in its decision." Evidently he withdrew on April 8 when these cases were reached; the Minutes show that he was absent from April 9 until April 21, 1874.[144]

SEQUELAE

Conrad v. Waples[145] and *Burbank v. Conrad*,[146] though argued separately, were considered together and decided on March 25, 1878. Each had to do with ground within the decree against the property of Charles M. Conrad. In the former, the sons of Conrad

---

[142] See supra, p. 816.

[143] 20 Wall. 92. May 4, 1874. As to the intervenors: since, as had been settled in Day v. Micou, confiscation of real property did not disturb a lien, their claims, even if well founded, afforded no ground for intervening. Claims of Marcuard, 20 Wall. 114. The confiscation of *Ten Lots of Ground, Property of Conrad*, and of *Six Lots of Ground, Property of Hatch*, 154 U.S. 596, 22 L. Ed. 326, was sustained on the basis of *Slidell's* case. In *Conrad's Lots*, 20 Wall. 115, it had been alleged as error that the Circuit Court had confirmed the sale and awarded Conrad only the net proceeds: but now that point fell to the ground. In Kenner v. United States, 154 U.S. 595, 22 L. Ed. 325, the de-

cree of confiscation had been sustained, and that was affirmed.

[144] It seems fair to conjecture that he took this moment to study the problem in what became "the Cruikshank Case," pending in the Circuit Court at New Orleans. See infra, p. 1378. The indictment, entitled United States v. C.C. Nash *et al.*, was being tried before Woods, J., from February 23, 1874, until on March 16 the jury was found to be unable to agree. The second trial began on May 18, Bradley and Woods being that day present on the bench.

Bradley's diary for 1874 contains no entry prior to May 4.

[145] 96 U.S. 279.

[146] 96 U.S. 291.

sued in the federal court to recover from Waples. It was shown that on May 6, 1862—father and sons being within the Confederate lines and engaged in rebellion—the father had conveyed this property to his sons in settlement of a debt. On that same day, General Butler proclaimed the restoration of national authority at New Orleans. An act of sale was recorded in New Orleans on May 31. At the trial, proof of the sale was excluded, on the view that it could not take effect within the Union lines. Judgment was for Waples.

Burbank, it will be recalled, had purchased an undivided half interest in a Conrad lot. In a suit in the Louisiana courts, the sons claimed title under a conveyance from the father, on June 3, 1862, within the Confederate lines. But this transaction had not been recorded at New Orleans until 1870—long after Burbank had purchased. The Louisiana court held that "As to the United States, it was immaterial whether [the Conrad sons] had recorded their title or not; the property in question belonged to them . . . ."[147]

Justice Field spoke for the Court. The Confiscation Act of July 17, 1862, did not abrogate conveyances made before its passage. As to the facts in *Conrad v. Waples*: while dealing *with* the enemy was unlawful, "no consideration of public policy could be subserved" by denying effect to this transaction *between* enemies. "The act of sale made on the 6th of May, 1862, was unaffected by the subsequent confiscation proceedings, and should have been admitted in evidence." The judgment below in favor of Waples was reversed.

As to the unrecorded transaction: an innocent second purchaser for value would have been able to defeat the sale to the sons. But "the United States never stood in the position of the second purchaser of the property sold by the elder Conrad"; the United States "had caused his estate in land, whatever it was, to be seized and condemned; that was all it took, and that was all that passed to Burbank—"nothing more and nothing less." Judgment for the sons was affirmed.

Justice Clifford wrote a dissent applicable to the two cases. He started with the proposition that title to real property is governed by the law of the place; after New Orleans was reoccupied, that meant the law of the United States. But in 1861 Congress had forbidden intercourse with the enemy; therefore acts passed within the enemy lines could not take effect in New Orleans. He would not adopt a view that would "render the Confiscation Act a public snare and a delusion."

That tells something about the rock-bound character of Nathan Clifford. He would adhere to the rules of the law as he understood them—even where that would result in giving efficacy to a statute whose constitutionality had been established over his dissent.

---

[147] 27 La. Ann. 152 (1875).

Chief Justice Waite's Docket Book shows that he too voted against the majority. Evidently he saw no good in placing his disagreement on record.

Burbank found the statute to be a snare in another transaction. A libel filed on August 7, 1863, against *Six Lots of Ground, Property of Thomas J. Semmes,* resulted—after various irregularities—in a judgment of the Supreme Court in 1875, sustaining confiscation.[148] Long before that, however, Burbank was in trouble over his purchase at the confiscation sale. The libel had described six lots: in one square, lot 14, a portion of lot 18, and lots 14 [*sic*], 16, and 17; there was one other lot in another square. The decree of condemnation was to lots as "fully described in the libel on file." The "five certain lots" on the one square were sold by the Marshal to Burbank on June 13, 1865, for $10,500.[149]

The deed to Burbank executed by Marshal Bullitt purported to convey lot 14, the portion of lot 18, and lots *15*, 16 and 17. Burbank took possession from C. A. Weed,[150] who had been occupying Semmes' house and grounds under the military authority.

---

[148] Semmes v. United States, 91 U.S. 21. The case was submitted on October 15, 1875, and decided ten days later. The judgment of Bradley, J., Fed. Case No. 16,299 (1872), was affirmed.

On May 2, 1865, one Bloom filed a petition in the District Court, showing that *he* was the owner of the property in one of the two squares identified in the libel. On May 31 the court opened its decree of April 5 so far as to restore to Bloom his own property; whereupon there was a second advertisement, and on June 13 the sale to Burbank.

In October 1865 Semmes accepted a pardon, conditioned that he "shall not by virtue of this warrant claim any property or the proceeds of any property that has been sold by the order, judgment or decree of a court under the confiscation laws . . . ." Transcript of record, 49. Then President Johnson by proclamations of September 7, 1867, and July 4, 1868, granted amnesty without such conditions annexed.

On March 4, 1868, Semmes suggested to the District Court that since the decree of May 31, 1865, had been reopened, Semmes' property had never been condemned by any subsequent decree; now, it was contended, he was protected by the amnesty. On

June 27, 1868, Durell, J., decreed "that the libel be dismissed and the libelled property restored . . . ." Transcript of Record, 42, 48, 51.

The Government removed this to the Circuit Court, where on June 20, 1872, Bradley, J., held that the District Court could not, three years after it had rendered its decree, sit as a court of error and reverse it. Its original decree would stand. Pardon and amnesty did not invalidate judicial confiscation and sale; besides, acceptance of the pardon on condition was a bar to defendant's claim. Fed. Case No. 16,299.

Semmes will be mentioned in connection with Butchers Union Co. v. Crescent City Co., 111 U.S. 746 (1884), infra, p. 1381.

[149] Transcript of Record in Burbank v. Semmes, 10 (plan); 11–12 (libel); 30–31 (decree and sale). Lots 16, 17, and 18 were long strips with narrow frontage on Annunciation Street; lot 16, was on the corner of Annunciation and Edwards, running along the latter until it touched lot 15, which, with lot 14, fronted on Edwards. Without lot 15, Burbank's purchase would be in two parts.

[150] Mentioned in connection with the Slaughter House monopoly. Infra, ch. 21, n. 7.

On December 27, 1869, Semmes began suit against Burbank in a State court, seeking a judgment that he was the owner of lot 15. He showed that after purchasing lots 14, 16, and 17 in 1857, he had in 1858 acquired the front portion of lot 15 in exchange for the rear portion of lot 14. This exchange was not recorded.

The trial court gave judgment for Semmes, and the State Supreme Court affirmed.[151] Burbank went up to the Supreme Court, which had jurisdiction where the State court had decided against a claim of authority exercised under the United States.[152]

Counsel for Burbank argued that at the confiscation sale the lots "were put up and sold by the marshal as the property of T. J. Semmes" in that certain square; the sale was of "one property," in block; "not the slightest indication existed on the ground of the division of the property into lots"; it was assessed and taxed as one property. Under these circumstances, the numbers and precise measurements were "nonessential elements in the description . . . ."[153]

The Court did not accept that view. Justice Clifford's opinion recounted the history of the confiscation proceedings, up to the affirmation by the Court in 1875, and next traced the present suit to recover lot 15. Then he stated the controlling proposition: "it is clear that the Marshal could only make a valid title to the property described in the decree of condemnation, as that was all that became vested in the United States . . . ." "Viewed in the light of these suggestions,"[154] the judgment below must be affirmed.

Waples—having lost the Conrad lots, as recorded above—went into the Court of Claims and sued for $7,400 purchase money, alleging that there had been a warranty of title. (This was an alternative to the course of L. Madison Day in asking Congress to pass a statute for his relief.) Here claimant must show that he had a right, based upon contract, such as would entitle one to recover against a defendant not clothed with sovereign immunity. The Court of Claims dismissed the petition,[155] and Waples appealed to the Supreme Court. Charles W. Hornor for the appellant was joined by L. Madison Day (who had a personal interest in the outcome). Justice Field gave the Court's response;[156] his words carried a personal allusion. He observed gratuitously that the libel had made scattered allegations about Conrad, "the district attorney evidently regarding him as a person of so much consequence that he must have been called to some official position by the Confederate Government . . . ." Plaintiff's position, he said, "is

---

151 28 La. Ann. 694.
152 Sec. 709, Revised Statutes.
153 Brief for E. W. Burbank, by Durant and Hornor, 7–8.
154 This recalls one of Clifford's

mannerisms, early noted. Supra, p. 78.
155 16 Ct. Cls. 126 (1881).
156 Waples v. United States, 110 U.S. 630 (1884).

without even plausible foundation." A purchaser was bound to know that the decree carried nothing more than what the United States had taken on the confiscation. "This would be true with reference to any layman, but with special force may it be applied to the plaintiff, who as district attorney directed the seizure and conducted the proceedings to the decree."

In another proceeding initiated by himself, Waples paid $6,000 for the confiscated lots of General Harry T. Hays. The property had been mortgaged to E. A. Bradford for $6,000 in 1860; the court directed that the mortgagee share in the distribution of the proceeds. In 1876 Hays died; Waples' life interest being terminated, the heirs sued for possession. Waples, however, contended that by payment to the mortgagee the United States had been subrogated to his rights under the mortgage, that Hays' title had been extinguished and that the court's decree had given Waples a title in fee. Waite, C. J., for the Court, said No: "Waples got all the title the United States undertook to convey; that is to say, an unincumbered right to the use and enjoyment of the property during the life of Hays."[157]

In 1882 Waples published *A Treatise on Proceedings in Rem*, in which much attention was given to the Confiscation Act of 1862. In his critique of the cases the Court fares about as well as did Waples himself in the decisions of the Court.

DISTRICT JUDGE FOR VIRGINIA

FOR SCANDALOUS ADMINISTRATION of the Confiscation Act of 1862, the federal District Court for Virginia was outstanding. The Supreme Court's rebuke in *McVeigh v. United States* will be recalled.[158] In proceedings to confiscate McVeigh's home in Alexandria, when counsel appeared to make his answer and assert his claim, District Judge Underwood, on motion of District Attorney L. H. Chandler, struck the answer and claim from the files as "irregular and improperly admitted." Thereupon it was recorded that "McVeigh, having been duly called came not but made default"; the court ordered "that the libel in this cause be taken pro confesso," and upon hearing three witnesses [whose testimony is not recorded] the property was condemned. The Marshal was directed to publish notice and thereupon to sell to the highest bidder. Marshal John Underwood carried out these directions, and on April 11, 1864, sold the real estate for $2850.

---

[157] Waples v. Hays, 108 U.S. 6 (1882). Doubtless the mortgagee was the Edward A. Bradford, leading New Orleans lawyer, who in 1852 was President Fillmore's first nominee for the vacancy on the Court that eventually was filled by John A. Campbell. See supra, note 128.

[158] 11 Wall. 259, Mar. 6, 1871. Supra, p. 798.

The transcript does not name the purchaser: but it soon appears that a title in fee was vested in Mrs. Maria J. Underwood, wife of the Judge.

A writ of error was sued out to bring the case before the Circuit Court where, on November 28, 1864, Chief Justice Chase affirmed— and at once allowed a writ of error to remove the case to the Supreme Court.[159] There, as we have seen, it was held that it would be "a blot on our jurisprudence and civilization" to allow the decree to stand. The cause was remanded to the Circuit Court, "with directions to proceed in it according to law." This was on March 6, 1871.

McVeigh was a man of property. His residence, on St. Asaph Street between Duke and Prince Streets, had a frontage of 89 feet and a depth of 123 feet; the brick stable stood on a separate lot. This was only one "among the twenty-odd cases . . . in which valuable property of this unfortunate [party] was confiscated and sold without a hearing . . . ."[160]

On remand, *McVeigh v. United States* came before the Circuit Court at Richmond at October term 1871. Hugh L. Bond—appointed in 1870 to the new office of Circuit Judge—was on the bench. The Government was represented by District Attorney Henry H. Wells, Republican candidate for Governor in 1869. The former District Attorney, L. H. Chandler, appeared for Mrs. Underwood, contending that her rights under the judicial sale could not be divested by the reversal of the decree. John Howard, for McVeigh, argued that the proceedings, after the point where McVeigh was denied a hearing, were absolute nullities—that Mrs. Underwood's title was void—and that his client should now be allowed to answer the libel. The Judge agreed, and upon a hearing the libel was dismissed.[161]

But the Underwoods were in possession. An action to eject, brought in the Corporation Court of Alexandria, resulted in a judgment against the Underwoods, and they appealed to the Supreme Court of Appeals of Virginia.

Here we take as our guide the report of that court, in 23 Grattan 409, at March term 1873.

The Underwoods, it will appear, had a second title to the house. McVeigh had been a partner in a mercantile firm at Alexandria. After the war came and he removed to Richmond, presently creditors of his firm, in Massachusetts and at Baltimore, attached McVeigh's property, but refrained from bringing it to a sale. When, however, news came that confiscation proceedings had been started in the federal

---

[159] Transcript of Record in McVeigh v. United States, 13–19.
[160] Brief of John Howard for Defendant in Error, in Windsor v. McVeigh and Gregory v. McVeigh, at

1. The *Gregory* case, decided on May 3, 1875, is reported in 23 Wall. 294. *Windsor*, substantially identical, was decided with it. See infra, n. 168.
[161] Ibid., at 23–24.

court, the creditors rushed to Washington. (Not until ten years later, in *Day v. Micou,* was it established that confiscation would not disturb prior liens on real property.[162]) They learned that a little group had been formed to buy McVeigh's various properties. The leaders were Oakes Ames and John B. Alley, Republican Congressmen from Massachusetts and experienced moneymakers. Judge Underwood was a participant. The creditors asked the Judge to defer the confiscation proceedings. He refused, but—as one of the creditors later testified— "said he thought the parties buying under the confiscation act would pay us something for our judgments, to obtain a more perfect title, and make it sure if the confiscation act should be set aside."[163] And so it was arranged. The creditors obtained a judgment in the (Unionist) State court at Alexandria, and bought the attached property at a sale. An auction was held covertly—"there was hardly even a form of sale" —and Alley purchased on behalf of "the same ring" that purchased at the confiscation sale. As a creditor testified, "we were assured by Judge Underwood and by Alley and Ames, . . . the confiscation sales were valid and binding, and that our attachments were of no value; that the confiscation would be sustained by the court; and we thought, under the circumstances, that it was necessary for us to save ourselves by accepting their offer to buy our judgments . . . . The parties above mentioned, said that if they failed on the confiscation title they would fall back on the attachment title, and they were willing to pay us something for our judgment and lien; and they paid us in full, except $700."[164]

On April 23, 1873, the Supreme Court of Appeals entered judgment: the judgment below was affirmed, and defendant in error would recover damages and costs; this should be certified to the Corporation Court.

Underwood and Erasmus D. Foree—who had been appointed trustee for Mrs. Underwood's interest—sued out a writ of error to take the matter to the Supreme Court. Then on December 7, 1873, Underwood died.

The first writ of error was dismissed, for the reason that plaintiff in error had caused it to run to the wrong Virginia court.[165]

---

[162] 18 Wall. 156 (1874). See supra, pp. 814–16.

[163] 23 Gratt. (Va.) at 441.

[164] The creditors' attachments covered some property not purchased by the ring; the members were paying their proportionate share of the creditors' judgment.

[165] Underwood and Foree v. McVeigh, 131 U.S. App. cxix, 21 L. Ed.

952. The writ of error had been directed to the Corporation Court, not to the Supreme Court of Appeals.

We have come upon a covert leading to hide-and-seek. The explanation may be found in Gregory v. McVeigh, 23 Wall. 294, decided May 3, 1875, and in Atherton v. Fowler, 91 U.S. 143 (1875).

Section 709 of the Revised Statutes

Foree went back and started again.[166] In the meantime, *Windsor v. McVeigh*[167] and *Gregory v. McVeigh*[168] had been docketed, seeking a reversal of other judgments of ejectment in the Corporation Court of Alexandria. On December 11, 1876, those judgments were affirmed.

Before we turn to the Court's holding in matter of law, the transcripts of record are worth scanning for persons and dates. In McVeigh's actions to recover his home from the Underwoods, and to recover other houses from Windsor and Gregory, the striking of the appearance and answer of counsel, and the default decree, had in each

---

provided, in words derived from Section 25 of the Judiciary Act of 1789, that "A final judgment or decree in any suit, in the highest court of a State in which a decision in the suit could be had," might, where a claim of federal right had been denied, be taken to the Supreme Court on writ of error. In order to bring up the record, the writ should—as had been said in Hunt v. Palao, 4 How. 589 (1846)—be "directed to the court which holds the proceedings as part of its own records, and exercises judicial power over them."

Philip Phillips, counsel for McVeigh and an expert on Supreme Court practice, pointed out that when the Virginia Court of Appeals decided the *Underwood and Foree* case it had not sent the record back to the Corporation Court; it had merely directed that its judgment be certified to the lower court.

The Court accepted that view, and on March 23, 1874, dismissed the writ.

[166] The Docket shows that a new writ of error directed to the Supreme Court of Appeals, was filed by Foree on October 16, 1875.

[167] 93 U.S. 274, docketed Oct. 12, 1874; decided Dec. 11, 1876. A motion to dismiss was denied on May 3, 1875. See Gregory v. McVeigh, in footnote 168.

[168] 93 U.S. 284, docketed Oct. 16, 1874; decided Dec. 11, 1876, and reported under Windsor v. McVeigh.

On April 9, 1875, Phillips and Howard submitted motions to dismiss in *Gregory* and *Windsor*. These were denied for reasons set out by Waite, C.J., in Gregory v. McVeigh, 23 Wall. 294, on May 3, 1875.

(1) It was argued that the so-called sentence and condemnation of McVeigh's property was an absolute nullity, and that it should be treated as nonexistent, even though it was attacked in a collateral proceeding. This the Court rejected: there was a proceeding in the District Court, and its validity was drawn in question. There *was* a federal question to be considered. (It was considered and decided in Windsor v. McVeigh, 93 U.S. 274.)

(2) At any rate, it was argued, the writs of error to the Corporation Court should be dismissed. The Supreme Court of Appeals was the highest State court in which a decision of these cases could be had. Either it had acted upon the judgment of the Corporation Court, or it had not. If it had, the writ should have been directed to the highest court. If it had not exercised its jurisdiction, of course the Supreme Court of the United States had no jurisdiction.

The opinion by Waite, C.J., rejected that argument. By Virginia law there were two modes of obtaining leave to bring such cases as these to the State's highest court; through petition to that court, and through a petition to a judge thereof. Counsel for Gregory and Windsor had petitioned each and every judge, and all had refused on the ground that the judgment of the Corporation Court was "plainly right." In that situation, resort to the State's highest court was precluded by State law. In such circumstances, the Corporation Court was the highest in which a decision could be had.

case been on March 10, 1864. Marshal John Underwood's sale of the home, and also that of the house acquired by Windsor, had been on the same day and per his deputy W. A. Duncan. (We shall hear more of Duncan in a moment.) Who at the same time made the sale to Gregory does not appear. The certificate of the accuracy of the transcript in *Gregory* was signed on February 2, 1874, by Clerk Ed. J. Underwood. That in *Windsor* was signed on April 1, 1874, by a new Clerk, Jno. R. Popham. Upon Judge Underwood's death in January, President Grant had appointed Robert W. Hughes (1821–1901) to the District Judgeship. The new Judge was a post-bellum Republican, of a very different sort from his predecessor. When the writ of error issued to take *McVeigh v. United States* to the Supreme Court in December 1868, service was made upon the then District Attorney, S. Ferguson Beach. Counsel to Underwood and Foree, to Windsor and to Gregory, in resisting ejectment proceedings, was S. Ferguson Beach.

We come to the hearing of the *Windsor* and *Gregory* cases on the merits.

Beach argued with some subtlety that "the order of the . . . district court striking the answer of the claimant . . . did not render the subsequent sentence of condemnation absolutely void—it rendered it voidable, only, for error—and until actually avoided by proceedings in error, it was a valid judgment of a court of competent jurisdiction, and, as such, a firm and solid basis of title." He recalled *United States v. Leroy M. Wiley* in the Southern District of New York in 1863:[169] there too the answer of counsel for the claimant was struck. The *Wiley* case had been "published in the principal newspapers of that day," and although afterwards reversed, it "was a conspicuous precedent, and one regarded as of high authority when the order was made in this case of United States vs. McVeigh." Since the condemnation of the property held by Windsor had never been reversed or reviewed, the title should have been sustained by the court below.[170] The same could be said of the property occupied by Gregory.

Justice Field gave the answer of the Court:

> The doctrine invoked by counsel, that, where a court has once acquired jurisdiction, it has a right to decide every question which arises in the cause, and its judgment, however erroneous, cannot be collaterally assailed is undoubtedly correct as a general proposition; but, like all general propositions, is subject to many qualifications in its application. . . .

---

[169] Fed. Case No. 15,960a (1863); reversed in the Circuit Court by Nelson, J., Fed. Case No. 15,961 (1865). See supra, pp. 789–90.

[170] Brief of S. F. Beach for Windsor, of eight pages, dated Nov. 14, 1876.

Here, Justice Field declared, was such an exception. When the court denied a party an opportunity to be heard, it transcended its legal power and ceased to exercise jurisdiction. Its sentence was void, and even in a collateral proceeding was entitled to no respect.

Justices Miller, Bradley and Hunt noted dissent.

Windsor v. McVeigh was decided on December 11, 1876. Phillips and Howard were now anxious to see the Underwood-Foree matter settled promptly on the basis of *Windsor*. Upon notice to their opponents, they united two motions: that the writ of error be dismissed, and that the judgment below be affirmed. On April 16, 1877, the Court observed that the only federal question had now been decided, and affirmed the judgment of the Virginia Court of Appeals.[171]

Justice Field's opinion in *Windsor v. McVeigh* has been widely cited and applied where a court has gone beyond the bounds. An almost instant application was in *Avil v. Alexandria Water Company*, in the Circuit Court in Virginia.[172] Among the items of McVeigh's property confiscated after the denial of a hearing were ten shares of stock in the local water company. At the Marshal's sale they were bought by William A. Duncan, the Deputy Marshal already mentioned.[173] In 1866 the company denied Duncan's title and refused to pay dividends to him. Duncan assigned to his brother-in-law, thereby creating diversity of citizenship. The latter sued the company in the federal court, where the jury under proper instructions returned a verdict for the defendant.

McVeigh's name figures prominently in the Virginia reports, from 20 Grattan in 1871 to 94 Virginia in 1896. Notable is *McVeigh's Executor v. Howard*,[174] in 1891—a controversy over what was due for professional services that culminated in winning over Windsor and writing *finis* to Foree.

DISTRICT JUDGE FOR ALABAMA

RICHARD BUSTEED, born in Ireland in 1822, came as a young man to the United States and presently settled in New York City. There he worked as a typesetter, became a Methodist preacher, and in 1846 was admitted to the bar. He came to public notice in defending against extradition proceedings—in which connection he has been mentioned in the discussion of habeas corpus.[175] He supported Douglas for the Presidency in 1860.

---

[171] Minutes; see Foree v. McVeigh, 23 L. Ed. 1010.
[172] Fed. Case No. 679, C.C.E.D. Va., Apr. 1877.
[173] Supra, p. 827.
[174] 87 Va. 599.
[175] Supra, ch. 10, n. 47.

In August 1862, at the behest of William Cullen Bryant, Lincoln made him a Brigadier General—and presently asked his commanding officer to "assign him the position best adapted to his case . . . ." In March next Busteed left the army. The President in November appointed him to be District Judge in Alabama, and on January 20, 1864, the Senate confirmed.[176] At the time of the appointment, Attorney General Bates' estimate was that Busteed was " 'a slight, unmeritable man.' "[177]

Federal forces occupied Mobile in April 1865. Thereupon the office of the Clerk of the District Court began to function; Judge Busteed opened court at the December term. From that moment until he resigned in 1874, his conduct constantly brought discredit upon himself and upon federal justice.

In *Morris and Johnson v. United States*[178] the Court had a sample of his work.

An information filed by the District Attorney at November term 1866 showed that Thomas H. Watts (sometime Attorney General in the Confederate Government, and Governor of Alabama) had supplied cotton to James A. Farley, Confederate agent; this had been stored in Johnson's warehouse. By the surrender of General Taylor to General Canby on May 4, 1865, the property of the Confederate Government was turned over to the United States. Morris and Johnson removed 120 bales of the Watts cotton from the warehouse, sold it, and appropriated the proceeds to their own use. The prayer was that Morris and Johnson be summoned to show cause why judgment should not be rendered against them for the value of the cotton as ascertained by the court.[179]

Morris and Johnson answered that the latter had a warehouseman's lien for more than the value of the 120 bales, and that he was so holding them at the time of the surrender; that the bales were removed to save them at a moment in April when the Confederates were about to burn all the cotton in Montgomery. Johnson had given Morris a half interest in the cotton in consideration of an advance of money.

On December 17, 1866, Judge Busteed entered a judgment condemning the cotton, and against Johnson and Morris in the sum of $30,000 and costs. In execution the Marshal levied on more than

---

[176] *Collected Works of Abraham Lincoln*, V, 361; VI, 14; VII, 15. Sketch in Appletons' *Cyclopaedia of American Biography*.

[177] *Diary of Edward Bates*, entry for Nov. 19, 1863. Other unfavorable references appear in the entry for December 26. The quotation is from *Julius Caesar*, Act IV, scene 1, l. 12.

[178] 7 Wall. 578. Docketed on Dec. 4, 1867; submitted on Apr. 9, 1869; decided Apr. 15, 1869. A further development, 9 Wall. 605 (1870), will appear.

[179] Transcript of Record, 1–4.

twenty lots, property of Morris, and raised over $31,000. In anticipation, the Judge had made an order of distribution: 5 percent to District Attorney Smith and 1 percent each to the Marshal and the Clerk, as reasonable fees for their services; after all charges had been deducted, one half of the remainder would go to E. R. McCroskey, an informer, and the other half would be held in the registry of the court, subject to the order of the Secretary of the Treasury.

An "appeal" was taken to the Supreme Court—which would have been appropriate if this had been a condemnation of maritime prize,[180] but not in a case under the Confiscation Acts. The error was Busteed's. On December 27, 1866, the Clerk at Montgomery had telegraphed to the Judge at Mobile: "Morris & Johnson have filed writ of error & bond. . . . May I enter your approval of the bond? . . ." The reply was: "The defendants are not pursuing the appropriate remedy as I think now; . . . they must appeal, according to the course of the proceedings in admiralty . . . ."[181]

William P. Chilton,[182] appellants' counsel, told the Court that "this is a novel, and, I may say, a most remarkable proceeding": an action for conversion of property of the United States—tried as a suit in admiralty, without right to trial by jury—although as the Court found, the cotton at the time of the conversion was property of the Confederate States—invoking both the Confiscation Act of 1861 for the *use* of the cotton in aid of the rebellion and the Act of 1862 on the ground of the *rebel status* of Watts and Farley—where there had been no seizure, which those statutes made a jurisdictional prerequisite, and, indeed, as stated in the bill of exceptions, where the bales had been "removed out of the State before the institution of those proceedings."[183]

The record showed that Watts and Farley had been pardoned in 1865.

The Chief Justice said that, without adverting to principles settled in *Union Insurance Co. v. United States*[184] and *Armstrong's Foundry*[185]—decided on March 25, 1868, affirming the right to trial

---

[180] An Act to regulate Prize Proceedings, of June 30, 1864, sec. 13. 13 Stat. 310.

[181] Pamphlet of twenty-eight pages of documents, filed on Mar. 3, 1870, by petitioners in *Ex parte* Morris and Johnson, 9 Wall. 605, at 26–27.

[182] Formerly a Justice and Chief Justice of the Supreme Court of Alabama, and a Representative in the Confederate Congress. He died in 1871, and there is a memorial in 25 Ala. ix–xi.

[183] Brief for Appellant, in eight pages. He added the observation that the order of distribution rewarded an informer who had not been mentioned in the proceedings, and although for conversion of government property there was no statute authorizing any one to become an informer.

[184] 6 Wall. 759. See supra, p. 791.

[185] 6 Wall. 766. See supra, pp. 791–92.

by jury in cases of seizure on land, and the efficacy of a pardon before forfeiture had been adjudged—the case failed: at most, it showed only an unlawful conversion of property; and neither of the Confiscation Acts contemplated a proceeding "where there existed no specific property or proceeds capable of seizure and capture." The decree was reversed and the cause remanded, "with directions to the District Court to cause restitution to be made to the appellants, of whatever sum of money they have been compelled to pay under that decree."[186]

But when the mandate went down, Judge Busteed did nothing about it. So Morris and Johnson brought an original proceeding in the Supreme Court, a petition for a writ of mandamus to compel obedience to the Supreme Court's direction.[187] And this was disclosed: what had been wrongly exacted had already been distributed, to District Attorney, Marshal, Clerk, the award to the informer, and the remainder held for the United States had been deposited in a bank. The bank had failed. The informer had disappeared. The District Attorney objected to answering questions calculated to show that he had received a large part of the award to the informer, and the Judge had held "the inquiries were not pertinent to the issue before him."[188] The Judge professed himself to be at a loss to know what to do.

Philip Phillips filed the petition on February 8, 1870, at the same time serving notice on Judge Busteed "at his room in the Metropolitan Hotel." He argued his motion on April 22, with no opposition, and on April 30 Justice Swayne gave the Court's response. He said that the District Court's duty was "simple and obvious, and its power ample," adding concise directions.

The similar case of *Morris's Cotton*,[189] reversed and remanded with directions to issue a writ of restitution, in December 1869, only points to the same confusion.

A saying was passed about in Alabama, in post-war days when pleasantries were few: evidently Lincoln really didn't expect to bring the South back into the Union—else he never would have made Dick Busteed the federal Judge for Alabama! *The Nation* commented, in December 1873: he "was, at the outbreak of the war, one of the roughs of the New York bar—a man without learning or character, an active Tammany politician, and a noted brawler in court. . . . Since [he became a Judge] he has been a standing nuisance. . . . Of late he has had the good sense to keep his court closed and spend his time at the North . . . ."[190]

---

[186] Morris and Johnson v. United States, 7 Wall. 578, 580 (1869).

[187] *Ex parte* Morris and Johnson, 9 Wall. 605 (1870).

[188] Petition for Mandamus, filed Feb. 8, 1870, at 9.

[189] 8 Wall. 507.

[190] 17:418. Dec. 25, 1873.

For a District Judge to fail to reside in his district has been declared to be "a high misdemeanor."[191] In the 43rd Congress, the House Judiciary Committee was sure that Judge Busteed was guilty of that offense, whatever view might be taken as to whether other misdoings would support impeachment. After his resignation on October 20, 1874, the matter was dropped.[192]

DISTRICT JUDGE FOR KANSAS

KANSAS WAS ADMITTED to the Union in 1861, and President Lincoln twice had occasion to appoint a District Judge for that State. Archibald Williams (1801–63) of Quincy, Illinois, was well known and highly regarded by the President: they had served together in the legislature, had met in the same cases, and had supported one another in politics. This was a proper appointment.[193]

But Williams died in September 1863, and next month Mark W. Delahay (1817–79) was promoted from Surveyor General for Kansas to the Judgeship. Lincoln had known him for some years as a politician, in Illinois and after 1855 in Kansas; in 1859 he had been Delahay's guest during a short visit to Leavenworth to encourage local Republicans, and next year had advanced one hundred dollars to enable him to come to the convention at Chicago.[194] This appointee disgraced himself.

What follows deals with one case before the Supreme Court: *Thomas A. Osborn et al. v. United States*,[195] decided in 1876, resulting from the corrupt conduct of Judge Delahay and officers of his court in proceedings under the Confiscation Act of 1862. The Transcript of Record runs to 657 pages and—like the transactions with which it is concerned—is hard to trace.

---

[191] Secs. 551, 552, Rev. Stats. Derived from the Judiciary Act of 1789, 1 Stat. 73, and an Act of Dec. 18, 1812, 2 Stat. 788.

[192] Cong. Rec., 43–2, 324–26. Jan. 7, 1875.
The allegations on which action was based are in H.R. Misc. Doc. No. 109, referred to the Judiciary Committee on February 2, 1874; that committee's report, calling for impeachment, is H.R. Rep. No. 773, of June 20, 1874—both of the 43d Cong., 1st Sess.

[193] This is amply documented in the *Collected Works of Abraham Lincoln*;

the four volumes on *Lincoln* day-by-day, *1809–1861*, compiled by Harry E. Pratt, (the first two), Benjamin P. Thomas, and Paul M. Angle; Beveridge, *Abraham Lincoln, 1809–1858*; and by the *Diary of Orville Hickman Browning*.

[194] *Collected Works of Abraham Lincoln*; Paul M. Angle, *Lincoln* day-by-day, *1854–1861* (Springfield: Abraham Lincoln Assn., 1933); Beveridge; King, *Lincoln's Manager, David Davis* (Cambridge, Mass.: Harvard University Press, 1960), 139.

[195] 91 U.S. 474.

In the spring of 1863 the then District Attorney instituted suits, Nos. 140 and 141 on the court's docket, against bonds secured by mortgages executed by citizens of Kansas, the property of Edward S. Brown, a citizen of Virginia. The suits, which were consolidated, concerned a total of 48 such bonds. In May 1863, in default of appearance, the court condemned the property; the debtors were ordered within five months to pay into court the moneys due.

When the debtor had made payment, a United States Commissioner—such as David J. Brewer[196]—would enter on the margin of the register where the mortgage had been recorded a certificate of the confiscation and of satisfaction, and would release the property from the lien.

Besides the suits against Brown's property there were ninety-nine other confiscation proceedings. Judge Williams entered a scale of fees to be paid to officers of the court in such cases; he designated a banking house as the place of deposit of moneys paid into the registry of the court. This latter action was in accord with Rule 42 of the Rules of Practice in Admiralty, which prescribed that withdrawals be by check, signed by the Judge and countersigned by the Clerk, "stating on whose account and for whose use it is drawn, and in what suit and out of what fund in particular it is paid. . . ."

No censure attached to Judge Williams' conduct.

In October 1865 Brown went to Kansas, and next April presented his petition to the District Court: he alleged that the bonds had not been liable to confiscation—but if the decree was valid, he set up a pardon. District Attorney Emery moved to strike the petition, and Judge Delahay so ordered. Brown took his case to the Circuit Court, where it was heard at May term, 1868, by Justice Miller.[197]

The pardon as alleged contained conditions: among them, that Brown "pay all costs which may have accrued in any proceedings instituted or pending against his person or property before the date of the acceptance of this warrant," and that he "shall not, by virtue of this warrant, claim any property, or the proceeds of any property that has been sold" by judicial decree under the Confiscation Acts. Justice

---

[196] Brewer (1837–1910) is here mentioned only because he became a Justice of the Supreme Court in 1889, serving until his death. Certificates by him, executed on Apr. 11, 1864, appear in the Transcript in Osborn v. United States, at 637–38. Otherwise he does not figure in the case.

Brewer, whose name crops up here, and Henry B. Brown, who was noticed in connection with the Transcript in

Miller v. United States, supra, p. 803, were members of the Class of 1856 at Yale and, in alphabetical order, sat in the same pew at chapel. Brown was close to the appointment to the Court when President Harrison's choice settled upon Brewer; one year later he followed him.

[197] Brown v. United States, Fed. Case. No. 2032, decided June 1, 1868.

Miller observed that the effect of pardons had been "fully and ably argued before the Supreme Court," and while questions were pending,

> I feel at liberty to state my belief that there is no difference of opinion among the justices upon the proposition that they restore to the recipients of them all the rights of property lost by the offence, unless the property had, by judicial process, become vested in other persons, subject also to such other exceptions as the pardon itself prescribes.

The Circuit Court remanded with directions that the petition be admitted, and if it were found that Brown had been pardoned and had complied with the conditions, he would be entitled to all the property or money remaining within the control of the court, less the costs up to the time of offering the petition.

In October, Judge Delahay directed the court's officers to bring into court the moneys received in the proceedings.

But the order went unobeyed. On May 31, 1870, the Circuit Court, held by Justice Miller and Circuit Judge Dillon, appointed a special commissioner to examine the officers and make report. Six weeks of inquiry led to findings that called for judicial action. Examination of *all* confiscation cases had been involved, since the moneys from divers cases had been mixed. The *Brown* confiscation proceeds had been drawn upon, allegedly for general expenses of the court, and had been appropriated by Marshal McDowell. The original orders establishing fees had been mutilated, and higher figures inserted. The Judge had written checks to various officers, and simultaneous deposits to his own account were found. District Attorney Emery had failed to appear when called.[198]

On November 29, 1872, the Circuit Court ordered the parties involved (Judge Delahay not being included) to deposit in the registry of the Circuit Court specified sums which appeared to be due. A special examiner was appointed to take testimony offered on behalf of any who would contest the amounts ordered to be paid. And a special master was named, to consider the commissioner's report and the evidence now to be taken, to hear arguments, and to report on the liability of the parties concerned.

The special master concluded that "the question of liability on the part of M. W. Delahay" was not before him; he did, however, understand that he was not to confine his inquiry "to the whereabouts of Brown's money" to the exclusion of misdealings with other confiscation funds. He commented on the conduct of the bankers, although he was not to fix their liability. From the fact that they had paid Delahay

---

[198] Transcript of Record: report at 419-25, and appended papers at 425-516.

interest on the District Court account—had allowed his own account to remain overdrawn for months—and had transferred funds to his account—an inference arose that the bankers were at least aware of the frauds, if not in complicity. The report fixed the amounts of indebtedness of the various parties.[199]

On June 9, 1873, the Circuit Court, held by Judge Dillon *and Judge Delahay*, entered its decree.[200] The report of the special master and the decree of November 29, 1872, were confirmed with modifications. The parties were held liable for their dealings with funds in cases 140 and 141, and in respect of "undistinguishably mixed moneys" arising in those cases; but this did not relieve them of liability in other confiscation cases, "as to which other cases this court has no jurisdiction to make any orders or decrees." [It was only Brown's cases, 140 and 141, that were before the Circuit Court.] As to the bankers: the question of their liability was left open for further order, "with leave to any person in interest to apply hereafter for such decree or order against them as may be just and proper." The District Attorney would, at the suggestion of the petitioner (Brown) bring suit on the official bond of any officer who failed to make payment. The sums found due were fixed:

from former Marshal McDowell	$11,646.04
from former Marshal Osborn	3,750.22
from former District Attorney Emery	775.67
from former Clerk Hanks	262.29

—with 7 percent interest from April 26, 1866, to date of payment.

Five others had paid the sums fixed in the decree of November 29, 1872, and had not contested the proceedings: they were discharged from further liability.

The three first named above prosecuted a writ of error to the Supreme Court, where it was docketed on October 21, 1873.

The case was submitted on December 13, 1875: this was the time when it would have been called for oral argument. Richard M. Corwine and others were on the brief for Osborn *et al.* They said that the cause presented "novel and interesting questions," and made what they could of unsubstantial points. The brief for the United States was the work of Edward S. Brown himself: as against the misdemeaning officers he had all the right on his side, and presented his claim effectively. He wrote: "This case stands a foul blot on our judicial

---

[199] Ibid., 518–20, appointment of examiner and master; 521–640, the further testimony; 640–49, report of special master.

[200] Ibid., 653–55.

history. There is nothing comparable to it, except, perhaps, the case of the mandamus against Judge Busteed. 9 Wall. 605, *Ex parte* Morris and Johnson."

On February 7 Justice Field spoke for the Court, affirming the decree. On the effect of a pardon, he cited and affirmed what Justice Miller had said in the Circuit Court. The United States had not seen fit to object, and it was no concern of these officers that property adjudged forfeited was held subject to possible restitution. As to the condition attached to the pardon, that Brown should not claim proceeds of property that had been *sold*: these *bonds* had not been sold, even when payment had been forced by sale of the security. The court could, by summary proceedings, compel the restoration of what had been illegally withdrawn from the registry; that power was most fittingly applied to previous officers of the court.

Long before this, on December 10, 1873—shortly after the conclusion of the case in the Circuit Court—Judge Delahay had resigned.[201] Besides being dishonest, he was incompetent.

SIX DISTRICT JUDGES LEAVE THE BENCH

WITHIN TWELVE MONTHS, Judge Underwood had died and Delahay and Busteed had resigned in disgrace.

And three others quit the bench under discreditable circumstances. On November 28, 1873, Judge Charles T. Sherman of the Northern District of Ohio resigned, after a Congressional investigation of the New York Stock Exchange brought out that he had demanded $10,000 for his alleged effectiveness in the incorporation of an exemption of brokers in a tax statute. "I caused it to be fought through the conference committee and retained in the bill . . . ." His explanation to the Committee on Ways and Means was that he had agreed to be helpful, and had engaged his brother-in-law, Judge Bartley, and his friend, Richard C. Parsons; that he was endeavoring to make sure that they were properly compensated.[202] (Parsons was Marshal of the Supreme Court at the time of his alleged services; he resigned that post on December 11, 1872, having been elected to represent a Cleveland district in Congress.)

---

[201] The House of Representatives had informed the Senate that it impeached Judge Delahay, and would in due course exhibit articles. Report of the select committee in charge, H.R. Rep. No. 92, 42d Cong., 3d Sess., Mar. 3, 1873.

[202] New York Stock Exchange Investigation. H.R. Misc. Doc. No. 98, 42d Cong., 3d Sess. The taking of testimony and report were between February 14 and 22, 1873. Commented upon in *The Nation*, 16:126, Feb. 20, 1873.

Judge William Story of the Western District of Arkansas, appointed in 1871 when the place was created, resigned in 1874, when the House Judiciary Committee, in an investigation looking to impeachment, had taken evidence of wrongful diversion of public funds.[203]

The resignation of Judge Durell of the District Court for Louisiana in 1874 brought an abandonment of proceedings for his impeachment. Already the subject of complaints, he had put an end to all further usefulness by his "midnight order" of December 5, 1872, directing the Marshal to take possession of the State House.[204] The effect of this unwarranted intrusion was to bring the Kellogg "Custom House" government into power in that troubled State.[205]

In 1872 New York had purged itself of three corrupt judges who had served the Tweed ring. At the moment the appointive system of the United States Government, however, did not seem to offer a bright promise. "There is no question that the scandalous appointments made

---

[203] Cong. Rec., 43–1, 5316. June 20, 1874.

[204] Cong. Rec., 43–2, 319–24. Jan. 7, 1875.

In H.R. Rep. No. 732, 43d Cong., 1st Sess., of June 17, 1874, the Judiciary Committee had reported of Judge Durell:

Thus a Federal judge, on an action brought . . . to preserve evidence of the offer and exclusion of colored votes at a State election, . . . , of his own motion, in the night, issued an absolute order to prevent the assembling of a State legislature, when he neither had jurisdiction of the subject matter of such election nor of the persons declared to be elected, nor of the board by which the declaration of the election had been made . . . ."

The committee also reported that the Judge had appointed a close friend to be "official assignee in bankruptcy," and that in the handling of bankruptcy proceedings the Judge was either a party to corruption or grossly negligent in the discharge of his duties.

[205] See Kellogg v. Warmouth, Fed. Case No. 7667, Dec. 6, 1872, recognizing "the Herron board of returning officers" as entitled to the protection of the court. The "midnight order" was in aid of this board.

Ex parte Warmouth, 17 Wall. 64, argued before the Supreme Court on December 12, 1872, and decided on December 16, was an original action for a writ of prohibition against Judge Durell. Chief Justice Chase said:

We are all of opinion that when a final decree shall have been rendered in the circuit court in this case, an appeal will lie to this court. We are also of opinion that this court has no jurisdiction in this case to issue a writ of prohibition until an appeal is taken.

Henry M. Hart and Herbert Wechsler, *The Federal Courts and the Federal System*, (Brooklyn: Foundation Press, 1953), at 282, comment:

The Supreme Court at one time seems to have considered that its power, in the exercise of appellate jurisdiction, to issue mandamus or prohibition existed only when the writ was in aid of the proper disposition of a case then pending in the Supreme Court. Ex parte Warmouth . . . . In re Massachusetts, 197 U.S. 482 (1905), recognized the propriety of issuing the writ in aid of the disposition of a case pending in a lower federal court if the case was one over which the Supreme Court had a power of direct review. . . .

of late years to the Federal bench did a good deal to defeat the attempt
to get rid of an elective judiciary in this State," commented *The Nation*
at the close of 1873.[206]

MORE ABOUT BROWN'S KANSAS MORTGAGES

MANY MATTERS are interrelated in the tangled web out of which
cases rise to the Supreme Court. *Brown v. Hiatts*,[207] decided on
February 10, 1873, and *Brown v. Kennedy*,[208] one month later, have
their roots in the dense record we have consulted in *Osborn v. United
States*.

In September 1859, and in May 1860, Edward S. Brown came
and made his loans to people at Leavenworth. These were for twelve
months, with interest at 20 or 30 percent. (Kansas then allowed the
parties to agree upon any rate.) The amount of the bonds ranged from
$100 to something over $1,000; a few were for larger amounts.

Hiatt and wife on May 29, 1860, executed a bond for $2,400
at 20 percent, secured by a mortgage on their half section, and also as
collateral a judgment against *P* and a farm mortgage by *K*. War came
and intercourse between belligerents ceased.

Early in 1863 Hiatt drew the District Attorney's attention to
the Virginian's many claims; the county records were searched, and
proceedings to confiscate were begun. When the Hiatt bond was
included in the libel, he swore that his debt had been extinguished,
because Brown had accepted the judgment against P and the mortgage
by K in full settlement.[209] The District Attorney believed him, dismissed the proceedings against Hiatt's property, and filed a libel against
the K mortgage which resulted in its confiscation.

After the war Brown returned, as we know, and brought suit to
foreclose the Hiatt mortgage. He denied that he had accepted the
collateral in discharge of the debt. (The *P* judgment had proved worthless, and the *K* mortgage had now been confiscated.) When the case
reached the Supreme Court, the conclusion upon the record, as
expressed by Justice Field, was this:

> [Hiatt] concocted a scheme to defraud the complainant, and invented
> the shallow story of an agreement with him to take the collaterals in

---

[206] 17:418. Dec. 25, 1873.
[207] 15 Wall. 177. On one point the
Court disagreed with the opinion of
Judge Dillon in the Circuit Court,

Fed. Case No. 2011 (1870), and for
that reason reversed.
[208] 15 Wall. 591.
[209] Transcript of Record in Osborn
v. United States, at 210–12.

satisfaction of the loan, although they were less than the loan in amount by several hundred dollars. By barefaced and impudent falsehood, and the production of a fabricated letter purporting to be from the complainant, he induced the district attorney to believe that the bond and mortgage . . . had been paid . . . , and that the collaterals belonged to the complainant, and as his property their confiscation was decreed. Having thus led the public prosecutor to treat his own property as belonging to another and to be confiscated as such, he must suffer the consequences of his own folly and crime. . . .

Besides losing the *K* mortgage, Hiatt suffered judgment for the amount of his bond, plus interest at the rate stipulated to the date of the judgment—excluding the war period from April 27, 1861, to April 2, 1866.

In the second of the cases cited, Kennedy and wife on May 27, 1860, gave Brown their bond for $1,200 at 20 percent secured by a mortgage on their quarter section. When proceedings were brought to confiscate "the estate, property, claim, credits and rights" in the debt, Kennedy admitted that it was payable; he said he had been able and willing to pay when it fell due, but could find no agent representing Brown; he asked to be excused from paying interest after maturity.[210] Pursuant to the confiscation decree, Kennedy made payment into court.

On his return, Brown sued to foreclose. He lost in the Circuit Court, held by Justice Miller and Judge Dillon, and appealed to the Supreme Court.[211] He argued that inasmuch as the bond and mortgage were under his control in Virginia, they could not have been seized in Kansas. Justice Strong replied for the Court that the warrant was directed as well against the debt as against the written evidence of it. The marshal returned that he had attached bond, mortgage and credit—and that was what the decree expressly condemned. The opinion noted that Brown had acquiesced in the decree of condemnation, since he had petitioned the District Court to pay him the proceeds under it.

In this instance certainly Brown did not have justice on his side.

---

[210] Ibid., at 175–76.
[211] The holding by the Circuit Court is noted at the end of the report of Brown v. Hiatt, Fed. Case No. 2011.

The suits to foreclose the mortgages by Kennedy and Hiatt were matters of equity which, like cases of admiralty and maritime jurisdiction, went to the Supreme Court by an *appeal*, which brought the entire matter before the Court—to be distinguished from actions brought up on *writ of error*, where there was "an assignment of errors" on points of law, for which the Court was asked to reverse. This explains Justice Field's statement of what the Court found to be the facts. See supra, p. 35.

ABANDONED AND CAPTURED PROPERTY ACT

EXECUTIVE CLEMENCY, coupled with the Court's view that "in the eye of the law the [pardoned] offender is as innocent as if he had never committed the offense,"[212] when applied to the Abandoned and Captured Property Act,[213] led to a result which Congress sought to undo by imposing a new rule of decision upon the Court—an enactment which the Court, in turn, declared to be unconstitutional. This we shall examine.

Explanation begins with four cases which, in the order of docketing, were first, *United States v. Klein*,[214] the most significant case, second, *Anderson*;[215] third, *Padelford*;[216] and fourth, *Pargoud*.[217]

United States v. Anderson, at the request of Attorney General Hoar, received prompt consideration. The Government advanced various contentions limiting the application of the statute, all of which the Court rejected. They seem implausible, and need not be explained. Nelson Anderson, a free person of color, resident in Charleston, South Carolina, and by occupation a cotton sampler and drayman, owned cotton which he reported to the military authorities; by them it was shipped to New York and sold. Anderson's unbroken loyalty was established in the Court of Claims, which awarded him the net proceeds, $6,723.36. The Supreme Court affirmed.

Justice Davis wrote an opinion that made the statute coherent and understandable. Congress had appreciated the plight of those in the South who "adhered with fidelity to the national cause." It had foreseen that, as the enemy retreated, there would be abandoned and captured property of uncertain ownership which should be collected and disposed of. "In a spirit of liberality it constituted the Government a trustee for so much of this property as belonged to the faithful Southern people," and authorized recovery by loyal persons in the Court of Claims. Section 3 permitted suit to be brought "at any time within two years after the suppression of the rebellion." The President by proclamation of August 20, 1866, had declared that armed resis-

---

212 *Ex parte* Garland, 4 Wall. 333, 380 (1867). Supra, pp. 240–42.

213 Act of Mar. 12, 1863, 12 Stat. 820, explained supra, p. 787. The early case of Mrs. Alexander's Cotton, 2 Wall. 404 (1865), was stated supra, pp. 38–39.

214 United States v. Klein, 13 Wall. 128. Filed on Dec. 11, 1869, and, after delays because of its importance, decided on Jan. 29, 1872.

215 United States v. Nelson Anderson, 9 Wall. 56. Filed on Dec. 14, 1869, advanced for argument, and decided on Feb. 28, 1870.

216 United States v. Padelford, 9 Wall. 531. Filed on Mar. 25, 1870, advanced for argument, and decided on Apr. 20, 1870.

217 Pargoud v. United States, 13 Wall. 156. Filed on Apr. 1, 1870, argued with *Klein*, and decided on Apr. 8, 1872.

tance had ceased everywhere;[218] and Congress had recognized the date thus announced.[219] It was from that day that the two years ran.

Two months later, *United States v. Padelford* also received prompt determination. This is the case that led to the collision between Congress and Court.

Padelford, at Savannah, had accepted President Lincoln's subsisting offer of amnesty—on January 18, 1865, four weeks after Sherman had completed his March to the Sea, and when the actual seizure of the cotton was imminent. Self-interest would lead one to embrace the inevitable if thereby one might save one's property. Aside from clemency, Padelford might be seen as a loyal Unionist: the Court of Claims found him to be so, unless such acts as becoming security on a Confederate officer's bond amounted to giving voluntary aid within the meaning of the statute. It gave judgment for the claimant and the United States appealed.

Chief Justice Chase said that the Court did not doubt that such an act did constitute giving aid to the rebellion. However, notwithstanding that the statute permitted only a *loyal* claimant to recover, Executive clemency was in law "a complete substitute for proof that he gave no aid or comfort to the rebellion." The opinion stressed the fact that Padelford had accepted amnesty *before* his cotton was seized: "no . . . right had accrued to the Government until actual seizure, which was after the pardon had taken effect"; "at the time of the seizure of the petitioner's property he was purged of whatever offense against the laws of the United States he had committed . . . ."

While reiterating that holding, the Chief Justice interjected a different proposition, "that if the property had been seized before the oath was taken, the faith of the Government was pledged to its restoration upon the taking of the oath in good faith. . . ." That dictum answered the question that would arise in *United States v. Klein*, still far down in the regular order of the docket.

In the early chapter on the work of the Court it was suggested that there was no adequate opportunity for the entire membership to scrutinize what went into an opinion and to reflect upon particular expressions.[220] From later developments, this appears to have been such an instance.

The *Padelford* decision was announced on April 30, 1870— the last day of the term. Congress was working toward adjournment;

---

[218] 14 Stat. 814.

[219] This recognition was given quite incidentally: by an Act of March 2, 1867, to increase the pay of army officers, an increase previously provided for non-commissioned officers was continued for three years after the close of the rebellion as announced by the President by the proclamation of August 20, 1866.

[220] Supra, pp. 69–70.

it was not too late, however, to add a rider to the bill to appropriate for the Legislative, Executive, and Judicial Branches, then before the Senate. On May 24, Drake of Missouri moved a proviso to follow the appropriation for payment of judgments of the Court of Claims: no pardon or amnesty from the President would be considered by that court, or by "the appellate court on appeal from said court," to establish loyalty as required by the Abandoned and Captured Property Act; in cases where judgments had been awarded on that basis, "the Supreme Court shall, on appeal, reverse such judgment."[221]

After considerable debate in the Senate, and a little in the House, this became the Act of July 12, 1870,[222] save that the direction to the Supreme Court was amended to read "shall, on appeal, have no further jurisdiction of the cause, and shall dismiss the same for want of jurisdiction." The thought was that this would bring it within the *McCardle* case.[223]

Drake waved the *Padelford* opinion before the Senate, and said that unless his proposal was adopted, "judgments will be recovered . . . in favor of men who were rebels throughout the war to the amount of more than ten million dollars . . . ."[224] Edmunds of Vermont—whose view on a constitutional question was always worthy of consideration—said that *Padelford* was to him "a most astonishing decision . . . ." Congress had taken "express pains . . . on the subject of captured and abandoned property, to provide that persons should not go into the Court of Claims unless they went in there upon proof of complete and constant loyalty . . . ." Drake's proposal, he said, rested upon an elementary proposition: "No pardon can take money out of the Treasury of the United States. It takes an act of Congress to do that." The Court of Claims was Congress' own agent to determine, according to rules it prescribed, what claims were to be paid; "we may, by the same right, direct how the Supreme Court shall proceed in the given case in the exercise of a jurisdiction which is merely appellate . . . ." To meet Trumbull's objection to commanding the Supreme Court to reverse an appeal, Edmunds offered and Drake accepted the language that appears in the statute, going to the jurisdiction of the Court.[225]

The proposition that "No Money shall be drawn from the Treasury, but in Consequence of Appropriations made by Law"[226] was the Constitution itself. But was this money *in* the Treasury? Following what had been said in *Anderson*, the Chief Justice in *Padelford* had construed the statute to mean that "the Government is a trustee, hold-

<hr />

[221] Cong. Globe, 41–2, 3751–52.
[222] 16 Stat. 235.
[223] *Ex parte* McCardle, 7 Wall. 506 (1869). See supra, pp. 464, 493.

[224] Cong. Globe, 41–2, 3810. May 25, 1870.
[225] Ibid., 3810–12, 3820–22, 3824–3825. May 25.
[226] Art. I, Sec. 9, cl. 7.

ing the proceeds of the petitioner's property for his benefit . . . ." The Government, he said, lost nothing by the judgment, "which simply awards to a petitioner what was his own."

THE COURT HOLDS A PROVISION UNCONSTITUTIONAL

THE TEST CAME IN *United States v. Klein*.[227] Appellee was administrator of the estate of Victor F. Wilson, a man of Northern birth who had been in business at Vicksburg since 1849.[228] Wilson had held in his warehouse cotton he had purchased in 1862; this was seized by the Confederates and used in their fortifications in the siege of Vicksburg. When in 1863 that place fell, federal authorities shipped the cotton North to Special Treasury Agent Mellen,[229] by whom it was sold. The net proceeds were $125,300. In February 1864 Wilson took an oath of allegiance under Lincoln's amnesty proclamation: "not because he had done anything to make it necessary that he should," it was later explained, "but because he was advised to do it as evidence of his entire willingness to adopt the policy of the government . . . ."

Pursuant to the Abandoned and Captured Property Act, the administrator filed a petition in the Court of Claims, representing that Wilson had given no aid to the rebellion.[230] Judgment was for the petitioner and the Government took an appeal, which was filed in the Supreme Court on December 11, 1869.

In the meantime, on October 12, 1869, the Government asked the Court of Claims to open the case, to consider a fact stipulated by opposing counsel: Wilson had been surety on the bonds of two Confederate officers. On December 22, 1870, the court held that the amnesty oath had relieved Wilson from the effect of such acts. The supplemental finding was certified as part of the record.

Here the Court of Claims was conforming to *Padelford*, and was not conforming to the Drake amendment. Now the validity of that enactment was before the Supreme Court.

For a season, progress in *Klein* was delayed by difficulties attending the *Legal Tender Cases*: this was the time when the new

---

[227] 13 Wall. 128 (1872), affirming 4 Ct. Cls. 559.

[228] What is related here comes from the Transcript of Record, and the Addition to Record containing supplemental findings by the Court of Claims.

[229] Mentioned above as one of Chase's subordinates who constantly served his political interests, pp. 517–

18.

[230] He had been made judge of a civil court set up by the military authorities; later he was Collector of Customs at Vicksburg by appointment of President Johnson. The affidavits of loyalty seem persuasive; two, by well-disposed freedmen who signed by their mark, told how the rebels had carried away the cotton.

majority were pressing for a determination of that matter, while Chase, Nelson, and Field found themselves unable to be in regular attendance.[231] Since *Klein* involved the validity of an Act of Congress, it too should await the return of the absentees.

On November 28, 1870, Attorney General Akerman asked the Court "to send back this cause to the Court of Claims with a mandate directing the same to be dismissed for want of jurisdiction, as now required by law." The same motion was then made in *Pargoud v. United States*, the appeal of an admitted rebel whose pardon had come after the seizure of his cotton.[232] (For the next year, *Klein* and *Pargoud* would keep company.) Four days later the Government asked that the motions go over. On January 5, 1871, the supplemental findings in *Klein* were filed. On January 20, at the Attorney General's request, *Klein* and *Pargoud* were set down for argument—on March 13. But then postponements followed, pending the time when the absentees were brought back to the Bench and the *Legal Tender* question had its final argument.

On April 19 that matter was concluded, and on the twentieth and twenty-first, *Klein* and *Pargoud* were heard. Solicitor General Bristow and Akerman were opposed by a battery of counsel: from Cincinnati, T. D. Lincoln, anti-slavery Republican who had had "a friendly acquaintance" with Wilson over many years, and T. W. Bartley, pronounced Democrat who called upon the Court to avert this "violation of the plighted faith and honor of the nation"; and J. M. Carlisle, Philip Phillips, and T. J. Durant, practicing at Washington.

Nine months later—on January 29, 1872—it was announced that in *United States v. Klein* the motion to dismiss was denied, and the judgment below was affirmed. The Chief Justice spoke for the majority of six; Miller (Bradley concurring) dissented on the matter of the applicability of the pardon.

The Chief Justice—using a pretty strong hand in imputing to Congress an intention to make no change in ownership of the proceeds of abandoned and captured property—spelled out the right of a disloyal owner to recover upon receiving clemency. The Confiscation Act of July 17, 1862, had by its Section 13 authorized the President

> at any time hereafter, by proclamation, to extend to persons who may have participated in the existing rebellion . . . pardon and amnesty, with such exceptions and at such time and on such conditions as he may deem expedient for the public welfare.

---

[231] See supra, pp. 753, 755-57.
[232] Minutes for that day.
The jurisdictional difficulty Pargoud had already experienced in reaching the Supreme Court was related supra, note 44.

That was in effect when Congress passed the Abandoned and Captured Property Act of March 12, 1863: thus the proceeds were left subject to such action as the President might take under the Act of 1862. Then President Lincoln's proclamation of December 8, 1863, had referred to the provision in the Act of 1862, and had offered "a full pardon"

> with restoration of all rights of property, except as to slaves, and in property cases where rights of third parties shall have intervened . . .

upon taking and maintaining inviolate the prescribed oath.

The opinion concluded that

> The restoration of the proceeds became the absolute right of the persons pardoned, on application within two years from the close of the war. It was, in fact, promised for an equivalent. . . .

The notion that the Government bargained for the citizen's return to his allegiance as the contractual equivalent of the restoration of his property was not flawless. And Chase's further assertion, that a refusal thus to restore would have been as "cruel and astounding" as a failure to maintain the freedom conferred by the Emancipation Proclamation, was not carefully measured. The more Chase wanted a result, the less rigorous was his thinking.

The Drake proviso was found to have overpassed "the limit which separates the legislative from the judicial power." The prescribed rule of decision also impaired the effect of a pardon and so infringed the constitutional power of the Executive. It was "impossible to believe that this provision was not inserted . . . through inadvertence . . . ."

"A soft answer turneth away wrath." If Congress took umbrage at what the Chief Justice did, it would first have to disclaim the blameless intention he insisted on attributing to it.

Justice Miller, dissenting, hastened to agree that the Drake proviso was unconstitutional. But as to the Abandoned and Captured Property Act, he could not bring his mind to concur in the proposition that the statute left in the disloyal owner any interest whatever in the property or its proceeds. He recalled the unanimous agreement in the explanations given in *Anderson* and *Padelford*. But now, where the property had been seized and sold and the proceeds paid into the Treasury *before* the disloyal owner was pardoned, "the pardon does not and cannot restore that which has thus completely passed away." In this Justice Bradley concurred.

Presently *Pargoud* was decided in favor of the claimant.[233] His

---

[233] Pargoud v. United States, 13 Wall. 156 (1872).

counsel had contributed to the winning of the decision in *Klein*. The remaining point was that he had not been loyal nor had he sufficiently averred a pardon: now the Court held that the President's grant of unconditional amnesty, by the proclamation of December 25, 1868, was a public act of which the courts would take notice—and that sufficed to support recovery of the proceeds of his cotton.

On a heedless view one might take these decisions as text for a complacent observation that as the war receded its penalties were being remitted, thanks to Executive clemency and a benign Court. But listen to a deeper note: between *Klein* and *Pargoud* came the decision in *Blyew v. United States*,[234] an early construction of the Civil Rights Act of 1866. Section 3 gave federal courts jurisdiction "of all causes . . . affecting persons who are denied or cannot enforce in the courts . . . of the State" the rights secured by that statute. An old blind colored woman had been murdered; Kentucky would not allow her kinsmen, the only witnesses, to testify at the trial of a white man. But the victim was "beyond being affected," and the incompetent witnesses were not "affected" either.[235] Here was a forewarning of developments in years to come: while reconciliation between North and South progressed, the Court would be making some constructions of the law that were anything but benignant toward those for whose protection they had been adopted.

CLEMENCY AND THE RECOVERY OF PROPERTY

IN A WIDE RANGE OF MATTERS, the supervening effect of President Johnson's proclamation of December 25, 1868, became a problem. He there granted

> unconditionally . . . to all . . . who directly or indirectly participated in the late insurrection or rebellion, a full pardon and amnesty for the offence of treason against the United States, or of adhering to their enemies during the late civil war, with restoration of all rights, privileges and immunities under the Constitution and the laws . . . .[236]

When John Knote sued in the Court of Claims, certain of his personal property had been confiscated under the Act of 1862 and the proceeds had been paid into the Treasury. He claimed that by virtue of the proclamation of 1868 he was entitled to receive the money.[237] The Supreme Court said No. This was in 1877—ten years after *Ex parte*

---

[234] 13 Wall. 581, argued on Feb. 20 and 21, 1871, and decided on Apr. 1, 1872.

[235] See supra, chapter 14, note 166.

[236] 15 Stat. 711. See supra, p. 788.

[237] Knote v. United States, 95 U.S. 149, affirming 10 Ct. Cls. 397.

Garland[238]—and principles had now been settled. In the course of a full exposition Justice Field made these points: clemency created no right to compensation for punishment already undergone; nor did it restore what had already been vested in others under a judgment.

> So, also, if the proceeds have been paid into the Treasury, the right to them has so far become vested in the United States that they can only be secured to the former owner . . . through an Act of Congress. . . .
>
> Where, however, property condemned, or its proceeds, have not thus vested, but remain under control of the Executive, or of officers subject to his orders, or are in the custody of the judicial tribunals, the property will be restored or its proceeds delivered to the original owner, upon his full pardon. . . .

He gave as an example the recent case of *Osborn v. United States*: Brown, by virtue of his pardon, had been entitled to the moneys belonging to the registry of the District Court for Kansas which Judge Delahay had allowed unlawfully to be withdrawn.[239]

Money is not officially received into the Treasury until a "covering" warrant has been signed by the Secretary, as prescribed by the Act establishing the Department.[240] In carrying out the Abandoned and Captured Property Act, Secretary Chase had held large sums under his control, not covered into the Treasury: therefrom he paid expenses of administration, and also made restitution where it was apparent that a seizure had been unwarranted. His successors, Fessenden and McCulloch, continued the practice. In the 40th Congress, Representative C. C. Washburn of Wisconsin—who as major general commanding at Memphis had striven to suppress frauds and abuses in border trafficking—introduced Joint Resolution No. 19, to require that all moneys received from sales of abandoned and captured property "shall immediately be paid into the Treasury . . . ." He found "a startling state of affairs": disloyal claimants were being paid, and millions of dollars were being disbursed, by Departmental procedures outside the cognizance of Congress.[241] Fessenden, now a Senator, defended what had been done, and explained the mechanics of "covering into the Treasury."[242] The joint resolution became law on March 30, 1868.[243]

---

[238] 4 Wall. 333 (1867). Supra, pp. 240–42.

[239] 91 U.S. 474 (1876). Supra, pp. 832–36.

[240] The Act of September 2, 1789, in Section 4, Duties of the Treasurer, provided that "all receipts for moneys received by him shall be endorsed upon warrants signed by the Secretary of the Treasury, without which war-rant, so signed, no acknowledgment for money received into the Treasury shall be valid." 1 Stat. 65, 66. See the opinion of the Court of Claims in Menominee Tribe of Indians v. United States, 67 F. Supp. 972 (1946).

[241] Cong. Globe, 40–2, 1761–63. Mar. 9, 1868.

[242] Ibid., 1211–16. Feb. 17, 1868.

[243] 15 Stat. 251.

In *Haycraft v. United States*[244] a Mississippian who had not accepted the earlier proffers of amnesty nor received a pardon, invoked the proclamation of December 25, 1868, as a basis for recovering the proceeds of cotton seized under the Abandoned and Captured Property Act. He sued in the Court of Claims in 1872—but the opportunity to recover under that statute had lapsed on August 20, 1868, two years after the end of the rebellion. Counsel, T. W. Bartley and others, argued that the proceeds had been held by the Treasury "like a debt or legacy to fall to a person on a future contingency," and that on December 25, 1868, the grasp of the law was released. Chief Justice Waite for the Court replied that only Congress could determine whether relief would be granted.

DISPARAGING THE DEEDS OF CONFEDERATES

THE DEEDS TO BE CONSIDERED were to interests in property, made by Confederates and disavowed by their heirs.

In *Bigelow v. Forrest*[245] in 1870 the Court—rejecting the contention that the purchaser of land under confiscation proceedings received a title in fee simple—said that he took only an estate for the life of the person for whose offense it had been seized; but it was not "practical" to speculate where in the meantime the legal title was vested. In *Day v. Micou*[246] in 1874 the Court held that if the offender's property had been mortgaged, the interest conveyed upon confiscation was subject to that burden.

Then came *Wallach v. Van Riswick*,[247] decided in 1876. Wallach had joined the Confederate Army; in 1863 his land in the District of Columbia, already mortgaged to Van Riswick, was condemned; at the confiscation sale, Van Riswick purchased whatever interest passed thereby. Returning after the war, Wallach accepted a substantial sum from Van Riswick and, joined by his wife, gave a deed purporting to convey the land in fee, warranting the title. Upon Wallach's death in 1872, his heirs claimed the title; they sued to redeem the mortgage and to be put in possession of the property. Failing in the District of Columbia court, they appealed.

Representing the Wallach heirs were Albert Pike, ex-Brigadier General, C.S.A., and his son Luther. (It will be seen in a moment that General Pike's children had an appeal pending, very similar to that of the Wallachs and one year behind it on the Court's docket.)

---

[244] 22 Wall. 81 (1875).
[245] 9 Wall. 339. Supra, pp. 797–98.
[246] 18 Wall. 156. Supra, pp. 814–16.
[247] 92 U.S. 202. With it was decided Chaffraix v. Shiff, 92 U.S. 214, from the Circuit Court for the District of Louisiana.

With a tremendous show of erudition the Pikes contended that under the Confiscation Act and the Joint Resolution, condemnation left in the offender no interest of which he could dispose; that the estate had been vested in the United States for the offender's life, with reversion to his heirs. The brief concluded,

> When there is indeed the guilt of Treason and Rebellion, no punishment or forfeiture that affects the Traitor and Rebel himself alone, can be too severe: but none that visits by express intention on the heads of his children any degree of penalty or forfeiture for his offence, can be other than cruel, inhuman and shameful.

T. A. Lambert and T. J. Durant, counsel for Van Riswick, argued that confiscation simply carved out of the fee a life estate, leaving in Wallach a fee simple in reversion, which he was free to sell. They said, "It is true the statute . . . first confiscates the fee; but the amendment [the Joint Resolution interpreting the statute] . . . provides that it shall be so construed as to work no forfeiture of the *offender's* real estate beyond his natural life. . . ." Furthermore, even admitting that Wallach had no title when he executed the deed in 1866, the general amnesty of December 25, 1868, reinvested him with the title, with the result "that he, in his lifetime, was estopped, and that his heirs after him are estopped, from denying the validity of that conveyance."[248]

They quoted from the Congressional Globe for the 37th Congress, concluding,

> In vain do we look in the act itself, in the circumstances which justified its passage, or in the contemporaneous debates of Congress, for any indication, however remote, of an intention to interfere with the owner's control of that residuum of estate which still continued in him by way of reversionary interest . . . .[249]

Asperity marked the printed exchange between Durant, Southern Unionist whose argument would soften the effect of the Confiscation Act, and Pike, touchy Confederate general and publicist, who would maximize the consequence of rebellion.

Oral argument was heard on December 2 and 3, 1875. As Chief Justice Waite's Docket Book records, at conference on Saturday, the fourth, there was a unanimous vote to reverse. The Chief Justice assigned the case to Justice Strong, whose opinion was approved on Monday, January 3, and announced one week later.

It was "incredible," wrote Justice Strong, that Congress intended

---

[248] Brief for the Appellee, of Feb. 26, 1875, 3, 7.

[249] Supplemental Brief, 14.

849

that confiscation should leave in the offender an estate "which he could sell and convey," such that "his power to aid the public enemy thereby remained." The Joint Resolution was "introduced for the benefit of the children and heirs alone; a declaration that the children should not bear the iniquity of the fathers." The amnesty of 1868 "could not restore what the United States had ceased to hold"—and moreover it came after the deed had been executed.

At the next term, Luther Pike was back in court with a case wherein he and the other children of General Pike were parties.[250] Under circumstances paralleling those in Wallach's case, the general's property had been confiscated and Wassell had purchased. The children, claiming to be owners of the reversion, sued in the federal court in Arkansas to compel the tenant for life to pay the taxes and take care of the property.[251] Circuit Judge Dillon dismissed the bill "upon the sole ground that the plaintiffs, during the life of their father, are not his heirs, and are not now . . . possessed of any estate in this property."

On appeal, Chief Justice Waite said for the Court that inasmuch as the children of Albert Pike were apparently next in succession to the estate, and "as there is no one else to look after the interests of the succession," they should be permitted "to do whatever is necessary to protect it from forfeiture or incumbrance." "Without undertaking to direct specifically as to the form in which the protection asked shall be secured," the case was remanded for further proceedings in conformity to the opinion.

For some years sons and daughters of the Confederacy continued to be able to avoid the acts of their fathers because, by the providence of the 37th Congress, the rebel's estate "was separated entirely from that of his heirs after his death, and the heirs are not estopped by his warranty from asserting their rights."[252] Then decisions were made establishing that the rebel's heirs, at his death, took by descent from him and not by gift from the United States.[253] That had involved a closer analysis.

The outcome was recorded in *Illinois Central R.R. Co. v. Bosworth*,[254] in 1890. Abel W. Bosworth was a Confederate soldier; his Louisiana land was confiscated in 1865 and E. W. Burbank[255] purchased for $1,700. Later that year Bosworth was pardoned.

---

[250] Pike v. Wassell, 94 U.S. 711. Argued Apr. 11 and decided May 7, 1877.

Robert L. Duncan, in *Reluctant General: The Life and Times of Albert Pike* (New York: E. P. Dutton, 1961), relates some details of the confiscation and consequent impoverishment. Pp. 265–68.

[251] Pike v. Wassell, Fed. Case No. 11,164 (E.D. Ark. 1873).

[252] French v. Wade, 102 U.S. 132 (1880).

[253] Avengo v. Schmidt, 113 U.S. 293 (1885); Shields v. Shiff, 124 U.S. 351 (1888).

[254] 133 U.S. 92.

[255] See supra, p. 813.

In 1871, Bosworth and wife deeded all their right in the property to Edgar for $11,666.

In 1872, Burbank quitclaimed to Edgar for $5,000.

Illinois Central was lessee of a railroad company to which Edgar had sold the property with full warranty.

Upon Bosworth's death in 1884, his children claimed the fee simple and sued for possession. They won the judgment of the Circuit Court, and the Illinois Central took the case to the Supreme Court.

Thomas J. Semmes and other counsel for the Illinois Central said, We distinguish *Wallach v. Van Riswick*: Wallach was still a rebel under disability and the war had not ended when he purported to sell his interest; Bosworth had been pardoned and the war was over when he conveyed all that had not been sold and vested in another. On the effect of the pardon, they relied on Justice Field's opinion in the *Knote* case. Admitting that "there are some expressions in the cases" that were against them, they argued that their contention here was consistent with the holdings in all the cases.[256] To allow the heirs to enjoy, perhaps, the purchase money received by the parents, and to take the land besides, "would be a stench in the nostrils of common honesty."[257]

Counsel for the sons set out a string of quotations from the opinions to show that confiscation of the rebel's land "left in him no estate or interest"; pardon did not enable him to "deprive his heirs of the benefit secured solely to them by the joint resolution of Congress."[258]

On January 20, 1890, the Court gave judgment for the Illinois Central. In a lucid opinion Justice Bradley said

> it is not necessary to be over curious about the intermediate state in which the disembodied shade of naked ownership may have wandered during the period of its ambiguous existence. It is enough to know that it was neither annihilated, nor confiscated, nor appropriated to any third party. . . .

The Court need not be "trammelled by any technical rule of the common law or the civil law on the subject." It was what Congress had enacted that controlled, and looking at the substance of things,

> a portion of the estate, limited in time, was forfeited; the residue . . . remained untouched, undisposed of . . . . [It remained] ready to devolve to the heirs of the owner upon his death, or to be revived by

---

256 Brief in Behalf of Plaintiffs in Error, by Girault Farrar, Semmes, and James Fentress.

257 Argument of James Fentress, 14.

258 "Brief of Defendants and Appellees," at 30–31.

any other cause that should call it into renewed vitality or enjoyment. . . .

A pardon, removing disabilities and restoring all rights not absolutely lost, was such a cause. The pardoned rebel was restored to the suspended power of control and disposition.

Other heirs renewed their claim, but were turned away by two decisions in 1892—thirty years after the statute had been enacted. One opinion[259] was written by Justice Field, the sole remaining member of the Bench before which the first cases had been brought; the other[260] was by Justice Brown, who as a Deputy Marshal had conducted the confiscation sale in the case wherein the constitutionality of the statute was established.[261]

However wearisome the narrative, it leads to significant reflections. Congress in a moment of zeal laid hold upon an extraordinary power—resulting for the Court in a succession of suits between private parties over estates in real property. For every suit decided by the Court there were many titles clouded in uncertainty. While black-letter antiquities were cited in the briefs, the Justices looked to what was "most rational," without being captivated by theories about "the dead fee."

A CONTRACT PAYABLE IN CONFEDERATE NOTES IS ENFORCED

DURING FOUR YEARS of Confederate dominance, legal relationships of all sorts had been created. Now that that authority had been overthrown, how far should those relationships be recognized and enforced? It was not by deductions from some absolute premise, but by reasoned evaluations that the Court reached sound decisions.

Chief Justice Chase's opinion in *Thorington v. Smith*[262] opened the way. At Montgomery, Alabama, in 1864, Smith purchased Thorington's land for $45,000; $35,000 was paid in Confederate notes, and for the balance a promissory note was given, to be a lien upon the land.

In October 1865, the note remaining unpaid, Thorington sued in the federal court to enforce the lien. Smith answered that it had been agreed that the debt would be discharged in Confederate notes, which were of far less value than lawful money of the United States.

---

[259] Jenkins v. Collard, 145 U.S. 546.

[260] United States v. Dunnington, 146 U.S. 338.

[261] Supra, p. 803.

[262] 8 Wall. 1 (1869). The dates of the arguments as given in 19 L. Ed. at 362 are incorrect.

At Montgomery, Alabama, Jack Thorington was the law partner of William P. Chilton, mentioned supra, p. 830. In the Transcript of Record, it appears that the defendants were William D. Smyth and John H. Hartley, no longer resident in Alabama.

In January 1867, Busteed, J., gave judgment for the defendant, and Thorington appealed.

When on March 18, 1869, the case was called, Philip Phillips argued for the appellant. No counsel appeared on the other side. A reargument was ordered; this took place on October 7, when again only Phillips appeared. The decision was announced on November 1, 1869. The decree below was reversed and the cause remanded with instructions to proceed in conformity with the Court's opinion.

The Chief Justice began with a discussion of various types of de facto government—and this has been widely quoted in works on international law. The Confederate Government had exercised paramount force; the status of a belligerent had early been conceded to it. Within its military lines, "obedience to its authority, in civil and local matters, [was] not only a necessity but a duty. Without such obedience, civil order was impossible." Its notes "became almost exclusively the currency of the insurgent States" and must be regarded as "imposed on the community by irresistible force." Transactions "in the ordinary course of civil society," only remotely promoting the ends of the unlawful government, should be enforced by the courts "to the extent of their just obligation." Evidence should have been received to prove the sense in which the word "dollars" was used, "in order that justice may be done between the parties, and that the party entitled to be paid in these Confederate dollars can recover their actual value at the time and place of the contract, in lawful money of the United States."

This was hailed by a conservative Southern journal "a triumph" of that "sublime system of jurisprudence, which the Federal Supreme Court invariably carries into execution, when it is unhampered by the legislation of Congress."[263] But that failed adequately to recognize that the case had reached the Court only by reason of the diversity of citizenship that had been created before the suit was brought. If a State court on its own view of public policy were to hold that contracts for Confederate money were unenforceable, no federal question would be presented and the Supreme Court must refuse to review.[264]

WAR BONDS AND ARMY SUPPLIES

WE RECALL *Texas v. White*:[265] a contract to supply the Military Board with goods for the prosecution of the rebellion was unenforceable. There the purpose was manifest and the conclusion simple.

---

[263] *New Orleans Bee*, Nov. 4, 1869.
[264] Bethell v. Demaret, 10 Wall. 537 (1871), discussed infra, p. 857.

[265] 7 Wall. 700 (1869). Supra, p. 646.

Before the war, Louis Hanauer was a merchant in Arkansas; then he became a supply contractor for the Confederate Government, with residence at Memphis, Tennessee. He was a party to two litigations wherein the Court must look more closely at the doctrine of unlawful consideration for a contract.[266]

In 1861 Hanauer took Woodruff's note for $3,099; on this in 1868 he brought an action of debt in the Circuit Court for the Eastern District of Arkansas; jury trial was waived. The court, held by Justice Miller and District Judge Henry C. Caldwell, found that the consideration had been "war bonds" issued under an ordinance of Arkansas' secession convention; both parties knew that they had been issued to support the war; at the time of the transaction the bonds had a value locally not much less than what appeared on the face. They "were not used, or intended to be used, by [Woodruff] in support of the war . . . ."

The Judges certified a division of opinion.[267] Was the consideration void on ground of public policy, so that no action could be maintained? If not, what was the measure of damages? The transcript filled only two pages of print.

The case was submitted to the Court without oral argument, on November 3, 1870. The brief of A. H. Garland[268] for Hanauer maintained that the illegality complained of must exist in the particular contract sought to be enforced—which was not the situation here. Woodruff got something of great value to him; the bonds were like money, which he used for his own business affairs. He should not be allowed to repudiate now. By the time the brief was filed, the Court had decided *Thorington*: Garland added, "That settles all that . . . could be controverted" in the present case.

As in *Thorington*, no counsel appeared to argue that the transaction was illegal.

On January 23, 1871, Justice Nelson, then presiding, announced that the Court was equally divided; the case was remitted to the Circuit Court, to enable it "to take such action therein as it may be advised."[269]

There we leave the Woodruff matter for the present, to look at *Hanauer v. Doane*.[270]

---

[266] Hanauer v. Woodruff, 10 Wall. 482 (1871) and 15 Wall. 439 (1873); Hanauer v. Doane, 12 Wall. 342 (1871).

[267] Hanauer v. Woodruff, just cited.

[268] Whose right to practice in a federal court had been established on January 14, 1867, in *Ex parte* Garland, 4 Wall. 333. Supra, pp. 240–42.

[269] 10 Wall. 482. He added that "This direction is in conformity with the opinion of this Court in Silliman v. Bridge Co., 1 Black, 582," the intractable *Albany Bridge Case* in 1862. Cited supra, p. 51.

[270] Hanauer v. Doane, 12 Wall. 342 (1871).

"Questions upon illegal contracts," said Chief Justice Marshall in *Armstrong v. Toler*[271] in 1826, "have arisen very often, both in England and in this country; and no principle is better settled than that no action can be maintained on a contract, the consideration of which is either wicked in itself, or prohibited by law." But, he went on to say, how far that principle should be applied to contracts "the direct and immediate consideration of which is not immoral or illegal, is a question of considerable intricacy . . . ." In that case, *A* had imported goods illegally; so too had *T*, by the same ship but not in a joint enterprise. Subsequently at *A*'s request he paid what the Government imposed on *A*'s goods in lieu of confiscation. In *T*'s suit to recover, *A* contended that their contract was for an illegal consideration, and unenforceable. Judgment for the plaintiff was sustained by the Supreme Court: the undertaking to pay the charge was an independent and subsequent matter, distinct from the unlawful importation. It would have been otherwise if *T* had been a party to *A*'s scheme or had knowingly given assistance in its execution. Marshall's discussion was cited in many cases—including *Hanauer v. Doane*.

Doane sued on two notes originally given by Hanauer to Hunter, in payment for items for personal use—and for goods supplied by Hunter for the use of the rebel army—and for due bills issued by Hanauer to other suppliers of such goods and taken up by Hunter upon Hanauer's promise to reimburse. District Judge Caldwell instructed the jury that mere knowledge by Hunter of the intended use of the goods by the Confederates, or of the purpose for which the due bills had been given, would not taint the transaction: only if Hunter himself had some concern in supplying the army or if his purpose was to aid the rebellion would the notes be unenforceable. The jury found for the plaintiff, and Hanauer brought error.

The Supreme Court reversed, in an opinion by Justice Bradley. The closely written notes jotted down on his copy of the transcript bear witness that his treatment was not impressionistic, but based upon principle. He consulted the standard works, and even went to *Pothier on Obligations* and Justinian's *Institutes*, and made a discriminating examination of the leading cases. No man should furnish another with the means of committing a heinous crime. "No crime is greater than treason." A citizen who sold goods to the agent of the rebel government

> cannot be permitted to stand on the nice metaphysical distinction that,
> although he knows that the purchaser buys the goods for the purpose

---

[271] 11 Wheat. 258.

of aiding the rebellion, he does not sell them for that purpose. The consequences of his acts are too serious and enormous to admit of such a plea. . . .

Armstrong v. Toler was inapplicable: there the unlawful act had already been committed, and the loan merely enabled the wrongdoer to pay the fine.

Justice Strong noted dissent.

That was on November 27, 1871. Back in Arkansas, in October, the remanded case of *Hanauer v. Woodruff* had been considered by the Circuit Court, held by Circuit Judge Dillon and District Judge Caldwell.[272] Again a division of opinion was certified to the Supreme Court: this time it was asked whether the consideration of the note was void on ground of public policy or illegal by force of the Constitution and laws of the United States. The case was submitted on March 19, 1873, and promptly decided on April 7. Again eight Justices participated—the same as in 1871 save that Hunt had replaced Nelson—and this time there was a decision to which all agreed.

Justice Field wrote the opinion. If the bonds which had been the consideration of Woodruff's promissory note to Hanauer were illegal under the Constitution, of course it would also be contrary to public policy to enforce the note. The Arkansas war bonds showed on their face that they were issued for the purpose of overthrowing the Government: they could never be considered by a court of the United States to be a meritorious consideration.

"An ingenious argument" had been presented by A. H. Garland that the contract between Hanauer and Woodruff had been apart from the contract imported by the Arkansas bond; also that this case came within *Thorington v. Smith*. Neither ground could be sustained. A note given for a loan of money or a sale of goods would be held unenforceable if the court found that the lender or the vendor had known that the money or goods were for use in aid of the rebellion: that was *Hanauer v. Doane*. And *Thorington* was not controlling: that had to do with a currency "imposed by irresistible force" and necessary for "the commonest transactions in the daily life of millions of people," whereas to deal in war bonds was voluntarily to support the rebellion.

Justice Miller concurred in a brief statement. "I assented with much reluctance to the opinion in the case of Thorington v. Smith," and only "to prevent the grossest injustice" to millions of people. "I am content that [it] shall be so limited, modified and explained" as to make it inapplicable to any forseeable situation.

---

[272] Transcript of Record in Hanauer v. Woodruff, 15 Wall. 439 (1873).

SUPREME COURT JURISDICTION TO REVIEW STATE DECISIONS

SCORES OF CASES were arising in State courts to test whether some obligation, valid when contracted, remained enforceable, having regard to the downfall of the Confederacy and to measures related to that culmination. A State court might hold the obligation unenforceable and place its ruling simply on the ground of public policy. In that event, no question was presented that would permit the Supreme Court to review[273]—even though the Court might be enforcing a different conclusion in cases coming from the inferior federal courts. To be within the Supreme Court's jurisdiction to review, the State decision must be one wherein a claim of right under federal law had been denied. *Bethell v. Demaret*[274] in 1871 brought up as error the Louisiana court's decision that promissory notes made in 1862 for a loan of Confederate currency were unenforceable because they were given for an illegal consideration. The Supreme Court, finding that no federal question was involved, granted a motion to dismiss.[275]

Next year the Court reiterated that conclusion in *West Tennessee Bank v. Citizens' Bank.*[276]

In 1868 Louisiana, in the course of its reconstruction, adopted a new constitution. By Section 127 it declared that contracts wherein the consideration was Confederate notes or bonds were "void, and shall not be enforced . . . ." *Delmas v. Insurance Company*[277] brought up as error a judgment where the State court, in obedience to that command, had declared that such a contract, made prior to the new constitution, was unenforceable. The defeated party came to the Supreme Court. Justice Miller's opinion conceded that a State decision holding such a contract void on general principles of public policy would not be reviewable by the Court. Here, however, the State had made a law, and the question was whether thereby the Contract Clause of the federal Constitution had been infringed. The conclusion was that it had: accordingly the judgment must be reversed.

---

[273] Section 25 of the Judiciary Act has been quoted and explained on p. 45.
[274] 10 Wall. 537. The decision below is reported at 21 La. Ann. 620.
[275] John A. Campbell had made the motion. Opposing counsel said that the contract had been valid by the law as construed at the time it was made; "under the settled jurisprudence of the United States, it is clear that no subsequent action . . . of the Judiciary of the State . . . could impair its obligation"—citing Gelpcke v. Dubuque, 1 Wall. 175 (1864). The significance of *Gelpcke* will be dwelt upon in Chapter 17, Municipal Bonds I: Conflict in Iowa.
[276] 13 Wall. 433, decided Jan. 22, 1872.
[277] 14 Wall. 661 (1872).

Similar positions were taken in cases on the enforceability of promissory notes given for the purchase of slaves. We shall consider four decisions of the Court, all announced by Justice Swayne: *Palmer v. Marston*[278] and *Sevier v. Haskell*[279] on April 1, 1872, and, coming three weeks later, *White v. Hart*[280] and *Osborn v. Nicholson*.[281]

First *Palmer*, on writ of error to the Supreme Court of Louisiana. In 1867 that court had held that a suit to enforce an obligation arising from the purchase of a slave was defeated by a plea of failure of consideration, slavery having been abolished by sovereign authority.[282] Then came the constitution of 1868, which by its Section 128 declared that contracts for the sale of slaves were void and unenforceable. The State court went right ahead in holding that such contracts were unenforceable for the reason it had given in 1867; whether Section 128 could be reconciled with the Contract Clause had "considerable speculative interest," which the court declined to pursue. Thus Palmer was defeated in his suit to recover on Marston's promissory note of 1863; he brought error to the Supreme Court. Justice Swayne observed that the decision below "was governed by the settled principles of the jurisprudence of the State"; no federal question was involved, and the writ must be dismissed.

Sevier[283] met the same fate. The Supreme Court of Arkansas at December term 1867 had adjudged that an obligation undertaken for the purchase of slaves *was* valid and enforceable. Then, notwithstanding a provision in the constitution of 1868 declaring that no judgment should be rendered to enforce such a contract, the State court maintained its original holding. The record, said Justice Swayne, did not disclose the court's reasoning: it might well have held that the State constitution's provision was in conflict with the federal Contract Clause. At any rate, the record showed no claim that a federal right had been denied, and the writ of error must be dismissed.

Georgia too had a constitution of 1868, with a provision that no judgment should be given to enforce a contract for a slave. *White v. Hart*[284] brought up a judgment of the Supreme Court of that State absolving the maker of a promissory note of 1859 given to purchase a slave.[285] The Georgia court had reasoned that the constitution of 1868 had been adopted at the dictation of Congress; it was therefore to be considered as if it were an Act of Congress; and while a State was

---

[278] 14 Wall. 10.
[279] 14 Wall. 12.
[280] 13 Wall. 646.
[281] 13 Wall. 654.
[282] Wainwright v. Bridges, 19 La. Ann. 234.

[283] Sevier v. Haskell, 14 Wall. 12, refusing to review the decision of the State court. 25 Ark. 152, 26 Ark. 133.
[284] 13 Wall. 646.
[285] 39 Ga. 306.

858

restrained by the Contract Clause, Congress was not. Justice Swayne's opinion pronounced the reasoning "clearly unsound." Georgia had by its rebellion been out of its normal relations but not out of the Union; Congress had taken measures whereby it had been restored to its proper place; that had involved the submission of a new constitution, and it was upon that basis that Georgia had been restored. It was now estopped to assail the Congressional action by which "condonation by the National Government" had been received. Coming then to the promissory note of 1859: it had been enforceable down to the new constitution; to withdraw the remedy was to impair the obligation. The judgment must be reversed.

In the Circuit Court for the Eastern District of Arkansas, Osborn sued Nicholson on a promissory note made in March 1861 for "a negro boy named Albert," aged about twenty-three, warranted to be a slave for life.[286] District Judge Caldwell denied recovery in an elaborate and fervent opinion. Where slavery had existed it was only by force of positive law, contrary to natural right. A state might destroy such property merely by repealing the law by which it was established. Now the Thirteenth Amendment had abolished slavery, and Arkansas "in the exercise of her undoubted rights" over the institution and all its incidents, had made void all contracts for the sale of slaves. The Contract Clause was never intended to sanction slavery or to restrain such legislation as this. Finally, the Fourteenth Amendment, in its Section 4, enacted that

> neither the United States nor any State shall assume or pay any debt
> or obligation incurred in aid of insurrection or rebellion against the
> United States, or any claim for the loss or emancipation of any slave;
> but all such debts, obligations and claims shall be held illegal and void.

That, said Judge Caldwell, "cuts its way through all vested rights and obligation of contracts based on slave codes . . . ."

On writ of error the case was filed in the Supreme Court on May 17, 1870, and reached for hearing on November 8, 1871. Philip Phillips appeared for Osborn and Garland filed a supporting brief. For Nicholson a brief was submitted by Watkins and Rose.[287]

Justice Swayne was not given to spectacular displays of moral indignation—and he was devoted to the most ample protection of all

---

[286] Osborn v. Nicholson, Fed. Case No. 10,595 (1870).

[287] George C. Watkins (1815–72), sometime chief justice, had been a zealous secessionist. Uriah M. Rose (1834–1913) had opposed secession.

He attained such standing in his profession as to be elected president of the American Bar Association in 1901. His statue was placed in Statuary Hall of the national capitol.

that could be read into a contract. "It may safely be asserted," he said, "that this contract, when made, could have been enforced in the courts of every State of the Union . . . ." A supervening loss occasioned by vis major, fire, or the paramount power of a sovereign, fell upon the owner at the time of loss. He cited a case exactly in point, in the Queen's Bench.[288] There was nothing in the Thirteenth Amendment to authorize the taking of one man's property and giving it to another: such a deprivation would be without due process of law, a violation of the fundamental principles of the social compact, and beyond the legislative power of State or Nation. The judgment below must be reversed. Chase, C. J., noted dissent.

Ordinarily to deny enforcement of a certain type of contract on grounds of public policy serves as a deterrent in the future. That was not true here, inasmuch as slavery had been abolished. To absolve the purchaser from his promise and shift the loss to the seller would not achieve a clear triumph of justice, since it could hardly be said that to purchase a slave had been less blameworthy than to sell one. Moreover, the note might now be held by a stranger who had taken it for value.[289]

The resulting situation in Louisiana was that an out-of-State

---

[288] Mittelholzer v. Fullarton, 6 Adolphus & Ellis' Q. B. Reports, n.s. 989. *M* had sold to *F* the services of apprentice laborers who had been slaves; the Government of British Guiana declared them free. Held: *F* must complete his payments.

[289] On April 5, 1869, in the short-lived First Session of the 41st Congress, Sumner introduced S. 254, "to prevent the courts of the United States from enforcing contracts concerning slaves." It was referred to the Judiciary Committee. Cong. Globe, 41–1, 492. Nothing came of this initiative.

Next day Gideon J. Pillow (1806–1878), late Brigadier General, C.S.A., wrote from his law office at Memphis, praising Sumner. He found the bill perfectly logical: if, as the Republicans contended, slavery had been wrong, then a contract for slaves ought not to be enforced. Pillow explained the situation, and his own interest and desire in the matter:

I am myself sued for $150.000 & a Decree was had against me for it,—on slave contracts,—The suit is now pending in the Supreme Court of Arkansas . . . .

If not pressed through Congress, your measure of *relief & justice* will come too late. There are now in suit in the Southern States, I should think, not less than 250 million of these claims. Some of the State courts are enforcing such contracts & some are deciding them *invalid*. But the greater number are enforcing them.

. . . You will observe that the new Constitution of Arkansas declares such contracts *void* & denies to its courts jurisdiction of all such contracts. Your Bill I think should declare such contracts *invalid*—& *void* as in conflict with the principles of the Constitution of the U. S.—expressly give jurisdiction to the Federal Courts—authorize the judges of the Supreme Court, to grant writs of Error & Supersedeas in all such cases, without giving *other bond & security*, than for *costs*—otherwise the Decrees of the State Courts will be executed—(though the case is taken up by writ of error)—for want of Bond & security. The holder of a note given for a slave could sue in the federal court and have a recovery, whereas such holders as must look to a State court would be empty-handed. That led to *Boyce v. Tabb*,[290] decided in October 1873. Boyce had given such a note in 1861; Tabb sued on it in the federal court and won a judgment. Philip Phillips, as Boyce's counsel, asked the Supreme Court to reverse on the following line of argument. By Section 34 of the Judiciary Act, "The laws of the several States . . . shall be regarded as rules of decision in trials at common law in the courts of the United States . . .": therefore the federal court should have conformed to the decisions of the Louisiana court and denied recovery. Not so, said Justice Davis for the Court, citing *Swift v. Tyson*,[291] a memorable precedent of 1842 where Justice Story had explained that "laws" in Section 34 meant only statutes and not judicial decisions.

Let this signal proximity to a dark forest upon which we must enter when we reach chapter 17, dealing with municipal bonds.

THE COURT'S VIEW ON PUBLIC ACTS WITHIN THE CONFEDERACY

WHEN THE CHIEF JUSTICE was on his circuit in North Carolina in June 1867 he made an important decision in *Shortridge v. Macon*.[292] Plaintiff, a citizen of Pennsylvania, sued on a note given in 1860. Macon's defense was that he had been compelled to pay into the Confederate Treasury under the Sequestration Act of August 30, 1861. The Chief Justice replied that although the United States had treated the insurgents as belligerents, as was recognized in the *Prize Cases*,[293] it had never renounced its jurisdiction over the whole territory and all the citizens of the republic, "or admitted the existence of any government de facto, hostile to itself within the boundaries of the Union."

> Those who engage in rebellion must consider the consequences. If they succeed, rebellion becomes revolution, and the new government will justify its founders. If they fail, all their acts hostile to the rightful government are violations of law, and originate no rights which can be recognized by the courts of the nation whose authority and existence have been alike assailed. . . .

---

parties will be *unable* to give the necessary bond & security for supersedeas, to stay execution. Sumner Papers, Harvard Univ. Lib.

  Approbation from Gideon Pillow was not such praise as would assure Sumner that the principle of his S.

254 would achieve justice between the opposing interests.
[290] 18 Wall. 546.
[291] 16 Pet. 1. See infra, pp. 938–39.
[292] Fed. Case No. 12,812.
[293] 2 Bl. 635 (1863).

It followed that payment even under compulsion to the receiver under the sequestration statute was no discharge.

While the federal judiciary would follow the National Government's policy of refusing to recognize the "so-called central government" of the Confederacy, the opinion in *Texas v. White*[294] asserted most impressively the indestructibility of the States, whose acts, necessary to peace and good order—in such matters as domestic relations, inheritance, property transactions, and remedies for injuries to person and property—must be regarded as valid, while acts in furtherance of the rebellion would be held void.

The Supreme Court maintained the proposition that official action emanating from the Confederate Government would not be recognized. In *Hickman v. Jones et al.*,[295] from the federal court for Alabama, plaintiff had sued the Judge[296] of the District Court of the Confederate States, officers of the court, members of the grand jury, and Clay, editor of the *Huntsville Confederate*, for having maliciously caused him to be arrested, imprisoned and prosecuted for treason against the Confederate States. The record of the trial of Hickman's action before Busteed, J., abounded in errors for which the judgment for the defendants must be reversed. Along with pointing out these errors, Justice Swayne's opinion announced these propositions: "The rebellion was simply an armed resistance . . . ."; the United States dealt only with the military authorities of the Confederacy and not with its government; the statute creating this court was void and the court a nullity; the forms of law by which it clothed its proceedings gave no protection to its officers.

United States v. Keehler[297] was a suit on the official bond of a postmaster in North Carolina who, upon an order of the Post Office Department of the Confederacy, pursuant to a statute, had handed over the balance due to the United States. Justice Miller said that, whatever weight might be given to exertions of irresistible power, and whatever effect might be allowed to the legislation of the individual States while in insurrection—"questions which we propose to decide

---

[294] 7 Wall. 700 (1869). Supra, pp. 639–40, 646.
The Chief Justice's language was quoted and applied in United States v. Insurance Companies, 22 Wall. 99 (1875), holding that insurance companies chartered by the Georgia legislature during the war were valid corporations, entitled to sue under the Abandoned and Captured Property Act for the proceeds of cotton captured at Savannah in 1864.
[295] 9 Wall. 197 (1870).

[296] William G. Jones had been commissioned United States District Judge for Alabama in 1859; he resigned on January 11, 1861—the day that the Alabama convention adopted its Ordinance of Dissolution. When the Provisional Congress of the Confederate States passed its Judiciary Act, President Davis appointed him to the District Court for Alabama. Robinson, *Justice in Grey*, passim.
[297] 9 Wall. 83 (1870).

only when they arise"—the Confederate statute and order here relied upon were of no avail.[298]

AN EXECUTOR'S CONVERSION INTO CONFEDERATE BONDS

Horn v. Lockhart[299] grew out of a family dispute over the administration of the father's estate. John Horn died in Alabama in 1858. His only son, appellant here, was his executor. Daughters, Sarah Lockhart and others, appellees, were citizens of Texas who as legatees had sued in the federal court for Alabama, alleging that the executor had received sound funds and invested in Confederate bonds; they prayed for an accounting. Justice Bradley in the Circuit Court, reviewing what had been done in the sale of land pursuant to the will, concluded that the executor had not shown a sufficient excuse for his failure to collect the money prior to the outbreak of the war. Horn had received Confederate notes, which he kept "until March, 1864, when, under laws then existing, he deposited $7,900 thereof, as executor, in the Confederate States depository office" in exchange for Confederate bonds. Horn's explanation was that he was confronted by the Act to reduce the currency, of February 17, 1864, whereby notes not converted into bonds would incur a heavy penalty. What he had done was lawful for executors under the Alabama statutes, and had been approved by the probate court in the final settlement of May 1864. Justice Bradley said that what took place in conformity with existing laws should stand good, except "such transactions as were directly in aid of the rebellion . . ."—which this conversion was.

The judgment was that the executor must pay complainants the amounts found due by the probate court, not in Confederate bonds as there ordered, but in lawful money of the United States, with interest from the date of that settlement.[300] An appeal to the Supreme Court was filed on November 10, 1871. On March 5, 1873, when the case was called, Philip Phillips appeared for Horn, while the reply for the appellees was made on printed brief by John T. Morgan, Brigadier General, C.S.A., and Senator from Alabama from 1877 to his death in 1907.

---

[298] In United States v. Thomas, 15 Wall. 337 (1873), an action on the official bond of the surveyor of customs at Nashville, it was held that such bond did not impose absolute liability; that an officer was not liable for moneys taken from him by forcible seizure by a public enemy without any fault or neglect on his part.

[299] 17 Wall. 570 (1873).

[300] Transcript of Record, decree at 140 and opinion at 133–39.

The Justices had trouble with this case. At the moment they had before them *Hanauer v. Woodruff*, wherein on April 7 it was held that war bonds were not a good consideration for a promissory note.[301] Justice Field's opinion, distinguishing the *Thorington* case, observed that war bonds "did not constitute any forced currency which the people . . . were obliged to use." Horn, however, had converted into bonds in order to avoid a penalty, and in accordance with Alabama law for executors. On April 28 the Court ordered a reargument at the October term.

This was held on October 21 and 22, 1873, Phillips and Morgan both appearing. Justice Clifford presided: Chase had died on May 7. Evidently Swayne was first designated to write the opinion— yet in the outcome he was one of three dissenters, and Field spoke for the majority. Justice Clifford wrote on the front of his copy of the transcript, "Affirmed—Jus Swayne," and later crossed out that designation and wrote below it, "Jus Field."[302] Bradley made like annotations on his transcript.[303] So while a majority stood fast for affirming, apparently further study caused Swayne to shift.

Justice Field saw "but one answer" to the basic question. The bonds were issued to aid in prosecuting the war; the investment was a direct contribution. "No legislation of Alabama, . . . no judgment of its tribunals and no decree of the Confederate Government, could make such a transaction lawful." He went on to observe (as had Chase in *Texas v. White*) that what the insurrectionary States had done by way of preserving order, protecting property, enforcing contracts, settling estates and the like, where not hostile to the National Government, would be respected. In the present instance, only the investment in Confederate bonds was struck down.

Swayne, Davis, and Strong recorded dissent, without assigning

---

[301] 15 Wall. 439. Supra, p. 856.

[302] Clifford's unmistakable handwriting appears on many in the Library of Congress set of Records and Briefs. When he was presiding, and accordingly must take account of the time allowed to counsel, he would keep notes as this: "Phillips—20 p[ast] 1"; "Morgan—10 p 2"; and for the concluding argument next day, "Phillips 5 p 12."

[303] He made six foolscap pages of notes. After abstracting "The laws . . . authorizing Executors to take Confederate money & invest in Confederate bonds," as set out on pages 76–84 of the transcript, he wrote, ap-

parently on reflection and in determined handwriting,

☞ Now with regard to all these laws, authorizing or sustaining the action of the executor, I have this to say: if the investing of money in Confederate bonds was an act to aid the rebellion, *it was void*, and cannot be sustained by any law. The rights of the legatees cannot be taken from them by any such process . . . .

That comment took account both of the authority of the United States and of the rights of the parties.

a reason. Perhaps on studying the record they did not agree with the decision below that the executor should be faulted for failure to collect before the outbreak of the war.

THE CONFEDERATE SEQUESTRATION ACT

Williams v. Bruffy[304] holds a variety of attractions. It put beyond doubt the proposition that when the Government of the United States prevailed over that of the Confederacy, the latter's Sequestration Act of August 30, 1861,[305] vanished into nothingness. Yet when this great case was first considered in conference, the Court found itself unsure of its jurisdiction. When an affirmative conclusion was reached on that point, the Court, in order to justify its authority, gave a novel and ingenious reading to that invaluable grant, Section 25 of the Judiciary Act of 1789.[306] In observing the implication of its holding on this point we shall catch a distant glimpse of Justice Brandeis displaying his pertinacious resourcefulness in statutory interpretation, in a case in 1928.[307] And when we find that after the Supreme Court had ruled, and had sent its mandate down to Virginia's highest court, the latter declined to obey, we shall seem to be carried back to old Virginia and the anxious situation in *Martin v. Hunter's Lessee*[308] in 1816, when the nationalism of John Marshall's Court and the jealous particularism of that of Spencer Roane were poised in dubious balance.

In March 1861 Williams' mercantile house at Philadelphia sold goods to the amount of $578.59 to George Bruffy of Harrisonburg, Rockingham County, Virginia, terms six months. On April 17 came Virginia's ordinance of secession. On January 1, 1862, in compliance with the Sequestration Act, Bruffy paid the amount of the debt to the Confederate receiver. Failure to do so would have been a high misdemeanor. Bruffy died during the war.

In August 1866 Williams brought suit against the administrator in the Rockingham Circuit Court. Payment under the Confederate statute was set up as the defense. Judgment, on April 18, 1871, was for the defendant. Under Virginia law, the mode of seeking review by the Supreme Court of Appeals was by petition for a writ of supersedeas. On September 12, 1874, that court denied the writ on the ground that the judgment below was "plainly right." Waite, C.J., allowed a writ of error, and on August 21, 1875, the case was docketed in the Supreme Court.

---

[304] 96 U.S. 176 (1878); 102 U.S. 248 (1880).
[305] Supra, p. 779.
[306] Supra, p. 45.

[307] King Mfg. Co. v. Augusta, 277 U.S. 100, 132–33; infra, p. 869.
[308] 1 Wheat. 304.

Inasmuch as the United States Government had fought the war to preserve the Union under the Constitution, it would be easy on a superficial view to suppose that controversies resulting from the war presented a federal question. The Supreme Court made a much more refined analysis. In *New York Life Insurance Co. v. Hendren*,[309] decided on May 8, 1876—while *Williams v. Bruffy* was waiting on the docket—a Virginia court had given judgment for a local beneficiary under a life insurance policy issued by a New York company, premiums having been paid during the war to the local agent, down to the death of the insured. The trial court refused to instruct that the war had dissolved the agency and that payments to the agent did not bind the company. The Supreme Court of Appeals had affirmed. Was a federal question presented? Counsel for the defendant in error moved the Supreme Court to dismiss for want of jurisdiction. In conference, all of the Justices except Bradley voted to dismiss.

The case below, said Waite, C.J., in announcing that decision, had been decided on the basis of "the general laws of war, as recognized by the law of nations": "it nowhere appearing that the Constitution, laws, treaties or Executive Proclamations of the United States were necessarily involved in the decision, we have no jurisdiction. . . ."

Bradley, dissenting, reasoned that when the insurer claimed that the policy had been dissolved by the war, it claimed an immunity under the Constitution. "It is under the authority of the Government of the United States that the party is not only shielded, but prevented from the execution of his contracts. If he performed them, it would be a violation of his obligations to his government." It was "highly expedient" that questions of this sort be subject "to the final adjudication of the Judicial Department of the General Government."

When Enoch Totten prepared his first brief as Williams' counsel before the Supreme Court, he wrote somewhat generally that the Confederacy's "acts were all in furtherance of the rebellion, or intended to defeat the just rights of citizens, and are therefore void . . . . Every instant of the existence of the Confederate organization was a violation of the Constitution and Laws of the United States . . . ."[310]

Henry Wise Garnett, for Bruffy, opened his brief with the proposition that "There is no question raised by the record that can give this Court jurisdiction." He quoted the headnote in *New York Life Insurance Co. v. Hendren*, and other helpful statements. On the merits, he argued that whatever residents within the Confederacy had done in obedience to its laws was entitled to "perfect legal immunity," provided only that it was not contrary to the lawful usages of war.

---

[309] 92 U.S. 286, dismissing for want of jurisdiction a writ of error to re-view 24 Grat. (Va.) 536.

[310] Brief for Plaintiffs in Error, 5.

THE COURT DOUBTS, THEN SUSTAINS ITS JURISDICTION

WHEN THE CASE was called on November 20, 1877, only Totten appeared to argue. At the Court's ensuing conference, the preliminary matter of jurisdiction was discussed, and the Chief Justice recorded the vote on that question: Hunt and Miller in the affirmative, the other six in the negative. (At that moment, there was one vacancy: the nomination of John M. Harlan, vice Davis, was pending in the Senate.) On Monday, December 3, the Chief Justice announced that on account of the importance of the question, a reargument was ordered before a full Court: "While the whole case will be open, the attention of counsel is asked particularly to the question of jurisdiction. . . ." A day would be fixed as soon as the existing vacancy was filled.[311]

On December 10 Justice Harlan took his seat, and on February 14, 1878, *Williams v. Bruffy* was argued—each side having an additional half hour and being represented by two counsel. William A. Maury of the District of Columbia, not engaged in the case, was allowed to file a brief. (He denied the jurisdiction.)

Section 25 of the Judiciary Act of 1789,[312] reenacted by the statute of February 5, 1867,[313] with a modification not here material, had now been carried into Section 709 of the Revised Statutes. Did Williams' case involve "a statute of, or an authority exercised under" the State of Virginia? Or had some "title, right, [or] privilege" under the Constitution been denied? Totten had filed a Supplemental Brief in which he maintained both of those points, substantially as Justice Field presently affirmed them on behalf of the Court. Totten had also invoked the Fourteenth Amendment: "No State shall . . . *enforce* any law which shall abridge the privileges . . . of citizens of the United States." In the opinion for the Court that ground was not mentioned.

This time when the case was considered in conference—on February 25, according to Chief Justice Waite's Docket Book—there was agreement that the Court did have jurisdiction, and that the judgment below should be reversed.

We take time out for passing comment. February 25, 1878, fell on Monday, whereas Saturday was the regular day for conference. Perhaps the Court took a long holiday, over Washington's Birthday and the Saturday that followed? Not so: Friday the twenty-second was an ordinary working day; the Docket Book shows much business done at Saturday's conference; and in addition to the regular proceedings in

---

[311] Minutes of the Court.   [312] Supra, p. 45.   [313] 14 Stat. 385.

Court on Monday there was a conference devoted to several cases involving questions on jurisdiction. One of these was *Ford v. Surget*, soon to be introduced.

Justice Field delivered the opinion in *Williams v. Bruffy* on March 25, 1878. First he established the basis on which the Court could take the case. "No State shall enter into any Treaty, Alliance, or Confederation": the Confederacy, set up in defiance of that constitutional prohibition, could not be regarded as having any rightful existence. It followed that "whatever efficacy the [Sequestration Act] possessed in Virginia must be attributed to the sanction given to it by that State." Then came this broad interpretation: "Any enactment, from whatever source originating, to which a State gives the force of law is a statute of the State, within the meaning of the clause cited relating to the jurisdiction of this Court. . . ." There were several ways in which a State might make laws, and the Court would not give "a narrow construction" to the word "statute."

Treating the Confederate enactment as a law of Virginia, it did impair the obligation of the contract between Williams and Bruffy. Also, since it discriminated against citizens of loyal States, it denied a privilege secured by Article IV, Section 2.

"The defendant, however, takes the ground that the enactment of the Confederate States is that of an independent nation, and must be so treated in this case." Counsel for Bruffy had made much of the opinion of the Supreme Court of Appeals of Virginia in *Newton v. Bushong*[314] to the effect that the Confederacy had held the status of a government de facto, and that what was done in obedience to its paramount power should be treated as rightly done; in particular, that a legatee resident in a loyal State could not recover from an executor in Virginia who had delivered the fund to the receiver under the Sequestration Act. The greater part of Field's opinion was devoted to a denial that the Confederacy had attained the status of a de facto government. He quoted with approval what Chase had said in *Shortridge v. Macon*.[315]

Justice Clifford concurred solely on the point that acts in aid of the rebellion were void. The reason for his unwillingness to join in Field's argument denying that the Confederacy was a government de facto will appear presently.[316]

Williams v. Bruffy is said to have been "the first case in which the phrase 'a statute of any State' in the jurisdictional provision was

---

[314] 22 Grattan 628. The opinion was written by Judge Waller R. Staples, sometime Commissioner to the Provisional Congress, and there- after a Representative throughout the war.

[315] *Supra*, p. 861.

[316] *Infra*, p. 873.

considered and construed." This statement was made by Justice Van Devanter in *King Manufacturing Co. v. City Council of Augusta*,[317] in 1928. The immediate question then was, Did "a statute" include a *city ordinance*? Congress by the Judiciary Act of 1925,[318] in order to enable the Court to keep up with its docket, had reduced the categories wherein the exercise of appellate jurisdiction was *mandatory*, leaving it largely to the Court's discretion to take such cases as appeared, on a petition for a writ of certiorari, really to merit its determination. In an endeavor to exclude attacks upon municipal ordinances from the mandatory jurisdiction, Justice Brandeis (Holmes lending his accord) went back to *Williams v. Bruffy* and to the briefs in that case: he insisted that Justice Field in his broad proposition was concerned merely to show how the enactment of the *Confederate Congress* could be treated as a statute of a *State*, and that his words ought not now be taken to mean that a municipal ordinance should be regarded as "a statute." The effort did not persuade the other members of the Court in 1928,[319] and the ruling then made has been maintained.[320]

THE COURT EXECUTES ITS JUDGMENT

THE DISPOSITION IN *Williams v. Bruffy* in 1878 was in the customary form: the judgment of the court below was reversed, and the cause was remanded for further proceedings "in conformity with the opinion of this Court."[321]

But on October 18, 1880, Enoch Totten was back at the Supreme Court bar with a sad story and a petition for relief: the Virginia Court of Appeals on last April 24 had declared that it "must decline to take any further action with respect to the mandate" from the Supreme Court.[322] No counsel appeared for the respondent.

The Court took until November 22, and then spoke in an opinion

---

[317] 277 U.S. 100, 107 (1928).

[318] 43 Stat. 936.

[319] Judge Henry J. Friendly cites this as an example of Brandeis' "architectural skill in marshaling all possible considerations favorable to his view," intimating also that it was an instance where, "with his magnificent freedom from doubt," Brandeis pressed his contention "a bit too hard." Mentioned in the course of "Mr. Justice Frankfurter and the Reading of Statutes," in *Felix Frankfurter: The Judge* (New York: Reynal and Co., 1964), 30 at 33 and footnote 15.

[320] In Jamison v. Texas, 318 U.S. 413 (1943), where the appellee asked for a reconsideration of the ruling in King Mfg. Co. v. Augusta, the Court saw "no reason" to do so. Frankfurter, J., acquiesced, although he thought that Brandeis and Holmes had been right.

[321] Minutes, Mar. 25, 1878. The more proper and considerate formula, when remanding to a *State* court, is for "further proceedings *not inconsistent with* the opinion of this Court."

[322] Williams v. Bruffy, 102 U.S. 248, and the Minutes for Oct. 18, 1880.

by Justice Field. He set out the Virginia court's statement of its reasons,[323] and showed in unimpassioned language that they were quite untenable. In any event, the highest appellate court in Virginia had affirmed the validity of the judgment below—there was a federal question involved—and the jurisdiction of the Supreme Court had been invoked. "And when this Court has once acquired jurisdiction, it may send its process, in the enforcement of its judgment, to the appellate court of the State, or to the inferior court whose judgment is reversed." Inasmuch as the Court of Appeals found itself embarrassed, the Supreme Court would now recall its mandate, and would itself enter judgment, reversing the judgment of the Rockingham County Court, and adjudging that Bruffy's administrator pay Williams $578.57, with interest from April 2, 1866 (the day when the President had declared the war to be at an end in Virginia), and $124.61 costs.[324]

In this disposition the Court was following action taken in *Martin v. Hunter's Lessee*[325] in 1816, when the Virginia court had refused to yield obedience to the Supreme Court's mandate. In 1873 it had followed the same course in bringing to an end a protracted litigation where the Supreme Court of Missouri had proved intractable.[326]

In 1884 Justice Field recounted the history of *Williams v. Bruffy* in speaking for the Court in *Stevens v. Griffith*,[327] on writ of error to the Supreme Court of Tennessee. There an executor, holding funds he could not remit to legatees in Illinois by reason of the war, had paid to a Confederate agent under a judgment pursuant to the Sequestration Act. That had been held a good defense. Now the Tennessee court must reverse its stand.

AN ACT OF WAR UNDER CONFEDERATE AUTHORITY

WASHINGTON FORD OWNED two hundred bales of cotton at his plantation in southwestern Mississippi; on May 5, 1862, James Surget burned them. On October 1866 Ford sued in the circuit court of the county, alleging damages of $120,000. Surget's defense was that by an Act of the Confederate Congress of March 6, 1862, military com-

---

[323] The explanation was that when in 1874 it refused to grant the writ to bring up the judgment of the County Court, the judgment below became "irreversible, and placed beyond the control and jurisdiction of this court." Now, "If . . . the mandate of the Supreme Court of the United States shall be entered on the records of this court, it must be inoperative

and of no effect . . . ," because State law afforded no authority for further exercise of appellate jurisdiction.

[324] Minutes, Nov. 22, 1880.

[325] 1 Wheat. 304. Supra, p. 865.

[326] Tyler v. Magwire, 17 Wall. 253, decided Mar. 17, 1873. See infra, p. 1454.

[327] 111 U.S. 48.

manders had been charged to destroy cotton when, in their judgment, it was about to fall into the hands of the enemy; that on May 2, 1862, General Beauregard had issued such an order as to cotton along the Mississippi River; and that it was in obedience to that order, as passed down, that Surget had committed the alleged trespass. Upon the verdict of a jury, judgment was for the defendant, which was affirmed by the Supreme Court of Mississippi.[328]

On writ of error the case was filed in the Supreme Court on October 11, 1873.[329] That was more than a year and ten months prior to the filing of *Williams v. Bruffy*.[330] But then counsel caused the Mississippi case to be passed, again and again, until upon request it was restored to the call of the docket, and heard on December 20 and 21, 1877.

That was one month after the first hearing in *Williams v. Bruffy*: the Court was in a quandary about its jurisdiction, and was awaiting a reargument of the case from Virginia, which came on February 14, 1878.[331]

We have seen that on Monday, February 25, the Court conferred on its jurisdictional problems, and then reversed the Virginia court's judgment in *Williams*. Then what about its jurisdiction in *Ford v. Surget*? Bradley wrote on the back page of the brief for the defendant in error, "N.Y. Life Insu. Co. v Hendren 2 Otto."[332] Doubtless what Waite had expressed for the Court in that case was now drawn into the discussion. If, as there held, no federal question was raised where the State court merely applied "general public law" in deciding what was the effect of war upon a contract, albeit that one party was in a loyal and the other in a rebel State, it might be argued that a fortiori no federal right was involved where the Mississippi court had passed upon the defense of an act of lawful belligerency in an action for trespass between two of its own citizens, themselves co-belligerents. Yet over against that view was the consideration that in this case—unlike *Hendren* but like *Bruffy*—Surget relied upon a Confederate statute and official action in pursuance of it.

Bradley had dissented in *Hendren*. In *Williams v. Bruffy* he had made a note reasoning that plaintiff had claimed a right under the Constitution which the State court had denied. Now in *Ford v. Surget* his analysis included this proposition:

> The plaintiff resisted the justification on the ground of its re-pugnancy to the Constitution of the United States. Did he not thereby

---

[328] 46 Miss. 130.
[329] Ford v. Surget, 97 U.S. 594 (1878).
[330] Supra, p. 865.

[331] Supra, p. 867.
[332] 92 U.S. [2 Otto] 286 (1876). Supra, p. 866.

claim a right, privilege or immunity under the Constitution . . . —not in his declaration for the trespass—but in answer to the justification made by the defendant?

When the Justices were polled on the question of the Court's jurisdiction, Miller and Waite voted No. Strong refrained from voting. Harlan, Hunt, Bradley, Field, Swayne and Clifford voted Yes. That appears both in the Chief Justice's Docket Book and in Bradley's indorsement on his transcript. Thus the Court would take jurisdiction.

Then on the merits, how should the Court rule on the Mississippi court's decision sustaining Surget's plea in justification? The vote, as recorded both by Waite and by Bradley, was as follows:

Affirm	Reverse
Bradley	Harlan
Field	Hunt
Clifford	Strong
Waite	Miller
	Swayne

Justice Harlan was designated to write the opinion.

But then Waite's Docket Book shows that six weeks later, at conference on Saturday, April 6, the case was "Brot back." And then at a conference on Monday, April 15, the Court's vote was changed to "Affirmed." Presumably it was on April 6 that the Chief Justice crossed out the mark that placed Harlan in the column "Rev.," and recorded him as being in the column "Aff." Bradley, too, noted the change.

The Court's judgment in *Ford v. Surget* was announced seven months later, on November 4, 1878—three weeks after the Court had come in for the October term. Now there was no dissent when Justice Harlan delivered an opinion that affirmed the judgment below.

On the matter of jurisdiction, this case was found indistinguishable from *Williams v. Bruffy*. "If we regard substance . . . , the defense rested upon [an Act of the Confederate Congress]," and the State court's action sustained the validity of that statute and "enforced it as the law of Mississippi."

On the merits, the opinion advanced by steps already established. The country declared to be in insurrection was enemy territory, and all residing there were, for purposes connected with the prosecution of the war, to be treated as enemies. No Acts of the Confederate Congress could be allowed any validity against the United States or its citizens residing outside the insurrectionary territory. The Confederate Army, however, was conceded belligerent rights as understood by the law of nations. The cotton in this case was liable to be seized or destroyed by the Union army. Logically a military order for its preventive destruction must be regarded as a lawful act of war, "for which the person executing such military orders was relieved from civil responsibility at the suit of the owner voluntarily residing at the time within the lines of the insurrection." In so deciding the Court gave no force to the Confederate statute: even without any such legislation a Confederate commander "had the right, as an act of war, to destroy private property" under the circumstances shown in this case.

Thus the Confederate statute enforced by the State court—the basis upon which jurisdiction was asserted—proved on the merits to be inconsequential, while upon general principles of public law, the facts set out, considered in connection with the belligerent rights conceded to the Confederacy, afforded a defense to the action.

Justice Clifford filed a long concurring opinion, concluding that the Confederate States must be regarded as having constituted a de facto government: otherwise, service on a Confederate privateer might be viewed as piracy, and soldiers who had killed in battle might be indicted for murder. Clifford would avoid any such doctrine as would tend to "renew and inflame public discord." Recent opinions for the Court had spoken of confiscation proceedings under the Confederate statute as being void, but such remarks "were wholly unnecessary to the decision." Here one sees why Clifford had not accepted Justice Field's discussion of that topic in *Williams v. Bruffy*.[333]

"Viewed in the light of these suggestions," the decision of the Mississippi court was free from error.

IN RETROSPECT

A REPRESENTATIVE SELECTION of decisions on various consequences of the rebellion have now been examined. Over a number of terms, cases such as these made a significant fraction of the business at hand. The Court was performing its share in the labor of restoring the national house to order. This was a useful contribution, necessary at that period, yet of transitory importance. Some incidental rulings on matters of practice have had significance. But the major problems were, mainly, such as the nation would not meet again.

Confiscation disturbed real property in an unprecedented way, leaving concealed uncertainty for the Court presently to resolve. It placed temptation in the path of District Judges and court officers, to which, as has been seen, some yielded. In a few situations the Court might disallow what had been wrongly done and order restitution—but it did not and does not have any disciplinary power over the inferior

---

[333] Supra, p. 868.

judicial establishment. That in some Southern districts the administration of federal justice was not entitled to public confidence is an item to be set on one side of the account—over against many items in the record of violations of federal law.

The Court measured the effect of Executive clemency in a generous spirit. When in consequence it was suddenly subjected to interference by Congress, it stood its ground with quiet dignity.

The Court displayed restraint in asserting jurisdiction over controversies arising out of measures of the Confederacy. In very large part, it remained for the courts of the Southern States to rule upon private rights—in such fields as torts, contracts, and trusts—as affected by the war.[334] Where there was diversity of citizenship, the party from out-of-State might go into the federal court, with resort to the appellate jurisdiction of the Supreme Court. But the State courts were not bound to conform to federal rulings on matters not governed by the Constitution or laws of the United States. When it appeared that a claim of federal right had been asserted, and had been rejected by the highest State court wherein the matter could be brought, then indeed the Supreme Court did speak. Yet, as one sees in *Ford v. Surget*, the scope of "belligerent rights" as conceded to the Confederacy was as ample as reason justified.

In this chapter of its annals the Court performed well.

---

[334] Professor Neill H. Alford, Jr., in "The Influence of the American Civil War Upon the Growth of the Law of Decedents' Estates and Trusts," *Am. J. Legal Hist.*, 4:299–354 (1960), has illuminated the developments in one such field.

CHAPTER XVI

Consequences of the Confederacy II: The Cotton Tax, and a Church Schism

THE ACT OF MARCH 7, 1864,[1] to increase the internal revenue, laid taxes upon the production of two commodities: distilled liquor and cotton. That upon the latter was at two cents per pound. Cotton would in the main be such as was brought in from insurrectionary districts. At that moment it commanded a high price, and by summer it more than doubled the figure for March.[2]

The statute gave a drawback, in the amount of the tax, on the exportation of goods manufactured of cotton.

With the end of hostilities, a relief from burdens was in order. The purpose of the Act of July 13, 1866,[3] was to reduce internal taxation. On the production of cotton, however, the tax was increased to three cents. Again there was a drawback, equal to the tax.

As the bill came from the Committee on Ways and Means, the figure stood at five cents.[4] Thad Stevens would have raised it to eight cents: "I think there is very good reason why this one article should pay a very large portion of the taxation which we are obliged to raise. . . ." If only the Constitution did not forbid duties on exports, he said, such a tax at ten cents could have been laid, producing $200

---

[1] 13 Stat. 14. The tax of two cents per pound was maintained by the general Internal Revenue Act of June 30, 1864, 13 Stat. 223.

[2] Annual Cyclopaedia for 1868, at 207, sets out the price for middling cotton, the first week of each month, from 1864 through 1868. Various quotations may be found, but the figures cited above will be accepted for the discussion that follows.

The price for March 1864 was 66; it rose to 165 for August.

[3] 14 Stat. 98.

[4] Cong. Globe, 39–1, 2187, 2434. Justin S. Morrill of Vermont, presenting the bill, said that although the South, "never fruitful in taxable resources, . . . have less now than ever," still it should be required to make this much of a contribution. P. 2435, May 7, 1866.

million annually: thereby the country would be protecting home manu-facturers while "selling abroad just as much cotton as we do now."[5]

Attempts to substitute a rate lower than five cents failed—and so the bill was sent to the Senate.

There the Finance Committee reported the measure with an amendment, to reduce the tax to two cents. Henderson of Missouri failed in an effort to abolish the tax. It was, he argued, a *direct tax*, not apportioned according to the population. Furthermore, it was a *tax on exports*. On both grounds it was unconstitutional. And it was impolitic —falling on those who now needed encouragement, discouraging immi-gration from North to South, and impeding recovery of the nation's position in world trade. His motion received only 10 votes from Democrats and moderate Republicans, to 24 Republican nays.[6] The reduction from five to two cents met no opposition.

The House refused to concur. John Augustus Griswold, iron manufacturer from Troy, New York, cited the *London Economist* of April 7: "The world will be glad enough to get American cotton at a rate which will pay the [five-cent] tax to the Government and a fair profit to the grower."[7] Stevens, always positive, said that even "a tax of ten cents would not stop the sale of a pound of it. . . . The burden of the tax is borne by foreign purchasers, and not by our own people."[8]

The vote to refuse concurrence was 84 (all except one being Republicans) to 47 (about two-thirds of whom were Democrats).[9]

The conference committee on the revenue bill proposed, among the compromises, that the tax be three cents a pound: with that pro-vision the bill became law.[10]

In the autumn there appeared in the press the reply Senator Reverdy Johnson had made to an inquiry from Alabama: "My opinion is that the tax . . . is unconstitutional, and I believe the Court will so decide."[11]

Presently a suit to test the tax was started in Tennessee, by Farrington against Saunders, Collector; the outcome was that the Supreme Court, after twice hearing argument found itself equally divided; accordingly the Circuit Court's judgment sustaining the tax

---

[5] Ibid., 2473–74. May 8.
[6] Ibid., 3390. June 25.
[7] Ibid., 3445. June 27.
[8] Ibid., 3445–47.
[9] Ibid., 3447–48.
[10] 14 Stat. 98. The tax was paid within the district, and the bales were marked, before removal, save that they might, after being marked, be re-moved to the control of the collector

in another district upon giving bond. The normal method is described in Miltenberger v. Cooke, 18 Wall. 421 (1874).
[11] Letter of Sept. 20, 1866, to Charles L. Scott of Wilson County, Ala. *Augusta Chronicle & Sentinel*, Oct. 16, 1866; *Cairo Democrat*, same day.

was affirmed. This litigation will, in a moment, come under close scrutiny.

Long before that indecisive result in the Court, however, economic and political developments had culminated in the abolition of the tax.

REPEAL OF THE COTTON TAX, AND A CLAIMS AGENCY

IN THE AUTUMN OF 1866 the New York Chamber of Commerce reiterated its call for repeal. The tax depressed the South and indirectly stimulated cotton culture in countries that had been adapting to meet the deficiency that had existed during the war.[12]

The message of Governor Patton to the Alabama legislature, on November 12, 1866, stated the Southern case against the tax.[13] At the then current price of cotton, the levy took about 20 percent of the producer's profit, and would become more onerous if the price fell. It took from the South in order to give to Northern manufacturers: "Upon all cotton fabrics or yarns, manufactured for export, the manufacturer receives from the United States treasury a gratuity of three cents per pound. . . . It is a munificent bounty ruthlessly wrung from the hard earnings of the freedmen . . . ," inasmuch as they raised cotton on their own account or were indirectly affected as hired workers. "A law which paralyzes our energies, and represses the development of our resources, is injurious to the whole country." That theme recurred in numerous Southern editorials. While concern for the effect upon the freedmen was protested rather too much, the tax did bear heavily upon them too, and was a matter of complaint by Republican party organizations in the South.

David A. Wells, Special Commissioner, in his elaborate report on the revenue in December 1866, recommended "that the tax of three cents per pound on cotton be allowed to stand, looking to the session of Congress to be held in 1867–'68 for its abatement or repeal, if circumstances shall then render it necessary."[14]

By the Revenue Act of March 2, 1867,[15] the tax was reduced to two and one-half cents. The Ways and Means Committee had recommended no change. But then James G. Blaine carried the Committee

---

[12] Ann. Cyc., 1866, 261; *National Intelligencer*, Oct. 6, 1866.
[13] Ala. House J. (1866–67) 21; Sen. J. 20.

[14] S. Exec. Doc. No. 2, 39th Cong., 2d Sess., at 5–6.
[15] 14 Stat. 471.

of the Whole in an effort to do away with it altogether;[16] the full House, however, reversed that action.[17] In the Senate, a like amendment supported by Henderson received 19 votes for to 19 against, and so was lost.[18] Reverdy Johnson affirmed his opinion that the tax was unconstitutional.[19] The reduction to two and one-half cents was the best the opponents could do.

By November 1867, cotton had fallen to half its price one year before. Commissioner Wells now called for repeal.[20] So, too, did such Northern Republican journals as the *Chicago Tribune*[21] and the *Cincinnati Gazette*.[22]

The Second Session of the 40th Congress met on December 2, 1867. Next day Schenck of Ohio reported a bill to exempt cotton from internal taxation;[23] it expressed the unanimous judgment of the Committee on Ways and Means. The Committee thought it inexpedient to make the repeal applicable to the 1867 crop: seemingly a large portion had passed from the growers, so that immediate remission would bestow a gratuity upon cotton factors. And if it appeared that Congress was disposed to refund taxes already paid, word would be flashed to agents all over the South to buy up the claims of "many freedmen and others knowing little of their rights . . . ."

The bill became the Act of February 3, 1868, exempting from internal tax cotton grown after 1867—and from customs duty all foreign cotton imported after November 1, 1867.[24]

The two months between introduction and enactment saw protracted and illuminating debate, and three conferences before the Houses reached agreement. Divergent positions were soon disclosed.

James Brooks, purposeful Democrat and free trader from New York City, called for repeal with instant effect; he professed to speak for the unrepresented South, black and white.[25]

John Covode, Pennsylvania Republican and director in the National Manufacturing Association, said that high cotton was good for wool growers: he opposed repeal, and reproached Schenck for deserting his own constituents.[26] Others, more influential than Covode, were guided by a similar concern for protection.

---

[16] Cong. Globe, 39–2, 1479. The vote was 63 to 54, on February 22, 1867. The *Kennebec Journal* of Augusta (Maine), with which he had been associated, urged repeal in editorials on December 28, 1866, and March 1, 1867.

[17] Ibid., 1548, Feb. 25. In the full House, repeal received 63 votes to 94 nays.

[18] Ibid., 1929. Mar. 1.

[19] Ibid., 1921.

[20] *National Intelligencer*, Nov. 25, 1867.

[21] Nov. 23, 1867, and Jan. 9, 1868.

[22] Jan. 6, 15, and 24, 1868.

[23] Cong. Globe, 40–2, 13–14.

[24] 15 Stat. 34.

[25] Cong. Globe, 40–2, 14. Dec. 3, 1867. From him, this was a new-found solicitude for blacks.

[26] Ibid., 14–15.

Garfield supported the bill "on the ground of national policy."[27] Some cotton was being held by speculators, in anticipation of repeal with immediate effect, while some cotton had already borne the tax. In regard to the latter,

> I am told a large combination has been formed with a man who once ran for the vice presidency of the United States at its head, and notices have been circulated among the planters that they will undertake to restore the tax already paid for half of the proceeds. . . .

This first brought to the attention of the House the scheme of Herschel V. Johnson (1812–80) of Georgia—pre-war Senator and Governor, Vice Presidential candidate on the Douglas ticket in 1860, and Confederate Senator. He had formed a company to recover, for a contingent fee of 50 percent, what had been paid as cotton tax. Garfield cautioned the House:

> If we repeal the law, to take effect immediately, it will open the way for an equitable demand upon us to refund the tax already collected on the crop of 1867. . . . These circulars are scattered broadcast through the South at this time, and men who are in charge of the matter are urging their friends to press upon all the members of Congress to hurry the bill through now . . . .

Let the repeal apply to future crops.

Next day Windom of Minnesota produced, and the Clerk read, the text of Johnson's solicitation with the tendered contract. He had been informed that promoters professed already to control claims to the amount of $20 million.[28]

The same document was read in the Senate on January 7.[29] One statement was that "We are assured by our friends at the North that the Court of Claims will certainly pronounce this tax unconstitutional, and that if we hasten to get the claims before Congress we will succeed. . . ."

Griswold of New York explained that whereas cotton had seemed well able to bear the tax when he had supported the bill in June 1866, today it was in the weakest position of all products of the soil. He favored repeal as to future crops—but believed "that not one third of the cotton producers of the present year would derive any advantage" if Brooks' substitute were accepted.[30]

Brooks' proposal was rejected, 41 yeas to 120 nays.[31]

---

27 Ibid., 17.
28 Ibid., 29. Dec. 4.
29 Ibid., 355.

30 Ibid., 27–28. Dec. 4.
31 Ibid., 36. Dec. 4.

William Lawrence of Ohio moved to add a provision, "That the Court of Claims shall not have or entertain jurisdiction of any claim to recover back any taxes which have been paid or may be paid on cotton." At that point debate was not in order, and the motion was lost, the vote being 69 to 93.[32]

Then Schenck's measure was carried by 146 to 20.[33]

When Senator Sherman, for the Committee on Finance, reported in favor of the bill, other voices were raised. Reverdy Johnson wanted to make repeal applicable to the current crop—at least so far as it remained in the hands of the producer. Morrill of Vermont, Fessenden of Maine, and other Senators whose constituents relied heavily upon protection, wanted to maintain the tax. Cameron of Pennsylvania could "see no reason why we should at one swoop take $27,000,000 from [the South's] payments . . . , and particularly when that is the only sum they do pay . . . . I am sure they do not pay anything like what it costs to keep them in the Union . . . ."[34] After days of debate, the Senate by a narrow margin accepted an amendment by Conkling merely to exempt cotton grown during the year 1868.[35] Then a proviso offered by Morrill was accepted, to suspend the duty on imported cotton for one year from April 1, 1868. Thereupon the bill was passed and sent back to the House.[36]

Ultimately, as stated above, repeal was achieved only in exchange for putting cotton on the free list.[37] This was the Act of February 13, 1868.[38]

A SUIT TO TEST CONSTITUTIONALITY

HERSCHEL V. JOHNSON was not the only Southerner who set up an agency to recover payments made in obedience to the cotton tax. So, too, did another Georgian, Henry W. Hilliard of Augusta.[39] And at Memphis, Tennessee, a Cotton Tax Association was formed with

---

[32] Ibid.

[33] Ibid.

[34] Ibid., 357. Jan. 7, 1868.

[35] Proposed on Dec. 16, adopted on Jan. 7. Ibid., 208, 355.

[36] Ibid., 356–58. The vote on passage was 24 to 12; 16 were recorded as absent.

[37] The Senate, to whose position the conference report had come, accepted without division. Ibid., 861. Jan. 30. The House accepted by vote of 106 to 43. Ibid., 898. Jan. 31.

[38] 15 Stat. 34.

[39] (1808–92). Born in North Carolina; educated in South Carolina; professor in the University of Alabama, and later a Whig Congressman from that State. He opposed secession, later commanded "Hilliard's Legion." After the war he practiced law at Augusta and then at Atlanta. Unsuccessful as a Republican candidate for Congress in 1876, he was appointed Minister to Brazil by President Hayes.

like purpose; William M. Farrington,[40] Robertson Topp,[41] and Samuel Tate[42] were its executive committee.

To challenge the tax, this association brought the suit of Farrington against Rolfe S. Saunders, Collector of Internal Revenue for the Eighth District of Tennessee. This was begun in the Law Court of Memphis on August 15, 1867. Defendant removed the case to the federal Circuit Court, on the ground that he was being sued for an act done under a revenue law of the United States.[43] The case was submitted on an agreed statement of facts: Farrington had been the owner of 148 bales of cotton, weighing 66,858 pounds, upon which Saunders had demanded and collected a tax of $2,005.74 under the Act of July 13, 1866. On September 23, 1867, District Judge Connally F. Trigg held the statute to be valid.[44]

A writ of error took the case to the Supreme Court, where it was docketed on December 6.

---

[40] Wholesale grocer, cotton factor and commission merchant; sometime postmaster of Memphis. A man of many interests, he was an incorporator of the Memphis City Railroad, president of the De Soto Insurance and Trust Co., and president of the Union and Planters' Bank.

He appears in Farrington v. State of Tennessee, 95 U.S. 679 (1878). The charter provided that the bank "pay . . . an annual tax of one-half of one per cent, on each share . . . in lieu of all other taxes." Held: an additional tax on shares in the hands of stockholders was barred by the Contract Clause. Strong, Clifford, and Field dissented: the limitation on taxing the corporation did not preclude a tax on the shares of the individual stockholders—citing Van Allen v. Assessors, 3 Wall. 573 (1866), supra, p. 46.

[41] Lawyer, long a leading citizen of Memphis. Formerly president of the Memphis & Ohio Railroad, running to Paris, Tenn., near the Kentucky line. In 1867 it was leased, and in 1872 was purchased by the Louisville & Nashville.

[42] For fourteen years prior to his resignation in 1868 he was president of the Memphis & Charleston Railroad—which eventually became a part of the Southern Railway. In 1862 the lines came under the control of the

Union Army. Three days before the capture of Memphis, the officers and the rolling stock were moved South, and remained under Confederate control until the end of the war. In Memphis & Charleston R.R. v. United States, 108 U.S. 228 (1883), it was held that, the corporation being under the actual control of the United States, the internal revenue law applied; its income was taxable, notwithstanding that it came from property used within the Confederate lines.

Tate was subsequently receiver of the Meridian & Selma, and president of the Memphis & Little Rock Railroad.

[43] As the law then stood, suit to recover moneys exacted under the internal revenue laws could not be *commenced* in the federal Circuit Court unless there was diversity of citizenship; but where suit was brought in a State court it might be *removed* into the federal court by the defendant. Collector v. Hubbard, 12 Wall. 1 (1871). Such removal was authorized by the statute of March 2, 1833, 4 Stat. 633 (enacted at the time of South Carolina's attempt at nullification), and by the revision of internal revenue law by the statute of July 13, 1866, 14 Stat. at 171.

[44] The Transcript of Record contains only nine pages; no opinion was filed.

Trigg (1810–80), a Unionist from

THE CONSTITUTIONAL PROBLEM

THE CONSTITUTION imposed these requirements:

The Congress shall have Power To lay and collect Taxes, Duties, Imposts and Excises . . . ; but all Duties, Imposts and Excises shall be uniform throughout the United States . . . . [Art. I, Sec. 8.]

No Capitation, or other direct, Tax shall be laid, unless in Proportion to the Census or Enumeration . . . . [Art. I, Sec. 9, cl. 4.]

No Tax or Duty shall be laid on Articles exported from any State. [Art. I, Sec. 9, cl. 5.]

In the Constitutional Convention, "Mr. King asked what was the precise meaning of *direct* taxation? No one answered." So James Madison recorded in his *Notes on the Convention*.[45]

In *Hylton v. United States*[46] in 1796, Congress had laid a specific tax on carriages, which was contested as unconstitutional. Samuel Chase, J., was *inclined* to the view that only a poll tax and a tax on land were "direct." Paterson, J., said that it was "a questionable point" whether anything other than a capitation tax or a tax on land was "direct"; *perhaps* "the immediate product of land, in its original and crude state, ought to be considered as the land itself . . . ." Iredell, J., started with the major premise that Congress had "the power of taxing all taxable objects, without limitation," save that there could be no duty on exports. It was "manifestly absurd" to tax carriages in proportion to population: hence this tax could not be considered "direct." To sustain the present exaction it was unnecessary, and improper, to pronounce whether any tax other than on land or on polls was "direct" within the meaning of the Constitution. Wilson, J., had joined in the decision in the Circuit Court: he said that he remained of the opinion that the tax was constitutional.

Paterson had sat in the Constitutional Convention of 1787. So too had Wilson, and in the Pennsylvania convention that ratified. Chase had participated in Maryland's convention, casting an adverse vote. Iredell, in North Carolina's convention, had been conspicuous for his detailed defense of the Constitution.

Eastern Tennessee, was appointed on July 17, 1862—in succession to Judge West H. Humphreys, who had accepted appointment as District Judge under the Confederate Government, for which he was impeached, and convicted on June 26, 1862.

In 1865, in the unreported case of John Baxter, Judge Trigg held invalid the test oath prescribed by Congress for practitioners in federal courts. William M. Robinson, Jr., *Justice in Grey* (Cambridge, Mass.: Harvard University Press, 1941), at 166, 296–297, 596–97.

[45] Gaillard Hunt, ed. (New York: Putnam, 1908), II, 208.

[46] 3 Dall. 171.

The views expressed in the *Hylton* case were accepted and reaffirmed by the Court in *Pacific Insurance Company v. Soule*[47] in 1869. By successive enactments since 1861, Congress had taxed incomes. The Act of July 13, 1866—which laid the three-cent tax on cotton—went on to impose many other exactions, inter alia a tax of 5 percent on the dividends paid by banks and insurance companies. This provision[48] was attacked by the Insurance Company's suit against Soule, Collector, in the Circuit Court for California. The Judges certified questions to the Supreme Court.

The case was reached for oral argument on January 14, 1869. John A. Wills[49] appeared for the plaintiff. He filed, moreover, a brief by William O. Bartlett against the income tax. Weight was placed on the contention that inasmuch as rents from real estate were included, the tax was in effect a tax on land, and therefore direct.[50] Attorney General Evarts, opposing, said that *Hylton* was "conclusive" on the point at issue.

Swayne, J., for a unanimous Court, said simply that if a tax upon carriages was not "direct," "we can see no ground upon which a tax upon the business of an insurance company" could be so classed. Consider the consequences if the tax in question were apportioned according to population: in a State where insurance companies were numerous and rich, the tax would be light; where none existed, the tax could not be collected; where they were few and poor, it would bring annihilation. "The consequences are fatal to the proposition."

That decision was announced on February 1, 1869.

FARRINGTON v. SAUNDERS

AT THE ADJOURNED SESSION in October, 1869, Attorney General Hoar asked that a day be set for a hearing of the case from Tennessee. The Court fixed the first Tuesday of the next term.[51]

Concern in the South ran high: more than forty millions of cotton tax had been collected in the fiscal years 1867 and 1868. But more important than the amount involved, said the *New Orleans Times*, was the matter of "the future powers of the Federal Government to impose a tax upon a certain raw product of some of the States . . . ."

---

[47] 7 Wall. 433.
[48] 14 Stat. 137, 140.
[49] Supra, p. 753.
[50] Bartlett's argument against the constitutionality of the income tax had already been brought to public notice through the press. The *New*

York Herald advanced it in the issue of April 9, 1868. Bartlett was a confidant of the elder James Gordon Bennett; it was through him that President Lincoln had dealt with that sinuous moulder of public opinion.
[51] Minutes for Oct. 18, 1869.

> If cotton . . . can be thus taxed, and not corn, wheat, hay or oats,—the product of the other twenty-six States,—then are these eleven States placed outside of the pale of constitutional equality . . . .[52]

On December 7 and 8, 1869, *Farrington v. Saunders* had its first argument. As in *Insurance Company v. Soule*, these eight Justices were on the Bench: Chase, Nelson, Grier, Clifford, Swayne, Miller, Davis and Field.

Philip Phillips opened for the plaintiff in error.[53] Within the meaning of the Constitution, all taxes must be *direct*, and apportioned according to population, or *indirect*, and uniform throughout the United States. The legislation of Congress, down to 1861, showed a recognition of these propositions:

> 1st. That a tax on lands and houses and a capitation tax are direct.
>
> 2d. That taxes on specific articles of consumption or expense are indirect.
>
> 3d. That an ad valorem tax on personal property, without reference to consumption, is of the same character as an ad valorem tax on land, both being direct.

On that basis, a tax on the production of cotton, without reference to its use or consumption, was *direct*, and could be levied only by apportionment.

Moreover, this was a tax on *exports*. About three-fourths of the entire crop was sent abroad. It had been a great practical concern, in the framing of the Constitution, to make sure that taxation by the General Government could not oppress particular States. As Marshall had said in *Brown v. Maryland*[54] the Court should look, not merely at words, but at the substance.

Attorney General Hoar and Assistant Attorney General Wal-

---

[52] Leading editorial of Jan. 3, 1870. Other expressions of concern, in late 1869, are recorded in the *Milwaukee News* (a Democratic organ), Oct. 15; *Atlanta Constitution*, Dec. 19; *Louisville Courier-Journal*, Dec. 26–27; *Jackson Weekly Clarion*, Dec. 30.

[53] The summary that follows is based upon his brief of seventeen pages, filed on December 7, 1868.

[54] 12 Wheat. 419 (1827). A licensing statute had imposed an annual tax on importers of foreign articles.

Did this offend the Constitution's provision that "No State shall, without a Consent of Congress, lay any Imposts or Duties on Imports . . . ."? Taney, for Maryland, had defended the exaction as a tax on an occupation. That, Marshall observed, was "treating a prohibition which is general, as if it were confined to a particular mode of doing the forbidden thing." To tax the occupation was to tax the importation.

bridge A. Field[55] said that while, perhaps, "a tax laid upon the whole profits of land might be deemed equivalent to a tax upon the land itself," this was not such a tax: it fell upon a particular product, after it was ginned and baled and thus derived its value partly from land and partly from labor. In this it was like many another taxable article. The tax fell ultimately upon the consumer, and was *indirect*.

This was an excise on production: it did not become a tax on exports by reason of the circumstance that the major portion of the product eventually was sent abroad.[56]

Benjamin R. Curtis, closing for the plaintiff in error, displayed his remarkable ability so to develop the elements of a case as to lead most persuasively to his conclusion.[57] No weighty presumption of validity, he said, should be accorded this statute, passed in the heat of party feeling aroused by the war. Assume that this was an *excise*: it must be "uniform throughout the United States." Yet here the operation of the cotton tax was as definitely confined within geographical limits as if Congress had legislated for the eleven Southern States. That denied the Constitution's promise of "protection against geographical discrimination in taxation."

Next, this was a tax on exports. "When the Constitution provided that no tax should be laid on exports, did it not confer the privilege upon everybody who had something which he desired to export, of exporting it without the payment of a tax?"

Finally, this was a direct tax. No distinction could be drawn between a tax on land and a tax on the crop the moment it was severed: in either case the tax must be paid from a part of the crop.

Additional briefs, adverse to the tax, were filed. One by John A. Campbell, of nineteen pages, came down through centuries of taxation from the Code of Manu, Athens, and Rome, to conclude that history demonstrated that this tax was "direct."

Albert Pike and his partner, Robert W. Johnson, insisted in a headstrong argument of sixty-six pages that whether a tax was "direct" was a question, not of law, but of the science of political economy. They quoted Adam Smith, Bentham, Jean B. Say, Ricardo, John Stuart Mill, and others. "However the nature of the Union is regarded now, under the interpretations of Force and Congress," there still could be no departure from the firm principle that direct taxation must be according to population. The Government was "morally estopped to

---

[55] (1833–99), a Justice and Chief Justice of the Supreme Judicial Court of Massachusetts from 1881 to his death. O. W. Holmes, Jr., was his colleague and successor.

[56] Summary based on their brief of twenty pages, filed Dec. 3, 1868.

[57] Summary based on Argument of Hon. B. R. Curtis, printed as a pamphlet of eighteen pages. His oral arguments were admirably concise.

deny" the representations to that effect made in the Federalist Papers, upon which ratification of the Constitution was based.

Judge James Hughes of Indiana, recently of the Court of Claims, and Judge William L. Sharkey of Mississippi, submitted an energetic brief of twenty-eight pages. They said that "the southern people are anxious to know whether they are living under a government which may constitutionally compel them to bear all its burthens," and that the Court was their "last hope, to inform them whether they are the mere slaves of a majority . . . ." Sharkey added a supplement, at pages 29 to 43, arguing earnestly "that the Act under consideration was not passed by a constitutional Congress," inasmuch as ten States were denied representation.

Robertson Topp, of the Cotton Tax Association of Memphis, filed an argument of forty-four pages. Fitting together the pertinent words of the Constitution with remarks by those who framed it and those who debated it in State conventions, he offered an explanation of what was really intended. "Duties" referred to "*stamp* duties, and nothing else." The word "stamp" had become so odious that, out of prudence, it was omitted—like the word "slaves." "Imposts," without question, were imposed upon articles imported. "Excises," in the original understanding, "applied to manufacturers, and *nothing else*." These three, the Constitution declared, must be "uniform throughout the United States." Then there was one other category, "taxes": they were subject to the other great rule, that they must be apportioned according to the population. In the thought of the framers, if imposts and excises proved inadequate to the needs of the Government, resort might be had to "taxes." That meant that "the rule of apportionment must be observed, which involves assessments and valuations, *a general system*, . . . which would reach the property of all the citizens, in all the States . . . ." If a "tax" could not be so apportioned, then it was not permitted by the Constitution. There was no permissible exaction that was not laid with uniformity or by apportionment—and certainly one imposed on cotton, produced in only eleven States, could not be "uniform throughout the United States."

And then there was another objection: publications of the Government "furnished the evidence, that cotton was an article of *export*—was in fact *exported*—and was *taxed*. By this they are estopped. The Congress that passed the Act, knew it was an article of export. . . ."

Topp had essayed to discredit the *Hylton* case by establishing that the four Justices who decided it—themselves all parties to the enactment of the Constitution—had not understood its true meaning. Here was a rather interesting example of what, with ingenuity and a strong purpose, one may perhaps devise to give a novel and superficially plausible interpretation to a constitutional text.

886

A REARGUMENT IS ORDERED

THIS WAS THE MOMENT when the Court was caught up in the struggle over the legal tender question; Justice Grier resigned, two new appointments were to be made.[58] On March 14, 1870, Justice Strong was seated; the nomination of Bradley remained pending in the Senate. On that same day, the Chief Justice announced that *Farrington v. Saunders* would stand over for further argument on the second day of the December term.

Only seven Justices sat during the adjourned session in October: the Chief Justice was recovering from a stroke, and Nelson also was absent. On November 21 Justice Clifford announced that *Farrington v. Saunders* was reassigned for the first Tuesday in February 1871.

An Additional Brief in defense of the tax was filed by the new Attorney General, A. T. Akerman, and the new Assistant Attorney General, Clement H. Hill. The meaning of "direct taxes," they said, had now been pretty well settled: that meant a capitation tax, or an analogous tax directly upon land—such as *could* be apportioned according to population without injustice or absurdity. What had been said to that effect in the *Hylton* case[59] had now been approved by *Insurance Company v. Soule*,[60] and by the Chief Justice's remark in *Veazie Bank v. Fenno*.[61] "If the term 'direct taxes' is extended farther, and is applied to taxes like the income tax, which cannot be apportioned without producing great inequality and injustice, the General Government is virtually deprived of all power to levy such taxes."

The nature of an "excise," the brief continued, was well understood at the time of the adoption of the Constitution: it was a duty upon products before they passed into the possession of the public. The cotton tax was an excise—like a duty on hops, or on iron dug up and smelted, where the value was in part the result of labor. Such taxes might affect land indirectly, but yet they were not direct taxes on land. An analogy was seen in *Society for Savings v. Coite*[62] and *Provident Institution v. Massachusetts*:[63] there the Court had held that a State might lay a tax on savings banks, measured by a percent of total deposits, even though the deposits were in part invested in United States securities, which the State could not tax.

The cotton tax was not a tax on exports within the condemna-

---

[58] Supra, p. 730.
[59] 3 Dall. 171 (1796). Supra, p. 882.
[60] 7 Wall. 433 (1869). Supra, p. 883.
[61] 8 Wall. 533 (1869). Supra, pp. 711–12.

[62] 6 Wall. 594 (1868). Supra, pp. 49–50.
[63] 6 Wall. 611 (1868). Supra, pp. 49–50.

tion of the Constitution. The test was, Could the owner have avoided the tax by not exporting? Here the answer was No.

On February 7 oral argument began, before a Bench of eight Justices: Nelson, Clifford, Swayne, Miller, Davis, Field, Strong and Bradley. William M. Evarts opened for the plaintiff in error. He was followed by Assistant Attorney General Hill. Next day Akerman continued, and Benjamin R. Curtis concluded.

Of course this case was important, said Evarts,[64] inasmuch as it touched the constitutionality of an Act of Congress: but a mere $2,500 was involved, and if any further suit was brought it too would be for a "trivial" amount. The tax had been repealed. So the Justices were in "that most serene position" of rendering "a judgment that is wholly judicial" without "any considerable results" at stake. He dwelt upon the theme that the Convention of 1787 had made the taxing power proof against abuse by special interests. He would not attempt, by "any nice philological criterion," to establish "the precise meaning of the different words" in the clauses on taxation; rather he would seek guidance "of the intelligence and of the patriotism of the framers."

> If the Court please, we say, then, that this tax thus laid is repugnant to the Constitution, and that if it be regarded as an export tax—as a tax on an article exported or a duty laid on an article exported—it is, in the very words of the Constitution, a prohibited tax. If it be a direct tax it is not apportioned; if it be an indirect tax it is not uniform.

Evarts was holding aloof: however the Court might classify the tax on cotton, it would still offend the framers' firm principle,

> that no tax should be laid to which the constituents of the people who voted for it should make no contribution . . . .

The speech as heard by the Justices must have been more effective than it seems in silent print. Knowing that Evarts was a powerful advocate, we must bear with his cumbersome syntax. In this argument, one of his sentences ran to 284 words. There were reasons to remain noncommittal; he may have felt restrained by the consideration that two years before, when Attorney General arguing *Insurance Company v. Soule*, he had urged the Court to follow *Hylton v. United States*.

Hill in opening observed that "the eminence and ability" of counsel arrayed against the Government belied the suggestion that this was a trivial case.[65] It was notorious

---

[64] His oral argument is included in *Arguments and Speeches of William Maxwell Evarts*, edited, with an introduction, by his son, Sherman

Evarts, 3 vols. (New York: Macmillan Co., 1919), in II, 366–98.
[65] Argument of Mr. C. H. Hill, Assistant Attorney General . . . in the

that an effort is now being made to obtain a decision from this court as a foundation for an attack upon the national treasury . . . .

His oral argument followed the Government's Additional Brief. In concluding, Hill took a line calculated to lodge in the minds of the Justices. Would the construction he had been giving to these clauses of the Constitution have prevailed at the time of its adoption? He was willing to admit, No. In order to persuade the reluctant, language had then been used disparaging the powers of the General Government. But in the course of national development, broad interpretations had been made to meet new exigencies. He read anew the grant of the power to tax. If that were to be shackled in accordance with the arguments adduced against the Government in this case, "how could we ever collect a very great revenue?" How could the Government provide for the general welfare and common defense in a great emergency? He urged the Court to be mindful of the needs of an expanding future.

It does not appear that Attorney General Akerman's remarks were printed. From what was said in rebuttal, he must have stressed such points as the presumption of validity to be accorded to Acts of Congress, the vagueness of the term "direct taxes," and the impracticability of apportioning taxes by population.

While Curtis always spoke with marked deference, his concluding argument seems to convey an impression that he did not feel confident that his suggestions would prevail. Doubtless he sensed—if indeed he did not know—about where each of the Justices stood.

Herschel V. Johnson prepared, and put into print, a forty-page brief, opening with the observation that it had now been decided by the sword that there remained "no mode of redress for States, by State action, against wrongs of which they may complain. . . . Whither, then, shall an aggrieved and oppressed minority turn, when a majority, frenzied by party zeal, . . . shall violate the Constitution? . . . To whom, but to this HONORABLE COURT? . . ." If redress was not found there, despair might lead to popular revolution. He went on to argue that the tax, however categorized, "has not the shadow of a foundation on which to stand."[66]

On January 7, 1871, he had written to Messrs. Farrington, Topp, and Tate at Memphis: he expected to be in Washington for the hearing of *Farrington v. Saunders.* Further,

---

Case of Farrington vs. Saunders . . . . Feb. 7, 1871.

[66] The brief, printed at Augusta by the *Chronicle & Sentinel* press, is among the Herschel V. Johnson Papers in the Duke University Library. So too are the letters to and from Johnson, now to be quoted.

Having a deep interest in the question involved, . . . , I beg to tender my professional services, if agreeable to you. I am preparing my argument & I feel sure that I can demonstrate to any unprejudiced Court the unconstitutionality of the Law. I will add, that I hope to meet, in Washington one or more of your firm, in order to make arrangement for full co-operation between you & the Company I represent.

The entire performance seems presuming. Johnson was not then a member of the Supreme Court bar: he was admitted on Akerman's motion on February 6, one day before the argument commenced. How did he suppose his "demonstration" might be arranged, and wherein could he improve on the performance of Evarts and Curtis? He did not even ask leave to file his brief as friend of the Court: it seems to have figured merely in the public impression that he had taken part in the argument.

AFFIRMATION BY A DIVIDED COURT

On February 20 it was announced that, the Court being equally divided, the judgment below was affirmed.

Bradley noted on his copy of the transcript what developed at conference:

> Field says "direct tax"
> Davis says "export"
> Nelson "both"
> Clifford "both"
>
> Affirmed by division

Justice Davis was the movable member of the Court in the crucial cases of large political significance. He had taken his stand with the Democratic members in *Milligan*,[67] and presumably would have stood with them if *Ex parte Yerger* had been carried to a final judgment.[68] He had reverted to the Republican side in the *Test Oath Cases* in 1867,[69] and remained there when Frank Blair's attack on the test oath for voters was turned back by an equally divided Court on January 31, 1870.[70] He stood with Miller and Swayne, dissenting, in *Hepburn v. Griswold* on February 7, 1870[71] and remained with them throughout the fight that went on until the statute was upheld in the *Legal Tender Cases* on May 1, 1871.[72] Now in the *Cotton Tax Case*

---

[67] 4 Wall. 2 (1866). Supra, p. 207.
[68] Supra, p. 584.
[69] Cummings v. Missouri, 4 Wall. 277, and *Ex parte* Garland, 4 Wall. 333. Supra, p. 240.

[70] Supra, p. 616.
[71] 8 Wall. 603 (1870). Supra, pp. 713–14.
[72] 12 Wall. 457. Supra, p. 759.

on February 20, 1871, he was aligned with Nelson, Clifford, and Field, yet was not in complete agreement with any one of them. A fortnight later, on March 6, when the Court rejected Virginia's complaint against West Virginia, Davis in dissent spoke also for Clifford and Field.[73] Then in *Miller v. United States*, where the validity of the Confiscation Act was affirmed by the majority and denied by Clifford and Field, Davis agreed to sustaining the statute but found reversible error in the proceedings below.[74]

Johnson explained to James S. Walker of La Grange, Georgia, who was cooperating with him in the western part of the State, that "The ablest and best of the Judges, were decidedly in our favor. This fact will give us much power before Congress." (Let it be noted that although the alignment within the Court had not been announced, Johnson felt sure that he knew what it was.) He thought it inadvisable to try to bring the question up again:

> The decision w^d have been in our favor, if Judge Chase had been on the bench; but I have no idea he will ever preside when this question is up. He believes the law unconstitutional, but is unwilling, I fear, to bear the responsibility of so deciding. He is a politician and desires to be President and presidential aspirants are not brave to express unpopular opinions.[75]

It seems fortunate that Chase was absent and that thereby a ruling by the Court was averted. His powers were not up to the mark, while his meditations were still disturbed by his great ambition. The tax had already been repealed. It had been enacted as a means of recovering reparations from the South: that it arose in that setting was not conducive to a sober consideration of the meaning for the future of the Constitution's clauses on the taxing power.

THE CLAIMANTS LOOK TO CONGRESS

IN THE LETTER to Walker introduced above, Johnson explained how he hoped to persuade Congress to refund the cotton tax money:

> Success depends mainly, I think, upon our ability to concentrate an amt sufficiently large to enable us to impress on Congress the conviction, that our cause is just & righteous. Hence, we are so anxious

---

[73] Virginia v. West Virginia, 11 Wall. 39. Supra, p. 627.

[74] 11 Wall. 268. Supra, p. 802.

[75] Letter of July 18, 1871. Letterpress copy in the H. V. Johnson Papers, Duke Univ. Lib.

A portion of the letter appears in Professor Percy S. Flippin's biography, *Herschel V. Johnson, State Rights Unionist* (Richmond, Va.: Dietz Printing Co., 1931), at 303–04.

for our agents to be active & persevering. If we can secure contracts enough, I have strong hope of success, *finally*. Our friends must be patient; for such a big enterprise cannot be completed in a day.

But many were holding back because of the contingent fee of 50 percent of what might be recovered:

> One of our greatest difficulties in getting "Constituents" is that many very large claimants stand aloof, upon the idea that if *we* succeed *they* will get back their money, almost by magic & without much expense. They want us to shake the tree, & they pick up the fruit. . . . If *we* fail, my opinion is, that not one dollar of the Cotton tax will ever be refunded. . . . We expect it will cost us, first and last, 33⅓ to 50 per Ct. of our half to push our enterprise to success. I doubt if individual claimants, if they could succeed at all, which I do not believe, can get the services of agents at Washington on better terms than we offer. . . . I say this much to you, if it will aid you in overcoming the erroneous views of the reluctant.

Johnson was sending similar messages to other Georgians at this time.

While they were in Washington on the occasion of the reargument of the *Farrington* case, on February 14, 1871, Topp and Johnson made a contract on behalf of their respective agencies.[76] This recited that the Memphis Association had "contracted conditionally for litigation about two and a half millions of dollars;" it was believed that it would be necessary to contract conditionally for the expenditure of that much more; Johnson & Co. desired to cooperate and to bear its fair share. Let it be assumed that the Memphis Association was agent for about thirty million dollars in claims, and Johnson for about six million: the two parties would in the event of recovery make a faithful report of the interests they respectively represented, and share the expenditures pro rata on that basis. Not more than the five million dollars already contemplated would be committed except by agreement of the parties.

On March 22 Topp wrote from Memphis:

> We are by no means discouraged by the Court quailing and failing to do their duty. We purpose to apply to next Congress. . . .[77]

In the meantime, during the recess of Congress, the delegations from the Southern States were to be united; the legislatures would be called upon to petition Congress.

---

[76] Signed copy in the H. V. Johnson Papers, Duke Univ. Lib.

[77] Among the H. V. Johnson Papers, Duke Univ. Lib.

We think Missouri, Kentucky, Maryland & Delaware will go with us. This will give us 30 Senators, 100 Reprs. For the balance, enough to carry the bill we must do that which is necessary for success.

In the autumn, Henry W. Hilliard wrote from Augusta:

> I am ready to cooperate with you fully in all the steps taken in regard to our Cotton claims. Please consider it settled . . . .
>
> I have given so much time to this business and represent so large an interest, that I must succeed or lose heavily. . . .
>
> What a deplorable condition the country is in; Radicals triumphant; and the friends of Constitutional liberty divided and disorganized. . . .[78]

Hilliard's anticipation was "enhanced by the consciousness that one [he] so highly esteemed" as Johnson would share in "the rewards of our labor." Actually, it should be recalled, Johnson's most recent position in the matter of constitutional liberty had been that "much as I deprecate military government, it is far preferable to such a government as will probably be inaugurated under [Congressional Reconstruction]." "The whites, in Georgia, are largely in the ascendant . . .": let them not seek to escape confiscation "by becoming false to their race, and by playing the part of pall-bearers at the funeral of the Constitution . . . ." It was useless to look to the Supreme Court: "That tribunal is not equal to the occasion. It bows to the black surges of fanaticism."[79]

The 42d Congress met in its Second Session on December 4, 1871. Representative E. I. Golladay of Tennessee, Democrat, sometime Colonel, C.S.A., introduced a bill to refund the cotton tax money.[80] Representative George C. McKee of Mississippi, Republican, sometime Colonel, U.S.A., introduced a more adequate bill for the same purpose.[81] They were referred to the Ways and Means Committee, and

---

[78] Letter of Nov. 10, 1871. H. V. Johnson Papers, Duke Univ. Lib.

[79] Letter of July 11, 1867, to John G. Westmoreland and others, reprinted in the *Southern Watchman* of Athens, Georgia, July 24, 1867, from the *Atlanta Intelligencer.*

Johnson's name stood first in the committee that framed the address by the Conservative Party of Georgia, in convention on December 5 and 6, 1868: it called upon the people to "organize for self-protection and ceaseless opposition to the direful rule of *negro supremacy* which is sought

to be enforced on us and our children . . . ." When secession was removed, "all that the United States, under the Federal Constitution had a right to do . . . was to restore those [previously existing] governments and constitutions back to the people." *Montgomery Daily Mail,* Jan. 12, 1868; Ann. Cyc. 1868, 309–10.

[80] H. R. 700. Cong. Globe, 42–2, 196. Dec. 18, 1871.

[81] H. R. 1592. Cong. Globe, 42–2, 1114. Feb. 9, 1872. It provided for a bond issue to raise the means, and a commission to adjudicate claims.

never emerged. (McKee should be remembered as one of the "cowards, dogs and scoundrels" of McCardle's editorial on "The Immortal Eight."[82]) On the unconstitutionality of the cotton tax, declared the *Columbia Daily South Carolinian*, "the South is a unit; a very large preponderance of the Northern Democracy, if not the entire party, is of the same opinion."[83] The Southern legislatures did, indeed, memorialize Congress. A consideration adverse to refunding was the fact that claims in large amounts had been bought up by speculators; even so, said the *Jackson Clarion*, all classes would share in "the recuperating influence of the restoration of a large amount of capital . . . ."[84]

Johnson and Topp were busy in Washington. To provide for the adjustment of any conflicts of interest "should Congress pass a law for the restitution of said tax money," an additional contract was drawn.[85] The Memphis Association published a notice of February 27, cautioning their constituents not to listen to rival agencies: "One of the undersigned has been in Washington all winter, and will remain there to attend to the interest of those we represent. Our friends must rest assured that all things necessary will be done . . . ."[86]

The *Washington Chronicle* of April 25 recorded that yesterday the Ways and Means Committee had considered the refund of the cotton tax; Johnson had made an argument. "The committee arrived at no conclusion . . . ."

No report was made to the House.

In the Second Session of the 43d Congress, on December 14, 1874, Representative William A. Smith of North Carolina, Republican, introduced a bill which referred to the cotton tax, and to the heavy indebtedness of the States wherein it was collected: the Secretary of the Treasury and the Attorney General would confer with the creditors of those States, and ascertain on what terms the indebtedness of each could be adjusted; if in the opinion of those officers a fair settlement could be made, the amount of cotton tax collected from the State would be paid toward such settlement.[87]

---

[82] Supra, p. 421.
[83] Feb. 25, 1872.
[84] *Weekly Clarion*, May 9, 1872.
[85] Of Jan. 15, 1872. It was open to others engaged in the endeavor: H. W. Hilliard and R. L. Mott appear as signatories.
[86] *Jackson Weekly Clarion*, Feb. 29, 1872. The notice was to be carried for one month.
[87] H.R. No. 3956. Cong. Rec., 43–2, 71. If the amount was insufficient to discharge the entire debt, payment should first be made of debts contracted previous to January 1, 1861, and then on those contracted after May 1, 1865. If a surplus remained after discharging the entire debt, it would be paid to the proper State authorities, to be used for the support of free schools.

This was a period when the State debt was a matter of major concern in the public life of North Carolina. Ann. Cyc. 1872, 1873, and 1874, under "North Carolina."

The Judiciary Committee returned an adverse report.[88]

There is a long story of unsuccessful attempts to induce Congress to refund the cotton tax money: they are set out in House Report No. 1017, in the Third Session of the 65th Congress in 1919, wherein the proceedings in *Farrington v. Saunders*, as derived from the transcript of record and briefs, were summarized. A new and futile turn was attempted in 1922, when Representative L. A. Scott of Tennessee introduced a joint resolution to authorize and request the Supreme Court "to rehear on its merits and redecide" the case of *Farrington v. Saunders*: he conceded that this was an "extraordinary" proposal.[89]

Fifty years—twenty-five Congresses—had elapsed since Johnson and Topp staged their movement for the refunding of what the 39th Congress had seen fit to impose on the Cotton States. Whatever favorable considerations could then be adduced had long since lost their force.

SLAVERY AND SEPARATION WITHIN THE CHURCHES

THE METHODIST EPISCOPAL CHURCH, formally organized in 1784, started from an anti-slavery position. Then as slavery became an established institution in the South, particularly upon the introduction of the cotton gin, church members there came to regard it as normal. Meanwhile abolition sentiment grew in the North, and was expressed in church conferences. For a time, Northern moderates joined with Southern delegates to suppress agitation. But then a crisis arose in 1844 when Bishop James O. Andrew of Georgia married a widow who owned slaves. At the general conference that year, after heated debate, it was voted by a considerable majority that he be requested to desist from performing his episcopal functions so long as he remained a slaveholder. That led to a separation, and the formation in 1845 of the Methodist Episcopal Church, South.[90] The new branch then had about 330,000 white and 125,000 black members.

---

[88] Cong. Rec., 43–2, 756. Jan. 26, 1875.

[89] Cong. Rec., 67–2, 3826–34, in support of his H.R.J. Res. No. 251. Mar. 13, 1922.

[90] In Smith v. Swormstedt, 16 How. 288 (1853), is narrated the action of the General Conference of the Methodist Episcopal Church in 1844, when it provided for a distinct organization in the slaveholding States, in case the annual conferences of those States elected to separate. The holding of the case is that the General Conference was competent to authorize the separation, and that on being accomplished it carried with it a division of the common property. The subject of the suit was the Methodist Book Concern, established at Cincinnati, whose capital fund was devoted to publication, and whose profits were devoted to the care of travelling preachers. The Court's decree provided for the equitable division of the property.

The Baptist denomination, from New England beginnings, had spread widely; growth in Virginia and the Carolinas at the period of the Revolution was phenomenal. Freedom of the individual conscience and separation of church and state were basic tenets. Members were grouped in independent congregations, with no hierarchical authority; representatives met in periodic conventions. After twenty years of struggle over slavery, in 1845 a peaceful separation took place. A Southern Baptist convention was then organized, with a constituency of about 350,000. Many slaves had been admitted; sometimes they sat in a congregation with whites and sometimes in meetings of their own.

Thus two great communities based upon conscience found that compromise and the stifling of dissent would not avail to preserve their union—sixteen years before that method failed in the national political community.

THE PRESBYTERIAN CHURCH

THE PRESBYTERIAN DENOMINATION, firmly planted in the Middle Colonies, adopted a national constitution at the close of the Revolution, and held its first General Assembly in 1789.[91] Repeatedly the church condemned slavery—notably in the statement of 1818 that "We consider the voluntary enslaving of one portion of the human race by another as a gross violation of the most precious and sacred rights of human nature, utterly inconsistent with the law of God . . . ."

---

[91] Constitutional documents include the Confession of Faith, Form of Government, Book of Discipline, and Directory for Worship.

The Minutes of the General Assembly of the Presbyterian Church, from 1854, are the authentic source. What was available from earlier times the Rev. Samuel J. Baird gathered into his *Collection of the Acts, Deliverances, and Testimonies of the Supreme Judicatory of the Presbyterian Church to the Present Time* (1854). A revised edition of 1856 was commonly known as the *Assembly's Digest*.

In the litigation presently to be traced, reference was frequently made to these materials. Numerous quotations are to be found in the prevailing and dissenting opinions in Watson v. Avery, 65 Ky. (2 Bush) 332 (1867), and Gartin v. Penick, 68 Ky. (5 Bush)

110 (1868). Also in the report of State of Missouri *ex rel.* Watson v. Faris, 45 Mo. 183 (1869).

The Annual Cyclopaedia for 1862 and thereafter, under "Presbyterians," traces developments with which our account will be concerned. McPherson's *History of the Rebellion*, 2d ed. (Washington: Philp and Solomons, 1865), at 461–548, collects a mass of items on "The Church and the Rebellion." Material on the Old School Presbyterians is at 461–70. Many of the individuals to be mentioned are remembered in the Dictionary of American Biography.

A mass of extracts from source materials, pertinent to the issue in Watson v. Jones, are detailed in the Transcript of Record, Addition to Record, briefs and oral arguments in that case.

By "a plan of union" in 1801, Presbyterians worked in concert with Congregationalists where they came together, in New York, Ohio, and on the frontier. Out of that emerged a "New School," yielding a relaxed adherence to the established doctrines of the church and concerning itself with such matters as abolition and temperance.[92] Controversy arose, culminating in a triumph of the conservatives at the General Assembly of 1837, where the western synods were exscinded. Thereafter the New School had a vigorous existence in free territory.

Our concern is with the Old School church, whose strength lay in communities of Scotch-Irish and Scottish descent, in both free and slave States. When the Civil War came it had about 300,000 members, in some 3,600 congregations.

The constitution placed each congregation under the spiritual government of a *session*, made up of the pastor and ruling elders. The next higher body was the *presbytery*, consisting of the minister and one ruling elder from each congregation. A *synod* was composed of the minister and elder from each congregation within a larger district—often a State. The *General Assembly* consisted of delegations from the various presbyteries. An "appeal" lay from each judicatory to that next above. Moreover, each superior body had power to review the records of those below it and to approve or censure. "To the general assembly also belongs the power of deciding in all controversies respecting doctrine and discipline;" of reproving error, of repressing schismatical disputation, "and in general of recommending and attempting reformation in manners, and the promotion of charity, truth, and holiness throughout all the churches under their care."

It is evident that this constitution did not make a separation of legislative, executive, and judicial functions.

THE CIVIL WAR

THE GENERAL ASSEMBLY OF MAY 1861, on the initiative of Dr. Gardiner Spring of the Brick Presbyterian Church in New York City, adopted resolutions declaring "our obligation to promote and perpetuate, so far as in us lies, the integrity of these United States, and to strengthen, uphold, and encourage the Federal Government in the exercise of all its functions under our noble Constitution . . . ." Thereupon the Southern representatives withdrew.

---

[92] Mention of this development was made in footnote 92 of chapter 1, where Salmon P. Chase represented the trustees of Lane Theological Seminary, who had engaged Lyman Beecher and another, professors of the "New School."

In December a convention met at Augusta, Georgia, and established the Presbyterian Church of the Confederate States of America.

At the Assembly of May 1862, Dr. R. J. Breckinridge[93] of the theological seminary at Danville, Kentucky, submitted a long paper declaring that "This whole treason . . . is utterly contrary to the dictates of natural religion and morality . . ."; it was the duty of all persons to sustain the Government in suppressing it. By vote of 206 to 20, this was adopted as an official "deliverance."[94]

The Assembly of 1863 reaffirmed the deliverance of 1818 in condemnation of slavery. The *True Presbyterian*,[95] published in Louisville, deplored this descent from spirituality to politics: "the Presbyterian Church must have reached her lowest point of humiliation, and therefore it may be expected that from this time she must begin to ascend to higher and more Scriptural views . . . ."

The fact that emancipation had been proclaimed was reflected in the action of the Assembly of May 1864. Stanley Matthews[96]

---

[93] Robert Jefferson Breckinridge (1800–1871) was of the distinguished Kentucky family that was divided by the war. Before the war he had labored for emancipation; now he became a mainstay of the Union cause. He was temporary chairman of the Baltimore convention in 1864 where Lincoln was renominated. See Sandburg's *Lincoln* (New York: Harcourt, Brace and Co., 1939), III, 78–81.

William C. P. Breckinridge, colonel, C.S.A., and later a Representative from Kentucky, was his son. So too was Lieutenant Joseph C. Breckinridge, U.S.A. John C. Breckinridge, Vice President of the United States, Southern Democratic candidate for President in 1860, and major general and Secretary of War in the Confederacy, was the clergyman's nephew.

[94] Among those voting yea was the Rev. George Junkin, formerly president of Lafayette College, of Miami University, and from 1848 to 1861 of Washington College of Lexington, Virginia. While opposed to slavery, he was a vigorous opponent of abolitionism. One of his daughters was the first wife of Stonewall Jackson.

Junkin will be mentioned infra, p. 904.

Among those voting nay were Dr. Stuart Robinson of Louisville, sometime colleague of Dr. Breckinridge at the Danville seminary, and from 1858 to 1881 pastor of the Second Presbyterian Church of Louisville; also he edited the *True Presbyterian*. Suspected of disloyalty, he removed to Toronto in 1862. His journal was suppressed by the military authorities in 1864.

Another nay vote came from Dr. Samuel B. McPheeters of the Pine Street Presbyterian Church at St. Louis. When for his pro-Southern sympathies McPheeters was in December 1862 ordered by a provost marshal to leave the country, President Lincoln interfered: "the U. S. government must not, as by this order, undertake to run the churches." But when later the Unionist portion of the congregation succeeded in removing the minister from his pastorate, and his adherents appealed to the President to restore him, Lincoln replied that "I will not have control of any church on any side." *Collected Works of Abraham Lincoln*, ed., Roy P. Basler (New Brunswick, N.J.: Rutgers University Press, 1953), VI, 20, 33–34, Dec. 27, 1862, and Jan. 2, 1863; VII, 85–86, Dec. 22, 1863.

[95] The organ of Dr. Stuart Robinson; see footnote 94 above.

[96] Matthews (1824–89) was identified in chapter 1 at p. 14 as Justice Swayne's successor on the Court. He

reported from the Committee on Bills and Overtures a recital of "the early and unequivocal instructions of our Church" in condemnation of slavery; the report concluded that

> the time has at length come, in the providence of God, when it is His will that every vestige of human slavery among us should be effaced, and that every Christian man should address himself with industry and earnestness to his appropriate part in the performance of this great duty.

The report went on to notice "the President's declared policy not to consent to the reorganization of civil government within the seceded States upon any other basis than that of emancipation."

The report was adopted with near-unanimity.

At the Synod of New York and New Jersey, Dr. Henry J. Van Dyke[97] offered resolutions to censure the General Assembly for its action on the subject of slavery, and particularly for the sentiment about the reorganization of civil government in the South. His proposal was rejected as "a perversion and misrepresentation" of the Assembly's statement.

The Synod of Kentucky pronounced the Assembly's recent deliverance "unnecessary, unwise, and untimely"—but not a sufficient ground for seceding. It called for "great mutual forbearance."

POST-WAR DEVELOPMENTS

CONFLICT WITHIN THE CHURCH seems rather to have become more intense when hostilities in the field had ceased. The General Assembly of May 1865 declared and gave effect to its view that rebellion to support slavery "was not only a great sin, but wholly unwarranted." It repelled the criticism by the Kentucky synod, and reproached it for having done nothing to sustain the Government in suppressing the rebellion.

A majority of the Presbyterian ministers in Kentucky and Missouri thereupon drew up a "Declaration and Testimony against the Erroneous and Heretical Doctrines and Practices which have obtained and been propagated in the Presbyterian Church in the United States of America during the last five years." The document recommended

---

had been colonel of an Ohio regiment when in 1863 he was elected to the Superior Court of Cincinnati. He will appear presently as counsel defending the Cincinnati school board in the discontinuance of Bible reading in the public schools. Infra, n. 97.

[97] (1822–91), pastor of the First Presbyterian Church in Brooklyn. He was much concerned with doctrine and discipline. He will be mentioned infra, pp. 901, 904.

that "all ministers, elders, Church Sessions, Presbyteries, and Synods who approve of this Declaration and Testimony give their public adherence thereto . . . ."

The Presbytery of Louisville adopted this Declaration on September 2, 1865, by vote of 19 to 1.

In the Kentucky synod in October 1865, Dr. Breckinridge proposed severe condemnation of the presbytery for its "open rebellion." After days of debate, that was rejected by 102 to 25 votes. Then the synod defined its position: it held the pronouncements of the Assembly to have been "unwise, unconstitutional, and unscriptural"; even so, it would not produce a schism; it disapproved the Declaration; and it called upon all under its care "to study the things which make for peace."

When the General Assembly met in May 1866 it showed its temper in its choice of a moderator. Dr. Robert L. Stanton of the Danville faculty, who stood for unyielding adherence to the deliverances on loyalty and on slavery, received 158 votes. Dr. Phineas D. Gurley—whose church Lincoln had attended—favored great forbearance in the application of the deliverances: he had the support of 75. Only 18 voted for Dr. Samuel R. Wilson of the First Church of Louisville, a leader in the "Declaration and Testimony" party. The Assembly decided, by 201 to 50, to exclude from voting the representatives from Louisville, pending an investigation. Wilson and Dr. Stuart Robinson of the Second Church of Louisville—recently returned from a war-time sojourn at Toronto[98]—presented a protest in vindication of their presbytery.

Upon deliberation the Assembly condemned the "Declaration and Testimony" as slanderous and schismatical; its adoption by any church court was declared to be an act of rebellion. All signers, and all who had voted for it, were summoned to answer before the next Assembly; in the meantime they were barred from sitting in any court higher than the session.

The Assembly of 1866 also considered a "petition and memorial" from Avery and others, ruling elders of the Third or Walnut Street Church of Louisville: this complained that the Presbytery of Louisville designed to discredit their election; the peace of the church and their congregational rights were in danger; they asked that the Assembly interpose its authority. The Assembly acknowledged the petitioners as ruling elders, and enjoined all church courts "to respect and sustain their authority as such."

This declaration by the Assembly had been sought for its bearing upon the pending suit of *Avery et al. v. Watson et al.*, brought in

---

[98] Supra, n. 94.

the Louisville Chancery Court on February 1, 1866. To this litigation, and to the ensuing case of *Watson v. Jones*, carried from the federal Circuit Court to the Supreme Court, we shall soon return.

When the Synod of Kentucky met at Henderson in October, the clerk—pursuant to the action of the General Assembly—omitted from the roll call the names of those who had subscribed to the Declaration and Testimony. Then the moderator called the names of *all* elected to the synod. Of those present, 59 adhered to the Assembly and 99 supported the Louisville Presbytery. The upshot was that the *opponents* of the Assembly organized the meeting. The *friends* of the Assembly remained after adjournment, and organized themselves as *the* Synod of Kentucky. The main part of those who thus broke from the national body presently followed Dr. Robinson into the Southern church.

Also in October 1866 the Synod of Missouri likewise fell apart over the question of obedience.

The Synod of New York and New Jersey excluded Dr. Van Dyke from their meeting, in that he had signed the Declaration.

The Assembly of 1867 declared its readiness to receive back in fellowship such errant members and congregations as would submit to established authority by the next meeting.

The Old School and the New School Presbyterians had come to feel a need to restore the union that had been broken in 1837. That was effected in 1870. William Strong, shortly thereafter appointed to the Supreme Court, was one of the committee of conference that framed the Plan of Reunion. "The Presbyterian Church in the United States of America" was the title selected for the restored union.

The Southern organization had already assumed the title "The Presbyterian Church in the United States."

This narrative suggests the large context in which the litigation arising in one congregation at Louisville is to be viewed.

AVERY v. WATSON IN THE LOUISVILLE CHANCERY COURT

IN THE AUTUMN OF 1865 the Walnut Street Church was deep in controversy. The Rev. William T. McElroy was the acting pastor: to the majority of the congregation his ministry was unwelcome. The *session* consisted of the acting pastor and Elders Watson, Gault, Martin, and Hackney. Watson and Gault were bent upon making McElroy the regular pastor, notwithstanding that a meeting of the congregation had rejected such a recommendation. Elder Hackney presented to the session the petition of many members, adverse to retention. Deacon

Avery was prominent among these opponents. McNaughton carried a petition to the *presbytery*—which pronounced it to be unsuitable to be received, inasmuch as it concerned matters pending before the session.

After the congregation refused to call McElroy as their pastor, he preached a sermon censuring those who had not favored him, causing a large number thereafter to absent themselves. McElroy voted in the presbytery to adopt the "Declaration and Testimony," but that action does not figure in the record as a ground of complaint against him.

The session charged Hackney and Avery with unchristian conduct; Hackney was suspended from participation in the session. McNaughton also was charged. The trial of the first two was commenced. Elder Martin retired, and presently moved away.

The Synod of Kentucky met in October 1865. McNaughton, Hackney, and Avery severally petitioned for relief. The synod appointed a committee of visitation, and directed that a meeting of the congregation be called to elect additional elders.

Undeterred when Watson and Gault and Trustees Fulton and Farley barred the church doors, the congregation did meet. Avery, McNaughton, and Leech were chosen to be additional elders. But Watson and Gault refused to associate with them.

On February 1, 1866, Avery and associates brought ₐa suit against Watson and associates in the Louisville Chancery Court, praying for an order that the edifice be opened for congregational and session meetings, and that Trustees Fulton and Farley be removed.

At a meeting of the *presbytery* in April 1866, both Watson and Avery appeared to represent the Walnut Street Church—the former by designation of the old session and the latter by designation of the session composed of Elder Hackney and those newly elected. A committee reported in favor of seating Watson. Before acting on that report the presbytery adjourned to resume in June.

Meanwhile the General Assembly convened in May. As already noted, it considered a "memorial and petition" from Avery and others, and reached this decision: all church courts were enjoined to respect their authority as ruling elders of the Walnut Street Church.[99]

On June 2, counsel for Avery filed with the Chancery Court the text of the General Assembly's decision, to be read as evidence in the pending suit.

Pursuant to adjournment, the Louisville presbytery met in June. As we know, it was dominated by "Declaration and Testimony" men. Avery was rejected and Watson was seated as a delegate.

---

[99] Supra, p. 90.

A minority in the presbytery, adhering to the General Assembly, organized as a separate body, and seated Avery.

When the Synod of Kentucky met at Henderson in October, the Declaration men took charge. What the Louisville presbytery under control of their party had done in the Walnut Street matter was approved.

Upon the final hearing of *Avery v. Watson* in the Chancery Court, it was adjudged that Avery, McNaughton, and Leech were ruling elders and together with Hackney, Watson and Gault constituted the session; the management of the church property was committed to their care, "under the regulations of the Presbyterian Church in the United States of America."[100]

WATSON v. AVERY IN THE COURT OF APPEALS

THE DEFEATED PARTIES went to the Court of Appeals, and won a reversal at Summer Term, 1867.[101]

Kentucky's highest court was composed of four Judges, elected by district. At this period, three were Democrats, one a Unionist. In the church controversy, they divided on party lines.

Judge Mordecai R. Hardin spoke for the court. The "sole inquiry" was whether Avery *et al.* were ruling elders and therefore members of the session. They claimed through an election called pursuant to an order of the synod, whose action had been approved by the Assembly. While that which had been done by an ecclesiastical tribunal on a matter within its competence must be respected, it nevertheless pertained to the civil court to inquire whether the tribunal had acted within the regulations and constitutional restraints the church itself had established.

The Form of Government was examined critically. It provided explicitly for successive "appeals" from a lower to the next higher judicatory. But there had been no "appeal" in the present matter: "The session of the church had in fact rendered no decision to be reviewed in any superior judicatory." Where the mode of appellate review was so "clearly prescribed," it did not seem permissible to derive from other general language an "original and concurrent jurisdiction in the synod and general assembly" over the appointment of elders, which was expressly vested in the congregation.

---

[100] The Chancellor in this phase was Henry Pirtle (1798–1880), concurrently professor of constitutional law, equity, and commercial law in the University of Louisville. He had compiled the two-volume *Digest of Decisions, Court of Appeals, Kentucky* [1792–1832] (1832).

[101] Watson v. Avery, 65 Ky. (2 Bush) 332.

This view was said to be in accord with the opinions rendered by "Rev. George Junkin, of Pennsylvania, Rev. H. J. Vandyke of New York, and Rev. Stuart Robinson and Rev. S. R. Wilson of Kentucky, whose depositions, taken by the defendants, show them qualified by experience and study to testify to a knowledge of the laws and usages of the Presbyterian Church."[102]

Judge Rufus K. Williams, dissenting, dwelt upon the unseemly facts in the case—the session's "utter disregard" of the dissatisfaction of a majority of the congregation, its "persistent refusal to call a congregational meeting," and the manifest "indelicacy, if not partiality and prejudice," shown by McElroy, Watson, and Gault in using their power as the session court to accuse and then sit in judgment on those who differed with them.

Opposing counsel agreed that both synod and General Assembly did have jurisdiction over the controversy: the question was whether their actions should be pronounced null because they had proceeded otherwise than upon a formal appeal. In Judge Williams' view,

> A secular court can not review the regularity or irregularity of an ecclesiastical court, in matters strictly spiritual, as in the election and ordination of elders or any other office-bearers.

To appreciate the import of the concluding remarks in this dissenting opinion one needs to recall what was going on in that autumn of 1867. The Reconstruction Act of March 23, 1867, was being carried into effect: constitutional conventions dominated by Radical Republicans were in sight.[103] In this season of "rampant, radical, revolutionary ideas," wrote Judge Williams, the decision of his brethren would "open a door . . . fraught with danger to all the southern churches and their church property":

> when these soon to be newly-created courts take cognizance of the ecclesiastical proceedings of the different church tribunals, and . . . by a monstrous injustice strip them of their property, they may quote the opinion of the Kentucky court . . . in the important controlling fact that it has recognized the power of a civil court over the heads of the church courts to expound the church constitution. . . .

The danger Judge Williams had in mind took concrete form in a provision in Virginia's "Underwood constitution," completed in April

---

[102] Junkin and Robinson were identified supra in footnote 94. Wilson and Van Dyke have appeared in the text as prominent signatories of the Declaration and Testimony.

[103] Supra, chs. 8, 9, and 10.

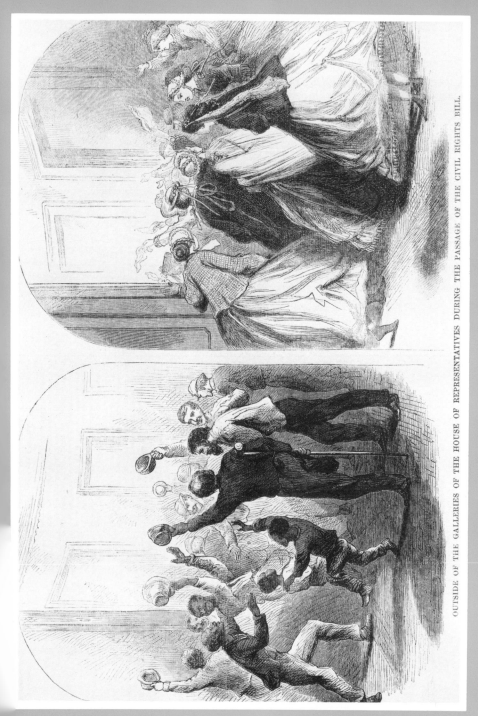

OUTSIDE OF THE GALLERIES OF THE HOUSE OF REPRESENTATIVES DURING THE PASSAGE OF THE CIVIL RIGHTS BILL.

From *Harper's Weekly*, April 28, 1866.

JAMES F. WILSON, Iowa.   GEORGE S. BOUTWELL, Mass.   JOHN A. LOGAN, Ill.

BENJAMIN F. BUTLER, Mass.   THADDEUS STEVENS, Penna.   THOMAS WILLIAMS, Penna.   JOHN A. BINGHAM, Ohio.

Managers of the Impeachment of the President, 1868.
(Library of Congress)

James A. Garfield.
(Library of Congress)

Henry Winter Davis.
(Library of Congress)

George S. Boutwell.
(G. A. F. Corporation)

Samuel Shellabarger.
(Library of Congress)

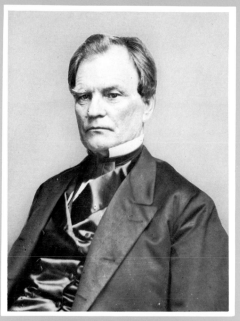

Benjamin F. Wade.
(Library of Congress)

Timothy O. Howe.
(Library of Congress)

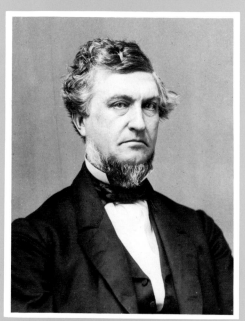

Zachariah Chandler.
(Library of Congress)

Simon Cameron.
(Library of Congress)

James M. Ashley.
(Library of Congress)

Burton C. Cook.
(Library of Congress)

James G. Blaine.
(Library of Congress)

Henry J. Raymond.
(Library of Congress)

Garrett Davis.
(Library of Congress)

James R. Doolittle.
(Library of Congress)

Frank P. Blair, Jr.
(U.S. Signal Corps)

Herschel V. Johnson.
(Library of Congress)

Ira Harris.
(U.S. Signal Corps)

Frederick T. Frelinghuysen.
(Library of Congress)

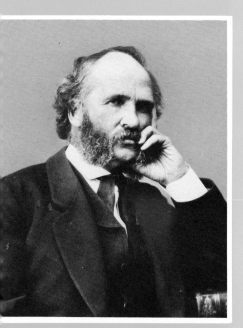

James W. Grimes.
(Library of Congress)

Charles D. Drake.
(Library of Congress)

John William Wallace, the Reporter.
(Pennsylvania Academy of the Fine Arts)

Mrs. Myra Bradwell.
(Chicago Historical Society)

Ward Lamon, U.S. Marshal.
(Library of Congress)

Richard C. Parsons, the Marshal.
(Library of Congress)

1868 and adopted (omitting certain clauses) in July 1869. It contained this disposition on "Church Property":

> The rights of ecclesiastical bodies in and to church property conveyed to them by regular deed of conveyance shall not be affected by the late civil war, nor by any antecedent or subsequent event, nor by any act of the legislature purporting to govern the same, but all such property shall pass to and be held by the parties set forth in the original deeds of conveyance, or the legal assignees of such original parties holding through or by conveyance, and any act or acts of the legislature in opposition thereto shall be null and void.[104]

The *Richmond Dispatch* sounded the tocsin:

> The northern Methodist Church, which can do no good in Virginia, . . . is trying to obtain a foothold here. The people cordially detest the whole concern—bishops, preachers, and horse-stealers (if this last class does not include the other classes). . . . Yet these Radical parsons . . . would, if they could, steal the churches themselves. Their excuse is that these churches are deeded to the "Methodist Episcopal Church." . . . But since that Church took to politics, and blazed the way for the present Radical party, our people have established one of their own, which they call "Methodist Episcopal Church, South."[105]

The new constitution aimed to deliver this church property "to wolves in sheep's clothing hailing from the North."

CONTINUED CONTEST

Avery v. Watson had been filed on February 1, 1866. On July 23—after other interlocutory orders had proved inadequate—the marshal by order of the Chancery Court took possession of the church property and held it for use as directed of a majority of the session wherein Avery, McNaughton and Leech were included. From that day, the party in affiliation with the General Assembly had the use of the church building.

On May 1, 1867, the Chancellor entered his decree in favor of the plaintiffs. That remained in force during the appellate proceedings.

In June 1867 the Rev. John S. Hays, adherent to the General Assembly, was installed as pastor. Membership increased rapidly.

---

[104] Art. XI, Miscellaneous Provisions.

[105] July 29, 1868.

Accord prevailed among the worshippers at Eleventh and Walnut Streets.

Meanwhile in a house at Ninth and Chestnut, Watson, Gault, and others of the minority were ministered to by Dr. Lunsford P. Yandell,[106] an eminent physician, sometime in the Confederate service, who was also of the Presbyterian clergy.

On November 22, 1867, the Court of Appeals reversed the judgment below in so far as it held that Avery, McNaughton and Leech were elders and committed the control of the property to them in conjunction with the old elders; the cause was remanded "for proper corrective proceedings" respecting control of the property.

Appellants filed a copy of the opinion and mandate with the Chancery Court on February 21, 1868, and moved for an order of restitution.

In opposition, on February 28, plaintiffs' counsel filed a supplementary petition: they asked that defendants be enjoined from any further proceedings to obtain possession. The petition averred that subsequent to the original decree, Watson and his associates had voluntarily withdrawn from the Walnut Street Church and from the Presbyterian Church in the United States of America, and hence had no interest in the property; that the plaintiffs and those united in interest with them were the only beneficiaries of the trust on which the property was held; that therefore the attempt by Watson and associates, under an order of *restitution* to themselves *as elders and trustees*, was a fraud upon the rights of the true beneficiaries. The petition charged that Watson and associates intended to use the property exclusively for a small faction, denying the rights of all others. (This is rather similar to the bill which presently we shall find counsel filing in the federal court in the suit of *Jones v. Watson.*)

In March the Chancellor granted an injunction against Watson and others, forbidding any further proceedings on their motion of February 21 for an order of restitution.

Defendants then obtained a summons against the Chancellor. Upon hearing his answer the Court of Appeals held that its mandate must be entered, before the Chancellor could suspend execution, even for a good cause. This ruling was made on June 26, 1868.[107]

Thereupon counsel for Avery *et al.* presented, and the Chancellor granted, a motion to dismiss their supplementary petition of February 28, without prejudice. They had been baffled, but only to fight better.

---

[106] (1805–78)—a man whose varied distinctions, in paleontology, and as a practitioner and professor of medicine at Louisville and Memphis, are recorded in D.A.B.

[107] 66 Ky. (3 Bush) 635.

In September, Chancellor T. B. Cochran directed that possession be restored to the old trustees, or a majority of them.

JONES v. WATSON IN THE FEDERAL CIRCUIT COURT

WILLIAM A. JONES—theretofore a member of the Market Street Methodist Episcopal Church—had joined the Walnut Street Church on March 8, 1868. His wife, and her mother, Mrs. Lee, were admitted at the same time. They came at a moment when the congregation was perplexed: the advice of the presbytery had just been sought about what to do in the light of the adverse decision of the Court of Appeals.

Jones was employed by the Bible Society of Louisville during May and June; thereafter he was out of work, and small sums were advanced to him from the church treasury. On July 1 he rented a house in New Albany, Indiana—just across the river from Louisville—and next day settled his family there. He intended to find a job and make his permanent residence in that community. Living there would be cheaper, and the health of his family would be improved. He intended to remain a member of the Louisville church; he was continuing to attend services when practicable. He further deposed:

> Shortly before I left I was told by several persons that when I removed over to Indiana I could bring a suit in the federal court at Louisville, and try the title of our church property, and believing that those members who went to hear Mr. Hays preach justly owned the property, and that if Watson and Gault got possession they would turn Mr. Hays and his friends out of the church, and by that means break up our Sabbath school and congregation, I made up my mind that I would bring the suit if I could . . . .[108]

Actually, it seems this expedient was not indispensably necessary to enable the church to get into the federal court. In the congregation there were several aliens, British subjects; indeed one, on going for a visit to Scotland, had left with an elder a power of attorney to permit suit to be brought.[109]

Jones had the services of very able counsel. Among them was John M. Harlan (1833–1911), lately Attorney General of Kentucky; he was familiar with the needs of the Walnut Street congregation, having represented Avery in the suit against Watson. Another was Benjamin H. Bristow (1832–96), then United States District Attorney, vigorously enforcing the Civil Rights Act.

---

[108] Transcript of Record, 127.
[109] Ibid., 89, 90 (deposition of Mc-   Naughton); 92 (deposition of Rev. Hays).

On or about July 17, 1868, counsel filed in the Circuit Court at Louisville the complaint of Jones, his wife, and Mrs. Lee, citizens of Indiana, against various defendants, all citizens of Kentucky: Watson and Gault, who without right claimed to be elders of the church; Fulton and Farley, who without right claimed to be trustees, and who recognized the pretensions of Watson and Gault; "Trustees of the Third or Walnut Street Church, in Louisville," a Kentucky corporation; and the three individuals then rightfully in office as such trustees, and Hackney, ruling elder, who, notwithstanding their duty to protect the members from the unlawful attempts of Watson and his associates to obtain possession, "refuse to take any legal steps to that end, upon the ground, as they allege, that it would prove unavailing and useless for them to do so." An injunction was sought against the first four defendants.

The complaint was amended to reflect an election of other elders and trustees by the group worshipping under Dr. Yandell.

The court temporarily restrained defendants from attempting to take possession of the property and from interfering with the Rev. Mr. Hays' preaching.

Depositions were taken upon interrogatories and cross-interrogatories, pointing in part to the standing of plaintiffs to maintain the suit. Exhibits were entered, including numerous excerpts from the minutes of various judicatories, to establish the circumstances of the cleavage between those bodies that accepted and those that repudiated the authority of the General Assembly. A transcript of the record in Avery's suit against Watson was also introduced.

District Judge Bland Ballard announced certain preliminary rulings on October 12, 1868. He said that "the learned presiding judge of the court [Justice Swayne], who heard the oral arguments, and who was compelled to leave for home, concurs in the general conclusions . . . ," although they had not been put into writing before he left.

The jurisdiction of the court and the right of the complainants to maintain their suit was affirmed on the authority of a number of cases cited, notably *Dodge v. Woolsey*, sustaining federal jurisdiction of a nonresident stockholders' suit to prevent a violation of the rights of a corporation which its directors refused to resist.[110] He also cited *Briggs v. French*, where Justice Story had observed that "It is every day's practice for a citizen of one State to remove to another State, to become a citizen of the latter, in order to enable him to prosecute suits . . . in the courts of the United States."[111]

---

[110] 18 How. 331 (1856).
[111] 2 Sumner 251, Fed. Case No. 1871, in the Circuit Court for Massachusetts in 1835. If the change of residence was real, the motive was immaterial.

On May 11, 1869, the court gave judgment for the complainants. While, as had already been acknowledged, the federal court could not enjoin those named in the Kentucky court's judgment from taking possession of the property according to that judgment,[112] it could and did perpetually enjoin all defendants from interfering with the use of the property by members of the Walnut Street Church submitting to the authority of the Presbyterian Church in the United States of America.

WATSON v. JONES IN THE SUPREME COURT

AN APPEAL was docketed on December 4, 1869. Recorded as counsel for the appellant were Thomas W. Bullitt, who had represented Watson and associates in this case below as well as in the Avery suit, and Jeremiah S. Black.[113] Bristow and Harlan were recorded as counsel for the appellees.

When the case came to be argued, on March 9 and 10, 1871, seven Justices were on the Bench. The Chief Justice and Nelson were absent. Bullitt opened, followed by Harlan. Next day Bristow continued, and Bullitt closed.

Bullitt's argument fell into two parts. First, the relations between State and federal courts: he contended on several grounds that the Circuit Court had intruded upon the field occupied by the Kentucky courts.

> The suggestion that a conflicting decree may be effectually executed without interfering with the possession or jurisdiction of the State Court, by means of a declaration of uses and an injunction, seems to us . . . a subterfuge of the flimsiest material.[114]

---

[112] Act of Mar. 2, 1793, 1 Stat. 334. The writ of injunction shall not be granted by any federal court "to stay proceedings in any court of a State."

[113] Thomas Walker Bullitt, born in 1838 at the ancestral home at Oxmoor, near Louisville, had studied for the bar in Philadelphia, and was in practice there with his brother, John Christian Bullitt until, on the outbreak of the war, he returned to Kentucky and joined the Confederate army. In Morgan's raid into Ohio in July 1863 he was taken prisoner. After the war he practiced at Louisville with another brother, Joshua Fry Bullitt—who, while Chief Justice of the Kentucky Court of Appeals, had in the summer of 1864 been arrested and held on a charge of holding high office in the Sons of Liberty. See supra, chapter 5, note 50.

What contribution Black made to preparing the case does not appear. The Case File in the National Archives contains a letter he wrote to the Clerk on December 6, 1869: "A record from Kentucky will be sent to you to be docketed—probably has arrived already. It is important that no time be lost. . . ." He offered his bond for the Clerk's fees.

Here, as in *McCardle*'s case docketed two years earlier, Black was impatient to check the advance of Radicalism.

[114] Brief for Appellants, 21. Only Bullitt's name appears.

This part of the argument concluded:

> By whatever process of reasoning it is reached, the effect is that the Federal Circuit Court has sat as a Court of Review and Appeal upon a decree of the Court of Appeals of Kentucky, and reversed its decision.[115]

If the Court accepted this first branch of his argument, it would not need to pronounce upon the second large question, the extent of the authority which the law allowed to ecclesiastical courts. Relying heavily upon the pertinence of precedents in the Scottish courts and the Privy Council, he submitted this proposition:

> that . . . where a right of property depends upon an adherence to religious doctrine, or is affected by an act or judgment of an ecclesiastical tribunal, the civil court will *examine* into such doctrine *as a matter of fact*, for the purpose of determining which party maintains the original principles of the society, and will examine into the act or judgment of the ecclesiastical court, for the purpose of determining whether it is in *contravention* of the fundamental law of the church . . . .[116]

Bullitt started with a rigid version of the powers of the ascending judicatories. Then he traced the pronouncements of successive General Assemblies, condemning slavery and demanding "adherence and loyalty" to a particular civil government—then the "Declaration and Testimony" seeking to bring the Church back to her ancient purity—and finally the "*ipso facto* order" of 1866 whereby any presbytery that seated an adherent to that document would be automatically dissolved. The Court should recognize that the higher judicatories had departed from the principles of the society. The appellants had not withdrawn from the true Church: they had been "*unlawfully and unjustly excluded.*"

Harlan's oral argument was transcribed and printed.[117] He detailed the controversy within the Walnut Street congregation and the bringing of the present suit. Justice Bradley jotted down notes of what was said:[118]

. . . .

> The present suit does not involve any questions decided in Avery v Watson
>
> Mr. Harlan then argues the question on the merits—contending
> I. That the complainants have a clear equity to the relief sought

---

[115] Ibid., 28.
[116] Ibid., 42.
[117] Argument for Appellee by John M. Harlan, Louisville, Ky., a pamphlet of eighty-three pages.
[118] On his copy of the Transcript of Record.

II. That the decision of the Genl Assembly of the Presbyterian Church is conclusive on all questions of Ecclesiastical order and discipline in that Church: and that the Civil Courts ought not to question it—ought not to set their own judgment against that of the Genl Assembly.

Next day Bradley resumed his summarizing:

Mr. Bristow
    I. Jurisdiction
    II. Competency of plffs to sue
. . . .
    Dodge v Woolsey, 18 How. 341, 344. Stockholder of another State may sue. . . .
    question of practice and not of jurisdiction
. . . .
What is the Constitution of the Presbyterian Ch?
    Brief 17
Dr. Breckenridge in the Critic.

At page 17 of the Brief of B. H. Bristow and John M. Harlan, of Counsel for the Appellees, one finds statements by Presbyterian clergymen on the constitution of the Church. Dr. Breckinridge had written in the *Presbyterian Critic* for 1855, at pages 348–50, that

> Theoretically the General Assembly is the general gathering of all the Presbyterian congregations connected with us, all forming one church; and as such has all the inherent power over the whole body that any part has over itself.

Virtually identical language was quoted from the *Church of God* (1848) at page 92, a book by Dr. Stuart Robinson, now leading the Declaration and Testimony party.

> Deliverances of Assembly in civil matters objected to
> These deliverances examined.
> Deliverances of Southern Assembly on same matter on the other side, and no objection to joining that assembly.
> These deliverances examined.

Bradley noted the points made in the concluding arguments for the appellants:

Bullitt
    Sup. Court of Ky. went into the matter of the election of officers, and decided against the election of Avery & als

That decision they [appellees] do not pretend to controvert or question

That decision is conclusive that they had no right to admit these complts [Jones, wife, and mother-in-law] to the Church

Ten days later, on March 20, Bristow presented himself with his commission as Solicitor General, which was recorded.[119] Actually it bore date of December 9, 1870.

On April 3 Justice Clifford, presiding, announced that the Court would adjourn on Monday, May 1, to resume on October 16. Also that it would not sit on Good Friday, one week hence.

It was not to be expected that the Court would take hold of its thorny Church Case at this moment when there was so little time for deliberation.

DECISION IN *WATSON v. JONES*

"MARCH 11, 1872 *Affirmed Miller*": Justice Bradley noted on his transcript the decision of *Watson v. Jones* in conference. A year and a day had elapsed since the oral argument. Justice Miller gave the reason when on April 15 he delivered the opinion of the Court:[120]

The novelty of the questions presented to this Court for the first time, their intrinsic importance and far reaching influence, and the knowledge that the schism in which the case originated has divided the Presbyterian churches throughout Kentucky and Missouri, have seemed to us to justify the careful and laborious examination and discussion which we have made of the principles which should govern this case.

The Court in delaying had hoped

that since the civil commotion, which evidently lay at the foundation of the trouble, had passed away, that charity, which is so large an element in the faith of both parties, and which, by one of the apostles of that religion, is said to be the greatest of all the Christian virtues, would have brought about a reconciliation. But we have been disappointed. . . .[121]

---

[119] Supra, ch. 14, n. 178.
[120] 13 Wall. 679.
[121] The General Assembly of the Southern Presbyterians, meeting at Louisville on May 18, 1870, had rejected the idea of eventual reunion with the Northern church: it declared itself the only surviving heir of the true faith; there were impassable barriers to official intercourse between the two Churches. Overtures for conference had been brought by Dr. Van Dyke and William E. Dodge. Ann. Cyc. 1870, 622. (Dodge's advocacy

Appellants' objection to the intervention of the Circuit Court was first to be considered. Questioning of the good faith of complainants' claim to Indiana citizenship had apparently been abandoned. But it was insisted that the pendency of the litigation started by Avery in the Kentucky courts precluded the entertainment of the *Jones* suit in the Circuit Court. That one court had already obtained jurisdiction of a subject matter did not, however, necessarily exclude adjudication by a court of concurrent jurisdiction of matters having a very close connection with that which was before the first.[122] In *Avery*, as the Kentucky Court of Appeals had said, "the sole inquiry" was "whether Avery, McNaughton, and Leech are also ruling elders." In the *Jones* suit, the question was "which of the two bodies shall be recognized as the Third or Walnut Street Presbyterian Church"; the claim of Avery and others to be ruling elders was "a very subordinate matter," depending on circumstances "which did not exist when [the *Avery* suit] was brought." Avery had later filed a supplementary petition containing much the same matter as the Jones' bill—but that had been dismissed without prejudice prior to the *Jones* suit.[123]

The Circuit Court had "carefully framed" its decree, which did not interfere with the marshal of the Chancery Court, nor did it restrain

---

of moderation, when a member of Congress at the time of the passage of the Reconstruction Act of March 2, 1867, has been recorded, supra at pp. 272–73.

Earlier in 1870 conventions of the Southern Baptists and Southern Methodists had refused to cooperate for the reunion of their respective denominations.

The *New Orleans Bee* in an editorial on May 18, 1870, "An Important Sign of the Times," anticipating the debate that would take place in the Southern Presbyterian Assembly, said that "There seems to be a decided preference on the part of the Southern clergy and people for separate organizations." The partition of the Baptists and the Methodists in 1845 had been regarded by political leaders as the entering wedge of the breach that came in 1861; and although the Civil War was ended, "who can say that a political UNION of the Northern and Southern people now exists?"

[122] Here Miller quoted from and applied Buck v. Colbath, 3 Wall. 334 (1866), in which he had spoken for

the Court. In an attachment suit in a federal court, Buck, federal marshal, had levied upon property *not* belonging to the defendant. Colbath, the true owner, sued Buck in trespass in a State court. A judgment for damages was sustained by the State's highest court, and Buck brought error under Section 25 of the Judiciary Act. Held: the marshal was subject to an action in a State court for levying on property not liable to attachment. It would have been otherwise had he been executing an order to seize that particular property. And even property wrongfully seized could not have been replevied while under the control of the court.

The respect which one court owed to the authority of a court of concurrent jurisdiction was of preeminent importance in a federal system, said Miller, where courts "whose powers are derived from entirely different sources" exercised jurisdiction which was "concurrent as to the parties and the subject-matter of the suit."

Miller's discussion in Buck v. Colbath has been often cited and quoted.

[123] Supra, p. 906.

Watson from receiving possession of the property. Yet the trustees of a Presbyterian church were "mere nominal title holders," subject to the rules of the parent Church and holding office "under the control of the church session." And the decree of the Circuit Court simply required Watson and his associates "so to use the possession and control to which they may be restored as not to hinder or obstruct the true uses of the trust . . . ."

Coming to the merits, Justice Miller extracted from the record the factual situation to which principles of law must now be applied.

Questions before the civil courts concerning the rights of property of ecclesiastical bodies fell under three heads. Sometimes property had been left in trust for the support of some specific form of doctrine. Here the general principles of equity in dealing with charitable trusts were applicable: "though the task may be a delicate one . . . , it will be the duty of the court . . . to inquire whether the party accused of violating the trust is holding or teaching a different doctrine . . . ."

Second, property might be held by an independent congregation owing no fealty to any higher authority. If the principle of the congregational government was that the majority ruled, then in the event of a schism the majority retained the property.[124] If the congregation had vested powers of control in officers, then those who adhered to the acknowledged organism were entitled to the use of the property.

The present instance was of a third sort, where the congregation was a subordinate member in a hierarchical organization under a supreme judicatory. Justice Miller outlined the Presbyterian system of government.

> In this class of cases we think the rule of action which should govern the civil courts, founded in a broad and sound view of the relations of church and state under our system of laws . . . is, that, whenever the questions of discipline or of faith, or ecclesiastical rule, custom or law have been decided by the highest of these church judicatories . . . , the legal tribunals must accept such decisions as final . . . .

For a civil court to sit in judgment would amount to "an appeal from the more learned tribunal in the law which should decide the case, to one which is less so."

In this country, where men enjoyed "the full and free right to entertain any religious belief,"

---

[124] In Bouldin v. Alexander, 15 Wall. 131 (1872), there had been a schism within the Third Baptist Church in Washington, D.C. "In a congregational church, the majority, if they adhere to the organization and to the doctrines, represent the church," said Strong, J., for the Court.

The law knows no heresy, is committed to the support of no dogma, the establishment of no sect. . . .

Miller turned to cases to sustain his statement that the Court's view was in accord with "the preponderant weight of authority in this country." Particularly to be noticed was *Chase v. Cheney*, decided by the Supreme Court of Illinois at January term 1871.[125] Bishop Whitehouse, High Church Episcopalian, had charged the Rev. Charles E. Cheney, Low Church, with an ecclesiastical offense, in that in performing infant baptisms he had omitted to declare that the infant thereby became "regenerate." Melville W. Fuller, for Cheney,[126] obtained an injunction from the Superior Court. Before the Supreme Court of Illinois, Fuller made an "earnest and able and elaborate argument" to persuade that court to examine the question of the church court's jurisdiction, and to hold that it had been organized in defiance of church law. The court refused, and ordered the injunction dissolved.

Shall we maintain the boundary between Church and State, and let each revolve in its respective sphere, the one undisturbed by the other? . . .

Quoting the guaranty in the State constitution,[127] the court answered,

. . . Freedom of religious profession and worship can not be maintained, if the civil courts trench upon the domain of the church, construe its canons and rules, dictate its discipline, and regulate its trials. . . .

Justice Miller found this a "very important case" in support of the position taken in his opinion.

Justice Clifford (Davis, J., with him) dissented: it was improper for the Circuit Court to act while the church property was under the control of the Chancery Court.

---

[125] 58 Ill. 509.

[126] The participation of the future Chief Justice is described in Willard L. King's *Melville Weston Fuller* (New York: Macmillan Co., 1950), at 69–72.

Cheney (1836–1916) is included in the Dictionary of American Biography. In 1873 he joined in establishing the Reformed Episcopal Church.

S. Corning Judd, chancellor of the Episcopal Diocese of Illinois, conducted the prosecution in the church court, and appeared against Fuller in

the State courts. There is a memoir in Proc. Ill. State Bar Assn. (1896), Pt. II, 178. He will be mentioned infra, p. 1006.

With Judd in the State courts was his brother-in-law, William C. Goudy, who later figures in Munn v. Illinois, 94 U.S. 113 (1877), and other leading cases as an opponent of rate regulation.

[127] The constitution of 1870 in Article II, Bill of Rights, in Section 3, secured "The free exercise and enjoyment of religious profession and worship, without discrimination . . . ."

A CENTURY LATER

Watson v. Jones remains a high authority. Of recent years the Court has heard in Justice Miller's language "a clear constitutional ring,"[128] and has followed its guidance in a controversy that could be carried to the Court only because a mandate of the Constitution was involved.

This was in *Presbyterian Church in the United States v. Hull Church*, in 1969.[129] As at the time of the Civil War, so again the General Assembly had taken a stand—on such issues as civil rights and the war in Viet Nam. Two local churches in Georgia, holding such outspeaking on public questions to be a departure from the doctrine and practice in force at the time of their affiliation, chose to withdraw from the parent church; they sued in the Superior Court for an injunction to forbid it to trespass on local church property. The State courts took the view that if "a fundamental or substantial abandonment of original tenets or doctrines" were proved—and here a jury so found—the implied trust on which the parent church held title would be terminated. Judgment was for the local bodies.[130]

The Supreme Court reversed, and remanded for further proceedings not inconsistent with the Court's opinion. It held that

> the departure-from-doctrine element of the Georgia implied trust theory requires the civil court to determine matters at the very core of religion—the interpretation of particular church doctrines and the importance of those doctrines to the religion. Plainly, the First Amendment forbids civil courts from playing such a role.

The First Amendment had become a limitation upon the States through the Fourteenth Amendment.

The Justices who joined in the opinion in *Watson* did not dream that they were speaking the constitutional law of another century. The Fourteenth Amendment was new and untried: the Court had just heard the first argument in the *Slaughter House Cases*, wherein they were asked to hold that it condemned Louisiana's abattoir monopoly.[131] As recently as 1869 the Court had reiterated that Amendments First to Eighth "were not designed as limits upon the State governments . . . ."[132] When *Watson* was being decided, Stanley Matthews

---

[128] Brennan, J., for the Court in Presbyterian Church in the United States v. Hull Church, 393 U.S. 440, 446 (1969).

[129] Supra, n. 128.

[130] 224 Ga. 61 (1968).

[131] *The Slaughter House Cases*, 16 Wall. 36 (1873). Infra, ch. 21.

[132] Twitchell v. Pennsylvania, 7 Wall. 321. Infra, ch. 21, n. 47.

—author of the Assembly's statement about effacing every vestige of slavery[133]—was engaged in a controversy in the Ohio courts wherein he was contending that compulsory Bible reading in the public schools was against law.[134] The Justices at Washington would hardly have guessed that the new Amendment made *that* a matter within their cognizance.

Justice Reed, speaking for the Court in *Kedroff v. St. Nicholas Cathedral*[135] in 1952, traced the steps by which the principle in *Watson* came to be recognized as a constitutional rule. It was brought in the federal court, and carried to the Supreme Court, simply on the basis of diversity of citizenship. That was at a time when the rule in *Swift v. Tyson*[136] prevailed: in diversity cases the federal courts took an independent view, unaffected by local prejudices that might prevail in the judge-made law of the State wherein the action arose.[137] That will be explained and amply illustrated in the chapters on Municipal Bonds.[138] And, Justice Reed explained, *Watson* was decided long prior to "judicial recognition of the coercive power of the Fourteenth Amendment to protect the limitations of the First Amendment against state action." That remarkable development will be noted in connection with the unfolding of the post-war Amendment.[139] Although federal jurisdiction in *Watson* depended on nothing more than diversity of citizenship, the Court's response gave it a great significance: the opinion, said Justice Reed, radiated "a spirit of freedom for religious organizations, an independence from secular control or manipulation, in short, power to decide for themselves, free from state interference, matters of church government as well as those of faith and doctrine."

An element of Miller's strength was his ability to express authentic values of the American scheme of government. That he did in *Watson v. Jones*—and through developments that were unimaginable to the Justices at that moment, his utterance was ultimately raised to the dignity of a rule of constitutional law.

---

[133] Supra, p. 898.

[134] Infra, p. 1312.

[135] 344 U.S. 94.

[136] 16 Pet 1 (1842). Overruled in Erie R.R. v. Tompkins, 304 U.S. 64 (1938). Infra, p. 939.

[137] The local prejudice that dominated the Court of Appeals of Kentucky was made manifest in Gartin v. Penick, 68 Ky. (5 Bush) 110 (1868).

Robertson, J., said that the "extraordinary declarations of presumptuous dogmas" by the General Assembly marked it "as an intermeddling and revolutionary partisan in an unconstitutional, unholy, and bloody work of abolition by armies, and even servile war and insurrection." At 130.

[138] Infra, chs. 17, 18.

[139] Infra, pp. 1318–20.

CHAPTER XVII

Municipal Bonds I: Conflict in Iowa

W<small>E MUST NOW</small> examine a matter long obscured with the passing of time. For a season, cases on municipal bonds bulked larger than any other category of the Court's business. Chiefly these were bonds issued to purchase stock in order to encourage the building of a railroad. In our period the Court decided some two hundred cases on these railroad aid bonds. When as often happened the railroad never came, or fraud and bribery in the bond issues came to light, or statutory prerequisites had been ignored, or people simply became disenchanted, communities would refuse to pay taxes, interest would be stopped, and then bondholders would sue to compel payment. Normally the plaintiff resided out-of-State and thus could resort to the federal court, where a more sympathetic hearing was to be expected than in State courts held by judges popularly elected for brief terms.[1]

---

[1] By the "assignee clause" in Section 11 of the Judiciary Act of 1789, 1 Stat. 73, 78–79, Congress sought to provide that a mere collusive assignment to create diversity of citizenship would not avail to bring a controversy within the jurisdiction of the federal courts: it excluded "any suit to recover the contents of any promissory note or other chose in action in favor of an assignee" unless suit might have been brought by the assignor, except in cases of foreign bills of exchange. But neither that nor later versions of the assignee clause (as by Sec. 1 of the Act of Mar. 3, 1875, c. 137, 18 Stat. 470; Sec. 1 of the Act of Aug. 13, 1888, c. 866, 25 Stat. 433) applied to the owner of a bearer bond, or of coupons therefrom, issued by a municipal corporation. Such instruments passed by delivery without formal assignment, and the owner sued in his own right, not as assignee of the right of another. Thomson v. Lee County, 3 Wall. 327, 331 (1866); City of Lexington v. Butler, 14 Wall. 282, 293 (1872); Thompson v. Perrine, 106 U.S. 589, 592 (1883); Ackley School Dist. v. Hall, 113 U.S. 135, 140 (1885); Lake County Comm'rs. v. Dudley, 173 U.S. 243, 250 (1899).

If in any case, however, it appeared that a party was not the owner of the bond or coupons on which he claimed, but had been made the assignee of the rights of others in order to create diversity of citizenship or to

XVII: *Municipal Bonds I*

The Supreme Court's decisions on the validity and enforcement of railroad aid bonds led to lively resistance in Iowa and then in Missouri; more limited conflicts occurred elsewhere in the Mid-West, and even in up-State New York. The clash with Iowa in the '60's, and that with Missouri in the '70's, were comparable to the well-known episodes of defiance by the Virginia court under Spencer Roane in the time of Marshall, by Georgia in the Jackson Administration, and by the Wisconsin court on the eve of the Civil War.

This matter, long ignored, looms like a wilderness—trackless even to knowledgeable students of the Supreme Court. The best-known landmark is *Gelpcke v. Dubuque*[2] (presently to be discussed), decided in 1864, where the Court refused to follow the Iowa court when, overruling an earlier holding, that court had declared that taxation to aid railroads was contrary to the State's fundamental law. It seems commonly to be assumed that the rest of the bond cases fall into this pattern and illustrate the Court's stand against "judicial repudiation." That comes far short of the whole truth. The Court went much further: enforcing bonds which the State court had held invalid without overruling any decision; construing State statutes—on the powers of municipal officers, on debt limits, on the privileges of railroad corporations, etc.—contrary to the construction given them by the State courts; and exercising unrestrainedly that independence in matters of "general jurisprudence" which a later Court abandoned as "an unconstitutional assumption of powers by the Courts of the United States which no lapse of time or respectable array of opinion should make us hesitate to correct."[3] It will be found that in a number of important matters the Court eventually confessed previous error, and thereupon overruled some of its own precedents on which investors had relied.

One estimate of the Court's work, often cited, is this, made by an experienced practitioner in 1891:

> As we look back over the record, we can plainly see that the firm moral fibre displayed in the opinions upon bond cases has been of incalculable value to the whole country. Whatever hardship may have resulted from individual decisions, the sum total of the court's labors

---

make up the amount requisite to suing in the federal court, it was the duty of the court to dismiss. Sec. 5, Act of Mar. 3, 1875, supra; Williams v. Nottawa, 104 U.S. 209 (1881); Farmington v. Pillsbury, 114 U.S. 138 (1885); Waite v. Santa Cruz, 184 U.S. 302 (1902).

Under the original Judiciary Act, in order to give diversity jurisdiction, the matter in dispute must exceed $500;

the Act of Mar. 3, 1887, substituted $2,000; the Act of Mar. 3, 1911, $3,000; the Act of July 25, 1958, $10,000.

[2] 1 Wall. 175.

[3] Erie R.R. v. Tompkins, 304 U.S. 64 (1938), adopting the language of Holmes, J., dissenting, in Black & White Taxicab Co. v. Brown & Yellow Taxicab Co., 276 U.S. 518, 533 (1928).

in this department stands as an enduring monument, for which our people can never be too profoundly grateful.[4]

That was the judgment of Frank W. Hackett, well acquainted with the bond cases, and it should be added, son of a wealthy investor in municipal bonds, whose interests he had defended before the Court.[5]

Justice Miller, who lived in Iowa and presided over the Circuit where the conflict was most acute, put a different estimate on the Court's performance in the field of municipal obligations:

> Our court or a majority of it are, if not monomaniacs, as much bigots and fanatics on that subject as is the most unhesitating Mahemodan in regard to his religion. In four cases out of five the case is decided when it is seen by the pleadings that it is a suit to enforce a contract against a city, or town, or a county. If there is a written instrument its validity is a foregone conclusion.[6]

He wrote this in 1878, when the Court had carried its doctrine to a high point, far beyond the position that it would not recognize an overruling decision that would invalidate.

A practical view of the situation at the close of our period may be found in publications prepared by counsel and distributed by conservative bankers specializing in municipal bonds. The authors were experienced, and what they conceded was in accord with the facts. One, dated January 1889, gave this account:

> During the years following the war, many municipalities, especially in some of the western states and territories, became careless and extravagant in the issue of bonds for all sorts of authorized, and occasionally unauthorized, purposes. They were frequently voted with little or no restriction, in aid of all sorts of railroad schemes, in many cases for railroads never built, and in some cases apparently never intended to be built. Instances might be given where bonds were issued to an amount greater than the assessed value of all the taxable property within the . . . subdivision issuing them. . . .
>
> Probably no question in American jurisprudence has been more persistently and thoroughly litigated than the validity of municipal bonds issued in aid of railroads. . . .
>
> The correctness of the principle that taxation could be made, and bonds issued in aid of private railroad corporations has

---

[4] "A Recent Decision of the Supreme Court upon Municipal Bonds," *Harv. L. Rev.*, 5:157, 158.

[5] See infra, p. 944; the son appeared as counsel in Hackett v. Ottawa, 99 U.S. 86 (1879).

[6] Letter of Feb. 3, 1878. Charles Fairman, *Mr. Justice Miller and the Supreme Court, 1862–1890* (Cambridge, Mass.: Harvard University Press, 1939), 232.

been ably and vigorously contested by several leading elementary writers and jurists, but the legality at least of the principle is now too well established for further controversy. That the doctrine has led to extravagant municipal bonding, which in many cases has been disastrous, and in more than one instance has resulted in municipal bankruptcy, cannot be denied. Our federal reports, especially from 1860 to 1880, are filled with cases where municipalities have attempted to avoid the payment of this class of bonds. It is not surprising that municipalities have resisted the payment of bonds, issued perhaps under misrepresentations, in anticipation of benefits, usually largely overestimated, or in aid of roads never built. The effects . . . have been to create a growing conservatism on the subject of contracting municipal indebtedness, and increasing the statutory and constitutional restrictions on the issue of such bonds, and in many states absolute constitutional prohibitions against the granting of aid in any form to railroad or other similar corporations. . . .[7]

This handbook concluded with a sort of checklist of points to be established by competent proof, preliminary to putting bonds on the market. It has long since been elementary that the legality of an issue should be assured by the opinion of competent bond counsel.[8] Until near the close of the period with which we are concerned, however, the Court had no idea that the way to promote a stable market was by inculcating an awareness that a purchaser should attend to such precautions. Its zeal was directed toward protecting the bondholder if he, or any predecessor in title, had bought without actual knowledge of invalidity.

---

[7] *The Law of Municipal Bonds*, by James A. Burhans of the Chicago bar, prepared for and published by S. A. Kean & Co., Bankers, Chicago and New York. At 2–3, 19–21.

[8] In *Fundamentals of Municipal Bonds*, published by the Investment Bankers Association of America (Washington, 1959) one may read in the chapter on "The Municipal Bond Attorney" by David M. Wood (of Wood, King, and Dawson, of New York) that

The practice of submitting state and municipal issues to independent counsel . . . grew out of the wide-spread defaults which occurred, largely upon railroad aid bonds, in the late 1870's and early 1880's. . . . Some municipalities and counties . . . issued bonds in aid of projects often in amounts which equalled, or even

exceeded, their entire assessed valuations.

The result was inevitable. Wide-spread defaults upon these bonds occurred. . . .

In order to assure investors in public securities that the bonds were legally issued, the dealers in municipal bonds began the practice of employing lawyers of outstanding reputation in the field of municipal law and of the highest reputation for integrity to examine the proceedings under which the bonds were authorized to be issued, and to render an opinion as to the validity of the bonds. The experiment succeeded. . . .

From *Fundamentals of Investment Banking* (Englewood Cliffs, N.J.: Prentice-Hall, Inc., 1946, 1947), p. 55.

When it became the standard practice of bond houses to obtain the opinion of a specially qualified attorney, municipal bonding underwent a profound change. This was explained in the brochure of another firm of bankers, published in 1890:

> Many cases of repudiation of railroad-aid bonds (which . . . comprise by far the greater part of the defaults in the history of Municipal Bonds) have been brought about through the claim of illegality of issue. It is a matter of record that the proceedings bearing upon such issues were formerly loosely conducted, while purchasers were equally lax in giving the legal papers touching the same the attention and investigation which their importance demands, and which is invariably given them today. . . . Perfect equity between debtor and creditor demands . . . that the authority to issue shall be unquestionable, and bond-houses and other large fiduciary institutions of today meet this requirement by retaining attorneys of ability, who instead of taking for granted, as in former times, that everything had been "properly done, happened and performed," now insist on all steps being taken in strict conformity with law. . . .

It contrasted "the premiums now commanded by the better class of [municipal] bonds" with the discounts which formerly prevailed and were a warning of the risk involved. It added:

> Railroad-aid Bonds.—These we decline to handle, for, although when legally issued they are undoubtedly collectible, the chances of litigation are so great that we should not ask our clients to buy into a possible lawsuit.[9]

The brochure of still another house, published in 1889, observed that among safe investments, municipal bonds had come to rank second only to the Government's obligations.

> If the courts will enforce bonds issued in aid of railroads, where the benefit to the taxpayer is so doubtful, there need not be the slightest apprehension of bonds issued for strictly municipal or public purposes . . . .[10]

The statement merits rereading. That normal borrowing by local governments had been made secure was, of course, commendable. It

---

[9] Eben H. Gay, *Municipal Bonds,* prepared for and published by N. W. Harris & Co., Bankers, Boston. At 39–40, 45.

[10] *Judicial Decisions on Municipal Bonds,* published by W. J. Hayes & Sons, Cleveland. At 5, 43.

was the extraordinary exertions of the Court in respect of one exceptional type of obligation that was called in question. Do the decisions stand as a monument to the Court's moral fibre? Or were the Justices so prepossessed as to render adjudication "a farce whose result is invariably the same, namely to give more to those who have already, and to take away from those who have little, the little that they have"?[11]

To acquire such familiarity as permits an informed conclusion must be a tedious business; judgment should be held in suspense while one explores widely to make sure of one's bearings. There is a notable dearth of monographs.[12] Historians have dwelt upon many aspects of the frontier. They have concerned themselves with agrarian discontent— the farmer's burden of debt, the medium in which he must repay, his fight to curb the railroad lobby. Congressional support of the transcontinental route, and land grant policies, have received attention. But no comparable interest has been directed toward the experience of municipal bonding to build scores of roads which, if they exist on the ground today, are imbedded deep in the corporate structure of some one of the operating companies. Histories of the various railroads often follow a romantic theme,[13] and even the more serious ones tell of builders rather than of those who supplied the means. One must find the sources for oneself.

Of unique importance is John F. Dillon's *Law of Municipal Corporations*, which in its first edition appeared in 1872. The author had been Justice and Chief Justice of the Supreme Court of Iowa, 1862 to 1869; then for ten years he "filled the office of Circuit Judge in the Eighth Circuit with such distinguished ability" as to be mentioned in those words by Chief Justice Waite.[14] Judge Dillon knew *everything* about municipal bonds: but his treatise was properly limited to the discussion of points of law.

---

[11] Justice Miller's comment. Fairman, *Mr. Justice Miller*, 231.

[12] For Missouri, mention should be made of Edwin L. Lopata, *Local Aid to Railroads in Missouri* (1937), a doctoral dissertation at Columbia University; and E. M. Violette, "The Missouri and Mississippi Railroad Debt," (Columbia: Missouri Historical Soc., 1921), reprinted from the *Missouri Historical Review*.

[13] For example, *The Katy Railroad and the Last Frontier* (Norman: University of Oklahoma Press, 1952), by V. V. Masterson, is dedicated "to the memory of Robert S. Stevens, Indian Territory pioneer . . . ," whose notable achievements the book extols. In the history of municipal railroad aid, Stevens is memorable, inter alia, as the consignee of 127 out of 229 $1,000 bonds, corruptly issued by the officers of Cass County, Missouri—a fraud that led to a celebrated lynching in April 1872. George H. Preston, *A History of the Cass County, Missouri, Bond Swindle* (St. Louis: Southwestern Book and Publishing Co., 1873), 71; Cass County v. Green, 66 Mo. 498 (1878).

[14] In Douglass v. Pike County, 101 U.S. 677 (1880), a leading municipal bond case.

APPROACH TO AN UNFREQUENTED FOREST

Gelpcke v. Dubuque,[15] as a unique case, has been discussed in juristic writing, because it presented a puzzle whether a sound justification could be found for what the Court did.[16] Specialists in federal jurisdiction have been interested in a few decisions, such as *Riggs v. Johnson County*,[17] holding that a federal court has power to enforce its judgment notwithstanding that this operates upon one who has been enjoined by a State court; *Amy v. Supervisors of Des Moines County*,[18] holding further that officers who refused to obey the court's mandamus to levy a tax could be held personally liable in damages; and *Amy v. Watertown*,[19] where city officials by systematic resignations over many years had avoided paying the bondholder until at last the statute of limitations barred his claim. Such specialists, however, have been gathering specimens for their own purposes and have not been concerned to penetrate the forest.

Herman Gelpcke, Fred. W. Kentgen and Adolphus Reicheldt, partners in banking in New York, in negotiating with Dubuque represented also clients in Germany to whom they had sold bonds; their counsel said that at stake was "five millions of property securely treasured upon the banks of the Delaware, the Hudson, the Thames and the Rhine."[20] America was then a borrowing nation; to a considerable extent municipal bonds were sold to Europeans—who, fed upon stories of the enormous promise of the West, might not comprehend how a municipality was in financial distress.

Henry Amy—whose name led all the rest in the annals of litigation to enforce railroad aid bonds—was a Belgian who came to New York in 1850 and entered the employ of Meyer & Stucken, bankers dealing in municipal bonds. In 1859 he established the firm of Amy & Heye, succeeding to the business of his former employers. In 1865, in association with Gustavus L. Hoppenstedt, he established the house of H. Amy & Co., which he headed until his death in 1901.[21] He first appears in the United States Reports in *Amey* [sic] *v. Allegheny City*[22] in 1861, and in more than a dozen instances thereafter even beyond

---

15 Supra, n. 2.
16 Infra, pp. 936–40.
17 6 Wall. 166 (1868). Infra, p. 963.
18 11 Wall. 136 (1871).
19 No. 1, 130 U.S. 301, and No. 2, 130 U.S. 320 (1889).
20 Argument of S. V. White, xxiii, in submitting the *Gelpcke* case to the court. Stephen Van Culen White

(1831–1913), then practicing law at Des Moines, shortly thereafter moved to New York City, where he engaged in banking and was a member of the Stock Exchange. He was a Republican Congressman, 1887–89.
21 Obituary in *Boston Evening Transcript*, Jan. 12, 1901.
22 24 How. 364.

Amy v. Watertown in 1889.[23] This is not surprising when one takes note of his business card:

> H. Amy & Co., Bankers
> 19 & 21 Nassau Street, New York.
> Transact a general banking business.
> Deal in investment securities.
> Buy all descriptions of UNCURRENT Bonds,
> also Bonds REPUDIATED by CITIES
> and COUNTIES.[24]

In short, he specialized in the venturesome business of trying to collect where normal efforts had failed.

Frequently the holders of these bonds were themselves chief promoters of the railroad being aided. Perhaps they had formed a construction company which contracted to build the roadbed for the railroad of which they were directors, or by some other means had contrived to pass the bonds through the hands of a third party in whose shoes they then could stand with the rights of a bona fide purchaser without notice of any illegality. "It is worthy of parenthetic remark . . . , as one of the anomalous incidents to the transfer of railroad bonds, that a purchaser of a different description is seldom, or never seen." Such was the observation of Chief Justice Sherwood of Missouri, in a case where a banking house and a member of the bar contended—unsuccessfully—that they had purchased without knowledge that the bonds had been fabricated by corrupted county officers in the notorious "Cass County Swindle."[25] Again, the bondholder might be one who had bought an uncurrent or repudiated issue at a sharp discount. As was said in the brochure of a conservative bank, "the buyer of such a security could but appreciate the chance he was taking."[26]

In *Mercer County v. Hackett*,[27] decided a week after *Gelpcke*, the Supreme Court threw the weight of its authority behind the proposition that the bonds of a municipality—where it had been given power to issue them—were *negotiable*, and thus in the hands of a bona fide purchaser were proof against defenses of fraud or illegality. Justice Grier observed that "this species of bond is a modern invention, intended to pass by manual delivery, and to have the quality of negotiable paper; and their value depends mainly upon this character."

This new type of security was the subject of the following

---

[23] Infra, pp. 1045–47; Manning v. Amy, 140 U.S. 137 (1891).

[24] For example, *Commercial & Financial Chronicle*, 22: 192, Feb. 19, 1876.

[25] Cass County v. Green, 66 Mo. 498 (1878).

[26] Gay, *Municipal Bonds*, 37, supra, n. 9.

[27] 1 Wall. 83 (1864), infra, pp. 944–45.

encomium in *A Practical Treatise on the Law of Municipal Bonds,* published by William N. Coler in 1873:

> It is the offspring of the same heroic principle that has within a century enlarged the borders of our civilization with a rapidity unknown to history, and conferred upon our people every public blessing which the genius of an enlightened age has produced.[28]

Municipal issues, it was said, now equalled in amount "the securities of the nation and all the States combined."[29] These are the words of a lawyer and dealer[30] who was so sanguine that in that year of panic he was contracting to supply foreign investors with securities yielding 9.5 percent in gold[31]—and who before long was himself a bankrupt.

A more prudent attitude was disclosed in the brochure published in 1885 by another bond house,[32] which could say that "In an experience of over twenty years, neither ourselves nor any investor through us, so far as we know, has lost a dollar through default or repudiation of any municipal bonds handled by or purchased through us." It hastened to add,

> We do not handle bonds issued for railroad aid, for the reason that this class of securities has been most fruitful of litigation.

"Probably ninety-five percent. of the losses arising from investments in municipal bonds," it said, "have been caused by want of information as to the laws, both constitutional and statutory, governing their issue."

> We invariably require full official certified records of proceeding of authorities in matter of issue, have said records examined by the most competent attorneys, and have uniformly declined bonds where the least taint or irregularity has been shown. . . . In addition to this, we in every case where it is practicable, make a personal inspection of the municipality, talk with the people, see that the contemplated improvement is desirable and necessary, and that the citizens are in favor of it. . . .

One example, presently to be examined, of culpable failure to examine the law: a Pennsylvania banking house purchased county bonds issued to aid a railroad (which turned out to be a monumental failure) on the urging of their local attorney who, it seems, relied upon a

---

[28] P. xi.
[29] P. 26.
[30] W. N. Coler & Co., 17 Nassau Street, New York.
[31] Transcript of Record in Lewis v.

Commissioners, 105 U.S. 739 (1882), at pp. 16–19.
[32] *Digest of Laws Governing the Issue of Municipal Bonds* (Chicago: S. A. Kean & Co., Bankers) at pp. 3, 4.

pamphlet issued by the company itself representing that counties were authorized to support it by a tax of one half of 1 percent of the assessed value of all property—whereas the charter as enacted provided for a tax of only one twentieth of 1 percent. Controversy between the county and these bankers ran on for decades.[33] Clients seem generally to have looked to their attorneys to tell them, Where can a handsome profit be made? Can payment of these bonds be enforced?—rather than, Were they issued in conformity with law? Is there a fair prospect that payments will be made when due?

Judgment about these bond decisions should be suspended until the entire experience can be critically examined.

THE *SHARPLESS CASE* IN PENNSYLVANIA

WHILE THE STORM OVER railroad aid had its center in Iowa and then in Missouri, there had been significant disturbances in States farther to the East. We can best approach the subject by way of Pennsylvania, Ohio, Indiana, and Illinois.

A starting point is *Sharpless v. Mayor of Philadelphia* in 1853,[34] apparently the most cited of all decisions by the Supreme Court of Pennsylvania.[35] This was a suit by citizens to restrain a subscription to railroad stock, to be paid by an issue of $1,000,000 in city bonds. "This is, beyond all comparison, the most important cause that has ever been in this Court since the formation of the government"—so spoke the Chief Justice, Jeremiah S. Black, in a memorable opinion that set forth every consideration, pro and con, relevant to a conclusion.

> The fate of many most important public improvements hangs on our decision. If all municipal subscriptions are void, railroads . . . must stand unfinished for years to come, and large sums, already expended on them, must be lost. Not less than fourteen millions of these stocks have been taken by boroughs, counties, and cities within this Commonwealth . . . . It may well be supposed that a large amount of [railroad aid bonds] are now in the hands of innocent holders . . . .

Now to hold them invalid would be a "deadly blow" at improvement, would have a "disastrous effect . . . on the private fortunes of many honest men, at home and abroad," and would "do much to lessen the influence of our institutions on the public mind of the world."

But, he continued, "The reverse of this picture is not less appalling":

---

[33] Infra, p. 1091.
[34] 21 Pa. St. 147.

[35] This is supported by a count in *Shepard's Pennsylvania Citations.*

If the power exists, it will continue to be exerted, and generally it will be used under the influence of those who are personally interested, and who do not see or care for the ultimate injury it will bring upon the people at large. . . . The selfish passion is intensified by the prospect of immediate gain: private speculation becomes ardent, energetic, and daring, while public spirit—cold and timid at best—grows feebler still when the danger is remote.

If only a few of the roads then projected turned out as unfortunate as *all* had proved in the past, the burden would prove unendurable. He apprehended that

this plan of improving the country, if unchecked by this Court, will probably go on until it results in some startling calamity, to rouse the masses of the people.

The court, however, must deal with this strictly as a *judicial* question: "However clear our convictions may be, that the system is pernicious and dangerous, we cannot put it down by usurping authority which does not belong to us." That a statute violated "the spirit of our institutions," or appeared wrong and unjust, was not a ground on which judges could hold it invalid. Nor could they say that legislation authorizing municipal aid to railroads would tax the citizen for a *private* purpose. "A railroad is a public highway for the public benefit," even though conducted by a private corporation exacting "a uniform, reasonable, stipulated toll from those who pass over it . . . ." The duty of the State extended to education, the promotion of arts, the stimulation of commerce, the construction of highways. It might accomplish its ends "through the agency of an individual or corporation." That railroads, like canals and turnpikes, served a public end was illustrated when land was taken by the power of eminent domain, whereas no such power could be invoked to build a tavern, a mill or a blacksmith shop.

While Pennsylvania's judges would in no wise shift their responsibility to the judges of other States, still it was noted that several other courts had held that aid to railroads was for a *public* purpose, for which taxes might be laid. These decisions disclosed "a manifest triumph of reason and law over a strong conviction in the minds of the judges that the system they sustain is impolitic, dangerous and immoral."

Two judges concurred in Black's conclusion; two dissented.

In this unhappy spirit the Pennsylvania court, by a bare majority, sustained railroad aid. Bondholders to the extent of "fourteen millions" had already purchased other municipal issues: on the very threshold of municipal aid to railroads, that consideration weighed heavily upon the judicial mind. State constitutions of that day had provided no firm ground on which a court could take a stand against such improvidence.

928

The most that could be said was that private property could be taken only for a *public* purpose: it was regarded as fundamental that the legislature could not take A's property to give to B. A court might, perhaps, reason that the State constitution gave the legislature only "legislative power," and go on to assert that such power was limited by principles of justice, of which the courts could judge.[36] Even so, aid to canals and turnpikes had long been familiar, and railroads seemed to present an analogous case. For a court to declare that railroad aid was ultra vires would have gone counter to the current of the moment, and would have seemed a bold assertion of judicial power. Only two of the five Pennsylvania judges were prepared to take that stand.

In the companion case of *Moers v. City of Reading,*[37] counsel for the city, arguing for the validity of railroad aid, included William Strong—who subsequently, as a Justice of the Supreme Court, bore a considerable part in enforcing municipal issues.

In 1857—four years after *Sharpless*—Pennsylvania's constitution was amended to limit the debt-contracting power of the State, and absolutely to prohibit legislation authorizing municipalities to take stock in or lend their credit to any private corporation. And the State Supreme Court weakened the position of municipal railroad aid bonds by denying them the quality of negotiability—thereby leaving them shorn of that indisputability which commercial law accords to negotiable instruments in the hands of bona fide purchasers.[38]

DEVELOPMENTS IN OHIO, INDIANA, AND ILLINOIS

THE OHIO COURT in 1852, in what appears to have been a friendly suit, held that municipal aid to railroads did not offend the constitution of 1802. Stress was laid on the millions already invested.[39] The statute in question had been snapped through a few days before the completion of the constitution of 1851, which declared that the General Assembly shall never authorize a municipality to become a stockholder or to loan its credit to a corporation. The schedule, however, saved laws in force, "not inconsistent with this constitution." And the court went on to hold, by a 3 to 2 division, that notwithstanding the prohibition, municipalities could go on subscribing so far as authorized by statutes already enacted.[40] Again, it held that as to bona fide holders, the municipality was

---

[36] Taylor v. Porter, 4 Hill (N.Y.) 140 (1843).
[37] 21 Pa. St. 188 (1853).
[38] Diamond v. Lawrence County, 37 Pa. St. 353 (1860). Infra, n. 98.

[39] Cincinnati, W. & Z. R.R. v. Comm'rs of Clinton County, 1 Ohio St. 77.
[40] Cass v. Dillon, 2 Ohio St. 607 (1853).

estopped to set up irregularities in proceedings which the statute directed to be taken preliminary to the issue of bonds.[41] Here counsel for the bondholders included Noah H. Swayne—who later, on the Supreme Court, stood first among the supporters of the bondholding interest. "Skillful avoidance" of the constitutional prohibition was at times practiced by the legislature.[42]

Indiana's constitution of 1851 declared that "No county shall subscribe for stock in any incorporated company, unless the same be paid for at the time of such subscription . . . ." This emerged from the State's bitter experience with public aid to railroads and canals in the 1840's.[43] The Indiana court held, however, that it was competent for the legislature to authorize a *city* to take railroad stock to be paid for by an issue of bonds.[44]

In Illinois, a decision in 1858 sustained a provision in the General Railroad Law of 1849 authorizing cities and counties to issue bonds to take stock in railroads.[45] That was consistently followed. However, as the court observed in 1872, "the passion for subscriptions by the municipalities to every conceivable project presenting itself in a corporate form, was so violent, and prevailed so extensively throughout our State, as to demand a speedy, prompt and efficient remedy."[46] Accordingly, the constitutional convention of 1870 framed a provision that no municipality should aid a private corporation by subscription or donation, save for subscriptions then permitted by law if voted by the people prior to the adoption of the constitution. Further, municipal indebtedness must not exceed 5 percent of the assessed value of taxable property. While even these prohibitions left room for controversy, their application gave rise

---

[41] State *ex rel.* Smead v. Trustees of Union Township, 8 Ohio St. 394 (1858).

[42] In Pleasant Township v. Aetna Life Ins. Co., 138 U.S. 67 (1891), there had been a combination of statutes each authorizing a particular township to build its own railroad, along a line such that the several petty links could be joined for operation by one lessee railroad company. The Ohio Supreme Court condemned this scheme as unconstitutional. Aetna, which had purchased bonds prior to that adjudication, brought suit to enforce them in the federal court. Justice Brewer's opinion held, however, that none of the decisions of the federal Supreme Court went so far as to sustain the bondholder in so unmeritorious a situation. To Justice Brewer

from Kansas, this sort of thing seemed an old story.

[43] Traced in Lafayette, M. & B. R.R. v. Geiger, 34 Ind. 185 (1870).

[44] City of Aurora v. West, 9 Ind. 74 (1857).

[45] Prettyman v. Supervisors of Tazewell County, 19 Ill. 406.

[46] Schall v. Bowman, 62 Ill. 321. Justice Breese recalled that "Many of those who vote these subscriptions, it was well known to the convention and to everybody else, did not possess a dollar of their own, or own any property to be taxed, but having the voting power, they could so use it in furthering such enterprises, producing, as they do, many jobs and contracts by which they would profit as individuals, with none of the burdens of the tax payer."

to no serious breach in the relations between the State and federal judiciary.[47]

What has been said is enough to show that it was with grave misgiving that the courts sustained municipal aid to railroads; that experience led to constitutional prohibitions; but that then "the ingenuity of the lawyer and the legislator" (Justice Brewer's phrase)[48] was constantly at work to find some means of circumventing.

THE SUPREME COURT IN *KNOX COUNTY v. ASPINWALL*

COMMONLY A STATUTE authorizing counties or cities to aid in railroad construction imposed prerequisites: that an initiating petition be filed, that a certain majority of the voters approve, that the outlay must be within a prescribed limit, and perhaps that certain progress have been shown before bonds were delivered. But how would these requirements be enforced? The great case of *Knox County v. Aspinwall*[49] in 1859 presented this issue: Could the county set up, in defense to a suit by a bona fide purchaser, that the bonds had been issued in disregard of statutory prerequisites—in this case, without giving the prescribed notice of the election? (The importance of adequate notice, especially in a backwoods Indiana county, is not to be overlooked.[50]) Normally, of course, the unauthorized act of an agent does not bind the principal; a corporate officer who acts without authority does not bind the corporate body—as the Court had declared a month before, holding that a bank was not liable for an engagement by its cashier in excess of his authority.[51] Failure to comply with the statute's prescriptions on the issue of railroad aid bonds would be decisive against the county board's authority, said the Court, "were it not for the question that underlies it: and that is, who is to determine whether or not the election has been properly held, and a majority of votes of the county cast in favor of the subscription?" Could compliance be put in issue in any suit on the bonds? Or did the statute mean that the board itself, ascertaining before

---

47 Infra, pp. 1048–52.
48 Pleasant Township v. Aetna Life Ins. Co., supra, n. 42.
49 21 How. 539.
50 The Indiana statute of January 15, 1849, authorizing county aid to the Ohio & Mississippi Railroad, to run across the southern part of the State (now part of the Baltimore & Ohio line between Cincinnati and St. Louis), directed that sheriffs forthwith give notice of an election to be held on the first Monday of March then next. Knox County (county seat, Vincennes) extends more than thirty miles along the Wabash River, and is about twenty miles wide; its population in 1850 was 11,084. The giving of effective notice under such circumstances would be difficult. The proposal was to subscribe $200,000.
51 United States v. City Bank of Columbus, 21 How. 356 (1859).

it acted that prerequisites had been met, thereby made a determination on which innocent holders could rely? The Court concluded that the question was committed to the board.

That one who deals in bonds issued in pursuance of a valid public law may rely upon what that law declared, is a sound proposition. But the opinion did not point to any peculiar provision in this Indiana statute making the board the final judge of compliance; rather it implied generally that the governing body of any municipal corporation was "fit and competent to be the depositary of the trust."[52]

In this spirit Justice Nelson went on to give "another answer," broader than the first: this was that whenever the face of the bond recited that it was issued in pursuance of a statute, "the purchaser was not bound to look further for evidence of a compliance with the conditions of the grant of the power." This amounted to saying that whenever the governing body of a city or county issued bonds reciting that they had authority, then true or false, the municipality was bound as against a bona fide purchaser.

Several comments are in order. First, it is a maxim of prudence that the Court will not decide more than the case in hand requires.[53] Here having placed its decision on one ground, it went on gratuitously to state "another answer," much more far-reaching. Second, this other answer made new law peculiar to municipal bonds. From the outset, these became a specially indulged category.[54] Third: When one considers the exertions put forth by promoters, and the eager hopes aroused among the people at the prospect of getting a railroad, one sees how great was the danger that magistrates would be overpersuaded, deceived,

---

[52] The Court pointed out that it did not mean that the board's determination would be conclusive in a direct proceeding to inquire into the facts *before* the interest of third parties had attached.

Justice Daniel alone dissented: "the Commissioners being known to be mere agents, it was the duty of those who dealt with them to ascertain the extent of their powers."

[53] Justice Brandeis developed this proposition in his concurring opinion in Ashwander v. T.V.A., 297 U.S. 288, 341 (1936).

[54] The Court based this part of its opinion on the recent English case of Royal British Bank v. Turquand, 6 E. & B. 327 (1856). The Court of Exchequer there held that where by the relevant public documents the directors have power to bind the company, but certain preliminaries are required to be gone through on the part of the company before that power can be duly exercised, one who deals with the directors is entitled to presume that the preliminaries have been observed and that the directors are acting lawfully. Quite so: the internal affairs of a private corporation are hidden from the outsider. With a municipal corporation authorized to issue bonds upon compliance with certain preliminaries, the practical situation is distinguishable: the petition, the giving notice, the election, and the canvass of returns are matters of record open to the world. It was a long jump from *Royal British Bank* to *Knox County* on the banks of the Wabash.

or corrupted. At a juncture when enormous obligations were being assumed by frontier communities, the Court's *Aspinwall* decision put taxpayers in an extremely vulnerable position and encouraged laxity on the part of purchasers.

Finally—perhaps the most striking observation—one needs to acquaint oneself with the plaintiffs who passed as bona fide purchasers. In this instance they were William Henry Aspinwall (1807-75)—who had already made a fortune from the monopoly of transportation between the East and West coasts via Panama—and his business associates, including Joseph W. Alsop and Samuel L. M. Barlow. These men were the promoters of the company to which the Knox County bonds had been issued—the Ohio & Mississippi Railroad between Cincinnati and St. Louis, subsequently incorporated into the Baltimore & Ohio. Alsop became president of the Eastern Division, Barlow of the Western Division, of the O. & M. Having agents vigilant at every point, they had the means of knowing everything it was to their interest to know. These were the innocent holders for value in whose suit the Court pronounced its momentous decision.[55]

When Aspinwall and associates took their judgment to the Knox County board, they could not get execution: the board (disregarding the Indiana statute) refused to levy a tax. And rather than seek to enforce that duty through the State courts, the judgment creditors asked the federal Circuit Court to compel the levy by its writ of mandamus. The writ was granted.[56] And the Supreme Court sustained what the court below had done as having been "necessary for the exercise of its jurisdiction" within the meaning of Section 14 of the Judiciary Act of 1789.[57] For a federal court to grant mandamus against a federal officer was familiar; this, however, is said to have been "the first instance in which a federal court ever issued a writ of mandamus to a State officer in the history of this government."[58]

Such was the state of the law when railroad tracks were first laid in the trans-Mississippi West.

---

55 While the S. L. M. Barlow Papers in the Huntington Library do not speak to this Knox County case, they do show that Barlow and his associates were able to maintain a close watch over the affairs of the Ohio & Mississippi, including the issue of railroad aid bonds by the city of Cincinnati.

56 Aspinwall v. County Comm'rs, Fed. Case No. 593 (1859).

57 Board of Comm'rs v. Aspinwall, 24 How. 376 (1861).

58 Miller, J., dissenting in Riggs v. Johnson County, 6 Wall. 166 (1868).

Senator Judah P. Benjamin of Louisiana had represented Aspinwall in earlier litigation before the Supreme Court; he could not participate in persuading the Supreme Court to advance to this new ground in imposing its authority over the State, for the reason that some days earlier he had quit the Senate and gone South to defend State sovereignty.

RAILROAD PROMOTION WEST OF THE MISSISSIPPI

THE FACTUAL SITUATION bore certain marked features. In 1862 Congress passed an act to aid in the construction of a railroad from the Missouri River to the Pacific: the Union Pacific and other branches of this national system brought special problems to the Supreme Court, not to be considered at this point. Other Western trunk lines were projected, to connect with lines from the Eastern seaboard. And then each State had a number of local railroads which if they survived were presently absorbed into some system. In the East, railroads had been built between established communities, whose commerce was ready to be tapped. In the West, railroads were pioneer works, running through land yet to be filled. Congress granted to the States, in aid of the construction of roads between named points by companies designated by the legislature, alternate sections in a strip of public land along the right of way. (In Iowa, the railroads were given about one-eighth of the State's entire area.) But to lay tracks took capital—which must come from the East or from Europe. If people along the line would pledge their credit to an extent sufficient to "grade, bridge and tie" the road, perhaps the promoters could get the iron rails and equipment—hopefully, from some railroad to which the new road would be a "feeder"—and bring off a success. Failure, which was frequent, commonly left the people with nothing but their indebtedness.

Promoters played one community against another; bidding became frantic. Not all citizens saw a profit from such a subsidy: business men at the county seat, and landowners along the line, stood to gain; farmers in a remote corner might oppose. Unskilled laborers might foresee jobs, with little burden to themselves in taxes. A community constantly augmented by newcomers might feel little moral involvement in obligations assumed in years past, especially where there was nothing to show as consideration. And when one railroad had come, its charges might seem extortionate; then competition by a rival would be sought. We shall see communities concerting measures to evade old obligations at the same moment they are whooping to contract new ones. An editor may praise a judicial decision that taxation to aid a railroad violates an indefeasible right of the individual—and at the same time urge surrounding communities to tax themselves to build a railroad to his town. The same session of a legislature may pass one law to hinder enforcement of old bonds and another law to permit a new round of municipal subsidies. Only when this mystery has been unfolded may one safely reach conclusions.

934

GELPCKE v. DUBUQUE

BY WAY OF this introduction we come to the leading case of *Gelpcke v. Dubuque*, decided on January 11, 1864.[59] In 1856 that city voted to subscribe $250,000 in each of two railroads. Dubuque was then the scene of wild speculation. It was the only river town between Rock Island and St. Paul—some three hundred miles—that had a railroad from the East; emigration to northern and central Iowa poured through it. Then came the panic of 1857. Moreover, the river was tapped at two other points. Much of Dubuque's trade was lost; business houses closed. In 1860 the city failed to meet the interest on its bonds.[60] Gelpcke sued in the federal court for interest on bonds issued to the Dubuque Western Railroad.

In 1862, in the *Wapello County* case,[61] the Supreme Court of Iowa, repudiating the view upon which it had acted theretofore, held that under the State constitution the citizen could not be taxed to aid a railroad. Thereupon the federal court, in Gelpcke's suit, accepted the State court's new construction and accordingly held the Dubuque bonds unenforceable. Gelpcke asked the Supreme Court to reverse that judgment.

The Court had long adhered to the principle that "if the highest judicial tribunal of a State adopt new views as to the proper construction of . . . a statute, and reverse its former decisions, this court will follow the latest settled decisions." These are the words of Justice Swayne, speaking for the Court in 1862.[62] Now in *Gelpcke* in 1864 the Court, again speaking through Justice Swayne, declared an exception—based, it was said, "upon the plainest principles of justice"—for the situation where the latest adjudication held municipal bonds to be invalid. The Court now adopted as its own what Chief Justice Taney had once said, obiter, in a separate opinion:

> the sound and true rule is, that if the contract, when made, was valid by the laws of the State, as then expounded by all the departments of its government, and administered by its courts of justice, its validity and obligation cannot be impaired by any subsequent act of the Legislature of the state, or decision of its courts, altering the construction of the law.[63]

---

[59] 1 Wall. 175.
[60] *Dubuque Times*, May 8, 1864, tracing the history of the debt.
[61] State *ex rel.* Burlington & Missouri R.R. v. County of Wapello, 13 Iowa 388.
[62] Leffingwell v. Warren, 2 Bl. 599.
[63] Ohio Life Ins. & Trust Co. v. Debolt, 16 How. 416, 432 (1853).

Justice Swayne was content to let the matter rest simply on Taney's assertion. He concluded, sententiously,

> We shall never immolate truth, justice, and the law, because a State tribunal has erected the altar and decreed the sacrifice.

Justice Miller protested against this "advance . . . in the direction of a usurpation of the right, which belongs to the State courts, to decide as a finality upon the construction of State constitutions and State statutes . . . in a case where there is no pretense that the constitution, as thus construed, is any infraction of the laws or Constitution of the United States."

> Thus we have two courts, sitting within the same jurisdiction, deciding upon the same rights, arising out of the same statute, yet always arriving at opposite results, with no common arbiter of their differences. There is no hope of avoiding this, if this Court adheres to its own ruling . . .

because, he recalled, where it was not contended that the State court had infringed federal law, the Supreme Court had no authority to send down its writ of error to force the State court into conformity.

The majority were making this exception to general principle to meet the particular situation where the State court by overruling a precedent had rendered municipal bonds invalid. Justice Miller conceded that

> The moral force of this proposition is, unquestionably, very great. And I think, taken in connection with some fancied duty in this Court to enforce contracts, over and beyond that appertaining to other courts, has given the majority a leaning towards the adoption of a rule, which in my opinion cannot be sustained either on principle or authority.

The decision of the majority had been marked by "language as unsuited to the dispassionate dignity of this Court, as it is disrespectful of another court of at least concurrent jurisdiction over the matter in question . . . ." He warned of resulting judicial conflicts "which, if they shall occur, will weigh heavily on that court which should have yielded to the other . . . ."

Those conflicts will fill this and the following chapter.

THE COMPLEXITY OF *GELPCKE*

THIS AT THE outset may be said of Justice Swayne's opinion: that what the Court was doing was not nearly so simple as his brisk treatment made it sound. The Iowa court had seriously weighed the consideration that by overruling a decision it would extinguish interests acquired in faith of it. Respect for such interests is not, however, an imperative that overrides every other concern of the law. "State courts, like this [Supreme] Court, may ordinarily overrule their own decisions without offending constitutional guaranties, even though parties may have acted to their prejudice on the faith of earlier decisions"—so wrote Justice Brandeis in 1930, pointing to the exceptional nature of *Gelpcke v. Dubuque.*[64] Presently we shall find the Supreme Court sustaining a certain contention by a bondholder in his suit against an Iowa city,[65] and then learn that in 1892 the Court declared that that case was overruled—notwithstanding the reliance that through the years investors had placed upon it.[66] Indeed Chief Justice Taney's statement, the proposition upon which *Gelpcke* was decided, was itself an item in a line of cases on the obligation of statutory tax-exemptions for corporations, a series wherein the Court eventually excluded what at the outset it had declared to be included within the protection of the Contract Clause.[67]

Whether the Iowa court had done well or ill in overruling a precedent is not the issue in a critique of *Gelpcke v. Dubuque.* The question is, On what rational basis can one justify the Supreme Court's refusal to follow the State court's decision on a matter of State law? For years afterward the Justices were at a loss to find any adequate justification—and so too were the commentators.

The quotation from Taney assimilated the impairment of a contract by judicial decision to impairment by a statute. The Contract Clause, however, forbids the State to *pass any law* impairing the obligation of a contract. The Court consistently has held that its power under the Contract Clause was "for the restraint of unconstitutional legislation by the States, and not for the correction of alleged errors by their judiciary."[68] Indeed the Justices who decided *Gelpcke* were clear that the overruling by the Iowa court did not offend the Contract Clause.[69]

---

[64] Brinkerhoff-Faris Trust & Sav. Co. v. Hill, 281 U.S. 673, 682 n. 8.

[65] Rogers v. Burlington, 3 Wall. 654 (1866). Infra, pp. 997–98.

[66] Brenham v. German-American Bank, 144 U.S. 173.

[67] In Gordon v. Appeal Tax Court, 3 How. 133 (1845), it was said that where a price had been paid for a corporate franchise, thereafter to lay a tax upon the privilege would be impermissible. In New Orleans City & L. R.R. v. New Orleans, 142 U.S. 192 (1892), in such a situation, a subsequent tax was sustained and the *Gordon* case was distinguished; this new

view was affirmed in St. Louis v. United Rys. Co., 210 U.S. 266 (1908).

[68] Grier, J., in Commercial Bank v. Buckingham's Exr's., 5 How. 317, 343 (1847); followed in Tidal Oil Co. v. Flanagan, 263 U.S. 444 (1924), where Taft, C.J., cited nineteen instances where the Court had so held.

[69] Were it otherwise, *Wapello* and the State court decisions that followed it would themselves have been reviewable in the Supreme Court under Sec. 25 of the Judiciary Act as instances where a claim of constitutional right had been rejected. But

What the Court did in *Gelpcke* must, then, look for its justification to the provision of Article III of the Constitution: the judicial power of the United States "shall extend . . . to controversies . . . between citizens of different States . . . ." In such a controversy the law of the State is to be applied; the federal judiciary has cognizance only by reason of the diversity of citizenship. Within what ambit does the federal judiciary act in this situation? That is an historic question. Some have reasoned that the Constitution made the Supreme Court the head of a unified national judicial system, and that its rulings, even on questions of State law, in cases within "the judicial power of the United States" became precedents binding upon the State courts.[70] On the theory of those commentators, *Gelpcke* made a rule not for federal courts alone: the Iowa court ought to bow and abandon its own view of the constitutional law of Iowa.

Quite different was the analysis of Oliver Wendell Holmes in his twelfth edition of Kent's *Commentaries on American Law*, in 1873. He there added a note to report the Court's new line of decision in bond cases, commenting that "This principle, if sound, seems to stand, not on the Constitution, as the . . . language might indicate, but on the general grounds of justice on which it was put by Taney, C.J. . . . ." He went on to state the reasoning of Justice Miller in dissent, with evident agreement.[71]

The Court's position in *Gelpcke* was that it had an independent judgment, not a supreme authority. In *Swift v. Tyson*[72] in 1842 it had held that the federal judiciary would exercise an "independent judgment" on questions of "general law" (as distinguished from such matters as "the rights and titles to real estate, and other matters immovable and intraterritorial")—declining to follow a State court's decision where it appeared erroneous. It disclaimed, however, any power to impose its view upon the State court: this was a field, it said, where "the federal courts and the State courts, each within their own spheres, deciding on their own judgment, are not amenable to each other."[73] In 1883 Justice

---

when counsel for bondholders pressed that construction upon the Court, their cases were dismissed for want of jurisdiction: Railroad Co. v. Rock, 4 Wall. 177 (1867); Railroad Co. v. McClure, 10 Wall. 511 (1871). See infra, chapter 18, note 34.

[70] That thesis is defended in the massive discussion by Professor W. W. Crosskey, *Politics and the Constitution in the History of the Supreme Court*, 2 vols. (Chicago: University of Chicago Press, 1953), chapters 20–26. Professor Henry Schofield had reached a like conclusion in "Swift v. Tyson: Uniformity of Judge-Made Law in State and Federal Courts," *Ill. L. Rev.*, 4:533 (1910).

[71] Vol. I, *419 n. 1 (a) and *342 n. 1.

[72] 16 Pet. 1.

[73] Delmas v. Insurance Co., 14 Wall. 661 (1872).

Bradley, "in order to obviate any misconception that may arise from language and expressions used in previous decisions"—including *Gelpcke* and a host of other municipal bond cases—arrived at this explanation: out of considerations of comity and good sense, the courts of the United States endeavored to avoid conflict with the decisions of the State courts; since, however, the object in giving them jurisdiction in diversity cases "was to institute independent tribunals . . . unaffected by local prejudices and sectional views, it would be a dereliction of their duty not to exercise an independent judgment in cases not foreclosed by previous adjudication."[74] That was the Court's most persuasive justification.

Ten years later, however, Justice Field professed that he had seen a new light; he was now persuaded that "Supervision over either the legislative or the judicial action of the States is in no case permissible except as to matters by the Constitution specifically authorized or delegated to the United States."[75] Presently Justice Holmes came to the Court, and the views he had intimated in his note on Kent of the duty of the federal judiciary to follow State decisions on State law appeared in dissenting opinions.[76] At last in *Erie R.R. v. Tompkins*[77] in 1938, the Court overruled *Swift v. Tyson* and renounced as unconstitutional the pretension there made. Since that time, *Gelpcke* has been in limbo.[78]

---

[74] Burgess v. Seligman, 107 U.S. 20, 33.

[75] Dissenting in Baltimore & O. R.R. v. Baugh, 149 U.S. 368, 401 (1893), where the Court applied its own view of the so-called fellow-servant rule to an industrial accident.

[76] Muhlker v. New York & H. R.R., 197 U.S. 544, 573 (1905); Kuhn v. Fairmont Coal Co., 215 U.S. 349, 370 (1910); Black & White Taxicab Co. v. Brown & Yellow Taxicab Co., 276 U.S. 518, 533 (1928).

[77] 304 U.S. 64.

[78] Gelpcke v. Dubuque and Swift v. Tyson may be bracketed as cases where the Supreme Court asserted its independence of State court rulings on State law. Yet in another aspect they stand in contradiction. In Swift v. Tyson the Court had to construe Sec. 34 of the Judiciary Act: "The laws of the several States shall be regarded as rules of decision . . . in the courts of the United States . . . ." Here "laws" refers only to statutes, not to judicial decisions, said Justice Story; the latter "are, at most, only evidence of what the laws are, and are not themselves laws." In Gelpcke v. Dubuque the Court said that when the Iowa court overruled a precedent it was making new law which—no less than would have a statute—impaired the contract. Justice Holmes discussed the doctrinal difference in his dissenting opinion in Kuhn v. Fairmont Coal Co., 215 U.S. 349, 370 (1910).

Gelpcke v. Dubuque and Swift v. Tyson worked as a team in the municipal bond cases.

In *Gelpcke*, it should be remarked, the Court was not exercising an "independent judgment": the federal court must refuse to follow the Iowa court, not because the latter had reached the wrong answer on the question of municipal aid, but because it had overruled a precedent and thereby destroyed acquired rights. The Supreme Court made clear, however, that it regarded the earlier Iowa decisions as being "sustained by reason and authority."

One can only speculate what remedy, if any, might be found in the event a State court's overruling decision ever threatened great injustice such as the Court saw in the Iowa decision of 1862.[79]

WHAT THE IOWA JUDGES HAD DONE

OF THE EARLIER IOWA decisions, overruled by the State court in 1862, Justice Swayne in *Gelpcke* made this characterization: they "cover the entire ground;" "they exhaust the argument;" "we could add nothing to what they contain." On scrutiny this proves to be quite unwarranted.[80] First came *Dubuque County v. Dubuque & Pacific R.R.*,[81] in 1853. Pursuant to an election, the county was going ahead with the issue of bonds when, momentarily and insincerely reversing its position, it challenged the railroad company to show that the county could lawfully carry out the transaction. The State court, by two judges against one, obligingly said what both parties were waiting to hear: that the issue was valid. The majority found authority in a provision of the law governing counties, for submitting to the voters any proposal for an extraordinary expenditure to construct "any road or bridge." Said the majority, "a road" includes a railroad. Then disposing of suggested constitutional difficulties: the legislature was not abandoning its own "legislative power" by leaving such expenditures to a popular vote; and the specific prohibitions that the *State* must not become stockholder in any corporation, or incur indebtedness over $100,000, did not limit what the legislature might authorize a *county* to do.

The two judges at that time filed no opinion to support their decision; not until five years later did one become available—a slender effort of less than five pages.[82]

---

[79] In 1922 Congress amended the Judicial Code to extend the Supreme Court's jurisdiction to any suit wherein it was claimed that a change of ruling by a State's highest court "would be repugnant to the Constitution of the United States." In a case brought under this provision, Taft, C.J., said for a unanimous Court: "The mere reversal by a State court of its previous decision . . . , whatever its effect upon contracts, does not . . . violate any clause of the federal Constitution." He said that "Certain unguarded language in Gelpcke v. Dubuque, 1 Wall. 175, 206; Butz v. City of Muscatine, 8 Wall. 575, 583 [infra, p. 1000], and in Douglass v. Pike County, 101

U.S. 677, 686–87, [infra, pp. 1080–81], and in some other cases has caused confusion, although those cases did not really involve the contract impairment clause of the Constitution." Tidal Oil Co. v. Flanagan, 263 U.S. 444, 454, 455 (1924). See also Great Northern Ry. v. Sunburst Oil & Refining Co., 287 U.S. 358, 364 (1932).

[80] The Iowa cases were listed and examined by Justice Miller in his dissenting opinion in *Gelpcke*.

[81] 4 G. Greene 1.

[82] When in 1858 Judge Greene published the fourth volume of his Iowa Reports, wherein his opinion appeared.

The third judge filed a cogent dissent. On the question of statutory authority, he held that "road" had not been intended to include a railroad; indeed the legislature had rejected a proposal to authorize county aid for "work of internal improvement." And as a matter of the constitutional law of Iowa, he held that one could not be compelled to bear taxation for railroad aid: "it does not contribute in any way to the support of government, nor is it promotive of that welfare and security for which governments are established."

At that moment, he remarked, "but few of the counties in comparison to the entire number interested" had voted to take stock.

In cases thereafter, later judges differed among themselves: over what deference they should pay to the first ruling—over the merits of the constitutional issue—over statutory construction—over the consideration due to a bona fide purchaser. When the power to issue such bonds was next actually challenged,[83] in 1857, two judges said that "whatever doubts we may tacitly entertain," it was now "impossible to recede." The third, Chief Justice Wright, said that notwithstanding all the considerations that urge acceptance of what has been done, he must dissent on both the constitutional and the statutory points. In several cases that followed, county bonds were upheld while individual differences continued to be expressed. Then in 1862, when two new members joined Judge Wright, a unanimous court planted itself firmly in this ground: the Iowa constitution—whose Bill of Rights concluded with the statement that "this enumeration of rights shall not be construed to impair or deny others, retained by the people"—recognized that the citizen did have rights beyond those expressly safeguarded. Freedom from compulsory contribution to railroads was such a right. On the basis of this provision the Iowa judges found the law of their State to be different from that expounded in such cases as *Sharpless v. Mayor of Philadelphia.*[84] In thus deciding according to their best understanding they unavoidably visited a hardship on innocent creditors: they appealed to the moral sense of the people to take such measures as would save the good faith of the State. By the time the federal Supreme Court decided *Gelpcke*, the new Iowa ruling had been affirmed in five more cases; it could, therefore, be called "settled."

Those two Iowa judges of 1853 had produced great mischief. Upon inadequate argument they had pronounced on the State's most consequential question. They had fudged to find statutory authority; they had ruled upon constitutionality after a skimpy examination of the problem. They left a precedent with no record of how they had reasoned or on what points they had passed. This, and the unsteady decisions that ensued prior to 1862, were the adjudications which the Supreme Court

---

[83] Clapp v. County of Cedar, 5 Iowa 15.   [84] Supra, n. 34.

of the United States said had established the law which the federal courts would now enforce.

REACTION IN DUBUQUE

THE PEOPLE OF Dubuque accepted in good spirit the Supreme Court's decision in *Gelpcke*. The *Daily Times* reported: "When the news of the decision came, it went over the city like a plague, and created a great sensation. But the people soon became cool, and concluded to wait for further advices before getting very nervous over the matter." It foresaw a satisfactory compromise. The story was put under the buoyant headline, "We are Coming, We Dubuquers, $600,000 More."[85]

The town's Democratic daily, the *Herald*, reported that "a vast degree of interest was felt" in the decision, "and though it was expected yet it created a feeling of despondency . . . . But we apprehend no very serious results, and although it is a heavy burden yet it was incurred knowingly and willingly, and there is no doubt at all that means will be devised" for a settlement.[86]

The city was taking it in stride.

Three days later the *Herald* published a dispatch that had come by mail from its special correspondent in Washington. On January 11, the day the decision in *Gelpcke* was announced, he had written: "To-day the Supreme Court will decide two cases against your city. . . ." Evidently he wrote earlier in the day than the Court's announcement—yet he knew what was coming. (Actually there were three Gelpcke suits, on different debts.) This illustrates the unguarded way in which the Court's business was treated at that period.

The correspondent gave a partisan twist to the decision. He understood that the Court was going further than ever before "in ignoring the rights of State Courts to construe their own local constitutions and statutes." Continuing in that vein,

---

[85] Jan. 13, 1864. The editor was paraphrasing a patriotic song, then popular:

> We are coming, Father Abraham,
>   three hundred thousand more,
> From Mississippi's winding
>   stream and from New England's shore . . . .

The poem, written by James S. Gibbons, anti-slavery advocate, had first appeared in the *New York Evening Post* of July 16, 1862, in response to Lincoln's call for 300,000 volunteers, dated July 1.

The *Dubuque Times* was a sturdy Union paper, owned and edited by George T. Stewart, who had read law in Justice Swayne's office. Presently he referred to Swayne as "one of most eminent jurists, and purest patriots of the nation"—quoting from a letter in which Swayne hailed the prospect that an abolition amendment would be added to the Constitution. Apr. 24, 1864.

[86] Jan. 13, 1864.

This is what might naturally be expected. When State lines are being obliterated by the other departments, the Judiciary must be expected to sympathize.

The people will after awhile begin to feel the practical evils of consolidation. . . .

He told of other instances of the Government's oppression: the War Department had requisitioned a boarding house it really did not need; the privacy of a government clerk's home had been violated to found a charge of disloyalty. This was reported under the headings "The Decision in the Gelpcke Case—Dissent of Judge Miller—Trampling Down State Rights—Tyranny at the Capital."[87] The *Herald* was an intemperate journal that expressed violent and unreasoning anti-War sentiments.

The text of Justice Swayne's opinion was printed in the *Herald* of April 9—three months after the decision was rendered; Justice Miller's dissent appeared in the *Times* of April 21. In this period, newspapers commonly reacted on the basis of a very imperfect understanding of the Court's decision.

The City's debt to Gelpcke, and to the German bondholders he represented, was promptly compromised. The city turned over its shares in the Dubuque & Sioux City Railroad (successor after a receivership to the Dubuque & Pacific to which the bonds had been issued) and undertook a manageable payment in money.[88] Dubuque County made a similar arrangement.[89] "Thus a great incubus . . . has been removed. . . . Real estate . . . is worth twenty per cent. more to-day than it was yesterday," the *Times* reported, with praise for "the liberality and patience of Mr. Gelpcke."[90]

Dubuque's situation stands in marked contrast to many to come. Here was a commercial center, where men were sensitive about their city's reputation in business and financial circles. It might be quite otherwise in a rural setting. Here the railroad gave promise of success—an unusual feature.[91] When Dubuque came to terms with Gelpcke, interest was still a minor part of its indebtedness; where resistance ran on for

---

[87] Jan. 16, 1864.

[88] *Dubuque Times* and *Dubuque Herald*, May 7 and 8, 1864.

The Dubuque & Sioux City (soon to become part of the Illinois Central lines) was reporting earnings of more than 4 percent on its entire stock and debt; it had a valuable land grant; its prospects were good. *Dubuque Herald*, July 20, 1864. Its president, Platt Smith, was a lawyer, one of Gelpcke's counsel before the Supreme Court. The history of the road is traced in the *Herald* of July

12 and 13, 1870, the moment it had been completed to the Missouri River; also in Carlton J. Corliss, *Main Line of Mid-America, the Story of the Illinois Central*, (New York: Creative Age Press, 1950), 141–54.

[89] *Times*, May 3 and 7; *Herald*, May 3 and 7, July 20, 1864.

[90] May 3, 1864.

[91] Compare with Washington County, one hundred miles southwest; aid had been voted for the second and third divisions of the Mississippi & Missouri Railroad; "neither

years, interest commonly exceeded principal. Finally, Dubuque compromised only with Gelpcke and those he represented; about half of its debt remained to make trouble.[92]

OTHER LEADING CASES AT THAT MOMENT

CONTEMPORANEOUS WITH *Gelpcke* were three other decisions on railroad aid bonds: *Mercer County v. Hackett*,[93] *Von Hostrup v. Madison City*,[94] and *Meyer & Stucken v. City of Muscatine*.[95] Each had been brought in a federal court on the basis of diverse citizenship; each had waited on the Supreme Court docket through the two years which was then the normal delay. In each the municipality sought to evade payment on bonds issued in the early or middle 1850's; in each the Court applied the doctrine in *Aspinwall*[96] to reject complaints of irregularity and of fraud attending the issue. Such defenses would have had far greater merit had they been asserted by way of taxpayers' suits to prevent the bonds being issued in the first place.

William H. Y. Hackett (leading lawyer and banker, Presidential elector in 1864, and one of the wealthiest citizens of Portsmouth, New Hampshire) sued on bonds issued in aid of the Pittsburg & Erie, an enterprise that failed before any road was built. The county offered evidence to show gross fraud by the railroad in obtaining the bonds; also that they had been paid out to contractors and laborers at less than par value (contrary to the requirement by which the legislature sought to secure to the county its money's worth). Upon like allegations, the Supreme Court of Pennsylvania had granted the county an injunction as to bonds not already negotiated.[97] Against a bondholder suing in the federal court, however, such a defense was precluded by the *Aspinwall* doctrine protecting holders of negotiable instruments. But, Mercer County contended, these bonds are not negotiable: see *Diamond v. Lawrence County*,[98] where in 1860 our court held that railroad aid bonds were not governed by the law merchant. Woodward, J., had there observed that they were temporary, local in origin, not issued for ordinary municipal purposes, not arising out of the daily business of mankind. He had recalled "how recklessly railroad officers abused the overwrought confidence of the public, and what burdens of debt resulted

---

was ever built, yet our bonds were taken and sold, and we are called upon to pay them." D.C. Cloud, sometime Attorney General of Iowa. *Washington Gazette*, Dec. 17, 1869.
[92] *Dubuque Herald*, Jan. 14 and July 15, 1864.
[93] 1 Wall. 83 (1864).

[94] 1 Wall. 291 (1864).
[95] 1 Wall. 384 (1864).
[96] Supra, n. 49.
[97] Mercer County v. The Railroad, 27 Pa. St. 389 (1856).
[98] 37 Pa. St. 353, supra, at n. 38. Lawrence County was next south of Mercer, and their cases were similar.

to the people." He asked, "What then is equal justice both to purchasers and people . . . ?" and answered, "enforcement of the bond to the extent of the money it actually brought to the company, but no entanglements of communities in the meshes of commercial law."[99]

In this the Pennsylvania bench was unanimous. Of these five Judges, Woodward had concurred and another had dissented when the *Sharpless* case affirmed the permissibility of railroad aid, seven years earlier;[100] three, including William Strong, had come to the court since that time.

George Washington Woodward (1809–75) was a man of strong opinions and rugged speech. President Polk had nominated him for the Supreme Court in 1845, but some Democrats had joined the Whigs to defeat the appointment. Thereupon Robert C. Grier—like Woodward, then a judge on an inferior Pennsylvania court—was nominated and confirmed.

Now in *Mercer County v. Hackett* it was Justice Grier who spoke for the Supreme Court, declaring that it would not follow the State court's determination of the character of a Pennsylvania railroad aid bond. He said this was a matter to be governed by mercantile law, not by usages peculiar to any place. (In *Swift v. Tyson*[101] in 1842 the Court had declared that it would make an independent judgment on the rule to be applied in the case of what was unquestionably a negotiable instrument; here it was making an independent judgment on whether an instrument of this particular type was negotiable. But in this field the Court at that time did not pause to consider nice distinctions.) Grier— whose language could be as rough as Woodward's—said that "we doubt not the facts stated as to the atrocious frauds which have been practiced in some counties"; however, "the epidemic insanity of the people, the folly of county officers, the knavery of railroad 'speculators,' " could be considered only in a suit to enjoin before the bonds had been negotiated.

Justice Miller dissented without opinion.

In *Von Hostrup* the Court illustrated the liberality of its construction of municipal powers to aid railroads. Madison, Indiana, on the Ohio River, had authority to take stock for building a railroad "to said city." It issued bonds and took stock in a railroad distant by forty miles and more, which would run *to* an existing railroad that ran *to* Madison. Counsel, including Reverdy Johnson and Jeremiah S. Black, warned that such a fashion of building *to* Madison might bring great abuses. But Justice Nelson said the Court would not give the charter "a very narrow and strained construction" that "would defeat the manifest

---

[99] A constitutional amendment in 1857 had forbidden further issues. Supra, p. 929.

[100] Supra, pp. 927–28.
[101] Supra, n. 72.

object." In cases like this "something may be trusted to the wisdom and integrity, as well as the interest, of the body appointed to execute the power." Here the Court was treating the town fathers of Madison with an indulgence it might not have shown to the Congress.

Meyer & Stucken sued Muscatine on bonds issued for stock in the Mississippi & Missouri Railroad. The city's main defense had now been rejected in *Gelpcke v. Dubuque.* But Muscatine had another point: unlike Dubuque, it had no express authority to aid a railroad; it denied that power could be spelled out of the general provisions of its charter. There one found the grant of the usual municipal powers—as to schools, streets, fire protection, etc.—and then this clause: the city had power "to borrow money for any object in its discretion . . . ." As Justice Miller, dissenting, cogently observed, that could mean one or other of only two things: if the discretion was unlimited, then the council had permission to go into business, speculate in the market, or "organize mining companies in Colorado." That must be rejected. Then the only permissible view was that the borrowing must be confined to the execution of the specified municipal powers—and aid to a railroad was not among them.

Justice Swayne, for the majority, got over that difficulty in just two sentences. He eked out authority by citing a general statute of 1855 that fixed the interest to be paid where a railroad company received municipal bonds. But, Justice Miller replied, that statute should be read as applicable only to issues by cities and counties on which the power to aid railroads had been otherwise conferred. He said:

> To infer from this Act that the Legislature intended to make valid the bonds of the City of Muscatine, issued without any authority, is a stretch of fancy, only to be indulged in railroad bond cases . . . . Is this the language in which an Act of such importance, and affecting so many persons and so much property, would be framed? . . .

Surely if the house of Meyer & Stucken had consulted competent counsel before buying, it should have been advised that the law was *not* adequate to sustain the issue.

Of course the city on its side was restrained by no such prudent counsel when in 1855 it launched its bonds: no, it gave itself over to rejoicing at the advent of a railroad, with an oratorical display followed by a banquet where tables were loaded with pyramids of cake and twenty kinds of meat—"turkey, quail, chicken, venison, tongue, ham, beef, oysters . . . ."[102] That was a typical performance for such an occasion.

---

[102] William E. Hayes, *Iron Road to Empire. The History of the Rock Island Lines* (n.p., 1953), 38–39. The coming of the Mississippi & Missouri, later Chicago, Rock Island & Pacific, is narrated in this book; also in

XVII: *Municipal Bonds I*

The Supreme Court, Judge Dillon wrote in 1872, in respect of railroad aid bonds,

> has upheld and protected the rights of such creditors with a firm hand, disregarding, at times, it would seem, principles which it applied in other cases, and asserting the jurisdiction and authority of the federal courts with such striking energy and vigor as apparently, if not actually, to trench upon the lawful rights of the states and the acknowledged powers of the state tribunals; yet, upon the whole, there is little doubt that its course has had the approval of the profession in general and of the public, which neither appreciates nor cares for fine distinctions, and it will be well if it shall teach municipalities the lesson that if, having the power to do so, they issue negotiable securities, they cannot escape if these find their way into the hands of innocent purchasers.[103]

The *Aspinwall* decision had declared a special rule. *Gelpcke* introduced a very special rule. The *Von Hostrup* case illustrated how far the Court would lean away from a "narrow and strained construction" of a city charter. Muscatine was adjudged liable with never a thought that the extent of municipal powers was peculiarly a concern of the State or that the Supreme Court should display any deference in dealing with such legislation. Doubtless because in *Gelpcke*—the least forgotten of the bond cases—the State court had overthrown a precedent, the impression has persisted that throughout these decisions the Supreme Court was vindicating public honesty against the State courts' repudiation. Sometimes that feature was present, but often the Court was enforcing some much more advanced pretension.

POPULAR RESENTMENT: EXPERIENCE WITH THE MISSISSIPPI & MISSOURI

BEFORE GOING FURTHER with the judicial history of railroad aid in Iowa it will be useful to examine how that matter appeared to the people upon whom the Supreme Court's mandates were to be enforced. There is much one should know that can never be learned from the Reports. One reads, over and over, that evidence of fraud or of irregularities cannot be heard to defeat an innocent holder: one wonders what frauds, if any, there had been—how substantial were the irregularities?

Dwight L. Agnew's articles in the *Iowa Journal of History*: "Iowa's First Railroad," 48:1–26 (1950); "The Mississippi & Missouri Railroad, 1856–1860," 51:193 (1953); and "The Rock Island Railroad in Iowa," 52:203 (1953).

[103] *Treatise on the Law of Municipal Corporations* (Chicago: James Cockroft & Co., 1872), sec. 416.

Were communities the victims of deceit—or only of their own folly? A run over the line of the Mississippi & Missouri, with a visit to one among a dozen defiant counties, will enable one to hear what the people have to say.

In 1854 the Iowa legislature gave a charter to the Mississippi & Missouri Railroad Company, to build from Davenport (on the Mississippi) to Council Bluffs (on the Missouri River, opposite Omaha). The managers were substantially the same group who had succeeded in building the road from Chicago to Rock Island in less than two years. Now they proposed to carry the line right on across Iowa. Henry Farnam (1803–83), engineer, and his associate, Thomas Clark Durant (1820–85), daring promoter and speculator, were the real doers. John A. Dix (1798–1879), respected political and military personage, was named president. It was supposed that his influence would prove effective in obtaining land grants from Congress. The corporation made a contract with the partnership of Farnam & Durant whereby the latter would construct the road as far as Grinnell, 120 miles west of Davenport; municipal bonds passed to the partnership as a part of the consideration. (It was a common practice for the board of directors of a projected railroad to contract with a firm made up of their own leaders, who in consideration of bonds, stock, and land grants undertook to construct the road. This device later became notorious in the relations between the Union Pacific Railroad and the Credit Mobilier: the resources of the former were exhausted by diversion to the latter. By that time, Durant had abandoned the Mississippi & Missouri and had moved on to become vice president of the Union Pacific and president of the Credit Mobilier.[104])

---

[104] Of such an arrangement, Field, J., said in Wardell v. Union Pacific R.R., 103 U.S. 651 (1881), "It hardly requires argument to show that the scheme thus designed to enable the directors, who authorized the contract, to divide with the contractors large sums which should have been saved to the Company, was utterly indefensible and illegal. Those directors, constituting the executive committee of the board, were clothed with power to manage the affairs of the Company for the benefit of its stockholders and creditors. Their character as agents forbade the exercise of their powers for their own personal ends against the interest of the Company. . . . It is among the rudiments of the law that the same person cannot act for himself and at the same time, with respect to the same matter, as the agent for another, whose interests are conflicting. . . ."

A kindred abuse occurred when directors bought land along the projected line. For example, John F. Tracy (President of the Chicago, Rock Island & Pacific), Ebenezer Cook (Davenport banker, vice president of the Mississippi & Missouri and secretary of the C., R.I. & P.) and B. F. Allen (Des Moines banker, and like Tracy and Cook a member of the Executive Committee of the C., R.I. & P. board) in 1868 formed a company to purchase land necessary for the future use of the railroad. The facts are set out in Allen v. Withrow, 110 U.S. 119 (1884), where

Muscatine, on the river south and west of Davenport, was a new city which competed earnestly for a connection with the Mississippi & Missouri. In the outcome a *branch* line was started from Davenport, aimed via Muscatine toward Oskaloosa, a trading center on the Des Moines River, 120 miles south and west. On November 20, 1855, the first train to operate in Iowa made the run from Davenport to Muscatine. It was in consideration of this achievement that the city of Muscatine, about December 31, 1855, issued the bonds on which Meyer and Stucken later brought suit.

On December 31, 1855, the *main* line of the M. & M. reached Iowa City, fifty-five miles west of Davenport. A dead engine was pushed over shaky rails to win at the last minute the city's offer of $50,000 in bonds. This suggests the breathless expectancy that marked the coming of a railroad. Who cared about regularity in issuing bonds when such a race was on?

In 1856 Farnam built the first railroad bridge across the Mississippi, at Davenport, thus connecting the Chicago & Rock Island with the Mississippi & Missouri.[105]

Agents for the M. & M.—among them Hiram Price, its secretary, a Davenport banker and later Congressman—worked hard to drum up support along the projected line. Cities and counties subscribed to

---

plaintiff attempted to prove a trust by Tracy.

Much earlier, when the course of the M. & M. was being planned, Farnam had written to Durant, "I fear that notwithstanding Mr [Ebenezer] Cook told you they [Cook and another director] had no interest in lands along the line of the Road, that the moment we talk of changing a location he is on end in a twinkling." Letter of Aug. 7, 1856, in Leonard Collection, State University of Iowa Library, quoted in Agnew, "Iowa's First Railroad," note 102 above, 19.

B. F. Allen, mentioned above as a director of the C., R.I. & P., was in 1867 appointed receiver in a case pending in the federal Circuit Court for Iowa; in that capacity he converted to his own use railroad bonds among the trust funds. Of this one reads in Blennerhasset v. Sherman, 105 U.S. 110 (1882), where his attempt when insolvent to defraud his creditors was condemned and disallowed.

[105] The bridging of the Mississippi

led to litigation brought by steamboat interests based at St. Louis. In the federal Circuit Court for the Northern District of Illinois, a suit by owners of a steamboat that collided with a pier ended when a jury divided on the question whether the bridge had been shown to create an unreasonable obstruction to traffic by river. Abraham Lincoln appeared for the defendant railroad company. Beveridge, *Abraham Lincoln, 1809–1858*, 2 vols. (Boston and New York: Houghton Mifflin Co., 1928), I, 598–605.

Then in a suit in the federal court for Iowa, to abate the bridge as a public nuisance, Love, D.J., ordered the removal of so much of the bridge as lay on Iowa's side of the river; but the Supreme Court reversed and ordered the bill dismissed. Nelson, Wayne, and Clifford, J.J., dissented. Mississippi & Missouri R.R. v. Ward, 2 Bl. 485 (1863). Compare with Gilman v. Philadelphia, 3 Wall. 713 (1866), supra, p. 51.

$1,145,000 of the stock—[106] surely a formidable undertaking by a few prairie communities.

Much of the Iowa bond trouble was to arise right there, along the line of the M. & M., by reason of the managers' failure to perform their promises.

In large part these bonds were transferred to contractors or creditors;[107] Thomas C. Durant (a director in the M. & M.) and his kinsmen became large holders. Soon they will appear conspicuously as bona fide purchasers, suing the counties and cities that had issued the bonds to aid Durant's project—a project he mismanaged and then quit, unfinished. Small wonder that these suits were resisted bitterly.

Hard times came in 1857; construction slowed to a crawl. By 1858 the branch line through Muscatine was pushed another thirty-five miles to Washington, seat of the county of that name. There it stopped, leaving a resentment in communities that had voted aid for a branch that in promise was to run on to Oskaloosa. We shall return to Washington presently. Muscatine had voted some of its bonds for a division to run northwest to Cedar Rapids; that line was never built. The main line from Davenport via Iowa City reached Grinnell in 1862, fifty miles short of Des Moines, the new capital. Farnam dropped out. The management could not get ahead. Compare this with the prospects held out when the venture was launched: for example, the statement of President Dix in 1854 that the road would reach the Missouri River by the first of January, 1856.[108] When the managers failed in their undertakings, the cities and counties refused to pay on their bonds. By 1865, ten years after work began, the company had 183 miles of road with a bond debt of $40,000 per mile. In contrast, the Rock Island's 181 miles had been laid across Illinois in two years, at a cost of $25,000 per mile.[109] Durant and his associates, says the historian of the Rock Island lines, had given a "dismal performance for the people of Iowa who had placed their hopes and their fortunes in the Mississippi and Missouri."[110] The company became insolvent; in July 1866 the road was sold on foreclosure to the Chicago, Rock Island & Pacific, a new corporation which consolidated the road in Illinois with the unfinished line in Iowa.[111]

If one will run ahead to take one's stand at the month of May

---

[106] *Public Aids to Transportation.* Federal Coordinator of Transportation. Part II, 153 (1938).

[107] *Public Aids to Transportation,* cited above, shows that bonds for $687,000 were so transferred, while $203,000 in bonds went to raise $178,530 in cash. Disposition of the rest could not be traced.

[108] Morgan Dix, *Memoirs of John*

A. Dix, 2 vols. (New York: Harper and Brothers, 1883), I, 307.

[109] Hayes, *Iron Road to Empire,* 68.

[110] Ibid., 64.

[111] Stockholders — municipalities among them — were allowed sixteen cents on the dollar; even that fund, however, was subject to the claims of judgment creditors — the Durants among them — who held defaulted

1869, relevant events may be viewed in perspective. First, the Rock Island track reached Council Bluffs on the eleventh of that month— barely in time to avoid the forfeiture of a land grant. The M. & M. had had a contract with the Union Pacific that would have made it that road's eastern connection, had its track reached Council Bluffs in time to meet the needs of the U.P., building westward. That position, how- ever, had been won by the Chicago & North Western, which by leased lines had crossed the Mississippi on a bridge built at Clinton in 1865,[112] and had reached Council Bluffs in January 1867.

Second: on May 10, at Promontory Point—1,084 miles west of Omaha—the Union Pacific made its junction with the Central Pacific of California. Representing the U.P. at this triumphal moment was its vice president and general manager, Thomas C. Durant. The elation was not shared by the communities that had gone into debt to aid Durant's earlier venture: the great new transcontinental highway did not pass by their door.

Third: on May 15, in *Durant v. Washington County*[113] and related cases before the federal Circuit Court at Des Moines, Justice Miller "announced the decision . . . relative to county and city officials who failed to levy taxes to pay bonds. They must levy the tax and obey the order of the court or be placed in the custody of the Marshal until they agree to obey . . . ."[114] The contumacious officials represented cities and towns along the path of the M. & M. In the five years since *Gelpcke v. Dubuque*, the judicial conflicts of which Justice Miller there warned had indeed come to pass—as will presently be traced. By 1869 numerous communities, in southeastern Iowa as well as along the path of the M. & M., stood in organized defiance of the authority of the federal courts.

JAMES GRANT: FOREMOST AMONG BONDHOLDERS' COUNSEL

AN INCIDENT IN the story of that resistance is *Benbow v. Iowa City*.[115] The city had issued to the Mississippi & Missouri, on March 1, 1856, one hundred $500 bonds for twenty years, bearing 10 percent interest. After 1861 it made no payments. Benbow, a citizen of Indiana, owner of eleven bonds, sued in the federal court and in October 1864

---

municipal bonds to which the M. & M. had added its guaranty. Chicago, R.I. & P. R.R. v. Howard, 7 Wall. 392 (1869); In the Matters of Howard, 9 Wall. 175 (1870).

[112] The Clinton Bridge, Fed. Case No. 2900 (C.C.D. Ia. 1867); 10 Wall. 454 (1870).

[113] See Fed. Case No. 4191.

[114] *Washington* (Iowa) *Gazette*, May 21, 1869.

[115] 7 Wall. 313 (1869).

recovered a judgment for $2,276.90. A year later an alternative writ of mandamus was issued, commanding the mayor and aldermen to "levy a specific tax . . . sufficient to pay said judgment . . . and collect the said tax and pay the same, or to show cause to the contrary." In May 1866, return was made: respondents answered that they had levied a tax "sufficient in amount to pay the said judgment and . . . other claims" and had "duly certified said levy to the proper officers for collection." (That is, the mayor and aldermen answered with a generality that they had done all that was needed of them, and let it go at that—the rest pertained to others.) James Grant, counsel for Benbow, demurred. Justice Miller, holding the Circuit Court, heard argument by Grant against George W. McCrary and another and then, in an opinion not reported, held the return sufficient. A writ of error was taken, to bring that question to the Supreme Court.

James Grant (1812–91) should here be identified as the most masterful among bondholders' counsel.[116] A North Carolinian opposed to slavery, he had come to Chicago and practiced law from 1834 to 1838, when he moved to Davenport, Iowa. There he was elected to the legislature, to the constitutional convention, and to the office of district judge. Moreover he was a founder and the earliest president of the Chicago & Rock Island, whose projection into Iowa was the disappointing Mississippi & Missouri.[117] Grant's was an independent mind—alert, original, and idiosyncratic. This led him into a diversity of enterprises whereby he became wealthy. He had scholarly tastes, and enjoyed an excellent law library, which he made available to others.[118] Grant was devoted to material progress, as in the building of railroads; he was powerful in managing the interests of his many clients; and even by the standard of Western lawyers he was unusually forthright. In the *Benbow* case, it will appear, he went beyond the bounds and suffered a most unusual reproof from the Supreme Court.

Benbow v. Iowa City, as one reads in the Reports, resulted in a unanimous ruling that the mayor and aldermen had not been properly responsive in their return: they should have stated fully what had been done to obey the mandamus that a sufficient tax be laid, collected, and paid to this judgment creditor. The Court was not going to tolerate evasion by municipal officers in these bond cases.

But there had been an inward tension that the Reports did not even suggest. On the Court's Minutes for March 30, 1868, there stands this item: "Ordered by the Court that the brief filed by Counsel for the

---

[116] Dowd, "James Grant, a Model American," *Green Bag*, 21:556 (1909).
[117] Hayes, *Iron Road to Empire*, 1–32.

[118] As Judge Dillon acknowledged in dedicating the second volume of his Circuit Court Reports to Judge Grant.

plaintiff in error be stricken from the files & returned by the Clerk to him because of improper expressions contained in it." What lay behind this most unusual—perhaps unprecedented—order?

Benbow went on the docket on July 11, 1866, to await its turn on the calendar. On December 3 Grant's brief was received at the Clerk's office, although the rule required only that it be filed six days before the case was reached on the call.[119] On March 19, 1868—no appearance having been made for the City—Grant submitted the case on his written argument alone. Thereupon it was circulated to the Justices, who read it and then made the order set out above.

On December 24, 1868, *Benbow* was again submitted on a revised brief.

Fortunately the Clerk did not fail to file in the Court's library a copy of the offending production. It is set out below: italics are here added in order to identify the "improper" paragraphs; the revised argument consisted of no more than the second and third paragraphs of the original.

ARGUMENT

It must be apparent to this court, that the tribunal below, which made this judgment, is utterly "demoralized" on the subject of paying Iowa county and city, railroad bonds [italics added]:

Leaving out of consideration the formal objections to the return, that it is not sealed, signed, nor sworn to, it purports to obey the writ, and undertakes to say wherein it has obeyed it. The demurrer shows, as the strongest argument we can make, that the writ commanded a specific levy of a tax sufficient to pay this judgment, to collect said tax and to pay said judgment.

The return is, that the defendants "have levied a tax, not a specific tax, of one per cent," without saying on what amount of valuation, "sufficient to pay this judgment and other claims:" It does not state the amount or nature of such other claims, whether judgment or simple contract, whether for interest or other similar bonds, or for debts not entitled to this levy, under the ordinance, which authorized this debt: The mandate ordered a levy and collection of the tax; the return made six months after the date of the levy, does not aver a collection of the tax, but that the levy has been delivered to the proper officer to collect, who is he? The mandate is to collect and pay; the return is silent on these two clauses of the writ. It is no return.

We have probably no right to refer to an opinion below, which is not set out, but we may justly say, that the court below fills our way, in collecting these bond debts with obstacles. In all other causes,

---

[119] The print bears date of 1866, at the Daily Democrat Printing House. The *Daily Davenport Democrat* (whose editorial policy favored bond-holders) was described as "Shylock Grant's organ" by the *Muscatine Journal* (whose policy supported resistance), May 5, 1870.

we can get a writ in vacation. In mandamus cases the state court practice is not adopted and we must first make a demand after judgment; then we must await until the succeeding term, before we can get an alternative writ, which is a mere clerical duty; then the defendant is allowed until next term to answer; then the writ is mandatory only to one class of officers, and if any inferior officer under the Mayor and Alderman has any duty to perform, the court below holds, that another alternative writ and another return must be made as to him, and then, in spite of repeated decisions here, if every possible point is not covered by an exact adjudication precisely in point, the decision is against us, and we have to come here and when in this court, we must tarry two or three years for a decision.

It is time that this matter was ended. We hope, we have cases enough here now to determine all possible points, which can be made to evade the payment of these debts; and we hope that we may have these questions settled, so as to trouble this court no more with them.
[Italics added.]

GRANT, for Plaintiff in Error.

The Clerk returned the original brief as directed, and presently received this acknowledgement:

Davenport, 11 April 1868

To D. W. Middleton Esq
   Washington D C.
Dear Sir
   I have received the order of the court in the case of Benbow v Iowa City.
   I have already apologized to Judge Miller & will certainly do so to the court, and if I ever have the good fortune to get through this difficulty without broken shins, will tell you a good story.
               Your Obt Svt

James Grant[120]

He did get through and, as has been seen, won his point.

When this sensation first broke on the members of the Court, Justice Miller wrote to Grant substantially as follows:

Washington D C
March 29 1868

Hon. James Grant,
   Dear Sir
   You will receive from the Clerk of the Supreme Court in a day or two an order of the Court in the case of the United States at the relation of Benbow v. The Mayor and Aldermen of Iowa City.
   I wish to say to you now in reference to that order, that it was

---

[120] Letter in the file of papers in | Benbow v. Iowa City, in the National Archives.

not made at my suggestion, or request. It was the spontaneous action of the other members of the Court.

I cannot refrain however from expressing to you the surprise and the pain which I felt when I read the brief, and I am induced to write you this letter, in the hope that it may turn out that you were not aware of the contents of the brief, or that you could not for some reason have fully comprehended the force of the language used.

But for this hope, self respect would forbid me take any notice of remarks which every member of the Court considered to be discourteous and offensive.

The record shows that I was the court of which you speak as being "demoralized," and as "filling your way in collecting these bond debts with obstacles."

I say that the brief filled me with surprise. If there is any member of the bar of my entire circuit outside of my own city, for whom I entertained stronger feelings of respect, and friendship than yourself, I do not know it, and it has been a pleasure to me to believe, as I think I had a right to do, from all your intercourse with me, that this feeling was in some measure reciprocated.

You can well imagine then what must be my surprise and regret to find in a brief filed in this Court in your name, language used in a public manner open to all the world, of a character so offensive in reference to my judicial conduct, that no Judge remembers any thing so discourteous in this Court.

It has been my pride that in a judicial service of now near to six years, I have never had the slightest ill feeling with counsel, nor has any reproach affecting my honor as a judge before this, ever come to my hearing. I must leave my personal and official character to make the only reply that I shall ever make to the charges of your brief; but I could not in view of our relations to each other omit to call your attention to this matter.

In the meantime I have the honor to be
very respectfully yr obed servt
Sam. F. Miller[121]

The terms of Grant's apology are not known. Presumably it reached Justice Miller at Little Rock, where he had gone to hold the Circuit Court after the Supreme Court adjourned on April 6. On May 15 Grant, attending the Circuit Court at Des Moines, sent this letter to Justice Miller by the hand of District Judge Love:

Dear Judge,

I received your kind note on Saturday [May 9] & should have answered it, but expected to see you here.[122]

I am much obliged to you for your acceptance of my apology

---

[121] Justice Miller's draft copy, in author's possession.

[122] After Little Rock the Justice had next held court at Topeka.

and I should regard it as a great calamity of my life, to lose your friendship & esteem.[123]

He went on to bespeak the Justice's attention to a chancery suit that would probably soon be brought; his clients would wish it to be heard by the Justice as well as by Judge Love, sitting at chambers.

DIALOGUE IN A DISAPPOINTED COMMUNITY

WASHINGTON COUNTY—ALREADY introduced as one against which Thomas C. Durant recovered a judgment[124]—was slow to yield to the federal court. When at last on September 10, 1869, the supervisors were in the course of levying a tax to satisfy the judgments in favor of Durant and others, the sheriff arrested them for contempt of the State District Court, which had enjoined the levy. Then District Judge Love, in the federal Circuit Court, directed the United States District Attorney to bring habeas corpus proceedings. The writ issued; the supervisors were brought before the federal court, and discharged from State custody. (The court, it appears, was acting under a statute passed to meet South Carolina's attempted Nullification.[125]) They were sent home with a stern admonition that the decree of the Supreme Court must be obeyed. The board of supervisors then levied the tax.[126]

Excitement led to recrimination: Who was to blame for the county ever getting into this predicament? Here is the story that emerged—the narrative of a typical situation.[127]

At an election on August 7, 1854, the people had voted to take $50,000 in M. & M. stock, delivery of bonds to be only "as fast as the work progresses towards completion within the limits of said county." (Note how vague the definition.) On March 1, 1858, after a sharp con-

---

[123] Letter in author's possession. Writing on February 12, 1871, to his brother-in-law, Ballinger, Miller commented, "Grant is a man of great energy, and great reputation, but of hasty and crude judgment." This was apropos of Galveston, Houston & Henderson R.R. v. Cowdrey, 11 Wall 459 (1871), wherein Ballinger and Grant were on opposing sides.

[124] Supra, p. 951. It lies next south of that in which Iowa City is located.

[125] Act of Mar. 2, 1833, which extended the benefit of the writ to cases where one was detained "for any act done, or omitted to be done, in pursuance of a law of the United States, or any order, process, or decree, of

any judge or court thereof . . . ." 4 Stat. 634.

[126] Statement derived from *Washington* (Iowa) *Gazette*, Sept. 24 and Oct. 29, 1869; *Washington County Press*, as quoted in the *Muscatine Journal*, Sept. 23, Oct. 21 and 29; *Burlington Hawk-Eye*, Sept. 19; *Keokuk Gate City*, Oct. 8.

Prior to the time Judge Love acted, the Supreme Court of Iowa had abandoned the effort to defeat the process of the federal courts. *Ex parte* Holman, 28 Iowa 88, decided Oct. 11, 1869. Infra, p. 972.

[127] *Washington Gazette*, Dec. 24, 1869. The quotations that follow are from this source.

test, the people voted an additional subscription of $100,000, delivery of bonds being "conditioned that said road be completed and in good running order to the town of Washington . . . by the first day of September, 1868 . . . ." The railroad management kept demanding bonds; the County Judge[128] kept refusing, on the ground that the work had not progressed well enough to meet the conditions, and on the further ground that the company was asserting a claim to hold the shares as security until the bonds were paid.

> This [refusal by the County Judge] resulted in one of the largest indignation meetings ever held in the county, held on one of the worst days of that winter; the court room was packed full. The Judge was called on for a statement of facts, which was given by him as above. . . . On taking his seat, he was beset by a torrent of abuse by a score or more present, but the better judgment of some on the other side was finally heard and after a debate lasting four or five hours, the meeting adopted by a small majority a resolution endorsing the position of the Judge. . . . Finally, the railroad Co., in May, 1858, yielded all points contended for by the Judge. . . .

In June and July, 1858, the Judge, being satisfied that conditions had been met, delivered the bonds and received the stock.

When one reflects on the usages of a pioneer community—how informal and close to the people was its administration—one understands how fragile was the restraint of legality when both promoters and public were impatient to have something done. And once the bonds were negotiated, the doctrine of the *Aspinwall* case cut off any defense of fraud or irregularity.

In the dialogue over Washington County's indebtedness one hears the common rationalizations. A conservative lawyer and officer of the local insurance company chides the "repudiators": consider, he says, your condition before the railroad came. "Here you were in the wilderness, forty miles from the river, with no communication but teaming . . . . You had no money to build the road. . . . A large majority of the people said *borrow* the money. Pledge, or allow the railroad company to borrow on the *honor* and *credit* of the county. It was done . . . . This alone is what secured the road. The people have had the benefit of it for twelve years; it has doubled, tripled, quadrupled the value of their property and business. . . ." Let us, he said, pen up in the pillory the demagogue—"so officious and loud-mouthed"—who had led the people into this mischief and dishonor. A debt of $150,000 had, through default, grown to $300,000; the opportunity for an advan-

---

[128] This officer was the governing authority of a county until, by the Code of 1860, the Board of Supervisors was established.

tageous compromise had been lost; and the people had been "wantonly fleeced" out of thousands more in fees to attorneys. "After long, fruitless, and most expensive resistance" it was plain that the only way out was to pay the debt.[129]

But then from Dutch Creek township, on the western edge of the county, came a rustic retort. The railroad was the adventure of the company, not of the community: "they wanted US to help THEM with OUR county bonds to build THEIR road, and the income is theirs." Further, the bonds had been obtained by false pretenses:

> In order to secure a majority, they sent their private emissaries chiefly in the western part of the county and to make the promise through them that the road would be built right along, to Oskaloosa and Ft. Des Moines. It was this promise that induced the voters in the western part of the county to cast their vote in favor of it. Have they carried out that promise? No . . . . Without that promise they never would have got a majority . . . and that promise was a pretense. . . .[130]

Back at the county seat, the chairman of the Board of Supervisors, a banker, pointed out that the courts had been just as open to enjoin the contracting of the debt at the beginning as they were now to enjoin payment; he asked,

> why should honest men let a road be finished, . . . and our land increased in value . . . , and then come in and sue out an injunction and lead the people to believe that somebody has been acting the rogue, when the worst that can be said is that our partner was too sharp for us, or was dishonest and squandered our interest . . . .[131]

TRIBUNE OF THE PEOPLE

THE POPULAR CASE for avoiding the bonds, as set forth in 1869 by one of its foremost advocates, D. C. Cloud of Muscatine, made two points. First, most of the bonds were purchased prior to the publication, in 1858, of the majority opinion stating reasons for the judgment in 1853 in favor of the Dubuque & Pacific Railroad Company.[132] So purchasers acted upon what they had *heard*: they "did not act upon any knowledge derived from an adjudication . . . ; in other words, [so he argued] they were not 'innocent purchasers.' "[133]

---

[129] *Washington Gazette*, Jan. 7, 1870.
[130] Ibid., Jan. 28, 1870.
[131] Ibid., Feb. 4, 1870.
[132] Supra, p. 940.
[133] Letter of Dec. 7, 1869, to the

Chicago Post, reprinted in the *Muscatine Journal*, Dec. 13, and in the *Washington Gazette*, Dec. 17, 1869. It was an extended statement, aimed at counteracting the unfavorable comments in the Chicago press.

Second, the people were "swindled." For example,

Louisa county subscribed $100,000 stock to the "Philadelphia, Fort Wayne and Platte River Railroad Company," in 1856, at a time when the nearest point upon which any work was being done on said road was at least 200 miles distant. Yet in order to get possession of the bonds of this county, the company began work in the county, called for and got the full amount, suspended work, and until the present time have done nothing on the road. They disposed of the bonds for a small consideration (some as low as 23 cents on the dollar,) and the county got nothing for them. The railroad company guaranteed the payment of the principal and interest of the bonds, and put the proceeds in their pockets.

The truth as to the inept handling of the *Dubuque & Pacific* case in 1853 was that the *judgment* (although not the majority *opinion*) was then duly recorded, and it was notorious that it involved a holding that county railroad aid was permissible. The proceeding, to be sure, had been friendly and ill-contested. *But D. C. Cloud was at that moment the Attorney General of Iowa; if, as he later asserted, "most all those people who pretended to any legal knowledge contended that such power did not exist," why did he not at that time appear as friend of the court to assert and defend those limitations that might be derived from the Iowa constitution and statutes?* It was in 1853 (when it would have been most unpopular), rather than in 1869, that that voice was needed.

As to swindling: a few months later Cloud, as counsel for Muscatine and Louisa counties, had occasion to make the most of it when he asked Justice Miller, in chambers, to enjoin the collection of taxes to pay judgments on railroad aid bonds. And that judge—as well disposed to the popular cause as any judge ought to be—made this rigorous response:

it may well be doubted whether the bill shows any fraud or failure of consideration which should be a defence to the bonds either in law or equity. When the allegations are examined closely they seem to amount to [no] more than a failure of the railroad company to which the bonds were first issued, to comply with certain promises made at the time of the transaction.

If, however, they could be held sufficient as allegations of fraud or failure of consideration, there are two very sufficient answers to them in this application.

1. They are no defence to the bonds in the hands of innocent holders.

2. They were proper defences, if good at all, to the action in

which the judgments were rendered, and cannot be set up against the enforcement of these judgments now.[134]

"Failure of the railroad company . . . to comply with certain promises . . .": pretty generally, it appears, this is the substance of what was popularly denounced as "fraud." Judge Dillon wrote:

> The misrepresentations which have oftentimes induced the issue of the bonds, and the disappointment arising from the over-estimated benefits of the roads to the localities which aided their construction, make the attempts to avoid payment of the bonds not unnatural, and more excusable than they would otherwise be. . . .[135]

Bribery of county officers is commonly suggested by the facts, and doubtless was not infrequently practiced. Instances have been authenticated.[136] (It may be added that improper influencing of State legislators, to procure what the railroads wanted, is spoken of in the press as a commonplace.)

LEE COUNTY ENCOUNTERS THE FEDERAL JUDICIARY

COMING NOW TO the judicial history of railroad aid in Iowa, this can best be traced by keeping Lee County most particularly in view. It was deepest in debt, and deepest too in the struggle with the federal judiciary.

Lee County lies in the southeast corner of the state, a wedge between the Mississippi and the Des Moines rivers. Its chief city, Keokuk, was important and aspiring. In 1856 the county voted—2537 to 937—to subscribe $150,000 to each of three railroads and to issue bonds therefor. (Moreover, the city of Keokuk voted a like provision for two of those projects.) The venture proved largely a disappointment. The line from Keokuk up the Des Moines valley performed a useful function; by 1866 it had covered the 162 miles to Des Moines. After a foreclosure it became part of the Rock Island lines. The second project, running north from Keokuk, made the 25 miles to Fort Madison, the county seat, and there it stopped. In 1869 it was acquired

---

[134] Muscatine v. Mississippi & Missouri R.R. *et al*, Fed. Case No. 9971 (Sept. 1870). The word *no*, inserted in the quotation, is necessary to make sense in the context; obviously it was intended by Justice Miller.

[135] *Municipal Corporations*, sec. 416a, second ed., (New York: James Cockroft Co., 1873).

[136] For example, Smith v. Sac County, 11 Wall. 139 (1871); Cass County v. Green, 66 Mo. 498 (1878).

by the Chicago, Burlington & Quincy as a feeder.[137] A third, to run west from Fort Madison, proved a total disappointment.[138]

At the outset, Francis Semple entered upon what turned out to be a career of opposition. (The United States Marshal's levy on his mule, fourteen years later, became a memorable incident in the long struggle.) On behalf of dissenting taxpayers, Semple sued to enjoin, and won a judgment that the mode of submission had been illegal.[139] Promptly the legislature passed a Curative Act—responding, let it be noted, to the pressure of "scores" of leading citizens from Lee and other counties.[140] A challenge to this new statute was rebuffed.[141] Thereupon the bonds were issued.[142] In vainest hope, the matter was carried to the Supreme Court of the United States, on the fantastic contention that there was a contract between the State and its citizens, embodied in the State constitution, which had been impaired by the legislature. This was dismissed for want of jurisdiction.[143] Then, in July 1860, a third effort was begun to enjoin the levy of a tax; this culminated successfully in a decision by the State Supreme Court on October 18, 1862—wherein the decision in *Wapello*, four months previously, was affirmed and applied.[144] Elsewhere municipal officers were similarly enjoined. Thereafter boards of supervisors and city coun-

---

[137] *Keokuk Gate City*, Mar. 13, 1869; *Burlington Hawk-Eye*, Mar. 13 to 18, 1869.

[138] *Keokuk Constitution*, Dec. 21 and 28, 1869.

[139] McMillan v. Lee County, 3 Iowa 311 (1856). The three projects had been tied together, so that each would fail unless all were carried.

[140] *Keokuk Gate City*, Oct. 6, 1869.

[141] McMillen [*sic*] v. Boyles, County Judge, 6 Iowa 304 and 391 (1858). Filing an elaborate brief to sustain validity was Joseph M. Beck —who eleven years later, as Judge of the Iowa Supreme Court, played a colorful part in attempting to defeat enforcement of the bonds in the federal court. Infra, pp. 968–69.

[142] Lee County v. Rogers, 7 Wall. 181 (1869).

[143] The Court's Minutes show this disposition, per Taney, C.J., on April 30, 1860. In Semple's brief in Thomson v. Lee County, 3 Wall. 327 (1866), he related this effort and said that dismissal was "on the ground that the contract impaired was politi-

cal only, and not within the [Contract Clause] which was held to apply to pecuniary contracts only." Brief for Defendant in Error, 20. Perhaps the Chief Justice made some such explanation orally when the case was dismissed.

[144] McMillan v. Boyles *et al.*, 14 Iowa 107, per Lowe, J.

Ralph P. Lowe (1805–83), ex-Governor and now Judge, had been spokesman for the court in *Wapello*, writing a strong and carefully reasoned opinion to hold that it violated the State constitution to tax a citizen to contribute to a railroad, in that case under a statute authorizing counties to take stock.

Yet in Hanson v. Vernon, 27 Iowa 28 (1869), where a new statute authorized townships and incorporated towns and cities to aid the construction of a railroad by taxation to make an outright gift, Lowe, now back at the bar, was leading counsel for the defense of this form of aid. Infra, p. 978.

cils, barricaded behind injunctions, refused to levy taxes to pay on railroad aid bonds.

The second case of *Knox County v. Aspinwall*,[145] in 1861, had established that a federal court should grant mandamus where that was necessary to compel taxation to satisfy its judgments. Circuit Courts had acted accordingly.[146] Now numerous holders of Iowa municipal bonds claimed that remedy. But here a new feature was present: the Iowa courts had already issued injunctions not to levy such a tax. And it is a principle of wide application among courts of concurrent authority, that the jurisdiction that first attaches will not be disturbed. At base, certainly it was competent for the Supreme Court of Iowa to restrain Iowa municipal authorities from levying a tax for what was held to be an illegal object. The Supreme Court of the United States had never held that the *Wapello* decision infringed the federal Constitution or laws—it had held only that the federal courts would not follow it. Now would federal courts respect the Iowa injunctions—or would they, on the contrary, order supervisors and councilmen to levy taxes notwithstanding that the State court had forbidden them to do so? Federal and State judges might find themselves competing at battledore and shuttlecock.

That issue came before two Circuit Courts. Inasmuch as Justice Miller resided in Keokuk, and District Judge James M. Love was also a resident of Lee County, they were "interested" within the meaning of a statute of 1839, which directed that in such a situation the Judges would certify the suit "to the most convenient court in the next adjoining State . . . ."[147] Accordingly cases involving Lee County or Keokuk were transferred to the Northern District of Illinois, where they came before Justice Davis and District Judge Thomas Drummond.[148] The same issue, in cases arising elsewhere—notably where municipalities had aided the Mississippi & Missouri—was heard in the Circuit Court for the District of Iowa. Both courts declined to issue a peremptory man-

---

[145] 24 How. 376, supra, p. 933.

[146] *High on Extraordinary Legal Remedies,* second ed., (Chicago: Callaghan and Co., 1884), at sec. 394, observed that "The jurisdiction by mandamus in this class of cases [*i.e.,* to enforce payment of judgments on municipal bonds] has been more frequently exercised in the federal than in the state tribunals. And while doubts have been expressed as to the power of the circuit courts of the United States to issue the writ of mandamus to municipal officers, com-

manding them to levy a tax in payment of judgments upon municipal obligations, the right is now clearly established, both upon principle and authority."

[147] 5 Stat. 322.

[148] United States *ex rel.* Moses v. City Council of Keokuk, 6 Wall. 514 (1868); United States *ex rel.* Thomson v. Keokuk, 6 Wall. 518 (1868); Board of Supervisors of Lee County v. United States *ex rel.* Rogers, 7 Wall. 175 (1869).

damus where the return set up the State court's injunction. The bondholders took their suits to the Supreme Court.

As reported in the press, "The bar generally says it is the first
time in the history of the Court that such a question of conflict has
occurred, and look with a good deal of interest to its determination."[149]

FEDERAL COURT MANDAMUS AND STATE COURT INJUNCTION

THE LEADING CASE is *Riggs v. Johnson County*, decided January
13, 1868.[150] (Here the bonds had been issued in 1853 to the Lyons
Iowa Central Railroad, projected to run from Lyons on the Mississippi
River to Council Bluffs; later the plan was changed to take it instead
through Cedar Rapids, in the county north of Johnson. The transaction
was regarded as "an unmitigated swindle."[151]) James Grant represented
the bondholders. Opposing were Henry Strong, well trained and able
lawyer from Keokuk; Orville H. Browning of Quincy, Illinois, then the
Secretary of the Interior; and the venerable Thomas Ewing of Ohio, old
as the Supreme Court itself. Could it be said that the jurisdiction of the
federal court continued, after it had reached judgment, until that judgment had been satisfied—that mandamus was simply a further step in
the original proceeding, and would not be controlled by the consideration that a State court had enjoined? Or, taking a technical view, should
one reason that an application for mandamus was a new proceeding;
that here it had been commenced after the State court had acted; and
that the federal court, out of respect for the State court, should decline to
award this additional remedy? The majority, speaking through Justice
Clifford, took the larger view: mandamus was essential to the exercise of
federal jurisdiction, and no State process could bar the way. Justice
Miller wrote a dissenting opinion, in whose conclusions Chase, C.J., and
Grier, J., concurred.[152]

---

[149] Washington dispatch of Dec. 17, 1867, to the *Chicago Tribune*, re-printed in *Keokuk Gate City*, Dec. 24, 1867.

[150] 6 Wall. 166. United States *ex rel.* Thomson v. Henry County, 6 Wall. 210, coming from the Circuit Court for the Northern District of Illinois, was decided on the same day. Walkley v. Muscatine, 6 Wall. 481; Moses v. Keokuk, 6 Wall. 514; and Thomson v. Keokuk, 6 Wall. 518, were decided on April 6, 1868.

Numerous suits in the courts be-low were governed by the *Riggs* case.

[151] *Iowa City Republican*, reprinted in the *Muscatine Journal*, Aug. 19, 1869.

[152] In 1870, in Supervisors of Wash-ington County v. Durant, 9 Wall. 415, the Court declared that it was "im-material whether the injunction of the [State] court was before or after the judgment obtained by the relator in the Circuit Court of the United States, or whether before or after the

But when the writ issued, if municipal officers obeyed, would they not be punishable by the State court? Such resistance was not to be expected, said Justice Clifford; in any event, the federal courts had statutory authority to release on habeas corpus.

One's eye may be arrested at the spectacle of Clifford, sturdy old Democrat, boldly advancing the national flag, while Miller, the Republican, would yield ground to the State courts.[153] Occasionally considerations present in a particular situation—especially economic considerations—prove more compelling than the general tendency of a judge's mode of thought. Municipal bond cases were a very special category.

The resisters had only begun to fight. In Lee County, whose experience was typical, "anti-bond" meetings were held. Lawyer-politicians came to argue what the crowds now wanted to hear: that the bonds were invalid and a fraud upon the people. Resolutions were adopted: the State judges were praised "for their manly, dignified and unswerving position"; Congress should curb the powers of the federal judiciary; the board of supervisors should abandon its proposal to compromise, and should fight to win. The mass meeting pledged to indemnify supervisors for any damage.[154] (On these occasions people were very brave about urging their officers to go to jail.) The board changed its position to comply.[155] (In Keokuk, where more responsible urban thinking prevailed, the city council set about effecting a compromise.[156])

When the Circuit Courts acted in pursuance of the *Riggs* decision, local boards very generally persisted in refusing to levy a tax. On behalf of judgment creditors of Lee County, James Grant asked the court for Northern Illinois to apply two remedies: proceed against the supervisors for contempt, and appoint the federal Marshal for Iowa a receiver to levy and collect a tax to pay the judgments. Justice Davis answered that the bondholders severally might have either, but not

---

institution of the suit. It is not a question which court first obtained possession of the case." Mayor &c of Davenport v. Lord, 9 Wall. 409, had been to that effect. Cf. Hollman v. Fulton, per Beck, J., infra, n. 181.

[153] Contrast, at that same time, Crandall v. Nevada, 6 Wall. 35, p. 1302; also Provident Institution for Savings v. Massachusetts, 6 Wall. 611, supra, pp. 49–50, where Miller dissented.

[154] For example, *Keokuk Gate City*,

Aug. 20, 1868; also Mar. 4 and 11, June 20, July 8. Also *Keokuk Constitution*, Feb. 2, Mar. 18, 1868.

[155] *Gate City*, Sept. 15, Oct. 4, 1868.

[156] *Gate City*, June 10 and 24, July 15 and 23, Sept. 30, Oct. 7, 1868. The vote, on July 1, was 332 for compromise, 23 against: an exceedingly light vote for a city of 12,500 population. The election "elicited scarcely any interest, as but few persons were opposed to it." *Keokuk Constitution*, July 2, 1868.

both. On behalf of certain litigants, the appointment of a receiver was elected.[157] Here the case to watch is that of Evans Rogers. Other bondholders were allowed a writ of attachment to bring the supervisors before the court at Chicago to answer for their contempt. The leader among these bondholders was J. Edgar Thomson.[158]

The Circuit Court for Iowa, however, would do no more than proceed against the municipal officers to compel them to perform their duty. The court, said Justice Miller, was not and could not properly be authorized itself to levy a tax; that was "a function peculiarly and exclusively legislative."[159]

Thus the bondholders' advance had two prongs. Lee County carried to the Supreme Court the question in Evans Rogers' case. The answer came promptly. Under the Court's rule 20, if counsel on both sides chose at the outset to submit on printed briefs, foregoing oral argument, the Court would decide "without regard to the number of the case on the docket." Filed on January 6 and submitted on February 11, the *Evans Rogers* case was decided on March 1, 1869: the action of the Circuit Court for Northern Illinois was affirmed.[160]

The problem was somewhat delicate, and continued to be troublesome; its essentials should be explained. By the Process Act of 1828, as extended to Iowa, the power of a federal court in respect of final process was measured by what the State had established for its own courts.[161] The Iowa Code, under "Action of Mandamus," provided that "The court may . . . direct that the act required to be done may be done by . . . some . . . person appointed by the court . . . ."[162] On the basis of this provision of Iowa law, the Supreme Court concluded, the Circuit Court for Northern Illinois had authority for appointing the United States Marshal for Iowa to levy and collect a tax

---

[157] The *Gate City* of October 10, 1868, reported the argument on the sixth and the court's decision on the seventh.

[158] United States *ex rel.* Thompson v. Lee County, Fed. Case No. 15,589 (Jan. 1869). Thomson's name was commonly misspelled.

[159] Rusch v. Des Moines County, Fed. Case No. 12,142 (Oct. 1868).

[160] Supervisors v. Rogers, 7 Wall. 175. Justice Miller took no part.

The counties of Des Moines, Henry, and Louisa, being interested in the same question, joined in paying counsel's fee. Proceedings of Lee County Board of Supervisors, Jan. 9, 1869, reported in the *Gate City*, Jan.

16, 1869.

[161] United States *ex rel.* Moses v. Keokuk, 6 Wall. 514 (1868).

[162] Sec. 3770, Revised Code of 1860. As Justice Miller explained in Rusch v. Des Moines County, Fed. Case No. 12,142 (October term, 1868), the function of mandamus had been expanded by the codifiers of 1860. Although the provision quoted has been perpetuated, it is significant that the Iowa Code Annotated cites no case where it has been construed or applied, while Shepard's Iowa Citations points to nothing besides the federal cases cited in this and the next chapter. Infra, p. 1039.

in Lee County.[163] Subsequently, where in other States—that peculiar enactment being absent—judgment creditors asked to have an appointee sent in to collect what was due, the Supreme Court rejected the claim.[164]

While the *Evans Rogers* maneuver was going on, supervisors watched apprehensively on the field of battle immediately before them: What now would the federal courts do to them for their defiance? At this juncture their courage was braced by the Iowa Supreme Court. In a bond case there—an appeal by Durant and others in their struggle with Washington County—Judge Beck's opinion for the court reviewed the entire matter, and reasserted that *Wapello* was right and *Gelpcke* was wrong.[165] The State Court—so people allowed themselves to believe—would give firm support to the supervisors.

In January 1869, at the suit of J. Edgar Thomson, Judge Drummond at Chicago granted an attachment against the Lee County supervisors (save one who had voted against resistance).[166] Plaintiff, it was recalled, had recovered judgment in 1864; unable to get execution, he had obtained an alternative writ of mandamus in July 1868; when that was ignored, a peremptory writ had been granted; now that was defied, the supervisors contending that the State court's injunction was of higher obligation than the judgment of the Supreme Court of the United States. Such a view, said Judge Drummond, "was exploded by the issue of the late Rebellion." That thrust cut deep.

NEWSPAPER COMMENT ON THE JUDICIAL CONFLICT

THE *Chicago Tribune* hastened to declare that

> Judge Drummond's decision is clearly in the pathway of law and order and in the interests of commercial morality. Now if the authorities of Iowa shall do so foolish a thing as to offer resistance to the decree, it will be the bounden duty of the executive branch of the government to employ force to execute it, and as much force as may be necessary. In such a conflict, all the moral and material energies of thirty-six States will be arrayed on the side represented by Judge Drummond, which is simply the side of law, as interpreted by its authorized tribunals.[167]

---

[163] Without specific mention, this rejected the reasoning by which Justice Miller had found the section of the Code inapplicable.

[164] Infra, p. 1041.

[165] McClure v. Owen, 26 Iowa 243,

decided Dec. 17, 1868.

[166] United States *ex rel.* Thompson v. Lee County, Fed. Case No. 15,589. Supra, p. 965.

[167] Jan. 12, 1869. At the same time the text of Judge Drummond's opin-

The *Chicago Post*, more gently, conceded that many excellent citizens of Iowa conscientiously believed they were resisting injustice; "their idea is to fight the matter along in the courts, and thus somehow to get a reversal of the rulings of the Supreme Court of the United States." That hope, said the *Post*, was futile; "we beg to assure them that those who teach otherwise are not their friends, but their practical enemies."[168]

In Keokuk, at the center of the storm, the *Gate City* commented that "outside parties, especially the Chicago papers, are prodigal of advice and counsel . . . ." If no forcible resistance was made—and certainly none was contemplated—"we are equally certain that the Federal Government will not interfere to enforce the decisions of its courts . . . ." Hopefully it concluded, "the whole matter will resolve itself into a technicality of jurisdiction," to be settled amicably; "and our word for it, our State Supreme Court will be allowed to have its own way."[169] Ardently Radical, the *Gate City* had been fulminating against the Southerners who had rebelled against the national authority; now it was disturbed at the suggestion that Iowans were being led into a like sin. Its publisher, James B. Howell (1816–80), a lawyer turned editor, had been an early and advanced Republican, and a bitter critic of Johnson's reconstruction policy; in 1870 the legislature elected him to the Senate for an unexpired term. The *Keokuk Constitution*, Democratic and free from such taint of inconsistency, warned anew of "the encroachment of federal power upon the reserved rights of the states," "so numerous and flagrant since the radical party has been in power." "If our state Judges now back down, and permit our County Supervisors to be arrested and carried beyond the state to be punished by a Federal Judge for obeying the mandate of the Supreme Court of Iowa . . . , they will be guilty of an act of . . . cowardice . . . ."[170]

Elsewhere in Iowa the press was divided. Some newspapers took the line that regardless of the moral and legal case against the bonds, the time had come when the boards of supervisors ought to yield. "The question has been fairly decided against them by the highest court known to our law," said the *Davenport Gazette*. "The whole power of

---

ion was set out in full. On January 13 a long editorial pursued the theme.

It was greatly to the interest of Chicago as a rail center that tributary projects in Iowa be supported and completed. In an article on "Iowa East and West Railways" on March 10, 1869, the *Tribune* detailed the flourishing condition of five such roads.

The *Tribune*'s comment of January 12 was reprinted in the *Keokuk Gate City* of the fourteenth.

[168] Quoted in *Keokuk Gate City*, Jan. 22, 1869.

[169] Jan. 22, 1869.

[170] Jan. 16, 1869.

the Federal Government can be, and will be invoked in aid of the court."[171] Said the *Burlington Hawk-Eye*,

> Iowa, having shed much of her best blood to establish the supreme authority of the general Government, and to explode the baneful doctrine of "State-rights," so-called, will not now array herself against that supreme authority . . . . We warn the people against assuming a position which will not only insure defeat, but painful humiliation.[172]

Encouraging resistance, the *Dubuque Herald* said that "Iowa is on the brink of rebellion"; "we do not believe that the supreme court of the state will back down"; "we calmly await" that array of national power that the *Chicago Tribune* was threatening.[173] That came easily from a strongly partisan Democratic journal. Yet the *Nashua Post*, a Republican weekly, in like vein said that the Supreme Court of the United States was paramount only as to federal law; the *Lee County* case involved only questions of Iowa law and "must be settled by Iowa courts"; to attempt to override Iowa law was "an insult to the State . . . ." The State's motto was invoked: "Our Liberties We Prize and Our Rights We Will Maintain." The Lee County supervisors "may surrender their persons to the officers of Judge Drummond's Court, but for the honor of the State we trust they will never compromise their manhood." So wrote the editor, Andrew Felt, a Radical in politics.[174] But the editor of the *Gate City* admonished, "Come Andy, it won't do for any of us to get mad. Our success depends upon preserving our tempers."[175] The anti-bond men of Iowa did not mean to imitate the "exuberant expressions of meridional speech."[176]

CONFRONTATION AT FORT MADISON

LIVELY ACTION IN J. Edgar Thomson's case came on Tuesday, March 2, 1869—the day next after the Supreme Court held, in the *Evans Rogers* case, that the federal court might even send in its own appointee to levy a tax upon the people. The Lee County supervisors met, as usual, in the county court room at Fort Madison. There federal Deputy Marshal Fulton arrested them on the writ of attachment from the Circuit Court at Chicago. Then the sheriff served on the marshal a writ of habeas corpus issued by Judge Beck of the State Supreme Court (who

---

[171] Quoted in *Keokuk Gate City*, Jan. 16, 1869.

[172] Jan. 14, 1869. Reprinted in the *Gate City* of the sixteenth.

[173] Jan. 14, 1869.

[174] Quoted in the *Gate City*, Feb. 12, 1869.

[175] Feb. 12, 1869.

[176] Justice Holmes' phrase. Gandia v. Pettingill, 222 U.S. 452, 458 (1912).

resided at Fort Madison). The judge entered and went on the bench. The marshal responded, citing his authority and declining to produce his prisoners; he purposed to take them to Chicago. Counsel for the supervisors asked the judge to direct the sheriff to take the prisoners away from the marshal's custody. The judge overruled that motion: his eyes saw the prisoners present before him; the marshal disclaimed any intention to remove them while the hearing was pending; the judge concluded that they were under his jurisdiction, "so far as may be necessary to the continuance of the investigation."

Such were the histrionics of habeas corpus.[177]

For two days the cause was argued, by counsel for the supervisors against counsel for Thomson, who sustained the marshal's authority.

On March 6 Judge Beck ordered that the petitioners be discharged. He delivered a long opinion. May a State court release one held under claim of federal authority? That was an old question, on which there had been conflicting views. Taney's opinion in *Ableman v. Booth* in 1859 had held No:[178] but that was uttered in connection with the Fugitive Slave Act, at a time when, said Judge Beck, the Court was under the influence of the slave power; like *Dred Scott*, it should now be forgotten. Coming then to examine the authority of the federal court in the present instance, he found that the State court had acquired jurisdiction of the subject matter (the duty of the county officers to levy the tax) in the third injunction suit by Lee County taxpayers, resulting in the decision of October 1862,[179] before Thomson first brought suit. All Lee County bondholders were bound by that decision. *Riggs v. Johnson County*[180] was held inapplicable, inasmuch as the State court injunction there had been obtained after Riggs had recovered his judgment.

Judge Beck's conclusion was that in the premises the attachment by the federal Circuit Court was void. He ordered that the prisoners stand discharged.[181]

Counsel for Thomson then read a telegram from Judge Drum-

---

177 The events were narrated in the *Keokuk Gate City*, March 3 to 11, 1869, and in the *Constitution*, March 3 to 7.

It seems that prior to this *Lee County* proceeding, the Johnson County supervisors, when before the Circuit Court at Des Moines, had contemplated defiance; but that an informal approach to Judge George G. Wright brought a plain intimation that he would not interfere; that the supervisors thereupon gave bail. Conversation with United States Marshal Clark, reported in the *Dubuque Herald*, Jan. 21, 1869.

178 21 How. 506.

179 McMillan v. Boyles, 14 Iowa 107. Supra, n. 144.

180 6 Wall. 166 (1867). Supra, n. 150.

181 Hollman v. Fulton. Opinion in full in *Keokuk Gate City*, Mar. 30, 1869.

mond: the marshal was to disregard any such order; he was to summon a posse and bring the supervisors, by force if need be. But would a posse come when the marshal called? He tried, and found no response; he was obliged to acquiesce. So the supervisors went free—and promptly ordered a printing of 1,500 copies of Judge Beck's opinion, to be sent throughout the country, to designated officials and to the press.[182]

The entire proceeding, it should be emphasized, had been marked by calm and courtesy. Judge Beck pointed out that if the full State bench sustained his ruling, the federal Supreme Court could review. And in that event, "that Court's mandate will be obeyed by my brothers, (for I know I can speak for them,) and I know that I will render it cheerful obedience, while my mind may continue to doubt its correctness." His opinion had the air of an appeal to Philip sober. He regretted the difference resulting from the *Gelpcke* decision; particularly did he deplore Justice Swayne's "disrespectful allusion" to the Iowa court—"a barbed arrow that will long rankle . . . ."[183]

Would the State's full bench, when presently the case reached it on appeal, support Judge Beck's bold action? If it did so, it would come squarely into collision with the judicial power of the United States. This had become, as Judge Dillon later recalled, "a controversy to which the attention of the whole country was attracted."[184]

Manton Marble's *New York World* led in spreading alarm over Iowa's bond controversy. Bitterly opposed to Lincoln's Administration throughout the war,[185] and now to the course of the Radicals, the *World* set the tone for Democratic criticism. In *Twitchell v. Pennsylvania* the Supreme Court had just reaffirmed that the Fifth and Sixth Amendments apply only to the federal Government and do not limit the States;[186] the *World* in an undiscriminating editorial proclaimed that this was a recognition of State Rights as a great fundamental—"it is a good thing that the Supreme Court defends it from assault."[187] A few days later the *World* made much of the Lee

---

[182] *Keokuk Constitution*, Mar. 7, and *Gate City*, Mar. 11, 1869.

[183] Joseph M. Beck (1823-93) was for twenty-four years a Judge of the State Supreme Court: a Republican in politics, devout churchman and Sunday School teacher, deeply devoted to all that tended to make his State progressive, just and temperate. "A very Gibraltar of convictions," recalled ex-Chief Justice Wright in memorial proceedings. "A man of much more than ordinary mental power [and] of strong predilections

. . . ," said Chief Justice G. S. Robinson. "Sometimes his sympathies led him to the limits of a sound legal discretion." 89 Iowa iv to xi (1894).

[184] King v. Wilson, Fed. Case No. 7810 (C.C.D. Ia. 1871).

[185] Sandburg, *Abraham Lincoln: The War Years*, 4 vols. (New York: Harcourt, Brace and Co., 1939), II, 581-83; III, 52-58.

[186] 7 Wall. 321, decided Apr. 5, 1869.

[187] Apr. 7, 1869.

County collision between Judge Beck and the federal Circuit Court at Chicago. In "Iowa Defends Itself" the editor pointed to a supposed contradiction: whereas the Supreme Court was deciding a case on the basis of State Rights, the lower federal court was overriding a State judge. This excess had been committed in purported enforcement of the rule in *Gelpcke v. Dubuque.*

> So stands the issue. On the one side the State of Iowa attempting to protect the property of its citizens, and on the other the Federal government seeking to take it away. How the matter will end one does not need much discernment to discover; but in the substantial matter of the public good—and this, after all, is the only use of any courts, governments, or laws—the right is most indubitably with Iowa. This State alone of the thirty-seven in or out of the Union is free from debt, and not only free from debt but actually with a surplus in her treasury.
>
> . . . . [T]hough our fears are much to the contrary, we cannot but hope the State will stand stoutly out for the protection of her people against the rapacity of wild-cat corporations. Bond-subsidy to all sorts of joint-stock concerns is a great evil of the day, and it would be well for Iowa to take such steps as may let us know if the United States Supreme Court really does mean to say that a State constitution shall not protect those who are to live under it against such virtual robbery. . . .[188]

The *World* could not believe that *Gelpcke v. Dubuque* was meant to be carried to such an extreme.

The *World*'s editorial was picked up by Iowa newspapers.[189]

MOVEMENT TO SUBMIT TO THE FEDERAL JUDICIARY

WHEN THE FEDERAL Circuit Court for Iowa held its May term (1869), "the court room was full of supervisors anxious to know what the court would do with them." Justice Miller gave this answer:

> We are of the opinion that it is our duty to hold these gentlemen in prison or in the custody of the United States Marshal until they

---

[188] Apr. 12, 1869.

[189] The *Keokuk Constitution*—whose editor was in political accord with the *World*—set out the editorial at length on April 17, 1869. On April 24 it repeated much of the language, attributing this time to the *New York* *Herald.* The *Burlington Hawk-Eye* of May 1 quoted in part as coming from the *Herald.*

One learns not to be surprised at such inexactitude in newspapers of that period, as they picked up and repeated bits from hither and yon.

obey the mandate of this court. We feel happy to say that the Court will cheerfully act upon the suggestion offered by counsel for relators, namely: that those who shall agree to obey the mandate of this court in good faith before the next term, may be permitted to go on their bail already given and their cases for contempt will be continued until that time.[190]

That was accepted. Every supervisor and councilman "came into open court personally or by his attorney, pledged himself to go home and levy the tax at an early day . . . ." So reported one of counsel for the bondholders, adding, "from all this it would look as though this Railroad Bond war was virtually at an end; and it will be matter of lasting regret that it was not ended long ago and in a different way, by an amicable compromise of the bonds . . . ."[191]

When *Ex parte Holman*,[192] the appeal from Judge Beck's order, was decided on October 11, 1869, the Iowa Supreme Court held that a State judge had no authority to interfere with the process of a federal court. Chief Justice Dillon spoke for the majority. (In a moment he will reappear as the new United States Circuit Judge.) Judge Beck, dissenting, stood by his original holding. Inasmuch as the highest State court *sustained* the claim of federal right, no review by the Supreme Court was provided.

Three years later, in *Tarble's Case*,[193] the vexed habeas corpus question was settled—against the pretension of the State courts.

Ex parte Holman fell as a sobering reality: it meant that the Iowa Supreme Court had quit the contest. The *Davenport Gazette* commented approvingly:

> It is, we think, a matter of just congratulation to every right minded citizen of the State that the court found a legal exit from the impending trouble, and that the State has Judges who have the courage to make what may be, in some quarters, but ought not to be anywhere in Iowa, an unpopular decision.[194]

In some quarters indeed it was unpopular. The *Keokuk Constitution* said that the Judges had shown themselves to be "mere braggadocios, without nerve to stand up to their previous decisions." For months the editor had been filling his pages with wild exhortations to resist "the usurpation and assumptions of the Supreme Court of the

---

[190] *Keokuk Gate City*, May 19, 1869, quoting the *Des Moines Register*.

[191] H. Scott Howell, in *Keokuk Gate City*, May 20, 1869.

[192] 28 Iowa 88.

[193] 13 Wall. 397 (1872). Infra, pp. 1421–26.

[194] Quoted as "wise and timely" by the *Washington Gazette*, Oct. 22, 1869.

United States" which were "the evidence of the growing disposition of the federal government to absorb all power unto itself, and to trample upon and belittle the reserved rights of the States and the people . . . ."[195] Now he was preparing his own retreat by throwing the blame on the Iowa Judges' "cowardice." If only they had used all their power, he declared, "the matter would end and end forever." The Governor was "a coward and a traitor" because he did not call out the militia to protect the citizens from "Federal usurpation."[196]

The *Dubuque Herald* conceded that the court "could come to no other [decision] than it did." Thereupon, however, it began abusing it as being "more responsible . . . than any other party" for the plight of the indebted communities; it was in reliance upon the court's earlier decisions that they had conducted costly litigation, and had exasperated creditors whom they might have placated. Now the court made "a labored but ineffectual apology for its previous course."[197] Thus Democratic editors were seeking to discredit the bench of Republican judges.

When Judge Love held the federal Circuit Court in late October 1869, he observed that "It is now quite evident that there is no branch of the State government which has either the disposition or the power to resist the lawful process of the United States courts . . . ." He said this in admonishing another crowd of supervisors who were being released upon promising to levy taxes. He impressed upon them "how groundless has been the assertion that the executive arm of the [federal] government would not be extended to aid and sustain the courts of the Union in this controversy."[198]

There were signs tending to show that resistance was being abandoned. Among newspapers shifting their position was the *Des Moines Register*, which now counselled counties to "go to work in good faith and honestly to compromise and pay the bonds."[199] Some communities were doing just that. Thus the *Dubuque Herald* reported that "Our board of supervisors and our city council . . . have devoted their energies to effecting settlements and compromises whenever it was possible to do so. Now, behold the result. *Dubuque County is entirely clear of all this debt*," while the city was constantly making settlements.[200] Davenport was compromising; $130,000 of indebtedness had been settled for new bonds and some cash.[201]

The city of Burlington had a debt of nearly $700,000; judgments were being recovered, and some were already being enforced by

---

195 May 22, 1869.
196 Oct. 29, 1869.
197 Oct. 21, 1869.
198 *Keokuk Gate City*, Nov. 4, 1869.

199 Quoted disapprovingly by the *Muscatine Journal*, Nov. 2, 1869.
200 Oct. 20, 1869.
201 *Davenport Democrat*, Nov. 3, 1869.

mandamus—notably at the suit of Henry Amy & Co.[202] On October 18, 1869, the people by a vote of 340 to 58—a very light vote—authorized the compromise and funding of the city debt. Offers were sent to all known creditors. The influential *Hawk-Eye* newspaper spoke approvingly: "We are unable to see . . . the prospect of gain in those counties which continue their resistance to the processes of the United States Supreme Court in the matter of railroad bonds. . . ." It was not to be doubted that the Court "will sustain every action necessary to enforce the judgment of its own inferior courts." "The day of payment cannot be put off forever, though the ingenuity of lawyers may delay it" —while costs mounted and Iowa's good name was tarnished.[203]

Lee County's debt was $1,000,000, of which $600,000 was then due: judgments for $200,000 had been rendered, and the balance could speedily be put in judgment. The supervisors, some of whom had been shirking responsibility,[204] at last urged the people to authorize the Board to seek a settlement.[205] The election on November 13, 1869, returned 1,576 votes Yes, 1,204 No—a majority of 372 for compromise. But outside of Jackson Township (Keokuk and environs) the tally was only 415 in favor to 1,151 against. In rural townships voters remained overwhelmingly opposed to payment.[206] (A year earlier, Keokuk had voted to compromise.[207])

MORE TRIBUNES, AND A CONVENTION

MUSCATINE COUNTY OWED about $300,000; the city of Muscatine owed nearly as much—all on account of aid to the disappointing Mississippi & Missouri venture. The Board of Trade urged the city council to ask the voters for authority to compromise. But there were leading

---

[202] United States *ex rel.* Henry Amy v. City of Burlington, 154 U.S. 568, 19 L. Ed. 495 (1870).

Drawing upon the *Burlington Hawk-Eye* for 1869 and 1870, *passim*, it may be said that the largest item in the city's aid had been for the Burlington & Missouri River R.R. (subsequently part of the Chicago, Burlington & Quincy). About half of the debt was accumulated interest. For a population of say 15,000 this came to about $46 per capita. It was about 21 percent of the assessed valuation of taxable property—say about 8 percent of the actual value. In addition there should be considered the railroad aid debt of Des Moines

County, wherein Burlington lies: it was reported to be $940,000—say $35 per capita, or nearly 6 percent of the assessed valuation.

[203] Oct. 28, 1869.

[204] "Tax Payer" wrote: "Let us . . . tell the truth, and not be all for settlement when we are at Fort Madison, then as soon as we get home, to save a little political capital for future use, clamor for all to vote 'No' [on settling the debt]." *Keokuk Gate City*, Nov. 5, 1869.

[205] Gate City, Oct. 28, 1869. They proposed an issue of twenty-five year 6 percent bonds.

[206] *Gate City*, Nov. 26, 1869.

[207] Supra, p. 964.

men resolved to frustrate that effort. There was D. C. Cloud, sometime carpenter who had prepared for the bar by years of night study, and presently had been elected Attorney General;[208] now he had turned his efforts to anti-monopolistic agitation. He told the people that they were suffering from the federal courts "an oppression worse than any despotism on earth."[209] And the Attorney General then in office, Henry O'Connor: with Hibernian ardor he assured the citizens that if only they would "leave the railroad tax unpaid," then "the bondholders will never be able to collect a dollar of this tax."[210] And John Mahin—publisher of the *Journal*, Representative in the General Assembly, and unflinching fighter for the causes he espoused: all along he had been preaching that "The bondholders can be kept out of this money till doomsday by legal means. . . . Our State Courts will stand by the people if the people will stand by them. . . ."[211] Now that the State Court had given up the struggle, Mahin urged the people still to fight on—"never [to] give their money to swindlers without stout resistance. . . . It makes no difference how high the Court may be which decrees the payment of these bonds."[212]

At the prompting of these men a mass meeting voted to call a convention of indebted counties to be held at Muscatine on December 15, 1869. The purpose was to reverse the trend toward submission and to concert resistance.

The convention[213] was attended by delegations from eleven counties, whose indebtedness for railroad aid was estimated at some $4,000,000 to $5,000,000. (Often records had been kept so carelessly that no exact figure could be set.) Chosen to preside was that upholder of moral causes, Rev. Josiah B. Grinnell of Poweshiek, recently a Radical in Congress, founder of the town and college that bear his name. Chairman of the committee on resolutions was Samuel J. Kirkwood of Johnson County, Republican war-Governor and Senator, and railroad president. The resolutions—far more restrained than the speeches—called for legislation to correct the Supreme Court's "encroachments," and for "equal taxation" of railroads. Citizens were urged not to pay the bond tax; counties were urged not to settle "without general consultation."

The most interesting remarks came from Rush Clark of Johnson County—prominent lawyer, sometime Speaker in the General Assem-

---

208 Supra, p. 958.
209 *Muscatine Journal*, Nov. 17, 1869.
210 Ibid.
211 Ibid. July 30, 1869.
212 Ibid. Nov. 1, 1869.
213 Reported in the *Muscatine Jour-* *nal* for the evening of Dec. 15, the *Davenport Democrat* of Dec. 16, the *Keokuk Gate City* and the *Washington Gazette* of Dec. 17, the *Keokuk Constitution* of Dec. 17 and 18, and in numerous other papers, in and out of Iowa.

bly (and subsequently, from 1877 to his death in 1879, a Representative in Congress). He told about the taxpayers' suit he had recently brought in the local court to restrain the Board of Supervisors from collecting the tax. His theory was this: "the Supreme Court of the United States . . . did not go so far as to say that the bonds were a valid debt upon the individuals of the county, but only that the corporation, Johnson county, was bound for the bonds she had issued . . . ." The taxpayer was entitled to a day in court before *his* property could be affected—and that (he argued) raised a new issue for the *State* court finally to decide. This theory inspired great expectations.[214]

The convention gave rise to a good deal of comment, within and outside the State. "Who would have thought during the war, that before the end of the decade, the loyal J. B. Grinnell would be found presiding over a convention of Nullifiers, and that ex-Gov. Kirkwood . . . [would be] advocating the doctrine of Calhoun":[215] that was one prevalent thought. The *Milwaukee Evening Wisconsin,* under the caption "A Bit of Rebellion in Iowa," said "They went into this bond business with their eyes open"; now they should, "like honorable men, get out of the scrape as cheaply as possible, consistent with honor and their duty as good citizens."[216] The *New York Times* under the title "Repudiation in Iowa," gave a carefully detailed history of the bond controversy; the editorial was particularly scornful that any leader could now call for repudiating bonds whose issue he himself had actively supported. Iowa was "advancing in the career of prosperity and wealth" with marked rapidity; "it has no State debt"; "it has a population of great enterprise, intelligence and moral purity"; now it must lead its wayward counties and cities back "to the path of honor, and justice, and moral obligation."[217]

Rush Clark's suit, and like proceedings elsewhere, ran on for some months; hope was thus sustained, and settlement deferred.

Of course such a suit would not affect a marshal collecting a tax under the order of a federal court. But for that too the leaders had an answer. As D. C. Cloud explained to a mass meeting:

> He thought no man could be found in the country sufficiently depraved to bid in the property to be offered at public sale . . . . He said that the U.S. Marshal would probably bid in the property for the judgment creditor. The moment that he bids it off his duty as United States Marshal, so far as that property is concerned, is at an end.—If he attempts to hold the property as agent of the bondholders

---

[214] His letter of October 4, 1869, to the *Iowa City Republican,* was widely reported.

[215] Letter to the editor, *Davenport Democrat,* Jan. 4, 1870.
[216] Dec. 18, 1869.
[217] Jan. 31, 1870.

he does so as an ordinary citizen. We can replevy the property from his possession. . . . Our State Courts will return the property to us with damages. . . .[218]

INCONSISTENT ACTION BY IOWA'S LEGISLATURE AND COURT

ANOTHER HOPE WAS that the legislature would comply with the request of the Muscatine convention: that new "equal taxation" of railroads would bring a large sum, out of which the indebted counties would be relieved.[219] This did not command the necessary support. Would the legislature memorialize Congress to amend the Judiciary Act, to require the federal judiciary to respect State decisions on State law? Again the answer was No: that proposal ended in an adverse report in the lower house. At no time was the legislature disposed to experiment with interposing the shield of the State.

The State was speaking equivocally. The General Assembly of 1868 had passed two statutes, here to be put side by side. Chapter 67, the Act of April 2, set up a procedure whereby, upon a favorable popular vote, a municipality might settle with its creditors and pay by an issue of new bonds.[220] Yet Chapter 48, an Act of March 22, had provided that upon a favorable popular vote, a township, town or city might give aid to a railroad by levying a tax not to exceed 5 percent of the assessed valuation of property. When this measure was under consideration, a correspondent at Des Moines reported that "every town, or at least every county seat, wants a railroad," and many legislators were convinced that municipal giving was "the only way." Others felt mistrustful, but might confine their efforts to seeking safeguards.[221] Of course the railroad lobby pressed for the new law; it was powerful and resorted to "a good deal of 'scullduggery.'"

How remarkable it seems that at a moment when—following the Supreme Court's decision in *Riggs v. Johnson County* on January 13, 1868[222]—communities already indebted were stirred over the impending mandamus to pay, and when mass meetings were declaring

---

[218] *Davenport Democrat*, June 2, 1870.

[219] *Keokuk Gate City*, Jan. 21, Feb. 19, Mar. 5 and 22, 1870; *Washington Gazette*, Feb. 11, 1870. A bill, Senate File No. 99, was introduced for that purpose.

[220] It was under that statute that most of the efforts to compromise

mentioned above were being carried out.

[221] *Keokuk Constitution*, Feb. 13 and Mar. 11, 1868. Immediately below the latter item in the newspaper is the report of a meeting of citizens in Lee County protesting that the previous issue of railroad aid bonds had been a great fraud.

[222] Supra, p. 963.

the bonds to be an "iniquitous and fraudulent obligation,"[223] the legislature would inaugurate a new round of railroad aid. How singular, too, that the legislature would go in the teeth of the *Wapello* decision, reaffirmed half a dozen times, that taxation to aid a railroad violated a right secured by the State constitution, at a moment when many were crying out that the federal Supreme Court's disregard of those adjudications was an outrage upon the State.

Inconsistency and contradiction all about add to the complexity of this entire matter.

This new railroad aid statute of 1868 was held unconstitutional in *Hanson v. Vernon,* decided by the Iowa Supreme Court in April 1869.[224] Chief Justice Dillon said that it was of no constitutional significance that this statute authorized a *gift* to a railroad, whereas earlier cases had dealt with subscriptions to stock. The essential point was that taxation was permissible only for a public purpose. Wright and Beck, JJ., agreed.

Cole, J., dissented. He twisted the earlier cases to mean only that the legislature had not authorized the issue of bonds; the denial of constitutional power he dismissed as dictum. The legislature, he contended, was the sole judge of what purpose was "public." This shift is to be watched.[225]

The wonder grows when one looks into the facts out of which *Hanson v. Vernon* arose. It was an appeal from the District Court of Henry County, in a suit to enjoin the trustees of Center Township from laying a tax—of 2.25 percent on the assessed valuation—to make a gift to the projected Keokuk Northern Railroad, as permitted by the recent statute. An injunction was denied, and the objectors appealed. Henry County (immediately north of Lee) was at that moment deeply involved in an effort to avoid payment of railroad aid bonds amounting to about $400,000. *J. Edgar Thomson v. Henry County* had been a companion case to *Riggs v. Johnson County,* where on January 13, 1868, the federal Supreme Court had sustained a mandamus to compel the collection of a levy.[226] Center Township comprises the county seat and environs. And yet at that place, at that juncture, a majority had voted to compel all taxpayers to contribute to another railroad venture.[227]

---

[223] *Keokuk Gate City,* Mar. 4 and 11, 1868.

[224] 27 Iowa 28. On the effect of this decision, the *Keokuk Gate City* reported: "Our Iowa exchanges along the line of prospective railroads all indicate that these railroads will be built, despite the decision of the Supreme Court . . . . There is enter-

prise enough in this State to build the railroads needed without the questionable and vexatious expedient of voting a tax. . . ." May 1, 1869.

[225] Infra, p. 990.

[226] Supra, p. 963.

[227] One reads of the favorable vote in the *Keokuk Constitution* of July 8, 1868—side by side with the report of

Hanson v. Vernon was a test case; attorneys interested in like proceedings were heard on the constitutional issue. Among those supporting the new aid was Ralph P. Lowe, who as a Judge seven years earlier had spoken for the State Court in affirming and reaffirming that the municipal bonds were void;[228] he was a credulous man of malleable mentality. Beside him was Henry Strong, who a year before had been arguing to the Bench at Washington that the Circuit Court could not grant mandamus to compel Henry and Johnson counties to levy a bond tax.[229]

Iowa's next biennial legislature, in 1870, has already been mentioned as having refused to comply with the requests of the Muscatine convention.[230] It passed two statutes now to be noticed, each of which became law on April 12. To please the people burdened with railroad aid bonds it enacted, by Chapter 90, that the penalties imposed upon delinquent taxes "shall not apply upon taxes levied by order of any court to pay judgment on city or county indebtedness . . . ." That meant that a delinquent taxpayer would incur nothing more than the payment of ordinary interest. And to please the people who still wanted to give aid to railroads, the legislature—going squarely against *Hanson v. Vernon*[231]—by Chapter 102, substantially reenacted the statute of 1868 there pronounced invalid. In so doing it was "speculating upon the effect of certain changes in the constitution of the Supreme Bench of the State"—in the words of Judge Dillon, who in December 1869 had become United States Circuit Judge.[232]

The former of these enactments was promptly held invalid by Judge Dillon in the federal Circuit Court—the forum where bondholders were recovering the judgments at which the statute was aimed.[233] It was plain that the Contract Clause of the federal Constitution barred any substantial impairment of the remedy as it existed when the bonds were issued. The Supreme Court had recently had occasion to enforce that principle in municipal bond cases from Illinois.[234]

The fate of the reenacted aid law must await litigation. By the

---

the "Lee County Citizens' Anti-Railroad Bond Meeting" not twenty-five miles distant, which urged "vigorous and untiring legal opposition to the bonds."

Thereafter there was a meeting of Center Township taxpayers opposed to the tax recently voted, "for the purpose of determining what action is necessary to be taken to defeat the payment of said tax." *Keokuk Constitution*, Aug. 21, 1868.

[228] Supra, n. 144.

[229] Supra, p. 963.

[230] Supra, p. 977.

[231] Supra, n. 224.

[232] 9 Am. L. Reg. (n.s.) 489, 503 (1870).

[233] United States *ex rel.* Lansing v. Treasurer of Muscatine County, Fed. Case No. 16,538, decided in May 1870.

[234] Von Hoffman v. City of Quincy, 4 Wall. 535 (1867); City of Galena v. Amy, 5 Wall 705 (1867).

time it came to be argued before the State Supreme Court, new men would occupy the places once held by Judges Dillon and Wright.

DEFIANT TAXPAYERS' LAST STAND

FOR THE EMBATTLED counties, the first six months of 1870 were filled with incidents—and nowhere more so than in Lee County. The leading counsel for the bondholders offered to settle for a new issue of 6 percent bonds payable in twenty-five years, with an annual tax to meet interest and, after ten years, additional taxation to make an adequate sinking fund. The Board of Supervisors took this under consideration. But then the anti-bond party—following the Rush Clark will-o'-the-wisp[235]—sought and obtained an injunction restraining the County Treasurer from levying the taxes as the federal court had commanded. The treasurer, and the treasurers of other counties, were thus placed between the horns, just where the board of supervisors had been two years earlier, prior to *Riggs v. Johnson County*. But now James Grant, for the bondholders, made it clear that if there was any more hesitating, he would proceed to collect the entire amount of the judgments, through the federal marshal—which would add enormously to the ultimate cost to the taxpayers.[236] The Lee County Treasurer decided to proceed with the collection, by offering for sale personal property of the delinquents.

There was much agitation. The editor of the *Keokuk Constitution* incited resistance by comment such as this:

> There is a point . . . in the affairs of men where patience ceases to be a virtue, and outrages upon individual rights will not be *peaceably submitted to* even when attempted under a bastard decision of a corrupted or profligate judge or court. If these bondholders and their attorneys attempt to press their tyranny too far, they may find it to be unhealthy for them to lay round loose in this country; and if any personal collision is provoked—which every good citizen will regret —no body will be to blame for it but the bondholders and their attorneys.[237]

A representative of the creditors sent in to bid "received an anonymous note . . . advising him to 'keep scarce!' " At a farm where a sale was to be held, the property could not be found. Although "the sales were *largely attended* . . . , . . . the property offered . . . did not appear to be the kind the farmers wanted . . . ."[238] A threshing machine was bid off for the judgment creditor; but then, although hundreds were pres-

---

[235] Supra, pp. 975–76.
[236] *Keokuk Gate City*, Mar. 5, 1870.

[237] Apr. 5, 1870.
[238] *Keokuk Constitution*, May 3, 14, 1870.

ent, no one would help to move it, and it had to be abandoned.[239] Francis Semple,[240] ever resisting at the bar and on the stump, published a notice that his mule was to be sold for his tax:

> As the parting with our Jack will be extremely tearful and solemn, the presence and sympathy of our friends will be thankfully received and duly appreciated.
>
> F. Semple, Wife and Babies.[241]

All this seemed less amusing when, before the Circuit Court at Des Moines, James Grant "read the editorial articles and Semple's 'mule' letter from the *Constitution* as the basis for his application for the appointment of the United States [Marshal as] tax collector."[242] At the same time the collectors for Johnson and Muscatine counties told the court that they had been frustrated; they asked the court's assistance. On May 19 Judge Dillon made answer. The Supreme Court, he pointed out, had established the power and duty to appoint an officer of the court to make the collection, when local officers could not or would not do so. On the showing made, it was the court's duty to give that relief. As to Lee County, the relators were entitled to have the Marshal directed to act at once; as to the others, the Marshal would await further instructions. The Court's words were calm but emphatic, designed to convince the people that all hope of escape was "wholly illusory."[243]

---

[239] *Washington Gazette*, May 27, 1870.

[240] Supra, p. 961.

[241] *Keokuk Constitution*, May 11, 1870.

[242] Ibid., May 17, 1870.

[243] United States *ex rel.* Lansing v. Muscatine County, Fed. Case No. 16,538. It was on this occasion that the court held, further, that the recent statute to remove the penalty for tax delinquency was unconstitutional. Supra, p. 979.

Inasmuch as Judge Dillon did not reside in Lee County, when he held court matters affecting that county could be decided. Compare the disqualification of Justice Miller and Judge Love, supra, p. 962.

The *Muscatine Journal*, which had been preaching resistance, now chided the County Treasurer for stating that he apprehended violence. "Thousands of citizens will make affidavit, if necessary, that there is no danger in this county to any officer in the legitimate and peaceable discharge of his duty . . . ." It concluded with the fatuous remark, "We think it would have been sufficient for him to have answered in the U.S. court that he was enjoined by a court of the State, and that the injunction must be dissolved before he could proceed to collect the tax." May 17, 1870.

In Johnson county, the *Iowa City Republican* said: "If we understand the temper of the people of this county, they only intend to seek redress for wrongs done them of whatever kind, through the courts of the country. This is an undeniable, a guaranteed right . . . ." Quoted in the *Muscatine Journal*, May 17. But the *Republican* kept on saying that the marshal might as well stay away, because the people were not going to pay. Quoted in the *Muscatine Journal*, June 2.

Later at the May term, an order was made as to Louisa County, that the Marshal proceed to collect the tax.[244]

A motion having been made to vacate the order as to Lee County and to reinstate the County Treasurer, on May 28 Judge Love suspended collection by the Marshal until argument could be heard on July 1.[245] That gave the Board one more month in which to bring about compliance.

At the same May term, bondholders were rolling up more judgments against about fourteen counties and cities—to a total greater than $260,000, it was reported.[246] And the Supreme Court had been pronouncing, over and over, that the mandamus of the federal court must be obeyed, notwithstanding a State court's injunction. Cases decided between March 28 and April 30 were: *Mayor of Davenport v. Lord;*[247] *Supervisors of Washington County v. Durant;*[248] same *v. Mortimer;*[249] and two cases of *Supervisors of Poweshiek County v. Durant.*[250] The tide was running strong.

The *Keokuk Gate City,* the more moderate of the two local papers, now abandoned the fight. In its issue of May 24 it listed straws to which hope could no longer cling:

> The State of Iowa should have made the cause its own. . . .
> No relief can come from the Courts.
> Doubtless it is equally useless to look for relief from Congress. . . .[251]
> Nor let any think that the Marshal will not be sustained by the Executive Department in the levy and sale, if resistance is attempted. That is a vain expectation.[252]

---

[244] *Washington Gazette,* June 3, quoting the *Wapello Republican;* statement of facts in Letz v. Clark, Fed. Case No. 9971, C.C.D. Ia., Sept. term 1870.

[245] *Keokuk Constitution,* June 7 and 12; *Muscatine Journal,* June 2.

[246] *Keokuk Constitution,* July 15, 1870.

[247] 9 Wall. 409.

[248] 9 Wall. 415.

[249] 154 U.S. 571, 19 L. Ed. 734.

[250] 9 Wall. 736, and 154 U.S. 576, 19 L. Ed. 813.

[251] The publisher, James B. Howell, at that moment a Senator, and George W. McCrary, both Keokuk Republicans, introduced bills to amend Sec. 34 of the Judiciary Act, to provide that the laws of the several States *and the latest settled adjudications of the highest judicial tribunals* construing such laws would be regarded as rules of decision in the federal courts. H.R. 2150 of June 9, S. 1002 of June 20, 1870. The former died in committee; the latter was reported adversely and postponed.

In August, at the Democratic convention for the 1st Congressional District, Thomas W. Clagett, publisher of the *Keokuk Constitution,* caused the adoption of a resolution calling for legislation to the same effect. *Constitution,* Aug. 13, 1870.

This was all quite futile.

[252] May 24, 1870.

XVII: *Municipal Bonds I*

Early in June the supervisors for Lee published an address to the taxpayers, seeking to demonstrate the county's plight.[253] They said, in part:

> As a Board of Supervisors, we have done acts, changed policy, and deferred settlements as we have been instructed by public meetings of citizens. We have had no other desire than to please, and obey the instructions of the people. We followed our State Court decisions when in our favor, but are powerless now, and the responsibility of all future actions is with the citizens; and if the Railroad Bond taxes are paid just as other taxes are paid, the United States Marshal will not come here to collect; if not he will.

That was all very true: far from giving leadership, the supervisors had been docile while mass meetings determined the course of events. Even now they took care to have the County Attorney append his concurrence: he had been forced upon the board by the sentiment of an anti-bond rally where he had appeared as chairman of the committee on resolutions.[254]

About $400,000 in interest coupons was now due and could soon be put in judgment. Bondholders had been willing to settle for new bonds to the full amount of principal and interest; but citizens and many members of the board had bitterly opposed payment in full. Now, it seemed, some bondholders had withdrawn their offers and expected to enforce payment as rapidly as possible.

By their vote in November 1869, the people had authorized the supervisors to make a settlement.[255] But thereupon there had been much agitation, as a result of which the power had not been exercised. Now the board called upon the people to hold more meetings and manifest their desires. "We await the result of your deliberations."

Recall how in the *Aspinwall* case Justice Nelson had magnified the board of supervisors as a body "fit and competent to be the depositary of the trust . . . confided to it."[256] In actuality, the statement of the supervisors of Lee came much closer to the truth: at every juncture, they "had no other desire than to please," according to the popular sentiment of the moment.

On June 28 the Lee County board announced that the people with great unanimity were resolved to obey the federal court; for the past month the payment of the tax had been proceeding quietly. The board voted to issue twenty-five year 6 percent compromise bonds; a

---

[253] *Keokuk Constitution,* June 12, 1870.
[254] *Keokuk Gate City,* Aug. 21,

Sept. 15, 1868.
[255] Supra, p. 974.
[256] Supra, p. 932.

commission was appointed to negotiate with creditors.[257] But that was not final action; a settlement could yet be defeated, and opponents were very active.

At this point a group of influential citizens called up a powerful reserve. In a note stating that there was still "an undecided feeling in the minds of many of our taxpayers," they invited Justice Miller to give his advice. Reluctantly, one may be sure, and with careful reservation of all questions of law, he gave to his "neighbors and friends [his] opinion on an aspect of the matter not based on any view affecting [his] future judicial conduct." It must be conceded, he said, that outside Iowa "the belief is generally entertained that this county is resisting, by force, the due administration of law by the Federal Courts, and that this is construed into a resistance of the Federal Government." Such an opinion was disastrous in many ways to the prosperity of the county—as by discouraging immigrants and investment.

> The want of success thus far during the course of many years litigation in obtaining the support of the Supreme Court of the United States to any of the propositions advanced as defences to these bonds, should have a serious influence on the minds of those interested in the final result. This, however, is a conclusion which, whatever its merits, it does not become me to press.

For these and other reasons, Justice Miller was of opinion that the true interests of the citizens of Lee County—"and I think of the bondholders, also"—would be served by a speedy adjustment on the best terms to be had.[258] The letter was, of course, widely noticed.

THE PRESIDENT WILL SUPPORT THE COURTS

THEN AN ADDITIONAL force was thrown into the battle: a letter from President Grant. The Judges in their opinions had kept asserting that it was the duty of the Executive to support the federal courts. Yet the man in the White House remained characteristically taciturn. The *Muscatine Journal* said it had learned "directly" that no troops would be sent to collect taxes.[259] That brought a reaction from the *Davenport Democrat* and the *Dubuque Herald*, Democratic journals favorable to the bondholders' cause and at the same time resentful at Radical treatment of the Southern States. "The last organized resistance to Federal authority . . . is that now going on in this State," said the former.[260] "The

---

[257] *Keokuk Gate City* and *Keokuk Constitution*, July 3, 1870.
[258] *Keokuk Gate City* and *Keokuk Constitution*, July 12, 1870.
[259] Jan. 22, 1870.
[260] Feb. 17, 1870.

laws should be enforced in Iowa no less than in South Carolina," said the latter.[261] Were the Iowans merely engaged in a manful defiance of "monstrous judicial tyranny" unparalleled "in the history of this, or any other civilized country," as some editors were telling people?[262] Or, as Judge Drummond had said, was this the "hydra-headed" spirit of the late Rebellion against the United States, reappearing in "the patriotic State of Iowa"?[263] Although the *Muscatine Journal* asserted that neither Judge Drummond nor Judge Love nor Napoleon Bonaparte ever supposed that bayonets could collect a judgment,[264] still the use of federal troops became something of great symbolic importance. The President's attitude on that point seemed to be the test between defiance of the United States and mere defiance of evil judgments.

It was in this context that on June 11, 1870, General John A. Dix, sometime president of the Mississippi & Missouri, sought an expression from the President. Grant replied:

> Executive Mansion,
> Washington, D.C., June 20, 1870.
>
> To Gen. J. A. Dix:
>   Dear Sir:—Yours of the 11th inst., stating that the report had been circulated in Iowa, that I had stated that I would not enforce the laws for the collection of taxes to pay railroad bonds, if resisted by the citizens, is received. It is hardly necessary for me to deny such a statement. I would hardly invite a community to resist the laws which I am sworn to execute. I do, however, emphatically deny the report, and state further that if it becomes my duty to use force to execute the laws of Iowa, or any other State, I shall do so without hesitation.
> Very respectfully, your obedient servant.
> U. S. Grant.[265]

The substance of this correspondence was reported in late June; the text appeared in Iowa newspapers at various times in August. To men who had borne so faithful a part in the Civil War, doubtless this struck home.

Early in August the Iowa Supreme Court rejected Rush Clark's contention that the federal court's judgments did not reach the individual taxpayer.[266] Judge Wright said, "the county must be accepted and treated as plaintiff's agent or representative, and whatever binds the county binds him." Judge Beck dissented.

---

261 Feb. 11, 1870.

262 *Keokuk Constitution*, Jan. 6, 1870.

263 United States *ex rel*. Thompson v. Lee County, Fed. Case No. 15,589 (1869).

264 Nov. 6, 1869.

265 Published in the *Gate City* and the *Constitution* on August 13.

266 Clark v. Wolf, 29 Iowa 197; *Keokuk Gate City*, Aug. 4 and 6.

SUBMISSION—AND DENUNCIATION OF THE SUPREME COURT

"THE WAR IS OVER," the *Davenport Democrat* announced on August 2. As is the way with stubborn struggles, the end when it came seemed sudden. "[A]ll hands have surrendered and the debts will be arranged." That was generally true, although pockets of resistance held out for some time.[267] For months thereafter, county boards and city councils would be busy with compromises, with settlements in new long-term bonds and cash.

Defiance of the judicial power of the United States had collapsed.

When in 1869 its judgments came to press hard upon the indebted municipalities, the Supreme Court became the object of newspaper censure of a pattern rather familiar in American history. When Judge Drummond, pursuant to the Court's ruling, ordered the arrest of Lee county supervisors, the *Keokuk Constitution* (Democratic) declared that

> The encroachments of federal power upon the reserved rights of the States have been so numerous and flagrant since the radical party has been in power, that the just balance of power between the States and the federal government . . . has well nigh been entirely lost sight of.

Citizens should be warned of the near approach "to the gulf of federal absolutism."[268]

On that occasion its rival, the *Gate City* (Radical Republican), breaking six months of editorial silence on municipal bonds, published under the caption "Conflicting Decisions" a detailed history of the subject. In the interpretation of State law, it said, federal jurisdiction was not paramount—it was only concurrent with that of the State courts;

> to prevent . . . unseemly conflict, the Supreme Court of the United States in its earlier and better days, when it was both more modest and more courteous, adopted the principle that they would follow the decisions of the Supreme Courts of the States in matters arising under their Constitutions and Laws. . . .

---

[267] *Keokuk Gate City*, Aug. 12, 18, 19, Sept. 7 and 8; *Keokuk Constitution*, Aug. 17 and 30; *Muscatine Journal*, Sept. 13; Letz *et al* [taxpayers of Louisa county] v. Clark [United States Marshal,] Fed. Case No. 9971, decided Sept. 6, 1870.

[268] Jan. 16, 1869. Later it said of the bond decisions, "No higher-handed outrage was ever perpetrated upon a free people. No more dangerous blow was ever struck at civil liberty." Oct. 29, 1869.

Now it called upon the Court to abandon its error and return to "its true, peaceful and courteous spirit."[269]

Reacting to this article, the *Burlington Hawk-Eye* (Republican) said that in the conflict that had now developed, "consistency, equity, and common sense are on the side of the Supreme Court of the United States"; whoever urged resistance to its authority was "an unsafe counsellor and should not be listened to."[270] The *Davenport Gazette* (Republican) said that "the sober second thought of the people" would bring submission.[271]

The *Iowa City Republican* published a letter on the topic "Have We a State Government?" Considering the control now being exerted over county supervisors, it was asked,

> Is it not clearly an outrageous and dangerous usurpation of power by the Federal Judiciary; a tyranny which if fastened upon us would be infinitely worse than that fastened upon France by Napoleon?

The *Muscatine Journal* (Republican) quoted the above "sober and truthful" expression, and added its own reflection:

> In this country we have been so accustomed to look with veneration and respect upon the judiciary (the character of most of our judges in times past having warranted it), that we are now almost ready to accept whatever they say or do without question.

Recent encroachments "should cause public meetings to be held in every town and hamlet in our State . . . ."[272]

It was remarkable to find Republican editors publishing articles on "State Rights"; warning that in enforcing the new Fifteenth Amendment, Congress had gone too far—"this disposition to centralize power should be checked;"[273] and even lamenting those "earlier and better days" when the Court had been worthy of "veneration and respect." When a Radical editor and legislator declared "It is no use to ask justice or the observance of law at the hands of this tribunal,"[274] the conservative *Davenport Democrat* exclaimed,

> Pretty loud! It reminds us of those more prosperous days of the Republic, when earnest radicals prayed for the death of that noted Chief Justice, Roger B. Taney, and when radicals hoped, prayed, and

---

[269] Jan. 20, 1869.
[270] Jan. 22, 1869.
[271] Quoted disapprovingly by the *Gate City*, Jan. 27, 1869.
[272] Nov. 4, 1869.
[273] For example, *Muscatine Journal*,

Feb. 5, 9, 16, 23, Mar. 10, June 9, 1870.
[274] Ibid., Jan. 14, 1870, apropos of Butz v. Muscatine, infra, p. 1000. John Mahin, the editor, was a Representative in the General Assembly.

wrought early and late for the purification, as they termed it, of the Supreme Bench, which meant a full Radical representation therein. They have got their wish. The Supreme Bench is radical to the core— therefore 'loyal,' patriotic, high toned, learned, stupendous legal ability; perfect purity of character, with all the christian graces! Such a bench! and yet a radical quill driver out here in Iowa has become so suddenly disgusted as to feel it his duty to stand up and impeach the concern as utterly unworthy of confidence; as barren of justice—lawless and despicable! Bless us, how these radical brethren do love each other![275]

Actually the bond question cut across party lines. Republicans and Democrats appeared together on anti-bond platforms and committees. The creditors' interest would be defended by the Democratic newspaper in one town, and by the Republican in another. In tax-burdened counties, candidates might vie over which was the more tough in resisting collection. At election time, blame for all the trouble might be placed on a Supreme Bench of Republicans in Washington— or on the Democratic State Court that had hastened railroad aid bonding on Iowa in 1853.

Very significantly, neither party chose to make repudiation of railroad aid a State-wide issue.

A Republican politician active in the anti-bond forces—author of the bill to remove the penalty for bond tax deficiencies[276]—portrayed the Court as having

> always been on the side of capital and power, American slavery was once its master; it is now obeying the behests of capital and railroad bondholders.[277]

A Democratic politician in the same movement put the same thought in a partisan context:

> in these latter days neither the congress . . . nor the Supreme Court . . . have any regard whatever for the rights of any class of citizens than the bondholders, bankers and other money shavers and leaches [sic] on the body politic, who produce nothing themselves nor add a dollar to the general wealth of the community in which they live. . . .[278]

When in December 1869 Senators Trumbull and Drake introduced bills that would have stripped the Court of power to interfere

---

[275] Jan. 22, 1870.
[276] Supra, p. 979.
[277] State Senator Samuel McNutt of Muscatine, addressing the Musca-

tine convention. *Keokuk Constitution*, Dec. 18, 1869.
[278] Thomas W. Clagett, editor, in the *Keokuk Constitution*, Apr. 16, 1869.

with Reconstruction,[279] Radical anti-bond editors in Iowa hastened to make common cause. The *Gate City* supported measures "to control the lofty ambition of that aristocratic tribunal, which seeks to exalt itself over the nation and absorb all power and jurisdiction into its own hands." Let not the Iowa delegation in Congress be awed "by the long robed toggery that keeps up a solemn state in one of the chambers of the Capitol."[280]

The *Muscatine Journal* (Republican) joined in endorsing Trumbull's bill, condemned the Court for invalidating the Legal Tender Act in *Hepburn v. Griswold*,[281] and dwelt upon the theme that the power of the federal judiciary had increased, was increasing, and ought to be diminished.[282] In *Dred Scott*, it said, the Supreme Court had threatened to spread the black pall of African slavery over the whole country. Recently, "in the case of the little steamboat Ad Hine" the Court by "arbitrary" construction had swept away the jurisdiction of State courts over navigable inland waters. Of late there had been numerous instances of usurpation. And now "the State of Iowa is . . . in an expensive and irritable controversy on account of what many good lawyers believe an unwarranted exercise of power by the United States judiciary." How foresighted did Jefferson now seem in his apprehensions about the federal judiciary!

One of the most unsatisfactory aspects of editorial treatment of the Supreme Court, through the years, has been the tendency to resort to indiscriminate condemnation for alleged enormities in matters where the readers (and perhaps the writer) had no understanding of the particulars. Here, in the matter of *The Hine v. Trevor*,[283] if—to readers whose sporting interest in steamboats was comparable to what later generations have had in privately-owned baseball clubs—the editor had explained that the Court's decision meant that errors imputed to a steamboat would now be judged by a disinterested federal umpire applying a universal body of rules, would informed readers have agreed that that was "dangerous to the civil and political liberties of the people"?

A NEW ROUND OF RAILROAD AID

THE COURSE OF Iowa's "irritable controversy" took another strange turn when in October 1870 the State Supreme Court, transformed in composition, said that for the future municipal aid to railroads was con-

---

279 Supra, pp. 587–88.
280 Dec. 10, 1869.
281 Supra, ch. 14.

282 Dec. 15, 1869, and Feb. 11, 1870.
283 4 Wall. 555 (1867), per Miller, J.

stitutionally permissible after all. This was in *Stewart v. Board of Supervisors of Polk County.*[284] Overruling *Hanson v. Vernon,*[285] the court sustained the statute of 1870 whereby townships, towns, and cities might vote as much as a 5 percent tax as a gift to a railroad.[286] This was the work of Judge Cole[287] (the dissenter in *Hanson v. Vernon*) aided by two Judges newly come to the court.[288] Beck, J., dissented.

The court said, however, that it was adhering to *Wapello*[289] and the cases that followed it holding county and city bonds invalid. So it was permissible to tax people for a gift to a railroad, but not to tax where the municipality received stock in return for its bonds.[290] (This gave the supporters of railroad aid what they wanted, yet permitted the indebted municipalities still to maintain that their bonds were invalid by State law.)

In the federal Circuit Court, Judge Dillon, in evident disgust, said that this result was "anomalous"; nevertheless, as was the duty of a federal judge, he would follow the latest State decision.[291]

---

[284] 30 Iowa 9.

[285] Supra, n. 224.

[286] Supra, pp. 977, 979.

[287] Chester Cicero Cole (1834–1913), after twelve years on the bench, in 1876 returned to private practice. Shortly thereafter he was the subject of disbarment proceedings pressed by the Iowa Bar Association, on the charge that he had encouraged a client to attack the honesty of Circuit Judge Dillon, in the hope of inducing a favorable decision in the matter of a foreclosure of the Central Railroad of Iowa; Cole's answer admitted that the charges against Judge Dillon were false. *Central Law Journal,* 7:420, Nov. 22, 1878, and 10:438, June 4, 1880—two among numerous articles recording the widespread indignation at the attack upon Judge Dillon. To the same point were articles in the *Albany Law Journal,* 16:94, 126, 212, of August 11 and 18 and September 22, 1877—critical of *The Nation,* which in articles between July 12 and Nov. 29, 1877, gave credence to the charges.

It was shortly after this episode that Chief Justice Waite took occasion to express the Court's confidence in Judge Dillon, in the words quoted above, p. 923—that he had "filled the office of Circuit Judge in the Eighth Circuit with such distinguished ability . . . ." Douglass v. Pike County, 101 U.S. 677, 679. In 1879 Dillon had resigned, to the great regret of the bar of his circuit, to become professor of law in Columbia Law School, for which he had Justice Miller's unqualified endorsement.

[288] Judge Dillon's appointment to the federal bench in 1869 produced one vacancy. It was an appointee (next after Dillon's immediate replacement) who spoke for the Court in the *Stewart* case. Judge Wright also left the bench upon his election as United States Senator; his appointed successor joined in the *Stewart* decision.

[289] Supra, n. 61.

[290] As a practical matter, perhaps a single contribution, taken from people who had voted on it, would cause less pain than a taking by inches over ten or twenty years.

[291] King v. Wilson, Fed. Case No. 7810 (Jan. 1871), denying an injunction sought by citizens of other States owning land taxed by an Iowa township for railroad aid. The opinion reviewed the history of the Iowa statutes and decisions.

It is to be remarked that, in the continued abuse of the Supreme Court, very little was ever said to suggest that the citizen ought to have judicial protection against any compulsory contribution to a railroad company. The air had been filled with allegations of "fraud" and "swindle"—which, even if proved, could not avail against an innocent purchaser. There had been much ado over the fact that no opinion had been published in 1853 to support the decision upholding county bonds.[292] Most of all, there was an outcry that in *Gelpcke v. Dubuque* the Supreme Court, by a change of the rules, had refused to follow the latest holding of the State court. Very seldom was it argued that *Wapello* should have been respected because it was right. When in May 1870 the Supreme Court of Michigan decided that taxation for railroad aid was not for a public purpose and hence was unconstitutional[293]—a decision by Judge Cooley that came with powerful impact —some Iowa editors claimed this as a vindication, in articles under such headlines as "The Invasion of Private Rights Under the Guise of Law." But really that was not the position for which the indebted counties had been fighting. Pretty generally, people thought it was right to compel their neighbors to contribute to a work that would enhance the value of all property. When there was no statute by which that could be enforced, very strong social pressures were applied to induce every man to subscribe according to the amount of his possessions.[294]

The statute of 1870 permitting a 5 percent tax for railroad aid was, the *Dubuque Herald* said, "wise in its purpose and eminently just in its application."[295] *Stewart v. Polk County*, sustaining it, would "be received with great favor in some parts of the State; with just as positive disfavor in others," said the *Gate City*. The editor's own view was that it was "a big mistake."[296] The *Keokuk Constitution*, disapproving, commented that "the railroad corporations of Iowa by their agents in both branches of the legislature" had enacted the statute, and then "by their agents upon the Supreme Court bench" had pronounced it constitutional.[297] The *Davenport Democrat* discussed the decision in a wishy-washy editorial that concluded,

---

[292] Supra, p. 940.

[293] People *ex rel.* Detroit & Howell R.R. v. Township of Salem, 20 Mich. 452. Infra, p. 1011.

[294] For example, when Washington, Iowa, saw the prospect of being "on one of the greatest thoroughfares in the world" and becoming "the Pittsburg of the West," it was urged that there be a black list of all "sharks" and "cormorants" who refused to bear their share. *Washington Gazette*, Jan. 21 to Feb. 18, and Nov. 4, 1870.

So in Muscatine, there was discussion whether to "spot" those who failed to subscribe to railroads that would make theirs "the leading river city in the State." *Muscatine Journal*, Apr. 23 to May 9, 1870.

[295] May 1, 1870.

[296] Oct. 15, 1870; June 23, 1871.

[297] Jan. 14, 1871.

Yet, looking at the vast resources of the State, its almost illimitable wealth when under proper improvement, it is more than probable that the gains achieved through this questionable law, will more than over-balance the swindles that will arise under it. So let us hope—even though some day we may be deceived.[298]

The Iowa story had now come full circle. Everywhere men were hastening to take advantage of the new statute. In Dubuque—home of the *Gelpcke* case, and still $1,000,000 in debt—two new railroads were being promoted. "Yesterday," the *Herald* reported, the presidents of these enterprises "circulated the petition for the submission of the question of a tax to aid the roads, required under the new law, and in passing down one side of Main Street, from the corner of 5th to the corner of 2nd streets, over one hundred signatures were obtained, but four or five to whom application was made refusing."[299]

In the next county down river, there was the prospect that a railroad would be built from Milwaukee, entering Iowa at Sabula and running west to Kansas. A visitor reported that "the people of the townships for the first twenty or thirty miles, have, with great unanim-ity, commenced the work of securing the tax. . . ."[300]

Citizens of Muscatine wanted to encourage the building of a railroad in Illinois, to come to their city;[301] the statute of 1870, how-ever, said nothing about giving extraterritorial aid. According to the *Journal*,

> If this could have been done it would not only have been an easy way to raise the money, but an equitable one, as each property owner would then pay his share in exact proportion to his interest.[302]

With this may be compared the same journal's comment two months later, in praise of the Michigan court's decision wherein municipal aid to railroads was condemned as exacting a contribution for what was not properly a public purpose. Said the editor:

> No one can, after mature deliberation, doubt the correctness and justice of this principle. It lies at the very foundation of our boasted liberty and free enjoyment of the fruits of our labor. In any State or county where this principle of liberty is denied the people are merely vassals, subject to being stripped of that which is next to life itself—property.[303]

---

[298] Dec. 10, 1870.
[299] May 4, 1870.
[300] *Milwaukee Sentinel*, Dec. 10, 1870.

[301] Supra, n. 294.
[302] Apr. 22, 1870.
[303] June 24, 1870.

XVII: *Municipal Bonds I*

Washington County in 1871 owed about $400,000, chiefly on account of aid to the Mississippi & Missouri.[304] In May of that year promoters appeared, with a plan for a Burlington & Northeastern line that would afford a second outlet to the East—on condition that a 3 percent tax be voted. The president of the new corporation "thought that the present system of raising aid should be taken advantage of, as the day might come when the law would be repealed."[305] A local banker, conspicuous in resisting the old bonds, now was foremost in drumming up support for the new subsidy; he warned that "if we failed to vote the tax, and the route south of Skunk River did, then we would certainly lose the road."[306] (One learns to expect that every project will have its own Skunk River alternative, to quicken the hesitant; perhaps in the end a "branch line" would still take the route via Skunk River.) Now the State Senator from Washington urged haste to proceed under the new law;[307] a year before he had been a leader in the anti-bond convention, and then in the legislature had made a major speech on behalf of the bonded counties. He blamed the Supreme Court for its *Gelpcke* decision, which saddled on Iowa counties a six million dollar indebtedness. "But you say [that in such situations] the people voted on the proposition. I care not for that. The citizens of a county possess no legislative power, and can confer no authority . . . not conferred by statute." "The question is one of legality"—not of moral obligation.[308]

When Washington County held its election, there were 177 votes for tax aid, 423 against. That was the death of a worthy project, lamented the local editor; the farmers were to blame for killing it.[309] Three months earlier, this editor had been telling his readers that the people were being "robbed by judicial decisions in favor of owners of the county and city railroad bonds. But the time will come," he predicted, "when [these] scoundrelly decisions of . . . the Supreme Court of the United States . . . will be overthrown, and the judges who acquiesced in them will be damned in the estimation of all honest men."[310]

What with disenchantment at paying an old piper and the allure of each new one, the people were sadly confused.

---

[304] *Washington Gazette,* Apr. 7, 1871.

[305] Ibid., May 26, 1871. This was James H. Gear, Burlington merchant; thereafter Speaker in the legislature, Governor, Congressman, and Senator.

[306] *Washington Gazette, June* 2, 1871.

[307] Ibid.

[308] *Keokuk Gate City,* Mar. 22, 1870, reporting the speech of Granville G. Bennett—later a Justice of the Supreme Court of the Territory of Dakota, and a Delegate to Congress.

[309] *Washington Gazette,* July 28, 1871.

[310] Apr. 21, 1871.

J. EDGAR THOMSON—HONORED GUEST

THIS ACCOUNT MAY conveniently be broken off just as it reaches a rather dramatic climax. The villain in Lee County's story had been J. Edgar Thomson (commonly "Thompson" in law reports and in newspapers)—the chief holder of the county's bonds and of Keokuk's as well. He had been portrayed as the man who had made himself a millionaire by buying up fraudulent bonds "at a heavy shave"—who had "succeeded in getting that [Supreme] Court to render some most rascally decisions in his favor"—who had induced "a corrupt Congress to give him" millions of acres of public land, and then had had "the brazen impudence to refuse to pay" the State property tax.[311]

But this J. Edgar Thomson (1808–74) was none other than the president of the Pennsylvania Railroad, a powerful man then bent upon expansion. (With the panic of 1873 the management would be forced to turn inward toward consolidation and a tightening of control.) On June 10, 1871, on one of his prospecting excursions, he visited Keokuk.[312] (A year earlier he had been dared to come there in person, to bid on Francis Semple's mule.[313]) Chief among those accompanying him was Thomas A. Scott (1823–81), first vice president of the Pennsylvania Railroad, and president of the subsidiary Pennsylvania Company organized in 1870 to operate all leased and controlled lines west of Pittsburgh. Another of the party was Andrew Carnegie (1835–1919), once Scott's personal telegrapher, later his successor as superintendent of the Pittsburgh division; since 1865 he had been engaged in bridge building and steel production. These men,

---

[311] *Keokuk Constitution*, May 8, 1870. The last jibe refers to Thomson v. Pacific R.R. Co., 9 Wall. 579, decided April 30, 1870, where the Court had rejected the claim that the property of a railroad chartered by Congress was exempt from State taxation. Attorney General Hoar appeared on behalf of Thomson *et al.*, complaining stockholders.

[312] The account that follows draws upon the *Keokuk Gate City* from 1868 through 1871.

On Thomson's death *The Nation* pointed to his monumental accomplishment over twenty-five years;

    and though, like all men engaged in the tremendous game of competition which the conduct of

these great enterprises involves, he exposed himself often to censure, one marvels at the close of his career at the small amount of it he drew forth. His life reveals to us in great part where it is that the highest order of administrative ability in this country and in our day goes, . . . and places in a somewhat comic light the attempts that are now being made to commit the railroads of the country to the supervision of . . . the philosophers of the Granges.

18:356, June 4, 1874.

[313] *Keokuk Constitution*, May 14, 1870.

and their associates, were at the moment planning to project their system west of the Mississippi. The *New York Tribune* in a survey in 1869[314]—a climactic year for the Pennsylvania—had recorded that, "with the connections it now has, [this] is the most extensive railroad corporation in the world. [Its "Panhandle line" ran from Pittsburgh to Columbus; thence its allied "Ben Smith Roads"] carry it to Chicago and St. Louis, and furnish it, besides, with very important feeders, among which are the Toledo, Peoria and Warsaw . . . ."[315]

This T., P. & W. ran across Illinois to Hamilton on the Mississippi river, opposite Keokuk. When the Keokuk & Hamilton Bridge, built by Carnegie's Keystone Bridge Company, went into service in June 1871, the Pennsylvania had a through line between Keokuk and New York City, with one change of cars at Columbus.[316]

Thomson and party had come to Keokuk, it was reported, to study whether that city should become "the base of their railroad operations from the Mississippi west."[317] Specifically that meant support of the Missouri, Iowa & Nebraska, projected to run along the Iowa-Missouri boundary and on to a junction with the Union Pacific in Nebraska. People of Keokuk imagined that "manifest destiny" would make their town "the most important point on this great thoroughfare."[318]

But it was feared that Thomson and his associates "have gathered the impression that Keokuk and its Council are hostile to them and their interests . . . ." That idea must be dispelled; "much of what Keokuk is to be" depended upon satisfying this Pennsylvania

---

[314] The issue of February 25, 1869, contained a detailed account of "The Great Railroad War" then being fought for strong positions in the Mid-West and for dominance of areas beyond; the chief contestants were Jay Gould's Erie, Commodore Vanderbilt's New York Central, the Pennsylvania under Thomson, and the Baltimore & Ohio under John W. Garrett.

[315] Ben Smith was president of the Columbus, Chicago & Indiana Central; his "chain of connecting railroads" included two that ran on from Indianapolis to St. Louis.

[316] "Pullman Palace Cars" were available all the way; the time table called for just under forty-eight hours.

Keokuk had two other routes toward the East: over the bridge on the Toledo, Wabash & Western and thence by way of Cleveland; and to Burlington and then Chicago over the Chicago, Burlington & Quincy.

[317] *Gate City*, June 10, 1871. There had been a visit to Keokuk in June 1869 by Thomson, Ben Smith, presidents of other railroads in the Pennsylvania system, and men interested in construction west of the Mississippi, including Francis M. Drake, president of the Missouri, Iowa & Nebraska. The *Gate City* said that there emerged an "arrangement unanimously come to, to put the road through to the Missouri river, promptly." June 18 and 19, 1869. *Keokuk Constitution*, June 18 and 20, 1869.

[318] *Gate City*, Nov. 27, 1870; Aug. 9, 1871.

group. "Let these gentlemen say just what it wants Keokuk to do and then let Keokuk do it." "The impressions with which Thompson and Scott go away from here at this time" would be decisive.

When presently an intermediate stretch of forty miles of the M., I. & N. was completed, the toast was "Keokuk, once the Gate City of Iowa, now the Gate City of America. May she become the Gate City of the World."[319]

THE SUPREME COURT'S CONSTRUCTION OF MUNICIPAL POWERS

MUNICIPALITIES ARE CREATIONS of the State. Their powers, and their debt limits, are established by State law—especially by a charter. The construction of these municipal powers and limitations has a much wider application than the immediate business of aid to railroads.[320]

We are examining what the federal Supreme Court did in this field which, in principle, is governed by the law of the State. The jurisdiction of the federal courts arose from the circumstance that a litigant, the bondholder, was a citizen of another State.

We may say at the outset that the Court went wrong. That may be stated flatly, inasmuch as the Court itself came to admit it.

We start from horn-book law:

> It is a general and undisputed proposition of law that a municipal corporation possesses, and can exercise, the following powers, and no others: First, those granted in *express words*; second, those *necessarily or fairly implied* in, or *incident* to the powers expressly granted; third, those *essential* to the declared objects and purposes of the corporation—not simply convenient, but indispensable. . . .

So Judge Dillon wrote in *The Law of Municipal Corporations*, first published in 1872.[321] A corporation's charter, he continued, is "its organic act."

> Neither the corporation, nor its officers, can do any act, or make any contract, or incur any liability, not authorized thereby. All acts beyond the scope of the powers granted are void. . . .

The reason for thus limiting municipal liability was obvious, said the great Chief Justice Shaw of Massachusetts in 1839: "if this liability

---

[319] *Gate City*, Sept. 29, 1871.
[320] Touched upon in the discussion of Von Hostrup v. Madison City, 1 Wall. 291 (1864), and Meyer v. City of Muscatine, 1 Wall. 384 (1864), supra, pp. 945–46.
[321] Sec. 55.

were to extend to unlimited and indefinite objects, the citizen, by being a member of a corporation, might be deprived of his most valuable personal rights and liberties." This point was "of the highest importance . . . where corporations have been extended and multiplied so as to embrace almost every object of human concern."[322] Municipalities are subordinate units which, subject to legislative control, perform specified local functions; their powers are not to be read with the liberality that is appropriate to the construction of the State or the federal Constitution.

These were, and are, fixed principles. It is useful to establish them, because, once one enters upon the Court's decisions on municipal bonding, the beacons become obscure.

Burlington's charter authorized it "to borrow money for any public purpose" upon a two-thirds vote of approval. In 1856 the corporation issued $75,000 of twenty-year 10 percent bonds, which it *loaned* to the Burlington & Missouri Railroad.[323] In *Rogers v. Burlington*[324] in January 1865, able counsel presented a sharp issue on that charter provision: aid to a railroad was not within that grant of municipal powers; and in any event, a power "to borrow" did not include a power *to lend*. Rejecting that defense, Justice Clifford for a majority of five said that

> the decision in the case of Gelpcke v. Dubuque, although the opinion of the Court contains a reference to other statutes, was chiefly founded upon the construction of a provision in the charter of that city expressed in the same words . . . . Decision, also, in the case of Meyer v. Muscatine,[325] is to the same effect. . . .

The further point—that the city had loaned, not borrowed—was brushed aside as without substance: in effect, Clifford said, the city was borrowing from those who took the bonds.

Justice Field wrote a crackling dissent in which the Chief Justice and Justices Grier and Miller joined. "Borrowing money and lending credit are not convertible terms." He pointed to an important recent decision to that effect by the New York Court of Appeals.[326] (That highly respectable court was applying to its municipal bond cases the principles of law generally applicable to the situation, with no indulgence for this particular activity. This course presently brought it into collision with the Supreme Court of the United States.[327]) One serious

---

[322] Spaulding v. Lowell, 23 Pick. 71, 74.

[323] That line, running west across the State, in 1872 became a part of the Chicago, Burlington & Quincy.

[324] 3 Wall. 654. Evans Rogers sued

on interest coupons on such bonds.

[325] 1 Wall. 384 (1864). Supra, p. 946.

[326] Gould v. Town of Sterling, 23 N.Y. 439, 456 (1861). Infra, p. 1053.

[327] Infra, pp. 1052–58.

objection was that where the railroad company disposed of bonds at a discount, the benefit the voters had sought to confer would not be realized.

On the larger point, that the bonds had been issued for a purpose ultra vires of the charter, the dissent did not dwell, because,

> When the authority to borrow money is made to cover a case of lending credit, it is vain to contend that the "public purpose" prescribed by the charter is limited to any of the purposes for which such charter was created.

Twenty-six years later, when of the nine participants only Justice Field remained, the Court—stressing decisions that had been made after the departure of Swayne and Clifford—declared that *Rogers v. Burlington* must be regarded as overruled.[328]

One should take account how lightly the majority in *Rogers* were treating the limitations on municipal powers, and how loosely they dealt with earlier rulings. Here an ordinary power to borrow for a public purpose was held to mean, not merely to incur indebtedness on a note or on warrants in anticipation of revenues, but also to emit negotiable securities to circulate throughout the world, with all that that involved in commercial law; that this might be done, not merely for the usual municipal purposes envisaged by the charter, but also to aid a private corporation to build its railroad; and that this power to borrow extended to loaning bonds to a company that could dispose of them on such terms as it saw fit to accept.

Dubuque's charter contained precisely the same provision on borrowing as did Burlington's. In *Gelpcke v. Dubuque*, however, there was also a statute expressly authorizing the city to aid two named railroads by issuing bonds; what it might have done by virtue of its charter alone, Justice Swayne there said, was "not now in question." Burlington, on the other hand, acted without any such statute; but, Justice Clifford now said, *Gelpcke* "was chiefly founded" upon the charter provision, and so was controlling. Muscatine's charter gave the corporation authority "to borrow money for any object in its discretion;" but in *Meyer v. Muscatine*, Justice Swayne had found the power to issue bonds in another statute taken "in connection with the provision of the charter."[329] But now in *Rogers v. Burlington*, Justice

---

[328] City of Brenham v. German-American Bank, 144 U.S. 173 (1892).

[329] 1 Wall. 384 (1864). Supra, p. 946. Justice Miller had said in his dissent, "what is wanting in original power to issue these bonds is supposed to be supplied as a ratification or confirmation of them, by the Act of January 25, 1855 . . . ," Relating to the Interest on City and County Bonds.

Clifford was announcing a rule—allegedly resulting from *Gelpcke* and *Meyer*—for the federal judiciary's construction of municipal charters generally, without any connection with related statutes.

This was without any regard, too, for what the State courts might have held about the construction of the State statute from which the municipality derived its powers. Two years before the decision in the *Rogers* case, the Supreme Court of Iowa had considered the Burlington charter as it bore upon this same bond transaction, and—without overruling any precedent—had held that it did not authorize aid to a railroad, and did not permit a loan of credit.[330] Apparently that was not cited when *Rogers* was argued; but if it had been, doubtless the Supreme Court would have paid no heed.[331]

The Court went astray again in refusing to respect limits on municipal taxation.

By the charters of Burlington and Muscatine it had been enacted that the city council would have power to impose taxes, not exceeding 1 percent upon the taxable property in any year. That stood as fair warning to all who became creditors of the city.

The Iowa Code, when it came to the title Execution, provided (Sec. 3275) that where a judgment had been rendered against a city or county, "a tax must be levied as early as practicable, sufficient to pay off the judgment with interest and costs." This was part of the general law, first enacted in 1851. The specific limitations as to Burlington and Muscatine had been enacted later, in 1852 and 1853 respectively. Such being the law, those cities thereafter issued railroad aid bonds, and presently defaulted.

Butz recovered a judgment against Muscatine, and Amy and Learned against Burlington; then they sought mandamus to compel the levy of a tax. Could a judgment creditor insist that "a tax must be levied . . . ," without regard to any tax limit? James Grant fastened upon those words as an independent and overriding command.

In *Learned v. Burlington*,[332] at the circuit in 1863, Justice Miller held that the duty to levy a tax was limited by the 1 percent maximum of the charter. Otherwise, he pointed out, a city council, simply by exercising its power to enter into contracts, could render the limit nugatory, and "impose upon the property-holders a tax unlimited in amount or duration." He added that "the wisdom of such limitation had been amply vindicated by events . . . ."

---

[330] Chamberlain v. City of Burlington, 19 Iowa 395 (1864).

[331] Chamberlain v. Burlington was cited a year later in argument—and went unnoticed in the decision—of

two cases where the Court followed *Rogers*: Mitchell v. Burlington, 4 Wall. 270 (1867), and Learned v. Burlington, 4 Wall. 275 (1867).

[332] Fed. Case No. 14,687.

Also in 1863, when the question first came before it, the Supreme Court of Iowa reached the same result: Section 3275 did *not* confer a power to tax otherwise than had elsewhere been provided by law.[333]

Butz v. Muscatine[334] brought this question to the Supreme Court of the United States. James Grant's brief for the bondholder showed that he had not been chastened by the Court's reproof in *Benbow v. Iowa City*.[335] He said that Justice Miller's position was "not at all tenable." He derided his remark about "the wisdom" of limiting taxation; the "wise" thing for a Judge, said Grant, was "not to construe laws against their plain meaning to suit the changing opinions of the hour . . . ." Of the opinion of the Iowa court in 1863 (where Grant had met defeat in his attempt to fasten liability on Davenport, his own city)[336] he exclaimed, "why, what a jumble of nonsense . . . ." It "has no logic in it."[337] Such contemptuous expressions were quite out of the ordinary in arguments addressed to the Supreme Court.

In deciding *Butz* a majority of the Court gave Grant what he sought. Justice Swayne refused "blindly" to follow the Iowa court in its construction of Iowa statutes. The tax limit was brushed aside as applicable only to "the ordinary course of . . . municipal action." There was "no room for doubt": for a judgment creditor a tax must be laid regardless of that limitation. "Here the remedy was taken away; not by a subsequent repeal [as had been condemned in *Von Hoffman v. Quincy*[338]], but by subsequent judicial decisions."

But that was not fair and square. In *Von Hoffman* the Court had held, rightly, that a tax limit enacted in 1863 was constitutionally inapplicable to bonds issued between 1851 and 1856. In *Butz* the limit was already on the statute books when the bonds were issued—and the State court, as early as it had occasion to pronounce upon the question, held that the limit did apply. In truth, no remedy was "taken away" from Butz: only in hope did he ever have the remedy he claimed—and that on the basis of a construction which the Supreme Court itself, four years later, found to be "certainly remarkable."[339]

---

[333] Clark, Dodge & Co. v. Davenport, 14 Iowa 494. Adhered to in Coy v. Lyons, 17 Iowa 1 (1864); Oswald v. Thedinga, 17 Iowa 13 (1864); Porter v. Thomson, 22 Iowa 391 (1867).

[334] 8 Wall. 575. Docketed Sept. 13, 1868; decided Dec. 20, 1869.

[335] Supra, pp. 952–53.

[336] Clark, Dodge & Co. v. Davenport, 14 Iowa 494.

[337] Argument for Plaintiff in Error, 5–7. Serious typographical errors tend to confirm the impression that when he struck off his brief for an appellant, Grant did not wait to count to one hundred, or even to ten.

[338] 4 Wall. 535 (1867). Supra, p. 979.

[339] Supervisors of Carroll County v. United States *ex rel*. Reynolds, 18 Wall. 71 (1873), infra, p. 1001. Grant, for the defendant in error, had said that the question "has been settled by the court and requires no argument now."

Justice Miller filed a sharp dissent, in which Chief Justice Chase concurred, pointing out how far the Court was advancing beyond the ground claimed in *Gelpcke v. Dubuque.*

The *Butz* decision was applied a month later in *Amy v. Burlington* and *Learned v. Burlington.*[340]

Muscatine had been host to the convention of bond-burdened counties on December 15, 1869.[341] *Butz v. Muscatine* was decided on December 20. When in the *Journal* of that evening the editor suggested that the Supreme Court was ready to help a "sharper" take "the last shirt off the greenhorn's back," he was unaware of what had happened that day in Washington. Not until January 14 did he report this "latest and most alarming act of encroachment" which had "just come to our knowledge."

> Here is an instance of the State Courts giving construction to State laws by uniform decisions, which laws no one will say are contrary to any law of Congress, and yet the Federal Court steps in and nullifies it! By what right, or shadow of right, can it do this? . . .
> . . . It is no use to ask justice or the observance of law at the hands of this tribunal. It has determined to carry its point, which is to make us pay these unjust demands, though it may divest us of all our property. . . .

On May 5, 1870, the *Journal* published Justice Miller's dissent, explaining that it had been obtained "at some trouble and expense." This illustrates how the action of the Court was often learned only belatedly—and sometimes in garbled form—even in the community immediately affected.

The twist in Justice Swayne's opinion in *Butz* is shown by placing it beside that of Justice Strong in *Supervisors of Carroll County v. United States ex rel. Reynolds,*[342] in 1873. There was a limit on the taxing power of a county, and a judgment creditor sought mandamus to compel the levy of a tax, contending that Section 3275 on Execution operated independently of any limit. Justice Strong, examining the problem closely, said that it would have been "certainly remarkable" if the legislature had intended such a grant yet left it to inference and tucked away in a section of a statute on Executions. "We do not propose, however, to discuss the question now. It has already been answered, and we must accept the answer. The Supreme Court of Iowa has decided in several cases that section 3275 confers no independent power . . ." to levy a tax—first in 1863, prior to the issue of Reynolds' warrants. While this placed the decision, rightly, on the duty of the

---

[340] 154 U.S. 568 (1870).   [341] Supra, p. 975.   [342] 18 Wall. 71.

Supreme Court to respect the State court's construction of a local statute, it was clearly implied that the Iowa court had been right—which meant that Justice Swayne's construction had been wrong. *Butz* was distinguished on the ground that the bonds there had been issued before the State court's ruling.

Justices Clifford and Swayne dissented; in their view, the Supreme Court should stick to its original opinion even though the State court gave a different construction.

HOPE SPRINGS FROM RUMOR:
MARSH v. FULTON COUNTY

As 1871 DAWNED, the Iowans were in an acquiescent mood. Throughout the area that had been seriously disaffected—about a dozen counties, in a strip along the eastern side with a tongue pointing west along the Rock Island (formerly Mississippi & Missouri) tracks—people now were pretty well resigned to paying their way out of their misadventure. On January 6 the Lee County board resolved that "all reasonable and diligent efforts shall be made to compromise [the railroad bond] indebtedness on fair and reasonable terms."[343] That was typical.

And then suddenly rumor came of a marvelous happening in the Supreme Court whereby "that rascally decision" in *Gelpcke v. Dubuque* had at last "kicked the beam," so that true justice thenceforth would be found on the other side of the balance; that, it was supposed, must mean that bondholders could no longer collect—even that payments already made by way of compromise could be recovered.[344] The *Keokuk Constitution* had it from "a leading lawyer of Carthage, Illinois," who had it from "Skinner & Marsh, attorneys of Quincy," who had "just received notice from Washington," that in *Marsh v. Fulton County* the Supreme Court had "reversed its former rulings." As other Iowa newspapers took up the tale, this almost "seemed too good to be true."[345] The *Burlington Hawk-Eye* pronounced it "huge folly" thus to give "new life to the repudiating spirit, which had become wellnigh extinct." It could not see "the least probability that the Supreme Court will reverse its repeated decisions . . . ."[346]

In *Caleb P. Marsh v. Fulton County*,[347] on February 13, 1871, the Supreme Court did with unanimity decide against a holder of

---

[343] *Keokuk Constitution*, Jan. 14, 1871.

[344] *Keokuk Constitution*, Mar. 21, 1871, "Important Decision by the Supreme Court of the United States

on the Bond Question."

[345] *Washington Gazette*, Apr. 21, 1871, quoting the *Muscatine Journal*.

[346] Apr. 8, 1871.

[347] 10 Wall. 676.

railroad aid bonds: that in itself was an extraordinary event. A commentator branded the case "an illegitimate child, which has by some means stolen into the family";[348] it was plainly "wrong," another asserted.[349]

Important for the law it laid down, the case is even more instructive when one learns from the transcript and briefs how easily diversity of citizenship was established, and how a straw man who had paid nothing could be given the semblance of an innocent purchaser. So palpable was the reek as doubtless to impel the Justices to let this case go against the bondholder.

The case, on Marsh's behalf, was submitted to the Court by Orville H. Browning and Onias C. Skinner, both of Quincy: the one had recently been a member of Johnson's Cabinet, the other had from 1855 to 1858 sat on the Illinois Supreme Court. Skinner & Marsh had represented the plaintiff in the federal Circuit Court.

Caleb P. Marsh of New York, in whose name the action was brought, was Attorney Marsh's brother. (Let it be interjected that while this litigation was going on, Caleb Marsh was engaged in a larger transaction which presently brought him to the attention of Congress and the entire nation. In 1870 he arranged with Secretary of War Belknap to be given the appointment as post-trader at Fort Sill, Indian Territory; the actual commission was issued to Marsh's nominee, who pursuant to contract paid Marsh $12,000—later $6,000—annually; one-half of each payment Marsh sent to Belknap, "Simply because I felt like doing it. It gave me pleasure to do it. I sent him the money as a present always, gratuitously."[350] Thus was Marsh related to one

---

[348] G[aspar] C. Clemens, *The Law of Corporate Securities as Decided in the Federal Courts* (St. Louis: W. J. Gilbert, 1877), 40. The author was a Kansas practitioner, experienced in representing the bondholder interest.

[349] Leonard A. Jones, *A Treatise on the Law of Railroad and other Corporate Securities, including Municipal Bonds* (Boston: Houghton, Osgood and Co., 1879), in note to Sec. 282. By accepting and holding the shares of the Central Division, the County, he wrote, should have been held estopped to deny the validity of its bonds. The author was a Boston lawyer who had turned to the writing of practical treatises.

[350] *Proceedings of the Senate sitting for the Trial of William W. Belknap,*

late Secretary of War . . . , 44th Cong., 1st Sess. (1875–76), vol. 4, pt. 7, at 238.

Allegation of corruption appeared in the *New York Tribune* of February 16, 1872. Four years later, when the 44th Congress convened with a Democratic majority in the House, articles of impeachment were brought, specifying seventeen occasions when Belknap had received money, usually $1,500, from Marsh. Although Belknap resigned earlier in the day than the bringing of the impeachment, the Senate sustained its jurisdiction. As the vote to convict was never greater than 37 to 25 on any article, the proceedings failed for want of "the concurrence of two-thirds of the Members present,"

of the more discreditable happenings in Grant's second Administration.)

In February 1853 the Illinois legislature had chartered the Mississippi & Wabash Railroad Company, to build a road between Warsaw, on the Mississippi River, and the east line of the State.[351] In November the Fulton voters approved a subscription of $75,000, to be paid in bonds when the company had made certain progress in raising capital. Discouragements were such that, as one director testified, "I consider the road, as an entire line, abandoned from July, 1856, and a majority of the stockholders about Canton [in Fulton County] considered it so; and we turned our attention to [a north-south road]."[352]

In February 1857 the legislature, "for the purpose of . . . securing the early construction of certain portions" of the line, voted to amend the charter to create three separately controlled entities, the Western, Central, and Eastern Divisions. Now events follow very rapidly. On September 1 the Clerk of the County Court issued bonds to the amount of $15,000—thirty bonds for $500, payable in ten years, with coupons for 7 percent interest annually—to the *Central Division* of the Mississippi & Wabash. On October 9 the Board of Supervisors filed in the State court a bill against the Mississippi & Wabash, the Clerk, and others, to restrain the issuance of $60,000 in bonds, and to recover the bonds already issued or compensation therefor. This was *Supervisors of Fulton County v. Mississippi & Wabash R.R.*, which presently the Supreme Court of Illinois decided in favor of the County.[353] When the suit was filed, the circuit court issued a temporary injunction; upon the hearing this was dissolved and the bill dismissed. Instanter the County appealed—but also on the instant, it will be seen, affected bonds were negotiated.

At January term 1859 the State Supreme Court reversed the lower court's decree; the issue was adjudged to have been invalid. First, because "the great enterprise, originally contemplated, has dwindled to a mere local road fifty miles in length, having no important termini, the stock in which, as appears by the record, would be of a nominal value only." Second, the election in November 1853 had been an undivided proposition of subscribing to stock in the Mississippi & Wabash *and* in the Petersburg & Springfield: "the law never intended

---

[351] The western terminus would be close to Keokuk, Iowa (to which Samuel F. Miller had recently come); that city voted a subscription. As chartered, the road would run via Bloomington, Illinois (David Davis' residence). Transcript of Record, 7; Argument for Defendants in Error, 3.

[352] Transcript, 27.

[353] 21 Ill. *338.

that two roads should be coupled together, and the people forbidden to vote for one if they did not also vote for the other, the one road being really a bribe for votes for the other."[354]

Now come to Caleb P. Marsh and his bonds, illegally issued according to the State Supreme Court. The Clerk had issued the thirty bonds for $500 on September 1, 1857, to the Central Division, M. & W. Most of these were promptly paid over to Edgar P. Buell, then resident in Fulton County, who had a contract to build a part of the Central Division.[355] Buell sold to James Thompson, another local man, for the latter's hotel property: some of the bonds were passed before the temporary injunction was issued, most of them the instant it was vacated by the circuit court—notwithstanding that an appeal had been taken. Thompson "knew of the suit . . . within a day or two after it was commenced." Thompson kept his bonds and coupons—which latter the County at all times refused to pay—until shortly before the bonds matured. Then he sold them to Caleb Marsh of New York, represented by William Marsh—his brother, agent, and attorney. The consideration was a promise in writing to pay "66 2/3 cents on the dollar . . . when the money was made on the bonds or collected. . . . It was understood, at the time of making the bargain, that payment of the bonds would be resisted."[356] As counsel for the County later pointed out, this "looks very like a convenient bargain for lawyers' ser-

---

[354] This case invites one to take a sentimental excursion through Lincoln country; one may fancy that "old Fiddler Jones" of Edgar Lee Masters' *Spoon River Anthology* would have recalled Fulton county's early efforts to bring a railroad. The proposed Petersburg & Springfield, coming from the south, must have passed close by the site of New Salem, where Lincoln had read law while tending store and post office.

When Lincoln set out on his Senatorial campaign in 1858 he spoke twice in Fulton County as he made his way toward Ottawa for his first debate with Douglas. Fulton County then had no railroad; he was going up the Illinois river by steamboat. Entry for Aug. 17, in Paul M. Angle's record of day-by-day activities, *Lincoln 1854–1861* (Springfield: The Abraham Lincoln Assn., 1933).

When the Civil War ended, Fulton County was still awaiting its railroad. By that time the Mississippi & Wabash

had been consolidated with the Toledo, Peoria & Warsaw, which was about to complete its track from the Mississippi River to the east line of the State—where it joined the Columbus, Chicago & Indiana Central. Supra, p. 995. Fulton County would then, it was boasted, be on what "must ultimately be one of the principal branches of the great Pacific Railway." *Canton Weekly Register*, Dec. 4, 1865.

[355] Buell figures prominently as a contractor and as a railroad officer in western Illinois and in Missouri. In Ashcraft's *Railway Directory* for 1868 he appears as President and Chief Engineer of the Alexandria (Missouri) & Nebraska City R.R.; Superintendent of the Mississippi & Wabash R.R.; and a director in the Toledo, Peoria & Warsaw.

[356] Deposition of Thompson, Transcript of Record in Marsh v. Fulton County, 27.

vices, . . . and to secure some one to play 'innocent purchaser' . . .,"[357] on bonds Thompson could never enforce in a State court.

The "sale" being made, Skinner & Marsh filed in the federal Circuit Court the action of Caleb P. Marsh against Fulton County. Judge Samuel H. Treat instructed the jury "that it appeared from the evidence that the said bonds and interest coupons . . . were made and issued by the clerk . . . without authority; and that their verdict should be for the defendant."[358]

On writ of error the case was filed in the Supreme Court on August 30, 1870. Counsel agreed to submit on their printed arguments; a prompt decision could be expected.

Browning and Skinner actually misrepresented to the Court the procedural law in Illinois—as by insisting that the chancery proceedings brought in 1857 "cut no figure" from the moment the lower court dissolved the temporary injunction.[359] In this and other respects their effort was unavailing, inasmuch as S. Corning Judd,[360] for the County, met them at every turn. By terse paragraphs, effective typographical devices, and insistence that these experienced counsellors needed to "rub up their spectacles" to find the controlling statutes and decisions, he took care that the Justices were not led astray on the facts of the case or on Illinois law. His main points were two: that there had been

---

[357] Argument for Defendants in Error, by S. Corning Judd, 12.

[358] Transcript, 32.

[359] Brief for Plaintiff in Error, 19–21. Opposing counsel pointed out (Argument, 47) that the Illinois court, proclaiming what theretofore had been the rule, had stated at September term 1870 that "In cases where the court below award a temporary injunction, which is continued to the final hearing, and is then dissolved and the bill dismissed, and the party prays for and perfects his appeal under the order of the court, such appeal suspends the decree dissolving the injunction, and therefore leaves it still in force." "But," it added, "if the injunction is dissolved by an interlocutory order, and the cause afterwards proceeds to a final hearing, such appeal will not revive the judgment." Bressler v. McCune, 56 Ill. 475.

[360] Chicago practitioner; during the Civil War, when residing in Fulton County, he had been Grand Commander of the Order of American Knights for Illinois, and in 1864 Democratic candidate for lieutenant governor.

In memorial proceedings, it was recalled that "He was a strong, independent man in his prime," and "unquestionably the ablest ecclesiastical lawyer in the State." Proc. Ill. State Bar Assn. (1896), Pt. II, 178. As chancellor of the Episcopal Diocese of Illinois he conducted (in the ecclesiastical court and in the courts of Illinois) proceedings initiated by Bishop Henry J. Whitehouse (High Church) against the Rev. Charles E. Cheney (a Low Church rector). Associated with him was his brother-in-law, William C. Goudy (1824–93)— who later figures in Munn v. Illinois, 94 U.S. 13 (1877), and other leading cases as an opponent of rate regulation. In the church litigation, Judd was opposed by Melville W. Fuller. Chase v. Cheney, 58 Ill. 509 (1870). This case has been mentioned in connection with Watson v. Jones, 13 Wall. 679 (1872), supra, p. 915.

no authority to issue the bonds, for reasons established by the Illinois Court in 1859; and that, moreover, plaintiff did not have the standing of an innocent purchaser for value.

The Supreme Court, a fortnight after submission, announced that it affirmed the Circuit Court's decision in favor of the County.[361] Justice Field's opinion followed closely what the State Court had said in 1859, on the "fundamental change" from the railroad for which the people had voted to the "Central Division" for which the bonds were issued. The power "never existed" to do what the county clerk here had done—issue bonds to a wholly different company. Even supposing Marsh to be an innocent purchaser, still what the Court had recently held in *The Floyd Acceptances* would control:

> in each case the person dealing with the agent, knowing that he acts only by virtue of a delegated power, must, at his peril, see that the paper on which he relies comes within the power under which the agent acts. And this applies to every person who takes the paper afterwards; for it is to be kept in mind that the protection which commercial usage throws around negotiable paper cannot be used to establish the authority by which it was originally issued.[362]

Of course, *Marsh v. Fulton County* did not unsettle the line of municipal bond cases. That might have been perceived from the fact that the Court was unanimous: a conversion in mass was beyond rational belief.

For a while anxious telegrams were sent to Washington: had the bond cases really been overruled? To one such inquiry Justice Miller answered, "I know of no such decision."[363] To another he replied:

> I do not know of any decision of our Court overruling those heretofore made in regard to county bonds.
>
> A case was decided recently from Illinois in regard to county bonds issued for railroad subscriptions, in which the bonds were held to be void; but it was on grounds having no relation to any question involved in Iowa bonds, so far as I know.
>
> On the contrary, the Court has just decided that the Supervisors

---

of Des Moines county are personally liable for their refusal to obey the mandamus issued to them.[364]

Miller's concluding paragraph was a reference to *Amy v. Supervisors*, a decision still more recent than *Marsh*. In that suit by Henry Amy against individual supervisors it was held that such an officer could be held personally liable in damages to the extent of the injury resulting from his refusal to obey a mandamus to levy a tax.[365] The grip of that decision was compelling.

IN CONCLUSION

IOWA NOW RANKED sixth among the States in railroad mileage—surpassed only by Illinois, Pennsylvania, New York, Ohio, and Indiana.[366] New track was coming into service at a rate better than fifty miles a month. In well over half the State's area the rich prairie sod still awaited the coming of the settler. When some leading journals were making a momentary sensation of the Iowans' resistance to the federal courts, Horace Greeley's *Tribune* published an editorial to magnify the strength of Iowa's human and natural resources. "During the war her people were so patriotic that no assessments were made to purchase substitutes, nor were the regiments of any of the other States more wholly composed of volunteers." Her free school system and higher education were amply supported. "The liberality and the independence of the people" had given the vote to all men without regard to color. Those who settled Iowa had enjoyed "advantages in means, culture and enterprise superior to what their fathers possessed. . . . Hence it is that greater progress in a few years has been made in whatever is of a substantial and valuable character than in many years was made in Western New York, Ohio, or Indiana."[367]

The prospect of legislation to control railroad charges came closer when the General Assembly of Illinois passed a series of such measures in April 1871. But, as a correspondent had reported during

---

[364] Des Moines *Iowa State Register*, Apr. 13, 1871, quoting the *Mt. Pleasant Journal*.

[365] 11 Wall. 136, decided Mar. 27, 1871. At the same time, in Farr v. Thompson, 11 Wall. 139, it sustained a recovery against a city councilman of Racine, Wis.

[366] The State Treasurer reported at the end of 1870 there were 2,683 miles of track. (Elsewhere one finds larger figures.) This was made up of

twenty railroads, some quite new, eleven of which had less than one hundred miles. The *Burlington Hawk-Eye* of April 13, 1871, thought that this evidence of prosperity pointed to a 50,000 majority for Grant's reelection in 1872; actually his majority proved to be 60,000, or almost 2 to 1.

[367] Editorial, "The State of Iowa," Jan. 4, 1869.

the session of the Iowa legislature of 1870, "the railroad interest in our State has suddenly grown to almost herculean proportions. . . . These corporations, backed up by indefinite resources in the States east of us, can, when they combine forces, exert a tremendous influence." The railroad lobbyists "hang around committee rooms, and darken both chambers with their presence . . . . They have their friends and co-workers in both houses who are ready to . . . follow their advice on all occasions." The railroad companies were "determined to defeat" bills to control their tariffs or increase their taxes.[368] For the moment, people generally were more concerned to get more miles of track than to get lower rates.

The Justices in Washington seem to have been surprised that resistance to payment of railroad aid bonds continued to be pressed, term after term—in cases from the West, the South, sometimes even from the East—long after it had been supposed that "there is hardly any question connected with this species of securities, that has not been discussed and decided by this Court."[369] One observation, however, is notable: so far as Iowa was concerned, such contests virtually came to an end in 1871.[370]

---

[368] *Burlington Hawk-Eye*, Mar. 8 and 25, 1870. This was a newspaper notably partial to the railroad interest.

[369] Davis, J., in Thomson v. Lee County, 3 Wall. 327 (1866); he said the same thing a year later in Campbell v. City of Kenosha, 5 Wall. 194; similarly Swayne, J., in San Antonio v. Mehaffy, 96 U.S. 312 (1878).

[370] In 1873 there was the case of Supervisors of Carroll County v. United States *ex rel*. Reynolds, 18 Wall. 71, already noted, supra, p. 1001, where the Court sustained the County's contention.

CHAPTER XVIII

Municipal Bonds II: From 1870

THUS FAR THE Court had made only a limited entry upon contested territory. In *Gelpcke* the *overruling* of a decision on which investors might have relied was treated as analogous to a law impairing the obligation of a contract. Subsequent decisions in Iowa bond cases had enlarged and thrown bulwarks around that position.

Soon, however, the Court advanced until presently, after battles in various sectors, it had occupied a much wider domain. The leaders in this movement were Justices Swayne, Clifford, and Strong. Dissent within the Court came from Justice Miller, joined from time to time by Field, Chase, Davis, and Bradley.

This chapter will explore some of the salient points. The going will not be easy: an informed judgment can be reached only through unflagging attention to transcripts and briefs, and to the details of State statutes and the holdings of State courts.

THE WISCONSIN AND MICHIGAN COURTS RULE AGAINST RAILROAD AID

A PROFOUND SENSATION was produced when in 1870 the Supreme Courts of Wisconsin and Michigan gave judgments against the validity of municipal aid to railroads. In Wisconsin the court had to take account of its own precedents permitting taxation for the purchase of railroad stock.[1] Now it said that whereas municipal authority to become part

---

[1] Clark v. City of Janesville, 10 Wis. 136 (June term 1859), and Bushnell v. Beloit, 10 Wis. 195 (Jan. term 1860). Objections had been rested upon particular constitutional provisions (forbidding *the State* to loan its credit or to contract a debt for works of internal improvement), and upon general principles of law and policy as well. To the latter the

owner of a railroad might be deduced from its power to build the road for itself, such reasoning would not sustain an outright gift. This was in *Whiting v. Sheboygan & Fond du Lac R.R.*, where Chief Justice Luther S. Dixon spoke for the court. The State might condemn land for a public use, upon payment of just compensation; and that public power might be exercised on behalf of a railroad. Still, a railroad was essentially a private corporation: that it was permitted to take land by eminent domain was an exceptional indulgence—it was not to be regarded as supporting a larger proposition that taxation to aid a railroad was permissible as being a public purpose.[2]

Had it not been for the precedents, he later explained, two of the three judges would have been disposed to deny the power to tax even to make a subscription; as it was, the court drew a line against the further step of taxing to make a gift.[3]

This was promptly noted with approval by Judge Dillon in the *American Law Register*: it was in accord with his own recent opinion for the Iowa court in *Hanson v. Vernon*.[4]

In May 1870 came the decision of the Michigan court in the *Salem Township* case.[5] A statute of 1864 had authorized certain townships, upon vote of the people, to pledge their credit to aid a railroad. Now the Detroit & Howell company sought mandamus to compel the township to issue bonds that had been approved by such a vote. In Michigan there had been no adjudication on taxation for railroad aid. After hearing eight days of argument the court held the statute invalid. Judge Thomas M. Cooley wrote a notable opinion for the majority of three; one judge dissented. The judgment was placed upon "the first and most fundamental maxim of taxation"—that it could be imposed only for a *public purpose*; the building of a railroad to be owned and

---

court had replied that "it seems rather late to raise the objection" that the practice should be repudiated as "evil and pernicious." 10 Wis. at 220.

[2] 25 Wis. 167 (Jan. term 1870, denying a rehearing, after decision reached at June term 1869). Paine, J., dissented: he could not agree that, so far as public purpose was concerned, a distinction could be drawn between taxation and eminent domain.

In Curtis v. Whipple, 24 Wis. 350 (1869), the court had held invalid a statute authorizing a town to tax to make a gift to a private school; mere incidental benefits to the community would not justify a compulsory contribution. Now the court held that this same reasoning forbade taxation

to make a gift to a railroad company. Decisions sustaining taxation to purchase railroad stock were distinguished: the building of a railroad was a work such as a municipality might have been authorized to pursue as sole owner; from that could be deduced authority to become a part owner. As stockholder it would share in ownership and control—not so if it were only a donor.

[3] Phillips v. Town of Albany, 28 Wis. 340 (1871).

[4] 9 (n.s.):156 (Mar. 1870). On Hanson v. Vernon, see supra, pp. 978–79.

[5] People *ex rel.* Detroit & Howell R.R. v. Township of Salem, 20 Mich. 452.

operated by a private corporation was not "public" within that test. The statute being obnoxious to that first principle, the court found it "superfluous" to consider whether it violated express provisions of the State constitution as well.

The dissenting judge held that inasmuch as a railroad had been held public for purposes of eminent domain, that was decisive for aid by taxation.

The Michigan bench presided over by Chief Justice James V. Campbell enjoyed a wide esteem. (In historical perspective, it was indeed a strong court.) Cooley had attained distinction by the publication in 1868 of his *Treatise on the Constitutional Limitations which rest upon the Legislative Power of the States of the American Union*— one of the most influential of treatises on American law. Accordingly the *Salem Township* decision commanded respectful attention throughout the land. Judge Dillon and Judge Isaac F. Redfield hastened to praise it in editorial notes in the *American Law Register*.[6] *The Independent*, until recently a sectarian journal, struck a moral note in commenting on *Salem*. The municipalities that had issued bonds should make them good. As a general principle, taxation should not be imposed to aid private enterprise. Sometimes, however, the building of a railroad would bring such great public good as to justify an exception —as in the case of a railroad to the Pacific. The article did not distinguish between national, State, and municipal aid.[7]

The Nation first gave a noncommittal report of *Salem*. The result, it said, "is widespread consternation . . . . Abuse of the court, however, is kept to one or two of the less decent newspapers, while the majority of the press and the people recommend that steps be taken to amend the constitution . . . ."[8] Presently it published an article on "Railroad Subsidies" by Charles Francis Adams, Jr. (1835–1915), of Massachusetts' new Board of Railroad Commissioners. The Michigan court, he said, should not have set itself against "the reasoning of a score of courts and the decisions of twenty years." In America, railroads were an absolute necessity. "The railway is our pioneer—it made the settlement of our country possible." Public aid, "much as it has been abused, has been productive of more good than evil."[9] By force of his name, his independence, and his self-assurance, Adams' conclusions always carried respect.

But Justice Davis, from close acquaintance with conditions in Illinois, had recently expressed this practical judgment:

---

[6] 9 (n.s.):501 and 504 (Aug. 1870). Redfield had sat on the Supreme Court of Vermont from 1835 to 1860, and was the author of *A Practical Treatise upon the Law of Railways* and other leading works.

[7] June 22, 1870.

[8] 10:360. June 9, 1870.

[9] 11:219. Oct. 6, 1870.

The railroad mania in this State, supported by subscriptions of towns, cities & counties is fearful & will lead to bankruptcy unless stopped. I know of nothing that will stop it except hard times & a consequent inability to negotiate bonds. . . .[10]

In Iowa, anti-bond editors hailed the *Salem* decision as a vindication; particularly did they notice that it was winning praise from newspapers that recently had traduced the Iowa court for a like decision.[11]

The statute involved in *Salem* was of only limited application. An Act of March 22, 1869, however, had provided generally that any township, city or village might pledge its aid, by loan or donation, to a railroad company, to the extent of 10 percent of the assessed valuation, upon approval of a majority of those voting on the proposition. This statute was held invalid in *People ex rel. Bay City v. State Treasurer,* on October 18, 1871.[12] Judge Cooley explained that in *Salem* the decision had been placed on a fundamental ground which, the court had supposed, could not be misunderstood. Now it said explicitly that such legislation violated the State's due process clause, and was inconsistent with other constitutional provisions. Specifically, the State was forbidden to lend its credit or subscribe to any corporation, or to be a party to any work of internal improvement; in adopting the Constitution of 1850 the people had supposed—so the court said—that public aid was being totally forbidden. The State must not do indirectly through municipalities what it was prohibited to do outright.[13]

---

[10] Letter written from his home, Bloomington, July 26, 1869, to his brother-in-law, Judge Julius Rockwell. Davis Papers, Ill. State Hist. Soc.

Justice Breese of the Supreme Court of Illinois has been quoted to a like effect in Schall v. Bowman, 62 Ill. 321 (1872), supra, ch. 17, n. 46.

[11] *Muscatine Journal,* June 16, 1870; *Keokuk Constitution,* June 8, 1870, and July 22, 1871; *Keokuk Gate City,* Aug. 16, 1870.

[12] 23 Mich. 499. Bay City had issued $100,000 in bonds, which it deposited with the State Treasurer for delivery when the railroad had completed the requisite construction. Now it sought to compel the return of the bonds on the ground that the statute was invalid.

[13] Judge Campbell and Judge Cooley each wrote a history of Michigan, and each dwelt upon the recurrent mania for internal improvements. "These schemes [of the 1860's] were pushed through the Legislature against the opposition of the governors, who were called upon to consider them, and the executive objections were sustained by the Supreme Court, which held the laws void. Every constitutional amendment which sought to validate them has been rejected." James V. Campbell, *Outline of the Political History of Michigan* (Detroit: Schober & Co., 1876), 571–72. The *Salem* decision was a "conspicuous landmark" in the struggle to maintain prudence in public affairs, wrote Cooley. *Michigan, A History of Governments,* rev. ed. (Boston and New York: Houghton Mifflin & Co., 1906), 293.

For a season after the *Salem* decision there was an earnest clamor. Some $6,000,000 in railroad aid bonds was said to be involved; the greater part was being held by the State Treasurer to await the performance of precedent conditions. The Governor summoned the legislature, seeking a constitutional amendment to surmount the decision. That movement failed. And yet, as Judge Cooley wrote in an opinion in 1881,

> Notwithstanding that [*Salem*] decision the municipalities which had issued bonds in conformity with the invalid legislation, generally recognized their obligation to provide payment, and proceeded to do so without dissent on the part of the people. In some cases suits were brought in the federal courts and recovery had. In some other cases suits were brought in the State courts and judgments allowed to pass by default or on confession. . . .[14]

Thus the climate in Michigan did not cease to be favorable to railroad building: 1871 saw more miles of track completed than in any previous year. The *Chicago Railroad Gazette* commented:

> The extraordinary activity in construction in this State is the more remarkable because it has not been encouraged in any way by the votes of aid from municipalities. When the decision of the Supreme Court in 1870 put an end to such subsidies . . . it was prophesied that there would not only be a great decrease, but almost a total cessation in railroad construction . . . . But there never was so much . . . activity in construction as in 1871 . . . . There has been a large amount of local aid, it is true, but it has come in the shape of voluntary private subscriptions . . . .[15]

"PUBLIC PURPOSE"—FOR TAKING BY EMINENT DOMAIN, AND FOR TAXATION

BOTH JUSTICE COOLEY in Michigan and Chief Justice Dixon in Wisconsin had drawn a contrast between the "public purpose" that would permit a compensated taking of private property and the "public purpose" that would justify the casting of a tax upon the entire community. This touched upon a body of thought that derived from the writings of civilians, such as Grotius, which had guided judges in the formative period of American law. Public convenience and necessity would sustain the taking of private property for fair compensation to permit

---

14 City of Port Huron v. McCall, 46 Mich. 565—in a situation where the city attorney, as instructed by the city council, confessed judgment in suits upon railroad aid bonds.
15 Quoted in Ann. Cyc. 1871, 513.

the building of a public highway. The flooding of private land by a mill dam had also been upheld, "for the better use of the water power, upon considerations of public policy and the general good . . . ."[16] On the other hand, a statute authorizing a private road to be laid over the land of an unwilling owner had been condemned as beyond the scope of "legislative power."[17] When railroads came it had been indispensable that they be enabled to exercise the State's power of eminent domain for the projection of their lines; as Cooley wrote in the *Salem Township* opinion,

> the business of transporting persons and property for long distances by rail, which has been found so essential to the general enjoyment and welfare, could never have existed if it were in the power of any unwilling person to stop the road at his boundary, or to demand unreasonable terms as a condition of passing him. . . .

But it did not at all follow that because the building of a railroad met the test of public interest for the exercise of this power, it might also be aided by the power of taxation:

> each of these has its own peculiar and appropriate sphere, and the object which is *public* for the demands of the one is not necessarily of a character to permit the exercise of the other.

Thus the Wisconsin and Michigan courts had declared the constitutional law of their respective States. And unlike the Iowa court, neither had overturned any precedent.

THE SUPREME COURT REFUSES TO FOLLOW THE STATE COURT

AFTER THE WISCONSIN court's decision in *Whiting v. Sheboygan & Fond du Lac R.R.*,[18] an issue was raised whether the federal court would conform. If it refused, then the county notes could still be enforced—by transfer, if need be, to a purchaser in some other State. In

---

16 Shaw, C.J., in French v. Braintree Mfg. Co., 23 Pick. 216, 220 (Mass. 1839).

17 Taylor v. Porter, 4 Hill 140 (N.Y. 1843). In this influential case the court construed the State constitution's grant of "legislative power" as being limited by principles of justice—and then went on to find support in the specific guaranties that

rights should not be taken "unless by the law of the land" or "without due process of law." This illustrates how easily fundamental principles of justice and specific constitutional provisions may shade into one another.

Consider Loan Assn. v. Topeka, 20 Wall. 655 (1875), infra, pp. 1101–06.

18 Supra, n. 2.

Olcott v. Fond du Lac County,[19] decided in the Circuit Court for the Eastern District of Wisconsin in 1870, Circuit Judge Drummond made this answer: the federal court in applying the State's law should consider a judicial interpretation as being incorporated into the written law; the exception made in *Gelpcke* did not include the instant case, since there had been no overruling.

A writ of error brought this up to the Supreme Court, where Matt. H. Carpenter, Senator from Wisconsin, appeared for the plaintiff. He argued boldly that what had been *understood* to be the law entered into the contract and should be enforced by the federal judiciary. This he derived from the *Gelpcke* decision.[20] "It is not necessary," he contended, "that the precise point should have been directly involved in a cause and expressly decided by the courts." What had been assumed by the courts, what could be inferred from their opinions—on these too a business man might rely, and the federal courts should protect him accordingly.[21]

Carpenter proceeded to a congenial conclusion from the language the State court had used in deciding a variety of questions. Especially did he draw upon decisions declaring railroads to be *public* highways for the exercise of the State's power of eminent domain:

> it is evident that a railroad is either a highway, held by the corporation in trust for the public use, or it is a mere private property, owned by the stockholders in absolute right. One of these theories must be true; and whichever is held to be true, it will follow that the other is untrue.[22]

---

[19] Fed. Case No. 10,479. Reversed in Olcott v. The Supervisors, 16 Wall. 678 (1873).

[20] Argument for Plaintiff in Error, 13.

[21] Ibid., 20. He relied also upon Havemeyer v. Iowa County, 3 Wall. 294 (1866), a case certified from the Circuit Court for Wisconsin, where Carpenter had argued with success for the bondholder, [William F. Havemeyer, capitalist and mayor of New York City]. The county had issued bonds in 1853 under a railroad aid statute which was not published until after the bonds were issued. If this was a *general* law, then under the State constitution it did not take effect until it was published. The State officers charged with publishing the statutes had classed this and similar statutes as *private*. In 1858, in a controversy where both parties treated such a statute as *private*, the State court had tacitly assumed that it was. Hewitt v. Town of Grand Chute, 7 Wis. 282. In 1859, when the question was actually litigated, the State court decided that such an act was *general*. State *ex rel*. Cothern v. Lean, 9 Wis. 279. (Moving a county seat—not railroad aid—was involved.)

When the question of the validity of Havemeyer's bonds was brought before the Supreme Court, the answer, by Swayne, J., was that "We can look only to the condition of things which subsisted when they were sold. That brings them within the rule . . . in Gelpcke . . . ."

[22] Brief, 28. This mode of reasoning is commented upon, infra, pp. 1023–24.

He would thus make it appear that his client's case rested upon a great principle: it was "of the highest importance" that railroads be *"subject at all times to governmental control, like other highways . . . ."*[23] (As a politician, Carpenter had indeed been calling for public control of railroads;[24] but as an advocate he had been representing the bond-holders' interest, and here he was putting his client's case in its most persuasive guise.)

Speaking for five of the eight Justices who participated, Justice Strong held the county notes to be enforceable, in an opinion that adopted Carpenter's argument.[25] In the State court's *Fond du Lac* decision, "the meaning of no provision of the State constitution was considered or declared. What was considered was the uses for which taxation generally, taxation by any government, might be author-ized . . . ." Without citing *Swift v. Tyson*,[26] Justice Strong was enlarg-ing its principle when he declared that "The nature of taxation, what uses are public and what are private, and the extent of legislative power, are matters which, like questions of commercial law, no State court can conclusively determine for us."

Still "another consideration" led to rejecting the Wisconsin court's decision. Here Justice Strong enlarged the principle of *Gelpcke v. Dubuque*. Prior to the issue of the Fond du Lac notes, the State court had made various pronouncements about "public purpose" in taxation (in cases dealing with various particular matters, such as a bounty to encourage enlistments in the Union army); also it had sustained legisla-tion giving the power of eminent domain in order that water power might be created or a canal or railroad built. By projecting these expo-sitions one constructed law to fill a gap, and by that law the Fond du Lac notes were valid. When the Wisconsin court rejected the law as thus inferred, its action was to be assimilated to that of the Iowa court when it overruled a case in point. (To be sure, Justice Strong did not explain so baldly as this what the Supreme Court was doing.)

The Court repudiated the Wisconsin court's distinction between taxing to make a gift and taxing to take stock: there was "no substan-tial difference in principle."

Submitted on able briefs, and considered and decided together with the *Fond du Lac* case, was *Chicago, B. & Q. R.R. v. County of Otoe*.[27] By a special act the Nebraska legislature had authorized the County Commissioners to issue $150,000 in bonds to any railroad that would secure to Nebraska City (on the Missouri River, facing the

---

[23] Brief, 28.

[24] E. Bruce Thompson, *Matthew Hale Carpenter, Webster of the West* (Madison: State Historical Society of Wisconsin, 1954), 202–3.

[25] Olcott v. The Supervisors, 16 Wall. 678 (1873).

[26] 16 Pet. 1 (1842). See supra, pp. 938–39.

[27] 16 Wall. 667 (1873).

southwestern corner of Iowa) a direct connection to the East. Thus to a railroad corporation in another State, an outright donation would be made, without a vote by the people.[28] Circuit Judge Dillon and District Judge Dundy, holding the Circuit Court, certified a division of opinion.[29] Counsel attacking the statute argued that this was taking A's property and giving it to B—something it had always been said no American legislature could do.

Justice Strong, for the same majority of five, sustained the statute at each questioned point. No direct conflict with any Nebraska decision was involved.[30]

In both *Fond du Lac* and *County of Otoe*, Justice Miller announced that he, Chief Justice Chase and Justice Davis dissented. They filed no opinion.

When these cases were first put to a vote in conference, the result in each stood four to four. Justice Bradley noted on his copy of the *Fond du Lac* transcript, "*Affirmed* by Divided Court. Feby 19, 1873."[31] Some Justice, originally voting with Miller, Chase, and Davis, on further consideration changed his mind.

Apparently this was Bradley. Two terms before, early in his service on the Court, he had jotted down this comment:

I agree with Miller's dissenting opinion
1 Wallace *Gelpcke* v *Dubuque* . . . .[32]

He wrote this on his copy of the Transcript of Record in *Railroad Co. v. McClure*[33]—a municipal bond case from the Supreme Court of

<hr>

[28] It was among the agreed facts that the statute had been drawn by the attorney for the railroad—which doubtless was common enough with municipal bond statutes.

[29] Chicago, B. & Q. R.R. v. Otoe County, Fed. Case No. 2667 (1871).

[30] Justice Bradley wrote on his copy of the Transcript:

The act of Feby 15 1869, quoted in the Case authorizes the issue of the bonds without further submission to vote

Was the act constitutional? I think it was. I think it is within the *legislative* power to authorize local communities to aid in the construction of works of public improvement which may benefit the place.

The provision of the Nebraska Constitution referred to does not inhibit this ["The property of no person shall be taken for public use without just compensation therefor." Art. I, Declaration of Rights, Sec. 13].

[31] So too did Clifford on the Transcript now in the Library of Congress set. Bradley's Transcript in Otoe County has a note that (at the first conference) that case was "Affirmed by divᵈ Court."

[32] The remainder of his sentence is set out in the latter part of footnote 34, p. 1019.

[33] Mississippi & Missouri R.R. Co., Clark Durant *et al.* v. McClure *et al.*, 10 Wall. 511. Argued Nov. 9, 1870, and decided Jan. 23, 1871. This was a substantially longer interval than was then normal—which suggests that there was considerable discussion.

See supra, ch. 17, n. 69.

Iowa, where the Justices in conference must have threshed over *Gelpcke v. Dubuque* even though that case was not directly involved.[34] On first contact, then, it was Bradley's view that the federal judiciary should have respected and followed the Iowa court's overruling decision. Reflecting further while *Olcott v. Supervisors of Fond du Lac*

---

[34] McClure and others, taxpayers in Washington County, Iowa, had sued in the local District Court to enjoin the county officers from collecting taxes to pay interest on bonds issued to the Mississippi & Missouri R.R. Co. and held by Thomas C. Durant and others close to that enterprise. (On the railroad troubles of that county, see supra, pp. 951, 956–58.) The court granted a perpetual injunction. James Grant took an appeal to the State Supreme Court, arguing only one point: that on the basis of what had been decided by the Supreme Court of the United States [doctrine of the *Gelpcke* case], the decision below *impaired the obligation of a contract*. The court responded that, under the Iowa constitution, municipal railroad aid bonds were void— hence there had been no contract. McClure *et al.* v. Owen *et al.*, 26 Iowa 243. Dec. 17, 1868.

Railroad Co. v. McClure was taken to the Supreme Court under Section 25 of the Judiciary Act as a case where a claim of right under the federal Constitution (namely, under the Contract Clause) had been denied by the State court. (On Section 25 of the Judiciary Act, see supra, p. 45.) Justice Swayne, speaking for a unanimous Court, held that the case must be dismissed for want of jurisdiction. "The question of the validity of the bonds is not one of federal jurisdiction." Neither by its constitution nor by any statute had Iowa *passed a law* impairing the obligation of the bonds. The Court's review of decisions by State courts was strictly confined by the terms of Section 25. He pointed out that if the basic issue in this case had been presented in an appeal from a federal Circuit Court, under Section 22 of the Judiciary Act, "this question and all others arising from the record would have been open for examination."

See supra, p. 839n.

This was Grant's second defeat in his attempt to gain direct review by the Supreme Court of a State court's decision holding municipal railroad aid bonds to be invalid. Mississippi & Missouri R.R. Co. v. Rock, 4 Wall. 177 (1867), was his earlier failure. See supra, p. 938.

Bradley's jotting apropos of the *McClure* case, quoted in the text above, continued: ". . . but not with his [Miller's] opinion in Bridge Proprietors Case same book." In Bridge Proprietors v. Hoboken Land & Improvement Co., 1 Wall. 116 (1864), the proprietors, complainants below, under a New Jersey statute of 1790 had an exclusive privilege to maintain a "bridge" over the Hackensack River for ninety-nine years. A statute of 1860 authorized the Hoboken Co. to build a railroad from Hoboken to Newark, with power to build a railroad bridge over the river. The Chancellor decreed "that the complainants are not entitled to restrain the defendants from building the bridge, or structure complained of . . . ." The decree of the Court of Errors merely affirmed.

Proprietors sought review by the Supreme Court, contending that the statute of 1860 impaired the obligation of their contract of 1790.

Bradley, as counsel for the Hoboken Co., denied the jurisdiction of the Supreme Court. How could it be seen that the validity of the statute of 1860 had been drawn in question for repugnancy to the Contract Clause, and that the State court had rejected that claim? The record did not establish the points required by Section 25; judgment for the defendant might have been on some wholly independent ground. In particular, to hold that a railroad viaduct was not a "bridge" within the meaning of the exclusive grant of 1790 would be

County was before the Court—it was under consideration for more than four months—he wrote this conclusion:

> On a more careful examination of, and reflection upon, this case, I am of opinion,
>
> 1. That a State legislature, unless restrained by special constitutional prohibitions is competent to authorize public donations as well as public subscriptions to Railways and other schemes of public improvement.
>
> 2. That bonds issued by the State or under its authority for such purposes, are valid and binding contracts.
>
> 3. That no decision of a State court, any more than an act of State legislation, made after the issue of such bonds, can affect their validity.
>
> 4. That it is the right of the Federal Courts to judge for themselves, on all questions of general policy, and the general principals [*sic*] of constitutional, commercial or common law.
>
> 5. That the decisions of State courts furnish rules for decision binding on the federal courts only in matters of local legislation peculiar to the State, or upon usages and rules of property on which rights have arisen.
>
> 6. I, therefore, think that the judgment in this case should be reversed.

Justice Bradley did not share the great preoccupation for the holders of municipal bonds that ruled the action of Swayne, Clifford, and Strong. He did come to display a marked devotion to the proposition in his point four: the authority of the federal courts to enforce their own conceptions of "general law" in cases of diversity of citizenship.[35]

In his *Fond du Lac* opinion Justice Strong threw out a dictum

---

merely a construction of that statute —a decision wholly unrelated to the Contract Clause.

But the Court, per Miller, J., sustained its jurisdiction. In order to vindicate the Contract Clause, the Court must be free to inquire whether there had been a contract, and whether a subsequent law had impaired its obligation. It sufficed, to bring the case within Section 25, that upon the whole record the Court could see that a provision of federal law had been relied upon, and that that claim had been denied. Here, if the statute of 1790 prohibited the kind of structure defendants were about to build, then the statute of 1860 impaired that right: it was proper to take jurisdiction and to consider what the statute of 1790 had granted.

Proceeding to the merits, the Court held that the railroad viaduct did not invade the grant of 1790.

In Knox v. Exchange Bank, 12 Wall. 379, decided in November 1871, Miller, J., for a unanimous Court restated what had been held in Railroad Co. v. Rock, Railroad Co. v. McClure, and Bridge Proprietors v. Hoboken Co.

[35] See supra, pp. 938–39.

that could be projected into the future. Expanding on the theme that a railroad was an undertaking of great public concern, he said this:

> The railroad can, therefore, be controlled and regulated by the State. Its use can be defined; its tolls and rates for transportation may be limited. Is a work made by authority of the State, subject to its regulation, and having for its object an increase of public convenience, to be regarded as ordinary private property?

When the actual test came, four years later, the Court, after a mighty struggle at its bar, did sustain the power of a legislature to regulate railroad rates: but Justice Strong joined Justice Field in protesting that the decision "practically destroys" the rights of railroad companies.[36]

DISAGREEMENT WITH THE MICHIGAN COURT

A YEAR AFTER *Fond du Lac* the Court met the like question from Michigan: Should the federal judiciary respect the *Salem* and *Bay City* decisions? The Circuit Court had answered No,[37] and a majority of the Supreme Court agreed. This was *Pine Grove Township v. Talcott.*[38]

James A. Garfield—who while serving in Congress occasionally appeared before the Court—argued the cause for the Township. He stressed that the *Bay City* case had held invalid the very statute now in question, not on general principle alone (as in the *Salem* judgment) but as offending specific provisions of the State constitution. Opposing counsel, led by Jeremiah S. Black, said that there was nothing in Michigan's constitution to make this bond case different from those from Iowa and Wisconsin.

Justice Swayne wrote for the majority. It was "an axiom of

---

[36] Chicago, B. & Q. R.R. v. Iowa, 94 U.S. 155 (1877).

[37] Talcott v. Pine Grove, Taylor v. City of Battle Creek, Fed. Case No. 13,735, C.C.W.D. Mich., decided Jan. 16, 1872. Sitting with Circuit Judge H. H. Emmons were the District Judges for the Eastern and Western Districts. The Circuit Judge wrote an opinion of some 18,000 words; each District Judge concurred in a short opinion. Judge Emmons' opinion soon reached the conclusion that "We have nothing to decide upon principle": the issue had been settled by the Supreme Court. But then—

despite "much doubt" as to the propriety of doing so—he went on to argue at length the constitutionality of railroad aid, and to show wherein the decision of the Supreme Court of Michigan had been "revolutionary in doctrine" and wrong.

Michigan lay within the Sixth Circuit, over which Justice Swayne presided. Emmons' opinion supplied an elaborate support for the views Swayne was expressing somewhat dogmatically from the Supreme Court bench.

[38] 19 Wall. 666, decided May 4, 1874.

American jurisprudence" that a statute was not to be held invalid unless repugnancy to the constitution was clear; the judicial function called for "delicacy" and "caution." He proceeded to make an independent examination of the Michigan constitution, concluding that the statute really was not in conflict with it. The judgments of the Michigan court were "not satisfactory to our minds. We think the dissenting opinion in the one first decided is unanswered." What had been declared in the *Fond du Lac* case was "conclusive of the case before us."

As in that case, Justices Miller and Davis dissented without opinion. Death had now removed Chief Justice Chase. Waite, his successor, and Justice Bradley, took no part in *Pine Grove Township*. "As I have grown older in the Court, I have grown more averse to dissents," Miller had written in 1871.[39] Certainly a powerful appeal to the wisdom of a later day might have been written. Here, brushing aside the rulings of the State's highest court, the Justices in Washington were declaring what was the constitutional law of the State. The basic question—whether municipal taxation to aid railroads was permissible—was a matter of unique consequence to the people, whichever way it was settled. No provision of the Constitution of the United States dictated the answer; not even the excuse of an overruling State decision was present in the situation.

From their beginning, State courts had on occasion based a decision on what was conceived to be some fundamental principle of public right, without relying upon any constitutional text. Sometimes the federal Supreme Court reasoned in the same way.[40] How far this mode of thought can be approved makes an absorbing topic in jurisprudence. But, sound or not, what was there in the Constitution of the United States to warrant the Supreme Court in rejecting the Michigan and Wisconsin decisions? With what propriety could Justice Strong declare that the extent of legislative power in a State was a matter which, "like questions of commercial law, no State court can conclusively determine for us"? So far as the United States is concerned,

---

[39] Charles Fairman, *Mr. Justice Miller and the Supreme Court, 1862–1890* (Cambridge, Mass.: Harvard University Press, 1939), 61.

[40] For example, Loan Association v. Topeka, 20 Wall. 655 (1875), infra, pp. 1104–05.

In the great case of Fletcher v. Peck, Marshall, C.J., had said, "It may well be doubted whether the nature of society and of government does not prescribe some limits to the legislative power . . . ." 6 Cranch 87, 135

(1810). Johnson, J., had there joined in striking down the Georgia statute —not because of any provision in the Constitution, but "on a general principle, on the reason and nature of things . . . ." At 143. "That government can scarcely be deemed free, where the rights of property are left solely dependent upon the will of a legislative body . . . ," said Story, J., for the Court in Wilkinson v. Leland, 2 Pet. 627, 657 (1829).

should not a State court's determination of the State's fundamental law —whether drawn from express text or found to be implicit—be respected save only where such construction may collide with something that the United States Constitution has made supreme?[41] By what authority did Justice Swayne instruct Judge Cooley and his brethren on the deference they owed to the Michigan legislature? Was not the Supreme Court of the United States blind to that "delicacy" and "caution" it should practice—not only in judging the action of Congress and of the Executive, but also in respect of the constitutional organs of the several States?

An exploration of these topics might fill a book—and then other books might be written in reply. Surely it is true, at any rate, that in *Fond du Lac* and *Pine Grove Township* the Court gave rough treatment to sensitive relations between State and federal judiciaries. If a reasoned justification was possible, then certainly it should have been elaborated with the greatest care. If none was possible, then the Court should never have acted as it did.

It would have been practically impossible to have railroads without permitting them, upon payment of compensation, to condemn a right of way. The Michigan court had recognized that such a taking was for a "public purpose" in a decision in 1852.[42] From this inescapable proposition did it follow, as the night the day, that a tax levy, further to benefit the railroad company, must likewise be lawful? Substantially, that is what Justice Swayne's opinion said. To bring the Michigan situation within the rationale of *Gelpcke v. Dubuque,* he made these points: the Michigan court had denied that its holding on eminent domain was decisive of the constitutionality of taxation for railroad aid; moreover, when the legislature passed statutes permitting railroad aid, the court had not "lifted its voice against it." Of course it could not lift its voice until a suit had been brought: here the reproach was so utterly unreasonable as to reflect on the Justices who made it.

The censure for not equating "public purpose" for taxation with "public purpose" for eminent domain had a semblance of plausibility. Judge Cooley had given the answer, however, in the *Salem* opinion, in a comment that still rings true:

> Reasoning by analogy from one of the sovereign powers of government to another is exceedingly liable to deceive and mislead. An ob-

---

[41] As was the situation in the unusual case of West Virginia v. Sims, 341 U.S. 22 (1951), supra, p. 624, where the State court had discovered in a provision of the State constitution a disability to the performance of obligations under a compact with other States entered into in accord with the Compact Clause of the United States Constitution.

[42] Swan v. Williams, 2 Mich. 427. James V. Campbell, later the Chief Justice, appeared for the railroad.

ject may be *public* in one sense and for one purpose, when in a general sense and for other purposes it would be idle or misleading to apply the same term. All governmental powers exist for public purposes, but they are not necessarily to be exercised under the same conditions of public interest. . . .

"Delusive exactness" in the use of words and phrases has been a source of fallacy, as Justice Holmes often pointed out;[43] law, in becoming civilized, depends upon differences of degree.[44] In *Munn v. Illinois* in 1877 the Court sustained regulation of businesses "affected with a public interest,"[45] and presently conceptual thinking turned that into a tight category that deceived and misled, until at last the Court opened it to the light of reason.[46] Carpenter's mode of argument— that what a phrase means in one context it must mean elsewhere—[47] no longer carries conviction.

In the jurisprudence of Michigan, the *Salem Township* case remained a firm authority.[48] Municipalities ceased to vote aid; as has been noted, those that had issued bonds commonly met their moral obligation.[49] Thus the Supreme Court heard little more from Michigan on that score. In the early '80's there came a group of cases—from townships in one county and from one city—wherein the holding in *Pine Grove Township* was challenged anew and, upon mature reconsideration, the Court affirmed it.[50] Of the minority in the earlier cases, only Justice Miller remained, and he refrained from noting dissent.

CONTINUING CONFLICT WITH THE WISCONSIN COURT

FOR THE WISCONSIN court, *Olcott v. Fond du Lac County* was the culmination of disagreements with the federal Supreme Court, running

---

[43] Louisville & N. R.R. v. Barber Asphalt Paving Co., 197 U.S. 430, 434 (1905); dissenting in Truax v. Corrigan, 257 U.S. 312, 342 (1921).

[44] LeRoy Fibre Co. v. Chicago, M. & St. P. Ry., 232 U.S. 340, 354 (1914); dissenting in Schlesinger v. Wisconsin, 270 U.S. 230, 241 (1926).

[45] 94 U.S. 113.

[46] Nebbia v. New York, 291 U.S. 502, 533 (1934).

[47] Supra, p. 1016.

[48] Thomas v. City of Port Huron, 27 Mich. 320 (1873); Dodge v. Van Buren Circuit Judge, 118 Mich. 189 (1898), rebuking caustically a judge who had held otherwise; Attorney General v. Pingree, 120 Mich. 550 (1899).

[49] Supra, p. 1014.

[50] Taylor v. Ypsilanti, 105 U.S. 60 (1882), followed in New Buffalo v. Cambria Iron Co., 105 U.S. 73 (1882). Besides *New Buffalo*, there were other cases from Berrien County (southwesternmost in Michigan): Edwards v. United States *ex rel.* Thompson, 103 U.S. 471 (1880); Township of Lincoln v. Cambria Iron Co., 103 U.S. 412 (1881); and Township of Chickaming v. Carpenter, 106 U.S. 663 (1883)—unsuccessfully raising a variety of objections to enforcement of municipal bonds.

back some fifteen years. They began with *Ableman v. Booth*,[51] where the State court vainly attempted to release one held for violating the Fugitive Slave Act. Booth's counsel, Byron Paine—a State-rights anti-slavery man—had promptly been elected to the supreme bench. There he and his brethren found other points of conflict: about the release of a federal prisoner by the State court's writ of habeas corpus;[52] about the demand of a citizen of another State to remove his case into a federal court;[53] and, our present concern, about the respect to be accorded to the State court's rulings in municipal bond cases.[54]

In a clash next to be considered, over the affairs of the city of Kenosha, one observes uncertainties typical of municipal bonding, and marks too the misapprehension and looseness which at times characterized proceedings in these matters in the Supreme Court.

Wisconsin's constitution declared, in substance: it shall be the duty of the legislature to provide for the organization of cities, and *to restrict their power of taxing, borrowing and loaning so as to prevent abuses.*[55] The legislature passed two acts for Kenosha, on March 22 and 23, respectively, in 1853. For simplicity, call them *A* and *B*. Act *A* said: to aid in the construction of the Kenosha & Beloit Railroad the city may issue not to exceed $150,000 in bonds, and levy taxes to pay. In July 1853 these bonds were issued and delivered.[56]

It was "City orders or scrip" issued in 1856 under statute *B* that led to judicial conflict. That was a statute to amend the city charter by empowering the council to tax "for any purpose which may be considered essential to promote or secure the common interest of the city" and to "borrow . . . for such purposes, any sum of money for any term of time, at any rate of interest not exceeding ten per centum . . . ." Under that spacious grant the city voted to subscribe *another* $150,000 to aid the same railroad. In *Foster v. Kenosha* in 1860 the State court restrained the collection of a tax to meet this subscription: statute *B* was invalid because the legislature could not, consistently with the constitutional mandate quoted above, confer such

---

[51] 21 How. 506 (1858).

[52] Tarble's Case, 13 Wall. 397 (1872), infra, pp. 1421–24.

[53] Moseley v. Chamberlain, 18 Wis. 700 (1861); Knorr v. Home Ins. Co., 25 Wis. 143 (1869).

[54] One such instance, Havemeyer v. Iowa County, 3 Wall. 294 (1866), has been noted, supra, n. 21.

[55] Constitution of 1848, Art. XI, Sec. 3.

[56] Their enforceability, notwith-standing difficulties not here material, was affirmed in Knapp v. Grant, 27 Wis. 147 (1870). (The bonds had been issued before the statute was published; accordingly they were affected by the objection considered in Havemeyer v. Iowa County, 3 Wall. 294 (1866), supra, n. 21. In Knapp v. Grant that objection was found to have been removed by ratification of the issue in statutes of 1857, 1862 and 1868.)

unrestricted power to borrow for other than necessary municipal purposes.[57]

Campbell, a citizen of Illinois holding 570 city orders issued under statute *B*, in 1864 resorted to the federal Circuit Court for Wisconsin. At the hearing before Justice Miller and the District Judge, statutes *A* and *B* were read in evidence, but an objection to introducing the action of the city council was sustained on the ground that the statute purporting to authorize such action had been held unconstitutional. Assigning this as error, Campbell took his case to the Supreme Court. He won a reversal, in a decision now to be critically examined.[58]

William P. Lynde for the plaintiff, and John W. Cary for Kenosha, were experienced railroad lawyers practicing at Milwaukee. The former gave the Supreme Court to understand that the scrip held by his client was part of the indebtedness expressly authorized by statute *A*: "We feel convinced that we might safely rest upon that act . . . ." The State court's condemnation of statute *B* in *Foster v. Kenosha* was inapplicable, he said, because in that suit the authority of the City "UNDER THE SPECIAL ACT [*A*] WAS NOT BEFORE THE COURT. . . . THE QUESTION OF THE LEGALITY OF THESE CITY ORDERS OR SCRIP HAS NEVER BEEN BEFORE THE SUPREME COURT OF WISCONSIN."[59]

Cary's brief, in reply, was explicit that "The bonds authorized to be issued under this act [*A*], were issued to said railroad company . . . which bonds are now outstanding. . . . This act [*A*] . . . has no reference to the matter in dispute . . . as the scrip was not issued under or in pursuance of it." Plaintiffs scrip had been issued under *B*; in *Foster v. Kenosha* the State court, enforcing an *express* provision of the constitution, on the earliest occasion and without overruling any precedent, had pronounced *B* invalid.[60] But neither Cary's brief nor anything said on oral argument availed to shake the Court's acceptance of Lynde's statement of the situation under Wisconsin law.

Justice Davis wrote a relaxed opinion. These municipal bond

---

[57] 12 Wis. 616. The court said it would not determine in this proceeding what the consequences would be for scrip already issued. That was proper, obviously: the court should not, in a suit between taxpayer and city, pronounce upon the rights of holders of obligations who were not before the Court.

[58] Campbell v. Kenosha, 5 Wall. 194 (1867).

[59] Brief for Plaintiff in Error, 8–10. Foster v. Kenosha, he advised the Court, "did not apply to the scrip": the State court had there said, *"Whether this would render the scrip of the city . . . void . . . ,* WE WILL NOT ATTEMPT TO DETERMINE IN THIS PROCEEDING." See supra, note 57.

Adding to the confusion, the Bill of Exceptions (Transcript, 237) followed by Lynde's Brief, 6, spoke of the Act of March 23 where the Act of March 22 was meant.

[60] Brief and Points of Defendant in Error, 3, 8–10.

cases, he said, had been numerous of late and—reassuringly—"there are very few questions connected with them that have not been decided."[61] (Twenty years later the Court would be deciding twice as many such cases as at the term when Davis spoke.)

The question, he said, was "an important one; but, in our opinion, easily solved . . . ." Following Lynde's brief, he said that the scrip could be sustained under statute *A*, where a subscription of $150,000 had been authorized. But as to Cary's insistence that the City had acted under statute *B*, which the State court had pronounced invalid: whatever might be the merit of that point, Justice Davis viewed a subsequent amendment of the city charter (enlarging the powers of the city's Railroad Commissioner in respect of the Kenosha & Beloit Railroad, and directing the City Treasurer to redeem city scrip) as amounting "by fair implication" to a curative act.

It followed that plaintiff was entitled to a new trial.

But when in 1870 the Wisconsin court decided *Fisk v. Kenosha*,[62] it had occasion to make a critique of Justice Davis' opinion. The Supreme Court had acted under the misapprehension that it was better informed about Wisconsin statutes than the State court had been. As to Justice Davis' first ground: in truth the power under statute *A* had been exhausted by an issue of $150,000 in bonds long before Campbell's scrip had been emitted.[63] And as to the alternative ground that by amending the city charter the legislature had cured the invalidity of statute *B*: there was nothing about the amendment to indicate that the legislature had paid any more attention to the constitution's command that it restrict municipal taxing and borrowing to prevent abuses—the defect for which *B* had been adjudged invalid in 1860. (In this field where so much was done out of order, the Court was prone to sustain curative statutes, without sensitive regard for the consideration that the legislature might be trying to make lawful a result that was beyond its constitutional power.[64])

This emphatic statement by the Wisconsin court at its June term came too late even to be considered in Campbell's controversy with Kenosha: upon remand, a second trial had brought a judgment for the plaintiff, which on April 4, 1870, the Supreme Court had affirmed. On this second occasion Cary had struggled to retrieve what he had lost on the first. As Chief Justice Chase said, he had

---

[61] Compare with other reassuring remarks, supra, p. 1009.

[62] 26 Wis. 23.

[63] Fisk v. Kenosha was a suit on scrip such as Campbell had held. The court pointed out that plaintiff's counsel, an old resident of Kenosha and an able lawyer familiar with the facts, made no claim or suggestion that statute *A* was applicable.

[64] See notes 149 and 164 below.

labored with much zeal and ability to satisfy the Court that, upon the former hearing, "One important and controlling fact was misapprehended, or did not sufficiently appear in the case at that time." But we are not convinced that there was any such misapprehension, or that any important fact escaped the observation of the Court.[65]

Accordingly the judgment for Campbell was affirmed.

On the same day—April 4, 1870—the Court entered another judgment against the city, this one in favor of Lamson, holder of coupons detached from bonds which Kenosha had issued in the sum of $100,000 to aid the Kenosha & Rockford (formerly Kenosha & Beloit, in the *Campbell* case, *supra*).[66] The opinion was by Justice Nelson; Miller, J., noted dissent. What occurred in the argument and decision of *Lamson*'s case calls for more probing.

Reporter Wallace's headnote, faithful to Nelson's opinion, announced this holding:

> Where bonds issued to bona fide holders for value, are valid by the judicial decisions of a State when issued, subsequent decisions in the same State cannot destroy their validity in such hands. Gelpcke v. City of Dubuque (1 Wallace, 175), affirmed.

Anyone relying upon the decision thus reported would understand that (just as in *Gelpcke*) there had been a State court ruling—then the bond issue in faith of that ruling—and subsequently some decision overruling what had earlier been established. *But that was not true.*

Judge Byron Paine of Wisconsin, in the course of a long excoriation of the Supreme Court, made this critique of its *Lamson* decision:

> the court professes to bring this within the doctrine of [*Gelpcke v. Dubuque*], by stating generally that, at the time the bonds were issued [1857], "the decisions of the court of the State favored the validity of the law [under which they were issued]." This is wholly untrue in point of fact. There was no [such] prior decision or assumption by this court . . . . The cases referred to by the reporter [*Dean v. Madison*, 7 Wis. 688 (1858); *Clark v. Janesville*, 10 Wis. 136 (1859)] as supporting the statement of the court involved no such question. And, what is an equally significant fact in answer to the purpose for which they are here referred to, they were both made sometime after the bonds then involved were issued.[67]

---

[65] Kenosha v. Campbell, 131 U.S. App. xcvii, 19 L. Ed. 711. The Court did, however, deny the motion by Campbell's counsel for 10 percent damages, under the Court's Rule 23, which provided for such a penalty where a writ of error appeared "to have been sued out merely for delay."

[66] Kenosha v. Lamson, 9 Wall. 477.

[67] Paine, J., said this in the course of a dissenting opinion in Knorr v. Home Ins. Co. of New York, 25

By reconstructing this matter, going back to the transcript and briefs, one finds a revelation of how the Court was functioning.

The bonds had been issued on September 1, 1857; they recited that they were issued in pursuance of a statute of March 2, 1857 (which amended the city charter, and perpetuated the spacious grant of power to tax and borrow for *any* purpose, aside from activities specifically provided for in the charter).[68] By *Foster v. Kenosha* (1860), which condemned the earlier charter provision (of 1853), bonds issued under this unrestricted grant would be invalid. (Kenosha had overextended its borrowing; by 1862 the legislature was authorizing it to make settlements in bonds at low interest for not over half the amount of its indebtedness.) Lamson was seeking to enforce payment of old interest coupons maturing between 1862 and 1867.

John W. Cary argued that the issue of the bonds had been ultra vires: that was established by *Foster v. Kenosha* in 1860, which "was the first adjudication of the [Wisconsin] court on this question, and stands to-day as the final and settled judgment . . . ."[69]

Matt. Carpenter, for Lamson, could be counted on to extract the uttermost in persuasive force from the materials available in any situation. While in *Lamson*'s case he stopped short of actual misrepresentation, he did make it easy for the Court to plunge on into error.

In his brief, Carpenter told the Court that

> These bonds, when made in September, 1857, were perfectly valid upon the authority of Dean vs. Madison, 7 Wis. and Clark vs. Janesville, 10 Wis.; were circulating in market and passing from hand to hand, with the full sanction of our Supreme Court, until the decision in Foster v. Kenosha; and henceforth they were not worth the same amount of blank paper, in the State court.[70]

But in point of time, *Dean v. Madison* was decided in 1858 and *Clark v. Janesville* in 1859: the bonds of 1857 were not issued in faith of those decisions. To be sure, Carpenter had taken care to mention their dates; but at the outset he had asserted confidently that "I shall

---

Wis. 143, 163. That case was decided at June term, 1869; Paine wrote his dissenting opinion, however, late enough to take note of what the Supreme Court had done on April 4, 1870. The issue in *Knorr* was, whether the out-of-State corporation doing business in Wisconsin should be permitted, under Section 12 of the Judiciary Act of 1789, to remove to the federal court a suit commenced in a State court by a Wisconsin citizen.

Paine, J., held that the Judiciary Act was to that extent invalid. Dixon, C.J., held that it was valid. Cole, J., who wrote the majority opinion, while agreeing with Paine's view, acquiesced in the application of the statute in this case in order to avoid loss and embarrassment to the parties.

[68] Supra, p. 1025.
[69] Brief and Points of Plaintiff in Error, 9–11.
[70] Brief for Defendant in Error, 9.

show *that at the time these bonds were issued"* [his italics], "the rule of decision in the Supreme Court of our State" rejected the view which by *Foster v. Kenosha* in 1860 made the bonds invalid.[71] And later on he told the Justices that they should not respect *Foster v. Kenosha* because "It was pronounced after these bonds were issued, and totally reverses the rule of decision upon this subject, existing in the courts of the State, at the time the bonds were issued. Gelpcke v. Dubuque . . . ." But Carpenter's brief cited *no* Wisconsin ruling "existing at the time the bonds were issued."

And in point of substance, he wrung from the two cases on which he relied a good deal more than fairly they imported. *Dean v. Madison* held that to acquire land for a cemetery (an express municipal function) the city might issue bonds (here $10,000); it rejected plaintiff's contention that by the State constitution a municipality could not be authorized to create a public debt for any purpose. The limitation on *State* indebtedness did not apply to municipalities; and as to the mandate that powers of cities to tax and borrow should be restricted to prevent abuses, "We cannot discover that the legislature restricted in the charter the power of the common council to contract debts, and some provisions . . . obviously contemplate that debts will be contracted . . . . We therefore conclude that the ten thousand dollar indebtedness, contracted by the city to purchase cemetery grounds, is free from all constitutional objection." Carpenter professed to see a great contradiction when, two years later, the court held that while a city's power to tax and borrow for "strictly municipal" purposes need not be restricted, a license to borrow any sum for any object not among the enumerated municipal functions—in particular, aid to a railroad—was inconsistent with the constitution's command that the power of cities to tax and to borrow be so restricted as to prevent abuses.

The second case on which Carpenter relied, *Clark v. Janesville*, while involving other points, turned on the question whether a city charter was a "general law"—which, by the constitution, would not be in force until published. Two Judges held that it was, one Judge that it was not. The dissenter, enlarging on the theme that municipal bonding for railroad aid was permissible, found evidence in the constitution's direction to the legislature to restrict the power so as to prevent abuse. In Janesville's charter, he said, "The power to take the stock was subject to the will of the people directly affected by the indebtedness; and this was all the restriction the legislature deemed necessary to impose

---

[71] Ibid., 5.

upon its exercise in the present instance." And there was "nothing in the opinion of the majority in conflict" with this statement.[72]

Magnifying the discrepancy between the holding in *Foster v. Kenosha* and sentences plucked from the earlier opinions, and representing that inferences from what was said in decisions of 1858 and 1859 proved the existence of a "rule of decision" in 1857 when the bonds were issued, Carpenter boldly claimed that the situation in *Lamson* fell within the rationale of *Gelpcke*.

And Justice Nelson, writing for the Court, accepted all this implicitly, in just two sentences:

> at the time this loan was made, and these bonds were issued, the decisions of the court of the State favored the validity of the law. The last decision cannot, therefore, be followed.

He did not even bother to cite the decisions to which he attributed controlling force; Wallace supplied them in a footnote, with "Rep." to show that it was his own addition.

Confidence is shaken whenever it is patent on the face of the printed report that the Justices made a mistake about some element in a matter before them. Still more damaging is a discovery *dehors* the report that they had acted on the basis of some hidden error; one wonders how often they failed to get things straight. And how paradoxical that the Court professed to sustain the purchasers' supposed reliance upon decisions which actually had not been made, while its own decision was not worthy of men's confidence.

How far the *Kenosha* rulings of April 4, 1870 (in *Campbell*'s case, and then in *Lamson*'s) are attributable to undue submissiveness to powerful counsel, or to a general laxness—how far to a prepossession in favor of bondholders—how far (if at all) to the turmoil of that moment over reopening the legal tender question[73]—*quaere*. Earlier in that term, in *Butz v. Muscatine*, the Court had made another bad mistake when—disdaining "blindly" to follow the Iowa court—it had disregarded a debt limit plainly posted in the statutes.[74] The Supreme Court was putting out slovenly work, while reproving State courts for alleged shortcomings.

---

[72] Ibid., 8.
In Bushnell v. Beloit, 10 Wis. 195, at January term 1860, supra, n. 1, a unanimous bench sustained the power of the legislature to authorize a municipal corporation to subscribe to railroad stock and to issue bonds therefor. Clark v. Janesville had involved the same basic question, and the opinions there show that the two cases had been considered together.
[73] Supra, pp. 738–39.
[74] Supra, p. 1000.

BOND EMISSION IN DISREGARD OF
PENDING LITIGATION

MOVING NOW TO a new topic, it has been seen that in *Olcott v. Fond du Lac County*,[75] on March 31, 1873, the Supreme Court refused to follow the Wisconsin court's determination[76] that it was beyond the powers of the legislature to authorize taxation to make a *gift* to a railroad. In so refusing the Supreme Court had reversed the judgment of Circuit Judge Drummond.[77] But the County had set up another answer to Olcott's claim, an answer not mentioned in the Court's opinion: the defense of *lis pendens*, that the bonds had been issued in disregard of litigation pending in the State court to prevent their issue. This was a feature often present in municipal aid to railroads: a suit would have been brought (commonly by taxpayers) and a temporary injunction granted; then upon a hearing the judge (acting perhaps under pressures of the moment) dissolved the injunction; and instantly thereupon the clerk (perhaps also under pressure) delivered the bonds to the promoters, notwithstanding prompt action by counsel to appeal to the State Supreme Court. Would the purchaser of such a bond have a perfect title, despite a decision on appeal that the issue was not lawful and that the injunction should never have been dissolved?

If at that period it had been understood that regularity, substantial popular support and an adequate tax base must be shown before municipal bonds were put into circulation—if approval by competent counsel had been essential to marketability—such craftiness would have been unavailing, regardless of the technical issue whether at the very hour of the issue the municipal officers were under an injunction.

Litigation had been pending when the bonds in *Marsh v. Fulton County*[78] were issued, but without adverting to that point the Court had held them invalid on other grounds. But then in *Olcott v. Fond du Lac County* the Court enforced the bonds, without discussing the defense of *lis pendens*. Did that signify that the point had been considered and rejected—or had the Justices overlooked it?

Circuit Judge Drummond wondered. He had before him suits by Marcy and others over bonds of Warren County, Illinois[79]—cases

---

[75] 16 Wall. 678. Supra, pp. 1016–17.

[76] Whiting v. Sheboygan & Fond du Lac R.R., 25 Wis. 167 (1870). Supra, pp. 1010–11.

[77] Olcott v. Fond du Lac County, Fed. Case No. 10,479. C.C.E.D. Wis., Oct. 1870.

[78] Supra, ch. 17, n. 347.

[79] George O. Marcy of Massachu-

setts, Augustus F. Post of New York, and the Portsmouth Savings Bank of New Hampshire, in July and August 1873 had brought their suits on coupons from the bonds. These reached the Supreme Court as Warren County v. Marcy, 97 U.S. 96 (1878), and companion cases.

similar to *Olcott v. Fond du Lac.* What inference ought he to draw from the Supreme Court's silence?

The Supreme Court of Illinois in 1872, in a suit brought by one Abner C. Harding, a taxpayer, had held that Warren County should be enjoined from issuing the bonds, because of its failure to give the requisite thirty days' notice of the election on the proposal to subscribe.[80] Actually the bonds had been issued in 1871: they had been delivered to the railroad two days after the trial judge—erroneously, it was held on appeal—had dissolved a temporary injunction. The bonds bore a recital importing compliance with law; hence a federal court must doubtless protect those who qualified as bona fide purchasers, notwithstanding the irregularity in the election. But now Warren County, in defense against the claim of Marcy and the other bondholders, answered that it was during the pendency of the suit in the State courts—culminating in a permanent injunction—that the bonds had been issued.[81]

The situation was explained in a letter to Justice Davis by Charles B. Lawrence, of counsel for Warren County. (Lawrence had just ceased to be a Justice of the Illinois Supreme Court; he had not participated when the *Warren County* case was before that court.) Writing from Chicago on February 12, 1874, he related the events on which the County based its contention that "the bonds were issued in fraud of the court and the parties," to which plaintiff had replied that he was an innocent purchaser without actual notice.

---

[80] Harding v. Rockford, Rock Island & St. Louis R.R., 65 Ill. 90.

Notices of an election to be held on September 23 were first published in a newspaper on August 27; they were posted for periods varying from 30 to 20 days, and in one township not at all. At the special election, 1,775 voted for and 975 against the subscription; at the most recent general election the total vote had been 4,731. Warren County v. Marcy, 97 U.S. 96.

The plaintiff, Abner C. Harding (1807–74), was a lawyer, a distinguished brigadier general in the early part of the war, an advanced Republican in the 39th and 40th Congresses, and a wealthy banker and railroad builder.

[81] By Judge Drummond's special finding, events in Harding's suit to enjoin the county from issuing the bonds were as follows:

July 18, 1870—taxpayers' suit was filed; upon giving bond, an injunction was issued, which remained in force until January 23, 1871—when on defendant's motion and over complainants' objections, the injunction was dissolved.

January 25, 1871—the bonds were executed and delivered to the railroad company.

January 27, 1871—complainant prayed an appeal from order dissolving the injunction; trial court refused.

Thereupon the cause went to final hearing;

February 2, 1871—court entered final decree dismissing bill.

From that decree, complainant perfected an appeal to the State Supreme Court, resulting in a reversal and a permanent injunction. 65 Ill. 90.

Transcript of Record in Warren County v. Marcy, 33–34.

To this replication we demurred and the demurrer was argued before Judge Drummond last week.

Judge Drummond says he fully agrees with us that these bonds were issued subject to whatever decree the court might render in the suit pending in the Circuit Court of Warren County at the time of their issue, and that our defence is therefore complete.

He says that this is his individual opinion but that in the case of Olcott vs. Board of Supervisors 16th Wallace, 768, the identical question was involved, and although nothing whatever is said about it in the opinion and no person could discover from the report of the case that it was presented by the record, yet Judge Drummond says it was in fact in the record, and he thinks it must have been passed upon by the Supreme Court. Under the authority of this supposed decision he would feel constrained to decide the demurrer against us, but he says, if you say that this question of *lis pendens* was not in fact considered by the Supreme Court in that case he will then follow his own judgment and sustain the demurrer.

Justice Davis had dissented in *Olcott* and doubtless would remember. Would he please advise Judge Drummond?[82]

From Springfield, where he was holding court, on February 16 Drummond sent a like inquiry to the Circuit Justice. "Was anything said in Olcott v. Fond du Lac about the effect of the pendency of the proceedings in the State Court. I mean of course among the Judges did any of you think that had influence on the question?"[83]

Justice Davis indorsed the letters "Recd. & ansd Feby 1874"; but what he wrote does not appear.

What happened, however, was that at the July term of the Circuit Court Davis and Drummond heard argument, and then entered an order that the court "take time to consider."[84] On January 5, 1875, the court, held by Judge Drummond, entered judgments for the respective plaintiffs, with such special findings as would clearly present the element of *lis pendens* to the Supreme Court.

It was more than three years later when, in due course, the Court reached *Warren County v. Marcy* and companion cases—argument opening on April 10, 1878, continuing throughout the eleventh, and closing on the twelfth.

George F. Harding, a well-educated lawyer, appeared for the County. He labored under a heavy handicap. Courts had decided, time and again, that "the doctrine of *lis pendens* does not apply to negotiable paper." Even so, Harding insisted,

---

[82] Davis Papers, Ill. State Hist. Soc.
[83] Ibid.

[84] Transcript of Record in Warren County v. Marcy, 29–30.

Not a case in the books can be found, in which this exception was sustained, where the paper did not exist at the time when the suit was brought, and where the suit was brought, as in this case, to prevent it coming into existence.[85]

Admittedly the necessities of commerce forbade that one who took a negotiable instrument would be affected by perhaps many suits against many previous holders in many courts. But an exception to that exception should be recognized—so Harding argued—in the present situation where a suit had been pending to enjoin the creation of the instrument in the first place: for here

the purchaser need take notice of but one suit involving but one question, in but one court, and of known parties; and could satisfy himself by inquiring of the parties on the spot. To protect himself . . . the purchaser need only go to the one court, where alone the corporation can be sued . . . .

In ten minutes . . . Marcy could have, at the wire, sent a dispatch, and within two hours received an answer, which would have forbid the purchase. . . .

It would be easy to require proof on this point, of the party selling paper open to such impeachment. . . .[86]

"People cannot protect themselves by an appeal to the courts," he warned, "unless the Court shall hold the decree therein to be effectual." Otherwise, in actual practice, a false clerk could issue bonds apparently regular, "and when once issued no power on earth can defeat [them] in the hands of the wily broker and capitalist, who, to play his part, shuts his eyes and ears and takes no notice, not if the people fill the world with their clamor!"[87] Already, Harding told the Court, "the law has gone too far in the interest of the capitalist and note broker; and the rights of the citizen, the tax payer, the shareholder, the laborer, have been struck down."[88]

Opposing counsel took their stand on the proposition that the doctrine of *lis pendens* was not applied to negotiable securities. Also, going into technical matters, they said that, in respect of the suit to enjoin that had been carried through the Illinois courts, taxpayer should be faulted under that State's rules of chancery practice—it was because his attorney had failed to make the proper moves that the bonds had been issued.[89]

---

[85] Brief and Argument, 45–46.
[86] Ibid., 8–9, 54–55.
[87] Ibid., 61.
[88] Ibid., 24.
[89] "When his injunction was dis- solved, 23 Jan'y, 1871, he did not have his bill dismissed by the court for want of equity, as it was competent for him to do, under the chancery practice in Illinois, and then

The argument for the County had been unusually energetic and cogent; but it proved unavailing. Bradley recorded on his copy of the Transcript the votes as the Justices were polled at conference, in the inverse order of seniority:

Aff.	Rev.
Hunt	Harlan
Bradley	Field
Strong	Miller
Swayne	
Clifford	
Waite	

The Chief Justice selected Justice Bradley to write the opinion. That insured a workmanlike discussion of the issues. Here was an occasion of crucial importance. All along opponents of railroad aid had been chided for contesting bonds after the benefits had been received —they should have made their challenge before the bonds were put into circulation. But here they had done just that—and now the Court was going to say that this timely effort was unavailing. The opinion should give some good reason.

Bradley started with the general proposition that one who deals with property is bound at his peril to take notice of pending litigation affecting title. The foundation had been traced in an opinion by Chancellor Kent,[90] one which "deserves the careful study of every student of law." The Chancellor had recognized that "the safety of commercial dealing would require a limitation of the rule" where negotiable paper was concerned. That limitation was firmly established. Bradley pointed to procedural measures whereby, perhaps, vigilance might preclude its abuse. That brought him to the critical issue:

> The only thing calculated to raise any doubt, in the present case, is the fact that the bonds in question were not in existence when the suit to prevent their issue was brought. . . .

---

take an appeal, and *thus keep his injunction in force.* It is true, that four days after his injunction was dissolved, he prayed an appeal from the order dissolving the injunction, but this was refused, for the obvious reason that in no case does an appeal lie from an interlocutory order of the court. The whole case must first be disposed of. Ten days after the injunction was dissolved, the bill was dismissed and an appeal was taken, but that did not revive the injunction; to keep that in force, the bill should have been dismissed *at the time the injunction was dissolved.* . . ." Brief for Defendant in Error, Portsmouth Savings Bank, by Isaac G. Wilson and Sanford B. Perry, 36. Charles M. Osborn's brief for Marcy made the same point, at 35–36. On this see Bressler v. McCune, 56 Ill. 475 (1870), cited supra, ch. 17, n. 359.

[90] Murray v. Ballou, 1 Johns. Ch. 566 (N.Y. 1815).

To this he answered:

> But we see no good reason for limiting the exception to paper or securities previously in existence. . . . Its object is to protect the commercial community by removing all obstacles to the free circulation of negotiable paper. If, when regular on its face, it is to be subject to the possibility of a suit being pending between the original parties, its negotiability would be seriously affected, and a check would be put to innumerable commercial transactions. These considerations apply equally to securities created during, as to those created before, the commencement of the suit; and as well to controversies respecting their origin, as those respecting their transfer. Both are within the same mischief, and the same reason.

Justice Bradley had found it "unnecessary now to inquire" into procedural niceties about how to avoid any moment when in a pending suit an injunction was not in force. He recalled that in *Lexington v. Butler*[91] in 1872, the city had issued bonds under a judgment of mandamus obtained by the railroad company; on appeal that judgment was reversed, and the company was enjoined from parting with the bonds and was ordered to deposit them; yet in disobedience they were circulated, and the Supreme Court enforced them in the hands of a purchaser without notice. The defense of *lis pendens* had there been rejected, although Justice Clifford's opinion did not mention the point.

In *Warren County v. Marcy*, Waite, Bradley, and Hunt, upon a comparison of injustices, were unwilling to make an exception to discourage an abuse commonly practiced by the collusion of railroad promoters and municipal officers. The position of Clifford, Swayne, and Strong on such a question could not be in doubt. Miller, Field, and Harlan (successor to Davis in 1877) noted dissent without filing an opinion.

While in *Warren County* the Court, as Chief Justice Waite later observed, refused to charge the purchasers with constructive notice of a pending suit,

> it has never been doubted that those who buy such [negotiable] securities from litigating parties, with *actual* notice of the suit, do so at their peril and must abide the result the same as the parties from whom they got their title. . . .

He was speaking in *Scotland County v. Hill*,[92] in 1884. At the very moment the case of Warren County, Illinois, was being decided in the Supreme Court, in Scotland County, Missouri—eighty miles away—

---

[91] 14 Wall. 282. [92] 112 U.S. 183.

popular resistance was mounting as the federal court moved to enforce bonds which the county clerk had spirited away to Illinois to avoid service of an injunction, and there had delivered to the railroad at the office of Hill's bank. And even if Hill's suspicion had been aroused by this irregular conduct, unquestionably he could recover on such bonds if they had passed through the hands of an innocent holder.[93]

SUCCESSFUL EVASION OF THE COURTS

CONTEMPT OF LAW in issuing municipal bonds was at times offset by contempt of law in evading their collection. And as it resulted from the Court's adherence to principle in *Warren County* that the former went unreproved, so it might happen that for a like reason citizens banded together would succeed in defeating enforcement. Here recalcitrance in Beloit and in Watertown, Wisconsin, made history.

Samuel C. Morgan had recovered judgment in the federal court against the Town of Beloit on coupons from bonds issued for railroad stock.[94] Through concerted action, there was never a board of supervisors in being when there was process to be served. The supervisors had levied no tax, and by systematic resignations had so contrived

---

[93] Scotland County v. Hill, 132 U.S. 107 (1889). Infra, n. 280.

[94] A statute had authorized the town to subscribe and issue bonds to "a railroad company authorized to construct a railroad from . . . Racine [on Lake Michigan, westward] to . . . Beloit." In 1853 the town issued bonds for $100,000 in the stock of the Racine, Janesville & Mississippi R.R. Co., (chartered to build "from Racine . . . by way of Janesville . . . to the Mississippi river"), upon that company's undertaking to build eastward from Beloit a connecting line. (Inasmuch as the chartered route ran from east to west via Janesville, whereas Beloit lies thirteen miles due *south* from Janesville, this undertaking was *ultra vires*—as to the company and as to the town as well.) The Beloit bonds were passed to a construction company, from which Morgan purchased at seventy cents on the dollar. The Racine, Janesville & Mississippi became insolvent; in 1853 the town stopped paying interest.

Out of Beloit's misadventure, five cases reached the Supreme Court:

four were decided at December term 1868, all in favor of Morgan. No. 320, not reported, affirmed judgment on his basic claim. No. 91, argued with it, rejected the Town's prayer for a determination that the bonds were void, for the illegality noted above and on other grounds. This was Beloit v. Morgan, 7 Wall. 619. No. 118 held that under the Wisconsin statutes, mandamus lay against the Town Clerk to compel *him* to perform the duty the supervisors had evaded: Morgan v. Town Clerk, 7 Wall. 610. No. 281 held that a bill in equity would lie to compel the *City* of Beloit (carved out of the town in 1856) to pay the share charged upon it by the act of its incorporation: Morgan v. Beloit City and Town, 7 Wall. 613.

No. 17, the most difficult, went over to the next term. This is Morgan v. Town of Beloit and Ruble *et al.*, 19 L. Ed. 508, discussed in the text.

What is here explained is based on the Transcripts and the Briefs in these related cases.

that no mandamus or attachment could be made effectual. On Morgan's behalf a bill was filed against the Town, naming as co-defendants Simon Ruble (a repeating resigner) and a few other selected inhabitants; it asked the Circuit Court to take this extraordinary action: to appoint a master with instructions to collect out of the property of these named individuals a sum sufficient to satisfy the judgment. (Whether they in turn could cause their fellow-townsmen to contribute would be their problem.) Matt. H. Carpenter represented the claimant in this formidable endeavor. His doughty rival, Edward G. Ryan, represented the Town.

The Circuit Court, held by District Judge Andrew G. Miller, dismissed the bill. An appeal to the Supreme Court was docketed in July 1867; as the Court's business was then moving, a decision might be expected in the spring of 1869.

After the case was argued, on February 23, 1869, the Court put it over for a reargument of the difficult question. As has been related, Evans Rogers, in his effort to collect his judgment against Lee County, Iowa, had won an order directing the Marshal to levy a tax. That case, submitted on February 11, was decided on March 1, 1869.[95] Thus the Justices had considered the *Rogers* matter, and doubtless had decided it in conference, when *Morgan v. Town of Beloit and Ruble et al.* was argued. In Iowa, it will be recalled, there was a Code provision on which the requested mode of execution could be based; Wisconsin had no such statute.

Rogers claimed something authorized by statute; for Morgan, the remedy at law had yielded no results, and now he asked that equity create something more. In Rogers' case it was contemplated that the Marshal would collect a tax from all property-owners; Morgan asked that his judgment be satisfied out of the property of a few he had picked to be defendants. It was significant that the Justices saw enough merit to order a reargument.[96]

Carpenter dwelt upon the frustration of justice through the town's combined effort; upon a few precedents from States in New England where recovery had been allowed against an inhabitant for a neglect of duty by some entity of local government that had no corporate funds; and upon an appeal to the spirit of equity jurisprudence which historically had fashioned redress in some situations where remedies at common law were inadequate. As in the then contemporary litigation over the bonds of Kenosha,[97] here too Carpenter displayed his resourcefulness in argument. Ryan, opposing, was no less skillful. The New England cases, he pointed out, had no relevance to Wisconsin

---

[95] Supra, ch. 17, n. 160.
[96] Which occurred on Dec. 8, 1869.

Only Carpenter appeared.
[97] Supra, pp. 1025–31.

towns, which did have a corporate treasury and were liable to pay judgments. "And Equity will not devise a new ground of jurisdiction, to enforce a cruel remedy, because a speculator in public faith is unlucky in his legal remedies."[98]

On January 31, 1870, Chief Justice Chase announced that the judgment denying the remedy was affirmed by an equally divided court. As was the Court's wont in such a situation, no opinions were filed and no disclosure was made how the individual members stood.[99]

An equal division encourages another try. James H. Rees of Chicago had judgments against the City of Watertown, and he too had been unable to collect.[100] (Rees had bought, about 1861, railroad-aid bonds issued in 1856, interest whereon had been in default since January 1858; it seems that even upon their issue they could be purchased at ten cents on the dollar, "for reason that [they] were so largely in excess of the resources of the city to pay."[101]) Mandamus to enforce the judgments had been issued against three successive boards; but when the Marshal arrived, resignations had produced incapacity to act. Now counsel filed a bill praying that the Circuit Court direct the Marshal "to seize and sell so much of [the taxable property within the town] as may be necessary to raise the amount due to your orator and the costs of this action and pay it over to him . . . ."[102] This was dismissed (Circuit Judge Drummond and District Judge Hopkins being divided[103]), and an appeal was taken.

It is always worth watching when the Court has come to the verge of established judicial power and is considering some bold new step. Counsel for Rees urged this in the name of federal supremacy:

> The theory of the bill is as simple as it is radical. It is this: The complainant having established a clear legal right at law, and having demonstrated that he has no remedy at law, it is the duty of the court of equity to devise and enforce an effectual remedy, which

---

[98] Brief, 8.

[99] Participating were Chase, Nelson, Grier, Clifford, Swayne, Miller, Davis, and Field. This was Grier's last day on the bench. Supra, p. 717.

[100] Rees v. Watertown, 19 Wall. 107 (1874).

[101] Transcript in Rees v. Watertown, 17. Testimony of Theodore Prentiss—attorney, man of business, and former mayor.

Statements herein rely also upon the papers in Amy v. Watertown (No.

1), 130 U.S. 301 (1889), and Amy v. Watertown (No. 2), 130 U.S. 320 (1889).

[102] Transcript, 7.

[103] Ibid., 18–19. Hopkins, J., expressed an opinion against the right claimed; Drummond, J., in view of the equal division in the Supreme Court in Morgan v. Beloit, concurred in this dismissal. John F. Dillon, *The Law of Municipal Corporations*, 2d ed., 2 vols. (New York: James Cockroft and Co., 1873), sec. 693n.

must be done through its own officers, because there are no others in existence capable of it.

. . . .

    We are aware of the gravity and delicacy of the questions presented. For on our part we assert the right of a United States court to take possession of a city and sell it in its own way, without regard to state laws or state officers. And on the other side, the claim is that the United States court is powerless in this case to execute its judgment except through instrumentalities provided by another sovereign, and that, these being withdrawn, the city may safely and effectually repudiate its debt. . . .

When the Marshal had collected enough to satisfy the complainant, the court might leave it to the citizens "to settle the equities between themselves at their leisure . . . ."[104]

    Counsel for Watertown replied:

    But it is clearly a mistake that equity gives a remedy to every party in difficulty, unless his difficulty be covered by some specific ground of equitable jurisdiction. "The true nature and extent of equity jurisdiction, as at present administered, must be ascertained by a specific enumeration of its actual limits in each particular class of cases falling within its remedial justice." Story's Equity Jurisp. 62.[105]

He repeated Ryan's thrust in the *Beloit* case, that equity would not devise a new and cruel remedy to aid a speculator[106]—especially one who was "expecting *in this case a ten fold return.*"

    The Court's decision in *Rees v. Watertown*, on March 2, 1874, was that relief must be denied.[107] Said Justice Hunt:

    A court of equity cannot, by avowing that there is a right but no remedy known to the law, create a remedy in violation of law, or even without the authority of law.

Although the municipal corporation had failed to pay Rees what was his due, "it does not follow that this Court may order the amount to be made up from the private estate of one of its citizens. This summary proceeding would involve a violation of the rights of the latter . . . ."

    To afford perspective, Justice Hunt recalled the anti-rent agitation that had shaken New York (from 1838 until 1846, when a new

---

[104] Appellant's Brief, 4, 9.
[105] Respondent's Brief, 5.

[106] Supra, pp. 1039–40.
[107] 19 Wall. 107.

constitution brought reform). Combinations of tenants had resisted process "so effectually that for some years no landlord could gain possession of his land." Neither then nor now would a temporary obstruction of the law justify the judiciary in creating some rough new remedy in the name of equity.

To make their contention seem less stark, counsel had asserted in their bill that really it was the citizens of Watertown who owed the debt, and that all their taxable property should be regarded as a trust fund; the city officers were said to be trustees for the benefit of creditors.[108] Justice Clifford, dissenting, found this convincing; he said that equity would not suffer a trust to be defeated through the misconduct of a trustee; also, quite simply, that he would not sanction the fraudulent repudiation of an honest debt. Justice Swayne also dissented.[109]

With his habitual clarity of perception, Justice Bradley endorsed on his copy of the transcript a note rejecting the loose theory that the taxable property of all the citizens was a trust fund. He wrote, in part:

> As to the jurisdiction of Chancery—that court can only be resorted to by creditors in pursuit of their claims when there is a fund belonging to the debtor, to be administered, or assets which cannot be reached by legal process, such as property held in trust for the debtor, or debts due to him, or property of his which has been fraudulently assigned or concealed. If there are other cases depending upon the want of an adequate remedy at law, they are never directed at the appropriation of any thing but legal or equitable assets of the debtor.
>
> In this case there are no assets belonging to the City, either legal or equitable which the Complainant proposes to reach. The property of the people is not such assets. It does not belong to the City in any sense. It is subject to the sovereign power of taxation, it is true; but the court cannot exercise that power. It can only act as a court of law, by its process of mandamus and attachment, upon the persons having the proper official character for levying of taxes. If it cannot find such persons, it is powerless to afford a remedy.
>
> What results may follow from legislative neglect or inability to provide the proper machinery for levying taxes,—which is practical repudiation—is not for us, at this time, to decide. It is not in the province, or power of the court to supply that machinery.

---

[108] Transcript, 7.

[109] Since Morgan v. Beloit four years earlier, Chase, Nelson, and Grier had gone, and Strong, Bradley, and Hunt had been added. Waite, C.J., joined the Court on March 4, 1874—two days after Rees v. Watertown was decided.

Fifteen years later, Bradley would employ the same rigorous sort of analysis when, as spokesman for the Court, he returned to the affairs of Watertown in litigation by another bondholder, Henry Amy.[110] The decision in *Rees* was firmly adhered to by the Court.[111]

WATCHFUL WAITING AT WATERTOWN

A CREDIBLE ACCOUNT of "The Watertown Railway Bond Fight" was written, long afterward, by a citizen who had known men and events at firsthand.[112] Before the Supreme Court the fight ran for twenty years, from *Rees* in 1874 to *Metcalf v. Watertown*[113] in 1894. From this account and what may be gathered from the Records and Briefs, one may satisfy the curiosity aroused when one reads the Reports: How did this city get into so much trouble?

In aid of the Watertown & Madison Railroad, in 1856 the City issued $200,000 in 8 percent bonds payable in 1877. ("The voting was largely done by laborers on the railroads, not residents of the city."[114]) The aid was viewed as a loan; the company undertook to pay the interest and principal. (Construction of this road was further supported by the mortgaging of farms[115] and by stock subscriptions by individu-

---

[110] Amy v. Watertown (No. 1), 130 U.S. 301 (1889); Amy v. Watertown (No. 2), 130 U.S. 320 (1889).

[111] Pending when *Rees* was decided was a like suit by Walter S. Hubbell against the nearby Town of Waterloo, Wisconsin. The Court denied relief; the case—No. 66, decided Nov. 17, 1874—was not reported. *Rees* was followed in Heine v. Levee Comm'rs, 19 Wall. 655 (1874); Barkley v. Levee Comm'rs, 93 U.S. 258 (1876); and Thompson v. Allen County, 115 U.S. 550 (1885).

[112] William F. Whyte, in *Wisconsin Historical Society Proceedings for 1916*, 268–307, being Paper No. 177.

[113] 153 U.S. 671.

[114] Transcript in Rees v. Watertown, 17. Testimony of Prentiss, former mayor.

[115] Professor Frederick Merk's *Economic History of Wisconsin During the Civil War Decade* (Madison: State Historical Society of Wisconsin, 1916) has a chapter on "Railroad Farm Mortgages." He writes:

During the years 1850 to 1857, while the first fever of railroad construction was at its height, approximately 6,000 Wisconsin farmers mortgaged their homesteads to the extent of from $4,500,000 to $5,000,000 in order to purchase railroad stock. . . .

Disillusion came only too quickly. The farmers learned that the railroad companies were disposing of their mortgages in the eastern money markets at from 50 to 75 per cent of their face value. They discovered that the interest on the mortgages was not being cancelled and that eastern holders were threatening foreclosure. Rumors of extravagant and fraudulent contracts and stories of corruption, rapidly leading the roads into receivership, leaked out. In 1857 came the crash of the panic and every railroad in the State sank at once into hopeless ruin. The bubble had burst! The farmers of Wisconsin had burdened themselves with debt and as compensation

als along the way.) The city had previously issued $80,000 in bonds to aid the Milwaukee & Watertown. With the reorganizing and consolidating that followed the panic of 1857, the citizens discovered that successor companies—presently the Milwaukee & St. Paul, of which Russell Sage and his lawyer, Nathaniel A. Cowdrey[116] were directors—refused to honor the undertaking on which the aid had been given.[117] The people's sense of injustice was heightened by the discovery that the promoters of the La Crosse & Milwaukee (immediate successor to the Milwaukee & Watertown) had been dispensing enormous sums in bribing the governor and legislators to give them a big land grant that was coming to the State from Congress. (The mayor who had signed the bonds and another townsman who was president of the Watertown & Madison were among the distributees.[118]) While the citizenry debated what to do about the unexpected burden that had fallen upon them, interest for 1858 and thereafter went unpaid.

"The year 1868 saw the beginning of a turmoil which lasted without cessation for more than ten years." Judgments aggregating $65,000 had been recovered. Rees had his writ of mandamus, but the city officers "declared that they would not obey it; and that the state of feeling was such among the citizens, a large proportion of whom were Germans, that they could not attempt to obey it without great danger of personal violence."[119] A system was contrived whereby the mayor and a portion of the aldermen would function for an instant and then sign resignations, effective at once;[120] the remaining aldermen as the Board of Street Commissioners would then govern throughout the year.

With the Supreme Court's *Rees* decision in 1874, bondholders

---

had only the worthless stock of bankrupt corporations. At. 243–44.

[116] Cowdrey (? –1885) graduated from Yale Law School in 1847. He assisted Professor Henry Dutton in *A Revision of Swift's Digest of the Laws of Connecticut* (1848–53). Practicing in New York City, he figures prominently, as counsel and as a party, in far-flung railroad litigation.

[117] Watertown had also in 1856 issued $200,000 in bonds to the Chicago, St. Paul & Fond du Lac. The successor Chicago & North Western redeemed these bonds "and the city was never harmed by the transaction . . . ." Whyte, *Wisconsin Historical Society . . . 1916*, 277–78.

[118] Ibid., 285–86.

[119] Transcript in Rees v. Watertown, 3. Complainant's bill.

Whyte recalled that Wisconsin received a large influx of "settlers from Northern Europe . . . who were wholly ignorant of the wiles of the promoter in whose unscrupulous grasp they were as mere babes in the woods." *Wisconsin Historical Society . . . 1916*, 268.

[120] "The members being provided with written resignations, could perfect their resignations after the United States marshal was actually in the council room, before he could serve [the writ] on them . . . ." Transcript in Rees v. Watertown, 7. Complainant's bill. (This is not to affirm that any marshal ever did manage to get so close.)

saw the wisdom of compromise. That was what the better element among the citizens had desired all along. But now a Union League of obstreperous leaders and their followers managed "for fifteen years to play a sinister role in the city's affairs," proposing "all sorts of impracticable schemes to obstruct" a settlement.[121]

Rees had at any rate recovered a judgment; generally bondholders had not been able to go even that far. Wisconsin law required that process be served on the mayor. Deputy marshals had quailed and failed at catching a mayor in being. The federal court and the State Supreme Court had held service upon anybody else to be ineffective.[122] Meanwhile the statute of limitations was ticking away.

In *Amy v. Watertown (No. 1)*,[123] suit had been brought on coupons maturing between 1858 and 1871. A first attempt in 1873 had proved abortive when the City appeared specially and moved to set aside the service as not in accord with the statute. Ten years later these steps were repeated, with the same result—and this time a writ of error brought the question of service before the Supreme Court.

Wisconsin law said: to sue the city, process must be served on *the mayor.*

And Congress, by the Conformity Act of 1872 had prescribed:[124]

> The practice, pleadings, and forms and modes of proceeding in civil causes, other than equity and admiralty causes, in the circuit and district courts, shall conform, as near as may be, to the practice, pleadings and forms and modes of proceeding, existing at the time in like causes in the courts of record in the State within which such circuit or district courts are held.

Certainly that meant that, in the manner of serving process, a federal court must conform to State law. Agreeing with the State court's construction of the State statutes, the Supreme Court held that Amy had not effectively served his writ; the Circuit Court had been right in holding that its jurisdiction had not been engaged.

In the companion case of *Amy v. Watertown (No. 2)*[125] the same plaintiffs sued on three bonds, and on coupons that matured subsequently to those in *No. 1*. Here the City had voluntarily appeared in

---

[121] Whyte, *Wisconsin Historical Society . . . 1916*, 295–96.

[122] Perkins v. Watertown, Fed. Case No. 10,991 (C.C.W.D. Wis. 1873); Robinson v. Watertown, 59 Wis. 513 (1884) and 69 Wis. 230 (1887).

[123] 130 U.S. 1 (1889). Plaintiffs were Henry Amy and Gustavus L. Hoppenstedt, partners in H. Amy & Co., specializing in repudiated municipal bonds. Supra, pp. 924–25.

[124] Act of June 1, 1872, 17 Stat. 196, by its sec. 5, which became Rev. Stats., sec. 914.

[125] 130 U.S. 320 (1889).

the Circuit Court, in order to plead a defense which, if successful, would be definitive. This was the statute of limitations: in Wisconsin, suit on bonds or coupons must be brought within six years.

But, plaintiffs' counsel answered, such a statute should be so applied that—quite aside from the express exceptions (as where the debtor was out of the State, or was citizen of a country at war with the United States)—time would not run against a plaintiff so long as he was the victim of concealed fraud on the part of the debtor. Then they labored on the theme that where officers and citizens have conspired to prevent plaintiff from making service of process, their action was as bad as, and should be assimilated to, concealed fraud. But, said Justice Bradley for a unanimous Court,

> Fraud is not the proper term to apply to such conduct. It may be morally wrong. It may be dishonest: but it is not fraudulent in the legal sense of the term.
> Inability to serve process on a defendant has never been deemed an excuse for not commencing an action within the prescribed period. . . . If this is an omission, the courts cannot supply it. That is for the Legislature to do. . . .

"The effect of this decision," wrote the Watertown chronicler,[126]

> was, of course, overwhelming. At one stroke it outlawed every bond against the city which had not been reduced to a judgment, and these latter amounted to only about one-third of the total.

One Wisconsin creditor, long scornful of compromise, in 1891 accepted $15,000 in settlement of claims for $600,000.

Only after the lapse of twenty years would the bar of the statute fall upon judgments that had been recovered in the federal court in Wisconsin. The Supreme Court so held, in 1894.[127] Watertown now

---

[126] Whyte, *Wisconsin Historical Society . . . 1916*, 305.

[127] Metcalf v. Watertown, 153 U.S. 671. Wisconsin's Revised Statutes of 1858 had a limitation of twenty years on judgments "of any court of record of this State," and of ten years on judgments "of any court of record of any State . . . , or of any court of the United States." Metcalf sued in 1883 on a judgment recovered in the federal Circuit Court for Wisconsin in 1866. The statute was construed to mean that as to the judgment of any court—State or federal—sitting

in Wisconsin, the limitation was at twenty years. (Wisconsin Revised Statutes of 1878, operating prospectively, had expressly so provided.)

Only on this final point was Watertown unsuccessful in its bond cases before the Supreme Court.

Pereles v. Watertown, Fed. Case No. 10,980 (C.C.W.D. Wis. Apr. 1874), was concerned with "An act to limit the time for the commencement of actions against towns, counties, cities and villages, on demands made payable to bearer," which took effect on April 3, 1872. Laws 1872,

reverted to normal government. It settled the balance of its indebtedness by twenty semi-annual installments with 5 percent interest.

Of the Justices who had participated in *Rees* in 1874, Justice Field alone remained when Watertown's last case was decided.

TWELVE DECISIONS IN 1876 TO BE SCRUTINIZED

AT OCTOBER TERM 1875 a run of railroad-aid bond cases came before the Court—a dozen of which, all reported in 92 U.S., will here be considered. By subjecting them to a rigorous examination, a just appraisal may be made of what the Court was doing in this field. Some of the questions were peculiar to one State, some were of general application. Each suit came up from a federal Circuit Court, where it had been brought on the basis of diversity of citizenship.

One cluster of five—*Town of Venice v. Murdock*[128] and companion cases[129]—arose in Cayuga County in up-State New York, which in 1852 had been authorized to aid the building of a local railroad with terminus at Lake Ontario. Here one is reminded that railroad-aid bonding was not confined to the West. Also one finds the Supreme Court in conflict with a State court of high authority and independence, and one that certainly was mindful of the interest of investment banking. Municipal subsidies became barred on January 1, 1875, by constitutional amendment; but litigation out of the past went on for a long time.

Four of the cases arose in Illinois, one of which, *Town of Coloma v. Eaves*,[130] would stand as "probably the fullest statement of the

---

p. 56. This barred suit at *six* years after money became due, "provided that any such action may be brought within one year after this act shall take effect . . . ."

Pereles brought suit on July 31, 1873 on Watertown bonds issued on August 1, 1853 and payable on August 1, 1863.

The Circuit Court observed that the bonds when issued "would necessarily have to find a market in distant places, where money was more abundant than in a new country"; a holder would hardly know of this reduction in the time within which suit might be brought. As to this cause of action, the statute impaired the obligation of the contract and was unconstitutional.

Representing Watertown through-

out this litigation was Daniel Hall, a local attorney: a spokesman for reasonable compromise, but designer of the measures that "served to protect the city from the rapacity of its creditors and the mandates of the courts." He was described as being "of the New England Puritan type," a man "of refinement and culture," sometime Speaker in the Legislature. Whyte, *Wisconsin Historical Society . . . 1916*, 284–92.

[128] 92 U.S. 494, decided Mar. 27, 1876.

[129] Town of Venice v. Woodruff; Same v. Matson; and Same v. Edson, 92 U.S. 502 note; Town of Genoa v. Woodruff, 92 U.S. 502.

[130] 92 U.S. 484, decided Mar. 27, 1876.

settled doctrine of this Court."[131] Illinois had sworn off railroad aid by its constitution of 1870—subject to a proviso, however, that was productive of much uncertainty. (Great resolutions of this sort commonly left some hole through which much aid could still be pulled.) For some years after 1875, this State made the largest contribution to the Supreme Court's municipal bond business. Conflicts with State court rulings, while considerable, never approached in severity the clashes which the courts of Iowa and of Missouri had with the Supreme Bench in Washington.

Two of the cases to be scrutinized came from Kansas,[132] one from Missouri,[133] States from which more was presently to come.

By mid-February 1876, all of these bond cases had been presented; from late March to the close of the term on May 8, opinions were announced. It was a season of concentrated study and of sharp division. In three instances, bonds were held invalid—twice with unanimity, once over the dissent of Justices Strong, Clifford, and Swayne. In nine the bonds were enforced, always over the dissent of Justices Miller, Davis, and Field.

DECISIONS THAT THE MUNICIPALITY HAD *NO POWER*

IF THE MUNICIPALITY had *no power* whatever to grant aid, its bonds would be invalid, and unenforceable even in the hands of a bona fide purchaser.[134] So far, all the Justices agreed. *Town of Concord v. Portsmouth Savings Bank*,[135] from Illinois, and *Harshman v. Bates County*,[136] the case from Missouri, were found, without dissent, to fall within that rule. (The Court soon pronounced each of these decisions to have been erroneous.[137])

Town of Concord was the earliest to be argued, and thus took on a special importance in the Court's renewed study of the entire

---

[131] Harlan, J., in Northern National Bank v. Porter Township, 110 U.S. 608, 616 (1884).

Others from Illinois here to be examined are Town of Concord v. Portsmouth Savings Bank, 92 U.S. 625, and County of Moultrie v. Rockingham Savings Bank, 92 U.S. 631—both decided on Apr. 10, 1876; and Town of Elmwood v. Marcy, 92 U.S. 289, decided May 8, 1876.

[132] Marcy v. Township of Oswego, 92 U.S. 637, and Humboldt Township v. Long, 92 U.S. 642, decided on May 8, 1876.

[133] Harshman v. Bates County, 92 U.S. 569, decided on May 8, 1876.

[134] St. Joseph Township v. Rogers, 16 Wall. 644 (1873), per Clifford, J., for the Court.

[135] Note 131.

[136] Note 131.

[137] *Town of Concord* was overruled by Fairfield v. Gallatin County, 100 U.S. 47 (1879), infra, p. 1050; Harshman was overruled by Cass County v. Johnston, 95 U.S. 360 (1877), infra, pp. 1077–80.

problem.[138] The briefs prepared by Chicago counsel pointed to a factual situation that was abnormally untidy even for a municipal bond case: the route of the railroad had been shifted, whereupon the town voted to rescind; the bonds had been altered, after execution, by a supervisor—who received money from the railroad company. And yet counsel for the bondholder relied confidently on the strength of the recitals. When the time came they submitted their case without oral argument; they even asked that damages be added by reason of the frivolous nature of the appeal.[139] The Town retained George H. Williams (who until the previous May had been the Attorney General of the United States) to make an oral presentation.

Williams' two-page memorandum of points to be presented concluded with one that had not theretofore figured in the litigation: "The bonds in question were prohibited by the Constitution of the State of Illinois, and are therefore void."

Illinois' constitution of 1870 had declared: no municipality shall make a *subscription* or a *donation* to a railroad; a proviso, however, saved *subscriptions* authorized under existing laws. Concord's officers had attempted to carry out a *donation* in 1871 pursuant to a popular vote in 1869 under a statute of 1867. This difficulty, presented in Williams' oral argument on November 12, led the Court to make an order on December 6, 1875: "It has been contended in the argument here, that the bonds in question were prohibited by the Constitution of the State of Illinois and are therefore void. A reargument upon that point is ordered."

On each side, counsel prepared new briefs. Each now resorted to the *Debates and Proceedings of the Constitutional Convention*. The evidence extracted therefrom was sparse and not very significant; it rather tended to strengthen the argument from the text itself, which would make the Concord bonds invalid.

Counsel for the bondholder came on to appear against Williams at the reargument, on January 27, 1876.

Justice Strong rendered the Court's opinion in favor of the Town, on April 10. He noted the "very able and ingenious argument" aiming to show that the proviso was as wide as the prohibition. That, however, must be rejected: "No matter what may have been the intention of the mover of the proviso, the intent of the framers of the article and of the people adopting it, must be gathered from the article itself." To the Court, the text seemed clearly to mean that only existing powers to

---

[138] Consideration of Humboldt Township v. Long, and County of Moultrie v. Rockingham Savings Bank, submitted on briefs, was on Dec. 4, 1875, postponed to await the oral argument in *Town of Concord*—as appears from entries in Chief Justice Waite's Docket Book.

[139] Brief for Defendant in Error, 23.

subscribe had been saved; power to *donate* had been cut off. Hence the bonds were invalid.

The practice of resorting to legislative history as an aid in construing a provision of law—a topic that calls for the greatest circumspection—although not unknown at the time with which we are concerned,[140] is largely a development of later years.

Chief Justice Waite's Docket Book records that when he polled the Justices after discussion in conference, Swayne and Clifford voted to affirm the Circuit Court's judgment for the bondholder. This surely is to be attributed to their concern to enforce bonds, rather than to any refined difference over textual interpretation. They refrained, however, from recording dissent. The Chief Justice showed discrimination when he assigned the writing of the opinion to Justice Strong—who normally voted with Swayne and Clifford in bond cases.

Remarkable to relate, Illinois counsel in *Town of Concord* did not mention—evidently because they did not know—that the State Supreme Court had already ruled on the scope of the constitutional proviso. That court, in a decision made in 1874 but not reported until 1877,[141] had rejected as "narrow and technical" the construction which the federal Justices, all unknowingly, later found to be clear beyond doubt. Here—as was not uncommon in those days—the publication of reports was tardy; and counsel had failed to learn of the decision in their own State court. (In *Fairfield v. Gallatin County*[142] in 1879, the Court overruled *Town of Concord*. It explained that the Illinois court's decision "was not called to our notice"; now being better informed, the Court would apply its general principle that a State court's construction of its own written law "is accepted as the true interpretation, whatever may be our opinion of its original soundness.")

Harshman v. Bates County,[143] the case from Missouri, was found to present another instance of *no power*. To quote the headnote of the report of the Circuit Court's decision,

> A township voted stock in company A, which afterwards, under the general law of the State, consolidated with company B, and formed a new company C. *Held*, that the subsequent subscription by the township to company C, by virtue of the prior vote to company A, was

---

[140] For example, at the same term, Justice Hunt, dissenting alone in United States v. Reese, 92 U.S. 214 (1876), had invoked the record in Congress to give the Enforcement Act of 1870 a precision which—had it been adopted by the Court—would have saved the validity of that statute to punish inspectors of elections who refused to count the votes of citizens because of their race.

[141] Chicago & Iowa R.R. v. Pinckney, 75 Ill. 277. Sept. term 1874.

[142] 100 U.S. 47.

[143] 92 U.S. 569. (1876).

unauthorized, and bonds which on their face recited these facts, were void, even in the hands of a bona fide holder for value.[144]

Judge Dillon held it to be within the principle of *Marsh v. Fulton County*.[145]

The Supreme Court accepted that view, which was all that was needed to affirm the judgment below. But Justice Bradley's opinion made a much bigger—and gratuitous—pronouncement: first of all, that the entire Township Aid Act violated the State constitution. That came as a complete surprise to the lawyers and judges and the people of Missouri. Merely to have affirmed what had been decided below would have affected only a $90,000 issue. But to hold the Township Aid Act unconstitutional suddenly released the obligation of some $3,000,000 in bonds. To the townships it came as a windfall, from a quarter where such a gift was least to be expected.

This uncalled-for ruling led to tangled and unhappy consequences—a distinct episode presently to be traced.[146]

A majority of the Court found *no power* in a third case, *Town of Elmwood v. Marcy*.[147] An election had been held in March 1869, on making *two* subscriptions to the same railroad: the one was authorized by law, the additional subscription was not. Both were carried (by a preponderance of about 5 to 2). In April the Legislature purported to validate the election for the additional amount. The bonds were issued. But when, shortly thereafter, the project was abandoned, the townsmen considered themselves to have been victimized; payment of interest was stopped.[148] In litigation arising out of the additional and unauthorized issue, the Illinois court—drawing upon propositions established before the bonds were issued—declared that the subsequent curative act was of no avail.[149] Now in Marcy's suit Justice Davis, for the majority, applied the proposition that "we have always followed

---

[144] Harshman v. Bates County, Fed. Case No. 6148 (C.C.W.D. Mo. 1874). Per Dillon, J.; District Judge Krekel dissented.

[145] 10 Wall. 676 (1871). Supra, pp. 1002–08.

[146] Infra, pp. 1069–75.

[147] 92 U.S. 289 (1876).

[148] Elmwood lies in Peoria County, in north central Illinois—about fifty miles from Bloomington where, about the time the subscriptions were voted, Justice Davis had observed that "The railroad mania in this State . . . is fearful . . . ." Supra, pp. 1012–13. The Dixon, Peoria & Hannibal was to come from northern Illinois, south

and southwest to the Mississippi. "Soon after the receipt" in April 1869 of the bonds of Elmwood [and other town bonds] "said company . . . made a lease for ninety-nine years . . . to the Chicago, Burlington and Quincy Railroad Company . . . and the capital stock of said Dixon, Peoria and Hannibal Railroad Company is, and has ever since been, of no market value." Transcript of Record, pp. 13–14. After July 1871 the Town refused to pay interest.

[149] Marshall v. Silliman, 61 Ill. 218 (Sept. term 1871), followed by Wiley v. Silliman, 62 Ill. 170 (Sept. term, 1871): holding a curative act invalid

the highest court of the State in its construction of its own constitution and laws"—except in the *Gelpcke* situation. Strong, Clifford and Swayne, dissenting, thought that the Illinois court had deviated from its own leading case and ought not to be followed.

CASES WHERE PREREQUISITES HAD NOT BEEN MET: CONFLICT WITH THE NEW YORK COURT OF APPEALS

FUNDAMENTAL DISAGREEMENT among the Justices came where the board or council did have authority to issue bonds, but only upon certain conditions—as to notice of an election, as to assent by residents or

---

as to Brimfield and Elmwood respectively—towns six miles apart that had made unauthorized subscriptions to the same railroad. These were proceedings to enjoin the collection of taxes and to compel the surrender by the railroad and the cancellation of such bonds as it still held.

It had been established in Town of Keithsburg v. Frick, 34 Ill. 420 (1864) that the legislature could not *compel* a municipality to incur a debt for railroad aid. It could authorize a debt to be incurred by vote of the people: but here the election had been an utter nullity, ineffective as an expression of consent. Or the legislature could authorize municipal officers in their discretion to incur a debt: but this curative statute had not left the matter to discretion. It had declared an ineffective election to be binding —and so in effect had imposed a debt without consent.

Looking to developments in the Supreme Court after Elmwood v. Marcy: the Court came to take a different view of curative acts in Illinois, as may be seen in Bolles v. Town of Brimfield, 120 U.S. 759 (1887). Brimfield's unauthorized vote for an additional subscription to the Dixon, Peoria & Hannibal, noted above, was declared to be valid and binding by an act of March 31, 1869. This had been found to be *ultra vires*, however, in Wiley v. Silliman, supra. Presumably the Supreme Court's decision in *Elmwood* would govern cases on curative acts under like circumstances.

In Leslie v. Urbana, Fed. Case No. 8276, C.C.S.D. Ill. 1879, Drummond, J., followed Marshall v. Silliman and Wiley v. Silliman, in deference to *Elmwood*. On that judgment being carried up for review, it was affirmed by an equally divided Court, on March 2, 1880. Waite's Docket Book shows that Bradley, Field, Miller and Waite voted to affirm; Harlan, Strong, Swayne, and Clifford to reverse.

Presently the question of following the Illinois court's doctrine on curative acts was considered anew, by a Court that had been renewed in membership. In Anderson v. Township of Santa Anna, 116 U.S. 356 (1886), the Court declined to accept the construction of Illinois decisions on which Elmwood v. Marcy had been based: now it gave effect to a curative act such as had there been held invalid. The vote in conference was 7 to 2: Gray and Miller differed from their brethren. No dissent was noted in the Reports.

Shortly thereafter, in Bolles v. Town of Brimfield, cited above, the Court, on the authority of Anderson v. Santa Anna, held valid bonds which had been held invalid by the Illinois court in Wiley v. Silliman in 1871. No dissent was noted. The Chief Justice's Docket Book, however, records that at conference Gray, Field, and Miller differed from Blatchford, Matthews, Harlan, Bradley, and Waite.

This experience may be compared with that of New York, note 164 below.

by taxpayers, as to the issue being limited to a certain figure or to a certain percent of assessed valuation, and so forth. What if bonds were issued and were held by bona fide purchasers, where in fact the prerequisites had not been met?

We may start with cases from New York, of which *Town of Venice v. Murdock*[150] was representative. A statute of 1852 had authorized towns to borrow by issuing bonds and with the proceeds to take stock in the railroad; however, the town's supervisor and commissioners

> shall have no power to do any of the acts authorized . . . until . . . the written assent of two-thirds of the resident persons taxed in said town, as appearing on the assessment roll . . . shell have been obtained . . . and filed in the Clerk's office of Cayuga county, together with the affidavit of such supervisor or commissioners, or any two of them, . . . to the effect that the persons whose written assents are thereto attached and filed . . . comprise two-thirds of all resident taxpayers of said town on its assessment roll . . . .

(New York, in its "town bonding," prescribed such written assents instead of an election.) The drafting was pointed: *the officers shall have no power . . . until . . . .*

Murdock sued on eleven instruments purporting to be $1,000 bonds: Were they valid? How was it to be ascertained whether the requisite two-thirds had assented? That was the question.

This had long been a great cause to the people of Cayuga. The projected road was to have run from the vicinity of Ithaca northward to Lake Ontario. It failed to materialize, and in 1857 the Town had quit paying interest on bonds issued in 1853. It contended that there had been no power to issue the bonds. Litigation brought by local bondholders in the State courts resulted in victory for the Cayuga towns.[151] But then the bonds were transferred to out-of-State purchasers, and now the contest was renewed in the federal court. One bondholder had won before Circuit Judge Woodruff in March 1873.[152] But the concerted effort in four other cases was reserved for the Circuit Justice. The record reads:

> At a circuit court held at the village of Canandaigua, in and for the northern district of New York, on the seventeenth day of June,

---

[150] 92 U.S. 494, supra, p. 1047.

[151] Starin v. Town of Genoa, Gould v. Town of Sterling, 23 N.Y. 439, Sept. term 1861. Infra, p. 1055.

[152] Town of Venice v. Opher Edson, unreported. The record of the trial at Utica on March 21, 1873, is found in the Transcript for Town of Venice v. Edson, decision reported in 92 U.S. at 502, note following Town of Venice v. Murdock.

one thousand eight hundred and seventy-three, before the Hon. Ward Hunt, associate justice of the Supreme Court of the United States, came the parties . . . by their attorneys . . . .[153]

The language suggests the pleasant rural setting to which the representative of federal justice had now come to hear a decisive case tried by well-prepared country lawyers. Justice Hunt had been appointed to the Supreme Bench in December 1872. Formerly a Judge of the New York Court of Appeals, he already knew the "bonding" problem at first hand.[154]

Plaintiff's counsel read the bonds, now twenty years old: each bore an indorsement that pursuant to written assent of two-thirds of the resident taxpayers, filed in the County Clerk's office, the bonds were executed this second day of March, 1853; each statement was signed: King, Supervisor, and Wood and Smith, Commissioners. The signatures of King, Wood, and Smith were proved.

Those officers had been elected at town meeting on March 1, 1853—and next day executed the bonds. What did they actually know of the facts they recited? Their certificate made reference to assents on file.

The County Clerk now in office (in 1873) was called. He produced, from the files in his office, the old assents—pieces of paper headed "We, the undersigned," etc., on which 259 names were signed. With these papers was an affidavit, dated October 30, 1852, by one Mills, then Supervisor, and one Jones, then Assessor, declaring "that the persons whose names are subscribed to the foregoing written assents hereto attached comprise two-thirds of all resident tax-payers of said town . . . on its assessment roll . . . ." (Did that signify [1] that Mills and Jones *each knew* that every name written was a true signature of a taxpayer, and [2] that such 259 taxpayers comprised two-thirds of the total?)

The New York Court of Appeals had concluded in *Starin v. Genoa*[155] in 1861 that such an affidavit was to be taken to relate merely to the matter of computation, leaving the verity of the purported signatures to be proved in court, if need be.

Now in the trial before Justice Hunt, counsel for the defendant argued that the signatures to the assents must be proved to be genuine; that the authority of King, Wood, and Smith to execute the bonds

---

[153] Quotations will be from the Transcript of Record in Town of Venice v. Murdock.

[154] He had joined in the decision of People v. Mead, 36 N.Y. 224 (1867), where it was declared that Starin v. Genoa, 23 N.Y. 439 (1861), had settled the law. Supra, p. 1053; infra, p. 1055.

[155] 23 N.Y. 439. Supra, p. 1053; infra, p. 1055.

could not rest on their own recital. This was rejected, doubtless in deference to Supreme Court rulings. Then counsel for the defendant "offered to show that some of the signatures to said assents were not genuine and that others were duplicates, and that in point of fact the same never were signed by two-thirds of the resident tax-payers . . ."; but Justice Hunt, "after expressing great doubts on the subject, excluded the evidence offered . . . ." Under the judge's instruction the jury returned a verdict for Murdock, and so too for the plaintiffs in the cases that followed.

On writ of error the towns went to the Supreme Court, where the same counsel renewed the contest.

This fight in Cayuga County was an old story in the annals of New York. In 1857 Venice, and other towns that denied the validity of bonds issued in aid of the same project—Genoa, Scipio, and Sterling —were sued in the State courts by local bondholders. This resulted in *Starin v. Town of Genoa, Gould v. Town of Sterling*, wherein the Court of Appeals in 1861 held that the bondholder, to recover, must prove affirmatively that the requisite assents had in fact been obtained: the officers' certificate did not, under the statute, prove the fact.[156]

Thereupon the bondholders turned to the Legislature; a bill was introduced in 1864 to make the officers' affidavit "conclusive evidence of the facts therein stated."[157] That failed through the opposition of the chairman of the Senate Judiciary Committee—Charles J. Folger, later Judge and Chief Judge of the Court of Appeals. (Judge Folger consistently opposed the "accursed mildew of town bonding."[158]). The same bill failed again in 1870. The bondholders carried another case to the Court of Appeals: the Judges responded that, notwithstanding the views being expressed by the Supreme Court of the United States, the New York court would adhere to its own ruling in 1861.[159] That was in March 1867.

Promptly the bonds were transferred to citizens of other States —to Murdock of Iowa, who purchased on August 1, 1867; to Woodruff and Macauley of Indiana, and others. They could—and did—sue in the federal court on the same bonds, and by the same counsel who had represented the local bondholders.[160]

---

[156] 23 N.Y. 439; followed in People v. Mead, 24 N.Y. 114 (1861), another case from Genoa.

[157] This account is based upon the documented narrative in the brief for plaintiff in error in Town of Venice v. Murdock. Counsel on each side in that case had represented their respective clients before the Legislature.

[158] Article on Folger in D.A.B.

[159] People v. Mead, 36 N.Y. 224, Mar. 1867—adhering to what had been decided in Starin v. Town of Genoa, Gould v. Town of Sterling, 23 N.Y. 439, Sept. term 1861; People v. Mead, 24 N.Y. 114, Dec. term 1861. Judge Ward Hunt joined in the decision of 1867.

[160] In Town of Venice v. Woodruff, 62 N.Y. 462 (1875), the referee had

Such was the background of *Town of Venice v. Murdock and companion cases*, which the Supreme Court must now decide.

"We find ourselves unable to yield our assent" to the views of the New York court, said Justice Strong for the majority. "They ignore the paramount purpose for which the bonds were authorized by the Legislature . . ." which "must have contemplated that the bonds would be offered for sale; and it is not to be believed that they intended to impose such a clog upon their saleableness . . . ." To the Supreme Court, ready marketability seemed the overriding consideration. The Court of Appeals, said Justice Strong, had not really been construing the New York statute; rather it had been expressing views on general principles of law—views with which the Supreme Court and the courts of other States did not agree.

Justices Miller, Davis, and Field noted dissent. (They were waiting until the last day of the term, when Miller would deliver an opinion dealing with their difference with their brethren.)

Thus the position which the Court of Appeals had been defending since 1861 was in 1876 at last outflanked.[161] The New York judges had been applying to town bonds the ordinary rules of law

---

found that the bonds had been issued without the assent of the requisite two-thirds of the taxpayers—hence were void; the court held, however, that it could not properly restrain their transfer, merely to protect the town from the danger that they would be enforced in the federal court.

[161] At the outset, in 1858 the New York Court of Appeals had affirmed the permissibility of municipal aid to railroads. Town of Rome v. Village of Rome, 18 N.Y. 38. But the New York judges, like those of Pennsylvania (supra, pp. 944–45), had sought to confine the danger inherent in such a decision. "Every step required to confer the power must be shown to have been taken in strict conformity to the statute," said Chief Judge Church. People v. Hurlburt, County Judge, 46 N.Y. 110 (1871). The Bonding Act of 1869 made the determination of the County Judge final as to compliance with requirements; but the Court of Appeals could review on writ of certiorari, and in the cases here cited did so, with salutary effect, correcting looseness in the enforcement of the prerequisites: People

v. Smith, County Judge, 45 N.Y. 772 (1871); People v. Knowles, County Judge, 47 N.Y. 415 (1872); People v. Spencer, County Judge, 55 N.Y. 1 (1873); People v. Smith, County Judge, 55 N.Y. 135 (1873).

In this the Judges were defending what they regarded as a basic value: as Judge Andrews declared in the retrospect of twenty years,

> The bonding acts are subversive of the just rights of the minority, who do not consent to the issue of the bonds, and we are not disposed to relax the stringency of the rule we have heretofore adopted . . . Town of Wellsborough v. New York & Canada R.R., 76 N.Y. 182 (1879).

By the constant holdings of the Court of Appeal,

> there can be no *bona fide* holders of bonds, within the meaning of the law applicable to negotiable paper, which have been issued without authority. . . . Unless issued in the way pointed out by statute, they cannot bind the town. Cagwin v. Town of Hancock, 84 N.Y. 532 (1881).

applicable to negotiable paper executed by an agent. That meant—as was recognized by the federal Circuit Court for Northern New York, in a town bond decision in 1876—that

> The bonds, having been issued by agents acting under a special power, would not be obligations of the corporation, unless they were issued within the limitations and conditions imposed upon the exercise of the power, and it would devolve upon a purchaser to ascertain whether or not the agents were acting within the terms of their authority. . . .

After spelling out what that involved (in accord with what the New York court had been holding), the federal judge explained why a Circuit Court of the United States was constrained to depart from those general principles of law:

> But, the adjudications of the Supreme Court of the United States have invested municipal bonds . . . with anomalous and peculiar immunities, and it is now too late to apply the ordinary doctrines of the law of commercial paper . . . [citing *Gelpcke* and a number of other cases, some of which have been examined *supra*].[162]

Justice Strong's opinion in *Town of Venice v. Murdock* professed concern for the presumed intent of the Legislature: but the Legislature, as noted above, had refrained from declaring any such intent although pressed to do so by the bondholders. Note the assurance with which the Supreme Court construes the New York statute as certainly *meaning* what the Court itself prefers, while rejecting the construction given by the Court of Appeals as having been derived, not from the statute itself, but from the preference of the judges. With what right could the Supreme Court, within the Constitution's scheme of Federal-State relations, impose its own policy in the premises? For

---

[162] Miller v. Berlin, Fed. Case No. 9562, decided January 18, 1876—which happened to be at the time when Town of Venice v. Murdock was under consideration in the Supreme Court. The author of the opinion was District Judge William J. Wallace (1837–1917), who in 1882 (when Judge Samuel Blatchford went to the Supreme Court) entered upon a twenty-five-year period of service as Circuit Judge.

The Town of Berlin (a hamlet in the Taconic range on the eastern border of New York) had been authorized, by a statute "framed with great care," to loan its credit to the Lebanon Springs R.R. The prerequisites were similar to those in Town of Venice v. Murdock. It was conceded that the requisite number of assents had not been obtained. Judge Wallace observed: "The inspection of the records of the clerk's office, by the person to whom the bonds were offered for sale, would have shown that the commissioners were attempting to bind the municipality in utter defiance of the conditions upon which they were to exercise their authority. . . ." In obedience to "an unbroken line of decisions" in the Supreme Court, however, decision must be for the coupon-holder.

New York, the policy of bending the law to facilitate the market of town bonds had not seemed compelling: in 1874 the people had voted to amend their constitution to put an end to the whole business of town bonding in aid of private enterprises.[163]

One more encounter lay ahead. The Court of Appeals was also strict in dealing with the power of the legislature to cure infirmities. The Supreme Court, however, enforced bonds declared valid by a statute which the Court of Appeals had held to be ultra vires.[164]

TOWN OF COLOMA v. EAVES—THE LEADING CASE

In *Town of Coloma v. Eaves*,[165] Justice Strong set out the reasoned basis of the majority's position that a recital of compliance with statutory prerequisites was binding upon the municipality. It was the "fullest statement of the settled doctrine,"[166] and became by far the most cited of the opinions in the municipal bond symposium in 92

---

[163] Effective January 1, 1875, "No county, city, town or village shall hereafter give any money or property, or loan its money or credit to or in aid of any individual, association or corporation . . . ." Amending Sec. 11 of Art. VIII of the Constitution of 1846. The vote was 337,891 for, 194,234 against.

[164] It was the result of various decisions of the Court of Appeals that the legislature might authorize a municipality to issue railroad-aid bonds—upon the decision of the elected officers, or by decision of the taxpayers: but that the legislature could not *compel* such issue without consent so expressed. People v. Batchellor, 53 N.Y. 128 (1873). (Cooley noted, however, that there had been some inconsistency in the cases. *Constitutional Limitations*, note 1 at *231–33, pp. 285–87 of 5th ed., 1883.) Hence it was held in Horton v. Town of Thompson, 71 N.Y. 513 (1878), that the legislature could not by curative act give validity to an issue where (1) the consent of the taxpayers had been given to an issue on different terms, and (2) the curative act did not leave the matter to the decision of the elected officers. The Supreme Court, however, enforced such bonds, notwithstanding the decision of the Court of Appeals. Town of Thompson v. Perrine, 103 U.S. 806 (1881); Town of Thompson v. Perrine, 106 U.S. 589 (1883). No dissent is shown in either of these cases; however, the Chief Justice's Docket Book shows that on the first case, Field and Miller had differed from their colleagues, and that on the second, Miller refrained from voting.

In Perrine v. Thompson, Fed. Case No. 10,997, C.C.S.D. N.Y. 1879—the decision affirmed at 103 U.S. 806 —Wallace, D.J., said of the plaintiff, "Quite likely he bought them mainly with the object of bringing suit upon them in this court, and intending, if he collected, to pay over a portion of the recovery to some other person . . . ." Nevertheless he had acquired a good title and the motive was not material.

On curative acts, compare this experience of New York with that of Illinois, note 149 above.

[165] 92 U.S. 484. Affirming the decision of Blodgett, J., in the Circuit Court for the Northern District of Illinois.

[166] Northern National Bank v. Porter Township, 110 U.S. 608, 616 (1884), quoted above, p. 1048.

U.S. Reports.[167] Indeed the opinion was devoted so singly to the statement of doctrine that it omitted to specify the precise point of the alleged invalidity: to discover that one must go to the Transcript of Record.

Coloma will not be discovered on any ordinary map of Illinois. It lies in the northwestern corner of the state, about 110 miles west of Chicago—a small township in Whiteside County, on the Rock River, just upsteam from the point where the river flows between the cities of Sterling and Rock Falls.

The charter of the Chicago and Rock River Railroad Company, enacted on March 24, 1869, authorized cities, towns, and townships along the route to subscribe to stock: but "no such subscription shall be made until the question has been submitted to the legal voters . . . ."

Eaves, a citizen of Kansas, sued on coupons due July 1, 1873, and January 1, 1874, attached to bonds dated January 1, 1872, payable to the Chicago and Rock River Railroad Company or bearer in 1881, with interest at 10 percent. The bonds carried a recital, by the supervisor and the clerk, that they were issued under the statute and "in accordance with the vote of the electors . . . ."

At the trial, defendant offered testimony—excluded by Blodgett, D.J.—that the election on July 28, 1869, was called to vote on subscribing $50,000 to the stock of the *first division* of the railroad (between Amboy and Rock Falls, a distance of twenty miles), and that the vote (123 to 4) was *so recorded* in the clerk's office. Also, that no dividends were ever paid, and that the stock was of no value. Also, that before the supervisor and clerk delivered the bonds they "had heard and understood that an application was to be made by some citizens and tax-payers . . . for an injunction," and that they then took the bonds to the railroad office in Amboy "under an arrangement with some of the officers . . . to prevent the service" of process.[168]

Actually construction through Coloma was completed within a few weeks after the delivery of the bonds; then, the effort behind the Chicago & Rock River having been spent, its 47 miles of road was absorbed by the Chicago, Burlington & Quincy.[169]

---

[167] In *Shepard's United States Citations* it has twice as long a list as does Marcy v. Township of Oswego, the next most often cited of the bond cases in 92 U.S.

[168] Transcript of Record, 22–25.

[169] Ibid., 25.

The I.C.C. report on the valuation of the Chicago, Burlington & Quincy, 134 I.C.C. 1, 343–44 (1927), relates that after the C. & R.R. made an abortive start with one construction company, a second was engaged by contract of September 7, 1871, its consideration including the township bonds. Then this construction company, by contract of October 5, 1871, with the C., B. & Q., agreed to transfer to the latter all it was to receive from the C. & R.R.; the C., B. & Q. would supply sufficient funds to complete the road, and would lease it for

The election as conducted and recorded was for a proposition different from what the statute authorized and the bonds imported: Did the recital cure the variance?

The duty of ascertaining whether the statute had been followed, said Justice Strong, must be vested somewhere, to be settled once for all; it must be presumed that this was to be done by the officers who were to conduct the election, certify the result, and issue the bonds. That led to the following rule:

> Where legislative authority has been given to a municipality or to its officers to subscribe for the stock of a railroad company, and to issue municipal bonds in payment, but only on some precedent condition, such as a popular vote favoring the subscription, and where it may be gathered from the legislative enactment that the officers of the municipality were invested with power to decide whether the condition precedent has been complied with, their recital that it has been, made in the bonds issued by them and held by a *bona fide* purchaser, is conclusive of the fact, and binding upon the municipality; for the recital is itself a decision of the fact by the appointed tribunal. . . .

Indeed, Justice Strong observed, *Knox v. Aspinwall* and a few other cases had gone so far as to assert that a purchaser had a right to *assume* that the conditions had been complied with from the fact that the subscription had been made and the bonds had been issued. That proposition had "never been overruled . . . , whatever doubts may have been suggested . . . ." Other objections were said to be without merit[170]

Justice Bradley said, "I dissent from the opinion . . . so far as it may be construed to re-affirm" the proposition in *Aspinwall* that the mere execution of bonds by the responsible officers was conclusive proof that conditions had been met. That he chose the word "dissent" suggests that the larger proposition was being actively supported within the Court.

Miller, Davis, and Field again noted dissent.

---

operation. C., B. & Q. supplied $600,000 cash for construction, and received 47 miles of road, completed in October 1872 and thereafter operated by C., B. & Q.

The C. & R.R. had received $250,000 in township bonds.

[170] The explanation supplied above, that the vote was to subscribe to stock of the *first division* of the C. & R.R., renders comprehensible Justice Strong's concluding remark, distinguishing Marsh v. Fulton County, 10 Wall. 676 (1871), supra, pp. 1002–08. "There the subscription was for the stock of a different corporation [the *Central Division* of the M. & W.] from that for which the people had voted; here it was not." (It does not appear what the C. & R.R. may have done to make its *first division* appear to be a separate entity.)

COUNTY OF MOULTRIE v. ROCKINGHAM BANK: NO CHECK ON LOOSE CONDUCT

ILLINOIS' NEW CONSTITUTION, with its ban on railroad aid, became law on July 2, 1870.[171] In *County of Moultrie v. Rockingham Savings Bank*,[172] the disorderly proceedings must be brought to the test of that prohibition. As Justice Bradley noted on the cover of his copy of the Transcript,

> Question whether the subscription to stock in the case was made before the Constitutional amendment was passed prohibiting the same— Ordered but not actually subscribed

Justice Strong's opinion for the majority of the Court answered in the affirmative and announced judgment for the bondholder. The case might be passed hastily with the comment that it established nothing of importance, was seldom cited and was never controlling in any other case.

Yet if one will take time to probe the record and the briefs, the case becomes enlightening—about the manner in which bond issues were induced, and about the Court's method in such instances.

Suit had been brought in 1874 on coupons attached to bonds which recited that they were issued in pursuance of a subscription of $80,000 to the Decatur, Sullivan & Mattoon Railroad, made by the board of supervisors *in December 1869*, in conformity with the act of incorporation of March 26, 1869.[173] The defense now was that the informal proceedings in December 1869 had *not* effected a subscription, and that the entry into force of the constitutional prohibition on July 2, 1870, had barred completion. Admittedly, "no subscription

---

[171] It was on that basis that the Court held that the Town of Concord had had *no power* to issue bonds on which the Portsmouth Bank sued. Supra, pp. 1048–50.

[172] 92 U.S. 631. Submitted on Dec. 1, 1875; decided on Apr. 10, 1876.

[173] The I.C.C. report on the valuation of the Illinois Central Railroad, 46 Valuation Reports 1, 320 (1933), shows that the Decatur, Sullivan & Mattoon constructed thirty-two miles of track, between Hervey City (near Decatur) and Mattoon. (Sullivan, county seat of Moultrie County, lies midway on this road.) It was consolidated with the Chicago & Southern Illinois in 1872; that was set aside by the federal court in 1876. Next year the D., S. & M. was sold at foreclosure. Eventually it became a part of the Peoria, Decatur & Evansville branch of the Illinois Central system. "Probably no segment of the Illinois Central Railroad has experienced more vicissitudes or suffered a closer acquaintance with the bankruptcy courts than has this line . . ." made up from "no fewer than twenty-eight distinct companies . . . ." Carlton J. Corliss, *Main Line of Mid-America: The Story of the Illinois Central* (New York: Creative Age Press, 1950), 289.

was in fact made . . . upon the books of said railroad company until the month of July, 1871."[174]

The critical point, then, was what the Justices would make out of the doings in December 1869.

On examining the findings of District Judge Samuel H. Treat—more minutely than they are set out in the United States Reports—one observes the laxness, and the conflicts of interest, that characterized the transaction of the county's business. Alfred N. Smyser, the county clerk, was at the same time secretary *pro tem.*, and then president, of the D. S. & M. R.R. John A. Freeland, who as chairman of the county board signed and delivered the bonds, was a company director.

Among Judge Treat's findings one reads:[175]

> that on the 16th day of December, A.D. 1869, the board . . . passed some kind of informal resolutions to the effect that the county . . . [in addition to a donation of $75,000] . . . would subscribe eighty thousand dollars . . . to the capital stock . . . and that said resolutions be referred to John R. Eden, an attorney, to put in form before the same should be recorded on the records . . . ; that afterwards, in the spring or summer of 1870, A. N. Smyser, the county clerk . . . , without any further action or direction of the board . . . , entered upon the record the following order or resolutions: . . .
>
> December special meeting, A.D. 1869. . . .
>
> The following orders, pledging the county to subscriptions . . . were adopted . . .
>
> . . . that . . . the county of Moultrie subscribed [*sic*] to the capital stock of the Decatur, Sullivan and Mattoon Railroad Company the sum of eighty thousand dollars . . . .
>
> *And it is further ordered, that the chairman of the board . . . shall issue and deliver to said railroad company the bonds aforesaid whenever the said railroad company shall have completed and equipped their said line of railway through the said county of Moultrie.* [Italics added.]
>
> . . . .
>
> A. N. Smyser, Clerk

Eden[176] did prepare the resolutions, and deliver them to Smyser. But in recording them—so the trial court found—[177]

> the said A. N. Smyser, then clerk of said board . . . and president of said railroad company, without any authority from said board

---

[174] Finding of the Circuit Court. Transcript, 12.

[175] Ibid., 10–11.

[176] John R. Eden was a resident of the county seat, who represented the County in its litigation with the Bank. Sometime a member of Congress, in 1868 he had been Democratic candidate for governor.

[177] Transcript, 10–12.

. . . added on the record of said order or resolution, and without the knowledge and consent of the said Eden, the following: [the paragraph in italics set out above, *purporting to authorize the chairman of the board of supervisors to issue and deliver the bonds*].

Upon the incorporation of the D. S. & M. (by statute of March 26, 1869) the persons named in the charter met and elected temporary officers—president and secretary. It was found, further, that there was

no regular meeting of stockholders held . . . until the 13th day of July 1870, for the purpose of electing the board of directors to succeed the one named in the charter; that at said time the books of subscription were opened . . . .

Also, that no subscription was in fact made until July 1871 when the chairman of the board, without any express authority, subscribed in order to vote at a company election.

Supposing that what had been done by the supervisors at their December special meeting 1869 amounted to an *offer* to subscribe, had it been *accepted* by the company before the constitution's ban fell on July 2, 1870? To show that it had, plaintiff had introduced a contract of April 15, 1870, between the D. S. & M. by its temporary officers, and one Brink and others, who undertook to build the road for $325,000 in bonds; it was contemplated that payment would include "one hundred and fifty-five thousand dollars in Moultrie County bonds." Counsel for the bank pointed to this as showing acceptance.[178]

On December 25, 1872, a committee of the board of supervisors, after taking advice of counsel, reported to the chairman of the board that the subscription was "in accordance with law." The trial judge found that the chairman of this committee of three "was also an agent in the employment of said company."[179]

Completion of the road through Moultrie County was reported on December 30, 1870; next day the bonds were issued over the signatures of Smyser, clerk [and president of the railroad company] and Freeland, chairman of the board of supervisors [and a company director].

What then had been the situation on July 2, 1870, when the ban fell: (1) had the county subscribed? The subscription books were not open until July 13, 1870, and the county did not subscribe *on the books* until July 1871. Alternatively, (2) had the county made a contract to subscribe? So to hold would involve finding an *offer* in the "informal resolutions" of December 1869—oral, unformulated, and

---

[178] Brief, 12.   [179] Transcript, 13–16.

unrecorded until sometime "in the spring or summer of 1870"—and an *acceptance* in the fact that the company, in the contract it made with Brink in April 1870, mentioned "the Moultrie County bonds" as a part of the consideration.

Here Justice Strong drew upon *Nugent v. Supervisors*,[180] where it had been held that manual subscription on the company's books was not necessary to make the county a subscriber; in that case "there was not only the resolution, declaring the subscription made, but there was an acceptance by the railroad company, and notice of acceptance." Could the *Moultrie* facts be squeezed into that mould? Justice Strong said that they could: "the action of the Board of Supervisors in December, 1869, was in substance and effect a subscription." Without addressing himself to the task of sustaining that proposition, Justice Strong virtually abandoned it by hastening on to say, "And if this conclusion could not be reached, . . . it could not be doubted that the action of the Board was at least an undertaking to subscribe, and this was assented to or accepted by the railroad company"—as was shown by the provision in the contract with Brink. And then there was "another consideration that is worthy of notice": the bonds recited that they were issued in pursuance of a subscription made in December 1869 and in conformity with the statute. A bona fide holder could rely on the recital.

When, after discussion in conference, the Chief Justice polled the Court, he recorded Hunt, Strong, Swayne, and Clifford voting to affirm; Bradley, Field, Davis, and Miller would reverse. The judgment for the bondholder was "Affirmed by casting vote Ch J." When, after the opinion had been written the judgment was announced, only Miller, Davis, and Field recorded dissent.

Let it be noted how little it took to fasten indebtedness upon the county. First, the offer: "some kind of informal resolutions" that the county *would* subscribe. This rested in words spoken. Written resolutions were to be framed: but even supposing that they were to be inserted upon the record without being seen and adopted by the board of supervisors, they were not inserted until "the spring or summer of 1870"—which might have been after July 2 when power to subscribe was cut off. "Some kind" of words at the December meeting fell short of an *offer* to subscribe *communicated to* the company. Of course the company had knowledge of whatever the board did—if by no other means than that the board's clerk was the company's officer: but knowledge, whether obtained in open meeting or by means of that reprehensible conflict of interest, would not suffice unless the board intended to communicate an offer. The trial court did not so find, and

---

[180] 19 Wall. 241 (1874). Miller and Davis, JJ., dissented without opinion.

the Court simply assumed it. Furthermore, contrary to principle, it found acceptance not in anything communicated to the offeror, but implied by something in the company's contract with somebody else.

As a precedent, the *Moultrie County* case was virtually suppressed. It was tucked in under *Nugent v. Supervisors*,[181] and the two were cited together as establishing a rule that

> If the body or agency having authority to make such a subscription passes an ordinance or resolution to the effect that it does thereby, in the name and on the behalf of the municipality, subscribe a specified amount of stock, and presents a copy of that ordinance or resolution to the company for acceptance as a subscription, and the company does, in fact, accept and notifies the municipality or its proper agent, to that effect, the contract of subscription is complete . . . .[182]

That is an accurate statement of *Nugent*, but it is not what had happened in *Moultrie County*.

This illustrates that there may be a remarkable divergence between (1) the facts to be found in the record, (2) the construction the Court gives to those facts, and (3) the proposition which the case is subsequently said to support.

TOWNSHIP BONDS IN KANSAS

IN THE COURSE of growing up, Kansas adopted several measures for municipal bonding—in particular, statutes of 1865 and 1868 authorizing counties and cities to aid railroads; one of 1870 to enable townships to subscribe; and in 1872 legislation permitting municipal gifts even to manufactories and other enterprises that might contribute to public improvement. All of these measures eventually came before the Supreme Court.

Marcy v. Township of Oswego[183] and *Humboldt Township v. Long*,[184] decided on May 8, 1876, concerned bonds reciting that they were issued "in accordance with" the statute of 1870. The authority was limited by this proviso:

> the amount of bonds voted by any township shall not be above such an amount as will require a levy of more than one per cent. per annum on the taxable property of such township to pay the yearly interest on the amount of bonds issued.

---

[181] Supra, p. 1064.
[182] Per Waite, C.J., in Bates County v. Winters, 112 U.S. 325

(1884).
[183] 92 U.S. 637.
[184] 92 U.S. 642.

To be workable, that must refer to the latest assessed valuation—although counsel for the bondholders would not concede so much.[185] Interest on Oswego's issue of $100,000 would be $7,000, whereas 1 percent of the assessed value of taxable property would be only $3,520.[186] Humboldt had issued $75,000 at 7 percent, which would mean $5,250 a year, while the assessment rolls showed only $415,000 of taxable property.[187]

In *Knox v. Aspinwall* in 1859[188]—the precedent upon which so many bond decisions relied—Justice Nelson had said that the ascertainment of the outcome of an election on subscribing "was necessarily left to the inquiry and judgment of the Board itself . . . ." But here, as Justice Miller said in his dissenting opinion, the material facts were "all public, all open, all accessible." It was a matter of simple arithmetic, not of judgment: look at the assessment rolls.

Counsel for the bondholders, however, planted themselves confidently on the cases holding that a bona fide purchaser could rely upon the bond's recital. "The argument is in a nut shell," wrote James Grant, citing *Aspinwall*.[189] There was, however, a new feature in the Kansas township cases which, it was urged, took them out of the rationale of the decisions that a municipal corporation was bound by a recital made by its elected governing board. In Kansas the *township* bonds were issued after proceedings conducted entirely by the *county* board; they were executed by its chairman and its clerk. Should Humboldt Township be bound by recitals made by the governing board of Allen County, a wholly different municipal unit? As the brief for the Township explained, "Each County is divided into three Districts, each District elects a County Commissioner. The voters of Humboldt Township could not have possibly participated in the election of two of the Commissioners who constituted a majority of the Board and as to the third he may have been a nonresident of the Township and may not have had a dollar's worth of property in the Township . . . . It may be a matter of entire indifference to them, how much Humboldt Township is indebted . . . ."[190] Under the Kansas statute, whenever fifty voters in a Township petitioned the County Board, the latter called an election;[191] if "three-fifths of the electors voting at such election vote for

---

[185] Argument of G. C. Clemens [author of *Law of Corporate Securities as decided in the Federal Courts* (1877), in ch. 17, n. 348, for Defendants in Error in the *Humboldt Township* case, 15–17; Argument of Alfred Ennis and A. L. Williams for Plaintiff in Error, Marcy, 4–7.

[186] Transcript, 5–6.

[187] Ibid., 11.

[188] 21 How. 539. Supra, pp. 931–33.

[189] Further Argument for the Bondholders, 2—a brief he filed in the *Humboldt Township* case, on behalf of "various holders of bonds" interested in the outcome.

[190] Argument, 16.

[191] In *Humboldt* there was a further point, that a special election on the issue had been called on 19 days

the subscription," the Board would order the Clerk to make it in the name of the Township.

By contrast, under the Illinois statute in *Coloma*, it was the township's own officers who received the petition, called the election, determined the result, issued the bonds and made the recital indorsed thereon: this was the town's own business. If aught was done amiss, at any rate it was done by agents the voters had chosen. But in *Oswego* and *Humboldt* it was otherwise.

With this explanation—not found in the Reports—one can understand what Justice Miller meant when he described the property owner in these Kansas townships as "helpless":

> I say helpless, advisedly, because these are not his agents. They are the officers of the law, appointed or elected without his consent, acting contrary, perhaps, to his wishes.
>
> Surely, if the acts of any class of officers should be valid only when done in conformity to law, it is those who manage the affairs of towns, counties and villages in creating debts which not they, but the property owners, must pay.

This, of course, was in a dissenting opinion; Justices Davis and Field concurred with him.[192]

AN IRRESISTIBLE CURRENT OF DECISION

SUCH WAS THE performance of the Court at what, for municipal bond litigation, was a memorable term. One notes that preoccupation with marketability was dominant over all other considerations. One marks the liberty the Court took with a State's written as well as its common law, in a field where the Court had jurisdiction only because the parties were of diverse citizenship—a diversity that perhaps had been expressly contrived, as in the cases from the Town of Venice.

It was three years later, apropos of a case comparable to those above, that discriminating counsel made this comment:

> The Court yesterday decided Calhoun Cy. against us—Swayne delivered a most lame opinion. Miller, Bradley and Harlan dissented.

This was Philip Phillips, reporting to an associate in Mississippi on the loss of the suit of *Supervisors of Calhoun County v. Galbraith.*[193] And again,

---

notice, whereas the statute prescribed "not less than thirty days."

[192] Appended to Humboldt Township v. Long, 92 U.S. 642, but applicable generally to the cases wherein they had noted dissent.

[193] 99 U.S. 214, argued on Apr. 2 and decided on Apr. 14, 1879.

The decision by Swayne was a most slovenly one—but on the question arising out of these municipal bonds—the current is set so strong against all defenses it is impossible to resist it. There is no use to attempt the rehearing of the case.[194]

This should not be dismissed as the aspersion of a disappointed advocate. Phillips stood in the inner circle of Supreme Court practitioners—appeared as frequently as any, in a wide variety of causes—enjoyed the confidence of the Court, and was sophisticated and dispassionate in his professional judgments.[195]

Justice Miller, in the freedom of his most intimate correspondence, had recently commented that

the feeling which has control of the court against all municipalities who contract any asserted obligation in [bonds] amounts to a mania. If I were a practicing lawyer today, my self respect, knowing what I do of the force of that feeling, would forbid me to argue in this

---

[194] Writing to H. A. Barr of Oxford, Miss., on Apr. 15 and May 21, 1879. Phillips' Letterbook (1878–1880), pp. 177, 203. Ms. Div., L.C.

Calhoun County was authorized by statute to take stock and to pay for it in bonds "made payable to the President and Directors of the Grenada, Houston and Eastern Railroad Company, and their successors and assigns"; it issued bonds payable to the Company *or bearer*, thus giving them the properties of commercial paper.

The opinion by Swayne, J., held that

The statutory requirement . . . is only directory. The defect is one of form and not of substance. The irregularity was committed by the servants of the County, and the County is estopped to take advantage of it. The recital in the bonds . . . is also conclusive. . . .

There had been two elections: at the first the bond issue had been defeated; at the second it won a majority. It was argued that the first submission had exhausted the power. Justice Swayne replied:

We cannot recognize any restriction . . . in this respect, without

adding to the statute what it does not contain. Our duty is to execute the law, not to make it. Such an interpolation would involve the "judge-made law" which Bentham so earnestly denounces. . . .

That Swayne, of all the Justices—in a bond case, among all the matters on which the Court passed judgment —should have condemned "judge-made" law, must be put down to densest obfuscation.

Mississippi's constitution of 1868— the much-derided "mongrel constitution" (see pp. 424–29)—had imposed this restraint upon prodigality:

The legislature shall not authorize any county, city, or town to become a stockholder in, or to lend its credit to, any company, association, or corporation, unless two-thirds of the qualified voters . . . shall assent thereto. (Art. XII, Sec. 14.)

The Court held that this did not preclude subscriptions by a mere majority of voters, at an election subsequent to the constitution, under a statute that antedated it.

[195] Phillips has been characterized supra, p. 568.

court any case whatever against the validity of a contract with a county, city or town under any circumstances whatever. It is the most painful matter connected with my judicial life that I am compelled to take part in a farce whose result is invariably the same, namely to give more to those who have already, and to take away from those who have little, the little that they have.[196]

HARSHMAN v. BATES COUNTY: SURPRISE FOLLOWED BY CONFUSION

THE COURT'S *Harshman* opinion, already noticed,[197] brought a chain of reactions in Missouri, culminating in agitation in the summer of 1878 to strip away the growing powers of the federal judiciary. *Harshman* was a suit where an argument of counsel fired backwards, with devastating effect—though from the Reports one would not guess what had happened.

Missouri's constitution of 1865 declared:

> The General Assembly shall not authorize any county, city, or town to become a stockholder in . . . any company . . . unless two-thirds of the qualified voters shall assent thereto. (Article XI, Section 14.)

It is not surprising that no mention was made of the *township*, which in 1865 was merely an unincorporated subdivision of a county; it was a unit for holding elections, and chose a constable and justices of the peace.

It came to be seen, however, that townships were a source that might be tapped: a projected railroad might fail to win the approval of a county, where yet the inhabitants of townships along the route would be willing to aid. This led to the statute of March 23, 1868, "to facilitate the construction of railroads"—commonly known as the Township Aid Act. Upon petition, the county court must call a township election;

> and if it shall appear . . . that not less than two-thirds of the qualified voters of such township, voting at such election, are in favor of such subscription, it shall be the duty of the county court to make such subscription in behalf of such township, according to the terms and conditions thereof . . . .

---

[196] Letter of Jan. 13, 1878, to his brother-in-law, William P. Ballinger of Galveston, Texas. Fairman, *Mr. Justice Miller*, 231.

[197] Supra, pp. 1050–51.

(Did subscription by a *township* need to comply with Article XI, Section 14? If so, did *two-thirds of the voters voting* satisfy that constitutional requirement?)

Under the statute, an election was held in Mount Pleasant Township of Bates County, on May 3, 1870, on a proposal to subscribe $90,000 of stock in railroad company *A*;[198] it won a two-thirds vote of those voting. It would have been in order thereupon to make the subscription—but from the record, it appeared that that had not been done.[199]

The managers saw that if the route could be altered to make a bulge to the west, additional benefits would be forthcoming from the community thus served. To achieve this, two steps were taken in quick succession. On July 18, 1870, corporation *B*[200] was created, to connect this community with Railroad *A*. Then on October 4, 1870, companies *A* and *B* were consolidated to form Railroad *C*[201] under the Railroad Consolidation Act of March 24, 1870, whereby the consolidated road would take "all the . . . rights [and] privileges . . . which belonged to either of the companies . . . ." Thereupon the managers of the bulging Railroad *C* demanded that the Bates County Court make the subscription and deliver the bonds which, on May 3, had been voted for Railroad *A*; the County Court complied.[202]

When the thing proved a fiasco,[203] payment of interest was stopped. Then Harshman sued on his coupons.

Counsel for Harshman argued: it was the *duty* of the county court to make the subscription: Township Aid Act. And Company *C* was entitled to all the *rights* and privileges of Company *A*: Railroad Consolidation Act.

Opposing counsel said: under the Township Aid Act, the county

---

[198] Lexington, Chillicothe & Gulf R.R. Co., chartered to run southward from Lexington. Mount Pleasant Township was about eighty miles south of Lexington.

[199] But in Bates County v. Winters, 112 U.S. 325 (1884), supra, n. 182, upon a second trial in that case, it had been made to appear that a subscription to Railroad *A* had been presented and accepted on June 17, 1870. One learns not to be surprised at uncertainty and informality in such matters.

[200] Pleasant Hill Division of the Lexington, Chillicothe & Gulf R.R. Co.

[201] Lexington, Lake & Gulf R.R. Co.

[202] In their brief for Defendant in Error in Harshman v. Bates County, Glover and Shepley suggested that this was done "perhaps under the influence of these managers, perhaps honestly thinking the court was compelled to make the subscription." If the Township had held the stock in *A*, it could and presumably would have been voted *against* the consolidation. Brief, 12–13.

[203] "Now as a matter of fact, . . . not a rail of iron is laid . . . nor are the cars running . . . on any part of said road south of the City of Lexington, . . . no work has been done on this road for over two years." Brief for Defendant in Error by Ross and Bassett, 5.

court could make only *such subscription* as had received the voters' assent, *according to the terms and conditions thereof.* And Article XI, Section 14, which was "intended and supposed" to apply to "every possible . . . political subdivision," forbade any legislation whose effect would be to make a municipality to take stock in any company unless two-thirds of the voters assented thereto.[204]

This latter view was adopted by Judge Dillon in the Circuit Court.[205] He held that the constitutional provision applied to townships, but assumed as unquestioned that it was satisfied by the vote of two-thirds of those voting. His decision that the bonds were invalid rested on the ground that a vote for *A* did not warrant a subscription to *C.*

On going up to the Supreme Court, to escape the force of this reasoning, Thomas K. Skinker, of counsel for Harshman, took a hazardous line: the vote was immaterial, he contended, because Article XI, Section 14 spoke only of "counties, cities, and towns"; it had no application to a township. *"This case is, therefore, to be determined without reference to that section."*[206] Thus the Railroad *Consolidation Act* could *compel* the subscription to be given to Railroad *C*, even though the voters had not assented thereto. "The Legislature has full control over the townships." So true was that, he argued audaciously, that in framing the Township Aid Act they were not even trying to conform to Article XI, Section 14: look, they called for only two-thirds of the *voters voting*, whereas Article XI, Section 14 meant two-thirds of *all registered voters.* "The difference is so manifest as to strike the most casual reader." "If [Article XI, Section 14] applies to townships, [this discrepancy] will certainly invalidate the [Township Aid] act," after "millions of bonds have been issued and are now afloat."[207] Counsel implied confidently that the Court must recoil from so catastrophic a consequence.

But the Court did not recoil. Justice Bradley's opinion held, in a few sentences, that the two-thirds majority of voters voting, required by the Township Aid Act, did not satisfy the constitution's requirement of "two-thirds of the qualified voters:" that meant two-thirds of *all* qualified voters. To this extent the Court adopted what Harshman's counsel had *conceded.* But then, coming to the question whether

---

[204] Brief of Glover and Shepley, 9.

[205] Harshman v. Bates County, Fed. Case No. 6148 (W.D. Mo. 1874).

[206] Brief and Argument of T. K. Skinker, 16.

[207] Pp. 20, 22. He cited as relevant the Missouri court's construction of a somewhat similar constitutional provision: no county seat should be removed "unless two-thirds of the qualified voters of the county, at a general election, shall vote in favor of such removal"; this had been held to require two-thirds of *all* registered voters. State v. Sutterfield, 54 Mo. 391. Oct. term 1873.

townships fell within Article XI, Section 14, it was held that they *were* included—agreeing here with counsel for Bates County. It followed that the Township Aid Act was invalid. Harshman lost his cause, on a point volunteered by his own counsel.

Unmentioned was the larger consequence that in the federal courts, which would follow the Supreme Court, all other Township Aid bonds would be held unenforceable.

Justice Bradley went on to "another objection": that whereas the township had voted to subscribe to *A*, the county court had subscribed to *C*. That was the point on which the controversy had been conducted, and Judge Dillon had cited *Marsh v. Fulton County*[208] as controlling. Justice Bradley, agreeing with the Circuit Court, said that "the law authorizing the consolidation of railroad companies does not change the law of attorney and constituent." The county court was the township's agent only to subscribe to Railroad *A*; when *A* was extinguished, so too was the agency.

The *Harshman* decision was an unguarded performance[209]—

---

[208] Supra, pp. 1002–08.

[209] It is instructive to trace how this case went wrong.

Argument was on February 15, 1876. Discussion at conference on Saturday, February 26, must have run in terms of the problem as Judge Dillon's opinion had presented it. As the Chief Justice recorded, Strong, Swayne, and Clifford voted to reverse. The Chief Justice first selected Justice Davis to write the opinion. The latter asked to be excused, in this undated note:

I really have not time to write the opinion in Harshman v. Bates County. I have three cases to write opinions in, & I must go to Maryland for a day to transact some personal business, or I cant go to the Centennial [at Philadelphia], which I am very desirous of doing.

Besides, I believe that an opinion in this case would come much better from you, being the head of the Court, than any one else. The division in the Court on this question, it seems to me, fixes you as the proper person to write on the subject.

If you cannot write it, I wd suggest Judge Bradley as I think

he voted to affirm. He could not but write satisfactorily on this subject, considering his status on the Bond Cases.
Waite Papers, L.C.

Bradley was asked to write the opinion. Evidently he became possessed by the idea, propounded by Skinker, that the provision in the Missouri constitution required two-thirds of *all registered voters*. He made *that* the principal reason why judgment should be for the County.

His opinion was presented at conference on May 6, when a batch of opinions were being cleared for delivery on May 8, the concluding day of the term. Although Clifford, Swayne, and Strong had voted on February 26 to sustain the Bates bonds, they recorded no dissent now. It seems highly probable that Bradley's brethren did not perceive what would be the effect of the opinion on other bonds.

Among Waite's papers is this reply of June 16, 1876, from the Clerk's Office to Waite, then in New York:

Yours of the 15th inst recd. I enclose copy of the opinion in case of Harshman vs Bates County—delivered by Mr Justice Bradley which is the only

XVIII: *Municipal Bonds II*

and an ill-starred one.[210] Whereas the Court had been showing a marked prepossession in favor of bondholders, here suddenly it spoke the doom of some three millions in township bonds[211] when "another objection" sufficed to dispose of the small Bates County issue. Its pronouncement on the meaning of the State constitution was impetuous. In 1869, when the Township Aid Act was new, the Missouri court had ruled against all constitutional objections that counsel had thought

---

opinion in relation to Missouri municipal bonds that I have been able to find.

A postscript noted that on the docket were Cass County v. Johnston, Same v. Shores, and Same v. Jordan.

Apparently the Chief Justice had heard repercussions—and did not remember exactly what it was the Court had done about Missouri bonds.

Also among Waite's papers is a letter of July 26 from "an old man with a family dependent on me" who was dismayed at the report that his Buchanan County bond was not good.

Cass County v. Johnston, mentioned in the letter from the Clerk's Office, was argued on October 29 and 30, 1877. The outcome of conference on November 3 was that Harshman v. Bates County would be overruled —as it was when the decision in Cass County v. Johnston was announced on November 12. Infra, pp. 1076–79.

On October 8, 1877, Justice Miller, in the course of a letter to his brother-in-law, William P. Ballinger, in Texas, made this comment:

He [Justice Bradley] is a queer man. As Judge Strong said the other day, "If there is a principle on which a case can be decided that no one else has thought of it has for that reason a charm for him. . . ."

It seems highly probable that Strong's remark had reference to the mischievous decision in *Harshman*.

(For a fair understanding of Miller's unflattering remark, it should be said that he had set his heart on having Ballinger on the Court, as successor to Justice Davis—and that Bradley, Circuit Justice for the Fifth Circuit, "with his usual eccentricity," had spoken well of Ballinger but recommended some one else. The place went to Harlan.)

Bradley had a strong mind, trained by rigorous professional discipline. It was remarkable how he would hold judgment in suspense until he was satisfied that he had found the truth. But, being self-reliant and not deferential to the opinions of others, he could make a mistake all by himself —and so he did in *Harshman*.

[210] Its construction of the Missouri constitution was overruled at the following term. Cass County v. Johnston, 95 U.S. 360. Infra, pp. 1076–79.

And as a strict holding that a vote for Railroad *A* would be no authority to subscribe to Railroad *C, Harshman* was explained and distinguished by Bradley himself in his opinion for the Court in County of Scotland v. Thomas, 94 U.S. 682 (1877): in *Harshman*, the county court was the mere agent of the township to execute precisely what had been voted; but where the county court was acting for the county on its own judgment, it might subscribe to a consolidated road serving the same purpose as that for which the popular vote had been given. In Livingston County v. First National Bank of Portsmouth, 128 U.S. 102 (1888), the township had voted aid to one railroad company, and the county court had subscribed to a consolidated company which built "the very road intended": the Court declined to follow "the rigid rule" of Harshman v. Bates County, leaving that case to stand on its peculiar facts.

[211] Edwin L. Lopata, *Local Aid to Railroads in Missouri* (New York: no pub., a Columbia University thesis, 1937), 120; 3 *Cent. L. J.* 363, 367 (1876); *Com. & Fin. Chron.,* 22:591 (1876); 1 *Railway Age* 1 (1876).

worth argument. This was in the *Linn County* case, where at the suit of a railroad company a reluctant county was compelled to deliver bonds pursuant to a township vote.[212] While the phrase "two-thirds of the qualified voters" was not there drawn in question, doubtless this was universally taken to call for nothing more than two-thirds of the voters who voted, which is what the Act of 1868 required. Thereafter the Missouri court had confidently applied the statute in eight more cases.[213] Meantime, as Judge Dillon recalled,

> A hundred cases—and I do not think I exaggerate—have been brought on these township bonds in the federal courts of this state, and prior to the decision of Harshman v. Bates County, none of the able lawyers defending these cases ever made the point that the Act of March 23, 1868, was unconstitutional. . . .[214]

Bonfires were lighted when word of the *Harshman* decision reached the indebted areas; a band serenaded the local counsel who had fought the case.[215]

On the other side, when a year and a half had gone by, a disapproving lawyer, "Res Judicata," wrote that

> The decision surprised everybody, and none more than the bond makers and their attorneys. They had never sought and never dreamed of such a result. . . . [Township bonds] had been favorite objects of investment, and bond maker and bond-holder reposed alike in the confident belief that all questions touching their validity had forever been put at rest by the decisions of our own supreme court. . . .
>
> The surprise and amazement . . . was followed by the refusal of most of the counties involved to pay interest either on their township or county bonds. Universal repudiation became the order, and excited controversy ensued as to the scope and meaning of the "Harshman decision."[216]

The *Commercial and Financial Chronicle* of New York, in its survey of "Investments in September [1876]," gave practical advice. It said that while municipal issues would probably continue to be favorites with bond purchasers,

---

[212] State *ex rel.* North Missouri Central R.R. v. Linn County Court, 44 Mo. 504.

[213] Cited in Cass County v. Johnston, 95 U.S. 360, 366 (1877).

[214] Westermann v. Cape Girardeau County, Fed. Case No. 17,432. C.C.E.D. Mo., Sept. 1878.

[215] Missouri newspaper reports, quoted by Lopata, *Local Aid to Railroads in Missouri*, 120, and *Com. & Fin. Chron.*, 22:591, June 17, 1876.

[216] *St. Louis Missouri Republican*, Dec. 24, 1877, quoting from the *Columbia* (Mo.) *Herald*.

the drift of recent events, including the repudiation by towns and counties in Missouri, is such as to induce careful examination of the constitutional provisions and statute laws under which the issues of bonds are made. For a large buyer it may be worth while to have the services of a lawyer regularly employed to "search the title," and for a small purchaser, the bankers who negotiate the loans should be able to give all desired information.[217]

Here one sees that it had not yet become an established practice to obtain the opinion of competent bond counsel before municipal bonds were put upon the market. But even a cautious lawyer would not have foreseen what happened in *Harshman v. Bates County.*

Suppose it had been the Supreme Court of Missouri that pronounced this judgment of unconstitutionality, and that the judgment had then been invoked in a federal court to defeat the suit of a bondholder: undoubtedly the Supreme Court of the United States, citing *Gelpcke,*[218] would have refused to "follow every such oscillation." Just as in *Olcott v. Supervisors of Fond du Lac County,*[219] there had been "expositions of the law of the State" on comparable matters— where in other connections the requirement of a majority of voters had been held to mean only a majority of those who came to vote[220] —on which a purchaser was entitled to rely. As in *Pine Grove Township v. Talcott,*[221] it could be said that when these bonds were being issued no department of the State government had "lifted its voice against them." But in *Harshman* it was none other than the Supreme Court of the United States which, disregarding its own lofty pronouncement, had "erected the altar and decreed the sacrifice" of millions in Township Aid bonds.

THE MISSOURI COURT FALLS INTO LINE—BUT THE SUPREME COURT REVERSES ITS STAND

WHEN THE SUPREME Court in Washington had given Missouri townships such a godsend, could their own State court be far behind in generosity? In *State v. Brassfield,*[222] decided on April 16, 1878, the Missouri court held the Township Aid law to be unconstitutional, for the reason Justice Bradley had given.

This, however, did not bring the two benches into accord: the

---

[217] *Investors' Supplement*, Sept. 30, 1876.

[218] Supra, pp. 935–44.

[219] Supra, pp. 1016–17.

[220] These decisions were paraded in Chief Justice Waite's opinion for the

Court in Cass County v. Johnston, 95 U.S. 360 (1877), where *Harshman* was overruled. Infra. pp. 1077–79.

[221] Supra, p. 1021.

[222] 67 Mo. 331.

Supreme Court, in *Cass County v. Johnston*,[223] on November 12, 1877, had already overruled *Harshman*, Bradley and Miller, JJ., dissenting. Each court was now defending the position on which the other had first taken its stand.

In the eighteen months between the *Harshman* decision and its overruling—so the Missouri court commented resentfully on May 6, 1878—

> ample opportunity was afforded to mere schemers and speculators to procure the bonds declared to be worthless, for a song . . . .

These were the words of Judge Elijah H. Norton, a State-rights Democrat, whose name will recur in the account of mounting hostility to the federal judiciary. He was speaking for the court in *Webb v. Lafayette County*, reinforcing the position the court had announced three weeks earlier.[224] Judge William B. Napton dissented from what his brethren were now doing. At the outset, there had been no doubt that the Township Aid Act was valid;

> and in the faith of this construction, bonds, to the amount of millions of dollars, were purchased by our citizens, and the only effect of the present decision is to annul their titles whilst the citizens of other States and foreigners may still proceed to get judgments and collect them.

This was true because the federal courts would follow *Cass County v. Johnston*, the most recent ruling of the Supreme Court.

The *St. Louis Missouri Republican*, a moderate and ably edited Democratic newspaper, commenting on "Judicial Disagreement,"[225] deplored asperity "calculated to bring the respective courts into many such conflicts of opinion in which each in expressing its own conclusions will tend more and more to harshness of criticism" which would lessen public confidence in both of the courts.

Of course it came very hard when the Supreme Court took back what it had given so unexpectedly in *Harshman v. Bates County*—and nowhere was it more aggravating than in Cass County, Bates' neighbor on the western border of the State. Cass stood near the top in the issue of Township Aid bonds, and perhaps at the very top in bitterness over the experience with railroad aid. In 1872 two corrupt county judges had been induced secretly to make an order whereby

---

[223] 95 U.S. 360.
[224] Webb v. Lafayette County, 67 Mo. 353, 371 at 372. Hough, J., concurred in this dissent.
In State v. Brassfield, 67 Mo. 331,

Napton, J., noting dissent, said that he agreed with the opinion of Waite, C.J., for the Court in Cass County v. Johnston.
[225] May 30, 1878.

$229,000 in bonds were issued, quite unlawfully and without benefit to the county. These were distributed at a meeting in a St. Louis hotel; bonds for $127,000 were deposited with an express company in Illinois, directed to Robert S. Stevens, railroad promoter, to whose enterprises, including the St. Louis & Santa Fe and the Tebo & Neosho, Cass and other counties in the western half of Missouri had trustfully contributed. Lesser amounts went to others—$55,000 to County Attorney Cline, organizer of the scheme; $12,000 to Jehiel C. Stevenson, presiding justice of the county court, who had signed the bonds. But suspicions had been aroused; through dramatic exertions some of the participants were captured and the bonds traced and recovered. Stevenson and Cline, on bail, and a third man were taken from a train by masked men and shot, on April 24, 1872. The "Gunn City tragedy" drew national attention to the desperate state of affairs in Cass.[226]

THE *CASS COUNTY* CASE, WHEREIN *HARSHMAN* WAS OVERRULED

Cass County v. Johnston was concerned, not with the "bloody bonds," but with issues on behalf of townships; so too was the suit of Jordan, decided with it.[227] Those on which Johnston sued had been issued pursuant to an election on April 20, 1868, to aid the St. Louis & Santa Fe Railroad. The County contended that, inasmuch as the company became incorporated on that same April 20, the petition and the order for the election, in respect of a company not yet existing, had been void. Jordan's suit was on bonds that had been issued to the *Pleasant Hill & Lawrence Branch* of the Pacific Railroad, whereas the township had voted to subscribe to the stock of the *Pacific Railroad*, "preparing to build a railroad . . . to be known as the Pleasant Hill and Lawrence branch . . ."; the County contended that there was a fatal discrepancy between what had been authorized and what had been done.

---

[226] George H. Preston, *A History of the Cass County, Missouri, Bond Swindle, with Personal Sketches and a Graphic Account of the Gunn City Tragedy* (St. Louis: Southwestern Book and Publishing Co., 1873); Lopata, *Local Aid to Railroads in Missouri*, 105–7; Ann. Cyc., 1872, p. 551. Also Cass County v. Amos Green, 66 Mo. 498 (1878), decreeing the surrender of 55 bonds Cline had sold to Kansas City bankers who in turn sold to a local lawyer and a newspaper publisher—none qualifying as innocent holders.

[227] Cass County v. Jordan, 95 U.S. 373. In a third case, Cass County v. Shores, 95 U.S. 375, suit had been brought on refunding bonds purporting to bind the *county*, although issued for the benefit of certain *townships*; the question was whether the county court had authority to bind the county, and the Court held that it had. J. C. Stevenson, involved in the "bloody bonds" matter, had signed the bonds on which Johnston and Shores sued.

The Circuit Court rejected the answer set up against Jordan's suit,[228] and that against Johnston as well—decisions presently affirmed by the Supreme Court.

These cases had been filed in the Supreme Court *prior* to the time when *Harshman v. Bates County* was argued. Inasmuch as Johnston and Jordan sued on Township Aid bonds, the *Harshman* decision gave the County a new defense. And on the bondholder side, here was an opportunity to seek an overruling of *Harshman*. A mighty effort was made. Thomas K. Skinker, for Jordan, undertook to persuade the Court that what in arguing *Harshman* he had said was "manifest" to the most casual reader was not true at all:

> In the Harshman case, the Court was led by counsel into the assumption that there is a broad difference between the language of the Constitution and the act of 1868 in respect of the number of voters whose assent is necessary to obtain. . . . More thorough examination leaves no room to doubt that the proposition is erroneous, and that where the assent of a two-thirds majority of the voters is necessary, this requirement is complied with if two-thirds of those who voted gave their consent. This is the established doctrine.[229]

Senator John B. Henderson and associates, in a tightly packed brief on behalf of Johnston, opened their critique of *Harshman* with this comment:

> This case was submitted near the close of the last term.[230] It was imperfectly considered. Only one short oral argument was made, and the brief filed in the case for the bond-holder was well calculated to mislead the court as to the rulings of the local courts on the questions involved. . . .[231]

And James Grant—whose bold advocacy had won so much for holders of Iowa and Illinois municipal bonds—chided the Court because

> all these debts are wiped out and extinguished by the casual remark of this court, unconsidered, and not argued . . . in the case of Harshman v. Bates County.

---

[228] Jordan v. Cass County, Fed. Case No. 7517 (1874), and No. 7518 (1875).

[229] Brief, 13.

[230] It was argued on February 15, 1876, and decided in conference on February 26. As Waite's docket shows, at that time Strong, Swayne, and Clifford voted to reverse. Humboldt Township v. Long, Elmwood v. Marcy, and Marcy v. Oswego Township were also decided in conference on February 26. Bradley's opinion received approval on May 6, and was delivered on May 8.

[231] Brief "On Township Bonds of Missouri," filed by Henderson, George H. Shields, and James Grant, at p. 34.

He professed disbelief that the Court had really intended

> to invalidate millions of dollars not apparently in a cause, without
> first requiring that on so grave a question, counsel should be heard.[232]

A reproach of culpable judicial practice, such as this, touches a
sensitive spot—it is quite different from an argument merely that the
Court had reasoned to the wrong conclusion.

Chief Justice Waite, for the majority, responded that it had been
"incidentally decided" that the Township Aid law violated the Missouri
constitution; now that the question had been "directly presented," the
Court, drawing on what might be inferred from State decisions, concluded that the statute was valid. Justice Bradley (Miller, J., concurring) adhered to his opinion in *Harshman*. "I concede that if the
Supreme Court of Missouri has given a contrary construction to the
clause, which has become the settled law of the State, we should be
governed by it. But I do not understand that this has been done."

Five months later—as has been explained—the Missouri court
in the *Brassfield* case declared the Township Act law unconstitutional,
adopting Bradley's construction and declining to follow the Supreme
Court.[233]

It was not to be doubted what the federal Circuit Courts in
Missouri would do. The certain answer came in *Foote v. Johnson
County*,[234] decided on April 20, 1878, just four days after the Missouri court had spoken in *Brassfield*. The federal court, said Judge
Dillon, must follow the Supreme Court's second thought, notwithstanding the State court's ruling: he cited *Gelpcke*, *Pine Grove*, and *Olcott
v. Supervisors*.

The federal and State judiciaries were now in conflict, at close
quarters: both courts had been sitting in Jefferson City at the moment
their opposing decisions were announced.

The *Missouri Republican* conceded that it was "certainly singular" that the Missouri court, after enforcing the Township Aid Act for
years, had suddenly discovered unconstitutionality.

> But it is not more inconsistent than that the United States supreme
> court should after this very question was presented to it determine
> it in two contradictory ways. . . . The fact shows that confusing
> inconsistencies are to be found in the federal supreme court as well
> as in the state tribunal, and the former is quite as unstable a guide
> as the latter.

---

[232] Brief for Defendant in Error,
Johnston, at 5.

[233] Supra, p. 1075.
[234] Fed Case No. 4912. W.D. Mo.

The editor foresaw collisions when the federal courts gave judgments for bondholders and the State courts enjoined the levy of taxes to pay them.[235]

Missouri was now caught up in the same sort of struggle that Iowa had experienced a decade earlier.

Foote v. Johnson County gave off political overtones. Sitting with Judge Dillon was District Judge Arnold Krekel: German-born Republican leader; president of the convention that framed the proscriptive constitution of 1865; appointee of President Lincoln. Counsel for the plaintiff was Senator John B. Henderson, one of the State's leading Unionists. Henderson had of late gone about urging local authorities to settle with creditors; he was said to be "a holder of a large amount of township bonds."[236] Henderson had published an article in the *Central Law Journal* supporting the Supreme Court's decision in *Cass County v. Johnston*.[237] The plaintiff, Elisha Foote, had been a judge in western New York, and later (1868–69) Commissioner of Patents; he was Henderson's father-in-law. On the other side, Thomas C. Reynolds, retained by Johnson and other counties, had been Lieutenant Governor and then Governor in the rebel administration that purported to represent Missouri during the Civil War. Johnson, Cass, Bates, and other heavily indebted counties in western Missouri were overwhelmingly Democratic in politics.

Earlier than this, in the period when *Harshman* was a ruling case, Foote had lost just such a suit against Pike County. So too had Joseph M. Douglass. So too Smedley Darlington had lost a township bond suit against Jackson County. Each filed his writ of error in the Supreme Court, and during the two and a half years of waiting, *Cass County v. Johnston* had overruled *Harshman*.[238] So when *Foote*, *Douglass*, and *Darlington* came to be heard, the bondholders had the victory in *Cass County* on which to rely. But, counsel for the Counties replied, since then the Missouri court has held the Township Aid Act

[235] "Judicial Conflict." Apr. 22, 1878.

[236] *Missouri Republican*, Dec. 10, 11, 21, 1877.

[237] 5:499 and 518, Dec. 14 and 21, 1877, by "J.B.H." This journal had been established at St. Louis in 1874, under the editorship of Judge Dillon.

[238] Discussion herein rests upon transcripts of records and briefs in Douglass v. Pike County, 101 U.S. 677; and Foote v. Pike County and Darlington v. Jackson County, decided with it at 101 U.S. 688. They were argued on January 5, 6, 1880,

and decided March 29, 1880. In the Circuit Court for Eastern Missouri, *Douglass* was decided on April 7, 1877; *Foote* on September 18, 1876. Foote sued on only $1,220 in coupons; his case could not have been taken to the Supreme Court had not District Judge Treat professed a difference of opinion with the Circuit Judge. In the Circuit Court for Western Missouri, Darlington's suit on bonds issued on behalf of Kaw Township (Kansas City) was decided on April 24, 1877. Jackson and Pike were both heavily bonded for railroad aid.

invalid, in a suit where for the first time it ruled on the particular point involved. Only two months ago, they reminded the Court, in *Fairfield v. Gallatin County*[239] you overruled *Concord v. Portsmouth Savings Bank* in order to follow the Illinois court's first ruling on the constitutional question: let the same effect now be accorded to the Missouri decision.

In *Douglass v. Pike County*, Chief Justice Waite went over the ground again to show that in *Cass County* the Court had followed faithfully the law as it appeared to be in the light of pertinent State decisions. Now the Missouri court had announced a new rule: but, as had been said in many cases, in the federal courts the rights of the parties would be determined according to "the law as it was judicially construed to be when the bonds in question were put on the market as commercial paper."[240] Now the Court was unanimous: evidently Bradley and Miller had no disposition to differ from their brethren.

An impulse from the Supreme Court runs with controlling effect throughout the complicated mechanism of the federal system. When, perhaps through haste, some faulty action is taken, vibrations may continue despite an attempt to still the error. The consequences of *Harshman* serve to illustrate. One may doubt whether, but for that initial mistake, the Missouri court would ever have invalidated the Township Aid Act.

COUNTY BONDS: FURTHER COMPLEXITY AND CONFLICT

THE MOST PROTRACTED of the judicial disagreements in Missouri had to do with bonds issued by a county court, binding the county itself (not on behalf of a township), without a vote of the people— and commonly, as it turned out, for railroads that did not materialize. Here enters the act of March 23, 1861:

> It shall not be lawful for the county court of any county to subscribe to the capital stock of any railroad company, unless the same has been voted by a majority of the resident voters who shall vote at such election under the provisions of this act.[241]

---

[239] 100 U.S. 47, decided November 10, 1879: it held that a donation to a railroad company, authorized prior to the coming into force of the constitution of 1870, had *not* been forbidden by that constitution—following the decision in Chicago & I. R.R. v. Pinckney, 74 Ill. 277 (1874), unknown to the Court when it held otherwise in Concord v. Portsmouth Savings Bank, 92 U.S. (1876). Supra, p. 1050.

[240] Douglass v. Pike County, 101 U.S. 677 (1880).

[241] Sess. Acts 1860–61, 60.

That sounds unqualified: no county subscription—hence no bonds—without such approval at an election.

In the railroad-building enthusiasm that followed the Civil War, that statute was rather ignored—until, at a time of disillusionment, it was invoked by the State court to invalidate issues made in disregard of it.[242]

The constitution of 1865, to assure a further restraint of municipal aid, made the provision already discussed at length, requiring the assent of two-thirds of the qualified voters.[243] The next session of the legislature revised the general railroad law to declare that

> It shall be lawful for the county court of any county . . . to take stock . . . in . . . any railroad company . . . ; *provided* . . .

—and there the constitution's requirement of the assent of two-thirds of the qualified voters was inserted verbatim.[244]

There was a little case in the Missouri Reports, however, that seemed to teach that once authority had been given to aid a railroad, a subsequent general limitation would not efface it.[245] That proposition was now established in the leading case of *State ex rel. Missouri & Mississippi R.R. v. Macon County Court*, in 1867. That railroad's charter, enacted on February 20, 1865, authorized the county court of any county to take stock and issue bonds. A few months later came the new constitution, and then the general railroad law quoted above. The Missouri court held that a county court was free to take stock and issue bonds, without regard to the constitutional limitation and the statute to implement it.[246]

Enthusiasm for railroad building then ran high; on learning of the *Macon County* decision, the populace "gathered en masse in the courthouse and proceeded to make glad over the outcome."[247] But as it turned out, the Missouri & Mississippi was a monumental failure.

---

[242] "Strange as it may seem, that act, though cited by counsel, was never discussed until the year 1878 . . . ." Sherwood, C.J., in State *ex rel.* Barlow v. Dallas County, 72 Mo. 329 (1880).

[243] Supra, p. 1069.

[244] Gen. Stats. 1866, ch. 63, sec. 7, p. 338.

[245] City and County of St. Louis v. Alexander, 23 Mo. 483 (1856). A special act of March 1, 1851, permitted St. Louis to take stock in a certain railroad; a general statute of March 3, 1851, enacted that "the

city shall not at any time become a subscriber . . . ." Held: the later law did not repeal the special act.

[246] 41 Mo. 453. The Macon County Court had made a subscription of $175,000 on April 2, 1867. Then a taxpayers' convention took steps that caused the county clerk to halt. The railroad company brought mandamus, and won a judgment ordering the county court to deliver the bonds.

[247] E. M. Violette, *The Missouri and Mississippi Railroad Debt* (Columbia: Missouri Historical Society, 1921), 12–18.

Soon we shall find the Supreme Court passing upon efforts by Macon County to avoid enforcement of its bonds.[248]

When the Civil War was ended and order was restored, the people of Missouri returned eagerly to the projecting of railroads. In five years from 1867, local aid flowed abundantly, while mileage nearly trebled. Then aid all but stopped; building declined sharply, even before the panic broke in 1873.[249] Discontented taxpayers discovered invalidity in subscriptions; payment on bonds was cut off.

For several years the Missouri court, adhering to its *Macon County* decision of 1867, went right on in holding that when a railroad charter antedating the constitution had authorized county courts to give aid—and there were dozens of such charters—a power was thereby vested that could be exercised without submitting the matter to a popular vote.[250] The judges had been captivated by the notion that the particular grant in a railroad charter was not affected by a general prohibition.

Accepting these Missouri decisions as "settled law," the Supreme Court at its terms of 1876 and 1877 gave judgment against four Missouri counties on bonds issued, without popular vote, subsequent to the constitution of 1865, under charter provisions antedating it.[251]

Then on June 27, 1878, a break appeared in the front of the Missouri court. Chief Justice Sherwood announced it to be his view that the Act of 1861[252] spoke without qualification—that it governed the *means* by which subscriptions might be made, even under a pre-existing charter—and that county bonds issued after the 1861 statute without approval at an election were invalid. This was in *State v. Garroute*, concerning bonds issued by the county court of Greene County;[253] two other judges joined in holding the bonds invalid on

---

[248] Infra, pp. 1093–95.
[249] Lopata, *Local Aid to Railroads in Missouri*, 71–73.
[250] Kansas City, St. Joseph & Council Bluffs R.R. v. Alderman, 47 Mo. 349 (1871); State *ex rel.* St. Joseph & Iowa R.R. v. Sullivan County Court, 51 Mo. 522 (1873); State *ex rel.* Baker, Attorney General v. Greene County Court, 54 Mo. 540 (1874).
[251] Callaway County v. Foster, 93 U.S. 570 (1876); Scotland County v. Thomas, 94 U.S. 682 (1877); Henry County v. Nicolay, 95 U.S. 619 (1877); Ray County v. Vansycle, 96 U.S. 675 (1878).
[252] Supra, p. 1081.
[253] 67 Mo. 445.

The bond issue here held invalid was the very same whose validity had been affirmed in State *ex rel.* Baker, Attorney General v. Greene County Court, 54 Mo. 540 (1874).

The subscription was made to the Kansas City & Memphis R.R. That company found its destination, not in the Tennessee city, but in the bankruptcy court.

Chief Justice Thomas A. Sherwood (1834–1918) was a conservative Democrat, opposed to subsidies and governmental interference in private enterprise. See D.A.B.

He resided in Springfield, county seat of Greene County. The people there had been demonstrating against paying on the bonds; the decision in

another point: that the railroad company, by entering into a consolidation, had extinguished any privilege under the original charter. The report gave the impression that soon there would be three judges supporting this new view of the statute of 1861. And so it proved.

This decision against these county bonds, on June 27, 1878, should be seen in conjunction with the decision on April 16 in *State v. Brassfield* where the Missouri court held Township Aid bonds invalid for reasons first given by the Supreme Court in *Harshman*.[254]

In Washington, the Supreme Court held to its course. Only one of the Missouri judges, it observed, had professed this new view of the statute of 1861; "we do not think it necessary to discuss the question."[255]

In 1880, in *State ex rel. Barlow v. Dallas County*,[256] Chief Justice Sherwood announced that two of his brethren now joined him in holding that the statute of 1861—"It shall not be lawful for the county court . . . to subscribe . . . unless the same has been voted by a majority of the resident voters . . ."—applied to the issue of bonds even under pre-existing charters. The line of cases beginning with *Macon County* in 1867 was overthrown. It resulted that many issues of county bonds were now invalid, in the eyes of the Missouri court.

The Supreme Court had to take cognizance of this development, in *Ralls County v. Douglass*[257] in 1882. Without any aspersions, Chief Justice Waite said simply that "the bonds involved in this suit were all in the hands of innocent holders when the law of the State was so materially altered by its courts." He repeated what had been said after the Missouri court had ruled against Township Aid bonds in the suit by by this same plaintiff in error, Joseph M. Douglass, against Pike County.[258] With that the Court treated the matter as "no longer an open question."[259]

STORM OVER THE FEDERAL JUDICIARY

BY THE SUMMER of 1878, judgments of the federal courts were pressing insistently at many points. More than seventy Missouri coun-

---

Garroute caused "great rejoicing not only in Greene but in the other Southwestern counties having similar railroad debts. . . ." *Missouri Republican*, May 7, July 10, 1878.

254 Supra, p. 1075.

255 Waite, C.J. in Schuyler County v. Thomas, 98 U.S. 169 (1878). Also Cass County v. Gillett, 100 U.S. 585 (1879); Benton County v. Rollins, 154 U.S. 665, (1880).

256 72 Mo. 329.

257 105 U.S. 728.

258 Supra, p. 1081.

259 Waite, C.J., in Dallas County v. McKenzie, 110 U.S. 686 (1884). Also City of Louisiana v. Taylor, 105 U.S. 454 (1882); Green [Greene] County v. Conness, 109 U.S. 104 (1883); Scotland County v. Hill, 132 U.S. 107 (1889).

ties had incurred debt for railroad aid. Some were making no trouble. Bright examples were Audrain (county seat, Mexico), which took pride that it had "never been a party to any suit" on bonds and had "never been a day behind time" with interest,[260] and Boone (county seat, Columbia), whose citizens were "not a repudiating people" and gave "a pretty general acquiescence" to the view that judgments of the Supreme Court should be obeyed.[261] But for the greater part, mass meetings were passing resolutions, and expedients were being devised and even tested—for example, that chattels seized on execution be replevied in a State court;[262] that there be a concerted refusal to bid at execution sales;[263] and that county judges resign to avoid levying taxes.[264] (At the next legislature, a bill to make a county officer's resignation effective upon filing—which had facilitated evasion in Wisconsin[265]—was stopped by the governor's veto[266]) The situation was comparable to that in Iowa ten years earlier. But in Missouri the affected area was wider—yet one infers that generally feeling was less intense and resistance less determined. Arrangements with creditors were being considered, and here and there settlements were being made.

In some counties the people had special reasons for indignation, as where the county court had been corrupted and, moreover, no railroad had been built. Such was the case in Henry (county seat, Clinton) in the west: it remembered a deathbed confession that its county court had been bribed when, without an election, it issued bonds to aid the proposed Clinton & Memphis branch of the Tebo & Neosho.[267] It was on these bonds that Albert H. Nicolay,[268] New York broker, had recently won a judgment in the Supreme Court.[269] To stay the

---

[260] *Missouri Republican*, Jan. 6, 1879; also May 20, 1878 and Nov. 13, 1879.

[261] Ibid., Mar. 20 and May 9, 1878; also Apr. 29, June 24, 1878.

[262] Ibid., Aug. 27, Nov. 28, 1878.

[263] Ibid., Dec. 7, 1877; Apr. 1, 11, 12, May 22, June 11, Nov. 28, Dec. 2, 1878; Mar. 6, 1879.

[264] Ibid., May 29, 1878; Feb. 3, 1879.

[265] Supra, pp. 1038–43.

[266] *Missouri Republican*, May 10, June 13, 1879.

[267] Ibid., Mar. 16, 1878.

[268] Albert H. Nicolay & Co., Stock Auctioneers and Brokers, No. 43 Pine Street, New York, dealers in "first class municipal bonds." Advertisement in the *Commercial & Financial Chronicle* of the period, passim.

[269] Henry County v. Nicolay, 95 U.S. 619, decided Nov. 5, 1877. James Grant appeared for the bondholder.

The Court held that the charter of the T. & N., granted in 1860, was not controlled by the limitation of the constitution of 1865. Supra, p. 1069. Nor did that limitation control the issue of bonds to the C. & M. Branch, under a statute of 1868 "to Aid in the Building of Branch Railroads," inasmuch as the original charter gave power to construct the branch. (In this the Court was following Missouri decisions.) The bonds being regular on their face, it was no defense that proceedings to acquire them were not regular, unless purchaser was shown to have had notice.

This was followed in a similar case

execution of the Circuit Court's judgment, pending resort to the Supreme Court, a number of citizens signed the supersedeas bond. But the judgment was affirmed—"and now," it was reported, "the county has no alternative but to pay the judgment or allow execution to issue on the bond against the citizens. There is another judgment for $7,500 against the county on its railroad bonds, and to pay this a tax of 15 cents is levied." The tax rate for 1878 amounted to $1.05 for county purposes, plus .40 for the State. The former included .65 for federal court judgments on bonds: .50 to pay for the Nicolay appeal bond, plus .15 for the other judgment under mandamus of the Circuit Court.[270]

St. Clair County (immediately south of Henry) had subscribed $250,000 to the same scheme—its sole venture in railroad aid—and, waiving a stipulation for its own protection, had handed over all of its bonds without waiting for any work to be performed. Against this county, too, Nicolay recovered a judgment on bonds issued to the Tebo & Neosho to the use and in the name of the Clinton & Memphis.[271] Twice masked men carried away the tax books;[272] for years, county court judges were being sentenced to jail for contempt of the federal court. Not until 1910 was the debt compromised.[273]

In the Eighth Congressional District (around Kansas City, wherein Cass County was included) it was learned, during the campaign of 1878, that one of the candidates for Representative in Congress had accepted a large "attorney's fee" for bribing the State's Attorney General to cause the dismissal of a suit wherein Cass taxpayers were seeking to restrain the issue of bonds in aid of the Clinton & Memphis, and for the candidate's further services in corrupting the county court.[274] This bit of work for the "Memphis railroad gang" was associated with the other job that culminated in the lynching at Gunn City and in frustrating the disposal of the "bloody bonds" through a Kansas City banking house.[275]

In 1878 the people of Scotland County, in northeastern Mis-

---

of Cass County v. Gillett, 100 U.S. 585 (1879). James O. Broadhead, infra, p. 1088, appeared for Cass County.

[270] *Missouri Republican*, May 22, Sept. 23, 1878.

[271] Nicolay v. St. Clair County, Fed. Case No. 10,257 (C.C.W.D. Mo. 1874). James Grant for the plaintiff.

[272] *Missouri Republican*, Dec. 16, 19, 24, 1877; Sept. 11, 1878; May 26, 1879.

[273] Lopata, *Local Aid to Railroads in Missouri*, 88, 102, 125–26, 136.

[274] *Missouri Republican*, Aug. 20, Sept. 9, 10, Oct. 9, 1878. The item last named is a letter publishing that accusation, from John C. Gage, attorney for the County in Cass County v. Johnston, 95 U.S. 360 (1877), and in other bond cases.

[275] Supra, p. 1077. Cass County v. Amos Green, 66 Mo. 498 (1878).

souri, were facing stiff taxation to meet judgments on bonds, under exasperating circumstances. In 1877 the Supreme Court, following indulgent holdings by the State court when railroad aid was popular, had held Scotland bonds to be valid.[276] The bonds had been delivered in contempt of a local court where a suit to enjoin was pending; the county court had sent an agent to Illinois to evade service and make delivery there. In 1878 the Missouri bench, taking a stricter view than had their predecessors, held the issue ultra vires and affirmed the injunction.[277] But the bonds had long since been in circulation, and judgments on them were being enforced by the federal court. The local Taxpayers' Association, in February 1878 and thereafter, by direct action frustrated the execution of the court's mandates.[278] One bondholder brought an action for conspiracy against fifteen of the members, claiming the amount of his judgment, interest, and exemplary damages; in 1885 the Supreme Court, overruling the Circuit Court, held that such an action could be maintained.[279] That decision, however, had no effect upon actual events.

Inasmuch as the Scotland bonds had been carried away and sold to Hill, an Illinois banker who qualified as an innocent purchaser, the County was unable to escape payment. After a third defeat on that issue in the Supreme Court, in 1891,[280] the County next year compromised with its creditors.[281]

A convention of indebted counties called for early June 1878

---

[276] Scotland County v. Thomas, 94 U.S. 682. The opinion was written by Justice Bradley. He had stated the problem in a note on his copy of the transcript:

Where a railroad charter gives authority to towns & counties to subscribe, is that authority abrogated by a subsequent consolidation with a railroad company of another State—not authorized when the charter was granted: Though legislature had power to alter.

Justice Miller noted dissent.

[277] Wagner v. Meety, 69 Mo. 150 (Oct. term 1878).

[278] *Missouri Republican*, Feb. 13, May 29, Dec. 30, 1878; Feb. 3, June 21, 23, Dec. 29, 1879.

[279] Findlay v. McAllister, 113 U.S. 104. Miller and Field, JJ., noted dissent.

[280] Scotland County v. Hill, 112

U.S. 183 (1884); Scotland County v. Hill, 132 U.S. 107 (1889); Scotland County v. United States ex rel. Hill's Exrs., 140 U.S. 41 (1891).

Justice Harlan's opinion in the case in 132 U.S. observed that

The bonds were delivered to the railway company at the office of the bank in Warsaw, Illinois, of which Hill was president. And it is, perhaps, true that Hill had then heard of the Wagner suit, and knew or suspected that Mety's purpose in bringing the bonds to Warsaw was to deliver them to the company before the injunction could be served upon him. But he had no connection with the conspirators . . . .

Warsaw is on the Mississippi River, about forty miles east of Memphis, county seat of Scotland County.

[281] Lopata, *Local Aid to Railroads in Missouri*, 124.

proved to be a small and tame affair, quite different from the Iowa convention in December 1869.[282] A committee on its behalf issued an address calling for a return by the Supreme Court to the principle that a State court's construction of its own constitution and laws would be respected. "We desire simply that that rule shall govern in these bond cases . . . ." Apparently nothing came of this demonstration;[283] perhaps its thunder was stolen by a political party better organized for producing sound effects.

This was the State Convention of the Democratic party, which met on July 10, 1878. Its chairman, James O. Broadhead, seized the occasion to reply to what ex-Senator John B. Henderson had been saying as he pressed the claims of bondholders. It was not true, said Broadhead, that the Missouri judiciary was meditating a rebellion against the federal judiciary. A conflict had indeed arisen between the Missouri court and the federal judiciary; but "the rebellion is the other way," in that the Supreme Court had refused to be bound by State decisions on the construction of the State constitution and laws. "The State has it in its own hands," said Broadhead, "to determine how far and to what extent judgments of the Supreme Court of the United States or federal tribunals in this State shall be enforced against municipal corporations." If the federal marshal could find no county property on which to execute a judgment, his authority was exhausted. "Nor has the federal court any authority to levy a tax to pay that judgment." If there was anything for which the Democratic party deserved the thanks of the people, it was because "they are resisting the efforts which have been made to break down the barriers of constitutions and establish in their place a consolidated despotism at the federal seat of government."[284]

Broadhead's professional distinction was such that, when next month the American Bar Association was organized, he was chosen to be its first president. Of course what he had said at the political conclave sounded different from what as an advocate before a federal court he might say on behalf of a client.[285]

---

[282] Supra, pp. 975–76.

[283] *Missouri Republican*, June 3, 6, 10, Aug. 27, 1878; Jan. 13, 1879.

[284] Ibid., July 11, 1878.

[285] As counsel for the City in Jarrott v. Moberly, Fed. Case No. 7223 (C.C.W.D. Mo., Apr. 17, 1878), a suit on coupons from "Moberly Machine Shop Bonds," Broadhead had recently urged the federal court to sustain a demurrer based upon the doctrine the Supreme Court had im-

posed in Loan Association v. Topeka, 20 Wall. 655 (1875), infra, pp. 1101–05, that a statute authorizing a municipality to issue bonds in aid of a manufacturing enterprise was void, as involving taxation for what was not a *public purpose*.

He was of counsel for plaintiff in error in Douglass v. Pike County, 101 U.S. 677 (1880), urging the Supreme Court *not* to reconsider its decision in Cass County v. Johnston, albeit the

The State Convention, borrowing a plank from the Indiana Democracy, declared that the jurisdiction then being exercised by the federal courts was "unwise and hurtful to the true interests of the people"; that it should be restricted "to such matters as are clearly contemplated by the Constitution . . . ."[286] By overwhelming vote the next legislature memorialized Congress in a resolution that incorporated this part of the Democratic platform.[287] At that moment there was a great deal of Democratic agitation to cut down the powers of the federal judiciary.

The Convention renominated by acclamation Judge Elijah H. Norton,[288] whose position as an anti-bond judge was now well established. Among three candidates he received 55 percent of the vote— rather better than others on the Democratic ticket; his nomination had proved "especially satisfactory" to counties heavily in debt.[289]

While there was a general disposition to obstruct bondholders, the people of the debtor counties, in the main, would not go to the point of actual defiance of the federal courts. As will appear, neither would the State's highest court.

LITIGATION ALONG THE MISSOURI & MISSISSIPPI

IN PURSUING THE experience with railroad aid, one surmounts one range of problems only to behold another. The Missouri & Mississippi Railroad Company, chartered on February 20, 1865, was to build from Macon County (centered about fifty miles from the northern and sixty miles from the eastern boundary), northeast to the corner of the State, and southwest to the Missouri River.[290] Municipal authorities might subscribe and issue bonds, "and levy a tax to pay the same not to exceed one-twentieth of one percent upon the assessed value of taxable property for each year." There was the root of trouble: 1/20 of 1 percent, a mere five mills on the dollar. Macon County had a total assessed valuation of about $5,000,000. A tax thus limited would produce about $2,500 a year—enough to service say $26,000 in twenty-year bonds bearing 7 percent interest. Macon issued $350,000 in bonds. Clark, in the corner of the State, subscribed $200,000; Knox, $285,000; Chariton, $100,000; one township in Howard, $100,000;

Missouri court had subsequently held the Township Aid Act to be invalid. In the companion cases of Foote v. Pike County and Darlington v. Jackson County, ex-Senator Henderson was on the same side as Broadhead.

[286] Ann. Cyc. 1878, 441 (Indiana) and 587 (Missouri).

[287] Ibid., 643.

[288] Supra, p. 1076.

[289] Ann. Cyc. 1878, 579; *Missouri Republican*, Aug. 8, Nov. 13, 1878.

[290] Violette, *The Missouri and Mississippi Railroad Debt* (1921) tells its story.

in all, more than $100,000,000 for a 120-mile project which in the end produced fifteen miles of operating line. The charter antedated the constitution of 1865 and—as the State court in 1867 held unanimously in the memorable case of *State ex rel. Missouri & Mississippi R.R. v. Macon County Court*, dwelt upon above[291]—a county could validly subscribe without any reference to the voters.

When the affair turned out badly, resistance fed upon indignation at the absence of popular assent. Disaffection over the Missouri & Mississippi in Missouri may be likened to that over the Mississippi & Missouri in Iowa some years earlier.[292]

We shall examine three important litigations concerning bonds issued in aid of the Missouri & Mississippi: *Johnston against Clark County*, *Huidekoper against Macon*, and *Harshman against Knox*. In the end, each county lost.

In the *Shortridge* decision in 1874, where local bondholders were seeking to compel the Macon County Court to levy a tax adequate to pay interest, the Missouri court held that in respect to these bonds the rate of 1/20 of 1 percent had set the limit of the County's taxing power.[293] When the charter was enacted and thereafter, the general law authorized the levy of taxes to pay interest and provide a sinking fund: here, however, the very statute authorizing the issue had made its own special provision—for the protection, not of bondholders, but of taxpayers. Such was the holding.

Johnston, a citizen of Iowa, recovered a judgment in the federal court against Clark County, on bonds issued under the M. & M. charter. The proceeds of the five-mill tax proving inadequate, he sought mandamus to compel the county court to pay the balance due out of general funds.[294] This was the same Johnston on whose behalf the doughty James Grant won the victory over Cass County in November 1872.[295] Now Grant was opposed by George W. McCrary; they submitted on briefs. The latter relied upon the State court's decision in *Shortridge*, and upon the strong line of reasoning by which it could be supported. Grant replied that plainly the County was obligated to pay, and that the special provision for a five-mill tax had been intended as an additional security, to increase the bonds' value in the market. In a decision announced on January 7, 1878, the majority, speaking through

---

[291] 41 Mo. 453. Supra, p. 1082.

[292] Supra, pp. 947–51.

[293] State *ex rel.* Aull and Pollard v. Shortridge *et al.*, Justices of Macon County Court, 56 Mo. 126. Mar. term 1874.

[294] United States *ex rel.* Johnston v. Clark County, 96 U.S. 211 (1878).

[295] Cass County v. Johnston, 95 U.S. 360, where Harshman v. Bates County had been overruled and Township Aid bonds had been saved. Supra, pp. 1076–79.

Justice Strong, accepted and followed Grant's argument. The Chief Justice, Miller, and Bradley dissented.[296] Waite said:

> I think the Act under which the bonds were issued limited the power of taxation for their payment, and that the holders are chargeable with notice of the limitation. The debt authorized was one payable from a particular fund. If the fund is deficient, the Legislature alone has the power to grant the necessary relief.

E. M. Violette, who studied the Missouri & Mississippi experience painstakingly, had the benefit of consulting Thomas K. Skinker, the St. Louis attorney who had been retained in the litigation. The statutory "one-twentieth of one percent," in Skinker's opinion, may have resulted from a clerical error in transcribing an intended 1/2 of 1 percent in a draft bill. The railroad directors published a pamphlet naming the higher rate. The Huidekopers, Pennsylvania financiers, purchased Macon County bonds on the advice of their attorney, "Joseph Shippen, then of St. Louis, who is said to have been misled by the pamphlet...."[297]

That a counsellor might form his opinion of the law on the basis of a pamphlet issued by promoters gives point to something Chief Justice Waite said in *United States ex rel. Huidekoper v. Macon County*:[298]

> While there has, undoubtedly, been great recklessness on the part of the municipal authorities in the creation of bonded indebtedness, there has not unfrequently been gross carelessness on the part of purchasers .... Every purchaser of a municipal bond is chargeable with notice of the statute under which the bond was issued ....

The promoters of the Missouri & Mississippi were simply men of local prominence—lawyers, farmers, merchants—with no experience

---

[296] The decision was by 5 to 3. As the Chief Justice's Docket Book shows, Justice Harlan—newly come to the Court, vice Justice Davis—took no part.

On the same day, Justice Strong announced the unanimous decision in United States *ex rel.* Johnston v. Clark County, 95 U.S. 769. It appeared that Johnston's bonds, executed in 1871, were not issued until January 1, 1874. He sought by mandamus to compel the levy of the five-mill tax for the years 1871 and following. Held: until

the bonds were issued, there was no authority to levy the tax.

[297] Violette, *Missouri and Mississippi Railroad Debt*, 6–8. Skinker represented Huidekoper in the *Macon County* litigation, 99 U.S. 582 (1879) and 109 U.S. 229 (1883), presently to be discussed, as well as in suits against other counties. Inasmuch as Skinker and Shippen were associated in the *Macon County* litigation, it is reasonable to believe that he was reliably informed.

[298] 99 U.S. 582 (1879).

in railroading and no substantial resources. Municipal aid was their reliance. Apparently their idea was that if the route could be graded, bridged and tied, some moneyed interest could be found to supply rails and equipment and put the railroad in operation.

BONDHOLDERS IN SEARCH OF A REMEDY

THE RELIEF JOHNSTON sought against Clark County, to which the Court held him to be entitled, ran in these terms: that the county court give him a warrant on the county treasurer for the unpaid balance, *so that he may be enabled, on its presentation, to have it paid in its order out of general funds in the county treasury.*[299] The *Missouri Republican* forecast that

> The result will be that as fast as moneys come into the treasury from the regular county tax, they will be paid out to the judgment creditors, and there will be no means of defraying the county's regular expenses. It will be forced, therefore, to increase the levy till it will yield revenue enough to pay the ordinary expenses and the interest on the bonds too.[300]

That was on the assumption that the Supreme Court's judgment would be made effective.

Clark county taxpayers, however, resolved to "resist to the last extremity, by all legal and other means" the collection of any tax for the M. & M. bonds, "issued by a corrupt county court in opposition to the emphatically expressed will of the people, for which the county has had not one foot of road completed, or received the slightest benefit in any way."[301] Presently the local circuit court granted an injunction to restrain the county court from issuing and the treasurer from paying the warrant to which the Supreme Court had declared Johnston was entitled.[302] Soon, however, the people were induced to cease opposing and to look toward a compromise, which in 1881 was concluded on the very favorable terms of thirty cents on the dollar, in 6 percent renewal bonds.[303]

Whether the right declared for Johnston would be extended to a Missouri bondholder suing in the State courts was answered No by *State ex rel. Watkins v. Macon County Court,* decided in October

---

[299] United States *ex rel.* Johnston v. Clark County, 96 U.S. 211, decided Jan. 7, 1878. Supra, p. 1090.

[300] Jan. 28, 1878.

[301] *Missouri Republican,* May 13, 1878.

[302] Ibid., Sept. 13, 1878.

[303] Violette, *Missouri and Mississippi Railroad Debt,* 44–45.

1878.[304] The Missouri court adhered to its *Shortridge* decision, disapproved *Johnston v. Clark County*, and refused to compel the County to pay Watkins more than the proceeds of the five-mill tax. This, of course, involved no direct collision with the judicial power of the United States.

Of the counties that had aided the Missouri & Mississippi, Macon and Knox remained belligerent.

Huidekoper, finding himself unable to collect a judgment on his Macon County coupons, asked the federal court to compel the levy and collection of a tax specifically for that purpose. From a denial there he went to the Supreme Court. This had been on the docket eight months before Johnston's case against Clark County came up. In the latter, however, once counsel agreed to submit without oral argument, they had their decision within a month. Then a second Huidekoper case was docketed—one in which he had sought, and won, a writ directing the Macon County Court to give him a warrant payable out of general funds then or thereafter in the treasury—the same remedy that had been granted Johnston. The two Huidekoper cases were heard together, and decided on March 3, 1879.[305]

The specific tax was denied. When the bonds were issued and at all times thereafter, the Chief Justice observed, Macon County's power to tax for general purposes was limited by law to 1/2 of 1 percent.

> We have no power by mandamus to compel a municipal corporation to levy a tax which the law does not authorize. We cannot create new rights or confer new powers. . . .

(The Chief Justice's Docket shows that when the Justices were polled at conference on January 11, 1879, Clifford voted to reverse. In partisan sympathies, Clifford was an undeviating Democrat: at this period he was refusing to enter the White House, because in his judgment Hayes was not rightfully the President. Yet so fixed was his attitude on municipal bonds that he would use federal judicial power to mandamus a municipal corporation to tax where State law had conferred no authority to do so.)

In the second case, where Huidekoper sought a warrant payable

---

[304] 68 Mo. 29; *Missouri Republican*, Nov. 1, 1878.

[305] United States *ex rel.* Huidekoper v. Macon County Court, 99 U.S. 582; Macon County Court v. Huidekoper, 99 U.S. 592.

The first *Huidekoper* case was docketed on Mar. 3, 1876.

Johnston v. Clark County was docketed the following November 3; on December 10, 1877, counsel stipulated to submit on briefs; judgment was rendered on January 7, 1878.

The second *Huidekoper* case was docketed October 12, 1878.

out of general funds, the Chief Justice announced that "a majority of the Court adheres to the decision" in *United States ex rel. Johnston v. Clark County.*[306] Thus the bondholder would have what the special tax of 1/20 of 1 percent produced, *plus* whatever he might be able to collect out of the County's tax for general purposes. (On consulting the Chief Justice's Docket Book, and comparing with the division in Clark County, thirteen months before, Harlan now participated, and went with the majority; Bradley, Miller, and Waite maintained their position; and Field now came over to them.)

Obedient to the Court's judgment, on August 28, 1879, the county court gave Huidekoper a warrant on the general funds. It continued to levy the special tax of 1/20 of 1 percent—year after year until 1911, when the debt was finally compromised. Pursuant to other judgments, other such warrants on the general funds were issued, to Huidekoper and other bondholders.[307] The county officers, however, contrived to bar collection. There was a good deal of litigation. The County lost in an attempt to induce the Court to overrule its holding that the M. & M. bonds were payable out of general funds.[308] Huidekoper won a decision that the County could be compelled to levy taxes for the full 1/2 of 1 percent permitted by law; also that a pro rata distribution must be made among holders of warrants of even date, "whenever any reasonable amount has accumulated."[309]

The Missouri court, while insisting that "we adhere to the former rulings of this court," held that the mandamus of a federal Circuit Court directing the county court to issue warrants payable out of general revenue must be respected as the adjudication of a court of competent jurisdiction.[310]

In 1892 the Supreme Court denied, upon the authority of *United States ex rel. Huidekoper v. Macon County*[311] in 1879, a new application by a bondholder for an order to direct the levy of a special tax beyond the 1/20 of 1 percent fixed by statute.[312]

Meanwhile propositions for compromise were rejected by the voters—in 1879, 1894, and 1904, but with less determination as the years went by. A new generation succeeded to the Huidekoper claim. By a more and more artificial under-assessment of property for taxa-

---

[306] Supra, pp. 1090–91.

[307] Violette, *Missouri and Mississippi Railroad Debt*, 67 et seq.

[308] Macon County Court v. Huidekoper, 109 U.S. 229 (1883), infra, pp. 1097–98.

[309] Macon County Court v. United States *ex rel.* Huidekoper, 134 U.S. 332 (1890).

[310] State *ex rel.* Hudson v. Tram-

mel, County Treasurer of Macon County, 106 Mo. 510 (1891).

[311] 99 U.S. 582, supra, n. 305.

[312] United States *ex rel.* Jones v. Macon County Court, 144 U.S. 568. Per curiam statement by Fuller, C.J. Of those who had participated in the case relied upon, only Justice Field remained. Thomas K. Skinker and Joseph Shippen represented the applicant.

tion, and through the systematic circulation of warrants in place of money, the County managed to starve the bondholders, whose claim mounted to $2,150,000. In a suit in equity against the County Court, Clerk, Treasurer, and banks of Macon County, for conspiracy to defraud the bondholders, in 1911 the federal court—withholding the imposition of a judgment—suggested that the parties settle for $750,000, about 35 percent of the debt. An arrangement to settle on that basis was overwhelmingly approved by the voters.[313]

We take up the affairs of Harshman, the chief holder of Knox County bonds issued to the Missouri & Mississippi. He had the Circuit Court's mandamus for warrants on the County's general funds; Knox, like Clark and Macon, went to the Supreme Court.

Normally such a plaintiff in error would file a supersedeas bond, thereby causing the Circuit Court's judgment to be stayed pending the decision of the Supreme Court. By the Court's Rule 29, the amount of such bond "where the judgment or decree is for the recovery of money not otherwise secured, must be for the whole amount of the judgment or decree, including just damages for delay, and costs and interest on the appeal . . . ." Commonly where the county had lost in the Circuit Court, a considerable number of local citizens would sign the bond, which was subject to approval by the Judge.

In the Court's Minutes is an unusual entry which, when taken in context with newspaper reports and other items, explains what would otherwise be obscure. Harshman sought to enforce two judgments which together came to something over $10,000. By reason of objections to the bond given below, on December 2, 1879, the Court gave the County until "the first Monday in January next" to file a new bond in the amount of $20,000. But this time sureties could not be found.[314] Accordingly on January 27, 1879, on motion, it was ordered that the supersedeas be vacated. It followed that in February the County Court was directed to issue warrants to Harshman.

THE COTTEY ACT: THE LEGISLATURE SEEKS TO OBSTRUCT

SENATOR L. F. COTTEY of Knox was at that moment pushing through the legislature a measure calculated to arrest the execution of judgments. By the Cottey Act of March 8, 1879,[315] a county court should levy no taxes—other than State taxes and taxes for schools and current

---

[313] Violette, *Missouri and Mississippi Railroad Debt*, 65–93.

[314] *Missouri Republican*, Jan. 13, 1879.

[315] Laws 1879, p. 185.

county expenses—without an order of the Missouri circuit court, which order that court would grant only if satisfied that collection "will not conflict with the constitution and laws of this State." Any county officer offending would be liable to a fine of not less than $500 and loss of office. That would seriously clog the channel for collecting on municipal bonds, even if it were held that enforcement of a federal court's judgment would not conflict with the State's constitution and laws. And if it were held that examination of the grounds for such judgment was in order, then any one of the several points of disagreement between the federal and the State judiciary might be made a bar to collecting a tax.

A companion statute of March 19, 1879,[316] directed that the county revenue be apportioned into separate funds; not more than one-fifth of the total might be allowed for contingencies. The evident object was "to place [county revenues] beyond the reach of processes issued by United States courts for the payment of judgments on railroad bonds...."[317]

The Cottey Act was instantly challenged in matters pending in the Circuit Courts for the Eastern and Western Districts.[318] Circuit Judge Dillon and District Judges Treat and Krekel sat together, and early in April, 1879, the statute was held unconstitutional as interfering with the judicial powers of the United States and impairing the obligation of contracts.[319]

In Knox county, the members of the county court "now found themselves standing between two fires." "If the object of the legislature is to provoke a direct conflict between the judiciary of the State and that of the nation," it was reported, "it could hardly have devised a scheme that will more promptly accomplish that object." In Buchanan, Cape Girardeau, and other counties as well, the members of the county courts now had to decide what master they would serve. What was done in Knox, Senator Cottey's home county, would have great significance. Mass meetings throughout that county called for a refusal to obey the mandate of the federal court. "But the judges, after weighing the matter carefully, decided otherwise, and issued the warrant...."[320]

Harshman, and other judgment creditors holding warrants, now

---

316 Laws, 1879, p. 191.
317 Missouri Republican, June 4, 1879.
318 Missouri Republican, Mar. 13, Apr. 1, 8, 9, 1879.
319 United States ex rel. Foote v. Johnson County, Fed. Case No. 15,-489, W.D. Mo., and United States

ex rel. Douglass v. Lincoln County, Fed. Case No. 15,503, E.D. Mo. Infra, p. 1099.
320 Missouri Republican, Mar. 10, 11, 13, 19, 21, 1879; Violette, Mississippi and Missouri Railroad Debt, 47; Ann. Cyc. 1879, 645.

met other obstructions. The county collector would accept warrants in payment of taxes; a system developed whereby those paid in warrants for supplies and services marketed them to taxpayers, with the result that little money came into the treasury. Harshman brought an action against the collector and his sureties, to make them responsible for his inability to collect his warrants for over $10,000. The Court held, however, that the defendants were under no obligation to the County's creditor; moreover the County had settled with the collector and that was a discharge.[321]

The writ of error taken by Knox County in the matter of Harshman's demand for payment of his judgments out of general funds (in addition to the special five-mill tax), had been docketed on July 2, 1878. Three other cases presenting the same issue became companions with it. They were decided together on November 13, 1883, by affirmance of the judgments of the Circuit Court—simply by reference to what had already been decided on substantially the same issue in *Johnston v. Clark County* in 1878,[322] and then in *Huidekoper v. Macon County* in 1879.[323] A page sufficed for the Chief Justice's opinion.[324]

How could it have taken five years to attain this reaffirmation? By comparing the entries in the Minutes with the transformation in the membership of the Court at that period, one may reconstruct what transpired. On December 21, 1880, when in its turn *Harshman* was first heard, the majority that had decided *Johnston* and *Huidekoper* had disappeared: Justice Strong had resigned, Swayne was on the point of following; Clifford and Hunt were absent by reason of disability, and would never return. But the dissenters—Waite, Miller, and Bradley—remained. Almost a year later, on December 5, 1881, it was ordered that *Harshman* be reargued when the Court reached *Knox County v. United States ex rel. Davis*, a case presenting the same question, then far down on the docket. By this time, Justices Woods and Matthews had succeeded Strong and Swayne. By October 26, 1883, when *Harshman, Davis*, and three similar cases were argued, Justices Gray and Blatchford had succeeded Clifford and Hunt. Upon a new argument, would this Bench overrule what had twice been decided? The Chief Justice's Docket Book shows that when, in conference on

---

[321] State of Missouri *ex rel.* Harshman v. Winterbottom, 123 U.S. 215 (1877).

[322] United States *ex rel.* Johnston v. Clark County, 96 U.S. 211, supra, pp. 1090–91.

[323] United States *ex rel.* Huidekoper v. Macon County, 99 U.S. 582, supra, p. 1093.

[324] Knox County v. United States *ex rel.* Harshman; Same v. United States *ex rel.* Davis; Same v. United States *ex rel.* Wells; Macon County v. Huidekoper; Baker, Treasurer of Knox County v. United States *ex rel.* Davis, 109 U.S. 229.

November 5 the Justices were polled, the four newcomers, Harlan, and Field voted to affirm; Miller voted to reverse; blanks appear for Bradley and the Chief Justice—evidently they refrained from vain dissent. Hence the mode of expression by which the Chief Justice announced that *Harshman* and the companion cases were decided in accordance with the *Johnston* and *Huidekoper* decisions: "It was conceded in the argument that all the judgments now under consideration must be affirmed, unless these cases are overruled. This a majority of the Court are unwilling to do . . . ."

The Court has sometimes been held at fault for what is supposed to have been inexcusable delay. Such a reproach should be taken with caution: as in the incident above, there may have been an adequate reason.

SUCCESSIVE COUNTY POSITIONS ARE LOST

IN 1881, HARSHMAN had recovered a third judgment against Knox County on M. & M. bonds, this one for $77,374.46. In framing the petition in this instance, however, Thomas K. Skinker made a *new* allegation: that the bonds sued on had been issued pursuant to an election wherein two-thirds of the qualified voters had acted under the State's general railroad law. (The point was that if bonds were issued under *that* authority, *not* under the provisions of the M. & M. charter, they would have the benefit of this provision of the general law: that the county court should "levy a special tax . . . to be kept apart from other funds, and appropriated to no other purpose than the payment of such subscription.") The recital on the face of the bonds, however, declared that they were issued under the authority granted in the M. & M. charter.

Inasmuch as the County did not deny the debt—(which it supposed could be collected only out of the five-mill tax authorized in the M. & M. charter)—it suffered judgment by default. This was on March 28, 1881.

When thereupon Harshman sought mandamus to compel the levy of a tax sufficient to pay his judgment, allegedly recovered on the basis of the general railroad law—and the County Court made return admitting the debt but denying that it rested upon other authority than the charter *as recited in the bonds*—the Circuit Court must decide whether this was a sufficient return. Circuit Judge McCrary and District Judge Treat concluded that, under these circumstances,

> we are at liberty to look into the terms of the contract upon which the relator's judgment was rendered, and if there is a variance be-

tween the contract and the allegations of the petition, we will presume in favor of the contract until it is shown that the recitals therein were the result of mistake or inadvertence. . . .

Accordingly judgment was for the County.[325]

Harshman's counsel, Skinker and Henderson, went to the Supreme Court and, four years later, won a reversal. The Court, per Matthews, J., held that, in allowing judgment to go by default the County had admitted what the petition alleged—that these bonds had been issued under the general railroad law.[326] While no dissent was recorded, the Chief Justice's Docket Book shows that, in conference, Blatchford and Miller voted to affirm.[327]

A suit by the County to go back and set aside the default judgment on the ground that proper service had not been made—a wholly unmeritorious contention—resulted in a denial by the Supreme Court in 1890.[328]

At the end of its rope, the County arranged to pay by installments. Harshman's judgment for some $77,000 was satisfied in 1884: with interest it came to about $135,000. By a compromise accepted that year, while "voted bonds" were paid at par, "unvoted bonds" were paid at sixty-five cents. Harshman's earlier judgments for some $10,000, with interest, were settled for about $20,000. Refunding bonds were issued, and in 1899 were liquidated, with the customary ceremony on burning the last bond.[329]

The Cottey Act of March 8, 1879, had been held invalid by the Circuit Court one month after enactment, as was recounted above.[330] This was in a suit by Joseph M. Douglass against Lincoln County.[331] That and two other cases from Lincoln, and two from Ralls County, were carried to the Supreme Court and decided together on May 8, 1882. On that occasion the Chief Justice said: "all laws which have been passed since the bonds were issued, purporting to take away from the

---

[325] United States *ex rel.* Harshman v. County Court of Knox County, 15 Fed. 704. C.C.E.D. Mo., Mar. 23, 1883.

[326] Harshman v. Knox County, 122 U.S. 306. May 27, 1887.

[327] And Dillon, in revising his *Law of Municipal Corporations*, inserted a note to argue that the Court had misapplied the principle of estoppel: the question of the extent of the county court's power and duty to levy a tax arose for the first time in the mandamus proceeding. 5th ed., sec. 1508,

note 1.

[328] Knox County v. Harshman, 133 U.S. 152.

[329] Violette, *Mississippi and Missouri Railroad Debt*, 56–63.

[330] Supra, p. 1096.

[331] United States *ex rel.* Douglass v. Lincoln County Court, Fed. Case No. 15,503, C.C.E.D. Mo., Apr. 7, 1879. At the same time the same bench decided a parallel case from the Western District, United States *ex rel.* Foote v. Johnson County, Fed. Case No. 15,489.

county courts the power to levy taxes necessary to meet the payments, are invalid . . . ."[332] Without specific mention, the Cottey Act was thus brushed aside.

This instance illustrates a quality for which Chief Justice Waite was outstanding. Thanks to simple good sense and courtesy, he avoided any needless utterance, any intrusion of personality, susceptible of arousing resentment. The Circuit Judge had already demonstrated wherein the statute was invalid. What Waite said was adequate for the occasion, without further inflaming the Court's relations with Missouri.

In *State ex rel. Cramer, Prosecuting Attorney v. Hager et al., Judges of Cape Girardeau County Court*,[333] the Missouri court sustained an injunction against the collection of a tax ordered by the federal court, where the procedure prescribed by the Cottey Act had not been followed. Sherwood, J., undertook to show that the change in remedy did not "essentially affect the right embodied in the contract."[334] This opinion was delivered on March 21, 1887. But when on May 27, 1887, the Supreme Court decided *Seibert, Collector of Cape Girardeau County v. United States ex rel. Lewis, Administrator of the Estate of Elisha Foote*,[335] Matthews, J., said "we are unable to concur" in the Missouri court's view. The bonds had been issued under the Township Aid Act, where it was provided specifically that a special tax would be collected "in the same manner as county taxes . . .": but the Cottey Act directed that taxes to pay bonds must be treated in a different manner from other county taxes. "It is in this vital point that the obligation of the contract with the relator has been impaired . . . ."

---

[332] Ralls County Court v. United States *ex rel.* Douglass, 105 U.S. 733.

[333] 91 Mo. 452 (1887).

[334] Judge Sherwood would not yield ground to the federal judiciary. In 1881—in a case in which the Cottey Act was not involved—his brethren held that where a county court, obeying the mandamus of a federal court, had levied a tax, the State judiciary would not interfere, notwithstanding that the federal court's judgment enforced bonds which in the eyes of the State judiciary were invalid. State *ex rel.* Wilson v. Rainey, 74 Mo. 229. This was an action between a county collector and a recalcitrant taxpayer, growing out of a tax levied in 1878; the taxpayer had been following the Rush Clark theory on which Iowans had once vainly relied. Clark v. Wolf,

29 Iowa 197 (1870), supra, p. 985. The Missouri court cited and followed that case. Sherwood, C.J. dissented:

when [the federal courts] render judgments on bonds which our laws, and our constitution, as expounded by us, pronounce void, . . . I will not so far bow the knee to Federal usurpation as to become an aider and abettor in the collection of what I regard, and what this court have said are unlawful and unjust claims. . . . Henceforth, a Federal court with a State court attachment, will trample our laws and our constitution into the dust and accomplish the realization of the wildest dreams of the lovers of consolidated power!

[335] 122 U.S. 284.

Thereafter the Missouri court, in cases on bonds antedating the Cottey Act, bowed without question to the Supreme Court's decision.[336]

RETROSPECT

HERE ENDS THE examination of decisions on railroad aid bonds. The selection—superabundant though it may seem—has been confined to a fraction of the cases, exposing some of the major problems as they arose in a few States most deeply involved. Enough has been set forth to support a judgment on the work of the Court.

Gelpcke v. Dubuque has been put in its setting. Opinions may differ whether, given the circumstances, the Court did well to rule as it did in that case. But certainly it must be faulted for those advances beyond that position that have now been recounted. Preoccupation with the protection of bondholders caused a majority of the Justices to be insensitive to all other considerations in these complex situations. What is more, slovenly work concealed egregious deviations even from professed principles. It would be unwarranted to say that at any rate the Court was enforcing common honesty. So simple an explanation would ignore the misrepresentation, fraud, and illegality that often procured a bond issue, and the carelessness or the sharp discount that commonly attended a purchase.

Eventually this wasteful experience ran its course. The regularity and confidence essential to sound municipal borrowing was attained by such developments as the rise of bond counsel, and prudent inquiry into the legality, feasibility and public support of a proposed issue. One cannot say that this flowed directly from teachings inculcated by the Court. Rather it came to be realized that even after a bondholder had pursued to the end the remedies afforded by the federal judiciary, he might at long last be brought to a negotiated settlement with an indignant community.

"PUBLIC PURPOSE"—*LOAN ASSOCIATION v. TOPEKA*

THAT MUNICIPAL AID was not allowed to spread from railroads to other privately owned enterprises was largely the result of the Supreme Court's decision in *Loan Association v. Topeka*, in 1875.[337]

"The city of Topeka, young and ambitious capital of a growing

---

[336] State *ex rel.* Hamilton v. Hannibal & St. Joseph R.R., 113 Mo. 297

(1893); State *ex rel.* Scotland County v. Ewing, 116 Mo. 129 (1893).
[337] 20 Wall. 655.

western State, desirous to maintain its supremacy and to achieve the ascendancy over its rival sister competitors, seeks to develop a manufacturing interest within its limits; seeks to obtain the prestige of fostering the largest manufacturing establishment of its kind in the Union": so ran the brief filed by counsel for the Citizens' Savings and Loan Association of Cleveland, Ohio. To that end, upon vote of the people, Topeka gave $100,000 in bonds to the King Wrought-Iron Bridge Manufactory in consideration of its undertaking to establish a factory there. That enterprise was the work of Zenas King of Cleveland, who in 1871 had reorganized it as a corporation, "in which he enlisted the cooperation of a number of leading Cleveland capitalists and others of prominence in industrial affairs."[338]

Topeka had acted in accord with a statute of 1872 authorizing cities "to encourage the establishment of manufactories and such other enterprises as may tend to develop and improve such city . . . ."

When, after the first year's interest had been met, Topeka ceased payment, suit was brought in the Circuit Court for Kansas.[339]

Impatient Iola, eighty miles to the south, had not waited for authority: it had gone ahead with an election, and then in 1871 the legislature had passed a statute, reciting and legalizing the election and authorizing the city to issue bonds to the amount of $50,000 to erect buildings to be used in manufacturing Zenas King's iron bridges, and as a foundry and iron works.

Commercial National Bank of Cleveland v. Iola in the Circuit Court for Kansas was an action on coupons attached to these bonds.[340] It became an addendum to the Supreme Court's decision in the *Topeka* case.[341]

The question in *Iola*, said Circuit Judge Dillon, was

Whether the legislature may thus compel or coerce the citizen to aid in the establishment of purely private enterprises or objects because

---

[338] Wm. R. Coates, *A History of Cuyahoga County and the City of Cleveland* (Chicago and New York: American Historical Society, 1924), III, 75–7. King (1818–92), born in Vermont, had left the farm to seek opportunity in Ohio. His wrought iron bridge, for which he held patents (see King v. Hammond, Fed. Case No. 7797, C.C.N.D. Ohio, 1871) came to be used for "spanning rivers and minor streams in all parts of the country, from Maine to Texas." *Cleveland Plain Dealer*, Oct. 26, 1892. At the time of the *Loan Association* decision, the company was manu-

facturing "over three hundred spans each year," and had annual sales of "nearly a million dollars." William Payne, *Cleveland Illustrated; A Pictorial Handbook* (Cleveland: Fairbanks, Benedict & Co., 1876), 181.

[339] Citizens' Sav. Assn. v. Topeka, Fed. Case No. 2734, C.C.D. Kan. decided June 11, 1874. It was alleged that it was after such payment of interest that plaintiff became owner of the bonds and coupons, for value.

[340] Fed. Case No. 3061, C.C.D. Kan., decided June 6, 1873.

[341] 154 U.S. 617; 22 L. Ed. 463; 14 S. Ct. 1199.

these will or may incidentally promote the general good of the community or locality. . . .

He answered that the courts were all agreed that taxation could be only for a *public* purpose; he concluded that although railroads had generally been held to meet that test, certainly a factory did not. Judgment was for the defendant.

At that moment, it was estimated, "over $2,000,000 of bonds had been issued in Kansas to aid private enterprises, such as hotels, manufactories, etc., and . . . preparations to issue large amounts of similar bonds were making."[342] In raw Western communities the urge to enter into this sort of promotion was compelling. One notes the responsibility a federal Judge bore in putting a stop to it.

Topeka, when coupons next fell due after the *Iola* decision, declined to pay, and presently the Savings and Loan Association brought suit. This presented squarely the validity of the statute of 1872. Judge Dillon held for the defendant, on the authority of *Iola*.

In November 1874 the *Topeka* and *Iola* cases were docketed in the Supreme Court. Counsel agreed to submit on printed briefs. This is not surprising: the issue was clean cut; the Justices were familiar with the ground; and by submitting without oral argument, the cases would have prompt attention.

Alfred Ennis, for the banks, argued

> It is *not* claimed that there is any constitutional *restriction* or *limitation* upon the legislature of the State of Kansas prohibiting the enactment of the laws under consideration. *No* constitutional provision *has been pointed out* which these laws *infringe or are repugnant to. No such provision exists.*
>
> The judiciary, a co-ordinate branch of the government, possessing *no greater* or *higher powers* than the legislative department, *cannot* declare a legislative enactment invalid for any cause, *except* that such enactment infringe or be repugnant to the State or Federal constitution.[343]

There followed some seventy quotations, reinforced by a host of additional references, to the effect that judges may not nullify a statute "on the vague ground that they think it opposed to a general latent spirit supposed to pervade or underlie the constitution";[344] "it is necessary that we be pointed to the clause";[345] "we must be able to lay our finger

---

[342] Note to Citizens' Sav. Assn. v. Topeka, Fed. Case No. 2734 (1874).

[343] Argument of Alfred Ennis for Plaintiff in Error, 23.

[344] Walker v. Cincinnati, 21 Ohio St. 14, 41 (1871).

[345] Stockton & Visalia R.R. v. Stockton, 41 Cal. 147, 162 (1871).

on the part of the constitution violated."[346] Judge Dillon's opinion he deprecated as being

> the Archimedean lever, with which the effort is being made to lift the great weight of the bona fide bonded indebtedness from off these *would-be-honest*, but over *self*-burthened cities.[347]

Counsel for Topeka, replying, said that

> In Kansas, where the line between legislative and judicial authority is not yet definitely settled, we have many illustrations to show that all enactments, though called laws, are not so, even where no constitutional provision, express in its terms, has been violated.[348]

Kansas, unlike most States, had in its constitution no provision to the effect that private property may not be taken for public use without just compensation; and, the brief continued, of course the like provision in the federal Bill of Rights did not apply to the States. Did it result that a statute authorizing private property so to be taken could be sustained? Surely not. "That taxes can only be levied for public purposes seems to be too well settled to require any extended argument." Then

> Who shall determine what is a public purpose? The Courts. It is essentially a judicial question. . . .[349]

Submitted on December 8, 1874, *Topeka* and *Iola* were considered at the Saturday conference (the twelfth). The Chief Justice recorded in his Docket Book that Hunt and Clifford voted to reverse—all others to affirm. The writing of an opinion was assigned to Justice Miller. On February 1 it was read from the Bench.

He took hold with that firm grasp that marked his treatment of a case where some fundamental of government was to be vindicated. The question was "not new," nor was it "difficult of solution." The courts of almost every State had considered the validity of taxation for railroad aid; universally it had been recognized that the critical issue was whether this was for a *public purpose*. "[T]he strongest advocates for the validity of these laws never placed it on the ground of the unlimited power of the State Legislature to tax the people"; it had always been recognized that a tax "purely in aid of private or personal objects" would be an "unauthorized invasion of private rights."

Then came this classic passage:

---

[346] Tyler v. The People, 8 Mich. 320, 333 (1860).
[347] Argument, 58.
[348] Argument of Ross Burns and A.

L. Williams for Defendant in Error, 10.
[349] Ibid., 12.

It must be conceded that there are such rights in every free government beyond the control of the State. A government which recognized no such rights, which held the lives, the liberty and the property of its citizens subject at all times to the absolute disposition and unlimited control of even the most democratic depository of power, is after all but a despotism. It is true it is a despotism of the many, of the majority, if you choose to call it so, but it is none the less a despotism. . . .

The theory of our governments, state and national, is opposed to the deposit of unlimited power anywhere. The executive, the legislative and the judicial branches of these governments are all of limited and defined powers.

There are limitations on such power which grow out of the essential nature of all free governments. Implied reservations of individual rights, without which the social compact could not exist, and which are respected by all governments entitled to the name. No court, for instance, would hesitate to declare void a statute which enacted that A and B who were husband and wife to each other should be so no longer, but that A should thereafter be the husband of C, and B the wife of D. Or which would enact that the homestead now owned by A should no longer be his, but should henceforth be the property of B.

So, too, of taxation: "To lay, with one hand, the power of the government on the property of the citizen, and with the other to bestow it upon favored individuals to aid private enterprises and build up private fortunes" was "not legislation" but only "a decree under legislative forms."

In the case at hand, there was "no difficulty in holding" that a gift to attract a bridge company was not for a public purpose. "No line can be drawn in favor of the manufacturer which would not open the coffers of the public treasury to the importunities of two-thirds of the business men of the city or town."

Two recent decisions "by courts of the highest character" illustrated this proposition. In *Allen v. Inhabitants of Jay*,[350] in 1872, the Supreme Judicial Court of Maine had enjoined the collection of a tax to attract a factory to the town. And in *Lowell v. Boston*,[351] in 1873, the Massachusetts court held invalid a statute, enacted after the Boston fire of 1872, authorizing the city to issue bonds to be loaned to owners of land burned over, to enable them to rebuild. (In each State there were pertinent constitutional provisions, not present in the Kansas constitution: and yet, Justice Miller might have remarked, the Maine and Massachusetts courts treated those provisions as illustrative of a fundamental principle, rather than as directly controlling the decision.)

---

[350] 60 Me. 124.   [351] 111 Mass. 454.

Justice Clifford dissented. "Except where the Constitution has imposed limits upon the legislative power, the rule of law appears to be, that the power of legislation must be considered as practically absolute . . . . [I]n my judgment, there is much more to be dreaded from judicial decisions which may have the effect to sanction the fraudulent repudiation of honest debts, than from any statutes passed by the State to enable municipal corporations to meet and discharge their just pecuniary obligations."

Clifford's dutiful mind recoiled from the large style Miller sometimes displayed in dealing with fundamental issues.[352]

SOME RELATED CASES

THE LOAN ASSOCIATION's suit had been brought in the federal court and carried to the Supreme Court, simply on the basis of diversity of citizenship, not by reason of any claim under the Constitution or laws of the United States. Although the opinion applied what Miller later referred to as "principles of general constitutional law,"[353] the Court was speaking as the State court might well have done if the issue had arisen there; no provision in the Constitution of the United States was considered, nor anything in the constitution of Kansas. The courts of that State had not passed upon municipal aid to private industry: there was no such ruling to consider. In time, however, the proposition that taxation can be only for a public purpose came to be embraced within the Fourteenth Amendment's protection. Then the taxpayer could assert that as a federal right, as against the government of his own State.[354]

Very shortly after *Loan Association* was decided, the Supreme Court of Kansas did have occasion to pass upon a somewhat similar problem.

In 1874 an invasion of grasshoppers brought desolation to western Kansas, where settlers had scarcely established themselves. Then a severe winter left farmers generally in financial straits. What relief the State should afford was the great question before the legislature. On February 1, the day that *Loan Association* was announced, a member

---

[352] Consider Crandall v. Nevada, infra, pp. 1302–07, in this connection.

[353] In Davidson v. New Orleans, 96 U.S. 97, 105 (1877), explaining *Loan Association*.

[354] Jones v. City of Portland, 245 U.S. 217 (1917), reviewing the decision of the Supreme Judicial Court of Maine; Green v. Frazier, 253 U.S. 233 (1920), from the Supreme Court of North Dakota; Milheim v. Moffat Tunnel Improvement Dist., 262 U.S. 710 (1923), from the Supreme Court of Colorado. Allbritton v. City of Winona, 303 U.S. 627 (1938), where an appeal from the Supreme Court of Mississippi was "dismissed for the want of a substantial federal question," will be noticed infra, p. 1113.

was saying in the House at Topeka that while he supported relief legislation, he feared that

> There are many people who . . . when they have enjoyed all its benefits, raise a howl against those who voted bonds. Our experience in railroad bonds ought to teach us something. The most blatant demagogues who had howled themselves hoarse in favor of repudiating railroad bonds, were the men who had caused them to be saddled upon the people. He had hopes for the future of the state. We had from the first been subject to trial. The motto of our state seal is appropriate—*Ad astra per aspera*. But we shall yet come out all right.[355]

One measure of relief that became law on February 20, 1875, authorized townships, upon an election, to issue bonds and levy taxes for relief purposes. On March 8 the Township of Osawkee [now Ozawkie] in Jefferson county voted to issue $6,000 in relief bonds. (This was not in the grasshopper county: it was twenty miles northeast of Topeka, and less than forty from the eastern boundary.) Taxpayers sued to enjoin further action; losing in the district court, they went to Supreme Court at Topeka.

Brewer, J., spoke for the court.[356] [This is David J. Brewer, who in 1889 became a Justice of the Supreme Court.[357]] The purpose of the statute, he observed, was not to provide food for the hungry or clothing for the naked:

> It contemplates a class who have fields to till and stock to care for, and purposes to help them with seed for their fields and grain for their stock, that thus they may pursue with better prospects of success their ordinary avocations. It taxes the whole community to assist one class, and that not for the purpose of relieving actual want, but to assist them in their regular occupations. . . .

On the basis of the propositions laid down in *Loan Association v. Topeka*, and in cases there cited, this was unconstitutional.[358]

---

[355] *Topeka Commonwealth*, Feb. 2, 1875. In the same issue the decision in *Loan Association* was announced, as learned from Mr. Ennis. The text of the two opinions was published on February 25.

[356] State *ex rel.* Griffith v. Osawkee Township, 14 Kan. 418. Jan. term 1875.

[357] Brewer (1837–1910), nephew of Justice Field, had read law with David Dudley Field and at the Albany Law School. Coming to Kansas, he sat on inferior courts, on the State Supreme Court for fourteen years, and as federal Circuit Judge from 1884 until his appointment to the Supreme Court.

[358] This was followed by similar decisions where Brewer, J., spoke: McConnel v. Hamm, Treasurer, 16 Kan. 228 (1876), and Central Branch, Union Pacific R.R. v. Smith, Treasurer, 23 Kan. 745 (1880).

At the next term after *Loan Association*, on January 4, 1876, Alfred Ennis submitted to the Court the case of *Otis v. Cullum*.[359] Frank A. Otis & Co. had purchased eighteen of Topeka's $1,000 bonds for $12,852. Now judgment was sought against the seller (the Topeka bank, of which Cullum was receiver) for failure of consideration. The Court denied recovery: the purchasers had gotten exactly what they intended to buy; the seller had given no warranty, nor acted in bad faith.

The unreported case of *Caroline A. Brough v. City of Topeka*, No. 811 at October term 1879, was, as Justice Bradley noted on his copy of the transcript, "brought to reverse Loan Assn v. Topeka No opinion." On December 1, 1879, the same counsel as in *Loan Association* submitted on their respective printed arguments. At conference on Saturday, the sixth, all save Swayne and Clifford voted to affirm the decision of the Circuit Court. On Monday, December 8, 1879, the Chief Justice announced that judgment. No opinion was filed.

A CAVEAT ON DOCTRINAL INTERPRETATION

ALONG WITH BEING cited and applied by many courts, *Loan Association* has received marked attention in refined intellectual circles. Perhaps Justice Miller would be a little surprised. By the Chief Justice's designation, he had a splendid opportunity: so to express the Court's decision as most effectively to arrest the tendency to bond and tax in order to subsidize manufactories. Jurisdiction resting only on diversity of citizenship, his function here was to speak as a judge of the State court might speak. Appleton, C.J., in *Allen v. Inhabitants of Jay*,[360] had said at the outset, "Taxation, by the very meaning of the term, implies the raising of money for public uses, and excludes the raising if for private objects and purposes." Wells, J., in *Lowell v. Boston*,[361] had said that "this distinction is fundamental. It underlies all government that is based upon reason . . . ." The text of the constitutions was confirmatory.

Miller expressed the same thought, in the vernacular to which he and his contemporaries had been accustomed in their formative years. Kentucky's constitution of 1799, under which his political ideas had been formed, opened its Bill of Rights with this affirmation:

> That the general, great, and essential principles of liberty and free government may be recognized and established, we declare:
> Section 1. That all free men, when they form a social compact, are equal . . . .

---

[359] 92 U.S. 447 (1876).   [360] Supra, n. 350.   [361] Supra, n. 351.

The article closed with the statement that everything contained therein was "excepted out of the general powers of government . . . ."

In each of the two constitutions of Iowa under which he had lived, the Bill of Rights concluded with a pregnant reservation:

> This enumeration of rights shall not be construed to impair or deny others, retained by the people.

"Implied reservations of individual rights, without which the social compact could not exist, and which are respected by all governments entitled to the name" was, then, no more than a striking expression of what had been axiomatic.

A just government did not lodge absolute power anywhere. This came down in a noble tradition from the mother country—from *Dr. Bonham's Case*,[362] from Locke's *Second Treatise on Government*, and the like. It had been cherished by the colonists, to whom a statute "against common right, as well as against magna charta" was void,[363] and in the early years of the republic, as evidenced by many affirmations such as Marshall's in *Fletcher v. Peck*, that the State was restrained "either by general principles which are common to our free institutions, or by the particular provisions of the Constitution of the United States."[364]

"Principles of general constitutional law," and the specific guaranties of the State's Bill of Rights, belonged in one universe of thought—as becomes evident if the matter is considered reflectively.[365]

---

[362] 8 Rep. 118a (1610), where Lord Coke had uttered the dictum that "when an act of parliament is against common right and reason, . . . the common law will control it and adjudge such act to be void."

[363] Bowman v. Middleton, 1 Bay (S.C.) 252 (1792), with respect to an Act of Assembly of 1712.

[364] 6 Cranch (1810). All this is traced in Edward S. Corwin's "The 'Higher Law' Background of American Constitutional Law," *Harv L. Rev.*, 42:149 and 365 (1928, 1929).

[365] Compare two New York opinions, eight years apart.

In 1835, Judge Samuel Nelson wrote:
> We have no bill of rights [in the constitution of 1821]; though many of the principles usually found in such an instrument are incorporated in the provisions of the Constitution. The enumeration was designedly omitted, because unnecessary, and tending to weaken, if not endanger those unnoticed. . . . It is now considered an universal and fundamental proposition, in every well regulated and properly administered government, whether embodied in a constitutional form or not, that private property cannot be taken for strictly private purposes at all, nor for public without a just compensation . . . . These and other vested rights are held sacred and inviolable, even against the plenitude of power of the Legislative Department. . . .

The People v. Morris, 13 Wendell 325. In the result, no statute was invalidated.

In 1843, the same court derived a like restraint from the very words of New York's constitution. The grant of "legislative power" should be read

In the opening part of his opinion in *Sharpless*, Black, C.J., had said categorically that "the words of the constitution furnish the only test" and that "all arguments, based on general principles outside of the constitution, must be addressed to the people, and not to us." But in a moment he was saying, "neither has the legislature any constitutional right . . . to lay a tax, or to authorize any municipal corporation to do it, in order to raise funds for a mere *private* purpose. . . . Taxation is a mode of raising revenue for *public* purposes. When it is prostituted to objects in no way connected with the public interests or welfare, it ceases to be taxation, and becomes plunder."[366] What he had repelled at the door had flown in at the window.

Presently it was recognized that the Fourteenth Amendment in its amplitude secured the individual from being taxed for any purpose not "public"[367]—and so this "principle of general constitutional law" became anchored to a constitutional text.

It has sometimes been remarked with an inflection of surprise that in *Loan Association* no reference was made to the Fourteenth Amendment. It was scarce two years since the Court had first had occasion to consider that new ordering of relationships; initial contact had exposed a dilemma—the Court might give it too little meaning, or too much.[368] How injudicious it would have been, then, to draw the Amendment into the *Topeka* case and to intimate what application it might have. The City had won below, and now stood on its victory; its

---

as limited by principles of justice; it did not extend to "despotic power." The court went on to find additional support in the constitution's guaranties that rights would not be taken "unless by the law of the land" or taken "without due process of law." In particular, a statute authorizing a private road to be laid over privately owned land without the owner's consent was held invalid. Taylor v. Porter, 4 Hill 140.

In the famous case of Wynehamer v. The People, 13 N.Y. 378 (1856), compare the rejection of the suggestion "that there exists in the judiciary some vague, loose and undefined power to annul a law" on grounds of natural equity and justice (Selden, J., at 430; similarly Comstock, J., at 391), with what was later found to be the "plain and obvious meaning" of the constitution's due process clause. (Comstock at 398, Selden at 434).

[366] Sharpless v. Mayor of Philadelphia, 21 Pa. St. 147, 162, 168–69 (1853). Supra, pp. 927–29.

[367] As Justice Stone pointed out, speaking for the Court in Carmichael v. Southern Coal & Coke Co., 301 U.S. 495, 515 (1937), citing cases, when it was held that that test had been met by Alabama's tax to create an Unemployment Compensation Fund: in the light of the nation's recent experience it was now clear that relief of unemployment had become a public purpose.

[368] *Slaughter-House Cases*, 16 Wall. 36 (1873), infra, 1349–60. The word "dilemma" reflects the language of Stone, J., in Colgate v. Harvey, 296 U.S. 404, 445 (1935), and of Jackson, J., in Edwards v. California, 314 U.S. 160, 183 (1941). They were referring to the Privileges and Immunities Clause, which was the feature chiefly considered in *Slaughter-House*.

counsel made no suggestion that it had or needed any protection from the Amendment. For the Court, it sufficed to speak as the Kansas court might speak—and as it did, per Brewer, J., a few weeks later.

It would wrench Miller's words out of historical context to imagine him to have been a forerunner of the defenders of economic laissez faire, on the Court and in the country, in the latter part of the nineteenth century and for nearly four decades of the twentieth. He was affirming that no man should be taxed—not even by vote of the majority—to make a lure for private businesses. He maintained, as he had said in a dissent (Chase, C.J., and Field, J., concurring)—

> We do not believe that any legislative body, sitting under a State constitution of the usual character, has a right to sell, to give, or to bargain away forever the taxing power of the State. . . .
>
> The result of such a principle, under the growing tendency to special and partial legislation, would be, to exempt the rich from taxation, and cast all the burden of the support of government, and the payment of its debts, on those who are too poor or too honest to purchase such immunity.[369]

In *Woodson v. Murdock*[370] a few weeks prior to *Loan Association*, the majority of the Court had given effect to a Missouri statute whereby, in consideration of a payment of $5,000,000, the Pacific Railroad was released from the lien for a much larger indebtedness to the State, notwithstanding a provision in the constitution of 1865:

> The general assembly shall have no power, for any purpose whatever, to release the lien held by the State upon any railroad.

Justice Miller (and Davis, J.) dissenting, had said, in part,

> of what avail are constitutional restrictions of legislative power, or legislative restrictions of municipal power, if they are disregarded by the Legislatures and municipalities?

. . . .

---

[369] Washington University v. Rouse, 8 Wall. 439, 443 (1869). Home of the Friendless v. Rouse, 8 Wall. 430, was decided with it. The Court, reversing the judgments of the Supreme Court of Missouri, had construed charter provisions for exemption from taxation as contracts for perpetual exemption, within the protection of the Contract Clause.

In New Jersey v. Yard, 95 U.S. 104, 114 (1877), he reiterated that as his personal view.

[370] 22 Wall. 351, decided Nov. 16, 1874.

Some decades earlier, Woodson—a lawyer, and now Governor of Missouri—and Miller—then a physician, and now a Justice of the Supreme Court—had shared a log cabin office in the village of Barbourville, Kentucky. They had participated in the local debating society, where "the rights which are respected by all governments entitled to the name" had been thoroughly discussed.

These instruments . . . , supposed to be the peculiar pride of the American people, and the great bulwark to personal and public rights, must fall rapidly into disrepute if they are found to be efficient only for the benefit of the rich and powerful, and the absolute majority on any subject will seek to enforce their views without regard to those restrictions on legislative power which are used only to their prejudice.

Only by "the ingenuity of casuists and linguists"—Miller's phrase, in *Woodson v. Murdock*—could expressions used in *Loan Association* be made to place him in incongruous association with later Justices to whom "liberty of contract" prevailed over the enactments of a legislature.[371]

---

[371] To one most influential scholarly exponent of conservatism, the opinion in *Loan Association* seemed highly objectionable. William Graham Sumner (1840–1910), professor of political and social science at Yale, heard of Loan Association v. Topeka from David A. Wells (1828–98), opponent of the protective tariff and economic advisor to President Cleveland. They met on a train in 1887, and Wells unfolded to Sumner his desire to contrive a suit that would test before the Supreme Court the constitutionality of the protective tariff; he hoped that *Loan Association* would lead to a decision that it was unconstitutional to tax consumers, beyond the needs of the Government, in order to give a subsidy to producers. On returning to New Haven, Sumner read the *Loan Association* opinion, and then wrote:
Dear Wells,
I looked up Topeka vs Loan, & I must say it rather took my breath away. I do not consider it a sound decision at all. It is an outgrowth of this extra-legal way of looking at things of wh. the Sup. Ct has shown several examples within 10 yrs. The Court is trying to do abstract justice—to set things right generally. I do not believe in it. I go with Clifford in his dissent. The Court has no right to bring in great *a priori* principles wh. underlie all free gov'ts. They only deal with laws & constitutions. This time it makes for us.

Next time it will make for others. We may, however, properly play this card for all it is worth. I hope you will bring it out in relation to the tariff. I am sure that the answer of the Ct if called on to decide a tariff case wd be what I told you on the cars. A bigoted republican like Miller, cutting loose from written law, & finding whatever he wants to find in the great underlying principles of free gov't can easily squirm out of any application of his own doctrines wh. he does not like. . . .
Sumner's conclusion was, "There is enough in it for a splendid contest on one side, but the Sup Ct wd never face the question of declaring the tariff unconst." Letter of June 6 or 7, 1887. Wells Papers, L.C.
The idea of "implied reservations of individual rights, without which the social compact could not exist," belonged among the "speculative assumptions and dogmatic deductions" which Sumner found pernicious. *Folkways* (Boston: Ginn and Co., 1906), 33. Applying Darwinian methods to the study of the ways of primitive peoples, Sumner saw social institutions as the gradual product of painful adjustment. In the mature work, *The Science of Society*, 4 vols. (New Haven, Conn.: Yale University Press, 1927) by Sumner and A. G. Keller, it was pointed out that "No person but an *a priori* theorizer would wish to assert that

"PUBLIC PURPOSE" RESPONDS TO THE TIMES

IN 1936 MISSISSIPPI adopted its Balance Agriculture With Industry Plan. The legislature authorized municipalities to tax for the purchase of land and the construction of buildings to be leased to private manufacturers—the object being to relieve unemployment and promote economic welfare. The State court sustained the statute, distinguishing *Loan Association*, and saying "We must not permit ourselves to be subjected to the tyranny of symbols"—such as the charge that it was "a step towards socialism"—nor be guided "by what Dean Pound designates as 'an idealized political picture of the existing social order.' " This was in *Albritton v. City of Winona*.[372] An appeal to the Supreme Court was "dismissed for want of a substantial federal question."[373]

From this beginning came municipal financing of industrial development now permitted in more than half of the States. By statute, after constitutional amendment where that was needed, local govern-

---

peoples have been moved by . . . rational considerations to establish government and authorities. The reason that such arrangements embody is the rationality of any product of evolution that represents expedient adjustment . . . ." "Law, as we view it, is a sort of crystalization or precipitation of the mores." I, 460, 653.

But Sumner was the defender of "The Forgotten Man," representative of "the sober, honest, industrious, economical men and women, who attend no meetings, pass no resolutions, never go to the lobby, are never mentioned in the newspapers, but just work and save and pay." Sumner, *The Forgotten Man and Other Essays* (New Haven, Conn.: Yale University Press, 1911); H. E. Starr, *William Graham Sumner* (New York: Henry Holt and Co., 1925), 287. And surely Miller, in *Loan Association*, in Washington University v. Rouse, and in Woodson v. Murdock, supra, was also speaking for "the forgotten man."

The late Professor Robert G. McCloskey's *American Conservatism in the Age of Enterprise* (Cambridge, Mass.: Harvard University Press,

1951) deals perceptively with Sumner as "the schoolmaster, the grammarian," of that tradition.

Returning to Wells' and Sumner's desire to challenge the protective tariff before the Supreme Court: the "flexible tariff" provision in the Act of 1922 afforded an opportunity to resist payment of an increment specifically to enable domestic producers to compete on terms of equality with foreign producers in the American market. In J. W. Hampton, Jr., & Co. v. United States, 276 U.S. 394 (1928), it was held that this declared motive did not render the tax unconstitutional. Speaking for the Court was Chief Justice Taft—who remembered Sumner as the teacher who "had more to do with stimulating my mental activities" than any other. It is said that "Taft, for a little while, wondered whether Sumner might not be right" about the tariff. Henry F. Pringle, *The Life and Times of William Howard Taft*, 2 vols. (New York: Farrar and Rinehart, 1939), I, 34.

[372] 181 Miss. 75 (1938).

[373] W. S. Allbritton *et al.* v. City of Winona, Mississippi, 303 U.S. 627 (1938).

ments have been authorized to issue bonds and with the proceeds to acquire facilities to be leased to private corporations, in order to bring new industry to the community and thereby increase employment and promote economic stability.

Test cases have been concerned with issues of State constitutional law, chiefly of "public purpose." Abuse might, of course, give rise to some "substantial federal question" in the future.

Thus a new form of municipal bonding, of enormous magnitude, was set on foot—a century after the disastrous experiences examined in the two foregoing chapters. To point to similarity and contrast, mention will be made only of the region with which those chapters were chiefly concerned.

In Nebraska, a project to acquire a packing plant for lease was in 1957 held impermissible as not for a public purpose.[374] Then the Industrial Development Amendment of the constitution was adopted in 1960, and in 1962 in *State ex rel. Meyer, Attorney General v. County of Lancaster,*[375] a test case on a proposed issue of $3,000,000 in revenue bonds for the construction of an industrial plant survived constitutional challenge.

The Supreme Court of Kansas in 1961 sustained legislation of that year in a suit involving a municipal issue of $130,000 in industrial development revenue bonds to purchase a site and build a plant to be leased to a textile business.[376] It quoted what the court had said in 1871 in *Leavenworth County v. Miller,*[377] in sustaining municipal aid to railroads: "The ultimate object . . . is to increase the facilities for travel and transportation from one part of the country to the other, . . . a public purpose." Concluding, "Notwithstanding there are members of this court who entertain serious misgivings and doubts as to the wisdom and propriety of the act under consideration—it nevertheless is held not to violate the constitution on any of the grounds asserted."

Presently Topeka issued $3,700,000 in revenue bonds to finance the introduction of a department store.

Missouri's constitution was amended in 1960 to provide that

> By vote of two-thirds of the qualified electors thereof voting thereon, any city or incorporated town or village within any county . . . which has less than four hundred thousand inhabitants according to the last preceding federal decennial census, may become indebted for and may purchase, construct, extend or improve plants to be leased

---

[374] State *ex rel.* Beck, Attorney General v. City of York, 164 Neb. 223.
[375] 173 Neb. 195.

[376] State of Kansas *ex rel.* Ferguson v. City of Pittsburg, 188 Kan. 612.
[377] 7 Kan. 479.

or otherwise disposed of pursuant to law to private persons or corporations for manufacturing and agricultural development purposes . . .

provided that the indebtedness incurred shall not exceed ten percent of the value of taxable tangible property as shown by the last assessment. A statute pursuant to that amendment was enacted in 1961, and sustained in 1962 in a test case relating to El Dorado Springs' proposal to construct a plant to be leased to a printing company.[378]

Iowa's statute of 1963 was sustained next year in a declaratory-judgment action concerning the plan of Mt. Pleasant, in Henry county, to issue $650,000 in revenue bonds to acquire a plant for lease by an outside industry.[379] The court took judicial notice that

> for many years there has been a continuing and discouraging decline
> in the population of the rural area surrounding Mt. Pleasant, agricul-
> ture is no longer as dominant and significant a factor in the Iowa
> economy as it was a few generations ago and that many people are
> moving from Iowa farms and smaller towns because of a lack of ade-
> quate opportunities to earn a living.

Considerations which had led the Supreme Court to uphold taxation to provide compensation for unemployment[380] would sustain this plan for industrial development.

These latter-day happenings occurred on old camp ground of railroad-aid controversy. Mt. Pleasant, seat of Henry county, had seen bonds issued in 1868, and enforcement resisted in 1869. Close to El Dorado Springs is Vernon County, Missouri, which incurred a debt of $317,000 for railroads, and bitterly repented; in 1968 its seat, Nevada, issued $15,500,000 in bonds to bring a manufacturing plant. Springfield, Missouri, issued $6,250,000 in bonds to bring a manufacturer of radios: it is the seat of Greene County, foremost among those resisting enforcement ninety years earlier.

Salient differences between present and past become evident when one examines, for instance, the Official Statement of $60,000,000 City of Fort Madison, Iowa, 1967 Series Industrial Development Revenue Bonds, to bring about the construction of a chemical fertilizer plant to be operated by a wholly owned subsidiary of a great oil company. The bonds are payable solely from revenue and rental income. Leading bond counsel found the issue valid and legally binding. The lease was, in the opinion of other counsel, binding upon the

---

[378] State *ex rel.* City of El Dorado Springs v. Holman, State Auditor, 363 S.W.2d 552.

[379] Green v. City of Mt. Pleasant, 256 Iowa 1184 (1964).

[380] In Carmichael v. Southern Coal & Coke Co., 301 U.S. 495 (1937), supra, n. 367.

parent oil company. The underwriters purchased at par plus accrued interest. By contrast, railroad aid bonds had been general obligations of the municipality. The community hoped it would get a railroad; it looked to promoters who had few resources of their own. Now the industrial development lessee normally is an established enterprise with ample resources. For the municipality, the inducement is that the arrangement will assure employment by an expanding company. The transactions are carried on deliberately, without the breathless anticipation that marked the project of a railroad.

Indeed the community can remain quite composed. With slight risk it has issued bonds enjoying tax-exemption—the generating cause of this huge development—and in the outcome will receive benefit from employment and economic stability. The lessee may, as in Iowa, be required to contribute the equivalent of what is lost in revenue when the municipally owned site is taken off the tax rolls.

The reason for using Fort Madison as an illustration should be obvious: it was there that in 1869 Judge Beck released on habeas corpus the Lee County supervisors in custody of the federal marshal for their failure to satisfy J. Edgar Thomson's judgment.[381]

---

[381] Supra, pp. 968–70.

CHAPTER XIX

The Thirteenth Amendment and the Civil Rights Act

THE SUBMISSION AND adoption of the post-war Amendments received mention in earlier chapters as events in the course of Reconstruction. Now a close view must be taken of some of the debates in Congress.

With the passing of a century has come an aroused conscience that justice has not been made secure to black citizens. Eagerness now to make effective what the Constitution promised has produced an outpouring of writings, often of distinguished skill, pointing to paths toward that attainment. Some of these studies go to historical origins and, through reinterpretation, report the discovery of high moral purposes which, though lost awhile, are now offered as authentic. In some of these works of great good will it seems as though fervor to hasten justice now has, however unwittingly, been given ascendancy over devotion to cold truth. Much depends on what pieces of evidence one selects from the record, and what meaning and weight one attributes to them.

Every office—such as advocate, judge, legal reformer, scholar—has its appropriate confines and duties, although in periods of moral stress the canons become obscured.[1] In contributing to a scholarly

---

[1] Lincoln distinguished between "my view of *official* duty" and "my oft-expressed *personal* wish that all men every where could be free," in his letter of August 22, 1862, to Horace Greeley, responding to the latter's editorial of the nineteenth, "The Prayer of Twenty Millions." Actually the President, one month earlier, had drafted an Emancipation Proclamation, which he held under advisement. Lincoln was doing his own praying. And he did find it proper, one month later, to issue the Preliminary Emancipation Proclamation, followed by the operative proclamation of January 1, 1863. *Collected Works of Abraham Lincoln*, ed. Roy P. Basler (New Brunswick, N.J.: Rutgers University Press, 1953), V, 336, 388, 433; VI, 28. See infra, note 54.

history of the Supreme Court, the proper aim seems clear: to seek the truth, representing every significant aspect fairly and evenhandedly, to the best of one's understanding. It is important thus to identify the objective.

In approaching this most knotted topic in our constitutional history, perhaps a reminder may be permitted. We do well to proceed as seekers, with open mind. There is need for patience and candor in taking account of all considerations, in whatever direction they may bear. We shall hear members of Congress voicing a wide range of opinion about the place black people were expected to occupy in the life and law of America. It is to be remembered that this was the true reflection of the diversity of thought and sentiment among the American people during that period of five years within which three amendments were added to the Constitution. In seeking to comprehend the factual situation at that distant moment, we all need to invoke Paul's admonition against haughtiness of opinion: "Be not wise in your own conceits."

THE THREE POST-WAR AMENDMENTS

THE THIRTEENTH AMENDMENT, coming into force in December 1865, brought this new ordination:

> Section 1. Neither slavery nor involuntary servitude, except as a punishment for crime whereof the party shall have been duly convicted, shall exist within the United States, or any place subject to their jurisdiction.
> Section 2. Congress shall have power to enforce this article by appropriate legislation.

The words of Section 1 were derived from the Ordinance for the government of the Northwest Territory, enacted by the United States in Congress assembled in 1787, and continued in force by the First Congress under the Constitution. The States carved from that territory carried forward the prohibition when they came to make their own constitutions: Ohio, Indiana, Illinois, Michigan, Wisconsin. In the 29th Congress (1845–47), when President Polk sought an appropriation for settling the war with Mexico, Representative David Wilmot of Pennsylvania in association with Brinkerhoff of Ohio[2] introduced a proviso—that it would be a "fundamental condition" that "neither slavery nor involuntary servitude . . ." should ever exist in any territory

---

[2] Identified above as an advocate of the appointment of Chase to the Chief Justiceship in 1864. Supra, p. 13.

so acquired. Southern opposition in the Senate defeated that condition —and thereafter the Wilmot Proviso was a battle cry in resisting the expansion of slavery. The words of prohibition were written into the constitutions of Iowa, California, Minnesota, Oregon, and Kansas; and Congress employed them when it forbade slavery in the territories by the statute of June 19, 1862 (thereby contradicting Taney in *Dred Scott*).

While the words of Section 1 were thus old and familiar, they would be scanned anew, searchingly. And Section 2 was new: How far might Congress go with "appropriate legislation"? Might it efface whatever seemed a "badge of slavery"—even to elevating the status of Negroes who had been free all along, and displacing legislation of States where slavery had never existed?

Congress exercised its new power in the Civil Rights Act of 1866. That will come under close scrutiny.

Of the Fourteenth Amendment, the following provisions (in Section 1) will be our immediate concern. *No State* shall [1] "make or enforce any law which shall abridge the privileges or immunities of citizens of the United States"; but what they were remained for judicial inference, since they had never been expressly defined.

Further, [2], "nor shall any State deprive any person of life, liberty, or property, without due process of law . . . ." Out of the long catalog of the federal Bill of Rights—freedom of religion, of speech, and of the press, the right of assembly, freedom from unreasonable search and seizure, and so forth—this one clause was repeated for imposition as a limitation upon the States.

Section 1 of the Amendment concluded, [3] "nor deny to any person within its jurisdiction the equal protection of the laws." Even in so straightforward a command there was latent uncertainty. Did "equal protection" forbid exclusion on racial grounds from testifying in a cause wherein one was not a party? What about service on juries?

By Section 5, Congress was given power to enforce by appropriate legislation. The framers did not foresee that it would be the Court, not Congress, that most concerned itself with the application of the provisions of Section 1.

"The right of citizens of the United States to vote," the Fifteenth Amendment added in 1870, "shall not be denied or abridged by the United States or by any State on account of race, color, or previous condition of servitude." Congress promptly passed the Act of May 31, 1870, to enforce the right of citizens to vote.[3] In our period, the Court's concern with this statute was momentary and rather disap-

---

[3] 16 Stat. 140.

pointing.[4] The Voting Rights Act of 1965 eventually made provision for really serious enforcement.[5]

ANTE-BELLUM BACKGROUND

WE APPROACH THE changes thus introduced by way of a survey of certain features of the constitutional system as it was established before the Civil War.

The powers delegated to the federal government, Madison wrote in No. XLV of *The Federalist*, "are few and defined." In this respect, he assured apprehensive readers, the change from the Articles of Confederation consisted "less in the addition of NEW POWERS to the Union, than in the invigoration of its ORIGINAL POWERS." Powers remaining with the States were "numerous and indefinite," extending "to all the objects which, in the ordinary course of affairs, concern the lives, liberties and properties of the people, and the internal order, improvement, and prosperity of the State." The Constitution opens with a declaration that "We the People of the United States, in Order to form a more perfect Union, establish Justice, . . . promote the general Welfare, and secure the Blessings of Liberty to ourselves and our Posterity, do ordain and establish this Constitution . . . ." The "true office" of this statement, Story wrote in his *Commentaries on the Constitution*, was "to expound the nature and extent and application of the powers actually conferred . . . and not substantively to create them."[6] Thus Congress had no general authority to enact whatever

---

[4] In United States v. Reese, 92 U.S. 214 (1876), the Court, per Waite, C.J., took an exceedingly strict line with the penal section of the statute: it found it not "appropriate legislation" for enforcing the Amendment. Sections 1 and 2, in referring to voting, had done so "without distinction of race, [etc.] . . ."; Section 4 imposed a penalty for hindering any citizen "from voting at any election as aforesaid." Held: too broad, because not specifically limited to hindering *on account of race*, etc.

In United States v. Cruikshank, 92 U.S. 542 (1876)—the Grant Parish case, infra, pp. 1378–79—it did not appear that the "banding" and "conspiring" laid under Section 6 of the Act of 1870 had been with intent to prevent the victims from exercising rights on account of their color.

Ex parte Siebold, 100 U.S. 371 (1880), held that Section 22 of the Act, penalizing "any officer of any election" at which a Representative in Congress was to be voted for, was applicable to a *State officer* conducting such an election.

Ex parte Yarbrough, 110 U.S. 651 (1884), the *Ku-Klux Case*, sustained the validity of Section 5508, Revised Statutes (derived from Section 6 of the Act of 1870), penalizing conspiracies to injure or intimidate citizens in the exercise of civil rights, in a case where Y. *et al.* were charged with combining to intimidate B.S., a colored citizen, in the exercise of his right to vote for a Representative in Congress.

[5] 79 Stat. 437.

[6] Sec. 462 (1833).

would tend to establish justice or secure liberty: it could exercise only the powers enumerated (chiefly in Article I, Section 8), including the power "to make all Laws which shall be necessary and proper for carrying into Execution" the other granted powers.

Slavery was recognized in the Constitution,[7] albeit only by circumlocution. Representation and direct taxation would be based on "the whole Number of free Persons" and "three fifths of all other Persons." Persons "held to Service or Labour in one State," escaping to another, must be delivered up to the party "to whom such Service or Labour may be due." Congress must not, prior to 1808, prohibit the importation of "such Persons as any of the States now existing shall think proper to admit."

The phrase "privileges and immunities" originated in the Articles of Confederation: "The better to secure and perpetuate mutual friendship and intercourse," the free inhabitants of each State would enjoy "all privileges and immunities of free citizens in the several states," and in particular the right to free ingress and regress, and all the privileges of trade and commerce, subject to the same requirements as applied to local citizens. The framers of the Constitution compressed the thought into the provision of Article IV, Section 2, clause 1:

> The Citizens of each State shall be entitled to all Privileges and Immunities of Citizens in the several States.

That meant, as Chancellor Kent said in his *Commentraies on American Law*, that if citizens of one State remove to another "they are entitled to the privileges that persons of the same description are entitled to in the state to which the removal is made, and to none other. The privileges thus conferred are local and necessarily territorial in their nature."[8] In short, a citizen from out-of-State would have the benefit of the laws as he found them, without discrimination against him as an outsider.

That simple idea was beclouded by an opinion Justice Washington rendered on the circuit in 1823, in *Corfield v. Coryell*.[9] Plaintiff's vessel, out of Philadelphia, had sailed into New Jersey waters and

---

[7] That was inescapable: only so could there continue that Union of the States whose independence as the United States of America had been declared in 1776. The constitution-makers could not even ignore the peculiar institution: on the apportionment of representation and some other matters, dispositions had to be arranged around that ugly but immovable fact.

In 1843, William Lloyd Garrison carried the Anti-Slavery Society of Massachusetts to the point of declaring that the Constitution was "a covenant with death and an agreement with hell": but this looked to a dissolution of the Union, not to any present possibility of amending the Constitution to abolish slavery.

[8] II, 71 (1832).

[9] Fed. Case No. 3230, E.D. Pa.

taken oysters, defying a State law that restricted such fishing to residents. Defendant had seized it. Did the statute infringe Article IV, Section 2? Justice Washington held that it did not: sharing in this natural resource was not among the "privileges and immunities." Doubtless trying to be helpful, the Judge essayed a comprehensive exposition of the clause, beyond what was needed for the case at hand:

> We feel no hesitation in confining these expressions to those privileges and immunities which are, in their nature, fundamental; which belong, of right, to the citizens of all free governments . . . . What these fundamental principles are, it would perhaps be more tedious than difficult to enumerate. They may, however, be all comprehended under the following general heads: Protection by the government; the enjoyment of life and liberty, with the right to acquire and possess property of every kind, and to pursue and obtain happiness and safety; subject nevertheless to such restraints as the government may justly prescribe for the general good of the whole. The right of a citizen of one state to pass through, or to reside in any other state, for purposes of trade, agriculture, professional pursuits, or otherwise; to claim the benefit of the writ of habeas corpus; to institute and maintain actions of any kind in the courts of the state; to take, hold and dispose of property, either real or personal; and an exemption from higher taxes or impositions than are paid by the other citizens of the state; may be mentioned as some of the particular privileges and immunities of citizens, which are clearly embraced by the general description of privileges deemed to be fundamental: to which may be added, the elective franchise, as regulated and established by the laws and constitution of the state in which it is to be exercised. . . .

The reference to "professional pursuits" was unguarded (for example, it is familiar that a State may say that residence is a condition to admission to practice law in its courts), and that to the "elective franchise" was plainly wrong (for it is obvious that citizens from all about may not come in on election day and vote). The great confusion, however, lay in saying that the clause secured those "privileges and immunities which are . . . fundamental; which belong, of right, to the citizens of all free governments." That could be taken to mean the "natural rights" which *ought* to be accorded by any government properly called "free."[10]

It would have sufficed for Justice Washington to say, simply, that the visitor had no constitutional right to share in the public

---

[10] In Hague v. Committee for Industrial Organization, 307 U.S. 496, 511 (1939), Roberts, J., spoke deprecatingly of Justice Washington's description; he concluded, "The section, in effect, prevents a State from discriminating against citizens of other States in favor of its own."

patrimony, such as oyster beds, the common property of the citizens of New Jersey;[11] presumably he meant that anything so special and peculiar was not included, because it was not "fundamental."

Doubtless Justice Washington's words, as reported, far over-leaped his thought. One should not suppose—because it would have been preposterous—that he meant that when the Framers carried forward the obligation assumed in the Articles of Confederation they widened it to charge each State to accord to citizens from sister States whatever the Supreme Court might hold to be "fundamental" in "free governments," regardless of whether the State made any such provision for its own citizens. At any rate, it would have taken much more than a dictum from a Justice on circuit to establish such a proposition.

Later Justice Curtis, advisedly, said that "any merely abstract definition" of the "privileges and immunities" of Article IV, Section 2 "could scarcely be correct: and a failure to make it so would certainly produce mischief"—(which is what Justice Washington's opinion did). "It is safer, and more in accordance with the duty of a judicial tribunal, to leave its meaning to be determined, in each case, upon a view of the particular rights asserted and denied therein."[12]

One denial of rights guarantied by Article IV, Section 2—a dramatic episode that shook the North—occurred in South Carolina in 1844. Colored citizens of Northern States, seamen on ships sailing to South Carolina ports, were systematically held in jail until the time for their ship's departure. The government of Massachusetts sent Samuel Hoar, an eminent lawyer, to Charleston for the purpose of challenging this practice. The South Carolina legislature requested the Governor to expel "the Northern emissary." A mob surrounded the hotel where Hoar was staying, and he was compelled to leave without performing his mission. Reference to this indignity cropped up constantly when Congress came to consider, in the light of the outcome of the war, what further safeguards should be written into the Constitution.

THE FIRST TEN AMENDMENTS (1791)

IN OBEDIENCE TO a popular sentiment that had imperilled the adoption of the Constitution, the 1st Congress promptly framed a Bill of Rights to lay restraints upon the General Government. As John Marshall related in his *Life of George Washington*, "The formidable

---

[11] In McCready v. Virginia, 94 U.S. 391 (1877)—where much was said in argument about Corfield v. Coryell—it was held that the State was free to prohibit to citizens of other States the right it accorded to its own citizens to plant oysters in its tide-waters.

[12] Conner v. Elliott, 18 How. 591, 593 (1856).

minorities in several of the conventions, which in the legislatures of some powerful states had become majorities, and the refusal of two states to complete the union, were admonitions not to be disregarded, of the necessity of removing jealousies however misplaced, which operated on so large a portion of society."[13] Ratification of ten Amendments was completed in 1791.

Marshall recalled this history in 1833 when, speaking for a unanimous Court in *Barron v. Baltimore*,[14] it was held that the federal Bill of Rights had provided "security against the apprehended encroachments of the general government—not against those of the local governments." "[S]o far from the States which insisted on these amendments contemplating any restraint or limitation by them on their own powers," said Justice Barbour in 1840,[15] "the very cause which gave rise to them was a strong jealousy on their part of the power which they had granted in the Constitution." "They are exclusively restrictions upon federal power," said Justice Daniel for the Court in 1847;[16] it was useless "to attempt to shake or disturb that doctrine," he added in 1858.[17]

Thus when the Fourteenth Amendment was being framed, it was clear to anyone acquainted with *Barron v. Baltimore* and its reaffirmations, that the guaranties of freedom of speech and of the press, right of assembly, grand jury, trial jury, due process of law and the rest, specified in Amendments I to VIII, were not applicable to the States. In so far as such rights were secured in any State, it was by virtue of its own laws. Normally the State constitution did contain an enumeration of such guaranties, often in language identical with the federal provision.

THE STATE OF THE LAW IN 1865

A FEW ILLUSTRATIONS will show how the law stood when the 39th Congress assembled.

If *Congress* were to pass a statute that forbade the people peaceably to assemble, or to petition the Government for a redress of grievances, that would go squarely in the teeth of the First Amendment. For a *State* to forbid the people to assemble and petition would *not* infringe the First Amendment; ordinarily it would infringe some

---

[13] V, 208 (1807).

[14] 7 Pet. 243, 250.

[15] Holmes v. Jennison, 14 Pet. 540, 587.

[16] Fox v. State of Ohio, 5 How. 410, 434.

[17] Withers v. Buckley, 20 How. 84, 90. Other affirmations are found in Lessee of Livingston v. Moore, 7 Pet. 469, 551 (1833); Smith v. Maryland, 18 How. 71, 76 (1855); Pervear v. Massachusetts, 5 Wall. 475, 480 (1867).

guaranty in the *State* constitution. For a *State* to forbid the people to assemble and petition the *United States Government* in respect of some matter of *federal* cognizance, again, would not infringe the First Amendment; but it would offend a basic principle whose classic statement was made by Chief Justice Marshall in *McCulloch v. Maryland*: "the government of the Union, though limited in its powers, is supreme within its sphere of action. . . . It is of the very essence of supremacy to remove all obstacles to its action within its own sphere . . . ."[18] Whether the obstacle be viewed as a hindrance to the action of the United States, or as an interference with a person's enjoyment of some right derived from the United States, the principle applies. Maryland's law had embarrassed the Government's power to charter a bank that would serve its purposes: it had also embarrassed the bank's enjoyment of its rights under the charter. When Georgia imprisoned Samuel A. Worcester, missionary to the Indians, for residing in the Cherokee country without a license from the State, it denied rights to which he was entitled under the treaties and laws of the United States; at the same time, Georgia was defying the authority of the United States, and especially that of the Supreme Court.[19] When South Carolina attempted Nullification it obstructed the enforcement of the revenue laws, but it also interfered with the right of individuals to import.

As the United States may call upon its citizens to comply with its lawful commands, so "the citizen also has correlative rights" to enjoy all the benefits that flow from national citizenship. The State may not "impede or embarrass the constitutional operations of that government, or the rights which its citizens hold under it . . . ." So spoke Justice Miller for the Court in *Crandall v. Nevada* in 1868—a leading case presently to be examined.[20] This was said a few months *before* the Fourteenth Amendment went into effect; the basic principle was old, although the language rang with the assurance derived from the recent triumph of the Union.

The principle extends to interference by an individual or by individuals in concert. When Congress makes it a crime to intimidate or to corrupt a witness or officer in a federal court, it is supporting the judicial power of the United States; but it is also protecting the interest of witnesses, of officers, and of litigants. So too of the Post Office, of the Treasury, of the armed services, of the civil service, the public lands, and so forth: the citizen's rights to the various benefits derived from the United States are his *federal rights;* and Congress, by penal statutes or other appropriate measures, may make him secure in the enjoyment of them.

---

[18] 4 Wheat. 316, 405, 427 (1819).
[19] Worcester v. State of Georgia, 6 Pet. 515 (1832).
[20] 6 Wall. 35. Infra, pp. 1302–07.

When he receives diplomatic protection abroad, the citizen is enjoying a federal privilege. An example is the recovery, under a provision in the Treaty of Ghent of 1814, of compensation for slaves emancipated by the British armed forces on the occasion of their occupation of American territory during the War of 1812. John Quincy Adams, as a peace commissioner, insisted on the incorporation of this provision; later, as Secretary of State, he successfully insisted upon its fulfillment.[21] An extreme case was the recovery, by international arbitration, of damages where slaves, on an American merchant vessel forced into a British port by stress of weather, had been liberated by the local authorities.[22] John Quincy Adams, a Representative in Congress and Chairman of the Committee on Foreign Affairs when this matter arose in 1841, opposed the slave-owners' demand for protection.

When citizens petitioned Congress to take steps against slavery, they were exercising a federal right—which however was frustrated when in 1836 the House adopted a rule that all petitions relating to slavery be laid on the table, unread. John Quincy Adams persistently presented such petitions and continued to denounce the rule until in 1844 it was repealed.

Communication through the Post Office is a federal privilege—which however for a time was abridged when in 1835 Postmaster General Amos Kendall countenanced the stopping of "inflammatory papers" by postmasters.

A new right under the Constitution was discovered and gratuitously announced by Chief Justice Taney in the *Dred Scott Case*,[23] in 1857: the right of the citizen to take his slaves no less than other property into any territory of the United States, and to be protected in such ownership by the federal Government. This meant that the drawing of a line to limit slavery in the territories, as had been done by the Missouri Compromise of 1820, was unconstitutional.

In the practical working of the constitutional system, in the three decades prior to the Civil War, there was much to demonstrate energy where slavery was to be protected—and many examples of ineffectiveness to secure the rights of slavery's opponents.

There had been little occasion, apart from the distorting subject of slavery, to dwell upon the distinction between the rights incident to State and those incident to federal citizenship. If Congress had

---

[21] Samuel F. Bemis, *John Quincy Adams and the Foundation of American Foreign Policy*, (New York: Alfred A. Knopf, 1949), 231–33.

[22] *The Creole*, Moore, *Digest of International Law*, II, 351–52.
[23] 19 How. 393.

denounced as crimes such acts as the preventing of a citizen from voting for a Representative in Congress, or that of combining to deny to any citizen the enjoyment of privileges secured by Article IV, Section 2—and if through the years there had been considerable litigation over such provisions—then perhaps the country would have become familiar with the incidents of dual citizenship. As it was, when Congress set about making the Union what it should be after the war, and undertook to make secure, to new citizens and old, the enjoyment of *federal rights*, against denial by State or by individual, inherent problems resulted which members of Congress, in the main, failed accurately to perceive.

ANTI-SLAVERY INTERPRETATIONS

ABOLITIONISTS OF DIVERSE convictions had all contributed to the moral awakening that made possible their common objective, the prohibition of slavery. They had been divided, however, in their attitude toward the Constitution and the Union. For Garrison and Phillips, the Constitution was "a covenant with death" which "should be annulled"—"My *curse* on the Constitution . . . ." Others, cherishing the Union, used their ingenuity to demonstrate that in truth the Constitution had given no sanction to slavery.

Attracted by the writings of the latter school, Howard Jay Graham has traced perceptively the philanthropic impulse that sprang up in the mid-'30's and was carried through the Northeast and Northwest, lodging notably in certain communities in Ohio.[24] John A. Bingham—who as a member of the Joint Committee on Reconstruction became the chief draftsman of Section 1 of the Fourteenth Amendment—and other members of Congress influential in its adoption came from some of these strongholds. "It now is beyond doubt," Graham writes, "that the evangelical abolitionists anticipated members of the Joint Committee by a full thirty years in developing the privileges and immunities—due process—equal protection phraseology as a bulwark for the rights of free Negroes and slaves."[25] "[I]n working out this theory, they began, not as lawyers or constitutionalists, but as moralists and evangelists. Their basic case was a compendious Biblico-moral, ethico-religious, natural rights argument confidently addressed to their countrymen as patriots, Christians, and 'free moral agents.' "[26]

---

[24] "The Early Antislavery Backgrounds of the Fourteenth Amendment," 1950 *Wis. L. Rev.*, 480 and 610.

[25] Ibid., 658.

[26] Ibid., 625.

"Systematic thinking and criticism were retarded by stereotyped rhetoric and habits of thought. More serious was the confusion of moral with civil rights—the failure to distinguish between socially desirable ends and the steps and means necessary for their legal or constitutional attainment. Rights were interchangeably regarded as preexistent human ideals and as socially implemented and enforceable privileges or immunities. In countless arguments what ought to be was mistaken and substituted for what was. Abolitionist theory was a monument to this imprecision." He adds, "To a generation more sophisticated in drafts-manship, all this seems incredible."[27]

A representative expression of this school is William Goodell's *Views of American Constitutional Law in its Bearing Upon American Slavery,* published at Utica, New York, in 1844. Goodell (1792–1878), a self-educated man, devoted his life to editing, writing, and lecturing in advocacy of various reforms; he was among the organizers of the Prohibition Party. The Declaration of Independence—"the Constitution of 1776," he called it—"as the *fundamental basis and ground work* of AMERICAN CONSTITUTIONAL LAW, remains unchanged, and in full force."[28] "By the united act of all the people, all men were declared to be equal and endowed with unalienable rights." "[B]y the power of that act, SLAVERY WAS ABOLISHED."[29] "[T]he minutely detailed *provisions* of the subsequently written Constitution" were no more than *"instruments"* of the Declaration.[30] The Constitution adopted in 1789 "must be construed to mean and intend what *it says* it means and intends"—to establish *justice* and to secure *liberty.*[31] Persons "held to Service or Labour," whether that be construed by the dictionary or by the spirit of 1776, he contended, did not mean *slaves.*[32] The United States guarantees to every State "a Republican Form of Government": since a republic is based on equality of rights for every citizen, slavery was repugnant to the guaranty and should be destroyed by Congress.[33] Supposing, arguendo, that slavery had survived 1776 and 1789: then surely the Fifth Amendment, adopted in 1791, released all in bondage by its provision that no person should be deprived of liberty without due process of law.[34] If Goodell had ever heard of *Barron v. Baltimore,* it would have made no difference. He was unimpressed with what the Justices said about the Constitution: "what if *they* have construed it *wrong*? Are *our* consciences to be bound by *theirs?*" "[C]onflicting constructions of statutes and parchments, . . . precedents arrayed against

---

[27] Ibid., 612, 613.
[28] Pp. 135–36.
[29] Ibid., 141.
[30] Ibid., 138.

[31] Ibid., 40–41.
[32] Ibid., 21, 81 *et seq.*
[33] Ibid., 47 *et seq.*
[34] Ibid., 57 *et seq.*

precedents, and technicalities against common sense, have made law a vast game of hazard . . . ."[35]

Prepossessed as he was with his own moral truth, Goodell could dismiss any inconvenient consideration as plain error.

AN ABOLITIONIST LAWYER'S REVISED VERSION OF THE CONSTITUTION

SIMILAR IN RESULT to Goodell's artless pamphlet was the systematic *Manual of the Constitution of the United States* produced by Timothy Farrar in 1867—too late to influence events, yet significant as a revelation of what a trained lawyer could bring himself to profess as the true reading of the past. Before we come to grips with the post-war Amendments it will be instructive to meet this example of what distortion can be practiced through a zeal to redress injustice.

Farrar (1788–1874), the son of a New Hampshire judge, had attended Dartmouth College, and read law in Daniel Webster's office. He practiced in New Hampshire—during three years as Webster's partner. From 1824 to 1833 he sat on the court of common pleas; later he was cashier of a bank. In 1844 he moved to Boston, where he practiced law, managed trusts, and engaged in literary and historical pursuits. In his opinions "he was always positive, not to say aggressive",[36] and—for all his practical background—on the subject of slavery he gave himself over entirely to theory. His pen, enlisted in the war effort, proved mighty enough to declare that "there can be no slaves in the land," even without the Thirteenth Amendment.[37] Of Section 1 of the Fourteenth Amendment—in the course of ratification when the *Manual* appeared—Farrar commented, "This will scarcely be claimed by anybody to delegate any thing new to the government, or to prohibit the States from doing any thing which otherwise they might rightfully do"[38]—so overpowering had been the national authority, so firmly secured the natural rights of all men, according to his fresh construction of the Constitution.

"We the People of the United States" ordained a Constitution, and in the "enacting clause"—falsely dubbed a Preamble, but in truth the "most mandatory section of the Constitution"—we declared "six express purposes, constituting the duties and limiting the powers of the national government . . .: '1. To form a more perfect Union; 2. establish justice; 3. insure domestic tranquility; 4. provide for the common

---

[35] Ibid., 155–56.
[36] Memoir in D.A.B.
[37] *Manual of the Constitution, of* *the United States of America* (Boston: Little, Brown and Co., 1867), 164.
[38] Sec. 448 of the *Manual*.

defence; 5. promote the general welfare; and, 6. secure the blessings of liberty to ourselves and our posterity.' "[39] It would be a "gross absurdity" to suppose that the government charged with such spacious duties was limited to the particular delegations of power elsewhere in the text, such as Article I, Section 8, "Congress shall have Power . . . ."[40] It was a "marvel," Farrar said, how Hamilton, writing in the *Federalist*, had depreciated the powers of Congress.[41] When "false and groundless assumptions" were put aside, it should be seen that "the plenary powers of general legislation for the public welfare, as embraced in the enacting clause, for the great purposes of government, are vested in Congress, and are limited only by the laws of God, the principles of free government, and the express or implied restrictions of the Constitution."[42] (Farrar had no difficulty in knowing what those laws, principles, and implied restrictions were.)

Clearly—so it was argued—a government charged with establishing justice and securing liberty could not tolerate slavery. The fact that "four millions of people, partly their [the people's] own posterity, mostly natural-born citizens of the United States," were still held in chattel slavery, was "a mortifying evidence of the incompetency of written laws, and the infidelity of human agencies, to counteract the selfishness, avarice, and injustice of men." The "voluntary abandonment" of duty had begun with the First Congress; this had persisted, even to Lincoln's position that his object was to preserve the Union, not to interfere with slavery.[43] Inconvenient passages in the Constitution were forced into line with the author's prepossessions. For example, Article I, Section 2 spoke of "free Persons" and "other Persons": "free" was ambiguous—it might describe those admitted as freemen of a municipal corporation. Or perhaps it was used in counterdistinction to persons who were indented to labor for a term—but that implied capacity to contract, which excluded the idea of slavery. In any event, both "free persons" and "other persons" were "people of the United States," citizens all. Nowhere did the Constitution admit the existence of slavery.[44]

"On any just principles of reasoning, it is impossible to consider the general government unauthorized to do any thing that the people assert they made it to do."[45] To accord with that enormous proposition, Farrar must debase the States. "It would have been impossible for any central government to manage all the minute interests of every petty locality . . . . As such [local] governments were necessary in

---

[39] Secs. 6, 64.
[40] Sec. 52.
[41] Secs. 288, 289.
[42] Sec. 302.

[43] Ch. X of the *Manual*.
[44] Secs. 131–41.
[45] Sec. 121.

some form, and as these were already formed, what could be more natural or desirable than to recognize and continue and guarantee the perpetual republican character of those organizations?" So for convenience and with misgivings, the State governments were tolerated, subject always to the mandate that they be "republican."[46] That required "strict adherence to the laws of God and eternal justice, the equal and invaluable rights of man."[47] Indeed the Constitution reserved to the States none of their original powers except "the right to appoint the officers of the militia . . . ."[48]

Individual rights figured largely in Farrar's exposition, especially as they ran against the States. At the outset, in making the Constitution the people reserved "many natural and civil common-law rights, which, of course, are placed beyond the reach of any subordinate government, and even of their own." Then the "privileges and immunities" of Article IV, Section 2: "whether originally natural, personal, or common-law rights, or civil and political rights, all became, by this guaranty, legal rights secured by the Constitution to every citizen of the United States"—even as against the State of which he was a citizen. But alas, "For more than three quarters of a century, . . . it stood a perfect dead letter in the Constitution . . . ."[49] And then the federal Bill of Rights: "In these, certain particular rights are plainly declared and recognized, as natural, legal, and subsisting rights of the people, and so made their constitutional rights. They . . . bind the government, and all subordinate governments,—every body, in fact, owing allegiance to the Constitution." For this he quoted, inter alia, Chief Justice Marshall, inappositely: "The Constitution of the United States is made for the whole people of the Union, and is equally binding upon all the courts and all the citizens."[50] He ignored the fact that what he was asserting had been squarely denied by the Court in 1833—save for a footnote, "*e con.*, see . . . *Barron v. Baltimore* . . . ."

Judge Farrar had shattered history to bits, and remoulded it according to his heart's desire. "Your book signalizes the great change in our history," Sumner wrote in appreciation; "Such a system of constitutional law would have found little favor only a short time ago. I trust it will be generally accepted now."[51] *The Nation*, under the

---

[46] Sec. 41.
[47] Sec. 219.
[48] Sec. 42.
[49] Secs. 34, 179–81.
[50] Secs. 440, 441. Marshall's sentence occurs in his opinion in Farmers' and Mechanics' Bank v. Smith, 6 Wheat. 131 (1821), which had nothing to do with the Bill of Rights. It held that the Contract

Clause (which in Sturges v. Crowninshield, 4 Wheat. 122 (1819) had been held to bar a State statute discharging a bankrupt from his indebtedness) applied where debtor and creditor were citizens of the same State.

[51] Letter of July 15, 1867, thanking Farrar for a copy of the *Manual. Memoir of Timothy Farrar, LL.D.*, by Rev. Samuel Lee, 17 (1875). Re-

headline "New Theories of Constitutional Law," considered this "ingenious and elaborate effort" to overturn what had prevailed since 1787.[52] The reviewer thought that the nation would not have been better served by Farrar's supposition than under the system that had theretofore existed:

> Even if we did, we could not justify ourselves in putting a meaning upon the words of the Constitution which we all know was not attached to them by a single man who helped to frame it, who voted for it, or who advocated it . . . . No instrument could endure such a mode of interpretation . . . . No confidence could be placed in any man's word, or in any of the bonds which hold society together, if such total disregard of precedent, and such amazing ingenuity in explaining away language or torturing it into meanings of which its authors never dreamed, should become general. . . .

This brought a retort from General John Wolcott Phelps (1813–1885), of Brattleboro, Vermont:

> The great mistake made by our war administration was that it did not assume the ground which is maintained by Judge Farrer [*sic*], viz., that the slave States, by becoming parties to the Constitution, were bound by the act to abolish slavery. This is the true issue before the country and the world . . . . Our present difficulties have arisen from the failure to assert and maintain this ground . . . .[53]

It is not surprising that Phelps rushed to Farrar's defense—so far as appears, without reading the *Manual*, or even knowing how to spell the author's name: Phelps himself had taken that stand, conspicuously, in 1861. A graduate of the Military Academy and long in the regular service, he had volunteered at the outbreak of the Civil War. As a brigadier general of volunteers, he was the senior officer present when two regiments debarked at Ship Island, Mississippi, in December 1861. From that toe-hold Phelps addressed a proclamation to the loyal citizens of the Southwest. He declared that the slave States that were parties to the formation of the Constitution were under the highest obligations of honor and morality to abolish slavery; that the subsequent admission of slave States had been in violation of the Constitution; that slavery must now be overthrown, and that the motto of his command would be "Free labor and workingmen's rights." Among his own troops, this caused considerable dissatisfaction. Phelps

---

printed from *New-England Historical and Genealogical Register*, XXIX, 225–33, July 1875.

[52] 5:250. Sept. 26, 1867.
[53] *The Nation*, 5:298–99. Oct. 10, 1867.

set about enlisting colored soldiers. All on his own, he was getting far ahead of the Administration. When directed to desist from recruiting and merely to employ colored men as laborers for hire, Phelps quit the army and went home. When Lincoln did find it proper, as a measure for the preservation of the Union,[54] to proclaim emancipation, Phelps wrote to Senator Sumner,

> Our president must play the dictator, the King; decide for himself and do what is right. In no other way can he inspire enemies with dread and friends with confidence. . . .
>
> I am convinced that moral considerations should have gone together with, and been placed before, military necessity as a reason for the act of abolishing slavery . . . .[55]

---

[54] Lincoln's first draft of an Emancipation Proclamation, of July 22, 1862, had at that time been sketched to the Cabinet for their reaction. At that moment the Second Bull Run campaign was in progress; its outcome was that Lee inflicted a severe defeat upon Pope, on August 29–30. McClelland was restored to command.

Lee crossed the Potomac and swept into Maryland. For several days prior to September 10 his headquarters were near Frederick. After the Battle of Antietam on September 17, Lee withdrew to Virginia.

On September 22, the President issued his Preliminary Proclamation of Emancipation: it gave notice that on January 1, 1863, all persons held as slaves in places which at that time should be in rebellion would be "forever free," and that the Executive with the armed forces would maintain that freedom. See supra, note 1.

As Chase recorded in his diary, Lincoln told the Cabinet,

When the rebel army was at Frederick, I determined, as soon as it should be driven out of Maryland, to issue a Proclamation of Emancipation such as I thought most likely to be useful. I said nothing to any one; but I made that promise to myself, and (hesitating a little)—to my Maker. The rebel army is now driven out, and I am going to fulfill that promise. . . .

David Donald, Ed., *Inside Lincoln's*

Cabinet. The Civil War Diaries of Salmon P. Chase (New York, London, Toronto: Longmans, Green and Co., 1954), 150.

Secretary Welles' memorandum of the Cabinet meeting included this passage:

[The President] remarked that he had made a vow, a covenant, that if God gave us the victory in the approaching battle, he would consider it an indication of Divine will, and that it was his duty to move forward in the cause of emancipation. It might be thought strange, he said, that he had in this way submitted the disposal of matters when the way was not clear to his mind what he should do. God had decided this question in favor of the slaves. He was satisfied it was right, was confirmed and strengthened in his action by the vow and the results. . . .

The Diary of Gideon Welles, 3 vols. (Boston and New York: Houghton Mifflin Co., 1911), I, 143.

[55] Letter of Feb. 16, 1863, quoted in Carl Sandburg's *Abraham Lincoln: The War Years*, 4 vols. (New York: Harcourt, Brace and Co., 1939), II, 25–56. The sentences above from that quotation have been corrected to conform to the original, in the Sumner Papers at the Houghton Library, Harvard University.

Ann. Cyc. 1861, 291–92, reports the Ship Island expedition, and gives at some length the substance of

Phelps and Farrar were in accord that, to do so great a right, it was morally imperative to deny the plain meaning of the Constitution as it had been known from the beginning.

THE VOCABULARY OF FREEDOM

A DEGREE OF imprecision is to be found throughout the deliberations on the constitutional settlement consequent upon the war. Fervent men spoke exultantly as they joined in achieving the nation's deliverance from the power of slavery. In the main they did not discern the obduracy of problems lying on the shady side of victory. Opponents of advance vociferated their objections, sometimes in measured criticism but generally in wild exaggeration—they were dogmatic about State rights and embittered about black men. Die-hards took a disproportionate amount of space in the Congressional Globe, and among the friends of freedom, some of the most outspeaking were not to be reckoned among the more helpful.

Slavery was a legal status: it was also an institution, an entire system of mores—economic, political, social, cultural, religious. It had been tolerated in 1787 as the price of Union. In later decades, after the cotton gin had made slavery seem ever more profitable, its defenders had become more audacious, its pretensions ever more disruptive of the public tranquility and disturbing to the national conscience.

In the 38th Congress, in advocating what became the Thirteenth

---

Phelps' proclamation. In *Butler's Book*, (Boston: A. M. Thayer and Co., 1892), 896–97, the author—Benjamin F. Butler, who as commander of the Army of the Gulf was Phelps' immediate superior—described him as an excellent officer: "He had but one fault: he was an anti-slavery man to a degree that utterly unbalanced his judgment." Benjamin P. Thomas and Harold M. Hyman, in their biography of *Stanton* (New York: Alfred A. Knopf, 1962), mention the Ship Island episode at p. 242.

Phelps was the subject of an exchange of letters between Reverdy Johnson and President Lincoln in July 1862. The former, who had gone to New Orleans as agent of the State Department, reported that Phelps' course of action was destructive of Union sentiment. Lincoln—without a word of approval for Phelps—replied that the people of Louisiana

"know how to be cured of General Phelps. Remove the necessity of his presence. . . ." *Collected Works of Abraham Lincoln*, V, 342–44.

By the Confederate Government, Phelps was declared an outlaw for having armed slaves against their masters.

Phelps was a candidate for the Presidency in 1880, by nomination of the American Antimason party, whose object was to "expose, withstand, and remove secret societies, Freemasonry in particular, and other anti-Christian movements, in order to save the churches of Christ from being depraved; to redeem the administration of justice from perversion, and our republican government from corruption." Ann. Cyc. 1880, 697.

There is a memoir in Appletons' *Cyclo. of Am. Biog.*, IV, 751.

Amendment, speakers inveighed against slavery as an "aggregation of enormities" (Representative James F. Wilson of Iowa);[56] condemnation ranged over its "divers and sundry grievous misdoings" (Senator Daniel Clark of New Hampshire).[57] Senator James Harlan tolled its wicked "incidents": denial of the law of God establishing the conjugal relation; disregard of the parental relation; denial of the right to hold property; the negation of legal rights and of redress for wrongs; even the attempt to separate the slave from human sympathy. Slavery had suppressed freedom of speech and press among whites, and had even made their education practically impossible.[58]

Senator Henry Wilson, in a speech entitled "The Death of Slavery is the Life of the Nation," said that

> If this amendment shall be incorporated by the will of the nation into the Constitution . . . , it will obliterate the last lingering vestiges of the slave system; its chattelizing, degrading, and bloody codes; its dark, malignant, barbarizing spirit; all it was and is, everything connected with it or pertaining to it, from the face of the nation . . . .[59]

Such heightened speech is easily understandable, coming from men eager to witness slavery's uprooting.

We shall discover, however, that when the 39th Congress came to consider the Civil Rights Bill, the extent of power generated by the Thirteenth Amendment became a sharply drawn issue. We shall hear Senator Cowan declare that it "was simply made to liberate the Negro slave from his master. That is all there is to it." The power of Congress was merely to afford a remedy—namely, by writ of habeas corpus. "That is all."[60] Doubtless that was too ungenerous a reading of the text. But how far did the amendment carry by its own force? What among the myriad evils now lay within the remedial power of Congress?

No doubt some of Senator Harlan's "incidents" amounted to "badges of servitude" that would fall within the ban of the amendment. But surely freedom of speech and press and education for Southern whites were not by the Thirteenth Amendment being placed under the guardianship of Congress. And Senator Wilson's affirmation that the amendment would obliterate the "spirit" of slavery can count for no more than a prayer. If the debates are invoked to aid in construing the amendment, there is need to distinguish between sanguine prophecies and cold propositions about legal consequences.

---

[56] Cong. Globe, 38–1, 1203. Mar. 19, 1864.
[57] Ibid., 1368. Mar. 31, 1864.
[58] Ibid., 1437–40. Apr. 6, 1864.

[59] Ibid., 1319, 1324. Mar. 28, 1864.
[60] Cong. Globe, 39–1, 499. Jan. 30, 1866.

An impressive argument has been made that the Thirteenth Amendment was designed to effect "a revolution in federalism"—that it "extended far beyond the personal burden of the slaves and the characteristics of immediate bondage"—that it "nationalized the right of freedom, and made the national Congress the organ of enforcement" —that indeed

> it was intended by its drafters and sponsors as a consummation to abolitionism in the broad sense in which thirty years of agitation and organized activity had defined that movement. . . .[61]

The substance of that thesis and the practical effect justly to be accorded to it must presently be examined. The word "revolution" is itself imprecise, and so too was the unschooled jurisprudence of the abolitionists.

Our immediate task is to see what the debates on the Thirteenth Amendment fairly import.

DEBATE ON THE THIRTEENTH AMENDMENT

THE 38TH CONGRESS, meeting for its First Session in December 1863, saw the introduction of a number of measures to abolish slavery. Representative Owen Lovejoy of Illinois, abolitionist, sought to achieve that result simply by statute: his bill "to give effect to the Declaration of Independence, and also to certain provisions of the Constitution," was sent to the Committee on the Judiciary, where it remained.[62] Representative James M. Ashley of Ohio introduced several proposals calculated to advance the cause of freedom, including one to amend

---

[61] Jacobus tenBroek, *Equal Under Law*, (New York: Macmillan Co., Collier Books, 1965), in Part Three, "The Consummation of Abolition— The Thirteenth Amendment," at 166, 167, 173, 196.

[62] Cong. Globe, 38–1, 20. Dec. 14, 1863. After a long recital invoking the Declaration of Independence and the Due Process Clause of the Fifth Amendment, it would enact that all persons held in slavery were freed, and would be protected, as all other free citizens are protected, from unreasonable search and seizure, would be allowed to sue and be sued, and to testify in the courts of the United States.

Lovejoy (1811–64) was a brother

of Elijah P. Lovejoy, the abolitionist clergyman and editor who was killed at Alton in 1837 when a mob attacked to carry away his press. In 1856 Owen Lovejoy won the nomination to Congress in the convention at Bloomington and—despite the misgivings of conservatives such as David Davis— carried the district by 6,000 votes.

Lincoln's prudent course, in Illinois and as President, had Lovejoy's understanding support. He died on March 25, 1864—and Lincoln said, "to the day of his death, it would scarcely wrong any other to say, he was my most generous friend." *Collected Works of Abraham Lincoln*, VIII, 366. See D.A.B.

the Constitution by prohibiting slavery. While this measure did not emerge from committee, Ashley should be kept in mind as the man who would manage the successful drive in the Second Session to carry the Thirteenth Amendment.[63] James F. Wilson of Iowa, chairman of the Judiciary Committee, introduced a joint resolution for a constitutional amendment to declare that "Slavery, being incompatible with a free Government, is forever prohibited . . . ." Presently this was reported favorably, and supported in a notable speech by its author.[64] In the Senate, John B. Henderson of Missouri offered a joint resolution, S.J. Res. 16, which as amended by the Judiciary Committee eventually became the Thirteenth Amendment.[65]

Sumner sought, in place of S.J. Res. 16, to substitute a constitutional amendment declaring that "all persons are equal before the law, so that no person can hold another as a slave."[66] In argument, "scorning all false interpretations and glosses," he insisted that slavery had always been unconstitutional: this he derived from the Preamble, the Republican Form of Government Clause, and the Due Process Clause of the Fifth Amendment. "And yet slavery still exists . . . How shall [it] be overthrown?" That *should* have been done by the courts.

> But alas! one of the saddest chapters in our history has been the conduct of judges . . . . Courts which should have been asylums of liberty have been changed into *barracoons*, and the Supreme Court of the United States, by a final decision of surpassing infamy [the *Dred Scott Case*] became the greatest *barracoon* of all. . . .

That failing, "By a single brief statute, Congress may sweep slavery out of existence." But now "An amendment of the Constitution may do what courts and Congress decline to do, or, even should they act, it may cover their action with its panoply. . . ."[67]

---

[63] Cong. Globe, 38–1, 19. Dec. 14, 1863.

[64] Ibid., 21, Dec. 14, 1863; 1199, March 19, 1864.

[65] Ibid., 145, Jan. 13, 1864.

[66] Ibid., 521, Feb. 8, 1864. Sumner's S. No. 24 was referred—not, as he desired, to his own Select Committee on Slavery and Freedmen—but to the Judiciary Committee, already charged with the consideration of Henderson's measure.

[67] Ibid., 1479–83, 1487–89. This was on April 8, 1864—immediately before the Senate voted on S. J. Res. 16, the Thirteenth Amendment as adopted. Sumner was telling at length why

he preferred his own formula, "all persons are equal before the law." He had found this in the French Constitution of 1793. "Equality" was a beautiful word derived from the Greek; he invited the "curious student" to turn to Herodotus. The phrase although "new in our country," was "already well known in history"; it has appeared in three French constitutions, and in the charters of Belgium, Italy, and Greece—it was "a well-known expression of a commanding principle of human rights."

Trumbull and Howard, of the Judiciary Committee, were visibly irked: they wanted to get on with

In the outcome, the Senate passed S.J. Res. 16 on April 8, 1864, by a vote of 38 to 6.[68] The majority included some conservative Republicans—notably Cowan of Pennsylvania—as well as Reverdy Johnson of Maryland and Nesmith of Oregon, Democrats. In the House, on June 15, the measure received a vote of 93 to 65—less than the requisite two-thirds. Several pairs were announced, and 23 were recorded as not voting. Ashley changed his vote from yea to nay, "for the purpose of submitting at the proper time the motion to reconsider."[69]

Early in the Second Session, on December 15, 1864, Ashley gave notice that on January 6 he would call up his motion. By the autumn elections it had become clear that the next Congress would propose an amendment if the 38th failed to do so. In Maryland a new constitution, incorporating the language of the Congressional measure, had been ratified in October. Missouri's convention, meeting on January 6, 1865, ordained abolition on the eleventh. President Lincoln's message to Congress on December 6 had asked, "may we not all agree that the sooner the better?" Enough Democratic opponents now shifted their position to permit the constitutional amendment to pass on January 31, 1865, by 119 yeas to 56 nays—8 not voting.[70]

Returning now to examine the record, of the 6 Senate Democrats who voted nay, 5 participated in the debates; of 38 Senators who

---

the business of abolishing slavery. Pp. 1488–89.

[68] Ibid., 1490.

[69] Ibid., 2995.

[70] Cong. Globe, 38–2, 531.

The *New York Tribune Almanac* for 1866, pp. 51–52, reporting the vote, distinguished between Unionists and Opposition:

For the Amendment:

    103 Unionists
     16 Opposition
    ———
    119

Against: 56 Opposition

Not voting: 8 Opposition

This reckons among the Unionists the New York Congressman, John Augustus Griswold, elected as a Democrat to the 38th Congress and as a Republican to the 39th and 40th. He voted yea on both occasions.

Looking at the 16 Oppositionists voting for the Amendment in January

1865, 11 had voted nay in June 1864; 2 had voted yea and thus were making no change; 2 had been recorded as not voting; 1 had not been recorded.

Still looking at the 16: 6 came from New York; 3 from Pennsylvania; 2 from Missouri; and one each came from Connecticut, Kentucky, Michigan, Ohio, and Wisconsin. They were all men of short service in Congress: 10 were in their first term, 6 in their second. Only one of the 16 had been reelected to the 39th Congress. Turning to the election figures, only 6 of the 16 had won his seat by a majority of as much as 2,000 votes.

Of the 8 recorded as not voting in January 1865, 6 had voted nay in 1864; 1 had been recorded as not voting, and 1 had been paired. These 8 abstainers were making their contribution toward the passage of the Amendment: suppose that as many

supported the amendment, 7 Republicans and Reverdy Johnson contributed significantly.[71] We begin with the opponents.

Senator Lazarus W. Powell of Kentucky said that the amending process could not touch rights of property. Any reasoning that would permit interference with the relation of master and servant would apply as well to the relation of husband and wife. He was "opposed to any amendment of the Constitution at this time." Even so, he proposed to add to the pending measure a proviso that no slave be emancipated until the owner had been paid. He offered another proposal: that the President be limited to one term of four years.[72]

His colleague, Garrett Davis, made the same contention, that slavery was a State institution, not subject to constitutional amendment. Instead he proposed: that the six States in New England be reduced to two; that no Negro could be a citizen of the United States; that the pending amendment contain a further provision that emancipated slaves be distributed among the States in proportion to their white population.[73]

Willard Saulsbury of Delaware professed that slavery was "in perfect accord with the ways of Providence to man." If property in slaves could be regulated by constitutional amendment, so too could the family relationships. He offered a constitutional amendment in twenty sections, to make slavery secure throughout the Union, south of 36°30′ north latitude [that is, below the line of the southern boundary of Missouri].[74]

Senator James A. McDougall of California, "in the name of

---

as 4 of these had voted nay, the result would be less than a two-thirds majority.

[71] Carl Sandburg quotes the classification of Senators made at this time by the Washington correspondent of the *Cincinnati Commercial*. Of interest here,

Best lawyer—Collamer of Vermont.
Best scholar—Sumner of Massachusetts
"Keenest" debater—Trumbull of Illinois.
Greatest bore that ever lived—Davis of Kentucky.
Most violent Copperhead—Powell of Kentucky.
Best looking man when sober—Saulsbury of Delaware.

The man who has least to say—Hendricks of Indiana.
Abraham Lincoln: The War Years, II, 556–57.

[72] Cong. Globe, 38–1, 1424, Apr. 5; 1444–47, Apr. 6; 1483–87, Apr. 8.

[73] Ibid., 921, Mar. 3; App., 104–8, Mar. 30; 1424–25, Apr. 5; 1488, Apr. 8.

[74] Ibid., 522–23, Feb. 8; 1364–67, Mar. 31; 1440–43, Apr. 6; 1489–90, Apr. 8.

Senator Anthony of Rhode Island commented: "If the Senator from Delaware has ever made any speech in this Chamber the whole staple of which was not upon the negro, it is one that I did not have the pleasure of listening to." P. 523, Feb. 8.

humanity," protested against "a policy for sacrificing the whole of the colored people": they would die off if liberated.[75]

Senator Thomas A. Hendricks of Indiana was not one to join in an exhibition of unreason. He said "I do not intend to discuss the merits or demerits of the proposition of general emancipation:" the time was not auspicious—the people were excited over the war—the requisite number of ratifications could not be obtained.[76]

On the affirmative side, Trumbull "as the organ of the Committee on the Judiciary" took the lead.[77] He said that the nation's troubles sprang from slavery. "If a large political party in the North attribute these troubles to the impertinent interference of northern philanthropists and fanatics with an institution in the southern States with which they had no right to interfere, I reply, if there had been no such institution there could have been no such alleged impertinent interference . . . ." He sketched the "hostile collision [of] the slaveholding aristocracy . . . and the free laboring masses of the North . . . ." He traced legislative and executive measures against slavery in the course of the war. "If . . . we are to get rid of the institution, we must have some more efficient way of doing it . . ."—by a constitutional amendment to prohibit it forever.

Could ratification be obtained from three-fourths of the existing 35 States? He calculated, hopefully: 21 States were free; initiatory steps toward abolition had been taken in Maryland, West Virginia, Missouri, Arkansas, Tennessee, and Louisiana; he trusted that Delaware could be added, to make the requisite 28.[78] By the adoption of the amendment,

---

[75] Ibid., 1490. Apr. 8.

[76] Ibid., 1456–57. Apr. 7.

[77] Ibid., 1313–14. Mar. 28.

[78] Trumbull also took account of the effect if one or more new States were admitted. Actually, Nevada came into the Union on October 31, 1864; its first legislature ratified the Amendment on February 16, 1865.

When Senator Hendricks had forecast that the requisite three-fourths could not be obtained, considering "in what condition" were the Southern States, Howard had asked, Whose fault was it if they were absent? Hendricks replied that the wrongfulness of secession would be no answer to the categorical requirement of the Constitution. Collamer of Vermont, intervening, indicated that he agreed "we must have three quarters of all the States"; moreover, "I believe we

will." Cong. Globe, 38–1; 1457–58, Apr. 7.

Ten months later, on February 4, 1865, Sumner introduced a concurrent resolution to declare that "the three fourths must be founded on the simple fact of representation in the Government of the country and the support thereof . . . ." This was laid on the table. Cong. Globe, 38–2, 588.

Joseph P. Bradley (who five years later was appointed to the Court) supported Sumner's resolution in a letter to Charles Knap, written at Washington, February 18, 1865. The gist of his opinion was this:

To admit for a moment that the wrongful secession of a State, or a number of States can embarrass the proceedings required to amend the Constitution, or to perform any function of the

We take this question entirely away from the politics of the country. We relieve Congress of sectional strifes, and, what is better than all, we restore to a whole race that freedom which is theirs by the gift of God, but which we for generations have wickedly denied them.

Reverdy Johnson, Maryland Democrat, made a memorable speech in support of the amendment. He explained at length why it would not be wise to rely upon the war power as a basis for universal emancipation. Next he rejected the contention of "a few wild men carried away by some loose and undefined notions of human liberty" that slavery had already been abolished by the Constitution and that all that was now needed was a pronouncement to that effect by Congress or by the Supreme Court. Hence there must be a constitutional amendment. He went on to answer the contention of Saulsbury, Powell and Davis that slavery was somehow beyond the scope of Article V's provision for amendment.

Then he asked, had the bondsman's long degradation rendered him unfit to accept the blessings of liberty? He answered with what, for him, was unwonted fervor:

Look to the illustrations which the times now afford . . . . He is willing to incur every personal danger which promises to result in throwing down his shackles and making him tread the earth which God has created for all as a man and not as a slave. It is an instinct of the soul. Tyranny may oppress it for ages and centuries . . . ; but the sentiment is ever there; it kindles into a flame in the very furnace of affliction, and it avails itself of the first opportunity . . . promising the least chance of escape . . . , and whether it succeeds or fails . . . , vindicates in the very effort the inextinguishable right to liberty.[79]

If Johnson had sensed from the opinions being ventilated that members contemplated that the proposed text would effect some veritable revolution in the federal system—other than what the words fairly imported—doubtless he would have addressed himself pointedly

---

Government, would be to enable disloyal and rebellious States to deprive the people of loyal and faithful States of their most valued privileges. . . .

Knap published this as a pamphlet of 11 pages. It appears in *Miscellaneous Writings of the late Hon. Joseph P. Bradley*, Charles Bradley, ed., (Newark, N.J.: L. J. Hardman, 1902), at 151–63.

Joel P. Bishop argued that it needed only three-fourths of the States actually participating in the Union to ratify the Thirteenth Amendment, in his *Commentaries on the Criminal Law*, third ed., 2 vols. (Boston: Little, Brown and Co., 1865), I, 276. Bishop had early become associated with the anti-slavery movement.

The same problem of ratification, in the case of the Fourteenth Amendment, was noted supra, pp. 255–57.

[79] Cong. Globe, 38–1, 1419–24. Apr. 5.

to that matter. He was ever the prudent counsellor, vigilant to fasten loose ends. But now Johnson offered no caveat about the meaning of the amendment.

Senator Timothy O. Howe of Wisconsin condemned the way in which the defenders of slavery, "by bluster, by threats, by menace," had imposed upon the nation; the time had come to submit "to the American conscience" the question whether slavery ought longer to be tolerated.[80]

John P. Hale, easy-going Senator from New Hampshire, could not refrain from replying to Saulsbury, despite his resolve not to make another speech against slavery. (He had been Free-Soil candidate for the Presidency in 1852.) In jocular remarks he said that although the defenders of slavery "die hard, very hard," the "day when the nation is to commence its real life . . . [is] near at hand."[81]

Senator Wilson's contribution, and that of Sumner, may be judged from what has been quoted. Key words from the speeches by Clark and Harlan have suggested the direction of their remarks. That substantially completes the favorable side of the Senate debate on the Thirteenth Amendment, save for a carefully prepared speech by the Senator who had introduced S.J. Res. 16.

John B. Henderson of Missouri, Virginia-born, had been a staunch Democrat through the election of 1860. His speech on April 7, 1864, he said, "does not spring from hatred of slaveholders, for, whether in honor or shame, I am a slaveholder to-day."[82] "Nine tenths, perhaps, of the loyal men of the country conscientiously believe that slavery is morally wrong and an evil in government." The time had come "to follow the dictates of right" by amending the Constitution. In the days of Jefferson and Jackson, the Democratic party had "advocated the largest liberty"; it should not object now to abolishing slavery. He remarked that "the tendency of our Government now is to centralize power, to destroy the powers of the States and make a nation supreme in all things"; this should not be allowed to continue after peace was won. Evidently appealing to the Democrats, he closed on this note:

> I will not be intimidated by the fears of negro equality. . . . Whether he shall be a citizen of any one of the States is a question for that State to determine. . . . So in passing this amendment we do not confer upon the negro the right to vote. We give him no right except his freedom, and leave the rest to the States.

---

80 Ibid., App., 111–18. Apr. 4.
81 Ibid., 1443. Apr. 6.
82 Ibid., 1459–65. He spoke with

care: "I have committed to writing the most of what I shall say."

I will not be deterred from doing an act of simple justice from
fear of the consequences. . . .

"We may not be able now to solve the many problems that universal
emancipation may present": he would do justice now, and meet them
as they came. (Two years later he would join in carrying the Civil
Rights Bill over President Johnson's veto.)

On April 8, Sumner made a last-minute protestation in favor of
the formula he had offered: "all persons are equal before the law, so
that no person can hold another as a slave." Trumbull replied that the
Judiciary Committee had considered the matter at length and had
reported what "a majority . . . thought . . . were the best words." Why
was the Senator "so pertinacious" about words "copied from the French
Revolution?" When Sumner persisted, Senator Jacob M. Howard of
Michigan (a member of the Judiciary Committee) spoke forthrightly:

> Now, sir, I wish as much as the Senator from Massachusetts . . .
> to use significant language, language that cannot be mistaken or mis-
> understood; but I prefer to dismiss all reference to French constitu-
> tions or French codes, and go back to the good old Anglo-Saxon
> language employed by our fathers in the ordinance of 1787, an ex-
> pression which has been adjudicated upon repeatedly, which is per-
> fectly well understood both by the public and by judicial tribunals,
> a phrase, I may say further, which is peculiarly near and dear to the
> people of the Northwestern Territory, from whose soil slavery was
> excluded by it. I think it is well understood, well comprehended by the
> people of the United States, and that no court of justice, no magis-
> trate, no person, old or young, can misapprehend the meaning and
> effect of that clear, brief, and comprehensive clause. I hope we shall
> stand by the report of the committee.[83]

The words of the proposed amendment had been written into
Michigan's first constitution of 1835, and in its then operative document of 1850. Howard had been the State's attorney general from 1855
to 1861; he was, moreover, a front-line Republican. He was satisfied
that the language had a well-established meaning, in law and in
popular understanding. This is what the amendment would make universal.

---

[83] Ibid., 1488–89. Apr. 8.
Howard pointed to uncertainties
latent in Sumner's language. For example, did "all persons" include
women? Would a wife "be equal to
her husband and as free as her husband before the law"? Inadvertently
Sumner's words might becloud well-
established propositions in various
fields of private law.

Howard had a scholarly command
of French literature and history; he
informed Sumner that the phrase he
cherished was not the language of the
decree by which slavery was abolished.

DEBATE IN THE HOUSE OF REPRESENTATIVES

ON MARCH 19, 1864, Representative Wilson reported from the Judiciary Committee his joint resolution for an amendment to declare that "Slavery, being incompatible with a free Government, is forever prohibited . . . ."[84] His explanation was sharply focused: "The proposition introduces no intricate question of constitutional law for discussion. It simply submits a question of fact for our determination . . . . Is slavery incompatible with a free Government? This is the true question involved; and no artful summonings of cunningly devised side issues, or of the ghosts of dead expediencies, can release any member of this body from passing upon this single issue. It is all there is in the case. . . ." He surveyed the many respects in which "an aristocracy" had attained "unlimited power, while the people were . . . denied the inestimable privileges which by right they should have enjoyed in all the fullness designed by the Constitution." "An equal and exact observance of the constitutional rights of each and every citizen, in each and every State, is the end to which we should cause the lessons of this war to carry us. . . ." The nation should now pronounce the dissolution of slavery.

Here Wilson's joint resolution drops out of view.

On March 28—the day when Trumbull opened debate on S.J. Res. 16 in the Senate—Thad Stevens offered in the House his own joint resolution, H.R.J. Res. 53, for a constitutional amendment to abolish slavery: the words were almost identical to Section 1 of S.J. Res. 16.[85] In presenting his text, Stevens did a characteristically audacious thing: he "demanded the previous question." Apparently he wanted to carry his measure then and there, without debate. Instantly his path was blocked by Holman of Indiana, Democrat.

William S. Holman (1822–97), then in the third of his sixteen terms in the House, typified an important segment of the Democracy. He came from southeastern Indiana—the Ohio line was near by, Kentucky lay just across the river. Like the man he rose to challenge, Holman was lanky and careless in his appearance, unconventional, astute, and inflexible in the pursuit of his principles. These included economy in public expenditures (whereby he won the title of "The Great Objector") and the preservation of a simple agrarian economy, with State sovereignty averting the "central despotism" the Radical party would impose.

---

[84] Ibid., 1199–1204. Supra, p. 1137.
[85] Ibid., 1325. There was a further provision, to annul so much of Article IV, Section 2, as provided for the rendition of persons "held to service or labour." In a moment he caused that to be struck.

The people of Indiana were of two minds about slavery. At the final division where the House passed the Thirteenth Amendment, the State's four Republicans voted yea, while five of its Democrats voted nay and two others who had failed of reelection abstained.[86]

The upshot of Stevens' move was that while Holman could not muster enough votes to table the joint resolution, Stevens could not find the requisite two-thirds to carry it; he obtained two postponements and there the measure disappeared.[87]

In the meantime, S.J. Res. 16 was passed by the Senate and sent to the House. Holman moved for a rejection at once, and lost by 55 yeas, 76 nays.[88] Debate followed, from May 31 to June 15, 1864. Supporters and opponents of the Amendment spoke in about equal numbers. The main contentions of the latter were that the abolition of slavery was beyond the scope of the amending power; that the aim at this moment should be to hasten restoration of the Union under the Constitution as it was—not to give the Southern people still further reason for resistance. Opponents also dilated on the repulsiveness of lifting the black man to equality with the white: that pointed toward social equality, miscegenation, Negro voting. Such comments, in the main, seem to have been intemperate efforts to make the proposal odious.

Of the speeches in opposition, that by Holman[89] appears to contain the passage most helpful to the thesis that the amendment was intended by its advocates and recognized by critics to have a far more powerful libertarian sweep than the words would naturally convey. He began by saying that "The merits of the amendment are of comparatively little moment. The more serious question is, shall the Constitution be amended at all. . . ." He answered No: the times were inauspicious. "If you amend the Constitution simply to render it hostile to the institutions of the South, you will not restore the Union." The purpose "in the secret councils of your ruling cabal is not for the Union," but rather to make sure that "if the Union cannot be restored with slavery abolished[,] the separation shall be eternal."

Then came this passage:

> But, sir, the amendment goes further. It confers on Congress the power to invade any State to enforce the freedom of the African in war or peace. What is the meaning of all that? Is freedom the

---

[86] One not voting was Daniel W. Voorhees of Terre Haute who, although seated in the 39th Congress, soon was replaced by the Republican contestant. Republicans voting yea included Colfax, the Speaker, and George W. Julian, the advanced opponent of slavery.

[87] Ibid., 1325; 1336; 1680.

[88] Ibid., 2612. May 31, 1864.

[89] Ibid., 2960–62. June 14, 1864.

simple exemption from personal servitude? No, sir; in the language of America it means the right to participate in government, the freedom for which our fathers resisted the British empire. Mere exemption from servitude is a miserable idea of freedom. . . . Then, sir, this amendment has some significance. Your policy, directed in its main purpose to the enfranchisement of a people who have looked with indifference on your struggle, who have given their strength to your enemies, and then the constitutional power to force them into freedom, to citizenship. If such be your purpose, why deceive a noble and confiding people? . . .

He cried out against the "visionary fanaticism" which, in order to elevate the African, "strikes down . . . the local sovereignty of the States, the only resistance this day to a central despotism . . . ."

What does this come to? The amendment, said Holman, meant more than the end of *personal servitude*: it meant the *enfranchisement of a people*. But in its primary sense, the word "enfranchisement" is not limited to voting: it signifies "liberation from imprisonment, servitude, or political subjection."[90] From the context, seemingly Holman was thinking of admission into *citizenship*—which is what the Civil Rights Act of 1866 did in its opening sentence. Perhaps he feared that a "fanatical" Congress might even attempt so deep an invasion of the rights of the States as to confer upon freedmen the right to vote. The substance of his charge, however, is this: that the amendment would not simply break the fetter and then leave the African to the local sovereignty of the State—no, Congress would "force" rights of citizenship upon him, and thereby "this new act of folly and madness" would bring a "fatal change" "in the relation of the States to the Federal Government."

One may say, then, that Holman foresaw (and utterly deplored) that the amendment, if adopted, would be followed by legislation such as did come in the Civil Rights Act of 1866. That leaves intact the problem of constitutional construction, what legal effects would result from the Thirteenth Amendment? Holman was warning that *any* consequence would be an undercutting of State sovereignty, "the cornerstone of the Republic."[91]

---

[90] *Oxford English Dictionary.*

> As low as to thy foot
>   doth Cassius fall,
> To beg enfranchisement
>   for Publius Cimber.

The conspirators were asking Caesar to release Cimber from an order of banishment.

[91] Anson Herrick, sometime office holder at New York City and editor of a weekly journal, was serving a single term in Congress. He spoke on the theme that the proposal was "a disunion measure"; there could be no reconciliation until "the glowing fanatics of the party now in power . . . cease to breathe threatenings and slaughter upon the southern people

XIX: *Thirteenth Amendment and Civil Rights Act*

If Holman had sat in the 39th Congress, one might compare his action on the Civil Rights Bill and on the Fourteenth Amendment with his lament over the implications of the Thirteenth; but he was not the Democratic candidate in his district, which was carried by a Republican.

One should not leave Holman's speech without noting that he was quite wrong in saying that Africans "looked with indifference on your struggle," and unjust in his reproach that slave people had "given their strength to your enemies."

Fernando Wood, ex-mayor of New York and one of the bitterest of Northern anti-war Democrats, made this comment:

---

for the *sin* of slaveholding . . . ." He said,

> Sir, the slavery issue, which this resolution seeks to finally settle in a summary manner by the immediate abolition of slavery, is legitimately merged in the higher issue of the right of the States to control their domestic affairs, and to fix each for itself the status, not only of the negro, but of all other people who dwell within their borders. That is the great question involved in the resolution now before the House.
>
> . . .

His plea was, do not raise "a barrier of insurmountable magnitude" to restoration of the Union as it was. Cong. Globe, 38–1, 2615–18. May 31, 1864.

Indeed it was true that each State had had exclusive authority over the status of all who dwelt within its jurisdiction; the Thirteenth Amendment would make a breach in that exclusive authority. The "great question" was whether such a breach should be made. To a dogmatic Democrat, that would be a monstrous thing. Herrick did not purport to consider what the particular consequences might be.

Robert Mallory, Unionist, represented a district surrounding Louisville, Kentucky; he was now in his third (and last) term. He had helped to hold his State in the Union; now he was striving to hold the Union under the Constitution as it had been. When M. Russell Thayer of Pennsylvania said that "now is the time to

uproot and destroy forever this prolific cause of all our sufferings," (ibid., 2980), Mallory rose to reply that it was "the most inopportune" time. What had begun as a war to save the Union had been turned into a war to destroy slavery. In the name of the loyal slave State of Kentucky, he protested.

> Now, let me ask you a practical question. What do you intend to do with the slaves you propose to set free? . . .

He answered his own question:

> you propose to leave them where they are freed, and protect them in their right to remain there. You do not intend, however, to leave them to the tender mercies of those States. You propose by a most flagrant violation of their rights to hold the control of this large class in these various States in your own hands. . . . Do you expect that the States will submit quietly to this outrage? You are not so infatuated. . . .

He concluded, "I believe that the only way to preserve this Union is to stand by the Constitution as our fathers made it . . . ." Ibid., 2981–83. June 15, 1864.

Mallory was attempting no nice construction of the proposed Amendment; its immediate effect would be to turn slaves into freemen—and he explained why this seemed highly inexpedient. The particular consequence he mentioned did indeed come to pass: the Freedmen's Bureau was intruded into the State of Kentucky.

This proposed alteration of the Constitution is therefore beyond the power of the Government, but the necessary consequences of it are revoltingly so. It involves the extermination of the white men of the southern States, and the forfeiture of all the land and other property belonging to them. Negroes and military colonists will take the place of the race thus blotted out of existence. Is this intended as the last scene of the bloody drama of carnage and civil war now being prosecuted? . . .[92]

Of course the Thirteenth Amendment did not contemplate the blotting out of the white men of the South. If their property was confiscable, it would be by reason of their rebellion and not by force of the amendment. The excerpt serves as a caution about treating the utterances of opponents as credible admissions against interest and serious interpretations of the effect of the amendment.

Of speakers supporting the proposal, none appreciated it in loftier terms than Ebon C. Ingersoll of Illinois, newly seated as successor to Owen Lovejoy, deceased.

I am in favor of the adoption of this amendment because it will secure to the oppressed slave his natural and God-given rights. . . . He has a right to till the soil, to earn his bread by the sweat of his brow, and enjoy the rewards of his own labor. He has a right to the endearments and enjoyment of family ties; and no white man has any right to rob him of or infringe upon any of these blessings.

He spoke also of the benefit to "seven millions of poor white people who live in the slave States . . . . Slavery has kept them in ignorance, in poverty, and in degradation. . . ."[93]

William D. Kelley, then in the second of his fifteen terms as Representative of a Philadelphia constituency, made a spirited rebuttal to Democratic objections.

What, asks the gentleman, are you going to do with the freed negroes? . . . I will trust the free negroes to the care of God, under our beneficent republican institutions. . . .

Kelley affirmed that

When the proposed amendment to the Constitution shall have been adopted . . . , that instrument will be perfect as the genius of man can conceive. . . .[94]

---

[92] Cong. Globe, 38-1, 2940-43, at 2941. June 14, 1864.
[93] Ibid., 2989-91. June 15, 1864.
[94] Ibid., 2983-85. June 15, 1864.

Words attributed to Kelley in Professor tenBroek's *Equal Under Law*, at 165, were in fact extracted from the remarks of the speaker who fol-

Kelley was notable as a self-made man; "all his early struggles and his innate perceptions of the rights of man made him an enemy to all forms of oppression."[95] But he did not have the genius to perceive the constitutional problems that lay beyond emancipation.

On June 7, 1864—eight days before the House voted on the joint resolution—the National Union [Republican] Convention met in Baltimore; it renominated Lincoln, on a platform that called for a constitutional amendment to "terminate and forever prohibit the existence of slavery . . . ." The Democratic Convention, in August, professed its aim "for a cessation of hostilities" and "to preserve the Federal Union and the rights of the States unimpaired . . . ." It nominated General McClellan.

In the election, Lincoln won 212 electoral votes to McClellan's 21 from Delaware, New Jersey, and Kentucky. That gives a distorted reflection: the popular vote was about 2,207,000 to 1,804,000. In States that provided for voting from the army, Lincoln did handsomely, save that Kentucky regiments preferred the Democratic party by more than 2 to 1. New York was carried by 50.5 percent; Connecticut and New Hampshire by about 52 percent; Illinois and Indiana by about 54 percent. Lincoln carried Pennsylvania by less than 52 percent—but would have won there even without the soldier vote of better than 2 to 1. He carried Ohio by nearly 57 percent—and would have succeeded even without the soldiers' preference of 4 to 1.[96]

The President's message of December 6, 1864, to the Second Session of the 38th Congress said that in the recent elections "the voice of the people" was "most clearly declared" in favor of the constitutional

---

lowed, Representative Joseph K. Edgerton of Indiana, a one-term Democrat. Enumerating "cardinal objections" to the joint resolution, Edgerton said:

> There can, . . . it seems to me, be no practical purpose to be accomplished by this attempt . . . at this time, except to indicate to the world, and especially to the men in arms against us, that the war on our part is to accomplish the very purpose with which they charged us in the beginning, namely, the abolition of slavery . . . , and the political and social elevation of negroes to all the rights of white men. . . .

Pp. 2985–88, at 2987.

It was a reflection upon the credi-

bility of the objector, and not an accurate statement of the purpose of the Amendment, to say that it was designed to produce political and social equality.

[95] John Sherman, *Recollection of Forty Years in the House, Senate and Cabinet*, 2 vols. (Chicago, New York, London, Berlin: Werner Co., 1895), II, 1078.

[96] Figures are based on what appears in *Historical Statistics of the United States, Colonial Times to 1957* (Government Printing Office, 1960), prepared by the Bureau of the Census with the cooperation of the Social Science Research Council; the *New York Tribune Almanac* for 1865; and the Annual Cyclopaedia for 1864—avoiding any significant discrepancy where such appears.

amendment pending in the House of Representatives. "I venture to recommend the reconsideration and passage of the measure at the present session."[97]

SECOND DEBATE IN THE HOUSE

REPRESENTATIVE JAMES M. Ashley of Ohio—already introduced as an animated member of the Radical wing of the Republican party—assumed the management of the proposed amendment at the Second Session.[98] Opening debate, he said that slavery, always "revolting and brutal," had become intolerable. He dwelt upon its inhumanity to its victims, and its debauching of the entire national life. In his opinion,

If the national Constitution had been rightfully interpreted, and the Government organized under it properly administered, slavery could not have legally existed in this country for a single hour . . . .

He challenged the Democratic position that the abolition of slavery was beyond the amending power. Ratification by three-fourths of those States not in rebellion would suffice. He volunteered that when the rebellion was suppressed, the inhabitants of the rebel States "will be under the exclusive jurisdiction of Congress . . . ." [Ashley was chairman of the Committee on the Territories, and presumably was thinking of the role that committee might play.] "The genius of history with iron pen is waiting to record our verdict . . . ," he concluded.[99]

Slavery was dead: so it was asserted by members on both sides of the House. Justin S. Morrill, Republican from Vermont, quoted Richmond journals which argued that it was better to liberate slaves to fight for the Confederacy than to lose them in defeat. He asked,

Can it be that the last Swiss Guard in the defense of slavery shall prove to be from the free States in Congress assembled? . . .[100]

---

[97] Cong. Globe, 38-2, App. 1, 3; *Collected Works of Abraham Lincoln*, VIII, 136, 148-49.

[98] Supra, ch. 1, n. 59, p. 268.

[99] Cong. Globe, 38-2, 138-41, Jan. 6, 1865.

[100] Ibid., 172-74. Jan. 9.

On January 6, Representative Godlove S. Orth of Indiana had said: "Slavery is dying . . . . No act of ours is necessary to accomplish this result, but . . . let us take care to provide by amendment of the Constitution that under no circumstances hereafter shall slavery exist in any of these States."

"Another and also a very important question is rapidly pressing upon us for solution": reconstruction, to enforce in each rebel State the guaranty of a republican form of government. With "personal freedom without distinction assured to every one of their citizens," and "every germ of aristocracy uprooted," it would be time to readmit the wayward sisters to the family circle.

"Some good people" were unnecessarily uneasy over "the question, 'What shall we do for or with the

Moses F. Odell, Democrat from Brooklyn, New York, spoke next:

> That slavery is dead is an admitted truth. . . .
>
> Now, I am in favor of giving it a constitutional burial; not by the irregularity of a proclamation by the President, of doubtful constitutionality . . . .[101]

He would vote for the amendment—as he had at the First Session. Odell was about to leave the House: the Republican he had defeated in 1862 had recaptured the seat in the 39th Congress.

Daniel W. Voorhees of Indiana, Democrat, could not close his eyes to events transpiring in the Confederacy: "Slavery can no longer exist . . . . Whether for better or for worse it is passing away. . . ." Even so, he said, he would vote against the amendment. He apprehended that the party in power would go on to make the liberated black "a voter, a juror, and eligible to office. . . ."[102]

Actually, Voorhees was out of town when the amendment came to a vote. He sat in the 39th Congress less than three months, when a contest was decided in favor of his Republican opponent.

"In my judgment the fate of slavery is sealed," said Holman of Indiana. Even so, "I oppose the amendment, because, admitting the full force of your arguments, it is unnecessary, a dangerous precedent without a benefit."[103]

"If the slave is to be used in this war let him be used in the cause of the Union," said Austin A. King, Missouri Democrat.[104] He would vote for the amendment. At the First Session his vote was nay—but since then he had suffered a chastening defeat at the polls.

Over fifty members had something to say before the vote was taken—about half of whom would not be returning for the 39th Congress.[105] An historic moment was at hand, and many wanted to put

---

freedmen?' May we not with equal propriety ask, 'What shall we do for or with the late owners of these freedmen?' " The wisest course, he thought —after the system that debased the one and enfeebled the other had ceased to exist—was "to leave both classes in the hands of God . . . , giving to each equal protection under the law . . . ." Cong. Globe, 38–2, 141–44.

Orth represented a district in western Indiana, north of the center of the State, holding it by a precarious 52 percent. In the 39th Congress, when convinced of Johnson's unyield-

ing stand, he became an advanced Radical.

[101] Cong. Globe, 38–2, 174–75. Jan. 9.

[102] Ibid., 180–81. Jan. 9.

[103] Ibid., 217–19. Jan. 11.

[104] Ibid., 195–99. Jan. 10.

[105] Some of those not returning had not been candidates for reelection.

In the reckoning of those not returning are included three who would temporarily occupy contested seats in the 39th Congress: James Brooks of New York, Alexander H. Coffroth of Pennsylvania, and Daniel W. Voorhees of Indiana, Democrats.

themselves on record—some to utter defiance, some to express accord with the doom of slavery. In the main these final words are of little significance in construing the Thirteenth Amendment.

Representatives from Kentucky were in a rather special position. Brutus J. Clay, Unionist from the bluegrass region, protested that "in reality this is a movement, not against the rebellious States, but against a loyal State now in the Union." He had told his people "that you would never interfere with the rights guarantied to the States . . . ."[106]

Answer was made by his nephew, Green Clay Smith,[107] whose district was in northernmost Kentucky, opposite Cincinnati. Smith had served as a brigadier general in the Army of Kentucky until the convening of the 38th Congress. He said that "While I have had all the prejudices concerning [slavery] that any man could have, . . . and while, as an abstract proposition, I cannot now altogether deny the principles in which I was educated, yet when I view the present condition of the country, . . . I lay aside those prejudices . . . ." "Whatever may have been my opinion four years ago," now he agreed with what the President had written to Colonel Hodges of Frankfort: "If slavery is not wrong, nothing is wrong."[108] To support abolition did not mean that one was "in favor of miscegenation, amalgamation, association, and all that kind of thing."

The proposed amendment, he said, was not directed against the interests of Kentucky:

> Slavery . . . has kept us back. Ohio, a younger State, . . . has outstripped us vastly . . . . And so with every State North. . . . The time has come, and I thank God for it, when we will wipe that institution out . . . .

---

[106] Cong. Globe, 38–2, 181–83. Jan. 9.

[107] Ibid., 234–38. Jan. 12.

Brutus Junius Clay (1808–78) was born at Richmond, Kentucky, the son of Green Clay (1757–1826), soldier and legislator. [Another son was Cassius Marcellus Clay (1810–1903), abolitionist, and minister to Russia under President Lincoln.]

Green Clay Smith (1826–95), also born in Richmond, was named for his maternal grandfather. His father, John Speed Smith (1792–1854) had been a member of Congress, and was holder of numerous other offices.

Green Clay Smith was reelected to the 39th Congress and sat during its First Session; he resigned to become

Governor of Montana Territory, in which post he served to the end of the Johnson Administration.

Thereafter he was ordained to the Baptist ministry, and became an evangelist. He was the Prohibition party's candidate for President in 1876, receiving less than 10,000 votes.

Addendum: Justice Miller also was born in Richmond, Kentucky—in 1816, under circumstances far less promising than attended members of the Clay family.

[108] A sentence from Lincoln's famous letter to Albert G. Hodges of the *Frankfort Commonwealth*, April 4, 1864. *Collected Works of Abraham Lincoln*, VII, 281.

With mounting fervor he affirmed his belief that the nation would, "by the blood which is now being spilt, be brought back to a stronger union, a more surely perpetual union, and a more glorious union than it was before." With slavery left behind, this would grow to be "a country of great men and great women, a country which will command the respect and admiration of the whole civilized world."

The speech had been impressive; the House gave additional time to hear more.

It was not by reasoned argument or by spiritual conversion that the amendment would be carried. It was a practical business of inducing about a score of Democrats to act in disregard of their party. Lincoln was prepared to exert the full weight of his office in that effort—in which he worked through Congressmen of such diverse outlook as Ashley[109] the abolitionist and James S. Rollins of Missouri, owner of many slaves. The latter, in June 1864, had voted nay; but in November

---

[109] An example of Ashley's activity is recorded in John G. Nicolay and John Hay, *Abraham Lincoln: A History*, 10 vols. (New York: Century Co., 1890), X, 84, and restated in Sandburg, *Abraham Lincoln: The War Years*, IV, 9–10.

During the war the monopoly enjoyed by the Camden & Amboy Railroad Company in New Jersey was threatened by rival interests that importuned Congress to enact an "air line" bill that would enable them to breach the exclusive grant from the State. See supra, pp. 724–25, 736–37, and Charles Fairman, "Mr. Justice Bradley's Appointment to the Supreme Court and the Legal Tender Cases," *Harv. L. Rev.*, 54:977 and 1128, at 983–87 (1941).

On January 18, 1865, Ashley reported to the President that if the Administration would prevent the enactment at that session of the "air line" bill, Camden & Amboy would "make the New Jersey Democrats help about the [constitutional] amendment, either by their votes or absence."

In fact, when the House voted on the Thirteenth Amendment, on January 31, there was one shift in the New Jersey delegation: Rogers (although he had made a speech against the amendment on January 7, Cong. Globe, 38–2, 150–54), now was recorded as not voting.

Mr. ROLLINS, of Missouri, stated that Mr. ROGERS, of New Jersey, had been confined to his room several days by indisposition.
Cong. Globe, 38–2, 530.

There seems to have been more to it than that. On March 1, 1866, in the House, Rogers was questioned pointedly by Thayer of Pennsylvania, Republican, and by Niblack of Indiana, Democrat, concerning his action on the constitutional amendment. Rogers reiterated that "If I could have been here, I would have cast my vote most unhesitatingly against it." He said he would not have joined in robbing a portion of the people of millions of dollars invested in slaves. "But slavery is dead now, and I am glad it is gone." Cong. Globe, 39–1, 1123.

Next day, Windom of Minnesota, Republican, twitted Rogers on the same matter: "I was informed at the time that he was pledged to vote for it, but that he was sick when it was passed . . . ." Rogers protested, "I never agreed, directly or indirectly, to vote for that constitutional amendment. . . ." Niblack then said, "I only regret that the gentleman was not able to give us more particularly and in detail the reasons why he did not vote on that subject. . . ." Cong. Globe, 39–1, 1158.

the people of Missouri had chosen delegates to a constitutional convention who were certainly going to abolish slavery. Responding to a pencilled summons, Rollins went to see the President: he told Lincoln that he had already decided to vote for the amendment—and thereupon was enlisted "to talk to *all* the border State men whom you can approach properly . . . ."[110]

On January 13, Rollins rose to make remarks, "in the nature of a personal explanation" why, this time, he would vote for the constitutional amendment. He asked, "Does any man in this House . . . believe that the institution of African slavery will survive this rebellion?" He subscribed to the statement in the Declaration of Independence, that all men are created equal: he added, "without distinction of race or of color." "I am no longer the owner of a slave, and I thank God for it." [He had had telegraphic news of the ordinance abolishing slavery, adopted by the Missouri constitutional convention on January 11.] He concluded, Let us all be thankful "that although we have had our trials, we have saved our country; that although we have been guilty of sins we have wiped them out, and that we at length stand up a great and powerful people, . . . 'redeemed, regenerated, and disinthralled by the genius of universal emancipation.' "

Rollins had spoken more than two hours—his time being twice extended at Ashley's request. At the conclusion there was "Loud applause on the floor and in the galleries . . . ."[111] This appeal, James G. Blaine recalled, had "special weight." "The tone and temper of the speeches exhibited assurance on one side and failing confidence on the other."[112]

On January 31, 1865, Ashley made his motion, to reconsider the vote of June 15. In anticipation, the galleries were crowded. A Democrat's effort to table was defeated, 57 to 111. That showed not quite the two-thirds strength necessary to propose a constitutional

---

[110] Rollins' district ran from Boone and Callaway counties in the central part of the State, along the north side of the Missouri River, and as far north as Pike and Ralls counties on the Mississippi—an area frequently mentioned in connection with railroad-aid bonds, supra, chapter 18.

In 1862, Rollins had won by 7,700 votes against 2,797 for Arnold Krekel, Emancipationist.

In 1865, January saw Krekel chosen president of the constitutional convention, and in March he became United States District Judge for Western Missouri.

Rollins, speaking on the objects of the war, had told the House on June 1, 1864, that "rather than see the negro, under the influence of a false philanthropy and a pertinacious fanaticism, taking the place of the white man, and made by law politically and socially his equal, . . . I would say let there be separation, hoping still, however, that . . . another generation . . . would bring about union once more . . . ." Cong. Globe, 38–1, 2577.

[111] Cong. Globe, 38–2, 258–263.

[112] *Twenty Years of Congress*, 2 vols. (Norwich, Conn.: Henry Bill Publishing Co., 1884, 1886), I, 538.

amendment. During the call, the absences of Rogers of New Jersey and Voorhees of Indiana were accounted for—two sturdy Democrats. The motion to reconsider then was put: yeas 112, nays 57—still less than two-thirds. Then the roll was called, and each defection by a Democrat was applauded. Speaker Colfax directed that his own vote be recorded. The last two names on the roll were noteworthy. Henry G. Worthington—Nevada's one Representative, recently arrived, voted yea. (The significance of that new State's admission, in relation to the constitutional amendment, had been foreseen.) And last was George H. Yeaman of Kentucky, Unionist: he had not voted in June—now he voted yea.[113] The count was 119 to 56, 8 not voting: enough, with little to spare.[114]

When at last the cheering had been quieted, the House, on Ingersoll's motion, adjourned "in honor of this immortal and sublime event."

One opponent, so far unmentioned, was Alexander Long, Democrat from Cincinnati: he made no speech, but on both occasions voted against the amendment. He would soon be going home, to practice law—and three years later to become agent for Chief Justice Chase in his candidacy for the Democratic nomination for President.[115]

THE IMPORT OF THE DEBATES

NOTHING LESS THAN an amendment of the Constitution would have sufficed for the eradication of slavery. The Emancipation Proclamation was based on the war powers of the Executive: its scope was limited, and its validity and effect would be subject to challenge. Moreover, when the nation came to free itself from this heaviest of burdens, only the most solemn form of attestation would have seemed appropriate.

[113] Yeaman represented a district along the Ohio River, opposite southwestern Indiana. In 1862 he had defeated a Democrat by vote of 8,311 to 3,087. In 1864, however, he had lost to a Conservative, receiving 5,786 to 6,974.

On January 9, in a prepared speech, he announced his decision to vote for the amendment—explaining his course to Southerners who would disapprove. "And since it is settled that slavery must die, . . . why keep the country in a turmoil . . . .?" "Events have taken the place of arguments . . . ." "I have emancipated myself from the unmanly fear of censure and saved myself from the embarrassments of a false position." Cong. Globe, 38–2, 168–72.

[114] Cong. Globe, 38–2, 531.

[115] Supra, ch. 11.

In 1862, Long had won his seat by a majority of 131 votes. In 1864 the Democrats of his district nominated a more attractive candidate—who was decisively defeated by Brigadier General Rutherford B. Hayes, who had spent his time "stumping the Shenandoah Valley."

However true it may have been that slavery was no longer viable, it could not be left simply to wither away. Only in obedience to an imperative mandate would the rebel States have made slavery unlawful; without a constitutional amendment, presumably many blacks would have been detained in servitude for years to come.

While Section 1 made universal what was already the law of many States, Section 2 added something essential: authority to enforce by appropriate legislation. Outstanding questions now would be, (1) What is the scope of the prohibition? (2) What is the extent of the legislative power to make the prohibition effective?

In a sense, indubitably the Thirteenth Amendment introduced a revolutionary change in the relation of the United States to the State governments. Never before had there been authority for federal intrusion between the State and its inhabitants in respect of the civil status of the latter; henceforth there would be warrant for entering to make sure that in fact "neither slavery nor involuntary servitude" existed. It was not merely authority to disallow State action found to contravene the prohibition: it was a power actually to interfere in order to bar the proscribed relationship between persons. To State-rights dogmatists, this shattered the premise which they regarded as fundamental to the Union. While that in itself seemed impious, indignation conjured up enormities that would follow, once the breach had been made.

To supporters of the amendment, there was glory enough in abolishing the institution which had long poisoned the nation's entire life. They rejoiced in the expectation that once the cause was eradicated, the baneful consequences would disappear. With a poor comprehension of social behavior, they did not perceive how enduring would be the mores that were entwined about it.

The debates seem not to support a conclusion that the men of the 38th Congress had a clear view of the ultimate results of the amendment. Indeed it would have been surprising if, when the war had not yet been ended, and when efforts were bent upon abolishing its cause, the participants had taken thought for the problems of another day. Planning was not a Congressional practice. Had the question been brought into focus, there could not have been agreement among two-thirds of the two Houses.

Attention was drawn above to the thesis that behind the Thirteenth Amendment there was a well-articulated purpose to give a "mandate to enforce . . . not just the liberty of the blacks but the liberty of the whites as well"; that this "included not merely freedom from personal bondage but protection in a wide range of natural and constitutional rights"; that indeed the amendment was intended by its drafters and sponsors to be "a consummation of abolitionism broadly conceived."[116] If one were privileged to treat this as a tract in progression from those of the moral reformers of a century before, one might pay respect to its spirit and pass by. But it may not be left at that. It was put forward as the authentic key to constitutional construction: a text derived from the Northwest Ordinance of 1787 should be given a special meaning drawn from antislavery agitation. But the Constitution binds a nation comprising citizens of many sorts—even men who may not hold entirely to the abolitionists' conception of equality. In so far as history may be relevant to the interpretation of the Constitution, all are equally entitled to have that history set forth as objectively as may be. There is no "higher law" superior to that.

If the thesis be taken seriously, when tested by the record it encounters formidable obstacles. Some of these will be recalled.

Representative Wilson, speaking for the Judiciary Committee, gave the first extended discussion of a constitutional amendment when he introduced his proposal: "Slavery, being incompatible with a Free Government, is forever prohibited . . . ." The proposition, he insisted, "introduces no intricate question of constitutional law for discussion."[117] That would have been untruthful if he had understood that the abolitionists' peculiar mode of interpretation would now be imposed. Wilson said that he excluded as irrelevant all "cunningly devised side issues."

Senator Henderson, who introduced S.J. Res. 16 to propose the amendment, said that "We give him [the slave] no right except his freedom, and leave the rest to the States."[118]

Senator Sumner did indeed speak in the dialect of the abolitionists: but the Thirteenth Amendment was none of his handiwork—he even delayed its passage in an effort to substitute his own measure. And Senator Howard—defending the language adopted from the Ordinance of 1787—said that "it is well understood . . . by the people of the United States, . . . no person . . . can misapprehend the meaning . . . ."[119]

When Ashley resumed the debate at the Second Session, he too reasoned like the abolitionists: but when he went among Democrats soliciting enough votes to carry the amendment, surely he was not representing that it would bring the "consummation of abolitionism broadly conceived."

---

[116] tenBroek, *Equal Under Law,* 157, 173, 196.

[117] Cong. Globe, 38–1, 1199, 1200. Supra, p. 1137.

[118] Ibid., 1459, 1465. Supra, p. 1142. It was pointed out above that in 1866

he supported the Civil Rights Bill; however, what is quoted above expressed his view on the effect of his proposal.

[119] Ibid., 1488–89. Supra, p. 1143.

Smith of Kentucky spoke most ardently of any Representative from a slave district who supported the amendment:[120] but in the 39th Congress he voted against the Civil Rights Bill—and at the end of the First Session accepted an appointment from President Johnson and vacated a seat which thereupon was filled by the Democrat Smith had defeated the year before.

In declaring his support for the amendment, Yeaman of Kentucky[121] said that on "the final destiny of the black man" he adhered to views he had expressed at the First Session. When the Wade-Davis bill was under discussion,[122] Yeaman had delivered an elaborate systematic address on "the elements and habits of political thought and influences that prepared men's minds and feelings" for the rupture that came in 1861. He viewed "the antagonism of race"—particularly where there was economic competition—as far more intractable than was realized by "the enthused democrat of the abolition school" who "makes his politics his religion." He insisted, "Dispose of the slavery question and the negro question remains. . . ."[123]

Evidently Yeaman's support of the amendment implied no acceptance of abolitionism broadly conceived.

Neither did that of Rollins of Missouri, whose weight in the scales seems to have been considerable.[124]

Mallory of Kentucky asked, "Does the mere abolition of slavery . . . by a constitutional amendment settle all the great questions springing up in relation to that institution?" Pointedly, "what are you going to do then with these liberated negroes?"[125] Other opponents asked the same question.

Grinnell of Iowa answered.

> What shall we do with them? . . . Cannot they who have supported themselves and their masters in the past take care of themselves? That, sir, is a question which we can well afford to leave unanswered, since the enslaved race are establishing their manhood and fighting our battles.[126]

Grinnell was an abolitionist, a clergyman and lawyer, and by his own description, a "radical." Speaking with this background, he said that the future status of the freedman could be left "unanswered."

Quite aside from utterances in debate, on a reckoning of num-

---

[120] Supra, p. 1152.
[121] Cong. Globe, 38–2, 172. Supra, note 113.
[122] Supra, pp. 97–98.
[123] Cong. Globe, 38–1, 2006–11, at 2010. Apr. 30, 1864. It was a re-markably inclusive and imaginative analysis—and anything but sanguine.
[124] Supra, pp. 1153–54.
[125] Cong. Globe, 38–2, 179. Jan. 9.
[126] Ibid., 199. Jan. 10.

bers it seems evident that when this constitutional amendment could be carried only by the accession of a group of Democrats to the united vote of Republicans whose opinions shaded from radical to conservative, there could not have been a consensus that the amendment for which they all voted would not only do what the words imported but would also impose the peculiar doctrines of the most radical among them. And in moral authority, the members of the 38th Congress, elected in 1862, came with no popular mandate to abolish slavery: the conviction that that step should be taken came gradually. The Presidential election of 1864 did carry a mandate for the proposed amendment—by 55 percent of the voters of the loyal States. The men of the 38th Congress did well to bow to that: but voters who chose Lincoln and the amendment cannot be said to have adhered to the peculiar doctrines of the abolitionists. The meaning of the text remained to be unfolded, by reasoned discussion.

Mallory warned that the Thirteenth Amendment would not settle all the great questions resulting from emancipation. Grinnell said that the problem could well be left unanswered, to await the 39th Congress—when "we shall have an overshadowing majority which will open a new page in our political history . . . ." Both were correct.

THE 39TH CONGRESS

ITS MANDATE EXPIRED, the 38th Congress closed on March 4, 1865. On April 9 came Lee's surrender. On April 15, Lincoln died.

Presently President Johnson set on foot what became "My Policy": Provisional Governors were appointed—conventions were summoned in the ex-rebel States—elections were held, new legislatures met, Black Codes were enacted—as has been recounted.[127] Congressional delegations were sent to Washington, to be on hand when the two Houses opened in December. As we know, they were not seated—a fact which the President resented, and presently made the ground for questioning the validity of action by the Congress.

When on December 4 the House chose a Speaker, 139 votes were cast for Schuyler Colfax of Indiana, Republican—36 for James Brooks, Copperhead from New York City (who on April 6 lost his contested seat to William E. Dodge, conservative Republican). That division reflects the outcome of the elections in November 1864. In the intervening thirteen months, a wholly new situation had developed—and Executive leadership had passed to a Union Democrat from Tennessee with whom neither the country nor even the Congressional leaders had

---

[127] Supra, pp. 105–17.

any distinct acquaintance. About half of the Congressmen were new; group affiliations had not yet solidified.

Of Senators from the 25 States represented in Congress, only 11 were Democrats: two each from New Jersey,[128] Delaware and Kentucky, and one each from Pennsylvania, Maryland (Reverdy Johnson), Indiana (Hendricks), California, and Oregon. Several nominal Republicans of conservative views presently began to act apart as friends of the President: notably Dixon of Connecticut, Cowan of Pennsylvania, and Doolittle of Wisconsin.

On that opening Monday, Sumner was ready with six bills, S. 2 to S. 7, to advance liberty and secure a republican form of government in various ways; S.J. Res. 1 to amend the Constitution; also three concurrent resolutions running to some 3,500 words. One of these would declare that the Thirteenth Amendment had been adopted by the ratification of the legislatures of three-fourths of the loyal States. The two other resolutions were "declaratory of the duty of Congress" in respect of the rebel States: numerous specifications were laid down, such as

> The complete suppression of all oligarchical pretensions, and the complete enfranchisement of all citizens, so that there shall be no denial of rights on account of color or race; but justice shall be impartial, and all shall be equal before the law.[129]

Sumner had a penchant for lofty declarations of this sort, albeit that they would have had no operative effect. Here he would settle the refractory problem of reconstruction, not by setting on foot an inquiry by a select group from which measures might emerge for general consideration, but by this prescription of generalities sprung from his own brain.

He had been forestalled by Thad Stevens, manipulator of men and master of practical legislative operations. On Friday, December 1, Stevens and other advanced Radicals had concerted a method for seizing control of reconstruction.[130] When the Republicans of the House

---

[128] Against John P. Stockton, seated on December 4, a protest was that day filed from members of the New Jersey Legislature. His seat was declared vacant on March 27, 1866. At the Second Session, in December 1866, Alexander G. Cattell, Republican, was seated.

William Wright died on November 1, 1866; Frederick T. Frelinghuysen, Republican, was appointed to the vacancy, and presently was elected, and served until March 3, 1869.

[129] Cong. Globe, 39–1, 2.

[130] Benjamin B. Kendrick, *The Journal of the Joint Committee of Fifteen on Reconstruction* (New York: n.p. 1914), 139–41.

It appears from the Introduction that the *Journal* was not printed until in 1884 the Senate made an order for 6,000 copies; that these were

met in caucus on Saturday evening, they approved—without fully understanding Stevens' strategy—a measure which he introduced on Monday, as soon as the House was organized: that a Joint Committee on Reconstruction be appointed to inquire into the condition of the rebel States and report whether they, or any of them, were entitled to be represented in either House. The result, when this was voted by House and Senate, was to give to the Joint Committee the initiative in establishing what the Southern States must do to gain restoration. As it turned out, the Joint Committee's most important work was in framing the Fourteenth Amendment.

APPROACH TO SENATOR TRUMBULL'S CIVIL RIGHTS BILL

ON DECEMBER 18, 1865, the Secretary of State certified that the Thirteenth Amendment had become a part of the Constitution.[131] Actually ratification had been completed by the action of the legislature of Georgia on December 6: it was the twenty-seventh to ratify out of the 36 States in the Union—and the eighth among the States that had joined the Confederacy.

It was related in an earlier chapter how Congress was concerned at the course of developments in the South—and how Senator Wilson on December 13 sought action "at once" on his bill for the protection of the freedmen in the insurrectionary States: he foresaw "great danger that at Christmas there will be bloody outbreaks."[132] His S. 9 would invalidate all laws whereby inequality in civil rights was imposed on the basis of color; anyone attempting to make or enforce such a law would be punishable by fine or imprisonment. He announced that "six eminent lawyers" had found his bill "clearly constitutional."

Sherman of Ohio and Trumbull of Illinois (chairman of the Judiciary Committee) expressed their sympathy with the purpose—which was quite sincere—but dissented as to time and manner. It would be prudent to wait until the Thirteenth Amendment was declared to be in force. Congress should not legislate "without having a full comprehension" of the matters involved, said Sherman; it should not be "left to the uncertain and ambiguous language of this bill." Legislation "general throughout the land" was needed, whereas Wilson's

---

never distributed, but that a copy was preserved at the Government Printing Office. Kendrick, a candidate for the doctorate at Columbia University, located the manuscript after it had been sold with Senator Fessen-

den's papers and had passed through several hands. It was published at pp. 37–129 of Dr. Kendrick's dissertation.

[131] 13 Stat. 774.

[132] Cong. Globe, 39–1, 39–42. Supra, pp. 122–23.

proposal was directed only at the States lately in rebellion.[133] Trumbull made like objections. The matter was "of too much importance" to be acted upon without consideration by a committee. He said,

> I trust we may pass a bill, if the action of the people in the southern States should make it necessary, that will be much more sweeping and efficient than the bill under consideration. . . .[134]

On December 19 Trumbull gave notice that he would soon "introduce a bill to enlarge the powers of the Freedmen's Bureau so as to secure freedom to all persons within the United States, and protect every individual in the full enjoyment of the rights of person and property and furnish him with means for their vindication. . . ." "I think it important that action should be taken . . . at an early day for the purpose of quieting apprehensions . . . lest by local legislation or a prevailing public sentiment in some of the States persons of the African race should continue to be oppressed and in fact deprived of their freedom . . . ."[135]

Actually this purpose led to two measures: S. 60, the Freedmen's Bureau Bill, and S. 61, the Civil Rights Bill—introduced on January 5, 1866.[136]

Wilson's bill came to naught—but not before there were further significant remarks. On December 20, Sumner called for instant enactment—and charged the President with an "attempt . . . to throw the mantle of official oblivion over sickening and heart-rending outrages . . . ."[137] Stewart of Nevada—a staunch Republican with a Mississippi affiliation who at this moment was striving mightily to promote moderation both South and North—praised the President's "pure and patriotic spirit" while calling for legislation to secure the freedmen "perfect equality before the law."[138] Wilson joined in, urging "a manly, generous, and earnest support" for President Johnson. Congress should pass, and the President would approve, legislation whereby "these freedmen, ground and degraded by two centuries of slavery, will in all respects be free . . . ."[139]

---

[133] Ibid., 41–42. Dec. 13.
[134] Ibid., 42–43. Dec. 13.
[135] Ibid., 77.
[136] Ibid., 129.
[137] Ibid., 90–95. He had also spoken of "whitewashing" on December 19, when the Senate received from the President a report on conditions in the Southern States, as well as the report of General Schurz on his trip through the South; gratuitously, the President included General Grant's more favorable and much more superficial impressions on a brief visit to the South. See supra, p. 124. Cong. Globe, 39–1, 78–80.
[138] Ibid., 109–11. Dec. 21.
[139] Ibid., 111–12.

Within a month, these Senators would join in passing the Freedmen's Bureau Bill—and a month after that they would be voting on whether to override the President's objections to it.

THE FREEDMEN'S BUREAU BILL

S. 60, FOR THE immediate protection of freedmen in the Southern States, and S. 61, to protect civil rights throughout the land, proceeded through the Senate in loose association, the former always in the lead. Some remarks apropos of the one had a bearing on the other: in particular, an exchange between Senator Hendricks and Senator Trumbull on January 19.[140]

The bill to extend the powers of the Freedmen's Bureau[141] provided, in its Section 7, that "it shall be the duty of the President . . . to extend military protection and jurisdiction over all cases affecting" persons discriminated against in States not in possession of full constitutional rights as parts of the Union, "and wherein, in consequence of any State or local law, ordinance, police or other regulation, custom, or prejudice, any of the civil rights or immunities belonging to white persons, including . . . [here were inserted the particulars enumerated in Section 1 of the Civil Rights Bill] are refused or denied to negroes . . . ."

Section 8 of the Freedmen's Bureau Bill began by defining a misdemeanor: any person who, under color of any State or local law, etc.—in a State not in possession of full rights in the Union—deprived any negro, on account of race, of any civil right secured to white persons, would be punishable by fine, or imprisonment, or both. [This language was modeled upon Section 2 of the Civil Rights Bill.] Section 8 continued: it would be the duty of the Bureau to take jurisdiction and determine offenses against the civil rights of negroes as defined in Sections 7 and 8. This jurisdiction would cease when the State had been fully restored to its relations to the United States.

These sections abounded in difficult questions—and Hendricks made a sharp attack upon them, as well as on other provisions. He understood that Trumbull based his bill upon the Thirteenth Amendment: but that amendment merely broke asunder the relation between master and slave—no new rights were thereby conferred; what civil rights the freedman had were fixed by State law. He mentioned the

---

[140] Ibid., 314–23.
[141] The text of the bill is set out in Edward McPherson, *The Political History of the United States of America during the Period of Recon-* struction, third ed. (Washington: James J. Chapman, 1880), 72–74. Further discussion appears supra, pp. 123–24.

right to testify, and the right to sit on a jury. Suppose that a minister, in obedience to State law, refused to solemnize a marriage between black and white: would he be subject to punishment by the Bureau?

Seeking to answer a host of these objections, Trumbull covered a wide field. The Bureau was "only designed to aid these helpless, ignorant, and unprotected people until they can provide for and take care of themselves." It was "a part of the military establishment"; the Government was entitled to exercise its war powers until its authority was "established firmly and upon a sure foundation . . ." The provisional governments recently set up remained subordinate to that authority—"the same authority that we have been exercising all the time in the rebellious States . . . ."

That was Trumbull's explanation of the Bureau's jurisdiction under Sections 7 and 8. He turned then to the matter of civil rights— what rights could be conferred in pursuance of the Thirteenth Amendment. S.60 would make temporary provision to secure those rights in the insurrectionary States; S.61, "somewhat akin to this," would extend to all parts of the country.

Here we come to Trumbull's exposition of what, in his view, might properly be done in conferring civil rights. The quotation will be long, but in the end it will all have pertinence—and major importance.

> But the Senator says that these sections, he supposes, derive their authority, in my opinion, from the amendment to the Constitution of the United States. Sir, I think that amendment does confer authority to enact these provisions into law and execute them . . . through the judicial tribunals in any State of the Union. What was the object of the constitutional amendment abolishing slavery? It was not, as the Senator says, simply to take away the power of the master over the slave. Did we not mean something more than that? Did we not mean that hereafter slavery should not exist, no matter whether the servitude was claimed as due to an individual or the State? The constitutional amendment abolishes just as absolutely all provisions of State or local law which make a man a slave as it takes away the power of his former master to control him.[142]

If the construction put by the Senator from Indiana upon the

---

[142] Trumbull's thought in these last two sentences becomes more clear when one recalls what Justice Miller had written, a few days earlier, to his Texas kinsman:

The laws proposed by Mississippi, Alabama, South Carolina &c do but change the form of the slavery. As it *was*, the individual slave belonged to, and laboured for the individual white man. As it is *proposed to be*, the whole body of the negro race in each state, must belong to and labour for the whole body of the white people of that state, under compulsion of law. Miller to William P. Ballinger, Jan. 11, 1866. Supra, pp. 124–25.

amendment be the true one, and we have merely taken from the master the power to control the slave and left him at the mercy of the State to be deprived of his civil rights, the trumpet of freedom that we have been blowing throughout the land has given an "uncertain sound," and the promised freedom is a delusion. Such was not the intention of Congress, which proposed the constitutional amendment, nor is such the fair meaning of the amendment itself. With the destruction of slavery necessarily follows the destruction of the incidents to slavery. When slavery was abolished, slave codes in its support were abolished also.

Trumbull went on to give his thought about State legislation abridging the liberty only of blacks:

> Those laws that prevented the colored man going from home, that did not allow him to buy or to sell, or to make contracts; that did not allow him to own property; that did not allow him to enforce rights; that did not allow him to be educated, were all badges of servitude made in the interest of slavery and as a part of slavery. They would never have been thought of or enacted but for slavery, and when slavery falls they fall also. The policy of the States where slavery has existed has been to legislate in its interest; and out of deference to slavery, which was tolerated by the Constitution of the United States, even some of the non-slaveholding States passed laws abridging the rights of the colored man which were restraints upon liberty. When slavery goes, all this system of legislation, devised in the interest of slavery and for the purpose of degrading the colored race, of keeping the negro in ignorance, of blotting out from his very soul the light of reason, if that were possible, that he might not think, but know only, like the ox, to labor, goes with it.

A new policy, Trumbull continued, resulted from the Thirteenth Amendment:

> Now, when slavery no longer exists, the policy of the Government is to legislate in the interest of freedom. Now, our laws are to be enacted with a view to educate, improve, enlighten, and Christianize the negro; to make him an independent man; to teach him to think and to reason; to improve that principle which the great Author of all has implanted in every human breast, which is susceptible of the highest cultivation, and destined to go on enlarging and expanding through the endless ages of eternity.

We interrupt for a moment. Surely Trumbull did not contemplate that Congress would pass any law to "Christianize the negro." Patently the First Amendment would forbid. His words misrepresented the idea he sought to express. This serves as a reminder: we are not entitled to take remarks in extemporaneous debate as necessarily expressing exactly what the speaker thought on some precise point he may not have had in mind.

Now resuming Trumbull's reply to Hendricks: he gives his conception of the power of Congress to enforce the Thirteenth Amendment:

> I have no doubt that under this provision of the Constitution we may destroy all these discriminations in civil rights against the black man; and if we cannot, our constitutional amendment amounts to nothing. It was for that purpose that the second clause of that amendment was adopted . . . . Who is to decide what that appropriate legislation is to be? The Congress of the United States; and it is for Congress to adopt such appropriate legislation as it may think proper, so that it be a means to accomplish the end. If we believe a Freedmen's Bureau necessary, if we believe an act punishing any man who deprives a colored person of any civil rights on account of his color necessary—if that is one means to secure his freedom, we have the constitutional right to adopt it. If in order to prevent slavery Congress deem it necessary to declare null and void all laws which will not permit the colored man to contract, which will not permit him to testify, which will not permit him to buy and sell, and to go where he pleases, it has the power to do so . . . . That is what is provided to be done by this bill. Its provisions are temporary; but there is another bill on your table, somewhat akin to this, which is intended to be permanent, to extend to all parts of the country, and to protect persons of all races in equal civil rights.

(An annotation should be appended to Trumbull's last clause: the Civil Rights Bill declared that "citizens, of every race and color . . . shall have the same right . . . as is enjoyed by white citizens . . . .")

Trumbull considered the matter of miscegenation:

> But, says the Senator from Indiana, we have laws in Indiana prohibiting black people from marrying whites, and are you going to disregard these laws? Are our laws enacted for the purpose of preventing amalgamation to be disregarded, and is a man to be punished because he undertakes to enforce them? I beg the Senator from Indiana to read the bill. One of its objects is to secure the same civil rights and subject to the same punishments persons of all races and colors. How does this interfere with the law of Indiana preventing marriages between whites and blacks? Are not both races treated alike by the law of Indiana? Does not the law make it just as much a crime for a white man to marry a black woman as for a black woman to marry a white man, and *vice versa*? I presume there is no discrimination in this respect, and therefore your law forbidding

marriages between whites and blacks operates alike on both races. This bill does not interfere with it. . . .

Next Trumbull pointed out that his two bills had nothing to say "about the political rights of the negro. On that subject it is known that there are differences of opinion . . . ." He had sought to find "points of agreement" with President Johnson's message to Congress. He had avoided the problem of reconstruction.

Trumbull concluded:

> I hope that the people of the rebellious States themselves will conform to the existing condition of things. I do not expect them to change all their opinions and prejudices. I do not expect them to rejoice that they have been discomfited. But . . . they say in their State conventions that slavery shall no more exist among them. With the abolition of slavery should go all the badges of servitude which have been enacted for its maintenance and support. Let them all be abolished. . . .

Let the people of the rebellious States be active in measures to elevate and improve the blacks, let them do justice and deal fairly with Union men in their midst, let them be themselves loyal, and before this Congress adjourned these once rebellious States would have been restored to their position in the Union.

The Senate passed the Freedmen's Bureau Bill on January 25, by vote of 37 to 10.[143] No Republican voted against it. (Cowan of Pennsylvania was absent. In debate he had made critical comments, culminating in an outburst against the Anti-Slavery Society—all of whose tracts and preachings, he said, would have been unavailing had it not been for the madness of the secessionists.[144]) In the House on February 6 the division was 136 yeas to 33 nays.[145]

The President's disapproval of the bill has been recorded in earlier chapters—also the insufficient vote in the Senate on overriding the veto—and Johnson's unseemly behavior before the crowd of his supporters at the serenade on February 22.[146]

---

[143] Cong. Globe, 39-1, 421.

[144] Ibid., 334, 340-45. Jan. 20, 22.

[145] Ibid., 688. Green Clay Smith of Kentucky, Thomas N. Stillwell, and others who presently would be classed as conservatives, voted for the bill. The only Republican voting against it was General Lovell H. Rousseau of Kentucky, victor over Robert Mallory, who had early abandoned his radical position.

[146] See supra, pp. 126, 344.

On overriding the veto the division was 30 yeas, 18 nays—less than the requisite two-thirds. Included in the nay vote were Cowan, Dixon, Doolittle, Norton, the two Senators from West Virginia, and even Stewart of Nevada and E. D. Morgan of New York. Cong. Globe, 39-1, 943. Feb. 20.

From that moment, the chance for accommodation between President and Congress hung precariously as he listened to conflicting counsels. Six weeks later, with the veto of the Civil Rights Bill, alienation became final.

At this juncture a reminder is in order. In focusing upon these debates in the First Session of the 39th Congress one leaves in obscurity important related happenings. Leading moderate Senators—Trumbull, Fessenden, and Grimes of Iowa (a member of the Joint Committee)— supposed that in their visits to the White House they were actually negotiating an understanding. John Sherman, another moderate, in a political speech on March 17, expressed confidence "that Andrew Johnson never will throw the power we have given him into the hands of the Copperhead party . . . ." Congress had passed the Civil Rights Bill, and "I believe the President will sign it."[147] But Johnson was giving ear to more engaging voices—such as the comment on the Freedmen's Bureau veto from Jerry Black, that it "made millions of good hearts glad and grateful," and that of Tom Ewing, assuring him that

> you will be sustained by nearly all of the legal profession and that thinking conservative portion of our people whose opinions make up all that is valuable and permanent in public opinion.[148]

This was an occasion for constant communication between members of Congress and their lieutenants at home. Whereas the Thirteenth Amendment had been generally popular among Northerners, the Civil Rights Bill, as James G. Blaine recalled, was legislation "of a different type," which, particularly in the Middle and Western States, touched upon deep feelings. Democratic leaders expected "that with the prejudices of the people supplemented by the patronage of the President a serious division would ensue, which would prove fatal to Radical ascendancy in a majority of the Northern States."[149]

When one follows the speeches made in Congress, one should know that there were conversations and calculations—perhaps of greater significance—going on outside.[150]

Americans living at the time of the Civil Rights Act of 1866 were not more broad-minded than those living a hundred years later. Nor were Senators and Representatives of a nobler mold.

---

[147] John Sherman's *Recollections of Forty Years*, I, 368–69.

[148] Jeremiah S. Black to Johnson, Feb. 20; Thomas Ewing to Johnson, Feb. 22. Johnson Papers, L.C.

[149] Blaine, *Twenty Years of Congress*, II, 180.

[150] Professor Eric L. McKitrick's *Andrew Johnson and Reconstruction* (Chicago: University of Chicago Press, 1960), chapter 10, "Johnson's Break with the Party," is excellent in tracing what members of Congress were doing and saying, and what they were hearing.

THE CIVIL RIGHTS ACT OF APRIL 9, 1866

S.61, THE CIVIL Rights Bill, was passed by the Senate on February 2.[151] In the House it remained under consideration in the Judiciary Committee until March—that is, until after the President had vetoed the Freedmen's Bureau Bill and had thereby demonstrated his unfriendly disposition toward the plight of the freedman. The President observed that slavery was "already effectually and finally abrogated"— hence, in his view, nothing more need be done by Congress. On the freedman's economic position he said:

> Competition for his services from planters, from those who are constructing or repairing railroads, and from capitalists in his vicinage or from other States, will enable him to command almost his own terms. He also possesses a perfect right to change his place of abode . . . . The laws that regulate supply and demand will maintain their force, and the wages of the laborer will be regulated thereby. There is no danger that the exceedingly great demand for labor will not operate in favor of the laborer.[152]

The danger in the theory of free labor, from the point of view of the white planter, was the invincible prejudgment that "You cannot make the negro work without physical compulsion." General Schurz, in his report to the President, wrote that

> I heard this hundreds of times, heard it wherever I went, heard it in nearly the same words from so many different persons, that at last I came to the conclusion that this is the prevailing sentiment among the Southern people. There are exceptions to this rule but, as far as my information extends, far from enough to affect the rule.[153]

Congress would not be stopped in its tracks by the Freedmen's Bureau veto. It would not leave the freedman to the laws of the State and the law of supply and demand.

The House debated the Civil Rights Bill and on March 13 passed it, with amendments, by vote of 111 to 38, with 34 not voting. The Senate concurred.[154] The President vetoed in a message of March 27. Should the bill pass, the objections of the President notwithstanding?

---

[151] Cong. Globe, 39–1, 606–7.
[152] Veto message, Cong. Globe, 39–1, 915–17. Feb. 19, 1866. See supra, p. 126.
[153] Schurz Report, Sen. Exec. Doc.

No. 2, 39th Cong., 1st Sess., p. 16. See ch. 3, n. 111.
[154] Cong. Globe, 39–1, 1367, in the House. Ibid., 1413–16, in the Senate, Mar. 15.

In the Senate, 33 answered yea, 15 nay.[155] In the House, the response was 122 yeas to 41 nays; not voting, 21.[156]

Thus on April 9, 1866, the Civil Rights Bill became law.[157]

In the history of the Supreme Court, Sections 1 and 2 are the matters of chief importance. Section 1 enacted:

> That all persons born in the United States and not subject to any foreign power, . . . are hereby declared to be citizens of the United States; and such citizens, of every race and color, without regard to any previous condition of slavery or involuntary servitude, . . . shall have the same right, in every State and Territory in the United States, to make and enforce contracts, to sue, be parties, and give evidence, to inherit, purchase, lease, sell, hold, and convey real and personal property, and to full and equal benefit of all laws and proceedings for the security of person and property, as is enjoyed by white citizens, and shall be subject to like punishment, pains, and penalties, and to none other, any law, statute, ordinance, regulation, or custom, to the contrary notwithstanding.

Section 2 provided a criminal sanction: "any person who, under color of any law, statute, ordinance, regulation, or custom," deprived any inhabitant of any right thus secured, by reason of race or color, would be punishable for a misdemeanor.

We shall come in a moment to the debates that preceded this enactment—and in order that they may be better comprehended, other sections should be noticed. Some of these were modeled upon the Fugitive Slave Act of 1850:[158] but whereas the purpose then had been to defeat and punish those who would "obstruct, hinder, or prevent" the return of the black man, now the purpose was to defeat and punish those who would interfere with proceedings for his protection. When Democratic Senators complained, Lane of Indiana replied that "It is an instance of poetic justice and of apt retribution that God has caused the wrath of man to praise Him."[159]

By Section 3, the inferior federal courts would have jurisdiction of offenses under the statute. [No appeal to the Supreme Court was provided until the House added an amendment to that effect on March 13, just before it passed the bill.] Any suit or prosecution in a State court against a person who was denied or could not enforce his civil rights could be removed by him to a federal court. Also, a suit or

---

[155] Ibid., 1809. Apr. 6. Voting to sustain the President, besides the Democrats, were Cowan, Doolittle, James H. Lane of Kansas, Norton of Minnesota, and Van Winkle of West Virginia. Dixon of Connecticut was absent.

[156] Ibid., 1861. Apr. 9.

[157] 14 Stat. 27.

[158] 9 Stat. 462.

[159] Cong. Globe, 39–1, 602. Feb. 2.

prosecution in a State court against one who acted under color of authority derived from the Civil Rights Act or the statute of 1865 creating the Freedmen's Bureau could be removed.

District attorneys, by Section 4, and marshals, United States Commissioners, and officers and agents of the Bureau, were directed to institute proceedings against all violators of the statute. The courts should appoint additional commissioners, to afford a speedy enforcement.

By Section 5, marshals and their deputies were required to obey and execute all warrants and precepts under the statute—under penalty of a fine of $1,000, "to the use of the person upon whom the accused is alleged to have committed the offence." All persons charged with the execution of process would have authority to "call to their aid the bystanders or posse comitatus," or such portions of the armed forces or militia as were necessary.

By Section 6, any person obstructing process under the statute —or rescuing or attempting to rescue one in custody—or harboring a person for whose arrest a warrant had been issued—would be subject to a fine not exceeding $1,000, or imprisonment up to six months, or both, upon indictment and conviction in a District Court.

The frame of this section was derived from the Fugitive Slave Act. In the memorable case of *Abelman v. Booth*,[160] the defendant in error had been charged with aiding a slave to escape: the Supreme Court of Wisconsin had sustained Booth's release on habeas corpus, holding the Act of 1850 to be unconstitutional;[161] and the Supreme Court had reversed for the reason that it was beyond the authority of any State court or judge to release one held under the authority of the United States. The opinion of Chief Justice Taney closed with this announcement:

> although we think it unnecessary to discuss these questions, yet, as they have been decided by the State court, and are before us on the record, and we are not willing to be misunderstood, it is proper to say that, in the judgment of this Court, the . . . Fugitive Slave Law is, in all of its provisions, fully authorized by the Constitution . . . .[162]

---

[160] 21 How. 506 (1859).

[161] In re Booth, 3 Wis. 1 (1854).

[162] This dictum covered with approval, inter alia, the provision that the master might apply to any court of record in his State, making satisfactory proof of the escape; the court should make a record of matters so proved, with "a general description of the person so escaping, with such convenient certainty as may be;" an authenticated transcript was made "full and conclusive evidence of the fact of escape, and that the service or labor of the person escaping is due . . . ." (Sec. 10.) At the place of capture, "In no trial or hearing under this act shall the testimony of such alleged fugitive be admitted in evidence . . . ." (Sec. 6.) The com-

Other sections of the Act of 1866 authorized the President to direct judge, district attorney and marshal to attend at any place for the more speedy trial of persons charged as violators. The President or his representative were empowered to employ the armed forces or the militia to enforce the statute.

Now we go back to trace how this came to pass, with attention directed primarily upon Sections 1 and 2.

DEBATE ON THE CIVIL RIGHTS BILL:
IN THE SENATE

ON JANUARY 29, 1866—four days after the Senate had disposed of S.60, the Freedmen's Bureau Bill—Trumbull opened debate on S.61. He offered an amendment, to insert at the opening of Section 1 a definition to make clear that persons of African descent, born in the United States, were citizens thereof.[163] (Whether this could be accomplished merely by statute was contested: while there is no need here to pursue the matter, it is material to note that many passages in the debates were addressed to that question.)

The first thing to notice about Section 1, as it stood, is that it had *two* clauses:

> [1] That there shall be no discrimination in civil rights or immunities among the inhabitants of any State or Territory of the United States on account of race, color, or previous condition of slavery; . . .[164]

That remained in the bill throughout its consideration by the Senate— and indeed until, on March 13, shortly before the passage of the bill by the House, that clause was stricken.

Section 1 continued, particularizing the civil rights secured— *the same as emerged in the statute*:

> [2] but the inhabitants of every race and color, without regard to any previous condition of slavery or involuntary servitude, except as a punishment for crime whereof the party shall have been duly convicted, shall have the same right to make and enforce contracts, to sue, be parties, and give evidence, to inherit, purchase, lease, sell,

---

missioner conducting the hearing was allowed $10 where he found for the claimant, $5 where he found the proof insufficient. (Sec. 8.)

The Civil Rights Act did not imitate these provisions.

[163] Cong. Globe, 39–1, 474–76. Trumbull's amendment was amended by the Senate, to read as appears in the statute; in that form it was adopted on February 1. At 575.

[164] Ibid., 474.

hold, and convey real and personal property, and to full and equal benefit of all laws and proceedings for the security of person and property, and shall be subject to like punishment, pains, and penalties, and to none other, any law, statute, ordinance, regulation, or custom to the contrary notwithstanding.

When one hears Senator Trumbull declare that "the very object of the bill is to break down all discrimination between black men and white men,"[165] it should be recognized that he was merely paraphrasing clause 1—which is something different from construing Section 1 after clause 1 had been deleted.

It should also be recognized that "civil rights" did not have a precise meaning. What would be the scope of an enactment that there should be "no discrimination in civil rights . . . on account of race"? That would be a matter of serious concern in the debates.

The Civil Rights Bill, Trumbull began, was "the most important measure" to come up since the adoption of the constitutional amendment declaring the end of slavery:[166]

> This measure is intended to give effect to that declaration and secure to all persons within the United States practical freedom. There is very little importance in the general declaration of abstract truths and principles unless they can be carried into effect . . . .

He observed that

> Since the abolition of slavery, the Legislatures which have assembled in the insurrectionary States have passed laws relating to the freedmen, and in nearly all the States they have discriminated against them . . . . The purpose of the bill under consideration is to destroy all these discriminations, and to carry into effect the constitutional amendment. . . .

Section 1 was "the basis of the whole bill. The other provisions of the bill contain the necessary machinery to give effect to what are declared to be the rights of all persons . . . ."

He explained the constitutional foundation. "I take it that any statute which is not equal to all, and which deprives any citizen of civil rights which are secured to other citizens, is an unjust encroachment upon his liberty; and is, in fact, a badge of servitude which, by the Constitution, is prohibited."

The people of the slaveholding States "have not regarded the colored race as citizens, and on that principle many of their laws making

---

[165] Ibid., 599. Feb. 2.   [166] Ibid., 474. Jan. 29.

discriminations between the whites and the colored people are based";
but it was competent for Congress to declare who are citizens, and this
bill would settle the question.

Next, What are the rights of citizens? Trumbull answered:

> The great fundamental rights set forth in this bill: the right to ac-
> quire property, the right to go and come at pleasure, the right to
> enforce rights in the courts, to make contracts, and to inherit and
> dispose of property. These are the very rights set forth in this bill
> as appertaining to every freeman.

Referring to Section 2—which imposed a penalty upon "any
person who under color of law . . ."—Trumbull said that

> When it comes to be understood . . . that any person who shall
> deprive another of any right or subject him to any punishment in
> consequence of his color or race will expose himself to fine and
> imprisonment, I think such acts will soon cease.

Most of the other provisions, Trumbull explained, "are copied
from the late fugitive slave act, adopted in 1850 . . .":

> The act that was passed at that time for the purpose of punishing
> persons who should aid negroes to escape to freedom is now to be
> applied by the provisions of this bill to the punishment of those
> who shall undertake to keep them in slavery. Surely we have the
> authority to enact a law as efficient in the interests of freedom, now
> that freedom prevails throughout the country . . . .

Latter day preoccupation with Sections 1 and 2 has distracted
attention from the bill's further provisions setting up machinery for
enforcement. Trumbull had taken pains to frame a measure which, he
trusted, would prove "efficient." There was little point in declaring
"abstract truths" if they were not carried into effect. Here one may recall
the situation in December, when Sumner had introduced his sheaf of
bills and declaratory resolutions, and his colleague Wilson had called
for instant enactment of S. 9, which would have afforded freedmen
only a temporary and ineffective protection against unequal laws in
States declared to be in insurrection. Trumbull had urged the Senate
to take time to enact a measure "that will be much more sweeping and
efficient . . . ."[167]

---

[167] See supra, pp. 125–26, 1162.
Sumner had then urged: pass Wilson's bill, pass any bill; "An avenging
God cannot sleep . . . ." It has been
pointed out that Sumner had introduced a bundle of measures which,
in his judgment, were ready for
adoption. Supra, p. 1160.

When Trumbull had completed his presentation, McDougall of California, Democrat, asked him to give his interpretation of "civil rights."[168] Trumbull replied that Section 1 gave the definition—and he ran over the particulars in clause 2. "This bill has nothing to do with the political rights or *status* of parties."

Senator Willard Saulsbury of Delaware took the floor.[169] The bill was "one of the most dangerous that was ever introduced . . . ." He developed that contention in a long and bitter speech.

First, it rested on no constitutional authority. Prior to the adoption of the Thirteenth Amendment there had been "free negroes all over the United States," and Congress had had no power to enact that they "should be the equals of the white man before the law . . . ." The effect of the amendment was nothing more than "putting them on an equality in reference to their *status* with the free negroes that then existed . . . ." "It bestows no rights further than to relieve [the former slave] from the burden of servitude and slavery. A man may be a free man and not possess the same civil rights as other men. . . ."

Saulsbury was prone, in any speech, to lapse into a rancorous harangue upon the course of national events. (McDougall, and Garrett Davis of Kentucky, were similarly inclined.) So now:

> I shall not follow the honorable Senator [Trumbull] into a consideration of the manner in which slaves were treated in the southern States, nor the privileges that have been denied them by the laws of the States. . . . The tears which the honest white people of this country have been made to shed from the oppressive acts of this Government in its various departments during the last four years call more loudly for my sympathies than those tears which have been shedding and dropping and dropping for the last twenty years in reference to the poor, oppressed slave—dropping from the eyes of strong-minded women and weak-minded men, until, becoming a mighty flood, they have swept away, in their resistless force, every trace of constitutional liberty in this country.

The Senator turned to particular provisions. "There shall be no discrimination in civil rights . . .": Saulsbury demanded, "What are civil rights?" It was "a generic term which in its most comprehensive signification includes every species of right" derived from government. *Voting* might be so classed. "Was it . . . to secure this right to negroes that the Senator amended his bill . . . by declaring that all persons of African descent born in the United States shall be citizens of the United States?" Saulsbury insisted, "the question is not what [Trumbull] means, but what the courts will say the law means . . . ."

---

[168] Cong. Globe, 39–1, 476. [169] Ibid., 476–80. Jan. 29.

Property, the Senator continued, was a subject that pertained exclusively to the State. The Union might have been dissolved with "society scarcely receiving a shock," while "the laws for the regulation of property . . . would have been in full force within the States . . . ." But under this bill, the State would be "invaded and defrauded of the right of determining who shall hold property and who shall not within its limits, who shall sue and be sued, and who shall give evidence in its courts. All these things are taken out of the control of the States by the paramount authority of this bill . . . ." Delaware would be prevented from protecting its people by keeping firearms out of the hands of blacks. From the provision allowing them to testify it would result that many crimes could not be punished in the State's courts: some deputy marshal would "go and arrest the judge," and the case could be removed into the federal court.

Saulsbury went over the bill's "machinery to carry it into effect." One complaint was that "an ignorant deputized agent," perhaps black, would "have the power to summon all the able-bodied men in any county . . . to aid him in arresting a white man for committing the simplest offense against a negro . . . . Verily, not only the negro is as good in law as the white man, but he is much more favored and better protected . . . ."

"Go sweep the whole field of legislation," he concluded, "and show me, if you can, any enactment so flagrantly unjust, so oppressive in its character, so violative of all rights of the citizen, as this."

The report of Saulsbury's criticism of the bill ran to well over twice the space needed for Trumbull's explanation and defense.

Senator Van Winkle, Unionist of West Virginia—a man of conservative and independent cast of mind—had interrupted Trumbull to challenge his proposition that it was within the power of Congress to enact that all persons born in the United States were citizens. Next day Van Winkle explained his "peculiar ideas."[170] A citizen was "one who is an integer of the body-politic or community." Men were divided into

---

[170] Ibid., 497-98. Jan. 30.

Peter G. Van Winkle (1808-72) came of an old Knickerbocker family; in early manhood he moved from his native New York City to Parkersburg. There he practiced law; was treasurer and then president of the Northwestern Virginia Railroad (subordinate to the Baltimore & Ohio); and was attorney and lobbyist for the B. & O. See D.A.B.

He was prominent in the movement for the creation of the State of West Virginia, and had a particular concern for the inclusion of the eastern counties through which ran the Baltimore & Ohio. These counties became the subject matter of the suit of Virginia v. West Virginia, supra, pp. 619-27.

Van Winkle was a delegate to the Southern Loyalists' Convention that met at Philadelphia on September 3, 1866. Supra, pp. 180-81. But at the impeachment trial of President Johnson in 1868 he voted to acquit—in disregard of strong pressure from home. Supra, p. 526.

separate national communities; the Declaration of Independence meant merely that "the rights of citizens of any community are equal to the rights of all other citizens of that community." Only by amending the Constitution could non-whites be accepted as citizens of the United States.

> We have the right to determine who shall be members of our community, and much as has been said here . . . about our obligations to the Almighty in reference to this matter, I do not see where it comes in that we are bound to receive into our community those whose mingling with us might be detrimental to our interests. . . .

He pledged that "if these dusky people shall . . . be admitted to the rights of citizenship" by constitutional means, he would treat them as citizens.

The contention made by objectors that it was not competent for Congress to admit these native-born non-whites to citizenship— either under the power "to establish an uniform Rule of Naturalization" or otherwise—need not be pursued here: the Fourteenth Amendment by its opening sentence disposed of the problem.

In the second day of debate, Senator Cowan did most of the talking.[171] The "original corporators" of this Government, he said, had never admitted to membership as freemen "the barbarian races of Asia or of Africa." And the Thirteenth Amendment had no such purpose: as "everybody knows," it "was simply made to liberate the negro slave from his master." Then what was it that Congress was authorized to enforce? "The breaking of the bond . . .; that is all. It was not intended to overturn this Government and to revolutionize all the laws of the various States . . . ."

The bill declared "there shall be no discrimination . . . among the inhabitants of any State . . . ." In Pennsylvania, said Cowan,

> We put the African children in this school-house and the white children over in that school-house, and we educate them there as best we can. Is this amendment . . . abolishing slavery to break up that system . . . ? . . . Are the school directors . . . to be punished . . . ? To me it is monstrous. . . .

Cowan agreed with Van Winkle that it would require further amendment of the Constitution to permit a measure such as this.

There was, he continued, "a great deal more in this bill that is exceedingly objectionable." He fastened upon this aspect of Section 2.

---

[171] Cong. Globe, 39–1, 498–503, 506, 507. Jan. 30. His speech was almost twice as long as Trumbull's presentation.

It is the first time I think in the history of civilized legislation that a judicial officer has been . . . subjected to a criminal punishment for that which may have been a conscientious discharge of his duty. . . .

Fessenden interrupted, and then five Senators were drawn into a somewhat confused colloquy:[172]

MR. FESSENDEN. Where is the particular provision of the bill to which the Senator now alludes?

MR. COWAN. All the way through.

MR. TRUMBULL. That particular provision is in the imagination of the Senator from Pennsylvania.

MR. COWAN. Is there not a provision by which State officers are to be punished?

MR. TRUMBULL. Not State officers especially, but everybody who violates the law. It is the intention to punish everybody who violates the law.

MR. COWAN. In the first place, all State laws making discriminations are swept away, and in the next place all persons who undertake to execute these laws are made criminals, and that includes the judge, the constable, the sheriff, the marshal, and everybody. That is my reading of it; I may be wrong; I have not had an opportunity of examining the bill thoroughly in all its details.

MR. STEWART. I will ask the Senator whether the fugitive slave law did not contain a precisely similar provision, and if it was not held good by the Supreme Court of the United States?

MR. COWAN. The fugitive slave law of 1850 the Senator means. I was always opposed to it, Mr. President.

MR. JOHNSON. The Supreme Court held it to be constitutional.

MR. COWAN. That may be; but I say I was always opposed to it; and I had always very grave doubts whether it was good law. Certainly, I never volunteered to execute it, and never made one of a *posse comitatus* to carry it out . . . . I am opposed to having any more such doubtful legislation, or such legislation as will not be acceptable to the people where the law is to operate.

Here, for the moment, the pursuit of Cowan's contention was abandoned. Later the problem of Section 2 reappeared, and Trumbull made his defense.[173]

---

[172] At p. 500.

[173] Infra, pp. 1194–95.

It is not clear precisely what Trumbull had in mind when he replied to Cowan that the bill would punish "not State officers especially, but everybody who violates the law. . . ."

It is not difficult to find provisions in the Black Laws already enacted when Trumbull spoke, under which private persons might perform acts which the Civil Rights Bill would condemn as discriminatory. For example, the Mississippi statute of

It is to be remarked that Trumbull did not reply to Cowan's assumption that the first clause, "no discrimination," forbade segregated schools. His silence does not prove acquiescence: where allegations were flying so fast it may have seemed impracticable to meet them all. Quite likely he would have said of schools—as in a moment he said of anti-miscegenation laws—that there would be no violation where the rule for one race was the same as that for the other.[174] To have said otherwise would have exposed the bill to active opposition in the North.[175] In debates on measures for the protection of the Negro, opponents were prone to make intemperate statements about the consequences: such remarks should not be taken as sober constructions, nor should the proponents' failure to deny every allegation be deemed an admission.

Howard of Michigan rejected Cowan's "absurd construction" that the Thirteenth Amendment accomplished nothing more than breaking the bondage.[176] On that view, the freedman "has nothing that belongs to him . . . except solely his naked person. And here, in this state, we are called upon to abandon the poor creature whom we have emancipated. . . ." Howard recollected the views within the

---

November 25, 1865, to confer Civil Rights on Freedmen provided (Sec. 7) that "every civil officer shall, and every person may arrest and carry back to his or her legal employer any freedman . . . who shall have quit the service . . . without good cause . . . ," receiving a fee therefor. Laws of 1865, 82, 84.

Another instance, presumably, would be where, under a statute applying to apprenticeship only of young persons of color, the master was authorized to inflict chastisement. Mississippi's statute of November 22, 1865, to regulate the relation of Master and Apprentice, as relates to Freedmen . . . , (Sec. 3), Laws of 1865, 86, 87; South Carolina's statute of December 21, 1865, to establish and regulate the Domestic Relations of Persons of Color, (Sec. 22), Acts of 1864–65, 291, 293. So too of the latter statute (Sec. 50), p. 296, where it provided that the master might "moderately correct" colored servants under the age of 18 years.

South Carolina's statute of December 19, 1865, to amend the Criminal Law, authorized "any person present" to arrest a person of color for a mis-

demeanor committed within his view—not so as to a white misdemeanant (Sec. 30), Acts of 1864–65, 271, 278.

That State's statute of December 19, 1865, to establish District Courts, created a separate jurisdiction for civil and criminal cases involving persons of color; the judge sat with a jury of four citizens (Sec. 15). Acts of 1864–65, 278, 282. By their participation in such proceedings, the jurymen would doubtless fall within Section 2 of the Civil Rights Bill.

It is pertinent in this connection to cite the holding in United States v. Price, 383 U.S. 787 (1966), that "Private persons, jointly engaged with state officials in the prohibited action, are acting 'under color' of law for purposes of the statute."

[174] Infra, p. 1180.

[175] Recall that even Sumner—when in March 1867 he sought to impose "a system of public schools open to all, without distinction of race or color," as a condition for the restoration of the Southern States—flinched from saying categorically that such was the meaning. Supra, p. 330.

[176] Cong. Globe, 39–1, 503–4. Jan. 30.

Judiciary Committee when the amendment was under consideration. The intention was "to give to Congress precisely the power . . . which is proposed to be exercised by the bill now under our consideration." The bill "simply gives to persons who are of different races or colors the same civil rights. That is its full extent; it goes no further . . . ."

Reverdy Johnson hoped "that the Senators who think they have the power to pass the bill"—he was not among them—would "make it as acceptable and as free from doubt as their wisdom will allow them to do."[177] Section 1, in its second clause, would enact that "the inhabitants . . . shall have the same right to . . . inherit, purchase, lease, sell, hold and convey real and personal property": that would forbid the State to distinguish between citizen and resident alien in respect of the ownership and transmission of real property—which ran counter to the law of many States. Again, Maryland and other States had statutes forbidding marriage between parties of different races. But Section 1, in its first clause, commanded "no discrimination":

> White and black are considered together, put in a mass, and the one is entitled to enter into every contract that the other is entitled to enter into. Of course, therefore, the black man is entitled to enter into the contract of marriage with a white woman; but the law of Maryland prevents it . . . .

And by Section 2, "he who prevents a black man from marrying a white woman under any law of Maryland is to be subject to the penalties . . . . That is the way I understand it. . . ."

Fessenden and Trumbull interrupted to reply: each said that there was no discrimination where every one was free to marry a spouse of his own color.

Johnson concluded:

> But whether I am wrong or not, upon a careful and correct interpretation . . . , I suppose all the Senate will admit that the error is not so gross a one that the courts may not fall into it. . . .

Senator Garrett Davis of Kentucky was, as he said, "wound up" and "obliged to run down."[178] He spoke at length on January 31, and on the two days thereafter.[179] "My position is that this is a white man's Government. It was made so at the beginning. . . . The negro had nothing to do with it . . . . I . . . reiterate the position that the

---

[177] Ibid., 504–7. Jan. 30.
[178] Ibid., 578. Feb. 1.

[179] Ibid., 523–30; 575–78; 595–600.

negro is not a citizen here according to the essential fundamental principles of our system; . . . he is not a foreigner, and no man . . . can be made a citizen by naturalization unless he is a foreigner . . . ."[180]

Senator Lot M. Morrill of Maine—certainly well disposed toward emancipated people—began his speech with an estimate of the mood of the moment:[181]

> If there is anything with which the American people are troubled, and if there is anything with which the American statesman is perplexed and vexed, it is what to do with the negro, how to define him, what he is in American law, and to what rights he is entitled. What shall we do with the everlasting, inevitable negro? is the question which puzzles all brains and vexes all statesmanship. Now, as a definition, this amendment [to Section 1, to establish the citizenship of the native of African descent] settles it. Hitherto we have said that he was a nondescript in our statutes; he had no *status*; he was ubiquitous; he was both man and thing; he was three fifths of a person for representation and he was a thing for commerce and for use. In the highest sense, then, . . . this bill is important as a definition. . . .

Until today, Morrill continued,

> There has been no time since the foundation of the Government when an American Congress could by possibility have enacted such a law, or with propriety have made such a declaration. . . .

Senator Davis had said the change was "revolutionary"; Morrill agreed: but "it was a change precisely in harmony with the general principles of the Government." Then turning to Senator Cowan,

> No proposition could possibly be made . . . more inaccurate than to say that American society, either civil or political, was formed in the interest of any race or class. Sir, the history of the country does not bear out the statement . . . . All the . . . varieties of the races of the nations of the earth have gathered here. . . .

Morrill's remarks were concerned only with the definition of citizenship.

---

[180] Ibid., 528.
[181] Ibid., 570–71. Feb. 1. A member of the Committee on the District of Columbia, in 1862 he had led in carrying the bill to emancipate slaves there; in the 39th Congress he had charge of S.1, which became the Act of January 8, 1867, giving equal suffrage in the District.

The speech aids one to take bearings. Not seven weeks had passed since the Thirteenth Amendment had been proclaimed to be in effect. It was in the preceding week that the Joint Committee on Reconstruction had begun to take testimony on the condition of the Southern States. Members of Congress did not foresee, much less have solutions for all the problems that would arise as four million new citizens adventured into the future: they were "perplexed and vexed" about what to do.

February 2 was the fourth and final day of debate. Davis of Kentucky had the floor, and presently he came to particular complaints.[182] The bill would conflict with statutes against miscegenation. "By the law of my State a negro who commits a rape upon a white woman is subject to death . . . ," whereas a white man was punishable by a term of years. Under this bill, the judges and officers who carried out the State's law would commit a federal offense. "This is an act for the benefit of the free negro . . ."; he harped upon that proposition.

Davis had filled about twelve columns of fine print in the Congressional Globe—considerably more than 9,000 words.

Trumbull took "a very few moments" to deal with "this long harangue," this "piling up of adjectives, and denouncing as outrageous a bill which contains but one single principle, and that to establish equality in the civil rights of citizens . . . ." He made sport of Davis' professed concern that the bill would override statutes against miscegenation: "I have answered that question two or three times."[183]

The Senators from Indiana engaged in an unhelpful exchange over the section authorizing the use of the armed forces "to prevent the violation and enforce the due execution" of the act. Hendricks, in unusually loose remarks, pictured "some white man who is running for his liberty because some negro has charged him with denying to him equal civil rights . . . ." Lane, whose strength lay rather in stump speaking, replied that this section was "more important than any other." "What white man fleeing . . . is in danger of having his rights stricken down?" The bill "simply places others on the same platform upon which he stands, and if he would invoke the power of local prejudice to override the laws of the country, this is no Government unless the military may be called in to enforce the orders of the civil courts and obedience to the laws of the country."[184]

Soon the vote was taken, and the bill was carried by 33 to 12. Cowan, Norton, and Van Winkle voted with the Democrats. This was on February 2, 1866.

---

[182] Ibid., 595–600. Feb. 2.
[183] Ibid., 599–600. Feb. 2.

[184] Ibid., 600–603. Feb. 2. See note 71 in chapter 20.

THE CIVIL RIGHTS BILL GOES TO THE HOUSE

BEFORE AND AFTER the Senate debate on the Civil Rights Bill, the Joint Committee on Reconstruction had been considering what further amendments to the Constitution seemed to be needed. One matter was the basis of representation, now that former slaves would be reckoned in "the whole Number of free Persons" and would thereby enhance the political weight of the Southern States.[185] Another concern was to secure the due protection of the rights of all persons. As to this latter, the upshot was that on February 13 the Joint Committee submitted to each House a proposal by constitutional amendment to empower Congress "to secure to the citizens of each State all privileges and immunities of citizens in the several States; and to all persons in the several States equal protection in the rights of life, liberty, and property."[186]

This proposal—which had been inspired by Representative John A. Bingham of Ohio, a member of the Joint Committee—was debated in the House on February 26 to 28. One major inadequacy in Bingham's draft was that these rights would not actually be made secure: they would be left dependent upon the shifting attitude of Congress. On February 28 the House voted to postpone further consideration— which was the end of that proposal.

Thus when on March 1 Wilson for the Judiciary Committee called up S. 61, the Civil Rights Bill,[187] the House had already been immersed in that subject.

He offered amendments. In Section 1 he would strike out "inhabitants" and insert "citizens of the United States." Then he would amend the second clause to declare that "such citizens . . . shall have the same right to make and enforce contracts, [etc.] . . . as is enjoyed by white citizens." The amendments were accepted without comment.

"Civil rights," Wilson explained, did not signify that all would vote—or sit on juries—or send their children to the same school. Civil rights were the rights to personal liberty and security, to acquire and enjoy property—the sort of rights this bill specified.

> Mr. Speaker, if all our citizens were of one race and one color we would be relieved of most of the difficulties which surround us. This bill would be almost, if not entirely, unnecessary . . . .
> It will be observed that the entire structure of this bill rests

---

[185] Supra, pp. 119, 131; infra, pp. 1261–65.

[186] Discussed infra, pp. 1271–74.
[187] Cong. Globe, 39–1, 1115–19.

on the discrimination relative to civil rights and immunities made by the States on "account of race, color, or previous condition of slavery." . . .

"We are establishing no new right, declaring no new principle," he emphasized; it was only because some States failed to respect the rights to which all citizens were entitled this "remedial and protective" legislation was needed.

The ever-combative Rogers of New Jersey took the lead in opposition.[188] "Has Congress the power to enter the domain of a State, and destroy its police regulations with regard to the punishment inflicted upon negroes?" He ran over typical discriminations made by statute: a judge who followed the law of his State would be liable to punishment under this bill. He stressed the breadth that might be given to the clause forbidding discrimination "in civil rights or immunities": it would include suffrage and much more.

Rogers recalled what Secretary Seward had declared to reluctant men of the South: that Section 2 of the Thirteenth Amendment was a *restriction* on the powers of Congress.[189] The purpose of Section 2, said Rogers, was merely "to enable Congress to lay the hand of Federal power . . . upon the States to prevent them from reënslaving the blacks . . . ." While extending freedom to the slaves, he said, let us not fail "to perpetuate the liberty which our fathers designed should be extended to the white men and the white women of this country forever and ever."

Rogers' speech provoked reaction on the Republican side—instanter by Burton C. Cook of Illinois, and by Thayer of Pennsylvania, who obtained the floor for the next day.

These two replies will be quoted at some length: there is going to be occasion presently to return to scan the words in context.

Cook was "astonished" at Rogers' "apprehension this bill is designed to deprive somebody in some State . . . of some right which he has heretofore enjoyed. . . ."[190] "We are not pointed to one single right now possessed by a single white man in this Government touched or impaired by the provisions of this bill."

"What is the situation of affairs for which we are called to

---

[188] Ibid., 1120–23. Mar. 1.
[189] The reference was to Seward's reproof to Provisional Governor Perry of South Carolina, November 6, 1865. Supra, p. 122.
[190] Cong. Globe, 39–1, 1123–25. Mar. 1.
Cook (1819–94), an experienced lawyer and politician, represented a district in northeastern Illinois. He carried his constituency by a preponderance of 3 to 2, in the first of his four elections to Congress. In 1860 he had seconded Lincoln's nomination, and in 1864 nominated him at the Baltimore convention.

legislate for four million human beings who have been set free from chattel slavery . . .?" In six of the ex-rebel States the legislatures had passed laws "so malignant," "so subversive of their liberties," that the responsible commanders had issued orders forbidding enforcement.[191]

> Vagrant laws have been passed; laws which, under the pretense of selling men as vagrants, are calculated and intended to reduce them to slavery again . . . . Then the question is, shall we leave the men who have been loyal during this struggle . . . to the operation of laws denounced as tyrannical by the military powers . . .?

He reproached Rogers for professing concern for the civil rights of freedmen while opposing "every earthly mode that can be devised for protecting them . . . ."

> Then the question that remains is simply this: can the Congress . . . provide that as between citizens of the United States there shall be no discrimination in civil rights or immunities, but they "shall have the same right to make and enforce contracts, [quoting the enumerated

---

[191] Evidently the six legislatures were those of Mississippi, South Carolina, Louisiana, Florida, Alabama, and Virginia—which had enacted their Black Codes before March 1 when Cook spoke. Georgia and North Carolina acted later in March; Texas not until October and November 1866.

Four of those legislatures had enacted vagrant laws. First, Mississippi's statute of November 24, Laws of 1865, 90. See supra, pp. 110, 114.

Alabama, by statute of December 15, Acts of 1865–66, 119, had amended its vagrancy law to include "a stubborn or refractory servant; a laborer or servant who loiters away his time, or refuses to comply with any contract for a term of service without just cause." Upon conviction before a justice of the peace, the vagrant might be sentenced to a house of correction or a jail, or be hired out or sent to labor on public works and highways.

This statute was repealed by an Act of February 15, 1867. Laws of 1866–67, 504.

South Carolina's comprehensive statute of December 21, to establish and regulate Domestic Relations of Persons of Color, and to amend the law in relation to Paupers and Vagrancy, Acts of 1864–65, 291 at 303, included in its definition of vagrants "All persons who have not some fixed and known place of abode, and some lawful and reputable employment; those who have not some visible and known means of a fair, honest and reputable livelihood; . . ." Trial might be by a magistrate "with the assistance of five freeholders," or by two magistrates with three freeholders. One convicted might be hired to a farmer, or sent to hard labor on streets, public roads or public buildings. Sections 95 to 99.

Virginia's Act providing for the punishment of vagrants, of January 15, Public Acts 1865–66, 91, included in its definition "All persons who, not having wherewith to maintain themselves and their families, live idly and without employment, and refuse to work for the usual and common wages given to other laborers in the like work in the place where they then are."

If Representative Cook had particular statutes in mind, it seems likely it was those of Mississippi and South Carolina.

rights] . . .? Has Congress the power to so enact that there shall be no discrimination in these things between the citizens of this Government? . . .

Cook's answer was,

> Now, sir, I am prepared, for myself, to say that when those rights which are enumerated in this bill are denied to any class of men on account of race or color, when they are subject to a system of vagrant laws which sells them into slavery or involuntary servitude, which operates upon them as upon no other part of the community, they are not secured in the rights of freedom. If a man can be sold, the man is a slave. If he is nominally freed by the amendment to the Constitution, he has nothing in the world he can call his own; he has simply the labor of his hands on which he can depend. Any combination of men in his neighborhood can prevent him from having any chance to support himself by his labor. They can pass a law that a man not supporting himself by labor shall be deemed a vagrant, and that a vagrant shall be sold. . . .

Congress, he concluded, should not "abandon these people and deliver them up to the operation of just such laws . . ."; any member of the House who thought otherwise "is strangely blind to the enactments passed by Legislatures touching these freedmen . . . ."

Next day Thayer took up the defense: that he was making a further reply to Rogers is evident from personal references and repeated exchanges between the two. M. Russell Thayer was a Philadelphia lawyer with a literary bent; his colleague Blaine recalled that he made "an uncommonly able speech."[192]

Thayer agreed with opponents' characterization that the Thirteenth Amendment was "a revolutionary measure": it had brought "a revolution which gave life, liberty, and hope to millions whose condition until then appeared to be one of hopeless despair." The Civil Rights Bill was "the just sequel" to the amendment:

> The bill which now engages the attention of the House has for its object to carry out and guaranty the reality of that great measure. It is to give to it practical effect and force. It is to prevent that great measure from remaining a dead letter upon the constitutional page of this country. It is to carry to its legitimate and just result the great

---

[192] The speech is in Cong. Globe, 39–1, 1151–55. Mar. 2. Blaine's comment is in *Twenty Years of Congress*, II, 175.

Thayer (1819–1906), a graduate of the University of Pennsylvania, had practiced law since 1842. He had won election to the 38th and 39th Congresses by exceedingly slender majorities—62 and 278. From 1867 to 1896 he sat on lower courts at Philadelphia.

humane revolution to which I have referred. The events of the last four years . . . have changed this large class of people . . . from a condition of slavery to that of freedom. The practical question now to be decided is whether they shall be in fact freemen. It is whether they shall have the benefit of this great charter of liberty given to them by the American people.

Then came a paragraph that arrests attention:

Sir, if it is competent for the new-formed Legislatures of the rebel States to enact laws which oppress this large class of people who are dependent for protection upon the United States Government, to retain them still in a state of real servitude; if it is practicable for these Legislatures to pass laws and enforce laws which reduce this class of people to the condition of bondmen; laws which prevent the enjoyment of the fundamental rights of citizenship; laws which declare, for example, that they shall not have the privilege of purchasing a home for themselves and their families; laws which impair their ability to make contracts for labor in such manner as virtually to deprive them of the power of making such contracts, and which then declare them vagrants because they have no homes and because they have no employment; I say, if it is competent for these Legislatures to pass and enforce such laws, then I demand to know, of what practical value is the amendment abolishing slavery in the United States? Tell me when you boast of the glorious character of that addition to your Constitution what benefit you have conferred upon the men who are liberated from slavery by it, if these things are to be done under the flag of the United States and in the face of the authority of the Federal Constitution.

Continuing, Thayer replied to Rogers' argument that Section 2 of the Thirteenth Amendment gave Congress power to do nothing more than "to prevent [the States] from reënslaving the blacks." Thayer answered,

For one, sir, I thought when I voted for the amendment to abolish slavery that I was aiding to give real freedom to the men who had so long been groaning in bondage. I did not suppose that I was offering them a mere paper guarantee. And when I voted for the second section of the amendment, I felt in my own mind certain that I had placed in the Constitution and given to Congress ability to protect and guaranty the rights which the first section gave them.

Twice thereafter Thayer returned to denounce "the tyranny of laws" by which a man "may be deprived of the ability to make a contract; may be deprived of the ability to sell or convey real or personal estate"—and he mentioned freedom to move at will, liberty to engage in ordinary occupations, the right to be a party or a witness in a court of justice. These were "laws which, if permitted to be enforced, would strike a fatal blow at the liberty of the freedman and render the constitutional amendment of no force or effect whatever. . . . That, sir, demonstrates the necessity of enforcing the guarantees of liberty and of American citizenship conferred by the Constitution."

Charles A. Eldridge of Wisconsin, a sturdy Democratic partisan, viewed the bill as "one of a series . . . arising out of a feeling of distrust and hatred . . . toward those persons who formerly held slaves"—it was "another of the measures designed to take away the essential rights of the States."[193] The bill "attempts to destroy the independence of the State judiciary." He quoted Section 2, and demanded, "by what provision of the Constitution is the Federal Government authorized to affix a penalty to the decision which the judge of a State court may make in the exercise of the judicial function" and "make him the mere creature of the Federal Government?" There was good reason, he maintained, for the State to discriminate on ground of color—as in the punishment for rape.

Eldridge had hoped that, when "the institution of slavery has been freely given up, . . . this subject would cease to haunt us . . . ." He was disappointed:

> Gentlemen refer us to individual cases of wrong . . . as an argument why we should extend the Federal authority into the different States to control the action of the citizens thereof. But, I ask, has not the South submitted to the altered state of things there, to the late amendment of the Constitution, to the loss of their slave property, with a cheerfulness and grace that we did not expect? . . .

He did not credit these stories about a general feeling of hostility on the part of former slave-owners. "The cases of ill-treatment are exceptional cases."

Anthony Thornton, a conservative Whig-turned-Democrat with a Southern background, was a trial lawyer from central Illinois, subsequently a judge of its highest court. He covered several points in a few minutes.[194] It was the exclusive right of the State to determine the

---

[193] Cong. Globe, 39-1, 1154-56. Mar. 2.

Eldridge, of Fond du Lac, represented a district in southeastern Wisconsin from March 4, 1863, to March 3, 1875. In the 38th and 39th Congresses his majorities were about 5,000, notwithstanding a poor showing in the soldier vote.

In the Congressional Globe for his first five terms his name was printed "Eldridge"; in the Congressional Record for the 43rd Congress it is "Eldredge," and is so recorded in the *Biographical Directory of the American Congress.*

[194] Cong. Globe, 39-1, 1156-57. Mar. 2.

status of its inhabitants. Under the Thirteenth Amendment, Congress could prevent the reenslavement of the freedman, and could protect his right to contract and to recover his wages; but "to go beyond that is to trench upon the rights of the States . . . ." He feared there was "something hidden, something more than appears in the language" of Section 1 of the bill: was it intended to include the suffrage? The bill was "a stepping-stone to . . . the overthrow of the local powers of the States."

Debate went over from Friday, March 2, to Thursday, the eighth. When it was resumed, the discussion took a turn that signalled a warning: Republicans unquestionably favorable to the objective of the bill began to stress constitutional difficulties.

Thomas T. Davis, Unionist from Syracuse, a lawyer concerned with large industrial enterprises, commonly practiced a circumspection which precipitate Republicans failed to appreciate. Now while "anxious to support" the bill, he had serious doubts about Section 2.[195] A judge who followed the laws of his State would be liable to conviction. That was an assumption of power "which perhaps the courts of the Federal Government may say [has] never been delegated by the States."

Then Bingham gave notice of the disposition for which he was going to press: that the bill be sent back to the Judiciary Committee with instructions, (1) to strike from Section 1 the provision that "there shall be no discrimination in civil rights"; also (2) to strike out all provisions for criminal proceedings, and in lieu thereof to give a civil action for deprivation of any right secured by the bill.[196]

Henry J. Raymond of New York was "heartily in favor" of the bill's two purposes:

1. To declare who shall be citizens of the United States . . . .
2. To provide for that class of persons thus made citizens protection against anticipated inequality of legislation in the several States.[197]

However, he would not vote to attain a desirable object "by means which seem to me unconstitutional." Section 2 whereby State judges and other officers could be punished for obeying State law "seems to me a direct violation of the rights of every State and of every State court."

Moreover, Raymond questioned whether "the condition of the southern States absolutely requires us to take . . . such strong, direct, punitive action as this, in order to secure the rights which this bill proposes to confer . . . ."

---

[195] Ibid., 1265–66. Mar. 8.
[196] Ibid., 1266. Mar. 8.
[197] Ibid., 1266–67. Mar. 8.

Raymond has already been identified: see supra, pp. 178–79, 219, 273–74.

> We have all sorts of evidence presented to us except that which seems to me entitled to weight. . . . We all know perfectly well that a war like this leaves behind it a great wreck, a great *debris* of order, peace, and respect for law. It is so in the South. . . .

When Raymond went on to minimize alarming reports from the South, Woodbridge of Vermont and Schenck of Ohio interrupted to disagree. The latter referred to matters being "proved by the evidence laid before the House by the committee on reconstruction." Raymond answered,

> The gentleman may have had an opportunity to peruse that testimony; I have not; and before I make up my mind about the condition of the southern States I should like to have an opportunity to read it. . . . I suggest whether it would not be worth while to wait until it has been printed, so that we may see on what ground we have to act.

Here a comment is in order. Raymond at that juncture was ready to believe all things and hope all things, in anticipation of such evidence of Southern self-restraint as would avert drastic action by Congress. Thus he seized upon the fact that testimony before the Joint Committee was not yet in print as a reason for putting aside the Civil Rights Bill.

Actually when the bill became law, the Joint Committee would not have completed its hearings—and the printed report with supporting testimony would appear still later.[198]

Raymond yielded to Columbus Delano, a Republican who had won a contested seat for a district in central Ohio. The structure of Section I was scrutinized.[199] There was a general declaration: "there shall be no discrimination in civil rights . . . ." "I suppose that what follows after this is a limitation . . ."—to contract, to sue, etc. "Then is added this clause, 'and to full and equal benefit of all laws and privileges [proceedings] for the security of person and property, as is enjoyed by white citizens.' . . ." That seemed "an enlargement or extension" of the enumerated specific rights. Would it not include jury service? Wilson answered No—but Delano thought it could be "fairly interpreted" to include that right. He went on to the competence to testify—apparently even in State courts; and to Section 2's threat of federal punishment of State judges. "I do not see how we can sustain the principles of this bill."

Delano wanted to see the rights enumerated in this bill enforced upon the States. To that end, let the Constitution be amended to assure

---

[198] See infra, ch. 20, n. 165.

[199] Cong. Globe, 39–1, 1267; App., 156–59. Mar. 8.

those rights, "giving to Congress power to enforce . . . where the States withheld them."

Next day Bingham resumed the critique.[200] "Doubting, as I do, the power of Congress to pass the bill," he would seek at least to remove "its unjust provisions." First, let there be "a final appeal of all questions of law arising under it to the Supreme Court . . . ."

Was it competent for Congress to declare—in the clause which Bingham would strike out—that there shall be "no discrimination in civil rights" in any State on account of race? "What are civil rights?" That classification was indeterminate: it might embrace voting and eligibility to office. He believed "that there is scarcely a State . . . which does not . . . make some discrimination on account of race . . . ." "I deny the power of Congress to make an error of judgment in a State officer a crime . . . ."

Bingham read the specific enumeration of civil rights in Section 1, from "to make and enforce contracts" to the end, and commented:

> I say, with all my heart, that that should be the law of every State, by the voluntary act of every State. The law in every State should be just; it should be no respecter of persons. It is otherwise now . . . . I should remedy that not by an arbitrary assumption of power, but by amending the Constitution . . . ; expressly prohibiting the States from any such abuse of power in the future. . . .

Bingham noticed the analogy between Sections 1 and 2 of the Civil Rights Bill and Sections 7 and 8 of the Freedmen's Bureau Bill. He thoroughly approved the latter, inasmuch as it applied to the insurrectionary States; he was satisfied that the Government had such power "within the insurrectionary districts during the time of insurrection and until the duly organized State governments were restored for the protection of life, liberty, and property, to all men alike. . . ." However, "I have always believed that the protection in time of peace within the States of all the rights of person and citizen was of the powers reserved to the States. And so I still believe."

Representative Samuel Shellabarger of Ohio has already been introduced.[201] He was a sagacious lawyer of straightforward speech. He remained not quite satisfied about the constitutionality of Section 1. For Congress to assume to *confer* rights to contract, sue, testify, inherit, and so forth, "would, it seems to me, be an assumption of the reserved rights of the States and the people." Section 1, however—aside from conferring citizenship—

---

[200] Ibid., 1290–95. Mar. 9. [201] See supra, pp. 288–89, 290–92.

neither confers nor defines nor regulates any right whatever. Its whole effect is . . . to require that whatever of these enumerated rights and obligations are imposed by State laws shall be for and upon all citizens alike without distinctions based on race . . . .

He illustrated its application:

> If you permit a white man who is an infidel to testify, so you must a colored infidel.
>   Self-evidently this is the whole effect of the first section. . . .

Was this within the legislative power of the United States? Shellabarger touched upon his conception of the rights that should pertain to United States citizenship:

> It does seem to me that that Government which has the exclusive right to confer citizenship, and which is entitled to demand service and allegiance, which is supreme over that due to any State, may, nay, must, protect those citizens in those rights which are fairly conducive and appropriate and necessary to the attainment of his "protection" as a citizen. And I think these rights to contract, sue, testify, inherit, &c., . . . are of that class which are fairly conducive and necessary as means to the constitutional end, to wit, the protection of the rights of person and property of a citizen. It has been found impossible to settle or define what are all the indispensable rights of American citizenship. But it is perfectly well settled what are some of these . . . . Two of these are the right of petition and the right of protection in such property as it is lawful for that particular citizen to own.

Without mentioning Bingham, Shellabarger answered the objection noted above:

> It must here be noted that the violations of citizens' rights, which are reached and punished by this bill, are those which are inflicted under "color of law," &c. The bill does not reach mere private wrongs, but only those done under color of State authority; and that authority must be extended on account of the race or color. It is meant, therefore, not to usurp the powers of the State to punish offenses generally against the rights of citizens in the several States, but its whole force is expended in defeating an attempt, under State laws, to deprive races and members thereof as such of the rights enumerated in this act. This is the whole of it.

Shellabarger would vote to send the bill back to the committee, because he believed that the bill's enumeration of rights might be somewhat

THE PRESIDENTIAL FEVER ON THE SUPREME BENCH.

Chief Justice. "Mark but my fall, and that that ruin'd me.
  Judge Davis, I charge thee, fling away ambition;
  By that sin fell the angels; how can man, then,
  The image of his Maker, hope to win by't?"—*Shakspeare.*

Cartoon by Nast from *Harper's Weekly*, April 6, 1872.
(*Library of Congress*)

REGISTRATION AT THE SOUTH—SCENE AT ASHEVILLE, NORTH CAROLINA.—[Sketched by A. W. Thompson.]

From *Harper's Weekly*, September 28, 1867.

Edwin L. Godkin of *The Nation*.
(Harvard College Library)

Horace Greeley of the *New York Tribune*.
(Library of Congress)

**William Cullen Bryant of the
New York Evening Post.**
(Library of Congress)

**Whitelaw Reid of the *Cincinnati Gazette*,
later of the *New York Tribune*.**
(Library of Congress)

**James Gordon Bennett, Sr., of the
New York Herald.**
(Library of Congress)

**John W. Forney of the *Washington
Chronicle*, Secretary of the Senate.**
(Library of Congress)

Judge James V. Campbell
of Michigan.
(Library of Congress)

Judge George G. Wright of Iowa.
(Iowa State Department of History and Archives)

Judge Luther S. Dixon of Wisconsin.
(State Historical Society of Wisconsin)

Judge Thomas M. Cooley of Michigan.
(Library of Congress)

Judge John F. Dillon of Iowa.
(Iowa State Department of History and Archives)

Judge Byron Paine of Wisconsin.
(State Historical Society of Wisconsin)

J. Edgar Thomson.
(Library of Congress)

Judge Thomas Drummond.
(Chicago Historical Society)

Judge Joseph M. Beck.
(Iowa State Department of History and Archives)

Thomas A. Scott
(Library of Congress)

James Grant.
(Iowa State Department of History and Archives)

Rush Clark.
(Library of Congress)

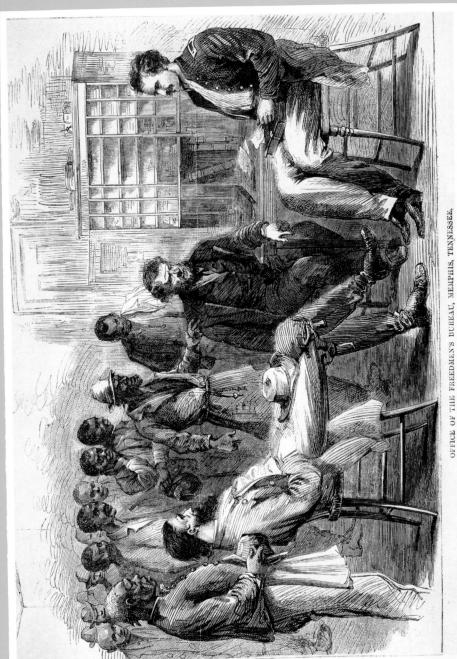

OFFICE OF THE FREEDMEN'S BUREAU, MEMPHIS, TENNESSEE.

From *Harper's Weekly*, June 2, 1866.
(Library of Congress)

Edward R. S. Canby.
(Library of Congress)

John M. Schofield.
(Library of Congress)

Edward O. C. Ord.
(Library of Congress)

George G. Meade.
(Library of Congress)

Winfield S. Hancock.
(Library of Congress)

Oliver O. Howard.
(Library of Congress)

William H. McCardle.
(Old Court House Museum, Vicksburg)

Judge John C. Underwood.
(Library of Congress)

Congressman John B. Alley.
(U.S. Signal Corps)

Congressman George C. McKee.
(Library of Congress)

Judge Richard Busteed.
(Library of Congress)

Governor William G. Brownlow.
(Library of Congress)

narrowed to remove constitutional doubts "without greatly impairing its value."

Shortly thereafter the House came to voting. Bingham's proposed instructions were overwhelmingly rejected. Then Wilson's motion to recommit was carried by 82 to 70, 31 not voting.[202]

On March 13, Wilson reported the bill with amendments—two of which should be clearly marked. The first was to *strike* from Section 1 the clause that read

> There shall be no discrimination in civil rights or immunities among citizens of the United States in any State or Territory of the United States on account of race, color, or previous condition of slavery.[203]

Wilson commented:

> I do not think it materially changes the bill; but some gentlemen were apprehensive that the words we propose to strike out might give warrant for a latitudinarian construction not intended.

Trumbull in the Senate, then Wilson in the House, had given assurance that State legislation on certain matters—voting, jury service, separate schools, miscegenation—would *not* be disturbed. Critics had replied that the courts might not observe such understandings. Now the "no discrimination" clause had been removed.

Further, the committee would add a new section, in response to the critics:

> That upon all questions of law arising in any case under the provisions of this act a final appeal may be taken to the Supreme Court of the United States.

Each amendment was adopted without division. Thereupon the bill was carried by 111 to 38, 34 not voting.[204]

On March 15 the Senate—after hearing Davis of Kentucky renew his protest "in despite of all opposition, of frowns or scoffs"— accepted the amendments without a record vote.[205]

---

[202] Cong. Globe, 39–1, 1296. Mar. 9. Joining in the majority were Democrats, Republicans of moderate tendency, and even some—notably Schenck—who were quite advanced.

[203] Ibid., 1366. The substitution of "citizens" in place of "inhabitants" had been made by the House on March 1. P. 1115. Supra, p. 1183.

[204] Ibid., 1367. Mar. 13.

[205] Ibid., 1413–16.

VETO AND RECONSIDERATION: THE SENATE

THE PRESIDENT HELD the bill for the full "ten days (Sundays excepted)" and on March 27 returned it to the Senate with his objections.[206] "In the exercise of State policy over matters exclusively affecting the people of each State," he wrote, "it has frequently been thought expedient to discriminate between the two races." But now this bill sought to fix "a perfect equality . . . over the vast field of State jurisdiction covered by these enumerated rights." That led him to inquire whether,

> if Congress can abrogate all State laws of discrimination between the two races in the matter of real estate, of suits, and of contracts generally, Congress may not also repeal the State laws as to the contract of marriage between the two races? . . .

And again,

> why, it may be asked, may not Congress repeal in the same way all State laws discriminating between the two races on the subjects of suffrage and office? . . .

From Section 2 he assumed that "members of State Legislatures who should vote for laws conflicting with the provisions of the bill," as well as judges who rendered and ministerial officers who executed judgments in antagonism with it, would be punishable in a federal court.

This bill, the President concluded, gave to the colored race "safeguards which go infinitely beyond any that the General Government has ever provided for the white race." (That comment was literally true, but uncandid: there had never been occasion to protect white men in their right to equal treatment in an unfriendly State ruled by men of a different race.)

After enough time to count to a hundred and to make careful preparation, on April 4 Trumbull opened the reconsideration with "a candid and dispassionate examination of the President's various objections."[207]

Of particular concern here is Trumbull's construction and defense of Section 2:

---

[206] Ibid., 1679–81.

[207] Ibid., 1755–61.
Senator Solomon Foot of Vermont died on March 28. At page 1761, Trumbull said, "The measure has been delayed for a week in conse-

quence of a sad calamity . . . ."
George F. Edmunds was appointed to succeed, and took his seat on April 5. Thus began a distinguished career in the Senate that ended with his resignation, effective November 1, 1891.

> Who is to be punished? . . . The person who, under the color of the law, does the act, not the men who made the law. . . .
>
> But it is said that under this provision judges of the courts and ministerial officers who are engaged in the execution of any such statutes may be punished; and that is made an objection to this bill. I admit that a ministerial officer or a judge, if he acts corruptly or viciously in the execution or under color of an illegal act, may be and ought to be punished; but if he acted innocently the judge would not be punished. . . .

Here Trumbull essayed to explain his conception of the mental element requisite to a conviction under Section 2:

> Sir, what is a crime? It is a violation of some public law, to constitute which there must be an act and a vicious will in doing the act; or, according to the definition in some of the law-books, to constitute a crime there must be a violation of a public law, in the commission of which there must be a union or joint operation of act and intent or criminal negligence; and a judge who acted innocently, and not viciously or oppressively, would never be convicted under this act. But, sir, if he acted knowingly, viciously, or oppressively, in disregard of a law of the United States, I repeat, he ought to be punished, and it is no anomaly to prescribe a punishment in such a case. . . .

Trumbull cited as analogous a provision in the Act of Congress of April 30, 1790, to define and punish crimes against the United States: after declaring void any judicial process, State or federal, against a public minister received by the United States, the statute went on to declare that any person suing out such process, whether as party or as attorney, and every officer concerned in executing it, would be liable to imprisonment not exceeding three years, and to a fine at the discretion of the court.[208]

After "replying with what patience I could command" to the President's objections, Trumbull went on to trace his exertions to avert any collision between Congress and the Executive over this bill. "I had frequent interviews . . . ; a copy was furnished him . . . , and a hope expressed that if he had objections to any of its provisions he would make them known . . . . He never indicated . . . the least objection . . . . The bill was framed, as was supposed, in entire harmony with his views . . . ."

---

[208] Sec. 26, 1 Stat. 117; Rev. Stats., sec. 4064. This was modeled upon the famous statute of 7 Anne, ch. 12, declaratory of the law of nations, enacted after the Russian ambassador had been arrested in 1708.

Trumbull called upon the Senate to override the veto and thereby make the Thirteenth Amendment effective.

Reverdy Johnson had been taking notes: next day—Thursday, April 5—he came to the President's defense with his unfailing professional skill.[209] There was grave doubt about the power of Congress to confer citizenship upon those who by State law were slaves at birth. Section 1, in conferring civil rights, struck at "what has hitherto been considered as the exclusive authority of the States," while Section 2 assumed "a power inconsistent with the independence and integrity of the State judiciary." Concluding, the President "must stand before the country a patriot, though he may be mistaken." The Senator hoped it would not be long before President and Congress were reconciled and "we shall be again together" in a restored Union.

Senator Cowan followed.[210] He hoped his words, "if they are not to convince anybody in the Senate, may go to the country and be reflected upon there." "Where do we get the power to pass this bill?" Not from the Thirteenth Amendment: "I have always been of opinion that the second clause [section] of that amendment amounted to just nothing at all. When slavery was abolished, it was abolished as perfectly by the first clause as by both together." Congress might punish kidnapping—or provide for the writ of habeas corpus—or give an action for damages: but to pass this Civil Rights Bill was beyond its power.

However, waiving that constitutional objection, he would examine particular provisions.

> I . . . am quite willing . . . that all the people of this country shall enjoy the rights conferred by this bill. . . . That all men should have the right to contract, I agree. . . . I might limit the right of a great many people to purchase and hold real estate, but as a general proposition I would allow them to purchase, hold, and lease, and to be entitled to their remedies for the defense of their property. There is no doubt in my mind about that.

But this should be done by *State* legislation: if Pennsylvania had not already granted those rights, no one would have cried longer or louder than he to cause them to be recognized.

But Cowan professed to believe that the Senators were under a misapprehension about the effect of the clause enumerating civil rights. He quoted the text, commenting,

> This portion of the first section confers upon all persons born in the United States the rights which are here enumerated, and it con-

---

[209] Cong. Globe, 39–1, 1775–80. Apr. 5.   [210] Ibid., 1781–85. Apr. 5.

fers those rights without any qualification and without any restrictions whatever . . . . The bill has been taken to mean to confer those rights as they are conferred upon white citizens in the several States. That is not so. . . .

Grammatically, he insisted, the text meant that Congress was conferring upon married women and upon minors an unqualified right to contract, "in direct defiance" of limitations imposed by State law.

Here Trumbull interrupted to protest, "Oh, no"—but he made no further attempt to contradict Cowan's statements. (Republicans, it will be seen in a moment, were seeking an early vote, while opponents needed a delay.)

Presently Cowan returned to his old objection to Section 2, "and that is, the substitution of an indictment for the writ of error." The Senator from Illinois had said that it followed the Act of 1790 which provided for punishing all concerned in executing process against a diplomatic minister received by the United States. Cowan exclaimed in derision,

What potency there must be in the recent amendment of the Constitution which has foisted the negro and set him upon the same platform as the envoy extraordinary and minister plenipotentiary of Great Britain or of all the Russias to the United States of America, . . . and the judge who decides against him is to be punished as a criminal!

Was Congress willing to enact such an absurdity as was involved in Section 2?

Here it is proposed on the part of the Congress of the United States, to pass a law overriding certain State laws. Is that denied? Will any Senator upon the floor deny the fact that this bill is intended to override and set aside the State laws? Why, sir, if it is not to have that operation, it is to have none at all. . . .

It was "atrocious and unworthy the Congress" to make it a crime for "an honest and conscientious judge" to execute the law of his State.

At the outset of his remarks, Cowan had drawn attention to a matter of great concern to the Democrats: Dixon of Connecticut and Wright of New Jersey were confined at home by illness; they could not safely be brought to the Senate chamber for a vote that night. He asked the Republicans to agree upon some hour next afternoon. McDougall of California, Hendricks, Guthrie of Kentucky, and Reverdy Johnson joined in this.

Trumbull replied, "I myself am willing . . . . I hope our friends will agree to it."

But then an ugly scene developed. Ben Wade of Ohio spoke out in his most offensive manner:

> I will tell the President and everybody else, that if God Almighty has stricken one member so that he cannot be here to uphold the dictation of a despot, I thank Him for His interposition, and I will take advantage of it if I can. [Manifestations of applause in the galleries.][211]

Wade plunged on, his remarks having no immediate relevance to the subject before the Senate. He said that "the quarrel [the President] has picked with Congress . . . is nothing more or less than on the question of recognizing and permitting rebels to occupy their old places on this floor . . . ." His thought went back to the Wade-Davis bill in the 38th Congress, and his effort then to establish the paramount authority of Congress over reconstruction.[212]

> It is not a presidential question. I argued then as zealously against Mr. Lincoln's interposition as I do now against Mr. Johnson's inter-position. . . . Sir, if there is any one question about which the American people are unanimous, it is against this one-man power— these monarchical attempts of your Presidents to beat down every other department of the Government and set up their own will as supreme over all. . . .

Thus Lincoln and Johnson were tied together for condemnation in this debate on the latter's veto of the Civil Rights Bill.

Guthrie of Kentucky renewed Cowan's request that the Senate grant a postponement—and, he added, "teach the Senator from Ohio that he is not the one-man power here."[213] He touched upon another matter wherein, the week before, Republican Senators had made a conspicuous display of their power and determination:

> I should not like it to go out . . . that the Senator from New Jersey (Mr. Stockton) was removed because his vote was wanted. I do not want it to go out . . . that we would not do a courtesy to sick Senators because we could pass a bill without their votes, when we could not if they were here. . . .

John F. Stockton (Democrat) had sat throughout the session until—giving effect to a protest by a minority of the members of the

---

[211] Ibid., 1786. Apr. 5. Senator William Wright died on November 1, 1866. He was succeeded by Frederick T. Frelinghuysen, Republican. See note 128.

[212] See supra, pp. 97–98.

[213] Con. Globe, 39–1, 1786. Apr. 5.

New Jersey legislature—[214] on March 27 the Senate, by vote of 22 to 21, declared the seat vacant.[215]

Trumbull responded to Guthrie's appeal: "I am satisfied that no good is to grow out of a struggle here to-night." Thereupon the greater part of the Republicans voted with the Democrats to adjourn.[216]

Next day Wade, in the same mood, set upon "some Senators" who had become "the mere slaves of an accidental Executive"[217]— meaning, in particular, James H. Lane of Kansas, who at that moment was forsaking his Republican associates to come to the support of the President.[218] Trumbull also reprobated the defection somewhat sharply.

Doolittle, already recognized as tending to adhere to the President, now announced that the speeches of Bingham and Delano in the House[219] had led him to devote "some days of study and most earnest reflection" to the bill, while it evidently was receiving "most earnest and serious consideration by the Executive."[220] His conclusion was that he could not conscientiously support it. He urged the Judiciary

---

[214] Ibid., 1, 1565.

The Constitution of the United States then provided: "The Senate . . . shall be composed of two Senators from each State, chosen by the Legislature thereof . . . ."

A statute of New Jersey provided that "United States Senators . . . shall be appointed by the Senate and General Assembly in joint meeting assembled . . . ."

A joint meeting on February 15, 1865, adopted a rule "That no candidate shall be declared elected unless upon receiving a majority of the votes of all the members elected to both Houses of the Legislature."

On March 15 that rule was rescinded: a plurality of the votes was declared to be sufficient.

A vote was taken, yielding Stockton 40; Ten Eyck, Republican incumbent, 37; scattered, 4. Stockton was declared duly elected.

Later, 38 members of the legislature filed a protest that only a majority would suffice.

[215] Cong. Globe, 39–1, 1677–79.

On January 30, Trumbull had reported the resolution of the Judiciary Committee, in favor of Stockton.

That came up for debate on March 22, 23, 26 and 27. Pp. 1564–73; 1589–1602; 1635–48; 1666–79.

On March 23, Morrill—who had been paired with Wright—declared himself free to vote, and voted against Stockton. Whereupon Stockton cast a vote in favor of himself. Pp. 1601–2.

On March 26 the Senate, without record division, agreed that Stockton's vote would not be received. P. 1648.

After further debate on March 27, the result was that Stockton was unseated by a majority of one.

Subsequently he was elected to succeed Frelinghuysen, and served from March 4, 1869 to March 3, 1875. His support of Justice Bradley's nomination has been mentioned. Supra, pp. 734, 737.

[216] Cong. Globe, 39–1, 1787. Apr. 5.

[217] Ibid., 1801–3. Apr. 6.

[218] Ibid., 1799–1800, 1802–5. Apr. 6.

Theretofore Lane had been a defender of the Negro. His defection brought censure from his former friends, in Congress and in Kansas. On July 11 he died of a self-inflicted shot.

[219] Supra, pp. 1189–91.

[220] Cong. Globe, 39–1, 1804–7. Apr. 6.

Committee to bring in a measure that would simply punish the carrying away or holding of a person in slavery.

Turning then to Wade's remarks about reconstruction, Doolittle said that President Johnson was merely carrying forward the policy Lincoln had established—and that that policy had had the indorsement of every member of Lincoln's cabinet, including the present Chief Justice.

Then there was a lively moment. Sumner interrupted to say that Chase never consented "to any proposition which was not founded on universal suffrage"—referring to Chase's letter of April 12, commenting on Lincoln's remarks at the serenade on April 11.[221] Trumbull "happened" to have the pertinent part of the speech, and a discussion ensued on the applicability of Lincoln's conduct to the present policy of his successor.

Senator Henderson said that a policy that was wise in 1863 might not be wise in 1865: Lincoln had called for Union men who would form a loyal State government while the Confederates were in arms; Johnson's call had been to ex-Confederates to "take the civil power into their hands" after secession had failed.[222]

Davis of Kentucky spoke—at great length, as his speech was published in the Appendix to the Congressional Globe.[223] The President was being denounced because he had refused to use his influence and power to establish Negro suffrage—which, Davis knew "from the best authority," had been pressed upon him "by Senators . . . and by a member of the Supreme Court . . . ." The President had shown "the very highest order of moral courage" in the use of the veto.

Davis saw in the bill "a studied want of clearness, a studied ambiguity:" its true purpose was "to consolidate all the reserved sovereignty and powers of the several States into the Congress and Government of the United States." "In many, if not most of the States, there are discriminations . . . against the negro race, made by their constitutions and statutes . . . ." He gave examples: in the punishment for rape—he recounted recent incidents; in competence to testify; in forbidding a black to contract marriage with a white. He went on to other discriminations made by "ordinance, regulation, or custom":

> On ships and steamboats the most comfortable and handsomely furnished cabins and state-rooms, the first tables, and other privileges; in public hotels the most luxuriously appointed parlors, chambers, and saloons, the most sumptuous tables, and baths; in churches not

---

[221] Supra, p. 102.

[222] Cong. Globe, 39–1, 1807. Apr. 6. See supra, pp. 103–05.

[223] Cong. Globe, 39–1, 1809; App., 181–85. Apr. 6. There were long quotations from the *Federalist Papers* and Kent's *Commentaries*.

only the most softly cushioned pews, but the most eligible sections of the edifices; on railroads, national, local, and street, not only seats, but whole cars, are assigned to white persons to the exclusion of negroes and mulattoes. . . .

"This bill," Davis said indignantly, "proposes to break down and sweep them all away, and to consummate their destruction, and bring the two races upon the same great plane of perfect equality, declares all persons who enforce those distinctions to be criminals . . . ." It was a "bold and iniquitous device to revolutionize the Government and to humiliate and degrade the white population, and especially of the late slave States, to the level of the negro race. Vain effort!" The people would "turn with loathing and horror" to overthrow the authors of this "enterprise not only against the instincts and customs of the whole white race, but also against the unchangeable laws of nature."

Saulsbury spoke to the point that "the bill will lead to revolution in blood"; no judge in Delaware would "attempt to execute such a flagrantly unconstitutional act as this. . . ."[224]

McDougall of California said that this revolutionary movement "if not checked must end in vast disaster"—even "a rougher tempest than has raged over the land for the last five years."[225]

Thereupon the call of the roll was ordered—the President pro tem. warning that there must be no disturbance in the galleries.

The result was 33 to override the veto, 15 to sustain it. Wright was present to vote nay; Dixon was absent. The bill had been carried by the requisite two-thirds majority.[226] But, James G. Blaine recalled,

The close vote . . . admonished the Republicans of their danger. If Mr. Dixon had not been confined to his house by illness, if Mr. Stockton had not been a few days before deprived of his seat, the Administration would have been able to rally seventeen votes in the negative, leaving but thirty-three to the Republicans out of a Senate of fifty members. . . .[227]

FURTHER PROCEEDINGS IN THE HOUSE

IN THE HOUSE, which was sitting on Saturday, April 7, Wilson announced that he intended, when the Civil Rights Bill was received from the Senate on Monday, to demand the previous question. "The bill has already been very thoroughly discussed."[228]

[224] Ibid., 1809. Apr. 6.
[225] Ibid., 1809. Apr. 6.
[226] Ibid., 1809. Apr. 6.

[227] *Twenty Years of Congress*, II, 183.
[228] Cong. Globe, 39–1, 1828.

Representative William Lawrence of Ohio had painstakingly prepared a defense of the bill, and later on Saturday he delivered it.[229] This was a well-educated lawyer—sometime reporter of the Supreme Court of Ohio, an editor of the *Western Law Monthly,* and a common pleas judge.[230] In effect he argued from a brief, with elaborate quotation and citation. The bill was "scarcely less" important for the people of the United States than was Magna Charta for Englishmen. "It does not confer any civil right," but "it does provide that as to certain enumerated civil rights every citizen 'shall have the same right in every State and Territory.' That is whatever of certain civil rights may be enjoyed by any shall be shared by all citizens in each State . . . ."

The bill conferred national citizenship: Lawrence developed the proposition that that carried with it "certain absolute rights which pertain to every citizen."

It is worse than mockery to say that men may be clothed by the national authority with the character of citizens, yet may be stripped by State authority of the means by which citizens may exist.

He quoted: "You take my life when you do take the means whereby I live."

The reasoning continued:

Every citizen, therefore, has the absolute right to live, the right of personal security, personal liberty, and the right to acquire and enjoy property. These are rights of citizenship. As necessary incidents of these absolute rights, there are others, as the right to make and enforce contracts, to purchase, hold, and enjoy property, and to share the benefit of laws for the security of person and property.

Now, there are two ways in which a State may undertake to deprive citizens of these absolute, inherent, and inalienable rights: either by prohibitory laws, or by a failure to protect any one of them.

He illustrated: (1) a State would *prohibit* if it enacted that naturalized citizens could not make contracts, etc.: (2) it would none the less *deprive* them if it simply enacted laws for the benefit of native-born citizens and made no provision whereby naturalized citizens could enjoy the same benefits.

Here an observation is appropriate. In another month, as we

---

[229] Ibid., 1832–37. Apr. 7.
[230] He was mentioned supra, pp. 163, 171, 289.
The *Western Law Monthly* was published at Cleveland, January 1859 to April 1863. Lawrence served as editor during its first three years. Reference to the Table of Citations in the *Digest of Federal Cases* shows that a number of cases there collected had appeared in *Western Law Monthly.*

shall see, the House would be debating the proposed Fourteenth Amendment, which in its Section 1 would guarantee (1) the privileges and immunities of citizens of the United States; (2) due process of law; and (3) equal protection of the laws. We shall not hear from Representative Lawrence in that discussion. But let it be noted that here he had stressed the point that "citizenship implies certain rights."

Lawrence went on to show that "there is a present necessity for this bill": the Southern legislatures had not conceded to blacks the civil rights enjoyed by whites. He quoted from testimony before sub-committees of the Joint Committee on Reconstruction, by Generals Terry, Custer, and Thomas, as well as orders from military head-quarters and other items, to show the need for federal protection of civil rights in the South.

Congress, Lawrence argued, had power

> to enforce the observance of the provisions of the Constitution, article four, section 2,[231] and the equal civil rights which it recognizes or by implication affirms to exist among citizens of the same State.
>
> Congress has the incidental power to enforce and protect the equal enjoyment of civil rights which are inherent in national citizenship. . . .

Lawrence came to the defense of Section 2 of the Civil Rights Bill, and gave a much more satisfactory exposition than it had theretofore received. Critics had said that a conscientious State judge, if he ever decided against a claim to an alleged civil right, might be fined or imprisoned. Lawrence answered: "A single case tried and finally decided by the Supreme Court of the United States would determine the right just as all great rights are settled." By the general principles of the criminal law, there would be no criminality "unless there be willful wrong." "And if an officer shall intentionally deprive a citizen of a right, knowing him to be entitled to it, then he is guilty of willful wrong which deserves punishment." The method of Section 2 was extraordinary, but appropriate to meet the needs of the moment:

---

[231] See supra, pp. 1121–23.

If critically examined, this "implication" that Article IV, Section 2, required equality of civil rights "among citizens of the same State" ran into difficulty. Kent, as Lawrence quoted, had explained that the provision meant equal treatment for "persons of the same description." *Commentaries on American Law*, II, 71. Whereupon Lawrence pronounced this dictum:

That is, distinctions created by nature of sex, age, insanity, etc., are recognized as modifying conditions and privileges, but mere race or color, as among citizens, never can. . . .

Lawrence was getting ahead of the law: in the context of the Fourteenth Amendment, "equal protection" did have that meaning. But this had not been the meaning of Article IV, Section 2.

The penal section . . . is made for a great emergency, when the rights of millions are imperiled or totally denied, as a temporary expedient, justified by the times and the circumstances, and which may be modified or abandoned when the necessity for it has ceased.

Seeking further to be helpful, Lawrence took note of Bingham's speech of March 9, which "has been extensively published in a mode to mislead the public judgment." As the bill had stood, it contained the clause commanding "no discrimination in civil rights"; Bingham had given it "an interpretation different from" that of the Judiciary Committee. "But for the purpose of obviating his objection this clause was stricken out and forms no part of the bill as it finally passed."

While by this time no member of the House remained open to persuasion, the speech stands as an impressive brief in support of the Civil Rights Act.

Presently the Fourteenth Amendment supplied an incontestable foundation.

On Monday, April 9, the bill and veto message were received and read. On the question of overriding the objections of the President, there were 122 yeas, 41 nays, not voting, 21.[232]

The Civil Rights Bill had become law.[233]

SECTION 2 HAS BEEN PERPETUATED

SECTION 2 OF THE statute was never "abandoned"—as Lawrence thought it might be—but, with alterations, has been carried forward through a century of statutory revision.[234] Some difficulties which critics foresaw have indeed perplexed the Court.

The Fifteenth Amendment, declaring that the right to vote should not be denied or abridged on account of race, was certified to be in effect on March 30, 1870.[235] To enforce that right, Congress passed the Act of May 31, 1870; therein by Section 16, the rights that had been enumerated in Section 1 of 1866 were secured to "all persons within the jurisdiction of the United States"; Section 17 followed the language of Section 2 of 1866 in penalizing the act of depriving of any right secured by the preceding section; and Section 18 expressly reen-

---

[232] Cong. Globe, 39–1, 1857–61.

Of the Republican critics mentioned above, Delano voted for the bill, Raymond against; Bingham was paired, in opposition.

[233] 14 Stat. 27.

[234] The transition is set out in a Comparative Table of Successive Phraseology, in an appendix to Justice Frankfurter's opinion in United States v. Williams, 341 U.S. 70, 83, 84 (1950).

[235] 16 Stat. 1131. See supra, pp. 557, 1119.

acted the Civil Rights Act of 1866 and declared that Sections 16 and 17 would be enforced according to its provisions.[236]

In the Revised Statutes of 1874, Section 17 above was recast in this language:

> Sec. 5510. Every person who, under color of any law, statute, ordinance, regulation, or custom, subjects, or causes to be subjected, any inhabitant of any State or Territory to the deprivation of any rights, privileges, or immunities, secured or protected by the Constitution and laws of the United States, or to different punishments, pains, or penalties, on account of such inhabitant being an alien, or by reason of his color or race, than are prescribed for the punishment of citizens, shall be punished by a fine of not more than one thousand dollars, or by imprisonment not more than one year, or by both.

This was substantially repeated in Section 20 of the Criminal Code of 1909[237]—with the insertion, however, of the adverb "*willfully* subjects," etc. That was in accord with what Trumbull and Lawrence, after the President's veto, had derived from general principles of criminal law.[238]

When Title 28 of the United States Code, Crimes and Criminal Procedure, was enacted in 1948, the former Section 20 became the present Section 242.

The objection to Section 2, as President Johnson asserted in his veto message, was that it "invades the judicial power of the State." In actual litigation in recent times, the challenge has been placed in a different setting. A statute so vague and indefinite that it fails to give fair notice of what acts will be punished offends the Due Process Clauses of Amendments Five and Fourteen.[239] But the civil rights enumerated in Section 1 and protected by Section 2 of 1866, and now the "rights . . . protected by the Constitution or laws of the United States" within the meaning of Section 242, are constantly being defined and refined in the course of Supreme Court adjudication: on many matters there may be uncertainty.[240] It is clearly recognized that, even as Senator Cowan said in 1866, it would be monstrous if a mistake on an unknowable point of law were to be "tortured into a crime."[241]

---

[236] 16 Stat. 140, 144.

[237] 35 Stat. 1092.

[238] Supra, pp. 1195, 1203–04.

[239] United States v. Cohen Grocery Co., 255 U.S. 81 (1921); Lanzetta v. New Jersey, 306 U.S. 451 (1939).

[240] For example, Trumbull insisted, over and over, that his bill would not disturb statutes against miscegenation; yet in Loving v. Virginia, 388 U.S. 1 (1967), the Court held such a statute to violate the Equal Protection and Due Process Clauses of the Fourteenth Amendment.

[241] Cong. Globe, 39–1, 500. Trumbull's invocation, at p. 1758, of Sec-

The Court has made it clear, however, that the intent required by the statute "is an intent to deprive a person of a right which has been made specific either by the express terms of the Constitution or laws of the United States or by decisions interpreting them."[242]

---

tion 26 of the Act of April 30, 1790, making it an offense to sue out process against a diplomatic officer, did not meet the problem. Whether an individual is such an officer, received by the United States Government, is certain and ascertainable.

[242] Screws v. United States, 325 U.S. 91, 104 (1945); Williams v. United States, 341 U.S. 97 (1951); United States v. Price, 383 U.S. 787 (1966). "Misuse of power, possessed by virtue of state law and made possible only because the wrongdoer is clothed with the authority of state law, is action 'under color of' state law." United States v. Classic, 313 U.S. 299, 326 (1941). The right there alleged to have been interfered with —namely, to vote for a Representative in Congress, and to have one's vote counted—was a right made specific by the Constitution and by decision of the Supreme Court: what this cause decided was that such interference at a *primary election* was punishable under the federal statute. The *Price* case holds that "Private persons jointly engaged with state officials in the prohibited action, are acting 'under color' of law for pur-

poses of the statute." 383 U.S. at 794.

In *Ex parte* Virginia, 100 U.S. 339 (1880), Coles, County Judge, stood indicted under Section 4 of the Civil Rights Act of 1875, 18 Stat. 335, in that in selecting jurors he had excluded citizens on account of race. In an original petition for habeas corpus, the State sought his discharge. Strong J., spoke for the Court:

We do not perceive how holding an office under a State and claiming to act for the State can relieve the holder from obligation to obey the Constitution of the United States, or take away the power of Congress to punish his disobedience.

The selection of jurors was "merely a ministerial act"—often assigned to officers who were not judges.

It is idle, therefore, to say that the Act of Congress is unconstitutional because it inflicts penalties upon state judges for their judicial action. It does no such thing.

It was held that Coles was properly detained for trial.

CHAPTER XX

The Civil Rights Act Reconsidered, and the Fourteenth Amendment

A CCOUNT MUST NOW be taken of *Jones et ux. v. Alfred H. Mayer Co. et al.*, decided by the Supreme Court on June 17, 1968—[1] by reason of what was there said about the Civil Rights Act of 1866. In pronouncing upon the legislative history of that century-old statute and upon the purpose entertained by the 39th Congress, the opinion raised issues that cannot be ignored in a history of the Supreme Court during the Reconstruction period.

Jones and wife complained that respondents had refused to sell them a home in the Paddock Woods community of St. Louis County for the sole reason that Jones was a Negro; they asked injunctive and other relief. Paddock Woods had been planned by Mayer as a complete suburban community; developer had laid out the streets; recreational facilities were provided; community services, such as garbage collection, would be maintained by a board of trustees to be appointed by the developer; the board would have authority to levy assessments and to collect them through the courts.

Complainants—petitioners in the Supreme Court—rested their case against such racially motivated refusal upon two grounds: (1) that it was prohibited by Section 1 of the Civil Rights Act, as reenacted and codified;[2] (2) alternatively, that the State was so much involved in

---

[1] 392 U.S. 409. On writ of certiorari to the U.S. Court of Appeals for the Eighth Circuit. Argued Apr. 1–2, 1868, and decided on June 17. The decision below, 379 F.2d 33 (1967), affirmed the judgment of the District Court for Eastern Missouri, 255 F. Supp. 115 (1966), granting respondents' motion to dismiss.

[2] Pertinent provisions were 42 U.S.

Code, Sections 1981 and 1982. These were derived from Section 1 of the Civil Rights Act of 1866, which was reenacted by the Act of May 31, 1870, 16 Stat. 140, 144, and then codified as Sections 1977 and 1978 of the Revised Statutes of 1874—whence they were carried into Title 42 U.S. Code.

Section 1981 enacts that all persons

Paddock Woods, by licensing, zoning, regulating and assisting, as to make the refusal amount to State action in violation of the Fourteenth Amendment.

Petitioners' brief in the Supreme Court argued that "the 1866 Act . . . uses the broadest imaginable language"; it was *not* passed "merely to overthrow the 'black codes' or discriminatory legislation." The Act gave Negroes equal rights to make and enforce contracts, and in particular the right to buy and lease property, the same as enjoyed by white citizens:

> it is clear that if this language is to be given any meaning at all, it must at least be interpreted to mean that a person cannot be refused the right to buy or lease property solely because of the color of his skin. . . .

Counsel submitted that "from the language of the statute, as well as from its legislative history, it is clear that Congress has created a law giving all persons the equal opportunity to participate in the housing market, regardless of race . . . ."[3]

The brief did not set out an account of the legislative history of the Civil Rights Act in substantiation of that flat statement.

THE DEPARTMENT OF JUSTICE FILES A BRIEF

A BRIEF FOR THE United States as amicus curiae, supporting the petitioners, calls for notice. Significantly, it put in the first place the submission that the Fourteenth Amendment, of its own force, prohibited the conduct described in the complaint: in the circumstances, the respondents were exercising State power and performing governmental functions.

Alternatively, the Government supported the contention that the challenged conduct was within the prohibition of Section 1978 of the

---

shall have "the same right in every State and Territory to make and enforce contracts, to sue, be parties, give evidence, and to the full and equal benefit of all laws and proceedings for the security of persons and property as is enjoyed by white citizens, and shall be subject to like punishment, pains, penalties, taxes, licenses, and exactions of every kind, and to no other."

Section 1982—securing other rights enumerated in Section 1 of 1866—was the one on which complaints particularly relied:

All citizens of the United States shall have the same right, in every State and Territory, as is enjoyed by white citizens thereof to inherit, purchase, lease, sell, hold, and convey real and personal property.

[3] Petitioners' brief, 13–16.

XX: *The Fourteenth Amendment*

Revised Statutes of 1874—drawn from Section 1 of the Civil Rights Act of 1866. (Section 1978 is now repeated verbatim by Section 1982 of Title 42, United States Code.[4])

The Government's argument was that the text of Section 1978 disclosed a purpose broad enough to forbid any substantial "fencing out" of an entire racial class, and that the legislative history confirmed that broad purpose:

> The Civil Rights Act of 1866 was written against the background of the so-called "Black Codes" of the Southern States . . . . But, however discriminatory they were, it does not appear that any of the Black Codes denied the capacity of the Negro to acquire and hold property, real or personal. . . . [Here standard histories were quoted, and also State legislation as reported in Congressional documents.]
>
> What, then, was the congressional purpose in securing to the freedman "the same right . . . as is enjoyed by white citizens . . . to inherit, purchase, lease, sell, hold, and convey real and personal property"? Were the legislators of 1866 knowingly indulging in a vain and empty gesture? Or were they ignorant of the true conditions of the South? . . .

Here Senator Trumbull's statement was quoted, that his purpose was to secure "practical freedom"; further, the vigorous opposition to the President's veto was said to be inconsistent with a view "that the measure merely solemnized what no one contested, that the colored man was now legally competent to own and acquire property."

> The actual problem was somewhat different: it was that many of the Southern States, while conceding the legal capacity of the Negro to hold all kinds of property and to engage in real estate transactions, severely limited the practical exercise of these new rights. . . . [Here a standard history is cited, and numerous illustrations found in Southern statutes reprinted in Congressional documents.]
>
> This was the evil to which Congress was addressing itself: not the absolute disabling of the Negro, but the serious practical abridgments placed on his freedom to contract and his rights with respect to property. The examples we have given were cited again and again in the debates on the Civil Rights Bill and on companion measures. Cong. Globe, 39th Cong., 1st Sess., pp. 39, 111, 474, 475, 516–517, 603, 1755, 1759. To be sure, there were occasional overstatements. The law of Mississippi was sometimes said to bar Negroes from holding real property anywhere in the State, (*e.g., id.* at pp. 1160, 1759); but, as often, it was correctly represented as applying

---

4 Set out in note 2 above.

only to rural areas. *E.g., id.* at pp. 39, 111. And provisions of local law nominally guaranteeing the Negro the right to acquire and hold property were brought to the attention of Congress. *E.g., id.* at pp. 1755, 1785. In sum, the authors of the Civil Rights Act of 1866 were obviously well aware of the true legal status of the freedman in the South and were concerned to combat *discrimination*, not *disabilities*. Practical equality of right was the aim of their work. See *id. at* 1117–1118, 1293, 1413. It is, therefore, no accident that the law they framed is formulated in those terms: the Negro shall "enjoy" "the *same* right" as whites.[5]

The brief reiterated that Section 1 of the Act of 1866 had been reenacted in 1870, and then codified in the Revised Statutes of 1874.[6] Thus Section 1978 was the product of two enactments *after* Congressional Reconstruction had so transformed the South as to remove the immediate need for a ban on discriminatory statutes. Further, Section 1's concluding phrase—"any law . . . to the contrary notwithstanding" —had been omitted in the revision of 1874. Thus disappeared whatever implication that phrase had made that Section 1 was aimed only at *governmental* and not at *private* discrimination. Then it was pointed out that

> It is of course contrary to the established rule governing the interpretation of the Revised Statutes of 1874 to go behind a clear text to an earlier version of the law. . . .[7]

---

[5] Brief of the United States as Amicus Curiae, 29–33.

[6] Ibid., 21–22, 33–34. See note 2 above.

[7] Ibid., 40. Citing United States v. Bowen, 100 U.S. 508, 513 (1880); Vietor v. Arthur, 104 U.S. 498, 499–500 (1881); Hamilton v. Rathbone, 175 U.S. 414, 419–21 (1899); Benson v. Henkel, 198 U.S. 1, 13 (1905); and United States v. Mosley, 238 U.S. 383, 388 (1915).

In *Bowen*, Justice Miller spoke for a unanimous Bench in saying

> The Revised Statutes must be treated as the legislative declaration of the statute law on the subjects which they embrace, on the first day of December, 1873. When the meaning is plain, the courts cannot look at the statutes which have been revised to see if Congress erred in that revision, but may do so when

> necessary to construe doubtful language used in expressing the meaning of Congress. . . .

Under the Revised Statues, only those pensioners who had *not* contributed to Soldiers' Home funds were required to surrender their pensions while inmates of the Home.

In *Vietor*, a matter of the applicable custom duty, the Court followed *Bowen*. In particular, a section of the Revised Statutes laid a certain duty on "stockings"; the Court held it applicable to stockings of worsted, declining to consider the contention that under earlier legislation they would have been dutiable as "knit goods . . . ."

In the *Hamilton* case, Brown, J., said:

> The whole doctrine applicable to the subject may be summed up in the single observation that prior acts may be resorted to,

The brief claimed further strength from this thought on statutory construction:

> It is no ground of objection that present conditions suggest new applications for the old words. As Mr. Justice Holmes observed for the Court in *United States* v. *Mosley*, 238 U.S. at 388, applying the broadly worded provision before him to circumstances far removed from those which prompted its enactment, "we cannot allow the past so far to affect the present as to deprive citizens of the United States of the general protection which on its face [the statute] most reasonably affords." . . .[8]

Undoubtedly it was for good reason that the Department of Justice placed its submission primarily on the Fourteenth Amendment, and dwelt upon the State-related features of the Paddock Woods community. Whatever the reasoning, it took greater hardihood to seek a reversal on the basis of Section 1978 of the Revised Statutes—now 42 U.S. Code 1982. If reversal were to be placed on statutory ground, the brief showed how to distribute the weight as widely as possible: the Act of 1866—the reenactment of 1870—the codification of 1874—the claim that this gave a clear text and so cut off any doubts arising from earlier legislative history—and the proposition, per Holmes, J., that the past should not so far affect the present as to deprive citizens of the protection of a broadly worded provision.

---

to *solve*, but not to *create*, an ambiguity. . . .
In particular, the Revised Statutes for the District of Columbia (1874) authorized a married woman to convey, devise, and bequeath "her property." The statute from which this provision was drawn had excepted such property as she had received by gift or conveyance from her husband. The Court found the code provision "clear upon its face," and held it applicable.

The *Benson* case held that the District of Columbia was a "district" within a section of the Revised Statutes derived from the Judiciary Act of 1789, although the District of Columbia was not then in existence.

On the *Mosley* case, see next footnote.

[8] Ibid., 24.

In United States v. Mosley *et al.*, 238 U.S. 383 (1915), the statute involved was Section 19 of the Criminal Code enacted in 1909, punishing conspiracy to injure or intimidate any citizen in the exercise of "any right . . . secured to him by the Constitution or laws . . . ." This had originated in Section 6 of the Enforcement Act of 1870. But Section 4 of that Act had provided a less severe punishment for the act of hindering or combining to hinder the exercise of the right to vote; and *that* provision had been repealed.

Mosley *et al.* had been indicted under Section 19 for conspiring to injure citizens in the exercise of their right to vote, by omitting to count their votes. The District Court had sustained a demurrer, on the ground that the code provision derived from Section 6 of 1870 should not be held to punish action covered by Section 4 of 1870, now repealed. In rejecting that view, Justice Holmes used the language quoted in the text.

BRIEF OF THE NATIONAL COMMITTEE AGAINST DISCRIMINATION IN HOUSING

ANOTHER AMONG THE several briefs by amici curiae—one from which the Court borrowed substantially—is that on behalf of the National Committee Against Discrimination in Housing, the National Association for the Advancement of Colored People, the American Jewish Congress, and the Anti-Defamation League of B'nai B'rith— hereinafter "the Anti-Discrimination brief." This set out boldly to seek reversal on the basis of Section 1982:

> This Court, which has never ruled on the specific issue of the applicability of this provision of the 1866 Act to private action, should now declare that the Act means what it says and is constitutionally applicable to bar racially discriminatory sales of real property.[9]

"Soon after the Thirty-Ninth Congress convened," the brief recited, a variety of bills were introduced for the protection of freedmen; mention was made of a resolution by Representative Benjamin F. Loan of Missouri directing the Select Committee on Freedmen [of which he was a member] to consider "legislation securing to the freedmen and the colored citizens of the States recently in rebellion the political and civil rights of other citizens of the United States."[10] Also Senator Wilson of Massachusetts introduced a bill, and Sumner introduced others, with similar objective. "Although these proposals died they are significant as showing a uniformity of approach by the draftsmen and supporters of the Civil Rights Act of 1866 to the protection of the rights as humans and the essential needs of the freed men."[11]

---

[9] Brief, p. 8.

[10] Ibid., 21.

Loan has been mentioned supra, p. 154.

The Select Committee on Freedmen was created at the opening of the 39th Congress on the initiative of Thomas D. Eliot of Massachusetts, who had the welfare of Negroes close at heart. The Speaker named Eliot as chairman, and six other Republicans of like outlook: Kelley of Pennsylvania, Orth of Indiana, Bingham of Ohio, Loan of Missouri, Grinnell of Iowa, and Paine of Wisconsin. There were two Democratic members, who had not sat in the 38th Congress: Nelson Taylor of New York (some-time Brigadier General in the Army of the Potomac) and Samuel S. Marshall of Illinois.

[11] Ibid., 21–22. See supra, pp. 1160–63. Compare with the Court's opinion, 392 U.S. at 429–30; and see infra, pp. 1223–24.

Emphatically, Loan, Wilson and Sumner were *not* "draftsmen" of the Civil Rights Bill: Trumbull was, and he would not have agreed that there was "a uniformity of approach" uniting himself with those two Senators. He had wanted "a more full comprehension," and a "more sweeping and efficient" measure than Wilson's hasty proposal. And when, in explaining his bill, he said there was "very little im-

Numerous excerpts from Trumbull's speeches were set out, including that about "the trumpet of freedom,"[12] and—in italics for emphasis—his statement that "the very object of the bill is to break down all discrimination between black men and white men."[13] Howard's remarks, in accord with that statement, were also quoted.[14] (The brief marshalled helpful comments without tracing the bill's chronology; it did not draw the Court's attention to the fact that throughout most of the debate there had been a "no discrimination" clause, stricken out at the very last.)

"Senate opponents of the measure held the same view of its thrust" as did Trumbull and Howard: "they conceded that . . . the bill applied to private persons as well as the state. This view was expressed, for example, by Senator Garrett Davis of Kentucky who said": and here followed an extract from Davis' resentful speech, just prior to the overriding of the veto, wherein he asserted that the preferential treatment whites had received in hotels, churches, and public conveyances would now be at an end. "Supporters of the bill made no effort to deny this sweeping characterization of what they intended."[15]

The brief passed from sentiments expressed during the debate to consider "The Meaning and Effect of the Act," reaching this conclusion:[16]

> The language of the Act makes it clear that it is aimed not just at "Black Codes" and other state laws imposing discrimination on the basis of race or previous condition of servitude but rather at any and every effort or development, whether by use of state power or by private power, to re-establish and re-impose on any group the incidents or practices of slavery. The use in the statute of the term "custom" makes it clear that its thrust is by no means limited to the exer-

---

portance in the general declaration of abstract truths and principles unless they can be carried into effect," he must have had Sumner in mind. Supra, p. 1173.

[12] Ibid., 23. See supra, pp. 1164–65. The same passage is quoted in the Court's opinion, at 440; and see infra, pp. 1236–38.

[13] Ibid., 28. See supra, p. 1173. The same statement is quoted in the Court's opinion, at 432; and see infra, pp. 1225–26.

The brief, at page 22, also quoted Trumbull's statement on December 19 that he thought it important that Congress act at an early date "for the purpose of quieting apprehensions . . .

lest by local legislation or *a prevailing public sentiment* in some of the States persons of the African race should continue to be oppressed . . ." —as tending to show that the subsequent Section 1 was aimed at *private* as well as at public discrimination. See supra, p. 1162. Quoted in the Court's opinion, at 432, n.54.

[14] Ibid., 25 and 28. See supra, pp. 1179–80. Howard's speech was cited in the Court's opinion, at 433, n.55.

[15] Ibid., 28–29. See supra, pp. 1200–01. Court's opinion, at 435, took note of Davis' speech and commented, "Those observations elicited no reply."

[16] Ibid., 38–39.

cise of state power.[17] And the discriminations it bars deal with far more than the right of access to state facilities. Clearly the guarantee against racial discrimination in the right to make contracts can have meaning only in terms of a limitation on the right of private individuals, the other parties to such contracts. And the civil right here in issue, to purchase and hold real property, is equally a right which can have no meaning if private individuals, who are the sellers of most real property, are free, either through conspiracies or individually, to nullify the right by refusing, on the basis of racial bigotry or discrimination, to sell property they have put on the market.

In the outcome, the effort spent on this brief as friend of the Court was abundantly rewarded.

BRIEF FOR THE RESPONDENTS

OUR CONCERN WITH *Jones v. Mayer Company* is confined to a single matter: the Court's pronouncement on the legislative history of the Civil Rights Act of 1866. Consider the words of Section 1, that all citizens, without regard to color, "shall have the same right . . . to . . . purchase, lease, sell, hold, and convey real and personal property . . . as is enjoyed by white citizens, . . . any law, statute, ordinance, regulation, or custom, to the contrary notwithstanding": did that mean that not only would they have *capacity* to purchase, but also that all others would be under a *duty not to refuse*, on account of color, to sell to a would-be purchaser?

Here counsel for the respondents labored under a handicap. He must sustain a *negative*—that notwithstanding remarks in debate decrying the numberless injustices then being practiced upon freedmen, Congress did *not* purpose in Section 1 to ban *private* as well as *governmental* discrimination. He must make that showing about a *statute of 1866* before a Court which, in its progressive application of the *Constitution* a century later, had set its face against racial discrimination.

The brief quoted Trumbull when he presented the bill:

> It will have no operation in any State where the laws are equal, where all persons have the same civil rights without regard to color or race. It will have no operation in the State of Kentucky when her slave code and all her laws discriminating between persons on account of race or color shall be abolished.[18]

---

[17] On the word "custom," see infra, pp. 1238-44.

[18] Respondents' brief, 14, quoting from Cong. Globe, 39-1, 476. Jan. 29.

And Wilson, opening debate in the House:

> If the States would all observe the rights of our citizens, there would be no need of this bill. . . .
>   It will be observed that the entire structure of this bill rests on the discrimination relative to civil rights and immunities made by the States "on account of race, color, or previous condition of slavery."[The quoted words came from the "no discrimination" clause, subsequently deleted.] . . .[19]

Thayer's speech was quoted, wherein he identified the objective at which the bill was directed, and launched into the colorful reiteration that it was "laws . . . , laws . . . , laws . . . ."[20]

Other quotations were adduced, from supporters and opponents, to show that it was discrimination attributable to the State that was forbidden—but these were not as helpful since they did not negate a purpose to do more.

Respondents' counsel noticed, *in quotation marks,* what the Anti-Discrimination brief had submitted, that

> "Racial segregation in housing is an immediate and pressing evil," and, that, therefore, the Court "should now declare that the Act means what it says and is constitutionally applicable to bar discriminatory sales of real property."[21]

(To say that the Act "means what it says" begs the question—but the phrase recurs, and the Court said that "Indeed, even the respondents seem to concede that, if §1982 'means what it says'—to use the words of the respondents' brief—then it must encompass every racially motivated refusal to sell or rent and cannot be confined to officially sanctioned segregation in housing. . . ."[22])

Respondents' brief had proceeded to argue that not only did the Congress of 1866 have no such intention, but that if Section 1 were given the construction for which petitioners and amici contended, "a Pandora's box of problems" would result. Personal property as well as real would be affected. And as to the latter, "even a single rented room in a residence and the proverbial shack in the woods would be subject to the statute. For it makes no distinction as to size or importance— something which the petitioners and their supporting *amici* frequently overlook when they emphasize the 'substantial' or 'significant' role of a

---

[19] Ibid., 15, quoting from Cong. Globe, 39-1, 1117, 1118. Mar. 1.

[20] Ibid., 19-20. See supra, pp. 1186-88.

[21] Ibid., 35, quoting Anti-Discrimination brief, 8.

[22] 392 U.S. at 421-22. But respondents' counsel was quoting, not conceding.

subdivision as justifying application of the statute. . . . We are not here considering whether Congress has the power, under either the Thirteenth or the Fourteenth Amendment, to enact some other kind of legislation, e.g., a fair housing law, that would by appropriate definitions recognize such distinctions."[23]

THE RESPONSE OF THE COURT

JUSTICE STEWART'S OPINION for the Court held

that §1982 bars *all* racial discrimination, private as well as public, in the sale or rental of property, and that the statute, thus construed, is a valid exercise of the power of Congress to enforce the Thirteenth Amendment.[24]

It was "unnecessary to decide whether that discrimination also violated the Equal Protection Clause of the Fourteenth Amendment." In this he spoke as well for Chief Justice Warren and Justices Black, Brennan, Fortas, and Marshall. Justice Douglas concurred briefly in an opinion that dwelt on "badges of slavery [that] remain today."[25]

Justice Harlan (White, J., joining with him) dissented:

For reasons which follow, I believe that the Court's construction of §1982 as applying to purely private action is almost surely wrong, and at least is open to serious doubt. The issues of the constitutionality of §1982, as construed by the Court, and of liability under the Fourteenth Amendment alone, also present formidable difficulties. . . .[26]

Then Justice Harlan took note that, while *Jones* was under consideration within the Court, Congress had largely covered the field by the comprehensive Civil Rights Act of 1968.[27] He said:

---

[23] Respondents' brief, 35–39. Counsel quoted what Joseph B. Robison—one of the counsel on the Anti-Discrimination brief—had written in an article on "The Possibility of a Frontal Assault on the State Action Concept," *Notre Dame Lawyer*, 41:455, 465 (1966):

It hardly needs to be said that, if the courts were persuaded to accept a broad interpretation of Section 1982, the effect would be tremendous. A strong factor working against such an interpretation is that it would do too much. It would instantly create a fair housing law for all states and territories, without any of the exceptions that are usually taken for granted. . . . Moreover, since the Act is not limited to real property, the provisions dealing with personal property might constitute a nationwide law against discrimination in all retail stores.

[24] 392 U.S. at 413.
[25] Ibid., 444, at 445.
[26] Ibid., 449, at 450.
[27] Pub. L. 90–284, 82 Stat. 73.

Moreover, the political processes of our own era have, since the date of oral argument in this case, given birth to a civil rights statute embodying "fair housing" provisions which would at the end of this year make available to others, though apparently not to the petitioners themselves, the type of relief which the petitioners now seek. It seems to me that this latter factor so diminishes the public importance of this case that by far the wisest course would be for this Court to refrain from decision and to dismiss the writ as improvidently granted.

Justice Harlan examined the legislative history of the act of 1866 at as great length as did Justice Stewart for the majority—twenty-four pages in each opinion.

Jones v. Mayer Company had been argued on April 1 and 2, 1968; it was decided on June 17. In the meantime, Congress passed the Civil Rights Act of April 11, which in its Title VIII[28] established what the Court described as "a detailed housing law, applicable to a broad range of discriminatory practices and enforceable by a complete arsenal of federal authority."[29] The Court found that the statute of 1968 did not displace that of 1866, which was "a general statute applicable only to racial discrimination in the rental and sale of property . . . ."[30]

Since the Act of 1866 spoke of both "real and personal property," evidently the holding in *Jones v. Mayer* applies to both.

And, inasmuch as the enumeration in Section 1 conferred at the start the right "to make and enforce contracts"—now Section 1981 of 42 U.S. Code—*parity of reasoning points to the consequence that racial discrimination in the making of contracts generally is barred.*

This awakens one to the fact that as we come to examine the Court's mode of dealing with the legislative history of the Act of 1866, we touch upon a subject much larger than the matter of Paddock Woods. Our concern, however, is not the implications of the *Jones* case for the future, but a question about long-ago: What in truth did the 39th Congress purpose when it passed that statute?

The Court sought to fortify its construction of Section 1 by a textual argument about its relationship to Section 2; for convenience, this will be adjourned for notice after the Court's treatment of the legislative history has been studied.

---

[28] Sections 801 to 819, 82 Stat. 81.
[29] 392 U.S. at 417. It forbade discrimination on ground of race, religion, or national origin in the sale or rental of a dwelling, but gave certain exemptions from its coverage.

Its housing provisions became applicable on January 1, 1969. Intervention by the Attorney General was authorized.
[30] Ibid., 415–17.

THE COURT'S VENTURE INTO HISTORICAL RESEARCH

FROM BEGINNING TO end the opinion marches boldly, with an air of absolute certitude. Unlike the Government's brief, which summoned its strength from a range of points, the opinion for the Court rested confidently upon the Act of 1866 and the broad "vision of the task before it" which inspired the men of the 39th Congress when they gathered in December 1865.

Section 1 is "plain and unambiguous." "On its face . . . [it] appears to prohibit *all* discrimination against Negroes in the sale or rental of property—discrimination by private owners as well as discrimination by public authorities." Respondents had seen "revolutionary implications of so literal a reading . . .": "Our examination of the relevant history, however, persuades us that Congress meant exactly what it said."[31]

This tone of assurance is maintained in spite of the fact that, as the dissenting opinion points out, "the precedents in this Court are distinctly opposed to the Court's view of the statute."[32] Thus in the *Civil Rights Cases*[33] in 1883, Justice Bradley said of the Act of 1866 that "This law is clearly corrective in its character, intended to counteract and furnish redress against State laws and proceedings, and customs having the force of law, which sanction the wrongful acts specified. . . ." In 1926 the Court, construing Section 1978 of the Revised Statutes (derived from Section 1 of the Act of 1866) and two other sections dealing with civil rights, said that they "do not in any manner prohibit or invalidate contracts entered into by private individuals in respect to the control and disposition of their own property."[34] And in 1948 the Court accepted the proposition that Section 1978 "does not invalidate private restrictive agreements so long as the purposes of those agreements are achieved by the parties through voluntary adherence to the terms": judicial enforcement, however, must not be granted, because that would deny "rights intended by Congress to be protected by the Civil Rights Act."[35]

---

[31] Ibid., 420–22.

[32] Ibid., 450.

[33] 109 U.S. 3, 16.

[34] Corrigan v. Buckley, 271 U.S. 323, 331. The Court dismissed for want of jurisdiction, because the construction of the statute was not substantially "drawn in question" by a denial below of an injunction to restrain the prospective breach of a racially restrictive covenant.

[35] Hurd v. Hodge, 334 U.S. 24, 31–34. The Court cited passages in the debates in the 39th Congress on the Fourteenth Amendment, to the point that the amendment would give constitutional force to the provisions of the Civil Rights Act, and that both were confined to governmental action.

This at any rate is true: the meaning which the majority found "plain" in 1968 was not the meaning that had seemed plain to their predecessors.

A disturbing fact which haunts an examination of the Court's opinion is the absence of any recognition that Section 1 of the Civil Rights Bill, as Trumbull introduced it, had *two* clauses: (1) the general prohibition, "there shall be no discrimination in civil rights . . . on account of race . . . ," and (2) the enumeration of particular rights to be enjoyed, without regard to race or color—to contract, to sue, etc.[36] The original text of Section 1 is set out on page 474 of the Congressional Globe—plainly in view, immediately beside a passage in column 1 which the Court quotes.

The general clause remained in the bill as it was debated and passed by the Senate—and throughout the debate in the House until, shortly before the vote on passage, the House accepted an amendment that it be *stricken out.*

Here let it be recalled that critics had asserted that by Section 1 Congress would transgress upon the domain of the State: not only in the particular matters enumerated in clause 2, but—what was even worse—by the undefined term "civil rights" in clause 1. They said that it could be read so broadly as to require that black men be admitted to vote, to hold office, to sit on juries—to override the State's school system—to invalidate its statutes against miscegenation, and the like. No matter that proponents professed that such results were not intended: they said that even so, such an interpretation was not so gross but what some court might adopt it. But note, these critics in parading their apprehensions never suggested that "no discrimination" might be stretched to forbid *private* as well as *official* action. Think for a moment what alarm they could have spread through the land if it had occurred to them to allege that possibility! Bitter partisans, such as Saulsbury, McDougall, Garrett Davis, and Rogers, would have put that forward specifically in the front line of their attack.

The Court's opinion makes no mention whatever of the presence throughout the debates, and the deletion at the last moment, of the categorical requirement of "no discrimination in civil rights . . . ." It had at the outset announced its firm conclusion, from both text and legislative history, that Section 1 forbade *"all* discrimination . . ."against Negroes in the sale or rental of property. From the Court's failure to mention, plus that announced conclusion, it results that whenever a Senator or Representative is quoted as saying that there will be *no discrimination,* the opinion gives one to understand that this evidences a clear Congressional purpose and understanding that *all*

---

[36] Cong. Globe, 39–1, 474. See supra, pp. 1172–73.

discrimination, *private* as well as *official*, would be banned. That is doubly misleading. (1) When a speaker was merely repeating language that then stood in the bill, it is unwarranted to represent that he was affirming something meaningful about the effect of the bill with that language removed. (2) It is unwarranted to represent that the prohibition of private discrimination was included, when such an aplication had not entered into the discussion.

"Our examination of the relevant history," one is at first inclined to suppose, had simply failed to take account of the presence and then the removal of the "no discrimination" clause. No one of the briefs had drawn attention to it. *Jones v. Mayer* was decided on the last day of the term: the Court is in a hurry at the close. One is inclined to suppose that the Court was not properly acquainted with the legislative history, since otherwise it must have been realized that such use of the quotations would be unfair—and one recoils from that alternative.

But then one must reckon with the fact that in 1966—just two years earlier—in *Georgia v. Rachel*,[37] the Court had had occasion to consider the Civil Rights Act of 1866, and Justice Stewart's opinion there told how the bill had contained both "a general provision" and "the specific enumeration of rights," and how, after "sharp controversy," the former was stricken:

> The legislative history of the 1866 Act clearly indicates that Congress intended to protect a limited category of rights, specifically defined in terms of racial equality. As originally proposed in the Senate, §1 of the bill that became the 1866 Act did not contain the phrase "as is enjoyed by white citizens."[38] That phrase was later added in committee in the House, apparently to emphasize the racial character of the rights being protected. *More important, the Senate*

---

[37] 384 U.S. 780, decided on June 20, 1966.

Rachel *et al.*, prosecuted as sit-in demonstrators, sought to remove to the U.S. District Court under Section 1443 (1) of 28 U.S.C. authorizing removal where defendant cannot enforce in the State court "a right under any law providing for the equal rights of citizens . . . ." This provision was derived from Section 3 of the Civil Rights Act of 1866, permitting removal where a right under Section 1 could not be enforced. Defendants had set up rights under the First Amendment and the Due Process Claues of the Fourteenth. The District Court remanded. While appeal was pending in the Court of Appeals,

Congress passed the Civil Rights Act of 1964: the court held that defendants should be allowed in the District Court to show a right within that statute.

The Supreme Court, on review, concluded that the Act of 1866 was "the model" for the phrase in the section on removal, and that the phrase referred to "civil rights stated in terms of racial equality." Hence a claim under the Civil Rights Act of 1964 was—but claims under the First Amendment or under the Due Process Clause were not—embraced within Section 1443 (1).

[38] At 791, citing Cong. Globe, 39–1, 474.

bill did contain a general provision forbidding "discrimination in civil rights or immunities," preceding the specific enumeration of rights to be included in §1.[39] Objections were raised in the legislative debates to the breadth of the rights of racial equality that might be encompassed by a prohibition so general as one against "discrimination in civil rights or immunities." There was sharp controversy in the Senate,[40] but the bill passed. After similar controversy in the House,[41] however, an amendment was accepted striking the phrase from the bill.[42] [Emphasis added.]

One even finds the Court's opinion of 1966 citing what Senator Saulsbury said at pages 476 and 477 as illustrative of the "sharp controversy" that led to the deletion of the "no discrimination" clause, while the opinion of 1968 uses Saulsbury's words at page 478 as a stepping stone to reach its conclusion that the bill as enacted would tolerate *no* discrimination, even in private dealing in property. As will be explained in a moment, it cited what Saulsbury (and others) said as showing that "when the Senate passed the Civil Rights Act . . . , it did so fully aware of the breadth of the measure it had approved."[43] The 1968 opinion goes on to say that "when the House passed the Civil Rights Act"—citing the page in the Congressional Globe next after that recording the vote to *strike out* the "no discrimination" clause—

It too believed that it was approving a comprehensive statute forbidding *all* racial discrimination affecting the basic civil rights enumerated in the Act.[44]

The Court had not altogether forgotten *Georgia v. Rachel* when the opinion in *Jones v. Mayer* was being written: the former was cited in footnote 25—dealing with the right of removal derived from Section 3 of the Act of 1866—with a direction to "See *Georgia* v. *Rachel*, 384 U.S. 780, 797–804." The discussion of the deletion of the "no discrimination" clause, quoted above, is at pages 791–92 of *Rachel*.

How, then, could the Court have thought proper in 1968, when

---

[39] Citing ibid.

[40] The footnote directs the reader to the debates "at 476–477 (remarks of Senator Saulsbury); 505–06 (remarks of Senator Johnson)."

Saulsbury's remarks have been summarized supra, pp. 1175–76, Johnson's at p. 1180.

[41] The footnote directs the reader to the debates "at 1121–1122 (remarks of Representative Rogers); 1157 (remarks of Representative

Thornton); 1271–1272 (remarks of Representative Bingham)."

Rogers' remarks have been summarized supra, p. 1184, Thornton's at pp. 1188–89, Bingham's at p. 1191.

[42] Citing, "See Bickel, The Original Understanding and the Segregation Decision, 69 Harv. L. Rev. 1, 11–29 (1955)." The pertinent provisions of Section 1 are there set out, and the legislative history of the bill is traced.

[43] 392 U.S. at 433.

[44] Ibid., 435.

the scope of Section 1 of the Act of 1866 was the critical issue, to make no reference to what seemed "important" in 1966 when only a superficial examination of the statute sufficed?

Besides its undue inference from statements about "no discrimination," the Court's opinion is disturbing in another aspect. Democrats in the debates in 1866 contended that the Thirteenth Amendment had only released the shackles, leaving the status of the freedman in other respects to be determined by the State; Congress could do no more than prevent any further enslavement. Supporters of the Civil Rights Bill answered that the Amendment went further than that: it authorized Congress to insure "practical freedom" by securing such rights as were enumerated in the bill against discrimination by the State. Far removed from that controversy was the line separating counsel in *Jones v. Mayer*: one side argued that Section 1 of the statute simply conferred *capacity*, while the other claimed that it also imposed upon all persons a *duty* not to discriminate on account of race. Yet the Court appropriates and quotes with emphasis sentences uttered to repel the Democrats' narrow construction—such as

> *The practical question now to be decided is whether they shall be in fact freemen. It is whether they shall have the benefit of this great charter of liberty* given to them by the American people.[45] [Emphasis by the Court.]

—as if such statements about the effect to be given to the Thirteenth Amendment could fairly be taken to construe Section 1 of the Civil Rights Act and to show that it forbade discrimination by private individuals. Truly, such quotations do not establish that a supporter of the bill of 1866 was affirming that it meant what the Court for the first time was asserting in 1968.

One seems to be dealing with a strongly purposeful opinion.

THE COURT'S OPINION: PURPOSE OF THE 39TH CONGRESS

CONTROVERTING WHAT TO the Court seemed plain from the start, that Section 1 "was meant to prohibit *all* racially motivated deprivations of the rights enumerated in the statute," respondents, the opinion observes, "rely heavily upon the fact that the Congress which approved the 1866 statute wished to eradicate the recently enacted Black Codes":

---

[45] Ibid., 434, quoting the remarks of Representative Thayer. The speech has been summarized at some length supra, pp. 1186–88.

but the Civil Rights Act applied throughout the country, "and its language was far broader than would have been necessary to strike down discriminatory statutes." Congress had numerous newspaper reports, official documents, and correspondence telling of private outrages and atrocities inflicted upon Negroes.

> Indeed, one of the most comprehensive studies then before Congress stressed the prevalence of private hostility . . . . The report concluded that, even if anti-Negro legislation were "repealed in all the States lately in rebellion," equal treatment for the Negro would not yet be secured.[46]

[This refers to the report of General Carl Schurz on his observations in seven Southern States, completed and submitted to the President in mid-November 1865.]

> In this setting, it would have been strange indeed if Congress had viewed its task as encompassing merely the nullification of racist laws in the former rebel States. That the Congress which assembled . . . in December 1865 in fact had a broader vision of the task before it became clear early in the session, when three proposals to invalidate discriminatory state statutes were rejected as "too narrowly conceived."[47] . . .

[The reference is to Senator Wilson's S. 9 and to two of Sumner's sheaf of proposals at the opening of the Session; the quoted words are from Professor tenBroek.[48] The reasons why these measures were regarded as impractical have been set out above.[49] They were not "rejected" after serious consideration, but like scores of others simply made no progress. That was not because Congress when it met in December 1865 was in so resolute a temper as to demand measures more drastic than what the Senators from Massachusetts had to offer. Trumbull said that the need was for "a bill that will be much more efficient to protect the freedman in his rights"—and his companion measures on the Freedmen's Bureau and on Civil Rights made a systematic response: the former to the immediate situation in States not yet restored to their normal relations with the Union, and the latter to the enduring need for general legislation. The fact that the offerings of Wilson and Sumner were allowed to wither was in no wise on the ground that only discriminatory *laws* and not private manifestations of prejudice would be condemned.]

---

[46] Ibid., 426–29.
[47] Ibid., 429.
[48] *Equal Under Law* (New York: Macmillan and Co., Collier Books,

1965), 177.
[49] See supra, pp. 122–23, 1160–63, and n. 11 of this chapter, where the proposals are considered.

It is upon this showing that the Court finds it "clear" that the Congress that assembled in December 1865 brought with it this "broader vision."

THE COURT'S OPINION: THE CIVIL RIGHTS BILL IN THE SENATE

As THE OPINION TAKES NOTE,[50] on December 19 Trumbull gave notice that he would introduce legislation which, he said, would "enlarge the powers of the Freedmen's Bureau . . . and protect every individual in the full enjoyment of the rights of person and property and furnish him with means for their vindication."[51] Prompt action was needed,

> lest by local legislation *or a prevailing public sentiment* in some of the States persons of the African race should continue to be oppressed and in fact deprived of their freedom . . . . [Emphasis by the Court.]

Let it be recalled that what Trumbull had in mind turned out to be *two* bills. The Freedmen's Bureau Bill, based on the power to suppress the rebellion and applicable to States and districts that had been involved therein, would make it the duty of the President "to extend military protection and jurisdiction" in cases where there had been discrimination against "negroes, mulattoes, freedmen, refugees, or any other persons," in respect of the civil rights there enumerated, "in consequence of any State or local law, ordinance, police or other regulation, custom, or prejudice . . . ."[52]

Its companion, the Civil Rights Bill, based on the Thirteenth Amendment, was designed for permanent application throughout the country—including the once-rebel States, which would presently be restored to their place in the Union and thus no longer be subject to an extraordinary regime. Section 1, in making provision to secure civil rights, made its meaning more clear by concluding, "any law, statute, ordinance, regulation, or custom to the contrary notwithstanding." And since, Trumbull observed, "A law is good for nothing . . . without a sanction to it,"[53] Section 2 straightway provided "That any person who under color of any law, statute, ordinance, regulation, or custom, shall subject . . ." a person so protected to the deprivation of any right secured by the Act would be liable to trial and punishment in a federal court.

Trumbull's thought seems clear. In a once-rebel State, where both a hostile government and "prevailing public sentiment" caused

---

[50] 392 U.S. at 431.
[51] Cong. Globe, 39–1, 77. Supra, p. 1162.

[52] See supra, pp. 1163–64.
[53] Cong. Globe, 39–1, 475. Jan. 29.

apprehension, he would charge the Bureau—which was on the ground, acting directly in individual situations—to protect blacks and whites against deprivation of their rights by governmental action or by "prejudice." The "public sentiment" in Trumbull's extemporaneous remarks and the "prejudice" in Section 7 of the Freedmen's Bureau Bill seem to correspond. Then in the Civil Rights Bill, it seems evident that there is a correspondence between the thought in Section 1, that these rights are to be secured, "any law . . . or custom to the contrary notwithstanding," and Section 2, which makes it an ingredient of the misdemeanor that the deprivation be "under color of any law . . . or custom." The meaning of "custom" will be considered hereafter; it is believed that the draftsman referred to customs followed by officialdom—for example, by the courts in their selection of jurors and in passing upon testimonial competence, and by officers who carried out the sentences imposed.[54]

With this explanation, Trumbull's utterance of the words "or a prevailing public sentiment," in his speech on December 19 when he said he would introduce "a bill" for two purposes, does little to establish that the Civil Rights Bill had the particular purpose for which the Court was contending—to forbid private discrimination in the sale of property.

Among its numerous quotations from remarks by Trumbull, the opinion sets out some of what he said on January 29 when he opened debate on the Civil Rights Bill; then the opinion goes forward with this comment:[55]

> Of course, Senator Trumbull's bill would, as he pointed out, "destroy all [the] discriminations" embodied in the Black Codes, but it would do more: It would affirmatively secure for all men, whatever their race or color, what the Senator called the "great fundamental rights:" . . .

—that was, to acquire property, to go and come at pleasure, to enforce rights in the courts, to make contracts, and to inherit and dispose of property.

> As to those basic civil rights, the Senator said, the bill would "break down *all* discrimination between black men and white men."[56] [Emphasis by the Court.]

---

[54] Infra, pp. 1238–44.

[55] 392 U.S. 431–32, quoting the debates at 474, where Trumbull said the bill was intended to secure "practical freedom." See supra, pp. 1172–75.

[56] Trumbull in the debates, on February 2, at 599. He was replying to Davis' "long harangue," and in particular to the contention that "This is an act for the benefit of the free negro, not the white man." Trumbull said its object is "to secure equal rights to all the citizens of the country . . . ."

[As Section 1 then stood, it expressly commanded "no discrimination in civil rights . . . on account of race . . . ."]

By reason of the opinion's treatment of the "Black Codes," the chronology should be brought into view.[57] Mississippi's measures became law between November 22 and December 2, 1865. So much had been done when Congress assembled.

When Trumbull introduced his Civil Rights Bill on January 5, two more States had completed their provisions, by bills that became law between December 19 and 21: South Carolina[58] and

---

[57] See the topic "The Legislatures Enact 'Black Codes,' " supra, pp. 110–17. Also ch. 19, notes 173 and 191.

The authentic place to find statutes is, of course, in the Session Laws of the respective States. To trace legislative history, one must go to the Senate Journal and the House Journal for the session. Local newspapers often carry accounts of legislative actions, and may publish speeches, during the session.

S. Exec. Doc. No. 6, 39th Cong., 2d Sess., is a letter from the Secretary of War to the President of the Senate, wherein are transmitted, at 170–230, Laws in Relation to Freedmen, compiled by command of General Howard, Commissioner of the Freedmen's Bureau. While approximately accurate, these reports vary materially from the authentic statutes, in punctuation and sometimes in more serious respects.

Walter L. Fleming's *Documentary History of Reconstruction*, 2 vols. (Cleveland: A. H. Clark Co., 1906, 1907), Vol. I at 273–312, reprints a selection of typical statutes. Edward McPherson's *Political History of the United States of America during the Period of Reconstruction*, third ed. (Washington: James J. Chapman, 1880), summarizes a much larger number.

[58] South Carolina Statutes at Large, Acts of 1864–65, contain (1) at 271, An Act of December 19, preliminary to the legislation induced by the Emancipation of Slaves. It gave to colored persons the right to acquire and dispose of property; to contract; to enjoy the fruits of their labor; to sue; to receive protection under the

law in their persons and property. They would have the rights and remedies enjoyed by whites, save as modified by statutes in the code.

(2) At 271–78, an Act of December 19, to amend the Criminal Law.

(3) At 278–91, an Act of December 19, to establish District Courts, with exclusive jurisdiction in civil and criminal cases involving persons of color.

(4) At 291–304, an Act of December 21, to regulate the Domestic Relations of Persons of Color, and to amend the law in relation to Paupers and Vagrancy.

See supra, pp. 110, 116, and ch. 19, n. 173.

Provisional Governor Perry, transmitting on October 27 the report of the commission to draft a code for Negroes (see supra, p. 116), had advised the legislature that until proper legislation was enacted, "the Federal authorities . . . will retain their military forces throughout the State"; but that when it was enacted, he felt assured that the President would declare that South Carolina was "entitled to her position once more as a member of the Federal Union" and then the seating of Senators and Representatives could not, "with any show of propriety," be denied. S.C. House J., Extra Sess. 1865, 24, 25.

Governor Orr's message of December 6 renewed this urging: "If [the freedman's] rights of person and property are not fully and firmly secured by our local legislation, we can not hope to be relieved of the presence of the Military and Provost Courts. The authorities of the United States will not remove their protecting hand

Louisiana.[59] Moreover, Alabama in December had enacted a statute to protect freedmen in their rights of person and property (giving a limited competence to testify), and a statute concerning vagrants (not confined to persons of color).[60] And Georgia had admitted the colored person as a witness in certain cases.[61]

While Trumbull's bill was pending, Florida enacted its laws in mid-January; in the latter part of February, Alabama completed its work, and Virginia passed its statutes; in March, Georgia adopted several statutes on domestic relations, and North Carolina its act concerning persons of color. (Not until August did the Texas legislature assemble; on November 10 it enacted a measure to define the rights of persons of color which substantially followed the enumeration in Section 1 of the Civil Rights Act, save that competence to testify was limited.[62])

. . . until we provide by our laws to give him full protection in all his civil rights. . . ." S.C. House J., Regular Sess. 1865, 61, 63.

[59] Louisiana Acts, Extra Sess. 1865, contain (1) at 14, an Act of December 20, to prohibit the carrying of fire-arms on premises or plantations without consent of the owner. (2) At 16, an Act of December 20 to prevent trespassing upon any plantation. (3) At 16, an Act of December 20 to amend the statute on crimes. (4) At 24, an Act of December 21 to punish the enticing away of laborers, servants, or apprentices. (5) At 28, an Act of December 21, relative to apprentices and indentured servants. (6) At 32, an Act of December 21 to punish the employment of a laborer or apprentice already employed.

Governor J. Madison Wells allowed to fail, by pocket veto, a bill to regulate labor contracts for agricultural pursuits. It began with a requirement that all laborers so engaged must "within the first ten days of . . . January of each year," make contracts for the ensuing year. "All labor contracts shall be made with heads of families," to embrace "all the members of the family able to work . . . ." Fines were prescribed for a wide range of acts and omissions, to be imposed by the employer. The bill thus allowed to fail was mild in comparison with a bill on a like subject introduced at the opening of the session. Every adult freedman or woman, it would have required, must provide self and family "with a comfortable home and visible means of support within twenty days after the passage of this act." Failing therein, the freedman or woman would be arrested and hired to the highest bidder for the remainder of the year. La. Sen. J., Extra Sess. 1865, 13. Nov. 29, 1865.

[60] Ala. Acts of 1865–66, 98 (of Dec. 9), and 119 (of Dec. 15).

[61] An Act to make free persons of color competent witnesses in certain cases, of December 15, Acts of the General Assembly, Annual Session, Dec. 1865 to Mar. 1866, 239. See infra, p. 1242.

[62] Texas Gen. Laws of 1866, 131. There were provisos: that nothing therein would repeal the law against intermarriage; or permit other than whites to sit on a jury, hold office, or vote.

Legislation at that session required that one car for freedmen be carried on every train. The school laws then enacted contemplated that only white children would be served.

A number of statutes were enacted, not specifically limited to colored persons yet obviously having them in view: on apprentices; on vagrancy; on contracts of labor.

Thus when Trumbull did his drafting, there had been only an alarming start on the enactment of laws to govern persons of color. Then from one legislature after another, more came forth while the bill was under consideration—producing a succession of exhibits showing what its immediate field of operation would be. Georgia was just completing its legislation when the Civil Rights Bill went from Congress to the President.

The Court's opinion speaks of "the recently enacted Black Codes," and says

> But the Civil Rights Act was drafted to apply throughout the country, and its language was far broader than would have been necessary to strike down discriminatory statutes.[63]

This seems to pose these alternatives: Did Congress purpose nothing more than "to do away with the Black Codes"—or did it *also* want to forbid "mistreatment of Negroes by private individuals and unofficial groups, mistreatment unrelated to any hostile state legislation"? The former seeming too inconsiderable a goal, one is invited to accept the latter.

Certainly when Trumbull framed his bill he was not aiming merely to knock down the discriminatory codes already in sight, and such others as might in the weeks ahead be put on the same line. He designed, in what seems apt language, an important statute of permanent and universal applicability. Of course it would "apply throughout the country": (1) the bill would override discriminatory laws on the statute books of a number of States that had remained loyal; and (2) even though the chief apprehension was for the colored people in States then undergoing Reconstruction, the day would come when those States would be subject only to federal laws of general applicability.[64] Trumbull would not attempt by federal authority to establish a body of substantive civil rights: that field was conceded to the States, and Congress had never intruded. He would, however, in the name of appropriate legislation to enforce the Thirteenth Amendment, impose a federal principle of racial equality in the enjoyment of State-created rights, to the extent expressed in Section 1. To affect the law of every State—"free" as well as those wherein slavery had existed—even in that limited respect, seemed at that time a major advance. Some Republicans, wholly sympathetic with the result, were troubled about the power

---

[63] 392 U.S. at 426–27.

[64] Some words spoken in the debates failed to express precisely the simple thought that the Act would be *in effect* throughout the United States, but would have *no effect* on the laws of a State which made no racial discrimination.

of Congress to attain it.[65] That concern was somewhat relieved by the elimination of the general "no discrimination" clause. Appreciated in this historical context, Trumbull's bill expressed a noble purpose: to ordain, under federal sanction, equality of black and white in the enjoyment of a wide range of rights under State law. (When the Fourteenth Amendment, with its Equal Protection Clause, came into force in 1868, the federal guarantee became wider and uncontestable.)

Whether, in addition to this accomplishment, the bill was intended to forbid private discrimination in the sale or lease of property, was the issue in *Jones v. Mayer.*

After reiterating Trumbull's statement that the bill would "break down *all* discrimination between black men and white men" [emphasis by the Court], the opinion comes to this conclusion about what Senators understood:[66]

> That the bill would indeed have so sweeping an effect was seen as its great virtue by its friends[67] and as its great danger by its enemies[68] but was disputed by none. Opponents of the bill charged that it would not only regulate state laws but would directly "determine the persons who [would] enjoy . . . property within the States,"[69]

---

[65] See supra, pp. 1189–93.

[66] 392 U.S. at 432–33.

[67] Ibid at 433, citing the remarks of Senator Howard, Cong. Globe, 39–1, at 504. See supra, pp. 1179–80. Presumably the citation referred to the passage where Howard said that the bill "simply gives to persons who are of different races or colors the same civil rights."

[68] Citing the remarks of Senator Cowan (debates at 500, see supra, pp. 1177–79) where in particular he defended separate schools; and the remarks of Senator Hendricks (debates at 601, see supra, p. 1182) where—speaking with disapproval of the fact that the bill would "recognize the civil rights of the colored people as equal to the civil rights of the white people"—he called for the deletion of the section authorizing the use of the armed forces to execute the statute. This was in the ill-considered remarks where he imagined "some white man who is running for his liberty because some negro charged him with denying him equal civil rights . . . ." He was making alarming suggestions about

measures to enforce the statute—not about the meaning of Section 1.

[69] Quoting words of Senator Saulsbury (debates at 478, see supra, pp. 1175–76). He said that many things were "taken out of the control of the States by the paramount authority of this bill . . .":

> Mr. President, this bill not only proposes to assume control over the laws which shall govern title to estates, but also to determine the persons who shall be entitled to enjoy estates and property within the States, and if you can do this as to a portion of that property, any particular species of it, you can do so as to the whole; and if you can regulate and govern in one particular, you can govern in reference to all the property and all the interests of the States. . . . Then also you can determine who shall not hold property within a State. . . . Such an assumption of power on the part of Congress ought to arouse the people of the whole country to

threatening the ability of white citizens "to determine who [would] be members of [their] communit[ies] . . . ."[70] The bill's advocates did not deny the accuracy of these characterizations. Instead, they defended the propriety of employing federal authority to deal with "the white man . . . [who] would invoke the power of local prejudice" against the Negro.[71] Thus, when the Senate passed the Civil Rights Act on February 2, 1866, it did so fully aware of the breadth of the measure it had approved.

Inasmuch as the bill then contained the general prohibition that "there shall be no discrimination in civil rights . . . on account of race . . . ," it is not significant that Senators said so too. The footnotes have explained the context in which quoted words were uttered. Saulsbury resented that the bill "invaded and defrauded" the State of its reserved rights. Van Winkle denied the power by statute to admit blacks to the *national* "community" of *citizenship*. Lane was defending the machinery for executing the statute in the event of "organized resistance" that might use "the power of local prejudice." The quotations do not sustain the conclusion for which the Court offers them.

---

a sense of impending danger. Let them take warning in time.

. . .

That does not suggest that he supposed that the bill would control *private* dealings; the inference, on the contrary, is irresistible that if he had recognized that to be a possibility, he would indeed have aroused the people.

[70] Quoting words of Senator Van Winkle (debates at 498, see supra, pp, 1176–77). The Senator's contention was that "I think it needs a constitutional amendment to make these people [of African descent] citizens of the United States." At 497. It is perfectly clear in his speech that he used the word "community" in the sense of *national body politic or community*. His remarks had no bearing on keeping colored people out of a local neighborhood.

[71] Quoting words of Senator Lane of Indiana (debates at 603, see supra, p. 1182). Hendricks had been imagining with somewhat wild exaggeration the possible consequences of the bill's provisions for enforcement, especially by the use of armed forces: did the Senators "want this to be a country governed by military power?" Lane, replying, said that "Where

organized resistance to the legal authority assumes that shape that the officers cannot execute a writ," it was proper to call the armed forces; "without that provision this act would be a mockery and a farce." Seemingly his reference to "the power of local prejudice to override the laws of the country" had reference to such "organized resistance" to the enforcement of the statute. Lane was not notable for precise statement; Hendricks, whose remarks were normally pointed accurately, had in this exchange spoken loosely.

Lane had been defending the bill against Hendricks' objection that it adopted the machinery of the Fugitive Slave Act of 1850. (See supra, pp. 1170–72.) Lane had replied that here "the purpose is changed. These provisions are in the interest of freemen and of freedom, and what was odious in the one case becomes highly meritorious in the other." P. 602. One recalls that it was familiar that "the power of local [anti-slavery] prejudice" had at times threatened "to override the laws of the country."

At any rate, the Senators were not discussing the meaning of Section 1 of the bill.

THE COURT'S OPINION: THE CIVIL RIGHTS BILL IN THE HOUSE

THE OPINION CONTINUES:[72]

    In the House, as in the Senate, much was said about eliminating the infamous Black Codes.[73] But, like the Senate, the House was moved by a larger objective—that of giving real content to the freedom guaranteed by the Thirteenth Amendment. Representative Thayer put it this way: . . .

In calling Thayer to witness, the Court makes a splice of excerpts from his notable speech of March 2: the two parts may be found in the much longer selection set out above in the account of the debate.[74] First the opinion quotes,

    [W]hen I voted for the amendment to abolish slavery . . . I did not suppose that I was offering . . . a mere paper guarantee. And when I voted for the second section of the amendment, I felt . . . certain that I had . . . given to Congress ability to protect . . . the rights which the first section gave . . . .

Then the opinion goes back two paragraphs in Thayer's speech, to the place where he said

    The bill which now engages the attention of the House has for its object to carry out and guaranty the reality of that great measure. It is to give to it practical effect and force. It is to prevent that great measure from remaining a dead letter upon the constitutional page of this country. . . . The events of the last four years . . . have changed

---

[72] 392 U.S. 433.

[73] There is a footnote:

    See, *e.g.*, [Cong. Globe, 39–1] at 1118–1119 [Wilson; see supra, pp. 1183–84], 1123–1125 [Cook; see supra, pp. 1184–86], 1151–1153 [Thayer, see note 74], 1160 [Windom, who referred to discriminatory legislation in several States]. See generally the discussion in the dissenting opinion, *post*, at 464–467.

There Justice Harlan had quoted extensively from Representative Wilson's introduction of the bill on March 1 [see supra, pp. 1183–84]; from Thayer on March 2 [see supra, pp. 1186–88; infra, pp.1231–32]; and a sentence from Bingham on March 9, debates at 1291—all to the effect that the bill was aimed at discriminatory State laws; also to Shellabarger's statement that "The bill does not reach mere private wrongs, but only those done under color of state authority." [See supra, pp. 1191–92.]

[74] See supra, pp. 1186–88, summarizing what Thayer said in the debates at 1151–55 on March 2.

[a] large class of people . . . from a condition of slavery to that of freedom. *The practical question now to be decided is whether they shall have the benefit of this great charter of liberty* given to them by the American people. [Emphasis by the Court.]

This mode of extracting omits the intervening paragraph where Thayer rang the changes in denouncing the "laws . . . laws . . . laws . . ." then being enacted by these "new-formed Legislatures of the rebel States." By the time Thayer spoke—March 2—six of the States had their statutes for blacks. Military commanders, he pointed out, had issued "peremptory prohibitions" against the application of their "oppressive" features. That, he said, showed the necessity of the Civil Rights Bill "for enforcing the guarantees of liberty" conferred by the Thirteenth Amendment.

It seems remarkable that an opinion bent upon demonstrating that Congress had "a larger objective" than merely to efface discriminatory laws should claim support from a speech that dwelt so heavily upon the theme that it was the discriminatory laws that demonstrated the immediate necessity for the Civil Rights Bill.

Moreover, as was earlier pointed out,[75] expressions such as Thayer's sentence underlined by the Court, whose purpose was to repel Democratic arguments for a narrow construction of the Thirteenth Amendment, cannot fairly be used to support the Court's contention that Congress purposed in Section 1 of the Civil Rights Bill to forbid private acts of discrimination.

The Court's opinion then moves to the speech Representative Cook made on March 1—which also has been reported at some length in the account of the debate.[76] The opinion relates that

Representative Cook of Illinois thought that, without appropriate legislation, any "combination of men in [a] neighborhood [could] prevent [a Negro] from having any chance" to enjoy these benefits. To Congressman Cook and others like him, it seemed evident that, with respect to basic civil rights—including the "right to . . . purchase, lease, sell, hold, and convey . . . property," Congress must provide that "there . . . be *no* discrimination" on grounds of race or color. [Emphasis by the Court.]

The quoted words should be placed in the context of Cook's speech. He was dilating upon the vagrant laws recently enacted in Southern States. These laws did indeed create a peril that a freedman without employment might be summarily convicted of vagrancy, where-

---

[75] See supra, p. 1222.
[76] 392 U.S. at 434. See supra, pp. 1184–86, summarizing what Cook said in the debates at 1123–25.

upon the right to his labor might be sold. And Cook was saying that a "combination of men in his neighborhood [could] prevent him from having any chance to support himself by his labor." Cook was not suggesting that the Civil Rights Bill would give the hapless freedman some remedy against the "combination of men":[77] he was pointing to the vagrant laws as typical of recent enactments—"so malignant in their spirit toward these freedmen, so subversive to their liberties"—which the Civil Rights Bill would render unenforceable.

When Cook said,

> Then the question that remains is simply this: can the Congress . . . provide that as between citizens of the United States there shall be no discrimination in civil rights or immunities?[78]

he was simply repeating the very words of the general "no discrimination" clause.

On the basis of its extracts from the speeches of Thayer and Cook, the opinion reaches this conclusion:

> It thus appears that, when the House passed the Civil Rights Act on March 13, 1866, it did so on the same assumption that had prevailed in the Senate: It too believed that it was approving a comprehensive statute forbidding *all* racial discrimination affecting the basic civil rights enumerated in the Act.[79]

For the passage of the bill the opinion cites page 1367 of the Congressional Globe. Yet plainly in sight on page 1366 it appears that formerly the bill had provided that

> there shall be no discrimination in civil rights . . . on account of race . . .

and that on March 13 the House had voted to *strike out* that clause.[80]

This leads back to the quandary already explained:[81] Can one go on supposing that the Court was unaware of the presence and the deletion of that clause?

Assume for a moment that the Court was aware, but that it concluded—as did Representative Wilson—that the deletion did not "materially" alter the meaning of Section 1. Even so, the need for the Court always to be frank must have caused it to point to the alteration, with an acknowledgement that the clause had been removed because some members were "apprehensive that the words . . . might

---

[77] See infra, pp. 1247–48, 1258.
[78] Cong. Globe, 39–1, 1124; quoted in context supra, pp. 1185–86.

[79] 392 U.S. at 435.
[80] See supra, pp. 1172, 1193.
[81] See supra, pp. 1220–22.

give warrant for a latitudinarian construction not intended."[82] Or, as the Court itself expressed it in 1966, "Objections were raised . . . to the breadth of the rights of racial equality that might be encompassed by a prohibition so general . . . ," leading to "sharp controversy" and then to "striking the phrase from the bill."[83]

THE COURT'S OPINION: PROCEEDINGS AFTER THE VETO

THE OPINION RECORDS President Johnson's veto of the bill on March 27, and says that

in the brief congressional debate that followed, his supporters characterized its reach in all-embracing terms. One [Senator Cowan] stressed the fact that §1 would confer "the right . . . to purchase . . . real estate . . . without any qualification and without any restriction whatever . . . ."[84] Another [Senator Davis of Kentucky] predicted, as a corollary, that the Act would preclude preferential treatment for white persons in the rental of hotel rooms and in the sale of church pews.[85] These observations elicited no reply. . . .

Cowan's remarks on April 5 have already been reported at some length:[86] he hoped his objections would be heard in the country—and he was endeavoring to delay a vote. He was clear that these civil rights should exist—by *State* law—although he himself would be inclined to "limit the right of a great many people to purchase and hold real estate." His points were (1) that *Congress* had no power to confer civil rights; and (2) that, grammatically, Section 1 conferred these rights upon married women and upon minors, in defiance of the limitations which State law imposed by reason of coverture and infancy. When he said, "without any qualification and without any restriction whatever," he referred to *capacity*: that was the point of his objection.

Then when he came to Section 2, his complaint was that the bill sought to override State laws by the "atrocious" method of threatening State judges with a criminal sanction:

Will any Senator . . . deny . . . that this bill is intended to override and set aside State laws? Why, sir, if it is not to have that operation, it is to have none at all. . . .

---

[82] Representative Wilson, Cong. Globe, 39–1, 1366. Mar. 13.

[83] Georgia v. Rachel, 384 U.S. 780, 791–92. See supra, p. 1221.

[84] 392 U.S. at 435, citing Cong. Globe, 39–1, 1781.

[85] Ibid., citing Cong. Globe, 39–1, App. at 183.

[86] See supra, pp. 1196–97.

Fairly treated, Cowan's remarks give no support to the Court's holding that the Act did more than merely confer capacity—that it actually forbade discrimination by private individuals as well as by public authorities. Cowan spoke severely of "loose notions prevailing upon the proper construction to be given to the laws," and of his apprehension that "a passionate, or a prejudiced [Federal] judge, who had some end or motive beyond that which ought to govern him in the execution of his official duty, would take advantage of this in order to widen the jurisdiction of the United States courts . . . ." It was "enough in this nineteenth century to make a man tremble for the fate of constitutional government."[87] Could he have been presented with the possibility that in the twentieth century Section 1 might be construed not only to confer capacity but also to impose a duty of nondiscrimination, and that words selected from his speech might be used to prove that such a result was intended by the 39th Congress, he would not have failed to foreclose it.

Garrett Davis' speech of April 6 has already been summarized.[88] It was his final outcry against breaching the system of racial inequality. He spoke of the luxurious appointments on public conveyances and in hotels that had been reserved for whites, and "in churches not only the most softly cushioned pews, but the most eligible sections of the edifices . . . ." *That comes the closest, of anything the Court quoted from the debates, to a specific statement that the bill forbade racial discrimination when property was put up for sale.* It is true that in some church buildings the pews were owned by individuals: the interest was classed as real property in some jurisdictions and as personal in others.[89] From this a contention might be raised that the Senator was speaking technically of this legal interest—although he bracketed it with "eligible sections" of the edifice, which argues against it. Had he said that an owner who put a farm or a house on the market would be under a duty to refrain from racial discrimination, the statement would be entitled to serious consideration: but the prediction that black people would be purchasing "the most softly cushioned pews" seems no more than another of the indignities in which Davis' speeches abounded.

Of this we may be sure: if he had imagined that the bill would control private transactions in property, he would not have kept the point hidden from January until April, to express it in a vague hint in the course of a long speech just before the vote on overriding the veto.

The Court's opinion adds, "These observations elicited no

---

[87] Cong. Globe, 39–1, 1782. Apr. 5.
[88] See supra, pp. 1200–01.

[89] Kent, *Commentaries on American Law*, III, 402.

reply."[90] But when it is realized to what lengths the supporters had gone to contrive a two-thirds majority, how vital it now seemed to vote at this hour before their opponents' strength could be increased by even one Senator,[91] it is no wonder that Davis' remarks elicited no reply. It was not fair to draw an inference. Had the Court known, surely it would not have claimed that point to support its argument.

And quite aside from the peculiar circumstances in this instance, resort to legislative history in aid of statutory construction would become less reliable if the Court made a practice of drawing inferences from a failure to deny statements made in such unreasoning partisan harangues as Senator Davis had made against the Civil Rights Bill. (It would certainly be unwarranted to accept as admitted every proposition found in a concurring or a dissenting opinion which the Court has allowed to pass unnoticed.)

THE COURT'S OPINION: TRUMBULL'S "TRUMPET OF FREEDOM" SPEECH

HAVING FOUND AT the outset that the language of the statute was "plain and unambiguous," and then having found that the debates made it "clear that the Act was designed to do just what its terms suggest,"[92] the Court said that

> The remaining question is whether Congress has power under the Constitution to do what §1982 purports to do: to prohibit all racial discrimination, private and public, in the sale and rental of property. . . .[93]

In the section of the opinion wherein the Court answers this question in the affirmative, there is only one quotation from the debates of 1866 that needs here to be noticed. It comes from Trumbull's "trumpet of freedom" speech on January 19. A long excerpt has been set out above, with a signal that presently it would appear to have importance.[94]

Trumbull was defending the constitutionality of the Freedmen's Bureau Bill—and incidentally of the Civil Rights Bill, which the Senate had not yet considered. Hendricks of Indiana had contended that the Thirteenth Amendment did no more than to break the "private relation between the master and his slave"; that it did not alter the public

---

[90] Seemingly in this remark it was following the Anti-Discrimination brief. See supra, p. 1213.

[91] See supra, pp. 1197–99, 1201.

[92] 392 U.S. at 436.

[93] Ibid., 437.

[94] Trumbull's speech is in Cong. Globe, 39–1, 319–23. The account of it above is at pp. 1164–67.

"relation between the slave and the State": "no new rights are conferred upon the freedman."[95] The Court quotes Trumbull's reply, that if the Thirteenth Amendment meant no more than that,

> the trumpet of freedom that we have been blowing throughout the land has given an "uncertain sound," and the promised freedom is a delusion. Such was not the intention of Congress, which proposed the constitutional amendment, nor is such the fair meaning of the amendment itself. . . .

Trumbull next made remarks—two paragraphs in the Congressional Globe—which the Court did not need to quote: the omission was indicated by periods.

After that, Trumbull continued:

> I have no doubt that under this provision . . . we may destroy all these discriminations in civil rights against the black man . . . .

He went on to say that under Section 2 of the Thirteenth Amendment, Congress was authorized to "adopt such appropriate legislation as it may think proper, so that it be a means to accomplish the end."

It is pertinent to the point now to be made—although it was not pertinent to the Court's discussion of the power of Congress under the Thirteenth Amendment—to recall something Trumbull said in the omitted passage: that

> Now, our laws are to be enacted with a view to educate, improve, enlighten, *and Christianize* the negro . . . . [Emphasis added.][96]

It is a categorical statement—yet unhesitatingly we reject it: Trumbull simply could not have meant it—it was a lapse of the tongue.

The example is a reminder that in tracing legislative history, one needs to comprehend the entire course of a debate, and to acquire sufficient acquaintance to judge of the credibility and animus of the participants; one should not simply go searching for quotable snippets.

Again, in the paragraph next after that from which the Court last quoted, Trumbull said, and reiterated, that "there is no discrimination" where "your law forbidding marriages between whites and blacks operates alike on both races. . . . Make the penalty the same . . . and then no one can complain."[97]

---

[95] Cong. Globe, 39–1, 318. Jan. 19. Supra, pp. 1163–64.

[96] Ibid., 322. An aside: if Congress in 1866 had had power and purpose to establish such a ministry to meet the needs of Reconstruction, it would not have been freedmen alone who were "standing in the need of prayer" —nor would the best exemplars all have been white.

[97] Ibid.

But a hundred years later, parties to a mixed marriage did complain[98] when the Virginia court sustained their conviction under that State's anti-miscegenation law. On appeal, a unanimous Court reversed. Expressions cited from the debates on the Freedmen's Bureau and Civil Rights Bills were said not to be controlling: they pertained to "specific statutes," while here the Court was concerned with "the broader, organic purpose of a constitutional amendment." Taking account of thinking about racial classifications that had matured "over the years," the Court concluded that the Virginia statute did make a discrimination that was obnoxious to the Equal Protection Clause; also that it deprived the parties of a fundamental liberty within the condemnation of the Due Process Clause.

The Court might appropriately have said, with its predecessors, that "it is a Constitution we are expounding";[99] that "we read its words, not as we read legislative codes which are subject to continuous revision . . . , but as the revelation of the great purposes which were intended to be achieved by the Constitution as a continuing instrument of government";[100] that in translating the "majestic generalities" of the Fourteenth Amendment, "changed conditions often deprive precedents of reliability . . . ."[101]

Quite otherwise was the situation in *Jones v. Mayer*. That was a matter of construing a *statute*—one that spoke from 1866. The Court insisted that it sought to discover what the members of Congress understood they were enacting: it purported to place its decision upon what it called "our examination of the relevant history . . . ."

It is this peculiar feature of *Jones v. Mayer*—the Court's studied pronouncement upon a matter of history, namely, the purpose entertained by the members of the 39th Congress—that has created the need to subject to this critical review that venture in historical research.

"ANY LAW . . . OR *CUSTOM* TO THE CONTRARY NOTWITHSTANDING"

A PRECISE POINT is now to be considered: the meaning of "custom" in Trumbull's two bills. The word was repeated in the debates, but its exact meaning was not drawn into the discussion. It became a factor, however, in the Court's argument to reach its conclusion in *Jones v.*

---

[98] Loving *et ux.* v. Virginia, 388 U.S. 1 (1967).

[99] Marshall, C.J., for the Court in McCulloch v. Maryland, 4 Wheat. 316, 407 (1819).

[100] Stone, J., for the Court in United States v. Classic, 313 U.S. 299, 316 (1941).

[101] Jackson, J., for the Court in West Virginia State Board of Education v. Barnette, 319 U.S. 624, 639, 640 (1943).

Mayer.[102] To afford understanding, there must be extensive quotation. (Emphasis throughout will be added.)

Section 1 of the Civil Rights Bill, as introduced and as enacted, provided that its beneficiaries "shall have the same right"

> to make and enforce contracts, to sue, be parties, and give evidence, to inherit, purchase, lease, sell, hold, and convey real and personal property, and to full and equal benefit of all laws and proceedings for the security of person and property, [as is enjoyed by white citizens,[103]] and shall be subject to like punishment, pains, and penalties, and to none other, any law, statute, ordinance, regulation, or *custom* to the contrary notwithstanding.

Then Section 2 caught up and carried forward this concluding phrase: in providing a penal sanction it enacted

> That any person who, under color of any law, statute, ordinance, regulation, or *custom*, shall subject, or cause to be subjected, any inhabitant of any State or Territory to the deprivation of any right secured or protected by this act, or to different punishment, pains, or penalties on account of such person having at any time been held in a condition of slavery . . . or by reason of his color or race, than is prescribed for the punishment of white persons, shall be deemed guilty of a misdemeanor, and, on conviction, shall be punished . . . .

Custom, it is believed, is here used in the sense of *official custom or usage*—not in the sense of private or unofficial community activity. Here it occurs as the last in a series of five words, the first four of which indisputably denote forms of official action; it is far more natural to read "custom" as closing a potential loophole in this series—rather than as making an abrupt vault into the disparate category of private action.

Custom and *usage* are commonly treated as synonymous, although the former bears the more precise nuance of a usage that has acquired the force of law or right.

In the Act of 1870 to enforce the Right of Citizens of the United States to vote,[104] and in the Act of 1871 to enforce the Provi-

---

[102] 392 U.S. at 422–24; dissenting opinion at 454–76, passim. See supra, pp. 1224–25.

[103] Inserted by the House on motion of Representative Wilson. Cong. Globe, 39–1, 1115. Mar. 1. See supra, p. 1183.

[104] Act of May 31, 1870, 16 Stat. 140. The Second Civil Rights Act, or the Enforcement Act. By Sections 16, 17, and 18 of this statute, Sections 1 and 2 of the Act of 1866 were re-enacted with some modifications.

sions of the Fourteenth Amendment,[105] *custom* and *usage* are used together as co-ordinate with *law*.

A statute of the First Congress provided that the acts of the legislature and the judicial proceedings of the courts in any State shall, when authenticated as therein provided, be given such faith and credit in the federal courts "as they have *by law or usage in the courts of the state . . . .*"[106] A supplementary act of 1804, on the attestation of other records, repeated the words underlined.[107]

The Act of May 26, 1824, relating to claims to land within the Louisiana Purchase of 1803, spoke of "any French or Spanish grant . . . which might have been perfected into a complete title, under and in conformity *to the laws, usages, and customs, of the government under which the same originated . . . .*"[108] A statute of 1828 made this applicable to claims to land in Florida, ceded by the Treaty with Spain in 1819.[109] In the leading case of *United States v. Arredondo*, sustaining a claim to land in Florida, Justice Baldwin observed that, besides legislative acts, "*There is another source of law in all governments—usage, custom . . . .* In England, and in the States of this Union which have no written constitution, it is the supreme law . . . .*"[110] In 1851 Congress enacted that claims to California lands based on title from the Spanish or Mexican government would be determined on the basis of " *. . . the laws, usages, and customs of the government from which the claim is derived . . . .*"[111] Over the years much litigation, in which leading counsel were engaged, arose out of these various statutes.

In establishing a rule for the selection of jurors for the federal courts, Congress directed that there be substantial conformity "to the *laws and usages*"—or, in another statute, "the *practice and usage*" in force in the State wherein the court sat.[112]

---

[105] Act of April 30, 1871, 17 Stat. 13. The Ku Klux Act. Section 1 gave a civil action against any person who, "under color of any law, statute, ordinance, regulation, custom, or usage of any State," deprived another of a right secured by the Constitution. Now Sec. 1983 of Title 42, U.S. Code.

[106] Act of May 26, 1790. 1 Stat. 122. Construed in United States v. Amedy, 11 Wheat. 392 (1826).

[107] Act of March 27, 1804. 2 Stat. 298, 299. The two statutes were embodied in Section 905 of the Revised Statutes.

[108] 4 Stat. 52. This was revived and extended by the Act of June 13, 1844. 5 Stat. 676.

[109] Act of May 23, 1828. 4 Stat. 284, 285.

[110] 6 Pet. 691, 714–15 (1832). The same Justice had more to say upon "custom and usage" in Strother v. Lucas, 12 Pet. 410, 436–37 (1838). This concerned a claim to land in the Louisiana Purchase, under the statute of 1824.

[111] Act of Mar. 3, 1851. 9 Stat. 631, 633.

[112] Act of July 20, 1840, 5 Stat. 394; of Mar. 19, 1842, 5 Stat. 471; of Mar. 3, 1849, 9 Stat. 403. The acts of 1840 and 1849 were embodied in Section 800 of the Revised Statutes.

XX: *The Fourteenth Amendment*

The 39th Congress at its Second Session passed an Act to abolish and forever prohibit the System of Peonage in the Territory of New Mexico and other Parts of the United States: "all acts, laws, resolutions, orders, regulations, *or usages*" under which it had been established or maintained were declared void.[113] Senator Wilson, the sponsor, recounted that the military authorities in New Mexico "had undertaken to enforce *this law or custom* . . . ." Senator Lane of Indiana explained that "By the laws of Mexico which were existing in New Mexico at the time of the conquest peonage was established. . . ." "*According to the custom of that country*," Senator Doolittle added, the system had continued since the acquisition of the territory by the United States.[114]

In the debate following the veto of the Civil Rights Bill, several Senators referred to "custom." First, Trumbull.[115] It was, he said, "a manifest perversion" for the President to assert that Section 2 would impose fine and imprisonment on legislators who passed a statute in conflict with the bill. "Not at all" was Trumbull's answer: Section 2 would punish only the person who, under color of law, did the forbidden act. He carried out the implication of the President's objection: "In some communities in the South *a custom prevails* by which different punishment is inflicted upon blacks from that meted out to whites for the same offense. Does this section propose to punish the community where the custom prevails?" Of course not.

Section 3 of the bill gave to the federal courts jurisdiction of "all causes . . . affecting persons who are denied or cannot enforce" in the State courts "any of the rights secured to them by the first section . . . ." The mere existence of a discriminatory statute or of "*a custom in the community*," Trumbull explained, would not give rise to federal jurisdiction: but if, when the matter was tested, the State court sustained the discrimination, then there would be a right to remove.

Senator Reverdy Johnson, in sustaining the President's action, asked, What is the effect of Section 2 of the bill?

In the first place, it assumes, what is true, that there is a statute, an ordinance, a regulation, or *a custom* inconsistent with the exercise of the rights secured by the first section, *an existing law, organic or statutory*, which declares who may sue, who may contract, ...[116]

Johnson uses the words in apposition: *custom* is one sort of law.

It has been explained that at this moment Senator Stewart of Nevada, valiantly and hopefully, was seeking a restoration of the Union

---

[113] Act of Mar. 2, 1867. 14 Stat. 546. Sec. 1990, Revised Statutes.
[114] Cong. Globe, 39–2, 1571, 1572. Feb. 19, 1867.

[115] Cong. Globe, 39–1, 1755 at 1758–59. Apr. 4.
[116] Ibid., 1778. Apr. 5.

on the basis of the Southern States abolishing racial discrimination on their own motion—in consideration of which they would receive generous treatment by Congress.[117] On April 4 he received from Alexander H. Stephens, and read to the Senate, Georgia's statute of March 17 wherein persons of color were accorded civil rights, approximating the enumeration in Section 1 of the Civil Rights Act.[118] Next day he pointed out that to be liable under Section 2 the defendant must commit the deprivation "under the color of a law."

> If there is no *law or custom* in existence in a State authorizing [a deprivation], it will be impossible for him to do it under color of any law. *This section is simply to remove the disabilities existing by laws tending to reduce the negro to a system of peonage. It strikes at that; nothing else. . . .*[119]

It is clear that to Stewart, *custom* is enforced by authority of the State. Also, the purpose of the Civil Rights Bill is simply to *remove the disabilities*: he says that "if all the southern States will follow this noble example, this civil rights bill . . . will be simply a nullity . . ."—it will have "no operation." By "doing a simple act of justice," as Georgia has done by its statute, the effect of the Civil Rights Bill will be "so easily avoided."

Stewart said categorically that the purpose of the Civil Rights Bill was simply *to remove the disabilities*: yet in *Jones v. Mayer* the Court found that its "clear and unambiguous" meaning was *also to impose a duty*. The Court attached "crucial" importance to the language, "the *same* right . . . as is enjoyed by white citizens." Georgia's statute enacted "That persons of color shall have the right to make and enforce contracts," etc., and would be subject to no different punishment, pain or penalty "than such as are prescribed for white persons . . ."—and Stewart pronounced this to be "precisely similar to the first section of the civil rights bill . . . ."

---

[117] Supra, pp. 128–29.

[118] Cong. Globe, 39–1, 1755. What he read was a version of an Act to define the term "persons of color," and to declare the rights of such persons. Acts of the General Assembly, Annual Session, Dec. 1865 to Mar. 1866, 239.

Section 2 declared

That persons of color shall have the right to make, and enforce contracts, to sue, be sued; to be parties, and give evidence; to inherit; to purchase, lease, sell, hold and convey, real, and personal property, and to have the full and equal benefit of all laws and proceedings, for the security of person and estate, and shall not be subjected to any other or different punishment, pain or penalty for the commission of any act or offence, than such as are prescribed for white persons, committing like acts or offences.

[119] Cong. Globe, 39–1, 1785. Apr. 5.

Stewart was an attentive and a very practical lawyer.

One more Senator is to be quoted, and at last there is a passage that lends a shade of credence to the idea that *custom* signified unofficial action within the community. This is Garrett Davis' speech, telling of "handsomely furnished cabins," "sumptuous tables," and "softly cushioned pews," all "established by ordinance, regulations, and *customs*."[120] That passage is not much on which to hang a construction of the Civil Rights Act.

It is useful to tarry for a moment with Georgia's civil rights statute of March 17. That was less a "noble example" than Stewart professed, considering the history that lay behind it. The Freedmen's Bureau by its Circular No. 5 of May 30, 1865, approved by President Johnson on July 2, directed that the assistant commissioners exercise jurisdiction in places where "the negro's right to justice before the law, in allowing him to give testimony," was not recognized.[121] In Georgia, instructions were issued denying the exercise of civil jurisdiction where, "under the *laws or customs* of this State," the testimony of freedmen was rejected.[122] On December 15, Governor Jenkins urged the members of the legislature, "before your contemplated recess," to provide "for the admission of the testimony of free persons of color, . . . with such limitations as your wisdom may devise." He explained the objective in view. "Many of our citizens now charged with crime or misdemeanor, will probably be remitted to the civil tribunals for trial . . . ."[123] On that day it was enacted "that free persons of color shall be competent witnesses" in civil cases where a colored man was a party, and in criminal cases where a colored man was defendant or

---

[120] Ibid., App. 181 at 183. Apr. 6. See supra, pp. 1200–01.

[121] By paragraph 7 of that circular,
In all places where there is an interruption of civil laws or in which local courts, by reason of old codes, in violation of the freedom guaranteed by the proclamation of the President and the laws of Congress, disregard the negro's right to justice before the law, in not allowing him to give testimony, the control of all subjects relating to refugees and freedmen being committed to this bureau, the assistant commissioners will adjudicate, either themselves or through officers of their appointment, all difficulties arising between negroes themselves, or between negroes and whites, or Indians, except those in military service, so far as recognizable by military authority, and not taken cognizance of by other tribunals, civil or military, of the United States.
H.R. Exec. Doc. No. 70, 39th Cong., 1st Sess. 180. And, as brought to the notice of officers in the field, at 10 (in Louisiana); 40 (in Alabama); 46 (in Tennessee); 61 (in Georgia); 77 (in Arkansas); 81 (in Florida); 102 (in South Carolina); 127 (in Virginia); 146 (in Texas); 170 (in Mississippi).

[122] Cir. No. 4 of the office for Georgia, Nov. 15, 1865. Ibid., 61, 62.

[123] Ga. Sen. J. 72 (1865–66); House J. 68–69.

where the offense charged was against a colored man's person or property, "any law, *usage, or custom* to the contrary notwithstanding."[124] However, it was not until the legislature accorded complete equality of black with white in respect of testimonial competence and punishment, by its act of March 17,[125] that officers of the Bureau were directed to cease to exercise judicial functions under the Bureau circular of May 30, 1865.[126]

Footnotes in other chapters cite instances where, by *judicial custom*, men of color were denied equality with whites in the administration of justice. In South Carolina in 1867, Judge Aldrich refused— the Civil Rights Act notwithstanding—to allow black men to be called for jury service. It was reported that he acted in defense of the "Jury Law of 1831": but there was no such statute; and if perhaps it was the colonial enactment of 1731, that merely confirmed "the ancient and approved method of drawing juries . . . ."[127] Again, the Chief Justice of Delaware will be quoted on the practice of the courts of that State: that prior to 1875 they did not accord to persons of color the same testimonial competence as to whites.[128]

Early in the Senate debate, Davis of Kentucky and Clark of New Hampshire had an exchange, with no thought of the meaning of "custom" as used in the Civil Rights Bill. The former asked, "Did you ever find a law declaring a horse to be property? . . . We have none in our State. It probably exists by *usage*." And the latter responded, "So it exists in my State by *custom*; but we recognize it as property by statute as well. . . ."[129] That reflects the natural, and one would have supposed the obvious meaning of "custom" as it appears in the Civil Rights Act.

This discussion has been needed in preparation for a salient point in the Court's opinion.

---

[124] An Act to make free persons of color competent witnesses in certain cases. Acts of the General Assembly, Annual Session, Dec. 1865 to Mar. 1866, 239.

[125] See note 118 above.

[126] Assistant Commissioner Tillson to General Howard, report of Nov. 1, 1866. Sen. Exec. Doc. No. 6, 39th Cong., 2d Sess., 48, 54–55.

[127] See notes 248 to 255 of chapter 10.

[128] See note 16 of ch. 21.

[129] Cong. Globe, 39–1, 529. Jan. 31.

Six years after the Civil Rights Act of 1866, Congress used the word "custom" in a sense different from that in the illustrations given above— but it made clear what that special sense was. The Act to promote the development of the Mineral Resources, of May 10, 1872, 17 Stat. 91, recognized "local customs or rules of miners," not inconsistent with the laws of the United States; claims to veins and lodes would be governed "by the customs, regulations, and laws in force at the date of their location." Secs. 2319 and 2320 of the Revised Statutes.

THE RELATION BETWEEN SECTIONS 1 AND 2;
THE GOVERNMENT'S BRIEF

WE HAVE REPRESENTED Trumbull's drafting to be well considered and coherent—in respect of the congruity between the Freedmen's Bureau and the Civil Rights Bills,[130] and in the correspondence between Sections 1 and 2 of the latter.[131] We now approach an examination of the Court's treatment of those matters.

In the *Civil Rights Cases*[132] in 1883, where the issue was the constitutionality of the Act of 1875, Justice Bradley's opinion for the Court came to the problem by way of the first Civil Rights Bill,

> originally passed April 9, 1866, and re-enacted with some modification in sections 16, 17, 18, of the Enforcement Act, passed May 31, 1870. That law, as re-enacted, after declaring [in Section 1] that all persons . . . shall have the same right . . . to make and enforce contracts, [etc.] . . . as is enjoyed by white citizens, and shall be subject to like punishment . . . and none other, any law, statute, ordinance, regulation or custom to the contrary notwithstanding, proceeds to enact [in Section 2] that any person who, under color of any law, statute, ordinance, regulation or custom, shall subject or cause to be subjected any inhabitant . . . to the deprivation of any rights secured or protected by the preceding section, above quoted, or to different punishment . . . by reason of his color or race . . . shall be deemed guilty of a misdemeanor . . . . This law is clearly corrective . . . , intended to counteract and furnish redress against State laws and proceedings, and customs having the force of law . . . .[133]

Justice Bradley regarded the clause "any law . . . or custom to the contrary notwithstanding" as "very important": it "gave the declaratory section [Section 1] its point and effect," while "the penal part [Section 2], by which the declaration is enforced, and which is really the effective part of the law," applied "only to those who should subject parties to a deprivation of their rights under color of any statute, ordinance, custom, etc. . . ."

So the Act of 1866 was intended to counteract State laws and proceedings, and customs having the force of law: and *the declaratory and the penal sections were in exact correspondence.* That seemed clear and unambiguous to the Court in 1883. It was not ruling on the point—there was no occasion to do so; it was, however, speaking precisely about a statute with which it had had years of experience.

---

[130] Supra, pp. 1224–25.
[131] Supra, p. 1225.

[132] 109 U.S. 3.
[133] Ibid., 16–17.

The Government's brief in *Jones v. Mayer* recognized that to attain the result there desired, the above construction must be breached. The declaratory Section 1 must be construed to have a wider scope that would prohibit wholly private acts of discrimination, while Section 2 punished only conduct "under color of law."

The brief took this approach:

> In the first place, symmetry is not the hallmark of Reconstruction legislation. In fact, almost every measure of the period juxtaposes provisions which bear only against officials with others which control private action. This is sufficient reason to resist the temptation to construe one provision by the next, even in the same Act. But if that approach were followed here, it would seem to lead in the opposite direction. Indeed, why expressly limit the application of the penalty to deprivations "under color of law" if the right involved itself runs only against official action?[134]

The answers seem apparent. As to "reconstruction legislation" generally, Congress coped with the situation by such measures as seemed appropriate and feasible within the Constitution as amended—by penalizing those who abused "under color," and such private wrongdoers as it seemed federal law might reach, and by affording a civil action where that might be useful to the victims. But in any event, there was no occasion for applying any disparaging generalization to the Act of 1866. It expressed the clear thinking of an able Senator. Its passage was not troubled by intra-party diversions or inter-party combinations.[135] When enacted it had undergone only three significant amendments: Trumbull's addition of the definition of citizenship, the deletion of the general "no discrimination" clause, and the insertion of the section giving an appeal to the Supreme Court.

Next, there need be no pother about "limiting" the penal section to deprivations "under color of law" *unless* one has posited that Section 1 had a wider scope. Absent that assumption, how would a critic more aptly draft Section 2? Surely when creating an offense the draftsman should define, inclusively and exclusively, what it is that is made punishable. The qualification, "under color of law," was an essential ingredient. How, without it, could the drafting of Section 2 have avoided vagueness? Someday the Government might even propound the idea that Section 1 forbade private acts of discrimination, and seek a conviction under Section 2!

---

[134] Brief of the United States as Amicus Curiae, 42–43.

[135] Compare the simplicity of the action on the Civil Rights Bill with the complexity that developed in the course of enacting the Reconstruction Act of March 2, 1867. Supra, ch. 6.

The brief then engages in conjecture to accommodate its initial assumption:

> At all events, it would not be remarkable if the Congress of 1866 had deemed it appropriate to confine criminal sanctions to State officials, bound by oath and duty to support the supreme law, while allowing only civil remedies against ordinary citizens. Or it may have been thought unnecessary to impose federal penalties where there were no laws condoning abridgment of the rights declared in Section 1 because, in that situation, it was assumed the State itself would punish the offender under local ordinances implementing the national law. See Cong. Globe, 39th Cong., 1st Sess., pp. 1758, 1785. Neither hypothesis suggests that the potential scope of Section 1 was restricted to acts "under color of law."[136]

That makes enormous demands upon one's credulity. First, Congress does its cogitating by oral speech, and what is said goes into the printed record. Unless some pertinent remarks are shown, there is no basis for supposing that it "deemed" anything. Or if it be suggested that the Judiciary Committees may have "deemed," still the supposition is unfounded unless some communication to the Houses is shown.

It is inexact to speak of Section 2 as confining criminal sanctions to "State officials, bound by oath": Trumbull said, "Not State officials especially, but everybody who violates the law."[137] It has been pointed out above that there were numerous situations in which a private individual might act under color of law.[138]

"While allowing only civil remedies against ordinary citizens": but on the supposition that Section 1 was intended to forbid private acts of discrimination, why did not Congress then and there provide a civil action? The failure so to do is perhaps the most patent of the objections to the theory of the Government's brief and of the Court's opinion.[139]

The brief affirms that Section 1 plainly forbade racial discrimination in the sale of property: otherwise the legislators of 1866 would have been making "a vain and empty gesture"—to suggest which would make "an unworthy accusation against the great emancipators of the 39th Congress. They were realists, not theorists."[140] And yet they

---

[136] Brief, 43–44.

A footnote at the close of this passage draws attention to a colloquy between Representatives Wilson and Loan on March 1, Cong. Globe, 39–1, 1120.

The Court's opinion, 392 U.S. at 425, footnote 33, made much of the line of thought in the paragraph from the brief quoted above, and of the colloquy to which it drew attention. See infra, pp. 1253–55.

[137] Cong. Globe, 39–1, 500. See supra, p. 1178.

[138] See the discussion in chapter 3 at pp. 100–17, and in chapter 19, notes 173 and 191.

[139] Considered infra, pp. 1258–59.

[140] Brief, 31.

affirmed their high purpose so indistinctly that it was not discovered for a century—failed to provide any remedy whereby it could be made effective—and may simply have "assumed the State itself would punish the offender."

Rays of hope perhaps leading them to this assumption are said to shine forth from pages 1758 and 1785 of the Congressional Globe. (Since nothing more specific is cited, one must do one's best to locate the source of this light.) Presumably on page 1758 it came from this sentence in Trumbull's speech after the veto:

> If an offense is committed against a colored person simply because he is colored, in a State where the law affords him the same protection as if he were white, this [Civil Rights] act neither has nor was intended to have anything to do with his case, because he has adequate remedies in the State courts . . . .

And on page 1785 presumably it was this sentence by Senator Stewart:

> I fully concur with the opponents of the bill that it would be much more desirable that the States should do it themselves [that is, secure to the freedmen personal liberty]; and I am anxious that propositions should be held out whereby they may do it . . . .

Until it is established that Trumbull and Stewart understood that Section 1 forbade private discrimination, there is no basis for supposing that they regarded one who did discriminate as an "offender"— and still less that they gave any reason for Congress to assume that "the State itself would punish" him. They said nothing about the State "*implementing* national law": they said simply that if the State would treat black like white, the national law would have no effect upon it. Stewart was specific: simply do as Georgia has done, and the standard of the Civil Rights Bill will have been met.

This portion of the Government's brief has been dwelt upon, for the reason that the Court embraced its arguments and repeated them with even greater assurance.

THE COURT'S OPINION: RELATION BETWEEN SECTIONS 1 AND 2

UPON QUOTING SECTION 1 of the Act of 1866, the Court made this comment:

> It is, of course, immaterial that §1 ended with the words "any law, statute, ordinance, regulation, or custom, to the contrary notwithstanding." The phrase was obviously inserted to qualify the reference

to "like punishment, pains, and penalties, and to none other," thus emphasizing the supremacy of the 1866 statute over inconsistent state or local laws, if any. It was deleted, presumably as surplusage, in §1978 of the Revised Statutes of 1874.[141]

That depreciates as "immaterial" words which Justice Bradley had pronounced "very important."[142]

Next the Court says that "obviously" the words were applicable only to the latter part of Section 1, the "like punishment" clause. Presumably the purpose of this construction was to remove the right "to . . . purchase . . . real and personal property," so far as possible, from the thought that the enumerated rights were secured merely against State laws, etc. But that minute gain for the Court's thesis ignores the fact that in Section 2 the "under color of law" qualification applies, first of all, to the deprivation of a secured right, and then to "different punishment." (In the Revised Statutes of 1874, the Title on Civil Rights brought together provisions from the Acts of 1866, 1870, 1871, and elsewhere; *enumerated rights* of Section 1 of 1866 entered into Sections 1977 and 1978. *Penal* provisions were gathered under the Title on Crimes: Section 2 of 1866 became Section 5510, which punished acts depriving citizens of civil rights under color of State laws. When the proximity and coherence that had linked Sections 1 and 2 thus disappeared, there was no need to retain the phrase "under color of law" in Sections 1977 and 1978.)

The opinion proceeds:

> The crucial language for our purposes was that which guaranteed all citizens "the same right, in every State and Territory in the United States, . . . to inherit, purchase, lease, sell, hold, and convey real and personal property . . . as is enjoyed by white citizens . . . ." To the Congress that passed the Civil Rights Act of 1866, it was clear that the right to do these things might be infringed not only by "State or local law" but also by "custom, or prejudice."[143]

That is supported by footnote 30, which sets out a tenuous line of argument. The Freedmen's Bureau Bill spoke of extending military protection and jurisdiction over certain areas in the South where—to quote the footnote as it quotes the bill—

> "in consequence of any State or local law, . . . *custom, or prejudice,* any of the civil rights . . . belonging to white persons (including the right . . . to inherit, purchase, lease, sell, hold, and convey real and

---

[141] 392 U.S. at 422–23, footnote 29.
[142] Civil Rights Cases, 109 U.S. 3,

17 (1883). Supra, p. 1218.
[143] 392 U.S. at 423.

personal property . . .) are refused or denied to negroes . . . on account of race, color, or any previous condition of slavery or involuntary servitude . . . ."

The Court declared this to be "significant for its recognition that the 'right to purchase' was a right that could be 'refused or denied' by 'custom or prejudice' as well as by 'State or local law.'" Then the Court adopted a quotation:

> Of course an "abrogation of civil rights made 'in consequence of . . . custom, or prejudice' might as easily be perpetrated by private individuals or by unofficial community activity as by state officers armed with statute or ordinance." J. tenBroek, Equal Under Law 179 (1965 ed.).

As a result of footnote 30, the argument can claim to have made this gain: that *custom*, by its momentary proximity to *prejudice* in Section 7 of the Freedmen's Bureau Bill—(thereby losing its coloration in "State or local law, police or other regulation or *custom*" in Section 8 of that bill)—has taken on the meaning of private or unofficial community activity. *Custom*, then, will be charged with that significance when it appears in Section 1 of the Civil Rights Act:

> Thus, when Congress provided by §1 in the Civil Rights Act that the right to purchase and lease property was to be enjoyed equally throughout the United States by Negro and white citizens alike, it plainly meant to secure that right against interference from any source whatever, whether governmental or private.[144]

Footnote 31 undertakes to buttress this assertion. Congressman Bingham, in expressing his objections to the Civil Rights Bill,

> charged that it would duplicate the substantive scope of the [Freedmen's Bureau Bill] . . . . Although the Civil Rights Act . . . made no explicit reference to "prejudice," . . . the fact remains that nobody who rose to answer the Congressman disputed his basic premise that the Civil Rights Act of 1866 would prohibit every form of racial discrimination encompassed by the [Freedmen's Bureau Bill]. . . .

This section of the opinion began with the object, so to exploit the word "prejudice" in Section 7 of the Bureau Bill as to impart to Section 1 of the Civil Rights Bill the meaning that it prohibited private discrimination in the sale of property. To explain fairly the remarkable

---

[144] Ibid., 423–24.

endeavor to make Bingham serve this object will take several paragraphs.

When Trumbull drafted his bills, the Freedmen's Bureau—on the basis of its ill-defined responsibility for "the control of all subjects relating to refugees and freedmen from rebel States"[145]—was busy with many matters: among them, food and shelter; medical care; labor contracts; settlement on abandoned and confiscated lands; schools; and protection against violence and unfair treatment by individuals and against abusive action by State and local governments. Trumbull sought by his Bureau Bill to extend its life "until otherwise provided by law," and to give it more specific authority to carry on its activities. Our concern is only with Sections 7 and 8.[146] The former described the situation wherein it would be "the duty of the President . . . , through the commissioner, to extend military protection and jurisdiction over all cases affecting such persons so discriminated against." The persons thus referred to were those who, by "State or local law, . . . custom, or prejudice," were refused or denied the civil rights belonging to white persons, including—and here were named the rights enumerated in Section 1 of the Civil Rights Bill, and also "the constitutional right of bearing arms." To repeat, Section 7 established the *duty of the President*: to extend military *protection* and *jurisdiction*. Evidently those two words had distinct meanings. The former looked to fostering and directing in a wide variety of matters: the Bureau was to serve as friend and tutor of four million freedmen. The latter spoke precisely of judicial proceedings before tribunals within the Bureau, which would try cases, civil and criminal, where the local courts could not be trusted to do equal justice. Certainly the agents of the Bureau would have occasions without number to step in and protect freedmen against individual and local prejudice. But before a tribunal of the Bureau could enter a judgment, there must have been proof of facts to warrant such judgment upon relevant rules of law.

Section 8 made it "the duty of the officers and agents of this bureau to take jurisdiction of" two categories of matters. (1) One who, under color of law, etc., subjected a protected person to the deprivation of a civil right secured to whites, or to different punishment, whether on account of race "or for any other cause," would be guilty of a misdemeanor. [This was similar to Section 2 of the Civil Rights Bill.] (2) Further, and much more broadly, the Bureau's officers and agents would have jurisdiction of "all cases affecting negroes, mulattoes, freed-

---

[145] Act of Mar. 3, 1865. 13 Stat. 507. It was "to continue during the present war of rebellion, and for one year thereafter."

[146] The text is set out in McPherson, *History of Reconstruction*, 72–74, supra, p. 1163.

men, refugees, or other persons who are discriminated against in any of the particulars mentioned in the preceding section."

The jurisdiction conferred by Section 8 was to cease in any State upon the restoration of its constitutional relations in the Union.

Now to Bingham's speech on which footnote 31 relied. The tenor of his constitutional objections to the Civil Rights Bill has already been explained.[147] He said,

> I hold, sir, that our Constitution never conferred upon the Congress . . . the power—sacred as life is . . . —to protect it in time of peace by the terrors of the penal code within the organized States . . . .

The power to protect the citizen in that respect belonged to the States.

> Now, what does this bill propose? To reform the whole civil and criminal code of every State government by declaring that there shall be no discrimination between citizens on account of race or color in civil rights or in the penalties prescribed by their laws. . . .

Bingham agreed that such inequality should not be tolerated in any State:

> but what power have you to correct it? That is the question . . . .

> Bingham had already told the House that the Civil Rights Bill "stands in strange contrast" to "that just and righteous bill known as the Freedmen's Bureau bill." He was going to read Sections 7 and 8 of the latter.

> But I beg leave to remark to the House, and I ask consideration of the fact, that the seventh and eighth sections of the Freedmen's Bureau bill enumerate the same rights and all the rights and privileges that are enumerated in the first section of this bill, and for a violation of those rights and privileges within any of the insurrectionary States they impose the same penalty, and no other, than that which is imposed by the second section of this bill. . . .

There one has the sentence on which footnote 31 relies. That sentence, plus the fact that nobody contradicted it, was adduced to demonstrate an understanding that Section 1 of the Civil Rights Bill would prohibit private discrimination in the sale of property. But no

---

[147] The footnote cited to 39 Cong. Globe, 39–1, at 1292. The speech, at 1290–93, has been summarized supra, pp. 1191–92.

one in the debate was then talking about "prejudice" or individual conduct. "The question," Bingham insisted, was whether Congress had power to enact, as he saw it, a "whole civil and criminal code" for every State. The Bureau Bill, which he applauded, would have applied only to insurrectionary States, and the jurisdiction conferred was to cease when a State was restored: in that he saw "the solemn conviction and declaration of Congress" that thereupon "our powers in the premises cease" and freedmen became "dependent for justice and their rights upon the civil administrators" of the several States.

What Bingham "charged" was no "charge" at all: it was nothing more than the observation—patent to any one who compared the two bills—that the rights mentioned in Section 7, and inferentially referred to in Section 8 of the Bureau Bill, were virtually identical with the rights enumerated in Section 1 of the Civil Rights Bill, and incorporated in its Section 2 as being "secured or protected by this act." And Bingham's "basic premise" *had nothing to do with individual prejudice*: it was that Congress had no constitutional authority over civil rights in the several States, save in the temporary situation of those recently in rebellion.

The Court's opinion now treats its thesis as having been established. It adduces corroboratory considerations:

> Indeed, if §1 had been intended to grant nothing more than an immunity from *governmental* interference, then much of §2 would have made no sense at all. . . .[148]

The thought here is that the qualification at the head of Section 2— "under color of any law, statute, ordinance, regulation, or custom"— is to be viewed, not as needed to make the sanction in Section 2 fit the right secured by Section 1, but rather as having been "carefully drafted to exempt private violations of §1 from the criminal sanctions it imposed." [The thought that "custom" means individual or unofficial community activity is here abandoned without notice. Even bold and resolute Judges would not carry their construction so far as to make private discrimination a misdemeanor. Congress had not gone so far in the Civil Rights Act of 1968.]

The opinion was now borrowing from the Government's brief.[149] In footnote 33, to support the sentence last quoted above, it recounts an exchange between Representative Loan of Missouri [a member of the Committee on Freedmen] and Wilson of Iowa, chairman of the Judiciary Committee. To quote from the Congressional Globe:[150]

---

[148] 392 U.S. at 424.
[149] See supra, pp. 1246–48.

[150] Cong. Globe, 39–1, 1120. Mar. 1.

MR. LOAN. Mr. Speaker, I desire to ask the chairman . . . why the committee limit the provisions of the second section to those who act under the color of law. Why not let them apply to the whole community where the acts are committed?

MR. WILSON . . . . That grows out of the fact that there is discrimination in reference to civil rights under the local laws of the States. Therefore we provide that the persons who under the color of these local laws should do these things shall be liable to this punishment.

MR. LOAN. What penalty is imposed upon others than officers who inflict these wrongs on the citizen?

MR. WILSON . . . . We are not making a general criminal code for the States.

The opinion, after an abridged statement of this exchange, derives the following conclusion:

Mr. Wilson's reply was particularly revealing. If . . . he had viewed acts not under color of law as not violative of §1 at all, that would of course have been the short answer to the Congressman's query. Instead, Mr. Wilson found it necessary to explain that the Judiciary Committee did not want to make "a general criminal code for the States." . . . Hence only those who discriminated "in reference to civil rights . . . under the color of . . . local laws" were made subject to the criminal sanctions of §2. . . .

The Court is resorting to "ingenious analytical instruments"[151] to make Wilson's language appear to sustain the theory it has excogitated. But from all he said it is clear that he saw a perfect unity between the declaratory section and the penal section. The former secured the enumerated civil rights against discrimination under color of law: that was all that was attempted—and the sanction of Section 2 was in exact correspondence with it. Thus his response to Loan's question: "We are not making a general criminal code for the States."

Read what Wilson had been saying throughout that day—March 1—when he was explaining and defending the bill.[152]

If the States would all observe the rights of our citizens, there would be no need of this bill. . . .

The trouble was that States did discriminate on ground of color:

---

[151] The phrase comes from the opinion of Justice Fortas for the Court in United States v. Price, 383 U.S. 787, 801 (1966). In Jones v.

Mayer the Court quotes, professing that it will not use such instruments now. 392 U.S. at 437.

[152] Cong. Globe, 39–1, 1115–19.

if the States . . . would but shut their eyes to these differences and legislate, so far at least as regards civil rights and immunities, as though all citizens were of one race and color, our troubles as a nation would be well-nigh over. . . .

He spoke of the singleness of thought that ran throughout the bill:

It will be observed that the entire structure of this bill rests on the discrimination relative to civil rights and immunities made by States on "account of race, color, or previous condition of slavery." . . .

As "the result of the recent war, and the enactment of the measures to which the events of the war naturally led us," hate on the part of the "controlling class in the insurgent States" had caused "laws barbaric and treatment inhuman" to be inflicted upon "our colored friends."

We should put a stop to this at once and forever. . . .
In order to accomplish this end it is necessary to fortify the declaratory portions of this bill with such sanctions as will render it effective. The first of these is found in the second section, and in these words:

and he quoted Section 2 in full. (That sufficed to make "the declaratory portions" *effective*.)

Toward the close of his exposition, Wilson told how discriminatory *governmental* measures had been "pushed out of the way" by military orders (which he quoted), and said that "a restoration of the ordinary forms of civil law" *must not* be permitted "to result in a subjection of our people to the outrages under the operation of State laws and municipal ordinances which these orders now prevent . . . ." He placed his justification of the Civil Rights Bill on the proposition "that we may protect a citizen of the United States against a violation of his rights by the law of a single State . . . ."

When read fairly, Wilson's language repels the Court's labored thesis.

Footnote 33 continues, following almost verbatim the Government's brief: it ventures to speculate that

Congress might have thought it appropriate to confine criminal punishment to state officials, oath-bound to support the supreme federal law, while allowing only civil remedies—or perhaps only preventive relief—against private violators. . . .

The opinion has to come down from its theory of the "broader vision" to the hard fact that Congress provided no remedy to enforce the alleged duty of nondiscrimination in private dealings. Here it brings its conjecture about what "Congress might have thought" into accord with what had been held at the beginning of the opinion: that the omission of Congress "does not, of course, prevent a federal court from fashioning an effective remedy...."[153]

Further conjecturing,

> Or Congress might have thought that States which did not authorize abridgment of the rights declared in §1 would themselves punish all who interfered with those rights without official authority. See *e.g.*, Cong. Globe, 39th Cong., 1st Sess., 1758, 1785. . . .

The citations are taken from the Government's brief—which, as was said above, presumably referred to remarks by Senators Trumbull and Stewart. The reason why the most likely passages seem irrelevant to *Jones v. Mayer* has been explained.[154] Stewart at page 1785 said specifically that "to remove the disabilities existing by laws" was "the whole scope" of the Civil Rights Bill.

Footnote 33 continues—and the Government brief bears no responsibility for what follows:

> Whatever the reason, it was repeatedly stressed that the only violations "reached *and punished*" by the bill, see Cong. Globe, 39th Cong., 1st Sess., at 1294 (emphasis added), would be those "done under color of State authority." . . .

The words "reached and punished" come from the speech of Representative Shellabarger: the passage from which they are extracted has been set out in the account of the debate.[155] Nothing that Shellabarger said warrants any inference that Section 1 was broader than Section 2, and that the former forbade other acts besides those which the latter punished. On the contrary, in the sentences immediately following, Shellabarger said:

> The bill does not reach mere private wrongs, but only those done under color of State authority; . . . its whole force is expended in defeating an attempt, under State laws, to deprive races and members thereof as such of the rights enumerated in this act. This is the whole of it.

A moment later, Shellabarger said: "The only doubt I have as to the constitutionality of this first section arises out of the question whether all these rights to testify, &c. . . . can be said to come within

---

[153] 392 U.S. at 414, footnote 13.
[154] See supra, p. 1248.

[155] See supra, pp. 1191–92.

the rule laid down by the Supreme Court in innumerable cases . . ."—
that the measure must appear "appropriate and plainly adapted to the
end." Section 2 gave Shellabarger no concern: "it is the ordinary case
of providing punishment for violating a law of Congress."

If Shellabarger—a prudent supporter who was concerned lest
the bill go beyond what was safely within the judicial test of "appropriate and plainly adapted" to carrying out the provisions of the Constitution—had imagined that Section 1 could be made to reach so far as
to control private dealings in property, he would have voiced an
insistent warning. As it was, he suggested that perhaps it would be
wise to reduce the number of rights enumerated, in order "to remove
doubts as to constitutionality."

The opinion offers Shellabarger's three quoted words as illustrative of what was "repeatedly stressed": but inasmuch as no other
speeches are cited, one cannot pursue the statement.

The result claimed for this portion of the opinion, culminating
in footnote 33, is that

> Hence the structure of the 1866 Act . . . points to the conclusion . . .
> that §1 was meant to prohibit *all* racially motivated deprivations of
> the rights enumerated in the statute, although only those deprivations
> perpetrated "under color of law" were to be criminally punishable
> under §2.[156]

That crowns an effort of marvelous fragility.

REFLECTIONS

THE EXAMINATION OF this opinion of the Court has been a most
unwelcome task. Our responsibility in contributing to the *History of
the Supreme Court* is to assess its performance in the period of Reconstruction—and *Jones v. Mayer* is "too recent to be called history."[157]
But the Court placed its opinion squarely on the alleged purpose of
Congress in 1866. Either one must bow to that determination, and
revise accordingly what had been written about the 39th Congress, or
else examine the opinion critically for what it might be worth as an
interpretation of history. The occasion arose late in the preparation of
the present volume: this new labor has imposed a large demand on
time, and has resulted in a swelling of the discussion of the Thirteenth
Amendment and the Civil Rights Act.

---

[156] 392 U.S. at 426.
[157] Justice Miller's comment about
the adoption of the post-war amendments, in the Slaughter House Cases,
16 Wall. 36 (1873).

In *Jones v. Mayer* the Court displayed a desperate earnestness to rid the law of any tolerance of racial discrimination in a matter which the Department of Justice rightly characterized as preeminent among "the causes of the racial tensions which beset the Nation at the present time . . . ."[158] One would not gratuitously say a word in disparagement of that effort.

The critique has been carried no further than was needed to disembarrass the field of history.

The extent to which Congress may rightly go in enforcing the Thirteenth Amendment is not here considered. In particular, no suggestion is made that it is confined to dealing with "State action." The issue has been simply what was purposed in the Civil Rights Act of 1866.

Why, if the men of the 39th Congress were inspired by the "broader vision," did they so weakly "let their currents turn awry, and lose the name of action"? Why did they fail to create an effective civil remedy to match this valiant purpose? The Court's opinion—like the Government's brief—could meet the challenge with nothing better than paltering conjecture: that "Congress may have thought"—without saying a word; and—always insisting that Congress really did have the "sweeping" purpose—that it would have been content with one of the trivial solutions offered. To maintain that the men of 1866 put their aim so high must result in "an unworthy accusation" that these "great emancipators" did indeed make "a vain and empty gesture"—to borrow words from the brief.[159]

Think for the moment of the poor African, whose untutored mind understood such straightforward things as that Mr. Lincoln had given him freedom, and that Congress said that he could make contracts, and go to court, and own land, just like the white man: but to instruct him that Congress had also put others under a duty not to discriminate, which might be useful to him if he could induce a federal court to "fashion an effective equitable remedy," would to him "have made no sense at all."

In *Jones v. Mayer* the Court appears to have had no feeling for the truth of history, but only to have read it through the glass of the Court's own purpose. It allowed itself to believe impossible things—as though the dawning enlightenment of 1968 could be ascribed to the Congress of a century agone.[160] Items from the Congressional Globe

---

[158] Memorandum for the United States as Amicus Curiae supporting the petition for certiorari, at p. 1.

[159] Government's brief, p. 31— using these phrases in arguing that the men of the 39th Congress would not

have been content to do so small a thing as merely to forbid *official* discrimination.

[160] Compare: *Through the Looking Glass*, chapter 5. The Queen had been telling Alice how to remember "things

may restore a sense of reality. President Johnson, in vetoing the Freedmen's Bureau Bill, had said unfeelingly that if the freedman found one community unsuited to his desires, "he can move to another."[161] To which Trumbull retorted, "they cannot read the fingerboards by the wayside; and where are they to go, and what is to be done with them?"[162] A few days earlier, Reverdy Johnson had reminded his colleagues of a fact by this question: "Why is it that [you have] separate places for the respective races even in your own Chamber? Why are they not put together?"[163] He was not proposing a change, but only calling attention to what was regarded as the normal arrangement. It would have been strange indeed if the Congress which first determined what rights should be secured to the four million propertyless freedmen beyond naked liberation from bondage, and which found it proper that black and white sit apart in its galleries, should have resolved that not only were they to have capacity to contract, to testify, to own property, etc., but also that all men would thenceforth be under a duty to refrain from racial discrimination in property transactions. Congressional thinking had not advanced so far. Moreover, a majority of voters in the North would not have supported legislation that intruded so far into their personal conduct.

Senator Trumbull did not purpose to frame a bill for every ill that remained after the abolition of slavery. Recall what he said at the conclusion of his "trumpet of freedom" speech, on January 19:

> I hope that the people of the rebellious States themselves will conform to the existing condition of things. I do not expect them to change all their opinions and prejudices. . . .[164]

If the 1860's are to be called to reprove the practices of the 1960's, let the lesson be restrained and truthful: that a Congress reflecting a wide range of opinion determined that the members of the emancipated race were now citizens of the national community, and secured to them the equal capacities and immunities that at the moment seemed appropriate. Measured from the situation six years earlier, this was a worthy achievement.

---

that happened the week after next." Presently,

"I can't believe *that*," said Alice.

"Can't you?" the Queen said, with a pitying tone. "Try again: draw a long breath, and shut your eyes."

Alice laughed. "There's no use trying," she said: "one *can't* believe impossible things."

"I daresay you haven't had much practice," said the Queen.

. . .

[161] Cong. Globe, 39–1, 915, 917.
[162] Ibid., 936, 939. Feb. 20.
[163] Ibid., 766. Feb. 9,
[164] Ibid., 323. Supra, p. 1167.

Concurrently with the debate on the Civil Rights Bill, Congress was moving toward the formulation of a Fourteenth Amendment to establish the rights of citizens of the United States and the equal protection of the laws—on the basis of which it was expected that restoration of the Union would take place.

THE JOINT COMMITTEE OF FIFTEEN

AT THE BEGINNING of the First Session, Thad Stevens had seized the initiative to set up a joint committee "to inquire into the condition of the States which formed the so-called Confederate States, and report whether they, or any of them, are entitled to be represented in either House of Congress . . . ."[165] His object was to prevent the seating of Southern delegations—then being urged by the President—until conditions could be settled by Congress. The six members from the Senate were led by William P. Fessenden of Maine—distinguished for moderation and high character. Jacob M. Howard of Michigan and Reverdy Johnson of Maryland were among his colleagues.[166] Thad Stevens led the group from the House, whose membership included John A. Bingham of Ohio, Roscoe Conkling of New York, and George S. Boutwell of Massachusetts. Johnson and two Democrats from the House represented the minority party.[167] "It was foreseen," Blaine recalled, "that

---

[165] Supra, p. 118.

It should be pointed out that it is unwarranted to attribute to the Civil Rights Bill a purpose of correcting the myriad injustices appearing in the testimony that eventually became available in the report of the Joint Committee on Reconstruction.

The Joint Committee resolved, on January 12 and 15, to proceed by four subcommittees to inquire into the conditions in the rebel States. Benjamin B. Kendrick, *Journal of the Joint Committee of Fifteen on Reconstruction* (New York: n.p., 1914), 47, 48.

The taking of testimony in the several subcommittees began on or about January 22.

The subcommittee on Tennessee called few witnesses, and completed its hearings on February 13. (The restoration of that State was being facilitated. It was readmitted to representation by joint resolution of July 24, 1866.)

On April 21 the Joint Committee voted that it was expedient that the taking of testimony be "concluded next week." *Journal*, 83.

However, the subcommittee for Florida, Louisiana, and Texas took testimony as late as May 19.

On April 30, Stevens announced to the House of Representatives "that it is designed, as soon as the testimony is printed, that a short report will be made by the committee . . . ." Cong. Globe, 39–1, 2287.

On April 7, Representative Lawrence, in anticipation of the vote by the House overriding the President's veto, read excerpts from the testimony of three witnesses. Cong. Globe, 39–1, 1833–35. Supra, pp. 1202–04.

[166] Cong. Globe, 39–1, 106. The other members were James W. Grimes of Iowa, Ira Harris of New York, and George H. Williams of Oregon.

[167] Ibid., 57. The others were Elihu B. Washburne of Illinois, Jus-

in an especial degree the fortunes of the Republican party would be in the keeping of the fifteen men who might be chosen."[168] These were explorers, selected to find the course of further constitutional amendment.

Their proposals dealt with four matters: a new basis for apportioning seats in Congress (leading to Section 2 of the Fourteenth Amendment); protection of the rights of citizens (Section 1); disqualification of former Confederates (Section 3); and war debts (Section 4).

To the understanding of the moment, a new basis of representation seemed much the most important. Yet within five years what Congress chose to do in that matter proved ill-conceived. The Due Process and Equal Protection Clauses of Section 1 became *the* Fourteenth Amendment; and the Supreme Court—not Congress—turned out to be the principal agency for its application. Inasmuch as it has been a point of controversy how faithfully the Court has acted in this respect, the workmanship of the 39th Congress in fashioning it will be drawn into question.

As an aid in judging the acuity of its perception in framing Section 1, it will be useful to examine how Congress went astray with Section 2.

SECTION TWO: THE PROBLEM OF THE BASIS OF REPRESENTATION

As THE CONSTITUTION stood, excluding words rendered obsolete by the Thirteenth Amendment,

> Representatives and direct Taxes shall be apportioned among the several States . . . according to their respective Numbers, which shall be determined by . . . the whole Number of free Persons . . . excluding Indians not taxed . . . .[169]

Freedmen would thenceforth be counted at their full number, and in consequence the representation from Southern States would become a substantially greater fraction of the House of Representatives. So too the weight of the South in the electoral college would be increased. As matters stood, only whites would be allowed to vote in the South; then delegations of ex-Confederates would join with their Northern Demo-

---

tin S. Morrill of Vermont, Henry T. Blow of Missouri, Henry Grider of Kentucky, and Andrew J. Rogers of New Jersey. The last two were Democrats.

[168] James G. Blaine, *Twenty Years of Congress*, 2 vols. (Norwich, Conn.: Henry Bill Publishing Co., 1884, 1888), II, 127.

[169] Constitution, Art. I, Sec. 2, cl. 3.

cratic allies in the House, and soon would control the Government. If this was to be averted the Constitution must be amended—but how?

One possibility was to declare forthrightly that *the right to vote shall not be denied or abridged on account of race, color, or previous condition of servitude.* That was what was eventually proposed as the Fifteenth Amendment, in 1869. But in 1866, Republican leaders thought that would not be practical politics. In only half a dozen States could the Negro then vote. At the autumn elections in 1865, Connecticut, Minnesota, and Wisconsin, while electing Republican governors, had rejected proposals to strike "white" from their voting requirements—by a majority of about 55 percent in each case.

Again, as was proposed by Representative Robert C. Schenck of Ohio, one might substitute as the basis of representation *the number of male citizens of the United States over twenty-one years of age, qualified to vote according to State law.* At first that idea was well received. Only as the State admitted its colored citizens to the suffrage could it have the benefit of their numbers in the allotment of seats in the House. But then Blaine of Maine objected that this would work to the disadvantage of Eastern States whose menfolk had gone West, leaving behind a disproportionate number of women and minors. California and other frontier States would be unduly favored.[170]

What the Joint Committee proposed was that representation continue to be based upon population—adding, however, this proviso:

> That whenever the elective franchise shall be denied or abridged in any State on account of race or color, all persons of such race or color shall be excluded from the basis of representation.

Stevens presented that to the House on January 22, 1866—and asked that it be passed "before the sun goes down."[171] He hoped that this as a separate amendment could be submitted to the States in time for ratification by legislatures then in session.

It fell to Conkling to make the proposal appear to be founded on principle: that each State would remain free to fix the qualifications for voting; but that if any race was found "so vile and worthless" that its members should be excluded, then none of such race should be counted.[172] Or, candidly, the "free" States could exclude Negroes at no significant sacrifice, while the States where Negroes were numerous must pay dearly for the same discrimination. Concededly a mass of freedmen could be excluded with impunity—as by a literacy test or property qualification—so long as the law was applicable to all.

---

[170] Cong Globe, 39-1, 141. Jan. 8, 1866.

[171] Ibid., 351.

[172] Ibid., 358. Jan. 22.

The House was not to be hurried. A respectable group, chiefly from Ohio and Illinois, rallied around Schenck's formula to base representation on adult male citizens qualified to vote. But on January 31 this was defeated, 131 against 29.

Thereupon the House, by 120 to 46, adopted the Joint Committee's proposal.[173]

It was a bitter thing, for men of Abolitionist conscience, that there might thus be written into the Constitution a provision admitting that suffrage might be denied on the ground of race. Here was a moral issue, and they rose to it.[174] It was idle to tell them that this was not a license but rather a penalty—like a statute recognizing murder by punishing it. Sumner, naturally, spoke for these men of principle. On February 6 he made a monumental effort that runs to 41 columns in the Congressional Globe. He resumed on March 7, filling 22 more.[175] As with his position on the Thirteenth Amendment, so now: amendment was unnecessary—Sumner found in the Republican Form of Government Clause, "when properly understood," authority to do what was needed. The Joint Committee's proposal was "a Compromise of Human Rights, the most immoral, indecent, and utterly shameful in our history"—"repeating in a new form that abomination which has blackened the name of Taney"—"a mighty House of Ill Fame, which it is proposed to license constitutionally for a consideration."[176] ("Every . . . vulgar epithet which polished cultivation could command," was Thad Stevens' resentful comment.[177])

Senator Yates found in the enforcement clause of the Thirteenth Amendment authority for his proposal to establish suffrage without regard to color simply by joint resolution. He repelled the suggestion that the Supreme Court would not sustain such legislation.[178] Henderson inquired: If the withholding of suffrage was a mark of slavery which could be removed under the power to enforce the amendment, could not woman suffrage be likewise established?[179]

Elizabeth Cady Stanton, Susan B. Anthony, and others urged Congress, while "placing new safeguards round the individual rights of four million emancipated slaves," to "extend the right of suffrage to woman, the only remaining class of disfranchised citizens, and thus fulfill your constitutional obligation 'to guaranty to every State in the Union a republican form of government.'"[180] These women were keeping watch in the congressional galleries. To the Abolitionists,

---

[173] Ibid., 538. Jan. 31.

[174] Joseph B. James, *The Framing of the Fourteenth Amendment* (Urbana: University of Illinois Press, 1956) at 67 notes some reactions.

[175] Cong. Globe, 39–1, 673–87, Feb. 6; 1224–32, Mar. 7.

[176] Ibid., 1225, 1226, 1228.

[177] Ibid., 2459. May 8.

[178] Ibid., App., 98. Feb. 19.

[179] Ibid., App., 120, 121.

[180] Ibid., 380. Jan. 23.

woman suffrage was extra luggage they were not willing to bear. To the Democrats, it was convenient to utter such taunts as "I prefer the white women of my country to the negro. [Applause on the floor and in the galleries promptly checked by the Speaker.]"[181] They intended to do nothing for either. Unquestionably those barred from the suffrage by reason of color stood in far greater need of protection than those barred by sex. But it displayed obliquity of thought to declaim loftily that "Republican Government" required "Equal Rights for All" in "the Human Family," while affecting utterly to ignore one half of that family.[182]

Senator Henderson, who had introduced the measure that became the Thirteenth Amendment,[183] now proposed as a Fourteenth this simple proposition: "No State, in prescribing the qualifications requisite for electors therein, shall discriminate against any person on account of color or race." This he defended in a speech of remarkable force and cogency.[184] "The States," he explained, might "prescribe an educational or property test, but any such test shall apply to white and black alike."

The Senators were not prepared to take that stand; Henderson's proposition received only 10 votes, with 37 against.[185] "It will not be five years from to-day before this body will vote for it," he asserted. (Actually it was not quite three years later when the Fifteenth Amendment was submitted to the States.)

Sumner's joint resolution, which he had modified to apply only to the insurrectionary States, to declare that there should be no "oligarchy, aristocracy, caste or monopoly," and that all persons were "equal before the law, whether in the court-room or at the ballot-box," received 8 yeas to 39 nays.[186]

Next the vote on the Joint Committee's recommended draft found 25 in favor, 22 opposed—far less than the two-thirds requisite for a constitutional amendment.[187] Uncompromising advocates of equality joined with Administration Republicans and Democrats in

---

[181] Ibid.
[182] Senator Sumner. Ibid., 673–87. The late Dr. W. E. B. Du Bois quoted long excerpts in *Black Reconstruction*, Harbor Classics ed. (New York: S. A. Russell Co., 1956), 192–98.
[183] Supra, p. 1137.
[184] Cong. Globe, 39–1, App., 115–24. Feb. 14. He spoke on his proposal also on March 9. Cong. Globe, 39–1, 1283.
[185] Ibid., 1284. Voting with him

were his colleague, B. Gratz Brown, and Zach. Chandler of Michigan, Clark of New Hampshire, Howe of Wisconsin, Pomeroy of Kansas, Sumner and Wilson of Massachusetts, Wade of Ohio, and Yates of Illinois.
[186] Ibid., 1287. Mar. 9. The yea votes came from the Senators who had voted for Henderson's measure, *minus* Henderson and Clark.
[187] Ibid., 1289. Mar. 9.

opposition. Thad Stevens later spoke of them as "the united forces of self-righteous Republicans and unrighteous copperheads."[188]

The foregoing has identified some of the interests engaged in the problem of finding a new basis of representation. For our purposes it suffices to say that the Joint Committee gave further thought, and on April 30 presented to both Houses a proposed amendment in five sections;[189] that this was accepted by the House[190]—accepted with amendments by the Senate,[191] in which the House concurred[192]— and that Section 2, as it went to the States and as it now stands in the Constitution, reads as follows:

> Representatives shall be apportioned among the several States according to their respective numbers, counting the whole number of persons in each State, excluding Indians not taxed. But when the right to vote at any election for the choice of electors for President and Vice President of the United States, Representatives in Congress, the Executive and Judicial officers of a State, or the members of the Legislature thereof, is denied to any of the male inhabitants of such State, being twenty-one years of age, and citizens of the United States, or in any way abridged, except for participation in rebellion, or other crime, the basis of representation therein shall be reduced in the proportion which the number of such male citizens shall bear to the whole number of male citizens twenty-one years of age in such State.

AN EXCURSUS: EXPERIENCE WITH SECTION 2

WE TAKE MOMENTARY leave of the 39th Congress, to examine how its handicraft stood the test of practice. Section 2 of the amendment was the part that was expected to bear directly on the future of the political parties. Thad Stevens had said,

> The second section I consider the most important of the article. It fixes the basis of representation in Congress. . . .[193]

---

[188] Ibid., 2459. May 8.

[189] By Stevens in the House, Cong. Globe, 39–1, 2286; by Fessenden in the Senate, at 2265.

[190] Cong. Globe, 39–1, 2545. May 10. The vote was 128 yeas, 37 nays, 19 not voting.

[191] Ibid., 3042. June 8. The vote was 33 yeas, 11 nays; 5 were absent.

[192] Ibid., 3149. June 13. The vote

was 120 yeas, 32 nays, 32 not voting.

The evolution of Section 2 has been traced by Horace E. Flack, *The Adoption of the Fourteenth Amendment* (Baltimore: Johns Hopkins Press, 1908), at 97–127; and by James, *The Framing of the Fourteenth Amendment*, passim.

[193] Cong. Globe, 39–1, 2459. May 8, 1866.

Each State remained free to prescribe who could vote: but if it denied or abridged, etc., the basis would be *reduced in the proportion which the number excluded bore to the whole number of adult male citizens.* This made no reference to denial *on ground of color*: members of Congress had that in mind, but the language was not so limited.

At the Second Session of the 41st Congress, in December 1869, the Select Committee of the House on the Ninth Census began to study how the census should be conducted in preparing for the reapportionment of seats in Congress.[194] Suddenly "the incongruities, the looseness, the haste"[195] that characterized Section 2 became apparent. By the Joint Committee's original proposal, if a State excluded Negroes from the suffrage (which would be found by reference to its laws), then all Negroes (whose total number would be shown by the census) would be excluded from the basis. But now, how could it be determined what number of adult male citizens were excluded on grounds other than rebellion or crime? Did the prescription mean, on *any* other ground? Even insanity? And insufficient length of residence?

James A. Garfield, a member of both Congresses, and now a member of the Committee on the Census, found it to be

> a curious fact—perhaps not new to every gentleman in this House, though it certainly was to me—that the provisions of the fourteenth amendment to the Constitution changes the representative basis of the national Legislature in a way that no one, so far as I remember, supposed it would when the amendment was before Congress.
>
> Everybody knew, of course, that there was a change, but none seemed to be aware how radical and sweeping that change was. . . . The fourteenth amendment, so far as it related to suffrage, was generally understood as referring exclusively to the denial of the right to vote on account of race or color. But the language of the Constitution is much broader. It is in substance that wherever the right to vote is denied or abridged in any State, not merely on account of race or color, but for any other reason than rebellion or crime, in that State the basis of representation shall be reduced proportionately. The committee found it necessary, in view of that provision, to inquire what were the other grounds in the several States on which the right to vote was abridged or denied except for rebellion or crime. . . .
>
> Without going into the matter more minutely, I will say in general that there are seventy or eighty grounds on which men are excluded . . . besides rebellion or crime. How far those different

[194] George D. Zuckerman, "A Consideration of the History and Present Status of Section 2 of the Fourteenth Amendment." *Fordham L. Rev.*, 30: 93 (1961).

[195] Representative Richard J. Haldeman, a member of the Select Committee on the Ninth Census. Cong. Globe, 41-2, 40. Dec. 8, 1869.

causes will operate to reduce the basis of representation is a grave question . . . .[196]

And how did the committee propose that the determination be made? The reply seems ludicrous. "After a very careful study," said Garfield, "the committee saw no better way" than to have the census taker *ask* every adult male citizen whether he was denied the right to vote for any reason other than rebellion or crime.[197] "It may be objected that this will allow the citizen to be a judge of the law as well as the fact, and that it will be difficult to get true and accurate answers," Garfield admitted; "I can only say that this is the best method that has been suggested."[198]

The takers of the census did inquire what adult male citizens were deprived of the right to vote otherwise than for rebellion or crime; but the Secretary of the Interior reported that "the Department is disposed to give but little credit to the returns . . . ." He pointed to "the numerous questions of difficulty and nicety which are involved."[199]

When Section 2 was framed, its proponents' great concern was the situation in the Southern States, which would not willingly allow colored men to vote. But then Congressional Reconstruction left the Southern States with constitutions that did not exclude black citizens. And with the Fifteenth Amendment, proclaimed to be in effect on March 30, 1870, *no* citizen could be denied the vote on ground of color.

When the census returns came in from the field in September 1870, it appeared that now it was the Northern States that more largely abridged the right to vote. Massachusetts, with its literacy test, disqualified 1 in every 84; South Carolina excluded only 1 in 284; Ohio denied the ballot to 1 in every 233; Louisiana to only 1 in 860.

Thus Section 2 made the Republicans somewhat shamefaced. "You made it to hold it *in terrorem* over the southern States," said Representative S. S. Cox, Democrat. "You thought to strike the South . . . ; but you have struck yourselves and now how you wriggle over it. [Laughter.] Oh! it is pitiful. . . ."[200]

Congressmen—having reckoned the consequences for State, for party, and for sectional influence—gave varied constructions to Section 2. Representative Horace Maynard of Tennessee, Republican, said that

The object . . . was to prevent the disfranchisement of the colored population. . . .

---

[196] Cong. Globe, 41–2, 38. Dec. 8, 1869.
[197] Ibid.
[198] Ibid., 181. Dec. 16, 1869.

[199] Cong. Globe, 42–2, 66. Dec. 11, 1871.
[200] Ibid., 82. Dec. 12, 1871.

. . . It means that, and that, I respectfully suggest, is all that it does mean . . . .

Now that the Fifteenth Amendment had utterly forbidden such discrimination against colored men, he thought that Section 2 had "no vitality."[201]

Representative Ulysses Mercur of Pennsylvania, Republican, was inclined to the same view: that Section 2

> did not mean to apply to that class of restrictions which every State, for its own security and its own protection, and for the purity of the ballot-box, saw proper to throw around it. . . .[202]

Michael C. Kerr of Indiana, Democrat, spoke with the authority of one who had sat in the 39th Congress:

> It was then never pretended by any one . . . that this section was intended to affect any States except such as might deny suffrage . . . on some ground of race, color, nationality, or other quality that inheres in and constitutes a part of the identity or individuality of the voter, . . . in contradistinction from a mere regulation concerning the exercise of the right, such as previous residence, or registration, or the payment of taxes. . . .
>
> . . . .
>
> This construction, not free from doubt, I agree, seems to me most in harmony with the spirit of the whole Constitution, the particular language of this section, and the rights and dignity of the States. . . .[203]

Representative Garfield adhered to the opinion he had expressed when the 41st Congress was preparing for the census: that Section 2 applied to *every* disqualification other than for rebellion or crime. But he saw a wide variance between the evil in view and the language employed:

> I do not believe that those who put it into the Constitution saw, at the time, the full scope and extent of its meaning. . . . Thus they made the back of the blade cut as sharp as the edge itself. . . .[204]

Shellabarger of Ohio had been a leader among those in the 39th Congress who sought to base representation upon the number of eligible voters. Now he saw no "insurmountable or very grave" diffi-

---

[201] Ibid., 65, 66. Dec. 11.
[202] Ibid., 79. Dec. 12. From 1872 until his death in 1887, Mercur was a Justice, presently Chief Justice, of the Supreme Court of Pennsylvania.
[203] Ibid., 106. Dec. 13.
[204] Ibid., 35 and 82. Dec. 6 and 12.

culty in applying Section 2.[205] A residence requirement was "a mere regulation to secure the purity of election; it does not go to the fundamental right at all." Quite otherwise was the literacy requirement in Massachusetts and the property requirement in Rhode Island: they were abridgments within the meaning of Section 2. Shellabarger gave this version of the intent of the framers, much wider than merely to protect against a color bar:

> The design . . . was that the poor man, the ignorant man, the colored man, should be secured, should be guarantied his right to vote . . . .
> In other words, we are not to have the old slave system—the learned man voting for the unlearned, on the theory that the latter are not competent themselves to vote. . . .

But, Shellabarger concluded, on the basis of the census returns, "I understand that, as a matter of fact, the numbers disfranchised are too small, perhaps, to result in any changes as to the representation of the several States . . . ." It seemed to be a matter of *de minimis*.

And so the 42nd Congress treated it in making the apportionment: no State was penalized by operation of Section 2. However, Senator Justin S. Morrill of Vermont intoned, "If not needed to-day, it may be to-morrow. It must not become a dead letter."[206] In that spirit, the Apportionment Act of February 2, 1872, carried in its Section 6 a warning that if any State should deny or abridge, etc., the number of its Representatives would be reduced.[207]

The experience with Section 2 of the Fourteenth Amendment is enlightening as one approaches the problem of Section 1. The search for a basis of representation was not nearly so elusive as the problem of framing effective guaranties of civil rights. Section 2 presented a problem of political mechanics—the sort of thing about which one expects politicians to be astute. And yet, after days spent in its design, it was so defective as to run right into a cul-de-sac. While Section 2 appears to have the precision of arithmetic, within five years even members of the Congress that framed it were in disagreement over its construction. The framers had been thinking about one evil—but their language was general, and soon had to be applied to a situation they had not foreseen. So it turned out with Section 1. In 1873, in the *Slaughter House Cases*,[208] Justice Miller said of the Equal Protection Clause that "It is so clearly a provision for that [Negro] race and that emergency, that a strong case would be necessary for its application to any other."

---

[205] Ibid., 81. Dec. 12.
[206] Ibid., 670. Jan. 29, 1872.
[207] 17 Stat. 28, 29. This became Sec. 22 of the Revised Statutes, and Sec. 6 of Title 2, U.S. Code.
[208] 16 Wall. 36. See infra, p. 1355.

In problems of constitutional history one needs to be wary lest one expect too much foresight of even sagacious men of another era.

SECTION I IN THE JOINT COMMITTEE

THE MEMBER OF the Joint Committee principally concerned with the section dealing with civil rights was John A. Bingham; from first to last the drafting bore the traits of his peculiar mode of thought. The recollections of several of his contemporaries will establish his standing. Blaine described him as "an effective debater, well informed, ready, and versatile. A man of high principle, of strong faith, of zeal, enthusiasm, and eloquence, he could always command the attention of the House."[209] John Sherman wrote that Bingham

> was regarded, next to Mr. [Thomas] Corwin, as the most eloquent member of the Ohio delegation, and, perhaps with one or two exceptions, of the House of Representatives. He studied law and was admitted to the bar in 1840. He served for sixteen years [1855–63, 1865–73] in the House of Representatives . . . and took a leading part in all the debates . . . . He was a man of genial, pleasing address, rather too much given to flights of oratory, but always a favorite with his colleagues . . . .[210]

Samuel S. Cox, Ohio Democrat who had served concurrently with Bingham, remembered him as a man "of rare elocution," "full of impulsive ardor . . . ."

> He lacked the reasoning faculty, but he could, as Thaddeus Stevens used to say in his sarcastic way, appeal to the "gathered wisdom of a thousand years," in his references to Anglo-Saxon privilege and prerogative with more frequency than any orator known in the history of that race. . . .[211]

George S. Boutwell, himself a member of the Joint Committee that drafted the Fourteenth Amendment, recalled that

> The part relating to "privileges and immunities" came from Mr. Bingham . . . . Its euphony and indefiniteness of meaning were a charm to him.[212]

---

[209] *Twenty Years of Congress*, I, 328.
[210] *Recollections of Forty Years*, 2 vols. (Chicago, New York, London, Berlin: Werner Co., 1895), I, 226–27.

[211] *Three Decades of Federal Legislation* (Providence, R.I.: J.A. and R.A. Reid, 1886), 75, 585.
[212] *Reminiscences of Sixty Years of Public Affairs*, 2 vols. (New York: McClure, Phillips Co., 1902), II, 41.

As special judge advocate before the military commission that tried the persons charged with the assassination of President Lincoln, Bingham argued that "Jefferson Davis is as clearly proven guilty . . . as is John Wilkes Booth," and that it lay within the power of the Chief Executive even to "string up the culprits without any court."[213]

The Joint Committee, as soon as it had charged a subcommittee to work on a basis for apportionment, turned to the problem of civil rights. On January 12, 1866, two texts were proposed. Bingham suggested:

> The Congress shall have power to make all laws necessary and proper to secure to all persons in every state within this Union equal protection in their rights of life, liberty and property.[214]

Then Stevens proposed:

> All laws, state or national, shall operate impartially and equally on all persons without regard to race or color.

Stevens' proposal—whatever it might mean—would work by its own force: courts would be bound to disregard invidious laws, and questions could be carried to the Supreme Court. Not so with Bingham's: *Congress* would be empowered—yet nothing would result save as it legislated, and anything that was enacted could be repealed. The need as he saw it was to arm Congress.

The two texts were referred to a subcommittee of five—(Fessenden, Stevens, Howard, Conkling, and Bingham)—which on January 20 offered a draft—(see diagram on pp. 1272–73)—that

> Congress shall have power . . . to secure
> to all citizens of the U.S., in every State,
> the same political rights and privileges;
> and to all persons in every State
> equal protection in the enjoyment
> of life, liberty and property.

After discussion, this was referred on January 24 to a committee of three—(Bingham, Boutwell, and Rogers). Bingham brought back on January 27 a proposal which, as amended by the Joint Committee, stood as follows (in diagram):

---

[213] Benn Pitman, *Assassination of President Lincoln and the Trial of the Conspirators* (Cincinnati: Moore, Wilstach and Baldwin, 1865), 351,

380. Quoted in the discriminating article on Bingham in the D.A.B.

[214] Kendrick, *Journal of the Joint Committee of Fifteen on Reconstruction*, 46.

	1866 February	March
Freedmen's Bureau Bill		
Civil Rights Bill		
XIV AMENDMENT:		
SENATE	2/13 S.30★ (Bingham's Amendment) introduced and tabled	
HOUSE OF REPRESENTATIVES	2/13 H.R.63■ (Bingham's Amendment) introduced by Bingham 2/26-28 Debated: Bingham Price Higby Woodbridge Kelley Bingham Hale Conkling Stevens Hotchkiss Postponed [and never taken up]	
JOINT COMMITTEE ON RECONSTRUCTION	1866 Jan. 12 Bingham: Congress shall have power . . . to secure to all persons . . . equal protection . . . of life, liberty and property. Stevens: All laws . . . shall operate impartially and equally . . . without regard to race . . . . Referred to subcommittee of 5 (Bingham a member) Jan. 20 Subcommittee reported: Congress shall have power . . . to (1) secure to all citizens of U.S. same political rights and privileges; (2) to all persons equal protection in . . . life, liberty and property.	Jan. 24 Referred to select co mittee of 3 (Bingh: chairman) Jan. 27 Bingham reported: Congress shall have p er . . . to secure (1) to all persons . full protection . of life, liberty property; (2) to all citizens of the same immun and equal poli rights and privile Motion to report to (gress. Lost: 5:5:5 Feb. 3 Bingham: substitute: Congress shall have er . . . to secure (1) to citizens of State all privi and immunities

THE FOURTEENTH AMENDMENT

April	May	June 1866
→		
4/30 S.78▲ reported by Fessenden	5/15 Fessenden not ready (ill) 5/23 Howard brought up 5/30 Howard: Amend § 1 to define citizenship REPUB. CAUCUS	6/4-8 Debated: Poland Howe Davis Hendricks Johnson Carried: 33:11:5
4/30 H.R.127● reported by Stevens	5/8-10 Debated: Stevens Raymond Finck Miller Garfield Eliot Thayer Randall Boyer Rogers Broomall Farnsworth Shanklin Bingham Carried: 128:37:19	6/13 Concur in amendments 120:32:32

citizens in the several States;
  (Art. IV, § 2)
2) to all persons in the several States equal protection of life, liberty and property.
  (Amend. V)
ubstitution agreed:
:6:2
mendment thus amend-
accepted:
9:4:2

Feb. 10
a motion to report
mendment to Congress
arried: 9:5:1
came:
0★
R.63■

April 21
vens' plan:
. No discrimination by
tes or U.S. as to civil
nts of persons because
race.

§ 2. No discrimination in suffrage after July 4, 1876.
§ 3. Until then, persons discriminated against not counted for representation.
§ 4. Debts.
§ 5. Congress empowered to enforce.
Bingham:
Add to ¶ 1:
  (1) nor shall any State deny any person equal protection of laws,
  (2) nor take private property without just compensation.
Lost: 5:7:3
Bingham:
Insert new § 5:
  privileges and immunities, due process, equal protection clauses [as finally adopted].
Carried: 10:2:3

April 25
Williams moved:
Strike out Bingham's § 5:
Carried: 7: 5: 3
Vote to report to Congress.
Carried: 7:6:2
Bingham:
Report § 5 as separate Amendment.
Lost: 4:8:3
Vote to report to Congress reconsidered.
Carried: 10:2:3

April 28   1866
Bingham:
Strike out § 1 of Stevens' plan; insert § 5: privileges and immunities, due process, and equal protection clauses.
Carried: 10:3:2
On report to Congress:
12 Repubs: 3 Dems.
Became:
S.78▲
H.R.127●

> Congress shall have power . . . to secure
> to all persons in every State
> full protection in the enjoyment
> of life, liberty and property;
> and to all citizens of the U.S. in every State
> the same immunities
> and equal political rights and privileges.

The drafting sounds agreeable—but what does it mean? Would Congress have power to legislate substantively on the whole field of "life, liberty and property"? Or only to secure "full protection" in the enjoyment of such rights as the State conferred? Why *full* protection? And why *immunities?* Article IV, Section 2, guaranteed "privileges and immunities." A competent draftsman would have seen that to select one word and omit the other would be taken as a signal of some significant distinction—yet none is apparent. *Immunity* connotes exemption from some duty or liability resting upon the generality of persons—for example, diplomatic immunity; it is ill-chosen where the intention is that all be treated alike.[215] Equal political rights: equal throughout the United States (supplanting State laws)?—or equal to all citizens within a State?

Fessenden, Stevens, Bingham, and two others were ready to report this to the Houses: five were not. The matter went over to February 3.

On that day Bingham moved a substitute:

> Congress shall have power . . . to secure
> to the citizens of each State
> all privileges and immunities of citizens in the
> several States (Art. 4, Sec. 2);
> and to all persons in the several States
> equal protection in the rights
> of life, liberty and property (5th Amend.).

Presently that text was adopted, by 9 votes to 4.

On February 10 it was voted—9 to 5—to report this to the two Houses as a proposal for a constitutional amendment.

---

[215] "What does the word immunity in your Constitution mean?"—Bingham posed the question in debate, and answered, "Exemption from un- equal burdens." Cong. Globe, 39–1, 1089. Feb. 28. *Immunity* from *inequality* was Bingham's way of securing *equality*.

FIRST DEBATE IN THE HOUSE OF REPRESENTATIVES

THE SENATE—DEEP in controversy over the provision on the basis of representation—put this measure on the table.

In the House, Bingham brought the joint resolution to a debate at the earliest opportunity—which was February 26 to 28. In the outcome it was postponed—without hope of further consideration.

Bingham, presenting the proposed amendment, said that "the interest of the country" required action "at an early day."[216] Evidently he thought that this draft should be acceptable to everyone not "opposed to enforcing the written guarantees of the Constitution."[217] For, he explained, "the amendment proposed stands in the very words of the Constitution . . . as it came to us from the hands of its illustrious framers"[218]—the Comity Clause (Article IV, Section 2, clause 1), and the Due Process Clause of the Fifth Amendment (of 1791). "[I]t has been the want of the Republic that there was not an express grant of power" to Congress "to enforce obedience to these requirements . . . . Nothing can be plainer" than that if Congress had had such power, and had exercised it, the rebellion "would have been an impossibility." His amendment would not "impose upon any State . . . or on any citizen . . . any obligation which is not enjoined upon them by the very letter of the Constitution." He derived this from the Supremacy Clause—the Constitution shall be "the supreme Law of the Land." "Could words be stronger . . . to enjoin upon every officer of every State the obligation to obey these great provisions of the Constitution, in their letter and their spirit?" But "these great provisions of the Constitution, this immortal bill of rights embodied in the Constitution, rested for its execution and enforcement hitherto upon the fidelity of the States." "[W]ithin the last five years" the officers of eleven States, "in utter disregard of [their] official oath," had violated these provisions. There, as Bingham saw it, lay the great defect which a constitutional amendment should cure.

This jumbled exposition rested upon the notion that the Supremacy Clause bound the State and its officers to conform to the Due Process Clause of the Fifth Amendment. (Ever since *Barron v. Baltimore* in 1833 it had been established that the federal Bill of Rights

---

[216] Cong. Globe, 39–1, 1034. Feb. 26.

[217] On February 13, when Brooks of New York, militant Democrat, showed a disposition to delay Bingham's progress, the latter said, "I want [the country] to understand who are opposed to enforcing the written guarantees of the Constitution." Cong. Globe, 39–1, 813.

[218] Cong. Globe, 39–1, 1034. Feb. 26.

did not apply to the States.[219] Abolitionists had contended, obstinately, that the Due Process Clause of the Fifth Amendment was a prohibition of slavery[220]—but on that view, the clause had been violated every day since it became effective in 1791, not only "within the last five years.") Further, Article IV, Section 2—"The Citizens of each State shall be entitled to all Privileges and Immunities of Citizens in the several States"—had not been fulfilled,[221] and Bingham located the seat of the trouble in the absence of an express grant of authority to Congress to enforce it. (Neither had there been an express authority to enforce the parallel provisions, on the rendition of fugitives from justice, and on the delivery of persons "held to Service or Labour"—and yet Congress in 1793 had passed one statute to enforce those provisions, and the Supreme Court had affirmed the "natural inference" that Congress had authority to do so.[222])

Next, Representative William Higby of California, Republican, expressed his understanding of the measure: it "will only have the effect to give vitality and life to portions of the Constitution that . . . have been entirely ignored and have become as dead matter in that instrument. . . . But by condensing it, . . . it will then become operative and beneficial."[223] Niblack, Democrat from Indiana, interrupted to inquire "whether the amendment . . . is intended or calculated to have any effect on the condition of the Chinamen in California." Higby answered in the negative: "The Chinese are nothing but a pagan race. They are an enigma to me . . . ." But, Niblack persisted, "If a China-man is one of the human race, why should he be degraded below the negro?" Higby explained: the latter "is not a pagan now. The negro is as much a native of this country as the gentleman or myself. . . ."

Higby's speech is a fair illustration of the level of understanding prevalent in Congress. Talk ran to evils in the past, to whether the rebel States were "in" or "out of" the Union, and to other matters foreign to the text before the House. The problems of the future lay in a mist which members did not endeavor to penetrate.

William D. Kelley of Pennsylvania, a leading Republican, supported the proposal on the basis of this understanding:[224]

> I hold that all the power this amendment will give is already in the Constitution. I admit that it has lain dormant. . . . The aroused people will demand that all the powers of the Constitution be exercised so that each State shall be guarantied a republican government,

---

[219] See supra, p. 1124.
[220] See supra, p. 1128. And see note 228 below.
[221] See supra, pp. 1121–23.

[222] Prigg v. Pennsylvania, 16 Pet. 539, 623 (1842).
[223] Cong. Globe, 39–1, 1054–57. Feb. 27.
[224] Ibid., 1057–63. Feb. 27.

and that the citizens of each State shall enjoy peaceably the privileges and immunities of citizenship in the respective States . . . .

But as some had questioned the power of Congress, and others the propriety of exercising it, Kelley supported the amendment, which would "more explicitly empower Congress to enforce and maintain" the rights of the people.

Kelley had spoken at great length—he was given an additional half hour—with a mass of quotations, on a point of his own, wholly irrelevant to the proposed amendment: the power of Congress under Article I, Section 4, in the matter of the "Times, Places and Manner of holding Elections for Senators and Representatives," and "the supervisory power of Congress over the suffrage regulations of the States" in respect of choosing Representatives. As Speaker Colfax reiterated, discussion "has taken a wide range"; he "would confine the debate to the constitutional amendment" whenever a point of order was raised.[225] Apparently members wandered from the subject before the House because they did not perceive the problem. This had started with Bingham's introduction: all that was needed was to enforce "the very letter of the Constitution," which somehow Congress had been unable to do, and from that want had come the war of the rebellion; but now this amendment was presented "for the purpose of giving to the whole people the care in future of the unity of the Government which constitutes us one people, and without which American nationality would cease to be."[226]

Robert S. Hale, conservative Republican from northern New York and a discriminating lawyer, called upon the House to desist from irrelevant matters and make a "scrutinizing examination" of the "extremely vague, loose, and indefinite provisions of the proposed amendment."[227] (Hale and Bingham had had private "conversations"; they knew more of one another's thinking than what had been said on the floor.[228]) It was not, as might be supposed from Bingham's

---

[225] Ibid., 1066, 1091. Feb. 27 and 28.

[226] Ibid., 1034. Feb. 26.

[227] Ibid., 1063–66. Feb. 27.

[228] Bingham, p. 1065, col. 1. Hale's speech attributes expressions to Bingham that had not been uttered in debate:

But the gentleman says there is, and there has been from first to last, a violation of the provisions of this bill of rights by the very existence of slavery itself; that the institution of

slavery itself has existed in defiance of the provisions of the bill of rights; that all the anomalies and all the enormities that have grown out of that institution have been equally in violation of it. . . .

At p. 1065, cols. 1–2.

Assuming that that was in Bingham's mind when he talked about enforcing "this immortal bill of rights," the Thirteenth Amendment had now put an end to slavery.

remarks, "a subject of the most trivial consequence." Hale read the text, and pointed out that it conveyed a sweeping new substantive power:

> It is not a mere provision that when the States undertake to give protection which is unequal Congress may equalize it; it is a grant of power in general terms—a grant of the right to legislate for the protection of life, liberty and property, simply qualified with the condition that it shall be equal legislation. . . .

Thad Stevens expressed surprise; to him it meant only that "Congress shall have power to correct . . . discrimination and inequality." And he supposed that State laws placing on married women disabilities not applied to those unmarried could not be considered discriminatory, because "where all of the same class are dealt with in the same way then there is no pretence of inequality." On that view, Hale replied, a State might treat whites as one class and Negroes as another: "the line of distinction is, I take it, quite as broadly marked between negroes and white men as between married and unmarried women." Before the House voted on an amendment "in such vague and general language," let the author "state where he apprehends that Congress and the courts will stop in the power they may arrogate to themselves under this proposed amendment." In Bingham's desire to protect the liberty of the citizen—"the negro, the late slave, as well as others"—Hale fully concurred. But in doing so let us not destroy the "individual freedom and the protection of personal rights we owe to our decentralized system." The "heretical and dangerous doctrine of State sovereignty" had at last been put down. Yet in the struggle there had been an inevitable tendency toward the accumulation of authority in the central government. Now "our tendencies ought all to be the other way." Hale appealed for delay, to permit "careful examination and dispassionate reflection."

Hale's speech, warning the House of the complexity of the matter, prompted Hiram Price of Iowa to reply. He was a layman, one of "the very few men" who did not claim to be a constitutional lawyer.[229] He took "a common sense view" of the proposal. "When I read it the first time I gathered from it this idea, and I have not changed my opinion in reading it half a dozen times over": it meant

---

[229] Cong. Globe, 39–1, 1066. Feb. 27.

Price (1814–1901) was a successful merchant at Davenport, a banker, promoter of railroads and president of one. He had given solid support to the raising of troops, was an earnest Methodist, and had been active in the prohibition movement in Iowa. Judge John F. Dillon was his son-in-law.

to give the same rights, privileges, and protection to the citizen of one State going into another that a citizen of that State would have who had lived there for years.

During the past quarter century, "if a citizen of a free State visiting a slave State expressed his opinion in reference to slavery he was treated without much ceremony to a coat of tar and feathers and a ride upon a rail."

Price's "common sense view" is noteworthy, because it is typical of many men's reaction to Section 1 of the Fourteenth Amendment: the words sounded excellent—how could anyone object?

Frederick E. Woodbridge of Vermont was a member of the Judiciary Committee. Now he expressed himself in copious phrases.[230] He asked, "What is the object of the proposed amendment?"—and answered:

> It merely gives the power to Congress to enact those laws which will give to a citizen of the United States the natural rights which necessarily pertain to citizenship. It is intended to enable Congress by its enactments when necessary to give to a citizen of the United States, in whatever State he may be, those privileges and immunities which are guarantied to him under the Constitution of the United States. It is intended to enable Congress to give to all citizens the inalienable rights of life and liberty, and to every citizen in whatever State he may be that protection to his property which is extended to the other citizens of the State.

This is quite a congeries of conceptions: the natural rights pertaining to citizenship, the inalienable rights to life and liberty, the privileges and immunities already guarantied, and as to property the same protection as the local law affords to local citizens. And—contrary to what Hale had argued—this amendment would involve no significant extension of national authority over matters theretofore controlled by the States. On the contrary, he concluded,

> The adoption of this amendment, Mr. Speaker, will be no shock upon the present well-arranged system, defining the powers of the General Government and the States, under which we have so happily lived. . . .

What supporters of the proposed amendment wanted was, in colloquial language, that the insurrectionary States behave themselves:

---

[230] Cong. Globe, 39–1, 1088. Feb. 28.

that they desist from abusing visitors—that they tolerate local dissent—that they accord the freedman equality in civil rights and hold open the door of opportunity. They were persuaded that simply by a fresh enactment of provisions already in the Constitution, and with no major distortion of the existing federal system, this great amelioration would somehow be accomplished.

On February 28, winding up the debate, Bingham made a fresh statement of his proposal:[231]

> The proposition pending before the House is simply a proposition to arm the Congress of the United States . . . with the power to enforce the bill of rights as it stands in the Constitution to-day. It "hath that extent—no more." . . .[232]

Whether Bingham's reference to "the bill of rights" was intended simply to mean the provisions from Article IV, Section 2, and the Fifth Amendment he had written into his proposal—or rather that its language reached out to embrace Amendments I to VIII, calls for later examination. Whatever he had in mind, he said that

> in the event of the adoption of this amendment, if they [State legislators] conspire together to enact laws refusing equal protection to life, liberty, or property, the Congress is thereby vested with power to hold them to answer before the bar of the national courts for the violation of their oaths and of the rights of their fellow-men. Why should it not be so? . . . Is the bill of rights to stand in our Constitution hereafter, as in the past five years within eleven States, a mere dead letter? It is absolutely essential to the safety of the people that it should be enforced.[233]

Talk about Congress marshalling a crowd of State legislators before the bar of a court to answer for passing a statute "in violation of their oaths and of the rights of their fellow-men" has the sound of tumbrels rolling over the cobblestones. Of course Congress does not "hold" anyone "to answer." It may define a crime—but it may not punish what has already been done. It is "the first essential of due process of law,"[234] guaranteed by the Fifth Amendment upon which Bingham drew for his new amendment, that an offense shall not be so vague that men can only guess what is forbidden. The Civil Rights Bill did provide for punishing those who under color of State law deprived

---

[231] Ibid., 1088–90.
[232] Ibid., 1088. On the matter of the Bill of Rights, see note 275 below.
[233] Ibid., 1090.

[234] Connally v. General Construction Co., 269 U.S. 385, 391 (1926); United States v. L. Cohen Grocery Co., 255 U.S. 81, 89 (1921).

men of the rights there secured: but Trumbull, contradicting the veto message, had insisted that there was no thought of reaching State legislators.[235]

Roscoe Conkling took the floor when Bingham concluded. In the Joint Committee he consistently "felt constrained" to oppose Bingham's proposal; now, with his *"quasi* consent," he would move to postpone.[236] First, however, he would yield the floor to Giles W. Hotchkiss, a Republican from Binghamton, New York. "Constitutions should have their provisions so plain . . . that the common mind can understand them," said Hotchkiss. As he understood the language proposed, it would "authorize Congress to establish uniform laws throughout the United States upon . . . the protection of life, liberty, and property. I am unwilling that Congress shall have any such power." But if, as he supposed, Bingham's object was "to provide against a discrimination to the injury or exclusion of any class of citizens in any State," then that should be provided outright and not left in peril of an "accidental majority of Congress."

Conkling's motion to postpone was carried by 110 to 37—the minority being Democrats who sought a more brusque rejection by laying the measure on the table.[237] *The Nation* reported that "members of the legal profession," "unimpeachable Republicans," had seen in the proposal "a dangerous centralization of power."[238]

Next day, March 1, the House turned to the Civil Rights Bill.[239] Although on April 9 it became law, grave doubts about its constitutionality made a civil rights amendment seem an urgent need.

THE JOINT COMMITTEE FRAMES AN AMENDMENT

IN THE LATTER half of April the Joint Committee, which had not met in a body for six weeks, resumed work on an amendment. It had made two false starts: its proposal on representation had met failure in the Senate on March 9, and the civil rights measure had been put aside by the House on February 28. Now Congress and the country were impatient. "We hear a great deal of the President's policy"—to readmit the rebel States at once—said *The Nation* on March 22, "but we never hear of the policy of Congress, because there is no such thing. The people are ready to keep the South out until it complies with certain conditions, but we want to know what these conditions are . . . ."[240] Then on the Civil Rights Bill the President and Congress

---

[235] Supra, p. 1195.
[236] Cong. Globe, 39–1, 1094. Feb. 28.
[237] Ibid., 1095.

[238] 2:291. Mar. 8, 1866.
[239] Supra, p. 1183.
[240] 2:358.

reached an outright break. "The time has arrived at which [Congress] must visibly *begin* to shape a policy," *The Nation* warned on April 12; "[the people] want some tangible proposition."[241] What Congress settled upon would become the Republican platform for the elections of 1866; the test would be whether it could win majorities in the North against the opposition of President Johnson and the Democratic party.

Two plans were laid before the committee. On April 16, Senator Stewart of Nevada argued for his project of "universal amnesty and universal suffrage," which he now cast as a constitutional amendment.[242] A month earlier it had been introduced as a legislative measure whereby Congress would offer to readmit any State that would provide for racial equality in civil rights and in suffrage, without however having to disqualify those qualified to vote in 1860. But that glimmering hope had vanished, and the Joint Committee would not seek to revive it.

The other plan had been framed by Robert Dale Owen, the English reformer who had been taking a useful part in working for Negro advancement. Stevens brought this before the committee on April 21.[243] A constitutional amendment would be proposed, with sections to provide as follows:

1. No racial discrimination in civil rights;
2. After July 4, 1876, no racial discrimination in the suffrage;
3. Until July, 4, 1876, a racial class discriminated against in the suffrage would not be counted for the basis of representation;
4. Rebel debts and claims would not be paid;
5. Congress would have power to enforce.

Whenever such amendment had become part of the Constitution, any rebel State that had ratified, and had modified its law to conform to Section 1, would be readmitted to representation.

Taking that as a starting point, the committee made drastic alterations. Bingham strove for a three-point provision on civil rights: privileges and immunities, due process, equal protection. This was accepted—then stricken—and at last restored.

When on April 30 the committee reported to the two Houses, its draft provided:[244]

1. Section 1 as it stands in the Constitution, without the opening sentence defining citizenship.

---

[241] 2:454.
[242] See supra, pp. 128–29, 131.
[243] Kendrick, *Journal of the Joint Committee*, 83–84.
[244] Cong. Globe, 39–1, 2286, by

Stevens in the House. This became H.R. J. Res. 127. On the same day, p. 2265, Fessenden reported the measure to the Senate, where it became S.J. Res. 78.

2. Substantially Section 2 as it stands—discussed above.
3. Until July 4, 1870, adherents to the late insurrection excluded from voting in federal elections.
4. Debts in aid of the war against the United States, and claims for slave labor, never to be paid.
5. Congress would have power to enforce.

Two bills were also reported. One—H.R.543, and in the Senate S.292—would declare that when the amendment had become part of the Constitution, any State that had brought its law into conformity "may"—not *shall*—be readmitted. The other—H.R.544 and S.293—would declare ineligible to hold federal office five categories of participants in the rebellion—from President down to colonel, and such as had treated prisoners unlawfully.[245]

The issues were now in the lap of Congress. Practical Republicans must consider whether the country would be satisfied that an adequate settlement had been staked out; some would be apprehensive lest the party go too far.[246] Adjusting the basis of representation came first in the priorities of the moment. Excluding the rebel leaders from any further domination was a kindred concern. Making life secure for loyal men, and in particular for freedmen, wherever they might be, was an essential: but this problem was obscure, and declamation abounded where hard analysis was wanting.

SECOND DEBATE IN THE HOUSE OF REPRESENTATIVES

ON MAY 8, THAD Stevens opened debate on the proposed amendment.[247] He took note of the growing impatience, but begged the House "to consider the magnitude of the task." The Founders in 1787 had been "compelled to postpone the principles of their great Declaration," expecting "their full establishment" at "a more propitious time." He had hoped to "found the repaired edifice upon the firm foundation of eternal justice. . . . But if full justice could not be obtained at once," he said, "I would not refuse to do what is possible." In that spirit he

---

[245] Cong. Globe, 39–1, 2286–87 in the House, 2265 in the Senate.
[246] In "The Late Session of Congress," *The Nation*, 3:90, August 2, 1866, Thomas G. Shearman wrote: The members from Indiana and Southern Illinois well knew that their constituents had barely

overcome their prejudices sufficiently to tolerate even the residence of negroes among them, and that any greater liberality would be highly repulsive to them. . . .
[247] Cong. Globe, 39–1, 2459–60.

introduced the Joint Committee's proposal. "It falls short of my wishes, but it fulfills my hopes."

He paraphrased Section 1, and commented:

> I can hardly believe that any person can be found who will not admit that every one of these provisions is just. They are all asserted, in some form or other, in our Declaration or organic law. But the Constitution limits only the action of Congress, and is not a limitation on the States. This amendment supplies that defect, and allows Congress to correct the unjust legislation of the States, so far that the law which operates on one man shall operate *equally* upon all. . . .

Without distinguishing between the three clauses, he said simply that discrimination against men of color would be banned. *Inequality* had been Stevens' concern from the start. Now *Congress* would be able to correct unjust State legislation: Stevens' thought ran to political rather than judicial action.

He assigned first importance to Section 2:

> The effect of this provision will be either to compel the States to grant universal suffrage or so to shear them of their power as to keep them forever in a hopeless minority in the national Government . . . .

Of Section 3 he said, "My only objection to it is that it is too lenient. . . . Still I will move no amendment, nor vote for any, lest the whole fabric should tumble to pieces."

On Section 4, concerning debts: "none dare object to it who is not himself a rebel."

Thad Stevens was the black man's devoted friend, in his own earthy, practical way. "In my judgment," he said, "we shall not approach the measure of justice until we have given every adult freedman a homestead on the land where he was born and toiled and suffered." He resented the "puerile and pedantic criticism" with which Sumner had "slaughtered" the Joint Committee's earlier proposal on the basis of representation. That, plus repudiation of the rebel debt, "would have gone far to curb the rebellious spirit" and bring universal suffrage.

Such was the crude pragmatism of the chairman of the House delegation on the Joint Committee: his remarks give no aid to latter-day subtleties in reconstructing Section 1 of the Fourteenth Amendment.

William E. Finck of Ohio—an obdurate Democrat—insisted that only when the Southern States had been restored could "the great questions of amendment be fairly discussed and voted upon."[248] He commented on Section 1:

> Well, all I have to say about this section is, that if it is necessary to adopt it, in order to confer upon Congress power over the matters contained in it, then the civil rights bill, which the President vetoed, was passed without authority, and is clearly unconstitutional.

Not so, Garfield replied.[249] He was "glad to see this first section here which proposes to hold over every American citizen, without regard to color, the protecting shield of law." Everyone knew that a mere statutory protection would be repealed the moment the Democrats returned to power. "For this reason, and not because I believe the civil rights bill unconstitutional," he welcomed the first section. He regretted that the proposal did not secure the Negro's right to vote. Section 3 was the only one "not bottomed clearly and plainly on principle": he wanted it to be stricken out.

Throughout the debate, opponent and supporter alike assigned to Section 1 the function of putting permanent support under the Civil Rights Act.

M. Russell Thayer of Pennsylvania spoke at length in advocacy of the measure.[250] One sentence sufficed to cover Section 1: "I cannot conceive that any loyal man can hold any other view upon that subject . . . ."

Benjamin M. Boyer of Pennsylvania, Democrat, made a long speech in opposition.[251] He disposed of Section 1 with the remark that it

> embodies the principles of the civil rights bill, and is intended to secure ultimately, and to some extent indirectly, the political equality of the negro race. It is objectionable also in its phraseology, being open to ambiguity and admitting of conflicting constructions.

His colleague, William D. Kelley, dared Boyer to denounce Section 1 back home: there was not a man in his district who would not say "those provisions ought to be in the Constitution if they are not already there."[252]

John M. Broomall, a thoroughgoing Republican from Pennsylvania, said "We propose, first, to give power to the Government . . . to protect its own citizens within the States, within its own jurisdiction.

---

248 Ibid., 2460–62. May 8.
249 Ibid., 2462–64.
250 Ibid., 2464–65.

251 Ibid., 2465–67.
252 Ibid., 2468.

Who will deny the necessity of this? No one."[253] The Civil Rights Act was "this proposition, in another shape." But Bingham had said that it was unconstitutional. "On so vital a point I wish to make assurance doubly sure."

George S. Shanklin, Kentucky Democrat, said that Section 1 expressed a single idea:[254]

> to strike down the reserved rights of the States, those rights which were declared by the framers of the Constitution to belong to the States exclusively . . . .

He urged, discharge the Joint Committee, abolish the Freedmen's Bureau, repeal the Civil Rights Act, and admit delegations from the Southern States.

Henry J. Raymond of New York had withheld his support from the Civil Rights Bill because of grave constitutional doubts. "And now, although that bill became a law . . . , it is . . . proposed so to amend the Constitution as to confer upon Congress the power to pass it."[255] He was happy to support Section 1, which "secures an equality of rights among all the citizens of the United States."

Of course, to identify Section 1 with the Civil Rights Act was not to affirm that it had no larger significance. But when speaker after speaker says that and nothing more, one surmises that nothing more specific was present in their thoughts.

George F. Miller of Pennsylvania dismissed Section 1 with the statement that "it is so just . . . and so clearly within the spirit of the Declaration of Independence . . . that no member of this House can seriously object to it."[256] Section 2, he reiterated, was the most important part of the proposal.

Thomas D. Eliot of Massachusetts was one who had found "ample power" to enact the Civil Rights Bill, but was happy "to incorporate into the Constitution provisions which will settle the doubt" others had entertained.[257]

Samuel J. Randall, Pennsylvania Democrat, said that "The first section proposes to make an equality in every respect between the two races"; he thought that was a matter that should be left to the States.[258]

Andrew Jackson Rogers, the pugnacious New Jersey Democrat, was a member of the Joint Committee and thus was unusually well informed. His conclusion, he said, differing from that of others, was that Section 1 was "the most dangerous to liberty"; it was "no more

---

[253] Ibid., 2498–2500. May 9.
[254] Ibid., 2500–1.
[255] Ibid., 2501–3.
[256] Ibid., 2510–11.
[257] Ibid., 2511–12.
[258] Ibid., 2530–31. May 10.

nor less than an attempt to embody in the Constitution . . . that outrageous and miserable civil rights bill . . . ."[259] He examined the opening clause. "What are privileges and immunities? Why, sir, all the rights we have under the laws of the country are embraced under the definition of privileges and immunities." To marry, to contract, to serve as a juror, to hold office—all these were included within that expression—and now if the Negro were denied any of those rights, "the Federal Government will step in" and the outcome would be "a revolution worse than that through which we have just passed."

Rogers was an intemperate partisan, but his perception was sharp. Discussion within the committee had not shown him that "privileges and immunities" had any precise meaning. Like the others, he looked to Congress as the organ by which Section 1 would be enforced.

John F. Farnsworth was an influential member from Illinois, a lawyer with advanced political views. His years in Congress had been interrupted by distinguished service in the army. He regretted that the proposed amendment did not put the Declaration of Independence into practice by giving the ballot to the Negro.[260] The value of Section 1, as he saw it, lay in its equal protection clause—"the very foundation of a republican government"; the other clauses were "surplusage."

So far the Congressmen have been saying that Section 1 would prevent discrimination against the Negro in respect of civil rights— would make certain the validity of the Civil Rights Act—would give renewed expression to principles already in the Constitution—was perhaps harmless surplusage. Opponents said it was ambiguous, and an invasion of the State's proper field. No one attempted to detail the function of each of the three clauses. Some participants in the debate made no mention of Section 1. Interest was chiefly in the political sections, 2 and 3.

Toward the close of the three-day debate, Bingham spoke on the amendment, and in particular of his own concern.[261] Section 1, he said, would fill a great want, demonstrated by the years of conflict.

> What is that? It is the power in the people, the whole people of the United States, by express authority of the Constitution to do that by congressional enactment which hitherto they have not had the power to do, and have never even attempted to do; that is, to protect by national law the privileges and immunities of all the citizens of the Republic and the inborn rights of every person within its jurisdiction whenever the same shall be abridged or denied by the unconstitutional acts of any State.

---

[259] Ibid., 2537–39.   [260] Ibid., 2539–41.   [261] Ibid., 2541–44.

Allow me, Mr. Speaker, in passing, to say that this amendment takes from no State any right that ever pertained to it. No State ever had the right, under the forms of law or otherwise, to deny to any freeman the equal protection of the laws or to abridge the privileges or immunities of any citizen of the Republic, although many of them have assumed and exercised the power, and that without remedy. . . .

Bingham purported to explain. Section 1 did not confer the suffrage. It would reach instances, such as had occurred in the past, where a State inflicted "cruel and unusual punishments" upon citizens "for sacred duty done"—meaning, apparently, punishment for acts of loyalty to the United States. He quoted the Privileges and Immunities Clause of Article IV, Section 2: among these privileges was "the right to bear true allegiance to the Constitution and laws of the United States, and to be protected in life, liberty, and property." He recalled Nullification in South Carolina: thereupon Congress passed legislation providing for the collection of the revenue and for the protection of revenue officers; but "No remedy was provided to protect the citizen." Why was that? Because the power to lay and collect taxes, and the power to pass laws necessary and proper for executing the other powers, were expressly given; but there was no power to protect citizens "against the infamous provision of the [Nullification] ordinance which required them to abjure the allegiance which they owed their country."

That great want of the citizen and stranger, protection by national law from unconstitutional State enactments, is supplied by the first section of this amendment. That is the extent that it hath, no more; and let gentlemen answer to God and their country who oppose its incorporation into the organic law of the land.

The burden of this confused discourse is that some States had abused citizens for doing what under the Constitution they were entitled or even in duty bound to do—but that Congress had been powerless to protect them. Section 1 would take away no right theretofor belonging to the States; it would simply enable Congress to supply a remedy against unconstitutional State action. Bingham wove in a reference to Article IV, Section 2. He was correct in the view that a citizen of, say, Massachusetts who went to South Carolina was there entitled to the benefit of the local laws, which would include protection of his various interests—his life, liberty, and property. But he was mistaken in relating Article IV, Section 2, to the citizen's "right"— actually his duty—to bear allegiance to the United States. That duty was inherent in the constitutional system, and rested on the citizen whether he was at home or elsewhere—without any reference to Article IV, Section 2.

Bingham also wove in a reference to "cruel and unusual punishments," borrowing words from the Eighth Amendment: but apparently the gist of the complaint was simply that citizens had been made to suffer for their loyalty to the United States. This illustrates the disconcerting way in which Bingham would pluck a constitutional phrase and toss it in at some point to which it had no relevance.

Bingham alluded to "the inborn rights of every person"—which sounds like the law of nature and the "unalienable rights" of the Declaration of Independence. Yet he reiterated that Section 1 would enable Congress to prevent the States henceforth from interfering with the citizen's performance of his "sacred duty" to the United States. It is no wonder that when the Court had to construe and apply the Fourteenth Amendment, some Justices held that it "was intended to give practical effect to the declaration of 1776 of inalienable rights, rights which are the gift of the Creator," while others held that the "privileges and immunities" it secured were those rights "which owe their existence to the Federal Government, its national character, its Constitution, or its laws."[262] When one studies Bingham carefully one learns that many of his utterances cannot be accepted as serious propositions.[263]

---

[262] Slaughter House Cases, 16 Wall. 36 (1873). See infra, pp. 1349–60.

[263] He was badly mistaken in supposing that Congress had lacked authority, and had "never even attempted," to protect citizens of the United States against unconstitutional acts of a State. Martin v. Hunter's Lessee, 1 Wheat. 304 (1816), and Cohens v. Virginia, 6 Wheat. 264 (1821), were memorable demonstrations to the contrary. In the latter case Chief Justice Marshall, sustaining the Court's jurisdiction, said that "No government ought to be so defective in its organization as not to contain within itself the means of securing the execution of its own laws. . . . Courts of justice are the means most usually employed . . . ." Certainly Congress could have resorted to additional means if "necessary and proper" to enforce rights arising under the Constitution, laws and treaties. Prigg v. Pennsylvania has already been cited on the power to enforce duties created by Article IV, Section

2. Supra, p. 1276. Corfield v. Coryell, supra, pp. 1121–23, illustrated how one who asserted a constitutional right would be protected if his claim proved to be well founded.

The Civil War itself was the most convincing demonstration of the power of the United States to compel States that refused to observe their duties under the Constitution.

Bingham was deep in error in treating Barron v. Baltimore as "a decision showing that the power of the Federal Government to enforce in the United States courts the bill of rights . . . had been denied." Cong. Globe, 39–1, 1089. What the Court actually held was "that the provision in the fifth amendment . . . is intended solely as a limitation on the exercise of power by the government of the United States, and is not applicable to legislation of the States." 7 Pet. 243, 250 (1833). See infra, p. 1124. If in the premises Barron had had a constitutional right, of course it would have been enforced.

The superficiality of comment on Section 1 may in a measure be explained by the preoccupation with Section 3 as proposed by the Joint Committee. Would it exclude from the suffrage even those who had received Executive clemency? It remained unsettled what the words meant.[264] To Section 3, Blaine recalled, "there was strong hostility from two classes—one class opposing it because it was a needless proscription, and the other, equally large, because it did not go far enough . . . ."[265] In Raymond's words, it looked like a measure "for the purpose of influencing and controlling the presidential election of 1868"; it would result in a majority of the Southern people being "misrepresented in Congress by men in whose election they had no voice or vote."[266]

An attempt to prevent Section 3 as it stood from remaining in the joint resolution was defeated. Then Republicans stood together in voting to pass the measure as it came from the Joint Committee: there were 128 in favor, 37 opposed.[267]

In the Senate, Section 3 would be transformed.

The capital's leading newspaper, the *National Intelligencer*, conservative and friendly to President Johnson, summarized what, in the editorial view, Section 1 would accomplish: "Give citizens equal rights in every State."[268] It said, in conclusion:

> As regards the first provision, no one, so far as we know, raises any objection. It is only, if we understand it correctly, undertaking to carry out what the Constitution now commands, and what was equally enjoined by the Articles of Confederation.

Later it said that "the efficient part" of the Amendment consisted of only two provisions, Sections 2 and 3. "This is the milk of the cocoanut."[269]

No one, so far as this Washington journal had heard, made any objection to Section 1; it sought to enforce commands dating back to the Articles of Confederation. Sections 1 and 4 were "mere side dishes."

THE JOINT RESOLUTION IN THE SENATE

BY REASON OF protracted illness, Fessenden—chairman, on the part of the Senate, of the Joint Committee—had to "pass over the recon-

---

[264] Cong. Globe, 39–1, 2460, where Blaine raised the question; 2463, 2503, 2537. See infra, p. 1296.

[265] *Twenty Years of Congress*, II, 207.

[266] Cong. Globe, 39–1, 2503.

[267] Ibid., 2545. May 10.

[268] May 15, 1866.

[269] May 17.

struction debate to somebody else."[270] The duty fell upon Senator Howard, who on May 23 brought up the joint resolution and said that, in the chairman's stead, he would present "the views and motives" which had influenced the Joint Committee, "so far as I understand those views and motives."[271] Howard, apparently, had not entered into the spirit of Bingham's drafting: three times in the committee he had voted against the author's work. Howard would have had Section 1 declare simply, No discrimination by State or federal government as to civil rights on account of color.[272]

Beginning with the privileges and immunities clause, Howard observed that it was not easy to define accurately what was meant by "citizen of the United States." (The Civil Rights Act of April 9 had defined that citizenship; on May 29 the Senate would add the definition at the head of Section 1 of the pending constitutional amendment.) Since, in the beginning, one State might have treated citizens of other States as aliens with reference to itself, the provision was made in Article IV, Section 2, that "The Citizens of each State shall be entitled to all Privileges and Immunities of Citizens in the several States." Howard said "It would be a curious question to solve" what those privileges and immunities were. But the clause must have been inserted "for some good purpose"; "some results beneficial to the citizens of the several States" must have been in view "or it would not be found there." Recently the Supreme Court, he recalled, had "very modestly declined to go into a definition."[273] "But we may gather some intimation of what probably will be the opinion of the judiciary" by considering what Justice Washington said on the circuit in *Corfield v. Coryell*. He read the long discussion, wherein Washington spoke of rights that are "fundamental," that "belong of right to the citizens of all free governments."[274]

Then Howard stated what he understood the privileges and immunities of citizens of the United States to be:

Such is the character of the privileges and immunities spoken of in the second section of the fourth article of the Constitution.

---

[270] Francis Fessenden, *Life and Public Services of William Pitt Fessenden*, 2 vols. (Boston and New York: Houghton Mifflin Co., 1907), II, 56, 61. He was present, however, when Howard presented the measure in the Senate on May 23.

[271] Cong. Globe, 39–1, 2764–68.

[272] On April 25 Howard had voted to strike Bingham's draft as an additional section, and then against accepting it as a separate constitutional amendment. On April 28 he voted against Bingham's motion to strike a "No discrimination . . ." section and insert Bingham's draft in lieu thereof.

On the final vote on the proposed amendment, all 12 Republicans voted yea and the 3 Democrats nay.

[273] Conner v. Elliott, 18 How. 591 (1856).

[274] See supra, pp. 1121–23.

To these privileges and immunities, whatever they may be—for they are not and cannot be fully defined in their entire extent and precise nature—to these should be added the personal rights guarantied and secured by the first eight amendments of the Constitution; such as the freedom of speech and of the press; the right of the people peaceably to assemble and petition the Government for a redress of grievances, a right appertaining to each and all the people; the right to keep and to bear arms; the right to be exempted from the quartering of soldiers in a house without the consent of the owner; the right to be exempt from unreasonable searches and seizures, and from any search or seizure except by virtue of a warrant issued upon a formal oath or affidavit; the right of an accused person to be informed of the nature of the accusation against him, and his right to be tried by an impartial jury of the vicinage; and also the right to be secure against excessive bail and against cruel and unusual punishments.

We pause to take note of the statement that among these privileges and immunities "which cannot be fully defined" Howard included the rights secured by the first eight amendments to the Constitution. That remark has given rise to much controversy.[275]

---

[275] There have been occasions in recent years when the debates on the framing of the Fourteenth Amendment have been sifted in search of material bearing on some one particular issue. A notable inquiry has been, Did the 39th Congress purpose by that amendment to make the federal Bill of Rights—Amendments I to VIII—applicable to the States? The affirmative was sustained by Justice Black in a dissenting opinion in Adamson v. California, 332 U.S. 46, 68 at 71 et seq. (1947). Reliance was placed chiefly on the statements of Representative Bingham and Senator Howard. Justice Douglas joined in that opinion. Justices Murphy and Rutledge expressed "substantial agreement" with the opinion, but were not prepared to say that the amendment was "entirely and necessarily limited by the Bill of Rights." At 124.

This view on the issue was maintained by those four Justices in Wolf v. Colorado, 338 U.S. 25 (1949).

The negative was sustained in Fairman, "Does the Fourteenth Amendment Incorporate the Bill of Rights? The Original Understanding." *Stan. L. Rev.* 2:5–139 (1949).

In twenty years much has been written, pro and con, on the historical question. No member of the Court has taken his stand with the minority of 1947. The Court has, however, found a number of the particular guaranties of the Bill of Rights to be made applicable to the States by force of the Due Process Clause of the Fourteenth Amendment. Among these, Gideon v. Wainwright, 372 U.S. 335 (1963), held that appointment of counsel for an indigent defendant in a criminal trial was among the "fundamental safeguards of liberty" protected against invasion by a State. Malloy v. Hogan, 378 U.S. 1 (1964), held that "the Fifth Amendment's exception from compulsory self-incrimination is also protected by the Fourteenth Amendment against abridgment by the States." Duncan v. Louisiana, 391 U.S. 145 (1968), likewise incorporated the right of trial by jury in all criminal cases which, were they to arise in a federal court, would be within the guaranty of the Sixth Amendment. Black, J., concurring, reaffirmed his stand in the Adamson case, while Harlan, J. (Stewart, J., joining with him), expressed disagree-

XX: *The Fourteenth Amendment*

Returning to Howard's explanation,

Now, sir, here is a mass of privileges, immunities, and rights, some of them secured by the second section of the fourth article of the Constitution, which I have recited, some by the first eight amendments of the Constitution; and it is a fact well worthy of attention that the course of decision of our courts and the present settled

---

ment with "the total incorporation view of the Fourteenth Amendment," and approved "the Court's selective incorporation approach."

The thesis that the 39th Congress purposed by the Fourteenth Amendment to make Amendments I to VIII applicable to the States necessarily includes the Seventh Amendment:

In suits at common law, where the value in controversy shall exceed twenty dollars, the right to trial by jury shall be preserved . . . .

State courts—unlike those of the United States—do have a mass of civil litigation where the value in controversy is small; and "trial by jury" has been understood to mean the unanimous verdict of twelve jurors.

Irving Brant, defending the thesis of incorporation, disposes of the Seventh Amendment with celerity:

That amendment was destroyed ages ago by the devaluation of money. Adopted to allay idle fears, long outmoded in federal practice, it is subject also to discard, as far as the Fourteenth Amendment is concerned, under the rule *de minimis*—the law takes no account of trifles.

The Bill of Rights: Its Origin and Meaning (Indianapolis, Kansas City, New York: Bobbs-Merrill Co., 1965), 487.

That seems a rather offhand way of snuffing out one of the "Bright Constellation."

It is true that in 1970, in Williams v. Florida, 399 U.S. 78, the Court, two Justices dissenting, put aside the understanding—explicitly affirmed in Thompson v. Utah, 170 U.S. 343 (1898)— that "trial by jury" as it appears in the Constitution is impressed with its historical meaning of "a trial by twelve jurors." Now it said

that the Court would "do [no] violence to the letter of the Constitution by turning to other than purely historical considerations to determine which features of the jury system, as it existed at common law, were preserved in the Constitution." It said that "the essential feature of a jury obviously lies in the interposition . . . of the commonsense judgment of a group of laymen, and in the community participation and shared responsibility that results . . . ." The case at hand was a trial in a State court for a noncapital offense, and it was held that a jury of six satisfied the Fourteenth Amendment.

Whatever might result from this line of thought as applied to trial by jury as guaranteed by the Seventh Amendment, account must still be taken of the specific amount of "twenty dollars." To treat that as *"de minimis,"* trifling, would require the Court to give some new translation to that figure—for surely the Court would not make bold to jettison the Amendment.

The Fourteenth Amendment and the Bill of Rights: The Incorporation Theory (New York: Da Capo Press, 1970), reprints from 2 *Stanford Law Review* the article by Fairman cited above; the companion article by Professor Stanley Morrison, "The Judicial Interpretation," *Stanford Law Review*, 2:140–73; the report of Adamson v. California and that of Duncan v. Louisiana; with an introduction by Professor Leonard W. Levy.

Apropos of Brown v. Board of Education, 347 U.S. 483 (1954), another particular problem of the Fourteenth Amendment, "The Original Understanding and the Segregation Decisions," was discussed by Bickel, *Harv. L. Rev.* 69:1 (1955).

doctrine is, that all these immunities, privileges, rights, thus guarantied by the Constitution or recognized by it, are secured to the citizen solely as a citizen of the United States and as a party in their courts. They do not operate in the slightest degree as a restraint or prohibition upon State legislation. . . .

After the semicolon, Howard spoke inaccurately. The privileges and immunities of Article IV, Section 2, are secured to "the citizens of each State" as limitations upon the action of other States. It is only the rights "recognized" in Amendments I to VIII that "[did] not operate in the slightest degree . . . upon State legislation." Returning to Howard's remarks on Amendments I to VIII,

States are not affected by them and it has been repeatedly held that the restriction contained in the Constitution against the taking of private property for public use without just compensation is not a restriction upon State legislation, but applies only to the legislation of Congress.

Now, sir, there is no power given in the Constitution to enforce and to carry out any of these guarantees. They are not powers granted by the Constitution to Congress, and of course do not come within the sweeping clause of the Constitution authorizing Congress to pass all laws necessary and proper for carrying out the foregoing or granted powers, but they stand simply as a bill of rights in the Constitution, without power on the part of Congress to give them full effect; while at the same time the States are not restrained from violating the principles embraced in them except by their own local constitutions, which may be altered from year to year. The great object of the first section of this amendment is, therefore, to restrain the power of the States and compel them at all times to respect these great fundamental guarantees. How will it be done under the present amendment? . . .

Take note how Howard is going to answer this question. Omitting, as though not present in his thought, that Section 1 would itself be enforceable by the courts, he will say if that these fundamentals are to be enforced, it must be by giving *Congress* power to enforce them:

As I have remarked, they are not powers granted to Congress, and therefore it is necessary, if they are to be effectuated and enforced, as they assuredly ought to be, that additional power should be given to Congress to that end. This is done by the fifth section of this amendment, which declares that "the Congress shall have power to enforce by appropriate legislation the provisions of this article." Here is a direct affirmative delegation of power to Congress to carry out all the principles of all these guarantees, a power not found in the Constitution.

Earlier Howard had found the content of "privileges and immunities" rather puzzling, and had passed on with the remark that the judiciary would settle it. Now he says that if the "great fundamental guarantees" are to be enforced, Congress must be given power to that end. He—like members of the 39th Congress generally—thought of giving power to Congress as the great need of the moment: evidently that, rather than the content of the fundamental guarantees, was uppermost in his mind.

The provisions for due process and equal protection—what has become *the* Fourteenth Amendment so far as litigation is concerned— Howard disposed of in one paragraph:

> The last two clauses of the first section . . . disable a State from depriving not merely a citizen of the United States, but any person, . . . of life, liberty, or property without due process of law, or from denying to him the equal protection of the laws of the State. This abolishes all class legislation in the States and does away with the injustice of subjecting one caste of person to a code not applicable to another. It prohibits the hanging of a black man for a crime for which the white man is not to be hanged. It protects the black man in his fundamental rights as a citizen with the same shield which it throws over the white man. . . . Ought not the time to be now passed when one measure of justice is to be meted out to a member of one caste while another and a different measure is meted out to the member of another caste . . . ?

Section 2, Howard admitted with regret, did not confer suffrage upon colored men. But the practical question was, "what will the Legislatures of the various States . . . do in the premises; what is it likely will meet the general approbation of the people who are to elect the Legislatures, three fourths of whom must ratify our propositions before they have the force of constitutional provisions?"

When he reached Section 3, Howard said frankly, "I do not believe, if adopted, it will be of any practical benefit to the country."

As soon as Howard sat down, a number of Senators were ready to propose changes. "The possibility of the main proposition being carried down by an overload of amendments," the *Chicago Tribune*'s correspondent reported, "was by no means remote. It became obvious that something had to be done to prevent a discouraging, demoralizing failure of what had required so much time and effort to mature, when it was determined, after due consideration in the course of Thursday [May 24], to call a caucus of *bona fide* Union Republican Senators . . ." to agree upon a line of action. Thereafter, the report continued, "Republican Senators will refrain from long speech-making . . . . They are fully impressed with the necessity of acting instead of wasting any more words upon an already thoroughly discussed and understood subject . . . ."[276]

When the Senate met on Wednesday, May 30, Howard presented the amendments agreed upon in the Republican caucus.[277] The major changes were two. (1) At the beginning of Section 1 would be inserted the definition of citizenship. (2) Section 3, instead of denying to rebels the right to vote prior to July 4, 1870, would be converted to bar from federal and State office all who, having taken an oath to support the Constitution, had thereafter engaged in the rebellion. Those changes, being adopted, entered into the Constitution.

As the correspondent had forecast, significant Senate debate on the Fourteenth Amendment was brief.

Senator Luke E. Poland of Vermont had served for seventeen years on that State's highest court; he was a respected lawyer. The proposed privileges and immunities clause, he said, "secures nothing beyond what was intended" by Article IV, Section 2, clause 1.[278] (Thus he *ignored* what Howard had said about the Bill of Rights.) With the rise of the slave power, that guaranty "became really a dead letter." Now that slavery had been overthrown, it was "eminently proper and necessary that Congress should be invested with the power to enforce this provision throughout the country . . . ." He spoke of the due process and equal protection clauses, rather noncommittally, as being in accord with "the very spirit and inspiration of our system of government." Congress, he said, had already shown its intention to uproot all partial State legislation by enacting the Civil Rights Bill.

If Poland spoke precisely, it was his understanding that the new privileges and immunities clause would mean no more than the old; from that it would result that it would impose no restraint upon a State in its treatment of its own citizens. Yet the due process and equal protection clauses unmistakably ran to all persons. Once again, as so often in studying the work of the 39th Congress, one is at a loss to know what the speaker really had in mind. It is to be noted that Poland, like the rest, contemplated action by Congress and ignored direct enforcement by the courts.

Senator Timothy O. Howe of Wisconsin, formerly on the highest bench of that State, was a pronounced Radical. He would have treated the Southern States as defunct, mere territories, for whose government Congress should provide.[279] Regretfully he accepted the milder settle-

---

[276] Dispatch of May 27, in the *Tribune* of June 1.

James, *The Framing of the Fourteenth Amendment*, discusses "Senate Parley" in ch. 10.

[277] Cong. Globe, 39–1, 2890–2900.
[278] Ibid., 2961–64. June 5.
[279] Ibid., App., 217–26. June 5 and 6.

ment. He spoke of Section 1 loosely, as being aimed at unequal laws such as the Black Codes. So far as he knew, no abridgment of the privileges and immunities of citizens of the United States was tolerated in any of the States then represented in Congress. He was "sorry for the necessity which calls upon us" to put Section 1 into the Constitution; evidently in his thought it was made necessary by the "diseased appetite" of Southern communities to deny "to a large portion of their respective populations the plainest and most necessary rights of citizenship."

Senator Davis of Kentucky protested at length against the outrageous regime the Radicals would impose upon the country.[280] The worst he could say against Section 1 was that its definition of citizenship would include the Negroes. The privileges and immunities clause was "unnecessary" because already covered by Article IV, Section 2. Due process was a matter for each State and was already assured by the State constitutions. Equal protection should be left to each State.

Hendricks of Indiana made the last speech before the voting.[281] He called Senator Howard's attention to textual uncertainties. Repeating criticism he had earlier made,[282] he said "I have not heard any Senator accurately define, what are the rights and immunities of citizenship." "What is meant by 'abridging' the rights and immunities of citizens? We do not know, the Senator from Michigan says."

Reverdy Johnson moved to amend Section 1 by striking out the privileges and immunities clause.[283] He said:

> I am decidedly in favor of the first part of the section which defines what citizenship shall be, and in favor of that part of the section which denies to a State the right to deprive any person of life, liberty, or property without due process of law, but I think it quite objectionable to provide [the privileges and immunities clause], simply because I do not understand what will be the effect of that.

Johnson's opposition is not to be classed with that of Garrett Davis, a wrangler, nor even with that of Senator Hendricks. Johnson saw constitutional provisions as they would appear when tested at the Supreme Court bar. He had participated in the Joint Committee, he had heard Howard's presentation—and he still did not understand what the effect of the clause would be. Coming from him, that amounted to a certificate that, for purposes of litigation, the privileges and immunities clause did not have a definite meaning.

No answer was attempted. Without record vote, the motion to strike was rejected.

---

[280] Ibid., App., 231–43. June 7.
[281] Ibid., 3039–40. June 8.
[282] Ibid., 2939. June 4.
[283] Ibid., 3041. June 8.

The entire amendment, as amended to conform to what had been fixed in the Republican caucus, was carried by vote of 33 to 11.[284]

Back in the House, Rogers of New Jersey protested against the Republican Senators writing a constitutional amendment "in a secret cabal with closed doors";[285] a few other inconsequential speeches were made; then by a vote of 120 to 32 the joint resolution was passed, on June 13.[286]

THE FOURTEENTH AMENDMENT BEFORE THE COUNTRY

IN EXPLAINING SECTION I during the summer campaign, Republican leaders repeated the undiscriminating sort of comment that had been heard in Congress. Senator John Sherman said that it was "an embodiment of the Civil Rights Bill, namely: that everybody . . . without regard to color, should have equal rights before the law."[287] Trumbull gave a similar explanation, adding that it was "an unnecessary declaration, perhaps . . . ."[288] Bingham, characteristically, added embellishments: Section I "is the spirit of Christianity embodied in your legislation. It is a simple, strong, plain declaration that equal laws and equal and exact justice shall hereafter be secured within every State of this Union by the combined power of all the people of every State. . . ." No longer could a State "take away freedom of speech," or "condemn men, as felons, to the penitentiary for teaching their fellow men that there is a hereafter, and a reward for those who learn to do well."[289] "The only effect," said Senator Howe, "is to enable the National Legislature . . . to enforce equal justice when the several States refuse to enforce it."[290]

Significantly, Northern Democrats complained of the bad tendency of Section I rather than of any specific legal effect. "Soon thereafter the negro will stand by your side at the polls," warned Senator Hendricks.[291] Orville H. Browning, conservative Republican who had recently become Secretary of the Interior, published a letter that served as a campaign document. "New and enormous powers will be claimed and exercised by Congress," he prophesied, "and the whole structure of our Government will perhaps gradually but yet surely be revolutionized. And so with the Judiciary. If the proposed amendments be

---

[284] Ibid., 3042. June 8.
[285] Ibid., App., 230. June 13.
[286] Ibid., 3149.
[287] *Cincinnati Commercial*, Sept. 29.
[288] *Chicago Tribune*, Aug. 2.
[289] *Cincinnati Commercial*, Aug. 27.
[290] *Chicago Tribune*, Aug. 14.
[291] *Cincinnati Commercial*, Aug. 9.

adopted, they may and certainly will be used substantially to annihilate the State judiciaries."[292] The draft of this letter had been approved at a White House conference by President Johnson, Attorney General Stanbery, Judge Sharkey of Mississippi, and others.[293] If Section 1 had been suspected of having any specific effect to which objection might usefully have been taken in order to arouse the voters, surely Browning would not have confined himself to such foreboding generalities.

These quotations are a fair sampling of what was being said to the voters in preparation for the autumn elections for Congressmen and for State officers—including legislators who would vote upon the ratification of the proposed amendment.[294]

RATIFICATION BY THE LEGISLATURES

WHEN THE LEGISLATURES convened, Republican governors urged prompt ratification, commonly in terms such as these by Governor Lucius Fairchild of Wisconsin: "The people of this state are thoroughly familiar with its provisions . . . ."[295] "I need not discuss the features of this amendment; they have undergone the ordeal of public consideration," said Governor Reuben E. Fenton of New York; "they are understood, appreciated and approved."[296] "No public measure was ever more fully discussed before the people, better understood by them, or received a more distinct and intelligent approval," Governor Oliver P. Morton told the Indiana legislature.[297]

The obvious rightness of Section 1 was another theme. "A simple statement of these propositions is their complete justification," said Governor Jacob D. Cox of Ohio.[298] "So manifestly an axiom of free government as to preclude the necessity of argument," was the comment of Governor Alexander H. Bullock of Massachusetts.[299]

Eleven legislatures ratified in January 1867, bringing the count to 17; February brought 3 more. Ratification by Massachusetts came after a delay of more than two months, caused by men of abolitionist

---

[292] Ibid., Oct. 26.

[293] *Diary of Orville Hickman Browning* (Springfield: Illinois State Historical Library, Vol. I [1850–64], Pease and Randall, eds., 1925; Vol. II [1865–81], Randall, ed., 1933), II, 101. Oct. 20.

[294] A wider selection is given in the article in *Stan. L. Rev.*, 2 (5), at 68–78, cited in note 275; also in Flack, *The Adoption of the Fourteenth Amendment*, ch. 3; and James, *The*

Framing of the Fourteenth Amendment, ch. 12.

[295] Wis. Sen. J. 32; Assembly J. 33. Jan. 9, 1867.

[296] N. Y. Sen. J. 6; Assembly J. 13. Jan. 2.

[297] Ind. Sen. J. 42 (1867); House J. 48.

[298] Ohio Exec. Docs., Part I, 282. Jan. 2, 1867.

[299] Mass. Acts and Resolves, 1867, 789 at 820. Jan. 4.

sentiment who were dissatisfied that the amendment failed to command universal suffrage. During the next year only Nebraska ratified. In March 1868, Iowa (whose legislature met biennially) gave its assent, followed shortly by seven reconstructed States. On July 21, 1868, Congress declared the Fourteenth Amendment to have been adopted.[300]

The Nation reported this accomplishment with the comment that "The Fourteenth Amendment has been so long before the people that the average reader has very likely forgotten just what it is."[301] (It gave a brief summary.) Notwithstanding the pronouncements that it had been thoroughly understood by the voters, we know that in truth it had not been understood even by its framers. A form of words had been made supreme law. That the leading clause of Section 1 would soon wither—that what had seemed a lesser clause would become, for purposes of litigation, the most interesting feature of the Constitution —that Congress would take little part in the unfolding of the amendment—that the Court would become the agent for enforcing Section 1, but that the Justices would never wholly agree upon its meaning: these are among the surprising observations about the Fourteenth Amendment.

---

[300] The actions of the several legislatures, in ratifying or rejecting the amendment, are explained in greater detail in the article in *Stan. L. Rev.*, 2 (5), at 81–132, cited in note 275.

The painful course by which the Southern States came to ratify the amendment was traced in chapters 6 to 12 above.

[301] 7:61. July 23, 1868.

CHAPTER XXI

Privileges of Citizens of the United States: The Slaughter House Cases

To KNOW THE laws, it was written of old, is not merely to hold to their words, but to comprehend as well their force and power.[1] A peculiar wisdom is needed to expound the *Constitution*—a charter intended to endure for ages to come and to be adequate to the unfolding needs of a nation.[2] Its underlying *reason* may govern situations not present to the mind when the text was framed;[3] the particular application with which a general provision was identified at the outset should not so limit its future operation as to produce a public inconvenience—notably when this would deny that perfect equality of rights among citizens which the Constitution contemplates.[4] Interpreted by the Court in this spirit, a concise and felicitously drafted Constitution had sufficed, down to the triumph over slavery.

Theretofore the Court's major work in constitutional law had been to establish the line between the authority of the Nation and the concerns remaining to the States. The Bill of Rights protected the individual only against the National Government, and complaints on any such ground had been exceedingly rare. But now the Court had a new mission: to test, by the standards of the post-war Amendments, the conduct of the State as it exercised its own proper powers upon those within its jurisdiction. Exacting tasks for judicial prudence lay ahead.

---

[1] *Scire leges non hoc est verba earum tenere, sed vim et potestatem.* Digest, I. 3. 17. The sentence comes from Celsus. It was, Kent wrote, the doctrine of "the most illustrious commentators on the Roman law." *Commentaries on American Law*, I, 462.

[2] Marshall, C.J., for the Court in McCulloch v. Maryland, 4 Wheat. 316, 407, 415 (1819).

[3] Marshall, C.J., for the Court in Dartmouth College v. Woodward, 4 Wheat. 518, 644 (1819).

[4] Taney, C.J., for the Court in *The Genesee Chief*, 12 How. 443, 454–460 (1851).

CRANDALL v. NEVADA

"No State can be justified in any device to tax the transit of travel and commerce between States." So one read in President Johnson's message of December 4, 1865: he called upon Congress to guard against "every obstacle to . . . free circulation . . . ."[5]

A case was already in the making. Nevada's first legislature, casting about for ways to support the government, had included in its Revenue Act of 1865 a tax of one dollar upon every passenger leaving the State by public conveyance.[6]

Crandall, agent for the Pioneer Stage Company at Carson City, had refused to file a statement of the number of passengers carried out of State during April, as required by the statute. In the court of a justice of the peace he was committed for contempt—only "constructively," the local newspaper explained.[7] A writ of habeas corpus was sought in

---

[5] The paragraph in full was as follows:

The Constitution confers on Congress the right to regulate commerce among the several States. It is of the first necessity, for the maintenance of the Union, that that commerce should be free and unobstructed. No State can be justified in any device to tax the transit of travel and commerce between States. The position of many States is such that, if they were allowed to take advantage of it for purposes of local revenue, the commerce between States might be injuriously burdened, or even virtually prohibited. It is best, while the country is still young, and while the tendency to dangerous monopolies of this kind is still feeble, to use the power of Congress so as to prevent any selfish impediment to the free circulation of men and merchandise. A tax on travel and merchandise, in their transit, constitutes one of the worst forms of monopoly, and the evil is increased if coupled with a denial of the choice of route. When the vast extent of our country is considered, it is plain that every obstacle to free circulation of commerce between the States ought to be sternly guarded against by appropriate legislation, within the limits of the Constitution.

Cong. Globe, 39–1, App., I, 3.

Johnson's message was written by George Bancroft, historian, former Secretary of the Navy, diplomat, and Democratic politician.

The most unpopular of the monopolies at which the paragraph was aimed were those enjoyed by the Camden & Amboy and the Baltimore & Ohio on the route between New York and Washington. Supra, pp. 724, 735.

[6] The Ways and Means Committee of the Senate, in reporting a general financial plan, recommended:

Property taxes, to yield	$225,250
Tax of 1% on proceeds of mines	50,000
Stamp tax, similar to that of U.S. Govt. ..	70,000
Capitation tax on passengers leaving State	10,000
Poll tax of $4 on males aged 21 to 60	20,000
	$375,250

Golden Hill Evening News, Jan. 21, 1865.

[7] *Carson Daily Appeal*, June 7, 1865.

the Nevada Supreme Court, on the ground that the exaction was unconstitutional.[8]

The court observed that only if it upheld the tax could review be had in the Supreme Court. Considering what the several Justices had said in pertinent cases, the Nevada judges concluded that the preponderance of opinion was that, in the absence of any expression from Congress, such action by the State should be sustained. It was ordered that the petitioner be remanded.[9]

A writ of error was docketed in the Supreme Court on December 27, 1865, on the same day, and immediately preceding, *Ex parte Milligan*. But whereas the latter was advanced for argument, and was decided on April 3, 1866, *Crandall* awaited its turn, and was decided on March 16, 1868.[10]

Meanwhile the Stage Company lost interest: no brief was filed, no counsel appeared on its behalf.[11]

---

[8] *Ex parte* Crandall, 1 Nev. 291 (April term, 1865).

[9] See note 11, infra.

[10] Crandall v. Nevada, 6 Wall. 35.

[11] Curiosity stimulated by a motion to dismiss, argued by Philip Phillips on December 20, 1867, led to an inquiry into the circumstances under which this memorable case came to the Supreme Court.

As agent for the Pioneer Stage Line at Carson City, Crandall did business at the office of Wells, Fargo & Company; he was also agent for the latter. The significance of this will appear. The *Carson Daily Appeal* for July 4, 1865, carries, over Crandall's name, Pioneer's advertisement of two stages daily, from Virginia City, via Carson City, to Sacramento; next below is the advertisement of the Wells Fargo Fast Freight Line, also carrying passengers, between the same points. (Virginia City, north of Carson City, was then Nevada's chief town, and the most important stop on the overland line between Salt Lake City and Sacramento. The distance between Carson City and Sacramento was 145 miles.)

On the first Monday in April, 1865, the sheriff of Ormsby County demanded of Crandall a statement of the number of passengers carried out of State by Pioneer during the preceding month, as required by the Revenue Act of March 8, 1865. Upon failure to comply, the sheriff brought Crandall before a justice of the peace on May 1. Conviction followed, with judgment that he be confined in the county jail for one day.

Thereupon, on May 1, Chief Justice Lewis granted a writ of habeas corpus to bring Crandall before the Supreme Court. The minutes show that the matter was argued on May 1 and 2; decision was reserved.

On May 31, 1865, the Chief Justice delivered the court's opinion, sustaining the statute. It concluded:

The time having expired during which the petitioner could be held under the commitment of the court below, no order can be made remanding him to the custody of the sheriff, but our views here may be a guide in subsequent cases of this character.

So it appeared in the transcript certified to the Supreme Court by the Clerk of the Supreme Court of Nevada. And so it appears in *Ex parte* Crandall, 1 Nevada 294, at 314.

On that record, the case sought to be carried to the Supreme Court was moot: Crandall had been discharged.

On November 9, 1865, however, the Clerk made a further certificate, to an amendatory order purporting to have been made by the State court

The question was one of first impression—and of first importance. Most nearly resembling it among Supreme Court adjudications

on May 31: that Crandall be remanded to the custody of the sheriff, to be dealt with pursuant to the order of the justice of the peace; it was further ordered that the concluding paragraph of the opinion be expunged, and the new disposition substituted.

Rule No. 8 of the Supreme Court, Return to Writ of Error, etc., contained this requirement:

2. No cause will hereafter be heard until a complete record, containing in itself, without references *aliunde*, all the papers, exhibits, depositions, and other proceedings which are necessary to the hearing of this court, shall be filed.

Rules of Dec. Term 1858, 21 How. v, vii.

Would the Court, when Crandall v. Nevada was reached, hear it on this state of the record?

Among the Case Files for matters before the Supreme Court, preserved in the National Archives, that for Crandall v. Nevada contains several items worthy of notice. First, a letter of December 9, 1865, to Clerk Middleton from A. Ford of the law office of Ford & Baldwin, 84 Broadway, New York City:

I have been requested by Messrs Wells Fargo & Co of this City to file the enclosed printed points "with the Clerk of the U. S. Supreme Court", and transmit them for that purpose.

I don't know, if any, what fees are required on filing, if you will advise me I will remit the amount forthwith.

There is also a two-page printed document, containing Facts in the Crandall case, and then Points of Argument. At the foot the source is indicated as "William Crandall P. P. [per proxy]."

The Clerk replied on December 18:

. . . The record of the case is here, but has not been docketed for want of security as required by the rules of this Court.

If you will send me draft of Messrs Wells, Fargo & Co for $200, the amount required I will at once enter the case.

By Rule No. 10, Security for Costs —Printing Records—Attachment for Costs, the Clerk was directed to take a bond or a deposit in the amount of $200, to secure his fees.

On December 26, Wells, Fargo & Co., New York and California Express and Exchange Company, also of 84 Broadway, New York, sent their check for $200 "for fee in the filing of 'Ex parte Crandall.' "

The Clerk replied on December 27: ". . . the case is now entered on the docket—No 349."

(By December Term 1866 it had advanced to become No. 237; at December Term 1867, when it was decided, it was No. 85.)

Philip Phillips was retained by the State of Nevada.

No counsel had appeared for the plaintiff in error. Evidently the Stage Company was not sufficiently concerned to go to that expense. Evidently Wells Fargo's interest was not such as to induce a further outlay. (Presumably this was by reason of the impending completion of the transcontinental railroad, passing through Nevada. After that event, Wells Fargo's advertisement in Carson City was that its express for California and the East left daily at 5:30 P.M. "making close connections with the Trains East and West." *Carson Daily Appeal*, Dec. 30, 1869.

In anticipation of the time when the Court would reach the *Crandall* case, Phillips must choose a course of action. He might move to dismiss by reason of the defective form of the record: if the attempted patch was not accepted, the case was moot. If a ruling on the merits of Nevada's tax was desired, it was advisable to raise

was the *Passenger Cases* in 1849.[12] New York and Massachusetts had imposed taxes on aliens arriving from abroad; the income was denominated "hospital moneys" by the former, and "for the support of foreign paupers" by the latter. These exactions were held unconstitutional by five Justices in five separate opinions; Taney, C.J., and Daniel, Nelson, and Woodbury dissented. New York's statute also reached citizens from other States, but that was not involved in the litigation. While Taney would permit a State to indemnify itself for "sanatory precautions" incident to the arrival of foreigners, he took occasion to say that it would be otherwise as to American citizens coming from other States:

> We are all citizens of the United States; and, as members of the same community, must have the right to pass and repass through every part of it without interruption, as freely as in our own States . . . .[13]

that objection in advance, before preparing to argue the merits. Under Rule 16,

> Where there is no appearance for the plaintiff in error when the case is called for trial, the defendant may have the plaintiff called, and dismiss the writ of error, or may open the record, and pray for an affirmance.

In short, under this rule counsel could have the matter dismissed, or could present an argument and seek a decision on the merits.

Presumably on instructions from the Nevada State authorities, a decision on the merits was sought. And, prudently, on Friday, December 20, 1867, Phillips moved to dismiss for want of jurisdiction. (The motion is in the Case File.) On Monday next, Chase, C.J., delivered a short opinion, concluding that "We think that the order thus certified must be taken as a part of the record . . . ," just as when a court below was called upon to certify something that had been omitted. Thus jurisdiction was sustained. 131 U.S. App. lxxxiii, 18 L. Ed. 744.

When on February 19, 1868, Crandall v. Nevada was reached, argument on behalf of the State was presented by Thomas J. D. Fuller and

Phillips. Fuller (1808–76), a Democrat, had represented a Maine district in Congress from 1849 to 1857 (overlapping Phillips' service of one term as a Congressman from Alabama). Next he was Second Auditor of the Treasury under Buchanan; thereafter he practiced in Washington.

This long note suggests that Crandall v. Nevada had a dubious title to be taken as a "case or controversy" within the jurisdiction of the Court. Also, Nevada might have had the case dismissed—in which event the Crandall matter would have disappeared save for entries hidden in the Docket and Minutes. It was by choice that a decision on the merits was sought —resulting in a defeat for Nevada, and an extraordinary pronouncement by the Court. Further, this footnote serves to show that it may prove revealing to resort to sources beyond the range of materials conventionally used in writing about the Court. Finally, the significance of the Rules is illustrated. Those here quoted are from the then current Rules as revised and corrected at December Term 1858. Another revision was adopted on May 1, 1871, and the next on January 7, 1884.

[12] 7 How. 283.
[13] At 492.

Evidently the Justices of 1867 were perplexed and divided about the doctrine to be implied from the Commerce Clause where Congress had remained silent. Through the years there had been a wide diversity of opinion. In this *Nevada* case, only the State's side was presented. There was unanimity that, although it was represented to be a legitimate tax upon a business, this exaction should be condemned. Justice Miller undertook the preparation of an opinion to support that result. He summarized the import of previous decisions, and said that "in view of the principles on which those cases were decided" it was "not easy" to maintain that the Nevada tax infringed the Commerce Clause.

But the Court did not concede that its ruling must be based on the Commerce Clause. Here he drew from Taney's remarks in 1849 a line of thought adequate to reach a proper decision. Miller wrote:

> The people of these United States constitute one nation. They have a government in which all of them are deeply interested. This government has necessarily a capital . . . , where its principal operations are conducted. . . . That government has a right to call to this point any or all of its citizens to aid in its service . . . . The government, also, has its offices of secondary importance in all other parts of the country. . . . In all these it demands the services of its citizens . . . , and no power can exist in a State to obstruct this right that would not enable it to defeat the purposes for which the government was established.
>
> . . . .
>
> But if the government has these rights on her own account, the citizen also has correlative rights. He has the right to come to the seat of government to assert any claim he may have upon that government, or to transact any business he may have with it . . . . [H]e has a right to free access to its sea-ports . . . , and this right is in its nature independent of the will of any State over whose soil he must pass in the exercise of it.

These principles, Justice Miller concluded, must govern the present case. The judgment of the Nevada court was reversed.

Justice Clifford (Chase, C. J., concurring with him) agreed with the result, but could not accept the expansive reasoning: judgment should have been placed on the Commerce Clause.

> I am clear that the State legislature cannot impose any such burden upon commerce among the several States. Such commerce is secured against such legislation in the States by the Constitution, irrespective of any Congressional action.

Presently the Court overcame the hesitation about the Commerce Clause which had led to Miller's accommodating opinion in *Crandall*; it held that, in the silence of Congress, a tax falling on the interstate movement of persons or goods was invalid. Thereafter *Crandall* came to be treated as a holding on the Commerce Clause.[14]

There was nothing in the record to suggest that the stage company's passengers were engaged on business for or with the Government. Justice Miller might well have dwelt upon a wider proposition in Taney's remarks: that a member of the national community is privileged to pass and repass throughout the land, even on purely private affairs.

Four months after the decision in *Crandall*, the Fourteenth Amendment, expressly recognizing the privileges and immunities of citizens of the United States, became a part of the Constitution.

When in 1941 the Court unanimously condemned California's statute that forbade the bringing in of nonresident indigents, four of the Justices thought it proper to place the decision on the Privileges and Immunities Clause of the Amendment. "[T]he migration of a human being," said Justice Jackson, does not "fit easily into my notions as to what is commerce"; it is of a higher order, said Justice Douglas, than the "movement of cattle, fruit, steel and coal across State lines."[15]

---

[14] The Case of the State Freight Tax, 15 Wall. 232 (1873), held that such a tax offended the Commerce Clause, noting that the majority in *Crandall* had decided on other grounds. Railroad Co. v. Maryland, 21 Wall. 456 (1875), reaffirmed the proposition in *State Freight Tax*, citing that and *Crandall* together; it held, however, that the State's stipulation in the charter for a portion of the railroad's earnings was not invalid. Justice Miller dissented from that holding.

In Henderson v. Mayor of New York, 92 U.S. 259 (1876), Miller explained that *Crandall* had come at a time when doctrine was unsettled; thereupon for a unanimous Court he pronounced invalid an exaction of $1.50 for each passenger from out-of-State, set as being in commutation for a costly security against the passenger becoming a public charge. In his *Lectures on the Constitution of the United States* (New York and Albany: Banks and Brothers, published in 1891, after his death), Miller treated *Crandall* as a case on the Commerce Clause. Pp. 462–64.

In Helson v. Kentucky, 279 U.S. 245, 251 (1929), it was said that, insofar as the *Crandall* opinion conceded that the Nevada tax did not in itself amount to a regulation of interstate commerce, it "has not been followed," citing Henderson v. Mayor of New York.

[15] Edwards v. California, 314 U.S. 160, where the Court condemned on the basis of the Commerce Clause, overruling Mayor of New York v. Miln, 11 Pet. 102 (1837). Jackson, J., spoke for himself. Douglas, J. (Black and Murphy, JJ., with him) said: "I cannot accede to the suggestion [in Helson v. Kentucky, supra, note 14, and Colgate v. Harvey, 296 U.S. 404, concurring opinion of Stone, J., at 444 (1935)] that the Commerce Clause is the appropriate explanation of Crandall v. Nevada. . . ."

CHANCE MEETING WITH
THE FOURTEENTH AMENDMENT

OFTEN IT IS instructive to inquire, Why was it that something, seemingly to be expected, failed to happen? One might have supposed that it would be a case on behalf of Negroes, or the suit of some citizen from the North complaining of treatment in the South, that first raised the Fourteenth Amendment at the bar of the Supreme Court. Instead it was a suit by Southern whites, complaining against Carpetbag legislation; the right they would vindicate was not a political but an economic liberty—namely, to carry on the business of slaughtering cattle, free from a monopoly conferred by the legislature upon a favored group of incorporators. This was all out of accord with what members of Congress had had in mind in their debates. To understand why the foreseen failed to occur, one must take account of developments subsequent to the submission of the proposed Amendment in June 1866.

By the time the Amendment went into effect, in July 1868, Congressional Reconstruction had done its work. The once-rebel States were controlled by Unionists of varied antecedents. Their new constitutions proclaimed political equality. Moreover, the Border States that had not seceded were moving into line. In Missouri it was now the Southern sympathizers who sought the poor privilege of equality. Testimonial competence without regard to color—the great touchstone of the moment—was soon yielded in Missouri, West Virginia, and Maryland, and dilatorily by Kentucky and Delaware: by constitutional provision, by statute, or at least by bowing to the civil rights legislation of Congress.[16]

---

[16] Missouri: Gen. Stats. 1866, in ch. 114, sec. 8, on incompetency, omitted the former provision on Negroes. West Virginia: Acts of 1866, ch. 89, p. 85; Code of 1870, ch. 130, sec. 24. Maryland: Constitution of 1867, Art. III, Sec. 53. "No person shall be incompetent, as a witness, on account of race or color, unless hereafter so declared by Act of the General Assembly." Kentucky: Gen. Stats. 1873, ch. 37, sec. 28. The federal Civil Rights Act, as it gave such competence to Negroes, had been held invalid by the State court in Bowlin v. Commonwealth, 2 Bush 5 (1867). Delaware: Rev. Stats. of 1852 as amended (1874), ch. 52, omitted the basic disqualification of Negroes, because "not enforced by the Authorities of this State, being in conflict with acts of Congress." In 1880, in State of Delaware v. Neal, Comegys, C.J., said: "Ever since the last civil rights bill was passed by Congress [in 1875], negroes have been admitted as witnesses in all cases, civil and criminal, tried in our courts; whereas before they could give no evidence in any such cases against a white person except in case of crime, and to prevent a failure of justice, when no white person was present at the time of the transaction competent to give

XXI: *Privileges of Citizens of the United States*

Of the Northern States that had bordered on slavery, those most influenced by Southern sentiment—Indiana and Illinois—were responding to events. In 1866 the Indiana court held invalid, under the Privileges and Immunities provision of Article IV, a constitutional command of 1851 that "No negro or mulatto shall come into, or settle in the State . . . ."[17] Illinois in 1865 admitted the testimony of the Negro against the white.[18] Various racial discriminations remained, on the statute books and by judicial decisions, in the Northern States; a complainant, given resources and determination, could early have brought litigation that might have reached the Supreme Court. But no such case came up.

On the side of Congressional action, the Civil Rights Act of 1866 had been sustained and applied on the circuit in conspicuous decisions by Justice Swayne[19] and Chief Justice Chase[20] in 1867.

---

testimony." The State of Delaware vs. William Neal. Opinions of Court of Oyer and Terminer, at p. 14 (1880). Separately published in connection with Neal v. Delaware, 103 U.S. 370 (1881), and filed with the Record and Briefs in that case.

[17] Smith v. Moody, 26 Ind. 299. The constitutional provision was stricken out by an amendment in 1881.

[18] Laws of 1865, p. 105.

[19] In United States v. Rhodes, Fed. Case No. 16,151: on October 10, 1867, denying a motion in arrest of judgment, he had concluded, "We entertain no doubt of the constitutionality of the act in all its provisions." Defendants had been convicted in the federal court under the Civil Rights Act of 1866, in that, being white men, they had on May 1, 1866, burglarized the house of N. T., a United States citizen of the African race, denied the right to testify against the defendants in the courts of Kentucky.

This was denounced as an "unworthy perversion of a high judgment seat" in a bitter speech by Senator Garrett Davis of Kentucky, on January 14, 1868. Cong. Globe, 40–2, 492–99.

[20] *In re* Turner, Fed. Case No. 14,247. In the Circuit Court for the District of Maryland, he released on habeas corpus a Negro girl who, when Maryland's emancipation became effective in November 1864, had been indentured under a statute that made the lot of a Negro apprentice much harder than that of a white. For the petitioners, Stockwell and Nathan M. Pusey argued that, by force of the Civil Rights Act, the law for white apprentices must be applied. "The respondent said he wished to retain the girl, but did not feel sufficient interest in the case to spend any money on it."

The Chief Justice held that the restraint amounted to "involuntary servitude" within the condemnation of the Thirteenth Amendment, and that it was invalid under the equal rights provision of Sec. 1 of the Civil Rights Act. This was on October 13, 1867— before the Fourteenth Amendment with its equal protection clause had been adopted.

It had been reported that there were many hundreds of incidents of unjust apprenticing in Eastern Maryland. *The Nation*, 4:3, Jan. 3, 1867. Now that journal commented, "to Judge Chase fairly belongs the honor of having been in at the death of the 'peculiar institution.'" 5:325, Oct. 24, 1867.

Times would come when that statute, as reenacted and amplified, would be closely scrutinized; but for the moment the federal judges were enforcing it unhesitatingly.

This observation that what might have been expected failed to occur does not explain why the unexpected did. The New Orleans slaughter house litigation was fortuitous. In 1869 the Louisiana legislature carried through a corrupt job, which was nothing rare at that time and place. This was in a city where the extraordinary skill of ex-Justice John A. Campbell was available to the victims; it was his resourcefulness that injected the claim of constitutional right that carried the case to the Supreme Court and won the assent of four out of nine Justices. Some different incident might have become the no-less-improbable first case on the Fourteenth Amendment.

MINOR v. BOARD OF EDUCATION OF CINCINNATI

HINDSIGHT DISCOVERS VARIOUS possibilities in the newspapers of the day. In "Religion in Common Schools," the *New York Tribune* of January 28, 1869, drew attention to "the claim advanced by certain Roman Catholics and certain also of other persuasions for a partition of Public School Moneys in the interest (as they hold) of Religion." After stating the arguments advanced for that claim, the *Tribune* gave reasons for supporting the existing public school system. Ample resources for religious instruction existed in the churches and Sunday Schools; moreover,

> At present, the reading of a brief extract from the Christian Scriptures is a part of the daily routine in our schools: the Catholic version being used where Catholics predominate. Hebrews and other non-Christians might plausibly object to this as unfair, yet we have never heard of their doing so . . . .

The editorial called upon men of all creeds "to stand by our Common School system, and not allow it to be pulled to pieces. . . ."

In Cincinnati, on November 1, 1869, the board of education resolved,

> That religious instruction, and the reading of religious books, including the Holy Bible, are prohibited in the common schools of Cincinnati, it being the true object and intent of this rule to allow the children of the parents of all sects and opinions, in matters of faith and worship, to enjoy alike the benefits of the common-school fund.

Accordingly the existing prescription of Bible reading with "appropriate singing" as an opening exercise was repealed.[21]

Next day Minor and thirty-six others filed suit in the Superior Court "on behalf of themselves and many others, citizens and taxpayers of Cincinnati." Their petition alleged that the reading of the Bible had been a daily exercise since 1829; that the text books then in use contained selections from the Bible inculcating religious truths, and that the rule just passed would exclude them;[22] that a large majority of the school children received no religious instruction or knowledge of the Bible except what was communicated in the city schools; that such instruction was necessary to good citizenship, and was required by the Northwest Ordinance of 1787 and by the Ohio constitution. Wherefore they prayed for an injunction.[23]

---

[21] *The Bible in the Public Schools. Arguments in the Case of John D. Minor et al. v. The Board of Education of the City of Cincinnati . . . with the Opinions and Decision of the Court* (Cincinnati: Robert Clarke & Co., 1870). At p. 6. Also, Board of Education v. Minor et al., 23 Ohio St. 211 (1873); Ann. Cyc. 1869, 552.

The existing regulation, adopted in 1852, was as follows:

The opening exercises in every department shall commence by reading a portion of the Bible by or under direction of the teacher, and appropriate singing by the pupils. The pupils of the Common Schools may read such version of the sacred scriptures as their parents or guardians may prefer, provided that such preference of any version, except the one now in use [the King James version], be communicated by the parents and guardians to the principal teachers, and that no notes or marginal readings be allowed in the schools, or comments made by teachers on the text of any version that is or may be introduced.

The Bible in the Public Schools, supra, at 7; 23 Ohio St. 211–12.

It did not appear that this option had ever been tested in practice.

The Bible in the Public Schools, with a new introduction by Robert G. McCloskey, was reprinted by the Da Capo Press, New York, in 1967.

[22] By stipulation, *McGuffey's New Eclectic Readers*, 1st to 6th, were made a part of the record as texts long in use.

There was a special local interest: they were published by a Cincinnati firm.

[23] *The Bible in the Public Schools*, supra, at 6–10.

The Northwest Ordinance declared that "Religion, morality, and knowledge being necessary to good government and the happiness of mankind, schools and the means of education shall forever be encouraged." "The constitution and government" of States formed in the Northwest Territory "shall be republican, and in conformity to the principles contained in these articles . . . ." Arts. III, V.

Ohio's constitutions—that of 1802 and that of 1851—had drawn from that language. The Bill of Rights of 1851, Art. I at Sec. 7, spoke of an indefeasible right to worship according to the dictates of conscience; no person should be compelled to support any form of worship against his consent; no preference should be given by law to any religious society, nor any interference with the rights of conscience permitted.

Religion, morality, and knowledge, being essential to good government, it shall be the duty of the General Assembly to pass suitable laws to protect every religious denomination in the

The division within the board was reported to have been:

	For exclusion	Against
Catholics	10	..
Free Thinkers	8	1
Protestants	3	13
Jews	1	1

On the Superior Court sat Judges Hagans[24] (Methodist), Storer[25] (Episcopalian), and Taft[26] (who had rejected his Baptist background to become a Unitarian).

While the resolutions were pending, a meeting in opposition was held—the largest gathering since the war; fifteen hundred were turned away. Rufus King, William M. Ramsey, and George R. Sage, all leaders at the bar, were the speakers. They warned that there was a coalition between infidels, who denied the authority of the Bible, and Romanists, whose aim was a division of the school fund. The former, said Ramsey, would treat as a delusion the Bible which Milton and Sir Walter Scott, John Harvard and Jonathan Edwards and Benjamin Franklin had trusted as the word of God. Sage said that the Bible had been an essential part of instruction in the common schools since long before the Declaration of Independence. The nation must be either Christian or Infidel—and he who chose the latter was more deadly than the vilest rebel.[27]

These were the counsellors who would represent the plaintiffs.

Retained by the board were lawyers of even more memorable distinction: Stanley Matthews (an elder in the Presbyterian church);

---

peaceable enjoyment of its own mode of public worship, and to encourage schools, and the means of instruction.
It was around the quoted passage that the Cincinnati controversy was fought.

[24] When the National Convention, to amend the Constitution to declare the nation subject to the authority of the Bible, met in Cincinnati in February 1872, "the Hon. M. B. Hagans, Judge of the Superior Court of Cincinnati," was listed among those joining in the call. On being chosen to preside he said, "I firmly believe the vast majority of the people of the United States approve . . . the purpose of this movement. . . ." *Cincinnati Commercial*, Feb. 1, 1872.

[25] Bellamy Storer (1796–1875) in his youth had been active in the "Fly-

ing Artillery," a band who went from town to town to stimulate revivals. Coming from Maine to Ohio, he had been a leading Whig, and served in Congress, 1835–37. Judge of the Superior Court, 1854 to 1872, and professor in the Cincinnati Law School, 1855 to 1874.

[26] Alphonso Taft (1810–91), after studying law at Yale, had settled in Cincinnati. He sat on the Superior Court from 1865 to 1872, and served as Attorney General of the United States from June 1876 until the Grant Administration closed in March 1877. William Howard Taft, President and Chief Justice, was his son.

[27] The *Christian Statesman*, Oct. 15, 1869, at 29–31, reported at considerable length.

George Hoadly (a great-great-grandson of Jonathan Edwards); and Johann Bernard Stallo (born in Germany of a family of schoolmasters, devoted to the pursuit of science and the popular dissemination of learning, a follower of Jefferson, and an organizer of Cincinnati Germans in the suppression of the rebellion).

Crowds filled the courtroom and gallery, day after day, as argument went on—running to 325 pages in the 420-page report. Ramsey[28] said that Ohio's constitution meant that "religion was to be taught in the schools even as it was to be taught in the churches." It was said, to be sure, that the Jew's Testament was in Hebrew, and that the Catholic did not accept the King James version. "To all this I answer: 'De minimis non curat lex.'" The right of conscience must receive "a sensible, practical construction." He adopted "every word of Webster" in his argument in *Vidal v. Girard's Executors.*

Much was made over that great case in the Supreme Court in 1844.[29] Stephen Girard had devised the residue of his estate to the Mayor, Aldermen, and Citizens of Philadelphia in trust, to establish a school for "poor white male orphans"; the boys should be taught "the purest principles of morality," free from the excitement of sectarian controversy; no ecclesiastic should ever be admitted within the premises. Daniel Webster, on behalf of the heirs, sought to defeat the trust: it was "derogatory to the Christian religion" and "contrary to the public law and policy of Pennsylvania." For three days he made "an address to the prejudices of the clergy" (Justice Story's comment). In the outcome, Story, J., for a unanimous Court, said that while Christianity was, in a qualified sense, a part of the common law of Pennsylvania, Girard's trust was not "inconsistent with the Christian religion, or . . . opposed to any known policy of the State . . . ."[30]

Stallo,[31] opening the case for the board, pointed to what the Supreme Court of Ohio had laid down in *Bloom v. Richards,*[32] in 1853: Judge Thurman had there said that it was not true that one religion was a part of the law, and all others only tolerated; rather, that every individual was protected in his belief or disbelief, not by mere tolerance, but by an indefeasible right of conscience, which the constitution of Ohio put beyond the control of government. Stallo asked, had

---

[28] The *Bible in the Public Schools,* supra, at 25–58.

[29] 2 How. 127. On appeal from the Circuit Court for Eastern Pennsylvania. Jurisdiction was based on diversity of citizenship.

[30] Long afterwards, Girard's trust was back in the Supreme Court: in Pennsylvania *et al.* v. Board of Directors of City Trusts of the City of Philadelphia, 353 U.S. 230 (1957), it was held that the Board was an agency of the State, and that for it to refuse to admit Negro boys solely because of their race was a violation of the Fourteenth Amendment.

[31] *The Bible in the Public Schools,* supra, at 59–105.

[32] 2 Ohio St. 387.

the Christian church ever welcomed new truth? It had opposed Galileo, Copernicus, Kepler, and Newton, and now it was at war with zoologists. This exchange followed:

> Judge Storer: Do you allude to the man who thinks that our ancestry runs back into the animal creation?
> Stallo: I allude to the followers of Charles Darwin.

Counsel suggested that the case was turning into a controversy whether the schools were to be allowed to find truth from such as Darwin, or must stick to the truth as presented in the McGuffey readers.

George Hoadly,[33] on the same side, made an able argument on the theme that a court of law could not properly assume control of the board's discretion in such matters as what views of science should be presented, what readers should be adopted; that it was incompatible with the judicial function to pass upon religious questions such as must result if the court ordered that the Bible be read.

Sage,[34] for the plaintiffs, said that

> The Bible is essential to religion, and religion is essential to good government, and both are, therefore, under the protection and foster-ing care of the government. . . . It follows as a legal proposition that the truth and inspiration of the Holy Scriptures, and the divinity of the religion which they teach are not to be questioned in a court of justice.

Stanley Matthews,[35] closing for the board, said that the McGuffey readers, with their selections from the Bible, were not used as instruction in religion but as exercises in English, on the same foot-ing as Hamlet's soliloquy and Macbeth's speech to his drawn dagger. By our republican institutions, he said, in the presence of the law,

> every citizen, without respect to religion, race, color, condition, or any of the accidents of human life, was absolutely and perfectly equal. I admit that there has been up to this time only an approxima-tion to the model, to the ideal. We have not yet arrived at the full fruition and realization of that dream, but we are approaching it; we have nearly arrived at it. The adoption of the Fifteenth Amend-ment to the Federal Constitution[36] will bring into the full realization of the fundamental law that all citizens are absolutely, in all respects, equal before the law, in civil rights, in religious rights, in all the rights

---

[33] *The Bible in the Public Schools,* supra, at 106–48.
[34] Ibid., at 149–206.
[35] Ibid., at 207–87.

[36] Proposed by Congress on Feb-ruary 26, 1869, it had been ratified by twenty States when Matthews spoke, in early December 1869.

that spring from the possession of human life—in every thing which makes a man, a man. . . .

Rufus King,[37] closing for the plaintiffs, told the court that "McGuffey's Readers are enough for my case. They were, fortunately, put in evidence, and your Honors will find marked . . . what is denominated by all dictionaries, . . . religious and moral instruction . . . ." The common schools were maintained expressly to teach "religion, morality, and knowledge."

Judgment was announced in February 1870: the board was permanently enjoined from carrying out its resolutions. In the constitution's provision for the protection of "religion, morality, and knowledge," Judge Hagans and Judge Storer found a mandate that the Bible must be taught in the public schools.[38]

---

[37] *The Bible in the Public Schools,* supra, at 289–349.

[38] *The Nation* of February 17, 1870, 10:98, commented:

The theological discursus of the Court cannot but be regarded as unfortunate . . . , as there is hardly one of its propositions which will bear examination, or which a Catholic, Jew, or Rationalist will not vehemently dispute. . . . We are now fairly in for one of the most exciting questions the country has ever had to deal with. The case, of course, goes up on appeal.

As the journals of that time testify, the country did become greatly excited over the action of the Cincinnati board. No such startling assault upon the Protestant religion had ever before been attempted, said the *Dubuque* (Iowa) *Times,* November 24, 1869. The *Muscatine* (Iowa) *Journal,* November 3, commented that if "the bigotry and intolerance" of the school board ever became the prevalent sentiment, then "we may expect the re-enactment of the terrible scenes witnessed in France during the revolution fitly called 'the Reign of Terror,' when an attempt was made to blot out in bloodshed the Bible and the Christian Sabbath . . . ." The *Keokuk Gate City* saw beneath the surface a Catholic attack upon the public schools, and the *Burlington Hawk-Eye* deplored "heated and vio-

lent" discussion but said that certainly "the majority must rule;" each journal, however, quoted a wide range of opinions. (*Gate City,* Nov. 14, 30; Dec. 5, 25; *Hawk-Eye,* Nov. 11, 14.) Inter alia, *The Advance* (of Chicago, Congregationalist): "We have no right to insist that our wishes shall be gratified in religious respects, against the scruples of others, and in connection with institutions supported by a public tax on all property . . . ." *The Standard* (of Chicago, Baptist): "Germany sends us infidels and Ireland sends us a bigoted, persecuting priesthood . . . . Under the influence of the infidels the Sabbath is in danger of being secularized; under the influence of the priests all that redeems our public schools from entire secularization is also in danger . . . ." *The Western Watchman* (of St. Louis, Catholic): "We are glad at this discomfiture of the Puritans . . . because we hope that . . . a compromise may be agreed upon—one founded on an equitable distribution of the school money among the various denominations . . . ."

In Cincinnati, after arguments had closed, Rev. W. C. McCune of the Lincoln Park Presbyterian Church preached a sermon to condemn, in particular, the part taken by Judge Matthews, "an elder with a national reputation in the Presbyterian Church." He must have realized that "his professional interests are best

Judge Taft, dissenting, held that religious freedom meant

> absolute equality before the law, of all religious opinions and sects
> . . . . The government is neutral, and, while protecting all, it prefers
> none, and it disparages none.

Ninety-three years later the Supreme Court of the United States adopted those expressions as its own when in *Abington School District v. Schempp*[39] it held that prescribed reading of the Bible in the public schools was forbidden by the Fourteenth Amendment.

On writ of error the board took the case to the Ohio Supreme Court, where, three years later, it won a reversal.[40]

The Cincinnati controversy was a matter of prime concern to the association seeking a constitutional amendment to recognize Almighty God as the author of National Existence, Jesus Christ as the Ruler of Nations, and the Bible as the fountain of law. It met in national convention at Pittsburgh on March 3 and 4, 1870. Its president, William Strong, had excused himself: he had just become a Justice of the Supreme Court.[41] Rev. H. H. George of Cincinnati was reported to have told the convention of the experience in his city:

> The enemies of the Bible have been defeated, it is true, in the Superior Court. But the Supreme Court of the State has granted a writ of error. Suppose . . . their defeat [in the appellate court] . . . . Will they rest the case there? No! . . . They will carry the conflict to the United States Supreme Court. Judge Taft had told him that the case could go there on the principle that the decision in Ohio, if affirmed by the Supreme Court of the State, was contrary to the

---

promoted by retaining his popularity with Christians, and with those who act with them in this case, and he certainly foresaw that this popularity would be impaired by taking sides against these classes in this matter." The preacher went on to quote numerous propositions in Matthews' argument, which were pronounced to be grievously erroneous.

The sermon concluded with a warning to infidels and Roman Catholics that while their rights were conceded, "if you persist in this attempt to wrest from our children this Bible, to prohibit all religious instruction, during all their school life, then . . . we will resist you unto the end."

The sermon was reprinted in extenso in the *Cincinnati Daily En-*

quirer, Monday morning, December 13, 1869.

[39] 374 U.S. 203, 215 (1963).

[40] Board of Education v. Minor *et al.*, 23 Ohio St. 211 (1873).

[41] Letter of Feb. 26, 1870. *The Christian Statesman* of Mar. 15, 1870. See supra, p. 722.

That journal, the organ of the association, reported that "Jews and others in the Eastern cities" had been opposed to his confirmation because of his support of the Christian amendment; Strong had "submitted that not he, but they were open to the charge of intolerance." The journal rejoiced that Strong "occupies now so influential a position in the courts of the land . . . ." 3:113, April 1, 1870.

U. S. Constitution. Now, if the question is decided by the national constitution, where is the clause in that document that will secure us the Bible in our schools? . . .

The speaker's conclusion was that although Chief Justice Chase and his brethren were Christian men, they were "under oath to judge by the written Constitution," without regard to personal feelings or popular sentiment. And so judging, they "must decide against the Bible." It followed that "We can have no security for it but a Constitutional recognition of the Bible as the fountain of our laws."[42]

As this clergyman had understood Judge Taft, in the event that the Supreme Court of Ohio affirmed the judgment, the board could take this case to the Supreme Court on the ground that a claim under the federal Constitution had been denied. It would be exceedingly interesting to know exactly what Judge Taft did say, and what constitutional claim he had in mind. So far as appears in the report, no such point had been made in the pleadings or even suggested in the argument. Pretty surely the clergyman had failed precisely to apprehend.[43]

However, as will be brought out presently, Justice Bradley on the circuit, in June 1870, spoke of "the entire equality of all creeds and religions before the law" as being embraced within the meaning of the Fourteenth Amendment.[44] Perhaps Stanley Matthews or one of his associates perceived that such a claim might be made, or conceivably Judge Taft thought of it, after the *Minor* case had been submitted.

At any rate, here was a *latent* issue under the new Amendment —which perceptive and resourceful counsel might have pressed with fair prospects of success.

When, on June 24, 1873, the Ohio bench unanimously reversed the judgment of the Superior Court,[45] it held that the State constitu-

---

[42] *The Christian Statesman* of March 15, 1870. 3:105

[43] I took occasion, on September 18, 1964, to call at the office of the Clerk of the Supreme Court of Ohio. Starting from the docket where Board of Education v. Minor appeared (No. 342, Dec. term 1869, Minute Book No. 1-A 1868-70, p. 212), resort was had to the files where the papers should be. Evidently they had been extracted from their normal place. Possibilities of misfiling, suggested by the docket entries, were pursued without avail.

[44] Infra, note 98.

[45] Board of Education v. Minor *et al.*, 23 Ohio St. 211.

Two months earlier—on April 14, 1873—the United States Supreme Court in the *Slaughter House Cases*, 16 Wall. 36, had given its earliest construction of the Fourteenth Amendment. Infra, p. 1349. Made alert by George's version of Judge Taft's statement about going to the Supreme Court, I had wondered whether the Ohio court had delayed its decision in the *Cincinnati* case in order to find what the Supreme Court had to say about the Fourteenth Amendment. On looking at the Ohio court's docket I found, however, that the *Cincinnati* case was decided with no unusual delay.

tion did not require religious instruction in the public schools; further, the legislature having placed school management under the exclusive control of the board of education, the judiciary had no authority to interfere with the exercise of its discretion.[46]

APPLICATION OF THE PRECEDING DISCUSSION

THIS CONTROVERSY AT Cincinnati has been elaborated to suggest a significant line of reflection. Many a contrariety in American life of that day contained the makings of a case on the new Fourteenth Amendment. A suit over a matter of religious liberty would have started with much in its favor: the First Amendment protected that basic value against abridgment by Congress, and a telling argument could have been made that the post-war Constitution surely *ought* to bar abridgment by the State. (The precise formulation by which that result could be achieved is not here under discussion.) Or where a defendant had been convicted in a State court of a serious crime, and there was some plausible contention that the proceedings had in some respect been defective, pertinacious counsel *might* have invoked the Fourteenth Amendment's guaranty of due process of law.[47] Numerous other pos-

---

[46] When the National Convention to secure the Religious Amendment of the Constitution met in Philadelphia in February 1874, its proceedings recorded that

The principal assaults within the year upon the Christian elements of our political organization have been the decision of the Supreme Court of Ohio, reversing the decision of the Superior Court of Cincinnati, and sustaining the expulsion of the Bible from the schools, and the attempts to overthrow Sabbath law and order in New York, Chicago, St. Louis and other smaller cities and towns. . . .

The association was "laboring for the protection of our best institutions against these irreligious and communistic assaults . . . ." At p. 78.

Justice Strong was no longer the president of the association. The call for the convention in 1872 had been issued in his name with this identification: "United States Supreme Court, President of the National Association." *Cincinnati Commercial*, Feb.

1, 1872. The *Albany Law Journal* drew attention to the impropriety of a Justice of the Supreme Court presiding over an association agitating for that purpose, in opposition to the separation of state from religion. 5:72, Feb. 3, 1872.

[47] Glance at Twitchell v. Pennsylvania, 7 Wall. 321: a motion for a writ of error—to review a sentence of death affirmed by the State Supreme Court—was argued on April 2 and denied on April 5, 1869. Upon circumstantial evidence, Twitchell had been convicted of the murder of his mother-in-law. The details were atrocious. Accused had borne a good character; he maintained his innocence. The trial aroused high interest, and was reported at length—in the New York papers as well as at home in Philadelphia.

Under the Pennsylvania statute, it was not necessary "to set forth the manner in which, or the means by which," death was caused. The writ of error was sought on the ground that this violated the Fifth Amendment (indictment by a grand jury) and the

sibilities come to mind when one reads the newspapers of that day. That the Court's first case arose in the slaughter houses of New Orleans, and was concerned with an alleged liberty to engage in a common calling—to be free from an unreasonable monopoly in business—was attributable to two special factors: (1) that relief from Carpetbag legislation was not to be expected from a Carpetbag State judiciary; hence the aggrieved party must base his claim on some federal ground; and (2) that ex-Justice John A. Campbell was there, uniquely qualified to devise such a line of thought as might captivate the minds of the Justices. While he persuaded only four of the nine, this effort made the Amendment seem from the start to face toward economic liberty, "laissez faire."

For many years in the adjudications of the Court, "liberty" had a particular significance—"liberty of contract," free from wage and hour legislation and the like; "property" covered courses of business conduct, including the rates that a public utility might charge; and "without due process of law" could be described with substantial accuracy as signifying "in any manner which a majority of the Supreme Court strongly disapprove."

Only slowly was it reflected in the law of the Court that "liberty" has a moral and spiritual content. It was as late as 1925 that the Court tentatively gave this recognition:

> For present purposes we may and do assume that freedom of speech and of the press . . . are among the fundamental personal rights and "liberties" protected by the due process clause of the Fourteenth Amendment from impairment by the States.[48]

After that proposition had been applied to various restraints of speech and press, the Court, upon great deliberation, in 1943 held invalid the compulsory salute to the flag and recital of the pledge of allegiance, in

---

Sixth ("to be informed of the nature and cause of the accusation").

The writ of error was refused, per Chase, C.J., on the ground that, as held in Barron v. Baltimore, 7 Pet. 243 (1833), and cases following it, the federal Bill of Rights did not apply to the States.

Evidently it did not occur to defense counsel to put up an argument on the Fourteenth Amendment, which had been in effect for more than eight months.

[48] Gitlow v. New York, 268 U.S. 652, 666. There had been a conviction under New York's Criminal Anarchy Law of 1902 [enacted shortly after President McKinley had been assassinated in New York State] for the publication of a pamphlet, "The Left Wing Manifesto." There was "no evidence of any concrete result flowing from the publication of the Manifesto or of circumstances showing the likelihood of such result"—the statute as construed penalizing the mere utterance. When the Supreme Court affirmed, Holmes and Brandeis, JJ., dissented.

a suit brought by affected members of the Jehovah's Witnesses, whose religious scruples were outraged by this requirement.[49] Whereas for decades the typical claim under the Amendment had been that government should not dictate how the individual managed his business, now it was being urged that government should not prescribe how he might speak, what he must or must not hear, and what he was to read and to profess. It was after much further consideration of the relation between state and religion that in 1962 the Court disallowed a mandate that prayers be read by public school classes.[50] This was followed the next year by the holding that compulsory Bible reading was inconsistent with the Fourteenth Amendment.[51] Judge Taft, as reported, had spoken of taking the question to the Supreme Court—and at last that had been done.

APPROACH TO THE *SLAUGHTER HOUSE CASES*

SEVERAL CASES, PRIOR to that of the New Orleans butchers, involved or suggested questions under the Fourteenth Amendment. In *Worthy v. Commissioners*[52] the Privileges and Immunities Clause was first invoked in the Supreme Court; but Section 25 of the Judiciary Act required that the alleged right must have been "specially set up or claimed" in the State court, and on that ground the Supreme Court dismissed for want of jurisdiction. *Northern R.R. v. People of the State of New York*[53] was dismissed because the judgment attacked actually did not rest upon the statute alleged to violate the Due Process Clause. In *Steines v. Franklin County*[54] the due process point had been injected only on a motion for a rehearing, the granting or denying of which was a matter of discretion not subject to review by the Supreme Court. *Bartemeyer v. Iowa*[55] was a made-up case challenging the State's prohibition law. On this first effort the Court contrived to dismiss by adopting a very stiff construction of the statute governing writs of error—as will be explained in context when the second effort is considered.[56] In *Pumpelly v. Green Bay Company*,[57] coming up

---

[49] West Virginia State Board of Education v. Barnette, 319 U.S. 624 (1943).

[50] Engel v. Vitale, 370 U.S. 421.

[51] Abington School District v. Schempp, 374 U.S. 203 (1963), cited supra, p. 1316.

[52] 9 Wall. 611 (1870), a contest for the office of sheriff in a county of North Carolina; on the ground that he was disqualified by Section 3 of the Fourteenth Amendment and by a North Carolina statute, plaintiff in error had been denied the office to which, he alleged, he had been elected.

[53] 12 Wall. 384 (1871).

[54] 14 Wall. 15 (1872). Subsequently a case based on diversity of citizenship was made to renew the issues under State law. Ritchie v. Franklin County, 22 Wall. 67 (1875).

[55] 14 Wall. 26 (1872).

[56] Infra, pp. 1417–20.

[57] 13 Wall. 166 (1872).

from a federal Circuit Court, recovery was allowed for land flooded by a State-authorized dam. This was done as an application of the State's own constitutional requirement of fair compensation where private property was taken for public use; Justice Miller's opinion, however, was soon being quoted as descriptive of what the State *must* do to satisfy the Fourteenth Amendment.[58] In *Osborn v. Nicholson*[59] the Court, Chase, C.J., dissenting, rejected a contention that the Thirteenth and Fourteenth Amendments barred the enforcement of a note, valid when made, for the purchase of slaves. To decide otherwise, said Swayne, J., would take one man's property and give it to another, while conferring no benefit on those formerly in bondage.

It was unfortunate that some relatively simple cases, close to the contemplated field of the Amendment, did not first engage the Court's attention. The meaning of the text must be unfolded; reflection was needed, to consider what readings were admissible, and the consequences to which each would lead. As it was, the earliest invocation was a cry from far afield; it asked relief against a piece of unjust legislation such as might occur wherever local government was in the hands of spoilsmen. The evil was not such as had been envisaged in the debates on the Amendment. The statute, however, was represented as infringing upon the citizen's liberty to follow his calling, and the Amendment *could* be made to reach it. Four of the Justices responded to the call. Five refused to venture into the unknown; in their wariness against distorting the federal system, they gave the Amendment a minimal construction. "Criticism of this case has never entirely ceased," said Justice Moody in 1908, "nor has it ever received universal assent by members of this Court."[60] This at least may be said with assurance: the problem in *Slaughter House* proved too big for wise solution in the Court's initial groping with the Amendment.

THE ABATTOIR STATUTE

BY WAY OF background we relate how by a corrupt job there came into being the Crescent City Stock Landing and Slaughter House Company, hereinafter "the Crescent City Company."

In March 1869 the Louisiana legislature passed Act No. 118, to protect the health of the city of New Orleans, to locate stock landings

---

[58] By Field, J., dissenting, in Munn v. Illinois, 94 U.S. 113, 144 (1877), and Spring Valley Water Works v. Schottler, 110 U.S. 347, 380 (1884); by Harlan, J., dissenting, in Louisiana v. Mayor of New Orleans, 109 U.S. 285, 294 (1883); and by the Court, distinguishing, in Mugler v. Kansas, 123 U.S. 623, 667 (1887).

[59] 13 Wall. 654 (1872).

[60] Twining v. New Jersey, 211 U.S. 78, 96.

and slaughter houses, and to incorporate the Crescent City Company, at whose establishment alone, after June 1 next, the landing and slaughtering of cattle would be permitted.[61] Slaughtering as theretofore conducted, on the banks of the Mississippi above the intake of the city water plant, had been a menace to health. Chief Justice Ludeling recited noisome details when the State Supreme Court sustained the statute as a sanitary measure.[62] Thus public health and a monopoly were two faces of one statute. "The butchers and stock dealers," reported the *Picayune,* "while they bow to the popular decision that they ought not to remain above the city, have not succumbed to the claim that they shall pay tribute to this incorporation."[63]

It was in accord with municipal development throughout the country that slaughtering be brought under public control and confined to a remote location. The Metropolitan Board of Health of New York, acting under a statute of 1866, had been sustained by the local Supreme Court in ordering butchering to be removed to abattoirs outside of the metropolitan district.[64] The Court of Appeals sustained the statute in 1868, in an opinion by Chief Judge Ward Hunt.[65] (The New Orleans Slaughter House case would be one of the earliest in which Hunt participated when he came to the Supreme Bench in 1873; and as it turned out, his vote was decisive.) A Massachusetts statute of 1870 incorporated a company to whose facilities all within six miles around Boston might be required to resort. The seemliness of this statute, in its drafting and its administration, was in marked contrast to the regime at New Orleans.[66] Comparable statutes for Milwaukee and San Francisco were sustained by the State courts in 1866 and 1867 respectively.[67]

The vice of the Louisiana statute was that it was procured by bribery and was designed for the special benefit of the incorporators— "the seventeen" in Campbell's indignant phrase. In his argument before the Supreme Court in 1873 he insisted that, contrary to the theory of Chief Justice Ludeling's opinion on the validity of the statute, protection of the public health had not been the true motivation. Rather, he said,

---

[61] Act of Mar. 8, 1869. Acts of 1869, 170.

[62] State of Louisiana *ex rel.* Belden, Attorney General v. Fagan *et al.,* 22 La. Ann. 545 (1870). Infra, p. 1327.

[63] *New Orleans Picayune,* Dec. 26, 1869.

[64] Cooper v. Schultz, 32 How. Pr. 107 (1866). The action of the board was "eminently wise and proper," and in line with measures being taken in large European cities, commented *The Nation.* 3:273, Oct. 4, 1866.

[65] Metropolitan Board of Health v. Heister, 37 N.Y. 661.

[66] Acts and Resolves 1870, ch. 365. Infra, n. 161.

A statute of 1871, to permit authorities of towns of more than 4,000 inhabitants to control slaughtering, was sustained in Inhabitants of Watertown v. Mayo, 109 Mass. 315 (1872).

[67] City of Milwaukee v. Gross, 21 Wis. 241; *Ex parte* Shrader, 33 Cal. 279.

Our hypothesis is, that a person we will call Durbridge, had lands on the west bank of the river he desired to sell. That his "brain conceived this measure." That he communicated it, and it was found to have money in it. That $60,000 was subscribed to pay the expenses of its passage. That 6000 shares of stock—paid up stock (so called) were placed in the charge of a committee. That the seventeen resolved themselves into a committee to go in person to see the bill carried. That money and stock were distributed to the members of the legislature, and that the bill passed. That this very corporation defended itself successfully against Durbridge in a suit for stock. That there was turpitude in the procurement of the charter, and this turpitude was proved in open court and his suit defeated.[68]

Indeed turpitude was brought to light. In the distribution of the bribes, the promoters could not trust one another: in defense to a suit by Durbridge for his portion of the shares of stock, the Company exposed its own shame and answered that another participant had already made off with them.[69] The trial judge found:

> The evidence shows that members of the House of Representatives were bribed for their votes, and members of the Senate were also bribed for their votes. It further shows that other parties occupying official positions in the city of New Orleans were bribed; and I think the evidence is irresistible that the Governor's signature to that bill was obtained by the same soft sawder.[70]

He found that persons with the *New Orleans Times* and *Republican* newspapers had received shares from this "wholesale bribery concern."[71]

The trial court refused to aid the participants, and the State Supreme Court dismissed Durbridge's appeal with the curt statement that

> we are satisfied, from an examination of the testimony, that the ground from which this action springs was a fund created for the purpose of corrupting and improperly influencing members of the Legislature . . . .[72]

---

[68] Brief upon reargument, p. 35.
[69] Testimony in the *New Orleans Bee*, June 2, 1871; *Picayune*, Dec. 23, 1871.
[70] *New Orleans Bee*, Mar. 19, 1872.
[71] Oral opinion, the *Bee*, Mar. 14, 1872.
The books of the Crescent City Company showed that C. A. Weed, proprietor of the *Times*, held 800 shares; Michael Hahn, editor of the *Republican*, held 250. *Bee*, Mar. 20, 1872. The books also showed cash payments of $92,990 by the company's president, Franklin J. Pratt; he alleged that this was for counsel fees. *Bee*, Mar. 22, 23, 1872.
[72] Durbridge v. Slaughter House Co., 27 La. Ann. 676 (1875).

While this corruption belongs to the history of the Crescent City Company, it could not be made an issue in the controversy between the butchers and the company.[73]

THE BUTCHERS SUE THE CRESCENT CITY MONOPOLY

RETURNING TO 1869, when the statute was enacted: on June 1, all stock dealers and all butchers, if they would stay in business, must resort to the facilities of the Crescent City Company, facilities that were hurriedly being improvised. On May 26, in the Sixth District Court for the Parish of Orleans, came counsel for the Butchers' Benevolent Association to seek an injunction. This body, incorporated in 1867, comprised some four hundred butchers; its purpose was to maintain a place for slaughtering cattle, and in other ways to serve the interests of its members. Alleging a combination to engross the trade, its bill prayed that Crescent City be enjoined from interfering with existing arrangements. This was supported by the affidavit of Paul Esteben, president of the Association. (Esteben is a man to watch: before two years had passed he would be on the other side.)

Counsel for the petitioners—of whom John A. Campbell and John Quincy Adams Fellows will appear throughout the litigation—took care to write into the bill the point of federal law on which they would take the case to the Supreme Court:

> Your petitioners represent that the first clause of the 14th amendment of the Constitution of the United States prohibits the States to abridge the privileges and immunities of citizens of the United States, and secures to all protection from State legislation that involves [sic., invades?] the rights of property, the most valuable of which is to labor freely in an honest avocation . . . .[74]

---

[73] As the Louisiana Court held in State *ex rel.* Belden, Attorney General v. Fagan *et al.*, 22 La. Ann. 545 (1870).

[74] Transcript of Record in Butchers' Benevolent Assn. v. Crescent City Live Stock Landing and Slaughter House Co., p. 3.

To facilitate citation, let it be explained in advance that six "Slaughter House Cases" were filed in the Supreme Court on August 30, 1870. Three were dismissed, on motion of plaintiff in error, on October 19, 1876. The three remaining were those decided on April 14, 1873, and re-ported in 16 Wall. 36. These comprised:

(1) Butchers' Benevolent Assn. v. Crescent City Live Stock Landing and Slaughter House Co., No. 476 when docketed, No. 8 when decided. This was the Benevolent Butchers' suit to enjoin enforcement of Act No. 118.

(2) a cross suit instituted by the Company, and taken to the Supreme Court as Butchers' Benevolent Assn. v. Crescent City . . . Co., No. 480 when docketed, No. 10 when decided.

(3) a suit instituted by the Attorney General of Louisiana against

The Commerce Clause was also invoked, inasmuch as large interstate shipments would be limited to the Crescent City landing. This contention, however, was not put forward in the effort before the Supreme Court.[75]

A preliminary injunction was granted at once; Crescent City would show cause on June 5 why in their view the injunction should be set aside.

For weeks Franklin J. Pratt, president of Crescent City, and his associates had been keeping close watch, to see whether dealers and butchers would muster enough strength to do battle. Within an hour after their adversaries were detected in the Sixth District Court, Crescent City's attorneys came before the Fifth District Court with a bill to enjoin Butchers' Benevolent and its members from thwarting the monopoly.[76] Again, an injunction was issued. Such was the way in which contests were conducted in the Louisiana courts at that moment. Opponents would cause one another to be restrained on *ex parte* applications, and what was done in one court could perhaps be punished as contempt by another. The newspapers deplored this practice as "Farcical Administration of Law"[77] and "Abuse of Injunctions"— and yet it was noted that the same sort of thing was going on in New York in struggles such as that to gain control of the Erie Railroad.[78] From the outset, the Slaughter House litigation was a crafty business.

Counsel on both sides were outstanding men. Campbell had proved to be a useful Justice of the Supreme Court, from 1853 to 1861. Fellows had been a leading pro-slavery Unionist; in 1864 he was the conservative candidate for governor. Among their associates in the Louisiana courts was Edward Bermudez, later the State's chief justice. (Edward Douglass White, future Chief Justice of the United States, graduated from Bermudez' office in 1868.)

Representing Crescent City were William H. Hunt and his brother Randall: although authentic Southerners, they had remained

---

Fagan, Esteben, and other dealers and butchers, the Live Stock Dealers' and Butchers' Assn., and Charles Cavaroc. This was docketed in the Supreme Court as Esteben . . . v. State of Louisiana *ex. rel.* Belden, No. 479 when filed, No. 9 when decided.

The claim of right under the federal Constitution was made in the answer to these two latter suits, Transcript in No. 10, p. 6; Transcript in No. 9, p. 23.

[75] Infra, p. 1340.

[76] Testimony of William H. Hunt,

counsel for Crescent City, in Transcript in No. 8, pp. 16–18.

[77] *Bee*, Mar. 30, 1869.

[78] *Picayune*, Jan. 14, 1870.

An Act of March 16, 1870, created an Eighth District Court for the Parish of Orleans, with exclusive jurisdiction to issue writs of injunction, mandamus and quo warranto. To the new judgeship, Gov. Warmoth appointed an energetic young supporter, Henry C. Dibble—who soon became entangled with the federal Circuit Court in the *Slaughter House* controversy.

loyal to the Union, and after the war had cooperated with the Republicans. (The former was appointed to the Court of Claims in 1878, and later served as Secretary of the Navy under Presidents Garfield and Arthur.) With them was Christian Roselius, distinguished as practitioner, scholar, and dean of the local law faculty (now Tulane).

On July 21, 1869, while the suit and the counter suit already mentioned were pending, Esteben, William Fagan, and numerous others incorporated as the Live Stock Dealers' and Butchers' Association, to acquire land and erect buildings for slaughtering. Their articles of association provided that this establishment would be located "on the tract of land known as Delery Place, owned by Cha's Cavaroc," on the left bank, down-stream.[79] The *Bee*—English version of *L'Abeille de la Nouvelle Orléans*—welcomed this move by dealers and butchers to resettle their businesses and families below the city; it would satisfy the only point on which the public had opposed them. The character of the parties, it was reported, gave assurance of success.[80]

Now Live Stock Dealers and Butchers went into the Seventh District Court and obtained an injunction to restrain Crescent City from interfering with their plans. Thereby they began another case that went to the Supreme Court, only to be dismissed on their own motion, on October 19, 1871, as the outcome of a compromise with Crescent City.

As one of the gods might descend to rescue a favorite Greek or Trojan warrior caught in a tight spot, so throughout Reconstruction did State governments come to the aid of their partisans. Thus Simeon Belden, Louisiana's Attorney General, appeared on July 27 in the accommodating Fifth District Court and on behalf of the State obtained an injunction to restrain Paul Esteben, William Fagan, and others, using the name "Live Stock Dealers' and Butchers' Association," from breaching the monopoly statute, and to restrain Cavaroc from letting them have his place for their slaughtering. This restraint upon Cavaroc's use of his land was a feature upon which Campbell would dwell when he came to argue that the statute had imposed an "involuntary servitude" comparable to the burdens maintained under the *Ancien Régime* in France, when one man's land was held in subservience to the pleasure of another. This suit by the *State ex rel. Belden* became the third of the *Slaughter House Cases* decided by the Supreme Court in 1873.

Cavaroc went into the Third District Court and obtained an injunction whereby the State, the city and the police were forbidden to interfere with his rights of ownership. He built stock yard facilities,

---

[79] Articles of incorporation, in Transcript in No. 10, pp. 16–19.

[80] July 25, 1869.

in accordance with the directions of the dealers and butchers. (Cavaroc was a New Orleans banker. Upon the compromise made in March 1871, he became president of the Crescent City Company; Crescent City's seat of operations was moved across the river to the Cavaroc place.)

In December 1869 came decisions in the several District Courts making permanent the opposing injunctions, on the basis of rulings that Act. No. 118 was—or was not—constitutional. Here was glorious disorder.

Opposing counsel agreed that, out of more than two hundred suits brought by or against the company, each side would select three to be appealed; meantime, all other proceedings would be stayed.[81]

Six cases, then, were taken to the State Supreme Court under "suspensive appeals"; that is, the operation of the respective injunctions was suspended, pending the judgment of that court.

Argument was heard on January 27 and 28, 1870. On April 11, Ludeling, C.J., announced the decision: the statute was sustained.[82] On that basis the judgments in the District Courts were respectively affirmed or reversed. On May 9, rehearing was refused.

On April 29 the *Picayune* reported a rumor that Live Stock Dealers were negotiating to go over to the side of the monopoly; it commented that after having "constantly and generously stood by" the former, it would be indignant if the rumor proved true.

FEDERAL JUSTICE IS INVOKED

ON MAY 13, 1870, writs of error were allowed by Justice Bradley, who at that moment was holding court at Galveston.[83] That would carry the controversy up to the Supreme Court where, unless the matter was taken out of order, a decision was to be expected in perhaps two years.

"A writ of error," the Judiciary Act provided, "shall be a supersedeas and stay execution" if taken within ten days, upon giving "sufficient security, that the plaintiff in error shall prosecute his writ to

---

[81] Transcript in No. 9, pp. 27–28.

[82] State *ex rel.* Belden, Attorney General v. Fagan *et al.*, 22 La. Ann. 545. Wyly, J., dissented: slaughtering might, in the interest of health, be confined to a designated area, but the creation of a monopoly was ultra vires.

[83] J. Q. A. Fellows had gone to Galveston on that mission. The

Picayune, May 14; the *Bee*, May 15. The latter concluded, too sanguinely.

The case will be heard in the Supreme Court in Washington in December next. The Supreme Court of the State of Louisiana and Mr. Chief Justice Ludeling are completely divested of any further jurisdiction in these cases.

effect, and answer all damages and costs if he fail to make his appeal good." That suspended the power of the State Supreme Court to take any further action: but where did it leave the parties?

Campbell and his associates took the position that the writs of error put a stop to all proceedings; that the several District Court injunctions remained in suspense. On that advice, their clients went right ahead with their butchering at the Cavaroc location. They did not propose, the *Bee* reported, "to abandon their business to a set of interlopers;" indeed, it said wishfully, there was "no little anxiety among the supporters of the monopoly."[84] The *Bee* was particularly attentive to the interests of the butchers, who were largely French-speakers.

The *Picayune* reported, encouragingly, that the new facilities were complete and most convenient—as clean as a lady's parlor.[85]

Opportunely, Justice Bradley reached New Orleans on May 26, 1870, and next day took his place on the bench of the Circuit Court, with Circuit Judge William B. Woods at his side.[86] The occasion is noteworthy. The new Circuit Justice, Wayne's successor in this respect, had held office a mere two months; Woods had been Circuit Judge scarcely five months, by appointment under the Act to Amend the Judicial System, of April 10, 1869.[87] They came as strangers, Northerners, although Woods had shifted his domicile from Ohio to Alabama on leaving the army. They brought the justice of the United States to the South's great metropolis. "This city is the chief cotton market of the world," the travel guide reported. "Not unfrequently from a thousand to fifteen hundred steamers and flatboats may be seen lying at the Levee, that have floated down the stream hundreds of miles with the

---

84 "The Slaughter-House Litigation," May 29, 1870.

85 Apr. 10.

86 Bradley's diaries are among his papers in the New Jersey Historical Society at Newark. They are not loquacious. In that for 1870 he recorded:

Wed., May 25 . . . .
    12 m. Sailed from Galveston for New Orleans—accompd wife & Judge [J.S.] Black & wife & daughter &c
    Thurs., May 26 11 am Arrived at N Orleans
        Stopped at St Charles Rooms E & F
        Did not attend court
        Judges Woods & Durell called

Fri., May 27 Held Circuit Court with Judge Woods—
    Confiscation Cases argued by T.A. Clark & others—gave 6 hours to one side & 5 hours to other
    Sat., May 28 Confiscation Cases argued by C M Conrad & al . . . .

. . . .

    Wed., June 8 Live Stock Dealers Asso v Crescent City &c

. . . .

    Fri., June 10 Opinion in Slaughter House Case
    Sat., June 11 Supplemental decision in Slaughter House Case
    5 PM Started for home

87 Supra, pp. 487–88, 559–60.

rich produce of the interior country."[88] Following the flag, adventurers had flocked to New Orleans, attracted to the richness of the prize. Some had profited handsomely in confiscation cases.[89] Indeed a number of those instances came before Justice Bradley at this time. New Orleans' motley crowd who exploited their adherence to the Republican party attained special notoriety even for the days of Reconstruction. When Campbell said that the slaughter house monopoly had been awarded to men mostly inexperienced in the business, some of them bankrupts, some not domiciled in Louisiana, none of whom merited favor by reason of any service to the community,[90] he touched upon a sore point, however irrelevant it was in law. New Orleans had had a culture of its own, distinct even from the rest of the South. Now its habits had been rudely broken, its standards corrupted. "The public sense is becoming so depraved," the *Picayune* lamented, "men who would scorn bribes themselves, so unhesitatingly offer them to others," that the community was being debased by their effrontery.[91] But not all of the corruptionists carried a carpetbag: Durbridge, for example—who, according to Campbell, had conceived the scheme for a monopoly—had done business in New Orleans since 1846.[92]

Before Justice Bradley in chambers, on June 1, opposing counsel made statements of their respective positions in the uncertain state of affairs. Inasmuch as the writs of error were being interpreted as suspending the execution of the statute, counsel for Crescent City asked that Live Stock Dealers and Butchers be required to give a much larger bond, adequately to secure the former for unpaid fees accumulating during the pendency of proceedings in the Supreme Court. On Friday, June 3, Justice Bradley announced his conclusions. Contrary to his first impression, it appeared from decisions in the Supreme Court that, after the granting of the writ of error, that matter became cognizable there alone. As to the effect of the writs of error upon injunctions previously entered, "parties must take the law at their peril, as I cannot, sitting here, make any judicial determination which will bind them."[93]

Crescent City took instant action on its own responsibility. On the evening of Friday, June 3, an order was obtained from Judge Henry C. Dibble of the Eighth District Court—created in March 1870, with exclusive jurisdiction to issue writs of injunction—directing the

---

[88] *Appleton's Hand-book of American Travel* 1869, 390.
[89] Supra, ch. 15.
[90] Transcript in No. 10, p. 6.
[91] Editorial, "When Will We Have Relief?" Feb. 24, 1869.

[92] Transcript in No. 8, pp. 30–38.
[93] Butchers' Assn. v. Slaughter House Co., Fed. Case No. 2234, 1 Woods' Circuit Court Reports 50. *New Orleans Times*, June 2, 3, 4, and 5; *Bee*, June 3, 4.

Metropolitan Police Board to prevent slaughtering, and the offering for sale of meat that had been slaughtered, elsewhere than at Crescent City's abattoir. The police, energized by Governor Warmoth, obeyed with alacrity: they went into the markets and seized thousands of dollars worth of meat, holding it until it spoiled in the June heat. This destruction of the Sunday supply of fresh meat, the *Bee* reported, "created great excitement among all classes of the population and the parties instigating and procuring the seizure were unsparingly denounced. . . . Many members of the bar indeed consider the action of the Slaughter-House Company . . . as highly disrespectful and contemptuous toward Mr. Justice Bradley and his colleagues in Washington."[94]

Attorney General Belden was already taking parallel action in the name of the State: on June 2 he had moved to remove from the Fifth to the Eighth District Court his suit against Esteben, Fagan *et al.*, the Live Stock Dealers and Butchers, wherein the injunction had now been affirmed. His purpose was to obtain enforcement.

Now the dealers' and butchers' only hope for immediate relief lay in the federal Circuit Court.

LIVE STOCK DEALERS AND BUTCHERS SEEK AN INJUNCTION IN THE CIRCUIT COURT

ON MONDAY, JUNE 6, Campbell and Fellows filed the bill of *Live Stock Dealers' and Butchers' Assn. v. Crescent City . . . Co. and Board of Metropolitan Police.*[95] Complainants as citizens asserted rights under the Constitution, especially under the Fourteenth Amendment; also under the Civil Rights Act of 1866. In particular, they were entitled to pursue their avocations (described in detail), to have the equal protection of the laws, and to be exempt from involuntary servitude and vassalage. These rights had been invaded by Act No. 118 of 1869: the bill traced the litigation in the State courts, culminating in the judgments of the Supreme Court sustaining the statute, and the prompt taking of writs of error "whereby the judgments of the Supreme Court and the District Courts became and are superseded," so that any further action thereon was in derogation of the laws of the United States and the authority of its courts. Notwithstanding this, Crescent City Company had obtained from the Eighth District Court, "the extraordinary writ, called in the proceedings an injunction," by which the Metro-

---

[94] "The Butchers' Controversy," June 9, 1870.
[95] Fed. Case No. 8408, 1 Woods 21, decided June 10 and 11, 1870. The text of the bill is set out in the *Bee*, June 7.

politan Police Board were commanded, etc., whereupon police officers had seized meat to the value of $20,000, so that it spoiled. The relief sought was that defendants be enjoined to suspend all proceedings against complainants; that complainants be protected in their rights to carry on their businesses, subject to no condition more severe than what was applicable to any other party, defendants included; and that the Eighth District Court be directed to transfer the record of its proceedings into the federal court for its review.

Allowing two days' notice to the respondents, the Circuit Court set June 9 for the hearing. Campbell appeared on the one side, William H. Hunt and Roselius on the other. Justice Bradley, presiding, went to the basic issues—expeditiously, tentatively, and with marked consideration toward these able counsellors.[96] The bill opened a wide field: the new Amendment must be unfolded, and applied to this unforeseen type of situation. The report does not set out the propositions on which counsel respectively insisted. One can see from Justice Bradley's opinion that he was feeling his way in a problem "of great delicacy and embarrassment." Judge Woods' headnotes supplement the opinion and clarify passages that seem puzzling.

This was, Judge Woods noted, "the first case" in which the Fourteenth Amendment was fully considered, and it is revealing to observe certain interpretations that needed to be established at the outset.

> 1. The first section of the fourteenth amendment of the constitution applies as well to white as colored persons, as citizens of the United States; and is intended to protect them in their privileges and immunities, as such citizens, against the action, as well of their own state, as of other states in which they may happen to be.

Apparently counsel for the defendants had argued that Section 1, or perhaps only the Privileges and Immunities Clause, should be construed narrowly as operating merely to lift black citizens as a category to the same plane with whites.

---

[96] The *Bee* had commented on May 29:

Judge Bradley conducts the business of the court to the satisfaction of the Bar. His manners are exceedingly urbane. He has none of the boorishness of some other Judges. Judge Bradley comes here with a fine reputation as a jurist, and his promptitude in dispatching business shows that he thoroughly understands his duties. We are happy to say that the Bar repose unlimited confidence in the impartiality and learning of Mr. Justice Bradley. Judge Woods, also, is well spoken of at the Bar. It must be a pleasure to plead before our new Judges.

Further,

2. These privileges and immunities do not consist merely in being placed on an equality with others; but embrace all the fundamental rights of citizenship.

That reflects a point in the opinion where Justice Bradley wrote,

It was very ably contended, on the part of the defendants, that the fourteenth amendment was intended only to secure to all citizens equal capacities before the law. That was at first our view of it. But it does not so read. . . . What are the privileges and immunities of citizens of the United States? Are they capacities merely? Are they not also rights?

Apparently the contention had been that so long as no category of citizens was disqualified—so long as all citizens stood upon the same level—the State was free, so far as the Privileges and Immunities Clause was concerned, to designate which among them would be licensed for a particular calling.

The court, however, held that the clause ran directly to the individual citizen and secured to him certain fundamental rights;

3. One of these fundamental rights is that of pursuing any lawful employment in a lawful manner; or, in other words, the right to choose one's own pursuit, subject only to constitutional regulations and restrictions.

These initial headnotes indicate the range of the discussion, which was reflected in the opening paragraph of the opinion Justice Bradley delivered on Friday, June 10:

This application brings up the question whether the civil rights bill[97] applies to such a case as the present, and whether the fourteenth amendment to the constitution is intended to secure to the citizens of the United States of all classes merely equal rights; or whether it is intended to secure to them also absolute rights? And if the latter, whether the rights claimed by the complainants in this bill are among the number of such absolute rights?

(At the outset he put the Civil Rights Act aside as inapplicable, apparently because no claim by persons of color was here involved; next morning, however, he modified his expression.)

---

[97] Referring to the Civil Rights Act of 1866. Woods' footnote: "The act of May 31, 1870 [16 Stat. 141] which reënacted the civil rights bill, had not come to the knowledge of the court when this opinion was delivered."

"Before proceeding to examine the technical points," he would discuss "the main question" of the validity of the Louisiana statute. And he was prepared to find that the words of the Amendment carried wider than the mark at which the framers had aimed:

> It is possible that those who framed the article were not them-selves aware of the far reaching character of its terms. They may have had in mind but one particular phase of social and political wrong which they desired to redress. Yet, if the amendment as framed and expressed, does in fact bear a broader meaning, and does extend its protecting shield over those who were never thought of when it was conceived and put in form, and does reach social evils which were never before prohibited by constitutional enactment, it is to be presumed that the American people, in giving it their *imprimatur*, understood what they were doing, and meant to decree what has in fact been decreed.

He distinguished the function performed by Article IV, Section 2, of the Constitution: "Each [State] was prohibited from discriminating in favor of its own citizens . . . ." But the new Privileges and Immunities Clause "not merely requires equality of privileges but it demands that the privileges and immunities of all citizens shall be absolutely unabridged, unimpaired."

> There is no more sacred right of citizenship than the right to pursue, unmolested, a lawful employment in a lawful manner. . . .
> This right is not inconsistent with any of those wholesome regulations which have been found to be beneficial and necessary in every state.

The opinion took note of permissible types of regulation.

> The legislature has an undoubted right to make all police regulations which they may deem necessary (not inconsistent with constitutional restrictions) for the preservation of the public health, good order, morals, and intelligence; but they cannot [interfere with liberty of conscience, nor with the entire equality of all creeds and religions before the law. Nor can they][98] under the pretense of a

---

[98] The words in brackets appear in the opinion as published at the time in the *Chicago Legal News* 3:17; they were omitted from the revised text as published on 1 Woods' Cases in the Fifth Circuit 21.

When he spoke, Bradley was making an early exploration of the new Amendment; this comment had no application to the slaughter house problem, and advisedly it was later excised. Note, however, that the statement was relevant to the problem of Bible reading in the schools, recently raised at Cincinnati. Whether that situation was present in Bradley's mind, actively or subconsciously, *quaere*.

police regulation, interfere with the fundamental privileges and immunities of American citizens. . . .

In the instant case, the statute was represented to be a police regulation and nothing more. "But this pretense is too bald for a moment's consideration." It conferred "a monopoly of a very odious character," of the sort which, if the Crown had attempted to grant it, would have been void at common law.[99] But the legislature might alter the common law, and a monopoly might be legal though impolitic.

Was the monopoly here such as would contravene the fundamental rights protected by the Amendment: that was "the precise question for us to decide."

> When the question was first presented, our impressions were decidedly against the claim put forward by the plaintiffs. But the more we have reflected on the subject, the more we are satisfied that the fourteenth amendment . . . was intended to protect the citizens of the United States in some fundamental privileges of an absolute and not merely a relative character. . . .

And the present seemed a "flagrant case of the violation of the fundamental rights of labor . . . ."

What, then, could the court do? After having decided so much, Justice Bradley faced what supplied a short answer to most of Campbell's petition. A statute of 1793,[100] supplementary to the Judiciary Act, provided:

> nor shall a writ of injunction be granted to stay proceedings in any court of a State.

This was "an objection which cannot be surmounted." Congress could, as a means of enforcing the Amendment, authorize the Circuit Courts to enjoin judicial proceedings in such a situation as this, but it had not done so. Plaintiffs' only remedy lay in going from the highest court of the State, by writ of error, to the Supreme Court.

At the opening of court next morning, Justice Bradley made an announcement concerning his statement the day before that in his view the Civil Rights Act had no application to the instant case.

> This portion of the opinion was not written at the time, and was somewhat hastily expressed. Our attention had been chiefly given to

---

[99] He cited The Case of Monopolies, 11 Coke's Reports 84 (1603).

[100] 1 Stat. 334. The prohibition had reference only to such proceedings as might already have been brought in a State court. Fisk v. Union Pacific R.R., Fed. Case No. 4830 (CCSD NY 1873), per Blatchford, D.J.

the main question—the true construction of the fourteenth amendment. On a more careful examination, considering that the civil rights bill was enacted at the same session, and but shortly before the presentation of the fourteenth amendment was reported by the same committee, was *in pari materia*, and was probably intended to reach the same object, we are disposed to modify our opinion in this respect, and to hold, as the counsel on both sides seem to agree in holding, that the first section of the bill covers the same ground as the fourteenth amendment, at least so far as the matters involved in this case are concerned.

In pursuance of that announcement, the court decreed that plaintiffs were entitled to carry on their landing, slaughtering, and vending business under the same regulations as governed the defendants; defendants were restrained from bringing any *new* suit or otherwise interfering with plaintiffs' pursuit of their lawful business.

ENSUING DEVELOPMENTS

IN EFFECT, JUSTICE Bradley had declared that the Constitution was on the side of the complainants, even though the Circuit Court could not fully impose that conclusion upon the existing situation. The *Picayune* and the *Bee* hastened to maximize the importance of the pronouncement. "Death Blow to the Slaughter-House Company," cried the latter; Justice Bradley's opinion was "one of the most luminous expositions of American constitutional law which ever emanated from any court"; no utterance of Marshall or Story had ever surpassed "this splendid production."[101]

The *Times*,[102] on the other side, heaped derision on the Justice: he had shown such ignorance of federal jurisdiction as would have caused the rejection of any "young applicant for admission to our bar." That journal's services had been bought by the monopoly: the proprietor held eight hundred shares of Crescent City stock and occupied a dwelling in common with the company's president.[103] Though corruptly inspired, the *Times* scored some telling points. One was that Justice Bradley had gone far out of the normal path of judicial duty to make his pronouncement. Another was that the Fourteenth Amendment—framed "with the sole purpose and intent of abolishing all distinctions of color"—would in Bradley's view bring "a vast and indefinite extension of the power and authority of the judicial depart-

---

[101] June 11, 12, 1870.
[102] Editorials on June 11, 12 and 14.

[103] *Bee*, June 19, 1870, and Mar. 20, 1872. Supra, p. 1323.

ment of the Government." He would "convert our judges into constitution makers and amenders, with full power to lay down and proclaim what are the 'civil rights' of men . . . ."

In the Eighth District Court, the Attorney General was pressing for the enforcement of the injunction against Esteben, Fagan, the Live Stock Dealers and Butchers. Campbell and Fellows attempted to remove the cause into the federal Circuit Court on the ground that their clients' rights could not be enforced in the State court: Durell, federal District Judge, ruled against them,[104] and Judge Dibble held their effort to be a contempt and fined each counsellor $100.[105]

On June 28, Judge Dibble ordered the enforcement of the *preliminary* injunction issued at the time the Attorney General instituted the suit—in order "to retain the object in dispute in the exact position it occupied in relation to the parties when the appeal was granted." He referred to "the unpleasant difference between the state court and the United States circuit court sitting here"; it had been argued that he ought to take no action inconsistent with the ruling of Justice Bradley. But the federal court had no power to interfere with his proceedings, and it was his duty to follow the Supreme Court of Louisiana so long as its judgment had not been reversed.[106]

The monopolists procured the publication of an *Avis au Public* wherein fifty-two butchers declared their complete satisfaction in dealing with the Crescent City Company.[107]

"The practical result" of the action of the Eighth District Court,

---

[104] Stafford and others, butchers, also laid a complaint that Weed, Pratt, and others of the monopoly were violating the Civil Rights Act: Durell, federal District Judge, held that nothing shown amounted to an offense against that statute. *Bee*, June 16 to 26.

[105] Minutes of the Eighth District Court, June 21, 1870, set out at pp. 12–13 of the Transcript of Record in State of Louisiana *ex rel.* Belden, Attorney General v. Fagan *et al.*, No. 122, which is Exhibit B, annexed to affidavits X and Z, submitted to the Supreme Court at Adjourned Term commencing October 31, 1870, in support of the motion for a supersedeas in Fagan *et al.* v. State of Louisiana *ex rel.* Belden, Attorney General, No. 479.

[106] At pp. 26–29 of Exhibit B, cited next above.

"Oh! I said I thought he [Justice Bradley] had made a very great fool of himself." Testimony of Judge Dibble in examination before United States Commissioner in the matter of Stafford *et al.* v. Weed *et. al.*, mentioned in footnote 104. *Bee*, June 18, 1870. The *Bee* characterized Dibble as "a boy of 23 or 24 summers."

Actually, Dibble was about two years older than that. Born in Indiana, he had been a cabin boy on the Mississippi, a newsboy in Chicago; he entered the Union army at 16, and lost a leg at the siege of Port Hudson, Louisiana, in 1863. Thereafter he graduated from the University of Louisiana, and was admitted to the bar in 1865. A supporter of Governor Warmoth, he had been active in drafting the statute creating the Eighth District Court, and in March 1870 had received the appointment as Judge. *Picayune*, Jan. 21, 1872.

[107] *Bee*, June 19, 1870.

the *Bee* admitted, was that the butchers "must yield to the monopolists . . . until the Supreme Court of the United States shall have reversed the decision of the Supreme Court of the State of Louisiana . . . , or issued a writ of prohibition to the Eighth District Court. The Supreme Court does not assemble until October . . . ." "Pending so much uncertainty . . . , we learn that quite a number of butchers . . . have gone to work at the establishment of the Slaughter-House Company . . . till the issue is finally determined."[108] It made comparisons between the charges by the monopoly and what would have been charged at the Cavaroc abattoir: the former were more than three times as great.[109]

A MOTION TO STAY PROCEEDINGS

THE SUPREME COURT met in its Adjourned Term on October 31, 1870. On the earliest motion day—Friday, November 4—Campbell presented his motion to enforce a stay by enjoining all proceedings to carry out the challenged statute. The matter was put over for two weeks, when the Court heard Campbell and Philip Phillips against Jeremiah S. Black and Thomas J. Durant.[110]

On December 2, Justice Clifford spoke for the Court in denying the motion: "this Court possesses no power to grant any relief to the plaintiffs under the Act of Congress [the Judiciary Act] on which these motions are founded."[111]

Justice Bradley dissented, "with some diffidence." "The judgment of this Court disclaims all jurisdiction over the acts of the subordinate State Courts and thereby, in my judgment, surrenders a very important power necessary to the effective support of its appellate jurisdiction."[112]

---

[108] June 26, 29.

[109] July 3, August 3.

[110] Phillips was expert in matters relating to the practice of the Supreme Court.

Black had been present in New Orleans when federal jurisdiction was invoked. Supra, n. 86. It is worth noting that Black, who a year and a half earlier, in *Ex parte* McCardle, supra, p. 433, had been doing his utmost to arrest Reconstruction, was now engaged in the service of one of its offensive manifestations, in association with Thomas J. Durant, spokesman for Southern Unionists.

[111] *Slaughter House Cases*, 10 Wall. 273.

Chase, C.J., and Nelson, J., were absent throughout this period; consequently Clifford, J., was presiding. It was customary for the presiding Justice to speak for the Court on points of procedure.

[112] Phillips, in the concluding paragraph of his brief, had urged that, aside from pertinent provisions of the Judiciary Act, "the Court by virtue of its appellate power would still be authorized, as are the Courts in England, to exercise a judicial discretion on the peculiar circumstances of the case in arresting by its order all proceedings subsequent to the decree and pending the appeal." He added, hopefully, "No stronger case

BACK IN LOUISIANA

THERE WAS NO joy in New Orleans when the telegraphic news arrived—except among the monopolists and their adherents. A week went by before the *Bee* made editorial comment on the decision, "on one of the side issues," it said. But in conclusion the editor spoke frankly: "It follows that the butchers must submit to the operation of the State law until it shall be set aside after the final hearing on the merits . . . ."[113]

Now occurred an episode that reveals the true quality of government in Louisiana. The legislators took this occasion to make a show at repealing the Crescent City charter. A bill to that effect passed by overwhelming votes: 90 to 5 in the House, 32 to 1 in the Senate. Governor Warmoth vetoed, on the pious ground that the Contract Clause forbade. Then on the question of passing the bill notwithstanding the Governor's objections, the House vote was only 58 yea to 37 nay: that was less than two-thirds, and the bill failed. The *Picayune* gave this explanation: "The purchase [of the charter] was remembered, and the [legislators] sought to make another haul by threatening repeal. But the slaughter-house corporators thought it too dear to buy a whole House and a whole Senate to retain their monopoly, but preferred to trust to a veto and a third part of one house. The result was the astounding vote of yesterday. Thirty-five men who had voted

---

for the exercise of this discretion could be presented, than the one now before the Court." *Slaughter-House Cases. Motion to Enforce the Supersedeas on Writ of Error. Brief of P. Phillips,* at p. 19.

Justice Bradley, speaking for the Court in Hovey v. McDonald, 109 U.S. 150 (1883), said: "This Court, in the Slaughter-House Cases, 10 Wall. 273, decided that an appeal from a decree granting, refusing or dissolving an injunction, does not disturb its operative effect. . . . It was not decided that the court below had no power, if the purposes of justice required it, to order a continuance of the *status quo* until a decision should be made by the appellate court, or until that court should order the contrary. This power undoubtedly exists, and should always be exercised when any irremediable injury may result from the effect of the decree as

rendered; but it is a discretionary power, and its exercise or non-exercise is not an appealable matter."

Reynolds Robertson and Francis R. Kirkham. *Jurisdiction of the Supreme Court of the United States,* second ed. by Richard F. Wolfson and Philip Kurland (Albany: Matthew Bender and Co., 1951), at sec. 441, note that although "the dearth of reported authority" had left the subject unfamiliar and obscure, the Court and individual Justices had, on proper occasions and on proper terms, made orders staying all proceedings in an inferior State court, until the Supreme Court had acted on a pending case—citing Ohio River Contract Co. v. Gordon, 244 U.S. 68 (1917); Natural Gas Co. of West Virginia v. Public Service Commission, 294 U.S. 698 (1935); and United States v. Moscow Fire Ins. Co., 308 U.S. 542 (1939).

[113] Dec. 10, 1870.

for the repeal of the monopoly turned around and voted to retain it! Further comment is needless."[114] But in candor it admitted that "some of our most respected citizens" were trafficking with those in power.[115]

Another item goes to show that things were rotten in the State of Louisiana. Then pending in the federal Circuit Court was *Jackson et al. v. Ludeling et al.*, a suit to recover control of a railroad worth say two million dollars, from those who in a sneaky foreclosure had purchased it for $50,000. Chief Justice Ludeling had done the bidding. John A. Campbell appeared for the complainants, William H. Hunt for the respondents. Hunt dwelt upon "the high character and spotless integrity" of his client; Judge Woods was persuaded to sustain the transaction.[116] On appeal, however, Justice Strong for a unanimous Court described it as "a great wrong perpetrated by the agency of legal forms." Ludeling had been "the active agent of the combination"; he had perpetrated "a gross fraud" by inducing "a flagrant breach of trust." The Court decreed that the sale be cancelled and that defendants make an accounting.[117]

OPPONENTS COMPROMISE AND COMBINE

For the really substantial interests engaged in the *Slaughter House* litigation, the Supreme Court's denial of interim relief, on December 2, 1870, proved decisive. Quietly the leading parties—the Crescent City Company, the Live Stock Dealers' and Butchers' Association (Paul Esteben, president), the principal dealers, and Cavaroc—worked out

114 Feb. 26, 1871. On February 18 it had reported that "the lobbies were crowded to overflowing by brokers and others more or less interested in the Slaughter-House."

115 Mar. 1, 1871. It recalled, too, that "our own people held aloof when members of the Convention were chosen" [as elsewhere, ch. 9], and thereby had facilitated the advent of the existing political regime.

116 *Bee*, June 16, 1871; Apr. 5, 1872.

117 Jackson v. Ludeling, 21 Wall. 616 (1874). Subsequently the Court, on a construction of the Louisiana Civil Code, allowed the *mala fide* possessors to recover for improvements they had made. Jackson v. Ludeling, 99 U.S. 513 (1879). Justice Field wrote a sturdy dissent, concluding that "just in proportion to the value of this property is the temptation to get possession of it, and if plunderers can, when compelled to restore it, be allowed for their expenditures and alleged improvements, there will be an added incentive to plunder."

Appellants in these two phases of the litigation were represented by Campbell and his partner, Henry M. Spofford (1821–80), a New Englander who, after graduating at the head of his class, and then tutoring, at Amherst College, had gone to Louisiana, been admitted to the bar, and from 1854 until his resignation in 1858 had sat on the Supreme Court. In 1877 he claimed a seat as Senator from Louisiana; his opponent, William P. Kellogg, Republican, was however seated by the Senate.

Appellees were represented by William H. Hunt in 1874; in 1879, argument was by J. S. Black, Matt. H. Carpenter, and Ludeling himself.

a settlement that was accepted on March 14, 1871.[118] Cavaroc became president of the Crescent City Company. That company purchased from Live Stock Dealers and Butchers the left-bank abattoir (on the site they had acquired from Cavaroc a year before). Live Stock Dealers and Butchers received a block of shares in Crescent City; its men were placed on the board of directors. It was agreed that all proceedings, including those before the Supreme Court, would be dismissed. Live Stock Dealers and Butchers arranged to terminate the services of counsel, paying $3,000 each to Campbell's firm, to Fellows', and to Cotton & Levy. Then Live Stock Dealers and Butchers liquidated, distributing its assets among its members.

Butchers' Benevolent Association, be it noted, did not figure in this settlement, except as Paul Esteben purported to commit it. The agreement to end litigation, dated March 14, 1871, was signed "Paul Esteben, President of the Butchers' Benevolent Association, and as President of the Live-Stock Dealers' and Butchers' Association."[119] The butchers were expected to go along with the dealers who had conducted the negotiations.

Not much publicity was given to the compromise: there was nothing about it that would command public sympathy. The *Times*, whose owner was a party to the arrangement, said in an inconspicuous paragraph that henceforth the slaughter house would be run "to the advantage of all concerned."[120] The new management—representing dealers rather than butchers—enforced the old scale of charges.

On October 19, 1871, when the Court had resumed its work, Mr. Fellows appeared and moved for the dismissal of *three* cases, by reason of the compromise: the one brought by Live Stock Dealers and Butchers, that by the Imbau firm of dealers (now represented on the Crescent City board), and a third by the owners of the Steamer B. L. Hodge.[121] (This vessel, bringing cattle to New Orleans, had been constrained by the statute to land its cargo at the privileged wharf and to pay the prescribed fee. Here the point on the Commerce Clause dropped out of the litigation.)

Fellows did *not* move to dismiss the other three cases: the two suits taken up by Butchers' Benevolent Association, and the cause originated by the Attorney General against a large array of parties. Some of the "Gascon butchers" still wanted to fight.

---

[118] The papers are included in a forty-seven-page document, "In the Honorable the Supreme Court of the United States, December Term, 1872 [*sic*]. Motion to Dismiss. The following pages contain the motion made by the defendants in error to dismiss, with documents and affidavits in support, as well as the affidavits against the motion, filed by the plaintiffs in error."

[119] Motion to Dismiss, at p. 6.

[120] Mar. 16, 1881.

[121] Minutes of the Supreme Court.

The parties to the settlement were taken aback; they called upon their counsel in Washington to ask the Court "to postpone the trial of the case, and order further investigation into the question of compromise or no compromise."[122] Accordingly J. S. Black sought and, over Campbell's opposition, was on November 15 granted a delay.[123] On December 14, counsel for defendants in error filed a suggestion "that all matters in controversy have been finally settled between the parties, and the plaintiffs in error are desirous that their writs of error should be dismissed, as will more fully appear by the within agreements . . . filed with the motion . . . ."[124] Counsel aimed to show that the situation fell within the reason of *Lord v. Veazie*,[125] where Chief Justice Taney had pronounced the Court's condemnation of feigned litigation, when there was "no real conflict of interest" between the parties.

The three remaining *Slaughter House Cases* came up for argument on January 11, 1872. The Court granted an additional hour to each side, and heard Fellows and Campbell, opposed by Matt. Carpenter and Durant. The entire day was devoted to the case, and Campbell concluded his argument on the twelfth. In addition to affidavits already filed, he produced that made by Sylvan Verges, in open court and witnessed by Middleton, the Clerk: Verges, now president of Butchers' Benevolent Association, declared that Esteben, the former president,

---

[122] J. P. Hornor, local counsel, to T. J. Durant, Nov. 30, 1871. Motion to Dismiss, pp. 6–10. Hornor continued:

The action of Mr. Fellows in dismissing but three out of the six cases . . . , and attempting to try the other three, took the Slaughter-House Company by surprise, as they believed the whole litigation closed and settled, and were not aware of Messrs. Fellows and Campbell's intentions to press the trial of the other three cases until the day of the date of my first letter to you on this subject, viz: 11th November, 1871.

[123] Minutes, Nov. 13, 14, and 15, 1871.

[124] Motion to Dismiss, p. 3. Durant also filed a twelve-page Brief of Counsel of Defendants in Error on Motion to Dismiss.

[125] 8 How. 251 (1850). L. deeded property to V. with a covenant that it carried certain rights—which act-

ually were claimed by third persons. Thereupon V. sued L. on the covenant, and the District Court "gave judgment for the defendant *pro forma,* at the request of the parties, in order that the judgment might be brought before this [Supreme] court." Counsel for the third persons entered a motion to dismiss, and filed documents and affidavits which satisfied the Court that it was a feigned case. A judgment thus procured, said Taney, was "a mere form"; the writ of error was dismissed.

In 1869, upon a third party's intervention and motion to dismiss, in American Wood Paper Co. v. Heft, 131 U.S. App. cxii, 19 L. Ed. 378, depositions were taken, whereupon the Court concluded that the controversy was a sham, and dismissed it.

In 1862, J. S. Black had appeared for third persons, and upon evidence filed with the Court won a dismissal in Chamberlain v. Cleveland, 1 Bl. 419.

had acted without authority when he purported to give the Association's consent to the dismissal of these suits; that the Association had never assented, and that the meeting where butchers were alleged to have accepted the compromise was not the action of the Association.[126]

The Court, having heard arguments on the merits as well as on the suggestion to dismiss, took the cases under advisement.

THE COURT ORDERS A REARGUMENT

ON APRIL 15, 1872, the Court continued the cases for further argument at the next term. While no ruling was announced on the motion to dismiss, the action taken implied that it was being rejected.

Eight Justices had participated; Justice Nelson had taken almost no part in the Court's work for the past two years.[127] When a year later the matter came to judgment, these eight would divide equally, and the outcome would turn on Nelson's successor.

The argument and postponement of the *Slaughter House Cases* attracted little attention in New Orleans. Thanks to some butchers who refused to knuckle under, the controversy had been kept alive:[128] but it had ceased to be a topic of consuming public interest.

At that juncture the people had more exciting things to think about, including conflicts that presently reached the Supreme Court. In New Orleans a Committee of Fifty-One—leading citizens of various antecedents, John A. Campbell among them—were working to bring a reform in municipal affairs, then suffering from "the treachery, duplicity and tyranny" of the State administration. The Republicans had divided into warring factions, one for and one against Governor Warmoth.[129] There were two legislatures. On January 12, 1872—a day when Campbell was arguing the *Slaughter House Cases* in the Supreme Court—Mayor Flanders was calling upon President Grant to declare New Orleans under martial law: "Any hour may bring a collision which would only end in a scene of bloodshed."[130] A committee from the House of Representatives arrived in late January, heard a mass

---

[126] The affidavit, dated January 12, 1872, appears in Motion to Dismiss, at pp. 46–47.

[127] See supra, p. 753, and infra, p. 1451.

[128] To Verges, who said he spoke for "two thousand butchers," the new management was as obnoxious as the old: "We look upon this company as a crushing monopoly . . . . We intend to fight its iniquities as long as we possibly can, in hopes that we will

yet rout it, horse, foot and dragoon." *Bee*, Mar. 24, 1872.

It would be interesting to know what arrangements Campbell and Fellows had made with the butchers for a fee for the further prosecution of the controversy; to them the effort was greatly in the public interest.

[129] Ann. Cyc., 1871 and 1872, under "Louisiana."

[130] *Bee*, Jan. 13, 1872.

of testimony, and reported on the miserable situation without recommendation of any federal action.[131] Another matter in January 1872, of public interest especially to people of color, was a decision by the Supreme Court of Louisiana in *Sauvinet v. Walker*,[132] sustaining the State's equal rights legislation and Judge Dibble's award of $1,000 punitive damages against the owner of a coffeehouse. The action of the Supreme Court in 1876,[133] affirming the judgment of the State court, will be considered presently.

On November 28, 1872, Justice Nelson resigned, just before the December term. In his place, on December 3, President Grant nominated Ward Hunt, lately Chief Judge of the New York Court of Appeals. Also on December 3, the Court ordered that the three *Slaughter House Cases* be passed, to be taken up for argument on three weeks notice to counsel. The nomination was confirmed on December 11; Hunt took his seat on January 9, 1873. On December 16 the Court set Monday, February 3, for the pending cases.

THE REARGUMENT

ON THE DAY appointed a full Bench, after other business had been disposed of, turned to Nos. 8, 9, and 10, the butchers' cases. Counsel were granted four hours on each side, twice the normal allowance. Campbell opened, continuing on Tuesday, February 4. Senator Matt. H. Carpenter and Thomas J. Durant, for defendants in error, used the rest of that day. On Wednesday, J. Q. A. Fellows closed the argument.

Consideration of the *Slaughter House* litigation has been obscured by the interpretation and critique of latter-day wisdom: it will be rewarding for a while to sweep all this aside, to view the matter simply as it appeared to the participants. They could not possibly imagine the corpus of Fourteenth Amendment law which, accumulating through the decades, has come to impose itself upon men's minds

---

[131] After months of the most tangled partisan evolutions, at the election in November 1872, William Pitt Kellogg was the Republican candidate for governor. Under the Act of March 31, 1870, to enforce the right of citizens to vote, 16 Stat. 140, Kellogg brought suit against Governor Warmoth and his Board of Returning Officers, based on alleged exclusion of voters, to Kellogg's prejudice. Kellogg v. Warmouth *et al.*, Fed. Case No. 7667 (1872). [The name was often spelled Warmouth.] There-

upon the governor filed an original proceeding in the Supreme Court for a writ of prohibition or certiorari directed to District Judge Durell, holding the Circuit Court. This was argued on December 12, 1872, and decided on December 16. The Court responded that, until a final decree had been rendered, it had no jurisdiction. *Ex parte* Warmouth, 17 Wall. 64.

[132] 27 La. Ann. 14.

[133] Walker v. Sauvinet, 92 U.S. 90 (1876).

as though it should always have been obvious. Conversely, we would do well to concede that the Justices must have been acquainted with what had been going on, under the dome of the Capitol and in popular understanding throughout the country. If then they show no cognizance of purposes that have since been attributed to the men who carried the Amendment into the Constitution, we should take heed and proceed with caution. For the moment let us take them as we find them, seeking modestly to understand before we presume to criticize.

From his original bill of complaint to his final argument, Campbell displayed a confident authority in presenting *Slaughter House* as a great cause. In the earliest of his briefs in the Supreme Court he dwelt upon the transformation effected by the Thirteenth and Fourteenth Amendments:

> Conscience, speech, publication, security, freedom, and whatever else is essential to the liberty, or is proper as an attribute of citizenship, are now held under the guarantee of the Constitution of the United States. We have found in the bill of rights in the Constitution of Louisiana but a cobweb, through which the seventeen made an easy passage. Nor have we been greatly disappointed at this fact. The case shows that the expectation existed at the beginning that protection must be found in the tribunals of the United States under the amendments to the Constitution. . . .[134]

The question raised at this juncture was of first magnitude: "None more so has been presented to the Court."[135]

Campbell based his effort almost as much on the Thirteenth as on the Fourteenth Amendment. The prohibition, "Neither slavery nor involuntary servitude," derived from the Northwest Ordinance of 1787, had "a wider and more enduring purpose" than merely to forbid black slavery. "Whenever a law . . . makes a discrimination between classes of persons, which deprives one class of their freedom or their property" to serve the interest of others, it imposes an involuntary servitude. In Roman and in modern Civil Law (including the system prevailing in Louisiana), the relationship whereby certain land was in some respect burdened for the benefit of the owner of other land, was known as a *servitude*. Campbell instanced *thirlage* in Scots law, whereby dwellers in a district must resort to one mill: in 1799 Parliament had provided a release. A like relation was the *banalité* in prerevolutionary France, whereby a lord might hold a monopoly "of the oven, mill, wine-press, SLAUGHTER HOUSE, forge and the like:" all that was abolished in 1791. "The privilege granted these *seventeen*" by the Slaughter House charter

---

[134] Brief in the six cases at December term 1869, p. 37.

[135] Brief on reargument, p. 3.

was another servitude: the inhabitants of three parishes "are deprived of what was a common right, and bound under a thraldom."[136]

This was really a play upon the word "servitude"—yet Campbell developed his theme to reach this conclusion:

> The general principle of the law is that every person has individually, and the public have collectively, a right to require that the course of trade should be free from unreasonable obstruction. . . .[137]

The Fourteenth Amendment was "a more comprehensive exposition of the principles which lie at the foundation of the 13th."[138] National citizenship had been made primary; "with an imperial authority" the Amendment secured to every citizen his privileges and immunities. "The comprehensiveness of this amendment"—the "breadth of the language"—"the long drawn history" and the "discussions, contests and commotions" of which it was the culmination—all these, he said, "demonstrate that the weighty import of its ordination is not to be misunderstood . . . ."[139]

Campbell spun his conception of the privileges in which a citizen of the United States should now be secure. They included freedom to travel throughout the land, "to cultivate the ground, or to purchase products, or to carry on trade, or to maintain himself and his family by free industry. The capacity to acquire and hold property is also recognized in the Constitution. These positive rights live in the consciousness of the peoples, and are called the people's rights—the common right— the common law, and are the product of the common mind of the people, living and working as individuals . . . ." "All these things grow out of these two amendments, and are held under the safeguard of the nation. These things being secured, all the other things would follow. But the amendments secure the more important and the most imperiled of the consequential rights . . . ."[140]

While he was not so specific, Campbell's argument seems to lead to this: that as the courts had shaped the common law in accord with the needs of society, henceforth the Court should find authority in the Fourteenth Amendment to recognize whatever was "consequential" to national citizenship. (But there would be this difference: that whereas the development of the common law remained subordinate to legislation, the Court's interpretations would become the law of the Constitu-

---

136 Brief on Reargument, pp. 5–10.
137 Brief at December term 1869, p. 6; Report of Argument on 3d and 4th February, 1873, p. 24.

138 Brief on reargument, p. 10.
139 Ibid., pp. 17–19.
140 Ibid., pp. 20–22.

tion.) Campbell did not pursue his conception beyond its immediate application to the situation at New Orleans.

This to be sure was advocacy with a specific purpose; yet it was the production of a contemplative and resourceful mind. (Justice Miller, while rejecting Campbell's line of thought, observed that his research had been equalled only by his eloquence. In Field, Campbell's argument kindled a fervid sympathy; in Bradley it struck accord with views long held on the relation of the law to "the unimpeded, unrestrained, free development of the *individual man.*"[141]) Campbell did not rest his argument on words spoken in the 39th Congress—he did not glance in that direction. He viewed the Amendment in the larger context of the progress of liberty, and the "mighty revolution" that had lately taken place within the nation: citizenship had been made "a word of large significance, and comprehended great endowments of privilege, immunity, of right . . . ."[142]

The briefs filed by Thomas J. Durant for Crescent City were undistinguished. The slaughter house statute, he said, was a measure of police, and concededly the police power resided in the States: he cited the language of old cases where the Court had discussed what States might do without encroaching upon the Commerce Clause.[143] But this ignored that the Fourteenth Amendment had done something new: it had imposed a federal standard upon those very matters that belonged to the States. The Amendment, he asserted, had "no other meaning than to place the blacks on a footing of political and civil equality with the whites." "The contemporaneous discussions and debates at the time of the amendment show that no other object was in view, nor can it be made to embrace any other without sacrificing its spirit."[144] He did not elaborate.

Retained as counsel by Crescent City, but not taking part in oral argument, was Charles Allen, Attorney General of Massachusetts from 1867 to 1872. This was an able and discriminating lawyer; later for many years he sat on the Supreme Judicial Court of his State. Allen's brief is the one set out in 21 Lawyers' Edition of the United States Reports at 399–402 as presenting the case for the defendants in error. It made a powerful challenge to Campbell's expansive mode of thought.

---

[141] Reference is made to three of my biographical studies of Bradley, identified supra, ch. 14, note 132. The quotation is from an address at Newark in 1848, used in the lecture reprinted in *Mr. Justice*, at p. 78, edition of 1956; p. 74 of edition of 1964. Bradley's background in the civil law and in English legal antiquities is explained in "The Education of a Jus-

tice," at pp. 230–35, and in "What Makes a Great Justice?", passim.

[142] Brief on reargument, p. 39. He said he could not read the Fourteenth Amendment "as a measure of hostility; as a form of words to establish the supremacy of a party—a party platform . . . ." P. 18.

[143] Brief on first argument, pp. 6–8.

[144] Brief on reargument, pp. 7, 10.

XXI: *Privileges of Citizens of the United States*

Did the Fourteenth Amendment strike at legislation such as that under review? He answered concisely:

> So far as can be judged by public debates upon the subject, it was certainly never intended or contemplated that this Amendment should receive such a construction. Have Congress and the whole nation been deceived, misled, mistaken? Have they done that which they did not intend to do?

If the language were taken in its broadest sense—abridge *no* privilege —it would

> prohibit any State from abridging any existing privilege of any citizens of the United States, or from enforcing any law already enacted which abridges any privileges or immunities of citizens. . . .

He pointed to the startling consequences: that would bar the enforcement of a mass of laws for regulating employments, for restraining lotteries and the liquor trade, for fixing hours of labor and for prohibiting the employment of children, women and men in particular occupations for more than a certain number of hours. It would "bring within the jurisdiction of this court all questions relating to any of these or kindred subjects, and deprive the Legislatures and State courts of the several States from regulating and settling their internal affairs." (As the Fourteenth Amendment later came to be applied, many of those consequences did indeed come to pass, through the fostering of economic "liberty" and "property" under the Due Process Clause. This culminated in a memorable check to the Court in the constitutional crisis of 1937.)

"The true method of constitutional interpretation," Allen's brief continued, was to read the Amendment in relation to "the state of things in which it had its origin." The design was "simple and well known":

> It was to assure to all citizens and persons the same rights enjoyed by white citizens and persons. Every citizen should enjoy the same rights as white citizens. Every person should enjoy the same protection of the laws as white persons.

The contrast between the mood of Allen's brief and that of Campbell's argument anticipates the difference between the majority and the minority of the Court when *Slaughter House* came to be decided.

Matt. Carpenter led for Crescent City, in 1872 and on the

reargument in 1873. Apparently what he said was not transcribed; doubtless it was powerful, for the Justices remembered him as having been well prepared and luminous on every occasion.[145]

On the reargument, J. Q. A. Fellows, for Butchers' Benevolent Association, filed a twenty-three-page brief entitled "History, Object, Aim and Intent of the 13th, 14th and 15th Amendments, and of the Contemporaneous Legislation." This was put in by way of reply to assertions minimizing the Amendment. Fellows' brief was not reflected in Wallace's report or in Lawyers' Edition. Because it expresses all that an advocate attacking the monopoly statute saw fit to claim from the Congressional debates, the brief is entitled to attention.

The Civil War, Fellows began, was the culmination of a contest *"as to the unrestricted right of every man to the fruits of his own labor."* When the fighting was ended, it was found that the old spirit of oppression still prevailed. Something more was needed; the 39th Congress took measures to "secure to mankind the fruits which the immense sacrifice of life and treasure had placed within their reach." Fellows traced the debates on the Civil Rights Bill and the Amendment. He quoted Trumbull, Sumner, Bingham, Kelley, Hale, Stevens, Garfield, Raymond, and Poland. Then,

> As the result of this examination, the only conclusion to be arrived at, as to the intention of Congress in proposing the amendments, and especially the first section of the Fourteenth Amendment, and the interpretation universally put upon it by every member of Congress, whether friend or foe, the interpretation in which all were agreed, was, in the words of Mr. Hale, "that it was intended to apply to every State which has failed to apply equal protection to life, liberty and property"; or in the words of Mr. Bingham, "that tne protection given by the laws of the States shall be equal in respect to life, liberty and property to all persons"; or in the language of Mr. Sumner, that it abolished "oligarchy, aristocracy, caste, *or monopoly with peculiar privileges and powers."*
>
> In other words, that the aim, object and intent was to make sure to all men that those rights of life, of liberty, and of property, of

---

[145] After Carpenter's death in 1881, Justice Miller wrote of him that "He was the only man I have ever known, who while filled with learning, and brilliant with genius never omitted ample and careful preparation . . . ." Fairman, *Mr. Justice Miller,* 117. And Justice Bradley: "He was extremely happy in possessing the court at once with the pith and gist of his case

. . . . Although to do this must have cost him an immense amount of labor and exact investigation, his address did not betray them, except in the result, his manner and style having all the outward appearances of being perfectly off-hand and spontaneous." Frank A. Flower, *Life of Matthew Hale Carpenter* (Madison, Wis.: D. Atwood and Co., 1883), 171n.

the right to labor freely, and the enjoyment of the fruits of their own industry, which has been contended for in blood for centuries, and ever since the first contest for the rights of man began.[146]

Members throughout the debates had said that men should receive equal protection in the enjoyment of life, liberty and property: but such a general sentiment does not decide concrete cases. Fellows was displaying the best of his gleanings—and the result was scarcely helpful. Others with other purposes have plucked many other sentences from the profuse record. The point here is that a competent advocate, urging an expansive interpretation, combed through the debates and, with specific citations, drew the attention of the Justices to so much as he saw fit to claim for his side.

Fellows closed the argument on February 5, 1873. On April 14 the decision was announced: the judgments of the Supreme Court of Louisiana were affirmed, per Miller, J; Chase, C. J., and Swayne, Field, and Bradley dissented.

Carpenter wired to his clients:

The banded butchers are busted. Matt.[147]

THE OPINION FOR THE COURT

JUSTICE MILLER SKETCHED the progress of the litigation since it came on the docket.[148] He now passed upon the motion to dismiss, which had been "much pressed by counsel." In the materials filed the Court did not find satisfactory evidence that the compromise had been

---

146 Fellows' brief, cited in text, at pp. 21–22.

147 Flower, *Life of . . . Carpenter*, 135n.

148 The following sentence seems to call for explanation:

On account of the importance of the questions involved in these cases they were, by permission of the Court, taken up out of their order on the docket and argued in January 1872.

Actually the *Slaughter House Cases*, from docketing on August 30, 1870 to argument on January 11 and 12, 1872 (as Nos. 60, 61 and 62), had been moving in their normal order. Compare:

Tarble's Case, 13 Wall. 397, had been docketed on July 19, 1870—argued on November 14, 1871—and (as No. 54) was decided on March 4, 1872.

The Pennsylvania College Cases, 13 Wall. 190 [statute authorizing merger of Washington College and Jefferson College did not infringe Contract Clause] were docketed on July 25, 1870—argued on January 8 and 9, 1872—and (as Nos. 55, 56 and 57) were decided on February 12, 1872.

Nicholson Pavement Co. v. Jenkins, 14 Wall. 452, was docketed on September 6, 1870—argued January 12, 1872 [the day the argument in *Slaughter House* was concluded]—and (as

binding upon the plaintiffs in error now before the Court. "They have a right to be heard, and the motion to dismiss cannot prevail."

He then separated the essential matters from the large assertions that had been made. There could be no question of the propriety of confining the slaughtering business to a remote locality. *Under the statute, the butchers remained free to practice their calling: they must simply use the appointed facilities.*[149] Had it been the City itself, rather than a private corporation, on which the Legislature cast the same duties, with the same privileges, no serious question of constitutionality could have been raised. But surely the Legislature might choose the means: he recalled *McCulloch v. Maryland*, where Marshall had sustained the authority of Congress to incorporate a private bank in order that it might perform a public function.[150] The charges to be made by the company were limited by the statute, "and we are not advised that they are on the whole exorbitant or unjust." (It was not until 1890 that the Court, in the development of the Due Process Clause of the Fourteenth Amendment, held that a party affected was entitled to a *judicial* determination of the fairness of utility rates fixed by public authority.[151])

No. 63) was decided on January 29, 1872.

According to the Docket and the Minutes, the only respect in which *Slaughter House* was taken up out of order was at the point that follows.

On November 7, 1871—early in the Adjourned Term—an order was announced:

That all cases continued at this term after Monday next, the 13th instant, will be put at the foot of the calendar of the next term unless otherwise specially ordered by the Court.

On November 14 Black moved that the three remaining *Slaughter House Cases* be continued; this was then argued. On November 15 the motion was granted. Black's object was to obtain time to assemble material to show that the remaining cases had been compromised, and should be dismissed. On December 14, Exhibits A and B were filed, and at the same time a motion was filed to dismiss. Although no special order is recorded for bringing up the cases, they were (as Nos. 60, 61 and 62) argued on January 11 and 12, 1872—both on the motion to dismiss and on the

merits. Presumably this is the point to which Justice Miller's sentence referred.

The cases were held under advisement until, on April 15, they were continued to the next term for reargument.

Without this explanation, a very attentive reader might have found a discrepancy between Justice Miller's statement and the chronological account that has been given in the text. This footnote has illustrated, once again, the use of the Minutes and the Docket for observing in close focus what the Court had done in its control of its calendar.

[149] The statement needs to be underlined because, in the denunciation of the monopoly, its truth tends to be lost to view. Certainly those who procured the charter saw to it that the prescribed charges were higher than they should have been. Yet it would be the consumers rather than the butchers on whom the burden would come to rest.

[150] 4 Wheat. 316 (1819).

[151] Chicago, M. & St. P. R.R. v. Minnesota, 134 U.S. 418.

The proposition, said Miller, is reduced to these terms:

can any exclusive privileges be granted to any of its citizens, or to a corporation, by the Legislature of a State?

Campbell's examples of monopolies established by a monarch in derogation of the rights of his subjects were inapposite to the situation where some exclusive privilege had been granted by a representative legislature.

The statute had been sustained so far as the constitution of Louisiana was concerned; there remained the contention that it violated the Constitution of the United States, at four points: involuntary servitude—privileges and immunities—equal protection—due process of law.

Miller dwelt upon the gravity of the occasion: nothing so important had come before the Court during the official life of any of its members. (He might have said, nothing since *Dred Scott*, for Justice Clifford had come to the Court after that momentous decision.)

We have given every opportunity for a full hearing at the bar; we have discussed it freely and compared views among ourselves; we have taken ample time for careful deliberation . . . .

Here a note, pertinent to later criticism: everything that counsel or Justices then regarded as significant had been brought into consideration.

Appeal to the Thirteenth Amendment was dismissed as far-fetched: it applied only to *personal* servitude.[152] The dissenters made no serious contest on this point.

The pervading purpose of the three post-war Amendments had been to bring freedom and security to the slave race; but for that, said Justice Miller, they would not have been suggested. Early legislation (the Black Codes) in States being restored by President Johnson had forced upon the 39th Congress a conviction that a further Amendment was needed for the protection of "the unfortunate race who had suffered so much."[153]

The Fourteenth Amendment opened with a definition which—overturning what Taney had said in *Dred Scott*—admitted members of

---

[152] He instanced the burdensome Negro apprenticeship which the Chief Justice had struck down in Matter of Turner, on the circuit in Maryland. Fed. Case No. 14,247 (1867), supra, p. 1309.

[153] He made brief reference to the "onerous disabilities and burdens" which that legislation had laid upon the colored race, and the belief "that their lives were at the mercy of bad men, either because the laws for their protection were insufficient or were not enforced." See supra, pp. 282-84.

that race to [1] *citizenship of the United States and* [2] *of the State*.[154] Then came the command that no State abridge "the privileges and immunities of *citizens of the United States.*" The Amendment, further, gave Congress authority to enforce its provisions by appropriate legislation.

Theretofore "the entire domain" of the rights of citizens within a State had lain "within the constitutional and legislative power" of the State, subject to a few federal constitutional limitations, such as that against laws impairing the obligation of contracts.

The Constitution, in Article IV, Section 2, had declared that

> The Citizens of each State shall be entitled to all Privileges and Immunities of Citizens in the several States.

Miller sought to give clarity to that provision:

> Its sole purpose was to declare to the several States, that whatever those rights, as you grant or establish them to your own citizens, or as you limit or qualify, or impose restrictions on their exercise, the same, neither more nor less, shall be the measure of the rights of citizens of other States within your jurisdiction.

Such had been the scheme of the Constitution. Now that the Amendment, after defining the *two* citizenships, had commanded that no State abridge the rights of *citizens of the United States*, was it purposed thereby that "the entire domain of civil rights heretofore belonging exclusively to the States" should henceforth be "subject to the control of Congress," and that the Supreme Court become "a perpetual censor upon all legislation of the States, on the civil rights of their own citizens"? "[S]o great a departure from the structure and spirit of our institutions" must be rejected, "in the absence of language which expresses such a purpose too clearly to admit of doubt."

At this point a reminder is in order. "Civil rights" has come to have a particular connotation: the rights of members of a racial minority to personal safety, to participation in the political process, to

---

[154] The Constitution had expressly recognized that there was a citizenship *of the United States* (by its provisions on eligibility to be President, Senator, and Representative), but had not defined it. Some had argued that *State* citizenship was primary, and *United States* citizenship derivative. Taney in *Dred Scott* had taken the view that a Negro could not become a citizen within the meaning of the Constitution—not by the action of a State, nor by naturalization by Congress; the Court did not rule upon that proposition.

The Civil Rights Act of 1866 declared who were citizens of the United States; the Fourteenth Amendment repeated that definition, and added, "and of the State wherein they reside."

opportunities for advancement. Justice Miller was referring to something quite different—the vast field wherein the State legislated on such matters as family relationships, the acquisition and disposition of property, business associations, and the regulation of occupations. Article IV referred to this field, and simply required that the State give equal treatment to the sojourner; his rights were fixed by that relation. But the new phrase, "privileges and immunities of citizens of the United States," must have its own substantive content. If, moved by disapproval of the arrangements at New Orleans, the Court were to hold that the butchers had been denied a privilege of United States citizenship, would not similar complaints in a wide variety of other situations call for redress by the Court? Whatever reasoning would enable the Court to afford a remedy, the same reasoning would permit Congress to prescribe a rule. Afterknowledge of Congressional lethargy in acting under the Fourteenth Amendment, even for the protection of those for whom it was most immediately designed, should not dull apprehension of the consequences Justice Miller was considering.[155] The Court wisely

---

[155] When *Slaughter House* was argued in January 1872 there was pending in the Senate a measure by Senator Sumner to enact that citizens of the United States, without distinction of race, were entitled to impartial enjoyment of accommodations or facilities furnished by common carriers; innkeepers; theaters and other places of public amusement; public institutions of learning supported or authorized by law; and incorporated church organizations, cemetery associations, and benevolent institutions. This was offered as an amendment to House Bill No. 380, to remove political disabilities imposed by Section 3 of the Fourteenth Amendment. Cong. Globe, 42–2, 244, Dec. 20, 1871; p. 381, Jan. 15, 1872.

The Nation commented:

Now, there can be no question as to the propriety of forcing common carriers to afford all citizens accommodation on an equal footing, and there is the same thing to be said with regard to licensed innkeepers. Men must travel on their lawful occasions, and the means of travel are now . . . great monopolies, to which everybody must resort *nolens volens*. In travel-

ing, too, one must often use inns, and in large numbers of places there is only one inn, and in most places there are only a few . . . .

So far, Sumner's measure had *The Nation*'s support. As to cemeteries, it thought that compulsion was inexcusable; as to theaters, it hoped for "admission through improvement in the moral sense of the community . . . ." 14:65–66. Feb. 1, 1872.

On January 8, 1874, *The Nation* spoke of further debate at the First Session of the 43rd Congress:

As to the inexpediency of this kind of legislation, vastly larger numbers of Northern people are now convinced of it than we would have believed possible a few years since when Mr. Sumner began pushing this measure . . . . But if anything could prevent these numbers from becoming larger, it would be such things as the behavior of [a Southern Representative who asserted that the black man could never be the equal of the white]. 18:17.

The Civil Rights Act of March 1, 1875, 18 Stat. 335—passed after Sumner's death—was substantially his measure, reduced to apply only to

pauses to inquire, what would be the logical implications of the course we are asked to take?

If the new clause did not cover "the entire domain" of rights established by the State, what then was its meaning? Evidently some alternative must be indicated. In recoiling from consequences they considered too subversive of the federal system, the majority felt driven to a construction that made the clause trivial. As the Amendment distinguished two citizenships, so there pertained to each its own body of privileges and immunities. The "privileges and immunities of citizens of the United States" were only those that pertained to citizens of the United States *as such*—rights that "owe their existence to the Federal Government, its national character, its Constitution, or its laws." To illustrate, there was the right to resort to the offices of the Government, to have access to the ports, to use the navigable streams. (But these were rights such as had been recognized in *Crandall v. Nevada*[156] in 1868, four months before the Fourteenth Amendment went into force.) Also there was the right to be protected on the high seas and in foreign countries. (But there had been no need to prohibit the States from interfering with the enjoyment of such protection, beyond the reach of State power.) The opinion also mentioned the right to assemble, to petition, to have the writ of habeas corpus as among the "rights of the citizen guarantied by the Federal Constitution." (But whatever flowed from the Constitution had been enforceable all along, with no need for reiteration.)

Certainly Justice Miller and those for whom he spoke would never have propounded so vacuous a construction if they had not felt compelled thus to avoid what Justice Frankfurter later referred to as "the mischievous uses to which that [privileges and immunities] clause would lend itself if its scope were not confined to that given it [by the Slaughter House Cases]."[157]

The argument on the Due Process Clause had "not been much pressed," said Justice Miller; and "under no construction . . . that we

---

carriers, inns, and theaters and other places of public amusement. This was held invalid in the Civil Rights Cases, 109 U.S. 3 (1883).

The next Civil Rights Act was that of 1957, 71 Stat. 634. It authorized the Attorney General to seek a declaratory judgment or injunctive relief to restrain the deprivation of the right to vote; it also created the Commission on Civil Rights, with power to investigate allegations of such denials.

[156] 6 Wall. 35. Supra, pp. 1303–07.

[157] Concurring in Adamson v. California, 332 U.S. 46, 59 at 61 (1947). He was agreeing with the majority in rejecting the contention of four Justices that the Privileges and Immunities Clause and other provisions of Section 1 of the Fourteenth Amendment, "separately and as a whole," were intended to make the federal Bill of Rights (in particular, the Fifth Amendment) binding upon the States.

have ever seen, or any that we deem admissible," could the restraint upon the butchers be held to be a deprivation within that clause.

The claim under the Equal Protection Clause was dismissed with what proved to be a most unlucky prediction: "We doubt very much whether any action of a State not directed by way of discrimination against the negroes as a class, or on account of their race, will ever be held to come within the purview of this provision."

"Unquestionably," Justice Miller concluded, the experience of the Civil War had "given great force to the argument" for strengthening the national government. But however that sentiment had contributed to the adoption of the post-war Amendments, the Court did not read in them "any purpose to destroy the main features" of the federal system. The Court must maintain "the balance between State and federal power" with a steady hand.

JUSTICE FIELD FOR THE DISSENTERS

WHEN THE COURT has been put to a hard choice, there will be much that can be said in dissent. Field observed that the butchers had abstract justice on their side, and that he would "endeavor to show that the position has some support in the fundamental law of the country."

The pretense that the Louisiana statute was a sanitary measure was "shallow." In only two of its requirements could it be so qualified: that for landing and slaughtering at a designated place below the city, and that for the inspection of animals before slaughter.

Otherwise the statute was without justification.

> If exclusive privileges of this character can be granted to a corporation of seventeen persons, they may, in the discretion of the Legislature, be equally granted to a single individual. . . .

If for twenty-five years, then in perpetuity; if for this pursuit, then for even the most simple occupations. Indeed, on the theory of the majority opinion, "there is no monopoly, in the most odious form, which may not be upheld."

This sort of reasoning might pass as legal logic, but it was, rather, the flight of an agitated mind.[158] Durant's brief for Crescent

---

[158] Compare this observation, in Justice Miller's opinion for the Court in United States v. Lee, 106 U.S. 196, at 217 (1882):

Hypothetical cases of great evils may be suggested by a particularly fruitful imagination in regard to almost every law upon which depends the rights of the individual or of the Government, and if the existence of laws is to depend upon their capacity to withstand such criticism, the whole fabric of the law must fail.

City had used the same method of exaggeration to reach the opposite pole: "If it can be said with truth that any man has a common-law—natural—right to keep a stock landing or slaughter-house, so it may be equally well said that every man has such a right to build and carry on a railroad, to be a banker, have a ferry, carry letters for pay, &c. ...."[159]

Projection to an extreme was particularly inappropriate for testing validity as against the Fourteenth Amendment, whose effect has been to confine the State's exercise of its own powers within the bounds of reason. "This is a question of degree—and therefore cannot be disposed of by general propositions."[160] Field himself put it accurately, years after *Slaughter House*, in sustaining the State's power to select those who would be allowed to sell liquor at retail: notwithstanding "the right of every citizen of the United States to pursue any lawful trade or business, under such restrictions as are imposed upon all persons of the same age, sex, and condition," this was "subject to such reasonable conditions as may be deemed by the governing authority of the country essential to the safety, health, peace, good order and morals of the community."[161]

If, Justice Field's opinion continued, the new Privileges and Immunities Clause meant no more than the majority conceded,

> it was a vain and idle enactment, which accomplished nothing, and most unnecessarily excited Congress and the people on its passage. . . .

In that he was certainly right. But then it was incumbent on him to answer,

---

[159] Brief for Defendant in Error in Esteben v. State of Louisiana, No. 479 (December term 1869) at p. 8.

[160] Holmes, J., speaking for the Court in Pennsylvania Coal Co. v. Mahon, 260 U.S. 393, 416 (1922). The question was whether a statute, forbidding the mining of coal in such a way as to cause the subsidence of a dwelling, amounted to a taking of property without due process of law. The majority held that it had gone "too far." Brandeis, J., dissented.

[161] Crowley v. Christensen, 137 U.S. 86 (1890).

Field's words in *Slaughter House*, that "all grants of exclusive privileges [in the pursuit of the ordinary avocations] are against common right, and void" were wide enough to condemn Massachusetts' well-contrived statute of 1870, whereby all engaged in slaughtering within six miles of Boston might be required to resort to the facilities of a corporation at Brighton. Act to incorporate the Butchers' Slaughtering and Melting Association, Acts and Resolves 1870, ch. 365. Supra, n. 66. This could be done by the State Board of Health if, upon notice and hearing, it was found requisite to the public health. Charges would be fixed by the Board. Enforcement was subject to effective judicial control. How the legislation arose out of the conference of interested parties is recounted in the Official Record of the State Board of Health in the case of John M. Tyler *et al.* v. John P. Squire *et al.*, Cambridge, 1874.

What, then, are the privileges and immunities which are secured against abridgment by State legislation?

Justice Field recurred to the privileges and immunities of Article IV, Section 2, and to the gloss Justice Washington had given on the circuit in 1823[162]—an utterance which, in the absence of anything more authoritative, had been repeated over and over. The citizen from out-of-State was entitled to such rights as were "fundamental" (but not, the court held, to take oysters from the waters of the State). He was free to pass through or to reside "for the purposes of trade . . . or otherwise," to hold property, to have the protection of the local law— "subject nevertheless to such restraints as the government may justly prescribe for the general good . . . ."

Justice Field accepted that as "a sound construction." The clause, he said, secured "the right to pursue a lawful employment in a lawful manner, without other restraint than such as equally affects all persons." Then, he reasoned, Suppose that a State were to create "a monopoly of any known trade . . . [for example, making shoes] in favor of her own citizens, or any portion of them:" by Article IV, Section 2, "non-resident citizens could claim equality of privilege, . . . and thus, as respects them, the monopoly would cease." From the proposition that no State could "exclude at any time, citizens of other States from participation in particular branches of commerce or trade," Justice Field advanced to this further proposition:

> Now, what the clause in question does for the protection of citizens of one State against the creation of monopolies in favor of citizens of other States, the 14th Amendment does for the protection of every citizen of the United States against the creation of any monopoly whatever. . . .

Thinking went astray at the fantasy about a State creating a monopoly, say in shoe-making. If it conferred such a monopoly upon *all* of its citizens, that would plainly be a violation of Article IV. Of course no State ever enacted that only *some* of its citizens could make shoes for all of its inhabitants: but upon that absurd supposition, was it true that citizens of other States could come in and—what was forbidden to the generality of local citizens—make shoes, and so break the monopoly? Justice Field's assertion was a large dictum, unwarranted, and it seems, unsound.

Rights under Article IV, Section 2, were merely relative, not absolute: Justice Bradley had that in mind when, on the circuit at

---

[162] Corfield v. Coryell, Fed. Case   No. 3230 (C.C.E.D. Pa.). See supra, pp. 1121–22.

New Orleans, he said, by way of contrast, that "the Fourteenth Amendment . . . was intended to protect the citizens of the United States in some fundamental privileges of an absolute and not merely a relative character."[163] Since Article IV promised the visiting citizen nothing more than pot-luck, it was faulty reasoning to say that as a consequence *of that provision* one reached the proposition that the Fourteenth Amendment guaranteed adequate substantive fare to every citizen of the United States in his own or in any other State.[164]

Justice Field's opinion took a new turn:

> All monopolies in any known trade or manufacture are an invasion of these [Fourteenth Amendment] privileges, for they encroach upon the liberty of citizens to acquire property and pursue happiness, and

---

[163] Supra, p. 1334.

[164] Justice Field's hypothetical monopoly will be pursued a little further, simply to test his mode of reasoning.

One ought to avoid dogmatism about Article IV, Section 2—partly by reason of the paucity of decided cases, partly because that provision can hardly be kept in isolation from the Commerce Clause.

Take Ward v. Maryland, 12 Wall. 418 (1871): the State imposed a discriminatory license fee upon nonresidents who sold by sample the products of other States. Evarts argued that this was invalid under the Privileges and Immunities provision of Article IV, and also under the Commerce Clause. The Court condemned it on the former ground, but observed that if States could lay such discriminatory taxes upon citizens of other States, the commerce power would be "of no value." Justice Bradley condemned the tax on both grounds.

Contemplating Justice Field's hypothetical monopoly of shoemaking: certainly the State could not have prevented the introduction of shoes in foreign and interstate commerce, and *in that way* the monopoly would indeed have been broken.

Vary his hypothetical situation, and imagine a State-created monopoly in lotteries. That is not fantastic: in 1868 the Louisiana State Lottery Company was created, with the "ex-

clusive privilege" of conducting a lottery, for a period of twenty-five years. (This was enacted by the same Legislature which, at its Second Session, in 1869, chartered the Crescent City Company.) The Lottery Company was to pay the State $40,000 per annum, and would be "exempt from all other taxes or licenses of any kind whatever." The validity of this was affirmed by the Louisiana Supreme Court: Louisiana State Lottery Co. v. Richoux, 23 La. Ann. 743 (1871) as to the exclusive right; Louisiana State Lottery Co. v. New Orleans, 24 La. Ann. 86 (1872) as to the exemption from taxation.

One reads of this monopoly in the United States Reports. A statute of March 1879 declared that the grant was repealed; but thereupon by the constitution of 1879 the charter was "recognized as a contract binding on the State"—and on that basis the Court held that the tax exemption was protected by the Contract Clause. New Orleans v. Houston, 119 U.S. 265 (1886).

Apply Justice Field's reasoning to Louisiana's lottery monopoly: would it be true that "non-resident citizens could claim equality of privilege . . . , and thus, as respects them, the monopoly would cease"? Surely Article IV, Section 2, would not enable citizens of other States to come in and engage in what to the generality of local citizens was forbidden.

were held void at common law in the great *Case of Monopolies,* decided during the reign of Queen Elizabeth.

This referred to *Darcy v. Allen,* in the King's Bench in 1603.[165] D. held an exclusive grant from the Crown to import and sell playing-cards; he sued A. for invading the privilege. A. pleaded the custom of the city of London, that as a freeman he could buy and sell all things merchantable. The court held: the grant was a monopoly, and against common law; not by the Crown, but only by Parliament, could a man be restrained from exercising a trade. Field told of the Statute of Monopolies of 1624 which (with exceptions) declared the illegality of such royal grants.

Then,

> The common law of England is the basis of the jurisprudence of the United States. . . .

It had been cherished by the colonists, and upon their separation from the mother country it was incorporated into their law.

Field cited three great works, each of 1776, and each supporting the freedom of individual initiative: the Declaration of Independence, Adam Smith's *Wealth of Nations,* and (of special relevance to Louisiana) the French king's decree abolishing monopolies, prepared by Turgot. Now the Fourteenth Amendment, he wrote,

> was intended to give practical effect to the declaration of 1776 of inalienable rights, rights which are the gift of the Creator, which the law does not confer, but only recognizes. . . .

The argument came to this climax:

> If the trader in London could plead that he was a free citizen of that city against the enforcement to his injury of monopolies, surely under the 14th Amendment every citizen of the United States should be able to plead his citizenship of the republic as a protection against any similar invasion of his privileges and immunities.

That sentence should be scanned. The proposition comes to this: that since the English court of common law held that it pertained not to the Crown, but only to the Legislative Power, to create a monopoly in trade, now it was a privilege of the citizen of the United States that he should not be injuriously affected by State legislation making such an exclusive grant.

---

[165] The Case of Monopolies, 11 Coke's Reports 84b; Sir Francis Moore's Cases 671.

As a demonstration, that fell flat.

As an argument to show that exclusive grants in trade were impolitic and contrary to the economic thought of the past century, Justice Field's paragraphs were effective. Campbell's briefs were full of just such appeals to history. But whereas an advocate seeks to persuade, it is the function of a Judge to decide—and one expects that his reasons will be tenable.

Field, in the ardor of his condemnation of the malodorous situation in New Orleans, was bent upon scoring points. The paramount need of the occasion, however, was for cool heads—straight thinking—as clear prevision as could be attained. What was the Court going to make out of the Amendment?

The essence of Field's response was that it promised to every citizen the realization of the inalienable rights of the Declaration of Independence—"rights which are the gift of the Creator; which the law does not confer, but only recognizes."

If it meant all that, the Supreme Court was going to have a boundless field of action.

Chase, C.J., Swayne, and Bradley concurred in Field's dissent.

JUSTICE BRADLEY'S OPINION

IF ONE READS it afresh in the light of a century's experience, Justice Bradley's opinion seems to have pointed the way toward what might have been a practicable and beneficial construction of the new Privileges and Immunities Clause. The reason for saying this will be explained at the close of the chapter. As his opinion is traced, in summary and quotation, one may look beyond the slaughter house to discern the implication he would draw from "the Privileges or Immunities of Citizens of the United States": not redundant, as in the opinion of the majority, nor unmeasured, as in Field's rhetoric.

Solution of the case at hand depended, he began, upon two questions:

> First. Is it one of the rights and privileges of a citizen of the United States to pursue such civil employment as he may choose to adopt, subject to such reasonable regulations as may be prescribed by law?

(In answering that in the affirmative he would develop his major premise—the import of the new clause.)

> Second. Is a monopoly, or exclusive right, given to one person to the exclusion of all others, to keep slaughter-houses, in a district

1360

of nearly twelve hundred square miles, for the supply of meat for a large city, a reasonable regulation of that employment which the Legislature has a right to impose?

(This would yield his minor premise: that under the circumstances it was not a reasonable regulation. This is the sort of inquiry with which one has long been familiar in Fourteenth Amendment cases. While agreeing on a general principle, the Justices may differ on whether some State measure, ill-devised as it seems, should be held to be beyond the limit of tolerance.)

Bradley then identified a third question:

> Lastly: can the Federal Courts administer relief to citizens of the United States whose privileges and immunities have been abridged by a State? Of this I entertain no doubt. Prior to the 14th Amendment this could not be done, except in a few instances, for want of the requisite authority.

His conclusion was that "Our jurisdiction and our duty are plain and imperative."

Certainly Bradley did not apprehend what enormous demands the years would bring: indeed he greatly underestimated. Yet he did throw a beam of light upon the course for the future.

"The first of these questions," he began, "is one of vast importance, and lies at the very foundations of our government." It was now settled, by the Amendment, "that the citizenship of the United States is the primary citizenship in this country...."

> A citizen of the United States has a perfect constitutional right to go to and reside in any State he chooses, and to claim citizenship therein, and an equality of rights with every other citizen; and the whole power of the nation is pledged to sustain him in that right. He is not bound to cringe to any superior, or to pray for any act of grace, as a means of enjoying all the rights and privileges enjoyed by other citizens. And when the spirit of lawlessness, mob violence, and sectional hate can be so completely repressed as to give full practical effect to this right, we shall be a happier nation, and a more prosperous one than we now are. ...

Included in the bundle of national privileges and immunities, in Bradley's view, was "the right of any citizen to follow whatever lawful employment he chooses to adopt (submitting himself to all lawful regulations) ...."

"In this free country, the people of which inherited certain traditionary rights and privileges from their ancestors, citizenship means

1361

something. It has certain privileges and immunities attached to it which the government, whether restricted by express or implied limitations, cannot take away or impair." These included "the rights which have been wrested from English sovereigns at various periods . . . ." He quoted from Magna Charta: No freeman shall be taken, etc., but by the law of the land—which had been expounded as rendering life, liberty and property inviolable, except by due process of law. The right to the writ of habeas corpus was another fundamental. The "life, liberty and the pursuit of happiness" of the Declaration of Independence were the equivalent of Blackstone's "absolute rights" of the individual: to personal security, liberty, and private property.

The Constitution declared some of the most important of the privileges of citizens. He mentioned several secured as against the States, and a number that were limitations upon the federal Government. "It was not necessary to say in words that the citizens of the United States should have and exercise all the privileges of citizens; the privilege of buying, selling and enjoying property; the privilege of engaging in any lawful employment for a livelihood; the privilege of resorting to the laws for redress of injuries and the like. Their very citizenship conferred these privileges . . . ."

To the minor question, Bradley made this answer:

> To compel a butcher, or rather all the butchers of a large city and an extensive district, to slaughter their cattle in another person's slaughter-house and pay him a toll therefor, is such a restriction upon the trade as materially to interfere with its prosecution. It is onerous, unreasonable, arbitrary and unjust. . . .

Lastly, he defined the nature of the task, as he saw it, and explained why it seemed quite manageable.

> It is futile to argue that none but persons of the African race are intended to be benefited by this amendment. They may have been the primary cause of the Amendment, but its language is general, embracing all citizens, and I think it was purposely so expressed.
>
> The mischief to be remedied was not merely slavery and its incidents and consequences; but that spirit of insubordination and disloyalty to the National Government which had troubled the country for so many years in some of the States, and that intolerance of free speech and free discussion which often rendered life and property insecure, and led to much unequal legislation. The Amendment was an attempt to give voice to the strong national yearning for that time and that condition of things, in which American citizenship should be a sure guaranty of safety, and in which every citizen of the United States might stand erect in every portion of its soil, in the full enjoy-

1362

ment of every right and privilege belonging to a freeman, without fear of violence or molestation.

That perceptive summary of the "national yearning" is in accord with what members of Congress, hazily and hopefully, had seemed to be saying when they supported the Amendment.

Would it result from such a construction that Congress, through its power to enforce, would be "interfering with the internal affairs of the States, and establishing therein civil and criminal codes of law for the government of the citizens and thus abolishing the State governments in everything but name"? Would it lead the federal courts to assume "the supervision of State tribunals on every subject of judicial inquiry" on the plea that some federal privilege had been abridged? In Bradley's view, "no such practical inconveniences would arise." "Very little, if any, legislation on the part of Congress would be required . . ."; the Amendment, like the Contract Clause, "would execute itself." That is, the point would arise in a suit, and would be settled by final reference to the Court. "As the privileges and immunities protected are only those fundamental ones which belong to every citizen, they would soon become so far defined as to cause but a slight accumulation of business in the Federal Courts." "But," he said in conclusion,

> even if the business of the National Courts should be increased, Congress could easily supply the remedy by increasing their number and efficiency. The great question is: what is the true construction of the Amendment? When once we find that, we shall find the means of giving it effect. The argument from inconvenience ought not to have a very controlling influence in questions of this sort. The national will and national interest are of far greater importance.

JUSTICE SWAYNE'S OPINION

SWAYNE JOINED IN the dissenting opinions of Field and Bradley, and added one of his own. The discussion was not acute. "No searching analysis," he said, was needed to discover the meaning of Section 1 of the Amendment. "Its language is intelligible and direct. Nothing can be more transparent. Every word has an established meaning. There is nothing to construe."

This throws more light upon Justice Swayne than upon the Amendment.

Chief Justice Chase said nothing beyond joining in Field's dissent. This was one of the last decisions in which he participated: he died three weeks later, on May 7, 1873.

MYRA BRADWELL'S CASE

On Tuesday, April 15, 1873, the Court announced its decision in another case on the Fourteenth Amendment: *Myra Bradwell v. State of Illinois.*[166] The holding was that it was *not* a denial of a privilege of United States citizenship for Illinois by its highest court to refuse a license to practice law to a woman otherwise qualified, on the ground of her sex. Justice Miller spoke for the Court. Of the minority in *Slaughter House,* Bradley, J., concurred specially in an opinion in which Swayne and Field joined. The Chief Justice dissented without opinion.

Myra Bradwell (1831–94) edited the useful *Chicago Legal News.* She had read law under the guidance of her husband, a practitioner and then judge in Chicago; the examiners certified to her professional attainments. But the Supreme Court of Illinois denied her a license, on the ground that a married woman would not be bound by contracts such as the law creates between attorney and client. Then upon a rehearing, after the applicant had "earnestly and ably" contested that point in a brief, the court held "that the sex of the applicant . . . is, as our law now stands, a sufficient reason for not granting this license."[167] When the legislature, said Lawrence, J., confided to the discretion of the court the making of rules on admission to practice, certainly there was "not the slightest expectation that this privilege would be extended equally to men and women." "Courts of justice were not intended to be made the instruments of pushing forward measures of popular reform." If this change was to be made, let it be done "by that department of the government to which the constitution has entrusted the power of changing the laws."

> In the view we have taken of this question, the argument drawn by the applicant from the constitution of the United States has no pertinency.

"Of the qualifications of the applicant we have no doubt," said the court—and to facilitate application to the legislature, filed a full opinion. "If the legislature shall choose to remove the existing barriers, . . . we shall cheerfully obey . . . ."

On the contention that she had been denied a privilege of citizen-

---

[166] 16 Wall. 130.

With the decision in *Slaughter House* and other cases being announced on Monday, for want of time this case had gone over.

[167] In the matter of the application of Mrs. Myra Bradwell, 55 Ill. 535 (1869).

ship, her case was taken to the Supreme Court, and docketed just a month behind the cases from New Orleans. It was argued on January 18, 1872,[168] by Senator Carpenter; no counsel appeared to oppose.

While Chicago lawyers could not fail to respect "our Myra's" remarkable attainments, their profession was inclined, the Illinois court had remarked, "if not to stand immovable upon the ancient ways, at least to make no hot haste in measures of reform . . . ." Her serious effort to win recognition as a lawyer was commonly treated as somewhat whimsical.

Carpenter took pains to distinguish this claim from a proposal of "female suffrage, which, it is assumed, would overthrow Christianity, defeat the ends of modern civilization, and upturn the world."[169] The Court, he recalled, had recently said that it was among the inalienable rights that "all avocations . . . are alike open to every one . . .";[170] it had spoken of attorneys being admitted upon "sufficient evidence of the possession of the requisite legal training and . . . that their private and professional character is fair."[171] Undoubtedly the Court would hold void a rule that whites only could practice law: was it less objectionable to say, men only? The Fourteenth Amendment spoke of the privileges of citizens of the United States—and women were citizens too.

The Court let the case wait while it attended to the butchers.

For the majority in *Slaughter House* it was easy to say that the practice of the law was not a matter inherent in United States citizenship, but was governed by the law of the State.

But it was not so easy for Justices who had joined in Field's affirmation that "equality of right, with exemption from all disparaging and partial enactments, in the lawful pursuits of life, . . . is the distinguishing privilege of citizens of the United States." Bradley (Field and Swayne concurring) said that, as to women citizens, the privilege did not extend "to any and every profession." He found repugnance between the institution of the family and "the idea of a woman adopting a distinct and independent career from that of her husband." No matter that many women were unmarried:

> The paramount mission and destiny of women are to fulfill the noble and benign offices of wife and mother. This is the law of the Creator. And the rules of civil society must be adapted to the general constitution of things, and cannot be based upon exceptional cases.

---

[168] *Not* 1873, as indicated in 21 L. Ed. 442, 443. Occasionally such dates in Lawyers' Edition are inaccurate or incomplete.

[169] Brief, p. 2.

[170] Cummings v. Missouri, 4 Wall. 277 (1867), per Field, J. Supra, pp. 240–42.

[171] *Ex parte* Garland, 4 Wall. 333 (1867), per Field, J. Supra, pp. 240–42.

"The humane movements of modern society" to open avenues for woman's advancement, said Justice Bradley, "have my heartiest concurrence." But not every citizen was qualified for every calling, and it remained "the prerogative of the legislator to prescribe regulations" for admission to callings requiring special skill and confidence.

As a demonstration of man's superior fitness for the law, this opinion was not a shining example.[172]

In fact, the Illinois legislature had spoken, a year before the Court rendered its decision. On March 22, 1872, it enacted:

> That no person shall be precluded or debarred from any occupation, profession or employment (except military) on account of sex: *Provided*, that this Act shall not be construed to affect the eligibility of any person to an elective office.[173]

Mrs. Belva Ann Lockwood (1830–1917) graduated from the National University Law School in 1873, and was admitted to the District of Columbia bar. After the three years required by the Rules of the Supreme Court, she applied for admission to practice there. Albert G. Riddle made the motion, on November 6, 1876. Chief Justice Waite—having had notice—was ready with the Court's answer. He said that

> By the uniform practice of the Court from its organization to the present time, and by the fair construction of its rules, none but men are permitted to practice before it as attorneys and counsellors. This is in accordance with immemorial usage in England, and the law and practice in all the States until within a recent period, and that the Court does not feel called upon to make a change until such a

---

[172] Cf. Lucetta, in *Two Gentlemen of Verona*:
I have no other but a woman's reason:
I think him so, because I think him so.
Cf., also, Peckham, J., for the majority in Lochner v. New York, 198 U.S. 45 (1905), striking down a statute establishing a ten-hour day for bakers: "We do not believe in the soundness of the views which uphold this law." Over the years the Justices became bold in asserting their personal convictions and prejudices as the true meaning of the Fourteenth Amendment—leading to a constitutional crisis in 1937, and a chastening for the Court.

On a notable occasion in 1876, when in South Ottawa v. Perkins, Justice Bradley expressed the opinion of a minority of the Court, Mrs. Bradwell in her journal defended Bradley's view, with none of the "timidity" he had supposed "unfits" a woman for the law. Upon a rehearing he became the spokesman for the Court. 94 U.S. 260 (1877).

[173] Laws of 1871–72, p. 578, in force July 1, 1872. The Illinois court recalled Mrs. Bradwell's case, and the enactment of the statute, when in 1881 it held that a woman was eligible to the office of master in chancery. Schuchart v. The People *ex rel.* Hall., 99 Ill. 501.

change is required by statute or a more extended practice in the higher courts of the States.[174]

Mrs. Lockwood brought about the enactment of such a statute on February 15, 1879.[175]

On March 3, 1879—the first day thereafter when the Court was in session—Mr. Riddle made his motion anew, and Mrs. Lockwood became the first of her sex to be admitted to the Court's bar. As candidate for the Presidency on the National Equal Rights ticket in 1884 and 1888 she received some hundreds of votes.

Myra Bradwell went on doing a lawyer's work in publishing her journal, one of whose merits was the prompt publication of the Illinois session laws. Law reform for equality in the treatment of men and women had her effective support. She made no attempt to take the benefit of the statute of 1872; but years later the Illinois court, on its own motion, upon the basis of the original application, directed that a license to practice law be issued to her. And on March 28, 1892, upon motion of Attorney General W. H. H. Miller, Myra Bradwell was admitted to the bar of the Supreme Court.[176] (Death on January 22 had

---

[174] Minutes, Nov. 6, 1876.

The "fair construction" of the Rules involved no profound study. In the beginning, on February 5, 1790, it had been

Ordered, That (until further orders) it shall be requisite to the admission of Attorneys or Counsellors to practice in this Court, that they shall have been such for three years past in the Supreme Courts of the State to which they respectively belong, and that their private and professional character shall appear to be fair.

That was substantially the rule in force when Mrs. Lockwood applied—and remains so today, save that "fair" has been replaced by "good." [Originally "fair" meant "free from blemish," but in the latter part of the nineteenth century it acquired the connotation of merely "passable, average." See *Oxford English Dictionary*.]

On August 8, 1791, the Chief Justice announced "that this Court consider the practice of the Courts of King's Bench and of Chancery, in England, as affording outlines for the practice of this Court; and that they

will, from time to time, make such alterations therein as circumstances may render necessary."

On February 5, 1795, the Court gave notice to the *gentlemen of the Bar* that thereafter the Court should "be furnished with a statement of the material points of the case" from the counsel on each side.

[175] 20 Stat. 292. A statute of one sentence, to direct that any woman [otherwise qualified] shall upon motion be admitted to practice before the Supreme Court.

[176] On the occasion of her death in 1894, the *American Law Review's* appreciation in memoriam was discriminating. 28:278–83.

A gentle and noiseless woman, her tenderness and refinement making her character all the more effective, Mrs. Bradwell was one of those who live their creed instead of preaching it. She did not spend her days proclaiming on the rostrum the rights of woman but quietly, none the less effectively, set to work to clear away the barriers.

Her surviving children, a son and a daughter, were both lawyers.

removed from the Bench the author of the remarkable concurring opinion of 1873.)

SOME CONTEMPORARY COMMENT

JUDGE THOMAS M. COOLEY's *Treatise on the Constitutional Limitations* was published in 1868. In 1871, preparing a second edition, he inserted a footnote to his statement that the national government could not, through any of its departments, assume any supervision of the police regulations of the States, so long as they did not obstruct the exercise of any authority confided to the nation. Now he added this footnote:

> A claim has recently been advanced at New Orleans, that the Civil Rights Bill, in connection with the fourteenth amendment . . . , has so far enlarged the jurisdiction of the Federal Courts, as to authorize them, at the suit of citizens of a State, to review one of its statutes purporting to establish a police regulation, and to adjudge it void if in their opinion it wrongfully abridged the right of citizens to follow a lawful employment: and this claim has been sustained by Mr. Justice *Bradley* . . . .

The matter was pending before the Supreme Court and perhaps it was not proper to comment; but if the claim were to be upheld, "an innovation will be made in our system which ought not to be made without careful consideration and deliberate intention."[177] Evidently he did not approve.

Next Cooley prepared a fourth edition of Story's *Commentaries on the Constitution*, which appeared in 1873. He had written supplementary chapters on "The Emancipation of Slaves," "The Fourteenth Amendment," and "Impartial Suffrage Established," to give an exposition of the three Amendments adopted since the third edition in 1858. Finally he supplied an Appendix, to report "two exceedingly important cases"—*Slaughter House* and *Bradwell*—decided "while the last of the foregoing sheets were passing through the press." That implies very strongly that when one reads "The Fourteenth Amendment" one will find Cooley's own analysis, written quite independently of the *Slaughter House* decision. And there in Section 1937 he distinguished between the privileges of State citizenship and those of United States citizenship. "The difference is in a high degree important. . . . [T]he privileges which pertain to citizenship under the general government are as

---

[177] Footnote 3 at p. *574.

different in their nature from those which belong to citizenship in a State as the functions of the one are different from those of the other. . . ." He gave illustrations of the privileges of United States citizenship: protection from wrongful action by foreign authorities; the privilege of a passport; use of the navigable waters; the benefits of the postal laws. "[T]he duty of protection to a citizen of a State in his privileges and immunities as such is not by this clause [of the Fourteenth Amendment] devolved upon the general government, but remains with the State itself where it naturally and properly belongs."

This pristine view—remarkably in accord with that taken by the majority of the Court—is offered merely to show what to one disinterested and discriminating constitutional lawyer seemed the natural construction of the new Privileges and Immunities Clause, prior to the delivery of the opposing opinions within the Court,[178] and long before the ground had become covered with commentaries. Cooley had a definite philosophy about constitutional construction, which he had set out in a famous chapter. A constitution derived its force from ratification: one should act on the supposition that those who ratified accepted the text "in the sense most obvious to the common understanding"; in construing, one should not look "for any dark or abstruse meaning"; he cautioned against giving "a controlling force" to remarks in the debates of its framers, especially where to do so would give a meaning different from what the words would "most naturally and obviously convey."[179] It is not surprising that when a mind so organized read the Fourteenth Amendment—and saw that two citizenships were identified, and that then a provision was made for the privileges of United States citizenship—the conclusion was that the privileges incident to State citizenship were not included.

---

[178] One cannot say positively that Cooley did not change what had already been set in type, or even run through the press, in order to bring his comment into accord with the Court's opinion. It is believed, however, that that should be rejected. (1) His statement would have been uncandid if he had done so. (2) He was not so obsequious as to parrot the Court. His mind was his own, and his authority was well established. (3) He had already signalled danger, as he saw it, in Justice Bradley's opinion at New Orleans.

[179] His Chapter IV was "On the Construction of State Constitutions" —appropriately so entitled, in a *Treatise on the Constitutional Limita-* tions which Rest upon the Legislative Power of the States of the American Union: it was the *State* constitution wherein almost all of the limitations were to be found. Much of what he said, however, was applicable to the construction of the federal Constitution. At pp. *66–67 he warned against being governed by words some particular member or members of a constitutional convention used in debates: "the few remarks made concerning [a clause] . . . might have a tendency to lead directly away from the meaning in the minds of the majority. . . ." He distinguished constitutional construction from the interpretation of a statute, for in the latter "it is the intent of the legislature we seek."

In the third edition of his *Treatise*, published in 1874, Cooley noted that the Fourteenth Amendment "received a very careful examination at the hands of the Supreme Court" in *Slaughter House*, and indicated that he still approved.

Cooley's views are not presented as the height of wisdom about the Amendment, but as the considered product of an eminently respectable mind, free from any captivation of fancy.

The *American Law Review* of July 1873[180] invited "special attention" to the *Slaughter House* decision—"of untold importance to the future relations" of State and Nation. Continuing,

> It is noteworthy that, while the executive department keeps Casey in New Orleans,[181] and sends its soldiers to regulate the internal politics of Louisiana, the judicial department remits to the people of that state, to its courts and legislature, the custody of the privileges and immunities of its citizens.

This was rather superficial—the sort of comment one might find in a newspaper. The *Review* was then being edited by O. W. Holmes, Jr., and Arthur G. Sedgwick (1844–1915). The note is *not* in the style of the former, and *is* in that of the latter.[182]

Holmes was then nearing the completion of his twelfth edition of Kent's *Commentaries on American Law*. In that work he took no notice of *Slaughter House*. The Fourteenth Amendment—with which in later years his name would be closely linked—he mentioned only to note that it recognized the principle that nationality was based on place of birth.[183]

---

[180] 7:732.

[181] James F. Casey was President Grant's brother-in-law—Collector of the Port of New Orleans—and prominent in the Custom House faction of the Republican party. In the months before this comment was written, Governor Warmoth, with Democratic adherents, had been contending for the power to govern, against Acting Governor Pinchback and Governor-elect Kellogg. Casey figured conspicuously in the operations of the latter party, and appealed directly to the President. Grant gave his support to that side.

[182] Each had gone from Law School into the office of Chandler, Shattuck and Thayer, at Boston. Sedgwick's interests, however, ran to journalism; presently he became assistant editor of *The Nation*. There he contributed an article on "Monopolies and the Fourteenth Amendment," commenting adversely upon Bradley's *Slaughter House* opinion on the circuit. 11: 361–62, Dec. 1, 1870. "If the decision is sustained, every moneyed corporation in the country is in danger of destruction. Whenever a court can be satisfied that the exclusive privilege granted by the State or the United States inures rather to private than to public advantage, the franchise will be set aside as in violation of the Fourteenth Amendment. . . . It seems hardly possible that the Supreme Court will sustain Judge Bradley . . . ."

[183] Vol. II, *49 note 1.

XXI: *Privileges of Citizens of the United States*

The Nation discussed *Slaughter House* and *Bradwell* under the caption "The Supreme Court Righting Itself." The decisions showed

> that the Court is recovering from the war fever, and is getting ready to abandon sentimental canons of construction. In the principal case there is, indeed, this drawback—that it is rendered by a divided bench; but no impartial lawyer, we fancy, will hesitate to say that the strength of the Court, as well as of the argument, was on the side of the majority. . . .

The consequences of the larger interpretation, which Justice Miller had exposed, would have been "monstrous."[184]

Back in New Orleans, and elsewhere in the South, the *Slaughter House* decision received ill-tempered comment. It meant, said the *Picayune*, that white men were excluded from any benefit from the Amendment; "State rights receive a sort of faltering support, and white folks are permitted to breathe in African society."[185] The *Times* (under new management) concluded that "Negro citizenship is the only citizenship worth having for the purpose of invoking the strong arm of national authority against local usurpation and oppression . . . ."[186] At that moment the decision was overshadowed by a local happening: on April 13, Easter Sunday, a pitched battle had been fought between blacks and whites in Grant Parish in central Louisiana, wherein scores of the former were killed by shooting or by the burning of the building to which they had fled. Out of this arose *United States v. Cruikshank*,[187] wherein the Fourteenth Amendment, upon further examination by the Court, proved to be a more profound disappointment to Negroes than it had to butchers. Its protection to the Negro was only that *no State* could deny his rights; it did not "add anything to the rights which one citizen has under the Constitution against another," said Chief Justice Waite.

An often-cited critique of the *Slaughter House* decision is that by William L. Royall in the *Southern Law Review* in 1878.[188] At first glance it might seem surprising to find a prominent Virginia lawyer chiding the Court for its failure more broadly to protect the individual against his State government. Actually Royall was bent on liberating Virginia from Republican domination, and in particular on turning

---

[184] 16:280. April 24, 1873. It seems probable that this was written by Sedgwick, mentioned above. Myra Bradwell's contention was called "ridiculous"—"interesting as showing the effect produced by legal study on the female mind."

[185] Apr. 23, 1873.
[186] Apr. 24, 1873.
[187] 92 U.S. 542 (1876).
[188] "The Fourteenth Amendment: the Slaughter House Cases," 4 (n.s.): 558–84. Oct. 1878.

back the Readjuster Movement to repudiate the State debt. He had been retained by bondholders; his name is foremost in litigation before the Supreme Court in that behalf.[189] His article has the semblance of a brief for the interests he had at heart.

"Ninety-nine out of every hundred educated men," he said, "upon reading this [first] section [of the Fourteenth Amendment] over, would at first say that it forbade a state to make or enforce a law which abridged any privilege or immunity whatever of one who was a citizen of the United States . . . ." (Charles Allen's brief had pointed out the enormous consequences if the provision were taken "in the broadest sense."[190])

Royall shifted from what educated men (supposedly) would understand to what the members of the 39th Congress (supposedly) intended. Here is the point on which his article has been most influential:

> It is a little remarkable that, so far as the reports disclose, no one of the distinguished counsel who argued this great case . . . , nor any one of the judges who sat in it, appears to have thought it worth while to consult the proceedings of the Congress which proposed this amendment, to ascertain what it was that they were seeking to accomplish.

It is always arresting to hear that for want of a key, the Court has failed to interpret the Constitution aright. But if Royall had thought it worth while to consult the briefs filed in *Slaughter House* he would have found that J. Q. A. Fellows had made such a survey, and at much greater length than that which Royall himself was about to offer. "I believe that an attentive examination of the proceedings," Royall continued, "will satisfy any impartial mind, to the point of mathematical demonstration, that the framers of the amendment intended to accomplish that which the minority of the court held that the language meant." But when one knows that Fellows' survey of the Congressional debates had been laid before the Court, the omission of the dissenting Justices to invoke the debates appears to have been deliberate—which seems significant.

---

[189] As counsel, or as party with appearance *pro se*, in Hartman v. Greenhow, Treasurer of City of Richmond, 102 U.S. 672 (1881); Antoni v. Greenhow, 107 U.S. 769 (1883); *Ex parte* Crouch, 112 U.S. 178 (1884); *Ex parte* Royall, 112 U.S. 181 (1884); Poindexter v. Greenhow, 114 U.S. 270 (1885), and six cases decided with it; Moore v. Greenhow, 114 U.S. 338 (1885); Royall v. Virginia, 116 U.S. 572 (1886), and three other cases decided at the same time; *Ex parte* Royall, 117 U.S. 241 (1886); Stewart v. Virginia, 117 U.S. 612 (1886); *Ex parte* Ayres, 123 U.S. 443 (1887); McGahey v. Virginia, 135 U.S. 662 (1890).

[190] Supra, pp. 1346–47.

In eleven pages Royall set out quotations from the Congressional Globe. He concluded that there was "perfect unanimity" that the purpose was "to incorporate the Civil Rights Bill bodily into the Constitution." But the Civil Rights Act of 1866 provided that citizens of the United States without regard to color would have the same right to contract, to sue, and to inherit, hold and convey property, etc., as was enjoyed by white citizens—which fell a long way short of securing for all citizens "practical effect to the declaration of 1776 of inalienable rights, rights which are the gift of the Creator," which according to Justice Field's opinion had been the intent of the Amendment.

"The truth is," Royall continued, "that when this Amendment came before the Court for construction, the minds of patriotic men were filled with alarm at the centralizing tendency of the government . . . ." (Certainly that had been a stock complaint of Democratic partisans, and the apprehension had been shared by moderate men, such as Justice Davis.[191]) "The great argument made against an enlarged construction . . . was the argument *ab inconvenienti*" which "ought to find no place in a court of justice where the language . . . contains no ambiguity." "Privileges and immunities" had previously been "defined with sufficient certainty." To show how the clause should have been applied, Royall asked, "Is there a man who could contend that a state ought to make or enforce a law giving to sixteen monopolists the odious privilege granted by the Legislature of Louisiana . . . ?" Such enactments went against right and justice: it was "exactly these laws the Constitution ought to forbid [the States] to make."

Royall had "no criticism" of the Court's decision that the Fourteenth Amendment was inapplicable in *United States v. Cruikshank,*[192] because it was "not by any law of Louisiana, but simply by unlawful and riotous interference by individuals" that the evil had been done.

It is remarkable that so infirm an article should have passed current at face value.

On January 30, 1880, Royall began the publication, at Richmond, of a new daily, the *Commonwealth*. This was devoted to the promotion of Conservative politics, the payment of the State debt in full—and, it soon appeared, the nomination of Justice Field as Democratic candidate for the Presidency. When on Monday, March 1, 1880, the Supreme Court in a memorable group of opinions[193] held that by virtue of the Fourteenth Amendment the colored citizen on trial was

---

[191] As expressed in his letter of April 22, 1868, to Judge Rockwell, supra, p. 484.

[192] 92 U.S. 542 (1876). See infra, pp. 1377-79.

[193] Strauder v. West Virginia, 100 U.S. 303; Virginia v. Rives, 100 U.S. 313; *Ex parte* Virginia, 100 U.S. 339.

entitled to a jury from which members of his race were not excluded on ground of color, that Congress might authorize removal to a federal court in the event such discrimination was practiced, and that a State judge who excluded jurors on account of their color was punishable under the Civil Rights Act of 1875—Justices Field and Clifford dissenting throughout—Royall explained to his readers that "this [Fourteenth] amendment, which is the vital one, was actually coerced into the Constitution."

> Though it was not supposed that it would ever receive the wide construction which is now given to it [by the decisions on March 1], yet thinking men looked upon its provisions with alarm, until [the decision in *Slaughter House*]. . . . This was considered to have emasculated the Fourteenth Amendment, and the apprehensions of thinking men were at once allayed.
>
> . . . This same Republican court sees now . . . that the limitation which its [*Slaughter House*] decision put upon the powers of Congress, so far freed the country from congressional domination, as that the Democrats are about to take possession of the Government.
>
> It has, therefore, made the decisions that were rendered on Monday. These decisions mean that the Republican party intend to hold on to the reins of Government, and to retain the acts of Congress which now enable them to perpetuate their power. They are revolution. They are a complete overthrow of our Constitutions. . . .

"Remember," the editor concluded, "that Judge Field raised his voice in solemn protest" against these recent decisions.[194]

At the Democratic National Convention in late June, Justice Field fared poorly; General W. S. Hancock was nominated on the third ballot.

In late July, the *Commonwealth* ceased publication.

Royall as an advocate and politician had certain objectives: what he wrote about the Fourteenth Amendment should be read with caution as self-serving statements.

WALKER v. SAUVINET (1876)

LOUISIANA'S CONSTITUTION OF 1868 had declared that all persons should have equal rights upon any public conveyance and in all places of business or of public resort. To enforce this guaranty, a statute of 1869 gave a civil action for damages. Then a statute of 1871 specified that trial should be by the court, or by jury at the request of either party: but if a jury failed to agree, the judge should decide forthwith.

---

[194] Fri., Mar. 5, 1880.

Out of these statutes arose *Walker v. Sauvinet*.[195] It held that trial by jury in suits in State courts was *not* a privilege of United States citizenship such as the States were forbidden to abridge.

Charles S. Sauvinet, born in Louisiana of parents of foreign origin, had the complexion of a white man but was reputed to be of color. On that ground, before the war, he had been denied the right to vote. He served as a captain in the Union Army; then had been elected an alderman at New Orleans; and in 1871 was sheriff of Orleans Parish. By invitation he accompanied two white men into The Bank, Walker's coffeehouse. At the bar he was refused service; the bartender simply reiterated, "Never mind, it is all right."

Sauvinet brought suit in the Eighth District Court, held by Dibble, J. When a jury was being chosen, a colored man was challenged for cause, on the ground that as such he would be interested and prejudiced. That was overruled. The court refused to charge that "the jury must find that plaintiff is a man of color or he cannot recover."[196] The judge sustained the relevant provisions of State constitution and statutes. When the jury failed to reach a verdict, he found for the plaintiff and awarded $1,000 as exemplary damages. On a motion for a new trial, one ground rejected was "that by the fourteenth amendment of the Constitution of the United States certain inalienable rights are guaranteed to the defendant which the laws of the State cannot deprive him of, among which is the trial by jury."[197] The Supreme Court of Louisiana affirmed, two judges dissenting on the ground that the damages were excessive.[198]

When on writ of error *Walker v. Sauvinet* was presented to the Supreme Court there was, quite literally, a conflict between the conception that a citizen of the United States might stand erect in the exercise of all the privileges enjoyed by other citizens, and the conception that the Fourteenth Amendment imposed such a particular of the federal Bill of Rights as the Seventh Amendment.[199] In practice, trial

---

[195] 92 U.S. 90, decided Apr. 24, 1876.

[196] Transcript of Record, p. 30.
At the trial Sauvinet testified upon cross-examination:

Q. Are you a colored man?
A. Whether I am or not is a matter that I do not know myself.

. . . .

Q. Has it not been your custom to let it be generally known and understood that you are a white man?
A. I should answer that I am very much astonished that I should want to be proven a white man, when a few months ago I was called a negro. . . . [Everybody knows] that I am not a white man, because I was refused all the rights inherent in that title; and how can a man be a white man and be refused that? Transcript, pp. 17–18.
Other factual details mentioned in the text are found in the Transcript.

[197] Transcript, p. 35.

[198] 27 La. Ann. 14 (1871).

[199] "In suits at common law, where

by a jury of the vicinage was an invaluable device for assuring that equality of rights was *not* enjoyed by colored citizens.

J. Q. A. Fellows appeared for Sauvinet. As counsel for the New Orleans butchers he had filed the brief on the history and objects of the post-war Amendments.[200] Now he told the Court that "It is hardly to be conceived, that the first section of the fourteenth amendment, can be found to have so large a scope, as to prohibit a State legislature from passing the law in question."[201]

The brief of T. J. Durant and C. W. Hornor on behalf of Walker *made no mention of any right to trial by jury*. That fact is meaningful. Under "Assignment of Errors" it was said, first, that the statute of 1871 abridged the privileges and immunities secured by the Fourteenth Amendment. Here is the elaboration:

> These acts [of 1869 and 1871] have in direction intention to compel all persons engaged in business to sell their commodities whenever called upon to do so, and whether willing or not. Such compulsion is an abridgment of the right of the citizen, who has the natural right to sell or keep his commodities as best suits his own purpose; and this compulsion is a violation of the XIVth amendment of the Constitution.[202]

Thus counsel sought to do battle on the proposition that the proprietor of a place of public resort had a constitutional right to choose whom he would serve. (Recently Congress by the Civil Rights Act of March 1, 1875, had enacted expressly to the contrary.[203])

The second assignment was that the power to enforce the Thirteenth, Fourteenth, and Fifteenth Amendments belonged exclusively to Congress and had been exercised, notably by the Civil Rights Act of 1866 and the reenactment in 1871.[204] Finally the Court was invited to consider alleged errors in which no federal question was involved. Evidently the argument ranged widely.

Chief Justice Waite's opinion for the Court said that "So far as we can discover from the record, the only federal question decided by

---

the value in controversy shall exceed twenty dollars, the right of trial by jury shall be preserved . . . ."

The Supreme Court of Louisiana, in denying a rehearing, had said, "We are not aware of the existence of any constitutional provision making it imperative upon the legislature to accord a trial by jury in all civil cases. . . ." Transcript, p. 41.

[200] Supra, pp. 1348–49.

[201] Brief for Defendant in Error, pp. 4–5.

[202] Brief for Plaintiff in Error, pp. 2–3.

[203] 18 Stat. 335. Held to be too broad, and invalid, in the Civil Rights Cases, 109 U.S. 3 (1883).

[204] Brief for Plaintiff in Error, pp. 2, 3. Prigg v. Pennsylvania, 16 Pet. 539 (1842), was cited as a "complete illustration" of the principle to be applied.

either one of the courts below" was in their rejection of the claim to trial by jury. But the Seventh Amendment, "as has been many times decided, relates only to trials in the courts of the United States," citing what the Court, per Clifford, J., had decided in *Edwards v. Elliott* at the preceding term.[205] So far as the Fourteenth Amendment was concerned, the States "are left to regulate trials in their own courts in their own way." The Due Process Clause "does not necessarily imply that all trials in the State courts affecting the property of persons must be by jury. This requirement of the Constitution is met, if the trial is had according to the settled course of judicial proceedings." That had been satisfied in this case.

Other points assigned as error could not be considered, "as the record does not show that they were brought to the attention of either of the courts below."

Clifford and Field, J.J., dissented from the opinion and the judgment, without indicating the point of disagreement.[206]

In this case, as in *Slaughter House*, one observes advocates crossing over to take positions the reverse of what, as politicians, they had held a decade earlier. Fellows, once Conservative Unionist, was asserting Sauvinet's right to equal treatment without regard to race, whereas Durant, erstwhile Free State leader, had written a brief to deny it.[207]

DEVELOPMENTS AFTER *SLAUGHTER HOUSE*

A MARKER ON THE ground of the Grant Parish Courthouse bore this legend:

> On this site occurred the Colfax Riot in which three white men and 150 negroes were slain. This event on April 13, 1873 marked the end of carpetbag misrule in the South.

---

[205] In Edwards v. Elliott, 21 Wall. 532, from the highest court of New Jersey, decided on November 30, 1874, Clifford, J., had said:

Objection is also taken to the validity of the State law, upon the ground that it is in conflict with [the Seventh Amendment].

Two answers may be made to that objection, either of which is decisive: (1) That it does not apply to trials in the State Courts. [Citing Barron v. Baltimore, 7 Pet. 243 (1833); Twitchell v. Pennsylvania, 7 Wall. 321 (1869), and other cases.]

(2) That no such error was assigned in the Court of Errors, and that the question was not presented to, nor was it decided by, the Court of Errors.

[206] It is conceivable that there was some question whether procedure under the statute of 1871, which mutilated the trial by jury in one category of litigation, could be said to afford equal protection in the right to a trial according to "the settled course of judicial proceedings."

[207] See supra, pp. 94–95, 270, 290, 303.

Without critical examination of this recital, the event is taken as a point from which to trace certain developments.

Cruikshank and others were found guilty on counts under the Act of May 31, 1870,[208] to enforce the rights of citizens of the United States, in that at Grant Parish they had banded together to deprive L. N. and A. T., colored citizens of the United States, of the free exercise of certain rights (allegedly) secured to them by the Constitution and laws of the United States. On a motion in arrest of judgment, Justice Bradley and Judge Woods certified a difference of opinion,[209] whereby the case was taken to the Supreme Court.

Justice Bradley went to New Orleans to sit in the Circuit Court and deliver his opinion.[210] Congress had power to enforce the Thirteenth Amendment, and for that purpose had enacted the Civil Rights Act of 1866. This secured to *all* citizens the benefit of such protection of person and property as State law accorded to white citizens, "whose privileges were adopted as the standard." But the power of Congress under the Thirteenth Amendment did not extend to penalizing the commission of ordinary crimes against colored people: there must be a design to injure the victim *by reason of his color*. The indictment had failed to add that allegation.

As to the Fourteenth Amendment: the power of Congress to enforce its provisions did *not* extend to legislation directly to enforce *all* the privileges and immunities of citizens of the United States; that

---

[208] 16 Stat. 140.

[209] United States v. Cruikshank, Fed. Case No. 14,897, June 27, 1874.

[210] His diary for 1874 shows that he had been following his circuit from May 14 [ten days after the adjournment of the Supreme Court] to June 10 when he returned to Washington. He had been at New Orleans from May 17 to 23; the jury to try Cruikshank had been empanelled on May 18.

Back at Washington, for a fortnight "I was at work re-vamping & printing an opinion in the Grant Parish case—preparatory to the motion in arrest of judgment. Also finished up opinion in Brown v. Guild & al. [Doubtless related to Brown v. United States, *Ex parte* Bridges, Fed. Case No. 1862, C.C.N.D. Ga. 1875.]"

On Wednesday, June 24, "7 AM I started for N. Orleans via Lynchburg, Knoxville . . . . This was the hottest day I have known . . . ."

He arrived at New Orleans on Friday at 11 P.M.; went into court at noon on Saturday and delivered his opinion, and at 4 P.M. started for Washington, arriving on Tuesday, June 30. Next day, "Prepared opinion in Grant Parish Case for printing." On July 3 he sent off copies: to his brethren of the Court; to members of the Senate Judiciary Committee; to Representative Luke P. Poland (Rep., Vermont) of the House Judiciary Committee; to Attorney General Williams, Secretary of State Fish and Secretary of the Navy Robeson; to Judge Woods and the District Judges of the Fifth Circuit; to District Attorney Beckwith and to R. H. Marr, senior counsel for the defense; to the *Chicago Legal News*, the *Albany Law Journal*, and the *Central Law Journal* at St. Louis; to five newspapers (not named)—two at Washington, two at New Orleans, and one at New York; and to a few acquaintances, and close friends, such as Cortland Parker and George Harding:—42 copies in all.

subject matter embraced the citizen's "political inheritance derived from the mother country, . . . his birthright, and it is the duty of the particular State of which he is a citizen to protect and enforce" such rights. The duty of Congress was to enforce the prohibition that "No State shall . . . abridge . . . ," as it did by allowing appeals from the State courts to the courts of the United States.

Two years later the Supreme Court agreed that the conviction of Cruikshank and others could not stand.[211]

As federal judicial protection of the freedmen crumbled, white Conservatives moved closer to the recovery of domination.[212] Governor Kellogg maintained a precarious hold, thanks to the support of the Grant Administration. But when the election in November 1876 produced a conflict over the returns, the Democratic candidate, General Francis R. T. Nicholls, set up a government in opposition to the pretensions of S. B. Packard, the Republican. Nicholls declared that he would "carry out faithfully and impartially the amendments to the Constitution" and that he was "utterly opposed to class legislation." On March 1, 1877, Grant's secretary advised Packard that the President "feels it his duty to state frankly that he does not believe public opinion will longer support the maintenance of State Government in Louisiana by the use of the military, and that he must concur in this manifest feeling."[213]

President Hayes on April 20 directed that the federal troops stationed in New Orleans be withdrawn. Thereupon the Packard legislature dispersed; some of its members entered the Nicholls legislature, with the result that the Senate comprised 20 Democrats and 16 Republicans, the House 64 Democrats and 42 Republicans.

It was an objective of the Democratic party to replace the con-

---

[211] United States v. Cruikshank, 92 U.S. 542, argued Mar. 30 and 31 and Apr. 1, 1875, and decided Mar. 27, 1876.

The discussion of *Cruikshank* here is confined to the purpose of the present chapter on *Slaughter House*.

I have long been acquainted with Justice Bradley's letters on the problem of enforcing the Fourteenth Amendment, early expressions from which found their way into Justice Goldberg's concurring opinion in Bell v. Maryland, 378 U.S. 226, 286 at 309–10 (1964). On July 19, 1874, Bradley wrote to Senator F. T. Frelinghuysen, his intimate friend for more than forty years: "My own mind is rather in the condition of

seeking for truth, than that of dogmatically laying down opinions . . . ." This was three weeks after he had delivered his opinion in *Cruikshank* on the Circuit Court.

All this must await examination in due time.

[212] United States Attorney J. R. Beckwith wrote to Attorney General Williams on October 7, 1874: "The armed White league organizations in the South from which most grave and serious danger and consequences may be apprehended sprung into life or received their only vitality from the action of Justice Bradley in [the Cruikshank case] . . . ." National Archives.

[213] Ann. Cyc. 1877, 455–67.

stitution of 1868, framed in pursuance of the Reconstruction Acts. In 1879 a convention composed of Democrats and Republicans in the proportion of about 3 to 1 framed a constitution which was adopted in December by a popular vote of somewhat better than 3 to 1.

BUTCHERS' UNION CO. v. CRESCENT CITY CO. (1884)

THE CONSTITUTION OF 1879 provided that the local authorities of parishes and municipalities "shall alone have the power of regulating the slaughtering of cattle and other live stock . . . ; provided, no monopoly or exclusive privilege shall exist in this State . . . ." Further, "the monopoly features in the charter of any corporation now existing in this State, save such as may be contained in the charters of railroad companies, are hereby abolished."[214]

Crescent City Company sued in the State courts to restrain the New Orleans city council from exercising the powers conferred by the new constitution, on the ground that their privilege under the statute of 1869 was exclusive and irrevocable. The Louisiana Supreme Court decided adversely to that contention, at May term 1881.[215] A writ of error was filed in the Supreme Court on July 26, 1881. But then, as it neared the call of the docket, the case was dismissed on January 22, 1884, on motion of counsel for plaintiff in error.[216]

In the autumn of 1881 the city council, after the State Supreme Court had decided the injunction suit in its favor, adopted ordinances declaring that "it shall be lawful for any person or corporation" to maintain slaughter houses within limits prescribed. Butchers' Union Company, established in 1880, went about the preparation of a slaughter house. Crescent City on November 23, 1881, sued in the federal Circuit Court to restrain Butchers' Union on the ground that plaintiff had an exclusive right under the statute of 1869 which was protected by the Contract Clause. (Thus Crescent City raised the very point of constitutional law on which it had suffered defeat in the suit against the city, then pending in the Supreme Court.) On May 8, 1882, a

---

[214] Arts. 248, 258.

A memorial with about 350 signatures was presented to the convention, urging the abrogation of the statute of 1869, because it was enacted "in the interest of a few persons at the expense of citizens generally, at a time of the greatest profligacy," and because its effect was to "paralyze and to a great extent destroy trade in this line . . . ." *Proceedings of the Constitutional Convention convening at New Orleans, April 21, 1879,* p. 79.

[215] Crescent City Live Stock Landing and Slaughter-house Co. v. City of New Orleans, 33 La. Ann. 934 (1881).

[216] Supreme Court Docket and Minutes.

decree for a permanent injunction was entered by Circuit Judge Don A. Pardee.[217] (Judge Woods had been promoted to the Supreme Court in December 1880, as successor to Justice Strong, resigned; Pardee was appointed to the vacancy.[218])

The appeal of Butchers' Union to the Supreme Court was argued by B. R. Forman; the monopoly was defended by Thomas J. Semmes, former Confederate Senator who had worked with the Republicans after the war. Both had served in the constitutional convention. Now counsel for Crescent City must minimize the scope of the police power.

The Court had recently affirmed in leading cases that a legislature may not divest itself of power to protect the public health, safety and morals.[219] Forman relied upon these decisions. A fertilizer company might be required to move when its operations became obnoxious: "Is the State more concerned with stinks and sweet smells than with cheapness of food to its citizens?"

> A few large shareholders in the . . . company have, since 1869, controlled the cattle market in New Orleans. Their influence in the management of the slaughterhouse enables them to get better facilities, more eligible pens, readier attention, and facilitates combinations to keep up the price of animals intended for slaughter. Is it not the duty of the State to take precautions against the continuance of this state of things . . . ?[220]

It will be noticed that he pointed to the consuming public, not to the butchers, as those who had been wronged by the creation of the monopoly.

Semmes, in reply, recalled the distinction Justice Field had made in *Slaughter House,* between those provisions of the statute of 1869 which were properly police regulations and those "other particulars" granting "the special and exclusive privileges by which the health of the city is in no way promoted." Very well, Semmes now argued, the

---

[217] 9 Fed. 743; Transcript of Record, p. 27.

[218] Don Albert Pardee (1837–1919), born in Northern Ohio, attended the United States Naval Academy, read law, and in 1861 was commissioned a major in the 42nd Ohio, of which Garfield was lieutenant colonel and colonel. Most of his service was in the lower Mississippi Valley. On leaving the army he opened an office in New Orleans; by election and reelection he held the office of district judge for twelve years; he was a delegate to the convention of 1879. Appointed Circuit Judge by Garfield in 1881, he held that office until his death—a period of thirty-eight years.

[219] Boston Beer Co. v. Massachusetts, 97 U.S. 25 (1878)—prohibitory law; Fertilizing Co. v. Hyde Park, 97 U.S. 659 (1878)—prohibiting operations of fertilizer plant within village limits; Stone v. Mississippi, 101 U.S. 814 (1880)—prohibition of lotteries.

[220] Brief for Appellant, p. 13.

inalienable nature of the power of police afforded no justification for destroying features of the charter that were quite distinct from the protection of public health.[221]

On May 5, 1884, the decision of the Court was announced: the abolition of the monopoly was sustained; the judgment of the Circuit Court was reversed.[222] All the Justices agreed to this result.

Justice Miller had been designated to speak for five of the Justices. Surveying recent decisions, he said that a State legislature could not by contract limit the exercise of police powers to the prejudice of the general welfare, at least in regard to public health and public morals. On that basis the challenged provisions of the State constitution and the city ordinances were sustained.

In *Slaughter House* the dissenters had maintained that the exclusive grant in the statute was beyond the power of the legislature, hence void. Now Field and Bradley, the two of that group remaining on the Court, would not abandon their old contention and agree to Miller's statement that the grant had been valid but always subject to be set aside by an exercise of the police power. Each wrote a specially concurring opinion; Harlan and Woods, appointed since *Slaughter House*, joined in that by Bradley.

These concurring opinions, which came to be quoted as though they bore the stamp of the Supreme Court, exerted a powerful influence in constitutional development during half a century.

Some of the pronouncements in Justice Field's opinion, on matters wholly unrelated to the case before the Court, suggest that he hoped to achieve some immediate objective—considering that the Democratic National Convention would meet two months thereafter, on July 8, 1884.[223]

---

[221] Brief for Appellee, p. 18.

[222] Butchers' Union Slaughter-House, etc. Co. v. Crescent City, etc. Slaughter-House Co., 111 U.S. 746.

On May 28, 1884, Butchers' Union sued Crescent City for malicious prosecution of the suit just decided by the Supreme Court. The trial court gave judgment for $12,500 damages plus $2,500 attorneys' fees; the Louisiana Supreme Court affirmed. It held "that the prosecution of a suit which had no foundation, except in the assumption that our decree [in Crescent City Co. v. New Orleans, 33 La. Ann. 934] was not law, was without probable cause; and that neither the advice of counsel, nor the opinions of judges of a co-ordinate court [9 Fed.

743] that our decree was error, could furnish any cause whatever for the prosecution of such suit." 37 La. Ann. 874 (1885).

This was taken to the Supreme Court, which reversed on the ground that the decree of the Circuit Court (notwithstanding that it was adverse to the judgment of the Louisiana court, and notwithstanding that it was reversed by the Supreme Court) should have been accepted as conclusive evidence of probable cause. Crescent City Live Stock Co. v. Butchers' Union Co., 120 U.S. 141 (1887).

[223] His prospects, dubious at best, were diminished when the Democratic State Convention in California on

Field began by declaring his devotion to the reserved power of the States to make regulations for the health, peace and safety of society. "When such regulations do not conflict with any constitutional inhibition *or natural right*, their validity cannot be successfully controverted. The General Government was not formed to interfere with or control them." [Italics supplied.] But to grant a monopoly was an abuse of power: he expanded on that theme.

Then came a lofty appreciation of the Declaration of Independence:

> As in our intercourse with our fellow-men certain principles of morality are assumed to exist, without which society would be impossible, so certain inherent rights lie at the foundation of all governmental action, and upon a recognition of them alone can free institutions be maintained. These inherent rights have never been more happily expressed than in the Declaration of Independence, that new evangel of liberty to the people: "We hold these truths to be self-evident"—that is, so plain that their truth is recognized upon their mere statement—"that all men are endowed"—not by edicts of Emperors, or decrees of Parliament, or Acts of Congress, but "by their Creator, with certain inalienable rights,"—that is, rights which cannot be bartered away, or given away, or taken away, except in punishment of crime—"and that among these are life, liberty, and the pursuit of happiness; and to secure these"—not grant them, but secure them—"governments are instituted among men, deriving their just powers from the consent of the governed."

Field gave a practical application in this highly quotable passage:

> Among these inalienable rights, as proclaimed in that great document, is the right of men to pursue their happiness, by which is meant the right to pursue any lawful business or vocation, in any manner not inconsistent with the equal rights of others, which may increase their prosperity or develop their faculties, so as to give them their highest enjoyment.

He came to the Fourteenth Amendment, and his idea of how it ought to be treated:

> The 1st section . . . was, among other things, designed to prevent all discriminating legislation for the benefit of some to the disparage-

---

June 10 declared its preference for Tilden for President (or if he declined, then Thurman) and for Hendricks for Vice President—and then resolved that it "unanimously repudiates the presidential aspirations of Stephen J. Field," requiring that delegates pledge to use their "earnest endeavors" against him. Carl B. Swisher, *Stephen J. Field* (Washington: The Brookings Institution, 1930), 304–5; Ann. Cyc. 1884, p. 104.

ment of others, and when rightly enforced as other prohibitions upon the State, not by legislation of a penal nature but through the courts, no one will complain. . . .

One would never suspect from this that the particular purpose of the Amendment had been to secure the civil rights of men of color. Field referred sympathetically to complaints that had been made over the disability imposed by Section 3 and over the Civil Rights Acts to enforce Section 1:

> The disfranchising provisions of the 3d section naturally created great hostility to the whole Amendment. They were regarded by many wise and good men as impolitic, harsh and cruel; and the manner in which the 1st section has been enforced by penal enactments against legislators and Governors has engendered wide spread and earnest hostility to it. . . . The appropriate mode of enforcing the Amendment is, in my judgment, that which has been applied to other previously existing constitutional prohibitions, such as the one against a State passing a law impairing the obligation of contracts, or a bill of attainder, or an *ex post facto* law. The only provisions deemed necessary to annul legislation of this kind have been such as facilitated proceedings for that purpose in the courts; no other can be appropriate against the action of a State. Thus enforced, there would be little objection to the provisions of the 1st section of the Amendment. . . . If the 1st section . . . is thus applied as a restriction against the impairment of fundamental rights, it will not transfer to the Federal Government the protection of all private rights, as is sometimes supposed . . . . The principal, if not the sole, purpose of the prohibitions is to prevent any arbitrary invasion by State authority, of the rights of person and property, and to secure to everyone the right to pursue his happiness, unrestrained, except by just, equal and impartial laws.

In its immediate partisan context, this expressed just the sentiments that Democrats delighted to hear.[224] If the Fourteenth Amend-

---

[224] The disqualification from office-holding imposed by Section 3 (supra, p. 260) remained a sore point with the Democrats. The parallel matter of the iron-clad oath (supra, pp. 260–61) was being agitated in Congress at the moment Field was writing: the Act of May 24, 1884, 23 Stat. 22, repealed Sec. 1756 of the Revised Statutes (the iron-clad oath); also Sec. 820 (the test oath for jurors and grand jurors in the federal courts); and amended Sec. 1218 so as to permit ex-Confederates to hold military office—*except* such as had held a commission at the outbreak of the Civil War and had thereafter served the Confederacy. Representative S. S. Cox was foremost in the effort to remove all proscriptions. In his *Three Decades of Federal Legislation*, (Providence, R.I.: J. A. and R. A. Reid, 1886), he had much on that subject—and suggested that "a learned and unprejudiced court" might well hold that a pardon from the President would overcome the disability imposed by Section 3; the concluding sentence ("But Congress may

ment could be "rightly enforced" according to Field's ideas, it would be tolerable and even beneficial.

In its enduring significance, the opinion became "the fountain head" of a line of decisions which, in the name of "liberty of contract," struck down statutes to redress the inequality between the power of working men, women and children and that of their employers.[225]

Justice Bradley's concurring opinion is easily summarized:

> The right to follow any of the common occupations of life is an inalienable right; it was formulated as such under the phrase "pursuit of happiness" in the Declaration of Independence . . . .

---

by a two-thirds vote of each House, remove such disability.") would be construed to give "a power of grace for cases wherein executive clemency might be refused." P. 601.

Justice Field would have had nothing done about Section 1 more than to permit review of State action by the federal courts. He was alluding to matters where he had been in disagreement with the Court—notably *Ex parte* Commonwealth of Virginia and J. D. Coles, 100 U.S. 339 (1880). (This was mentioned supra, pp. 1373–74.) Coles, County Court Judge, had been indicted for violating the Civil Rights Act of 1875, in that he had excluded citizens from service as jurors because of their black color. Denying a petition for habeas corpus, the Court, per Strong, J., had said:

> We do not perceive how holding an office under the State and claiming to act for the State can relieve the holder from obligation to obey the Constitution of the United States, or take away the power of Congress to punish his disobedience.

Field, J. dissenting (Clifford, J., with him), had said, "The proceeding is a gross offense to the State . . . ."

What Field wrote, in dissent, in this and in related cases on Acts of Congress to enforce the Fourteenth and Fifteenth Amendments, decided on March 1 and 8, 1880, figured prominently in *Some Account of the Work of Stephen J. Field . . .* , at 177–216. This compilation, published in 1881, had evidently been prepared for use as campaign literature in the event Field received the Democratic nomination for President in 1880. See supra, pp. 510n., 1373–74.

[225] Much has been written on this topic. Here one comment will suffice, that of Roscoe Pound in "Liberty of Contract," *Yale L. J.*, 18:454, in 1909:

> Turning now to the actual state of the decisions, let us look first at the cases in which the idea of liberty of contract has been invoked to defeat legislation. The fountain head of this line of decisions seems to be the opinion of Mr. Justice Field in Butchers' Union Co. v. Crescent City Co., in which he restates the views of the minority in the Slaughter House Cases. This opinion has been one of the staple citations in causes involving liberty of contract. In it he took a vigorous stand against legislative interference with the "right to follow lawful callings." Although it did not represent the views of the Federal Supreme Court, this opinion had a far-reaching influence in the State Courts. It produced a reactionary line of decisions in New York on liberty to pursue one's calling [Matter of Jacobs, 98 N.Y. 98; People v. Marx, 99 N.Y. 377], and through these cases its echoes are still ringing in the books. Mr. Justice Field was eminently the man to lead this belated individualist crusade. . . .

It was because the dissenting Justices in *Slaughter House* held this to be a "privilege of a citizen of the United States" that they had condemned the Louisiana statute.

> 2. But if it does not abridge the privileges and immunities of a citizen of the United States to prohibit him from pursuing his chosen calling, and giving to others the exclusive right of pursuing it, it certainly does deprive him (to a certain extent) of his liberty . . . . And if a man's right to his calling is property, as many maintain, then those who had already adopted the prohibited pursuits at New Orleans were deprived by the law in question of their property as well as their liberty without due process of law.
>
> 3. But still more apparent is the violation, by this monopoly law, of the [Equal Protection Clause] . . . .

Chase and Swayne, dissenters in *Slaughter House*, had now been succeeded by Waite and Matthews, who stood beside Miller. Davis and Strong, of the majority in 1873, had been replaced by Harlan and Woods, who joined Justice Bradley. Gray, like his predecessor Clifford, stood with the majority. The net change after eleven years was zero.

Justice Peckham in 1897 quoted Bradley's language in the course of an opinion for the Court: this was in *Allgeyer v. Louisiana,* where the application was remote.[226] Then in 1905 he made that proposition from *Allgeyer* his first citation in *Lochner v. New York,*[227] where a bare majority struck down a ten-hour work day for bakeries. Thus Bradley's words were projected far beyond his thought.[228] In

---

[226] 165 U.S. 578. The Court there invalidated a statute that penalized the doing of any act by a person within the State to effect marine insurance on property therein in a company not qualified to do business in Louisiana. The State must not so interfere with the individual's "liberty" in carrying on his business.

[227] 198 U.S. 45.

[228] He was not one who would judge on the basis of a concept of liberty where in fact those on one side were not free. Thus he spoke for the Court in Railroad Co. v. Lockwood, 17 Wall. 357 (1873), denying that a common carrier may contract out of its common law liability. "It is a favorite argument in the cases which favor the extension of the carrier's right to contract for exemption from liability, that men may be permitted to make their own agreements, and that it is

no concern to the public on what terms an individual chooses to have his goods carried." Not so. "The carrier and his customer do not stand on a footing of equality. The latter is only one individual of a million. . . ." And in his "Outline of my views on the subject of the Granger Cases," Bradley wrote: "As to railroads, it is hardly necessary to say that there are in this country no more absolute monopolies of public service than they are. The public stands on no equality with them." Accordingly the Court should uphold the legislative regulation of rates. Waite, C.J., made use of this study in writing for the Court in Munn v. Illinois, 94 U.S. 113 (1877), and railroad regulation cases decided with it. Charles Fairman, "The So-Called Granger Cases, Lord Hale, and Justice Bradley," *Stan. L. Rev.,* 5:587 (1953).

May 1937 Justice Butler quoted Bradley's *Butchers' Union* remarks to argue that a statute authorizing peaceful picketing and publicity in labor disputes should be held invalid under the Fourteenth Amendment: but now Butler was speaking for a minority[229]—the Court had just turned a new leaf.[230]

POSTSCRIPT

UNITED STATES CITIZENSHIP, Bradley wrote in his *Slaughter House* dissent, "is not an empty name"—"citizenship means something"—it carries "certain incidental rights, privileges and immunities of the greatest importance"—it is "a sure and undoubted title to equal rights in any and every State in this Union . . . ." A citizen "is not bound to cringe . . . or to pray for any act of grace, as a means of enjoying all the rights and privileges enjoyed by other citizens." "[T]he whole power of the nation is pledged to sustain him in that right" to equal treatment.

His ideas were never fanciful or undisciplined; he abhorred fuzziness. What he expressed in *Slaughter House* was in accord with a deep current of thought. The object of law and government in America, he had once said, was "the unimpeded, unrestrained, free development of the *individual man*"; every member of society should be protected in "the enjoyment of all the natural liberty compatible with mutual security."[231] "Unrestrained monopolies," however, "as to those things which the people must have and use, are a canker in any society, and have ever been the occasion of civil convulsions and revolutions. A people disposed for freedom will not tolerate this kind of oppression at the hands of private corporations or powerful citizens."[232]

The "liberty" and "property" secured by the Fourteenth Amendment, as the Court came to give them content, were self-regarding rights, serving the individual's material prosperity. Bradley's conception of the privileges of citizenship embraced rights of a more humane order, according to the citizen an effective participation as a member of the national community. Only natural persons would share these privi-

---

[229] Senn v. Tile Layers Protective Union, 301 U.S. 468, 483 at 487. Joining in the dissent were Van Devanter, McReynolds, and Sutherland, JJ.

[230] Notably in West Coast Hotel Co. v. Parrish, 300 U.S. 379, decided March 29, 1937, sustaining a minimum wage law. This overruled Adkins v. Children's Hospital, 261 U.S.

525 (1923), which had struck down a minimum wage law for women and children on the reasoning of Lochner v. New York.

[231] See note 141.

[232] The language comes from Bradley's "Outline of my views . . . ," cited in note 228 above.

leges[233]—whereas the benefits of "liberty" and "property" flowed in large measure to business corporations.

His thought remains capable of sound development: those conditions to which one is entitled by virtue of being a citizen of the United States—the protection and dignity that are his due, the opportunities, associations and relationships that ought to be open to him. The conception is not static. As the nation experiences change—in its transportation, commerce and industry—in its political practices—in the way in which people live and work and move about—in the expectations they entertain about the quality of American life—surely the privilege of membership in this national community must broaden to include what has become essential under prevailing circumstances.

The Fourteenth Amendment, in Bradley's apt interpretation, expressed a national aspiration that "every citizen of the United States might stand erect in every portion of its soil, in the full enjoyment of every right and privilege belonging to a freeman, without fear of violence or molestation." After a century, the nation is stirred anew by a yearning to attain that goal.

---

[233] Bank of Augusta v. Earle, 13 Pet. 519, in 1839 had established that corporations were not entitled to the privileges and immunities of Article IV, Section 2, and Paul v. Virginia, 8 Wall. 168 (1869), had repeated that proposition.

An aside: in 1839, while reading for the bar, Bradley made his first visit to Washington, and was present in the Court room during some of the argument in *Bank of Augusta*.

CHAPTER XXII

The Chief Justiceship of Chase

F ROM DECEMBER TERM 1865 until the errant States were gathered back in their proper relation in the Union, under a Constitution so amended as to promise security for the future, the Court moved from one anxious passage only to confront another. As the leaders of the 39th Congress read the omens, measures inconsistent with acceptance of the situation as it was upon the ratification of the Thirteenth Amendment would find an unfriendly majority on the Supreme Bench. That apprehension was well founded.

The new and untried President had affirmed in April that

> [Traitors] must not only be punished, but their social power must
> be destroyed. If not, they will still maintain an ascendancy, and may
> again become numerous and powerful . . . .[1]

But then in accord with an Executive prescription the rebel communities went through a minimal transformation that left power exactly where it had been all along. By constitutions and statutes enacted during the autumn and winter of 1865–66, the black man was consigned to an inferior order, under a "white man's government." He was

---

[1] Remarks on April 21, 1865, to a delegation of citizens from Indiana, introduced by Governor Morton. Edward McPherson, *The Political History of the United States of America during Reconstruction*, 3d ed. (Washington: James F. Chapman, 1880), 44.

On the same day Senator Trumbull was writing to the President from Chicago:

The control of state organiza-
tions in the rebel states must not be left in the hands of those who undertook to take their states out of the Union, but must be given to new men having no sympathy with the slaveholding aristocracy of the South who have hitherto lorded it over the masses, if we mean to have permanent peace, & good feeling between the masses North & South.

Johnson Papers, L.C.

to remain a menial servant; public education was not contemplated; no prospect was held out that he would ever be allowed to qualify for participation in government.[2]

Upon adoption of the Amendment forbidding slavery—so the President told the incoming Congress—"it would remain for the [secessionist] States . . . to resume their places in the two branches of the national Legislature, and thereby complete the work of restoration." We would be "once more a united people."[3]

But Congress, not content to leave it to the States to "provide adequate protection and remedies for the freedmen," enacted the Civil Rights Bill, notwithstanding the President's objections. It carried, over a veto, a second Freedmen's Bureau Bill, establishing in the insurrectionary States "military jurisdiction over all cases and questions concerning the free enjoyment" of the civil rights secured to men of color. In order to establish civil liberty and equal protection upon an impregnable foundation, and to counteract the augmented power in the electoral college and in the House of Representatives that would result to the slave States from the Thirteenth Amendment, Congress proposed a Fourteenth. Ratification was a condition to readmission to representation: this would be an earnest for the future, and make it possible to meet the Constitution's requirement of "three fourths of the several States."[4]

At a meeting with his Cabinet on May 1, 1866, the President declared his opposition to the plan reported the day before by the Joint Committee on Reconstruction "for restoring the States lately in insurrection to their full political rights" on the basis of their accepting and conforming to the proposed Fourteenth Amendment.[5] The members of the Cabinet were required to declare their stand. Then the President caused a full account to appear in the press.

> He insisted . . . that Senators and Representatives ought to be at once admitted into the respective Houses, as prescribed by law and the Constitution. . . . He remarked, in general terms, that if the organic law is to be changed at all, it should be at a time when all the States and all the people can participate in the alteration.

This was read in Congress, and accepted as a challenge.[6]

A few days after the Fourteenth Amendment was submitted for ratification, Justice Nelson in chambers gratuitously affirmed that upon

---

[2] Supra, pp. 108-17, 1226-28, ch. 19, n. 173.

[3] Message to Congress, Dec. 4, 1865. Cong. Globe, 39-1, App., 1, 2. Supra, p. 118.

[4] Supra, pp. 121-33, 1159-1205, 1260-1300.

[5] Supra, pp. 131-33.

[6] National Intelligencer, May 2; Cong. Globe, 39-1, 2333-34, May 2; Orville H. Browning's account of the President's report of the meeting, Diary of Orville Hickman Browning (Springfield: Illinois State Historical

compliance with the Executive prescription, an insurrectionary State "was entitled to the full enjoyment of all her constitutional rights and privileges."[7]

The issue in the election of 1866 was whether to support Congress and the Amendment, or to stand with the President and the insurrectionary States. The outcome was an overwhelming endorsement of the former. Yet when the Second Session convened in December, the President's message offered no prospect of accord on other than his own terms. Of the ten States awaiting restoration, two had already repelled the Amendment, and the others promptly followed suit. "There should be no faltering," was the word from the White House. "Masterly inactivity" was the Southern watchword; the Amendment was dead, and there was nothing Congress could do about it.[8]

At this juncture, on December 17, 1866, Justice Davis delivered the opinion of the majority of the Court, to support the ruling made in April that the trial of the Indiana conspirators by military commission had been in excess of the powers of the Executive. In doing so he made an unnecessary pronouncement confining the powers of Congress as well. The language in effect condemned the jurisdiction established by the Freedmen's Bureau Act to protect the civil rights of the blacks. The President instantly acted on that view by ordering the release of Dr. Watson in Virginia, who after a deliberate killing had been exculpated by the local magistrates.[9]

More than that, the opinion cast an ominous shadow over deliberations progressing in Congress on the question, What shall be done about the recalcitrant States? When Justice Davis saw how his masterpiece was being received, he protested in private that there was "not a word said in the opinion about reconstruction." But in the same breath he insisted that it would have been worth nothing for the future if the Court had "cowardly toadied to the prevalent idea, that the legislative dept of the govt can override everything. . . . Congress claims omnipotent power . . . . I have no faith in the purposes and aims of the extreme men of the dominant party, & they control legislation. . . ." If endowed with sufficient genius and power, "I wd resign my office & try if I could not by a great missionary effort wake up the common people of the West to a sense of their danger."[10]

Library, Vol. 1 [1850–64], Pease and Randall, eds., 1925; Vol. II [1865–81], Randall, ed., 1933), 74; Eric McKitrick, *Andrew Johnson and Reconstruction* (Chicago: University of Chicago Press, 1960), 351–52.

[7] *In re* Egan, Fed. Case No. 4303, June 22, 1866. Supra, p. 148. The Amendment had been proposed on

June 13. The legislature of Tennessee ratified on July 19, whereupon that State was readmitted to representation on July 24.

[8] Supra, pp. 182–83, 253–57.

[9] Supra, pp. 207–22.

[10] Letter of Feb. 24, 1867, to Judge Rockwell. Supra, pp. 232–34.

It was a delusion to suppose that those sentiments toward the dominant party in Congress had not shone through the opinion. Jerry Black in his Jackson Day tribute hailed "the words that burn all over that opinion," which as he said "confines their power by limits inconveniently narrow."[11]

Congress would, however, break out of what the Democrats cheerfully called the "dead-lock." It would replace the all-white regimes that then were "the State" by newly constituted governments erected by the suffrage of citizens without regard to color. Before this step was taken it had become abundantly clear that the existing governments would not themselves permit blacks to attain the suffrage on meeting nondiscriminatory qualifications, even as part of a settlement such as Senator Stewart's "universal suffrage and universal amnesty" of March 1866,[12] or the "North Carolina Plan" of January 1867.[13] The Congressional prescription was formulated in Sections 5 and 6 of the Act of March 2, 1867, to provide for the more efficient government of the rebel States.[14]

When shortly it was recognized as impracticable to look to initiative within the affected States to effect the prescribed transformation, the incoming 40th Congress provided the machinery by the Supplementary Act of March 23, 1867.[15] It would not entrust the conduct of registration and elections to the all-white administrations then in office—nor would it place local loyalists in charge: "no one in possession or out of possession is to be prejudiced by any action of ours."[16] The statute assigned the task to "the commanding general in each district," because that gave the best prospect that the will of Congress would be faithfully executed.

Chief Justice Chase provided Senator Wilson with a draft for this supplementary bill.[17]

Notwithstanding the view in some Southern quarters that the prudent course was to accept the legislation and make the best of it,[18] the attractive possibility of extracting a judgment of condemnation from the Court could not be put aside. The first attempt was in *Mississippi v. Johnson*, seeking to enjoin the President from carrying out the two Acts of Congress. Such an application had no precedent in the history of the republic. The Court was unanimous in sustaining the

---

[11] Toast at the Jackson Day dinner. *National Intelligencer*, Jan. 9, 10, 1867. Supra, pp. 222–23.
[12] Supra, pp. 128–30.
[13] Supra, pp. 275–81.
[14] Supra, pp. 295–307.
[15] Supra, pp. 313–24.

[16] Blaine's comment, supra, p. 319. "We want neither black nor white oligarchies," Sherman had said a month earlier, in the 39th Congress. Supra, p. 261.
[17] Supra, p. 324.
[18] Supra, pp. 366–78.

objection of Attorney General Stanbery that the motion should not even be entertained.[19] The Chief Justice said:

> The Congress is the Legislative Department of the Government; the President is the Executive Department. Neither can be restrained in its action by the Judicial Department; though the acts of both, when performed, are, in proper cases, subject to its cognizance.

That was on April 15, 1867.

Next came Georgia's suit to restrain Stanton and others:[20] The Court was asked to protect the existing polity "composed exclusively . . . of white male citizens above the age of twenty-one years" against the statutes whereby "many thousands of black men" would be allowed to participate in government. Attorney General Stanbery moved for a dismissal for want of jurisdiction. He argued,[21]

> suppose that what is proposed to be done is done, and all that is future and contingent becomes actual and past, and a constitution is framed under these laws and is accepted and ratified by Congress as the constitution of Georgia, and then an appeal is made to your Honors not to prevent, but to restore, to keep, to preserve the right of the contesting State organization as the State Government of Georgia—what sort of a question would your Honors then encounter? Just the same that you encountered in the Dorr case, Luther vs. Borden,[22] precisely. . . .

In that case from Rhode Island, the Court had been asked to decide which of two was the rightful government, and Taney had replied that that was "a question to be settled by the political power," not by the judiciary.

On May 13, 1867, the Court ruled in accord with Stanbery's argument: it dismissed Georgia's bill for want of jurisdiction.

If Congressional Reconstruction was to be stopped by mandate of the Court, such a judgment must be won at December term, 1867. Jeremiah Black was in charge, and his hopes were fixed on *Georgia v. Grant, Meade et al.*[23] and *Ex parte McCardle.*[24] The former went awry when the Court declined to grant a preliminary injunction without personal service being made upon the respondents. In *McCardle,* the Court granted Black's request to advance for an early argument. It rejected Trumbull's dilatory motion to dismiss. But then it refrained from sprinting to announce a judgment before Congress could pass a

---

[19] 4 Wall. 475. Supra, pp. 381–83.
[20] 6 Wall. 50. Supra, pp. 384–93.
[21] Oral argument, in the *National Intelligencer,* April 27, 1867.

[22] 7 How. 1 (1849). Supra, p. 395.
[23] Supra, pp. 433–37.
[24] Supra, pp. 437–41.

statute, and bowed when the grant of an appeal was withdrawn with effect upon pending cases. Promptly however, in *Ex parte Martin and Gill*, it offered the suggestion that review was still available through the old method of habeas corpus aided by certiorari.[25] In short, it forbore to perform a feat that would prove its valor, not needed for the protection of any man's life or liberty, but greatly desired by Governor Jenkins, Black, Judge Sharkey, Charles O'Conor, Editor McCardle, and many others, for their own purpose.

In these instances, truly the disclaimers of jurisdiction seem the right rulings; and where it was a matter of discretion, the Court's exercise seems sound. In *McCardle*, where the facts were somewhat complicated, there has been uncertainty about the path of duty. But surely Reverdy Johnson's statement in the Senate,[26] and James M. Carlisle's informed vindication in the press,[27] are worthy of our acceptance.

And if, indifferent to jurisdictional niceties, one were to inquire whether the Court was faithful to the call of "justice," could it be affirmed that it should have lent itself to Black's carefully prepared design to keep the ante-bellum past upon the throne?

Ex parte Yerger[28] was brought to save a killer from sentence and punishment. The Court sustained its jurisdiction in habeas corpus, notwithstanding that Congress had abolished the direct appeal. Counsel joined in an arrangement whereby their client would presently be released—at the same time precluding a decision on the constitutionality of Section 3 of the Reconstruction Act, and avoiding a crisis involving Court, Congress, and President, just as Congressional Reconstruction was drawing to a close.

Texas v. White, in 1869, was the occasion for affirming that the Constitution contemplates "an indestructible Union, composed of indestructible States."[29] It was useful to establish a doctrine on what had been a much-debated point, and in particular to discredit Stevens' talk about "conquest." The immediate application was that Texas had standing to maintain this suit, although it had not yet been restored to representation and, according to the Reconstruction Act, its government should "be deemed provisional only." The case has received marked attention from historians. It did not make a major contribution to decisional law: only rarely has it been cited in the United States Reports.[30]

---

[25] Supra, pp. 471–78.
[26] Supra, p. 468.
[27] Supra, pp. 479–80.
[28] Supra, pp. 565–90.
[29] 7 Wall. 700, 725. Supra, pp. 619, 635–40.

[30] For example, McReynolds, J., cited this "cause of momentous importance" for its statement that the maintenance of the States was as much within the design of the Constitution as the maintenance of the

The Legal Tender Act, pronounced invalid as to preexisting debts in *Hepburn v. Griswold* in February 1870 was, upon a fresh argument before a full Bench, sustained in May 1871 as a constitutional exercise of the powers of Congress.[31] The aspersion that the Court was "packed" is refuted by the facts. The untoward experience—which Charles Evans Hughes characterized as a "self-inflicted wound"[32]— is traceable to the determination of Chase and some of his brethren to hasten to a judgment of condemnation, in disregard of the peculiar circumstances of the moment. Notably Grier's performance at the conference on November 27, 1869, should have brought a recognition that this would be an improper act of power.[33] It was doubly culpable thus to affront the spirit of the Constitution by hastily clutching the power of judicial review, in order to invalidate an Act of Congress for being "inconsistent with the spirit of the Constitution."

"Brother Grier," Justice Miller had commented in a letter of January 19, 1868, "is getting a little muddy . . . ."[34] On November 17, 1869, George Harding had reported conversations with Nelson, Swayne, and Davis: "They are greatly exercised at his not resigning— They declared they were going to crowd him about December 1 '69. . . . Congress will also crowd him if he dont resign . . . ." On December 9 the Chief Justice and Nelson conveyed to Grier the insistence of his brethren that he leave the Bench.[35]

Near the end of Chase's service the Court applied the Fourteenth Amendment to the complaint of the New Orleans butchers.[36] The problem was utterly novel, and the resulting alignment within the Court such as had never occurred theretofore. Justice Field for four Justices took a line which, when projected, led to the dogma of "the

---

National Government, when he dissented from the decision sustaining the Social Security Act in respect of its provisions to promote State unemployment funds. Steward Machine Co. v. Davis, 301 U.S. 548, 598–99 (1937). Sutherland, J., quoted the same passage in his dissent in the same case, at 611.

Lurton, J., quoted "the strong and memorable language" about "indestructible States" when, in Coyle v. Smith, 221 U.S. 559, 579 (1911), the provision locating the State capital, in the statute admitting Oklahoma to the Union, was held unenforceable.

Brewer, J., cited it in 1905 in holding that the federal excise tax *could* be imposed upon a State in respect of its retail liquor business, South Carolina v. United States, 199 U.S.

347, 453; also in 1909 in holding that Congress *had no power* to make it a crime to keep an alien woman for purposes of prostitution "within three years after she shall have entered the United States." Keller v. United States, 213 U.S. 138, 149.

[31] Supra, pp. 713–19, 738–63.

[32] *The Supreme Court of the United States* (New York: Columbia University Press, 1928), 50.

[33] Supra, ch. 14.

[34] Charles Fairman, *Mr. Justice Miller and the Supreme Court, 1862–1890* (Cambridge, Mass.: Harvard University Press, 1939), 164. Referring to Grier's opinion in League v. Atchison, 6 Wall. 112 (1868).

[35] Supra, pp. 716–17, 730.

[36] Supra, pp. 1324–63.

liberty of contract,"[37] to *Lochner v. New York* in 1905,[38] and on to that "culmination of the constitutional restraints of due process on state action in the field of business and economics"[39] ending in the "Supreme Court crisis" of 1937. Justice Miller, for the majority, cried out in protestation: "the one pervading purpose found in [the post-war Amendments], lying at the foundation of each, and without which none of them would have been even suggested, [was] the freedom of the slave race, the security and firm establishment of that freedom, and the protection of the newly made freeman and citizen from the oppressions of those who had formerly exercised unlimited dominion over him." Although the Civil War had brought a recognition that "the true danger to the perpetuity of the Union" lay in the powers of the States rather than in that of the Nation, it was not the purpose of the Amendments "to destroy the main features of the general system."[40]

It would be presumptuous for any modern critic to pretend that if he had been present in 1872–73 he would have known how to give a permanently satisfactory answer to the problem Judge Campbell's imagination had contrived.

The foregoing paragraphs have marked anew the thread of the turbulent current that swept through the years of Chase's Chief Justiceship. All the while the Justices were attending to a host of other matters that were borne along on quieter waters. Some of these will now be pointed out.

POSITION OF THE OUT-OF-STATE INSURANCE CORPORATION: *PAUL v. VIRGINIA*

CONSTITUTIONAL PROBLEMS NOT related to the war and restoration should be introduced with a forewarning. Many will be beginning cases, where the Court first took hold of an emerging problem to which it would return again and again. To pursue the doctrine of each of these cases would anticipate major concerns of the Chief Justiceship of Waite. The purpose at this point is to round out the account of the present volume by illustrating anew the wide variety of matters on which, at all times, the Justices were at work. In the main, the constitutional decisions to be noticed came late in Chase's tenure, and it does not appear that he contributed significantly to them.

In the First Session of the 39th Congress, on June 29, 1866,

---

[37] Supra, pp. 1366, 1386.
[38] Supra, p. 1387.
[39] Words of Chief Justice Stone, in *Proceedings of the Bar and Officers* *of the Supreme Court of the United States in memory of George Sutherland, December 18, 1944*, 101 at 104.
[40] 16 Wall. 36 at 82.

Representative Burton C. Cook reported from the Judiciary Committee a bill for the creation of a Bureau of Insurance, which was ordered to be printed, and recommitted.[41] There was no further action upon it by the House.

In the 40th Congress, at the First Session, two more such proposals ended in the Judiciary Committee.[42] At the Second Session, a Bureau of Insurance bill by Senator George H. Williams, similar to the bill of 1866, went to the Committee on Commerce which, "after carefully considering it," reported adversely; thereupon it was postponed indefinitely.[43]

The Stockholder, a recently established financial journal in New York City, explained the details of the 1866 measure in its issue of July 24.[44] The bureau, under a commissioner, would be established within the Treasury Department. Insurance corporations contemplated under the laws of any State must file a statement of various pertinent facts, and must deposit with the Commissioner, to secure faithful performance, United States bonds in amounts graduated according to the type of insurance and the company's assets. Upon receiving the Commissioner's certificate, the corporation would be authorized to transact business, without being subject to State or local taxation at more than 1 percent of the net premiums received. Annual reports must be made; the amount of individual risks was controlled.

The editor pronounced this judgment:

> We are strongly of opinion that this is a class of legislation which Congress would do well to let alone. . . .

Perhaps the federal Government might control the "new business of telegraphing, unknown when the constitution was made, as also that of express companies," under the *postal* power. But, he concluded,

> There are matters enough with which Congress can legitimately concern themselves without interfering with those functions which are rightfully and better performed by the several states.

---

[41] Cong. Globe, 39–1, 3490.

[42] Cong. Globe, 40–1, 126, by Eldridge of Wisconsin, and 332, by Pile of Missouri, on Mar. 15 and 25, respectively.

[43] Cong. Globe, 40–2, 816, Jan. 29, and 1669, Mar. 4, 1868.

The *Richmond Dispatch* of Jan. 31 commented that the federal Government "cannot exercise as much vigilance in the premises as the States."

Aside from creating a demand for Government bonds, the bill's only purpose was to expand "the rigor of the power of the General Government. . . . The great point now is to increase the machinery and the number of offices and sinecures at Washington, so that the harvest for office-hunting party hacks may be abundant. . . ."

[44] 4:585.

The *New York Evening Post* was speaking in the same tone.[45] The war, it said, had brought an enormous increase in the activities of the Government: an "expensive and useless" Department of Agriculture had been created;[46] an ill-advised attempt was being made to extend the life of the Freedmen's Bureau;[47] a bill to establish a Bureau of Education was pending.[48] And now came "this outrageous and unconstitutional attempt to multiply bureaus" by needlessly adding one to supervise insurance.

> We shall next hear of the general government controlling and directing baths, laundries, retail groceries and water closets.

The editor and publisher of the *Evening Post*, William Cullen Bryant, has already been presented as an extreme doctrinaire in his hostility to governmental action.[49]

In late November 1866 representatives of life insurance companies gathered in New York City and formed the Chamber of Life Insurance of the United States.[50] William Barnes, Superintendent of Insurance for the State of New York, spoke by invitation. He discouraged the idea of a federal bureau with adequate powers—apparently on constitutional grounds, and certainly because of opposition in some States. "Life insurance companies cannot find any better tribunals than the State legislatures, which, however, need to be enlightened . . . ," so as to act for the interest both of the companies and of the public.

The president of one of the companies spoke much more sanguinely about a federal bureau. He said that the business needed "a general plan which would secure uniformity of action throughout the country." Elizur Wright, retiring insurance commissioner of Massachusetts, believed that Congress could be induced to act, notwithstanding influences that would oppose this "as another attempt at centralization."[51] The *Evening Post* reported the meeting, in an editorial

---

[45] "Congress and the Insurance Companies," July 5, 1866.

[46] "Act of May 15, 1862, creating this agency, under a Commissioner, "to acquire and to diffuse among the people of the United States useful information on subjects connected with agriculture." 12 Stat. 387.

[47] Supra, pp. 125–27, 1163–67. The bill was carried over a veto, and became the Act of July 16, 1866, 14 Stat. 173.

[48] H.R.276, framed in a select committee of which Garfield was chairman, was passed by the House on June 19, 1866. Cong. Globe, 39–1,

3270. At the close of the Second Session the Senate passed the bill, whereby a Department of Education, under a Commissioner, was created. Act of Mar. 2, 1867, 14 Stat. 434.

[49] Supra, pp. 344–45.

[50] The *National Intelligencer* of November 24, 1866, gave a report, with extensive quotation. In an editorial note it said that it opposed the proposal for a national bureau as "another step in the direction of centralizing power, which Radicalism is upholding . . . ."

[51] On Wright see the D.A.B. He has already been identified as a sincere

declaring that the idea of a national bureau of insurance was "an absurdity."[52]

When Wright returned to Boston he sent the *Post* a rebuttal of its editorial.[53] He said that since the national government had been preserved at so great a cost, surely now it could "secure to us free trade among the States." Without federal regulation there would be "thirty-six little nations," each enforcing its sovereign will through its own bureau, "with tape of every hue to be found in the rainbow."

The burden of his argument may be kept in mind, for contrast with what Justice Field will say for the Court in the momentous decision of *Paul v. Virginia,* three years later.[54]

> I will not here pretend that the corporation has any right out of the State which controls it, and will even concede that the individual citizen of another State, and of the United States, cannot represent or act for it in any way without the consent, express or implied, of the one or the other government. But the other citizen who desires to take a policy in a company chartered out of his own State, has a right, as a citizen of the United States, to have commerce between the States so regulated that he can freely do it. In order to regulate commerce so as to secure him this freedom of trade, Congress may permit a citizen of the United States to represent a corporation out of his State, in spite of State prohibition, because this permission is a logical necessity under the constitutional power to regulate inter-state commerce.
>
> Commerce is an exchange of values, not of mere materials which may happen to be more or less valuable. Common sense and the dictionaries, I think, settle it that life insurance is a branch of commerce, an exchange of values. If it be only an *incident* of commerce, it is placed under the control of Congress, if I am not mistaken, by the concession of more than one State judiciary.

The Virginia legislature on February 3, 1866, enacted that no out-of-State insurance company should do business in Virginia without a license, to obtain which it must deposit State or certain other bonds to an amount varying from $35,000 to $50,000 according to the capital employed. No such deposit was required of a domestic insurer. And no person should without a license act as agent for a foreign company, under penalty of from $50 to $500.

Samuel B. Paul of Petersburg applied for a license to act as agent for certain foreign companies, and tendered the license tax; he met refusal, because his companies had not deposited bonds.

---

and effective reformer. Supra, pp. 722–23.

[52] "The Life Insurance Convention," November 23, 1866.

[53] Letter of November 26, published in the *Evening Post* of December 1.

[54] 8 Wall. 168 (1869). Infra, pp. 1400–01.

For having written a contract on behalf of four New York fire insurance companies he was fined $50 in the circuit court, notwithstanding claims of right under the Privileges and Immunities Clause of Article IV, Section 2, and the Commerce Clause. On October 12, 1866, the State's highest court held the judgment to be "plainly right."[55] Paul sued out a writ of error, and filed his case in the Supreme Court on November 16, 1867.

In the meantime the National Board of Fire Underwriters had been organized. At the annual meeting in April 1869 it was voted to support Paul's appeal to the extent of $15,000. The Committee on Legislation and Taxation reported its "strong hopes of obtaining a decision . . . on the ground . . . that underwriting is inseparable from, and constitutes a part of, the commerce of the country"; on that proposition there was "no diversity of opinion among the members of the Board"; the committee thought "that the unanimous opinion of so large a body of intelligent men, familiar with the subject, should give it weight worthy to influence the judgment of the Supreme Court as to the interpretation of Commercial Law."[56]

James M. Carlisle and Benjamin R. Curtis presented the challenge to the Virginia legislation when argument was heard on October 12, 1869.

The Justices did not feel any need for long reflection. On November 1 the judgment below was affirmed, per Field, J., by a unanimous Court.

For *jurisdictional* purposes—as when Article III spoke of "Controversies . . . between Citizens of different States"—an incontrovertible presumption had come to be recognized whereby a corporation of one State was deemed to consist only of citizens of that State; thus the corporation was treated, in respect of jurisdiction, as if it were a citizen of the State by which it had been created. Justice Field traced the evolution of decisions. But when Article IV declared that "The Citizens of each State shall be entitled to all Privileges and Immunities of Citizens in the several States," the promise ran "only to natural persons, members of the body politic . . . , not to artificial persons created by the Legislature, and possessing only the attributes which the Legislature has prescribed."

"Now, a grant of corporate existence is a grant of special privileges to the corporators, enabling them to act for certain designated

---

[55] Transcript of Record in Paul v. Virginia, 23. No opinion was filed. Counsel for the defendant in error cited Slaughter v. The Commonwealth, 13 Grat. 767 (1856), as substantially in point.

[56] Alden L. Todd, *A Spark Lighted in Portland. The Record of the National Board of Fire Underwriters* (New York: McGraw-Hill Pub. Co., 1966), 18–20.

purposes as a single individual . . . ." Such a creation of local law could carry on business in other States only as a matter of comity, "upon such terms and conditions as those States may think proper to impose."

> They may exclude the foreign corporation entirely; they may restrict its business to particular localities, or they may exact such security for the performance of its contracts with their citizens as in their judgment will best promote the public interest. The whole matter rests in their discretion.

Justice Field expanded on the theme that it would be intolerable if a State could not protect itself from "a flood of corporations from other States . . . ."

He turned to the second contention: that the Commerce Clause secured to the New York insurance companies the right to effect insurance in Virginia through an agent there upon terms as favorable as could a Virginia company. Justice Field rejected that succinctly:

> The defect of the argument lies in the character of their business. Issuing a policy of insurance is not a transaction of commerce. . . . The policies do not take effect—are not executed contracts—until delivered by the agent in Virginia. They are, then, local transactions, and are governed by the local law. . . .

Insurance is not commerce: so pat a sentence lodged and stuck.

Paul v. Virginia was cited in the United States Reports more than a hundred times in the next hundred years, as one or other of its holdings was put to the test in hard cases. Field's propositions were unqualified, and experience deals harshly with absolutes. As to the statement that the State was wholly free to exclude foreign corporations according to its own discretion, Justice Holmes in 1926 marked the erosion that meandering lines of decision had produced:

> But it has been held a great many times that the most absolute seem-ing rights are qualified, and in some circumstances become wrong. One of the most frequently recurring instances is when the so-called right is used as part of a scheme to accomplish a forbidden result. . . . Thus the right to exclude a foreign corporation cannot be used to prevent it from resorting to a federal court . . . ; or to tax it upon property that by established principles the State has no power to tax . . . ; or . . . to interfere with interstate commerce . . . .[57]

---

[57] Fidelity & Deposit Co. of Maryland v. Tafoya, 270 U.S. 426, 434. A New Mexico statute provided for suspension of foreign insurance company's license if it paid any fee to nonresidents on policies covering risks within the State: held, violative of the Fourteenth Amendment.

The proposition that insurance was not a part of interstate commerce withstood a well-mounted attack in 1913,[58] but fell in *United States v. South-Eastern Underwriters Association*[59] in 1944. Insurance companies that combined to fix rates in several States were held to be punishable under the federal Anti-trust Act.

Over the years after *Paul v. Virginia*, State supervision of insurance became highly developed; evils Wright had expected from regulation by numerous "little nations" were largely avoided. When the logic of the *South-Eastern Underwriters* decision threatened this existing system, Congress promptly enacted that "the continued regulation and taxation by the several States of the business of insurance is in the public interest...."[60]

DUCAT v. CHICAGO

AT THE TIME of *Paul v. Virginia* there existed nothing comparable to the present loose-leaf "services" whereby one may learn what are the issues involved in cases pending on the Court's docket. In a brief dated November 8, 1870, Samuel W. Fuller, representing the plaintiff in error in *Ducat v. Chicago*,[61] opened with this statement:

> This case was brought here for the purpose of presenting to the Court the same questions which were raised and decided in ... Paul v. The State of Virginia .... The parties and counsel in this case did not know of the pendency of that, until after it was argued and submitted to the Court, at the December Term, 1868 ....[62]

He did not propose to challenge what had been decided, but suggested differences that might lead the Court to distinguish between the Illinois statute and that of Virginia. A large number of similar cases awaited the outcome of this: counsel were submitting without oral argument, and were anxious to have a decision on the merits.

Justice Nelson gave the Court's prompt response. The only notable difference, he said, was that the requirement imposed by Illinois was more onerous.

---

[58] New York Life Ins. Co. v. Deer Lodge County, 231 U.S. 495. Roscoe Pound appeared for the plaintiff in error.

[59] 322 U.S. 533.

[60] Insurance Regulation Act of Mar. 9, 1945. 59 Stat. 33. This was sustained and applied in Prudential

Insurance Co. v. Benjamin, 328 U.S. 408 (1946).

[61] 10 Wall. 410, submitted on Dec. 21, 1870, and decided on Jan. 9, 1871.

[62] Brief, p. 1. Fuller was a prominent lawyer at Chicago, who frequently had cases in the Supreme Court.

As to the nature or degree of discrimination [between foreign and domestic corporations], it belongs to the State to determine, subject only to such limitations on her sovereignty as may be found in the fundamental law of the Union. We find no such limitations in this case.

In years to come the Court would have numerous occasions to determine what limitations should be "found in the fundamental law...."

STATE TAXATION AND ORIGINAL PACKAGES: *WOODRUFF v. PARHAM*

WHEN ON APRIL 12, 1869, Benjamin R. Curtis concluded the argument in *Paul v. Virginia*, John A. Campbell opened the case of *Waring v. Mayor of Mobile and others*,[63] including Parham, City Tax Collector. Philip Phillips replied. Then Campbell began argument in the related cases of *Woodruff v. Parham*[64] and *Hinson v. Lott, Tax Collector for the County of Mobile*.[65] It was an extraordinary coincidence that the Court was thus addressed by two former Justices in succession. Curtis had resigned in 1857, being succeeded by Clifford. Campbell had resigned in 1861 and gone home to Mobile. Now he stood at the bar to argue that the Supreme Court of Alabama had erred in denying his clients' claims of constitutional right to exemption from certain taxes laid under authority of the State.

Waring had purchased from the consignees bags of salt brought into the harbor as ballast by foreign vessels that came for cargoes of cotton; then he had sold the salt in the original packages. The question was whether he was liable to the city tax of one-half of one percent of gross receipts, notwithstanding the command of Article I, Section 10, Clause 2:

> No State shall, without the consent of Congress, lay any Imposts or Duties on Imports or Exports, except what may be absolutely necessary for executing its inspection Laws ....

In *Brown v. Maryland* in 1827 Marshall, C. J., had said for the Court that

> while remaining the property of the owner, in his warehouse, in the original form or package in which it was imported, a tax upon it is

---

[63] 8 Wall. 110, decided Oct. 25, 1869.
[64] 8 Wall. 123, decided Nov. 8, 1869.
[65] 8 Wall. 148, decided with Woodruff v. Parham.

too plainly a duty on imports to escape the prohibition of the Constitution.[66]

But Waring, said Justice Clifford for the Court, was not the importer: he was the second vendor, and merchandise once sold, even though it remained in the original package, was taxable as other property.

It was not a very significant decision, since it turned upon an appreciation of an unusual set of facts.

Woodruff v. Parham[67] was quite another matter. It passed upon a question which, Justice Miller said, "is before the Court now for the first time"; the conclusion was in disregard of language Marshall had used in *Brown v. Maryland*; and the importance of the decision is attested by the scores of instances in which the Court has cited and followed it.

Mobile, in accord with its charter, had taxed, *inter alia*, sales at auction. Woodruff had sold at auction goods in original packages brought into Alabama from other States of the Union. He claimed that these were "imports" within the protection of Article I, Section 10, Clause 2. The Court rejected that contention.

"Imports," said Justice Miller, referred only to goods from foreign countries. This was deduced from a comparison of the language of related constitutional provisions. It was confirmed by the history of the period of the Confederation, and by resort to the debates in the Convention of 1787 and in the State conventions that followed. And, Miller added confidently,

> If we examine for a moment the results of an opposite doctrine, we shall be well satisfied with the wisdom of the Constitution as thus construed.

A merchant at Chicago buys in New York and sells at wholesale in original packages: surely he should not escape taxation by the State and local governments that protect him. In Massachusetts, one wholesale dealer purchases in New York and his neighbor purchases in Boston: there was no reason why only the latter bear taxes "which Massachusetts levies with equal justice on the property of all the citizens."

But there was a dictum by Marshall in *Brown v. Maryland*. After holding that the license tax on the occupation of an importer amounted to a tax on imports, he had gone on to hold that it was also inconsistent with the grant of power to Congress "to regulate commerce . . . ." Then he had uttered this dictum: "we suppose the prin-

---

[66] 12 Wheat. 419, 442.   [67] Supra, n. 64.

ciples laid down in this case, to apply equally to importations from a sister State. . . ." Perhaps Marshall's "casual remark" was intended to apply only to what had just been said apropos of the Commerce Clause: if so, said Miller, the Court now would concur that taxation discriminating against goods because produced in another State would offend that constitutional provision. But if Marshall had been intimating that goods from a sister State were "imports," exempt from nondiscriminatory taxation, the mature thought of the Court was to the contrary.

In *Hinson v. Lott*,[68] one section of a statute of 1866 required that dealers who offered for sale liquor not produced in Alabama must first pay a tax of fifty cents per gallon. The contest had to do with barrels of whisky brought in from other States; the argument had been addressed solely to the one section of the statute. But the Court read the statute as a whole; other sections provided collection of an equal tax upon production by local distillers. Thus one exaction was the complement of the other, and there was no discrimination.

The decree for the collector was affirmed.

Justice Nelson dissented in both *Woodruff* and *Hinson*. He argued at length that "imports" should be taken to include goods from another State.

A VINDICATION OF THE POWER OF CONGRESS

The Daniel Ball,[69] a steamer of 123 tons burden and a draft of two feet, plied the Grand River in Michigan, over the forty miles between Grand Rapids and the port of Grand Haven, where the river empties into Lake Michigan. Goods and passengers were carried, some bound thence to Chicago and Milwaukee. Goods and passengers from other States were carried upstream. An Act of Congress in 1838 required a license to transport by steam vessel upon the navigable waters of the United States. For failure to comply, the vessel had been libelled for the statutory penalty. The District Judge, subordinating his own opinion to that of other Judges, ruled that for this transportation wholly within the boundaries of Michigan no license was required.[70] The Circuit Court reversed, and the owner appealed to the Supreme Court.

---

[68] Supra, n. 65.
[69] 10 Wall. 557, submitted on Nov. 22, 1870, and decided on Jan. 23, 1871.
[70] *The Daniel Ball*, Fed. Case No. 3564.
District Judge Withey, of the Western District of Michigan, took

account of two unreported decisions in 1856 or 1857 by Wilkins, D.J., in what was then the District Court for Michigan: he had said, of the same situation, that "This commerce . . . was altogether internal, and subject only to the control and government of the state of Michigan." Other

Justice Field made its response in a concise opinion of enduring importance. So far as the vessel carried what was destined for or had come from another State, it was engaged in interstate commerce:

> The fact that several different and independent agencies are employed . . . , some acting entirely in one State, and some acting through two or more States, does in no respect affect the character of the transaction. To the extent in which each agency acts in that transportation, it is subject to the regulation of Congress.

But it had been argued that such a holding would permit Congress to assume the entire control of the commerce of the country.

> We answer that the present case relates to transportation on the navigable waters of the United States, and we are not called upon to express an opinion upon the power of Congress over interstate commerce when carried on by land transportation. . . .

When Justice Field read this opinion, on January 31, 1871, it was particularly appropriate that the Court thus guard its language. Then pending before the Third Session of the 41st Congress was the old "air line" measure to grant a federal charter for a railroad from Washington, across Maryland, Delaware, Pennsylvania, and New Jersey, to New York City. This had figured in the efforts that led to carrying the Thirteenth Amendment.[71] It had entered into the cogitations of Senators in 1870 when the nomination of Justice Bradley was pending. Cameron of Pennsylvania had a personal interest in the passage of the bill, and sought unsuccessfully to extract a statement that Bradley "did not think the Constitution prohibited Congress from chartering a railroad"; and Chandler of Michigan, sponsoring the bill, also desired "written evidence."[72]

Now on February 6, 1871, Chandler called up his S.526, hoping for passage that afternoon.[73] "We ought not to miss this opportunity," Sumner agreed; the proposal had been before Congress "as many as eight years." "The simple question now," said Sherman, a supporter, was the authority of Congress under the Commerce Clause. Morton of Indiana warned against "the exercise of a dangerous power . . . ."

Judges in districts bordering the Great Lakes and navigable tributaries were understood to agree with that opinion. Moreover, the Government had for more than ten years acquiesced in Judge Wilkins' ruling. For the sake of uniformity, Judge Withey dismissed the libel, leaving it to the Government to appeal if it saw fit.

[71] Supra, p. 1153n.
[72] Supra, pp. 724–25, 736–37.
[73] The account that follows summarizes proceedings on February 6 and 7. Cong. Globe, 41–3, 988–91, 1015–20.

Stewart of Nevada said that "at all times a large majority . . . believed we had the power; but the bill has been talked down . . . . Let us pass this bill, and then all the monopolies . . . will fight it. They will carry it to the Supreme Court of the United States, and the question will have to be settled there before they are satisfied. . . ." The Senators from Maryland now voiced the opposition. Howe of Wisconsin, a supporter, did not hope to live long enough "to see the Congress . . . act upon this measure." (He was not yet fifty-five.) And in a moment the bill was again laid on the table, by vote of 25 to 21.

On March 3, 1871, the 41st Congress came to an end.

THE CLINTON BRIDGE

AT THE TIME of the decision of *The Daniel Ball*,[74] Oliver Wendell Holmes, Jr., was preparing the twelfth edition of Kent's *Commentaries*. He appended a note to mark the significance of that case: "a pretty liberal view is taken by the Supreme Court of what constitutes commerce between the several states, at least when it consists of transportation on the navigable waters of the United States."[75] Furthermore, he noted, a similarly expansive view of the authority of Congress over transportation by land had recently been expressed in *The Clinton Bridge*,[76] where Justice Miller had been speaking from the bench of the Circuit Court for Iowa at its October term, 1867. In sustaining an Act of Congress declaring a bridge over the Mississippi to be a lawful structure and recognizing it as a post route, Justice Miller observed that the railroad had now become as important as the steamboat, that rails were being connected to form "the great highways of our Union," and that federal control was needed, as in 1787, to protect commerce among the States from local shackles.

> For myself, I must say that I have no doubt of the right of Congress to prescribe all needful and proper regulations for the conduct of this immense traffic, over any railroad which has voluntarily become part of any of those lines of inter-state communication, or to authorize the creation of such roads, when the purposes of inter-state transportation of persons and property justify or require it.

The bridge at Clinton, Justice Miller continued, "constitutes a part of an unbroken iron track from the Atlantic seaboard to the Missouri

---

[74] 10 Wall. 557, decided Jan. 23, 1871.
[75] Kent, *Commentaries on American Law*, 4 vols. (Boston: Little, Brown and Co., 1873), I: *439, n.1.
[76] Fed. Case No. 2900.

river . . . . Within two or three years, it is confidently believed, this track will be without break from the Atlantic to the Pacific ocean, and will carry the commerce of continents. . . ." That was quite accurate. The bridge at Clinton, built in 1865, was the means whereby the Chicago & North Western reached Council Bluffs in January 1867, where it made contact with the Union Pacific, which in May 1869 made its junction with the Central Pacific of California.[77]

The Clinton Bridge was the short title of the suit of *Gray v. Chicago, Iowa and Nebraska Railroad Co.*, a bill in equity brought in March 1861, culminating in a decision by the Supreme Court on December 19, 1870, wherein the Circuit Court's judgment for the defendants was affirmed.[78] Captain Richard C. Gray of Pittsburgh, Pennsylvania, had a large interest in transportation by steamboat on the Mississippi. For his suit to abate the bridge as an obstruction to navigation he engaged Judge James Grant[79] of Davenport. Associated with him was Timothy D. Lincoln of Cincinnati, who had recently handled the litigation against the Rock Island bridge, forty miles to the south.[80] Defending the bridge, besides local counsel, was Timothy O. Howe, Senator from Wisconsin. Defendants' answer was filed in November 1864; thereafter a voluminous body of evidence was taken.

Meanwhile the defendants had gone ahead and built the bridge.[81] Then they sought a Congressional declaration that it was a lawful structure. A bill to authorize a bridge from Quincy, Illinois, to Missouri had been introduced by Senator Trumbull in the First Session of the 39th Congress, on March 27, 1866.[82] In the course of its passage through the two Houses this was amended until it became an omnibus bill authorizing eight bridges at and above St. Louis, and one across the Missouri. This was the Act of July 25, 1866.[83]

But the friends of the Clinton bridge failed to gain inclusion in that statute. Representative John B. Alley[84] of Massachusetts, who as

---

[77] See p. 951.
[78] 10 Wall. 454. The defendant was absorbed into the Chicago & North Western.
[79] He figured largely in chapter 17, Municipal Bonds in Iowa.
[80] See pp. 13, 844.
[81] Gray v. Chicago, I. & N. R.R., Fed. Case No. 5713, C.C.D. Ia., Oct. term, 1864, illustrates the unruly conduct of the parties to this contest. Plaintiff obtained from the District Judge, while the Circuit Court was in vacation, an injunction against proceeding with the bridge. Under the statute, this expired at the commencement of the next term of the Circuit

Court, not being continued by that court. For work done thereafter, plaintiff, without notice to the defendants, procured from the District Judge an order for their arrest. The Circuit Court, held by Justice Miller, ruled that there was no ground for commitment, there having been no injunction in existence at the time of the alleged violations.
[82] Cong. Globe, 39–1, 1665.
[83] 14 Stat. 244. A succinct history of Congressional legislation on bridging is given in Newport & Cincinnati Bridge Co. v. United States, 105 U.S. 470 (1882).
[84] See p. 825.

chairman of the Committee on the Post Office and Post Roads had charge of the bill in the House, made extraordinary exertions to carry an amendment in favor of the Clinton bridge.[85] One objection was that whereas the bill called for construction with spans of not less than 160 feet, those of the existing structure at Clinton were only 120 feet in length. Representative John Hogan[86] of St. Louis, protector of his city's interest in river traffic in opposition to Chicago's interest in railroads to the West, charged that the applicants had "their agents . . . stockholders . . . feed attorneys here to vote upon this measure and rob the people of the West of the great, God-given right to navigate freely the great Mississippi river." Representative Elihu B. Washburne of Galena, Illinois—a lead mining town fifty miles north of Clinton, which had a major concern for traffic by water—called Alley's amendment "one of the most impudent and one of the most outrageous measures that this House was ever called upon to sanction . . . ." And Representative James K. Moorhead of Pennsylvania produced a letter from his constituent, Captain Gray, warning that the Clinton bridge was a menace to steamboats with barges, and that "a few such bridges will effectually stop cheap transportation." The outcome was that Alley's amendment received only 54 yeas to 66 nays.[87]

At the Second Session of the 39th Congress it was a different story. On January 10, 1867, Representative Alley reported from his committee a bill to declare the Clinton bridge a lawful structure and a post route.[88] In spite of Washburne's outcry against "gag rule" and the Chicago & North Western's "stupendous and remorseless monopoly," and reference to the "case now pending in the United States court in Iowa for damage," the bill was carried at that sitting of the House by vote of 101 to 43.[89]

In the Senate, Kirkwood of Iowa called up the bill on February 21.[90] Senator Howe said that inasmuch as "Congress reserves to itself the power so to alter or amend this act as to prevent any material obstruction of that river hereafter, it will always have the control, being the judge of what is a material obstruction . . . ." The promoters, he said, had invested $480,000; the bridge had stood there two years and the committees of the two Houses reported that it was not a material obstruction.[91] Notwithstanding remonstrance by Senator Henderson, the bill was then passed by 30 yeas against nays from Henderson and his colleague B. Gratz Brown, and Buckalew of Pennsylvania.[92]

This became the Act of February 27, 1867,[93] the subject of

---

[85] Cong. Globe, 39–1, 3811–18. July 14.

[86] See p. 152.

[87] Cong. Globe, 39–1, 3817.

[88] Cong. Globe, 39–2, 391.

[89] Ibid., 398.

[90] Ibid., 1669.

[91] Ibid., 1762, 1763.

[92] Ibid., 1765.

[93] 14 Stat. 412.

Justice Miller's remarks in *The Clinton Bridge* at the October term of the Circuit Court.

Howe, for the defendants, moved that the suit be dismissed for want of jurisdiction: the statute had taken away the court's power to proceed. Not so, replied Grant and Lincoln: Congress had not intended to make its law apply to the pending litigation; and if it were otherwise, the statute would be unconstitutional as an invasion of the judicial power. Whereupon the court held that the statute indeed did govern, by furnishing a rule of law by which the case must be decided; but it did not deprive the court of jurisdiction. The situation was within the *Wheeling Bridge Case*, where Pennsylvania had brought an original suit for relief from an obstruction; and after the Court had rendered a decree for the complainant, Congress in 1852 enacted that the existing structure was lawful: thereupon the Court held it to be competent for Congress in the exercise of its power over commerce to declare the rule by which the matter was to be governed.[94] Upon the authority of that case, Justice Miller overruled Howe's motion. Then on the merits the bill was dismissed.

An appeal was argued by T. D. Lincoln on December 7, 1870. His contentions were that the statute was prospective, not affecting the pending suit; that otherwise it would be an unconstitutional interference with the judiciary; that a bridge was not, in any fair sense, an instrument of commerce. The Court next day "declined hearing further argument in this cause";[95] this was one of the infrequent occasions where an appeal is seen to be so plainly unmeritorious that there is no need to hear the appellee. On Monday, December 19, Justice Nelson delivered the opinion, recounting and following the *Wheeling Bridge Case*.[96]

Here, as in the recent appeal of *McCardle*,[97] the Court was acknowledging the authority of Congress on a point where the exercise of legislative power came into close proximity with the exercise of judicial power.

SALESMEN FROM OUT-OF-STATE

Since 1852 it had been the law of Maryland that no person, not a permanent resident of the State, should sell, offer or expose for sale, within the city of Baltimore, products of other States, by sample or

---

[94] In Pennsylvania v. Wheeling and Belmont Bridge Co., the Court's decree in 1852, 13 How. 518, was held superseded by the Act of Congress in the decision of 1856, 18 How. 421.

[95] Minutes, Dec. 8, 1870.

[96] *The Clinton Bridge*, 10 Wall. 454.

[97] 7 Wall. 506, considered in ch. 10.

catalogue, without a license. This had gone unchallenged until in December 1868 Elias Ward offered to sell by sample six leather blinders for horse harness, without a license, for which the annual fee was $300.[98] For this he was convicted and fined $400 in the Criminal Court for Baltimore, notwithstanding his claim of right under the Commerce Clause and Article IV's clause on the Privileges and Immunities of citizens out-of-State. The Court of Appeals affirmed,[99] and on writ of error *Ward v. Maryland* was filed in the Supreme Court on March 17, 1870.

Ward was a resident of Newark, New Jersey, where the manufacture of leather products, particularly for the Southern trade, was a leading industry. Security for costs was executed before Anthony Q. Keasbey, the United States District Attorney for New Jersey.[100] William M. Evarts was retained to argue the defense. Evidently this was no casual case of a hapless itinerant. The Civil War had caused men to think more spaciously about the meaning of their Federal Union. That had been stimulated by the accent in *Crandall v. Nevada*, decided on March 16, 1868: "The people of these United States constitute one nation."[101]

A motion by Evarts to advance the case for hearing on April 4, 1871, was denied.[102]

In the order of call, argument was heard on the following November 21. Evarts' first point rested on the Commerce Clause. He cited *Cooley v. Board of Wardens*,[103] where in 1852 Justice Curtis for the Court had distinguished between subjects "imperatively demanding a single uniform rule," and other subjects that might conveniently be left to local regulation until Congress saw fit to occupy the field. In matters "in their nature national," where yet Congress had remained silent, State regulations would be disallowed. Evarts said that "The recent cases in this Court seem to assume that if the subject of State taxation and regulation, presented therein, had been of *commerce*, the legislation complained of would have been beyond the authority of the State"[104]—citing *Paul v. Virginia*[105] and *Ducat v. Chicago*.[106]

Further, the statute was "flatly repugnant" to Article IV, Section 2: commercial dealing that was lawful for Marylanders was made

---

[98] Ward v. Maryland, 12 Wall. 418. Argued on Nov. 21, and decided Dec. 11, 1871.
[99] 31 Md. 279.
[100] Transcript of Record, 11–12.
[101] 6 Wall. 35. Supra, p. 1306.
[102] Ward v. Maryland, 12 Wall. 163, on Mar. 6, 1871. Clifford, J.,

observed that the State had not sought an early hearing; and the defendant was not in jail.
[103] 12 How. 299.
[104] Brief of Plaintiff in Error, 4.
[105] Supra, n. 54.
[106] Supra, n. 61.

"unlawful for citizens of other States, unless upon onerous conditions...."

The Attorney General of Maryland replied that the enactment concerned the "completely internal commerce of the State," something not within the grant of power to Congress.[107]

Justice Clifford, for the Court, held the law invalid on the ground that Ward was privileged under Article IV, Section 2, to sell in Baltimore any goods that permanent residents there might sell, "without being subjected to any higher tax or excise than that exacted by law of such permanent residents."

Justice Bradley concurred, but went further: the tax also violated the Commerce Clause,

> and it would be so, although it imposed upon residents the same burden for selling goods by sample as it imposed on non-residents. Such a law would effectually prevent the manufacturers of the manufacturing States from selling their goods in other States unless they established commercial houses therein, or sold to resident merchants who chose to send them orders. . . .

He wanted to make it clear that, insofar as the Court's opinion might imply otherwise, he disagreed.

Four years later, in *Welton v. Missouri*[108]—a case where only the Commerce Clause was invoked—the Court held invalid a tax upon peddlers dealing in goods not produced within the State. The statute made no distinction as to the citizenship of the peddler; actually, as the Transcript of Record shows, Welton was a resident of Missouri.

Ward v. Maryland was constantly cited as though it had been based upon the Commerce Clause.

TAXES ON CARRIERS

REACHING FROM LAKE Erie to Delaware Bay, Pennsylvania occupied a commanding position in its exactions upon railroads within its borders. Leading decisions on three Pennsylvania taxes display the Court's initial response to problems with which it would be struggling for decades to come. In the *Case of the State Freight Tax*[109] the

---

[107] Statement, Points and Authorities of the Defendant in Error, 7.

[108] 91 U.S. 275, decided Jan. 17, 1876. Followed in Morrill v. Wisconsin, 154 U.S. 626, 23 L. Ed. 1009 (1877), on a similar statute.

[109] 15 Wall. 232.

carrier had been commanded to pay two, three, or five cents, according to the category of the goods, on every ton of freight; there was no apportionment by mileage. As applied to freight carried across, or into, or out of Pennsylvania, did this offend the Commerce Clause?

In *State Tax on Railway Gross Receipts*,[110] another statute demanded three-fourths of one percent of the corporation's gross receipts. Consistently with the Commerce Clause, could this be applied to gross receipts from carriage across, into, or out of the State?

The legislature required a domestic corporation doing business within Pennsylvania to retain five percent of the interest due to holders of its bonds and pay over to the Treasury. In *State Tax on Foreign-held Bonds*[111] the question was whether this could be enforced as to bonds held by nonresidents.

These cases made a large demand upon the thinking of the Court when it was in the middle of its December term, 1872. In each the two-hour rule was waived.[112] *Freight Tax* and *Gross Receipts* were argued together on February 5 and 6, and decided on March 3, 1873; *Foreign-held Bonds* was heard on February 10, 11 and 12; the decision was announced on March 10.

Justice Strong for the Court held the *Freight Tax* invalid: it was a tax on transportation, an exaction for allowing goods to pass from State to State; it was not saved by the consideration that the same charge was laid upon internal commerce.

Swayne and Davis, JJ., dissented: the tax was imposed on the business, and tonnage was simply the measure of its extent; there was no discrimination against freight that moved between States.

Justice Strong also spoke for the Court in upholding the *Gross Receipts Tax*. This was viewed as a tax on the corporation, measured by the amount of its business; it came out of the fruits after they had become mingled in the general property of the carrier. Or it might be justified as a tax upon the franchise.

Justice Miller dissented in an opinion in which Field and Hunt concurred. It was obvious that a tax on gross receipts must come directly out of the freight transported.

> I lay down the broad proposition that by no device or evasion, by no form of statutory words, can a State compel citizens of other States to pay to it a tax, contribution, or toll, for the privilege of having their goods transported through that State by the ordinary channels of commerce. . . .

---

[110] 15 Wall. 284.   [111] 15 Wall. 300.   [112] See p. 62.

In 1887 Justice Bradley for a unanimous Court reviewed the attempted distinction between a tax on tonnage of freight and a tax on gross receipts from freight, and pronounced it "not tenable."[113]

In *State Tax on Foreign-held Bonds*, the Cleveland, Painesville & Ashtabula Railroad Company denied the right of the State to tax the interest of nonresident holders of the company's bonds. The Court agreed. The subjects of taxation, said Justice Field, could only be persons, property, or business. A debt owed to a nonresident had its situs where he resided, and could not be thought of as property in Pennsylvania. It was true that the bonds were secured by a mortgage on the road, which lay partly in that State. But a mortgage there was only a security for payment, and could not be made the basis for this exaction. To enforce it would be to impair the obligation of the contract between the railroad and its creditor.

Justice Davis filed a short dissent, in which Clifford, Miller, and Hunt, JJ., joined. A Pennsylvania statute of 1844 had declared that "all mortgages [and] money owed by solvent debtors" were among the subjects of taxation. That was in force when the bonds in this case were issued, and the State court had held that it authorized the imposition of the tax in controversy.

Justice Field had covered a large subject with his usual air of certitude. In years to come his opinion was often cited, being followed, distinguished, questioned, and explained. In 1898 the proposition that the interest of a nonresident mortgagee could not be taxed was overruled.[114]

Osborne v. Mobile[115] challenged an ordinance that required every express company and railroad company doing business within the city to pay for an annual license: $500 if its business extended outside of Alabama, $100 if through the State, and $50 if confined to the city. Osborne was the local agent of the Southern Express Company, a Georgia corporation whose business was within and beyond Alabama. The State court sustained the exaction as an occupation tax; it did not regulate commerce: "The company can conduct its business as it pleases . . . ."[116]

The Express Company engaged Benjamin R. Curtis and Clarence A. Seward to present their case to the Supreme Court; Philip Phillips appeared for the city. Argument was heard on January 24 and 27, 1873; the decision was not rendered until April 28.

Chase, C.J., for a unanimous Court sustained the tax. It was, he

---

[113] Philadelphia & S. Mail S.S. Co. v. Pennsylvania, 122 U.S. 326, 342.
[114] Savings & Loan Soc. v. Multnomah County, 169 U.S. 421.

[115] 16 Wall. 479.
[116] Osborne v. Mobile, 44 Ala. 493 (1870).

said, "as important to leave the rightful powers of the State . . . unimpaired as to maintain the powers of the Federal Government in their integrity." It was difficult to draw the line, but this case came "directly within the rules laid down" in the *Gross Receipts* case. The tax here was no more a tax on interstate commerce than would be a tax on drayage where a licensed drayman might sometimes haul goods for transport beyond the limits of the State. (This is an example of the misleading mode of reasoning by saying that the case to be decided is like some other situation, and then resting judgment on the easier analogue.)

Fifteen years later, *Leloup v. Mobile*[117] presented a municipal license tax of $225 per year on telegraph companies; the State court had sustained it on the authority of *Osborne*. But, said Justice Bradley for a unanimous Court, "In view of the course of decisions which have been made since that time," certainly such a tax must be regarded as repugnant to the Commerce Clause.

Thomas Reed Powell's conclusion about the work of the Justices at the time of *Railway Gross Receipts* and *Osborne* was that "They seemed to be feeling their way in the dark."[118] Did wisdom lie in Justice Strong's formal method of asking whether the *subject* named in the tax law was within the field reserved to the State?[119] Or was Miller on the right path when he said that the distinction between a tax on freight and a tax on the gross receipts from freight was nothing but a matter of words, and that the Court should be looking, not to the name but to the practical effect, and to the underlying *purpose* of the Constitution?[120]

As we leave the Justices here in the spring of 1873 with an appreciation of the difficulties of their task in applying the Commerce

---

[117] 127 U.S. 640 (1888).

[118] "Indirect Encroachment on Federal Authority by the Taxing Powers of the States," a series of eight parts in 31 and 32 *Harv. L. Rev.* (1918–19), in Part V, 32:234 at 244. He was, as Justice Frankfurter wrote in 1956, unmatched as "critic of the Court's work during the last half century." *Harv L. Rev.*, 69:797, 799.

[119] Cf. Marshall, C.J., in McCulloch v. Maryland, 4 Wheat. 316, 429–30 (1819): "If we measure the power of taxation residing in a State, by the extent of sovereignty which the people of a single State possess, and can confer on its government, we have an intelligible standard, applicable to every case to which the power may

be applied. . . . We are not driven to the perplexing inquiry, so unfit for the judicial department, what degree of taxation is the legitimate use, and what degree may amount to the abuse of power. . . ."

[120] Cf. Holmes, J., in Galveston, H. & S.A. Ry. v. Texas, 210 U.S. 217, 225, 227 (1908): "Regulation and commerce among the States are practical rather than technical conceptions, and, naturally, their limits must be fixed by practical lines. . . . Neither the state courts nor the legislatures, by giving the tax a particular name or by the use of some form of words, can take away our duty to consider its nature and effect. . . ."

Clause of 1787 to expanding railroads and awakening business, perhaps we may take a more understanding view of their puzzlement over the *Slaughter House Cases*,[121] where a new Amendment had been invoked to meet a situation that had not been remotely within the contemplation of the framers of 1866.[122]

THE LIQUOR BUSINESS

THE "MAINE LAW"—an energetic statute forbidding the manufacture and sale of liquor, carried through the legislature in 1851 by Neal Dow, mayor of Portland[123]—became a cry of battle in many States. Interests hostile to temperance legislation were eager to gain some protection from the Court. *McGuire v. Massachusetts*[124] in 1866 denied a liquor dealer's claim that his federal "license" under the Revenue Act was a good defense to the State's prosecution for violation of its prohibitory law. At the next term in the *License Tax*

---

[121] 16 Wall. 36, decided Apr. 14, 1873.

[122] See pp. 1349–63.

[123] As mayor, Dow ordered certain liquor for the City Agency, which was stored in the city hall. In 1855 a warrant was sworn out for his arrest for violating the statute. Nathan Clifford prosecuted, William Pitt Fessenden defended. The complaint was dismissed on the ground that the city had authorized the purchase. This episode was the occasion of an anti-prohibition riot. See article on Dow in D.A.B.; Philip G. Clifford, *Nathan Clifford, Democrat (1803–1881)* (New York and London: G. P. Putnam's Sons, 1922), 262.

[124] 3 Wall. 387 (1866).

At December term 1864, counsel for the plaintiff in error asked that the case be advanced. On January 3, 1865, this was denied, because it did not seem a matter of sufficient importance to be given priority over prior cases on the docket.

At the following term, on Friday, February 9, 1866, the Attorney General of Massachusetts and Attorney General Speed asked that the case be advanced, because of the volume of litigation arising on the question involved. Caleb Cushing for the plaintiff in error opposed. The Court took

time to consider.

On Tuesday the thirteenth, when the Court next sat, it set Monday the nineteenth for the argument.

Then on Friday the sixteenth, Cushing asked to discontinue the writ of error: he professed that he did not have time for proper preparation, and said that one of his associates was ill. He asked also to withdraw the appearance of all counsel.

On Monday the nineteenth the Court denied the motion for leave to discontinue. Counsel might withdraw: but the Court warned that the defendant in error could then ask for an affirmance. The Chief Justice made what sounds like a wry remark, that the Court believed that Cushing "has underrated his power and overrated his need of preparation . . . ." 3 Wall. 382, and Minutes of the Court.

Cushing elected to proceed, and the Court fixed Monday the twenty-sixth. Actually the hearing came on the twenty-seventh and twenty-eighth.

A month later, on March 26 Justice Nelson delivered a terse opinion affirming the judgment of the State court.

Cushing's performance in this matter gives the appearance of trifling with the Court.

Cases[125] the Court sustained federal indictments for failure to pay the excise, against Evarts' argument that there was repugnancy between the commands of the two sovereigns, and that "there can be no doubt of the supremacy of the State legislation." In *Pervear v. Massachusetts*[126] the Court said No to the theory that when the State fined and committed to the house of correction one who, having paid the federal excise, made prohibited sales of liquor, it imposed an excessive, cruel and unusual punishment in violation of the Constitution: the Eighth Amendment did not apply to the States, and moreover the sentence could not be so characterized.

Downham v. Alexandria Council[127] challenged an ordinance imposing a license tax upon dealers in beer by cask, not manufactured within the city: counsel argued that this violated both the Commerce Clause and the Privileges and Immunities Clause of Article IV. But, said the Court, for aught that appeared in the record, Downham's beer might have been manufactured elsewhere in Virginia: only "a possible but not an actual question" had been shown. That did not meet the requirement of Section 25 of the Judiciary Act, and accordingly the writ of error must be dismissed for want of jurisdiction.

Bartemeyer v. Iowa[128] has been mentioned as having ineffectively presented an early invocation of the Fourteenth Amendment in answer to a prosecution under a prohibition law.[129] In 1851 the legislature passed a Prohibitory Liquor Law which, as amended, was incorporated in the Revised Laws of 1860. (This was only a revision, not new legislation.) The statute forbade the selling and the keeping for sale of liquor. On March 8, 1870, at Davenport, Bartemeyer was charged with making such a sale. In the circuit court he admitted the sale of one glass of whisky, but pleaded that this was no crime because he was the owner of that liquor "prior to the day on which the law was passed . . . ." On that admission the trial court found him guilty. The Supreme Court of Iowa affirmed, notwithstanding appellant's claim on the basis of the Fourteenth Amendment and on other grounds.

On August 24, 1871, a writ of error was allowed by William E. Miller, Associate Justice of the Iowa court. On November 22 the case was docketed. And then on February 1, 1872, counsel submitted on their printed arguments, expecting thereby to have an early decision. On February 26, however, the Justice Miller who sat on the Supreme Bench at Washington announced that the writ of error was dismissed because not properly before the Court: to satisfy Section 25 of the

---

[125] 5 Wall. 462 (1867). There were nine cases from four Districts: United States v. Nancy Swain, from Massachusetts, was an indictment for retailing liquor without a license; the others concerned lotteries.
[126] 5 Wall. 475 (1867).
[127] 10 Wall. 173 (1870).
[128] 14 Wall. 26 (1872).
[129] P. 1320.

Judiciary Act the writ should have been allowed by the Chief Justice of the Iowa court or by a Justice of the Supreme Court of the United States. Swayne, J., joined by Chase and Bradley, pronounced that view "unwarrantably narrow."[130]

Doubtless there was more to this than meets the eye. On January 11, 1872, the Court had heard argument in the *Slaughter House Cases*; on April 15 it continued that litigation for further argument.[131] The eight Justices then participating would eventually be evenly divided. Now *Bartemeyer's* case disclosed an attempt upon a very skimpy record to elicit a judgment that the Fourteenth Amendment condemned the Prohibitory Liquor Law. Evidently those Justices who felt appalled at the magnitude of what was already before the Court were anxious to prevent consideration being overwhelmed by this additional matter of prohibition.

Bartemeyer was not so easily stopped. Application was now made to Justice Miller, the writ of error was allowed by him on April 1, and on May 29, 1872, the record was filed again with the Supreme Court. And early in the next term, on December 17, counsel filed their agreement to submit on their printed briefs.[132]

The case from the dramshop was considered in connection with the *Slaughter House Cases*,[133] although it was left unsettled when they were decided on April 14, 1873. Not until March 4, 1874, did the Court rid itself of *Bartemeyer*, and then it once again refused to rule

---

[130] The pertinent words were that the writ of error must be allowed "by the chief justice, or judge or chancellor of the court rendering . . . the judgment or decree complained of, or by a justice of the Supreme Court of the United States . . . ." 1 Stat. 86. Justice Miller's opinion for the Court construed the words "judge or chancellor" to apply only to a State court held by a single judge or chancellor. He cited no previous ruling to that effect. The Chief Justice had recently spoken of "the proper judge of the State court." Gleason v. Florida *ex rel.* Attorney General, 9 Wall. 779, 783–84 (1870).

[131] See p. 1342.

[132] Counsel for Bartemeyer filed a thirty-six-page brief that relied upon the several clauses of the Fourteenth Amendment; the Civil Rights Act of 1866; the Commerce Clause; Article I, Sec. 9, cl. 6 (no preference to the ports of one State, etc.); and Article I, Sec. 10, cl. 2 (no duties on im-

ports). He rested heavily on Wynehamer v. The People, 13 N.Y. 378 (1856), where a prohibition statute had been held to violate the due process clause of the New York constitution because it applied to property already acquired. See ch. 17, note 401.

Henry O'Connor, Attorney General of Iowa, replied in a brief of a scant six pages. He found no issue that had not been "again and again decided," so that it would be "superfluous, if not impertinent," to argue at length the State's side of the question.

O'Connor was prepared to deliver an address on "Temperance." *Daily Davenport Democrat*, Mar. 7, 1870, p. 4, col. 2; Mar. 9, p. 1, col. 2. But his official performance as vindicator of the Prohibitory Law was meager indeed.

[133] As Justice Field observed in his concurring opinion in Bartemeyer v. Iowa, 18 Wall. 129, 141 (1874).

on the merits.[134] The factual foundation consisted of Bartemeyer's admission that he had sold one glass of whisky, to which was added his argumentative plea that he was guilty of no offense because he was the owner of that liquor prior to the day on which the law was passed. He seemed to refer to the Revised Laws of 1860. It was "absurd," said Justice Miller for the Court, to suppose that an ordinary retailer could have proved that he owned that certain glass of whisky prior to the original enactment of 1851, and without that there was no ground for counsel's large argument that his client's property had been taken without due process of law in violation of the Fourteenth Amendment.

> If it be said that this manner of looking at the case is narrow and technical, we answer that the record affords us on its face the strongest reason to believe that it has been prepared from the beginning, for the purpose of obtaining the opinion of this Court on important constitutional questions without the actual existence of the facts on which such questions can alone arise.

The Court would not "make any advances to meet them until we are required to do so by the duties of our position."

Inasmuch as counsel had argued that the Prohibitory Liquor Law was in "flagrant violation of the fundamental privileges and immunities of an American citizen," the Justices who had been in the minority in *Slaughter House* added statements to the effect that they had there spoken in defense of free pursuit of a lawful occupation—not of an unlawful one.

INTERGOVERNMENTAL IMMUNITIES

IN *Dobbins v. Commissioners of Erie County*[135] in 1842 the Court had held, in an opinion by Justice Wayne, that an officer of the United States was constitutionally exempt in respect of his salary from a State tax on the "profits arising" from "all offices and posts of profit." A State tax so applied would be an "interference with a constitutional means" adopted by the federal Government for exercising its powers.

The converse situation was presented in *Collector v. Day*,[136] decided in April 1871. Congress by its Revenue Acts of 1864, 1865, 1866, and 1867, had taxed the "income of every person residing in the United States . . . whether derived from any kind of property, rents, interest, dividends, or salaries, or from any profession, trade, employment or vocation . . . ." Day, a Probate Judge of Massachusetts, paid under protest the tax upon his salary, and then sued the Collector

---

[134] 18 Wall. 129.   [135] 16 Pet. 435.   [136] 11 Wall. 113.

to recover. The Circuit Court, held by Justice Clifford and District Judge Lowell, held for the plaintiff[137] and the Collector brought error. The case was docketed in December 1870 and at once, on motion of the Attorney General, was set down for argument.

The hearing came on February 3, 1871, before a Bench of eight, Nelson, J., presiding. John C. Ropes, Assistant Attorney of the United States for Massachusetts,[138] made the opening argument. He had presented the case below, and had written an acute brief to which Attorney General Akerman merely appended his signature. Opposing was Dwight Foster, the State's Attorney General during the war, and a Justice of the Supreme Judicial Court from 1866 until his resignation in 1869. He made effective use of a line of cases on the respective powers of the two sovereigns; *Dobbins*, he said, was "the precise converse" of the present case. The Attorney General closed the argument.

On April 3 Justice Nelson delivered what proved to be his last utterance for the Court.[139] "The supremacy of the General Government, . . . so much relied on in the argument of the counsel for the plaintiff in error, in respect of the question before us, cannot be maintained. The two governments are upon an equality . . . ." Judge Day stood on as firm ground as did the federal officer in the *Dobbins* case. It was true that in *Veazie Bank v. Fenno*[140] "a majority of the Court" had sustained a federal tax that annihilated the exercise of a power theretofore conceded to the States; but even in that case it had been said that the administration of justice by the State was not a proper subject of the taxing power of Congress. The judgment for Day was affirmed.

Justice Bradley dissented in a statement that struck a new note. "No man ceases to be a citizen of the United States by being an officer under the State Government. I cannot accede to the doctrine that the General Government is to be regarded as in any sense foreign or antagonistic to the State Governments, their officers or people . . . ." Taxation by a State was a very different thing: it must not be allowed to interfere with the powers of the Government in which all the other States and their citizens were no less interested. "Where are we to stop in enumerating the functions of the State Governments which will be interfered with by federal taxation?" If a State incorporated a railroad, would that be viewed as an agency whose bonds must be free from federal taxation?

---

[137] Day v. Buffinton, Fed. Case No. 3675.

[138] Already introduced as one of the two original editors of the *American Law Review*. P. 74.

[139] Supra, p. 753. This was at the time when a reargument of the legal tender question was pending, and truancy was high.

[140] 8 Wall. 533 (1869), where Nelson (joined by Davis) had dissented. Pp. 711–12.

The mills of the Court keep grinding. After the exemption from taxation allowed in *Dobbins v. Commissioners* and *Collector v. Day* had been carried to excessive lengths in the 1920's and '30's, the Court in 1939 repudiated their doctrine.[141] The force of Justice Bradley's dissent, said Frankfurter, J., concurring, had "gathered . . . strength with time."

TARBLE'S CASE

EDWARD TARBLE,[142] AGED seventeen, lived near Madison, Wisconsin. He came to town and on July 27, 1869, enlisted in the army. He gave his name as Frank Brown and swore that he was twenty-one years of age. Within half an hour after enlistment he disappeared, returning on August 9. In the meantime he had been reported as a deserter; now he was held to await proceedings.

On August 10 Abijah Tarble, the father, petitioned the court commissioner for Dane county for a writ of habeas corpus, alleging that the son was under age and had not had parental consent. The recruiting officer, respondent, made return, protesting that the State commissioner had no jurisdiction, and stating the authority on which Tarble was held. After hearing testimony and argument, on August 16 the commissioner ordered the prisoner discharged.

Counsel for the recruiting officer petitioned the State Supreme Court for a writ of certiorari. This was granted, and the record was sent up.

Abijah Tarble was represented by Philip L. and John C. Spooner;[143] the firm of William F. Vilas[144] had appeared for the respondent before the commissioner.

At the hearing before the Wisconsin court on January 11, 1870, the United States District Attorney, Gerry W. Hazelton,[145] moved for

---

[141] Graves v. New York *ex rel.* O'Keefe, 306 U.S. 466.

[142] The account that follows is based upon the Transcript of Record in Tarble's Case, 13 Wall. 397, decided on March 14, 1872; the transcript supplies details not recounted in Justice Field's statement of the case.

[143] The son and junior partner, (1843–1919), was a brevet major at the close of the Civil War, and a Republican Senator 1885–91, 1897–1907.

[144] (1840–1908), a lieutenant colonel at the close of the war; a Democrat, member of President Cleveland's

Cabinet from 1885 to 1891, and a Senator 1891–97.

A headnote of an opinion by Attorney General Bates of October 16, 1861, is as follows: "It is not a part of the official duties of a District Attorney to resist applications for the discharge of enlisted minors, under writs of *habeas corpus* issued out of State courts, but the Secretary of War has power to employ the District Attorney for that purpose, if he shall deem it proper." 10 Ops. Atty. Gen. 146.

[145] A Representative in Congress, 1871–75.

a dismissal; presently by leave he withdrew his motion and the cause was then argued. On April 2 the court affirmed the order of the commissioner, Dixon, C.J., dissenting.[146]

To say that Judge Byron Paine (1827–71) wrote the opinion for the court is to certify that it made an energetic defense of the authority of a State court to discharge from federal custody upon its own judgment that the detention was unlawful. That had been the ground on which he had distinguished himself as an advocate in the controversy culminating in *Ableman v. Booth*,[147] where habeas corpus and State rights were the means whereby he had battled to render the Fugitive Slave Act unenforceable in Wisconsin. That had called forth Taney's assertion of the duty of submission to the authority of the United States. The Chief Justice declared that

> after the return is made, and the State judge or court judicially apprised that the party is in custody under the authority of the United States, they can proceed no further. They then know that the prisoner is within the dominion and jurisdiction of another Government, and that neither the writ of habeas corpus, nor any other process issued under State authority, can pass over the line of division between the two sovereignties.

Paine's advocacy of the cause of Booth led to his elevation to the Wisconsin bench, where at this moment he was in the midst of other losing battles with the Supreme Court in Washington; that over municipal bonds has been recounted in detail.[148]

The writ of habeas corpus, wrote Judge Paine, was "the aegis of personal liberty." Full power to issue it was a part of the sovereignty of the States at the adoption of the Constitution, and that instrument did not abridge the power or exempt federal officers from its operation. Nevertheless, the Supreme Court had made its pronouncement in *Ableman v. Booth*. Some courts, like that of Iowa, had admitted the doctrine only where the detention was under the judgment of a federal court.[149] Others, like that of Michigan, had taken it to apply even where the detention was by the mere ministerial officers of the federal government under color of authority.[150] Judge Paine thought there was "no solid distinction" between the two situations; if the doctrine of *Ableman v. Booth* was true at all, it applied to both. He quoted words from Taney's opinion, as set out above: the only proper acceptation of that language, he said, was that if the party was in custody under *lawful* authority of

---

[146] 25 Wis. 390.
[147] 21 How. 506 (1858).
[148] Pp. 1024–31.

[149] *Ex parte* Anderson, 16 Iowa 595 (1864), per Dillon, C.J., in chambers.
[150] In the Matter of Jacob Spangler, 11 Mich. 298 (1863).

the United States, then indeed the State court should proceed no further. But to desist upon a mere *claim* of authority was "incommensurate with the high character and function of the writ itself, and with a due respect to the sovereign power of the State, to relieve against any imprisonment of its citizen within its borders which is without authority of law. . . ."

It appeared from the evidence that Tarble was under eighteen years of age. "His enlistment was therefore unauthorized by any act of Congress. . . ."

On writ of error allowed by Chief Justice Dixon, Tarble's case was docketed on July 19, 1870. When in order it was called on November 14, 1871, only Solicitor General Bristow stepped forward. "Whatever doubt or difficulty may have existed with reference to the question presented in this record would seem to have been removed by the unanimous opinion of this court" in *Ableman v. Booth*. If that opinion meant no more than the Wisconsin court conceded—that a State court must desist at the point where the *lawful* authority of the United States was shown—it was "wholly unnecessary," for in such a situation neither federal nor State court could discharge from custody.[151]

On March 4, 1872, Justice Field spoke for the Court in a powerful opinion.[152] It was a reasoned reaffirmation of *Ableman v. Booth* in all its force. If it were competent for any judicial officer of a State to release one held under the authority or claim of authority of the United States, the same might be done by every such officer, and the exercise would be limited only by the legislative power of the State. And while the Wisconsin court's opinion did indeed disclaim any right to interfere where a party was in custody under judicial sentence of a federal court that had jurisdiction in the premises, yet as had been shown in the *Booth* case, the pretension had been carried to the point of ordering the discharge of a prisoner convicted under an Act of Congress that the State judge deemed unconstitutional. Then in that case the Wisconsin court had "directed its clerk to refuse obedience to the writ of error issued by this [Supreme] court under the Act of Congress, to bring up the decision for review."

Justice Field recalled the experience of raising an army to suppress the late rebellion:

---

[151] Government brief, 6, 7.

[152] *Tarble's Case*, 13 Wall. 397.

Justice Bradley noted on the cover of his copy of the transcript: "Miller," and then crossed it out and wrote "Field." This either corrects an error or indicates a reassignment, and the latter seems far more likely. Certainly it was preferable when a Justice of Democratic affiliation would write so forthrightly that he, rather than a pronounced nationalist, speak for the Court in this case.

It is manifest that the powers of the National Government could not be exercised with energy and efficiency at all times, if its acts could be interfered with and controlled for any period by officers and tribunals of another sovereignty.

The opinion set out a guide for the orderly resolution of the issue where a State judge was called upon to grant habeas corpus to release from the custody of a federal officer.

Justice Field concluded: "This limitation upon the power of State tribunals and State officers furnishes no just ground to apprehend that the liberty of the citizen will thereby be endangered. The United States are as much interested in protecting the citizen from illegal restraint under their authority, as the several States are to protect him from the like restraint under their own authority, and are no more likely to tolerate any oppression. . . ."

Chief Justice Chase dissented, alone and briefly. He was back on the old camp ground in the war against the Fugitive Slave Act, a war that had long since ceased. To deny the power of State courts to adjudicate in habeas corpus proceedings the issue of the jurisdiction of a federal court or the authority of a federal officer, he said, was "to deny the right to protect the citizen . . . against arbitrary imprisonment in a large class of cases . . . ." He conceded that a State court might err: but "if it does, the error may be corrected here. The mode has been prescribed and should be followed."

Those words meant that the Government would have to litigate its claim to custody up to the highest State court wherein the matter could be heard, and if rebuffed there it might bring error to the Supreme Court under Section 25 of the Judiciary Act.[153] That would indeed have threatened its "energy and efficiency."

Among the State courts that treated *Ableman v. Booth* as precluding their issue of habeas corpus only where the detention was under judgment of a federal court was the Supreme Judicial Court of Massachusetts. In *McConologue's Case* in 1871 Justice Gray said that the practice of a State court issuing the writ where a minor was illegally enlisted was "too well settled" by judicial opinion and practice "to be now disavowed, unless in obedience to an express act of congress, or to a direct adjudication of the supreme court of the United States."[154]

After the *Tarble* decision, Chief Justice Chase wrote to Albert G. Browne, Reporter of the Massachusetts court, as follows:

---

[153] See chapter 2, footnote 51.
[154] 107 Mass. 154, 160. In support he cited, *inter alia*, the opinion of

Attorney General Stanbery in *Gormley's Case*, 12 Ops. Atty. Gen. 258, of October 4, 1867.

I thank you for sending me the proof-sheets in McConologue's case. The decision of the Supreme Court of Massachusetts was, in my judgment, unquestionably sound law.

I am sorry to read the last sentence of your note to the case, that "the practice in this commonwealth has since conformed to the decision in Tarble's case . . . ."

My health did not permit me to give my views in that case as fully as I should have otherwise . . . felt it my duty to do, nor to participate at all in the discussion in conference, of which, indeed, there was little or none before the opinion was written.[155]

The Chief Justice's failing health had prevented him from acting effectively. Discussion in conference—which is peculiarly a responsibility of the Chief Justice—had, in his view, been inadequate. These points are significant, but not surprising.

Further, he was "sorry" that the judiciary of Massachusetts were conforming to the ruling of the Supreme Court: that means that he would have welcomed insubordination by State judges in the matter of a ruling to which he personally did not agree.[156] But two years earlier he had been insisting with all his power that it was the duty of all the Justices to accept as final the invalidity of the Legal Tender Act as asserted by the majority in *Hepburn v. Griswold*.[157] As Justice Miller observed, Chase had an "imperious will" and "liked to have his own way."[158]

Preoccupation with a transient situation may distort a judge's analysis of a larger issue. When *Tarble's Case* arose the entire matter of State-federal relations was moving into a new setting. The Fourteenth Amendment had just been adopted: national citizenship was made primary; States were bound under federal sanction to accord a wide but as yet not precisely defined body of rights to the individual. By a statute of February 5, 1867, Congress had thrown open the habeas corpus jurisdiction of courts and Judges of the United States: they "shall have power to grant writs of habeas corpus in all cases where any person may be restrained of his or her liberty in violation of the constitution, or of any treaty or law of the United States . . . ."[159] Without being fully aware of the significance of what it was doing, Congress had here made a great enactment for securing liberty. While, in the special circumstances of the *McCardle* case it took back so

---

[155] Robert B. Warden, *An Account of the Private Life and Public Services of Salmon Portland Chase* (Cincinnati: Wilstach, Baldwin and Co., 1874), 799.

[156] Recall his own unwillingness to bow to the ruling in *Ex parte Garland*, with which he disagreed. Supra, p. 767.

[157] Chapter 14.

[158] Pp. 26–27. And see pp. 766–67, 1476–77.

[159] 14 Stat. 385. The immediate occasion has been explained. See pp. 448–49.

much of the statute as gave an appeal to the Supreme Court,[160] the basic grant remains a part of the law today.[161]

Habeas corpus, in Justice Holmes' words, "comes in from the outside, not in subordination to the proceedings, and although every form may have been preserved, opens the inquiry whether they have been more than an empty shell."[162] Whether the petitioner be in State or federal custody, the Judicial Code's chapter on Habeas Corpus affords an inquiry "from the outside" to see whether the substance of justice as protected by the Constitution was denied in the proceedings —such as whether the petitioner was convicted on a confession involuntarily extracted, whether he was denied the right to counsel, whether the jury was unfairly selected, whether the evidence against him was obtained by unlawful search and seizure, and whether he was not allowed adequate facilities to seek a review.[163]

Certainly the Chief Justice was mistaken in imagining that State habeas corpus was needed to relieve men from arbitrary arrest under pretension of federal authority. He was not sufficiently reflective to perceive that the civil rights then being secured by Amendments to the Constitution and by new laws of the United States might on occasion be systematically denied, even by State officers low and high, and that —if his view prevailed—those who were held to answer for such denials might resort to the local courts for release on habeas corpus, and that those local courts would be free to discharge on their own view that what had been done by federal authority to protect the citizen in his constitutional rights was invalid, even that federal civil rights legislation was unconstitutional.

DECISIONS HOLDING FEDERAL LEGISLATION INVALID

ON EIGHT OCCASIONS while Chase was Chief Justice the Court found that Congress had gone beyond its powers. Four of these have been explained. In *Gordon v. United States*[164] one section of the Court of Claims statute authorized appeal to the Supreme Court while another

---

[160] Act of March 27, 1868, 15 Stat. 44. See pp. 464–69. Resort to the Supreme Court by appeal was restored by an Act of March 3, 1885, 23 Stat. 437.

[161] 28 U.S.C., Sec. 2241.

[162] Frank v. Mangum, 237 U.S. 309, 346 (1915). This was in a dissenting opinion in which Justice Hughes joined, where the Court did not make the writ available to a petitioner who had been convicted of murder in a State court amid surroundings such that neither the prisoner nor his counsel would have been safe had the jury failed to convict. But larger views came to rule the Court, widely opening the inquiry.

[163] Ch. 153 of Title 28, U.S. Code (1964). The refinement in method to which this has given rise is examined in "Federal Habeas Corpus," *Harv. L. Rev.*, 83:1038–1280 (1970).

[164] 2 Wall. 561 (1865). Pp. 52–54.

declared that no judgment under the statute would be paid until an appropriation had been made upon an estimate by the Secretary of the Treasury. The Court, two Justices dissenting, declined to exercise a jurisdiction so conditioned. Thereupon Congress repealed the latter section. It is still true that no money judgment against the United States by any court can be paid save as Congress has appropriated the money, but the appropriation is general and comprehensive.

Ex parte Garland[165] in 1867 held invalid the test oath required as a condition to practicing as an attorney in the federal courts. The decision was by five to four.

Passing over for the moment two very minor instances, we recall *Hepburn v. Griswold*[166] in 1870, holding the Legal Tender Acts unconstitutional as applied to preexisting debts. Fifteen months later that was overruled.

Passing two more, we have seen that in *United States v. Klein*[167] the Court held invalid a proviso of 1870 directing that no pardon or amnesty be considered by the judiciary in cases under the Abandoned and Captured Property Act. That holding had the support of the entire Court, although Justices Miller and Bradley were of opinion that, on a proper view of the law, one who did not have the status of a loyal citizen when seizure was made was not entitled to recover the proceeds.

That leaves four cases to be noticed. Most important of these was *United States v. Dewitt*[168] in 1870, which held one section of a statute unconstitutional as "a police regulation, relating . . . to the internal trade of the States"—a matter not within the competence of Congress.

In February 1867, when the Second Session of the 39th Congress neared its close, the Ways and Means Committee brought in H.R.1161 to revise the Revenue Law, in order to afford the country as much relief as seemed prudent.[169] One item was to transfer naptha, then taxed at ten cents per gallon, to the exempt list: the petroleum industry, then in a slump, had been further depressed by taxation.[170]

---

[165] 4 Wall. 333, discussed in ch. 5.
[166] 8 Wall. 603. Ch. 14.
[167] 13 Wall. 128 (1872). Pp. 843–46.
[168] 9 Wall. 41.
[169] Its effort led to the Revenue Act of March 2, 1867, 14 Stat. 471. This has been referred to in the account of the cotton tax, in chapter 16.
[170] The development of the petroleum industry, in the late 1850's, had ruined whaling as the basis for domestic lighting. But then many wells were suddenly brought into production; the expiration of a patent in Great Britain facilitated extraction from Scotch shales. Exports fell; wells of low yield were put out of business. On May 7, 1866, Garfield of the Ways and Means Committee asked that the rules be suspended to permit the passage of a joint resolution to exempt crude petroleum from internal taxation. Justin S. Morrill, chairman, explained

Representative Schenck agreed, but saw a need to introduce a penal provision forbidding the mixing for sale of naptha and illuminating oil, or the offering for sale for illuminating purposes of a petroleum product inflammable below a certain fire test. Illuminating oil, he explained, was then taxed at twenty cents per gallon; sometimes naptha, being cheap, was mixed with illuminating oil, and the public, unknowing, would purchase "a mixture almost as explosive as gunpowder." It would be useful to make naptha cheaper for industrial use; but "just in proportion as you make it cheap . . . you increase the temptation to mix it with illuminating oil and make a compound which is destroying lives and property. . . ." A moment's discussion led to inserting the word "knowingly."[171]

The end of the 39th Congress was at hand; Schenck's amendment went unquestioned in the Senate, and became Section 29 of the Revenue Act of March 2, 1867.[172]

In the Eastern District of Michigan, Henry C. Dewitt was indicted for offering for sale oil within the statutory description. To this there was a demurrer. The Judges certified a division of opinion: Did Congress have power to enact Section 29? The case was docketed on July 8, 1868. When it was called on November 25, 1869, Assistant Attorney General Walbridge A. Field[173] appeared for the Government. A brief for the defendant was filed by John A. Wills and others.

When in the meantime the Revenue Act of July 20, 1868, removed every tax on mineral oil and its products,[174] Section 29 could more easily be viewed to its disadvantage, stark naked, as no more than "a police measure . . . within the reserved powers of the several States."[175]

On February 21, 1870, Chief Justice Chase gave the Court's answer. Congress had acted ultra vires. The Commerce Clause implied "a virtual denial of any power to interfere with the internal trade and

---

the need for prompt action: "employés have become riotous, and are destroying large numbers of the wells. . . ." Instantly the rules were suspended and the measure passed. Next day Senator Cowan of Pennsylvania asked for prompt concurrence; he explained the local situation. The Senate passed the joint resolution at once, and it was signed into law on May 9, 1866. Cong. Globe, 39–1, 2433, 2446–47. 14 Stat. 355.

[171] Cong. Globe, 39–2, 1259–60. Feb. 14, 1867. At that point Schenck withdrew his amendment, in order to introduce it at a proper place in the

bill. It was adopted without debate on February 21, page 1436.

[172] 14 Stat. at 484.

[173] (1833–99). He had been Assistant United States Attorney for Massachusetts under Richard Henry Dana, Jr., and then was Assistant Attorney General under Hoar. He sat on the Supreme Judicial Court from 1881 until his death; at the close he was Chief Justice, in which office he was succeeded by O. W. Holmes.

[174] By its concluding section 109. 15 Stat. 167.

[175] Brief for Defendant in United States v. Dewitt.

business of the separate States," save as might be necessary and proper to exercise some other power. Section 29 was not a means toward exercising the power to lay and collect taxes: any such relation was "too remote." This was a police regulation, and could be applied only in the territories and the District of Columbia, where Congress had powers of general legislation.

The case had a sequel. In 1867 Dewitt had received a patent for what was called "Aurora oil." In *Patterson v. Kentucky*[176] in 1879, plaintiff in error had been indicted for selling such oil, which an inspector, pursuant to a State statute, had marked "unsafe for illuminating purposes." Defendant claimed that, as assignee of Dewitt, he had a federal right under the patent to sell the article anywhere in the United States. The Court answered that the patent right to vend must be exercised in subordination to the police regulations of the State.

In the century since the *Dewitt* decision Congress has gone far, by aptly drawn statutes invoking the commerce and taxing powers, to protect the health, safety and welfare of the national community.

TWO MINOR INSTANCES OF INVALIDITY

Reichart v. Felps,[177] in 1868, found that, fifty-six years earlier, Congress had committed a transgression. Virginia in 1784 had yielded to the United States her claim to the Northwest Territory on condition that the possession and title of those who had professed to be her citizens would be confirmed. In 1788 the Congress of the Confederation enacted that the Governor should make the appropriate determinations, and confirm in fee. The Governor issued a patent to Jarrot, under whom Felps claimed title. But then Congress, by an Act of February 20, 1812,[178] caused a board of revision to examine into the validity of claims to lands confirmed by the Governor; in accordance with the board's report, the confirmation to Jarrot was disallowed, and presently the land was sold to Reichart. He brought an action of ejectment in the Illinois courts; the highest court of that State upheld the title of Felps. Inasmuch as it thereby denied Reichart's claim of title under the United States, writ of error lay to the Supreme Court.[179]

Having established the Court's jurisdiction in two sentences, Justice Grier settled the merits in a page. Congress had no power to nullify titles confirmed by the authorized agents of the Government. He did

---

[176] 97 U.S. 501.
[177] 6 Wall. 160.
[178] 2 Stat. 677.
[179] This situation, where a decision for either claimant involved a denial

of the other's claim of a federal right, was noticed in the discussion of *Roosevelt v. Meyer*, 1 Wall. (1863), in the chapter of the Legal Tender Cases, at p. 697.

not cite the provision of the Constitution that had been violated: doubt-less this was the Due Process Clause of the Fifth Amendment—but perhaps respect for a vested title seemed so much a matter of first principle that no need to point to the Constitution was perceived.

In *The Alicia*[180] in 1869 a transitional provision in the Act of June 30, 1864,[181] to regulate prize proceedings would have resulted in the Court exercising original jurisdiction inconsistently with Article III, Section 2, clause 2.[182] Chase, C.J., said that Congress had acted "inadvertently," and explained wherein lay the objection.

It is useful to interject that the 38th Congress had passed this statute with no debate in either House. On behalf of the Judiciary Committee, Senator Foster said that the bill was approved by the Navy Department after being prepared "under the very close supervision of the judge of the district court and the attorney for the district of the State of Massachusetts, both of whom are very familiar with prize law."[183] Judge Peleg Sprague, on the District bench since 1841, and Richard Henry Dana, Jr., were indeed highly competent.

For breach of blockade *The Alicia* had been condemned by the District Court for Southern Florida in January 1865. Appeal was taken to the Circuit Court, in accord with the law as it then stood. The appeal had the effect of vacating the decree below; the Circuit Court acquired full jurisdiction and could proceed as freely as if the cause had originated there.[184] But then Congress, as noted above, passed the statute of 1864 on prize proceedings. Section 13 provided "That appeals from the district courts . . . in prize causes shall be directly to the Supreme Court . . . ." That was free from difficulty, and desirable in a category of such wide importance. Then came a provision concerning prize causes pending in a Circuit Court: on the application of all parties they would "be transferred by that court to the Supreme Court." But inasmuch as there was no subsisting decree in such a case, the effect would be to bring to the Court a matter of first instance. "We must decline, therefore," said the Chief Justice, even to docket and dismiss the case; "but this opinion may be *certified to* [the Circuit Court] for information."

---

[180] 7 Wall. 571.

[181] Sec. 13 of the statute, 13 Stat. 306, 311.

[182] "In all Cases affecting Ambassadors, other public Ministers and Consuls, and those in which a State shall be Party, the supreme Court shall have original jurisdiction. . . ." Otherwise its jurisdiction is appellate.

[183] Cong. Globe, 39–1, 3250–51, June 25, 1864.

[184] "There was no longer any valid or operative decree in the court below," said Nelson, J., in a prize appeal to the Circuit Court. The Sunbeam, Fed. Case No. 13,614, C.C.S.D. N.Y., May 1863.

In years to come *The Alicia* would be cited in situations where a lower court had certified, not specific questions of law, but the whole case pending before it.[185]

REMOVAL INTO A FEDERAL COURT, AND A DISREGARD OF THE SEVENTH AMENDMENT

The Justices v. Murray,[186] decided on March 14, 1870, resulted in this holding:

> that so much of the 5th section of the Act of Congress, March 3d, 1863,[187] entitled "An Act Relating to *Habeas Corpus*, and Regulating Proceedings in Certain Cases," as provides for the removal of a judgment in a state court, and in which the cause was tried by jury, to the Circuit Court of the United States for a retrial on the facts and law, is not in pursuance of the Constitution, and is void.

In attempting to allow a retrial the Congress had infringed the second clause of the Seventh Amendment:

> no fact tried by a jury shall be otherwise examined in any Court of the United States, than according to the rules of the common law.

The constitutionality of removal had been affirmed in *Mayor v. Cooper*[188] in 1868; in that instance, however, defendants had exercised their right prior to judgment. If the national government could not provide the means to remove to a federal court, Justice Swayne had there said, every federal officer, civil or military, "would be liable to harassing litigation in the State courts. However regular his conduct, neither the Constitution nor laws of the United States would avail him, if the views of those tribunals and the juries which sit in them, should be adverse. . . . Such a government would be one of pitiable weakness . . . ."

Robert Murray, United States Marshal for the Southern District of New York, and William Buckley, a deputy, had been sued by Albert J. Patrie in a New York court for illegal arrest and imprisonment over

---

[185] Baltimore and O. R.R. v. Interstate Commerce Commission, 215 U.S. 216, 224 (1909); Wheeler Lumber Bridge & Supply Co. v. United States, 281 U.S. 572, 577 (1930).
[186] 9 Wall. 274.

[187] 12 Stat. 755, 756. Sections 1 and 2 of this statute, on suspension of the writ of habeas corpus, figured largely in the discussion of *Ex parte Milligan* in chapter 5.
[188] 6 Wall. 247.

several days in late August and early September 1862.[189] Patrie was charged with "discouraging volunteer enlistments" and other "disloyal practices against the United States." The action for arresting him was tried "like an ordinary action for an assault and battery and false imprisonment, upon the general denial, without any special justification. . . ."[190] Patrie recovered a verdict for $9,000 and costs.

After the entry of judgment, defendants sought to remove the case to the federal court under the Act of 1863. They filed affidavits which alleged that what was done was under an order issued by authority of the President on August 8, 1862, directing all Marshals "to arrest and imprison any person or persons who might be engaged by act, speech or writing, in discouraging volunteer enlistments, or in any way giving aid and comfort to the enemy, or in any other disloyal practices against the United States." They further stated that before the arrest they were informed and believed that Patrie had done these things.

Patrie by affidavit denied that he had committed any act within the provisions of the President's order.

The Judge holding the Special Term at which this motion was argued held in a reasoned opinion that the 5th Section of the Act of 1863, in authorizing removal after judgment, was in violation of the Seventh Amendment. That judgment was affirmed by the full bench at the General Term, December 1864.[191]

Application was then made to Justice Nelson in the Circuit Court for the order to remove the case, as provided in the Act of 1863. That was granted; but the clerk of the State court refused to make a return.[192] On October 16, 1866, Justice Nelson allowed an alternative

---

[189] This was a moment when the strength of the Union was at a low ebb. On August 30 General Lee had reported to President Davis: "This army [of Northern Virginia] achieved to-day, on the plains of Manassas, a signal victory over the combined forces of Gens. McClellan and Pope. . . ." Lee invaded the North. On the Union side there was no general who commanded confidence. Rumors, fault-finding, gloom prevailed. On August 19 Greeley published in the *New York Tribune* his editorial, "The Prayer of Twenty Millions," with a list of complaints. Attorney General Bates recorded that Lincoln "seemed wrung by the bitterest anguish—said he felt almost ready to hang himself." *Collected Works of Abraham Lincoln,* ed. Roy P. Basler (New Brunswick, N.J.: Rutgers University Press, 1953), V, 404n.

The statement that an act was done under an order issued by authority of the President did not signify that the President had actually issued such an order. Resentment at the arbitrary arrests made at this period caused Secretary Stanton to call a halt on September 9.

[190] Quoting the opinion of Judge Miller at the Special Term of the Supreme Court of New York for the Third Judicial District in Patrie v. Murray and Buckley, 43 Barbour's N.Y. Supreme Court Reports 323, 327 (July 1864).

[191] 43 Barbour 337.

[192] Murray *et al.* v. Patrie, 5 Blatch-

writ of mandamus. To that a return was made, denying the jurisdiction of the federal court. Justice Nelson issued a peremptory mandamus on November 20, 1866.

From that judgment a writ of error was carried to the Supreme Court, where the record was filed on December 18.

On February 24, 1869, the case was called. Before the eight who then comprised the Court, Amasa J. Parker[193] made an oral argument for the Justices of the Third Judicial District; Attorney General Evarts submitted on a printed argument.

On March 4, 1869, President Grant succeeded Johnson; Evarts retired and on March 11 Hoar entered upon the duties of the Attorney General.

On March 15 the Court ordered a reargument on the first Tuesday of the next term (which would be December 7, the day next after the December term began. This did not mean that it was expected that the case would actually be heard so soon.) On December 17 the Court announced that it desired that argument be addressed to two questions. Was an act of Congress providing for removal after judgment by a State court consistent with the Constitution? Did the provision of the Seventh Amendment apply to facts heard by a jury in a State court?

At the time of that announcement the Court was experiencing remarkable events. *Hepburn v. Griswold* had been decided in conference; in consequence of what there transpired, Justice Grier on December 15 had resigned, effective on January 31. Hoar had been nominated to be a Justice on December 15, and had been rejected on February 3, 1870. Strong and Bradley had been nominated on February 7.[194]

The Justices v. Murray was heard on February 16 by a bench of seven, Parker arguing for the plaintiffs in error and Assistant Attorney General Walbridge A. Field for Murray.

On March 14 Justice Nelson spoke for the Court in reversing the judgment he had entered in the Circuit Court; the cause was remanded with directions to dismiss all the proceedings in the court below.[195]

---

ford 343 (July 1866); Fed. Case No. 9967. Murray and Buckley were represented by Samuel Blatchford and Clarence A. Seward; Patrie by Amasa J. Parker. The further course of events was traced with particularity by Blatchford when District Judge, in Fisk v. Union Pacific R.R., 6 Blatchford 362, at 370, 375, 382–86 (1869), Fed. Case No. 4827 at 152, 154, 157–58.

[193] He has been introduced as counsel for the petitioner in the *Egan* case before Justice Nelson in chambers in 1866. Ch. 4, n. 61.

[194] As recounted at pp. 677, 729–30.

[195] The Court entered a note:

The alternative and peremptory *mandamus* against the Supreme Court of New York was allowed by consent of the counsel for the defendants, with a view to present the question raised and decided in the case. The Circuit Court had refused to issue it against the court, and

Evidently the Court had not found this to be an easy case. Counsel for Murray had argued that the concluding clause of the Seventh Amendment should be construed in connection with the first: "In suits at common law, where the value in controversy shall exceed twenty dollars, the right of trial by jury shall be preserved . . . ." The meaning of the concluding clause was that "no fact tried by a jury in such manner as is prescribed by the first clause, shall be otherwise re-examined in any Court of the United States . . . ." A jury trial in a State court need not be in accord with the provisions in the Constitution. The Amendment "was not intended to prevent one full trial, both of law and facts, in any case arising under the laws of the United States in a court of the United States."

It was admitted, said Justice Nelson, that the Amendments constituting the Bill of Rights were limitations only upon the Federal Government and not upon the States: that had been acknowledged since *Barron v. Baltimore*[196] in 1833, and had been recognized as recently as *Twitchell v. Pennsylvania*[197] at the last term. But, admitting that, could a federal court be authorized to reexamine what had been found by a State jury? From the beginning, State courts had been allowed a large concurrent jurisdiction in matters embraced within "the judicial Power of the United States." It was believed that the purpose of the second clause of the Seventh Amendment had been to quiet apprehension lest Congress allow a reexamination of what a State court jury might have found in a case that lay within federal judicial cognizance.

Accordingly so much of Section 5 of the Act of 1863 as allowed removal after judgment must be held invalid.

---

only against the clerk. This is stated to prevent the case from being cited as an authority for the power, and without intending to express any opinion on this subject.

Recently in Hough v. Western Transportation Co., Fed. Case No. 6724 (1864), Drummond, J., in the Circuit Court for the Northern District of Illinois had ruled, as stated in the headnote, that

The United States circuit court has no power to issue a writ of mandamus to a state court for the removal of a cause. Congress undoubtedly could give them such power, but it has not done so.

The remedy is by appeal to the supreme court of the state, and thence by writ of error to the United States supreme court.

Chief Justice Fuller, *In re* Blake, 175 U.S. 114 (1899), observed that the writ of mandamus was not to "be used to perform the office of an appeal or writ of error," and that "it only lies, as a general rule, where there is no other adequate remedy." He recalled how the federal judiciary had in this respect been zealous to avoid jealousies and collisions between the States and the General Government—explaining The Justices v. Murray, and citing Hough v. Western Transportation Co.

[196] 7 Pet. 243, 250.

[197] 7 Wall. 321 (1869). Explained in ch. 21, n. 47.

DISTINCTION BETWEEN INVALIDITY AND INAPPLICABILITY

Collector v. Day[198] is sometimes reckoned among the decisions holding an Act of Congress invalid. The Revenue Acts laid a tax on "income of every person," yet the Court held that that could not be applied to Day's salary as a State judge. But the Court was not finding fault with the statute: it merely said that, by reason of a doctrine deduced from the Constitution, the statute could not be applied to salary paid for performing a function of the State.

United States v. Baltimore and Ohio Railroad Company,[199] decided in April 1873, is another instance not properly to be accounted as condemning a federal statute as unconstitutional. Section 122 of the Internal Revenue Act of June 31, 1864,[200] provided that

> any railroad . . . company indebted for any money for which bonds have been issued . . . upon which interest is stipulated . . . , or any such company that may have been declared any dividend . . . shall be subject to and pay a duty of five percentum on the amount of all such interest, or . . . dividends . . . , whenever and wherever the same shall be payable, and to whatsoever party or person the same may be payable, including non-residents, whether citizens or aliens; and said companies are hereby authorized to deduct and withhold from all payments on account of any interest, or . . . dividends . . . , the tax of five percentum; . . . [the company being thereby discharged as to that amount to the payee, and accountable to the assessor].

The City of Baltimore, as authorized by a State statute, had issued bonds and had advanced the proceeds to the Baltimore and Ohio, to enable it to expand and so bring more business to Baltimore; the company in return gave a mortgage and undertook to pay interest and principal to the city. The company contended that it should not make any withholding for the federal assessor, because the tax was actually imposed on the payee—in this case the city, which stood in the place of the State of Maryland; hence payments due were immune to federal taxation. Justice Hunt, for the majority, sustained that contention. Bradley, J., concurred in the result: without pronouncing whether Congress could tax the property of municipal corporations, he thought

---

[198] 11 Wall. 113 (1871). See supra, pp. 1419–21.

[199] 17 Wall. 322.

[200] 13 Stat. 284. An amendment, not essential here, was made by Section 9 of the Act of July 13, 1866, 14 Stat. 138.

that no such attempt had been made by the Revenue Acts. Clifford and Miller, JJ., dissented: they would not extend the doctrine of *Collector v. Day* so far as to exempt from federal taxation the property that a municipal corporation held for profit.[201]

The sections of the Revenue Act involved in these two cases remained enforceable, save in the particular situations to which the Court's rulings applied.[202]

Ordinarily Congress legislates in general terms. If one believes that for some reason an enactment cannot rightly be applied to him, and is unable to persuade the Executive to accept that view, resort may be had to the Judiciary for a determination. It is not to be expected that Congress recognize every such exception in advance. Justice Bradley, dissenting in *Collector v. Day*, said that there was no foretelling how far its doctrine might be carried; and the *Baltimore and Ohio* decision confirmed that remark.

REVIEW OF JUDGMENTS OF THE COURT OF CLAIMS

THE STATUTE OF March 3, 1863, authorized the Court of Claims to hear and determine "claims founded upon any law of Congress, or upon any regulation of an Executive Department, or upon any contract, express or implied, with the Government of the United

---

[201] In Barnes v. The Railroads, 17 Wall. 294, decided on March 3, 1873, five weeks prior to *Baltimore and Ohio*, the question was whether the tax imposed by Section 122 could be collected as to dividends from earnings in 1869, declared payable in 1870, having regard to the provisions of Section 13 of the Act of March 2, 1870, 13 Stat. 281, so amending Sections 116 and 119 that the tax to which they applied would be imposed on income only through the year ending on December 31, 1869, and would be levied on March 1 of each year including 1870. The problem involved a very close comparison of interrelated sections as amended. The majority, per Clifford, J., concluded that Section 122 imposed the tax on the railroads, although they were authorized to withhold its amount, and that it was rightly collected on earnings of 1869. Strong, J. (who

had decided contra in the Circuit Court, Fed. Case No. 11,087) dissented, and was joined by Chase, C.J., Davis and Field, JJ. See infra, p. 1452.

In Stockdale v. Atlantic Ins. Co., 20 Wall. 323, 329 (1874), Justice Miller remarked that "It is, perhaps, fairly inferable from the report" of *Barnes* and then of *Baltimore and Ohio* "that among those who composed the majority in the *Barnes* cases, there were some shades of difference in the precise grounds on which the validity of the taxes rested."

[202] In Stockdale v. Atlantic Ins. Co., cited just above, Justice Miller observed that in a situation where a dividend "is for any special reason exempt from such tax, as in the case of the City of Baltimore on her stock," the railroad company was not liable to make payment to the assessor.

States . . . .["203] When Congress removed what had been held to be a bar to the exercise of appellate review,[204] the Supreme Court entered upon the exercise of what Justice Miller characterized as "this unaccustomed jurisdiction, . . . embarrassed by the . . . absence of precedent and settled principles by which the liability of the Government may be determined." As spokesman for the Court in several early cases, Miller stressed two themes: adherence to the limits set by Congress, and insistence upon requirements for protecting the Supreme Court in the performance of its new duty. The words quoted come from *Gibbons v. United States*,[205] whose teaching was that unauthorized acts of officers, even though done for the benefit of the Government, were not to be construed as creating an implied *assumpsit* to make compensation. Congress had reserved such claims for its own determination.

In *The Floyd Acceptances*,[206] Russell & Co. had had contracts to furnish supplies to the Army in Utah; they were to be paid on final delivery (save for a partial payment in one contract), by the quartermaster at St. Louis or by his draft on the Assistant Treasurer of the United States at New York. Performance, however, involved a large outlay, and as an accommodation, bills of exchange drawn by the firm, payable at a New York bank, were accepted by Secretary of War John B. Floyd.[207] It was not expected that these drafts would be paid by the Government—only that they would be used to raise money, and would be taken up by Russell before or at maturity. The Quartermaster's Department had paid Russell according to the contracts, and it did not appear that anything remained due. But more than a million

---

[203] 12 Stat. 765.

[204] Supra, pp. 52–54, 1426–27. Gordon v. United States, 2 Wall. 561 (1865); 14 Stat. 9.

[205] 8 Wall. 269 (1869).

[206] 7 Wall. 666 (1869).

[207] (1806–63), sometime Governor of Virginia; served in Buchanan's Cabinet to the end of 1860, when he resigned on the ground that the President declined to order a withdrawal from Fort Sumter. The Secretary of the Interior, Jacob Thompson of Mississippi, resigned on January 8.

Presently it appeared that $870,000 of Floyd's acceptances had been substituted for Indian trust funds in the Department of the Interior; the President had called for Floyd's resignation on that account, before it was tendered on other grounds. J. S. Black, also of that Cabinet, said that

"There is no evidence against [Floyd] of anything worse than reckless imprudence; not a cent from any money proceeding from those premature acceptances could be traced to his hands; . . . he had no connection . . . with the abstraction of the Indian trust funds . . . ." *Essays and Speeches of Jeremiah S. Black, With a Biographical Sketch.*, Chauncey F. Black, compiler (New York: D. Appleton and Co., 1885), 13. On February 12, 1861, a Select Committee of the House of Representatives reported that the Floyd acceptances were "unauthorized by law and deceptive and fraudulent in character" and irreconcilable with "faithfulness to public trusts." H.R. Rep. No. 78, 36th Cong., 2d Sess., 19–20.

See D.A.B. on Floyd and Thompson.

dollars in Floyd's acceptances remained unpaid, and the holders sued in the Court of Claims. Failing there, they appealed to the Supreme Court.

Caleb Cushing and Jeremiah S. Black were among the counsel for the appellants. The latter—who as Attorney General in Buchanan's Cabinet had been Floyd's colleague and acquainted with his doings— now told the Court that

> this act was valid and binding, the act of the Secretary being the act of the Government; and it is no matter whether he exercised the power well or ill, properly or improperly, lawfully or unlawfully. We deny that the power was abused in this case; but if it was, then the Government which gave him the power must suffer for his misconduct.[208]

Attorney General Evarts led for the Government in reply. It was fundamental, said Justice Miller for the Court,

> that the protection which commercial usage throws around negotiable paper, cannot be used to establish the authority by which it was originally issued. . . .

Authority for the Secretary's acceptances must be found in written law—the Constitution or the statutes. Looking there, the conclusion was that "there can be no lawful occasion for any department of the government, or for any of its officers, or agents, to accept drafts drawn on them . . . ." What the Secretary had undertaken here was "a loan of the credit of the government volunteered by him, without consideration and without authority." Indeed a statute of 1823 had enacted that "no advance of public money shall be made in any case whatever . . . ."[209] The conclusion, after "a careful and earnest investigation," was that the claims must fail.

Nelson and Clifford, J.J., dissented. They held that by the Secretary's acceptance the Government became bound to apply all moneys due or that might become due on the contracts. They would have granted a new trial, throwing on the Government the onus to show what amount, if any, was due.

Presently when there was occasion to reiterate that even with commercial paper issued by delegated authority a holder bore the onus of establishing the delegation, citation was made[210] to *The Floyd Acceptances*, coupled with *Marsh v. Fulton County*[211] which had

---

[208] Oral argument, set out in his *Essays and Speeches*, 470–88, at 472.

[209] Act of Jan. 31, 1823, 3 Stat. 723, perpetuated as Sec. 3648 of the Revised Statutes.

[210] By Field, J., in Moffat v. United States, 112 U.S. 24, 32 (1884), and in Merchants Bank v. Bergen County, 115 U.S. 384, 391 (1885).

[211] 10 Wall. 676 (1871). See supra, pp. 1002–08.

been based upon it. *Marsh* was the almost unique instance where the Court had found a want of authority to issue railroad-aid bonds. Black, in arguing for the holders of the Floyd acceptances, had invoked the line of decisions wherein the Court, "with inflexible severity" had enforced municipal bonds, notwithstanding dubious antecedents:[212]

> You have seen the inside of many cases where the contest was upon the validity of bonds given by municipal corporations to railroad and other improvement companies; and I think you know that not one in twenty of those securities would stand the test of an inquisition into the special circumstances attending every particular case. The application to them of the doctrine laid down by the Court of Claims would make them nearly all as worthless as so much waste-paper.

Black referred to six then recent decisions—with which, let it be recalled, he had had a noteworthy connection.[213] They were all in accord with the reluctant opinion he had written as Chief Justice of the Pennsylvania court when in the *Sharpless* case three of the five judges sustained municipal bonding in aid of railroads.[214] And three of the six recent decisions had rejected arguments he himself had made at the bar of the Supreme Court. All of the decisions were in accord with Justice Nelson's consequential opinion in *Knox County v. Aspinwall*.[215]

Miller consistently lamented that in municipal bond cases, "while this principle of law [in *The Floyd Acceptances*] is not expressly contradicted, it is held that the paper, though issued without authority of law and in opposition to its express provisions, is still valid."[216] That carries us back to chapters 17 and 18.

---

[212] Argument set out in his *Essays and Speeches*, 470 at 473–74.

[213] (1) Curtis v. County of Butler, 24 How. 435 (1861). Edwin M. Stanton, for the bondholder, relied upon the opinion of Black, C.J., in Sharpless v. Mayor of Philadelphia, 21 Pa. St. 147 (1853), see supra, pp. 927–29. The Butler County bonds, Black argued unsuccessfully, were invalid because only two of the three commissioners had executed them.

(2) Woods v. Lawrence County, 1 Bl. 386 (1862), where the Court recalled but again rejected Black's argument in the *Curtis* case.

(3) "Kennett v. Mercer County," by which he meant Mercer County v. Hackett, 1 Wall. 83 (1864). Supra, p. 945.

(4 and 5) "Gelpcke v. City of Muscatine," by which he meant Gelpcke v. Dubuque, 1 Wall. 175 (1864), supra, pp. 935–44, and Meyer v. Muscatine, 1 Wall. 384 (1864), supra, pp. 944–46.

(6) Von Hostrup v. Madison City, 1 Wall. 291 (1864), in which he had argued, unsuccessfully, that the bonds were invalid for want of power to issue them. Supra, pp. 944–47.

[214] Sharpless v. Mayor of Philadelphia, cited in note 213.

[215] 21 How. 539 (1859), see supra, pp. 931–33.

[216] Dissenting opinion in Humboldt Township v. Long, 92 U.S. 642, 648 (1876), Davis and Field, JJ., joining with him. See supra, pp. 1066–67.

RULES GOVERNING APPEALS FROM THE COURT OF CLAIMS

BY THE ACT of March 17, 1866,[217] Congress repealed the section of the Act of 1863 that had produced the Supreme Court's objection to hearing appeals.[218] Promptly on April 3 the Court announced "Regulations under which appeals may be taken from the Court of Claims to the Supreme Court."[219] The salient feature of the Court's three rules was that the transcript must bring up

> The finding of the facts and the conclusion of law to be stated separately, and certified to this Court as part of the record. . . . See Burr v. Des Moines Company, 1 Wall. 102 [1864].

In the *Burr* case, where in the Circuit Court a jury had been waived, the writ of error brought up a "large mass of evidence of twenty pages," and Justice Miller for the Court had explained why the writ was being dismissed:

> The statement of facts on which this Court will inquire, if there is or is not error in the application of the law to them, is a statement of the ultimate facts or propositions which the evidence is intended to establish, and not the evidence on which those ultimate facts are supposed to rest. . . . It must leave none of the functions of a jury to be discharged by this Court, but must have all the sufficiency, fullness and perspicuity of a special verdict. . . .

"In practice" however, Justice Miller said in retrospect in 1872,[220] "it was found that the Court of Claims did not, in many cases, make the necessary findings of facts until after they had rendered their decree, and complaints were made here that the findings were often insufficient to present the law points on which parties . . . desired a review in this Court."

To correct those evils, the Court on April 30, 1870, promulgated Additional Rules IV and V.[221] The immediate occasion was *United States v. Alonzo Child*, remanded that day: the order in that case specified the points on which findings were to be made, and

---

[217] 14 Stat. 9.
[218] Supra, pp. 52–54, 1426–27.
[219] Minutes for that day; 3 Wall. vii. Section 5 of the Act of 1863 provided that appeals might be taken "under such regulations as the supreme court may direct."
[220] In Mahan v. United States, 14 Wall. 109.
[221] Minutes for that day; 9 Wall. vii.

directed that they "be returned to this Court with all convenient speed."[222]

With minor alterations in 1873, 1879, and 1883, these rules sufficed to govern appeals from the Court of Claims until, in a general revision of the Rules of the Supreme Court in 1925, those applicable to the Court of Claims were there incorporated.[223]

LIMITS ON THE COURT OF CLAIMS' ACTION

United States v. Alonzo Child, just mentioned, and the claim of Theodore Adams, presently to be considered, grew out of General Frémont's conduct of affairs at St. Louis in 1861, particularly in the administration of Major Justus McKinstry, Chief Quartermaster of the Department of the West. President Lincoln removed Frémont, and the Secretary of War appointed a commission, of which David Davis was chairman, to examine and report on claims arising from Frémont's regime.[224] By a Joint Resolution on March 11, 1862, Congress provided for the payment of claims allowed by the commission.

United States v. Adams[225] concerned a claim for mortar-boats built on the order of General Frémont. It appeared that this had been submitted to the commission, that an allowance had been made for less than Adams demanded, and that he had accepted what was so allowed. He might instead have trusted to an application to Congress, or might have gone to the Court of Claims at the time when it had no authority to render a judgment. After the Act of 1863 gave the Court of Claims that power, Adams there sought and obtained a judgment for an additional amount. The Supreme Court reversed and directed that the petition be dismissed. Acceptance of what the commission found due barred further recovery; otherwise, said Justice Nelson, the Government would never know when a claim had been finally settled.

When the further findings in the *Alonzo Child* case[226] came up, it appeared that although claimant had not "submitted" his claim to the commission as to an arbitrator for conclusive determination, yet

---

[222] Minutes for April 30, 1870. The case is reported, under the title United States v. Adams, at 9 Wall. 661. The claim of Alonzo Child and that of Theodore Adams had to do with matters heard by the Commission on War Claims at St. Louis, to be mentioned in a moment.

[223] Reynolds Robertson and Francis R. Kirkham, *Jurisdiction of the Supreme Court of the United States* (St. Paul: West Publishing Co., and

Kansas City, Mo.: Vernon Law Book Co., 1936), sec. 211.

[224] The Report of the Commission on War Claims at St. Louis is H.R. Exec. Doc. No. 94, 37th Cong., 2d Sess. Major McKinstry was convicted by court-martial of neglect and violation of duty, and dismissed in January 1863.

[225] 7 Wall. 463 (1869). There were other phases, reported at 6 Wall. 101 (1868), and 9 Wall. 554 (1870).

[226] Supra, pp. 1440–41.

he had accepted the amount the commission allowed to be due, and had signed a receipt "in full of the above account." The Court, per Miller, J., held that to be a complete discharge; the judgment of the Court of Claims allowing further recovery was reversed.[227]

In *United States v. Alire*[228] the Court of Claims had adjudged that the petitioner was entitled to a warrant for military bounty-lands, and had directed that its decree be remitted to the Secretary of the Interior. The Supreme Court, reversing, held that the petition must be dismissed: the statute authorized only money judgments against the United States. In *Bonner v. United States*[229] petitioner's contention had been that Virginia's cession of its western lands to the United States in 1784 had been subject to a trust that certain lands be held for that State's veterans; that the United States had violated the trust; and that the Court of Claims should decree that satisfaction be given in land or in money. Justice Davis for the Court pointed out that the claim was not based upon an act of Congress, nor upon a contract; if the Government was liable it could be only for a breach of trust, and Congress had not authorized the Court of Claims to exercise the jurisdiction of a court of equity. Claimant's only remedy lay in an appeal to Congress.

Private property, the Fifth Amendment declares, shall not be taken for public use without just compensation. In *United States v. Russell*[230] three steamboats had been impressed where "impending public danger [was] too urgent to admit of delay"; the officers who issued the orders "were not trespassers," said Justice Clifford for the Court; the transaction was contractual, and "the Government . . . is bound to make full compensation to the owner for the services rendered." The employment under these circumstances was not within the meaning of a statute of 1864 enacting that the jurisdiction of the Court of Claims should not extend to "the appropriation of property . . . by the army or navy, engaged in the suppression of the rebellion . . . ."

Two claims cases at this period had to do with the treaty-making power. Amos Kendall (1789–1869), Postmaster General under Jackson, had in 1843 agreed with the Western Cherokees to press their claim against the Government; he stipulated that he was to receive, directly from the United States, five percent of what was collected. By a treaty of 1846 the Cherokees were to receive more than eight million dollars, which would be held in trust and paid to the individual members. Congress appropriated accordingly, with a provision that no part of the money would be paid to any agent. In *Kendall v. United States*,[231]

---

[227] 12 Wall. 232 (1871). Chase, C.J., and Clifford, J., dissented.
[228] 6 Wall. 573 (1868).

[229] 9 Wall. 156 (1870).
[230] 13 Wall. 623 (1871).
[231] 7 Wall. 113 (1869).

affirming the judgment of the Court of Claims, it was held that the Government was free to make the treaty and to settle with the Indians without consulting the agent or incurring any liability to him. *Meade v. United States*[232] concerned the treaty of settlement with Spain in 1819. By one article the United States exonerated Spain from claims by American citizens, and undertook itself to make satisfaction to them. A commission was set up for that purpose, by which Meade's claim was rejected. The Court examined the complicated circumstances and held that the decision of the commission was conclusive and a bar to recovery.

The Court of Claims figured incidentally in Chapter 15's discussion of the recovery of proceeds under the Abandoned and Captured Property Act.[233] *United States v. O'Keefe*[234] was the case of a British subject who sued under that statute. Congress by an Act of July 27, 1868, had conceded to the citizen of a foreign government the right to sue in the Court of Claims if his government accorded in its own courts a like privilege to citizens of the United States.[235] Justice Davis for the Court examined the proceeding by Petition of Right as it had become "crystalized in the common law of England," and concluded that while it was "formal and ceremonious, it is, nevertheless, a practical and efficient remedy," equivalent to suit in the Court of Claims; accordingly O'Keefe had standing to bring his suit.

Carlisle v. United States[236] was the suit of another British subject, who claimed under the Abandoned and Captured Property Act the proceeds of cotton taken in Alabama. He had, however, manufactured and marketed saltpeter, evidently aware that it would be used in the prosecution of the rebellion. Justice Field quoted and applied what had been said in *Hanauer v. Doane*:[237] he must be taken to have intended the consequences of his act. But if, although an alien, Carlisle could take the benefit of President Johnson's proclamation of December 25, 1868,[238] then what had been decided in *Padelford*,[239] *Klein*,[240] and *Pargoud*,[241] would permit him to pursue his claim

---

232 9 Wall. 691 (1870).

233 Supra, pp. 840–88.

234 11 Wall. 178 (1871).

235 15 Stat. 243.

236 16 Wall. 147 (1873). The Docket shows that this case had been filed on December 11, 1871; on January 24, 1873, counsel submitted without oral argument. On Monday, March 10, the Court ordered oral argument "upon the question whether the amnesty proclamations of the President apply to domiciled aliens as well as to citizens." That took place on April 3. Decision was announced on April 14—immediately before that in *Slaughter House*.

237 12 Wall. 342 (1871). Supra, pp. 854–56.

238 15 Stat. 711. Supra, p. 846.

239 9 Wall. 531 (1870). Supra, pp. 840–42.

240 13 Wall. 128 (1872). Supra, pp. 840, 843–45.

241 13 Wall. 156 (1872). Supra, pp. 840, 844–46.

without proof of loyalty. Upon that point, said Justice Field, "we entertain no doubt." "The alien, whilst domiciled in the country, owes a local and temporary allegiance, which continues during the period of his residence." Carlisle owed "fidelity and obedience to the Government of the United States," and for throwing his lot with the Confederates "would be subject like them to punishment under the laws they violated, but for the Proclamation . . . of December 25, 1868. That Proclamation in its comprehensive terms, includes them and all others in like situation. . . ." For dismissing Carlisle's petition, the judgment of the Court of Claims was reversed. Justice Field's opinion has figured prominently in works on international law and in diplomatic correspondence.

When in 1863 Congress waived sovereign immunity to the extent of permitting the United States to be sued on claims founded upon a statute, or upon a contract, express or implied, it produced "a novel feature in our jurisprudence," as Justice Miller observed in *Gibbons*.[242] Evidently it was important that the Supreme Court exercise a supervisory control over the principles to be applied, while holding itself aloof from the business of finding facts.

BUSINESS OF THE COURT

"THE JUDICIAL POWER" of the United States, declares Article III of the Constitution, shall extend to certain categories of "Cases" and "Controversies." It defines the original jurisdiction of the Supreme Court, and grants it appellate jurisdiction of all other matters of federal judicial cognizance "with such Exceptions, and under such Regulations as the Congress shall make." It was a matter of jealous concern, when the Constitution was adopted, to mark "the precise limits, beyond which the federal courts cannot extend their jurisdiction," as Hamilton wrote in No. LXXXIII of *The Federalist*. It was inherent, then, that the Supreme Court must always be concerned with the question of jurisdiction before it came to the merits of a dispute.

Beginning with Section 17 of the Judiciary Act of 1789, the Court had received statutory grants of rule-making powers, "for the orderly conducting of business" before it and presently for the conduct of business in all federal courts.[243] The Court will also be concerned, then, with rules of practice.

A few examples will point to significant observations.

---

[242] Gibbons v. United States, 8 Wall. 269 (1869). Supra, p. 1437.

[243] Pertinent references are set out in Justice Gray's opinion in Hudson v. Parker, 156 U.S. 277, 281 (1875).

Section 25 of the Judiciary Act has been presented as the invaluable means whereby one whose claim of federal right has been rejected by the courts of a State may carry his contention to the Supreme Court.[244] This may, however, be viewed from the obverse side, as placing a narrow limit on bringing error from a State court. When, after the war, litigants came crowding to the Supreme Court, there was increasing occasion to insist upon the negative aspect of Section 25. Thus in a case in 1872, in dismissing a writ of error to the Supreme Court of Iowa, Chief Justice Chase restated the jurisdictional requirement, and remarked:

> It does not appear from the record that any such question was either made or decided.
>
> Much expense to suitors would be spared if counsel would attend to the principle above stated, and . . . frequently laid down, before advising their clients to resort to the appellate jurisdiction of this court from the decisions of the State courts.[245]

How scrupulous was the Court in applying Section 25 was illustrated six weeks later in *Klinger v. Missouri*.[246] Plaintiff in error had been convicted of murder by a Missouri court. The transcript of record showed ten assignments of error, only one of which could possibly raise a federal question: that over Klinger's objection one Park had been excluded from serving as a juror. Park had declined to take the loyalty oath prescribed by the State constitution, that he had always been truly and loyally on the side of the United States. Examined under oath, he said he had sympathized with the Confederate cause during the rebellion, and that now that sentiment was even stronger than it had been then. Before the Supreme Court, counsel for Klinger insisted that the loyalty oath for jurors was unconstitutional, and that its imposition upon Park violated Klinger's rights. But, said Justice Bradley for the Court, the record did not show whether Park had been excluded because of his refusal to take the oath, or on the independent and valid ground that he avowed himself to be a still more bitter rebel than ever before. Justice Bradley then stated this proposition:

> where it does not appear on which of the two grounds the judgment was based, then, if the independent ground on which it might have

---

[244] Supra, p. 45.

[245] Hurley v. Street, 14 Wall. 85. The contention that counsel for the plaintiff in error wanted to argue was that the statute of Iowa, under which their client's land had been sold for delinquent taxes, contravened the Fifth Amendment. But the Court had reiterated, as recently as Twitchell v. Pennsylvania, 7 Wall. 321 (1869), that that Amendment bound only the Federal Government and not the States. Supra, ch. 21, n. 47.

[246] 13 Wall. 257, decided Apr. 1, 1872.

been based was a good and valid one, sufficient of itself to sustain the judgment, this Court will not assume jurisdiction of the case . . . .

It could not with certainty be said that the Supreme Court of Missouri had sustained the constitutionality of the juror's oath; the writ of error must be dismissed.

The rule thus "firmly fixed" had been "reiterated in a long line of cases since that time," said the Court in 1935.[247]

Under Section 22 of the Judiciary Act, review by the Supreme Court, in actions at law tried in the inferior federal courts, was by writ of error. And the Court's Rule 4 directed that the Judges in those courts

> shall not allow any bill of exceptions, which shall contain the charge of the court at large to the jury in trials at common law, upon any general exception to the whole charge. But the party excepting shall be required to state distinctly the several matters of law, in such charge to which he excepted; and that such matters of law, and those only, shall be inserted in the bill of exceptions, and allowed by the court.[248]

Throughout the period we are examining, faulty bills of exceptions were a constant hindrance to the Justices—and it is to be remembered that every Justice made an independent examination of the papers in every case, prior to conference. Grier, J., in a characteristic utterance in 1867 was "protesting against attempts at mystifying the merits of a case" by "the bill of exceptions (so-called) . . . ."[249]

In 1869 a case from the Northern District of Illinois was the occasion for this censure by Justice Field:

> The bill of exceptions in this case is made up without any regard to the rules . . . . It . . . covers ninety-six printed pages of the record, when the exceptions could have been presented with greater clearness and precision in . . . five . . . . In its preparation counsel seem to have forgotten that this Court does not pass, in actions at law, upon the credibility or sufficiency of testimony; that these are matters which are left to the jury . . . .

He went on to say that "the practice in some districts—quite common of late—of sending up to this Court bills . . . filled with superfluous

---

[247] Fox Film Corp. v. Muller, 296 U.S. 207, 210.

[248] The Rules as revised and corrected at December term, 1858, are in 21 How. v-xvi. This was repeated in the Rules of May 1, 1871, and of

January 7, 1884.

[249] Evans v. Patterson, 4 Wall. 224, from the Circuit Court for the Western District of Pennsylvania. The single assignment of error was found to be without merit.

matter—must be condemned." And the Judge in the trial court, before he signed a bill of exceptions, should make sure that it was "freed from all matter not essential . . . ."[250]

Long after Field was gone, other Justices pointed to what he had said on that occasion.[251]

And only one week after this censure, Justice Swayne was making the same protest in another case from the same Circuit Court, where the Justices must go "winnowing away the chaff" in a bill of exceptions that covered a hundred and twenty-seven printed pages.[252]

"We have felt very much inclined," said Justice Miller in 1872, in still another case from the Northern District of Illinois, "to dismiss the writ of error or affirm the judgment, without an attempt to look up the questions of law which might possibly be involved," where all of the evidence had been set out in the transcript, and where counsel, submitting on printed briefs, had attempted to argue the entire case "as if the verdict concluded nothing . . . ."[253] The Court did, however, extract two questions of law, which it "examined carefully." The result was that the judgment below was affirmed.

Briefs, as has been observed all along, varied widely in quality. Many showed little perception of the needs of the Justices to whose minds they were addressed, in such requisites as a succinct statement of the case, identification of the points to be made, citations to pages in the record and to the authorities relied upon, adequate excerpts from State statutes involved, and such perspicuous organization of the argument as would enable the reader quickly to comprehend.

Add to that the consideration that in six years since the end of the war the number of cases docketed had nearly doubled. At Decem-

---

[250] Lincoln v. Claflin, 7 Wall. 132, decided Feb. 8, 1869.

[251] Taft, C.J., in Krauss Bros. Lumber Co. v. Mellon, 276 U.S. 386, 391 (1928); Van Devanter, J., in Alexander v. Cosden Pipe Line Co., 290 U.S. 484, 490 (1934).

[252] Laber v. Cooper, 7 Wall. 565, decided February 15, 1869.

[253] Gregg v. Moss, 14 Wall. 564. The transcript illustrates how error or ineptitude can cause judicial effort to be lost. In this case there had been four trials below. The first resulted in a verdict for a certain sum in damages. But a new trial was granted, which resulted in a hung jury. A third trial produced a verdict like that in the first. But again a new trial was granted, which resulted in a verdict for the defendant. The bill of excep-

tions, at pp. 15–43, set out all the evidence. This was signed by District Judge Henry W. Blodgett.

Chicago v. Greer, 9 Wall. 726 (1870) was another case from the Northern District of Illinois, where the Court, per Strong, J., censured for failure to observe Rule 4.

Woodruff v. Hough, 91 U.S. 596 (1876) was "another one of those cases, so common from that circuit, in which . . . this Court is expected to retry the case as if it were both court and jury," said Miller, J.

And in Hall v. Weare, 92 U.S. 728 (1876), Justice Strong's opinion began with "This record has been brought up in a shape of which we can hardly speak in too strong terms of disapproval. . . ."

ber term 1871, the Justices determined to prescribe with particularity how a brief must be organized. Accordingly on November 26, 1872—the last day of the adjourned term—an amended Rule 21 was promulgated, greatly expanding the provisions on "Briefs."[254] At the same time the Clerk was directed to have printed copies sent "to each of the counsel of record in all cases now pending and not yet argued."

Elaboration is found in the opinion of Chief Justice Chase in *Portland Company v. United States*,[255] an appeal from the Court of Claims, decided on January 20, 1873. He began:

> From time to time, the Court has adopted rules of practice intended to facilitate the presentation of causes by counsel and their consideration by the Court. Finding that these rules, through the inattention of the bar, had failed in a great degree of their intended effect, we promulgated at the last term . . . an amended twenty-first Rule, the 4th section of which required that the brief should contain . . .

and the Chief Justice went on to detail what was expected. "The necessity of strict compliance with these rules, especially in view of the greatly augmented business of the Court, is evident. . . ." Then came the imposition of the penalty of which the amended Rule had forewarned:

> In the case before us, this rule has been totally disregarded on the part of the appellant.
> *We shall, therefore, in this case dismiss the appeal.*[256]

The burdensome task of reading through the mass of evidence brought up on an appeal in equity or in admiralty was explained at the outset.[257] In *Mann v. Rock Island Bank*[258] in 1871 Miller, J., pronounced this an "obstruction to public justice," and said that

> We do not feel that this burden should be further increased . . . in writing and delivering opinions which, if they attempt to go into examination of the facts to justify the decision of the Court, will be equally tedious and useless.

---

[254] Minutes for November 26, 1872. The amended rule appears in 4 Wallace at xi-xii. The date is inaccurately stated as November 16.

[255] 15 Wall. 1.

[256] The Docket shows that this appeal from the Court of Claims, 5 Ct. Cl. 441, had been filed on April 11, 1871, by T. J. Durant. On November 22, 1871, the Court granted him leave to withdraw his appearance, and

Thomas H. Talbot took his place. On January 8, 1873, the cause was submitted.

Talbot, as an Assistant Attorney General under Hoar was experienced at the Supreme Court bar. It seems probable that what looks like a bad mark resulted from his late entry in the case.

[257] Supra, pp. 35, 75n.

[258] 11 Wall. 650.

The Steamboat St. John,[259] decided on April 1, 1872, was a libel for damages resulting from a collision. Judge Blatchford in the District Court had entered a decree;[260] on appeal to the Circuit Court Judge Woodruff had affirmed;[261] and now the Supreme Court had heard a further appeal. Justice Bradley, in affirming, stated the facts in say six hundred words, and concluded:

> The case is purely one of fact, and it can serve no instructive purpose to review the evidence in detail. We have carefully examined it, and are satisfied that the result reached by the circuit and district courts was correct.

In January 1872 the House of Representatives passed H.R.891, a bill "further to regulate the appellate jurisdiction of the Supreme Court and to prevent delays therein."[262] It had been drawn by Justice Miller and accepted by his brethren. Review in equity and admiralty cases would be confined to questions of law, upon findings of fact by the court below; the jurisdictional limit for bringing a case to the Supreme Court would be increased from $2,000 to $5,000, and in admiralty cases where there had been two hearings below, the matter involved must exceed $10,000. It went through the House easily, only to perish in the Judiciary Committee of the Senate. Concurrently Miller had supported the proposal in an article on "Judicial Reforms," appearing in legal journals.[263] On April 23, 1872, a fortnight before the Court adjourned, he surveyed the situation in a letter to a kinsman:

> Our Court has decided one third more cases since it met in October than it ever did and our docket is left with about 450 cases. This is at least 150 more than we ever left before.
> My bill which passed the House hangs fire in the Senate Committee which is a Committee of all the talents and all the politicians and all the elements of discord, and is the greatest nuisance of its kind in either House of Congress.[264]

He recognized that "the effect of my bill [would be to leave] the people of the Southern States at the mercy of their district judges in finding of facts which is made conclusive. The same objection is urged here by Mr. [Philip] Phillips and other lawyers interested in cases coming from from that region. But I do not see how to avoid the difficulty. The one important feature on which all our court is agreed, and the only one

---

[259] 154 U.S. 586, 20 L. Ed. 645.
[260] Fed. Case No. 12,223 (1868).
[261] Fed. Case No. 12,224 (1870).
[262] Cong. Globe, 42–2, 712–13, 732–36. Jan. 30 and 31, 1872.

[263] 2 U. S. Jurist 1; 6 Western Jurist 49, in Feb. 1872.
[264] To his brother-in-law, William P. Ballinger, of Galveston, Texas. Fairman, *Mr. Justice Miller*, 403.

which seems to be without objection in Congress, is to relieve this court from that business. It is a necessity. . . ."[265]

In 1866, during the First Session of the 39th Congress, Miller had hoped most earnestly for the passage of Senator Harris' bill to create an intermediate appellate court within each circuit, and to reduce the flow of cases into the Supreme Court; that was the effort with which Chase had unhelpfully intermeddled for his own purposes.[266] In 1872 Miller recognized that even if H.R.891 were to be enacted by the 42d Congress, it would be "a very imperfect remedy" for the "vast increase" in the volume of litigation that was coming to the Court; only the creation of intermediate appellate courts would meet the need. Actually that step was not taken until 1891.[267]

More decisions meant more opinions, and there was opposition to any swelling of the Reports. From time to time the Justices considered what might well be done. Evidently the most eligible possibility was to write more concise opinions. Among Justice Davis' papers is a reckoning of the average number of pages per opinion by the several mem-

VOL. X

Name of Justice	Whole no. of pages occupied by opinions	No. of opinions or dissents	Average no. of pages of each
Clifford	$101\frac{3}{8}$	10	$10\frac{1}{10}$
Chief Justice	$8\frac{1}{4}$	3	$2\frac{2}{3}$
Nelson	18	15	$1\frac{1}{5}$
Swayne	43	8	$5\frac{3}{8}$
Miller	$33\frac{3}{4}$	11	3
Davis	$23\frac{1}{4}$	7	$3\frac{2}{7}$
Strong	38	7	$5\frac{3}{7}$
Bradley	18	7	$2\frac{4}{7}$
Field	$30\frac{1}{2}$	8	$3\frac{3}{4}$

VOL. XI

Clifford	90	10	9
Nelson	$17\frac{1}{4}$	5	$3\frac{2}{5}$
Swayne	$35\frac{2}{5}$	10	$3\frac{1}{2}$
Miller	$31\frac{1}{8}$	8	$3\frac{7}{8}$
Davis	$28\frac{1}{2}$	10	$2\frac{4}{5}$
Strong	$53\frac{3}{4}$	9	$5\frac{5}{9}$
Bradley	$59\frac{2}{5}$	11	$5\frac{4}{11}$
Field	$37\frac{1}{2}$	8	$4\frac{5}{8}$

[265] Ibid., 403–4.
[266] Supra, pp. 160–72.

[267] Circuit Court of Appeals Act of March 3, 1891. 26 Stat. 826.

bers.[268] It was drawn from 10 Wallace (concluding the reports for December term, 1869, and beginning those for the following term) and 11 Wallace (continuing for the December term, 1870—which also ran on through 12 and into 13 Wallace).

Before any refined conclusions were drawn from these figures it would, of course, be proper to consider such matters as the importance of the various cases, and the record of each Justice's attendance.[269] There can be no doubt that Justice Clifford was inexcusably prolix. A small saving was accomplished by the omission of less important opinions, such as that by Justice Bradley, just quoted, in *The Steamboat St. John*.[270]

SOME OBSERVATIONS DRAWN FROM THE MINUTES

THE COURT CONVENED on Monday, December 2, 1872, and continued until May 1. This was Chase's last term, and by following the Minutes one may find a basis for some useful generalizations.

On December 9 the Chief Justice read from the Bench a letter he had received from Justice Nelson, dated at Cooperstown, November 28: "The mail that carries these lines to you, carries my resignation of the office of Associate Justice of the Supreme Court." "Age and infirmities" had dictated this action. This was anything but hasty. Since the Court met in adjourned session on October 31, 1870, Nelson had attended only forty-eight days, never after April 19, 1871.

Ward Hunt of New York was commissioned on December 11, 1872, and took his seat on January 9.

The resignation of Richard C. Parsons, the Marshal, was read on December 16; he had just been elected to Congress. The Court made an order that the Marshal be required to reside at Washington, and that "he is expected to engage in no other business than attention to the duties of the Marshalship." The appointment of John G. Nicolay was then announced. Parsons had been engaging in discreditable lobbying in Congress.[271]

Twelve cases at this term were disposed of "by a divided court." Chase's year of illness and recuperation, and Nelson's absence, overlapping in part that of Chase and continuing for a year thereafter, had

---

[268] Davis Papers, Ill. State Hist. Soc.

[269] Notably the long absences of the Chief Justice and of Justice Nelson. Two of Nelson's opinions in 11 Wallace were in cases decided in December 1867 and March 1869.

[270] Such omitted opinions are included at their chronological place in Lawyers' Edition; they were published in appendices to 131 U.S. and 154 U.S.

[271] Supra, p. 836.

been causing a number of cases to be dispatched in that indecisive way, or else to be repeatedly postponed.

In six of the above, Nos. 15 to 20—reported together as *Barnes v. The Railroads,* already identified in a footnote[272]—judgments of affirmation by a divided court on December 16, 1872, had been "rescinded and annulled" on December 20. Then upon reargument the decisions below were reversed on March 3 by a majority of five, Chase, Davis, Field, and *Strong* dissenting. (In mentioning dissenters in the paragraphs that follow, italics will indicate the Justices who filed opinions.)

Also in *National Bank of Washington v. Texas,* where on March 17, 1873, an equal division resulted in affirming the decree of the District of Columbia court, this action was on May 1 rescinded and annulled; at the following term the decree was reversed.[273] This incident was recounted in the discussion of the litigation that followed *Texas v. White.*[274]

The question in *State ex rel. Wagner v. Stoll* and in *State ex rel. Robb v. Gurney* was whether bills of the Bank of the State of South Carolina were receivable in payment of taxes, having regard to the language of the bank's charter in 1812 and the controverted effect of subsequent legislation. The bank was unable to pay in specie. The State court had sustained county treasurers in refusing to accept the bills. On March 13 and 14, 1873, W. W. Boyce and B. R. Curtis sought a reversal, against Daniel H. Chamberlain, Attorney General. On March 31 Justice Hunt spoke for the Court, affirming the judgments below. Davis and Strong, JJ., noted dissent. But then on May 1 the action of March 31 was rescinded, and a reargument ordered. That took place on the following October 20 and 21; Andrew G. Magrath, former federal and Confederate District Judge, replaced Boyce. And on November 3, 1873, Justice Hunt delivered the Court's opinion: the case having been "re-argued with greater care," the conclusion was that the bills were receivable.[275] Bradley, J., dissented.

On April 18, 1873, the Court, per Chase, C.J., affirmed the judgment of the Supreme Court of Iowa in *Northwestern Union Packet Co. v. Home Insurance Co.*—after having adjudged at the last term that the writ of error must be dismissed, and having subsequently rescinded that disposition.[276]

At this period there was enough of this deciding, rescinding, and after further argument reaching a new decision, to suggest looseness in

---

[272] 17 Wall. 294. Supra, note 201.

[273] 20 Wall. 72, decided Apr. 20, 1874.

[274] Supra, pp. 650–51, 653–55.

[275] 17 Wall. 425.

[276] The decision of the State court is reported in 32 Iowa 223 (1871). Dismissal of the writ of error, on January 29, 1872, is reported in 154 U.S. 588, 20 L. Ed. 463. No opinion has been found for the affirmance on April 18, 1873.

the performance of counsel and lack of adequate understanding on the part of the Court.

Now looking at combinations of Justices in dissent: if one extracts from the Minutes for this term the instances where more than one member recorded disagreement with the action of the Court, the variety of groupings will be striking. One will also observe the sort of issues over which such differences arose. What this may signify will be considered presently.

Gray v. Darlington[277] held that a certain advance in the value of bonds was not taxable as "gains" under the Internal Revenue Act. Chase, Clifford, and Bradley dissented.

Canal Co. v. Hill[278] taught that in construing an agreement a court should look to the surrounding circumstances and not merely at the form. In particular, it was held that the grant of a right to draw as much water as will pass through an aperture of given size and position in a canal was a grant of a certain quantity of water; and under the circumstances in this case the grantee was entitled to take that amount, through an enlargement of the aperture if necessary. Davis and *Strong* dissented.

United States v. Thomas[279] exculpated a collector of customs who had surrendered public money on demand of a rebel force. *Miller* dissented, because he found the ruling irreconcilable with precedents the Court had left standing; Swayne and Strong also dissented.

Of ten cases at that term concerning municipal bonds, Justice Miller dissented in four: Field joined in one of those dissents,[280] *Field* and Chase in another;[281] in the other two, Miller was joined by Chase and Davis.[282]

Miller v. New York[283] held that a reserved power to amend a corporate charter enabled the legislature to change the directorate by providing for seven instead of four public members. Field and *Bradley* dissented.

In *Taylor v. Taintor*[284] an accused had been allowed by his bondsman to go to another State; while there he was extradited to a third State. Held: the bondsman was not exonerated. Clifford, Miller, and *Field* dissented.

---

[277] 15 Wall. 63 (1872).

[278] 15 Wall. 94 (1872). Cited on the use of extrinsic evidence in Zeckendorf v. Steinfeld, 225 U.S. 445, 457 (1912).

[279] 15 Wall. 337 (1873).

[280] Kenicott v. The Supervisors, 16 Wall. 452 (1873).

[281] Lynde v. The County, 16 Wall. 6 (1873).

[282] Railroad Co. v. County of Otoe, 16 Wall. 667 (1873), and Olcott v. The Supervisors, 16 Wall. 678 (1873). These two cases, decided on the same day, were discussed supra, pp. 1016-20.

[283] 15 Wall. 478 (1873).

[284] 16 Wall. 366 (1873).

As has been recorded, in the *Case of the State Freight Tax*,[285] *Swayne* and Davis dissented, while in *State Tax on Railway Gross Receipts*,[286] *Miller*, Field, and Hunt dissented.

In *State Tax on Foreign-held Bonds*[287] there was dissent by Miller, *Davis*, and Hunt.

Railroad Co. v. Johnson[288] repeated the holding that the Legal Tender Act was valid. Chase, Clifford, and Field noted dissent.

Magwire v. Tyler (as it appears in all the original papers and in the Court's records)—being *Tyler v. Magwire*[289] as it appears in Wallace's *Reports*—was the concluding phase of a dispute over land at St. Louis, Missouri, which had already received much attention from the Court.[290] In 1869 it had held that Magwire was owner entitled to possession by a grant to B, through C; this rejected Tyler's claim of title by the grant to B, through L. The judgment of the Supreme Court of Missouri was reversed, with a direction for "further proceedings, in conformity to the opinion of this Court."

But the State court did not allow Magwire to have the fruits of this victory; it held that only by starting anew by an action at law could Magwire pursue his claim to eject Tyler. Upon a new writ of error, Justice Clifford for the Supreme Court said that its decision in 1869 had "disposed of every material question at issue in the record between the parties"; "the whole case had been decided . . . ." For the subordinate court "to evade . . . the judgment of this Court" would contravene the Constitution and the laws of Congress. Thereupon, as authorized by Section 25 of the Judiciary Act in a situation where a cause had already been once remanded, the decree was that Magwire recover possession and that this would be executed by the Court's own Marshal.[291]

It is noteworthy that in this unusual exhibition of federal judicial power over the highest court of a State, the Court's spokesman was Justice Clifford, a confirmed Democrat, while Swayne, Strong, and Bradley, all Republicans, recorded dissent.

In *Goddard v. Foster*, plaintiff in error and his former business representative abroad had litigated in a jury trial in the Circuit Court what was due to the latter for services rendered subsequent to the

---

[285] 15 Wall. 232 (1873), supra, pp. 1412–14.

[286] 15 Wall. 284, supra, pp. 1413–14.

[287] 15 Wall. 300, supra, pp. 1413–14.

[288] 15 Wall. 195.

[289] 17 Wall. 253 (1873).

[290] Magwire v. Tyler, 1 Bl. 195 (1862), affirming the authority of the Secretary of the Interior to set aside a Spanish survey and to order a new

one; Magwire v. Tyler, 8 Wall. 650 (1869), establishing that title was in Magwire and not in Tyler; Magwire v. Tyler, 8 Wall. 668 (1869), modifying the language of the direction to the State court consequent on the decree earlier that year.

[291] Tyler v. Magwire, 17 Wall. 253, 292 (1873), cited in connection with Williams v. Bruffy, supra, p. 870.

termination of their protracted dealings under a written agreement; this involved the construction of several writings. The Court affirmed the judgment below, and Strong and Hunt noted dissent.[292]

United States v. Baltimore and Ohio Railroad Co. has been explained above as a case concerning, not the validity of the Internal Revenue Act, but only its applicability in a particular situation.[293] *Clifford* and Miller dissented.

In *Tweed's Case*[294] the plaintiff had contracted with the Treasury Agent to collect abandoned and captured cotton and send it to New Orleans, in consideration whereof he would receive three-fourths of what he collected. He had sent cotton, but contended that it was not abandoned or captured, but other cotton which he had purchased on his own account. He sued the Treasury Agent for the additional quarter of the cotton. The Court accepted that view of the transaction and affirmed the judgment for Tweed. Davis and *Bradley* dissented: plaintiff was not free to proceed under government protection into the affected district and then abandon the agreement and purchase on his own account.

In *Lapeyre v. United States*,[295] an appeal from the Court of Claims, the owner of cotton in enemy territory had shipped it to New Orleans where on June 26 he executed a bill of sale to the Treasury Agent and received back three-fourths of the cotton, as provided in a statute of 1864. Unknown to both, on June 24 the President had executed a proclamation removing the restriction on trade; this proclamation was not published until June 27. The majority held that the proclamation became effective on the date of its execution, and allowed Lapeyre to recover for the quarter of his cotton. Miller, Field, Bradley and *Hunt* dissented, holding that a proclamation became effective only when it had been made known "by some public or official notice of its existence."

In the much-cited case of *Crapo v. Kelly*[296] a ship owned by insolvent citizens of Massachusetts and there registered was, while on the high seas, transferred by a Massachusetts court to assignees for the benefit of creditors, pursuant to local law. Later the ship entered the port of New York and was attached in a suit by a New York creditor. The Court of Appeals upheld the attachment. The Supreme Court, per Hunt, J., held that it had jurisdiction to review the New York judgment,

---

[292] Goddard v. Foster, 17 Wall. 123 (1873). Controversy over what was due under the agreement had been determined by Foster v. Goddard, 1 Bl. 506 (1862).

[293] 17 Wall. 322 (1873), supra, pp. 1435–36.

[294] 16 Wall. 504 (1873).

[295] 17 Wall. 191. The Court heard argument on Jan. 14, 1873, and again on Apr. 2, before deciding on Apr. 15.

[296] 16 Wall. 610 (1873), reversing Kelly v. Crapo, 45 N.Y. 86.

in order to consider the contention that it failed to give "full faith and credit" to the judicial proceedings in Massachusetts, as required by Section 1 of Article IV of the Constitution—what has been called the "lawyer's clause." Justice Hunt went on to reason that personal property of Massachusetts residents when on the high seas was to be regarded as if it were within the territory of Massachusetts, and that the assignment had been instantly effective, before the ship had come within the reach of New York. Justices Field and *Bradley*, dissenting, reasoned that the transfer of the ship by operation of Massachusetts law could have no extraterritorial force in another State save by that State's comity, and such "comity is never exercised to the prejudice of the citizens of the State which accords it."

When in *Davis v. Gray*[297] the Court entertained jurisdiction of a suit by the receiver of a railroad company against the Governor of Texas to enjoin the execution of a law alleged unconstitutionally to deprive the company of a grant, Chase and *Davis* dissented on the ground that this was in effect a suit by an individual against a State within the prohibition of the Eleventh Amendment. The Court later conceded that "the case goes to the verge of sound doctrine, if not beyond it . . . ."[298]

This catalog of instances where two or more Justices disagreed with the Court concludes with the *Slaughter House Cases*,[299] the subject of chapter 21. There the majority was led by *Miller*, speaking also for Clifford, Davis, Strong, and Hunt. The minority comprised Chase, *Swayne*, *Field*, and *Bradley*. This cut squarely across the cleavage of party affiliations. The issue corresponded to nothing that had ever come before the Court; the grouping of the Justices conformed to no previous division.

REFLECTIONS ON THE FOREGOING

WE HAVE FOUND that in only twenty out of about 170 reported decisions was there dissent by as many as two Justices. That shows a very large measure of accord. And where there was dissent, the combinations were diverse. At earlier terms, in controversies born of the war and reconstruction, Justices sometimes divided along the line of party cleavage, with Davis taking an intermediate position and Chase following his own peculiar meditations. In the scores of municipal bond cases, Swayne, Clifford, and Strong took one stand while Miller took

---

[297] 16 Wall. 203 (1873).
[298] Per Miller, J., in Cunningham v. Macon & Brunswick R.R., 109 U.S. 446, 453 (1883).
[299] 16 Wall. 36 (1873).

another, joined occasionally by Field or by one or more other colleagues. Aside from those categories, where in the wide variety of issues there was dissent, there was also a wide variety in the dissenters.

Of the cases coming up from the lower federal courts, many were of federal cognizance only because the litigants were citizens of different States: the issue would commonly be one of private law, such as a matter of contract or of tort, of commercial law or of equity jurisprudence. At December term 1872, for example, there was a question of negligence in *Parrott v. Wells, Fargo & Co., The Nitro-Glycerine Case*.[300] Defendants had transported a box from New York to California; on arrival its contents were leaking, and an employee by direction attempted to open the box for inspection; an explosion resulted, damaging the premises leased by Wells Fargo and other premises as well. Defendants had no knowledge or reason to suspect that the box contained nitro-glycerine. Justice Field's opinion held that defendants were not liable for the damages to premises not governed by their lease. "No one is responsible for injuries resulting from unavoidable accident, whilst engaged in a lawful business." The opinion was widely cited, and after it had been included in casebooks on torts became a part of the learning of every law student. In *Mutual Life Insurance Co. v. Terry*[301] a widow sued on a policy that excluded recovery where the insured "died by his own hand." In the Circuit Court, Miller, J., had charged the jury that to avoid this provision it lay upon the plaintiff to show that the insured's "reasoning powers were so far overthrown . . . that he could not exercise his reasoning faculties on the act he was about to do . . . ."[302] Judgment for the plaintiff was sustained by the Supreme Court in an opinion by Justice Hunt, Strong, J., dissenting. This case, too, was widely cited. At this period the Court had occasion rather often to pronounce on questions of life insurance.

On such matters of "general law" the Supreme Court at that time exercised an independent judgment, uncontrolled by the view prevailing in the courts of the State wherein the cause of action arose;[303] the lower federal courts were bound to follow, but to the State courts such rulings were no more than the utterances of a respectable bench of Judges. Aside from the cases on municipal railroad-aid bonds, this sort of work was unlikely to produce deep feeling within the Court.

In times more recent, much has been written about "conservative" and "liberal" Justices, about "activists" and practitioners of

---

[300] 15 Wall. 524 (1873).

[301] 15 Wall. 580 (1873).

[302] Terry v. Life Ins. Co., Fed. Case No. 13,839, C.C.D. Kans., 1871. Dillon, J., was sitting with Justice Miller.

[303] See the discussion of Swift v. Tyson, 16 Pet. 1 (1842), overruled by Erie R.R. v. Tompkins, 304 U.S. 64 (1938), supra, pp. 938–39.

"judicial self-restraint." The developments within the Court giving rise to these characterizations result from a variety of causes. Doubtless an important factor has been the Fourteenth Amendment, which makes it a duty of the Justices to give meaning to its promise of "due process," "liberty," "property," and "equal protection." An application which a critic may deplore as giving constitutional force to individual preconception, an enthusiast may hail as an admirable display of judicial creativity. For present purposes it is enough to say that systems that have been devised to explain such latter-day phenomena may not safely be projected back to the period with which we are concerned.

Chief Justice Taft revered the Court, was joyful in exercising to the full the authority of his office, and conceived it to be the Chief's function to be "a leader . . . in *massing the court*."[304] Chase did not seek fulfilment in that conception. It was a meaningful sentence that he wrote to John Van Buren on March 25, 1868, when the possibility of winning the Democratic nomination to the Presidency was in view:

> In fact it is only as a Circuit Judge that the Chief Justice, or any other Justice of the Supreme Court has, individually, any considerable power; and even then it is not active power, but only authority to declare what the law is by which the active power of others should be regulated.[305]

The "active power" that fascinated him was only that of the Chief Executive. On the Court he wanted to have his own way on certain matters, such as invalidating the Legal Tender Act.[306] It was a great satisfaction to declare his theory of Reconstruction in *Texas v. White*.[307] He wanted to uphold the test oath, and was troubled with misgivings that his associates had been concerting a decision behind his back—even as he was negotiating with friends in Congress for legislation concerning the Court about which he had not consulted them.[308] The authority that belonged to Marshall, and later to Taney, rested in considerable measure on the admiration that each inspired in his brethren; Chase, so far as appears, gave little thought to binding his colleagues to himself.[309] In much of what was done in their common labors he seems to have taken no deep interest.

---

[304] Henry F. Pringle, *The Life and Times of William Howard Taft*, 2 vols. (New York and Toronto: Farrar and Rinehart, 1939), II, 1044.

[305] Chase Papers, L.C.

[306] Supra, ch. 14.

[307] Supra, pp. 638–40.

[308] Supra, pp. 152–58, 161–72.

[309] Only rarely does one come upon a letter not strictly on business and written in a relaxed mood, where Chase allows himself to express a warmth of personal regard for an associate—such as that to Field on April 30, 1866, supra, p. 18, and that to Davis, after a period of estrangement, on June 24, 1867, supra, ch. 11, n. 7.

THE POST-WAR COURT

CHASE'S ASSOCIATES BROUGHT varied qualities and limitations to the work that opened before the Court as it emerged from the war. Grier's unwillingness to leave had long survived his usefulness. What had formerly been a somewhat wholesome forthrightness toward counsel and litigants degenerated into acrid comment upon the action of the Court in matters wherein he dissented. Words of disapproval in the *Myra Clark Gaines* case in 1868 had to be retracted when they proved "offensive to my brethren,"[310] and next year—apparently in respect of *Ex parte McCardle* or *Texas v. White*—he apologized to the Chief Justice and withdrew words "that may *bear a construction* which would hurt your feelings. I am sure I had no *such* intention."[311]

Also Justice Nelson—with no want of grace, however—clung to his office even when he contributed only the embarrassment of an empty chair—long after the statute of 1869 offered assurance of salary for life, and after any hope of preventing the overthrow of *Hepburn* had played out. "Judge N.," Justice Davis wrote on November 30, 1870, "is nearly 80, & I could see last winter that his constitution was breaking up."[312]

"Judge Clifford," Davis continued, "has presided with great dignity & to the satisfaction of the bar & bench. He really has more administrative ability than the Chief Justice." But in presiding he filled

[310] Gaines v. New Orleans, 6 Wall. 642. The effort to establish Myra Clark Gaines as the legitimate daughter and heir of Daniel Clark (1766–1813), sometime Delegate in Congress from the Territory of Orleans, reached the Court on many occasions. Shepard's Citations points to 13 such cases connected with the one cited above, between 1839 and 1891. In Gaines v. Hennen, 24 How. 553 (1861), Wayne, J., had covered the ground in an enormously long opinion, sustaining her claim. Taney, Catron, and Grier dissented, and the latter had expressed, in English and Latin, his astonishment "that a will can be established by the dim recollections, imaginations, and inventions of anile gossips, after forty-five years . . . ."

The case decided in 1868 concerned owners of other property claimed by Mrs. Gaines, and brought up a record of nearly 8000 pages. Davis, J., speaking for the majority, followed the decision in 1861. Grier, Swayne, Miller, JJ., dissented, and apparently Grier had found some even more forceful language to express his dismay.

His letter withdrawing his opinion is in the Chase Papers, L.C. Letters concerning its disappearance are among the Papers of the Clerk's Office, preserved in the National Archives: Wallace to Middleton, June 8 and 14, 1868, and reply of June 16.

[311] Letter of April 28, 1869, to Chase: he had sent Chase's note to Wallace and had asked him to make the amendments requested. "I can write with difficulty even with a pencil so must be brief." Chase Papers, L.C.

[312] To his brother-in-law, Judge Rockwell. Davis Papers, Ill. State Hist. Soc.

only a temporary role. Clifford belonged wholly to the past: he would resist all efforts to change the ways of the Court to meet the needs of the future.

In Justice Swayne's early years on the Bench, when the work consisted chiefly in ordinary matters of private law, his familiarity with the common law seemed impressive. In 1864 Davis had pronounced him "by all odds the best lawyer" among Lincoln's appointees.[313] But when the Court came to face greater challenges that preeminence was not maintained. In 1869 Swayne was going to hold the Circuit Court in Texas, where he would hear a railroad foreclosure suit in which William P. Ballinger, Miller's brother-in-law, represented the stockholders.[314] He inquired of Miller what to expect. On June 17, 1869, came this characterization:

> He is not a man much affected by the justice of a case as distinguished from the principles of law which ought to govern it and his judgment is just of that kind which is much influenced by plausibilities. His judgment is not clear, nor is he very self-reliant, though not likely to show this latter trait. He will examine such a case as yours fully and thoroughly. He is much governed by authorities and is fond of the older decisions especially of the English courts. He is more familiar with the authorities than any judge on our bench, and has a just estimate of their relative value. . . .
>
> . . . .
>
> He is very fond of the literature of the profession in which he believes himself to be remarkably well read. . . . Nor will he be insensible to injustice if it be patent and gross. He and I were alone politically last winter, and had much close consultation.[315]

While this evidently was written by no loving hand, the estimate seems just. Swayne was in his sixty-ninth year when Chase died, and his further service did not add to the vigor of the Court.

Miller had kept growing. His masterful self-confidence had been proved; his instinct for the values of the American constitutional system was sound; and he was devoted to the Court and zealous to promote its usefulness. He had come to speak with an authentic voice.

Justice Davis had never become deeply committed to the Court; at moments when he felt some special call to be helpful to the country, it always involved his leaving the Bench. He described his feeling about

---

[313] Supra, p. 12.
[314] Cowdrey v. Galveston, Houston and Henderson R.R., this phase not reported, but mentioned in the press, *Baltimore Sun*, Aug. 9, 13, 17, and 20, 1869. Later phases reported in Fed. Case No. 3293 (1870); 11 Wall. 459 (1870); and 93 U.S. 352 (1876). This was an additional assignment for Justice Swayne.
[315] Fairman, *Mr. Justice Miller*, 233–34.

his duty on the Court to his brother-in-law, Judge Rockwell in Massachusetts, in the letter of November 30, 1870, from which quotation has already been made:

> I have got pretty well down to work, though the first two weeks it went pretty hard. I have not the same zest for the employment that I had six or eight years ago, and as I never did like hard study, the work is not always agreeable. I believe I write the shortest opinions of any one on the bench, & if I had to elaborate opinions & write legal essays as some Judges do, I would quit the concern. I like to hold trial court, but this work on an appellate bench is too much like hard labor.[316]

But so long as he remained, Davis brought frank warm-heartedness and practical sense.

Justice Field had a somewhat prickly personality, an alert mind, and a designing foresight about the power of the Court to affect the course of affairs. He would exert a potent influence for years to come.

Justice Strong was a thoroughly competent lawyer and a colleague of sincere kindliness; he was not inclined to seek leadership and was far too independent to be a follower. He had had few opportunities to write memorable opinions.

To Bradley, service on the Court was a supreme vocation. As has been amply illustrated, he was outstanding in ability and in self-reliance; in his early years on the Court he held himself somewhat aloof. With Miller and Field, he would be one of the pillars.

When Ward Hunt arrived as a replacement he was suddenly plunged into an accumulation of controversies on which the Court had been divided. His most important action was to cast the decisive vote in the *Slaughter House Cases.* Hunt was an able Judge but not one of great power. Personally he made an addition to the amenity of the group.

If in the light of this survey one reflects on the cleavage in the *Slaughter House* decision, it may be remarked that the majority was led by Miller who stressed the maintenance of the federal system and "the security and firm establishment" of the freedom of the black citizens for whom the amendment was made; and those who stood with him, one may say with varying emphasis, were men of staid mentality with no urge to reorder the scheme of government. Of the dissenters, Bradley was of a speculative yet highly disciplined mind; he had an understanding of the function the Amendment might be made to serve. Field had his own vision of its use. But Swayne's judgment

---

[316] Davis Papers, Ill. State Hist. Soc.

was "not clear," "influenced by plausibilities;" he supposed that "Nothing can be more transparent" than the language of Section 1. And Chase is to be credited with no adequate comprehension. In 1866, on the day when the draft of the Joint Committee was introduced in the Houses, he thought it proposed "rather too big a contract;" he would have limited the Amendment to what was contained in Sections 2 and 4. "Prohibiting the States from interfering with the rights of citizens," and "granting express legislative power to Congress to enforce the new constitutional provisions," in his view, went beyond what was expedient.[317] That does not sound like farsighted statesmanship.

AN OPINION FOR THE SECRETARY OF STATE

IN 1793 THE SECRETARY of State, by direction of the President, addressed a request to the Justices of the Supreme Court. Questions were frequently arising, involving the law of nations and the construction of treaties, "under circumstances *which do not give a cognizance to the tribunals of the country*": would the Justices be available to give their advice? Chief Justice Jay conveyed their reply: "the lines of separation drawn by the Constitution between the three departments of the government" seemed to point to the impropriety "of our extrajudicially deciding the questions alluded to . . . ."[318] This has been regarded as a wise precedent.[319]

On November 26, 1872, Secretary of State Fish addressed a request to Chief Justice Chase, in accord with a conversation they had had "a day or two since." He inclosed the draft of one article of a contemplated convention with Great Britain and other powers "from whose dominions emigrants are constantly coming," for the better protection of steerage passengers, who often were subjected to "gross wrongs . . . during their passage across the ocean . . . ." Commonly the immigrants were bound for the Western States, had little money, and could not delay for the ordinary course of criminal proceedings. Thus "redress becomes almost hopeless."

To remedy this evil the draft article would provide for a hearing before two commissioners, one a federal officer and the other to be designated by the consul of the country to which the ship pertained.

---

317 The letter of April 30, 1866, to Justice Field, cited in ch. 1, n. 55.
318 *Writings of Thomas Jefferson*, Paul L. Ford, ed., 10 vols. (New York: G. P. Putnam's Sons, 1892–99), VI, 351–52; *Correspondence and Public Papers of John Jay*, Henry P. Johnston, ed., 4 vols. (New York: G. P. Putnam's Sons, 1890–92), III, 486–89.
319 Muskrat v. United States, 219 U.S. 346, 353 (1911); Chicago & Southern Air Lines v. Waterman S. S. Corp., 333 U.S. 103, 113 (1948).

The accused would be able to confront and to cross-examine the witnesses against him. The resulting record might be given in evidence before a grand jury or upon the trial of the accused, with like effect as if the witnesses were present.

"The growing importance of the question as one of humanity as well as of public policy" led the Secretary to submit it to the Chief Justice and "to ask that so far as it may be consistent with your judicial position, you will advise me" whether the provisions would contravene the Constitution.[320]

The Secretary had in mind the Sixth Amendment:

> In all criminal prosecutions the accused shall enjoy the right to a speedy and public trial, by an impartial jury of the State and district wherein the crime shall have been committed, . . . and . . . to be confronted with the witnesses against him . . . .

Chase replied on December 10. He had consulted "the two senior Associates"—at that time, Clifford and Swayne.

> We all doubt the constitutionality of the provision which authorizes the examination of witnesses before the Commissioners and the use of their depositions on the trial of citizens of the United States, charged with the offences described in the treaty. I incline to the opinion, that the clause providing for the right to be confronted with witnesses before the Commissioners, is a substantial compliance

---

[320] Exchange of letters in Chase Papers, L. C.

Background is supplied by papers in the National Archives, General Records of the Department of State, Drafts of Treaties, vol. 3, Great Britain, where printed drafts and handwritten notes on the proposed convention are preserved.

The design was to regulate a wide range of matters for the protection of steerage passengers. But how should the requirements be enforced? That was the subject of Article XXIII. A handwritten memorandum records that

> The main difference between the several governments is in the framing of the 23d Article.
> The Government of the United States has frankly stated the insuperable reasons which compel it to decline creating mixed courts, that the exercise of jurisdiction by such courts within the

territory of the United States would be in conflict with the Constitution.

> This explanation has been accepted by Great Britain and North Germany. An attempt is made on the part of the United States in the following proposed substitute for Article XXIII, in the American Draft to frame a system which shall give to the European powers a supervision over every step in the examination of cases arising under the Convention, thus confining the exclusive exercise of the powers of the national court to the final act of giving judgment.

Thus arose the proposal of the system of the two commissioners.

For locating this file and making it available on microfilm, I am obliged to the Historical Office of the Department of State and to the National Archives.

with the constitutional provision on the subject, but my associates incline, and quite decidedly, the other way.

There is, of course, no objection as to any stipulation for such testimoney to be used in civil suits, not criminal proceedings.[321]

The Secretary's objective was commendable, but not the method of approach. Certainly it was improper for Justices thus to give what Chase termed "our impressions," even with the reservation that these might, "of course, be changed upon argument and full consideration . . . ." A Justice owed it to his office and to the full Court to refrain from such a gratuitous and unconcerted commitment. The Secretary was not without the means of obtaining counsel: from the beginning the heads of the Executive Departments had been authorized to call upon the Attorney General for guidance. Evidently, however, he wanted the greater assurance that would come from an opinion from the Chief Justice.

Apparently what he learned put an end to the project. The papers in the Department of State were endorsed "Filed January 20/73."

The opinion of the Chief Justice is subject to the further criticism that it was imprecisely drafted. He reported grave doubt on the use of depositions "on the trial *of citizens of the United States,* charged with offences described in the treaty." He should have written, "on the trial *in courts of the United States* of persons charged with offences described in the treaty"—for it is not to be doubted that the constitutional protections on trials in federal courts are applicable as well to alien defendants.[322] And certainly the draft convention contemplated the trial of such persons.

Doubtless the Secretary recognized that legislation by Congress— not merely the ratification of the projected convention—would be requisite to the exercise of the new jurisdiction by the courts of the United States.

PRESIDENTIAL ASPIRATIONS FOR 1872

As WAS HIS wont when writing to Judge Rockwell, Justice Davis turned to politics in his letter of November 30, 1870, quoted above.[323]

---

[321] The draft article also provided for civil proceedings, *in rem* and *in personam*, for infractions of the convention.

[322] In Wong Wing v. United States, 163 U.S. 228, 238 (1896), the Court found it evident that the Fifth and Sixth Amendments protected *all* persons within the territory of the United States; and in Russian Volunteer Fleet v. United States, 282 U.S. 481 (1931), Hughes, C. J., observed that "an alien friend . . . as such was entitled to the protection of the Fifth Amendment," citing *Wong Wing* and other decisions.

[323] Supra, pp. 1459, 1461. Davis Papers, Ill. State Hist. Soc.

At the moment he was so busy with his work on the Court that he mingled little with politicians and heard "but little of the current gossip in that direction."

> It is the prevailing opinion that the Republicans will renominate Genl Grant, and he is certainly administering the Govt so that that end shall be secured at any rate. There is a good deal of disintegration going on in the party, but whether it will amount to enough to overthrow it at the next Presidential Election is questionable. I dont think it will. . . . It will take, I imagine, some time longer to break the Republican party down but it will gradually break down by its own corruption & maladministration. . . .

Chief Justice Chase had suffered a paralytic stroke on August 16, 1870. The entire right side of his body was affected, and for a time he lost the power of speech.[324] He was absent from Court throughout the adjourned term opening on October 31, and the December term that followed. Davis' letter spoke of that subject:

> The reports that we get of the Chief Justice are not favorable, and there is a belief here—on what it is based I do not know—that he will never resume his judicial duties. It is believed almost universally, that his family are contriving to keep his exact condition concealed from the public. . . . If it be true, I cannot account for their conduct except on the idea that his true condition if known might hurt his political prospects, & his family live in hopes he will ultimately get well, & certainly in season to be the Democratic candidate for the Presidency. . . . Chase is the most ambitious man, except Douglas, that I ever knew personally. As long as the Presidency is not reached, every thing else that he has obtained is as dust and ashes. . . .

Justice Miller had been writing in a like vein to his brother-in-law in Texas. On November 6 he reported that the indications were that Chase would recover; whether he could serve efficiently on the Court was doubtful.

> But I do not think he will resign unless he is provided with something else. That is not now probable. The paralytic stroke places him out of the list of probable candidates for the Presidency, and thereby removes any inducement for Grant to propitiate him or to send him to Europe which is the only alternative to his remaining a figure head to the court. His daughters, especially Mrs. Sprague will never consent to his retiring to private life. . . .[325]

---

[324] Jacob W. Schuckers, *The Life and Public Services of Salmon Portland Chase* (New York: D. Appleton and Co., 1874), 620. This goes on to describe his slow recovery.

[325] Fairman, *Mr. Justice Miller*, 251.

The Chief Justice returned to the Bench for the adjourned term in October 1871, and attended faithfully to the close of the regular term on May 6, 1872. He spoke for the Court in various small matters where one or two paragraphs sufficed. In *United States v. Klein*,[326] holding invalid the attempt to Congress to limit the effect of the President's proclamation of amnesty, he wrote the opinion, as well as in a few other cases relating to the war. In *Tarble's Case*[327] he dissented in three paragraphs; he noted his disagreement where the Court allowed a seller of slaves to recover from the purchaser.[328] In *Clinton v. Englebrecht*[329] he discussed the powers of a territorial government, and held that territorial courts were not courts of the United States within the meaning of the Constitution and that in selecting juries they must follow the statutes of the territory.

Aside from what he may have contributed to the decision of other cases in conference, that substantially summarizes the share borne by the Chief Justice in the labor of the Court.

Kate Chase Sprague was determined to convince the world that her father was fully restored and quite fit for the Presidency. To that end invitations were issued for a reception at her home on Thursday, April 25, 1872. The newspapers devoted hundreds of words to the extravagant affair. The effusive column of "Miss Grundy" reported that the Chief Justice was "so much his old self that except for a few pounds less flesh he scarcely bears a trace of his long and severe indisposition."[330] But what knowing eye was deceived? Senator Carl Schurz remembered that "his futile efforts to appear youthfully vigorous and agile were pathetically evident."[331]

The week that followed saw Schurz at Cincinnati, the moving spirit in the Liberal Republican convention called as an "uprising of honest citizens" to "take such action as their convictions of duty and of public exigencies may require." The call had been issued in January, 1872, by an assembly of the Liberal Republicans of Missouri. As has been recorded above, there had been a disintegration of the Republican party in that State; the Liberal wing which advocated repeal of

---

[326] 13 Wall. 128 (1872), supra, pp. 843–46.

[327] 13 Wall. 397, supra, pp. 1421–26.

[328] White v. Hart, 13 Wall. 646, and Osborn v. Nicholson, 13 Wall. 654, decided on Apr. 22, 1872. Supra, pp. 858–60.

[329] 13 Wall. 434 (1872).

[330] *New York World*, Apr. 28, 1872. The report, dated April 26, added that "last evening [he] walked from [his country-place, a short distance beyond the city limits] to his daughter's house."

The account in the *New York Herald* for Sunday, April 28, reported that "Among the most gratifying things of the evening was the sight of the Chief Justice, who, like his daughter, seems to have discovered the fountain of youth, for he appeared as robust in health and alert in intellect as ten years ago . . . ."

[331] *The Reminiscences of Carl Schurz*, 3 vols. (New York: McClure Co., 1907–8), II, 187.

the disqualifications imposed by the constitution of 1865 and the Democrats effected a fusion and put the Radicals out of power.[332] Now these Liberal Republicans proclaimed the need for national reconciliation and purification through such measures as complete amnesty and equal suffrage, reduction of the tariff, and civil service reform that would put an end to the use of federal patronage for the control of elections.

The appeal evoked a mounting response, from men sincerely concerned for reform—also from practical politicians who saw in this their best hope of displacing Grant. At Cincinnati, Stanley Matthews, George Hoadly, and J. B. Stallo early announced their support.[333] A varied group of prominent New Yorkers accepted the invitation, hoping that the movement would "spread through all the States and influence every political party"; Horace Greeley was the second among the signatories. In Illinois, Senator Trumbull and his friend, Horace White of the *Chicago Tribune*, joined in the movement. So, too, did Leonard Swett,[334] and Jesse W. Fell of Bloomington: they were already at work for Davis.

On February 22 the Labor Reform convention at Columbus, Ohio, named Davis for President and Joel Parker, Democratic Governor of New Jersey, for Vice President, on a platform whose first plank called for legal tender paper money. Thomas Ewing was on hand on Davis' behalf: he reported that "They are determined to lead off with nominations acceptable to the Democracy," but would not directly seek a combination. "Finding postponement impracticable, I devoted myself to an effort to get them to nominate you. . . ."[335]

This Labor nomination came somewhat inopportunely. Davis thanked the convention for the "unexpected honor" and, on the inspiration of James E. Harvey, a newspaper man who was advising him, commented enigmatically that "The Chief Magistracy of the Republic should neither be sought nor declined by an American citizen."[336]

---

[332] Supra, p. 617.

[333] They were introduced above as counsel for the school board in the litigation over the abolition of compulsory Bible reading in the schools. Supra, pp. 1312–13.

[334] Swett was one of the lawyers in Davis' circuit in Illinois who pressed Lincoln to appoint Davis to the Court. Supra, p. 4. In 1871 Swett became a manager of efforts to promote Davis for the Presidency. Willard L. King, *Lincoln's Manager, David Davis* (Cambridge, Mass.: Harvard University Press, 1960), 277. Chapter 22,

"Candidate for President, 1868–1872," deals with the Liberal Republican movement with particular reference to Davis.

[335] Letter from Lancaster, Ohio, February 22, informing Davis of what he had observed and done at Columbus the day before. It appeared that the ticket would be Davis and Joel Parker, which "will be accepted by the Democracy beyond a doubt." Davis Papers, Ill. State Hist. Soc.

Ewing has been identified supra, pp. 9, 230.

[336] Davis Papers, Ill. State Hist.

On February 28 Jeremiah S. Black wrote from New York City where, in the light of the action of Columbus, he had been consulting "several people." He told Davis that

> If Cincinnati repeats this nomination you will be President.
>
> In the mean time it is not necessary that you should commend yourself to the Democracy by saying that you are sound. We will try to prove that by more indifferent witnesses. . . .
>
> I have said and I shall probably say again unless forbidden that if you were President you would stand by the Constitution through thick and thin using all your legitimate power to preserve protect and defend it . . . .[337]

Of course no one could enter upon the office of President without taking the oath prescribed by Article II of the Constitution. But to one acquainted with Black, his quotation of the words conveyed his own special meaning: it was that that would "satisfy leading men everywhere that you are democrat enough for us."

Admirers of Chief Justice Chase felt, once again, that he was the man for the occasion. Judge M. C. C. Church of Parkersburg, West Virginia, identifying himself as "Secretary of the Democratic Republican Executive Committee," broached the matter by a letter to politicians who might be interested:

> The friends of Chief Justice Chase, with his consent, and with a full knowledge of the present political situation are of opinion that now is a favorable time to bring forward his claims for the Presidency. At a recent meeting of some of these friends in Washington where the matter was fully canvassed the enclosed call was drawn up and is now being circulated for signatures. . . .

It appeared that "the Liberal Republican movement . . . is in danger of being deflected into a channel which will destroy . . . the great ends for which conservative men throughout the Country are laboring. We wish in time to arrest disorganization and place a Platform and a Name before the Country which will hold the opposition until we have time to thoroughly organize." The battle at Cincinnati, the statement continued, would be fought between the friends of Justice Davis and those of the Chief Justice, "each representing widely differing political views. . . ." John Quincy Adams, Jr., was thought to be "the proper person to be associated with the Chief Justice as second on the Ticket."

Soc. Willard King names Harvey as the source of this suggestion. The sentiment originated with William Lowndes, when in 1821 he was nominated for the Presidency by the South Carolina legislature. See the article on Lowndes in the D.A.B.

[337] Davis Papers, Ill. State Hist. Soc.

A copy of this appeal, dated at Parkersburg, March 18, was sent to George W. Morgan of Mount Vernon, Ohio, a Democratic member of the House of Representatives who in fact was actively supporting Justice Davis. The paper was placed in Davis' hands.[338]

John Quincy Adams (1833–94) was the eldest son of Charles Francis Adams (1807–86), war-time Minister to Great Britain. The son had served one term in the Massachusetts legislature and had been the unsuccessful Democratic candidate for Governor in 1867 and in 1871.

It was fatuous for this group of enthusiasts to dream of settling so much with such an absence of substantial support.

Chase's response to the prospectus Church submitted was in a familiar pattern:

> Its first sentence seems to place me in the position of a man desiring a nomination for the Presidency. I do not desire it. . . . If those who agree with me in principle think that my nomination will promote the interests of the country, I shall not refuse the use of my name. . . .
>
> I doubt the expediency of the remark in regard to the tendency of the Liberal Republican movement. Nothing that I have seen seems to warrant a doubt of the patriotism of its promoters.
>
> Nor am I willing to be put in the attitude of rivaling Judge Davis. He is my friend, and I hold him in the highest esteem as a man of honor and ability. I differ from him on some important points of principle, but do not question the integrity of his convictions; nor, I think, does he question mine.
>
> And, finally, I doubt the expediency of suggesting any name for the second office. Let this be left to the Convention. Many will agree with you as to your first choice who will not agree with you as to your second.
>
> I inclose a draft, which will show more clearly my views.[339]

As the assembly at Cincinnati drew near, Charles Francis Adams and Lyman Trumbull stood out as likely nominees most in accord with the ideals of Liberal Republicanism, while, it was reported, "a good deal of very noisy work is being done for Justice David Davis" by his friends, Democratic and Republican.[340] Adams, with admirable independence, declared that he would not "consent to peddle . . . for

---

[338] Ibid. Morgan (1820–93) had been a Brigadier General in the Union Army from 1861 to 1863, when he resigned, partly by reason of his dissatisfaction with the use of colored troops. He was Democratic candidate for Governor in 1865.

[339] Letter of March 26 to Church. Warden, *An Account of the Private Life and Public Services of Salmon Portland Chase*, 728; Letterbook in Chase Papers, L.C.

[340] *The Nation*, 14:281. May 2, 1872.

power. If the good people who meet at Cincinnati really believe that they need such an anomalous being as I am (which I do not), they must express it in a manner to convince me of it. . . ."[341]

Representative George W. Morgan, introduced above, sent Justice Davis a copy of a message he had sent to James E. Harvey, who would be working for Davis at Cincinnati:

> The excentric [sic] letter of Mr. Adams shows that he has too light an estimate of the condition of our country, to be a safe pilot . . . . But aside from Ohio, 700,000 Irish voters would cast their ballots against him.
>
> The connection of Judge Trumbull with the McArdle [sic] case[342] would lose him 40 per ct. of the whole democratic vote . . . .
>
> My belief is that Judge Davis would poll the entire democratic vote, for the Milligan case[343] is a tie which binds our people to him. . . .[344]

Representative Fernando Wood of New York was sending Justice Davis bulletins of his efforts in support. One was, "I had a long & quite a *satisfactory* interview with Gov. Fenton last night. He will see you today or tomorrow . . . ."[345] Wood, Mayor of New York from 1861 to 1863, had been on the extreme pro-Southern wing of the Democratic party.[346] Reuben E. Fenton, Republican Governor of New York from 1865 through 1868, had then been elected to the Senate. He had built up a powerful machine, only to see leadership wrested from him by Roscoe Conkling, who controlled patronage under President Grant. This situation, rather than zeal for reform, was the basis for Fenton's interest in the Liberal Republicans.

Judge James Grant[347] of Davenport, Iowa, was bestirring himself in Justice Davis' behalf. He sent to Jesse Fell, for communication to Davis, a letter he had received from William A. Graham, sometime Governor of North Carolina, Secretary of the Navy under Fillmore, Senator at Washington and also at Richmond: he had opposed secession, and worked for an early peace. Graham considered Justice Davis "the most available candidate to beat Genl Grant and at the same time

[341] Letter of April 18 to David A. Welles. This was published. Ann. Cyc. 1872, 777.

[342] *Ex parte* McCardle, supra, ch. 10.

[343] Supra, ch. 5.

[344] Copy of letter of April 26 to James E. Harvey, who apparently was already on the ground, inclosed in letter of that date, written at Mount Vernon, Ohio, to Justice Davis. Davis Papers, Ill. State Hist. Soc.

[345] Davis Papers, Ill. State Hist. Soc. In a note marked "*Private* Monday April 21 2.pm" he reported that he had just arrived from New York with important information. Presumably this was on Monday, April 22. The note about meeting Fenton was dated "Thursday Morning," presumably April 25.

[346] Supra, pp. 256, 306–07, 312, 318–19.

[347] Supra, pp. 951–56.

a fit person to fill the office. As regards the South he is the least liable to objection of all persons who cooperated with the North . . . ." Graham mentioned in particular the *Milligan* opinion.[348]

Edward M. Yerger, it may be recalled, having escaped a trial for his killing of Major Crane in 1869, had quit Mississippi and entered upon a newspaper venture at Baltimore.[349] From the office of the *Baltimore Evening Journal* he wrote to Justice Davis on April 25, 1872:

> This letter will be handed to you by Col Wiegel of this city, who has recently been elected a delegate from Maryland to the Cincinnati Convention. He sympathizes with me politically and desires to make your acquaintance. His familiarity with the politics of Maryland may be useful to your friends.[350]

Representative S. S. Cox, Ohio Democrat, sent Davis a note on March 8: "I want you to read this debate, all through. . . . I am not a friend of any person for Prest; but I am not an enemy of the human race; nor of yourself in particular. When I return to Washn. I desire to confer with you."[351] Pretty surely the debate to which Cox referred was one that had taken place in the House of Representatives on March 5, 1872.[352] It had been precipitated by R. T. W. Duke of Virginia, Conservative, and continued by Cox: their speeches were full of the stock complaints about Carpetbaggers and blacks. Replies were made by Garfield (who was in charge of the Deficiency Appropriation Bill, the matter before the House), by Henry L. Dawes of Massachusetts, and by Joseph H. Rainey of South Carolina, a Negro, who made a very proper answer to Cox.

Some of the company into which Davis was being drawn was hardly suitable for a Justice of the Supreme Court.

On the eve of the Liberal Republican convention, Horace White of the *Chicago Tribune*, Samuel Bowles of the *Springfield* (Massachusetts) *Republican*, Henry Watterson of the *Louisville Courier-Journal*, dining with Murat Halstead of the *Cincinnati Commercial*, hit upon a scheme to embarrass Davis: each sent to his paper an adverse editorial, which Halstead would print in the *Commercial*. The effect was disheartening to the Davis forces, just as the delegates convened on May 1.

---

[348] Letter of James Grant to Fell, April 16, with copy of letter of Graham, from Hillsboro, North Carolina, dated April 11. Davis Papers, Ill. State Hist. Soc.

[349] Supra, pp. 590–91.

[350] Davis Papers, Ill. State Hist. Soc.

Colonel William H. Wiegel of Baltimore had been on the staff of the Freedmen's Bureau there. Report of the Assistant Commissioner for Maryland, S. Exec. Doc. No. 6, 39th Cong., 2d Sess., 89, 94.

[351] Davis Papers, Ill. State Hist. Soc. Cox has been identified supra, pp. 186, 191, 645.

[352] Cong. Globe, 42–2, 1438–45.

Stanley Matthews presided over the organization. Schurz was chosen for permanent president. He deprecated the cry of "Anybody to beat Grant." "We do not merely want another, but we want a better President than we have."[353] His prescription sounded like Adams or Trumbull.

On the first ballot, Adams received 203 votes; Horace Greeley, 147; Trumbull, 100; Governor B. Gratz Brown of Missouri, 95; Justice Davis, 92½; Governor Andrew G. Curtin of Pennsylvania, 62; Chief Justice Chase, 2½; Senator Charles Sumner, 1. Brown withdrew in favor of Greeley. On other ballots Davis' vote declined; that for Adams advanced, but Greeley's mounted faster. After the sixth ballot had been recorded, the convention swarmed to Greeley. Governor Brown was named for the second place.

The Nation commented:

> We suppose that a greater degree of incredulity and disappointment than was caused by the nominations at Cincinnati has not been felt in this country since the news of the first battle of Bull Run. The country had been led to believe that the candidate most dangerous to Mr. Adams, Mr. Trumbull, and the good men of the Convention, was Judge Davis, and almost no one outside the hall of the Convention was fearing that it was to Mr. Greeley and Mr. Gratz Brown that the Convention was to fall a prey. . . .[354]

Justice Davis advised the Labor Reformers that, in view of what had happened at Cincinnati, he found it "proper to retire absolutely from the presidential contest . . . ."

Edwin W. Stoughton (1818–82), a New York lawyer with some practice before the Supreme Court, was writing frequently to Justice Davis during this period: on February 23, March 9, April 19, May 8, and then a long personal letter on August 6.[355] The first three swelled to the theme that Davis would be the choice of both Liberal Republicans and Democrats. That of May 8 recounted how at Cincinnati "There was no fair play towards you . . . ." Fenton's men had been "packed and managed . . . for the benefit of Greeley." On June 23, Stoughton was about to call upon Justice Nelson at Cooperstown. "I *very much wish to talk with you . . . .*"

The letter of August 6 lays bare what, one infers, had been in Stoughton's mind all along: he wanted to be Nelson's successor on the Court. He had learned from Nelson that "If he does not . . . recover

[353] *Speeches, Correspondence and Political Papers of Carl Schurz,* Frederic Bancroft, ed., 6 vols. (New York and London: G. P. Putnam's Sons, 1913), II, 354, 358–59.
[354] 14:297. May 9, 1872.
[355] Davis Papers, Ill. State Hist. Soc.

he will resign. . . ." Stoughton reasoned, "In the event of Grant's defeat [it would be assumed] that Judge Nelson would not resign before March unless he was sure of a fit successor; and I think that were it understood that he would resign in view of my appointment, [friends of Stoughton would endeavor] to secure the pledge of Genl Grant to that effect. Now I cannot write or talk to Judge Nelson on the subject, but as I feel confident he would do all he properly could to put me in his place . . . , I am anxious . . . that he be advised of the plan I have suggested, if you think it proper to do so . . . . Of course in writing to Justice Nelson at this time, the most entire delicacy for his feelings can be observed . . . and I am persuaded he would be glad to see me in his place."

However—as Stoughton's better judgment had foreseen in his letter of June 23—it was Grant who carried the election. Then when Nelson resigned on November 28, it was in accord with the recommendation Senator Conkling had already made that Ward Hunt was appointed.[356]

The Republican National Convention in June renominated Grant, and chose Senator Henry Wilson of Massachusetts for the second place.

The Democrats in July made Greeley and Brown their nominees.

What started as a movement for quality and integrity in the national administration had gone far astray. As an editor Greeley had made a worthy contribution; but his record of erratic judgments, his eccentricities and unconventional appearance, made his candidacy appear simply implausible. Grant, with all his shortcomings, seemed on the safer side.

---

[356] In the diary of Hamilton Fish, then Secretary of State, the entry for Tuesday, December 3, 1872, records what transpired at a meeting of the Cabinet:

President calls attention to appointment to be made of a Judge of the Supreme Court in place of Nelson resigned. Says parties are recommending Judge Woodruff, Evarts & Pierrepont, that a year or so ago, when it was thought Nelson would resign, very numerous recommendations were made of Ward Hunt, that he had made up his mind at that time to appoint him, he would like to gratify Judge Pierrepont, but thinks a majority of the Bar & the Public of N.Y. prefer Hunt. He appeals to me. I say . . .

that in the City I think a majority of both classes would prefer Pierrepont. . . . (The President . . . on Saturday referred to his former intention & repeated it in effect, leaving it contingent only in case Conkling had changed his opinion in regard to Hunt.) . . .

Fish Papers, L.C.

Lewis B. Woodruff (1809–75), appointed Circuit Judge for the Second Circuit in 1869, has been referred to above, p. 1053. He was Justice Bradley's brother-in-law, each having married a daughter of Chief Justice Hornblower of New Jersey.

Edwards Pierrepont was introduced supra, pp. 516, 534. In May 1875 he became Attorney General in Grant's Cabinet, and served one year.

Greeley carried only six States: Georgia, Kentucky, Maryland, Missouri, Tennessee, and Texas. His popular vote was 2,843,000 to 3,596,000 for Grant. He died on November 29, 1872—before the Electoral College had acted.

So far as concerns the Court, the memorable aspect of the contest of 1872 was registered in Thomas Nast's cartoon, "The Presidential Fever on the Supreme Bench," in *Harper's Weekly* for April 6, 1872. The Chief Justice, at whose feet lies a paper, "A life long Chase after the Presidency," admonishes Justice Davis, clutching the Labor Reform nomination, in a paraphrase of Cardinal Wolsey's words to Thomas Cromwell in *Henry VIII*:

> Mark but my fall, and that that ruin'd me.
> Judge Davis, I charge thee, fling away ambition . . . .

NUNC DIMITTIS

ON MAY 6, 1873, Chief Justice Chase suffered another paralytic stroke, from which he died next day.

Harper's Weekly, surveying his varied accomplishments, stressed that "he was conspicuous in all free-soil and antislavery movements," and then "placed himself in the front of the defenders of the union." It concluded,

> Hence it is not so much the Chief Justice or the eminent politician, the lawyer or the orator, for whom the country grieves, as for the friend who sustained it in its moment of trial, for the voice that was always cheerful in the period of danger, for the heart that ever beat true to the cause of freedom. It is by such labors that the citizen endears himself to his country. And in return, if he have faults, the country hides them in a decent veil, and dwells tenderly upon his patriotic services.[357]

The Nation took note of the Chief Justice's passing in a long article by Charles C. Nott, Judge and eventually Chief Justice of the Court of Claims, 1865–1905. The late Chief Justice's "burning ambition" to attain the Presidency, with his "thinly disguised electioneering tours for the purpose of keeping himself before the people," cast "the chief dimness on a most honorable record."

> The nine annual terms through which he has presided constitute a judicial period of little less importance than that period of constitu-

---

[357] 17:434. May 24, 1873. Concerning a successor, it hoped he would be one who "will find all his powers engaged and his ambition fully satisfied with the proper duties of his office." 17:866, October 4, 1872.

tional interpretation which it was the fortune of Chief-Justice Marshall almost exclusively to fill. For many years to come the decisions of these nine terms will be referred to by lawyers, legislators and constitutional students more than any others. . . .

In that examination, Chase's judicial services would be "highly esteemed" as tending to "the maintenance of those principles which are the basis of national integrity . . . ."[358]

Rutherford B. Hayes, in camp in Virginia in 1862, had recorded in his diary that "I am very glad Governor Chase is Chief Justice."[359] Now Governor of Ohio, and still keeping a diary, on May 18, 1873, he recorded his preference for measured appreciation rather than fulsome eulogy of the late Chief Justice:

> Chase possessed noble gifts of intellect, great culture, and a commanding presence. When this is said, about all that is favorable has been said. He was cold, selfish, and unscrupulous. His conduct to Lincoln and Stanton, his . . . contempt for the great office he held and his willingness to degrade it, should have made lawyers, at least, chary of praise. I have heard him speak of himself and his associates on the bench as old women, and he always preferred the title of Governor to that of Chief Justice. He often expressed preference for the place of Senator to that of Chief Justice. Political intrigue, love of power, and a selfish and boundless ambition were the striking features of his life and character.[360]

However severe that may be as a conclusion, Hayes' statement of what he had observed is hardly to be questioned.

In 1864, when William M. Evarts was an aspirant for the Chief Justiceship, he had written, "I do not feel any public duty that requires me to wish for, or aid in, the appointment of Gov. Chase. On the contrary, if I were the appointing power, I should think many reasons dissuaded from it."[361] Ten years later, Evarts by invitation was delivering a eulogy of the late Chief Justice before the alumni at the Dartmouth commencement:[362] Chase had now taken his place beside Daniel Webster as the graduates whom that college most delighted to honor.

---

[358] 16:330–31. May 15, 1873.

[359] Supra, ch. 1, n. 58.

[360] *Diary and Letters of Rutherford Birchard Hayes* (Columbus: Ohio State Archeological and Historical Soc., 1922–26), III, 242–43.

[361] Letter of October 15, 1864, to Richard Henry Dana, Jr. Other sentences of this letter were quoted in chapter 1, note 60. Brainerd Dyer, *The Public Career of William M. Evarts* (Berkeley, Cal.: University of California Press, 1933), 156.

[362] *Eulogy on Chief Justice Chase, delivered by William M. Evarts, before the Alumni of Dartmouth College, at Hanover, June 24, 1874.* Hanover, N.H., J. B. Parker, 1874. Reprinted in Schuckers, *Chase*, 635–62.

When Evarts came to the appointment to the Chief Justiceship, he dwelt upon the "immeasurable honor" that redounded to a President, and the "vast benefits to his countrymen," from a thoroughly worthy selection. No act of John Adams had been greater than his appointment of Marshall.

> There is no doubt that Mr. Chase greatly desired this office, its dignity and durability both considered, the greatest gratification . . . that our political establishment affords . . . .

One need not question that Evarts himself held that estimate, but certainly Chase did not.

The Chief Justice of the Supreme Court should exercise a "gracious authority, as first among equals, to adjust, arrange, and facilitate the coöperative working of its members." Evarts spoke of the varied fields with which a Justice must be concerned: "the tangled mazes of affairs which form the body of private litigations"; the law of nations; "the . . . public law of our political system, . . . where the bounds of State and Federal authority . . . require accurate and circumspect adjustment"; and the "final arbitrament on all conflicts . . . by which the great coördinate departments of the Government are to be confined to their appropriate spheres . . ."; in all these functions "the adequacy of the Chief Justice was unquestioned."

Two matters received special consideration. The Chief Justice's conduct in presiding over the trial of the impeachment of the President, Evarts was happy to defend. And as to the validity of the Legal Tender Act, while he professed "a firm approval of the final disposition of the constitutional question . . . ," he expressed "regret that the just result was not reached by less uncertain steps. . . ."

When Ebenezer R. Hoar in Massachusetts received a copy of his kinsman's address, he replied that "It is certainly able and ingenious . . . . But . . . I do not believe the sound judgment of this generation or the judgment of history will agree with your estimate of Chase, who was insincere, selfish and intriguing, and did more than any one else to degrade and ruin the office of Chief Justice."[363]

Justice Strong acknowledged receipt of a copy in a letter which Evarts preserved. He pronounced the remarks "just and discriminating," then made his own comment on Chase:

> I cannot but think . . . he was greater as a statesman than as a judge. He was not a thoroughly trained and learned lawyer, nor was

---

[363] Moorfield Storey and Edward W. Emerson, *Ebenezer Rockwood Hoar, A Memoir*, (Boston and New York: Houghton Mifflin Co., 1911), 242–43.

he at home in habits of close legal reasoning, though there was a class of subjects, semi political, either constitutional or arising out of legislation during or following the war, in discussing which he showed great power. And one of the elements of his strength was that he was always "thoroughly persuaded" before he acted, and always followed his convictions. This may account for the fact that sometimes he was imperious in his conduct towards subordinates. It may be that he was not conscious of his imperious manner.

It was unfortunate, Strong continued, that upon accepting the Chief Justiceship "he did not give up entirely his ambition for the Presidency," which "amounted to a passion." Inevitably it had aroused suspicion that his aspiration affected his legal judgments. "Thus he suffered, and thus, to some extent, the Court suffered with him."

Strong took note of Evarts' remark about "uncertain steps" in arriving at the decision in the *Legal Tender Cases*. It was not unprecedented "to allow in a second case a reargument of a question which was decided in a former case. The propriety of such an allowance in cases involving constitutional questions, especially when the first decision was made by a Court almost equally divided, and when upon the decision the powers of the government depend, is sufficiently obvious." It was well known that "the Chief Justice was himself anxious to reverse several that were given by his predecessors." "The only thing extraordinary was the multiform effort to prevent a hearing of the case of Knox and Lee on all the questions involved in it."

"I am anxious to preserve," Justice Strong concluded, "my just reputation as an upright man and I am particularly solicitous for the good opinion of men like yourself. I wish also to protect the Court, so far as I can from unjust imputations."[364]

IN CONCLUSION

INSOFAR AS THE years of Chase's Chief Justiceship may be said to stand out as a distinct period in the annals of the Court, it was not by reason of any profound impulse he imparted. Such influence as he exerted was confined to those few categories in which he took some particular interest.

The years between the attempted secession and the restoration of normal relations within the Union had an essential unity. The situation was not contemplated in framing the Constitution: no text declared

---

[364] Letter written at Washington, September 10, 1874. The Library of Congress has a typewritten copy, sent by Sherman Evarts, February 3, 1922, of the original then in the Evarts Papers at Woodstock, Vermont.

what should be done in the event of a breach of the order there "ordained and established." The President met the ordinances of secession with proclamations of blockade. In the *Prize Cases*[365] his authority to do this was recognized: he was bound to meet the threatened dismemberment of the Union "without waiting for Congress to baptize it with a name." The dissenters quoted Article 2: "The Congress shall have Power . . . To declare War . . ."; they said that until it had acted, the President had been conducting no more than "a personal war," to which the courts could not properly give effect. Here at the outset one observes a cleavage in the mode of approach. Some Justices would start with a recognition that another branch of the Government had been obliged to meet a situation as it was in fact; it was in that light that they would judge what had been done. Other Justices would say that whatever might have obtained "in a material sense," "in contemplation of law" it was immaterial what "the magnitude and dimensions of the resistance" had been. The majority comprised Justices Grier and Wayne, pre-war appointees, and Swayne, Miller, and Davis; in dissent, Nelson spoke also for Taney, Catron, and Clifford.

One may say, broadly, that this difference in outlook persisted throughout the controversies over measures of war and of restoration. What the Court pronounced "in contemplation of law" was profoundly affected by the outlook of the individuals who sat on the Bench and did this contemplating.

The propriety of any action within the system of the Constitution is to be judged in the light of its allocation of competence. On August 31, 1861, General Frémont, commanding the Western Department, declared the emancipation of slaves held by rebels in Missouri; he reached his decision overnight, "without consultation or advice with any one." When the President countermanded this action, the friends of liberty cried out in praise of the General.[366] When on September 22, 1862, the President issued his Preliminary Emancipation Proclamation, Justice Nelson wrote despairingly to Justice Clifford,

> *Proclamations* and *orders* thicken upon us from Washington. The plunge of emancipation is taken in one, and military deportation in the

---

[365] 2 Bl. 635. docketed December 2, 1862, and decided March 10, 1863. Supra, ch. 11, n. 86.

[366] Edward McPherson, *The Political History of the United States, during the Great Rebellion*, 2d ed. (Washington: Philip and Solomons, 1865), 245–47.

Whittier wrote,
Thy error, Fremont, simply was

to act
A brave man's part, without the statesman's tact,
And, taking counsel but of common sense,
To strike at cause as well as consequence.

The Political Works of John Greenleaf Whittier (Boston: Houghton, Mifflin and Company, 1882), 321.

loyal States, in the other—no man can see the end— The darkness deepens—[367]

Nelson wrote at a moment when arrests by subordinates of the Executive had gotten out of hand.[368] Presently General Burnside in Ohio took it upon himself to move against Vallandigham, most harmful among the Copperheads, and approved a sentence that he be confined for the duration. As a result, the President was charged with countenancing measures tending towards despotism. He sought to extricate himself from the embarrassment by sending Vallandigham to the Confederates. Counsel petitioned the Court to direct a writ of certiorari to the Judge Advocate General, to send up the record; his objective was to elicit a judgment condemning what had been done. There was no dissent when Justice Wayne, upon a careful exposition, concluded that the remedy sought did not lie within the jurisdiction granted to the Court.[369]

One might continue, taking other conspicuous incidents during the war and the restoration, and hasty conclusions might be drawn— perhaps that Frémont should be commended because he struck a blow for freedom; that Justice Nelson should be faulted for having doubts about Executive emancipation, but that he was right in condemning arbitrary arrests; that the Court was shirking when it did not come to Vallandigham's rescue. One might praise the virtue of Henry Winter Davis, who would stop appropriations until the Executive conformed to "the fundamental principles of the Government."[370] Yet he claimed for Congress "a plenary, supreme, unlimited political jurisdiction, paramount over courts, subject only to the judgment of the people," in the treatment of the rebel States[371]—an extreme expression of Radicalism, which according to general impression must be censured. The pretentious language seems to illustrate what Justice Davis reprobated in his letter justifying the breadth of his opinion in *Milligan*: that it would have been "worth nothing for future time" if it had failed to condemn the claim of Congressional omnipotence.[372] But we live under a Constitution that creates separate Branches, and invests each with defined powers; it expects universal respect for the order thus established. It is in that context that all actions should be judged.

---

[367] Letter of Sept. 25, 1862. Clifford Papers, Me. Hist. Soc.

[368] Supra, n. 189.

[369] *Ex parte* Vallandigham, 1 Wall. 243 (1864). Supra, ch. 5, n. 49.
It was cited by Chief Justice Waite in 1877 for the proposition that "We have only such appellate jurisdiction as has been conferred by Congress, and in the exercise of such as has been conferred we can proceed only in the manner which the law prescribes." United States v. Young, 94 U.S. 258.

[370] Supra, pp. 190–91.

[371] Supra, p. 98.

[372] Supra, p. 232.

Because the issues of the war and reconstruction were unprecedented, because the factual situations were complicated and awkward, because preconception has been deep-seated and discriminating analysis has been difficult, superficial and inconsistent judgments have been allowed to pass current.

It seems patent on calm reflection that at the close of hostilities it was in order to make a new start, one that laid a firm foundation for the future of the Union. This work would be, in the highest sense, "political," not "judicial." This appears true in the abstract. Its truth is more evident when one says that the commissions held by Samuel Nelson, Robert C. Grier, Nathan Clifford, Noah H. Swayne, and the rest, did not vest in them final authority to pass upon the basis upon which the restoration of the secessionist States was to be effected.

Reconstruction was a matter wherein accord between the President and the Congress was most urgently needed. But when Congress assembled, the President insisted that restoration had been completed, awaiting nothing but the seating of the delegations from the rebel States. In dealing with Presidential intransigence and the unyielding situation that developed in the South, "the magnitude and dimensions of the resistance" forced Congress to measures not remotely contemplated at the beginning.

It is to the credit of the Justices that, despite a wide range of personal sentiment, they acted together like Judges in declaring their incompetence to enjoin the Chief Executive from enforcing a statute, or to rule upon the contention that the "State of Georgia" was entitled to remain a community "composed exclusively . . . of white male citizens."[373]

In principle it did belong to the judiciary to determine whether an individual litigant had been deprived of liberty or property without lawful authority. Congress had reason to fear, however, that the Court would not confine itself to the narrow issue, but would seize the occasion to declare broadly that the means Congress had taken to restore the Union were unconstitutional. Jere. Black was a mighty general who in *Ex parte McCardle* had as his objective nothing short of the preservation of the South as it had been.[374] Once the danger inherent in *McCardle* disappeared, Congress evinced nothing but consideration for the effectiveness of the Court.[375] Then suddenly *Ex parte Yerger* gave fresh alarm, and once again Trumbull proposed a declaration that reconstruction was a "political" matter. Attorney General Hoar managed to avert any untoward action. Soon Mississippi and Texas, having complied with the terms set by Congress, were in February and

---

[373] Supra, p. 387.   [374] Supra, pp. 433, 456–57.   [375] Supra, p. 487.

March, 1870, restored to their normal relations within the Union.[376] Congressional Reconstruction had been completed.

In its seeming hostility toward the Court, Congress had been guarding the key to its position as it faced the President and the South: only with governments organized without discrimination on ground of color, and after acceptance of the Fourteenth Amendment, would the secessionist States be readmitted to representation. That reasoned statement expresses the essence of a situation wherein a multitude of unreasoning utterances had been made on each side of the contested line.

Suppose that the Justices, while deciding every case as actually it was decided, had uttered no dictum, and had avoided all remarks and all personal intercourse, conveying any menace to the authority of Congress over reconstruction: it seems reasonable to doubt whether any legislation hostile to the Court would have been seriously considered by Congress. Of course the antecedents of the Justices were known and their personal sentiments could be assessed: but if their conduct had inspired confidence that they would respect the limitations on the Court's competence, a different atmosphere would have prevailed. And if one were to suppose that the dissent of Justice Miller in *Ex parte Garland* had been the opinion of the Court, the likelihood that there would have been no breach in the comity between Court and Congress seems high indeed. *Garland* is here referred to for the profession with which Miller closed: he had brought "to the examination of the grave questions of constitutional law . . . those principles alone which are calculated to assist in determining what the law is, rather than what, in my private judgment, it ought to be."[377]

It was a relief to the Court when the strain of reconstruction was at an end and thoughts were directed to problems of national expansion. The mystery of the Fourteenth Amendment had been broached. When the Court met in October 1873 it would have on its docket the first of the cluster of the so-called *Granger Cases*, wherein it must consider whether State laws regulating the charges of railroads and warehouses were violative of the new Amendment.[378] It would have before it a load of cases which for the first time surpassed eight hundred. And presently it would receive as its new Chief a man of unpretentious dignity who would devote himself singly to the duties of his office and prefer his brethren to himself.

Here we take leave of the Court, to resume when it next convenes "at the time and place appointed by law."

---

[376] Supra, p. 589.
[377] 4 Wall. 333, 399 (1867). Supra, p. 244.
[378] Winona & St. Peter R.R. Co. v.

Blake, 94 U.S. 180, was decided with Munn v. Illinois, 94 U.S. 113, and other cases, on March 1, 1877. Chief Justice Waite spoke for the Court.

Table of Cases

1483

Index

A NOTE ON THE BOOK

This book is set in Linotype Times Roman. Composition by
Maryland Linotype Company, Baltimore, Maryland. Printed
and bound by The Kingsport Press, Kingsport, Tennessee.
Paper is English Finish Laid manufactured by Oxford Paper
Company, Rumford, Maine. Slipcases made by Miro Pack-
aging and Sales Corporation, Long Island City, New York.
Woodcut of seal of the Supreme Court by Fritz Kredel.

Typography and binding design by
WARREN CHAPPELL